SECOND HANDBOOK of RESEARCH on TEACHING

SECOND HANDBOOK of RESEARCH on TEACHING

A Project of

The American Educational Research Association

Edited by ROBERT M. W. TRAVERS, Editor

RAND McNALLY & COMPANY
Chicago

Preface

The term *handbook* has been used to designate a great many different kinds of publications. In engineering and in the physical sciences, handbooks typically are compilations of numerical constants of the kind that frequently enter into the calculation of results or the design of equipment. But handbooks in the behavioral sciences have had entirely different content and generally have emphasized discussions of research methods and the outcomes of major programs of research. The original *Handbook of Research on Teaching* represented the first venture of its kind in education and followed the pattern already set in the behavioral sciences. The remarkable success achieved by that volume indicated that it had been cast in a format highly useful to readers. After reflecting on the success of what has become known as the "Gage Handbook," my first impulse was to produce a new handbook that simply continued where the original volume had left off and covered work that had taken place in the intervening years. Although such a plan appeared attractive, a consideration of the recent knowledge available for inclusion in the new volume made it quite clear that this knowledge could not be elegantly organized into the structure of chapters previously used. Immense change has taken place in the intervening years, but some of the change has occurred so gradually that those who have been participating in it have hardly been aware that they have been moving slowly, but in-exorably, into a world of new techniques, new ideas and new research endeavors. Let us consider what some of those changes have been.

At the time when the original *Handbook* appeared, research on the technology of both classroom management and teaching equipment was in its infancy. Sociology had barely begun to have the impact on educational thought that it has today. The term *behavior modification* had not been introduced to educational circles. The name of Piaget was almost unknown to American psychologists. The computer had not extended its terminals to schools. The potential use of educational programs below the level of the kindergarten remained largely ignored. In brief, much of what is exciting and interesting in the contemporary educational scene did not exist. The new *Handbook* had to be structured to accommodate the wealth of new and intriguing research-related ventures that have appeared. Since such innovation did not fit well into the plan of the original *Handbook,* the editorial board evolved a new organization of chapters.

Two broad trends are also evident in the development of education through research. One of these is a trend to develop a technology of education as, historically, most technologies have emerged—quite independent of the scientific disciplines. Steam engines, the smelting of metals, the manufacture of glass, die casting, printing, paper manufacture and other technologies fundamental to our civilization evolved long before the academic disciplines could provide them with any scientific base. To some degree, the existing technology of education has shown a similar pattern of development, and many of the contemporary research and development organizations sponsored by the federal government seek to develop a technology of education on a similar basis.

A second trend is seen in those who seek to develop education through the application of ideas derived from the framework of the organized sciences or through the extension of these sciences to the development of an understanding of educational phenomena. The impact of such outstanding laboratory scientists as Jean Piaget and B. F. Skinner is evident in many chapters of this volume, but the influence of many less well-known scientists is also evident. For example, the chapters on motor-skill learning and physical education show the close relationship that exists between the thinking of the many laboratory scientists exploring problems of motor-skill acquisition and the practical task of the physical education instructor. The chapter on motor-skill learning (Chapter 25), written by experimental psychologists, illustrates the kind of scientific base that many aspects of educational practice may be expected to have in the future. Much of the knowledge summarized in many of the chapters comes from the research of those who, themselves, have little direct concern with education but whose work is providing the foundation for many contemporary developments in education.

The *Handbook* might have been limited to reviewing the available knowledge that has some implications for teaching, but an attempt has been made also to make the volume a handbook of ideas. Research related to teaching is a large though ill-defined area that at present is experiencing a surge of new ideas. The ideas that are being explored, even more than the knowledge developed to date, may be of interest to the contemporary reader since the ideas represent the very foundations on which an edifice of knowledge may be built. For this reason chapters on the new technology of education have been included. The area of educational technology is one that has intrigued some of the sharpest minds in education, but it is one too new to represent the kind of solid body of useful knowledge that an advanced technology can offer. At this time it can be described more aptly as a spring of fresh ideas which may encourage many who drink of that spring to pursue development that may help to bring fresh approaches to education.

One of the chapters that offers ideas rather than established knowledge is that by Holland and Doran (Chapter 9) on instrumentation in classroom research. Not much has been done to learn what is happening to pupils through the use of modern instruments developed in the biological and physical sciences; much more could also be done to understand the behavior of pupils by an implementation of the kind of telemetry developed for recording the behavior of astronauts. Although a great deal is known about the emotional responses of astronauts as they encounter the hazards of space exploration, little is known about how the pupil responds to the many nagging frustrations that he encounters in schools. Gaming and simulation represent another area where ideas that ultimately may have impact are emerging.

The structure of the *Second Handbook* also differs from the structure of the first due to the changed way in which professors in colleges of education specialize. Ten years ago one could find a person expert in such broad fields as the sociology of education or research methods, but today there are few, if any, who would claim expertise in such broad areas. Indeed, the modern expert not only confines his interest and activity to a quite narrow area, but he often claims expertness only in a particular approach to that narrow area. For example, consider the area of moral development, an area in which there has been a great expansion of research and an emergence of extensive research literature. Among research workers investigating moral development one can find some who structure their thoughts in terms of an operant model and others who structure their thoughts along Piagetian lines. The person willing to and interested in providing a broad and eclectic review of the entire area is not likely to be found. The specialization that has long characterized research workers in the physical sciences is now quite apparent in education and related branches of knowledge. The result of this is that generally chapters have had to cover much narrower topics than in the earlier *Handbook*. They also tend to be written by individuals who admit to examining their area from a particular point of view. It is not that these authors are blind to other viewpoints, but only that they take the position that they wish to pursue their own convictions and discover where they will lead.

A common reaction of authors to their task calls for comment. A majority of the authors, after they had completed a review of the relevant literature, expressed disappointment about the lack of substantive research in the area in which they had agreed to write a chapter. In many cases, after reviewing the literature, the author made the decision that the material was such that he could not write a chapter bringing the findings together—the complaint being that the research consisted of a patchwork of unrelated items that neither fitted together nor yielded a useful set of generalizations. Faced with such a problem, the typical response of the author was to begin to consider why the research had not been productive and how a productive program of research should be planned. A search for ideas that might form the basis of a worthwhile program of research then became the foundation for the chapter. In some areas covered in this volume, many excellent reviews of research have already been published. In such cases, the authors of the corresponding chapters concluded that their task should not be to provide just another review article.

Instead, most of these authors decided to refer the reader to the previously published reviews and then direct their own contributions toward a discussion of the research issues. The result is a volume in which there is considerable emphasis placed on a consideration of how research should be undertaken if it is to be productive. Not all chapters are of this character; there are some that summarize developing and growing programs of very important research.

An interesting point to report in connection with the complaints of authors concerning the quality of material reviewed is that although there has certainly been an improvement in the statistical design of studies over the last decade, a corresponding improvement in conceptual design is often not apparent. Of what avail is it to apply excellent statistical design to the execution of poorly conceived research? Perhaps the emphasis on statistical design in graduate training programs in education needs to be balanced by an effort to train students in the knowledge acquired in the behavioral sciences on conceptualizing problems.

The reaction of the authors reflects a disappointment in the advance in substantive knowledge of teaching during the last decade. Indeed, in looking over the collected chapters, one cannot help but be concerned about the lack of progress that has been made in relation to the large sums of money invested in the enterprise by the federal government. The latter statement is, of course, not true of every area of research related to teaching, for there are some, such as the early education area, in which considerable advances have been made. However, the heavy emphasis in this volume on what is wrong with educational research must not be attributed to any author's particular love for hammering at issues of method, but it reflects the general level of inadequacy of much of the research that has been undertaken. Those who participated in the first *Handbook* would never have guessed that, a decade later, authors of the *Second Handbook* would be having even greater difficulty in finding significant research to report than did their predecessors.

This experience in the development of the *Second Handbook* suggests that the time is ripe for taking a fresh look at the policies that guide the development of educational research. That such policies have been seriously misguided seems to be the consensus of many invited to contribute chapters—a consensus reached reluctantly after exhaustive examinations of the research available in the various areas studied by these authors.

Research on teaching does not cover a well-identified set of areas of study as does, for example, research on bridge design or research on internal combustion engines. For this reason, considerable judgment is involved in deciding what to include in a handbook such as the present one. The editorial board decided that the scope should be broad, but they did not hold out any hope that the *Second Handbook* would be comprehensive. Even after an editorial board, with the varied backgrounds of the present one, had listed all the problems and topics that could come to mind in the course of a meeting, there still would be other problems and other topics that different editorial boards might list. The *Second Handbook* may help to define the scope of the concept *research on teaching,* but it cannot define it to the satisfaction of all who may read it.

The boundaries of any handbook in the social and behavioral areas are also determined by other conditions related to the production of the materials involved. Editorial boards inevitably list some chapters for which authors cannot be found. Experts exist in these fields, but none may be willing to write a chapter to meet the production schedule. For example, the original outline of this *Handbook* included a chapter on research on group dynamics and its implications for teaching. Although there are many persons who have competence in this field of inquiry, none was found willing to prepare a chapter. The boundaries of knowledge covered are also influenced by the fact that authors have individualistic interpretations of the outlines provided. Authors inevitably give special emphasis to those aspects of knowledge in which they have special interest. Some gaps in coverage are also produced by prospective authors who fail to deliver manuscripts. The adequacy, or inadequacy, of the coverage of the *Second Handbook* is the result of a long contest between the editor and circumstances that tend to restrict what is included.

It is impossible to acknowledge all the help that has been given by individuals and institutions in the preparation of the *Second Handbook*. Some authors received extensive support from their institutions by having graduate assistants assigned to them. Western Michigan University provided me with the time necessary to undertake an editor's share of the work and a graduate assistant to work on the planning phase. Edward Schwab, who filled the latter role, contributed much more than can ordinarily be expected of a graduate assistant. The tedious task of checking the references was undertaken by Reiko Schwab. Furthermore, this kind of an enterprise would never reach completion without an efficient manager to keep track of the immense amount of detail that such a project entails. The latter task was undertaken by Sherry Bate, whose contribution calls for special acknowledgment. Finally, thanks must be expressed to Debora Wohlford, whose editorial and other skills contributed so much to the final publication phase of the volume.

Robert M. W. Travers
Western Michigan University
Summer 1972

Contents

PART III: Research on Special Problems of Teaching

CHAPTER 1

A History of the Impact of Research on Teaching

GERALDINE JONÇICH CLIFFORD
University of California, Berkeley

THE SCIENTIFIC MOVEMENT IN EDUCATION

The scientific movement in education has been part of the history of public schools in the United States for the whole of the twentieth century. Moreover, it has been a continuous movement, both in its activities and the expectations surrounding it. Four changes in the movement have been observed, however. The least of these has been in terminology: in its first four decades its investigations and products were commonly called "the science of education" or "educational science," terms later replaced by the more modest "educational research." The second change has been a broadening of its investigators, as social scientists joined psychologists in the study of educational issues—a change probably more apparent than real in that educational psychologists and their research "styles" have remained dominant (Cronbach & Suppes, 1969, pp. 135, 212; J. A. Johnston, 1970, p. 9).

A third change has been the sharp increase in research expenditures, largely through the entry of federal support; it was estimated that appropriations for research and development for 1966 through 1968 alone equaled three-fourths of all funds ever made available (United States Office of Education [USOE], 1969, p. 170). The fourth permutation in the scientific movement has been a greater questioning of its impact upon schools. This was one consequence of the increased expenditures, forcing a reckoning of the value received for the funds spent and promising what one observer (MacDonald, 1966, p. 604) judged as the most potentially embarrassing revelation in American educational history. This concern with impact also involved the general demand upon schools for "accountability."

Earlier students of education also occasionally had wondered if science made any difference in school operations. As early as 1921 Edward L. Thorndike commented that between his discoveries of certain facts of individual differences and their implementation in classroom management, he expected the "usual lag of thirty to fifty years" (Jonçich, 1968, p. 560). But what is remarkable is how long unquestioned, unexamined and unshaken was that optimism which had reigned at the outset of the scientific movement: that "to *know* the right is

1

to *do* the right," that "a progressive society" would certainly put to use its available science.

Much of that typically nineteenth-century faith in progress and knowledge (especially in scientific knowledge) gave way to twentieth-century skepticism. Consequently, much faith in educational research was lost, but many hopes remained.

One of the earliest hopes for research was its power to professionalize teaching and to win greater professional autonomy. Charles Judd and Ellwood P. Cubberley, investigators who remained close to school leaders, were representative exponents of this view. As Judd saw it, "The whole community must be shown by scientific methods that the school is a complex social institution, and that its conduct...requires constant study and expert supervision" (1918, p. 3). Cubberley thought it possible to change school administration "from a job depending upon political and personal favors to a scientific service capable of self-defense...." (1916, p. 328). Consequently there would be fewer such "blots upon the profession" as recounted in Dinsmore's *Teaching A District School: A Book for Young Teachers,* where a teaching post was secured by offering "a quart of whisky to the 'right' man" (1908, p. 18).

One of the complaints of educational research has been that it helped freeze classroom practices. It was argued, for example, that new school tests supported customary teaching practices in English composition (Lyman, 1929, p. 197). This stabilizing of practice was, however, an initial hope of educational science. Under a system where the formal legal power rested with laymen, with schools buffeted by competing interest groups and vulnerable to every fad, then (1889–1906) United States Commissioner of Education William T. Harris described the line of educational progress as a zigzag, moving from one extreme to the other. Hence the American school oftentimes appeared in need of the peaceful cove of scientific protection.

The stature of science in America was, in 1900, regnant in the university. And it was into the universities that the avantgarde moved pedagogy. Educators had concluded that "the department of education's place in the university must depend upon its ability to win the respect of those other departments in which the spirit of science largely prevails." Or, as a Cornell University speech professor succinctly put it in 1915, "Research is the standard way into the sheepfold" (Winans, p. 17). Into these research centers came undergraduate teaching courses and advanced-degree programs in school curriculum, teaching methodologies, school administration, educational psychology, and whatever other "scientific" fields might emerge to illuminate educational problems and train professionals. The day when "a little learning and 'a way with children' sufficed for a teacher" was considered over; there was growing "a body of scientific knowledge of children and of the laws of their development," the best corrective to the "shallow speculation and sentimentality" which mark the quack (Bennett, 1917, pp. 357f).

Within 15 years' time two doctoral degrees became available in education: the Ph.D., available since Clark University granted one in 1891, and the Doctor of Education, advertised as the "advanced professional degree." The two degrees became virtually indistinguishable (Buswell, McConnell, Heiss, & Knoell, 1966, p. 114; Wilder, 1966, pp. 153–175), however, as the line between "the professional" and "the scientific" grew indistinct through the vaulting ambitions of the professional and the activism of the scientist. A similar desire to partake of the scientist's prestige later led professional associations of science educators to support such projects as Physical Sciences School Curriculum Physics.

The high hopes held for the scientific movement did not, however, exclude reformers. Some assumed that change would proceed toward the "one right way" which science would discover—although teachers were reminded that a "genuine professional education continues all through life" (Bennett, 1917, p. 359). Science also held within itself "such growth...as that which comes to a tree in spring" (Bryan, 1895, p. 163); hence, schools in harmony with science held the possibility of a never-ending reordering of themselves. John Dewey told the Progressive Education Association in 1928, "Command of scientific methods and systematized subject-matter liberates individuals; it enables them to see new problems, devise new procedures, and, in general, makes for diversification rather than set uniformity" (Dewey, 1929, p. 12).

The presumption that research would improve schools was only one among science's several aims until a combination of events caused it to become central to whatever societal concern existed within educational science. The angst of the depression years and its release of radical thought shifted greater emphasis to research's role as "an agent of change" (Cronbach & Suppes, 1969, pp. 66–68).

By the 1960s some no longer perceived the chief threat to effective education as residing primarily outside the school—in greedy politicians, silly faddists, self-serving pressure groups, and other "enemies of the public schools." Rather, the threat was felt to be within the school, and much of what was "wrong with American education" lay with "the educational establishment," the "interlocking directorate," the securely tenured teacher, with racist white principals and school counselors, and in the "intellectually vapid" schools of education. The public discovered what a Rand Corporation consultant called the "urgent pathologies" of American schools: reading problems, unresponsiveness to community needs, unmet demands for ethnic and bilingual education, an inadequate vocational education, and neglect of the disadvantaged (Welch, Dec. 1970, p. 4).

When the Cooperative Research Act was passed by the United States Congress in 1954, the legislation's declared goal was to improve education at every level and in every subject area through educational research, development, demonstration and dissemination activities. In 1970 President Richard Nixon proposed a National Institute of Education "as a focus for educational research and experimentation in the United States." To the goal of improving the quality of public education he added those of enhancing equality and invigorating the ideal of local control of schools: "the decade of the 1970's calls for thoughtful redirection to improve our ability to make up for environmental deficiencies among the poor;...to begin the serious, systematic search for new knowledge needed to make educational opportunity truly equal;...to see to it that the flow of power in education goes toward, and not away from the local community" (Nixon, 1970, p. 28). Thus, though an unquestioning optimism had been routed and an insistent, widespread dissatisfaction with American schools had surfaced, something important had *not* changed: the scientific movement in education was not to be abandoned and its mission, if somewhat redirected, remained undiminished.

DETERMINING IMPACT: THE HISTORIOGRAPHIC DILEMMA

To establish the facts of the impact of educational research upon teaching itself, to advance quite certain proof, and to reconstruct a relationship of cause and effect is a near impossibility. If either the praise (including contracts, royalties, promotions) or the blame accorded educational research depended on the existence of hard data on its impact upon schools, there would be little of either.

Problems of Evidence

Two characteristics of the writing on the history of education (Cremin, 1965a) are pertinent to reconstructing the impact of research on teaching. First, it is predominantly a history of ideas. Second, most is history viewed from the top of the educational hierarchy. The two are, of course, related: when the perspective is that of the intellectual, it tends to dwell on theories and to cast its illumination upon pinnacles—the extraordinary "great statesmen" of education. If the recitations were instead those of teachers or students, better light might fall on school practices, on classroom life, on the ordinary event; indicating what typically happens in schools would provide better information for determining research effects. *Both* the histories of educational ideas, like Bowers's *The Progressive Educator and The Depression* (1969), and those "narrowly institutional" histories which are actually too rare, are needed.

This tendency of educational history to omit school culture is particularly misleading when the telling deals with the more "progressive" parts of the story, i.e. with change. Hence, the chronicler specifies the charges against the formerly tyrannical schools, illustrates the pedagogical sins of the old-fashioned teacher, paints an outline of the "bad old schooldays." The detailing of reformed practices, however, is typically sketchy, and change is reducible mostly to statements of ideals. Therefore the data are especially meager when research impact is sought in change.

Educational historiography has been faulted with being promotional and parochial (Bailyn, 1960). The error of promotionalism was exorcised in studies such as Katz's *The Irony of Early School Reform* (1968). Opportunities for determining impact should increase as historians turn to writing exposés—providing that exposure looks inside the schoolroom. Redress of the error of parochialism is more complex. As historians take a more comprehensive view of education (by looking to the family, other social groupings, the media, the work site, the community itself), and as they turn from the ideas of educators to broad social forces and society-wide phenomena for clues to educational development, there is danger

of further ignoring teaching behavior. Yet such histories may enhance our determination of research impact by placing schools (and such activities as research) in perspective. Our purposes, then, require both the interpretive insights from broad-gauge historiography and those narrower data on schoolroom practices.

The insufficient data on teaching practices are not caused solely by historiographic styles. The very structure of American educational control hampers all reporting. Consider the prized decentralization of administration, the absence of comprehensive coercive data-gathering power in the federal Office of Education, the built-in tensions between professional and lay responsibilities that encourage covertness and "public-relations" data, intense social sanctions against "snooping" and "French-style school inspectors," the egg-crate construction of school buildings and the "campus-like" suburban model; these all discourage confidence in the completeness, representativeness and validity of school data—and especially data on teaching practices.

An estimated 150,000 local school districts functioned in 1900. The movement to unified and consolidated districts reduced that by nine-tenths, or to only 15,000 local school districts, by 1970. Given fewer reporting districts and great increases in prescriptive state school legislation (and then federal programs with reporting requirements), more available and reliable information seems possible. But the tremendous increase in numbers of classrooms and teachers also created more opportunities for variation. Moreover, the average length of education completed by teachers increased from 12 years of schooling to 17 years between 1900 and 1970. The better-educated teacher was probably not more likely to "teach by the book"; the latter-day, professionalized teacher was probably not more closely supervised than formerly; and the 1970 principal was probably not the functional equivalent of the head-teacher of 1900. While socioeconomic and educational advances were creating a larger, more observant and confident body of parental classroom monitors, their data remained mostly isolated, impressionistic and political.

The teaching of reading affords a dramatic example of insufficient data on impact. More research has been done here than in any other curriculum area; the better studies in the sociology, psychology, and teaching of reading numbered some 4,000 by 1960 (Russell & Fea, 1963, p. 865). Yet Wilder found no diffusion studies undertaken to authenticate impact (1966, p. 3). Neither the annual summaries in *Reading Research Quarterly* nor the decennial surveys (Traxler, 1941, 1946, 1955, 1960) looked for implementation. *Reading Teacher* began its regular feature, "What Research Says to the Teacher," in 1948 without asking what teachers say back. Numerous other journals began research-reporting columns without treating impact; a perusal of *Arithmetic Teacher, Elementary English,* and *Social Education*—all with annual summaries—left the impact question untouched.

School superintendents were reported as uncertain of the meaning of "educational research" and unable to articulate its impact; when asked of familiar innovations in practice and programs they made such comments as, "Obviously, someone must have done some research on it," or "We know it was tried out before we introduced it." When asked to identify research and development activities having national influence, 64 percent could not answer and only 3.1 percent specified even one research project (Ross, 1958; USOE, 1969, p. 146).

Attempts to locate and evaluate research impact on teaching continually encounter the "evidence" of assertions. Some are negative—"Barring a few rare exceptions," teachers of industrial arts proceed uninfluenced by research (Worthington, 1963, p. 18)—without identifying the exceptions and without substantiation for the whole. Some assertions are positive, stating that some unspecified research fostered exciting, innovative practices, challenged existing with superior alternative methods, or certified present practices (Cook, Hovet, & Kearney, 1956, p. 224). Sometimes the message of the assertion is mixed, as when one observer indicated that attempts to apply psychological findings to schooling are constant, the implication being that some were successful attempts, yet later stating that the lag between research and practice is "one of the saddest features" of educational psychology (Amatora, 1957, pp. 175, 179). Finally, assertive statements are made concerning cases where examples are offered that dispute or make ambiguous the overall conclusion of the study. Consider a survey (Gibson, 1967) which suggested that research, development, and revision appeared "in all dimensions" of the social studies; the example of basic research offered was investigations of political socialization. But the subsequent discussion conceded that the research had no effect in that schools paid less attention to citizenship education in the lower grades while the research strongly indicated that the ability to effect political socialization decreases with age.

While far less common than assertions about impact, examples and illustrations are taken more seriously. Later sections of this chapter will discuss some of these, but two cases here will indicate why most examples also constitute "soft data" on research's impact on teaching. In her comprehensive survey of primary reading, Chall stated that, "It soon became clear that the findings of research in beginning reading ... are not an important factor in influencing decisions about beginning reading instruction" (1967, p. 288). Aside from other "clues" and her intuition, Chall's evidence consisted of the fact that, in extensive school visitations, no teacher or administrator said that he was impelled to change a practice by reading a research report or consulting research findings. The possibility is that research impact was too narrowly conceived—i.e. by reference only to changing practice. If professionals read research it may be used to retain as well as to change some teaching practice. Moreover, not reporting such research effect does not constitute proof: research may have been read and it or its effect forgotten or simply not volunteered. The question also arises as to whether it is necessary to limit research, and hence research impact, to "raw" research—to "reports of experiments" and "descriptions of findings."

Another kind of example is reference to particular bodies of investigations in a teaching field. Russell considered Ruth Strang's studies in his "Reading research that makes a difference," and maintained that Strang's research "widely influenced reading instruction" and "clearly pointed to the need for developmental reading instruction" in secondary and higher education (Russell, 1961, p. 76). It remains soft data because Russell did not establish that developmental reading instruction actually eventuated, nor did he prove that, where inaugurated, it was due to research since, arguably, the upward extension toward universal education caused higher incidences of reading problems in high schools and colleges and attempts to overcome this practical problem possibly resulted in instructional innovation (Chall, 1967, p. 289).

Some other types of "examples" have only the credibility of "conventional wisdom"— as advancing the theory that the social-psychological research of Kenneth Clark encouraged the Supreme Court's *Brown* versus *Topeka* decision (1954) and generated innovative programs for educating the disadvantaged. There is also evidence that has a certain "face validity"—as the assertion that research-based, standardized tests conferred greater weight on test results and thereby more strongly conditioned teacher behavior than did the use of teacher-made examinations.

Problems of Interpretation

It has been contended that historical inquiry did not flourish in a century dominated by empirical and statistical research modes, that penetrating historical questions were accordingly left unasked (Cronbach & Suppes, 1969, pp. 56–58). The asking of such historical questions about research impact requires examination of several assumptions. One has already been challenged: the supposition that research would necessarily have effect and of a salutary kind. Another assumption remained dominant: that research impact *must* be measured in change —"against the standard of that which might have been" (Jonçich, 1968, p. 574). This attitude was perhaps inevitable; research flourished because the society talked of change, the era was dominated by philosophical reformism, and the American school's mission was evangelical. After 1950 mere change often seemed insufficient; talk was heard of "revolutionary" change, of a "mass reformulation" of teaching and learning (John Goodlad, in Haskew & McLendon, 1968, p. 365).

This history, however, recognizes the corroborative and the conservative functions of research which align it with the characteristics of bureaucratic public institutions. "People are more conservative in their attitude toward educational innovations than ... in any other field of activity," reminded the superintendent of the Boise, Idaho, schools in 1915, schools being "the last institution to respond to the changing demands of modern life" (Meek, 1915, p. 57).

The 1970 presidential message on educational research contended that, "We must stop pretending ... that we are significantly applying science and technology to the techniques of teaching..." (Nixon, 1970). The adverb "significantly" raises another issue in interpreting research impact: what *is* the test of significance in history? how *does* one assign weights in qualitative research?

It can be argued that, in the magnitude of American public education, ostensibly minor changes may loom significant; vast economic and social resources are recommitted when an adjusting of detail spreads (Oettinger, 1969, p. 3). For example, the junior high school was described as "a new institution created in recognition of the changes in pupil nature which occur at the beginning of and throughout adolescence" (Caldwell & Courtis, 1925, p. 114). Not much actual research on adolescence preceded the appearance of the junior high school in 1910. One cannot say, however, that it was insufficient research. There was much enthusiasm about what was uncovered; G. Stanley Hall's *Adolescence* (1904) was a monumental work and that generation apparently believed that it knew enough. However else it is evaluated, the junior high school qualifies as historically significant.

Another case is handwriting instruction, once a costly item in the curriculum, often employing penmanship teachers and supervisors for a subject which occupied many school hours. Researching the teaching of handwriting and devising scales to measure achievement were common activities from 1910 to 1920. Before midcentury the subject withered in time and prominence and specialist teachers became rare (T. L. Harris, 1960, p. 617). If research merited even partial credit for these reallocations of teacher and student energies, its impact was significant.

Another issue concerns how research effects upon attitudes are to be interpreted. Is it impact if teachers only think they act from scientific principles? How great must be the discrepancy between teacher attitudes and teacher behavior for attitudes to be discounted as evidence of research impact? Ralph Tyler has argued that research values ought to be measured by increased understanding, and that "we can easily recognize values of this sort" (Banghart, 1960, p. 92). The now-widespread view that learning is many-sided and education is complex is a reconception that evidences research impact irrespective of data on practice.

In fields where teacher attitudes appeared unaffected by research and opposition to research was manifested, the issue is moot.

A 1963 survey of attitudes of music teachers showed little change over 30 years (Horner, 1965, pp. 4, 217), and the challenge that music educators become "research-minded" (Jones & Evans, 1951) was blunted by the belief that psychological influences foster "utilitarian" teaching aims—violating a cherished belief in "music for music's sake" (Funchess, 1949, p. 349). Similar identifications of research with "usefulness" and "relevance," and resistance to studies of pupil interests were reported present in teachers of literature; several authorities declared their opposition to research because "good literature justifies itself" (Temp, 1964, p. 195). Art education also depended upon a discipline of unabashed, qualitative valuation; opposition to analysis and inquiry seemed strong among practicing artists who also taught (Beittel, 1960, p. 77; Hausman, 1963, pp. 1101f). Even science education had skeptics: "In physics teaching, as in most human endeavors, it's the loving that counts," concluded an editorial in *The Physics Teacher* (Swartz, 1969, p. 438).

The reading field appeared otherwise. A wide conviction existed that science determined the teaching methods to be used with the basal readers; most teachers believed that school readers were based on "definite scientific proof" (Chall, 1967, p. 300). Wilder's investigations showed the same belief held by 66 percent of the teachers and 58 percent of the principals in his sample; in contrast, less than one in five reading experts held this belief (Wilder, 1966, pp. 108, 141, 234).

The inability of science to certify that some one teaching method is superior—as in the remedial teaching of arithmetic (Wilson, 1941, p. 55)—does not prevent inconclusive research from being accepted as confirming evidence. Schoolmen have also erroneously assumed that research has generated the use of teacher aides, ability groupings and elementary departmentalization (USOE, 1969, p. 147).

In military training the discrepancy between official policy and practice is probably less than anywhere else in education, perhaps with the exception of the religious orders. When a military development unit prepares teaching manuals, films and models based on behavioral research, the directives, regulations and the supporting social system of authority increase our confidence that impact was actually being observed irrespective of teacher attitudes (Lavisky, 1969). The compulsion system and bureaucratic efficiency of public education are more doubtful, however, and attitudes and preferences *do* matter. A discrepancy between articulated teacher beliefs and teaching practices in providing for individual differences, recognizing pupil experiences, and relating to student interests has been documented with one sample of elementary teachers (Oliver, 1953). Teaching practices in social studies often were found incompatible with the theory offered in teacher training (Duffey, 1954)—such theory many times being "informed" by research. But such investigations are too few and incomplete, and the doubtful impression persists that teachers come to an awareness, acquire values and assume a teaching posture roughly consonant with the concerns of 70 years of educational and psychological research (Sieber & Wilder, 1965). This impression itself has probably confounded attempts to apply research and to ascertain impact.

One of the main problems of interpretation is to establish that research *itself* caused change, stabilized practice, or increased understanding. Summaries of various disciplines occasionally admitted that numerous factors dictated classroom practices. Thus the modern social studies program was described as an outgrowth of recommendations dating from the National Education Association's (NEA's) Committee of Ten (1893), the Committee of Seven of the American Historical Association (1899), and the Committee on Social Studies of the 1918 Commission on the Reorganization of Secondary Education (Gross & Badger, 1960, p. 1297). Similar national committees were credited with influencing virtually every

field. But their reports were laced with a popularized, digested educational science. Of the reportedly influential 1920 Committee on Science Education, Powers wrote that the Committee's psychology was shaped by Thorndike's: a functionalist, stimulus-response psychology stressing habit formation and specific learning tasks and urging teachers to inform students of learning outcomes (in Whipple, 1932, I, p. 75).

If influences other than research could have exerted *research* impact, then conversely, what appears to have emanated from science may have originated elsewhere. Practices which have been "researched" need not have grown out of research (Bereiter, 1965, p. 96). Recognition of the "lack of any fixed relation between a mark and the ability which it is supposed to measure" originated not in that research which disclosed great inconsistencies in grading practices, but in every school where it was observed that "some teachers are chronically severe markers while others are notoriously easy" (Bennett, 1917, p. 153). Both awareness of individual differences and provisions for them preceded the relevant research. Desires to adjust to each pupil's differing achievements and to accommodate differences among students prompted many reorganizations before 1917. However much support they received from the retardation research of Ayres and Thorndike, the achievement and ability studies of Bonser, Thompson, and Courtis, and the surveys of Judd and Strayer, these reorganizations date back at least to 1870 when St. Louis's superintendent, W. T. Harris, inaugurated six- to eight-week terms to reduce the penalty of nonpromotion and to place the makeup work close to the need (Bennett, 1917, p. 128).

The foregoing suggests that a history of the impact of research on teaching must be content with indicating how teaching may have been associated with scientific ideas rather than with proving that they actually have been so associated or that the association was prepotent. What follows, therefore, is an indication of the cases for and against the impact of the scientific movement on teaching. An outline of a general theory concerning the interaction of research and practical experience with other educational and social tensions will follow that, and the chapter will be concluded by considering some of history's "lessons" for future educational research.

THE CASE FOR THE IMPACT OF EDUCATIONAL SCIENCE

The Rhetorical Case

Midway through this century, the National Research Council and the National Academy of Sciences contrasted the separation of research psychologists from schoolmen with the situation during the years 1890–1920, when basic research "assisted importantly in the shaping of educational developments, theories and methods" (National Research Council, 1958b, p. 4). The Committee on Educational Research of the National Academy of Education described the schools reported in the 1938 Yearbook of the National Society for the Study of Education as "profoundly influenced" by educational psychology (Cronbach & Suppes, 1968, p. 45).

Such positive evaluations of the earlier period are not made only by nostalgic observers looking back at the past; often the participants themselves perceived the effects of science about them. Psychology and the measurement movement received much credit, for, due to their influence, "teachers are at last beginning to act on the belief that children differ...," while the Detroit schools' use of a million standardized tests annually exhibited "the spirit and practical use of scientific research" (Caldwell & Courtis, 1925, pp. 109, 124). In 1930 Carleton Washburne noted that recommendations for the placement of arithmetic topics were being made according to requisite mental age and arithmetic ability scores because grade level meant little when pupils and

schools varied as much as research showed (Whipple, 1930, p. 669). A three-volume research summary in science education claimed that these studies were "of paramount value and significance in the teaching of science..." (Curtis, 1931, p. 4).

Not all who perceived scientific impact thought it beneficial. Psychologist William McDougall lampooned "sarbon"—stimulus-response bond (S-R bond)—learning theory, regretted its status as "the indispensable key to practical as well as to theoretical problems," and lamented "its presence in every school" as a false science of human nature (1930, pp. 32, 48).

Some observers also saw research impact continuing in the middle period. The school surveys which revealed high levels of retardation had finally forced a lowering of promotion standards, and teachers passed their students more frequently (Boyer, 1935, p. 12; Friedman & Kelley in Rivlin & Schueler, 1943, p. 617). Buswell thought "much improvement" in the teaching of arithmetic had resulted from a few excellent research studies done between 1920 and 1940 (1951, p. 283). About physical education instruction Rarick claimed that "many of the concepts which have come from recent research are being put into practice"; the clearest exception was in boxing, where neither research nor sporting deaths halted the increase in boxing programs (1960, pp. 974, 977). A University of Michigan psychologist described college teaching as increasingly grounded upon research (McKeachie, 1954).

There were spokesmen, too, for the view that research impact could not be found until one looked to the 1950s. The chairman of the President's Science Advisory Committee set the beginning of educational research and development impact at about the time of curriculum-development projects in high-school physics (Zacharias, 1964, p. vii). Sidney Pressey was even more pessimistic; he felt that until the advanced placement program, schooling was little affected by the years of research and experimentation on individual differences and independent study (1969, p. 353).

The Search for Evidence

Evidence in the curriculum and materials of the school. A noteworthy characteristic of the scientific movement was that some who investigated also edited schoolbooks, authored texts for teachers, consulted with schoolmen, and conducted lectures and workshops. In the reading field the experts' connections with publishing helped to establish the presumption that the books were based upon science, and pupils' textbooks and teachers' methods were united in the basal reading series with their detailed teachers' manuals (Wilder, 1966, pp. 54, 55). But the historic dominance of teaching by the textbook was more general. In 1962 textbooks were reported still the prime determinants of what students studied (NEA, 1962, p. 23).

Reportedly the modern textbook author was becoming surrounded by an atmosphere of educational science (Buswell & Judd, 1925, p. 138; Woolbert, 1927, p. vii). Investigations of the words used by adults, the problems they solved, and the needs they recognized, together with studies of pupil interests, their relative difficulties with mastering different tasks, and their problems in understanding pushed textbooks, workbooks and drill sheets toward reform. The textbook enthusiasts hailed the changes in content, in attractive appearance, and in adjustment to the tastes and abilities of children as great and far-reaching. Spelling books were reduced from some 40,000 words of the 1850 version to the 3,000–4,000 words of the 1920 speller (Caldwell & Courtis, 1925, p. 120f). Word-usage research was used to discredit the study of grammar (Pilgrim, 1966, p. 23). Word problems in arithmetic were often recast, using a simpler vocabulary. After 1921 E. L. Thorndike's *The Teacher's Word Book* replaced the earlier word-usage lists of Ayres and Buckingham,

and test makers, school encyclopedia writers, and authors of children's fiction could adjust their work to psychological principles (Jonçich, 1968, p. 393).

Later textbooks also showed less "mental gymnastics" content, more problem-solving situations rather than memorization tasks, and a search for life-like situations to introduce concepts and provide practice. The same deductions from research which removed "phthisic" and "quassia" from spellers reduced the incidence of such arithmetic problems as "What is the quotient of one ten-thousandth divided by ten thousand?" By 1919 E. P. Cubberley credited the scientific movement with the fact that "we do not now teach a third as much arithmetic or grammar as we used to do; the facts in geography and the dates and battles of history are made much less prominent than they used to be; and bone and muscle and nerve physiology and the memorization of the Constitution have been displaced by hygiene and community civics" (1919, p. 444).

Comparisons of textbooks do not adequately illustrate the potential influence of whole learning theories. Consider the connectionist psychology of Thorndike, whose ideas on arithmetic teaching may have "constituted a pedagogical revolution as far-reaching and as important" as the "new math" reforms of forty years later; indeed, Thorndike's work represented a more serious and thorough attempt to ground teaching practices in a comprehensive learning theory than did the "new math" (Cronbach & Suppes, 1969, p. 97). The *Thorndike Arithmetics* (1917b, 1924), like his *Psychology of Algebra* (1923)—which originated in courses on "the psychology of the elementary school subjects" at Columbia's Teachers College—were systematic, extensive applications of psychological formulations.

Teachers' guidebooks into the new educational landscape, such as *School Efficiency* (Bennett, 1917) and *Then & Now in Edu-*

cation (Caldwell & Courtis, 1925), enjoyed debunking the mental discipline arguments bolstering the old curriculum, its formalized teaching methods and its arid textbooks (Cameron, 1918). Bennett (1917, p. 116) reminded his readers that teachers had taught under authoritative statements that learning arithmetic trains a pupil to reason. Unlike "the old days [when] it was thought not to matter much what the child studied so long as he did not like it," the modern course of study was subjected to requirements that 1) its values be stated in *specific,* preferably measurable form so the outcomes could be shown to have occurred, and 2) it be fitted to the growth and development of individual pupils (Caldwell & Courtis, 1925, p. 120). Some research indicated that abstract ideas of number develop out of many concrete experiences, while other studies sought to discover the character of effective drill; teaching methods which increased the use of arithmetic in practical situations were thereby encouraged (Kinney, in Rivlin & Schueler, 1943, pp. 52f). Meanwhile, research on pupil readiness for arithmetic and studies of difficulty in learning the various number combinations were credited with producing more teaching materials and systematic study in the primary grades (Buswell, 1960, pp. 66f).

The situation was similar elsewhere. A 1906 survey (F. S. Hoyt, p. 473) found substantial agreement on this ranking of the goals of English grammar instruction: it disciplines the mind, prepares for the study of other languages, gives command of an indispensable terminology, enables one to improve his usage, and aids in interpreting literature. Two decades of research on the transfer of training and numerous studies of the disciplinary value of formal grammar were credited with a subsequent "decline in confidence in formal grammar as a disciplinary subject" (Lyman, 1929, p. 23) and a new emphasis upon "functional grammar." This functional grammar was itself "researched" (Stormzand & O'Shea,

1924, p. 224), although the research was not cited, for the Committee on the Reorganization of English (1917) simply asserted that "It is a mistake to regard English as merely a formal subject" (Hosic, 1917, p. 26). English textbooks, meanwhile, became increasingly graded and differentiated, so that the fifth-grader and college sophomore were no longer assigned the same book—as was common in the nineteenth century (Carr, 1927).

Reading, more than grammar or arithmetic, was closest to basic psychological questions—exemplified by Thorndike's reconception of reading as reasoning rather than word-calling, and by Judd's popularization of a psychology of "the higher mental processes." Favoring a learning theory which stressed the formation of discrete stimulus-response connections, Arthur Gates gave impetus to the diagnosis and remedial treatment of reading difficulties; his researches explained most reading failures as the result of groups of specific related factors rather than by such "worthless" general explanations as bad attitude, restlessness, laziness or low intelligence (Russell, 1961, p. 75). Subsequently diagnostic test batteries and specially prepared remedial materials were employed by many public schools.

Reading research accumulated before World War II and reading surpassed arithmetic as the most important subject in the elementary-school curriculum. Grouping children within a classroom either by reading test scores or teacher inspection became a commonplace device for accommodating pupil variability—even when arithmetic teaching remained on a class-wide basis. The assignment of different children to different activities was supported by a line of research which included the Buswell and Judd studies of the reading process, Thorndike's study of reading errors, and Gates's on visual techniques. The thrust of this research was toward an instructional program which decreased oral reading, emphasized comprehension, and expanded word recognition approaches—constituting what Russell called "a revolution in teaching materials and in methods..." (1961, p. 74f).

Investigations in science education began in 1904 when school children in Passaic, New Jersey, were queried on their knowledge of common plants and animals (Chambers, 1904). In 1910 the first reported science learning study compared the relative effectiveness of two approaches to teaching secondary-school zoology. Most of the several hundred studies of the next four decades were comparable to those in other fields: status studies of pupil interests, analyses of adults' science needs, experimental studies of the results of using motion pictures or laboratory drawings, attempts to identify the teachable elements of the scientific method (Curtis, 1950). Researches of the 1920s were credited with bringing about two changes in teaching practices: Gerald Craig's investigations separated elementary science from nature study and turned teaching emphasis toward science principles, and S. R. Power's science vocabulary studies reduced the vocabulary loads of high-school texts and identified the critical scientific terms—these studies causing an impact "easily traceable" in subsequent textbooks and research (Curtis, 1950, pp. 63f). An article in the *Music Educators Journal* declared that "the superiority of an inductive approach" in concept development had made that approach "a cornerstone of educational theory" (Olsen, 1968, p. 59).

The work of Jean Piaget in cognitive development and the espousal by psychologist Jerome Bruner of "inquiry" approaches to teaching-learning were thought central to whatever part psychological research would play in latter-day curriculum change. One probable vehicle for carrying such research into classrooms was via new curriculum materials. For the preparation and dissemination of those materials a combine of scholars or scientists, federal or foundation officials, and a publisher was usually assembled. In the case of the Physical Science Study Committee (PSSC), over 250 scientists, teachers and specialists were involved, development cost $4.5 million in federal funds, and 20 percent of all secondary-school students were reported using PSSC materials within seven years of the project's beginning (Marsh, 1964). By 1968 one-half of all chemistry students were reported using the CHEM Study course and sales of text materials in Biological Sciences Curriculum Study (BSCS) Biology and School Mathematics Study Group (SMSG) Mathematics were reported at several million copies (USOE, 1969, pp. 144f).

It was said that because of past failures in upgrading teacher skills such curriculum project committees reputedly tried to make the materials as self-contained and "teacher-proof" as possible (Oettinger, 1969, p. 102). The movement for standardized tests also hoped to eliminate subjectivity and variability; some textbook authors had made their products so foolproof that misuse was believed impossible. Noting that the preferred method of teaching subtraction had gone back and forth, Wilson (1941, p. 44) rejected the idea that the teaching method was the critical factor. "The proper placement of the teaching of the process with reference to the maturity of the child, the development of an adequate drill service, or even the setting up of proper standards of proficiency when the process is taught may be more important"; the "curriculum scientist" thought *he* could handle these tasks. Despite such reasoning, however, "teacher-development" activities were often prominent. The budget of PSSC financed over 100 teacher-retraining courses and thousands of teachers attended summer institutes and other workshops—indicating at least some teacher interest in furthering the impact of "research" on teaching.

Evidence in the teachers' perceptions of pupils. Of the ideal school desk for 1917 it was written: "The use of light-colored woods finished in bright tones and glossy surface is not in good taste or in harmony with the studious purposes of the classroom unless perhaps in primary grades" (Bennett, 1917, p. 54). That this advice now sounds quaint may testify to what Getzels calls a change in the very environment of learning, as the ideal school shifted from a teacher-centered to a learner-centered focus. Having altered their conception of the learner, teachers increasingly acted as if pupils were dynamic expressers of needs, attitudes, values, interests and conflicts rather than the psychologically "empty organisms" they had previously been assumed to be (USOE, 1969, pp. 139f). These views, combined with such results from learning research as Thorndike's on reward and punishment, have eliminated the earlier charge that teachers by the tens of thousands daily used "the rule of the rod and the sway of the switch" (Bennett, 1917, p. 270).

A psychology of personality emerged to add its influence. Speech teachers found arguments for the social purposes of speech buoyed by personality studies. They were given "conclusive evidence" that speech disorders could trigger personality disorders, that speech is itself "a phase of personality," that because personality is largely the result of social interaction, "any limitation in the means of expression and communication correspondingly stifles and distorts personality" (Murray, 1954, p. 8). A popular speech text, *Modern Speech,* added to those ancient aims of rhetoric—improving one's faculty to order and organize one's ideas and express them with effectiveness—these modern goals of speech teaching: furthering the student's growth in poise and confidence, self-control, emotional balance, sense of humor, courtesy and tact (Irwin & Roseberger, 1951, p. iii).

Chall found American teachers more knowledgeable and confident about child psychology than British teachers (1967, p. 285). Frequently the materials to which American teachers had access were indeed confidently framed. Bennett's *School Efficiency* (1917) was immodestly offered to

teachers as a bridge between theory and practice. A typical textbook in reading (A. J. Harris, 1962) contained many such authoritative conclusions as that the satisfactory teaching of reading requires $1\frac{1}{2}$ hours daily in the first grade, or that the study of prefixes, suffixes and roots is most beneficial in vocabulary building with bright children. A guide to developments in elementary-school mathematics (Glennon & Callahan, 1968) liberally used such phrases as "The classroom teacher can be quite confident that...."

Such authoritativeness furthered a certain precison in talking of, and perhaps in dealing with, pupils. The language of numbers, employed by educational research and especially by the testing movement, *seemed* precise. As the decades passed, increasingly more aspects of student life were described quantitatively: data on I.Q. and achievement levels in the various subjects, scores on measurements of cognitive style and attitudes, statistics on probable achievement according to race or social class. By 1963 even the art teacher could discover the kindergartner's art vocabulary by reading the periodical, *Art Education.* A criticism arose that, from knowing a pupil in this way, schools then inferred what could be expected of him and taught or counseled accordingly; the tests were determining students' fates rather than merely describing them. Research into the "Pygmalion" phenomenon (Kranz, Weber, & Fishell, 1970; Rosenthal & Jacobson, 1968) followed decades of disagreement about test usage. What the argument and the research suggested was that teachers altered their behaviors toward their pupils according to whether they perceived them as having high, average or low academic potential.

During the twentieth century the view that the variation among pupils was an important psychological fact became popular; numerous plans to accommodate these differences evolved. One approach, as has been discussed, was to eliminate from the curriculum much of the useless, difficult and ab-

struse material at which the less motivated
and slower learner often failed. More
direct programs were also instituted: programs that held standards constant but increased the instructional time for slow
students; programs that maintained a uniform time allotment but varied the course
of study according to ability; contract plans
that allowed students to select certain portions of the curriculum to complete at their
own pace (Cook, 1958). The merits of
acceleration (skipping grades) were debated, for research was unable to prove
whether it was advantageous (Carter, 1960,
p. 586; Norris & Noonan, 1941, p. 78). Any
interest in gifted pupils was remarkable,
however, given the popular prejudice within
public education against a privileged class or
intellectual elite (Thorndike, 1941, p. 421).
Widely held misconceptions about the
gifted—their proneness to ill-health, early
death, and insanity, a great "imbalance"
between their intellectual and social abilities
—were challenged by the researches of Leta
Hollingworth and Lewis Terman. Becoming a teacher of a gifted class became a
prized assignment in the 1950s.

Those perceived as the disadvantaged received earlier and more abundant attention.
By 1913 special provisions for the mentally
retarded were reported in 108 districts
(Wallin, 1917, p. 49). When the problems
of the poor were explained as the results of
educational and/or cultural disadvantage,
there was research available to support special programs. Basic research included
studies of the effects of deprivation on
animals and humans. Between these and
the moving personal accounts of disadvantage were social-psychological studies of
children's attitudes and self-images, of family structure, of motivational systems, of the
mechanisms of prejudice. And, when it was
declared that the 1970s required "a thoughtful redirection to improve our ability to
make up for environmental deficiencies of
the poor," there *was* research upon the early
childhood years, making it possible for the
President of the United States to say that

his administration's commitment to an expansion of preschool education "was based
on new scientific knowledge about the
development of intelligence...in the first
five years..." (Nixon, 1970). There was,
too, the model of Israel, where researchers
had already been involved in improving
child-care services (Smilansky, 1962, p.
280).

THE CASE AGAINST THE IMPACT
OF EDUCATIONAL SCIENCE

The Rhetorical Case

William Bagley looked back on the expectations he had had in 1900—that within three
decades the teacher's art would depend as
much upon scientific principles as did the
physician's—and was surprised at the small
effect educational science had had on schools
(1934, p. 194). In 1948 another early participant, W. W. Charters, was worried about
how little educational research had been
translated into action (Foshay, 1955, p. 169).
Considering the great impact research had
had upon industry and agriculture, the
director of the Bureau of Educational Research at the University of Minnesota
lamented the virtual absence of research
impact in education (C. Hoyt, 1953, p. 59).
Such assertions mounted after 1950. Stephen
Corey claimed that "relatively few decisions
about instructional materials or methods are
based upon scientific evidence" (1954, p.
465). Julian Stanley agreed, believing that
most teaching decisions issued from "col-
loquial, anecdotal, or administrative considerations" (1957, p. 201). Notwithstanding
many changes made in the high-school
curriculum, a Florida professor concluded
that the great bulk of research gained no
classroom implementation; a Columbia
Teachers College professor concurred
(Ahrens, 1956, p. 366; Beach, 1954, p. 351).

After the decline of the action-research
movement—which prompted many negative
assessments of impact and will be discussed
later in the chapter—researchers themselves

expressed disappointment. "One looks in vain for discoveries that have had any impact on the enterprise which educational research was intended to serve," said Carl Bereiter, concluding that "a field of endeavor that never changes anything but itself is more appropriately regarded as an art or a sport than as a science" (1965, pp. 95, 96). To supplement essentially impressionistic reports (Fattu, 1960; Griffiths, 1959) of the minimal effect of research upon educational understanding, and its even slighter impact upon school functionings, there were disheartening clues in the large-scale Sieber and Lazarsfeld study (1966) of the research enterprise. As educational research entered its eighth decade, its reconstruction was called for on the grounds of scant evidence of impact as measured by improved daily school operations (Shulman, 1970, p. 371).

The reformation promised by federal funding was also found deficient. Sixteen years after its passage, the Cooperative Research Act (1954) was discounted as having generated no *known* effects on improved schooling (Wolf, 1970a, p. 1). The research unit of the federal Office of Education was consistently criticized by schoolmen as not having contributed products that made "a visible difference" (Gallagher, 1970, p. 2). Research in higher education had a short history, but strong resistance to applied social research was reported in some administrative and faculty circles (Trow, 1962).

Experts in social studies teaching were especially critical of a field where most of the techniques tried or advocated were not based on research (Gross & Badger, 1960, p. 1305). In their zeal to create and implement new curricula, many teachers and school systems were charged with having failed to consult research (Gibson, 1967, I, p. 225). The then-president of the National Council for the Social Studies, Richard Gross, viewed elementary-school social studies as frozen in a 30-year-old mold and the high-school courses dominated by committee recom-

mendations dating to 1893 (in Gibson, 1967, II, p. 36). The same was said of science education to 1960; despite fifty years of research, the pivotal influences emanated from nonscientific sources: the Committee of Ten, the 1916 Commission, and various yearbooks (Smith & Anderson, 1960, p. 1216). Frederick R. Smith maintained that, if measured by research impact on teaching, few, if any, fields of instruction in public education would fare well (in Massialas, 1962, p. vii). And he could easily find agreement among other experts, ranging from those in the latter-day glamour area of compensatory education to those in spelling where the research history was long and the sex appeal was gone.

Of the various programs for disadvantaged students, one observer claimed they suffered alike from one basic difficulty: "they [the programs] are based on sentiment rather than facts" (Gordon, 1967, pp. 7f). Addressing the American Psychological Association in 1966, Albert E. Myers declared that the impact of research on educational action-programs for the poor "seems to me to be small, microscopic, infinitesimal; there may be none." He also warned against expecting conclusive information on impact because of governmental requirements that these programs be evaluated—such evaluations usually constituting mere exercises in report writing (Myers, 1970, pp. 371, 374).

Little impact was expected in the fine arts, given their smaller formal commitment to rebuilding practice on a scientific base. One observation described art education as having "to its discredit, a history of neglecting findings proper to its own advancement" (Beittel, 1960, p. 77). The situation still resembled that of twenty years earlier when Schultz, Ross, and Moore lamented the persistence of old ways despite knowledge of individual differences and the possibility of moving art topics from logical to psychological bases (1941, p. 62). The same was said of music education: learning theory went unapplied, while traditional methods prevailed (Thorpe, 1958, p. 163). An example was the omission or relaxation of musical training in the later elementary and early secondary years, in contradiction to the continuity found in developmental studies (Horner, 1965, p. 51). Hendrickson (1960, p. 909) pointed out that modern curriculum and instructional materials in music bore "little resemblance to their origins in the colonial singing school and in early public-school work"; the development, which had been gradual, however, he attributed to forces other than research.

Literature was another subject where resistance to research was obvious. Hence, virtually every aspect of literature education remained in need of research, with teaching almost entirely dependent upon opinion and tradition (Pooley, 1941, p. 465). This situation appeared unchanged in 1960 according to a survey in *Encyclopedia of Educational Research* (Pooley, 1960). More surprising was the assertion, also in 1960, that research had had little influence upon either the behavior or the thinking of science teachers (Watson & Cooley, p. 298). But an optimistic note was sounded for the larger language field in 1962, when it was predicted that 30 years of discoveries by linguistic scientists would surely "revolutionize the teaching of English," a prediction supported by the attention given to linguistics in conventions, committees, journal articles and textbooks (Link & Schuster, p. 294). Indeed, Carroll (1963, p. 1094) thought foreign language teaching had already profited from linguistic science, although educational research had had little impact on teaching methods, but had contributed primarily to knowledge of test construction, foreign-language aptitude and bilingualism. And despite their special implications for instructional technology, the advances in communications research and the creation of programs, schools, and departments of communications in various universities had little impact on school practices (Saettler, 1968, p. 320).

In arithmetic, the subject which once occupied more than half the elementary-school day, the evidence indicated that teaching had been altered by the work of those like Thorndike. As Gestalt and other field psychologies became popular alternatives to S-R behaviorism, they influenced the recommendations of two arithmetic yearbooks (Reeve, 1935; 1941) of the National Council of Teachers of Mathematics. The third such yearbook (in 1960) declared it almost a certainty, however, that classroom practice had *not* caught up with those earlier recommendations (Grossnickle, 1960, p. 3).

Concepts described as originating in research affected physical education in that programs better related to the facts of child and adolescent development were designed. However, one specialist who judged these concepts "theoretically sound" reported that they were not yet implemented and that the experiences of successful teachers and the beliefs of outstanding performers remained the bases for most teaching methods (Rarick, 1960, p. 981f). The situation was similar in vocational education; those who read research in the journals failed to see the advantages of the methods promoted by some "cloud-nine researcher" (Worthington, 1963, p. 18).

By stabilizing the curriculum, textbooks had done much to cause a great similarity among American schools. Educational science, however, deserved less credit than did the acumen of textbook publishers, who knew better how to profit by tendencies to imitate and to repeat that which is familiar. Gross thought that textbooks in social studies had changed primarily in size, cost and pictures (Gibson, 1967, II, p. 37).

The Search for Evidence

Evidence in the old curriculum. Reflecting on improving schools through research led to the tired observation that "We might ask why we bother at all, since there is ample evidence that our research in the past has led to little change" (MacDonald, 1966, p. 603). The evidence was perhaps "ample," but not "hard." As Oettinger (1969, pp. 91f) pointed out, even the simple problem of how many schools, students or teachers used Harvard Project Physics could not be solved conclusively with the varied interpretations given to "use," "availability," "entirety," etc. Even though Horn provided explicit examples to illustrate what he considered research's failures to affect spelling instruction, more conclusions issued from the indirect evidence in textbooks on teaching.

Forty years of "intensive psychological research" on spelling preceded Samuel Streicher's conclusion that research failed to quiet the conflicting opinions that determined practice (Rivlin & Schueler, 1943, p. 757). Even after six decades of research the advantages of a 5-words-daily plan over a 25-words-weekly plan could not be shown (Singleton, Diederich, & Hill, 1961, p. 332). But the nation's foremost spelling expert, Ernest Horn, disagreed: spelling research was more nearly adequate than research in any other subject, and demonstrable shortcomings in teaching reflected inadequate knowledge of the available research, failure to apply it intelligently, or erroneous interpretation rather than insufficient research (1944, p. 6). Horn (1950, p. 1256) exposed practices of "dubious worth" such as stressing the hard spots and grouping words to teach them. Research, however, showed the superiority of giving pretests so that students could locate their own errors; it also showed that grouping produced generalizations promoting spelling errors in other words. In his 1960 review, Horn again identified many instances where research had been ignored.

Considerable research had established word usage levels and the spelling and comprehension difficulties of vocabulary and sentence constructions. Yet a study of all secondary science textbooks in print at mid-century showed great variations in difficulty among any one text's various passages, no progression in difficulty from a text's earlier to later passages, and showed that texts intended for students at a similar level were not comparable (Mallinson & Buck, 1954, p. 64). Apparently only occasional consideration was given to difficulty levels in constructing and standardizing textbooks.

Given evidence of the presence of listening abilities and their improvement under instruction, Russell (1964, p. 264) considered it "high time that more curriculum specialists and teachers of English made a serious beginning on the teaching of listening abilities."

Indirect evidence of too little research impact also came with congressional passage of the Vocational Education Act of 1963, providing that 10 percent of each year's appropriation be reserved for funding research and development projects. Meanwhile, Yee (1970, p. 5f) observed that educational psychology texts seldom supply suggestions for application of the principles they propound; he also found teachers' textbooks—in reading, science and social studies—inadequate in translating psychological concepts into teaching behavior. Chall (1967, p. 188) quoted studies reporting that the majority of teachers gained their opinions on reading from their teachers' manuals and basal readers rather than from their preservice methods courses, student-teaching or subsequent reading. One small survey of graduates from nearly 100 teacher-training institutions concluded that the run-of-the-mill program failed to develop concepts of or favorable attitudes toward research (McComas & Uxer, 1968). The fact that many campus schools were disbanded, further isolating the more research-aware college staff from the practical classroom world, was judged a contributing factor to the regrettable state of teacher education (Rising, 1969). Nevertheless, it seems improbable that methods books and journal articles had *no* effect upon teachers' opinions (including opinions on the value of research), particularly in fields without dominating basal series. Thus it appeared worthwhile for the historian to evaluate the position of research in books and journals for teachers.

A random, nonsystematic sampling was

made of books published in the last 20 years in the broad language-arts teaching area. The occasional, nonspecific commentaries upon research impact in the sample were predictably both favorable and unfavorable. More provocative was the information gained from inspection. For example (Hunnicutt & Iverson, 1958), in a section devoted to research studies "which have had far-reaching influence," a statement about the predominance of "assumption and conjecture" undermines the importance of research. Teachers' books have not increased the impact of research to any extent (Dawson & Zollinger, 1957; A. J. Harris, 1962; Pilgrim, 1966; Shane, Mulry, Reddin, & Gillespie, 1962; Strickland, 1957; Tidyman & Butterfield, 1959), for, while occasionally mentioning research, they rarely detail a study or cite one in a footnote, the references and citations usually being to national committee reports and yearbooks, state and local "frameworks" and courses of study, and other "authoritative summaries"—i.e., other textbooks. Their indexes commonly had no entry for "research." One book on language-arts teaching totaled 513 pages with appendices and bibliography; research, in seven curriculum "areas," was discussed on a total of 23 pages, much of it in overlapping references and citing as research surveys of existing practices. Offering references only to other secondary sources, another text described it as time-consuming and laborious work to consult research directly; the impression given was that it was also useless labor. In yet another, the first footnote citation to empirical research located was on page 209; it reported a study of 800 children comparing two methods of teaching reading and finding equivalent results. Equally chastening was the observation that a ten-year research and development project merited but a few lines of general description.

A large portion of the research reported, especially in quantitative or tabular form, was "status" research: the average sentence length or total speaking vocabulary of the 4½-year-old; the average reading rates (words per minute) at various grade levels; the vocabulary loads in various first-grade reading books; the fact that the concept "legislator" is learned primarily at school, while the term "divorce" becomes known in out-of-school experiences. Was such research applicable? Were these data about which the teacher could *do* something?

There were also indicators of limited research impact in science education, which should be thought sympathetic to research. A textbook in elementary science, published by the Center for Applied Research in Education, was frankly a compendium of the author's judgments of good practices, good examples, and agreed-upon aims; although one of the two bases given for a science curriculum was children's growth and development (the other was the needs of society), no research was cited from developmental studies (Vessel, 1963, pp. 52f).

The Physics Teacher, a journal published since 1963 by the American Association of Physics Teachers, was a potpourri of news on science, occasional articles explaining why physics should be taught, short biographical and historical pieces, and "look-what-we-did" reports; despite its section, "The Research Frontier," the journal did not seem interested in educational research —this in a time when enrollments in physics were declining. If one judged by a selection of "outstanding high school physics programs," competence in using educational research was not highly rated among teacher qualifications (Reitz, 1969). A committee to select 10 outstanding physics programs did not ignore the enthusiasm of the staff —one teacher was described as a "revered and respected teacher"—or the summer institutes variously attended; but the persistent desideratum was the amount of undergraduate and graduate *physics* preparation received: "...an impressive background in physics and mathematics"; "the three physics teachers...present a combined background of almost 150 semester hours in physics"; "the two physics teachers...well over 100 semester hours"; "an exceptional training in physics," etc. (Reitz, 1969). The *Journal of Biological Education,* published in Britain, made no mention of research while defining the journal's aims as elevating the teaching of the biological sciences and adjusting its methods and content to the new age.

"Practical" teachers' magazines, which are used primarily by younger teachers (NEA, 1970), are a veritable wasteland for research. The formats of the *Instructor* and *School Arts* lent them to descriptive pieces of great brevity; one or two pages was insufficient space for describing research and discussing its implications. The various state educational journals were ordinarily repositories of news items, conference calls, inspirational pieces, memoirs and occasional descriptions of "new" programs. The *State Education Journal Index,* an annotated reference, occasionally entered articles under "research" or "educational research" or "learning"; these were slim reportings of action research, status studies in reading, one-page descriptions of Educational Resources Information Center (ERIC—the federal research reporting service) published in *New Mexico School Review, Idaho Education News, Indiana Teacher;* and there were far fewer entries under "research" than found on "school finance" or "public relations."

Evidence in issues of teaching-learning. Late in the nineteenth century doubt accumulated about the doctrines of mental discipline, formal discipline, the transfer of training—the frequently compounded views that mental capacities can be trained to operate better generally, that education strengthens mental powers when it exercises on abstract subjects, that direct training in one area transfers its effects elsewhere (Kolesnik, 1962). Pre-1915 investigations confirming this doubt helped to popularize educational science. Many people felt that scientific evidence destroyed doctrines of mental and formal discipline; even conser-

vative schoolmen and psychologists sharply downgraded their expectations of the values in transfer of training. Hence, continuations of these practices in the schools indicate a failure to teach according to "known scientific fact." Writing in 1929, a prominent expert noted critically that "in spite of researches indicating the limited value of grammar as formal discipline, drill in grammar is still the predominating language work of Grades 6, 7, 8" (Lyman, 1929, p. 69).

The same complaint was heard in music. In 1936 it was predicted that knowledge about, rather than experience with, music would remain prevalent as long as music continued to be taught for the sake of mental training (Mursell, 1936, p. 5). English teaching received continuing criticism on this score; in 1947 Loban (p. 523) charged that, notwithstanding research findings, vast numbers of students were still being taught *about language* rather than being given guided practice in genuine communication. By 1960, while most teachers probably conceded that mental discipline was unsubstantiated, they still credited grammar study with having "instrumental value" as a basic tool to improve usage, understand literature, or learn a foreign language; all this was despite research summaries which "consistently concluded that there is no shred of evidence to substantiate the continued emphasis on grammar prevalent in most classrooms" (Searles & Carlsen, pp. 461f). Apparently a prediction from 1905—that a belief in formal discipline might prevail, "first, because the truth in it is so vital, so far-reaching, and so evident to every generation; and, second, because the error in it is so subtle, so plausible, and above all so natural" (Lewis, 1905, p. 281)—held true.

Variations among students in aptitude and achievement had ramifications for several pedagogical issues: grading and grouping systems, marking practices, promotion and retardation policies, and adjustments in teaching methods. A criticism of the research of Piaget was that he frustrated educational planning by providing such meager information about individuals (Watson & Cooley, 1960, p. 302). Through the greater part of this century probably the most critical mark by which to identify the scientifically progressive school was its provision for individual and group differences. Yet the evidence indicated that by this standard schools consistently fell short. As Bertha Friedman (in Rivlin & Schueler, 1943, p. 147) viewed schools, virtually all elementary classrooms and some high schools persisted with rigid grade-level arrangements. While the extent of teachers' disregard for test data was unknown, one study found that American teachers *reported themselves* as not liking intelligence tests, thinking poorly of standardized achievment tests, and favoring promotion based on a satisfactory school record and personal recommendations of teacher and principal (Edman, 1968, pp. 87, 196). Experiments in grouping were not based on supportive research; the research appeared so inconclusive and was so poorly regarded that disagreements persisted, as did variations in practice (Carter, 1960, p. 586; Dunfee, 1967, p. 28; Norris & Noonan, 1941, p. 79; USOE, 1969, p. 147).

Controversy about the appropriate pupil-teacher ratio never subsided. In the turbulent 1960s—when problems of drugs, student disorders, community conflict, racial animus, and virtual bankruptcy all impinged upon schools—polls of teachers usually located their first problem as too large classes and their first suggestion for improving education was reduction in class size. In this they simply echoed the long-standing position of the organized profession. In evaluations of experimental educational programs for the urban poor in the 1960s, Myers (1970) found class size a far more potent interest than was research; "I have even had teachers tell me there is nothing that they feel they have to know more about and the only obstacle was the size of the class" (p. 371).

The impact of research on this issue was negligible in two ways. First, professional attitudes remained fixed in the assumption that class size was a critical factor despite considerable research evidence to the contrary. Second, neither teacher preferences nor research was determining class size; this was being done by school enrollment figures and the financial standing of the school's community (Jamison, in Rivlin & Schueler, 1943, pp. 143f). Research studies have had a similar lack of effect upon the question of time. In 1969, to make a subject "teachable," it was still considered feasible for a teacher to recommend that the time allotment be doubled (Goldstein, 1969, p. 72).

Evidence in the "post-Sputnik" innovations. After projecting its results to cover nearly 34 million students, a United States Office of Education survey concluded that the great majority of students were studying subjects relatively unaffected by curriculum innovations; even in the areas of most common innovation, roughly half of the students were using "relatively old materials" (USOE, 1969, p. 147). But what of students exposed to the new materials? Were they experiencing the impact of research?

Innovations in science education were felt largely to ignore studies of children's science interests in a trend away from a child-centered and toward a content-centered curriculum (Dunfee, 1967, p. 18). Even though Thorndike (1912, pp. 177f) had cautioned against them years before, the claims for the laboratory-discovery method were passed along, virtually unchallenged by the studies which showed at least equal results obtained with demonstration methods of teaching (Powers, 1950, p. 1139). A laboratory approach was given substantial emphasis in all the new secondary science programs, especially programs showing students the tentative qualities of science in its endless search for understanding; this stemmed from the participating scientists' immediate knowledge of what scientists do. But, as one science educator pointed out, few of the projects included any substantial evaluation of pupil achievement or consideration of basic learning questions, since these curricula were based not on research but on scientists' intuitive and experiential senses of teaching; the exception noted was one elementary science program unique in its concern with psychology, including Piaget's, and less preoccupied with "inquiry" than with the importance of ordering content (Novak, 1969, pp. 379f). Ausubel (1966, p. 176) characterized BSCS Biology's overall approach to high school science as "psychologically and pedagogically unsound." The director of SMSG conceded that the originators' exploratory studies and evaluations of SMSG Mathematics were not properly designed and executed experiments (Begle, 1968, p. 243). Apparently, the new curricula were less dependent upon the accumulated research, and less scientific in their development and dissemination, than many schoolmen realized (USOE, 1969, p. 146). Not that schoolmen were simply "guiltless victims"; a 1968 study of 1000 schools using BSCS Biology found that the program's orientation around laboratory work was "not characteristic of BSCS classes," and that the experts' pamphlets and films were little used (Novak, 1969, p. 379).

Another much-discussed educational "innovation" was team teaching. Interest had mounted rapidly, jumping from no entries in *Education Index* during the period from 1955 to 1957, to over 200 during the next decade. Predictably school practice lagged behind; roughly 10 percent of the school districts reported some use of team teaching in a 1966 survey (USOE, 1969, p. 144). Nevertheless, intense enthusiasm and confidence was evident (Goldstein, 1969, p. 73). Confidence in the great effectiveness of team teaching, if based on research, rested on extremely slight evidence; the considerable literary interest in team teaching was not accompanied by a corresponding volume of research activity—only one report in five years in the *Journal of Educational Research* and none in the Office of Educa-

tion's Cooperative Research Project *Bulletin*. Articles describing team teaching in operation omitted specification of empirical evaluations of results (Fraenkel & Gross, 1966, pp. 335f).

Evidence in the action-research movement. The series "What Research Says to the Teacher" was a joint project of two departments of the National Education Association: the Department of Classroom Teachers and the American Educational Research Association. Its avowed purpose was to bridge the gap between research and practice, recognizing the obstacles placed before the utilization of science by heavy teaching burdens and the technical character of much research reporting. This effort by the NEA can also be characterized as the research establishment's attempt to maintain confidence in conventional educational research activities—which were under severe challenge by the rising support for action, or classroom, research.

Claims that the use of research somehow depended upon getting the feel of research by doing one's own, as well as the claim that classroom experimentation alone endowed research with concreteness (Abelson, 1933; Maehling & Rankin, 1939; Zyve, 1931), had agitated some leaders of the NEA as far back as the 1930s—perhaps back to John Dewey's speech in 1928 on "The Sources of a Science of Education" (Dewey, 1929). In the 1950s, however, a new movement was underway. From 1950 to 1953 over half the articles on the methodology of educational research listed in *Education Index* dealt with action research; thereafter a separate action-research entry competed with, or surpassed in space, traditional research listings. Before peaking in the early 1960s, action research effectively threatened the legitimacy of educational research as it had been known for some 75 years.

The action-research literature often located its origination in the failure to implement "laboratory research" findings

(Ahrens, 1956; Corey, 1953; Corman, 1957; Kowitz, 1960; Laing, 1959; Shumsky & Mukerji, 1962; Wann, 1953). Action research, nonetheless, had other appeals, especially to those who wrote for *Educational Leadership* (the journal of the Association for Supervision and Curriculum Development—perhaps the principal remaining home of the latter-day supporters of progressive education). Action research's values lay in participation and in the democracy of group planning. One project described itself as the result of holding "certain views regarding ways of working with people" (Hughes, 1955, p. 490). What action research offered was the interchange of ideas and the recognition of group dynamics (Worthington, 1963, p. 19). Action research was also characterized as the opportunity for the creative growth of teachers among bureaucratic rigidities, complexities, conformist traditions and monotonous routine (Columbro, 1964).

The recognition of midcentury America as a society in need of cooperative work appealed to the progressivist's historic search for community. To Abraham Shumsky action research was a way of "activating the social and spiritual life" of the school, and a way of creating a "social setting where people can work together, dream together of a better community" (1956, p. 182). Noting how central "group interaction" had become to the rhetoric of action research, Harold Hodgkinson compared action research to the works of Kurt Lewin, where "science and sociability" also came together (Hodgkinson, 1957, pp. 138f). While action research was consistent with this century's attempt to improve schools through science, it reflected even more that other historic quest for the active, social pedagogy envisioned in the progressive philosophy. As Hodgkinson observed, why should teachers not be urged to exploit the methods they had so long supposedly been encouraging in their students: problem-solving through working together on a piece of research.

Evidence in the research enterprise. The considerable literature critical of educational research offered other indirect evidence of too little impact even while it indicated some commitment to research which *would* make a difference. Thus Hilgard (1964, pp. 416f), by calling attention to the six chapters in the 1942 Yearbook of the National Society for the Study of Education (NSSE) on the educational implications of psychological research, disputed the contention that the earlier educational psychologists ignored application. But, had teachers reciprocated this interest, even to the extent of reading NSSE publications? The media which reported research were often dismissed as inadequate for classroom application. One complaint was of dreary or vague writing (Muskopf & Robinson, 1966, p. 76). Few teachers could become personally involved in the *Review of Educational Research* (Hodgkinson, 1957, p. 139). An anthology for teachers described the usual bibliography in teacher education as one where "spiteful tracts compete against bloodless surveys" (B. Johnston, 1971, p. xi). The research's infrequent offers of "implications for practice" were *bloodless,* tending toward anemic language and bland "principles"—e.g., that giving the learner tasks both suited to his background and challenging would "appear...helpful" (Ojemann, 1957, p. 99). Another complaint was about research buried in dissertations (Temp, 1964, p. 197). While researchers saw the publication of an occasional dissertation in a research monograph series as widening their audience (Early & Odland, 1967, p. 178), this seemed useless given the poor understanding of research in professional populations, the tiny proportions of teachers or administrators in research organizations (Borg, 1951; Marland, 1960), the reports that under one-half of a large sample of teachers read even one professional book a year (Hawkinson, 1941) and that administrators rated research publications least useful as a source of knowledge (USOE, 1969, p. 151).

Another charge leveled at educational research was insufficiency—the implication being that if there were ample research, there would be impact (Beittel, 1960; Carter, 1960; Gibson, 1967; Greene, 1941; Knower, 1960; Pooley, 1941; B. O. Smith, 1960; Strang, 1962). Scanty investigation of the effects of various teaching methods marked such fields as art education (Moore, 1941) and literature, where the average from 1920 to 1960 was one study per decade (N. B. Smith, 1963). Where comparative studies of methods were profuse they were often useless in "comparing the incomparable"—as in not comparing the "Socratic method" with another where students received direct instruction in logical thinking (Shaver, 1962, p. 14). Even teachers of speech found little help from research in developing diagnostic and remedial procedures in speech pathology (Travis, 1950, p. 1247).

Complementing the charge of insufficient research was that of inconclusiveness or inconsistency of findings (Early & Odland, 1967; Knight, 1930; Pilgrim, 1966; Shaver, 1962; Tanner, 1969). Although Mallinson and Buck (1954, p. 78) considered much science education research superfluous because it simply substantiated already accepted results, most others disagreed. Inconclusiveness was particularly striking in research on reading. Since no phonics research was definitive (Russell, 1961, p. 76), since comparative methods research said "nothing consistently" (Chall, 1967, p. 87), research at best confirmed prior preference. If teachers knew that modern science and scholarship no longer expected or required definitiveness, they themselves did not appreciate relativism; schoolmen with any interest in educational research wanted a science that added a degree of predictability to the chancy world of everyday classroom experience.

Inconclusive results were attributed to the fragmentary and directionless character of much research (Bereiter, 1965, p. 98; Gray,

1960, p. 1087; Jonçich, 1962, p. 10; H. K. Smith, 1968). Failure to meet the scientific standard of replication was the reason given for teachers' needs personally to confirm research in elementary mathematics (Riedesel, 1968). The replication by one researcher of his own or another's research was unlikely since the majority of investigators were one-time-only scientists. William Brownell's 1950 survey of arithmetic research showed that 615 of 778 authors never reported more than one study, and only 53 persons reported more than three each (in Buswell, 1951, p. 283). In other school subjects, to 1947, the following percentages of authors reported one piece of research each, and subsequently produced no more: reading, 76 percent; spelling, 82 percent; English, 82 percent (L. J. Smith, 1951). Research was a lesser activity even of the members of the American Educational Research Association, according to a 1968 membership survey (Roaden & Worthen, Oct. 1970, pp. 3f). Because a large share of research was done by graduate students seeking advanced degrees (Funchess, 1949; Horner, 1965, p. 217; Watson & Cooley, 1960, p. 310), fragmentary and uncoordinated research of low impact potential was predicted.

Summaries of relevant research frequently excluded what Massialas (1962) called "I-used-such-and-such-classroom-aids-and-I-got-favorable-results-research" (p. 10). Nevertheless, much of what remained was inadequate in design and execution. An editor of the *Review of Educational Research* estimated that 90 percent of the papers published in educational journals did not merit reporting as research (Michael, 1963, p. 443). Harsher still was the assessment of philosopher Michael Scriven (1960, p. 426): "By minimum acceptable research standards, 95 percent of the work … that is concerned with causal analysis is, by either theoretical or practical standards, invalid or trivial." Goodlad (1966, p. 18) found most curriculum "experiments" to be trial-and-error refinements of seldom-questioned assumptions.

Expediency and lack of imagination, more than "relevancy," dictated the use of standard curricula, regular teachers and intact classes in many studies; the monotonous frequency of samples of 36 students might have increased teacher-identification with the experimental conditions (J. MacDonald, 1966, p. 602; Shulman, 1970, pp. 376f), but diminished reliability and validity (Buswell et al., 1966, p. 68).

By 1930 enough arithmetic investigations had accumulated to characterize the issues studied as brief, inconclusive and trivial (Buswell, in Whipple, 1930, pp. 412f). A review of one year's curriculum research in social studies found 25 of 27 studies essentially descriptive or "status" reports, and a larger survey was equally discouraging (Cox, Johnson, & Payette, 1968, p. 557; Metcalf, 1963). This condition persisted in instructional research in all subjects, including vocational education (Brandon, 1969, p. 42), prompting the observation that "Unfortunately, imagination-free, trivial research only reinforces this vision of the researcher as a eunuch; he is useful to have around, but he's not one of the boys" (Myers, 1970, p. 373).

In 1928, in asking the profession to be patient with science, E. L. Thorndike (1928) argued that "The more general and fundamental our researches concerning learning are, the more productive they will be in the end for the curriculum" (p. 575). Three decades later the National Research Council (1958a, p. 1) endorsed this principle, but regretted that researchers had neglected basic studies of school learning. Assessments of the research establishment were discrepant on this issue: criticism blamed research for being *both* too specific to be generalized and too generalized to be specific (Gross & Badger, 1960, p. 1305; Shulman, 1970, p. 377; H. K. Smith, 1968; W. C. Wolf, 1970b, p. 11). On the one hand, studies were dismissed as yielding findings applicable only to isolated situations; on the other hand, those dealing with teaching methods in general were faulted for not spelling out

their implications for a given teaching area. Where one observer criticized researchers as too quick to generalize, another scored them for timidity in generalizing.

History shows that research need not be without deficiencies or be sophisticated in design and execution—even by the standards of its own time—to have discernible impact; Thorndike's was a case in point (Cronbach & Suppes, 1969, pp. 109f; Jonçich, 1968, pp. 262f). Attributions of deficiencies to educational science apparently functioned both as reasons *and excuses* for its failure convincingly to have affected practice.

CONCLUSIONS: SOME NOTES TOWARD A HISTORY OF THE IMPACT OF RESEARCH ON TEACHING

To employ a distinction made by John Tukey (1962), this search for the impact of research on teaching was closer to an exploratory than to a confirmatory study. It was more a reconnoitering than an exploration in depth, because the scantiness and impressionism of prior historical scholarship on this question created little advance knowledge. The problems of data-gathering and issues of definition (explained early in this chapter) pointed toward collecting information even suspected of being relevant as well as those data most pertinent to adjudicating specific ideas and sharp hypotheses. Describing this as an exploratory analysis does not, however, dictate that conclusion-drawing be left only for another time and place; even the information gleaned from more or less random data-gathering needs to be interpreted. The process of ordering facts also furthers an implicit interpretation. Stating conclusions makes the results explicit.

Impact: By Diffusion, Not Dissemination

In the early decades of the scientific movement, dissemination of research findings was a casual matter; ordinarily articles were written, textbooks published, workshops arranged, surveys commissioned and courses authorized at the instigation of the individual researcher, editor or administrator. As research and dissatisfaction with its relative impact accumulated, concerted efforts were made at dissemination by instituting annual research summaries, regular research-reporting columns in journals, yearbook treatments, and dissertation reviews in alumni newsletters. Later came the dissemination mechanisms—data banks, films, demonstrations, brochures, games for policymakers—attendant upon federal sponsorship of research and development projects (USOE, 1969, pp. 4f). However much deliberate dissemination strategies promote future research impact, the conclusion for the past is otherwise: that discrete, observable, chartable dissemination activities were far inferior in operation to the processes of *cultural diffusion,* to that obscure, ambiguous, often involuntary transaction system whereby innovations and ideas are spread widely throughout some extended subsociety or the whole culture.

Other commentators have drawn similar conclusions. J. W. Getzels has argued that the significant influence of research operated not piecemeal, study by study, but in a cumulative altering of those conceptions of human behavior in which schools are imbedded. His example was the transformation from teacher-centered to child-centered classrooms, to which dynamic and gestalt psychology, psychoanalytic and group-dynamics theorists all contributed (Getzels, Lipham, & Campbell, 1968, pp. 9–16; USOE, 1969, pp. 139f). The Committee on Educational Research agreed that practical developments emerged not from isolated findings but from some "prevailing view." In arguing that research exercised influence *in*directly, the Committee also recognized the step of popularization, or "domestication," of research ideas: "as concepts flow out beyond the circle of specialists they are given a looser, somewhat metaphorical application" (Cronbach & Suppes, 1969, pp. 129f).

My analysis probably goes further with the concept of cultural diffusion. It devolves from a view of education giving heavy weight to the characteristics of the United States as a mass society, with the special implications this has had for the research and teaching professions. Mindful of popular charges that teachers are carriers of "middle-class culture" and of the intriguing, even persuasive, arguments of younger historians that American public education has been governed consistently by elites who favor their own and seek social control over the discordant cultures of the poor and the different (Katz, 1970; Tyack, in press), nevertheless, the middle class expanded in both size and meaning as the United States better qualified itself as a mass society.

Unlike physical scientists, educational researchers have been close to mass man in their origins and experiences. The huge corpus of American teachers and administrators has not been an elite. They have differed from other professionals who deal with dependent clients in that they perform a nearly universal service. Therefore, among other factors, in their heterogeneity and in their daily dealings with all of the children of all of the people, the press of the whole culture has been greater upon schoolmen, the points of interaction with mass society more numerous. The opportunity for a degree of insulation for the research and dissemination components of the profession has been sufficiently attenuated so that two consequences have ensued: first, educational research has been thrown into and filtered through the marketplace of ideas more than, for example, medical, economic or engineering research has been; and, second, the research itself has been more rooted in what Joseph Novak (1969) called "the available culture."

Consider two illustrations of cultural diffusion—of research exercising impact by what Martin Trow (1962, p. 22) called "working through the slow erosion of old assumptions and pieties" by operating as new ideas in the larger world. Although evident in the mental hygiene movement, and after 1950 in Erik Erickson's influence upon child psychology, Freudian psychology was neglected in educational psychology. But an Americanized, domesticated version of Freudianism nonetheless has been present in educational theory, in shoptalk about students, explanations of teacher behavior, discussions of discipline (Reinoehl, in Rivlin & Schueler, 1943), and in the vocabulary of daily discourse. Unlike Dewey, who entered the schoolhouse in textbooks and curriculum study-groups, Freud entered in the persons of middle-class schoolchildren, in any teacher who read the latest novel or saw a modern stage play, in any mother who protested that her son would "get a complex" if held back.

Darwinian science furnishes another example, perhaps one even more pervasive since the attempts of religious fundamentalism to combat or come to terms with the theory of evolution made Darwinism less a middle-class cultivation than was Freudianism. Decades of research and debate about environmental and hereditary influence on scholastic aptitude were owed to Darwin. So, too, were the professional assumptions that an active learner interacts with perceived stimuli and that the classroom should be a rich *environment* for learning (viz in Henry, 1947).

The Interpenetration of Influences

Committees and commissions are often listed as influencers of school programs (viz Gross & Badger, 1960). Russell and Fea (1963, p. 865) added these other determinants of methods of teaching reading: opinions of parents or other teachers, personal experiences of teachers, hortatory journal articles, how-we-did-it accounts of action research and more scholarly descriptions of research. A sociologist (Wilder, 1966, p. 5) has concluded that, *in the absence of* clear or rational empirical evidence, such factors as ideology, sentiment, tradition, administrative ruling, or a bookseller's persuasiveness

determine how a given group of children is taught. Clearly, knowledge, scientific or otherwise, is only one of many pressures operating on policy. Questions of strategy— whether to use ability or heterogeneous groupings—were supported or attacked upon educational, philosophical and social as well as "psychologically scientific" grounds.

It is doubtful that the historic acceptance of research as a foundation for school practice was seriously a function of its empirical credentials. More persuasive is Frederick J. McDonald's proposition that scientific utility depended less upon evidences of validity, prescriptiveness or practicality than upon research's "consistency with the thinking of influential educational and social theorists, and more subtly on the zeitgeist" (McDonald, 1964, p. 3). What was considered "good science" changed, partly because standards of research methodology progressed; but because education remained more than a technical activity, *to be acceptable, educational science also needed intangible qualities of philosophical or social significance.*

Examining hundreds of statements on research and school practice discloses great emotionalism and what psychologist John B. Carroll (1964, p. 341) called the "overnormativeness" of some research itself. Hortatory and defensive "analyses" abound. Therefore, evidence becomes both what is said and *how* it is said. Consider the reviews of research in physical education which, in lamenting the low intellectual and scholastic reputation of physical education teachers, diminish the issues raised by the research (Esslinger, 1950), or science education articles which lost sight of research in their efforts to obtain for science a larger place in schooling. Also revealing were the frequent discontinuities between the research cited and the conclusions drawn. Science education (Voss, 1967) displayed too the polemical tendencies long noted in reading—open admission that research impact was substantial only upon those already disposed toward its findings (Mathews, 1966, p. 194).

Surveying a research summary in music education (Hendrickson, 1960) and noting the nuances of the commentary strengthen the impression that research impact has been greatly facilitated under two conditions: when it has concerned a *neutral* issue—few issues in education are neutral—or when it has *substantiated* existing opinion or experience. Thus, teachers accepted the principle of gearing instruction to students' maturational states; they accepted developmental psychology because they thought they themselves had observed these developmental data (Jones & Evans, 1951, p. 23). Conversely, research that contradicted personal or group opinion won neither notice nor acceptance. Research on class size illustrated this: because teaching includes class management as well as instruction, and because teachers perceived class size to be positively related to complexities and problems in management, they disregarded research findings.

The Warrant of Legitimation

It was noted earlier that, reform sentiments to the contrary, one expectation of educational science was that it would stabilize practice, provide technical advice and *legitimate* some accepted practices. Prior to any research, efforts were made to reduce technical grammar study (Harris & Gilbert, 1907). A 1936 Curriculum Commission of the National Council of Teachers of English reiterated that all teaching of grammar other than the functional use of sentences be stopped—*now* with scientific certification that the utility of grammar knowledge per se could not be proved (Greene, 1941, p. 456). Similarly it was pointed out that research "afforded some justification" for the existing trend toward less individual laboratory work in science, conforming to a pedagogical philosophy stressing "real" problem solving over the "artifices" of the laboratory (Brechbill, in Rivlin & Schueler, 1943, p.

713). An analysis of research's contributions to the individualization of teaching noted that the accumulation of scientific facts on individual differences were "utilized to further the purposes of those who wish to individualize..." (Courtis, 1938, p. 202). An emphasis on word meaning and advocacy of a later start to reading instruction antedated the research by 20 or more years (Chall, 1967, p. 89; Wilder, 1966, p. 40).

Similar expectations of the serviceability of science to an emerging consensus on good practice and efficient management promoted the school survey movement. Ordinarily called in first by boards of education to improve the administration of municipal school systems (Judd, 1938), imported teams of experts studied many phases of school operations and made lengthy recommendations. After the Cleveland survey (1915–1916), however, the movement settled down and lost its threatening aspect; measurement techniques improved, the predispositions of survey experts became known quantities (the names Hanus, Cubberley, Strayer, Judd, Kendall, Elliott and Ayres reappeared frequently), and a consensus of opinion united "progressive" administrators. Thereafter it was often a superintendent, ambitious to secure some given end, who persuaded the citizens of the board to hire outsiders to survey some more limited aspect of school operations—hoping, indeed expecting, that the desired recommendations would ensue. The conclusion of the Secretary of the Carnegie Foundation for the Advancement of Teaching, while directed at surveys of higher education, pertained generally: "Useful as educational surveys may be, their effect in many cases has been principally to corroborate conclusions arrived at long before..." (Savage, 1937, p. iv). In seeking research impact on educational organization—supervision, staffing, building needs, pupil-assignment systems—some of the surest successes lay in the survey movement; the effects of research upon teaching practices were more uncertain.

School survey research spanned the distinction between research *selected* to support a preexistent practice or purpose and research *designed* to prove a point (Chall, 1967, p. 314; Geyer, 1936; Jonçich, 1962, p. 10). The famed Eight-Year Study of the Progressive Education Association appeared less concerned with determining *whether* subject-matter college entrance requirements stifled high-school modernization than with promoting experimental schools. Not surprisingly the period of most active research interest on the effects of class size was the 1920s (Otto & Von Borgersrode, 1950, p. 212), coinciding with heightened progressivist efforts at shaking loose the classroom structure. Myers (1970, p. 372) only found instances where a researcher was asked to justify a decision already made by an administrator of education programs for the poor, and not to provide information to help *make* a decision. At other points, however, research virtually ignored practice: the widely seen high-school declamation program was little researched (Travis, 1950, p. 1334).

There is yet another aspect of legitimation by research. A profession requires that its expertise be a foregone conclusion. The research enterprise grew in the service of certifying such professional expertise for educators. But once established, expertise must be maintained—at least in a democratic, change-oriented society. It is arguable that research survived less for its substantive support of educational practice or innovation than simply as an activity *expected* of an expert group (Jonçich, 1968, p. 559).

Educational Science and Pedagogical Philosophies

A survey (Moore, 1941, p. 58) of the social forces and shifting educational philosophies which governed school art education neatly periodized the preceding century in terms of these determinants of practice: 1821–1850, theories of mental discipline;

1851–1870, commercial and industrial purposes; 1871–1900, "cultural" values; 1901–1920, creative expressionism; 1921–1938, developing good taste and discrimination. The latter two were elements within the several-sided progressivist philosophy (Cremin, 1961); the creativity theme was particularly identified with certain private, experimental schools (caricatured as "Auntie Mame" or Summerhillian), while "good taste and discrimination" conformed to the complex theme of utilitarianism, meaningfulness and conformity with personal experience.

Explicit references to progressivism and recognition of its influence upon research were common in the research literature—especially where attempts were made at drawing practical implications and in the secondary research reviews. Noteworthy, however, was the apologia of the National Society for the Study of Education's 1930 Committee on Arithmetic (in Whipple, 1930): "Some readers may feel that this Yearbook is too conservative, that it lacks a bold and daring spirit of progressivism" (p. 2). The author, F. B. Knight, was an unromantic Iowa educational psychologist, reporting the Committee's "conscious attempt to avoid the urging of any point of view not supported by considerable scientific fact"; it supported only changes based on a "sober psychology of learning and of human nature, rather than changes based on a psychology which in its enthusiasm stubbornly refuses to view all the factors involved" (p. 2). In Knight's distinction between two types of "psychologies," and in later references to "pseudo-science," there was recognition of the great difficulty schoolmen had in distinguishing between empirical research and a philosophy draped with scientific allusions and calling itself "experimentalism" or "instrumentalism" (Esslinger, 1950, p. 820). With 40 years of additional experience, another Iowan, D. P. Scannell, conceded that many of the important questions of arithmetic instruction are simply not researchable issues but matters decided by philosophical or normative considerations (1969).

Ernest Horn's research life spanned much of the scientific movement, and he developed a healthy cognizance of the limited impact of spelling research when its findings were inconsistent with powerful dictates, philosophical or otherwise. In 1944 he wrote, "It was inevitable that twenty years of emphasis upon learning in a natural setting should be reflected in theories for the teaching of spelling." These found expression principally in proposals to teach spelling incidentally, and in learning words in context, not in lists; the research evidence contested incidental learning and consistently supported the list method (Horn, 1944, p. 10).

Where investigations were compatible with progressive ideology, as in Thorndike's 1917 study of errors in paragraph reading, there was "research that made a difference" in practice (Russell, 1961, p. 74). On the other hand, however, even with deficient arithmetic learning still the chief source of high levels of nonpromotion in the elementary schools, research fell off. Dewey's general attack on formalism and the "new practical point of view" had effectively shrunk the market for such research (Buswell & Judd, 1925; Jonçich, 1962; McLaughlin, 1918).

Changes in educational conceptions of the nature of the learner actually antedated an accumulation of research; the little relevant "fact-letting" present before 1900 was that from certain physicians and G. Stanley Hall's child-study movement—both products of a modern love for children that took shape around the 17th century and crested in Victorian sentimentalism (Ariès, 1962; Boas, 1966; Kessen, 1965; Ryerson, 1961). The kind of child-centered classroom model (in which Getzels saw a measure of research impact) had become desirable within 15 years of the publication of John Dewey's *School and Society* (1900). "The whole idea of children's seats being screwed immovably

to the floor in rigid lines is repugnant to the modern spirit of school study and government," wrote a professor at the College of William and Mary—not ordinarily considered an outpost of progressivism—and his book for teachers included photographs of schools already conforming to that modern spirit (Bennett, 1917, p. 57). When two exponents of modernism identified the progenitors of newer instructional policies, they appropriately listed psychological laws of learning *behind* the theories of Rousseau, the experiences of Pestalozzi, the prophetic vision of Horace Mann, and the activities of the kindergarten pioneers (Caldwell & Courtis, 1925, p. 117). Even philosophy might lack influence, however, as shown by the persistence of rows of desks fixed to the floors in New York City's schoolrooms 40 years later.

The teaching of social studies was probably the most naturally fertile ground for the broad progressive vision. And Dewey's influence proved pervasive there. The research—"expected to emphasize the testing, clarification, and refinement of his theory" —simply failed to appear (Metcalf, 1963, p. 933). Where progressivism prospered, research was a straggly weed; it could not adjust well to that area called "curriculum's foggy bottom" (Ploghoft, 1965). It was not needed. Latter-day research even avoided social studies—that field which had long since come to terms with progressive theories and contented itself with uncritical action research (Fraser, 1965; Massialas, 1962).

Early in 1957 it was still possible to claim that "current practice in the general organization of elementary social studies programs represents no break with the past," and to write of the expanding fusion of social studies and science (Fraser, 1957, p. 133). By the end of 1957 the launching of the Sputnik caused the reestablishment of science as an independent subject. It also generated a few social studies curriculum innovations compatible with post-Sputnik interest in gifted students and in cognitive development—projects, incidentally, fairly innocent of research testing. Moreover, social studies progressives, like other schoolmen, were rudely challenged to defend the profession's conduct of public education.

Science and the Political Sociology of the Education Profession

The flurry of curriculum revision in the 1950s and 1960s—the substitution of new slogans ("inquiry," "the structure of the disciplines," "modular scheduling"), talk of "breakthroughs" in teacher training and "massive retoolings" for "new modes" of instruction—illustrated the tendency of educational thinking to *seem* to "move by spasms of action and reaction" (Cronbach & Suppes, 1969, p. 161). But much of this reaction was chimerical, shallow, diversionary. Resistance lurked, though it was a resistance not specifically against social or political pressures or "what research tells us," just as earlier teachers had resisted textbooks and the ideas of articulate educators as well— see the long defiance of English teachers to pupil compositions (Lyman, 1929, p. 41).

Like most such resistance, that to research was seldom articulated. Most school administrators, at least, expressed the properly positive attitude toward research; indeed, some were accused of commissioning research in order to blunt other pressures (Cronbach & Suppes, 1969, p. 195). Safe studies were encouraged by an ambience of defensiveness, suspicion and fear. The action-research literature was uncritical of itself and not threatening to the profession (Hodgkinson, 1957, p. 141). Status studies were both easy and noncontroversial—who could object simply to gathering more information (Trow, 1962, p. 20)? Yet, when even information-getting seemed sufficiently threatening, the profession acted out its opposition. The American Association of School Administrators publicly opposed the National Assessment Program for nationwide school testing until changes were made that minimized exposure, and the Coleman study of

equality of educational opportunity was reportedly denied access to 45 percent of urban school districts (Wynne, 1970, p. 6). Another drive to domesticate threats appeared in organized professional action to change the National Teacher Corps (B. C. Watson, 1968). The research establishment was, then, only one of numerous hazards lurking about the public school.

Seemingly no analysis of the interaction of research and practice can ignore the anomalous position of the teaching profession. Teachers were not free professionals; the American system formally made them mere agents of lay decision-makers. Yet decentralized administration, a degree of bureaucratic anonymity, and professional rhetoric gave them considerable de facto power in the schoolhouse. While the near monopoly status of public education reduced competition, claims for accountability, and incentives to improve, it also increased responsibility; teachers *were* blamed for the discrepancy between their accomplishment and public expectations of an institution which was chronically overvalued. Millennialist expectations coexisted with dreary routine; exaltations of the teacher's calling alternated with refusals to sanction his competence by conferring formal autonomy. To overstate the case somewhat, teaching was alternately embattled and boring; when teachers were not demonstrating a need to defend what they were doing, they were resting on their oars (Chall, 1967, p. 7; Gates, 1962, p. 549). Critics of schools asked schoolmen to be what the critics were *not*: openminded, receptive to new ideas, eager to innovate, imaginative, willing to be guided by science. And amid the bustle after research knowledge, one suspected that the schools already knew more about better education than they ever put into practice (Cross, 1967, p. 3).

Educational science was once expected to help cement teachers into a cohesive, self-governing expert group. In one view, when that failed to happen, subsequent research could have relatively little impact on teaching: socializing a research commitment was insuperably difficult in a minimally prepared, highly transient, hard to organize occupational group dominated numerically by women whose cultural biases and cognitive styles ill-qualified them as research users (Jonçich, 1968, pp. 566ff; Rossi, 1965). In another view, the professional cement worked all too well: an "educational establishment" *was* created, and research was unable to loosen teaching from its new lockstep. Because research could upset the power status quo, its potential was reduced by inadequate funding, disinterest and taming (Wynne, 1970).

The applications of research could be frustrated either by too little power *or* by too little desire to change (Trow, 1962, p. 9); in education the two appeared simultaneously. Schools operated in a multijurisdictional tangle of authorities who felt "threatened, conservative, and broke" (Oettinger, 1969, p. 44). When the restiveness of school boards, citizens and teachers was not deterred by ideology or by limited imagination from making all but cautious changes, it was restrained by finances. Americans, teachers included, expect improvements and innovations to cost money and lose respect for those that do not. Salaries were the largest item on school budgets, but who could expect that to finance research teachers would willingly be paid less, or that those secured at less pay would better apply research? Consequently the hunt for additional funds strained the resources traditionally reserved for public education. What had once been a progressive, reformist taxing policy—taxes on real property made some sense in assessing wealth in an agricultural age of land speculation—had become regressive in a metropolitan society with millions of home owners. Except for some state and federal monies, public schools remained wrapped in obsolete tax traditions.

The inertia and conservatism in which schools were imbedded extended beyond school funding. Old committee pronouncements rang so contemporary because schools were slow to change (Ashbaugh, 1935, p. 224; Bidwell, 1968, p. 383). Newer insights could not be guaranteed implementation even where philosophy and psychology together supported reform; the haphazard use of reward in teaching showed that (NRC, 1958a, p. 17). Despite poor results found when pupils repeated a grade—*experiential evidence*—educators frequently justified nonpromotion on the unsubstantiated grounds that repeaters were a warning to other students (Friedman & Kelley, in Rivlin & Schueler, 1943, p. 617). While the military took steps to implement "systems engineering" in determining training requirements, and industry adopted many of these procedures, their use by public-school vocational education predictably lagged behind (Lavisky, 1969, p. 3).

Educational Science and American Society— Conservative, But Not Traditional

The importance of critical or reflective thinking was central to John Dewey's philosophical and psychological system. It was elemental to the problem-solving pedagogy of William Kilpatrick, and even to the exponents of the later "life-adjustment" education. The social studies curriculum was the natural habitat for critical thinking since science education seemed hidebound. Yet both research and practical efforts at teaching aimed at critical thinking were described as "scarce and unproductive" (Shaver & Oliver, 1964, p. 191). One compelling conclusion was that it was *not* desired of education; indeed subsequent social events indicated that discernible amounts of critical thinking by the student body were not appreciated by the schools' public.

The United States has been, in paradoxical ways, an unstable society, and change has been accepted in both rhetoric and practice. Yet it has also been a notably conservative society. As its principal agents for socializing youth into its core values, the schools have remained among society's most circumscribed instrumentalities. As much as classrooms took on the appearances of becoming child-centered, protesting students found them still authoritarian, and teachers everywhere talked far too much (Mayer, 1961). *The Lonely Crowd* found the modern school still one of society's agents for "the destruction of fantasy" (Riesman, Glazer, & Denny, 1950, p. 62).

If American society was conservative in expecting schools to teach and not "release" its youth, if its moralism was old-fashioned in its views of authority, discipline, competition and hard work, research seeking for impact somehow had to come to terms with that society. It also faced contending with teachers acting not only as society's agents of the status quo, but as themselves carriers of that culture. Teaching was both a mass profession and always something done briefly by millions of Americans. Hence, teaching was especially likely to partake of, and express, that vague but indisputable preference in American thought toward the practical and nonintellectual, and away from the theoretical and abstract.

While conservative and old-fashioned in critical areas, America was *not* a traditional society. Its disinterest in abstractions also made it impatient with reasoning out the consequences of its actions and with neat distinctions. Hence it committed itself both to universal education and to comprehensive schools, indiscriminately accommodating disparate students, programs, purposes and standards. *The whole history of American education seemed one of varying parts of social conservatism and generosity in conception, and opportunism and improvisation in execution.*

Consider the possible relationship of universal schooling to research impact. One line of nineteenth century school "reform" replaced ungraded schools with age-graded classrooms and standardized practice by adopting uniform textbooks and routinized procedures. What followed were the horrendous problems of nonpromotion, retardation and school elimination. To the findings

gained from research, teachers added their own experiences with schools now both standardized and universalized. Since the chief impetus for change remained that arising from everyday needs and pressures, a favorable climate was apparently created for research impact. Perhaps much of the difference between Thorndike's influence on arithmetic and his apparently small effect upon algebra instruction was that conservatism and subject-matter influence remained predominant in algebra with its lesser student variability and hence lesser motivation for change. While instruction ordinarily proceeds in groups, the needs of the individuals press upon teachers, and the scope for academic individualism was ordinarily greater in the undifferentiated arithmetic than in the differentiated algebra class (Cronbach & Suppes, 1969, p. 119; F. J. McDonald, 1964, p. 25).

As the century wore on, however, students came to seem less strange to teachers. As standards were changed, failure became less apparent. The humanitarianism of progressivism helped. So did an ordinarily expansive economy that made more demands on the fact of attending schools than on content mastery. The schools settled into a routine and into an attitude asking little of research. This torpor ended in the 1950s.

Two relevant characteristics were noted of the subsequent curriculum innovations: the cities led in their adoption, and they appeared most often in reading, mathematics and science education (USOE, 1969, p. 147). First, despite the romantic images of the little red schoolhouse and rural college, the cities have consistently led the educational advance. Earlier in this century they had the nation's most heterogeneous classes; by 1970 these were again filled with the children which the schools found hardest to teach. Second, after Sputnik, science education joined reading and arithmetic as a curriculum indispensable; they stood together under the new injunction that they be both scholastically respectable (demanding) and successfully mastered—so help was awaited from research.

Schools innovative in reading were found primarily serving the two ends of the socio-economic scale: inner-city schools and independent and suburban schools (Chall, 1967, p. 289). A social pressure operating upon the suburban schools was parental expectation of adequate preparation for elite colleges and selective universities. But everywhere in the society after midcentury one also found that social mobility, heightened parental ambitions and automation promised to continue universal schooling into higher education. Would the science of education then make some modest inroads in the colleges as professors confronted increasingly varied student bodies, encountered students strange to them in institutions too large to further personal relationships, and experienced the motivational problems familiar in "compulsory" forms of education?

When the journal *Improving College and University Teaching* began publication in 1953, it was a montage of assorted quotations, personal reminiscences, and homey advice. A description of a special program in pedagogy for Ph.D. candidates in history ignored the general literature on teaching and learning while acquainting students with the "better form of personal reminiscence" (Hill, 1954, p. 5). Federal support of the continuing education of former servicemen had already expanded college student bodies, but those ex-GIs were matured and motivated. Their presence challenged, if anything, the extracurriculum—the fun culture, parietal rules, dormitory society—not the classroom's assumptions or the academic and professional traditions which gave higher education some cohesion (Trow, 1970a). After campus disruptions began genuinely to threaten higher education, this journal became somewhat less personalistic as it prospered; an occasional study, such as an investigation of the time factor in test-taking, was reported. But as

with teachers at all levels, research competes with, and is strained through, the net of personal experience. And, among the more highly professionalized and "cultivated" college faculty, the existence of research on college teaching and on students insults the faculty's intelligence and sensibility and "threatens their role as intellectuals, as interpreters of their own social experience" (Trow, 1962, p. 16). So, need must struggle with the wish to resist.

In America's better colleges and universities there was a formally operating degree of independent faculty entrepreneurship and collegial self-government which has been denied to other teachers. Nevertheless, virtually all schools, excepting perhaps strictly controlled church schools, partook of the society's scruple that, whenever possible, acceptable behavior be secured by democratic, anti-authoritarian social consent. Consider the work of William H. Burton, where attempts to create a "science of supervision" were in dynamic tension with a "spirit of democratic supervision" that emphasized freedom, self-judgment and total participation. Predictably, research was used to support both sides, the measurement movement vying with Kurt Lewin's group dynamics (Button, 1970).

Administrative power to act ex cathedra, even when armed with research findings, was circumscribed by these democratic social sanctions (Trow, 1970b). This also restricted research impact, as did the other factors already discussed—internal and external, methodological and philosophical. That even the controlling precedents which framed educational research existed outside it should not be surprising, since educational practice predates research by the experiences of thousands of generations (Coladarci, 1960, p. 4).

The proposition is heard that 80 years of research *diminished* our knowledge of teaching-learning. It is possibly true that school operations in 1970 aroused less satisfaction than in 1900. Paradoxically, these testify to some *success* of research in having raised professional and public expectations. By knowing *something,* we know how much more remains to be understood about the infinite complexities that are teaching and learning. In this newer awareness, educational research certified some impact and received a warrant to continue and try to achieve more.

IMPLICATIONS: THE "LESSONS" OF HISTORY

The great lesson of history, wrote G. K. Chesterton, is that mankind never profits from the lessons of history. How disappointed, then, would be the philosophers of the Enlightenment and their heirs—the great literary historians of the nineteenth century who so deeply believed in history as the compass into the future. Hence, Santayana's prediction: "those who do not remember the past are condemned to relive it." Not so, would explode Henry Ford, whose "history is the bunk!" was a rejection of history as the imposition of the "dead hand of tradition" upon an innovating culture. The weight of contemporary opinion among professional historians is closer to Ford's skepticism than to the earlier progressivist and positivistic optimism. When Max Beerbohm quips that history repeats itself *because* "historians repeat one another," and the cynic defines history as "a lie agreed upon," they reflect a consciousness of subjectivity, phenomenological experience, and cultural relativism which causes most modern historians to flinch from drawing moral lessons —let alone predictions!—from their work. The more modest, but safer, attribution of value to history is that it "confers perspective." Allan Nevins writes of history as "a bridge connecting the past with the present" and as "an interpretive guide" (1962, pp. 14, 17). A yearbook committee of the National Society for the Study of Education acknowledges that the study of the educational past (in this case by autobiography and biography) "may enable us to escape from the provincialism and exclusiveness of our own ego and our own milieu" (McCaul, 1971, p. 4).

Yet the suspicion remains that in even the modern, "post-scientific" historian lurks the wish to instruct, the sympathy with Viscount Bolingbroke's characterization of history as "philosophy teaching by examples." If so, this chapter's statements about what we have "learned" about the impact of research on teaching in the past probably do have an *implicit* message for those who would expand research impact in the future. What follows, then, is a set of "moral lessons" to be learned from the past history of educational research, *provided that* a more comprehensive and exhaustive study, which should be undertaken, confirms most of the conclusions arrived at by this survey. These "lessons" have been arranged to follow one from the other and not by order of importance. Mixing summary with speculation, few are stated outright as predictions. Instead, cognizant of variety and individuality as two of history's most striking traits, and having a profound respect for the accidents and ironies of history, we merely follow Johann Herder (in Gardiner, 1959) in pursuit of the proposition that the contemplation of past achievements and failures has some *inspirational* power: "The more speedily [man] discerned his faults, the greater the promptitude and energy with which he applied to correct them: the farther he advanced, the more his humanity was formed; and this must be formed, or he must groan for ages beneath the burden of his mistakes" (p. 46).

The Continuity of Efforts

As specializations proliferate and the common culture is increasingly fragmented by new "heresies," it becomes harder to recognize the continuity of the educational research movement. Neither the value of individual achievements nor the participation in a collective effort is adequately known by researchers. Each researcher, hereafter, should know the history of educational research in general. In detail he should be held accountable for knowing the fuller past of what he is investigating and accountable for looking for any impact. Most dissertation "searches" of the relevant literature are travesties and ignore impact altogether, even when they ground justification of the proposed research in "practical" school needs.

The Efficacy of Unified Research

The work of Thorndike and his students possessed a unity; fundamental researches and the production of school materials alike were generated by an overarching learning theory. Other examples are rare, for the discrete study has been the byword. It has remained true that "too many reports consist of a series of tables and graphs with a weak submission of the problem to the public as one which requires further investigation" (Buckingham, 1939, p. 36). Fragmented research seldom has impact. It lowers the researcher's morale by denying him participation in research perceived as important, planned and ongoing. If research in departments of education, institutes, or under federal programs cannot become better unified, then much more justification in terms of coordinating individual studies with prior research can be demanded before dissertations are approved, research contracts funded, or research leaves awarded.

The Commitment to Impact

To the old American anti-intellectualism has been added a new nihilism: loss of faith in science. An insistence on doing research which makes a difference may, however, have other social support. Competition for scarce resources, a slowdown in the market for Ph.D's, and/or opinions placing teaching or "social service" above university research could buttress demands for accountability of educational research.

Research is difficult to impose, especially when "free thinkers" are drawn to teaching by the perception that schools are amiss. Hence impact depends upon co-opting teachers by conversion. Research *intended* to have impact is harder to ignore. It is more "seemly" and, as any successful politician knows, things must not only *be* right; they must also *seem* right. Currently the weakest section of research reports—that on practical implications—must be at least as elaborated as the specifications of research design; better still would be the requirement that the implications be tested.

The Scarcity of Impact Data

The commitment to research impact might necessarily proceed despite continued difficulties in securing valid and reliable impact data. Proposals to fund educational diversity, as in the voucher system, would increase the number of reporting units; this itself compounds data-gathering problems. Accountability systems would have to be far more sophisticated and "tamper-proof" than they have been to date to determine what is happening in education. *Then* begins the task of identifying the effects of this research in education.

The Product Motive

A rough relationship appears between a) a belief in research efficacy and b) the amount of research being done (viz the reading field) or the visibility of "innovation" (viz recent science curriculum projects). The easiest way to suggest impressive research and promote visibility is by producing school materials. Teachers probably remain the "ultimate consumers"; at least the grab for materials at inservice workshops seems unabated.

Possessing a scientific reputation and having new products do not, however, guarantee to a teaching field freedom from attack. The reading field has shown this, and perhaps now the sciences. Moreover, believing that science is on one's side is like "being right": it intensifies defensive feelings when one is experiencing criticism.

Research as the Enlargement of Understanding

Given the "product motive" and cultural expectations of change, it will be difficult to conceive of research impact as doing other than promoting change. But researchers and teacher-educators, at least, should recognize the conserving role of research: the "making sensible," the explaining of that which *is* in education. This seems an indispensable element in creating a "learned" or "liberal profession" out of one which has been, in turn, an amateur occupation and a mass practice. It is possible, of course, that an oversupply of teachers and a heightened entrance into teaching of thoughtful people could, if unassisted, support a new commitment to theory; but history would regard this a radical departure from past practice.

The Research Establishment

Some research has assumed the impact of prior studies; research on the "Pygmalion effect" assumes the impact of tests on teacher and counselor behavior, their responsiveness to data on the low achievement of poor children, etc. (Kranz, 1970). Most research, however, goes on without considering impact—disregarding even information of no-impact. To paraphrase Ignazio Silone, educational regimes come and go; bad habits remain.

Educational research has never been well financed; tighter restrictions on future funds will not drive out all the bad research. Neither will demands for accountability. Whatever its dimensions (probably larger), a research establishment will remain, sustained by status pressures, professionalism, individual idiosyncrasies, neglect and some mechanical principle which protects the continued existence of that which has once gotten started.

The Survival-Training Barrier

Prevailing styles of teacher preparation have not adequately introduced prospective teachers to accumulated research, spelled out enough of its implications, nor developed attitudes favorable to inservice interest in applied research. The pervasive culture of teacher training is one of, in Mencken's term, "empty technic," of vapid methods textbooks, a disinterested educational psychology, of a "survival-training" mentality among its participants. It blankets even special fields—speech pathology or remedial reading—where a degree of *careerism* might have been expected to have created a greater research consciousness.

A change could come with greater selectivity caused by an oversupply of teachers, from having more research-experienced people in teacher education because of an excess Ph.D. population, from heightened desires to improve public-school teaching in competition with nonpublic education. One obstacle to a more expensive, rigorous and selective professional course, however, comes with the new climate of "amateurism": to the old belief that teacher education drove out the best people is added a new belief that race, or social conscience, or alienation from middle-class values is now the desideratum for effective teaching. Also, attacks on tenure unsettle the reward system and work against that deep, prolonged, and specialized training which could promote research impact.

Intervention Research

If the aim of research is improving effectiveness or promoting change, intervention data are probably the only kind worth reporting to teachers, counselors and administrators. The research reported should be of the kind with which professionals can *do something obvious*. There is little merit to status research—unless the point is, for example, to clarify differences among groups so as to encourage the teacher to intervene. Most status research now functions as mere window-dressing and obfuscation.

Saliency and Quality in Research

Insufficient or inconclusive educational research does not much explain low impact. Although most research is both inadequate and ignored, an unsatisfactory piece of research may become influential. Application of, or deference to, research depends less upon its quality or completeness than upon such social and ideological factors as were earlier indicated: upon the zeitgeist of education and society.

Talent Takes Precedence

History seems to support the opposition of research leaders to the review of research proposals by public-school officials (Cronbach & Suppes, 1969, pp. 249f). Productive researchers have been predominantly very able people, rigorously trained and working in environments congenial to research. The action-research movement collapsed under its own triviality; except for a few dedicated exponents moved by a group-dynamics vision of inservice education and teacher involvement, little talent supported action research. High quality research, some of which has had impact, so far has depended more upon talent and critical perceptiveness than upon regular proximity to "the real world of the schools."

Impact and Elitism

The probability of research impact increases when professionals—teachers and researchers—themselves constitute an elite. More barriers to research implementation are owed to inadequate, incomplete professionalism than to the existence of a status-secure "educational establishment." The most elite, fully-professionalized segment in education—school administrators—appears more responsive to "progressive" influences than do teachers; a very conservative public appears least responsive (Sieber & Wilder, 1967).

Factors previously mentioned could advance elitism in the cadres of researchers and teachers. These seem, however, to be more than offset by other pressures: the democratization ethos, reassertions of cultural pluralism, the strivings of the "have-nots" to take the place of whichever of the disaffected children of the middle class "drop out." Thus the education profession will probably retain its roots in, and connections with, mass society.

Diffusion, The Mechanism

Concern with techniques of dissemination expands with commitment to research which makes a difference in teaching. But the principal process by which new ideas capture education remains that of cultural diffusion. Nonscientific pressures upon schools will not quit the scene and leave the content and the conduct of education to the development specialist, the "educational engineer." History will say, also, of future education that, "while research can doubtless inform that enterprise, it can never replace the political process that is its essence" (Cremin, 1965b, p. viii).

REFERENCES

Abelson, H. H. *The art of educational research: Its problems and procedures.* Yonkers, N.Y.: World Book Co., 1933.

Ahrens, M. R. Curriculum improvement through action research. *High School Journal,* 1956, 39, 364–369.

Amatora, M. A functional approach to educational psychology. *Educational Administration and Supervision,* 1957, 43, 175–181.

Ariès, P. *Centuries of childhood.* New York: Alfred A. Knopf, 1962.

Ashbaugh, E. J. What changes would be made in the curriculum if secondary education followed research? In *The application of re-*

search findings to current educational practices. Official report, American Educational Research Association. Washington, D.C.: National Education Association, 1935. Pp. 223–226.

Ausubel, D. P. An evaluation of the BSCS approach to high school biology. *American Biology Teacher*, 1966, 28, 176–186.

Bagley, W. C. *Education and emergent man.* New York: Nelson & Sons, 1934.

Bailyn, B. *Education in the forming of American society*. Chapel Hill, N.C.: University of North Carolina Press, 1960.

Banghart, F. (Ed.) *First annual Phi Delta Kappa symposium on educational research*. Bloomington, Ind.: Phi Delta Kappa, 1960.

Beach, N. L. Research goes into action. *Journal of Educational Research*, 1954, 47, 351–358.

Begle, E. G. SMSG: The first decade. *The Mathematics Teacher*, 1968, 61, 239–245.

Beittel, K. R. Art. In C. W. Harris (Ed.), *Encyclopedia of educational research*. New York: Macmillan, 1960. Pp. 77–87.

Bennett, H. E. *School efficiency; a manual of modern school management*. Boston: Ginn & Co., 1917.

Bereiter, C. Issues and dilemmas in developing training programs for educational researchers. In E. Guba, & S. Elam (Eds.), *The training and nurture of educational researchers*. Sixth Phi Delta Kappa Symposium on Educational Research. Bloomington, Ind.: Phi Delta Kappa, 1965. Pp. 95–110.

Bidwell, J. K. A new look at old committee reports. *The Mathematics Teacher*, 1968, 61, 383–387.

Boas, G. *The cult of childhood*. London: Warburg Institute, University of London, 1966.

Borg, W. R. Teachers as intelligent consumers of research. *School and Society*, 1951, 73, 357–359.

Bowers, C. A. *The progressive educator and the depression: The radical years*. New York: Random House, 1969.

Boyer, P. A. Promoting individualized instruction. In *The application of research findings to current educational practices*. Official report, American Educational Research Association. Washington, D.C.: National Education Association, 1935. Pp. 12–15.

Brandon, G. L. (Ed.) Research visibility: The vocational education curriculum. *American Vocational Journal*, 1969, 44, 41–56.

Bryan, W. L. Science and education. National Education Association, *Addresses and Proceedings*, 1895, 34, 161–165.

Buckingham, B. R. The value of research to teachers. In *The implications of research for the classroom teacher*. Joint Yearbook, American Educational Research Association and Department of Classroom Teachers. Washington, D.C.: National Education Association, 1939. Pp. 24–37.

Buswell, G. T. An experimental study of the eye-voice span in reading. *Supplementary Educational Monographs*, No. 17. Chicago: University of Chicago, 1920.

Buswell, G. T. Introduction. In N. B. Henry (Ed.), *The teaching of arithmetic*. The Fiftieth Yearbook of the National Society for the Study of Education, Part II. Chicago: NSSE, 1951. Pp. 1–5.

Buswell, G. T. Arithmetic. In C. W. Harris (Ed.), *Encyclopedia of educational research*. New York: Macmillan, 1960. Pp. 63–77.

Buswell, G. T., & Judd, C. H. *Summary of educational investigations relating to arithmetic*. Chicago: University of Chicago Press, 1925.

Buswell, G. T., McConnell, T. R., Heiss, A. M., & Knoell, D. M. Training for educational research. Cooperative Research Project No. 51074. Berkeley, Calif.: Center for the Study of Higher Education, University of California, 1966.

Button, W. W. H. Burton and democratic supervision. Unpublished manuscript, Faculty of Educational Studies, State University of New York at Buffalo, 1970.

Caldwell, O. W., & Courtis, S. A. *Then & now in education, 1845–1923*. Yonkers, N.Y.: World Book Co., 1925.

Cameron, E. H. Formal discipline, past and present. *Educational Review*, 1918, 56, 133–148.

Carr, W. G. The evolution of the junior high school textbook in English. *English Journal*, 1927, 16, 119–128.

Carroll, J. B. Research on teaching foreign languages. In N. L. Gage (Ed.), *Handbook of research on teaching*. Chicago: Rand McNally, 1963. Pp. 1060–1100.

Carroll, J. B. The analysis of reading instruction: Perspectives from psychology and linguistics. In E. R. Hilgard (Ed.), *Theories of learning and instruction*. The Sixty-third Yearbook of the National Society for the

Study of Education, Part I. Chicago: NSSE, 1964. Pp. 336–353.

Carter, H. D. Gifted children. In C. W. Harris (Ed.), *Encyclopedia of educational research.* New York: Macmillan, 1960. Pp. 583–593.

Chall, J. S. *Learning to read: The great debate.* New York: McGraw-Hill, 1967.

Chambers, W. G. Questionnaire methods of child study. National Education Association, *Addresses and Proceedings,* 1904, 43, 762–770.

Coladarci, A. P. Towards more rigorous educational research. *Harvard Educational Review,* 1960, 30, 3–11.

Columbro, M. N. Supervision and action research. *Educational Leadership,* 1964, 21, 297–300.

Cook, W. W. The gifted and the retarded in historical perspective. *Phi Delta Kappan,* 1958, 39, 249–255.

Cook, W. W., Hovet, K. O., & Kearney, N. C. Curriculum research. *Review of educational research,* 1956, 26, 224–240.

Corey, S. M. *Action research to improve school practices.* New York: Teachers College Press, 1953.

Corey, S. M. Editorial: Curriculum research. *Educational Leadership,* 1954, 11, 463–465.

Corman, B. R. Action research: A teaching or a research method? *Review of Educational Research,* 1957, 27, 544–547.

Courtis, S. A. Contributions of research to the individualization of instruction. In G. M. Whipple (Ed.), *The scientific movement in education.* Thirty-seventh Yearbook of the National Society for the Study of Education, Part II. Bloomington, Ill.: Public School Publishing Co., 1938. Pp. 201–210.

Cox, C. B., Johnson, W. D., & Payette, R. F. Review of research in social studies: 1967. *Social Education,* 1968, 32, 557–571.

Cremin, L. A. *The transformation of the school.* New York: Alfred A. Knopf, 1961.

Cremin, L. A. *The wonderful world of Ellwood Patterson Cubberley: An essay on the historiography of American education.* New York: Teachers College Press, 1965. (a)

Cremin, L. A. Preface. In M. L. Borrowman (Ed.), *Teacher education in America: A documentary history.* New York: Teachers College Press, 1965. Pp. vii–viii. (b)

Cronbach, L. J., & Suppes, P. (Eds.) *Research for tomorrow's schools: Disciplined inquiry for education.* New York: Macmillan, 1969.

Cross, K. P. When will research improve education? *The Research Reporter,* 1967, 2(4), 1–4.

Cubberley, E. P. *Public school administration.* Boston: Houghton Mifflin, 1916.

Cubberley, E. P. *Public education in the United States.* Boston: Houghton Mifflin, 1919.

Curtis, F. D. *Digest of investigations in the teaching of science in the elementary and secondary schools.* Philadelphia: P. Blakeston's Sons, 1926–39. 3 vols.

Curtis, F. D. Milestones of research in the teaching of science. *Journal of Educational Research,* 1950, 44, 161–178.

Dawson, M. A., & Zollinger, M. *Guiding language learning.* New York: Harcourt, Brace & World, 1957.

Dewey, J. *The school and society.* Chicago: University of Chicago Press, 1900.

Dewey, J. *Sources of a science of education.* New York: Liveright, 1929.

Dinsmore, J. W. *Teaching a district school: A book for young teachers.* New York: American Book Co., 1908.

Duffey, R. V. A study of the reported practices in 538 Temple University graduates and students in their teaching of social studies in the elementary school. Unpublished doctoral dissertation, Temple University, 1954.

Dunfee, M. *Elementary school science: A guide to current research.* Washington, D.C.: Association for Supervision and Curriculum Development, 1967.

Early, M., & Odland, N. Literature in the elementary and secondary schools. *Review of Educational Research,* 1967, 37, 178–185.

Edman, M. *A self-image of primary school teachers: A cross cultural study of their role and status in twelve cities.* Detroit: Wayne State University Press, 1968.

ERIC at your service. *Idaho Education News,* 1967, 22, 19.

ERIC to speed research data to educators. *Indiana Teacher,* 1968, 113, 66.

Esslinger, A. A. Physical education. In W. S. Monroe (Ed.), *Encyclopedia of educational research.* New York: Macmillan, 1950. Pp. 820–835.

Fattu, N. A. The role of research in education —present and future. *Review of Educational Research,* 1960, 30, 409–421.

Foshay, A. W. Action research as imaginative

hindsight. *Educational Research Bulletin,* 1955, 34, 169–171.

Fraenkel, J. R., & Gross, R. E. Team teaching: Let's look before we leap! *Social Education,* 1966, 30, 335–337.

Fraser, D. M. The organization of the elementary-school social-studies curriculum. In N. B. Henry (Ed.), *Social Studies in the Elementary School.* The Fifty-sixth Yearbook of the National Society for the Study of Education, Part II. Chicago: NSSE, 1957. Pp. 129–162.

Fraser, D. M. Status and expectations of current research and development projects. *Social Education,* 1965, 29, 421–434.

Funchess, L. W. Research is needed in music education. *Phi Delta Kappan,* 1949, 30, 349–350.

Gallagher, J. J. A national institute of education: Promise and problems. *Educational Researcher,* Sept. 1970, 21, 1–4.

Gardiner, P. (Ed.) *Theories of history.* Glencoe, Ill.: Free Press, 1959.

Gates, A. I. *The improvement of reading.* New York: Macmillan, 1927.

Gates, A. I. The future of research in reading. *Education,* 1962, 82, 545–554.

Getzels, J. W., Lipham, J. M., & Campbell, R. F. *Educational administration as a social process: Theory, research, practice.* New York: Harper & Row, 1968.

Geyer, D. L. Results of activity instruction: An interpretation of published findings. In *Reconstructing education through research.* Official Report, American Educational Research Association. Washington, D.C.: National Education Association, 1936. Pp. 170–176.

Gibson, J. S. *New frontiers in the social studies.* New York: Citation Press, 1967. 2 vols.

Glennon, V. J., & Callahan, L. G. *Elementary school mathematics: A guide to current research.* Washington, D.C.: National Education Association, Association for Supervision and Curriculum Development, 1968.

Goldstein, W. Is "English" still teachable? *Teachers College Record,* 1969, 71, 70–73.

Goodlad, J. I. *The changing school curriculum.* New York: Fund for the Advancement of Education, 1966.

Gordon, E. W. Is compensatory education failing? *College Board Review,* 1966–67, 62, 7–11, 25–26.

Gray, W. S. Reading. In C. W. Harris (Ed.), *Encyclopedia of educational research.* New York: Macmillan, 1960. Pp. 1086–1135.

Greene, H. A. English: Language, grammar, and composition. In W. S. Monroe (Ed.), *Encyclopedia of educational research.* New York: Macmillan, 1941. Pp. 446–461.

Griffiths, D. E. *Research in educational administration: An appraisal and a plan.* New York: Teachers College Press, 1959.

Gross, R. E., & Badger, W. Social studies. In C. W. Harris (Ed.), *Encyclopedia of educational research.* New York: Macmillan, 1960. Pp. 1296–1319.

Grossnickle, F. E. Introduction. In National Council of Teachers of Mathematics, *Instruction in arithmetic.* Twenty-fifth Yearbook. Washington, D.C.: The National Council of Teachers of Mathematics, 1960. Pp. 1–9.

Hall, G. S. *Adolescence.* New York: Appleton-Century-Crofts, 1904.

Harris, A. J. *Effective teaching of reading.* New York: David McKay, 1962.

Harris, A. V. S., & Gilbert, C. B. *New English lessons.* New York: Silver Burdett, 1907.

Harris, T. L. Handwriting. In C. W. Harris (Ed.), *Encyclopedia of educational research.* New York: Macmillan, 1960. Pp. 616–624.

Hart, J. K. Can a college department of education become scientific? *Scientific Monthly,* 1916, 3, 377–384.

Haskew, L. D., & McLendon, J. C. (Eds.) *This is teaching.* (3rd ed.) Glenview, Ill.: Scott Foresman, 1968.

Hausman, J. Research on teaching the visual arts. In N. L. Gage (Ed.), *Handbook of research on teaching.* Chicago: Rand McNally, 1963. Pp. 1101–1117.

Hawkinson, E. A. Selected difficulties of social studies teachers. Unpublished doctoral dissertation, University of Minnesota, 1941.

Hendrickson, G. Music. In C. W. Harris (Ed.), *Encyclopedia of educational research.* New York: Macmillan, 1960. Pp. 905–916.

Henry, N. B. (Ed.) *Science education in American schools.* The Forty-sixth Yearbook of the National Society for the Study of Education, Part I. Chicago: NSSE, 1947.

Hilgard, E. R. Postscript: Twenty years of learning theory in relation to education. In E. R. Hilgard (Ed.), *Theories of learning and instruction.* The Sixty-third Yearbook of the National Society for the Study of Education, Part I. Chicago: NSSE, 1964. Pp. 416–418.

Hill, H. B. The teacher training program for doctoral candidates in history at the University of Wisconsin. *Improving College and University Teaching,* 1954, 2, 5–6.

Hodgkinson, H. L. Action research: A critique. *Journal of Educational Sociology,* 1957, 31, 137–153.

Horn, E. Research in spelling. *Elementary English Review,* 1944, 21, 6–13.

Horn, E. Spelling. In W. S. Monroe (Ed.), *Encyclopedia of educational research.* New York: Macmillan, 1950. Pp. 1247–1264.

Horn, E. Spelling. In C. W. Harris (Ed.), *Encyclopedia of educational research.* New York: Macmillan, 1960. Pp. 1337–1354.

Horner, V. *Music education; the background of research and opinion.* Hawthorne, Victoria: Australian Council for Educational Research, 1965.

Hosic, J. F. Reorganization of English in secondary schools. Report by the National Joint Committee on English representing the Commission on the Reorganization of Secondary Education of the National Education Association and the U.S. National Council of Teachers of English. *Bureau of Education Bulletin,* 1917, No. 2.

Hoyt, C. J. Enabling research to answer. *Phi Delta Kappan,* 1953, 35, 59–62, 68.

Hoyt, F. S. The place of grammar in the elementary curriculum. *Teachers College Record,* 1906, 7(5), 1–34.

Hughes, M. M. et al. Iron county teachers study their problems scientifically. *Educational Leadership,* 1955, 12, 489–495.

Hunnicutt, C. W., & Iverson, W. J. (Eds.) *Research in the 3 R's.* New York: Harper & Row, 1958.

Irwin, J. V., & Roseberger, M. *Modern speech.* New York: Holt, Rinehart & Winston, 1951.

Johnston, B. (Ed.) *The literature of learning: A teacher's anthology.* New York: Holt, Rinehart & Winston, 1971.

Johnston, J. A. AERA members: A profile, 1969. *Educational Researcher,* December 1970, 21, 9–10.

Jonçich, G. M. Whither thou, educational scientist? *Teachers College Record,* 1962, 64, 1–12.

Jonçich, G. M. *The sane positivist: A biography of Edward L. Thorndike.* Middletown, Conn.: Wesleyan University Press, 1968.

Jones, A. N., & Evans, G. K. Areas of needed research in music education. *Education,* 1951, 72, 23–27.

Judd, C. H. *Introduction to the scientific study of education.* Boston: Ginn & Co., 1918.

Judd, C. H. Contributions of school surveys. In G. M. Whipple (Ed.), *The scientific movement in education.* Thirty-seventh Yearbook of the National Society for the Study of Education, Part II. Bloomington, Ill.: Public School Publishing Co., 1938. Pp. 9–20.

Katz, M. B. *The irony of early school reform: Educational innovation in mid-nineteenth century Massachusetts.* Cambridge: Harvard University Press, 1968.

Katz, M. B. From voluntarism to bureaucracy in American education. Paper presented at the meetings of the American Studies Association, Washington, D.C., September 1970.

Kessen, W. (Ed.) *The child.* New York: John Wiley, 1965.

Knight, F. B. Introduction. In G. M. Whipple (Ed.), *Report of the Society's committee on arithmetic, Part I. Some aspects of modern thought on arithmetic.* Twenty-ninth Yearbook of the National Society for the Study of Education, Part I. Bloomington, Ill.: Public School Publishing Co., 1930. Pp. 1–7.

Knower, F. H. Speech. In C. W. Harris (Ed.), *Encyclopedia of educational research.* New York: Macmillan, 1960. Pp. 1330–1337.

Kolesnik, W. B. *Mental discipline in modern education.* Madison: University of Wisconsin Press, 1962.

Kowitz, G. T. *Research for educational improvement.* Albany: Division of Research, New York State Education Dept., 1960.

Kranz, P. L., Weber, W. A., & Fishell, K. N. The relationships between teacher perception of pupils and teacher behavior toward those pupils. Paper presented at the meeting of the American Educational Research Association, Minneapolis, March 1970.

Laing, J. M. The practicality of small school action research. *High School Journal,* 1959, 43, 89–92.

Lavisky, S. HumRRO research and the army's training programs. Professional Paper 36–69. Alexandria, Va.: Human Resources Research Organization, 1969.

Lewis, F. C. A study in formal discipline. *School Review*, 1905, 13, 281–292.

Link, F. R., & Schuster, E. H. Linguistics in high school: A report of action research. *Educational Leadership*, 1962, 19, 294–299.

Loban, W. Studies of language which assist the teacher. *English Journal*, 1947, 36, 518–523.

Lyman, R. L. Summary of investigations relating to grammar, language, and composition. *Supplementary Educational Monographs*, No. 36. Chicago: University of Chicago, 1929.

MacDonald, J. B. Thoughts about research in schools. *Educational Leadership*, 1966, 23, 601–604.

Maehling, H., & Rankin, P. T. The interpretation and evaluation of research. *The implications of research for the classroom teacher*. Joint Yearbook, American Educational Research Association and Department of Classroom Teachers. Washington, D.C.: National Education Association, 1939. Pp. 38–52.

Mallinson, G. G., & Buck, J. V. Some implications and practical applications of recent research in the teaching of science at the secondary school level. *Science Education*, 1954, 38, 58–81.

Marland, S. P. Superintendents' concerns about research applications in educational administration. In R. F. Campbell, & J. P. Lipham (Eds.), *Administrative theory as a guide to action*. Chicago: Midwest Administration Center, University of Chicago, 1960. Pp. 21–36.

Marsh, P. E. Wellsprings of strategy: Considerations affecting innovations by the PSSC. In M. B. Miles (Ed.), *Innovation in education*. New York: Teachers College Press, 1964. Pp. 249–267.

Massialas, B. G. Research prospects in the social studies. *Bulletin of the School of Education, Indiana University*, 1962, 38(1).

Mathews, M. M. *Teaching to read: Historically considered*. Chicago: University of Chicago Press, 1966.

Mayer, M. *The schools*. New York: Harper & Row, 1961.

McCaul, R. L. Autobiography in American educational history. In R. L. Havighurst (Ed.), *Leaders in American education*. Seventieth Yearbook of the National Society for the Study of Education, Part II. Chicago: University of Chicago Press, 1971. Pp. 500–504.

McComas, J. D., & Uxer, J. E. Graduates' perceptions of research. *Improving College and University Teaching*, 1968, 16, 118–119.

McDonald, F. J. The influence of learning theories on education (1900–1950). In E. R. Hilgard (Ed.), *Theories of learning and instruction*. The Sixty-third Yearbook of the National Society for the Study of Education, Part I. Chicago: NSSE, 1964. Pp. 1–26.

McDougall, W. The psychology they teach in New York. In W. King (Ed.), *Behaviorism, a battle line*. Nashville: Cokesbury Press, 1930.

McKeachie, W. J. College teaching and student motivation. *Improving College and University Teaching*, 1954, 2, 39–41.

McLaughlin, K. L. Summary of current tendencies in elementary school mathematics as shown by recent textbooks. *Elementary School Journal*, 1918, 18, 543–551.

Meek, C. S. *Special report to the Boise public schools*, 1915.

Metcalf, L. E. Research on teaching the social studies. In N. L. Gage (Ed.), *Handbook of research on teaching*. Chicago: Rand McNally, 1963. Pp. 929–965.

Michael, W. B. Teacher personnel: A brief evaluation of the research reviewed. *Review of Educational Research*, 1963, 33, 443.

Moore, J. E. Art education. In W. S. Monroe (Ed.), *Encyclopedia of educational research*. New York: Macmillan, 1941. Pp. 58–65.

Murray, E. *The speech personality*. Philadelphia: Lippincott, 1954.

Mursell, J. L. Principles of music education. In G. M. Whipple (Ed.), *Music education*. Thirty-fifth Yearbook of the National Society for the Study of Education, Part II. Bloomington, Ill.: Public School Publishing Co., 1936. Pp. 3–16.

Muskopf, A. F., & Robinson, H. A. High school reading—1965. *Journal of Reading*, 1966, 10, 75–87.

Myers, A. E. The impact of evaluative research on educational programs for the poor. *Teachers College Record*, 1970, 71, 371–378.

National Education Association. *The principals look at the schools*. Report of the Project on the Instructional Program of the Public Schools. Washington, D.C.: NEA, 1962.

National Education Association. What teachers use professional periodicals? *NEA Research Bulletin,* December 1970, 48, 116–118.

National Research Council. *Psychological research in education.* Washington, D.C.: National Academy of Sciences, National Research Council, 1958. (a)

National Research Council, & National Academy of Sciences. *A proposed organization for research in education.* Washington, D.C.: Government Printing Office, 1958. (b)

Nevins, A. *The gateway to history.* (Rev. ed.) Garden City, N.Y.: Doubleday, 1962.

Nixon, R. M. Excerpts from the president's special message to congress on education reform. *New York Times,* March 4, 1970, p. 28.

Norris, D. E., & Noonan, N. I. Atypical children—I. Gifted children. In W. S. Monroe (Ed.), *Encyclopedia of educational research.* New York: Macmillan, 1941. Pp. 75–81.

Novak, J. D. A case study of curriculum change—Science since PSSC. *School Science and Mathematics,* 1969, 69, 374–384.

Oettinger, A. G. *Run, computer, run: The mythology of educational innovation.* Cambridge: Harvard University Press, 1969.

Ojemann, R. H. Social studies in light of knowledge about children. In N. B. Henry (Ed.), *Social studies in the elementary school.* The Fifty-sixth Yearbook of the National Society for the Study of Education, Part II. Chicago: NSSE, 1957. Pp. 76–119.

Oliver, W. A. Teachers' educational beliefs versus their classroom practices. *Journal of Educational Research,* 1953, 47, 47–55.

Olsen, R. G. On not forgetting what we've learned about learning. *Music Educators Journal,* 1968, 55(2), 57–59.

Otto, H. J., & Von Borgersrode, F. Class size. In W. S. Monroe (Ed.), *Encyclopedia of educational research.* New York: Macmillan, 1950. Pp. 212–215.

Pilgrim, G. H. *Learning and teaching practices in English.* New York: Center for Applied Research in Education, 1966.

Ploghoft, M. E. Social studies: Curriculum's foggy bottom. *Social Education,* 1965, 29, 539–540, 554.

Pool, R. A. ERIC—the teachers' new friend. *New Mexico School Review,* 1968, 47(6), 17, 28–29.

Pooley, R. C. English literature. In W. S. Monroe (Ed.), *Encyclopedia of educational research.* New York: Macmillan, 1941. Pp. 461–467.

Pooley, R. C. English literature. In C. W. Harris (Ed.), *Encyclopedia of educational research.* New York: Macmillan, 1960. Pp. 470–478.

Powers, S. R. Science education. In W. S. Monroe (Ed.), *Encyclopedia of educational research.* New York: Macmillan, 1950. Pp. 1133–1145.

Pressey, S. L. Education's (and psychology's) disgrace: And a double-dare. *Psychology in the Schools,* 1969, 6, 353–358.

Rarick, G. L. Physical education. In C. W. Harris (Ed.), *Encyclopedia of educational research.* New York: Macmillan, 1960. Pp. 973–995.

Reeve, W. D. (Ed.) *The teaching of arithmetic.* Tenth Yearbook, National Council of Teachers of Mathematics. New York: Teachers College, 1935.

Reeve, W. D. (Ed.) *Arithmetic in general education.* Sixteenth Yearbook, National Council of Teachers of Mathematics. New York: Teachers College, 1941.

Reitz, R. A. Outstanding high school physics programs. *The Physics Teacher,* 1969, 7, 486–489.

Riedesel, C. A. Every teacher is a researcher. *The Arithmetic Teacher,* 1968, 15, 355–356.

Riesman, D., Glazer, N., & Denny, R. *The lonely crowd.* New Haven, Conn.: Yale University Press, 1950.

Rising, G. R. The sorry state of mathematics teacher education. *The Arithmetic Teacher,* 1969, 16, 296–300.

Rivlin, H. N., & Schueler, H. (Eds.) *Encyclopedia of modern education.* New York: Philosophical Library, 1943.

Roaden, A. L., & Worthen, B. R. A profile of AERA members as researchers. *Educational Researcher,* Oct. 1970, 21, 3–5.

Rosenthal, R., & Jacobson, L. *Pygmalion in the classroom: Teacher expectation and pupils' intellectual development.* New York: Holt, Rinehart & Winston, 1968.

Ross, D. H. *Administration for adaptability.* New York: Metropolitan School Study Council, 1958.

Rossi, A. S. Barriers to the career choice of engineering, medicine, or science among American women. In J. A. Mattfeld, & C. G. Van Aken (Eds.), *Women and the scientific professions.* Cambridge, Mass.: MIT Press, 1965. Pp. 51–127.

Russell, D. H. Reading research that makes a difference. *Elementary English,* 1961, 38, 74–78.

Russell, D. H. A conspectus of recent research on listening abilities. *Elementary English,* 1964, 41, 262–267.

Russell, D. H., & Fea, H. R. Research on teaching reading. In N. L. Gage (Ed.), *Handbook of research on teaching.* Chicago: Rand McNally, 1963. Pp. 865–928.

Ryerson, A. J. Medical advice on child rearing, 1550–1900. *Harvard Educational Review,* 1961, 31, 302–323.

Saettler, P. *A history of instructional technology.* New York: McGraw-Hill, 1968.

Savage, H. J. Foreward. In W. C. Eells (Ed.), *Surveys of American higher education.* New York: Carnegie Foundation for the Advancement of Teaching, 1937. Pp. iii–v.

Scannell, D. P. Obtaining valid research in elementary school mathematics. *The Arithmetic Teacher,* 1969, 16, 292–295.

Scriven, M. The philosophy of science in educational research. *Review of Educational Research,* 1960, 30, 422–429.

Searles, J. R., & Carlsen, G. R. English: Language, grammar, and composition. In C. W. Harris (Ed.), *Encyclopedia of educational research.* New York: Macmillan Co., 1960. Pp. 454–470.

Shane, H. G., Mulry, J. G., Reddin, M. E., & Gillespie, M. C. *Improving language arts instruction in the elementary school.* Columbus, Ohio: Charles E. Merrill, 1962.

Shaver, J. P. Educational research and instruction for critical thinking. *Social Education,* 1962, 26, 13–16.

Shaver, J. P., and Oliver, D. W. Teaching students to analyze public controversy: A curriculum project report. *Social Education,* 1964, 28, 191–194.

Shulman, L. S. Reconstruction of educational research. *Review of Educational Research,* 1970, 40, 371–396.

Shumsky, A. Cooperation in action research: A rationale. *Journal of Educational Sociology,* 1956, 30, 180–185.

Shumsky, A., & Mukerji, R. From research idea to classroom practice. *Elementary School Journal,* 1962, 63, 83–86.

Sieber, S. D., & Lazarsfeld, P. F. *The organization of educational research in the United States.* Cooperative Research Project No. 1974. New York: Bureau of Applied Social Research, Columbia University, 1966.

Sieber, S. D., & Wilder, D. E. Teaching styles: Parental preference and professional role definition. *Sociology of Education,* 1967, 40, 302–315.

Singleton, C. M., Diederich, P. B., & Hill, W. The classroom teacher as a researcher. *Elementary English,* 1961, 38, 330–335.

Smilansky, M. Israel. *Review of Educational Research,* 1962, 32, 280–293.

Smith, B. O. A concept of teaching. *Teachers College Record,* 1960, 61, 229–241.

Smith, H. A., & Anderson, K. E. Science. In C. W. Harris (Ed.), *Encyclopedia of educational research.* New York: Macmillan, 1960. Pp. 1216–1232.

Smith, H. K. Needed: Research in high schools and colleges. *Journal of Reading,* 1968, 12, 203–204.

Smith, L. J. Research workers in selected school subjects. *Journal of Educational Research,* 1951, 45, 255–273.

Smith, N. B. Introduction. In N. B. Smith (Ed.), *The development of taste in literature.* Research bulletin, National Conference on Research in English. Champaign, Ill.: National Council of Teachers of English, 1963. Pp. 3–7.

Stanley, J. C. Controlled experimentation in the classroom. *Journal of Experimental Education,* 1957, 25, 195–201.

State education journal index. Fort Collins, Colorado, 1963.

Stormzand, M. J., & O'Shea, M. V. *How much English grammar?* Baltimore: Warwick & York, 1924.

Strang, R. Reactions to research on reading. *Educational Forum,* 1962, 26, 187–192.

Strickland, R. G. *The language arts in the elementary school.* (2nd ed.) Boston: D. C. Heath, 1957.

Swartz, C. E. The Hawthorne effect and

other mysteries. *The Physics Teacher*, 1969, 7, 429, 438.

Tanner, R. T. Discovery as an object of research. *School Science and Mathematics*, 1969, 69, 647–655.

Temp, G. Literature in the secondary school. *Review of Educational Research*, 1964, 34, 195–202.

Thorndike, E. L. *Education, a first book*. New York: Macmillan, 1912.

Thorndike, E. L. Reading as reasoning: A study of mistakes in paragraph reading. *Journal of Educational Psychology*, 1917, 8, 323–332. (a)

Thorndike, E. L. *The Thorndike arithmetics, books 1–3* [grades 3–8]. Chicago: Rand McNally, 1917, 1924. (b)

Thorndike, E. L. *Psychology of algebra*. New York: Macmillan, 1923.

Thorndike, E. L. Curriculum research. *School and Society*, 1928, 28, 569–576.

Thorndike, E. L. Gifted children in small cities. *Teachers College Record*, 1941, 42, 420–427.

Thorpe, L. P. Learning theory and music teaching. In N. B. Henry (Ed.), *Basic concepts in music education*. The Fifty-seventh Yearbook of the National Society for the Study of Education, Part I. Chicago: NSSE, 1958. Pp. 163–194.

Tidyman, W. F., & Butterfield, M. *Teaching the language arts*. (2nd ed.) New York: McGraw-Hill, 1959.

Travis, L. E. Speech pathology. In W. S. Monroe (Ed.), *Encyclopedia of educational research*. New York: Macmillan, 1950. Pp. 1243–1247.

Traxler, A. E. *Ten years of research in reading: Summary and bibliography*. New York: Educational Records Bureau, 1941, 1946, 1955, 1960.

Trow, M. Some factors which affect the use of social research in higher education. Paper presented at the meeting of the American Sociological Association, Washington, D.C., August 1962. (Modified version published as The role of social science in planning for higher education. *Proceedings of the symposium on undergraduate environment*. Brunswick, Maine: Bowdoin College, 1963. Pp. 13–21.)

Trow, M. Expansion and transformation of higher education. Paper presented at the meeting of the American Sociological Association, Washington, D.C., September 1970. (a)

Trow, M. Methodological problems in the evaluation of innovation. In M. C. Wittrock, & D. E. Wiley (Eds.), *The evaluation of instruction: Issues and problems*. New York: Holt, Rinehart & Winston, 1970. Pp. 289–305. (b)

Tukey, J. W. The future of data analysis. *Annals of Mathematical Statistics*, 1962, 33, 1–67.

Tyack, D. Centralization of control in city schools at the turn of the century. In J. Israel (Ed.), *Building the organizational society*. New York: Free Press, in press.

United States Office of Education. *Educational research and development in the United States*. Washington, D.C.: Government Printing Office, 1969.

Vessel, M. F. *Elementary school science teaching*. Washington, D.C.: Center for Applied Research in Education, 1963.

Voss, B. E. The impact of BSCS biology. *School Science and Mathematics*, 1967, 67, 145–148.

Wallin, J. E. *Problems of subnormality*. Yonkers, N.Y.: World Book Co., 1917.

Wann, K. D. Action research in schools. *Review of Educational Research*, 1953, 23, 337–345.

Watson, B. C. The taming of a reform. *Phi Delta Kappan*, 1968, 50, 99–104.

Watson, F. G., & Cooley, W. W. Needed research in science education. In N. B. Henry (Ed.), *Rethinking science education*. The Fifty-ninth Yearbook of the National Society for the Study of Education, Part I. Chicago: NSSE, 1960. Pp. 297–312.

Welch, J. D. C. Perspectives. *Educational Researcher*, December 1970, 21, 3–4.

Whipple, G. M. (Ed.) *Report of the Society's committee on arithmetic*. Twenty-ninth Yearbook of the National Society for the Study of Education. Bloomington, Ill.: Public School Publishing Co., 1930.

Whipple, G. M. (Ed.) *A program for teaching science*. Thirty-first Yearbook of the National Society for the Study of Education, Part I. Bloomington, Ill.: Public School Publishing Co., 1932.

Wilder, D. E. The reading experts: A case study of the failure to institutionalize an applied science of education. Unpublished doctoral dissertation, Columbia University, 1966.

Wilson, G. M. Arithmetic. In W. S. Monroe (Ed.), *Encyclopedia of educational research.* New York: Macmillan, 1941. Pp. 42–58.

Winans, J. A. The need for research. *The Quarterly Journal of Public Speaking,* 1915, 1, 17–23.

Wolf, W. C., Jr. Educational reform White House style. *Educational Researcher,* 1970, 21, 1–2. (a)

Wolf, W. C., Jr. Look out practitioners. *Educational Researcher,* 1970, 21, 11. (b)

Woolbert, C. H. *The fundamentals of speech.* (Rev. ed.) New York: Harper & Brothers, 1927.

Worthington, R. M. Action research in vocational education. *American Vocational Journal,* 1963, 38(1), 18–19, 38.

Wynne, E. Education research: A profession in search of constituency. Paper presented at the meeting of the American Educational Research Association, Minneapolis, March 1970.

Yee, A. H. Educational psychology as seen through its textbooks. Paper presented at the meeting of the American Educational Research Association, Minneapolis, March 1970.

Zacharias, J. In Panel on Educational Research and Development, The President's Science Advisory Committee. *Innovation and experiment in education.* Washington, D.C.: Government Printing Office, 1964.

Zyve, C. Applications of measurement and research: The teacher and research. *The principal and supervision.* Tenth Yearbook, Department of Elementary School Principals. Washington, D.C.: National Education Association, 1931.

CHAPTER 2

Contemporary Models of Teaching

GRAHAM NUTHALL
University of Canterbury, New Zealand

IVAN SNOOK
University of Canterbury, New Zealand

INTRODUCTION—THE MEANING OF MODEL

The term *model* suffers from the ambiguity that comes from constant usage in a variety of contexts. In general, it can be said that a model may be used for imitation, description, explanation, prediction or persuasion. An artist imitates his model, and a model child is one to be imitated. A map of France and a diagram of the human body are *iconic* models which a lecturer may use to help him describe the landscape of a country or the physiology of human beings. A scientist may use *analogue* and *symbolic* models to explain data, to suggest predictions, or to simulate factors which cannot be manipulated in the real world. Finally, a model may be used to persuade people to adopt some policy or ideal: "melting pot" and "brotherhood of man" are examples of this kind of model (cf. MacIver & Holdaway, 1966).

Within education the term "model" is used in similarly diverse ways. Model teachers and model lessons are used as exemplars for teachers to imitate and as standards for evaluation. Educational practice has been described and justified, praised and condemned in terms of authoritarian, democratic, child-centered and traditional models. It is not unusual to find the author of an introductory text in educational psychology designing a model of the educational process which he uses to justify and structure the contents of his textbook (cf. De Cecco, 1968).

At a more sophisticated level, several of those involved in research on teaching have designed descriptive symbolic models of teacher-pupil relationships which are intended to coordinate in a single picture those elements of observation, research and educational folklore which they consider significant (cf. Smith, 1968; Strasser, 1967). Since these models seem to have characteristics of simplicity and abstraction and the promise of explanatory and predictive significance, they appear to be very like the popular notion of a model in the physical sciences.

It would provide an instructive commentary on the aspirations and concerns of teaching researchers to collect together all such models and make an analysis of the areas of agreement and disagreement which they display. However, if we had taken this approach in writing this chapter, we believe we would have seriously misrepresented the content and style of much of the research and debate on teaching which is an important part of the contemporary educational scene. Examination of the research literature indicates that very few of these descriptive models have stimulated any research investigation or been the focus of continued discussion. To take these models seriously as valid representations of our current knowledge about teaching would be to run the risk of depicting research on teaching as a well-developed area of empirical knowledge based on generally accepted primary concepts and well-established methods for gaining and organizing data.

It is in fact the very physical science appearance of these models which detracts from their usefulness as a means of representing and interpreting the significant research which has been conducted. Whether we like it or not, it is clearly false to represent research on teaching as the development of a new empirical science along the lines of the established physical sciences. The guiding force of much of the research on teaching has not been the discovery and systematic accumulation of empirical knowledge, and certainly not the gradual refinement of seminal models and larger theoretical structures. Rather, the greatest amount of research and discussion has been generated by debate and controversy over certain highly provocative pedagogical concepts and claims about how teaching ought to be viewed.

1. A Model as Interpretive Framework

To claim that formal descriptive models, such as those depicted by Smith (1968) and Strasser (1967), do not represent or interpret contemporary research on teaching, is not to claim that the notion of a "model of teaching" is irrelevant to our understanding of that research. On the contrary, if we discard the popular notion of a model as a formal symbolic representation of variable relationships and entertain, instead, a conception of "model" as a more general and influential point of view with certain significant functions in guiding and structuring research, then it becomes evident that there have been models of teaching which have dominated recent investigation and analysis of teaching procedures.

Recent writers on the history and philosophy of science have pointed out that one of the major functions of a model in the development of science is to persuade and foster conviction that one way of looking at and structuring data is better than any alternative view (cf. Kuhn, 1962; Polanyi, 1958). These models serve as *interpretive frameworks* (Polanyi, 1958) and tend to carry with them their own concepts, their own rules for collecting and structuring data, and most significantly their own criteria for deciding which research questions are worth asking. The extent to which these scientific models constitute more or less adequate representations of reality is still a matter of dispute (see Scheffler, 1967). It safely can be said, however, that important scientific models are not justified solely by the weight of evidence, nor does one model replace another purely by reference to universally accepted data. They are themselves methods of interpreting and organizing the empirical evidence, and they compete for the allegiance of researchers by reference to such nonempirical considerations as "simplicity," "elegance" and "theoretical beauty."

Without claiming that research on teaching constitutes a "developing science" which is groping towards the discovery of those general laws and explanatory principles which characterize the physical sciences, much of the investigation and analysis of teaching which has been carried out has been empirical and rigorously logical. The way in which educational researchers have organized themselves into a "scientific community" and have attempted to interpret the scientific method in the solution of teaching-method problems, can be illuminated and understood by identifying those "interpretive frameworks" which they have used in directing their activities and structuring their data—in short, by identifying the "models of teaching" by which they have organized their work.

2. The Nature of a Model of Teaching

Our purpose in writing this chapter has been to identify those conceptual structures which have functioned as models in recent research and debate on teaching methods. We make no apology for the fact that the models which we have been able to identify do not *look like* the types of models which Maccia, Maccia and Jewett (1963) and Brodbeck (1959) claim are the way models in the social sciences ought to be conceived. Our concern has been primarily with understanding research on teaching *in its own terms.*

Working from this point of view, there appear to have been three distinct models of teaching which have provided the stimulus and structure for recent teaching research. Each of these models consists of a set of associated ideas and concepts more or less organized around a larger conception of what teaching ought to be like, and how it ought to be viewed.

If there is any single characteristic which defines these models, it is that they each have, at their center, an assumption that all significant variation in teaching is a function of variation along a single dimension. This assumption makes it possible for an investigator to see questions about teaching methods as evaluative "either . . . or" questions. When the investigator conducts research or analysis within the context of a model, he no longer needs to worry about the multitude of teaching methods that might be considered, but can confine his attention to simplistic comparisons between competing alternatives. In this way each model serves to simplify and organize the process of research, and provides the grounds for interpreting and generalizing the empirical data which are obtained.

We have labeled the three dominant models as the *behavior-control model,* the *discovery-learning model,* and the *rational model.*

The *behavior-control* or *behavior-modification* model consists of that set of concepts and claims about teaching which has arisen from the attempt to apply the interpretive framework of behavioral psychology to the classroom. Generally, it might be called the stimulus-response view of teaching, and it incorporates within its boundaries the theoretical residue of the programmed instruction movement and the present claims of behavior-modification advocates.

The *discovery-learning* model incorporates those views of teaching which place greatest emphasis on the self-directed activity of the student. It might be seen as the contemporary successor to the authoritarian-democratic model, but incorporates some of the present-day concern for creativity and the terminology of cognitive psychology, and it finds some of its strongest proponents in the recent curriculum reform movements.

The *rational* model owes a lot of its impetus to the recent application of analytic philosophy to educational issues. It stands as the major nonpsychological model, generating its own type of quasi-empirical research. Central to this model is the claim that teaching must be concerned with rationality and that the practice of teaching must be influenced by the logic of argument and justification.

Unlike major models which have been influential in the physical sciences, these models do not compete with each other as alternative views of the same body of established data. Since there is little, if any, established data about teaching which is widely accepted, they compete with each other as alternative ways of viewing the practical activity of teaching.

For this reason there are few logical or empirical connections between the models. What is considered "good teaching" in one model is not the same thing as that which is considered bad teaching in another model. Nor is there any sense in which empirical evidence can be used to prove the validity of one model or demonstrate its superiority over another model. It is not even possible to claim that one model has the quality of having generated more research than another, because, as the following discussion of the models will indicate, advocates of the different models do not agree about what constitutes appropriate research.

Yet despite all this, advocates of one model tend to see advocates of another of the models as competitors. Not, however, as competitors for scientific truth or respectability, but as competitors for the allegiance of the educational community. Each model is fundamentally a claim about how teaching *ought* to be understood and interpreted.

3. The Structure of This Chapter

The body of this chapter is divided into four sections. In the first section we have attempted to provide a brief description of the contemporary *practice* of teaching without reference to any interpretation of that practice. The purpose of this section is to provide the reader with a background against which the details of the three models will stand out more clearly. These models have become so much a part of our thinking about teaching that we are inclined to forget that they are interpretations and what goes on in classrooms is something else again.

In the following three sections we provide descriptions of the three models, attempting to represent each view as sympathetically as possible and to reflect something of the enthusiasms and concerns of its protagonists.

The chapter is concluded with an attempt to summarize the functional significance of these models and to point up the dilemma which faces researchers who work within the interpretive framework which a model provides.

SECTION ONE:
THE PRACTICE OF TEACHING IN CONTEMPORARY CLASSROOMS

In any consideration of the contemporary practice of teaching, it is probably easiest to start from the distinction that is usually drawn between a) the interaction of teacher and students with the subject matter or skills that constitute the curriculum, and b) the management of the classroom as a social institution functioning in the larger context of the school and educational community.

If we refer to the first as *instruction,* and to the second as *classroom management,* then it is generally true that most of the available observational data are concerned with teaching as instruction. For this reason most of this section is concerned with a summary of the available data about teaching as instruction, with a brief summary of teaching as classroom management included at the end to round out the picture.

1. Teaching as Instruction: Major Lesson Forms

First let us consider the kinds of activities which are found in the typical school classroom. Herbert (1967) has suggested that most of what we refer to as classroom teaching (instruction) consists of lessons in which teacher and students interact with each other and with some form of subject content. There are three basic forms which these lessons, or parts of these lessons, might take.

The first form is one in which the teacher is in control of the treatment of subject matter. The teacher is lecturing, performing, demonstrating or exhibiting materials. In the second form both teacher and pupil have some control over the treatment of subject matter. Usually this involves verbal interaction with variations in the degree to which teacher or students control the course of the interaction. In the third form the students are displaced from the direct control of the teacher and are engaged in assigned or unassigned exercises, practical work, or study. In this last form of lesson the teacher's control is indirect.

The lecture form of lesson needs no illustration. Detailed analysis of explanatory lectures in twelfth-grade social studies classes has been reported by Rosenshine (1968) and by Hiller, Fisher, and Kaess (1969). Observation suggests that it is not a common form of lesson, especially in the lower grades.

More common are the lesson forms which involve some student participation. The following extract from a twelfth-grade class on government is typical of a lesson in which there is minimal student participation. The teacher is discussing "democracy."

Teacher:	Democracy, a government by the people . . . a government in which the supreme power is retained by the people and exercised either directly, absolute or pure democracy. Where do we have absolute or pure democracy in the world today?
Student I:	Switzerland?
Teacher:	Switzerland. Switzerland is exercised as a pure democracy . . . one of the few places in the world, but not the only place. Why can it be exercised there, whereas it could not be here, as a pure democracy? You see any reason for it being exercised in Switzerland?
Student II:	Too much population.
Teacher:	That's right. Population is an important element . . . .

Flanders (1970) and others who have been engaged in classroom observation studies for some years have noted that in the traditional classroom teachers do a lot of talking. Even when the lesson is concerned with nonverbal materials the teacher provides a verbal commentary. The following extract was recorded in a tenth grade biology class as the teacher sliced sections of the stem of a plant.

Teacher:	The pith is a vulnerable part as far as the plant is concerned, because it still has some small amount of food stored in it, and this is inviting as far as insects are concerned. If I can hold this up to the light at the angle there is a small hole, you should be able to see an opening where this pith, or the pith in this wood cut was destroyed by insects. They've been eating it. . . . See these lateral lines here, the rays, Sally, can you see them? Okay, these rays are responsible for lateral conduction. Lateral conduction from the pith, also from the cortex. These tiny lines running throughout. Most . . . you can see them clearly on this cut. And here's another spot where they show up well. Responsible for lateral conduction. . . .

Perhaps the most common form of lesson to be found in the contemporary traditional classroom is the one in which both the teacher and students have a significant part to play in the direction of the discourse. The following illustration is taken from a recording of a science lesson in a third grade classroom.

Teacher:	Yesterday we said that the black-backed gull was found in many different places. What were some of these places? Christine?
Christine:	Down in the parks.
Teacher:	Down in the parks.
Peter:	By the river.
Teacher:	Down by the river.
Mark:	And at the beach.
Teacher:	Beach.
Simon:	They follow up especially fishing boats.
Teacher:	Right. Now why are they found in these places? Julian?
Julian:	Because they are looking for food and scraps.

Teacher: All right. Let's look at the
              food they'd find in these
              places. . . .

This form of interaction is extremely common in the recordings which have been made in observational studies of the classroom.

2. Teaching as Instruction: The Frequency of Different Lesson Forms

It is difficult to generalize about how frequently a student is exposed to these different lesson forms, because clearly there are variations between different subject areas and between different grade levels. The data obtained by Herbert (1967), Gump (1967), and Adams and Biddle (1970) suggest that on the average, teachers spend about:

(a)   18 to 22 percent of the time lecturing, or lecturing and demonstrating or exhibiting materials;

(b)   20 to 30 percent of the time engaged in the question-answer type of recitation or discussion with students (often interspersed with short lectures);

(c)   14 to 23 percent of the time combining demonstration or exhibition of materials with question-answer type discussion;

(d)   between 25 and 45 percent of the time supervising students who are engaged in individual seat or laboratory work.

3. Teaching as Instruction: The Rules of the Game

The question-answer type of verbal interaction between teacher and students, which has been illustrated above, is the lesson form which springs to mind most readily when classroom teaching is mentioned. Bellack and Davitz (1963) have provided a succinct description of this form of verbal interaction in a set of "rules of the classroom game." They characterize the game as one in which the object is to engage in verbal discourse about subject matter. The teacher obeys a set of rules which stipulate that *he* must do most of the talking and must structure the specific form and content of the verbal game at any one time. If he plays in the way expected of a teacher he will spend most of his time asking questions and commenting on pupil responses. From time to time he will spend time structuring the content and providing summaries of previous discourse.

The rules for the pupils are much more restrictive. The pupil's primary task is to answer questions, to reply when called on. The pupil must respond as though the teacher always asks questions which a pupil *should* be able to answer. He may not respond evaluatively but may, under certain conditions, ask the occasional question.

The pupil is expected to pay attention to the progress of a lesson even though he will not be expected to respond more than six or seven times in an hour. When he is asked to respond his response will be repeated, praised or commented on by the teacher. Most of his time will be taken up listening to other pupils' responses and the teacher's comments to those responses.

The evidence gathered by Hoetker and Ahlbrand (1969) strongly suggests that this classroom language game has had a long and persistent history. Records of observational studies from the turn of the nineteenth century indicate that the game has not changed substantially in approximately 60 years. What may have changed is the nature of the questions asked by teachers. It is probable that the frequency of questions calling for recall of information and repetition of practiced responses has declined, and the frequency of questions requiring pupils to give opinions, make and draw conclusions has increased proportionately. The research of Smith and Meux (1962) indicates that about $\frac{2}{3}$ of teachers' questions require recall or reporting of known information and about $\frac{1}{3}$ are questions which require pupils to perform logical operations such as making comparisons, drawing inferences and constructing explanations.

What is the purpose of this apparently laborious and complex pattern of verbal interaction? Underlying it there is a kind of pedagogical folklore, a set of rationalizations for practices that have survived the passing pressures imposed by parents, administrators, curriculum innovators and teacher-training programs. Some of the elements of this folklore are:

    (a) pupils must be kept active and busily engaged in intellectually relevant activities;

    (b) teachers should avoid telling pupils when pupils can tell themselves;

    (c) questions stimulate pupil thinking and pupils should be made to think about the subject matter;

    (d) it is the teacher's duty to monitor pupil understanding of subject matter by asking further appropriate questions.

Jackson (1968), through interviews with selected teachers, has been able to probe more deeply into the folklore of good teachers. His study suggests that teachers respond directly and personally to their pupils, seeing signs of the success of their teaching in the appearance and responses of the pupils. Teaching is going well when the pupils are responding with enthusiasm, when they look alert and interested. Teachers see a virtue in maintaining some degree of informality in their classrooms so that lessons can follow lines of interest rather than the structure imposed by subject matter. Teachers feel constricted and that their work is being undermined when they have to meet the demands of examinations and external curricular pressures.

4. Teaching as Classroom Management

Whatever "rules of the game" may be seen as relevant and desirable in conducting instruction in the classroom, it is clear that they are overlaid by other "rules of the game" which are imposed on the situation by the social context of the classroom. In its simplest terms this social context creates a situation in which, generally, one teacher is brought into contact with 30 pupils, assigned authority over them and given responsibility for their conduct. Many of the teacher's activities in the classroom represent his use of this authority in creating what is thought to be the "well-managed" classroom.

How much of the teacher's time is taken up in management activities is indicated in a study reported by Gump (1967). He found that on an average the teachers he observed spent:

    (a) 51 percent of their time in instructional activities;

    (b) 23 percent of their time structuring and organizing the behavior of the pupils;

    (c) 14 percent of their time admonishing, giving permission, and dealing with deviant behavior;

    (d) 12 percent of their time in other activities including dealing with individual problems.

Unfortunately there has been little observational study of classroom management procedures. The work of Smith and Geoffrey (1968) and Kounin (1970) suggests that there are other more subtle characteristics of a teacher's activities which affect management (cf. Kounin's "with-it-ness"), but no general observational data are available on these characteristics. Clearly teachers do set up rules of conduct, impart to pupils expectations about desired behavior, and administer rewards and punishments. How they normally do this has not been extensively studied.

Given this descriptive sketch of the practice of teaching, it is now possible to examine the way this practice is viewed and interpreted by the three models of teaching. What is the teacher *really* doing? How *should* the teacher be behaving? How are differences between teachers to be interpreted? What aspects of the teacher's practice need to be conceptually isolated and investigated? What psychological or logical prescriptions are relevant to an evaluation of the teacher's performance?

The answers to these and further related questions form the substance of the three models of teaching which are described in the following three sections. The exponents of these models do not generally appeal to the known facts about the practice of teaching as justification for their position, but the reader will be better able to evaluate each model if this picture of the practice of teaching is kept in mind.

SECTION TWO:
THE BEHAVIOR-CONTROL MODEL

What we have termed the "behavior-control" model is that set of concepts and claims about teaching which was generated by the growth of the automated (programmed) instruction movement and the consequent attempts to apply modern behavioral psychology to education. Unlike other technological advances in education, the introduction of teaching machines by Professor Skinner heralded much more than the launching of a new piece of audio-visual hardware.

While Pressey in the late 1920s saw his original teaching machine as a mechanical aid which might signal the coming of an industrial revolution in education (Pressey, 1926, 1932), Skinner in the 1950s was claiming that the teaching machine had introduced the considerable power of scientific psychology into the management of teaching (Skinner, 1954). Behind Skinner's teaching machines lay the concept of a true science of instruction with a vision of the boundless advances that only an empirical science could bring.

This vision caught the imagination of many educators and coincided with the interests of a further group of psychologists with experience in military training research. Sharing a common background in

behavioral psychology, this latter group was able to demonstrate that, with the application of modern techniques of job-analysis, psychological research methods could contribute directly to the improvement of classroom instruction.

As the movement has developed, theory and research have bypassed the limitations of the teaching machine (and its computerized counterparts) and laid claims to the foundation of a "behavioral science of instruction" (cf. Glaser, 1965b). While Skinner has pursued his own specific theoretical concerns (Skinner, 1968), others have taken over his vision of "education as the most important branch of scientific technology" and attempted to prescribe the methods of investigation and kinds of knowledge which will make this a reality (cf. Anderson, Faust, Roderick, Cunningham, & Andre, 1969).

1. The Behavior-Control Description of Teaching

The label "behavior-control" has been applied to this model because underlying many of the concepts and ideas expressed by its protagonists is the notion of teaching as a method of *controlling* the behavior of students and the conditions of learning.

Teaching is approached as a *management* procedure which ought to be accomplished as quickly and as efficiently as possible. Objectivity, precision and economy are the prime methodological virtues. For Skinner the validity of his argument rests on the demonstration of his ability to control behavior (Skinner, 1968). For Stolurow it is the "new concept of instruction as a communication and control process" which is going to provide the solution to the educational crisis (Stolurow, 1965).

Within this context the initial emphasis is not on teaching as such but on the objectives of a teaching task. It is claimed that the *essential task* of teaching is to get students to perform precisely delineated responses (Taber, Glaser, & Schaefer, 1965).

Further, one of the major reasons that there has been a failure to put teaching on a sound scientific basis in the past has been that teachers have failed to consider their objectives in precise behavioral terminology. The progress which is evident in the psychological laboratory has been dependent on precise behavioral specification, and progress in teaching will depend on the same kind of precision.

For this reason description of teaching goals in terms of such vague and non-measurable concepts as "understanding," "awareness" and "appreciation" must be replaced by descriptions of goals in terms of what the student is expected to *do*. Specific responses must be delineated and desired rates of responding calculated.

There appear to have been two distinguishable lines of development in the application of behavior-control theory to the problem of teaching. On the one hand there has been the elaboration of the theory to the problem of *instruction* in subject-matter areas. This elaboration is, to a large extent, a generalization of programmed instruction principles to subject-matter instruction in general. Alongside this development there has been an extension of the "applied analysis of behavior" to include teaching as a special case of behavior *modification*. In this behavior modification version of the model the teacher's task is seen as one in which control is exercised over the rate of occurrence of such generalized behaviors as "attending," "sitting still" and "studying."

Instruction with subject matter. In the "instruction" version of the behavior-control model the task of the teacher is to form associative bonds between subject-matter stimuli and appropriate student responses. As Taber, Glaser and Schaefer express it, the primary objective of the teacher's work is to produce the requisite changes in student behavior and to bring this behavior under the discipline or control of appropriate subject-matter stimuli (Taber, Glaser,

& Schaefer, 1965). In an example given by Gagné, the student learns a response—stating orally the appropriate numeral which is the sum of two numbers—to a specific stimulus—two numerals connected by the sign + (Gagné, 1965a).

Despite the emphasis on the precise definition of teaching objectives in this version of the model, there is very little precision in the description of what teaching should be like. Skinner claims that students learn without teaching. Teaching is not the creation of learning nor the stimulus to it. Teaching is the arranging of conditions which *expedite* the required learning (Skinner, 1968).

The problem of describing what teachers should do is to some extent avoided by extending the behavioral analysis to the students' situation before and during instruction. Designing instructional procedures is seen as a problem in designing ways of getting students from what they "know" before instruction starts (the behavioral repertoire at entry), through the instructional situation (intermediate behaviors), to the overt goals of teaching (the terminal repertoire).

Given an adequately precise delineation of the students' entering and terminal behavioral repertoires, and of the student behaviors needed to progress from entry to termination, the problem of how to teach is largely solved. As Glaser has claimed, *definition* of the stimulus, response and structural characteristics of the subject matter and of the involved behavioral repertoires "will determine what to teach and, correspondingly, how it is to be taught" (Glaser, 1965b, p. 772).

The elaborate development of techniques for prompting and fading prompts in the frames of programmed text materials is the one example, in this version of the behavior-control model, of a relatively precise approach to teaching techniques. Markle's book on programming techniques, *Good Frames and Bad* (1964), is the classic treatment of this set of procedures.

One of the side effects of the emphasis on student entering behaviors is the attention that has been paid to individual differences. Both Glaser (1969) and Stolurow (1965) have been careful to emphasize that the efficient design of instructional procedures must depend on precise measurement of the characteristics and capabilities of the individual student. Since each student has a unique history of learning experiences, his repertoire of responses and style of learning will probably be unique. And since efficient instruction must be tailored to fit the student's existing repertoire of responses, it is evident that efficiency implies individualization. The work of Stolurow and his associates with the SOCRATES (System for Organizing Content to Review and Teach Educational Subjects) computer-based system and the work completed at the University of Pittsburgh Oakleaf Project represent applications of this theoretical position. Each is an attempt to prescribe individualized instructional treatments. The element of control is maintained alongside the notion of individual differences.

The behavior-modification version. The alternative behavior-modification version of the behavior-control model is much more concerned with overt student behavior. In this version teaching is viewed primarily as the management of the classroom. Emphasis is placed on the teacher's control and modification of those behaviors which characterize the smooth and efficient classroom program. By means of the precise manipulation of conditioned ("token") reinforcement, disruptive behaviors (moving out of seats, talking out) can be eliminated and desired behaviors (attending, studying, responding accurately) can be elicited with increased frequency.

The teacher as "behavior-modifier" is urged to view teaching in the same way as the experimental psychologist views an operant conditioning task in the laboratory (cf. Hanley, 1970). Having identified the target behavior in need of modification,

the teacher should obtain an observational record of the normal rate of occurrence of that behavior. Then, by the manipulation of appropriate contingent stimuli (reinforcers), he can begin a systematic modification program. Generally the manipulation of reinforcers involves the giving or withdrawing of positive stimuli (money, candy, free time) or of tokens which can be exchanged for positively valued goods or activities. The teacher's task is completed when her observational records show that the desired modification in the performance of the target behavior has been accomplished. To be successful the teacher should define the target behavior precisely, inform the students of the rule which is being followed in managing the reinforcement contingencies, and use considerable skill in identifying and using effective reinforcers.

This behavior-modification version of the model is, in many respects, much closer to Skinner's operant theory than is the instruction version of the model. It involves fewer assumptions about the nature of appropriate operant responses, and like Skinner's demonstrations with pigeons, appeals directly to the criterion of observable success for justification.

2. Behavior-Control Assumptions about Learning

This model of teaching might well have been given the alternative title of "the learning theory model," because protagonists of this model tend to see the practice of teaching as an exercise in the *application* of well-established learning principles to the attainment of educational goals.

For Skinner the problem of applying behavioral science to teaching is not the problem of analyzing the kinds of learning that occur in the classroom, but the problem of finding ways to make established knowledge about learning work in the classroom context. According to Homme and Tosti (quoted in Hanley, 1970), teachers use reinforcement and have a knowledge of the principles of behavioral control. The major difficulty lies in the fact that operant principles are not applied, or if they are applied, they are applied only sporadically.

In the behavior-modification version of the model, the operant theory is maintained in its pure form. Learning is known to be the product of the consequences of behavior. These consequences are reinforcing stimuli. Behavior can be modified (learned) by appropriately manipulating the contingent consequences of that behavior.

In the instruction version of the model, the nature of learning has been seen as more problematical. In the early versions of programmed instruction, the relevant consequences of a student's behavior were taken to be information about whether the response was right or wrong. This knowledge of results was equated with reinforcement.

More recently this concept of reinforcement and the notion that there is only one major type of learning have been acknowledged as needing revision.

Stolurow has suggested that the one-to-one S-R conception is inadequate for many training tasks. Many-to-one, one-to-many and many-to-many relationships are more likely to be involved. Further, to assume that the connection between S and R is always some kind of meaningless bond oversimplifies the logic inherent in most subject matter.

Gagné's book, *The Conditions of Learning* (1965b), was an attempt to expand the concept of learning outside the narrow confines of a simplistic S-R interpretation. Gagné takes the learning tasks that have interested experimental psychologists and develops them as hierarchically ordered types of learning. His listing identifies signal learning (classical conditioning) as the simplest, proceeds through stimulus-response, chaining, verbal association, multiple discrimination, concept, and principle learning, to problem-solving at the top of the hierarchy. While Gagné's analysis of learning introduces a considerable complex-

ity to the behavior-control model, it remains tied to the major conceptual concerns of other writers in the area. Gagné still emphasizes that the task of the teacher is the *management* of learning. The nature of this management is largely self-evident in situations where desired student behaviors *and* kinds of learning have been adequately defined in the terminology of behavioral science.

3. Research Related to the Behavior-Control Model

Possibly because of its behavioral science origins, research has been an important adjunct to the development of the behavior-control model of teaching. It would be claiming too much to say that research has assisted the development of the model because much of the critical research has been theoretically more damaging than helpful. But there have been a considerable number of relevant research studies which have contributed substantially to the elaboration of the model and have assisted in publicizing the model to the educational world.

When Skinner first published his descriptions of working teaching machines and suggested some of their potential, he drew forth an immediate hostile reaction from those who felt that there must be a fundamental antagonism between machines and human education. The immediate questions raised were: Can machines *teach* in any meaningful, humane way? Are these machines going to replace human teachers?

The first research studies were attempts to tackle the issues raised by these questions. Skinner and his associates took it as their first task to demonstrate that these machines did in fact teach (Holland, 1959; Keisler, 1959; Porter, 1959).

This kind of research was, however, rapidly swamped by a flood of studies which attempted to compare machine (or program) and teacher. Granted that the machine could teach (in some sense of teach), could it teach as well as the classroom teacher or some traditional method? Just how many of these studies have been completed it is difficult to assess. A review by Hartley (1966) located 112 studies conducted in England and the United States. Since the greatest activity in this area probably occurred between 1960 and 1965, it is doubtful if the number is now considerably larger than this.

The results of these studies have not helped to answer the question which was asked. According to Hartley, when criterion test results are considered, about 37 percent of the studies showed the program to be significantly superior, about 49 percent showed no significant differences, and 14 percent showed the conventional method (lecture, teachers, etc.) to be significantly better. In a review of similar comparative studies conducted with the teaching of mathematics, Zoll (1969) found that in 13 studies, three showed programmed methods to be superior, three showed the traditional methods to be superior, and the other seven studies revealed no statistically significant differences.

Since empirical research is not a form of democracy influenced by majority vote, the tabulation of these findings serves to indicate nothing more than the futility of attempting to provide a general answer to the question. The theory of instruction has not been developed by this research except in the limited sense that researchers have been forced to consider reasons (excuses) for the failure of their comparative hypotheses.

Fortunately another kind of research which has been much more productive of useful theory and knowledge about teaching, has been stimulated by the behavior-control model. This research includes those studies in which specific aspects of the teaching process as it is conceived in the behavior-control model have been scrutinized. Investigators have looked at the need for immediate reinforcement, the kinds of reinforcers which work in a behavior-modification program, the need for overt responding, the effects of different kinds of prompts, and so on. The section headings of a recent book on research on teaching edited by Anderson, et al. (*Current Research on Instruction*, 1969) indicate the nature and scope of this research. These headings are: Instructional Objectives, Prompting and Fading Techniques, Student Response, Reinforcement and Feedback, Facilitation of Concept Learning, Organization and Sequence, and Evaluation of Instruction. These form the major areas of concern in the behavior-control model of teaching.

4. The Behavioral Science Base and Its Critics

Much of the power and purpose of this model lies in its claim to be the way in which behavioral psychology can be introduced effectively into the management of teaching. It is currently popular to revere the role of science in human affairs and to revere the potential role of psychological science in education. The serious critic of the behavior-control model hardly dares to attack the intentions of its protagonists, but he can criticize either the way the model distorts the educational enterprise or the kind of psychological science that it has espoused.

The former kind of criticism centers around the apparent products of applying behavioral terminology to educational objectives and procedures. Are understanding, thinking and appreciating reducible to observable student responses? Can teaching be reduced to the elicitation and reinforcement of responses? The argument is not specific to the behavior-control model of teaching but is a special case of the general argument against the reductionist intentions of the behavioral psychologist.

The second kind of criticism—that the psychological theory of the behavior-control model is the wrong kind of psychology—is again a special but more sophisticated anti-reductionist criticism. For instance, Ausubel, in his theory of meaningful verbal learning, presents a series of arguments against assuming that behavioral psychology can be translated readily to school learning. In his view much of the content of education cannot be reduced to simple S-R connections. The meaningfulness of the content of school curricula distinguishes it from the content of most experimental learning tasks. Some of his research has been directed to demonstrating that the laws which apply to rote verbal learning do not apply to the learning of meaningful educational materials (Ausubel & Blake, 1958; Ausubel, Stager, & Gaite, 1969).

From a rather different point of view, Rothkopf also has attacked the notion of interpreting educational tasks in simple behaviorist terms. Rothkopf asserts that the precision and objectivity of experimental studies lie in their description of the experimental hardware (trials, exposure time, time intervals, tokens, nonsense syllables) and not in their description or control of psychological processes. It may be clear in the laboratory context how physical stimuli and responses are operationally defined and controlled. But it is not at all clear what psychological processes underlie these events, and it is completely unclear how one is to identify relevant psychological variables in educational contexts where the laboratory-based operational definitions do not apply (Rothkopf, 1968).

Basic to these criticisms is the fundamental problem which must confront any attempt to translate a laboratory-based conceptual system into the context of the larger outside world. Do you alter the conceptual system so that it fits the existing realities of the outside world? Or do you attempt to remake the outside world so that it comes to look like the laboratory situation? The protagonists of the behavior-control model, impressed with the elegance and power of laboratory-based experimental psychology, have attempted the latter solution. They have applied the reductionist's "simplicity filter" (Griffin, 1967) and have asserted that a science of teaching can be developed if the educational task is remodeled so that it looks like the laboratory experiment. The teacher is to be the experimenter and the pupils are his experimental subjects.

Critics, including Ausubel and Rothkopf, have stated that this remaking of the educational task changes not only its shape but also its nature. They would claim that scientific method and scientifically respectable concepts can be applied to research on teaching without the necessity for this gross distortion of real educational problems.

Another type of criticism comes from those who find the traditional operant conditioning model conceptually and theoretically inadequate. Still working from within the view that teaching must be based on the experimental psychology of learning, they emphasize the power of alternative theoretical positions such as those developed in the areas of perception and psycholinguistics. Unimpressed by the "justification by demonstrable effects" espoused by the behavior-modification school, they tend to dismiss the operant model as disproved by other influential psychologists. A recent paper by Anderson (1970) is an example of this type of criticism.

SECTION THREE: THE DISCOVERY-LEARNING MODEL

While the behavior-control model is an attempt to let behavioral psychology structure the nature of teaching, the discovery-learning model represents an attempt to give psychological respectability to the inspired performance of the master teacher. The advocate of the discovery-learning model tends to rest his case on the evident excitement and inspiration of those moments in the classroom when teacher and pupil achieve together some significant insight into the nature of things. The psychological theory which is used to support the discovery-learning model is not precise and rigorously experimental but consists rather in a loosely grouped amalgam of ideas from cognitive psychology, child development and the study of creativity.

Proponents of the discovery-learning model want to claim that their view of teaching is both a "new pedagogy" and a historically rich tradition. Some are concerned to show that the antecedents of their ideas are clearly evident in the writings of Rousseau, Montessori and Dewey. Taba (1963) identified descriptions of discovery-learning dating back to 1904, and Hendrix (1961) found similar evidence in a book published in 1823. Glaser (1966) claims that the inductive method (which he associates with discovery-learning) is a "long standing procedure, recognized in society for its excellence," and he quotes Mechner (1961) as stating that through the ages great teachers and great writers have known, intuitively, the principles of inductive teaching.

On the other hand, writers like Bruner (1961) see the use of discovery learning as an innovation desperately needed in our school system to replace the current emphasis on rote learning and restricted thinking. Suchman (1961) writes on the "new pedagogy" in which retention is subordinated to thinking and in which the teacher must abandon his "traditionally directive mode" and structure the environment so that the child is led to "exciting new discoveries."

Both of these views can be seen as valid when it is realized that the discovery-learning model represents a new mode of relating the very old humanist-Gestalt tradition in psychology to the practice of teaching. Those who dislike the notions of control and prediction in human affairs, and prefer solutions which allow for individual initiative and freedom, have found the discovery-learning model to be an appropriate expression of their values.

But the major reason for the prominence of the discovery-learning model in recent educational debate has been the incorporation of this model of teaching into several well-publicized new curricula in mathematics, science and the social studies. As Taba has indicated, the curriculum projects which started out to remodel the subject-matter content of traditional school programs have produced a major renewal of emphasis on teaching methods (Taba, 1963). It would be unusual to find a carefully prepared new curriculum which did not incorporate in some way the objective of students discovering for themselves some major concepts or principles.

1. The Discovery-Learning Model View of Teaching

The literature on discovery-learning suffers (if it can be said to suffer) from a surfeit of descriptions and illustrations of the discovery method. Psychologists (Bruner, 1966; Friedlander, 1965), curriculum writers and theorists (Taba, 1963), and experienced teachers (Davis, 1966; Hendrix, 1961) have all been involved. Clearly it is difficult to provide a succinct summary of these diverse points of view.

Those who have been involved in the development and use of curriculum materials tend to produce a picture which is closely tied to particular subject matter and to practical procedures. Hendrix (1961) and Davis (1966) both provide illustrations of a two-stage process. In the first stage pupils are asked to solve problems or discuss examples for which their prior knowledge is appropriate and adequate. In the second stage the problems or examples are changed, slowly or abruptly, so that the known procedures become either cumbersome or impossible to apply. During this stage the successful student "discovers" a new method or principle which enables him to handle the new problems more efficiently or correctly. Davis refers to this second stage as "torpedoing."

Both Taba and Hendrix are at pains to point out that saying or telling students the new procedure or principle is not only not part of the teaching procedure, but may be positively harmful if the students are not ready for it. The fear is that students will learn to "parrot" what they are told.

A rather different and more elaborate description of the discovery-learning teaching procedure has been reported by Worthen (1968). In an experiment comparing discovery and expository methods, teachers using the discovery method were required to follow carefully prepared curriculum materials, and instructed to perform in the following manner:

(a) The teacher was not to act as the primary source of knowledge but was to give the impression that he depended on the students to help him work the problems.

(b) The teacher was to avoid indicating anything about the generalizations to be discovered before nearly all students had discovered them for themselves.

(c) The teacher was to prevent sharing of ideas among students.

(d) If the students reached false conclusions or generalizations the teacher was not to tell them that they were wrong, but was to "trap" them by asking them to do examples in which the false generalization could be seen to be false.

In addition to these teacher instructions, the materials used were organized so that instances (problems) were presented first before principles (heuristic rules) were mentioned.

Rather different descriptions of the discovery method have been provided by writers who have attempted to isolate the psychological processes involved in the discovery process (e.g., Bruner, 1961).

Bittinger (1968) has suggested that the only common theme running through all of the different descriptions is the emphasis on the teacher *not* telling the students the principle or generalization or rule which they are supposed to learn. What the teacher is to do when he is not telling the student is not always agreed on. For some it is a matter of presenting material in an example-to-rule sequence. It is implied that this must involve the students in a process of induction, and the process of induction is what distinguishes the discovery method from the usual expository nature of classroom teaching where deduction is the rule (Glaser, 1966).

For others induction is not enough to ensure that discovery learning occurs. Hendrix (1961) claims that the fallacy in the inductive method lies in its confusion of pupil verbalization of a rule with the "advent of discovery itself." For Hendrix the big new breakthrough in pedagogy lies in the separation of discovery from the verbalization of generalizations. Appropriate teaching for "nonverbal awareness" of new generalizations is an art with a difficult technique. The teacher must use carefully prepared materials and must reward students for looking for a "short cut" or obtaining an "insight." The teacher must above all else be sensitive to those nonverbal signs which indicate moments of discovery in individual pupils. According to Davis (1966), this sensitivity must include an awareness that pupils may well discover new and unique procedures which are as good as the conventional ones. The best discovery learning occurs in situations where there is more than one right answer.

It is acknowledged that this kind of teaching is very difficult, and it is claimed that expository teaching is so common in the traditional classroom because it is so much easier and more rewarding to teachers. The traditional teacher finds it hard to tolerate errors and is happier when his teaching leads straight to the one correct solution.

It should be clear from these descriptions that the goals of discovery teaching generally are agreed upon, but there is a variation in the means advocated to achieve these goals. The definition provided by Young (1906) makes this point clearly: "It is the function of the teacher and of the text *so to present* the things to be done, *so to prepare* the problems to be solved, *that* they require real discovery on the part of the pupil" (p. 70) (author's emphasis).

2. Discovery Learning

Much of the justification given for the discovery-learning view of teaching lies in the nature of the learning it is supposed to foster. The claims made are wide-ranging and diverse, but they usually have this in common: they provide attractive alternatives to the passive, rote, meaningless incorporation of isolated facts which (it is claimed by proponents of the discovery-learning model) is the standard fare of ordinary classrooms.

In most discussions of the topic, the processes of discovery and learning are assimilated to each other and often to the process of thinking (cf. Taba, 1963). Thus it is true to say, in one sense, that the objective of discovery methods of teaching is discovery, not learning. But since the act of discovery is taken to imply a particularly powerful kind of learning, the objective is learning in this specialized sense.

According to Bruner (1966), discovery is a matter of rearranging or transforming evidence. It is a type of thinking. This type of thinking occurs in such a way that the individual discoverer goes "beyond the information given" to new insights and generalizations. Suchman (1961) sees it rather differently. For him the experience of discovery involves the *sudden* assimilation of perceived data into the existing framework of a conceptual system. Friedlander (1965) describes the process as one in which the student, led by the "momentum" of the information which has been presented to him, makes correct inferences.

When discovery has occurred, then that which has been discovered is a very special kind of knowledge. This knowledge is something which stays with the student longer than knowledge gained in other ways, it is more easily transferable to other situations, and has a more important place

in the student's mind. In fact, Bruner (1961) has claimed that discovery guarantees that what is learned has been learned effectively. According to Hendrix (1961), *only* those generalizations which have emerged from a student's own discovery experiences can play a "dynamic part in the learner's later behavior."

When a student is led to discover a generalization, he does not learn only that generalization; he also learns from the process of discovery itself. The psychological processes involved are said to be similar to the processes involved in any problem-solving situation. Hence, when discovery methods are used, the student learns how to explore a situation for himself (Bruner, 1966), how to go beyond the information given in a situation, and how to behave in a scientific manner and think in an inductive style (Wittrock, 1966). The student is said to develop an "organizing scheme" for his own cognitive activity and an expectation that learning is something which is primarily self-directed (Taba, 1963).

Clearly the view of learning which is involved in these claims is quite different from the view of learning that underlies the behavior-control model. The behavioral psychologist would find it difficult to recognize any learning in this situation at all. There are no trials and presentations of the thing to be learned. In the discovery process it may not be at all certain exactly *what* an individual is learning, which makes it extremely difficult to determine *how,* or even *if,* learning and forgetting are taking place.

The psychological theory which tends to be used by advocates of the discovery-learning model is derived from experimental investigation of concept attainment and problem-solving (cf. Bruner, Goodnow, & Austin, 1956), from studies of creative thinking, and from the research on intellectual development initiated by Piaget and his co-workers. It is especially important for many of the advocates of the model that Piaget's theory has given respectability and logical rigor to the view that maturation and unguided individual experience are important components of intellectual development. While Piaget's views do not give any exact theoretical support for the discovery-learning process, his elaborate conceptual structure emphasizes inner-directed development and endorses the claim that human responses are more than the product of reinforcement contingencies.

The connection between Piagetian psychology and discovery-learning methods has been partly established by the personal interest of influential writers such as Bruner (1961, 1966) and Taba (1964) in both areas.

It would be doing an injustice to the proponents of the discovery-learning model, however, if we were to give the impression that they advocated that all learning should involve student discovery. It is acknowledged that discovery procedures are difficult and time-consuming, and that students cannot be expected to rediscover the entire content of the culture for themselves. What is claimed is that discovery learning is the most powerful and effective kind of learning and must be used where what is being learned has major significance. Thus, for Bruner, Taba and others, each discipline contains certain very powerful and pervasive organizing concepts and principles. To learn a discipline effectively requires that these concepts be firmly implanted in the minds of students, preferably from an early age. Discovery methods are the methods par excellence for the learning of these major organizing concepts.

One further point about the discovery-learning model view of learning needs to be emphasized. It is the association often made between discovery and meaningfulness. Discovery is, of necessity, a very individual thing. When a child discovers something for himself, he makes use of his own ways of viewing and structuring the world around him. Guided by the teacher, he employs his own developed skills of searching and ordering data, and his own particular set of meanings and feelings about his experiences. The product of his discovery will be something uniquely his own. It follows that discovery learning is always highly meaningful learning. Curiously, however, it is rarely claimed that discovery-learning methods should be highly individualized procedures.

3. Research Related to the Discovery-Learning Model

A large number of research studies have been conducted in which some version of the discovery-learning method has been the object of investigation. An excellent review of these studies has been published by Wittrock (1966), and the reader is referred to that review for details.

Most of this research has been designed in the way that one would expect from the nature of the discovery-learning model. Typically, the favored method (the discovery method) has been compared with its theoretical opposite (the traditional expository or deductive method). Since the objective of the discovery method is usually the learning of some rule or generalization, the criterion tests used involve measures of immediate or delayed ability to use the rule on familiar examples, to transfer the use of the rule to unfamiliar examples, or to verbalize the rule itself.

The earliest studies quoted by Wittrock date back to the turn of the century, but there is still a growing research literature on the problem. In 1968 *The Journal of Educational Psychology* devoted an entire monograph supplement to a study by Worthen. Evidently those convinced that the discovery-versus-expository view is an important way of conceptualizing teaching have not been convinced that the issue is yet settled. It is still necessary to find the experimental evidence which demonstrates convincingly that the discovery procedure is superior.

In addition to this kind of discovery-versus-expository research, Wittrock's review indicates that the discovery-learning model has also generated other kinds of studies in which more attention has been paid to the details of the learning processes involved. Kersh (1958, 1962) has looked at the motivational effects of discovery methods. Craig (1956) and Corman (1957) have investigated the effects of varying amounts of guidance by the teacher in stimulating discovery, and Wittrock (1963) has looked at the interaction between amounts of guidance and direct and transfer learning criteria.

It is interesting to note that, as this research has become more sophisticated and less concerned with the simple method A versus method B problem, it has become more removed from the classroom with respect to the nature of the learning tasks and the teaching methods involved. It has become laboratory research on the problems of transfer learning, verbal mediation and task instructions rather than research on teaching in the traditional sense. In other words it has become less dominated by the model, and more specifically concerned with the psychological processes implicated in the model.

While one might hope that this sophistication of research interest would evolve into a soundly based area of empirical knowledge about teaching, the fact remains that studies such as that reported by Worthen (1968) are still considered significant.

4. Critics of the
Discovery-Learning Model

Wittrock (1966) has made it clear that from an experimental psychologist's point of view there is considerable conceptual confusion in the typical description of the discovery-learning model. He points out that it is seldom made clear whether "discovery learning" refers to a *method* or to an *objective*. In making this criticism, Wittrock, understandably, has failed to see that these two aspects (method and objective) are assimilated to each other in the discovery-learning model. To ask that they be conceptually distinguished is to impose another model of learning (the behavioral psychology model)

where such a model is inappropriate. That the discovery-learning view of learning makes it very difficult to do the kind of research with which the behavioral psychologist is familiar should not be surprising.

Other critics have claimed that discovery-learning methods are too time-consuming, that the methods may not suit all kinds of students, and that forcing students to discover for themselves may prevent them from obtaining adequate amounts of rewarding experiences. It has also been claimed that, in addition to discovering knowledge, students need also to be able to evaluate and interpret the fruits of others' work.

Friedlander (1965) has voiced a series of doubts about the rationale underlying the discovery-learning model. He points to the frequency of student failure and error which is a necessary part of discovery teaching. Such errors may produce considerable confusion in the minds of students when teachers are unable to respond individually and immediately to the occurrence of these errors in the classroom. He has suggested that we need to face up to the "hopelessly chaotic chains of inferences and deduction" which may arise when students are asked to reason for themselves. It is unreasonable to assume that students have the powers of judgment and evaluation needed to assess their own intuitive leaps or reasoning.

Friedlander also claims that there is no hard evidence that insights which a student develops on his own are remembered any better than insights which are learned from others. Wittrock (1966) has drawn attention to the fact that research has not isolated the effect of discovery itself on learning.

Finally, Friedlander draws attention to the problems that face a teacher attempting to use discovery methods in the ordinary classroom. There are usually wide differences in the meanings which teacher and students attach to their perceptions and experiences. Students work at different speeds and think in different ways. These disparities between teacher and students, and between student and student, in cognitive experience and style, may provide insuperable barriers to coherent learning when the teacher opens up the classroom to the unstructured methods of discovery learning.

Ausubel (1961) points out that there is no necessary connection between discovery methods and the meaningfulness of learning, any more than there is a necessary connection between expository methods and rote learning. It is a misleading oversimplification to assume that all expository methods must lead to meaningless and useless learning. For Ausubel, meaningfulness is a quality of the relationship between the materials to be learned and the way these are incorporated into the learner's cognitive structure. There is no one method of teaching by which meaningfulness can be assured.

Perhaps the central point of these criticisms is that the claims made by the proponents of the discovery-learning model have been overgeneralized. Few would want to claim that discovery-learning methods are not in some circumstances highly valuable. Critics cannot deny the force of some of the practical examples cited by Hendrix (1961) and Davis (1966). What they do claim is that discovery methods cannot be used in all situations, and may not be the best methods for most classroom learning tasks. They are denying that the discovery-learning model has the generality and persuasive force that its proponents would hope for it.

SECTION FOUR:
THE RATIONAL MODEL

Whereas the previous two models are psychological in origin and orientation, the rational model emerges from philosophy. The main exponents of this model today are those who write from within the analytic movement in philosophy. On the surface, what they are doing is analyzing the concepts of "teaching" and "learning" and related terms such as "conditioning," "indoctrination" and "education." They would probably deny that they are presenting a model for the practice of teaching and may even be loath to admit that their work has much in common with that of the traditional philosopher. However, when their writings are viewed in the context of historical and contemporary concerns and in the light of the research interests they have fostered, the conclusion is that they do expound a definite model of teaching and that this model can be traced to concerns which have marked philosophical endeavor over the centuries.

Underlying this model are certain basic assumptions. Man is viewed as a rational being whose behavior cannot be completely understood in terms associated with animal life or machines. His rationality not only limits the extent to which his behavior can be understood by such analogies but also prescribes limits as to what can be legitimately done to him. Rationality implies a moral thesis about how man is to be treated.

Thinking and language are regarded as the traits which are distinctively human. Man, the rational animal, is also man the symbol-using animal. Language must play the key role in teaching since its connection with thinking and with rationality is so intimate.

1. The Rational Model
Description of Teaching

The other two models assume that there is a logically tight connection between teaching and learning. Proponents of the rational model agree that there is some connection but reject a conceptual one. The reason for this is that they regard teaching as a human *activity*. It is goal-oriented and intentional. This means that it is not always successful and learning does not necessarily follow. It also implies that not all activities which bring about learning can be called teaching; only intentional activities can qualify as teaching activities. Furthermore, since teaching is the activity of a human agent working upon pupils who are also human agents, there are moral limits to what may count as teaching. Thus Scheffler (1960) argues that at all stages the pupil's reason must be engaged and the teacher must submit himself to the independent judgment of the pupil. Changes in behavior are not sufficient for saying that teaching has occurred. These changes must have been brought about intentionally and by rational means. Teaching involves the interaction of rational agents; teachers and pupils are united in being responsible to a rational order. The teacher's prime task is to ensure that when a change occurs in the beliefs or behavior of the students, it occurs for reasons which the student himself accepts.

There are, then, important distinctions between teaching and training and between teaching and conditioning. Training is concerned with performance; it is successful if the student's performance is judged satisfactory (Green, 1964b). Teaching, however, is concerned with beliefs and rational action. It is successful only to the extent that the student can justify his beliefs and give reasons for his actions. Conditioning bypasses the agent's rationality and seeks only to alter his behavior. It takes no heed of him as an agent. This distinction between behavior and human action is one of the principal tension points between psychology and philosophy. Traditionally, psychologists have sought to explain behavior in terms of prior experiences or states of the organism. Philosophers have insisted that the unique feature of human action is that it is goal-oriented: adequate explanation has to be in terms of the aims, intentions and purposes of the individual (Peters, 1958). Whether a person has been taught or merely conditioned to do something is to be determined by the reasons he can give for doing it. Reasons for acting are related to some human goal. Teaching, therefore, is designed to bring about changes in the capabilities of pupils to perform human actions for themselves (Kaufman, 1966).

In this view teaching is regarded as a predominantly linguistic affair. Thinking and language are viewed as closely linked, and since the rational model is concerned with thinking, it is also concerned with language. Traditionally, intelligent behavior was thought to be behavior preceded by thinking. McClellan (1967) has argued that Skinner is a target for the humanists precisely because he denies this causal efficacy of thought. However, contemporary analytic philosophers do not part company with Skinner on this point. Following Ryle (1949), they do not regard thought as a mysterious process accompanying action, nor do they regard intelligent behavior as behavior necessarily preceded by deliberation. They do, however, reject Skinner by claiming that human speech cannot sensibly be described as operant behavior (Chomsky, 1959). Insofar as it is language and not simply noises in the throat or mouth, it is indissolubly linked to thinking. Since teaching people to think is regarded as the particular concern of schools, mastery of language is also seen as very important. In a seminal article, B. Othanel Smith (1956, p. 342) went so far as to assert that teaching cannot occur without the use of language. More recently, Hirst has argued that the central function of education is to bring about thinking by means of language (1966).

We have already indicated in the early part of this chapter that teaching as it is actually carried on is a linguistic affair. It is difficult to determine whether the stress placed on language in the rational model has its origin in the philosophy of human action or in the realities of classroom practice over the centuries. Fortunately it is not important to decide this question. What is important for understanding the significance of this model is to realize that once teaching was seen as a linguistic operation the way was open for using philosophical as distinct from psychological categories in educational research and the training of teachers.

Those who were captivated by the linguistic character of teaching realized that many of the activities of teachers in ordinary classrooms are described by terms which are logical rather than psychological. Teachers define terms, explain phenomena and events, justify views and conclusions, and prove theorems. To define a term is more than to say a few things about it. There are criteria for an adequate definition and these criteria are worked out by philosophers: they are conceptual, not empirical. The same is true of notions of proof, justification, and explanation: these have been the particular concern of philosophers. So a new link was forged with traditional philosophical concerns and a new way of analyzing teacher behavior was at hand.

2. The Rational Model
Description of Learning

In our consideration of the previous model we pointed out that a pupil might discover an answer without being able to justify it or even express it. He might also "discover" a wrong answer. Similarly, if teaching is the control of behavior, including verbal behavior, one can be taught to give wrong answers as readily as right answers. In these cases are we to say that the student has learned what he was being taught? The discovery-learning proponents have a certain difficulty in answering the question when it is related to a discovery. The behavior-control people are forced to answer yes.

On the rational model, the answer is *no*. Proponents differ among themselves as to the correct analysis of "learn," and would agree that a person who has come to believe something false can be said, in some sense, to have learned it. However, they would also argue that for humans such "learning" is essentially defective. As Castell (1967, p. 160) puts it, such a usage is a "primitive and pedagogically uninteresting sense of learning." The learning at which teaching aims is not definable as a change in behavior and it cannot be identified with some emotional reaction on the part of the learner.

Teaching aims at knowledge. A student has learned when he *knows,* and knowing cannot be identified with giving answers, even correct answers. Contemporary philosophers argue that a person knows P only if three conditions are fulfilled: 1) he believes P, 2) P is true, 3) he believes P on good grounds. In terms of learning, it follows that a person's ability to give a certain verbal response to a question is not a sufficient condition for saying that he knows the answer. First, he may not really believe that this is the answer; he may be giving the answer which the teacher wants or responding to some irrelevant feature such as the amusement of the class. Second, his answer may be wrong and even if the teacher accepts it, the student cannot be said to know it; what is false cannot be known. And third, the answer may be correct but the student unable to show that it is correct; he cannot justify it and therefore does not really know it. Scheffler (1965, p. 9) argues that if the third requirement seems too stringent for school learning, we can revert to a weak sense of "know" in which the ability to justify what one claims to know is not required. While this does seem to take account of the realities of classroom teaching, there is little doubt that supporters of the rational model pose something like the strong sense as the ideal and are unwilling to say that learning has taken place unless the student has come to "know" in the strong sense.

As we argued earlier, proponents of the rational model are not interested simply in an analysis of the term "learning." They see the learner, as well as the teacher, as rational agents. Learning, therefore, should not be a process to which the student is subjected but an activity which he performs. It is an activity by which, with the help of the teacher, he comes to know (Castell, 1967, p. 160). To be sure, Scheffler (1965, p. 10) and others deny that learning is an activity but this is because of a semantic point. These philosophers would, we believe, support the notion that if learning is occurring the pupil himself must (logically) be actively engaged in the process of acquiring knowledge.

Learning is contrasted with conditioning, which suggests the stamping in of responses by means of reinforcement (Vesey, 1967). Of course the behaviorist can argue that giving reasons is another form of behavior and this can be brought about by the same methods as the behavior itself. The defender of the rational model answers simply that mouthing reasons is not the same as giving reasons and that the notion of "giving a reason" essentially resists behavioral analysis; it is a distinctively human action.

With such concepts of teaching and learning, exponents of this model have been firm supporters of the traditional academic disciplines for it is only by means of these that justification is made possible. Hirst has gone so far as to argue that there is a conceptual link between rationality, knowledge and the disciplines (1965). To be rational is to be able to justify one's claims and beliefs. To justify a claim is to relate it to other established claims and to a particular set of critical standards. These are found in the disciplines. Thus, a claim about the past can be justified only in terms of a body of historical knowledge, which in turn is dependent on certain precise methods for assessing the documents which are the resources of the historian. A student cannot be said to know that the Great War began in 1914 simply because he can give that answer whenever a certain question is asked. He must also have some ability to verify the statement; he must have been "initiated" into the tradition of historical scholarship (Peters, 1966). The structure of the disciplines becomes important not because discovery of basic principles is facilitated (discovery model) or because it is possible to break up learning into discrete and manageable units (behavioral model), but because an understanding of this structure is necessary for the validation of claims. Unless justification is possible, the result will

not be knowledge, and teaching and learning in the ideal sense will not have occurred.

Bantock greatly extended this point in order to argue that since a teacher always teaches *something* to someone, research on teaching is misguided. Since there is no teaching but only teaching geography, physics, or history, educational researchers should cease to study teaching and instead study the teaching of a particular subject (Bantock, 1961). In a crushing reply Jane Roland Martin pointed out that the fact that there are differences between two activities does not mean that there are no similarities; research can be concerned with the similarities as well as with the differences. She pointed out that it is an empirical matter whether this approach will be fruitful or not. The question cannot be decided by conceptual analysis (Martin, 1963). It is instructive to view this exchange as an example of a model being stretched so much that another person working within that model has to draw attention to its limitations.

3. Research Related to the Rational Model

One of the features which makes the rational model distinctive is its rejection of many of the assumptions underlying behavioral science. Hence, its research concerns are radically different from those of the other two models. Its tools are linguistic and logical analysis. To those who say that this kind of activity is not really research, proponents of the model reply that these critics are victims of the "empiricist-practicalist" ideology which regards the experimental testing of hypotheses as the only significant intellectual work (Komisar & Nelson, 1968, p. 9).

Bellack and Davitz (1963) acknowledged that the conceptual background of their extensive studies of classroom verbal interaction was derived from the work of Wittgenstein. The concept of a language game with identifiable rules for playing the game is one which is familiar to analytic philosophers (see the discussion of Bellack's "rules of the classroom game" in Section I above).

Perhaps more clearly related to the rational model is the work of Smith and his associates (1962, 1967). The studies directed by Smith were purely observational studies based on extensive tape recordings of classroom discourse in which the question of pupil learning was deliberately left aside. In the first study (Smith & Meux, 1962), classroom discourse was analyzed in terms of "logical operations"—those logical actions by which the teacher shapes the classroom discourse, such as explaining, defining, classifying, evaluating and opining.

In the second study (Smith, Meux, Coombs, Nuthall, & Precians, 1967), attention was focused on the teaching strategies which evolve as different aspects of the subject-matter content of lessons are discussed. The concern was with the manipulation of subject-matter topics and the semantic units that make up those topics.

While the work of Bellack and Smith and their co-workers has received some attention from others engaged in observational studies of classroom discourse, and has served as a model for the development of later observational systems (e.g., Nuthall & Lawrence, 1965), others more closely allied to the rational model of teaching have followed a different line of investigation. They have begun to elaborate the criteria by which the logical operations of teaching might be evaluated and improved.

They began by applying the work of philosophers directly—papers dealt with such concepts as explanation, assumption-finding, and generalization (Ennis, 1961; Henderson, 1967; Phenix, 1967; Swift, 1961). More recently educational philosophers have taken account of the pedagogical setting and have done more to relate these logical categories to the psychological dimension (Martin, 1970; Soltis, 1965). They have recognized that although teaching and learning are distinct conceptually, teaching is aimed at learning. In Komisar's terms (1968), the teacher engages in intellectual acts which, in the pedagogical setting, have the notion of success built into them. There are formal and logical criteria for an explanation, but in the teaching situation the teacher cannot be said to have explained X to pupil P, however faultless the explanation, unless pupil P has come to understand X. Jane Martin's book (1970) represents an important development here. It relates the concepts of explaining and understanding to the work of the teacher in a way that earlier accounts did not.

Since an underlying purpose of this stress on the logical dimensions of teacher activity was to improve the student's powers of thought, attention has also been given to the formulation of tests of critical thinking. The work of Ennis is significant in this area. He attempted a conceptual analysis of critical thinking which departed from the earlier psychological interpretations by concentrating on the logical dimension—on the logical criteria required for getting the answers correct (Ennis, 1967).

Again, as with the work of Smith and Bellack, the empirical implications of the work on critical thinking have not been extensively developed. Those working within the rational model have not found empirical studies congenial to their major concerns.

4. Criticism of the Rational Model

The rational model has been criticized by being either ignored or misunderstood. Clearly there is continued debate about critical issues among the proponents of the rational model, but their concerns have not been taken seriously by those committed to the empiricist-practicalist ideology.

The work of Smith and his co-workers is frequently referred to, but systematic criticism is difficult to find. The observational system that evolved from their work has been used in empirical studies of classroom learning (cf. Wright & Nuthall, 1970), but the conceptual background of the work has met with little response.

Educational research has traditionally been psychological in orientation, but if analytic philosophers continue to direct their attention to teaching and continue to publish books like those of Ennis (1969) and Martin (1970), then the next decade will see the rational model come in for its fair share of critical attention.

CONCLUSIONS

We have claimed in the first section of this chapter that the major contemporary models of teaching are pervasive views of teaching which act as interpretive frameworks for assimilating information, for conceptualizing differences between teaching methods, and for posing and answering research questions. It was our conclusion from an examination of contemporary research and debate about teaching that three models have dominated the present scene. These models we have called the behavior-control model, the discovery-learning model and the rational model.

It is now possible to have a general look at the way in which these models have generated and exerted an influence over the kinds of research which have been undertaken.

1. The Function of the Models in Generating Research

A feature of a major scientific model is that its assumptions are not subject to test within the discipline or area in which the model functions. The model suggests hypotheses which are testable and the way data should be collected to test these hypotheses. The research, then, does not verify the model; it verifies statements derived from the model.

In an important sense this is true of the major models of teaching. Each of the models has suggested research hypotheses relevant to teaching, but the outcomes of this research have not affected the status of the models themselves. No one has asked the question, which of the three models is the correct model? Nor has anyone attempted to collect evidence which might indicate that, for example, the behavior-control model ought to be replaced by the rational model. By virtue of adopting one model in preference to another, those involved in the research make it impossible for agreement to be reached on what evidence would be relevant to answering such a question.

For example, it is a matter of concern to those who work within the framework of the behavior-control model whether delay of reinforcement has an effect on the learning of responses in the classroom. This is a research problem generated by the conceptual framework of that model. But studies which are undertaken to determine the effects of delayed reinforcement have no bearing on whether the behavior-control model is a valid model or not. The results of such studies might force a reinterpretation of the concept of reinforcement in the classroom, but are not likely to persuade anyone to drop the model in favor of some other model.

However, it is also true that arguments are developed and research studies undertaken which attempt to demonstrate that a favored method of teaching has the right to claim the allegiance of all educators. Proponents of the rational model attempt to demonstrate through analytic argument that teaching *must* be a rational activity. Proponents of the discovery-learning model attempt to provide empirical evidence that discovery methods are better than expository methods. The important quality of this research and argument is that it is intended primarily to *persuade* the educational community. It is prejudiced research because those who undertake it delineate not only the view of teaching which they favor, but also the alternative traditional method of teaching which they are against.

The major models of teaching operate as models in that they define how teaching should be viewed. And, in this definition, they stipulate not only what is good teaching, but also what is bad teaching or what should not be considered teaching at all. It is for this reason that the research generated by a particular model is not generally useful outside the context of that model.

The importance of these models of teaching lies in the fact that each has stimulated a considerable body of research and argument about teaching. Each has given teachers a point of view which is capable of guiding, in some sense, their activities in the classroom. Teachers have become concerned about the definition of behavioral outcomes, have become enthusiastic about discovery learning, problem-solving skills and creativity, and have developed an interest in the quality of their questions and the promotion of critical thinking.

But the hope that there would develop a single, universally accepted body of empirical research on teaching has not been realized. No matter how impeccable the research designs, nor how sophisticated the statistical analyses, the research remains, for the most part, tied to the models. It finds a place in conference papers and textbooks so long as the model retains its power to command the allegiance of some significant section of the educational community. When the model loses its persuasive power it is likely to disappear from view, taking with it the research it generated. For example, it may well be that by the time this *Handbook* is published, research on discovery learning will have lost its interest as the discovery-learning model fades from view in the face of the debate and research being generated by the open classroom.

It is for this reason, we believe, that when, in the early 1960s, the curriculum reform sponsors came to the educational psychologists for information about how to teach effectively, they met with two responses. Either they were met with the embarrassed acknowledgement that educational psychologists could help them analyze their problems but could tell them nothing about how to teach (Cronbach, 1965), or they were sold a particular model of teaching, i.e. the discovery-learning model.

2. The Paradox of Research on Teaching

Some readers of this chapter may be disturbed to find that the conclusions we have drawn about the nature and function of models in contemporary research on teaching sound very much like a restatement of the conclusions which Wallen and Travers made in their chapter on teaching methods research in the first *Handbook* (1963).

Wallen and Travers found that most of the teaching research which they reviewed consisted of comparisons of two contrasting methods. They pointed out that, for all the sophistication in statistical techniques employed, these studies did not provide a "unified body of scientific research." They concluded, optimistically, that the "era of research comparing one teaching method with another seems to be coming to a close."

Our analysis of contemporary models of teaching suggests that that era has not yet come to a close. The models employed have become more psychologically and logically sophisticated. The current models appear to be more scientific than the progressive-traditional and authoritarian-democratic models of the 1930s and 1940s, but their function in promoting research has been much the same.

If our analysis of the current situation is correct, then it points up a fundamental dilemma which is faced by a person attempting research on teaching. We have suggested that research which is generated by an influential model of teaching is necessarily tied to that model. Research generated by different models cannot form a unified body of empirical knowledge which exists independently of the models.

On the other hand, research which has attempted to avoid models completely tends to be either misunderstood or ignored. The current emphasis on observational studies has produced a proliferation of observational systems and frequency counts of the minutiae of teacher and student behaviors in their daily situations. It shows few signs of being any more successful in providing empirical knowledge of value to teachers than the research which has been generated by the major models of teaching. For example, the observational studies of Bellack and Davitz (1963) and Adams and Biddle (1970) have produced a considerable body of numerical data which has been very largely ignored except by those conducting further observational studies. Without some model to guide interpretation, no one is quite sure what such data might mean or how it can be put to significant use. A model is, after all, an *interpretive* framework.

The researcher is thus faced with a dilemma: if he works within the context of a model of teaching, his data have little significance outside the 'sphere of influence' of that model. If he spurns a model, he runs the risk of having data which no one knows what to do with.

In the face of this dilemma, two routes remain open. First, researchers may conclude that teaching is a practical activity which can never become the object of meaningful empirical research, and revert to more fundamental psychological, sociological and philosophical studies of selected aspects of teaching (cf. Newsome, 1964). The models followed will be those which are current in the basic disciplines, and whether the research contributes to the advancement of teaching becomes an unimportant consideration.

Second, researchers may conclude that the deficiencies of model-dominated research are the result, not of models per se, but of inadequate models. They may attempt, therefore, to develop functional models of teaching which are more suited to the complex phenomena of classroom teaching. It may be the case, for example, that the research generated by a former model of teaching such as the authoritarian-demo-cratic model has not been integrated into the contemporary stream of research, not because the model is no longer of interest but because the concepts involved in the model were inadequately defined and the methods of interpreting data too narrowly conceived (cf. Anderson, 1959). It is possible to conceive of functionally significant models of teaching which do provide appropriate interpretive frameworks, but developing such models will require a more sophisticated analysis of the whole enterprise of research on teaching.

REFERENCES

Adams, R. S., & Biddle, B. J. *Realities of teaching.* New York: Holt, Rinehart & Winston, 1970.

Anderson, R. C. Learning in discussions: A resumé of the authoritarian-democratic studies. *Harvard Educational Review,* 1959, 29, 201–215.

Anderson, R. C. Control of student mediating processes during verbal learning and instruction. *Review of Educational Research,* 1970, 40, 349–369.

Anderson, R. C., Faust, G. W., Roderick, M. C., Cunningham, D. J., & Andre, T. (Eds.) *Current research on instruction.* Englewood Cliffs, N.J.: Prentice-Hall, 1969.

Aschner, M. J. The language of teaching. *Teachers College Record,* 1960, 61, 242–252.

Ausubel, D. P. Learning by discovery: Rationale and mystique. *Bulletin of the National Association of Secondary School Principals,* 1961, 45(269), 18–58.

Ausubel, D. P., & Blake, E. Jr. Proactive inhibition in the forgetting of meaningful school material. *Journal of Educational Research,* 1958, 52, 145–149.

Ausubel, D. P., Stager, M., & Gaite, A. J. H. Proactive effects in meaningful verbal learning and retention. *Journal of Educational Psychology,* 1969, 60, 59–64.

Bantock, G. H. Educational research: A criticism. *Harvard Educational Review,* 1961, 31, 264–280.

Bellack, A. A., & Davitz, J. R. *The language of the classroom.* USOE, Cooperative Research Project No. 2023. New York: Teachers College, Columbia University, 1963.

Bittinger, M. L. A review of discovery. *The Mathematics Teacher,* 1968, 61, 140–146.

Brodbeck, M. Models, meaning and theory. In L. Gross (Ed.), *Symposium on sociological theory.* Evanston, Ill.: Row, Peterson, 1959. Pp. 373–403.

Broudy, H. S. Teaching machines: Threats and promise. *Educational Theory,* 1962, 12, 151–156.

Bruner, J. S. The act of discovery. *Harvard Educational Review,* 1961, 31, 21–32.

Bruner, J. S. Some elements of discovery. In L. S. Shulman & E. R. Keislar (Eds.), *Learning by discovery: A critical appraisal.* Chicago: Rand McNally, 1966. Pp. 101–113.

Bruner, J. S., Goodnow, J. J., & Austin, G. A. *A study of thinking.* New York: John Wiley, 1956.

Castell, A. Pedagogy follows learning theory. In B. P. Komisar & C. J. B. Macmillan (Eds.), *Psychological concepts in education.* Chicago: Rand McNally, 1967. Pp. 158–166.

Chomsky, N. Review of B. F. Skinner, *Verbal Behavior. Language,* 1959, 35, 26–58.

Cooper, J. Criteria for successful teaching. *Proceedings of the Philosophy of Education Society of Great Britain, 1966,* 5–18.

Corman, B. R. The effect of varying amounts and kinds of information as guidance in problem solving. *Psychological Monographs,* 1957, 71 (Whole No. 431).

Craig, R. C. Directed versus independent discovery of established relations. *Journal of Educational Psychology,* 1956, 47, 223–234.

Cronbach, L. J. Issues current in educational psychology. In L. N. Morrisett & J. Vinsonhaler (Eds.), *Mathematical learning.* Monographs of the Society for Research in Child Development, 1965, 30(1), 109–126.

Davis, R. B. Discovery in the teaching of mathematics. In L. S. Shulman & E. R. Keislar (Eds.), *Learning by discovery: A critical appraisal.* Chicago: Rand McNally, 1966. Pp. 114–128.

Dearden, R. F. Instruction and learning by discovery. In R. S. Peters (Ed.), *The concept of education.* London: Routledge & Kegan Paul, 1967. Pp. 135–155.

De Cecco, J. P. *The psychology of learning and instruction.* Englewood Cliffs, N.J.: Prentice-Hall, 1968.

Ennis, R. H. Assumption finding. In B. O. Smith & R. H. Ennis (Eds.), *Language and concepts in education.* Chicago: Rand McNally, 1961. Pp. 161–178.

Ennis, R. H. A concept of critical thinking: A proposed basis for research in the teaching and evaluation of critical thinking ability. In B. P. Komisar & C. J. B. Macmillan (Eds.), *Psychological concepts in education.* Chicago: Rand McNally, 1967. Pp. 114–148.

Ennis, R. H. *Logic in teaching.* Englewood Cliffs, N.J.: Prentice-Hall, 1969.

Flanders, N. A. *Analyzing classroom behavior.* New York: Addison-Wesley, 1970.

Friedlander, B. Z. A psychologist's second thoughts on concepts, curiosity, and discovery in teaching and learning. *Harvard Educational Review,* 1965, 35, 18–38.

Gagné, R. M. The analysis of instructional objectives for the design of instruction. In R. Glaser (Ed.), *Teaching machines and programed learning, II: Data and directions.* Washington, D.C.: National Education Association, 1965. Pp. 21–65. (a)

Gagné, R. M. *The conditions of learning.* New York: Holt, Rinehart & Winston, 1965. (b)

Glaser, R. *The new pedagogy.* Pittsburgh, Pa.: University of Pittsburgh, Learning Research & Development Center, 1965. (a)

Glaser, R. Toward a behavioral science base for instructional design. In R. Glaser (Ed.), *Teaching machines and programed learning, II: Data and directions.* Washington, D.C.: National Education Association, 1965. Pp. 771–809. (b)

Glaser, R. Variables in discovery learning. In L. S. Shulman & E. R. Keislar (Eds.), *Learning by discovery: A critical appraisal.* Chicago: Rand McNally, 1966. Pp. 13–26.

Glaser, R. The design and programing of instruction. In H. T. James et al., *The schools and the challenge of innovation.* Supplementary paper No. 28. New York: Committee for Economic Development, 1969. Pp. 156–215.

Gowin, D. B. Teaching, learning and thirdness. *Studies in Philosophy and Education,* 1961, 1, 87–113.

Green, T. F. Teaching, acting, and behaving. *Harvard Educational Review,* 1964, 34, 507–524. (a)

Green, T. F. A topology of the teaching concept. *Studies in Philosophy and Education,* 1964, 3, 284–319. (b)

Green, T. F. The concept of teaching: A reply.

Studies in Philosophy and Education, 1966, 4, 339–345.

Griffin, D. R. Lecture delivered at the 10th International Ethological Conference in Stockholm, 1967. Quoted by K. Z. Lorenz, Innate bases of learning. In K. H. Pribram (Ed.), *On the biology of learning.* New York: Harcourt, Brace & World, 1969. Pp. 75–76.

Gump, P. V. The classroom behavior setting: Its nature and relation to student behavior. Final Report, Project No. 2453. Lawrence, Kan.: Midwest Psychological Field Station, University of Kansas, 1967.

Hanley, E. M. Review of research involving applied behavior analysis in the classroom. *Review of Educational Research,* 1970, 40, 597–625.

Hartley, J. Research report. *New Education,* 1966, 2, 29–35.

Hay, W. H. On Green's analysis of teaching. *Studies in Philosophy and Education,* 1965, 4, 254–263.

Henderson, K. B. Thoughts about Phenix's "An analytic view of the process of generalization." *Studies in Philosophy and Education,* 1967, 5, 341–346.

Hendrix, G. Learning by discovery. *The Mathematics Teacher,* 1961, 54, 290–299.

Herbert, J. *A system for analyzing lessons.* New York: Teachers College Press, 1967.

Hiller, J. H., Fisher, G. A., & Kaess, W. A computer investigation of verbal characteristics of effective classroom lecturing. *American Educational Research Journal,* 1969, 6, 661–675.

Hirst, P. H. Liberal education and the nature of knowledge. In R. D. Archambault (Ed.), *Philosophical analysis and education.* New York: Humanities, 1965. Pp. 113–138.

Hirst, P. H. Language and thought. *Proceedings of the Philosophy of Education Society of Great Britain, 1966.* Pp. 63–75.

Hoetker, J., & Ahlbrand, W. P. The persistence of the recitation. *American Educational Research Journal,* 1969, 6, 145–167.

Holland, J. G. A teaching machine program in psychology. In E. Galanter (Ed.), *Automatic teaching: The state of the art.* New York: John Wiley, 1959. Pp. 69–82.

Jackson, P. W. *Life in classrooms.* New York: Holt, Rinehart & Winston, 1968.

Jordan, J. A. Jr. Socratic teaching? *Harvard Educational Review,* 1963, 33, 96–104.

Kaufman, A. Teaching as an intentional serial performance. *Studies in Philosophy and Education,* 1966, 4, 361–389.

Kaufman, A. On some philosophic grounds for understanding teaching. *Studies in Philosophy and Education,* 1967, 5, 347–357.

Keislar, E. R. The development of understanding in arithmetic by a teaching machine. *Journal of Educational Psychology,* 1959, 50, 247–253.

Kersh, B. Y. The adequacy of "meaning" as an explanation for superiority of learning by independent discovery. *Journal of Educational Psychology,* 1958, 49, 282–292.

Kersh, B. Y. The motivating effect of learning by directed discovery. *Journal of Educational Psychology,* 1962, 53, 65–71.

Komisar, B. P. Teaching: Act and enterprise. In C. J. B. Macmillan & T. W. Nelson (Eds.), *Concepts of teaching: Philosophical essays.* Chicago: Rand McNally, 1968. Pp. 63–88.

Komisar, B. P., & Nelson, T. W. Introduction: Conceptual analysis of teaching. In C. J. B. Macmillan & T. W. Nelson (Eds.), *Concepts of teaching: Philosophical essays.* Chicago: Rand McNally, 1968. Pp. 1–10.

Kounin, J. *Discipline and group management in classrooms.* New York: Holt, 1970.

Kuhn, T. S. *The structure of scientific revolutions.* Chicago: University of Chicago Press, 1962.

Maccia, E. S., Maccia, G. S., and Jewett, R. E. (Eds.) *Construction of educational theory models.* Cooperative Research Project No. 1632. Columbus: Ohio State University, 1963.

MacIver, D. A., and Holdaway, E. A. An analysis of the use of models in education. *Alberta Journal of Educational Research,* 1966, 12, 163–188.

Markle, S. M. *Good frames and bad.* New York: John Wiley, 1964.

Martin, J. R. Can there be universally applicable criteria of good teaching? *Harvard Educational Review,* 1963, 33, 484–491.

Martin, J. R. *Explaining, understanding and teaching.* New York: McGraw-Hill, 1970.

McClellan, J. E. B. F. Skinner's philosophy of human nature: A sympathetic criticism. In B. P. Komisar & C. J. B. Macmillan (Eds.), *Psychological concepts in education.* Chicago: Rand McNally, 1967. Pp. 224–247.

Mechner, F. *Programming for automated in-*

struction. New York: Basic System, 1961. (mimeo.)

Miller, G. A., Galanter, E., & Pribram, K. *Plans and the structure of behavior.* New York: Holt, Rinehart & Winston, 1960.

Nagel, E. *The structure of science: Problems in the logic of scientific explanation.* London: Routledge & Kegan Paul, 1961.

Newsome, G. L. Jr. In what sense is theory a guide to practice in education? *Educational Theory,* 1964, 14, 31–39, 64.

Nuthall, G. A. A review of some selected recent studies of classroom interaction and teaching behavior. In *Classroom behavior,* American Educational Research Monograph, No. 6. Chicago: Rand McNally, 1970.

Nuthall, G. A., & Lawrence, P. J. *Thinking in the classroom.* Wellington: New Zealand Council for Educational Research, 1965.

Peters, R. S. *The concept of motivation.* London: Routledge & Kegan Paul, 1958.

Peters, R. S. *Ethics and education.* London: Routledge & Kegan Paul, 1966.

Phenix, P. H. An analytic view of the process of generalization. *Studies in Philosophy and Education,* 1967, 5, 245–266.

Polanyi, M. *Personal knowledge.* New York: Harper & Row, 1958.

Porter, D. Some effects of year long teaching machine instruction. In E. Galanter (Ed.), *Automatic teaching: The state of the art.* New York: John Wiley, 1959. Pp. 85–90.

Pressey, S. L. A simple apparatus which gives tests and scores—and teaches. *School and Society,* 1926, 23, 373–376.

Pressey, S. L. A third and fourth contribution toward the coming "industrial revolution" in education. *School and Society,* 1932, 36, 668–672.

Price, K. On "having an education." *Harvard Educational Review,* 1958, 28, 320–337.

Rosenshine, B. To explain: A review of research. *Educational Leadership,* 1968, 26, 303–309.

Rothkopf, E. Z. Two scientific approaches to the management of instruction. In R. M. Gagné, & W. J. Gephart (Eds.), *Learning research and school subjects.* Itasca, Ill.: Peacock, 1968. Pp. 107–132.

Ryle, A. G. *The concept of mind.* New York: Barnes and Noble, 1949.

Scheffler, I. *The language of education.* Springfield, Ill.: Charles C Thomas, 1960.

Scheffler, I. *Conditions of knowledge: An in-*troduction to epistomology and education. Chicago: Scott Foresman, 1965.

Scheffler, I. *Science and subjectivity.* Indianapolis: Bobbs-Merrill, 1967.

Skinner, B. F. The science of learning and the art of teaching. *Harvard Educational Review,* 1954, 24, 86–97.

Skinner, B. F. *The technology of teaching.* New York: Appleton-Century-Crofts, 1968.

Smith, B. O. On the anatomy of teaching. *Journal of Teacher Education,* 1956, 7, 339–346.

Smith, B. O. Logic, thinking, and teaching. *Educational Theory,* 1957, 7, 225–233.

Smith, B. O. A concept of teaching. In C. J. B. Macmillan, & T. W. Nelson (Eds.), *Concepts of teaching: Philosophical essays.* Chicago: Rand McNally, 1968. Pp. 11–16.

Smith, B. O., & Ennis, R. H. (Eds.) *Language and concepts in education.* Chicago: Rand McNally, 1961.

Smith, B. O., & Meux, M. O. *A study of the logic of teaching.* Urbana, Ill.: University of Illinois, Bureau of Educational Research, 1962.

Smith, B. O., Meux, M., Coombs, J., Nuthall, G., & Precians, R. *A study of the strategies of teaching.* Urbana: University of Illinois, Bureau of Educational Research, 1967.

Smith, L. M., & Geoffrey, W. *The complexities of an urban classroom.* New York: Holt, Rinehart & Winston, 1968.

Soltis, J. F. The subjective dimension of explanation. In *Proceedings of the Philosophy of Education Society,* 1965. Pp. 13–18.

Stolurow, L. M. Model the master teacher or master the teaching model. In J. D. Krumboltz (Ed.), *Learning and the educational process.* Chicago: Rand McNally, 1965. Pp. 223–247.

Strasser, B. A conceptual model of instruction. *Journal of Teacher Education,* 1967, 18, 63–74.

Suchman, J. R. Inquiry training: Building skills for autonomous discovery. *Merrill Palmer Quarterly of Behavior and Development,* 1961, 7, 147–169.

Suchman, J. R. The child and the inquiry process. In A. H. Passow (Ed.), *Intellectual development: Another look.* Washington, D. C.: Association for Supervision and Curriculum Development, 1964. Pp. 59–77.

Swift, L. F. Explanation. In B. O. Smith & R. H. Ennis (Eds.), *Language and concepts in education.* Chicago: Rand McNally, 1961. Pp. 179–194.

Taba, H. Learning by discovery: Psychological and educational rationale. *Elementary School Journal,* 1963, 63, 308–316.

Taba, H., Levine, S., & Elzey, F. *Thinking in elementary school children.* U. S. Office of Education, Co-operative Research Project, No. 1574. San Francisco: San Francisco State College, 1964.

Taber, J. I., Glaser, R., & Schaefer, H. H. *Learning and programmed instruction.* Reading, Mass.: Addison-Wesley, 1965.

Vesey, G. Conditioning and learning. In R. S. Peters (Ed.), *The concept of education.* London: Routledge & Kegan Paul, 1967. Pp. 61–72.

Wallen, N. E., & Travers, R. M. W. Analysis and investigation of teaching methods. In N. L. Gage (Ed.), *Handbook of research on teaching.* Chicago: Rand McNally, 1963. Pp. 448–505.

Wertheimer, M. *Productive thinking.* New York: Harper, 1945.

Wittrock, M. C. Verbal stimuli in concept formation: Learning by discovery. *Journal of Educational Psychology,* 1963, 54, 183–190.

Wittrock, M. C. The learning by discovery hypothesis. In L. S. Shulman & E. R. Keislar (Eds.), *Learning by discovery: A critical appraisal.* Chicago: Rand McNally, 1966. Pp. 33–75.

Worthen, B. R. Discovery and expository task presentation in elementary mathematics. *Journal of Educational Psychology,* Monograph supplement, 1968, 59, No. 1, Part 2.

Wright, C. J., & Nuthall, G. Relationships between teacher behaviors and pupil achievement in three experimental elementary science lessons. *American Educational Research Journal,* 1970, 7, 477–491.

Young, J. W. A. *The teaching of mathematics.* New York: Longman's Green, 1906.

Zoll, E. J. Research in programmed instruction in mathematics. *Mathematics Teacher,* 1969, 62, 103–110.

CHAPTER 3

Theory Constuction for Research on Teaching[1]

RICHARD E. SNOW[2]
**Stanford Center for Research
and Development in Teaching**

Many factors influence the development of research in an area. New instruments, like electron microscopes or computers, make new kinds of investigations possible. Developments in related disciplines, like animal learning and analytic philosophy, gradually infiltrate the thinking of researchers. Social problems, like poverty and race relations, impress new concerns upon investigators. This chapter deals with a factor different from any of these. It concerns the theoretical formulations in a field that shape its research and development.

The purposes of this chapter are several. At a specific level, it seeks not merely to describe the influence of theories in research on teaching, but rather to provide, albeit sketchily: a) an outline of the process of theory building, including a consideration of some useful heuristic techniques; b) a classification of types of theories and models potentially useful in research on teaching; c) a review of criteria for the evaluation of theories and models; and d) some admonitions as guides for future theorizing.

A more general intent of this chapter is to suggest that building theories and models is not only respectable but extremely useful, perhaps even indispensable, in pursuing research on teaching. Some writers, including Nuthall and Snook (see Chapter 2), seem to reject model building on the grounds that it is largely irrelevant when compared to the practice of researchers over past decades. On the contrary, the practice of researchers in past decades may be irrelevant when reviewed with improved models of the phenomena under study. To be sure, there is not now general agreement on the best ways to build improved theories and models, or to apply them in improving research. Only an outline of some distinctive features of theory-building processes can be provided here, in the hope of enlisting interest in theorizing among a wider circle of researchers. It will remain for later writers to crystallize the forms of theory and theory

[1] The preparation of this chapter was supported in part by funds from the United States Office of Education, Department of Health, Education, and Welfare. The opinions expressed in this publication do not necessarily reflect the position, policy or endorsement of the Office of Education (Contract No. OE-6-10-078, Project No. 5-0252-0501.)

[2] The author wishes to acknowledge the significant contributions of N. L. Gage to the development of this chapter.

building deemed most suitable for research on teaching.

The process of theorizing is itself a complex phenomenon deserving extended scientific study. Theory is examined here primarily from a psychological perspective. Of course, the role of theory in any scientific discipline deserves philosophical analysis (e.g., Turner, 1967) and sociological study (e.g., Barber & Hirsch, 1962; Merton, 1955, 1957), as well as psychological examination. While I have tried to maintain some sensitivity to these orientations in constructing this chapter, I am only a psychologist; the view of theory and research represented here, and the examples chosen may display very poorly the perspectives of philosophers, other social scientists and educationists. It is hoped that the reader will take due account of this bias and find no gross distortions as a result of it.

PRECURSORS OF THEORY

There appear to be almost as many definitions of *theory* as there are people concerned with theory. And, in a real sense, this entire chapter is an elaborated definition of theory. In its simplest form, a theory is a symbolic construction designed to bring generalizable facts (or laws) into systematic connection. It consists of a) a set of units (facts, concepts, variables) and b) a system of relationships among the units. These are defined and interpreted in statements that are understandable to others and that make predictions about empirical events. As an illustration,

The road map is an artificial, symbolic, and reduced representation (a theory) of the terrain, and the schooled reader of the map may act in a reasonable way (behave factually) over that terrain with the help of the map. The rules for interpretation of the map correspond in a rough way to definition in theory construction (Mandler & Kessen, 1959, p. 133).

Theorizing, i.e., constructing such systems, is a basic aspect of human behavior. As Kaplan suggests:

Human behavior not only supplements pure reflexes with learned habits, but also rises above habit to novel responses in unfamiliar situations, achieving creative solutions to problems never before confronted. These novel responses constitute the behavioral correlate of theorizing. A theory is a way of making sense of a disturbing situation so as to allow us most effectively to bring to bear our repertoire of habits, and even more important, to modify habits or discard them altogether, replacing them by new ones as the situation demands. In the reconstructed logic, accordingly, theory will appear as the device for interpreting, criticizing, and unifying established laws, modifying them to fit data unanticipated in their formulation, and guiding the enterprise of discovering new and more powerful generalizations. To engage in theorizing means not just to learn by experience but to take thought about what is there to be learned. To speak loosely, lower animals grasp scientific laws but never rise to the level of scientific theory. They learn *by* experience but not *from* it, for *from* learning requires symbolic constructions which can provide vicarious experience never actually undergone (Kaplan, 1964, p. 295).

The popular view of theorizing shows the scientist pondering his observations, generalizing from data, forming these generalizations into systems of concepts and relationships, and conducting crucial experiments designed to test deductions from the systems thus created. In short, theory is first the product of the individual scientist's ingenuity. If a theory then is shown to account for a set of phenomena more completely or more simply than its predecessors, if it is borne out in independent examination, and if it leads to major new insights and extensions, it may gain acceptance in the wider research community. This acceptance is determined not only by the theory's merit but by the community's readiness to accommodate to it, and to assimilate its implications. Major theoretical advances in a science come eventually to be regarded as the Great Events, and their originators as the Great Men, in the history of a science (Boring, 1963).

The Great Events of a science are what Kuhn (1962) called scientific revolutions.

Each such revolution consists of a change of *paradigm*. For Kuhn, paradigms refer to major scientific achievements that serve "...for a time implicitly to define the legitimate problems and methods of a research field for succeeding generations of practitioners." The term suggests "that some accepted examples of actual scientific practice—examples which include law, theory, application, and instrumentation together—provide models from which spring particular coherent traditions of scientific research." For an achievement to be thus regarded, it must be "sufficiently unprecedented to attract an enduring group of adherents away from competing modes of scientific activity.... [and] sufficiently open-ended to leave all sort of problems for the redefined group of practitioners to resolve" (Kuhn, 1962, p. 10). The three general models for research on teaching described in Chapter 2 by Nuthall and Snook appear to be paradigms in Kuhn's sense; the earlier review by Gage (1963) of "paradigms for research on teaching" also suggested that the term is interchangeable with "model." Boring views the paradigm as "more complex than the model, less concrete, and, as Kuhn thinks of it, less fully conscious, being in large measure carried in the stream of the zeitgeist, the current of credence, which is so often not recognized by he [sic] who shapes his thinking in respect of it" (1963, p. 9).

The zeitgeist, literally "spirit of the times," was Goethe's term for a multiplicity of climates of opinion, though Boring preferred "current of belief or credence" (1963, p. 13). It refers to "the total body of knowledge and opinion available at any time to a person living within a given culture" (Boring, 1955, p. 106). For the scientist, it is the source of the puzzles that motivate him to theorize, the metaphors that inspire his theorizing, and the mental habits that shape the result.

The theorist thus affects the current of credence of his discipline and is in turn affected by it. To study the role of theory in research on teaching, one can concentrate on the individual's research and theoretical work in the development of paradigms or on the paradigms themselves and their influence on the subsequent theory and research of individuals. Whether the Great Men are to be considered the cause or the consequence of the Great Events is itself a topic of considerable interest, but one well beyond the scope of this chapter (see Boring, 1963).

A first order of business must be to dispense with the term *paradigm* as too global for the purposes of this chapter. There now appears to be considerable uncertainty about its several meanings (see Shapere, 1971). While the concept may be useful in studying the history and philosophy of science, the concern here is more with the day-to-day interplay of theory and research in the development of a scientific field which, if not in its infancy, is hardly adolescent. As used by Kuhn (1962), paradigm apparently includes *metatheory, model* and *metaphor* as well as *theory*. Distinctions between these terms will be needed.

Metatheory and Theory

A metatheory is a theory concerned with the development, investigation or description of theory itself. It specifies the rules with which a theory is constructed and written down. While a metatheory may be explicitly formulated using some particular philosophical or logical system (e.g., Woodger, 1939), it may also arise through accumulation of individual pieces of research to be formalized much later. In behavioral and social science, metatheories appear usually to be families or categories of theories that develop when an original theory spawns descendants or deviationists. Often methodologies attain the status of metatheory. They prescribe the form that theories based on that metatheory or methodology can take and constrict the researcher's modes of thought, explicitly and perhaps also unconsciously. Consider some examples:

(1) The term *S-R Psychology* implies more than a specific behavior theory; it

represents both a family of theories taking a particular form and, beyond this, a method-ological position regarding behavioral sci-ence that may be a foundation even for research which does not pursue behavioral as opposed to cognitive or other theories. The original work of Pavlov and of E. L. Thorndike led to that of Hull, Guthrie, Skinner and Tolman and, more recently, to the mathematical learning theories that may in many respects constitute a new metatheory. For reviews of these learning theories see Hilgard and Bower (1966).

(2) Freud, followed by Adler, Jung and others, produced a general form for psycho-analytic theory within which specific posi-tions differ in detail. For a review here see Hall and Lindzey (1957).

(3) The three "models" reviewed by Nuthall and Snook in Chapter 2 are simi-larly metatheoretical families in this sense.

(4) Factor analysis is a methodology which has prescribed the nature of theory and research on individual differences for decades. Spearman's initial work on intelli-gence branched to different extensions by Holzinger, Thomson, Thurstone and, more recently, Guilford and Cattell. These works differ in interpretation and in methodologi-cal detail but are clearly cut from the same metatheoretical cloth.

(5) Fisherian experimental design and the associated analysis of variance methods similarly, though perhaps less obviously, mold the structure of our thinking about human behavior. When Campbell and Stanley (1963) said that their "chapter is committed to the experiment: as the only means for settling disputes..., of verifying educational improvements, and ... of estab-lishing a cumulative tradition ..." (p. 172), they were promoting predisposition toward a distinctive form of research and thus of theory. Their emphasis on quasi-experi-ments loosened considerably the traditional Fisherian conception of admissible experi-mental work. But the basic metatheoretic choice, namely the decision to manipulate stimulus variables systematically as opposed

to sampling them representatively from real environments or using correlational ap-proaches, was left largely unexplicated.

(6) The decision to study behavior through nomothetic as opposed to idio-graphic approaches represents still another metatheoretic choice deserving careful at-tention.

Formal influences of the zeitgeist on the researcher often act through metatheory in the form of graduate courses and textbooks on "contemporary" theory, research meth-odology and statistical analysis. A research-er's metatheoretic choices are thus often made for him. Only by exposing and ex-amining the implications of such choices can a balanced view of research alternatives in an area be achieved. An example of this kind of analysis of metatheory is the com-parison by Cronbach (1957) of correlational and experimental psychology. Another is the discussion by Brunswik (1956) of repre-sentative versus systematic design of psy-chological experiments.

In short, a metatheory provides a kind of syntax or grammatical structure within which a particular theory can be developed and stated. It offers a distinctive medium of communication that often defines a dis-tinctive community of researchers. And it ultimately provides the means by which alternative forms of theory are compared. Of the terms used in this chapter, "meta-theory" is admittedly the least precise and may suffer from the same difficulties as Kuhn's "paradigm" concept. The term may be particularly bothersome to those philoso-phers who would apply it only to the anal-ysis and evaluation of theories after their construction. The domain represented by this term is itself worthy of considerable further study, as the current interest in Kuhn's ideas seems to signify.

Model and Theory

The term *model* also has many defini-tions, both in science and in everyday life. In current usage it sometimes seems to stand for humble theory, as if the author regarded *theory* as too lofty a term for the miniature system being presented. Also, *theory* is often used in a generic sense with individual theoretical constructions referred to as models. The terms may be regarded as synonymous when used to label theoretical constructions expressed in formal postulational style (see Kaplan, 1964).

When philosophers of science use the phrase "a model of a theory," they mean a second deductive system, similar to that of the theory, constructed to interpret the calculus of the theory. The theory and the model have the same formal structure but different epistemological structures (Braithwaite, 1953; Turner, 1967). This use of models, although important, appears limited to work done *after* a formal theory is in hand. In research on teaching, we need models that promote theoretical developments beforehand and thus must accept a more general definition. Also, *model* should not necessarily imply an exact one-to-one correspondence or isomorphism between two theories, as Brodbeck (1963) would have it. Her conception of isomorphic theories, in which one well-developed theory is used as a model for theory in another area as yet undeveloped, offers an important *use of theory* but not a satisfactory definition of model. This use of theory is discussed later, as a heuristic technique called *theory translating*.

In the present context, it seems most useful to consider models as well-developed descriptive analogies used to help visualize, often in a simplified or miniature way, phenomena that cannot be easily or directly observed. Each model is thus a projection of a possible system of relationships among phenomena, realized in verbal, material, graphic or symbolic terms.

Chapanis (1961) distinguished two basic kinds of models—replica models and symbolic models. Replica models are usually material or pictorial representations made with a change in spatial or temporal scale. Symbolic models tend to be intangible, using abstract verbal, graphic or symbolic representation to stand for conceptual systems. Both kinds of model are useful, and often a particular model may combine replica and symbolic aspects. Ahmavaara (1957) contrasted mechanistic and abstractive representation. Mechanistic models attempt to visualize the connecting operations arrayed between input and output variables, usually by graphic-schematic means, while abstractive models characterize formal relationships between input and output variables symbolically, without speculative visualization of connecting mechanisms. He suggested that most theoretical work in psychology relied on mechanistic representation, although factor analysis provided one major abstractive representation system. In addition to factor analysis and related techniques, the past two decades have seen the development of powerful abstractive representations in the form of mathematical models for aspects of social behavior (Simon, 1957) as well as learning, thinking and problem solving (see Snyder, 1968). These mathematical models typically are not simply quantitative representations fit to empirical findings. They are rational equations with parameters representing presumed key structural and operational features of the phenomenon being modeled.

Correlated but not coincident with these distinctions is the distinction between geometric and algebraic representation. While replica models are almost always mechanistic and either tangible or geometric, symbolic models are not necessarily abstractive and algebraic. Good examples of symbolic, abstractive, but geometric models are physical force fields, atomic structures, and the double helix representation of the DNA molecule. Examples of geometric models in behavioral science that are also symbolic and abstractive are Lewin's (1936) life-space topology and more recently Allport's (1967) use of geometric concepts in the initial organization of his theory of enestruence. One can probably generate examples for all possible combinations of these forms.

A model—whether replica or symbolic, mechanistic or abstractive, geometric or algebraic—can be used in seeking to explain some phenomenon by simplification and analogy to already understood systems. An excellent example of the use of several kinds of models to characterize the present state of understanding in an area is the collection of memory models edited by Norman (1970). Also, Dember and Jenkins (1970) used simple physical constructions to contrast alternative factor theories of intellectual organization. Gregory (1953) even used alternative computer models (analogic versus digital) to explain metatheoretic differences between two general types of psychological theory (field theory versus association theory). As London (1949) put it,

Fundamentally, all explanation proceeds in terms of models . . . with modular apparatus ranging from the mathematical rigor of the closely articulated symbolical, at the one extreme, to the free looseness of the suggestive metaphor and simile, at the other. But no matter how constructed or arrived at, every model serves to bring order of some kind to nature or, rather, our comprehension of her (p. 165).

Modeling thus provides a versatile tool for theory construction.

Metaphor and Theory

A metaphor is a compressed simile, usually a substitution of one kind of object or idea for another, to suggest a likeness or analogy between them. Models are scientific metaphors in this sense, but artistic uses of metaphor come close to the intended meaning here also. Metaphors are basic heuristics for theoretical speculation in science. Brodbeck (1963) noted that,

Where knowledge is scarce speculation abounds. Social science not surprisingly witnesses a plethora of speculative "models" or guesses about isomorphisms. . . . [As an example] the notion of society as an organism, though repeatedly discredited, has a way of cropping up in one form or another. In its Spenglerian form, society is likened to a plant, complete with a seasonal life cycle (p. 90).

Another famous speculation of this sort is, "ontogeny recapitulates phylogeny" (see Hall, 1904).

These heuristic devices are here referred to as *metaphors;* the term *model* is reserved for more formal systems related to organized data, as discussed above. The development of metaphors can be an important form of theorizing, not to be ignored or criticized when used with a realistic perspective. Metaphors may be the ratiomorphic roots of theory, where art and science are indistinguishable mixtures of fact, fantasy, intuition and reasoning in the theorist's mind from which spring the scaffolding of formal models and, eventually, fullblown theories.

Metaphor, model and metatheory all are regarded as precursors of theory. As Turner (1967) noted, "Models, analogues, and scientific metaphors play an all but indispensable role in theoretical invention" (p. 229). Conceptions of theory and theory construction that do not include reference to these precursors may be satisfying in a logical sense, but will not be useful in understanding the ways in which theories are developed and used by human beings.

GRADES OF THEORY

But what really constitutes a theory? How shall we know one when we see, make or use one? The formal characteristics of a theory can be specified, following Braithwaite (1953), N. R. Campbell (1920), and Turner (1967), as including a) *presumptive hypotheses or axioms*—explicitly stated postulates without direct evidential support from which empirically testable theorems can be derived; b) *a calculus*—a set of equations or logical formulae that specify operations performed on variables in the language of the theory; c) *a dictionary* —empirical definitions for the terms of the theory and the rules used to verify derived theorems; and d) *a model*—a set of propositions, usually in the form of some theoretical or material analogue, that interprets the calculus of the theory. But these offer a philosopher's abstract view of "formal" theory. Earlier a looser definition of model was favored. Following Boring (1963), it seems useful also to admit many kinds of statements to the category called *theory*. The development of research on teaching will be best served, it is suggested, by defining several grades of theory, including not only the formal theory to which all science aspires but also less rigorous formulations of potential value in developing research. Thus, based partly on Boring's (1963) 14 types of theoretical statements, six grades of theory are here distinguished. The six grades reflect an abstract judgment as to the probable long-range importance of each kind of theoretical statement for behavioral and social research in general and for research on teaching in particular. But this is not to say that some particular statement classed here as of lower grade may not prove to be far more valuable in the long run than some particular statement from a higher grade level.

The higher grades of theory are directly related to work on a model. Some theories may be the products of such work, while some models may be produced to serve a theory already in hand, as Turner's (1967) description of theory suggests. Whether models are indispensable for all kinds of theory is certainly arguable (see Braithwaite, 1953, and Suppes, 1962, in addition to Turner, 1967). Whether theories of some type arise primarily from metatheoretic developments, from metaphors or from observation directly is also an open question. Each grade of theory deserves brief description before the interplay of research and theoretical work can be discussed in detail.[3]

[3] It should be noted that all but one of the grades of theory were defined before the rather too convenient A through F designation was recognized; the label for B-theory is somewhat strained. Readers are invited to substitute more preferred terms to avoid some of the unfortunate associations connected with letter grades.

A-Theory (Axiomatic Theory)

A theory is said to be axiomatized or axiomatic if it "possesses a set of primitive or undefined concepts with the help of which all its remaining concepts can be defined, and a set of primitive statements or postulates [axioms] from which all the remaining statements [theorems] can be derived as consequences" (Woodger, 1939, p. 66). For Turner (1967) this means giving the theory a formal model. Kaplan (1964) calls this "hierarchical theory."

The term *axiom* is synonymous with *postulate,* but is preferred for its brevity and convenience in declension. Unfortunately, in English it is often taken to mean "self-evident truth." Usage here follows Woodger (1937):

For in connexion with axiom-systems the question of self-evidence does not arise. All that is intended by the distinction between 'axioms' and 'theorems' is that the former are not 'proved' in the system, whereas the latter are all deducible from the former in accordance with those syntactical rules of the system which are called the 'rules of inference.' At the outset the choice between axioms and theorems is to some extent arbitrary. The ideal is to choose a number of statements (as small as possible) which will be consistent among themselves and will suffice for the derivation of all remaining statements of the system (p. 4).

Any rigorous theory can be axiomatized. However, except for Hull's (1943) system, statistical learning theory (Bush & Mosteller, 1955; Estes & Suppes, 1959), measurement theory (Lord & Novick, 1968), and scattered other developments (e.g., Luce, 1959), attempts at axiomatization are still rare in contemporary psychological theory and virtually unknown in education. The inference usually drawn from inspecting this literature is that axiomatization requires extensive skill in mathematics or symbolic logic, making it inaccessible to most educational researchers. The formal systems of mathematics and logic are indeed useful in theory building (see Woodger, 1939). But axiomatic theories can also be strictly verbal. Zetterberg (1954; see also Blalock, 1969) provided an example for sociologists using a variation of Durkheim's theory of division of labor. He recommended four steps for producing axiomatic theory: a) list primitive terms or *basic concepts,* undefined but for examples; b) define *derived concepts* using combinations of basic concepts; c) formulate *hypotheses* to contain only derived concepts; and d) divide hypotheses into axioms and theorems such that the axioms are consistent and independent, and all theorems are derivable therefrom. These derivation rules may be expressed mathematically or in ordinary language. Verification of the theory then proceeds by selecting hypotheses for empirical examination. Favorable results validate derived hypotheses as well as those given direct test.

Zetterberg saw five advantages in axiomatic theory. Such theory provides the most parsimonious summary of research findings, yields the highest plausibility for a given amount of supporting data, helps to locate critical research problems, delimits the area in which sources of failure of the theory are to be located, and assures clear distinction between definitions and hypotheses. Woodger added that axiomatization permits the use of symbols and the powerful techniques of modern logic, providing the only proper means of comparing the essential features of alternative theories.

Thus, the highest form of theory imposes demands and yields values not often met in educational and psychological theory. Not to aspire to such a level in theoretical work would be shortsighted, as would denigration of work at lower levels.

B-Theory (Broken Axiomatic Theories)

Two kinds of B-Theory can be identified: formal theories "on the way out," and growing theories for which complete formalization has so far been sacrificed in favor of inventiveness.

Some axiomatic theories are broken by continuing research. Evidence for them is recognized as insufficient or contradictory, but they remain useful because they remain productive of hypotheses and offer some modicum of understanding. Researchers knowingly retain such theories until they can be supplanted or improved upon. As Dallenbach (1953) noted, "Theories...pass from the scientific stage not because they have been discredited but because they have been superseded or by-passed—pushed off the stage and replaced by other theories" (p. 34).

Axiomatization assumes a good deal of prior logical analysis, though not necessarily psychological analysis. Some theories may not yet be fully axiomatized because their authors refuse to sacrifice interesting substantive features for logical or mathematical conventions. Restle (1959) contrasted purely abstract models, in which the mathematical form of the model bears no real meaning in terms of an underlying psychological theory (e.g., Bush & Mosteller, 1955), and those where the equations arise primarily from psychological considerations (e.g., Estes & Burke, 1953). Abstract models are sufficient for many purposes, but he doubted that they can fit more complex learning situations without richer bases in psychological theory. While starting from substantive considerations may make advances more difficult, at least partial algebraic models can be abstracted from these bases for intensive study.

Also, as Kaplan (1964) noted:

Knowledge grows not only by accretion and the replacement of dubious elements by more sound ones, but also by digestion, the remaking of the old cognitive materials into the substance of a new theory. Hierarchical [axiomatic] theories are typically improved by replacing some of their postulates with others, or by formulating a new set from which we can deduce the old one and other significant consequences as well (p. 304).

During this digestive process the system would be classified as B-Theory.

Even this view of progress in psychological theory may not be sufficiently eclectic to meet needs for theory in education. Assuming there existed, say, four fully formalized psychological theories, each representing domains of behavior relevant to education, the educational theorist might still be well advised to borrow useful portions of each for recombination in the educational arena. B-Theory often results from eclecticism; it is likely to be the highest form of theory found in research on teaching for some time to come.

C-Theory (Conceptual Theories and Constructs)

New concepts are proposed to simplify the explanation and description of relationships among observed variables. So Tolman (1936) suggested the use of hypothetical constructs as variables intervening between observed stimuli and responses. Some constructs can be given operational definition, some cannot. As research and theory proceed their nature becomes elaborated. Their validity is examined by comparing results using alternative operational definitions and by tracing their implications in various empirical settings (Cronbach, 1971; Cronbach & Meehl, 1955). Key issues in this process involve both the separation of new constructs from others in the domain and their demonstration using alternative methods of measurement (Campbell & Fiske, 1959). With consistent validation the construct takes its place in a network of related concepts invoked regularly to account for findings in some domain. Kaplan (1964) calls this "concatenated theory"; findings are explained in this type of theory by explicating their place in the pattern. Evolutionary and psychoanalytic theory are good examples of this type. Other examples of conceptual networks in the process of validation might be Atkinson and Feather's (1966) theory of achievement motivation, and Festinger's cognitive dissonance theory (1957).

Eventually, when a concept receives ex-

tensive validation over years of use it may become reified—it gains thinghood as a "real" entity. Boring (1963) offered "gravitation" as an example of reification in physics; "intelligence" is perhaps the most prominent example in psychology and education. Premature reification has been the unhappy consequence of much factor analytic research on personality.

D-Theory (Descriptive Theories and Taxonomies)

The processes of classification and discrimination are basic to the development of conceptual networks. Systematic descriptions of phenomena produced through use of these processes are thus important in theoretical work. They are theories, according to Boring (1963) who places Skinner's position (see Skinner, 1950) at this level, but they are classified below C-Theory because they do not introduce new hypothetical constructs for explanatory purposes.

The taxonomic work of Bloom (1956) and Krathwohl, Bloom, and Masia (1964) provides excellent examples of D-Theory in education. Guilford's (1967) *Structure of Intellect* must similarly be placed here, along with Gagné's (1970) listing of types of learning. Spence (1959) and Melton (1964) have discussed the importance of formulating a taxonomy of human learning and its function in advancing theory and research in the psychology of learning.

E-Theory (Elementisms)

Some kind of analysis, logical or empirical, is usually a first step in theory development beyond initial hypotheses. Attempts are made to reduce the definition of variables and relations between them to the most elementary units possible. In basic psychology this reduction often reaches a physiological level of discourse. Factor analytic subdivision of complex constructs similarly seeks primary units for theoretical work. Guilford's (1967) studies of mental abilities have produced such hypothesized elements which then are candidates for classification in his taxonomy of abilities. A list of technical skills of teaching was experimentally developed by McDonald and Allen (1967) by defining elements of teaching skill that could be modeled by a master teacher on video tape and reliably recognized by judges working from the definition.

The analysis of phenomena into elements or components has been a key to the advancement of science, particularly physical science. And Gage (1963) has espoused such an analytic approach to research on teaching. For Boring, elementisms were explanatory theories, one step above descriptive theories in psychology. While such analytic work is clearly valuable for research on teaching, descriptive taxonomies composed of organizations of hypothesized elements are here regarded as at least one step closer to the kinds of syntheses ultimately needed in understanding educational phenomena. Education, and particularly its teaching aspect, may eventually be best conceived as a fusion of elements with emergent and evolutionary properties, never completely reducible to original elements. The specification of behavioral objectives or performance criteria, the identification of individual steps in programmed instruction, the delineation of teaching acts, etc., are vital steps in research and theory development, but they hardly constitute integrated understanding of the nature of educational outcome, the course of meaningful learning, or the process of teaching.

The values of reductive versus constructive explanation in psychology have been discussed by Marx (1963); also see Jessor (1963) on the problem of reductionism. There is clearly room for both in the study of educational phenomena.

F-Theory (Formative Hypotheses)

The formulation of hypotheses is probably the first step in problem-solving of any kind. Thus, hypotheses are the basic ideas and expectations with which research on teaching begins. Some hypotheses have no support, while others have rationalized support. Some hypotheses can be tested while others cannot. But all have some claim to a role in theorizing if they are productive of research. Of course, testable hypotheses are our prime concern. But even those that find no support serve useful functions if they generate related findings. As one example, a review of literature by Baker and Crist (1971) found no support for the hypothesis that favorable teacher expectations promote IQ growth (Rosenthal & Jacobson, 1968). However, studies examining this hypothesis have suggested that teacher expectations may influence classroom behavior and achievement and have begun to sketch the possible mechanisms mediating such expectations. Thus the original Pygmalion hypothesis, while technically wrong in the narrow sense, may yet prove to be valuable in developing related research.

Hypotheses that cannot be tested also deserve a place in the F-Theory category. As Boring (1963) noted, some hypotheses cannot be formulated without using terms for which an operational definition is currently impossible. Sometimes new technologies make formerly impossible operations possible. Telemetry now permits physiological monitoring of teachers *in situ*. Video-tape recording has made possible repeated re-analyses of the same teacher performance so as to obtain detailed measures of literally dozens of different variables in that performance, where previous classroom observation techniques precluded such meticulous analysis. These measures made possible the testing of many previously untestable hypotheses. The dissemination of presently untestable hypotheses may even hasten development of the needed technology. Thus, provision should be made for the preservation and dissemination of potentially fruitful hypotheses, whether presently testable or not.

STEPS IN THEORY CONSTRUCTION

The processes involved in theorizing may well vary for different levels of theory, even though each level must involve some kinds of connections between conceptual (or theory) language and empirical (or data) language. Lower levels of theory (D, E and F) may be characterized by relatively simple summarization of empirical relationships without substantial inferences or deductive logic. Marx (1963) calls this inductive theorizing, where the emphasis is on the acquisition of facts. As facts about the phenomenon of interest accumulate, generalized distinctions, categories and principles may be induced, but such theoretical constructions typically follow, rather than precede, the development of facts. Some advocates of this mode of theorizing avoid formal inferential structures and terms altogether (e.g., Skinner, 1950; Sidman, 1960), though it can be argued that they are using an implicit theory deductively to guide empirical work.

Theory at the C and perhaps B levels may be similar to that described as functional theory by Marx (1963). Here there is continuing interaction between provisional theoretical concepts and data gathering, coupled with reluctance to move too far away from inventive experimentation toward axiomatic theory building. The mode is eclectic; the researcher builds or borrows what constructs he needs to account for findings, returning frequently to empirical activity to test implications, and dropping and adding concepts as the data dictate. A-level theory is called deductive theory by Marx (1963). Its connections with empirical activity are more spaced; the theory is formally constructed from massed data; its mathematical and logico-deductive structure is elaborated; a program of research is conducted to test derived hypotheses; and findings are used to make improvements in the theory.

For thinking about the processes of theorizing in somewhat more detail, the schematic diagram shown in Figure 1 is proposed. Readers may note the similarity between this diagram and some of those used in describing theoretical models of memory mechanisms (the figure is patterned after that of J. S. Reitman, 1970). The parallel is deliberate, since it seems likely that human theory building processes will in the end be found similar to other human learning and memory processes, and vice versa. As Gregory (1953) has pointed out, a "theory of how the brain works must be commensurable with ... theory (if any) of how it is *possible* to gain knowledge of the world" (p. 193). The figure suggests how metaphor, model and metatheory can be seen as interconnected steps in a sequence of operations leading from observational inputs to theoretical outputs. Whether all, or any, of these steps are essential in theory production is debatable. But each appears in the process often enough to deserve special attention as a regular, if not necessary, component. For brevity, the sequence is referred to as the MMM continuum.

Recognizing Metaphors

Man is constantly observing his environment, labeling objects, events and ideas and relating them one to another. Spearman's (1927) basic definition of human intelligence included three functions: the eduction of relations between known facts; the eduction of correlates, given a known fact and a known relation; and apprehension—knowing what one knows and what one does not know. Man exercises the eduction functions to increase apprehension because he needs to know and because it is fun. The first cognitive products of this exercise are metaphors. They provide an initial comprehension, and often an illusion of comprehension, of man's environment. Some metaphors are trivial and expendable, others are essential to learning, some are judged great works of art. Black (1962) characterized types and functions of metaphor as follows:

substitution-metaphors and comparison-metaphors can be replaced by literal translations ... by sacrificing some of the charm, vivacity, or wit of the original, but with no loss of *cognitive* content. But "interaction-metaphors" are not expandable. Their mode of operation

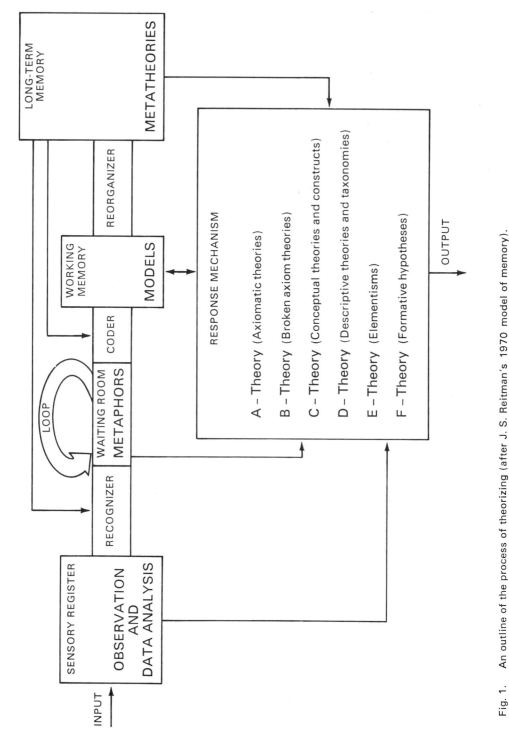

Fig. 1. An outline of the process of theorizing (after J. S. Reitman's 1970 model of memory).

requires the reader [or listener or viewer] to use a system of implications ... as a means for selecting, emphasizing, and organizing relations in a different field. This use of a "subsidiary subject" to foster insight into a "principal subject" is a distinctive intellectual operation (though one familiar enough through our experiences of learning anything whatever), demanding simultaneous awareness of both subjects but not reducible to any comparison between the two (pp. 45–46).

Some individuals, notably artists (of any medium), become particularly adept at capturing insights into the human condition in profound metaphors. The base of scientific creativity also, it is suggested here, is found in the production of metaphor. For the budding scientist (and the budding science), however, undisciplined metaphor making is difficult, perhaps because formal philosophical treatises make it seem illicit. As Wallach (1967) has argued, man's view of the nature of science has tended to concentrate on the formal analysis of implications given by nature; the function of playful generation and expression of conceptual possibilities in both scientific and artistic creativity has only recently been realized.

The paucity of theory in research on teaching may reflect an absence of metaphor making. The author (Snow, 1970) has elsewhere advocated using a heuristic, called "The Teacher as ..." device, for promoting theoretical thinking about teaching. This device is essentially a metaphor-making machine in which likely looking subsidiary subjects, to use Black's terms, that arise from observations or introspections are added to complete sentences starting with "The teacher" or "Teaching" as the principal subject. By creating an analogy between some aspect of teaching and other known things, concepts or roles, it is possible to elaborate ideas about teaching by playing out the analogy's implications. Such analogies are not meant to be closely reasoned or binding in detail, but merely to serve suggestive, hypothesis generating purposes. For example, one might consider

"The teacher as a Bayesian sheepdog." The resulting image is of a barking collie propelling his bulging flock along a path by successive statistical estimation and adjustment of the flock's average direction, while racing to keep diverging individuals contained within the group. Such an image may sum up some features of classroom teaching as it is observed in schools today. Jackson (1968) has used such metaphors, characterizing the teacher as traffic cop, judge, supply sergeant and time-keeper.

Other metaphors of interest (Snow, 1970) might be the teacher as a *Whole Earth Catalog,* a collection of puzzles, paradoxes, interesting activities and experiences like that published by Portola Institute (1969); the teacher as a General Problem Solver, the computer simulation of human problem-solving processes by Newell and Simon (1961) that allows detailed observation by students of ordinarily covert mental events in a teacher-model; the teacher as a critic, whose role is to interpret the world for students and vice versa.

The theoretician may start with metaphors such as these, producing them as a kind of image game, without much disciplined direction or general plan. He may take them explicitly or implicitly from the stream of the zeitgeist. Or he may construct them systematically to depict recognized patterns in reported data or his own observations. The metaphor captures key aspects of the phenomena of interest for the theoretician. It succinctly may schematize important insights into data and provide apt labels for these patterns of observation. It frequently overgeneralizes and is easily criticized because other persons, when told the metaphor, are likely to focus on irrelevant aspects until the theoretician's insight is explained to them. One can argue that the successful theoretician simply engages more in metaphor making than other researchers, so he is more likely to turn up some useful ideas. Or it may be that he is more skillful in constructing useful metaphors or in knowing one when he sees it. Perhaps proficiency in both quantity and quality marks the creative theoretician. In any case, it is conceivable that theory and research in teaching could benefit substantially if researchers of all persuasions engaged more extensively and intensively in metaphor making. Such activity might produce a store of interesting metaphors, some of which could lead to new ideas for concepts and variables of value.

Coding Models

But metaphors are hardly sufficient and perhaps not always necessary. They merely provide one basis for more formal theoretical constructions. The important features of the metaphor's structure must be translated or coded into some formal representation system. The representation system used may be verbal, but more frequently is graphic-pictorial, geometric or symbolic-mathematical. When completed, this abstraction process provides a model.

Model construction requires analytical skills to abstract important aspects of behavior in the form of a model, to derive implications from the model, and to identify predictions from it. March (1970a, 1970b) has described a course of instruction designed to develop such model-building skills, using as instructional examples social science models for individual and collective choice behavior, exchange, adaptation, diffusion and structure. Morris (1970) has added discussion of three components that deserve attention in learning to build models: a) a process of enrichment or elaboration through which overly simple models are chosen as starting points to evolve richer models reflecting the complexity of actual situations; b) a process of analogy or association in which well-developed logical structures from other fields are chosen as the starting points for the elaboration process; and c) a process of looping or alternating between model modifications and data and between model assumptions and deductions from it.

To show how this process might proceed in research on teaching, consider again the example of "The teacher as a Bayesian sheepdog." The key features of this metaphor are: a two-dimensional space in which a direction vector represents the teacher's chosen path and a flock of points represents pupils; a measure of average flock direction which the teacher estimates periodically; the difference between average flock direction and the teacher's direction vector, which the teacher tries to minimize; and a measure of flock density which the teacher tries to maximize. Using the pedagogical analogs of circling movements, feints and charges along with iterative sampling and estimation of location and direction, the teacher moves his or her class through a field, physical or psychological.

This metaphor might first have been conceived in thinking about an elementary teacher's discipline problems on a walk in the park, but it is also applicable, and perhaps more useful, as a representation of the teacher's cognitive activities in group discussion. Suppose the two dimensions are chosen to represent elapsed time and level of conceptual complexity reached in some domain of knowledge. An example of high conceptual complexity might be "recognizing the complex network of causes for the Civil War." The teacher's goal is to move all learners to the highest conceptual level in a fixed amount of available time. Through questions, probing comments, and explanations, along with supportive and reinforcing moves, the teacher seeks to keep the group together, leaving no one behind, and to estimate the group's progress up the levels of one dimension as a function of time remaining on the other dimension. Suppose we wish to study one particular aspect of the teacher's behavior, e.g., ideation rate—the speed with which the teacher introduces new ideas or shifts from one idea to another in discourse.

The metaphor becomes a model when such distinctive features are coded as components of a more formal system. First attempts at this coding step frequently involve some form of visual schematizing or graphing. Figure 2 shows estimated levels of conceptual complexity (Y) and time (T) as continuous variables, with an example of a teacher's planned path, the class without extensive further research. With simpler models, however, it is often possible to code directly into mathematical terms. For the sheepdog model, we might start by stating teacher ideation rate (I) as some function of estimated variance in learner

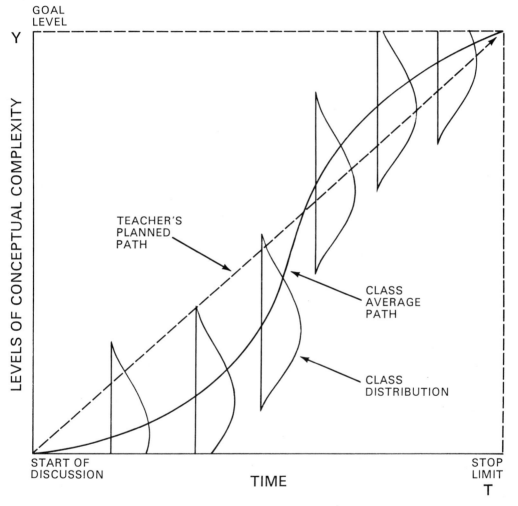

Fig.2.   Graph of the hypothetical relation of levels of conceptual complexity *(Y)* and time *(T)*, showing the teacher's planned path, the class average path, and the class distribution at several points in time.

average path, and some successive class distributions on conceptual level also depicted. Models of complex phenomena sometimes cannot be taken beyond this geometric step conceptual level (V) and the difference between the teacher's subjective estimation of the class-average conceptual level and the teacher's planned direction (D). That is,

$$I_{t+1} = f(V_t, D_t)$$

where:

I_{t+1} = teacher ideation rate at time $t + 1$,

V_t = teacher estimated variance of class conceptual level at time t,

D_t = the teacher's estimate of average learner conceptual level ($\overline{Y}$) at time t minus the teacher's planned conceptual level at time t.

Suppose our first attempt at specifying the function assumes a parsimonious model where the correlation between V_t and I_{t+1} is negative and linear, the correlation between D_t and I_{t+1} is negative and linear, and the correlation between V_t and D_t is zero. Then our model might be a linear regression equation

$$I_{t+1} = c - b_1 D_t - b_2 V_t$$

where b_1 and b_2 are regression coefficients and c is a constant representing the I intercept. These values could then be estimated in tryouts of the equation.

This simple mathematical model is purely hypothetical and almost certainly wrong. Relations among the variables would probably not be simple linear functions. V_t and D_t would probably not be independent of one another; both might also be complex functions of previous states of I, the starting conceptual level for students (which was set at zero above), and many other variables. And b_1 and b_2 might well vary across time. Further, actual tests of the model would have to wait upon the invention of new measurement techniques, since obtaining a measure of periodic teacher estimates of $\overline{Y}$ and V_t *in vivo* would be no easy matter. Having advanced a model that requires this measure, however, one might justify the effort involved in developing the needed measurement technology.

Even erroneous models may guide theory by suggesting kinds of data worth collecting. Experimentation with the model should show what improvements are needed. Suppose our simple model could not be made to fit experimental data because of the

problems listed above. Going back to the drawing board, we might try simple flow-charting techniques to examine further the processes presumed to be operating in the sheepdog model. If our earlier data would suggest that systematic individual differences among teachers occur in this situation, we would try to represent hypotheses about these differences also in our flow-charting. Figures 3, 4 and 5 show possible layouts for three hypothetical teachers, A, B and C, respectively.

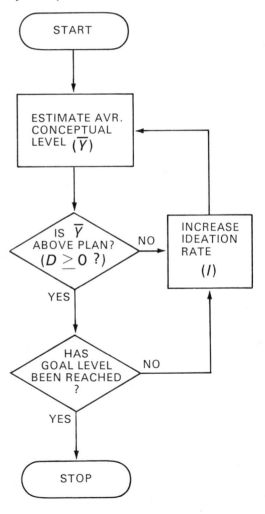

Fig. 3.   Flowchart representing behavior of Teacher A.

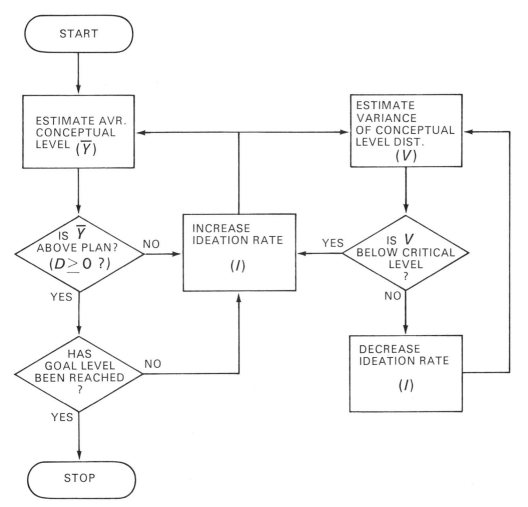

Fig. 4.   Flowchart representing behavior of Teacher B.

Teacher A, in Figure 3, pursues the teaching goal with singleness of purpose. She ignores the variance in conceptual levels in her class and continues to increase her ideation rate until the goal is reached for the above-average students. She hopes to drive the class average to her goal before the time is up, let us say, to gain the largest possible headstart on new material scheduled for the next class meeting.

In Figure 4 Teacher B pursues the same primary course, but includes consideration of class variance. When his estimate of class variance exceeds a certain minimum, he recognizes that some students may be falling behind, decreases his ideation rate, and perhaps inserts some kind of recycling or alternative explaining technique. This procedure may delay the more advanced students but it insures that slower members of the group will have the opportunity to catch up periodically. Aside from this allowance, however, Teacher B appears to be as interested as Teacher A in reaching the goal level, presumably for the same reason.

Teacher C, in Figure 5, differs in attitude

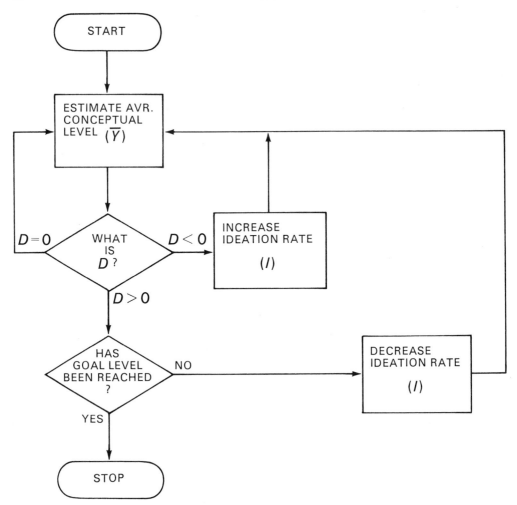

Fig. 5.   Flowchart representing behavior of Teacher C.

from A and B. She wishes not to reach the goal level ahead of time for she has planned each meeting so that it will end on key points of closure. Hence, she reduces ideation rate whenever the class average is above her planned path. Like Teacher A, she ignores class variance, although it should be clear from Figure 5 that the addition of V estimation components would create a hypothetical Teacher D. We have not depicted the fact that all teachers stop when the bell rings. Other components, of course, could be added to all of the flowcharts.

To press the model further, let us try to code these schematizations in mathematical terms. All three teachers must be described using relations among variables as functions of time. Hence the simple algebraic expressions tried earlier must be replaced by differential equations.

For Teacher C we have,

$$\frac{dI}{dt} = \begin{cases} + c \text{ when } D < 0 \\ 0 \text{ when } D = 0 \\ - c \text{ when } D > 0 \end{cases}$$

where c provides a constant added to or subtracted from the ideation rate I. Expressed as an equation for continuous variables,

$$\frac{dI}{dt} = -cD.$$

But Teacher A never decreases I. For her,

$$\frac{dI}{dt} = \begin{cases} + c & \text{when } D < 0 \\ 0 & \text{when } D = 0. \end{cases}$$

For Teacher B the matter is not quite so simple. Since the variance estimate is the key to determining whether I increases or decreases, we shall base our equations primarily on V. We assume that class variance decreases logarithmically with ideation rate; that is,

$$\text{Log } V = -aIt + c$$

or

$$V = e^{-aIt+c}.$$

Then, we can express this as a differential equation

$$\frac{dV}{dt} = -aVI.$$

We also assume that for each V there is a critical ideation rate. When V is below this level, ideation rate increases are facilitative; above it, ideation rate increases are debilitating because of the disparity among student conceptual levels and teacher anxiety about the impossibility of individualization. This critical level is defined as some function of V.

$$I_x = f(V)$$

which we assume for simplicity to be linear. Then we assume that when ideation rate is above this critical level the teacher will want to decrease the rate; when ideation rate is below this level the teacher will want

to increase the rate. This assumption can be written mathematically as

$$\frac{dI}{dt} = -b(I - I_x).$$

These equations are obscure without knowledge of advanced calculus[4], but they can be comprehended by tracing time paths for V and I, given initial values V_0 and I_0 for time t_0. In Figure 6 three hypothetical starting points and their respective time paths are displayed. It is apparent that success depends primarily on the teacher's starting point with respect to V and I. If V is very high while I is low, for the starting point identified as (I_0, V_0), the teacher's further reduction in I leads only to cognitive disorganization; the wide dispersion of students defeats attempts to get the group together, and the teacher effectively gives up. Starting at point (I'_0, V'_0), the teacher is above the critical level for V but with a substantially higher starting I. As ideation rate is reduced and class dispersion is brought under control, V drops below the critical level and the teacher can then concentrate on increasing I to advance the group toward the goal. For starting point (I''_0, V''_0), however, the group is already relatively homogeneous (below the critical level), so the teacher can move directly to advanced ideation rates and conceptual levels.

While such a formulation hardly represents a finished model, it should be clear how our conceptualization has been advanced. By iterative attempts at model improvement, using one or more representation systems, and comparisons with data collected according to model specifications, we might well arrive at a level of detail in describing teacher cognitive functions in group discussion not dreamed of beforehand. Further, it might be possible to extend the model by relating its parameters to larger networks of variables. What personal

[4] The assistance of Professor Janet Elashoff in checking the equations is gratefully acknowledged.

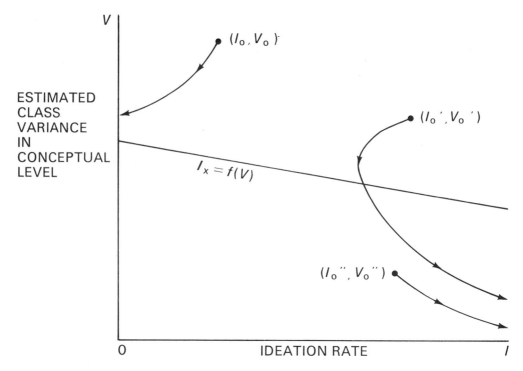

Fig. 6. Graph of the hypothetical relation of ideation rate *(I)* and estimated class variance in conceptual level *(V)*, showing the critical ideation rate and the resulting time paths for three alternative starting points.

characteristics might correlate with Y in learners or with I in teachers? What kinds of teacher-training practices or homogeneous grouping practices might influence characteristics of the model? What learning outcome variables might be influenced by characteristics of the model? This is a crude example dealing with a very small aspect of teacher behavior, but it serves as one illustration of the model-building process. This example also provides a base for later discussion, for teacher B actually represents a direct translation of a model by H. A. Simon (1964) concerning the relation of motivation and learning in students.

Mathematical models are extremely powerful tools, not only for systematizing research on individual theoretical formulations but also for controlling comparisons between competing formulations. An example of this use of modeling, comparing all-or-none learning versus incremental learning hypotheses, has been provided by Atkinson and Calfee (1965). Yet such models are still relatively new in behavioral and social science and almost unheard of in educational research. Excellent introductions to this field are available. Snyder (1968) discussed developments and applications in educational psychology without overburdening the reader with mathematics, and Coleman (1964) provided a general review of mathematical sociology. The use of computer simulation models, for which the flow charts of Figures 3, 4 and 5 provide beginning examples, is similarly new. Helpful introductions have been provided by Feigenbaum and Feldman (1963), W. R. Reitman (1965), and Snyder's (1968) chapters on this topic.

Organizing Metatheories

Figure 1 suggests that metatheories are organized, and sometimes reorganized, collections of theoretical models. They influence the recognizing and coding operations that produce metaphors and models, perhaps by constricting the perception and the model-building tools of the theorizer. Consider again the sheepdog example. The computer flowcharts represent forms prescribed by the collection of admissible operations available for use in computer programming. With computer simulation as an approach, we automatically give our model a distinctive character, even though we might have constructed our particular model using a wide variety of alternative layouts. As noted earlier, a metatheory provides a kind of grammar or medium of communication. Once a particular medium is chosen, we are free to express ourselves with any one or a combination of the admissible statements of that medium. Our mathematical constructions were similarly limited. Perhaps the contrast of algebra for the linear regression equations and the later use of differential calculus for time functions reflect a metatheoretic choice within a more general family of mathematical models.

Models are assembled and modified gradually through continuous interaction with ongoing observation and data analysis. Perhaps metatheories are also best conceived as built up from pieces (successful models) as research proceeds. Certainly major forms or categories of theory are not created overnight. Yet at any given moment metatheory seems imposed from "above." The zeitgeist, the "school of thought," the invisible college, the individual mentor, perhaps also the nature of the problem, force particular metatheoretic positions on the researcher often before the first study is designed.

Some metatheoretic choices are formalized and clearly delineated, available to the researcher as logical alternatives. Others appear to have arisen as stylistic differences among theorists that shade into one another. Coan (1968) performed a factor analysis of ratings of outstanding psychological theorists and defined six primary dimensions to characterize the apparent metatheoretic divisions. The largest dimensions, labeled subjectivistic versus objectivistic, and holistic versus elementaristic orientations, correspond to distinctions made by Brunswik (1952) in his analysis of theoretical frameworks in psychology. Organizing the six factors into a bipolar hierarchical structure, the construction shown in Figure 7 was obtained. The result displays nicely at least some of the metatheoretical choices to be made in pursuing psychological theory. And it would appear that the major dimensions characterize some salient differences in educational research traditions as well as those of psychology. Nuthall and Snook offered a grouping of theoretical approaches that shows some analogous choices for research on teaching. A more detailed subdivision of approaches to the study of teaching, perhaps patterned on Coan's work, would be useful but beyond the scope of this chapter. Barclay (1971) has proposed such a structure for the study of counseling.

The need for new metatheory arises out of the inadequacy of existing metatheory. When hypotheses too frequently fail to be confirmed, when results of investigations are insignificant or inconsistent, and when findings with theoretical or practical value appear too seldomly, a field of research becomes ripe for the emergence of new metatheories. Investigators become frustrated, discouraged and restless. Questions are raised as to the value of further work along the same apparently futile lines.

The field of research on teaching has exhibited such conditions at various periods in its brief history. In the first five decades of the twentieth century much of what little research on teaching occurred sought correlations between independent teacher traits measured with tests, inventories and rating

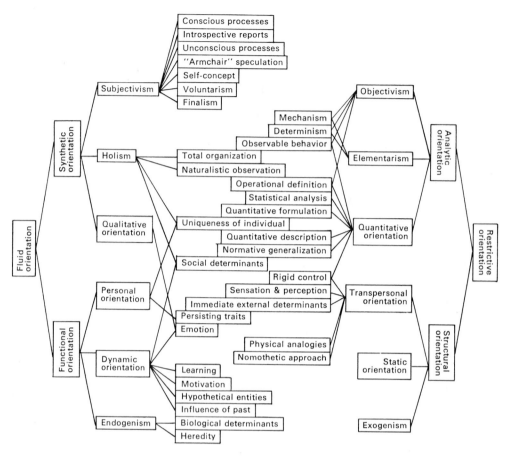

Fig. 7. A bipolar hierarchy of theoretical variables, showing relatively specific variables in the center with more general and mutually opposing trends shown on the left and right sides (after Coan, 1968).

scales as independent variables, and criteria of teacher effectiveness measured with rating scales. Results were unsatisfactory, in the various senses mentioned above.

During the 1950s and 1960s workers using this approach were joined by others seeking correlations between teacher classroom behavior, measured through systematic observation, and student achievement, adjusted for pretest measures. Chapter 5 reviews these *process-product* studies. After concluding that the results to date were not particularly promising, Rosenshine has suggested various improvements for future re-

search within this same general approach.

Will new research incorporating these suggestions prove fruitful? Or will it fail to increase the degree to which student achievement can be understood, predicted and controlled on the basis of variations in teacher behavior? Perhaps a more radical shift in metatheory is needed.

One such shift was proposed by Cronbach (1957) as a unification of experimental and correlational approaches to research. The educational implications of this shift have been discussed by Cronbach and Snow (1969) as a search for interactions between environmental variables, including teaching methods and styles, and student aptitude variables, including learning abilities and styles. The conception is basically Darwinian; research on teaching would seek the principles by which learners and learning environments can be matched to optimize educational outcomes. As Shulman (1970), Walberg (1970) and others have noted, progress in this direction requires, and may produce, distinct changes in the ways one describes teaching-learning environments.

Another shift derives from Skinner's approach to the experimental analysis of behavior. As advocated by Sidman (1960), one searches first for lawfulness in the behavior of *individual* organisms as a function of manipulable experimental variables, paying particular attention to within-individual variation over time. The approach is essentially idiographic; generalization across persons is secondary—attempted only when individual data justify it. In this view, both teaching and research on teaching become individualized experimentation with, and invention of, behavior modification techniques (see Becker, 1971; Becker, Engelmann, & Thomas, 1971).

These and other possible shifts represent metatheoretic choices that may lead to new varieties and models for research on teaching. An important reason for concern with metatheory is to make these choices explicit. The simple fact that some metatheories or methodologies have not been tried in research on teaching may be reason enough to try them. Diversity of approach should increase the likelihood of theoretical advance.

AIDS IN THEORY CONSTRUCTION

Metaphors, models and metatheories are general aids for the production of theory; there are also many special devices that can be distinguished. It is not possible here to review all of the more specific aids and heuristic devices used or potentially useful in invention, discovery and theory construction. Some of these devices bear relation to those discussed by Polya (1957) within the context of mathematical problem-solving. Others may derive from earlier treatises on the subject of heuristics but a tracing of such sources has not been attempted here (see Polya, 1957, for contributions by Bolzano, Descartes, Leibnitz, and others). Some selected techniques may be particularly helpful in theoretical work related to research on teaching and they deserve at least brief discussion.

Analyzing

A basic problem in theory building is the identification of appropriate units of analysis. Several different kinds of units are possible and it may not be clear at the outset which kinds will be most useful. The theorist does well to try different units in initial conceptual work before making choices. Dubin (1969) has discussed this problem in detail, suggesting five types of analytic units applicable in building social theory. These appear to be relevant to theory construction in education also.

Each type of unit is described in terms of properties of "things," usually persons or social groups, as follows: a) *enumerative* units are properties that are general characteristics regardless of other conditions, e.g., sex or age of people, or size or purpose of a social group; b) *associative* units are enumerative units that include a zero value, e.g., amount of productive skill or income for a person, or degree of stability or leadership for a social group—Dubin judged the distinction between enumerative and associative units to be important because theorists tend to ignore variables that happen to have zero value in the initial settings studied, forcing their entry later as intervening variables; c) *relational* units are properties determined by relations among properties, e.g., interaction properties like subordination and status, or combination properties like sex ratio and ethnocentrism—most theory building in behavioral science uses relational units and sometimes produces tautologies when the nature of these units is not kept clear; d) *statistical* units are properties that summarize the distribution of a property, e.g., homogeneous grouping, median income, middle class, underprivileged; e) *summative* units are global describers, e.g., other-directed personality, extended-kinship system, underdeveloped economy. In addition, Dubin dealt with certain combinations of units and methods for inventing new units through extending, subdividing, or factor analyzing existing classification systems.

Translating

Existing theories and models may be similar to the kinds of theory needed in a new domain. If, on close inspection of such situations, an analogy appears to hold, some form of substitution of one theory for another, in part or whole, may be possible. This process can be called *theory translation*.

Some examples have already been given in earlier sections of this chapter. The diagram of Figure 6, together with the differential equations used to characterize teacher ideation rate, were borrowed directly from Simon's (1964) formulation of motivation in learning. The concepts of class variation in conceptual level (V) and teacher ideation rate (I) were substituted for Simon's concepts of level of difficulty in learning material and rate of activity, respectively. The MMM continuum in Figure 1 was a translation from J. S. Reitman (1970).

These examples show the use of analogy to guide theory translation. It is possible that significant development of theory and research related to teaching might be obtained through wider use of this technique. However there is no guarantee that the procedure will provide more than interesting mental exercises for the theorist. Maccia, Maccia, and Jewett (1963) compiled several attempts to model educational theory on theories drawn from other unrelated disci-

plines. While the translations could clearly be executed, they seemed not to generate many interesting hypotheses, perhaps because the translations remained at a rather global level of analysis. In a critical review of this work, Jacobson, Stimart, and Wren (1971) argued that such efforts can be justified only if the translations suggest new hypotheses that would not have been otherwise available.

Schematizing

As Polya (1957) noted, figure drawing is often a useful heuristic device in mathematics, even when the problem is not basically a geometric one. More generally, it can be suggested that geometrizing and nonmetric figural representation frequently offer important visualizations of complex concepts. Many of the paradigms reviewed by Gage (1963) employed forms of crude visualization if not actual geometry. In some theoretical developments the creation of new geometries is an initial step. A fascinating example of geometrizing in process is Allport's (1967) work in which a quasigeometry is developed to characterize space and time relationships in both the inner and outer functioning of a behaving organism. Possibly Allport's geometry could be adapted to represent features of teacher-learner interactions; an analogous adaptation of another schema, Brunswik's (1952) lens model, has been proposed elsewhere (Snow, 1968).

Schematizing has also been used effectively by Blalock (1969) to portray various kinds of causal relationships among variables. He showed the way in which

$$X \rightarrow Y \rightarrow Z$$

implies different relationships than does

where "an arrow linking a given pair of variables indicates that there is assumed to be a *direct* causal link between these variables..." (p. 15). Blalock also diagrammed other causal models as shown in Figure 8. In Figure 8d, the intervening variables can be regarded as dependent variables in relation to $X_1, X_2, X_3 \ldots X_i$, and as independent variables in relation to Y. An example of this pattern in research on teaching might connect teacher-training variables (e.g., microteaching with video-taped models, video-taped feedback, and a programmed instructional manual) serving as $X_1, X_2,$ and $X_3,$ to various kinds of teacher behavior (e.g., higher order questioning, use of students' ideas) serving as intervening variables I_1 and I_2, which in turn might influence various kinds of outcomes in students (e.g., ability to solve problems, attitude toward the subject) serving as the dependent variables Y_1 and Y_2.

Schematizing can make explicit aspects of the situation the investigator may otherwise have only dimly perceived and can suggest relationships among variables that might not otherwise have been considered. Some forms of schematizing provide formal means of representing and manipulating the structure of a theory. An approach using linear directed graphs, called *digraph theory,* is one such form. Stinchcombe (1968) has shown some examples of this approach in sociological theory.

Miniaturizing

It is fashionable now to speak of miniature theories, suggesting that small portions of a domain can be covered by separate subtheories more easily than one could build a theory dealing with the domain as a whole. The aim is to divide by a kind of heuristic pluralism and eventually to conquer. Continuing research and theoretical analysis suggest distinctions between, say, several kinds of learning, so separate theory-building efforts become concentrated within categories (see Melton, 1964). Perhaps these categories are further subdivided so that separate subtheories are advanced for special learning tasks administered under strictly specified conditions.

The technique claims three main advantages (Zetterberg, 1954): general theories are more likely to emerge when a few miniature theories exist in a field; evidence supporting a miniature theory will also support more inclusive theories; and miniature theories more readily suggest tractable research studies.

There have been few attempts at miniaturizing in the field of teaching. The microteaching skills approach (Berliner, 1969; McDonald & Allen, 1967) may represent one example. But the work has not progressed to the point of theory construction. Dyadic interaction as in tutoring has been proposed as one miniature area worthy of theoretical attention. Simulations of different kinds of teaching situations may provide an avenue toward important subdivisions. To the degree that miniature theories can be constructed for aspects of teaching, they may then allow the fashioning of progressively more general theory as research combines and contrasts propositions derived from each. Spence (1959) once outlined how he expected higher-order theories of learning to incorporate separate miniature systems, building up from a base in conditioning theory. One might hope for similar patterns in the development of theories of teaching.

Taxonomizing

The creation and manipulation of taxonomy produces D-theory but can be used to guide higher-order theory building as well. Gage (1964) has shown how the crossing of several category systems may lead to clearer delineation of theoretical domains for research on teaching. Teaching was analyzed in four ways, using a) types of teaching activities, b) types of educational objectives, c) components of the learning process, and d) families of learning theory. By selecting categories from each of these lists,

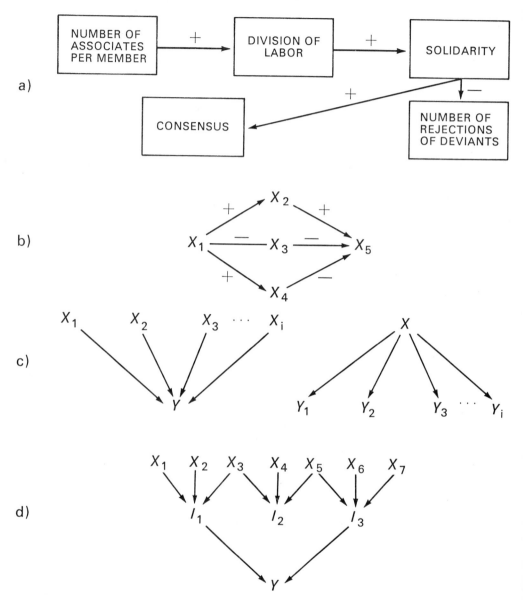

Fig. 8.   Schematized causal relationships among variables (after Blalock, 1969).

one can define individual domains that may deserve attention. Given an educational objective and a particular learning theory, say, the taxonomy can be used to suggest what teaching activities directed at what components of learning are likely to be worth research and, eventually, useful in practice.

Melton (1964) discussed the importance of taxonomy for the development of learning theory and research. Spence's (1959) vision, noted above, of a general learning theory constructed from several smaller theories, implied not only a taxonomy but also a scale of increasing complexity along which the categories of learning tasks could be arrayed. Work on accumulating the general theory moved from simple to complex tasks. Gagné's (1970) types of learning similarly assume that each level represents a combination of elements from the levels beneath it. Units of analysis, variables, categories of tasks, situations, etc. can often be ordered in this way. These hierarchical taxonomies offer the added advantage of comparison across domains. In Table 1 four such structures are arrayed beside one another to suggest a correspondence between levels. The product dimension of Guilford's (1967) *Structure of Intellect* seems to fit fairly well with Gagné's (1970) types of learning; the lack of clear correspondence at two levels might be taken to suggest the addition of two product categories in Guilford's array. The arrays from Bloom (1956) and Krathwohl et al. (1964) also appear to show correspondences. Do such parallels suggest psychological similarities between levels of learning, cognitive abilities, and cognitive and affective educational objectives? While the idea is appealing, one may easily be misled by superficial similarities in labels when underlying processes actually differ markedly. Apparent connections between taxonomies, however, may at least guide and help justify empirical exploration of their implications.

Comparisons of taxonomies often fail to find congruences and this result may also suggest research to resolve the issue. The Bloom (1956) ability categories do not match Guilford's (1967) categories of cognitive operations, for example.

EVALUATIONS OF THEORY

In a general sense any research that is suggested or guided by a theory provides evaluation of that theory. To the extent that a theory is useful in organizing existing data meaningfully in a field and is productive of useful hypotheses for further research, the theory is judged to be valuable. To the extent that it is not useful in these ways, it is rejected. At the present state of knowledge in research on teaching, and in all social and behavioral science, the primary criterion for the evaluation of theory is *usefulness,* not *truthfulness.* To be sure, the theories discussed here are expected to provide specific predictions that "come true," and theories that do not consistently provide such predictions will be rejected, at least within some margin of error. And these theories are expected to provide a system into which both new data and new hypotheses can fit. As Kaplan (1964) noted,

this function is more than a matter of what the older positivism used to call "economy of thought" or "mental shorthand", and what today is expressed in terms of the storage and retrieval of information. It is true that the systematization effected by a theory does have the consequence of simplifying laws and introducing order into congeries of facts. But this is a by-product of a more basic function: to make sense of what would otherwise be inscrutable or unmeaning empirical findings.... In providing meaning, the theory also attests to truth. A hypothesis may be as much confirmed by fitting it into a theory as by fitting it to the facts (p. 302).

But the main emphasis here is on meaningfulness; the ultimate truthfulness of theories is rarely discussed and cannot really be determined anyway. Marx (1963) has noted the impasse involved in attempts at empirical versus logical verification of theory. Besides, it is wasteful to argue whether, for example, both wave and quantum theories of light are true—perhaps both cannot be true, but both can be very useful for particular purposes. It is suggested that theories for research on teaching, even if contradictory, be judged on the basis of usefulness in this same way.

Several specific criteria for evaluating theories and models have been proposed.

TABLE 1

A COORDINATION OF FOUR TAXONOMIES

Source	Gagné's (1970) Types of Learning	Guilford's (1967) Cognitive Ability Products	Bloom's (1956) Knowledge Levels	Krathwohl's et al. (1964) Affective Levels
Levels	Problem-solving	Implications	Knowledge of the universals and abstractions in a field	Characterization
	Principle Learning	Transformations		
	Concept Learning	Systems		Organization
	Multiple Chaining		Knowledge of ways and means of dealing with specifics	Valuing
	Association	Relations		
	Chaining	Classes		Responding
	Response Learning	Units	Knowledge of specifics	
	Signal Learning			Attention

The following listing represents a combination of ideas on the potential shortcomings of models from Kaplan (1964) and Lachman (1960), and criteria for assessing theories of instruction offered by Gordon (1968).

1. The statement of a theory should make explicit its postulates (axioms and theorems) and the definitions of terms involved in these postulates. It should minimize the number of undefined primitive terms and attempt operational definition of all relevant variables. For an extended discussion of this requirement with reference to instructional theories, see Gordon (1968).

2. The statement of a theory should make explicit the boundaries of its concern and the limitations under which it is proposed. While the scope of applicability of a theory or model is ultimately an empirical question, delineation of the range of phenomena to which the system is supposed to be applicable is a responsibility of the author. This delineation serves as a guide and incentive to research and to subsequent improvements in the system. A related criterion, called *deployability,* refers to the degree to which terms in a model can be applied successfully in new settings; the more deployable a model, the greater the potential scope of the associated theory (see Lachman, 1960).

3. A theory should have internal consistency as a logical system. This require-

ment seems obvious but needs emphasis. Often attempts at explicating the logical system within a theory will expose inconsistencies and point to needed improvements.

4. A theory should be consistent with existing empirical data. The empirical sources of the theory should be clearly documented in detail. Data from related fields of theory and research should be reviewed to show that the theory is congruent with other known facts.

5. A theory should be capable of generating specific hypotheses and predictions. This requirement relates in part to that expressed in item 1, above. Postulates must be explicated in such a way that hypotheses are clearly derivable. But more is implied here; two theories that meet other criteria may still differ markedly in the quality and quantity of predictions and hypotheses that can be derived from them. Other things equal, we should prefer the theory that most enriches research on teaching with interesting hypotheses.

6. A theory should be testable. This requirement is met if theorems are stated in such a way that it is possible to collect data to disprove them. As pointed out in Gordon (1968), tautologies and truisms like, "pupil classroom behavior is a function of teacher personality," are not testable in their usual form. Theories and models containing variables that are not yet operationalized may still be useful, as suggested earlier, but the ultimate responsibility for testing remains with the user.

7. A theory should be parsimonious. The simplest of alternative explanatory propositions should always be accepted; the burden of proof should rest on those preferring the more complex alternative. As Marx (1963) has argued, the law of parsimony is misunderstood if applied to the construction or testing of complex hypotheses; it was never meant to restrict the advance of research. It applies only to the acceptance of propositions. Theories should become more complex only as indicated by evidence.

8. A theory should be quantifiable. While it is recognized that many theories and models today represent verbal-qualitative constructions, the ultimate need for theories that express quantitative relationships among variables must be stressed. The precision and power of mathematical methods that can be brought to bear in a quantitative theory or model greatly enhance its usefulness. With quantification, ambiguities and contradictions can be exposed and the degree to which the system meets other criteria listed here can be more readily determined.

However, misunderstanding of the emphasis on quantification, rigor and parsimony, particularly in model building, often leads to unfortunate shortcomings in the resulting product and its use. These shortcomings, discussed at length by Kaplan (1964), form the basis for additional rules listed below.

9. Unnecessary symbolization should be avoided. The substitution of symbols for verbal expressions may provide economy for some individuals but often serves only as obfuscation for others. Symbolization is valuable only as a means to use logico-mathematical methods. As Kaplan (1964) put it,

By the use of the symbols a proposition is given the form of a scientifically useful statement, but not always the content. To introduce "x" as an abbreviation for a longer—and especially, a more prosaic—expression, then to say that $y = f(x)$, may be to present something which has the appearance of mathematics without the reality (p. 278).

10. Unnecessary formalization should be avoided. Formal models can always be built but they are not always useful, so model building should not be undertaken for its own sake. The formalization of theories and models is valuable only as a means to scientific progress. The empirical content of this progress should dictate the nature of the theoretical tools we build, not logical form. And overemphasis on rigorous form may work against the production of fruitful

theories by hampering the budding Freud or Darwin.

11. Oversimplification should be avoided. Theories and models are always simplifications of the phenomena they address. The process of simplification makes the phenomena wieldy by paring them down to essential components. But some theories and models are oversimplified—Kaplan would prefer the term "undercomplicated"—to the point of leaving out essential components. The criticism that laboratory research cannot be generalized to classroom behavior must rest on this issue; so must the view that rote-learning studies are irrelevant for education. Granted we may not know all the components that are important to include, but at least we should not exclude components that are known to be important.

12. Theorizing by means of models requires vigilance. Dangers involved in thinking with models have been discussed by Kaplan (1964) as "map reading" and "pictorial realism." Models contain irrelevant features as well as essential components and it is easy to be misled into unprofitable research or theorizing by mistaking one for the other. One must be able to distinguish the essential features of the model. Even with these features distinguished, it is easy to mistake them for those of the phenomenon of which they are a model. Models are not literal representations; more than one model can picture the same phenomenon even though the models are themselves incompatible. Perhaps it would be beneficial to build at least two models in every instance; different representations would isolate essential features in bold relief and emphasize that no one represents reality.

THEORIES OF LEARNING, TEACHING, CURRICULUM AND INSTRUCTION

Space limitations prohibit attempts at describing all, or even major, extant theories and models that have relevance for educational practice. And it is not clear that such a cataloging would be useful at the present time. Even a superficial scanning of the literature shows amazing diversity both in the use of the terms *theory* and *model,* and in the nature of the formulations so identified.

The diversity of relevant theories and models is exhibited in collections like those edited by Hilgard (1964), by Hyman (1968), and by Macdonald and Leeper (1965). Then there are individual models for school learning (e.g., Carroll, 1963; Hunt, 1971), models for guiding educational research (e.g., Siegel & Siegel, 1967; Walberg, 1970), models for guiding research on teaching (e.g., Gage, 1963; Snow, 1968), and outlines for theories of curriculum and instruction (e.g., Biber, 1967; Bruner, 1966; Wagener, 1970). There are also influences on theory from new views of philosophy related to psychology (e.g., Buhler, 1971) and from demands that psychology needs its own philosophy (Wolman, 1971). And there are new critical views on the relevance and uses of any kind of theory in education (Schwab, 1970).

Some of these constructions bear close resemblance to the forms of theory described in this chapter; some do not, though it is likely that most could be forced to fit roughly. The purpose of this chapter has been to offer some beginning tools for this kind of work, not to advance some grand framework as *the* form for theory in education. Much more comprehensive analyses are required of the roles of theories and models in contemporary education than is possible here. But such analyses are being pursued (see, e.g., Belth, 1970). When a catalog of theories and models is eventually assembled, some improved integration of theory-building procedures may be apparent. Such a catalog may start simply, following the pattern of Simon and Boyer's (1970) compendium of classroom observation instruments. Hopefully it will reach the kind of study of educational theory envisioned for psychological theory by Koch (1951) and begun by the series of volumes edited by Koch (1959). Similarities and differences between the forms and roles of theory for learning, teaching, curriculum and instruction then should be clarified considerably.

One rule regarding this last issue should be asserted now, however. Most writers on the topic seem to agree that theories for these different areas will have somewhat different forms and that they should be developed in parallel; work on theories of teaching, for example, cannot be made to wait on the elaboration of theories of learning (Gage, 1964). But the principle of parsimony should be a guide for this work. Since a theory of teaching must incorporate conceptions of learning, it must be to some degree more complex than theories of learning. But how much more complex and in what ways? One strategy for theory building in teaching, as well as in other aspects of education, may be to formulate *minimum* theories by addressing the question: What minimum set of specific propositions must be added to a given theory of learning to equip it for use in describing and prescribing teaching practice in a given domain? By demanding such specification, theory development on a broad front should be promoted more efficiently, with increased hope of eventual successful integration.

RECAPITULATION AND CHALLENGE

By way of summary, the MMM continuum can itself be taken as an informal model of theorizing and a framework for a brief review of this chapter. Following the schematic diagram of Figure 1 (and paralleling the discussion of J. S. Reitman, 1970), the process begins with a continuous stream of observations entering a sensory register. Through selective attention and data analysis, some observations are accumulated to form hypotheses and analytic distinctions, some are crystallized into metaphors by a recognition or naming mechanism, and some are ignored and thus lost from the system. Metaphors are discovered easily, sometimes frivolously; so many more are available at any given time than the system can use. They are retained in a waiting room or storage until chosen for use. Those not chosen are recycled in storage until chosen or forgotten. Occasionally metaphors suggest hypotheses or constructs directly. Some metaphors are chosen for coding as relatively formal models. What metaphors are recognized initially, and what ones are chosen for coding as models, is determined in part by metatheoretic predispositions residing in long-term memory and in part by a continuing flow of observation about the phenomenon being studied. Models are coded into a working memory using one of several representation systems. That for formal models involves a logical or mathematical calculus. Research conducted on working models produces theoretical propositions and, in turn, suggestions for model improvement. Transactions between theory and model can be formal and direct, as in the case of axiomatic theory, or relatively informal, as in the case of most conceptual theories and constructs. Models and theories are organized into metatheories which provide permanent storage for significant features of current as well as outmoded models and theories. Metatheories can be used to suggest outlines for new theories by identifying combinations of metatheoretic choices not yet explored.

Several aids and heuristic devices exist to help in theory and model construction. These can be labeled: analyzing, translating, schematizing, miniaturizing and taxonomizing. The evaluation of theories and models focuses on their usefulness rather than their truthfulness. Specific criteria for evaluation are: explicitness of postulates and definitions, explicitness of boundaries and limitations, internal consistency, correspondence with existing data, fertility for hypothesis generation, testability, parsimony and quantifiability. Four admonitions for modeling, concerning the necessity for symbolization, formalization, simplification and vigilance can also be emphasized.

Two general admonitions provide a fitting challenge with which to close. First, successful theorizing should influence future research. But it is noteworthy that such influence is seldom attained unless the theorist first demonstrates the value of his theory through his own research. Many theories die, not because of any demonstrated lack of merit, but because even their creators failed to pursue their ideas with continued research to show their value. And if even the theorist fails to invest solid effort, it is not surprising that other researchers do not take the theory seriously.

Second, successful theorizing often ignores the prescriptions of past metatheories. Estes's (1957) observation in this regard may serve as well for research on teaching as it does for psychology:

the steepest obstacle to theory construction in psychology is not the complexity of behavior. It is the mountain of stereotypes deposited by centuries of prescientific attempts to comprehend behavior and capped by the pronouncements of the academicians who have always known in advance, apparently by divine inspiration, exactly what kind of theory is possible and proper for psychology. This barrier must be undermined by uncertainty before it can be toppled by experiment. Once it is down, our experimental subjects will be able to tell us, through the medium of their behavior, what kind of theory psychology is entitled to (p. 617).

The original intent in undertaking the writing of this chapter was to outline the role of theories in research on teaching. The result realizes only the first half of that intent—an outline for theory construction. The influence of these theories on research can be elaborated only as research on teaching becomes guided by and directed toward theory construction. It is hoped that the present chapter will prompt researchers to try theory building and help them in the process. Perhaps then, in the *Third Handbook of Research on Teaching,* someone can complete the task to which this chapter was originally assigned.

REFERENCES

Ahmavaara, Y. *On the unified factor theory of mind.* Helsinki: Svomalainen Tiedeakatemia, 1957.

Allport, F. H. A theory of enestruence (event-structure theory): Report of progress. *American Psychologist,* 1967, 22, 1–24.

Atkinson, J. W., & Feather, N. T. (Eds.) *A theory of achievement motivation.* New York: John Wiley, 1966.

Atkinson, R. C., & Calfee, R. C. Mathematical learning theory. In B. B. Wolman, & E. Nagel (Eds.), *Scientific psychology: Principles and approaches.* New York: Basic Books, 1965. Pp. 254–275.

Baker, J. P., & Crist, J. Teacher expectancies: A review of the literature. In J. D. Elashoff, & R. E. Snow (Eds.), *Pygmalion reconsidered.* Chicago: National Society for the Study of Education, 1971. Pp. 48–64.

Barber, B., & Hirsch, W. (Eds.) *The sociology of science.* Glencoe, Ill.: Free Press, 1962.

Barclay, J. R. *Foundations of counseling strategies.* New York: John Wiley, 1971.

Becker, W. C. *An empirical basis for change in education.* Chicago: Science Research Associates, 1971.

Becker, W. C., Engelmann, S., & Thomas, D. R. *Teaching: A course in applied psychology.* Chicago: Science Research Associates, 1971.

Belth, M. *The new world of education.* Boston: Allyn & Bacon, 1970.

Berliner, D. C. Microteaching and the technical skills approach to teacher training. Technical Report No. 8, October 1969, Stanford, Calif.: Stanford Center for Research and Development in Teaching. ED 034 707.

Biber, B. A learning-teaching paradigm integrating intellectual and affective processes. In E. M. Bower, & W. G. Hollister (Eds.), *Behavioral science frontiers in education.* New York: John Wiley, 1967. Pp. 111–155.

Black, M. *Models and metaphors: Studies in*

language and philosophy. Ithaca, N.Y.: Cornell University Press, 1962.

Blalock, H. M., Jr. *Theory construction: From verbal to mathematical formulations*. Englewood Cliffs, N.J.: Prentice-Hall, 1969.

Bloom, B. S. (Ed.) *Taxonomy of educational objectives: The classification of educational goals. Handbook I—cognitive domain*. New York: David McKay, 1956.

Boring, E. G. Dual role of the *Zeitgeist* in scientific creativity. *Scientific Monthly*, 1955, 80, 101–106.

Boring, E. G. The role of theory in experimental psychology. In R. I. Watson, & D. T. Campbell (Eds.), *History, psychology, and science: Selected papers by E. G. Boring*. New York: John Wiley, 1963. Pp. 210–225.

Boring, E. G. Eponym as placebo. In R. I. Watson, & D. T. Campbell (Eds.), *History, psychology, and science: Selected papers by E. G. Boring*. New York: John Wiley, 1963. Pp. 5–25.

Braithwaite, R. B. *Scientific explanation: A study of the function of theory, probability, and law in science*. Cambridge, England: Cambridge University Press, 1953.

Brodbeck, M. Logic and scientific method in research on teaching. In N. L. Gage (Ed.), *Handbook of research on teaching*. Chicago: Rand McNally, 1963. Pp. 44–93.

Bruner, J. S. *Toward a theory of instruction*. Cambridge, Mass.: Belknap Press of Harvard University, 1966.

Brunswik, E. The conceptual framework of psychology. *International encyclopedia of unified science*, 1952, 1(10).

Brunswik, E. *Perception and the representative design of psychological experiments*. Berkeley, Calif.: University of California Press, 1956.

Buhler, C. Basic theoretical concepts of humanistic psychology. *American Psychologist*, 1971, 26, 378–386.

Bush, R. R., & Mosteller, F. *Stochastic models for learning*. New York: John Wiley, 1955.

Campbell, D. T., & Fiske, D. W. Convergent and discriminant validation by the multitrait-multimethod matrix. *Psychological Bulletin*, 1959, 56(2), 81–105.

Campbell, D. T., & Stanley, J. C. Experimental and quasi-experimental designs for research on teaching. In N. L. Gage (Ed.), *Handbook of research on teaching*. Chicago: Rand McNally, 1963. Pp. 171–246.

Campbell, N. R. *Physics, the elements*. Cambridge, England: Cambridge University Press, 1920.

Carroll, J. B. A model of school learning. *Teachers College Record*, 1963, 64, 723–733.

Chapanis, A. Men, machines, and models. *American Psychologist*, 1961, 16, 113–131.

Coan, R. W. Dimensions of psychological theory. *American Psychologist*, 1968, 23, 715–722.

Coleman, J. S. *Introduction to mathematical sociology*. New York: Free Press of Glencoe, 1964.

Cronbach, L. J. The two disciplines of scientific psychology. *American Psychologist*, 1957, 12, 671–684.

Cronbach, L. J. Test validation. In R. L. Thorndike (Ed.), *Educational measurement*. Washington, D.C.: American Council on Education, 1971. Pp. 443–507.

Cronbach, L. J., & Meehl, P. E. Construct validity in psychological tests. *Psychological Bulletin*, 1955, 52, 281–302.

Cronbach, L. J., & Snow, R. E. *Individual differences in learning ability as a function of instructional variables*. Final report to USOE, March 1969, Stanford University, School of Education, Contract No. OEC 4-6-061269-1217.

Dallenbach, K. M. The place of theory in science. *Psychological Review*, 1953, 60, 33–39.

Dember, W. N., & Jenkins, J. J. *General psychology: Modeling behavior and experience*. Englewood Cliffs, N.J.: Prentice-Hall, 1970.

Dubin, R. *Theory building*. New York: Free Press, 1969.

Estes, W. K. Of models and men. *American Psychologist*, 1957, 12, 609–617.

Estes, W. K., & Burke, C. J. A theory of stimulus variability in learning. *Psychological Review*, 1953, 60, 276–286.

Estes, W. K., & Suppes, P. C. Foundations of linear models. In R. R. Bush, & W. K. Estes (Eds.), *Studies in mathematical learning theory*. Stanford, Calif.: Stanford University Press, 1959.

Feigenbaum, E. A., & Feldman, J. *Computers and thought*. New York: McGraw-Hill, 1963.

Festinger, L. *A theory of cognitive dissonance*. Evanston, Ill.: Row, Peterson, 1957.

Gage, N. L. Paradigms for research on teaching. In N. L. Gage (Ed.), *Handbook of research on teaching.* Chicago: Rand McNally, 1963. Pp. 94–141.

Gage, N. L. Theories of teaching. In E. R. Hilgard (Ed.), *Theories of learning and instruction.* The Sixty-third Yearbook of the National Society for the Study of Education, Part I. Chicago: NSSE, 1964. Pp. 268–285.

Gagné, R. M. *The conditions of learning.* (2nd ed.) New York: Holt, Rinehart & Winston, 1970.

Gordon, I. J. (Ed.) *Criteria for theories of instruction.* Washington, D.C.: Association for Supervision and Curriculum Development, 1968.

Gregory, R. L. On physical model explanations in psychology. *British Journal of Philosophical Science,* 1953, 4, 192–197.

Guilford, J. P. *The nature of human intelligence.* New York: McGraw-Hill, 1967.

Hall, C. S., & Lindzey, G. *Theories of personality.* New York: John Wiley, 1957.

Hall, G. S. *Adolescence: Its psychology and its relations to physiology, anthropology, sociology, sex, crime, religion, and education.* Vol. I. New York: Appleton, 1904.

Hilgard, E. R. (Ed.), *Theories of learning and instruction.* The Sixty-third Yearbook of the National Society for the Study of Education, Part I. Chicago: NSSE, 1964. Pp. 54–77.

Hilgard, E. R., & Bower, G. H. *Theories of learning.* New York: Appleton-Century-Crofts, 1966.

Hull, C. *Principles of behavior.* New York: Appleton-Century Co., Inc., 1943.

Hunt, D. E. *Matching models in education.* Monograph Series No. 10. Toronto: Ontario Institutes for Studies in Education, 1971.

Hyman, R. T. (Ed.) *Teaching: Vantage points for study.* Philadelphia: Lippincott, 1968.

Jackson, P. W. *Life in classrooms.* New York: Holt, Rinehart & Winston, 1968.

Jacobson, M. D., Stimart, R. P., & Wren, G. T. Models and educational research. *American Educational Research Journal,* 1971, 8, 311–320.

Jessor, R. The problem of reductionism in psychology. In M. H. Marx (Ed.), *Theories in contemporary psychology.* New York: Macmillan, 1963. Pp. 245–256.

Kaplan, A. *The conduct of inquiry: Method-

ology for behavioral science.* San Francisco: Chandler, 1964.

Koch, S. Theoretical psychology, 1950: An overview. *Psychological Review,* 1951, 58, 295–301.

Koch, S. (Ed.) *Psychology: A study of a science.* Vols. 1–6. New York: McGraw-Hill, 1959.

Krathwohl, D. R., Bloom, B. S., & Masia, B. B. *Taxonomy of educational objectives: The classification of educational goals. Handbook II—affective domain.* New York: David McKay, 1964.

Kuhn, T. S. *The structure of scientific revolutions.* Chicago: University of Chicago Press, 1962.

Lachman, R. The model in theory construction. *Psychological Review,* 1960, 67, 113–129.

Lewin, K. *Principles of topological psychology.* New York: McGraw-Hill, 1936.

London, I. D. The role of the model in explanation. *Journal of Genetic Psychology,* 1949, 74, 165–176.

Lord, F. M., & Novick, M. R. *Statistical theories of mental test scores.* Reading, Mass.: Addison-Wesley, 1968.

Luce, R. D. *Individual choice behavior.* New York: John Wiley, 1959.

Maccia, E. S., Maccia, G. S., & Jewett, R. E. *Construction of educational theory models.* Columbus, Ohio: Ohio State University Research Foundation, 1963.

Macdonald, J. B., & Leeper, R. R. (Eds.) *Theories of instruction.* Washington, D.C.: Association for Supervision and Curriculum Development, 1965.

Mandler, G., & Kessen, W. *The language of psychology.* New York: John Wiley, 1959.

March, J. G. Making artists out of pedants. In R. M. Stogdill (Ed.), *The process of model-building in the behavioral sciences.* Columbus, Ohio: Ohio State University Press, 1970. (a)

March, J. G. Problems in model-building. In R. M. Stogdill (Ed.), *The process of model-building in the behavioral sciences.* Columbus, Ohio: Ohio State University Press, 1970. Appendix. (b)

Marx, M. H. The general nature of theory construction. In M. H. Marx (Ed.), *Theories in contemporary psychology.* New York: Macmillan, 1963.

McDonald, F. J., & Allen, D. W. Training

effects of feedback and modeling procedures on teaching performance. Technical Report No. 3, 1967. Stanford, Calif.: Stanford Center for Research and Development in Teaching, ED 017 985.

Melton, A. W. (Ed.) *Categories of human learning*. New York: Academic Press, 1964.

Merton, R. K. A paradigm for the study of the sociology of knowledge. In P. F. Lazarsfeld, & M. Rosenberg (Eds.), *The language of social research*. New York: Free Press, 1955.

Merton, R. K. *Social theory and social structure*. Glencoe, Ill.: Free Press, 1957.

Morris, W. T. On the art of modeling. In R. M. Stogdill (Ed.), *The process of model-building in the behavioral sciences*. Columbus, Ohio: Ohio State University Press, 1970. Pp. 76–93.

Newell, A., & Simon, H. A. GPS, A program that simulates human thought. In H. Billing (Ed.), *Lernende automaten*. Munich: Oldenbourg, 1961. Reprinted in E. A. Feigenbaum, & J. Feldman (Eds.), *Computers and thought*. New York: McGraw-Hill, 1963. Pp. 279–296.

Norman, D. A. (Ed.) *Models of human memory*. New York: Academic Press, 1970.

Polya, G. *How to solve it: A new aspect of mathematical method*. Garden City, N.Y.: Doubleday, 1957.

Portola Institute. *Whole earth catalog*. Menlo Park, Calif.: Portola Institute, Inc. 1969.

Reitman, J. S. Computer simulation of an information-processing model of short-term memory. In D. A. Norman (Ed.), *Models of human memory*. New York: Academic Press, 1970. Pp. 117–148.

Reitman, W. R. *Cognition and thought*. New York: John Wiley, 1965.

Restle, F. A. A survey and classification of learning models. In R. R. Bush, & W. K. Estes (Eds.), *Studies in mathematical learning theory*. Stanford, Calif.: Stanford University Press, 1959. Pp. 415–427.

Rosenthal, R., & Jacobson, L. *Pygmalion in the classroom: Teacher expectation and pupils' intellectual development*. New York: Holt, Rinehart & Winston, 1968.

Schwab, J. J. *The practical: A language for curriculum*. Washington, D.C.: National Education Association, 1970.

Shapere, D. The paradigm concept. *Science*, 1971, 172, 706–709.

Shulman, L. S. Reconstruction of educational research. *Review of Educational Research*, 1970, 40, 371–396.

Sidman, M. *Tactics of scientific research: Evaluating experimental data in psychology*. New York: Basic Books, 1960.

Siegel, L., & Siegel, L. C. A multivariate paradigm for educational research. *Psychological Bulletin*, 1967, 68, 306–326.

Simon, A., & Boyer, E. G. (Eds.) *Mirrors for behavior: An anthology of classroom observation instruments continued*. Philadelphia: Research for Better Schools, Inc., 1970.

Simon, H. A. *Models of man*. New York: John Wiley, 1957.

Simon, H. A. The construction of social science models. In G. A. Miller (Ed.), *Mathematics and psychology*. New York: John Wiley, 1964. Pp. 137–146.

Skinner, B. F. Are theories of learning necessary? *Psychological Review*, 1950, 57, 193–216.

Snow, R. E. Brunswikian approaches to research on teaching. *American Educational Research Journal*, 1968, 5, 475–489.

Snow, R. E. Heuristic teaching as prosthesis. In R. E. Snow (Ed.), A symposium on heuristic teaching. Technical Report No. 18, 1970, Stanford, Calif.: Stanford Center for Research and Development in Teaching. Pp. 104–110. ED 046 893.

Snyder, H. I. *Contemporary educational psychology: Some models applied to the school setting*. New York: John Wiley, 1968.

Spearman, C. E. *The abilities of man, their nature and measurement*. New York: Macmillan, 1927.

Spence, K. W. The relation of learning theory to the technology of education. *Harvard Educational Review*, 1959, 29, 84–95.

Stinchcombe, A. L. *Constructing social theories*. New York: Harcourt, Brace & World, 1968.

Suppes, P. Models of data. In E. Nagel, P. Suppes, & A. Tarski (Eds.), *Logic, methodology and philosophy of science*. Stanford, Calif.: Stanford University Press, 1962. Pp. 252–261.

Tolman, E. C. Operational behaviorism and current trends in psychology. *Proceedings, 25th Anniversary Celebration of the Inauguration of Graduate Studies at the University of Southern California*. Los Angeles: University of Southern California Press, 1936.

Turner, M. B. *Philosophy and the science of behavior.* New York: Appleton-Century-Crofts, 1967.

Wagener, J. W. Toward a heuristic theory of instruction: Notes on the thought of Michael Polanyi. *Educational Theory,* 1970, 20, 46–53.

Walberg, H. J. A model for research on instruction. *School Review,* 1970, 78, 185–200.

Wallach, M. A. Creativity and the expression of possibilities. In J. Kagan (Ed.), *Creativity and learning.* Boston: Houghton Mifflin, 1967. Pp. 36–57.

Wolman, B. B. Does psychology need its own philosophy of science? *American Psychologist,* 1971, 26, 877–886.

Woodger, J. H. *Axiomatic method in biology.* Cambridge, England: Cambridge University Press, 1937.

Woodger, J. H. The technique of theory construction. *International encyclopedia of unified science,* 1939, 2(5).

Zetterberg, H. L. *On theory and verification in sociology.* New York: Tressler Press, 1954. See also the enlarged third edition of this book, New York: Bedminster Press, 1965.

CHAPTER 4   Social and Political Influences on Educational Research[1]

RICHARD A. DERSHIMER
American Educational Research Association

LAURENCE IANNACCONE
University of California, Riverside

The purpose of this chapter is to examine the influences which move educational researchers to select topics or areas for study. Or, posing it as a question: who defines the problems studied by researchers?

Since there is little research on the subject, this chapter necessarily remains in the realm of speculation. However the colloquium held by the American Educational Research Association in November, 1968, showed that the study of scientific behavior in general yields results clearly applicable to researchers in education.

A review of that literature points out that few scientific researchers, if any, select their problems at random. They are influenced by several factors, such as the "excitement of the chase," current scientific paradigms and theories, chance observations the scientists happen to have made, the dramatic nature of some phenomena, and the intellectual stimulation derived from work on complex tasks. Researchers are influenced by what

their colleagues find important and vital; they respond to society's opinion of their work. They are sensitive to the interests of granting agencies or persons, and they are influenced by their institutions' support and provisions available for certain research tasks.

We begin this chapter with a description of these influences as they appear in the field of educational research. Then, after reviewing the available literature, we shall explore the shifts in these influences over the past half century. Finally, we shall examine today's influences, their nature and importance, and the focus of researchers' responses to them.

OPERATIVE INFLUENCES ON EDUCATIONAL RESEARCHERS AS SCIENTISTS: A REVIEW

Educational researchers are social and behavioral scientists, subject to most, if not all, of the influences and forces that operate on physical, chemical and natural scientists (Dershimer, 1970). It is the relationship among these forces and their order of in-

[1] Special thanks are due to Miss Mary Wolfe and Miss Donna Durgin for their assistance in editing this chapter.

113

tensity in which the educational researcher differs from the "hard" scientist and from his counterparts in the basic disciplines (Corwin & Seider, 1970). It is important to review these influences individually before we move to an analysis of the peculiar nature of educational research.

The Challenge to the Intellect

Storer (1966) sees scientists essentially as "gamesmen," highly stimulated by intellectual challenges. Frequently the prestige of fields and specialties in academic circles is determined by the degree of intellectual challenge presented by the substantive and methodological problems; in fact, the preference rating is often highly correlated with the use of complex mathematics.

Until recently this situation insured a rich supply of manpower to the hard sciences, particularly the physical sciences. Presently, however, more and more young people are turning to social service and using much different criteria in selecting careers. Causes and outcomes of this shift are difficult to assess at the present time.

The Desires of Clients

A client is defined as the direct purchaser of the services of individuals or institutions (Merton, 1968). Local school districts increasingly call upon researchers to design programs or evaluations; this, in turn, creates demand for more research specialists. State agencies also are calling for assistance in the assessment of the quality of educational programs. Lately the federal government itself is contracting for evaluations or massive statistical studies such as the volume entitled *Equality of Educational Opportunity* (Coleman, 1966).

The Influence of Institutions

Scientists and administrators have been aware for many years of the effects of organizational characteristics on the produc-

tivity of researchers (Parsons, 1962).[2] Pelz and Andrews (1966), for example, document that individual productivity and initiative among scientists is encouraged by flexible organizational arrangements that permit scientists to freely interact among themselves and with engineers and product developers.

Few of these studies of organizational variables, however, pertain to education. Complex research and development (R & D) organizations that characterize the natural and physical sciences are virtually unknown in education. Until very recently, almost all of educational research was performed by individual professors located in schools of education. Guba (1965) and Hagstrom (1970) describe both the subtle and overt influences that have made it difficult for research to flourish within this environment.

Since the mid-1960s the federal government has created several types of institutions for educational R & D. The research and development centers located on university campuses and the independently incorporated regional educational laboratories are the best known among these. But while these new organizations appear to provide a more congenial setting for research and development they have not yet had sufficient time to demonstrate their effectiveness.

The Effect of Colleagues

Educational researchers, like most other scientists and scholars, are socialized or acculturated in graduate training and eventually form or perpetuate collegial social circles with well-defined cultures (Hagstrom, 1970). In the final analysis, colleague groups not only determine what is current knowledge, but they evaluate individual efforts to expand or transform that knowledge (Crane, 1970).

[2] Some scientists take the strong position that researchers can be "enslaved" to their institutions. See Holden, C. Public interest: new group seeks definition of scientist's role. *Science*, 1971, 173, 131–132.

In education the problems are compounded because, at present, the collegial groups are more loosely formed than in some of the other applied fields, e.g., medicine. It must be said, however, that in applied fields the criteria for valid knowledge are not as well defined or as systematically applied as in more basic fields of study. Many of the "newcomers" prefer to relate primarily to public school practitioners.

The Demands of Society

Applied researchers are supposed to be more conscious of the social utility of their work than are basic researchers and scientists (Storer, 1966). But in *The Double Helix* (Watson, 1968), Watson reveals that even a budding Nobel prizewinner can dream of winning widespread recognition— and from others than scientists.

This issue has implications beyond any direct influence exerted on scientists. As a field or set of issues gains importance in the public eye, more resources are provided to it under private and public auspices. Educational research has benefited from this trend. Crystallization of the national concern which followed Sputnik in the late 1950s produced the first round of federal support for R & D: the Cooperative Research Act, research into the use of technology under the National Defense Education Act, and the creation of the Course Content Improvement Program in the National Science Foundation. Awakened social awareness of the plight of the poor and of minorities in the 1960s led to the second round, better than a doubling of research funds. Although there was little discussion about how research might alleviate any of these public concerns, the result was that the study of education, within a few short years, grew to be as well funded as any aspect of the social or behavioral sciences.

For many years students of education have been aware of the importance of these influences, especially those of the academic colleagues and the practitioners. Consider the comments of Dewey that appeared in *The Sources of a Science of Education* (1929). He asked, "From what sources shall we draw so that there shall be steady and cumulative growth of intelligent, communicable insight and power of direction?" (p. 10). His answer was that... "educational *practices* provide the data, the subject-matter, which form the *problems* of inquiry. [They] ...are also...the final *test of value* of the conclusions of all researches" (p. 33). Dewey believed that "mature" sciences are the sources from which material is derived to deal intellectually with these problems.

Dewey identified the human sciences, especially psychology and sociology, as particularly relevant, but was concerned lest the research in education be dominated by the armchair social scientist. "Remoteness ...is found whenever there is a lack of vital connection between the field-work practice and research work" (p. 43). He saw the dangers of the other extreme, too: "The problem here is not, however, a onesided one. It concerns the teacher and administrator, the field worker, as well as the researcher. Special conditions are required if the material of school practices is to be presented to others in such shape as to form the data of a problem" (p. 45).

Dewey's discussion did not extend beyond the conceptual dilemma to the psychological and social pressures on the educational researcher, but it can easily be extended to include them. His statement suggests that the central system of pushes and pulls on the educational researcher may be usefully thought of as a dynamic tension between the demands of the disciplines and the client systems. Just as no one discipline, not sociology, psychology or economics, exhausts the range of disciplines for the educational researcher, likewise no one set of clients, as local school districts, classroom teachers, or state educational departments or foundations, exhausts the range of clients. It is, however, in the tension between these two sets of demands, those from the disciplines and those from the clients, that the educational researcher finds his research problems. Despite the manner of his individual response to the intellectual challenges of specific problems, as a group member his choice has been influenced historically by the dynamic of these demands. That pendulum swing, in turn, responds to larger social forces, translated partly through institutional settings and partly through professional organizations.

The researcher's colleagues from the disciplines and his clients in the field appear to be influenced in like manner. The prevailing wisdom of influential groups in society is expressed through political decisions at federal, state and local levels, and is customarily indicated through fiscal incentives and aids. Only recently in education it has been at the federal level where the government has been most innovative in attempting to improve the schools, although the states and localities remain most important for institutionalizing new directions. Schools of education are hardly immune to political decisions about their field, and neither are colleague networks nor client groups. It cannot be assumed, moreover, that the educational researcher is himself merely a pawn in this process. Most researchers are aware of political and fiscal realities and are sensitive to those issues which command public attention.

HISTORY OF THE CAUSAL INFLUENCES

No detailed review of the history of educational research is intended here. Rather, we shall focus on two of the major forces which can most readily be documented as particular to educational research: the demands of the disciplines, and the demands of the practitioners. Societal directions, translated in terms of political pressures and institutional decisions over long periods of time, have so moved the points of convergence between demands of colleagues and clients that it is difficult to ascertain at any given point which is predominant.

One way of tracing these shifts is by an examination of power relationships among important educational associations over the last hundred years. The National Education Association (NEA) is a good barometer to use. In its early years, first as the National Teachers Association and after 1870 as the NEA, its formal and informal leadership developed in large part from academicians, school administrators and state association leaders with an eastern private school and college orientation. Thomas Hill and Charles Eliot, presidents of Harvard; Nicholas Murray Butler, President of Columbia; John D. Philbrick and Henry Barnard, state superintendents of Connecticut; and Thomas W. Valentine and Daniel B. Hagar, presidents, respectively, of the New York and Massachusetts Associations were among educators active in the NEA prior to 1900.

As the character of public education changed, however, so did the NEA (Schmid, 1964). While the 1870 Association—or federation, actually—together with the National Association of School Superintendents and the American Normal School Association, did not produce immediate major changes in the power structure, it did indeed lay the groundwork for a new coalition of the midwestern administrator and the normal school administrator and teacher. Over the years there ensued a struggle between scholars and clients, a struggle defined both in terms of leadership and in terms of the issues to which the NEA would devote its energies.

One of the most colorful aspects of this evolutionary struggle appears as the history of the National Council of Education (NCE). Membership was by invitation only from current members; thus, before the turn of the century, the NCE had become the most prestigious policy-forming group within the NEA. By 1898 the Council controlled the NEA's investigative committees and funds. Research sponsored and supported by the NEA reflected this control beyond the turn of the century. Yet, at the same time, charges began to be leveled that the Council had too many noncontributing members and that the NEA's studies were too little concerned with the problems of practitioners. In 1907 Carol Pearse, manager of a coalition of midwestern school superintendents and urban classroom teachers, forced through a policy which made initiation of expenditures from the permanent fund a sole prerogative of the NEA's Board of Trustees controlled by the new client leadership. Moreover, in 1908 he drastically altered the Council's characteristics by leading a movement which packed its membership, expanding it from 51 to 120.

The NEA was not an isolated phenomenon; practitioners predominated in almost all educational associations, a development congruent with the times and with the demands of society. Callahan and Button (1964) have listed a series of societal elements which, at this time, were changing the concept of the role of the chief school administrator. Among these were the difficulties of the expanding school populations, largely immigrant; a need for more schooling for educators because of the expanded high school; growing economic needs in education coupled with a climate of suspicion about public expenditure and a developing tax-saving ideology. Added to these were other effects of industrialization: the prestige of the captains of industry (until they became the gods that failed in 1929), and the muckraking climate produced by those politically moderate critics of the American scene whose preferred solution to the problems they exposed was the application of modern business methods to public life. Against this backdrop of social unrest and educational challenge the efficiency movement must have seemed a panacea—or at least a businesslike solution—to all the problems of schools.

These same points of view and leadership groups shaped the growing schools of education. Callahan (1963) has documented the atheoretical, often trifling topics which, especially in the twenties and thirties, were major sources of teaching and research in

education during the first half of this century. Most of the research in educational psychology displayed a similar concern for the trivial and immediately practical.

Thus, at the turn of the century, norms shifted—those norms by which educational research problems were defined along the continuum suggested by Dewey's view of the sources of a science. Collegial influence on educational researchers waned, while the demands and outlooks of clients (practitioners and those in schools of education who serviced and supported them) increased (Cronbach & Suppes, 1969). With minor variations this state of affairs continued until Sputnik and the accompanying social changes of the 1960s.

RECENT DEMANDS OF SOCIETY

There can be no doubt that society has shifted its expectations of its schools. Sputnik led to the view that schools could be used as one of the instruments in the United States' competition with the Soviets; in the 1960s schools were viewed as an instrumentality to alleviate poverty and to aid in desegregation. While these altered views have been generally beneficial, they have led to considerable confusion in the directions of educational research.

The Soviet space challenge of the 1950s amplified the criticisms of the educational quality voiced by men like Hyman Rickover and Arthur Bestor. From this dissent came reformers who led a new curriculum movement. Organizational projects such as the Physical Sciences Study Committee and the Biological Sciences Curriculum Study, national in scope, were designed to improve the academic-scientific quality of the schools.

This reinforcement of the importance of the scholars gained momentum when, in the mid-1950s, the U. S. Office of Education (USOE) initiated the Cooperative Research Program (although with poor funding in its formative years). At first it favored small, unsolicited projects. The traditional educational researcher was encouraged by the USOE staff to build upon his past research. After Francis Ianni became director of the program, however, the staff sent out a new message: attack problems, define issues in ways acceptable in substance and methodology to scholars with recognizable credentials from the disciplines. During Francis Keppel's years as commissioner the circle of formal and informal advisors who formerly consisted mostly of educational psychologists and test and measurement specialists was expanded to include more social scientists and educational practitioners.

It was not just in the R & D programs that changes in constituencies were occurring. The Elementary and Secondary Education Act required a new educational coalition which included, in addition to the traditional educational organizations, social action groups concerned with the problems of poverty, blacks and urban schools (Bailey & Mosher, 1968). Both Keppel and Harold Howe II, as USOE Commissioners, attempted to consolidate these constituencies in a variety of ways; many of the spokesmen for these new groups were recruited to serve on advisory committees and on the USOE staff itself. While such a consolidation was only partially successful, their effect was such that by 1970 the federal government was clearly prepared to implement some definite educational policies.

Such was not the history of educational R & D in that same decade. As the 1960s waned, the USOE was increasingly hard pressed to show what the research money was producing. Federal officials sought and rearranged policies and programs to obtain viable, useful products: new uses for technology, new courses of study, new instructional systems. The shift in emphasis to development meant a shift in operating style in the USOE; by 1970 virtually the entire budget for educational R & D, with the exception of the small grant program, was spent on programs devised within the bureaucracy.

As a result, the educational R & D effort of the federal government was shaped essentially without an external contituency. Such a configuration implied an absence of the checks and balances that operated in other federal agencies as a countervailing force against the internal turmoil of bureaucracy.

What were these checks and balances? Writing in the fifties, Kaufman (1956) noted that institutions of American public administration have been organized and operated to pursue successive value orientations. The quest for representativeness dominated most of the nineteenth century. At the end of the century, the reaction to the political machine, especially in the troubled cities, produced the reform movement and the doctrine of neutral competence.

Each new doctrine, with its accompanying operational change, laid on over its predecessor, resulted in a fragmentation in governmental doctrine and operations. Theodore J. Lowri (1969) saw such increasing fragmentation, together with the growing need to buy the support of vested interests, as weakening the government's capacity to plan and act despite the rise of executive leadership. In turn, this lessened capacity itself has contributed to the demand for responsiveness and accountability in government and to the "quantum leap" in the use of external advisory groups.

Educational R & D in the 1970s found itself in a dilemma: it was being shaped as a mission-oriented, centrally controlled program by a government which was experiencing increasing difficulty in the management of existing programs in the traditional areas of defense, health and welfare. Furthermore, Congress and many segments of the educational enterprise itself who otherwise were opposed to federal control were in effect urging the bureaucracy to shape educational practices and policies by how federal R & D funds were spent.

Government influence was felt in a variety of ways. In a few short years it created what amounted to a parallel system of university research centers and product development centers, as well as a national dissemination network, the Educational Resources Information Center (ERIC). While the system was far from complete (Levien, 1971) and suffered from some serious omissions, it nevertheless provided more opportunities for certain kinds of educational research and especially development than traditional educational institutions ever had done (Bailey, 1970).

Both Keppel and Howe favored having private industry enter the educational R & D market. Keppel hired Louis R. Bright, a research engineer from Westinghouse Learning Corporation, as the first Associate Commissioner for Research. In various ways, including the active sponsorship of conferences, the USOE encouraged industries to seek grants and contracts from it. Although the expected funding level was lower than anticipated and the heightened war effort diverted industrial interest, the principle was established: private industry could be used to expand the institutional setting for educational R & D.

These trends have produced three secondary effects. First, new recruits, such as engineers, systems specialists and behavioral scientists with industrial and military orientation have entered the educational research community. The second effect has been that increased specialization has driven researchers and practitioners still further apart. The third effect has been to sharpen differences between scholars and problem-oriented clients.

Although the poor academic reputation of most schools of education had hindered the educational research participation of scholars and scientists from other disciplines, new institutions and new sources of funds were intended to attract more psychologists, sociologists and other social scientists to the study of education (President's Science Advisory Committee, 1964). Such an approach has been reinforced generally by the community of researchers. To illustrate, the National Academy of Education, a mixture of educationists and social and behavioral

scientists, was created; the American Educational Research Association established two new divisions, one for historians and one for social scientists; the National Research Council created the Committee on Basic Research in Education to assist in attracting new scholars outside the educational establishment into the field. Such events increased the legitimacy of education as a scholarly area of study.

But while the traditional disciplines were beginning to "rediscover" education, they themselves were beginning to transmute. Basic research was increasingly characterized in Washington as "game playing"; Congress served notice to scientists to find better ways to justify their requests for federal funds. Simultaneously the government challenged researchers to produce more results, to solve more problems. The sweep of concern for the poor and for minorities was intensified by the U.S. involvement in Indochina; scholars were attacked by the young, their own minorities and their liberals. Educational research was influenced by this ferment.

Educational research traditionally has been weak in its theoretical formulation (Bloom, 1966). Hopes for the alleviation of this chronic condition brightened as the increase of researchers from economics, political science and anthropology offered new links to bodies of knowledge previously overlooked. At the same time, however, a counterforce appeared, pressing researchers into finding solutions for immediate problems.

Although these pressures were felt in all scientific and scholarly fields, they caused additional problems in education for two reasons. First, education possessed neither a solid nor an expanded base of knowledge when the government began its financial support; second, educational R & D had not yet won the kind of backing from the practitioners that was necessary for adequate, sustained financial support. For years education had suffered not only from one reform movement after another, but also from a seemingly unending series of innovations, none of which had much, if any, foundation in the knowledge of individual or group human behavior. Pressure for immediate solutions threatened to perpetuate these problems, although hopefully at a more highly intellectual and sophisticated level.

CONCLUSION

The result of these changing conditions has brought educational researchers as a group into interaction with a bewildering array of other groups, all of whom have an influence in defining the problems confronting education. Most researchers reside within the establishment and are exposed to and influenced by the controversies and aspirations of the practitioners. Some are involved in military and industrial training and thus affected by its now-popular techniques and styles. Many more see themselves as academicians and are therefore subject to the current vicissitudes of the scholar. Should such a scholar devote his career to solving those immediate problems that continually impede learning? Or should he follow his conscience, his ingenuity, his intellectual competence and enthusiasm into fields of basic, long-range research?

Not only are the reference groups for educational research badly fragmented, but the major forces in education itself are likewise unstable. Still true today is Dewey's assertion of many years ago that educational research is partially rooted in problems found in the field and articulated, at least initially, by those who experience them. Yet under the present conditions of confusion and violent change in education, it is obvious that researchers will have difficulty identifying the most crucial, the most promising areas for study.

However, in this jumble of reforms, counter-reforms, demands and reactions, lies hope for the students of education. A process must be observed in action to understand it; the time to study an institution is not when

it is dormant. Public education—and educational research—in this nation and in others may well be in its most fruitful period. What is needed is a commitment to try many different ideas.

The debate in education over whether the emphasis should be placed on basic research or applied research is hackneyed. In a field with as little viable, supportable knowledge as education, all phases of R & D must be supported and improved. Society has benefited as much and probably more by the findings of men like Binet and Piaget as it has from the applied researchers who produce technologically useful research. What is needed is not another pendulum swing from client-centered to academic-oriented research, or one from research to development, but a continued dynamic tension and increasing interaction among them. The practitioner must learn to respect more highly than he has in the past the contributions of the researchers who are engaged in the disciplined inquiry into the behavior of individuals, groups and institutions. The scholar must respect those who are using research methods as well as they can to improve educational processes. Together they must insist that governmental agencies do likewise. Until the practitioners, researchers, developers and bureaucrats develop this kind of understanding and cooperation, educational R & D will not make the contribution of which it is capable, the contribution that is so badly needed.

REFERENCES

Bailey, S. K. Emergence of the laboratory program. *Journal of Research and Development in Education,* 1970, 3(2), 5–17.

Bailey, S. K., & Mosher, E. K. *ESEA, The Office of Education administers a law.* Syracuse: Syracuse University Press, 1968.

Bloom, B. S. Twenty-five years of educational research. *American Educational Research Journal,* 1966, 3, 211–221.

Callahan, R. E. *Education and the cult of efficiency.* Chicago: University of Chicago Press, 1963.

Callahan, R. E., & Button, H. W. Historical change of the role of the man in the organization: 1865–1950. In D. E. Griffiths (Ed.), *Behavioral science and educational administration,* The Sixty-third Yearbook of the National Society for the Study of Education (NSSE), Part II. Chicago: NSSE, 1964. Pp. 73–92.

Coleman, J. S., et al. *Equality of educational opportunity.* Washington, D.C.: U.S. Government Printing Office, 1966.

Corwin, R., & Seider, M. Patterns of educational research: Reflections of some general issues. In R. A. Dershimer (Ed.), *The educational research community: Its communication and social structure.* U.S. Office of Education report, Project No. 8-0751. Washington, D.C.: U.S. Office of Education, 1970.

Crane, D. The nature of scientific communication and influence. *International Social Science Journal,* 1970, 22, 28–41.

Cronbach, L., & Suppes, P. (Eds.) *Research for tomorrow's schools.* London: Macmillan, 1969.

Dershimer, R. Professional educational organizations. In R. L. Ebel (Ed.), *Encyclopedia of educational research* (4th ed.). New York: Macmillan, 1969. Pp. 1008–1017.

Dershimer, R. (Ed.) The educational research community: Its communication and social structure. U.S. Office of Education report, Project No. 8-0751. Washington, D.C.: U.S. Office of Education, 1970.

Dewey, J. *The sources of a science of education.* New York: Liveright, 1929.

Guba, E. (Ed.) *The training and nurture of educational researchers.* Sixth Annual Phi Delta Kappa Symposium on Educational Research. Bloomington, Ind.: Phi Delta Kappa, 1965.

Hagstrom, W. Educational researchers, social scientists, and school professionals. In R. A. Dershimer (Ed.), *The educational research community: Its communication and social structure.* U.S. Office of Education report, Project No. 8-0751. Washington, D.C.: Office of Education, 1970.

Kaufman, H. Emerging conflicts in the doctrines of public administration. Politics and Government Series, Reprint No. 146. Indianapolis: Bobbs-Merrill, 1956.

Levien, R. National Institute of Education: Preliminary plan for the proposed institute. Washington, D.C.: HEW Report 657, 1971.

Lowri, T. J. *The end of liberalism.* New York: W. W. Norton, 1969.

Merton, R. *Social theory and social structure.* (Enlarged ed.) New York: Free Press, 1968.

Parsons, T. The institutionalization of scientific investigation. In B. Barber, & W. Hirsch (Eds.), *The sociology of science.* New York: Free Press, 1962.

Pelz, D., & Andrews, F. *Scientists in organizations.* New York: John Wiley, 1966.

President's Science Advisory Committee, Panel on Educational Research and Development. *Innovation and experiment in education.* Washington, D.C.: U.S. Government Printing Office, 1964.

Schmid, R. D. *A study of the organizational structure of the National Education Association, 1884–1921.* (Doctoral dissertation, Washington University) Ann Arbor, Mich.: University Microfilms, 1964. No. 64-8279.

Storer, N. *The social system of science.* New York: Holt, Rinehart & Winston, 1966.

Watson, J. *The double helix.* New York: Atheneum Press, 1968.

CHAPTER 5 The Use of Direct Observation to Study Teaching[1]

BARAK ROSENSHINE
University of Illinois

NORMA FURST
Temple University

The research on teaching in natural settings to date has tended to be chaotic, unorganized and self-serving. The purpose of this chapter is to ease the reader into the maze of instrumentation and research which has focused on teaching in natural and semi-natural settings. There seems to be no simple route through the chaos which has developed. A model for assessing the state of the art as well as some examples of paradigm research will be offered, and we will also make an attempt to clarify and classify the existing knowledge and to delineate research problems which appear relevant at this time. Many of the conclusions and classifications in this chapter may and probably will soon be outdated, but undoubtedly many of the major research problems will still be unresolved.

THE DESCRIPTIVE-CORRELATIONAL-EXPERIMENTAL LOOP

Before discussing the present state and prospects for the future of the study of teaching, we shall introduce a fairly complete paradigm or model for studying teaching in natural settings or classrooms. Although the references used to illustrate the paradigm are recent ones, the model has been proposed many times before but seldom followed. The paradigm contains at least these elements:

1. development of procedures for describing teaching in a quantitative manner;
2. correlational studies in which the descriptive variables are related to measures of student growth;
3. experimental studies in which the significant variables obtained in the correlational studies are tested in a more controlled situation.

The sequence of these steps is not fixed—one might use the results of experimental studies to develop new observational instru-

[1] This work could not have been accomplished without the help of Barbara Rosenshine. Frank Sobol provided invaluable editorial assistance.

To the best of our knowledge the *Mirrors for Behavior* volumes noted in this chapter are not available in microfiche at this time. However the abstracts are still for sale from Research for Better Schools, 1700 Market Street, Philadelphia, Pennsylvania 19103.

ments. These steps are not isolated from one another; research at each step should influence modifications of research at other steps. These steps represent the criteria against which efforts labeled "research on teaching in natural settings" will be judged in this chapter.

The context within which this stepwise research takes place can vary, and different contexts have been proposed for this descriptive-correlational-experimental loop. Three overlapping contexts for instructional research will be discussed below. These three are tentatively labeled classroom-focused research, teaching-skills research and curriculum-materials research. Although these three contexts for research are not unique, they were chosen to represent some of the more comprehensive applications of the research model.

Classroom-Focused Research

One approach to the descriptive-correlational-experimental loop has been the study of classroom teaching as it exists. Most of the studies of the relationship between instructional activities and student growth fall within this area.

One of the clearest explications of classroom-focused research using the descriptive-correlational-experimental model is a description of the activities which have taken place in the Canterbury (New Zealand) Teaching Research Project (Nuthall, 1971). Nuthall described a four-stage cycle. In the first stage the investigators develop ways to categorize classroom interaction. In the second stage correlational studies are conducted to determine which kinds of behaviors are worth pursuing further and which behaviors are probably irrelevant for student growth. In the third stage the correlational results are tested in experimental studies to determine the effects which specific manipulations have on both subsequent classroom interactions and student growth. In these experimental studies instructional behavior

is very much controlled, even though the research takes place in regular classrooms.

Nuthall proposed that the results of the correlational and experimental studies be used to suggest and modify further descriptive, correlational and experimental studies in which new variables are observed in new ways in natural settings. "In the final stage, explanatory theory is developed which accounts for the relationships uncovered in experimental studies. This theory becomes embodied in the descriptive system so that the variables which have proved significant in the correlational and experimental studies can be identified by any user of a descriptive system" (Nuthall, 1971, p. 3).

The Canterbury Teaching Research Project. The studies being conducted at Canterbury University, New Zealand (on an annual research budget of less than $15,000), are examples of research within this classroom-focused approach. The descriptive system used at Canterbury was developed from the work of Smith and Meux (1970), Kliebard, Hyman, Bellack, and Smith (1966), and from the descriptive research conducted in New Zealand (Nuthall & Lawrence, 1965). This was followed by a correlational study (Wright & Nuthall, 1970) conducted in existing classes of eight-year-old children in which the instructors were both regularly assigned teachers and student teachers. The results of this correlational study and results of previous descriptive studies were used to design two sets of experimental studies.

The first set of experimental studies (Hughes, 1971) focused upon the control of student participation. The studies were conducted for two purposes: 1) to replicate experimentally the finding by Wright and Nuthall of a significant relationship ($r = 0.54$) between student achievement and the procedure in which a teacher follows a student's answer by redirecting the question to another student for comment, and 2) to expand upon this finding by introducing other participation variables presumably related to achievement. In some of the experiments the manipulated variables included whether the student was called upon to respond to questions in a random sequence, in a predictable sequence, or not at all. In another experiment half of the students were never called upon, and the rest were called upon in a random sequence. The procedure followed was one in which the teacher taught material through short lectures, then asked questions (and redirected questions when this was part of the design), and provided confirmation of the correctness or incorrectness of the answer. (No significant differences were found among any of these procedures on the adjusted posttest achievement scores, but other potentially relevant variables, such as student overt attention unfortunately were not studied as part of these investigations.)

The experimental studies by Church (1971) involved more complex variations than those of Hughes but illustrate one technique for controlling these variations within a classroom setting. In these studies the lessons were on the topic of electricity, and the model set of lessons against which variations were compared consisted of three 50-minute lessons containing 253 "episodes" (an episode being a content-oriented teacher question and all the verbal moves by teacher and students which are associated directly with that question).

In the first two studies, each involving three classrooms, student participation was manipulated. In the first study low participation was obtained by asking each student in the experiment to answer orally no more than eight of the 240 questions asked during the lesson; in the second study high participation was obtained by asking the students to answer questions orally and to write down answers to 85 questions. As in the studies by Hughes, these two treatments did not yield results that were significantly different from the model lesson.

Subsequent studies, each involving a minimum of three classes, have used a) open

questions (less structured, more vague) followed by questions redirected to other students and the termination of episodes with correct responses, b) open questions followed by redirection of questions and/or presentation of correct responses, and c) open questions followed by prompting information during episodes.

The analysis of data in Church's studies is far from complete, but there appear to be variations in class mean scores under conditions of different treatments. One of the clearest findings is that one cannot vary a behavior such as "open questions" and expect the rest of the interaction to remain constant. Rather, as these variables are introduced, variation will occur in the amount of content covered per unit of time, the frequency of teacher information, the number of episodes per unit of time, and the type of responses that students give. Additional studies are currently being conducted in which the frequency of questions, responses or feedback is being manipulated.

The studies in which variables such as a, b or c (above) are manipulated become quite complex because asking open questions leads to variation in other parameters (e.g., content covered, time taken, frequency of teacher ·information, number of episodes). Despite this complexity, Church and Hughes were able to handle the problems so that not only were the lessons within any treatment quite similar, but the results for a treatment across different classrooms were consistent. Studies conducted in such a controlled manner have the potential to yield systematic information not only on causes of student achievement but also on the contingent variations in classroom activities which can be expected when teacher behaviors have been varied.

The uniqueness of these experimental studies (Church, 1971; Hughes, 1971) is that in each study the experimenters taught almost identical lessons to existing classes, modifying the lessons only to introduce the experimental variations, and monitoring the tape recording of the lessons to insure high implementation of the treatment and fidelity to the content. The lessons took place in classroom settings and involved regular instructional material, with the experimental variable being the controlled change in teacher-student interaction. Thus, while these research settings approached the degree of control usually associated with laboratory studies, they appear to have much more generalizability for classroom instruction.

It is the design, then, rather than the particular results which merit the most attention for future research on teaching. The design and implementation of these experimental studies represent something quite different from the usual study in which Method A is taught to one class and Method B is taught to another. The usual method-comparison studies generally do not clarify all the variables that are different in the two situations. In contrast, the designs employed by the students at Canterbury allow us to learn a great deal about the effect of certain variables which are manipulated in classroom settings. As Nuthall has summarized, "We hope to develop an experimental method which is responsive to the full complexity of the classroom situation, and which will provide the kind of data which reflects the important characteristics of contemporary classroom teaching" (Nuthall, 1971, p. 22).

This sensible approach has seldom been used. Rather, investigators have taken parts of this approach and acted as if the parts were sufficient. Developers of descriptive systems have seldom moved to correlational studies; investigators who conducted correlational studies have seldom moved to experimental studies; investigators who conducted experimental studies have not used their results to develop new descriptive systems or to conduct further correlational and experimental studies. Whether the work at Canterbury will lead to new descriptive systems and new correlational studies remains to be seen.

It is difficult to find other examples of research which proceeded from descriptive to correlational to experimental studies. The best example is the work of Flanders. His observational system was developed and refined about 1957, and was followed by two correlational studies (see Flanders, 1965), which were followed by an experimental study (Amidon & Flanders, 1961). Unfortunately we were unable to find other examples. Even the work of Flanders did not loop back, and there is no clear evidence of the results of his correlational studies being used to modify the observational system (Flanders, 1969) or to lead to new experimental studies.

The Teaching-Skills Approach

Another approach to the descriptive-correlational-experimental loop can be seen in those studies in which the experimental focus is the training of teachers in specific skills. Perhaps the closest example to this approach is the work of Gage. One idea Gage (1963) suggested was that investigators focus upon specific aspects of the teacher's task rather than on all parts of teaching at once. He decided that the ability to explain new material was of sufficient interest to serve as the first aspect, and he and/or his students have completed eight correlational studies based on three independent sets of data (Belgard, Rosenshine, & Gage, 1971; Dell & Hiller, 1971; Fortune, Gage, & Shutes, 1966; Hiller, Fisher, & Kaess, 1969; Pinney, 1970; Rosenshine, 1971b; Shutes, 1970; Unruh, 1971).

All of these studies represent the type of correlational research which Nuthall and others have also suggested, although one modification in these studies has been the addition of data obtained through the use of rating systems completed by students and/or observers. Another student of Gage (Miltz, 1971) used the results obtained in these correlational studies with some ideas of his own to develop teacher-training materials on how to explain. These materials were validated in an experimental study in which one group of student teachers studied and practiced the ideas on how to explain, and another group did not receive this instruction. All teachers then taught a criterion lesson. The teachers who used Miltz's training materials received higher ratings in explaining ability from a group of judges than the untrained teachers, and objective counts of their behavior showed that the trained student teachers exhibited more of the intended behaviors than the untrained teachers. Unfortunately no data on student growth were obtained; nevertheless, the procedure used by Miltz is noteworthy because it is partly intuitive and partly data-based, and because an attempt was made to validate the training materials. Hopefully subsequent correlational and experimental studies will refine the training materials. The same procedure can be used to develop similar materials for other teaching skills.

Gage (1971) maintained his emphasis upon the study of specific skills of teaching when he advocated that research focus upon developing "tools of the trade" for teachers. These tools would be analogous to the tools, devices, formulas, strategies, tactics and algorithms available to engineers, physicians, lawyers and journalists, to name a few. The objective of these tools is to make teaching more manageable and to help ordinary people teach well.

The research which Gage and Miltz (Miltz, 1971) conducted is an example of the use of tools of the trade. Other potential examples are teaching skills such as higher-order questioning, reinforcing students, probing, diagnosing learning difficulties, as well as rules for the use of these skills and aids in performing them.

A problem to date with the development of tools of the trade is that the development is seldom completed. Just as it is relatively easy to develop new observational systems, it has been fairly easy for educators to develop lists of teaching skills. Unfortunately the teaching skills, like the observational systems, are seldom validated against measures of student growth. Yet there is enormous potential value in research on tools of the trade. As a result of the operationally

oriented approach to teacher training within the last decade, there exist a large number of teachers who have already received training in a variety of skills. Fortified with acceptable criterion measures, investigators could use existing observational systems to study the behaviors of these teachers and relate the skill-relevant behaviors to the measures of growth, and they could also compare the behavior and the outcomes for trained and untrained groups of teachers.

The Curriculum-Materials Approach

Rosenshine (1971a) suggested that settings in which special curriculum programs are being used represent an area for descriptive, correlational and experimental research. Curriculum models can refer to a set of instructional materials and instructions for their use which are "packaged" for dissemination (such as the Biological Sciences Curriculum Study [BSCS] Program) or to specific instructional procedures (such as the Bank Street Program [Bissell, 1971]). In this context a curriculum-materials approach does *not* refer to the practice of providing a teacher with a textbook and a curriculum guide developed by a committee in the school district. Rather, as in the BSCS and Bank Street programs, the emphasis is upon curriculum packages containing well-formulated strategies for implementation which have been previously tested in special situations and revised in accordance with earlier information. Such models or packages appear to be particularly useful settings for study because the programs incorporate ideas developed from research, the inventions and intuitions of experienced teachers and subject-area specialists, and the feedback data developed in the early tryout phases of the program.

Although curriculum-materials packages are prevalent today, this invention was probably developed independently numerous times in the past. The curriculum-materials package developed about 1910 by Montessori (E. Evans, 1971) is a superb example of this invention. The Montessori method includes specific, self-correctional materials (e.g., the brown stair, the pink tower, the golden beads), specific instructions for teacher interactions with the child (e.g., vocabulary development has a three-period sequence: naming, recognition and pronunciation), and general instructions for teachers (e.g., collaborative work with the child, avoidance of "don'ts," emotional support). The instructional materials, sequencing, provision for corrective feedback, and specific and general instructions to teachers contained in the Montessori materials are quite different from the usual practice of providing a teacher with only a set of books, a syllabus and vague objectives. The major advantage of the Montessori program or any other curriculum-materials package is that it may enable a teacher to accomplish ends which would not be accomplished without these materials.

The research loop which Rosenshine endorsed consisted of a) training teachers to use a certain package of materials, b) using observational systems to describe instructional activities on variables considered important for the implementation of the specific program and also on variables considered to have general educational importance, c) studying the relationship between instructional activities and student growth (on a variety of outcomes) *within* those groups of teachers who are supposed to be using the experimental treatment, d) changing training procedures and/or materials on the basis of these studies, and e) conducting new studies to determine the effects of the modifications and to determine the new relationship between instructional activities and student growth.

The advantage claimed for this approach is that curriculum-materials packages represent potential experimental treatments and also provide a teacher with means to accomplish more than he could without the materials. Whether these materials and instructions are suitable, whether they are used properly, and whether the outcomes are the ones which are expected are the research questions. Although there has been much development of curriculum-materials packages, there has been relatively little study of the research questions.

Curriculum studies in early childhood education. The value of instructional research within curriculum-materials packages might be assessed by discussing three studies in early childhood education. Despite the number of national curriculum programs at all levels which were developed in the 1960s, the clearest example of this research appears to be in early childhood education.

The first study, the Planned Variation program, lasted three years (1969–1972) during which time eight different Head Start model programs were studied. Each of the programs had been developed independently and tested previously in regular classrooms. The eight models represent the existing range of well-formulated approaches to early childhood education (Bissell, 1971, p. 5).

The primary focus in the first year of the study was on "the extent and nature of implementation achieved by the different models," and "the effects on children, on their families, and on programs of the experience provided by the different models" (Bissell, 1971, p. ii). In the fall of 1969 and again in the spring of 1970, observers rated the teachers in each model program as "high," "medium" or "low" implementers of their assigned model. The specific criteria were not given in the report, but separate, specific criteria were developed for each of the eight Head Start models.

Although examples of descriptive systems designed to monitor implementation will be presented later in this chapter, this type of descriptive research is rare at the present time. The documentation of implementation appears useful to any curriculum study or experimental study in which different treatments are being administered. Within the context of the Planned Variation research, differences in the level of implementation appeared to be extremely important during the first year of the study (Bissell, 1971). In the fall of 1969 only 5 percent of the 61 observed programs were coded as high implementation. By spring, 1970, 41 percent of the programs were coded as high implementation. The change from fall to spring probably reflects both the advisory function of the program sponsors and the experience of the teachers and children within the program. One cannot estimate the representativeness of these figures; these data have not been collected before. Taken alone, the figures are important for illustrating the difficulty of implementing new programs according to the intentions of the program developers, the futility of treating all programs within a model as appropriate exemplars of that model, and the uselessness, at least for this sample, of comparisons among the student gain measures obtained in any model. Without data on implementation, comparative data on outcomes seem meaningless.

The children's gains on a measure of academic achievement, on measures of general cognitive development, and on response styles were compared only for those 20 classes which were coded as high implementation. There were some interesting differences across program models, but the small sample size and the fact that these results are only the first in a three-year study preclude further discussion at this time. As new reports in this study and in similarly designed studies are presented, it will be interesting to note the programs which are easiest to implement according to the specifications of the developers, the differences in student gain across classes which obtain high implementation of their model, and the differences in student gain across all classes.

In two small studies involving no more than 24 classes, an effort was made to determine the relationship between variables specified in a program and student cognitive gain (Siegel & Rosenshine, 1972). In these studies, all classes were using the Direct Instruction System for Teaching (DISTAR)

program, a commercial version of the Bereiter-Engelmann program. The purpose was to determine whether the teacher behaviors that were considered important for successful program implementation were functionally related to student gain. Accordingly, eight teacher behaviors which were strongly emphasized in the training manuals and in the training program were selected, and specific rating scales were developed for each behavior. Three of the eight behaviors yielded significant correlations with student gain across both studies: the extent to which the teacher required 100 percent response from all students, the extent to which the teacher corrected errors by repeating the entire task and testing the child to be sure that he could then make the correct response, and the extent to which the teacher followed the specified lesson format. These findings are quite tentative and need to be cross validated both in correlational studies and in experimental studies in which teachers who have low frequencies of these behaviors receive additional training. The present studies represent the use of observational systems to validate the importance of variables emphasized within a program. In these studies all of the teachers were coded as high implementers of the program, and the differences in behavior which were obtained were within this restricted range. It will be interesting to expand this form of research to include teachers who are coded as moderate or low implementers of the program.

A third approach to the monitoring and study of curriculum-materials programs is exemplified by the preliminary data from a three-year study of Project Follow Through programs (Soar, 1971, 1972). These programs were monitored as they were implemented in their kindergarten and first-grade forms. Eight classrooms were observed in each of the seven programs, and, in addition, two comparison classrooms were selected for each program, yielding a total of 70 observed classrooms. Soar did not focus on the degree of implementation, nor did he use the program manuals to dictate the selection of variables. Rather, the research staff used four observational systems: the Reciprocal Category System (Ober, #61[2], an expansion of the Flanders system, #5), the Teacher Practices Observation Record (Brown, #36), the Florida Taxonomy of Cognitive Behaviors (K–1 Form) (Brown et al., #37), and the Florida Climate and Control System. The system by Ober is a counting system, and the others are sign systems. The Florida Climate and Control System was developed by Soar and his associates as an outgrowth of previous work (Soar, 1966, 1972).

Two types of analyses were conducted using each of the instruments separately. Before the analyses were made, the data obtained with each instrument were reduced by a factor-analysis procedure. The first analysis included a study of variance to determine whether the factors discriminated across the programs, and preparation of multiple-range tests to identify the differing programs. The second analysis correlated the factor scores with measures of class mean residual gain. These techniques are useful to determine whether a large number of educational variables discriminate among classes and are correlated with student growth. Inspection of the clusters of variables which discriminate across programs is a form of monitoring. The variables correlated with student growth across all programs appear to be particularly potent, general, instructional variables which are relevant (in a correlational sense) to many types of programs.

The results obtained by Soar and his colleagues must be considered preliminary, but they can serve as interesting hypotheses for further study. One conclusion Soar (1972) reached was that factors which best discriminated among programs were not usually the best predictors of student growth. In general, the factors which identified more general kinds of teacher-student interactions discriminated among programs well but did not predict student growth as well as some of the factors which seemed more subtle in nature. For example, a factor which contained loadings on whether activities are directed and controlled by the teacher was the most powerful in discriminating among programs. This factor indicates that the programs did differ on major components considered important, but the correlations between that factor and student growth were only moderate. Another factor, which represented occasional, tight, coercive attempts by the teacher to restrain students, yielded a stronger (negative) correlation with student growth. This second factor appears to reflect general teaching procedures rather than specific program variables.

Instructional research within curriculum programs. The ideas used in the studies described by Bissell (1971), Siegel and Rosenshine (1972), and Soar (1972) can be brought together into a fairly complete package of methods of instructional research within the context of curriculum-materials programs. The three studies are all examples of different types of research within the same context—that of curriculum-materials programs which had previously received extensive trial and modification within special settings. The three studies took place while the curriculum-materials programs were being implemented in semi-natural settings. The specific procedures used in each of the studies can easily be faulted, but the procedures can also be seen as illustrations of general, methodological ideas to be refined and used in future studies in natural settings.

---

[2] A number such as this was assigned to each observational system in *Mirrors for Behavior* (Simon & Boyer, 1967, 1970a, 1970b). The *Mirrors* volumes and the numbering system will be discussed later in this chapter. (Future citations from these volumes appearing in this chapter will usually be made only by system author and assigned number. For the more complicated references the entire Simon & Boyer citation will be given.)

The procedures exemplified by these studies (although they are not unique contributions of the specific investigators because others have also incorporated these ideas) are: monitoring programs to determine the extent to which they are being implemented according to the intentions of the developers; conducting correlational studies to determine the relationships between program-specific variables and student growth; and conducting correlational studies to determine the relationships between general instructional variables and student growth. To these three procedures one might add the monitoring of opportunity to learn the criterion material (or to learn attitudes) whenever possible. All these procedures together would make a potent package for instructional research within the context of curriculum-materials programs.

Even though each of the programs (or a single curriculum package compared to "traditional" instruction) represents an experimental treatment, there is still a need for further experimental studies within this context. For example, the program-specific and/or general-learning variables which are found to be significant in correlational studies will need to be validated and examined in experimental studies. Experimental studies here refer to the training or retraining of teachers until they attain frequencies or patterns of behaviors shown to be significantly correlated with the student-growth measures of interest. The experimental questions would be whether the teachers modified their behaviors while teaching, and whether student growth was enhanced by the different instruction.

This package for instructional research within curriculum development and its inevitable variations would appear to be most usable within large-scale programs of research and development. However, individual researchers or research organizations might do well to limit themselves to the pieces which are most important to them and which can be managed, rather than to risk finding themselves overwhelmed with data.

Hilgard's Paradigm

In 1964 Hilgard published a chapter on research and development in educational practice which remains relevant today. Hilgard abstracted six steps from a continuum which he saw as starting in pure science research and ending in advocacy and adoption of educational practices. The steps are:

1. Research on learning with no regard for its educational relevance;
2. Research on learning which deals with human subjects and with content that is nearer to that taught in schools;
3. Research on learning employing school-age children as subjects and using school subject matter as the material;
4. Research directly on school learning which is conducted in special laboratory classrooms with selected teachers and students;
5. Tryout of the results of prior research in normal classrooms with typical teachers;
6. "Packaging" materials for wider use and developing programs for advocacy and adoption.

Hilgard argued that there are research tasks at each of these "steps," and as one moves to steps 4, 5 and 6 there is a need for collaborative work among learning psychologists, subject-matter experts, skilled teachers and social psychologists. He also argued that one does not move directly from basic research to application: "In the process of application something more than the theory is always involved. Thus, one does not move directly from astronomy to navigation without concern for tides, prevailing winds, and the location of lighthouses..." (Hilgard, 1964, p. 402).

While describing the contributions of pure science, Hilgard cautioned readers not to overlook *invention*, "which is by no means limited to scientists. Some promising advances in education have come about as the inventions of skilled teachers, and a technology of instruction needs to examine and conserve the values of these inventions" (Hilgard, 1964, p. 411). Unfortunately, in practice we seldom examine inventions but tend to adopt, advocate and disseminate them.

As it is discussed in this chapter, research in natural and semi-natural settings enters at steps 4, 5 and 6. Procedures for describing classroom interaction, and the correlational and experimental studies described above, all appear to be useful supplements to the research which Hilgard suggested for steps 4 and 5. Research at these steps utilizes both the discoveries obtained at steps 1, 2 and 3 and the inventions introduced at steps 4, 5 and 6.

Hilgard's paradigm offers something else of value—the possibility of placing new educational ideas within a context of this research continuum. Regrettably, as Hilgard and others have noted, educational psychologists have tended to work at steps 1, 2 and 3 and then to jump by inference to step 6 without being sufficiently patient at steps 4 and 5. These practices are continuing. For example, the work of Piaget and Bruner is frequently cited as justification of dissemination efforts which began at step 6. Although little research on behavioral objectives can be found at steps 4 and 5, a great deal of advocacy exists at step 6. Unfortunately, as we shall see, much of the work in the use of the observational systems has entered at step 6 with little grounding in previous steps, and few of the authors of these systems have attempted to use them as part of a descriptive-correlational-experimental loop, or as part of the research and development which takes place at steps 4 and 5 of the continuum of Hilgard.

Summary

The descriptive-correlational-experimental loop and the development of explanatory theory to account for the results are not particularly new ideas. However these ideas have seldom been used by any research and development team. The possibility that this cycle of research will take place in the future cannot be predicted, but the work which has been done in the past decade provides investigators with more tools and more ideas for accomplishing this work than ever before. Descriptive instruments abound, and a technology for creating these instruments is developing. The contexts for conducting this research—controlled classroom situations, teachers trained in specific skills, and teachers using curriculum-materials packages—are becoming clarified, and a good deal of developmental work has been accomplished in teacher training and the development of curriculum-materials packages.

INSTRUMENTS FOR THE OBSERVATION OF TEACHING

Since the publication of the first *Handbook of Research on Teaching,* there has been a proliferation of instruments for quantifying events observed during classroom instruction. This section begins with an estimation of the number of instruments, includes an attempt to distinguish among types of instruments, continues with a discussion of the functional relationships between instrument form and measures of student (cognitive or affective) growth, and concludes with some suggestions for using varied instrument forms in future research.

The Number of Classroom Observational Instruments

Classroom observational instruments exist in abundance. More than one hundred category systems[3] (and sign systems) can be identified easily. The anthology, *Mirrors for Behavior* (Simon & Boyer, 1967, 1970a,

---

[3] The term *system* is misleading. *Category instrument* would be a better term, but *category system* is the common term.

1970b), contains 92 observational systems. Of these, 76 have been used for observation of instruction in schools or schoollike settings, but only 73 will be considered in this chapter because three of the systems are entered twice: once as an observational scale for students, and again as a scale for teachers.

By consulting five readily available sources, 48 additional, nonoverlapping category systems can be added to the 73 in *Mirrors*. Eight other category systems are available from the review by Medley and Mitzel (1963); the anthology of procedures for assessing environments of preschool programs (Dopyera & Lay, 1969) yields 16 systems; a short review of the research (Rosenshine, 1970a) contains 7 more systems; and finally, more than 20 new category systems not included in these references appear among the abstracts of papers delivered at the AERA annual meetings of 1970 and 1971. Thus, by consulting only six references, one can easily locate more than 120 different classroom observational category systems.

Even 120 systems are clearly an underestimation. A diligent search for the experimental, teacher-training and correlational studies which used frequency counts to assess the behavior of teachers and/or students would yield considerably more systems.

Although no known anthology of rating forms for observing teachers exists, a conservative estimate of the number of rating instruments would be in the hundreds. As part of a survey conducted in 1966, the American Council on Education obtained 133 rating forms used by students to evaluate college courses and instructors (Kent, 1966). The safest generalization Kent could make about these instruments was that they are diverse. The number of student rating forms which have been developed since the survey by the American Council on Education is probably as large as the number developed earlier. To these rating forms can be added the instruments used to assess student-teaching activities in laboratories and classrooms and instruction by regular teach-

ers in public schools. One can also add the rating forms used in research studies of student growth, and those used to describe learning environments or to monitor specific programs or research projects. Thus the number of category systems is much smaller than the number of rating forms which have been developed and used for the same purposes.

Types of Instruments

Although it was once possible to distinguish different types of observational instruments, now, "Things fall apart; the centre cannot hold" (Yeats, "The Second Coming"). As more instruments are developed, and as authors incorporate the ideas of others, distinctions among types of instruments become blurred.

There appear to be three elements which distinguish various observational instruments: the recording procedure, the scope and specificity of items, and the format used to code individual events. Perhaps a discussion of these elements will clarify the differences among instruments.

Differences in recording procedures. The scale used to record the frequency of the behavior or instructional event is one distinction among the various observational instruments. When an event is recorded *each time it occurs,* the instrument is labeled a *category system;* when an event is recorded *only once if it occurs within a specified time period,* regardless of how often it occurs during that period, the recording instrument is called a *sign system.* Observers using *rating* instruments are expected to estimate the frequency of specified events or constellations of events only once, usually at the end of an observational session. The estimations are usually made on a five- or seven-point scale one end of which represents high frequency (usually containing phrases such as "most of the time" or "strongly agree"), and the other end represents low frequency ("seldom" or "strongly disagree"). In practice, these distinctions are blurred. For example, if the time interval is a very short one, the frequencies of events recorded by a sign system approximate the frequencies recorded by a category system. (Both category systems and sign systems seem to be types of counting systems, but no general term is available to distinguish these two types from rating systems. For brevity, and because category systems are more widely used, the term *category system* will frequently be used in this chapter to refer to both category systems and sign systems.)

Differences in items. The items appearing on rating forms were once characterized as broad, requiring much inference on the part of the observer and reader. Ratings on teacher warmth, overall effectiveness, clarity, or enthusiasm require high inference. Similarly, the items which appeared in category and sign systems (e.g., teacher gives directions, teacher asks convergent question) were more specific and appeared to require less inference by the observer and reader (cf. Gage, 1969; Rosenshine, 1970a, 1970b, 1971c; Rosenshine & Furst, 1971).

As more observational systems have been developed and published, the distinctions made by these authors appear to have collapsed. Low-inference, behaviorally specific items have appeared in rating scales (e.g., see items in Anderson & Walberg, 1968; Jason, #51;[4] Solomon, Bezdek, & Rosenberg, 1963; Steele, House, & Kerins, 1971; Walberg, 1969). Moderate-inference items have appeared in category systems and sign systems (e.g., "teacher use of students' ideas," "teacher criticizes," "teacher listens carefully to student"). High-inference items have appeared in sign systems (e.g., terms such as "responsive," "receptive," and "harsh" appeared in the work of Galloway, #44, and Heger, #84).[5]

Several developments not discussed in the references above illustrate the diversity of items which can be used with different scales. First, it now appears that *all items* currently used in category and sign systems can also be used in rating systems. The transformation can be accomplished by selecting any of the items and asking an observer or a student to estimate the frequency of occurrence using a scale ranging from two points (e.g., yes and no) to any manageable number of points. One instrument which uses a rating scale (strongly agree to strongly disagree) and contains items developed from a cognitive taxonomy (Bloom, 1956) was said to require "low-inference student judgments" (Steele, House, & Kerins, 1971). Thus rating systems are no longer limited to high-inference items.

A second development has been the inclusion of high-inference items in category systems and sign systems. For example, Galloway (#44) and then Heger (#84) introduced a series of general descriptive terms which accompany the tally of each verbal event in the Flanders instrument (#5). In Heger's instrument, a verbal event such as "content presentation by teacher" is also coded as + if the observer believed the teacher was "spirited," "responsive" and "congenial," or as − if the observer believed the teacher was "monotonous," "unresponsive" and "uncongenial." Almost all the adjectives used under the + and − codes could be labeled as high inference.

The procedures Galloway and Heger developed for using high-inference variables within a category system appear applicable to all behavioral items in all observational systems. One could use their procedure to convert the items in any rating system into a sign system or some other form of counting procedure. For example, an observer could use a 30-item rating instrument and make a rating every five minutes, or he could use the instrument as a sign system and check only those events which occur during a five-minute (or a longer or shorter) period.

---

[4] See footnote 2, p. 129.

[5] Observer agreement can be just as high when category systems or rating scales are used (see Ryans, 1960).

The recent additions of relatively specific items in rating scales and relatively broad items in counting scales illustrate again that one cannot characterize an observational instrument simply on the basis of the scale being used. Although a researcher now has greater flexibility in devising or modifying an instrument, research will be needed to determine the functional value of the modified instruments.

Differences in format. "Multiple coding" of items (Flanders, 1970) has been appearing in category systems developed after 1968. The idea is not recent, but the interest in it is. Multiple coding means that an instructional event is coded according to any number of dimensions. For example, in the instrument developed by Moore (1968), each event is coded four ways, according to a) the dominant activity (e.g., lecture, supervised study), b) the speaker and communication (e.g., teacher answers question, student asks question), c) the communication content (e.g., fact, definition, criticism), and d) the major instructional objective under consideration. This four-dimensional system could easily be expanded to 15 or 20 dimensions by including dimensions used in other systems, such as the number of students attending to the interaction, the level of conceptualization, and the cognitive style (Gallagher et al., #7); type of pedagogical move and substantive-logical meaning (Bellack et al., #4); or teacher roles and student activities (Perkins, #63). In another system (Caldwell & Honig, n.d.) there is a separate dimension for rating the event with qualifiers such as "ineptly," "with intensity" or "complexly."

The presumed advantage of coding a single event according to a number of dimensions can be obtained in other ways. Soar (1972) reported on the value of the simultaneous use of four category and sign systems.

The technique of subdividing gross categories is similar to multiple coding. For example, some investigators find the category "use of student ideas" to be too large, so they subdivide it into "repetition of student idea," "summary of what student said," and "comparison of student's idea with another idea." In coding, two numbers are usually entered: one for the major category and one for the subdivision. Thus the same event is coded twice, as in multiple coding. It is possible to extend the idea of subdivision so that it equals multiple coding. The distinction between multiple coding and subdivision might be illustrated by using an analogy from analysis of variance. In multiple coding the design is crossed so that each behavior can be coded in each of the multiple-coding dimensions. In subdivision, the design is nested so that certain subdivisions appear only under certain larger categories. Of course there is nothing to prevent the development of category systems in which some variables are crossed and some are nested.

These variations within category systems raise some fascinating problems. How many dimensions are appropriate for coding a single event? Which combinations of category systems and category-system dimensions are functional for which ends? Unfortunately there has been little study of these problems.

Some Functional Differences

There are two types of functional differences between observational system designs. In all the studies mentioned in this section the validation criteria were measures of student cognitive gain.

Category versus sign. Only one study was found in which the same items were used, but on different scales, to code identical classroom events (Ragosta, Soar, Stebbins, & Soar, 1971). The results suggest the possibility that the type of scale used might influence the results. In this study, an existing category system (Brown et al., #37), which was based on the *Taxonomy of Educational Objectives* in the cognitive domain (Bloom, 1956), was modified for use in kindergarten and first grade. The original instrument was developed as a sign system in which each item on the instrument was recorded as 0 or 1 for each observational period. However, Ragosta et al. (1971) were also concerned with the repetition of cognitive interchanges, and this repetition is best coded in the format of a typical category instrument in which *every interchange* is coded. Because they were afraid that the relative frequency would be lost if a strict sign procedure were followed, and because of the research question itself, the investigators decided to use both recording procedures at the same time to code the same observed transactions. When the counting procedure was used, levels of thinking were recorded every three seconds or whenever the thought process changed. When the sign procedure was used, each category was scored 0 or 1 for each five-minute period. One difference between the two coding procedures is that events which occur infrequently receive more weight with the sign procedure because the range of frequencies possible is limited by the number of time periods (12 in this case). Conversely, events which occur very frequently receive proportionately less weight with the sign system.

Because there were a large number of items in the category system, the data on each scale were factor analyzed. The six factors generated for each scale were similar but not identical. Several items with low frequency counts on the category scale appeared on one factor; these items were dispersed among several factors in the analysis of the data from the sign scale. Teacher scores on each of the six factors derived from either procedure were correlated with two measures of student growth. Only two factors derived from the category scale were significantly correlated with one of the growth measures, whereas four factors derived from the sign scale were significantly correlated with one of the growth measures, and a fifth factor just failed to be significant at the 5 percent level.

In the example above, the category scale provided a closer approximation to reality, and the sign scale distorted the nominal events by giving a greater degree of emphasis to infrequently occurring behaviors. Yet the distortion appeared to predict student gain better than the more "accurate" approximation.

One should be cautious in extrapolating from a single example; it might be useful to conduct additional studies in which identical items are used and the method of recording the occurrence of behaviors is varied. In the example above, a category scale and a sign scale were used; in other studies rating scales could also be used. Studies of this type are useful if measures of student growth are available; the use of category, sign and rating scales on the same items without obtaining student growth measures to validate the predictability of the results might create confusion.

Category systems versus rating systems. An estimation of the functional value of category systems and rating systems can be obtained from studies of teacher behavior which include both category systems and rating scales *and* measures of student achievement. The results for each instrument in these studies are somewhat more difficult to compare than the results in the study by Ragosta et al. (1971) because both the items and the scale differed in the two types of instruments. However, in six of the studies (or sets of studies) the bivariate correlations or F-ratios were higher for rated behaviors than they were for counted behaviors (Fortune, 1967; Gage et al., 1968; Morsh, 1956; Morsh, Burgess, & Smith, 1955; Solomon, Bezdek, & Rosenberg, 1963; Wallen, 1966; Wallen & Wodtke, 1963). The raters were classroom students or observers. Measures of observer agreement were comparable to those obtained using category systems. The results are too varied to attempt a synthesis of the findings, but they suggest that ratings are a useful source of information about an instructional program.

Another estimation of the predictive validity of rating systems and category systems can be obtained by comparing the results of studies in which variables in both rating and category systems were used to predict student achievement. In studies reviewed by Rosenshine and Furst (1971; Rosenshine, 1971c), the most consistent results and the highest correlations and F-ratios were obtained from the variables in rating systems. For example, even though the low-inference correlates of "clarity" are presently unknown, ratings on variables referring to the clarity of the teacher's presentation were significantly related to student achievement in *all* studies in which such a variable was used (Belgard, Rosenshine, & Gage, 1971; Fortune, 1967; Fortune, Gage, & Shutes, 1966; Solomon, Bezdek, & Rosenberg, 1963; Wallen, 1966). The results on "clarity" are particularly robust because the investigators used different rating instruments. Furthermore, some investigators used student ratings, some used observer ratings, and the student ratings were given before the criterion test in some studies and after the test in others.

It would be a misinterpretation of this section to consider the above array of results as evidence for rating systems and against category systems; the systems themselves are too diverse to permit such an interpretation. Rather, the major generalization which might be permitted is that some observational systems which distort reality appear to be more predictive of student achievement than the systems which more closely represent the actual events. This generalization may be refuted by future studies. Still, the research to date on direct observation in natural settings suggests that the phenomena are so varied that one cannot present one set of items, method of scaling or format as inherently superior to another.

All observational systems distort actual events. Even category systems create distortions through their unit of measure. When time is the unit, as it is in most category systems, the interval can misrepresent the frequency of continuing events which occur longer than the time interval, such as teacher lecturing or student talk.

That is, if a student gives an answer which continues for 10 seconds, the answer can be scored as one, two, five or 10 units depending upon the time interval in the observational system. The fact that a difference in the time interval can modify the total frequencies in any category or the tallies in a dyadic matrix has been empirically demonstrated by Collet and Semmel (1971). Investigators who use units other than time, such as an episode, a cycle or a move, obtain a different form of distortion because they assume that all units are of the same length.

No judgment is made here on the value of distorting actual events when using an observational system. One cannot begin to anticipate the types of items which are most functional with various types of distortions. This problem needs further research. At the same time, the functional value of observational systems which purport to provide a detailed image of actual events may not be as great as was once assumed. Yet these are empirical questions. Leaping from one set of untested assumptions to another is hardly worthwhile.

Strategies for the Use of Observational Instruments

Given the variation which exists in the items, scale and format of observational instruments, given the lack of any consistent set of functional relationships between classroom events and student growth, and given the limited results which suggest that systems which distort actual events have some functional value, it seems unwise to limit research to a single observational system or type of system. Even if one's approach to direct observation is grounded in abundant and well-honed theory and research, the problems of instrumentation are sufficiently complex that it cannot be assumed that the items, scales and formats chosen for an instrument will be the most functional ones for the situation.

The optimal strategy at this point would

be to use a variety of instruments in every study. Broad items and rating scales could be used to probe for sets of variables which appear to be significant correlates of outcome measures; narrow, focused items and category systems could be used to help identify the specific components of the significant items in the rating scales. If a single category or sign instrument is too narrow or too complex for use, a number of these instruments could be used simultaneously.

As more studies are conducted using general and specific items and a variety of scales, we may begin to learn the functional value of the items and scales. For an approach to the problem using computerized retrieval systems, see Sobol (1971).

Mirrors for Behavior

The first reference one would consult at present to obtain descriptions of systems to observe classroom transactions would be the volumes of *Mirrors for Behavior* (Simon & Boyer, 1967, 1970a, 1970b).[6] Documents on 92 observational systems have been included in the 17 volumes of this anthology published to date. These volumes have been used as the major reference for most of the category systems discussed within this chapter because the category systems contained in *Mirrors* appear to be representative of the hundreds of systems which have been developed and are being developed, and because the volumes are in major educational libraries. Whenever possible in this chapter, references to observational instruments contained in *Mirrors* are made by citing the number that was assigned to the instrument in the anthology.

The first volume of *Mirrors* contains the editors' overview, summary charts, and the outlines of 26 category systems (called observational instruments by the editors). Volumes II–VI contain the 26 observational systems and reports by the original developers of the instruments. These reports

vary from a brief introduction outlining the categories (e.g., Amidon, #1) to the entire hardback edition of the book by Bellack et al. (#4) reporting their research (Volume VI). Volumes VII through XIII contain materials on an additional 53 systems. One of these is a rating scale; one is both a rating scale and a category instrument; and the rest use categories or sign scales. Volume XIV contains new materials by the authors of two previously listed instruments— Flanders (#5), and Simon and Agazarian (SAVI) (#18)—and an article by Romiett Stevens dated 1912, included for "historical interest." The next volume, entitled *Summary,* contains outlines of the 79 systems introduced in the previous volumes. Thus all the systems summarized in Volume I are repeated in the *Summary.* The next two volumes in the series, entitled Volume A and Volume B of the Supplement Edition, contain material on 13 additional category systems. None of the volumes in the series itself is for sale; they were distributed to major educational libraries around the world and to the authors of the category systems which were included. Summaries of these systems are for sale. The first 26 systems appeared as the January 1968 issue of the magazine *Classroom Interaction Newsletter,* and the next 52 systems were published as the Spring 1970 special edition of that magazine. Unfortunately these two summary volumes have been labeled Volumes A and B, the same labels as the supplementary volumes containing materials on the systems numbered 80 to 92.

Although the policy in selecting the first 26 systems in *Mirrors for Behavior* was to limit the systems to those designed for observation in school settings, the systems published subsequently in *Mirrors* are a potpourri of systems designed for classroom, group dynamics, counseling, industrial and other situations. Thus, for someone whose primary interest is education in school settings, the summary tables beginning with Volume VII will be confusing because all the systems are included, regardless of the

---

[6] See footnote 1, p. 122.

use for which they were designed. For example, although 62 systems are listed as having "affective" dimensions, only some of these instruments were designed for use in classrooms. Although the current number of instruments in *Mirrors* is 92, only 73 will be considered in this chapter, the ones designed as classroom observational instruments.

SOURCES OF VARIABLES

In order to provide a clearer understanding of observational instruments, we have organized the 73 category systems in *Mirrors* around two themes. In this section the instruments are classified according to the source of the variables which the authors chose; in the next section the same instruments are reclassified according to the author's purpose in developing the instrument. These two sections provide the data for the subsequent section, an attempt to assess the current use of observational instruments to study teaching.

Classification of Sources

Four classifications were developed to group the instruments according to the source of the variables which the authors selected:

1. *Instruments with explicit theoretical or empirical base* contain variables derived from specified, established theory or research, such as the work of Dewey, Menninger, Neal Miller, Piaget or Sullivan.

2. *Instruments with implicit theoretical or empirical base* contain variables the author claimed to have derived from empirical research, such as learning theory or research in group dynamics. The author did not specify the research base.

3. *Modifications or syntheses of existing category systems* are instruments created from previously developed classroom observation instruments, such as those by Flanders, B. O. Smith or Taba.

4. *Author-originated category systems* contain variables the author believed to be important in classroom interaction. The author did not specify the origin of these variables.

Although each of the 73 category systems is listed in one of the four classifications, few instruments contain variables derived exclusively from one source. This listing is not definitive; it is a first attempt to explain the sources of the variables. The information on sources includes citations from and references to the original reports on the instruments. Most of the instruments surveyed were described in the volumes of *Mirrors for Behavior*. It is advisable to read the original texts whenever possible.

1. Instruments with Explicit Theoretical or Empirical Base

Of the 73 classroom observational systems in *Mirrors*, 15 seem to have been derived from an explicitly stated theoretical or empirical base. The indefinite tone of the preceding sentence is intentional; although the authors explicitly stated that the systems were derived from other works, the line of development is not always apparent when one inspects the actual category system.

The 15 systems are presented in Table 1. Each system is accompanied by a quotation from the author citing the sources. These quotations are included so that the reader can decide for himself how to classify each system in terms of the source of variables. Readers may dispute whether the sources cited by the authors represent an accepted theoretical or empirical base. Nevertheless, the references in Table 1 indicate that some authors of category systems did search outside current classroom practice for new variables. Only one author (Spaulding, 1965, #22) drew his variables from research on student growth in school settings.

Of the 15 systems in this group, the one developed by MacDonald and Zaret (#54) presented the greatest problem in classification. Although they claimed that their system was derived from Rogers and

TABLE 1

CLASSROOM CATEGORY SYSTEMS WITH EXPLICITLY STATED
THEORETICAL OR EMPIRICAL BASE

Author	Mirrors Number	Source
Aschner & Gallagher*	#3	"... we have developed five primary sets of groups of categories for the classification of what is said and done in the classroom. Four of these—*cognitive memory, convergent thinking, evaluative thinking,* and *divergent thinking*—represent our adaptation of Guilford's model of the operations of intellect" (Simon & Boyer, 1967, Vol. 2, #3, p. Aschner-Gallagher System - ii).
Bellack et al.	#4	"A functional conception of pedagogical discourse was developed based on Wittgenstein's 'language-game' approach" (Kliebard, 1966, p. 235).
Spaulding	#21	"The term 'coping' and many of the ideas implicit in CASES have come from the work of Lois Murphy, especially from her book, *Methods for the Study of Personality in Young Children*" (Simon & Boyer, 1967, Vol. 5, #21–22, Spaulding - 2).
	#22	"STARS is the direct result of this comprehensive factor analytic study of approximately 113 categories of teacher-child transactions in a sample of 21 elementary school classrooms" (Simon & Boyer, 1967, Vol. 5, #21–22, Spaulding - 5).
Taba	#23	"... the strategies she recommends are derived from a variety of psychological research and theory (Sigel, 1966; Piaget, 1962; Bruner, 1965) all of which points to the need for carefully planned steps in the development of children's own concepts and generalizations" (Simon & Boyer, 1967, Vol. 5, #23, p. Taba [Generalization] - 5). (See also Taba, Levine, & Elzey, 1964.)
Wright & Proctor	#26	"This division of the cognitive aspect is in keeping with Cassirer's (1953, p. 9 - 345) consideration of thought as 'thing-concepts' and 'relation-concepts' ... the categories of the Process frame developed under the above considerations are in keeping with the broad division of the problem solving process reached empirically by Duncker (1954, p. 45)."
H. H. Anderson	#30	"It was our purpose to test several hypotheses and to use certain constructs developed by Mary P. Follett ... and published in 1924 under the ... title of *Creative Experience: ...*" (Simon & Boyer, 1970, Vol. 7, #30, p. 30.2 - 3).
Brown	#36	"... system which measures the instructional practices of a teacher in terms of agreement-disagreement with John Dewey's experimentalism" (Simon & Boyer, 1970, Vol. 8, #36, p. 36.2 - 1).
Brown et al.	#37	"Based upon the [Bloom] *Taxonomy of Educational Objectives: Cognitive Domain,* it [the Florida Taxonomy of Educational Objectives] is a sign system comprised of items organized in a somewhat hierarchical order, from the more simple to the more complex of cognitive activities" (Simon & Boyer, 1970, Vol. 8, #37, p. 37.2 - 1).
Denny	#41	"... categories of classroom behavior suggested by psychological literature relating to creativity development and the creative personality, and ... prior empirical studies of pupil creative development (Rusch, Denny, & Ives, 1965, 1967). Further validity data were provided by examining relationships to teacher characteristics (Turner & Denny, 1969)" (Simon & Boyer, 1970, Vol. 8, #41, p. 41.1 - 4).
Fuller	#43	"These dimensions were selected because of the considerable agreement which exists that these are important dimensions of interpersonal behavior (Wiggins, 1968)" (Simon & Boyer, 1970, Vol. 9, #43, p. 43.1 - 4).

continued on next page

TABLE 1 (Cont'd.)

TABLE 1 (Cont'd.)
CLASSROOM CATEGORY SYSTEMS WITH EXPLICITLY STATED
THEORETICAL OR EMPIRICAL BASE

Author	Mirrors Number	Source
MacDonald & Zaret	#54	"One such approach found ... among the writings of Rogers, Schachtel, and Rokeach, etc., gives promise for providing a conceptualization of the power, usefulness, and generality needed. Essentially, this is the idea of arranging behavior on a process continuum of openness as contrasted with compensatory and/or defensive behavior" (Simon & Boyer, 1970, Vol. 10, #54, p. 54.1 - 1).
Solomon	#72	"A scheme of cognitive growth can be advanced [which] incorporates and adds to the developmental stages of Piaget and the imagery related stages of Bruner" (Simon & Boyer, 1970, Vol. 13, #72, p. 72.1 - 2).
Tyler	#75	Based upon Menninger's *Theory of Psychoanalytic Technique* (1958) (Simon & Boyer, 1970, Vol. 13, #75, p. 75.1 - 2).
Waimon	#76	"The system used was based on Neal Miller's basic components of learning: 'drive, cue, response, reward' " (Simon & Boyer, 1970, Vol. 13, #76, p. 76.2 - 4).
Bemis, Luft, & Liberty	#82	"A series of pupil behaviors was subjectively judged as belonging in one of the three lowest levels of the affective domain (Krathwohl, Bloom, & Masia, 1964). . . . Sullivan's (1953) social-psychological theory of personality served as the basis for selection of two categories of teacher behaviors" (Simon & Boyer, 1970, Vol. A, #82, p. 82.1 - 2–4).

* *Mirrors for Behavior* is disorderly in that when developers (authors) have systems for observing teacher *and* student behaviors' the *Mirrors* editors sometimes counted these as two systems, other times, as one. In all cases but one, the authors were the same. The exception is the two systems developed for PLAN (Program for Learning According to Needs). The Student Observation System (SOS) was written by Lipe, Steen, and Quirk. The Teacher Observation System (PLAN-TOS) was written by Steen, Quirk, and Lipe. SOS has Mirrors #87; TOS has Mirrors #92.

Sometimes these systems have authors only (e.g., Flanders), sometimes they have names only (e.g., McRel or MidContinental Regional Educational Lab), and sometimes they have names and authors (e.g., PLAN-TOS, Steen, Quirk, & Lipe).

Rokeach and contains the "process continuum of openness as contrasted with ... defensive behavior," this open-closed dimension of teacher behavior is expressed by only two cells, one containing all "open" teacher interactions and one containing "closed" interactions. Of course there are many subcategories within these two cells which allow the rater to make low-inference coding, but the reader is forced to make high-inference interpretations of all results. In addition, the other two cells in their system came directly from the work of Aschner and Gallagher (#3). Therefore the system might be placed in this group because of the direct reference in their text to the work of Rogers and Rokeach, it might be classified as a modification of a previous system, or it might be classified as author-originated.

2. Instruments with Implicit Theoretical or Empirical Base

The authors of 10 of the 73 category systems referred to theories or research as the source of their variables, but the linkage between the research and the variables was not as clear as in the instruments previously described. The references are summarized in Table 2. Three authors wrote that some of their variables were derived from current theories of learning (Hough, #9; Withall, #24; Wallen et al., #77); one focused upon group dynamics concepts (Simon & Agazarian, #18); and one referred to both theory and research in interpersonal relations (Flanders, #5). In one study the category system was based upon an extensive review of political controversy in a democratic society (Oliver & Shaver, 1966, #16).

The remaining systems in Table 2 differ from these six in that the source of their variables was the literature on instruction (Joyce, #11; Jason, #51; Jones, #86; Spaulding, #91). The category system used by Spaulding might be separated from the

TABLE 2

CATEGORY SYSTEMS DERIVED FROM IMPLICIT RESEARCH OR THEORY

Author	Mirrors Number	Implicit Source
Flanders	#5	"This model is based on a psychology of superior-subordinate relationships, adapted to fit classroom conditions" (Flanders, 1965, p. 2).
Hough	#9	". . . [In this system] the categories have been developed so as to focus on observable behaviors that are commonly associated with principles of learning drawn from learning theory. The testing of hypotheses regarding the effects of instructional behavior on student learning (hypotheses generated from learning theory) seems to be the major contribution of this system" (Simon & Boyer, 1967, Vol. 3, #9, p. Hough (System) - 2).
Joyce	#11	"Instructional Flexibility Training uses three frames of reference." Each frame of reference enables practitioners to view teaching in terms of important theoretical positions. Together, the three frames of reference provide a balanced view of teaching (Simon & Boyer, 1967, Vol. 3, #11, p. Joyce-Hodges - 2).
Oliver & Shaver	#16	Category system developed from authors' analysis of social science writings in order to yield "selected concepts one might employ to frame and analyze political controversy in a democratic society" (Oliver & Shaver, 1966, p. 56).
Simon & Agazarian	#18	References in the review of research are to studies in group dynamics, particularly the conceptualizations of Gibb, and of Howard and Scott (Simon & Boyer, 1967, Vol. 3, #18).
Withall	#24	". . . [The] current theories of learning, . . . gleaned largely from the field-theorists . . . guide the study" (Simon & Boyer, 1967, Vol. 5, #24, p. Withall (B) - 1).
Jason	#51	"The process of designing the Medical Instruction Observation Record required heavy dependency upon prior research studies. The many lists of teacher characteristics available in the literature were analyzed and compared [and] . . . a single list of the most commonly agreed upon traits and attributes emerged. . . . The listed observable characteristics were then combined into sub-groups on the basis of similarity" (Simon & Boyer, 1970, Vol. 10, #51, p. 51.1 - 2–3).
Wallen et al.	#77	"[One unique feature is] the nature of the variables themselves and their direct (though not rigorous) tie to current general theories of learning and instruction" (Simon & Boyer, 1970, Vol. 13, #77, p. 77.1 - 1).
Jones	#86	"Upon the bases of both theory and empirical results, a new instrument—the SACC—was devised, which was intended to be somewhat more analytical than the simplest (and most used system—Flanders), yet less costly than the most complex" (Simon & Boyer, 1970, Vol. A, #86, p. 86.1–1).
Spaulding	#91	Following an extensive review of research on classroom research and student perceptions of their teacher, Spaulding isolated a number of variables which appeared to warrant further study, presented them, and justified the category system in terms of the variables (Simon & Boyer, 1970, Vol. B, #91).

other three because Spaulding derived his variables from an extensive review of the research on instruction.

The Hough system (#9) was difficult to classify. The system is primarily a modification of the Flanders system, but it was classified in this group because Hough claimed that his modifications were made in order to describe "those behavior patterns which are associated with many of the more commonly accepted principles of learning facilitation" (9–1.10). (Despite Hough's claim that his system provided for the testing of hypotheses generated from learning theory, no research was found in which this system was used for "the testing of hypotheses regarding the effects of instructional behavior on student learning" [9–1.10].)

3. Modifications or Syntheses of Existing Category Systems

At least 24 of the 73 classroom category systems in *Mirrors* represent modifications, syntheses and/or expansions of existing systems. In half of the instances (Table 3) the new instrument was a modification of a single existing instrument. In these cases the refinements consisted of subdivisions of gross categories into more specific categories of behaviors. The nature of these modifications is suggested in Table 3.

A second procedure for creating new category systems has been to synthesize two or more systems. The systems that were developed in this manner are listed in Table 4. Modifications are relatively simple to recognize in most systems. For example, Amidon (#1) subdivided the Flanders system (#5) and incorporated variables from the work of Hughes and Miller, Taba, and Aschner and Gallagher. Sometimes the original sources are more difficult to recognize, as in the systems of Ribble and Schultz (#65) and of Altman (#28).

In Tables 3 and 4 the existing system most frequently cited as a source of a new instrument is the system developed by Flanders (#5, 1965). Several reasons may

account for the popularity of this system. First, the instrument is relatively easy to learn to use. Second, several manuals and kits are readily available for training observers (Amidon & Amidon, 1969; Amidon & Flanders, 1967). Third, the system includes a matrix to record dyadic sequences, and this structure appeals to many users. Fourth, more research has been conducted with this instrument than with any others (cf. Amidon & Hough, 1967; Flanders, 1970).

Table 4 includes a variety of category systems. In most cases the new instrument was created by combining one which focused on cognitive interactions with one which emphasized affective interactions. However, not all instruments created in this manner are similar; distinctions can even be noted in instruments which were developed from the same "original." In some instances the modifications are so great that another reviewer might wish to classify the new instruments as author-originated systems.

Looking at the variety of instruments in Tables 3 and 4 resulting from modifications of existing systems, one wonders whether these modifications are of any psychological or educational merit.

4. Author-Originated Category Systems

Twenty-four classroom category systems in *Mirrors* are labeled as author-originated because the reports on the systems did not contain references to established theory or empirical research or because the systems did not seem to be descendants of prior systems (Table 5).

The system developed by Openshaw and Cyphert (#17) and the system developed by Schalock et al. (#69) were classified as author-originated even though the authors stated that they based their system upon previous category systems. This decision was made because the systems which they developed seemed to be quite different from the previous ones, and because it is difficult

TABLE 3

EXPANSION OF ONE SYSTEM

Author	Mirrors Number	System Expanded	Nature of Expansion
Amidon & Hunter	#2	Flanders	Divided questions into narrow and broad; acceptance and rejection subdivided.
Flanders	#6	Flanders	Subdivided most categories.
Miller & Hughes	#14	Hughes	Regrouped categories into various responsive-directive categories.
Moskowitz	#15	Flanders	Subdivided categories by adding more; added code for English or foreign language.
A. Anderson	#29	Flanders	Subdivided some categories.
Dodl	#42	Flanders	Added three categories in teacher-talk: sustains student response; closed or open question; control interruption.
Galloway	#44	Flanders	Added rating scale to each category to code noncognitive, nonverbal affect.
Mid-Continent Regional Educational Laboratory	#58	Flanders	Subdivided all categories according to topic or goal of interaction.
Ober	#61	Flanders	Added new categories and created a mirror-coding for student behavior.
Withall, Lewis, & Newell	#78	Withall	Subdivided Withall categories.
Wragg	#79	Flanders	Added notation for interactions in foreign language.
Shrable & Minnis	#90	Taba	Added new format to include matrix and teacher responses to students.

TABLE 4

SYNTHESIS AND/OR MODIFICATION OF TWO OR MORE SYSTEMS

Author	Mirrors Number	Names of Systems Synthesized
Amidon	#1	Aschner & Gallagher, Flanders, Hughes, Taba
Honigman	#8	Aschner & Gallagher, Flanders, Hughes
Wright	#25	Flanders, Wright & Proctor
Altman	#28	Flanders, Fleisher & Zimmer, Karplus & Thier
Cooperative Educational Research Laboratory, Inc.	#40	Aschner & Gallagher, Bales, Bloom, Flanders, Taba
Hunter	#49	Aschner & Gallagher, Flanders, Hughes
Perkins	#63 & #64	Flanders, Kowatrukal, Lamb, McKinstry, Sears
Ribble & Schultz	#65	Bellack, Taba, Withall
Roberson	#67	Bloom, Galloway, MacDonald & Zaret
Schalock et al.	#69	Aschner & Gallagher; Bales; Bellack; Flanders; Hughes; Moustakes, Sigel, & Schalock; Smith; Taba
Schusler	#70	Adams & Biddle, Flanders, Kowatrakul, Taba
Anderson & Bingman	#80	Flanders, Ober, plus addition of separate level for cognitive coding
Heger	#84	Flanders, Galloway

TABLE 5

AUTHOR-ORIGINATED CATEGORY SYSTEMS: ANCESTRY UNCLEAR

Author	Mirrors Number	Characteristics of System
Gallagher et al.	#7	Two dimensions for cognitive coding, one for focus of activity.
Hughes (Gilstrap)	#10	Teacher behavior divided into six types. Origin appears to have been the investigator's inspection and study of classroom behavior. References are mainly to group dynamics.
Lindvall et al.	#12	Categorization of types of student activity for Individually Prescribed Instruction. System for individualized instruction.
Medley	#13	Fairly simple categorization of a few affective and cognitive dimensions, and retention of sequential nature of interaction, plus coding of on or off task.
Openshaw & Cyphert	#17	Began as synthesis of several systems, but ancestry is not traceable. Multidimensional, many subdivisions. Complex, but seldom cited; apparently never used by others.
Smith, Meux, et al. (Logic)	#19	Interchanges are divided into 13 cognitive categories. Began by trying to apply categories from works on logic, but those ready-made classifications were inapplicable to the classroom.
Smith et al. (Ventures)	#20	Larger maneuvers on the subject matter, labeled Ventures, were subdivided into nine types.
Adams & Biddle	#27	Very complex, multidimensional; social psychology background, but references not given.
Barnes	#33	Classification of teacher questions into 10 types. Although many of the classifications are similar to other systems (e.g., closed reasoning, open reasoning), the classifications have not been brought together in this way before.
Clements	#39	New classification of questions, most similar to Smith (#19).
Galloway	#44	Added new factor to Flanders (#5), but the factor is unique. Factor contains ratings on affective tone of each interaction.
Herbert	#46	Elaborate system to code behavior in team teaching situation. Section on "lesson form" is new; focuses on groupings and interaction of students and teacher.
Honigman & Stephens	#48	Developed for individualized instruction. Has more categories and broader variables than Lindvall et al. (#12).
Jansen	#50	Developed to code all materials and activities of class.
Kowatrakul	#52	Six categories of student attention to task; three dominant classroom activities.
Matthews & Phillips	#55 #56	Generally a Flanders-type system for teacher behavior, but subdivided into "lesson related" and "non-lesson related." Student behavior also divided into 9 categories.
Parakh	#62	System is a variant of those which classify cognitive interactions into three or more levels. The four modes of student talk are like others, but not derived from them. The use of two factors seems unique, but is fairly similar to a subdivision of Flanders (#5).
Schalock et al.	#69	Extremely comprehensive system containing six levels, with three to 23 divisions within each level.
Stukat	#74	Classroom activities divided into a number of categories.
Balzar & Evans	#81	Categories on major purposes, with subdivisions for content development. Similar to others, but no discernible ancestry.

TABLE 5 (Cont'd.)

AUTHOR-ORIGINATED CATEGORY SYSTEMS: ANCESTRY UNCLEAR

Author	Mirrors Number	Characteristics of System
Brophy & Good	#83	Multidimensional system for coding interactions between teacher and individual students. Includes coding for type of question, level of question, student answer, and teacher reaction.
Lipe, Quirk, & Steen PLAN-SOS PLAN-TOS	#87 #92	Student observation scale contains 23 behaviors grouped into eight major categories. Teacher observation scale contains 21 behaviors grouped into six major categories. The major focus is upon the teacher and student activity.
Morsh	#88	Thirty-three items descriptive of student and teacher behavior.
Puckett	#89	Fourteen items grouped into five categories, all referring to student responses to teacher questions.
Spaulding	#91	Very elaborate system to code multiple dimensions; it is surprising that the system has received so little attention.

to identify the original sources of items in their instruments.

One might question the inclusion here of some of these instruments, such as those developed by Galloway (#44), Matthews and Phillips (#55, #56), Parakh (#62), and Balzer and Evans (#81), because they reflect the category system of Flanders and other systems on levels of cognitive interaction. These are borderline cases, and another reviewer might place them in the classification for authors who synthesized two or more systems.

Many of these author-developed systems are quite elaborate and are the results of several years of work. Each of the two systems by Smith (Smith, Meux, et al., #19; Smith et al., #20) was developed over a three-year period, and the systems by Gallagher et al. (#7), Openshaw and Cyphert (#17), Adams and Biddle (#27), Herbert (#46), Schalock et al. (#69), and Brophy and Good (#83) took at least one year to develop and have been published separately as books.

Summary

In Table 6 the 73 classroom category systems in *Mirrors* are summarized according

to the source of their variables. Perhaps the main generalization from this table is that the systems have been developed from a variety of sources. Author-developed systems and systems which are modifications of existing systems appear to predominate; however a sufficient number of systems have been developed on the basis of explicit theory or research to refute the contention that all category systems were developed from the authors' fantasies.

TABLE 6

ORIGINS OF CLASSROOM CATEGORY SYSTEMS IN *MIRRORS*

Developed from established theory or empirical research outside of education	
Explicitly stated theory or research	15
Implicitly stated theory or research	10
Developed from existing classroom category systems	
Modification of one system	12
Modification and/or synthesis of two or more systems	12
Developed by author	24

Discussion

The four classifications used in this summary of sources of variables were developed to illustrate the process by which category systems are currently being developed. However the problems of constructing a category system are so large that any category system represents personal judgment no matter what origins are cited for the variables. An investigator who wants to develop a category system based on Dewey, Menninger, or laboratory research on reinforcement must still make decisions on the unit of measure, the number of variables, the number of different behaviors to include in one variable, the number of dimensions and the scale to be used in recording the behavior. The original research or theory does not provide a basis for making these decisions. Thus, although one can separate the authors who apparently drew their variables out of the air from the authors who developed their variables from painstaking reading and thought, the resultant category systems may not reflect these differences because of the additional decisions which must be made in creating a system. Because of these additional problems, all category systems are the products of personal judgment and intuition —some less than others.

It is almost impossible to inspect a variable in a category system and determine the source used by the developer. Even when an author decides that, if a teacher has 50 percent of behavior X and 32 percent of behavior Y, the percentages "fit" or "do not fit" the theory of Piaget or Dewey, it is almost impossible to determine the appropriateness of this fit.

Let us illustrate the difficulty of linking the coding of a classroom event to a particular source of the category used to code it. Suppose a child gave an "unusual" response and the teacher said, "John, that's an interesting idea." How would this teacher's response be coded in different systems which purport to be derived from different sources? Here is a list of six categories from six different category systems, purported to come from six different sources into which this interaction could be coded. It is an interesting problem to try to identify the source of

each category and to name the system and the source of the variable.

1. Teacher entertains even "wild" or far-fetched suggestions;
2. Routine agreement;
3. Teacher accepts or uses ideas of students;
4. Sanctions-search;
5. Exits-approved;
6. Evaluate without public criteria.

The answers are: 1.) Brown (#36) from Dewey; 2.) Aschner and Gallagher (#3) from Guilford (1965); 3.) Flanders (#5) from theory and research in interpersonal relationships; 4.) Joyce (#11) from sources in instructional theory; 5.) Medley (#13), author originated; and 6.) Miller and Hughes (#14), expansion of Hughes's hypothesis taken from Group Process literature.

It probably is impossible for anyone to match most of the categories to sources of the categories. Labeling the teacher response as "sanctions-search" or "exits-approved" seems as much like Dewey's theories of education as does "teacher entertains even 'wild' or far-fetched suggestions." Furthermore, labeling Brown's instrument (#36) as derived from Dewey overlooks Brown's use of sign system coding and his method for combining variables, both of which are different from the procedures developed by Joyce (#11) and by Medley (#13).

No matter how excellent the origins which one claims for a category system are, these systems cannot be validated on the basis of their sources. The systems represent hypotheses that certain variables and certain ways of coding instructional transactions are related to student growth. Interesting hypotheses with the most prestigious sources cannot substitute for generalizations developed from experimental and correlational studies of student growth in classroom settings. Even stable and well-established generalizations developed in laboratory studies or in special classroom situations cannot be accepted wholesale as principles for learning in school settings (for an elaboration of these ideas, see Shulman, 1970).

Unfortunately, in this area as in so many areas in the social sciences, one cannot find evidence of cumulative research within school settings like the research suggested by the descriptive-correlational-experimental loop. We would like to find observational systems in which the variables were based on research in school settings. Only two have been found—the category system by Spaulding (1965, #22) and the rating system developed by Davidoff (1970).

CLASSIFICATION OF PURPOSES AND USES OF OBSERVATIONAL SYSTEMS

Another way of viewing observational systems is to classify them according to the author's dominant purpose in developing them. Such a classification can provide an overview of the major emphases in this area and of the relative amounts of energy being devoted to each goal.

Four classifications were developed to summarize the purposes of the authors of the instruments in *Mirrors*. These four purposes are:

1. To describe current classroom practice;
2. To train teachers;
3. To monitor instructional systems;
4. To investigate relationships between classroom activities and student growth.

Although classification of systems by the author's purpose is useful, such classification can also be misleading because category systems have been used by the authors and by other investigators for many purposes. For example, the instrument developed by Flanders (#5) has been used for all four purposes.

Purposes and uses overlap, and a separate classification according to uses would have been illuminating. However there was no way to obtain adequate information on the variety of ways these instruments have been used. Still, whenever information was available on uses other than the author's dominant purpose, it was included below. In addition, other observational systems not mentioned in *Mirrors* were included in order to round out the discussion of the four dominant purposes.

The four classifications and the placement of the instruments in these classifications are meant to be suggestive rather than assertive. The reader is invited to inspect the original reports in the volumes of *Mirrors* (not the Summary volumes) and ascertain for himself the authors' purposes.

1. To Describe Current Classroom Practice

The largest number of category systems is classified under the tentative title, "descriptive." Anyone who reads the dominant purposes of the systems in *Mirrors* becomes overwhelmed by the tens of systems whose avowed purpose is to describe, analyze or observe. At least 37 of the systems in *Mirrors* appear to fall under this classification.

In nine systems the words "describe" or "description" appear in the early pages of the reports (Bellack et al., #4; Gallagher et al., #7; Hough, #9; Openshaw & Cyphert, #17; Fuller, #43; Herbert, #46; Jason, #51; Withall, Lewis, & Newell, #78; Jones, #86). Some of these systems were designed "to describe the patterned processes of verbal interaction that characterize classrooms in action" (Bellack, #4, p. 1), "to provide a structure which...can describe present classroom behavior" (Gallagher et al., #7, p. 2), "to more precisely describe the classroom behaviors that are ...implicitly described in commonly accepted principles of learning and instruction" (Hough, #9, p. 10), and to facilitate "the gathering of data descriptive of classroom communication between teacher and pupils" (Jones, #86, p. 1).

In seven systems the words "analyze" or "analysis" appear in the early pages of the reports (Simon & Agazarian, #18; Smith et al., #20; A. Anderson, #29; Jansen,

#50; Stukat, #74; Tyler, #75; Wragg, #79). In these systems the purposes were "to analyze verbal communication in a way that reflects the major patterns of verbal and non-verbal interaction" (Simon & Agazarian, #18, p. 3), "to analyze classroom discourse into strategies" (Smith et al., #20, p. 1), "to throw light on instruction through an analysis of the material used by pupils in their work" (Jansen, #50, p. 2.5), and "to start with an analysis of the teacher's behavior in the instructional situation" (Stukat, #74, p. 1).

If the reader cannot distinguish between description and analysis, he is invited to examine three category systems which claim to provide both. The first system "is an analytic and descriptive one" (Smith, Meux, et al., #19, p. 11), the second meets "the need to describe and analyze the effects of teacher verbal and non-verbal messages" (Galloway, #44, p. 4), and the third is for "classification, quantitative description, and analysis of verbal behavior of individual pupils" (Parakh, #62, pp. 6–7).

If a reader is uncomfortable with the terms *describe* or *analyze,* he might select category systems which purport only to help people observe. One of these systems "provides a framework for observing and recording the cognitive behavior of the teacher and students" (Brown et al., #37, p. 1), one is a "vehicle for systematically observing classroom behavior" (Wallen et al., #77, p. 2), another is for "systematic observation" (Balzar & Evans, #81, p. 3), and one "establishes a conceptual framework for observation and recording of the symptomatic behaviors of the teacher and class thereby providing a means for the evaluation of the classroom interaction process" (Heger, #84, p. 6).

The reader who prefers simpler outcomes may use a system which "measures the instructional practices of a teacher" (Brown, #36, p. 1), "categorizes the behavior of teachers and students" (Roberts, #68, p. 1), helps to "determine the teacher's (cognitive) level of presentation" (Solomon, #72, p. 5),

or one which "gives an accurate record of the amount, kind, and direction of verbal interaction and is adaptable to both [sic] teacher-directed, pupil-directed and small group activities in a regular classroom" (Simon & Boyer, 1970, Vol. 12, #70, p. 70.1–15).

Researchers who want more than description from a category system can select from among those which "meet the need for a classroom observational instrument that deals with the affective, control, and cognitive dimensions in a relatively balanced way" (Honigman, #8, p. 31); which "help you to better understand the actions of a teacher" (Hughes [Gilstrap], #10, p. 1); which "seek as broad an understanding as possible of the observable characteristics of classroom activities" (Adams & Biddle, #27, pp. 5–6); or which "represent an effort to develop a conceptually sound, relatively exhaustive measure of teacher behavior and the contextual variables which influence it" (Simon & Boyer, 1970, Vol. 12, #69, p. 69.1–4).

The long listings of descriptive, analytical and observational purposes seem to confirm that the developers of these systems feel description is both necessary and sufficient for improving classroom instruction. However a concern for either the descriptive-correlational-experimental loop paradigm or the Hilgard continuum requires researchers to assume that description is *not* sufficient.

Differential and relational descriptive systems. Although the above systems were designed for description, very little descriptive data appeared in the *Mirrors* volumes. Most of the data there were gathered in the course of obtaining interrater agreement. A few reports included more data than just mean scores and standard deviations.

The purpose of two category systems was to study differential behavior. Clements (#39) developed his descriptive instrument in order to find differences in types of teacher questions, lengths of answers for each question type, and the varying sequences of types of questions from grade to grade, teacher to teacher, and lesson to lesson. Brophy and Good (#83) were interested in learning whether the teachers behaved differently toward high-achieving and low-achieving students.

Other investigators developed category systems so that they could describe the relationship between sets of classroom events. The system developed by Kowatrakul was used "to make an empirical survey of the relationships of six categories of student behavior to three classroom activities and four subject areas" (#52, p. 1-1). The system developed by Dodl was used to determine, "if and when pupils do ask questions in the classroom, what kinds of questions are they; of whom are they raised? From what sources do they stem? More importantly, what do teachers do in evoking and handling these questions?" (Simon & Boyer, 1970, Vol. 9, #42, p. 42.2 – 1).

Simple versus complex descriptive systems. At first glance it appears that relatively simple category systems were designed mainly for teacher feedback purposes, whereas investigators interested in describing the classrooms chose more complex category systems. Certainly the systems developed by Bellack et al. (#4), Gallagher et al. (#7), Smith, Meux, et al. (#19), Smith et al. (#20), and Adams and Biddle (#27) are examples of highly complex descriptive systems. The authors all discussed building their categories to capture the complexities of the classroom. One identifying feature of these systems is the elaborate preparations necessary for using them. One cannot walk into a classroom and code; instead, audio-tape and video-tape recordings are necessary, and typed transcripts must be prepared for some of the analyses. Adams and Biddle (#27) reported that it took from 10 to 20 hours to code an hour of audio tape using their system.

However, only 12 of the 37 systems labeled as descriptive require video tape, audio tape, transcripts or anything other than live coding. If a system can be used "live" without transcribing and recording, then an hour of observation yields an hour of data and the observation time is the coding time. This might be taken as an indication that the system is less complex than one which requires hours of coding for each hour of class time. However this distinction does not appear to hold. Some seemingly complex systems, such as those by Schalock et al. (#69) or Openshaw and Cyphert (#17), were said by their authors to be codable without recording equipment. On the other hand, some of the simpler systems take hours to decode even when detailed manuals are available. For example, Flanders's (#5) categories are easy to learn, and observations are made "live"; yet adequate interpretations of matrices may be complex and time-consuming.

Often the complexity of a system lies in the pretentious justifications given and not in the category system itself. Perhaps the best example is in the report written by Wragg (#79). He stated, "it is essential that foreign language lessons should be subjected to systematic analysis, so that the nature of spontaneous interaction both in the native and foreign languages can be better understood" (Simon & Boyer, 1970, Vol. 13, #79, p. 79.1 – 1). Yet all he did was use the simple Flanders categories and add a 1 before each category if the interactions were in a foreign language.

Another example of a grandiose description for a rather simple system was presented by MacDonald and Zaret (#54). They stated that in order to understand the nature of teaching one needs a "...dynamic conceptualization which deals with human behavior in terms of a general dimension ...that can move freely among the levels of the teacher as a behaving person, the interactive context, and the children as behaviors" [*sic*] (Simon & Boyer, 1970, Vol. 10, #54, p. 54.1 – 1). Operationally, their dynamic conceptualization was the division of teacher responses to student answers into two types (transition-oriented and role-expectancy–oriented) and the learner's subsequent responses into two types (productive and reproductive).

Description is the predominant purpose given by the authors and the predominant use made of the instruments. This type of research was intended to provide a set of concepts and some baseline data on teaching in natural settings. Although these descriptive studies should lead to correlational and experimental studies, to date they have not. For the most part, descriptive studies have led only to further descriptive studies and attempts to "analyze" teaching by recording whether certain intuitively selected activities were present.

2. To Train Teachers

At least 10 category systems in *Mirrors* appear to have been developed primarily for teacher training. In teacher-training situations category systems are used in one or more of three ways: 1) to provide a teacher with feedback on his behavior, 2) to give a teacher a set of procedures by which to categorize instructional activities, and 3) to provide a teacher with behaviors and activities which he can model during instruction. A clear example of a category system planned for teacher training is the system developed by Amidon (#1). In the introduction to this system Amidon wrote,

"In the four years that Interaction Analysis has been used with student teachers at Temple, the work of Hughes, Taba, and Gallagher and Aschner, among others, has been introduced as well, and in this paper some aspects of these systems which have been found useful will be added to Interaction Analysis in an attempt to combine into one category system the items found particularly helpful in the training of student teachers" (Simon & Boyer, 1967, Vol. 1, #1, p. Amidon – 6).

In the same vein, when Hunter (1970) discussed the four modifications of the Interaction Analysis system which she helped make, most of the reasons for the modifications focused on teacher training. For example, one revision was made because "it became clear to me that certain additional categories would be useful for practicing teacher talk" (Hunter, 1970, p. 17), and another revision was made to include two categories on student behavior while working with science materials "because there had been considerable stress in the training sessions for teachers upon permitting children to explore materials and to talk with each other while doing so" (Hunter, 1970, p. 18). Other examples of category systems developed primarily for giving feedback to teachers are those developed by Joyce (#11), Moscowitz (#15), Barnes (#33), Waimon (#76), Puckett (#89), and Shrable and Minnis (#90). In general the instruments developed primarily for teacher training have tended to be simpler than the ones developed for the description of teaching.

Several authors have attempted to develop systems which the teachers could use to monitor their behavior without depending on outside observers. The clearest example of a self-monitoring system is the one developed by the Cooperative Educational Research Laboratory, Inc. (#40), which "offers the teacher a simple and efficient method for recording and classifying verbal statements made in a classroom" (#40, p. 1). Self-feedback also appears to be the major purpose of the systems developed by Amidon and Amidon (1969), Ober (#61) and Roberson (#67).

It is within teacher training that the distinction between the author's stated purpose and the actual use becomes most blurred. If a system is developed for the training of teachers but is not used for that purpose to any extent, how does one classify it? The system by Puckett (#89) is an example. If a system is used only for one or two semesters and only at the author's institution, then how is it classified? There are no answers.

Difficulties in system classification. Several systems were classified as developed to describe classroom practice because the authors said that was their primary aim. However, in many cases the authors may have wanted to describe teaching to teachers or to provide feedback to teachers, so these systems could have been classified under teacher training. The systems developed by Hough (#9), Simon and Agazarian (#18), Galloway (#44), MacDonald and Zaret (#54), Wragg (#79) and Heger (#84) could have been classified as instruments for either teacher feedback or description. The distinction between category systems whose purpose was description and those whose purpose was teacher training is not clear because any system could be used to provide feedback to teachers.

Category systems have been used often in teacher training. By using category systems as part of the training, college educators have been able to modify teacher behavior in predetermined ways. However, one might question the logical or empirical basis of the teacher training formulated on the particular "shoulds" of these instruments.

The use of observation in natural settings as part of teacher training or as criterion variables in the performance-based training of teachers will not be discussed here because this topic is amply treated in Chapter 30.

Can teachers study their own behavior? Several writers have suggested that teachers use classroom observational systems to study their own behavior. Simon and Boyer expressed the opinion of many when they wrote:

These instruments contain a wide variety of categories which are descriptors of behaviors. These descriptors of behavior can be used as prescriptions for skills to be acquired by people to help them become what they want to be. And this, for us, is their greatest fascination.... (Simon & Boyer, 1970a, Vol. 15, Summary, p. 33).

Flanders (1970) presented a variation of this idea when he suggested that the inquiry behaviors of a teacher include five

steps: 1) specifying the pupil behavior desired in the class, 2) identifying the patterns of teaching behavior considered likely to fit such pupil behavior, 3) practicing the teacher behavior patterns, 4) designing a way to test the relationships between targeted pupil behavior and designated teacher behavior, and 5) carrying out the plan in the classroom and testing the results. The suggestions that teachers should study their behavior, that they need terms to describe their behavior, and that teachers should attempt to obtain certain patterns of instructional activities seem reasonable. However, if teachers "become what they want to be," or if they exhibit the desired patterns, will student learning automatically be increased?

In the last chapter of his book, Flanders suggested some limitations to his inquiry approach. He stated that

there probably is a point at which higher levels of teacher responsiveness begin to erode the efficient learning of problem-solving skills and principles. A different point may exist for other measures of pupil growth such as positive attitudes, creativity, memory tasks, and other kinds of educational outcomes (Flanders, 1970, p. 403).

Flanders elaborated this point with the suggestion that the use of simple bivariate relational procedures may grossly underestimate the complexity of valid functional relationships, which may be nonlinear depending upon the sample and the range of teacher behavior available in the sample. Furthermore, he argued that if there were a relatively narrow but high level of indirectness in some classrooms, the relationship between indirectness and student growth might be positive for some outcomes, negative for others, and a reverse-U for still others. This possibility has been demonstrated in one study (Soar, 1968) and strongly suggested in another study (Sprague, 1970). Although few studies exist on this question, there is the possibility that if a teacher moves to a high level of indirectness, this behavior will enhance student growth on some measures and depress student growth on others. This question needs further study.

Although arguments exist for the importance of a teacher choosing his own classroom transactions, there is a lack of data on the relationship between these desired transactions and transfer variables such as measures of student growth. In addition, it is possible that some modifications of teacher behavior may be negatively correlated with some outcome measures.

What then is the value of teachers studying their own behavior? Our position is that such training will not be productive unless transfer outcome measures such as reading comprehension, creativity, problem-solving skill and students' attitudes toward learning are included in the research design.

3. To Monitor Instructional Programs

One of the more important purposes of category systems is to monitor the implementation of educational programs. At least 15 category systems were developed to monitor the implementation of specific instructional programs. Four systems in *Mirrors* were developed to record the transactions of teachers and students within specific programs which stress individualized instruction or students working on different activities at the same time. There are: a) the system developed by Lindvall et al. (#12) for Individually Prescribed Instruction; b) the system developed by Honigman and Stephens (#48) focused mainly on the students; c) the two category systems for the Program for Learning in Accordance with Needs (PLAN), one for observing students (Lipe, Steen, & Quirk, #87) and one for observing teachers (Steen, Quirk, & Lipe, #92); and d) the two systems developed by Spaulding, one for observing students (#21) and one for observing teachers (#22).

Five systems in *Mirrors* were developed to monitor specific programs in science education (Altman, #28; Hunter, #49; Matthews & Phillips, #55 and #56; Balzer

& Evans, #81), and two were developed to monitor activities relevant to self-directed learning in science (McReL, #58; Anderson & Bingman, #80). Two systems were developed to monitor special programs in mathematics (Wright, #25; Wright & Proctor, #26), and two were developed to monitor specific social studies programs (Oliver & Shaver, #16; Taba, #23).

Ribble and Schultz developed a new category system to obtain data on the "congruence between a teacher's stated objective and the classroom behaviors the teacher chose to implement the objective" (#65, p. 1-4). This system appears to be another use of monitoring except that in this case the external criteria were the teacher's stated objectives rather than the objectives of the developers of a curriculum.

In addition to the category systems collected in *Mirrors,* other observational instruments have been developed to monitor specific educational practices and/or methods and materials packages (e.g., Hall, 1969; Moon, 1971; Resnick, 1971; J. Smith, 1970). Several questionnaires have also been developed to monitor programs. The Biology Classroom Activity Checklist, a questionnaire to be completed by students, was designed "to classify a teacher's practices according to the extent to which they conformed with the practices recommended in the Biological Sciences Curriculum Study literature" (Kochendorfer, 1967, p. 71). The Preschool Environment Inventory, a questionnaire to be completed by observers, was designed to embody the "Bank Street College view of what is salient in the education of young children" (Stern & Gordon, 1967, p. 1) and has been used to monitor instruction designed according to the Bank Street model.

Monitoring instructional implementation. The use of systems to monitor instruction in order to determine whether the intentions of the program developer are being implemented appears to be a valuable addition to the research literature. This concept is not new—Medley and Mitzel (1963) discussed the research of Wispé (1951), who used an observational system to monitor whether teachers were really conducting their classes in a "permissive" or "directive" manner—but the monitoring of specific instructional procedures is an excellent alternative to studies where one vague method is compared to another vague method (Wallen & Travers, 1963). Such procedures were used by Oliver and Shaver (1966) and by Rogers and Davis (1970).

Curriculum-materials programs are monitored to determine whether the instruction is implemented according to the program specifications or the intentions of the developers. Category systems or rating systems are used to focus upon the activities considered important for high implementation of the program. For example, in the Oral Language Program developed and disseminated by the Southwestern Cooperative Educational Laboratory (Olivero, n.d.; Reeback & Osterreich, 1971), performance standards were set for teachers using the program. The fidelity of teacher behavior to those standards was assessed by Quality Assurance Specialists who observed and rated teachers on an observational rating schedule designed for the program. Teachers who did not meet the standards could attend special in-service workshops, but "ultimately, if the teacher is unable or unwilling to perform, he or she will be asked to stop using the Oral Language Program" (Olivero, n.d., p. 8).

Similar monitoring to insure high implementation of the program has been part of at least two programs developed at the Southwest Regional Laboratory for Educational Research and Development. As part of the initial development of their First-Year Communication Skills Program, "observation was conducted to determine the extent to which the classroom instruction of the teachers...was consonant with the procedures prescribed in the teacher's manual.... SWRL observers recorded the instructional interaction using specially developed scales" (Niedermeyer, 1970, p. 2). As a result of the observational data, a new teacher-training procedure was developed to help the teachers learn program-specific behaviors as well as general instructional skills considered important for successful implementation of the program. The teacher training was followed by observation and subsequent modification of the teacher-training program.

Aside from monitoring the degree of implementation of a program, monitoring information is useful in instructional research in two ways. One is to determine the extent to which the variables considered important for implementation are related to measures of student growth. The research by Kochendorfer (1967) is regrettably the only example found in which such a relational study was undertaken. A second use of monitoring is to determine significant differences in student growth between programs which are well implemented and comparison situations. This research has occurred at the Southwest Regional Laboratory and the Southwestern Cooperative Educational Laboratory. As was suggested at the beginning of this chapter, the combination of both types of studies could be very useful in improving both the curriculum materials and the process of instruction.

The curriculum implementation monitoring practices of these laboratories—reported earlier within the context of the research on Head Start Planned Variation (Bissell, 1971)—are relatively new. Only a few other examples were found, and most of these were dated 1969 or later. Unfortunately none of the national curriculum programs five years old or older has developed and used descriptive instruments for monitoring curriculum implementation. The instrument developed for the Individually Prescribed Instruction program (Lindvall et al., #12) has not received extensive use; to date, results have been reported for only four classrooms (Lindvall & Cox, 1970). The student questionnaire developed by Kochendorfer (1967) has seldom been used to monitor implementation of the BSCS curriculum. The student questionnaire developed by J. Smith (1970) was designed to monitor implementation of the Earth Science Curriculum Project, and hopefully it is being used both for that purpose and for correlational and experimental studies.

Comparison monitoring. Investigators have used a variety of category systems to compare transactions in classes using special curriculums with transactions in other classes. Among studies of science programs few significant differences between programs were found in three studies (T. Evans, 1969; Hunter, 1969; Vickery, 1969), but highly significant differences were found in two studies (Moon, 1971; Moore, 1968). All of these investigators used category systems in their observations. Highly significant differences were found in two more comparison studies involving new science curriculums and using student questionnaires (Anderson, Walberg, & Welch, 1969; Kochendorfer, 1967). Few significant differences were found when category systems were used to compare instructional procedures in a mathematics program (Wright, 1967) and in an English program (Furst & Honigman, 1969). Other investigators analyzed variability among transactions *within* programs only. Significant differences were found among teachers in the same science program (Gallagher, 1970), and although the statistical significance of the differences was not analyzed, there was a strong trend favoring differences among teachers in a science program (Parakh, 1967) and in reading programs (Harris & Serwer, 1966; Harris et al., 1968).

In summary, a major advantage of category systems designed to monitor specific curriculum programs is that these systems can yield program-specific information which can be used to revise the operation of the program to conform to the intentions of the developers. When one wishes to compare the outcomes of Program A with those of Program B, category systems designed to monitor instructional programs can determine the extent to which Program A or B has been implemented in accordance with the intentions of the developers. If in practice the instructional activities within Program A represent low implementation of the program, it would be unreasonable to say that Program A has actually been implemented.

When descriptive systems are used to monitor implementation of a program, it is important that data be obtained on student growth in both the curriculum program and comparison groups. Without data on outcomes the researcher may assume that congruence between the instructions given to teachers and the actual activities in the classrooms assures the achievement of the expected student outcomes. In an evaluation report, Matthews & Phillips (1970) concluded on the basis of data collected using their category instrument that "classroom conditions considered desirable for child-structured learning can be established by techniques and materials associated with 'Science One'" (p. 17). Unfortunately such a statement implies that desirable conditions are equal to effective conditions. However it is absurd to expect a one-to-one relationship between desirable conditions and desirable outcomes. The next research steps should include studying the relationship between desirable conditions and desirable outcomes, and comparing the instructional activities and outcomes of one curriculum package with the instructional activities and outcomes of another one.

4. To Investigate Relationships Between Classroom Activities and Student Growth

Observational instruments in the fourth classification were developed expressly to study the relationships between classroom activities and measures of student growth. For example:

The purpose of this observational schedule is to gather some objective information concerning teacher-pupil behaviors which relate to pupil creative growth (Denny, #41, p. 1).

In addition to the category system developed by Denny, seven other category systems in *Mirrors* were developed to determine relationships between instructional activities (i.e., teacher and student behaviors as monitored by the category system) and student growth: Flanders (#5), Perkins (1965, #63, #64), Wallen et al. (#77), Bemis, Luft, and Liberty (#82), Morsh (#88) and Spaulding (#91). More than seven systems may exist, but one cannot tell by reading the articles collected in *Mirrors*.

The systems developed by Aschner and Gallagher (#3), Taba (#23) and Parakh (#62) might be added to the list, because these authors also conducted correlational studies using their systems and measures of student growth. However, the small number of classrooms studied and the use of students as the statistical unit of analysis suggest that the criteria for adequate statistical analyses were not met.

Two authors conducted experimental studies using their systems (Miller & Hughes, #14; Oliver & Shaver, #16), but again the use of students as the unit of analysis makes the results difficult to interpret.

In sum, how many authors developed a descriptive system and then attempted to validate the variables within the system by conducting a correlational or experimental study? Of the 73 classroom observational systems in *Mirrors,* there are seven clear cases in which authors conducted such studies, and five more cases in which the studies have marginal external validity. By the most generous criteria, 12 of the 73 systems have been used *by their developers* in a correlational or experimental study.

Apparently only one system in *Mirrors* has been used by both the author *and* other investigators in correlational and experimental studies—the system developed by Flanders (#5); this system has been used in more correlational and experimental studies than any other classroom observational instrument found to date (an early version of the Observation Schedule and Record [OSCAR, Medley & Mitzel, 1959]

which did not appear in *Mirrors,* has also been used by the authors and other investigators in correlational studies). At least seven systems not used in correlational or experimental studies by their authors were used in such studies by other investigators. These are the systems by Medley (#13), Smith, Meux, et al. (#19), Withall (#24), Brown (#36), Brown et al. (#37), and Ober (#61). The use of one in four of the systems in *Mirrors* in a study of student growth is encouraging; the fact that few of these systems have been used in more than one study is discouraging for the development of cumulative knowledge.

There have not been enough reviews of the results of correlational studies involving observational systems and measures of student growth. No review was found in which gain in creativity was the criterion, although classroom studies exist in this area (cf. Denny, 1968; Soar, 1966; Wallen, 1964; Wallen & Wodtke, 1963). A review in which student attitudes toward school, subject matter and/or teacher are the criterion measure(s) will be particularly difficult to write because several investigations have shown that such attitudes tend to *decrease* across a school year (cf. Flanders, Morrison, & Brode, 1968; Rhodes, 1971). One attempt has been made to gather all the correlational studies in which student achievement was the criterion measure (Rosenshine, 1971c), and the variables which yielded the most significant and/or consistent results across studies have been summarized separately (Rosenshine & Furst, 1971). As new studies appear and old studies are re-read, the significance of some of these variables will change. The variables below and the order in which they are presented represent a slight modification of the earlier summary (Rosenshine & Furst, 1971).

Correlational studies on teaching behavior and student achievement. Nine variables appear to have yielded the most significant and/or consistent results across the 50-odd studies in which naturally occurring behavior was related to measures of student growth (adjusted by regression for relevant pretest measures). These are:

1. *Clarity.* Teacher clarity, as assessed on rating scales by students or observers, yielded significant results in all seven studies in which the variable was used ($rs = 0.37$ to 0.71). Unfortunately, it is not clear just what is meant by clarity, and future investigators might well attempt to determine the more specific behaviors which comprise a high rating on clarity. "Organization" appears to be related to clarity, and ratings on "organization" may be influenced by the confusion and/or coherence in a lesson.

2. *Variability.* Rosenshine (1971c) placed a number of variables from different studies under the general terms "variability" or "flexibility." However, additional research needs to be done to determine whether this classification contains variables which are indeed related. Significant results ($rs = 0.24$ to 0.54) on at least one achievement measure were obtained in four separate studies in which observer or student questionnaires were used to determine the extent to which the teacher was "flexible in procedure" or "adaptable versus inflexible," or the amount of extra materials, displays and resource materials which were in the classroom. Significant results were also obtained in a study in which the observer counted the variety of materials, equipment, types of materials and variety of tests used; and in another study in which the teachers completed a daily checklist on the number of different materials and activities used during lessons.

Other investigators have used category systems to study whether teachers who used a greater variety of cognitive levels of discourse obtained greater achievement from their students. To date, significant results have been obtained in two of four studies.

3. *Enthusiasm.* The teacher's enthusiasm has been studied primarily through observer ratings on paired adjectives such as "dull versus stimulating," observer estimation of the teacher's "vigor and power," and student ratings of the teacher's involvement or excitement in the lesson. Such variables were found to be significantly related to at least one measure of student growth in all six studies in which such variables were used on questionnaires ($rs = 0.36$ to 0.62), and all nonsignificant results were in a positive direction. Significant results were also obtained in studies in which the teacher's movements, gestures and voice inflections were counted, but the specific cognitive components of enthusiasm are yet to be determined.

4. *Task-oriented and/or businesslike.* Teacher behavior which might be classified as task-oriented, achievement-oriented and/or businesslike has been assessed through student or observer rating scales in which teacher behavior was estimated as "evading versus responsible," or "erratic versus steady." Teachers were rated on these scales as to whether they emphasized the stimulation of thought or the acquisition of information and skills, and whether teachers were more concerned that students learn something than that they enjoy themselves. Significant results on at least one achievement measure were obtained in six of the seven studies in this area ($rs = 0.42$ to 0.61).

5. *Criticism.* Criticism by teachers and its effect on student achievement have been investigated in 17 correlational studies by counting the frequencies of general and specific forms of criticism. Significant, negative relationships were found in six of the studies ($rs = -0.38$ to -0.61). When only the direction of the relationship was considered, 12 of the 17 studies yielded negative correlations. When comparisons were made among types or intensities of criticism, the seemingly harsher type of criticism yielded a higher negative correlation in 10 of the 17 studies. In no study was there a significant correlation between mild forms of criticism (e.g., telling a student his answer was wrong, or providing academic directions) and student achievement.

6. *Teacher indirectness.* Teacher indirectness has usually been studied using the Flanders system (#5). Specific variables have included "use of student ideas," "praise plus use of student ideas," and the indirect/direct ratio, or a ratio of the behaviors "praise" plus "use of student ideas" to the behaviors coded as "giving directions" and "criticism." Significant results were seldom obtained, but positive correlations favoring "use of student ideas" were found in seven of eight studies ($rs = 0.17$ to 0.40), and positive correlations favoring a higher indirect/direct ratio were found in 11 of 13 studies ($rs = 0.12$ to 0.51).

7. *Student opportunity to learn criterion material.* A measure of the student's opportunity to learn the criterion material appears to have value not only as a correlate of student achievement, but also as a covariate in studies of student growth. Unfortunately this variable is difficult to measure. When it was measured by coding transcripts of lessons to determine the extent to which the criterion material was covered, the results were significant in both studies ($rs = 0.4$ to 0.5). However both studies were conducted in settings in which the total instructional time was 60 minutes or less; coding of typescripts seems unreasonable in settings in which instruction occurs for nine or 10 months of the year.

In a third study, when the coding was modified somewhat so that only the topics and subtopics in a common unit were coded, no significant relationship between the topics covered and student achievement was found.

Opportunity to learn has also been measured in studies of instruction for periods longer than four 60-minute sessions by asking the teachers to estimate the number of students who had the opportunity to learn each of the items on the criterion test (Husén, 1967), or by asking teachers to estimate the amount of emphasis they gave to 40 specific topics which were covered in a standardized reading test (e.g., locating places on maps and globes, identifying synonyms and antonyms for words in context) (Chang & Raths, 1971). In Husén's international study this procedure did *not* yield significant correlations within a country (although significant rank-order correlations were obtained across countries ($rs = 0.5$ to 0.9). Chang and Rath's procedure did discriminate between schools in which students were above average and below average on the Iowa Tests of Basic Skills. Thus, although the concept of opportunity to learn has been useful in studying transcripts, there has been insufficient research involving this variable when standardized achievement tests were used to measure student growth.

8. *Use of structuring comments.* Structuring statements which provide an overview for what is about to happen or has happened have been identified and counted at the start and end of lessons, and at the start and end of sequences of questions. Investigators used diverse definitions, but whatever the definition, significant results were obtained in all four studies in which structuring statements were counted. In three studies in which the students or observers rated the adequacy of the beginning *or* ending of the lesson, significant results were obtained ($rs = 0.35$ to 0.69). Although it is hazardous to group these seven studies under a common title, the results suggest that teacher use of structuring statements merits further study.

9. *Multiple levels of questions or cognitive discourse.* Only three studies were found in which the investigators classified questions (or cognitive discourse) into three or more levels and retained these classifications in the statistical analysis. Significant results were obtained in all three studies. It should be noted that when investigators have counted questions which they coded into only two types (e.g., factual versus "higher level"), significant results or trends have seldom been obtained. Similarly, when investigators have coded questions into

multiple types (or levels) but collapsed them into two forms for statistical analysis, significant results have seldom been obtained. Thus multiple classification of interactions according to cognitive level, and retention of the classifications in the statistical analysis, appear promising for future research.

Summary. At first glance the above list of the strongest findings may appear to represent educational platitudes. Their value can be appreciated, however, when they are compared to the equally virtuous and sensible behaviors which have *not* shown significant and/or consistent relationships with student achievement *to date.* These variables, taken from larger reviews (Rosenshine 1970c, 1971c), include nonverbal approval (counted), praise (counted), warmth (rated), the I/D ratio, or ratio of all indirect teacher behaviors (acceptance of feelings and ideas, praise and questions) to all direct teacher behaviors (lecture, directions and criticism) (counted), questions or interchanges classified into only two cognitive types (counted), student talk (counted) and student participation (rated).

Inspection of the list of findings shows that the most significant results have been obtained using rating scales, but not all items on either a rating scale or a category instrument have yielded significant or consistent results. In addition, there have been relatively fewer investigations in which cognitive aspects of instruction have been studied, and a predominance of concern with coding and rating affective variables. One would expect that when the criterion measure is student achievement, greater attention would be given to including instruments which focus upon cognitive interactions. Perhaps future investigators will use more of these readily available instruments.

Experimental studies. As yet there has been no review of experimental classroom studies in which descriptive instruments were used to monitor classroom activities, and in which measures of student growth were also obtained. It is difficult to estimate the number of experimental studies which exists. In a preliminary review of studies in which student achievement was the criterion (Rosenshine, 1970b), 15 studies were presented, and 15 to 20 additional studies have since been discovered. Reviews of other studies in which student attitudes, creativity, or other important outcomes were the criteria have not been found. Given the large number of workshops and in-service training programs which have been held to train teachers to modify their behavior in a variety of ways, and given the resources available to many regional educational laboratories which have conducted some of these workshops, it is unfortunate that the training has not been followed by experimental studies on student growth measures of interest in which the trained teachers served as the experimental group. Hopefully such studies will appear in the future.

The studies which have been collected dampen some of the correlational results described above (and in Rosenshine & Furst, 1971; and Rosenshine, 1971c). In six studies teachers were trained to use types of discourse which called for cognitive interactions on levels higher than fact stating. In all studies the observational results showed that the interactions of the experimental teachers were significantly different from those of the control teachers, although some of the teachers would not be considered high implementers of the desired procedure. In five of the six studies there were no significant differences on the measures of student achievement, even when the tests were constructed by the experimenters.

Six experimental studies were found in which teachers were trained to increase their use of praise and other positive behaviors, as well as to decrease their use of criticism and other negative behaviors. The teachers appeared to have implemented their training successfully and were different from the control group on relevant measures of classroom interaction. No significant differences in student achievement were found in five of the studies; the experimental teachers obtained significantly higher achievement in one study (Clark & Walberg, 1968).

The two studies in which student participation was manipulated and no significant differences were obtained were cited earlier (Church, 1971; Hughes, 1971).

Descriptive instruments appear to be particularly useful in the monitoring of experimental studies. Hopefully these instruments will be used in more of these studies, and the results will be made available to the educational audience.

Difficulties in Classifying Systems by Authors' Purposes

It is not enough to describe observational category systems on the basis of the authors' purposes. It is important to know the uses to which an instrument has been put. For example, the system developed by Flanders (#5) has been used extensively in teacher training, in research on student growth, and in describing teaching, and has also been used to monitor specific programs. The systems developed by Aschner and Gallagher (#3), Medley (#13), Smith (#19), Withall (#24), Brown (#36), Brown et al. (#37), and Ober (#61) have been used in studies of student growth by other investigators. More complete information about the uses to which any one system has been put is extremely difficult to find, but there does not seem to be any reason not to use any system for all four purposes.

The distinction between the category systems which are for teacher training and the ones which are descriptive is a tenuous one. Many training sessions consist only of teaching teachers how to use a system to code classroom activities. The four classifications used above may be an oversimplification. All category systems provide descriptive

data; hence, the systems that were labeled "descriptive" are in fact the ones which did not fit neatly into the other classifications of teacher training, student growth research or monitoring. Even this last sentence is inadequate. One would like to divide the category systems whose primary use has been descriptive into those which broke new ground in conceptualizing classroom interaction and those which represent only minor modifications of previous systems. But one cannot always make such a judgment on the basis of the available reports.

AN ASSESSMENT OF THE USE OF OBSERVATIONAL SYSTEMS TO STUDY TEACHING

The use of observational systems to study teaching will be assessed by first discussing the dominant purposes of the category systems in *Mirrors*, then commenting on the user's bias when interpreting descriptive results, and finally making some suggestions for cumulative research.

Dominant Purposes

Authors of category systems in *Mirrors* describe their purposes as follows:

To describe teaching	36 systems
To train teachers	11 systems
To monitor instruction	16 systems
To relate instruction to student growth	7 systems
Not classifiable	3 systems

There may be a parallel between this distribution of purposes for the classroom category systems and the cognitive activities which users of the category systems have noted in the classrooms they observed. Investigators have usually noted that the majority of classroom interactions was on the lowest cognitive levels (cf. Gall, 1970), such as fact stating, recalling and describing, and that relatively few interactions required the development of generalizations, relationships or evaluations using explicit criteria. One can agree with this observation and also note that most of the category systems were developed to describe classroom interaction or to give feedback to teachers—these purposes appear to be on low cognitive levels analogous to fact stating. In practice, the development of instruments for the analysis of teaching has come to mean no more than a description of some aspect of instruction along with an interpretation which objectifies the author's bias.

But description alone has not improved our understanding of functional relationships between classroom events and student growth. Only one system in 10 has been used by its author to discover relationships between instructional activities and student growth, or to test hypotheses by monitoring an experimental study or by implementing a curriculum package. At best, only one system in six has been used *by anyone* in a study involving student-growth measures.

Use of systems by others. Clear data on the use of these instruments by others are difficult to obtain. One estimation of use might be provided by counting the category systems which were included in the abstracts of papers presented at the 1970 and 1971 meetings of the AERA. Only six of the 73 systems in *Mirrors* were used in studies by investigators other than the author. These systems were: Aschner and Gallagher (#3), Bellack et al. (#4), Flanders (#5), Joyce (#11), Medley (#13) and McRel (#58). In contrast, the authors of at least 30 *new* systems presented papers in which their own observational systems were used to obtain descriptive data (no more than two or three of these new systems were validated by student-growth measures).

It appears that for every six systems that are written, only one author proceeds to do any correlational or experimental study involving student growth. In addition, for every investigator who uses an existing system for any purpose, five or six others write new, unvalidated systems.

Teachers Should . . .

When investigators develop observational systems to describe teaching, to monitor programs or to train teachers, the descriptive data collected are seldom treated as indifferent statistics. Certain biases, expressed as statements of "teachers should," are implicit or explicit in most of the reports. For example, investigators reporting their descriptive results may note a high percentage of interactions on the factual level and/or a low percentage on the evaluative level, and state that the evidence suggests teachers should learn to modify their behavior toward fewer factual interchanges. Although authors sometimes insist that their systems are descriptive and not prescriptive, the evidence of their reports has shown that certain variables become "dos" and others become "don'ts" fairly quickly (for an elaboration of the prescriptive nature of many descriptive systems, see Mitchell, 1969.)

A dramatic example of how a category system designed to provide relatively objective description can be translated into prescription was found in two articles on the Galloway system (#44), one by Galloway (1968) and the other by a supervisor (Lail, 1968) who used the system in teacher training and supervision. Galloway believed that "teachers convey information to students through non-verbal behavior" (Galloway, 1968, p. 172) and hoped that his instrument could help teachers "become more knowledgeable of non-verbal cues" (Galloway, 1968, p. 175) and of inconsistencies between their verbal and nonverbal behavior. In the report by Lail on the use of this instrument to describe the teaching of intern teachers, the descriptive picture available from this instrument acquired evaluative and prescriptive qualities. The following conclusions were based on data gathered with the system by Galloway:

Teacher A is a teacher who uses indirect methods in a rather mechanical way. Insofar as her verbal behavior goes, she is in a dismal rut. While she is trying to give pupils a sense of accomplishment, she is not succeeding. This teacher needs to learn to ask questions of a broader nature and to handle student responses in a different manner....

Teacher B . . . is bound by an inflexible mode of behavior. His major method is to ask a narrow question, followed by a student's answer, followed be either criticism or unconvincing praise, depending upon the factual correctness of the answer....

...How can Teacher C be helped to improve her teaching methods? Greater effort toward giving genuine praise and more use of pupils' ideas would make this teacher even more effective than she already seems to be (Lail, 1968, pp. 179–180).

Lail's language was extreme but refreshingly honest. The summary is a clear instance of judging descriptive data against one's own ideals of what should occur in a classroom.

A complete list of educational "shoulds" can only be guessed at, but at least three "shoulds" appear to be current. They are:

1. Teachers and students should be humane in their interactions with each other.
2. Classroom activities should be on higher cognitive levels, such as hypothesizing, evaluating, generalizing, synthesizing, comparing and contrasting.
3. Students should spend time initiating activities.

The reader may add, modify, and delete items as he chooses. The major point is that although an observational category system may provide neutral, objective description of classroom transactions, the people who interpret the data usually make judgments about effective teaching. At present the judgments can be only guesses about what is good, true and beautiful in classrooms—research in this area has barely begun.

Proving versus improving hypotheses. Much research time and money have been spent trying to prove the value of some of these gross "teacher shoulds." Arguing the importance of humane classrooms, interactions on higher cognitive levels, or student-initiated activities seems unproductive; the debates on good guys and bad guys have continued for years with scant empirical data. Observational systems appear to have been used more to document desired behavior than to test hypotheses. Those studies which used both observational systems and student-growth measures have tended to focus more on proving hypotheses than on probing the relationships between classroom events and student growth.

In place of studies attempting to prove that humane, warm or indirect teachers obtain more student learning than direct teachers, we hope for studies which attempt to improve our understanding of these gross variables. Instead of lumping all teacher criticism or all student talk into one variable, we hope for studies which probe the relationships of many types of teacher criticism to student growth, and many types of student talk to student growth. A few such studies have been conducted.

For example, from a larger sample of 150 high-school social studies teachers, Sprague (1970) selected a sample of 16 teachers who had indicated on a questionnaire that they spent 25 percent or more of their time discussing controversial issues. Direct observation confirmed that student talk occurred an average of 47 percent of the time (the students of the indirect teachers in Flanders's study [1965, p. 76] talked 27 percent of the time). Sprague did *not* compare achievement or attitudes in these classes with achievement or attitudes in less talkative classes; instead, she divided these 16 classrooms into three groups according to the type of student talk. Of the three groupings she established—1) expository, 2) student inquiry followed by probing student or teacher comments, and 3) student inquiry not followed by probes—the inquiry-probing situation appeared to be most functional for both student achievement and student attitudes, even though the sheer amount of student talk was not much different among the three groups.

Observational Instruments as Tools

Observational instruments offer the potential for categorizing and labeling instructional activities at different levels of specificity. If these instruments are seen as tools for testing hypotheses, perhaps the repetitions among the numerous, various systems will not seem so endless and we can hope to find which patterns of variables and methods of displaying classroom events are most useful for selection, modification and adoption in the studies which cycle through the correlational and experimental loop. Hopefully studies which contain outside criteria relating classroom phenomena to student growth will begin the development of cumulative knowledge which can improve the education of children.

METHODOLOGICAL ISSUES AND SUGGESTIONS

In this final section the emphasis is on methodological issues which have developed during the last 10 years, and on suggestions for refining observational systems and for designing and analyzing future correlational and experimental research. Many of the ideas are expansions of ideas from previous articles on this topic (cf. Amidon & Simon, 1965; Bellack, 1968; Davis & Tinsley, 1967; DeLandsheere, 1969; Flanders, 1970; Flanders & Simon, 1969; Furst, 1971; Gage, 1969; Hough & Duncan, 1970; Medley & Mitzel, 1963; Rosenshine, 1970a, 1970c; Rosenshine & Furst, 1971).

The earlier articles were written in the hope that observational instruments would be used in correlational and experimental studies where the criterion was student gain, and that such studies would embody a cycle of probing and refinement which would improve both instruction and student growth. Unfortunately this research has not been done to any great extent. Instead, as has been demonstrated, the major use of observational instruments has been to describe teaching and train teachers in skills of undocumented value. Such activities are necessary but not sufficient.

Educational Settings and Criterion Measures

Educational settings may be divided into four types: 1) traditional settings with relatively little control by the investigator over the type of materials or the method of instruction; 2) curriculum-materials packages in which the instruction is organized around specific materials or procedures such as the Biological Sciences Curriculum Study or the Bank Street model; 3) short-term units in which all teachers receive the same materials and directions but instruction takes place within regular classroom settings; and 4) semi-natural settings in which students are brought together specifically for the purpose of the study for a short period of time such as five minutes or four one-hour lessons.

The advantages and disadvantages of conducting research in different settings depends upon the research question being asked and the criterion measures being used. If one is interested in conducting correlational or experimental studies in which the criteria are measures of student growth, each setting may offer a unique contribution. However, if one is also interested in studying relationships between high-inference and low-inference variables, or in comparing observations made by an observer with those made by the students, then again each setting offers unique advantages.

Traditional settings. In the most frequently used setting for correlational studies, a standardized pretest (or pretests) is given to students in a number of classrooms at the start of a semester, observational information is obtained during the year, and a posttest is administered at the end of the year.

A major criticism of this design is that the skills sampled on these tests may not correspond to the skills which were taught in the classrooms. For example, the more widely used standardized reading tests in the elementary grades sample a child's ability to recognize and understand implied facts and relationships, to detect the main purpose of a paragraph or a selection, and to deduce the meaning of words or phrases from context (Chang & Raths, 1971). Although reading comprehension skills such as these comprise 50 percent of the usual reading test, the student may have spent relatively little time in class on these skills. Some teachers may have devoted most of the reading instruction time to teaching correct pronunciation, other teachers may have stressed reciting rules of syllabication, devising alternative endings to a story, or relating a story to everyday life. Differences such as these between the skills measured by the standardized tests and the skills stressed by different teachers may account for the claims of some teachers that the standardized tests are not "valid." (We might reverse the argument and question the "validity" of the skills selected by some teachers or emphasized in different instructional and/or curriculum packages.)

Even apparently similar standardized achievement tests have yielded different measures of class mean residual gain so that correlations between teacher behavior and student achievement were different with different instruments. For example, Snider (1965) used both the New York State Regents Exam and the Cooperative Physics Test as his criterion instruments, yet teacher behaviors related to residual gain measures on one instrument were not significantly related on the other. In another study (Chall & Feldmann, 1966) teacher ratings found to be significantly related to student achievement in reading on the Stanford Achievement Test were not significantly related to scores on the Fry Reading Test or the Gates Reading Test.

Currently we have the problem of teachers teaching for various goals, some or none of which may be related to the criterion test, and researchers trying to see which teacher behaviors are related to goals that neither the teachers nor the students perceive. However, alternative designs can be devised to obtain better congruence among the curriculum, the teachers' behaviors and the criterion instruments. These new designs focus on increasing the investigator's control over the teaching situation. The paradox is that the new situations may not represent naturally occurring teaching as it presently exists. Given the diverse goals of teachers, curriculum developers, students and test developers, no adequate procedures have yet been devised to study the relationship between instructional activities and student growth in the typical, fairly uncontrolled classroom situation.

Other settings. Administrative problems and the lack of similarity between instructional goals and criterion measures have led some investigators to modify the traditional settings by using curriculum-materials packages, short instructional units and/or ad hoc "classes" of students. These elements provide greater control over instructional content by supplying the materials and giving the teachers some examples of the criterion measures upon which they can focus the instruction. The entire instructional period can be observed and tape recordings can be made. Studies which include these elements offer an opportunity to focus attention upon specific aspects of the teacher's role, such as the ability to explain new material. Thus investigators do not have to contend with "noise" such as the teacher's managerial and disciplinary functions. In similarly controlled situations the teacher's managerial and disciplinary functions can be studied separately for their effects on learning and, after promising variables in these areas have been isolated, the entire instructional procedure can be studied.

However, a move to situations which provide greater control and/or reduced focus does *not* solve two problems. First, in the modified situation, although the criterion has been changed, the problem of the relevance of standardized achievement tests to instruction has not been solved; it has been avoided by substituting different tests. Second, if greater control of cognitive interactions is provided, affective outcomes are still uncontrolled. Teachers may still be teaching for attitudes A, B, and C very well, although their class is being tested on attitudes X, Y, and Z. Perhaps the study of more than one outcome at a time in these modified settings is inappropriate.

A concern for specificity and control of the instructional setting has been incorporated in a number of studies in which the instructional period ranged from 15 minutes to eight one-hour lessons (e.g., Flanders, 1965, 1970; Furst, 1967; Rosenshine, 1971b; Wright & Nuthall, 1970). These studies have been summarized in the overview of relational studies above, and specific information on each study is available elsewhere (Rosenshine, 1971c). Surprisingly, the correlation coefficients and F-ratios on variables in these studies were not higher than the ones obtained on similar variables studied in less controlled, traditional settings.

One can only speculate on why stronger results have not been obtained in these more controlled studies. Perhaps there has been insufficient focus and control. For example, when the relevance of the instructional interaction to the criterion test was investigated in two of these studies (Rosenshine, 1971b; Shutes, 1970), the results were positive and significant ($rs = 0.4$ to 0.5). In a third study (Bellack et al., 1966) wide variation existed in the content covered across classes. In two studies (Fortune, Gage & Shutes, 1966; Rosenshine, 1971b) the teach-

ers were given half the posttest items before instruction, yet there was no difference in student achievement between the items given and the ones which were withheld. Apparently providing teachers with identical materials and telling them something about the cognitive posttest do not insure the adequate coverage of the content.

Even if the instructional setting is controlled, it is still important to be concerned with the types of cognitive processes which the teachers will use. In one short-term study (Wright & Nuthall, 1970) the teachers were given outlines of the material to cover each day and were told that the test would be factual. Yet some teachers asked open-ended questions or responded to student answers with a further question designed to raise the cognitive level of the student response. Thus, in a well-designed study, even though teachers were told that the tests would be on skills X, Y, and Z, some teachers taught skills A, B, and C.

Additional control in these more focused studies would be possible if the teachers' behavior were stabilized through training so that the observed behavior is a more accurate reflection of the teachers' intentions or the intentions of those who prepared the instructional material. Curriculum developers and teacher educators would have to work together on this problem, or curriculum experts will continue to develop instructional packages without clearly specifying teacher behaviors, and teacher educators will continue to train teachers in teaching skills without clearly specifying the instructional situations in which they will be used.

Stabilizing teacher behavior raises questions about the likely decrease in variation across teachers on the variables of interest. Only two studies have been located in which the variables observed were ones in which the teachers had received extensive training (Baker, 1969; Siegel & Rosenshine, 1972). Surprisingly, significant correlations between some of the variables of interest and measures of student growth were obtained in both studies ($rs = 0.3$ to 0.9) despite the fact that almost all the teachers received high observer ratings on the specific behaviors. Further studies in this area are needed, but these two studies suggest that even after training there may remain significant variability across teachers on behaviors of interest. Another procedure for studying the effects of stabilizing teacher behavior would be to use a comparison group of teachers who did not receive this specific training.

The main advantage in conducting correlational studies in short-term settings in which teachers are using common materials may be that the audio-tape and video-tape recordings of total instructional activities can be made available for study by various investigators. The main disadvantage of such studies may be that the procedures used to increase the internal validity also limit the external validity, or generalizability of the results to typical classroom settings.

Selection of Variables

Four suggestions are offered for the selection of variables in future studies: 1) use of variables available in existing observational category systems and rating systems, 2) use of a greater variety of variables, 3) use of high-inference and low-inference variables together, and 4) use of more variables derived from laboratory studies. It is most important to test *all* variables using the criteria of student learning.

(1) Using variables from existing observational systems. It is not difficult to select a large number of variables for use in an observational instrument because more than 200 category systems and more than 200 rating instruments are readily available. Although many of the variables in different instruments duplicate or overlap each other, a large pool of variables for observing instruction exists. This pool is greatly enlarged when we consider the variety of units of measurement and contexts into which these variables may be coded. Given the large number of existing variables and the small number of published studies, it seems appropriate to test these variables against measures of student learning before developing additional observational instruments.

(2) Using a greater variety of variables. Classroom observational systems which focus on cognitive interactions have been developed, but few researchers have used these systems to determine which cognitive variables are related to measures of student achievement. More research on cognitive variables seems warranted. Variables which have been used in correlational studies and which should be studied more thoroughly include subdivision of questions, probing responses to student answers, variation of activities and of the cognitive level of discourse, and use of structuring statements. The variable, opportunity to learn criterion material, as measured by teacher self-reports, has also been correlated with student achievement. The inclusion of this variable in an observational instrument may prove to be valuable.

Several other cognitive variables have seldom been included in descriptive instruments or used as part of correlational or experimental studies. These variables include the relevance of the materials to the ability of the class, the amount of time a teacher spends preparing a class to do future classwork, the procedures a teacher uses to assign and respond to homework, the textbooks and supplementary materials, the organization of major sections of the lesson and the sequencing of these sections, the sequencing of activities through the school year, the cognitive learning style of individual students, and the influence of the school environment. In fact, most of the cognitive variables which are discussed in textbooks on educational psychology and teaching methods have not been included in observational systems or in classroom research.

The study of a larger variety of variables

can also be accomplished by the use of more complex category systems for coding classroom events. Some existing category systems make distinctions between discussion and laboratory periods, but further subdivisions within these categories have rarely been made. Current observational instruments disregard the materials being read, the assignments students write, the teacher's use of written or oral material, and the physical features of the room, such as seating arrangements and lighting. These additional classroom events and characteristics might be profitably incorporated as variables in research on student growth. Suggestions for coding concurrent events were discussed previously in the section on procedures for coding.

(3) Using high-inference and low-inference variables together. Variables such as clarity, task orientation and enthusiasm are high-inference items which have not been specified as denotable, countable behaviors. Yet they have greater predictive validity than most low-inference items. One probable reason for the lack of specificity in these variables is that investigators have seldom used *both* high-inference and low-inference measures in the same study to discover, for example, which specific behaviors comprise a high rating on clarity or enthusiasm.

The use of both high-inference and low-inference items in future studies may be profitable. Rating scales allow a student or observer to process many cues before he makes a decision, whereas someone using a category system would not be able to perform such processing. At the same time, the low-inference category systems provide specific details which would not be available to an investigator using only high-inference measures. One way to combine the two observational procedures would be to use student questionnaires as the source of the high-inference measures and tape recordings of the instructional period as the source of the low-inference measures.

(4) Using variables from laboratory research. The lack of common variables between laboratory and classroom research may exist because studies of instruction in classrooms have focused on instruction mediated by a teacher, whereas studies in laboratories have not. In effect, two separate disciplines are being developed to study meaningful human learning—one contains a minimum and the other a maximum of verbal interaction. Although some overlap exists between the two disciplines in areas such as reinforcement and feedback, there has been little attempt to combine the two. Occasionally bridges are built. Nuthall (1968) used programmed materials to investigate the effects of classroom instructional strategies identified by Smith and Meux (1970), and Worthen (1968) designed a study to test whether the laboratory studies on discovery learning could be replicated in a natural classroom setting. Perhaps more variables developed in the laboratory will be applied to classroom research and vice versa. For example, many of the ideas on "test-like events" could be used in correlational and experimental classroom research.

Summary. In discussing the variables used in observational systems, Travers (1971) emphasized the importance of deriving variables for observational systems from experimentation rather than inspiration. He suggested that it might be profitable to study teaching using data-based variables such as those developed by Piaget, by Guilford, by investigators of information processing, and by investigators of achievement motivation.

It seems prudent to be suspicious of variables which do not have any data base. As the section on sources has shown, few of the variables which are included in observational systems developed to describe teaching have a data base. However, one cannot consider data-based variables from settings other than classrooms as prescriptions for teacher behavior; rather, they form hypotheses for correlational and experimental studies in the classroom.

At the same time, some variables have a fairly strong data base within classroom instruction. As mentioned above, variables such as clarity, enthusiasm and task orientation have excellent correlational data bases from classroom studies. It is quite possible that as research continues, a number of data-based variables which are relevant to education will be developed in studies in school settings. Soar suggested this possibility as he discussed some preliminary findings from his instructional research within the Follow Through Planned Variation program. He noted that "at this point the theory from which we derive our hypotheses can provide general direction, but it is too primitive to focus us very sharply" (Soar, 1971, p. 7). He also claimed that in his analyses to date, factors which have emerged as powerful predictors of student learning describe aspects of classroom interaction for which there is relatively *little theoretical expectation*.

By the term *theory* Soar apparently meant the logically and empirically developed discoveries on the instructional variables which facilitate student growth. The theory was probably derived from research at steps 1, 2 and 3 in Hilgard's paradigm. However, as one moves to steps 4, 5 and 6, new, unanticipated variables emerge. As soon as these new variables are validated and refined against measures of student learning in both correlational and experimental classroom studies, the variables and the interrelationships among them will contribute to a technology of instruction. However, the proliferation of observational systems without validation against measures of student growth has led to the current chaos which is a pretense of research.

Various Methodological Issues

A number of methodological issues in this type of research have been discussed elsewhere (cf. Biddle, 1967; Flanders, 1970; Flanders & Simon, 1969; Gage & Unruh, 1967; Mitchell, 1969; Rosenshine, 1970a,

1970c; Rosenshine & Furst, 1971). Some recent developments and some issues which have received comparatively little attention follow.

Identifying sequences of instructional events. When a category scale (but not a sign or rating scale) is used, it is possible to record events sequentially and to use the information in data analysis. In one study the sequencing of events was logically constructed as part of the category system (Wright & Nuthall, 1970). When coding from transcripts the investigators created separate categories for teacher questions which a student answered after the first "teacher utterance," after "two utterances," and after "two or more utterances," and the correlations with achievement obtained for each type were significantly different.

Two empirical procedures for identifying sequences are now available. Flanders (1965) introduced matrix recording for displaying events as dyads, and Amidon and Flanders (1967) and Flanders (1970) discussed the inspection of a matrix to identify larger dominant sequences of events. Collet and Semmel (1971) have developed a computer program to isolate recurring category chains of any specified length as well as to identify precedent and consequent families of chains. In addition, the computer program provides for the potential identification of nonfunctional categories within chains. The number of chains (including chains derived from multidimensional systems) which can be identified appears to be limited only by the capacity of the computer. Another attempt to describe the sequence of classroom events was made by Bellack et al. (1966) when they combined their pedagogical move categories with teaching cycles and used Markov chaining techniques to analyze the cycle occurrences.

Systems specific to subject matter. Although several systems have been developed for specific subject areas, almost all of these systems can be used in other subject areas.

This point was discussed elsewhere (Rosenshine, 1970a), and the statement remains generally true for observational systems found after the 1970 review. For example, an investigator wrote that although the Instrument for the Analysis of Science Teaching was developed for the observation of teaching behaviors in elementary-school classrooms using *Science—A Process Approach*, "after the initial development of the IAST, the instrument was found to be applicable ... in curriculum areas other than science and in other levels of education as well" (Hall, 1969, p. 3).

However, since the 1970 review, two multidimensional category systems were found which contain a dimension truly specific to a subject area. The system developed by Moore (1968) was designed to determine the extent to which high-school physics teachers were exhibiting behaviors consistent with the Physical Sciences Study Committee (PSSC) objectives and with non-PSSC objectives. Moore developed eight objectives unique to PSSC physics and six objectives unique to non-PSSC physics. These objectives are included as the fourth dimension of a multidimensional system, and the content of each observed interaction is coded as to whether it is congruent with a PSSC objective, a non-PSSC objective, or none of the objectives. This procedure of developing a dimension for the objectives of a specific curriculum is unique and can be useful to future investigators. Hopefully this technique will be used with existing observational systems.

Another investigator (Tannenbaum, 1970) developed a multidimensional system which contains two dimensions specific to reading instruction. In the first dimension each interaction is coded under one of four basic skills (e.g., language analysis, reading comprehension), and in the second dimension each basic skill is subdivided into five to seven subskills. Thus language analysis was divided into consonants, vowels, vocabulary, word structure and syntax, and appropriate subdivisions were made in the second di-

mension for reading-comprehension activities. The third dimension coded the grade level of the materials being used. This use of two subject-area dimensions and a grade-level dimension could easily be added to existing category systems (or sign systems). The procedures for developing truly subject-specific dimensions used by Moore and by Tannenbaum also seem useful for monitoring students' opportunities to learn. If observers determine that little time is being devoted to the subskills of reading comprehension, and if students do poorly on standardized tests of reading comprehension, then perhaps it is the instruction which is not "valid."

Issues in reliability. Even within the limited area of classroom observational instruments the term *reliability* has been given several meanings. Therefore an effort will be made to avoid the term itself but to describe three types of evidence usually associated with reliability.

Observer agreement is the most common form of reliability, and issues in this area have been discussed by Mitchell (1969). He noted that the agreement coefficient is usually based on whether two (or more) observers were similar in their tally of *total events* of each type, but agreement is seldom based on whether *each event* was coded the same way by the observers. This problem may become acute if investigators interested in the sequencing of events use matrix cells or clusters of cells in their analyses when the coefficient of observer agreement is based solely upon column (or event-type) totals. A second problem, which might be labeled *inter-investigation agreement,* occurs when different investigators use the same observational system. An important question is whether different investigators, all of whom used the Aschner-Gallagher system (#3), for example, also used the same ground rules to code "divergent questions" or "convergent questions." If the ground rules are different across different investigations, then the problem of inference becomes serious.

Medley and Mitzel (1963, pp. 309–321) argued against using measures of observer agreement as the sole estimation of reliability and presented a detailed exposition of methods for determining whether a behavior differentiated across classes (or situations). They argued that although two coders could agree on the number of factual questions a teacher asks, these frequency counts would have little predictive value if all teachers were similar on this behavior. Without information on whether a variable differentiates across classrooms, it is difficult to interpret reports which contain nonsignificant correlations with a measure of student growth. McGaw, Wardrop, and Bunda (1972) have refined Medley and Mitzel's procedures and have discussed means of measuring differentiation in situations where teacher behavior is expected to vary, as in the variable flexibility (Flanders, 1969). At the same time, it seems inappropriate to delete some variables from an observational instrument even if they do not differentiate across classrooms; data on teacher praise or student attention to task are still important for describing what is going on in classrooms.

A third type of reliability, "representativeness," has received relatively little study. Insufficient attention has been given to determining whether a sample of observed classroom transactions is a trustworthy representative sample of total behavior. Decisions to make two, four or more observations on each teacher in a study have little empirical basis. Limited available data (Emmer & Peck, 1971; Moon, 1971) indicate that the intraclass coefficient (reliability for *individual* teachers across visits) is not particularly high for individual cognitive or affective variables, and these coefficients depend upon the variable being observed ($rs = 0.0$ to 0.7).

The importance of representativeness depends upon the purpose of the study. If the purpose is to compare the behaviors of one *group* of teachers with the behaviors of another group, then the number of observations necessary to obtain a representative group mean may be small. But if the purpose is to relate instructional activities in individual classes to outcomes obtained in these classes, then the problems of representativeness are perplexing and in need of further study.

The potential influence of the observer(s) is an additional problem in determining the representativeness of a classroom observation. Teacher behavior that occurs when an observer is present may or may not be similar to what occurs when an observer is not present. One study has been completed in which 10 teachers were observed during scheduled observation periods and unscheduled periods, and the teachers did not know when classroom verbal interaction was being recorded (Samph, 1969). The results showed differences in teacher behavior across these observation conditions. However, ethical considerations will probably preclude replications of this study. Even if investigators obtained teacher permission to activate a microphone whenever they wished, one would still wonder whether the teachers and students would behave differently if there were no microphone.

An issue not yet discussed is the point at which various measures of reliability must be obtained. If an author of an observational instrument has a set of hypotheses or variables which he considers important, he would spend his time most profitably by first determining the predictive validity of the variables and *then* attempting to train others to observe events according to his categories. The predictive validity may diminish or increase as soon as reliable observational data are used in a statistical analysis, but at least the researcher would know whether the variables are worth studying. Many writers of observational instruments reverse these two steps; they obtain observer agreement and neglect the study of predictive validity.

Frequently writers of dissertations in the field of classroom interaction have limited time and resources which prohibit the gathering of both types of data. When these limits apply, we advocate the collection of data on validity without the reliability data, so long as audio- or video-tape recordings accompany the report. Then these materials could be placed in a data bank, and measures of observer agreement and subsequent reanalyses could be made by other researchers.

Data analysis. There are four issues in determining the relationships between instructional activities and measures of student growth (or gain scores): selecting variables for analysis, adjusting posttest scores, stratifying the sample and using various procedures for determining the existence of functional relationships.

(1) Selecting variables for analysis. It is easier to develop an instrument than to analyze all the data that an instrument can generate. Even a relatively simple, 10-category system like Interaction Analysis (Flanders, #5) can yield many variables which could be correlated with student growth. Hundreds of variables can be selected from the 100-cell matrix by using single cell frequencies, combining cell frequencies, or forming ratios of one set of cells to another. If an investigator expanded the simple system by subdividing all or some of the categories, he could easily obtain a 42 x 42 cell matrix which would yield thousands of variables for analysis. When multidimensional systems are used (e.g., Bellack et al., #4; Gallagher et al., #7), and each "move" or "topic" is coded with four or five digits, each of which represents a dimension, then the number of discrete variables becomes as large as or larger than the number which can be obtained using a one-dimensional system with dyadic coding.

Investigators have usually made a priori selections of single cells, clusters of cells, combinations of categories, and ratios of categories, and have analyzed only these variables. The number of variables which has been statistically analyzed is conservative compared to the number of variables available. For example, although Flanders and Soar both used the 10-category Flanders matrix (#5) to code classroom behavior, Flanders (1970) selected only 15 variables, and Soar (1966) selected only 39 variables for statistical analysis.

This conservatism is understandable because, as the number of variables increases, the risk of spuriously significant results also increases. Cross-validation of results is one solution to this problem. Whether statistically significant results are obtained in a single study is not as important as whether the results are consistent across a series of studies. If researchers cross-validated their results as a matter of course, the concern about "false positives" would be obviated; spurious results should fall out across the studies.

One consequence of conservatism in selecting variables for analysis is the danger that investigators will lose or ignore potentially useful data. For example, the data available from many behavioral units often are reduced to a single variable, such as a composite or ratio, for analysis. Perhaps ratios, composites, and factors are better predictors of student gain than any of their components, but this possibility has seldom been tested empirically.

The problem of losing potentially useful data through the combination of a number of variables into ratios, composites or clusters might be overcome by conducting a two-step analysis. In the first step the investigator could develop his hypotheses and parsimoniously select a limited number of variables for statistical analysis. In the second step hundreds of variables could be formed from the data and subjected to analysis. For instance, in the second step, an investigator using the Flanders system could analyze every cell, combinations of cells from the matrix or an expanded matrix, every cell and combination of cells that includes Category 3 (use of student ideas), and a variety of estimations of indirectness, directness and ratios of the two. The important question in such post hoc analyses is whether any of these new variables predict student achievement as well as or better than the variables chosen originally. These analyses could be conducted by the original investigator, or by other researchers if sufficient data were presented in the complete report. If the post hoc analyses revealed that certain variables were better predictors than the ones originally selected, the correlational importance of these new findings could be cross-validated by reanalyzing the data from another study.

The danger of finding false positives through this two-step method is decreased by emphasizing cross-validation of results, and by considering correlational research to be only one part of the series of research efforts in a descriptive-correlational-experimental loop. A major purpose of correlational studies is to obtain consistently "strong" variables which can be further tested and refined within experimental settings. As was noted above in the section on results obtained in classroom experimental studies, some of the variables found to be consistently positive and/or significant in correlational studies have not held up in experimental studies to date.

(2) *Adjusting posttest scores.* Although regression procedures have been used to adjust posttest scores for measures of initial standing, the computational procedures and the variables selected as covariates have differed from study to study. Just which covariance procedures or other statistical procedures are most appropriate to adjust posttest measures for initial standing has been a topic of considerable recent discussion (cf. Coats, 1966; Cronbach & Furby, 1970; Lord, 1963, 1969; Wallen & Wodtke, 1963). No guides are available yet to plan an adequate statistical design to adjust for differences among classes in initial standing, or even to determine the most meaningful covariates.

One likely, but frequently overlooked, covariate is "opportunity to learn." In studies in natural settings, classes have been treated as if all students had equal opportunity to learn criterion material. The "opportunity to learn criterion material" has been assessed by asking the teachers to estimate the percentage of students in their class who had an opportunity to learn material of the type illustrated by each test item (Husén, 1967). A similar procedure was used to assess the amount of emphasis teachers gave to various topics within the instructional program (Chang & Raths, 1971). They divided the items on the Iowa Tests of Basic Skills, Form 1, into skill classifications and converted these skill classifications into questionnaire items. Items included "deducing the meaning of words from context," "identifying and recognizing implied facts and relationships," "how to carry tens in addition," and "comparing distances of yards, feet, and inches." Twenty questionnaire items were randomly selected from the pool of items corresponding to test questions which differentiated the children in two schools; 20 nondiscriminating items were also selected. Teachers were asked to rate the amount of emphasis they had given to each item during the year and to score the items from 1 (very little emphasis) to 4 (very much emphasis). Across the two schools teacher responses on the 20 discriminating items were significantly different, but they were not different on the 20 nondiscriminating items.

The effectiveness of the procedures developed by Chang and Raths (or modifications of the procedures) is still to be determined in other samples. Can they be adapted to other skill areas such as the application of biological laboratory principles? Are the procedures useful in correlational designs as well as analyses of variance? Is there substantial correspondence among teacher reports, student reports and observer reports of the skills stressed? Studying these questions seems more important than creating yet another category system or training teachers in a skill of dubious effectiveness.

When short-term studies are conducted

the transcripts or recordings of the entire sessions can be inspected to estimate the extent to which the instructional material was covered. But whether a measure of opportunity to learn is best used as a covariate, a stratifying variable or a dependent variable remains to be determined. Research on this question is lacking.

(3) Other statistical procedures. An alternative method for statistically analyzing classroom events was suggested by Gage and Shutes (Shutes, 1970). They suggested developing a scoring scheme for hierarchical teacher behaviors. For example, a hierarchy might be developed in which the relevance of the instruction to the criterion test is considered first, then the cognitive level of the interactions, and then the affective level of the interactions. High positive affective behaviors by the teacher might not influence student cognitive growth if the instruction is not relevant to the test and if the cognitive level of the interactions is low; to account for this possibility, the scoring scheme would give less weight to teacher affective behaviors. These same ideas could be used to establish multiple cutoff points, so that teachers are eliminated from the sample at the point where they fail to meet certain instructional criteria, such as coverage of content or feedback to students on the correctness of their responses. The usefulness of the cutoff points could be determined by correlating the order in which teachers were eliminated with the student gain measure(s).

It is also possible that certain teaching behaviors are variously effective for different content and objectives and for different students. Unfortunately, few studies have been designed to give this information. Some investigators are beginning to approach these concerns. Grannis (1971) suggested using matrix arrangements to display classroom observational data in terms of the congruence between two constructs. For example, one matrix contains types of knowledge organization (traditionally prescribed, rationally prescribed, and constructed) on one side, and the same constructs for the classroom social order on the other side. In this procedure the diagonal of the matrix represents the hypothesized optimal blend of the two constructs. The analysis would then determine whether teachers who are coded as being on the diagonal for the two constructs have classes which gain more than the classes of teachers who are various distances from the diagonal. Grannis and his associates created a large number of matrices representing different constructs, and they use them as part of classroom observation and data analysis.

(4) Analysis of subgroups. Despite the doctrine of individual differences in education, studies still have been designed as if one set of instructional behaviors were effective for all students. Almost all the experimental and correlational studies have focused upon the relationship of teacher behavior to the *class mean.* Few investigators have focused on the personality or learning style of subgroups of learners, or have stratified classes according to the initial knowledge or aptitude of the students. (For a discussion of analyses of main effects and interaction effects, see Walberg, 1970. For an example of the study of subgroups within a class, see Anderson, 1970.)

(5) Alternative procedures to obtain the same ends. To date the analysis of data has been based on the assumption that there is just one set of effective instructional behaviors. Perhaps a variety of instructional procedures exists for attaining the same educational goals. These behaviors may differ in overt properties and thus may be coded differently by an observer, but they may engender the same implicit behaviors in students. Consider a simple example in which Teacher A provided a summary of the class discussion, pointing out the contributions of each student, and Teacher B asked a student or students to provide the summary. Under the conventions of most category or sign systems, the behaviors of

the two teachers would be coded differently. Perhaps the behaviors are different, but they might be equally functional.

For example, teacher probing of student responses might be equivalent to the use of student ideas; homework questions requiring higher level processing might be equivalent to the higher level teacher questions in classroom interactions; requiring students to respond at frequent intervals might be equivalent to class discussion and frequent questions; teacher disapproval which is followed by eliciting student clarification of what the student said might be equivalent to teacher use of student ideas. These comparisons have not been made. Similarly, various composites of specific behaviors may account for a high rating given to a teacher on high-inference variables such as clarity or enthusiasm.

One approach to determining whether seemingly different instructional activities yield the same outcomes can be illustrated by a two-factor analysis of variance design. Suppose that one variable of interest was the use of summary statements by the teacher at the end of an episode, and that the sample of teachers was stratified as high, middle and low on this variable. A second variable of interest might be the frequency of questions requiring interpretation; the teachers could be classified as high, middle and low on that variable. The residual gain scores on outcomes of interest would be entered as the cell scores, and the research question would be which cells (or combinations of cells) contained particularly high and low residual gain scores. In effect, the design could show functional and dysfunctional combinations of behaviors which might be obscured in a one-way multivariate analysis of variance or a discriminate analysis. This approach need not be limited to two variables, nor to analysis of variance. (For an approach to this problem using regression, see Walberg, 1971.)

This approach was used by Conners and Eisenberg (1966) when they classified 38 Head Start teachers as high or low according to the number of interactions coded as focusing upon intellectual activity, and classified them again according to the number of interactions coded as emphasizing property and materials. The gain scores were entered in the cells. There were no differences between teachers classified as high on intellectual activity and low on property and materials, or teachers classified as low on both variables. However, teachers who were low on intellectual activities and high on emphasis of property and materials obtained gain scores which were grossly below the teachers in the other cells. If the analysis had been limited to whether the frequency of intellectual activities discriminated among teachers on the gain measure, then the results clearly would have favored high frequencies of intellectual activities. When the two-way analysis was made, the results suggested that teachers who were low on the frequency of intellectual activities and also low on property and materials had apparently found a successful alternative procedure to enhance student learning (unfortunately this alternative procedure was not described in the report).

Collections of Data, Materials and Tests

A researcher who wanted to follow the suggestions made in this chapter would likely have problems in obtaining suitable instructional materials and instruments to measure outcomes, and would probably encounter administrative difficulties in obtaining observational records of instructional activities and scores on the outcome measures. Suggestions for the creation of data banks, materials banks and test banks are offered to assist students and others who would like to conduct empirical studies but are uncertain how to proceed.

Data bank. A data bank would be a collection of studies in which classroom transactions were available in the form of audio tapes, video tapes and/or transcripts, and pretest and posttest scores were supplied for all classrooms which participated in the study. Users and developers of observational systems could take a study from the data bank, code the instructional transactions using the system they had chosen or developed, and then determine which variables and dimensions of their system yielded functional relationships between the frequency of occurrence of behaviors or sequences of behaviors and various measures of student growth. By using a series of studies, developers of a new system could validate, refine and cross-validate their system until they learned which variables and combinations of variables were most predictive of student growth. In addition, one could compare existing systems for predictive validity. Any number of existing systems of different variables and different forms could be tested in this manner.

The idea is not unique, not even to education. The *Standard Test Lessons* developed in 1925 by McCall and Crabbs served as the data bank for the validation of the major readability formulas constructed in the 1940s. Data for a bank exist in many correlational studies in which the transactions were recorded on audio tape or video tape; unfortunately, little use has been made of the data. A few investigators saw this opportunity: Furst (1967) used the classroom tapes and class mean achievement measures which had been collected by Bellack et al. (1966) to code both cognitive and affective variables; Hiller, Fisher, and Kaess (1969) applied a new analysis to the lectures collected by Gage et al. (1968); Rosenshine, Crill, and McAdams (1971) tested the predictive validity of one set of gross categories and subdivided categories using the materials made available from the study by Wright and Nuthall (1970). Most authors of new systems have not sought existing materials to test the predictive validity of their systems; perhaps they will be more likely to do so if existing materials and new materials are gathered, documented, and made available for distribution from a single location.

The closest approximation of a data bank was developed by Flanders (1969), in which matrices, achievement data and attitude data for five studies were gathered; any investigator can reanalyze the matrices and cross-validate the findings across studies. However in those studies the coding was done live, so that any reanalysis would be limited to the data which Flanders retained. The data on transactions and student growth measures in a bank need not be limited to naturally occurring instructional activities. Data from experimental studies (e.g., Carline, 1970; Millet, 1969; Rogers & Davis, 1970) could also be included.

Materials bank. There is a need for a bank of instructional materials and criterion tests associated with the materials which assess student attainment of various cognitive, attitudinal and personal outcomes. Materials can be collected for instruction at various grade levels. The materials can range in length from short packets for five- or fifteen-minute instructional sessions, to the pamphlet and tests prepared by Bellack et al. (1966) for instruction in four one-hour periods, to the materials and tests prepared by Flanders (1965) for two weeks of instruction, to the six-week instructional unit prepared by Worthen (1968). A materials bank can also include the units written for some of the national curriculum programs. Davidoff (1970) and LaShier and Westmeyer (1967) both used materials and criterion tests from the BSCS curriculum.

The materials in the curriculum packages could be used in experimental studies in teacher-training programs to help validate the skills being taught to in-service and pre-service teachers. Validating training skills is important because many of these behaviors seldom appear in natural classroom settings. In addition, these experimental studies themselves will generate more observational records and outcome data to be contributed to the data bank.

An existing materials bank is described in Chapter 7.

Test bank. One of the most consistent complaints in education has been about the scarcity of tests or situations to measure student growth on outcomes of interest, particularly on outcomes other than those assessed by standardized achievement tests. At the same time, many seemingly excellent tests have seldom been used, modified or normed. The tests on affective goals which are illustrated throughout the *Taxonomy of Educational Objectives: Affective Domain* (Krathwohl, Bloom, & Masia, 1964) seldom appear in the research studies of those who decry standardized achievement tests. A test on student sensitivity to social issues which also appears to contain items on critical thinking (Taba & McGuire, 1942) has lain dormant since the test was constructed. A seemingly excellent test on the ability to ask questions in the social studies (Wallen, Durkin, Fraenkel, McNaughton, & Sawin, 1969) has not been used even by those who claim that questioning is an important skill.

Fortunately, since 1970 efforts have been made to collect these unpublished tests and to publicize them. The ERIC Clearinghouse in Tests and Measurements is collecting many of these instruments and making bibliographies available. For example, an annotated bibliography of tests of self-concept was developed in conjunction with the ERIC Clearinghouse in Early Childhood Education (Coller & Guthrie, 1971). The Center for the Study of Evaluation prepared a list of more than a hundred major goals of elementary education, categorized all published standardized tests in terms of which objective they most closely met, and evaluated each test on a number of criteria in terms of appropriateness for grades 1, 3, 5 and 6 (Hoepfner et al., 1970). A second volume provided the same evaluation of preschool and kindergarten tests (Hoepfner, Stern, & Nummedal, 1971). When these published and unpublished tests have been assembled in various centers, investigators will have much easier access to these valuable, necessary tools of research.

Summary. Surprisingly, neither the data bank nor the materials bank has been developed to date. Not only have many people suggested the creation of banks, but many people already have deposits to make. It is an idea whose time came at least by 1967.

The data bank appears to be essential for validating and refining the myriad observational systems which are being developed, and all three banks will make it possible to begin the sharing of ideas and the cooperation of psychologists, curriculum developers and classroom researchers which Hilgard envisioned. Without a data bank to validate and refine observational systems, we will remain bound to the assertions of observational category system developers; with a data bank, we might be able to develop cumulative knowledge. Without a data bank, many of the ideas suggested in this chapter and in other articles are useless. A data bank, a materials bank and a test bank will provide the tools which system developers and teacher educators can use to validate and refine their "shoulds."

THE ETERNAL NOTE OF SADNESS (ARNOLD, 1848)

It is possible that the patterns of effective teaching for different ends are so idiosyncratic that they will never be isolated; it is possible that studying teaching in natural settings is unproductive because the settings are not functional for the desired outcomes; it is possible that descriptive systems and research within the descriptive-correlational-experimental loop will be unproductive; it is also possible that linear and nonlinear curriculum approaches and the monitoring of these approaches will be unproductive. At the moment there has not been enough research to make any firm statement about any of these concerns.

Until the reward system in American research circles changes, until regional educational laboratories engage in testing their assumptions about the mirrors of behavior instead of publishing 17 volumes of them, until educators concern themselves with improving rather than proving hypotheses, and until we stop getting letters from colleagues who indicate more interest in statistics than students when they say ". . . it is more fruitful for us to sharpen our categories and make the coding reliable than to try to explore the subtleties of what makes one or two teachers outstanding. . .", we shall not learn the answers.

REFERENCES

Amidon, E. J., & Amidon, P. *Skill development in teaching work manual.* Minneapolis, Minn.: Association for Productive Teaching, 1969.

Amidon, E. J., & Flanders, N. A. The effects of direct and indirect teacher influence on dependent-prone students learning geometry. *Journal of Educational Psychology,* 1961, 52, 286–291.

Amidon, E. J., & Flanders, N. A. *The role of the teacher in the classroom.* Minneapolis, Minn.: Association for Productive Teaching, 1967.

Amidon, E. J., & Hough, J. B. (Eds.) *Interaction analysis: Theory, research, and application.* Reading, Mass.: Addison-Wesley, 1967.

Amidon, E. J., & Simon, A. Teacher-pupil interaction. *Review of Educational Research,* 1965, 35, 130–139.

Anderson, G. J. Effects of classroom social climate on individual learning. *American Educational Research Journal,* 1970, 7, 135–152.

Anderson, G. J., & Walberg, H. J. Class climate and group learning. *International Journal of Educational Sciences,* 1968, 2, 175–180.

Anderson, G. J., Walberg, H. J., & Welch, W. W. Curriculum effects on the social climate of learning: A new representation of discriminant functions. *American Educational Research Journal,* 1969, 6, 315–328.

Arnold, M. Dover Beach. Paper presented at the meeting of the National Aesthetic Research Association, London, June 1848. (Laleham, England: Parish Yard.)

Baker, E. L. Relationship between learner achievement and instructional principles stressed during teacher preparation. *Journal of Educational Research,* 1969, 63, 99–102.

Belgard, M., Rosenshine, B., & Gage, N. L. The teacher's effectiveness in explaining: Evidence on its generality and correlation with pupils' ratings and attention scores. In I. Westbury & A. Bellack (Eds.), *Research into classroom processes.* New York: Teachers College Press, 1971. Pp. 182–191.

Bellack, A. A. Methods for observing classroom behavior of teachers and students. Paper presented to the conference on Methods of Determining Criteria for the Evaluation of Comprehensive Schools, sponsored by Padagogisches Zentrum, Berlin, November 1968. ED 040 113.

Bellack, A. A., Kliebard, H. M., Hyman, R. T., & Smith, F. L., Jr. *The language of the classroom.* New York: Columbia University Press, 1966.

Biddle, B. J. Methods and concepts in classroom research. *Review of Educational Research,* 1967, 37, 337–357.

Bissell, J. S. *Implementation of planned variation in Head Start. I. Review and summary of the Stanford Research Institute interim report: First year of evaluation.* Washington, D.C.: U.S. Department of Health, Education, and Welfare, Office of Child Development, 1971.

Bloom, B. S. (Ed.) *Taxonomy of educational objectives, the classification of educational goals, handbook I: Cognitive domain.* New York: David McKay, 1956.

Caldwell, B. M., & Honig, A. S. Approach, a procedure for patterning responses of adults and children: Coding manual. Unpublished manuscript, undated. Little Rock: University of Arkansas, Center for Early Development and Education.

Carline, J. L. *An investigation of the relationship between various verbal strategies of teaching behavior and achievement of elementary school children.* (Doctoral dissertation, Syracuse University) Ann Arbor, Mich.: University Microfilms, 1970. No. 70-10,327.

Chall, J. S., & Feldmann, S. C. *A study in depth of first-grade reading—An analysis of the interactions of professed methods, teacher implementation, and child background.* U.S. Office of Education Cooperative Research Project No. 2728. New York: The City College of the City University of New York, 1966. ED 010 036.

Chang, S. S., & Raths, J. The schools' contribution to the cumulating deficit. *Journal of Educational Research,* 1971, 64, 272–276.

Church, R. J. The effects of systematic changes in standard four science lessons. *Educational Research Newsletter,* 1971, 4, 15–30.

Clark, C. A., & Walberg, H. J. The influence of massive rewards on reading achievement in potential urban school dropouts. *American Educational Research Journal,* 1968, 5, 305–310.

Coats, W. D. *Investigation and simulation of the relationships among selected classroom variables.* U.S. Office of Education Research Project No. 6-8330. Ann Arbor: University of Michigan, 1966. ED 029 170.

Coller, A. R., & Guthrie, P. D. *Self-concept measures: An annotated bibliography.* Head Start Test Collection, ERIC Clearinghouse on Tests and Measurements. Princeton, N.J.: Educational Testing Service, 1971. ED 051 305.

Collet, L. S., & Semmel, M. I. The analysis of sequential behavior in classrooms and social environments: Problems and proposed solutions. Paper presented at the meeting of the American Educational Research Association, New York, February 1971. (Ann Arbor: College of Education, University of Michigan.)

Conners, C. K., & Eisenberg, L. *The effect of teacher behavior on verbal intelligence in Operation Headstart children.* U.S. Office of Economic Opportunity Headstart Contract No. 510. Baltimore, Md.: Johns Hopkins University School of Medicine, 1966. ED 010 782.

Cronbach, L. J., & Furby, L. How we should measure "change"—or should we? *Psychological Bulletin,* 1970, 74, 68–80.

Davidoff, S. H. The development of an instrument designed to secure student assessment of teaching behaviors that correlate with objective measures of student achievement. Paper presented at the meeting of the American Educational Research Association, Minneapolis, March 1970. ED 039 170.

Davis, O. L., Jr., & Tinsley, D. C. Cognitive objectives revealed by classroom questions asked by social studies student teachers. *Peabody Journal of Education,* 1967, 45, 21–26.

DeLandsheere, G. *Comment les maitres enseignent: Analyse des interactions verbales en classe.* Liège, Belgium: Ministere de L'education Nationale et de la Culture, 1969.

Dell, D., & Hiller, J. E. Computer analysis of teachers' explanations. In I. Westbury & A. Bellack (Eds.), *Research into classroom processes.* New York: Teachers College Press, 1971. Pp. 209–217.

Denny, D. A. Identification of teacher-classroom variables facilitating pupil creative growth. *American Educational Research Journal,* 1968, 5, 365–383.

Dopyera, J., & Lay, M. *Assessing the program environments of Head Start and other preschool children: A survey of procedures.* Addendum to Final Report to Office of Economic Opportunity, Head Start Evaluation and Research Contract #OEO 4120. Syracuse, N.Y.: Syracuse University, 1969.

Emmer, E. T., & Peck, R. F. Dimensions of classroom behavior. Paper presented at the meeting of the American Educational Research Association, New York, February 1971. ED 052 224. (Research and Development Center for Teacher Education, University of Texas at Austin.)

Evans, E. D. *Contemporary influences in early childhood education.* New York: Holt, Rinehart and Winston, 1971.

Evans, T. P. A category system for teacher behaviors. *American Biology Teacher,* 1969, 31, 221–225.

Flanders, N. A. *Teacher influence, pupil attitudes, and achievement.* U.S. Office of Education Cooperative Research Monograph No. 12, OE-25040. Washington, D.C.: Government Printing Office, 1965.

Flanders, N. A. *Teacher influence patterns and pupil achievement in the second, fourth, and sixth grade levels.* U.S. Office of Education Project No. 5-1055. Ann Arbor, Mich.: University of Michigan, School of Education, 1969. 2 vols.

Flanders, N. A. *Analyzing teaching behavior.* Reading, Mass.: Addison-Wesley, 1970.

Flanders, N. A., Morrison, B. M., & Brode, E. L. Changes in pupil attitudes during the school year. *Journal of Educational Psychology,* 1968, 50, 334–338.

Flanders, N. A., & Simon, A. Teacher effectiveness. *Classroom Interaction Newsletter,* 1969, 5, 18–37.

Fortune, J. C. *A study of the generality of presenting behaviors in teaching pre-school children.* Unpublished manuscript, University of Massachusetts, 1967. ED 016 285.

Fortune, J. C., Gage, N. L., & Shutes, R. E. The generality of the ability to explain. Paper presented at the meeting of the American Educational Research Association, Chicago, February 1966. (Amherst: College of Education, University of Massachusetts)

Furst, N. F. The multiple languages of the classroom. Paper presented at the meeting of the American Educational Research Association, New York, February 1967. (Philadelphia, Pa.: Temple University, College of Education)

Furst, N. F. Systematic classroom observation. In L. Deighten (Ed.), *Encyclopedia of education.* New York: Macmillan, 1971. Pp. 168–183.

Furst, N. F., & Honigman, F. K. A study of pupil-teacher interaction in experimental communications courses compared with traditional junior high school classes. Paper presented at the meeting of the American Educational Research Association, Los Angeles, February 1969. (Philadelphia, Pa.: Temple University, College of Education)

Gage, N. L. Paradigms for research on teaching. In N. L. Gage (Ed.), *Handbook of research on teaching.* Chicago: Rand McNally, 1963. Pp. 91–141.

Gage, N. L. Teaching methods. In R. L. Ebel (Ed.), *Encyclopedia of educational research.* (4th ed.) New York: Macmillan, 1969. Pp. 1446–1458.

Gage, N. L. Tools of the trade: An approach to enhancing the teacher's ability to make a difference. In *How teachers make a difference.* U.S. Office of Education, Bureau of Educational Personnel Development. Washington, D.C.: U.S. Government Printing Office, 1971.

Gage, N. L., et al. *Explorations of the teacher's effectiveness in explaining.* Technical Report No. 4. Stanford, Calif.: Stanford University, Stanford Center for Research and Development in Teaching, 1968. ED 028 147.

Gage, N. L., & Unruh, W. R. Theoretical foundations for research on teaching. *Review of Educational Research,* 1967, 37, 358–70.

Gall, M. D. The use of questions in teaching. *Review of Educational Research,* 1970, 40, 707–721.

Gallagher, J. J. A "topic classification system" for classroom observation, and Three studies of the classroom. In *Classroom observation.* American Educational Research Monograph No. 6. Chicago: Rand McNally, 1970. Pp. 30–73, 74–108.

Galloway, C. M. Nonverbal communication. *Theory Into Practice,* 1968, 7, 172–175.

Grannis, J. C. Autonomy in learning: An exploration of pupils' and teachers' roles in different classroom environments to develop criteria and procedures for evaluation in project Follow Through. Second Progress Report. Unpublished manuscript, 1971. (New York: Institute for Pedagogical Studies, Teachers College, Columbia University)

Guilford, J. P. The structure of intellect. *Psychological Bulletin,* 1956, 53, 267–293.

Hall, G. E. *The instrument for the analysis of science teaching: A system for measuring teaching behavior.* Austin, Texas: University of Texas, Research and Development Center for Teacher Education, 1969. ED 041 843.

Harris, A. J., Morrison, C., Serwer, B. L., & Gold, L. *A continuation of the CRAFT project comparing reading approaches with disadvantaged urban negro children in primary grades.* Cooperative Research Project No. 5-0570-2-12-1. New York: City University of New York, Division of Teacher Education, 1968. ED 010 297.

Harris, A. J., & Serwer, B. L. *Comparison of reading approaches in first-grade teaching with disadvantaged children (the CRAFT project).* Cooperative Research Project No. 2677. New York: City University of New York, Division of Teacher Education, 1966. ED 010 037.

Hilgard, E. R. A perspective on the relationship between learning theory and educational practices. In E. R. Hilgard (Ed.), *Theories of learning and instruction.* The Sixty-third Yearbook of the National Society for the Study of Education, Part I. Chicago: NSSE, 1964. Pp. 402–415.

Hiller, J. H., Fisher, G. A., & Kaess, W. A computer investigation of verbal characteristics of effective classroom learning. *American Educational Research Journal,* 1969, 6, 661–675.

Hoepfner, R., and others. *CSE elementary school test evaluations.* Los Angeles: University of California, Graduate School of Education, Center for the Study of Evaluation, 1970.

Hoepfner, R., Stern, C., Nummedal, S. G., and others. *CSE-ECRC preschool/kindergarten test evaluations*. Los Angeles: University of California, Graduate School of Education, Center for the Study of Evaluation, 1971.

Hough, J. B., & Duncan, J. K. *Teaching: Description and analysis*. Reading, Mass.: Addison-Wesley, 1970.

Hughes, D. C. The effects of certain conditions of pupil participation and teacher reacting on the achievement of form 2 pupils. *Educational Research Newsletter*, 1971, 4, 12–14.

Hunter, E. Talking in first grade classrooms. *Urban Review*, 1969, 4, 39–43.

Hunter, E. Some reasons for modifying existing category systems. *Classroom Interaction Newsletter*, Spring 1970, 6, 17–23.

Husén, T. (Ed.) *International study of achievement in mathematics: A comparison of twelve countries*. Vol. 2. New York: John Wiley, 1967.

Kent, L. Student evaluation of teaching. *Educational Record*, 1966, 47, 376–406.

Kliebard, H. M. Dimensions of meaning in classroom discourse. *Journal of Teacher Education*, 1966, 17, 233–244.

Kochendorfer, L. H. The development of a student checklist to determine classroom teaching practices in high school biology; Classroom practices of high school biology teachers using different curriculum materials; and Use of the biology classroom activity checklist in identifying specific classroom practices of individual teachers and students. In A. E. Lee (Ed.), *Research and curriculum development in science education: 1. The new programs in high school biology*. Austin, Texas: University of Texas, Science Education Center, 1967. Pp. 71–78, 79–84, 85–89.

Krathwohl, D. R., Bloom, B. S., & Masia, B. B. *Taxonomy of educational objectives, the classification of educational goals, handbook II: Affective domain*. New York: David McKay, 1964.

Lail, S. S. The model in use. *Theory into Practice*, 1968, 7, 176–180.

LaShier, W. S., Jr., & Westmeyer, P. The use of interaction analysis in BSCS laboratory block classrooms. *Journal of Teacher Education*, 1967, 18, 439–446.

Lindvall, C. M., & Cox, R. C. *The IPI evaluation program*. American Educational Research Association Monograph No. 5. Chicago: Rand McNally, 1970.

Lord, F. M. Elementary models for measuring change. In C. W. Harris (Ed.), *Problems in measuring change*. Madison: University of Wisconsin Press, 1963. Pp. 21–38.

Lord, F. M. Statistical adjustments when comparing preexisting groups. *Psychological Bulletin*, 1969, 72, 336–337.

Matthews, C. C., & Phillips, D. G. Child-structured learning in science in the Atlanta Public Schools January-February, 1969. Unpublished manuscript, 1970. (Tallahassee, Fla.: Florida State University, Department of Science Education)

McCall, W. A., & Crabbs, L. M. *Standard test lessons in reading: Teacher's manual for all books*. New York: Columbia University Teachers College, Bureau of Publications, 1925.

McGaw, B., Wardrop, J. L., & Bunda, M. A. Classroom observation schemes: Where are the errors? *American Educational Research Journal*, 1972, 9, 13–27.

Medley, D. M., & Hill, R. A. Dimensions of classroom behavior measured by two systems of interaction analysis: OSCAR and Flanders. *Educational Leadership*, 1969, 26, 821–824.

Medley, D. M., & Mitzel, H. E. Some behavioral correlates of teacher effectiveness. *Journal of Educational Psychology*, 1959, 50, 239–246.

Medley, D. M., & Mitzel, H. E. Measuring classroom behavior by systematic observation. In N. L. Gage (Ed.), *Handbook of research on teaching*. Chicago: Rand McNally, 1963. Pp. 247–328.

Millet, G. B. Comparison of four teacher training procedures in achieving teacher and pupil "translation" behaviors in secondary school social studies. Paper presented at the meeting of the American Educational Research Association, Los Angeles, February 1969. ED 027 256.

Miltz, R. J. Development and evaluation of a manual for improving teachers' explanations. Unpublished doctoral dissertation, Stanford University, 1971.

Mitchell, J. V., Jr. Education's challenge to psychology: The prediction of behavior from person-environment interactions. *Review of Educational Research,* 1969, 39, 695–721.

Moon, T. C. A study of verbal behavior patterns in primary grade classrooms during science activities. *Journal of Research in Science Teaching,* 1971, 8, 171–177.

Moore, J. R. An analysis of teacher and pupil verbal behavior and teacher procedural and evaluative behavior in relation to objectives unique to PSSC and non-PSSC physics curricula. Paper presented at the meeting of the National Association for Research in Science Teaching, Chicago, February 1968. (Ypsilanti, Mich.: Eastern Michigan University)

Morsh, J. E. *Systematic observation of instructor behavior.* Development Report No. AFPTRC-TN-56-52. San Antonio, Tex.: Air Force Personnel and Training Research Center, Lackland Air Force Base, 1956.

Morsh, J. E., Burgess, G. G., & Smith, P. N. *Student achievement as a measure of instructor effectiveness.* Project No. 7950, Task No. 77243. San Antonio, Tex.: Air Force Personnel and Training Research Center, Lackland Air Force Base, 1955.

Niedermeyer, F. C. *Developing exportable teacher training for criterion-referenced instructional programs.* Inglewood, Calif.: Southwest Regional Laboratory for Educational Research and Development, 1970. ED 040 164.

Nuthall, G. A. An experimental comparison of alternative strategies for teaching concepts. *American Educational Research Journal,* 1968, 5, 561–584.

Nuthall, G. A. Teacher verbal behaviour and pupil learning. Unpublished manuscript, 1971. (Christchurch, New Zealand: University of Canterbury, Department of Education)

Nuthall, G. A., & Lawrence, P. J. *Thinking in the classroom.* Wellington: New Zealand Council for Educational Research, 1965.

Oliver, D. W., & Shaver, J. P. *Teaching public issues in the high school.* Boston, Mass.: Houghton Mifflin, 1966.

Olivero, J. L. *Developing the oral language program.* Albuquerque, N.Mex.: Southwestern Cooperative Educational Laboratory, undated. ED 041 861.

Parakh, J. S. A study of teacher-pupil interaction in high school biology classes: Part II.

Description and analysis. *Journal of Research in Science Teaching,* 1967–68, 5, 183–192.

Perkins, H. V. Classroom behavior and underachievement. *American Educational Research Journal,* 1965, 2, 1–12.

Pinney, R. H. Presentational behaviors related to success in teaching. (Doctoral dissertation, Stanford University) Ann Arbor, Mich.: University Microfilms, 1970. No. 70–10,552.

Ragosta, M. N., Soar, R. S., Stebbins, L. B., & Soar, R. M. Sign versus category: Two instruments for observing levels of thinking. Paper presented at the meeting of the American Educational Research Association, New York, February 1971. (Gainesville: Institute for Development of Human Resources, College of Education, University of Florida)

Reeback, R. T., & Osterreich, H. *Progress report on the oral language program.* Albuquerque, N.Mex.: Southwestern Cooperative Educational Laboratory, 1971.

Resnick, L. B. Teacher behavior in an informal British infant school. Paper presented at the meeting of the American Educational Research Association, New York, February 1971. (Pittsburgh: University of Pittsburgh)

Rhodes, F. Team teaching compared with traditional instruction in grades kindergarten through six. *Journal of Educational Psychology,* 1971, 62, 110–116.

Rogers, V. M., & Davis, O. L. Varying the cognitive level of classroom questions: An analysis of student teachers' questions and pupil achievement in elementary social studies. Paper presented at the meeting of the American Educational Research Association, Minneapolis, March 1970. (Lexington, Ky.: University of Kentucky)

Rosenshine, B. Evaluation of classroom instruction. *Review of Educational Research,* 1970, 40, 279–300. (a)

Rosenshine, B. Experimental classroom studies of teacher training, teaching behavior, and student achievement. Unpublished manuscript, 1970. (Urbana, Ill.: Bureau of Educational Research, University of Illinois) (b)

Rosenshine, B. *Interpretative study of teaching behaviors related to student achievement.* Final report, U.S. Office of Education Project No. 9-B-010. Philadelphia: Temple University, 1970. ED 051 116. (c)

Rosenshine, B. New directions for research on teaching. In *How teachers make a differ-*

ence. U.S. Office of Education, Bureau of Educational Personnel Development. Washington, D.C.: U.S. Government Printing Office, 1971. (a)

Rosenshine, B. Objectively measured behavioral predictors of effectiveness in explaining. In I. Westbury, & A. Bellack (Eds.), *Research into classroom processes*. New York: Teachers College Press, 1971. Pp. 51–98. (b)

Rosenshine, B. *Teaching behaviors and student achievement*. Windsor, Berkshire, England: National Foundation for Educational Research in England and Wales, 1971. (c)

Rosenshine, B., Crill, E., & McAdams, R. Empirical validation of a new category system: One example. Paper presented at the meeting of the American Educational Research Association, New York, February 1971. ED 052 138.

Rosenshine, B., & Furst, N. F. Research on teacher performance criteria. In B. O. Smith (Ed.), *Research in teacher education: A symposium*. Englewood Cliffs, N.J.: Prentice-Hall, 1971. Pp. 37–72.

Ryans, D. G. *Characteristics of teachers, their description, comparison, and appraisal*. Washington, D.C.: American Council on Education, 1960.

Samph, T. Observer effects on teacher behavior. Paper presented at the meeting of the American Educational Research Association, Los Angeles, February 1969. (Syracuse, N.Y.: Center for the Study of Teaching, Syracuse University)

Shulman, L. S. Reconstruction of educational research. *Review of Educational Research*, 1970, 40, 371–396.

Shutes, R. E. *Verbal behaviors and instructional effectiveness*. (Doctoral dissertation, Stanford University) Ann Arbor, Mich.: University Microfilms, 1970. No. 70–1603.

Siegel, M. A., & Rosenshine, B. Teacher behavior and student achievement in the DISTAR program. *Chicago Principals Reporter*, 1972, 62, 24–28.

Simon, A., & Boyer, E. G. (Eds.) *Mirrors for behavior: An anthology of classroom observation instruments*. Vols. 1–6. Philadelphia: Research for Better Schools, 1967. ED 029 833.

Simon, A., & Boyer, E. G. (Eds.) *Mirrors for behavior: An anthology of classroom observation instruments*. Vols. 7–14 and *Summary*. Philadelphia: Research for Better Schools, 1970. ED 031 613. (a)

Simon, A., & Boyer, E. G. (Eds.) *Mirrors for behavior: An anthology of classroom observation instruments*. Supplementary Vols. A and B. Philadelphia: Research for Better Schools, 1970. ED 042 937. (b)

Smith, B. O., & Meux, M. O. *A study of the logic of teaching*. Urbana, Ill.: University of Illinois Press, 1970.

Smith, J. P. The development of a classroom observation instrument relevant to the earth science curriculum project. Paper presented at the meeting of the National Association for Research in Science Teaching, Minneapolis, March 1970. (Seattle: College of Education, University of Washington) ED 037 372.

Snider, R. M. *A project to study the nature of effective physics teaching*. U.S. Office of Education Cooperative Research Project No. S-280. Ithaca, N.Y.: Cornell University, 1965. ED 003 826.

Soar, R. S. *An integrative approach to classroom learning*. Final Report, Public Health Service Grant No. 5-R11 MH 01096 and National Institute of Mental Health Grant No. 7-R11-MH 02045. Philadelphia: Temple University, 1966. ED 033 749.

Soar, R. S. Optimum teacher-pupil interaction for pupil growth. *Educational Leadership Research Supplement*, 1968, 26, 275–280.

Soar, R. S. Advantages of multiple systems over a single system. Paper presented at the meeting of the American Educational Research Association, New York, February 1971. (Gainesville: Institute for Development of Human Resources, College of Education, University of Florida)

Soar, R. S. An empirical analysis of selected Follow Through programs: An example of a process approach to evaluation. In I. J. Gordon (Ed.), *Early Childhood Education*. The Seventy-first Yearbook of the National Society for the Study of Education. Chicago: NSSE, 1972.

Sobol, F. T. A model teacher observation system. Unpublished doctoral dissertation, Stanford University, 1971.

Solomon, D., Bezdek, W. E., & Rosenberg, L. *Teaching styles and learning*. Brookline, Mass.: Center for the Study of Liberal Education for Adults, 1963. ED 026 556.

Spaulding, R. L. *Achievement, creativity, and*

self-concept correlates of teacher-pupil trans-actions in elementary schools. Cooperative Research Project No. 1352. Hempstead, N.Y.: Hofstra University, 1965. ED 024 463.

Sprague, N. F. Structure and process of inquiry into social issues in secondary schools. Vol. 3. Social issues classroom discourse: A study of expository, inquiry-nonprobing, inquiry-probing classes. Ann Arbor, Mich.: University of Michigan, 1970. ED 052 124.

Steele, J. M., House, E. R., & Kerins, T. An instrument for assessing instructional climate through low-inference student judgments. American Educational Research Journal, 1971, 8, 447–466.

Stern, V., & Gordon, A. Development of observation procedures for assessing preschool classroom environment. Head Start Evaluation and Research Center. Progress reports of research studies 1966 to 1967. Document 4, 1967. (New York: Research Division, Bank Street College of Education) ED 021 626.

Taba, H., Levine, S., & Elzey, F. F. Thinking in elementary school children. U.S. Office of Education Cooperative Research Project No. 1574. San Francisco: San Francisco State College, 1964. ED 003 285.

Taba, H., & McGuire, C. Evaluation of social sensitivity. In E. R. Smith, & R. W. Tyler (Eds.), Adventure in American education. Vol. 3. New York: McGraw-Hill, 1942. Pp. 157–244.

Tannenbaum, A. J. The taxonomic instruction project: An introduction to taxonomic instruction. U.S. Office of Education Cooperative Research Project Nos. 6-2528, 7-1295, 422273. New York: Columbia University Teachers College, Research and Demonstration Center for the Education of Handicapped Children, 1970.

Travers, R. M. W. "The limitation of variables derived from common language." In Perspectives on recent research, American Educational Research Association Cassette Tape Series. Washington, D.C.: AERA, 1971.

Unruh, W. R. The modality and validity of cues to lecture effectiveness. In I. Westbury, & A. Bellack (Eds.), Research into classroom processes. New York: Teachers College Press, 1971. Pp. 191–201.

Vickery, R. L. An examination of possible changes of certain aspects of teacher behavior resulting from adoption of individ-ualized laboratory centered instructional materials. (Doctoral dissertation, The Florida State University) Ann Arbor, Mich.: University Microfilms, 1969. No. 69–13,288.

Walberg, H. J. Predicting class learning: An approach to the class as a social system. American Educational Research Journal, 1969, 6, 529–542.

Walberg, H. J. A model for research on instruction. School Review, 1970, 78, 185–200.

Walberg, H. J. Generalized regression models in educational research. American Educational Research Journal, 1971, 8, 71–91.

Wallen, N. E. Relationships between teacher characteristics and student behavior—Part II. U.S. Office of Education Cooperative Research Project No. 2096. Salt Lake City: University of Utah, Department of Educational Psychology, 1964. ED 001 257.

Wallen, N. E. Relationships between teacher characteristics and student behavior—Part III. U.S. Office of Education Cooperative Research Project No. 2628. Salt Lake City: University of Utah, 1966.

Wallen, N. E., Durkin, M. C., Fraenkel, J. R., McNaughton, A. H., & Sawin, E. I. The Taba curriculum development project in social studies: Development of a comprehensive curriculum model for social studies for grades one through eight inclusive of procedures for implementation and dissemination. Final report. U.S. Office of Education, Bureau of Research, Project No. 5-1314, Grant No. OE-6-10-182. San Francisco: San Francisco State College, 1969. ED 040 106.

Wallen, N. E., & Travers, R. M. W. Analysis and investigation of teaching methods. In N. L. Gage (Ed.), Handbook of research on teaching. Chicago: Rand McNally, 1963. Pp. 448–505.

Wallen, N. E., & Wodtke, K. H. Relationships between teacher characteristics and student behavior—Part I. U.S. Office of Education Cooperative Research Project No. 1217. Salt Lake City: University of Utah, 1963. ED 001 250.

Wispé, L. G. Evaluating section teaching methods in an introductory course. Journal of Educational Research, 1951, 45, 161–186.

Withall, J. The development of a technique for the measurement of social-emotional climate in classrooms. Journal of Experimental Education, 1949, 17, 347–361.

Worthen, B. B. A study of discovery and expository presentation: Implications for teaching. *Journal of Teacher Education,* 1968, 19, 223–242.

Wright, C. J., & Nuthall, G. A. Relationships between teacher behaviors and pupil achievement in three experimental elementary science lessons. *American Educational Research Journal,* 1970, 7, 477–491.

Wright, E. M. J. *Teacher-pupil interaction in the mathematics classroom, a sub-project report of the Secondary Mathematics Evalu-* ation Project. Technical Report 76-5. St. Paul, Minn.: Minnesota National Laboratory, Minnesota State Department of Education, 1967.

Zahorik, J. A. Classroom feedback behavior of teachers. *Journal of Educational Research,* 1968, 62, 147–150.

Zahorik, J. A. Teacher verbal feedback and content development. *Journal of Educational Research,* 1970, 63, 419–423.

CHAPTER 6

Techniques of Observing Teaching in Early Childhood and Outcomes of Particular Procedures

IRA J. GORDON
University of Florida

R. EMILE JESTER
University of Florida

Our search of research literature revealed few attempts to observe and describe in quantifiable fashion both teacher and pupil behavior and even fewer examples of attempts to relate observed behavior in a teaching setting to pupil performance in other settings. Therefore this chapter will include materials which are data-based and contain at least some type of systematic description of teacher behavior even though the interaction of such behavior with pupils or the effects of that behavior on pupil growth may be missing. We decided to confine our search to material published since the Sears and Dowley (1963) chapter in the previous handbook (Gage, 1963) and in Swift's (1964) review, with the exception of the Reichenberg-Hackett (1962) article which has been used to some degree as a basis for the day-care setting by more recent investigators.

Rashid states, "There is a sharp break between the professional literature describing preschool programs and that describing practices in the primary grades" (Rashid, 1969, p. 5). She indicates that preschool research has not been concerned with the explication of the interaction between teacher and pupil behavior in an attempt to provide specific transactional relationships.

Since the field was so ill defined and poorly organized, our first step was to organize a system for categorizing what we found. Wright (1960) presents a digest of methods for categorizing observational child study. We developed Table 1 as an outline for this chapter by modifying his Table 3.2 (Wright, 1960, p. 74). The rows titled along the left side of the table are the procedures taken from Wright. The columns titled along the top are settings where observational procedures might be used at the preschool level.

Specimen description means detailed sequential recording of all that is taking place in a situation. This may be accomplished by audio- or video-tape recording or by continuous note-taking. Following the recording, a coding or scoring scheme is imposed on the record as contrasted to coding during the initial collection of data. Statistical analysis is done only after the original records have been coded. Wright (1960) calls this an open method because the coding follows the moment-to-moment recording. A distinguishing characteristic of open and

TABLE 1
OBSERVATION TECHNIQUES AND BEHAVIOR SETTINGS

Observation Techniques	Behavior Settings				
	Home and Mother	Head Start and Follow Through Research	Experimental Preschool	Nursery, Kindergarten	Day Care
Specimen description			Scott (1969) Braun & Lasher (1970)	Reichenberg-Hackett (1962) Kounin (1970)	
Time/signs	Gordon (1969) Herman (1970) Gordon & Jester (1970)	Soar (1970) Miller et al. (1969, 1970) Katz (1968) Katz, Peters & Stein (1968)	Spaulding (1963, 1967, 1968)		
Time/ categories	Hess et al. (1968) Brophy (1970)			DiLorenzo, Salter & Brady (1969)	
Event sampling		Miller et al. (1969, 1970)			Prescott, Jones & Kritchevsky (1967)
Trait rating	Schaefer (1969) Schaefer & Furfey (1967)	Beller (1969) Conners & Eisenberg (1966) Harvey et al. (1966)			
Level of Cognitive Interaction		Soar (1970)	Spaulding (1969)		

closed systems is that an open system preserves the raw data so that it is available for other coding systems while the closed system imposes a coding scheme at the time of initial data collection. In the latter, the observer simply notes specific behaviors as they occur. Examples of closed methods are time and event sampling and trait rating. In the closed system, efficiency of basic data recording is gained at the loss of the raw data. We have further divided Wright's classification of Time Sampling into sign and category systems. Sign systems preserve some elements of the raw data since behaviors are listed in the observer's record

and he usually makes some sort of frequency count of the occurrence of specific behaviors. Category systems, however, destroy the discrete behavior by grouping under a label.

In event sampling the observer records "behavioral events of a given class [as arguments]" (Wright, 1960, p. 74) by means of immediate coding. Use of the trait-rating procedure usually requires longer periods of observation time followed by the observer making a somewhat subjective judgment of an underlying trait possessed by the person being observed.

We added one additional type of observation to Wright's list and included it in Table 1. Since education is concerned not only with the interpersonal relationship between teacher and pupil, or among pupils, but also with the content being conveyed, we added a category for those studies which described the level of abstraction of *what* was being taught as well as *how* (setting or instructional procedure) it was being taught. Table 1 illustrates that the bulk of studies is of the time-sampling type which may reflect the psychological rather than the pedagogical background of investigators. Either educators have not concerned themselves with analysis of the content, or they have failed to develop ways to report in quantitative terms what is occurring in preschool settings. Except in the experimental analysis of behavior where specific behaviors are counted, psychologists have been more prone to investigate how learning is taking place or the social setting for learning than what is being learned.

The behavior settings for observation reflect not only the kind which existed prior to 1965 (kindergarten, nursery school, daycare center), but also show the impact of the social setting since that date. The first setting is a mixture of two types: either experimental-laboratory settings in which mothers without instruction in how to teach are observed teaching their children (Brophy, 1970; Hess, Shipman, Brophy, & Baer, 1968), or home-visit settings in which another person, either professional or paraprofessional, teaches the child (Radin & Weikart, 1967), or the mother is taught and observations are made as to the behavior setting and her role as teacher (Gordon, 1969; Gordon & Jester, 1970; Herman, 1970). The second major setting is Head Start and Follow Through research, and the third is the preschool which is designed as experimental or in which experiments are conducted. The last two categories are the more traditional settings for preschool education.

The rest of this chapter is organized around Table 1. We will discuss the studies within each observation system across the settings. The material, therefore, will be basically methodological.

SPECIMEN-DESCRIPTION APPROACHES

Four studies make use of the specimen-description approach to the observation of preschool settings. A pioneer attempt to develop a systematic look at nursery schools serving four-year-old children in a middle-sized southern town was conducted by Reichenberg-Hackett (1962). She studied 10 nursery classrooms. These groups represented different social classes and were segregated by race so that there were six variations: white upper-middle, white middle-middle, white lower-middle, Negro upper-middle, Negro middle-middle and Negro lower-middle classrooms. The data were collected by a team of two observers who took 10-minute turns in detailed anecdotal recording so that there was a total of 4½ hours per teacher from three sessions of 1½ hours each. The data were divided into episodes and categorized by a different team of workers than those who collected the information. All records were analyzed at least twice and sometimes as many as four times to arrive at 96 percent agreement among analysts. Only teacher behavior was categorized. This study, therefore, does not yield data on the interaction between teacher behavior and pupil behavior. It is presented here because it served as a stepping-stone for later categorizations which appear in Prescott, Jones, and Kritchevsky (1967). The three major categories of teacher behavior were: teacher approach, motivating techniques, and a combination of activities, lessons and values. The subcategories appear on Table 2.

The data across these 10 classrooms indicate a wide range of behaviors within all of these categories. Ninety-five activities were observed although no single classroom included all of them. Only major ones such as development of an adequate self-concept,

TABLE 2

TEACHER BEHAVIOR IN CLASSROOM ACTIVITIES

I. Teacher approach
   A. Communicative
      1. Verbal communication
      2. Nonverbal communication
   B. Noncommunicative
      1. Child-centered (preparation of materials)
      2. Neutral
      3. Subjective (centered on self)
      4. Silent supervision

II. Motivating techniques
   A. Encouragement (both pre- and postchild response)
   B. Management: socialization discipline
   C. Discouragement: suppression of spontaneity, regimentation
   D. Combination of management with either encouragement or discouragement

III. Activities
   A. Classroom activities
   B. Lessons: didactic instructions
   C. Values: a combination of activities and lessons subjectively assessed after group discussion by coders and reference to early childhood literature

Note: Categories derived from W. Reichenberg-Hackett, "Practices, attitudes and values in nursery group education," *Psychological Reports*, 1962, 10, 155–158.

personal responsibility, consideration for well-being of others, emotional stability and belongingness, and intellectual growth were presented in the study. Teacher activity and lessons directed toward intellectual growth were observed less than 10 percent of the time. The majority of values observed related to either emotional development or the socialization process.

There was no relationship between Parent Attitude Research Instrument scores and the classroom behavior of the teachers. Although teachers differed widely, the differences were not a function of either race or social class. Both Negro and white teachers in each social group were found who were very high on encouragement and low on discouragement. Other teachers were found who were essentially neutral with little encouragement within each social group. Some anecdotal data as well as children's drawings on the "Draw A Man Test" suggested to Reichenberg-Hackett that there were relationships between the teacher's motivating techniques and child performance in executing a task; however the finding was only suggestive.

Based upon the psychological-ecological views of Barker and Wright (1954), Scott (1969) observed five head teachers in classrooms for five-year-old disadvantaged children. Observers recorded their data directly into steno masks attached to portable tape recorders. Two records were taken on three of the teachers, three on one, and one on the other. The behavior settings were morning greetings and large-group activity. The unit of analysis was a behavior episode (Wright, 1967). Sixteen categories were developed for the analysis of the settings. Some categories were: length of episode, total number of overlapping episodes, form of transition (whether or not a new episode merged with the one preceding or an ending was abrupt), mechanisms used (verbal, physical, gesture), and level of affect. After coding, the data were converted to percentages to eliminate the factor of varying length.

The five teachers who were studied were selected by supervisors for their position at one of the two ends of a continuum of effectiveness. However Scott does not define any of the criteria the supervisors used for determining effectiveness, nor are any data presented to indicate whether teacher effectiveness was related to pupil outcomes. Scott reported three differences between effective and ineffective teachers. Effective teachers seemed 1) to sustain their behavior longer in a continuous flow, 2) to have had more episodes ending in attainment of their goals (although the category system does not indicate the means for assessment of goal attainment), and 3) to have shown more positive and less negative emotional tone than ineffective teachers. Her findings may simply reveal circularity of reasoning since the supervisors may have used the level of affect, the smoothness of episodes, and the attainment of goals as their criteria for effectiveness. Since we do not have this information, the major value that this study contributes is the demonstration that a specimen-description method can be used to gather data leading to the differentiation of teacher behavior as a function of setting (greeting and large-group activity), and someone's criteria of effectiveness.

Braun, Holzman, and Lasher (1969) developed a specimen-description system as a part of their project in training teachers for disturbed preschoolers. Their original data were obtained in only two classrooms in the Boston area. An observer made 10-minute observations at the same time each day and wrote down all teacher talk and behavior. A coding system was developed in which the basic unit of analysis was the sentence. Each sentence was categorized as teacher's actions, teacher's verbalizations to and about whom the teacher talks, or degree of responsibility teacher takes toward a child (Braun & Lasher, 1970, p. 137). The first two categories, actions and verbalizations, are rather clear-cut. The third, degree of responsibility, was divided into a six-point scale: 1) approaching, waiting, sitting with the child, 2) asking for information, 3) stating own ideas and feelings, 4) asking children to comply, 5) working on the same materials with the child, and 6) statements about a child's feelings or motives.

Rather than studying the effect of these teacher actions on child behavior, the investigators applied their coding system to a study of the influence of the children and the effect of other variables such as training, presence, and role of other adult and home visits upon teacher behavior. Three classrooms were studied, each consisting of two adults and four or five children. An experienced teacher was present in only one of the classrooms. Video tape recordings were made of classroom behavior. Child behavior was coded into five categories: 1) direct physical aggression toward a peer, 2) physical aggression toward a teacher, 3) disrup-

tive use of materials, 4) dangerous play, and 5) interfering noise. In each classroom one of the teachers was responsible for visiting the home. The data indicate that the teachers generally gave their greatest attention to the most disruptive children, and that secondarily teacher attention was positively related to visiting the home. Again, the major value of this study lies not so much in its findings, although the correlations are interesting, but in its methodology. It was possible to perform a reasonable content analysis, divide units into meaningful categories, and analyze relationships between these categories of child behavior and teacher situation.

Kounin (1970) was the fourth investigator to use specimen description. Only his kindergarten study is relevant to this review. He investigated the *ripple effect* in the management of classroom discipline. This term refers to how a teacher's technique for handling the misbehavior of one child affects the subsequent behavior of others. Kounin studied kindergartners because 1) children do misbehave in kindergartens and teachers do correct them for misbehavior; therefore, desists are ecologically prevalent and not unexpected; 2) children in this group would have had little direct experience with teachers, thus permitting a study of the impact of desists relatively uninfluenced by previous relationships with teachers; 3) special subgroup formations which might affect the reactions of pupils in unknown ways would be relatively absent (Kounin, 1970, p. 7).

Fifty-one student observers collected descriptive records of classroom behavior focused on the misbehaving child, the way the teacher corrected it, and its effect on the overt behavior of witnesses. Twenty-six kindergartens in 20 schools in Detroit were observed. The observers were trained to record what the misbehaving child and audience children were doing immediately before the teacher intervention. They noted the full content and manner of the teacher's intervention, the child's immediate reaction, and a two-minute record of the behavior of the child nearest to the one who was target for the teacher's action. Four hundred and six incidents were recorded by observers who took notes during the event and wrote a detailed record immediately following. Three dimensions of teacher technique emerged: *clarity, firmness* and *roughness. Clarity* meant the amount of information in the message which told the misbehaving child exactly what he was to stop or what he was to do. *Firmness* referred to the amount of emphasis in the teacher's voice or manner, and *roughness* to the expression of anger or exasperation. Effects on the children were categorized into *no reaction; behavior disruption,* in which the child showed apprehension or restlessness or decreased involvement in the required activity; *increased conformance,* the ripple-effected child became more conforming, stopped his own misbehavior and paid more attention; *increased nonconformance*—in this case, he engaged in a misbehavior; and *ambivalence,* which was coded "when the child showed increased conformance in one act and increased nonconformance in another act following the desist" (Kounin, 1970, p. 10). Kounin's data demonstrate that the teacher's behavior has an effect on "audience" children as well as the children to whom the teacher directs the behavior. The outcome for the audience children is similar to that for the target children. The three categories of teacher behavior produced the following effects on the audience children: clarity produced more conformity; firmness tended to lead to better behavior; and roughness had little effect on conformance but seemed to produce more anxiety and apprehension along with other disruptive behavior in the audience child.

Kounin then attempted to take into account the audience child's behavior prior to his observation of the teacher with another child. That is, rather than simply seeing the teacher's behavior as though it were functioning on a neutral child, he recognized that the audience child's own immediate behavior might relate to his subsequent behavior. Audience children's behavior was categorized into *deviancy-free* or *deviancy-linked* behavior. In the former case children were doing legitimate work. In the latter they were either misbehaving or watching the misbehavior of the child who was stopped by the teacher. The latter group of children reacted with both more conformance and nonconformance, and with more ambivalence than did the deviancy-free children. As Kounin (1970) stated, "Conformance, nonconformance, or ambivalence have the property of *direction*—they are ripple effects that are directed toward conformance, or misbehavior, or both" (p. 11). When the three variables of clarity, firmness and roughness were examined, clarity affected both groups of children, whereas firmness affected only the deviancy-linked children. Both served to increase conformity and decrease misbehavior.

Kounin's (1970) observations were made on the first four days of the school year. The data were also analyzed to see if teachers' techniques had any longitudinal effect or whether they wore off and, further, whether the same technique used on the second, third and fourth day of school produced the same effect it had on the first day. There were differences as a function of time. There were fewer reactions on the second through fourth days than on the first day. Further, on the first day most of the children were influenced by the teacher's behavior, whereas only a minority of children were influenced on the subsequent days. There was a significant difference between the type of reaction on day one and the following days. On the first day more children showed conformance and behavior disruption and fewer showed nonconformance. This may suggest that the action of the teacher has a lessening effect on audience children with the passage of time, although such studies obviously need replication. Though not directly relevant to the age group reviewed here, it might be noted that when these same categories of behavior and effects were studied in school-age and high-school children, Kounin (1970) concluded:

> ... the techniques of dealing with misbehavior, as such, are not significant determinants of how well or poorly children behave in classrooms, or with how successful the teacher is in preventing one child's misbehavior from contaging others (author's emphasis) (p. 70).

One might also say that this general conclusion is also true of the Kindergarten Study where there were considerably more "no observable effects" consequent to desist events during the second through fourth day than on the first day of school (p. 71).

Using specimen description techniques, Kounin's studies of the upper grades led to a far more elaborate category system for the analysis of the total ecology of the classroom, but unfortunately these later categories were not reapplied to the kindergarten data. Such a study would prove valuable. One of the special contributions of Kounin's work is, in contrast to the experimental analysis of behavior experiments, his focus on the nontarget child and his concern for the total ecology of the classroom. His categories offer the researcher an opportunity to examine a wide range of classroom variables to pupil achievement and personality measures similar to Soar (1970).

TIME / SIGNS APPROACHES

HOME AND MOTHER SETTINGS

A series of studies was done as a part of the Parent Education Projects at the University of Florida. Time sampling was used for investigating the behavior of adults in the home while a parent educator was teaching the mother a series of activities for use with children between 3 and 24 months of age (Gordon, 1967, 1969). The general technique was to use a paraprofessional as the agent for education in the home. The paraprofessional was trained in time-sampling observation techniques and she completed a Parent Educator Weekly Report at the termination of each visit. Since she was a participant observer, the normal time-sampling technique of rapidly coding discrete behaviors was not possible. The time unit was the total home visit and ranged from 15 to 60 minutes in duration. Because the behaviors which the parent educator was asked to record were not categories but specific items, we have placed these studies in the time/signs cell. Ideally, the teaching behavior of the mother and of the parent educator toward the infant would be the behavior to be observed. Since we were dealing with paraprofessional participant observers, we developed a schedule to record only certain verbal behaviors and other behaviors that might indicate the mother's involvement in the project. This yielded two types of scales: verbal and attitude.

Verbal Behavior

The extent and nature of the verbal interaction was measured by the items on Table 3. The maximum possible mother score for one home visit is 15. The means include all tallies, so that the maximum positive is 11; the maximum negative is 4. Jester and Bailey (1969) divided the items into the two categories shown on the table for their study of the relationship between total verbalization in the home and infant performance. The Parent Educator Weekly Report form allowed for recording the presence of other adults and indicating their behavior on the items on Table 3. We could thus investigate the relationship between maternal verbal behavior and all adults' present behavior (both process variables), and child performance on tests (product variables).

Out of a possible maximum frequency of 15, the mothers in both the first and second years averaged about 7.5. This is not a true measure of frequency, but of variety. The verbal interaction measure may drastically conceal the true amount of verbal interaction in these homes. Since the parent edu-

TABLE 3

ITEMS FROM THE WEEKLY REPORT USED IN ESTIMATES OF VERBALIZATION IN THE FLORIDA PARENT EDUCATION PROJECT

Growth-Producing (Social Interaction)	Nongrowth-Producing
1. Look directly into his face 2. Talk words rather than sounds 3. Tone of voice sounds soft and loving 4. Use the baby's name when speaking to him 5. Repeat sounds the baby makes in a question-ing way 6. Listen to the baby when the baby talks 7. In a few words, order or tell the baby to do or not to do things 8. Explain and describe things when talking to the baby Additional items for mother index: How many words are there in most of the sentences spoken to the baby by the mother-ing one? 0 1 2 3 4 5 6 7 8 9 9. Tally 1 if 1, 2, 3 10. Tally 2 if 4, 5, 6 11. Tally 3 if 7, 8, 9	1. Talk about him as though he were not there 2. Tone of voice sounds cross and angry 3. Talk sounds rather than words (example: coo, goo) 4. Interpret to others what the baby says

Note: Adapted from J. Bailey and R. Jester, "Hearing-speech scores on the Griffiths Mental Development Scale as a function of language usage in the home." In I. J. Gordon (Ed.), *Reaching the child through parent education: The Florida approach*, Gainesville, Fla.: Institute for the Development of Human Resources, University of Florida Research Reports, 1969, p. 25.

cator was a participant observer, she could not be expected to use any type of observation which required frequent check marks at any fixed, small time interval. She therefore completed the items shown in Table 3 following a complete home visit. This means that a mother might have used the baby's name when speaking to him any number of times during the visit, but she would only receive a score of 1. The best way to interpret this score is to assume that it means the average mother on the average home visit did not avail herself of all the categories of interaction covered on the measure, but might have had a high frequency of a particular behavior.

Of interest is the low mean on what had been assumed would be nongrowth-producing types of verbal interaction. Here it was possible for the maternal score to be 4.0. The means never even reached an average of one occurrence per home visit. Generally, these homes used a high mixture of positive ver-

bal interaction and little variety of nongrowth-producing interaction in the first two years of life.

At age one the infants were administered the Griffiths Mental Development Scale and were scored on the five subscales of that test: locomotor, personal-social, hearing and speech, eye and hand, and performance. The mean score for the experimental groups was about 100 with a standard deviation of about 15. The only subscale of the Griffiths test which correlated with the verbal observations was the hearing and speech subscale. It correlated in the low 20s with the total amount of verbal interaction and the amount of adult positive verbal interaction. When the second-year data were examined, correlations between verbal interaction scores of mothers in the second year with child scores on the Bayley scales at age two for a group which received home visits in the second year only ($n = 15$), were 0.64 for total verbal to Bayley Mental scales, 0.52

for adult positive verbal to Bayley Mental scale, and 0.53 in adult positive verbal to child task-oriented behavior during the test. Thus, the data from a relatively primitive signs instrument, used by paraprofessional participant observers, were of an order to demonstrate a reliable relationship between verbal behavior in the home of an infant observed when the home was a teaching setting and performance on a standardized measure of mental development.

Herman (1970) studied a selected sample of 39 black families from the larger Parent Education Project group on whom there were complete data for all of the various schedules. These were Bayley scores for the children, attitude test scores for the mothers, and weekly reports on the mothers used in the larger study. She investigated the differential effects of maternal attitude and behavior upon child performance as a function of the sex of the child. The group was divided into high- and low-scoring males and females on the basis of the Bayley Mental, Bayley Motor and Bayley Task-oriented scale scores. A stepwise discriminant function analysis was then done using the Bayley scales as criteria and the maternal measures as predictors. Her measure of verbal interaction was the same as that in Table 3. Generally she found that maternal verbal behavior significantly influenced performance on both the Bayley Mental and Motor scales for the boys. The mothers of high-scoring boys ($n = 12$) were significantly higher in positive verbal behavior than were the mothers of the low-scoring boys ($n = 11$). However, for the girls, only on the motor scale did positive verbal behavior serve to differentiate high- from low-scoring girls. The mothers of high-scoring males on both mental and motor scales engaged in significantly more positive verbal behavior than did the mothers of high-scoring females. The mothers of low-scoring males engaged in significantly less positive verbal behavior (0.05 level) than did the mothers of girls scoring low on the motor scale.

For the total group ($n = 39$) the correlations between the positive verbal scale and the Bayley Mental and Motor Scales were 0.31 and 0.41 respectively.

The above studies using the observed verbal behavior of the mother in the home during home intervention indicate a reliable but low correlation between her verbal behavior as measured on the schedule and the performance of her child at ages one and two on standard intelligence tests. It must be remembered that the observation schedule used did not have the capability of the frequency count so that the amount of variability is very low. Even with the gross instrument it seems clear that the relationship is reliable. The study also demonstrated that it is possible to train paraprofessionals to be reliable data-collectors even when they are participant observers, provided the instrument does not require a large number or a high frequency of discriminations.

Based upon these data and the need for much finer measurement, infant research is now under way in which the same type of verbal data is being collected on a similar population but through the utilization of video tapes of every sixth home visit (Gordon & Jester, 1970). The observation schedule being used in this project is a modified Parent Educator Weekly Report on which items are completed by the parent educator on a yes-no basis for the nonvideo-taped home visits. They are used for frequency count analysis of the video-taped visits.

Observed Attitudes

The parent educator was trained to observe the items on Table 4 while making a home visit. Items A through G on Table 4 were completed by the parent educator at the termination of a visit. We reasoned that a mother who could repeat the exercises, knew what she was doing, watched the parent educator demonstrate, and brooked few interruptions would be considered as displaying a positive attitude. Further, a

TABLE 4

ITEMS FROM PARENT EDUCATOR WEEKLY REPORT USED FOR ATTITUDE INDEX IN THE PARENT EDUCATION PROJECTS

Series Information
A) How did the mothering one react to your instructions?
  1. Looked at you while you were talking, and/or asked questions_____.
  2. Did other things while you were showing her how to do the exercise (examples of other things: straightened baby's clothes, looked around the room, did housework) _____.
  3. Walked out of the room while you were explaining things to her_____.
  4. Refused to do an exercise_____.
  5. Laughed at and/or scoffed at instructions _____.
  6. Other_____What?_____.
B) Mothering one's ability to repeat exercises:
  1. Could repeat exercises the parent educator had explained to her_____.
  2. Could do part of the exercise by herself but needed your help_____.
  3. Couldn't repeat exercises you had explained to her_____.
D) When the mothering one goes over last week's exercises with her child she:
  1. Doesn't know what she's doing_____.
  2. Knows what she is doing_____.
E) When the mothering one goes over last week's exercises with her child she:
  1. Tries them on the child more than once if it doesn't go well the first time_____.
  2. Gets discouraged or is satisfied after doing them once even if it doesn't go well the first time_____.
  3. Does them more than once even if it goes very well the first time_____.
F) How many interruptions were there during training that made the mothering one stop the exercise for a time?
  None_____, 1_____, 2_____, 3_____,
  4_____, 5_____, more_____.
G) What kinds of interruptions were there?
  1. Mothering one had to care for another child_____.
  2. An adult wanted something_____.
  3. The phone rang_____.
  4. Visitors came_____.
  5. The baby had to be fed_____.
  6. The baby went to sleep_____.
  7. Other_____.
  8. None_____.
Missed Appointments and Delays

TABLE 4 (Cont'd.)

ITEMS FROM PARENT EDUCATOR WEEKLY REPORT USED FOR ATTITUDE INDER IN THE PARENT EDUCATION PROJECTS

C) How many trips did you make before you got to see the mothering one for this visit?_____
D) Did the mothering one leave a message for you on any of the trips?
  Yes_____ No_____
E) When you finally got to see the mothering one:
  1. She said nothing about missing her appointment_____.
  2. She gave a confusing explanation_____.
  3. She gave an understandable explanation _____.

Source: I. J. Gordon, *Early child stimulation through parent education*. Final report to Children's Bureau, Grant #PHSR-306, 306(01), Gainesville, Fla.: IDHR, College of Education, University of Fla., 1969.

mother who missed appointments for other than reasons of illness or who seemed to be avoiding the parent educator would be scored as displaying a negative attitude in addition to negative behaviors observed during the home visit. The items were converted into an attitude index so that we could test this index against other observed behaviors and child performance.[1]

The mean for mothers on the attitude index (range from $+1$ to -1) was about 0.6 for the various experimental groups in the project with a standard deviation of about 0.2. Herman (1970) found that the attitude index contributed more than any other variable to the differentiation among all the children ($n = 39$) who scored high or low on the Bayley Mental Scale at age two. Mothers of high-scoring children had more positive attitudes ($p < 0.05$) than mothers of low scorers. It was the second variable to appear in the discriminant function analysis differentiating high and low males on the Mental Scale and was the fourth variable differentiating males on the Motor Scale, in both cases adding significantly to the prediction.

[1] This index was developed by John Maurelli based upon a pilot study by Susan Herman.

The attitude index differentiated between high-scoring boys and girls on all three scales with mothers of high-scoring males reflecting a more positive attitude than mothers of high-scoring females. Attitude scores were reliably correlated with Mental ($r = 0.34$, $p < 0.05$) and Motor ($r = 0.38$, $p < 0.05$) Scale scores. Again we can say that this type of observation schedule, as limited as it is, was adequate to demonstrate a relationship between maternal behavior and child performance on standardized tests. Perhaps the finding of most methodological importance was produced by dividing the group by sex. This procedure clearly revealed the differential pattern of relationships between observed maternal behavior and child performance of girls by both the verbal output and the attitude of the mother. In order to follow up these findings, the new infant project (Gordon & Jester, 1970) is using similar attitude items on the weekly observation report and, in addition, we have developed an adult infant interaction schedule which is a modification of the gross verbal observation plus some additional data.

We have excluded from consideration some natural history investigations of maternal behavior even though some of the observation schedules have become somewhat sophisticated. We have done this because our intent was to focus only on behavior in a teaching setting and not on the whole issue of socialization. It is important, however, that investigators of maternal teaching behavior look at the general literature in socialization to enable them to extract items which might appear on new observation schedules. For example, Schaefer (1959) developed a circumplex model of maternal behavior based upon attitude ratings rather than on observation. He then used those items as a guide for observers as they taught infants and toddlers in ghetto homes in Washington, D.C. (Schaefer, 1969), and found rather high relationships between ratings on maternal behavior and child performance. We will treat his data

later in our discussion of ratings. The idea here is that investigators of maternal teaching behavior can borrow items from natural history investigators, such as Schaefer's (1959), Gewirtz and Gewirtz's (1968), or Rubenstein's (1967) and convert them into observational schemes to assess the transactional relationship between adult and infant in a teaching setting. For example, in our new infant investigation (Gordon & Jester, 1970) Schaefer's schedule based upon global observations and inference has been converted into a time/signs schedule used by the parent educator on her weekly visits and as a frequency measure for the analysis of video tape. This schedule allows the possibility of two dimensions, control and warmth, to be studied on the basis of the observation of the behavior of the mother while teaching as distinct from its previous use in either a natural setting or while looking at the behavior of the mother when someone else was teaching her child.

CLASSROOM SETTINGS

Two studies of classroom observation, each using the time/signs approach, investigated phases of Head Start activities and one examined the extension of Head Start into the public school through Follow Through. Katz (1968), in her study of two types of Head Start classrooms, used the point-time sampling technique originally developed by Kowatrakul (1959) and Sears (1963) at Stanford. In this technique the observer looks at the behavior of the target person only long enough to be sure what the behavior is, and then checks off the behavior in the appropriate cell. The earlier work by Sears and her students led to the development of the student point-time sampling form. Katz then developed a Teacher-Behavior Survey Instrument. The observer records teacher behavior in six major dimensions: contact, teaching, feedback, control, nurturance and dominant tone. The observer also categorizes a rough description of the type of activity going on in the classroom, such as blocks, nutritional, circle time and dramatic play. The first five dimensions are far more objective than is the sixth. In the dimension of "contact," for example, the observer records what the contact is with an individual child or with a small group, whether the teacher or the child initiates the contact, and whether it is verbal or nonverbal. In the second category, teaching, the behaviors somewhat resemble the interaction process analysis categories. They are presented on Table 5.

The area of feedback is distinguished from the control area in that the former is

TABLE 5

TEACHING CATEGORIES FROM KATZ

A : *Gives directions:* tells child what to do, or how to do something related to a task, activity, or routine.

B : *Sets standards of performance:* tells the child what a completed task is expected to be like ; some description of desired terminal behavior.

C : *Gives knowledge and information:* facts about the world, concepts, functions of events, insight into cause-effect relations, etc.

D : *Solicits ideas and information from the child:* asks leading questions or probes the child intending to stimulate him into giving his own ideas, opinions, experiences, etc.

E : *Demonstrates and gives examples:* shows how some skill is executed, demonstrates task, skill, gives examples of concepts, labels events, in order to illustrate some knowledge or learning she intends as the purpose of the interaction.

F : *Encourages the child's activity or interest:* makes positive comment upon the child's expressed interest, gives permission to pursue activity, plays with child in order to encourage his enjoyment and/or interest.

G : *Helps with task or activity:* any teacher behavior giving child direct assistance with task or activity, e.g., arranging materials, helping to carry equipment to suitable place, holding down paper to make cutting or pasting easier for the child to do.

H : *Offers choice of alternative activities to the child:* this involves explicit statement to the child of what choices are suggested, asking the child whether he would like one among several alternative activities.

Source : Lilian Katz, A study of the changes in behavior of children enrolled in two types of Headstart classrooms. Unpublished doctoral dissertation, Stanford University, 1968, p. 85.

intended to let the child know how well he is doing while the latter is much more a power assertion (Katz, 1968, p. 86) on the part of the teacher. Feedback includes such behavior sets as praises performance, clarifies task steps, analyzes and evaluates performance, and emphasizes processes. There are eight items in this dimension. Control consists of six items such as states behavior expectation, calls for attention, stops behavior by nonverbal means. The nurturance dimension includes personal approval, affection, reassurance and support, and consists of six items. It is interesting to note that Katz presents a control dimension as distinct from a nurturance dimension. This corresponds somewhat to Schaefer's (1959) circumplex model, and to Soar's (1966) two dimensions of control and warmth. The more subjective dimension is what Katz calls "dominant tone." Here the observer does not make an entry for each point in time, but only one for each observation. It includes such items as the teacher being tense or serious, relaxed or hostile. These are clearly judgmental items requiring immediate inferences from the observer.

The Child Behavior Survey Instrument (Katz, Peters, & Stein, 1968) includes the categories: task absorption, attention to teacher, social work (engaged in cooperative work with other children), intent on nonpermitted work, aimless movement, disruptive behavior, and, finally, a subjective mood category. Katz reported very low frequencies in the feedback dimension of teacher behavior. There was also some difficulty in maintaining observer reliability over time for the teacher observations. The significant question is what relationships exist between observed teacher behavior and observed pupil behavior and in what fashion teacher behavior influences pupil behavior. Children were observed 14 times during the first, third and sixth weeks. The teachers were observed during the second, fourth, and fifth weeks for a total of 100 observations per teacher. The observers were two college sophomores who had received approximately 15 hours of training on the teacher instrument and 20 hours training on the child instrument. Katz (1968) originally set out to test hypotheses about two types of classrooms, but she was unable to do this because the classrooms were not true to type. Although it is hard to extract conclusions from her data, Katz concluded that "even in six weeks, the teacher who makes demands, who structures the children's activities, but who is parsimonious with her rewards, cannot only fail to facilitate growth in the children, but she can engender an increase in those behaviors which are likely to interfere with later school adjustment" (Katz, 1968, p. 77). Her two main instruments seem useful but further work to handle the problem of reliability is needed.

Another attempt to differentiate among approaches to Head Start classrooms is being conducted by Miller et al. (1969, 1970). An observational system has been developed to assess teacher and pupil behavior of children in classes categorized as Bereiter-Engelmann, DARCEE, Montessori and traditional. Fourteen classes were observed, two being Montessori and four classes in each of the other classifications. The classes were composed of 4-year-old children in the area of Louisville, Kentucky. A monitoring schedule was developed for live observation, and video-tape samples were collected for tape analysis. Tallies were made every 15 seconds with the special requirement that "no more than one instance of any particular technique be tallied in any 15 second period" (Miller et al., 1969, p. 99). The tally sheet consisted of type and size of group, type of activity, media and teaching technique. The techniques were: 1) MANP—manipulatory, hands, consisting of all activities in which the teacher handles something in order to show children how something is done or how it works; 2) I-V—verbal explanation or information consisting of verbal instruction by the teacher or by one child to another; 3)

X—exemplary, any instance of showing in order to teach; 4) MO—motor activity, not to be used simply when children and teacher are moving around, but only when the motor activity is "instruction"; 5) RP—role playing, or dramatization; 6) PG—physical guidance, when a child is taken manually through an activity such as tracing letters; 7) CON—conversation, when an adult is conversing with a single child, or when a sustained conversation is going on between children (Miller et al., 1969, pp. 101–103).

The video tally sheet, in addition to these items, included a section called Standard Setting. The signs were: cites a principle, cites another child, states reinforcement contingency, cites teachers, challenges.

Miller et al. (1970) found program differences in the classroom operations and concluded:

Bereiter-Engelmann and DARCEE *teachers* did more teaching of all kinds and used more verbal instructions than Montessori and Traditional teachers; exemplification, as a technique, was significantly high in Bereiter-Engelmann; teachers in Traditional classes used manipulation of materials more than any other technique. In Bereiter-Engelmann and DARCEE classes, *children* worked in groups, engaged in the same kind of activities; in the Montessori and Traditional classes children were engaged in different activities, either individually or moving around in various groups, the composition of which fluctuated rapidly. Children in Bereiter-Engelmann and in DARCEE classes did more reciting, children in Montessori more manipulating of materials, and children in Traditional more role playing (p. 34).

Two other findings emerge. First, although there was variability among teachers within any model, the four to eight weeks of training did seem to shift teachers toward the program norm. Second, the children were assessed on a variety of measures in the spring. The DARCEE program seemed to have the most impact on children's motivation to achieve, as measured by a variety of motivational tasks such as a curiosity box, replacement puzzle, behavior inventory and the Stanford-Binet face sheet. DARCEE children were rated better in verbal-social participation by their teachers than were the children in other programs when rated by their teachers. On arithmetic measures the Bereiter-Engelmann children scored highest in the arithmetic test which was taken from the Bereiter-Engelmann program. The DARCEE children scored second; they had also received some numerical training. The Montessori and traditional children had no such training.

Since this project is continuing, not all analyses are complete, but several interesting facts emerge. First, a monitoring observation schedule was successful in differentiating teacher behavior in relation to program emphasis. There were mean differences between groups of teachers that related to the program they were supposed to be conducting. Second, child performance was related to the programs in ways one might have expected from the philosophical positions and operational procedures of these programs. However, the process of analysis was not a direct measure of teacher behavior to child performance, but an indirect one in which both teacher behavior and child performance were related to the model. Since not all teachers resembled each other within the model, there is a certain degree of slippage in interpreting in this fashion.

A further and more sophisticated approach to the problem is being conducted by Soar (1970), who is gathering midyear data on several systematic observation schedules across seven of the Follow Through projects. His questions are similar to those of Miller et al. (1969, 1970), that is, is it possible to determine through observation the reliability with which a program implements what it intends to do through teacher behavior, and second, are there any significant relationships between teacher behavior and child performance?

Soar began by using instruments that had already been developed, and modified these in a pilot period before gathering further data. Although his instruments fall in more than one cell on Table 3, we will treat all but one here. He observed in a total of 70 classrooms, 8 for each of the 7 models, and in 14 comparison classrooms drawn from the same schools in which the Follow Through projects were operating. Three teams of observers were used. A team of two observers spent a day in each classroom, one using the Teacher Practices Observation Record and the other using the Florida Affective Categories (Soar, 1970). They made a tape recording, observed for 30-minute periods, and then switched instruments. Since the Florida Affective Categories is undergoing considerable revision, only the Teacher Practices Observation Record (TPOR) data will be reported here. The TPOR was developed by Brown (1968) as an observation schedule to see how closely a teacher's behavior aligned with Dewey's experimentalist position. It consists of 62 items, half of which reflect the experimental position and half the nonexperimental position. It is divided into seven main dimensions: nature of the situation, nature of the problem, development of ideas, use of subject matter, evaluation, differentiation, and motivation and control. Soar factor-analyzed the Teacher Practices Observation Record on the basis of the data from the 70 classrooms and identified several major factors. He labeled Factor 1: "Teacher directed activity versus pupil selected activity." Two of the seven models fall at completely opposite extremes on this factor with Bereiter-Engelmann extremely high and the Educational Development Corporation form of the British Infant School approach extremely low (see Table 6).

Soar's data (1970) indicate that there are several Teacher Practices Observation Record factors which identify teacher behavior with reference to a program. In this respect we have a verification of Miller's findings (1970) that training a teacher in a particu-

TABLE 6

TEACHER PRACTICES OBSERVATION RECORD, ITEMS ON FACTOR 1— TEACHER-DIRECTED ACTIVITY VERSUS PUPIL-SELECTED ACTIVITY

Positive Loading

T occupies center of attention
T makes some *thing* as a *thing* center of *p*'s attention
T has *p* spend time waiting, watching, listening
T organizes learning around *Q* posed by *T*
T prevents situation which causes *p* doubt or perplexity
T asks *Q* that *p* can answer only if he studied the lesson
T accepts only one answer as being correct
T expects *p* to come up with answer *T* has in mind
T expects *p* to "know" rather than to guess answer to *Q*
T accepts only answers or suggestions closely related to topic
T collects and analyzes subject matter for *p*
T provides *p* with detailed facts and information
T relies heavily on textbook as source of information
T immediately reinforces *p*'s answer as "right" or "wrong"
T has all *p* working at same task at same time
T holds all *p* responsible for certain material to be learned
T evaluates work of all *p* by a set standard
T motivates *p* with privileges, prizes, grades
T approaches subject matter in direct, business-like way

Negative Loading

T makes *doing something* center of *p*'s attention
T has *p* participate actively
T organizes learning around *p*'s own problem or *Q*
T has *p* make his own collection and analysis of subject matter
T makes a wide range of information material available
T encourages *p* to put his ideas to a test
T has *p* work independently on what concerns *p*
T approaches subject matter in indirect, informal way

Note: Adapted from Robert S. Soar, "Follow Through Model Implementation." Interim report on project #EOG-0-8-522471-4618(100), Gainesville, Florida: IDHR, College of Education, University of Fla., 1970, p. 40.

lar program tends to lead to more uniform behavior by teachers assigned to or working in specific clear-cut, well-defined programs.

On such factors as teacher evaluation and control in subject matter interaction, for example, the Bereiter-Engelmann project is significantly different from the other six Follow Through projects (see Table 7).

TABLE 7

TEACHER PRACTICES OBSERVATION RECORD, ITEMS ON FACTOR 3— TEACHER EVALUATION AND CONTROL IN SUBJECT MATTER INTERACTION

Positive Loading

T makes *p* center of attention
T remains aloof or detached from *p*'s activities
T discourages or prevents *p* from expressing self freely
T expects *p* to "know" rather than to guess answer to *Q*
T passes judgment of *p*'s behavior or work
T stops *p* from going ahead with plan which *T* knows will fail
T has all *p* working at same task at same time
T holds all *p* responsible for certain material to be learned
T evaluates work of all *p* by a set standard
T motivates *p* with privileges, prizes, grades
T imposes external disciplinary control of *p*

Negative Loading

T gives *p* time to sit and think, mull things over

Note: Adapted from Robert S. Soar, "Follow Through Model Implementation." Interim report on project #EOG-0-8-522471-4618(100), Gainesville, Florida: IDHR, College of Education, University of Fla., 1970, p. 49.

The second classroom live-observation instrument was the Florida Affective Categories, which was a modification of Soar's South Carolina Observation Record (1966). This instrument has now undergone considerable revision as a result of the first year's study, but the affective section remains the same. The observer watches for five minutes and then enters a sign in the cell for teacher or pupil. He observes teachers for the first five minutes, pupils for the second five, etc., for 15 minutes each. Soar (1970) found some significant differences among the programs on some of the Florida Affective Categories factors represented by the items on Table 8.

TABLE 8

AFFECTIVE ITEMS FROM FLORIDA AFFECTIVE CATEGORIES

Negative Affect

TEACHER

Says "stop it," etc.	Waits for child
Uses threatening tone	Frowns
Rejects child	Ignores child
Blames	Points finger
Criticizes	Shakes finger
Makes threat	Pushes or pulls
Humiliates	Spanks
Yells	Other
Other	

PUPIL

Says "no," etc.	Makes face
Teases	Frowns, pouts, withdraws
Laughs	Uncooperative, resistant
Tattles	Interferes
Commands or demands	
Makes disparaging remarks	Threatens
Makes someone "feel small"	Takes property of others
Finds fault	Damages property of others
Threatens	Picks at child
Blames	Pushes or pulls
Cries	Holds
Starts fight	Hits
	Hurts someone with something
Other	Other

Positive Affect

TEACHER

Says "thank you," etc.	Accepts favors for self
Agrees with child	Waits for child
Gives individual attention	Gives individual attention
Accepts favors	Sympathetic
Sympathetic	Listens carefully to child
Praises child	Smiles, laughs
Draws all into group	Pats, fondles, hugs child
Other	Other

PUPIL

Says "thank you," etc.	Pats, fondles, hugs toy or doll
Asks permission in friendly manner	Helpful, shares
Agrees with another	Leans close to another
Chooses another	Chooses another

TABLE 8 (Cont'd.)

AFFECTIVE ITEMS FROM FLORIDA AFFECTIVE CATEGORIES

Offers to compromise, share, cooperate	Smiles, laughs with another
Defends another	Does something for someone
Enthusiastic, happy	Sympathetic
Praises another	Pats, fondles, hugs another
Other	Agreeable, cooperative
	Enthusiastic, happy
	Other

Note: Adapted from Robert S. Soar, "Follow Through Model Implementation." Interim report on project #EOG-0-8-522471-4618(100). Gainesville, Florida: IDHR, College of Education, University of Fla., 1970, p. 19.

The audio tapes were analyzed by the Reciprocal Category System, which is a modification of the Flanders Interaction Process Analysis by Ober (1968). Nine additional categories have been added so that a matrix with four major quadrants is produced: teacher to teacher, teacher to pupil, pupil to teacher, pupil to pupil. Table 9 represents a summary of the categories. To use this system the coder listens to an audio tape and enters a category number describing the teacher's or pupil's verbal behavior every three seconds. This number is paired with the following entry and entered into cells. Soar factor-analyzed these data and emerged with eight factors. The factors consist of combinations of cells from the matrix and are not necessarily items from Table 9. Although difficult to interpret, the factors are worth noting because they differentiate among the various Follow Through projects; however, at this date it is not possible to identify them until sponsor clearance and release are obtained.

A second facet of Soar's work (1970) was to examine the relationship between pupils' gain scores on the several readiness and achievement measures and the observed classroom behavior dimensions. His teams had observed in 35 kindergarten classrooms on which pupil data were available on four

TABLE 9

SUMMARY OF CATEGORIES FOR THE RECIPROCAL CATEGORY SYSTEM

Description of Verbal Behavior

"Warms" (Informalizes) the Climate: Tends to open up and/or eliminate the tension of the situation; praises or encourages the action, behavior, comments, ideas, and/or contributions of another; jokes that release tension not at the expense of others; accepts and clarifies the feeling tone of another in a friendly manner (feelings may be positive or negative; predicting or recalling the feelings of another are included).

Accepts: Accepts the action, behavior, comments, ideas, and/or contributions of another; *positive reinforcement* of these.

Amplifies the Contributions of Another: Asks for clarification of, builds on, and/or develops the action, behavior, comments, ideas, and/or contributions of another.

Elicits: Asks a question or requests information about the content, subject, or procedure being considered with the intent that another should answer (respond).

Responds: Gives direct answer or response to questions or requests for information that are initiated by another; includes answers to one's own questions.

Initiates: Presents facts, information, and/or opinion concerning the content, subject, or procedures being considered that are self-initiated; expresses one's own ideas; lectures (includes rhetorical questions not intended to be answered).

Directs: Gives directions, instructions, orders, and/or assignments to which another is expected to comply.

Corrects: Tells another that his answer or behavior is inappropriate or incorrect.

"Cools" (Formalizes) the Climate: Makes statements intended to modify the behavior of another from an inappropriate to an appropriate pattern; may tend to create a certain amount of tension (i.e., scolds someone, exercising authority in order to gain or maintain control of the situation, rejecting or criticizing the opinion or judgment of another).

Silence or Confusion: Pauses, short periods of silence, and periods of confusion in which communication cannot be understood by the observer.

Note: Adapted from Robert S. Soar, "Follow Through Model Implementation." Interim report on project #EOG-0-8-522471-4618(100), Gainesville, Florida: IDHR, College of Education, University of Fla., 1970, p. 31.

measures, and 33 in which an additional six measures were available. Three Reciprocal Category System factors, flexibility of teacher-pupil activities in accepting climate, drill versus pupil initiation, and teacher acceptance versus teacher correction were all significantly related to several of the pupil measures. Drill correlated negatively with pupil gain scores on six abstract language measures. Flexibility correlated positively with the same six measures, plus an alphabet measure. Teacher acceptance correlated negatively on all seven pupil variables. Soar (1970) explained this by saying that gains in concrete skill reflect drill and corrective feedback while gains in abstract skill reflect flexibility. His earlier work (Soar, 1966) also indicated that the teacher behavior which fosters concrete reading-learning is different from that which fosters abstract problem solving. The correlations are low, in the 0.20s and 0.30s, but they are stable. One Florida Affective Categories factor, teacher neutral control versus teacher support in task settings, produces correlations with pupil gain measures ranging from the 0.30s to the 0.60s, which means that the more supportive teachers produced more pupil gain. The items on this factor are shown in Table 10.

TABLE 10

FLORIDA AFFECTIVE CATEGORY ITEMS FROM FACTOR 6— TEACHER NEUTRAL CONTROL VERSUS TEACHER SUPPORT IN TASK SETTINGS

Items Reflecting Neutral Control:
    Teacher supervises pupil closely
    Teacher immobilizes pupils
    Social group without adults
    Cognitive plan, teacher problem
    Pupil parallel play

Items Reflecting Teacher Support:
    Pupil gives information
    Pupil intermittent work
    Teacher positive nonverbal

Note: Adapted from Robert S. Soar, "Follow Through Model Implementation." Interim report on project #EOG-0-8-522471-4618(100), Gainesville, Florida: IDHR, College of Education, University of Fla., 1970, p. 63.

As Soar (1970) points out, a classroom is a complex mix of many influences. What is measured by each observation schedule accounts for only a small portion of variation in pupil achievement. The combination of five factors from three instruments indicates that future studies must go into more multivariate observational systems and analyses.

Experimental Preschool Settings

The next cell in Table 1 is the use of time/signs observations methods in experimental preschools. An experimental preschool is either a specially designed preschool program or a nursery or kindergarten program that is so designed that researchers can enter and conduct small studies with teachers and children. One such program is the Education Improvement Program directed by Robert Spaulding at Duke University. Spaulding applied the classroom behavior-analysis methods previously used (Spaulding, 1967) in preservice training of elementary-school teachers to the observation of teacher-pupil behavior in a special program for disadvantaged preschool children. Two instruments were developed: the Coping Analysis Schedule for Educational Settings and the Spaulding Teacher Activity Rating Schedule. The former consists of 13 categories of behavior; 12 reflect the person's relation to his external environment. The categories are: aggressive behavior; negative (inappropriate) attention-getting behavior; manipulating, controlling and directing others; resisting authority; self-directed activity; paying close attention, thinking, pondering; integrative sharing, helping; integrative social interaction; integrative seeking and receiving support, assistance and information; following directions passively and submissively; observing passively; physical withdrawal or passive avoidance; and the one that is not focused externally, responding to internal stimuli (Spaulding, 1968, pp. 5–6). This instrument can be used either on a continuous time-flow basis or with a time-sampling approach.

The second instrument arose out of a factor-analytic study of approximately 113 categories of teacher behavior from 21 elementary classrooms (Spaulding, 1963). It consists of eight major categories of teacher operant behavior with 21 subcategories. The general transactional categories are: approval, either verbal or nonverbal; disapproval, either verbal or nonverbal; structuring; restructuring; information; and listening and observing. In addition there are two social behavior management categories used in conjuction with disapproval. These are the removal of child from social setting and withholding an object or privilege. In Spaulding's system behavior can be coded either continuously or in time blocks of five to 10 seconds.

Observer training for both instruments takes about two to three weeks and produces reliability indices in the 0.80s. As in the case of other interaction process-analysis systems, it is possible to use both instruments together to develop a view of the transaction between teacher and pupil behavior. Spaulding is particularly concerned in using these two instruments to enable teachers to modify classroom pupil behavior.

Time/signs systems have been used to obtain a systematic picture of transactions in the classroom. Miller (1969) and Soar (1970) are interested in linking classroom process variables to pupil product measures. Katz (1968) and Spaulding (1963, 1967, 1968) have related teacher process variables to pupil process variables. Miller et al. (1969) and Katz (1968) attempted an indirect connection between program identification and teacher and pupil behavior; Soar (1970), in addition to this, has also shown the direct relationship between teacher behavior and pupil academic gains regardless of program. What also emerges are some observation schedules which have elements common to both teacher and pupil behavior. This suggests to us that new instruments combining commonalities into schedules might give the field more generalizable tools and still leave a base as a result of the research done with separate instruments.

TIME / CATEGORIES APPROACHES

MOTHER AS TEACHER SETTING

Perhaps the most thorough investigation of the relationship between maternal teaching behavior and child performance is that conducted over several years by Hess and his colleagues at the University of Chicago (Hess et al., 1968; Brophy, 1969). Three mother-child teaching interaction cognitive tasks were designed (Block Sorting, Etch-A-Sketch and Toy Sorting). In each situation an audio tape recording was made of the procedures used by the mother in teaching the child and the responses made by her child. The focus was upon instructional information-giving techniques rather than socialization. The sample consisted of black mothers from the Chicago area: 40 middle class, 40 skilled working class, and 40 unskilled working class, all with father present, and 40 unskilled working class with father absent. The children in each group of mothers were equally divided between boys and girls. Twelve maternal interaction variables were established for scoring the video tapes (see Table 11).

Two types of child variables were studied: process variables in the teaching setting and product variables following the teaching. The process variables are listed in Table 11, the product variables were scores on the cognitive tasks and the Stanford-Binet test. When the correlations between maternal and child interaction variables are examined, it is possible for any single maternal variable to be correlated against all 10 child variables. Nine of the 12 maternal variables correlated with at least five of the 10 child interaction variables. Most of the correlation coefficients, although reliable ($p < .05$), are in the high teens and low twenties. Two of the nine correlated with

TABLE 11

MATERNAL CHILD INTERACTION VARIABLES

Maternal	Child
Orientation	Resistance
Requesting block placement	Errors
	Labels
Requesting labels	Verbal participation
Specific instructions	Inhibition
Specific feedback	Spuriously successful placement
General verbal specificity	Nonmeaningful placement
Affirmation / negation ratio	Interruptive distraction
Praise and engagement	Test period inhibition
Coercive control	Test period nonmeaningful placement
Attention demand	
Response quality demand	
Affectionateness	

Note: Categories derived from Robert Hess et al., *The cognitive environment of urban preschool children*, Chicago: Graduate School of Education, University of Chicago, 1968.

seven child variables: frequency of requesting child to place blocks, and specific feedback. Three were relatively unrelated to child performance: affirmation/negation ratio, praise and engagement, and affectionateness. When the means and standard deviations on these three variables are examined, it is clear that affirmation/negation ratio is an extremely variable item with a mean for both sexes combined of approximately 48 and a standard deviation of more than 20. Praise and engagement, on the other hand, is a relatively narrow-range variable with a mean of 20 and a standard deviation of 1.6. Affectionateness has a mean of 20 and a standard deviation of not quite 4. The lack of relationship for at least two of these is not because of a lack of variability in maternal behavior.

When we focus on the child variables, four of them—test-period nonmeaningful placement, nonmeaningful placement, errors, and labels—correlate with at least eight of the 12 maternal variables. Verbal participation, inhibition, interruptive distraction, and test-period inhibition correlate with three or less. There is a reliable relationship between maternal teaching activity and child performance activity when both are observed in the same setting, that is, a process-process relationship.

Hess et al. (1968) reported the correlation between maternal behavior and child Stanford-Binet score for only the block-sorting task. Child score correlates reliably with eight of the maternal interaction variables. The correlations are relatively low, the highest two being 0.37 for orientation and 0.35 for requesting block placement. It is interesting that the Stanford-Binet score correlates with all three of the variables which contribute least to the pattern of child behavior in the situation: affirmation/negation ratio, praise and engagement, and affection. However Hess et al. (1968) do not report either the correlation between Wechsler Adult Intelligence Scale and Stanford-Binet, or the maternal process variables and child product variables as measured by the Stanford-Binet.

As a part of the Hess et al. (1968) study, Brophy (1969) reanalyzed the data on the block-sorting task and added more categories in order to continue the assessment of social-class differences in maternal-teaching behavior. He was particularly concerned with preresponse instructions compared to postresponse feedback; that is, did the mother verbalize and engage in specific instructions before the child attempted the task, and what kind of feedback did she use immediately after the child's behavior? He found the most consistent differences were between the middle-class and lower-class mothers in the preresponse instruction variables. Middle-class mothers engaged much more in what was labeled "proactive" rather than "reactive" behavior. Proactive maternal behavior may be thought of as initiated by internal events, whereas reactive behavior is structured by the stimuli in the task. Brophy contrasts his theoretical position with that of reinforcement theorists who investigate reactive behavior. He claims that more attention should be paid to instructional processes which occur as cues and orientation information for the child. He points out that those mothers who use only postresponse activities are not necessarily very efficient so that the study is not an investigation of the relative merits of two approaches to learning, but highlights the importance of further investigations of the mother's orientating behavior toward the child.

The middle class mothers were the only group to consistently spend much time on initial orientation to the task, to make the relevant block attributes more salient to the child's perceptual field by helping him to focus his attention on them, or to give pre-response instructions which specify the response process by including the appropriate verbal labels. The performance of the middle class mothers on these variables was far from perfect by ideal standards, but as a group they did tend to recognize the need for such behavior and to supply it at least some of the time.... The most typical procedure among these [lower-class] mothers was to attempt to show the child what to do with a quick demonstration and then to settle into a pattern of getting the child to respond, and attempting to teach through corrective feedback.... The feedback, although relatively better, was not consistent and specific enough to overcome these other deficiencies and produce adequate learning (Brophy, 1969, p. 14).

NURSERY SCHOOL SETTINGS

DiLorenzo, Salter, and Brady (1969) investigated a group of prekindergarten programs for both disadvantaged and advantaged children in eight New York state communities for the period 1965 to 1968. By the third year of the project they had developed an observational schedule—which approached a signs/category system, although it was not nearly as sophisticated as those we have previously described—divided into six aspects: classroom organization, use of supporting staff, discipline, structuring program, encouraging language development, and reacting to pupil needs. The complete list is presented in Table 12. Only two of these produced clear-cut differences in teacher practices among the communities. It was possible to assign three communities to a high structure group, two to moderate, and three to low with respect to program orientation. The same three communities which were highest on structure were also highest on part 4, which DiLorenzo et al. called cognitive-language orientation, and the same low communities ranked low on this part. The report lacks many details, such as length of observation time, number of observations, schedule of observations, and observer training and reliability. However, they stated that anecdotal descriptions of the programs combined with these observations indicate that the emphasis in the three high-rated communities could be called cognitive-language orientation. In these classrooms the teachers spent more time on inference-making, comparisons, and conceptualizing relationships as well as stressing skill development and language usage. These teachers also seemed to use more planned sequence-type activities. "The observers repeatedly checked activities, such as number activities, language activities, readiness activities, and concept development in all the classrooms" in the three high-rated locations, "whereas, these activities were never checked for the classrooms in" one of the low-rated communities. "The frequency and duration of these activities were quite limited in" the other two low-rated communities (DiLorenzo et al., 1969, III-9).

Using the same logic as Miller et al. (1969), DiLorenzo related pupil outcomes to community rather than directly to teacher behavior. No differences were found among programs or between experimental and control groups on a learner self-concept test which they developed using a projective model. When the separate communities were compared with their own control groups, only 10 of 25 comparisons were significantly different. The schools stressing cognitive language accounted for eight of these, all on Stanford-Binet IQ Test scores. Although there are a number of problems with both the design and the data presentation, the conclusion seems to fit with other studies; that is, observed teacher behavior can be used to identify program elements which relate to pupil intellectual behavior or academic achievement.

EVENT SAMPLING

HEAD START SETTINGS

No studies were found which used conventional event sampling—that is, a decision beforehand to watch only for certain types of situations such as the display of aggression or the introduction of new material. However, many of the investigators previously mentioned include on their observation forms some place for recording activity such as free play, large-group activity, or teacher working with small groups as a part of their schedules. For example, Miller et al. (1969, 1970) include a partial list of activities consisting of 37 items which may be found in a Head Start room. We saw earlier that Reichenberg-Hackett (1962) was able to identify as many as 95 activities. Soar (1970) and Miller et al. (1969) both list the variety of groupings which might be found in a classroom, varying from pupils engaged in individual work, to small groups with or without the teacher present, to large groups and total class activities. Miller et al. (1970) compared four programs on the basis of group arrangements. The Montessori classrooms make considerably more use of small groups than do any of the other three approaches. The order is: Montessori, traditional, Bereiter-Engelmann, DARCEE. The difference between Montessori and all the others is significant ($p < 0.001$). Further, in both the Mont-

TABLE 12

TEACHER PRACTICES SECTION OF CLASSROOM OBSERVATION SCHEDULE

Teacher Practices

Listed below are series of descriptions of six aspects of teacher behavior. Under each category check that description which best fits the practice of the teacher in the class observed.

1. *Classroom Organization*
( ) a. The teacher plans most activities for the group as a whole. During free play, she singles out individual children for special attention.
( ) b. The teacher works with individual children, small subgroups, and the entire group, shifting the organizational pattern for different activities and according to the needs of the children.
( ) c. The teacher plans the program for the group as a whole. At any given time during the day, all children are engaged in the same activity.

2. *Use of Supporting Staff*
( ) a. The teacher aide works with small groups and individuals; she may join in whole-class activities as a participant.
( ) b. The teacher aide performs housekeeping functions and assists in maintaining discipline.
( ) c. The teacher aide has responsibility for specific portions of the educational program (e.g., storytelling) in addition to working with small groups and individuals.
( ) d. The teacher aide performs housekeeping functions only.
( ) e. The teacher and the teacher aide function as a team, shifting responsibilities according to the needs of the children.

3. *Discipline*
( ) a. The teacher is constantly admonishing the children for misbehavior; she threatens and cajoles to get attention and cooperation, but her efforts are not fully successful.
( ) b. The teacher exercises control through reiteration of her expectations of "good" and "grown-up" boys and girls. Conforming behavior is rewarded by privileges and priority in participation.
( ) c. The teacher maintains discipline through the pace of her program and personal enthusiasm, and by quickly reprimanding those who depart from the group pattern.
( ) d. The children follow routines, exercise responsibility for their own behavior, and cooperate readily with a minimum of teacher direction. The teacher reinforces desirable behavior and is alert to potential problems and areas of conflict.

TABLE 12 (Cont'd.)

TEACHER PRACTICES SECTION OF CLASSROOM OBSERVATION SCHEDULE

( ) e. A laissez-faire attitude pervades the classroom; the teacher places few if any restrictions on the children's behavior.

4. *Structuring Program*
( ) a. The children engage in a variety of activities without discernible objectives and unrelated to apparent needs.
( ) b. The teacher emphasizes diverse experiences for general enrichment. She relies primarily on children's responses to determine her teaching goals and strategies at a given time.
( ) c. The teacher emphasizes specific instructional goals. She focuses attention on the objective through defining the time period for the activity, using special materials, and prescribing the child's responses.
( ) d. The teacher gives equal attention to enrichment experiences and instructional activities for specific learnings.

5. *Encouraging Language Development*
( ) a. There is no special provision for language activities. Language development is incidental to a general enriched-experience program.
( ) b. The teacher makes provision for language development through discussions, question and answer periods, and planned exposure to new concepts through books, pictures, and other special materials.
( ) c. The teacher gives the children controlled practice in the use of selected terms and concepts in order to establish specified language patterns.

6. *Reacting to Pupil Needs*
( ) a. In planning and carrying out her program, the teacher fails to take account of the developmental status of the children and their particular needs.
( ) b. Classroom activities are appropriate to the age range and developmental status of the children, but the teacher is insensitive to the children's responses so that teaching opportunities are lost.
( ) c. The teacher is sensitive to the needs and reactions of the children and modifies her behavior accordingly in both large-group situations and individual encounters. The teacher is flexible; she has a capacity for listening and does not domineer.

Source: L. DiLorenzo, R. Salter, and J. Brady, *Prekindergarten programs for educationally disadvantaged children.* Final report project #3040, USOE. Albany, N.Y.: N.Y. State Education Dept., Office of Research & Evaluation, Dec. 1969.

essori and traditional programs, there was a good deal more shifting of children from one group to another during the observation period than in the other two programs. Groups of children who were engaged in the same kind of activity were observed more frequently in Bereiter-Engelmann and DARCEE than in Montessori or traditional. This means that children who were classified as being in a group in the Montessori or traditional classrooms may have been engaged in parallel activities, while group work in the Bereiter-Engelmann and DARCEE classrooms was shared or at least focused on a single topic. Soar (1970) presented no data about the effects of grouping arrangements in his study.

It is unfortunate that although so many researchers in the observation of classroom behavior at the school level have included information about the physical arrangements, these data do not seem to be used to the fullest extent as a part of the basic analysis. We were unable to detect whether teacher or pupil behavior shows a variation in one-to-one contact, small-group contact or large-group teaching. We cannot extract from these studies whether there is a relationship with teacher and pupil behavior and subject matter to be learned, the activity to be conducted, and/or the size and composition of the group. We have only the grossest indications about many of the ecological factors present in the preschool classroom.

Day-Care Center Settings

Prescott, Jones, and Kritchevsky (1967) examined the relationship between space and teacher behavior although the complex relationships suggested above were not explored. Prescott's group based their observation on the work of Reichenberg-Hackett (1962). They studied 50 day-care centers in Los Angeles County of which 30 were commercial, five nonprofit, and 15 Board of Education. Four visits of about 1½ to two hours apiece were made to each center, two

in the morning and two in the afternoon. Each teacher was observed by two or more observers with no more than three observers present in the center at one time. The observers recorded two 20-minute observations each hour and then rotated to another classroom in the center. The observers focused on teacher behavior. The study has been classified in the event-sampling section because of the way data were analyzed rather than because of the teacher-behavior orientation. A unit of teacher activity was defined as "an act on the part of the teacher which involves discernible contact with an object or person" (Prescott et al., 1967, p. 65). The Reichenberg-Hackett (1962) noncommunicative category was used with only one change; that is, in addition to "child centered neutral" and "silent supervision," "conversation with persons other than children" was included and the subjective "teacher focusing upon herself" was eliminated. In addition to the subcategories of "verbal" and "nonverbal" within the communicative category, targeting toward an individual child as a subgroup or as one of a group of children was added. The encouragement category was divided into: "supporting-extending," in which the teacher had to follow up on the self-initiated activity of the child; "responsive," which is a follow-up of a brief nature merely showing awareness of child activity; "routine" and "approval-nurturance," in which the teacher either recognized a child's accomplishments or helped the child handle negative feelings.

Rather than using a single management category, the data were divided into several categories and subcategories (see Table 13).

Note that there are similarities between this set of categories and both Kounin's (1970) and those reported in the signs section of this chapter. This similarity may indicate that with some careful work in the next few years we will be able to produce a reliable and viable taxonomy of teacher-management behavior in the preschool setting which can serve as a baseline

TABLE 13

CATEGORIES USED IN OBSERVING DAY-CARE CENTERS

Teacher Direction	Initiation and goal setting by teacher
Teacher Suggestion	In which children cannot determine choice
Teacher Approval	For behavior that meets a teacher social standard
Guidance	Including routine mechanics of management
Direct Guidance	Teacher specifically requests action
Indirect Guidance	Teacher expects obedience but may couch it in question form
Manipulative Guidance	"Nice people don't do that."
Distraction/Redirection	The stopping of behavior without calling attention to misbehavior
Restriction	Teacher behavior in conflict with child's wishes
Simple Restriction	Teacher warns or otherwise enforces and that firm enforcement has limits. Teacher makes limits very clear. May show anger.
Firm Enforcement	Of limits, absence of intent to hurt
Belittling/Disparaging	Teacher shows no acceptance of child's feelings or ideas
Neutral Activities	Teacher behavior has no intent to manage, such as an exchange of information or a care of physical needs

Note: Categories derived from E. Prescott, E. Jones, with S. Kritchevsky, "Group day care as a child-rearing environment," Pasadena, Calif.: Pacific Oaks College, 1967, report to Children's Bureau, U.S. Dept. of HEW, pp. 69–73.

for many studies rather than continue the development of separate scales by individual investigators. Prescott et al. (1967) extended the Reichenberg-Hackett categories to include one called "development of verbal skills" in which the teacher activity was designed to develop "the child's ability to listen, to express himself, or understand by means of verbal communication" (Prescott et al., 1967, p. 74). This consisted of: 1) repetitive activities such as group recitals, 2) expressive activities initiated by the teacher, 3) interpretive activities, in which the teacher helps the child put his thoughts into words, and 4) informational activities in which the teacher explains labels or meanings of words.

In addition to the teacher behaviors, observations were categorized under the heading of Lessons Taught and a global indication of children's responses. The lessons taught were: physical skills—large muscle activity, eye-hand coordination, verbal-physical coordination; social skills—rules of social living, dealing with other children, consideration of rights and feelings; intellectual attainment—formal skills, knowledge and awareness of world, sense of pleasure, awe, wonder; self-responsibility—self-sufficiency and independence, creativity and experimentation, control and restraint, dealing with strong emotions; other—can't decide, no lesson taught.

The children's responses were: 1) children are disinterested, bored, hyperactive, restless, lethargic, 2) children are somewhat disinterested, 3) children generally are involved, moderately interested, 4) children are involved and interested, and 5) children are exceptionally involved and genuinely interested (Prescott et al., 1967, p. 77).

In addition, structural variables and organization characteristics were recorded, such as the number of people, type of activity, time of day, type of physical space, size of the center, pupil characteristics (age, socioeconomic status), and administrative framework, as well as staff background characteristics. Our concern here, however, is not with the huge mass of data collected and reported by Prescott, but in those data and relationships specific to systematic observation.

Reliabilities are reported for observations in each category varying from the high sixties to the high eighties. They also compared whether or not ratings changed as more information was accumulated on a particular teacher and found that differences were mostly accounted for by six or eight observations, but they used 10 as their sample to be on the safe side. Sixteen hundred and four observations were then reported for these 50 day-care centers in order to achieve what they call their major purpose, which was "to obtain an overview of the functioning of the day care center as a working unit, based on observation of teacher-child interaction within a variety of settings which contain certain features and are peopled by individuals of varying characteristics" (Prescott et al., 1967, p. 97). The value of adding direction to the communication category is indicated by their finding that over three-quarters of all teacher behavior was directed to an individual child, even though these were group settings. About half of each teacher's time was spent in guidance (25 percent) and encouragement (20 percent) and only 7 percent was spent in restriction. A fifth of the teacher's time was spent in noncommunicative activities and the remainder of her time was equally divided between the neutral and teacher-direction categories. Although the categories were double-coded for teacher's active development of children's verbal skills, only a mean 15.4 percent of all teacher behaviors were so categorized. Most of this behavior was directed toward individuals.

In each day-care center Prescott ranked three lessons in each of the 10 observations as rank 1 (primary), rank 2 (secondary) or rank 3 (tertiary) based on the degree to which the lesson was the major emphasis of the teacher during the observation period. The ranks were based on observation of time the teacher was actively teaching. Ranking does not reflect the great amount of time in which children were learning but a teacher was not directly teaching. Indeed, they report "the majority of teachers taught no primary lessons, as

rated, in more than half the observations .... many teachers set up a rich environment for children to pursue their own activities and then withdraw to observe unless help is needed" (Prescott et al., 1967, p. 105). Their data show what a teacher taught on 10 primary, 10 secondary and 10 tertiary lessons in each of the 10 observations. When the totals for these three ranks (calculated from Prescott et al., 1967, p. 107) are combined, 553 episodes dealt with self-responsibility, 487 with social skills, 445 with intellectual skills, and 254 with physical skills out of a total of 1,739. There were 1,604 observations, so that 4,812 (1,604 x 3) were possible. The difference represents the number of times no lesson was taught (2,932) and inability to classify (141). As we would expect for a preschool day-care operation, the greatest amount of direct teaching is in the social-emotional area (approximately 60 percent of the lessons) followed by intellectual skills (approximately 25 percent) and physical skills (approximately 15 percent).

Fifty-two variables (including teacher behavior, lessons taught, children's responses; some presage variables such as teacher attitudes, training, space; and some global ratings of tempo and teacher verbalization) were factor-analyzed. For the 52 variables and the 104 teachers, four patterns were extracted: pattern 1, encouragement/restriction; pattern 2, conformity to routine; pattern 3, group teaching; and pattern 4, independence. Each pattern includes a mixture of teacher behavior and lessons taught. The variables which load on each seem self-explanatory and closely related to the pattern label. The third pattern emphasizes group-centered versus individual-centered teaching, yet we noted earlier that more than 75 percent of the teachers' behaviors were directed toward an individual child. Pattern 4, independence, includes such variables as low number of lessons taught, noncommunicative behavior, self-sufficiency lessons, and lessons in dealing with strong emotion. It is important to note that the stability of the conclusions drawn on the basis of this analysis are questionable since there were 52 variables and 104 teachers.

The Prescott study presents data on both presage-process interactions and process (teacher)–process (child) interaction, but no information on the effects of either setting or teacher variables on child performance or personality as measured by tests or observation outside the day-care classroom. They related teacher behavior to children's responses by including children's response as one of the variables in the matrix from which the four factors were extracted. Children's responses loaded positively (0.70) on pattern 1, encouragement, but did not load on any of the other three patterns. This means that the children were more likely to be exceptionally interested and involved in an atmosphere of encouragement; children were more likely to be disinterested, bored and restless in an atmosphere of restriction.

Data are presented on center relationships as well as teacher-pupil relationships. When the centers are compared and the variables factor-analyzed, four patterns emerge which characterize centers. Only one factor, freedom-restraint, relates both to teacher pattern 1 and to children's responses. Children's responses load at 0.71 on center pattern "freedom-restraint." Further, children's responses and teacher pattern 1 are positively related to the quality of space. There are relationships between activity settings, time of day, age of children, the size of the center and children's process responses. Free choice is more likely to elicit high interest, and it elicits few very low or low child responses. On the other hand, teacher-directed activities toward an individual elicit almost a quarter of the child responses in the low category. Interestingly enough, juice and lunch time do not have the same positive quality shown in free play or free choice. Younger children are less likely to be seen as interested. Responses vary by size of center; no children were ranked as very highly interested in any of the 14 centers with more than 60 children.

In summary, a category system built originally on specimen description procedures along with setting categories arrived at a priori, or such independent variables as child's age, was used to assess 50 day-care centers. Patterns of teacher behavior were identified as well as patterns of center operations and some process-process relationships were found among teacher behavior, center organization, and pupil level of interest. Since this is the most comprehensive study of group day care, it is disappointing that no product measures on children were secured and that the only measure on the children is that of interest in the setting. This is particularly disappointing because Prescott and her colleagues end their report with a series of recommendations about the organization and operation of day-care centers which unfortunately rest far more on theoretical grounds than upon solid empirical data. Although one may subscribe to their recommendations philosophically, it will take a good deal of further study and much tighter logic to demonstrate the relationships among the mix of variables such as teacher behavior, classroom organization type, amount of lessons taught, and product variables such as child behavior and achievement.

TRAIT-RATING SCALES

HOME SETTINGS

We have selected only one observation of parent behavior to include in the home cell. Our focus was on maternal behavior observed during a teaching setting, which eliminates all of the general natural-history studies. Schaefer and Furfey (1967) and Schaefer (1969) investigated the effects of a home-tutoring program beginning at 15 months of age and continuing to age three on a group of underprivileged Negro infants in Washington, D.C. Thirty experimental and 30 control infants were selected from one of the most deprived sections of the city. The experimental infants were tutored at home an hour a day, five days a week, by volunteer tutors. These tutors observed the behavior of the mother during the tutoring session and completed structured rating scales on the basis of their observation. The structured rating scales reflect Schaefer's long years of work on maternal attitudes and maternal behavior. The infants were tested at 14, 21, 27 and 36 months on either the Bayley or the Stanford-Binet tests and at 36 months on the Johns Hopkins Perceptual Test. In addition to IQ scores, the behavior of the infant in the testing situation was also observed, by means of the Bayley Infant Behavior Profile. On the basis of a factor analysis of profile items, Schaefer used a dimension, task-oriented behavior, as a product measure. Maternal behavior at 16, 30 and 36 months as rated in the home setting was reliably correlated with child behavior at 36 months. The correlations between hostile involvement on the mother's part and the child's hostility, belligerency or irritability are all over .40. The correlations between hostile detachment of the mother and child's hostility, belligerence, negativism and irritability are all over 0.45. The relationships between maternal hostile involvement, hostile detachment, low interest, low involvement, low verbal expressiveness and Stanford-Binet scores at 36 months are all over −0.35. The child's own hostile behavior correlates better than −0.42 to the Stanford-Binet scores at 36 months, and higher than at least −0.49 to the Johns Hopkins test. The pattern thus presented by Schaefer seems to indicate an interrelationship between affective and intellectual behavior in which the mother's negative affect relates positively to the child's negative affect and negatively to the child's intellectual performance. The child's negative affective behavior also relates negatively to his intellectual performance (Schaefer, 1969). Schaefer's results are in line with those reported from the Florida Parent Education Project in which there was, especially for the boys, a high degree of positive relationship between observed maternal positive affective measures and child intellectual performance at age two (Herman, 1970).

HEAD START SETTINGS

Conners and Eisenberg (1966) studied 38 teachers in a six-week summer program. The Peabody Picture Vocabulary Test was administered to the pupils at the beginning and end of the program. Observers recorded episodes of the teachers' classroom activities and then rated the teachers on three dimensions, such as "warm," and nine values. These values were subjective judgments on the parts of the raters and included such items as valuing intellectual growth. They reported relationships between these two dimensions, as "warm" and "high on valuing intellectual growth," and the growth in children's vocabulary on the Peabody Picture Vocabulary Test. They also reported some affective relationships, but the material is such that the grounds for making judgments are not clear. The inherent weakness of rating scales—that they rely so highly on observer judgment—might possibly have had a serious effect upon these data.

Harvey, White, Prather, and Hoffmeister (1966) studied presage-process variables, the relationship between teacher's personality or beliefs and his classroom behavior, but did not explore the relationship between teacher behavior and pupil outcome. They studied 30 women teachers who were divided into three groups of 10 on the basis of their scores on "This I Believe," a sentence completion test designed to reflect the teacher's conceptual system. Ten teachers were identified as "concrete," defined by such attributes as "high absolutism, high normative statements, ethnocentrism, and religiosity." Ten of the 168 teachers tested fit the other extreme of abstractness because their responses "implied a high degree of novelty and *appropriateness, independence without negativism, high rela-*

tivism and contingency of thought, and the general usage of multidimensional rather than unidimensional interpretive category" (Harvey et al., 1966, p. 374). Another 10 were at the next lower level of abstraction. The 30 teachers represented 10 of the most concrete, 10 of the most abstract, and 10 of the next most abstract. All had prior teaching experience. Each teacher was observed for approximately 2½ hours by two different observers a week apart. The observations took place in the normal classroom. The observers had been trained in seven sessions and their interobserver-reliability coefficient was almost 0.70. The behavior they saw was rated on 26 behavioral dimensions on a six-point scale. These dimensions are shown in Table 14. On 22 of the 26 dimensions the high-abstract teachers scored higher than the low-abstract teachers. These differences were significant in 14 of the 26 dimensions. The teachers rated as abstract differed from those rated concrete on 20 of the 26, and differed sig-

nificantly on eight. The results showed that the "This I Believe" test served as a predictor of the rated behavior of preschool teachers. The larger question, of course, of the effect on the child was unanswered.

A Head Start study was conducted by Beller (1969) to examine the effects of teachers' behavior on children's performance with a problem-solving task. Two independent measures of teacher effectiveness were used. First, out of a group of 18 teachers the Head Start supervisor identified three as "good and effective" on her criteria (warm, child-oriented, well-prepared program) and three others who were not. Second, as an independent check, all 18 teachers were observed by a team of six observers who collected 12 observations in each classroom. They event-sampled dependency sequence, and placed the observed behavior into categories of child-teacher interaction and teaching-style scales which Beller had previously developed. There were 10 scales: controlling children, closeness to children, individual child-oriented, approval-oriented, encouraging exploration, enjoying teaching, work-play distinction, flexible classroom arrangement, flexible curriculum, and control of materials by children. The scales were scored on a nine-point continuum after the sixth and twelfth observations. The supervisor's "effective" teachers were different in the prediction direction on eight of the 10 scales (not on encouraging exploration and flexible curriculum).

All the children in the six classrooms were given a problem-solving task (finding an object hidden under one of three boxes) in which the conditions of reinforcement were what Beller called "intrinsic nonsocial," that is, reinforcement was solving the problem and knowing one had solved the problem. Beller (1969) found that pupils of

TABLE 14

RATING DIMENSION ON THE "THIS I BELIEVE" TEST

1. Warmth	13. Ingenuity
2. Perceptiveness	14. Utilization of resources
3. Flexibility	
4. Relaxed	15. Task effectiveness
5. Attention to individual	16. Diversity of activity
	17. Smoothness
6. Involvement	18. Consistency
7. Enjoyment	19. Functional explanation of rules
8. Enlistment child participation	
	20. Nonfunctional explanation
9. Encourage individual responsibility	21. Unexplained rules
	22. Rule orientation
10. Encourage expression of feelings	23. Determination of procedure
	24. Need for structure
11. Encourage creativity	25. Punitiveness
12. Teach new concepts	26. Anxiety

Note: Categories derived from O. J. Harvey et al., "Teachers' belief systems and preschool atmospheres." *Journal of Educational Psychology*, 1966, 57 (6), 378.

teachers who made less distinction between work and play, who interacted affectionately with the children, who were more flexible in their classroom arrangement, and more flexible in programming their instruction, performed better on our problem-solving task under conditions of intrinsic reinforcement than did children of teachers with opposite characteristics (p. 8).

Supervisor judgment has often been used as a criterion of teacher effectiveness and has been severely criticized as lacking objectivity. In the Beller study, however, the supervisor indicated what her criteria were; these criteria were independently checked by means of observation and were found to be valid discriminators between the two sets of teachers. One could argue whether the term "good and effective" is valid. The agreement between observations and supervisor rating only indicated that both were able to see the same discriminating behaviors. However, Beller's further check by means of pupil performance marks the study as containing far more information than the majority of studies reviewed in this chapter. That is, the behavior of teachers in dependency sequences in Head Start and Get Set classrooms predicted the behavior of their children in a problem-solving, learning situation. It is of special importance that Beller's scales are a mixture of affective and classroom-organization dimensions with heavy emphasis on the affective domain. Nevertheless, although there were no ratings of teachers "teaching" except in the encouragement of exploration, teacher affective behavior was found to be predictive of pupil cognitive problem-solving behavior. Distinctions between affect and cognition did not seem to be relevant here. One of the implications from Beller is the importance of the affective domain in its influence upon intellectual learning for very young children. In this regard, his classroom study supports and goes along with Soar's (1966, 1970) classroom work and also relates to that of Gordon (1969) and Schaefer (1969) with even younger children.

The event-sampling and trait-rating studies, which include mixes of presage-process-product findings, seem to indicate that at least for preschool children observations of teaching behavior must include a wide range of the ecological variables and data on the interpersonal relationships between teacher and pupil, and on the personality, attitudes and the belief system of the teacher or parent acting as teacher.

This may be one place or one issue in which the function of age becomes an important variable. The long history of classroom studies of teacher personality in relation to pupil achievement have generally borne little fruit. However, when we turn to the young child, the studies presented above, although far from conclusive and but a mere beginning, indicate that this dimension may be more important than it has seemed to be for older children.

LEVEL OF COGNITIVE INTERACTION

Although we have indicated above that for young children there are relationships between adult affective behaviors and child cognitive behaviors, we need a good deal more work to extricate and examine the adult cognitive behaviors and the cognitive teaching behaviors which occur in the classroom and in home-learning settings, and their effects upon the child. As we indicated at the beginning of this chapter, the research emphasis has been on the process of instruction in the noncognitive domains and in the setting for instruction. When we reach this last set of cells the data seem even more striking. There are only two studies which present observation-schedule possibilities for dealing in any sophisticated fashion with cognitive behavior outside of general language behavior, and in only one of these are there data about relationships between the observed cognitive level of operation in the classroom and independent measures of pupil performance.

There are hints in many of the studies

above, and there are indirect data. For example, as a part of the larger Hess et al. study (1968), data were collected on maternal language behaviors. They found that the mother's level of language abstraction was significantly related to child performance, but for our purposes such data do not fit within the realm of systematic observation. Maternal language was measured outside the teaching situation and was a presage-product measure. While we may assume that the mother, since she used a good deal of abstraction, used it in the presence of the child, we still lack a direct measure of mother as teacher in which maternal language is assessed.

Similarly, Prescott et al. (1967) indicated that about 15 percent of all teacher behavior was directed at the improvement of verbal skills, but there was no careful presentation of the ways teachers did this nor any data relating the results.

Spaulding's (1967, 1969) Teacher Activity Rating Schedule has a cognitive section. Teacher behavior is noted in such items as: presenting concrete data, presenting concepts in verbal form, presenting two or more rules in generalizations (all three of which are connected with induction), asking for deductions, labels, giving labels and generalizations, listening to or observing with pupils giving labels, operating inductively or deductively such as expressing a rule, stating a generalization, and listing names in rote fashion (Spaulding, 1969, pp. 11–12). These are not organized in any hierarchy but fall under his general categories of structuring and restructuring, information and listening, so that the encouragement of pupil cognitive behaviors by the teacher is spread across his scale in a nonhierarchical fashion.

Soar developed a modification of the Florida Taxonomy of Cognitive Behavior (Brown et al., 1968) which was a translation of Bloom's Taxonomy (1956). The Florida Taxonomy consists of observational items in the seven levels of cognitive activity: 1)

memory, 2) translation, 3) interpretation, 4) application, 5) analysis, 6) synthesis, and 7) evaluation. Soar developed his form to be more applicable to kindergarten and first grade. Based on the observation of Head Start kindergarten classrooms, he changed a number of the items but maintained the hierarchy and the overall construction and rationale of the original Bloom and Florida Taxonomies. He submitted his data to factor analysis (see earlier description of his project). Each factor contains both teacher and pupil behaviors so that it is possible to have items on a factor that apply only to a teacher or only to pupils, or to both. Soar identified six factors: information giving and receiving, molecular learning tasks, complex versus simple information processing, nonsubstantive similarities and differences, learned tasks, and evaluation, and pupils interact—teacher intervenes. He indicated that "the data from the cognitive taxonomy seem in many ways the least clear of all the systems. It was the most subjective to code, and the analysis was the most difficult to interpret" (Soar, 1970, p. 11). This led him to continue his modification of the schedule, moving further away from some of the original Bloom rationale, but still preserving the hierarchical structure. One of his problems may have been that the items contained on his scale, although observable when translated into kindergarten terms, did not occur with much frequency because the emphasis in so many preschool programs was not on teacher cognitive behaviors. Further, observers using the cognitive taxonomy listened to audio tape and tallied once every three seconds. Many of the preschool classrooms were organized so that considerable cognitive activity occurred in small groups or by individual pupils, which would not have been recorded on audio tape. Video tape or live observation may yield a much richer collection of data which might then be more amenable to classification into the taxonomy. Nevertheless, Soar found reliable correlations between the "evaluation" factor of the cognitive taxonomy (which consists of: pupil sounds letters; pupil reads; teacher compares with criteria, rule or plan; pupil compares with criteria, rule or plan) and two of the reading subtests on the Follow Through evaluation of pupil growth measures in kindergarten. Growth during the school year was related at about the $r = 0.30$ level across 35 kindergarten classrooms with scores on this factor.

The Teacher Practices Observation Record, described earlier as a sign system, also yielded a cognitive factor called "logical thinking" in Soar's first year of evaluating Follow Through kindergartens. It consisted of such items, among others, as: T involves p in uncertain or incomplete situation; T asks p to support answer or opinion with evidence; T helps p discover and correct factual errors and inaccuracies; T questions misconceptions, faulty logic, unwarranted conclusions; and T encourages p to put his ideas to a test.

The "logical thinking" factor correlated reliably with pupil-gain scores in kindergarten in the numerical concept activation, and the total of these subtests of the national Follow Through evaluation tests. These data from Soar are just a beginning step into the whole realm of the observation and measurement of identifiable cognitive activities in the preschool setting. The sparsity of such information indicates the challenge which remains.

CONCLUSIONS

It is evident that systematic observation of the teaching-learning situation in the preschool years is in its infancy. An extensive search of the literature, including the numerous studies using a behavior-analysis framework, yielded only the twenty-odd references shown on Table 1. The blank spaces on that table reveal that we need more studies in day-care and nursery-school settings, more time-sampling studies, and far more attention to the level of interaction.

Further, a review of the work reveals another essential weakness. If we conceptualize a model of instruction that describes the relationships among presage variables (pupil-entering characteristics, teacher-entering characteristics, demographic characteristics), process variables (teacher and pupil behavior in the setting, organization and content factors), and goal or product variables (immediate and long-range effects of pupils in both cognitive and affective domains) (Gordon, 1968), then it is evident that these studies, although contributing both to our methodological and substantive knowledge, fall short. The investigations using specimen description either describe teacher process variables and attempt to relate them to teacher presage variables (Reichenberg-Hackett, 1962) or to pupil process variables (Braun & Lasher, 1970; Kounin, 1970), or to some external judgment of effectiveness (Scott, 1969).

The investigators using time-sampling approaches also most often select only a portion of the total transactional instructional system. Gordon's group (Gordon, 1969; Gordon & Jester, 1970; Herman, 1970) related parental presage variables (attitude, self-concept demographic data), parent process variables (a very limited observation of maternal behavior during teaching sessions), and child test performance; Hess's group (Brophy, 1970; Hess et al., 1968) analyzed the relationships among parent presage (social class), parent and child process, and child performance (IQ and cognitive task) variables. Both efforts represent beginnings with need for refinement of observational tools and child performance measures, and clarification of presage variables as so gross a label as social class.

The classroom investigators using time sampling studied mainly process (teacher behavior)–product (pupils' test performance) interaction. Soar (1970) analyzed teacher and pupil processes, including cognitive level of interaction and pupil test performance, drawing direct relationships between process and product measures. Miller et al. (1969, 1970) and DiLorenzo et al. (1969) interposed program labels between their process and product measures which may obscure the results. Katz (1968) and Spaulding (1969) described only teacher process–pupil process interactions.

Prescott's large-scale study of day-care centers, using a combination of specimen-description and event-sampling approaches, yielded relationships between presage (setting and teacher variables) and teacher and pupil process measures, but did not investigate products. The pupil process measure was very weak, a rating of interest.

Schaefer's (1969) analysis of trait-ratings showed relationships between maternal affect behavior during tutoring with child affect and cognitive measures during testing. The classroom studies revealed relationships between teacher presage (belief system) and teacher process variables (Harvey et al., 1966), and teacher process–pupil product measures (Beller, 1969).

What we have, then, are threads of relationships which can be sewn together from different studies. We need more comprehensive investigations.

A third conclusion we can draw is the need for common instrumentation. A number of observation schedules seem to use similar items. We would suggest a further analysis of these studies to produce observation items and schedules which demonstrate some reliable relationship, even of a response-response type, with other measures. Thus we might develop a pool of both teacher and pupil process measures which have been found to relate either to each other or to presage and/or product measures. Future investigators would then be able to either replicate these relationships or develop more total instructional system studies built on the already developed techniques and their findings.

Although the picture looked discouraging as it unfolded in our investigation, these early efforts offer promise to increase our knowledge of the nature of preschool teaching and learning and its effects upon the child.

REFERENCES

Barker, R. G., & Wright, H. F. *Midwest and its children.* New York: Harper & Row, 1954.

Beller, E. K. Teaching styles and their effects on problem-solving behavior in Headstart programs. In E. H. Grotberg (Ed.), *Critical issues in research related to disadvantaged children.* Princeton, N.J.: Educational Testing Service, 1969. Seminar #6. Pp. 1–22.

Braun, S. J., Holzman, M. S., & Lasher, M. G. Teachers of disturbed preschool children: An analysis of teaching styles. *American Journal of Orthopsychiatry,* 1969, 39, 609–618.

Braun, S. J., & Lasher, M. G. *Preparing teachers to work with disturbed preschoolers.* Cambridge, Mass.: Nimrod Press, 1970.

Brophy, J. Mothers as teachers of their own preschool children: The influence of socioeconomic status and task structure. Unpublished manuscript, The University of Texas, 1969.

Brophy, J. E. Mothers as teachers of their own preschool children: The influence of socioeconomic status and task structure on teaching specificity. *Child Development,* 1970, 41, 79–94.

Brown, B. B. *The experimental mind in education.* New York: Harper & Row, 1968.

Brown, B., Ober, R. L., Soar, R. S., & Webb, J. N. The Florida taxonomy of cognitive behavior. Gainesville, Fla.: Institute for the Development of Human Resources, 1968. (mimeo)

Conners, K., & Eisenberg, L. The effect of teacher behavior on verbal intelligence in Head Start children. Final report. Baltimore: Johns Hopkins Hospital, 1966. (mimeo)

DiLorenzo, L., Salter, R., & Brady, J. *Prekindergarten programs for educationally disadvantaged children.* Final report, Project #3040, U.S. Office of Education. Albany, N.Y.: New York State Education Department, Office of Research and Evaluation, 1969.

Gewirtz, H. B., & Gewirtz, J. L. Visiting and caretaking patterns for kibbutz children:

Age and sex trends. *American Journal of Orthopsychiatry,* 1968, 38, 427–443.

Gordon, I. J. *A parent education approach to provision of early stimulation for the culturally disadvantaged.* Final report, Fund for the Advancement of Education. Gainesville, Fla.: University of Florida, Institute for the Development of Human Resources, 1967.

Gordon, I. J. (Ed.) *Criteria for theories of instruction.* Washington, D.C.: Association for Supervision and Curriculum Development, National Education Association, 1968.

Gordon, I. J. *Early child stimulation through parent education.* Final report to Children's Bureau, Grant #PHSR-306, 306(01). Gainesville, Fla.: University of Florida, College of Education, Institute for the Development of Human Resources, 1969. (mimeo)

Gordon, I. J., & Jester, R. E. *Instructional strategies in infant stimulation.* Mimeo statement of Grant #NIH-MH-17347-01. Gainesville, Fla.: University of Florida, College of Education, Institute for the Development of Human Resources, 1970.

Harvey, O. J., White, B. J., Prather, M. S., & Hoffmeister, J. K. Teachers' belief systems and preschool atmospheres. *Journal of Educational Psychology,* 1966, 57(6), 373–381.

Herman, S. The relationship between maternal variable scores and infant performance in a Negro experimental stimulation training population. Unpublished doctoral dissertation, University of Florida, 1970.

Hess, R. D., Shipman, V. C., Brophy, J. E., & Baer, R. M. *The cognitive environment of urban preschool children.* Chicago: University of Chicago, Graduate School of Education, 1968.

Jester, R. E., & Bailey, J. Hearing-speech scores on the Griffiths mental development scale as a function of language usage in the home. In I. J. Gordon (Ed.), *Reaching the child through parent education: The Florida approach.* Gainesville, Fla.: Institute for the Development of Human Relations, University of Florida Research Reports, 1969. Pp. 21–31.

Katz, L. G. A study of the changes in behavior of children enrolled in two types of Head Start classes. Unpublished doctoral dissertation, Stanford University, 1968.

Katz, L. G. Teaching in preschools: Roles and goals. *Children,* 1970, 17, 42–48.

Katz, L. G., Peters, D. L., & Stein, N. S. Observing behavior in kindergarten and preschool classes. *Childhood Education,* 1968, 44, 400–405.

Kounin, J. S. *Discipline and group management in classrooms.* New York: Holt, Rinehart, & Winston, 1970.

Kowatrakul, S. Some behaviors of elementary school children related to classroom activities and subject areas. *Journal of Educational Psychology,* 1959, 50, 121–128.

Miller, L., et al. Experimental variation of Headstart curricula: A comparison of current approaches. Annual report on Research Grant #CG8199, OEO, Louisville, Ky.: University of Louisville, June 1969.

Miller, L., et al. Experimental variation of Headstart curricula: A comparison of current approaches. Progress report #5, Grant #CG8199, OEO, Louisville, Ky.: University of Louisville, January, 1970.

Ober, R. L., et al. The development of a reciprocal category system for assessing teacher-student classroom verbal interaction. Paper presented at the meeting of the American Educational Research Association, Chicago, February 1968.

Prescott, E., Jones, E., with Kritchevsky, S. Group day care as a child-rearing environment. Report to Children's Bureau, U.S. Department of Health, Education and Welfare. Pasadena, Calif.: Pacific Oaks College, 1967. ED 024 453.

Radin, N., & Weikart, D. A home teaching program for disadvantaged preschool children. *Journal of Special Education,* 1967, 1, 183–187.

Rashid, M. The teacher, teacher style and classroom management. In E. H. Grotberg (Ed.), *Critical issues in research related to disadvantaged children.* Princeton, N.J.: Educational Testing Service, 1969. Seminar #2. Pp. 1–27.

Reichenberg-Hackett, W. Practices, attitudes and values in nursery group education. *Psychological Reports,* 1962, 10, 151–172.

Rubenstein, J. Maternal attentiveness and subsequent exploratory behavior in the infant. *Child Development,* 1967, 38, 1089–1100.

Schaefer, E. S. A circumplex model for maternal behavior. *Journal of Abnormal and Social Psychology,* 1959, 59, 226–235.

Schaefer, E. S. Home tutoring, maternal behavior and infant intellectual development.

Paper delivered at the Symposium on Cognitive Stimulation in Infancy, American Psychological Association, Washington, D.C., September 1969.

Schaefer, E., & Furfey, M. Intellectual stimulation of culturally deprived infants during the period of early verbal development. Informal progress report, 1967. (mimeo)

Scott, M. Some parameters of teacher effectiveness as assessed by an ecological approach. Nashville, Tenn.: George Peabody College for Teachers, Demonstration and Research Center for Early Education, 1969. DARCEE papers and reports, 3, 3. (mimeo)

Sears, P. S. *The effect of classroom conditions on the strength of achievement motive and work output of elementary school children.* Cooperative research project No. OE 873. Stanford, Calif.: Stanford University, 1963.

Sears, P. S., & Dowley, E. M. Research on teaching in the nursery school. In N. L. Gage (Ed.), *Handbook of research on teaching.* Chicago: Rand McNally & Co., 1963. Pp. 814–864.

Soar, R. An integrative approach to classroom learning. Final reports on Grant 5-R11MH-01096 to University of South Carolina and Grant 7-R11MH02045 to Temple University. Philadelphia, Pa.: Temple University, 1966.

Soar, R. Follow through model implementation. Interim report on Project #OEG-0-8-522471-4618(100), U.S. Office of Education. Gainesville, Fla.: University of Florida, College of Education, Institute for the Development of Human Resources, 1970.

Spaulding, R. Achievement, creativity and self-concept correlates of teacher-pupil transactions in elementary school classrooms. Cooperative research project No. 1352. Urbana, Ill.: University of Illinois, 1963.

Spaulding, R. L. *An introduction to the use of the Coping Analysis Schedule for Educational Settings (CASES) and the Spaulding Teacher Activity Rating Schedule (STARS).* Durham, N.C.: Duke University, Education Improvement Program, 1967.

Spaulding, R. L. *Classroom behavior analysis and treatment using the Coping Analysis Schedule for Educational Settings (CASES) and the Spaulding Teacher Activity Rating Schedule (STARS).* Durham, N.C.: Duke University, Education Improvement Program, 1968.

Spaulding, R. L. *Classroom behavior analysis and treatment.* Durham, N.C.: Duke University, Education Improvement Program, 1969.

Swift, J. Effects of early group experience: The nursery school and day care nursery. In M. L. Hoffman & L. W. Hoffman (Eds.), *Review of child development research.* New York: Russell Sage, 1964. Pp. 249–288.

Wright, H. F. Observational child study. In P. H. Mussen (Ed.), *Handbook of research methods in child study.* New York: Wiley, 1960. Pp. 71–139.

Wright, H. F. *Recording and analyzing child behavior with ecological data from an American town.* New York: Harper & Row, 1967.

CHAPTER 7 The Assessment of Teacher Competence

JOHN D. McNEIL
University of California, Los Angeles

W. JAMES POPHAM
University of California, Los Angeles

A focus on pupils reveals far more about the effectiveness of teachers than does direct study of teachers themselves. Discovery of the effective teacher through observation of pupils is not unlike the practice of physical scientists who determine the presence of an agent by measuring objects quite apart from that agent. For example, the existence of the planet Neptune was first discovered because of perturbations noted in Saturn's orbit. Support for the position that the ultimate criterion of a teacher's competence is his impact upon the learner has been offered by a number of individual researchers as well as professional associations (e.g., American Educational Research Association [AERA], 1952; Astin & Lee, 1966; Biddle & Ellena, 1964; Cohen & Brawer, 1969). But reservations in accepting pupil change as the chief criterion of teacher effectiveness have arisen both from technical problems in assessing learner growth and from philosophical considerations. Chief among the former are concerns about the adequacy of measures for assessing a wide range of pupil attitudes and achievement at different educational levels and in diverse subject-matter areas (Flanders, 1965), failure to account for in-structional variables that the teacher does not control (Musella, 1970; Smith, 1967), and unreliability in the results of teacher behavior, that is, inconsistent progress of pupils under the same teacher (Lawler, 1964).

Philosophical differences, of course, underlie questions about the selection of desirable changes to be sought in learners (B. B. Brown, 1966). Value differences also are seen in the preferred methodologies of teacher competence researchers, e.g., the importance of securing accurate descriptions of what teachers do, not what they should do (Bellack & Davitz, 1965), the need for knowledge about those teaching behaviors by which pupil gain can be maximized (Rosenshine, 1968), and the weighting of different effects of a teacher in a given classroom.

It is clear that various views exist about what teacher effectiveness is, and there are numerous applications of the construct. In the sections to follow we will delineate many of the research activities of those with particular bents and attempt to cast these efforts into a framework by which their relevancy can be shown to both a) practitioners who must make on-the-job decisions about teachers and b) investigators seeking knowledge about teaching. In so doing we hope to illuminate practices that are sapping fruitful inquiry as well as confusing decision-making procedures.

DELIMITATIONS

The Teacher

A teacher is a person engaged in interactive behavior with one or more students for the purpose of effecting a change in those students. The change, whether it is to be attitudinal, cognitive or motor, is intentional on the part of the teacher. This designation distinguishes the teacher from instructional materials such as films, books and other prepackaged learning sequences. Also a teacher is not simply one who engages in any of the numerous activities that may or may not be associated with the act of teaching—setting goals, preparing lessons, marking papers, defining, explaining, clarifying, maintaining order, problem-solving and encouraging participation. For instance, the part-time clerk hired to mark examination papers would not, by this definition, be considered a teacher. Restrictions in the term *teacher* are necessary inasmuch as the problems associated with the assessment of teacher effectiveness are not entirely methodological but partly conceptual.

So long as investigators equate "good teacher" with "good person," the problems associated with teacher effectiveness are unmanageable and efforts addressed to the subject are likely to be unproductive. Those who are satisfied with the notion that a good teacher is a good person, simple and true, will not advance knowledge or practice. As a step in the direction of more useful refinement of the key term *teacher,* consider a linguistic structure found in the Spanish language, illustrated by the word order in expressions such as *doctor bueno* versus *buen doctor.* The first signals one who can be of specific help to a client, e.g.,

an individual to contact if an appendix is to be removed. The second is an excellent human being who just happens to be a doctor but whose competency in medical skills is not indicated.

Another necessary delimitation stems from the difference between teaching and curricular responsibilities. The teacher is not equivalent to the curriculum maker, i.e., the one who formulates and decides upon instructional ends. The task of making curriculum involves many individuals, not just the teacher. The public, politicians and even pupils themselves influence decisions as to what shall be taught. Although teachers often interpret and operationalize the goal statements decided upon by others, classroom teachers are generally not responsible for selecting the goals of a school system. It is true, however, that in order to bring about the changes in learners which have been set by the public's representatives in legislatures and boards of education, teachers may decide to diagnose individual learners with respect to prerequisite skills that are logically and empirically linked to mandated intents. Diagnoses and subsequent setting of en route or enabling objectives are instructional activities which may contribute to teacher competency in achieving objectives of the school. But the person who decides upon an instructional goal, whether it is a state legislator, a school board member, or Mrs. Jones who teaches the fourth grade, should not *by virtue of that goal selection* be considered a teacher. A decision regarding ends is one thing. Accomplishing ends is another. A teacher by our definition *must* attend to the latter.

Systematic behavior modification programs such as Individually Prescribed Instruction (Lindvall & Cox, 1970) suggest that aspects of the teaching role may be discharged by instructional material developers, and that the position of classroom teacher could be converted to manager. Such programs are contingent upon the availability of reproducible instructional sequences that achieve intended growth with a specified population of learners. When growth is produced by materials, the classroom manager should be assessed by the percentage of cases in which he selects the right instructional package for the right pupil. Teaching responsibilities in such situations are based on the teacher's appropriate selection and delivery behavior which, of course, may subsequently be assessed by what happens to the learners.

Distinction in Purposes for Inquiry

To make sense of the diverse inquiries undertaken in the name of teacher effectiveness we must make distinctions in purpose. The administrator is looking for knowledge of teacher effectiveness in order to make a better decision in situations such as hiring or firing a teacher. The instructional supervisor or teacher himself wants to know what instructional procedures are most likely to prove useful in achieving certain instructional ends with given students. The researcher's purposes include satisfying a desire to describe accurately what teachers do, searching for associations between theoretically or empirically derived variables and learning, and demonstrating the power of a given factor or instructional operation to make a practical difference upon the outcome sought.

Measures of Personal Attributes, Processes and Outcomes

Finally, we must differentiate between measures of teacher effectiveness which are *outcome-based* as opposed to *process-based*. As indicated previously, the test of a teacher's effectiveness is his accomplishment of the goals of education as displayed in the pupil's behavior following instruction. The single most important deficiency in research on teaching effectiveness is the failure to use outcome measures as a criterion and, instead, to rely upon a priori measures of a teacher's personal attributes, such as his personality or education, his background,

or the measures of instructional processes such as his instructional strategies or his verbal behavior in the classroom. When one considers the idiosyncratic backgrounds of teachers and pupils, the great range in typical instructional objectives, and the immense variation in the environments where teaching occurs, it is unlikely that any processes or personal attributes on the part of teachers will invariably produce pupil growth. In particular, those considering the teacher effectiveness arena must keep the process versus outcome distinction clearly in mind. Inadvertent mixing of the two procedures has rendered many teacher effectiveness investigations confusing if not misleading.

RESEARCH AND THE PROBLEM OF ASSESSING TEACHER EFFECTIVENESS

Use of Process Criteria

Although recognizing that the best criterion by which to judge teacher competence is a modification in the learner, many researchers have succumbed to the difficulties associated with assessing such results and have opted to use more readily available criteria. By studying certain procedures employed by teachers and then assuming that these processes are related to pupil growth, the investigator gets at a readily accessible process criterion and hopes it reflects an outcome criterion.

An illustration of a common weakness in research investigation using process criteria appears in the work of Sprinthall, Whiteley, and Mosher (1966). In this study a relationship was detected between teachers' responses on psychological tests of cognitive flexibility and teacher classroom behavior classified as cognitively feasible. Then, because cognitive flexibility was *assumed* to be related to teaching proficiency, it was concluded that effective teaching and cognitive flexibility are related.

Similar criticisms of those who used only process criteria have been made by Saadeh

(1970). In his carefully reasoned analysis of the work of Ryans (1960) and Smith (1961), Saadeh argues that a valid criterion of effectiveness in teaching must be based upon pupil outcomes, not teaching process alone. Saadeh chides these and other investigators who jump, often arbitrarily, from a desirable product criterion to less defensible process criteria.

Tool Refinement Studies

Systems for guiding the observation of teachers and teachers and pupils interacting are legitimate tools for obtaining a more accurate account of what is taking place during the teaching act, and the use of such tools in analyzing aspects of the interaction may have implications for improving instruction. Sometimes, however, these systems are used for passing judgment upon those observed. Category sets and rating scales are two kinds of tools most used for these purposes. A recent two-part anthology, *Mirrors for Behavior,* features a collection of 79 observation instruments for classifying the relationship between teacher-pupil roles and the dynamics of instruction (Simon & Boyer, 1970). The compilers of the systems which appear in this collection were interested in instruments which revealed a number of different teaching behaviors, on the premise that an increased number of teaching behaviors would make a wide variety of teaching strategies possible and hence more diverse pupil outputs. It is clear that an effort was made to select instruments that would draw attention to variables believed important to the advancement of new goals (intellectual, social and emotional) for learners.

Examination of these instruments leads us to conclude that the tools are most useful for describing the teaching act rather than for identifying instructional variables of great power or for judging effective teachers. By way of illustration we refer to one sophisticated scheme in the collection, that produced by Bellack and his associates

(Bellack & Davitz, 1965). Use of this scheme has led to provocative hypotheses regarding the common dimensions of teaching acts. The system requires that classroom interaction be tape-recorded for later analysis by coders. Eight potential category types are available to the coders for every statement, indicating the type of speaker, type of pedagogical move, the kind of content, and the logical meaning of the content. The system has been used in collecting data about teachers in high school (lessons in economics), indicating that cycles of teacher and pupil behavior are rather consistent from classroom to classroom, almost as if teachers and pupils are playing a game with well-defined rules. From his data, Bellack was able to derive "rules of the classroom game"—not with the idea that these rules necessarily *should* be followed, but offering the possibility that one might want to consider the effect of breaking the rules—or general teaching patterns, chiefly found in the asking and answering of questions.

Large numbers of classifications for analyzing teacher behavior have accrued as a result of the popular emphasis upon categorical systems. However, the relationship of these categories to pupil growth has not been clearly demonstrated. Problems associated with these classification tools are numerous. Indeed, the rapidly growing library of observational systems may in some ways be a barrier to scientific advances because the systems tend to be used only by their authors or immediate associates. Other researchers are prone to develop their own systems with the result that it is difficult to compare findings.

The general technical problems in using a classroom observation system are described elsewhere in this volume. Typically, those instruments which require less inference from the observer have a greater amount of agreement among users, and the more reliable systems are those in which the dimensions are clearly defined and the cues to be used by observers are well-specified. Reliability is also higher when a) the observers have had training, b) there is agreement on what is to be coded, and c) there are fewer things for the observer to do during the observation. Validity of the observer's report seems to be enhanced by items that require little judgment, e.g., "teacher asks a question" as opposed to "teacher accepts pupils' sentiments."

Recommendations for development of a second generation of category systems have been made by Rosenshine and Furst (1971). Among their suggestions are those for a) modifying coding procedures so that the tendency for each observer to make his own ground rules when viewing unforeseen behavior is reduced, b) describing the context of classroom events when certain behavior is elicited, largely through an allowance for coding a greater range of events, c) selecting variables from many sources, e.g., those designing observation systems might use more of the primary variables from laboratory studies and instructional materials research. Also there should be more attention to cognitive variables, thereby balancing the heavy emphasis those instruments now place upon affective dimensions.

Some idea of the focus in existing systems is gained by noting that 62 of the instruments in *Mirrors for Behavior* possess affective categories while only 48 have cognitive categories. Other classes such as psychomotor activities, sociological structure and physical environment are less frequent. Many of the categories, of course, reflect the bias of the instruments' designers. Those who value divergent thinking, for example, tend to provide for the collection of data which show the amount of divergent thinking allowed. There are two additional indicators that designers of observation systems often have personal hatchets to hone regarding their categories as ends rather than descriptive constructs. First, they make little use of promising instructional variables from empirical studies in the laboratory or associated with instructional product development, e.g., prompting, pacing,

sequencing and advanced organizers. Second, they seldom seek evidence that the categories are associated with specific changes in learners. It is almost as if the authors of the new tools want an increased number of teachers to instruct according to the categories treated in their observation schemes regardless of the consequences to learners which may follow from the use of such practices.

There are, however, voices of optimism regarding the role that observational tools can play in yielding knowledge about effective instruction. Reviewing research in the area, Flanders and Simon (1969) stated that progress in research of teacher effectiveness is being made and that it is no longer necessary to concur with earlier summarizers who concluded that no single, specific, observable teacher act has yet been found whose frequency or present state of occurrence is invariably and significantly correlated with student achievement. Flanders and Simon contend that this progress is due partly to the availability of more sophisticated techniques for analyzing verbal communication. To illustrate their point they marshaled a set of widely separated studies which purported to show support for a relationship between teaching process and subsequent learner behavior, observing:

...that *the percentage of teacher statements that make use of ideas and opinions previously expressed by pupils is directly related to average class scores on attitude scales of teacher attractiveness, liking the class, etc., as well as to average achievement scores adjusted for initial ability* (Flanders & Simon, 1969, p. 1426).

Similarly Campbell and Barnes (1969), after years of failure and discouragement, stated that, "We have isolated the first of many microelements which will eventually be utilized in a quantified theory of instruction," and "we can now give a teacher something definite, both in the form of a diagnosis and subsequent prognosis to utilize in improving his teaching." The research cited by these authors in support of their optimistic conclusions was chiefly studies where the Flanders Interaction Analysis System was used (e.g., Amidon & Flanders, 1961; Beller, Weber, & Amidon, 1965; G. I. Brown, 1960; Campbell, 1968; Davidson, 1968; Flanders, 1965; LaShier, 1966; Nelson, 1966; Powell, 1968; Soar, 1967). More specifically, Campbell and Barnes concluded that their studies show that microelements involved in the indirect/direct ratios (indirectness) do affect achievement and attitude development in almost every subject area at almost every grade level from kindergarten through ninth grade.

On the other hand, there are those who believe that the verdict is not in and is not likely to be in for some time even on the relationship between a teacher's behavior as measured by the Flanders Interaction Analysis System and pupil achievement. After making a careful examination of the studies cited by Campbell and Barnes, Rosenshine questioned the validity of the conclusions drawn (Rosenshine, 1970). The essence of his analysis follows:

... if one goes beyond the summaries which Campbell & Barnes read and checks the original reports, then one sees flaws in all of the "results" they cited. ... In short, the Campbell & Barnes review, which is based on secondary information, yields conclusions inconsistent with the original data (p. 445).

Learner Performance Criteria

Let us remember that those interested in teacher effectiveness have different purposes and consequently vary in their interpretation of the problem. Some persons would be satisfied to know whether or not a teacher is getting desired results with the results themselves indicating effectiveness, not the process used. Others want to know how to increase the probability of getting desired results. Researchers of the latter persuasion are searching for lawful teaching behavior, i.e., validated procedures for achieving instructional ends. Their assumption is that

effective teaching will be recognized when lawful relationships are established between instructional variables and learner outcomes —that certain procedures in teaching will then, within certain probability limits, be labeled as effective or ineffective. Further, laws would be of practical use in answering the questions of how we should prepare a teacher and how we can help a teacher make more of a difference. To date there are no such laws, only a few leads or practices that are more likely than others to maximize the attainment of selected instructional ends.

Whereas researchers such as Gage (1968) hope to establish scientific laws for teaching, others are more in agreement with Dewey (1929), who held that it is an error to believe that scientific findings can be transformed into rules of action. Dewey limited the value of scientific conclusions and findings from laboratory experiments to such activities as helping the teacher make his practice more intelligent, flexible and better adapted to dealing with individual situations. He thought scientific findings could do this by drawing the teacher's attention to certain observations which would otherwise escape him; by enabling the teacher to interpret what goes on before him in the classroom—taking into account more remote consequences originally hidden from view and hence ignored in action; and by seeing more relations, therefore having more possibilities and alternatives. Whereas Dewey's concern was to emancipate the teacher from the need to follow tradition and special precedents, others want to establish new precedents for the teacher, only justifying them on scientific grounds.

Whether one is seeking laws or more limited associations, he is likely to engage in process-product research. Variations are obviously found in the conduct of this kind of research, but the most common practice is to associate teacher behavior with student outcome measures via a correlation study. The independent variables are usually scored from either a frequency count of specific observable teacher actions or check marks on a rating scale that calls for an observer making inferences about the teacher. Measures of the independent variable are then compared with measures of the dependent variable such as students' test scores on cognitive measures or indicators of changes in attitudes. The dependent measures are often adjusted for the learner's initial attitude, achievement or aptitude.

There is a paucity of experimental studies where researchers randomly selected an experimental group from a population of teachers, equipped members of the group with specific performance competencies and then measured the extent to which these teachers (as opposed to their controls) both a) performed differently in their classrooms and b) enhanced the cognitive or affective growth of students.

There are even fewer experimental studies *within* classrooms, even though the results of within classroom studies should be of great importance to the individual teacher interested in knowing the power of certain instructional variables as applied to his particular situation. Two illustrations of within classroom studies are those of Dalis (1970) and Page (1958). The Dalis study involved a single teacher who arranged for his students to receive "secret messages" prior to the commencement of instruction. The messages were actually statements regarding what the student was expected to learn (the variable being different degrees of specificity in the instructional objective). The study illustrates how a teacher can control for extraneous factors, even his own bias toward method and students, to produce reliable and valid evidence about the practical importance of a particular instructional technique. The Page study, which has been widely cited, remains an exemplar of a good experimental design for the conduct of within-classroom studies involving a large number of teachers and subject matters, therefore producing conclusions about instructional practice that have wide generality.

The development of knowledge would be better served if results from correlational studies suggesting the presence of a variable of practical importance were followed by experimental investigations, manipulating the variable in order to detect a causal relation, not mere association. Hasty and unwarranted extrapolation from correlates to cause has made suspect much process-product research.

Searching for a scientifically grounded set of answers to the problem of how to teach, Gage and his associates have employed a promising strategy for the conduct of process-product research (Gage, 1968). This strategy is characterized by an analytical approach to the study of the teaching act—with opportunity for examining both very specific teaching practices and specific effects of these practices. Discrete components or technical skills are selected for empirical verification. Among so-called teaching skills are the following: a) establishing appropriate frames of reference or points of view, b) achieving closure, or pulling together major points, linking old and new knowledge at appropriate places within a teaching lesson as well as at the end, and c) using questions—eliciting the kinds of thought processes and behavior desired, such as simple recall, concept formation or evaluation. By this strategy teaching is analyzed into limited and rather well-defined components that can be taught, practiced, evaluated, predicted and controlled in new ways. Gage and his associates are making teaching skills the basis for research on teacher effects and are also showing how an investigator can control for the ability of pupils and difficulty of topic, thereby attributing results to the differences among teachers. For example, they have attempted to determine the generality of explaining ability, that is, the degree to which the ability to explain one topic was correlated with the ability to explain another topic, and the degree to which the ability to explain a topic to one group of pupils on one occasion was correlated with the ability to explain the same topic to another group of pupils on another occasion. To this end they were able to design a study so that 60 learners were systematically shared among 40 teaching interns who instructed them in groups of five for a series of 15-minute lectures, the learners then being tested with 10-item examinations. By carefully rotating pupils and lecture topics, the researchers were able to conclude that the interns were somewhat consistent in their ability to explain the same topic to different learners on different occasions, but were not consistent in their ability to explain different topics.

The investigators admit that 15-minute explanations may be too large a unit of teaching behavior to yield valid, lawful knowledge and that a mean score on a 10-item test of comprehension may still be too large and complex a dependent variable. "But, compared with the massive, tangled, and unanalyzable units that have typically been studied in the past—in research on the lecture method, the discussion method, and class size, for example—such units seem precise and manageable indeed" (Gage, 1968, p. 606).

The scarcity of experimental classroom studies in which variations in instructional procedures have been manipulated and effectively measured has been documented by Rosenshine and Furst (1971), who expressed the opinion that in order to furnish conclusions which can be applied to teacher education programs, experimental studies should have: a) the teacher as the statistical unit of analysis, b) random assignment of teachers or classes to treatment, c) observational data on the fidelity of teacher behavior to the treatment, and d) student performance assessed by a variety of end-of-course tests. In their extensive search of the literature, Rosenshine and Furst found no more than ten studies which satisfied all four criteria.

In contrast to the absence of experimental studies, we have a plethora of process-product studies which attempt to relate observable teacher behaviors to student outcome measures—correlational studies, again. Failure of the investigators to use the same operational definitions of a term and to carry out the required experimental study make it difficult to derive conclusions from this research which would be of generalizable value. In their review of 50 such studies, Rosenshine and Furst (1971) teased out several categories of independent variables which they judged strong enough to warrant attention of researchers. Among their categories were these: a) clarity of presentation, including organization; b) variability including various levels of discourse, various levels of tasks, and a variety of materials and techniques; c) enthusiasm, including movement, gesture, and voice inflection; d) task orientation, including businesslike and achievement orientation of teacher; e) student opportunity to learn; f) teacher use of student ideas, including such behaviors as acknowledging the student's idea, modifying the idea, and praise; g) criticism, including disapproval, rejecting behavior and giving of academic directions; h) teacher's use of structuring comments, including use of review and signals in making transitions within a lesson; i) types of questions, including "what," "where," "why," and "how," as well as those believed associated with convergent and divergent behavior; and j) perceived difficulty of the course, including strictness in demanding high standards, challenge and ability of the class.

One general criticism of process-product inquiry is that the investigators have used deficient operational definitions of variables within the categories and rubrics such as those above, e.g., lack of agreement and specificity of behaviors which make up clarity in presentation. Other serious criticisms are directed at the failure to use appropriate dependent measures, e.g., lack of sensitivity in tests, and at the failure to show either theoretical or empirical linkage between the independent and dependent variables.

It is probably unrealistic to expect future researchers on teaching to carry out studies that overcome all the sources of invalidity noted by Campbell and Stanley (1963). However, they can approximate the standards set in that work. Also, it has been suggested (Rosenshine & Furst, 1971) that process-product research would improve if investigators:

1. Give more attention to the prior learning of students. It may be that pretest scores account for 70 to 80 percent of the posttest variance, leaving 20 to 30 percent of the potential influence to the teacher and other factors. Increasing the number of predictor variables such as socioeconomic status and home pressure for academic achievement also may help identify true teacher influence.

2. Account for the stability of teacher behavior across occasions. That is, observe how the teacher acts in a range of situations, e.g., during lecture, student independent study, student reporting and testing. Also, determine the frequency of certain teacher behavior when observer(s) are present and absent.

3. Collect evidence of the teacher's effectiveness one year to the next. Such evidence might be useful in generalizing about the stability of teacher effects.

4. Design studies in which teacher behavior is studied over a short period of time—15 minutes of instruction in each of 10 daily lessons. Use microteaching, for example, to allow for greater specification of criterion measures, control of instructional content, and more accurate recording and analyses of teaching behavior.

5. Consider likely possibilities for finding "disordinal interaction"—seek teaching behavior that will produce superior results with one type of learner but inferior results with learners of different characteristics.

6. Confirm the power of selected teacher behavior by systematically having teachers vary their practice in accordance with the prediction, and collect evidence of the results.

MAKING DECISIONS ABOUT TEACHERS

Decisions involve evaluating alternative courses of action and making a choice. Decisions that require judgments about teachers are made by many—teacher educators, school personnel officers, administrators, supervisors and teachers themselves. Wise choices about teachers are made only when adequate data are at hand for judging. Decision-makers would profit from complete and dependable information about each teacher involved in the decision: a) a description of the teacher's particular teaching situation (pupils, structure of school, community, etc.), b) the reasons for placing the teacher there, c) the instructional procedures used by the teacher and why those procedures were selected, and d) the instructional intents of the administrator and the teacher, as well as essential data evidencing the teacher's effects upon pupils. Complete data are typically not available, possibly because those making the decisions have not given enough thought to what is required for making warranted decisions about a teacher and, accordingly, have not arranged for the collection of such data. A second reason that data are not available is that researchers often do not pursue their investigations with awareness of the practical decisions that must be made by those working with teachers and the scientific conclusions that would be helpful in making these complex decisions.

One special problem occurs because it is not generally recognized that most decisions regarding a teacher require more information than those facts which relate to the teacher's effectiveness. There are many teacher variables that are probably not relevant to teaching—to teaching competence—but are important in making the decision, say, to hire a teacher. Work habits, years taught, degrees held, grades received and ethnic background are pedagogically weak variables. Such characteristics and qualities of teachers can be important for political and other reasons and their inclusion in making the decision may be justified. However, this is not to say that knowledge of the presence or absence of these variables in a given teacher should be sufficient for making a decision about him. Every decision that has to do with the position of teacher and the person who is to perform the role of teacher should take into account evidence showing an individual's competency to produce changes in learners. Another special problem arises from overlooking the distinction between making a decision and providing information to be used in the making of the decision. Discussion of this problem will be treated in subsequent sections of this chapter.

Dissatisfaction with Practices of Teacher Evaluation

Professionals and laymen alike are unhappy with what is loosely called the evaluation of teachers. Results of a national survey conducted in 1963 among teachers, principals and superintendents revealed that although three out of four superintendents and principals expressed confidence in their school system's program of evaluation, over half the teachers responding did not (NEA, 1964). From the respondents in the same survey it was learned that only about half the school systems followed formal procedures in evaluating their teachers, that written ratings or evaluations were required in three-fourths of the schools for probationary teachers and in two-thirds for continuing teachers, and that the principal was nearly always responsible for evaluation but often shared that responsibility with other officials. In most school systems with 25,000 or more pupils, continuing teachers were evaluated less often than once a year. Approximately 40 percent of the secondary school teachers were not observed even once for a period of five minutes while teaching. Adverse comments as stated by the respond-

ing teachers were that the evaluations were not accurate and that the administrative staff was too busy to do an effective job of evaluating. Some principals also criticized their program. Their dissatisfaction was that lack of time prevented them from making judgments and that the evaluations were not well communicated—teachers did not inquire about their evaluations and thus did not know in what areas improvement was expected.

In a more recent survey there is information that most school systems now have established formal procedures for evaluating teachers (Stemnock, 1969). However, there is little change reported with respect to frequency of evaluations and observations. In this new survey administrators have these four opinions about the impact contract negotiations are having or might have on teacher evaluation: 1) greater care is being taken by evaluators in conducting and recording their evaluation; 2) there is more teacher involvement in the evaluation; 3) there is a tendency to protect the less competent teacher and make it more difficult to dismiss him; and 4) teacher organizations should start policing their own ranks. Nine out of 10 teacher respondents in the 1969 survey indicated they approved regular evaluation of teachers and they were almost unanimous in agreeing that the principal should be responsible for the evaluations. Nearly 93 percent of responses from the teachers favored undertaking evaluation for the purpose of assisting the teacher to improve his teaching competency compared to 54 percent of the responses also favoring evaluations for the purpose of making it possible to dismiss poor teachers; and only 17 percent of the responses were in favor of using evaluation for determining advancement on the salary scale.

There are indicators that leaders of teachers' organizations differ in their reactions to evaluation of teachers. As President of the National Education Association, Helen Bain has argued that teachers should have the legal right to make policy decisions regarding licensure and standards of teaching before they can be held accountable (Bain, 1970). David Selden, President of the American Federation of Teachers, has suggested that teacher evaluation is a red herring, for it turns teachers against themselves rather than against other forces which are obstacles to quality of instruction. He fears abuses by administrators of the evaluative power. As an alternative to evaluation, Selden wants improved working conditions, higher teacher salaries, reduced class size and reduced teaching hours (Selden, 1970). Albert Shanker, President of the New York Federation of Teachers, has pointed out that the famous 1969 contract between New York teachers and the New York City Board of Education carried a statement of intent to develop objective measures of teacher competency:

The Board of Education and the union recognize that the major problem of our school system is the failure to educate all of our students and the massive academic retardation which exists especially among minority group students. . . .

The Board and the union . . . agree to join in an effort, in cooperation with universities, community school boards and parent organizations, to seek solutions to this major problem and to develop objective criteria of professional accountability (Buder, 1969, Sec. E, p. 6).[1]

Shanker was also quoted as being concerned about the problem of weeding out the unfit teacher, saying, "There are, within a system of this size, some people who obviously shouldn't be there."

While one can understand the desire of teachers' organizations to protect their members, it would seem that the moral stakes are too high for a teachers' association to let this protection motive render impotent the process of teacher evaluation. If the task of the labor group is the production of transistor radios, then one feels more comfortable about such protective tendencies than

when the object is the modification of human beings. Ethical considerations will hopefully incline teachers' organizations to play leadership roles in promoting defensible assessment of teacher proficiency.

A major reason for a school system's failure to act against incompetents is the lack of objective criteria for evaluating performance. Virtually all teachers on tenure receive satisfactory ratings. Rather than attempt to prove at a hearing that a teacher is unsatisfactory and risk being charged with abuse of discretion, a principal merely encourages the teacher to transfer to another school—shifting the locus of the problem rather than solving it.

Student disaffection is only one source triggering demands for appropriate techniques for evaluating professors in colleges and universities. An analysis of the major results of an extensive survey by the American Council on Education has been reported by Astin & Lee (1966). This report gives a description of the techniques now being used in evaluating college teachers in different types of undergraduate schools—providing a basis for a clinical appraisal of current practice. A damning finding from the summary is that while most institutions claim that teaching effectiveness is a major factor determining a faculty member's value to the institution, the kind of information most likely to reveal effectiveness in teaching is least likely to be used. The primary considerations in evaluating his teaching ability are the professor's scholarly research and publication, not information based on classroom visits, systematic student ratings, student performance on examinations or similar sources.

Teacher evaluation in programs for the education of teachers has been singled out as particularly deficient. Evaluation for purposes of improvement is wanting. College supervisors seldom have pre-observational conferences with novice teachers before a lesson is presented. Often there is conflict between the expectations of the college supervisor and the supervising teacher in the

---

[1] © 1969 by The New York Times Company. Reprinted by permission.

classroom where the novice is teaching. Neither of these two supervisors is likely to be explicit in defining the competencies which the student teacher must acquire from training. Performance tests to accompany objectives have rarely been prepared. It is true that the newer model programs for teacher education developed under the auspices of the USOE (National Center for Educational Research and Development, 1969) include measureable objectives for prospective teachers, but specification of teaching skills to be displayed following training has raised a bigger issue— the validity of the skills required. There is a danger that new teachers are learning practices which are not only irrelevant but harmful to pupil progress. In some instances teachers are learning contradictory skills at different institutions. For example, the Far West Regional Laboratory uses a minicourse to train teachers to repeat answers less often; but the Northwest Regional Laboratory has a training program in Flanders Interaction Analysis which has as one measure of the preferred "indirect teaching" more teacher's repetition of pupil answers (Rosenshine & Furst, 1971). Generally, evaluation of student teachers is based upon the most subjective of factors. By way of example, Sorenson asked 163 student teachers to "list the things you would tell your best friend to do in order to get a grade of 'A' from your present training teacher." The responses indicated that a high rating was perceived as more dependent upon 1) doing as one was told, 2) fawning or cultivating the supervisor— having coffee with her, 3) preparing lesson plans in advance, 4) keeping absolute control of the class at all times, 5) using an inductive approach in teaching, 6) giving extremely explicit directions and 7) being original (Sorenson, 1967).

Analysis of Discontent

Much unhappiness regarding assessment of teachers is for curricular rather than instructional reasons. The teacher may be labeled ineffective not because his pupils failed to achieve, but because the achievement was in directions that were not valued by the rater. For instance, whereas most people expect teachers in the elementary school to equip children with skills of reading, arithmetic and compliance behavior, others want children to acquire processes and attitudes associated with inquiry and critical questioning behavior. As we indicated previously, the determination of instructional ends is a curricular matter, not an instructional one. It is quite possible for one to be an effective teacher (able to produce specified changes in learners) even when the intended results lack validity in the eyes of others. Practically, however, any teacher runs a high risk of being rated as ineffective who does not have a precise agreement with those who are to evaluate him regarding the desirability of the outcomes sought.

In his description of management control theory and its impact upon practice, Cook (1970) concluded that evaluation is being either defined as or related to the providing of information for decision making. Cook says that this interpretation causes evaluation to move from the act of making a judgment itself as in the past (good-bad, effective-ineffective, pass-fail) to providing the person who has to make such judgments or decisions with the information needed to make them. Thus the evaluator escapes from the value question. The practical input of this view of teacher assessment is that it permits teachers to participate in the collection of information about the instructional results attained by themselves and their colleagues and to provide these data to principals who in turn can use such information, along with other data, in making decisions that require an overall assessment of the teacher (not just the teacher's instructional effectiveness).

Most teachers have been reluctant to make, as a matter of public record, evaluative statements about the instructional effectiveness of peers. They will, however, assist in the collection of evidence that both describes a colleague's procedures and measures the results of these procedures. The importance of collecting such evidence must be stressed. Administrators are not getting this kind of information now and consequently, in making decisions about teachers, are relying upon data which is often peripheral to instruction.

The matching of data to purpose will also improve teacher assessment. When one is interested in the improvement of teaching, observations and analyses of the teaching act are helpful. When one must decide upon the selection or retention of a teacher, data showing the results of instruction are more useful. A principal need not personally observe a teacher in order to help the teacher improve. In lieu of personal observations the principal may rely upon delegation—letting others on the staff, who for reasons of technical qualifications, i.e., possession of subject-matter knowledge and skills of supervision, observe and analyze the instruction. When the purpose is instructional improvement, the data from the observation (accurate records of what took place with pupils, analyses, results, new strategies formulated) need not be reported to the principal as information bearing on decisions related to a rating of competence. In fact, for purposes of teacher improvement it is better when teachers feel free to reveal their weaknesses and to try to achieve objectives in areas where they have strong doubt about their competency. Freedom to fail with impunity will permit the teacher to strive more imaginatively for improved teaching tactics.

When the purpose is accountability, the principal has several options. He can again rely on delegation, only this time make clear to all that the results from instruction must be objectively reported to him. He may choose to join a team of faculty members who will collect the evidence. We believe that a principal should discharge his responsibility for holding the teacher accountable by using product specifications rather than activity specifications. The latter is the practice of seeing whether a teacher is following a procedure as directed, the former is specifying what the results (products) of instruction should be in terms of learner performance and then seeing the results that follow. Product specification is the preferred way to collect information about a teacher's effectiveness. Activity specification is most useful in collecting information that might explain the results and thereby contribute to instructional improvement.

We have said that many considerations besides teacher effectiveness enter into decisions such as whether to hire, to grant tenure, to fire. The teacher's relations with staff and the community, his own personal development and promise for growth, are a few items taken into account by decision-makers. However, the practice of assessing a teacher without having valid data regarding his ability to effect changes in pupils seems wanting. The collection of these essential data requires effort. In contrast, information about the teacher's personal characteristics, relations with other adults, appearance, political attitudes, etc., is plentiful and easily acquired as the teacher works in the school and the community. Also, whereas teacher competency is a universal value, appraisals of a teacher on the basis of factors unrelated to the progress of pupils allow the value preferences of individuals and local communities to operate. The point to be made is that professionals in education, researchers and decision-makers, must work at advancing the tools by which measures of teacher competency can weigh more heavily in the general appraisal of teachers.

A CRITIQUE OF WIDELY USED CRITERIA IN ASSESSING TEACHER COMPETENCY

A caveat introduces this discussion. Any single criterion of effectiveness is confounded by a number of factors. One factor stems from who is doing the measuring; a second is the kind and quality of instrument used; a third is faithfulness in applying the instrument as its designer intended; and a fourth is the purpose for applying the criteria—how the data are to be used.

Student Ratings

The use of student ratings of instructors is growing, particularly at the college level. Increasingly colleges and universities are introducing policy requiring student evaluations of professors before they can be promoted. These evaluations, which may carry equal weight with faculty committee evaluations, range from formal written documents to conversations with department chairmen. The most common method employed in student ratings is the opinionnaire. Samples of these forms appear in publications such as those by Bannister, Sutherland, and Brown (1961), Fitch (1965), Orange Coast Junior College (1968), Overturf (1966), Rayder (1968), Schmidt (1968). Most forms ask the student simply to rate his instructor on various attributes. Open-ended questions and opportunity for making suggestions are sometimes provided.

The validity of student ratings is a problem. Considerable halo effect is found when students rate their teachers on several traits. As expressions of feeling, student ratings unquestionably have validity. They can be useful indicators that learners have or do not have favorable predispositions to teacher and the course. As one wag observed, "The purpose of teacher evaluations is not so much to give knowledge as to communicate emotion." In their classic review of quantitative studies of the effective instructor, Morsh and Wilder (1954) found evidence that if the instructor teaches for the bright students, he will be approved by them and there will be a positive correlation between ratings and grades; if he teaches for the weaker students, he will be disapproved by the bright students and a negative co-

efficient will be obtained. More recent research suggests that the student's sex, age and grade-point average, and the grade received from the instructor have little relationship to student ratings (Rayder, 1968). In an especially well-designed study, Davidoff provided strong evidence leading to the conclusion that student opinion of teacher behavior is very stable over time and that there is no consistent relationship between student opinion of teacher behavior and student gain (Davidoff, 1970). Contrary findings presented in a paper by Fortune (1966) are interpreted by Davidoff in terms of possible confounding of ratings by pupils with their perceptions of how well they achieved.

The many uses of student ratings—instructional improvement, teacher assessment, descriptions of teacher practice—make this measure a fruitful one. When one desires day-to-day observation of the teacher's behavior without the presence of outside observers, the use of student accomplices is an answer. Reliability of student observations can increase by having students focus on discrete observable behavior.

Self-Ratings

We would like teachers to be students of teaching, systematically assessing and revising their own teaching behavior. Theoretically, persons want to evaluate themselves in order to obtain an accurate picture of their own abilities (Festinger, 1954), but there are only a few studies indicating that some teachers are self-directing in their learning and expend effort in judging their behavior on the basis of the consequences of their teaching as revealed by the actions of pupils (Weiner & Kukla, 1970). Not having received training on how to focus on relevant aspects of their work, most teachers tend to criticize superficialities—personal mannerisms, appearance, voice and use of materials. Most teachers require others "to keep them honest" and help them with their instructional problems. An interesting hypothesis is that teachers are not likely to change their performance unless they themselves see a discrepancy between what they want to achieve and what they are actually achieving. It has not been demonstrated, however, that the teacher can better his results with pupils by privately viewing himself via video-taped lessons. This is true even if these lessons are accompanied by data of pupil performance and guide sheets for self-appraisal (Allen, McDonald, & Orme, 1966, pp. 1–28; Orange Unified School District, 1968; Waimon & Ramseyer, 1970). A summary of results from studies of the effects of self-viewing, or video tape or film is reported in the work of Salomon and McDonald (1970). These authors also presented findings about the attitudinal changes and information selections of teachers when faced with their own recorded teaching performance. When no model of "good teaching" was presented, satisfaction with one's own performance determined what was noticed on the screen, how it was evaluated, and any attitudinal change. The investigators concluded that self-viewing will not produce any desirable attitudinal and behavioral changes unless it provides information about the amount of departure from a desired standard which has been accepted as a standard by the viewer.

There is a tendency for instructors to overrate themselves and there are negligible relationships of self-assessment with other criteria such as student ratings and measures of student gain.

Administrator and Peer Ratings

Principals and supervisors sometimes use rating scales as a tool for measuring teaching effectiveness. It is not uncommon to find such vaguely worded items on these scales as the following under the heading *teaching techniques:* planning and organizing appropriately, methods and instructional skills, classroom control, awareness

of individual needs, concern for students and motivation. The compounding of instruction with political and other considerations is recognizable in instruments that call for evaluating the teacher on the basis of his staff relations, professional improvement, ethics, professional attitude, loyalty to the school, cooperation, enthusiasm for teaching, inservice activities, initiative and community activity.

Halo, lack of operational definitions, failure to control for sampling of teacher behavior, effect of observer on teacher performance—all such limitations make rating scales of doubtful worth in the hands of administrators, supervisors and peers.

Classroom Environment

In their search for correlates of effective teaching, some investigators have turned to analyzing aspects of the classroom itself. They reason that environment is linked to pupil achievement since pupils interact with elements other than the teacher in the classroom, yet the teacher may manipulate many of these elements. Thus, it is argued, a fair and relevant criterion of teacher effectiveness is the manipulation of environmental elements in the classroom. By way of illustration, there is an investigation reported by Anthony (1968), who searched the literature to find pupil behavior considered relevant for academic achievement. She then tried to find classroom characteristics which might be capable of influencing these behaviors. Subsequently, Anthony collected data on environmental factors (including academic adornments and concrete objects used by teachers and pupils) in 21 fifth-grade classrooms and found an association between environment and classroom average achievement.

We cannot generalize much from this single study, especially since there were no demonstrated causal relations between classroom characteristics and achievement. One wonders, too, about which characteristics might be associated with particular outcomes and given learners. Nevertheless, Anthony has provided a more valid definition of classroom environment than is usually found on rating scales and check lists. At least there is a logical consistency between her environmental factors and achievement sought. Too typically, classroom environment is viewed as an end—teacher's awareness of physical environment, care of property, management of pupils, teaching techniques and materials. The relation of the environment to more remote consequences is not questioned.

Systematic Observations

As indicated previously, observations are most beneficial for recording and analyzing the teaching act—not judging it. Data from systematic observations are necessary for designing alternative teaching tactics and for suggesting instructional objectives previously overlooked. Effective teaching cannot be proven by the presence or absence of any instructional variable—even those with high probabilities for effecting change, such as the teacher's provision of opportunities for learners to practice the desired behavior, giving knowledge of results to pupils, using reinforcers in accordance with a theory for shaping behavior and presenting information in a logical sequence. Warranted judgment of teaching competence rests upon information about how pupils are different as a result of instruction.

Personal Attributes

It appears that lack of success in predicting teacher effectiveness is due to the fact that decision-makers have tried to predict an unstable criterion variable from an illogical predictor. Without agreement on the specific outcomes for learners it is difficult to see how personality factors, course work and letters of recommendation could be expected to predict a teacher's success with pupils. Grooming, emotional stability, health, use of English, punctuality, humor, tact,

poise, friendliness, vitality, and acceptance of criticism are largely in the eyes of the beholder and, therefore, may predict retention in a teaching position (as contrasted with instructional effectiveness) if the one making the prediction is the same as the one who will later assess the teacher for retention purposes. Perhaps it is true that assessment of a teacher by predictive criteria tells more about the assessor than the teacher.

Further items often used to assess personal characteristics are seldom adequately defined and at times are not consistent with each other. Dress has been and increasingly is a matter of personal preference; except for extreme cases, emotional stability is something even psychologists have difficulty agreeing on; the factor of initiative seems to contradict the predisposition to accept regulations. Although ratings of personal attributes are not sufficient for evaluative purposes, they are popular. In a recent description of the nature of teacher evaluation throughout the nation, Ingils analyzed samples of teacher evaluation programs from 70 school districts in 38 states (Ingils, 1970). His analysis revealed a commonality of procedure and purpose. The common purposes were: 1) to improve the quality of instruction, 2) to assist the teacher in identifying areas that need improvement, and 3) to protect the competent teacher and eliminate the incompetent. Procedures for achieving these purposes were chiefly through ratings of teacher in the general categories of professional attitudes, teaching techniques and personal characteristics.

ALTERNATIVE CRITERIA

Contract Plans Using Student Gain

A recently employed alternative for assessing teacher competence involves the use of contract plans which are based on student gain. One recommended contract plan rests on the premise that the ends of instruction must be agreed upon before teacher competency can be assessed. The essence of this technique involves the development of a carefully selected set of objectives for the pupil. Supervisors and teachers agree in advance what they will accept as evidence that the teacher has been successful in changing the skills, competencies or attitudes of his students. An agreement is drawn up before the teacher instructs and is designed to counter the prevailing practice of trying to make an ex post facto judgment about the desirability of ends. Subsequently, evidence is collected to see how well the learners achieved the stated objectives as well as whether unintended outcomes have emerged. The plan need not exclude the use of analytical schemes in the observation of instruction but does relegate their use as aids in guiding one while making a descriptive record of the teaching act and in suggesting alternative teaching procedures. An excellent source of ways in which teachers and others can participate in the analysis of instruction is *Clinical Supervision* by Goldhammer (1969). On the recommended contract plan, teacher competency is judged in terms of the results the teacher gets with learners, not by the procedures he is following in the classroom. Only those methods which are found to be directly related to the attainment of desired outcomes are judged effective. Promising findings from research can, of course, be considered by the teacher in generating alternative teaching tactics. Contracts are prepared for varying periods of time—a single day's lesson, a semester plan, a year of instruction. This contract system demands that data by which to judge more clearly what the instruction has done to those who have been subjected to it be supplied, and, when coupled with instructional analyses, ought to enable a teacher to revise and better in some respect the procedures employed in previous work.

One district plan, for example, has teachers setting objectives for end-of-quarter instruction, objectives for which the teacher is held accountable. Results are reported to the administrator as a factor to be weighted in evaluating the teacher. Simultaneously during the quarter the teacher sets objectives for single lessons which are observed by peers who make systematic observations and help the teacher devise alternative teaching tactics when the results signal instructional deficiencies. The results from these short-term contracts with peers are not reported to the administration because the emphasis is on instructional improvement, not accountability. Personnel in the district believe that when the purpose is improvement a teacher should be encouraged to reveal his weaknesses—to try to reach objectives about which he is most doubtful. An underlying assumption is that participation in improvement sessions focuses upon producing changes in learners which will increase the probability of the teacher having success in reaching the longer-term objectives for which he is accountable.

Options in the system are many. Peers can report to the administrator the number of times teachers succeed or fail with certain learners when teaching to specific kinds of objectives, thereby shifting the emphasis from improvement to accountability. Also the system permits collecting evidence for a) unplanned effects of instruction as well as planned, and b) holding the teacher accountable for some objectives, but not for those of a high risk nature, that is, those which are desirable but likely to be unattainable.

Detailed descriptions of the previously mentioned contract system appear in a number of sources (Cohen, 1967; McNeil, 1971). The effects upon teachers and pupils of using the system with both student teachers and experienced teachers have been reported (McNeil, 1967; Moffett, 1967; Nwana, 1968; Smithman, 1970).

The strength of this particular contract plan is that it allows the individual teacher to establish outcomes and standards that are deemed most appropriate for a particular teaching situation. Prior learning of pupils, intelligence, dynamics of the classroom, etc., can be taken into account in setting expectations for which one is to be accountable. Instead of comparing teachers on the basis of normative criteria, for example, standardized tests, this contract plan permits the teacher to serve as his own control, similar to the practice of Bloom who used different but parallel achievement tests for his classes—tests that matched the objectives of the course—and was able to produce yearly gains (practical differences) in the number of students achieving mastery (Bloom, 1968). Information indicating that a teacher is increasing the achievement of his pupils year after year should be of value to the administrator who must make decisions about that teacher. This is the case at least when achievement is measured by pupil performance on instruments that indeed sample the behavior called for in the objective, e.g., ability to apply a concept in new situations, rather than by pupil response to test items that have been presented in rote drill.

Other kinds of plans have been presented to achieve teacher accountability—payment by results, merit plans, performance contracting, voucher systems and the like. Historical analyses of these varied manifestations show a) that there is no single way to make one accountable in teaching and b) that particular plans may be identified with failure without destroying the concept of accountability. Rusk, in his *History of Infant Education,* for instance, documented that in the last half of the nineteenth century British educational commissioners made it possible for managers of schools to claim a fixed amount of money for certain pupils who attended regularly but one-third of the sum thus claimable was forfeited if the scholar failed to satisfy an inspection in reading, one-third if he failed in writing, and one-third if he failed in arithmetic (Rusk, 1933). An adverse side effect of this plan was that teachers tended to concentrate on the pupils whose grant earnings depended on passing

the examinations. Treating "scientific management" in American schools from 1910 to 1930, Callahan also described administrative practices by which the quality of instructional effectiveness was indicated by a variety of measures, including pupil performance on a number of specific tasks, e.g., the ability to add at a speed of 65 combinations per minute with an accuracy of 94 percent (Callahan, 1962). Negative consequences associated with many of the accountability plans of this period were said to be increased lay influence on the curriculum, more limited freedom of the teacher, exposure of educator's lack of talent and funds necessary for developing effective teaching, and a disproportionate share of educator's time spent on accounting. Most criticism of early accountability plans has been linked with criticisms of the achievement-testing movement as it was known at the beginning of this century. That is, measures did not cover all outcomes desired in the educational program; many of the sweeping conclusions drawn from test data were fallible; there was too much concentration upon static educational objectives; and teacher and pupils concentrated their efforts upon those aspects that were to be tested—testing itself tending to enforce conformity. Such criticisms have had considerable influence in shaping the changes in newer accountability plans although there is current evidence, as seen in a special issue of the *Phi Delta Kappan,* that many of the difficulties in implementing accountability programs have not been overcome (Lieberman, 1970).

Performance Tests

It is invalid to rank a teacher as effective when the teacher has not been confronted with a comparable set of teaching conditions as have other teachers. Yet at times it is necessary to differentiate among teachers —to identify who excels or falls below his peers. The problem, then, is to design tests of teaching power by which teachers have an equal chance to succeed or fail. Performance tests or teaching power tests are responses to the problem (Popham, 1967, 1968, 1971). A number of teachers are given one or more identical objectives and a sample of the measures based on the objective(s) to be administered to pupils following instruction. The objectives may be cognitive, affective or psychomotor in nature. The teachers may also be given resource materials from which to plan a lesson designed to accomplish the objectives. The instructional tactics to be employed are left entirely to the teacher. In other words, only the ends are given, the means are up to the instructor. Often the objective is novel, both to pupils and teacher, thereby eliminating major "contamination" due to the learner's previous exposure to the subject. The teachers are allowed a specific period of time for planning the lesson and for teaching it. Groups of learners, perhaps only a few students per group, are assigned to the teacher as pupils. These learners are drawn from a common population of pupils and randomly assigned to a group. If prerequisite skills are required on the part of pupils, this stipulation is acted upon in making up the population from which the learners are drawn. Following the teacher's instruction a test is administered to measure pupil attainment of the objectives. Although the nature of the test may be inferred by the teacher from the objective, the actual test is not available to the teacher and, indeed, is usually administered by someone other than the teacher. The mean posttest score becomes the criterion of effectiveness. In some instances test scores may be adjusted for the initial abilities of the pupils. If relatively large learner groups are employed, the randomization of assignment is to be preferred. Noninstructional control groups may also be used to further substantiate the amount of learning that occurred as a result of instruction.

The reliability with which one can determine teaching competencies through the use of these performance tests can be increased by using a number of lessons and different kinds of objectives—different subject matter, different levels of expected behavior, etc. Also, the total number of pupils can be shared in the small groups so that no teacher teaches the same group of pupils more than one lesson and no group receives a particular lesson more than once.

Retention tests can also be given to learners, thereby adding another dimension to the teacher's ability to accomplish prespecified objectives. The utility of performance tests as measures of teaching effectiveness has been demonstrated in the work of Borgerding (1970), Justiz (1969), Morsh, Burgess, and Smith (1955), Popham (1967, 1971), and Taneman (1970). These studies suggest the conclusion that when there is reasonable control for extraneous factors (teacher familiarity with content and pupil populations) some teachers are consistently more successful than others in getting desired results. There is, however, need for verifying that teachers who can produce desired effects under conditions of teaching performance tests maintain their effect over time and in the presence of a greater range of conditions such as exist in conventional classrooms.

CRITERIA OF TEACHING EFFECTIVENESS IN THE MAKING OF DECISIONS

Decisions such as hiring, promoting and firing teachers require more information than that which bears upon teacher competency. In selecting a teacher the administrator has legitimate concerns about the likely future effect of the teacher upon a) morale of other staff members, b) community support, and c) impact upon operations that may be only indirectly related to pupil growth. Then, too, we know that administrators are understandably protective of their own interests and, therefore, seek data that go beyond descriptions of effectiveness in teaching. The financial cost of hiring a qualified versus a partially qualified teacher, the energy which might have to be invested in working with a teacher, and a minority group's reaction to the ethnic background of the teacher are examples of the concerns which weigh heavily in making decisions about instructors. What appears serious is that administrators have almost universally lacked information regarding teaching effectiveness in making decisions regarding teaching personnel while, logically, data indicating teacher competency should be of the highest priority in such decisions. Quite frankly, one is not sure that administrators would use this essential information even if it were available. It has been shown that principals prefer to hire teachers on the basis of expressive characteristics rather than instrumental characteristics (Bridges, 1968). This finding suggests that much work would have to be done with administrators before measures of teacher competency affect decisions involving selection and retention.

We know that administrators have seldom shown the willingness to terminate the services of a teacher on the grounds of incompetency, although teachers are sometimes dismissed for moral reasons and for gross insubordination. Administrators may be afraid that their judgment regarding competency will not stand up in court should the teacher demand a legal hearing on the grounds that dismissal should be "for cause only." Indeed, the administrator may fear that he may be charged with abuse of discretion because his decision is not supported by substantial evidence. Lack of evidence stems in large part from the administrator's failure to employ defensible criterion measures of effectiveness. One cannot defend the charge of incompetency via impressions gathered through hit or miss observations of a teacher inside and outside the classroom. Incomplete records of a teacher's professional activities and records of rumors do not serve one well in the courtroom. We would like to argue, too, that it is difficult to know how to proceed in correcting a teacher's instructional deficiencies if one lacks valid criterion measures and must rely upon only ill-defined complaints about room appearance, noise level, pupil referrals to the office, and the like.

Just as it is miseducative for an administrator to ignore data indicating teacher competency in making decisions about teaching, so is he at fault if he uses data from measures of competency which are not appropriate, thereby misleading himself and others into thinking he has data when in reality his information is wanting.

DESIRABLE ATTRIBUTES OF TEACHER COMPETENCY CRITERIA

In surveying the numerous measuring approaches which have been employed to identify the effective teacher it becomes apparent that for given purposes some criteria are better than others. Perhaps the best way to promote a better fit between one's purpose and the selection of a criterion measure will be to isolate a reasonable number of attributes on which the available criterion measures differ, then rate the measures according to these attributes. One should be able to make a more defensible selection among competing criterion measures by deciding which of the several attributes are important to his particular operational decision or research investigation, then contrasting alternative measures according to whether they possess these attributes.

General Attributes

Ideally, of course, all measuring devices would possess certain positive attributes such as *reliability*. We would always want to devise classroom observation schedules, for example, which were quite reliable. Obviously, in selecting among alternative measures one should be attentive to whether the approach yields a relatively consistent estimate of teaching competence.

There are other general attributes which can or cannot be built into measuring devices. General attributes may be present or absent in particular members of a class of criterion measures, such as administration rating scales, but not in all members of that class. Such an attribute would be whether the measure possessed an essentially *neutral orientation,* that is, could be profitably used by educators with a variety of instructional viewpoints. Certain measuring instruments, e.g., observation schedules and rating scales, are so wedded to a particular view of instruction that anyone with a contrary view would find it difficult if not impossible to use the instrument. For instance, one might conceive of a classroom observation form designated so that the observer was to attend only to phenomena of interest to an advocate of operant conditioning methods. Such a form would not possess a neutral orientation and, therefore, would be less serviceable to a large number of those who must attend to many other factors. Not that highly partisan measures have no value, especially for certain research purposes, but generally criterion measures that are more neutrally oriented are to be preferred.

Another general feature which should be sought whenever possible in teacher competence measures is that it yields information about the types of instructional situations in which a given teacher functions best. This attribute can be described as an *assignment indicator* and, if present, would obviously be helpful for researcher and decision-maker alike. One could conceive of performance tests which might be designed so that we could discover what types of instructional objectives a teacher can best achieve for particular kinds of learners. Criterion measures which would permit this identification of the optimal role for a given teacher would be most helpful indeed.

There are other attributes of useful criterion measures which are a function of particular measures rather than a given class of measures, for example, initial cost, reuseability, etc. But if a measure possesses *reliability,* a *neutral orientation,* and an *assignment indicator,* it has a running start toward being a useful measure for a variety of situations.

Six Attributes for Discriminating Among Criterion Measures

We can turn now to several attributes which are often present or absent in an entire class of criterion measures, for example, in (almost all) contract plan measures. These attributes are not always needed by all who are seeking a criterion measure, but for given situations one or more of these attributes will usually be requisite. Without implying any hierarchy of import, we shall briefly examine six such attributes, thus attempting to rate classes of criterion measures according to their possession of each attribute.

1. *Differentiates among teachers.* For certain situations it is imperative to discriminate among teachers. Who is best? Who is worst? Is teacher X better than teacher Z? Under what conditions will teacher A perform best? What are the separate effects of teacher A? To answer such questions a criterion measure must be sufficiently sensitive to differentiate among teachers. There are decisions where we do not have enough knowledge merely by knowing that a teacher has met a minimal level of proficiency. Both administrators and researchers, for instance, often encounter situations where they need a measure sensitive enough to assess variance in teachers' skills.

2. *Assesses learner growth.* The thrust of frequent discussions in this chapter has been to emphasize the necessity to produce criterion measures which can be used to assess the results of instructional process, not merely the process itself. In certain limited instances we may not be interested in the outcomes of instruction as reflected by modifications in the learner, but these would be few in number. Certain classes of criterion measures are notoriously deficient with respect to this attribute.

3. *Yields data uncontaminated by re-*

quired inferences. An attribute of considerable importance is whether a measure permits the acquisition of data with a minimum of *required* extrapolation on the part of the user. If all observations are made in such a way that beyond human frailty they have not been forced through a distorting inferential sieve, then the measure is better. A classroom observation system which asked the user to record the raw frequency of teacher questions would possess the attribute more so than a system which asked the user to judge the warmth of teacher questions.

4. *Adapts to teachers' goal preferences.* A desirable feature of teacher competence measures for certain selections is that they can be adjusted to the differing estimates of teachers regarding what should be taught in the schools, indeed, what schools are for in the first place. In our society there are divergent viewpoints regarding the role of the schools, and in given subject fields even more disagreement about the best goals for that subject. A measure of teaching skill will be more useful for given situations if it can adapt to such dissimilarities in goal preferences.

5. *Presents equivalent stimulus situations.* For some purposes we would like to have criterion measures which could produce results not easily discounted because certain teachers were at a disadvantage due to deficiencies in the situations in which they were operating. If we use gross achievement scores of learners as an index of one's teaching skill, then it is not surprising that a ghetto school teacher would be perceived as being in a less advantageous position than a teacher from a wealthy suburban community. There are times when we might like to use a measure which would permit the measurement of teaching proficiency when the stimulus situations were identical or at least comparable.

6. *Contains heuristic data categories.* In a sense this final attribute is the reverse of attribute number three above which focused on the collection of data uncontaminated by required inferences. At times we want data that simply state what was seen and heard in the classroom. At other times it would be useful to gather information—interpretations—which illuminate the nature of the instructional tactics. For the unsophisticated individual, in particular, measures which would at least in part organize his perceptions regarding strengths and weaknesses in teaching would in certain situations be most useful. Theoretical concepts which suggest linkages between events are cases in point. The teacher or supervisor who learns to both recognize instances of the psychological principle of reinforcement (a class of events which modify responses) and to apply this principle in classroom situations should be able to generate more alternative teaching strategies than before.

Now these six attributes should be considered by those requiring teacher competence measures to see which attributes are particularly important for the situation at hand. Thus an inspection of Table 1 may be useful when we have arranged the classes of certain measures previously considered along with the six attributes just examined. In the table a minus indicates a deficiency with respect to the attribute, a plus indicates that the attribute is well satisfied by that class of criterion measure. Absence of a plus or minus reflects no predominant presence or absence of the attribute in the class of criterion measures. The following instances are offered as illustrations of how the table might be used. Principal X wants to know which of several teachers can best teach the children in his school to pronounce given vowel sounds in unfamiliar words. He therefore will select a performance test that measures the ability to teach this reading skill, for differentiation sensitivity is necessary to answer the question. Supervisor Y wants to know how successful a teacher is in achieving a certain instructional objective of great importance to that particular teacher, and how to help the

TABLE 1

**CLASSES OF TEACHING COMPETENCE CRITERION MEASURES
WITH RESPECT TO SIX DESIRABLE ATTRIBUTES OF SUCH MEASURES**

Desirable Attributes of Teacher Competence Criterion Measures	Classes of Criterion Measures							
	Systematic Observation	Administrator Ratings	Student Ratings	Peer Ratings	Self Ratings	Personal Attributes	Contract Plans	Performance Tests
1. Differentiates Among Teachers	+					+		+
2. Assesses Learner Growth	−	−	−	−	−	−	+	+
3. Yields Data Uncontaminated by Required Inferences			−	−	−		+	+
4. Adapts to Teachers' Goal Preferences	−				+		+	−
5. Presents Equivalent Stimulus Situations		−	−	−				+
6. Contains Heuristic Data Categories	+							

teacher in the event the objective is not attained. The supervisor could use both a contract plan which allows for selection of an individual goal and a systematic observation which promises to provide a more meaningful record of teacher-pupil interaction patterns.

CONCLUDING REMARKS

An evaluation of a teacher is not equivalent to determining the teacher's instructional competency, i.e., the ability to effect desired changes in learners. Defensible decisions concerning teachers rest on many kinds of data. However, it is essential that among these data appears valid information about teacher competencies. There is evidence that this latter kind of information is now overlooked in favor of subjective impressions of the teacher which are concerned primarily with the teacher's personal attributes and instructional techniques. Effectiveness in teaching is best evidenced by criterion measures which detect pupil

growth as a result of the teacher's instruction. Contract plans and performance tests are two promising tools for collecting information about instructional effectiveness. There should be more inquiry centered on these tools, their development, uses and limitations. Measures of long- and short-range instructional objectives for a variety of outcomes are very much needed if two key purposes of assessment are to be fulfilled: instructional accountability and improvement.

It is clear that investigators have shown a lack of balance by directing most of their inquiries toward development of schemes for analyzing teaching and the conduct of studies that correlate process and product. In order to confirm the power of instructional variables derived from theory, analysis and statistical associations, we now need experiments showing that the teacher's use of these variables can indeed produce predicted effects in learners.

This is not to say that we expect scientific findings about teaching to be valuable as rules for action in the classroom. On the contrary, evidence cited in this chapter suggests that practice has been seriously weakened by the false belief that there are scientific conclusions which correspond to good teaching. Teacher educators err when they promote teaching skills that are approximately consistent with scientific conclusions as if these skills were certain, confirmed answers about how a teacher should proceed to effect desirable consequences in learners. Instead, such skills should be regarded as hypotheses to be tested. The practical utility of research should be seen as allowing all students of teaching—teachers, administrators and researchers—to be more flexible in planning, executing, analyzing and evaluating the teaching act.

REFERENCES

Allen, D. W., McDonald, F. J., & Orme, M. E. J. *Experiment II: Effects of feedback and practice conditions on the acquisition of a teaching strategy.* Stanford, Calif.: Stanford University, 1966.

American Educational Research Association, Committee on the Criteria of Teacher Effectiveness. Report of the committee on the criteria of teacher effectiveness. *Review of Educational Research,* 1952, 22, 238–263.

Amidon, E., & Flanders, N. A. The effects of direct and indirect teacher influence on dependent-prone students learning geometry. *Journal of Educational Psychology,* 1961, 52, 286–291.

Anthony, B. M. A new approach to merit rating of teachers. *Administrator's Notebook,* 1968, 17(1), 1–4.

Astin, A. W., & Lee, C. B. T. Current practices in the evaluation and training of college teachers. *The Educational Record,* 1966, 47, 361–375.

Bain, H. Self-governance must come first, then accountability. *Phi Delta Kappan,* 1970, 51, 413.

Bannister, J., Sutherland, J., & Brown, J. W. Evaluating college teaching. *Curriculum Reporter Supplement No. 1,* December 1961.

Bellack, A. A., & Davitz, J. R. *The language of the classroom.* USOE, Cooperative Research Projects No. 1497 and No. 2023.

New York: Teachers College, Columbia University, 1963–65.

Beller, E. K., Weber, W., & Amidon, E. J. Teacher behavior and intellectual functioning in deprived kindergarten children. Paper presented at the meeting of the American Educational Research Association, Chicago, February 1966.

Biddle, B. J., & Ellena, W. J. (Eds.) *Contemporary research on teacher effectiveness.* New York: Holt, Rinehart & Winston, 1964.

Bloom, B. S. Learning for mastery. *Evaluation Comment,* 1968, 1(2), 1–12.

Borgerding, J. C. Practice versus practice and reflection in the improvement of instruction. Unpublished master's thesis, University of California, Los Angeles, 1970.

Bridges, E. M. Preferences of principals for instrumental and expressive characteristics of teachers related to system type. Paper presented at the meeting of the American Educational Research Association, Chicago, February 1968.

Brown, B. B. Bringing philosophy into the study of teacher effectiveness. *The Journal of Teacher Education,* 1966, 17, 35–40.

Brown, G. I. Which pupil to which classroom climate? *Elementary School Journal,* 1960, 60, 265–269.

Buder, L. The problem of weeding out the unfit teacher. *The New York Times,* Sunday, July 6, 1969. Sec. E, 6.

Callahan, R. E. *Education and the cult of efficiency.* Chicago: The University of Chicago Press, 1962.

Campbell, D. J., & Stanley, J. C. Experimental and quasi-experimental designs for research on teaching. In N. L. Gage (Ed.), *Handbook of research on teaching,* Chicago: Rand McNally, 1963. Pp. 171–246.

Campbell, J. R. Cognitive and affective process development and its relation to a teacher's interaction ratio. Unpublished doctoral dissertation, New York University, 1968.

Campbell, J. R., & Barnes, C. W. Interaction analysis—a breakthrough? *Phi Delta Kappan,* 1969, 50, 587–590.

Cohen, A. M. Defining instructional objectives. *Systems approaches to curriculum and instruction in the open-door college.* Junior College Leadership Program Occasional Report No. 9, Los Angeles: University of California, School of Education, 1967. Pp. 25–33.

Cohen, A. M., & Brawer, F. B. Measuring faculty performance. *ERIC Clearinghouse for Junior College Information.* Washington, D.C.: American Association of Junior Colleges, 1969.

Cook, D. L. Management control theory as the context for educational evaluation. *Journal of Research and Development in Education,* 1970, 3(4), 13–26.

Dalis, G. T. Effect of precise objectives upon student achievement in health education. *The Journal of Experimental Education,* 1970, 39(2), 20–23.

Davidoff, S. H. *The development of an instrument designed to secure student assessment of teaching behaviors that correlate with objective measures of student achievement.* The School District of Philadelphia, Office of Research and Evaluation, March 1970.

Davidson, R. L. The effects of an interaction analysis system on the development of critical reading in elementary school children. *Classroom Interaction Newsletter,* May 1968, 13, 12–13.

Dewey, J. *The sources of a science of education.* New York: Liveright, 1929.

Festinger, L. A. A theory of social comparison process. *Human Relations,* 1954, 7, 117–140.

Fitch, N. *Evaluation of instructors in California junior colleges.* Berkeley: University of California, 1965.

Flanders, N. A. *Teacher influence, pupil attitudes, and achievement.* United States Office of Education Cooperative Research Monograph No. 12, OE-25040. Washington, D.C.: USOE, 1965.

Flanders, N. A., & Simon, A. Teacher effectiveness. In R. L. Ebel (Ed.), *Encyclopedia of educational research.* New York: Macmillan, 1969. Pp. 1423–1437.

Fortune, J. C. *The generality of presenting behaviors in teaching pre-school children.* Memphis, Tenn.: Memphis State University, 1966.

Gage, N. L. An analytical approach to research on instructional methods. *Phi Delta Kappan,* 1968, 49, 601–606.

Goldhammer, R. *Clinical supervision.* New York: Holt, Rinehart & Winston, 1969.

Ingils, C. R. Let's do away with teacher evaluation. *The Clearing House,* 1970, 44, 451–456.

Justiz, T. B. A reliable measure of teacher effectiveness. *Educational Leadership Research Supplement,* October 1969, 3(1), 49–55.

LaShier, W. S., Jr. An analysis of certain aspects of the verbal behavior of student teachers on eighth grade students participating in a BSCS laboratory block. *Dissertation Abstracts,* 1966, 26, 7168.

Lawler, E. S. Differing rates of progress of classes under the same and different teachers. *The Journal of Educational Research,* 1964, 58, 84–86.

Lieberman, M. (Ed.) 8 Articles on accountability. *Phi Delta Kappan,* 1970, 52, 194–239.

Lindvall, C. M., & Cox, R. C. *Evaluation as a tool in curriculum development: The IPI evaluation program.* American Educational Research Association Monograph Series on Curriculum Evaluation, No. 5. Chicago: Rand McNally, 1970.

McNeil, J. D. Concomitants of using behavioral objectives in the assessment of teacher effectiveness. *The Journal of Experimental Education,* 1967, 36(1), 69–74.

McNeil, J. D. *Toward accountable teachers: Their appraisal and improvement.* New York: Holt, Rinehart & Winston, 1971.

Moffett, G. M. *Use of instructional objectives in the supervision of student teachers.* (Doctoral dissertation, University of California, Los Angeles) Ann Arbor, Mich.: University Microfilms, 1967. No. 67–446.

Morsh, J. E., Burgess, G. G., & Smith, P. N. *Student achievement as a measure of instructor effectiveness.* Project No. 7950. Task No. 77243. Lackland Air Force Base, Texas: Air Force Personnel and Training Center, 1955.

Morsh, J. E., & Wilder, E. W. *Identifying the effective instructor: A review of the quantitative studies. 1900–1952.* Project No. 7714. Task No. 77243. Chanute Air Force Base, Ill.: Air Force Personnel and Training Research Center, 1954.

Musella, D. Improving teacher evaluation. *The Journal of Teacher Education,* 1970, 21, 15–21.

National Center for Educational Research and Development. *Model teacher education program.* Washington, D.C.: U.S. Department of Health, Education and Welfare, 1969.

National Education Association, Research Division. *Evaluation of classroom teachers.* Research Report 1964—R14. Washington, D.C.: NEA, 1964.

Nelson, L. N. Teacher leadership: An empirical approach to analyzing teacher behavior in the classroom. *Journal of Teacher Education*, 1966, 17, 417–425.

Nwana, E. M. *An investigation into an objective way of examining student teachers in practical teaching in West Cameroon teacher training institutions.* (Doctoral dissertation, University of California, Los Angeles) Ann Arbor, Mich.: University Microfilms, 1968. No. 68–16,566.

Orange Coast Junior College. *Instructor rating scale study, Orange Coast College, Fall Semester, 1968.* Costa Mesa, Calif.: Orange Coast Junior College, 1968.

Orange Unified School District. Teacher self-appraisal in-service program. Educational Resources Information Center (*ERIC*) *Abstract*, November 1968, No. 4.

Overturf, C. L. *Student rating of faculty at St. Johns River Junior College, with addendum for Albany Junior College.* Palatka, Fla.: St. Johns River Junior College, 1966.

Page, E. B. Teacher comments and student performance. A seventy-four classroom experiment in school motivation. *Journal of Educational Psychology,* 1958, 49, 173–181.

Popham, W. J. *Development of a performance test of teaching proficiency.* USOE, Final Report, Contract No. OE-6-10-254. Los Angeles: University of California, 1967.

Popham, W. J. The performance test: A new approach to the assessment of teaching proficiency. *Journal of Teacher Education,* 1968, 19, 216–222.

Popham, W. J. Performance tests of teaching proficiency: Rationale, development, and validation. *American Educational Research Journal,* 1971, 8, 105–117.

Powell, E. V. Teacher behavior and pupil achievement. *Classroom Interaction Newsletter,* May 1968, 23–25.

Rayder, N. F. College student ratings of instructors. Lansing, Mich.: Michigan State University, Office of Educational Services, 1968.

Remmers, H. H. *Introduction to opinion and attitude measurement.* New York: Harper & Brothers, 1954.

Rosenshine, B. To explain: A review of research. *Educational Leadership,* 1968, 26, 303–309.

Rosenshine, B. Interaction analysis: A tardy comment. *Phi Delta Kappan,* 1970, 51, 445–446.

Rosenshine, B., & Furst, N. Research in teacher performance criteria. In B. O. Smith (Ed.), *Reseach in teacher education: A symposium.* Englewood Cliffs, N.J.: Prentice-Hall, 1971. Pp. 37–72.

Rusk, R. R. *A history of infant education.* London: University of London Press, 1933.

Ryans, D. G. *Characteristics of teachers: Their description, comparison, and appraisal.* Washington, D.C.: American Council on Education, 1960.

Saadeh, I. Q. Teacher effectiveness or classroom efficiency: A new direction in the evaluation of teaching. *The Journal of Teacher Education,* 1970, 21, 73–91.

Salomon, G., & McDonald, F. J. Pretest and posttest reactions to self-viewing one's teaching performance on video tape. *Journal of Educational Psychology,* 1970, 61, 280–286.

Schmidt, R. (Ed.) *Insight: A view of the faculty through the eyes of their students.* San Marcos, Calif.: Palomar College, 1968.

Selden, D. Evaluate teachers? *AFT QUEST Paper 4.* Washington, D.C.: American Federation of Teachers, 1970.

Simon, A., & Boyer, E. G. (Eds.) *Mirrors for behavior II: An anthology of observation instruments, Vol. A.* Philadelphia, Pa.: Research for Better Schools, Inc., 1970.

Smith, B. O. A concept of teaching. In B. O. Smith, & R. H. Ennis (Eds.), *Language and concepts in education.* Chicago: Rand McNally, 1961. Pp. 86–101.

Smith, B. O. Teaching: Conditions of its evaluation. In Pi Lambda Theta, *The evaluation of teaching.* Washington, D.C.: Pi Lambda Theta, 1967. Pp. 65–84.

Smithman, H. H. Student achievement as a measure of teacher performance. Unpublished doctoral dissertation, University of California, Los Angeles, 1970.

Soar, R. S. Pupil needs and teacher-pupil relationships: Experiences needed for comprehending reading. In E. J. Amidon, & J. B. Hough (Eds.), *Interaction analysis: Theory, research, and application.* Reading, Mass.: Addison-Wesley, 1967. Pp. 243–50.

Sorenson, G. What is learned in practice teaching? *The Journal of Teacher Education,* 1967, 18, 173–178.

Sprinthall, N. A., Whiteley, J. M., & Mosher, R. L. A study of teacher effectiveness. *The*

Journal of Teacher Education, 1966, 17, 93–106.

Stemnock, S. K. *Evaluating teaching performance.* Educational Research Service Circular No. 3. Washington, D.C.: National Education Association, 1969.

Taneman, I. A teaching power test: A method of using pupil gain as a criterion in teacher education. Unpublished doctoral dissertation, University of California, Los Angeles, 1970.

Waimon, M. D., & Ramseyer, G. C. Effects of video feedback on the ability to evaluate teaching. *The Journal of Teacher Education,* 1970, 21, 92–95.

Weiner, B., & Kukla, A. An attributional analysis of achievement motivation. *Journal of Personality and Social Psychology,* 1970, 15, 1–20.

CHAPTER 8

The Technology of Instructional Development

EVA L. BAKER[1]
University of California, Los Angeles

THE PLACE OF DEVELOPMENT IN SCHOLARLY ACTIVITY

A number of writers both within and outside the educational research establishment have tried to provide rules to enable the discrimination of research from development enterprises and, in the attempt, have become embroiled in a series of definitional crises. Research has been defined in terms of its purpose and outcomes as free inquiry in pursuit of the understanding of phenomena (Cronbach & Suppes, 1969). Development, in fairly limited treatment, has been described as "the production of materials, techniques, processes, hardware and organizational formats for instruction. The basis for such development is our knowledge about learning, motivation, instruction and education" (National Center for Educational Research and Development, 1970, p. 3). The need for a scientific orientation in

development has been underscored by Wittrock (1967) and Cronbach and Suppes (1969). Cronbach and Suppes explain that the term *development* refers to the production of materials or procedures based on general ideas of what will be successful. The report asserts that deliberate inquiry must be an essential component of true development and should be focused on data necessary for design of the product, information for revision, and evidence to demonstrate the effects of the product.

Development in education is sometimes termed "instruction or educational technology." Lumsdaine (1964) distinguished between a hardware definition of technology and a more generic definition "as a derivative or application of an underlying science." He goes on to say that learning theory may function

as a primary "underlying science" from which applications to a technology of instruction might be anticipated. However, [there are] potential contributions of other kinds of theorization to instructional practice.... for example, theories of communication and cybernetics, perceptual theories, and branches of logistics or economics concerned with the

[1] The author wishes to express extraordinary gratitude to Mrs. Arlene Fink, who devoted much energy and scholarship to the preparation of this paper, and to Mrs. Adrianne Bank, Mrs. Edys S. Quellmalz and Mrs. Tobie Robinson, who variously made critical contributions.

utilization of instructional personnel and equipment. . . .

. . . Furthermore, there are aspects of psychotechnology not deriving from learning and behavior theory which have important educational applications. Examples are the application of psychometrics to aptitude and achievement testing and of statistical method and experimental design . . . (p. 373).

Some writers have attempted to reconcile the categories of research and development with the common classifications of basic and applied research. Glass (1969) points out that basic research is nomothetic and applied research is idiographic; yet the difficulty encountered in classifying any given study as either one or the other should be of little concern. Reagan (1967) and Gilbert (1962) have also considered the utility of basic and applied research distinctions. Reagan suggests that "research" and "development" should be substituted as primary descriptive rubrics for basic and applied research, while Cronbach and Suppes substitute conclusion-oriented and decision-oriented studies. Similarly, Brooks (1967) notes that the boundaries of science (research) and technology (development) are becoming increasingly blurred and that distinctions between society-limited and science-limited problems may become less important as research techniques are applied to each with equal vigor.

The problem of sequence of activities is also of concern to a number of writers. From a purely syntactical analysis, one would infer that all research efforts must precede development; we do not speak of educational D and R. A recent report of the National Center for Educational Research and Development (1970) considered models of research and development functions. Linear models, such as those described by Novick (1964), assume that functional dependencies exist among research and development activities. He describes states of activity as follows: a) basic research, experimental research, experimental development; and b) applied research, advanced development, basic evaluation, basic

testing, product development, product application.

Hilgard (1969) challenges the neatness of such paradigms, stating, "The greatest fallacy is that there is a linear flow from basic research to development. Sometimes this is the case, but usually there is a complex interaction. That is, the boys in development do not sit around waiting for the new ideas to come from basic research and then make use of them in designing products" (p. 41). He continues that a number of studies of transfer functions have indicated that necessity and not research fosters technological invention. Reverse flows from technology to research are often significant, and Hilgard illustrates his point by reminding us that the value of technology to research is itself very important: the microscope to biology, the telescope to astronomy, and the high-speed computer to anyone involved in research. Glaser (1966a) and Schutz (1970) describe research and development relationships which, through feedback loops, support Hilgard's remarks. Yet, on the other hand, Gideonse (1968) provides a different perspective on research and development (R and D) interrelationships, asserting that the activities of research, development and school operations are distinct "with quite different objectives or outputs." Gideonse also emphasizes the complex relationships among elements of his model and states that while the order of activities may proceed from knowledge through development to installation, "there may be just as strong a flow backwards as operational problems define development programs, which in turn reveal the need for certain basic information and theory" (p. 541). Lazarsfeld and Sieber (1964) note examples of such reverse flows in the field of reading.

Other models reduce the importance of development as an enterprise and emphasize the "linkage" function served by institutions or individuals. Farr (1969) suggests that knowledge linkers must be able to provide guidance to researchers in the selection of their problems and to understand the needs and mentality of the practitioner. Similarly, Havelock (1970) advocates the need for linkers or "change agents" to perform a necessary educational function. Chase (1970) asserts that the regional laboratories were planned "to overcome resistance to innovation by establishing collaborative relationships with the producers of knowledge on one side and the users of knowledge on the other..." (p. 116). Clearly, linkage models do not necessarily depend upon systematic development as an integral element. The linker may wish to inform the practitioner directly of new, basic knowledge. Glass (1969) questions the utility of the linkage function of transmitting *educational metaphors,* Getzels's (1969) term for the practical and widespread interpretation of scientific knowledge. Glass argues that the metaphoric approach to influencing practice is too uncertain, that knowledge thus transmitted is often distorted, and that the difficulty of subsequently modifying diffuse, premature acceptance of scientific conclusion is monumental. He cites the examples of popular conceptions of the relationships between laterality and reading achievement.

Multiple views, then, characterize the perception of the place and role of development vis-à-vis research and development models. In all instances the activity of development is clearly within the applied classification, yet many writers support the idea that development problems can provide stimulation for theoretical studies. Brickell (1967) provides a series of examples of the relationship of research to practice.

ANTECEDENTS OF
PRESENT DEVELOPMENT

Early History

Development, as a technology, traces its lineages to the early empiricists in education, although one might pursue the sources of empiricism in other fields. For instance, many attribute empirical orientation to the followers of Johann Herbart, who argued that subject-matter materials should be organized separately and scientifically to lead students progressively to greater mastery. Thayer (1965) credits the Herbartians with directing the attention of teachers to the way in which children learn. Joseph Mayer Rice, another influential figure, has been described both as the initiator of the progressive movement in education (Cremin, 1966) and the founder of empirical scholarship in education. He conducted analyses of children's spelling performance and found no relationship between time devoted to spelling and competence (Rice, 1897). His results were met with well-documented negativism from the educational establishment (Ayres, 1918), a fact which may support notions of the continuity of human experience.

The prodigious vitality of E. L. Thorndike cannot be overlooked, no matter how brief the review of educational development. Thorndike's unprecedented studies of animal learning were based on the assumption that the laboratory behavior of animals was a key to the general problem of human learning. Thorndike and Robert S. Woodworth conducted studies on the transfer of training which discredited the "disciplinary" value of particular studies (1901). Thorndike's interest in educational practice also led him to examine individual differences as revealed through the development of the notion of intelligence tests and their implications for classroom grouping. In *Principles of Teaching* (1906) he provided examples to help teachers contend with such practical problems as attention. Beyond his writings, Thorndike significantly influenced educational practice through his 40-year tenure at Teachers College, Columbia University. Martin Mayer (1961) has estimated that in 1961 three-quarters of the state superintendents and at least half of the big city superintendents in the country had been either Thorndike's students or students of persons he had trained. Thorndike affected practice not only metaphorically, to use Getzels's term, but through direct development. His interest in intelligence tests at a time when national compulsory education had become a reality affected important experimental programs, such as Helen Parkhurst's Dalton Plan, Mary Ward's program at San Francisco State Normal School, and Washburne's activities in Winnetka. Thorndike was also directly responsible for the development of children's texts in which he attempted to incorporate his theoretical and empirical formulations. Cronbach and Suppes (1969) point out that Thorndike's early arithmetic texts still influence contemporary arithmetic instruction.

As a result of Thorndike's efforts, the influence of those who adhered to the concepts of the "faculties" of the mind and formal discipline was weakened. This accelerated the acceptance of the utilitarian or "social efficiency movement" advocated by Franklin Bobbitt who, like Thorndike, was interested in an empirical analysis of human behavior. Bobbitt advocated a curriculum organized around a delineation of specific activities based on an objective examination of society. Human life, he contended, consisted of the performance of specific activities and that which prepares for life must provide experiences which relate to such specific activities. From the study of human activities one would determine the elements important to success in particular activities. These skills, understandings and attitudes would form the objectives of the curriculum. Bobbitt's contributions were many and profound. His advocacy of social utility as a criterion for judging school goals (Bobbitt, 1918) was reflected in subsequent curriculum planning, and various writers have attested to his influence (Eisner, 1967; Kliebard, 1968).

Other educators attempted to translate Bobbitt's ideas into meaningful instructional practices. Washburne (1929) devised an individually paced curriculum which was directed to common essentials such as reading, writing, science, social studies and arithmetic, and to self-expression objectives. Instruction in the common essentials was intended to be self-paced. Skills were divided into subtasks which were to be mastered. Each child worked until he was successful.

Interim Trends

The emphasis on research-based innovation waned during the thirties as excitement was siphoned off, for example, to psychoanalytic interpretations of the individual. Moreover, progressivists came to dominate instruction in schools of education. Empirical approaches were further hampered by an economic depression which served to inhibit the conduct of costly research. Intelligence testing, originally designed to permit individual differences to flourish, degenerated into a procedure for the tracking of students.

However, resurgence of interest in educational research occurred in the World War II period, primarily because experimental psychologists had to contend with the efficient instruction of diverse individuals for service. The training of a large number of people led to the necessity of developing replicable instructional devices and materials, and such development permitted research pursuits under relatively stable funding conditions. Work instituted in this period can still be favorably evaluated against much of present educational research (see, for example, Hovland, Lumsdaine, & Sheffield, 1949).

Programmed Instruction

Following World War II the path of development was broadened. Studies in operant conditioning procedures with infrahuman species (Skinner, 1954) led to experimentation with programmed instruction (Holland & Skinner, 1961) which depended heavily upon principles such as successive approximation and stimulus control. The roots of this orientation can be traced again to E. L. Thorndike, who wrote in 1912, "If, by a miracle of mechanical ingenuity, a book could be so arranged that only to him who had done what was directed on page one would page two become visible, and so on, much that now requires personal instruction could be managed by print" (p. 165). Members of the programmed instruction school developed their own lexicon for describing instructional events, and words such as "tact," "mand" and "mathetics" were exchanged with great solemnity. While early programming efforts faithfully adhered to given guidelines (Fry, 1963), such as the provision of cues and knowledge of results, perhaps the greatest contribution of the movement of contemporary development was the shift from evaluating the attributes of a given program to evaluating the effects it has on learner achievement. Thus, today's programmer is urged to attack his task with a modest but clear conception of technical omnipotence. He must assmue he is in control of the variables which account for learning. Failure of his students reflects upon his inadequate analyses of the requirements of the learning situation. This penultimate reliance on rational control has encouraged zealots to insist that everything which could be learned could be successfully programmed. Skinner (1948) attempted to illustrate the flexibility of operant orientation in *Walden II.*

In their enthusiasm, early advocates of programmed instruction made the error of paying imperfect attention to the content to which they were applying their techniques. Many programs were rife with examples of incorrect information. A further impediment to the success of original programming efforts was the mechanical devotion to routinized and unimaginative language. Although there were exceptions (see, for example, *Words,* by Susan Meyer Markle, 1962), the tedium effected by early instances of programmed instruction retarded their acceptance and use.

Recent Curriculum Development

The development of a new curriculum is clearly intended to alter practice. Eisner (1970) points out that the product of this activity is often a guidebook, planned for use on a relatively widespread basis. Much of the process of curriculum development cannot be properly considered in a chapter on the technology of development, since the defining element of technology is the production of replicable materials through relatively codified means. The bulk of school-initiated curriculum development until recently would fail both criteria: it rarely described replicable procedures and the manner of its production can hardly be recounted. Instead, most curriculum activity persists as anthropological "rites of convocation" (Beals & Hoijer, 1953) where the activity is sufficient in itself and useful materials are both rarely expected and infrequently realized. Walker (1970) has described the process of curriculum development as mainly a search for a common platform around which content and activities may be organized rather than as a technically oriented procedure.

The high renaissance of curriculum development was clearly during the late years of the 1950s when institutional and financial support permitted the task to be approached with a commitment not previously known. Curriculum development began at this period to emerge consciously as a team enterprise rather than the hastily coalesced activity of a few individuals. Scholars and teachers renovated offerings in the natural sciences, mathematics, English, and later in selected social sciences, consistent with most recent knowledge. Conclusions of disciplines became less important than the procedures which scholars used to discover and verify knowledge. The efforts of such projects were usually encapsulated in materials for teacher and students; however, the manner in which one was to use the materials was essentially left to the teacher. Flaws in the projects have been well documented by Goodlad, Von Stoephasius, and Klein (1966). Short-term workshops were focused on preparing teachers to understand the new knowledge included in the revised curriculum. Little systematic attention was paid to the conditions under which students might optimally learn. The effects of the curricula were erratically tested, and often evaluations were made after the point when changes in the materials might have been practical. Despite the drawbacks of content-oriented curricula, attention and financial support had been drawn to the necessity of devising valid and effective materials for school use.

Profit-making Development

Major forces in curriculum building, which have only recently shown signs of modifying their hold, are the publishers of instructional materials. Instruction in reading, for example, came to depend upon the commercial offerings available to the schools. Rarely did educators prescribe or even seriously influence the materials presented to them by publishers. Until recently both supplier and user tended to place inordinate confidence in the academic qualifications of the author himself. The publishers verified that a potential author was respected in his field, and educators and public alike continued to assume that well-respected people produce valid materials. School officials trusted the publisher's judgment in the selection of authors and often based their adoption decisions on the physical attributes of the materials, such as typeface and illustrations, and their costs. It is fair to say that materials were only intended to augment the teacher's presence in the classroom, and that it was assumed that teachers understood and could make optimal use of whatever materials were available to them. A thorough, if not historical, treatment of the place of text materials in schooling, including specifications for their design, is contained in the *Text Materials Study* (Cronbach, 1955).

Toward Current Development

The activities of the programmed instruction movement, of the curriculum development enterprise, and of the publishers coalesced and formed the present entity of educational development in the context of a growing sense that schools were not meeting the needs of society. The chain of events which led to current emphasis on development may be interpreted as follows: at the inception of programmed instruction, publishers recognized its market potential and thus supported the preparation and distribution of many programs. What made this situation more dangerous than usual was that programmed instruction, in contrast to ordinary textbooks, emphasized the self-instructional nature of the materials and encouraged teachers to rely on given materials to accomplish certain goals. Evidence that programs produced desired outcomes was rarely available. To remedy this situation, a joint committee of the Department of Audio-Visual Instruction, the American Psychological Association and the American Educational Research Association, under A. A. Lumsdaine's leadership, prepared a set of technical recommendations for the evaluation of programmed materials. Publishers were urged to support the claims made in the name of programmed instruction by presenting data on the validation of programs. The *Journal of Programmed Instruction* (1966) secured pledges from thousands of school districts to purchase only those materials which were accompanied by reports of their effects on students. Attention was also given in the Joint Committee report to the credibility of the materials presented in the program. The report broadened the extant conception of programmed instruction by defining a program as "a vehicle which generates an essentially reproducible sequence of instructional events and accepts responsibility for efficiently accomplishing a specified change from a given range of initial competences of behavioral tendencies to a specified terminal range of competences or behavioral tendencies" (Lumsdaine, 1964, p. 385). Thus programs were emancipated from a frame-by-frame organization and expanded to include simulation, gaming and other replicable teacher-mediated procedures.

The requirement for data-supported programs implied expensive development activities over extended time periods. Legislation (The Elementary and Secondary Education Act, Title IV, in 1965) authorized the birth of government-supported agencies to produce such properly validated materials. Hence, private producers were encouraged to modify their stance regarding validation of materials, and many commercial publishers have markedly expanded their former conception of field testing. A problem to be faced, of course, is the relationship between producers from the private and public sector.

THE PRESENT CONCEPT OF EDUCATIONAL DEVELOPMENT

The task of describing present development is complex, but Hemphill (1969) has made a useful conceptual distinction in describing what he considers to be educational development. Educational development is the

... process of creating new alternatives that contribute to the improvement of educational practice ... (p. 23).

The *product development* process seeks to bring about improvement ... by creating tools, things, or devices, which when used as directed, are known to yield desirable and specified outcomes ... (p. 24).

The *change support* process directly addresses improving the behavior of those who are engaged in the practice of education. It emphasizes direct intervention ... (p. 24).

Hemphill has devised a table (Table 1) to make explicit the characteristics of alternative strategies for development.

Schutz (1970) also refers to product orientation and change orientation as two major development emphases, although he contends that the more popular approach in education has been the change orientation which focuses on people rather than products. Perhaps for the sake of emphasis, Hemphill (1969) states that one of the assumptions of the product development orientation is that "when improved materials

TABLE 1

CHARACTERISTICS OF DEVELOPMENT OBJECTIVES RELATED TO THE DEVELOPMENT STRATEGY TO BE RECOMMENDED

Change Support Process	Product Development Process
1. Complex relationships among groups of people or organizations are involved.	1. Specific behaviors of the individual only are involved.
2. Technological tools cannot be utilized meaningfully.	2. Technological tools can be adapted to support use of the product.
3. The 'operator's' input is critical to its effectiveness.	3. Self-sufficient 'packages' can be made available.
4. Control of the environment within which the change is to take place is minimal.	4. Control of the environment within which the product is to be used is maximal.
5. Deviation from traditional educational practice is large.	5. Deviation from traditional educational practice is small.
6. The total system to which the change must be related contains many human subsystems.	6. The total system to which the product is related has few human subsystems.
7. Attitudes, beliefs, and opinions are germane to the change.	7. Objective facts and figures are germane to content of the product.
8. Outcomes are subject to general long-range evaluation only.	8. Outcomes are subject to evaluation in terms of immediate behavior changes.
9. Power (ability to control) of the developer relative to power of the system is minimal.	9. Power (ability to control) of the developer relative to power of the system is maximal.
10. General objectives develop as the change proceeds.	10. Specific objectives can be stated in detail and in advance.

Source: J. K. Hemphill, Educational Development. *The Urban Review,* a publication of the Center for Urban Education, October 1969, 4, p. 27.

are created, they need only to be made available in order to improve educational practice" (p. 24). This assumption may be made by those viewing with unseemly optimism the process of product development, but probably would not represent the position of those who have attempted to secure adoption of developed materials. Schutz (1970) argues for a merged orientation, employing both a product development and a change orientation, stating "a pure product or change support strategy is rarely reasonable" (p. 51). "The availability of outcome-referenced methods and materials comprising a product constitutes a base for planning and managing human resources to enhance the attainment of specified outcomes" (p. 54).

Although Schutz's position is eminently sensible and a full description of educational development would undoubtedly contain descriptions of both product development and change-support procedures, this chapter will not attempt the task. Change support involves comprehensive questions of organizational change, and various forms of innovations have idiosyncratic support requirements. The remainder of this chapter then will describe in detail those particular development activities associated with instructional products.

PRODUCT DEVELOPMENT PROCEDURES

Development procedures which are based on a systems approach have been described by a number of writers in education (Banathy, 1968; Borg & Hood, 1968; Briggs, 1970; Flanagan, 1967; Gilbert, 1962; Glaser, 1966a, 1966b; M. Johnson, 1969; Mager & Beach, 1967; McNeil, 1968; Popham & Baker, 1971; Schutz, 1970; Shoemaker, n.d.; Stowe, 1969). In general, these procedures attempt to prescribe routines for the development of instructional materials. Specific attention has been given to the development of programmed instruction by S. M. Markle (1969). The development proc-

esses described and advocated vary in emphasis and detail. Borg and Hood (1968) list a total of 27 steps under the following general rubrics: a) research and information collection, b) planning, c) preliminary development, d) preliminary field testing, e) main product revision, f) main field testing, g) operational product revision, h) operational field testing, i) final product revisions, j) dissemination and distribution, k) report preparation, and l) implementation. Gilbert (1962) presents a much more general scheme involving a) specific development, b) design and proving, c) training and follow-through.

Popham and Baker (1971), in an instructional program written in 1967 and later modified by Sullivan (1968), describe major stages of product development to include formulation, instructional specifications, prototype development and tryout, product development, product tryout, product revision, and operations analysis. Sullivan's paper also includes expected documents, review criteria and decisions to be made at each stage of development.

Schutz (1970) provides a comprehensive and integrative description of developmental work and further expands Sullivan's paper. Stages described are formulation, prototype, component, product, installation, and program. Schutz relates each stage to its "uncertainty focus," that is, the outcome of operations conducted within the particular stage described. For instance, during the formulation stage, activities such as specifying desired outcomes, identifying subordinate skills, and designing initial strategies for teaching should reduce some of the uncertainty with regard to specifications (see Table 2).

The Northwest Regional Educational Laboratory (n.d.) includes 37 steps in product development and installation, 31 of which are directly related to development. Major phases are a) concept stage, b) feasibility stage, c) operational planning stage, d) development stage, and e) installation stage. In the introduction to

TABLE 2

SWRL INSTRUCTIONAL PRODUCT DEVELOPMENT STAGES

Stage	Activity	Uncertainty Focus	Typical Duration of Tryout
Formulation	Specifying the desired instructional outcomes; identifying the skills required to achieve the outcomes; designing strategies for teaching the skills.	Specification parameters.	One to several experimental sessions.
Prototype	Testing instructional strategies by empirically investigating variations of materials and methods, and assessing the impact of each variation.	Product specifications.	One day to few weeks.
Component	Producing a segment of instruction and trying it out with a single learner or groups of learners in a natural setting to determine if the instruction accomplishes its objectives.	Instruction parameters.	One week to few months.
Product	Successively trying out and revising a combination of components in a natural setting until acceptable levels of performance have been attained.	Instructional effectiveness.	One to several "semester" units.
Installation	Integrating a product into programs which are combined with existing school instruction to determine procedures for widespread implementation.	User training.	One to several "semester" units.
Program	Involving those agencies which will be responsible for maintaining operational use of a program without the direct assistance of the development agency.	Program management.	One to several years.

Source: R. E. Schutz, The nature of educational development. *Journal of Research and Development in Education,* Winter 1970, 3 (2), p. 52.

Northwest Laboratory's description the writers indicate that the sequence of steps may be abrogated. Briggs (1970) has produced a comprehensive document on the training of developers. Both issues related to the development are raised in expository sections as well as practice provided in what the author feels are critical development skills.

The danger in the delineation and dissemination of stages, critical events or steps in development is that they may be over-zealously employed while incompletely understood. The qualifications (permitting abrogation of steps) in the Northwest Regional Laboratory's statement may be overlooked in the quest for regularity and linearity in the development process. The following section will describe major stages in development. An attempt will be made to indicate areas of difficulty and alternate solutions suggested by writers in the field. Where pertinent and available, research evidence to support procedures will be included. Although these activities will be presented sequentially, the earlier noted qualifications regarding lack of linearity of development by Gideonse, Hilgard and others should be kept in mind.

Formulation

It is impossible to describe the origin of ideas that lead to the pursuit of instructional development. Although procedures to foster the flow of ideas have been studied in a management context (Dean, 1968), McCrory (1964) states that "a design concept is created when, through the designer's powers of synthesis, a recognized need, and technical capability as represented by the state of the art are matched" (p. 62). Schutz (1970) contends that the motivation for development in education derives from what Glennan (1967) terms the "requirements-pull" rather than technology-push. According to Glennan, requirements-pull fits those projects which are undertaken because of clearly articulated needs. Technology-push projects develop, on the other hand, anticipating that a technological breakthrough will result in the potential for new resources. The existence of these resources should stimulate the development of new ways to meet needs. As Schutz points out, the technology-push perspective has yet to be seriously recognized in education.

Educational needs assessment. The determination of educational needs has historically been a curriculum question involving a consideration of what the ends of instruction should be (Goodlad et al., 1966; M. Johnson, 1969; R. W. Tyler, 1950). R W. Tyler (1950) proposes the use of the learner, the society and the subject matter as sources of generalizations from which educational needs might be inferred. Research studies undertaken to determine educational needs have employed various strategies. An investigation supervised by Campbell and Markle (1968) employed the critical incident technique (Flanagan, 1954) to identify "need symptoms perceived by educators." Research sponsored by the UCLA Center for the Study of Evaluation considered pupil performance on a diagnostic test and ratings of teachers on the relevancy of the items (Skager, 1969). The same institution also supported research by Baker (1970b) on the determination of educational needs where parents, students and teachers rated the importance of educational objectives in mathematics, and pupil performance data on a test measuring those objectives were also obtained. Cornell (1970) describes another performance-based approach to needs assessment.

The use of experts to contribute to the

formulation of educational goals has its pitfalls, as Jacobson (1970) points out, particularly in the definition of "expert." Obradovic (1970) describes the difficulty of involving community members in early development. Implicit in the determination of needs is some measure of educational priority. Stake and Gooler (1970) and Stake (1970) provide a discussion of the difficulties inherent in operationalizing value decisions. Use of Delphi techniques (Helmer, 1966) to resolve conflict in preferences also has applicability to choices among educational objectives.

Technology as the impetus for educational formulation. Schutz's discussion of the motives for educational development indicates that the perspective required for what Glennan describes as "technology-push" does not currently exist in the field. One would suspect that such a perspective would require the history of successful examples in order to develop. Technological breakthroughs, including extant film and television use, have not produced consequences which have seriously affected educational practice. Computer, video cartridge and holography development might provide the necessary climate to make technology-push a reasonable source of instructional development. But because these developments compete with the apparent pressure inherent in the requirements-pull basis for production selection, Glennan (1967) points out that organizations are usually less "comfortable" in the support of technology-push activities.

Use of research in product formulation. Borg (1969) has neatly described the dilemma facing those involved in formulating educational programs. Logic dictates that research questions must be answered prior to the initiation of development work. Yet it is impractical to delay action in areas of strong requirements until sufficient evidence accumulates (see Hilgard, 1968). Development in a teacher-training program which Borg describes proceeded on the ideas which were incompletely validated but appeared to have potential import. Borg reports that concern was shifted at the Far West Regional Laboratory from "what skills are essential to effective teaching" to the question, "how can we teach effectively the skills *we* have selected?" Such a formulation policy may be termed high-risk, for there is the clear chance that the developers selected teaching behaviors which were only speciously related to effective learning. But, as will be elaborated in a subsequent discussion of noneducational development work, arbitrary decisions, which are subsequently tested and redesigned, may sometimes be the only way to make significant advances in the field.

Beyond experimental research as a basis for product formulation, literature searches may also make significant contributions to formulation effects. Popham and Baker (1971) suggest that some assurance be made that competing instructional products do not exist, and imply that the proposed product should provide a major advance over current practice. The *Educational Product Information Exchange*, which publishes listings of instructional products, might be an aid in such a search, although evidence related to the effectiveness of the rated products is usually not summarized. Unfortunately, development has not come to the point in education where concurrent exploratory development of divergent solutions to instructional needs is characteristic of many enterprises.

Although educational needs are ubiquitous, instructional development may soon begin to rely more heavily on some of the same criteria applied to evaluate proposals in industrial product development, such as the probability of commercial success (Dean, 1968). Market surveys in various forms have been conducted by major book publishers, but educators have yet to exploit the potential of employing workable market-

analysis techniques. A brief description of product-concept testing is reported by Greenwald (1969) in five specific situations.

SPECIFICATION

The conscious use of specifications in product development perhaps derives from the fields of systems analysis, learning psychology and engineering. Systems analysis depends upon the expression of objectives of systems in terms of "precise measures of performance" (Churchman, 1968) so that the effectiveness of the system may be evaluated. Specification of outcomes is required by the operant conditioner, not only for the purpose of evaluation, but so that adequate stimulus control is exercised to insure that the range of relevant tasks is learned efficiently. Engineering typically employs specifications to delimit the tolerances of internal characteristics of products, such as the weight or thickness of wire. Specifications in the planning of instructional materials are used for all three reasons: to provide a basis for product evaluation, to promote efficient instruction, and to limit the physical attributes of the intended product.

Performance Specifications

A description of learner postinstructional performance forms the basis of most rules for instructional specifications (Baker, Gerlach, Schutz, & Sullivan, 1968; Briggs, 1970; Johnson & Johnson, 1970; Northwest Regional Laboratory, n.d.; Popham & Baker, 1971; Stowe, 1969; Sullivan, 1968). An inspection of documents from development projects shows them to include a description of the intended accomplishments of the project in terms of learner's measurable behavior (Far West Regional Laboratory, 1968; Flanagan, 1967; Smith & Rapp, 1969).

Complete specifications of performance describe a) the type of response desired, b) the content to which the response should generalize, c) standards for determining if performance has been adequate, d) prerequisite experiences of learner, and e) social and psychological characteristics of the learner.

Behavioral objectives. The term *behavioral objective* as a basis for development seems to be a source of unending confusion among both developers and critics. When rigidly interpreted (Mager, 1962), behavioral objectives describe an observable response to a single stimulus, for example, giving the dates of the Spanish-American War. Objectives of this type have been severely criticized as trivial, mechanistic and arbitrary in their circumscription of the development task. Such formulation of behavioral objectives is essentially equivalent to the verbal description of one and only one test item, thus requiring the preparation of many objectives for even a modest development project. In other cases, objectives may be specified with the eliciting stimuli vaguely implied, for example, "the learner is to discuss economic priorities in an essay." The information and guidance provided to the developer by this objective are minimal. In the rush to adhere to the perceived prevailing view, the use of specifications is often abused. Nonfunctioning specifications may accord their writer with a sense of modernity, but as Walker (1970) notes, objectives are often tacked onto projects as appendages and in no way aid early planning. Some writers have compounded the problem of objectives by narrowly interpreting "behavior" as activity. Inspection of development plans finds that verbal learning is properly considered as a behavior in "behavioral objectives," and limited notions of "behavior" are unsubstantiated in development practice.

Response descriptions. Consistent with the notion that the precise form of the learner's response is critical in the planning and evaluation of instruction, a number of materials designed to train would-be objectives writers have been produced (Cohen, 1970;

Mager, 1962; McAshan, 1970; Popham, 1969a). Clearly limiting the form of the response in the objective is presumably required to insure that practice within the instructional program will be consistent with evaluation measures (Popham & Baker, 1971). Edling (1968) goes so far as to state that the verb in a sentence describing the behavior is considered the most critical element in preparing a behavioral objective. One possible misinterpretation of such a statement developers may make during the specification stage is to decide on precisely the form that the test item should take. For instance, there are those who would distinguish between objectives which either call for the learner to mark a box or circle a letter in order to indicate the correct answer. There are probably few serious implications for instructional design in this particular decision, since the learner's skill in making marks is clearly less significant than his ability to discriminate.

A retreat from operationalizing the nonessential attributes of performance, e.g., whether a response is indicated by marking X's or circling letters, was provided by Sullivan (1969), in part derived from earlier work (Baker et al., 1968). Sullivan describes a classification for behavioral objectives which he contrasts with Bloom's well-known work (1956). Sullivan's "performance terms" are based on overt learner behavior and are derived from the list published by the American Association for the Advancement of Science (AAAS) for use with the series entitled, *The Psychological Bases of Science—A Process Approach* (AAAS, 1965). The performance terms described by Sullivan, "identify," "name," "describe," "construct," "order," and "demonstrate," appear to be somewhat vague. However, when these terms are allied with illustrations of sample objectives and test items they may provide sufficient clarity for the design of instruction.

Gagné (1970) has also classified behaviors. However, his initial emphasis appears to be on learning rather than on instruction.

Gagné describes the following categories of behavior: a) a simple connection, b) a chain or sequence, c) identification, d) a concept, e) a principle, and f) a higher order principle, or general principle. Gagné provides examples to illustrate what is meant by each of the categories, and the relationship of both Sullivan's and Gagné's work is evident. A more recent work by Gagné (1971) provides a more precise technical language.

Content specifications. An antidote to objectives stated either too broadly or narrowly may eventually be derived through use of content specifications. Baker (1969), Hively, Patterson, and Page (1968), and Kriewall (1969) have affixed different labels to an essentially similar concept. Objectives are formulated as desired responses to well-defined classes of stimuli. The parameters of content within which the learner is expected to respond homogeneously are made explicit. Thus, a universe of stimuli is defined and parallel examples can be sampled for either practice or evaluation. Although Hively developed his domain-referenced model primarily to serve the development of post hoc achievement testing, the notion of universe-defined objectives to guide development has also been employed (Baker et al., 1968; Rabehl, 1970).

A central problem inherent in this procedure is the production of generation rules for limiting the content in a particular subject-matter area. Bormuth (1970), P. E. Johnson (1970), and Hively et al. (1968) illustrate the use of rules in transformational grammar, physics and mathematics, respectively. Attempts to employ generation rules in a less well-structured discipline, such as English literature, have been made with limited success (Instructional Objectives Exchange, 1970). The generation rule itself may describe a procedure for generating a class of problems (Kriewall, 1969) or may specify all items in the set (Southwest Regional Laboratory for Educational Research and Development, 1969). Kriewall

(1969) presents sample computer programs which generate items to conform to specified parameters.

The labels for such limiting rules have been influenced by the purpose for which they were produced. Hively (1970), Nitko (1970) and Sension (1970), concerned with test production, use the item form in which the specified "content domain" is an essential part. Baker (1969) describes "content generality" in an effort to broaden severely limited conceptions of behavioral objectives. Kriewall (1969) describes "specified content objectives" in an effort to make clearer generic types of objectives, e.g., to solve algebra problems. Baker et al. (1968) and Hively (1970) also list some unresolved problems in the use of domain-referenced objectives, including questions of how domains are defined, validated and ultimately used.

Projects should also be designed with the participation of experts in the subject matters of concern. Even in projects where subject-matter specialists have provided the leadership, an alarming number of content-based errors exist. Writers such as Ausubel (1966) have sensitized the development community to the necessity for accuracy and organization in the content, although such concerns are obviously facilitated if the development project attempts to employ domain-referenced objectives. In any event, some review of specifications should be conducted by competent subject-matter scholars to avoid the production of materials which efficiently teach imprecise and disordered content.

Performance standards. The seriousness with which a development agency uses specifications can be readily tested by looking at the standards which have been explicated to estimate adequacy of the performance. Achievement of most objectives is not an on-off proposition. Specifications must describe how well performance is to be demonstrated, that is, where along a continuum of performance the successful learner is placed. Early performance standards or minimal levels in programmed instruction (Mager, 1962) were rather glibly stated to be "90-90," 90 percent of the students achieve 90 percent of the objectives. The false sense of comfort in the presumed objectivity of such performance levels was not easily shaken. For instance, in many agencies, when a multiple-choice test was used to estimate achievement, learners were required to obtain at least a 90 percent score before the program was disseminated. Yet 90 percent mastery of some of these tests meant very little. A great deal of subjectivity and happenstance were incorporated into the test items. It is more useful for a developer to be provided with information about high-priority item forms and essential discriminations among correct responses and distracters. Baker et al. (1968) have described a procedure which requires that the parameters of right and wrong answers be included in the statement of specifications.

The production of performance standards for constructed responses is likewise a taxing proposition. For instance, in the earlier example of essay writing in economics, performance standards must be generated which detail the essential attributes the essay must have in order for the response to be deemed satisfactory and the objective achieved. However, performance standards do not necessarily dictate the actual content of the response. Standards might relate to the process which the learner is to demonstrate in his performance, for example, citing data-based rather than authority-linked evidence in an essay.

Performance standards or criteria have obvious relationships to instructional activities planned for the learner. For instance, if data-based evidence is to be central to the evaluation of an essay, then some instructional provision for the use and interpretation of data is important in the materials themselves. Certain objectives seem to elude definitional criteria, such as rules for evaluation. Standards to judge a program goal, such as "clearly written English," may

indicate that the instructional technologist needs more rigor than is currently provided in the subject-matter field. Encouraging and exhorting subject-matter experts to articulate and resolve ambiguities of their field is likely to have little immediate effect on development. As a temporary substitute, performance standards may be instituted by example. Excerpts of "good English" are provided as models and negative instances are also used. For example, the *Publication Manual of the American Psychological Association* (1967) gives criteria for judging manuscripts and provides both positive and negative examples of good writing style. The *English Literature Collection* of the Instructional Objectives Exchange (1969) includes both definitional and exemplar criteria for the assessment of the stated objectives. Subjective determination of minimal performance levels has also been described (Crawford, 1970).

Group-performance levels. Following a description of standards so that the quality of individual performance may be evaluated, a second common concern of developers is the specification of the proportion of the learners who will be able to meet the performance standards. The problem of deciding whether 70 or 90 percent of the learners should be expected to satisfy the objectives is usually not the central problem. The group-performance level will usually be empirically determined and does not exist at an absolute, fixed point. The lower limits of acceptable group performance are defined by the results of existing practice. If 60 percent of the children are currently able to solve Class X mathematics problems satisfactorily, then the performance levels expected from the developed product must either demonstrably increase the number of children who are successful or radically reduce the cost of 60 percent success (Sherwin & Isenson, 1967). Development will continue until the increase in numbers of students reaching criterion following a revision is not commensurate with the cost of the revision. Decisions about the value of performance increments are considered subjectively and are experientially consonant with the mission of the development agency (Crawford, 1970).

En Route Behavior

After the objectives and standards of the program have been generated, the component skills requisite for the achievement of the objectives should be described. Since empirical evidence is scarce (Gagné, 1962) regarding what constituent behaviors are necessary for achievement, certain schemes may be employed in the analysis of objectives (see, for example, Gagné, 1968, 1970; Mechner, 1967). The purpose for en route or subtask specifications is to guide initial instructional design to maximize the success of first-draft attempts.

Entry Behaviors

Specifications also normally describe the competencies the learner is expected to demonstrate upon entrance to the program. These entry levels delimit the parameters of responsibility for the instructional-development team. Entry skills such as the ability to write with a pencil may be important to include when preparing materials for primary-age children but not for older children. Novices at specification writing unfortunately tend to list exhaustively all precedent behaviors tangentially applicable to the desired goals. Guidance for the description of entry behavior can be found in works by Johnson and Johnson (1970), Popham and Baker (1971), as well as in Gagné (1970).

Population Specification

Some idea of the characteristics of the anticipated learner should be included in the specifications. These include an explanation of his required entry skills as well as those attributes which may facilitate or otherwise modify the instructional design. The difficulty and potential controversy inherent in determining the critical attributes likely to interact with instruction subvert the absolute utility of describing personality or cultural characteristics of the learners, but characteristics such as expected attention span or media tolerance could be described to provide minimal design guidance for the developers. Determinists might argue that all such "population characteristics" should be properly described in terms of previous experience of the potential learner. Although adequate information regarding learner experience is difficult and time-consuming to obtain, the description of population characteristics in the specifications is included primarily to make use of developmental descriptions (Ilg & Ames, 1955) and experiential observations of the behaviors of the intended learners.

Research on Performance Specifications

While there appears to be a surfeit of guides for writing performance specifications, the research in support of such practice in development is yet to be found. Studies have been conducted on giving objectives directly to students prior to instruction with positive results obtained (Blaney & McKie, 1969; Dallis, 1969; Mager & McCann, 1961). But the influence of specifications on the purveyors of instruction has not been demonstrated in controlled experimental settings (Baker, 1969).

Additional Issues in Performance Specifications

Almost every procedure described above could be subjected to empirical verification to determine the contribution its use makes to the efficient production of valid instructional materials. Critics might also revile the aforementioned procedures for what they omit. For example, few development efforts actually specify desired affective consequences of the planned instruction beyond rather global and gratuitous statements of good intentions in the introduction. Second, product specifications should describe alternate manners in which students may demonstrate their attainment of objectives. Arguments that clear instructional planning results in the homogenation of students (Arnstine, 1964) would be partially vitiated by multiple options for students to demonstrate competence.

Prototype Specifications

Following the delineation of performance specifications, and concurrent with other development activities, specifications to guide the form of preliminary materials and procedures must be provided. In engineering, form and function are often integral. In education, appropriateness of certain presentation modes for either categories of tasks or learners has yet to be demonstrated. Prototype specifications should permit invention and experimentation in preliminary development. Thus, at this point, specifications should provide broad limits within which initial prototypes may be designed. These limits may include constraints in design and production resources or, in the user, ability to implement the product. Shoemaker (n.d.) has identified eight types of constraints to be considered in the preparation of training specifications, three of which appear to have import for instructional development: a) resources—time and money, b) facilities for both production and reception, c) probable life expectancy of the product. Geis (1970), in a broader description of resources and constraints in development, identifies two specific points relevant to product specifications: a) intended life span of the product, and b) maintenance by the receiving system. Examples of contraints are provided in an air defense and an educational problem by Carter (1966). Two particular issues are relevant in this phase of development: 1) the desired degree of replicability of the finished product, and 2) the basis for the initial selection of presentation mode.

Reproducibility. Systematic development, with its procedures for design and repeated testing, implies that the resultant product will perform with some expected degree of reliability. The product performs when aspects of its design measurably contribute to learner performance. Reliability requires that the materials or procedures be implemented as intended. One of the most critical points in product specification is maximizing the likelihood that the product will have replicable effects. "Reproducibility" was the term emphasized by Lumsdaine (1964) in his definition of instructional programs. A program was described as "an essentially reproducible set of instructional events" which is designed to change efficiently particular attributes of the learner's performance. Literal interpretation of the notion of reproducibility conjures up visions of mimeograph machines; yet the most direct way to assure replicability is to incorporate all critical stimuli, and provisions for responses to them, in materials provided directly to the learner. Thus, an instructor not employing designated procedures, e.g., sufficient number of repetitions with flashcards, has only limited negative effect on the performance of the learners. The live teacher is, in such cases, auxiliary to the main thrust of the program. An alternative, employed in some development, is to "program" the teacher's behavior to meet the criterion of reproducible events (Buchanan, 1963) by providing scripts from which the teacher is directed not to depart, or by engaging in instructional training of the teachers. Since teacher approbation is often a review criterion for newly developed instructional products, either the avoidance or automation of teachers may have negative consequences in terms of product acceptability.

The Southwest Regional Laboratory (SWRL) (1969) has managed a more liberal interpretation of "reproducible" in the design of its First Year Communication Skills Program. Rather than providing detailed lessons for teachers, SWRL emphasizes the specific goals of the program and provides materials which the teacher may use. The program is heavily ends-oriented, in that the achievement of the children on the reading tasks is central rather than the precise specification of the teacher's classroom behavior.

Presentation mode. Related to the need for reproducible instructional events is the problem of selecting the mode of presentation for the product. As noted earlier, teacher-mediated instruction has been the rule rather than the exception in our classrooms, and early instructional materials were primarily designed to augment an assumed instructional repertoire of the teacher. When products are conceived as mere adjuncts to teacher routines, the evidence of reproducibility of instructional events is difficult to compile. If success of materials depends upon the precise implementation of designated procedures by the teacher, the cost of both initial training and maintenance of desired teacher behavior must be calculated. To bypass the administrative and psychic hardship of extensive teacher training, many instructional products are being conceived in terms of instructional media. The specific attributes of computer-assisted or other instrument-based instruction are considered elsewhere in this volume.

Selection of media. The selection of media for instructional products is plagued by methodological problems. Early studies which focused on the comparison of different media produced findings which, while useful for particular decision-making situations involving the particular cases compared, as film A contrasted with tape Z, provided no basis for generalizing to the entire media class from which the cases were selected (e.g., films are better than tapes). Unfortunately, researchers sometimes formulated their conclusions in class-comparison terms (see Lumsdaine, 1963; and Lumsdaine & May, 1965, for amplified discussion). More precise studies have been conducted where media have been compared for their effectiveness in teaching particular tasks. For instance, Dwyer (1969) has conducted a series of investigations re-

garding the kind of illustration most appropriate to certain instructional situations. Again, there is still the problem of generalization from a single instance or rendering to a probably poorly defined class, such as "realistic" illustrations. Nonetheless, the narrowing of media comparison as a function of task is clearly a substantial improvement over previous research and has great promise. Edling (1968), summarizing research on the relationships of educational objectives and educational media, states, "There is little evidence to support the concept that given media, qua media, contribute to more or better learning than other media; i.e., there is no evidence as to what, or how much, is learned in 'non-media' situations" (p. 189). In the absence of definitive or even indicative evidence, those responsible for product design might well conduct evaluation studies of probable contending media to determine their relative effectiveness for the particular objectives of interest. Such experimentation is costly but may be justified under conditions where the product is expected to endure for a long period and/or where the need for a successfully designed program is great.

When inspecting the technical reports of agencies involved in development, one can frequently observe early media commitments which appear to be arbitrary decisions. The basis for decisions to use a medium, such as video tape, is rarely described and one imagines that novelty, availability of equipment for production, or the project leader's unexamined preferences contribute greatly to the decision.

Criterion-Test Development

Performance specifications must eventually be translated into test items. Certain advantages are gained if test items are produced and tried early in the development process, for data can be accumulated and interpreted against three separate criteria: a) the appropriateness of the items to measure the specified objectives; b) the suitability of the product for the intended learner population; and c) the adequacy of preliminary instructional planning.

Appropriateness of test items. Even when objectives are specified clearly, the internal attributes of items generated to measure them can show great variation. Questions involving appropriateness of items are properly interpreted as validity concerns. Validity, as traditionally conceived and demonstrated by test producers, may not have compelling relevance for items produced to assess specific instructional products. The utility of traditional validity and reliability estimates for such criterion-referenced items has been considered by Gagné (1969), Glaser (1963), Glaser and Cox (1968), Kriewall (1969), and Popham and Husek (1969). Gagné describes the need for producing "veritable" measures, shifting the focus from the validity of items to the validity of the objective itself.

The use of an item-form strategy, described by Hively (1970), Kriewall (1969), and Nitko (1970), further circumvents the item validity problem since items generated through such procedures are a priori valid.

No resolution of the assumed conflict in methodologies between criterion-referenced and more traditional tests has yet emerged, although problems of item sampling, item congruence and reliability have been considered.

Beyond questions of validity, early item testing permits verification of the feasibility of the test items themselves under both laboratory and classroom use. Objectives which sound reasonable during the planning stage may deteriorate into exercises which are impractical or absurd in the classroom. Without early testing such lack of feasibility might go unnoticed until development has reached advanced stages. A change in the basic testing concept at a later point could easily require costly instructional revisions.

Suitability of the product for intended population. A second major focus of early

item trials is to pretest the learner rather than assess the quality of the items themselves. Items should be administered to the intended learner population to determine the degree to which the learners already possess the anticipated criterion behaviors. Testing may also consider the target group's entry skills to verify preliminary assumptions regarding the group's prior experiences, and should, for instance, determine attitude as well as cognitive performance. Data obtained from such trials are used to justify or to question the requirement for the planned product and contribute to needs-assessment procedures mentioned earlier.

Adequacy of instructional analysis. If the early tests consist of items measuring subordinate tasks as well as criterion and entry skills, data may corroborate the appropriateness of early analysis of component skills. Such evidence that deficiencies in en route objectives (Baker et al., 1968; Gagné & Paradise, 1961) are associated with failure on criterion items permits instructional design to proceed more confidently.

Prototype Development

Given the performance specifications and a statement of constraints designed to inhibit wildly unfettered invention, the actual development of product prototypes is in order. McCrory (1964) describes the design concept as analogous to the hypothesis in experimental methodology. The prototype design represents an estimate of effective means to meet the need outlined in the specifications. The analogy does not hold, of course, when one considers the consequences of failure in both hypothesis testing and prototype development. In the former case, even failure represents a contribution to the realm of knowledge. The researcher is free to pursue, to modify or to discontinue his line of inquiry. In prototype development the investigators are committed to some degree of success.

The acceptance of prototype development

as a regular procedure in design is a clear admission of the inadequate knowledge base and state of the instruction art. It is a recognition that there is but limited understanding of how learning can best be facilitated and that present information is in no way generalizable either to all learners or to products which have not yet been developed. Thus, prototype design inherently requires empirical data to validate preliminary decisions.

Nadler (1967) suggests an empirical procedure to use during design development. Comparative formats, media and organizations may be tested during the prototype phase of development. However, one should not infer that the entire process is empirical. Even in the face of uncertain experimental results, certain instructional procedures have high credibility and can be employed in early prototype designs. The use of procedures such as prompting, confirmation and direct practice is frequently found in effective materials and, for many tasks, they represent a set of reasonably efficient first-draft techniques. Beyond the artistic interpretation of these and other instructional techniques, prototyping may involve the choice between competing alternative solutions to design problems. In such cases a short-term test of alternative instructional procedures can provide data to aid the decision-maker. One should not assume that the collection of data will automatically resolve one's problems, for both data and judgment are required. One would hope that such preliminary evaluations are made in as rigorous a context as cost will permit. Enthoven (1966) describes the problems of design in the military context and the recognition that data are always integrated with the designer's judgment and experience.

Development: Translation of Prototype Specifications

The activities of actual product development would seem fool's play in the presence of adequately defined specifications and well-tested prototypes. Aside from the dismaying predicament that specifications and prototypes are almost always subject to a range of interpretation, and not infrequently to substantial modification, the product-development stage bears more responsibility than merely the stamping out of pre-ordained materials. The product-development activity involves two basic commitments. One responsibility is to produce an operative first version of the entire product. This task is relatively minor in the case of a 30-minute sequence but grows to enormous proportions when a year-long program is under development. The second activity subsumed under product development is the collection and interpretation of data for the purpose of product revision.

During the prototyping stage two concerns are critical. The first is the planning and verification of the reproducibility of instructional events, and the second is the determination of instructional strategies to be integrated into the product. The subsequent development of an operational version of the product additionally requires attention to the sequencing of lessons or materials, the correlation and integration of multiple-program components, and identification of extra-instructional contingencies necessary to make the program work.

Sequencing. Sequencing can be examined from a variety of viewpoints. The subject-matter expert attends to the sequence of concepts in a program to assure that it does not violate the prevailing view of the subject matter's organization. A curriculum worker might be interested in the relationship of the sequence in a single instructional program to other parts in the curriculum. An operant psychologist might be concerned that the learner has an opportunity to demonstrate subordinate skills identified in a task analysis of the terminal objectives. He might also inspect procedures to determine if learner behaviors were being shaped in successive approximations to the desired tasks. Whatever the particular focus of the developer, and the argument may be made that all three viewpoints are important, the product-development stage requires attention to the total sequence of instructional materials.

A second related concern is the integration of parts of a particular program. It is not uncommon for programs to consist of a variety of semiautonomous materials, each of which contributes to its own objective. For example, guides for the teacher, booklets for the children, films and kits comprise only a portion of the materials employed in the Elementary Science Study program developed by the Educational Development Center (1969). The coodinator of development must verify that the program elements relate to each other, and that the point at which a given lesson is used is consistent with concurrent instruction in other program elements.

Extra-instructional contingencies. The production of lessons which have demonstrated instructional effects in the laboratory and the assurance that each program element is both internally sequenced and correlated with other program elements does not assure a successful program. What may be termed "delivery" technology must be considered. Materials must be packaged so that they are easily accessible and interpretable to users.

If instructional systems are heavily individualized, procedures to allow the program to be activated by the learner must be developed. The limits on teachers' tolerance for distribution of materials, data tabulation, and changes in ordinary routine need description. The development coordinator must identify training requirements for the teachers and determine if other support systems are necessary to promote the success of the program. If a technology can be produced which permits facile student use of the instruction, a critical development problem has been solved. The discovery of a format which efficiently transmits essential instruction fosters the subsequent revision of the product.

Data Collection and Use in Improvement of Instructional Products

The use of data to improve effects of instruction is essential in current conceptions of product development. Numerous writers in the field of development describe the necessity for data-based instructional decisions (Flanagan, 1969; Gagné, 1969; Glaser, 1966b; Hemphill, 1969; Lindvall & Cox, 1969; Lumsdaine, 1965; S. M. Markle, 1967; Schutz, 1970) and have included the use of data in development as a defining characteristic of an instructional program.

The testing of materials and procedures in early instructional design, described by Scriven (1967) as formative evaluation, is central to the product-development notion. Data must be employed to verify assumptions about the effects of particular instructional manipulations because of the limited knowledge base in instruction. Developers must be skeptical by nature and place only restricted confidence in their initial designs until corroboration is obtained.

Data-collection points. Information about the effects of instruction may be obtained at various points in the development procedure. During the prototype stage, the testing of single lessons or of short instructional sequences with a single learner or a small group of learners clarifies the extent to which instruction functions according to plan. S. M. Markle (1967) terms this phase as developmental testing, and describes the interaction of the programmer and the learner in a laboratory setting as clinical in effect. Particular problems associated with intensive developmental testing, according to Markle, are the cost of the procedure, the interpretation of the responses made by the developer, and the representativeness of the observed students. Other procedures to guide developmental testing have been described by Horn (1964).

Use of data for product improvement continues beyond the prototyping stage. As segments of program components are developed, they are tested in both laboratory situations, as described by S. M. Markle, and in classroom or other reality contexts.

While Grobman (1968) presents a detailed description of the general evaluation of curriculum projects, *Calipers,* a publication of the Southwest Educational Development Corporation (1969), offers a set of procedures designed specifically for testing the class of instructional products described in this chapter. The writers of *Calipers* have included a feedback loop from the data obtained in their recommended field test which provides revision inputs.

Types of data to employ in revision. A primary source of data for the revision of instructional programs is the performance of the learner who is exposed to the product. Two major categories of data have been employed in guiding revision: responses made during the process of instruction, and responses made to the criterion tests at the conclusion of instruction.

The use of rate of errors made during the process of instruction has characterized the development of programmed instruction (see S. M. Markle, 1967), but has been disputed as a meaningful basis for revision. While operant programmers insist that errors made by the learner during instruction represent a program failure as reported by Glaser (1966b), other programmers with alternative theoretical orientations (Crowder, 1960) have used errors diagnostically to determine the appropriate sequence for each learner in the program. Research on the relationship of error rate to terminal performance further indicates its fallibility as a single revision criterion. Baker, Schutz, and Sullivan (1967) demonstrated that even under conditions where the error rate was low, students did not necessarily reach criterion. Silberman, Coulson, Melaragno, and Newmark (1964) found that error rates could be reduced without affecting criterion performance. Anderson and Faust (1967) inferred that error rate is highly dependent on the presentation of a frame and may be unrelated to criterion performance.

Criterion test performance has also been used as a basis of test-program revision. Scriven (1967) reminds us that percentages per se are not important but rather that the nature of the error is. The earlier work of Gagné and Paradise (1961) supports this analysis and suggests that three possible explanations exist when a criterion task has not been mastered: a) a subordinate learning set has been omitted, b) a subordinate learning set has not been retained because of inadequate practice, or c) insufficient guidance in the integration of subskills has been provided.

Empirical support for improvement associated with revision cycles has been gathered by investigators using various media as the instructional vehicle. Gropper and Lumsdaine (1961), in revisions of televised lessons, found improvement associated with revision. Studies by VanderMeer (1964), VanderMeer and Montgomery (1964), and VanderMeer and Thorne (1964) in filmstrip production, support the use of learner responses to guide revisions. Baker et al. (1967) investigated instructional procedures which led to the inclusion of greater control of learner behavior by instructional material. Gropper (1967) found increases in performance on empirically revised instructional materials. Silberman et al. (1964), in an extensive study, and Baker (1970c), in a modest one, used student performance to improve program results.

A recurring problem with revision studies is the generalizability of the revision procedure to other programmers. This point was raised in an earlier review by Lumsdaine (1963).

Rosen (1968) conducted a study using programmers as an experimental unit. Two groups were given the same materials to revise: one group was directed to use an editorial or intuitive method of revision. The other was given data based on objectives and posttest items. Both revisions yielded higher student performance than the original program, and data-based revisions exceeded intuitive revisions in pupil performance. Sulzen (1970) and Baker (1970c) have also used programmers as the experimental unit in supporting studies related to empirical revision.

Methodological questions can be raised, however, about considering revision as a variable suitable for experimental investigation. Even studies which provided reproducible rules to guide revision were forced to invoke a wide range of instructional remedies for deficient performance. When revision alternatives are diverse, and multiple avenues are explored to attempt to improve programs, "revision" becomes as unmanageable a treatment as "instruction." Studies such as Rosen's (1968), that concern the stimuli presented to influence revision activities, seem to be much more fruitful enterprises than revision-no-revision comparisons. In addition, questions for investigation might concern the context in which judgmental data are obtained, the effect of structure on the revisions suggested by users, or the decision chains employed by those engaging in revision.

Procedures for Revision

Dick (1968) described the activities of individuals asked to revise lessons. Revisers frequently based their changes on frame-error rates and reviewer comments, while learner performance on a criterion test rarely influenced revisions.

One would expect, for revision to be a useful process, that a set of procedures would be articulated which would be transmissible from developer to developer. Silberman et al. (1964) attempted to isolate principles which seemed to have effectiveness. They identified the a) Gap Principle, b) Irrelevancy Principle, and c) Mastery Principle. The Gap Principle requires that all criterion and subordinate skills should be practiced, a dictum which supports the findings of Gagné and Paradise (1961). The Irrelevancy Principle implies the removal of all items not directly related to the criterion task. The Mastery Principle, also in concert with Gagné and Paradise, suggests that each subskill should be attained before the

learner is permitted to continue through the program.

Moore (1968) attempted to verify the principles identified by Silberman's work and found that introducing gaps reduced learning. Irrelevancies which did not require mastery did not negatively affect learning. In Baker's study (1970c), rules to guide the revisions of programmers were presented which, with the exception of directions to fade prompts, required the addition of information to the program. Gropper's investigation of revision (1967) found that a revised version of a program required almost twice as long to complete.

Problems in Empirical Revision

Beyond the incidental evidence obtainable from many development ventures on the utility of revision, experimental results have rarely supported the generalizability of certain procedures to other developers. The question of generalizability to other tasks and subject matters has only been touched briefly. The demonstration of the utility of revision cannot occur without knowledge of the costs in time and resources one is willing to expend for given types of results. Thus, even a single revision cycle, which results in improvement on relatively modest performance levels, may be appropriate in certain projects where the goals are not critical for all learners.

The difficulty in estimating the effects of particular revision modifications was illustrated by the work of Project Hindsight. Although Project Hindsight's primary and controversial conclusion that basic research provides little direct payoff for technology is not of interest here, Sherwin and Isenson (1967) provide a provocative thesis about the effects of revising and redesigning of existing components. Although their area of inquiry was military spending, some results may have special interest for the instructional designer.

Of the events analyzed by the Project Hindsight staff as having significant impact in either the reduction of cost in maintaining present performance levels, or the reliable rise of performance, a consistent finding was that rather modest revisions of a component, e.g., propeller function, resulted in greatly increased overall performance of the system.

The Project Hindsight staff hypothesizes that an interaction occurs so that the overall technology is improved far beyond the sum of modest revisions. One might translate this problem into educational concepts where performance on a phonics task was slightly improved by revision, analogous to Sherwin's work. If performance increments were found in addition on irregularly spelled words, one might explain such obviously inexplicable results in terms of a critical performance threshold: a slight increase in performance of phonics material might be sufficient to increase motivation and other positive affective dimensions so that attention to the entire program dramatically improved. Applications of such a hypothetical analysis would urge one to err in the direction of revision in the development of an instructional program.

Product Evaluation

Any discussion of the evaluation of materials regardless of orientation becomes unmanageable even if only a small percentage of relevant concerns are aired. A comprehensive treatment of educational evaluation has been recently provided by the Sixtyeighth Yearbook of the National Society for the Study of Education, Part II, in *Educational Evaluation: New Roles, New Means* (edited by R. W. Tyler, 1969), the *Review of Educational Research* on educational evaluation (edited by Denny, 1970), and in the AERA Monograph series on Curriculum Evaluation. Each of these publications has extensive bibliographies which enable detailed consideration of most facets of educational evaluation. In addition, publications from the UCLA Center for the Study of Evaluation (see Alkin, 1970) and the Center for Instructional Research and Curriculum Evaluation at the University of Illinois are sources of both analytic and experimental research on problems of evaluation. A series of papers edited by Wittrock and Wiley (1970) are particularly concerned with the evaluation of instruction. Other useful papers on the topic of evaluation are by Eash (1969), Engler (1970), Fitts (1962), Hartley (1963), Lundin (1970), McIntyre and Nelson (1969), Metfessel and Michael (1967), Popham (1969b), Travers (1969), and Tyler, Klein, and Michael (1971). No discussion of evaluation which could be presented in the space allotted could adequately summarize such works.

EXAMPLES OF EDUCATIONAL PRODUCTS

To support the previous delineation of development tasks, one would wish to present many descriptions of materials developed by such systematic procedures. The difficulty of knowing, that is, of being sure of, the procedures which actually guided the development of systematically validated materials inhibits the presentation of such an array. Instead, only two instructional programs will be described. These were selected because of the available documentation. Other major developmental enterprises, which purportedly have been well planned, are Individually Prescribed Instruction, developed and tested by the Learning Research and Development Center at the University of Pittsburgh and Research for Better Schools, and Project Plan, developed by the American Institute for Research.

Southwest Regional Laboratory's First Year Communication Skills Program

The Southwest Regional Laboratory for Educational Research and Development began its development of a communications skills program in 1966. Formulation of general goals and program thrust for the Laboratory was a policy matter for the Laboratory senior staff. Following the decision to emphasize reading, experts such as Edward Coleman joined the staff to participate in initial design. The first versions of instruction were oriented toward the linguistic requirements of the program, using, for example, a special transitional orthography. Relatively little attention was given to the instructional requirements of the materials beyond the notion that reading short story books with delightful illustrations would provide opportunities for practice. Following a series of brief trials of segments, modifications in the selection of words, book format and typography were made.

Instructional-support materials in the form of practice sequences, games, and lesson plans were developed. During this phase, clarity regarding specifications was obtained and 16 tentative objectives relating to decoding and comprehension were delineated. Materials and procedures were tried out on small groups of learners. Extensive reviews by reading experts, administrators and teachers were concurrently obtained.

Early briefings, a preliminary form of dissemination, were held with interested educators in the region. Field trials were initiated in 1967 and 1968 with modest teacher training, observation of classroom procedures, and techniques for obtaining evaluative comments of teachers. The staggered collection of data enabled modifications to be made in the program as the staff received them. Both teacher comments and interim criterion tests provided a basis for revision (Baker, 1968).

Concurrent with these field trials, another division of SWRL was collecting data and conducting and compiling analytic research in psycholinguistics to determine what improvements might be made in the words and language structures selected for use in the program. Research was also conducted by those in the development division on numerous instructional problems, for instance, response mode, group versus single responses, and class of illustration preferred by children. Preliminary experiments in adapting the program to Spanish-speaking children (McNeil, 1968) and to older nonreaders were pursued. Extra program materials, such as training for parents and intergrade tutors, were developed and tested (Niedermeyer, 1970; Niedermeyer & Ellis, 1970).

SWRL is now able to reformulate some of the content based upon more complete linguistic analyses. In addition, components for oral language training, spelling and writing are under development so that the original "communications" intent is preserved. The next generation of the SWRL program will combine more current thinking on the content in the materials with a demonstrably effective format. But if the context of intended use of materials shifts in an ensuing revision, for instance, from principally teacher-mediated to self-instruction, a new set of delivery problems will have to be resolved.

The First-Aid Training Course

A second program developed empirically under the direction of David Markle is the American Red Cross First-Aid Training course (1967). The author describes the procedures used in the development of the course focusing on the revision cycles. This project, sponsored by the American Telephone and Telegraph Company, used performance and informational test items as bases for revision. The project was tested on a limited number of classes and never has been demonstrated to be replicable across classes. Yet, as a brief example of the use of empirical procedures on development, the publication should be read.

ALTERNATE DEVELOPMENT PROCEDURES

The following section will explore the development procedures of noneducational enterprises. This discussion will consider problems demonstrating that many educational concerns are not unique and pervade all development ventures. A second purpose of this section is to underscore practices in noninstructional development which may have transfer value in the field of instructional product development. This section will focus on operating procedures rather than the theoretical implications for education of noneducational fields, a line of inquiry extensively explored by Maccia, Maccia, and Jewett (1963) and Maccia and Maccia (1966).

Pharmaceutical Development

The parallel of the fields of medicine and education is by now familiar. The terms "interns," "clinical," "diagnosis and prescription" have been readily adopted by educational language (Lindvall & Cox, 1969). Pharmacology is the profession which supplies the necessary products to remedy the physiological dysfunction of the individual (Maren, 1968). While the direct equation of ignorance with disease may be somewhat theatrical, the metaphor can be partially applied, for certain points of educational tangency are clear. First, in this field as in education, the ultimate benefactor of the pharmaceutical product is the individual. His responses to it, as his responses to instruction, may be highly idiosyncratic. While certain effects of treatment are readily observable (e.g., the reduction of inflammation or maintenance of an appropriate blood count) and might be analogous to easily measurable effects of instruction (e.g., recitation of number facts), other consequences of drugs are less easy to gauge (e.g., mood elevation or analgesic effects). For outcomes which can only be partially quantified, educational analogs abound.

Product selection. The theoretical basis for the applied field of pharmacology is much more secure than the roots of education and draws from both natural and bio-logical sciences. Pharmaceutical developers support basic and applied science with approximately 11 percent of their total budget (Pharmaceutical Manufacturers Association, 1969). Obviously, much applied research is conducted and it tends to be both problem-centered (e.g., how can cancer be cured?) and technique-oriented (e.g., what effects will drug X have on a variety of maladies?) (see Gilbert, 1962).

The selection of ideas for advanced development (Novick, 1964) is governed by a number of factors: the seriousness and prevalence of the disorder, the effectiveness of existing remedies, the human cost of failure, and the speed with which ameliorative effects can be shown (Lasagna, 1969). The market potential probably also intrudes at this point. Thus, in the selection of potential product areas, pharmaceutical firms might be able to employ a purely empirical strategy in investigating the effects of a high-incidence, low-cure-rate disorder if the disorder is acute and likely to show immediate effects from use of the product. Another exploration strategy would be appropriate under different conditions. For example, the development of more satisfactory treatment for epilepsy is retarded since existing drugs are fairly effective, and the emotional and physiological concomitants of drug failure inhibit testing on all but presently poorly controlled epileptics. Education might profit from the example of pharmacology in product selection, attempting to use highly empirical, trial-and-error procedures for short-term, high-need areas, and carefully controlled, extensively validated techniques for instructional areas where the cost of failure is high and effects are not easily observed, such as attitudes toward democracy.

A second factor in the formulation of products in pharmacology is the mission orientation of the developers. Pharmaceutical houses often undertake research and development in specialized areas. Concentration in a few areas, such as pulmonary disorders, permits the accumulation of staff who have competencies and interests consistent with the pursuit of such problems. Thus, the idea that resources of an institution would be spread over "physiological dysfunction" in the way that certain educational agencies are directed to "learning" is absurd. Regional laboratories have by and large cultivated specialized interests, for instance, the Southwest Regional Laboratory focuses on primary education. Some other development agencies have attempted in shotgun fashion to develop fragmented projects in widely disparate areas without the unifying force of a program as advocated by Hemphill (1969). Although the argument may be made that what is learned in disparate development tasks may build knowledge which may transfer to a variety of instructional situations and learners, diversified program interests weaken the development organization's ability to assemble a critical mass of personnel to engage in fruitful and continued development.

Specialization, an integral element of mission orientation, also dictates prolonged interest in further development of existing products. Thus, when a pharmaceutical institution is committed to a particular domain, continuing research is required to maintain the extant market share. The idea of "signing off" on either a project or area of interest is only rarely possible, since a competitor's theoretical or technological breakthrough could immediately render existing products obsolete, either through the development of a product at reduced cost, a product with greater performance, or one with fewer side effects. Research in areas of defined interest therefore tends to be programmatic and continuing.

Product specifications. In contrast to educational endeavors, elaborate specification of the outcomes or effects desired by the pharmaceutical product is not possible in the early stages of development. This is partially explained by the fairly clear notion of what the drug is expected to do,

e.g., reduce inflammation. However, criterion levels, that is, how much effect the drug is to have, side effects, and so on, are empirically determined as field testing proceeds (Lasagna, 1969). The actual form of the drug, perhaps analogous to the selection of media in instruction, is also empirically developed, and alternatives, such as injection, emulsion, etc., are tested for their effects rather than specified at the outset.

Organization of development. A pervasive problem in both pharmaceutical and educational development is the organizational structure of the institution. The necessity for project organization during research and early development is clear, so that development proceeds on a team basis to permit continuous work. Staff, consisting of relatively inexperienced personnel paired with more experienced researchers, must develop tolerance for failure since the rate of aborted projects is high. The more experienced personnel can, by example, teach perseverance without reward. Campbell and Stanley (1963) describe a similar educational phenomenon. Because the average time from the initial development of a drug through its placement on the market is approximately four to eight years (Lasagna, 1969), quick successes are neither promised nor expected.

Much of the actual pharmaceutical development is concerned with the problem of dosage. How much of a particular product at what intervals in what stages of the disease is appropriate? Various hypotheses are tested but the possible combinations are infinite. So even a field that can be quantified rather rigidly in terms of milligrams suffers from intuitive development decisions.

Product testing. Pharmacological development is particularly dependent upon empirical testing (Lasagna, 1969) and has been clearly advanced by its reliance on the use of infrahuman species for preliminary verification of drug effects. Of the multitude of procedures used in the empirical testing of pharmaceutical products, two emerge with substantial probability of impact on instructional development.

The first is the notion of *toxicity*. Maren (1968), Cronbach (1963) and others have described the negative consequences of instruction as unintended outcomes. In pharmacology, after animal tests and before any drug is tried for its rehabilitative effects on diseased humans, it is first tested on normal people to determine their tolerance for it. This practice is clearly conservative in that a sick person might respond positively to a drug which has negative effects on healthy individuals. Brooks and Bowers (1970) note that no technology should be permitted to develop "without evidence on possible side effects and merit of alternatives." In education routine testing of programs with the *primary* focus on the negative outcomes which they produce could have saved thousands of students from the drudgery of ill-formulated and ill-executed instructional sequences. One might speculate that much of routine educational offering would not survive an initial toxicity screening.

A related concern in pharmacology is directed toward the side effects which the drug produces. Side effects are not necessarily negative, so that a compound which relieves pain might also function as a mild stimulant. The careful description of side effects observed on particular patient populations is standard practice in pharmaceutical development and has straightforward implications in education.

The notion of side effects is perhaps most significant of all the implications of pharmaceutical development. Because past educational treatments were diffuse in both substance and impact, concern with side effects was limited. It was not sensible to conceive of "side" effects when primary effects could not be detected. However, as instructional procedures become increasingly well described, to some extent replicable, and more widely disseminated, careful consideration of the range of outcomes produced by educational products is demanded. Concomitant effects may either suggest themselves simply or require sophisticated brainstorming to uncover. For instance, a programmed sequence in arithmetic, which is well ordered and managed, might vastly improve students' computational skills. It might also lead children to expect correct answers from authority and to increase their tendency to conform. If the program were highly individualized, students might proceed very efficiently at their own rate; however, they could also develop an aversion to public learning, that is, a fear of being wrong in the presence of others. Another example, suggested by a colleague, relates to the use of food as a reinforcer in behavior modification programs. Recent physiological work indicates that children develop persistent blood-sugar needs based on their early diet patterns. Children given candy in such programs may grow to be learned, nondelinquent and overweight adults.

An example of possible side effects of both the positive and negative variety can be inferred from the case of "Sesame Street," the public television program directed toward preschool youngsters. Direct evaluation of the program goals indicated that children were making excellent progress toward the program's objectives. Predictably, the objectives, e.g., the ability to recognize letters, the ability to count, the ability to group objects along similar dimensions, etc., were excoriated by critics as trivial. A side-effects analysis of "Sesame Street" seems warranted. For instance, did the slick production tend to decrease children's tolerance for less exciting instructional programs in any media? Regardless of the absolute import of the objectives themselves, did children develop increased confidence in their ability to learn? Were approach tendencies toward learning situations accelerated? Did the passivity condemned by critics (the child as viewer not doer) have any discernible transfer to the child's manner of participation in other instructional settings? Did children display reluctance to make responses in the presence of a personal, responsive figure, like the teacher, since they had enjoyed the anonymity of friendly but distant television personalities? Questions of this nature will have to be explored with greater persistence and regularity as instructional programs of wide distribution develop.

One would hope that the consequences of rapid technological advance now being suffered will enlighten and caution the educator. The limits of progress can be readily seen in almost every systematic intervention affecting masses of people. The present array of distressing side effects, for instance, of environmental pollution, disaffection with government, drug use, etc., should induce the educational developer to depend heavily on early analysis and study of all the effects of instructional programs. As Brooks and Bowers (1970) point out, the preservation of future choice is essential in technological decisions. It is clear that side effects once generated are not easily undone.

A second point derived from pharmacological practices is the concern with which drugs are tested. Ideally, careful attention is paid to the detection of improper testing techniques, and the development institution tends to conduct and directly supervise preliminary testing. Because of the surreptitious, but no less damaging, nature of many educational effects, such care and scrutiny has not characterized educational product testing. Following Food and Drug Administration permission to conduct trials on humans, testing is often subcontracted to clinicians who specialize in supervising the test treatment of drugs by physicians. Sample patients with various characteristics and combinations of symptoms are especially chosen. A federal agency presumably has also *certified* such physicians as competent and suitable to conduct such field tests. While there may be questions regarding the ease of obtaining such certification, the idea if not the reality might be appropriated. An analogous certification board, if magically shielded from inexorable bureaucracy, would be ideal in education for the purpose of certifying those consenting school districts which have demonstrated the capacity to observe the rudiments of reasonable field test procedures. At present, the credibility of the effects of many long-term educational products is suspect since nonreactive verification of their replicability, i.e., that the procedures were used as intended, has been almost impossible to obtain.

Treatment of data. Of great potential contribution to the field of education is an examination of the data-analysis routines employed in pharmaceutical development. Data are routinely analyzed by the subcontracted test agency, interpreted and communicated in the form of technical reports to the primary developing institution. Upon receipt of the report, all data are independently reanalyzed by the development institution and results and interpretations are then compared with the original test agency's report. Discrepancies in results should be resolved by additional field trials. The introduction of independent verification of data anaylsis could provide a major injection of rigor into the empirical development of instructional products. This procedure, if followed, would serve to reduce the unwarranted inferences which now form a powerful substratum of the validation of instructional products.

Product evaluation. The Food and Drug Administration must ultimately evaluate all of the data and documentation surrounding the development of a product before it is permitted to be marketed (Lasagna, 1969). Because of the enormous strain such evaluation places on the agency, an independent board has been proposed where competent researchers on a year's tour of

THE TECHNOLOGY OF INSTRUCTIONAL DEVELOPMENT 273

duty would evaluate preparation by listing probable side effects and labeling them: possibly effective, probably effective, or effective for various symptoms. Such evaluation and publication would be periodic since claims for effectiveness might change under extensive use.

A parallel review board was recommended by the early researchers interested in programmed instruction (*Journal of Programmed Instruction,* 1966) for the evaluation of programmed materials. A similar plea was voiced in the report of the Joint Committee on Programmed Instruction (American Educational Research Association, 1964). Educational Products Information Exchange makes some effort in this regard but has neither the resources nor the routine data network and history that the pharmaceutical industry possesses. Until product testing under verifiable conditions and dissemination of data on educational programs are integrated into educational habit, there is little possibility of adopting such a review procedure however useful it might be to procurement personnel in school districts.

Summary of Implications of Pharmaceutical Development of Education

Procedures for pharmaceutical product selection are determined by the kind of need, the intensity of the disorder and the interval requisite to show effects. Thus, different early-development strategies are adopted for different problems. First, an analogous approach to developing instructional products would militate against the tendency of educators to employ the same procedures for radically different problems. Second, the concentration of resources in a few prime areas for the benefit of staff accumulation and continuing development might be adopted. Third, the notion of toxicity, where negative outcomes assume primacy in data inspection, has particular merit and would screen out many soon-to-

be-defunct educational innovations. Educators also might more conscientiously focus attention on the description of side effects of educational programs, such as those which might result from their interactions with particular learner characteristics. The subcontracting of testing to a certified school or school district and the independent reanalysis and interpretation of data is also a promising area for educational application.

The use of an independent review board to rate the effectiveness of educational programs under varying conditions is also recommended, but would be dependent upon the rigorous and habitual assembly of criterion data.

There is always the danger in parallel descriptions of substantially different activities that the enterprise takes on allegorical qualities and that the interpretation has meaning for the writer only. Yet pharmacology provides a singular number of procedural modifications which should improve current practices in educational development.

Nuclear Development

The parallel between pharmaceutical and instructional product development is sufficient so that the implications of operations from one field to another are reasonably expected. A second field, nuclear development, although seemingly remote from education in background, method and intent, also has in its development history distinct implications for instructional product development. This area was selected as another illustration of noneducational product development because of the available documentation of development activities and the enormous complexity of the required effort. A set of case histories of development of the laser, transistor and maser has been compiled by Townes (1968). The critical development of nuclear power also necessitated the development of hundreds of separate instances of technology, and thus provided a more comprehensive and elaborate view of development than would the explication of a single line of technical innovation, such as holography.

The Manhattan Project (Groueff, 1967; Groves, 1962), the code name for the project devoted to the development of the atomic bomb, functioned under distinct advantages when compared with ordinary development activity. First, the theory predicting the physical requirements for nuclear reaction was never in question. Second, the project demanded and received priority attention in most of its manpower and material needs. Finally, the commitment engendered by the competition with the Germans under wartime conditions and fed by the fear of the consequences of failure generated a widespread ferocity of purpose among the intellectual leaders of the project, a commitment of a nature ordinarily ascribed to fanatics.

Simultaneous consideration of alternatives. One of the central problems which plagued the workers on the Manhattan Project was the discovery of a workable process by which sufficient amounts of fissionable material could be obtained. The scientists involved in the project had five alternative processes through which the required quantity might be obtained. When initial screening allowed no differential judgments to be made, the first lesson of nuclear development was learned. Simultaneous development under different lines of inquiry should be supported. Only after continued development were two of the processes judged to be clearly inferior in potential. In the nuclear example cost-efficiency equations were meaningless, precisely because the value of success was incalculable. Analogously, the value of a literate, well-educated electorate is similarly inestimable. Moreover, clearly established national goals in education could be more readily achieved if premature decisions to cut off contending lines of development were deferred, as was done by the Manhattan Project.

Maximum independence among activities. A second point derived from an analysis of nuclear development resides in the project's implicit anticipation of large-scale production. Even when critical elements in the technology remained impervious to solution, for instance, the production of a "barrier" essential for the gaseous diffusion process of producing enriched uranium, predictions were made about other task requirements which enabled rapid mass production once the central problem had been solved. As an illustration, regardless of the type of barrier evolved, the gaseous diffusion process required pipes which were leakproof and which would not be corroded by gaseous uranium. Concurrent with pursuing the solution to the barrier problem, teams worked on the production of noncorrodible plating for pipes and for instrumentation to detect leaks in the system. The work proceeded on the assumption that the major barrier difficulty would somehow be overcome.

Independent attack on diverse but interacting components of a system certainly does not characterize current educational development. Part of the inhibition may be financial, for anticipation of success which never materializes can be costly. Perhaps the quality of the faith of educators may also be called into question. How many deeply believe that there are technical solutions to instructional deficiencies? Without such a commitment, separate pursuit of development solutions becomes a futile exercise, for failure, not success, guides expectations.

Manpower and management. A final lesson from the development procedures employed in the Manhattan Project can be inferred from the use of manpower which such complexities required. Here, individuals from many fields with various levels of training were thrown into constant and intense contact. Kuhn (1966) documents the effects of using a widely disparate personnel base in a major development effort.

Another important point was that the Manhattan Project was closely coordinated by intellectuals with management skills. Many educational development projects have been supervised by administrators with little understanding of the procedures used in development, or by developers with inadequate management skills. The solution would require the identification of individuals with both technical and managerial competence who would be willing to devote a major portion of time to the management of research-based development. Hemphill (1969) treats the broad issue of project management in educational development.

In summary, experience gained in nuclear development might be useful to education in three major ways: a) the simultaneous consideration of alternative solutions, b) maximum independence of work on components of a system, and c) management by those with both managerial and substantive skills.

ORGANIZATION OF PRODUCT-DEVELOPMENT ACTIVITIES

A continuing concern with all research and development ventures is the organizational structure under which the work proceeds. Hemphill (1969) has lucidly written of development organization at his agency. More extensive treatment of organization is included in Bright's volume (1964) on research and development. Walters (1965) has also written on management and organization of research and development. Lazarsfeld and Sieber (1964) produced a well-known work on the organization of educational research in which tangential reference to educational development activities occurs.

The critical question in terms of operations is whether development activity should be organized functionally, for in-

stance, with specification, revision and field testing performed by different individuals, or by project, where a team would essentially perform all requisite activities. The important factor seems to be project size so that within small projects responsibility might be concentrated on a few individuals, whereas in large projects functional organization might be more sensible. A comprehensive treatment of models for functional organizational structures has been produced by Hills (1968). A more particularized work for the field of educational development has been produced by Yaney (1970). An unusual investigation on the organization of research and development was summarized by Pelz (1967). He described eight creative tensions which seem to result in high technical achievement of engineers and scientists. Dimensions included the amount of autonomy permitted staff, degree of specialization, sources of intellectual stimulation, decision-making role and self-reliance.

PREPARING DEVELOPERS

The recruitment and training of staff committed to educational development, an enterprise requiring new competencies and commitment, is an unresolved problem.

Gagné (1969) writes of the "irreducible" characteristics desired of an educational technologist. These characteristics fall in three categories: values, knowledge and methodologies. Gagné emphasizes that a central value for educational developers to hold is the belief "in empirical evidence as a source of truth and a preferred basis for action." Glaser (1966a) has noted that it is probable that such empirically oriented development personnel have been trained as educational researchers and often act in both research and development capacities.

Focus of Training

Clark and Hopkins (1969) analyzed 1964 data on manpower estimates for the broad field of research and development. They found very few professionals who were systematically identified with educational development. Implications of their report, particularly anticipated shortages, are treated in the report of the National Center for Educational Research and Development (1970).

A relatively small number of universities support graduate programs specifically directed to the preparation of instructional product developers. Popham (1967) has written a description of one of the few doctoral programs in this field, initiated with the aid of a U.S. Office of Education grant. Kuhn (1966) points out that government programs provided the majority of stimulation and support given to university-based training in other emerging technologies. At present, federal support of graduate training programs in development is undergoing fluctuation. One assumes that as the technology builds credibility, funds for training will be made available. Where is training best accomplished with the few extant university programs available? Very likely, according to Evans (1969), the average educational developer has been prepared through a period of apprenticeship by his employing agency in on-the-job training. Shoemaker (1968) points out that such in-house training is generally unsystematic and usually inefficient. One must suspect that such inefficiency is due to the mission orientation of the institution and its interference with its training function.

Adaptability as a Desired Attribute of Developers

James W. Kuhn (1966) describes manpower lessons inferred from the study of management problems in the emerging nuclear power industry. His observations have great relevance for instructional product development in its current pretechnology state. Kuhn proposes a framework within which one can assess manpower in de-

veloping technologies. His assumption is that requirements in the early stages of a technology change in dramatic and largely unpredictable ways. The flexibility of the developer along any one of the three dimensions is critical to his ultimate usefulness in a rapidly accelerating field. Individuals with flexibility along Kuhn's hypothesized first axis demonstrate their ability to draw from diverse theories or experience to design solutions to given problems. Such persons would correspond in role to those responsible for prototype preparation in the product development activities described. Individuals with flexibility along a second axis might instead be able to fulfill a given function in a wide variety of problem areas. For instance, they would be able to prepare specifications in the humanities as well as in the sciences for preschool learners or for college students. However, those who exhibit flexibility along a third dimension are most prized by Kuhn (1966): "This axis is parallel to the flow of technological development; a man flexible in this direction is able to shift the center of his job concern as the emphasis of a technology progresses from concept to marketable product" (p. 198). These individuals are rare and are essential when the functional distinctions among development stages are not discrete. Manpower will be initially concentrated on developing alternative designs; later, as the technology develops, individuals will be needed for prototyping, field testing and implementation. Rather than being idle or dismissed as the development focus shifts, the developer with "parallel flexibility" is invaluable since he can alter his role as necessary.

If one accepts Kuhn's analysis, the next puzzle is how one identifies or trains individuals to have such flexible predilections. One might venture that the training or identification of concept synthesizers, Kuhn's first type, might be most difficult. However, training could be reasonably provided to promote flexibility in the second and third dimensions. Trainees could be given experiences at either one or two stages and thus develop a functional role, such as test-writer or revision-maker. In training people to demonstrate "parallel flexibility," opportunities would be given to supervise a variety of projects from initial phases to completion.

The type of training needed is, of course, relevant to the organization of the development institution. Organizations structured by functions would have greater need for developers with practice in the second axis. Project-centered organizations might better use developers prepared to exhibit parallel flexibility.

SUMMARY

A description of any educational activity always occurs in the light of the author's biases. Development, considered as a phenomenon, provides more possibility for interpretation for it encompasses the entire range of educational endeavor. Clearly, the field has not suffered from lack of interest, for the writings noted here represent only a fraction of the work which might properly be included. Yet one might hope for a different kind of attention and look forward to writings which did not prescribe, on the basis of faith alone, legions of procedures. Rather, the field of educational development requires inquiry into the kinds of development procedures which are effective in particular contexts for various classes of organizations. From the current state of the art, one would suppose that minimally such procedures would require specification, field testing and revision as the foundation for development work. The possible ways in which each of these points might be translated into practice must be explored. Work in an area such as operations research might provide feasible methodology for such investigations. To quote C. P. Snow (1966):

I am going to finish with a mixture of confidence and anxiety.... there are no perfect solutions to the problems we are discussing and often no good ones ... (p. 653).

We can't do everything; but that doesn't mean that we can do nothing (p. 652).

REFERENCES

Alkin, M. C. Products for improving education evaluation. Fifth report to U.S. Office of Education, *UCLA Evaluation Comment.* Center for the Study of Evaluation, University of California at Los Angeles, September 1970, 2(3), 1–15.

American Association for the Advancement of Science, Commission on Science Education. *The psychological bases of science—a process approach.* Washington, D.C.: AAAS, 1965.

American Educational Research Association, American Psychological Association, Department of Audiovisual Instruction, National Education Association: Joint Committee on Programmed Instruction and Teaching Machines. *Recommendations for reporting of information on the performance characteristics of programmed learning materials: Third interim report.* (Preliminary ed.) Los Angeles: University of California, 1964.

American Psychological Association, *Publication manual of the American Psychological Association.* (Rev. ed.) Washington, D.C.: American Psychological Association, 1967.

Anderson, R. C., & Faust, G. W. The effects of strong formal prompts in programmed instruction. *American Educational Research Journal,* 1967, 4, 345–352.

Arnstine, D. G. The language and values of programmed instruction: Part II. *Educational Forum,* 1964, 28, 337–346.

Ausubel, D. P. Crucial psychological issues in the objectives, organization, and evaluation of curriculum reform movement. Paper presented at the Conference on Vocational-Technical Education at the University of Illinois, sponsored by the American Vocational Association, May 1966.

Ayres, L. P. History and present status of educational measurements. In G. M. Whipple (Ed.), *The measurement of educational products,* 17th Yearbook of the National Society for the Study of Education, Part II. Bloomington, Ill.: Public School Publishing Co., 1918. Pp. 9–24.

Baker, E. L. Developing a research based kindergarten reading program. Inglewood, Calif.: Southwest Regional Laboratory for Educational Research and Development (SWRL), 1968.

Baker, E. L. Effects on student achievement of behavioral and nonbehavioral objectives. *Journal of Experimental Education*, 1969, 37(4), 5–8.

Baker, E. L. Defining content for objectives. Los Angeles: Vimcet Associates, 1970. (Filmstrip) (a)

Baker, E. L. Experimental assessment of the effects of the probe system. Paper presented at the meeting of the American Educational Research Association, Minneapolis, March 1970. (b)

Baker, E. L. Generalizability of rules for empirical revision. *AV Communication Review*, 1970, 18(3), 300–305. (c)

Baker, R. L., Gerlach, V. S., Schutz, R. E., & Sullivan, H. J. Developing instructional specifications. *Developing instructional products: A collection of working papers and training documents.* Inglewood, Calif.: SWRL, 1968. Pp. 221–272.

Baker, R. L., Schutz, R. E., & Sullivan, H. J. Internal control procedures in the development of instructional materials. *Technical reports: Research on procedures for the development of instructional materials.* Wright-Patterson Air Force Base, Ohio: Aerospace Medical Research Laboratories, Aerospace Medical Division, 1967.

Banathy, B. H. *Instructional systems.* Palo Alto, Calif.: Fearon Publishers, 1968.

Beals, R. L., & Hoijer, H. *An introduction to anthropology.* New York: Macmillan, 1953.

Blaney, J. P., & McKie, D. Knowledge of conference objectives and effect upon learning. *Adult Education,* 1969, 19, 98–105.

Bloom, B. S. (Ed.) *Taxonomy of educational objectives. Handbook I: Cognitive domain.* New York: David McKay, 1956.

Bobbitt, J. F. *The curriculum.* Boston: Houghton-Mifflin, 1918.

Borg, W. R. The balance between educational research and development: A question of strategy. *Educational Technology,* 1969, 9 (7), 5–11.

Borg, W. R., & Hood, P. The twenty-seven steps in the development program. Berkeley, Calif.: Far West Laboratory for Educational Research and Development, 1968.

Bormuth, J. R. *On the theory of achievement test items.* Chicago: University of Chicago Press, 1970.

Brickell, H. M. Role of research in the innovative process. *The role of educational research in educational change.* Bloomington, Ind.: National Institute for the Study of Educational Change, 1967.

Briggs, L. *Handbook of procedures for the design of instruction.* Pittsburgh: American Institutes for Research, 1970.

Bright, J. R. *Research, development, and technical innovation—an introduction.* Homewood, Ill.: Richard D. Irwin, 1964.

Brooks, H. Applied science and technological progress. *Science,* 1967, 156, 1706–1712.

Brooks, H., & Bowers, R. The assessment of technology. *Scientific American,* 1970, 222 (2), 13–21.

Buchanan, C. D. *Sullivan reading program.* New York: Webster Division, McGraw-Hill, 1963.

Campbell, D. T., & Stanley, J. C. Experimental and quasi-experimental designs for research on teaching. In N. L. Gage (Ed.), *Handbook of research on teaching.* Chicago: Rand McNally, 1963. Pp. 171–246.

Campbell, V. N., & Markle, D. G. Identifying and formulating educational problems. Final report, American Institutes for Research, Palo Alto. Berkeley, Calif.: Far West Laboratory for Educational Research and Development, 1968.

Carter, L. F. From research to development to use. *Organizations for research and development in education.* New York: Phi Delta Kappa, Inc. and the American Educational Research Association, 1966, 41–56.

Chase, F. S. The laboratories: 1970 and beyond. *Journal of Research and Development in Education,* 1970, 3(2), 104–120.

Churchman, C. W. *The systems approach.* New York: Delacorte Press, 1968.

Clark, D. L., & Hopkins, J. E. *A report on educational research, development, and diffusion manpower, 1964–1974.* Bloomington, Ind.: Indiana University Research Foundation, 1969.

Cohen, A. *Objectives for college courses.* Beverly Hills: Glencoe Press, 1970.

Cornell, T. D. A systematic approach to needs assessment. Tucson, Ariz.: EPIC Evaluation Center, 1970.

Crawford, W. R. Assessing performance when

the stakes are high. Paper presented at the meeting of the American Educational Research Association, Minneapolis, March 1970.

Cremin, L. A. *The genius of American education.* New York: Random House, 1966.

Cronbach, L. J. (Ed.) Text materials in modern education—a comprehensive theory and platform for research. *The text materials study.* Urbana, Ill.: University of Illinois Press, 1955.

Cronbach, L. J. Course improvement through evaluation. *Teachers College Record,* 1963, 64, 672–683.

Cronbach, L. J., & Suppes, P. (Eds.) *Research for tomorrow's schools—disciplined inquiry for education.* Report of the Committee on Educational Research of the National Academy of Education. London: Macmillan, Callien Macmillan, Limited, 1969.

Crowder, N. A. Automatic tutoring by intrinsic programming. In A. A. Lumsdaine, & R. Glaser (Eds.), *Teaching machines and programmed learning: A source book.* Washington, D.C.: National Education Association, 1960. Pp. 286–298.

Dallis, G. The effect of precise objectives upon student achievement in health education. Unpublished doctoral dissertation, University of California, Los Angeles, 1969.

Dean, B. V. Evaluating, selecting, and controlling research and development projects. AMA research study No. 89. New York: American Management Association, Inc., 1968.

Denny, T. (Ed.) Educational evaluation. *Review of Educational Research,* 1970, 40, 181–320.

Dick, W. A methodology for the formative evaluation of instructional materials. *Journal of Educational Measurement,* 1968, 5, 99–102.

Dwyer, F. M., Jr. Exploratory studies in the effectiveness of visual illustrations. A paper from Pennsylvania State University, Division of Instructional Services, December 1969.

Eash, M. J. Assessing curriculum materials: A preliminary instrument. *Educational Product Report,* 1969, 2(5), 18–22.

Edling, J. V. Educational objectives and educational media. *Review of Educational Research—Instructional Materials: Educational Media and Technology,* 1968, 38(2), 177–194.

Educational Development Center. *Introduction to the elementary science study.* New York: Webster Division, McGraw-Hill, 1969.

Eisner, E. W. Franklin Bobbitt and the "science" of curriculum making. *School Review,* 1967, 75, 29–47.

Eisner, E. W. The evaluation of research of curriculum materials. Paper presented at the meeting of the American Educational Research Association, Minneapolis, March 1970.

Engler, D. A publisher's use of the recommendations for instructional materials development. Paper presented at the meeting of the American Educational Research Association, Minneapolis, March 1970.

Enthoven, A. C. Choosing strategies and selecting weapon systems. In S. A. Tucker (Ed.), *A modern design for defense decision: A McNamara-Hitch-Enthoven anthology.* Washington, D.C.: Industrial College of the Armed Forces, 1966. Pp. 133–148.

Evans, J. L. In-service programs in instructional technology as a way to solve an identity problem, among other things. Symposium on instructional technologists presented at the meeting of the American Educational Research Association, Los Angeles, February 1969.

Farr, R. S. Knowledge linkers and the flow of educational information. An occasional paper from ERIC Clearinghouse on Educational Media and Technology at the Institute for Communication Research, Stanford University, Stanford, California, 1969.

Far West Regional Laboratory for Educational Research and Development. *Basic program plans, September, 1968.* Berkeley, Calif.: Far West Regional Laboratory for Educational Research and Development, September 1968.

Fitts, P. Factors in complex skill training. In R. Glaser (Ed.), *Training research and education.* Pittsburgh: University of Pittsburgh Press, 1962. Pp. 177–199.

Flanagan, J. C. The critical incident technique. *Psychological Bulletin,* 1954, 51, 327–358.

Flanagan, J. C. Functional education for the seventies. *Phi Delta Kappan,* 1967, 49, 27–32.

Flanagan, J. C. The uses of educational evaluation in the development of programs, courses, instructional materials and equipment, instructional and learning procedures, and administrative arrangements. In R. W. Tyler (Ed.), *Educational evaluation: New roles, new means.* The Sixty-eighth Yearbook of the National Society for the Study of Education, Part II. Chicago: NSSE, 1969. Pp. 221–241.

Ford, G. W., & Pugno, L. (Eds.) *The structure of knowledge and the curriculum.* Chicago: Rand McNally, 1964.

Fry, E. B. *Teaching machines and programmed instruction: An introduction.* New York: McGraw-Hill, 1963.

Gagné, R. M. The acquisition of knowledge. *Technical Review,* 1962, 69(4), 355–365.

Gagné, R. M. Elementary science: A new scheme of instruction. *Science,* 1966, 151, 49–53.

Gagné, R. M. Curriculum research and the promotion of learning. In R. Tyler, R. M. Gagné, & M. Scriven (Eds.), *Perspectives of curriculum evaluation.* American Educational Research Association Monograph Series on Curriculum Evaluation, No. 1. Chicago: Rand McNally, 1967. Pp. 19–38.

Gagné, R. M. Learning hierarchies. Presidential Address, Division 15, American Psychological Association, August 1968.

Gagné, R. M. Characteristics of instructional technologists. *NSPI Journal,* 1969, 8(5), 6–9, 16–18.

Gagné, R. M. *The conditions of learning.* (2nd ed.) New York: Holt, Rinehart and Winston, 1970.

Gagné, R. M. Domains of learning. Washington, D.C.: American Educational Research Association, 1971. (audio tape)

Gagné, R. M., & Paradise, N. E. Abilities and learning sets in knowledge acquisition. *Psychological Monographs: General and Applied,* 1961, 75 (14), Whole No. 518.

Geis, G. L. Premature instruction. *Educational Technology,* 1970, 10(4), 24–30.

Getzels, J. Disciplined inquiry for education. Address presented at the meeting of the American Educational Research Association, Los Angeles, February 1969.

Gideonse, H. D. Research, development, and the improvement of education. *Science,* 1968, 162, 541–545.

Gilbert, T. F. Mathematics: The technology of education. *Journal of Mathematics,* 1962, 1(1), 7–73.

Glaser, R. Instructional technology and the measurement of learning outcomes: Some questions. *American Psychologist,* 1963, 18, 519–521.

Glaser, R. Postscript. Organizations for research and development in education. Symposium sponsored by American Educational Research Association and Phi Delta Kappa. Phi Delta Kappa, Inc. and AERA, 1966. (a)

Glaser, R. Psychological bases for instructional design. *AV Communication Review,* 1966, 14, 433–449. (b)

Glaser, R. The design and programming of instruction. In H. T. James et al. (Eds.), *The school and the challenge of innovation.* Supplementary paper, No. 28. New York: Committee for Economic Development, 1969. Pp. 156–215.

Glaser, R., & Cox, R. C. Criterion-referenced testing for the measurement of educational outcomes. In R. A. Weisgerber (Ed.), *Instructional process and media innovation.* Chicago: Rand McNally, 1968. Pp. 545–550.

Glass, G. V. Educational knowledge use. Address presented at the Orientation Program for the U.S.O.E., 1969–70. Postdoctoral Fellows, Elkridge, Maryland, September 1969.

Glennan, T. K., Jr. Issues in the choice of development policies. In T. Manschak, T. K. Glennan, Jr., & R. Summers (Eds.), *Strategies for research and development.* New York: Springer-Velaz, 1967.

Goodlad, J. I. *The development of a conceptual system for dealing with curriculum and instruction.* Los Angeles: University of California, 1968.

Goodlad, J. I., Von Stoephasius, R., & Klein, M. F. *The changing school curriculum.* New York: The Fund for the Advancement of Education, 1966.

Greenwald, H. M. Product concept testing on film. *Business Management,* 1969, 35(6), 26–32.

Grobman, H. Evaluation activities of curriculum projects: A starting point. *AERA Monograph Series on Curriculum Evaluation,* No. 2. Chicago: Rand McNally, 1968.

Gropper, G. L. Does "programmed" television need active responding? *AV Communication Review,* 1967, 15, 5–22.

Gropper, G. L., & Lumsdaine, A. A. *The use of student response to improve televised instruction: An overview.* Studies in Television Instruction, Report No. 7. Pittsburgh: American Institutes for Research, 1961.

Groueff, S. *Manhattan project: The untold story of the making of the atomic bomb.* London: Collins, 1967.

Groves, L. R. *Now it can be told.* New York: Harper & Row, 1962.

Hartley, J. Some problems of internal and external evaluation of programs. *Journal of Programmed Instruction,* November 1963, III(2), 5–7.

Havelock, R. G. Needs of development and diffusion models. Paper presented at the meeting of the American Educational Research Association, Minneapolis, March 1970.

Helmer, O. *Social technology.* New York: Basic Books, 1966.

Hemphill, J. K. Educational development. *The Urban Review,* October, 1969, 4, 23–27.

Hemphill, J. K. Management and operation of educational laboratories. *Journal of Research and Development in Education,* 1970, 3(2), 65–80.

Hilgard, E. R. The problem of R & D within behavioral social sciences. *Journal of Research and Development in Education,* 1968–1969, 2(4), 37–48.

Hills, R. J. *Toward a science of organization.* Eugene, Ore.: Center for the Advanced Study of Educational Administration, 1968.

Hively, W. (Chm.) Domain referenced achievement testing systems. Handout to accompany chairman's introduction. Symposium presented at the meeting of the American Educational Research Association, Minneapolis, March 1970.

Hively, W., Patterson, H. L., & Page, S. H. A "universe-defined" system of arithmetic achievement tests. *Journal of Educational Measurement,* 1968, 5, 275–290.

Holland, J. G., & Skinner, B. F. *The analysis of behavior: A program for self-instruction.* New York: McGraw-Hill, 1961.

Horn, R. E. *Developmental testing: Trying out programmed instructional materials with individual students.* Ann Arbor: The Center for Programmed Learning for Business, 1964.

Hovland, C. I., Lumsdaine, A. A., & Sheffield, F. D. *Experiments on mass communication.* Princeton, New Jersey: Princeton University Press, 1949.

Ilg, F. L., & Ames, L. B. *Child behavior.* New York: Harper & Row, 1955.

Instructional Objectives Exchange. *English literature collection.* Los Angeles: University of California, Los Angeles, Graduate School of Education, 1969.

Instructional Objectives Exchange. *English skills.* Los Angeles: University of California, Los Angeles, Graduate School of Education, 1970.

Jacobson, J. A. Forecasting future developments in education. Paper presented at the meeting of the American Educational Research Association, Minneapolis, March 1970.

Johnson, M. The translation of curriculum to instruction. In P. H. Taylor, S. Morris, & J. K. Kerr (Eds.), *Journal of Curriculum Studies,* 1969, 1(2), 115–131.

Johnson, P. E. The origin of item forms. Paper presented at the meeting of the American Educational Research Association, Minneapolis, March 1970.

Johnson, S. R., & Johnson, R. B. *Developing individualized instructional material—a self-instructional material in itself.* Evaluation Edition. New York: Westinghouse Learning Corp., 1970.

Journal of Programmed Instruction. Schools that have responded with "educators" statement as of June 23, 1966. 1966, 5(8 and 9), 2, 14–19.

Kliebard, H. M. The curriculum field in retrospect. In P. W. F. Witt (Ed.), *Technology and the curriculum.* New York: Teachers College Press, 1968. Pp. 69–84.

Kriewall, T. E. Applications of information theory and acceptance sampling principle to the management of mathematics instruction, Part II. Report from the Project on Computer-Managed Systems of Mathematics Instruction. Madison, Wis.: The University of Wisconsin, Wisconsin Research and Development Center for Cognitive Learning, October 1969.

Kuhn, J. W. *Scientific and managerial manpower in nuclear industry.* New York: Columbia University Press, 1966.

Lasagna, L. The pharmaceutical revolution: Its impact on science and society. *Science,* 1969, 166, 1227–1233.

Lazarsfeld, P. F., & Sieber, S. D. *Organizing educational research—an exploration.* Englewood Cliffs, N.J.: Prentice-Hall, 1964.

Lindvall, C. M., & Cox, R. C. The role of evaluation in programs for individualized instruction. In R. W. Tyler (Ed.), *Educational evaluation: New roles, new means.* The Sixty-eighth Yearbook of the National Society for the Study of Education, Part II. Chicago: NSSE, 1969. Pp. 156–188.

Lumsdaine, A. A. Instruments and media of instruction. In N. L. Gage (Ed.), *Handbook of research on teaching.* Chicago: Rand McNally, 1963. Pp. 583–682.

Lumsdaine, A. A. Educational technology, programmed learning, and instructional science. In E. R. Hilgard (Ed.), *Theories of learning and instruction.* The Sixty-third Yearbook of the National Society for the Study of Education, Part I. Chicago: NSSE, 1964. Pp. 371–401.

Lumsdaine, A. A. Assessing the effects of instructional programs. In R. Glaser (Ed.), *Teaching machines and programmed learning, II: Data and directions.* Washington, D.C.: National Education Association, 1965. Pp. 267–320.

Lumsdaine, A. A., & May, M. A. Mass communication and educational media. In P. R. Farnsworth, O. McNemar, & Q. McNemar (Eds.), *Annual Review of Psychology.* Palo Alto, Calif.: Annual Reviews, Inc., 1965, 16, 475–534.

Lundin, S. C. The application of a system for curriculum evaluation and revision based on the results of defined universe testing. Paper presented at the American Educational Research Association pre-registration session, titled "Diverse models for curriculum development and analysis," Minneapolis, March 1970.

Maccia, E. S., & Maccia, G. S. Development of educational theory derived from three educational theory models. Final report. Project No. 5-0638. Columbus, Ohio: The Ohio State University Research Foundation, 1966.

Maccia, E. S., Maccia, G. S., & Jewett, R. E. *Construction of educational theory models.* Cooperative Research Project, No. 1632. Columbus, Ohio: The Ohio State University Research Foundation, 1963.

Mager, R. R. *Preparing instructional objectives.* Palo Alto, Calif.: Fearon Publishers, 1962.

Mager, R. F., & Beach, K. M., Jr. *Developing vocational instruction.* Palo Alto, Calif.: Fearon Publishers, 1967.

Mager, R. F., & McCann, J. *Learner controlled instruction.* Palo Alto, Calif.: Varian Associates, 1961.

Maren, T. H. Pharmacology: Its nature in medicine. *Science,* 1968, 161, 443–444.

Markle, D. G. An exercise in the application of empirical methods to instructional systems design. *Final report: The development of the Bell system first aid and personal safety course,* American Institutes for Research, Palo Alto, Calif. New York: American Telephone and Telegraph Co., April, 1967. (manuscript)

Markle, S. M. *Words: A programmed course in vocabulary development.* Chicago: Science Research Associates, 1962.

Markle, S. M. Empirical testing of programs. In P. C. Lange (Ed.), *Programmed instruction.* The Sixty-sixth Yearbook of the National Society for the Study of Education, Part II. Chicago: NSSE, 1967. Pp. 104–138.

Markle, S. M. *Good frames and bad: A grammar of frame writing.* (2nd ed.) New York: John Wiley, 1969.

Mayer, M. *The schools.* New York: Harper, 1961.

McAshan, H. H. *Writing behavioral objectives: A new approach.* New York: Harper & Row, 1970.

McCrory, R. D. The design method—A scientific approach to valid design. In J. R. Bright (Ed.), *Research, development, and technological innovation—an introduction.* Homewood, Ill.: Richard D. Irwin, 1964. Pp. 59–67.

McIntyre, R. B., & Nelson, C. C. Empirical evaluation of instructional materials. *Educational Technology,* 1969, 9(2), 24–27.

McNeil, J. D. A perspective of developmental projects. Paper presented to the Developmental Project Guidelines Conference, sponsored by the Minnesota Research Coordination Unit in Occupational Education, University of Minnesota, Minneapolis, June 13–15, 1968.

Mechner, F. Behavioral analysis and instructional sequencing. In P. C. Lange (Ed.), *Programmed instruction.* The Sixty-sixth Yearbook of the National Society for the Study of Education, Part II. Chicago: NSSE, 1967. Pp. 81–103.

Metfessel, N. S., & Michael, W. B. A paradigm involving multiple criterion measures for the evaluation of the effectiveness of school programs. *Educational and Psychological Measurement,* 1967, 27, 931–943.

Moore, J. C. Manipulating the effectiveness of a self-instructional program. *Journal of Educational Psychology,* 1968, 59, 315–319.

Nadler, G. An investigation of design methodology. *Management Science,* June 1967, 13 (10), B642–B655.

National Center for Educational Research and Development. *Educational Research and Development in the United States.* Washington, D.C.: United States Government Printing Office, 1970.

Niedermeyer, F. C. *Parent-assisted learning.* Inglewood, Calif.: Southwest Regional Laboratory, 1970.

Niedermeyer, F. C., & Ellis, P. A. *The development of a tutorial program for kindergarten reading instruction.* Inglewood, Calif.: Southwest Regional Laboratory, 1970.

Nitko, A. J. Some considerations when using a domain-referenced achievement testing system in instructional situations. A paper presented at the meeting of the American Educational Research Association, Minneapolis, March 1970.

Northwest Regional Educational Laboratory. Stages of product development and installation. Portland, Ore.: Northwest Regional Educational Laboratory (undated).

Novick, D. Quoted in J. R. Bright (Ed.), *Research, development, and technological innovation—an introduction.* Homewood, Ill.: Richard D. Irwin, 1964. Pp. 21–22.

Obradovic, S. M. New strategies in educational planning and research involving ethnic minority communities. Paper presented at the meeting of the American Educational Research Association, Minneapolis, March 1970.

Pelz, D. C. Creative tensions in the research and development climate. *Science,* 1967, 157, 160–165.

Pharmaceutical Manufacturers Association. *Annual survey report, 1968–1969.* Washington, D.C.: Pharmaceutical Manufacturers Association, 1969.

Popham, W. J. Instructional product development: Two approaches to training. *AV Communication Review,* 1967, 15, 402–411.

Popham, W. J. Program fair evaluation—summative assessment of instructional sequences with dissimilar objectives. *NSPI Journal,* 1969, 8(6), 6–9.

Popham, W. J., & Baker, E. L. *Systematic instruction.* Englewood Cliffs, N.J.: Prentice-Hall, 1970.

Popham, W. J., & Baker, E. L. Rules for the development of instructional products. *The staff development compendium.* New York: Van Nostrand-Reinhold Companies, 1971. Pp. 129–168.

Popham, W. J., Eisner, E. W., Sullivan, H. J., & Tyler, L. L. *Instructional objectives.* American Educational Research Association Monograph Series on Curriculum Evaluation, No. 3. Chicago: Rand McNally, 1969. Pp. 32–64.

Popham, W. J., & Husek, T. R. Implications of criterion-referenced measurement. *Journal of Educational Measurement,* 1969, 6, 1–10.

Price, W. J., & Bass, L. W. Scientific research and the innovative process. *Science,* 1969, 164, 802–806.

Rabehl, G. J. The Minnemast Experiment with domain referenced achievement testing. A paper presented at the meeting of the American Educational Research Association, Minneapolis, March 1970.

Reagan, M. D. Basic and applied research: A meaningful distinction? *Science,* 1967, 155, 1383–1386.

Rice, J. M. The futility of the spelling grind. *The Forum,* 1897, 23, 163–172.

Robeck, M. D. A study of the revision process in programmed instruction. Unpublished master's thesis, University of California, Los Angeles, 1965.

Rosen, M. J. *An experimental design for comparing the effects of instructional media programing procedures: Subjective vs. objective revision procedures.* Final report. Palo Alto, Calif.: American Institutes for Research in Behavioral Sciences, 1968.

Schutz, R. E. The nature of educational development. *Journal of Research and Development in Education,* 1970, 3(2), 39–64.

Scriven, M. The methodology of evaluation. In R. W. Tyler, R. M. Gagné, & M. Scriven (Eds.), *Perspectives of curriculum evaluation.* American Educational Research Association Monograph Series on Curriculum Evaluation, No. 1. Chicago: Rand McNally, 1967. Pp. 39–83.

Sension, D. B. Future uses for domain referenced achievement testing systems. Paper presented at the meeting of the American Educational Research Association, Minneapolis, March 1970.

Sherwin, C. W., & Isenson, R. S. Project Hindsight: A Defense Department study of the utility of research. *Science,* 1967, 156, 1571–1577.

Shoemaker, H. A. Outline for preparing specifications for a training project. New York: American Telephone and Telegraph Company, undated.

Shoemaker, H. A. *Memorandum for the record.* New York: American Telephone and Telegraph Company, August 1968.

Shugrue, M. F. *English in a decade of changes.* New York: Pegasus, 1968.

Silberman, H., Coulson, J., Melaragno, R., & Newmark, G. *Use of exploratory research and individual tutoring techniques for the development of programing methods and theory.* Final report. National Defense Education Act Project 7-14-0000-181. Santa Monica, Calif.: Systems Development Corporation, 1964.

Skager, R. W. *Student entry skills and the evaluation of instructional programs: A case study.* Los Angeles: University of California, Los Angeles, Center for the Study of Evaluation of Instructional Programs, Report No. 53, 1969.

Skinner, B. F. *Walden two.* New York: Macmillan, 1948.

Skinner, B. F. The science of learning and the art of teaching. *Harvard Educational Review,* 1954, 24, 86–97.

Smith, K. T., & Rapp, A. V. A lap on writing lap's. Paper prepared for in-service training programs in cooperation with Broward County Board of Public Instruction, February 1969.

Snow, C. P. Government, science, and public policy. *Science,* 1966, 151, 650–653.

Southwest Educational Development Corporation. Planning the systems approach to field testing educational products. *Calipers.* Austin, Texas: Southwest Educational Development Corporation, 1969.

Southwest Regional Laboratory for Educational Research and Development. *Teacher's manual—SWRL first-year communication skills program.* Inglewood, Calif.: SWRL for Educational Research and Development, 1969.

Stake, R. E. The countenance of educational evaluation. *Teachers College Record,* 1967, 68, 523–540.

Stake, R. E. Objectives, priorities, and other judgment data. *Review of Educational Research,* 1970, 40, 181–212.

Stake, R. E., & Gooler, D. Measuring educational priorities. A paper presented at the meeting of the American Educational Research Association, Minneapolis, March 1970.

Stowe, R. A. (Ed.) *Case studies in instructional development.* Bloomington, Ind.: Indiana University, Laboratory for Educational Development, School of Education, 1969.

Sullivan, H. J. Product development documentation and review guidelines. Inglewood, Calif.: Southwest Regional Laboratory for Educational Research and Development, 1968.

Sullivan, H. J. Objectives, evaluation and improved learner achievement. In W. J. Popham, E. W. Eisner, H. J. Sullivan, & L. L. Tyler (Eds.), *Instructional objectives,* American Educational Research Association Monograph Series on Curriculum Evaluation, No. 3. Chicago: Rand McNally, 1969. Pp. 65–99.

Sulzen, R. H. The formulation of a replicable means of empirical development or revision of automated programmed instruction. A paper presented at the meeting of the National Society for Programmed Instruction, Anaheim, California, April 1970.

Thayer, V. T. *Formative ideas in American education from the colonial period to the present.* New York: Dodd, Mead, 1965.

Thorndike, E. L. *Principles of teaching.* New York: A. G. Seiler, 1906.

Thorndike, E. L. *Education.* New York: Macmillan, 1912.

Thorndike, E. L., & Woodworth, R. S. The influence of improvement in one mental function upon the efficiency of other functions. *Psychological Review,* 1901, 8, 247–261, 384–395, 553–564.

Townes, C. H. Quantum electronics, and surprise in development of technology. *Science,* 1968, 159, 699–703.

Travers, R. M. W. Models of education and their implications for the conduct of evaluation studies. Unpublished manuscript, Western Michigan University, 1969.

Tyler, L. L. A case history: Formulation of objectives from a psychoanalytic framework. In W. J. Popham, E. W. Eisner, H. J. Sullivan, & L. L. Tyler (Eds.), *Instructional objectives,* American Educational Research Association Monograph Series on Curriculum Evaluation, No. 3. Chicago: Rand McNally, 1969. Pp. 100–129.

Tyler, L. L., Klein, M. F., & Michael, W. B. *Recommendations for curriculum and instruction materials.* Los Angeles: Tyler Press, 1971.

Tyler, R. W. *Basic principles of curriculum and instruction.* Chicago: University of Chicago Press, 1950.

Tyler, R. W. Introduction. In R. W. Tyler (Ed.), *Educational evaluation: New roles, new means.* The Sixty-eighth Yearbook of the National Society for the Study of Education, Part II. Chicago: NSSE, 1969. Pp. 1–5.

VanderMeer, A. W. *An investigation of the improvement of educational filmstrips and a derivation of principles relating to the effectiveness of these media: Study no. 2.* University Park, Pa.: Pennsylvania State University, 1964.

VanderMeer, A. W., & Montgomery, R. E. *An investigation of the improvement of educational filmstrips and a derivation of principles relating to the effectiveness of these media: Study no. 3.* University Park, Pa.: Pennsylvania State University, 1964.

VanderMeer, A. W., & Thorne, H. E. *An investigation of the improvement of educational filmstrips and a derivation of principles relating to the effectiveness of these media: Study no. 1.* University Park, Pa.: Pennsylvania State University, 1964.

Walker, D. F. *An empirical model of the process of curriculum development.* Palo Alto, Calif.: Stanford University, 1970.

Walters, J. E. *The management of research and development.* Washington, D. C.: Spartan, 1965.

Washburne, C. Winnetka. *School and Society,* 1929, 29, 37–50.

Wittrock, M. C. Product-oriented research. *The Educational Forum,* 1967, 31, 145–150.

Wittrock, M. C., & Wiley, D. E. *The evaluation of instruction: Issues and problems.* New York: Holt, Rinehart & Winston, 1970.

Yaney, J. P. Project management: Some current developments. *NSPI Journal,* 1970, 9 (3), 6–7.

CHAPTER **9** **Instrumentation of Research in Teaching**[1]

JAMES G. HOLLAND
University of Pittsburgh

JUDITH DORAN
University of Pittsburgh

Via the television we have recently watched men as they walked on the moon. Many aspects of their physiological and psychological states were monitored with occasional information passed on to the millions who watched as it was happening. This is in stark contrast to educational settings in which we seldom know much more than whether or not the student is present. The space flight was the culmination of a long history of development of methods and instrumentation in the physical, biological and behavioral sciences. Man was preceded into orbit by a chimpanzee named Ham who performed a set of complex learning tasks during flight. The tasks required automated control not simply because Ham was alone but because of the subtle contingencies of reinforcement which cannot easily be

done without proper instrumentation (cf. Rohles, 1966).

Progress in science has often depended on the development of new instruments. Consider the importance of the lens to astronomy, the cyclotron to modern physics or the electrical amplifier to physiology. It is unlikely that Pavlov would have demonstrated adequately the conditioned reflex without developing his harness and the controlled environment, but having done so he opened the way to investigation of an important phenomenon since others could repeat or elaborate his experiments with the same care for precise measurement and careful control. The greater objectivity and reliability of measurement made subsequent studies of the reflex cumulative. Similarly the study of learning and motivation saw a sizable advance with Skinner's (1938) operant analysis and the manifestation of that analysis in instruments and procedures. Skinner identified his measure of behavior (the operant) as the probability of an arbitrary response and searched for those events in the environment which control the probability (or frequency) of the response. These events which control behavior are

[1] Much of the time for the preparation of this chapter was made possible by the Learning Research and Development Center supported in part as a research and development center by funds from the United States Office of Education, Department of Health, Education and Welfare. The opinions expressed in this publication do not necessarily reflect the position or policy of the Office of Education and no official endorsement should be inferred.

principally contingent relationships describable in contingency statements like "if x, then y," or "if the child picks from a set of forms a form which is identical to a sample form, he has completed the task and is reinforced," or "if in his speech the child produces the subtle and complex pattern of inflective rhythm and sound frequency distribution, his social environment acts appropriately and his behavior is reinforced." The contingent relationships between discriminative stimuli, responses and reinforcing stimuli are rich in variety and subtlety even though the principles of reinforcement describing them are simple.

The power of Skinner's analysis and the pervasiveness of its influence are in large part attributable to the nature of the instrumentation he developed and the precise way that the instrumentation embodied the concepts. Skinner's standard experimental chamber and the use of electro-mechanical equipment for the automatic control of all contingencies made possible an analysis of behavior of such precision that the science of behavior could often deal with the behavior of individuals rather than average trends and could move from prediction to control of its subject matter. The precision of control and measurement provided by instrumentation led to discoveries not otherwise possible. A few milliseconds delay of reinforcement can result in changes in the form of the response, and seemingly minor changes in a reinforcement schedule will change the pattern of response frequency. Therefore, variable error would be large if these factors were not controlled with the precision good instrumentation makes possible.

In systems in which all stimulus presentation and reinforcement contingencies are automated, much of the strength of instrumentation comes in the communication among scientists. In the style of McLuhan, "the equipment is the message." When the conditions of an operant conditioning experiment are described, the critical aspects of the environment are detailed by describing the nature of the apparatus including the electro-mechanical control circuits. A schedule of reinforcement is in no way a description of behavior; it is a description of the wiring of the equipment and thus a description of the environmental conditions. A second investigator can exactly replicate the reinforcement contingencies or can add his own elaboration. Again, in the case of the science of learning, instrumentation has made possible identification and measurement of phenomena that would have been difficult or impossible without it. Instrumentation has also made the science more precisely communicable and hence cumulative, and the findings and approaches have gradually been extended both to research in educational problems and to the use of instrumentation in education (cf. Chapter 6 in this volume by Glaser & Cooley).

As educational research moves forward in the use of better instrumentation, precise, subtle relationships are discovered and new discoveries can more easily be converted into practice. "Equipment as message" is particularly important in the transmission of new educational techniques into practice. Teachers have taken learning courses as part of their training for years with at best modest success in identifying the behavioral characteristics of each individual learning task, identifying when each student has met each contingency and reinforcing it. Such a feat is impossible because of the subtlety and number of such behavioral events in the classroom on the one hand and of the size of the teacher-training problem on the other. But with the introduction of teaching machines, direct transmission of good teaching became possible.

The progress of technical development in education is all too slow, however. Consider the irony of a nation gradually turning over the conduct of a war to electronic devices placed in a field to detect movement of people; these devices telemeter information back to computers which in turn can direct fire at the electronically designated targets (Kirchener, 1971). By contrast, educational research is in a most primitive state, a contrast which is a sad commentary on the priorities of our society and which raises concern in an educational researcher who might contribute to the store of technical knowledge that in turn might be used under the same system of priorities which has given us electronic battlefields. On the positive side, the classroom researcher can now draw upon the sizable technology developed by the scientist working on problems of human learning in the laboratory as well as the rich store of technical devices developed for uses in other contexts. The aim of this chapter is to explore the possibilities not only of instrumentation already being used in classroom research but also of instrumentation being used in the experimental analysis of behavior in other contexts than education which might in turn be profitably used in classroom research.

THE PROBLEM—
THE PROCESS OF LEARNING

The core problem in a science of instruction is the process by which the individual student learns. Instrumentation has potential for each step of this process. The learner is exposed to some material or stimuli; he must interact with that material in some active fashion as writing, talking, thinking or reasoning; and the adequacy of the interaction must in some way be evaluated and reinforced. It is this basic learning cycle that the operant conditioning laboratories have demonstrated for us. This learning cycle stands at the basis of programmed instruction, contingency management, behavior modification and behavior therapy. Each of the separate components in this learning cycle can be instrumented. Controlled presentation of material is very commonly instrumented in audiovisual language laboratories and in audiovisual equipment in the classroom. Tape recorders, one-way mirrors and video cameras aid in the measurement of student responses in the classroom and language lab.

The principal focus of the present chapter, however, will be on the instrumentation of the total, contingent relationship including the control of the stimulus, the assessment of the response, the determination as to whether the response has met the criteria for reinforcement, and the delivery of reinforcement. Extensively discussed elsewhere are the areas of audiovisual instruction (cf. Allen, 1960, or Brown, Lewis, & Harcleroad, 1964) and educational television (cf. Chu & Schramm, 1967). Only instances in which elements are relatively new and not yet used in common practice, e.g., new stimulus presentation devices or new modes of recording responses, will be discussed. Primary emphasis will be given to systems in which instrumentation is used for the control of contingencies of reinforcement under controlled stimulus conditions. But the most important reason for concentrating on the contingent relations between the student's response and the material is that the basis for learning, when learning occurs, is in the contingent relationship among stimuli, responses, and the resulting reinforcement.

Conventional classrooms have presented material either via textbooks, lecture or audiovisual equipment. Traditionally, learning has been left to the unspecified activity of the student when exposed to the materials. But since Skinner's article, "The Science of Learning and the Art of Teaching" (1954), educators have become increasingly aware of the importance of students' responses. This process of constructing repertoires of verbal and nonverbal behavior in the student has benefited by the laboratory experimentation in the analysis of behavior, and it is the use of instrumentation in this process which is the most profitable line of research and development for those interested in furthering the ends of education.

Each of the various components of the learning cycles can be illustrated with a program to teach preschool children to classify an array of objects a variety of different ways (Holland & Doran, in press). A teaching program was developed to further the ability to classify on the basis of relationships that exist between or within classes. Photographs of a variety of stimulus materials included abstract shapes and pictures of objects which in a given slide could differ in color, size, function, etc. These were presented by a 35mm carousel projector onto a touch-sensitive display which is a computer interface device that transmits the location of a touch by the child to the computer. This device is constructed by using two sets of fine wires, some running in the vertical direction, others in the horizontal direction. The wires are covered by a flexible plastic material which serves as a projection screen and at the same time transmits the pressure of the child's touch to the wires underneath. The press of the child will bring the vertical and horizontal wires appropriate to a given location into contact with each other, completing a circuit which is specific to the location of the press (cf. Fitzhugh & Katsuki, 1971). Early items in the program familiarized the child with the categories to be included in later multiple-category items. Auditory messages were presented by a random-access auditory device. In late items in the program, the child was presented with a picture of an array of objects having a variety of different properties and permitting different classifications on the basis of color, shape, size, function, etc. The child was asked by the taped message presented through a speaker to "Touch all the things that are alike." He could then proceed to touch all of the objects of the given color, for example. If the child failed to touch an object within 15 seconds, the original message was repeated. When the child completed a set, for example, touched all the things that were blue, he saw a light flash. He was then instructed to "Find some more things that are alike." If he again selected objects that were blue, he would hear, "You already did that. Try again." Then he might touch all of the things that were green, for example. If he began touching several given objects but did not complete the set, after ten seconds he heard, "You didn't find all of them. Try again." When

he completed the greet set, the light flashed. He was again instructed to "Find some more things that are alike." He might then go on classifying on the basis of color, or he might shift to classifying on the basis of another dimension such as touching all of the circles, all of the large objects, all of the objects used for transportation, or all of the objects that were hot. In each instance, when the child completed a given set, the light flashed. When he finished all of the required attributes, a bell sounded and a marble which was exchangeable with other marbles for a toy at the end of the session was presented. If the child failed to classify on the basis of some attributes, the computer presented each uncompleted set independently with the message, "Find all the Xs." After completing all of the missed sets in this fashion, the original instruction was again presented, "Find all the things that are alike," and the child started again to classify the objects in a variety of different ways. The number of possible sets in a multiple-category item ranged from two to six. Items of the complexity described were eventually reached in a low error rate program of 160 items. The children, therefore, were able to complete even the difficult multiple-category items with a low error rate. To determine, in each instance, what subsequent message was to be presented and whether the contingency for reinforcement had been met required apparatus as sophisticated as a computer. With each touch by the child, the computer had to determine whether a permissible category was being followed, and, as the touches proceeded, whether it was a category already completed or not, and which categories remained or if all the possible categories had been completed.

The computer, then, successfully managed reinforcement contingencies for a task which would be difficult or impossible to arrange with more simple devices or without instrumentation. Keeping track of such contingencies would be extremely difficult for a teacher operating without instrumentation, particularly in view of the need for immediate feedback. The use of automatic equipment provided the careful control of contingencies which made possible the establishment of this rather sophisticated skill several years earlier than it normally appears in children. The control of these difficult contingencies would not have been possible without instrumentation; moreover, the program sequence could be put through several revisions because the precise instrumentation removed the ambiguity of early difficulties with the program. Hence, again, the instrumentation made possible the direct transmission of the procedure into practice in the admittedly improbable event that some kindergarten class has a computer at its disposal. This example illustrates the three components of all problems of instrumentation of reinforcement contingencies: first, the production of environmental events as in the presentation of the stimulus material via slides or tape and the presentation of the reinforcement through operation of the marble dispenser; second, "sensing" and "transducing" the response as in using the touch-sensitive display to provide a separate electrical signal for each area the child touches; and third, the "logic" or control circuit to determine when a designated set of events has occurred and to provide control signals for the consequent events in the environment, as in using the computer to determine when admissible sets of objects were touched by the child. The old-style educational researcher turned gadgeteer finds the nature of his difficulties dependent upon the state of the art in these separate problem areas. And as the technical developments in each area became more sophisticated they also became more easily used by the relatively inexperienced.

HOW TO START IN INSTRUMENTATION

Instrumentation is now difficult only when response sensing and transducing stray from the common push-button, touch-window or press-key variety and the stimulus presentation is other than printed page, picture or taped sound. In other words the control circuit or "logic" aspects are already highly developed and, with a little effort at learning, easy to use. The older and still useful relay circuitry can be obtained from numerous equipment houses in modular form. There are interchangeable panels containing relays, electrical timers, counters, intake panels from standard response sensors and output panels to common stimulus devices. From years of experience, major equipment houses have designed these panels to make them extremely easy to learn to use. Wires of various lengths with snap attachments on each end enable quick and easy wiring with a little trial and error when necessary. The few fundamentals that must be learned can be found in books written for behavioral scientists (cf. Cornsweet, 1963; Sidowski, 1966). The use of the modular interchangeable units from equipment houses can be easily learned from materials available from these equipment houses (cf. also Rohles, 1969).

In recent years transistors have become increasingly popular in control circuits. Relays continue to be adequate for most behavioral work and have the advantage of being less expensive and, when it is necessary to do wiring without using modular equipment, easier to use. The novice would have difficulty with transistors if he attempted to wire his own circuits without using modules prepared by companies for behavioral work. The greater speed and the lower voltages of transistors make electrical noise from extraneous sources and rapid transient signals within one's own equipment difficult problems. However, companies have solved most of these problems by preparing modular units for use by behavioral scientists. These modules are extremely easy to use, as suggested by their names "and" gates, "or" gates and "flip-flops." An "and" gate gives an output when two or more required events occur as an input. Hence, x and y, for example, must happen in order for there to be a signal output from an "and" gate. In the case of an "or" gate, either one event or the other will result in an output. Thus, simple logical statements about the environmental events that must happen are reflected directly in the wiring of modular transistor components. Transistorized circuits have the advantage of being quiet and requiring less space than relays. While they are more expensive than relays, they are still less expensive than the third alternative, computers. Equipment houses not only provide easy instructions on the use of equipment of this type but also occasionally conduct workshops to teach potential users transistor circuitry.

Small computers, while still more expensive than relays or transistorized modular equipment, have become sufficiently inexpensive so that it has become feasible to use these in the laboratory for control of experimental conditions (cf. Weiss, 1969; Uttal, 1969). With a bit of effort anyone can learn to program these, though in some instances programming can be a bit tedious. The computer is impractical for cases where the investigator only has one or two particular studies to carry out. However, the ease of changing from one experiment to another by changing programs and using the computer as the common control equipment makes this equipment practical for a highly productive laboratory. A large central computer is less often generally available and, when available, has practical shortcomings such as the temporal delays produced by time sharing which would be disruptive for most experimental purposes. There are, in addition, a few problems such as the classification program described above in which the logical operations are too extensive to be performed easily with anything less than a large computer.

In the majority of educational research applications, the sensing of the response and the presentation of stimulus events are simple, requiring only such things as the operation of electrical switches using projectors, tape recorders, etc. In other instances they are quite difficult because the technology is undeveloped. In these cases the investigator will find himself facing difficult problems in developing methods of sensing the response and designing appropriate transducers to get the information to his logic circuit. Solutions for such problems often require considerable experience in electronics or other areas (cf. Malmstadt, Enke, & Toren, 1962). When the major equipment problem is not in sensing unusual responses or presenting unusual types of stimuli there is no reason for the novice to feel intimidated by the equipment. Switching circuitry is now easily accessible and many stimulus presentation and response sensing devices are available. Major equipment houses advertise in the *Journal of the Experimental Analysis of Behavior* and the *American Psychologist;* in addition, the beginner can find his way to the appropriate companies by use of a buyer's guide published in the *American Psychologist* (Sidowski, 1969).

INSTRUMENTED INSTRUCTION

To survey a variety of learning tasks it will be convenient to classify them in terms of the predominant aspect to be established. Learning tasks differ as to whether different response forms or topographies are being shaped, whether new stimulus control is being established, whether hierarchical textual relationships or a rote series of unrelated associations is being taught. Each of these presents somewhat different problems for the programmer or the researcher and different problems for instrumentation.

SHAPING RESPONSE TOPOGRAPHY

When an especially difficult response topography must be shaped, extremely crude approximations are at first accepted for reinforcement and on subsequent occasions the criterion for differential reinforcement is gradually increased until the skilled response is shaped. To instrument for such procedures, provision for measuring the response and automatically making decisions as to its acceptability for differential reinforcement must be made. A demonstration of shaping response topography is provided by a procedure to develop rhythmic skill in young children (Skinner, 1961). The child strikes a key in synchrony with a series of auditory stimuli; a bell sounds or a light flashes when the key is struck close enough in time to the sound. At first the response is reinforced even if the beat is poorly matched, but gradually closer and closer approximation between response and stimuli is required until a nearly perfect match is obtained. Control for this procedure was obtained by modifying an ordinary phonographic turntable by adding a metal plate on which a paper disk could be overlaid. The paper disk had slits cut in it. These slits were swept by two metal contacts, one controlling the presentation of the stimulus, the other the allowable reinforcement contingency. The stimulus sequence was arranged by cutting a series of holes in the paper in a rhythmic pattern. When the metal contact passed over one of these holes, it made contact with the underlying metal disk, completing a circuit which presented the auditory stimulus; a second longer slit corresponded with each stimulus, preceding it somewhat in time and following it somewhat in time. If the child struck the key during the time that the appropriate contact passed over this slit, the bell and light would operate. A series of pairs of patterned slits in the paper could provide different rhythms and different tolerances for reinforcement.

A similar problem saw a different solution when Ihrke (1971) developed an instrument to train a student to perform rhythmic patterns. The rhythmic stimuli were presented by an ordinary tape player and the student responded on the keyboard of an electric organ. The test for the adequacy of the response was provided by an especially designed electronic rhythm monitor which compared signals from the prerecorded tape with those from the student's electric organ. The electronic rhythm monitor informed the student if his response was early or late. The margin of allowed error could be varied from 0.25 second to 0.1 second. Thus there are many potential solutions to provide essentially the same result. Skinner used a primarily mechanical system for control of the stimulus and reinforcement contingencies supplemented by a simple relay control circuitry, whereas Ihrke provided this control through an electronic device he designed.

Another example of the instrumentation of contingencies to shape response topography is found in Israel Goldiamond's (1965) somewhat controversial procedure to correct stuttering. Over a period of years Goldiamond worked with procedures to modify stuttering, using contingencies of reinforcement. Either the stutterer or an observer pressed a switch with each disfluency and a variety of contingencies were explored. In some experiments stuttering was punished with electric shock. In others, a period of fluent speech delayed the onset of electronic shock. In still other instances, he used the stimulus of a slight delay in feedback of the subject's response. Delay of a fraction of a second between utterance and hearing one's speech proved to be aversive and quite disruptive. However, his early experiments had only mixed success in modifying stuttering. The aversive stimuli, whether delayed feedback or electric shock, decreased stuttering but also decreased speaking rate. Gradually he developed a technique which was successful. He provided continuous delayed feedback with instructions that the stutterer prolong each utterance, stretching out each word and thereby decreasing the disruptive effects of the delay. When this was done, the stutterer no longer stuttered although his speech pattern was not a normal but a prolonged pattern. Goldiamond began with delays of 200 milliseconds and gradually, on successive days, decreased the delay until there was no longer any delay in the feedback and speech was at a normal rate without stuttering.

Thus Goldiamond moved from a form of speech that was free of stuttering though not normal in a gradual progression to a normal rate of speech without stuttering. At each stage, the delayed feedback interval set the limit for prolonging to avoid the disruptive effect of the delay, and the gradual progression shaped the response topography to a normal speaking pattern. It should be noted that while stuttering is corrected by this procedure in the laboratory or the clinic, there are problems as yet unsolved in the carry-over to social speech outside this laboratory or clinic. This, and the concern some therapists have with searching for underlying etiologies of stuttering, have restricted the practical use of the technique. Nevertheless, the key to his promising procedure was good instrumentation in both the delayed feedback apparatus and the control circuit. Moreover, the long history of exploration of various procedures relied on good instrumentation. There is a cumulative nature to this research that may yet see the eventual evolution of a procedure that works in practice and, given the procedure which works, it can be passed on intact as an instrumented solution to a practical problem.

Discrimination Training

With the advent of new developments in educational technology with the emphasis on carefully defined behavioral objectives, discrimination training has become an increasingly important part of educational systems from the preschool, where the emphasis is on the learning of many perceptual concepts, to the advanced sciences and medical training, where it is becoming increasingly apparent that learning "about" things through textbooks is not a substitute for acquiring the various perceptual repertoires that are necessary. Therefore, discrimination training has become an important area for educational research, both as a testing ground for the extension of basic learning principles to the classroom and in discover-

ing new basic information beginning from an applied educational problem.

Visual Discrimination Training

In discrimation training a simple arbitrary response such as a touch that operates an electrical switch is sufficient and control circuitry is simple standard equipment. Any challenge found is in arranging for the necessary variations in stimulus material, and even here the well-developed technology of photography and projectors makes this simple. A typical instrument of this type is shown in Figure 1 (J. G. Holland, 1962).

Fig. 1. Child working on an inductive reasoning program at a teaching machine. In the upper rectangular window is a logical series with elements varying in color and orientation. The child must select from the choices in the five bottom windows an element of the color and orientation appropriate to continue the series.

There are a top window and five small choice windows. The windows serve both as stimulus displays and response keys. The windows are transilluminated by a 35mm slide projector. When the top window is pressed, a small microswitch mounted behind it and along an edge is operated; the shutter then opens, exposing the projected images on the five small choice windows. Each of these choice windows has a small microswitch mounted along its lower edge inside the instrument. Photocells, mounted inside the projector near the slide frame, are operated by light passing through a hole-punch coding system (or the photocells may be mounted near the keys and operated by exposed areas on the film). The photocell coding system determines which of the five bottom windows will be scored correct. When a correct bottom window is pressed, the shutters close, the slide changes to present the next frame, a red light mounted at the top of the instrument flashes, and a gong sounds for reinforcement. If, however, an incorrect window is pressed, only the bottom shutter closes. The subject must then press the top window again to open the bottom shutter. He responds again to the same problem. If in this case he is correct, the slide changes, the light flashes and the gong sounds; but instead of receiving the next frame in the sequence, the projector presents the previous frame. If he is correct on this frame, the material advances to the frame he has previously missed. If he is then correct on his first choice, the material advances to the next frame in the sequence. Detailed construction information and photographic procedures are provided by Hively (1964) for a response and display unit for this type of machine.

A particularly useful form of recording has been used with this instrument (described in Sidman & Stoddard, 1967). A standard cumulative recorder common in operant conditioning work was modified by attaching the pen directly to the slide tray with a cord. With each initial correct response, the slide tray advances, moving the pen upwards on the paper. With time the paper moves horizontally under the pen. A series of correct responses gives a series of steps. The slope described by the steps gives the rate of correct responding, the distance between successive steps is a measure of the time taken by the subject for a given frame. On a correct response following an error the slide tray backs up one frame, producing a downward step of the pen. It is common in materials in which the subject hits a point at which he has great difficulty for the slide tray to move backward and forward past a given frame, recycling as he finally gets a slide correct, backs up to the previous slide, repeats the difficult slide, again missing it, backs up to the previous slide, etc. Such areas of difficulty are readily apparent and the data can be interpreted at a glance.

Some of the earliest programs on this machine, which trained Thurstone's reasoning and spatial factors, served as a vehicle for exploring the utility of programming principles such as gradual progression and low error rate in discrimination training (J. G. Holland, 1962; Bijou & Baer, 1963).

Subsequently numerous studies have used similar procedures to investigate errorless discrimination, both for its importance to learning theory and its practical significance in education. Sidman's laboratories have been especially productive and especially well equipped with control circuits based on transistor modules (Sidman & Stoddard, 1966, 1967). Their experimental subjects have included a severely retarded adult, retarded children, normal children and monkeys, as well as a variety of important variables concerning stimulus fading which have been investigated in the careful, analytic fashion expected of a well-equipped operant conditioning laboratory. One study is of special interest because of the potential educational usefulness. Touchette (1971) developed an errorless method for discrimination training which does not require the laborious development of a fading procedure. He simply began by presenting the set of stimuli to be discriminated with a red light superimposed on the correct alternative. The red light had previously been established as a discriminative stimulus and quickly prompted the response. On successive trials the time between the new stimuli being learned and the onset of the red light gradually increased automatically. Soon the child began responding before the red light appeared, always responding correctly. Learning by this method is rapid compared with most errorless procedures and much faster than learning with mistakes. If this procedure can be extended to a variety of teaching tasks it will be of great value. Again, automatic equipment makes this procedure possible. Manual control would not only be too laborious to be feasible, but it would involve too much chance for experimenter error.

Teaching discrimination skills involving visual materials often requires special effects. In some cases the task analysis demands the use of motion pictures which may be used much like any other stimulus material (Gropper, 1966; Schrag & J. G. Holland, 1965). Schrag and Holland instrumented a Physical Sciences Study Committee (PSSC) film teaching the concept of relativity. A movie projector was modified so that it is automatically stopped on a signal coded in the margin of the film and turns off the projector. The student reads a printed question which he can answer if he has properly observed the film or, in some instances, he makes predictions as to the outcome of an experiment and the film is used to confirm his prediction. The teaching of concepts of the relativity of motion required temporal variation of spatial events and hence film was indicated.

Another special problem arises when three-dimensional views are necessary. Such a case arises in medical education when training visual discriminations necessary for operative procedures. The authors have observed interesting use of projections of filmed stereo views of eye operations prepared by Kenneth Richardson of the Pittsburgh Eye and Ear Hospital for a sophisticated teaching machine using a computer for control. A recent technological development called *holography* offers another solution to the presentation of three-dimensional views (Barson & Mendelson, 1969).

In this procedure, a picture in depth with full three-dimensionality is made using a special photographic plate and laser light. When the resulting slide is projected by a laser beam, it represents an image possessing full three-dimensionality. This opens new possibilities for use of three-dimensional stimuli. It will be easy to store libraries of holography slides which would serve the purpose of the often needed but rarely practical three-dimensional models. Moreover, these can be used in instrumented instructional settings more easily than models because of the greater ease of automatic presentation and control of the stimulus. Teaching machine programs in biology, geometry or similar areas may use laser projectors to provide three-dimensional stimuli.

Video tape is now a convenient alternative to film and has been used in some interesting research on training teacher-trainees in discriminating the properties of good and poor teacher interaction. In one study (Johnson, 1968), trainees viewed their video tape with an accompanying programmed booklet that, through the questions asked, provided cues as to which aspects of the scenes to focus upon, gave the trainees an opportunity to report their observations, and gave corrective feedback as to the accuracy of the reports. Another group of trainees, who viewed the video tape without questions, performed on a posttest like the no-treatment control group. Johnson concluded that video-taping teacher-pupil interactions is a useful training device if the trainees are taught what to observe in the video tape. Resnick and Kiss (1970) and Reynolds and Millmore (1971) similarly demonstrated the usefulness of video-taped teacher-student interactions. The material chosen for the video tape showed appropriate contrast between adequate and inadequate performance and was programmed to establish such a discriminative repertoire in the trainees. They demonstrated that discrimination training was reflected in the teacher's behavior and that discrimination training provided the possibility of self-editing of behavior.

Auditory Discrimination Training

The problems faced in discrimination training of visual stimuli are paralleled by the problems faced in discrimination training of auditory stimuli.

Instrumented speech correction. An interesting example of the usefulness of instrumentation in research on auditory discrimination training is found in the "ear training" of children who have articulation difficulties. It is a common practice for school speech therapists to work with children in the third or fourth grades who misarticulate certain speech sounds. For example, a child might substitute the /th/ for the /s/ in his typical speech behavior. It is commonly found that such children not only misarticulate these sounds, but also fail to discriminate the sound from their substi-

tute sound. Children with demonstrated articulation and discrimination difficulties normally spend many hours with the therapist learning to discriminate these sounds in words. But now a machine form of discrimination training has been developed (A. L. Holland & Matthews, 1963). After completing a program which usually required about two hours, the discrimination problem was completely corrected and the articulation significantly improved without intervening articulation therapy.

The instrumentation used for this discrimination-training procedure is best seen in a film prepared on the technique (A. L. Holland, 1965). Figure 2 is a photograph of the subject's response panel which consisted of a box with three keys coded differently for the various response requirements in different phases of the discrimination procedure. The auditory material was presented via a stereo tape player which was modified so that one track served to present the stimulus and the second track presented

Fig. 2.   Child working at a teaching machine with an auditory discrimination program. The child presses one of three buttons in response to each discrimination problem. If the choice is correct, a counter advances, a light flashes, and the tape recorder presents the next item. If the choice is incorrect, the tape recorder rewinds to replay the item.

a coded signal to the equipment in the form of a pulse train to signal the control circuit as to which of the response keys was correct. After either an error or the lack of a response in a five-second period, the tape recorder rewound a sufficient distance and replayed the missed item. All events—the rewinding of the player, the recording of responses, and the presenting of reinforcement—were automatically controlled by relays and other electro-mechanical equipment. The child used the appropriate one of 11 programs for the sound he misarticulated. Each program followed a careful, gradual progression of tasks. The final task in a program had the child discriminate which of a pair of productions of the same word contained the correct sound compared with misarticulated sounds. Within this section of the program among the misarticulated alternatives were representations of all the possible misarticulations of the sound. Each of the 11 programs underwent repeated tests and revisions using the automated equipment. This enabled gradual refinement of the programs in a way that would have been difficult without well-instrumented procedures to pinpoint ambiguity and sources of difficulty. After completion of the development of the programs, an alternative form of instrumentation was devised to make the programs more widely available (A. L. Holland, 1969). The New Century Audio-Frame-System with "Write and See" was employed (see Figure 3). In this system a small cassette recorder of a type readily available is used for the presentation of stimuli and a simple added circuit detects a tone recorded at the end of each frame and stops the cassette. A response button lights when the cassette stops and a press on this button presents the next frame. The student uses a response booklet with portions printed in an invisible ink and a special pen which reacts chemically with the ink on the booklet. An incorrect response produces a pale yellow, but a correct response produces a distinctly different dark brown.

Fig. 3.   Child using the New Century Audio Frame System. At the end of each frame the cassette stops and a white button at the lower right of the machine lights. When the child is ready to hear the next frame she presses this button to advance the tape.

In addition to providing a handy solution to the difficult problem of articulation therapy, the sound-discrimination program illustrates a process with wide potential educational application. The reason discrimination training influences production is that the subject acquires the ability to discriminate correct and incorrect productions of his own speech, enabling rapid correction and automatic reinforcement of correct productions. Many important educational tasks have this property. Examples include singing, drawing from copy (or arts and crafts generally), articulation in second languages, handwriting and English composition. Teaching production often requires one-to-one tutorial help to identify the adequacy of the response. The programmed speech therapy, however, suggests that any of these tasks might benefit from instrumented discrimination training which would provide the means for the automatic reinforcement of discriminably correct productions.

Audiometric measurement. Another instance in which training fine auditory discrimination is important is the audiological testing of nonverbal or retarded children. Much of the attention given this area is summarized in the proceedings of a conference dealing with the topic (Lloyd & Frisina, 1965). One of the papers given at that conference by Spradlin and Lloyd (1965) reported the use of operant techniques and instrumentation to evaluate hearing in profoundly retarded children who could not be reliably tested with the usual methods. Their apparatus was equipped with a Davis Universal Feeder allowing the delivery of a variety of foods as reinforcers. Prior to training, they determined which food—such as M & M's, popcorn, cereal—was reinforcing for each child. Standard programming equipment controlled the presentation of the auditory stimuli and reinforcement. The child's button press was reinforced in the presence of the discriminative stimulus (S^D), initially a 500 cycles per second (cps) tone paired with a light. After responding came under the control of the tone and the light, the light was gradually faded to establish the tone as the S^D. After tone control was established at 500 cps, other tones varying in frequency and amplitude were presented to assess the child's auditory sensitivity. With their instrumentation and procedures, Spradlin and Lloyd were able to set up clear-cut contingencies for reinforcement, establish stimulus control and use this control to test hearing of children who could not be tested in other ways.

Compressed speech. An instance in which the emphasis is not so much on training to improve discrimination but on modifying the sensory input to increase efficiency is found in work on time compression of speech or *speeded speech.* Interest in speeding the presentation of the spoken word originated with the military problem of the overcrowding of the channels of communication to pilots. A number of methods to change the speed of speech have been developed. The simple direct changing of playback speed results in a change in pitch which severely limits the amount of time compression that can be used without loss of comprehension. Of the several electronic

devices developed to provide time compression of the spoken messages without changing frequencies, the most practical device involves a tape recorder with a rotating pickup head. As a recording is put through this device it is re-recorded by the rotating pickup head over only a part of the circumference of the rotary head. Thus, small sections of the original recording are omitted with regularity. The omitted segments are only a few hundredths of a second duration and therefore leave some of every phoneme intact. It has been shown (Jester & Travers, 1967; Orr, 1971) that speech may be compressed by 50 percent with no significant loss in comprehension. Although in a conventional classroom with its all too frequent custodial function, speeded presentations may not have a high priority. Nevertheless, it should be possible to increase the amount of material covered in a given day or to shorten the time students must spend in listening to lectures, thereby opening the way for more individualized activities or shortened school days. The technique also has potential use in later reviews of lecture material. The college student should find edited and time–compressed tapes useful before examination periods. One of the most interesting possibilities (Foulke, 1971) is in the presentation of verbal material to blind students who lack the use of the faster information channel of reading.

Tactual Discrimination

One of the more fascinating cases of instrumentation with implications for educational research is found in attempts to communicate through the skin (Geldard, 1968). His work is an ideal example of the development of basic research and the extension of that basic research into the solution of a practical problem. Years of research by Geldard and his associates on the psychophysics of the sensitivity of the skin to vibratory stimuli revealed the basic dimensions of vibratory stimulation suitable for a communication system through the skin.

Almost all of this research was supported by the military because of their interest in an alternate communication system for pilots whose eyes and ears were overtaxed. However, the potential for special education problems of such a communication system, especially with deaf children, is high but unfortunately will probably go unfulfilled until one finds a society not only sufficiently affluent but also with humanitarianism as a high priority. The original basic research on vibratory sensitivity used considerable instrumentation in the form of electrical amplifiers, electronic control circuits and electrically operated mechanical vibrators. The differential thresholds for duration, frequency, intensity and location of the stimuli were intensively studied. The first actual communication system developed by Geldard, *vibratese,* used a combination of five vibrators on the chest, three durations (short, medium and long) and three intensities (weak, medium and strong) as the basis for a 45-unit code. Subjects were able to receive an alphabetic code at a speed limited by the speed of the equipment itself and at about twice the proficiency of Morse code reception.

Later, with the development of a more compact, powerful vibrator, a new code was developed, the *optohapt alphabet,* with nine vibrators placed on the arms, torso and legs of the body and a system using typed copy in which each typed character was electronically scanned and transmitted from left to right in the representative spatial temporal pattern directly to the body. There was a nine-photocell scanner which scanned each letter from left to right. These were passed from nine photo amplifiers onto the nine photo-sensitive relays. From there impulses passed to the vibrators so that a "picture" of each letter moved across the body from left to right and subjects were able to "read" the transmitted letters. They did even better when a new character code was put into the typewriter with symbols that were more discriminable than the normal alphabet.

Consider the possibilities of yet another code, one based on the spoken phonics picked up by a microphone, put through a speech analyzer and, assuming the increasingly available integrated transistor circuits, transformed into code using the differing duration, intensity and location of stimulation. Perhaps then the age-old dream of the deaf hearing through their skin could become a reality. While this suggestion somewhat taxes the current technology, such a system should be possible in the near future.

ROTE ASSOCIATIONS

When all of the stimuli in a given domain have been well discriminated and all of the needed responses well differentiated, there may remain a problem in the association between stimuli and responses. A single individual association of this sort is easily learned and in most educational problems rote association has little if any role to play. When such problems do arise, there is a rich literature from the verbal learning laboratories. The principal problem in learning rote associations is interference among new associations. Hence, the length of the list of items to be learned is a major consideration, and similarity between stimuli and responses is a major variable leading to interferences among the elements. Spaced practice decreases such interference and hence becomes important when many rote associations must be learned. In most educational settings new associative elements should be few and, where necessary, new associations can usually be spaced so that the literature on rote association is seldom relevant. There are occasional exceptions to this such as learning the typewriter keyboard in beginning typing, some aspects of initial reading, and learning the alphabet.

A very worthwhile and well-designed example of the use of paired associate learning is illustrated in a program which teaches typing to beginners (Robins & Reed, 1958). They use a phonograph and a typewriter in which all of the keys are covered so that the subject never associates the letter name with a visual position. The subject begins with his fingers on the home keys and is taught just four keys at first, practices these for a while, then adds two more keys to his repertoire. Designed into the program are many required rest pauses and a gradual pyramiding of the number of letter-name–finger movement (striking a key) associates. Robins and Reed keep the number of new associations low while the student practices the old associations. The subject quickly learns keying to proficiency.

Another task which takes a rote form is a drill and practice type of computer-assisted instruction. Suppes (1966) described such a procedure in drilling students in arithmetic problems. A problem is presented to the subject on a cathode ray screen such as, $(6 \times 8) + 10 = \underline{\quad}$. The student responds using a teletype keyboard and types in the numerical answer. If the student's answer is wrong, it is indicated to him and the question is repeated. If a second error is made, the statement of error is followed by the printing of the correct answer. The problem is then repeated for a third time. The student may copy the correct answer. The computer then provides the next question. An elaboration on this procedure in spelling drills (Block, 1971) has the computer select differentially from the set of words, depending upon the subject's performance on the words. Hence, the words which he consistently spells correctly do not reappear while he is more frequently drilled on the words with which he has difficulty. Although the limited role found in education for rote learning limits the usefulness of drill and practice, the studies are valuable as explorations into computer control of research in learning.

The computer also has been used in some fundamental rote-learning research. Maitland (1971) explored the hypothesis that in learning a serial list of words the student imposes his own organization when he attempts to recall all the words on the list regardless of order. A random-access audio device under computer control repeated the list between free recall trials in the subject's own order on every trial. Judd and Glaser (1969) also used a computer in a rote-association experiment exploring the possibility of using latencies as a principle for branching in a computer program instead of errors. They had subjects press as quickly as possible one of a set of keys corresponding to the appropriate syllable. The results suggested that latencies might be useful but the number of variables affecting latencies makes their use difficult for this purpose. It is ironic that one of the highest levels of instrumentation, the computer, has found a useful role in research involving one of the most elementary and simplest aspects of basic psychology, rote learning.

MIXED CASES: DISCRIMINATION, RESPONSE DIFFERENTIATION AND ASSOCIATIVE LEARNING

In many of the more challenging teaching problems, the tasks are not neatly divided into discrimination, response differentiation and rote association. The problem rather represents a mix of functional categories. Language or reading are examples of such a mix. In learning a language the student must learn auditory discriminations for the sounds of the language, visual discriminations for the pattern of printed characters, higher level discriminations like discrimination of syntactic characteristics, and also various associations like grapheme-phoneme correspondences in reading. He must learn vocabulary words for objects and relationships. He must undergo response shaping for production of sounds and for writing.

Language Teaching

In research spanning all aspects of language teaching the equipment needs to be highly flexible. Garvey, Johansen, and Noblitt (1967) made good use of an extremely flexible machine, the Portable Laboratory

System (Figure 4) distributed by Appleton-Century-Crofts publishing company. In Figure 4 one can see the subject's console and the control unit. The subject faces a console with a viewing area slightly smaller than an IBM card. This area is divided into four window-keys behind which material printed on cards appears automatically. The windows can also serve as response areas. Beneath three of the windows are three button-operated electric switches which may also be illuminated. To the right is an opening to a reel of paper tape

quirements can differ from frame to frame. A few examples from the French program will illustrate the flexibility of the equipment. In teaching auditory discrimination the tape player presents a word or phrase, the alternative windows light up indicating that they would react to a press, under the windows is a card with the numbers 1 and 2, the subject presses one of these windows and hears either the same word or phrase or a mispronunciation of the word or phrase. After listening to both as many times as he wishes, he indicates his choice

Fig. 4.   Components of the New Century Portable Laboratory System. At the left is the student's console with four response windows, three response buttons and a write-in area at the right of the console. Alongside the console is a microphone with a voice-operated relay for vocal responses. At the right is the logic unit which controls all phases and operations.

for write-in responses. A microphone with a signal light around it serves to record the voice and operate a voice-operated relay. A tape player is capable of presenting four different messages with each frame. For all of the presentations, the features and response possibilities are controlled by the logic unit, which consists of circuits based on small quiet relays and an interchangeable plugboard for changing the nature of operation of the equipment. Each stimulus card contains a punched-hole code which operates photocells that indicate to the logic circuit which alternative is correct and what mode of operation is called for on the particular card.

With this flexible machine, response re-

by pressing one of the two buttons beneath the windows. If he is correct, he hears confirmation in the form of an appropriate French sentence. If he is incorrect he hears a buzzer and the original stimulus is represented and he must choose again. After finally answering correctly, he hears the usual confirmation and the machine presents the previous item. In a "production" frame a printed French sentence or phrase appears in the left window with an oral instruction such as "Transform to negative," the light on the microphone then comes on and after the student has formulated his response he speaks into the microphone. The voice-operated relay in the microphone signals the logic unit when speech is occurring and when it has ended. When the subject's response is completed, it is confirmed by audio presentation of the correct form and the program advances to the next frame. The next frame might be a visual discrimination frame. In that case, the card in the left window shows perhaps a question written in French, the alternative windows indicate written French answers. For example, the choice between a masculine or feminine answer could hinge on the ending of a word in the question. Lights appear on the alternative windows and the student presses a window to indicate his chosen answer. If the choice is incorrect, a buzzer indicates an error and feedback is presented by the tape, for instance, "The spelling tells you that it must be a man." The student then chooses again. If the answer is correct, he hears confirmation in the form of a complete sentence answering the question and, after the microphone lights, the student repeats the confirmation sentence. Thus the Portable Laboratory System allows many contingent relationships between the types of stimuli and the types of response requirements. With such adequate and flexible instrumentation, Garvey, Johansen and Noblitt (1967) were not only able to produce a French program and a procedure readily transferable to other settings but also to contribute to the process of language teaching. The program was intended to serve as a prototype for future language programs.

The Portable Laboratory System resulted from considerable collective experience of many who had worked with instrumentation in educational research, but Mace (1967) was responsible for much of the development of the equipment and has described the scenario of his "cut-and-try" experiences in the evolution of the Portable Laboratory System. His attempts to program English as a second language determined the features of the equipment. He described his experiences beginning with a simple carousel projector and coordinated tape recorder and, over a period of years, extending the

equipment to obtain greater control over the necessary response contingencies. After various tryouts with Chinese students learning English in his program, he gradually modified his equipment, adding stimulus lights to windows, adding the voice-operated relay and so forth until the details of the Portable Laboratory System were gradually shaped by interaction among the equipment, the experimental subjects and Mace, the modifier of the equipment. His scenario is characteristic of the evolution of instrumentation in any new and difficult area.

Reading

Reading is another skill in which the functional categories of learning are mixed. One instrument used in teaching beginning reading is the well-known "talking typewriter," first introduced in filmed reports (Moore & Anderson, 1960) which described a few children who learned to read using a typewriter with an adult sitting beside it. When the child struck a key, the adult said its letter name. Later the adult gave the phonic sound of the letter. In another phase a projector presented letters which the child matched by striking the appropriate key. In this phase the adult operated a hand switch to cut off the power to the typewriter if the child was about to strike an inappropriate key. The child moved on to words and sentences with the adult using the hand switch to cut off the power when needed and continuing to say the letter sounds or to pronounce the word. While this procedure seemed to have taught some very young children (around age four) to read, experimental controls were not in effect and the film reporting was not sufficiently detailed to permit one to ascertain which elements of the described procedures were effective.

Later a fully automated instrument was developed in which the letter name or appropriate sounds were produced automatically when a key was struck. This instrument, the Edison Responsive Environment, was experimentally evaluated at New York University's Institute for Developmental Studies (Richardson & McSweeney, 1970). The procedure was found seriously deficient for the teaching of reading and most particularly as an analytic research device. Richardson and McSweeney carried out a detailed analysis of the deficiencies of the instrument. When the child was freely exploring the keyboard in the first phase of the procedure, a press on any key produced the appropriate sound. This procedure was presumed to teach the associative relationship between the letter name and the visual letter form. But they pointed out that there was absolutely no contingent relationship between spoken sound and printed letter as far as the child was concerned. He did not need to attend to either; his task was to strike the keys. If he looked at the letter he was doing it on his own. To the extent that children learn such associations, and Richardson and McSweeney find many deficient in this regard, they do so not because of a controlled, instrumented procedure. The same criticism applies, of course, when sound-symbol correspondences are taught. In the third phase, when the child is expected to type material corresponding to the visually presented words or letters, the keyboard locks when he attempts to strike anything but a correct letter. They pointed out that a child can hunt until he finds the letter which is unlocked and finally type a perfect message without attending to either the presented material or the letter forms on the keys. Moreover, there is nothing in this procedure which requires any form of print-to-oral association since the tasks can be done by visual matching. It is possible, of course, that with a teacher present and with children already having the prerequisite discrimination skills which are not appropriately taught by this equipment, the talking typewriter might be a useful teaching aid. However, it is significant that it was only after the procedure was instrumented that its deficiencies were discovered; until then

the procedure seemed to work. But the matter of the necessary intervention of the adult is not identifiable.

Another approach to research on the teaching of reading is found in the Stanford research project on computer-assisted instruction (Atkinson, 1968) which uses the IBM-1500 instructional system. The system includes a cathode ray tube which can present alphanumeric characters, a random-access audio device which can present messages ranging in length from a few seconds to more than 15 minutes, and a light pen for student responses. When the light pen is placed on the cathode-ray tube, the coordinates of the touch are sensed and conveyed to the computer. A typical item from the reading program is presented in Figure 5. Part A is the main line item. If the child, on hearing "Touch and say the word that belongs in the empty cell," touches "ran" with his light pen, he is correct and moves on to Part D, which is simply a confirmation frame. If he touches any of the other alternatives, it is taken as a diagnosis that he needs work on initial consonants, final consonants or both. If he needs work on initial consonants he is branched to Part B; for the final consonants, Part C; and for both he is exposed in turn to both B and C. In any case, after a corrective branch he is returned to A, the initial item. Information on the nature of the subject's response is stored. The computer is a particularly useful device in giving good summaries of data following such experimental treatment.

The procedure has difficulties similar to those of the talking typewriter. These are not, however, intrinsic to the computer as a presentation device but rather to the program. If the program is analyzed in terms of the contingencies which must be met in completing the illustrated item in Figure 5, it can be seen that in Part A the subject can respond on the basis of a simple visual match once he is familiar with this item type, picking the alternative which matches all of the elements above with no reference to the sounds of the elements. (There is no

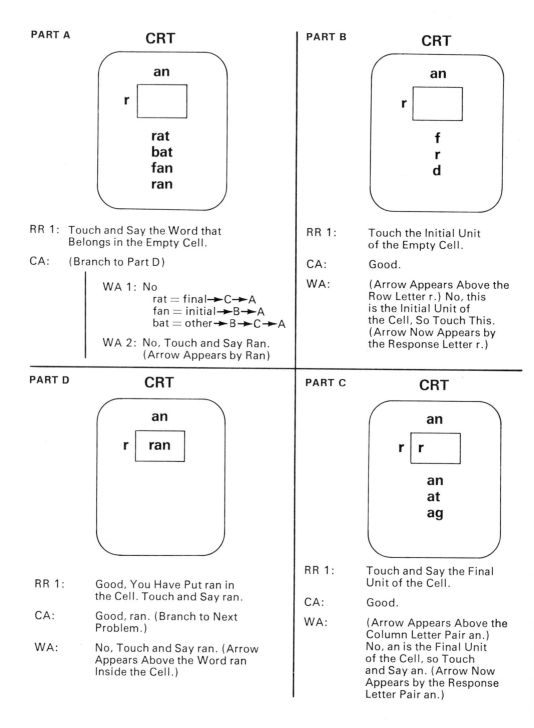

PART A

CRT

an

r ▢

rat
bat
fan
ran

RR 1:   Touch and Say the Word that
Belongs in the Empty Cell.

CA: (Branch to Part D)

WA 1: No
rat = final→C→A
fan = initial→B→A
bat = other→B→C→A

WA 2: No, Touch and Say Ran.
(Arrow Appears by Ran)

PART B

CRT

an

r ▢

f
r
d

RR 1:   Touch the Initial Unit
of the Empty Cell.

CA: Good.

WA: (Arrow Appears Above the
Row Letter r.) No, this
is the Initial Unit of
the Cell, So Touch This.
(Arrow Now Appears by
the Response Letter r.)

PART D

CRT

an

r ran

RR 1:   Good, You Have Put ran in
the Cell. Touch and Say ran.

CA: Good, ran. (Branch to Next
Problem.)

WA: No, Touch and Say ran. (Arrow
Appears Above the Word ran
Inside the Cell.)

PART C

CRT

an

r r

an
at
ag

RR 1:   Touch and Say the Final
Unit of the Cell.

CA: Good.

WA: (Arrow Appears Above the
Column Letter Pair an.)
No, an is the Final Unit
of the Cell, so Touch
and Say an. (Arrow Now
Appears by the Response
Letter Pair an.)

Fig. 5.   An item from the Stanford Reading Program (from Atkinson, 1968, p.229).

provision for monitoring the vocal response of the subject.) Should he make an error at this point and branch to either Part B or C he again can make a simple visual match without reference to the sounds of the letters in the word. When he eventually gets Part A correct and goes to Part D, he at least is exposed (now for the first time) to the sound of the word and even should he follow the instructions and actually repeat the word, there is no assurance that he will attend to the letter forms; his only required task is touching the center of the square with a light pen. In other words, while children may learn from this procedure through essentially unprogrammed or incidental learning, attention to sound-symbol relationships is not a reinforcement contingency in this procedure. Moreover, the chance level of responding on some of these items is one in four or one in three. We estimate, on the basis of the published data, that the poorest subject performed at chance level while the best subject performed at a near perfect level, but we have no way of knowing whether this child came to school already knowing how to read. The median subject was disappointingly halfway between these two extremes. But aside from the individual deficiencies in the program itself, the computer provides an extremely flexible device when coupled with appropriate student interface devices. The same equipment used by Atkinson, for example, could be a suitable substitute for the Portable Laboratory System which did an excellent job in teaching French (Garvey, Johansen, & Noblitt, 1967). The potential of good instrumentation for the analysis of the instructional process in teaching complex skills like reading and language is considerable.

Textual Material and the Write-in Machine

The popular view of a teaching machine is an instrument that presents short, incomplete statements with provision for the student to write an answer and then receive confirmation as to the correctness of the answer. Most of the early machines following Skinner's initial writing were of this type. Since much of what is traditionally taught in schools is textual, write-in machines could be very useful. The affluent educators in industry and the military have often used write-in machines, but the schools have used programmed texts due to economic considerations. Also, much debate has centered around whether write-in machines are useful for classroom presentation of material (cf. Stolurow & Davis, 1965). Most opponents of machines in the classroom have nevertheless considered machines appropriate in research where a greater degree of control is required for meaningful results. But even in the classroom the machine provides a useful function in controlling the contingencies required for the response. In programmed material the subject must read carefully, then think about or solve some problem in order to reach a correct answer. He fails to perform the critical behavior being taught when he reaches the correct answer for inappropriate reasons, as by peeking ahead at the answer or glancing at other items.

A procedure for determining the response contingencies is the blackout technique (J. G. Holland, 1967). All material in an item judged to be unnecessary for the correct answer is covered with black crayon. For instance, a long item in a statistics program describing combinations and permutations ended in the expression, "$3 \times 2 \times 1 = \underline{\quad}$." The blackout technique covered up many lines of material except this brief expression. Students had no difficulty, of course, providing the answer "6" without having read the rest of the item containing the information to be taught. The program, incidentally, was used in a study which failed to find an advantage for teaching machines. To determine if the blackout is valid, the error rates of subjects using blacked-out items are compared with the error rates of subjects using unchanged material. Kemp and J. G. Holland (1966) demonstrated that, for materials lacking appropriate response contingencies, there is no advantage for overt responding; similarly there would be no reason to expect machines to be important when there is no contingent relationship between reading or understanding the material and answering questions (nor is there much point in using such a program). However, they demonstrated that when such contingent relationships do exist, overt responding is superior and, therefore, machine use should be important to protect against misuses which bypass the work necessary to attain a correct answer. The control offered by write-in machines is needed not only in research but in the classroom as well when well-prepared programs are used.

The experimental control with machine presentation enables a thorough analysis of teaching materials. Regardless of whether the final form is programmed, the gathering of detailed information on each item provides the data for diagnosing and correcting the deficiencies in the material. Item data are important in the initial testing and revision of a program. An illustration of the improvement made possible by item

data is shown in Figure 6, which presents frequency distributions of error rates on three successive versions of a program. For each item a tally was made of the number of students missing the item and for each student a profile was made of his errors. These data permitted the detailed diagnosis of ambiguous items, of mistaken assumptions of the subject's previous knowledge, and of other sources of student confusion and error. In the figure, sizable improvement is shown between the first version and the second version of the program, and additional improvement by the third version. If teachers in training attempted programs, evaluated them with data, and modified procedures following analysis of the data, their teaching should improve greatly. Textbooks or other materials can similarly be tested in this manner quite aside from whether they will be subsequently published as programs.

Machine presentation adds greater precision to final validation data as well. Any program and most other educational materials should undergo thorough evaluation prior to any large-scale dissemination. Such

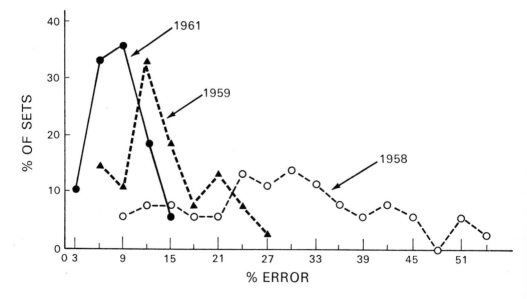

Fig. 6.   Frequency distributions for the error rates on three successive versions of a psychology program. Raw frequencies were converted to percentages to equate the areas under the curves.

evaluation should follow experimental procedures; published validation data should include a description of the population used, a complete description of the test instruments, performance on the tests and time required to complete the material (cf. J. G. Holland, 1961; Lumsdaine, 1965). When, in addition, the material is used in a well-instrumented form with adequate control of extraneous factors, the results are more precise. If another person replicates the described conditions including the machine use, he should obtain the same results. Validation data from machine presentations provide measurements comparable to those expected for many technological products like audio equipment, automobiles, and other physical equipment in which input-output characteristics can be precisely specified or for which a list of physical and operating characteristics can be obtained. Preparation of such specifications for programs requires the careful control made possible by machines.

The most important use of instrumentation for textual material is in the investigation of variables in teaching such material. A science of instruction for textual learning requires the same precision and care in the control of conditions as science in other areas. Elsewhere there has been a review of a sizable body of research on variables involved in programmed instruction, primarily of a textual nature (J. G. Holland, 1965).

BEHAVIOR MODIFICATION

In applications of the experimental analysis of behavior a variety of different terms is used to describe what is basically the same process. *Programmed instruction* has been discussed above. Other areas of behavior control are variously termed *contingency management, behavior modification,* or *behavior therapy.* Their fundamental principles and procedures are similar. They all begin with a behavioral analysis of the desired change followed by the design of contingencies of reinforcement. Usually it is

necessary to arrange for a gradual progression of the reinforcement contingencies and, if stimulus control is involved, for the appropriate presentation of stimulus conditions under which responses will be reinforced. But the term *behavior modification* is usually reserved for the change of non-academic behavior, the change of relatively gross behavior or styles of behavior such as deportment of a classroom or correction of alcoholism. Several applications discussed earlier might be classified behavior modification, but there are no underlying distinctions among the areas. Ironically, the area normally referred to as behavior modification or contingency management usually arranges contingencies with less precision and makes relatively little use of instrumentation.

Schwitzgebel (1970) made a strong case for instrumenting behavior modification to ensure the proper and lasting impact of useful behavior modification procedures. He pointed to such old, entrenched behavior-modification devices as the traffic light, the parking meter and the clock. He urged the psychologist-inventor not only to find solutions to important problems but also to insure the transmission of these solutions into the culture by designing instrumentation embodying the solution.

There has been much interest in recent years in behavior modification in educational settings. Although the work is still relatively limited, we can look forward in future years to a sizable increase in activity in this area. Moreover, we will see an increase in precision and an increase in the use of instrumentation.

An illustration of behavior modification in the classroom using simple instrumentation is provided in research on increasing the visual attention of deaf children to ongoing classroom work in a school for the deaf (Craig & Holland, 1970). The deaf child learns in the classroom only through vision. He must orient toward the teacher if the teacher is making a presentation or orient toward his books and paperwork when that is appropriate. In their baseline data, Craig and Holland found that the children in a seven-child classroom spent only about 20 percent of their time oriented toward the teacher or their paperwork. This measurement was made by sampling each child repeatedly for 10-second periods and noting where they were orienting. Next, a contingency management procedure was instituted to reinforce the students' attending behavior. A small box with a red light and a counter was mounted in front of each child. A hand switch held by an observer could operate each of these individually. Each child was sampled in turn and repeatedly throughout the hour session. The observer watched an individual child for 10 seconds and if, during that period, the child showed proper visual orientation, either toward the teacher or toward paperwork, the hand switch was pressed, the light flashed and the counter operated. At the end of the class hour the points on the counter entitled the subject to an equal number of M & M's. Proper attending behavior increased quickly to about 90 percent of the time.

This demonstration of behavior modification illustrates the basic elements of all such procedures. An explicit, identifiable behavior was designated (orienting toward the teacher); a procedure was established for identifying when the behavior was occurring (an observer sampled for 10-second periods); and a reinforcement procedure was established (operation of the light and the counter). In this instance the instrumentation was quite primitive but nonetheless adequate for the task. The adequacy of instrumentation in contingency management work most often depends on the adequacy with which the response is measured.

Monitoring and Feedback— Gross Behavior

Some methods of recording responses have now become so commonplace that they seldom merit mentioning and therefore are seldom more than casually noted in research papers. These include the use of a microphone in a room, and the use of TV monitoring, which are very often used for passive observation and perhaps as passive data-recording devices for subsequent analysis in a more formal fashion.

Microphones, audio amplifiers, TV monitors and similar monitoring devices also have been used to provide feedback. One of the earlier uses of the tape recorder was in self-therapy (Shor, 1955). Patients sitting alone talked into a recorder and later listened to their tapes. Slack (1959) extended this procedure with an "automated interviewing machine." With this machine the therapist monitored the recording and provided feedback with an electrical counter. Slack was able to monitor four therapy sessions simultaneously. Except for this gain in efficiency, there is no reason to believe that this procedure is superior to face-to-face work between therapist and client where reinforcement procedures have been frequently used but have not been instrumented.

A simple nonelectronic device potentially useful for feedback either to the teacher or to the student was developed by Montor (1970). His device, the United States Naval Academy Student-Response Monitor, has two major parts—an instructor's console and a student's response unit. The console, about the size of an average textbook, lists the students' names, and next to each name are five lights corresponding to potential answers. The student's response unit is a hand-held device with which the student can select one of five lettered positions. During an ongoing classroom presentation the instructor inserts questions to check whether the students are learning. This not only keeps the students alert but also gives the instructor feedback as to the adequacy of the presentation. The device also permits the student to communicate doubts or misconceptions privately while the presentation is underway. When it is used for formal examination, questions are reviewed one by one as they are answered.

Feedback can also be broadcasted to an

individual student through a small speaker worn in the ear. Recently, Vogel (1970) used an auditory feedback system in teaching group discussions. She was interested in improving small group discussion through individualized feedback which would not disrupt the group. The instructor monitored the discussion by means of a microphone placed in the center of the discussion group. While she watched and listened from a nearby sound-proof booth, the instructor could speak to any one of the students through that student's earphone. Thus, she could reinforce or prompt students with none of the other students hearing. A similar need is fulfilled by an inexpensive portable radio communication device to monitor teacher trainees during classroom instruction. Herold, Ramirez, and New-kirk (1971) transmitted voice messages by a miniature broadcasting unit using a transistorized FM radio and a small earphone. The system was free of wires, unobtrusive and portable. While the trainee conducted class, the observer gave guidance or provided feedback for the trainee's behavior. Thus reinforcement for adequate teaching behavior could be immediate without interrupting the class. The miniaturization of components which is currently undergoing rapid development makes possible such small, unobtrusive systems. A receiving unit can fit into a shirt pocket and the trainer's transmitter can be held easily in the hand or attached to the trainer's clothing.

A similar technique has been used in therapeutic situations (Sanders, 1966). A wire loop antenna circled the room. A patient in this area wearing a "behind the ear" type receiver heard the comments of the therapist with little sound leakage and without wires or large earphones. Sanders has used this system to supervise trainees during interviewing and testing and also with parents interacting with their children during play therapy sessions. Patterson, Jones, Whittier, and Wright (1965) have used this "bug-in-the-ear" device with a hyperactive child in the classroom. They differentially reinforced the child for sitting still during class by presenting a buzz through the earphone that indicated he had earned a piece of candy. The reinforcement was unobtrusive and unknown to other children in the room. Both the hyperactive child and other children received candy earned by this method, hence providing not only direct and immediate reinforcement to the hyperactive child sitting still but also insuring a supportive environment from the other children.

Video tape has also been used to provide feedback. Stoller (1967) taped group therapy sessions with schizophrenic patients and played them back as a basis for discussing with the patients the significant aspects of the group interaction. Similar classroom uses should be rewarding, especially for training in drama and speech or in teacher training. There is a report of the use of televised observation of classroom activities for purposes of data collection (Stukát & Engström, 1967). The total classroom was covered by three TV cameras and a set of microphones. Later they took time samples and classified the various forms of teacher and pupil behavior. This is an instance of useful passive recording, but the possibilities for using the procedure in a contingency management system should be apparent.

An interesting use of TV was provided by Lindsley's (1969) use of video and audio tapes separately in what he has termed *conjugate reinforcement*. The patient could continue viewing a therapist on video tape and continue hearing his voice on recorded audio tape only by pressing keys. The video and audio tapes each tended to fade at a rate that would make them disappear in a few seconds if there were no response. Responding maintained the intensity of the signals. Hence Lindsley could assess the reinforcing value of the voice or the view of the therapist. Similarly Lindsley (1964) evaluated the reinforcing value to an infant of a motion picture of his mother or father smiling. Movement on the part of an infant maintained the intensity of a projector light during the movie sequence.

MONITORING AND FEEDBACK—
SUBTLE RESPONSES

Within physiological psychology a voluminous literature has accumulated on measures which reflect some aspects of arousal, attention, emotion and affect. The knowledge and techniques of this area have as yet been little exploited for classroom research. Possible measures of interest are the galvanic skin response which measures the skin resistance which decreases with state of arousal or emotion, evoked potential and other electroencephalographic phenomena which can assess arousal and emotional state, eye pupil dilation which can be used as an index of interest in visual phenomena, and eye movements which can be used as an index of selective attention to visual displays. The extensive basic data on such measures as well as the accelerating trend toward miniaturizing equipment and telemetering the resulting measurements provide provocative opportunities in the measurement or even the shaping of attention, alertness and affect in educational settings.

A few have tapped the possibilities of monitoring physiological indices of arousal and attention. Levonian (1967) measured galvanic skin response while students watched a traffic safety film and demonstrated that long-term retention was better on the test items related to those points in the film showing high arousal, that is, lowered skin resistance. Carus (1969) measured the galvanic skin response in student teachers while they viewed video tapes of their performances in the classroom. Skin resistance changes indicated responses to the tape that were not reflected in the student teachers' verbal reports.

But these two studies hardly begin to represent the possibilities of monitoring the student's arousal states in an unobtrusive way in ongoing classroom or other educational situations. The high development of the miniature transistorized circuits and the techniques of telemetering information open new opportunities for unobtrusive monitoring. Mackay (1969) has suggested extensions of bio-medical telemetry to psychology. Radio transmitters have been made so small that pill-sized transmitters can be swallowed by humans or animals. Such techniques are used to monitor a number of biological events such as internal temperature changes, muscular activity, and pressure phenomena. Other miniature transmitters unencumbered by wires can telemeter the EEG (electroencephalogram), the EMG (electromyogram) or the EKG (electrocardiogram). Moreover, miniature transmitters can transmit voice or other signals.

Imagine a child sitting on the floor near a TV monitor. He wears a lightweight helmet with a device which measures eye movements. A beam of light reflected from the child's cornea is superimposed through a visual system onto the image he is viewing and is transmitted by a light cable to a video recorder. Over the other eye is a device which samples pupil diameter and transmits over a cable to another video recorder. Electrodes attached to the child are connected to an amplifying device for measuring the galvanic skin response. The child views an experimental educational film, perhaps one similar to "Sesame Street." From his eye movements we quickly learn what the child looks at on the screen— whether, for example, he looks at the printed word appearing below the character saying the word in the skit. From the pupil diameter we estimate his interest in events as they happen, and from the galvanic skin response we get an index of his excitement during the events. A microphone picks up his vocalizations and from time to time questions are inserted which sample his comprehension of the materials. If this instrumentation is used in developing a film, the material could be changed until arousal and interest were optimal and attention focused on the educationally important points. All of the elements described in this scenario are technically feasible and should be useful in a laboratory investigation of the variables important in successful educational materials.

Imagine another setting—an open classroom with the room divided into areas for different activities such as reading, artwork, games and science. Children move freely about the room and spend time in any area. To obtain information about how a child distributes his time in the room, whether he samples all activities and for what duration of time, a small transmitter which transmits a low intensity signal from generators in each area of the room is attached to the subject. A graphing device gives a pictorial representation of how each child spends his day. Also a small microphone and transmitter can record and transmit his vocal interaction with other students. This scene is also possible, and with slightly larger transmitters and small antennae, considerably greater range than a classroom is feasible. Schwitzgebel (1969) has designed and carried out exploratory work with a special belt which allows two-way voice communication both to monitor a subject's voice and to provide simple physiological data, as well as to give feedback to the subject. The belt will work outside of a room in a small locale although with some difficulties. Attempts to remove the belt can also be determined. He has suggested that the belt might be useful in monitoring people with such medical problems as diabetes or epilepsy and that it could also be used to monitor the movements and activities of parolees. It has recently been estimated that it would be technically feasible to monitor several hundred individuals in a single city wearing such belts (Schwitzgebel, 1970).

SOCIAL CONSEQUENCES OF INSTRUMENTATION

Hopefully by this time the reader is worried about ethical problems raised by such monitoring devices. In fact the question of the ethics of behavior modification might have occurred very much earlier in this chapter. There are two major areas of ethical concern which greatly restrict the use one would like to see for such instrumentation or perhaps would lead one to argue against the experimental development of such techniques. The first area is the familiar ethical consideration of informed consent and lack of deception in the treatment of experimental subjects. There are many instances in which the investigator might feel that to reveal that he was observing through a TV monitor, listening in on conversation, or making galvanic skin response measurements might hamper the spontaneity of behavior or otherwise influence the events being recorded. Under these circumstances the temptation is very great to monitor the behavior secretly. It is probable today that people regularly slip behind one-way mirrors to observe students in experimental classrooms and tomorrow will find the TV monitor a convenient way to peek at the class. Should even such relatively benign spying be carried out without the informed consent of the students and teachers being observed? Many experiments require that the subject not know the objective of the study; in some instances, the results would be distorted if the subject knew what was being measured or even if anything was being measured. Consider 1) investigating classroom cheating, 2) investigating pupils' use of standard English with teachers and black dialect with peers, or 3) determining the position on a school sociogram with relation to the school drug market. These and many other situations seem to require secret surveillance; but such surveillance would be a serious breach of the ethical requirement of informed consent by the subject.

There is, nevertheless, a well-developed and growing technology dealing with just such secret surveillance which is used extensively by agencies of the federal and local governments and by numerous private companies. Westin (1970) has summarized the state of art in the invasion of privacy by describing a host of gadgets including cameras, radios and video recorders. Coin-sized radio transmitters easily planted in briefcases, pockets, cars and elsewhere track an individual's movements. Very small radio transmitters can transmit conversations over short distances. The "radio pill" can be substituted in bottles of antihistamines and, when swallowed, enable tracking of a person throughout the day. TV camera monitoring has become commonplace in apartment elevators, lobbies, subway cars, prison cell blocks, stores and even on street corners. Moreover, there are techniques for hiding TV cameras in rooms, including the use of fiberoptics which can transmit images around corners. Techniques perfected by the military enable surveillance even in darkness. Surveillance of speech over long distances requires antennae, and there are ingenious devices for hiding antennae in the seams of clothing and in the thread which stitches a coat. Receivers can be concealed in belts and belt buckles. Microphones and transmitters come disguised as a variety of common objects including water coolers, desk sets, clocks and ashtrays. Also, a variety of techniques has been perfected for bugging rooms that an agent cannot enter.

The contrast between the dearth of good instrumentation in classroom or educational settings and the sizable use of technical resources for surveillance of American citizens or third-world citizens suggests the second and more difficult area of ethical consideration. Scientists are becoming increasingly aware that they can no longer ignore the probable uses of their work. The technological innovations described in this chapter are often used for other than the socially worthy objectives that the developer had in mind. They are more often used in the interest and for the goals of those who have extensive resources such as large corporate interests or the military and their domestic supporting agencies involved in

civilian surveillance. Miller (1970), in expressing concern about the possible problems of psychotechnology, made a distinction between proximal psychotechnology and distal psychotechnology. In proximal psychotechnology, the psychologist is in direct contact with the recipient of the technology. In these instances there is usually an adherence to an ethical code which includes the informed consent of the client. However, the strength of instrumentation that has been discussed in this chapter involves Miller's distal psychotechnology in which the technological innovation is transmitted to nonprofessional users. Teaching machines, classroom monitoring procedures, instrumented classroom behavior modification, and polygraphs of electroencephalogram and galvanic skin responses are all examples of distal psychotechnology. The strength of instrumentation is the ability to transfer well-developed and effective procedures into use by virtue of embodying the procedures in an instrument. Because nonprofessionals are the main users, Miller pointed out that the code of ethics no longer protects the interests of individual citizens against the use of distal psychotechnology. He suggested, rather, a code of priorities in developing technology. One of the priorities is the relative distributability of the new technology. Miller said, "A technique is distributable to the extent that its use need not be restricted to some privileged elite, but can be used by the general public" (p. 997). He suggested that the danger is not in control but in its nearly exclusive use by a privileged minority. The technology which, by its nature, can only be used by such an elite should have lower priority than the technology which can be used universally; and universal access to such technology should be assured by law and by codes of ethics. In other words, he suggested that "you should not be able to do unto others what they are unable to do unto you" (p. 1000).

Meyer (1970) also is concerned about the ultimate use of behavioral science and technology. After an examination of the potential uses of a variety of scientific results, he concluded that, in modern American society, technological development is almost always in the hands of the state and the well-to-do and not equally available to the poor. He consequently felt that a radical cannot in good conscience continue his work. An examination of the distribution of educational technology would seem to support Meyer's more pessimistic view. Robert McNamara, speaking as Secretary of Defense at the annual convention of the Veterans of Foreign Wars in New York (McNamara, 1967), described the Defense Department's educational establishment as the largest educational complex in the world. It is certainly the best financed and most able to use educational technology. McNamara also described the Defense Department as the world's most efficient educator as a result of its extensive efforts in teaching techniques and innovations in educational technology. He described the extensive use of closed-circuit television in Defense Department training including an entire individual-training network.

Indeed, some of the more outstanding examples of ideal instrumentation and innovative psychotechnology discussed in this paper were prepared for the military. The extensive work of Geldard in communication through the skin was stimulated by military concerns. The most outstanding program in French, prepared by Kate Garvey, was done as a prototype program in language training for the Defense Department in the hope that other languages could be similarly programmed. Scientists who contributed to the development of programmed instruction prepared an extensive Vietnamese language program at the American Institutes for Research on contract with the CIA. A document by the United States Continental Army Command (1968) described some of the utilization of behavioral and social science research projects supported under contract by the military. This document contains many references to pro-

grammed instruction used in officer training and in noncommissioned officer training which cover such things as "Training of Leaders of Small Infantry Units" and "Basic Principles of Small Unit Tactics." Programs are described which also cover numerous skills from aerial photography to maintenance and use of machine guns. The psychologists at Human Resources Research Organization (HumRRO) worked to increase the soldiers' willingness to fire their weapons more frequently and effectively (HumRRO, 1969) to solve a problem from earlier wars in which it was found that only 25 percent of the men under actual combat conditions fired their weapons. The new psychologist-developed training program was able to overcome man's reluctance to kill, increasing the number now firing their weapons under combat conditions to 55 percent (Marshall, 1966). That we can look forward to instances in which the recipient of the technology, far from giving informed consent, will instead be an unwitting victim of the technology is revealed by a Rand Corporation document (Gordon & Helmer, 1964) which projected as a major weapon system the behavioral control of mass populations. In this paper it was estimated that such a weapons system would be operational before 1980. Indeed, the United States Continental Army Command document cited earlier listed a number of case studies of psychological intervention programs in a variety of countries including a title as old as 1959 on "Psychological Operations: Cambodia."

The area of surveillance and privacy of information illustrates who is likely to use technology. J. Edgar Hoover publicly revealed embarrassing information gained by bugging the hotel rooms of Martin Luther King. He did so with impunity. On the other hand, Daniel Ellsberg, who released the Pentagon papers to the public, faces trial with charges totaling a possible 114 years in prison. Those in power can and do (cf. Westin, 1970) use technology to their advantage in subjecting citizens to surveillance, while not only do citizens not have the resources and access required for surveillance of the government, but, if by chance they obtain such information, they are prosecuted for their troubles. Plant management can and does (Westin, 1970) use TV monitoring of employees on the job, again hardly an example of a "distributable" technology.

These are only a few random examples to point out that presently technology is in the service of wealth and power. There are a few voices pointing the way toward a technology for the people. Hoffman (1971) and Powell (1971) both described a range of possible uses of technology by today's activists and revolutionaries. Powell is especially good on simple bugging procedures, radio-jamming techniques, weapons and sabotage. Hoffman's greater range included how to set up legal or illegal radio and TV broadcasting stations. Possible uses of educational technology should be looked at in terms of Miller's principle of distributability. Illich (1971) raised the interesting possibility of the creation of nets of training and communication as quite serious alternatives to schools. The telephone network is for Illich the ideal example of a technological net in which individuals can communicate with other individuals. Among his many ideas for technology in a grass roots system of education is wide distribution of small cassette recorders (easily extended into cassette-based teaching machines) and access via learning centers to a variety of educational tapes selected freely by the individual, or even the creation of tapes by individuals for use by their peers. He contrasted this type of distribution with large educational TV networks being constructed in Latin American countries. In other words, educational technology theoretically could go either way. It could be widely distributable or highly centralized. A survey in *Forbes* (Tools for Teaching, 1968) of industries involved in the exploration of innovation in education showed that almost all are developing large, centralized,

instrumented procedures. The *Forbes* survey described the linking of entire school systems to centralized computers and the merging of publishing houses with electronic companies to bring together standardized hardware and software components of central computers.

The old rationalization of scientific neutrality—that scientific and technological developments can be used for either good or bad—is inadequate, considering the realities of today. At the least we should give priority to developments which have the possibility of being distributable, as Miller suggested. But more is needed. If we are not to close our labs as Meyer has, we must at least attempt to convey our findings and technological developments widely with guidance for their use by all.

REFERENCES

Allen, W. H. Audio-visual communication. In C. W. Harris (Ed.), *Encyclopedia of educational research.* (3rd ed.) New York: Macmillan, 1960. Pp. 115–137.

Atkinson, R. C. Computerized instruction and the learning process. *American Psychologist,* 1968, 23, 225–239.

Barson, J., & Mendelson, G. B. Holography—A new dimension for media. *Audio-visual Instruction,* 1969, 14, 40–42.

Bijou, S. W., & Baer, D. M. Some methodological contributions from a functional analysis of child development. In L. P. Lipsitt, & C. C. Spiker (Eds.), *Advances in child behavior and development.* Vol. 1. New York: Academic Press, 1963. Pp. 197–231.

Block, K. K. Computer-assisted instruction. In A. Kent & H. Lancour (Eds.), *Encyclopedia of library and information science.* Vol. 5. New York: Marcel Dekker, 1971. Pp. 515–538.

Brown, J. W., Lewis, R. B., & Harcleroad, F. F. *A-V instruction: Materials and methods.* (2nd ed.) New York: McGraw-Hill, 1964.

Carus, F. E. *The use of closed circuit television (video-tape) and psycho-galvanic response to increase the rate of change in student teachers' classroom performance.* (Doctoral dissertation, University of California, Berkeley) Ann Arbor, Mich.: University Microfilms, 1969. No. 69–14,810.

Chu, G. C., & Schramm, W. *Learning from television: What the research says.* Stanford, Calif.: Stanford University, Institute for Communication Research, 1967.

Cornsweet, T. N. *The design of electric circuits in the behavioral sciences.* New York: Wiley, 1963.

Craig, H. B., & Holland, A. L. Reinforcement of visual attending in classrooms for deaf children. *Journal of Applied Behavior Analysis,* 1970, 3, 97–109.

Fitzhugh, R. J., & Katsuki, D. The touch-sensitive screen as a flexible response device in CAI and behavioral research. *Behavior Research Methods and Instrumentation,* 1971, 3, 159–164.

Foulke, E. The perception of time compressed speech. In D. L. Horton, & J. J. Jenkins (Eds.), *The perception of language.* Columbus, Ohio: Charles E. Merrill, 1971. Pp. 79–107.

Garvey, C. J., Johansen, P. A., & Noblitt, J. S. A report of the developmental testing of a self-instructional French program. Washington, D.C.: Center for Applied Linguistics, 1967.

Geldard, F. A. Body English. *Psychology Today,* 1968, 2(7), 42–47.

Glaser, R., & Cooley, W. W. Instrumentation for teaching and instructional management. In R. M. W. Travers (Ed.), *Handbook of research on teaching.* Chicago: Rand McNally, 1973.

Goldiamond, I. Stuttering and fluency as manipulatable operant response classes. In L. Krasner, & L. P. Ullman (Eds.), *Research in behavior modification.* New York: Holt, Rinehart and Winston, 1965. Pp. 348–407.

Gordon, T., & Helmer, O. *Report on a long-range forecasting study.* Santa Monica, Calif.: Rand Corporation, 1964.

Gropper, G. L. Learning from visuals: Some behavioral considerations. *AV Communication Review,* 1966, 14, 37–69.

Herold, P. L., Ramirez, M. III, & Newkirk, J. A portable radio communication system for teacher education. *Educational Technology,* 1971, 11(11), 30–32.

Hively, W. A multiple-choice visual discrimination apparatus. *Journal of the Experimental Analysis of Behavior,* 1964, 7, 387–389.

Hoffman, A. *Steal this book.* New York: Grove Press, 1971.

Holland, A. L. *Programmed auditory discrimination training for children who misarticulate.* Washington, D.C.: Office of Education, Bureau of the Handicapped, 1965. Sixteen-millimeter sound motion picture.

Holland, A. L. *Speech sound discrimination.* New York: New Century, 1969.

Holland, A. L., & Matthews, J. Application of teaching machine concepts to speech pathology and audiology. *Asha,* 1963, 5, 474–482.

Holland, J. G. Evaluating teaching machines and programs. *Teachers College Record,* 1961, 63, 56–65.

Holland, J. G. New directions in teaching machine research. In J. E. Coulson (Ed.), *Programmed learning and computer-based instruction.* New York: Wiley, 1962. Pp. 46–57.

Holland, J. G. Research on programing variables. In R. Glaser (Ed.), *Teaching machines and programed learning, II: Data and directions.* Washington, D.C.: National Education Association, 1965. Pp. 66–117.

Holland, J. G. A quantitative measure for programmed instruction. *American Educational Research Journal,* 1967, 4, 87–101.

Holland, J. G., & Doran, J. Teaching classification by computer. *Educational Technology,* in press.

Human Resources Research Organization (HumRRO). *Bibliography of publications.* Alexandria, Va.: HumRRO, September 1969.

Ihrke, W. R. A modular station for automated music training. *Educational Technology,* 1971, 11(8), 27–29.

Illich, I. *Deschooling society.* New York: Harper & Row, 1971.

Jester, R. E., & Travers, R. M. W. The effect of various presentation patterns on the comprehension of speeded speech. *American Educational Research Journal,* 1967, 4, 353–359.

Johnson, R. B. The effects of prompting, practice and feedback in programmed videotape. *American Educational Research Journal,* 1968, 5, 73–79.

Judd, W. A., & Glaser, R. Response latency as a function of training method, information level, acquisition and overlearning. *Journal of Educational Psychology Monograph,* 1969, 60(4), Part 2.

Kemp, F. D., & Holland, J. G. Blackout ratio and overt responses in programed instruction: Resolution of disparate results. *Journal of Educational Psychology,* 1966, 57, 109–114.

Kirchener, D. P. Antiguerrilla armament. *Ordnance,* 1971, 56, 127–130.

Levonian, E. Retention of information in relation to arousal during continuously-presented material. *American Educational Research Journal,* 1967, 4, 103–116.

Lindsley, O. R. Direct measurement and prothesis of retarded behavior. *Journal of Education,* 1964, 147, 62–81.

Lindsley, O. R. Direct behavioral analysis of psychotherapy sessions by conjugately programed closed-circuit television. *Psychotherapy: Theory, Research and Practice,* 1969, 6, 71–81.

Lloyd, L. L., & Frisina, D. R. (Eds.), *The audiologic assessment of the mentally retarded: Proceedings of a national conference.* Parsons, Kans.: University of Kansas Bureau of Child Research and the Parsons State Hospital and Training Center, 1965.

Lumsdaine, A. A. Assessing the effectiveness of instructional programs. In R. Glaser (Ed.), *Teaching machines and programed learning, II: Data and directions.* Washington, D.C.: National Education Association, 1965. Pp. 267–320.

Mace, L. The role of flexible laboratory equipment in verbal learning research. Paper presented at a colloquium at the Center for Research in Language and Language Behavior of the University of Michigan, Ann Arbor, Michigan, July 1967.

Mackay, R. S. Biomedical telemetry: Applications to psychology. *American Psychologist,* 1969, 24, 244–248.

Maitland, A. J. The effect of constancy in presentation order on word list acquisition in free recall. Unpublished doctoral dissertation, University of Pittsburgh, 1971.

Malmstadt, H. V., Enke, C. G., & Toren, E. C., Jr. *Electronics for scientists.* New York: W. A. Benjamin, 1962.

Marshall, S. L. A. *Men against fire.* (Rev. ed.) New York: William Morrow, 1966.

McNamara, R. S. World's largest school. *Training,* 1967, 4, 20–21.

Meyer, B. Can a radical be a scientist in our society? Paper presented at the meetings of the Eastern Psychological Association, Atlantic City, N.J., April 1970.

Miller, G. A. Assessment of psychotechnology. *American Psychologist,* 1970, 25, 991–1001.

Montor, K. Feedback, an aid to teaching. *Audiovisual Instruction,* 1970, 15(5), 89–90.

Moore, O. K., & Anderson, A. R. *Early reading and writing.* Pittsburgh: Basic Education, 1960. Sixteen-millimeter color and sound motion picture.

Orr, D. B. A perspective on the perception of time compressed speech. In D. L. Horton, & J. J. Jenkins (Eds.), *The perception of language.* Columbus, Ohio: Charles E. Merrill, 1971. Pp. 108–119.

Patterson, G. R., Jones, R., Whittier, J., & Wright, M. A. A behavior modification technique for the hyperactive child. *Behavior Research and Therapy,* 1965, 2, 217–226.

Powell, W. *The anarchist cookbook.* New York: Lyle Stuart, 1971.

Resnick, L. B., & Kiss, L. E. Discrimination training and feedback in shaping teacher behavior. Paper presented at the meeting of the American Educational Research Association, Minneapolis, March 1970.

Reynolds, J., & Millmore, M. Analysis of the teacher's role in individualized evaluation. Paper presented at the meeting of the American Educational Research Association, New York, February 1971.

Richardson, E., & McSweeney, J. An analysis of the E.R.E. "Talking Typewriter" as a device for teaching beginning reading skills. *Educational Technology,* 1970, 10(2), 81–88.

Robins, L., & Reed, H. *The living method typing course.* Long Island City, N.Y.: Crown, 1958.

Rohles, F. H., Jr. Operant methods in space technology. In W. K. Honig (Ed.), *Operant behavior: Areas of research and application.* New York: Appleton-Century-Crofts, 1966. Pp. 677–717.

Rohles, F. H. General instrumentation for the operant conditioning experiment. *American Psychologist,* 1969, 24, 250–254.

Sanders, R. A. The "Bug-in-the-ear": A device for training of clinical psychologists. Paper presented at the meeting of the Midwestern

Psychological Association, Chicago, May 1966.

Schrag, P. G., & Holland, J. G. Programming motion pictures: The conversion of a PSSC film into a program. *AV Communication Review*, 1965, 13, 418–422.

Schwitzgebel, R. L. A remote instrumentation system for behavior modification: A preliminary report. In R. D. Rubin, & C. M. Franks (Eds.), *Advances in behavior therapy, 1968*. New York: Academic Press, 1969. Pp. 1–9.

Schwitzgebel, R. L. Behavior instrumentation and social technology. *American Psychologist*, 1970, 25, 491–499.

Shor, R. E. Recorder self-therapy: A technique. *Journal of Counseling Psychology*, 1955, 2, 150–151.

Sidman, M., & Stoddard, L. T. Programming perception and learning for retarded children. In N. R. Ellis (Ed.), *International review of research in mental retardation*. Vol. 2. New York: Academic Press, 1966. Pp. 151–208.

Sidman, M., & Stoddard, L. T. The effectiveness of fading in programming a simultaneous form discrimination for retarded children. *Journal of the Experimental Analysis of Behavior*, 1967, 10, 3–15.

Sidowski, J. B. (Ed.) *Experimental methods and instrumentation in psychology*. New York: McGraw-Hill, 1966.

Sidowski, J. B. Buyer's guide. *American Psychologist*, 1969, 24, 309–384.

Skinner, B. F. *The behavior of organisms*. New York: Appleton-Century, 1938.

Skinner, B. F. The science of learning and the art of teaching. *Harvard Educational Review*, 1954, 24, 86–97.

Skinner, B. F. Why we need teaching machines. *Harvard Educational Review*, 1961, 31, 377–398.

Slack, C. W. An automatic interview machine for use in research, education, and psychotherapy. Unpublished manuscript, Harvard University, Department of Social Relations, 1959.

Spradlin, J. E., & Lloyd, L. L. Operant conditioning audiometry (OCA) with low level retardates: A preliminary report. In L. L.

Lloyd, & D. R. Frisina (Eds.), *The audiologic assessment of the mentally retarded: Proceedings of a national conference*. Parsons, Kans.: University of Kansas Bureau of Child Research and the Parsons State Hospital and Training Center, 1965. Pp. 45–58.

Stoller, F. H. Group psychotherapy on television: An innovation with hospitalized patients. *American Psychologist*, 1967, 22, 158–162.

Stolurow, L. M., & Davis, D. Teaching machines and computer-based systems. In R. Glaser (Ed.), *Teaching machines and programed learning, II: Data and directions*. Washington, D.C.: National Education Association, 1965. Pp. 162–212.

Stukát, K. G., & Engström, R. TV-observations of teacher activities in the classroom. *Pedagogisk Forskning*, 1967, 11, 96–117. Reprinted in A. Simon & E. G. Boyer (Eds.), *Mirrors for behavior*. Vol. 3. Philadelphia, Pa.: Research for Better Schools, 1970. Pp. 74.1–74.1–22.

Suppes, P. The uses of computers in education. *Scientific American*, 1966, 215(3), 206–220.

Tools for teaching. *Forbes*, 1968, 102, 38–44.

Touchette, P. E. Transfer of stimulus control: Measuring the moment of transfer. *Journal of the Experimental Analysis of Behavior*, 1971, 15, 347–354.

United States Continental Army Command. *Utilization of behavioral and social science research products*. CON Pam 70–1. Fort Monroe, Va.: U.S. Continental Army Command Headquarters, April 1968.

Uttal, W. R. Buggywhips, whalebones, and clipboards: Some notes on generating complex stimuli with small computers. *American Psychologist*, 1969, 24, 202–206.

Vogel, V. L. Teaching group discussion electronically. *Audiovisual Instruction*, 1970, 15(8), 67–69.

Weiss, B. Instrumentation for operant behavior research. *American Psychologist*, 1969, 24, 255–258.

Westin, A. F. *Privacy and freedom*. New York: Atheneum, 1970.

CHAPTER 10   Issues in the Analysis of Qualitative Data[1]

RICHARD J. LIGHT
Harvard University

Far better an appropriate answer to the right question, which is often vague, than an exact answer to the wrong question, which can always be made precise (Tukey, 1963, pp. 13–14).

My colleagues and statistics students sometimes seem a bit startled when I share with them my belief that data analysis is an art as much as it is a science. It must seem to them a bit incongruous that the same fellow who on one day interprets significance levels and suggests specific statistical techniques such as two-stage least squares should on another day question how "scientific" such a process is.

Yet this is an important question to raise. Those of us who spend time analyzing data sometimes do strange things. We first choose a model, often on the basis of its simplicity or tractability. Then, having fixed upon this model, we spend a great deal of time attempting to develop efficient and unbiased procedures which will assure the most sophisticated inferences possible from a set of data. Yet it should be well known that once a model has been chosen, a data analyst becomes a prisoner of the assumptions underlying that model. To give a frequently used example, the analyst who chooses a linear model to underlie his analysis will try various techniques to get a best "fit" of some observed data to this model; yet if the true relation among variables is not linear, this "best fit" still may not be very good. Even worse, a "fit" may be quite good and very misleading at the same time (cf. Himmelblau, 1970; Light, 1972).

Choosing a model to underlie the analysis of data can thus be viewed as either art or science; it depends largely upon the attitude of a particular researcher. Techniques exist for building directly into data analyses statistical procedures which discriminate

[1] Many colleagues have offered comments which helped to improve this manuscript. But I would like especially to thank those who helped with its actual development. Joan S. Bissell developed the section on iterative proportional fitting. Robert L. Brennan made contributions to the section on measuring agreement with no preassigned categories. Joe E. Crick performed many of the detailed computations. Finally, Paul V. Smith developed the material on combining 2×2 tables and on net weighted percentage differences, and he gave several critiques of earlier drafts. The discussion throughout this chapter includes many of his contributions.

Partial assistance for the preparation of this chapter was provided by a grant from the Spencer Foundation.

among competing models. These techniques can be viewed as relatively scientific. Yet by far the most common approach used by data analysts is first to choose a model, and then to try to obtain the best fit possible between a particular variation of this model and the data which are available. This is especially true in educational research where so little is known about the underlying processes involved in student learning, or about the interactions of student and teacher behavior. Here the initial selection of a model is unfortunately most often dictated by those techniques a researcher happens to know well or those techniques others have used with similar problems in the past.

I begin with this discussion because many researchers feel that if data which have a metric (i.e., continuous data) can be collected in a research effort, then these data are preferable to nonmetricized data (i.e., categorized data) which can be put into the format of a contingency table. In general, this is correct; data which have a scale can carry more information than categorized data on the same variable. But this general preference for scaled data has led to some excesses. Specifically, aspects of student and teacher behavior which have no obvious or necessarily correct scaling have been scaled by one means or another simply to fit one of the common techniques available for continuous measurements. The result is a double nonscience: the model chosen in the first place may be arbitrary, and even after the model has been chosen the variables are scaled or measured in an arbitrary manner. That is why I view some data analysis as art rather than science. A good analyst, who has insightful judgment both in selecting a model and scaling responses for different variables, can draw useful inferences from his research. A poor analyst, of course, cannot. This implies that when others read the results of a study of teacher effectiveness or school effectiveness, their confidence in the results may depend largely upon their confidence in the judgment of the particular researcher responsible for the study, and

not just the reported results themselves. More specifically, their confidence may be based upon how well, or how meaningfully, some of the variables in the study were scaled. Note that this problem of scaling is a different issue than taking measurements which are subject to error. Several studies (Cochran, 1968, 1970) have considered the implications of making specific kinds of measurement errors to common statistical procedures, such as regression analysis. I am concerned here, rather, with the case where measurement may be perfect once a variable has been scaled, but the scaling itself is open to question.

This problem of trying to fit human behavior to some metric is an important issue in data analysis, and especially so in educational research. More specifically, I believe that at the present time it often cannot and therefore should not be done. This implies that data on human behavior should instead be categorized into nominal scales, and that the analysis of this data should be based upon these nominal scales. In this chapter, I will present a number of techniques for data analysis which assume that measurements on variables fall into nominal categories. The presentation for each technique is organized so that a problem is first identified and then a measure or test statistic is discussed. Since this chapter is written for practicing researchers rather than professional statisticians, the mathematics will be kept to a minimum and the reader will be referred to other sources for details on the development of each procedure. Worked examples are provided as illustrations.

As an overview of what follows, the discussion will be divided into six parts. We begin in the first section by considering circumstances under which tables can be profitably used, and other circumstances when they can be badly misused. After distinguishing among alternative models for contingency tables, we then discuss in section two a variety of problems centered around the idea of measuring agreement, or reliability, for two or more observers.

These problems arise from situations particularly common to classroom observation, when the behavior of teachers and students is categorized. Subsumed under the general heading of agreement are special problems such as differentiating between level versus pattern of agreement, and distinguishing between "internal" group agreement versus agreement of an observer relative to a correct "standard."

The several techniques developed in the agreement section have a common underlying feature: they are based upon the analysis of *pairs* of responses. By simple counting of different kinds of paired responses, we are able to generate a wide variety of measures.

In the third section, we extend the simple pairs approach for nominal data to the problem of measuring statistical association between two or more variables. We consider the two and three variable cases in some detail. Test statistics are given for several independence hypotheses, and the behavior of these statistics is compared to that of the standard chi-square approach. We find that under some circumstances the statistics which come from a simple counting process are more powerful than the standard chi-square statistic.

In the fourth section a relatively simple geometric approach for comparing test statistics is presented. While the display techniques are developed in some detail to compare the pairs approach with the chi-square approach, these techniques are generalized to other statistical procedures.

In the fifth section we move to a set of specific problems which occur frequently in research on human subjects—problems involving dichotomous, nominal scale variables. A number of techniques are presented for analyzing 2×2 tables; for comparing them, combining them, rearranging them, and controlling for extraneous variables which might be influencing them. Examples from educational research problems are common here.

In the sixth and final section some new directions for research are proposed. The theme here is that any one of many social processes could "lead to" a particular set of data in a contingency table. Yet few procedures are currently available which enable a researcher to "go behind" a set of observed cell counts to better understand the model from which they arose. A rough scheme for beginning such new research is suggested.

THE CONTINGENCY TABLE FORMAT

When data on two or more variables can be assigned among nominal categories, it is often convenient to view the data in the format of a contingency table. The two-variable case is the easiest to illustrate. Each variable is divided into a set of nominal categories, say R for one variable and C for the other. The variables are then crossed, which gives a table with R rows and C columns. Contingency tables have been used both for ordered and unordered categories; we restrict our discussion here to *unordered* categories. Therefore the ordering of the R rows or the C columns has no internal importance.

Tables can be constructed so that each of the RC cells displays a frequency, n_{ij}, or a table can consist of a set of probabilities, $P_{ij}, i = 1, \ldots, R, j = 1, \ldots, C$. A researcher's hypotheses about the relation between two or more variables are generally expressed in terms of the P_{ij}, while sample data points collected from a predefined population are expressed as n_{ij}.

In general, the analysis of a table depends upon the manner in which the data points were assigned to the cells in the table. In a two-dimensional table there are three common designs: the marginal totals can be fixed for both variables, they can be fixed for one variable or they can be fixed for neither variable. Both margins fixed is called a *hypergeometric design*. One margin fixed is referred to as a *within-group multinomial design*. Neither margin fixed is a *complete multinomial design*.

The complete multinomial is the most frequently encountered research design. For example, we might take a sample of 300 college students and, after selecting the group, classify them by their major fields and by their preferred method of instruction. If we had decided in advance to sample fixed proportions from each major field, we would be using a within-group multinomial design. The hypergeometric design occurs quite rarely in practice. For our example we would have a hypergeometric design only if we both selected fixed proportions of our sample from each major field and also forced each of the 300 subjects to allocate himself into one of, say, five different course formats, each of which would accept exactly 60 students. The three different research designs are discussed in more detail later.

The notation using n_{ij}'s does not depend upon the research design which underlies a particular set of data. For example, Figure 1 gives the notation for a 3×2 contingency table; this notation is the same for all designs.

Note that in Figure 1 the $+$ subscript designates a sum over a dimension. Thus, in general, $n_{i1} + n_{i2} + \ldots + n_{io} = n_{i+}$ for the ith row. Also, $n_{1j} + n_{2j} + \ldots + n_{Rj} = n_{+j}$ for the jth column.

Further, $\sum_{i=1}^{R} n_{i+} = \sum_{j=1}^{C} n_{+j} = n$. This notation is generalizable to more than two dimensions, so that for three dimensions, n_{ijl} will represent the number of responses in the ith row category, jth column category and lth layer category.

	Group 1	Group 2	
1	n_{11}	n_{12}	n_{1+}
Response Type 2	n_{21}	n_{22}	n_{2+}
3	n_{31}	n_{32}	n_{3+}
	n_{+1}	n_{+2}	n

Fig. 1.   Notation using frequencies for a 3 X 2 contingency table.

Although the different research designs cannot be "discriminated" from the n_{ij}, the probability structure underlying any table will indicate which design it follows. For example, consider the probability structures defined in Figure 2.

Figure 2 shows that while for the no margins fixed design all the P_{ij} sum to 1.0, in the one margin fixed case the R P_{ij}'s within each of the C groups sum to one (thus the column marginals are fixed). In Figure 2, $P_{i.}$ represents the expected proportion of cases falling in row i. It always equals the sum of the expected values of the n_{ij} in row i divided by n. In Figure 2a, with no margins fixed, $P_{i.}$ equals the unweighted sum (not the average) of the P_{ij} in row i. In Figure 2b, with column margins fixed, $P_{i.}$ equals the average of the P_{ij} in row i weighted by the n_{+j}.

2a.   No Margins Fixed

	Group 1	Group 2	
1	P_{11}	P_{12}	$P_{1.}$
Response Type 2	P_{21}	P_{22}	$P_{2.}$
3	P_{31}	P_{32}	$P_{3.}$

$$\sum_{i=1}^{R} \sum_{j=1}^{C} P_{ij} = 1$$

2b.   One Margin Fixed

	Group 1	Group 2	
1	P_{11}	P_{12}	$P_{1.}$
Response Type 2	P_{21}	P_{22}	$P_{2.}$
3	P_{31}	P_{32}	$P_{3.}$

$$\sum_{i=1}^{R} P_{i1} = \sum_{i=1}^{R} P_{i2} = 1$$

Fig. 2.   Probability structures under two models for a 3 X 2 contingency table.

SOME RISKS IN USING CONTINGENCY TABLES

While I argued earlier that scaling data which have no obvious metric may be a bad idea, using contingency tables does not provide the "correct" scale. It simply enables a researcher to avoid an artificial scaling and, in that sense, to analyze data in a relatively more assumption-free format. There are several situations, however, in which using tables may mislead researchers very badly. We consider a few of these now, in the context of some questions which any researcher should ask about his data before analyzing it.

a) Are the variable(s) obviously ordinal? If so, then rows and columns should not be permuted. Treating ordinal data as if they were nominal can have a cost in terms of loss of information. If responses on a variable are ordinal but a researcher is hesitant to assign a metric, then categories such as "high," "medium" and "low" can be constructed, and procedures are available which are intermediate in power between those which assume a metric and those which simply set up nominal categories. A well-known problem here is the identification of cutoff points for defining the several ordinal categories. Unfortunately, little theory exists in this area.

b) Do the variable(s) have categories which discriminate among subjects on the basis of a single characteristic, or rather, do the categories represent hidden clusters of characteristics underlying a social *process?* If the latter, then seemingly simple tables may lead to severe misinterpretations. An example of this is given in Figure 3.

Suppose that the data in Figure 3 come from a school where sixth grade students are assigned to one of three "tracks" in which they learn mathematics. Let us call these tracks "H" (high), "M" (medium) and "L" (low). An educational researcher has reason to believe that students from disadvantaged backgrounds are being discriminated against in the assignment process. The assignment process consists of giving all students in the school a mathematics achievement test. Based on their scores, the assignment is supposed to proceed as follows: the top third of the students are assigned to track "H," the middle third to track "M," and the lowest third to track "L." Although the researcher, when beginning his study, expected that errors in assignments to track would tend to discriminate against disadvantaged students, Figure 3 indicates the exact opposite: 46 out of the 62 disadvantaged students who were incorrectly tracked were assigned to *higher* tracks than their achievement scores indicated, while this was true for only seven out of the 38 other students who were incorrectly tracked. The researcher concluded his hypothesis of discrimination against disadvantaged students was incorrect and that in fact the reverse was happening.

But Figure 3 gives an example of how measuring a "process" (which appears on the row; the process is the incorrect tracking) can obscure the true issue. In fact, we cannot tell anything useful about discriminatory assignments from the given data since Figure 3 does not indicate that, on the average, students from disadvantaged backgrounds tended to score lower on the

		Disadvantaged Students	Nondisadvantaged Students	
Tracking errors relative to measured achievement scores	Under-tracked	16	31	47
	Over-tracked	46	7	53
		62	38	

Fig. 3.   Relation between student type and tracking assignment errors.

math achievement test than did students from other backgrounds. Thus, since a "correct" assignment (using the achievement test as a basis for tracking) would have placed most of the disadvantaged students in the lower track, and most of the other students in higher tracks, it is essentially impossible to observe many disadvantaged students being incorrectly undertracked. The reverse is true for the remaining students. We can conclude from this discussion that, for this researcher's purpose, the data came in a form which was essentially meaningless, and that we should have taken a third variable, the relative performance of different types of students on the achievement test, into account if we wished to investigate discriminatory assignment.

c) Are the dimensions of the table meaningful? This is usually a difficult question to answer. In some research, measures of association are computed from contingency tables which were developed by crossing two or more variables. Yet the dimensions themselves may have no clear meaning. This happens when it is possible to reorganize the $R \times C$ table into a $1 \times RC$ table with no loss of information. For example, consider the data in Figure 4. There exists

into a single new dimension which appears in Figure 4b? If a liberal Republican has no more in common with either liberal Democrats or conservative Republicans than he has with conservative Democrats, then the two-way classification implies an independent existence for the two dimensions which they in fact lack. A rather analogous error in formal logic is called the "fallacy of misplaced concreteness." Dimensions employed in crossclassifications should have a firm theoretical basis and some empirical support apart from the data at hand. It might therefore be possible to argue that the arrangement in Figure 4b is actually more meaningful than the arbitrary cross-breaking of Figure 4a.

The Use of Qualitative Data in Educational Research

Let us now assume that a researcher has observed the caveats of the preceding section, and can develop a meaningful set of qualitative data. Given the problem of fitting a metric to some data, and given that categorized data often represent the only feasible option for describing student behavior, teacher behavior, and student-teacher inter-

		Republican	Democrat	
4a.	Liberal	12	22	34
	Conservative	34	32	66
		46	54	100

	Liberal Republican	Liberal Democrat	Conservative Republican	Conservative Democrat
4b.	12	22	34	32

Fig. 4.   Political affiliation and social attitudes of teachers.

in Figure 4a some association between the political affiliation and social attitudes of teachers. Yet, would any information be lost if we dissolve the two separate dimensions

action, how often are qualitative responses actually used in educational research and evaluation? The answer is that until recently they have been used too rarely.

Rosenshine (1970) gives an excellent summary of particular circumstances and work which relied upon such data. He notes that direct observations of classroom interaction were seldom obtained and analyzed.

A number of qualitative instruments for analyzing student and teacher behavior are available, however (see Gage, 1969; Solomon, Bezdek, & Rosenberg, 1963). Also, procedures for developing category breakdowns and several specific category systems have been proposed by Amidon and Simon (1965), Biddle and Adams (1967), Campbell (1968), Lawrence (1966), Nuthall (1968) and Simon and Boyer (1967).

We will not present here a thorough taxonomy of different category systems which have been developed for observing classroom behavior. Interested readers should consult Chapter 5 of this *Handbook* for detailed discussion and explanation of such systems. Perhaps wider appreciation of the advantage of using category systems, together with a full appreciation of the limiting assumptions which must be applied to the analysis of continuous data, will result in more widespread use of categorized data. For additional references on the value and details of category systems for human behavior, see Bloom and Wilensky (1967), Evans (1969), Fortune (1967), Gallagher (1968), Spaulding (1965), Vickery (1968) and Zahorik (1969). The last two references give examples of factorial category systems based upon classroom interaction, teacher style and teacher feedback. Two- and three-factor category systems can of course be translated into two- and three-dimensional contingency tables, and we focus throughout this chapter on such tables.

Finally, in recent research on preschool education, White (1969, 1971) gives a taxonomy of parents' behavior categories which are then crossed with children's behavior categories. The goal is to study combinations of parent behavior and child behavior which seem to result in positive cognitive and affective development. This research requires extensive observational study of sets of parents and children, but leads to a rich set of data giving behavioral descriptions which are then related to a child's later behavior. For the rest of this chapter, we will assume that a researcher is able to assign a set of data into a contingency table, and we now focus on a number of procedures for analyzing such data.

ANALYZING DATA IN TABLES

Chi-square and the Standard Test for Independence

By far the most common analysis for data in a contingency table is the Pearson chi-square test for independence. The hypothesis for chi-square tests is the null hypothesis, $H_0: P_{ij} = P_{i.}$. This hypothesis states that the responses in each column follow the same probability distribution over the rows. The chi-square test can be applied no matter what the research design underlying the data (both margins fixed, one margin fixed or neither margin fixed). Detailed treatments of the standard chi-square analysis appear in many texts (Kendall & Stuart, 1967; Snedecor & Cochran, 1967), so we give here only a brief summary.

Assume that n_{ij} represents the number of responses in the ith row and the jth column, $i = 1, \ldots, R;\ j = 1, \ldots, C$. Let $n_{i+} = \sum_{j=1}^{C} n_{ij}$, and $n_{+j} = \sum_{i=1}^{R} n_{ij}$. The total number of responses in the table is n.

The general formula for the chi-square test for independence is then:

$$(1)\quad \chi^2_{(R-1)(C-1)}$$

$$= \sum_{i=1}^{R} \sum_{j=1}^{C} \frac{\left(n_{ij} - \dfrac{n_{i+}n_{+j}}{n}\right)^2}{\dfrac{n_{i+}n_{+j}}{n}}.$$

This can be rewritten for easier computation as:

(2) $\quad \chi^2_{(R-1)(C-1)}$

$$= n \left(\frac{1}{n_{1+}} \sum_{j=1}^{c} \frac{n^2_{1j}}{n_{+j}} + \frac{1}{n_{2+}} \sum_{j=1}^{c} \frac{n^2_{2j}}{n_{+j}} \right.$$

$$\left. + \ldots + \frac{1}{n_{R+}} \sum_{j=1}^{c} \frac{n^2_{Rj}}{n_{+j}} - 1 \right).$$

Some texts suggest using a correction for continuity in special cases, such as the 2×2 table. But more recent work by Grizzle (1967) suggests that little is gained by using the correction. The major caution when using the chi-square test in (2) is that since it is an approximation to an exact test, the approximation may break down when the "expected" number of responses in several cells, under the null hypothesis, is very low, such as less than one. It is not uncommon in educational research to have a large table with several empty cells. So long as $n_{i+}n_{+j}/n > 1$, the fact that n_{ij} itself is zero is not important. But if the expected number of responses for some of these cells is less than one, the chi-square procedure should be applied with great caution. Details on this point are given by Lewontin and Felsenstein (1965).

While the test in (2) gives a significance test of the null hypothesis of independence, researchers often like to use a single measure of association, which gives an indication of the strength of the relationship between the two variables. It is possible to have a chi-square value which is very highly statistically significant, say beyond the 0.001 level, and yet have variables which are only slightly associated. This happens when there is a large sample size. Thus, since the computed value of chi-square for a given table is a linear function of the sample size n, simply multiplying every response in a contingency table by the constant θ will multiply the resulting chi-square value by θ. The data will then be judged as statistically significant at a much lower probability level (since the degrees of freedom will be unchanged), although the "structure" of the data in the table is unchanged. This suggests a need for a measure of association between two variables which will describe the structure of the data in a table and not be a function of the sample size (Costner, 1965).

Several such measures based upon chi-square have been proposed. The most commonly used measure is C_{χ^2}:

(3) $$C_{\chi^2} = \sqrt{\frac{\chi^2}{\chi^2 + n}}.$$

While C_{χ^2} has a value of zero when data indicate the two variables are independent, it reaches an upper limit under full association which depends upon the dimensionality of the $R \times C$ table. For example, for 2×2 tables, the upper limit of C_{χ^2} is 0.707. Thus, while an obvious scaling change which would adjust C_{χ^2} into a $0 - 1$ measure would be to take

$$\left(\frac{C_{\chi^2} \text{ observed}}{C_{\chi^2} \text{ maximum possible}} \right),$$

C_{χ^2} suffers from this slight scaling drawback. In general, for tables where $R = C$, the maximum value for C_{χ^2} is $\left(\frac{R-1}{R} \right)^{1/2}$.

To remedy this, the statistic V proposed by Cramer (1946) can be used:

(4) $$V = \sqrt{\frac{\chi^2}{n[\min(R-1, C-1)]}}.$$

V has the desirable property of always reaching 1.0 under perfect association, while it is zero under independence. For 2×2 tables only, a measure which varies between zero and one from independence to full association is ϕ;

(5) $$\phi = \sqrt{\frac{\chi^2}{n}}.$$

Note that the test of significance for each of these measures is the standard chi-square, and a given measure will thus become more "significant" as n increases.

Partitioning Chi-square
Into Components

It is often useful to partition the total chi-square in a table which is larger than 2×2 into single degree of freedom components. In this way relationships between the two variables in small portions of the table can be studied. Lancaster (1949, 1950) and Kimball (1954) have shown that as many partitions as there are degrees of freedom can be made, and they give formulas for the partitioning. In general the formulas are complex, but we give here a set of exact partitions for the 3×3 table. Since this table has four degrees of freedom, it can be divided into the four 2×2 subtables given in Figure 5. The partitions given are not the only ones possible. Rather than give formulas for all the different

analyses, it is simpler to observe that any potential analysis which is logically permissible can be brought to the form given in Figure 5 by rearranging the rows and columns in the original table. Note that this partitioning process should be decided upon in advance of the data collection and should not be based upon "peeking" at the data. It should be done in this manner because for large tables there are a large number of different ways of partitioning the degrees of freedom into single degree-of-freedom components. If the table is intentionally partitioned a posteriori to achieve components which, because of "peeking" are each known to have high association, the chi-square test, when applied to each component, is not a valid test, as no statistical penalty has been paid for the "peeking."

Total Table

n_{11}	n_{12}	n_{13}
n_{21}	n_{22}	n_{23}
n_{31}	n_{32}	n_{33}

The Four Partitions

a.

n_{11}	n_{12}
n_{21}	n_{22}

c.

$n_{11} + n_{12}$	n_{13}
$n_{21} + n_{22}$	n_{23}

b.

$n_{11} + n_{21}$	$n_{12} + n_{22}$
n_{31}	n_{32}

d.

$n_{11} + n_{12} + n_{21} + n_{22}$	$n_{13} + n_{23}$
$n_{31} + n_{32}$	n_{33}

Fig. 5.   Partitions of a 3 X 3 table into four additive X^2_1 components.

The computing formulae for the four tables in Figure 5 are:

$$(6) \quad \text{For (a)}: \chi^2_1 = \frac{n[n_{2+}(n_{+2}n_{11} - n_{+1}n_{12}) - n_{1+}(n_{+2}n_{21} - n_{+1}n_{22})]^2}{n_{1+}n_{2+}n_{+1}n_{+2}(n_{1+} + n_{2+})(n_{+1} + n_{+2})}$$

$$\text{For (b)}: \chi^2_1 = \frac{n^2[n_{23}(n_{11} + n_{12}) - n_{13}(n_{21} + n_{22})]^2}{n_{1+}n_{2+}n_{+3}(n_{1+} + n_{2+})(n_{+1} + n_{+2})}$$

$$\text{For (c)}: \chi^2_1 = \frac{n^2[n_{32}(n_{11} + n_{21}) - n_{31}(n_{12} + n_{22})]^2}{n_{3+}n_{+1}n_{+2}(n_{1+} + n_{2+})(n_{+1} + n_{+2})}$$

$$\text{For (d)}: \chi^2_1 = \frac{n[n_{33}(n_{11} + n_{12} + n_{21} + n_{22}) - (n_{13} + n_{23})(n_{31} + n_{32})]^2}{n_{3+}n_{+3}(n_{1+} + n_{2+})(n_{+1} + n_{+2})}$$

Each of these four components has a single degree of freedom. These four computed χ^2_1 values should add up to the single value which would be obtained from the total χ^2_4 in (2).

Example 1

To illustrate the partitioning of a 3×3 table into four single degree of freedom components, consider the data in Figure 6. Four hundred eight randomly selected college students were categorized on two variables. First, each student was assigned to one of three areas of academic concentra-tion—social sciences, natural sciences or humanities. Then each student was asked to indicate his preferred teaching style—seminar, lecture or small group project. Note that the overall test for independence between students' academic concentrations and preferred teaching styles gives a chi-square of 21.718, which, for four degrees of freedom, causes us to reject the hypothesis of independence beyond the 0.01 level of significance.

For the complete table, $\chi^2_4 = 21.718$, significant beyond 0.01. Now we partition the overall table in Figure 6 into the four 2×2 tables given in Figure 5.

		PREFERRED TEACHING STYLE			
		Seminar	Lecture	Group Project	
	Social Sciences	111	16	52	179
ACADEMIC CONCENTRATION	Natural Sciences	63	10	14	87
	Humanities	118	10	14	142
		292	36	80	408

Fig. 6.   Academic concentration by preferred teaching style for 408 college students.

(a)

111	16
63	10

$$\chi^2_1 = \frac{408[87(36 \cdot 111 - 292 \cdot 16) - 179(36 \cdot 63 - 292 \cdot 10)]^2}{179 \cdot 87 \cdot 292 \cdot 36(202 + 36)(179 + 87)} = 0.096$$

(b)

174	26
118	10

$$\chi^2_1 = \frac{(408)^2[14(111 + 16) - 52(63 + 10)]^2}{179 \cdot 87 \cdot 80(179 + 87)(292 + 36)} = 6.236$$

(c)

127	52
73	14

$$\chi^2_1 = \frac{(408)^2[10(111 + 63) - 118(16 + 10)]^2}{142 \cdot 292 \cdot 36(179 + 87)(292 + 36)} = 2.254$$

(d)

200	66
128	14

$$\chi^2_1 = \frac{408[14(111 + 16 + 63 + 10) - (52 + 14)(118 + 10)]^2}{142 \cdot 80(179 + 87)(292 + 36)} = 13.132$$

(a) is not significant at any reasonable level. Thus, focusing on this subtable which compares social scientists with natural scientists on their relative preferences between seminar versus lecture, we cannot reject the hypothesis of independence for the subtable.

(b) is significant at the 0.05 level. This subtable, which compares the relative preferences for seminar versus lecture of the humanities concentrators versus the other two groups taken together, enables us to reject the hypothesis of independence. We conclude that the relative preferences for the two groups differ.

(c) is not significant at any reasonable

level. This third subtable tests for the relative preferences of social science versus natural science concentrators when the teaching options are group project versus the seminar and lecture combined. Making this combination, we cannot reject the hypothesis of independence at any reasonable level of significance.

(d) is significant beyond the 0.01 level and compares the combined two science groups with the humanities concentrators as to their teaching preferences: group project versus nongroup project. In this comparison the independence hypothesis is rejected beyond the 0.01 level of significance.

To conclude this example, we note that the four single degree of freedom partitions are independent of one another, and that the four components add to the total chi-square with four degrees of freedom.

(a)   0.096
(b)   6.236
(c)   2.254
(d) 13.132
     ―――――
     21.718

The "Pairs" Approach to Qualitative Data

While there is little doubt that chi-square and its variations are the statistics most frequently applied to data in contingency tables, they suffer from the unattractive feature of lack of interpretability. Both the numerical value of a chi-square and the value of a measure of association based upon chi-square, such as ϕ, have no clear meaning to researchers. For example, for continuous data, when one or more independent variables is correlated with a dependent variable, the square of the zero order correlation coefficient gives the proportion of variance in the dependent variable which has been accounted for, or explained by, knowledge of the value(s) of the independent variable(s). An interpretation of the relation between two variables such as this one is often helpful to researchers, yet chi-square based measures lack it.

A whole series of measures is available, however, which can give some useful interpretation of qualitative data. These measures are based on the idea of taking pairs of responses and counting up the number of agreeing versus disagreeing pairs. An agreeing pair consists simply of both members falling into the same response category; a disagreeing pair occurs when the two members fall into different response categories.

By taking all $\binom{n}{2}$ pairs which can be identified from any set of n responses, we can construct statistics which measure agreement among two or more observers, association among two or more variables, and other useful statistics for qualitative responses. The attractive feature of these statistics is their heuristic interpretability as well as simplicity of computation.

We will use the "pairs" approach to measure both agreement and association among two or more variables. As these two issues are often entangled, we digress here to distinguish between the problems of measuring association versus agreement.

For nominal scale variables, we can define agreement between two responses as both of them falling into the same category. For two responses to be associated requires that the category of one response can be predicted from a knowledge of the other's category. Agreement, then, can be viewed as a special case of association, as illustrated in Figure 7.

In both tables of Figure 7, two teachers have each independently assigned 30 students to one of three behavioral categories—A, B or C. In 7a, note that knowledge about the category to which Teacher 1 has assigned any student gives us perfect knowledge about that student's category for Teacher 2. Thus, the two teachers exhibit perfect association in 7a. Yet, there is complete disagreement between the two teachers as to what the behavioral characteristics are of all 30 students. Table 7b, on the other hand, illustrates both perfect association and perfect agreement between the two teachers. Thus, agreement is only

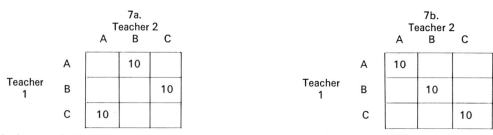

Fig. 7.   Illustration of difference between association and agreement.

a particular type of association. Note further that when measuring agreement between two observers (Goodman & Kruskal, 1954, refer to this as measuring reliability), the categories on the rows should have the same ordering as the categories on the columns. This enables us to define all responses on the main diagonal of a table as "agreeing" responses. It also implies that although any two rows can always be permuted, the two corresponding columns must be similarly permuted if the agreement property of the main diagonal is to be retained.

Note that chi-square based measures of association are quite inappropriate for measuring the agreement, or reliability, of categorization between two observers. In measuring agreement, we would essentially like to partition all n pairs of observations into two equivalence sets: those pairs which indicate agreement and those which indicate disagreement. The problem with applying chi-square to measuring agreement can be illustrated by the data in Figure 8. The data here are two teachers' assignments of 100 students into behavior categories A, B or C. Both tables 8a and 8b have the identical proportion of agreeing pairs and disagreeing pairs, as well as the same marginal structure. Yet the chi-square value in 8a is zero, indicating the agreements and disagreements are distributed over the table exactly as expected under a hypothesis of random agreement, while the chi-square in 8b is nonzero, indicating departure from a "random agreement" hypothesis. The reason for the nonzero chi-square in 8b is not that the observed agreement differs from the expected agreement under H_0; rather it is because the pattern of *disagreements* is different from expectation. This difference in the disagreeing cells should not affect a measure of agreement, and chi-square is therefore inappropriate for this problem. We now consider some alternative approaches.

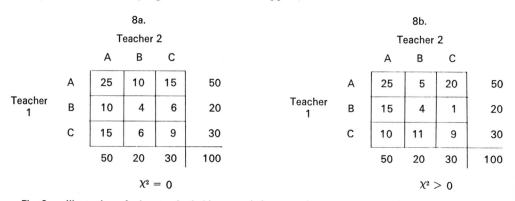

Fig. 8.   Illustration of why standard chi-square is inappropriate as a measure of agreement.

Measuring Level of Agreement
Between Two Observers

Assume that two observers independently assign n items among C categories. This results in a $C \times C$ table, with the row and column categories identically ordered. How can we define a measure of agreement between the two observers? The simplest measure would be to take the raw proportion of agreement $p = \dfrac{1}{n} \sum\limits_{i=1}^{c} n_{ii}$. This measure, however, is independent of the observed marginals.

Why is it usually desirable to have a measure which is conditional upon the observed marginals? The tables in Figure 9 offer one explanation.

they arise from tables having different marginal structures.

Cohen (1960) proposed a measure of agreement which depends upon the observed marginal totals. It is:

$$(7) \qquad K = \frac{p_0 - p_e}{1 - p_e}$$

where $p_0 = \dfrac{1}{n} \cdot \sum\limits_{i=1}^{c} n_{ii}$ and $p_e = \dfrac{1}{n^2} \sum\limits_{i=1}^{c} n_{i+} n_{+i}$.

Note that K essentially compares the observed entries on the main diagonal with the expected entries on this diagonal, where the expected number of entries is computed from the standard chi-square multiplicative model of independence. It thus avoids the problem of being affected by departures of

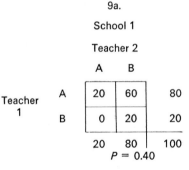

9a.

School 1

Teacher 2

Maximum conditional agreement

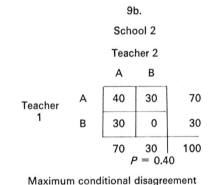

9b.

School 2

Teacher 2

Maximum conditional disagreement

Fig. 9.   Illustration of importance of conditioning level of agreement on marginal totals.

In 9a, the two teachers in School 1 agree on 40 percent of their student assignments. However, based on the marginal totals, they evidence the maximum possible agreement. In Figure 9b the two teachers in School 2 also agree on 40 percent of their assignments; yet given their marginal totals they evidence the maximum possible *disagreement*. The explanation for this seeming paradox is, of course, that in School 1 the two teachers differed in their pattern of marginal totals, while in School 2 the two teachers had identical patterns. This example, however, raises the question of how to analyze two measures of agreement when

observed n_{ij} from expected n_{ij} on the off-diagonal cells. K takes the value of zero when observed agreement equals expected agreement, and it takes the value 1.0 when all responses fall on the main diagonal. It becomes negative when the observed responses have less than "chance" agreement; its lower limit depends upon the marginals of the table.

The measure K was extended by Cohen (1968) and Fleiss, Cohen, and Everitt (1969) to permit differential weighting of different types of disagreements between the two observers. The general structure of this statistic is attractively simple, since it can be rewritten as a function of the number of agreements and disagreements in a table. Thus, we can rewrite K as:

$$(8.) \quad K = 1 - \left[\left(1 - \frac{\sum\limits_{i=1}^{c} n_{ii}}{n} \right) \div \left(1 - \frac{\sum\limits_{i=1}^{c} n_{i+}n_{+i}}{n^2} \right) \right].$$

In (8), the term $\sum\limits_{i=1}^{c} n_{ii}/n$ is simply the proportion of agreements observed, while the term $\sum\limits_{i=1}^{c} n_{i+}n_{+i}/n^2$ gives the expected number of agreements under H_0. Thus, K takes the general form $1 - \dfrac{d_0}{d_e}$, where d_0 indicates the observed proportion of disagreements, and d_e represents the expected proportion of disagreements. This enables us to interpret K as a measure of distance between the two observers, where distance is measured by counting up agreeing versus disagreeing pairs and is a function of the number of disagreeing pairs.

The statistical significance of an observed K can be tested using a normal approximation of the form:

$$(9) \quad Z = \frac{K - K_0}{\sqrt{\text{Var}(K)}},$$

where K is the computed agreement statistic, K_0 is a hypothesized value, and

$$(10) \quad \text{Var}(K) = \frac{p_0(1 - p_0)}{n(1 - p_e)^2} = \frac{p_0 d_0}{n d_e^2}$$

where

$$p_0 = \frac{\sum\limits_{i=1}^{c} n_{ii}}{n} \quad \text{and} \quad p_e = \frac{\sum\limits_{i=1}^{c} n_{i+}n_{+i}}{n^2}.$$

If the value of K_0 under the null hypothesis is zero (if we wish to test the hypothesis of

"random agreement conditional on the given marginals"), the test simplifies further to become:

$$(11) \quad Z = \frac{K}{\sqrt{\dfrac{p_e}{n(1 - p_e)}}}$$

which is approximately normal for large samples.

Example 2

To illustrate the computation and testing of K, we use the data in Figure 10.

Two hundred mother-daughter pairs were examined to find the level of agreement they demonstrated as to "the most important subject in school." Thus, each of the 400 people was independently asked to choose which among the four subjects—history, science, English or math—they considered most important. We now compute K from the data in Figure 10:

$$p_0 = \frac{1}{n} \sum\limits_{i=1}^{c} n_{ii}$$

$$= \frac{1}{200} [34 + 23 + 26 + 7] = 0.450$$

$$p_e = \frac{1}{n^2} \sum\limits_{i=1}^{c} (n_{i+}n_{+i})$$

$$= \frac{1}{(200)^2} [51 \cdot 92 + 44 \cdot 38 + 83 \cdot 56 + 22 \cdot 14]$$

$$= 0.283.$$

So,

$$K = \frac{p_0 - p_e}{1 - p_e} = \frac{0.450 - 0.283}{1 - 0.283} = 0.233.$$

Thus, there appears to be a moderate amount of mother-daughter agreement, above what we would expect from "chance," on most important school subjects.

Is the value $K = 0.233$ significantly dif-

Mother's Preference

		History	Science	English	Math	
	History	34	5	45	8	92
Daughter's Preference	Science	6	23	7	2	38
	English	10	15	26	5	56
	Math	1	1	5	7	14
		51	44	83	22	200

Fig. 10.   Data from mother-daughter pairs as to most important subject in school.

ferent from zero? Using the large sample approximation in (11),

$$S_0(\mathbf{K}) = \sqrt{\frac{p_e}{n(1 - p_e)}}$$

$$= \sqrt{\frac{0.283}{200(0.717)}}$$

$$= \sqrt{0.002}$$

$$\doteq 0.045$$

Testing $\mathbf{K}$,

$$Z = \frac{0.233}{0.045} \doteq 5.2,$$

which exceeds the critical value of Z at any reasonable level of significance. Thus, we reject the null hypothesis of "random agreement," and conclude that the observed agreement exceeds chance far beyond the 0.01 level of significance.

Note that in testing $\mathbf{K}$ either a one-tailed or a two-tailed test can be used in (11). The choice of procedure will depend upon whether a researcher "places his bets" on a level of agreement higher or lower than the expected level, or simply wishes to test for the presence versus absence of "random" agreement.

Measuring Level of Agreement Among Three Observers

The simple approach of taking pairs of observers' assignments to categories and counting up agreeing versus disagreeing pairs, has been extended to the case of more than two observers (see Light, 1971b). For example, suppose three observers each independently assign n items among C categories. This can be displayed in a three-dimensional contingency table. The general form of the agreement statistic here is once again $1 - \dfrac{d_0}{d_e}$.

Let n_{ijl} represent the number of items assigned by observer #1 to the ith category, observer #2 to the jth category, and observer #3 to the lth category; $i,j,l = 1,\ldots, C$. Then counting up all the sets of agreeing and disagreeing pairs yields the statistic:

$$(12) \qquad \mathbf{K}_3 = 1 - \frac{nA}{B},$$

where

$$A = \sum_{i \neq j} n_{ij+} \sum_{i \neq l} n_{i++} n_{++l} \sum_{j \neq l} n_{+j+} n_{++l}$$

$$+ \sum_{i \neq l} n_{i+l} \sum_{i \neq j} n_{i++} n_{+j+} \sum_{j \neq l} n_{+j+} n_{++l}$$

$$+ \sum_{j \neq l} n_{+jl} \sum_{i \neq j} n_{i++} n_{+j+} \sum_{i \neq l} n_{i++} n_{++l},$$

and

$$B = 3 \sum_{i \neq j} n_{i++} n_{+j+} \sum_{i \neq l} n_{i++} n_{++l} \sum_{j \neq l} n_{+j+} n_{++l}.$$

An approximate large sample estimate of Var $(\mathbf{K}_3)$ can be computed as:

$$(13) \qquad \text{Var}(K_3) = \frac{p_0(1 - p_0)}{n(1 - p_e)^2}$$

where $p_0 = 1 - \dfrac{A}{n^5}$ and $p_e = 1 - \dfrac{B}{n^6}$ with A and B defined just above. When testing the null hypothesis of no population agreement, $\text{Var}(K_3)$ becomes $\dfrac{p_e}{n(1 - p_e)}$. Again, K_3 divided by its estimated standard deviation is approximately normally distributed for large samples.

The pairs approach can be extended still further to derive a measure of *conditional* agreement. Thus, we may wish to ask the question, when three teachers each assign n students into C categories, "What is the agreement among the three teachers for only those students whom teacher #1 assigned to the first category?" Such measures of conditional agreement are available from Light (1971b).

Example 3

To illustrate the computation of the measure of agreement K_3 for three observers, suppose now that we have a set of 200 mother-father-daughter triplets. Each of these 600 people independently selects a response to the question, "Which is a more important goal for the daughter of the family—to do excellent work in school or to be popular with other girls?" In the notation of this section, the triplets of responses are distributed as follows (the subscript "1" indicates a preference for excellence in school; the subscript "2" indicates a preference for popularity), i referring to mother, j to father, and l to daughter in n_{ijl}.

$n_{111} = 23$	$n_{211} = 14$
$n_{112} = 41$	$n_{212} = 53$
$n_{121} = 18$	$n_{221} = 20$
$n_{122} = 4$	$n_{222} = 27$

To compute K_3 from (12), we first find the various required marginal totals. The single-face marginal totals are:

$n_{+11} = 37$	$n_{1+1} = 41$	$n_{11+} = 64$
$n_{+12} = 94$	$n_{1+2} = 45$	$n_{12+} = 22$
$n_{+21} = 38$	$n_{2+1} = 34$	$n_{21+} = 67$
$n_{+22} = 31$	$n_{2+2} = 80$	$n_{22+} = 47$

The double-face totals are:

$n_{++1} = 75$	$n_{+1+} = 131$	$n_{1++} = 86$
$n_{++2} = 125$	$n_{+2+} = 69$	$n_{2++} = 114$
	$n_{+++} = n = 200$.	

Now, computing from (12):

$$
\begin{aligned}
A = {}& (22 + 67)\ (86 \cdot 125 + 114 \cdot 75) \\
& \cdot (131 \cdot 125 + 69 \cdot 75) + (45 + 34) \\
& \cdot (86 \cdot 69 + 114 \cdot 131) \\
& \cdot (131 \cdot 125 + 69 \cdot 75) + (94 + 38) \\
& \cdot (86 \cdot 69 + 114 \cdot 131) \\
& \cdot (86 \cdot 125 + 114 \cdot 75)
\end{aligned}
$$

$$A = 1.257 \times 10^{11}$$
$$
\begin{aligned}
B = {}& 3(86 \cdot 69 + 114 \cdot 131)\ (86 \cdot 125 \\
& + 114 \cdot 75)\ (131 \cdot 125 + 69 \cdot 75)
\end{aligned}
$$
$$B = 2.604 \times 10^{13}.$$

Thus,

$$K_3 = 1 - \frac{nA}{B} = 0.034 .$$

If we observe that the within-family agreement exceeds chance by very little, as in this example, we may wish to test the observed value of K_3 to see whether we can reject the hypothesis that in the population the true level of within-family agreement is zero. To do this test, we first compute $\text{Var}_0(K_3)$ from (13).

$$\text{Var}_0(K_3) = \frac{p_e}{n(1 - p_e)}$$

where

$$p_e = 1 - \frac{B}{n^6} = 0.593 .$$

So,

$$\text{Var}_0(K_3) = \frac{0.593}{200(.407)} \doteq 0.0073$$

and the standard deviation is:

$$S_0(K_3) = \sqrt{0.0073} \doteq 0.085 .$$

Since we find,

$$z = \frac{K_3}{S_0(K_3)} = \frac{0.034}{0.084} \doteq 0.40,$$

we *cannot* conclude that the within-family agreement in the population will exceed the chance agreement suggested by the three observed marginal distributions (i.e., the marginal distribution of the fathers, mothers and daughters).

Examining Pattern of Agreement Between Two Observers

Both K and K_3 compare the observed level with the expected level of agreement in a table. But a researcher may be further interested in examining the pattern, or form, of the agreements. The K measures are insensitive to differences in patterns of agreement, as is illustrated in Figure 11. Both Figures 11a and 11b have $K = 0$. They also have identical marginal totals.

tures of observed frequencies from expected frequencies in all cells of a table) a *modified* chi-square statistic can be used to test the hypothesis that the true *pattern* of agreement is identical to what would be expected under chance. This statistic is:

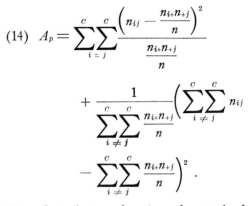

$$(14) \quad A_p = \sum_{i=j}^{c}\sum^{c} \frac{\left(n_{ij} - \frac{n_{i+}n_{+j}}{n}\right)^2}{\frac{n_{i+}n_{+j}}{n}}$$

$$+ \frac{1}{\sum_{i \neq j}^{c}\sum^{c} \frac{n_{i+}n_{+j}}{n}}\left(\sum_{i \neq j}^{c}\sum^{c} n_{ij}\right.$$

$$\left. - \sum_{i \neq j}^{c}\sum^{c} \frac{n_{i+}n_{+j}}{n}\right)^2 .$$

Note that A_p is a function of a total of $(C + 1)$ cells—the C cells on the agreement

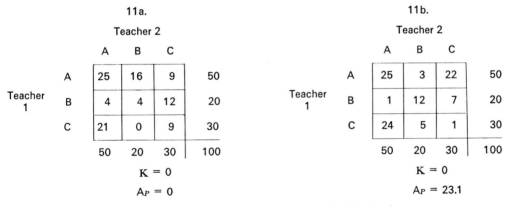

11a.

Teacher 2

		A	B	C	
	A	25	16	9	50
Teacher 1	B	4	4	12	20
	C	21	0	9	30
		50	20	30	100

K = 0

Ap = 0

11b.

Teacher 2

		A	B	C	
	A	25	3	22	50
Teacher 1	B	1	12	7	20
	C	24	5	1	30
		50	20	30	100

K = 0

Ap = 23.1

Fig. 11.   Illustration of different *patterns* of agreement with identical *levels* of agreement.

However, the distribution of the responses on the agreement diagonal is different for the two tables; in 11a the responses are distributed exactly as expected under the null hypothesis, while in 11b they have a different distribution.

Although we have previously discussed why the standard chi-square statistic is inappropriate for measuring *level* of agreement (because of its sensitivity to depar-

diagonal, and all the off-diagonal cells which it treats as a single "grand" cell. Under the null hypothesis that the "pattern" of agreement is that expected from the multiplicative model using the given marginal totals, A_p is asymptotically distributed as chi-square with C degrees of freedom. For table 11a, since the observed agreements are distributed exactly as expected under H_0, A_p is **zero**. In table 11b,

$$A_p = \frac{0^2}{25} + \frac{8^2}{4} + \frac{8^2}{9} + \frac{0^2}{62} = 23.1, \text{ which is}$$

significant beyond the 0.01 level for three degrees of freedom. Thus, by combining K and A_p for any table, a researcher should be able to develop a reasonable insight into how pairs of observers agree in their assignment strategies.

Example 4

To illustrate the test for "pattern of agreement," we return to the mother-daughter pairs data from Figure 10. From (14) we compute A_p:

$$A_p = \frac{(34 - 23.46)^2}{23.46} + \frac{(23 - 8.36)^2}{8.36}$$

$$+ \frac{(26 - 23.34)^2}{23.34} + \frac{(7 - 1.54)^2}{1.54}$$

$$+ \frac{1}{\left(\begin{array}{c} 20.24 + 38.18 + 10.12 + 9.69 \\ + 15.77 + 4.18 + 14.28 + 12.32 \\ + 6.16 + 3.57 + 3.08 + 5.81 \end{array}\right)}$$

$$\cdot \left[\left(\begin{array}{c} 5 + 45 + 8 + 6 + 7 \\ + 2 + 10 + 15 + 5 \\ + 1 + 1 + 5 \end{array}\right) - 143.4^2\right]$$

$$A_p = (4.74 + 25.64 + 0.33 + 19.36)$$

$$+ \frac{1}{143.4}(110 - 143.4)^2$$

$$A_p = 57.84$$

which, since A_p is distributed under the null hypothesis as χ^2_4, is significant beyond the 0.01 level. We thus conclude that the *pattern* of mother-daughter agreement differs from that expected by chance, given the observed marginal distributions.

Comparing Group Agreement with a Standard

The K measures have two properties. First, they assume nothing about a "true"— or correct—assignment of items to categories. The agreement they measure is purely internal consistency among assignments. Second, all observers are treated as having equal "weight." Thus, no one observer is singled out as the focus against which other observers' assignments should be compared.

But in social and educational research a common problem is to compare the categorizations of a group of students or observers with a "standard" categorization which is defined as being correct. This may happen when a teacher has categorized some responses and wishes to compare students' assignments with his own. A second common research setting occurs when one member of a group of members is singled out for special attention. Thus, in research such as that of Coleman (1961) or Kandel and Lesser (1969), responses are obtained from several members of a group of families, but the responses of the adolescent male, say, are the "special focus" of the study. In this situation we may wish to define a certain member of a group as the "standard" and compare the responses of the rest of the group with this standard.

A test for the joint agreement of m observers with the "standard" assignment is available. The layout for this problem can be viewed as a set of m contingency tables, each table comparing the responses of one of the m observers with the standard set of responses. Let $n^{(p)}_{ij}$ represent the number of responses in cell i,j of the pth table; $i,j = 1, \ldots, C; p = 1, \ldots, m$. If we designate the "standard" assignment on the rows and the pth observer's assignment on the columns, then for all m tables the row margins n_{i+} must be identical while the column margins will often differ.

A test statistic which for large samples is approximately normally distributed and which tests the null hypothesis that the joint group's assignments indicate "chance" agreement with the standard is G, given in (15):

$$(15) \quad G = \frac{t_m - E(t_m)}{(\xi t_m)^{1/2}}$$

a) $\quad t_m = \sum_{p=1}^{m} \sum_{i=j}^{c} n^{(p)}{}_{ij}$

b) $\quad E(t_m) = \frac{1}{n} \sum_{i=j}^{c} \left[n_{i+} \left(\sum_{p=1}^{m} n^{(p)}{}_{+j} \right) \right]$

c) $\quad \xi t_m = \frac{1}{n-1} \sum_{i=j}^{c} \left[n_{i+} \left(\sum_{p=1}^{m} n^{(p)}{}_{+j} \right) \right]$

$$+ \frac{1}{n^2(n-1)} Y - \frac{1}{n(n-1)}$$

$$\cdot \sum_{i=j}^{c} \left[n^2{}_{i+} \left(\sum_{p=1}^{m} n^{(p)}{}_{+j} \right) \right]$$

$$- \frac{1}{n(n-1)} \sum_{i=j}^{c} n_{i+}$$

$$\cdot \left[\sum_{p=1}^{m} \left(n^{(p)}{}_{+j} \right) \right]^2$$

where in (c) above:

$$Y = n_{1+} [n_{1+} \sum_{p} (n_{+1}{}^{(p)}) (n_{+1}{}^{(p)})$$

$$+ n_{2+} \sum_{p} (n_{+1}{}^{(p)}) (n_{+2}{}^{(p)}) + \ldots$$

$$+ n_{c+} \sum_{p} (n_{+1}{}^{(p)}) (n_{+c}{}^{(p)})]$$

$$+ n_{2+} [n_{1+} \sum_{p} (n_{+2}{}^{(p)}) (n_{+1}{}^{(p)})$$

$$+ n_{2+} \sum_{p} (n_{+2}{}^{(p)}) (n_{+2}{}^{(p)}) + \ldots$$

$$+ n_{c+} \sum_{p} (n_{+2}{}^{(p)}) (n_{+c}{}^{(p)})]$$

$$\vdots$$

$$+ n_{c+} [n_{1+} \sum_{p} (n_{+c}{}^{(p)}) (n_{+1}{}^{(p)})$$

$$+ n_{2+} \sum_{p} (n_{+c}{}^{(p)}) (n_{+2}{}^{(p)}) + \ldots$$

$$+ n_{c+} \sum_{p} (n_{+c}{}^{(p)}) (n_{+c}{}^{(p)})] .$$

G compares the observed agreements of each of the m respondents with the standard while recomputing the expected number of agreements for each respondent based upon his margin assignments $n^{(p)}{}_{+1}, \ldots, n^{(p)}{}_{+c}$; $p = 1, \ldots, m$. For testing, G will be approximately normally distributed around $E(t_m)$ under the null hypothesis of random agreement.

G is clearly useful for assessing the reliability of a typology among raters when a reference standard is available. It can also prove valuable for the study of role assignments in classroom interaction studies. Suppose that, based on a series of observations, an investigator has classified a group of classroom members into several role types. Without revealing his own assignments, he can then define the role types for the members of the group and ask each of them to make their own individual assignments for all members. With C role types, m group members, and the investigator's assignments as the "standard" margin, the G statistic can be used to search for better than chance agreement among the participants with the investigator's assignments. Since this aspect of role interaction studies is sometimes difficult to investigate, the G statistic might find frequent future use in documenting behavior typologies.

Example 5

To illustrate the use of G, assume that a "master" teacher classifies each of 100 reading students into one of three groups: normal, underachiever or dyslexic. Suppose also that each of two "teachers in training" independently categorizes the same students, and we wish to see whether the joint assignments made by the young teachers agree beyond chance with the assignments of the master teacher. The notation for this situation appears in Figure 12.

Assume now that the specific assignments for the three observers are given in Figure 13.

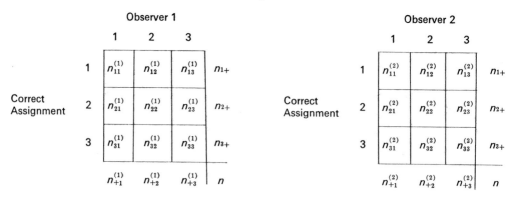

Fig. 12.   General notation for comparing several categorizations against a "standard."

TEACHER IN TRAINING #1

Normal   Underach.   Dyslexic

	Normal	Underach.	Dyslexic	
Normal	12	6	2	20
Underach.	4	10	16	30
Dyslexic	24	4	22	50
	40	20	40	100

MASTER TEACHER

TEACHER IN TRAINING #2

Normal   Underach.   Dyslexic

	Normal	Underach.	Dyslexic	
Normal	10	3	7	20
Underach.	14	15	1	30
Dyslexic	6	22	22	50
	30	40	30	100

MASTER TEACHER

Fig. 13.   Data for Example 5—A master teacher's categorization versus those of two teachers in training.

Computing t_m, $E(t_m)$, and ξ_{t_m} from the formulae in (15):

From 15a, $t_m = 91$

From 15b, $E(t_m) = 67$

From 15c,

$$\xi_{t_m} = \frac{1}{99}\,(6{,}700) + \frac{1}{990{,}000}\,(22{,}450{,}000)$$

$$-\frac{1}{9{,}900}\,(257{,}000) - \frac{1}{9{,}900}\,(235{,}000)$$

$$= 40.7 .$$

A test of the hypothesis of random agreement is given by:

$$G = \frac{91 - 67}{(40.7)^{1/2}} = \frac{24.0}{6.4} = 3.75 .$$

Whether to use a one-sided or two-sided test in this problem is up to a particular researcher, but in either case the value $G = 3.75$ is significant beyond the 0.01 level. We thus conclude that the joint categorizations of the two teachers in training agreed with the master teacher's categorizations more than we would have expected due to chance.

Measuring Agreement Between Partitions When No Categories Are Predetermined

Until now the various measures of agreement have been applicable only to problems for which the identity of the categories is predetermined, and the number of categories is constant for observers. For example, when observers are asked to rate students' behaviors, they place each of n students into a category which designates a behavior. But a different kind of problem involves asking two observers each to take n students, say, and then to sort these students into subgroups by some criterion. Thus, each observer assigns n "items" into categories, where each category has no "name" or description, but rather is defined simply as a set of items which an observer has grouped together. The total number of groupings can be specified in advance to be "C" for each observer, or the total number of groupings for each observer can be allowed to vary.

If we wish to measure the similarity or agreement between observers' groupings, we once again can arrange the data into a contingency table. Define a $C \times C$ table with Observer 1 on the rows and Observer 2 on the columns. There are n total responses for each observer. If the number of categories "used" by one observer differs from the number used by the other, a set of empty rows (or columns) can be specified to form a $C \times C$ table, where C corresponds to the larger number of categories used by either observer. In this table it is possible to permute rows without permuting columns, since the categories are not "named."

The procedure used to measure agreement here is a simple extension of the pairs idea. There are $\binom{n}{2}$ pairs of responses in the table. For each of these pairs we can examine the agreement or disagreement between the two observers in how they assigned this pair. There are two ways in which the observers could have agreed: they both could have assigned both members of the pair to the same category, or they both could have assigned both members of the pair to different categories. In either case, since the two observers agree, we assign a value of zero to that pair. There are also two ways in which the observers could have disagreed: the first could have assigned both members of a pair to the same category while the second observer assigned them to different categories, or vice versa. Whenever the two observers disagree on a pair, we assign a value of one to that pair.

A statistic discussed by Brennan and Light (1971) which gives the total number of disagreements for any particular set of data in the usual contingency table notation is:

$$(16) \quad D = \frac{1}{2}\left[\sum_{i=1}^{c} n^2_{i+} + \sum_{j=1}^{c} n^2_{+j} \right] - \sum_{i=1}^{c}\sum_{j=1}^{c} n^2_{ij}.$$

To test whether the computed value of D indicates that the two observers agree beyond chance in their groupings of the n responses, the test statistic A will be approximately normally distributed:

$$(17) \quad A = \frac{D - E(D)}{\sqrt{\mathrm{Var}\, D}}.$$

Note that *negative* values of A indicate agreement beyond chance, since D measures disagreements rather than agreements. To find $E(D)$,

(18) $E(D) = \binom{n}{2}(1 - S)$

where $S = P(Y) + P(Z)$, and

$$P(Y) = \sum_{i=1}^{C} \sum_{j=1}^{C}$$

$$\cdot \left[\frac{n_{i+}n_{+j}}{n^2} \cdot \frac{(n_{i+} - 1)(n_{+j} - 1)}{(n - 1)^2} \right]$$

$$P(Z) = \sum_{i=1}^{C} \sum_{j=1}^{C}$$

$$\cdot \left[\frac{n_{i+}n_{+j}}{n^2} \cdot \frac{(n - n_{i+})(n - n_{+j})}{(n - 1)^2} \right].$$

$\text{Var}(D)$ is computed as follows:

(19) $\text{Var}(D) = \binom{n}{2}(1 - S)(S)$

$$+ \binom{n}{2}\binom{n-2}{2}$$

$$\cdot [T - (1 - S)^2]$$

(19 cont.) $+ \binom{n}{2}\binom{n-2}{2}$

$$\cdot [U - (1 - S)^2]$$

where T and U are defined in (23) and (24). This formula (19) is developed from defining D in terms of all pairs of $\binom{n}{2}$ responses. Denoting these pairs as R_s, $s = 1, \ldots, \binom{n}{2}$, then:

(20) $D = \sum_{s=1}^{\binom{n}{2}} R_s$

and

(21) $\text{Var}(D) = \sum_{s=1}^{\binom{n}{2}} \text{Var}(R_s)$

$$+ 2 \sum_{s<t}\sum \text{Cov}(R_s, R_t).$$

We now define the following summations:

(22)

$$S_i^{(1)} = \sum_{i=1}^{C} [n_{i+}(n_{i+} - 1)(n_{i+} - 2)(n - n_{i+})]$$

$$S_i^{(2)} = \sum_{i=1}^{C} \sum_{i'=i+1}^{C} [n_{i+}(n_{i+} - 1)n_{i'+}(n_{i'+} - 1)]$$

$$= \prod_{i=1}^{2} n_{i+}(n_{i+} - 1) \qquad \text{for } C = 2.$$

$$S_i^{(3)} = \sum_{i=1}^{C} [n_{i+}(n_{i+} - 1)(n_{i+} - 2)(n_{i+} - 3)]$$

$$S_i^{(4)} = \sum_{i=1}^{C} [n_{i+}(n_{i+} - 1)(n_{i+} - 2)]$$

$$S_i^{(5)} = \sum_{i=1}^{C} [n_{i+}(n_{i+} - 1)(n - n_{i+})]$$

(22 cont.)

$$S_i^{(6)} = \sum_{i=1}^{C} [n_{i+}(n - n_{i+} - 1)(n - n_{i+})]$$

$$S_i^{(7)} = \sum_{e=1}^{C-2} \sum_{f=e+1}^{C-1} \sum_{g=f+1}^{C} \left[(n_{e+}n_{f+}n_{g+}) \left(\sum_{i \neq e,f,g}^{C} n_{i+} \right) \right]$$

$$= nn_{1+}n_{2+}n_{3+}n_{4+} \qquad \text{for } C = 4.$$

$$S_i^{(8)} = \sum_{i=1}^{C} \left[n_{i+}(n_{i+} - 1) \left(\sum_{a=1}^{C} \sum_{b=a+1}^{C} n_{a+}n_{b+} \right) \right]$$

$$= n_{1+}n_{2+}n_{3+}(n - 3) \qquad \text{for } C = 3.$$

All of the above equations are expressed in terms of n and the row marginal totals. By simply changing n_{i+}, $n_{i'+}$, n_{e+}, n_{f+}, n_{g+}, n_{a+}, and n_{b+} to n_{+j}, $n_{+j'}$, n_{+e}, n_{+f}, n_{+g}, n_{+a}, and n_{+b}, and by changing the index of summation from i to j, we have analogous formulae expressed in terms of column marginals; these can be denoted by $S_j^{(v)}$, $v = 1, \ldots, 8$. Then,

$$(23) \quad U = \frac{S_i^{(4)}S_j^{(6)} + S_j^{(4)}S_i^{(6)} + 2S_i^{(5)}S_j^{(5)}}{n^2(n-1)^2(n-2)^2} .$$

Further,

$$(24) \quad T = \frac{\sum_{w=1}^{3} \phi_w}{n^2(n-1)^2(n-2)^2(n-3)^2}$$

$$\text{for } C = 2,$$

$$= \frac{\sum_{w=1}^{7} \phi_w}{n^2(n-1)^2(n-2)^2(n-3)^2}$$

$$\text{for } C = 3,$$

$$= \frac{\sum_{w=1}^{9} \phi_w}{n^2(n-1)^2(n-2)^2(n-3)^2}$$

$$\text{for } C \geq 4.$$

The ϕ_w are defined in Figure 14.

The test statistic A in (17) is a one-tailed test. Although $\text{Var}(D)$ is tedious to compute, it can be programmed easily and, once programmed, can be applied to tables with both large C and large n.

Note that once again this test is a conditional test. The mean and variance of D for a table with given marginals are found by a raw counting process. We ask the question of how many possible table structures exist constrained by the observed marginal totals. We then identify each structure, find the value of D for this structure, and compute the exact probability of observing this structure. Once all possible values of D together with their exact probabilities are identified, expressions (18) and

Case	Use when:	Formula
ϕ_9	$C \geq 4$	$6 (S_i^{(3)} S_j^{(7)} + S_j^{(3)} S_i^{(7)})$
ϕ_8	$C \geq 4$	$12 (S_i^{(2)} S_j^{(7)} + S_j^{(2)} S_i^{(7)})$
ϕ_7	$C \geq 3$	$8 (S_i^{(8)} S_j^{(8)})$
ϕ_6	$C \geq 3$	$8 (S_i^{(8)} S_j^{(1)} + S_j^{(8)} S_i^{(1)})$
ϕ_5	$C \geq 3$	$16 (S_i^{(8)} S_j^{(2)} + S_j^{(8)} S_i^{(2)})$
ϕ_4	$C \geq 3$	$8 (S_i^{(8)} S_j^{(3)} + S_j^{(8)} S_i^{(3)})$
ϕ_3	$C \geq 2$	$16 (S_i^{(2)} S_j^{(2)})$
ϕ_2	$C \geq 2$	$8 (S_i^{(1)} S_j^{(1)})$
ϕ_1	$C \geq 2$	$4 (S_i^{(2)} S_j^{(3)} + S_j^{(2)} S_i^{(3)})$

Fig. 14. Computing formulae for ϕ_w for agreement in nonpredetermined categories.

(19) give the conditional mean and variance. Thus, the test in (17) takes the row and column marginals as given.

The value of the D statistic in testing the consistency of two raters with free groupings of items has been discussed, so we now suggest a somewhat more subtle use of this statistic. Suppose that children in kindergarten are customarily assembled into play groups given the names of birds, and that two years later the same children are assigned by a different teacher to second-grade reading groups identified by text use. We have data from several years.

We suspect that the cohesiveness of the kindergarten play groups has frequently been preserved, and that there has been a long-term persistence in the matching of a child's play group with the reader-group he found himself in two years later. Unfortunately, we face two difficulties: 1) we do not have any a priori way to know which bird-name is being matched with which reader, and 2) we know that there is a strong tendency to keep the kindergarten play groups at approximately equal sizes, while reading group sizes are determined largely by the unequal number of texts of the several types which are available.

We can then set up the following illustrative table:

integrity of the playgroups is preserved, not just that some nonrandom assignment process is at work. Thus if, say, all the wrens were always assigned to either Singer or Bank Street readers (in about equal proportions) while no one else was ever given them, we would have a nonrandom assignment, but not one that tended to preserve the integrity of the wren play group. A standard chi-square test will respond to nonrandom assignments which destroy the integrity of the groups, while the D statistic will respond only to integrity-preserving nonrandom assignments. The fact that categorical analyses can incorporate such fine distinctions between alternative theories is one of the strongest features recommending their use.

Example 6

As computations for the A statistic in most realistic situations are best done on a computer, we present here only a very small example. Two teachers are each asked to independently sort three children—A, B and C—into subgroups according to the teacher's judgment of their behavior similarity. It happens that both teachers choose to assign the three children into two groups; both use the active-passive dimension.

TABLE 1

KINDERGARTEN "BIRD-NAME" PLAYGROUPS

Second-grade Readers	Bluebirds	Cardinals	Robins	Wrens	Doves	
Harper & Row						197
Singer						99
Bank Street						84
Lippincott						80
D.C. Heath						40
	120	111	90	90	89	500

There is an important point to note about our hypothesis: we hypothesize that the

Teacher 1 puts children A and B into the same category and C into a different category. Teacher 2 places A and C together and B apart from the other two. The data are displayed in Figure 15.

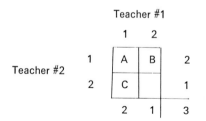

Teacher #1

Fig. 15. Assignments of subjects to subgroups when there are no preassigned categories.

Now we test the hypothesis of no more than chance agreement between the two teachers in their rating strategies. For Figure 15:

from (16), $D = 2$ (the observed number of disagreements in paired assignments);

from (18), $E(D) = \frac{1}{9}(6)(2) + (3)(0)$

$$= 4/3;$$

from (19), $\mathrm{Var}(D) = \frac{1}{9}[3(0 - \frac{4}{3})^2$

$$+ \ 6(2 - \frac{4}{3})^2]$$

$$= \frac{8}{9}.$$

This illustrates the calculations for a small example. If we used the large sample normal approximation given in (17), we would have:

$$A = \frac{2 - 4/3}{(8/9)^{1/2}} = \frac{0.67}{0.94} = +0.71 .$$

This would indicate *disagreement* between the two teachers, as A is positive. However, not only is the value of $+0.71$ not statistically different from zero at the 0.05 level of significance; there is also serious reason to question the applicability of using the normal distribution as a reference distribution for A, given such a small sample. For

larger problems, A is best evaluated using computer facilities.

The "Pairs Approach" to Measuring Association

We now leave the problem of agreement and focus on a somewhat different measurement problem very common in educational and social research. This is the problem of measuring association between two or more variables. We consider first the two-variable problem and later extend the procedure to three variables.

A rich array of measures is currently available to a data analyst wishing to measure the level of association between two nominal scale variables. Several such measures based on chi-square were discussed earlier. For excellent discussions of this problem, see Goodman and Kruskal (1954, 1959, 1963), Kendall and Stuart (1967) and Marx (1970). Yet it seems that new suggestions are constantly being offered. Perhaps Goodman and Kruskal put it best when they pointed out that there is no single best measure for all situations. Rather, a variety of situations may have generated data in different ways, and different techniques for describing the association between two variables may be most appropriate in different settings.

In this section we present and evaluate one particular approach to measuring association. It is based upon the "adding up of pairs" idea which underlies most of the agreement measures. It also has the attractive feature that it can be viewed as an analogue to the well-known r^2 for continuous data; it will offer a "proportion of variation explained" interpretation as a description of the relationship between two variables (see Dyke & Patterson, 1952, and Winson, 1948, for a discussion of the value of such an interpretation). Note that there is nothing "natural" about such an interpretation; it may be viewed as being quite arbitrary. But in some situations a researcher may find the approach helpful, since other approaches for nominal data do not work toward a measure with this interpretation.

The measure is developed by first defining the concept of variation for qualitative data. The total variation over two variables is then partitioned into additive components due to variation "within" and "between" the variables. This will lead to a measure which is related to the standard chi-square, yet can be given an interpretation which results from the partitioning of variation between the two variables.

We generally think of variation as involving the departures of a set of measurements from their mean. For qualitative responses the idea of a mean is unclear. However, in 1912 Corrado Gini noted that the standard expression for the sum of squares for measurement data, generally expressed as:

$$(25) \qquad S.S. = \sum_{j=1}^{n} (x_j - \bar{x})^2,$$

where $\bar{x}$ is the arithmetic mean of the n variables, can be alternatively written as:

$$(26) \quad S.S. = \frac{1}{2n} \sum_{i=1}^{n} \sum_{j=1}^{n} (x_i - x_j)^2.$$

This expression in (26) does not involve the arithmetic mean; it only requires examining all pairs of measurements. By appropriately defining the term $(x_i - x_j)$ in (26) for nominal data, it is possible to generate a sum of squares for such data.

Suppose n responses are distributed in some manner among I discrete categories. Each of these responses can be defined as an $I \times 1$ vector, X_i, $i = 1, \ldots, n$, consisting of I–1 zeros and a single one, where the position of the one identifies the category in which any response is located. Although the ordering of the categories in each of the $I \times 1$ vectors does not imply any true continuous ordering for the categories and is used purely as a coding device, the ordering of the categories must be identical for each of the n vectors.

The Euclidian norm of a vector is the square root of the sum of squares of its elements. Applying this to our notation, the sum of squares of n responses in I categories is the sum of the norms of $\dfrac{1}{\sqrt{2}} [X_i - X_j]$ taken over all $n(n-1)/2$ pairs.

Letting d_{ij} represent the norm of $\dfrac{1}{\sqrt{2}}$ $[X_i - X_j]$ for each pair of responses i,j, it is clear that:

(27) $d_{ij} = 1$ when the two responses in the i,j pair are in different categories;

$d_{ij} = 0$ when the two responses in the i,j pair are in the same category.

Substituting the d_{ij} of (27) for the $(x_i - x_j)$ of (26) leads to an expression for the sum of squares for n responses in I categories:

$$(28) \qquad S.S. = \frac{1}{2n} \sum_{i=1}^{n} \sum_{j=1}^{n} d^2_{ij} .$$

This expression (28) uses the idea of a single distance function between data in discrete categories as the sum of squares of the data. It defines the occurrence of two members of any pair falling into different response categories as a single unit of distance.

Partitioning variability into additive components. We now use the definition in (28) to develop a measure of association between two variables. In the formulae (25) through (28) we viewed the n responses as coming from a single "group." Assume now that data are available from G groups, and that this data can be viewed in the format of a contingency table.

We assume the one-way multinomial design—one margin fixed (the columns) and one margin left free to vary (the rows). Suppose the data consist of responses from G groups, where each response appears in one of I categories. The number of responses from the jth group in the ith category is denoted by $n_{ij}, i = 1, \ldots, I; j = 1, \ldots, G;$ and the total number of responses in the ith category appears as n_{i+}. The number of responses in the jth group may differ among groups and is denoted by n_{+j}. Thus, the total number of responses in the table is $n = \sum_{j=1}^{G} n_{+j} = \sum_{i=1}^{I} n_{i+}$.

Using this notation and the definition of the sum of squares given in (28), the total sum of squares for the n responses can be computed. It is found by examining all $\binom{n}{2}$ pairs of responses, counting a one when the members of a pair fall into different categories, and counting a zero when both members of a pair fall into the same category. This expression can be written for easy computation as:

$$(29) \quad T.S.S. = \frac{n}{2} - \frac{1}{2n} \sum_{i=1}^{I} n^2_{i+}.$$

This total sum of squares can now be partitioned into two additive components. The within-group sum of squares is found by identifying the $\binom{n_{+j}}{2}$ response pairs within each of the G groups, and summing (28) over all G groups:

$$(30) \quad W.S.S. = \frac{n}{2} - \frac{1}{2} \sum_{j=1}^{G} \frac{1}{n_{+j}} \sum_{i=1}^{I} n^2_{ij}.$$

Finally, the between-groups sum of squares is developed by applying (28) to all response pairs between groups, or, more simply, by taking the difference between the total and within-groups sum of squares. Thus, subtracting (30) from (29) yields the general expression for between-groups sum of squares:

$$(31) \quad B.S.S. = \frac{1}{2} \sum_{j=1}^{G} \frac{1}{n_{+j}} \sum_{i=1}^{I} n^2_{ij} - \frac{1}{2n} \sum_{i=1}^{I} n^2_{i+}.$$

Having made this partition, we can now define a measure of association between the two variables. If we take the ratio $B.S.S./T.S.S.$, we will have the proportion of variation in the response variable that is "accounted for" by knowledge of the grouping variable. Calling this measure of association R^2_Q, then, and canceling out the one-halves in both numerator and denominator:

$$(32) \quad R^2_Q = \frac{\sum_{j=1}^{G} \frac{1}{n_{+j}} \sum_{i=1}^{I} n^2_{ij} - \frac{1}{n} \sum_{i=1}^{I} n^2_{i+}}{n - \frac{1}{n} \sum_{i=1}^{I} n^2_{i+}}.$$

Significance testing for R^2_Q. A researcher may wish to test the hypothesis of no association: that the true value of R^2_Q in the population is zero. Letting P_{ij} denote the probability that a response in the jth group will be in the ith category, and also letting a "dot" represent the average value for any subscript, testing H_0 of no association is equivalent to testing the hypothesis that $P_{ij} = P_{i.}$. Light and Margolin (1971) have shown that $C = (I - 1)(n - 1)R^2_Q$ is distributed asymptotically as $\chi^2_{(I-1)(G-1)}$ under the null hypothesis. Thus, having computed R^2_Q, it is easy to test its statistical significance.

Example 7

A sample of 230 elementary-school students who had previously attended preschool programs was selected from a large city, and each student was categorized by the type of preschool instruction to which he had been exposed. The three instructional categories were Montessori Program, a highly structured curriculum, and a "traditional" curriculum. Each student was then asked to identify his favorite free-play activity; we will denote these four categories as A, B, C and D. The data appear in Figure 16.

CURRICULUM TYPE

		Montessori	Highly structured	Traditional	
	A	2	19	24	45
Student's Preferred	B	51	10	3	64
Activity	C	18	68	2	88
	D	12	13	17	42
		83	110	46	239

Fig. 16.   School curriculum type by favorite activity for 239 elementary-school children.

Computing R^2_Q from (32) for these data:

$$\frac{1}{n}\sum_{i=1}^{I} n^2_{i+} = \frac{1}{239}(45^2 + 64^2 + 88^2 + 42^2)$$

$$= 65.39$$

$$\sum_{j=1}^{G}\frac{1}{n_{+j}}\sum_{i=1}^{I} n^2_{ij} = \frac{1}{83}(2^2 + 51^2 + 18^2 + 12^2)$$

$$+ \frac{1}{110}(19^2 + 10^2 + 68^2 + 13^2)$$

$$+ \frac{1}{48}(24^2 + 3^2 + 2^2 + 17^2)$$

$$R^2_Q = \frac{(37.02 + 47.76 + 19.09) - 65.39}{239 - 65.39}$$

$$= 0.221.$$

Thus, we can interpret the data in Figure 16 as indicating that 22.1 percent of the variance in a student's preferred activity is "explained" or "accounted for" by knowledge of the curriculum type he has been exposed to. This can be further extended to an analogue with the simple correlation coefficient r for continuous data. With our categorized data, the simple correlation between curriculum type and student's preferred activity is $\sqrt{0.221} \doteq 0.47$.

To test the null hypothesis that the true correlation in the population is zero, we apply the test $C = (I - 1)(n - 1)R^2_Q$. This will be distributed under H_0 as chi-

square with $(I - 1)(G - 1) = 6$ degrees of freedom. For our data:

$$C = 3(238)(.221) = 158.26.$$

This value for chi-square is significant far beyond the 0.01 level, so we reject the null hypothesis of no correlation in the complete population.

Comparing C with the Standard Chi-square Approach

Both $C = (n - 1)(I - 1)R^2_Q$ and the standard chi-square statistic have the identical asymptotic distribution under the null hypothesis; both are $\chi^2_{(I-1)(G-1)}$. We now examine the relation between these two statistics.

The standard chi-square statistic can be written as:

$$(33) \quad \chi^2_{(I-1)(G-1)} = \sum_{i=1}^{I}\frac{n}{n_{i+}}\sum_{j=1}^{G}$$

$$\cdot \left(\frac{n_{ij}}{\sqrt{n_{+j}}} - \frac{n_{i+}}{n}\sqrt{n_{+j}}\right)^2$$

while we can also rewrite the B.S.S. from (31) as:

$$(34) \quad B.S.S. = \frac{1}{2}\sum_{i=1}^{I}$$

$$\cdot \sum_{j=1}^{G}\left(\frac{n_{ij}}{\sqrt{n_{+j}}} - \frac{n_{i+}}{n}\sqrt{n_{+j}}\right)^2.$$

Comparing (33) and (34) shows that chi-square is proportional to $B.S.S.$ up to the weighting factor of $\dfrac{n}{n_{i+}}$.

This is a general result. However, for the special case of $I = 2$, when there are only two response categories, $\chi^2 = n(I - 1)$ $B.S.S./T.S.S.$. In other words, when $I = 2$, C is identical to the chi-square statistic up to a constant.

A series of computer simulations (Light, 1969) indicates that the ordering of samples, generated from an underlying probability structure for an $I \times G$ table when I exceeds 2, is different for the two statistics, but they have a rank correlation of the order of 0.90.

Preference Regions in 3×2 Tables. Computer simulations have indicated that, while C and χ^2 are identical under H_0 when no association exists, C is more powerful for some departures from H_0 while χ^2 is more powerful for other departures. Thus, if a researcher believes that his data on two variables have some true association, and he further believes that he has some idea about what "form" that association takes, he should use the technique which gives the greatest power. Figure 16 gives results of power comparisons between χ^2 and C for 3×2 tables. Figure 17 is only applicable to the two groups by three responses case, but this case is common enough to warrant a careful investigation. Thus, if a researcher has data which consist of two groups with three categories per group, and he believes he has an idea of what the true probability structure of the table is (as given in his null hypothesis), he can consult Figure 17 for guidance as to which statistic to use.

Reading Figure 17. The figure gives combinations of group 1 and group 2 probability vectors for which the power of C may be expected to exceed the power of χ^2. Call these combinations C preference regions. To identify these regions, we hold one vector fixed, say the "group one" vector. The table includes 10 values of these fixed

vectors; they appear across the top of the table. Note that the first fixed vector is at the center of the simplex (1/3, 1/3, 1/3). Further, the next three fixed vectors represent a systematic movement towards a vertex. The following three vectors represent a systematic movement towards a side. Finally, the last three vectors represent points in the simplex somewhere between a vertex and a side.

Corresponding to each fixed vector, the body of the figure gives various probability combinations of the second vector for the C preference regions. The column on the left gives values of P_1 for the second vector, in steps of 0.05 from 0.05 to 0.95, inclusive. The body of the figure then gives a range of values for P_2 which designate the C preference region. Since $\overset{3}{\underset{i=1}{\Sigma}} P_i = 1$, no specification of P_3 is necessary. Further, we note that since the response categories have nominal scales, the designation of a particular category's P_i as P_1, P_2 or P_3 is left to the researcher. His only constraint is that this assignment must apply to both groups.

Examples from Figure 17:

a. *No interpolation*

Suppose a researcher has some data in a 3×2 table and believes that one group has an underlying vector of probabilities of $P_{i1} =$ approximately 0.333 for all $i = 1, 2,$ 3. Then the column under this fixed vector gives the sets of group 2 probability vectors corresponding to C preference regions. For example, if we expect that $P_1 = 0.05$ for group two, we see from Figure 17 that P_2 falling between 0.00 — 0.23 or 0.72 — 0.95 identifies the C preference region. Otherwise, if $0.24 \leq P_2 \leq 0.71$, χ^2 should be used.

b. *Interpolation*

In order to describe continuously bounded regions in a tabular reference format, 10 particular fixed group 1 vectors are given in Figure 17 together with discrete values of P_1 for the group 2 vectors. Therefore, Figure 17 gives preference regions for only a small number of the paired vector combinations which are possible in 3×2 tables. It

RICHARD J. LIGHT

Fixed Group 1 Vector

p_1	.333 .333 .333	.60 .20 .20	.80 .10 .10	.92 .04 .04	.40 .40 .20	.44 .44 .12	.48 .48 .04	.50 .35 .15	.60 .30 .10	.70 .25 .05
	Range of P_2 for which Power (C) > Power (χ^2)									
.05	.00–.23 .72–.95	.00–.27 .68–.95	.00–.27 .66–.95	.00–.32 .63–.95	.00–.28 .78–.95	.00–.25 .80–.95	.00–.25 .80–.95	.00–.23 .75–.95	.00–.23 .76–.95	.00–.24 .74–.95
.10	.00–.27 .65–.90	.00–.29 .63–.90	.00–.30 .62–.90	.00–.35 .55–.90	.00–.30 .71–.90	.00–.28 .74–.90	.00–.27 .76–.90	.00–.27 .68–.90	.00–.27 .70–.90	.00–.25 .69–.90
.15	.00–.28 .57–.85	.00–.30 .56–.85	.00–.85	.00–.85	.00–.32 .64–.85	.00–.30 .68–.85	.00–.30 .70–.85	.00–.29 .63–.85	.00–.28 .63–.85	.00–.27 .64–.85
.20	.05–.32 .48–.77	.00–.32 .47–.80	.00–.80	.00–.80	.02–.31 .58–.78	.03–.31 .63–.80	.03–.31 .65–.80	.00–.30 .57–.80	.00–.30 .57–.80	.00–.28 .57–.80
.25	.12–.32 .42–.65	.00–.75	.00–.75	.00–.75	.07–.28 .51–.71	.08–.29 .59–.73	.08–.29 .61–.75	.03–.30 .53–.74	.00–.31 .50–.75	.00–.35 .45–.75
.30	.18–.33 .35–.54	.00–.70	.00–.70	.00–.70	.17–.22 .47–.65	.17–.22 .56–.67	.17–.22 .58–.70	.07–.27 .48–.68	.01–.30 .45–.70	.01–.70
.35	.30–.33	.02–.65	.00–.65	.00–.65	.46–.55	—	—	.47–.60	.04–.28 .41–.65	.03–.65
.40	.25–.33	.07–.54	.00–.60	.00–.60	—	—	—	—	.13–.22 .37–.58	.08–.60
.45	.22–.32	—	.00–.55	.00–.55	—	—	—	—	.36–.51	.13–.55
.50	.18–.30	—	.00–.50	.00–.50	.26–.33	—	—	—	—	.24–.50
.55	.15–.29	—	.00–.45	.00–.45	.22–.33	—	—	—	—	.26–.45
.60	.13–.27	—	.02–.38	.00–.40	.17–.32	.22–.32	—	—	—	.27–.38
.65	.12–.35	—	.05–.32	.00–.35	.14–.29	.17–.30	.20–.34	.19–.24	—	—
.70	.09–.23	.14–.17	.10–.23	.00–.30	.12–.27	.14–.27	.15–.30	.14–.23	—	—
.75	.07–.22	.09–.17	—	.00–.25	.09–.23	.12–.23	.12–.23	.12–.22	.15–.20	—
.80	.03–.18	.06–.14	—	.05–.17	.06–.20	.08–.20	.08–.20	.08–.18	.11–.18	.13–.17
.85	.00–.15	.03–.13	—	—	.02–.15	.05–.15	.05–.15	.04–.15	.07–.15	.09–.14
.90	.00–.10	.00–.10	—	—	.00–.10	.00–.10	.00–.10	.00–.10	.01–.10	.04–.10
.95	.00–.05	.00–.05	—	—	.00–.05	.00–.05	.00–.05	.00–.05	.00–.05	.00–.05

Fig. 17. C versus χ^2 preference regions for 3 X 2 tables.

will often be necessary for a user of this table to interpolate on either the rows or the columns, and perhaps on both. In this event, a linear interpolation on either the rows or columns will generally yield preference regions within about 0.02 from the exact value. This happens because of the relative smoothness of the boundaries of the preference regions, and the fact that the 10 selected fixed vectors cover most of the simplex with a reasonably close spacing. Further, because of the nominal property of the response categories, it should generally be possible to permute the rows so that a minimum amount of interpolation is necessary.

If both vectors specified by the researcher would require interpolation across the top of Figure 17, no matter which was held fixed, another question that arises is which vector to fix? Since interpolation of an entire vector between two other vectors is more difficult than the interpolation of a particular P_1 between two other single P_1's, the vector which requires the least interpolation across the top of Figure 17 should be held fixed.

c. *Preference Regions Around Edges of Simplex*

Fortunately, there is no sudden change in the behavior of the preference boundaries at the outer limits of the simplex. Thus, extrapolation to these limits will yield good estimates of the true C preference regions. For example, if the fixed vector is approximately 0.40, and P_1 for the second vector is

$$\begin{matrix}0.40\\0.20\end{matrix}$$

estimated to be zero or very close to it, the limits of P_2 for the C preference region are approximately 0.00–0.26 and 0.85–1.00.

d. *Empty Spaces in Table*

An empty space in any cell of Figure 17 means that for that particular combination of a fixed vector and a P_1 for the second vector, there is no value of P_2 for which C is preferable to chi-square.

A GEOMETRIC REPRESENTATION OF $C = (n - 1)(I - 1)R^2_Q$

As a final comparison between C and chi-square in the two-variable case, we investigate the geometric structure of C versus χ^2 using barycentric coordinates. We focus again on the 3×2 table.

As soon as the n_{+j} for each group in a 3×2 table has been set, we can plot the numerical structure of each statistic, corresponding to each possible table configuration independent of cell probabilities. For example, consider the barycentric representation in Figure 18.

The triangle in Figure 18 corresponds to $n_{+j} = 3$ for both groups. The 10 points on

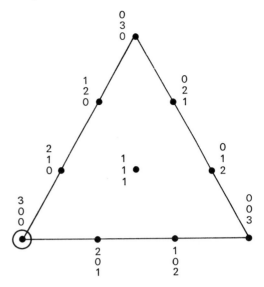

Fig. 18. Barycentric representation of responses in 3 x 2 tables when $n_{+j} = 3$ for both groups. Group 1 vector is held constant at $\begin{pmatrix}3\\0\\0\end{pmatrix}$.

the triangle indicate the 10 different group 1 outcomes which are possible. The dotted circle (on the figure) around the outcome $\begin{pmatrix}3\\0\\0\end{pmatrix}$ will be used to indicate that the group 1 vector should be held fixed at this outcome.

Using this display technique, we can examine the numerical values of either χ^2 or C over all possible configurations of one group while holding the other group fixed. Figure 19a shows that while holding one group constant at $\begin{pmatrix}3\\0\\0\end{pmatrix}$:

a) when the other group has structure 2,1,0 or 2,0,1 the χ^2 value is 1.2;

b) when the other group has structure 1,2,0 or 1,1,1 or 1,0,2 the χ^2 value is 3.0;

c) when the other group has structure 0,3,0 or 0,2,1 or 0,1,2 or 0,0,3 the χ^2 value is 6.0.

By connecting equivalued points in the triangle, we construct *iso-chis* (a set of equal

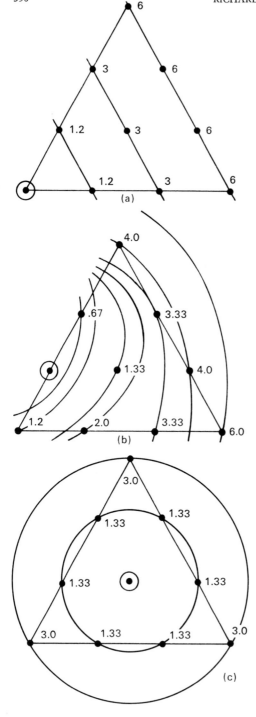

Fig. 19.   Chi-square values for $n_{+j} = 3 : j =$
1,2.

chi-square values), which give a picture of the statistic's ability to discriminate among various table structures. Note that Figure 19b holds one group fixed at 2,1,0 while Figure 19c holds one group fixed at 1,1,1, the center of the simplex. In this last case, the iso-chis consist of concentric circles, the inner circle indicating χ^2 values of 1.33, and the outer circle values of 3.0.

Focusing this approach on the C versus χ^2 comparison for $n_{+j} = 5$, we first define the barycentric triangle in Figure 20 to correspond to group vectors with five responses. We then plot the iso-chis and iso-C's with one group fixed at the vertex $\begin{pmatrix} 5 \\ 0 \\ 0 \end{pmatrix}$. The results appear in Figure 21.

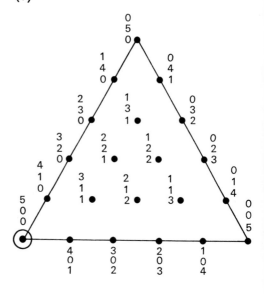

Fig. 20.   Barycentric coordinates for group with five responses.

The plots in Figure 21 indicate geometrically some differences between C and χ^2. Specifically, the iso-chis are straight lines while the iso-C's are curves, indicating a difference in the discriminations made by the two statistics. C makes some discrimination among points which lie along any given iso-chi. For example, while χ^2 cannot

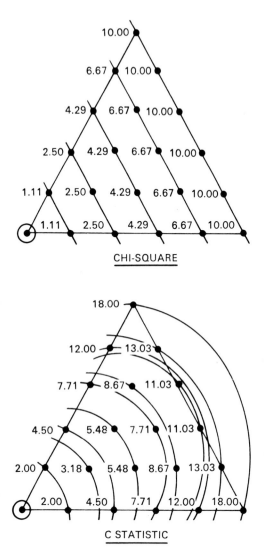

CHI-SQUARE

C STATISTIC

Fig. 21. Iso-chis and Iso-C's with fixed vec-
5
tor (0).
0

C discriminates among alternatives where χ^2 cannot, while for other points the reverse is true.

Extending the "Pairs Approach" to Three Dimensions

In general, the extensions from a two-dimensional table to tables with three and higher dimensions are not obvious since a variety of different hypotheses can be tested (Darroch, 1962; Lewis, 1962). However, assuming a relatively frequent multinomial model, we can extend the pairs approach to three dimensions.

Assume that data appear in an $I \times R \times C$ contingency table. Let I represent the number of response categories, R the number of rows and C the number of columns. The I categories within each of the RC cells should have a nominal scale, and the order in which they appear in all cells must be identical. We further assume that the model underlying this data has the row and column margins fixed, while the responses within each cell are allowed to vary. Thus, for example, if the response categories are children's behavior patterns, the rows might be schools and the columns might represent several grade levels. Then, within each grade level in each school, we observe children and classify their behavior among I categories.

For this model, let n_{ijk} indicate the number of observations in the j,k cell assigned to the ith response category; $i = 1, \ldots, I;$ $j = 1, \ldots, R;$ $k = 1, \ldots, C$. Once again, a sum over any subscript will be denoted by a $+$, so that $\sum_{i=1}^{I} n_{ijk} = n_{+jk}$, which indicates the total number of responses in the j,k cell. Note that n_{+jk} can differ over the RC cells; we assume that n_{+jk} for the j,k cell is under the control of the researcher. Further, $\sum_{j=1}^{R} n_{+jk} = n_{++k}$, representing the total number of responses in the kth column of the table. Finally, $\sum_{k=1}^{C} n_{++k} = n$, the total number

discriminate among the group 2 vectors 1,4,0; 1,3,1; 1,2,2; 1,1,3; and 1,0,4, C does make some discrimination. Depending upon the point in the simplex at which we fix one vector, we will find that for some points of responses in the entire table. The n's again represent frequencies; we let P_{ijk} represent the probability that a response in the j,k cell will fall into the ith category. To illustrate, the data format for a $2 \times 3 \times 4$ table appears in Figure 22. The total variation in the three-dimensional layout can be developed using the approach of (28), and this total can then be partitioned into additive components of variation. We now develop these components.

The total sum of squares comes from examining the total number of pairs of responses in the table and seeing how many of the pairs have responses falling into different categories. This expression becomes:

$$(35) \qquad T.S.S. = \frac{n}{2} - \frac{1}{2n} \sum_{i=1}^{I} n^2_{i++}.$$

We now partition this total variation into its components within and between groups. For the within-groups variation, summed over all of the RC groups:

$$(36) \quad W.S.S. = \frac{n}{2} - \frac{1}{2} \sum_{j=1}^{R} \sum_{k=1}^{C} \frac{1}{n_{+jk}} \sum_{i=1}^{I} n^2_{ijk}.$$

Again examining pairs, the overall between-groups variation is:

$$(37) \quad B.S.S. = \frac{1}{2} \left(\sum_{j=1}^{R} \sum_{k=1}^{C} \frac{1}{n_{+jk}} \sum_{i=1}^{I} n^2_{ijk} - \frac{1}{n} \sum_{i=1}^{I} n^2_{i++} \right).$$

The between- and within-groups variation in (36) and (37) is essentially analogous to (30) and (31) for the two-dimensional table except that now each of the RC cells in the entire table is viewed as a group. The $B.S.S.$ in (37) can be further partitioned, however, into additive components due to rows, columns, and a residual which we will view as an "interaction." Thus, the row variation becomes:

$$(38) \quad R.S.S. = \frac{1}{2} \left(\sum_{j=1}^{R} \frac{1}{n_{+j+}} \sum_{i=1}^{I} n^2_{ij+} - \frac{1}{n} \sum_{i=1}^{I} n^2_{i++} \right).$$

Column variation is:

$$(39) \quad C.S.S. = \frac{1}{2} \left(\sum_{k=1}^{C} \frac{1}{n_{++k}} \sum_{i=1}^{I} n^2_{i+k} - \frac{1}{n} \sum_{i=1}^{I} n^2_{i++} \right),$$

	C_1	C_2	C_3	C_4	
R_1	$\left.\begin{array}{l} n_{111} \\ n_{211} \end{array}\right\} n_{+11}$	$\left.\begin{array}{l} n_{112} \\ n_{212} \end{array}\right\} n_{+12}$	$\left.\begin{array}{l} n_{113} \\ n_{213} \end{array}\right\} n_{+13}$	$\left.\begin{array}{l} n_{114} \\ n_{214} \end{array}\right\} n_{+14}$	$\left.\begin{array}{l} n_{11+} \\ n_{21+} \end{array}\right\} n_{+1+}$
R_2	$\left.\begin{array}{l} n_{121} \\ n_{221} \end{array}\right\} n_{+21}$	$\left.\begin{array}{l} n_{122} \\ n_{222} \end{array}\right\} n_{+22}$	$\left.\begin{array}{l} n_{123} \\ n_{223} \end{array}\right\} n_{+23}$	$\left.\begin{array}{l} n_{124} \\ n_{224} \end{array}\right\} n_{+24}$	$\left.\begin{array}{l} n_{12+} \\ n_{22+} \end{array}\right\} n_{+2+}$
R_3	$\left.\begin{array}{l} n_{131} \\ n_{231} \end{array}\right\} n_{+31}$	$\left.\begin{array}{l} n_{132} \\ n_{232} \end{array}\right\} n_{+32}$	$\left.\begin{array}{l} n_{133} \\ n_{233} \end{array}\right\} n_{+33}$	$\left.\begin{array}{l} n_{134} \\ n_{234} \end{array}\right\} n_{+34}$	$\left.\begin{array}{l} n_{13+} \\ n_{23+} \end{array}\right\} n_{+3+}$
	$\left.\begin{array}{l} n_{1+1} \\ n_{2+1} \end{array}\right\} n_{++1}$	$\left.\begin{array}{l} n_{1+2} \\ n_{2+2} \end{array}\right\} n_{++2}$	$\left.\begin{array}{l} n_{1+3} \\ n_{2+3} \end{array}\right\} n_{++3}$	$\left.\begin{array}{l} n_{1+4} \\ n_{2+4} \end{array}\right\} n_{++4}$	n

Fig. 22.   Notation for 2 X 3 X 4 contingency table. Row and column margins are fixed. Responses are not fixed.

and finally the residual after $R.S.S.$ and $C.S.S.$ are subtracted from $B.S.S.$ is the interaction variation:

$$(40) \quad I.S.S. = \frac{1}{2} \left(\sum_{j=1}^{R} \sum_{k=1}^{C} \frac{1}{n_{+jk}} \sum_{i=1}^{I} n^2_{ijk} \right.$$

$$- \sum_{k=1}^{C} \frac{1}{n_{++k}} \sum_{i=1}^{I} n^2_{i+k}$$

$$- \sum_{j=1}^{R} \frac{1}{n_{+j+}} \sum_{i=1}^{I} n^2_{ij+}$$

$$\left. + \frac{1}{n} \sum_{i=1}^{I} n^2_{i++} \right).$$

Testing Hypotheses in the Three-Dimensional Table

There are a large number of hypotheses which can be tested in a three-dimensional table. The significance of single effects comprises one class, the significance of combinations of effects comprises another, and the interaction effect can be tested in several forms. For a good taxonomy of these hypotheses, see Lancaster (1969) or Lewis (1962).

Chi-square tests are available for assessing the independence of each pair of the three dimensions and for assessing the independence of the three dimensions taken together. They are primarily suitable for the case when the investigator cannot single out one of the three variables as the dependent variable and so is content with relatively general conclusions about the presence or absence of association in the table. The pairs approach, applicable when one dimension is a dependent or response variable, leads to tests of specific effects with a different focus from that of the standard chi-square procedures. We present here the hypotheses for which test statistics have been worked out using the pairs approach; let us call them the *dead dimension* hypotheses.

Probably the first question a data analyst asks when confronted with a multidimensional table is whether or not any information will be lost if the table is "collapsed" over a dimension. If the answer is no, this dimension may be called dead. Note that for a dimension to be dead, its combined main effect and interaction with other main effects must be nonsignificant. For example, a hypothesis that the row dimension is dead in the format of Figure 22 would be expressed:

$$(41) \quad H_{0_R} : P_{ijk} = P_{i.k} .$$

This hypothesis (41) states that the probability a response in a particular column falls into a particular category is independent of (the same for) all rows. Note that if this hypothesis is true, it implies that $P_{ij.} = P_{i. .}$.

The hypothesis that columns are a dead dimension is, symmetrically:

$$(42) \quad H_{0_C} : P_{ijk} = P_{ij.} .$$

This hypothesis indicates that the probability a response in a particular row falls into a particular category is independent of the columns. Note that H_{0C} being true implies that $P_{i.k} = P_{i. .}$.

To test these two hypotheses, Light and Margolin (1972) have shown that the following test statistics are asymptotically distributed as chi-square. For dead rows:

$$(43) \quad H_R = \frac{(I-1) \, C \, (R.S.S. + I.S.S.)}{\displaystyle\sum_{k=1}^{C} T.M.S._k}$$

which is asymptotically approximated by $\chi^2_{C(I-1)(R-1)}$ under H_0 where:

$$T.M.S._k = \frac{1}{n_{++k} - 1} \left(n_{++k} - \frac{1}{n_{++k}} \sum_{i=1}^{I} n^2_{i+k} \right).$$

For dead columns:

$$H_C = \frac{(I-1) \, R \, (C.S.S. + I.S.S.)}{\displaystyle\sum_{j=1}^{R} T.M.S._j} ,$$

which is asymptotically approximated by $\chi^2_{R(I-1)(C-1)}$ under H_0 where:

$$T.M.S._j = \frac{1}{n_{+j+} - 1} \cdot \left(n_{+j+} - \frac{1}{n_{+j+}} \sum_{i=1}^{I} n^2_{ij+} \right).$$

Notice that both of the statistics for the dead dimension hypotheses are functions of the interaction variation as well as the appropriate main effect variation. Thus, if the test statistic for either dimension indicates that the dimension is not "live," or statistically significant, the data in the table can be collapsed over that dimension, since leaving this dimension in the table offers no significant new information. Note further that accepting a dimension as dead does not require that there be no three-variable interaction present in the table, since the dead dimension hypothesis is a hypothesis about a *combination* of a main effect and its interaction component.

Suppose that a dimension is live. A data analyst may then wish to try to separate the interaction effect from the main effect to see if he can isolate the primary "contributor" to the significance of a dimension. To do this, he can test the additive interaction hypothesis:

$$(44) \quad H_{0_I} : P_{ijk} - P_{ij.} = P_{i.k} - P_{i..}$$

for all i, j, k.

This hypothesis has the interpretation that if we focus on a certain response category, then the effect of switching from any row to any other row is the same for all columns. A test statistic for H_{0_I} is:

$$(45) \quad H_I = (I - 1)(n - R - C + 1) \cdot \left(\frac{I.S.S.}{I.S.S. + W.S.S.} \right)$$

which is asymptotically approximated by $\chi^2_{(I-1)(C-1)(R-1)}$ under H_0.

But H_{0_I} only should be tested under special circumstances. Note that *I.S.S.*, which essentially is being tested for the significance of its departure from the population value of zero under the null hypothesis, is a func-

tion of n_{+jk}, the total number of responses in the j,k cell. But according to the within-cell multinomial model which underlies this analysis, the n_{+jk} is under the experimental control of the researcher. He can thus make *I.S.S* any value he wishes, just by appropriately fixing the n_{+jk} in various cells. Thus, the hypothesis H_{0_I} should only be tested in two circumstances. First, it can be examined in the special case of a balanced layout, where all n_{+jk} are equal. Example 8 (later in chapter) gives such a case. The results of this analysis will then tell a researcher something about the structure of the relationships among the several variables he is examining. Second, H_{0_I} can be tested when the n_{+jk} in the sample are proportional to the "true N_{+jk}" in the defined population. In this circumstance, the contingency table can be taken to represent a proportionate stratified sample from the population, and a test for the existence of interaction can be viewed as a test of how "things are" in the real world. In any other situation, a test of H_{0_I} should be made very cautiously, and perhaps not at all, since a researcher can achieve nearly any result he wishes by simply allocating sample points over the cells in a calculated manner. In summary then, both "dead dimensions" hypotheses can be tested in the general unbalanced layout, while the interaction hypothesis should be tested only for balanced designs, or designs which represent a proportionate stratified sample from a population.

Order of testing. Having presented the various test statistics for the two- and three-dimensional "pairs approach" to contingency tables, we can now suggest a procedure for examining a three-dimensional table. We assume that the within-cell multinomial model is appropriate.

When confronted with a three-dimensional table, the researcher should first test the two "dead dimension" hypotheses of (41) and (42). Suppose he finds both dimensions dead. Then he can conclude that the table consists of *RC* cells all with the same multinomial probability structure. Suppose he finds one dimension dead, say, the rows. Then he can collapse over the rows, and analyze the remaining two-dimensional table, consisting of columns by responses, with the test statistic for a two-dimensional table given in (32). If the researcher finds neither dimension dead, he then cannot collapse the table at all. However, if the n_{+jk} are equal, or they are proportional to the population distribution of elements, the possible presence of interaction can be tested by using (45). If interaction is found to be *absent,* then we conclude that the live dimensions are live because of their main effects, rather than interaction.

Measures of Association From the Three-Dimensional Table

In the two-variable contingency table, an attractive feature of using the pairs approach was that it led to a natural measure of association R^2_Q, which had a "proportion of variability explained" interpretation. For the three-dimensional table such a measure would also be useful, especially for the common situation where a data analyst is interested in determining which of two predictor variables is more importantly or highly related to a response variable. Thus, a separate measure of proportion of variation explained by each independent variable would be useful.

Such measures can be computed, but they must be interpreted with extreme care and used only in certain circumstances. The ratio R.S.S./T.S.S. is meaningful only if the columns dead dimension hypothesis has not been rejected. Symmetrically, C.S.S./T.S.S. should only be used if the rows dimension is concluded to be dead. These constraints are imposed because the expected value of the row sum of squares is a function of n_{+jk}, which the researcher sets. In other words, if either column effects or interaction effects exist, then different allocations of the n responses among the RC cells will yield different values for the ratio R.S.S./T.S.S.

This ratio will be insensitive to the n_{+jk} allocations only if the columns are a dead dimension, and should therefore only be interpreted in that event. By symmetric reasoning, C.S.S./T.S.S. can be interpreted as the proportion of variation in the response variable explained by the column variable only when rows are found to be dead.

One special case exists for which the two ratios have meaning even when the dead dimensions hypotheses are rejected. Suppose the three-dimensional layout represents a proportionate stratified sample from a larger population with known true N_{+jk}'s in the population, and n_{+jk}/N_{+jk} is constant for all j,k cells. Then the two ratios can be viewed as describing the proportion of variability in the response variable explained in the "real world" by the row variable and the column variable, respectively, even though the ratios are functions of the n_{+jk}.

As an example, suppose we had sampled college juniors who were themselves the children of college graduates. Each junior is classified by his mother's, his father's and his own major fields. We would expect that the two predictive dimensions—mother's field and father's field—would be associated in the real world, and that the n_{+jk}'s would be proportionate to the N_{+jk}'s. One partition of the total variation in the junior's major fields among the several predictor effects might be:

Variation in Field Due to	Percent of Total
Mother's major field	5%
Father's major field	25%
Interaction of mother's and father's field	45%
Residual variation	25%
	100%

Such a result is quite compatible with a nonsignificant two-way chi-square between mother's and son's field, even though two-thirds of the parentally determined variation in the junior's choice of fields is overlooked whenever the variable "knowledge of mother's field" is discarded.

To conclude our discussion of the pairs approach, note that there are some analogies between the entire pairs procedure for analyzing contingency tables and the standard analysis of variance for continuous data. The definition of a total sum of squares, and its partition into additive components, is a direct analogy to the analysis of variance. Further, Light and Margolin (1971) show that under the null hypothesis of no effects, the expected values of the several sums of squares components are equal. There are differences, however, such as the approximate asymptotic distributions of the test statistics, which for the analysis of variance are always F, while for the pairs approach they are always chi-square. The primary advantage of the statistics discussed here, in addition to their computational simplicity, is the ease with which they can be interpreted. For both the two- and three-dimensional contingency tables each test statistic and ratio of sums of squares has a precise interpretation, somewhat analogous to the interpretations researchers give to correlational analyses on continuous variables.

Example 8

We illustrate the three-dimensional pairs approach with the data in Figure 23. Note that the design is balanced. Three types of schools are represented on the rows—public, private and parochial. Five regions of the country are represented on the columns—northeast, northwest, southeast, southwest and midwest. Thirty children were selected randomly from each of the 15 cells. Each was then asked to select his favorite school subject from the four choices: history, science, English or mathematics.

From the data in Figure 23, we are interested in examining overall differences among school types, overall differences among regions of the country, and finally the presence of interaction between school type and region of country. We begin by

REGION

SCHOOL TYPE		Northeast		Northwest		Southeast		Southwest		Midwest		Σ =	
	Public	h*	7	h	3	h	4	h	10	h	9	h	33
		s	11	s	2	s	11	s	8	s	3	s	35
		e	8	e	16	e	2	e	7	e	12	e	45
		m	4	m	9	m	13	m	5	m	6	m	37
	Private	h	6	h	4	h	6	h	8	h	1	h	25
		s	10	s	12	s	15	s	14	s	19	s	70
		e	5	e	8	e	4	e	6	e	0	e	23
		m	9	m	6	m	5	m	2	m	10	m	32
	Parochial	h	10	h	8	h	18	h	12	h	15	h	63
		s	4	s	3	s	7	s	2	s	2	s	18
		e	8	e	8	e	0	e	7	e	3	e	26
		m	8	m	11	m	5	m	9	m	10	m	43
	Σ =	h	23	h	15	h	28	h	30	h	25	h	121
		s	25	s	17	s	33	s	24	s	24	s	123
		e	21	e	32	e	6	e	20	e	15	e	94
		m	21	m	26	m	23	m	16	m	26	m	112

(* h—history, s—science, e—English, m—mathematics)

Fig. 23.   Subject preferences for children in three types of schools and five geographic regions.

simply computing the raw sums of squares generated by the 450 responses:

$$T.S.S. = \frac{450}{2} - \frac{1}{900}$$

$$\cdot (121^2 + 123^2 + 94^2 + 112^2)$$

$$= 168.17$$

$$W.S.S. = 225 - \frac{1}{60}$$

$$\cdot \left(\begin{array}{l} 250 + 350 + 310 + 238 + 270 \\ + 242 + 260 + 302 + 300 + 462 \\ + 244 + 258 + 398 + 278 + 338 \end{array} \right)$$

$$= 150.00$$

$$B.S.S. = \frac{1}{2} \left[\frac{1}{30}(4500) - \frac{1}{450}(51150) \right]$$

$$= 18.17 .$$

We now partition the B.S.S. into its three additive subcomponents:

$$R.S.S. = \frac{1}{2} \left[\frac{1}{150} \right.$$

$$\cdot \left(\begin{array}{l} 33^2 + 35^2 + 45^2 + 37^2 \\ + 25^2 + 70^2 + 23^2 + 32^2 \\ + 63^2 + 18^2 + 26^2 + 43^2 \end{array} \right) - 113.6 \right]$$

$$R.S.S. = 8.51$$

$$C.S.S. = \frac{1}{2} \left[\frac{1}{90} \right.$$

$$\cdot \left(\begin{array}{l} 23^2 + 25^2 + 21^2 + 15^2 \\ + 17^2 + 32^2 + 26^2 + 28^2 \\ + 33^2 + 6^2 + 23^2 + 30^2 \\ + 24^2 + 20^2 + 16^2 + 25^2 \\ + 24^2 + 15^2 + 26^2 \end{array} \right) - 113.6 \right]$$

$$C.S.S. = 3.84$$

$$I.S.S. = \frac{1}{2} [150 - 121.36 - 130.69 + 113.7]$$

$$I.S.S. = 5.81$$

Having computed the sums of squares, we may now test the three hypotheses. First,

testing the dead row dimension hypothesis with H_R:

$$H_R = \frac{(3)(5)(8.50 + 5.81)}{3.69} = 58.18 .$$

Under H_{0_R} of dead rows, H_R has a chi-square distribution with $(C)(I-1)(R-1) = 30$ degrees of freedom. The computed value $H_R = 58.18$ is significant beyond the 0.01 level; we thus reject the dead rows hypothesis and conclude that we cannot collapse the table over the three rows. We also cannot interpret the ratio $C.S.S./T.S.S.$ as a proportion of variation explained.

Testing now for a dead column dimension:

$$H_C = \frac{(3)(3)(3.84 + 5.81)}{2.14} = 40.54 .$$

Under H_{0_C} of dead columns, H_C is distributed as chi-square with $(R)(C-1)(I-1) = 36$ degrees of freedom. Thus, the computed value $H_C = 40.54$ is not significant at the 0.05 level, and we cannot conclude that columns are live.

Finally, using H_I to test for interaction between school type and geographic region in terms of subject preference:

$$H_I = (3)(450 - 3 - 5 + 1) \left(\frac{5.81}{5.81 + 150} \right)$$

$$= 49.55 .$$

Under the null hypothesis of no interaction effects, H_I is chi-square with $(I-1)(C-1)(R-1) = 24$ degrees of freedom. The computed value of $H_I = 49.55$ is significant beyond the 0.01 level, and we conclude that a significant three-way interaction exists between the independent variables school type and geographic region and the dependent variable subject preference.

Errors of Classification and Contingency Table Procedures

Until now all the techniques discussed have assumed that responses on a nominal scale are correctly placed into categories.

In many research situations, however, this assumption may not hold. In educational applications especially, it is difficult to categorize human behavior into one among a set of categories. A question thus arises concerning the impact that errors of classification have on any estimates which a data analyst obtains from a contingency table. The major references in this area are the work of Assakul and Proctor (1965, 1967), Bross (1954) and Diamond and Lilienfeld (1962). An excellent summary of the effects of errors of measurement on both continuous and qualitative responses is given by Cochran (1968). We present here the main findings for qualitative data only.

Consider first the 2 x 2 table. Assume the model of two groups with fixed marginal totals n_{+1} and n_{+2}, and response marginal totals n_{1+} of ones (number of occurrences) and n_{2+} of zeroes (number of nonoccurrences) which are variable. Bross (1954) discusses the case where there may be classification errors within each group. For a single binomial population let p represent the observed proportion of ones, which comes from $p = P(1 - r) + (1 - P)s$, where P is the underlying correct proportion of ones, r represents the probability of incorrectly categorizing a one as a zero; and s represents the probability of incorrectly categorizing a zero as a one. If in either the standard chi-square test or the pairs approach for two dimensions we wish to compare the two groups, we essentially wish to estimate $P_1 - P_2$. Yet we only have available to us the estimate $p_1 - p_2$ which includes error. It can be shown that:

$$(46) \quad (p_1 - p_2) = P_1(1 - r_1 - s_1) - P_2$$
$$\cdot (1 - r_2 - s_2) + s_1 - s_2.$$

If the probabilities of misclassification are identical for the two groups, (46) reduces to:

$$(47) \quad (p_1 - p_2) = (P_1 - P_2)(1 - r - s).$$

Thus, if a data analyst has an approximate estimate of the probability of misclassification, he can estimate its impact on the search for a difference between two proportions. Note that in (47), when responses are subject to misclassification, the observed difference between proportions will underestimate the true difference. Also, when the null hypothesis $P_1 = P_2$ holds, the effect of misclassification on the standard significance tests will be to lower the power of the test, although the probability of a Type I error will be unaffected. From (46), however, we see that if the probabilities of misclassification differ for the two groups, the probability of making a Type I error in significance testing increases. Thus, as a general rule of thumb, the existence of misclassification errors is much more serious when the probabilities of misclassification differ among groups than when they are the same. A loss of power is a small price to pay relative to unwittingly increasing the level of significance.

In the multinomial case, for an $R \times C$ table with probabilities of misclassification on both variables, the relationships are much more complicated. Cochran indicates that the multiplicative null hypothesis, $P_{ij} = P_{i.}P_{.j}$, is correctly reflected by the observed probabilities only when the probabilities of row misclassifications are independent of those for column misclassifications. In situations where classification errors are serious enough to require some adjustment of the data, this condition will generally not hold, as it is highly restrictive. Further work needs to be done here (for some extensions, see Tenenbein, 1969).

2 x 2 TABLES

A format for data which is common in much research, but especially in educational research, is the 2 x 2 table. When two variables are being studied, and each variable is either a natural or an artificial dichotomy, the 2 x 2 table summarizes such data. An example of a natural dichotomy would be sex—male versus female. An example of an artificial dichotomy would be pass versus fail on a test. The latter is artificial in that by adjusting the level of achievement defined as passing, the form of responses in a table could be changed. Finally, educational data are often "broken at the median" in order to divide a set of responses into two subgroups of equal size. Thus, the responses in a 2 x 2 table could be either two natural dichotomies, two artificial dichotomies, or one of each. In the following several sections, we will consider some problems which frequently arise in the analysis of 2 x 2 tables. We will assume that regardless of how the categories were selected and divided, the resulting tables are meaningful representations of the intersections of two variables. In the concluding section of this chapter we will examine some implications of this assumption, but for now we focus on four problems:

1. restructuring cell estimates in a 2 x 2 table;
2. combining the results of several 2 x 2 tables;
3. comparing the association in several 2 x 2 tables;
4. developing multiple contrasts for sets of proportions.

1. RESTRUCTURING CELL ESTIMATES IN A 2 x 2 TABLE

It is sometimes difficult to visualize the "kernel" of association in a 2 x 2 table. This is often because the two categories on the rows and/or columns may not represent data which are broken at the median, and thus not have equal marginal totals for, say, the first and second columns. Similarly, the two row totals may be very unbalanced. Thus, in our earlier notation, it is fair to say that the form of the association between the variables in a 2 x 2 table will be clearest when $n_{1+} = n_{2+} = n_{+1} = n_{+2}$.

This rarely occurs, except in an ideally designed experiment. Since observational studies of students and teachers in their natural setting are especially common in educational research, we focus now on a procedure which will enable us to adjust the margins, and therefore also the cell entries, into a form which will permit a 2 x 2 table to display more clearly the bivariate association.

The particular method of cell adjustment which I present is called the *iterative proportional fitting method*. It is appropriate for making cell estimates in tables where we are given both the marginal totals and the association within the table.

The iterative proportional fitting method was developed by Deming and Stephan in 1940 for adjusting small sample observations to agree with a set of marginal totals obtained from census data. There are other procedures for cell estimation useful for particular classes of contingency tables, but they will not be described here. They are discussed by Bishop (1967), Fienberg (1968) and Mosteller (1968), and in careful detail by Fienberg (1970a, 1970b).

The main attractive feature of iterative proportional fitting in a 2 x 2 table is that the cross-product ratio $\frac{n_{11}n_{22}}{n_{12}n_{21}}$, which provides a measure of the interaction structure of the table, is preserved. While we only consider 2 x 2 tables, extensions to larger tables are given by Bishop (1967).

For example 9, which will illustrate this procedure, consider the data in Figure 24. We have here data on 234 males and 53 females; also we have observed a total of 29 high grades and 258 low grades.

In "standardizing" this table, we might be interested in arranging the table to have uniform margins, so that the four cells will be comparable in the sense of all being based on equal marginal totals. Thus, we wish to adjust the table so that $n_{1+} = n_{2+} = n_{+1} = n_{+2} = 1$, while still preserving the interaction structure.

Let's take a brief side-step and look at a 2 x 2 table similar to Figure 24. Figure 25 was derived from Figure 24 by doubling the number of males and multiplying the number of females by 10. Thus, the males and females obtain the same grades on the average as they did before; there are simply

RICHARD J. LIGHT

	Males	Females	Actual Totals	Required Totals
High Grades	18	11	29	1
Low Grades	216	42	258	1
Actual Totals	234	53		
Required Totals	1	1		

Fig. 24. Relationship between grades in school and sex.

more males and females. Should this increase in numbers change the basic association in Figure 25? A reasonable answer is that it should not.

We might think of a contingency table as having a basic nucleus which describes its association and think of all tables formed by multiplying elements in a complete row or a complete column by a positive number as forming an equivalence class—a class of tables with the same degree of association.

With this notion of an equivalence class in mind, let us look at Figures 26 and 27. They fall into the same equivalence class under this definition for any positive values of the r's and c's in Figure 27. That is, Figure 27 can be obtained by multiplying elements in row 1 of Figure 26 by r_1, multiplying elements in row 2 by r_2, multiplying elements in column 1 by c_1, and multiplying elements in column 2 by c_2. As previously indicated, the index of association which is invariant under these row and column multiplications is the cross-product ratio,

$$\frac{n_{11}n_{22}}{n_{12}n_{21}} = \frac{(r_1c_1n_{11})(r_2c_2n_{22})}{(r_1c_2n_{12})(r_2c_1n_{22})}$$

where $r_1, r_2, c_1, c_2 > 0$. In the numerical examples of Figures 24 and 25, the cross-product ratio is equal to $\frac{18(42)}{11(216)}$ or $\frac{36(420)}{110(432)}$ or 0.32.

	Males	Females
High Grades	n_{11}	n_{12}
Low Grades	n_{21}	n_{22}

Fig. 26. Prototype 2 X 2.

	Males	Females
High Grades	$r_1c_1n_{11}$	$r_1c_2n_{12}$
Low Grades	$r_2c_1n_{21}$	$r_2c_2n_{22}$

Fig. 27. Equivalent 2 X 2 after row and column multiplications.

Now let us return to our problem of converting each marginal in a 2 x 2 table to

	Males	Females	Actual Totals
High Grades	36	110	146
Low Grades	432	420	852
Actual Totals	468	530	

Fig. 25. Derivative of Figure 24.

the value of 1 while preserving the original association in the table. We begin with Figure 24 and perform the iterative proportional fitting procedure. First, we multiply each row of Figure 24 by the ratio of the desired final marginal to the initial row total in Figure 24—that is, we multiply each element in the first row by 1/29. Next, we multiply each element in the second row by the ratio of the desired final row margin to

the initial row total in Figure 24—that is, by 1/258. This gives us, to three decimals, Figure 28. Next we repeat the entire procedure on the columns, multiplying column one by 1/1.458 and column two by 1/0.542 and get as our result of the first iteration cycle Figure 29. We have now "messed up" the row totals and so we repeat the whole operation. After four cycles, we get Figure 30, the required table with uniform margins.

	Males	Females	Actual Totals	Required Totals
High Grades	0.621	0.379	1.000	1.000
Low Grades	0.837	0.163	1.000	1.000
Actual Totals	1.458	0.542		
Required Totals	1.000	1.000		

Fig. 28.   First iteration of Figure 24.

	Males	Females	Actual Totals	Required Totals
High Grades	0.426	0.700	1.126	1.000
Low Grades	0.574	0.300	0.874	1.000
Actual Totals	1.000	1.000		
Required Totals	1.000	1.000		

Fig. 29.   Second iteration of Figure 24—end of first cycle.

	Males	Females	Actual Totals	Required Totals
High Grades	0.361	0.639	1.000	1.000
Low Grades	0.639	0.361	1.000	1.000
Actual Totals	1.000	1.000		
Required Totals	1.000	1.000		

Fig. 30.   Figure 24 after four cycles of iterative fitting.

Clearly, we now see a nucleus of association that is hardly suggested by visual inspection of Figure 24, the original table. Because we have used only row and column multiplication in generating Figure 30, the cross-product ratio—and thus, the basic association in the new table—is the same as in the original table.

This simple example illustrates the use of the iterative proportional fitting method. The fact that this procedure provides the maximum likelihood estimates for cell entries has been proved by Bishop (1967). That this iterative scheme converges, providing the desired marginal values, has been proved by Bishop (1967) and by Ireland and Kullback (1968).

2. Combining the Results of Several 2 x 2 Tables

Another common problem facing researchers concerns optimal procedures for combining the results from several studies. We restrict ourselves here to 2 x 2 tables only, but the problem is general and needs much more work (Light & Smith, 1971).

Suppose we wish to study the dropout rate, by sex, in a number of Head Start centers. For each center, we classify the children by sex and by whether or not they completed the program. The table for the kth center would be given in Figure 31.

	Female	Male	
Dropped out	n_{11k}	n_{12k}	n_{1+k}
Completed	n_{21k}	n_{22k}	n_{2+k}
	n_{+1k}	n_{+2k}	n_{++k}

Fig. 31.   Dropout status.

We assume that the *column* totals were fixed in advance for each center—i.e., that the number of boys and girls in each program was known in advance. The null hypothesis is that the proportion of dropouts for boys and girls is identical or, equivalently, that sex and dropout status are independent. We wish to test this hypothesis by using all the data from all Head Start centers. Thus, we need a procedure for combining, or cumulating, data.

Perhaps our first thought might be to combine the data from all the centers into a single sex-by-retention 2 x 2 table, and then apply a chi-square test of independence to the single pooled table. That approach has two flaws: it has somewhat less power than the best technique, and it tacitly assumes that the relationship between sex and dropping out is identical in all centers. A better alternative is available.

To use this alternative, we define (for the kth table):

$$p_{1k} = n_{11k}/n_{+1k} \quad , \quad q_{1k} = 1 - p_{1k}$$
$$p_{2k} = n_{12k}/n_{+2k} \quad , \quad q_{2k} = 1 - p_{2k}$$
$$p_k = n_{1+k}/n_{++k} \quad , \quad q_k = 1 - p_k$$
$$d_k = p_{1k} - p_{2k}$$
$$w_k = n_{+1k}n_{+2k}/n_{++k}$$

Thus, to be clear: p_{1k} is the proportion of girls who dropped out, p_{2k} is the proportion of boys who dropped out, and p_k is the overall proportion of children who dropped out—all for the kth Head Start center.

The d_k is obviously the difference between the two proportions in the kth table. The w_k term is a "weight," and is larger for tables in which there are more children, several other things (which will be mentioned shortly) being equal.

A statistic proposed by Cochran (1954) to test for independence of child's sex and dropout status, using all the data from all the tables is:

$$(48) \qquad Y = \frac{\sum\limits_k w_k d_k}{\sqrt{\sum\limits_k w_k p_k q_k}} .$$

Under the null hypothesis of independence, the statistic Y is normally distributed with zero mean and unit variance—that is, it is a standardized normal deviate.

The Y statistic is generally more powerful than the alternative of simply pooling all the data into a 2 x 2 table and doing a chi-square test on the pooled table. It is *known* to be more powerful when the column totals tend to have the same proportion in all tables (i.e., the proportion of boys and girls is about the same in all centers), and it *may* be more powerful in certain other cases.

Radhakrishna (1965) studied the conditions under which Cochran's Y works relatively better than simple pooling of data. The test is as good or better than any alternative when the cross-product ratio in all tables is a constant.

Since the cross-product ratio for the kth table is

$$(49) \qquad n_{11k}n_{22k}/n_{12k}n_{21k} = \phi_k,$$

the test is uniformly most powerful when ϕ_k is identical for all tables.

The cross-product ratio, which is also sometimes called the "relative risk" or the "odds ratio," has a specific relationship to the "logit" transformation for proportions. The logit value of p_{jk} (where j is either 1 or 2) is defined as:

$$f_{jk} = \text{logit}(p_{jk}) = \text{Log}(p_{jk}/q_{jk})$$

(where Log is the natural logarithm, base e). If the difference between the logits of the two proportions in each table is always equal to the same constant, then the cross-product ratio is constant for all tables, and Cochran's Y is the best test.

This can be demonstrated by noting that for every table, k, when the difference between the logits of the two proportions is a constant, d, then $(f_{1k} - f_{2k}) = d$ for all k, and thus

$$(50) \quad \text{Log}(p_{1k}/q_{1k}) - \text{Log}(p_{2k}/q_{2k})$$

$$= \log\left(\frac{p_{1k}/q_{2k}}{q_{1k}/p_{2k}}\right)$$

$$= d.$$

Taking antilogs,

$$(51) \quad \frac{p_{1k}/q_{2k}}{q_{1k}/p_{2k}} = \dfrac{\dfrac{n_{11k}}{n_{+1k}} \dfrac{n_{22k}}{n_{+2k}}}{\dfrac{n_{21k}}{n_{+1k}} \dfrac{n_{12k}}{n_{+2k}}} = \frac{n_{11k}n_{22k}}{n_{21k}n_{12k}} = e^d.$$

Since d is constant for all tables, e^d is also constant, and the cross-product ratio is the same for all tables.

By looking at the logit formula, we can see that it transforms a proportion with a zero to one range into a new variable which can range from minus to plus infinity. If we transform the two proportions for each table and find that the difference between the transformed values is always the same in every table, then Cochran's Y is the best test.

But this result suggests a new question. Suppose there is a transformation, but not the logit transformation, which has the property that for our tables the difference between the transformed values is always the same; then what is the best test?

Radhakrishna (1965) shows that for several other possible transformations Cochran's Y is still the uniformly most powerful test, given that we redefine the weights, w_k, for each new transformation. He also indicates that even when we *do not know* what transformation will lead to constant differences between the proportions in a set of tables, the formula in (48) is still efficient, even for very small samples.

To digress for a moment, it might be helpful to try to visualize *why* such transformations have an effect on the choice of statistic, or, for that matter, why the "pooled" chi-square technique is not as efficient as Cochran's Y procedure.

We are interested in whether the boys' dropout rate is higher than the girls' (or vice versa). Notice that our question is strictly relative. Even though nearly all children may have quit in some centers while in others almost nobody quit, our question deals with the relative differences among boys and girls, ignoring (or getting rid of) the overall differences between centers. We can thus specify two possible cases which might describe the true situation over all the centers:

Case 1: The "truth" is that boys do drop out more than girls. Boys are not only more sensitive to dropout conditions in centers, but their relative sensitivity increases with the strength of those conditions. That is, centers with low dropout rates have a slightly higher dropout rate for boys than for girls, while those with high dropout rates have a much higher proportion of boys dropping out than girls dropping out.

Case 2: Again, the "truth" is that boys have a higher overall dropout rate than girls. But now there is something of a "threshold effect" in that the relatively greater sensitivity of boys is most noticeable when the overall dropout rate is slight. In other words, the best centers have the largest disparity between the dropout rates of the sexes even though they have the lowest overall dropout rates.

There are, of course, many other possible patterns, but let's focus on the above two. Now suppose we have two centers, one with a low dropout rate, and one with a high dropout rate (both centers have equal numbers of children, and the same ratio of boys to girls). Clearly, if case 1 is true, the statistic which weights the high-rate center most is better than one which weights the low-rate center most. This follows from the fact that, in case 1, discrimination is better in high-rate centers than in low-rate centers. On the other hand, if case 2 is true, then the statistic which weights the low-rate centers most is the more powerful choice.

If we can transform our proportions into values which have a constant difference for all tables, then we can compute a statistic (in terms of the transformed values) which weights all tables equally (or, more exactly, which weights them strictly in proportion to their n's, ignoring the overall dropout rates). That is essentially what Cochran's Y achieves.

Example 10

To illustrate the use of Cochran's Y statistic, we combine the results of the three 2 x 2 tables in Figure 32, and then test the departure of their combined value from the hypothesis of independence.

For Center 1:

$$p_{11} = 0.800 \qquad p_{21} = 0.864 \qquad p_1 = 0.823$$
$$q_{11} = 0.200 \qquad q_{21} = 0.136 \qquad q_1 = 0.177$$
$$d_1 = -0.064 \qquad\qquad w_1 = 14.194$$

For Center 2:

$$p_{12} = 0.613 \qquad p_{22} = 0.579 \qquad p_2 = 0.599$$
$$q_{12} = 0.387 \qquad q_{22} = 0.421 \qquad q_2 = 0.401$$
$$d_2 = 0.034 \qquad\qquad w_2 = 45.112$$

For Center 3:

$$p_{13} = 0.695 \qquad p_{23} = 0.526 \qquad p_3 = 0.629$$
$$q_{13} = 0.305 \qquad q_{23} = 0.474 \qquad q_3 = 0.371$$
$$d_3 = 0.169 \qquad\qquad w_3 = 23.113$$

From (48), Cochran's Y statistic is,

$$Y = \frac{4.512}{\sqrt{18.300}} = 1.055 .$$

Since under the null hypothesis of independence between dropout rate and child's sex Y is asymptotically distributed as a standard normal deviate, the computed value $Y = 1.055$ is not significant at, say, the 0.05 level. We thus cannot reject the independence hypothesis based upon the combined data from the three Head Start centers.

3. Comparing the Association in Several 2 x 2 Tables

We have now considered the basic problem of measuring association in a 2 x 2 table, and a procedure for combining the results of sets of such tables to obtain "overall estimates" of probabilities as well as a test for "overall" independence. Another frequent problem in research involves the comparison of two or more 2 x 2 tables. Do they represent samples from a single population, or can the tables be viewed as coming from more than one population? More specifically, a researcher may wish to test the

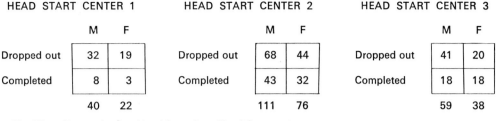

HEAD START CENTER 1   HEAD START CENTER 2   HEAD START CENTER 3

	M	F
Dropped out	32	19
Completed	8	3
	40	22

	M	F
Dropped out	68	44
Completed	43	32
	111	76

	M	F
Dropped out	41	20
Completed	18	18
	59	38

Fig. 32.   Data to be combined from three Head Start centers.

null hypothesis that all of the 2 x 2 tables have the same level of association. This problem has been studied by Berger (1961) and Goodman (1963) among others. We begin by discussing how to compare two 2 x 2 tables and then move to the more general problem of comparing association in K 2 x 2 tables. The techniques to be discussed apply to situations where the marginals are either fixed or variable.

a. *Comparing two 2 x 2 tables:* For notation, we use a slightly different scheme than the previous section. Let n_{ijk} be the number of items falling in the ith row of the jth column of the kth table, where $i,j,k = 1,2$. The layout then is given in Figure 33.

Also, let P_{ijk} represent the true probability that an observation in the jth column of the kth table will fall in the ith row. Then an estimate of P_{ijk} is given by $p_{ijk} = \dfrac{n_{ijk}}{n_{+jk}}$. Now suppose we define, from the observed data in the kth table,

$$(52) \quad d_{i+k} = p_{i1k} - p_{i2k} = \frac{n_{i1k}}{n_{i2k}} - \frac{n_{i2k}}{n_{+2k}}.$$

This d_{i+k} is an estimate of the true underlying value $D_{i+k} = P_{i1k} - P_{i2k}$. Further, define the term

$$(53) \quad \delta_{i++} = d_{i+1} - d_{i+2}$$
$$= \left(\frac{n_{i11}}{n_{+11}} - \frac{n_{i21}}{n_{+21}}\right) - \left(\frac{n_{i12}}{n_{+12}} - \frac{n_{i22}}{n_{+22}}\right).$$

This δ_{i++} gives an estimate of the underlying parameter $\Delta_{i++} = D_{i+1} - D_{i+2} = (P_{i11} - P_{i21}) - (P_{i12} - P_{i22})$. We can now state the precise null hypothesis for comparing two 2 x 2 tables:

$$(54) \quad H_0 : \Delta_{i++} = 0 \text{ ; or } D_{i+1} = D_{i+2}.$$

Note that $D_{i+k} = 0$ for any k implies independence, or no association, for the kth table.

The distribution of δ_{i++} is estimated from large sample theory, which assumes that the n_{+jk} are large enough so that

$$(55) \quad \frac{\delta_{i++} - E_{H_0}(\delta_{i++})}{S.E._{H_0}(\delta_{i++})}$$

is distributed as $N(0,1)$. The expected value of δ_{i++} under the null hypothesis in (54) is $D_{i+1} - D_{i+2} = 0$. The variance of δ_{i++} is found as follows:

$$\begin{aligned}
\text{Var } (\delta_{i++}) &= \text{Var } (d_{i+1} - d_{i+2}) \\
&= \text{Var}(d_{i+1}) + \text{Var}(d_{i+2}) \\
&= \text{Var}(p_{i11}) + \text{Var}(p_{i21}) \\
&\quad + \text{Var}(p_{i12}) + \text{Var}(p_{i22})
\end{aligned}$$

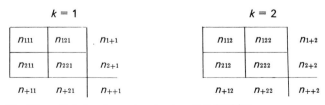

$k = 1$

n_{111}	n_{121}	n_{1+1}
n_{211}	n_{221}	n_{2+1}
n_{+11}	n_{+21}	n_{++1}

$k = 2$

n_{112}	n_{122}	n_{1+2}
n_{212}	n_{222}	n_{2+2}
n_{+12}	n_{+22}	n_{++2}

Fig. 33.   Notation for comparing two 2 X 2 tables.

which can be simplified to become:

$$\sum_{j=1}^{2}\sum_{k=1}^{2}\left(\frac{p_{1jk}p_{2jk}}{n_{+jk}}\right).$$

Thus, the standard error of δ_{i++} is,

$$(56)\quad S.E.(\delta_{i++}) = \sqrt{\sum_{j=1}^{2}\sum_{k=1}^{2}\left(\frac{p_{1jk}p_{2jk}}{n_{+jk}}\right)}$$

and so finally the test statistic for testing H_o in (54) becomes

$$(57)\, X_0 = \frac{\delta_{i++}}{\sqrt{\sum_{j=1}^{2}\sum_{k=1}^{2}\left(\frac{p_{1jk}p_{2jk}}{n_{+jk}}\right)}} \sim N(0,1).$$

Example 11

To illustrate the comparison of levels of association in two 2 x 2 tables, we return to the data for Head Start Centers 1 and 2 in Figure 32. We will compare the association levels in these tables using (57).

First, we summarize some useful data:

$n_{+11} = 40$ $p_{111} = 0.800$ $p_{121} = 0.864$
$n_{+21} = 22$ $p_{211} = 0.200$ $p_{221} = 0.136$
$n_{+12} = 111$ $p_{112} = 0.613$ $p_{122} = 0.579$
$n_{+22} = 76$ $p_{212} = 0.387$ $p_{222} = 0.421$
$d_{1+1} = -0.064$
$d_{1+2} = 0.034$
$d_{2+1} = 0.064$
$d_{2+2} = -0.034$

Now, comparing Centers 1 and 2 in Figure 32,

$$\delta_{i++} = d_{i+1} - d_{i+2} = -0.098 \text{ when } i = 1$$
$$= +0.098 \text{ when } i = 2.$$

Thus, note that since the test statistic X_0 in (57) is asymptotically distributed with δ_{i++} in the numerator, it does not matter which row we choose as the "i" in δ_{i++}. It is easily verified that $\delta_{1++} = -\delta_{2++}$ in general. Computing the test statistic:

$$X_0 = \frac{\pm 0.098}{\sqrt{0.0147}} = \frac{\pm 0.098}{0.121}$$

$$X_0 = -0.803 \text{ when } i = 1$$
$$= +0.803 \text{ when } i = 2.$$

Since a standardized normal deviate of 0.803 is not significant at any reasonable level, we cannot reject the null hypothesis of equal levels of association between child's sex and dropout rate in Head Start Centers 1 and 2.

b. *Comparing* **K** *2 x 2 tables:* In the generalization to **K** tables, where **K** > 2, the null hypothesis generalizes to,

$$(58)\quad H_0 : D_{i+1} = D_{i+2} = \ldots = D_{i+k}$$
$$= \ldots = D.$$

Thus, we now test the hypothesis that the level of association is identical for all **K** tables. The testing procedure, however, is somewhat different in this case. We want an estimate of D, say d, which utilizes all the d_{i+k}. As in the preceding section, we can do better than using a simple overall mean. We can weight each separate estimate d_{i+k}. Further, the more precise the estimate, the more weight we want to give it. Thus, we weight each d_{i+k} by its relative precision,

where $\text{precision}(d_{i+k}) = \dfrac{1}{\text{Var}(d_{i+k})}$, so that the smaller the variance for any estimate the greater its relative weight. Since,

$$(59)\quad \text{Var}(d_{i+k}) = \text{Var}(p_{i1k} - p_{i2k})$$
$$= \frac{p_{11k}p_{21k}}{n_{+1k}} + \frac{p_{12k}p_{22k}}{n_{+2k}},$$

then the precision of $d_{i+k} = t_k$ (say),

$$(60)\quad t_k = \frac{1}{\dfrac{p_{11k}p_{21k}}{n_{+1k}} + \dfrac{p_{12k}p_{22k}}{n_{+2k}}}$$

and our estimate of D is given by:

$$(61)\quad d = \sum_{k=1}^{K} d_{i+k}\left(\frac{t_k}{\displaystyle\sum_{k=1}^{K} t_k}\right)$$

which turns out to be the maximum likelihood estimate of D (Goodman, 1963).

Thus, finally, if we denote $\mathrm{Var}(d_{i+k}) = \dfrac{1}{t_k}$ by V_k, the test statistic to test H_0 in (58) is X^2, which can be shown to be distributed under H_0 approximately as

$$(62) \quad X^2_0 = \sum_{k=1}^{K} \left[\frac{(d_{i+k} - d)^2}{V_k} \right] \sim \chi^2_{K-1}.$$

A special case occurs when rather than simply testing to see if all K tables have the same level of association D, we test to see whether they all have the same *particular* level of association D_0. In this event, D_0 should be substituted for d in the statistic X^2_0 in (62). Further, the approximate reference distribution for $X^2_{D_0}$ then becomes χ^2_K instead of χ^2_{K-1}.

Example 12

To illustrate the comparison of levels of association in three 2 x 2 tables, we return once again to the three Head Start centers in Figure 32. We wish to test the null hypothesis of equal levels of association in the three tables, using (62). To do this, we refer to some of the summary data in Example 11 and add the following data corresponding to Head Start Center 3.

$n_{+13} = 59 \qquad p_{113} = 0.695 \qquad p_{123} = 0.526$

$n_{+23} = 38 \qquad p_{213} = 0.305 \qquad p_{223} = 0.474$

$D_{1+3} = 0.169$

$D_{2+3} = -0.169$

First, we compute the t_k from (60) for each of the three tables.

$t_1 = 106.916 \qquad t_2 = 187.074 \qquad t_3 = 98.483$

Thus $\sum_{k=1}^{3} t_k = 392.473$. From (61),

$$d = -0.063 \left(\frac{106.916}{392.473} \right)$$

$$+ 0.034 \left(\frac{187.074}{392.473} \right) + 0.169 \left(\frac{98.483}{392.473} \right)$$

$$= 0.041$$

The above calculation used data based upon $i = 1$. Had we used $i = 2$ as a base, we would have found the symmetric result $d = -0.041$.

Now, to compare the three Head Start centers:

$X^2_0 = 2.784$ for both $i = 1$ and $i = 2$.

Since X^2_0 is distributed asymptotically as chi-square with three degrees of freedom under the null hypothesis that all tables have an equal level of association, we cannot reject this null hypothesis at the 0.05 level of significance.

c. Comparing Two 2 x 2 Tables Using a Different Measure of Association: Sometimes a researcher facing two 2 x 2 tables rather than being interested in D_{i+k} as a measure of association in the kth table is more concerned with the relative difference

$$(63) \quad G_k = \frac{D_{i+k}}{P_{i2k}} = \frac{P_{i1k} - P_{i2k}}{P_{i2k}} = \frac{P_{i1k}}{P_{i2k}} - 1.$$

Since the hypothesis here is that the relative difference is identical in several tables, we should be clear about the very restrictive nature of this hypothesis. One of the two columns—we can arbitrarily rearrange our data to make it the second—is seen as a reference or "control" condition. The hypothesis is that, in all tables, the first column (the experimental condition) has a rate which is always a fixed fraction of the control condition. There can be a great variety of systematic differences between the proportions under the experimental and control conditions, none of which result in a constant *rate* of difference. Thus the hypothesis of equal G_k's posits that a very specific kind of difference exists uniformly for the two tables. An estimate of G_k is furnished by:

$$(64) \quad g_k = \frac{n_{i1k}}{n_{+1k}} \bigg/ \frac{n_{i2k}}{n_{+2k}} - 1 = \frac{n_{i1k}n_{+2k}}{n_{i2k}n_{+1k}} - 1.$$

We may wish in this situation to test the null hypothesis:

$$(65) \qquad H_0 : G_1 = G_2 .$$

To do this, Berger (1961) has worked out an estimate of the variance of g_k, which is:

$$(66) \quad \mathrm{Var}(g_k) = V_{g_k} = f^2{}_k \left(\frac{b_{1k}}{n_{+1k}} + \frac{b_{2k}}{n_{+2k}} \right)$$

where

$$f_k = g_k + 1 = \frac{p_{i1k}}{p_{i2k}}, \text{ and } b_{jk} = n_{1jk} n_{2jk}.$$

When the marginal totals n_{+jk} are large, V_{g_k} is a consistent estimator of the true variance of g_k.

Therefore, finally, a test statistic for H_0 in (65) is given by:

$$(67) \qquad X^2{}_G = \frac{(g_1 - g_2)^2}{V_{g_1} + V_{g_2}} \sim \chi^2{}_1 .$$

The following example gives an instance where the g approach is appropriate for a theoretical setting. Suppose there are two Head Start centers, and we have classified the children in each center into two groups —those with literate mothers and those whose mothers are not literate. Suppose, further, we believe that a fixed (but unknown) proportion, l, of all literate mothers will fail to teach their children the alphabet —regardless of which Head Start center their child is in. Finally, suppose we believe that those children of literate mothers who did not learn at home, and *all* the children of illiterate mothers, will fail to learn the alphabet in a proportion, m_k, which varies from center to center. This is our theory.

The proportion of children of literate mothers who did not learn the alphabet is thus lm_k in the kth center. We can then set up the following tables:

H.S. Center, $k = 1$

Mothers are:

Child knows alphabet:

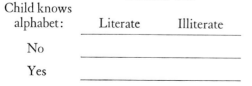

	Literate	Illiterate
No		
Yes		

H.S. Center, $k = 2$

Mothers are:

Child knows alphabet:

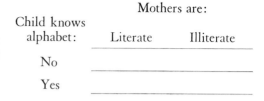

	Literate	Illiterate
No		
Yes		

Since by our model

$$n_{11k}/n_{+1k} = lm_k$$

and

$$n_{12k}/n_{+2k} = m_k$$

for both centers,

$$\frac{n_{11k}}{n_{+1k}} \Big/ \frac{n_{12k}}{n_{+2k}} = l ,$$

a constant, for both centers. Thus, even though the "failure to learn rates m_k" varies from center to center, and the numbers and proportions of children from literate homes also vary among centers, the ratio of the proportions not knowing the alphabet from groups with literate versus illiterate mothers should be constant in all centers if our theory is correct. A test of our theory is given by the hypothesis in (65). If the hypothesis of equal G_k is rejected, using (67), then we would be forced to conclude that our theory is incorrect.

d. *Comparing* **K** 2 × 2 *Tables Using* G: The method of comparing **K** tables to see whether their levels of association, using G as a measure, are identical, is a direct extension of the above procedures. The formal null hypothesis is:

$$(68) \quad H_0 : G_k = G ; k = 1, \dots, \mathbf{K} .$$

The test statistic for this null hypothesis takes the form:

$$(69) \quad X^2{}_G = \sum_{k=1}^{\mathbf{K}} \frac{(g_k - g)^2}{V_{g_k}} \sim \chi^2{}_{K-1} .$$

In this test statistic, g is an average of the g_k, weighted by their precision, where

$$(70) \qquad \mathrm{Precision}(g_k) = w_{g_k} = \frac{1}{V_{g_k}},$$

and so:

$$(71) \quad g = \frac{1}{w} \sum_{k=1}^{K} w_{g_k} g_k$$

$$\text{where } w = \sum_{k=1}^{K} w_{g_k}.$$

Once again here a researcher may wish to focus not only on the K tables having equal levels of association, but more specifically he may wish to test that the common level of association is specifically G_0. In this event, the statistic $X^2{}_G$ in (69) still applies, except that g in (69) should be replaced by G_0, and the resulting $X^2{}_{G_0}$ statistic will be distributed approximately as $\chi^2{}_K$ rather than $\chi^2{}_{K-1}$.

4. Doing Multiple Comparisons on a Set of Proportions

To conclude our discussion of data analysis for the case of two response categories, we move beyond the 2×2 table to consider situations where K independent binomial populations are to be compared. This layout can be expressed as in Figure 34.

null hypothesis that $P_{ij} = P_{i.}$ is rejected. Then we may ask ourselves *why* this happened, given that many alternative explanations could account for the rejection. For example, it is possible that $K - 1$ of the populations had the same binomial structure, while one population had a substantially different structure. Alternatively, perhaps all or most of the K populations have different structures. Finally, we may wish to compare one subgroup of populations against another subgroup, to see whether, when taken as subgroups, the two sets have different binomial structures.

To do this we may use results of Goodman (1964) and Marascuilo (1966), which extended the basic work of Scheffé (1959) and Tukey (1953). The null hypothesis preceding the multiple comparison is:

$$(72) \quad H_0 : P_1 = P_2 = \ldots = P_k.$$

If this hypothesis is rejected by the usual chi-square test with $K - 1$ degrees of freedom, we may next move to performing multiple comparisons. Marascuilo (1966) presents an alternative test to the standard chi-square, but points out that for moderate

POPULATION #

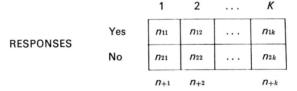

Fig. 34.   Data layout for multiple comparisons on proportions.

One hypothesis which researchers frequently test in this situation is the standard independence hypothesis H_0: $P_{ij} = P_{i.}$, or that the relative distribution of responses over the two response categories is identical for all K populations. The standard chi-square test, discussed earlier in this chapter, provides a test for this hypothesis.

However, it may also be of some interest to examine some *contrasts* among particular populations. In other words, suppose the

sample sizes the two approaches are nearly identical.

The form of the simple comparisons between pairs of populations is as follows: $(1 - \alpha)$ percent simultaneous confidence interval around each contrast is found from,

$$(73) \quad (p_l - p_m) \pm \sqrt{\chi^2{}_{K-1;\,(1-\alpha)}}$$

$$\cdot \sqrt{\frac{p_l q_l}{n_{+l}} + \frac{p_m q_m}{n_{+m}}}$$

where $l,m = 1, \ldots, \mathbf{K}$, $l \neq m$, and the p and $q = (1 - p)$ represent sample estimates of the population parameters P and Q.

Note that when $\mathbf{K}$ binomial populations are under study, it will be possible to make $\binom{\mathbf{K}}{2}$ paired comparisons. Further, the confidence intervals around different comparisons will have different sizes, because, although the term $\sqrt{\chi^2_{K-1; \, (1-a)}}$ in (73) will be constant for all the comparisons, the second term will vary since it is a function of the observed proportion in each population. Finally, note that the interpretation of a confidence interval such as in (73) is that if zero falls within the interval, we conclude that the two proportions being compared are *not* significantly different. Only when zero is excluded can we say, at the α level of significance, that we have compared populations with different binomial structures. As with any such multiple contrast procedure, its interpretation is that using this procedure at the level of significance α, the probability of any one or more contrasts being significant, when in fact H_0 of (72) is true, is at most α.

Cohen (1967) has proposed an alternative procedure to the one discussed above, which requires use of the arcsin transformation, but may be used when an observed sample proportion is either zero or one and also when sample sizes are quite small. Using the transformation $\phi = 2(\arcsin\sqrt{p})$, Cohen modifies (73) to become:

$$(74) \quad (\phi_l - \phi_m) \pm \sqrt{\chi^2_{K-1 \, : \, (1-a)}}$$
$$\cdot \sqrt{\frac{1}{n_{+l}} + \frac{1}{n_{+m}}} \, .$$

Similarly, in this analysis, if the transformed confidence interval excludes zero, the binomial populations are concluded to differ.

If a more complex contrast than a simple pairwise comparison is desired, Cohen notes that when

$$C = a_1\phi_1 + a_2\phi_2 + \ldots + a_k\phi_k \, ;$$

$$\sum_{k=1}^{K} a_k = 0$$

describes any contrast, the variance for that contrast is given by the expression:

$$(75) \qquad \mathrm{Var}(C) = \sum_{k=1}^{K} \frac{a^2_k}{n_{+k}} \, .$$

Thus, a $(1 - \alpha)$ confidence interval for any contrast can be found from:

$$(76) \quad C \pm \sqrt{\chi^2_{K-1; \, (1-a)}} \cdot \sqrt{\mathrm{Var}(C)} \, .$$

This enables us to compare, say, the combined effect of two binomial populations versus the single effect of a third binomial population.

Example 13

This example illustrates both procedures for multiple contrasts on binomial responses. The data in Figure 35 show the dropout frequencies for young children in three preschool programs—A, B and C.

PRESCHOOL PROGRAM

	A	B	C
Completed	63	115	79
Dropped out	19	79	21
	82	194	100

Fig. 35. Dropout frequencies for three preschool programs.

First, an overall chi-square test for independence over the complete 2 x 3 table gives a value $X^2_2 = 15.349$, which is significant well beyond the 0.01 level. Thus we conclude that the program type and dropout rates are related.

Now, we will compare the three programs pairwise, and set confidence limits around the difference between each pair of proportions. We begin with the first method,

$$p_A = 0.768 \quad p_B = 0.593 \quad p_C = 0.790 \, .$$

In each confidence interval the term $\sqrt{\chi^2_{(K-1);\,(1-a)}}$ will appear. Using $a = 0.05$ level of significance, for two degrees of freedom, this term will always be $\sqrt{5.991} = 2.448$. The three intervals from (73) are:

Program A versus Program B:

$$(0.768 - 0.593) \pm (2.448)\,(0.058)$$
$$= 0.176 \pm 0.143$$
$$= 0.032 < P_A - P_B < 0.319.$$

Since zero is excluded from this interval, the difference between the two proportions is significant at the 0.05 level.

Program A versus Program C:

$$(0.790 - 0.768) \pm (2.448)\,(0.062)$$
$$= 0.022 \pm 0.151$$
$$= -0.130 < P_C - P_A < 0.173.$$

Since zero falls within this interval, the two proportions cannot be concluded to be different in the population.

Program B versus Program C:

$$(0.790 - 0.593) \pm (2.448)\,(0.054)$$
$$= 0.197 \pm 0.132$$
$$= 0.065 < P_C - P_B < 0.329.$$

Thus, conclude that programs B and C have different dropout rates at the 0.05 level.

We now turn to the ϕ approach given in (74). First we find that:

$$\phi_A = 2.137$$
$$\phi_B = 1.757$$
$$\phi_C = 2.190$$

Using (74), the three sets of confidence limits become:

For A versus B:
$$(2.137 - 1.757) \pm (2.448)\,(0.132)$$
$$= 0.380 \pm 0.322$$
$$= 0.058 \text{ to } 0.702.$$

For A versus C:
$$(2.190 - 2.137) \pm (2.448)\,(0.149)$$
$$= 0.052 \pm 0.365$$
$$= -0.312 \text{ to } 0.417.$$

For B versus C:
$$(2.190 - 1.757) \pm (2.448)\,(0.123)$$
$$= 0.432 \pm 0.301$$
$$= 0.131 \text{ to } 0.733.$$

Thus the results of the two procedures are consistent. Preschool programs A and C have no difference in their dropout rates. Preschool program B differs from both A and C; it has a significantly higher dropout rate.

Taking Weighted Net Percentage Differences

We often encounter data for which there are several dichotomized dimensions. A particularly common and interesting case is where one of the dichotomies is a dependent variable and we must assess the relative importance of the several independent variables. In brief, we want to measure the net effect of an independent variable on the dependent variable while controlling for all the other independent variables.

The logic of this type of analysis is set forth by Lazarsfeld (1961) and will not be outlined here. James Davis (1964) developed a measure of the weighted net percentage difference in the dependent variable due to each independent variable. His measure W has a very appealing intuitive basis. Suppose we have data arranged as in Figure 36. Define the proportion scoring $\oplus$ on the dependent variable in the jth column in the kth table as p_{jk}. Then,

$$p_{jk} = n_{1jk}/n_{+jk}.$$

A measure of the effect of the independent variable j when the control variable k is held constant is:

$$d_k = p_{1k} - p_{2k}.$$

Notice that d_k is a difference in proportions (thus $100d_k$ is a percentage difference; hence the name of the statistic). The number of subjects *affected* by the d_k is n_{++k}, so W is defined as the weighted mean of the d_k, with the n_{++k} as weights:

$$(77) \qquad W = \frac{1}{n_{+++}} \sum_{k=1}^{2} n_{++k} d_k.$$

This defines W for a single control variable.

CONTROL

		+		−	
		Independent Variable		Independent Variable	
		+	−	+	−
DEPENDENT	+	n_{111}	n_{121}	n_{112}	n_{122}
VARIABLE	−	n_{211}	n_{221}	n_{212}	n_{222}

Fig. 36.   General format for weighted net percentage difference procedure.

But suppose we have several control variables; $k, \ldots, m$. Then, following the logic behind (77):

$$(78) \quad p_{jk} \ldots m = n_{1jk} \ldots m / n_{+j} \ldots m$$
$$d_k \ldots m = p_{1k} \ldots m - p_{2k} \ldots m$$

$$W = \frac{1}{n_{++} \ldots +} \sum_{k=1}^{2} \cdots \sum_{m=1}^{2} n_{++k} \ldots m d_k \ldots m .$$

The null hypothesis, that $D_k \ldots, m = 0$ for the complete population, can be tested in tables with large n's by

$$(79) \quad Z_W = \frac{W}{\sqrt{p(1-p)M}}$$

where p is $n_{1+} \ldots + / n_{++} \ldots +$ and $M = n_{++} \ldots + / (n_{+1} \ldots + n_{+2} \ldots +)$. For large samples, when the null hypothesis $D_k \ldots m = 0$ is true, Z_W is approximately distributed as $N(0,1)$ (Davis, 1964).

Example 14

Let us now turn to a hypothetical example that illustrates the use of the W statistic. It also demonstrates the importance of distinguishing between "simple" versus "net" (controlled) effects.

Suppose that the high schools of a city have suffered from widespread disturbances. As a result, two kinds of programs have been instituted in some schools. One program is based on the creation of student-parent-teacher review boards for disciplinary incidents. The second program is the introduction of uniformed police patrols into the high schools.

A newspaper conducted a survey among high-school students. Each student was asked whether or not his school had had a major disturbance in the past year, and whether it now has a review board and/or a police patrol. Finally, each student was asked whether he had been the victim of a disruptive incident in the last week.

Suppose the newspaper reported the results of their survey as follows:

POLICE MORE EFFECTIVE THAN BOARDS IN QUELLING HIGH SCHOOL INCIDENTS

In those schools with review boards but without police patrols, 36.4 percent of the students reported they had been victims of recent incidents. In schools without review boards, but where police patrolling has been put into effect, only 23.9 percent say they have been victimized. . . .

The (imaginary) raw data are shown in Figures 37 and 38. Notice that the column percentage is given just below each column in Figure 37, while the actual cell totals are given in Figure 38.

Careful study of the raw data indicates why the newspaper account has misleading implications. The report of recent incidents is much higher in those schools which originally suffered major disturbances. Re-

		NO DISTURBANCES		MAJOR DISTURBANCES	
		No Board	Review Board	No Board	Review Board
NO POLICE PATROL	Victim	213	4	76	412
	Nonvictim	1793	95	18	631
		(11 %)	(4 %)	(81 %)	(40 %)
POLICE PATROL	Victim	217	14	62	1627
	Nonvictim	848	99	39	2451
		(20 %)	(12 %)	(61 %)	(40 %)

Fig. 37. Hypothetical data on school disturbances.

		NO DISTURBANCES			MAJOR DISTURBANCES		
		No Board	Review Board		No Board	Review Board	
NO DISTURBANCES	Victim	213	4	217	76	412	488
	Nonvictim	1793	95	1888	18	631	649
		2006	99	2105	94	1043	1137
MAJOR DISTURBANCES	Victim	217	14	231	62	1627	1689
	Nonvictim	848	99	947	39	2451	2490
		1065	113	1178	101	4078	4179

Fig. 38. Raw data with column totals.

view boards have been set up primarily in those schools. Police patrols, however, have been instituted in many schools that originally had no major disturbances and these schools also have much lower rates of recent victimization. When we compare the incident rates for only those subtables which are *alike* in the presence or absence of earlier disturbances and police patrols, it is clear that the review boards are associated with *lower* recent incident rates.

Computing W for review boards, controlling for disturbances and police, we have:

$$W = \frac{1}{8599}[(0.11 - 0.04)(213 + 1793 + 4 + 95) + (0.81 - 0.40) \cdot (76 + 18 + 412 + 631) + (0.20 - 0.12)(217 + 848 + 14 + 99) + (0.61 - 0.40) \cdot (62 + 39 + 1627 + 2451)]$$

$$= \frac{1}{8599}(147.35 + 94.24 + 466.17 + 877.59)$$

$$= \frac{1585.35}{8599}$$

$$= 0.1843 .$$

Thus the weighted net percentage difference in victimization rates due to presence of review boards is an 18.4 percent point *improvement* (decrease in victimization rate).

We can test the significance of W by computing Z_W. The overall percentage reporting no incidents (p) is 30.52. The total number of students with review boards is 5333, and without is 3266. Thus

$$Z_W = \frac{0.1843}{\sqrt{\dfrac{0.305 \times 0.695 \times 8599}{5333 \times 3266}}}$$

$$= \frac{0.1843}{\sqrt{0.212 \times 0.00049}}$$

$$= \frac{0.1843}{\sqrt{0.0001}} = \frac{0.1843}{0.01}$$

$$= 18.43,$$

which is significant far beyond the 0.01 level.

We can also compute W for disturbances and for police patrols. The computations are omitted but the results are given below:

Due to	Weighted Net Percentage Difference in Victimization (A positive value indicates a decrease in victimization.)
Disturbances	−43.52%
Police Patrols	−2.96%
Review Boards	+18.43%

The conclusion, then, is that the introduction of police patrols has been associated with a slight net increase in the victimization rate. The only case where the patrols seem to have reduced the rate is in schools without review boards that have had disturbances, and then the reduction is not as great as apparently could have been achieved by review boards alone without police patrols (of course, we must be careful about making causal inferences here).

Thus, for this hypothetical example, the newspaper's statement was factual. But it contained a misleading implication. A useful basis for evaluating the relative importance of two independent variables in the presence of a third or prior "disturbing influence" is a net, or partial, statistic. Davis's weighted net percentage difference is such a statistic. Extensions of the procedure to dimensions with more than two levels, and a much lengthier discussion of uses for W, can be found in Spady (1971).

WORK WHICH NEEDS TO BE DONE

To conclude this chapter, I wish to present a brief discussion of work I believe needs to be done in the future. There are always two areas which fall under this heading—a) extensions or refinements of existing procedures, and b) entirely new areas of work. I would like to focus here on a generally new area, also discussed in Light (1971a).

Most procedures for data analysis accept a statistical model as given. For example, when dealing with continuous responses, a multiple linear regression model is generally assumed (e.g., Coleman Report, 1966; and Cicirelli et al., Westinghouse Learning Evaluation of Head Start, 1969). The purpose of the analysis is then to determine the effect of certain predesignated predictor variables on a dependent variable, such as children's cognitive achievement scores, or to determine the subset of a large pool of potential predictor variables which best explains the variation in the dependent variable. With qualitative data, a similar process occurs, although a specific statistical model may not need to be assumed. Thus, when faced with contingency table data such as the examples throughout this chapter, the data analyst generally thinks of a procedure which gives him the highest level of "explanatory power" to explore relationships among the qualitative variables.

But an important question really precedes

the data analysis, and if we had some means for exploring this question we could choose more effective procedures for analyzing data. This question deals with the system, or process, which generated the observed data. Most current work in data analysis focuses on choosing the most powerful means to milk a set of observed data. A preferable analysis, as yet unavailable, would attempt to first choose among several competing data-generating systems. We must develop procedures to do this.

Perhaps an example will best illustrate this point. Suppose an educational researcher collects data on 83 high school students and categorizes these data into the 2 x 2 table in Figure 39.

same 2 x 2 table will result, not only in number of children per cell, but also in terms of who the children in each cell are.

Notice that when there is fixed assignment to cells we must be very careful about the basis for our choice of dimensions in a crosstab. When there are four "cells" (types of persons or objects that are counted) there are three structurally different two-way tables that could be developed from these cells. Each table would, in general, show a different level of association. Some theoretical basis in the process which originally "typed" our subjects must be found for the dimensions we decide to use, or the implications from analyses done on the table we choose will be unclear.

FAVORITE SPORT

		(Playing) Basketball	(Watching) Horseracing
FAVORITE SUBJECT AREA	Sciences	7	53
	Humanities	15	8

83

Fig. 39. Favorite sport by favorite subject area for 83 high-school students.

Depending upon the questions this researcher is asking, he may compute various statistics from this table, such as a measure of association between the rows and columns, or a test of the hypothesis that $P_{ij} = P_{i.}$. Yet to really understand the data, he ought to first ask the question, "What system generated it?" Smith (1969) has suggested several data-generating systems, which we now summarize for illustration.

A. Fixed Assignments

Suppose each child is deterministically ordained to be a member of a particular cell. Then no matter how many times we sample a subgroup of n children from a larger population and assign them to one of the four cells in Figure 39, any particular child will always be in the same cell. Therefore, if we repetitively select the same particular n children in a series of trials, the

B. Fixed Occupancy

In (A) above, the outcome of any table was completely determined by the identity of the particular children selected in a sample. Now, assume that each cell has a maximum occupancy limit; that no more than $n_{ij}{}^{(max)}$ children can fit into any cell. Assume further that in any sample of n children, each child has the identical probability vector $(P_{11}, P_{12}, P_{21}, P_{22})$ of ending up in one of the four cells. Then if we view the assignment process of children to cells as being sequential, the first few children to be assigned are generally not affected by the cell occupancy limits, while later children may be constrained out of falling into certain cells. Thus, in (B) the occupancy limits have much to do with determining the cell frequencies.

The most obvious examples of such systems come from typologies of social activities such as sports or parties where minimum, maximum, or even fixed numbers of participants are required. Social-psychological typologies—such as dominant versus subordinate, or active versus passive—usually prohibit more than a certain percentage of a sample from falling into one category. After all, who would score every member of a group as a leader and none as a follower?

C. Pure Multinomial

This is the data generating system which most researchers assume when analyzing data from a contingency table. Here, all the children in a population are assumed to have identical probability vectors for cell assignments, and these probability vectors are unchanged in repeated sampling. This is, of course, the "no margins fixed" design which was discussed early in the chapter. Note that this pure multinomial model resembles (A) in that the children's probability vectors ultimately affect where they are to be placed, but it resembles (B) in that all children, before being assigned to cells, have identical probability vectors.

D. Mixed Multinomial

This model is simply a more complex version of (C): we now permit different children to have different probability vectors for their cell assignments. Once again, both margins are free to vary. An obvious research problem here is to separate children into groups depending upon their probability vectors. When a sample has been correctly decomposed into homogeneous groups, each with a common multinomial governing the behavior of its members, then the data are ideally suited to analysis by the C statistic derived from pairs that was discussed earlier.

E. Cohesive Subgroups

All of the four models above had in common the feature that each child, as an individual, was the unit of analysis. However, when facing data in a table, we must ask whether it could have arisen in such a manner that cohesive subgroups were assigned to cells together. In this event, the *complete subgroup* should ideally become the unit of analysis; a researcher may try to determine a probability vector for an entire subgroup rather than individual children. This model can be quite common in social research, such as in studies involving children who form cliques. Any analysis of enrollment patterns in a school should have to contend with this model. The general form of this model allows many subgroups to occupy a particular cell. However, we may postulate a special case of this model, say (E'), which limits a cell to a single cohesive subgroup of children. This special model (E') might be appropriate in research which specifies a cell in a contingency table as representing a classroom, and the children in the school being studied are "tracked," so that groups of children tend to stay together within classrooms.

I am sure that the reader can add many other possible data-generating systems to the six listed here. But why is this approach valuable? The answer is that a much deeper understanding of any process comes from an understanding of the system by which that process generates data, rather than just from the data themselves. This is particularly true when the purpose of a data analysis is to generate policy implications. These policy suggestions often take the form "change X and we can expect Y to change as follows...." Yet consider how much more powerful such arguments would be if a researcher knew that the appropriate target for intervention was a cohesive subgroup, say, rather than individual children.

In addition to strengthening policy suggestions, knowledge of which system generated a set of data would have implications for the analysis of these data. For example, if we knew we were in a model (A) situation, we would have perfect information about those children who were sampled relative to the variables which were categorized. If we knew we had a model (C) situation, we could estimate the probability vector common to each child by collecting all the data in a table and simply estimating four P_{ij}'s from these data. Finally, if the unit of analysis were the individual child, and we were particularly interested in estimating the probability vector for any particular child, the decision as to whether the data were generated from a model (C) or model (D) system is extremely important. A model (D) system would, of course, require many more samples than a model (C) to determine, with the same reliability, the probability vector of any particular child.

Let us examine the data in Figure 39 in the context of several of these models. If the data arose from a model (A) system, we would view the particular children in each cell as "belonging" to that cell. Note that if this is true, the dimensions of the table may be meaningless. Thus, no information would be lost if the 2 x 2 table was reformulated as a 1 x 4 table. This issue was discussed earlier in the chapter. One hint that the dimensions in a problem like this may in fact be not too useful is that while the columns focus on a child's favorite sport, perhaps the true "assigning factor" is the active or passive nature of the sport rather than the sport itself. Thus, there may be no reason to believe that children who favor basketball and the sciences are consistent in any way with those who favor basketball and humanities or those who favor horse-racing and sciences.

The data in Figure 39 might also have arisen via a model (E) system. Suppose classes at the school from which the data were collected were assigned according to both academic interests (sciences versus humanities) and leisure interests (sports preference). Then the students can be viewed as groups.

Finally, suppose the data arose from a model (D) system. Here each student is assumed to have a probability vector of preferences over the four cells, and these vectors may differ over students. But a researcher must then ask whether the data in the table accurately reflect these preferences. For example, it is possible that because of limitations on the size of a class, some students who really prefer humanities were assigned to the science cells. Thus, if the data were collected by studying an entire class as a unit rather than individual children, a researcher might draw incorrect inferences. Notice that in this example the limitations on class size which caused some students to be assigned to a subject other than their favorite one brings in model (B), the fixed occupancy limit model.

Ideally, then, knowledge of the system which generates data would give a researcher a better idea of how to analyze such data. Smith (1969) has also pointed out that such knowledge would clarify for researchers the kinds of questions they should ask about their data; information that would be useful under one data-generating system may be useless under different systems.

To illustrate, he suggested the following problem. Suppose we were asked to predict the probability that a particular child would be found in a particular cell. To begin with, we were not told for which child or for which cell our prediction was required. We did know the type of system that was at work, however, and we could ask any of the following three questions:

1. To which child does our prediction apply?
2. To what cell does our prediction apply?
3. How many other children will be located in the critical cell on the same trial?

For these three questions, the six models can be judged as to whether answers to these questions would be useful (Y), not useful (N), or possibly useful depending upon the particular answer (C). A summary of results appears in Figure 40.

As Smith points out, the crucial point when considering what model generated a set of data is to focus on system properties. "Some systems identify units, some do not. Some systems make one unit's destination dependent upon the allocation of the other units, but not on any specific subset of units. Other systems condition a unit's destination upon the destinations of specific other units." Any one of these systems, however, can be responsible for generating a set of data such as that of Figure 40.

In conclusion, then, we see that a wide variety of techniques is available to us when we wish to analyze, post hoc, a set of qualitative data. Many of the techniques discussed in this chapter are well known; several are less well known. What most of them share in common is their relative

Questions

Model	Identity of Child	Identity of Cell	Number of Other Children in Cell on the Same Trial
A: Fixed Assignment	Y	Y	N
B: Fixed Occupancy	N	Y	Y
C: Pure Multinomial	N	Y	N
D: Mixed Multinomial	Y	Y	N
E: Cohesive Subgroups (general)	Y	Y	Y(C)
E¹: Cohesive Subgroups (one subgroup per cell)	N	N	N

Fig. 40. Value of answers to questions about data under different models.

It is usually easier to pose and describe a problem than to solve it. I face this dilemma here, because I do not know how to tell the reader "what to do" to discriminate among data-generating systems. As a general statement, I believe that what we should do is to develop a set of procedures that would involve taking a single sample from a population and, based upon these data, suggest a design for a second sample. The two samples together would then suggest a design for a third sample. This procedure should continue until the researcher could make a reasonable guess at what model underlies his data. The criterion for the design of these sequential samplings would be that each stage should generate data such that a better discrimination could be made among competing models. Thus, once the alternatives were narrowed to two models, say, the next "stage" should strain the previous results as much as possible in a direction which would provide the best discrimination between the two models.

simplicity. Once these techniques are mastered, however, it will become necessary for research people to ask much more difficult questions—how did the observed data arise? what kinds of models could have generated such data? how do we choose from among several competing models? More work is needed on these issues.

REFERENCES

Amidon, E., & Simon, A. Teacher-pupil interaction. *Review of Educational Research,* 1965, 35, 130–139.

Assakul, K., & Proctor, C. H. Testing hypotheses with categorical data subject to misclassification. Mimeograph Series No. 448, North Carolina State University, Institute of Statistics, 1965.

Assakul, K., & Proctor, C. H. Testing independence in two-way contingency tables with data subject to misclassification. *Psychometrika,* 1967, 32, 67–76.

Berger, A. On comparing intensities of association between two binary characteristics in two different populations. *Journal of the American Statistical Association,* 1961, 56, 889–908.

Biddle, B. J., & Adams, R. S. Teacher behavior in the classroom context. In L. Siegel (Ed.), *Instruction: Some contemporary viewpoints.* San Francisco: Chandler Publishing Company, 1967. Pp. 99–139.

Bishop, Y. M. M. Multidimensional contingency tables: Cell estimates. Unpublished doctoral dissertation, Harvard University, 1967.

Bloom, R., & Wilensky, H. Four observation categories for rating teacher behavior. *Journal of Educational Research,* 1967, 60, 464–465.

Brennan, R., & Light, R. J. Measuring agreement when categories are not predetermined. Harvard Graduate School of Education, Laboratory of Human Development, 1972. (mimeograph)

Bross, I. Misclassification in 2 x 2 tables. *Biometrics,* 1954, 10, 478–486.

Campbell, W. J. Classroom practices. *New Zealand Journal of Educational Studies,* 1968, 3, 97–124.

Castellan, N. J., Jr. On the partitioning of contingency tables. *Psychological Bulletin,* 1965, 64, 330–338.

Cicirelli, V. et al. *The impact of Head Start: An evaluation of the effects of Head Start on children's cognitive and affective development.* New York: Westinghouse Learning Corp., 1969.

Cochran, W. G. Some methods for strengthening the common χ^2 tests. *Biometrics,* 1954, 10, 417–451.

Cochran, W. G. Errors of measurement in statistics. *Technometrics,* 1968, 10, 637–666.

Cochran, W. G. Effects of errors of measurement in correlational studies. *Journal of the American Statistical Association,* 1970, 65, 22–34.

Cohen, J. A coefficient of agreement for nominal scales. *Educational and Psychological Measurement,* 1960, 20, 37–46.

Cohen, J. An alternative to Marascuilo's "Large-sample multiple comparisons for proportions." *Psychological Bulletin,* 1967, 67, 199–201.

Cohen, J. Weighted kappa: Nominal scale agreement with provision for scaled disagreement or partial credit. *Psychological Bulletin,* 1968, 70, 213–220.

Coleman, J. S. *The adolescent society.* New York: Free Press of Glencoe, 1961.

Coleman, J. S. *Equality of educational opportunity.* Washington, D.C.: National Center for Educational Statistics (DHEW), 1966.

Costner, H. L. Criteria for measures of association. *American Sociological Review,* 1965, 30, 341–352.

Cramer, H. *Mathematical methods of statistics.* Princeton, N.J.: Princeton University Press, 1946.

Darroch, J. N. Interactions in multi-factor contingency tables. *Journal of the Royal Statistical Society,* 1962, B, 24, 251–263.

Davis, J. A. *Great aspirations.* Chicago: Aldine Publishing Company, 1964.

Deming, W. E., & Stephan, F. F. On a least squares adjustment of a sampled frequency table when the expected marginal totals are known. *Annals of Mathematical Statistics,* 1940, 11, 427–444.

Diamond, E. L., & Lilienfeld, A. M. Misclassification errors in 2 x 2 tables with one margin fixed: Some further comments. *American Journal of Public Health,* 1962, 52, 2106–2110.

Dyke, G. V., & Patterson, H. D. Analysis of factorial arrangements when the data are proportions. *Biometrics,* 1952, 8, 1–12.

Evans, T. P. A category system for teacher behaviors. *American Biology Teacher,* 1969, 31, 221–225.

Fienberg, S. E. The geometry of an R x C contingency table. *Annals of Mathematical Statistics,* 1968, 39, 1186–1190.

Fienberg, S. E. The analysis of multidimensional contingency tables. *Ecology,* 1970, 51, 419–433. (a)

Fienberg, S. E. An iterative procedure for estimation in contingency tables. *Annals of Mathematical Statistics,* 1970, 41, 907–917. (b)

Fleiss, J. L., Cohen, J., & Everitt, B. S. Large sample standard errors of kappa and weighted kappa. *Psychological Bulletin,* 1969, 72, 323–327.

Fortune, J. C. *A study of the generality of presenting behavior in teaching.* Final Report, ERIC: ED 016-285. Memphis, Tenn.: Memphis State University, 1967.

Gage, N. L. Teaching methods. In R. L. Ebel (Ed.), *Encyclopedia of educational research.* (4th ed.) New York: Macmillan, 1969. Pp. 1446–1458.

Gallagher, J. J. *Analyses of teacher classroom strategies associated with student cognitive and affective performance*. Final Report, Cooperative Research Project, No. 3325, ERIC: ED 021-808. Urbana: University of Illinois, 1968.

Gini, C. Variabilita e mutabilita, contributo allo studio delle distribuzion; e relazioni statistiche. *Studi Economico-Giuridici della R.; Universita di Cagliari*, 1912.

Goodman, L. A. On methods for comparing contingency tables. *Journal of the Royal Statistical Society*, 1963, A, 126, 94–108.

Goodman, L. A. Interactions in multidimensional contingency tables. *Annals of Mathematical Statistics*, 1964, 35, 632–646.

Goodman, L. A., & Kruskal, W. H. Measures of association for cross classifications. *Journal of the American Statistical Association*, 1954, 49, 732–764.

Goodman, L. A., & Kruskal, W. H. Measures of association for cross classifications, II: Further discussion and references. *Journal of the American Statistical Association*, 1959, 54, 123–163.

Goodman, L. A., & Kruskal, W. H. Measures of association for cross classifications, III: Approximate sampling theory. *Journal of the American Statistical Association*, 1963, 58, 310–364.

Grizzle, J. E. Continuity correction in the χ^2 test for 2 x 2 tables. *The American Statistician*, 1967, 21(4), 28–32.

Himmelblau, D. M. *Process analysis by statistical methods*. New York: John Wiley and Sons, 1970.

Ireland, C. T., & Kullback, S. Contingency tables with given marginals. *Biometrika*, 1968, 55, 179–188.

Kandel, D. B., & Lesser, G. S. Parental and peer influences on educational plans of adolescents. *American Sociological Review*, 1969, 34, 213–223.

Kendall, M. G., & Stuart, A. *The advanced theory of statistics*. (2nd ed.) London: Charles Griffin and Company, 1967.

Kimball, A. W. Short-cut formulas for the exact partition of χ^2 in contingency tables. *Biometrics*, 1954, 10, 452–458.

Lancaster, H. O. The derivation and partition of χ^2 in certain discrete distributions. *Biometrika*, 1949, 36, 117–129.

Lancaster, H. O. The exact partition of χ^2 and its application to the problem of the pooling of small expectations. *Biometrika*, 1950, 37, 267–270.

Lancaster, H. O. *The chi-squared distribution*. New York: John Wiley and Sons, 1969.

Lawrence, P. J. The anatomy of teaching. *Australian Journal of Education*, 1966, 10, 97–109.

Lazarsfeld, P. F. The algebra of dichotomous systems. In H. Solomon (Ed.), *Studies in item analysis and prediction*. Stanford, Calif.: Stanford University Press, 1961. Pp. 111–157.

Lewis, B. N. On the analysis of interaction in multi-dimensional contingency tables. *Journal of the Royal Statistical Society*, 1962, A, 125, 88–117.

Lewontin, R. C., & Felsenstein, J. The robustness of homogeneity tests in 2 x N tables. *Biometrics*, 1965, 21, 19–33.

Light, R. J. Analysis of variance for categorical data, with applications to agreement and association. Unpublished doctoral dissertation, Harvard University, 1969.

Light, R. J. Measures of response agreement for qualitative data: Some generalizations and alternatives. *Psychological Bulletin*, November 1971, 76, 365–377.

Light, R. J. Future directions in learning how to evaluate educational programs. In T. Sizer (Ed.), *The fiftieth anniversary volume of the Harvard Graduate School of Education*. Cambridge, Mass.: Harvard University Press, 1973, in press.

Light, R. J. Implications of statistical model selection to the outcome of an evaluation. In K. Hecht, & J. Fortune (Eds.), *Readings in evaluation methodology*, 1973. (forthcoming)

Light, R. J., & Margolin, B. H. An analysis of variance for categorical data. *Journal of the American Statistical Association*, September 1971, 66, 534–544.

Light, R. J., & Margolin, B. H. Analysis of variance for categorical data in three dimensions. Paper presented at the meeting of the American Statistical Association, Montreal, Canada, 1972.

Light, R. J., & Smith, P. V. Accumulating evidence: Procedures for resolving contradictions among different research studies. *Harvard Educational Review*, November 1971, 41, 429–471.

Marascuilo, L. A. Large sample multiple comparisons. *Psychological Bulletin,* 1966, 65, 280–290.

Marx, T. Choosing a measure of association. Unpublished qualifying paper, Harvard Graduate School of Education, 1970.

Mosteller, F. Association and estimation in contingency tables. *Journal of the American Statistical Association,* 1968, 63, 1–28.

Nuthall, G. An experimental comparison of alternative strategies for teaching concepts. *American Educational Research Journal,* 1968, 5, 561–584.

Radhakrishna, S. Combination of results from several 2 x 2 contingency tables. *Biometrics,* 1965, 21, 86–98.

Scheffé, H. *The analysis of variance.* New York: John Wiley and Sons, 1959.

Simon, A., & Boyer, E. G. (Eds.) *Mirrors for behavior: An anthology of classroom observation instruments.* Vols. 1–6. Philadelphia: Research for Better Schools, 1967.

Smith, P. V. Alternative models for contingency table data. Harvard University, Laboratory of Human Development, 1969. (mimeograph)

Snedecor, G. W., & Cochran, W. G. *Statistical methods.* (6th ed.) Ames, Iowa: Iowa State University Press, 1967.

Solomon, D., Bezdek, W. E., & Rosenberg, L. *Teaching styles and learning.* Chicago: Center for the Study of Liberal Education for Adults, 1963.

Spady, W. Simple techniques for multivariate analysis, or how to amaze your friends without the aid of a computer. *Interchange, Journal of the Ontario Institute for Studies in Education,* 1971, 1(3), 3–22.

Spaulding, R. L. *Achievement, creativity, and self-concept correlates of teacher-pupil transactions in elementary school classrooms.* Cooperative Research Project No. 1352, ERIC: ED 024-463. Hempstead, N.Y.: Hofstra University, 1965.

Tenebein, A. Effects of errors of misclassification on binomial data. Unpublished doctoral dissertation, Harvard University, 1969.

Tukey, J. W. The problem of multiple comparisons. Unpublished manuscript, Princeton University, 1953.

Tukey, J. W. The future of data analysis. *The Annals of Mathematical Statistics,* 1963, 33, 13–14.

Vickery, R. L. *An examination of possible changes of certain aspects of teacher behavior resulting from adoption of individualized laboratory centered instructional materials.* Unpublished doctoral dissertation, Florida State University, 1968.

White, B. L. Ethno-ecological study of the development of competence. Monograph 9A, Harvard Research and Development Center on Educational Differences, 1969.

White, B. L. An analysis of excellent early educational practices: Preliminary report. *Interchange, Journal of the Ontario Institute for Studies in Education,* 1971, 2, 3–18.

Winsor, C. P. Factorial analysis of a multiple dichotomy. *Human Biology,* 1948, 20, 195–204.

Zahorik, J. A. A teacher verbal feedback and content development. Paper presented at the meeting of the American Educational Research Association, Los Angeles, February 1969.

CHAPTER 11 Pitfalls in Research: Nine Investigator and Experimenter Effects[1]

THEODORE XENOPHON BARBER
Medfield State Hospital
Harding, Massachusetts

Much of our understanding of educational and psychological processes is based upon the results of experimental research. However, since experiments are designed and carried out by fallible individuals, they have as many pitfalls as other human endeavors.

In this chapter I will outline nine pivotal points in research where investigators and experimenters can go astray. By becoming sensitized to these pitfalls, those of us who are engaged in experimental research may be better able to avoid them in our own studies. Also, those of us who try to base our teaching methods or our practice of psychology on research results may be able to use experimental studies more wisely if we are sensitized to the many possibilities they contain for misleading results and conclusions.

Two questions are at the forefront of discussion: 1) At what pivotal points in the complex research process can the experimental study go astray and give rise to misleading results and conclusions? 2) What steps can researchers take to avoid these pitfalls? To answer these questions, I will first focus on those aspects of experimental studies that are under the control of the investigator and then on those aspects that are under the control of the experimenter.[2] I will begin by making a distinction between the investigator and the experimenter.

INVESTIGATOR ROLE AND EXPERIMENTER ROLE

Although the investigator and the experimenter can be the same person, their roles

[1] Writing of this paper was supported, in part, by a research grant (MH-19152) from the National Institute of Mental Health, U.S. Public Health Service. This chapter summarizes one part of a book that will be published by Aldine-Atherton, Inc. (Barber, in press). I am indebted to Robert Wesner, of Aldine-Atherton, for permission to summarize some of the material from the forthcoming book. I am also indebted to Maurice J. Silver for invaluable assistance in writing earlier papers (Barber & Silver, 1968a, 1968b) which began to specify the intricacies of the Investigator Analysis Effect and the Experimenter Unintentional Expectancy Effect.

[2] Experimental studies are also influenced by *the subject's* perception of the experimental situation and his needs or motivations for participating in the experiment. Although the subject's role in the experiment is very important, I will not discuss this aspect in the present chapter. A discussion of the role of the subject will be found in a forthcoming book (Barber, *Pitfalls in Research,* in press).

are functionally quite different, and it is rather common in recent research to find one person in the role of investigator and another person in the role of experimenter.

The *investigator* decides that a study is to be conducted, how it is to be designed and carried out, and how it is to be analyzed and interpreted. Thus, the investigator is responsible for the experimental design, the procurement and training of experimenters, the overall conduct of the study, the analysis of the results, the interpretations of the data and the final research report.

The *experimenter,* on the other hand, is the person who conducts the study—who tests the subjects, administers the experimental procedures, and observes and records the subjects' responses. Thus, strictly speaking, a person in the role of experimenter is responsible for the collection of the data but is not responsible for the experimental design, the analysis and interpretation of the data or the final research report.

Overview of Investigator and Experimenter Effects

Table 1 lists some of the major pitfalls that are associated with the investigator and with the experimenter. As shown in the top portion of Table 1, misleading results and conclusions in an experimental study can derive from the *investigator's* paradigm, from his experimental protocol, from his analysis of data and, possibly, from his fudging of data. As shown in the bottom portion of Table 1, misleading results and conclusions can also be produced by the experimenter's attributes, by his failure to follow the experimental protocol, by his misrecording of data, by his fudging of data and by his expectancies. Each of these effects will be discussed in turn.

Before we turn to the discussion of each effect, however, let us note two points:

1. The biasing effects and misleading conclusions that are associated with experimental research have been commonly attributed to the experimenter who carries out the study rather than to the investigator who designs and has the major responsibility for the study. Recent books (Friedman, 1967; Rosenthal, 1966; Rosenthal & Rosnow, 1969) which pertain to the artifacts or pitfalls in research tend to focus on the experimenter and tend to neglect the important roles of the investigator. I will attempt to redress this imbalance in the present chapter by focusing equally on the role of the investigator and the role of the experimenter. In focusing on the role of the investigator, it is necessary to mention some taboo topics that are not supposed to be talked about publicly—for example, the Investigator Fudging Effect.

2. I will first discuss, rather briefly, the first eight effects listed in Table 1. At the end of the chapter, I will discuss the ninth and final effect (the Experimenter Unintentional Expectancy Effect) in more detail. The Experimenter Unintentional Expectancy Effect will be discussed at greater length than the other eight effects because a) a large number of studies have been conducted which pertain to this effect (Rosenthal, 1963, 1964a, 1964b, 1966, 1968, 1969), b) it has received wide publicity during recent years, c) it has been widely accepted as the most important pitfall in experimental research, and d) since the studies which claimed to have demonstrated the Experimenter Unintentional Expectancy

TABLE 1

INVESTIGATOR AND EXPERIMENTER EFFECTS

Investigator Effects
  I. Investigator Paradigm Effect
  II. Investigator Loose Protocol Effect
  III. Investigator Analysis Effect
  IV. Investigator Fudging Effect

Experimenter Effects
  V. Experimenter Attributes Effect
  VI. Experimenter Failure to Follow the Protocol Effect
  VII. Experimenter Misrecording Effect
  VIII. Experimenter Fudging Effect
  IX. Experimenter Unintentional Expectancy Effect

Effect failed to avoid some of the other pit-falls in research, they can serve to illustrate concretely how experimental studies can lead to misleading results and conclusions.

I. INVESTIGATOR PARADIGM EFFECT

In Table 1 the Investigator Paradigm Effect is listed first. This effect appears to exert a powerful influence on every aspect of an experimental project including the results and conclusions. The investigator's paradigm, *his basic assumptions and way of conceptualizing the area of inquiry* (Kuhn, 1962), and his theories which are related to the underlying paradigm, determine not only what questions will be asked but also the kinds of data that will be considered relevant and how the data will be gathered, analyzed, interpreted and related to theoretical concepts (Chaves, 1968; Spanos & Chaves, 1970).

The effects of the investigator's underlying paradigm and associated theories on the conduct and outcome of his research can be illustrated in all areas of inquiry. Let us take an example from psychology. Katahn and Koplin (1968) have recently delineated two of the major underlying paradigms in present-day psychology. They pointed out that behavioristically oriented psychologists and those who prefer cognitive interpretations are working under two different paradigms. The behavioristic paradigm emphasizes objective descriptions of environmental events, operational definitions and controlled experiments whereas the cognitive paradigm emphasizes internal information processes and programming. Besides having different views of experiments and theory, the two paradigms also conceptualize the problems and goals of psychology in divergent ways. The investigator who adheres to the behavioristic paradigm seeks antecedent environmental and situational events that can be related to denotable behaviors. On the other hand, the investigator who adheres to the cognitive para-digm seeks to construct a model of internal processes and structures that can lead to the observed output. These contrasting paradigms lead to different questions and to different ways of designing and conducting a study. Furthermore, even if psychologists who adhere to these divergent paradigms obtain similar data—which is very unlikely since they will conduct quite different studies—their paradigms will lead to divergent interpretations of the data (Katahn & Koplin, 1968). Similarly, investigators who adhere to a third paradigm that is found in present-day psychology—the Freudian paradigm—will ask another set of questions (for example, questions pertaining to unconscious processes), will gather data in a different way (for example, by inferring unconscious processes from the verbal and nonverbal behavior of clinical patients), and will relate the data to a different frame of reference (the theoretical concepts that are derived from Freud).

Although much has been said during recent years about how experimenters bias their results, comparatively little has been said about how investigators bias their results. Investigators bias their results, in accordance with their paradigm and correlated theories, at practically all stages of the research process. At the very beginning of the research there is bias in the questions that are asked and the hypotheses that are formulated. The way the study is conducted—the experimental design, the choice of subjects, the selection and training of experimenters, the data analysis—are also biased by the underlying paradigm. Finally, the interpretations and conclusions that are drawn from the data are closely related to the underlying paradigm and associated theories (Dunnette, 1966).

Of course, investigators cannot carry out research without having some basic assumptions and a way of conceptualizing the area of inquiry. Although a paradigm and associated theories are necessary for the conduct of research, investigators can become more aware of their underlying paradigm and can try to make their assumptions more explicit (Barber, 1970b; Chaves, 1968; Spanos, 1970; Spanos & Chaves, 1970).

II. INVESTIGATOR LOOSE PROTOCOL EFFECT

A second effect associated with the investigator—the Investigator Loose Protocol Effect—pertains to the degree of imprecision of the experimental script or protocol which gives the step-by-step details of how the experiment is to be conducted. In rather rare instances, experiments do not have a formal protocol. In these cases the investigator has a general idea of how the experiment is to proceed, but the steps of the procedure are not planned or written out beforehand and the way the subjects are to be treated is not standardized.

An example of experiments that do not have a formal protocol can be taken from the area of hypnosis research (Barber, 1969a, 1970b). Prior to the advent of rigorous research in this area, investigators would implicitly follow a protocol which stated simply that they were to hypnotize one group of subjects but not another group. Nothing was stated as to what was to be said to the subjects, how the hypnotizing was to be done or how long the hypnotic procedures were to last. Of course it is difficult to draw conclusions from experiments based on such a loose protocol because the procedures can vary with the moment-to-moment predilections of the experimenter. A study based on such an imprecise protocol is unscientific in that science is based on the premise that the procedures of an experiment are specified in sufficient detail so that they can be replicated in other laboratories. If the protocol does not clearly specify the procedures, other laboratories cannot proceed to replicate them and to cross-validate the results.

In a somewhat more common case than the one described above, the experimental protocol has more precise specifications as to how the experiment is to be conducted, but there is still much missing and there is room for the experimenter to vary the procedure from subject to subject. For instance, experiments in education and clinical psychology are, at times, based on experimental protocols which state that certain kinds of subjects are to be tested and certain kinds of questions are to be asked, but the protocols do not state how the subjects are to be selected or what is to be done if the subjects do not understand the questions. This failure to plan for contingencies is also found in loose protocols that do not state what the experimenter is to do at various steps in the procedure—for instance, how he is to interact with the subject immediately before he begins the experimental procedure or how he is to carry out a specific test or interview procedure. The data from such experiments that are based on loose experimental protocols are often reported very precisely. However, since the "precise data" are based on a loose procedure that leaves much room for bias, they can be misleading.

Experimental studies in this area, reviewed by Barber (in press), have demonstrated that loose experimental protocols produce unreliable results. For instance, Feldman, Hyman, and Hart (1951) showed that experimenters obtain dissimilar data when there is a loose protocol (when they are permitted latitude in the way they word the questions during the interview). However, the same investigators also showed that experimenters obtain very similar data when the protocol is well structured (when the wording of the questions is clearly specified beforehand).

Raffetto (1967) has recently reported a study which illustrates an Investigator Loose Protocol Effect. The study was concerned with the effects of the experimenters' expectancies on reports of sensory experiences and "hallucinations" elicited in a sensory deprivation situation. Some of the experimenters were led to expect (by the investigator) that sensory deprivation produces many reports of sensory experiences and "hallucinations," while other experimenters were led to expect that sensory deprivation produces few such reports. After each subject had undergone a period of sensory deprivation, he was interviewed by an experimenter. During these postexperimental interviews, experimenters expecting many reports of sensory experiences and "hallucinations" elicited more reports of this kind than experimenters expecting few such reports.

Raffetto's data indicated that the experimenters influenced their subjects' reports because the experimental protocol was very loose—the interviews were not standardized and the experimenters could conduct their interviews in markedly different ways. As compared to experimenters expecting few reports of sensory experiences and "hallucinations," experimenters expecting many such reports more often encouraged their subjects to continue talking about their experiences, were much more active interviewers and held much longer interviews. In brief, the study indicated that when the investigator constructs a loose protocol, the experimenters' expectancies can affect the conduct of the study, and how the experimenters conduct the study can, in turn, affect the subjects' responses.

III. INVESTIGATOR ANALYSIS EFFECT

The investigator's responsibility extends beyond deciding what kind of study to undertake, what kind of data to gather, what kind of experimental design to use, and what the moment-by-moment procedure is to be. The investigator is also responsible for the way the data are analyzed, and this phase of the research process can easily lead to a major pitfall—the Investigator Analysis Effect.

In some experimental studies, data are collected on a variety of measures, and how the data are to be analyzed is decided *after* the investigator has perused them. After the investigator has studied the data, he may decide to analyze only certain parts of the data while neglecting others. When the investigator has not planned the data analysis *beforehand,* he may find it difficult to avoid the pitfall of focusing only on the data which look promising (or which seem to meet his expectations or desires) while neglecting data which do not seem "right" (or which do not meet his assumptions, desires or expectations). When not planned beforehand, data analysis can approximate a projective technique, such as the Rorschach, because the investigator can project into the data his own expectancies, biases or desires and can pull out of the data almost any conclusion he may desire.

There is also a broader issue that is related to data analysis. An investigator may analyze his data in appropriate ways and may obtain results which fail to confirm his hypothesis. The investigator may not report his negative results; instead, he may perform another study along the same lines and this time obtain results which confirm his hypothesis. If the investigator then publishes his positive results without reporting the fact that he had previously obtained negative results when conducting the same experiment, the reader is likely to draw a misleading conclusion—he is likely to conclude that the positive results are more stable, more easily replicable or more valid than they actually are.

Dunnette (1966) has noted that it is not too uncommon for investigators to bury their negative results. Along similar lines, McNemar (1960) pointed out that, at times, investigators "simply discard all data of an experiment as bad data if not in agreement with theory, and start over."

Another type of Investigator Analysis Effect appears to be more common than those mentioned above. In this case, the investigator performs a large number of statistical comparisons and finds that a small number (say 5 percent) are significant at the 0.05 level of confidence. He then reports the latter few correlations as significant without considering the fact that 5 percent of the comparisons will be significant at the 0.05 level by chance alone. Another example of this kind of effect is found when investigators "report from among a sizable number of computed comparisons only those that are significant [but the] reader is not told about this selection" (McNemar, 1960).

Scrutiny of studies for an Investigator Analysis Effect reveals that computational errors and inappropriate analysis of data are more common than one might suppose. For instance, Wolins (1962) found that faulty data analysis was not uncommon when he asked 37 investigators for raw data based on their recent journal articles. Of the 32 investigators who replied, 21 claimed that their data were either misplaced, lost or inadvertently destroyed. Finally, Wolins was able to complete seven reanalyses of data supplied by five investigators. Of the seven analyses, three involved gross errors. These errors were sufficiently great to change the conclusions which had been reported in the journal articles. For instance, in one analysis several F ratios near one (which were clearly nonsignificant) were reported to be highly significant, and another was incorrectly reported as nonsignificant due to the use of an incorrect error term.

I will return to the Investigator Analysis Effect toward the end of this chapter when I discuss the Experimenter Unintentional Expectancy Effect. I will show there that some studies which tried to demonstrate one of the pitfalls in research (the Experimenter Unintentional Expectancy Effect) ironically failed to avoid another pitfall (the Investigator Analysis Effect).

IV. INVESTIGATOR FUDGING EFFECT

For the sake of completeness, it is necessary to refer briefly to a taboo topic—the Investigator Fudging Effect. This effect is present when an investigator purposively reports results that are not the results he actually obtained.

Outright fraud (fudging of all of the data) appears to be very rare in experimental research. The kind of total fudging that was involved in the construction of the Piltdown man and in the notorious Paul Kammerer case appears to be very uncommon (Jastrow, 1935; MacDougall, 1958; Tullock, 1966). It also appears to be very uncommon for investigators to fudge a substantial proportion of their data as was done recently in a paper that was published in *Science* and in one that was published in the *Journal of Infectious Diseases* (the latter two cases of fudging are discussed by DuShane, Krauskopf, Lerner, Morse, Steinbach, Strauss, & Tatum, 1961).

Although the above type of fudging appears to be very rare, fudging of one or two numbers in the data may be somewhat more common. For instance, if an investigator finds that the statistical test of his hypothesis is approaching significance at, say, $p = 0.15$, he may fudge the p value by changing it to $p = 0.05$. To what extent this type of "small scale" fudging occurs is very difficult to document. However, the motivation for such fudging is sometimes present in experimental research.

As Reif (1961) has pointed out, there is often intense competition among investigators deriving from various factors which cause them to strive for prestige. Investigators commonly invest much time and effort in the study and they are not always neutral with respect to the results they obtain. Some investigators prefer that the results come out a certain way. Also, some investigators seem to believe that whether or not they report significant results can make a difference in their prestige, fame or career. For instance, an investigator may believe that if he reports nonsignificant results, he will not be able to publish the report, he will not receive a research grant or, if he is a doctoral candidate, he will not be granted the doctoral degree. Given this type of strong motivation to obtain significant results, it can be expected that some investigators may at times change one digit of a p value of, say, 0.15 to a p value of 0.05.

Since the hypothetical investigator discussed in the above paragraph is aware that he is violating a basic canon of scientific research—namely, to report the results correctly—he may attempt to rationalize his fudging to himself by arguing that the effect is actually there or that the results are "significant" even though they do not reach an acceptable level of confidence. He may rationalize to himself that reporting a $p = 0.05$ for his results is actually more representative of his data than reporting a nonsignificant $p = 0.15$.

As implied above, we might expect an Investigator Fudging Effect to occur at times when there is a strong motivation to obtain certain results. However, as C. P. Snow (1961) has noted, the motivation to fudge which may be present under these conditions is strongly counterbalanced by a very strong motivation to adhere to the basic canon of research by reporting the results correctly. The motivation to report the results correctly is very strong since the investigator knows that if he is caught fudging his data, he will immediately be expelled from the fraternity of scientists and, if he is even suspected of fudging, he will be treated as a pariah by his colleagues. Although the conscience of the investigator and the consequences of being caught are sufficiently strong to prevent fudging in the overwhelming number of cases, it might also be expected that, in a few cases, the countermotivation to fudge, which derives from the investment in and the importance of obtaining certain results, finally wins out.

EXPERIMENTER EFFECTS

Before I turn to the pitfalls associated with the experimenter, I would like to re-emphasize two points that were mentioned previously:

1. Even though the same person may be both an investigator and an experimenter, these two roles are functionally quite dif-
ferent. Furthermore, in much present-day research, investigators are highly paid professionals who design, analyze and report studies, whereas experimenters are often graduate or undergraduate students who test the subjects while having only a peripheral involvement in the overall plan of the study.

2. One of the major contentions of this chapter is that the bias that has often been attributed to the lowly experimenter who runs the study is at times actually due to the high status investigator who has major responsibility for the study. Recent books pertaining to the pitfalls or artifacts in experimental research (Friedman, 1967; Rosenthal, 1966; Rosenthal & Rosnow, 1969) have tended to focus on the pitfalls associated with the experimenter and have tended to downplay the many pitfalls that are associated with the investigator. Since I hope to have corrected this imbalance by pinpointing some of the many ways that investigators influence the results of their studies, I can now turn to the role of the experimenter and note some of the ways that he may affect the results.

V. EXPERIMENTER ATTRIBUTES EFFECT

There is evidence to indicate that experimenters differing in such personal attributes as sex, age, race, prestige, social status, ethnic characteristics, warmth, friendliness, dominance, etc. at times obtain divergent results when testing similar subjects. In fact, an Experimenter Attributes Effect has been found on a wide variety of tasks including intelligence tests, projective tests and other psychological and educational measures (Friedman, 1967; Johnson & Barber, in press [a]; Masling, 1960, 1966; Rosenthal, 1966, Chapters 4 and 5).

Although a rather large number of studies have shown an Experimenter Attributes Effect, it is difficult, nevertheless, to state at the present time which personal attributes of experimenters affect subjects' performances on what types of dependent variables or experimental tasks. As Johnson and Barber (in press [a]) have pointed out, when one study finds that a specific experimenter attribute affects subjects' performances on one type of task, other studies typically find that the same experimenter attribute does not affect subjects' performances on other types of tasks.

It needs to be underscored that the experimenter's personal attributes may interact in complex ways with the attributes of the subjects and with the specific dependent variables that are being measured in the experiment. For instance, the race of the experimenter may interact with the race of the subject and also with the type of experimental task (e.g., tasks which pertain to race or tasks which are not related to race). Although there is evidence to suggest a triple interaction between experimenters' personal attributes, subjects' personal attributes, and the nature of the task, no studies have been conducted which use experimental designs that incorporate the simultaneous assessment of all three sets of variables (Johnson & Barber, in press [a]). Consequently, all that can be said with confidence at the present time is that an experimenter's sex, age, race, prestige, anxiety, friendliness, dominance, etc. may *at times* affect how subjects perform in the experiment, but we can rarely predict beforehand what experimenter attributes will exert what kind of effects on subjects' performances on what kinds of experimental tasks. Clearly, much further research is needed here.

Until further research is conducted, an investigator who wishes to generalize his results broadly should have his study carried out by experimenters who differ on relevant personal attributes. The problem here is to decide beforehand on which relevant attributes the experimenters should differ. Certainly, if the dependent variable is related to race (e.g., attitudes toward integration, segregation or black-white relations), the investigator should use both black and white experimenters. Similarly, if the subjects' responses might be affected by the experimenters' sex, age, status, etc., the investigator should use sets of experimenters who differ on these attributes.

Since investigators rarely use various kinds of experimenters to conduct their studies, conclusions from studies should be stated more cautiously. The conclusions should include the proviso that the results may be limited to the specific kind of experimenter(s) who was used in the study. Of course, much of the emphasis on cross-validation of experiments in psychology and education derives from this consideration—namely, that an Experimenter Attributes Effect may have operated in the original study and that the results may not be valid when experimenters with different attributes conduct the same study.

VI. EXPERIMENTER FAILURE TO FOLLOW THE PROTOCOL EFFECT

Earlier in this chapter I mentioned the Investigator Loose Protocol Effect which refers to the *investigator's* failure to construct an experimental protocol that specifies clearly how the experimenter is to conduct the study. Let us now assume that the investigator has constructed a tight protocol which does not allow the experimenter much room to vary the procedure. The question now at issue is how often and under what conditions does the *experimenter* fail to follow the experimental protocol? Of course, if the experimenter deviates significantly from the specified experimental procedures, the study that is reported by the investigator is misleading—the study that was actually conducted is not the same as the one that is reported.

Although much has been written during recent years about how the experimenters' expectancies can unintentionally influence their subjects' responses, very little has been said about how the experimenters, by failing to implement the experimental protocol, can easily lead the investigator to present misleading results. In fact, with very few exceptions, studies which attempted to assess the effects of the experimenters' biased expectancies simply assumed that the experimenters carried out the procedures in the way they were supposed to. They rarely checked to determine if an Experimenter Failure to Follow the Protocol Effect was present. This important aspect of the research process—implementing the experimental protocol—has been surprisingly neglected.

In a recent study, Friedman (1967, chapter 5) attempted to determine how experimenters implemented the protocol. The study showed very convincingly that most experimenters have serious difficulties in following the experimental protocol closely even when the protocol is standardized and is not especially "loose." Friedman's data showed that experimenters vary in the way they greet their subjects, in the way they read the instructions and in the way they implement the specific experimental procedures. Not only do different experimenters vary, but the same experimenter tends to be inconsistent when testing different subjects. For instance, an unmarried male experimenter typically conducts the experiment somewhat differently when his subject is a pretty, single woman than when his subject is an older man. To what extent these apparently "small" variations in experimental procedures give rise to unreliable, invalid or unreplicable results remains to be determined. Although Friedman's data indicate that experimenters typically deviate in minor and apparently unimportant ways from the experimental protocol, they also suggest the possibility that some experimenters under some circumstances may deviate more markedly from the protocol.

An Experimenter Failure to Follow the Protocol Effect has been found in a rather large number of studies in which subjects were interviewed (Hyman, 1954). These studies found that a substantial proportion of interviewers deviated markedly from the protocol—skipping questions that were to be asked and holding discussions with the subject which were not part of the script (Johnson & Barber, in press, b). In fact, Hansen, Hurwitz, Marks, and Mauldin (1951) and also Kish and Slater (1960) found that interviewers varied the way they asked the questions even when they were told explicitly that they were to stick with precisely worded questions. Furthermore, Cannell and Kahn (1968) suggested that there appears to be a universal tendency for interviewers to introduce flexibility into their interviews. Apparently interviewers must be carefully supervised during training in order to instill in them the importance of following the protocol carefully.

This part of the research process—implementing the experimental protocol—requires much more careful scrutiny. When reinforcing words are not part of the experimental protocol, how often do experimenters reward their subjects for expected or desired responses by saying "good," "fine" or "excellent"? Under what conditions do experimenters change the procedures that are listed in the protocol or add new features to the prescribed procedures? Is the experimenter more likely to follow the protocol closely when the results he obtains are harmonious with the investigator's hypothesis and more likely to deviate from the protocol when the results are disconfirming the hypothesis? Very few studies have been conducted on this topic and further research should prove fruitful.

VII. EXPERIMENTER MISRECORDING EFFECT

The experimenter may faithfully follow the experimental protocol and yet may fail to record the subjects' responses correctly. Of course, if the errors in recording are biased (are not randomized), they can give rise to invalid results.

Investigators typically assume that their

experimenters correctly recorded the subjects' responses and they rarely check to see if the assumption is correct. Although the assumption is probably valid most of the time, there are data indicating that it is incorrect in some circumstances. For instance, Silverman (1968) and Johnson and Adair (1970) found that some experimenters misrecorded their subjects' responses and these misrecordings were in line with the results that the experimenters expected or desired. Laszlo and Rosenthal (1967) also found that experimenters made errors in adding their subjects' scores and that 75 percent of the errors were in the direction of the experimenters' expectancies or desires (Rosenthal, 1966, p. 13).

Recording errors are also found when the subjects are allowed to record their own responses. Sheffield and Kaufman (with reply by Rhine, 1952) claimed to have found psychokinesis and also clairvoyance when the subjects recorded their responses. Those subjects who believed in psychokinesis or in clairvoyance tended to misrecord their responses so as to show the phenomena; on the other hand, those subjects who did not believe in the phenomena tended to misrecord their responses in the opposite direction. (In reply, Rhine pointed out that these results do not bear on the validity of psychokinesis or clairvoyance since, in the studies he and others conducted on these topics, misrecording of responses was carefully excluded.)

VIII. EXPERIMENTER FUDGING EFFECT

Previously I discussed the *Investigator* Fudging Effect, which is very difficult to document because the investigator has practically complete control over the original data and can make only selected portions of it available for checking by other investigators. However, fudging on the part of the *experimenter* is not too difficult to document.

Of course, if the experimenter knows that he is being observed, he will not be likely to indulge in fudging. However, it is not too difficult to carry out studies in which the experimenter is not aware that possible fudging on his part is under scrutiny. For instance, some subjects can be used as stooges who give predetermined responses. A check can then be made later to determine if the experimenter's data are in harmony with the subjects' responses. This kind of check has been used in a substantial number of studies which involved interviewing of subjects. When such an attempt was made to check fudging in the interview situation, falsification of data was found more often than had been expected.

Hyman (1954) has described the study done by the American Jewish Committee in which 15 interviewers were hired for a special interviewing job. Each interviewer was to administer a standard questionnaire to one to four respondents who were actually stooges and who were particularly difficult to interview. For example, one stooge played the role of a hostile bigot—he had been instructed to be hostile, uncooperative and suspicious of the entire situation. Another stooge played the role of a punctilious liberal—he had been instructed to play the role of an individual who felt incapable of giving an unqualified answer to any question he was asked. Half of the interviewers fudged much of their data and *all* of the interviewers fudged at least some of their data. That is, each of the 15 interviewers at one time or another fudged data either by not asking a question but recording a response anyway or by recording a response when a respondent did not give an answer to the question.

The study described in the preceding paragraph, which involved an especially difficult interview situation, found more fudging than is usually the case. Wyatt and Campbell (1950) found that of 223 student interviewers, 123 (55 percent) either did not complete their interviews or fudged some of their data. Using college students as interviewers, Sheatsley (1947) and Guest (1947) also found some fudging occurring, but apparently to a lesser degree than in the two studies mentioned above.

Roth (1966) presented a series of testimonials from "hired-hand" experimenters who admitted that they had fudged their data. Roth then went on to present cogent arguments why some fudging may be typical among hired-hand experimenters —that is, experimenters who do not feel they have a stake in the research and who feel that they are "simply expected to carry out assigned tasks and turn in results which will 'pass inspection.' "

Roth argued that the behavior of hired-hand experimenters can be expected to be similar to that of a hired hand in a production organization. He described a series of studies which show that, to make their job easier, hired hands in a production unit typically cut corners on prescribed job procedures, fake time sheets and indulge in other forms of goldbricking. Roth pointed out that the product which the hired hand turns out is not his in any sense—he does not design it or decide how it will be produced or what is to be done with it afterwards. Given this alienation from the work, it can be expected that hired hands (working on a production unit or serving as experimenters) will typically deviate from the prescribed procedures and "cut corners" or fudge data.

Azrin, Holz, Ulrich, and Goldiamond (1961) inadvertently discovered that when an experiment is practically impossible to carry out a substantial number of experimenters (undergraduate and graduate students) fudge the data. At the beginning of their investigation, Azrin et al. were attempting to determine whether, in a natural nonexperimental setting, the type of statements made by unselected individuals would be influenced by statements made by experimenters. The experimenters were to strike up conversations with persons in a natural setting and, for a period

of time, were to record the number of statements made by the subject which expressed an opinion. After the base line for opinion statements had been determined, the experimenter was to reinforce the subject's opinion statements by agreeing with them, *to say nothing more,* and to record how many statements the subject subsequently made during a specified period of time which expressed an opinion. The aim of the study was to determine whether individuals would increase the number of their statements which stated an opinion if the experimenters reinforced their opinion statements by agreeing with them.

In one of these studies, Azrin et al. found that when four sophisticated investigators (presumably the authors themselves) tried to conduct the experiment, the experiment could *not* be conducted in accordance with the experimental protocol because all individuals who were approached broke off the conversation within a short period when the experimenter simply agreed with their opinions and refused to say anything more.

In another study in this series, 16 graduate students were asked to carry out the same experiment. Of the 16 experimenters, 15 reported that they completed the experiment successfully and 14 presented data which seemed to indicate that their subjects proffered more opinions after their opinions had been reinforced. However, one experimenter stated that he was unable to conduct the experiment because he was unable to maintain a conversation with his subjects without actively participating in the conversation. Subsequently eight of the remaining experimenters admitted that they also had similar difficulties and that they had deviated appreciably from the experimental protocol. Clearly, in this part of the investigation at least half of the experimenters showed an Experimenter Failure to Follow the Protocol Effect. Some of these experimenters may also have fudged part or all of their data, as indicated by a third study reported by Azrin et al. (1961).

In this third study, Azrin et al. asked

undergraduate students to carry out the same experiment. Again, the experimenters reported that they had succeeded in carrying out the study and their data indicated that reinforcement had influenced the subjects to give more opinions. However, much of the data had been fudged. Azrin et al. discovered the fudging as follows:

By coincidence, a student was enrolled in this third class who was also employed as a research assistant in a psychology laboratory. This student employee was assigned to question the other students informally and outside of class as to how they had conducted their experiments. The other students had no knowledge of this arrangement. Out of 19 students questioned, consisting of almost one-half of the class, 12 stated that they fabricated part or all of the data. This admission ... was readily made when the student was asked by the employee, "I'm having trouble with my experiment; can you tell me how you did yours?" Five of the remaining seven students questioned stated that they had deviated greatly from the prescribed procedure. Only two out of nineteen students stated that they had followed the prescribed procedure. Consequently, an attempt at an exact replication seemed pointless, since the data reports themselves were probably fabricated (Azrin et al., 1961, p. 29).

In brief, the studies by Azrin et al. indicated that when an experiment is practically impossible to conduct according to the experimental protocol, a substantial proportion of experimenters (undergraduate or graduate students) carry out the impossible study either by changing the experimental procedures (Experimenter Failure to Follow the Protocol Effect) or by fabricating the data (Experimenter Fudging Effect).

IX. EXPERIMENTER UNINTENTIONAL EXPECTANCY EFFECT

Experimenters commonly *expect* certain results; for instance, they expect that the experimental group will perform differently from the control group. Experimenters also commonly *desire* certain results—they would like to see the experimental hypothesis verified. In the 1960s Rosenthal (1963, 1964a, 1966) hypothesized that a) the experimenters' expectancies or desires are transmitted to their subjects by means of *unintentional* paralinguistic cues (such as variations in the experimenter's tone of voice) or *unintentional* kinesic cues (such as changes in the experimenter's posture or facial expressions), and b) the experimenters' expectancies or desires influence (or bias) *their subjects' responses,* that is, the subjects respond in such a way as to confirm the experimenters' expectancies or desires—Experimenter Unintentional Expectancy (or Desire) Effect.

Rosenthal carried out a large number of studies which concluded that an Experimenter Unintentional Expectancy (or Desire) Effect[3] had been demonstrated. Although the many studies carried out by Rosenthal and his collaborators have been widely accepted as showing the pervasiveness of the Experimenter Unintentional Expectancy Effect (or "Rosenthal Effect"), a close look at these studies indicates that most of them did not clearly demonstrate it. First of all, most of these studies did not clearly demonstrate that the expectancies or desires of experimenters *unintentionally* influenced their subjects' responses. Although some of the studies indicated that experimenters at times obtain results in line with their expectancies or desires, very few of the studies attempted to ascertain whether the experimenters *intentionally* or *unintentionally* influenced their subjects to respond in the way that was expected or desired. Secondly, most of the studies did not clearly

---

[3] Henceforth, I will refer simply to the Experimenter Unintentional Expectancy Effect instead of to the Experimenter Unintentional Expectancy (or Desire) Effect. However, the reader should keep in mind that, in practically all of the experiments that will be discussed below, the experimenters' expectancies were not separated from their desires.

demonstrate that the experimenters' expectancies or desires affected *the subjects' responses. Without in any way affecting the subjects' responses,* experimenters can bring the results in line with their expectancies or desires by deviating from the experimental protocol, by misrecording the data or by fudging the data.

As will be discussed below, many studies which claimed to have demonstrated that experimenters' expectancies *unintentionally* influence the subjects' responses are open to alternative interpretations, namely, that the results were due to one or more of the following: an Investigator Analysis Effect, an Experimenter Failure to Follow the Protocol Effect, an Experimenter Misrecording Effect, or an Experimenter Fudging Effect.

I will now present a rather detailed analysis of some of the studies which were interpreted as showing an Experimenter Unintentional Expectancy Effect. Some of these studies will be discussed at length because a) a large number of studies have been conducted which pertain to the Experimenter Unintentional Expectancy Effect and these studies have received wide publicity (Rosenthal, 1964a, 1966, 1967, 1968, 1969), b) investigators who claimed to have demonstrated the Experimenter Unintentional Expectancy Effect did not avoid the pitfalls which have been discussed previously in this chapter, and, consequently, c) studies which pertain to the Experimenter Unintentional Expectancy Effect can serve to illustrate some of the many pitfalls in research.

Experimenter Unintentional Expectancy Effect or Investigator Analysis Effect?

Several years ago Barber and Silver (1968a, 1968b) critically reviewed 31 studies which purported to show an Experimenter Unintentional Expectancy Effect. Ironically, 19 of these 31 studies seemed to show an Investigator Analysis Effect on the part of those investigators who were studying the

Experimenter Unintentional Expectancy Effect. To show how an Investigator Analysis Effect leads to misleading conclusions, I will now discuss two of these 19 studies, one by Rosenthal, Persinger, Mulry, Vikan-Kline, and Grothe (1964) and another by Persinger (1963).

Critique of a study by Rosenthal et al. (1964). In this study, which was designed to show an Experimenter Unintentional Expectancy Effect, 20 student experimenters were asked to test a total of 73 subjects on Rosenthal's person-perception task. When using this task, the subject is shown a series of photographed faces. The subject is asked to rate on a numerical scale whether each of the persons shown on the photographs has been experiencing success (high ratings) or has been experiencing failure (low ratings).

To induce the experimenters to expect high (or low) ratings from subjects on the person-perception task, all experimenters were told (by the investigators) that, on the basis of personality tests given to the subjects, it could be expected that certain of their subjects would give high ("success") ratings and other specified subjects would give low ("failure") ratings. (Since the subjects were *not* given the personality tests and since they were assigned to experimenters at random, the subjects should not differ in their ratings.) The dependent variable was the difference between the average ratings obtained by each experimenter from those subjects who he expected would give high ratings and those subjects who he expected would give low ratings.

The authors of the paper did not perform an overall statistical analysis to determine if the data were harmonious with the experimenters' induced expectancies for high and low ratings. Instead of determining first whether the data showed the hypothesized Experimenter Unintentional Expectancy Effect, the authors stated first that three of the 20 experimenters showed a "reversal of the biasing effect of expectancy, i.e., they obtained data significantly opposite to what they had been led to expect." The authors then analyzed the data for the remaining 17 experimenters and reported that these experimenters showed a significant Experimenter Unintentional Expectancy Effect.

There are several interrelated reasons why this conclusion—that the study showed an Experimenter Unintentional Expectancy Effect—cannot be accepted as valid: a) The authors concluded that the effect was present by excluding from the analysis the "negative" data (in the opposite direction) that were obtained by three of the 17 experimenters. b) The "negative" data were excluded from the analysis (which supposedly showed the Experimenter Unintentional Expectancy Effect) after the investigators had inspected the results and after they had determined that some of the data were "negative" with respect to the experimental hypothesis. c) The authors were *not* using the acceptable procedure of excluding data by means of a criterion that was determined *prior to* inspection of the data. d) The way the data were analyzed did not allow for the possibility that the study may have simply failed to show an Experimenter Unintentional Expectancy Effect.

Of course, no conclusions can be drawn from research reports that adopt the aforementioned procedures—that is, that conclude that the hypothesis was confirmed by a statistical analysis which included the data favorable to the hypothesis but did not include the data that were judged, after inspection of the results, to be significantly opposite to the hypothesis. (When the data of the study are analyzed appropriately using all 20 experimenters, the mean difference between the ratings obtained when the experimenters expected high ratings and when they expected low ratings is far from significant.)

Critique of study by Persinger (1963). In a thesis by Persinger (1963) which was supervised by Rosenthal, six experimenters were given reasons by the investigator why their subjects would give high ratings on the person-perception task, and six additional experimenters were given reasons why their subjects would give low ratings. Persinger hypothesized that the experimenters' expectancies would affect the ratings of those subjects with whom they were previously acquainted significantly more than those subjects with whom they were not acquainted. To test this hypothesis the investigator performed three different statistical analyses. These analyses yielded nonsignificant findings. A close study of the original report shows that after the investigator had failed to confirm his original hypothesis in three separate analyses, he changed the hypothesis. The revised hypothesis was that there is an interaction between the experimenters' expectancies, the sex of the experimenters, and whether or not they are acquainted with their subjects. The investigator performed two statistical analyses to test this revised hypothesis. One of the two analyses did not show the hypothesized interaction. The other, final, analysis showed a significant interaction which indicated that the expectancies of male experimenters (but not of female experimenters) affected their acquainted subjects more than their unacquainted subjects.

The final statistical analysis from this study was presented as a definitive finding —as showing that an Experimenter Unintentional Expectancy Effect had been demonstrated in interaction with the other variables (Rosenthal, 1968). However, this conclusion is invalid. The study did not show an interaction between experimenters' expectancies and other variables because the data analysis is faulty—that is, the conclusion is misleading because it is based on an Investigator Analysis Effect. It should be noted that the investigator did not confirm his original hypothesis in three separate analyses, he then went on to perform two analyses which pertained to a revised hypothesis, and one of the latter two analyses did not confirm the revised hypothesis. These kinds of analyses lead to misleading conclusions. If investigators keep changing their hypothesis and perform several statistical analyses on each hypothesis, sooner or later they will obtain a "significant" finding even when the data come from a Table of Random Numbers.[4]

Experimenter Unintentional Expectancy Effect or Failure to Follow the Protocol, Misrecording, and Fudging?

Two studies (Rosenthal & Fode, 1963a; Rosenthal & Lawson, 1964) were interpreted by their authors as indicating that experimenters' expectancies unintentionally influence the performance of rats. Although these studies have been widely quoted as indicating that the Experimenter Unintentional Expectancy Effect is found even when experimenters are testing animals, the results are open to a different interpretation, namely, that the studies showed an Experimenter Failure to Follow the Protocol

Effect, an Experimenter Misrecording Effect, or an Experimenter Fudging Effect.

In both of these studies the experimenters were undergraduate students enrolled in a beginners' psychology laboratory course. The experimenters were told by the investigator that they would receive practice in duplicating well-established experimental findings pertaining to rats. Half of the experimenters were told that their rats came from a bright strain and would learn quickly and the other experimenters were told that their rats came from a dull strain and would learn slowly. (The rats were actually drawn at random from a homogeneous animal colony and thus were equal in brightness.) In both studies the experimenters expecting fast learning from their rats reported significantly faster learning than the experimenters expecting that their rats were slow learners. Rosenthal (1966) interpreted this outcome as showing that the experimenters' expectancies unintentionally influenced the rats' responses. Rosenthal further hypothesized that experimenters expecting faster learning handled their rats differently from those expecting slower learning and that the tactual cues transmitted during handling mediated the Experimenter Unintentional Expectancy Effect.

However, there are alternative interpretations of these studies. As stated above, the experimenters were undergraduate students enrolled in a beginners' psychology laboratory. Students in introductory laboratory courses deviate from the experimental protocol and systematically misrecord the data to such an extent that most psychologists agree that the results from such laboratories cannot be trusted. In fact, the authors of these studies reported that failure to follow the experimental protocol and misrecording or fudging of data were occurring in their laboratories. In the Rosenthal and Fode (1963a) study, the student experimenters were rarely observed by the laboratory supervisor; however, during the brief period in which they were observed, there were

---

[4] Seventeen additional studies, which were interpreted as demonstrating an Experimenter Unintentional Expectancy Effect (Rosenthal, 1966, 1968), did not actually show this effect; instead, they seemed to show an Investigator Analysis Effect. These additional 17 studies, which further illustrate how investigators can derive invalid conclusions from inappropriate data analyses, are critically analyzed by Barber and Silver (1968a, 1968b). An additional 12 studies, which Rosenthal (1966) interpreted as showing an experimenter modeling effect (the subjects supposedly modeled their performance on the task after the performance of the experimenter) were also inappropriately analyzed—that is, they also showed an Investigator Data Analysis Effect (Silver, 1968). The critical reviews by Barber (1969b), Barber and Silver (1968a, 1968b), and Silver (1968) are well worth reading because they provide many examples of how investigators can derive invalid conclusions from inappropriate analyses of their data. Also recommended are the critical reviews of R. E. Snow (1969), Thorndike (1968), Claiborn (1969), and Hursch (1970), which showed that unreliable measuring instruments and serious deficiencies in data analysis negate the widely publicized conclusion—that teachers' expectancies influence their pupils' IQs—which was drawn in a study entitled *Pygmalion in the Classroom* (Rosenthal & Jacobson, 1968).

"five observed instances of cheating in which an *E* prodded an *S* [a rat] to run the maze" (p. 186). However, Rosenthal and Fode did not consider this type of cheating or failure to follow the protocol—prodding the rats to run the maze faster—especially important because it was not observed more often among experimenters expecting faster learning from their rats.

Regarding the second study (Rosenthal & Lawson, 1964), one of the authors subsequently stated (without presenting further details) that "several instances of data fabrication came to light" (Rosenthal, 1964a, p. 83). There is no reason to believe that the fudged data were used in the analysis. However, there is no way of knowing whether the remaining student experimenters in the introductory laboratory course who were not caught in the act of fudging the data and whose data were used in the analysis conducted the study honestly or dishonestly.

In brief, although these studies have been widely cited as showing that an Experimenter Unintentional Expectancy Effect is present even when the experimenters are testing rats, there is presumptive evidence that the results were due, not to an Experimenter Unintentional Expectancy Effect, but to an Experimenter Failure to Follow the Protocol Effect, an Experimenter Misrecording Effect, or an Experimenter Fudging Effect. Additional studies are needed to determine which of these kinds of effects play the most important role in biasing the results of experiments conducted in introductory laboratory courses.

Experimenter Unintentional Expectancy Effect: Negative Results

A rather large number of studies that tried to demonstrate an Experimenter Unintentional Expectancy Effect simply failed to show that experimenters' expectancies affect their subjects' responses.

Barber, Calverley, Forgione, McPeake, Chaves, and Bowen (1969) presented five studies which failed to demonstrate that experimenters' expectancies affect subjects' responses on Rosenthal's person-perception task. Strauss (1968) and Strauss and Marwit (1970) also failed to demonstrate a hypothesized Experimenter Unintentional Expectancy Effect on subjects' responses to the Rorschach. Zegers (1968) and Kennedy (1969) failed to demonstrate the effect in experiments on verbal conditioning. Timaeus and Lueck (1968) failed to demonstrate it in an experiment utilizing the Stroop color test. A rather large number of other studies which measured subjects' responses to a variety of experimental tasks also failed to show that experimenters' expectancies affected the subjects' responses (Becker, 1968; Friedman, 1964, p. 92; Jacob, 1968, 1970; McFall, 1966; McFall & Saxman, 1968; McGinley, McGinley, & Shames, 1970; Souren, van der Kloot, & van Bergen, 1969; Steinhelber, 1970; Wartenberg-Ekren, 1962; Wessler, 1968, 1969; Wessler & Strauss, 1968).

Experimenter Unintentional Expectancy Effect: Positive Results

A series of studies have apparently shown an Experimenter Unintentional Expectancy Effect. Zobel and Lehman (1969) found that experimenters' expectancies can influence the subjects' responses on a tone discrimination task and presented suggestive evidence that the expectancy effect can be mediated (probably unintentionally) by either verbal or facial cues from the experimenter. R. W. Johnson (1970) also presented data indicating that the experimenters' expectancies may be unintentionally transmitted to the subjects and that the subjects then respond in the direction of the experimenters' expectancies. McFall and Schenkein (1970) showed that experimenters' expectancies can be transmitted by verbal cues and can unintentionally influence the responses of some types of subjects (subjects who are high in need for achievement and in field dependence). Other studies (including Adair & Epstein, 1967; Blake & Heslin, 1971; Marwit, 1969; Marwit & Marcia, 1967; Masling, 1965; Minor, 1970; Rosenthal & Fode, 1963b, Exp. 2) also indicate that the experimenters' expectancies or desires can be communicated to their subjects by verbal, facial or gestural cues and that the subjects may then respond in such a way as to fulfill the experimenters' expectancies.

Experimenter Unintentional Expectancy Effect: Concluding Considerations

As stated earlier in this chapter, a large number of papers and books claim that experimental studies commonly show an Experimenter Unintentional Expectancy Effect. As stated above, this effect apparently has been demonstrated in some studies— experimenters at times unintentionally obtain results which confirm their expectancies (when they apparently follow the experimental protocol and do not misrecord or fudge the data). However, many studies which commonly have been cited as showing the effect either did not show it at all or were difficult to interpret due to the presence of an Investigator Analysis Effect. Also, some studies which seemed to show an Experimenter Failure to Follow the Protocol Effect, an Experimenter Misrecording Effect or, possibly, an Experimenter Fudging Effect were interpreted as showing an Experimenter Unintentional Expectancy Effect. Thus, it appears that the Experimenter Unintentional Expectancy Effect is more difficult to demonstrate and less pervasive than was implied in previous reviews (Friedman, 1967; Kintz, Delprato, Mettee, Persons, & Schappe, 1965; Rosenthal, 1963, 1964a, 1964b, 1966, 1967, 1968, 1969).

There are many reasons why the Experimenter Unintentional Expectancy Effect is rather difficult to demonstrate. First of all, to show that the experimenters' expectancies unintentionally influenced their subjects'

responses it is necessary to exclude the possibility that the experimenters obtained expected or desired results by deviating from the experimental protocol, by misrecording data, or by fudging data. Secondly, it is necessary to exclude the possibility that the results were made harmonious with the original expectancies or desires by the investigator's inappropriate analyses of the data. Even if these possibilities are excluded, it is still rather difficult to demonstrate an Experimenter Unintentional Expectancy Effect because, to demonstrate an Experimenter Unintentional Expectancy Effect, expectancies have to be transmitted from the investigator to the experimenter and from the experimenter to the subject. In fact, a seven-step transmission process must take place (cf. McGuire, 1968): 1) The experimenter must attend to the expectancy communication from the investigator. 2) The experimenter must comprehend the expectancy communication. 3) The experimenter must retain the communication. 4) The experimenter must then unintentionally emit cues which are capable of informing the subject of his (the experimenter's) expectancy. 5) The subject must attend to the cues from the experimenter. 6) The subject (consciously or unconsciously) must comprehend what the cues from the experimenter mean. 7) The subject (intentionally or unintentionally) must alter his responses so that they confirm the experimenter's expectancy. The transmission chain could break down at any one of these seven links. In the studies which have been conducted, the investigator tells the experimenter what results are expected or desired quite some time before the experimenter tests the subjects. At the same time, the investigator also tells the experimenter many other things besides what to expect —for example, he tells the experimenter how to obtain and how to test the subjects. When the experimenter is told what to expect, he may not pay close attention or may not comprehend the communication. Furthermore, by the time the experimenter runs his subjects he may forget what results are expected or desired. When the experimenter runs his subjects, he may fail to emit cues which inform the subject of the expected or desired results. Even if the experimenter emits such unintentional cues, the subject may not notice them or, if he notices them, he may not understand what they mean. Finally, even if the subject understands what the experimenter expects or desires, he may not alter his responses to fulfill the experimenter's expectancy. Instead, the subject may simply respond in his normal manner (not altering his responses) or may alter his responses so as to disconfirm the experimenter's expectancy—the "Screw You Effect" (Masling, 1966).

SUMMARY AND CONCLUSIONS

Since experimental research is carried out by fallible individuals, it is open to a wide variety of pitfalls. This chapter has focused on two sets of pitfalls, one set that is associated with the investigator (who designs, supervises and has major responsibility for analyzing and reporting the study) and another set that is associated with the experimenter (who tests the subjects and collects the data).

Recent books and papers in this area have heavily emphasized one of the pitfalls that is associated with the experimenter (the Experimenter Unintentional Expectancy Effect or "Rosenthal Effect") and they have tended to downplay the important role of the investigator. However, we need to become sensitized to the bias that is introduced by the investigator as well as the bias that is associated with the experimenter. Experimental studies are biased at their very outset by the investigator's paradigm and associated theories—by his underlying assumptions and his way of conceptualizing the area of inquiry (Investigator Paradigm Effect). Investigators also construct the experimental protocol, and the "looseness" or "tightness" of the specified experimental procedures can exert an important influence

on the experimental outcome (Investigator Loose Protocol Effect). Investigators also sometimes analyze their data in such a way that they obtain the results they desire or expect (Investigator Analysis Effect). Finally, some investigators are highly motivated to report certain results and, despite the scientific canon to present the results honestly, fabrication of some of the data may at times occur (Investigator Fudging Effect).

Present-day experimenters (who are often graduate or undergraduate students) can also bias the results of the research. At times the experimenter's personal attributes —his sex, age, race, prestige and personality characteristics—can affect the way his subjects perform in the experiment (Experimenter Attributes Effect). Experimenters sometimes deviate from the experimental protocol and carry out an experiment which differs from the one that was planned and reported by the investigator (Experimenter Failure to Follow the Protocol Effect). Also, some experimenters systematically misrecord their data (Experimenter Misrecording Effect) and a few experimenters may fabricate some of their data (Experimenter Fudging Effect). Finally, the experimenter's expectancies or desires are at times unintentionally communicated to the subjects, and the subjects sometimes alter their responses so as to confirm the experimenter's expectancies or desires (Experimenter Unintentional Expectancy Effect).

Experimental research can become a more reliable method for obtaining valid knowledge if the following changes are instituted:[5]

1. Investigators should become more

---

[5] Rosenthal (1966, Chapters 17–24) has also suggested a series of changes that should be made in the methods of experimental research. Although Rosenthal's discussion is concerned primarily with techniques for controlling the Experimenter Unintentional Expectancy Effect (and tends to downplay the many other investigator and experimenter effects that have been discussed in the present chapter), it is nevertheless stimulating and well worth careful reading. I am incorporating some of Rosenthal's suggestions into the 12 recommendations that I am listing here.

aware of their underlying paradigms and how paradigms influence every aspect of their research (Kuhn, 1962). Investigators should also try to make their assumptions (which derive from their underlying paradigms and associated theories) more explicit (cf. Barber, 1970b; Chaves, 1968; Spanos, 1970; Spanos & Chaves, 1970).

2. At the present time the same investigator who plans the study also has major responsibility for analyzing the data. Research studies would be less biased if the investigator who plans the study and who has an investment in the outcome is *not* the same person who has responsibility for the data analysis.

3. At times the same person plans the study (serves as investigator) and also collects the data (serves as experimenter). The investigator who plans the study and who has a strong commitment to the outcome should not be the same person who serves as experimenter and who collects the data.

4. Investigators should become more sensitive to the importance of the experimental script or protocol. A "loose" protocol that does not specify clearly how the experimenter is to carry out each phase of the study and that fails to consider the various contingencies which may arise can easily yield misleading results.

5. Investigators should give their experimenters more supervised practice in implementing the experimental protocol and in correctly and honestly recording the data. Before the formal experiment is conducted, the experimenters should carry out pilot studies under careful supervision.

6. In the training of researchers, additional emphasis should be placed on the complexities of data analysis. Researchers need to have a thorough understanding of the many kinds of data analyses that lead to misleading conclusions and the kinds of analyses that can be used appropriately with specified sets of data (cf. Barber & Silver, 1968a, 1968b).

7. The emphasis on "positive" results in graduate schools and in the training of researchers needs to be changed. Research should be judged on the validity of the design and procedures that are used to answer the questions that are posed rather than on the outcome—the results that are obtained (Rosenthal, 1966).

8. The present training ground for psychologists, the introductory psychology laboratory, is permeated with improper procedures—failing to follow the protocol, misrecording of data and fudging of data—and this early "training" may influence the investigator's later attitude toward the collection of data. Teachers of embryo psychologists and educators should place much more emphasis on the value of carefully following the prescribed procedures and carefully and honestly recording the data.

9. Investigators should check, much more often than they do at present, to see if their experimenters are faithfully implementing the experimental protocol and are carefully and honestly recording the data. This check could be made in various ways—by making tape recordings or video tapes of the experimenters carrying out the study, by using one-way mirrors to observe the conduct of the experiment, or by sending stooges, who give predetermined responses, to be tested by the experimenters.

10. Investigators should more often use sets of experimenters differing in personal attributes to collect the data. Too often experiments are carried out by one experimenter and the results may be influenced by the characteristics of that one experimenter.

11. More often than at present, experiments can be carried out "blind" (the data collector does not know what treatment the subject has received), the experimenter administering the experimental procedures can be a different person from the one who records the results, subjects can be given written or tape-recorded instructions, and automated equipment can be used both to administer the experimental procedures and to record the results (Rosenthal, 1966).

12. There are so many pitfalls in any one

experimental study that we should not take any one study too seriously. Before they are accepted as an integral part of the area of inquiry, the results of any experiment should be replicated by a variety of investigators who hold different paradigms or theories.

REFERENCES

Adair, J. G., & Epstein, J. Verbal cues in the mediation of experimenter bias. Paper presented at Midwestern Psychological Association, Chicago, May 5, 1967.

Azrin, N. H., Holz, W., Ulrich, R., & Goldiamond, I. The control of the content of conversation through reinforcement. *Journal of the Experimental Analysis of Behavior*, 1961, 4, 25–30.

Barber, T. X. *Hypnosis: A scientific approach.* New York: Van Nostrand-Reinhold, 1969. (a)

Barber, T. X. Invalid arguments, postmortem analyses, and the experimenter bias effect. *Journal of Consulting and Clinical Psychology*, 1969, 33, 11–14. (b)

Barber, T. X. *LSD, marihuana, yoga, and hypnosis.* Chicago: Aldine, 1970. (a)

Barber, T. X. *Suggested ('hypnotic') behavior: The trance paradigm versus an alternative paradigm.* Harding, Mass.: Medfield Foundation, 1970. (b)

Barber, T. X. (Ed.) *Pitfalls in research.* Chicago: Aldine-Atherton, in press.

Barber, T. X., Calverley, D. S., Forgione, A., McPeake, J. D., Chaves, J. F., & Bowen, B. Five attempts to replicate the experimenter bias effect. *Journal of Consulting and Clinical Psychology*, 1969, 33, 1–6.

Barber, T. X., & Silver, M. J. Fact, fiction, and the experimenter bias effect. *Psychological Bulletin* (Monograph Supplement), 1968, 70 (No. 6, Pt. 2), 1–29. (a)

Barber, T. X., & Silver, M. J. Pitfalls in data analysis and interpretation: A reply to Rosenthal. *Psychological Bulletin* (Monograph Supplement), 1968, 70 (No. 6, Pt. 2), 48–62. (b)

Becker, H. G. Experimenter expectancy, experience and status as factors in observational data. Unpublished master's thesis, University of Saskatchewan, 1968.

Blake, B. F., & Heslin, R. Evaluation apprehension and subject bias in experiments. *Journal of Experimental Research in Personality*, 1971, 5, 57–63.

Cannell, C. F., & Kahn, R. L. Interviewing. In G. Lindzey, & E. Aronson (Eds.) *The handbook of social psychology.* Vol. II. (2nd Ed.) Reading, Mass.: Addison-Wesley, 1968. Pp. 526–595.

Chaves, J. F. Hypnosis reconceptualized: An overview of Barber's theoretical and empirical work. *Psychological Reports*, 1968, 22, 587–608.

Claiborn, W. L. *An investigation of the relationship between teacher expectancy, teacher behavior and pupil performance.* (Doctoral dissertation, Syracuse University) Ann Arbor, Mich.: University Microfilms, 1969. No. 69-8619.

Dunnette, M. D. Fads, fashions, and folderol in psychology. *American Psychologist*, 1966, 21, 343–352.

DuShane, G., Krauskopf, K. B., Lerner, E. M., Morse, P. M., Steinbach, H. B., Straus, W. L., Jr., & Tatum, E. L. An unfortunate event. *Science*, 1961, 134, 945–946.

Feldman, J. J., Hyman, H., & Hart, C. W. A field study of interviewer effects on the quality of survey data. *Public Opinion Quarterly*, 1951, 15, 734–761.

Friedman, N. The psychological experiment as a social situation. Unpublished doctoral dissertation, Harvard University, 1964.

Friedman, N. *The social nature of psychological research.* New York: Basic Books, 1967.

Guest, L. A study of interviewer competence. *International Journal of Opinion and Attitude Research*, 1947, 1(4), 17–30.

Hansen, M. H., Hurwitz, W. N., Marks, E. S., & Mauldin, W. P. Response errors in surveys. *Journal of the American Statistical Association*, 1951, 46, 147–190.

Hursch, C. J. Review of R. Rosenthal & L. Jacobson, *Pygmalion in the classroom: Teacher expectation and pupils' intellectual development. Journal of Individual Psychology*, 1970, 26, 100.

Hyman, H. H. *Interviewing in social research.* Chicago: University of Chicago Press, 1954.

Jacob, T. The experimenter bias effect: A failure to replicate. *Psychonomic Science*, 1968, 13, 239–240.

Jacob, T. *The emergence and mediation of the experimenter bias effect as a function of "demand characteristics," experimenter "investment" and the nature of the experimental task.* (Doctoral dissertation, The University of Nebraska) Ann Arbor, Mich.: University Microfilms, 1970. No. 69-22, 279.

Jastrow, J. *Errors and eccentricity in human belief.* New York: Dover, 1935.

Johnson, R. F. Q., & Barber, T. X. Experimenter personal attributes effect: A methodological analysis. In T. X. Barber (Ed.), *Pitfalls in research.* Chicago: Aldine-Atherton, in press. (a)

Johnson, R. F. Q., & Barber, T. X. Pitfalls in research: The interview as an illustrative model. In T. X. Barber (Ed.), *Pitfalls in research.* Chicago: Aldine-Atherton, in press. (b)

Johnson, R. W. Subject performance as affected by experimenter expectancy, sex of experimenter, and verbal reinforcement. *Canadian Journal of Behavioral Science,* 1970, 2, 60–66.

Johnson, R. W., & Adair, J. G. The effects of systematic recording error vs. experimenter bias on latency of word association. *Journal of Experimental Research in Personality,* 1970, 4, 270–275.

Katahn, M., & Koplin, J. H. Paradigm clash: Comment on "Some recent criticisms of behaviorism and learning theory with special reference to Breger and McGough and to Chomsky." *Psychological Bulletin,* 1968, 69, 147–148.

Kennedy, J. J. Experimenter outcome bias in verbal conditioning: A failure to detect the Rosenthal effect. *Psychological Reports,* 1969, 25, 495–500.

Kintz, B. L., Delprato, D. J., Mettee, D. R., Persons, C. E., & Schappe, R. H. The experimenter effect. *Psychological Bulletin,* 1965, 63, 223–232.

Kish, L., & Slater, C. W. Two studies of interviewer variance of socio-psychological variables. *Proceedings of the American Statistical Association, Social Studies Section,* 1960, 66–70.

Kuhn, T. S. *The structure of scientific revolutions.* Chicago: University of Chicago Press, 1962.

Laszlo, J. P., & Rosenthal, R. Subject dogmatism, experimenter status and experimenter expectancy effects. Cambridge, Mass.: Harvard University, Department of Social Relations, 1967.

MacDougall, C. D. *Hoaxes.* (2nd ed.) New York: Ace Books, 1958.

Marwit, S. J. Communication of tester bias by means of modeling. *Journal of Projective Techniques & Personality Assessment,* 1969, 33, 345–352.

Marwit, S. J., & Marcia, J. E. Tester bias and response to projective instruments. *Journal of Consulting Psychology,* 1967, 31, 253–258.

Masling, J. The influence of situational and interpersonal variables in projective testing. *Psychological Bulletin,* 1960, 57, 65–85.

Masling, J. Differential indoctrination of examiners and Rorschach responses. *Journal of Consulting Psychology,* 1965, 29, 198–201.

Masling, J. Role-related behavior of the subject and psychologist and its effects upon psychological data. In D. Levine (Ed.), *Nebraska symposium on motivation.* Lincoln, Neb.: University of Nebraska Press, 1966. Pp. 67–103.

McFall, R. M. *"Unintentional communication": The effect of congruence and incongruence between subject and experimenter constructions.* (Doctoral dissertation, Ohio State University) Ann Arbor, Mich.: University Microfilms, 1966. No. 66-1809.

McFall, R. M., & Saxman, J. H. Verbal communication as a mediator of expectancy effects: Methodological artifact? *Psychological Reports,* 1968, 23, 1223–1228.

McFall, R. M., & Schenkein, D. Experimenter expectancy effects, need for achievement, and field dependence. *Journal of Experimental Research in Personality,* 1970, 4, 122–128.

McGinley, H., McGinley, P., & Shames, M. Failure to find experimenter-expectancy effects in IQ estimations. *Psychological Reports,* 1970, 27, 831–834.

McGuire, W. J. Personality and susceptibility to social influence. In E. F. Borgatta & W. W. Lambert (Eds.), *Handbook of personality theory and research.* Chicago: Rand McNally, 1968. Pp. 1130–1187.

McNemar, Q. At random: Sense and nonsense. *American Psychologist,* 1960, 15, 295–300.

Minor, M. W. Experimenter-expectancy effect as a function of evaluation apprehension. *Journal of Personality and Social Psychology,* 1970, 15, 326–332.

Persinger, G. W. The effect of acquaintance-ship on the mediation of experimenter bias. Unpublished master's thesis, University of North Dakota, 1963.

Raffetto, A. M. Experimenter effects on sub-jects' reported hallucinatory experiences un-der visual and auditory deprivation. Unpub-lished master's thesis, San Francisco State College, 1967.

Reif, F. The competitive world of the pure scientist. *Science,* 1961, 134, 1957–1962.

Rosenthal, R. On the social psychology of the psychological experiment: The experiment-er's hypothesis as unintended determinant of experimental results. *American Scientist,* 1963, 51, 268–283.

Rosenthal, R. The effect of the experimenter on the results of psychological research. In B. A. Maher (Ed.), *Progress in experimental personality research.* Vol. 1. New York: Academic Press, 1964. Pp. 79–114. (a)

Rosenthal, R. Experimenter outcome-orienta-tion and the results of the psychological ex-periment. *Psychological Bulletin,* 1964, 61, 405–412. (b)

Rosenthal, R. *Experimenter effects in behav-ioral research.* New York: Appleton-Cen-tury-Crofts, 1966.

Rosenthal, R. Covert communication in the psychological experiment. *Psychological Bul-letin,* 1967, 67, 356–367.

Rosenthal, R. Experimenter expectancy and the reassuring nature of the null hypothesis decision procedure. *Psychological Bulletin* (Monograph Supplement), 1968, 70 (No. 6, Pt. 2), 30–47.

Rosenthal, R. Interpersonal expectations: Ef-fects of the experimenter's hypothesis. In R. Rosenthal & R. L. Rosnow (Eds.), *Arti-fact in behavioral research.* New York: Aca-demic Press, 1969. Pp. 181–277.

Rosenthal, R., & Fode, K. L. The effect of experimenter bias on the performance of the albino rat. *Behavioral Science,* 1963, 8, 183–189. (a)

Rosenthal, R., & Fode, K. L. Psychology of the scientist: V. Three experiments in experi-menter bias. *Psychological Reports,* 1963, 12, 491–511. (b)

Rosenthal, R., & Jacobson, L. *Pygmalion in the classroom: Teacher expectation and pupils' intellectual development.* New York: Holt, Rinehart & Winston, 1968.

Rosenthal, R., & Lawson, R. A longitudinal study of the effects of experimenter bias on the operant learning of laboratory rats. *Journal of Psychiatric Research,* 1964, 2, 61–72.

Rosenthal, R., Persinger, G. W., Mulry, R. C., Vikan-Kline, L., & Grothe, M. Emphasis on experimental procedure, sex of subjects and the biasing effects of experimental hypoth-eses. *Journal of Projective Techniques and Personality Assessment,* 1964, 28, 470–473.

Rosenthal, R., & Rosnow, R. L. (Eds.), *Arti-fact in behavioral research.* New York: Aca-demic Press, 1969.

Roth, J. A. Hired hand research. *American So-ciologist,* 1966, 1, 190–196.

Sheatsley, P. B. Some uses of interviewer-re-port forms. *Public Opinion Quarterly,* 1947, 11, 601–611.

Sheffield, F., Kaufman, R. S., & Rhine, J. B. A PK experiment at Yale starts a contro-versy. *Journal of the American Society for Psychical Research,* 1952, 46, 111–117.

Silver, M. J. Experimenter modeling: A cri-tique. *Journal of Experimental Research in Personality,* 1968, 3, 172–178.

Silverman, I. The effects of experimenter out-come expectancy on latency of word asso-ciation. *Journal of Clinical Psychology,* 1968, 24, 60–63.

Snow, C. P. The moral un-neutrality of sci-ence. *Science,* 1961, 133, 256–259.

Snow, R. E. Unfinished Pygmalion. *Contem-porary Psychology,* 1969, 14, 197–199.

Souren, G., van der Kloot, W., & van Bergen, A. *Het Rosenthal-Effect.* Leiden, Nether-lands: Psychological Institute, Rijks Univer-sity, 1969.

Spanos, N. P. Barber's reconceptualization of hypnosis: An evaluation of criticisms. *Jour-nal of Experimental Research in Personality,* 1970, 4, 241–258.

Spanos, N. P., & Chaves, J. F. Hypnosis research: A methodological critique of ex-periments generated by two alternative para-digms. *American Journal of Clinical Hyp-nosis,* 1970, 13, 108–127.

Steinhelber, J. C. Bias in the assessment of psychotherapy. *Journal of Consulting and Clinical Psychology,* 1970, 34, 37–42.

Strauss, M. E. Examiner expectancy: Effects on Rorschach experience balance. *Journal of*

Consulting and Clinical Psychology, 1968, 32, 125–129.

Strauss, M. E., & Marwit, S. J. Expectancy effects in Rorschach testing. *Journal of Consulting and Clinical Psychology*, 1970, 34, 448.

Thorndike, R. L. Review of R. Rosenthal & L. Jacobson, *Pygmalion in the classroom*. *American Educational Research Journal*, 1968, 5, 708–711.

Timaeus, E., & Lueck, H. E. Experimenter expectancy and social facilitation: II. Stroop-test performance under the condition of audience. *Perceptual and Motor Skills*, 1968, 27, 492–494.

Tullock, G. *The organization of inquiry*. Durham, N.C.: Duke University Press, 1966.

Wartenberg-Ekren, U. The effect of experimenter knowledge of a subject's scholastic standing on the performance of a reasoning task. Unpublished master's thesis, Marquette University, 1962.

Wessler, R. L. Experimenter expectancy effects in psychomotor performance. *Perceptual and Motor Skills*, 1968, 26, 911–917.

Wessler, R. L. Experimenter expectancy effects in three dissimilar tasks. *Journal of Psychology*, 1969, 71, 63–67.

Wessler, R. L., & Strauss, M. E. Experimenter expectancy: A failure to replicate. *Psychological Reports*, 1968, 22, 687–688.

Wolins, L. Responsibility for raw data. *American Psychologist*, 1962, 17, 657–658.

Wyatt, D. F., & Campbell, D. T. A study of interviewer bias as related to interviewers' expectations and own opinions. *International Journal of Opinion and Attitude Research*, 1950, 4, 77–83.

Zegers, R. A. Expectancy and the effects of confirmation and disconfirmation. *Journal of Personality and Social Psychology*, 1968, 9, 67–71.

Zobel, E. J., & Lehman, R. S. Interaction of subject and experimenter expectancy effects in a tone length discrimination task. *Behavioral Science*, 1969, 14, 357–363.

CHAPTER **12** Critical Value Questions
and the Analysis of
Objectives and Curricula

JAMES B. MACDONALD
University of North Carolina, Greensboro

DWIGHT CLARK
University of North Carolina, Greensboro

Reviews of research over the past few years (e.g., Popham, 1969) have made it clear that separating objectives from curricular materials and either or both from instructional treatments is extremely difficult. The isolation of an objective (or statement of an objective) as a single variable which can be manipulated while other variables are held constant has not been a successful endeavor. Consistently it is revealed that variation in treatment, and often in material, results when objectives are altered.

The smallest viable empirical research unit with useful explanatory power would seem to be what is often called a *treatment* and which consists at least of objectives, materials, media and methods and all the isolatable subvariables within these areas. This does not lend itself to undue optimism if the Cronbach and Snow (1969) study is an accurate assessment of the present-day situation. Cronbach and Snow focused on a large-scale examination of studies that involved various treatments and found that there was no consistent and systematic empirical evidence to validate the contention that predictable effects upon individual

learning could be projected from present knowledge of treatment procedures. They conclude that it is only a matter of time and sophistication before this condition is righted. However, Jackson (1970) disputed this claim and raised a number of serious questions about the mind set which is displayed through this optimism as well as the logic which would lead one to expect positive results.

One of the clearly obfuscating elements in the present situation is a tendency to see schooling only in terms of summative evaluation and achievement "pay off." Thus, the higher, complex, lengthy and tortuous route by which curricula (objectives, materials, etc.) enter into classroom settings is treated as a mere "given" for instructional studies.

The separation of curriculum and instruction has been noted in the literature for a number of years, recently, for example, by Johnson (1967) and Macdonald (1966). Similar circumstances which underlie the distinction of these writers have been noted in more empirically oriented evaluative terms by Scriven (1967) when he clearly delineated between formative and summative evaluation. It is not entirely clear whether Scriven's differentiation rests primarily upon a critical philosophical analysis of curriculum development processes in schooling or whether he bases the distinction of formative and summative upon phenomenological and/or empirical grounds. It is the latter basis that provides the most distinct separation of the two.

Clearly, most curriculum development (and certainly all the more recent large projects) takes place in a social setting different from the instructional setting. The persons involved are rarely if ever even a small minority of the people who will be expected to make the curriculum viable in summative terms (i.e., students and teachers). The phenomenon of curriculum development thus involves a series of social roles, rewards, status and prestige opportunities that are not directly related to the summative aspects.

Further, curriculum products, in terms of goals, materials and suggested treatments, are placed into instructional settings which, as social subsystems, have a myriad number of variables which are either unknown or unpredictable during the developmental process. For example, anyone who has grappled for any time with two or more separate classes of 30 students with the same curriculum is well aware of important social variables which affect learning outcomes.

Furthermore, the individual variation in motivation, values, previous experience, aptitude and personal behavior patterns (regardless of group living situations) has been, and still is, a major influence upon what learning happens in the curriculum. The belatedly recognized need for in-service training expressed by many of the large project developers is a small indication of recognition of individual variables. When one considers the number of unique students and the fact that we may expect greater individual variation in students than staff because of added factors of immaturity, it soon becomes apparent that

a purely abstract linear and logical approach in moving from curriculum development to learning outcomes excludes more potential influences on learning outcomes than it includes.

Social system influences on performance (seen in individuals and groups in school) have been quite well documented by both Bloom (1964) and Coleman (1966). School system influences have not been as clearly established, but the organizational structure of the school, its communication network, the emotional climate and organizational goals which are contrary to or given more priority than curriculum goals are surely a source of other variables which influence learning outcomes. The recent phenomenon of conflict in some places between the school administration, teacher unions, and community pressure groups is further evidence of the existence of potentially influential variables on learning outcomes.

The logic of the curriculum research process necessarily has been linear and abstract. At this point it seems highly doubtful that the length of the linear chain of logic from systematic development to student learning has much validity in terms of time variation, level, and varying systems of the phenomena involved. We might well do better to shorten our logic chains and search for better research procedures.

Summative evaluation would appear to deal with the outcomes researched on the basis of treatments, and in light of the Cronbach and Snow data (1969), it appeared presumptuous of the authors to pursue research on summative or treatment data further. There are thus (at present) no consistent systematic research data which lead to useful generalizations about objectives and materials at the treatment or instructional level if we are concerned about the predictability of facilitating learning for an individual learner. Since there really appears to be little else as important as this concern in terms of summative evaluation, the balance of this chapter will be devoted to exploring the theory and research relevant to formative evaluation and/or curriculum development.

THE PROBLEM OF CURRICULAR OBJECTIVES

At the curriculum development level the source of objectives has been clearly explicated by many writers. Tyler (1950) is representative and, having been a key figure in the past 40 years, will serve well for a review of this material. (The reader is referred, however, to Smith & Moss [1970] for a recent, highly sophisticated development of this approach.)

Four elements or facets of concern are present and paraphrased here when Tyler talks about objectives: 1) the cultural heritage or subject matter or discipline, 2) the social needs for education, 3) the nature of learners and learning, and 4) a philosophy of education. It would appear that most curriculum people accept the idea that curriculum objectives are derived by looking at these four, or similar, disparate areas.

Beyond this agreement there has been little theoretical discussion and no empirical research in terms of how to proceed and what the effect of different procedures would be upon the formulation of objectives and materials. Generally, the approach has been to select a priority area and screen data from this area with the data from the other three areas.

Bobbitt (1918) was a well-known American pioneer of a social needs priority. Using job analysis techniques he identified a set of useful social functions and proceeded to construct a curriculum around these objectives. Bobbitt's position was that human life is a set of specific activities. Education for life should thus be preparation for specific activities. The activities should be those which show the abilities, attitudes, habits, appreciation and forms of knowledge needed. These would be the objectives of the curriculum.

A modern version of this general rationale with priority set in the disciplines of knowledge is the "behavioral objectives" approach. Again the attempt is to be highly specific about the behavior desired within each discipline, and these statements of behavior would become the objectives of the curriculum. Behavioral objectives proponents have gone a step further, however, in the sense that a philosophy of learning is part of the process. By necessity and the logic of this position, a reinforcement theory of learning has been incorporated into the process.

However, as Bode (1965) pointed out in relation to Bobbitt, and as Kliebard (1970) remarked in relation to the Tyler rationale, the selection of a beginning point is a statement of values. If one makes the wrong assumption or expresses the wrong ideal at the beginning, no amount of technical or scientific technique can convert an error into a sound principle. What in effect takes place is that a personal bias or preference is in operation under the guise of an objective and scientific determination.

Questions such as what courses to teach in schools (the scope of the curriculum) and what to do with the results of any discipline's work (sequence and selective school significance) are not answerable within the confines of a discipline or a social need or a learner preference. Somehow the three referents must be integrated through value judgments. It is this sort of process that has never been clearly explicated or researched.

Goodlad and Richter (1966) have attempted to reconceptualize this rational decision-making model to take into account the priority problem of values. They have made a compelling argument that values are the primary data source for selecting purposes for schooling and for all subsequent curriculum decisions. They propose a clear understanding of stated assumptions and values *before* turning to an analysis of society, knowledge, and the learner for screening. They further propose that these values be used as criteria (with others) at check points all during the development process and throughout the different levels of decision making.

Taylor and Maguire (1966) have proposed an interesting linear model which allows people, values and objectives to be conceptualized in matrix form. The connection between values and objectives is highlighted and the importance of the task of transferring values into objectives is held in a central position.

Empirical data have been useful in helping make some decisions about objectives. The work of Piaget (e.g., 1970) and others has provided cues which have implications for sequencing and content. Yet the crucial concerns of curriculum are not answered outside the applicative area of scientific data. Further, behavioral science data, and specifically data relevant for looking at the learning process, are value-laden. There are implicit philosophical/psychological orientations which clearly change the statement and the emphasis upon curriculum objectives.

It does not appear from the statements of many curriculum developers that they have been aware in the past that psychological data *are* value-laden. It makes a considerable difference, for example, if one is developing curriculum from the position of an experimental psychologist such as Gagné (1965) or from the perspective of a clinical psychologist such as Carl Rogers. From Gagné's position one can easily be oriented toward a stable, status quo, mastery position of the adult culture. However, from Rogers's viewpoint the major emphasis would be upon change and the preparation of youth for a dynamic, essentially unstable and somewhat unpredictable future. Objectives will be viewed much differently from these two positions.

What appears to be missing in the contemporary scene is an overarching social commitment concerning the role of the schools in society. Historically the American schools were said to be oriented toward developing character, citizens for a democracy, and vocational adequacy. Today even our dreams are considerably constricted to such things as the mastery of skills and information. Educators who even speak of character-building and democracy risk the ridicule of their contemporaries as romantics. Yet it appears patently clear that the beginning point for selecting and defining objectives must rest in some broad value commitment to the society we live in, whether this be, for example, democratic citizenship, individual character or potential, scholarly excellence or occupational competence. For the plain fact of the matter is that curriculum development is a continuous process of making human value judgments about what to include and exclude, what to aim for and avoid, and how to go about it—difficult judgments even when aided by technical and scientific data and processes.

Thus, we must recognize that the priority upon research and technology in education, when one considers the problems of objectives, is putting "the cart before the horse." Empirical examination requires a goal—any goal. We may empirically examine the process of deriving goals, but there is no way of creating the universe of values itself through an empirical process without committing oneself to a specific value position.

It is worth hypothesizing, as others have, that progress in education is illusory, cyclical and faddish because we have never resolved our value dilemmas satisfactorily. Twice in the twentieth century we have entered (and passed through) a curricular concern for the specification of objectives; twice in the twentieth century we have hit upon the basic generalizations, big ideas, or structure of the disciplines as our organizing referent. In each of the earlier incidences there appears to have been little or no progress in terms of their later counterparts (if the ahistoricity of contemporary curriculum developers is any valid indication).

MATERIALS, TEACHERS
AND MEDIA

There are two general views concerning the relationship of objectives to materials and media. Any material is, of course, in a general sense, a "media," although educators have been prone to restrict the concept of media to "hardware" and materials to "software." Philosophically there would seem to be little reason to worry about this distinction. It has heuristic value, perhaps, as a categorical process for stimulating single variable empirical research; but it would be difficult to separate even the teacher from the concept of material for learning, to say nothing of distinguishing between hardware and software. Recognition of this fact is witnessed by the growing concern for "treatments" and instructional systems.

An extremely informative and useful review of the present state of development of one general approach to the use of a systems idea in classrooms has been presented by Baker (1971). Among other things, Baker clearly specifies prerequisites to instructional management systems. These prerequisites include many of those concerns with which this chapter is attempting to deal, e.g., defining curricular objectives and developing related materials. It is clear from this review that a management systems approach is as dependent upon prior decisions as the more limited behavioral objectives approach.

The relationship, however, between materials (broadly or narrowly conceived) and objectives has not been sufficiently clarified. The predominant method of proceeding in curriculum has followed the logical sequence of first deciding upon the objectives and then selecting the materials. Nevertheless, reasonable hypotheses can be formulated to focus on the idea popularized by McLuhan (1967) that the *media* is the message. Were there strong supporting evidence to validate even the partial truth of this assertion the whole "rational" tradition in curriculum development would be forced into a fundamental re-evaluation.

The latter position raises the question of whether or not it is possible to define objectives in any realistic way outside the context of the material, media, and the context within which they must be accomplished. It is this position which has been implicit in the statement of what many critics have called vague and directionless objectives. It is, however, rationally possible and defensible to deliberately state objectives in a broad manner as a means of getting on with the business of creating the learning material from which the "real" objectives will emerge anyway.

The concept of operational definitions is inherent in the specification of objectives, and the question at stake in the above position is whether the operational specification should precede the development of materials or should emerge from pupil "operations" with material.

The latter position has some realistic, if disquieting, substance to the neat and tidy minds of curriculum technicians. Until technicians can state the universe of viable operational definitions for any given objective there is no way to know whether what has been selected is best or even a reasonable definition. Further, it is difficult to see how anyone could know before the fact what the total universe of potential objectives or operational definitions of these objectives could be in the context of the interaction of human beings with these educational materials.

Thus, to state as an objective that one wishes to teach a group to "appreciate Hamlet" may have considerable merit. The fact that the word appreciate is included in the objective may be misleading. It is perhaps better not to take the verb as a denotational statement but focus on the connotations of what appreciate means. The reading and discussion of Hamlet now provide a material setting out of which objectives may be specified as they arise from the people and encounter involved. When one wishes to evaluate the experience he might ask the students whether they got anything out of the exercise and, if so, what. A reasonably intelligent and experienced teacher (observer) would be able to judge the worth of the experience from this.

There are, to our knowledge, no empirical studies of the different objectives that are achieved by the two procedures named above. The only research that has been done has been biased by a pre-set list of objectives. This, of course, prejudices the case since one approach is compatible with the evaluation techniques utilized and the other is not. Would it not be worth the attempt to assess in depth the kinds of objectives and the depth of learning which is achieved in the latter case by means compatible with the approach? Until this is done, researchers are not researching the reality of educational phenomena; they are simply confining the range of concern to pre-formed conveniences.

THE EMPIRICAL STATE OF THE ART

The empirical state of the art of curriculum making has revealed the two major findings mentioned previously: 1) that the smallest defensible unit for research is a "treatment" (which includes objectives, materials, etc.), and 2) that there is presently very little known predictability of the effects of treatments in relation to individual learners.

Further, it is clear that very little empirical data are available concerning the curriculum-development process itself, or the process of implementing curriculum plans in instructional settings. Thus, we know next to nothing about the influence of social, psychological, political and cultural variables or the development of plans, and certainly no more about problems of their implementation. (It is, for example, interesting that very few studies provide any empirical data to substantiate the actual implementation of a plan being evaluated or compared with others.)

The most fundamental problem in curriculum—the derivation of objectives—has little or no research or theory to aid us. A secondary problem, the statement of objectives, is taken up by the behavioral objectives movement, which also provides little empirical evidence of its worth.

Essentially the empirical voyage has been grounded on the coral reef of values. One can only agree with Stake (1970) when he issued his plea for treating objectives as data and, in his review, discussed many potentially promising ways for improving the situation.

THE VALUE QUESTIONS

Historically, American educators have had little difficulty deriving statements of value at their most abstract levels. Thus the schools have been said to exist for common purposes such as facilitating individual self-realization, developing an intelligent and democratic citizenry, and preparing the young to be economically efficient and productive.

These broad statements perhaps have served a more useful political than educational purpose. That is, the generation and acceptance of broad goals has not especially facilitated the curriculum development process. These goals have, on the other hand, most probably been beneficial as a broad canopy which helpfully coalesced an extremely broad and diverse spectrum of people (and values) into a commitment to the school as a fundamental and increasingly more critical social institution.

The crux of value problems, however, rests in the decision-making process and the suggested events and/or behaviors that are involved. It is by no means clear, for example, what connection basic academic disciplines, or aspects within them, have to all or one of these value statements.

Thus, for example, there are no studies available to examine how the study of physics contributes (or can contribute) to the building of individual character, democratic citizenship or vocation. There have been no systematic large-scale attempts to operationalize aims of education in terms of content-area objectives. What literature relevant to this issue that does exist would tend to suggest more interdisciplinary kinds of programs.

It has never seemed productive or possible in the American experience to establish a central value for schooling, yet short of this there appears little hope of productive guidance for curriculum building from that level. This is indicative of the political and social contexts of education and it points toward the need for very careful analysis and study of the social connection and processes which encase curriculum decisions. At present, curriculum-developers are unable to clearly explicate the setting they find themselves in.

Within the institutional setting itself, traditional procedures have led curriculum developers to look toward three basic value referents for decision making: 1) society and its needs, 2) the cultural knowledge available, and 3) the learner and his learning. Two kinds of fundamental value problems immediately arise. One is concerned with priorities among the referents and the other deals with selection within each referent.

We believe the question must arise concerning the central priority of schooling. This is especially so if one hopes to proceed in a rational planning paradigm (itself a fundamental value position). It makes considerable difference where one begins when a linear reasoning process is in operation. Thus, when one begins with the learner, the kinds of social needs and cultural content that will be emphasized are in effect partially defined by the original value commitment (and the definition of its meaning). This appears to hold true for each of the basic referents.

The second value question rests upon the value position held within each referent.

Thus, questions of inclusion-exclusion are primary. What aspects of learners are legitimate for consideration in education—their character, cognitive ability, mental health, etc.? What needs of society are primary—intelligent citizens? workers? patriots? And, of course, what knowledge is of most worth—science? humanities? crafts?

The resolution of these value problems is not on the present horizon. We know little or nothing about how to proceed or what the total dimensions of the problems are.

Our traditional approach (regardless of the scientific social analysis of the 20s) has been an irrational one with respect to the value problems. We have simply asked the experts with knowledge to tell us what to teach and then have spent a considerable amount of time trying to modify and adapt this to data about learners and make it more socially useful.

This resolution of value problems has not been disastrous by any means, but it is clearly possible that it may become so in the foreseeable future. The sensibility of this approach as a resolution of value problems lay in our ability to be very efficient or effective in fulfilling irrationally selected goals. This is not at all the case now. With the advent of increased technology, growing ideas of behavioral management, and increasing sophistication in computerized and other systems approaches, the value problems are increasingly critical. We may well be approaching a situation in which value concerns about learners and learning, the nature of knowledge, and the nature of social living can become locked into certain unidimensional orientation without rational assessment and selection but merely by the effective and efficient achievement of ends.

What is needed most in curricula today is a generation of people who are willing and able to face up to, explicate and suggest ways of resolving the terribly complex, frustrating, but absolutely critical value questions.

In this sense curriculum is little different

from our broader society. In fact, the very concerns about technical thinking expressed within education have their corollaries throughout. The most fundamental problems today are moral ones, not scientific or technical. For example, should we build the SST (not can we)? Should we limit population? Should we settle national differences by violence? Should ethnic groups control their own curriculum development?

Fundamentally this is a problem of clarification of goals, and the crucial questions are how do we clarify goals and select the values we wish to pursue? Clearly, the fact that we can achieve a goal is no longer justification for valuing that objective. What, then, will we use for justification? Will rational processes alone suffice? Shall we become more dependent upon intuitive and emotive processes?

Whatever our solutions may be, it is not at all clear how empirical processes of study can help us, since little effort has been made to this point to clarify our goals, but a considerable challenge remains.

BIBLIOGRAPHY

Baker, F. B. Computer-based instructional management systems: A first look. *Review of Educational Research,* 1971, 41, 51–70.

Bloom, B. S. *Stability and change in human characteristics.* New York: John Wiley, 1964.

Bobbitt, F. *The curriculum.* Cambridge, Mass.: Riverside Press, 1918.

Bode, B. H. *Modern educational theories.* New York: Vintage Books, 1965.

Coleman, J. S., and others. *Equality of educational opportunity.* Washington, D.C.: U.S. Department of Health, Education and Welfare, Office of Education, 1966. ED 012 275.

Cronbach, L. J., & Snow, R. E. *Individual differences in learning ability as a function of instructional variables.* Final Report, Contract No. OEC-4-6-061269-1217, U.S. Office of Education, March, 1969. ED 029 001.

Gagné, R. M. *The conditions of learning.* New York: Holt, Rinehart & Winston, 1965.

Goodlad, J. I., & Richter, M. N., Jr. *The development of a conceptual system for dealing with problems of curriculum and instruction.* Report Contract No. SAE-8024, Project No. 454, U.S. Department of Health, Education and Welfare, June, 1966. ED 010 064.

Jackson, P. Is there a best way of teaching Harold Bateman? *Midway,* 1970, 10(4), 15–28.

Johnson, M., Jr. Definitions and models in curriculum theory. *Educational Theory,* 1967, 17, 127–140.

Kleibard, H. M. The Tyler rationale. *School Review,* 1970, 78, 259–272.

Macdonald, J. B. Structures in curriculum. *Proceedings of the Conference on Curriculum Leadership.* Madison, Wis.: Wisconsin State Department of Public Instruction, 1966. Pp. 28–46.

McLuhan, H. M., & Fiore, Q. *The medium is the massage.* New York: Bantam Books, 1967.

Piaget, J. *Science of education and the psychology of the child.* New York: Orion Press, 1970.

Popham, W. J. Curriculum materials. *Review of Educational Research,* 1969, 39, 319–338.

Scriven, M. The methodology of evaluation. In R. E. Stake (Ed.), *Perspectives of curriculum evaluation,* American Educational Research Association Monograph Series on Curriculum Evaluation, No. 1. Chicago: Rand McNally, 1967. Pp. 39–83.

Smith, B. B., & Moss, J., Jr. *Process and techniques of vocational curriculum development.* Minneapolis, Minn.: University of Minnesota, Minnesota Research Coordinating Unit for Vocational Education, 1970.

Stake, R. E. Objectives, priorities and other judgment data. *Review of Educational Research,* 1970, 40, 181–212.

Taylor, P. A., & Maguire, T. O. A theoretical evaluation model. *The Manitoba Journal of Educational Research 1,* 1966, 1(2), 12–17.

Tyler, R. W. *Basic principles of curriculum and instruction.* Chicago: University of Chicago Press, 1950.

CHAPTER 13 The Social Psychology of Teaching

CHARLES E. BIDWELL
University of Chicago

In this chapter I shall take a rather narrow and perhaps idiosyncratic view of teaching. The chapter will not treat the social psychology of education; this topic is much broader than mine and in any event has received recent comprehensive discussion (Backman & Secord, 1968; Boocock, 1966; Getzels, 1969; see also Miles & Charters, 1970). It also is not about the social psychology of teachers. Aspects of this topic (for example, the processes of becoming a teacher and variations in teachers' motives and conduct in different educational settings and at different career stages) are treated elsewhere in this handbook.

Rather, I shall consider teaching as a social process. It cannot occur except through interpersonal exchange, and these interpersonal relationships have both a social and normative structure and are contained within a broader social and moral order.[1] I shall discuss how variation in the social organization of schools may be related to variation in this process. (For an interesting earlier essay on this question from a rather different point of view, see Getzels & Thelen, 1960.) Thus I have limited my topic in several ways. First, I shall discuss teaching mainly as it occurs in schools, although I suspect that a good deal of what this chapter treats is applicable to teaching in other settings. Even so I shall be able to consider teaching only in fairly broad outline—most of the extant literature concerns teaching in the middle- and high-school grades, and anything like a full presentation of effects of varying school type and level, or student age, would itself demand a full essay.

Second, I shall not be concerned with the full range of the "teaching-learning" process. I shall be interested mainly in how we may understand *teaching* from a social-psychological perspective. What students do in reciprocal relations with teachers, for example, is pertinent to this topic, but the effects of teaching variables on students' learning processes is less so. Nonetheless, the outcomes of learning remain benchmark variables in studies of teaching. (For

---

[1] Certain aspects of the social organization of teaching are very nearly universal, for example, differences in power between teacher and student. Others are more specific to certain societies, periods, or types of schools —as the differentiation of curricula in modern high schools.

a fuller account of the reciprocal involvement of teachers and students in teaching-learning encounters, see White, 1969.)

Third, I shall not be much concerned with aspects of teachers' personalities, either as antecedents or as consequences of conduct in the teacher's role.

The problem for a social psychology of teaching, as here construed, is to trace relationships between the social organization of teaching and the conduct of teachers. This problem necessarily involves relations between social organizational and psychological variables, but as they operate in the teaching process. The bearing of varying bases of teacher specialization (e.g., student ability, subject matter or age) on teachers' definitions of acceptable academic performance is an example of such relations. What teaching does to teachers, for example, though of long-standing interest to sociologists (see Waller, 1932, pp. 375–440), is not directly pertinent. When traits of teacher personality enter the process, they do so as conditions affecting the relation between the social organization of teaching and the conduct of teachers.

PRELIMINARY OBSERVATIONS ON TEACHING

Teaching may be defined as a series of interactions between someone in the role of teacher and someone in the role of learner, with the explicit goal of changing one or more of the learner's cognitive states (what he knows or believes, or his skill in performing cognitive tasks) or affective states (his attitudes, values or motives). In its aims teaching is coterminous with socialization; it is distinctive in the social definition of the interpersonal relationships that it involves.

It is especially important to note that teaching is a rational process in that it is constituted of conduct planned to attain some specified goal of learner change (though of course unanticipated consequences may follow and unexpected bar-riers to goal attainment may arise). It also is formally organized in all but the simplest kinds of tutorial teaching. Teachers usually occupy organizational offices with designated responsibilities for a student clientele. They are accountable to superiors, form the main operating staff of schools, and have responsibilities, however residual and episodic (see Lortie, 1969), to fellow teachers. I shall examine relations between social organization and teaching activity as they occur in formally organized schools.

Social organizational variables may affect teacher-student interaction in several ways. In its simplest form, we can think of a teacher-student dyad, abstracted from its social environment, in which the interaction of teacher and student is face to face and unmediated by any human or nonhuman agency. Such teacher-student relations would approximate fairly closely the classical conception of primary social relations: face to face, marked by direct cooperation or conflict and allowing wide-ranging expression of sentiment. In such relations, social organizational variables enter as aspects of the teacher-student dyad: variations in the relative power of the teacher and student, the mixture of cooperation and conflict, and the like. The first portion of this chapter will consider the teacher-student dyad as if it could be separated from its social surroundings.

Although this discussion will help to clarify the nature of certain elements of teacher-student exchange, dyads insulated from a social context are empirically rare and are certainly rare in schools. Therefore I shall turn next to aspects of school and classroom social organization which, acting as contextual variables, may affect teacher-student interaction. For example, what difference does it make for a given teacher-student relation that the student is one of some 20 or 30, but the teacher is the only teacher in the class? I shall also consider teacher-student relations as they are affected directly by phenomena of the social organization of teaching situations that function in other than a contextual fashion. For example, what consequences may flow from variation in a teacher's official standing?

In these sections of the chapter, I shall proceed from a specific conceptual point of view, looking at teaching as personal influence. Thus I begin with this form of influence as it occurs in a simple social relation and then elaborate the formulation to include more complex social patterns. Following this discussion, I shall consider very briefly two additional conceptual perspectives that may complement the personal influence formulation in studies of teaching.

To this point I have talked about teaching and possible social organizational correlates of teaching without saying very specifically what I have in mind. Following my earlier comment on the two primary goals of teaching, it would appear that teaching incorporates activities of two principal kinds: attempts to change students' cognitions and attempts to change their moral commitments or affective states. This is a distinction, however, that cannot be sustained empirically with much ease for the two kinds of activities are interdependent. Attempts to alter cognition require that the teacher mobilize some sort of student motive to know and learn (the instrumental value of knowledge, the student's respect for or fear of the teacher, and so on). Changing moral commitments or affective states require that the student possess or acquire certain items of knowledge—the content of a nascent value or the nature of the person or object toward which an attitude may form, for example. This process also requires of the student certain cognitive skills; thus, as a case in point, before one can value something he must know about the thing and, more basically, be able to structure priorities of value.

Nonetheless one can scarcely deny that influencing or capitalizing on the learner's motivation is a fundamental task of teaching, whether for cognitive or for affective or moral aims. (On this point, discussed from a sociologist's view, see Bidwell, 1965; Hoyle, 1965; Waller, 1932, pp. 189–374.) It is also fair to say that there are substantial reciprocal effects from the cognitive aspects of teaching activities, as they are experienced by learners, on the learners' conceptions of self—with important consequences for further motivation to learn. Thus, in a highly original and by no means dated argument, Florian Znaniecki (1936, ch. 7) contended that in the schools of complex societies the essentially vicarious quality of the academic curriculum and teachers' stress on examination, certification and performance to a fixed standard foster among students a certain self-alienation, a tendency to regard the self as an object to be manipulated for external and for the most part distant future ends. This tendency results in a trained incapacity to take pleasure intrinsically in the play of intellect. (See also Friedenberg, 1959. For empirical evidence of the reciprocal relation between teaching for cognitive attainment and learner motivation and self-conception, see, for example, Brookover, 1943; Getzels, 1969; Getzels & Jackson, 1962.)

Thus a social psychology of teaching can begin fruitfully from an analysis of the relation between teaching and students' development of moral commitments. The formation and development in students of values, responsiveness to norms, and attitudes concerning intellectual content and processes are part of a more general set of processes involved in the relation between teaching and moral learning, that is, teaching as a process of moral socialization. I shall, in short, be concerned with the teacher's personal influence as it bears on students' moral commitments. The intellective side of learning will be noted only as it may affect this relationship. I assume, I hope not unreasonably, that any observed covariation of teaching and cognitive learning is substantially mediated by the teacher's influence on his students' moral commitments as they motivate cognitive activity—the relative value students place on school subjects or their adherence to teacher or peer norms defining levels or kinds of academic performance, for example. (Similar topics are treated from another vantage point by Glidewell, Kantor, Smith, & Stringer, 1966. For an important theoretical statement of the processes of moral learning, in many ways complementary to the viewpoint of this chapter, see Scott, 1971. See also the earlier discussion by Child, 1954.)

In another sense, too, the topic of this chapter is important. The impact of schools on students' moral commitments extends substantially beyond motivation to learn. One might argue that two chief functions of schools in modern societies are to foster, first, the development in students of motives that are adapted to the range of adult roles that they will enact (including but not limited to the motivation of intellectual activity) and, second, capacity for trust and solidarity in a highly differentiated society (cf. Slater, 1963). Both of these functions involve centrally the formation or elaboration of students' moral commitments. If we know something about teaching as moral socialization, we know something also about a major component of arrangements for socialization in modern societies. And from the point of view of formal organization for teaching, we know something about the interplay between conditions affecting organizational efficiency (e.g., the degree of scarcity of teachers' approval) and effectiveness (e.g., attainment of objectives of moral socialization). (On the concepts of efficiency and effectiveness in formal organizations, see Barnard, 1938.)

I can restate my earlier definition of teaching as a variety of social relationships. It is constituted of a cluster of activities, conducted by persons in the teaching role interacting with persons in other roles. Most salient among these other roles is the role of student. It is a set of activities that are normatively defined and open to sanction but that also involve norm setting and sanctioning for others (in the main, but not only, students). Sanctions are mechanisms for enforcing norms. They vary in content (i.e., the type of resource used to reward or punish—such as esteem, money, or physical pleasure or pain), and they occur with varying swiftness, rigor and exigence. The formal organization of most teaching situations, furthermore, affects sanctioning as it sets distinctive conditions under which teaching activities occur—for example, differences between teachers and students that follow from the teachers' and students' official standings, in the right to sanction and in the content and force of the sanctions used. (There is an important literature on the effects of varying teacher sanctions on students' conduct and learning, e.g., H. E. Anderson, 1966; Klugman, 1944; McKeachie, Lin, Milholland, & Isaacson, 1966; Polansky, 1954; Short, 1960; Thomas, Becker, & Armstrong, 1968.)

Sanctioning is central to the formation of moral commitment. A moral order is a social phenomenon; it defines right conduct in some system of social relations as a property of the collectivity in question. Moral conformity at some group-specific threshold is a sign of membership, an intrinsic aspect of collective identity, and a chief criterion of initial and continued acceptance. Its enforcement is a matter of collective interest and an aspect of the collectivity's activities (i.e., sanctioning).

Thus, becoming committed to some element of a moral order (that is, the willingness to incur costs for the sake of compliance, more particularly, such willingness when constraints on contrary action are absent) requires some mechanism for learning the collective significance of the moral element and the dependency of group membership on moral conformity. Sanctioning is this mechanism, and variation in the formation of moral commitments by learners must be affected by variation in the sanctioning activity of teachers. I shall pay special attention to sanctioning and sanctions in the following discussion.[2]

PERSONAL INFLUENCE

In its application to the study of teaching, the personal influence formulation has been given its fullest statement by Newcomb (1961) in his *ABX theory*. This formulation derives mainly from the work of Heider (1958) and Festinger (1957), but it shifts attention from intrapersonal to interactional congruence processes. In making this shift it borrows to some extent from Homans (1961). Later systematic refinements have been given by J. A. Davis (1963). The psychological processes presumed to be at work in personal influence are those said to maintain *cognitive consistency*. (For a review of fairly recent work on cognitive consistency, see Abelson et al., 1968. For more direct applications to processes of attitude change, see Rosenberg et al., 1960.)

There is some empirical evidence that certain effects of schooling on moral commitments arise from the action of personal influence (especially Newcomb, 1943; Wallace, 1966), but it comes from studies more concerned with student peer than with teacher influence. Indeed, the application of personal influence concepts to school

settings has come about because of a recently heightened interest in how students may socialize one another. (It is striking that although the greater proportion of work on schooling as socialization has been conducted in college settings, little of it deals with teacher effects; the student society is more often the focus. See the massive review of this literature by Feldman & Newcomb, 1969). The application of these concepts to teaching is a rather novel though not very startling idea. It may not have seemed profitable because of the social distance that usually separates students and teachers. (Indeed, the well-known studies of "authoritarian" and "democratic" styles of teaching or classroom organization can be viewed as an effort not so much to analyze this socially distant relationship as to find practical ways to reduce the distance. See R. C. Anderson, 1959, and Lewin, Lippitt, & White, 1939.) However, I shall try to show that pair relations in which social distance is comparatively great can be viewed as a type of personal influence situation that has a good deal of conceptual and practical interest.

The reluctance to study teaching processes may have arisen also from a narrow view of teaching essentially as an occupational technique or work process, in contrast with which student peer relations would seem to be richer and more rewarding to the social scientist. And the evidence for variable learning outcomes of differences of teaching method has been substantially negative and therefore also discouraging. (On this point, again with reference to colleges, see Dubin & Taveggia, 1968; McKeachie, 1963.) McKeachie notes that most of this literature remains unconcerned with the effects of different teaching modes on specified instructional results. The present discussion illustrates one way of thinking about consequences of such variation in teaching for changes in students' moral commitments. (Many of the variables treated in this chapter overlap those some-

---

[2] Because of the limits that I have set to my topic, I shall not have much to say about students' sanctioning of teachers. Clearly this phenomenon can be of the greatest import for teacher conduct, including teachers' subsequent evaluation and sanctioning of students. These processes may occur within teacher-student dyads, in a teacher's adjustment of his conduct to aggregate rates of pupil sanctioning (Gage, Runkel, & Chatterjee, 1963), or in alterations of school policies in response to varying student attainment or resistance (cf. Riesman, Gusfield, & Gamson, 1970). They may in part be mediated by the influence of students' sanctions on teachers' self-concepts (e.g., Jenkins & Deno, 1969) and by teachers' interpretations of student conduct as confirming or disconfirming their initial judgments with respect to the sources and meaning of students' acts (Johnson, Feigenbaum, & Weiby, 1964). A fuller account of teaching situations must be couched in the terms of such reciprocal social processes.

times used to analyze instruction as persuasion, e.g., the credibility of the speaker or the emotionality of the argument, cf. Hovland, 1963.) The "teacher competence" literature also takes the narrow technical view and has not been very useful. (For a summary, see Domas & Tiedeman, 1950.) I shall try to show that teaching is a complex social process that poses a wealth of questions for social psychological investigation.

In its outline, the personal influence perspective is simple. We begin with a pair of persons (A and B for Newcomb) who are drawn together by some sentiment or sentiments (a given sentiment need not be reciprocated), such as liking, respect or sympathy. The pair interacts, and each person discovers that the other holds certain values or beliefs or displays certain attitudes (Newcomb's X). If X is shared, the relationship becomes solidary and stable; it is in balance. If any X is not shared, the future of the dyad is more problematic. If the nonshared X does not represent an antagonism between the members of the dyad (e.g., if A likes classical music and B can tolerate it), the focus of the dyad may move to some other X that is shared so that balance is restored and solidarity can develop.

But if the nonshared X is antagonistic (e.g., B actively dislikes classical music), the dyad is likely to dissolve, as B searches for an A with whom a more viable sentimental tie may form—the process of selective interaction.

Certain conditions may work against its dissolution, however. First, the nonshared X may have low salience for at least one of the pair (e.g., B dislikes classical music but is not much interested in music at all), and the sentimental bond between A and B may be strong. Second, the bond may be strong, and A and B can limit their interaction to situations in which X does not become an issue between them (e.g., A never listens to classical music when B is around). Third, at least one of the pair may focus his sentiments only on the other's positively evaluated traits (e.g., B tells himself that he likes

A because A is a reliable friend or because A, as does B, enjoys sports, even though A has such strange musical tastes)—the process of selective evaluation. Fourth, B may misperceive A's "moral communication" (e.g., B regards A's liking for classical music as a liking for all kinds of music, some of which B also likes)—the process of misperception. (On the processes of selective interaction, selective evaluation, and misperception, see Backman & Secord, 1962.)

A fifth condition is the central process of personal influence. If the foregoing conditions do not obtain, that is, if B cannot bring his relation with A into balance in any other way and if his sentimental tie to A is strong, he may change his own commitment to X to conform to A's (in our example, B begins to like classical music, or at least to say that he does, and shared listening to such music with A may help to develop his taste for it).

This balance-creating shift is fostered by a tendency under unbalanced conditions for communication about the value, belief or attitude at issue to increase. At the very least, the partners are likely to discuss it more, so that as it becomes more salient the contrast between the moral antagonism and the positive sentimental bond between the pair is brought into relief.

However, it does not seem sufficient to consider such communications as all of a kind. Especially important is variation in the communicator's intent and therefore in the nature of the message—for example, whether it simply describes the moral orientation in question, attempts to persuade or demands compliance. What the intent is in specific dyads is probably a function of the strength of the sentimental bond and of the degree of status difference between the partners. One might guess, for example, that the more intimate the relation, the less frequent are demands for compliance and that the greater the status difference, the more often will the dominant partner make such demands. Status symmetry and intimacy also may foster fairly symmetrical communication-sending—each partner sending about the same number of messages, at least initially.

Such variations surely influence the socializing effectiveness of dyads, but they are not much attended to in the literature on personal influence. I shall return to questions of structural differentiation in teacher-learner dyads, but it will not be possible to consider relations between structural and communicative variation in the systematic fashion that is required. These covariations, however, must enter any reasonably rigorous analysis of personal influence processes in teaching situations. In any event, the more the intent is to persuade, the greater the likelihood that A will employ sanctions—withholding approval, for example, until B has come over to A's side.

Personal influence in
teacher-student dyads

How can this perspective be applied to teaching? For the moment, let us ignore any social organizational variables external to a simple teacher-learner dyad. What are the conditions that will make the teacher a source of personal influence? First, assume that the dyad came about because the teacher knows something or has some skill that the learner lacks and wants. I shall refer to this knowledge or skill as the *content* to be taught. This condition is especially favorable for the learner's developing such sentiments as admiration or respect for his teacher. There is nothing intrinsic to their relationship that favors any very strong sentiments about the learner on the part of the teacher. The teacher has greater resources of approval and is less sentimentally dependent than the learner, and thus is likely to initiate most of the persuading and sanctioning.

Second, assume that as they interact the teacher begins to make plain certain of his own moral commitments that are pertinent to the content that he is teaching—say, the importance of performing well or the social significance of his specialty. The teacher also may try to persuade and to sanction the learner to produce moral as well as content learning. Given the learner's desire to learn the content, these commitments of the teacher—his "moral communications" —are likely to have high salience for the learner.

If the learner shares them with his teacher, theirs is a balanced relationship. But suppose that he does not. What then is he likely to do? If his own moral commitments, alternative to the teacher's, are relatively weak or altogether absent, he is likely to comply readily. If he takes a strong but differing moral stand, his position is more difficult. He may change teachers if he can find another teacher of roughly equal quality who does not send such moral messages. But if the teacher market is limited, his options are relatively few; selective interaction is not then easily managed. Because of the close connection between the content taught and the teacher's moral communications, it is difficult for them to segregate the arenas of interaction between the moral and the content-centered. Moreover, because the relationship is a specific one focused on the activities of teaching and learning, selective evaluation also is difficult; the specificity of their relationship limits the traits of the teacher to which the learner's sentiments can be directed.

More probable means by which the learner can manage the unbalanced relation with his teacher are misperception, a change of his sentiments from positive to neutral or negative, or a change in his own moral commitments in the direction of those held by the teacher. However, the more frequent their interaction—and most teacher-learner dyads will have a relatively high rate of interaction—the more difficult is misperception, again because of the close connection between the content taught and the teacher's moral commitments.

Given the foregoing discussion, we come to the proposition that in unbalanced teacher-learner dyads, if the sentimental tie of learner to teacher is positive and strong, the learner will tend to adopt the teacher's moral commitments. Indeed, this effect should be more likely and more intense the stronger the sentimental tie. If the tie is weak, the tie itself is more likely to change. As it moves toward the negative, two results may follow. First, the learner's original moral commitment may become stronger, an outcome that the teacher is not likely to have anticipated. Second, his rate of content learning may decline so that the teacher's effectiveness is generally reduced.

One now can see certain important conditions under which a teacher's activities in a dyadic relation with a learner are likely to effect changes in a learner's moral commitments:

(1) a link between certain of the teacher's moral commitments and the content taught;

(2) communication of these commitments by the teacher;

(3) a strong positive sentimental tie from learner to teacher, which itself will be affected by the teacher's competence;

(4) a highly salient difference of moral orientation between teacher and learner;

(5) a moral difference characterized by absent or weak moral commitment on the learner's part;

(6) few other teachers whom the learner can accept; and

(7) a high rate of interaction between teacher and learner.

If these are the main dimensions of a view of teaching as personal influence, how do they involve elements of social organization? The foregoing discussion does not account for the unwillingness of the learner (person B) to tolerate an unbalanced social relationship. In point of fact, it does not make very good sense to posit some universal human need or striving for balance; all of us function perfectly well from day to day in unbalanced dyads. Part of the explanation, of course, lies in the varying salience of moral differences across pair relations; whatever my political values, those of my postman are not of much importance to me. But the more significant explanation derives from the sentimental tie; it does make sense to posit a general human tendency to want some continuing evidence from persons whom we like or respect that the sentiment is reciprocated. We want *their* liking, approval or respect, for instance. If a tie of this kind exists in a dyad and it is unbalanced, then the moral difference produces evidence that the sentiment is less than fully reciprocated—in the form of A's efforts to persuade B, in his more open disapproval of B's moral stance, or in B's anticipation of these events. In effect, B comes to the conclusion that A will reciprocate B's sentiment only if B becomes like A in moral commitment. It is B's efforts to obtain evidence of a reciprocal sentimental tie that generate the strain toward balance in his relationship with A.

In short, sanctions and sanctioning have a central explanatory role in the personal influence perspective.[3] Most powerful are those sanctions that both indicate and affect the solidarity of social relationships, such as approval, esteem and respect. I believe it is clear that in a teacher-learner dyad the greater amount of such "solidary" sanctions are in the teacher's hands and that sanctioning activities are most often those of the teacher.

Solidary sanctions show the learner especially clearly the collective (here the dyadic) significance of his conduct with respect to the collectivity's moral order, and allow him

---

[3] In point of fact, the centrality of sanctions in the personal influence perspective reflects the often implicit reliance of this perspective on a fairly simple reinforcement theory of learning. Adherents of this perspective assume that moral orientations that are punished will tend toward extinction, those that are rewarded will tend to persist. Moreover, they assume that sanctions in primary social relationships are very powerful rewards and punishments.

to see the gains or losses in membership status (expulsion or disapproval versus esteem, for example) that follow from greater or lesser moral commitment. And so, depending on the value that he sets on membership (here, the strength and sign of the sentimental tie), he will tend toward or away from commitment.

It is important to note that the sentimental tie of B to A can vary as the basis of B's evaluation of A varies, with significant consequences for the sanctions that A can employ. This variation depends primarily on the functional limits set to the relationship and therefore on the degree of purposefulness with which the relation formed. The more purposive is B, the more instrumental the relationship and the narrower its scope (i.e., the more functionally specific it is). Thus the more purposive is B, the more likely he is to evaluate A on the basis of A's competence to perform the task at hand (e.g., the teacher's command of his subject matter). As a result, the sentimental tie is likely to be one of respect or disrespect, depending mainly on the nature of this evaluation but also on the degree of voluntarism with which B entered the relation. Compulsory recruitment does not favor positive sentiments though they may later be earned by A.

The less purposive is B in entering the relation (i.e., the more functionally diffuse it is), the more likely the relationship is to form around relatively diffuse sentiments (e.g., love or liking), for it has an unclear functional base, is less likely to be clearly differentiated, and thus is more likely to have a broader scope. If recruitment to such relations is involuntary, positive sentiments rarely form (as in relations of inmates of prisons or asylums with staff), unless such relations evolve as sources of affective and social support for B in a situation that otherwise is psychically costly (on these matters, cf. Goffman, 1961; Street et al., 1966), or unless recruitment occurs as an extension or continuation of "primordial"

social ties (especially those of kinship), as in the recruitment of young children to the first years of school.

In complex societies, the high level of structural differentiation, which involves specialized occupations and organizations for providing various kinds of service to persons, makes social ties approximating the primordial unlikely between teachers and students except in the specific situation of nursery and primary education (cf. Durkheim, 1933). Thus, with this exception, we may expect the sentimental tie of student to teacher to vary chiefly along the continuum of respect-disrespect. (For interesting evidence that among high-school students sentiments about teachers are of this nature and derive from criteria centered on the teacher's office and not his person, see Rhea, 1968.)

Since the functional differentiation of teaching situations appears to be closely correlated with student age and curricular complexity (i.e., with school level), the ratio of love or liking to respect in relations of students to teachers should decrease with increasing student age and school level. Indeed, we may expect students to become more purposive (instrumental) and to have, at least above the school-leaving age, a greater range of choice as between schooling and other endeavors, or between teachers, courses, curricula and schools. Deviations from this pattern will require specific explanation, as, for example, efforts by teachers lacking in student respect to involve their students in more diffuse affective relations or the prevalance among students coerced into schooling of a fairly specialized variety of diffuse negative sentiments (cf. Stinchcombe, 1964).

The sentimental tie of B to A (student to teacher) and its structural underpinnings set certain limits to the sanctions that A can use. Leaving aside for the time any sanctioning power that may come from the formal definition of their situation, as the basis of solidarity varies so do the sanctions available to A. As the relation of A and B becomes more functionally differentiated, the sanctions available to A become those reflecting his specialized, competent evaluation of B's equally specialized performance (or, as is implied by the relation between content and moral commitment in teaching, other actions or traits of B that may have become pertinent to the functionally specific content of the relation). The power of these sanctions, limited then to varying degrees of approval of B's performance or related traits, will depend on the level of B's respect for A, as may the direction of their effect—disrespect causing the sanctions to be counterproductive.

As the relation of A and B becomes less functionally differentiated, the sanctions available to A have less to do with such instrumental considerations as his special skills (reflecting B's lack of purpose) and derive more from the affective quality of B's sentiments. The more intense the affect involved (e.g., love rather than liking), the broader the range of B's traits or conduct open to sanctioning, the more diverse the sanctions (e.g., not only approval but also reciprocated love, for example), and the greater their power. (For an argument that the specificity or diffuseness of the teacher-student relation may be influenced by a variety of social organizational attributes of schools, see Sugarman, 1968.)

Consequently, diffuse ties seem to have greater potential for a broad range of personal influence, though I would suggest that this influence need not be more potent than that found in narrower relations, especially when in the latter, B is clearly and strongly purposeful.

Aside from sanctions and sanctioning, the personal influence perspective in its current sociologically simple form has little to say about elements of social organization and therefore is not very helpful in relating the social organization of teaching to the conduct of teachers. That the teacher or learner may enact roles other than those directly implicated in the dyad, and that the dyad is in all but the most exceptional cases part of a complex role structure are points ignored; from this perspective the teacher-learner dyad exists in a social vacuum. Nor are the more complicated aspects of this dyad, which derive from the broader social setting, treated. Thus, though we may posit certain differentials in the sentimental tie or in control of sanctions, these are seen as based narrowly on differences of personal traits as between teacher and learner. Aspects, for example, of their formally organized relationships (e.g., differences of power-authority derived from the teacher's official status) do not intrude, nor do aspects of activity patterns in these broader social settings of which the teacher's and learner's activities are a part (e.g., scheduled examinations or a set school curriculum).

In brief, the personal influence perspective does not take into consideration external social structural influence on the dyad, though I shall try to show in a moment how this perspective can be expanded to incorporate certain of these social structural variables. Of course, such variables are of significance not only as they may affect discrete teacher-learner dyads, but also as they organize teaching viewed as an activity of larger social units (for example, as a function of school rather than simply of teachers as individual actors).

Norms and values are dealt with no more explicitly. This follows directly from its narrow focus on dyads, since they do not have moral orders as these are usually defined. Though partners in persisting dyads do develop fairly stable mutual expectations grounded in sentiment rather more directly than in culture, we must regard the moral commitments of the partners as externally derived—as consequences of their group memberships rather than of their dyadic relation. So, too, their sanctioning activities are likely to be externally constrained by the norms of the collectivity in which the dyad is located, while the sentimental ties that bind dyadic relations, in point of fact, also have cultural roots (in the value criteria of interpersonal judgments). Hence variations across dyads in pair-wise evaluations and sentiments and in sanctioning will be nonrandom in any collectivity, and the cultural variables affecting these variations must be introduced into a study that centers not on single dyads but on the patterning or distribution, in the present case, of teacher-learner relations (e.g., studies of school or classroom variations in teacher conduct and/or of learner performance).

Indeed, from a social organizational standpoint, even the treatment of sanctioning in the personal influence perspective is limited. Attention centers on the solidary sanctions. Yet, for example, if the teacher is a school official he also commands and must use the more authoritative and "rational" sanctions that his office entails (especially grades). Such sanctions may conflict in their effects with solidary sanctions, and reliance on the one may erode the potency of the other. In the long run it may also affect the sentimental base of a teacher-learner dyad. Moreover, these conflicts may vary with the type of school setting—especially its grade or curricular level and the age composition of its students. Thus the greater reliance in early school grades on diffuse teacher approval of students rather than more formal universalistic evaluation of their academic performance (cf. Dreeben, 1968; Parsons, 1959) suggests that conflicts between solidary and official sanctions will have a lower incidence in the early school grades than at more advanced school levels and with younger rather than older students.

Personal Influence, Social Organization, and Teaching

In what ways can the personal influence perspective be modified so that it may take better account of the social organization of teaching?[4] We can begin with a point al-

ready noted—that teacher-learner dyads are asymmetrical. They are relations of differential power and dependence (Emerson, 1962). Of particular import for this asymmetry are those of the teacher's characteristics that gain him the positive sentiments of learners. I have suggested that these attributes center, after the early school grades, especially on aspects of content competence—the degree to which the teacher is a master of his subject matter—and particularly affect learners' respect for the teacher. However, other of his traits may also contribute to learners' sentiments—his skill in the techniques of teaching, his age, his sex, or his official standing in the school (and perhaps derivatively in the community). Moreover, at any grade or school level both diffuse and more specific sentiments are likely to be present, though in differing proportions and perhaps with different bases.

It is most important to note that such factors as age (or more precisely status as an adult) and official standing are primary bases of students' diffuse sentiments for teachers in the first years of schooling. Durkheim (1961), writing about primary education in the France of some 60 years ago, described the child's awe for his teacher derived from the teacher's standing as an adult and a representative of the state. Dreeben (1968) discusses similar phenomena among primary-school pupils' respect for their teachers, and Parsons (1959) notes the effects of both age and sex roles

---

[4] My emphasis on social organizational correlates of teachers' personal influence does not deny the importance in teacher-student relationships of traits of teacher and student personality (cf. Getzels & Jackson, 1963). As I shall note, the largely negative findings on teacher personality and teaching activity do not address this question, while there is some evidence (Wispe, 1951) that student personality variables are associated with students' preferences for alternative modes of teaching (and thus perhaps with students' sentiments about teachers who use differing instructional procedures).

—the largely female primary-school teaching cadre allowing an extension of the diffuse solidarity of parent-child relations into the classroom. Such effects become more muted in later school grades as the curriculum becomes more complex and performance demands become more specialized and stringent.

Contemporary American writers make less of the official standing of the teacher than did Durkheim, but one might predict that teacher office will foster students' positive sentiments for teachers—an effect not limited to the early school grades—to the extent that in a society the government is symbolically central and enjoys a high level of popular legitimacy.

Waller (1932, pp. 49–67) also shows that in small communities relatively undifferentiated in social structure and culture, the teacher's statuses in and outside of the school tend to merge. There is no reason to doubt his finding, despite the date of his study, and it suggests another proposition: that the more differentiated in social structure or culture a school's community, the less bearing will a teacher's extraschool social position have on his students' sentiments.

But the phenomena of more general import are those having to do with student age, and therefore school-grade level, and with the complexity, or specialization, of the school curriculum. The older the student body, the more salient will be the sentiment of respect, while the teacher's age in itself will be less likely to foster respect. Older students, as they become more sophisticated and critical, also may be less likely than younger ones to respect the teacher by virtue of his office. Moreover, the more complex the curriculum and the more advanced its content, the more central to respect is the teacher's mastery of his subject matter. In part this phenomenon may be expected because the students have become a knowledgeable audience, in part because the specialized and rigorous demands of the curriculum on both teachers

and students tend to reduce the salience of other of the teacher's social identities (i.e., an effect of the greater centrality of technical achievement by both teacher and student in these situations), and in part because of norms widespread in modern societies that define specialist roles in universalistic and functionally specific ways.

From these considerations it follows that the lower the school grade, the younger the students, the more elementary the curriculum, or the less specialized the content taught, the greater the likelihood that *any* teacher will have substantial personal influence on students' moral commitments. Or, to put the same proposition in a different way, under any of these conditions, the more prevalent among a given teacher population will be such personal influence. Of course, these conditions tend to be associated with one another in most educational systems, further raising the probability of such patterns of interpersonal influence among a teaching force. The diffuse sentimental tie of student to teacher (e.g., love or liking), coupled with respect derived from teacher status (e.g., age or office), is posited as the principal intervening variable in these relationships.

On the other hand, as these conditions disappear, content-centered respect will become more central (though not exclusively so) as the sentimental base for student-teacher relations. Respect for the teacher initially will be problematic, to be earned by the teacher as he demonstrates his specialized skills in the content area that he teaches.[5] Now teachers' personal influence over students' moral commitments should be less prevalent and directly associated (via respect) with student evaluations of the teacher's content competence.

---

[5] How respect or other sentiments may be formed and the effects of sentimental ties on personal influence under the different conditions set by variation across teaching situations in the value taken by each of these conditional variables is complex and unknown. I cannot give systematic attention to this question, but it is an important one.

Graduate and professional schools may be limiting cases.

There are additional variables in the social organization of teaching that set conditions to this last proposition and may make it harder or easier for a teacher to become a source of personal influence for his students. Under certain circumstances teachers are not initially unknown to their students and enjoy either favorable or unfavorable reputations—reputations that may include subject-matter competence as well as other traits. For such reputations to emerge and persist, the teacher must have been in office for some time; hence the more stable a teaching force, the more likely are teachers' reputations to affect their capacities for personal influence (at least initially, since their subsequent conduct may either confirm or deny their reputations). Moreover, the student body must be organized so as to facilitate the formation of student cultures that include reputational information and that foster communication from "old hands" to novice students. Thus we might expect such factors as cohort recruitment of students, the organization of students into clearly bounded classes, high rates of student interaction (more probable in residential or para-residential schools), and the existence of a clearly established student leadership to favor the emergence, persistence and effectiveness of teachers' reputations.

The official standing of teachers may have an important effect on their reputations even when the foregoing conditions are unfavorable. When schools themselves are ranked by reputation, and most schools are ranked in this way, at least in local communities, the reputation of the school to which a teacher is appointed is likely to devolve upon him, affecting his own reputation (though perhaps only initially). Thus we might expect that the higher the prestige rank of a school, and perhaps also the firmer its rank (e.g., nationally as opposed to locally ranked schools), the greater prevalence of personal influence among its teachers on students' moral commitments. In point of fact, school reputation and teacher competence probably interact as they affect teachers' personal influence; it may require greater competence to attain a given level of personal influence in low- than in high-ranking schools, and student-observed failures of competence may count for less in high- than in low-ranking schools. Of course, students may be more demanding in higher-ranking schools, which would work to reverse the predicted relationship. (In this and subsequent arguments, unless otherwise noted, I make the simplifying assumption of comparable student bodies across teaching situations.)

For situations in which there is a close relation between the content taught and a teacher's moral commitments, an additional proposition can be derived. If the content taught is more specialized, a narrower range among the teacher's moral commitments should become salient (e.g., the medical school professor's commitment to research or clinical practice, but not his musical tastes). If the content is less specialized, a broader range of his moral commitments should become salient. Therefore, the less specialized the curriculum, the broader in scope and the more diffuse the teacher's personal influence. One might also argue to the same end that the less specialized the curriculum the greater the opportunity for the teacher to send a variety of moral communications to his students.

Although I shall not have much to say about teacher collectivities in relation to the teaching process, it is important to note that a further condition affecting a teacher's personal influence is the degree to which either his moral commitments or traits eliciting learners' sentiments (which, of course, may include his commitments) differ from those of other teachers. I have in mind here something of a figure-ground phenomenon. The more distinctive a teacher in his learner-valued trait, the greater the tendency for that value to be high. One thinks, for example, of the openness of the student to influence by a teacher who he believes is the only one of a faculty who is "really" competent, friendly or sympathetic, or consistent or firm in his values or attitudes. Nonetheless, it is entirely possible that the distinctiveness of a teacher, either in commitments or valued traits, may work to weaken the learner's sentiments toward him or to foster negative rather than positive sentiments if the teacher's unrepresentativeness raises questions of his social or normative acceptability. Perhaps effects favorable to the influence of the unrepresentative teacher will be more likely when the student's own beliefs or experiences or the school's reputation lead the student to give a low value to the faculty collectively, while unfavorable effects are more likely when these factors lead him to value the faculty highly. (Clearly here one must consider the student's possible identification with the faculty as a reference group.)

In any event, such figure-ground processes require that more than one teacher is clearly visible to a student, and therefore they should be more frequent as students gain experience in learning settings (present-past comparisons), in schools in which students are taught either serially or in teams by more than one teacher ("cross-sectional" comparisons), or in schools in which the faculty has a clear and consistent reputation among students (comparison of actual and imagined relations with teachers).[6]

The foregoing discussion may serve to illustrate how social organizational variables can be introduced into the personal influence perspective, resulting in a series of propositions about teaching as personal influence. These propositions are hardly exhaustive and not very rigorous, but the illustration must suffice.

_____

[6] It should be clear that in the foregoing analysis I have been discussing factors affecting students' definitions of the classroom situation as these in turn affect responses to teaching and the sentimental basis for such responses. (On "definition of the situation" see Thomas, 1928, pp. 42–43. For an application of this concept to schools, see Waller, 1932, pp. 292–317.)

Now we can consider in somewhat greater detail aspects of the teacher's official standing. (I shall leave aside interesting issues posed by variation in the broader formal organization of schools, for example, the degree to which they approximate a Weberian bureaucracy [Weber, 1946, pp. 196–244]. On certain of these issues see Bidwell, 1965.) In particular, the teacher's office gives him control over sanctions rather different from those of the solidary kind. I have suggested that the teacher's approval of the learner—of his performance, his moral commitments or any of a variety of his personal traits—is generally the most powerful of these sanctions. I have also argued that the close linkage in teacher-learner dyads between the salience of certain of the teacher's moral commitments and the content taught makes it likely that for the learner his teacher's approval of his performance in content learning also will reinforce adoption of the salient moral commitment.

The teacher's official sanctions, however, are not in the same direct sense (as are solidary ones) dependent for their potency on the learner's sentiments about the teacher. These sanctions, of which grades are the most central (though others may also be used—expulsion from the classroom or school or prizes and honors, for example) derive from the socially legitimate power, that is, the authority, of a school to control and reward the conduct of its students. Thus the teacher's use of official sanctions inheres not in his person but in his office. He can use them and students will respond to them because of the legitimacy of the school's power and the teacher's standing as a member of its staff.

Moreover, such official sanctions as grades are *formally rational;* in the ideal case they are applicable universally to formally defined categories of students (e.g., classroom groups or grade levels), specifically with reference to a given learning performance and without regard for social relations between teacher or learner other than those defined by their roles in the school.

Consequently, to the extent that teaching is conducted as an official function, the teacher's potency as a source of personal influence on students' moral commitments should be severely limited; sentiment and solidary sanctions would appear to be severely constrained in official teacher-student relations. Moral socialization as a task of teaching then would occur as formally planned indoctrination relying on an explicit moral curriculum with official rewards or punishments for "moral achievement."

Nonetheless, the distinction between formal and solidary sanctioning and between office-based relations and the sentimental tie cannot be sustained empirically in the study of teaching. In the first place, students must learn to respond to grades and other official teacher sanctions, and much of this learning takes place in the early years of school. Recall Dreeben's (1968) argument that the primary-school class is organized more on the basis of diffuse teacher-pupil solidarity than formally defined relationships. Parsons (1959) describes how in these classes pupils are rewarded more for the moral qualities of their conduct (for being "good" children and pupils) than for specific academic accomplishments.

Dreeben further suggests that the diffuse relation between teacher and student in the primary grades, with the corresponding scope and power of the teacher's approval of her pupils, provides the basis for their learning to respond to grading. In addition, the diffuse criteria for student conduct held by the teacher at this period should make it possible for students to learn to connect more differentiated forms of academic achievement with the moral approbation that comes from being a "good" student.

Now, although the school curriculum becomes more complex and intellectually demanding as students proceed through the school grades and levels, it does not follow that the significance for students of the teacher's approval necessarily decreases, though the range of its significance may narrow. Instead, we can view grades and other official school sanctions, in part, at least, as symbols of the teacher's approval—either the student's own teacher or the teacher collectivity (the faculty). These sanctions, nonetheless, do become more explicitly centered on academic performance.

If this argument holds, we may then regard teachers' approval and their formal sanctions as, to a degree, functionally equivalent and potentially reinforcing or conflicting in their consequences. This is true for both the academic attainments and the moral commitments of learners, at least in the postprimary years of schooling.

Let us consider first the results of this functional equivalence within the teacher-student dyad. If the teacher sends moral communications to the student, and if his moral commitments are salient for the student, then the teacher's formal evaluation of the student's content learning may reinforce the student's adoption of the teacher's moral commitment—independently of the teacher's moral persuasion or sanctioning of his student's moral stance. So, too, the teacher's direct approval of his student—whatever the trait or performance approved—also may strengthen the student's academic motives and serve to reinforce his attainment in content learning.

The complementarity of teachers' approval and formal sanctions suggests that content learning and moral learning may be dual outcomes of the same teaching activities when conditions favoring the teacher's personal influence obtain. However, the teacher's formal sanctions may weaken as well as reinforce approval. The learning of content and of moral commitment, for example, may not proceed apace. Consequently, the more closely related are the teacher's moral commitments and subject matter (a condition that, I have argued, favors the high salience of the teacher's commitment and therefore his personal influence), the greater his difficulty in maintaining personal influence when the learner's content performance is poor or the greater his difficulty in sustaining "objective"

evaluation and sanctioning of content learning when the learner's moral commitments
earn the teacher's approval. In the latter
case the teacher-learner dyad is in balance
with respect to moral commitment but it
is unbalanced from the teacher's point of
view with respect to the learner's content
performance. Given the conditions that I
believe obtain generally in teacher-learner
dyads, the teacher can solve this problem
by 1) sending the learner away (selective
interaction), 2) ignoring his morally valuable qualities (selective evaluation), or 3)
changing the evaluation and consequent
sanctioning of his content attainment.

The first solution is possible only if the
teacher is free to select his pupils. The
official standing of teachers more often than
not prevents this solution; it is most likely
to occur in such settings as universities (and
then often only in tutorial forms of teaching). When students are assigned to teachers,
whether in batches (as in classroom groups)
or individually, selective recruitment and
selective interaction are not possible.

The second solution is more probable
when the connection is weaker between the
teacher's moral commitments and his content specialty, while the third is more likely
when this connection is stronger. This connection probably is strongest when the
teacher's commitment is to conduct specific
to the content field of the teaching situation
(e.g., to the ethical responsibility of the
scholar, for the university teacher, in contrast to political or religious beliefs). If so,
commitment to the moral prescriptions of
school or academy and content attainment
may be alternative or complementary paths
by which a student can gain academic
success. (A limiting case here is the primary-
school classroom with its diffuse moral
order.)

The attenuation of a teacher's personal
influence when the learner's content attainment is poor arises also because the teacher's
negative sanctioning of content learning
may weaken the learner's positive sentiments about his teacher. I believe that this
tendency usually has two sources. First, the
teacher's disapproval of the learner's content
performance indicates that while the learner
may respect his teacher, the teacher is not
entirely favorable toward the learner. Now,
if the learner thinks fairly well of his own
content attainments, the teacher-learner relation is unbalanced. One solution for the
learner is to lower his estimate of the teacher's worth. If he can find an alternative focus
for evaluating the teacher, he may turn to
selective evaluation as a way to bring the
relation into balance, of course. If this
alternative focus is the teacher's moral commitment, then his personal influence may
gain in strength. Or, if the teacher is clearly
competent, that is, worthy of respect, the
learner may alter his evaluation of self.
This suggests that attenuation of the teacher's personal influence is more likely the
more specialized the teaching situation, and
therefore more likely if the content is "advanced" rather than "elementary." A similar
effect may occur if the teacher's competence
can be questioned (whether on the basis
of his own or the school's reputation or of
his learner-observed teaching).

Second, the formal sanctions that the
teacher will apply to the learner's content
performance, although they are surrogate
signs of approval or disapproval, nonetheless are not consistent with affectively
based solidarity in the dyad. They signify
that the teacher retains a certain emotional
distance or disengagement in the situation.
If the learner's sentimental tie to the teacher
is one of respect, the conflict between formal
sanctioning and solidarity will be muted.
But if the learner's sentiments are grounded
in his assumption of a more socially intimate
relationship (love, for example), the conflict
will be more intense. The learner may
resolve this conflict by using a mechanism
that I have not yet noted. He may change
the basis, but not the intensity, of his sentiment about his teacher—from the assumption of intimacy to the assumption of distance (e.g., from love to respect). This
solution, of course, is contingent upon his
finding in his teacher qualities that merit
this shift—for example, content competence

that he can respect. Or, he may resolve the conflict by lowering the intensity of positive sentiment or changing from positive to negative feelings. In this case the teacher loses personal influence and, indeed, if the sentiment becomes negative his efforts at moral persuasion may be counterproductive.[7]

COLLECTIVE ATTRIBUTES OF TEACHING

To this point, I have treated teaching as if it took place only in dyads, allowing social organizational variables to enter the discussion as defining the contexts or affecting the structure of these dyads. But what of the collective properties of teaching? If we allow the personal influence perspective to be applied only as in the foregoing pages, we assume that teaching in collective settings is organized as a set of discrete, though spatially close, pair relations. This assumption is usually wrong. At times in classrooms this form of social organization may be observed, as when elementary-school students are doing "seatwork," but as the growing number of classroom observers tell us, by far the larger proportion of a classroom teacher's day is spent performing before collective pupil audiences or in other ways acting as a member of the classroom collectivity. (For the most sensitive discussion of data from classroom observation, centered on elementary school classrooms, see P. W. Jackson, 1968.)

A full discussion of the relations between teaching as personal influence and the collective properties of teaching situations itself would require a long essay. (For a review of much of the pertinent literature from the small group point of view, see Bany & Johnson, 1964. To see the influence of group dynamics ideas on studies of class-

rooms, see Miles, 1964.) I can only suggest what some of these relations may be, and I shall restrict my discussion to the more typical situation of the one-teacher classroom. I shall ignore interesting problems in team teaching (on which the evidence with respect to learning is moot, cf. Lambert, Goodwin, Roberts, & Wiersma, 1965, though there has been some effort at social-psychological conceptualization, cf. Shaplin, 1964). I shall also ignore extreme variations attributable to student age and level of subject matter, ruling out of consideration teaching in nursery and primary schools and teaching adults.

As Getzels (1969, pp. 502–510) has argued in a cogent discussion of the social psychology of education, more refined approaches than the usual "democratic-authoritarian" or "permissive-directive" schemata are required to understand how the collective properties of teaching situations are related to teachers' conduct. The widespread but unreflective adoption of the more simple schemata by writers on "classroom technique" (e.g., Burton, 1952; Mursell, 1954) is no indicator of their analytical power. Getzels outlines several alternative and more refined approaches: ecological (Barker, 1963; Barker, Gump, Friesen, & Williams, 1970), linguistic (Bellack, 1965; B. O. Smith, n.d.; Wright & Proctor, 1961), or behavioral-descriptive (P. W. Jackson, 1964; Kounin, 1967; Kounin, Gump, & Ryan, 1961). It seems certain that neither efforts to find correlates of teacher personality in classroom activities, on which there is a large literature,[8] nor observation of classroom activity (cf. Medley & Mitzel, 1963)

---

[7] This conflict is potentially greatest in primary-school classes where pupils' sentiments reflect teacher-pupil intimacy. But in these classrooms formal sanctioning is relatively infrequent and is heavily loaded with more explicit teacher approval or disapproval.

[8] Central references in this literature include Callis (1953), Chappell and Callis (1954), Cook, Leeds, and Callis (1951), Della Piana and Gage (1955), Fuller (1951), Gough and Pemberton (1952), Harvey, Prather, White, and Hoffmeister (1968), Hedlund (1953), M. Hughes (1959), Leeds (1952), Michaelis (1954), Morsh and Wilder (1954), Oelke (1956), Ohlsen and Schulz (1955), Remmers (1963), Ryans (1960), Sandgren and Schmidt (1956), Schmid (1950), Sheldon, Coale, and Copple (1959), R. L. Turner (1965a, 1965b), Tyler (1954), Wallen and Travers (1963), Washburne and Heil (1960).

will succeed until personality variables or observational data are related to classroom social organization. Variation of teaching group size may be one social organizational variable (cf. Hare, 1962, p. 388; Thelen, 1949), especially when teaching diverges from the didactic (see McKeachie, 1963). Others may be distinctive patterns of communication among students and between teacher and students (see Bavelas, 1960; Leavitt, 1951), or composition with respect to ability, sex or traits of personality (see McKeachie, 1963; Thelen, 1963).

Lavin (1965, p. 161) holds that no current social-psychological formulation of teaching situations is sufficiently refined to capture the essential variation in crescive classroom social structures that provides the more powerful structural variables in teaching. Getzels (1969, p. 509; see also Getzels & Thelen, 1960) suggests that one might "conceive of the classroom as a miniature society or social system with differentiated role and personality relationships linked to differentiated educational goals."

I shall try to follow the leads given by Lavin and Getzels by outlining briefly the impact of teachers' pursuit of one such goal (the motivation of academic performance) as this pursuit is associated with a specific attribute of classroom social relations—their organization around interpupil competition. I shall indicate some of the ways in which this association bears on the teacher's personal influence, suggesting how the social organization of teaching situations may affect teaching activities. My example follows a line well established in social psychology (see, e.g., Cartwright & Zander, 1960, on effects of group cohesiveness on productivity) and in studies of classrooms (see Deutsch, 1960; DeVries, Muse, & Wells, 1971). But the results of variation in classroom group cohesiveness for students' academic performances are by no means clear. Thus in the Deutsch study classroom groups presumably high in interpupil cooperation acted in more coordinated and collectively task-centered ways than did

classrooms high in competition, but the learning rates of the two classroom situations were not significantly different.

To what extent may the classroom, viewed as a setting for a teacher's personal influence, show more marked differences in the association of social organization and learning outcomes? To what extent might content learning show greater or more consistent differences if the teacher's personal influence (e.g., as a source of student motivation) were considered explicitly as an intervening variable in this association?

School classes are organized formally into two strata: the teacher and the students. (More elaborate stratification is a crescive property of a given classroom—for example, differential sociometric status among its student members.) The upper stratum has only one member, the teacher. In this one-member stratum are found the various properties of the teacher's role that I already have noted: official standing (including the right to state or set performance standards), monopoly of formal sanctions, greater age, and, presumably, greater subject-matter competence. The lower stratum usually is homogeneous in age and, in schools tied to local attendance districts, relatively homogeneous in social origin. It is formally without authority and is usually not very competent, or at least not as competent as the teacher, in the content to be learned. It also is important that classroom membership most often is involuntary for both teacher and students—a matter of organizational rather than of personal decision.

This flat but asymmetrical status structure and the official responsibilities of the teacher produce certain distinctive patterns of group activity: the heavy involvement of the teacher in controlling student conduct; the centrality of the teacher in initiating interaction, receiving students' requests for help and advice, sending authoritative communications about the learning content and about students' classroom conduct, and evaluating and sanctioning students' academic performance; and the relative infrequency of lateral interaction and communication among students. The last of these classroom attributes varies substantially across classrooms and often within classrooms, but at the teacher's discretion. (On these characteristics of classrooms, see P. W. Jackson, 1968; Jackson & Lahaderne, 1967; and Smith & Hudgins, 1966.)

One further attribute of classrooms is very important. For the most part in western societies teaching centers on the individually evaluated performance of students. A result (Coleman, 1959; Waller, 1932) is the organization of the student members of the classroom as a competitive social order in which, moreover, the terms and results of competition are determined by the teacher. Even if the performance standard is not the same for all pupils but is dependent on each student's past performance or ability, variation in attainment still is open to interstudent competition and invidious judgment—the students, while "competing against themselves" may still compete with each other with respect to relative amounts of gain in accomplishment.

In the more usual situation, in which uniform performance standards are set by the teacher, grades or other direct and indirect forms of teacher approval of academic achievement are scarce. Although the currency of approval may become inflated (all students get good marks, for example), the teacher cannot allow this inflation without good cause, since performance standards and attendant sanctions are principal means of raising or maintaining students' motives to learn. Although it occurs more rarely, deflation of the approval medium also is possible but also problematic for the teacher; *relative* allocation of sanctions among students is presumed to foster student performance.

As a result, student competition approaches a zero-sum situation: gains by one student in positive sanctions result in losses by others. Given the homogeneity of the student stratum in most classrooms, this situation defines a problem common to the student membership and may result in their collective attempts either to inflate the currency of approval by pressing the teacher for lower performance standards that all may reach more easily (e.g., Waller's, 1932, famous "battle of the requirements") or by setting output-controlling norms that prevent any one student from gaining too much and, thus, any other from gaining too little (cf. Coleman, 1961). More rarely the teacher may be co-opted as a quasimember of the classroom student group (Gordon, 1957).

If the teacher does not set a common performance standard for all students in the classroom but lets the standard vary with their attainment or ability, competition for gain in accomplishment will tend to fragment relations with student peers, at least with respect to the academic tasks of the classroom, since there can be no collective solution to the problem of getting good grades. Under this condition, the teacher's authority is less likely to be eroded by collective student solutions to the problem of allocating scarce teacher rewards because student solidarity will not form around the task of deflecting or moderating the teacher's performance demands.

We also can consider the rarer situation in which performance standards are set not for individual students but for the whole classroom group—competition shifting to the interclass or interschool arena. Here rewards and punishments go to the pupil collectivity and presumably are shared equally by its members. The usual argument (Coleman, 1959) is that in such situations (which may be approximated in some Russian classrooms or in some schools operating under systems of "performance accountability") social relations among students are cooperative largely because of their joint involvement in the common welfare of the class, so that student peer norms tend to enforce maximum effort in the group's learning tasks. In addition, it is argued that the teacher becomes involved with students in more of an advising and leading than judging and sanctioning role. (Note that on this and the preceding variety of teaching situation only a modicum of empirical evidence is available, but see Deutsch, 1960, and DeVries, Muse, & Wells, 1971, for experimental evidence, and on the Russian case see Bronfenbrenner, 1962.)

In brief, I have described four patterns of classroom social organization: a) competition to a common standard with scarce or with b) "inflated" rewards; c) competition centered on differentially defined student gain; and d) cooperation for collective achievement and reward. Noting that the main outlines of formal classroom social organization do not vary across these patterns, how may each affect the teacher's personal influence?[9]

(a) Competition to a common standard: scarce rewards. In this situation a major task for the teacher is to prevent the formation of an oppositional student classroom culture—in part because of the dangers inherent in something like a "battle of requirements" and in part because of the power of peer relations to affect students' academic and postschool motives (cf. Alexander & Campbell, 1964; Bidwell & Vreeland, forthcoming; Boyle, 1966; E. Hughes, Becker, & Geer, 1962; McDill, Rigsby, & Meyers, 1969).

One tactic that teachers may employ is to reinforce competitive student relations, even outside of explicitly academic activities, by maintaining high but differential rates of solidary rewards (e.g., those centered on competitive behavior and invidious public comparisons of one student with another). This tactic, described sensitively by Henry (1955, 1957), keeps the student dependent primarily on the teacher for social support in the classroom. If the teacher commands

the positive sentiments of his students, this tactic makes him a source of strong personal influence for commitment to a norm of academic competition while at the same time weakening peer solidarity. Moreover, if the teacher's reinforcement of appropriately competitive conduct strengthens these sentiments (which seems likely when the teacher monopolizes solidary rewards), he may then become a powerful source of personal influence toward other moral commitments as well. In effect, this tactic fosters a decomposition of the classroom social structure into multiple teacher-student dyads in which the surviving peer relations are those predictable from the competitive task structure of the classroom.

There are certain limits to the use of this tactic, and it has certain consequences that the teacher may not anticipate. It appears to be most effective when the students' sentiments toward the teacher are diffusely affective (i.e., as these sentiments approach love more than respect). A diffuse sentimental base of the teacher-student relation gives to the teacher control over solidary sanctions in a broad range of situations —in episodes of disciplinary control, for example, as well as in those more explicitly concerned with teaching content. It also maximizes students' dependence on the teacher for the social support provided by these sanctions.

When students' sentiments are themselves more differentiated and specialized (e.g., approach respect more than love), the teacher is less able to monopolize social support and peers become more salient sources of approval and esteem, especially in extraacademic situations. Moreover, since respect centers on the teacher's content proficiency, efforts to sanction student conduct on bases other than strictly defined content achievement may weaken students' respect and generally lessen the teacher's personal influence. In point of fact, when respect is the prime sentimental tie of student to teacher, the teacher's sanctions are limited for the most part to sanctioning academic per-

---

[9] The following discussion centers largely on relations between teachers' use of power and crescive structures of classroom groups. For a summary of the pertinent literature and a distinctive theoretical view of the relation between power and group structure see Collins and Raven (1969).

formance; therefore the classroom remains open to the formation of an oppositional student subculture. Thus the tactic of "dividing and conquering" through personal influence should be effective more often in lower than in higher school grades, where indeed it is most often to be observed.[10] It may also be less likely if students have substantial extraclassroom bases for solidarity—in a local neighborhood or in team sports or other extracurricular activities (cf. Coleman, 1961; Gordon, 1957).

We thus have returned to the question of teacher-student opposition. While many factors may operate to mute tendencies toward such opposition (including extraclassroom variation in student solidarity and the degree of homogeneity in the students' social origins, for example), the sentimental tie of student to teacher is important among them. I argued earlier that the more competent in his subject matter is the teacher, the more likely he is to win the respect of his students individually. Now I also would argue that the more solidary the student classroom membership, the more likely is the sentiment to be visibly shared and normatively enforced (independent of possible reinforcing effects of teacher or school reputations).

Under these favorable conditions, the legitimacy of the teacher's performance demands—at issue centrally in "requirements battles"—is most likely to be granted and an explicitly oppositional student subculture is less likely to form (though one may still observe student adaptation to performance demands through cooperative priority-setting (cf. Becker et al., 1961). When respect for the teacher is low, student opposition will tend to be high. Recall that respect

will be affected by the *value* students set on the teacher's competence—including the possibility that competence is in itself of low value.

Note that when the teacher's performance demands are accepted as legitimate, he not only retains his personal influence but finds it reinforced by supportive student norms, though within the relatively narrow limits set by the pertinence of his moral commitments to his subject matter. Note also that rife student competition is not likely, since peer solidarities may take a relatively collegial form in which variation of attainment is defined by peers in functionally specific terms. (For evidence bearing on the strong personal influence of teachers under such conditions, see Gottlieb, 1961.)

(b) Competition to a common standard: inflated rewards. This teaching situation is apt to be, though it need not always be, an outcome of a "requirements battle." If the conditions of classroom social organization tend to restrict students' sentiments toward the teacher to respect, an inflation of the reward currency of the classroom will tend to weaken these ties and especially to preclude the development of respect as an element of the collective orientation of the student membership to the teacher. Possibly the teacher will shift from a more inflated to a less inflated reward (e.g., from marks to comments on students' work), but the new reward may remain relatively weak because of a patent contradiction between aspects of the teacher's evaluation of student performance. In some situations the teacher and students may agree that, say, grades are not legitimate and thus remove a given kind of sanction from consideration altogether.

But where the students' sentiments toward the teacher are more diffuse, as in the lower grades, the effect of inflated rewards for academic performance is especially to open students to teacher sanctions centered on extra-academic conduct; academic sanctions lose their value as well as

---

[10] There are also consequences, probably unanticipated, for student moral learning that I can only note: learning that performance standards are personal rather than impersonal, even in relatively specialized roles, that sentiments are manipulable for future extrinsic ends (self-estrangement), and that competitive relations cannot be impersonal and differentiated but must be diffusely personal even in apparently functionally specific situations.

their force. In the absence of a clear external object of classroom activity (as in interclass or interschool competition), moreover, the relations of students to the teacher are likely to be rather strongly dependent.

In this situation the teacher is apt to use diffuse forms of approval to solidify his ascendant position and to increase the level of students' content performance by means of sanctions centered on extra-academic conduct. The task for students is to please the teacher in a variety of ways, including content achievement, to gain a maximum amount of the teacher's approval.

Whether or not solidary sanctions are used by a teacher to induce competition among his students, the result for the students is to separate content learning from clear performance standards and to incorporate such learning into a more global self-definition of worth. The teacher's personal influence may be broad in scope, but his ability to induce his students' commitments to performance standards and related aspirations should be relatively weak. Such classrooms, therefore, should not be very effective in preparing students for later academic roles and for postschool roles involving performance to a standard.

These comments suggest that the teacher of the early school grades whose teaching is organized around common standards of student attainment, must balance fairly rigorous evaluation of performance with more diffuse forms of approval and must do so without letting diffuse approval erode the meaning of performance sanctions.

In higher school grades or levels, the appearance of diffuse sanctioning may be regarded as regressive, in particular as an attempt by a teacher to find ways of controlling student conduct and raising academic motives in the absence of student respect. Such an attempt, however, requires the teacher to be the object of student sentiments that are positive but more diffuse than is respect. Hence the inflation of performance rewards is likely to be accompanied by the teacher's attempts to present himself as a friend or compeer of his students. Our earlier discussion suggests that the more advanced or specialized the curriculum and the older the students, the less successful such efforts will be. Indeed they may further weaken students' respect and lead to a teaching situation in which the teacher has little personal influence. As a means of classroom control (to the extent that it is necessary) and as a device for raising students' academic motivation, the teacher then must rely on performance standards that his own actions have made meaningless to his students.

(c) Competition with respect to differential rates of student gain. I have argued that in these teaching situations student solidarity will be weak, but student relations will be more fragmented than conflict-laden. Since the teacher determines how much gain occurs in each case (even when standard achievement tests are used, he is a major source of approval of student gain), this situation makes students especially dependent on the teacher. If he holds the students' respect, he may have very strong content-linked personal influence. But because this influence will not be reinforced by a collective evaluation of his competence, given the absence of strong student solidarity, his influence may vary more from student to student than in the presence of strong student peer ties. Moreover, it may be more difficult for the teacher to establish his competence (reputational effects aside), since it is not embodied in a common performance standard and must be made evident through his presentation of subject matter. It cannot be grounded very firmly in his responses to students' public performances since these responses will be governed by students' gains rather than by their commonly measured attainments.

If students' sentiments toward the teacher are more diffuse, one again would expect the teacher to have very strong influence (now broad in scope) because the fragmentation of peer relations centers each student's classroom life directly on the teacher as an object of powerful affective attachment. Indeed, if these sentiments are negative, one would anticipate powerful reactive changes in students' moral commitments, given the central position of the teacher in the social organization of the classroom. Here, too, the strength of the teacher's personal influence should be variable across the members of the classroom group, a function of individual variation in the sentiments of his students.

(d) Extraclass competition, intraclass cooperation. This teaching situation would appear to favor the teacher's personal influence because the student classroom culture presumably is supportive rather than oppositional. The main sources of variation in the teacher's personal influence, then, should be across rather than within classrooms and, in the case of respect as its sentimental base, should occur as a function of the teacher's observed ability to foster the collective accomplishments of the group. Indeed, in such classrooms the grounding of respect may shift somewhat from content to task-leadership competence.

Now, however, more diffuse student sentiments may be less favorable to the teacher's personal influence if the requirements of task leadership (e.g., assigning work or criticizing contributions to the common task) appear inconsistent with the actions expected of an object of diffuse affective ties (i.e., expected of the teacher as a socioemotional leader). Here the teacher's personal influence may be greater the less he is a task leader, yet diffuse student sentiments are more likely to occur in classrooms in which task leadership must remain largely with the teacher (e.g., the early school grades).

Note also that in teaching situations of this type, the teacher (at least when he is the object of students' respect) may be less

distinctively the source of content-linked personal influence given the presumed strength and task-centered nature of student peer norms. In each of the other teaching situations peer solidarities either are weak or, if not in opposition to the teacher's influence, are centered substantially on moderating its impact. Indeed, in cooperative classrooms, a substantial portion of the teacher's influence over his students' moral commitments may be not direct but indirect —mediated by peer relations that are focused on the common academic tasks of the classroom group.

"Climate" studies

Studies of the vaguely named phenomenon "classroom climate" may be consistent with our expectations concerning the relationship between a teacher's personal influence and the cohesiveness of his classroom student group. Like their antecedents in education (e.g., Lewin et al., 1939; Ojemann & Wilkinson, 1939) and in industrial sociology (e.g., Roethlisberger & Dickson, 1939), more recent studies of classroom climates (e.g., Flanders, 1960; M. Hughes, 1959; Schmuck, 1966; Thelen, 1950, 1951; Withall, 1949) show an association between cooperative, in contrast to competitive or aggressive, activity by group members (students) and the degree to which the leader (teacher) tends to support rather than to dominate the task-centered activities of the student members.

These findings have been interpreted as indicating a flow of effect from the teacher's leadership style to the observed pattern of student interaction. The classroom climate studies have not sorted out the effects of such structural phenomena as the rate or direction of interaction and the rate and type of teacher sanctioning (e.g., the balance of approval and disapproval), nor do they provide clear evidence concerning sentimental ties between teacher and students. Nonetheless, these findings may show in the teacher's behavior reflecting differing opportunities, for the formation of such ties as classroom groups varies in cohesiveness. The findings, in brief, may describe settings that vary in the teacher's opportunity to exert personal influence. (An effort has been made, with negative results, to demonstrate a relationship between teacher personality and classroom climate [Lantz, 1965], but the teacher traits studied have no demonstrable bearing on personal influence processes.) Clearly any attempt to test this proposition must include measures of classroom social relationships that are more sensitive to sentimental bonds, sanctioning activities, and the collective properties of classroom groups than those used in the studies that I have cited or in the Stern-Pace (Pace, 1963; Stern, 1962; Stern & Pace, 1958) adaptation of the Murray Alpha-Beta press conception to the analysis of school climates.

Sociometric structures

I have tried to show how important it is to analyze the interplay between personal influence processes in teaching and the social organization of teaching situations. This analysis must involve not only the formal organization of these situations but also their crescive structures—especially since these structures form the more immediate setting in which teaching occurs. A further illustration of this sort of analysis is provided by considering, from the personal influence perspective, some of the sociometric literature on classrooms. There is a very large literature that reports the application of sociometric techniques to classrooms. Though much of this work is technically mechanical or highly derivative of the ideas of Moreno (1934), some findings merit attention. (For summaries of this and related literature, see Gronlund, 1959; Lindzey & Borgatta, 1954; Withall & Lewis, 1936.) There is substantial overlap between these findings and several ideas that I have already discussed,

although I have the opportunity here only to suggest a few points of convergence.

A bit of the sociometric work centers on the teacher's role. There is an apparent tendency for teachers' and students' ranking of students' sociometric status to diverge, but for the peer-accorded status of a student to be related to the rate of his interaction with the teacher (Gronlund, 1959, pp. 19–113), while teachers overrate those students who participate actively in class and who comply with the teacher's behavioral standards (Bonney, 1947). High peer-given status seems to be related to divergence from teacher standards—as a result of peer social support or as an indicator of compliance with oppositional peer norms (Bonney, 1947). However, teachers seem to be more sensitive to the classroom social relationships of students with low peer-given status than to their academic performance (Lippitt & Gold, 1959). The academic performance of high status students is more salient for teachers than is their participation in the classroom social structure. Apparently certain aspects of student conduct have much the same meaning for teachers as for fellow students.

Students' sex is an important variable affecting the association of their peer-given sociometric status and the teacher's interaction with them. In the Lippitt and Gold study, low status boys received teacher criticism while low status girls received support. Moreover, Meyer and Thompson (1956) have published evidence that boys generally receive more teacher criticism than girls, especially if the boys' conduct is stereotypically "masculine."

There also is evidence that academic performance and the utilization in performance of given levels of intellective ability are positively related to peer-accorded status, but as a function of students' more or less accurate perception of their sociometric rank. This is especially so for students of low status (Buswell, 1953; Schmuck, 1962). The flow of effect in these associations is not entirely clear; they may in part be artifactual, and there is some negative evidence (Sugimura, 1965). Nonetheless they suggest certain consequences of classroom sociometric structures for students' self-concepts and consequent intellective attainments.

How may these findings and our ideas about teachers' personal influence be related? Note that the findings are primarily from elementary-school classrooms and thus do not reflect much variation in the age- or curriculum-linked phenomena that I have reviewed. Moreover, conclusions from these findings have a very narrow empirical base. Still, one may speculate. The findings suggest that the teacher and peer support may not be functional alternatives. Students lacking peer approval or esteem will not always turn to teachers, or if they do, they may not receive what they seek, though "compensatory support" may occur in classrooms with strong teacher-student normative opposition or conflict.

But first, what of high status students? In nonoppositional classrooms these students may frequently enjoy both teacher and peer support; in fact the one may foster the other. If the teacher's approval does center on the students' academic performance, then to the extent that teacher approval is reciprocated by student respect, for the sociometric "stars" the teacher's influence will be strong but fairly narrowly centered on moral commitments having to do with the content taught. In point of fact, these conditions in the early grades could be highly favorable for the emergence of respect from more diffuse sentiments toward the teacher (especially since early in school a teacher's subject-matter competence is likely to appear secure in student eyes) and therefore for a parallel differentiation of students' moral commitments with respect to the content side of classroom activity.

Now, what of low status students? For low status girls the teacher may have sub-

stantial personal influence, but an influence that is based upon diffuse sentiments which are consequently of broad scope rather than upon respect. If the teacher is a woman, as is especially probable in elementary schools (and as was true of all teachers in the Meyer & Thompson [1956] study), she is likely to shape these students' moral commitments around "feminine" values and around affectively diffuse patterns of interpersonal response, with reinforcement of both deferent orientations, in school and out, and low academic achievement. For low status boys the classroom situation favors personal influence from neither teacher nor peers. Lacking teacher support, these students are less likely than high status boys to develop respect for the teacher, while there also is no basis for the maintenance of a positive diffuse sentimental tie. Indeed, continuing punishing sanctions by the teacher may lead via generalization into diffuse negative sentiments about teachers and thus to counterproductive effects of any of the teacher's efforts to "bring around" the attitudes and school and classroom conduct of these male students.

In point of fact, if student groups are fairly stable in a school (as in the assignment of student "batches" to successive classrooms), one might expect low status boys to develop subcultures in opposition to both teacher and broader peer norms. (Studies are clearly in order to examine systematically the covariation of the sex of students and teachers with phenomena such as these. I know of no example of such a study in the literature.)

In any event, the interpersonal classroom conduct of students appears to be more salient for teachers the lower the status of the student, whether male or female. Thus a high status pupil can misbehave, within limits, without endangering teacher approval since that approval has a more specific content-centered basis. This finding implies that the development of positive academic motives will occur especially among high status students, the result of teachers' personal influence as well as of the peer influence that more often has been analyzed. Indeed, these sources of influence should be complementary.

Although it seems to be commonsensical, this proposition rests on a very slender evidential base. But it suggests a still more tenuous proposition: that whatever the short-run mechanisms accounting for the correlation of sociometric status and intellective performance (among them presumably effects of status on pupils' morale and orientations to the school and its tasks) longer-run processes may include patterns of moral socialization to the academic role that are distinctive of the upper sociometric range of a student body. This socialization pattern should result in a self-concept well integrated with respect to intellective performance—a set of values, interests and aspirations that have been confirmed amply by the approval of both teachers and peers. It is interesting that Warren (1968), in a study of fourth-grade classes in a West German village, found evidence of under-utilization of pupils' intellective abilities associated with community norms that restrained teachers from providing for any student the sorts of support that the American sociometric findings indicate are forthcoming for high status pupils.

One might continue these speculations to consider the question of *streaming,* or ability grouping. Most of the published research on streaming, whatever its national setting, concludes that streaming has deleterious effects on the self-concepts and educational and occupational aspirations of students in lower ability streams, and thus tends to reduce their life chances, while heterogeneous ability groups appear to have little effect on the performance of the able and raise the performance of the less able—if there is any differential effect at all of varying mixtures of pupil ability (see, e.g., Ekstrom, 1961; Goldberg, 1966; B. Jackson, 1964; Lacey, 1966; Simon & Tyne, 1964; Svensson, 1962;

Thelen, 1963). These findings, by and large, rest on assumptions about the results on students' motives and conduct of interpersonal or intergroup comparison processes, of peer expectations and support, and of variations in teachers' expectations. These factors probably operate, but I think that it would also be interesting to consider how the teacher's personal influence may vary under different conditions of student grouping. (For ideas paralleling but more complex and systematic than those to follow, see Sørensen, 1970.) Indeed, I would guess that teacher expectations have their effect in part as a function of personal influence.

With ability grouping the bases of sociometric rank within classrooms are weakened as classroom groups become more alike internally in ability and its correlates (social class origins, etc.). Sociometric ranks may become more school-wide (as they do under the greater structural differentiation of the secondary school, cf. Coleman, 1961; Gordon, 1957). Teachers' expectations for pupil performance are likely to be fairly uniform for the classroom group, rather than cued by differential information about student ability, class performance or classroom conduct—factors that I suspect help to account for the correlation of classroom sociometric rank and teacher approval in the studies noted above. (Whatever the faults of the Rosenthal & Jacobson study, 1968, there is now more solid evidence that a teacher's expectations, his instructional procedures and learning outcomes are related and that expectations can center differentially on pupil groups as well as on individual students. See Beez, 1970.)

These factors should combine in high ability classrooms to foster teacher-student relations rather specific to intellective tasks (student respect reciprocated by content-centered teacher approval) and a supportive and solidary student classroom culture. If so, the teacher may become a potent agent socializing students to academic performance and reinforcing emerging student self-concepts centered on the academic side of the student role.

In low ability classrooms the teacher is less likely to become an object of respect, in part because of a tendency for him to use negative sanctions and in part because of the low salience for teacher and students of the content to be taught. Student sentiments toward the teacher should remain relatively diffuse, their sign depending largely on the degree to which low ability student groups are formed in the school around rebellious or oppositional peer norms. If the teacher does become a source of social support for his students, his resources are those of diffuse affect and he is not likely to have much influence on his students' academic motives. Nonetheless, he may be a powerful source of influence over other of their moral commitments (e.g., a "gentler of the masses" or perhaps a leader of "deviant" student groups within the school).

CONCEPTUAL ADDENDA

I should like to comment briefly on two aspects of teaching situations that are not directly pertinent to my topic because they have more to do with learning or with the relation between learning and the social organization of teaching situations than with the conduct of teaching per se. Nonetheless they must be introduced into any reasonably full analysis of the effects of teaching on learners' moral commitments. The first of these has to do with reference groups in teaching situations, the second with the teaching situation as something that may be called an activity structure.

Elements of the personal influence perspective on teaching clearly denote processes also involved in reference group phenomena, especially the functions of reference groups in setting moral standards and in sanctioning conduct or commitment in the light thereof (cf. Kemper, 1968; Merton, 1957, pp. 335–440). However, the applica-tion of reference group concepts to teaching situations is broader than is the application of the personal influence perspective. It includes, for example, processes of influence on moral commitments that may occur without either direct or mediated communication between persons: identification with role models and the vicarious, intrapersonal rehearsal of standard-setting and sanctioning by an actor who identifies but does not interact with a reference figure or group. It also points to the influence on students' commitments not only of individual teachers but of teacher groups—the effect, say, on a graduate student who identifies strongly with his department faculty and its collective level of commitment to the canons of scholarship.

These processes are potentially important in any analysis of the response of learners to teaching—either as processes complementary to or in conflict with teachers' personal influence or as conditions affecting this influence (e.g., the reinforcement of a teacher's personal influence by a learner's identification with teachers as a reference group).

The conception of teaching situations as activity structures derives especially from the work of Dreeben (1968) and is treated in Bidwell (1972). Its essence is that the pattern of daily activity in any social situation, including a teaching situation, can result directly in moral learning. This effect of activity structure occurs as the structure either exemplifies certain moral principles or gives moral meaning to the activities that it frames. (For a treatment of learning processes that may give rise to these effects, see Breer & Locke, 1965.)

If this conception gains support, at least under certain conditions (and there is as yet no evidence to bring to bear), it will mean that some effects of teaching situations may not be attributable to the teacher's influence even though one has controlled for alternative interpersonal influences (e.g., those of student peers). Instead, the characteristic social organization of the situation, in which both teacher and learner are involved, may have its own effects.

For example, let us suppose that learning science through laboratory work produces in students a commitment to the value of empirical investigation, while didactic teaching of science does not. Let us suppose further that science teachers more favorable to laboratory than to "blackboard" science are recruited or self-selected to science courses or departments as a function of emphasis on laboratory work in the curriculum. A study of the effects of the social organization of science teaching on students' commitments to the field could lead to erroneous conclusions about teachers' personal influence unless the effects of activity structure and teacher-student interaction were disentangled.

There is now a substantial body of findings apparently demonstrating that colleges or college fields of study have distinctive patterns of social organization, that they also have distinctive effects on students' values and aspirations, and that these effects can be attributed to interaction with teachers or peers (Astin, 1965; Bidwell & Vreeland, forthcoming; Brown, 1962; Thistlethwaite, 1959a, 1959b, 1960; Thistlethwaite & Wheeler, 1966). One wonders to what extent these observed effects are independent of the activity structures of the different colleges or fields of study.

It is also possible, of course, that the teacher's conduct is central to an activity structure, as in primary-school classrooms, in which case the study of activity structures may be largely the study of teaching, while other facets of the activity structure of the teaching situation are analyzed primarily as contextual properties that may set variable conditions to the teacher's personal influence. For example, Dreeben (1968, pp. 76–78) suggests that the age homogeneity of classrooms reinforces the universalistic quality of the teacher's sanctions and thereby helps students learn the norm of universalism. The teacher's activities are clearly central in this situation, and it might be

useful to study the moral learning of students in classrooms comparable in learning content, performance standards, and teachers' prescribed sanctioning practices, but in which students' sentimental ties to their teachers and the age homogeneity of the classroom are varied systematically.

Finally, teachers may deliberately construct activity structures, as they do when school curricula give teachers latitude to use alternative modes of instruction (e.g., projects, demonstrations and lectures in varying mixtures). I need only note that this is an example of a variety of teacher influences on students' moral commitments alternative to personal influence.

However, the effects of teachers' actions on activity structures need not be of this formal nature. Indeed, the daily conduct of the teacher in interaction with learners surely has important crescive consequences for the activity structure of the teaching situation. Here the teacher's personal influence may play a significant part as it alters the normative basis of interaction in the situation. I already have noted one example of such effects in the classrooms that Henry (1955) observed. To tease such effects out of the flow of events in teaching situations is not easy, for as traits of teachers affect students' sentiments toward them, activity structures are directly altered. Indeed, interaction, sentiment and influence are interdependent. But the student of teaching as personal influence must not err in assuming that classrooms are simple aggregations of dyads, cutting his concepts to fit problems of study design.

CONCLUSIONS

The personal influence perspective on teaching will be useful to the extent that it meets tests of logical soundness, economy and empirical validation. In the foregoing pages I have tried to show how from a few basic assumptions one can derive a number of testable propositions about teaching activities and teaching situations. Pertinent evidence with respect to these propositions is scanty, and I have centered on a limited range of teaching activities and effects—though I believe these activities to be central to any teaching situation. My aim has been advocacy—to foster applications of concepts of social psychology explicitly to teaching, believing that current preoccupation with student peer relations needs some correction, and to argue for one set of concepts that might be applied.

In testing the utility of the personal influence formulation of teaching (or any other), two strategies are available and both must be employed. One is to gather fresh evidence from studies specifically designed to verify its propositions. Here several tactics are in order: naturalistic observation (following the lead of Philip Jackson and others, but with a somewhat different set of observational categories), "natural experiments" (as may be provided, for example, by ventures in educational contracting and teacher accountability), and controlled experimentation in both natural and laboratory settings (well suited to the more micro-level focus of the personal influence perspective). I believe that survey research, for some time the methodological darling of American sociologists, will have limited use because it can tell us relatively little about interpersonal processes like those of personal influence.

The other strategy is the interpretation and integration of extant findings from various lines of research on teaching situations (e.g., on "classroom climates," on sociometric structures, on school and college "impact" or "outcomes," or on the ethnography of schools and classrooms). In this chapter I have suggested directions for such efforts from time to time, but I have not been able to pursue them. This will be a task of high importance.

Finally, the analysis of teaching from the personal influence perspective can have notable implications for educational policy. I can illustrate this by one example, the question of "equality" of educational provision

for the so-called "disadvantaged" social classes and ethnic minorities. Much sociological and social-psychological effort has been devoted to demonstrating imparities in access to education across elements of the populations of the United States and other modern nations (e.g., Douglas, 1964; Guthrie, Kleindorfer, Levin, & Stout, 1971; Pettigrew, 1964; Rogoff, 1961; Williams & Ryan, 1954), inequities in the measurement of academic ability and performance (e.g., A. Davis, 1948; Eells, Davis, Havighurst, Herrick, & Tyler, 1951; Haggard, 1954), and unequal exposure to interpersonal and organizational resources for education (e.g., Coleman, Campbell, Hobson, McPartland, Mood, Weinfeld, & York, 1966; Herriott & St. John, 1966; R. H. Turner, 1964, 1966).

Certain writers have argued or implied that the sources of these varieties of inequality are to be found more in social factors external to the school or in their penetration into the social organization of the school than in the school itself (e.g., Douglas, 1964; Havighurst & Davis, 1955; Hollingshead, 1949; Kahl, 1953; Kandel & Lesser, 1970; Maccoby & Gibbs, 1954; Sewell & Armer, 1966; Sewell, Haller, & Straus, 1957; Wilson, 1959, 1969).

Yet there is some evidence of a rising conviction that the school can become more active in reducing educational inequality—some people arguing for increasing access to current models of schooling or for refining such models (e.g., Guthrie et al., 1971), others for a reformulation of the social organization of schooling to provide a moral order within the school that will foster widespread integration of students of diverse background into the society (e.g., Janowitz, 1969).

To oversimplify, the arguments about equality of educational provision reflect au fond two quite different conceptions of equality: on the one hand, equality of access to provision for schooling (equality of opportunity), on the other, equality in gaining the outcomes or "goods" of schooling (if not actual parity of attainment at least equal chances to attain, unhindered by the constraints of social origins) once access to given types of schools or educational provision has been accomplished. Advocacy of equality of opportunity leads one away from concern with processes affecting education as these occur within educational settings. Belief that schools are relatively impotent in affecting students' motives or performance discourages concern with schools or teaching as instruments for reducing imparities of learning outcomes.

I believe that a view of teaching as personal influence indicates one set of processes of potential power to reduce differential chances for educational attainment that are linked to social origins. I have tried to show how certain social organizational conditions common to American schools make it difficult for teachers to become objects of student respect and sources of positive personal influence upon the formation of students' intellective values and attitudes. Moreover, I have tried to show that these conditions are characteristic especially of the experiences of students such as those of disadvantaged background.

That these conditions are so prevalent and may be so consistent in their bearing on students of varying social origin suggests one reason why schooling may be observed to have so little effect on students' motives and performance and why extraschool factors loom so large. Indeed, I have suggested that under these conditions respect for the teacher will characterize, and teacher support for students' intellective efforts center on, those pupils who in any event would do relatively well in school.

If one is convinced that educational equality demands more than equal access, then he may do well to explore in detail those conditions in the social organization of schools that will strengthen or weaken teaching as personal influence. He will not limit his attention, as some advocates of school reform are prone to do (cf. Coleman, 1966), to student peers as the only potent source of support for academic attainment.

In his emphasis on the moral order of the school and on the teacher as a leading figure in its formation, maintenance and communication, Janowitz (1969) points us in a promising direction. But I would add that we must know a good deal more than we do now about the interpersonal processes that make teaching and, for that matter, student peer relations, instruments of moral socialization if such efforts at school reform are to be at all successful.

REFERENCES

Abelson, R. P., et al. (Eds.) *Theories of cognitive consistency: A sourcebook*. Chicago: Rand McNally, 1968.

Alexander, C. N., Jr., & Campbell, E. Q. Peer influences on adolescent educational aspirations and attainments. *American Sociological Review*, 1964, 29, 568–575.

Anderson, H. E., Jr., White, W. F., & Wash, J. A. Generalized effects of praise and reproof. *Journal of Educational Psychology*, 1966, 57, 169–173.

Anderson, R. C. Learning in discussions: A résumé of the authoritarian-democratic studies. *Harvard Educational Review*, 1959, 29, 201–215.

Astin, A. W. Classroom environment in different fields of study. *Journal of Educational Psychology*, 1965, 56, 275–282.

Backman, C. W., & Secord, P. F. Liking, selective interaction, and misperception in congruent interpersonal relations. *Sociometry*, 1962, 25, 321–335.

Backman, C. W., & Secord, P. F. *A social psychological view of education*. New York: Harcourt, Brace & World, 1968.

Bany, M. A., & Johnson, L. V. *Classroom group behavior*. New York: Macmillan, 1964.

Barker, R. G. (Ed.) *The stream of behavior: Explorations of its structure and content*. New York: Appleton-Century-Crofts, 1963.

Barker, R. G., Gump, P. V., Friesen, W. V., & Williams, E. P. The ecological environment: Student participation in non-class settings. In M. Miles, & W. W. Charters (Eds.), *Learning in social settings*. Boston: Allyn & Bacon, 1970. Pp. 12–42.

Barnard, C. I. *The functions of the executive*. Cambridge: Harvard University Press, 1938.

Bavelas, A. Communication patterns in task-oriented groups. In D. Cartwright, & A. Zander (Eds.), *Group dynamics; Research and theory* (2nd ed.). Evanston, Ill.: Row, Peterson, 1960. Pp. 669–682.

Becker, H. S., et al. *Boys in white: Student culture in medical school.* Chicago: University of Chicago Press, 1961.

Beez, W. V. Influence of biased psychological reports on teacher behavior and pupil performance. In M. B. Miles, & W. W. Charters, Jr. (Eds.), *Learning in social settings.* Boston: Allyn & Bacon, 1970. Pp. 328–334.

Bellack, A. A. *The language of the classroom.* U.S.O.E., Cooperative Research Project No. 2023. New York: Columbia University Teachers College, Institute of Psychological Research, 1965.

Bidwell, C. E. The school as a formal organization. In J. G. March (Ed.), *Handbook of organizations.* Chicago: Rand McNally, 1965. Pp. 972–1022.

Bidwell, C. E. Schooling and socialization. *Interchange,* forthcoming.

Bidwell, C. E., & Vreeland, R. S. *College organization, social relations, and student change: A study of undergraduate socialization in Harvard College.* Chicago: University of Chicago Press, forthcoming.

Bonney, M. E. Sociometric study of agreement between teacher judgments and student choices: In regard to the number of friends possessed by high school students. *Sociometry,* 1947, 10, 133–146.

Boocock, S. S. Toward a sociology of learning: A selective review of existing research. *Sociology of Education,* 1966, 39, 1–45.

Boyle, R. P. The effect of the high school on students' aspirations. *American Journal of Sociology,* 1966, 71, 628–639.

Breer, P. E., & Locke, E. A. *Task experience as a source of attitudes.* Homewood, Ill.: Dorsey Press, 1965.

Bronfenbrenner, U. Soviet methods of character education: Some implications for research. *Religious Education,* 1962, 57, 545–561.

Brookover, W. K. The social roles of teachers and pupil achievement. *American Sociological Review,* 1943, 8, 389–393.

Brown, D. R. Personality, college environment, and academic productivity. In N. Sanford (Ed.), *The American college.* New York: John Wiley, 1962. Pp. 536–562.

Burton, W. H. *The guidance of learning activities.* (2nd ed.) New York: Appleton-Century-Crofts, 1952.

Buswell, M. M. The relationship between the social structure of the classroom and the academic success of the pupils. *Journal of Experimental Education,* 1953, 22, 37–52.

Callis, R. The efficiency of the Minnesota Teacher Attitude Inventory for predicting interpersonal relations in the classroom. *Journal of Applied Psychology,* 1953, 37, 82–85.

Cartwright, D., & Zander, A. Group cohesiveness; introduction. In D. Cartwright, & A. Zander (Eds.), *Group dynamics: Research and theory* (2nd ed.). Evanston, Ill.: Row, Peterson, 1960. Pp. 69–94.

Chappell, T. L., & Callis, R. The efficiency of the Minnesota Teacher Attitude Inventory for predicting interpersonal relations in a naval school. Columbia, Mo.: University of Missouri, Report No. 5, ONR 649(00), 1954.

Child, I. L. Socialization. In G. Lindzey (Ed.), *Handbook of social psychology.* Vol. 2. Cambridge, Mass.: Addison-Wesley, 1954. Pp. 655–692.

Coleman, J. S. Academic achievement and the structure of competition. *Harvard Educational Review,* 1959, 29, 330–351.

Coleman, J. S. *The adolescent society.* New York: Free Press, 1961.

Coleman, J. S., Campbell, E. Q., Hobson, C. J., McPartland, J., Mood, A. M., Weinfeld, F. D., & York, R. L. *Equality of educational opportunity.* Washington, D.C.: U.S. Government Printing Office, 1966.

Collins, B. E., & Raven, B. H. Group structure: Attraction, coalitions, communication, and power. In G. Lindzey, & E. Aronson (Eds.). *Handbook of social psychology* (2nd ed.), Vol. 4. Reading, Mass.: Addison-Wesley, 1969. Pp. 102–204.

Cook, W. W., Leeds, C. H., & Callis, R. *The Minnesota Teacher Attitude Inventory.* New York: Psychological Corp., 1951.

Davis, A. *Social class influences upon learning.* Cambridge, Mass.: Harvard University Press, 1948.

Davis, J. A. Structural balance, mechanical solidarity, and interpersonal relations. *American Journal of Sociology,* 1963, 68, 444–462.

Della Piana, G. M., & Gage, N. L. Pupils' values and the validity of the Minnesota Teacher Attitude Inventory. *Journal of Educational Psychology,* 1955, 46, 167–178.

Deutsch, M. The effects of cooperation and competition upon group process. In D. Cartwright, & A. Zander (Eds.), *Group dynamics: Research and theory.* (2nd ed.) Evanston, Ill.: Row, Peterson, 1960. Pp. 414–448.

DeVries, D. L., Muse, D., & Wells, E. H. The effects on students of working in cooperative groups: An exploratory study. Report No. 120. Baltimore: Johns Hopkins University, Center for Social Organization of Schools, 1971.

Domas, S. J., & Tiedeman, D. V. Teacher competence: An annotated bibliography. *Journal of Experimental Education,* 1950, 19, 101–218.

Douglas, J. W. B. *The home and the school.* London: MacGibbon & Kee, 1964.

Dreeben, R. *On what is learned in school.* Reading, Mass.: Addison-Wesley, 1968.

Dubin, R., & Taveggia, T. C. *The teaching-learning paradox: A comparative analysis of college teaching methods.* Eugene, Ore.: University of Oregon, Center for the Advanced Study of Educational Administration, 1968.

Durkheim, E. *The division of labor in society.* Glencoe, Ill.: Free Press, 1933.

Durkheim, E. *Moral education.* New York: Free Press, 1961.

Eells, K. W., Davis, A., Havighurst, R. J., Herrick, V. E., & Tyler, R. W. *Intelligence and cultural differences: A study of cultural learning and problem-solving.* Chicago: University of Chicago Press, 1951.

Ekstrom, R. B. Experimental studies of homogeneous grouping: A critical review. *School Review,* 1961, 69, 216–226.

Emerson, R. M. Power-dependence relations. *American Sociological Review,* 1962, 27, 31–41.

Feldman, K. A., & Newcomb, T. M. *The impact of college on students.* San Francisco: Jossey-Bass, 1969.

Festinger, L. *A theory of cognitive dissonance.* Evanston, Ill.: Row, Peterson, 1957.

Flanders, N. A. *Teacher influence, pupil attitudes, and achievement.* U.S. Office of Education, Cooperative Research Project No. 397. Minneapolis: University of Minnesota, 1960. ED 002 865.

Friedenberg, E. Z. *The vanishing adolescent.* Boston: Beacon Press, 1959.

Fuller, E. M. The use of teacher-pupil attitudes, self rating, and measures of general ability in the preservice selection of nursery school–kindergarten-primary teachers. *Journal of Educational Research,* 1951, 44, 675–686.

Gage, N. L., Runkel, P. J., & Chatterjee, B. B. Changing teacher behavior through feedback from pupils: An application of equilibrium theory. In W. W. Charters, Jr., & N. L. Gage (Eds.), *Readings in the social psychology of education.* Boston: Allyn & Bacon, 1963. Pp. 173–181.

Getzels, J. W. A social psychology of education. In G. Lindzey, & E. Aronson (Eds.), *The handbook of social psychology* (2nd ed.), Vol. 5. Reading, Mass.: Addison-Wesley, 1969. Pp. 459–537.

Getzels, J. W., & Jackson, P. W. *Creativity and intelligence.* New York: John Wiley, 1962.

Getzels, J. W., & Jackson, P. W. The teacher's personality and characteristics. In N. L. Gage (Ed.), *Handbook of research on teaching.* Chicago: Rand McNally, 1963. Pp. 506–582.

Getzels, J. W., & Thelen, H. A. The classroom group as a unique social system. In N. B. Henry (Ed.), *The dynamics of instructional groups.* Fifty-ninth Yearbook of the National Society for the Study of Education, Part II. Chicago: NSSE, 1960. Pp. 53–82.

Glidewell, J. C., Kantor, M. B., Smith, L. M., & Stringer, L. A. Socialization and social structure in the classroom. In M. L. Hoffman, & L. W. Hoffman (Eds.), *Review of child development research.* Vol. 2. New York: Russell Sage Foundation, 1966. Pp. 221–256.

Goffman, E. On the characteristics of total institutions. In E. Goffman, *Asylums.* Garden City, N.Y.: Doubleday 1961. Pp. 1–124.

Goldberg, M. L., Passow, A. H., & Justman, J. *The effects of ability grouping.* New York: Teachers College Press, 1966.

Gordon, C. W. *The social system of the high school.* Glencoe, Ill.: Free Press, 1957.

Gottlieb, D. Processes of socialization in American graduate schools. *Social Forces,* 1961, 40, 124–131.

Gough, H. C., & Pemberton, W. H. Personality characteristics related to success in practice teaching. *Journal of Applied Psychology,* 1952, 36, 307–309.

Gronlund, N. E. *Sociometry in the classroom.* New York: Harper & Brothers, 1959.

Guthrie, J. W., Kleindorfer, G. B., Levin, H. M., & Stout, R. T. *Schools and inequality.* Cambridge, Mass.: MIT Press, 1971.

Haggard, E. A. Social-status and intelligence: An experimental study of certain cultural determinants of measured intelligence. *Genetic Psychology Monographs,* 1954, 49, 141–186.

Hare, A. P. *Handbook of small group research.* New York: Free Press, 1962.

Hargreaves, D. H. *Social relations in a secondary school.* London: Routledge & Kegan Paul, 1967.

Harvey, O. J., Prather, M., White, B. J., & Hoffmeister, J. K. Teachers' beliefs, classroom atmosphere, and student behavior. *American Educational Research Journal,* 1968, 5, 151–166.

Havighurst, R. J., & Davis, A. A comparison of the Chicago and Harvard studies of social class differences in child rearing. *American Sociological Review,* 1955, 20, 438–442.

Hedlund, P. A. *Cooperative study to predict effectiveness in secondary school teaching: Third progress report.* Albany: University of the State of New York and State Education Department, 1953.

Heider, F. *The psychology of interpersonal relations.* New York: John Wiley, 1958.

Henry, J. Docility, on giving teacher what she wants. *Journal of Social Issues,* 1955, 11, 33–41.

Henry, J. Attitude organization in elementary school classrooms. *American Journal of Orthopsychiatry,* 1957, 27, 117–133.

Herriott, R. E., & St. John, N. H. *Social class and the urban school.* New York: John Wiley, 1966.

Hollingshead, A. *Elmtown's youth.* New York: John Wiley, 1949.

Homans, G. C. *Social behavior: Its elementary forms.* New York: Harcourt, Brace & World, 1961.

Hovland, C. I. Yale studies of communication and persuasion. In W. W. Charters, Jr., & N. L. Gage (Eds.), *Readings in the social psychology of education.* Boston: Allyn & Bacon, 1963. Pp. 239–253.

Hoyle, E. Organizational analysis in the field of education. *Educational Research,* 1965, 7, 97–113.

Hughes, E., Becker, H., & Geer, B. Student culture and academic effort. In N. Sanford (Ed.), *The American college.* New York: John Wiley, 1962. Pp. 515–530.

Hughes, M. M., & associates. *Assessment of the quality of teaching in elementary schools.* Salt Lake City: University of Utah Press, 1959.

Jackson, B. *Streaming: An education system in miniature.* London: Routledge & Kegan Paul, 1964.

Jackson, P. W. The conceptualization of teaching. *Psychology in the Schools,* 1964, 1, 232–243.

Jackson, P. W. *Life in classrooms.* New York: Holt, Rinehart & Winston, 1968.

Jackson, P. W., & Lahaderne, H. M. Inequalities of teacher-pupil contacts. *Psychology in the Schools,* 1967, 4, 201–211.

Janowitz, M. *Institution building in urban education.* New York: Russell Sage Foundation, 1969.

Jenkins, J. R., & Deno, S. L. Influence of student behavior on teachers' self-evaluation. *Journal of Educational Psychology,* 1969, 60, 439–442.

Johnson, T. J., Feigenbaum, R., & Weiby, M. Some determinants and consequences of the teacher's perception of causation. *Journal of Educational Psychology,* 1964, 55, 237–246.

Kahl, J. A. Educational and occupational aspirations of "common man" boys. *Harvard Educational Review,* 1953, 23, 186–203.

Kandel, D., & Lesser, G. S. Relative influences of parents and peers on the educational plans of adolescents in the United States and Denmark. In M. B. Miles, & W. W. Charters, Jr. (Eds.), *Learning in social settings.* Boston: Allyn & Bacon, 1970. Pp. 283–306.

Kemper, T. D. Reference groups, socialization and achievement. *American Sociological Review,* 1968, 33, 31–45.

Klugman, S. F. The effect of money incentives vs. praise upon the reliability and obtained scores of the Revised Stanford-Binet test. *Journal of General Psychology,* 1944, 255–269.

Kounin, J. S. An analysis of teachers' managerial techniques. *Psychology in the Schools,* 1967, 4, 221–227.

Kounin, J. S., Gump, P. V., & Ryan, J. J., III. Explorations in classroom management.

Journal of Teacher Education, 1961, 235–246.

Lacey, C. Some sociological concomitants of academic streaming in a grammar school. *British Journal of Sociology,* 1966, 17, 245–262.

Lambert, P., Goodwin, W. L., Roberts, R. F., & Wiersma, W. A comparison of pupil achievement in team and self-contained organizations. *Journal of Experimental Education,* 1965, 33, 217–224.

Lantz, D. L. Relationship between classroom emotional climate and concepts of self, others, and ideal among elementary student teachers. *Journal of Educational Research,* 1965, 59, 80–83.

Lavin, D. E. *The prediction of academic performance: A theoretical analysis and review of research.* New York: Russell Sage Foundation, 1965.

Leavitt, H. J. Some effects of certain communication patterns on group performance. *Journal of Abnormal and Social Psychology,* 1951, 46, 38–50.

Leeds, C. H. A second validity study of the Minnesota Teacher Attitude Inventory. *Elementary School Journal,* 1952, 52, 398–405.

Lewin, K., Lippitt, R., & White, R. K. Patterns of aggressive behavior in experimentally created "social climates." *Journal of Social Psychology,* 1939, 10, 271–299.

Lindzey, G., & Borgatta, E. F. Sociometric measurement. In G. Lindzey (Ed.), *Handbook of social psychology.* Vol. 1. Cambridge, Mass.: Addison-Wesley, 1954. Pp. 405–448.

Lippitt, R., & Gold, M. Classroom social structure as a mental health problem. *Journal of Social Issues,* 1959, 15(1), 40–49.

Lortie, D. C. The balance of control and autonomy in elementary school teaching. In A. Etzioni (Ed.), *The semi-professions and their organization.* New York: Free Press, 1969. Pp. 1–53.

Maccoby, E. E., & Gibbs, P. K. Methods of child-rearing in two social classes. In W. E. Martin, & C. B. Stendler (Eds.), *Readings in child development.* New York: Harcourt, Brace, 1954. Pp. 380–396.

McDill, E. L., Rigsby, L. C., & Meyers, E. D., Jr. Educational climates of high schools: Their effects and sources. *American Journal of Sociology,* 1969, 74, 567–586.

McKeachie, W. J. Research on teaching at the college and university level. In N. L. Gage (Ed.), *Handbook of research on teaching.* Chicago: Rand McNally, 1963. Pp. 1118–1172.

McKeachie, W. J., Lin, Y., Milholland, J., & Isaacson, R. Student affiliation motive, teacher warmth, and academic achievement. *Journal of Personality and Social Psychology,* 1966, 4, 457–461.

Medley, D. M., & Mitzel, H. E. Measuring classroom behavior by systematic observation. In N. L. Gage (Ed.), *Handbook of research on teaching.* Chicago: Rand McNally, 1963. Pp. 247–328.

Merton, R. K. *Social theory and social structure.* (Rev. ed.) Glencoe, Ill.: Free Press, 1957.

Meyer, W. J., & Thompson, G. G. Sex differences in the distribution of teacher approval and disapproval among sixth-grade children. *Journal of Educational Psychology,* 1956, 47, 385–396.

Michaelis, J. U. The prediction of success in student teaching from personality and attitude inventories. *University of California Publications in Education,* 1954, 11, 415–481.

Miles, M. B. The T-group and the classroom. In L. P. Bradford, J. R. Gibb, & K. D. Benne (Eds.), *T-group theory and laboratory method.* New York: John Wiley, 1964. Pp. 452–476.

Miles, M. B., & Charters, W. W., Jr. *Learning in social settings.* Boston: Allyn & Bacon, 1970.

Moreno, J. L. *Who shall survive? A new approach to the problem of human interrelations.* Washington, D.C.: Nervous and Mental Disease Publishing Co., 1934.

Morsh, J. E., & Wilder, E. W. Identifying the effective instructor: A review of the quantitative studies, 1900–1952. USAF Personnel Training Research Center, Research Bulletin No. AFPTRC-RE-54-44, 1954.

Mursell, J. L. *Successful teaching: Its psychological principles.* (2nd ed.) New York: McGraw-Hill, 1954.

Newcomb, T. M. *Personality and social change.* New York: Dryden Press, 1943.

Newcomb, T. M. *The acquaintance process.* New York: Holt, Rinehart & Winston, 1961.

Oelke, M. C. A study of student teachers' attitudes toward children. *Journal of Educational Psychology*, 1956, 47, 193–198.

Ohlsen, M. M., & Schulz, R. E. Projective test response patterns for best and poorest student-teachers. *Educational and Psychological Measurement*, 1955, 15, 18–27.

Ojemann, R. H., & Wilkinson, F. R. The effect on pupil growth of an increase in teacher's understanding of pupil behavior. *Journal of Experimental Education*, 1939, 8, 143–147.

Pace, C. R. Differences in campus atmosphere. In W. W. Charters, Jr., & N. L. Gage (Eds.), *Readings in the social psychology of education*. Boston: Allyn & Bacon, 1963. Pp. 73–79.

Parsons, T. The school class as a social system: Some of its functions in American society. *Harvard Educational Review*, 1959, 29, 297–318.

Pettigrew, T. F. *A profile of the Negro American*. Princeton: Van Nostrand, 1964.

Polansky, L. Group social climate and the teacher's supportiveness of group status systems. *Journal of Educational Sociology*, 1954, 28, 115–123.

Remmers, H. H. Rating methods in research on teaching. In N. L. Gage (Ed.), *Handbook of research on teaching*. Chicago: Rand McNally, 1963. Pp. 329–378.

Rhea, B. Institutional paternalism in high school. *Urban Review*, 1968, 2(4), 13–15, 34.

Riesman, D., Gusfield, J., & Gamson, Z. *Academic values and mass education*. Garden City, N.Y.: Doubleday, 1970.

Roethlisberger, F. J., & Dickson, W. J. *Management and the worker*. Cambridge: Harvard University Press, 1939.

Rogoff, N. Local social structure and educational selection. In A. H. Halsey, J. Floud, & C. A. Anderson (Eds.), *Education, economy, and society: A reader in the sociology of education*. New York: Free Press, 1961. Pp. 241–251.

Rosenberg, M. J., et al. *Attitude organization and change: An analysis of consistency among attitude components*. New Haven, Conn.: Yale University Press, 1960.

Rosenthal, R., & Jacobson, L. *Pygmalion in the classroom: Teacher expectations and pupils' intellectual development*. New York: Holt, Rinehart & Winston, 1968.

Ryans, D. G. *Characteristics of teachers, their description, comparison, and appraisal*. Washington, D.C.: American Council on Education, 1960.

Sandgren, D. L., & Schmidt, L. G. Does practice teaching change attitudes toward teaching? *Journal of Educational Research*, 1956, 49, 673–680.

Schmid, J., Jr. Factor analyses of prospective teachers' differences. *Journal of Experimental Education*, 1950, 18, 287–319.

Schmuck, R. Sociometric status and utilization of academic abilities. *Merrill-Palmer Quarterly*, 1962, 8, 165–172.

Schmuck, R. Some aspects of classroom social climate. *Psychology in the Schools*, 1966, 3, 59–65.

Scott, J. F. *Internalization of norms: A sociological theory of moral commitment*. Englewood Cliffs, N.J.: Prentice-Hall, 1971.

Sewell, W. H., & Armer, J. M. Neighborhood context and college plans. *American Sociological Review*, 1966, 31, 159–168.

Sewell, W. H., Haller, A. O., & Straus, M. A. Social status and educational and occupational aspiration. *American Sociological Review*, 1957, 22, 67–73.

Shaplin, J. T. Toward a theoretical rationale for team teaching. In J. T. Shaplin, & H. F. Olds, Jr. (Eds.), *Team teaching*. New York: Harper & Row, 1964. Pp. 57–98.

Sheldon, M. S., Coale, J. M., & Copple, R. Concurrent validity of the "warm teacher scales." *Journal of Educational Psychology*, 1959, 50, 37–40.

Short, J. F., Jr. Aggressive behavior in response to status threats. Paper presented at the meeting of the American Sociological Association, New York, August 1960.

Simon, B., & Tyne, A. (Eds.) *Non-streaming in the junior school*. London: P.S.W. Publications, 1964.

Slater, P. E. On social regression. *American Sociological Review*, 1963, 28, 339–364.

Smith, B. O. *A study of the logic of teaching*. U.S.O.E., Project No. 258–7257. Urbana, Ill.: University of Illinois, College of Education, Bureau of Educational Research, n.d. ED 015 164.

Smith, L. M., & Hudgins, B. B. Correlates of classroom functioning. *Genetic Psychological Monographs*, 1966, 74, 215–260.

Sørensen, A. B. Organizational differentiation of students and educational opportunity. *Sociology of Education,* 1970, 43, 355–376.

Stern, G. G. Environments for learning. In N. Sanford (Ed.), *The American college.* New York: John Wiley, 1962. Pp. 690–730.

Stern, G. G., & Pace, C. R. *College characteristics index.* Syracuse, N.Y.: Syracuse University, Psychological Research Center, 1958.

Stinchcombe, A. L. *Rebellion in a high school.* Chicago: Quadrangle Books, 1964.

Street, D., et al. *Organization for treatment.* New York: Free Press, 1966.

Sugarman, B. Moral education and the social structure of the school. *Journal of Curriculum Studies,* 1968, 1, 47–67.

Sugimura, T. Implicit reinforcement in the classroom as a function of grade and sociometric status. *Japanese Psychological Research,* 1965, 7, 166–170.

Svensson, N. E. *Ability grouping and scholastic achievement.* Stockholm: Almqvist & Wiksell, 1962.

Thelen, H. A. Group dynamics in instruction: Principle of least group size. *School Review,* 1949, 57, 139–148.

Thelen, H. A. Educational dynamics: Theory and research. *Journal of Social Issues,* 1950, 6(2), 2–95.

Thelen, H. A. (Ed.) Experimental research toward a theory of instruction. *Journal of Educational Research,* 1951, 45, 89–136.

Thelen, H. A. Grouping for teachability. *Theory into Practice,* 1963, 2, 81–89.

Thistlethwaite, D. L. College environments and the development of talent. *Science,* 1959, 130, 71–76. (a)

Thistlethwaite, D. L. College press and student achievement. *Journal of Educational Psychology,* 1959, 50, 183–191. (b)

Thistlethwaite, D. L. College press and changes in study plans of talented students. *Journal of Educational Psychology,* 1960, 51, 222–234.

Thistlethwaite, D. L., & Wheeler, N. Effects of teacher and peer subcultures upon student aspirations. *Journal of Educational Psychology,* 1966, 57, 35–47.

Thomas, D. R., Becker, W. C., & Armstrong, M. Production and elimination of disruptive classroom behavior by systematically varying teachers' behavior. *Journal of Applied Behavior Analysis,* 1968, 1, 35–45.

Thomas, W. I. *The unadjusted girl.* Boston: Little, Brown, 1928.

Turner, R. H. *The social context of ambition.* San Francisco: Chandler, 1964.

Turner, R. H. On neighborhood context and college plans (1). *American Sociological Review,* 1966, 31, 698–702.

Turner, R. L. The acquisition of teaching skills in elementary school settings. *Indiana University School of Education Bulletin,* 1965, 41, No. 1. (a)

Turner, R. L. Characteristics of beginning teachers: Their differential linkage with school-system types. *School Review,* 1965, 73, 48–58. (b)

Tyler, F. T. The prediction of student-teaching success from personality inventories. *University of California Publications in Education,* 1954, 11, 233–314.

Wallace, W. L. *Student culture.* Chicago: Aldine, 1966.

Wallen, N. E., & Travers, R. M. W. Analysis and investigation of teaching methods. In N. L. Gage (Ed.), *Handbook of research on teaching.* Chicago: Rand McNally, 1963. Pp. 448–505.

Waller, W. W. *The sociology of teaching.* New York: John Wiley, 1932. (Republished: New York, John Wiley, 1965.)

Warren, R. L. Some determinants of the teacher's role in influencing educational aspirations: A cross-cultural perspective. *Sociology of Education,* 1968, 41, 291–304.

Washburne, C., & Heil, L. M. What characteristics of teachers affect children's growth? *School Review,* 1960, 68, 420–428.

Weber, M. *From Max Weber: Essays in sociology.* (Translated, edited, and with an introduction by H. H. Gerth, & C. W. Mills) New York: Oxford University Press, 1946.

White, W. F. *Psychosocial principles applied to classroom teaching.* New York: McGraw-Hill, 1969.

Williams, R. M., Jr., & Ryan, M. W. (Eds.) *Schools in transition: Community experiences in desegregation.* Chapel Hill, N.C.: University of North Carolina Press, 1954.

Wilson, A. B. Residential segregation of social classes and aspirations of high school boys. *American Sociological Review,* 1959, 24, 836–845.

Wilson, A. B. *The consequences of segregation.* Berkeley: Glendessary Press, 1969.

Wispe, L. G. Evaluating section teaching methods in the introductory course. *Journal of Educational Research,* 1951, 45, 161–186.

Withall, J. The development of a technique for the measurement of social-emotional climate in classrooms. *Journal of Experimental Education,* 1949, 17, 347–361.

Withall, J., & Lewis, W. W. Social interaction in the classroom. In N. L. Gage (Ed.), *Handbook of research on teaching.* Chicago: Rand McNally, 1963. Pp. 683–714.

Wright, E. M. J., & Proctor, V. H. *Systematic observation of verbal interaction as a method of comparing mathematics lessons.* U.S.O.E., Cooperative Research Project No. 816. St. Louis, Mo.: Washington University, 1961.

Znaniecki, F. *Social actions.* New York: Farrar, 1936.

CHAPTER **14**   The School as a Workplace[1]

ROBERT DREEBEN
University of Chicago

The word *workplace* usually conjures up images of factories and craftsmen's shops, places where men mix with tools and things, manufacture products, and perspire. Schools are something else; even though children make noise, dirt and trouble, they are bound up with teachers in activities that are largely mental, bookish and abstract. The point is not to argue that schools are factories and shops after all, but rather that the analysis of social patterns advances more productively when ostensibly different phenomena are shown to be comprehensible in terms of a small set of theoretical propositions. To succeed in such abstract theorizing, of course, is any scientist's dream, and one seldom realized in the social sciences. Usually, however, we settle for less and find pleasure in showing that diverse patterns can at least be arrayed along a few dimensions. That is one reason to consider schools as workplaces: to show that there are concepts and perspectives derived from other areas of the world of work that, when

applied to the schools, make them more understandable.

Schools are organizations (as are other kinds of workplaces), which means that they are settings where a variety of occupations are brought together to create some product or provide some service. Organizations also contain work sites, places where particular activities, comprising some process of production, are carried out. Examples of sites are familiar: assembly lines in factories, wards and operating rooms in hospitals, classrooms in schools. In short, by considering certain structural properties of schools and classrooms, it becomes possible to understand the nature of educational work.

But why should one become preoccupied with theoretical notions about social patterns in the first place, and particularly with those pertaining to educational workplaces? The answer is straightforward; it is probably not possible to discover how teaching activities and the classroom experiences of children contribute to what pupils learn in schools (and in other settings) unless we can identify how different teaching activities in different settings create opportunities for and constraints upon learning. In plainer

[1] I wish to thank Mary Sullivan and Donald Soltz for their extremely helpful contributions to the writing of this chapter.

language, the study of workplaces can contribute to our knowledge about what is possible and how things work in schools.

This formulation is so obvious that one can properly ask, why bother with it? But perhaps some recent history (which also happens to be a replay of much ancient history) speaks to this point. *Informal education* and concern with *open classrooms* have burst upon the school scene, the subject of books, magazine articles, panegyrics —even invective has started to flow; schools of education and inspired advocates are already showing others "how to do it." Although informal education has yet to be defined with much clarity, most proponents claim that it entails the flexible use of space, setting children to tasks that interest them and that they can pursue at their own pace while relying on their own motivation (Silberman, 1970). But no one has yet addressed the question of whether these elements have some connection (except that they all sound like good, benign ideas), whether the combination becomes self-limiting under certain conditions, whether the scheme works (and under what conditions), in short, whether some outcomes become possible with this set of arrangements (not possible with others) or whether certain outcomes are easier or less costly to effect than with other arrangements.

As one might expect, a controversy over whether informal education is the same as, similar to, continuous with, or different from progressive education has already arisen. No convincing answer has come yet (nor is it likely to) because no one has known what progressive education is, either. For reasons not altogether clear, the history of education has consisted of a succession of programmatic efforts whose viability has usually been defended through appeals to plausibility, kindness, common sense, the eradication of existing evil, and one or another ideological principle; in short, everything but reasonably firm evidence that if teachers and parents do such-and-such, and if children are engaged in certain activities

in certain kinds of settings, then certain known results are likely to ensue. Educational thinking, unfortunately, does not seem to proceed along these lines; but during times when public questioning of the efficacy of the schools has become widespread, it seems not unreasonable to find out, not just assert, what teachers should do and how schools should be built if they are to become more effective or, if not more effective, if children are to become happier learning at prevailing rates and under existing conditions. It is toward this end that the consideration of schools as workplaces gains some justification.

This paper treats the school as a workplace from two perspectives: from the point of view of authority relationships in schools and school systems, and from the point of view of the spatial arrangement of classrooms (work sites). The central theme is that relationships of authority and arrangements of space shape the character of teachers' work activities. There is no attempt here to argue that these are the sole influences on work activities, only that they are central and crucial. The occupational characteristics of teachers (Dreeben, 1970a), for example, undoubtedly influence the nature of teachers' work as does the nature of curriculum materials (Bruner, 1966) and the aggregate social characteristics of pupils. But these topics are beyond the scope of the present effort.

EXTERNAL ENVIRONMENT OF SCHOOLS

In a strict sense the central administration of a school system represents the immediate external environment of schools within the system: the hierarchy of general policymakers and supervisors extending between the levels of system superintendent and school principal. Fundamental decisions about the allocation of the budget, hiring policies, building plans, negotiations with a variety of trade unions (including those of teachers), contractual arrangements with suppliers, political relationships with the relevant units of municipal, state and federal government, codes governing internal operations, relationships with organized and unorganized community groups, and general educational policy making all fall within the jurisdiction of the system-wide administration. Except in the smallest school systems, members of the top administrative echelon have little *direct* contact with teachers and little *direct* influence on the style and content of their daily work activities. School system administrators, like the managers of other kinds of large-scale organizations, in other words, concern themselves primarily with matters pertaining to the acquisition of resources, their internal allocation, and the setting of general lines of policy, but not with the day-to-day direction of the activities of workers (Parsons, 1963, pp. 59–96).

That the conduct of central office administrators does not directly influence the daily activities of teachers does not mean that administrative action has no effect on their work; quite the contrary is true. To the extent, for example, that significant portions of the budget are allocated to hiring more teachers to reduce class size, for providing special ancillary services, for modernizing buildings, and the like, the teachers' working conditions can be made more palatable. Similarly indirect is the nature of the relationships that school administrations strike with organized parents and political groups (Rogers, 1968) whose support, indifference or hostility can determine whether particular schools will be viable or strife-torn institutions: whether teaching and learning activities can occur, or whether chaos and hostility will prevail.

It is only in a narrow range of areas—not trivial ones by any means—that the direct impact of administrative action can be traced in the work of teachers: in matters pertaining to remuneration, to the selection and purchase of books and materials, to the assignment of pupils to classrooms and to the inclusion of particular courses in the curriculum. (This, of course, is an illustrative, not an exhaustive, list.)

That school systems are bureaucratically organized in many respects (Weber, 1947, pp. 329–333) is unmistakable; but it would be a gross distortion to regard school systems (and particularly schools) as bureaucratic in the same way, for example, that certain government agencies, certain parts of the military, and certain commercial and industrial organizations in which workers are ranked hierarchically to facilitate the "rational" accomplishment of routine and repetitive tasks for the production of tangible, measurable goods and services are considered bureaucratic. Certainly schools and school systems are bureaucratically organized in many important respects: they are hierarchical and governed by rules; workers are appointed to "offices" (or positions) according to criteria of merit, and the sequence of positions that workers occupy can constitute a career (actually several different careers). But the work of teachers can be properly understood only if the nonbureaucratic elements of schools are also identified. Among the most important of these nonbureaucratic elements is the teacher's immediate work site—the classroom, a setting subject to administrative direction (at least within the school hierarchy and under the authority of the principal) and yet significantly independent of such direction (Bidwell, 1965, pp. 1014–1016).

The term *nonbureaucratic* is residual and therefore cannot as such denote specific aspects of the external environment having consequences for the work of teachers. Accordingly, it is important to identify some of those aspects. First, the school system hierarchy does not serve as a direct transmission line for the communication of policy decisions designed to influence teachers' classroom activities or for the close supervision of those activities to gauge the accomplishment of school system goals, even though a school system can be viewed as an arrangement of hierarchical positions.

This is not to deny that some policy decisions pass down the line, nor to deny that supervision occurs. Rather, the statement indicates that the central *classroom* activities of teachers—instruction and classroom management—are not *primarily* determined by high level policy decisions; they cannot be viewed as "following orders," and the reasons are not hard to find. The educational goals of school systems tend to be vaguely defined and refer to present and future outcomes that defy easy measurement and specification into readily identifiable goal-directed activities. Much of the teacher's work, in short, derives its character from the exigencies of classroom, school and community events (Jackson, 1968), not from administrative directives.

Second, teaching activities tend not to be defined in terms of conformity to system-wide rules (though clearly certain types of teacher conduct have their origins in rules, e.g., taking attendance, monitoring students in public gatherings and the like). The reasons for the relative absence of rule domination are similar to those described above: activities difficult to codify in terms of sequences of means and ends are also difficult to subsume under general rules. That is, where work situations contain many unknowns and unpredictable exigencies, and where work entails significant loyalties to the needs of clients, work activities will be governed to a substantial degree according to the judgment of workers under the constraints of immediate situational demands (Gouldner, 1954, pp. 105–180; Perrow, 1970, pp. 75–89; Stinchcombe, 1959).

Third, the "quality control" function, to use a term with industrial overtones, tends to be highly attenuated in school systems. If, in fact, it is difficult to define educational goals and to design a "technology" to effect them, then the meaning of the supervisory rating of workers becomes difficult to interpret and not terribly instructive as far as the overall management of a school system is concerned. Thus, although the rhetoric of supervision has great currency in the vocabulary of school administrators, the practice of supervision and the definition of what it entails continue to be ill defined (Dreeben, 1970a, pp. 42–50). In sum, the facts that the administrative hierarchy does not serve primarily as a "line" for transmitting and effecting policy decisions, the relative unimportance of administrative rules for the classroom activities of teachers, and the attenuated nature of supervision constitute the more important non-bureaucratic elements that affect teaching.

One should not conclude from these assertions that teachers are essentially autonomous workers whose dealings with administrators are minimal and whose work is largely free of the conflicts usually engendered by hierarchical arrangements. Conflicts between teachers and administrators are legion and arise over such issues as the participation of teachers in the governance of schools and school systems, academic freedom, disciplinary policies, teacher ratings, closeness of supervision, red tape, the assignment of pupils and many more (Corwin, 1970, pp. 105–171). While the fact remains that the character of teachers' work in the classroom is not mainly determined through a bureaucratic apparatus, conflicts with the administration develop to a large extent from the ambiguous position of teaching as an occupation—it is not an autonomous profession nor is it a bureaucratized occupation; the prevailing conflicts frequently develop between the vaguely defined jurisdictional lines separating teachers and administrators.

The administrative hierarchy of a school system is not the totality of the teacher's external environment. It is perfectly obvious that in the American educational system, whose primary political units are states, municipalities, and other local units of government, the characteristics of communities and the problems they engender are likely to affect the work of teachers directly. Moreover, the recent growth of teachers' unions and the continuing activity of the National

Education Association (NEA) more than likely influence teachers' work activities. The difficulty with the general proposition that the characteristics of the surrounding environment affect the work of teachers is that very little systematic knowledge is available about the nature of community influence. Suggestive, though hardly systematic, evidence exists that some teachers have difficulty managing the disciplinary problems that arise in schools serving working class populations (Becker, 1952), though comparatively less has been said about disciplinary problems in middle-class schools. More important for this discussion, however, is the fact that classroom difficulties that supposedly originate in communities have been studied more in terms of teacher job satisfaction and propensity to transfer than in terms of work activities designed to cope with classroom problems. An important exception to this statement, however, is Kounin's work on disciplinary strategies (Kounin, 1970).

In recent years a great deal has been written, much of it in the public prints, union newspapers, and in books about education directed toward popular audiences, illustrating the problems posed by children from disadvantaged backgrounds and the frustrations experienced by the teachers of these children; but we are not yet able to disentangle the relative contributions of the children, the teachers, and the process of schooling itself to the creation of these problems nor to the ways in which teachers cope with them. In fact, strategies for coping with classroom problems have yet to be characterized in terms of general formulations of teachers' work.

The advent of teachers' unions (accompanied somewhat later and more slowly by the increasingly aggressive and militant action of the NEA) has led to changes in the economic circumstances of teachers and in their working conditions: the reduction of class size, the introduction of paraprofessionals, the release of teachers from onerous clerical obligations, and the introduction of grievance procedures have been some of the main areas of concern. And though it is not too much to surmise that the lot of teachers has improved—particularly economically—it is not yet possible to ascertain what impact these changes have had on the *character* of teachers' work: whether reductions in class size, for example, are related to changes in instructional and disciplinary strategies, to the reduction or change of characteristic classroom problems, to changes in work satisfaction; whether the introduction of paraprofessionals has in fact relieved teachers from tasks readily assumed by less skilled workers (and to what effect); or whether new patterns of classroom conduct have appeared among teachers and pupils with more than one adult present in classrooms at the same time.

The study of the impact of the external environment, both within school systems and from the external community on the work of teachers, has barely begun. The literature, to the extent that one exists, consists mainly of journalistic and popular accounts and a few scholarly studies that deal with a variety of events and phenomena that one would suppose are related. But for the most part, the work of teachers has remained unconceptualized as have those aspects of the environment that may in fact be related to the character of the work.

Issues pertaining to the relationship between the school's environment and the work of teachers are too numerous to catalogue here with any completeness; but to pose questions about schools that place the issues in the context of sociological inquiry pertaining to other kinds of organizations will at least open the agenda. Since schools are, in a sense, public utilities and not allowed to "go under" like many private organizations, by what means is the legitimacy of their services maintained, particularly in the light of evidence indicating that the effects of teaching activities cannot be clearly demonstrated? Certainly there are public reactions to the nature and quality of school services, but do these reactions take the form of "feedback" that in turn modifies the conduct of teachers? If so, by what means? and if not, why not? There is at least circumstantial evidence that many of these reactions take rhetorical, ideological and political forms; why these forms rather than direct feedback?

In recent years there has been much discussion about nonschool competitors to the public schools (Illich, 1971), alternative public schools (e.g., under voucher or accountability plans) and so-called "free schools." How likely is it that the character of public school teaching will change in response to the availability of alternatives, and how likely is it that teaching under the alternative plans will eventually come to resemble that prevailing in the public schools?

Do commitments made to outside organizations (e.g., unions, suppliers such as publishers, community groups, builders) affect the nature of teachers' work—what they are able to do and not do—and if so, in what ways? Does the social (i.e., racial, ethnic, religious, social class) composition of school districts affect the nature of teachers' work?

Schools, like other organizations, shield their workers from the impact of "intruding" events such as the introduction of educational "hardware" (Oettinger, 1969), the effects of changing rates of neighborhood in- and out-migration, political interference, school consolidations, changes in the market for teachers, the introduction of paraprofessionals and the like. By what means do schools cope with these changes, do they tend to maintain the *status quo ante,* and how do they guard against highly disruptive consequences? It is not suggested that all schools react the same way to changes that potentially affect the character of the teachers' working situation, but surely it is worth knowing the conditions under

which schools anticipate changes, plan in advance, coopt, react chaotically, and so on through the list of mechanisms by which organizations cope with the external environment and changes in it (Perrow, 1970; Rosenthal, 1969; Selznick, 1949, 1957; Thompson, 1967).

In sum, though everyday observation indicates that forces in the external environment, both in the school system and in the community, affect the work of teachers, neither these observations nor the existing research tells us *how* the environment affects their work. The situation is paradoxical. One can make a strong case, on the one hand, arguing that as public institutions the schools are highly vulnerable to many kinds of pressures originating in the external environment—to change the content of the curriculum, to introduce new hardware, to broaden the base of teacher recruitment, to change district boundaries, etc. On the other hand, schools appear to be among the most conservative and unbending of institutions, maintaining traditional ways of doing things in the face of intense pressures to change. Both contentions have important elements of truth, but no one can yet identify the conditions under which they are true.

THE STRUCTURE OF SCHOOLS

It is possible to make a reasonably convincing but weakly documented case that the public schools do not work very well; that is to say, *by virtue of their exposure to schooling,* children on the average do not show marked changes in those social and psychological capacities that schools are intended to influence. Consider the following kinds of supporting evidence. Over the past 10 years (at least) there has been mounting public criticism, by groups living in both socially disadvantaged and privileged circumstances, that children are learning very little in school. A number of investigators, in fact, have attempted to demonstrate empirically the chain of events linking socially disadvantaged conditions to low scores on tests measuring school-related abilities to poor school performance (Whiteman & Deutsch, 1968). Reviews of the literature on teacher effectiveness (Stephens, 1967) indicate low or equivocal relationships between a variety of teaching methods and educational outcomes. Surveys of reading test scores (by schools) published from time to time in major cities show substantial numbers of children, particularly in poor and ghetto areas, reading well below national grade-level standards. And, according to one massive survey of American schools (Coleman et al., 1966), the amount of variance in verbal learning accounted for by school and teacher characteristics, alone and in combination, does not reach very impressive levels (Bureau of Educational Personnel Development, 1970). (Keep in mind, however, that there has never been a large-scale longitudinal study that followed cohorts of children through school for at least several years to test propositions about the efficacy of schools rigorously.)

Compiling available evidence in this way does not make an overwhelming case; at the same time, evidence documenting the contrary argument, that schools have a substantial and positive educational impact, is difficult if not impossible to obtain. For the student of organizational structure, the inconclusiveness of evidence about the impact of an organization presents difficulties in understanding its structure. Presumably the structure of an organization has something to do with the nature, quantity and quality of its output; but if it is difficult to ascertain whether the schools in fact produce little or whether they actually produce a great deal that we are unable to measure, then it is not altogether clear what questions should be asked about structure.

If in fact the inconclusiveness of evidence is simply a function of the inability to measure or of the failure to undertake appropriately designed studies, then the examination of structure is largely a matter of taste. All questions are equally valid until the nature of what schools do is more definitively known. It is possible, of course, that schools have no (or negligible) *independent* effects on pupils, and that the only effects they do have appear when schools are considered in combination with other agencies. For the purposes of this paper, this possibility leads to a consideration of a variety of agencies producing joint effects, and this matter leads too far afield.

At least two assumptions about schools and schooling, however, justify asking less arbitrary questions about organizational structure. First, it is possible that schools resemble other organizations like mental hospitals, psychiatric social work agencies and churches (whose efficacy also remains in doubt), all of which are dedicated to changing or influencing complex and variegated patterns of human conduct. This assumption leads to considering the characteristics of "clients" and of the problems they present, and of the occupational resources—the technology—that workers bring to their jobs. It may be that none of these "people-changing" organizations has a viable technology for accomplishing its goals, or that any available technology, even if it is otherwise viable, cannot succeed in a large organizational setting.

Second, one can view schools in terms of structural "responses" to the problem of managing the lives of large numbers of children gathered in confined spaces for long-term instruction. This assumption leads to a consideration of ecological and architectural arrangements.

In any event, and whatever the assumptions, it is necessary to consider the nature of authority relationships in schools because they are hierarchical organizations and because managerial decisions at the minimum put constraints on teachers' work even if those decisions do not define its character. (Questions of architecture and ecology will be discussed later.)

RELATIONSHIPS OF AUTHORITY

The Affiliation of Teachers and Pupils

The manner in which workers are *attached* to an organization and the way others *with whom they have contact* are attached have important consequences for the conduct of workers. The reasons are clear: affiliation determines the nature and level of a worker's placement in the hierarchy and influences the availability of incentives and the nature of contacts between persons in different locations (Barnard, 1938, pp. 139–160). Teachers are affiliated with schools by hiring; hardly an earthshaking revelation, but nevertheless a problematic one. Not all workers associated with organizations are hired—doctors have hospital privileges and lawyers form partnerships, as do architects. Pupils, moreover, are affiliated to schools by conscription (Dreeben, 1970a, pp. 54–57). The variety of affiliative modes suggests that organization members face different constraints and opportunities in their working situations.

Being hired as a salaried employee means that one consents by contract to perform certain agreed upon activities, to accept subordination to hierarchical superiors in exchange for remuneration, and to follow the rules. It means that within agreed upon limits one is subject to the direction of others in the conduct of one's work according to rules binding on oneself and on one's superordinates. (Under arrangements like privilege and partnership, the element of subordination to hierarchical superiors is markedly less, hence the difference in opportunities and constraints.) Among the obligations that teachers assume on being hired is the instruction and control of groups of conscripts—pupils—whose membership is involuntary though not necessarily undesired. This means that teachers must be ready to confront the problems of establishing and maintaining the voluntary participation of pupils in school activities. The situation of the teacher is also affected by the fact that a school district is a catchment area whose social composition (and hence the school's composition) cannot readily be determined or changed by the school. Teachers, then, unlike free professionals, cannot select their clientele and cannot teach only those whom they like or only those who are interested in or responsive to school activities.

Schools, like universities and both mental and general hospitals, all of which include their clients as members of the organization for extended periods of time, depend on the voluntary compliance of their clients with the rules of the organization and on their voluntary participation in activities designed for their welfare (Lefton, 1970, pp. 17–36; Parsons, 1964, pp. 257–291). This means, given the description (above) of how teachers and pupils are affiliated with schools, that in exercising authority teachers must deal with problems of pupils' motivation, not simply in terms of complying with specific teacher requests, assignments and orders, but in terms of gaining pupils' commitment to the enterprise of schooling itself (Bidwell, 1970, pp. 37–69; Dreeben, 1968, p. 37), which entails the expression of goodwill and the establishment of trust. One must naturally distinguish between the voluntariness of membership and the voluntariness of compliance; involuntary members (pupils) may or may not comply voluntarily to the expectations of teachers. But the conscriptive affiliative arrangement creates the problem for teachers of trying to establish and maintain the voluntary participation of some and often many pupils.

The authority problems of school principals vis-a-vis their subordinates (teachers) differ substantially from the problems of teachers vis-a-vis pupils in part because teachers are affiliated to schools differently from pupils. The compliance of teachers is not really problematic if the terms of employment have really been settled in the labor contract. Violations of the contract (by either side), de facto changes in the contract not agreed to by one party or the other, or changes in external circumstances whose effect changes the meaning of the contract (e.g., assigning a teacher to a class with large numbers of children who are very difficult to manage) create problems of authority between employers (principals) and employees (teachers). (Principals, of course, are really managers, not legal employers; but by virtue of the provisions in the labor contract, they are agents of the employer.)

Whether principals can give orders in the bureaucratic sense (Weber, 1947, pp. 324–329) to teachers is debatable. Surely there are certain rules of school operation that they must enforce, rules pertaining more to the internal management of the enterprise than to classroom instruction (e.g., attendance, working hours, free time during the day), and clearly their position affords them both the right and obligation to supervise and judge the work of teachers (Lortie, 1969, p. 11). In these respects, principals occupy a position of bureaucratic superordination relative to teachers.

Teaching, however, is not routine and standardized work, and, moreover, it takes place simultaneously in many classroom locations scattered throughout a school building. The ecological characteristics of schools (a theme to be discussed later) do not resemble those of many factories, government bureaus and business firms whose workers are engaged in repetitive activities readily visible to their supervisors or where the product of their activities can be judged quantitatively and qualitatively. Principals, moreover, have many other responsibilities in addition to the supervision of teachers; and even though they attribute great importance to teacher supervision, they do not spend much time doing it (NEA, 1964, pp. 34, 36, 38). In effect, the situation makes it exceedingly difficult for principals to exercise their supervisory and judgmental functions even if one accepts the highly debatable assumption that there are valid criteria for judging the quality of teaching.

Thus, even though schools have many of the defining characteristics of bureaucracies, a consideration of the modes of affiliation of both pupils and teachers indicates that they do not operate like bureaucracies in some very critical respects. Hiring is an affiliative device that ordinarily makes the bureaucratic direction of work possible; but not in the case of teaching. In fact, the pressures and uncertainties entailed in the running of classrooms often make teachers want more administrative direction than they get (Dreeben, 1970a, pp. 66–75), though the evidence on this point is not completely consistent (NEA, 1964, pp. 41–43); and these same pressures and uncertainties make their work, by its nature, very difficult to direct administratively because principals cannot become well informed about the unique sequence of events in each classroom, nor are they competent to direct the work of teachers in all areas of the curriculum (Lortie, 1969, p. 12). Teaching, then, by virtue of the nature of the school hierarchy and of the characteristics of classroom activities, tends to be self-directed and isolated.

The Exercise of Teacher Authority

There has long been reluctance on the part of teachers and of those who have studied them to think of teaching in terms of relationships involving power and authority. Although the term "discipline" retains its currency, it also sends ideological shivers up the spines of those who think that teaching has some inherent connection with democracy. Aside from the question of ideological predilection, the difficulty with the concept of discipline (and its various euphemisms) is the narrow scope of problems it subsumes; and though one should not identify the concept of discipline with that of authority, it is still necessary to recognize that discipline, insofar as it refers to the problems of establishing and maintaining order in a classroom, is an important *element of* authority.

The most enduring tradition in the study

of authority relationships in teaching derives from Lippitt's pioneering work (on experimentally created boys' clubs) concerned with democratic and autocratic leadership styles (White & Lippitt, 1960). The democratic-autocratic distinction, under many synonymous guises (e.g., integrative versus dominative, teacher-centered versus pupil- or group-centered) has remained remarkably durable and remarkably unilluminating in the study of how classrooms operate. What is interesting about the distinction, however, is that it has been "rediscovered" several times by investigators working in different traditions of inquiry and under different assumptions: consider, for example, instrumental and social-emotional leaders (Bales, 1955, pp. 424–463), leaders who are liked and leaders who are respected (Homans, 1961, pp. 299–307). These distinctions were derived from studies of *small* groups whose members performed specific tasks having *clear outcomes* over *short time spans*. None of these properties characterizes classrooms. Of course, it is always an empirical question whether a conceptual distinction developed under one set of circumstances will apply to different circumstances; however, what appears so surprising among educational researchers is that so many have assumed the Lippitt distinction to hold and accordingly have failed to test its appropriateness to classrooms.

Work in the Lippitt tradition has proceeded on the tacit assumption that authority relationships can best be understood in terms of general teaching styles; and while there is nothing wrong with this formulation a priori, it has not proved fruitful empirically, perhaps because it ignores some of the structural parameters of classrooms (such as modes of affiliation). Neither does it take into account the collective nature of classrooms, the isolation of teachers with one group of pupils in a bounded space, the extended periods of time over which classrooms meet, and as one observer has noted, "the crowds, the praise, and the power..." (Jackson, 1968, p. 33). It fails, moreover, to entertain the possibility that teacher conduct can be formulated in terms of different strategies of response and action related to differing classroom situations.

It is not facetious to draw certain parallels between the circumstances of pupils in school and inmates in prison as long as one is entirely aware of the differences. But when there are substantial inequalities of power between those in authority and those not, and when some number of subordinates are present while preferring to be elsewhere, compliance can become a serious issue, particularly when those in authority do not have at their disposal adequate inducements to make *voluntary* compliance possible. Grades are not felt to be rewarding by all children, teachers are at times—perhaps often—unable to relieve classroom tedium, school can be uninteresting and teachers boring, and so on, not to mention the fact that some children detest school. In these circumstances, teachers can be impelled to make "deals" with some pupils by allowing them to escape the rigors of classroom life in exchange for their "agreement" not to disrupt the proceedings because teachers are obligated to carry on instruction, or at least to keep the peace, and preferably both. Teachers, like prison guards, may allow their authority to be subverted in the attempt to preserve their authority when neither coercion nor conventional inducements work (Sykes, 1958, pp. 40–62).

The issue here is not the efficacy of democratic and autocratic methods (or an ideological preference for one or the other), but rather the problem of how a teacher maintains order—classrooms cannot proceed in the midst of chaos—among many children, with at times inadequate inducements (the inability to keep them interested, to make the work provocative, to motivate them sufficiently, and the like), under crowded conditions with their potentialities for disruption. Even when the continued peaceful operation of classrooms is not seriously threatened by disruption, teachers must still adopt some strategy—knowingly or unknowingly—relating to the use of sanctions (positive and negative); in particular, balancing concern for the welfare of individual children against the welfare of the whole class when those interests conflict, gauging the possible diminishing returns of both rewards and punishments, and discovering precisely what actions are rewarding and punishing for individual children. These are questions of strategy, not of style; and it has only been very recently that investigators have begun to look at schools in these terms.

One important exploratory effort designed to consider problems of classroom management (not just discipline narrowly conceived) implicitly takes account of the spatial boundedness of classrooms—the extended time span of classroom activities, the need for teachers to decipher the course of events taking place before them, their need to manage a variety of events occurring simultaneously as well as to be aware of unexpected contingencies arising in classrooms (Smith & Geoffrey, 1968, pp. 96–128).

Smith and Geoffrey's work, though largely descriptive, explicitly acknowledges that if a teacher knows that events occurring at one point in time may have unpredictable consequences for events at an unpredictable future time, that if a teacher makes himself aware of what is going on and what informal social relationships obtain among pupils, that if past promises and threats are kept, and that if he establishes "rules of the game" and routines for classroom activities (so that disparate events can be tied back into an ongoing enterprise), it is possible to keep pupils engaged in classroom activities over time. These types of awareness and conduct do not appear to be part of the familiar language of authority with its emphasis on orders, sanctions, hierarchy and obedience. But the disparity in language is only illusory. A problem faced by all organizations is assuring the continuity of productive activities, and organizations will operate effectively if persons in positions of authority are able to keep things running without resorting to the use of sanctions and the exercise of power, thereby calling the legitimacy of their authority into question. In effect, Smith and Geoffrey are talking about getting work done in a way that avoids crises in authority, and the strategies they discuss appear well suited to the potentially volatile conditions of classrooms meeting over extended periods of time where a diversity of pupil interests and motivations is represented (not all of them congenial to the enterprise of schooling).

The recent work of Kounin on discipline and the management of classrooms is perhaps the single most important contribution to our understanding of the peculiarities of authority relations in classroom settings (Kounin, 1970); accordingly, his study merits some detailed consideration. He deals with the ways in which teachers cope with violations of classroom rules, in particular with "desists"—techniques designed to stop misbehavior—and with "ripple effects"—the impact of desists on those pupils who *observe* a teacher trying to stop the misbehavior of one of their number (Kounin, 1970, p. 2). The formulation treats types of desists (clarity, firmness, anger, humor); it compares desists with other kinds of disciplinary behavior (punishment, redirection of pupils into "legal activity"); and it considers the conditions affecting their use, including amount of harm resulting from the desist, pupils' motivation to learn, changes in pupil behavior, and liking the teacher. Consider, then, some of the empirical generalizations emerging from Kounin's data.

Among high-school students he discovered that pupil reactions to desists are related both to motivation to learn and to liking the teacher. When motivation and liking are treated simultaneously: highly motivated pupils behave better and pay more attention to the task in response to a desist; liking the teacher is associated with considering the teacher fair and siding with the teacher rather than with the deviate pupil; disliking the teacher is related to seeing the teacher as punitive, overreacting and angry. More generally, motivation appears related to task and behavioral conformity, while liking is related to evaluative judgments about the teacher (Kounin, 1970, pp. 33–34, 165). The *nature* of the desist (whether it entails punishment, firmness, anger or humor) has no effect on whether pupils *observing* the desist pay more attention to the task and behave better; the ripple effect is related to pupils' motivation but not to their liking the teacher (Kounin, 1970, p. 36). Pupils, moreover, who think their teacher is good at getting subject matter across and at getting a class settled down and working tend to like the teacher and express motivation to learn; they become anxious, restless and uninvolved, however, when the teacher's desist behavior is angry and punitive (Kounin, 1970, pp. 42, 54–55).

Discovering that characteristics of pupils (motivation and liking the teacher) but not teaching activities were related to the occurrence of ripple effects led Kounin to a different set of questions: do aspects of teacher conduct other than type of desist affect the behavior of pupils? A video-tape study of self-contained elementary-school classrooms (first and second grades) led to a reformulation of the problem of teacher effects by virtue of the fact that classrooms differed in the extent to which pupils were involved in their work or engaged in deviant activities.

Kounin measured how pupils' work involvement and deviancy, under recitation and seatwork conditions, were affected by a variety of teaching strategies, among them "withitness" (a most unhappy neologism), "overlapping," "smoothness" and "group alerting." However strange and ill-chosen, this collection of words nevertheless refers to some important and hitherto ignored aspects of classroom life: respectively, the extent to which teachers 1) explicitly communicate to pupils that they know what is going on; in particular that they can correctly identify culprits and stop infractions at the appropriate times; 2) attend to and deal with a second intruding event when they are already dealing with one, without becoming overly immersed in one at the expense of the other; 3) maintain a continuous flow of activities in a setting (such as a classroom) characterized by changes in activities, intruding events and frequent opportunities for teachers to become preoccupied with isolated episodes at the expense of ongoing events; 4) manage recitations in a way that keeps pupils engaged, usually by creating some uncertainty about the order in which they will be called on and by reducing the amount of waiting.

Overall, Kounin discovered positive relationships between these various strategies and both pupil work involvement and freedom from deviancy when pupils are involved in recitation and seatwork activities; some of these relationships are reasonably substantial ($r = 0.6$), some less so, and all tend to diminish somewhat when third variables are introduced by partial correlation (Kounin, 1970, pp. 169, 171–174). For present purposes, however, the reporting of results and the magnitudes of correlations (and the conditions under which those correlations vary) are not the main questions, though it is not unimportant that Kounin did find substantial relationships. More to the point is what this investigation says by implication about the work setting of teachers and how their work is shaped by the characteristics of the setting.

It would be strange to find an investigation of professional-client relationships (doctor-patient, lawyer-client) yielding the preceding peculiar set of four concepts used to analyze classroom events despite the fact that such relationships clearly entail problems of continuity and engagement. The reason appears to lie in the fact that classrooms are larger collectivities, that scattered events can arise from unexpected quarters at unexpected times, that classroom events come in rapid succession, and that pupils represent a far greater variety of interests and present a greater variety of problems to a teacher than individual clients seen one at a time can to a professional practitioner (Jackson & Lahaderne, 1967, pp. 204–206).

One can view these four concepts as strategies for dealing with characteristic classroom circumstances, such as: a dense collection of many people (mostly young children), a rapid flow of verbal exchanges between a teacher and pupils, easy opportunities for spontaneous expression (sought and unsought), and a program of activities planned by a teacher. Teaching in a crowd entails the possibility of disruption, particularly when pupils' interests, motivations and levels of maturity vary widely. To the extent that teaching involves a planned set of activities, a teacher must cope with the problem of seeing the plan through, keeping alert to the possibility of disruptions and dealing with them when they arise, subordinating them to the priority of the plan, and dealing with misconduct equitably. The teacher's position becomes vulnerable, as does the workability of the plan, if pupils are left unengaged in classroom activities (e.g., if they have to wait around with nothing to do), if minor disruptions become serious or widespread, and if teachers treat students unjustly (e.g., punish the wrong culprit). The strategies Kounin describes, then, represent attempts by teachers both to carry through an instructional plan and to protect the vulnerable parts of their situation; they must stay alert, avoid dwelling on misconduct to the point where doing so threatens the program, keep pupils occupied, and diagnose disruptions correctly both by following the origin and course of events leading up to them and by correctly identifying the participants.

The question of equitable treatment is particularly important and reflects the fact that classroom activities are public and continue over extended periods of time. Because pupils in a classroom are of roughly the same age, share similar responsibilities, have the same teacher, perform similar activities, and in general share comparable classroom circumstances so that their condition relative to one another resembles that of equality (Dreeben, 1968, pp. 13–17), it is particularly important that teachers avoid activities interpretable as favoritism or discrimination lest the legitimacy of their position be called into question. In short, equality among subordinates imposes constraints on the exercise of authority (Dreeben, 1970b, pp. 93–94); accordingly, for teachers to sustain their legitimate position in a situation requiring fair treatment based on the principles of equality, they must attend to the situation and act in ways (e.g., desisting) that avoid both the deliberately (favoritism, discrimination) and erroneously unequal treatment of pupils. They must, in Kounin's terminology, avoid "target mistakes"—catching the wrong culprit (Kounin, 1970, p. 82).

Summary

In the realm of authority relationships, the school as a workplace and the classroom as a work site pose problems for the conduct of teachers. These settings pose *tasks* for teachers: problematic situations for which they must devise strategies, more or less effective, for meeting organizational demands (from the administration), carrying out an instructional program, and coping with the regularities and irregularities of classroom events (Levinson & Gallagher, 1964, p. 38). In a number of crucial respects, schools differ from other organizations staffed by skilled white collar and/or professional workers, such as hospitals, law firms, universities, social work agencies, insurance companies and the like. They are not bureaucratic in the sense that central work activities are directed by rules or divided into routine, repetitive subactivities. Neither are they professional or craft organizations in which work activities are shaped by esoteric work traditions based on more or less sophisticated technologies in which workers' expert judgments are the primary criteria for making decisions

(Etzioni, 1961, pp. 40–54; Stinchcombe, 1959).

As a general rule workers (like teachers) engaged in a somewhat unpredictable environment and obliged to provide services for and heed the welfare of clients are not usually governed by bureaucratic rules. The vicissitudes of the classroom cannot be readily subsumed under general formulas prescribing conduct. At the same time and for the same reasons, supervisory direction and review, consistent with affiliation by hiring, do not typically obtain among teachers. Teachers, moreover, lack both a strong craft tradition and a highly developed technology (Dreeben, 1970a, chapter 4), unlike skilled craftsmen and free professionals, and accordingly have no coherent set of *occupational* (as distinct from organizational) guidelines, based on collectively codified work experiences developed over time or based on research, to cope with the situational demands of their work and to judge the appropriateness of their conduct.

Classrooms, where conscripted children are gathered in confined spaces over long spans of time, engender problems of compliance and order for teachers. From the teacher's perspective the central issue is engaging pupils in the instructional proceedings—keeping them interested, at work, and actively involved. The means for doing so, however, are not well understood so that one often finds teachers attempting to keep up with and control the rapid flow of events: in part the director of these events, in part their prisoner, but in any case deeply engrossed in them. Not surprisingly, under the circumstances, the teacher's exercise of authority resembles not that of the director who gives orders, the foreman who supervises, or the professional who attempts to apply his expertise to a problem; rather, it is an attempt to instruct (usually by talking, as will be discussed later), to identify and stop violations of rules of conduct, and to play fair—all under pressure. With the endemic uncertainty and unpredictability of classroom events, the teacher, in attempting to instruct and maintain order, becomes more the reactor to than the designer of classroom activities (Jackson, 1966).

SPATIAL ARRANGEMENTS IN CLASSROOMS

The association between work and authority has deep roots in the history of sociological thinking. Traditional grounds alone would have been sufficient to justify discussing how relationships of authority in schools shape the work of teachers, and of how the nature of their work shapes relationships of authority. But it is easy to forget, given the sociologist's traditional concerns, that not all conduct occurring in hierarchical work settings is best understood in terms of hierarchy, authority and power.

Educators, by contrast, are more likely to think of teachers' work as matters of instruction and curriculum, both topics extending beyond the scope of this paper. But perhaps because classrooms have been constructed according to such a familiar design and because that design has remained so stable (though not without some modifications in a relatively small number of schools), patterns of spatial arrangements in classrooms have largely gone unnoticed for a long time; they have not been considered problematic in terms of shaping the nature of teachers' work. In recent years questions about school architecture and the design of space have risen to educational consciousness—questions, for reasons not entirely clear, that have been heavily weighted ideologically. Proponents of open classrooms (Silberman, 1970) recommend the free use of space within classrooms and the extension of classroom space into corridors; the effect is supposed to be liberating and humanizing for teachers and pupils. Maybe it is; but it is also possible that teachers will encounter unfamiliar difficulties in managing large numbers of pupils in relatively unconfined spaces so that in fact they will have to devote even greater energies to keeping order, gaining attention, and keeping pupils actively engaged in classroom activities (Sommer, 1969, p. 105) than to encouraging pupils to follow their own interests, to inquire freely, and to work at their own tempos.

Some architectural critics of current building design see present arrangements as "mirroring" what they contend to be the authoritarian quality of classroom life (DeCarlo, 1969, pp. 20–21). One looks in vain, however, through this sometimes hortatory, sometimes polemical, literature either for propositions that link the design of space to the conduct of people or for cogent reasons *why* some particular prescribed change in spatial design will produce the changes in conduct its proponents claim for it.

If one has no ideological axe to grind, it seems reasonable to ask how people in a work setting are arranged spatially, how the boundaries of spaces are placed, where physical objects are located, what kind of objects they are, and whether patterns of people's conduct vary (and in what ways) with the arrangement of space (Hall, 1966; Walker & Guest, 1952; Woodward, 1965). Architects and educators, moreover, who have become advocates of flexible space out of ideological conviction may actually end up ensnared by their own logic, for if it is true, as some have argued, that the nature of educational activities should determine the spatial properties of learning areas, flexible space, designed to serve a variety of educational activities, may actually serve none well. There is perhaps a greater need at this time for description than for pronouncement.

Some Parameters of Classroom Life

The evidence to provide a detailed mapping of classroom arrangements and activities, identifying the dominant patterns and variations, does not yet exist. Yet the scattered descriptions that are available seem to indicate some modal consistencies that

may in fact have important implications for the nature of teachers' work. One begins, of course, with the familiar observation that most classrooms consist of four walls with rows of desks and chairs for pupils and a single desk for one teacher up front. They contain on the average about 30 pupils (plus or minus 15 at the extremes) and are crowded. Experience rather than systematic evidence indicates that this is the modal arrangement in the United States; experience, unfortunately, provides no satisfactory information about the frequency of this arrangement nor about the frequency of alternatives. Self-contained classrooms go back in history at least to the time of Boston's Quincy School built in 1847; they have been remarkably durable, for reasons scarcely understood.

Classrooms are characterized by high rates of interaction and frequent changes in activities. In one study of 32 lessons in 16 classrooms (grades 1, 6 and 11), some change in "activity" (not defined) was found to occur once every five seconds in an active classroom, every 18 seconds in a less active one; 371 "activity episodes" (not defined) occurred during the average lesson; and a change in who talked and who listened occurred 174 times each lesson (Adams & Biddle, 1970, pp. 29–30). Another investigator estimates about 650 individual interchanges (not defined) between an elementary-school teacher and her pupils in the course of a full day of teaching; about 1000 interchanges when the number of times a teacher talks to the class as a whole (rather than just to separate individuals) is considered (Jackson, 1966, p. 14). A study of four sixth-grade classrooms indicates that teachers initiate about 80 interchanges with individual pupils every hour, a figure similar in each class (Jackson & Lahaderne, 1967, p. 206). These are the findings of contemporary studies, but a recent review of past literature indicates that high interaction rates were far from unknown early in the century. A 1912 study, for example, showed that teachers asked

"...two, three, and four questions per minute..." in rapid-fire succession (Hoetker & Ahlbrand, 1969, p. 151).

Although no quantitative evidence is presented here on rates of interaction at other work sites, commonplace experience indicates that talk does not fly as fast and as constantly in business offices, law firms, doctors' offices, assembly lines, garages, farms and so on. There is undoubtedly substantial variation among classrooms in rates of interaction, but the fragmentary evidence now available suggests that classrooms are crowded places with lots of talk. But what of the patterns of talk?

Again, based only on suggestive evidence, one investigation showed that 75 percent of all classroom time was spent in aggregations consisting of a teacher and a group of more than 50 percent of the pupils (with the remainder either unorganized or in much smaller groups); that is, most of the classes were organized as a single, numerically dominant unit most of the time. Classrooms consisting of several small groups or of unorganized individuals appeared during the remaining 25 percent of the time (Adams & Biddle, 1970, p. 37). When the teacher is engaged with the large (50 percent plus) group, almost half the time (47 percent) is spent in the dissemination of information about subject matter; that is, somebody, mostly the teacher, tells everybody else about subject matter (Adams & Biddle, 1970, pp. 41, 45). The Adams and Biddle findings closely resemble those of Bellack and his colleagues who studied 15 teachers of tenth- and twelfth-grade pupils. Teachers speak (as measured by lines of transcribed typescript) almost three times as much as pupils (about 72 percent of the lines). Slightly less than 7 percent of that speech is devoted to responding to pupil-initiated talk; the rest consists of asking questions, focusing pupils' attention on topics, and commenting on and judging what they say (Bellack, Kliebard, Hyman, & Smith, 1966, pp. 43, 47). Almost two-thirds of the pupils' speech (amounting to about 27 percent of the total) is devoted to responding to teachers' questions (Bellack et al., 1966, p. 48).

Highly suggestive but by no means definitive evidence that runs back to the end of the nineteenth century indicates that teachers run classrooms; they do most of the talking and initiate most of the action. In the relatively short spans of time left to them, pupils mostly reply to questions and less frequently ask them. Evidence on the spatial distribution of talk locates most of it toward the front and center of classrooms (in both secondary schools and college classes). When the teacher talks, the chances are substantial that a large number of pupils will be addressed (not a small group), that the pupil who talks next will be sitting near the front or along a center strip, and that the teacher will be the following speaker (Adams & Biddle, 1970, pp. 63–68; Sommer, 1969, p. 118). Classrooms, in short, are run on the principle of the recitation (Hoetker & Ahlbrand, 1969, p. 146).

If systematic evidence about the past and about current practice, taking full account both of modal patterns and of variations, supports this generalization, we will have discovered a most remarkable phenomenon: the predominance of the recitation. Presumably there are many ways to teach a classroom full of children or to teach them in settings different in structure from classrooms, but for reasons as yet unknown these alternatives have not gained currency. Of course, one cannot dismiss out of hand the contention that the constraints of classrooms are of such a nature and of such intensity that only one teaching strategy is feasible given those constraints and that alternatives can emerge only against tremendous odds. But that is purely speculation.

There is apparently no inventory of information about elementary- and secondary-school classrooms documenting the extent to which either recitational teaching methods or alternative ones prevail; everything we know is based on a small number of studies of a small number of classrooms. With proper caveats, however, one can hazard some speculations about the prevalence of the recitation. Why should teachers have discovered this mode of instruction and classroom management? To what set of problematic conditions can the recitation be considered an adaptive response?

The physical design of classrooms, containing one badly outnumbered teacher crowded with some 30 children into a confined space, seems highly conducive to sporadic if not frequent disruption, particularly in the lower grades. The potentiality for disruption may arise from the pupils: because some are restless, immature, uninterested, unmotivated and the like; it may also be provoked by some teachers who are dull, threatening, ill-prepared, tired, or who cannot keep children occupied and interested. The teacher's primary task is to design and engage pupils in learning activities sufficiently engrossing that pupils find those activities substantially more attractive than proscribed alternatives (which often have attractions of their own). Under these circumstances, maintaining "the student's absorption in the task at hand" and getting his attention are tasks of great immediacy and importance both for instructional and managerial reasons (Jackson, 1968, pp. 85, 90).

Teachers' options for gaining attention and engagement are fairly circumscribed. They can command the front of the classroom and attempt to control the proceedings (both for instructional and management purposes) by doing most of the talking (lecturing, questioning and demonstrating) and by controlling pupil participation (presumably reducing its unpredictability) through rapid-fire questioning which limits pupils' engagement largely to occasions created by the teacher. As Kounin observed, teachers can maintain attention if they ask questions in a way that leaves pupils guessing about who will have to recite—identifying the pupil after the question has been asked, not before (Kounin,

1970, pp. 109–111). Moreover, to the extent that teachers wish to avoid empty time and maintain continuous classroom activity, they will attempt to manage the flow of events from the front of the class by asking questions and directing activities.

This, of course, is the recitation solution to the problems of carrying on an instructional program and maintaining order in a classroom having the social and spatial parameters described above. It is based on the premise that pupils actually lack the motivation or the interest to keep themselves engaged, or that teachers are afraid to rely on that motivation, or that they are unable to create it. The recitation, then, becomes a substitute for motivation, given the fact that the teacher's task is to establish and maintain attention.

The facts, moreover, that teachers are usually expected to cover a more or less standardized curriculum, and that pupils vary in motivation, ability and work tempo mean that they are likely to complete their assigned work at different times. Although this may not seem like a particularly problematic situation, it in fact requires an adaptive strategy because free time provides pupils with options that have implications for running a classroom. A pupil with free time, in a spatially bounded setting where others are still working on assigned tasks, may turn independently to different work (and thus remain occupied in approved ways), daydream, work on things unrelated to school, or make trouble. Most teachers will not tolerate the latter; others will not tolerate anything but the first. The teacher's task is to keep these pupils occupied, and this task becomes problematic in good part because the teacher is constrained by the demand (externally or self-imposed) to teach a standardized curriculum to "cover" the material (Bidwell, 1965, p. 974). In response, the teacher with foresight may have prepared additional materials with which early finishers can occupy themselves, though their desire to so occupy themselves cannot be taken for granted.

Another response, of course, is not to let the free time situation arise in the first place; and one way to accomplish that is to keep talking—to run the class on a recitation basis. In that way the constraint of the standardized curriculum can be met, the continuity of classroom activities maintained, and the problem of motivation side-stepped. But what are the alternatives to this solution?

One alternative is to divide pupils into several small groups based on interest, ability, attention span and the like, to prepare a variety of learning materials appropriate to these distinctions, and to change the composition of groups and the selection of materials according to shifts in interest, involvement and work tempo. There are teachers who work this way, but this strategy is enormously demanding of time (in preparation), concentration, energy and ingenuity. Unless teachers come to master an extraordinarily complex technology of instruction and management (and there is no evidence that they have), it does not seem that this alternative is likely to become predominant, though undoubtedly some teachers will continue to pursue it.

A second alternative is to bring one or more additional teachers into a classroom, one of the variants of the team-teaching idea. If the diversity of classrooms presents problems too complex and demanding for one teacher to manage, bring in more. Aside from the fact that this is an expensive alternative, even if class size were increased (in physical dimensions and number of pupils) to bring two or more teachers together, the pattern of teaching activities would have to change to accommodate new divisions of labor and authority and new status distinctions. This is not to say that multiple-teacher classrooms cannot work— the recent employment of paraprofessionals is a move precisely in this direction—but only that they have not yet been tried on a scale large enough to constitute a real alternative. Moreover, the recent experience with team teaching suggests that teachers were not able to solve the division of labor problems, at least not to the extent that team-teaching classrooms looked much different from conventional, self-contained ones.

Third, it is possible to open up classroom space by using larger areas of adjacent spaces hitherto considered to fall outside conventional classroom boundaries—the open classroom alternative. This arrangement provides flexibilities of space that presumably can be adapted to contain a variety of learning activities and a variety of pupil groups working at different tempos; it does not, however, automatically solve problems of low motivation and lack of interest (except insofar as those problems are attributable largely to the small range of learning activities readily carried out in the conventional, bounded classroom). Gaining pupils' attention and establishing control remain potential problems (and perhaps constitute greater problems) especially if classroom space covers a much larger area, and the richer instructional diet that gives rise to the need for more and freer space still requires a large investment of the teacher's time and energy. It may well be that bounded classrooms provide important resources for the control of classroom activities; management may become far more difficult in a large, loosely bounded space. And the expansion of space by no means guarantees the expected instructional advantages.

Finally, some writers have advocated the elimination of conventional classrooms (and schools) altogether (Illich, 1971), or the use of classrooms for a limited set of specialized learning activities while the rest take place under the auspices of one or another community institution not conventionally classified as a school (Newmann & Oliver, 1967).

Given the spatial constraints of self-contained classrooms and the need for teachers to gain and keep the attention of their pupils (both for administrative and instructional reasons), it is not surprising that the recitation has emerged as an adaptive solution because it can serve both as a means of disseminating knowledge and as a means of control at the same time in a setting whose major parameters are 1) spatial containment and crowding, 2) the inclusion of variously motivated children of different abilities and interests, and 3) the occupational and administrative injunction on teachers to teach—direct an instructional program. Though as noted earlier there is no adequate evidence on the frequency of prevailing alternatives to the recitation, one would expect them to take the form of teachers attempting to deal more with individual pupils and small groups, and using a variety of instructional techniques designed to cope with classroom variation (the first alternative to the recitation, mentioned above), not (or not yet) the forms of multiple teacher and open classrooms.

Although this discussion has proceeded mainly along ecological lines, it would be erroneous to advocate an architectural or spatial determinism. In fact, classrooms, at least from a sociological perspective, should be viewed in terms of both technological and ecological attributes. The recitational method is a technology—a way of marshalling means and resources to accomplish some end (whether or not the end is actually achieved, the efficacy of the technology is a distinct question). It is a technology that resides comfortably in a social setting having the organizational properties of classrooms—and comfort has no bearing on whether children learn anything or whether teachers are happy in their work. In recent educational history there have been no innovations in teaching technology of sufficient magnitude to render the self-contained classroom structurally obsolete; either the technology has changed to fit the constraints of the classroom, or the change proved compatible with existing classroom structure (Stinchcombe, 1965, pp. 153–160). The open classroom will prove to be an interesting test; it will provide some evidence about whether teachers, with current technology, turn it back into a self-contained classroom, or whether it represents a new form designed in response to strains engendered by the incompatibility between new modes of teaching (innovations in technology) and the constraining boundaries of conventional classrooms.

Classrooms and Occupational Life

Just as the characteristics of teachers' work are related to the internal spatial arrangements of classrooms, so certain aspects of their occupational life, particularly those pertaining to career development and the diffusion of technology, are related to the spatial placement of classrooms within schools. Perhaps the most important single property of classrooms, viewed from a school-wide perspective, is their spatial scattering and isolation throughout school buildings; and because teachers work in different places at the same time, they do not observe each other working. Even team-teaching arrangements, designed to expand the collaborative efforts of teachers, have not succeeded in making teachers' work activities in the classroom visible to each other even though team teaching does encourage collaborative planning. The implications of this spatial isolation are far-reaching.

If teachers do not observe each other directly, who does observe them? Pupils, certainly, and with great frequency. Administrators (principals, department heads) also observe them, but rather seldom. If patterns of visibility are construed in terms of who is available to help teachers and to judge their performance, then their isolation appears more than spatial. Pupils, by virtue of their subordinate position and their inexperience, cannot be of much direct help about how to teach and manage a classroom; certainly teachers cannot approach them with questions about what is going right and wrong and expect technically defensible answers. And although pupils can judge the performance of teachers (hold opinions, like and dislike), their judgments cannot be taken as determining criteria for advancement. The inexperience of pupils aside, when workers are hired the job of evaluation is undertaken by hierarchical superiors, not subordinates.

Administrators can legitimately judge and help by virtue of their hierarchical positions and their prior work experience, since they are virtually always former teachers. Their work schedules and job demands are such, however, that they spend very little time visiting classrooms, and when they do, much of what they see is bound to be understood partly out of the context of on-going classroom events that they have not observed.

Because of their work schedules and the spatial dispersion of classrooms, teachers have so few opportunities to see each other at work and accordingly cannot either judge or be helpful *on the basis of direct observation*. This is not to deny that teachers talk shop and talk about each other's problems; they cannot do so, however, on the basis of shared visible and audible experiences. They lack, moreover, written media for communicating about their work because the occupation has no counterpart to a scholarly research tradition (cf. university instructors) in which knowledge is circulated in books and journals, to a collective body of precedent (cf. lawyers) in court reports, to case records (cf. physicians) that document the accumulation of tests and prior medical decisions, and to published designs (cf. architects). And since most educational research is carried out by academics (and without the involvement of teachers) and is published in scholarly or technical journals, teachers tend not to become consumers of it.

The fragmentation of the colleague group, through spatial isolation and the absence of a written tradition of work reports, makes teaching a very solitary and private kind of work. Several observers (Jackson, 1968; Lortie, 1969) have reported that teachers look to the immediate classroom situation both as a source of satisfaction and for signs of their own accomplishment and competence. By implication, this inward-looking perspective on work augurs ill for the cumulative development of a codified body of knowledge about teaching that can be disseminated throughout the occupation. It means that teachers are left very much alone to determine what they are doing right and wrong and to discover what they must do to solve their problems and correct their errors at work. Furthermore, the absence of codified knowledge about teaching puts constraints on schools that train teachers; what precisely shall they train teachers to do, and how shall they design programs to train them, when ideas about the character of the work remain largely in the minds of individual teachers and not part of a publicly shared and reasonably systematic body of knowledge?

Both the spatial distribution of classrooms in schools and their internal arrangements affect the nature of teacher training, particularly practice teaching. Like teachers themselves, apprentices work in isolation from one another, each learning the job most directly from a single "cooperating teacher." Although practice teaching is the one phase of the career in which an individual receives frequent and direct supervision from an experienced teacher, the relationship with that teacher tends to be dyadic with the result that the apprentice is exposed mainly to one other person's perspective and mode of doing things. Unlike medical students who undertake much of their training in cohorts and small work groups and who have a great deal of contact with each other and with a variety of instructors (Becker, Geer, Hughes, & Strauss, 1961), teacher-trainees lack the kind of support and richness of communication that peers working collectively on the same problems can provide.

Internally, classroom structure limits the extent to which that setting can serve *both* as a work site and as a setting for the training of apprentices. Unlike hospitals and law firms, for example, where new recruits to medicine and law learn their trade as apprentices by performing work tasks of gradually increasing difficulty under close supervision, schools provide a less adequate setting—the classroom—for work and training activities to occur simultaneously. The self-contained, bounded, single-teacher classroom provides the apprentice with two main alternatives: to be observer-listener or teacher. Except for the brief periods of time when trainees are free to deal with individual pupils or small groups of them, the organization of the classroom (to the extent that the recitation model represents the predominant state of things) provides few opportunities to learn the variety of teaching activities that make up the job. The apprentice either does the whole job or watches someone else do it.

One observer has described teaching activities as "indivisible" (Lortie, 1969, p. 9), meaning that they cannot be readily broken down into component tasks. The recitation is a case in point; it is difficult if not impossible to determine where the instructional component leaves off and the classroom management aspect begins. And if one includes all the attempts to motivate, praise, blame, give instructions, lecture, help, chastise, and the like, it becomes nearly impossible to disentangle the threads. Perhaps teaching is not indivisible but only as yet undivided; occupational activities have not been analyzed to identify their components, and *a fortiori*, training experiences like practice teaching cannot be geared to mastering specific skills learned with repeated practice. It may well be, moreover, that the self-contained classroom militates against the identification of the components of teaching activities and accordingly against the development of a division of labor. The reason, of course, is that anyone assuming the position of teacher in such a setting must do the whole job whether or not the parts of the job can be identified. The training of teachers will

not *necessarily* be any different in open classrooms; whether the potential flexibility of that setting will be exploited will depend on teachers' concern with identifying and learning the components of their work. Once those components are identified, and if apprentices concern themselves with their mastery, then the open classroom is more likely to provide the potential flexibility claimed for it.

SUMMARY

It has not been the intent of this chapter to review that enormous, sprawling body of words constituting the literature on the nature and state of the art of teaching. The purpose has been to consider certain *organizational* properties of schools and classrooms that have implications for the character of teachers' work. This accounts for the concern with workplaces and work sites as the central focus, not with the whole range of teaching activities. Certainly the personal and social characteristics of teachers; the characteristics of pupils, families and neighborhoods; administrative styles; the nature of teacher training; and the opportunities and constraints of the curriculum as well as a host of other considerations affect teachers' work. Important as these considerations are, they were not the subjects of this particular chapter.

The main argument consists of the proposition that certain structural properties of school organization pertaining to relationships of authority and the spatial characteristics of classrooms pose certain problems for teachers, and that the nature of their work can be construed in terms of adaptive responses to those problems.

It would be a gross distortion to conclude from this chapter that teaching is merely teachers talking and keeping order, though much of it has been about those phenomena. It would be correct, however, to conclude that the nature of instructional activities and modes of maintaining order are both central to the enterprise of teaching and strongly affected by those aspects of school and classroom structure discussed here. If teachers saw their pupils one at a time (in tutorial) the way doctors and lawyers see their patients and clients, if pupils were not conscripted, or if teachers had a more viable technology at their disposal, it is reasonably certain that relationships of authority between teachers and pupils would be substantially different than they are. Similarly, if classrooms had different spatial arrangements, if more than one teacher (or other people with classroom responsibilities) were present, or if pupils were freer to use the internal space of learning areas differently, if teachers carried on several distinct instructional programs in a classroom, it is more than likely that alternative modes of teaching (alternate to the recitation) would appear, *if* the component activities of teaching were identified and teachers viewed variations in spatial arrangements as opportunities to combine these components in new ways, and if they wanted to do so.

There is a substantial amount of sociological evidence, based on research in a variety of work situations, that the activities comprising a particular type of work can be performed readily within a certain range of structural settings, but only with great difficulty outside that range (Stinchcombe, 1959). This is to say, settings, on the one hand, are constraining; on the other, though they provide opportunities for different kinds of conduct, there is no guarantee that these opportunities will be exploited. The difficulty with the ideologically inspired plans to change the nature of teaching, to make it more effective, more imaginative, more humane, is that they ignore the prevailing structural constraints of schools and classrooms and provide no clear guidelines for using the opportunities. The questions that need to be asked are: given existing structural arrangements in schools and classrooms, what are the alternative forms that teaching activities can take? What are the alternative structural arrangements that can serve educational purposes? And what opportunities and constraints do they create for the character of teachers' work?

REFERENCES

Adams, R. S., & Biddle, B. J. *Realities of teaching.* New York: Holt, Rinehart & Winston, 1970.

Bales, R. F. The equilibrium problem in small groups. In A. P. Hare, E. F. Borgatta, & R. F. Bales (Eds.), *Small groups.* New York: Alfred A. Knopf, 1955. Pp. 444–483.

Barnard, C. I. *The functions of the executive.* Cambridge: Harvard University Press, 1938.

Becker, H. S. The career of the Chicago public schoolteacher. *American Journal of Sociology,* 1952, 57(5), 470–477.

Becker, H. S., Geer, B., Hughes, E. C., & Strauss, A. L. *Boys in white: Student culture in medical school.* Chicago: University of Chicago Press, 1961.

Bellack, A., Kliebard, H. M., Hyman, R. T., & Smith, F. L., Jr. *The language of the classroom.* New York: Teachers College Press, 1966.

Bidwell, C. E. The school as a formal organization. In J. G. March (Ed.), *Handbook of organizations.* Chicago: Rand McNally, 1965. Pp. 972–1022.

Bidwell, C. E. Students and schools: Some observations on client trust in client-serving organizations. In W. R. Rosengren, & M. Lefton (Eds.), *Organizations and clients.* Columbus, Ohio: Charles E. Merrill, 1970. Pp. 37–69.

Bruner, J. S. *Toward a theory of instruction.* Cambridge: Harvard University Press, 1966.

Bureau of Educational Personnel Development. *Do teachers make a difference?* Washington: U.S. Office of Education, 1970.

Coleman, J. S. et al. *Equality of educational opportunity.* Washington, D.C.: U.S. Office of Education, 1966.

Corwin, R. G. *Militant professionalism.* New York: Appleton-Century-Crofts, 1970.

DeCarlo, G. Why/how to build school buildings. *Harvard Educational Review,* 1969, 39(4), 12–34.

Dreeben, R. *On what is learned in school.* Reading, Mass.: Addison-Wesley, 1968.

Dreeben, R. *The nature of teaching.* Glenview, Ill.: Scott, Foresman, 1970. (a)

Dreeben, R. Schooling and authority: Comments on the unstudied curriculum. In N. V. Overly (Ed.), *The unstudied curriculum: Its impact on children.* Washington: Association for Supervision and Curriculum Development, National Education Association, 1970. Pp. 85–103. (b)

Etzioni, A. *A comparative analysis of complex organizations.* New York: Free Press, 1961.

Gouldner, A. W. *Patterns of industrial bureaucracy.* Glencoe, Ill.: Free Press, 1954.

Hall, E. T. *The hidden dimension.* Garden City, N.Y.: Doubleday, 1966.

Hoetker, J., & Ahlbrand, W. P., Jr. The persistence of the recitation. *American Educational Research Journal,* 1969, 6(2), 145–167.

Homans, G. C. *Social behavior: Its elementary forms.* New York: Harcourt, Brace & World, 1961.

Illich, I. Education without school: How it can be done. *New York Review of Books,* January 7, 1971. Pp. 25–31.

Jackson, P. W. The way teaching is. In Association for Supervision and Curriculum Development and the Center for the Study of Instruction of the National Education Association, *The way teaching is.* Washington, D.C.: NEA, 1966. Pp. 7–27.

Jackson, P. W. *Life in classrooms.* New York: Holt, Rinehart & Winston, 1968.

Jackson, P. W., & Lahaderne, H. M. Inequalities of teacher-pupil contacts. *Psychology in the Schools,* 1967, 4(3), 204–211.

Kounin, J. *Discipline and group management in classrooms.* New York: Holt, Rinehart & Winston, 1970.

Lefton, M. Client characteristics and structural outcomes: Toward the specification of linkages. In W. R. Rosengren, & M. Lefton (Eds.), *Organizations and clients.* Columbus, Ohio: Charles E. Merrill, 1970. Pp. 17–36.

Levinson, D. J., & Gallagher, E. B. *Patienthood in the mental hospital.* Boston: Houghton Mifflin, 1964.

Lortie, D. C. The balance of control and autonomy in elementary school teaching. In A. Etzioni (Ed.), *The semi-professions and their organization.* New York: Free Press, 1969. Pp. 1–53.

National Education Association. Evaluation of classroom teachers, Research Report 1964-R14. Washington, D.C.: National Education Association, 1964.

Newmann, F. M., & Oliver, D. W. Education and community. *Harvard Educational Review,* 1967, 37(1), 61–106.

Oettinger, A. G., & Marks, S. *Run, computer, run: The mythology of educational innovation.* Cambridge: Harvard University Press, 1969.

Parsons, T. *Structure and process in modern societies.* Glencoe, Ill.: Free Press, 1963.

Parsons, T. Definitions of health and illness in the light of American values and social structure. In T. Parsons, *Social structure and personality.* New York: Free Press, 1964. Pp. 257–291.

Perrow, C. *Organizational analysis: A sociological view.* London: Tavistock Press, 1970.

Rogers, D. *110 Livingston Street.* New York: Random House, 1968.

Rosenthal, A. *Pedagogues and power.* Syracuse: Syracuse University Press, 1969.

Selznick, P. *TVA and the grass roots.* Berkeley: University of California Press, 1949.

Selznick, P. *Leadership in administration.* Evanston, Ill.: Row, Peterson, 1957.

Silberman, C. E. *Crisis in the classroom.* New York: Random House, 1970.

Smith, L. M., & Geoffrey, W. *The complexities of an urban classroom.* New York: Holt, Rinehart & Winston, 1968.

Sommer, R. *Personal space.* Englewood Cliffs, N. J.: Prentice-Hall, 1969.

Stephens, J. M. *The process of schooling.* New York: Holt, Rinehart & Winston, 1967.

Stinchcombe, A. L. Bureaucratic and craft administration of production: A comparative study. *Administrative Science Quarterly,* 1959, 4(2), 168–187.

Stinchcombe, A. L. Social structure and organizations. In J. G. March (Ed.), *Handbook of organizations.* Chicago: Rand McNally, 1965. Pp. 142–193.

Sykes, G. M. *The society of captives.* Princeton: Princeton University Press, 1958.

Thompson, J. D. *Organizations in action.* New York: McGraw-Hill, 1967.

Walker, C. R., & Guest, R. H. *The man on the assembly line.* Cambridge: Harvard University Press, 1952.

Weber, M. *The theory of social and economic organization.* Translated by A. M. Henderson, & T. Parsons. Glencoe, Ill.: Free Press, 1947.

White, R. K., & Lippitt, R. *Autocracy and democracy*. New York: Harper & Brothers, 1960.

Whiteman, M., & Deutsch, M. Social disadvantage as related to intellective and language development. In M. Deutsch, I. Katz, & A. R. Jensen (Eds.), *Social class, race, and psychological development*. New York: Holt, Rinehart & Winston, 1968. Pp. 86–114.

Woodward, J. *Industrial organization: Theory and practice*. London: Oxford University Press, 1965.

CHAPTER 15 Observations on Teaching as Work

DAN C. LORTIE
University of Chicago

Less than a generation separated the Pilgrim landing from the establishment of schools for colonial children; since that time, the schoolteacher has become a familiar figure on the American scene. The occupation has multiplied many times over and become the livelihood of more than two million Americans. Yet despite expansion and other developments (for example, the emergence and spread of the common school model during the nineteenth century), we find continuities which span three centuries. Features which have prevailed over that period include control by local citizens, salary payment for teachers and the grouping of students in classrooms. We can classify schools, in fact, as among our more traditional institutions; particular ways of doing things have come to be seen, in Sumner's phrase, as "right and natural," as not to be questioned. Organizational traditionalism is reflected in scholarly work in education; although schools have always been labor intensive, the arrangements used to mobilize the effort and talent of school personnel have occupied a marginal position in the study of schooling. Inquiry has concentrated on other issues (such as curriculum and the principles of learning) while patterns of school organization and characteristics of teacher work have been in the shade.

There is reason to believe, however, that changes are taking place today which alter ground-figure relationships in the study of public education. A new zeitgeist is emerging, a zeitgeist which forces institutional features of schooling to our attention. I shall argue that this new outlook enhances the significance of understanding the school as a place where people work. Teaching is so deeply implicated in the structure of schools that shifts in the structure imply shifts in the occupation of teaching; to think differently about schools is to think differently about teachers. Transitions in our collective outlook also affect our definition of knowledge, of what is valid and useful to know. As our knowledge changes—as we look more closely at the larger patterns around schooling—our conceptions of what is instructionally relevant and important to redesigning schools also change.

This chapter, then, is an attempt to identify how current changes affect the knowledge we need about teaching work and to relate such inferences to the current state of the field. The first section develops the idea of a changing zeitgeist and draws implications for studying the occupation. In section two, I shall review several topics from the occupational perspective and assess the directions taken by a variety of researchers. A last, brief section puts forth a few suggestions on how we might move to a more useful understanding of the teaching occupation.

THE CHANGING ZEITGEIST OF EDUCATION

Contemporary Threats to Educational Tradition

Charters (1963) has pointed out that the social status of the American teacher has become considerably more secular over the decades, reflecting urbanization and secularization in the society at large. We can extend that process to include the idea of modernization as historical conceptions of schooling give way to increasingly diverse orientations and alternatives. The proliferation of options is a critical aspect of modernization; the legitimation which used to derive from custom and usage no longer serves when alternatives abound. For today it seems that the buoyant confidence which carried the orthodoxies of the common school crusade well into the twentieth century is losing out to skepticism and, among some publics, disenchantment. It becomes possible for school decision making to shift to more "rational" types of thought —rational not in the sense of assurance that particular outcomes will follow particular procedures but rational in that the *attempt* is made to find the most appropriate fit between means and ends. For it is not necessary to assume the emergence of a "bright new day" to recognize that the hold of the past is weakening.

School effectiveness has always been constrained by the level of talent possessed by teachers and by the ways in which that

talent was mobilized to achieve school goals. Until recently people continued to believe in two basic strategies of mobilization developed during the nineteenth century. The first was limited bureaucratization in which administrators oversaw teachers and corrected for their deficiencies; the second was a peculiar form of professionalization in which primary emphasis was placed on ever-increasing amounts of formal schooling for classroom teachers. But these two principles seem to be losing at least some of their following today—growing disenchantment with schools is widening to include the ways in which they are organized. The waves of current protest, for example, reveal distrust of both bureaucratic controls and teacher professionalization; we can see that distrust in such battle cries as "decentralization," "responsiveness," "relevance," "community control" and "accountability." Whatever the ultimate fate of these particular demands may be, they apparently point to basic questioning of traditional forms by important segments of the public.

The pressure on tradition can be seen in several ways, and I shall discuss five of them here. They are a) the acceleration and broadening of attacks on public education, b) the proliferation of options within and outside the public school system, c) changing norms of interaction within schools as bargaining spreads, d) the growth and formalization of research, development and policy-planning in education, and e) the increased cosmopolitanism of public schools. Each of these trends undermines specific attributes of the traditional school order.

Attacks on public schools are part of their history, but there are special characteristics in the criticism which has occurred since the early 1950s. Onslaughts have accelerated in pace and their base of origination has expanded considerably. The Sputnik-induced outbursts were succeeded by the Civil Rights Movement, the protracted John Birch Society offensive, the urban crisis, and the broadside attacks of the "new romantics," political radicals and representatives of "moderate" foundation sentiment. In less than twenty years the schools have been damned successively (and sometimes concurrently) as soft on subject matter, as unjust to members of minority groups, as tools of international communism, as pathologically bureaucratic and unresponsive to the public will, as destructive of the human spirit, as perpetuators of class privilege and as conducted in mindless fashion. The wide spectrum of political opinion represented signals a contraction of the support base for public schools; hierarchical governance and teacher professionalization have featured prominently in the attacks, with romantics stressing the first and black critics the latter. Social scientists, moreover, have contributed to public disenchantment by questioning the equality of school practices, the rationality of decision processes and the knowledge base of practitioners. We do not yet know what the effects of this accelerated, cumulative criticism will be, but it does nothing to instill public confidence in traditional forms of schooling; one of the social functions of protracted criticism, moreover, is to prepare people for change.

We can see the dwindling power of tradition in the multiplication of alternative ways to operate public schools. Today curriculum consists of many different approaches to teach a given subject or grade; the range of options extends to all aspects of schooling, from building design to staffing patterns, from grouping students to new instructional technologies. The actuality of options (as I have argued elsewhere—Lortie, 1970) deeply influences decision-making processes, for even the decision to repeat previous patterns requires *justification* given the presence of alternatives. The need to find grounds for choice and for defending particular decisions alters the perspectives of those who govern schools, fostering the alignment of specific means with specific goals. The development of options encourages inquiry and evaluation as decision-makers seek to reduce uncertainty in their articulation of ends and

means; we observe this press, in fact, in the demands of federal government agencies and other donors who insist that provision for evaluation accompany their financial support.

Another threat to tradition rests in plans for basic revision in the way in which educational services are provided. Some conservatives and liberals have formed an implicit coalition to move schools from the public to the private sector—this is the essence of various voucher plans and performance contracting schemes. State legislatures are trying to break the mold of many decades by voting public tax monies to support private schools. Hundreds of independent, "free" schools are being established on an ideology which rejects the major tenets of public school systems. It is likely that the mere attempt to initiate such alternatives will affect public schools; should they succeed and flourish, the legally protected near-monopoly of public education will be broken.

Historians of the future may link current interest in alternative systems of schooling to a major change in public education—the emergence of teacher–school board conflict and movement toward collective bargaining. Relationships within school staffs used to be defined and regulated by familial kinds of norms; there used to be strong emphasis on mutual cooperation and concerted action by administrators and teachers. Teachers occupied a special status in the community as poor but respectable members of the middle classes; they probably benefited from the label "underpaid," for not too much is demanded of those whose services reputedly exceed their returns. But the sixties saw changes in both the familialism of staff relationships and the public image of teachers as underrewarded—strikes and increased benefits dramatized the changes. The previously "integrated profession" showed severe internal strains and the public watched its taxes rise. To the extent that relationships among school employees and between teachers and the public became calculative rather than normatively regulated, tradition was undermined, for the kinds of power plays and manipulations involved in collective bargaining played little part in the previous social order.

Collective bargaining means increased power by teachers to influence conditions of work and to affect the shape and nature of school organization. Plans for reordering public schools will require at least the acquiescence of teacher organizations and future planning will have to take greater account of teacher preferences and values. The specifics of teacher belief and sentiment, therefore, become important questions; the "zone of acceptance" of teachers is now an institutionalized feature of the action structure of public schools.

The composition of the intellectual establishment in public education changed somewhat during the sixties as a result of actions by the Kennedy and Johnson administrations. Research and development support expanded from a pittance to substantial levels as professors, school systems and newly created centers received federal monies. A new set of interests was vested as new careers opened up—careers in which rewards would follow successful advocacy of change in the schools. It is too early to assess the specific effects of developments in research and application, but it is very likely that the specializations and orientations they induced have contributed to the new zeitgeist. Scientific research sits comfortably with rationalistic perspectives; expanding research and development activities have drawn persons into education who lack the personal commitments to past practice of prior generations of educationists.

Localism was a proud feature of the common school model and persisted as school boards resisted state and federal influence. But that battle seems over in at least two respects; state and federal governments are taking over increasing proportions of school finance and, with it, greater influence over schools. But perhaps the less visible changes are as important. Campbell

and his associates (Campbell & Bunnell, 1963) have documented a general process of "nationalization" of educational affairs, a process which has accompanied increases in communication and travel. As far as teaching is concerned, we note that it and other educational roles are now considered fit objects for national planning—passage of the Education Professions Development Act signals this change. Although most teachers and school administrators probably continue to lead geographically restricted lives, local traditions are increasingly replaced by ideas of cosmopolitan origin.

Ramifications of the Weakening of Traditional Conceptions of Schooling

The weakening of traditional conceptions of schooling has ramifications for the study of teaching work. Topics which previously seemed important now appear less so as prior assumptions erode. Thus, doubt in the efficacy of hierarchical controls on teaching quality reduces our interest in specific questions about such supervision (e.g., how do teachers respond to central office versus principal supervision?). We need new questions to replace those which are losing their significance. It would be presumptuous of anyone, of course, to claim prevision of what specific issues will prove to be most important in the years ahead. But we can analyze some of the problems created by changing outlooks and identify approaches which will probably prove useful in resolving them.

Change and talk of change create an atmosphere of uncertainty among those interested in school events; this applies as well to persons doing research on them. It is probable that most researchers carry about implicit conceptions of how schools are and how they work; each of us has his skeletal empirical model. But perceiving change in thought and practice undermines confidence in those models as one is not quite certain whether personal condensations of reality still apply. The researcher experiences a heightened depictive dilemma, fearing, on one hand, that he will be misled by fads and overlook continuing patterns while, on the other hand, wondering whether trends are genuinely altering the reality. He knows that a given change can reverberate throughout the entire system yet finds no attention to such effects in what he reads and hears about specific innovations. Change increases the need for accurate reports on the empirical reality of schools and teaching—*representative* reports rather than "news" which is generally unique. Modern social science has "raised the ante" in what is considered representative and reliable; the student of school affairs is likely to feel flooded by information of dubious value.

Several commentators (Bidwell, 1965; N. Gross, 1956; Lortie, 1969) have noted that schools, in comparison with other types of institutions, have received little social scientific description useful to investigators. This exacerbates the depictive dilemma experienced in the field and may, in fact, reduce effective communication among researchers. (I suspect researchers may hold more diverse images of school reality than is generally recognized.) One of the urgent items of business in the study of teaching is the improvement of reporting on school and teaching events. We need information on trends throughout the country and we need sensitive, sociological accounts of the daily life of those engaged in school work. We need statistics gathered on germane questions through time; we need thorough accounts of specific innovations and their effects on other subsystems.

One of the ironies of change is that it increases the importance of understanding the status quo ante. Functional analysis has taught us, for example, that few well-established patterns prevail which have not gathered considerable "moss." Merton (1957) has argued persuasively that persisting attributes of social systems become entwined with other attributes in but partially understood ways. Analysts of organization and

work sense this, recognizing that a seemingly small change in one subsystem can have important consequences for other parts of the system. Yet the intuition is of little value unless one has studied the *particular* interconnections of a *particular* system; what latency means is that we cannot discern the linkages within a system without study of its specific nature.

It might be useful to give an illustration of how innovation can stimulate our curiosity into the prior social system. Asked to assess a program of computer-assisted instruction, an analyst might feel satisfied that he can compare cognitive outcomes attained in the program with those found in conventional classroom instruction. But he might have qualms—what other things occur in classrooms which do not in computer-assisted teaching? Are such events consequential? Previously unquestioned aspects of interaction with teachers and peers become important because they are being changed; it is one thing to make general assertions about the differences between human and man-machine interactions, but quite another to identify and measure their effects on students. To do so we must dig deeper into previously ignored aspects of the conventional situation, thus probing aspects of schooling which were previously ignored. This is indicative of the general tendency of change to increase our interest in the status quo.

There is further irony in that the prospect of a different kind of future can increase our dependence on understanding the past, for it is difficult to understand the prevailing system of schooling without attention to its historical development. It is always hypothetical that any given feature of a system is functional; it may be a "survival" which once solved important problems but persists after its utility has passed. But to make judgments about particular patterns is both complex and dangerous, and assessment is improved to the extent that the analyst is familiar with past as well as present problems in the system. Sensitive study of the development of educational institutions can help us to decide which patterns reflect enduring imperatives and which do not—knowledge of this kind is of great value when changes are being considered.

We can also benefit from historical analysis of other institutions. Several occupations, for example, have undergone challenges similar to those confronting teaching today. The potential replacement of certain teacher tasks by technological systems is anything but a novelty in the history of our economy. Under what circumstances have technological innovations become part of the tool kit of practitioners? Under what circumstances have they become capital goods to which workers were subordinated? Or what of the collective assertions called teacher "militancy"; under what conditions have previous efforts of this kind led to status enhancement or status loss? We have all too often overlooked history as a source of insight into organizational and occupational processes; change makes that oversight more serious.

Changes occurring in schools and educational thought have subtle effects on the meanings we attribute to different parts of the institutional reality; variables undergo redefinition as some gain new importance and others lose their previous rank. A major change taking place today is the broadening definition of what is considered to be instructionally significant. For as we become more aware of the traditional structure as but one of several alternatives, organizational aspects of schooling become variables of potential importance to instruction. The free school movement, for example, rejects much of the organizational paraphernalia of public schools; any success it attains will raise questions about the relationship between overall structure and learning. The teaming of teachers can alter the role of the principal, lessening its significance; what happens then to the definition of the role as "instructional leadership"?

Inquiry itself can lead to shifts in mean-

ing in the intellectual domain. Coleman (1966), for example, interprets his findings on the effects of racial separation and integration in terms of self-esteem and mastery feelings, linking these to groupings in schools and classrooms. Ways in which students are grouped rise in importance if his interpretations are accurate, and a matter which was previously thought to be "merely administrative" moves into the set of factors deemed relevant to instructional outcomes. The spread of various types of self-teaching (for example, programmed instruction) underscores a distinction previously made by philosophers but largely ignored by others—the distinction between teaching and learning.

Changes in practice also realign our intellectual priorities. It was not long ago that only sociologists were interested in teacher colleagueship; today, new kinds of staffing systems put issues of teacher interaction close to the heart of instructional affairs. I expect that if teaming arrangements persist and spread, educational research will show the same preoccupation with staff relationships we find in the study of hospitals and mental health organizations (Perrow, 1965). Changed social arrangements can also redefine the meaning of phenomena as, for instance, teacher turnover. That process has been discussed primarily in terms of its retarding effects on teacher professionalization. But when schools are organized on the basis of close and continuing staff relationships, we notice that many comings and goings disrupt teamwork and constrain cooperation. High turnover then becomes a matter of instructional importance.

As we broaden our conception of the instructionally relevant, we widen our view of what should be included in new instructional systems. Such broadening means that more and more aspects of school organization will be seen in "instrumental" terms, as means toward better instruction. The definition of environment for learning which is at the core of instruction will change and the search for ways to assess the relative effectiveness of one arrangement over another will spur inquiry into structural considerations. Research, evaluation and administration are likely to be brought into closer working relationships as decision-makers seek to reduce the increased uncertainty resulting from changed meanings and competing alternatives.

RESEARCH ON TEACHING AS WORK

I wish to preface my observations on recent research with a few comments on the perspective which underlies the approach taken to the review. The theoretical orientation is that of the sociology of work seen as a special case of the study of social institutions. Sociologists who study work generally share most of the predispositions of their colleagues in the discipline supplemented by a small number of particular emphases. One is the assumption, for example, that how persons earn their living has vital consequences for other facets of their lives; work provides the economic base and status expectations (for most people) which shape and constrain life styles. Another emphasis lies in the results which flow from common occupancy of similar work roles. There are cultural consequences as members of a common occupation frequently elaborate their shared experience, developing unique outlooks on their work world and, in some instances, the world in general. There are subcultural consequences as well, common effects whose bases are but poorly understood; but there is growing evidence that engagement in similar tasks induces similar states of mind (Breer & Locke, 1965). Sociologists of work see occupational life as an important source of values and sentiments and attitudes important to individuals and at times to the society as a whole.

The sociology of work comes closer to consisting of a series of problem areas than to an integrated theory or conceptual frame-work. Those engaged in it generally pay close attention to the characteristics of work settings and to repetitive relationships which occur there, including formal authority lines, relations of mutual dependence, informal associations and the like. Regularities of interaction are observed and the norms controlling them analyzed; we examine the interconnections between work processes and relationships with other persons. The delineation and analysis of tasks are of special importance; we inquire into the demands they make for technical and interpersonal and psychological capacities of various kinds and study the frustrations and satisfactions induced by particular task bundles.

Occupations are like communities in that they have a demographic-ecological base which influences their composition and the proclivities of those who enter and persist in a particular line of work. Certain key problems must be resolved if the occupation is to persist—it must recruit new members, train them in the tasks to be performed, absorb them into the group's subculture and reward them for mobilizing their energies and remaining within its ranks. These problems can be solved in a variety of ways; the specific strategies selected affect the kinds of people brought in, their level of technical capacity, the content of their beliefs and sentiments and the kinds of careers they are likely to experience within the occupation. In well-established occupations, therefore, we would expect correlations between the specific processes of perpetuation and the internal life of the occupation. The challenge is to trace such linkages—they are rarely self-evident.

Members of different occupations differ in the nature of their mutual bonds and in the extent to which they work together to shape work affairs. Established professions feature complex systems of entry, training, career allocation and so on; casual occupations have little or none of this. The associational life of an occupation and the forms it takes are important for the provision of its services to the wider society and as an indication of the fundamental commitments of the membership.

One could develop a list of topics studied by sociologists of work; those interested can find several excellent treatises on the subject (Caplow, 1954; E. Gross, 1958; Hall, 1969; Hughes, 1958; Nosow & Form, 1962). Of greater relevance here, however, is that most of us who engage in such inquiry share an interest in the systematic properties of any given occupation. We try to find the connections between seemingly diverse aspects of an occupation's life; linkages exist, in most instances, across demographic and cultural and technical domains to give an occupation its unique qualities. When we find these manifestations of system, our capacity to understand single events increases and we enhance our ability to estimate the likely effects of changes within the system. It is the latter advantage which, in my opinion, makes attention to the social system of teaching work of particular value to education today.

There are several reasons why one would not expect recent research on teachers to have attained great depth and breadth along the lines we have just sketched. The sociological study of teaching as work has been a modest enterprise; specialists in occupational and organizational inquiry are relatively new on the educational scene, while those not so engaged have rarely studied school affairs. Nor have change and its consequences drawn the attention they deserve—there seems to be a lag between most scholarly research and the pace of events in our society. What we know about teaching work is only partially based on direct attacks on the subject; we must use studies which were conceived in other terms.

Given a situation of changing contexts and limited inquiry, it is no simple matter to achieve a balanced assessment. I have tackled the problem by a series of short commentaries on topics which connect the study of occupations with empirical work reported in the literature. The period dealt with is, in most instances, 1964 to 1970 inclusively, with occasional exceptions. The focus is primarily on problems selected for study and general approaches to problems— my approach is broadly methodological rather than technical. The aim is general indication of where we currently stand in order to find leads that may move us closer to the kinds of knowledge which will prove valuable in the decade ahead.

Abstracts were prepared of approximately 150 articles and books touching on teachers.[1] Only data-based material is discussed here; although there have been efforts to synthesize what is known about schools as organizations and teaching as an occupation (some of which are important contributions), I decided to concentrate on what we might call "empirical building blocks" for such attempts. Discussion is also limited to published materials—dissertations are not included. It is certain that some omissions occurred in the review; some of my misgivings about these are allayed by the knowledge that there are several very useful reviews (Bidwell, 1965; Cohen, 1967; LeFevre, 1967; B. O. Smith, 1967) and one book (Dreeben, 1970) which bear on the topics I will discuss. I believe, however, that the research dealt with here consists of a reasonably good sample of the kinds of inquiry which have been undertaken in recent years.

On Statistical Information

Understanding a particular occupation requires that we find its unique place in the society's division of labor and that we know the kinds of people engaged in performing those functions. This is almost impossible to do without accurate data on the work settings and social characteristics of members of the occupation. The assessment and interpretation of trends and changes require regular collections of data

---

[1] These abstracts were prepared with the extremely able assistance of Sister Mary Sullivan.

comparable through time. Getting representative, country-wide data is beyond the resources of most individual researchers and local research agencies; advances depend, therefore, on efforts by government agencies and affluent national organizations. The two national groups which currently do most in this respect are the National Education Association (NEA) Research Division and the United States Office of Education (USOE).

The NEA materials provide the most important data readily available for work on the occupation, but they induce some degree of ambivalence. One is grateful that they exist—they are frequently the only source of information at hand. Yet frustration occurs as well, perhaps because they are often the only source of needed data. I should quickly add, however, that my personal impression is that the quality of NEA data has been improving steadily over the last few years.

Researchers who are unfamiliar with perceptions of political prudence guiding NEA efforts can only speculate that such inhibitions are at work in the Association's bulletins and reports. It is otherwise hard to understand the omission of particular items in the descriptions of teacher personal characteristics and sentiments. In Research Report 1967-R4 (NEA, 1967a), for example, an apparently careful national sample and questionnaire are used to study a variety of questions (including, for example, car ownership) while omitting information on religion, race and ethnicity. The data and cross-tabulations are presented with occasional use of one set of variables and occasional use of another; efforts to analyze the data are hampered. NEA reports sometimes omit interpretations needed by researchers who lack the ancillary information possessed by the Research Division. It is hard to imagine that NEA data banks do not include the information needed to resolve unanswered questions in the text of the comparative analysis of teachers for 1956, 1961 and 1966 (NEA, 1967b) (e.g., how

are we to account for the declining median age of classroom teachers?). One might urge the NEA to follow one or two courses: 1) the *complete* presentation of data with accompanying questionnaires, sample information, etc., with little interpretation or 2) full use of available data in answering general questions about the demographics, etc., of the occupation. Occasional reports on teacher opinion suggest that regular publication on a wider variety of such issues would be of enormous assistance; the time is past when researchers take the "status reports" published by commercial magazines seriously, yet there is special need for us to know (as mentioned above) the nature of teacher sentiment on a variety of questions.

Although its original mandate in the nineteenth century called for the regular production of statistics on education, there are problems with the regular data published by the USOE. There have been single studies of high importance (viz. the Coleman report, 1966, and Mason's work on the beginning teacher, 1961). One hopes that manpower functions undertaken with the passage of the Education Professions Development Act will lead to more emphasis on regular data gathering on schools and teachers, for the large gaps which prevail in our statistical information perpetuate the depictive dilemma of researchers and reduce the effectiveness of educational planning.

The Organizational Context

One of the striking features of teaching as an occupation is its inseparability from the organizational context of the school; in the United States it has been rare for individual teachers to sell teaching of the basic subjects to individuals. Teaching and schools have become entwined in myriad ways in the many decades of their mutual connection; we know relatively little of the many ways in which the occupation has been shaped by the peculiarities of American schools. Yet research on the relationship between teachers and their organizational setting has centered on a relatively narrow band of the theoretical possibilities.

One's first impression of recent empirical articles on this subject is of diversity—there is terminological variety (bureaucratization, teacher orientations, satisfaction, decision making, etc.) and a host of attitude tests and other instruments employed. Yet a small number of themes run beneath the apparent variety, principally, preoccupation with vertical authority relationships and teacher reactions to their work settings. The latter usually emphasize matters of satisfaction or dissatisfaction, a proclivity noted by Charters (1963) in his review of earlier work.

We can observe these twin interests in three inquiries which seem disparate—those of Hartley (1966), Hornstein, Callahan, Fisch, and Benedict (1968) and Flizak (1968). Hartley probed the connections between teacher satisfaction (along with effectiveness and conformity) and perceived degrees of bureaucracy in the school, and he elaborated the design by classifying teachers as local or cosmopolitan. He found some correlations, but the patterns remain somewhat puzzling. Hornstein, drawing on the general literature of work satisfactions, tested the likelihood that teachers prefer to have influence over organizational decisions; positive results were supplemented by findings that teachers preferred principals who were perceived as technically competent. Flizak developed a classificatory scheme for schools with authority as a major dimension and, having administered 10 different instruments, concluded that divergent authority settings produce divergent teacher orientations. Although one wishes that the dimensions measured by the instruments were clearer, the general finding is valuable. The three studies tend to converge on a central theme—the distribution and management of vertical authority are connected with the sentiments of classroom teachers. Perhaps future research can relate such sentiments to instructional outcomes, thus linking modes of authority to student learning.

Bridges (1964) and Trask (1964) undertook researches which lead to understanding important aspects of school dynamics. Bridges began with a focus on the psychological properties of principals (à la Rokeach) but found that teacher participation, as influenced by principals, depended more on school size and principal experience than on closed- or open-mindedness; he also found that although teachers generally preferred inclusion in decision making over exclusion, some "independent-minded" teachers were generally antipathetic to the principal. Teachers wanted principals to protect them from interfering parents and disruptive students; they were, moreover, considerably readier to comply with principal initiatives when they were somewhat remote from classroom immediacies. Trask's work supplements the picture we can draw from Bridges's findings; she demonstrated the variety of ways in which principals adjusted to the cross-pressures of honoring their responsibility to supervise teachers while respecting their autonomy. An NEA study (1969) of a large sample of teachers and schools confirms the problem of supervision for principals, revealing that many, in fact, sidestep evaluation of teachers, particularly those with experience; it reveals an interesting complication, however, in reporting that a high proportion of teachers say they want evaluation and supervision and want it from the principal. It may be, as Corwin (1965) argues, that professionalization is a militant process involving conflict between teachers and administrators, but there is little indication to date that teachers subscribe to an ideology which supports such conflict on a general basis. Much remains to be done in clarifying the perplexities presented by teacher sentiments toward principals; it is clear that direct application of the bureaucracy-professional dichotomy does not explain the case for public schools.

With one exception, there seems to be little attention to differences among schools on other than authority-related grounds. The exception is to separate out, in some researches, the peculiar nature of slum schools and their teachers. Wayson (1966) provides promising leads in a study suggesting that teachers who choose to remain in slum schools have redefined the psychic rewards which are meaningful to them. Sieber and Wilder (1967) point out that teachers and parents are particularly likely to conflict over teacher activities in lower-income areas. Smith and Geoffrey (1968) undertook a valuable case study of a classroom in a slum school—a study I shall refer to again. Yet it probably remains the case that the most influential depictions of teaching in city schools are those of individuals who, having undertaken the experience, write exposés of what transpires there. Kozol (1970) and others have continued the tradition of the *Blackboard Jungle* and *Up the Down Staircase,* a tradition which serves to generate blame rather than to explain recurrent patterns.

Charters (1963) has questioned the value of research preoccupation with teacher satisfaction and morale; one can also question the value of limiting organizational analysis to vertical authority and related questions on decision making. There continue to be, of course, significant issues in this area. Yet there are other ways in which teachers and schools interact, and schools differ on grounds other than their authority patterns. They come in different sizes and with different divisions of labor; their clienteles vary by socioeconomic level and by ethnic and religious background, by rural-urban or old versus new suburban settings, etc. Some schools are relatively well established, with traditions of academic excellence or athletic prowess; how do such contexts influence teachers and vice versa? Today we find more and more efforts to rearrange space and working relationships among teachers; therefore one would expect increasing variations along lines of teacher-teacher cooperation, etc. Surely these or other dimensions deserve considerable attention; much remains to be initiated in the study of teachers and their organizational setting.

Redefining the Teacher's Tasks

Perhaps it is because teaching is so very familiar, anything but arcane and esoteric; or, perhaps, it stems from the modest social status of the occupation, but whatever the reasons, the tendency has been to see the teacher's tasks as relatively simple and straightforward and, for scholars in education, among the less problematic and interesting areas for study. Pedagogical theories came and went without much attention to their interconnections with the daily actualities of classroom work; for many decades, there was practically no attempt to conceptualize the flow of events in classrooms, no serious attempt to codify existing practice, and no significant development of language to identify and clarify alternative actions for teachers. The sixties proved significant in this respect as sensitive scholars began long overdue research on the classroom itself (a few had begun earlier) and found that such inquiry was anything but simple and the reality considerably more involved than had generally been suspected.

The awareness of greater task complexity emerged from inquiry of rather diverse types. It came out of the inquiries of B. O. Smith, a philosopher, Bellack in curricular study, and Flanders's work on interactions. We see it in the work of Hyman (1967), Kliebard (1966) and Zahorik (1970). Glick (1968) and Yamamoto (1967) drew attention to group phenomena which have been overlooked in the study of classrooms. Two studies have been of special significance, however, in reshaping the image of teacher classroom activities, and both are based on intensive observation—the work of Jackson (1968) and Smith and Geoffrey (1968). Jackson and Smith, already well-established educational psychologists, observed and analyzed social psychological processes previously underplayed in educational research literature; it was clear that their attention to sociological realities was the outcome of observation and not the special pleadings of sociologists. And although the studies use somewhat different concepts and arrive at some different conclusions (Smith and Geoffrey are more optimistic about finding a rational basis for teaching decisions than is Jackson), both works contribute substantially to our understanding of classroom events and make us aware of the inadequacy of simple models of teaching tasks.

Jackson's and Smith and Geoffrey's studies are excellent starting points for inquiry that needs to be done on teacher tasks; from the perspective of the sociology of work, it is essential that we have as complete a picture as possible of similarities and differences among teachers of various kinds and within the different teaching roles found in modern schools. It is clear, for example, that the nature of a person's daily tasks plays a large part in forming his outlook on life; this theme stretches through the work of Adam Smith, William James, Thorstein Veblen and, most recently, the aforementioned research of Breer and Locke (1965). Those wishing to understand the shared beliefs, attitudes and sentiments of teachers are well advised, such authors tell us, to pay close attention to the repetitive demands work makes on people and the ways in which they come to adjust, in myriad ways, to those demands. There are several indications, in fact, that differences in roles among teachers are of great importance; Getzels and Jackson (1963) drew attention to subject matter in their review, and other researchers have commented on it in the course of reporting findings. Yet we have remarkably little inquiry into differences among teachers by level, type of clientele, subject matter, etc. (One suspects, for example, that role heterogeneity is an important factor playing on teacher bargaining representatives—the emphasis on salary and general working conditions may represent the relatively narrow common denominator of interest shared by teachers whose tasks are more diverse than usually recognized.) Our grasp of the occupation is obviously faltering until such time as we are able to make informed statements on such questions.

It is worth noting that the emergence of a more complex view of teaching has been associated with the readiness of researchers to engage in protracted observation—using both formal and informal approaches. A heartening development, moreover, is the increased use of video-taped transcriptions as occurs at Stanford's Center for Research and Development on Teaching. Sustained analytic work of this kind is highly promising and, if it continues, means that we shall learn a great deal more about teacher tasks and activities in the years ahead.

"Career" Processes in Teaching

It is a curious feature of our social scientific rhetoric that we lack a term which expresses the duality of occupational perpetuation and individual careers. For each is the other side of a common coin; to persist, occupations develop ways of recruiting and socializing and rewarding persons, while such patterns, seen subjectively, are paths individuals follow as their careers unfold. That is the reason the word career is placed in quotes above—I am using the term to refer to both aspects of the movement of persons into and through teaching. Deciphering the peculiarities of an occupation requires that we know the processes it has developed to perpetuate itself and the relationship between such processes and individual choice, such as how one learns the trade and various modes of "making it."

Our comments will be subdivided into six discrete subtopics. The various topics have received differential attention in the research literature and developments are uneven. Much of the work has been influenced by a concern with professionalization processes; one cannot miss the undertone of status anxiety which marks some of the studies. There is a general deficiency in this area which should be noted at the outset—namely, the absence of historical awareness on the part of almost all who study career phenomena. Most features of the career system in public schools have roots in decisions made during the nineteenth century, a fact which is apparent from a careful reading of Elsbree (1939). I believe this lack of historical sensitivity accounts, in part, for the tendency of researchers in this area to slight the societal context within which the teaching occupation has developed and to which it has necessarily adjusted.

Recruitment and Selection

Is it not odd that an occupation in which there is considerable talk about "attracting better people" has featured next to no research on processes whereby people move into it? Review reveals very few researches dealing with this question and, I fear, none which grapple with it in terms of the best available theory and conceptualization. We need research in this area which takes account of the various factors involved in occupational selection and is grounded in the realities of sex differences.

Ginzberg et al. (1951) have demonstrated how occupational selection involves economic, sociological and psychological dimensions which interact in the life history of individuals. One finds no attempts in the literature to encompass more than a single aspect of the question for teachers. The other problem we find in the few available studies is a reluctance to note from the outset (and thus take into account in designs) the fact that men and women experience different life contingencies and career realities. Studies of motives or values, for example, are not placed in the divergent contexts of the two sexes.

There are many issues of immediate importance which would be informed by knowledge in this area. To what extent is the orientation of men entering teaching shaped from the outset by the hope for promotion to administrative positions? How do fluctuations in the market affect decisions to enter teaching? This question is important today as we see important shifts in demand. Drucker (1970) has pointed out that careers in education rest on a demographic base; where are studies relating entry to teaching, etc., to shifts in the population? But there is little gain in belaboring the general point: we know next to nothing about the flow of people into teaching.

Formal Training and Its Effects

There is a ritualized quality about recent studies of teacher training; review of 20 such articles disclosed three major types of treatment: a) studies in which tests were given cohorts of trainees at succeeding points in their progress, b) discussions without empirical data and c) articles describing the merits of a particular program written by someone prominent in its operation. All in all, the outcome is disappointing. Studies based on intermittent testing generally fail to place either the tests or the findings in a meaningful theoretical context; the repeated use of the Minnesota Teacher Attitude Inventory (MTAI), for example, is rarely explained. The level of discussion in the nonempirical articles is rarely original or insightful; the descriptions of particular programs frequently suffer from evident overenthusiasm and rarely include systematic comparisons with other programs or earlier efforts in the same institutions. One hopes we will find better ways to disseminate information and evaluation than to have those responsible write them in so promotional a vein.

There are studies, however, which vary from these formulas and are of interest. Baker (1969) reports on a carefully conducted and modest experiment in which it was found that teachers who employed given principles of learning taught their students more. Kallenbach and Gall (1969), though tempering some earlier claims for the training efficacy of microteaching, argue most reasonably that its value lies in obtaining results similar to those obtained by considerably more expensive and troublesome alternatives. Young (1969) winnows out research on modeling processes involved in observing video-taped teaching in a thoughtful, useful way. Robbins (1969) asks good questions about training vis-à-vis altered conditions in the teaching role but unfortunately uses weak data of the old, "poll-the-practitioners" type.

Given the centrality of teaching preparation to schools and departments of education, one wonders at the paucity of important research on the topic. Research in education has long been criticized for its parochialism, and there seems to be a carrying over of self-imposed intellectual isolation in this area of research—the absence of comparative treatment is striking. There are, after all, numerous kinds of vocational preparation conducted in colleges and universities; where is the research contrasting practices and effects in teacher training with engineering or social work or forestry or law or clinical psychology or any number of other occupations? Dreeben (1970), for example, argues effectively that training in education is of relatively low impact; my findings (Lortie, 1966, 1968, 1969) based on interviews with teachers, suggest that this is indeed the case. If such be true, it is meat for considerable inquiry. Matters of fine detail might well wait until we learn considerably more about bases for the low permeation of teacher training; should research prove it to be considerably more influential than the preceding implies, researchers might then turn to discovering what lies behind the ambiguous reputation of teacher training with a variety of publics, including a significant proportion of classroom teachers (Hermanowicz, 1966).

The Riddle of Socialization

A fair amount of research on teacher socialization evolved during the later sixties; in fact, we now stand in the desirable position of having alternative explanations and emphases available for systematic testing. There are at least four distinct positions on the key processes involved in the transformation of a person into a classroom teacher. They are: a) an emphasis on early childhood, b) the presumption that peer influence is cardinal, c) a focus on the influence of persons with evaluative power and d) the view of students as socializing agents.

Benjamin Wright is the leading exponent of the early life emphasis; his psychoanalytic orientation leads him to examine teaching as the expression of psychodynamic processes initiated early in the teacher's life. In an article co-authored with Tuska (Wright & Tuska, 1968), for example, he interprets the ineffectiveness of practice teaching in terms of its continuation of passivity for the teacher-to-be, a situation which reinforces rather than corrects for fantasy elements which underlie the original choice of teaching. An interest in experience as a student has been shown by Lortie (1966, 1968, 1969), who suspects that the protracted exposure to potent models leads teachers-to-be to internalize (largely unconsciously) modes of behavior which are triggered in later teaching. Although the two hold different theoretical commitments, the implications of their positions are somewhat similar; each argues that to a considerable extent future teacher behavior is rooted in experiences which predate formal training.

Hoy (1967, 1968, 1969) has undertaken a series of interesting studies of the socialization of beginning teachers. For him, changes in teacher ideology grow out of interactions with fellow teachers. Edgar and Warren (1969), on the other hand, present strong evidence that beginning teachers are particularly sensitive to the views of those whose evaluations of them will have personal consequences. In this view, socialization is a function of internalizing values, etc., held by sanctioning colleagues.

The fourth position is reflected in research by Haller. In a highly imaginative study, Haller (1967) showed that protracted contact with children altered the sociolinguistic patterns of teachers, moving them in the direction of childlike rather than more adult forms of expression. Using this as evidence of student-to-teacher effects, he argues that teachers, in the beginning years, are shaped, in Skinnerian terms, by student responses.

This brief review is sufficient to indicate, I believe, that there are lively alternate explanations of the socialization process. I suspect that we shall find all emphases to be of some importance as inquiry proceeds, for socialization is undoubtedly a complex process not readily captured by a simple, one-factor frame of reference. One hopes it will not be long before we have sophisticated and comprehensive studies assessing the relative contributions of the several agencies and mechanisms.

Some Oddities of Professional Growth

Our era is one which lays heavy verbal emphasis on the importance of "continuing education." A few studies which report on aspects of such education among teachers suggest that the career system is somewhat anomalous in this regard. To wit:

1. Dillman (1964) had teachers (and members of some professions) rank activities in terms of their perceived contribution to teacher "growth." Among the findings is a negative correlation (0.55) between the attributed importance of activities by teachers and the actual distribution of time and energy teachers expend in the course of their regular work.

2. Amidon and Blumberg (1966) did a study of principals' and teachers' perceptions of school faculty meetings. They report that whereas principals think teachers feel free to speak, teachers feel inhibited; whereas principals are seen as noncommittal in their responses to teacher ideas, the principals see themselves as encouraging such ideas. Principals see the meetings in a favorable light, teachers much less so.

3. The NEA (1967c) studied payment arrangements in 307 school districts to find out what kinds of educative experiences were financially rewarded. One hundred percent of the systems recognize college courses, 82 percent in-service instruction and

67 percent travel. But 35 percent acknowledge research, 33 percent committee service in the school system, 29 percent professional writing, 22 percent attendance at professional meetings, 15 percent supervision of student teachers and 14 percent holding office in a professional association. One notes (NEA did not) that many more systems reward teachers for study under professors or school administrators while peer activities are considerably less likely to be reinforced. Does this reward system perpetuate a subordinate, passive intellectual stance for teachers contrasted to horizontal, collegial interchanges and personal responsibility?

Teacher Loss and Survival

Geer (1966) believes that the recurrent concern with persons leaving teaching reflects anxiety about professional status; her comment to this effect is made in an excellent essay on the problem of occupational commitment in teaching. Whatever accounts for the hardiness of this perennial, it surely is a prime instance of the lack of historical perspective in educational research, for few note that high turnover was built into American public schooling during the nineteenth century. It could hardly be otherwise when the position was designed to attract women rather than men and women had to leave upon marrying. Today, of course, married women do teach (they're the modal group), but we have the continuation of a related phenomenon in the interruption pattern associated with child rearing. But schools, during the formative period, accommodated to a high, regular rate of personnel turnover; I suspect that the self-contained classroom, in fact, was a prime facilitator of this revolving-door pattern.

We again encounter resistance to acknowledging the differences in life cycles of men and women as in the instance of recruitment/selection mentioned earlier. Rabinowitz and Crawford (1960), for example, documented the key role of sex in the career persistence of men and women. Yet we find later studies in which the two sexes are combined. White (1966), limiting his sample to female elementary teachers, shows that involvement differs sharply among those who persist a second year. A very careful study by Charters (1970) underlines the significance of life cycle factors in contrast to organizational factors. An NEA national sample study done in 1968 contains information useful to those interested in this topic and teacher mobility.

There are serious gaps, however, in our information on the movement of persons out of teaching. For example, of women who leave to have and raise children, which ones are likely to return? Men, it seems, are not too happy with classroom teaching after a given age, apparently somewhere around 40. What is the relationship between non-promotion and leaving education for a completely different kind of work? Myths abound on these and related topics, and valid knowledge would appear useful to those concerned with the retention of talent in the field.

Mobility

Two important studies on teacher mobility were undertaken during the latter half of the sixties—Griffiths, Goldman and McFarland (1965) on career mobility in New York City and Pedersen's study (1970) on teacher migration and attrition in Michigan. The first discloses some of the varieties of career orientations present among teachers and the informal mechanisms underlying "making out" in a particular school system; the pity is that others have not followed up with inquiries into other settings. Pedersen's study is unusual both in the wide range of variables considered and in the comprehensiveness of the data; it presents a statistical picture of high reliability that permits inferences on how allocative mechanisms work in teaching careers. One learns, for example, that larger and/or more prosperous communities attract and hold teachers more readily than the less favored; one observes that systems tend to be linked together in informal leagues. Both studies move us toward greater awareness of informal processes in the career system and their part in allocating resources. They contribute a note of realism which one hopes will be extended in subsequent research.

An Odd Gap: Teacher Attitudes, Values and Beliefs

Someone unfamiliar with the specifics of school and teacher literature might expect to find it replete with information on how classroom teachers see the world in general and their world in particular. For are teachers not critical agents in performing the socialization functions of schools? Is it not well established that American schools have a long tradition of including moral objectives on their agendas? Sophisticated observers of education, moreover, have commented frequently (before collective bargaining) on the "pocket veto" power of teachers (the latter phrase is Francis Keppel's), on their ability to quietly subvert plans and curricula, etc., in which they do not believe. Yet our neophyte reader of the research literature would find little inquiry dealing with values and viewpoints of teachers useful to understanding directions of student socialization or parameters of teacher acceptance and rejection of various schooling approaches. What he would find are materials at two extremes—sweeping generalizations about teachers as "upholders of middle-class morality" on one hand (a vague term which is rarely distinguished from general expectations in a highly industrialized society) and numerous studies measuring teacher subscription to highly specific, externally derived values as found in the MTAI and similar instruments. The very few exceptions (e.g., Jackson's [1968] insights into the phenomenology of teachers) make us realize how vital such knowledge is and, indeed, how misleading the implicit stereotypes of academic research are likely to prove.

Could such incuriosity about teacher views and values reflect an unconscious snobbery on the part of university-based researchers? Contacts between academic researchers and classroom teachers are likely to be supersubordinate relationships—the formal reward system of teaching, in fact, gives professors teaching employed teachers certain gatekeeper powers over salary levels, career opportunities, etc. Teachers are often the academic researcher's students —the capacity to learn from students, in all likelihood, is not widely distributed in any academic setting. Such circumstances do not prevail, of course, in inquiries undertaken by teacher organizations and agencies with full-time research staffs; perhaps we can expect more attention to teacher outlooks as people other than professors conduct research on the occupation.

There are methodological habits, however, which play a part in producing the gap in our knowledge of teacher viewpoints. One is the seemingly automatic reliance upon "instruments" which are so completely closed as to forestall the chance that teacher respondents will correct researcher assumptions and frameworks. This is coupled, moreover, with a proclivity to "discover" the effects of esoteric rather than basic, familiar variables of known general potency. Too many studies tell us of relationships between weak, exotic variables and researcher-centered dimensions of sentiment and values; in balance, we have too few studies which explore the subjective world of teachers in terms of *their* conceptions of what is salient. Basic demographic and personal characteristic variables have proved time and again in survey research to account for large proportions of attitudinal variance; we have yet to "map" the general outlines of teacher viewpoints and relate them to basic social variables. One does not object to the carefully targeted, theoretically designed study, but given our *general* ignorance of the world view of

teachers, we are not likely to interpret findings from such studies with the appropriate level of sophistication. We know too little of the general context to "place" smaller findings. In my opinion we have put certain fashionable carts before immature horses; we need research on the world view of teachers with approaches (open-ended interviews, observation, analysis of personal documents, etc.) that make the researcher come to terms with the value hierarchies of teachers. Once these have been identified, there will be no dearth of taxing theoretical work to be done.

Social Factors in the Classroom

Writing in 1966, Boocock was unable to find much information useful in differentiating teacher performance in the classroom. "While it is clear that the teacher and the methods he or she uses are important to the learning process, we cannot yet say just what it is that the effective teacher is or does" (p. 40). This is apparently still the case today, but one can take heart from the fact that we now have regular provision, in well-staffed research centers, for such inquiry. I should like to make a few observations on certain aspects of classroom affairs.

(a) Efforts to find a personality base for differences in classroom performance are apparently on the decline, but some writers continue the effort. Harvey, White, Prather, Alter, and Hoffmeister (1966), and Harvey, Prather, White, and Hoffmeister (1968), for example, present evidence that teacher beliefs, arrayed on the continuum of abstract to concrete, are associated with different levels of performance. Cogan (1963) relates the capacity of the teacher to be "inclusive" to student willingness to expend learning effort. Little has been done about investigating social characteristics and performance, but an exception is the continuing interest in the effects of upward mobility on teachers. Hart (1965), for example, shows that such teachers are harder on lower-class students.

Social characteristics may be more important than we currently believe—particularly in terms of matching teachers and students. There is little or no research reported on the compatibility of teachers and students along racial, ethnic and religious lines, although myths are developing (myths which can play an important part in social policy) on such compatibilities. Glazer and Moynihan (1970), for example, doubted that the New York City combination of Jewish staff and black and Puerto Rican students was fruitful, arguing that the differential perspectives of the teachers and students create dysfunctional strains. Which combinations seem productive and which do not in ethnic subdivisions among white children? Do arrogances and uncertainties in interaction found in the wider society stop at the classroom door, or do WASP students, for example, subtly patronize "ethnic" teachers? Many questions occur which do not appear in the research done during the sixties; one wonders whether norms of universalism in schools carry over to inhibit such research. It is unfortunate if they do; surely we can study what is the stuff of daily journalism and talk in the corner bar.

(b) A promising line of research rests in studying the relationships between career stages and orientations to classroom work. Such relationships, one presumes, are mediated by psychological states which result from career experiences and which influence classroom events. Take, for example, the state of mind which permits teachers to be "enthusiastic," a condition, asserts Rosenshine (1970), which is apparently associated with higher rates of student learning. Although one would expect personalities to differ in their capacity to express enthusiasm, one would postulate that the capacity also derives from feelings of satisfaction or frustration with teaching and other facets of one's life. Studies of teacher morale point to systematic variations by age, sex and marital status; older, single women, for example, invest more heavily in their teaching but report satisfactions lower than those re-

ported by less involved married women. Lortie (1972) found that older male teachers tend to displace their commitments and energy to avocational interests or other employment and to express bitterness in describing their school systems. If such regularities in the patterning of dissatisfaction lead to lessened capacity for enthusiastic teaching, there are instructional effects resulting from the way in which teacher career rewards are allocated. These negative effects may point toward the desirability of structural changes. All this remains hypothetical, but it illustrates that the way in which teaching work is organized may have considerably more direct instructional effect than has been recognized to date.

(c) Studies appeared during the sixties which indicated unequal treatment of students by teachers; these include Brophy and Good (1970), Hart (1965), Jackson and Lahaderne (1967), Rist (1970), and Yee (1968). Reported bases for differential treatment include the presumably "irrelevant" factors of student race, social class and sex. Such findings distress researchers who believe in the ideology of equitable treatment and who fear that schools may underscore injustices found in the society. One can interpret such indications of discrimination in various ways including, of course, the presumption that teachers are expressing prejudices held against blacks, the poor and boys. This is surely possible, although we do not know whether teachers hold more, less or similar levels of prejudice compared to others in our society; there may be other factors at work, however, which should be considered.

What occurs to teachers as the consequence of their position as initiators and upholders of the moral order in classrooms? It is clear that, given their organizational context, teachers must invent and enforce rules; Smith and Geoffrey (1968) are particularly helpful in showing this. If Durkheim's analysis of such phenomena is correct, upholding a moral order requires the regular, even dramatic reaffirmation of "the good" through censure of "the bad." Those who are the object of greater teacher reproof, moreover, may be less able and willing, for a variety of reasons, to conform to the typical rules developed in schools; teachers may fall into discriminatory interaction patterns as a consequence of role imperatives stemming from the group nature of classroom instruction. Thus correcting such inequities may lay less in "changing teacher attitudes" (a formidable task given their vast numbers) than in organizing instruction in ways which make fewer demands for rule proliferation and enforcement. It also suggests that training experiences should include greater attention to issues of distributive justice and relate legal understandings to the classroom situation.

(d) The norms of educational research (and social and behavioral science generally) stress the discovery of differences in phenomena and the search for antecedents or consequences of such differences. Thus we look for different kinds of schools and teachers and social arrangements. That such inquiry is essential (it takes on special value when options become available) is beyond doubt; it is possible, however, that we have unwisely ignored similarities within schooling and teaching and comparisons of modal ways in education with modalities elsewhere. One is restimulated to this view by reading Hoetker and Ahlbrand's article (1969) on the persistence of recitation in classrooms. They question our concentration on differences within classrooms, citing Flanders's findings to emphasize commonality rather than divergence.

Inquiry oriented to similarities within the classroom could focus on the issue of *general* performance by teachers compared to other categories of people at work. What mixtures of competition and cooperation, for example, obtain where average performance is high? What norms have developed to improve performance in some occupations and not in others? How do differences between occupations relate to issues of recruitment, socialization, the allocation of rewards, etc.? Such questions may well be settled by practitioners of pop social science unless serious research is undertaken and sustained; blind faith in private enterprise, for example, may simply decree that interpersonal competition between teachers is obviously the answer.

Prepared Ground: Collective Bargaining

There is one dramatic trend of the sixties which did receive close and sensitive scholarly attention—the development of large-scale collective bargaining within schools. Three important books appeared in a short period of time (Cole, 1969; Perry & Wildman, 1970; Rosenthal, 1969). Cole's study of the unionization of New York City teachers is first-rate, exemplifying the qualities argued for in the first section above. It is historically oriented, carefully conceptualized, uses survey research data in intelligent fashion, displays a sense of social structure, includes comparative analyses of teaching and other occupations and presents interpretations of the broader implications of unionization for the occupation. Rosenthal's study is particularly strong on political processes at work within both teacher organizations and their urban contexts and is based on comparisons of developments in five cities. Wildman and Perry fulfill a critical reportorial function based on surveys of numerous systems and provide essential orientation for researchers unfamiliar with the language and legalities of bargaining. Each book provokes new questions which should be important in the years ahead.

There is a growing number of articles, of varying importance, dealing with "teacher militancy." Two of special interest (Kratzmann, 1963; Paton, 1968) deal with the Canadian situation, providing a comparative context to the American experience and possible alternative models for the channeling of teacher assertions. Both authors argue that augmented teacher power can be combined with a sense of responsibility for its educational effects. Andreasen (1968) presents comparative data on members of AFT- and NEA-type organizations which suggest that the more aggressive groups get at least some of their impetus from the frustrations of men trapped in the peculiar career struc- ture of public school teaching.

There are opportunities for research of several kinds in the area of collective bar- gaining and associations; such inquiries can lead to better understanding of schools as organizations, the career dynamics of teach- ing and circumstances influencing the scope and consequences of teacher participation in policy making. For example, what effects does bargaining (particularly the grievance process) have on principal handling of authority, status, sense of colleagueship, etc.? Under what conditions do teacher representatives usurp functions previously performed by administrators? What kinds of teachers move into positions of associa- tional leadership, and how do their perspec- tives compare with those of rank-and-file teachers? Where does oligarchic governance occur, where not? In what kinds of bar- gaining situations can teacher organizations "afford" to show concern for purely educa- tional objectives? What are the antecedents of contracts which bureaucratize and crystal- lize previous practice versus contracts which permit structural flexibility?

It will also be important to watch develop- ments closely as the demand for teachers shrinks, providing school boards with op- portunities to counter teacher groups which they have not possessed in recent years.

EPILOGUE

It is difficult to avoid the impression that inquiry into teaching as work has missed important steps in its development; it is as if we were trying to chart particular acreage without a map of the general terrain. The lack of overview constrains our capacity to deal with change, for our image of "regular conditions," constructed from scattered in- stances of unrelated research, is blurred. It is not easy to separate trends from newly discovered patterns; we are likely to miss or exaggerate subtleties when prominent patterns of behavior and major variables are partially described and largely unanalyzed. Although we have noted a few instances where inquiry is doing well, the general impression formed in the course of this review is that our knowledge is uncoordi- nated and marked by large gaps. We are a long way from the resources we need to cope with a changing zeitgeist and its demands for inquiry-based guidance.

Despite long and widespread presence on the American scene, the social structure, social psychology and culture of schools and teachers remain largely unknown. Famili- arity seems to have bred incuriosity on matters which under more arcane circum- stances would have received patient descrip- tion and imaginative interpretation. It seems to be difficult for us to feel genuine puzzle- ment at something as "ordinary" as schools and teachers. Our relative indifference to the basic characteristics of our system of schooling means that we have little grasp on how various parts of the system con- tribute to the working of the whole.

There are ways, however, by which we can increase our research effectiveness. One such way lies in more thoughtful use of the principle of the division of labor within our research community. Earlier we dis- cussed the paucity of statistical data needed to understand the position and direction of the occupation and the inability of most researchers to tackle this problem. Would it not be possible for those already engaged in collecting such data (and some who do not, such as the teacher unions) to get together for rational planning on what organization should do what tasks? I sus- pect that many scholars in the field could generate insightful suggestions on how such data gathering could be improved and would be delighted to have the opportunity to share their views with federal agencies and national associations.

But we will not solve the depictive dilem- ma solely through obtaining better quantitative data. All of us will have to cooperate in finding more effective ways to share our observations on school processes and significant changes in them. We lack mechanisms for stimulating useful chronicles, case histories, close analyses of specific innovations, limited purpose surveys and the like for the enlightenment of the research community. Does the difficulty lie in an overly rigid definition of what constitutes publishable research? Have we fallen into an orthodoxy which requires that publication occur only when observations and findings fall into a particular format? It would be more than unfortunate if this is the case, for the expansion of research and development means that more and more investigators are having protracted contact with school realities. Surely the insights so gained should be made generally available.

The development of viable models of educational institutions will require researchers in education to engage in more original formulation and conceptualization. We have gone through a stage of importing concepts and models without sufficient attention to the special qualities of schools and teaching; note how gradually we have come to see the descriptive limits of the concept of bureaucracy. (A similar process has occurred with the idea of professionalism.) I know of no more effective strategy for dealing with this problem than the not-exactly-new method of systematic comparison; I should like to say a few words on its importance at the present juncture.

It is a truism that the quantity and quality of observations one can make on any object increase when it is juxtaposed with another. The research on teachers, however, is generally barren of role comparisons, both within the occupation and between it and other occupations. We have yet to see efforts to find characteristics generic to teachers after specific settings and tasks have been taken into account; for example, we find little research on persons who teach in commercial institutes, private schools, barber

colleges, Sunday schools and private music schools. Broadening our focus would help us to locate unique features in public school teaching; it would sensitize us to effects stemming from various organizational and task conditions.

There are several ways in which teachers could be effectively compared with members of other occupations. I would suggest one in particular—the method of pairing along single similarities. Teachers convey information; so do journalists, management consultants, certain kinds of advertisers. What imperatives flow from this function and how do they differ when we move across occupational lines? Teachers, like pediatricians and recreation workers, relate to persons younger than themselves; how does age discrepancy influence those engaged in such occupations? Police patrolmen share with teachers the need to make numerous discretionary judgments in the course of their work; what can we learn from comparing differences and similarities between the two occupations? Teachers are similar to mental health workers in seeking often elusive and intangible outcomes; what mechanisms can we trace to attempts to deal with this facet of their work? It is when we grapple with such questions that our curiosity about teaching is stimulated in fresh ways—they help us escape the clichés to which we are constantly exposed. Finding believable answers proves to require tough thinking and sensitive inquiry.

How are we to infuse our analyses of schools and teachers with greater awareness of historical and developmental processes? Would closer working relationships between behavioral scientists and historians bring this about?

A final word. The ultimate utility of research on the occupation of teaching will rest on the validity of findings on matters which relate to designing more effective arrangements for schooling. I cannot imagine a future in which scholarly resources are not less plentiful than potential lines of inquiry. The challenge is double-barreled

—we must find ways of combining the strengths of basic research with awareness of the points at which intervention can make a difference. There is considerable imagination called for in an applied field like education—the kind of imagination which can combine scholarly thoroughness and detachment with a sense of what is actionable. It is no simple matter to find effective levers of constructive action in an enterprise as massive as public schools. Economists have come to grips, however, with whole economies and have learned to think in terms of multiplier effects—they have located some of the points of intervention where decisions reverberate throughout the entire system. Given the emerging zeitgeist of education today, it seems we will have to develop that kind of understanding if research is to help education to adjust to new realities in a thoughtful, reasoned fashion.

REFERENCES

Amidon, E., & Blumberg, A. Principal and teacher perceptions of school faculty meetings. *Administrator's Notebook*, 1966, 15(3).

Andreasen, H. L. Teacher unionism: Personal data affecting membership. *Phi Delta Kappan*, 1968, 50, 177–189.

Baker, E. L. Relationship between learner achievement and instructional principles stressed during teacher preparation. *Journal of Educational Research*, 1969, 63, 99–102.

Bidwell, C. E. The school as a formal organization. In J. G. March (Ed.), *Handbook of organizations*. Chicago: Rand McNally, 1965. Pp. 972–1022.

Boocock, S. S. Toward a sociology of learning: A selective review of existing research. *Sociology of Education*, 1966, 39, 1–45.

Breer, P. E., & Locke, E. A. *Task experience as a source of attitudes*. Homewood, Ill.: Dorsey Press, 1965.

Bridges, E. M. Teacher participation in decision-making. *Administrator's Notebook*, 1964, 12(9).

Brophy, J. E., & Good, T. L. Teachers' communication of differential expectations for children's classroom performance: Some behavioral data. *Journal of Educational Psychology*, 1970, 61, 365–374.

Campbell, R. F., & Bunnell, R. A. (Eds.) *Nationalizing influences on secondary education*. Chicago: University of Chicago, Midwest Administration Center, 1963.

Caplow, T. *The sociology of work*. Minneapolis: University of Minnesota Press, 1954.

Charters, W. W., Jr. The social background of teaching. In N. L. Gage (Ed.), *Handbook of research on teaching*. Chicago: Rand McNally, 1963. Pp. 715–813.

Charters, W. W., Jr. Some factors affecting teacher survival in school districts. *American Educational Research Journal*, 1970, 7, 1–27.

Cogan, M. L. Research on the behavior of teachers: A new phase. *Journal of Teacher Education*, 1963, 14, 238–243.

Cohen, E. G. Status of teachers. *Review of Educational Research*, 1967, 37, 280–295.

Cole, S. *The unionization of teachers: A case study of the UFT*. New York: Praeger, 1969.

Coleman, J. S., et al. *Equality of educational opportunity*. Washington, D.C.: U.S. Government Printing Office, 1966.

Corwin, R. G. Professional persons in public organizations. *Educational Administration Quarterly*, 1965, 1(3), 1–22.

Dillman, B. R. Teacher activities and professional growth as perceived by physicians, lawyers, clergymen, and educators. *Journal of Teacher Education*, 1964, 15, 386–392.

Dreeben, R. *The nature of teaching*. Glenview, Ill.: Scott, Foresman, 1970.

Drucker, P. The new markets and the new capitalism. *The Public Interest*, 1970, 21, 44–79.

Edgar, D. E., & Warren, R. L. Power and autonomy in teacher socialization. *Sociology of Education*, 1969, 42.

Elsbree, W. S. *The American teacher*. New York: Greenwood Press, 1939.

Flizak, C. W. Organizational structure and teacher role-orientation. *Administrator's Notebook*, 1968, 17(2).

Geer, B. Occupational commitment and the teaching profession. *School Review*, 1966, 74, 31–47.

Getzels, J. W., & Jackson, P. W. The teacher's personality and characteristics. In N. L. Gage (Ed.), *Handbook of research on teaching*. Chicago: Rand McNally, 1963. Pp. 506–582.

Ginzberg, E., et al. *Occupational choice*. New York: Columbia University Press, 1951.

Glazer, N., & Moynihan, D. P. *Beyond the melting pot: The Negros, Puerto Ricans, Jews, Italians, and Irish of New York City.* Cambridge: MIT Press, 1970.

Glick, O. Educational process in the classroom. *School Review*, 1968, 76, 339–351.

Griffiths, D. E., Goldman, S., & McFarland, W. J. Teacher mobility in New York City. *Educational Administration Quarterly*, 1965, 1(1), 15–31.

Gross, E. *Work and society.* New York: Thomas Y. Crowell, 1958.

Gross, N. Sociology of education, 1945–1955. In H. L. Zetterberg (Ed.), *Sociology in the USA: A trend report.* Paris: UNESCO, 1956. Pp. 62–67.

Hall, R. H. *Occupations and the social structure.* Englewood Cliffs, N.J.: Prentice-Hall, 1969.

Haller, E. J. Pupil influence in teacher socialization: A socio-linguistic study. *Sociology of Education*, 1967, 40, 316–333.

Hart, J. W. Socially mobile teachers and classroom atmosphere. *Journal of Educational Research*, 1965, 59, 166–168.

Hartley, H. J. Educational bureaucracy, teacher orientation and selected criterion variables. *Journal of Educational Research*, 1966, 60, 54–57.

Harvey, O. J., Prather, M., White, B. J., & Hoffmeister, J. K. Teachers' beliefs, classroom atmosphere, and student behavior. *American Educational Research Journal*, 1968, 5, 151–166.

Harvey, O. J., White, B. J., Prather, M. S., Alter, R. D., & Hoffmeister, J. K. Teachers' belief systems and preschool atmospheres. *Journal of Educational Psychology*, 1966, 57, 373–381.

Hermanowicz, H. J. The pluralistic world of beginning teachers. In *The real world of the beginning teacher.* Report of the Nineteenth National TEPS Conference. Washington, D.C.: National Education Association, 1966. Pp. 15–25.

Hoetker, J., & Ahlbrand, W. P., Jr. The persistence of recitation. *American Educational Research Journal*, 1969, 6, 145–167.

Hornstein, H. A., Callahan, D. M., Fisch, E., & Benedict, B. A. Influence and satisfaction in organizations: A replication. *Sociology of Education*, 1968, 41, 380–389.

Hoy, W. K. Organizational socialization: The student teacher and pupil control ideology. *Journal of Educational Research*, 1967, 61, 153–155.

Hoy, W. K. Influence of experience on the beginning teacher. *School Review*, 1968, 76, 312–323.

Hoy, W. K. Pupil control ideology and organizational socialization: A further examination of the influence of experience on the beginning teacher. *School Review*, 1969, 77, 257–265.

Hughes, E. C. *Men and their work.* Glencoe, Ill.: Free Press, 1958.

Hyman, R. The language of the classroom: Implications for supervisors and teachers. *Journal of Secondary Education*, 1967, 42, 106–113.

Jackson, P. W. *Life in classrooms.* New York: Holt, Rinehart & Winston, 1968.

Jackson, P. W., & Lahaderne, H. M. Inequalities of teacher-pupil contacts. *Psychology in the Schools*, 1967, 4, 204–211.

Kallenbach, W. W., & Gall, M. D. Microteaching versus conventional methods in training elementary intern teachers. *Journal of Educational Research*, 1969, 63, 136–141.

Kliebard, H. M. Dimensions of meaning in classroom discourse. *Journal of Teacher Education*, 1966, 17, 233–244.

Kozol, J. *Death at an early age.* New York: Bantam, 1970.

Kratzmann, A. The Alberta Teachers' Association: A prototype for the American scene? *Administrator's Notebook*, 1963, 12(2).

LeFevre, C. Teacher characteristics and careers. *Review of Educational Research*, 1967, 37, 433–447.

Lortie, D. C. Teacher socialization: The Robinson Crusoe model. In *The real world of the beginning teacher.* Report of the Nineteenth National TEPS Conference. Washington, D.C.: National Education Association, 1966. Pp. 54–66.

Lortie, D. C. Shared ordeal and induction to work. In H. S. Becker et al. (Eds.), *Institutions and the person.* Chicago: Aldine, 1968. Pp. 252–264.

Lortie, D. C. The balance of control and autonomy in elementary school teaching. In A. Etzioni (Ed.), *The semi-professions and their organization.* New York: Free Press, 1969. Pp. 1–53.

Lortie, D. C. The cracked cake of educational

custom and emerging issues in evaluation. In M. C. Wittrock, & D. E. Wiley (Eds.), *The evaluation of instruction: Issues and problems.* New York: Holt, Rinehart & Winston, 1970. Pp. 149–164.

Lortie, D. C. Structure and teacher performance: A prologue to systematic research. In *How teachers make a difference,* U.S. Department of Health, Education and Welfare, Office of Education, Bureau of Educational Personnel Development, 1972.

Mason, W. S. *The beginning teacher, status and career orientations.* Washington, D.C.: U.S. Government Printing Office, 1961.

Merton, R. K. *Social theory and social structure.* (Rev. ed.) Glencoe, Ill.: Free Press, 1957.

National Education Association, Research Division. *The American public-school teacher, 1965–66.* Research Report 1967–R4. Washington, D.C.: National Education Association, 1967. (a)

National Education Association. Characteristics of teachers: 1956, 1961, 1966. *NEA Research Bulletin,* 1967, 45, 87–89. (b)

National Education Association. Professional growth of teachers in service. *NEA Research Bulletin,* 1967, 45, 25–27. (c)

National Education Association. Teachers' problems. *NEA Research Bulletin,* 1968, 46, 116–117.

National Education Association. Evaluation of teaching competence. *NEA Research Bulletin,* 1969, 47, 67–75.

Nosow, S., & Form, W. H. (Eds.) *Man, work, and society.* New York: Basic Books, 1962.

Paton, J. M. Trade union or professional association? The Canadian experience. *Phi Delta Kappan,* 1968, 49, 563–566.

Pedersen, K. G. Teacher migration and attrition. *Administrator's Notebook,* 1970, 18(8).

Perrow, C. Hospitals: Technology, structure and goals. In J. G. March (Ed.), *Handbook of organizations.* Chicago: Rand McNally, 1965. Pp. 910–971.

Perry, C. R., & Wildman, W. A. *The impact of negotiations in public education.* Worthington, Ohio: Charles A. Jones, 1970.

Rabinowitz, W., & Crawford, K. E. A study of teachers' careers. *School Review,* 1960, 68, 377–399.

Rist, R. C. Student social class and teacher expectations: The self-fulfilling prophecy in ghetto education. *Harvard Educational Review,* 1970, 40, 411–451.

Robbins, G. D. The impact of current educational change upon teacher education. *Journal of Teacher Education,* 1969, 20, 182–187.

Rosenshine, B. Enthusiastic teaching: A research review. *School Review,* 1970, 78, 499–514.

Rosenthal, A. *Pedagogues and power.* Syracuse, N.Y.: Syracuse University Press, 1969.

Sieber, S., & Wilder, D. E. Teaching styles: Parental preferences and professional role definitions. *Sociology of Education,* 1967, 40, 302–315.

Smith, B. O. Recent research on teaching: An interpretation. *High School Journal,* 1967, 51, 63–74.

Smith, L. M., & Geoffrey, W. *The complexities of an urban classroom: An analysis toward a general theory of teaching.* New York: Holt, Rinehart & Winston, 1968.

Trask, A. E. Principals, teachers and supervision: Dilemmas and solutions. *Administrator's Notebook,* 1964, 13(4).

Wayson, W. W. Source of teacher satisfaction in slum schools. *Administrator's Notebook,* 1966, 14(9).

White, K. The relation of career involvement to persistence in the teaching profession among beginning female elementary teachers. *Journal of Educational Research,* 1966, 60, 51–53.

Wright, B. D., & Tuska, S. A. From dream to life in the psychology of becoming a teacher. *School Review,* 1968, 76, 253–293.

Yamamoto, K. Analysis of teaching—Another look. *School Review,* 1967, 75, 205–215.

Yee, A. H. Source and direction of causal influence in teacher-pupil relationships. *Journal of Educational Psychology,* 1968, 59, 275–282.

Young, D. B. The modification of teacher behavior using audio video-taped models in a micro-teaching sequence. *Educational Leadership,* 1969, 26, 394–403.

Zahorik, J. A. Teacher verbal feedback and content development. *Journal of Educational Research,* 1970, 63, 419–423.

CHAPTER 16

Of the Impact of Theory of Knowledge on Thought about Education

KINGSLEY PRICE
The Johns Hopkins University

VIEW TO BE CONSIDERED

There is a widespread view, among those who are interested in education, that philosophy has an impact on thought about the subject. For some, this impact flows preeminently from ethics; for some, from metaphysics; for others, from theory of knowledge; and for others still, from several, or from all these regions.

In this essay, we shall not consider the view that impact flows from ethics and metaphysics to educational thought. We shall consider only the view that it flows from theory of knowledge. And in this connection, we shall not consider the view that it flows from some particular theory of knowledge by virtue of some peculiarly distinguishing feature of that theory, nor the view that it is attracted, as it were, to thought about education as this thought is specified by some particular school or movement. Rather, we shall be concerned, by noticing certain very general features of theory of knowledge and of thought about education, to determine what the impact might be that any such theory might exert upon any such thought, however each

might be specified by particular parties, sects, or authors.

What, then, is the impact of theory of knowledge, as such, upon thought about education, as such? In order to answer this question, we shall consider, at once, its central terms.

"THOUGHT ABOUT EDUCATION" DEFINED

Education consists in the activities of teaching and learning, and thought about education consists in the propositions men employ with respect to those activities. These propositions fall into two groups, and in one of them there are propositions of four kinds. In the first are propositions that attribute causes and effects to the activities of teaching and learning. They would advance the understanding of education by showing how it is enmeshed in a causality that is pervasive of human life. These propositions are found in books of educational psychology, sociology, history, etc. In the second kind are propositions about the curriculum—about the subject matter taught and learned. In the third and fourth, respectively, are propositions about the methods of teaching and learning the subject matter, and propositions about the purposes to which teaching and learning are, in fact, devoted. Propositions of these last three kinds are exemplified in all those books that describe the activities and purposes of education as they occur in particular times and places. But propositions of all four kinds describe educational practice in one way or another, either with respect to its surrounding causal companions, or with respect to its more inward nature. They constitute the descriptive aspect of thought about education.

Propositions in the second group advocate the adoption of certain educational practices. They occur in the thought of all those who advocate change in or preservation of the subject matter, the methods and the purposes of education. Unlike propositions referred to in the preceding paragraph, they describe nothing; but they fall into classes that correspond to the second, third and fourth kinds of propositions found in the descriptive aspect. However, in the second group, there can be no propositions that correspond to those of the first kind in the first group. The latter explain educational practice by describing its causal circumstances; but it makes no sense to advocate that this practice should be explained in any way whatever. The circumstances that explain teaching and learning are the circumstances they are, and do not alter to conform to our advocacy of one or other set of them. The propositions of this second group constitute the advocative aspect of thought about education.

"IMPACT" DEFINED

The term *impact* may be used to refer to any of several relations. It is sometimes used, first, to refer to the causal relation. Thus, one might say that a bullet has an impact on a target, and that a stage personality has an impact on his audience. In each case, one says that one thing causes something else—a new condition of the target, a new condition of the audience.

The other references of our term are all relations of a logical or quasi-logical sort. Sometimes, secondly, "impact" refers to the deductive relation—to the relation of premise to conclusion. The proposition that all students are rebellious and Stephen Dædalus is one has such an impact on the proposition that Stephen Dædalus is rebellious. Impact of this second kind is a relation such that if it relates one proposition to another, the second must be true if the first is true. Where one proposition has an impact of this kind on another, the former is a deductive basis for the latter; for perceiving its truth enables us to infer that the latter is true.

Thirdly, the term "impact" also refers, on some occasions, to the inductive relation between propositions. That Stephen Dædalus is rebellious has an inductive relation to the proposition that all students are rebellious. Seeing it to be true supports the probability of the proposition about all students. Where the truth of one proposition supports the probability of another, it is an inductive basis for that other; and the term "impact" sometimes refers to the fact that one proposition provides an inductive basis for another.

Fourthly, the term "impact" sometimes refers to the relation of presupposition between propositions. But the word "presupposition" refers to two quite distinct relations; and as a consequence, this fourth sense of "impact" resolves itself into two. To make these senses clear requires mention of two distinct characteristics of propositions—their form and their content.

The form of a proposition is what is common to it along with other propositions. "Canaries sing" and "men walk" possess the same form. The content of a proposition is what its form contains; it is what makes one proposition different from every other proposition. It is by virtue of its content that "canaries sing" differs from "men walk."

One proposition presupposes another provided that the content of the first depends on the truth of the second. The content of a proposition is determined by the concepts that make it up. The concepts "men" and "walk" quite clearly make up the proposition "men walk"; and it is by virtue of these ingredients that "men walk" differs from "men swim." For, if either were different, "men walk" would contain something altogether different from what it does in fact contain.[1] The truth of the proposition that expresses the concept "walk" determines, in this way, the content of the proposition "men walk"; and the content of "men walk" depends upon the truth of the proposition about the concept "walk." Thus, the relation of presupposition, in this first sense of the word, is the dependence that the content of every proposition has upon the truth of the propositions that describe its ingredients. Now, that one proposition has an impact on another sometimes means that the content of the other presupposes the truth of the first in the way just made out; and where "presupposition" has this meaning, "impact" has a fourth sense. It refers to the relation between the content of a proposition and propositions describing its ingredients such that the former depends upon the truth of the latter. Where one proposition has an impact of this fourth sort upon another, we shall sometimes say that its truth determines the meaning of the other.

But "presuppose" carries a second sense which provides a fifth use for "impact." On some occasions it refers to a relation between propositions such that the purpose for putting forward the one would collapse if the other were not true. A purpose for advancing a proposition is something that advancing it helps to accomplish. By asserting propositions like "the races ought to be integrated," "blacks and whites ought not to attend segregated schools," etc., some persons help with the task of racial inte-

gration; to integrate the races is, in some contexts, the purpose for asserting such propositions. Now, this purpose could not exist if there were not different races and if the different races were not segregated, for there could not be the task of integrating races if there were not different races that were segregated. A proposition of any kind presupposes, in this second way, all those propositions that must be true if the purposes for uttering it are not to collapse.[2] And presupposition of this second kind is the relation between propositions referred to by "impact" in the fifth sense of that word. To say that A has an impact on B, in this fifth sense, is to say that B presupposes A in the second way—that some purpose for uttering B could not exist if A were not true.

"THEORY OF KNOWLEDGE" DEFINED

What we mean by the phrase, "theory of knowledge," depends, of course, upon what we mean by "knowledge"; and this last term, we shall spend only a little time here explaining. It suffices for our purposes to say that knowledge of something consists in asserting[3] some proposition about it on good grounds. Theory of knowledge consists in a statement as to what constitutes the goodness of the grounds for asserting a proposition.

There are different theories of knowledge based upon different views as to what constitutes the goodness of grounds for assertion. According to the rationalists, being a true proposition and being a deductive basis for asserting a proposition is what constitutes the goodness of the grounds for asserting it. On this view, to know a thing is to assert[4] some proposition about it for the reason that we have deduced[5] that

---

[1] Or no proposition at all if walking should come to nothing intelligible.

[2] The purposes need not be valid or legitimate, but only intelligible, i.e., conceivable as things to be accomplished.

[3] Or be able to assert.

[4] Or be able to assert.

[5] But we must also not have forgotten how to deduce it.

proposition from some other proposition that we perceive to be true. According to the empiricists the trait of being true and of being empirical evidence for a proposition is what constitutes the goodness of grounds for asserting it. On this view, to know a thing is to assert[6] some proposition about it for the reason that we have secured[7] empirical evidence in its favor. Other theories of knowledge might be mentioned, but reference to these two will suffice to exemplify the meaning of the phrase.

VIEW TO BE CONSIDERED, MADE MORE DETAILED

Let us return to the view that theory of knowledge has an impact on thought about education. Now, since such thought has both a descriptive and an advocative aspect, our view amounts to the proposition that a theory of the goodness of grounds for assertion has an impact on both the phases of educational thought.[8]

But the term "impact" may carry any one of five different senses; and our proposition may amount to any one of five different propositions according as the term is endowed with one or other of those different senses. It may amount to the proposition that some theory of the goodness of grounds for assertion causes the descriptive and advocative aspects of thought about education, that it is a deductive basis for them, that it is an inductive basis for them, and so on for the other two senses of "impact."[9]

And in any particular context, the view could amount merely to holding some of the propositions to which one of these gives rise. That theory of knowledge causes the descriptive and advocative aspects, for example, gives rise to the proposition that it causes the descriptive aspect alone, and (more minutely even) that it causes propositions that describe the methods of instruction merely. But such cases of the impact of theory of knowledge on thought about education are clearly dependent upon its having an impact on the descriptive and advocative aspects generally; and here we shall examine each of the five major propositions to which, as we have seen, the five senses of "impact" give rise.

WHETHER THEORY OF KNOWLEDGE CAUSES THOUGHT ABOUT EDUCATION

Let us consider the proposition that theory of knowledge has an impact of the first kind on thought about education—that it causes its descriptive and advocative aspects. This view asserts that one proposition (the theory) causes other propositions —those that attribute to teaching and learning certain causes and effects, a curriculum, a method or set of them, and a purpose or set of purposes—together with those that advocate action to establish certain curricula, methods, and purposes.

The proposition expressing an impact of this first kind must be rejected. It makes no sense to hold that one proposition is the cause of others. To say that A causes B requires that both be things of such sorts that it is intelligible to attribute temporal locations to them. A cause must come before, or occur simultaneously with its

---

[6] Or to be able to assert.

[7] And we must not have forgotten how to secure the evidence. I do not consider, here, the place of authority in determining the goodness of grounds as analyzed by any of the schools of epistemologists.

[8] In fact, our proposition contains many more than these parts since each aspect of thought about education has several components upon each of which, according to our proposition, theory of knowledge has an impact. Fortunately, there is no need to write out all these propositions here.

[9] In fact, one who asserts our proposition, in any of the five senses distinguished, is committed, *prima facie*, to asserting that theory of knowledge has an impact on propositions of each of the kinds that make up the

descriptive and advocative aspects of thought about education–that it has an impact on descriptive and advocative propositions about the circumstances causally surrounding educational practice, curricula, method, etc. To make all these details evident would be both profitless and boring, each of which results is a good reason, however unusual in learned articles, for not doing so.

effect. But it is not intelligible to attribute temporal location to propositions; such a sentence as, "The proposition that John is tall occurred at four o'clock" is clearly incapable of carrying any significance. And the view that theory of knowledge has an impact on the descriptive and the advocative aspects of thought about education, where "impact" carries the sense of "cause," is a nonsensical view.

But although it is nonsensical, this view is similar to another which is not. This other doctrine is the view that belief in the truth of a theory of knowledge causes one to adopt certain beliefs with respect to the descriptive and advocative aspects of education. This second view seems to be what those assert who hold that one's theory of knowledge—his rationalism, empiricism, instrumentalism, etc.—cannot but turn up in the description he gives of educational phenomena, and in the advocacy he provides for educational practice.

This second view might be true. Surely, some beliefs do act as causes to one another, and one's believing in theory of knowledge of a certain sort might, in fact, influence him to believe certain propositions about education. One's philosophical belief in rationalism, for example, might cause in him the belief in the proposition that teaching and learning occur most effectively in highly authoritarian circumstances, that the de facto curriculum consists primarily in study of the classics, that the method of education is largely drill in reasoning, etc., and the belief that educational practices *ought to be* of these sorts.

It is important to notice, however, that it is *beliefs* that may be related as causes and effects, not the *propositions* that constitute the objects of those beliefs, and that, consequently, the question whether the belief in theory of knowledge has an impact of the first sort on belief in the two aspects of thought about education cannot be answered by considering the logical and quasi-logical relations that may connect theory of knowledge with thought about education.

Rather, that there is or is not such an impact can be ascertained, if at all, only by empirical investigation into the relations between beliefs like that of the biographer, the sociologist and the historian.

It is also important to notice that even though belief in a theory of knowledge should carry an impact of the first kind for belief in the two aspects of thought about education, we could not, so far, suppose that the descriptive or advocative propositions thus believed were true. Belief in rationalism with respect to theory of knowledge, for example, might cause belief in conservatism with respect to thought about education; but we cannot conclude from this causal influence that the descriptive and advocative propositions of which conservatism is composed are true or acceptable. Rather, that they are or are not can be supported only by an empirical examination of the facts that the descriptive propositions describe, and by moral reflection on the propositions advocated.

Ideologists and sociologists of knowledge are sometimes inclined to hold that behind thought about education lies a philosophical view which determines that thought. The effort to render this view precise easily resolves it into the view that belief in theory of knowledge causes belief in the propositions of educational thought. We have seen that such a view is itself susceptible of empirical inquiry, and even though true, would not assure the propriety of the beliefs about education caused by beliefs about the nature of knowledge.

WHETHER THEORY OF KNOWLEDGE IS A DEDUCTIVE BASIS FOR THOUGHT ABOUT EDUCATION

Consider, next, the view that theory of knowledge is a deductive basis for the descriptive and advocative aspects of education, the view that it has an impact in the second sense on thought about education. If theory of knowledge did provide such a deductive basis, its truth would determine the truth of certain propositions, in distinction from others, that describe and that advocate educational practice. If it were true, for example, that the only grounds for asserting a proposition lay in the fact that it could be deduced from another where that other is true, then some propositions like the following would also be true: that teaching and learning occur only where the community respects them, that the curriculum is made up from classical sources, that pedagogical method is authoritarian, that the purpose aimed at is the preservation of the status quo; that the curriculum, the method, and the purpose ought to be of these kinds; or both. But the truth of rationalism cannot determine the truth of these propositions about teaching and learning. For no proposition, by itself, can make another true unless it contains the terms that compose the other,[10] and rationalism does not contain the terms that compose the descriptions and injunctions stated.

Consider this parallel. "All students are rebellious, and Stephen Dædalus is one" cannot determine the truth of "Parnell is rebellious." The conclusion is about Parnell; and since he is not discussed in the proposition about students, that proposition can tell us nothing whatever about him, can yield no proposition whatever in which his name occurs. It may be true that Parnell is rebellious; but whether it is can never be ascertained by considering a proposition about students, rebellion, and Stephen Dædalus because Parnell is not referred to in it.

In the same way, the truth of rationalism cannot determine the truth of the descriptive and advocative propositions stated above. Rationalism discusses the truth of propositions and the way in which one makes a good ground for another. But nowhere does it refer to teaching and learning, community respect for it, the classics, authoritarianism in method, the status quo, etc. Consequently, it makes true no proposition whatever, that describe or advocate educational practices by use of these terms.

Just as rationalism cannot determine the truth of conservatism with respect to education, so a theory of knowledge of any kind whatever cannot determine the truth of educational thought of any kind whatever. No such theory contains the terms that compose the propositions that describe or advocate any practice of education. If we knew which theory of knowledge were true —rationalism, empiricism, etc.—we might be able to select from among the scientific, religious, and other doctrines available for being taught and learned, those that can be known as opposed to those that cannot; but we would not be able merely by consulting our true theory of knowledge to determine either those that are, in fact, taught and learned or even those that ought to be so treated. And theory of knowledge cannot have an impact, in the second sense of that term, on thought about education.

WHETHER THEORY OF KNOWLEDGE IS AN INDUCTIVE BASIS FOR THOUGHT ABOUT EDUCATION

Similar considerations show that theory of knowledge cannot have an impact on thought about education in the third sense of that term—that it can provide an inductive basis neither for its descriptive nor for its advocative aspect. In order that one proposition should constitute an inductive basis for another, the kinds of things referred to by the other must also be referred to by the first. But the kinds of things referred to in the propositions that describe and advocate educational practice are not referred to in any theory of knowledge; and any theory of knowledge must fail as an inductive basis for thought about education.

Consider this parallel. "The students, Stephen, James and John, are rebellious" is an inductive basis for "all students are rebellious"; its truth supports the probability of the latter proposition. But if the latter were about another kind of things

---

[10] Or terms that entail those that compose the other.

instead, if it were "all Irishmen are rebellious," the proposition about the students, Stephen, James and John, would lend it no credibility whatever. For students are one kind of things and Irishmen quite another. And for that reason the discovery that something is true about some of the former provides us with no basis whatever for the probability of a proposition about any or all the latter.

For like reason, theory of knowledge can never serve as inductive basis for either aspect of thought about education. That theory explains knowledge in terms of assertion, good grounds, etc.; thought about education refers to teaching and learning, the curriculum, etc. Now knowledge (assertion on good grounds) is a kind of thing altogether different from teaching and learning, the curriculum, etc. And to suppose that theory of knowledge provides an inductive basis for thought about education, to suppose that it carries impact for it in the third sense of that term, is to require that in proceeding from theory of knowledge to thought about education we commit the fallacy of changing the kinds.

Besides, theory of knowledge cannot possess a trait that must belong to every proposition that provides an inductive basis for another. Every such basis must possess empirical evidence. "The students, Stephen, James and John, are rebellious" would not constitute an inductive basis for "all students are rebellious" unless our observation showed it to be true.[11] In the absence of such evidence it remains a merely possible inductive basis for that proposition. But a theory of knowledge is a proposition to which all empirical evidence is irrelevant. We do not discover the truth or falsehood of rationalism or empiricism, etc., by observing people busily at work knowing— busily engaged in asserting, giving good grounds for asserting, etc. Rather, we do

---

[11] Or unless it could be deduced or were made probable by some proposition for which there is empirical evidence.

something quite different; we analyze language in which knowledge is expressed, or the concept of knowledge together with its kindred concepts, or something of that sort. And even if we disregard the fallacy of changing the kinds, the impossibility of empirical evidence for it precludes our holding that theory of knowledge has an impact of the third sort on thought about education.

WHETHER THEORY OF KNOWLEDGE DETERMINES THE MEANING OF THOUGHT ABOUT EDUCATION

Let us ask, now, whether theory of knowledge has an impact in the fourth sense on thought about education, i.e., whether its truth determines the meaning of the propositions that express that thought or whether those propositions presuppose that truth by virtue of their content. And let us consider, first, whether the theory has such an impact on the descriptive aspect. If it does, the concept treated by the theory must turn up as a constituent in the propositions used to describe teaching and learning. The concept treated by the theory is the concept *knowledge*. The theory tells us that this concept is constituted by that of assertion on good grounds, and it tells us what the goodness of the grounds consists in. So that if the concept "knowledge" occurs in the propositions used to describe education—if it helps to constitute the content or meaning of the description we give for education—the very meaning of those propositions is determined by the theory that explains the concept. In order to decide whether theory of knowledge has this impact on thought about education, we must discover whether the concept "knowledge" need occur in the propositions that describe the activities of teaching and learning.

Of these propositions, those of the first kind describe the causes and effects of those activities. The concept "knowledge" may occur in such propositions; consequently, theory of knowledge may determine their content. It is conceivable that knowledge should have an effect on teaching and learning. If it does, the relation is probably indirect. The mere existence of knowledge can hardly suffice to guarantee its influence upon the curriculum and the method or methods of instruction. It would ordinarily require, as well, the existence of a set of institutions—a priesthood, schools, or the like through whose activities knowledge could exert an influence on education. But given such a mechanism, it is quite possible that where knowledge exists, it should, in its character as knowledge, produce an effect upon teaching and learning by way of additions to the curriculum of subject matters known and of alterations in method suggested by appropriate knowledge. Moreover, it is quite conceivable that teaching and learning should bring knowledge into existence or should increase its bulk.

Of course, whether education does, thus, affect knowledge, and whether knowledge does influence education are matters to be decided only by empirical inquiry. Here, we deal with possibilities, and consequently, must recognize these two.

And so, it is quite conceivable that we should be required to make use of the concept "knowledge" in our descriptions of the causes and effects of education. And if we do make use of that concept in either way, then propositions of the first kind that describe education presuppose a theory of knowledge; for what we say about it—the meaning of our propositions about it—is determined by the account of knowledge offered by the theory.

Propositions of the second and third kinds, in the descriptive aspect, cannot make use of the concept "knowledge." To describe the curriculum as it is embodied in the activities of teaching and learning is to point out what these activities, in particular places and times, are directed toward achieving. It is to describe them as aimed at the student's mastery of certain cognitive subjects such as mathematics and history, of certain value subjects such as music and morality, and of certain attitudes and skills

such as those involved in religion, carpentry, etc. Some of these items may be objects of knowledge, but we cannot describe them as such in our description of the curriculum. No curriculum includes courses in knowledge; the very suggestion rings of nonsense in our ears. What we teach and learn is mathematics, history, and the like. The question whether the mastery of these subjects is the mastery of positive error, of what might be true or of what is known to be true—the question whether the crops that are grown in these academic fields are crops of knowledge—is a question quite foreign to a description of the curriculum. Consequently, the concept "knowledge" cannot be employed in propositions of the second kind.

Propositions of the third kind describe the methods employed in teaching and learning. These are general patterns within which teachers and students deal with one another and with things in order to bring about the student's mastery of the subject matter. The method for teaching and learning physics, for example, consists in lecturing and taking notes, in reading and discussing physics books, and in supervision of laboratory work. The method of teaching and learning piano technique consists in the teacher's bringing the student to adjust his body in a certain way at the instrument, and to practice various routines upon it under critical supervision, more or less extended. Now it is clear that these ways in which teachers and students deal with one another and with things are not cases of knowledge. It would be nonsensical to describe discussion, lecture, reading and experimentation as knowing although these method-governed activities might be preparatory to knowing; it would also be nonsensical so to describe the teacher's bringing the student to adjust his body in a certain way, the student's practice of routines, etc., although these activities might be preparatory to knowing how to perform on the piano. And the concept "knowledge" cannot enter into the propositions that make up the third kind in the descriptive aspect of education.

If knowledge is held to influence, or to be influenced by activities of teaching and learning, the explanation of those activities presupposes a theory of knowledge, and the latter has an impact of the fourth sort on the former. But propositions about the curriculum and about methods of teaching and learning cannot describe them by use of the concept "knowledge"; and on these second and third parts of the descriptive aspect, theory of knowledge has no impact of the fourth sort.

But it does on some of the propositions that make up those of the fourth kind in the descriptive aspect. These propositions attribute purposes to education as it is actually practiced in various places and times; and while some of these purposes may be described without presupposing theory of knowledge, others cannot. The purposes that are free from this presupposition are immediate. An immediate purpose is inherent in the teaching and learning of any subject; it consists in achieving the condition aimed at directly by teacher and learner—in the success of the methods employed. Thus, the immediate purpose of education in physics is the student's success in learning it—his mastery of physics; and the immediate purpose of education in any subject is a corresponding success or mastery with respect to it.

It is clear that the propositions that describe education as possessed of a certain curriculum—propositions of the third kind —require certain propositions of the fourth kind. They require propositions that attribute to education all the immediate purposes that inhere in its curriculum. If, for example, a particular set of educational activities is described as including the study of physics, it is necessary to describe it, also, as including the purpose of mastering that subject. But since the curriculum can be described without presupposing theory of knowledge, all that can be derived from it may also be so described; and the meaning

of propositions that describe education as possessed of immediate purposes cannot require the truth of any theory of knowledge.

But there is a second group of purposes that education adopts; and on some of these theory of knowledge does have an impact of the fourth sort. These purposes, although distinct from the mastery of any subject, can be attained only through the mastery of one or more. They lie remote from education but firmly joined to it through the immediate purposes that serve as their conditions. One often reads, for example, that the purpose of education in engineering is humanity's control of nature, the nation's military security or dominance, the student's economic success, etc. These purposes do not inhere in the courses that constitute the engineering curriculum; they are remote from the activities of teaching and learning the engineering art. But their attainment is possible only if those that do inhere in the courses of that curriculum are achieved.

If the description of education as possessed of remote purposes does not require the use of the concept "knowledge," the propositions that thus describe it do not presuppose a theory of knowledge. It is clear that many such propositions do not require the concept. That education in engineering is directed toward humanity's control over nature, toward military security or dominance, and toward economic success of the engineer exemplify this point. Thus, some propositions about remote purposes presuppose no theory of knowledge.

But others do. One often reads, for example, that however much education may be aimed at practical objectives, it is also directed toward pursuing knowledge, toward preserving it, toward increasing it, toward transmitting it from one age or generation to its successor, etc. The purposes are remote from education. For what teaching and learning aim at, immediately, is mastery of the subjects in the curriculum—of physics and chemistry, of history and literature, of swimming, driving, etc. But the realization of these immediate purposes may be described as leading to the achievement of those that are more remote. And some of these remote purposes cannot be attributed to education without the use of the concept "knowledge." For although we do not aim at securing knowledge when we study physics, it might be held that we do, in fact, secure it if that study is successful; and it might be said that the more the curriculum is mastered, the more knowledge is secured, preserved, increased and transmitted. Whether this purpose is achieved, of course, depends upon whether the subjects mastered are objects of knowledge as, some might say, physics is, and as astrology, many would say, is not. So that the meaning of the proposition that a remote purpose of education is the securing, preserving, increasing and transmitting of knowledge presupposes some theory of that subject; and such a theory has impact on thought about education insofar as the remote purposes it actually adopts count knowledge as one of these ingredients.

As for the advocative aspect of thought about education, it is now easy to see how it presupposes theory of knowledge. We presuppose nothing about the goodness of grounds for assertion (no theory of knowledge) when we advocate preservation of or alteration in the curriculum; when we advocate preservation of or alteration in methods of instruction; when we advocate immediate purposes; and when we advocate many that are remote. The reason is that our advocacy of all these things requires neither the use of the concept "knowledge" nor that of its kindred concepts, "goodness of grounds for assertion." Consequently, to argue for English literature from kindergarten onward, for the abolition of examinations, and for directing the activities of teaching and learning toward the establishment of general happiness—to advocate any such things is to advocate propositions whose content or meaning requires no theory of knowledge. But when we advocate that teaching and learning should bring

about, as a remote purpose, the securing, preserving, enhancing, transmitting or some other treatment of knowledge, the advocative aspect presupposes a theory of knowledge; for in such a case the content of the proposition advocated is determined by the concept "knowledge," and this concept by the theory. Here, rationalism, empiricism, instrumentalism, etc., have an impact on thought about education in the sense that they determine one, at least, of the remote purposes with whose achievement education is frequently charged.

WHETHER THEORY OF KNOWLEDGE DETERMINES THE TASK FOR WHOSE ACCOMPLISHMENT THOUGHT ABOUT EDUCATION IS ASSERTED

We come now to the question whether theory of knowledge has an impact of the fifth sort on thought about education. Impact of this kind occurs between one proposition and another provided that a task that uttering the other helps to perform would collapse if the first were not true. Now, theory of knowledge can have no such impact on the propositions that constitute the descriptive aspect of thought about education because these propositions, insofar as they are descriptive, play no role in the performance of any task whatever. That teaching and learning are influenced by community respect, that the curriculum includes history, that memorizing is the method for learning the alphabet, and that the schools in this city are directed toward developing democracy are propositions that describe the activities of teaching and learning. It is clear that when taken in this way, they play no role in the accomplishment of any task. One might hold that, as descriptions, they *are* the completed tasks of describing the facts they describe. But it is clear that, as descriptions, they can play no role in the accomplishment of tasks *other* than themselves. Consequently, the propositions that make up the descriptive aspect of thought about education help to perform no tasks that theory of knowledge might guarantee, and the latter has no impact of the fifth kind on the former.

But does theory of knowledge have an impact of this kind on the propositions that constitute the advocative aspect. Let us look at a characteristic of these propositions that has gone unnoticed hitherto.

This characteristic is the intelligibility of such propositions apart from their use in the performance of the tasks they advocate. Many propositions describe tasks located in the past and future, and some describe tasks whose performance we reject. Consider, for example, the propositions: "Charles I ought to have abdicated," "In the year 2000 nations ought to congratulate one another for having survived so long," and "We ought to win the war at any price." In such cases we refer to tasks whose performance, nonetheless, we do not advocate. For past and future tasks cannot be performed, and some of those not temporally remote lie beneath performance. Every advocative proposition, thus, refers to a task whose performance, in an act distinct from reference, it is also used to advocate.

Its reference to a task, quite apart from performance, makes an advocative proposition intelligible; its use to further the performance of that task makes it advocative. The proposition, "foreign languages ought to be taught in the lower schools," sets a task before us; its reference to that task is its intelligibility. The scholar, the advocate, and the opponent all find that reference in it. What makes the proposition advocative is its use—not merely to refer to the task, but to accomplish it. When one utters it in hearings before the school board, embodying it in certain cadences and tones of voice, surrounding it by certain gestures, etc., he is not merely referring to a task for the lower schools; he is endeavoring to accomplish the task by using the proposition as an instrument to bring the board to the appropriate decision. What makes a proposition advocative is that it is used to bring about the performance of a task; but this use requires

that the proposition devoted to it also refer to the task to be performed.

Our question whether theory of knowledge has an impact on the advocative aspect is not the question whether it has an impact on the mere intelligibility of the propositions in that aspect. Such propositions refer to tasks, and their references presuppose the truth of propositions that set forth the nature of their constituent concepts. These propositions have an impact on their intelligibility by way of determining their meaning. But we do not ask, here, how the references of advocative propositions are determined. We ask, rather, whether their being used to bring about the performance of the tasks they refer to—their peculiarly advocative use—presupposes a theory of knowledge. And this is the question whether the latter theory asserts the existence of something whose nonexistence would make it unintelligible to employ the propositions of the advocative aspect in an advocative way.

Does theory of knowledge assert the existence of something which is thus requisite for the intelligibility of using propositions about education in an advocative way? Let us notice that since the intelligibility of the reference of such propositions is not at issue, it is the intelligibility of the performance whose use they encourage we must consider.

But propositions that advocate a certain curriculum do not presuppose such a theory. They are uttered or written in order to secure the introduction of this subject matter, the elimination of that, or the preservation of the *status quo*. But to preserve, to eliminate and to introduce subject matter are tasks whose intelligibility in no way requires the existence of anything referred to by theory of knowledge. Physics and driving may be retained, eliminated or introduced into the curriculum quite independently of rationally binding evidence, empirical evidence, or any other thing mentioned by rationalism, empiricism, and the other theories of knowledge, for the performance of the tasks of spreading abroad the mastery of physics and of driving can be understood without reference to all such notions. The job of producing good drivers is that of fostering a skill, and clearly can be understood without adopting a view about knowledge and its grounds. And the task of fostering the mastery of physics can be understood without reference to the questions whether physics is mere superstition, probable belief, or assertion which can be justified.

And so, for all the tasks that advocated propositions about the curriculum might be used to accomplish. Their intelligibility does not presuppose a theory of knowledge.

Nor do those propositions advocate certain methods for teaching and learning. To urge that external authority be avoided, that successes should be rewarded, that examinations should be eliminated, etc., is to urge the performance of the appropriate tasks; and the intelligibility of these tasks is quite independent of any theory of knowledge. To hold that one does not understand the task of avoiding external authority, of rewarding the student's successes, or of eliminating examinations on the ground that he does not know what the good grounds for asserting any proposition are is clearly quite unacceptable.

Some authors, however, have put forward a different view. John Dewey seems to have held that the task of introducing the right method into teaching and learning would be unintelligible except in the light of theory of knowledge (1916, pp. 180–182). This method is that of developing the consequences of hypotheses, consulting experience to find whether the consequences are true, and accepting or rejecting the hypotheses according to the dictates of experience. An assertion embodies knowledge, Dewey held, if it is a hypothesis with good grounds, i.e., supported by the discovery that its consequences are shown true in experience (1960, pp. 217–222). And the method of teaching and learning a particular topic is simply the deliberate duplication of the

original procedure of hypothesis, deduction of consequences, verification, etc. The task of introducing such a method would be unintelligible unless his theory were true, he might hold, since the task consists simply of arranging the procedures of teaching and learning to conform to the method by which knowledge is secured. So, also, Plato seems to have held that the proper method for teaching and learning the sciences (he believed they were all mathematical in form) consisted in running through the proofs for each fact. And in that case, the task of introducing the right method of instruction would be unintelligible unless his theory of knowledge were true—the theory that the good grounds for assertion are true propositions from which the assertion can be derived by operations that are purely logical. One may interpret Dewey and Plato as having put forward different species of the view that the existential conditions of knowing—experimental conditions in one case, rational proofs in the other—have an impact on thought about education; one may interpret their work as advancing the view that the task of introducing the proper method into pedagogy would collapse unless the existential conditions of coming to know are as each says they are.

But although some authors may hold that advocacy of certain propositions about method presupposes theory of knowledge, that view is mistaken. The mistake flows from identifying the pedagogical conditions for learning something with the criteria for knowledge. The conditions for teaching and learning something do not alter with the cognitive status of the subject matter. The lighting of the room, the attitude of the instructor, the interest of the student—all these and many other circumstances may appear among the conditions for teaching and learning something; but they appear among these conditions whether the subject matter be a fabric of falsehood like the doctored histories of tyrannical states, or a body of knowledge as history and mathematics may be. Now, the criteria for knowledge lie in the goodness of the grounds for the propositions that express it. A historical proposition, for example, cannot express knowledge unless it is derived from documents that are authentic; and a mathematical proposition cannot express knowledge unless it has been deduced from another proposition in the same system.

Since one can learn a proposition of history or mathematics without receiving it from those propositions which were its good grounds, since to propagate a mistake and to propagate a truth require conformity to the same pedagogical conditions, these conditions cannot be identified with the criteria for knowledge. Consequently, one need not pass through the good grounds for knowing a proposition in order to teach and learn it. So that the intelligibility of the task of preserving, eliminating, or introducing methods into the practice of education—the methods advocated by Dewey, by Plato, or by any author—does not presuppose a theory of knowledge of any kind. That task would not collapse into absurdity if the theory advanced to support the method did not refer to genuinely existential conditions.

Of course, teaching and learning a truth are different from teaching and learning something which is not. In such a procedure, the good grounds for the truth must be assimilated by the student and their connection with the truth must be apprehended. In teaching and learning something else, the assimilation and apprehension of what makes the something true cannot occur. But the method of teaching and learning each is identical in both cases and theory of knowledge has no impact of the fifth kind on the task involved in advocating methods.

The verdict, with respect to its impact on the tasks involved in advocating purposes for education, is somewhat different. For the purposes that are immediate—the retention, the elimination or the reform of the lists of subject matters taught—theory of knowledge can offer no guarantee; the accomplishment of these purposes requires

no statements about the nature of knowledge, its grounds, etc. That driving ought to be taught, that military training should be eliminated, and that the programming of computers should be introduced—these propositions may be uttered in the course of trying to accomplish the tasks they set forth. But these tasks are no more than immediate purposes of teaching and learning; and they are intelligible without reference to theories that explain the concepts "knowledge," "good grounds," etc.

Moreover, the advocacy of some remote purposes—the use of propositions to bring about their achievement—is intelligible quite independently of any theory of knowledge. To employ the act of engineering for the benefit of mankind, for the enhancement of national security and for the success of the practitioner are purposes that are more remote from engineering than are those of acquiring the knowledge and skills on which the art is based. And these purposes do not presuppose the existence of anything that might be mentioned in theory of knowledge.

But there are certain remote purposes sometimes advocated in thought about education that do presuppose certain theories of knowledge. Sometimes the latter assert the existence of objects of certain sorts. Platonism asserts the existence of forms as the external reality to which propositions that are true may be known to refer, and it asserts that these forms are imbedded in a structure of such a kind that knowing something about some of the forms enables one to know others through it. So, also, empiricists have often asserted the existence of certain objects—sense-data, perceptions, etc.—about which we can be perfectly certain; and they have asserted that these objects are related to others—physical objects, minds, etc.—in such a way that knowing something about the former is good grounds for knowing something about the latter.

If educational propositions are used to foster the achievement of purposes that involve such objects, this advocative use presupposes the theories of knowledge which declare the existence of those objects. For if the objects did not exist, the use of propositions to foster the achievement of the tasks in which they are involved would be absurd. There cannot be a real task that involves nonexistent objects; and to use a proposition in the effort to realize it would be absurd, as it would also be absurd to use the telephone book to perform the task of finding Hamlet's number.

Some propositions in thought about education have been used to bring about tasks that presuppose theories of knowledge by requiring the existence of things those theories declare. Plato (*Republic,* 518d, 521c-d, 540a), for example, assigned to teaching and learning the task of "turning the eye of the soul" from the world of appearances to the world of forms in order that the learner should achieve the intrinsic value of knowledge and find, in it, the basis for governing the state well. But if appearances or forms did not exist, the performance of the task of turning the eye of the soul from the one to the other would disintegrate into absurdity; and if either did not exist, the use of many a proposition like those in the *Republic* and elsewhere to bring about the performance of that task would fail from the same absurdity. The proposition that advocates the remote purpose that Plato assigns to education presupposes a theory of knowledge, Plato's own, which construes this theory in terms of certainty about the forms and their logical connections; and this Platonistic rationalism has the impact on Plato's thought about education of providing objects which must exist if the performance of education's central task is not to collapse into nonsense. If the theory were not true, the advocacy would be absurd, for if there were no forms, the eye of the soul could not be turned to them from the world of appearances. One can imagine the assignment to education of the task of turning the student's attention toward sense-data—special objects which constitute, according to some empiricist theories, the ultimate evidence for all knowledge. Attention to them, one can imagine someone's saying, since it is a requisite for knowledge, is also essential to useful action, since the latter must flow from knowledge. The use of propositions to further such a task, should such a use ever occur, would also presuppose a theory of knowledge, for it would collapse into nonsense unless the theories that declare the existence of sense-data were true.

Theory of knowledge has no impact of the fifth kind on the descriptive aspect of education. The propositions that constitute it are used in the performance of no task other than description, upon whose performance such an impact might be exerted. Of the propositions that constitute the advocative aspect, only those involved in the advocacy of remote purposes for education may be influenced by theories of knowledge, and theories of this kind exert an impact of the fifth sort on propositions that advocate remote purposes only if these theories declare the existence of objects that are involved in the effort to accomplish the remote purposes advocated.

SUMMARY

Theory of knowledge, construed as an analysis of knowledge into assertion and good grounds for it, might be supposed to have an impact in one or more of five ways on thought about education. It cannot have a causal impact since one theory or proposition cannot cause another. Of course, belief in a theory of knowledge may cause belief in propositions about education; but whether it does is an empirical, not a philosophical, question. Theory of knowledge can have neither a deductive nor an inductive impact on thought about education. The former is about topics quite unrelated, logically, to those that occupy thought about education. But theory of knowledge may have an impact of a fourth kind on some parts of that thought, for the theory may determine the content of propositions that may turn up in the thought. If, in the effort to explain education, its causes or effects are put forward, and if knowledge is cited as one of these causes or effects, theory of knowledge determines what is said in such propositions by analyzing knowledge into the notion of assertion on good grounds and by whatever further analysis it presents of these two notions. Also, if education is described as aimed at remote purposes which involve knowledge, then for like reason a theory of that subject determines the content of the propositions that embody this description of education. Similarly, if a remote purpose for education is advocated which involves a reference to knowledge, its content, also, is determined by a theory of knowledge. Theory of knowledge can have no impact of the fifth sort on the descriptive aspect of thought about education. For these propositions only describe educational phenomena; whereas impact of the fifth kind occurs where theory of knowledge declares the existence of something whose nonexistence would lead to the absurdity of using a proposition not to describe but to bring about the performance of a task. Theory of knowledge can have an impact on no propositions that advocate the performance of tasks concerning the curriculum, and Plato and Dewey notwithstanding,

concerning method. But if it asserts the existence of special objects of knowledge, or special objects involved in good grounds for assertion, and if the task of achieving some remote purpose of education requires the existence of these objects, then theory of knowledge, to that extent, has an impact of the fifth kind on thought about education; for if it were not true, the use of propositions to encourage the accomplishment of that purpose would be absurd because the purpose, itself, would be unintelligible.

In this essay, we have seen that theory of knowledge can have no impact of three sorts on educational thought. We have also seen that it can have an impact of a fourth and fifth kind on certain parts, only, of that thought. And we have seen, further, that whether it has an impact of these kinds on those parts depends upon the particular propositions that constitute the parts—propositions which need not occur in those parts of every body of thought about education.

REFERENCES

Dewey, J. *Democracy and education*. New York: Macmillan, 1916.

Dewey, J. *The quest for certainty*. New York: Capricorn Books, G. P. Putnam's Sons, 1960.

Plato. *Republic*.

CHAPTER **17**   Changing Change: Innovating
a Discipline

ROBERT CHIN
Boston University

LOREN DOWNEY
Boston University

Knowledge-builders serve action. Activist-practitioners serve knowledge-builders. The collaboration between students of change and administrator-change agents is based upon common needs. The practitioner-administrator-change agent needs conceptual tools, mind holds, and handles for grasping and acting just as much as do the scholar, theoretician and empirical researcher. As collaboration has increased, with parallel efforts at times, a new discipline has begun to emerge. The new discipline is the study of changing behavior deliberately—the inducement of change in which concepts of change are embedded in a framework of bringing about change. The activist-practitioner has a need for a theory of deliberate action to help him functionally integrate and utilize the bits and pieces of extant knowledge. Collaboration with the student of change forces explicitness, helps organize present observations and provides mind holds and handles for action. In short, it leads to identification of the emergent characteristics of a theory of changing.

The objectives of this paper are as follows:

1. To review briefly and selectively the summaries of research findings on changing educational practices;

2. To specify one set of methodological requirements for knowledge seen as *selectively retained tentatives* in regard to principles and practices for changing;

3. To interrelate coherently the different theories, knowledges and practices of changing so as to provide a usable framework and guidelines for research in aspects of changing, change and innovation.

Delineation of the objectives might also state what we are not trying to do. We are not attempting to summarize the knowledges, researches and programs studying innovations and all the techniques associated with changing of management, teaching or reeducation. Nor are we summarizing these researches from other fields and practices as they relate to education.

The arrangement of the sections of this discussion are as follows: the first section will reference selectively summaries of literature on change and changing from studies in education and from other settings. We find it more helpful to refer to these rather than attempt a summary and integration. The second section will differentiate three types of knowledge. The focus will be on that type of knowledge which comprises the processes of changing. This categorization cuts across what is ordinarily thought of as basic versus applied knowledge. In order to build the type of desired knowledge, various activities at the theoretic level are needed to raise the empirical research to permit valid generalizing ability and to permit the derivation of sound and usable principles.

The final section details one of the specific problems, among the many, which we feel is central to the theoretic coherency. Simply put, the issue is that of defining change in some manner which allows systematic cumulation of knowledge to occur.

The underlying purpose is then to identify the emerging contours of a basic discipline of knowledge. We hope to advance the creation of a theoretic discipline and research on the unique characteristics of a theory of changing.

REVIEW OF RESEARCH SUMMARIES

The literature on changing, change, innovation and knowledge utilization is vast and elusive. It has developed rapidly (mainly in the past decade), comes from many fields of inquiry, both within and outside of education, and covers a great range of topics. It is also characterized by a wide variety of publication sources, research traditions and contributions to research knowledge. Concluding that the state of literature and the limitation of space would not permit a comprehensive and functionally integrated review, we shall present and describe selected major sources of research, information, summaries and compilations. Sources will be grouped under four kinds of literature: knowledge dissemination and utilization, educational change, innovation research and theory, and organizational change.

Literature on Knowledge Dissemination and Utilization

Two publications of the Center for Research on Utilization of Scientific Knowl-

edge, the *Bibliography on Knowledge Utilization and Dissemination* (Havelock, 1968) and *Planning for Innovation* (Havelock, 1969), are primary source materials in this area of change. They represent the cumulative efforts of more than six years of exploration, analysis and synthesis of the thousands of discrete pieces of knowledge central to the development of an emerging science of knowledge utilization.

The focus on knowledge utilization is chosen both as a way of organizing the material and as a central component of change. The scope is broad in tracking out the social, psychological, behavioral, and perceptual dynamics of various linkage systems within the overall national educational system deemed useful to interrelate, transform and make useful basic knowledge. The fields of agriculture, education, physical sciences, engineering and medicine, among others, are scanned to elicit and infer models in use. The collected theoretical and empirical knowledge is grouped into three general categories corresponding to the principles, models, methods and orientations of their authors. The three categories are 1) the Social Interaction Model, which includes studies of communication and influence, 2) the Research Development and Diffusion Model, and 3) the Problem-Solving Model, concentrating on the needs of the user and his processes. A fourth perspective is being developed as a possible unifying and integrating model, called the "linkage system." The first volume (Havelock, 1969), the report of the Planning for Innovation Project, with its organization of the frameworks of analysis in the literature on change, is of special interest to researchers and students of change.

The companion bibliography (Havelock, 1968) contains over 4,000 sources of literature from many content fields pertaining directly or indirectly to knowledge dissemination and utilization, innovation and technological change. Models viewing dissemination and utilization as a process and as a knowledge flow system between basic and applied researchers, practitioners and consumers were used to define relevant topic areas and key concepts for the literature search.

Literature on Educational Change

Another publication of the Center for Research on the Utilization of Knowledge authored by Havelock, entitled *A Guide to Innovation in Education* (1970), translates the research findings into practical work lines and, for the purposes of this discussion, provides in the appendix a directory of major information sources relevant to educational innovation and an annotated bibliography of major works in education. The directory is especially helpful because it lists addresses and describes the services offered by the information sources current as of April 1970. Included in the 45 pages of sources are newsletters, information services, libraries, directories and indices, and reference books, as well as consulting organizations, research and development centers, human resources, government agencies, professional organizations and other school systems.

The bibliography emphasizes change within the field of education and was designed to aid education practitioners on the subjects of change planning and knowledge utilization.

The *Guide* itself was developed as a handbook for change agents of education to guide the planning and day-to-day management of change. The format of the *Guide* follows a stage model of planned innovation and may offer ideas and conceptual springboards to researchers of change.

A more recent summary and analysis of the literature relevant to educational change is that by Maguire (1970) and the accompanying annotated bibliography by the same author (1970).

The first volume, which is designed for practicing school administrators interested in change, makes observations intended to join knowledge of the change literature

with knowledge of the educational setting. The observations are followed by a summary of the literature under the following headings: 1) definitions and types of change, 2) change models, 3) strategies and techniques, 4) people involved in change, 5) sources and barriers to change, and 6) research studies of the change process. The bibliography contains 495 annotated sources used in the review. References secured through the Educational Resources Information Center (ERIC) are listed with their ERIC accession number.

Another annotated bibliography focused upon the "how" of educational change is that by Kurland and Miller (1966). This describes 170 books, articles and bibliographies selected from the fields of anthropology, education, industry and technology, and international development, and from medical science, political science, rural sociology, sociology and psychology.

Literature on Innovation Research and Theory

One of the few reviews ordering theoretical and empirical studies through a descriptive taxonomy is provided by the monograph by Bhola (1965), which provides a taxonomy identifying five areas of inquiry reviewed through four levels of refinement of knowledge: 1) awareness, 2) knowledge of specifics, 3) models and paradigms, and 4) validated theories. The areas of inquiry are 1) philosophic considerations, 2) content of innovations, 3) nature of inventors, innovators, and adopters, 4) process and tactics of diffusion, and 5) measurement and evaluation. The 278 items discussed by Bhola would be of major interest to students of change.

Two other sources basic to an understanding of the diffusion and adoption of innovations are the volumes of Rogers (1962, 1971). The first of these volumes reviews over 600 publications in various fields subdivided into general and diffusion research studies. The second examines the

informal social group and the formally
organized system in terms of the effects on
the adoption behavior of members, thus
relating the concepts and theories of diffusion research to those of organizational
change.

Literature on Organizational Change

A major compendium of research results,
references, concepts, ideas and theories for
students of organizations and organizational
behavior has been edited by March (1965).
Chapters are classified into foundations,
methodologies, theoretical-substantive areas,
specific institutions and application. Charles
Bidwell's chapter on "The School as a
Formal Organization" provides knowledge
fundamental to changing schools. Discussions are mainly oriented toward scholars.

A source of equal interest to practitioners
and scholars is Baldridge's *Organizational
Change Processes: A Bibliography with
Commentary* (1970). The bibliography has
two major sections: "General Problems of
Analyzing Organizational Change" and
"Changes in Various Sub-Systems." The
first section discusses 1) reasons why organizational theorists have generally neglected the problem of organizational
paradigms, 2) deliberate action by authorities and partisans, 3) organizational conflict as a promoter of change, and 4) the
interrelation of organizational subsystems.
The second section discusses 1) changing
organizations by changing individuals, 2)
partisan groups of agents of organizational
change, 3) system changes planned by
authorities (long-range planning and decision making), 4) technology as a source
of organizational change, and 5) the organization and its environment.

A most central volume, edited by R.
Schmuck and M. Miles (1971), integrates
the applied behavioral techniques of organizational development with changing schools.
The book brings together much of the
available empirical work of the effects
of organization development on the im-

proved functioning of schools. They define
organizational development, contrast schools
with other settings, and present materials on
improving classroom group processes, using
group problem-solving procedures, and
changing classroom interaction. The chapters also examine how change agents are
organized, trained, enter and work in
schools.

A final item in this review, by Stuart and
Dudley (1968), lists approximately 650
sources dealing with educational innovation
from three broad social science perspectives:
social structure, social psychology and social
organization.

Summary

The preceding summaries and compilations of the literature on innovation, changing and change were selected primarily to
provide useful guides for those interested
in processing the study of change. Sources
were collected from four general areas of
change literature and selected to interest the
activist-practitioner as well as the scholar of
change.

THE EMERGENT DISCIPLINE

The emergent discipline is based on some
explicit assumptions, is differentiated from
other disciplines and types of knowledge,
has methodological requirements, and will
be based on more technical definitions of
change. Some issues not treated here are
normative-value issues, the "oughts" necessary for this discipline, the substantive
propositions already available, the issues of
research design and the signposts for
worthy exploration.

For the practitioner and researcher we are
attempting to search for the bare skeletal
structures of concepts and framework
around which a discipline of knowledge is
growing. We recognize that this discussion
offers many possibilities; we do not attempt
to legislate the right concepts and values of
the discipline. We do believe the following

assumptions are the requirements to fulfill for an adequately cumulating field of knowledge.

Initial Assumptions

What assumptions are being made in organizing the remainder of this paper? It is necessary to state some of these so that we can be explicit and also indicate what we are not discussing.

First, given the diversity of the content to be covered, how is it possible to have a discussion of changing separate from change in specific areas at all? It has to be an assumption of this discussion overall that there is a finite set of principles of changing and of change which can cover the specifics of change in different fields and arenas. Without this assumption, this discussion would be extremely abstract and idealized, and, more seriously, relevant only as an exercise in paradigm building.

If possible it would be preferable to differentiate the finite principles and basic knowledge into three forms: first, every change process is the same as every other; second, every change process is the same as only a set or class of change processes; and third, every change process is different from every other change process. Formulations of these sets of equally true propositions would be necessary. Strategically the second is most important. For example, the change processes in schools as an organization, while similar, are different from those of other organizations. The special features of a school organization in contrast to industrial organizations have been identified as: the ambiguity and diversity of goals, the low interdependence of staff, the vulnerability of schools to short-run demands from their environment, the inadequate provision of financing, the ritualistic use of procedures and the pressures toward "processing students" (Schmuck & Miles, 1971). But we do not have enough information for a comparative discipline of changing, however desirable such a discipline would

be. This is a future task. The practitioner-administrator does encounter unique cases and no theory or set of principles will appear to him to deal with the concreteness of the specific case.

A second assumption made in this discussion is that there is a need for a body of knowledge that directly attacks the issues of changing from the activist's stance. Whether the activist is the administrator, the program conductor, a teacher, a change agent or whatever, we assume that some principles and transformations of knowledge can and must be used in guiding his actions in producing change. In short, we assume there can be a discipline of changing which is serviceable for the change agent or activist-practitioner.

The third assumption is that the knowledge must be congruent and cumulative, and not a patchwork of random and motley assortments of propositional statements. Improvements in conducting the research and scholarly efforts are needed.

A fourth assumption is that the body of basic knowledge for the activist-practitioner will be integrated—a theoretic integration or a composite of well-researched generalizations, evaluated programs and experiences which include the distilled and formulated artful wisdom. Such basic knowledge is more evocatively and aptly described as the *selectively retained tentatives* (which is no more and no less than the description of any knowledge, including scientific knowledge).

Three Types of Knowledge

Three types of knowledge can be distinguished for the purposes of understanding and fostering research. Each of these types may be thought of as having some definable and denotative attributes, but there is no ultimate reality to these; they are selectively retained tentatives. These typologies are for heuristic purposes. The utility of this conceptual separation will depend upon how helpful they are in sorting out and suggesting other ideas to the user and in generating focused research. (We deliberately use symbols to denote these types of knowledge since the usual labels may not coincide exactly with the distinctions we are making.)

Type A is basic knowledge focused toward intervention and deliberate, intentional and planned change. It is a set of selectively retained tentatives based on theory and research on how to bring about change, and it has an action purpose.

Aspects of this emerging discipline of knowledge and practice have been explored under the labels of applied behavioral science, engineering in social science, clinical discipline, policy science, practitioners' discipline, change agents' strategies and models of changing, intervention theory, innovations adoption, knowledge utilization, techniques of interpersonal, group and organizational change, and revolution and revolutionary change.

Type B is the more accustomed basic knowledge focused toward understanding how change occurs, especially looking at changes, their correlates and their consequences. Sociologists study social change, development of societies and large and small subsystems. Psychologists and others study development and maturation developmentally. Educational researchers have studied innovation adoption and educational change.

Type C is the most accustomed knowledge in "basic research." It is focused toward understanding how the functional relationships of parts of a system fit, how the variables are interrelated both causally and especially correlationally. The basic social and behavioral science disciplines are the main formulations here. However, we dare hope that basic research is not restricted to Type C but is also a hallmark of Type A.

Type A basic knowledge is underdeveloped, and in the opinion of many researchers and theorists, does not exist, or at best is derived solely as applications of B and C. In the past few decades, both in creating and in reviving an older tradition

of application, there are signs of sufficient interest in studying application of social science and thus in Type A knowledge to make it a separate field or discipline of knowledge. Practitioner fields of administration and management, of social change and therapy, of human relations training and organizational development, and of programs and strategies to change societies as a whole as well as poverty, racism and other social problems, including educational practices and teaching, have all been applying basic knowledge from Type B and C in creating theoretical and conceptual formulations of planned change and techniques for deliberate change. And the interest in evaluation research has thrust attention on the creation of generalizations about techniques and programs leading to Type A knowledge.

Type A may develop into an autonomous field wherein it need not be bound by applying Type C basic social sciences solely, but may develop its own base from consideration of practices and from theory and research. Illustration: some theories and practices of therapy used to change the individual do not wait upon and are not bound by preexisting theories of personality (Type C) and theories of development of stages of growth (Type B). Theories and practices of teaching need not wait upon developed theories of learning (Type C) and cognitive development (Type B). Theories and practices of developing the economic and social system of a nation are not solely dependent upon fully developed theories of economic and sociocultural behavior (Type C) nor theories of developmental stages (Type B) of societies. Theories and practices of organizational change and renewal have not depended solely upon organizational behavior theory. Indeed, Type A knowledge may well be a contributor to Type C knowledge in the traditional basic social sciences as more systematic and conceptual work is done. "The best way to understand something is to try to change it" may indicate the way in which Type A contributes to Type C.

On the other hand, Type C basic social science has been much of the groundwork of Type A. Research on personality needs has led to procedures for altering needs, as in the work on achievement needs and as related to changing societies. Research on learning has evolved principles of reinforcement leading to practices of behavior modification. Dewey's approach to problem solving and learning, coupled with Lewin's situational field approaches to behavior, have led to the T-group and planned change techniques.

Obviously, there are difficulties in trying to separate these three types too rigidly. For example, the distinction centering around intentional, deliberate and planned change between Types C and B is blurred. In the study of social change are there not, in many cases, some actors and participants who have intentions to bring about change in some desired direction? Most probably there are if searched for. In these cases, the useful distinction for Type A is that the actors operate beyond the limitations of their own self-interest and desire, take some responsibility and purview for the overall sets of process—diagnosing, figuring out the various other groups and the forces involved —and create a style or strategy in dealing with these forces. Thus, the distinction between Type A and the others is the degree of conscious attention in Type A to the wide-range process of bringing about change versus the conscious purpose of how to bring about, or how to help bring about, the desired changes (cf. Downey, 1968).

Even so, there are many residual changes in social systems, or individuals and sub-systems, which either involve very limited scope of intentions, are outcomes which are unintended, or are by-products of some other intended outcomes. Such changes are often retrospectively found to have, or have attributed to, some inferred intentions of the acting parties either by the parties themselves or by an observer. Analyses of these attributions of determinants of actions and behaviors will be a useful future mode of analysis which reconciles, integrates and categorizes. Attribution theory in social psychology is growing and can be applied to change processes. However, our purposes in this disscussion will be of a less integrative nature.

Type A is our main concern in this discussion. Formulations of theories and the techniques, strategies and approaches to change, innovation and renewal require a value statement of direction, if not the substantive value to be striven for. For some the general desired outcome, the intention, is "increase in control by individuals over the conditions of existence, or alternatively an expansion of resources" (Coleman, 1971). For others, the desired outcome is the establishment of norms and values about the processes of change in major behaviors in the system, which allows the system to cope with internal as well as external impacts to produce a "healthy" or self-renewing system.

Type A must develop in directions which blur the usual distinctions between basic and applied knowledge. The main point of this discussion is: *Type A knowledge is basic knowledge seen as a set of selectively retained tentatives about the desired ends, processes and techniques in relation to these ends, and their outcomes in changing behavior and institutions. It uses theoretic-analytic tools and methods to order empirical observations, and makes explicit its bases of formulation as well as the quality of tentativeness of these formulations and generalizations.*

We shall delineate some of the activities and their mutual supportiveness for the theoretic-analytic and the empirical-descriptive. Another way to look at the purpose of this paper, then, is that it is trying to make suggestions for more theoretically oriented formulations about how to change —an applied behavioral science, a discipline of knowledge built on intervention theories, innovations, diffusion adoption, evaluation and achievement of goals.

There are three unique properties of Type A knowledge focused for the practitioner and change agent: the integrative and multi-level lenses of his conceptual framework, the actual or perceived strategic accessibility of the levers of action, and the morals-values-ethics issues. The study of each and their interactional effects on the others differentiates the heart of Type A knowledge.

Theoretic and Empirical Activities and Tools

In this section we distinguish between a set of ideas and activities for systematic knowledge building. What is ordinarily lumped together into theory is broken down into activities and tools: constructs, conceptual hypotheses, middle-range theory, conceptual schema (including grand theory), conceptual model and meta-theory. These are designations which are currently in practice in the formulating of systematic knowledge. The current emphasis in research is toward constructing middle-range theory, ever since it was pointed out that progress in research could not be made with the large, grand and conceptual analyses which are not tied to activities at the empirical-descriptive level.

The empirical activities are descriptions and observations, closer to the "facts" of the phenomena under study. Common sense facts and observations are the raw forms and give way to systematic descriptions of events and cases. Lurking within these are descriptive concepts, slices of the myriad phenomena of "reality." These descriptive concepts, more recently called the behavioral or observable manifestations of the constructs of the theoretic level, are the crucial stuff of knowledge. Without tie-in to the theoretic, research becomes "rank empiricism," accumulated empirical findings which are not organized to make sense no matter how refined and intricate the statistical manipulations. Empirical expectation and the experimental and quasi-experimental designs are the logic of proof and disproof, the "scientific method."

We have given special attention to the use of paradigms since paradigms are the ways in which an organized listing and categorization of the empirical findings and observations summarize and challenge the theoretic activities as to the task they must tackle in elevating the descriptive into useful theory. Paradigms are frequently used and currently popular as empirical substitutes for the theoretic activities (see Figure 1 for listing).

These distinctions in the theoretics and in the descriptives are most frequently found in Type B and especially C, the "basic disciplines," and, as we will develop in this discussion, are needed in Type A knowledge about changing. However, this discussion

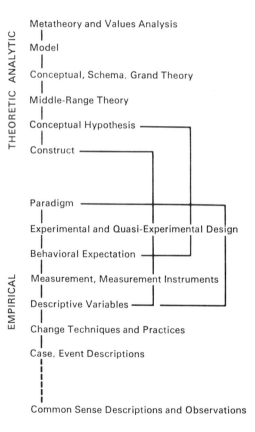

Fig. 1.   A paradigm of theoretic and empirical activities and tools for systematic knowledge building about changing behavior and institutions (Type A) (arranged by degrees of abstraction).

will not be able to fill in the levels for a complete theoretic-empirical system for knowledge about changing since such do not exist. Rather, we shall find fragments and unorganized heaps of Type A knowledge. The working out of the interconnections required for a cumulative discipline have not been achieved.

The conceptual models vary in breadth. The most general, and most inclusive, model is cast into systems-input-output terms. A given system (e.g., the educational system or a school district) is considered to have at any given time a set of resources held, and a set of transformation processes by which these resources create further resources. These created resources are of two kinds: outputs (in turn resources for other systems) and resources added to internal resources or to the transformation processes. The advantage of the model is that it represents a common ordering/classifying of specific factors in different content areas into outputs, transformation processes and so forth. What is not yet clear is whether the model is a set of constructs with middle-range theories and hypotheses or a convenient brokerage—transfer points of knowledge or analogical suggestions to serve specific studies in one area by exchanging ideas and properties from another content area. Either function would serve research well. At the very least such a model does provide at present a paradigm for creating taxonomies and formal listings. The issue of the use of the formal model is intrinsic to all models in knowledge building. Essentially a Type C conceptual schema, this schema is adapted readily to a Type A when changing this system is examined based upon unique dynamics and principles of changing and upon the study of change, deliberate or not. Type B knowledge also contributes.

The Type B conceptual model of input-transformation-output focuses on questions about these processes, for example, diagnosing and identifying deficiencies: in the internal resources and their allocation, in the transformation processes, in the input resources necessary to effect change in either or both of these, and so on.

In addition, Type A knowledge orients these questions to more concrete action issues such as the ways of estimating the relative advantages of remedying one deficiency or one inefficiency over another, the strategic access of the change agent to the variables identified as needing change, the procedures and strategies for altering these deficiencies and inefficiencies, and the inclusion of a principle of equifinality. This principle points out that there may be many ways to achieve the same ends or finals, and that these ways may be seen to be equal in effectiveness.

Changing in a Type B system requires a definition of change, the identification of the deliberate, intentional or planned change, and the accompanying processes.

A conceptual schema of more restricted scope that is the most explicit within intentional change (Type A) is Planned Change (we capitalize because the proponents of this conceptual model and attendant practices frequently use this term). This formulation focuses on the relationship between the change agent and client and restricts its scope by setting three relational conditions for Planned Change: there is mutual goal setting, movement towards equal power balance, and use of valid knowledge. In insisting upon the normative value positions the conceptual model limits its domain and specifies a value-ethical position for the change agent (e.g., Bennis, Benne, & Chin, 1961; Schein & Bennis, 1965).

In this schema the change agent is a trainer, facilitator, consultant, and/or process expert. The appropriate model is that of inter-system relations (Chin, 1961, p. 207).

Another Type A model revolves around advocacy. Here the change agent has intentions to bring about certain ends and participates in the change processes to accomplish these ends. His choices as an advocate are clear and he mobilizes his resources and skills for specific innovations and changes.

Frequently he is operating in the role of participant, program sponsor, administrator, and/or leader.

A survey and classification of models and strategies of deliberate changing categorize more than 20 specific ideas and practices into three major orientations: the rational-empirical, the normative-reeducative, and the power-coercive (cf. Chin & Benne, 1969). In this analysis the focus is on education. In the group labeled rational-empirical, based on views of the Enlightenment and Classical Liberalism, the emphasis is on knowledge and truth where basic knowledge is put to use in practice. They identify that much of the effort in education has been in this tradition and that the changing of education has followed in the same mode. The normative-reeducative embodies the views of therapists, human relations trainers and situation changers with roots in John Dewey, Freud and Lewin. The techniques are action research, problem-solving models, training labs, data collection feedback, and experiential learning methods.

In the power-coercive strategies, based on affecting the legal, economic and social conditions within which people act, there are power and political strategies. The techniques are administrative, or legal, or the use of political institutions, or, on the other hand, building countervailing power against established power.

The underdeveloped models and strategies of deliberate change are especially in two areas: power and the bottom-up deliberate change, and the strategies of revolution and revolutionary change. Many significant changes in structure, decentralization, community control, alternative schools, and others are deliberate changes.

APPROACHES
TO DEFINING CHANGE

The emerging position in conceptualizing change includes interaction of variables, the interaction of social system factors with an innovation, the interactions of the condi-

tions of a system with the social and psychological factors, the interaction of a change agent and the client system. While recognizing the necessity for interactions as the most adequate conceptual schema of determinants, still the end outcomes of the change are not necessarily interactional. They tend to fall into certain classifications.

In this section we shall describe the various definitions of change in use. The three types of definitions focus on 1) innovation definitions, 2) system definitions, and 3) emergent process definitions.

The central concern is to specify the concept of change in use in any theory or study, in creating middle-range theories that tie together because of a common definition of the outcome of change, in theories of testable propositions, and in techniques and procedures. *It is the most crucial task ahead for the study of change.*

Innovation Focused Definitions

The concept of innovation is seen as the central concept for one mode of study of change and of changing. An innovation is anything new—knowledge, idea or thing. The first and common approach to defining innovation is objective. The objective innovation is defined as "new" or something changed in a significant and substantial respect. No uniform criteria are available to specify new and what is meant by a significant and substantial respect. A second approach is quantitative—innovations which are ideas and practices or materials not yet adopted by a specified percentage, e.g., 10 percent or less. A third approach is to label a new total package practice as an innovation. For example, in education, a different technology of teaching, as computer aided instruction, team teaching, or modular scheduling is an innovation. Here the idea or practice is labeled as an innovation by the innovator. A fourth approach is in terms of defining an innovation by the critical factor of the *effects* on behavior. A fifth approach defines innovation as "perceived" as new.

"An innovation is an idea, practice or object perceived as new by the individual or group." It does not matter if the idea is objectively new; as long as the idea seems new and different to the individual, it is an innovation (Rogers, 1971; Zaltman & Lin, 1971).

The conceptual framework and/or paradigm for research on innovation includes invention, diffusion and adoption, communications and utilization. These substantial formulations of middle-range theory and research have been mostly of Type B knowledge. A systematic strategy of making use of these findings has been made possible in education by the proliferated systems of centers, regional labs, agencies and programs for diffusion, dissemination, communications and retrievals of new knowledge, practices and materials.

In general, innovation-focused definitions swing around a perceived difference that can be identified as having existed elsewhere and which are now present in the operating systems. They tend to be descriptive and range from common sense observations to descriptive catalogues. They are content-focused and emphasize visibility.

The global and descriptive nature of the term "innovation" and especially the brand labeling of an idea or practice as "innovation" has led to various discontents. The search is on for more systematic and theoretic dimensions of innovation.

Type A knowledge requirements provide some bases for deriving the dimensions of an innovation based on importance of the change to the actors and to the outcome of adoption of an innovation. A list of these dimensions so far proposed is as follows: 1) cost—financial, initial and continuing; 2) cost—social; 3) returns on the investment, including the short- or long-term returns and effects (there may be effects which are desirable, but no returns to the system which produced them); 4) efficiency—time saving, ability to reach the desired ends or to avoid distress or to obtain relief from a present state; 5) perceived risk and uncer-

tainty of failure of innovation and the resulting consequences; 6) communicability including clarity of results or outcomes, as well as communicability and transferability of the alterations in the transformation processes; 7) compatibility to existing activities; 8) complexity; 9) perceived relative advantage including visibility by demonstration; 10) structural radicalness which is related to the social systems' structures of communication, authority, and reward systems; 11) terminality—the time periods of closure for repeating cycles, e.g., school term, a class lesson module; 12) reversibility; 13) divisibility of innovation practice; 14) commitment, attitudinally or behaviorally required; 15) publicness versus privateness; 16) adoption variables such as decision-making bodies needed, number of gatekeepers for spread; 17) number of nodes of transmitting; 18) susceptibility to successive modifications; 19) gateway ability—opening gate for other innovations, i.e., foot in door; and 20) ego involvement (Zaltman & Lin, 1971). It is not yet clear whether these dimensions are perceived by the adopter or are intervening variables used to explain adoption/nonadoption.

It would be fallacious to say these are universal dimensions of any innovation. What we feel is that these dimensions can be used as the beginnings of the construct-theoretic system for the research. With each dimension some specialized conceptual hypotheses can be constructed, especially as these take into account the other approach of systems and emergent goals. There are middle-range theories about these dimensions from other fields of knowledge with either an objective analysis or a perceived judgment by the adopters of an innovation. For example, some of the Type A issues in this formulation are the discrepancies of perceptions by the various gatekeepers and/or decision makers on any one or several of the dimensions. The very fact of discrepancies and misperceptions may account for adoption of innovations rather than the objective properties of the various dimensions of the innovation. Consequently, the analysis of techniques for managing the perceptions must be a part of the basic knowledge needed for Type A.

Another major model built around innovation type definitions is that contained in the work of Havelock and his associates (Havelock, 1969). Their study of the various stages of a process of knowledge utilization has revealed the importance of a complex linkage system to coordinate the process. Propositions about the role relations in the linkage system abound in their work.

System Focused Definitions

Definitions of change are most frequently centered around some attributes of the client system. In this section, we shall quickly examine four slightly different approaches to defining change in terms of the client system.

Change defined in terms of relationships to goals of system. The most obvious definition of change is that which relates directly to the goals of the systems, namely, in education, the increases or decreases in students' learning. In addition, there may be shifts in balance among multiple goals as well as a shift in the priority and timing of goals. Any organizational system has more than one goal. In addition to production and output, the system has goals for members of its system. From time to time there are varying political and economic balances on a decision that must be made about the allocation of scarce resources to legitimate claimants for the resources. And finally, there may be new goals crystallized and claimed as equally valid. For example, there is increased claim to validity for the goal of schools in developing motivations and personal growth or identity, in juxtaposition to the goals of acquiring knowledge and skills. Definitions of change based on the goals of systems are very common, are generally limited to formal goals of the system, and

quite often ignore the intrinsic goals of functionaries.

Change defined as any substantive difference in the client system. The formalization of the categories of change here would be a large catalogue and would probably include almost all of the variables that have been identified and studied. Conceiving of the school as a system of interrelated subsystems, roles, methodologies, etc., almost any innovation will result in some substantive difference in some system variable.

Improvement in these dimensions is arbitrarily defined in terms of some larger possibilities in the service of some individual needs, or in terms of increased functioning of the collectivity, or in terms of an increase of some variable which is not necessarily embedded in a theoretical or conceptual network. For example, a school system may introduce differentiated staffing to improve the system's functioning. If seen as a substantive difference in the client system, the innovation may be deemed successful once the differentiation has taken place. However, if the innovation is defined differently it may represent trivial or irrelevant change. In any event, the definition of change on the given variable studied is not always placed in a theory of middle range, not to mention a conceptual schema with systematic propositions.

Change defined by some theoretical models. A different way of classifying definitions of change is by the use of some criterion of formal theory or model theory. We shall list two major classes of such definitions of change: those from the *system theorists* and those from the *developmental theorists.*

System theorists make a distinction between minor perturbations or dynamics of a system and major changes at the structural level. Thus, five levels of change can be distinguished on a continuum of system perturbation.

Beginning with the least amount of disturbance to the ongoing system we can identify the change level of *substitution*. This is where one element is merely substituting for another element already present. We often hope that, as in the case of the new and improved models of cars, people will look forward to substituting a later edition of a textbook or new media of communications for the old. A substitution change has little effect on the client system.

A second level is *alteration*. We alter some material in a textbook, hoping that the change will appear minor, and thus be readily adopted. For example, a new textbook may be designed to require small group activity as the text is used. Alteration changes like substitutions are easily made; however, they may lead to effects that are unanticipated. Returning to our example, a given teacher may accept the contents of the new textbook but find the small group activity associated with its use counterproductive to classroom objectives.

Perturbations and variations constitute a third level of change. Changes in the performance of a given client system sometimes lead only to temporary shifts in the system but not to a change in the structure of the system itself. For example, scheduling classes on 20-minute modules will disrupt the routines of teachers accustomed to 40-minute periods. Most teachers, however, will adjust to the new class arrangements within a relatively short time. From a long-range point of view, such changes are temporary oscillations in the relationships. Thus a sociological theorist would consider changes of this sort not real, or permanent changes, but merely variations in and around the equilibrium of a system.

Restructuring changes are disruptive in terms of the systems equilibrium. They are changes which lead to modifications and reorganizations of the fundamental structure of the system itself. Change of this order is basic social change of the system. An example would be the actual participation of students or laymen in the governance of schools.

A final level is *value-orientation* change. These are alterations and shifts in the fundamental value orientations which define and shape specific behaviors. Reorientation of values of the kind which define other values guiding behavior would represent fundamental change. The major effect this level of change has on the system can be seen through the example of staffing a school with teachers who value student growth more than system maintenance.

The preceding five levels of change are definitions within systems theory. The essential conceptual point in defining change from the system theorists' view is that there is an increase in the values of the parameters representing small increases cumulating, or perturbations and oscillations leading to "step-jump" in functional relations of the variables toward a new order of stable state relationships. The straws that break the camel's back, the increases which lead to a new gestalt, reflect the "step-jump" of the system or what also has been called the change in structure or restructuring of the system. Mathematically, and in physical systems, this change is noticeable and measurable. In living systems and in the conceptual models applied to human and social affairs in education, we have a different and unexplored problem of detecting such jumps, or change. System theorists have acknowledged the difficulty of conceptualizing change in system terms. However, using open system models for defining change has assured that change conceptions are built into the model and not just added as extra-system attributes.

Another set of definitions of change can be formulated from the work of *developmental theorists*. There has been less attention to conceptualizing change in developmental terms than in system terms, even though developmental theorists are directly concerned with change. Indeed, the central concepts of the developmentalists have assumed change as an ongoing process underlying all of the activities and functions of living organisms.

Developmental models are characterized by some common attributes and postulations. These have been identified as direction, the identifiable states or phases, forms of progression from one state or phase to another, and the forces and the potentialities of the system. Each of these characteristics of the developmental models may be used as ways of defining change (Chin, 1961).

If we assume an ongoing process of growth, or natural maturation, then there is a tough requirement for a definition of change based on intervention or deliberate change. There must be an increase in some attribute over and beyond that which would have occurred through maturation or development. So we need to see if anything can be attributed to deliberate change in addition to natural growth of the system.

There are several possible patterns of defining deliberate change within formal developmental theory. One common pattern can be termed *decay-arresting*. When there is some alteration of the processes underway so that the decay and/or moving away from the desired goals is arrested, then a form of change is being specified. Monitoring and feedback systems would exemplify this type.

Many theories of growth and movement of stages are based on phase oscillations. This leads to a pattern of *pendulum change*. Regressive appearing behavior occurs and recurs in phases when new problems are encountered. A change program that is tied with an increase in rational problem-solving behavior may only be reflecting the oscillation of a phase of action of the system as it slowly swings through its developmental stages.

If there is a growth process underway, then what the intervention produces in the client system may be the growth curve which was already present resulting in *disguised growth*. Measurement of an increase in reading ability without taking into account the factor of maturation and growth is an example.

A less common form of growth can be termed *borrowed ahead*. In this form the increase in growth during the period under scrutiny may be followed by slower periods of growth so that the average of the two, so to speak, just about equals the underlying natural growth increase. Bandwagon innovations often follow this pattern.

Another pattern common to bandwagon innovations is the *injection elevation change*. If with an intervention there is a dramatic increase in the functions under study, but after this period the change dampens out, then there is an overall increase in the level but no change in the growth. There is an increase during the period of direct study, but when the special study is over the growth rate returns to its previous state and continues on, albeit at a displaced level.

When a change resulting from an intervention program results in a difference in the system that is expressed in its rate of development, the pattern can be called *alteration in growth rate*. The increase is discernible in the rate of growth and not merely in the direct increase in functioning. Conceptually, alterations of the system of this order would unequivocally represent change.

A final and common pattern in schools is the *shift in direction* type. As a result of an intervention there is a disruption of the direction of movement of the systems; some new or lower priority goals are now reconstituted and made more salient. Such shifts and alterations of direction represent a significant alteration of the system and can be easily called change, conceptually.

Change defined by methodological processes of a system. There are other definitions of change based on some altering of the methodological and operating processes, such as problem solving, innovating processes, decision making, communication and planning, as well as those processes related to "an adaptive organization," with feedback and steering mechanisms built in between its purposes and its environment.

Alterations in these processes is a definition of change. The consequences of these alterations are in how the system functions in managing its own change and changing activities.

In a way, these definitions of change are based on a theoretical model in the same sense as those in the preceding section. Some sort of ideal state of these internal management processes such as "healthy," "adaptive" person, "actualizing," etc., is assumed as a methodological norm. These views based on a value are then used as the basis of evaluating events: change occurs in the increase in these norms and ways of working.

Problem-solving processes and the concept of organizational health fall into this class of defining change. Bennis and others in organizational theory also have conceptualized change in terms of the methodological processes. The newly emerging field of techniques and practices devoted to this type of deliberate and planned change is called *Organizational Development*.

Emergent Process Focused Definitions

The emergent process definitions of change are elusive. In their pure form the definitions of the ends of the change are not stated; an engagement and relationship with a change agent, facilitator or consultant is contracted and a "process" of exploration and work is developed to help the client system identify its shifting and emergent ends. The change desired is "changingness"—a processual flow, an attitude toward change. It may be only at the end, and in retrospect, that the changes are specifiable and denotable.

The open-endedness of this approach makes research difficult; at times, however, the need to specify "what you are doing and what your goals are," and the desire to examine empirical evidence of the effectiveness of the expenditure of energy and costs has forced out, however reluctantly, a set of change goals and their definition. Under these circumstances, the tendency is to spec-

ify methodological process goals of the system as these affect the management of change, resistance to change, and receptivity to further changes. The change sought is self-renewal or organizational health which is a condition of responding effectively to the exigencies of the system's environment.

The more complex definition is: altering or building the cultural values and norms governing the institutionalization of the norms and procedures which regulate the change processes in key factors of the social system and its environment. Achieving specific changes, adopting innovations, etc., are the way stations and plateaus. A "goal" is to have the client system proactively identify, install and manage those changes it deems relevant to present and future normative criteria of its members.

In the more formalistic terms of definitions of developmental models, the definition of change here is in ever increasing change after the outside intervention is withdrawn. When the changingness is present, there are internally generated deliberate changes, with intentions exhibiting the criteria of Planned Change, i.e., the use of knowledge, mutual goal-setting, and moving towards equal power balance.

Interrelations with theoretic-empirical. The definitions are cast into the level of models and that of conceptual schemas primarily. The development of middle-range theory for Type A knowledge is beginning to shape from the work in Types B and C. The most obvious set of issues is operationalizing these constructs and theoretics by tying them down into descriptive concepts and generating empirical expectations. The field of deliberate change is stocked with constructs and variables. The measuring instruments for them have to be standardized. A necessary task then is for the use of standardized "instruments," many yet to be created. We need to avoid rank empiricism of random construction and mass use of instruments by tying in the theoretics, especially middle-range theories.

The dimensions of any definition must be developed into taxonomies, taxonomies into paradigms, and paradigms into theories of segments of the paradigm, or the dimensions must be cast into a conceptual framework of changing (Type A) and new taxonomies, paradigms, and middle-range theories be derived from them.

CONCLUSION

It is hoped that this formalistic discussion helps the further development of the emergent discipline. At the heart of this new field of study is the need to change the definitions of change to fit Type A knowledge. Will the discipline of deliberate, intentional, planned change have to follow along the lines laid down by this discussion? We do not know. We do think that the discipline, if it is to be a discipline of knowledge—of selectively retained tentatives useful for guiding action—will have to come to grips with the issues we have raised. Our discussion is not a program for progress, rather it is intended as a set of standards (tentatively held) by which progress can be estimated. The strategy of progress will have to be with empirical studies, propositions, hypotheses, and middle-range theories. The fact that we did not choose to refer to the already growing body of such propositions is not to denigrate it. Our self-appointed task was to find some thoughts, ideas, and approaches to help our understanding, and hopefully to encourage others to assist in the advancement of the emerging discipline of deliberate Planned Change.

REFERENCES

Baldridge, J. V. *Organizational change processes: A bibliography with commentary.* Stanford, Calif.: Stanford University, Stanford Center for Research and Development in Teaching, 1970. ED 036 908.

Bennis, W. G., Benne, K. D., & Chin, R. (Eds.) *The planning of change.* New York: Holt, Rinehart & Winston, 1961.

Bennis, W. G., Benne, K. D., & Chin, R. (Eds.) *The planning of change.* (2nd ed.) New York: Holt, Rinehart & Winston, 1969.

Bhola, H. S. *Innovation research and theory.* Columbus, Ohio: The Ohio State University, School of Education, 1965.

Chin, R. The utility of system models and developmental models for practitioners. In W. G. Bennis, K. D. Benne, & R. Chin (Eds.), *The planning of change.* New York: Holt, Rinehart & Winston, 1961. Pp. 201–214.

Chin, R., & Benne, K. D. General strategies for effecting change in human systems. In W. G. Bennis, K. D. Benne, & R. Chin (Eds.), *The planning of change.* (2nd ed.) New York: Holt, Rinehart & Winston, 1969. Pp. 32–59.

Coleman, J. S. Conflicting theories of social change. *American Behavioral Scientist,* 1971, 14, 633–650.

Downey, L. W. Prototype instructional materials and processes for preparing administrative personnel to understand and cope with planned change. In J. Culbertson et al., *The design and development of prototype instructional materials for preparing educational administrators.* U.S. Office of Education, Bureau of Research, Project No. 5-0998, 1968. Pp. 43–85. (Reprints available from author.)

Havelock, R. G. (in collaboration with A. Guskin). *Bibliography on knowledge utilization and dissemination.* Ann Arbor, Mich.: University of Michigan, Center for Research on the Utilization of Knowledge, 1968.

Havelock, R. G. (in collaboration with A. Guskin). *Planning for innovation: A comparative study of the literature on the dissemination and utilization of scientific knowledge.* Ann Arbor, Mich.: University of Michigan, Center for Research on the Utilization of Knowledge, 1969.

Havelock, R. G. *A guide to innovation in education.* Ann Arbor, Mich.: University of Michigan, Center for Research on the Utilization of Knowledge, 1970.

Kurland, N. D., & Miller, R. I. *Selected and annotated bibliography on the process of change.* Albany, N.Y.: New York State Education Department, 1966.

Maguire, L. M. *An annotated bibliography of the literature on change.* Philadelphia: Research for Better Schools, Inc., 1700 Market Street, Suite 1700, 1970. (a)

Maguire, L. M. *Observations and analysis of the literature on change.* Philadelphia: Research for Better Schools, Inc., 1700 Market Street, Suite 1700, 1970. (b)

March, J. G. (Ed.) *Handbook of organizations.* Chicago: Rand McNally, 1965.

Rogers, E. M. *Diffusion of innovations.* New York: Free Press, 1962.

Rogers, E. M. Social structure and social change. *American Behavioral Scientist,* 1971, 14, 767–782.

Rogers, E. M., & Shoemaker, F. F. *Communications of innovations: A cross-cultural approach.* New York: Free Press, 1971.

Schein, E. H., & Bennis, W. G. *Personal and organizational change through group methods.* New York: John Wiley, 1965.

Schmuck, R. A., & Miles, M. B. (Eds.) *Organization development in schools.* Palo Alto, Calif.: National Press Books, 1971.

Stuart, M., & Dudley, C. *Bibliography on organization and innovation.* Eugene, Ore.: University of Oregon, Center for the Advanced Study of Educational Administration, 1968. ED 019 722.

Zaltman, G., & Lin, N. On the nature of innovations. *American Behavioral Scientist,* 1971, 14, 651–673.

CHAPTER 18

Research on Organized Programs of Early Education

E. KUNO BELLER
Temple University

INTRODUCTION

If one defines educational programs as organized manipulations of experience intended to change or maintain patterns of intellectual, emotional and social functioning, it becomes clear that, implicitly or explicitly, all societies have educational programs for the entire first part of the life span. This raises an interesting question: why have most societies remained vague and implicit in formulating and formalizing educational procedures for the first few years of life? In modern Western culture, until very recently, the education of most children for the first five or six years of life has been left to their mothers. Parents, particularly mothers, shaped their infants' experience depending on their own educational backgrounds, social class, personalities and belief systems. Formalized education beyond the home has been limited to the occasional employment of tutors and to institutional group care for orphaned or neglected children.

Educational principles applicable to infants and young children were formulated long before organized programs of early education such as nursery school and kindergarten came into existence. The essays on early education by John Locke and Jean-Jacques Rousseau in the seventeenth and eighteenth centuries had enormous and lasting impacts on subsequent approaches to preschool education. Locke's empirical views of the foundations of knowledge and his associational theory of learning have been considered the historical basis for adult-centered approaches to early childhood education. Essentially, this orientation considers the child an immature organism who must be taught the skills and values of his adult culture. Reward, punishment, and other consequences or contingencies of behavior are used as the major incentives and conditions of reinforcement in the educational process. J. B. Watson, E. L. Thorndike and B. F. Skinner have developed further the theoretical foundations for this approach in the twentieth century (Kessen, 1965).

Locke has often been considered the father of the notion of the child's mind as a container of the impressions built up from sensory experiences of the outside world. However, Locke emphasized the need for individualizing educational programs by adapting them to early or "constitutional" mental inclinations of each child and the important role of the child's active curiosity and inquisitiveness in his intellectual development. Essentially, it was David Hume rather than Locke who conceived of the child's mind as a passive recorder of impressions governed by contingencies and by the laws of association. As indicated earlier, this approach to learning and development forms the basis for preschool programs, emphasizing the direct teaching of skills and values held by the adult culture.

Rousseau ushered in a new era for early childhood education by proposing that adult society must not impose its own values on the child but must let the child learn through discovery and through exercise of his own body and senses. Rousseau objected to direct teaching of skills and abstract ideas in advance of the child's having developed the necessary functions to understand rather than mirror mechanically through memory and imitation what he is being taught. A child's thoughts are made up of images and not ideas. Unlike ideas, images do not bear inherent or logical relationships to one another. Clearly these formulations were historical forerunners of Piaget's profound insights of sensory motor development two centuries later. Within the realm of early childhood education Rousseau's emphasis on sensory motor functioning was applied by Johann Heinrich Pestalozzi, a Swiss who constructed a curriculum for developing the three elementary divisions of knowledge—form, number and words (Kessen, 1965). While preserving the importance of sensory experience and activity in early education, Pestalozzi believed that nature must be organized for the child so that he can benefit from his sensory impressions. Maria Montessori continued this trend of educating the young child by regulating his sensory motor interactions with selected objects in the environment. A central set of ideas permeating this approach was that the child is an active, inquisitive

organism who can discover knowledge through guided exercise of his senses and his body.

Although Rousseau placed much emphasis on the role of experience in the child's education and development, some writers (e.g., Kohlberg, 1968a) consider him the forerunner of hereditary, instinctual and innate approaches to development and learning as formulated by Arnold Gesell and found in some of Sigmund Freud's writings. Rousseau's formulations about early education were not concerned with the heredity-environment issue. However, there is another historical link between Rousseau and Freud which has had profound implications for a contemporary trend in preschool education embodied in the United States in progressive, child-centered or traditional nursery programs, in England in the infant schools, and on the European continent in anti-authoritarian preschool programs. Both Rousseau and Freud dealt with the negative consequences of prematurely imposed restrictions and values of the adult culture on the child. While Rousseau was concerned with nurturing the child's zest for learning by expanding his opportunities for unaided or autonomous exploration of his environment, Freud indirectly advocated a greater understanding of the child's infantile emotional needs and greater adult support of the child in his active struggle to find a balance of the conflicting demands within himself, as well as the conflicting pressures from within and from the outside world. Contemporary traditional preschool programs in the United States and the infant schools in England share the common objective of providing a responsive environment in which the child holds an active position, enabling him to make choices. Both attempt to offer the child assistance rather than make him accept (passively) through direct teaching the values and knowledge of his environment.

Even though past differences have continued to exist between philosophies of education, a common trend has been to advocate the articulation and institution of educational programs for children at earlier ages. Several other historical developments have contributed to this trend. One impetus has come from the emancipation of women and their desire for pursuing professional careers with reduced interruption from time needed for rearing their own children, and another from a greater tendency to turn to the rapidly maturing social and behavioral sciences rather than to rely on traditional sources of institutionalized authority for advice on the goals as well as on the techniques for rearing children from earliest infancy. In a recent paper Schaefer (1970) recommended the development of a new discipline of Ur-education, a label suggested for the earliest and most basic education of the child. Fortunately, the last decade has witnessed not only the formation of a wide range of organized programs in early education, but also a series of research studies investigating the immediate and long-range impact of such programs. The present chapter will be devoted to a discussion of major studies during the past decade.

EDUCATIONAL PROGRAMS FOR INFANTS

CHILD-ORIENTED PROGRAMS

One of the earliest child-oriented programs for infants from underprivileged families was carried out by Schaefer (1969). A major goal of Schaefer's project was to foster intellectual development of children of lower socioeconomic status parents through a program of tutoring infants in the acquisition of verbal skills and language development. The program consisted of home tutoring offered to experimental subjects between 15 and 36 months of age, one hour a day, five days a week. Sixty-four male infants were selected by a door-to-door canvass in two lower-class neighborhoods. The children were all pretested on the Bayley Scales of Infant Development one

month prior to the onset of the study. The check on mean IQ scores on this test for the control and experimental groups before the onset of the study showed no significant differences between the children assigned to the two groups. However, comparisons between the groups revealed small differences favoring the controls on family variables that might be expected to influence the child's intellectual development. In order to minimize bias in family attachment to tutors and to achieve continuity of the tutoring experience, tutors were rotated to different subjects.

Schaefer trained college graduates to function as tutors. The program emphasized verbal stimulation, the provision of varied experiences, and the development of positive relationships with the infant. Tutors were encouraged to interact informally with infants and to instruct when the opportunity arose. For example, the child was to be slowly introduced to a puzzle by presenting it to him when he could be interested in it. Children were never pressed to play with the puzzle. The puzzle was first presented intact. The object depicted in the puzzle was named and the child was asked to touch the object and repeat the name. Later the tutor might present the puzzle intact, name the represented object, take one puzzle piece out, show it to the child, have the child touch it, describe his actions, put the piece back in place, with assistance if necessary. Verbalizations eliciting and describing actions were used as a supplementary technique, e.g., "Push it in," "Boom, it went in," "Where's the head?"

In order to assess the effectiveness of his program Schaefer used the Bayley Scales at 14 and 21 months, the Stanford-Binet Test at 27 and 36 months, a Preposition Test, the Peabody Picture Vocabulary Test, and the Johns Hopkins Perceptual Test, and ratings of task-oriented behavior during testing at 36 months. After the base line testing at 14 months the infants were retested at 21, 27 and 36 months. Schaefer was interested in obtaining measures of the mothers' attitudes toward their infants in order to assess the effect of home factors on the intellectual and emotional development of infants.

Schaefer found highly significant differences between his experimental and control infants on his measures at 36 months of age. Although the differences were in favor of experimental subjects, these differences were due more to a decline in performance on the part of the control infants than an increase on the part of experimental subjects, i.e., the IQ of the experimental subjects at the ages of 14 and 36 months was 105 and 106 while the comparable IQ at 14 and 36 months for the control subjects was 108 and 89.

Schaefer found significant correlations between maternal attitudes toward the infants and measures of the children's cognitive and emotional functioning. Negative maternal attitudes such as withdrawal, punishment, irritability, hostile involvement and detachment, and low verbal expressiveness assessed at 16, 30 and 36 months yielded median correlations of -0.38, -0.34, and -0.40 with the infant Stanford-Binet score at 36 months of age. Comparable median correlations between maternal attitude and scores on the Johns Hopkins Perception Test at 36 months of age were -0.36, -0.48, and -0.56. Correlations between maternal attitude and the infant's performance on the Preposition Test at 36 months were of the same magnitude, except that low verbal expressiveness on the mother's part correlated most highly with this test at 36 months, i.e., -0.60 and -0.53. Maternal attitudes were uncorrelated with scores on the Peabody Picture Vocabulary Test. Turning to measure of noncognitive behavior, Schaefer found maternal attitudes correlated significantly with task orientation on the cognitive tests. Negative maternal attitudes yielded a median correlation of $+0.42$ with the child's emotional functioning at 36 months of age, i.e.,

hostility, belligerence, negativism and irritability. The same child measures correlated quite highly with the child's task orientation (median $r = -0.65$). Finally, median correlations between the child's emotional functioning at 36 months and performance on the Stanford-Binet, the Johns Hopkins Perception Test and the Preposition Test were -0.55, -0.61, and -0.39, respectively. Thus, although Schaefer set out to investigate primarily the effect of educational tutoring in the area of language and concept formation of the child's intellectual development, he discovered a series of impressive relationships of maternal attitudes to socioemotional and cognitive functioning of infants. As a result of these findings Schaefer has become convinced that a comprehensive approach to the study of early childhood education is more necessary than the employment of isolated educational techniques with the child away from his home setting.

A program similar to the one just discussed was carried out by Painter (1969). The goal of her program was to accelerate the spontaneous development of deprived infants and prevent anticipated cognitive and language deficits. Half of 20 children, eight to 24 months of age, were assigned to a control group and the other half to an experimental group. The latter received an hour of structured tutoring in their homes five days a week for a period of one year. In contrast to Schaefer's tutors, the tutors in this study came from a variety of educational backgrounds and were put to work after a week of intensive training which was continued throughout the study. The program emphasized language and conceptual development. Both training aspects were highly structured. In language training each child was presented with 1) beginning language, 2) elaborative language, 3) the breaking down of "giant word units" and 4) the encouragement of internal dialogue. In conceptual training, the concepts of 1) body image, 2) space, 3) number, 4) time and

5) categorical classification were emphasized. Some examples of activities used were dramatic play, rhymes, songs, imitation of tutor's speech, whispering solutions to problem-solving tasks, mirror games where the child labeled his body parts, and resting games. Language development was encouraged in all activities.

Scores of experimental and control infants did not differ at the onset of the program on the Cattell Infant Test, but at the end of the tutoring period the experimental group achieved an average of 10 Stanford-Binet IQ points above the control group. Painter included other tests such as the Illinois Test of Psycholinguistic Abilities, the Merrill Palmer Scales, and various items from other tests and found that her experimental subjects performed better than the control subjects on 25 of the 26 variables measured, with eight of these attaining statistical significance.

In contrast to Schaefer, Painter did not attempt to measure the infants' home environment nor to discover relationships between the home and the infants' emotional and intellectual development. It is therefore not surprising that Painter's study and her findings led her to a very different conclusion than the one reported by Schaefer. (Painter concluded that the tutorial programs for infants had made it clear that infants are capable of serious work for at least one hour a day and that infants might benefit even more from group programs away from home designed to offer physical care and an educational program free of the problems encountered in tutorial programs at home.) Schaefer concluded that successful and lasting educational programs for infants must include their families.

A third child-centered program was carried out under the direction of Palmer (1968, 1969, 1972). The goals of the program were to determine whether intellectual training early in life has demonstrable effects on children's ability to perform in the first grade, whether one age or another is more responsive to the program, whether duration of the effects varies with the age at which training takes place, and finally, whether the program would counteract the educational disadvantage of deprived lower-class black children in their cognitive development.

One hundred and twenty two-year-olds, 120 three-year-olds and 70 control children participated in this program. The children were randomly assigned to two experimental programs and one control program. One experimental program consisted of a highly structured, intensive concept-training curriculum while the other consisted of a less formalized discovery program. In the concept-training program the tutors talked more, followed a specific assignment plan with the children, and employed sequences of teaching increasingly difficult concepts to the children. Each task was carefully defined in relation to concept, series, stage and level. "Concepts" referred to bipolar dimensions of the child's environment believed to be essential for subsequent complex learning (e.g., up and down, in and out, hard and soft, etc.). "Series" referred to several related concepts which could be ordered into one training series as with sensual tactile concepts where stage one is wet and dry, stage two is hard and soft, etc. "Stages" were defined as sequences of training, e.g., for the development of form concepts simple trial and error puzzle work was employed in stage one, while visual discrimination and more complex trial and error work were used in stage two. "Level" referred to arbitrarily defined strata of relative complexity across training series. The trainers for the concept group were instructed to present each concept in the same four steps: 1) demonstrate and label actions related to the concept; 2) have the child perform an action related to the concept; 3) have the child perform such an action at the educator's demand in a choice situation to determine the child's knowledge of the concept; and 4) ask the child to label objects appropriately while the educator performed a task related to the concept. In the discovery group the tutors gave the same amount of individual attention but the child was left to his own initiative for selecting activities during the instructional period.

In contrast to the more structured program the instructors refrained from labeling and direct teaching, although the same materials were available during the teaching periods. A list of toys used in the concept-training groups was posted weekly so that the same toys could be used from week to week in the discovery group. Moreover, possible activities with the toys were also listed. Procedures were suggested to the instructors of the discovery group for involving reluctant discovery children who did not take initiative in selecting their own activities. For example, the teacher was instructed to take out the puzzle and the pieces and hand them to the child, but to go no further. With regard to the use of Play Dough, the instructor was encouraged to open the box, take out one can of dough and show the child how it could be molded. Blocks are a third example. The instructor was instructed to take out some blocks, informing the child that he was going to play with blocks, and build a tower or house and label it, without asking the child to use the blocks. The same group of instructors rotated in both programs and changed approximately every three weeks.

Early results indicate significant superiority of experimental subjects over control subjects on a number of measures of intellectual functioning both at the end of the eight-month experimental program and one year after the program ended. However, differences between the two experimental groups, that is, concept training versus discovery training, were minimal. After training, the experimental groups performed better than the control group on such tests as the Stanford-Binet Intelligence Test, language comprehension, perceptual discrimination, motor behavior, delayed reaction and persistence at a boring task. When retested a year later the experimental groups maintained their superiority on all but four of the assessment measures. A comparison between the two experimental groups yielded significant superiority of the concept training group only on a few measures, e.g., the concept familiarity index, which is highly loaded with items taught in the curriculum, motor performance, ability to follow instructions in sequence, and simple form discrimination. Palmer interpreted the comparable outcome of the concept-training and discovery groups as follows: a) the two-year-old is highly capable of learning a great deal with only two hours per week of instruction, but b) what he is taught is not so important as the conditions under which he is taught, specifically, the nature of the adult-child relationship. In his most recent progress report, Palmer (1972) presents findings of follow-up testing of his experimental and control children at age four years and eight months. The initial findings were essentially upheld. Palmer interprets some trends in his latest findings as indicating that the discovery program might be more effective for younger children, while concept training might be more effective in older children, that is, children three years or older.

It is interesting that in this well-controlled and carefully executed study the difference between educational techniques was far less important than the difference between intensive educational intervention, which was true of both programs, and no intervention, which applies to the control group. However, it would have been valuable to have had noncognitive measures of the children in the two experimental programs since it is conceivable that the distinction between a highly structured adult-initiated program and a permissive child-initiated program might have affected attitude toward learning and socioemotional functioning more than intellectual performance alone.

PARENT-ORIENTED PROGRAMS

The Florida Parent Education Program

This program has been directed by Gordon (1969) and is one of the pioneer parent-oriented educational programs for infants. Major goals of the program were to enhance intellectual and personality development of the child, and to produce changes in the mother's self-esteem and in her conviction that she could affect what happened to her and her child. An important feature of this program has been the use of paraprofessionals, or women from the community who were trained to function as educators. The parent educators received a five-week intensive training program which concentrated on principles of child development, skills in interviewing, techniques of recording information and specific exercises or games to be played with infants which had to be taught to the mothers.

Gordon attempted to build his instructional program on Piaget's concepts of development. Thus, early games were constructed to be sensory motor, manipulative, and exploratory, i.e., letting the baby pick up objects while describing to him what he was doing, the way things felt, etc. At later stages games had specific reference to more "pre-operational" activities such as the development of object permanence. For example, an object would be attached to a string and hidden from view, requiring the baby to pull the string to bring the object into view; or an object would be partly, and later fully, hidden under a blanket while the baby was watching and then the child was asked to find it.

Each mother was visited once a week. The parent educator demonstrated the activities which the mother was to carry out with her infant. The tasks were concretely and specifically spelled out in detail. However, the parent educator was instructed to emphasize to the mother the importance of treating the tasks as games and fun. Parent educators were instructed to test each infant on task competence before demonstrating to the mother how the task was to be performed. An attempt was made to make clear to the mother that the actual sequence of tasks depended on the individual child and if a task was failed it should be broken down into simpler components.

The subjects of the study were indigent mothers and their babies born between June 15, 1966, and September 30, 1967, at the public health center for small town and rural families in central Florida. Although Gordon started with 276 mother-infant pairs, their attrition rate was high and resulted in a final sample of 193 mother-infant pairs. Mothers were assigned to experimental or control groups on the basis of geography. The activity with all experimental mothers was the same but the timing of the instructional program was varied for different experimental groups. One group received home visits from the time the infants were three months old until they were two years old; a second group received visits from three months to one year; a third group received visits from the time the infant was one year until the infant was two years old; finally, a control group was tested without being tutored.

Gordon collected a large set of data on the mothers and the children. The data on each mother were based on the Parent-Educator Weekly Report, the Rotter Social Reaction Inventory, the Markle-Voice Language Assessment, estimate of mother's expectance, the Mother How I See Myself Scale, and a final observational report. The data on the child included the Parent-Educator Weekly Report, a final observational report, tests of performance, the Goldman Race Awareness Test, and the Griffith and Bayley Infant Scales. Apparently the collection and analyses of data were carried out and reported in parts by different associates and students who participated in this large research program.

One major finding in Gordon's study was that at the end of the first year of life, experimental infants were slightly but significantly ahead of control infants on total scores of the Griffith Mental Development Scales. When the children were retested at 24 months of age with Bayley Scales of Infant Development, no significant differences were found between any groups. However, while at 21 months of age experimental infants did not differ significantly from control infants on task-orientation scores on Bayley items, a later comparison at 27 months yielded significant differences on the same scores in favor of the experimental infants.

In his latest progress report, Gordon (1972) presents findings of a follow-up study of all his experimental and control groups when the children passed their fourth birthday. His findings at this time are based on three measures: the Stanford Binet Test, the Peabody Picture Vocabulary Test, and the Leiter International Performance Scale. In his latest longitudinal follow-up study Gordon found stronger and more consistent effects of his experimental intervention than he had found in his earlier assessments. The largest and most significant effects on all three tests occurred in children who received intervention for two or three consecutive years. Children who received intervention only during the third year of life performed better than control children on the Stanford Binet and Leiter Scales, although these differences did not reach statistical significance. Discontinuous intervention during the first and third years of life and intervention during only the second year had no positive effects.

Gordon and his associates found a multitude of relationships between specific maternal behaviors and performance of infants on a variety of measures. For example, Gordon found sizable correlations between verbal interaction scores of mothers and infant baby scores at age two for the group which received home visits the second year only. Correlations between maternal verbal scores and the child's performance on the Bayley Mental Scale and the child's task-orientation behavior during the test ranged from $+0.52$ to $+0.64$ ($n = 15$). Analyses

of data carried out by Herman (1971) showed that maternal behavior correlated significantly with the performance of 31 infants on the Bayley Motor ($r = 0.41$) and Mental ($r = 0.31$) Scales. Herman also reported that mothers of high scoring males on both mental and motor scales engaged in significantly more positive verbal behavior than did the mothers of low scoring boys and of high scoring females. Scott and Lally (1969) report significant sex differences in the infants' response to the program. For example, trained males performed significantly better than untrained males on the hearing subtest of the Griffith Mental Development Scales. Trained female infants scored significantly higher than untrained female infants on all but the performance subtest. Thus, it seems that girls benefited more consistently from the training program than male infants.

Gordon also reports some interesting findings with regard to effects of the educational program on the mothers. Mothers for whom pre- and post-information was obtained moved toward greater internal control of a reinforcement orientation. These mothers reported that they now felt greater control and more influence over what was happening in their own lives than they did when they entered the project. However, this change was significant only for mothers trained as parent educators while the majority of mothers who had not been trained as parent educators continued to evidence orientation toward external control.

Verbal Interaction Mother-Child Home Program

This program has been developed and carried out under the direction of Levenstein (1970, 1971; Levenstein & Levenstein, 1971; Levenstein & Sunley, 1968). A major goal of this program was to help low-income families to assume the same function of education which the middle-class parent carries out informally in raising his children. The immediate goal of the educational program was to increase conversation and communication between mother and child by using toys and books. The long-term goal was to help the mother become more effective in guiding the cognitive and intellectual growth of her child. Levenstein selected social workers rather than educators or psychologists to carry out the educational program. She believed that the social worker's background provided the most appropriate values and skills for the intervention program she conceptualized. The major function of the educator was to serve as a toy demonstrator helping the mother to become the effective educator. A set of verbal interaction stimulation material (VISM) was selected and used as a major vehicle for the educational intervention. The toys were such that they did not lend themselves to solitary play by the child but needed interaction with someone else for full enjoyment and learning. Mother-child interactions which were demonstrated by the home visitor emphasized the following points: giving information by describing the label, form, color and size of the object; describing toy manipulations such as building, matching, etc.; eliciting responses from the child through questions; describing the social interaction; encouraging reflections through questions; encouraging divergence by rewarding independence and curiosity; getting the child interested in books by eliciting verbalizations about illustrations and rewarding the child for his comments; and finally, building the child's self-esteem through frequent positive reinforcements in the form of verbal support and helping. During the early sessions the toy demonstrator interacted with the child more than the mother but gradually drew the mother into the activities. During the later sessions the home visitor attempted to shift interaction between adult and child entirely to the mother. This course was indicated because of Levenstein's conviction that the mother is the key person who must serve as the principal agent for helping a child acquire language and other cognitive skills.

To get the mother to assume this role the visitor or toy demonstrator emphasized the need for the mother to play and carry out demonstrated interaction with the child between sessions. Family counseling was added to the toy demonstration program as an additional activity. This was possible because the toy demonstrators were social workers.

The general hypothesis was that the verbal-intellectual competence of lower-class children would rise as a result of the program. A subhypothesis was that increases in intellectual achievement would be greater among two-year-old children than among three-year-old children because of the beginning symbolic language development at that age.

Fifty-four children, 20 to 43 months of age and drawn from two housing projects for low-income families on Long Island, New York, served as subjects. Eighty percent of the subjects were black. Children in the experimental and control groups were equated on social class on the basis of the Hollingshead Index. Thirty-three families in the experimental group received two half-hour visits weekly for a period of seven months. One control group, consisting of nine subjects, received weekly visits from a social worker who carried out the interview with the mother without providing verbal stimulation for the child. To control for the effect of leaving VISM with the mothers in the experimental group, the control mothers received toys other than VISM. The 11 children making up a second control group received only initial and posttests without any intervening home visits. The children all received the Cattell Infant Scales, the Stanford-Binet Test, and the Peabody Picture Vocabulary Test at the beginning and end of the program. The Peabody Picture Vocabulary Test was also given to the mothers of the infants at the onset and end of the study.

Levenstein found that experimental children manifested a gain of 17 points on the Cattell and Stanford-Binet Scales, which was significantly greater than comparable gains of one and two points by the control groups. The experimental group also manifested a gain of 12 points on the Peabody Picture Vocabulary Test, which was significantly greater than a four point loss of the first control group but not significantly different from a 4.7 gain of the second control group. The second hypothesis, namely a differential gain between two- and three-year-old children, was not supported by the data. The mothers' IQs did not show significant changes. Although there was some indication of mothers' positive attitudes toward the program, no significant differences were found in the kinds of major life events and in the incidence of mothers' employment. Two further findings reported more recently by Levenstein have been that the training of low-income, high-school–educated aides to function as educators resulted in the same effectiveness of the program as that achieved with social workers in the first year of the study; secondly, one- and two-year follow-ups of the infants after termination of the experimental intervention showed that gains over initial testing remained significant in spite of modest declines.

In her most recent report, Levenstein indicated a change in her control group composition. A third control group was added which received the verbal instructional stimulus materials for play with the infant without any home-visit toy demonstrations. Apparently this new control group which was added in 1967 showed a significant gain of eight IQ points over an eight-month period. No follow-up data were presented by Levenstein for this group. Follow-up data for the first control group which consisted of visitors who left toys in the home showed a 10 point increase in IQ during the year following the experimental program and a significant increase of 18 IQ points when tested 30 months after the original pretest.

The picture that seems to emerge from these findings is that the control groups which include either regular home visits and leaving toys, or leaving VISM only, manifest either immediate or delayed significant gains. This leaves only one control group, namely the one which received neither home visits nor toys, as the one which manifested no significant gain either after the eight-month period or after 30 months following the initial testing.

One of Levenstein's techniques was carried out a decade earlier by Irwin (1960), who instructed a group of working-class mothers to read to their infants 15 minutes daily to increase the amount of speech-sound stimulation. The mothers pointed out objects in pictures, made up stories and talked more to their infants. A control group received no systematic stimulation. After 18 months of the program the infants in the experimental group were significantly superior to the control infants in phoneme frequency.

Thus it seems that specific techniques of the home visitor, or even the choice of specific toys, are less important than a broadened range of opportunities for stimulation provided systematically by an experienced adult.

DARCEE Infant Program

A third program which is primarily parent-oriented is the intervention study with mothers of infants conducted at the Demonstration and Research Center for Early Education of the John F. Kennedy Center for Research on Education and Human Development at the George Peabody College, under the direction of Forrester, Harge, Outlaw, Brooks, and Boismeier (1971). Although the program has focused on infant growth and development in the physical and psychosocial areas of the infant's functioning, the overriding goal was to enable the parents to become a more effective educational change agent with their small children. The program has focused on the parent rather than the child because of the conviction that the parent is the most available sustaining agent to turn the home-visit program into a lasting experience. To accomplish the goal of making the parent an effective educational change agent, an attempt was made to move the parent to take increasing initiative in planning for her child. To implement this a further subgoal was to help the parent develop better coping skills in her daily life experiences, not only as a mother. It was hoped that a broader approach such as that would increase her ability to guide and shape the child's behavior rather than merely cope with it from moment to moment.

With regard to procedure and techniques, one home visitor worked directly in each home for at least one hour per visit for a maximum of 24 visits. Some overall guiding principles for carrying out procedure in the home were 1) to focus on the parent rather than the child, 2) not to exclude any family member from lessons during the home visit in order to promote rapport and spread the benefit of the experience to other members of the family, and 3) to employ materials which are easily available or simple to construct and to make use of such objects as discards around the home, e.g., plastic containers and coffee cans. Great stress was placed on encouraging the parent to use positive reinforcement, because it is believed that most lower-class parents are convinced of the validity of punishment as the most effective way to change a child's behavior. Beyond these general guidelines the approach to each home was highly individualized. Cultural as well as individual differences received a great deal of attention.

The implementation phase included six sessions or six cycles of home visits from April to November, 1970. One-week evaluation and planning activities preceded each of the six sessions. Focus and procedure over the six sessions shifted and changed in the following ways: in session one, initial visits focus on physical care, but social and cognitive components of basic routines are pointed out to the mother. Information

regarding infant growth and development is offered to the parents. During the next session emphasis is placed on improving the mother's ability to observe and record the baby's progress, behavior and development, and to make suggested play materials. The mother's observations are directed toward such events as teething, infant vocalizations and verbalizations, and the appearance of new behaviors in the infant. During the third session mothers are encouraged to carry out between-visit activities with the infant and to select appropriate toys or playthings. The home visitor deals to a considerable extent with the need for rewarding, reinforcing, disciplining and gaining the infant's attention. During the fourth session the home visitor systematically fosters the increasing involvement of the mother in the content of activities. During the fifth session each mother is asked to verbalize to the home visitor some of the things she has observed about her infant during the between-semester break. Some of the observations reported by the mothers dealt with motor development, new behavior, discipline, toilet training, environmental change, materials they had made, eating habits, social habits, provision of new playthings and father involvement. During the sixth and final session the home visitor reviewed the project with the mother and outlined expectations the mother may have for the child after 18 months of age.

Subjects of the study were 20 white and black mothers and their infants from low-income homes recruited from well-baby clinics. The infants were between seven and nine months of age. An equal number of mother-infant dyads were in comparison groups.

The Bayley Scales of Infant Development, the Griffith Mental Development Scales, and the Uzgiris-Hunt Scales were the three major instruments used in the evaluation of the program's effectiveness. All these scales were administered individually, prior to the onset of the training program and again at the end of the program. The interval between pre- and posttesting was eight months. The maternal behaviors were observed during testing. The homes were rated using the Caldwell Inventory of Home Stimulation. Data have been made available at this point for statistical analysis of pre-post changes on all the infants' measures (Forrester et al., 1971). The experimental infants exceeded the control infants on their performance on the Mental Scales of the Bayley and on the locomotion and performance scales of the Griffith. Although the focus of the study was on the education of the parent as a change agent for the child, findings obtained on the parent are not yet available.

Educational Intervention Program

The next program to be discussed is an educational intervention program with mothers by Karnes, Teska, Hodgins, and Badger (1970). A major goal of this program has been to forestall developmental deficiencies characteristic of disadvantaged children at three and four years of age by training mothers of infants to be the primary intervention agent. Mothers were met weekly and provided with a sequential education program. The mothers were helped to produce their own toys, for example, cutting out magazine pictures which the infant identified by naming and pointing, pasting these pictures in a scrapbook, and then occasionally reading the book to the infant. Other activities involved nested cans, snap beads, interlocking cubes of clay, a form box with masonite shapes in various colors and sizes. When working with the children mothers were told to instruct only when the infants were attentive. When the child did not want to carry out the activities the mother was instructed to put the toys away and wait until later. Activities were sequenced throughout the two-year period. For example, matching skills acquired in the first year in object motor games were incorporated into classification activities during the second year. Form perception in-

troduced during the first year with the form box and the masonite shapes was reinforced the second year with masonite templates.

A portion of each meeting was devoted to discussion which emphasized the need for a positive working relationship between mother and child and frequent use of positive reinforcement. An attempt was also made to foster a sense of dignity and worth in the mother through self-help capabilities, both in the family and in the community at large, by discussions on child discipline, birth control, community involvement, etc. The mothers were divided into two groups and met weekly over a seven-month period for the first year and weekly over an eight-month period during the second year. The staff workers made one or more monthly home visits to the experimental mothers.

The experimental group consisted of 20 mothers recruited primarily by 80 community and staff referrals. Fifteen of these 20 mothers continued to the end of the second year. Fourteen of the 15 mothers were black. The average age of the infants at the onset of the program was 15 months. None of the experimental children had attended a day-care center prior to or during the two-year study. The control group consisted of 15 infants who were selected from a larger study and matched with the experimental group on the basis of socioeconomic status, educational level and size of family.

Comparisons between experimental and control groups were based on posttesting only. The Stanford-Binet and the Illinois Test of Psycholinguistic Abilities were used as measures. The children were approximately 38 months of age at the time of posttesting. The children who received intervention significantly exceeded the control group children on the Stanford-Binet and on the Illinois Test of Psycholinguistic Abilities. A comparison of the experimental children with their older siblings showed that the experimental group exceeded their siblings on both the Stanford-Binet and on the Illinois Test of Psycholinguistic Abilities. Karnes points out that it is difficult to single out the component which might have been responsible for the improved functioning of the experimental children. Since the control group mothers received no attention during the same period in which the experimental mothers were in the training program, it is possible that the effect may have been due to the increased attention the mothers received and gave to their infants rather than the special activities and techniques that were devised for the experimental mother-infant pairs.

Prenatal Home-Visit Program

Lally (1971) has investigated the impact of a home-visit program which started during the mother's pregnancy and continued until six months after the infant was born. Paraprofessional home visitors designated as child-development trainers disseminated information necessary for the growth and development of the fetus and young infant. During the prenatal phase weekly home visits were designed to aid the expectant mother to understand her own nutritional needs and to prepare her for the arrival of her new infant. The home visitor helped each mother select adequate food for her baby. After the infant was born the child-development trainer continued to help the mother in the area of infant feeding but also began to introduce cognitive stimulation exercises which the mother would later practice with her child. The exercises were oriented toward the development of object permanence, the development of a concept that an object exists independently of the child's own actions, activities such as peek-a-boo, following of moving toy objects and finding hidden toys. Other areas of exercise dealt with the use of objects as instruments in attaining goals, with ways of acting on objects, with forming a distinction between act and external result, with developing the concept of space, with developing the sense organs and with development of gestural imitation as well as verbal learning. The Infant Intervention Program for

infants six months or older was composed of two groups of mothers, those who entered the program during pregnancy and continued to receive home instruction for six months following birth and those who entered when their infants were approximately six months old. Data were reported for infants of 23 mothers in the intervention groups and the 35 infants of mothers who entered the program when their infants were six months old. All mothers were from black lower-class families. Seventy-seven percent of the mothers were unmarried; none had a high-school diploma. The vast majority of mothers were under 20 and living with their parents when their infants were born.

At six months of age, when entering the Infant Intervention Program, all children were tested by means of the Cattell Infant Intelligence Scale. The children from the home-visit program received an average IQ score of 114 while the infants who had no prior home visit received an average IQ score of 104. The difference between the two groups was statistically significant. While this is only a first report of the findings, it is important because it offers results from an educational program—the home-visit program—which went further back than any other programs in the history of the child's development.

GROUP PROGRAMS FOR CHILDREN UNDER THREE

A major goal of pioneer group infant programs was to demonstrate that an infant will not be harmed by spending some of his time away from his mother and home. This explicit and often repeated objective was necessary because of the much-publicized findings of mental and physical growth retardation of infants cared for in orphanages (Goldfarb, 1945; Spitz, 1946). These findings have led to public decrees and decisions to eliminate infant group care wherever and whenever possible. Thus, it was necessary for such pioneers as Caldwell and Richmond (1964) and Keister (1970) to formulate, as one of the basic objectives of their undertaking, that group care for infants will not have damaging effects on the infant when his development is compared to infants reared at home. A second related objective was that educational group programs for infants will provide supplemental services, not substitute mothering, and will support the parent-child relationship in whatever way possible. The other objectives, especially with regard to furthering the child's development, did not differ from those described for tutorial programs earlier in this chapter.

The educational program and teaching techniques were dictated largely by two concerns: first, with separating the child from his mother, and second, with the accepted notion that infants benefit from a continued stable relationship with a nurturant adult. Thus, careful safeguards were taken to insure that every child accepted into the program maintained a continuing relationship with members of his own family so that he would not experience identity confusion or question the relative status of family members and educators in his life. Care was taken to provide the infants, especially those between six and 18 months, with organized routines similar to those they experienced at home. For the youngest group an attempt was made to assign most of the care for a given child to the same staff member throughout the day and week. Special emphasis was placed on having the same person attend basic physical needs such as feeding, putting the child to sleep, being there when the child awakened, etc. This emphasis required a ratio of approximately one adult to four infants. Beyond object constancy there was also concern to provide concentrated individual contact between infant and adult by giving individual attention to each infant for at least 15 to 30 minutes each day in the form of holding him, rocking him, taking him for a walk, playing structured learning games, etc. Regarding educational experiences, each daily schedule contained some activities that were carefully planned by the teaching staff and others that involved completely free selection of activity and expression of interest by the children. As a result, alternating opportunities were provided for child and teacher in each choice of activities and materials, e.g., reading books, labeling objects, playing sensory games, playing group games, etc. An attempt was made to match teaching activities and experiences to the child's current level of cognitive organization as determined both by tests and systematic observations of each child. Other concerns in the teaching program were to minimize unnecessary restriction on early exploratory attempts, e.g., keeping toys within the infant's reach or removing obstacles to exploration as much as possible. In order to optimize the infant's perception and awareness of his surrounding objects, furniture was occasionally moved to maintain the child's perceptual alertness to his environment.

The groups consisted of 10 infants between 6 and 18 months of age and 15 infants between 18 and 36 months of age. Although the children were separated into age groups, the age separation was never rigid and during each day planned opportunities were provided for contact between older and younger children. Attendance in the program varied from half days to full days, five days a week. Caldwell and Richmond (1964) have provided a careful chart for educational activities and routines in an infant nursery.

Finally, in order to maintain continuity between home and nursery, parent involvement included a brief orientation to infant development, monthly conferences with the staff and social work as needed by the family. Volunteer positions in the center were offered to mothers as an opportunity to observe the staff as they cared for very young children as well as an opportunity for the staff to learn about the mother-child relationships.

Moderate but statistically significant gains on the Bayley Mental and Motor Development Scales were found for children attending the nursery. The gains were not related to the child's sex, his ethnic background or the age at which he entered the program. The last finding was unexpected since Caldwell (1970) anticipated that earlier educational intervention would be more effective than later educational intervention. A comparison of mother-child attachment patterns in children attending the nursery and children reared at home revealed that children 30 to 36 months of age, following one year or more of participation in the program, did not differ significantly from comparably home-reared children. Age of entry in the program was not related to rated level of personal and social adjustment. These findings were interpreted by Caldwell as demonstrating that there was no negative effect associated with entering the nursery at an early age (Caldwell, Moselle, & Honig, 1968).

Caldwell compared 23 infants who had received their primary care from their mothers and 18 infants who had attended the Children's Center between 12 and 30 months on their performance on the Cattell Infant Intelligence Scales. Although the home-reared infants were significantly superior at 12 months of age, the Center infants were slightly, but significantly, ahead at 30 months of age. The changed positions of the two groups were due to a decline in the Developmental Quotients of the home-reared infants and a simultaneous rise of Center-reared infants during the 18 month period between the first and second testing.

Another study was recently reported (Honig & Brill, 1970) on 12-month-old infants who had participated in the program started by Caldwell and Richmond described above. This study was unique because it investigated effects on the development of cognitive functions as defined by Piaget and measured by means of Piagetian Infancy Scales specially constructed for the purpose of this study.

The sample consisted of 32 one-year-old

black infants from lower-class families. The 16 experimental infants attended either a morning or afternoon enrichment program for six months at the Syracuse University Children's Center. The 16 control group infants received no intervention.

The experimental infants performed significantly better on Piagetian Infancy Scales than the control infants. A more detailed analysis, however, revealed that the experimental infants performed significantly better only on two of the six Piagetian Scales, one of which was Object Permanence involving behavior such as finding an object after successive visible displacements and following an object through a series of increasingly invisible displacements. The second scale on which the experimental infants were significantly superior to the control infants dealt with developing means for achieving desired environmental ends. Specifically, this task involved the using of a stick to obtain a distant object. The particular contribution of this study was that it marked the beginning of the use of assessment procedures which fit into a theoretical system of cognitive development rather than the usual IQ assessment which most other investigators working with very young infants have been forced to employ. The advantage of using the former is that it makes it possible to relate specific elements of the educational program to specific outcome variables in a systematic and theoretically meaningful way.

It is clear that all the organized programs in infant education have had the common objective of preventing and forestalling retardation of the intellectual and language development in infants from lower-class families. Most programs have been concerned more with prolonged and sustained than immediate effects and with modifying not only the infant but also his environment. To date, all educational programs for infants which have evaluated the impact on cognitive development have found significant evidence for their effectiveness. Although in several programs the effect has lasted for more than a year after the program terminated, not enough time has elapsed for any of them to follow up children into elementary school. Several studies have exerted a major effort to modify the infant's family, particularly by training the infant's mother as an effective change agent. Although these programs demonstrated their effectiveness in measurable changes in the infant's intellectual and language development, attempts to find more direct evidence of changes in the mother have had little success as yet. Schaefer (1969) and Herman (1971) succeeded in obtaining measures of maternal attitudes which yielded substantial relationships with the intellectual functioning of infants. These findings point toward further efforts to measure the infant's immediate environment so as to close a missing link between changes in the mothers resulting from parent-oriented programs and changes in the mothers' infants.

A wide variety of personnel have been used to carry out the instructional programs with infants. Similarly, training and procedures for teaching staff have varied widely. Several of the investigators, e.g., Gordon (1969) and Levenstein (1971) have attempted to evaluate the effectiveness of personnel with different backgrounds and the degree of implementation of the programs by their staff. However, the study of teacher variables has not yet been sufficiently detailed to lend itself for generalization. This shortcoming is understandable since these programs have been started very recently and have not afforded the investigators enough time to explore this particular area. Nevertheless, teacher variables, especially personality traits which affect the adult's interaction with the child, are likely to be particularly important in the implementation as well as evaluation of educational programs for infants. One might, therefore, expect that in the near future this area will receive a good deal more attention in studies of the impact of educational programs for infants and very young children.

There has been a great deal of overlap as well as difference in strategies used by educational programs for infants. The dimensions on which programs have been comparable stand out rather clearly. One of these has been the degree of structure and formality with which instructions have been carried out, another the sequential progression in instructional materials, concepts and skills. It is difficult to draw conclusions concerning the effectiveness of variations of these instructional dimensions because it has not been a primary concern of study for most of the infant programs to date. Three of the programs, Gordon (1969), Levenstein (1971) and Palmer (1968) have reported results of comparisons between different techniques within their programs and none has found differences which would point to the superiority of one technique over another in the long run. Although these equivocal findings do not throw light on the differential effectiveness of particular techniques, they do have important implications which will be discussed shortly. A great deal of resourcefulness and imagination has gone into the construction of curricula and materials, and for that reason an attempt has been made to describe in some detail the curricula used in each of the studies that have been discussed.

The largest overlap among studies has occurred with regard to the use of instruments for assessing impact of programs on the cognitive development of infants. The Bayley Scales for Infant Development and the Cattell Infant Test have been used most often and therefore offer an excellent opportunity to pool findings from different studies for the evaluation of impact of educational programs on infants. The Illinois Test of Psycholinguistic Abilities and the Peabody Picture Vocabulary Test have been used most often for the evaluation of effects of language training, and the former has been more successful in picking up effects of instructional programs. There is less overlap among programs in the use of instruments for the evaluation of effects of specific instructional techniques. Both general as well as specific measures are needed. General instruments or scales are needed for two reasons: first, to provide a common base of assessment criteria so as to make the findings from different studies comparable, and second, to yield criteria of impact which apply to a wider variety of situations in which effects of educational programs can be assessed. Critics have pointed out that a general measure of intelligence, like the Stanford-Binet provides, is both too product-oriented and misses the specific effects of particular techniques or programs. Notwithstanding the validity of such criticism in specific instances, a need remains for a measure which applies to a wide range of situations in which intellectual competence and achievement are of central concern. For this latter purpose the Stanford-Binet Test presently, and probably the Bayley Scales of Infant Development in the near future, meet this demand better than any other available criterion measure. Nevertheless, to date, infant education studies have not used, have not used often enough, or have not consulted specific measures to evaluate directly the effect of special techniques in their programs. The value of specific measures can be seen clearly in the evaluative phase of Palmer's program where it became evident that the concept-training program produced superior functioning only in specific skills reflecting the effect of practice, whereas measures of intellectual functioning applied to new situations and new problems revealed effects of the discovery program to have been at least as large as the effects of the more specific concept-training program.

It is reasonable to expect that the vastly increased research studies in areas of cognitive as well as socioemotional functioning in early infancy within the near future will yield a host of new specific criteria for assessing impact of special educational conditions or programs on cognitive functioning in infants.

Finally, one finding which has important implications runs throughout several infant studies, particularly with reference to the issue of selecting a control group. A finding which occurs repeatedly is that comparison between different experimental groups and between specific programs and control conditions (of sheer availability of instructional materials or an "educator") yielded no significant differences. These findings are of particular interest because they have emerged from impact studies of educational programs for infants. Infants are at once more sensitive and less differentiated than older children. It may well turn out that the conventional use of "attention" as a control and "highly specific instruction" as an experimental program is less valid or fruitful in educational research on infants and young children than for later phases of development.

LONGITUDINAL IMPACT STUDIES

Does exposure to preschool education affect the child's intellectual development? There was a time when this question was more or less academic because preschool education was available almost exclusively to children of parents who could afford to pay for private schools or of parents who lived near a university which had a laboratory preschool program for purposes of training and research. The question was also academic in another sense. I make reference to the controversy of the 1940s when psychologists and educators took sides on the heredity-environment issue regarding the origin and development of intelligence. During the intervening years conditions have changed radically. Questions concerning the impact of preschool education on intellectual development are no longer academic in either sense. Preschool education is rapidly becoming institutionalized for all segments of our society. In the face of this massive reality, the question is no longer whether organized educational programs for children under six are available to most children. With regard to the heredity-environment issue the problem lies not with finding an answer to this question but with the question itself. The question represents a serious oversimplification which invites withdrawal from the more complex issues pertaining to the development of intellectual functioning and the flight toward analogues and simpler questions which appear more amenable to objective scientific study. These consequences of oversimplifying the question manifested themselves in two types of escape. One line of escape was to concentrate on the study of intellectual development in twins. This approach is at best an analogue of the broader question of heredity and intelligence because, as has been pointed out, it repeatedly touches on only a very small segment of the complex problem, leaving other questions, such as the nature of the environment and experience, and the link between biological development and psychological development, unanswered. The second line of escape was well expressed by Harold Stevenson in the introduction to the Sixty-Second Yearbook of the National Society for the Study of Education (NSSE) approximately a decade ago. "Child psychology of the past decade differs greatly from that of earlier years. Longitudinal studies, observational methods, and a developmental orientation have largely been replaced or supplemented by short-term experimental studies of the effects of particular variables on child behavior" (1963, p. 2). Without any intent to minimize the importance of short-term experimental studies dealing with isolated, well-controlled variables, it is clear from what has already been reviewed and discussed that the opposite statement can be made with regard to major approaches to the study of organized programs in early education and their effects on later development. The major studies in early education today and over the past five years have been carried out in the complex setting of the day-care center or nursery-school setting. They have attempted to investigate intellectual and social development as a complex, multivariable problem which re-quires refined observational techniques over longer phases of the life-span than the laboratory approach referred to earlier permits.

An unfortunate consequence of the single variable approach to the complex problem of investigating the impact of preschool education on later development has been evident in a recent study (Cicirelli et al., 1969) which has attempted to answer the question of whether or not Head Start has made a lasting impact on the intellectual development of children. The question of the researcher of the effects of early educational experience on a child's intellectual and social development must specify characteristics of the child, or learner, including his extended life situation such as family background and cultural setting; it must state the educational components and the configurations of the educational situation in order to investigate the interaction between the educational program and the child on intellectual development. If one wants to investigate whether the educational experience at a certain age has a more or less lasting effect on the later development of the individual, then it is necessary to take into account the subsequent experiences of the child which may enhance or interfere with beneficial effects of the earlier educational experience. In short, the relevant question is not "does preschool education help?" but rather, who benefits from what, and under what circumstances is the effect sustained? Several recent studies illustrate the necessity for such an approach, especially to the study of the effect of early education on later development. For example, one investigator found that children whose parents were voluntary participants in Head Start programs sustained gains better than children whose parents had been actively recruited for participation in the program (Holmes & Holmes, 1969). Another investigator found that children of parents who had a high level of participation retained gains better than children of parents who did not have a high level of participation in Head Start (Bittner, Rockwell, & Matthews, 1968). These two studies clearly indicate that the child's extended environment, namely his parents, is a vital factor in determining how lasting the benefits of the educational experience will be. We shall see later in the chapter that other child variables such as the age at which the child enters school, his motivation and his attitudes are important for the sustained effect of this experience on later intellectual and socioemotional development. An example of the importance of controlling the subsequent educational experiences and context becomes evident from the report of a study which found that Head Start children who entered a middle-class public school appeared to sustain their advantage over non-Head Starters, whereas similar Head Starters who moved on to a slum school did not (Hyman & Kliman, 1967).

The importance of long-term studies of the effects of early education on later development has become clear from a variety of studies. For example, one study which investigated cognitive competence and level of symbolization found that Head Start children did not differ significantly from non-Head Start children at the beginning of kindergarten, but did at the end of kindergarten (Sigel & McBane, 1969). The investigators suggest that the Head Start experience enabled children to better assimilate new information in kindergarten, and this might have been responsible for the belated effect. Another study which investigated the effectiveness of Head Start found no significant differences in a follow-up of Head Start children and controls at the end of first grade (Steglich & Cartwright, 1965) but found an increase in the number of superior Head Start children at the end of the second grade. Still another study investigating oral language ability of Head Start children found greater gains at the end of the second grade than at the end of the first grade (Hubbard, 1967).

The importance of a long-term follow-up of the impact of early childhood education can be seen from the results of several studies.

THE PHILADELPHIA STUDY

In one study (Beller, 1969a, 1972) three groups of children who entered school at different ages were followed up in their performance on several different measures of intellectual functioning and academic achievement. Group I attended an experimental nursery program for disadvantaged lower-class children; group II entered kindergarten without any previous educational experience; and group III entered first grade without having previously participated in an educational program. The three groups of children were followed up from the time of entry to the end of fourth grade. The initial sample consisted of 171 children. Although over 60 percent of the children had moved to 80 different schools in the city, all children were followed up individually each year. The sample attrition was no greater than 10 percent since the final sample size in the fourth grade was 153 children. The children recruited for the four nursery classes came from lower-class black families and were between three years seven months and four years six months of age. The program encompassed four nursery groups, each of which was located in a different public school within a large urban slum area. The program was supervised by the Department of Early Childhood Education at Temple University. Each nursery group consisted of 15 children with one head teacher and one assistant teacher. The program extended for four hours each morning for a week. During afternoons and on the fifth day of the week the teachers were engaged in program planning, continuation of their in-service training, making home visits, working closely with parents, home-school coordinator and the social worker.

The program was a traditional one which was concerned with the child's curiosity for discovery and with the child's creativity, stressing the warm, nurturing personalized handling of the child by his teachers. An emphasis was placed on developing a program geared to each child's readiness rather than premature introduction of concepts and practices in skills which might have a negative influence on the child's interest, cooperation and attitudes. The program attempted to establish a proper balance of self-initiated and structured activities. The structured part of the program was designed to extend the child's knowledge of the world and help him develop the kinds of perceptual discriminations and foundation skills that would facilitate his readiness to benefit from educational programs when he enters formal schooling. The content of the program concentrated on training—in language facility, auditory and visual discrimination, listening and paying attention, conceptualization, information about the environment, motor coordination and control, and self-esteem.

In all, the program was child-centered in the sense that an adult provided the child with opportunities to choose from a variety of learning resources, and learning was shaped around a child's needs and preferences. The adult accepted and appreciated divergent reactions of the child and permitted the child to arrange his own individualistic sequences rather then urging the child to follow prescribed ways.

Following the nursery experience the children were assigned to regular kindergarten classes in which the class size was increased from 15 to 25. However, the four schools provided much assistance and aid to the kindergarten teachers who continued the education of the children coming from the nursery as well as others who had not had the nursery experience. From the classrooms which were attended by the nursery children a new group of children was selected to match the nursery group with regard to age and sex. The same process was used in the first grade. The principals in the four original schools agreed to keep the three groups of children, that is, those who entered school at nursery, those who entered school at kindergarten, and those who were selected as a third group which entered school at first grade, in the same classroom with the same teacher to the end of the second grade so as to provide maximally homogeneous backgrounds for the three comparison groups in the study. Although the children were not selected randomly, they came from the same backgrounds and, as it turned out later, did not differ significantly with regard to their Stanford-Binet, Peabody Picture Vocabulary or Draw a Man IQ scores when they entered school.

Three types of measures were obtained with regard to intellectual functioning. The first set of measures consisted of three intelligence tests, the second of classroom marks from the first through the fourth grades, and the third of a set of attitudes toward learning in school as judged by the child's classroom teacher. All individual administrations of intelligence tests were carried out annually by different waves of testers who had no knowledge of which experimental group a child belonged to. The teachers of the children, especially after the first grade, had no knowledge of when the children entered school. With regard to the three intelligence tests, we found that the three groups of children did not differ from each other at the time at which they entered school. A differential and sustained gain of the three groups to the end of the fourth grade was consistent and significant when evaluated by an analysis of variance (see Figures 1 and 2). Inspection of Figure 1 reveals another interesting finding. Although the average Stanford-Binet IQ score of the three groups was approximately the same when they entered school, the direction of change from the first to the second testing differed from group to group. That is, the nursery children who started school at age four gained most, the kindergarten children who started a year later gained half as much, and the first-grade group lost approximately two points between the first and second testing. The differences between changes for nursery and first-grade groups were statistically significant. Thus, it seems that the initial boost in intellectual performance changes markedly the later the child experiences his first exposure to an educational group program. Another difference can be seen in the change from initial to final testing. The increase from first to final testing for the nursery group differed significantly from the decline for the first-grade group from initial to final Stanford-Binet Scores (see Figure 1).

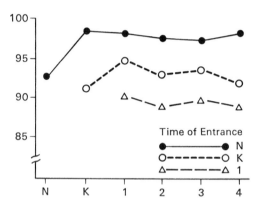

Fig. 1. Average Stanford-Binet IQ scores across grades of groups entering school at nursery (N), kindergarten (K) and first grade (1) (sizes of groups ranged from No. = 46 to No. = 58).

The findings that emerged from the performance on the Goodenough Draw a Man Test differed radically from those on the other two tests (see Figure 3). To the end of the first grade this test did not show any effect of the timing of educational intervention. However, following the first grade there was a significant decline in the performance proportional to the timing of school entry. The decline was much smaller in the children who had preschool education, especially the group which attended the nursery program or started school earliest. These differences were statistically significant when evaluated by a step-wise regression analysis.

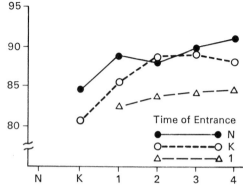

Fig. 2. Average Peabody IQ scores across grades of groups entering school at nursery (N), kindergarten (K) and first grade (1) (sizes of groups range from No. = 46 to No. = 58).

Timing of school entrance affected marks on arithmetic, reading, spelling, social studies and science in a consistent way. Children, especially girls, with preschool experience were consistently and significantly ahead from the first to the fourth grades, on all subjects except science. However, performance generally declined over time, and this decline reached significance in reading and arithmetic. Thus, effect of time of school entrance on the level of intellectual

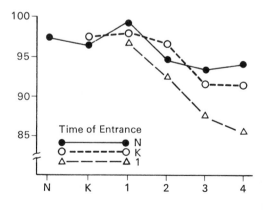

Fig. 3. Average "Draw a Man" IQ scores across grades of groups entering school at nursery (N), kindergarten (K) and first grade (1) (sizes of groups ranged from No. = 46 to No. = 58).

achievement was more consistent and lasting for performance on the Stanford-Binet and Peabody intelligence tests than on achievement in the classroom.

The present study went beyond the assessment of academic achievement and intellectual functioning, and obtained data on social and emotional functioning of three groups of children. The first area for social functioning dealt with the child's dependency, aggression, autonomous achievement striving, and dependency conflict or mistrust. These areas of functioning were assessed up to the end of the first grade by means of two independent observers who rated the children. An analysis of these ratings revealed that by the end of the first grade, the nursery group, who entered school earliest, was highest in autonomous achievement striving and lowest in their mistrust of their teachers. The difference with regard to autonomous achievement striving and mistrust is particularly important since autonomous achievement striving correlated positively and mistrust negatively with intellectual performance and academic achievement into the fourth grade.

Several other areas of socioemotional functioning were assessed in the fourth grade. One of the areas assessed was impulse control by means of the Kagan Reflective-Impulsive Test. Boys without preschool experience made up a significantly higher percentage of impulsive children than boys with preschool experience. A third area of the child's social functioning was assessed by means of a Piaget test for maturity of moral judgment. The test consisted of 18 Piaget items which measured moral realism. An analysis of these data revealed that by the end of the fourth grade, boys with preschool experience exceeded boys without preschool significantly in maturity of moral judgment. The fourth area of socioemotional functioning, assessed by means of the Pierce-Harris test, was self-concept. The three groups of children were compared on their positive self-concept answers on a selected number of items on

which the three groups differed by a predetermined minimum of 10 percent. Only comparisons for the three groups of girls are presented here because their differences, although in the same general direction, were simpler and more uniform than those of the boys. It becomes immediately apparent from inspection of these items in Tables 1, 2 and 3 that the girls who had experienced educational intervention earliest presented generally positive self-images while the girls who had no preschool presented an overwhelming negative self-concept. The girls who entered school at kindergarten, that is, the intermediary year between nursery and first grade, offered a mixed picture with regard to self-concept. It is apparent from these findings that impact of preschool education was as pronounced in the area of social and emotional functioning as it had been in areas of intellectual functioning and academic achievement.

Probably the most dramatic finding of the study occurred when we used a motivational variable as moderator to re-examine effects of preschool experience on later intellectual functioning and academic achievement as a result of the child's motivation. We divided the children on the basis of their autonomous achievement scores in the first grade into high and low group, and we compared the groups on the basis of the age at which educational intervention started. The findings of this analysis are plotted in Figures 4 and 5. We found that for the children who were high on autonomous achievement striving in the first grade, timing of educational intervention had no significant effect. Those children who started school later caught up with the ones who started earlier. The outcome was radically different in the low autonomous achievement groups. In these groups the timing of educational intervention had a significant and highly substantial effect on the child's intellectual performance. Children who entered school later performed much more poorly on intelligence tests than children who started school earlier (see Fig-

TABLE 1

HIGH PERCENTAGE RESPONSES OF NURSERY GIRLS TO SELF-CONCEPT ITEMS

Questions	Groups[1]		
	Nursery (N = 22)	Kinder-garten (N = 20)	First Grade (N = 29)
1. I am cheerful (52)[2]	91 %	85%	72%
2. I am not clumsy (64)	91	80	72
3. In games and sports I play instead of watch (65)	77	65	52
4. When I try to make something, everything does not seem to go wrong (61)	77	55	59
5. It is not usually my fault when something goes wrong (13)	73	50	59
6. I do not lose my temper easily (68)	59	40	45
7. I do not think bad thoughts (78)	100	85	72
8. I am well behaved in school (12)	95	80	76
9. I do not behave badly in school (12)	86	85	69
10. I often volunteer in school (42)	100	95	76
11. I do not usually want my own way (39)	77	65	55
12. I am not unpopular (11)	82	65	66
13. I am popular with boys (57)	41	30	14
14. I have many friends (51)	100	90	90
15. It is not hard for me to make friends (3)	91	70	72
16. I do not pick on my brothers and sisters (32)	91	75	59
17. I am an important member to my family (17)	73	45	69
18. My family is not disappointed in me (59)	91	80	83
19. When I grow up I will be an important person (9)	95	85	76
20. I am shy (6)	59	51	41
21. I am nervous (28)	50	30	28
22. I get nervous when my teacher calls on me (7)	45	30	31
23. I get worried when we have tests (10)	73	45	59

[1] Grouping based on year entering school.
[2] ( ) Original item numbers indicating position in the test.

TABLE 2

HIGH PERCENTAGE RESPONSES OF KINDERGARTEN GIRLS TO SELF-CONCEPT ITEMS

Questions	Groups[1]		
	Kinder-garten (N = 20)	Nursery (N = 22)	First Grade (N = 29)
1. I am smart (5)[2]	85%	73%	72%
2. I am not always dropping and breaking things (75)	80	73	55
3. I am good in making things with my hands (19)	85	68	66
4. I am a good reader (70)	90	77	79
5. I can give a good report in front of the class (30)	90	73	76
6. I have a pleasant face (43)	70	55	62
7. I am not unhappy (50)	85	73	72
8. I do not cry easily (76)	80	68	66
9. I do not worry a lot (37)	65	55	41
10. My friends like my ideas (33)	100	86	72
11. My classmates think I have good ideas (49)	90	50	66
12. I am a leader in games and sports (63)	60	27	38
13. I am not different from other people (77)	75	55	48

TABLE 2 (Continued)

HIGH PERCENTAGE RESPONSES OF KINDERGARTEN GIRLS TO SELF-CONCEPT ITEMS

Questions	Groups[1]		
	Kinder-garten (N = 20)	Nursery (N = 22)	First Grade (N = 29)
14. I do not wish I were different (60)	95	64	65
15. In school I am a dreamer (31)	45	32	17
16. I hate school (45)	20	9	10
17. I cannot draw well (23)	30	18	14
18. I am not an important member of my class (27)	60	50	50
19. I feel left out of things (40)	45	32	38

[1] Grouping based on year entering school.
[2] ( ) Original item numbers indicating position in the test.

TABLE 3

HIGH PERCENTAGE RESPONSES OF FIRST-GRADE GIRLS TO SELF-CONCEPT ITEMS

Questions	Groups[1]		
	First Grade (N = 29)	Nursery (N = 22)	Kinder-garten (N = 20)
1. I cause trouble to my family (14)[2]	24 %	9 %	10 %
2. I am always dropping or breaking things (75)	45	27	20
3. I am clumsy (64)	28	9	20
4. I am unlucky (36)	48	36	40
5. I am not strong (15)	69	55	40
6. I don't have lots of pep (55)	52	32	25
7. I worry a lot (37)	59	45	35
8. I am not cheerful (52)	28	5	15
9. I am not a happy person (2)	27	5	15
10. My looks bother me (8)	31	18	5
11. I am unpopular (11)	34	18	35
12. I am not popular with boys (57)	86	59	70
13. I am not popular with girls (69)	28	9	10
14. It is hard for me to make friends (3)	28	9	30
15. My friends don't like my ideas (33)	28	14	0
16. I am among the last to be chosen for a game (46)	59	41	40
17. People pick on me (58)	45	32	25
18. I get into a lot of fights (56)	33	14	25
19. I have bad thoughts (78)	28	0	15
20. I dislike my brother (72)	34	18	15
21. I pick on my brothers and sisters (32)	41	9	25
22. I behave badly at home (25)	31	14	15
23. My parents do not expect too much of me (38)	24	41	35
24. In games and sports I watch instead of play (65)	48	23	35
25. When I grow up I will not be an important person (9)	24	5	15
26. I do not volunteer in school (42)	24	0	5
27. In school I am not a dreamer (31)	17	32	45
28. I am not shy (6)	41	39	55

[1] Grouping based on year entering school.
[2] ( ) Original item numbers indicating position in the test.

ures 4 and 5). However, children who started school earliest, that is, the two groups of children who attended nursery school, although different in their autonomous achievement striving, were not significantly different in intellectual achievement. In short, children who started preschool earliest were least affected by adverse motivational factors. It is evident from the findings presented so far that the evaluation of the impact of the preschool experience is likely to be more fruitful and meaningful if it is long term rather than short term, if it uses multiple criteria for evaluating areas of intellectual and socioemotional functioning, and finally, if the distinction between children exposed to the same program (that is, if the question, who benefits from what?) is taken seriously.

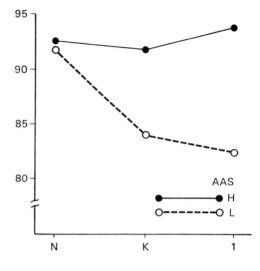

Fig. 5. Average Peabody IQ scores of high (H) and low (L) autonomous achievement striving (AAS) groups entering school at nursery (N), kindergarten (K) and first grade (1) (sizes of groups ranged from No. = 11 to No. = 20).

THE EARLY-TRAINING PROJECT

Another major longitudinal as well as experimental intervention study that pursued the effects of early organized education to the end of the fourth grade was the early-training project for disadvantaged children in Nashville, Tennessee, carried out by Gray and Klaus (1970). The goals of this study were to investigate the feasibility and effectiveness of conducting a preschool intervention program designed to offset the progressive retardation in cognitive development in deprived and educationally disadvantaged children. Specifically, the authors wanted to counteract the following characteristics in deprived preschool children: low motivation to succeed, poor delay of gratification, development of restricted and concrete language, poor perceptual discrimination, distrust of strangers and a poor self-concept.

The program was constructed to counteract the above deficiencies in deprived children on a preventive basis. A series of specific measures was selected to test the effec-

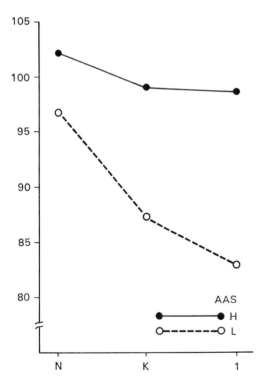

Fig. 4. Average Stanford-Binet IQ scores of high (H) and low (L) autonomous achievement striving (AAS) groups entering school at nursery (N), kindergarten (K) and first grade (1) (sizes of groups ranged from No. = 11 to No. = 20).

tiveness of the program. There were two treatment groups and two control groups in the program. The first treatment group was made up of 20 children who attended three 10-week summer preschool sessions and had weekly home visitors continue the educational program for the remainder of the year; the second treatment group had 20 children who attended two 10-week summer sessions and had two years of home visits prior to entering first grade; the first control group consisted of 18 children who served as a local control group and the second control group was made up of children located in a city similar to Nashville but 60 miles away. All subjects were black children from lower-class families.

In the experimental summer programs each group of 20 children had four teachers who worked with small groups of about five children each. Most of the four-hour daily program was spent in activities with the small-group teacher, alternating with brief sessions with the total group. The materials and curricular activities were not radically different from those used in more conventional nursery schools and kindergartens. The major difference consisted of the way in which the materials were used, the sequencing of activities, and the attempt to focus on those attitudes and aptitudes which the educational program intended to develop. An example of the sequencing of activities from simple to more complex levels can be seen in the way in which wheels and tricycles were used. Tricycles, for example, were used to increase language in children. At first they were used to set up a situation in which a child could obtain the desired object if he asked for it. Later it was made necessary to identify the particular tricycle the child wished. Still later, requests were made that the child take turns in using the tricycle to facilitate his learning of mutual interaction with other children. In the second summer session the tricycles were used in a miniature traffic situation. The children learned to respond appropriately to traffic signs and to play traffic officer.

To test the effectiveness of the program the Stanford-Binet and the Peabody Picture Vocabulary Test were used to assess intellectual functioning from the onset of the program to the fourth grade. The Illinois Test of Psycholinguistic Abilities was used to measure language functioning and the Metropolitan Achievement Test was used to measure academic achievement. Selected scales of the Pierce-Harris Self-Concept Test were used to measure self-concept in the four groups of children.

The investigators reported the following results from their latest analysis (Gray & Klaus, 1970). Though there was a general decline in all four groups from the first to the fourth grade on the Stanford-Binet scores, the groups which received preschool education were significantly superior to the two control groups to the end of the fourth grade (see Figure 6). The two treatment groups did not differ significantly from one another, which meant that earlier intervention did not have an appreciable effect. The two control groups were generally not different from one another except for the fourth grade, at which time the local control group was superior to the distal control group. The results of the Peabody Picture Vocabulary Test showed a pattern that was similar to the one that was obtained from the Stanford-Binet (see Figure 7). The scores showed a rise up to the first grade and then a leveling off and a slight decline in the fourth grade. The experimental groups were superior to the control groups through the second grade, but not thereafter. On the Illinois Test of Psycholinguistic Abilities the groups with preschool education remained superior to the control groups on a number of subtests through the first grade. With regard to the Metropolitan Achievement Test, children with preschool education outperformed the children in the control groups up to the second grade at which time the differences were no longer significant. Again the investigators found an appreciable difference between the local and distal control groups, favoring the local group. With regard to the self-concept test,

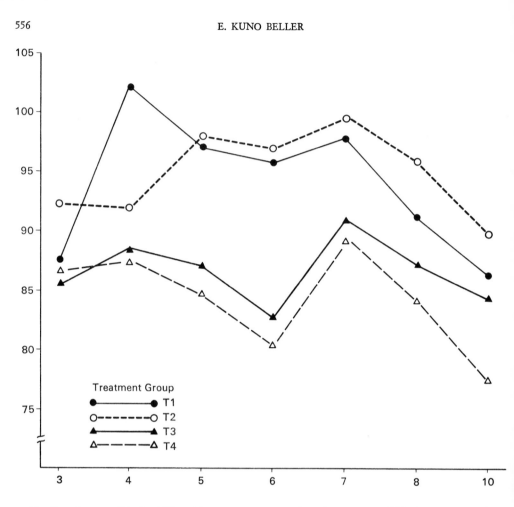

Fig. 6.   Average Stanford-Binet IQ scores across grades of one group (T1) that received three summer preschool programs, group (T2) that received two summer preschool programs, and two groups (T3 & T4) that received no summer preschool programs (sizes of groups ranged from No. = 18 to No. = 23). (Drawn from data presented in Table 2, p. 913, of an article by S. Gray and R. A. Klaus published in the December 1970 issue of **Child Development**. Copyrighted by the Society for Research in Child Development).

initial significant differences were found in favor of the experimental groups on two of the seven scales, namely, the dimensions of happiness and satisfaction. However, when the test was given again at the end of the second grade, the differences between the experimental and control groups disappeared.

The investigators were interested in the *vertical diffusion* of the preschool program on younger and older members of the children who participated in these programs.

Comparison between younger siblings of experimental and control children revealed a significant difference on the Stanford-Binet. No such effect was found in older siblings. The superiority of the younger siblings was evident especially in the first experimental group where the home visitor had spent more time than in the second group, and in siblings closer to the age of the experimental subjects. Gray and Klaus interpret these findings as a vertical diffusion. The superiority of the local over the distal control group is interpreted as *horizontal diffusion,* based on the observation that parents of local control children interacted a great deal with parents of the experimental, which of course did not apply to parents of the distal control group.

A comparison of the Philadelphia and Nashville studies makes it apparent that the outcome of the two studies bore certain basic similarities. In both studies the Stanford-Binet emerged as the more stable and discriminating measure of effects of early childhood education, while the effects on academic achievement were less sustained.

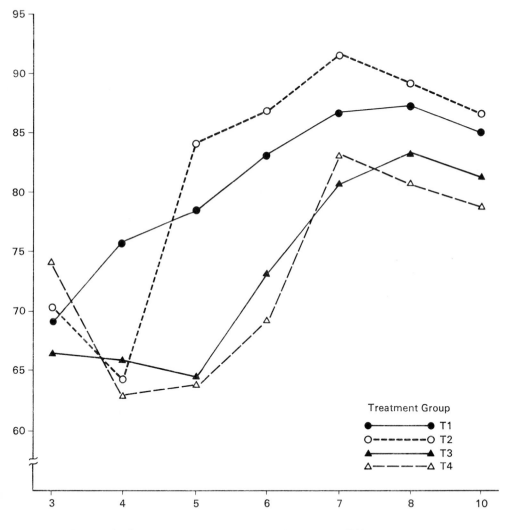

Fig. 7.   Average Peabody IQ scores across grades of one group (T1) that received three summer preschool programs, a second group (T2) that received two summer preschool programs and two groups (T3 & T4) that received no summer preschool programs (sizes of groups ranged from No. = 18 to No. = 23). (Drawn from data presented in Table 4, p. 915, of an article by S. Gray and R. A. Klaus published in the December 1970 issue of **Child Development.** Copyrighted by the Society for Research in Child Development.)

A difference between the two studies was a parallel decline in all groups of the Nashville study but not the Philadelphia study on Stanford-Binet performance. This difference may have been due to the fact that the children in the Philadelphia study received one or two full years of preschool education which resulted in a more powerful effect over time. The same applies to the measured effects of preschool education on academic achievement in the two studies. Moreover, it would be interesting to find out whether the pronounced sex differences in effect of preschool education on later academic achievement in the Philadelphia study were to some extent present in the findings of the Nashville study.

THE YPSILANTI PRESCHOOL PROJECT

Another major longitudinal as well as experimental intervention study to investigate effects of preschool education was carried out under the direction of Weikart (Weikart, Deloria, Lawson, & Wiegerink, 1970). The goal of this program was to compensate for functional mental retardation in children from disadvantaged families. Weikart selected children from educationally and economically deprived backgrounds who tested within the range of "educable mentally retarded." The children were carefully selected to be homogeneous in socioeconomic background and level of mental functioning before being assigned to the experimental or control group. The children were all between three and four years of age when they entered the program. The program was carried out over a period of five years. Each year a new wave of children was sent through a two-year preschool program. The total number of children in the program consisted of 123 children, 58 in the experimental and 65 in the control groups. The experimental children attended preschool five half-days a week for the regular school year. In addition, teachers visited each experimental child in his home for a 90-minute session each week. The purpose of this visit was to engage the mother in the process of her child's education and to gear activities specifically to the individual child. The teacher suggested activities that the mother could carry out with the child and pointed out household activities involving the child that could be structured to include the goals of the curriculum.

The program in the nursery was a cognitively oriented curriculum attempting to incorporate Piaget's theories as the basis for constructing activities for the children. Weikart (1971b) describes his curriculum as one which focuses on underlying processes of thinking and emphasizes the fact that learning comes through the child's actions, not through repetition of what he has been told. "Learning by the child is a product of his active involvement with the environment structured by the teacher" (p. 5).

Following Piaget's theory the curriculum incorporated four levels of cognition: object, index, symbol, and sign. The four areas of content were classification, seriation, temporal relations, and spatial relations. With these general guidelines in mind, it was left up to the teacher to develop the program in her own way, responding to the specific needs of the children. The pace of the learning process was determined by the child, although the teacher structured the child's activities.

Sociodramatic play was used as a teaching device to develop concentration and attention skills, to integrate scattered experiences, and to expand the child's imagination without depending explicitly on concrete experiences. An important goal of the program was to help the child increase impulse control by initiating planning, which was to precede activities, and by following activities with an evaluation of the outcome.

Weikart employed Stanford-Binet and Peabody Picture Vocabulary Tests to measure effects of the preschool educational program on intellectual functioning, the Illinois Test of Psycholinguistic Abilities to measure effects on language development, the California Achievement Test to measure effects of academic achievement, and rating scales as well as a pupil behavior inventory to measure effects on socioemotional development. The children were retested annually until the end of the third grade.

Analysis of the data yielded the following results. Preschool experience had a significant effect on the intellectual performance of children as measured by the Stanford-Binet Test. Children with preschool experience were superior to control children at the end of nursery, kindergarten and first grade, but the effect of preschool education disappeared by the second and third grades. These results are presented in Figure 8. Measures

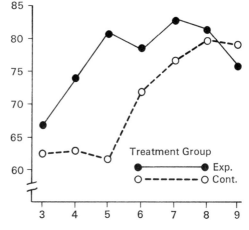

Fig. 9. Average Peabody IQ scores of children (Exp.) who experienced two years of nursery school and children (Cont.) who did not experience two years of nursery school (sizes of groups ranged from No. = 13 to No. = 60). (Drawn from data presented in Table 4-3, p. 67, of a report by D. P. Weikart, D. J. Deloria, S. A. Lawser, and R. Wiegerink published in August 1970.)

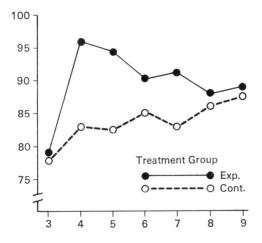

Fig. 8. Average Stanford-Binet IQ scores of children (Exp.) who experienced two years of nursery school and children (Cont.) who did not experience two years of nursery school (sizes of groups ranged from No. = 13 to No. = 63). (Drawn from data presented in Table 4-1, p. 65, of a report by D. P. Weikart, D. J. Deloria, S. A. Lawser, and R. Wiegerink published in August 1970.)

of the Peabody Picture Vocabulary Test yielded findings similar to those on the Binet test (see Figure 9). Effects of preschool education were much less pronounced on measures of the Leiter International Performance Scale. On this test ex-

perimental children were superior to control children only at the end of the nursery years. The same was true for the effect of preschool education on language development as measured by the Illinois Test of Psycholinguistic Abilities since, with the exception of one subtest—the Auditory Vocal Association Test—the experimental and control groups differed significantly in favor of the experimental group only at the end of the nursery year and thereafter not until the end of the third grade. Preschool education affected academic achievement as measured by the California Achievement Test both in the first and the third grades. It is interesting that the difference between the experimental and control groups almost doubled in favor of the experimental group from second to third grade. There was evidence that preschool experience was much more effective for the experimental girls than for the experimental boys. As a result of a regression analysis, Weikart found that other independent variables predicted later achievement as well as preschool education. For example, home background, reflected by mothers' education, the cognitive home environment scale, and the inventory of attitudes in family life in children accounted for an important amount of variance in the achievement scores for each of the three grades. In addition, entering cognitive performance as assessed by the Stanford-Binet and the Leiter International Performance Scale correlated more highly with achievement scores and accounted for more of the achievement variance than preschool attendance in each of the three grades. Weikart concludes from these findings that effects of preschool on later achievement were significant and important, though smaller than the effects attributable to certain aspects of the home environment and a child's level of intellectual functioning at the outset of preschool experience.

In his latest paper (Weikart, 1971a) Weikart reports findings of marked differences between the experimental and control group children with regard to their grade placement in elementary school. Eighty-three percent of the experimental children, compared with 61 percent of the control children, were placed in the expected grade; 17 percent of experimental children compared with 39 percent of control children were placed either in special education classes or retained a grade. These data extend to seven years after the end of the preschool program, as long a follow-up as any of the original preschool program follow-up studies have accomplished to date.

Weikart used the pupil behavior inventory for classroom conduct, academic motivation, socioemotional state and personal behavior to measure effects of preschool education on socioemotional development. He found that comparisons favored experimental children only at the end of the first grade and not at the end of kindergarten, second or third grade. In other words, the effect of preschool experience on these measures was delayed since it did not appear at the end of nursery or kindergarten. The same was true for measures of social development and emotional adjustment as assessed by the Ypsilanti Rating Scales, the only difference being that the effect of preschool experience here emerged significantly both at the end of first and second grades but disappeared by third grade.

It appears that Weikart found effects of preschool education on intellectual functioning to be immediate but that they lasted only a short period after preschool, that is, to the end of the first or second grade. Without considering differences in their quality of elementary-school education it would seem that preschool experience had a similar but less lasting effect on the children in the Ypsilanti study than the Nashville or Philadelphia programs. It is possible that the difference or less lasting effect in the Perry preschool program had something to do with their choice of mentally retarded educable population of children. The initial Stanford-Binet scores of the children in Weikart's study were approximately 10 points below those of the Philadelphia and Nashville studies. It would seem that the effect of the preschool program on academic achievement as measured by the California Achievement Test was more pronounced than impact of preschool education in any other area of the child's later functioning. It is unfortunate that the studies in Philadelphia, Nashville and Ypsilanti used different achievement tests so that slight variations between studies on such tests may have been due to the type of measure used. However, both Philadelphia and Nashville found the effect of preschool education on achievement to last at least up to the third grade and decline to a level of insignificance after that. It will be most interesting to see whether the effect on academic achievement which seems to be stronger in the Ypsilanti study than in the two other studies will be maintained into the fourth grade. Caution is in order because of the findings which resulted from a regression analysis and which indicated that other variables such as home background and initial performance levels on the Stanford-Binet and on the Leiter International Performance Scale turned out to be better predictors of achievement than preschool education. There is a further reason for caution, namely, that another experimental preschool program which used a population of deprived children with a base line average IQ of 75 failed to find sustained effects of their experimental preschool program on the California Achievement Test (Hodges, McCandless, & Spicker, 1967). It is interesting that the later study also found the effect of the preschool program to dissipate by the end of the second grade when the control group children caught up with the experimental children.

Another point of interest is that the effect of the preschool program on socioemotional adjustment in Weikart's children was delayed and did not last more than one year after preschool. It is possible that the same factor, namely the low level of intellectual functioning in these children, had its counterpart in a slowness of responding emotionally to the educational program and a difficulty in sustaining their gains and building on them once the intervention program had ended.

PROGRAMS IN EARLY EDUCATION

An attempt has been made to describe essential characteristics of the various educational programs which have been limited to infants and others which have carried out longitudinal studies of their effects. For the most part these programs did not differ from one another on the basis of a set of guiding principles with regard to the education and development of a young child. Differences were more of a content nature, such as whether the program was primarily oriented towards parent or child, whether the teaching was of a tutorial nature or was organized in a group, whether the program extended over several weeks or months or a major portion of the year, whether the child

was below three or between three and six, and whether the teacher was a professionally trained educator, a social worker, or a paraprofessional. We are now turning to a discussion of programs which are distinguished by different guiding concepts of development and principles of education. Since our major concern remains with studies of the effectiveness of educational programs, the discussion of the nature of the program itself will remain somewhat limited to a description of the underlying values and principles regarding development and education of the child, the role, style, and techniques of the teacher, and finally, the unique aspects of the curriculum of the program. The discussion will deal first with studies of the effectiveness of single programs when these were compared with a control or comparison group. Subsequently, we shall turn to a discussion of several attempts in which several different experimental preschool education programs were evaluated simultaneously and compared with each other.

The Montessori Program

Dr. Montessori first developed her system with mentally deficient children. Her success in increasing the abilities of these children made her wonder whether the same methods would not also increase the learning abilities of normal children.

According to Dr. Montessori the fundamental principle of education is the liberty of the pupil. Liberty is activity. Free activity is balanced by order and control, not by the teacher, but rather from the organization of the environment. This means the designing of materials which enable the child to learn through activity, which can be used with minimal instruction, which are self-correcting rather than requiring the teacher's judgment of success, and which the child is free to select at his own pace.

Education should be for "independence" and individual differences should be accepted by the teacher. The development of the child is seen as coming from within. The motivation to learn is present at the start of life, and the presence of appropriate activities will arouse this motivation. The development of the child's mind and his ideas derive from sensory experience. Intelligence is the ability to classify. Classification consists of analyzing an object and extracting a determined attribute therefrom. If this capacity for the selection of single attributes is not acquired, association by means of similarity, synthesis and all the higher work of intelligence becomes impossible. The Montessori materials were developed from this theory of knowledge.

The Montessori materials involve operations basic to classification. They are presented to a child in a certain sequence so as to enable the child first to make discriminations of same or different and to match in terms of sensory qualities such as color, pitch, or size; then to order qualities along some dimensions such as big to small; and eventually enable the child to differentiate and integrate sensory dimensions, as, for example, loudness and pitch. An important element in the conception of education and development is that the training of classification and the necessary operations to make classification are possible through direct sensory experience with minimal training through verbal labeling and description.

The teacher's personality or style must represent a blend of tolerance, empathy, matter-of-factness and task orientation. The teacher must not encourage too much of an emotional relationship between the child and herself because this will interfere with task orientation and the fostering of independence in the child. The child must learn to control his emotionality in the service of confidence and self-sufficiency. De-emphasis and control of emotionality will make it easier for both the child and the teacher to exercise mutual regard and helpfulness toward each other.

For Montessori, the teacher's role is that of a directress because she directs the psychic activity of the child. The teacher is also an observer who tries to understand children's behavior without intervening.

There is free movement in the classroom with each child working on his own task. Desks are abolished. Montessori does not approve of using external rewards and punishments because there is an inner force in the child that supplies a greater impetus than these artificial incentives.

The teacher is to work with each child individually on a task. Her lessons are to have the characteristics of conciseness, simplicity and objectivity. By objectivity, Montessori means that the lesson is oriented to objects and that the personality of the teacher disappears. The teacher is not expected to push the child or make him feel that he has made a mistake.

Montessori also sees discipline as a principal aim of education, but she does not mean by this external rewards and punishments. Instead, she feels the child's ability to regulate his own behavior must be developed very early. She states that a room where children move about usefully, intelligently and voluntarily without rough acts is very disciplined. The aim of the teacher is to discipline for activity, for work, for thought, but not for immobility, passivity and obedience.

An essential part of the learning experience is the Montessori materials which were designed to enable various sensory discriminations and classifications on the part of the child. The didactic material was created so that it contains within itself the control of errors and therefore makes auto-education possible.

The curriculum includes exercises for all of the senses; agricultural labor, pottery and other manual labor; reading and writing; and practical life experiences appropriate to the age of the child.

Banta (1966) conducted a study in which two different classrooms were compared in order to throw light on the question, "Is there really a Montessori method?" The classrooms served lower-class black children in Cincinnati, Ohio. Seventeen children were enrolled in one class and 20 children in the other. The average age in both classes was 42 months. Banta found that, although both classes had similar Montessori materials available to the children, the teachers were very different and the behavior of the children in each class was different. One teacher interpreted Montessori to say that structure and controls are necessary before freedom can be permitted. The other teacher believed that the child must experience freedom and encounter his impulses, and then gradually participate in setting limits and imposing controls. Thus, one class emphasized structure preceding freedom while the other emphasized freedom preceding structure. Banta observed the use of the didactic material in each classroom. Three criteria were used for judging whether or not the child was using didactic materials correctly: 1) the materials used were designed in such a way that they provided feedback to the child concerning error or success, 2) the teacher had individual or group instructions in the use of the material, and 3) the children used the materials in the didactically correct way. Banta reports that the average time of using these materials didactically for both classrooms was 12 percent. Banta himself comments that this was a much lower percentage of use of didactic materials than might be expected. Didactic activity varied greatly from one classroom to the other. In the highly structured classroom didactic activity ranged from 10 percent to 21 percent and in the less structured classroom from 1 percent to 7 percent. Finally, Banta reports that children in the structured setting initiated didactic activity by themselves and sustained such activity without teacher assistance 90 percent of the time. By comparison, in the less structured classroom only 56 percent of the didactic activities were self-initiated and unaided.

The implication of the study is that one needs to get a sample of Montessori classrooms if one wants to generalize concerning the effect of the Montessori method on the development of children.

Kohlberg (1968b) used available data from a Head Start project to evaluate the impact of a Montessori classroom and two non-Montessori classrooms on cognitive functioning in preschool children. Although there were too many confounding factors for empirical generalization, Kohlberg offered some important distinctions between perceptual and conceptual development as these apply to central concepts and educational practices of the Montessori program. Kohlberg found, among other things, that 10 children in a year-round Montessori program gained 17 IQ points over a four-month period. However, the same children failed to show any change on several Piaget conservation tests. Since Kohlberg also found a correlation of $r = 0.65$ between change in attention during the IQ tests and change in IQ for the 10 subjects, the investigator interpreted his finding to mean that the Montessori program primarily affected the development of attention which in turn affected performance on IQ tests. The failure of the 10 children to show a concomitant change in a Piaget task is taken to mean that the Montessori method primarily affects one aspect of classification, namely sensory discrimination. A conceptual task such as conversation requires mental operations which go beyond perceptual discrimination and therefore cannot be expected to change as a function of continued practice with perceptual discrimination.

Another study carried out recently (Beller & Kurtz, 1970) tends to support Kohlberg's conclusions. This study investigated conservation of length with 24 six-year-olds drawn from two different kindergartens with a child-centered, progressive program resembling the British infant school in some ways. The average IQ scores of the children based on the Peabody Picture Vocabulary Test in the two groups were 122 and 115, and did not differ significantly from one another. The outcome of this study was that a significantly larger number of non-Montessori children were able to solve the conservation task.

Dreyer and Rigler (1969) carried out a very careful and comprehensive study of the effects of Montessori preschool education on the cognitive performance of nursery-school children. The study has two aims: first to determine whether the parents who chose to send their children to a Montessori program were different from those who sent their children to a traditional nursery, and secondly, to determine the cognitive consequence of the two different educational programs on children in the two groups. In order to answer the first question the investigators administered a number of questionnaires to the mothers and fathers of all the children in the Montessori and traditional nursery programs. The questionnaires were designed to assess parental ideology, including authoritarianism, traditional family ideology, dogmatism, ennui, acquiescence, activism, importance placed on knowledge, independence, and achievement orientation. Parental values were also assessed with regard to fun morality versus work morality and entrepreneurial versus bureaucratic orientation. The parents were asked whether they preferred instrumental or expressive traits in their children. Instrumental traits were defined as ability to defend oneself, self-control, finishing what one starts, seriousness about things, and ability to play by oneself. Expressive traits were defined as obedience to parents, popularity, cheerfulness and consideration of others. Finally, parental attitudes toward child-rearing practices were analyzed around the two basic dimensions of autonomy versus control and love versus hostility. Fifty-four mothers and 54 fathers of children enrolled in the Montessori program, and 37 mothers and 37 fathers of children enrolled in the traditional nursery were compared on their attitudes of value orientation and parental

control as described above. Not a single one of 21 comparisons yielded significant differences between the parents of children enrolled in the two different programs. Thus, it was evident that there were no differential factors among the 182 middle-class mothers and fathers associated with preference for a Montessori or non-Montessori program.

In order to compare the children from the two groups, seven pairs of boys and seven pairs of girls were matched on Stanford-Binet, IQ, age, and socioeconomic status. Four tests were administered to the children. The children from the two groups did not differ with regard to the number of correct responses on the Children's Embedded Figure Test. However, the children from the Montessori group responded significantly faster. The Picture Construction Test, one of the nonverbal tests of the Minnesota Test of Creative Thinking, was used to assess the children's creativity. The children from the non-Montessori classroom received a significantly higher creativity score than the Montessori children. The authors adapted the subtest of the Illinois Test of Psycholinguistic Abilities to assess a concept selected by a child in his verbal description of the world. It was found that children from the Montessori program give significantly more often physical characteristics and significantly less often functional characteristics in their description of the objects presented to them. Finally, each child was given an opportunity to make a drawing of his own choice without any further instruction. The drawings were later analyzed for the presence of people versus the presence of geometric designs. The children from the Montessori group drew many more geometric forms and many fewer human forms or people. These differences were statistically significant. The investigators interpreted their findings as indication that Montessori children respond to the emphasis in their program upon the physical world and upon a definition of school as a place to work; the traditional nursery-school children respond on their part to the social emphasis and opportunity for spontaneous expression of feelings. Commenting on the behavior of the children during the test situations, the examiners reported that the Montessori children were highly task-oriented, whereas the other nursery children felt it to be an opportunity to socialize with the examiner.

A more recent study carried out by Beller, Zimmie, and Aiken (1971) provides strong support for the direction of the findings which have been discussed so far. This study was interested in the effect of different preschool programs on levels of play in children. Piaget distinguished between sensory-motor and symbolic play. For purposes of the study the investigators distinguished between two levels of sensory-motor play. Practice play involves repetition of a sensory-motor schema for the pleasure of its exercise without effort of adaptation. Combinations are composed of the same activities as in practice play but are distinguished by the building of combinations of such activities. On both levels the activities have been well mastered and present no problem of adaptation to the child. Two levels of symbolic play were distinguished. Symbolic play refers to acts involving the use of a simple symbol, whereas complex symbolic play refers to a sequence of symbolic activities involving an interrelated set of symbols.

The study was carried out in three different nursery programs. The first program was material-oriented and consisted of two Montessori classrooms, the second of two "adult-centered" classrooms, and the third of two "child-centered" classrooms. In the Montessori classrooms the children's activity was in a sense controlled by the materials which they attempted to use in correct ways. This emphasis on the correct use of materials in the Montessori environment led the investigators to hypothesize a lower incidence of symbolic play, particularly complex symbolic play, among the children attending the Montessori program. In the

child-centered nursery, materials were available to the children without restrictions on how they should be used. Children were free to spend their time as they chose. The teacher made herself available and attempted to assist the child while the child was engaging in spontaneous self-directed activity. It was expected that, because of the different emphasis, symbolic play, particularly complex symbolic play, would appear more often in the child-centered nursery than in the Montessori program. The adult-centered program was expected to fall somewhere in the middle since the emphasis was more on conformity to adult standards which were relatively neutral regarding symbolic or concrete use of materials.

Twelve children were selected from each of the three different programs. The children were equated for age, that is, three- and four-year-olds, for sex and for IQ as determined by the Peabody Picture Vocabulary Test. The data were collected by means of six 15-minute observations of each child in the same situations in all three programs. The first major finding was a significantly lower incidence of any kind of play behavior in the Montessori environment than in the other two environments. The second major finding was that practice play, as well as combinations, occurred significantly more often in the adult-centered nursery than in the other two nursery programs. Nevertheless, the relative rank of practice play was higher than other types of play for the children in the Montessori program. Both simple and complex symbolic play occurred significantly more often in the adult-centered and child-centered nursery programs than in the Montessori program. Finally, complex symbolic play occurred significantly most often in the child-centered nursery program. All these studies warrant the conclusion that Montessori nursery programs tend to facilitate discrimination learning, while child-centered programs, with an emphasis on self-initiated and self-directed spontaneous activity on the part of the children, appeared to be most conducive to creativity and free symbolic expression in the play behavior of children.

THE EDUCATIONAL DEVELOPMENT CENTER PROGRAM

This program represents the philosophy of the British Infant Schools in the United States. The goals and objectives of the Educational Development Center in Newton, Massachusetts, have much in common with the Montessori approach. The goals of the program are to develop initiative and self-direction, curiosity and commitment, imagination, openness to change, an ability to challenge ideas, self-respect and respect for others.

With regard to the role of the teacher, the emphasis is not on teaching but on the teacher's assisting the children in the learning process. In contrast to Montessori, the teacher is expected to take a more active role in the learning process of the child. The teacher helps to develop the child's mental process by posing questions and by helping the child to verbalize and formulate his ideas and thoughts. The teacher "will have to work alongside some children and become involved herself, whilst with others, a short discussion, the right question at the right time or the offering of advice or help may suffice" (Brown & Precious, 1968, p. 31). Thus, in the Educational Development Center approach, the teacher is expected to be more active and interact more often with the child than in the Montessori approach.

With regard to the teacher's style and personality, the Educational Development Center emphasizes that the teacher must be ready to concede that she is not always right. If she does not know the answer to a question, it is advisable that she be honest, admit her lack of knowledge, and suggest a way that both she and the child together can find the answer to the question. It is accepted that if a teacher had difficulties in her own childhood, she might find it difficult to cope tolerantly with failure, inadequacy, aggression and quarreling. In addition to expecting self-awareness, the teacher must have a sense of humor and must be flexible as well as innovative. This emphasis on the personality characteristics of the teacher goes beyond technique and curriculum. The emphasis on the teacher's personality and subtle interactions between teacher and child places greater emphasis on an emotional climate than on technique of teaching. This emphasis is reflected in suggestions for the handling of discipline. The discipline of the group is based on mutual respect between teacher and child. A look, a gesture, moving closer to the child or showing an increased interest in what he's doing may be more effective than prohibition, criticism or the citing of rules. Such functioning on the part of the teacher requires a relaxation and an emotional reserve as well as self-confidence.

The Educational Development Center and Montessori programs share a common emphasis on the importance of structuring the physical environment in such a way that it can provide both stimulation for the child to engage in a learning process and corrective feedback to reinforce the child directly in his unaided independent achievement striving. In both approaches, emphasis is placed on freeing the child from the tyranny of time and letting the child follow his own rhythm in engaging and disengaging from a task and in completing a task. However, the two approaches are far apart in the selection and structuring of the environment as a stimulus for the child's learning. Montessori's program, for the most part, adheres to preselected sets of learning materials which enable the child to progress from simple to more complex levels of sensory discrimination, integration and experience. The Educational Development Center starts with the assumption that there is no sacred body of information to which all children everywhere must be exposed. Children's responses to the environment provide the starting point for learning.

Activities most often arise from the needs and interests of the group rather than from a prescribed curriculum. The teacher presents a varied and flexible learning environment responsive to a wide variety of individual interests and talents. It is expected that the teacher will feel free to allow each class to develop in its own way and will be flexible and innovative about curriculum. The choice of materials and the choice of curriculum are dictated by each child's interest at the moment rather than by prescribed steps in the learning process. Teacher and child create their own relevant learning environment. Similarly, specific subject matter is not considered as important as *how* things are learned. There is much greater emphasis on the role of verbal learning and on the role of language in the learning process than is true for the Montessori program. An open dialogue that is carried on between teacher and pupil and among children themselves is the essence of good education. "The teacher's voice is one of the most important items of her 'stock-in-trade,' not because it must be loud and commanding but because it is in constant use to converse and explain and help" (Brown & Precious, 1968, p. 27).

As indicated earlier, the emotional relationship between teacher and child is of the essence. The teacher must give appropriate help to each child when she perceives difficulties and hurdles in which she can help the child. These difficulties may arise in the social, emotional or intellectual functioning of the child. But even then she must offer her help without intrusion—in the form of raising the right question at the right time and acting from a position of perspective rather than of power and authority. Here Montessori and the Educational Development Center converge in their expectations from the teacher.

Evaluative results of this preschool program to date are not yet available in the United States although the program is being tried and implemented in many places across the country. However, results are available from an extensive study carried out in Great Britain, where the program originated and has been in effect for many years. The study has been carried out by Gardner (1966). Two types of schools were selected for comparison: experimental infant schools, which were of the child-centered type, and conventional schools, which were teacher-centered. The schools were differentiated from many reliable sources through observations, questionnaires, and through the advice of qualified authorities in the school district. The experimental infant schools were distinguishable by means of the following characteristics: 1) they devoted a daily period of never less than an hour to free choice of activity by the children, 2) none of them had a compulsory period for reading or arithmetic until the children were six, or very nearly six, 3) they all tended to teach other subjects by informal methods, linking these with the interests of the children rather than treating them in isolation. Common characteristics of the experimental junior schools were that: they all devoted a considerable amount of the children's time to activities designed to make full use of their interests and purposes, they all taught English and arithmetic both in the context of the child's spontaneous activities and interests as well as a time set aside for these subjects, and finally, all of the experimental junior schools showed a balance between physical education, arts and sciences, creative work and skills.

The conventional or control infant schools were organized entirely on a subject-matter basis and teaching was formal with heavy emphasis on routine and discipline. Although teachers did not break away from established tradition they were often generous with their time in conducting games or sports out of school activities. The curriculum consisted of generally well-balanced periods. There were a good many extra-curricular activities going on in these schools. Relationships between teachers and children were happy and the teachers were interested in their work and in the children's progress. All the schools were "good schools" of their type. Experimental and conventional schools were paired on a one-to-one basis by equalizing conditions such as urban-rural, size of school, etc. Within the paired schools children were matched for age, sex, intelligence and socioeconomic status. Testing was carried out toward the end of the year, specifically, the end of infant school or junior school. Most of the paired classrooms consisted of 20 or more children.

Gardner reports results of the analysis of seven pairs of infant schools. Comparisons yielded significant differences in favor of the experimental schools for measures of concentration, listening and remembering, ingenuity, free drawing and painting. Superiorities were equally divided among conventional and experimental schools on measures of neatness, handwriting and mechanical arithmetic. Measures of reading were available only for two pairs of schools and here the conventional schools were superior to the experimental schools.

Twelve pairs of experimental and conventional junior schools served as subjects for comparisons. The children were all tested at the end of junior school when they were approximately 10 years of age. The children in each of these schools had been in the same type of school for both infant and junior school so that once the child started in experimental infant school he continued in an experimental type junior school; the same was true for children in the conventional schools. Comparisons in which the experimental schools clearly exceeded the conventional schools were found in measures of listening and remembering, interest, ingenuity, free drawing and painting, English papers and original compositions and, finally, neatness, care and skill. Comparisons in which the experimental schools were somewhat ahead of the conventional schools were measures of concentration on an uninteresting task, ability to solve a social problem, moral judgment,

general information, reading and handwriting. The conventional schools were somewhat ahead on both mechanical arithmetic and arithmetic problem-solving. It is clear from these findings, with the exception of certain specific skills such as reading at the end of infant school and arithmetic at the end of junior school, the experimental or child-centered educational programs resulted in superiority of most attitude as well as attainment measures.

The author also carried out a study comparing five pairs of conventional junior schools in which students in one of each pair had attended an experimental infant school while students in the other had attended a conventional infant school. Here the author found that in four out of five pairs the children who had attended experimental infant schools were superior in concentration on tasks of their own choice, on listening and remembering, on writing an original story and on free drawing. In three out of five pairs, children from the experimental infant school showed superiority in ingenuity, essays and original themes in English, writing an original poem and mechanical arithmetic. The experimental children also exceeded their peers who had attended a conventional infant school on ratings of friendliness and response to strangers who gave the test.

These findings, if replicated, present strong evidence in favor of the impact of child-centered early education as compared to the conventional type of preschool education. However, it must be emphasized that these findings were obtained in England against a background of different culture mores, norms and habits than might apply to American culture. Therefore, these findings cannot be taken to represent evidence of the impact of the Educational Development Center program in the United States. However, the current extensive efforts of planned variation in Follow Through in the United States encompassing the program on a large scale should yield results within the near future which can then be examined in the light of the wider perspective of comparable results in Great Britain.

ACADEMIC PRESCHOOL

The academic preschool is a program which has been widely used since its inception by Bereiter and Engelmann (1966). It is a highly structured, skill-oriented preschool program. The major objectives of this program have been to develop effective use of language, basic color concepts, to master and distinguish between verbal and visual symbols, and to acquire the basic skills of arithmetic—counting, adding, subtracting and multiplying. The program also aims at developing an ability in the child to apply his skills in a variety of situations and to increase his self-esteem and confidence through tangible academic achievements. Although the program was not intended to be confined to the education of disadvantaged children, it was developed especially for children who have failed to learn certain language skills which they need for success in school. Lower-class disadvantaged children in our society acquire inappropriate language patterns and although they learn to communicate their desires, they are not taught to use language as a learning tool. Thus, when the disadvantaged child reaches school he cannot make as effective a use of language skills as his middle-class advantaged classmate.

The academic preschool was designed as a crash program of language remediation to help the four- and five-year-old disadvantaged child to catch up to middle-class children.

The academic preschool is a half-day program. The role of the teacher is that of an initiator and evaluator of the child's learning behavior in highly compressed, intensive, and relatively short teaching sessions. The essential curriculum consists of three 20-minute periods during which language, reading and arithmetic are taught. Each subject is taught by a different teacher who specializes in one of these subjects.

Children are congregated into small groups according to their ability and given 20-minute periods of intensive training which are interspersed with less structured activities. The physical facilities are constructed to suit the program. The preschool includes a large classroom and several small rooms for direct instruction. Since the program does not provide for gross motor and expressive activities, certain facilities that one usually finds in a nursery school such as sandbox, jungle gym, seesaw and easels for painting are not present.

Teaching is carried out at an intensive, fast pace. The teacher directs her efforts at the level of the lowest performing child in the small group to insure that everyone can move with the program. Each concept is taught until every child in the group can use it correctly. New concepts are introduced with as many examples as possible. The instructional program is prescribed and each lesson is worked out beforehand in a step-by-step format. The teacher resembles a cheerleader as the children chant in unison the correct answers. These methods are utilized to keep motivation, participation, and arousal level at a maximum during the learning phase.

Learning is considered work and not play. Children are discouraged, criticized, or even isolated if they fail to participate fully and indulge in distractions. Children are rewarded with food and praise for answering correctly and for exhibiting maximum effort. Incorrect answers are corrected immediately. Children are called upon to recite and perform constantly. A special attentional device used by the teachers in this system is to change the pace of teaching, the loudness of their voices, and provide surprises as often as possible. These devices are used to avoid monotony and satiation in the children during the learning phases. Clearly it takes a teacher with a special personality and style to make such a teaching venture successful.

Since the program is focused toward a highly specialized curriculum, a brief description of the instructional program follows: with regard to language, children are first taught to describe and classify objects, after which they progress to usage of tense variation, action verbs, conditional and conjunctive statements, and the description of complex objects and events. Arithmetic deals with work on basic number concepts, simple counting operations, adding, subtracting, multiplying, and performing simple algebra problems. Unlike most other preschool programs, the Bereiter-Engelmann method stresses the need to teach reading as part of the curriculum. The authors use a modified initial teaching alphabet in which children are taught to spell and blend words phonetically. After this has been mastered, children are taught to read stories based upon words they have learned. Stories are taken home after they are mastered as a reward for achievement.

Bereiter and Engelmann report that after two years in the academic preschool, children made greater gains on the Stanford-Binet and the Wide Range Achievement Test than children in comparison groups who had not received the intensive academic training. By the time the experimental children entered first grade they achieved nearly at second-grade level in reading, arithmetic and spelling.

The academic preschool program was also used with a group of middle-class children. It was found that children in that group reached a higher reading and spelling level than those attending a month or so of preschool who were not specially trained to read and spell. The significant differences between the two groups of children at the end of the program led Bereiter and Engelmann to affirm their contention that all children, disadvantaged as well as advantaged, can benefit from their direct instructional methods.

Several studies that have attempted to apply the Bereiter-Engelmann method for the purpose of language training have reported mixed results. One study was carried out by Classen, Spear, and Tomaro (1969)

in which 50 percent of 30 children coming from low-income families were assigned to a concentrated language training program during an eight-week summer Head Start project, while the other 15 children were assigned to a more conventional, socially oriented program in which language training was purely incidental within the context of other activities. The authors found no significant differences between experimental and control groups on IQ scores. However, children who received intensive language training were significantly superior on the Illinois Test of Psycholinguistic Abilities to children who attended the control program. The authors concluded that focused programming produces results which are superior to conventional programming in those skills which were the focus of the program.

Other attempts to apply the Bereiter-Engelmann program were less successful. Bruce Rusk (1968) compared eight classes of 15 children who had received six weeks of the Bereiter-Engelmann structured curriculum with eight classes of 15 children who had attended a relatively unstructured program. Even though the children were tested on the Engelmann Concept Inventory for which the experimental group received special training, the latter were not significantly superior to children who had attended relatively unstructured programs. Adkins and others (1967) attempted a modified Bereiter-Engelmann language curriculum by moving more slowly through steps of the program and requiring less disciplined behavior from the children. When the children who had received this program were compared with Head Start children who attended a verbal enrichment program, no significant differences were found in the language performance of the two groups.

Stern and Keislar (1968) investigated one aspect of the Bereiter-Engelmann curriculum experimentally. Forty lower-class disadvantaged black children attending Head Start were assigned to four different groups.

In the first group children were required to echo sentences in response to pictures, in the second group sentences were modeled to one picture as children were expected to produce their own sentences to a similar picture, in the third group children simply listened to descriptions and stories about pictures, and the fourth group was a control group which had no language training. The investigators were interested in determining whether echoing, which has been used as a method of teaching in the Bereiter program, would be equal to or different from the other methods of language training. Children received pre- and posttests on the Peabody Picture Vocabulary Test, on the Expressive Vocabulary Inventory, on an Echoing Response Inventory and on a Parallel Production Test. The language program extended over a three-week period. Two of the tests, namely, the Expressive Vocabulary Test and the Echoing Response Test, yielded no changes from pre- to post-testing. On the Peabody Picture Vocabulary Test and on the Parallel Production Test the children from the "parallel prompting" group and the children from the "listening group" showed consistently greater gains than the children from the "echoing prompting" and "control" groups. The superiority of the parallel prompting group over the echoing prompting group was significant. The important conclusion to be drawn from this study is that listening alone produced results as good as the parallel prompting method and, if anything, was better than the echoing prompting method of language training.

The three programs which have been discussed in some detail in this section were evaluated in several research projects in which all three of these programs were compared with regard to their impact on cognitive and socioemotional functioning of children. Therefore, the next section will provide a broader and probably more meaningful perspective of these programs and the evaluation of their impact than the isolated studies which have been reported so far.

COMPARATIVE IMPACT RESEARCH

We shall now turn to a series of studies in which three or more different preschool programs were compared with regard to their impact on cognitive and socioemotional development. The majority of these projects are long-term follow-up studies in different stages of completion. Even though considerable caution in the interpretation of findings is indicated to date, these studies are unique in the history of research on organized programs on preschool education and for that reason will be discussed notwithstanding the fact that the results are incomplete.

THE RESEARCH AND DEVELOPMENT PROGRAM

Karnes (1969) and her associates carried out a study to evaluate the differential effects of five preschool intervention programs at the end of preschool and the end of kindergarten. The programs were selected to represent levels of structure along a continuum from a traditional nursery to a highly structured preschool program. Degree of structure was defined rather unconventionally as the degree of specificity and intensity of the teacher-child interaction. It was expected that the effects of preschool education on language functioning would increase with increased structure.

Five programs were selected for study. Two programs, traditional and community-integrated, represented the less structured end of the continuum; Montessori represented an intermediate point of structure; and the Ameliorative and Direct Verbal programs fell at the high end of the structure continuum.

Ninety-one children were assigned to three double-class units to cover each of the three points of the continuum. The children were selected from economically depressed neighborhoods and assigned in a stratified, random sample to the three different class-room pairs in such a way that an equal number of children above IQ's of 70, 90, and 100 were assigned to each of the programs.

The traditional nursery-school program had the goal of promoting the personal, social, motor and general language developments of the children. Teachers were oriented to provide incidental and informal learning and to encourage children to take initiative in the learning process. Otherwise the curriculum was the same as is usually encountered in nursery programs, i.e., art work, play, indoor play focused on doll play and housekeeping, a block corner, a small toy center which featured puzzles, beads, puppets and books. Other daily routines such as juice time, rest periods, supervised toileting and storytelling completed the schedule.

The Montessori program described earlier was administered by a local society which took full responsibility for setting the standards and selecting the usual Montessori materials for the preschool program.

The Direct Verbal program was supervised by Bereiter and Engelmann, and was the same as the one described earlier in this chapter.

The Ameliorative program was specially designed by the authors. The basic concepts and specific learning tasks in this program were selected to prepare each child for a successful academic performance in early elementary school. The teachers in this program were instructed to adapt their methods to language deficits of individual children as diagnosed by the Illinois Test of Psycholinguistic Abilities. Manipulative and multisensory materials were used to elicit verbal responses necessary for language development.

Each class was divided into three groups on the basis of Stanford-Binet IQ, with one teacher for each group. The daily schedule was divided into three 20-minute structured learning periods. Mathematical concepts, language arts, reading readiness, science and social studies were offered during these learning periods. A large room where the 15 children could gather for group activities was available. Instruction, however, took place in relatively small cubicles off the main room. Each cubicle offered materials appropriate to one of the three areas to be taught, and each teacher moved from one cubicle to another with her group of five children. In order to maximize motivation and opportunities for the reinforcement of learning, the same teacher remained with her group of children throughout the three structured learning periods, during juice breaks and field trips. In this program no use was made of outdoor play equipment or traditional toys such as dolls, trucks and cars. Concepts taught during the structured period were reinforced during all periods of the program. The goals of the social studies and science curriculum were to teach vocabulary and classification, and to provide experiences appropriate for the development of sensory discrimination. The mathematics curriculum attempted to teach basic number concepts, manipulative skills and useful vocabulary. The language arts in reading readiness relied heavily on the use of books to teach a child the basic elements and motor habits associated with language and reading readiness skills. However, language training was extended throughout all periods of the day, and the manipulation of concrete materials was utilized maximally in the process of language training.

Before we turn to the findings reported from this study, certain differences between the programs need to be pointed out since they are relevant to the evaluation. The quality and intensity of training varied from program to program, and the ratio of adults to children was not equal between the programs. For example, an in-service training program for traditional teachers was conducted prior to the opening of the preschool classes. However, the Ameliorative program received weekly in-service training sessions for teachers throughout the program. Similarly, the Direct Verbal program received weekly supervision from Bereiter and Engelmann in addition to daily discussions among staff members. No special in-service training programs or supervisory meetings were described by the authors for the Montessori and community-integrated programs. Moreover, the pupil-teacher ratios in the Montessori and community-integrated programs were less favorable than in the three programs directly supervised by the authors of the study, i.e., five to one for the traditional, Ameliorative and Direct Verbal program, in contrast to a ratio of eight to one for the Montessori program and a ratio which varied from six to one to 10 to one for the community-integrated preschool program. A third difference between groups was that the special programs for the Direct Verbal and Ameliorated groups continued during kindergarten while all others moved into regular kindergarten groups without any additional training. The Direct Verbal group continued under the same special program of Engelmann-Bereiter materials and procedures throughout kindergarten. The Ameliorative group moved to a regular kindergarten but received regularly supplemented training, continuing the special Ameliorative program throughout kindergarten.

At the end of the preschool year the children were evaluated by means of the Stanford-Binet Test, the Peabody Picture Vocabulary Test, the Illinois Test of Psycholinguistic Abilities, the Frostig Visual Perception Test and the Metropolitan Readiness Test. The findings of the evaluation at the end of preschool can be summarized as follows. The Ameliorative group was superior to all four groups on the Frostig Visual Perception Test. The authors attribute the superiority of the Ameliorative program in its effect on visual perceptual functioning, measured by the Frostig and by certain subtests of the Illinois Test of Psycholinguistic Abilities, to planned conjunction of verbalization with productive manipulative experiences in this program.

Both Ameliorative and Direct Verbal groups were superior to all other groups on the number readiness subtests of the Metropolitan Test. On the Stanford-Binet and on the total Illinois Test of Psycholinguistic Abilities, the Direct Verbal group was superior to the Montessori and community-centered groups but not to the children who had received the traditional program. Finally, no significant differences were found on the Peabody Picture Vocabulary Test. Thus, as measured by the Stanford-Binet, the three programs supervised by the authors of this study falling on the opposite ends of the structure dimension did not differ significantly from each other in areas of heaviest concentration of training.

At the end of kindergarten the Direct Verbal group was superior to the other four groups on the Stanford-Binet and on total Illinois Test of Psycholinguistic Abilities performance. The same group shared its superiority with the Ameliorative group on the number readiness test of the Metropolitan Test, while the Ameliorative group alone was superior to the other four groups on the reading readiness subtest of the Metropolitan. With regard to the last finding, the authors conclude that the special preschool training in reading offered by the Direct Verbal group only was not effective since the children in the Ameliorative group who received only readiness, but not direct training in reading, outperformed all other groups on the reading readiness subtest. As indicated earlier, it is difficult to ascribe superiority in performance of the Direct Verbal group and the Ameliorative group to the type of educational program since these two programs received more intensive and supplementary education than the other three groups during the kindergarten year.

Continued evaluation of the differential impact of preschool education at the end of first grade was limited to the three groups initially supervised by the authors, namely the Direct Verbal, the Ameliorative, and the traditional groups. Although the Direct Verbal and the Ameliorative groups were superior to the traditional group on the Stanford-Binet, these differences were not significant at the end of the first grade. The same findings obtained for the general Illinois Test of Psycholinguistic Abilities score and for the Visual Perception Score on the Frostig, that is, the Direct Verbal and Ameliorative groups were ahead of the traditional group, but none of these differences was significant. However, the Direct Verbal and Ameliorative groups were significantly ahead in certain achievement areas such as reading readiness and arithmetic as measured by the California Achievement Test and the Metropolitan Test.

This study was extremely well planned in certain respects. Unfortunately, differences in training and supervision of teachers, pupil-teacher ratios, and amount of supplementary education throughout kindergarten make it difficult to attribute any of the reported differences to type and content rather than amount of training and teacher supervision.

Ypsilanti Curriculum Demonstration Project

In 1966 David Weikart began an experimental preschool program in which three different curricula were carried out in different classrooms by separate teaching staffs. Each of the three curricula was carefully planned and implemented with the same intensity as the original program. Again, small groups of eight children were exposed to the program for periods of two years, and, as before, each year a new wave started which served as a replication sample of the program of the previous year. Each program was once again a half-day program in which each child was visited once a week by his teacher for a 90-minute period to offer instruction and continuity of the program in the child's home. The children were drawn from the same population by means of the same criteria as in the original study described earlier—that is, from a range of IQ's between 50 and 85, with no discernible organic involvement. Children were randomly assigned to one of the three programs.

The three programs were a cognitive program and a Bereiter-Engelmann language program, both of which were described earlier, and a unit-based program.

The unit-based curriculum followed traditional nursery-school goals and techniques. The curriculum focused on the development of the whole child with an emphasis on social and emotional growth. Activities, discussions and field trips were organized around broad themes such as circus animals and holidays. For example, the theme "Thanksgiving" provided a base for many activities. A picture of a turkey precipitated discussions of the different attributes of the turkey (it is a bird, it has feathers, a head, eyes, feet, beak, etc.). Coloring and drawing turkeys led to discussions of colors. Cutting turkey figures out of construction paper increased manipulative skills. Further activities extended into discussions and preparations of different foods. The basic approach to intellectual development was learning by experience and discovery through play. This involved fostering curiosity and creativity and experimenting with new materials.

The goals of the program were to encourage spontaneous conversation and activities among the children. To reach this goal the teacher took cues from the children concerning their needs and desires. Children were encouraged to take initiative in conversations and actions by means of praise and reinforcement. The atmosphere of the nursery was characterized by a permissive relationship between the teacher and the children as well as among the children themselves. There was a firm belief that "play is the child's work."

Although this program had many similarities to the Educational Development Center program described earlier, the teacher took a much more active role in structuring the daily program.

Results of both short- and long-range

impact of these very carefully planned and implemented programs on intellectual functioning and academic achievement have become available. Gains during the initial year for three waves of the program ranged from 17 to 30 IQ points on the Stanford-Binet. An unexpected finding was that these gains were equally large from all three programs. Although there tends to be some decline after the children enter kindergarten and elementary school, the substantial gains seem to be holding up to the end of the second grade. The findings are equivalent, if not more dramatic, on the California Achievement Test given to the children at the end of the first and second grades. Although caution is indicated because the samples are still small and the replications for elementary school not yet complete, a weakness has begun to emerge with regard to the long-range effect of the Bereiter-Engelmann language program. Children who received this program did less well at the end of the second grade on the Stanford-Binet Test, and did markedly worse than children from the other two programs on the California Achievement Test. Weikart (1971c) states, "these preliminary data suggest very strongly that the magic of the programmed approaches is almost purely illusory" (p. 17). A programmed approach does not equip the child to solve complex educational problems any better than other preschool programs such as the open framework or the child-centered program. The findings of highly similar outcomes of different research programs have led Weikart to the conclusion that the operational conditions of experimental programs are far more potent in affecting outcome than the particular curricula. Children profit intellectually and socioemotionally from any curriculum that offers a wide range of experiences. Weikart sees the primary role of curriculum as mobilizing and focusing the energy of the teacher, providing a rationale for selecting activities for the children as well as a rational base for the supervision of teachers. Looking toward the future, Weikart suggested that it might be more fruitful for researchers to spend more time studying the teaching process and the learning experiences of the child through classroom observation rather than through delayed results on achievement tests.

I would add to these observations another common characteristic of successful preschool programs—an intensive relationship between teacher and child which has offered, especially to the disadvantaged child, greater stability from day to day than he has experienced in most instances with adults in his home. This stable relationship also has the mix of order and variety which the teacher offers to the child in her daily contact with him.

EXPERIMENTAL VARIATION OF HEAD START CURRICULA

Miller and her associates (1970a, 1970b, 1970c, 1971) have been carrying out an experimental and longitudinal study comparing four types of preschool programs followed by two types of kindergarten programs for disadvantaged children. The objectives of the study have been to assess program components, that is, teacher behavior and pupil behavior as well as teacher-pupil interaction; to assess program effects on cognitive, motivational and social development; and to relate treatment dimensions to changes in cognitive and socioemotional functioning in the child.

Four types of Head Start programs were implemented by these investigators and three were directly supervised by them. One of these programs was a Bereiter-Engelmann program which emphasized the training of linguistic and numerical skills by the use of verbal instruction, imitation and reinforcement. This program de-emphasized sensorial stimulation and manipulation. The second was a Demonstration and Research Center for Early Education program which emphasized the training of verbal and conceptual skills, and attitudes and motives related to learning by means of verbalization, reinforcement, manipulation of materials and modeling. The third was a Montessori program stressing training of persistence, independence, self-discipline and conceptual skills through the use of sensorial stimulation, manipulation of materials and self-selection. The fourth program was a traditional Head Start program emphasizing training of socioemotional functioning, language and curiosity by means of manipulation of materials, sensorial stimulation, role-playing and self-selection. Verbal instruction and reinforcement were emphasized in both the Bereiter-Engelmann and Demonstration and Research Center for Early Education programs but not in the Montessori and traditional programs.

Children were assigned to four classes each of the Bereiter-Engelmann program, the Demonstration and Research Center for Early Education program, and the traditional program, and to two classes of the Montessori program. The children were assigned randomly within their geographic areas to Head Start classes, and were tested in the fall eight weeks after the start of school and again in the spring at the end of the school year. Teaching dimensions were assessed through samples of observation and video-taping of both teachers and children. The observations were later analyzed by means of Bales and Flanders Categories for Interaction Analysis.

The authors also obtained a middle-class and a lower-class control group consisting of a nonpreschool group similar to the experimental sample and a middle-class group in a private preschool.

An outstanding contribution of this study to those who have attempted to investigate experimentally the effects of different preschool education programs has been the investigation of program components, that is, actual differences in the behavior of teachers and children within and among the four experimental programs. The authors obtained time samples through direct observation, as well as video-taping in the 14 Head Start classrooms which made up the study.

The outcome of the study was that, in spite of variation among teachers within programs, the salient characteristics which were expected for each of the four programs by far outweighed their individual differences and produced great homogeneity within programs rather than between programs. Specifically, in the Bereiter-Engelmann class the teachers were significantly high in verbal instruction, exemplification, modeling of academic information, amount of positive and negative feedback, and in the use of recitation from children as a method of teaching. Teachers in the Demonstration and Research Center for Early Education were significantly high in verbal instruction, conversation with children and contingent positive reinforcement. Teachers from both Bereiter-Engelmann and the Demonstration and Research Center for Early Education did more teaching of all kinds and used more verbal instruction than Montessori and traditional teachers. Verbal recitation of children was found more often in Bereiter-Engelmann and the Demonstration and Research Center for Early Education programs. Montessori children were significantly high in manipulation of materials while traditional children exceeded children in other programs in role-playing. With regard to group formations, it was found that children in Bereiter-Engelmann and the Demonstration and Research Center for Early Education classes worked more often in groups in which children carried out the same kinds of activities. In Montessori and traditional classes children were engaged in different activities either individually or as part of subgroups within the major group. Finally, the teachers in the Bereiter-Engelmann program were more oriented to the group than to individual children. Although children were taught in small groups in both the Bereiter-Engelmann and the Demonstration and Research Center for Early Education programs, the teacher-child interaction in the latter program involved mostly individual children.

The authors emphasized that their findings of large differences in the techniques used by teachers in the different programs proved that it is possible to train teachers within an eight-week training program to acquire special techniques which they actually apply in their daily teaching. However, a closer examination of the reported findings reveals this generalization may be truer for certain techniques than others. The teacher behavior in the traditional and Montessori programs did not meet expectations as fully as teacher behavior in the Bereiter-Engelmann and Demonstration and Research Center for Early Education programs, which used more skill-oriented techniques than the traditional and Montessori programs. The latter put more stress on the complex emotional interplay between teacher and child than, for example, the Bereiter-Engelmann program. Not unrelated is the differential emphasis on short-range versus long-range goals with regard to child variables in the different programs.

The different preschool programs affected different areas of functioning in children. The outcome as measured by Stanford-Binet and Preschool Inventory Tests showed that children in experimental programs improved more than those in the control group. When one compares changes from pre- to posttesting, there does not seem to be any appreciable difference in gains among the experimental groups. With regard to socioemotional and motivational measures, the children in the Demonstration and Research Center for Early Education program showed generally greater gains than children in other programs—particularly in such areas as achievement motivation, independence, timidity, resistance to distractions and inventiveness. These findings suggest that children in the former program were emotionally more engaged as well as aroused than children in the latter programs.

In order to determine effects of the programs on achievement, four tests were given to a sample of children in each class at the end of the school year. As predicted, children in the programs who were oriented toward the development of specific skills achieved significantly higher scores on these tests. Children in the Bereiter-Engelmann program performed highest on arithmetic and sentence production. However, the Basic Concept Inventory, which was developed by Engelmann in connection with the Bereiter-Engelmann program and which was also administered at the end of the preschool program, did not differentiate between programs.

Following the prekindergarten experimental programs the authors provided for a modified continuation of the experimental program and a modified control group arrangement. Half of the children from the four experimental groups and from the control group were channeled into a Follow Through kindergarten and the other half into a regular kindergarten. The Follow Through kindergarten was designed as an experimental program with a highly academic and individualized program structured as a token economy. The children received intensive training in reading, handwriting and arithmetic. A school day was divided into earn and spend periods. During the earn periods the children were reinforced with tokens and verbal praise. Their accumulated tokens could be used to gain access to various kinds of activities and things to play with. The classes were divided into small groups which worked on common lessons but each child worked on his own and at his own rate. The regular kindergarten program was the one conducted by the city schools and was not intended as a preparation for first-grade work. Neither written materials nor prereading exercises was a formal part of the program. The emphasis of the program was on providing a variety of activities to reach individual and unique needs of a wide range of children.

The two kindergarten programs differed also in other respects which were not matters of type of program but intensity and length of educational experience. For example, the adult-child ratio in the Follow Through kindergarten was approximately one to six as opposed to a ratio of one adult to 30 children in the regular kindergarten. The regular kindergarten lasted two and a half hours per day while the Follow Through kindergarten extended for four hours a day. The teachers in the regular kindergarten taught different morning and afternoon classes while the Follow Through teachers taught only one-half day and one class. The situation is further complicated by the fact that the experimental Follow Through kindergarten was very similar in many respects to the experience of the Bereiter-Engelmann and the Demonstration and Research Center for Early Education programs and very dissimilar in many respects to the Montessori, traditional and control preschool programs. These differences were not symmetrically counterbalanced since the regular kindergarten program was most likely dissimilar to all four prekindergarten programs including the control group experience. All these uncontrolled differences complicate interpretation of follow-up findings.

The authors analyzed the separate and combined interacting effects of prekindergarten programs on the children's performances on the Metropolitan Readiness Test at the beginning of first grade. In the first positive findings there was a difference in the main effects of the Head Start program regardless of subsequent kindergarten programs. Here it was found that children who participated in the Bereiter-Engelmann program were inferior to all other children on word-meaning scores and inferior on listening and copying, while children from the traditional programs performed highest on these subtests. When children from the Follow Through kindergarten were compared with children from regular kindergarten, it was found that Follow Through children were superior to children who had regular kindergarten on total-readiness scores and on most of the subtest comparisons. When a similar analysis was carried out for chil-

dren who entered kindergarten without any preschool experience, the Follow Through children were again superior on total scores to children who had received regular kindergarten. However, subtest comparisons yielded superiority of the Follow Through kindergarten children only on matching, alphabet and copying subtests. Analysis of interacting effects between prekindergarten experience and type of kindergarten, as well as the child's sex, showed that male control children who had no previous Head Start experience and participated in the regular nonacademically oriented kindergarten were vastly inferior to males who had no Head Start experience and participated on the highly focused, academically oriented Follow Through kindergarten training.

One of the most striking findings in the study emerged when children were matched on readiness scores based on post-Head Start Preschool Inventory Scores in each of three preschool programs, i.e., Bereiter-Engelmann, Demonstration and Research Center for Early Education, and traditional, and then compared on the outcome of their kindergarten experience as measured by Metropolitan Readiness Scores. Here it was found that although traditional children entered Follow Through and regular kindergarten with lower readiness scores than children from the Bereiter-Engelmann and Demonstration and Research Center for Early Education programs, they performed as well or better than children from the other two programs at the end of both Follow Through or regular kindergarten. By contrast, children from the Bereiter-Engelmann preschool program, while holding their own at the end of the Follow Through kindergarten, performed much lower than any other group on the total Metropolitan Readiness Score at the end of regular kindergarten.

The authors conclude from their findings that children benefited more from the Follow Through kindergarten than from the regular kindergarten. While the empirical evidence supports such conclusions, the added conclusion by the authors that this difference was due to the type of education, namely, "the token economy Follow Through kindergarten," is not defensible on the basis of other relevant differences between the two types of kindergartens pointed out earlier, i.e., a more intensive achievement-oriented program, better pupil to teacher ratio, more intensive training and supervision for the Follow Through teachers, and a more exhausting daily teaching load for the regular kindergarten teachers. A second conclusion of the authors was that traditional Head Start preschool experience resulted in best long-range effects as measured by several specific Metropolitan subtests regardless of type of kindergarten experience and as measured by total Metropolitan Readiness Tests when traditional Head Start was followed by the intensive achievement-oriented Follow Through program. Conversely, the Bereiter-Engelmann Head Start program had the poorest long-range effect on several Metropolitan subtests regardless of the type of kindergarten program, and the lowest scores on the total Metropolitan Test when children from Head Start programs participated in the regular kindergarten program. A third main conclusion was that for males entering the regular kindergarten program, any type of Head Start appeared to be better than none. And finally, a conclusion which seems to be questionable is that "for children entering this Follow Through program there is no evidence that there was an advantage in having had Head Start at all" (Miller, Dyer, et al., 1971). It is reasonable to expect that an intensive achievement-oriented program would make up for relatively minor pretraining procedure differences, especially for its effect on academic achievement tests. However, this conclusion is based on a sample of four girls and nine boys which represents too small a sample and an unreplicated finding to make such a sweeping statement. Considering that the children from the two highly skilled and achievement-oriented prekindergarten pro-

grams entered the Follow Through kindergarten with a distinct advantage in the achievement areas and failed to maintain their advantage even though they experienced continuity of training in the same areas might lead one to conclude that intensive training for specific skills can well be delayed from nursery to kindergarten. That such a delay may benefit children could be concluded from the fact that at the end of Follow Through kindergarten children from the traditional Head Start program outperformed children from other Head Start programs on the total Metropolitan Readiness scores by one standard deviation, whereas children from the Bereiter-Engelmann Head Start program at the end of regular kindergarten scored one to two standard deviations below children from other Head Start programs.

Notwithstanding differences in interpretations, Miller's study is one of the most productive experimental studies in preschool education, and, when finished, is likely to produce a host of interesting and important findings on the impact of preschool education on cognitive and socioemotional development.

IMPLEMENTATION OF PLANNED VARIATION IN HEAD START

A large comprehensive study of the impact of preschool education (Bissell, 1971) was carried out as a pilot study to 1) collect base-line data for subsequent longitudinal analysis, 2) to document implementations of eight different preschool models, and 3) to undertake preliminary analysis of program effects. The criteria on which the model was selected for study was that it must have been tested in a school representing a well-formulated strategy for preschool education and that the sponsor of the model must have been implementing a program for elementary-school children based on the model's principles as part of the Follow Through program. Eight models were grouped into three categories on the basis of their primary orientation toward children's learning: 1) preacademic models which foster development of preacademic skills and place heavy emphasis on systematic reinforcement and drills on individualized programmed instruction; 2) cognitive discovery models which promote the growth of basic cognitive process by helping children develop the appropriate verbal labels and concepts while they engage in sequence exploration; 3) discovery models which view learning as part of the humanistic growth of the whole child with emphasis on free exploration and self-expression.

In order to investigate the implementation of the different models, the Office of Child Development initiated one- to three-day sight visits by consultants to describe teacher-training efforts and to assess the success of implementation and the level of teacher performance. The sponsor of each model arranged for making his own assessments and prepared reports on the same points as those just described. As a third method, questionnaires were constructed and given to the teachers to describe the sponsors' training efforts and educational objectives for the children in the program. Finally, the Stanford Research Institute Classroom Observation Instrument assessed time allotment, type of material, what children do, child grouping, types of control systems and the types of effective environments found in the classrooms of the different models.

Four areas were selected for the study of the effects of the preschool educational programs on the children. For the assessment of academic achievement a number of subtests were selected from the New York University Early Childhood Inventory; for the study of general cognitive development, the Caldwell Preschool Inventory and the Stanford-Binet tests were chosen; to study style of responding to cognitive demands the Hertzig-Birch scoring of responses to the Binet was selected; and for the study of response style the Maccoby Motor Inhibition Test was employed. To measure effects of

the preschool program on parents the authors decided to use the Eight Block Sort Test by Hess and Shipman and a Parent Questionnaire which was constructed by the Stanford Research Institute.

The sample consisted of 1,569 children enrolled in planned-variation classes and 1,078 children enrolled in regular Head Start classes. The programs are spread across the entire United States with the largest concentration in the South (42.7 percent), the second largest in the East (23.4 percent), the third largest concentration in the Middle West (21.2 percent), and the remainder distributed in northern and western parts of the United States. Seventy-two percent of the children were between four-and-a-half and five-and-a-half years of age when they entered Head Start. Other controlled factors in this study were ethnic composition, the proportion of children with prior preschool experience, the proportion of children with siblings who had prior preschool experience, and the proportion of parents who were actively involved in the preschool program and the study.

Although the analysis of the data is not complete, a good many important and interesting findings have been reported. With regard to implementation of programs it was found that 67 percent of the teachers began low in meeting the criteria of the model. By the end of the year 75 percent of the teachers had met a high or medium level of implementation. Success of implementation and the choice of curriculum were found to be related. The largest number of teachers rated high or medium level in implementation of standards was found in the preacademic models. The largest proportion of teachers rated low in meeting the criteria of their model were found in the discovery program. This finding supports a similar trend reported earlier in a study carried out by Miller, who found that components of the Montessori and traditional programs did not meet the expected criteria as fully as components in the preacademic, achievement-oriented preschool programs.

Bisell suggests that cognitive development and discovery models take more time to implement. The study yielded a further finding which throws additional light on this issue. The higher success in program implementation for preacademic achievement models was correlated with a higher amount of teacher training provided by these sponsors. Thus, it seems that easier and faster implementation of curriculum and other components of a more highly structured and skill-oriented educational program is a combined function of both more specific teaching skills, specific objectives, and the more frequent training provided by program sponsors. These differences might be due to a greater emphasis on teaching technique in the preacademic program and a greater emphasis on teaching style in the discovery programs. Teaching style is less easily developed by direct training and is more likely to be determined by the teacher's personality and accumulated experience with children.

Successful operation of programs was more likely to be reported where Head Start facilities and materials were more adequate, and where the teachers felt that the curriculum was useful and the sponsor of the model offered adequate educational counseling.

All children made intellectual gains as a result of their preschool education. The criterion for gain was a comparison between the actual gains children made from fall to spring testing with expected gains based on scores obtained from children with the same ethnic background and the same chronological age in the fall as the children enrolled in the preschool program had in the spring. Measured against these criteria, the gains of both the Planned Variation and regular Head Start children were significant, that is, larger than what would be attributed to expected maturational development. Comparisons between programs revealed that children enrolled in programs of the three types of models made somewhat larger (and statistically significant) gains

than children enrolled in regular Head Start programs. There were no statistical differences in the gains of children enrolled in the three different model programs. Professional backgrounds of teachers related to cognitive gains of children enrolled in regular Head Start programs, but no such relationship was found in Planned Variation programs. These findings can be interpreted to mean that the general background training of teachers was superseded by specific teaching techniques required by the various educational models.

Preschool programs had overall, as well as specific, effects on response-style measures of children. Children became significantly less impulsive on the Maccoby Measure from fall to spring when the gain was measured against expected maturational effects in the same way as was done for cognitive gains explained above. The largest gain was found in children enrolled in discovery classes. A significant decrease in failure measures on the Hertzig-Birch criteria was found for children in both Planned Variation models and regular Head Start programs when compared to expected maturational effects. The largest gains on this measure were found in children who attended preacademic Planned Variation preschool models. Decreases in extended, that is, nonrelevant responses on the cognitive tests were found both in planned variation and regular Head Start programs and were significantly greater than expected by maturation alone. The largest proportional decrease was found in nonverbal extensions among children enrolled in preacademic programs. These changes are interpreted to mean that children enrolled in these preschool programs had learned what a question is and what an appropriate answer is on cognitive tests. The changes also suggest that children have learned to focus on essential components of a schoollike test and to cope efficiently with such components.

A number of significant changes were found in mother-child interaction measures. The verbal communication of mothers became more task-related. The mothers' use of praise rather than blame showed a marked increase. Particularly pronounced were gains in children's success on the problem-solving task where the significance was determined by comparing changes in these areas with increases expected from maturational changes for low-income children with comparable backgrounds. While changes were approximately equal for mothers of Planned Variation and regular Head Start children, children attending Planned Variation programs had significantly greater increases in task success than children attending regular Head Start programs. Within the Planned Variation program the largest gain in the use of praise was made by mothers of children enrolled in cognitive discovery and preacademic classes.

An analysis of responses to the parental questionnaires showed that parents' responses corresponded with orientations of models, particularly in their reaction to the question, "What difference has Head Start made in your life this year?" Parents of children enrolled in Planned Variation programs emphasized changes in the parent-child relationship and in self-development of the child and parent. Parents of children enrolled in regular Head Start programs tended to express satisfaction with having found a place to look after their child. In response to the question, "What are the things you like most about Head Start?" parents of children enrolled in preacademic programs stressed relationships among children and relationships between teachers and children as the aspects which they appreciated most. These findings were interpreted by the investigators to mean that the parents understand and internalize the orientation of different Head Start models. Answers to questions oriented toward parental contact and involvement with the child's preschool program suggested that parents of children enrolled in regular Head Start programs participated more in the program than parents of children enrolled in Planned Variation programs.

Although these are only initial findings, they demonstrate the fruitfulness of widening the scope in impact research on educational programs, especially for young children. The findings from the Planned Variation Study were particularly meaningful because they could be examined in a wider context of available relevant data. For example, the question as to whether programs were differentially successful was not simply evaluated against the criterion of outcome but was examined in the light of variations in physical facilities available within programs and in the context of relationships between teaching staff and sponsor of the particular program. The employment of outcome measures was sufficiently varied to enable the investigators to answer the question, "What are the benefits of different programs?" rather than "Does program A have more effect than program B or no program?" For example, the child's ability to monitor his own behavior improved most in discovery programs, that is, programs in which a child is permitted to take initiative with regard to starting and terminating an activity, selecting the direction of his own activities and making more decisions on his own than in other programs. Efficiency in "test-taking behavior" improved most in preacademic programs in which the child had more opportunity to practice responding to structured tasks and received more praise, approval and other benefits for such behavior than in other programs. Parental attitudes were studied not only with regard to their being more or less positive toward their own children but whether the content of these attitudes changed in the direction of the educational program in which the child participated. Thus, the Planned Variation study illustrates clearly a full regard for the complexity of impact research on educational programs of young children just as the Westinghouse report (Cicirelli et al., 1969) illustrated the opposite extreme, namely, an oversimplified approach to impact research.

AN ANALYSIS OF
THE TEACHING PROCESS

The discussion so far has dealt with organized programs in early education and their effects on cognitive and socioemotional development. Although an attempt has been made to describe components of each program such as major goals, teacher role, technique of teaching, patterns of teacher-child interaction, and curriculum content, no attempt has been made to relate any one of these factors specifically to outcome variables such as changes in the cognitive and socioemotional functioning of children enrolled in different programs. The discussion will now turn toward a focus in this direction. Our major concern will be with patterns of teaching and their relationship to selected child variables. We may distinguish between a teacher's role, style and technique. The teacher's role may be defined as behavior which concerns the duties, responsibilities, and functions expected of the teacher (Katz, 1969). For example, in her maternal role the teacher concerns herself with the gratification of the child's needs and with the protection of the child from physical or emotional injury and harm. In her role as a socializer the teacher addresses herself to developing socially acceptable conduct and attitudes in a child. The instructional model of the teacher refers to the development of cognitive skills, strategies and interests in a child. Thus, it is clear in each _of these instances that the term "role" refers to an expected effect of the teacher's functioning on the child.

A distinction has been made between teacher style and technique of teaching (Beller, 1970). Technique of teaching refers to strategies and methods employed by a teacher to accomplish her objectives. For example, a teacher may use varying amounts of reward or punishment, praise or criticism, she may instruct large or small groups of children or concentrate on working with individual children, she may provide factual information or create opportunities for the child to discover such information on his own. She may use techniques of questioning, suggesting or active directing of children's activities. A teacher may use programmed instruction in which specific steps and alternatives are worked out in advance and in which the teacher functions essentially as a monitor of a prepared program. Alternately, the teacher may let the child select the content and determine the steps of progression in the acquisition of knowledge.

Style refers to belief systems, attitudes and other personality characteristics of teachers which are not planned components of her role functioning. Characteristics such as relaxed or tense, warm or cold, intimate or detached, sensitive or insensitive, outgoing and friendly or reserved and suspicious are often not subject to training over a short period of time. Techniques are more often associated with the implementation of skill-oriented and programmed instruction. The opposite approach, namely that of providing a responsive environment to child-initiated and -selected activities, requires much more complex interaction in which style variables such as spontaneity, receptivity and others mentioned above play an increasingly important role as part of the teaching process.

The relative emphasis and importance of technique and style may vary from one program to the next. However, all programs require more or less specified variations of each. While the sponsor of the program determines to a certain extent which aspects of teacher functioning are to be emphasized, other factors may effect variations in patterns of teaching. Two major factors which shall be singled out here for discussion are the environment of an educational program and staff variables. Examples of environmental determinants are size, location, activity, setting, and social climate of the program. Examples of staff variables are training, personality, and role concepts.

The Teaching Environment

Prescott et al. (1967) reported that teachers of medium-sized centers more often used encouragement as a technique, emphasized pleasure, creativity and interaction with other children, and manifested a low frequency of restrictive rules of social living and control of children. Teachers in large centers were found to make more frequent use of control and restraint and of direct guidance to emphasize rules of social living; they also tended to be adult- rather than child-centered. Teachers in adult-oriented centers which focused on transmitting the social values of their culture exhibited more restrictive discipline than teachers in other centers. A major difference between large and small centers involved the effective relationship between adults and children. Large centers were found to leave the staff less free for warm and accepting relationships with children. Staff members in small centers, by contrast, related more closely and intimately with the children.

The program and activity setting have been found to be important determinants of teacher behavior. For example, parts of the program dealing with essential routine activities evoked greater amounts of direction and restriction as well as more concern with control and rules of social living. In contrast to highly organized group activities, free choice settings and free play evoked the highest incidence of encouragement.

Teacher Variables

Training, personality and role concept have been found to be important determinants of teacher functioning. Prescott et al. (1967) found that teachers with little or no training used restriction more often than indirect guidance. Certified teachers who had a great deal of training showed most concern with the child's getting along with his peers and being considerate of the rights and feelings of others. These teachers were less concerned with control and restraint. As the teachers' amount of training increased, their attitudes toward authority became less arbitrary and their attitudes of warmth increased.

Teachers' role concepts have been found to be related to various aspects of their behavior. Prescott et al. (1967) reported that adult-centered teachers who aspired to teach children ways of behavior which were valued by adults have higher expectations for mastery of cognitive skills than child-centered teachers. These teachers also more frequently used their authority arbitrarily, exhibited low warmth, and used more restrictive discipline. Similarly, teachers concerned with rules of social living and with control were found to be irritable and unfriendly. Teachers who were child-centered used encouragement frequently and restriction infrequently, and emphasized pleasure and creativity in their activities with children.

Two major studies have dealt with relationships among teacher personality, belief systems and preschool atmosphere. Harvey, White, Prather, Alter, and Hoffmeister (1966) investigated the hypothesis that concrete teachers, when compared to abstract teachers, would be found to impose more structure and predetermined goals on children, would be less tolerant of student deviation and would react more strongly and invariantly to such deviations. These investigators selected 30 female teachers in a Head Start training program from a pool of 186 and separated them into three groups of 10 teachers according to scores received on a test which measured concreteness and abstractness of belief systems. The teachers were also given a conceptual systems test as an additional measure of the concreteness and abstractness of their ideas. On the basis of test results highly concrete teachers were characterized as expressing high absolutism, high frequency of platitudes and normative statements, high ethnocentrism, high religiosity, assertion of superiority of American morality and expression of highly positive attitudes towards institutional reference. These teachers also tended to believe more in divine fate control and had a low tolerance of complexity and uncertainty. Teachers grouped at the highest level of abstractness gave responses that indicated a high degree of novelty and appropriateness, independence without negativism, high relativism and contingency of thought, and the general usage of multidimensional rather than unidimensional interpretive categories. These teachers showed a high tolerance of complexity and uncertainty and tended not to believe in divine fate control or religious fundamentalism. Each teacher was observed for approximately two and a half hours by two trained observers and on two occasions one week apart. The teachers were rated on 26 behavioral dimensions by the observers. The dimensions were selected to reflect differences in the extent to which teachers fostered independence, creativity, diversity of interest, enjoyment and intrinsic motives among students. Each dimension was rated on a six-point forced-choice scale. A Tryon cluster analysis cohered the data into two major clusters, dictatorialness and task orientation. The data supported the hypothesis since concrete teachers were found to be significantly more dictatorial and less task-oriented than the more abstract teachers. The more abstract teachers were warmer, more perceptive of children's needs, more flexible in meeting needs, maintained more relaxed relationships with the children, encouraged greater responsibility, free expression of feelings and creativity, were less rule-oriented, invoked unexplained rules less often and were less punitive than the more concrete teachers. These findings would not have been predicted on the basis of amount of teaching experience since the more concrete teachers had greater teaching experience than the more abstract teachers.

In a second study Prather (1969) compared teachers who were identified as being abstract with teachers who were identified as having concrete belief systems. The teachers were divided into being more abstract or concrete. Classrooms were rated on a series of dimensions such as warmth toward children, degree of perceptiveness of the children's wishes, and flexibility in meeting the interests and needs of the children. A classroom analysis of these dimensions yielded three teacher factors: resourcefulness, dictatorialness and punitiveness. Comparisons of teachers on the three factors revealed that abstract teachers were more resourceful, less dictatorial and less punitive than concrete teachers. Although quantitative details were not available in the report of this study, they are included here because reported findings appear to replicate very closely the more fully reported study by Harvey et al. (1966).

A more recent study (Tuckman, Forman, & Hay, 1971) interrelated both environmental and personality factors in their combined effect on teacher innovativeness. These investigators attempted to apply Kurt Lewin's formula $(B = FPE)$ (1935) to demonstrate that it more clearly explains behavior than either the personality of the teacher or the environmental setting of the program. The major hypothesis of the study was that in open climates abstract teachers would be more innovative than concrete teachers, whereas the reverse would hold true for closed climates. Teacher innovativeness was defined by whether a teacher received a mini grant for an innovative proposal through the New Jersey Teachers Innovation Program. Level of abstractness of teachers was measured by a set of scales of the Interpersonal Topical Inventory, and openness was measured by teacher ratings on an Organizational Climate Descriptive Questionnaire. The sample included 304 teachers who had submitted proposals for innovation grants over a two-year period. Of these, 50 percent had received grants.

The outcome of the study was as follows. Teachers receiving grants and teachers not receiving grants did not differ significantly on the following control variables: sex, age, level of education, class size, years in the school building and years in teaching. Innovative teachers were more abstract than noninnovative teachers in open climates while the obverse was found in closed climates. In other words, abstractness of teacher and perceived openness of climate may be considered conjointly to predict teacher innovativeness.

The studies just reviewed give continuous support to the notion that an evaluation of teacher functioning must include not only the techniques the teacher employs but also her personality and the teaching situation in which she functions. The discussion will now turn to an examination of the research of the effect of teaching techniques and strategies on the socioemotional functioning of young children.

TEACHING TECHNIQUES

Effects on Socioemotional Functioning

A review of the literature makes it evident that very little investigation of relationships between techniques of teaching and socioemotional functioning in preschool children has been performed over the last three decades. The fruitful period from 1930 to 1945, during which major experimental work and systematic research in this area was carried out, is badly in need of continuation and follow-up. For example, Jack (1934) and Page (1936) found that nonparticipating children could be helped to become ascendant through training. Keister (1937) showed that children with initially very immature and undesirable responses to failure could be trained to respond in more mature and effective ways. Chittenden (1942) demonstrated successful training procedures to increase cooperative behavior in dominating children. Thompson (1944) constructed two types of educational programs for preschool children to study their effect on social and emotional development. In curriculum A the teacher was instructed to develop particularly warm relationships with each child, and to help the children develop their self-initiated activities by giving them information and help whenever the teacher felt that such information would be to the child's advantage. Teachers in curriculum B were instructed not to emphasize the development of warm friendship with particular children, and to confine their participation in the children's play experiences to responding to the children's requests for help and information. Thompson found that children in group A were more constructive when faced with possible failure, more ascendant, showed more participation, more leadership and less destructive behavior than children in group B.

Appel (1942) investigated techniques for controlling aggression in nursery-school children ages two to four. Nonpunitive methods of controlling aggression such as diversion, separating children and interpreting the wishes and feelings of one child to another were most effective. In contrast, arbitrary decisions and punitive methods such as disapproval and moralizing were ineffective. Purely rational methods such as having three- and four-year-olds "talk it over" were also ineffective. Kounin and Gump (1961), who investigated the comparative influences of punitive and nonpunitive techniques upon children, found support for the hypothesis that punitive techniques would create or activate more aggression and tension than nonpunitive techniques. These investigators also found that children who were exposed to punitive techniques would be more unsettled and conflicted about the meaning of misconduct than children of teachers who used nonpunitive techniques of discipline. In a more recent study, Kounin (1970) investigated the effects of the three types of teaching techniques on behavior disruption. He found that clarity resulted in increased conformity, firmness was associated with better behavior on the part of the children, and roughness led to an increase of disruptive behavior. Prescott et al. (1967) report that teachers who employed strict discipline received more negative responses from the children than teachers who employed encouragement as their main technique. The negative effects of teachers' punitive techniques are further supported by Katz (1968), who found that teachers who made demands and structured children's activities without being supportive and generous with rewards seemed to result in an increase of behaviors which were likely to interfere with later school adjustment.

Two studies have been carried out recently in which relationships between teacher variables and activity levels of children were investigated. Prather (1969), whose study was discussed earlier, found that a student's activity level as well as involvement in classroom activities were positively correlated with a teacher's abstract belief system and a teacher's resourcefulness, and negatively correlated with the teacher's dictatorialness and punitiveness. Children's cooperation, helpfulness and level of achievement correlated in the same direction with these teacher variables but less consistently than activity levels. Schoukert and Kouchton (1968) focused their study on relationships between techniques of teaching and low levels of activity or fatigue in children attending day-care centers. The study was carried out with 19 preschool children, two to six years of age, attending a special day-care program operated by the University of Tennessee. A special program was instituted in which two different situations were scheduled on alternate days and made to differ along the same lines as the programs constructed by Thompson described above. In one situation the teacher was instructed to help the child in his relations with other children and in his use of play materials to the extent demanded by the child's social and emotional needs. In the other situation the teacher was instructed to confine her interaction with children to responses to requests from children and to routine activities. Children were divided into older and younger groups for purposes

of this study. Data of the children's reaction were obtained during two-hour observations. The authors found that young girls showed significantly more fatigue under conditions of nonguided teacher participation. Under the same conditions the other children showed a nonsignificant but strong trend in the same direction.

Although the two investigators defined their teacher variables and the child variables differently, there appears to be a good deal of similarity between the last two studies. Both investigators found that teaching characteristics such as encouragement, helpfulness and sensitivity to needs of individual children were associated with increased activity levels of children. The similar relationship reported by the two studies is of particular interest since they employed different procedures, i.e., one used an experimental teaching program and direct observation with mostly prekindergarten children, while the other used observational ratings in existing kindergarten and first-grade classrooms. These differences between the two studies make the common finding more salient.

Effects on Cognitive Functioning

A component of the teaching process which has received a great deal of attention during the last decade has been verbal communication. Two main reasons can be singled out for the increased interest in researching this area of teaching. First, the fields of linguistics and language development have experienced accelerated growth during this period and have stimulated educational research in this area. A second reason has been a trend to consider defective and impoverished language development a central factor in the failure of lower-class disadvantaged children to benefit from educational instruction in elementary and secondary school.

The work of Basil Bernstein (1961) has aroused a great deal of interest in the role of verbal communication as an important component of the teaching process, particularly in the education of disadvantaged children. Bernstein distinguished between two types of verbal communication which characterize middle- and lower-class language styles: restricted and elaborated verbal codes. Restricted language is condensed and interferes with conceptualization because it lacks specificity and exactness. The condensed language used by lower-class children is not conducive to articulated and differentiated conceptualization. Elaborated codes, which are more common in communication of middle-class children, permit the expression of a wider and more complex range of thought and facilitate articulation of both cognitive and affective content. Hess and Shipman (1965) were among the first to apply Bernstein's formulation to the educational process. They suggested that a restricted verbal code of communication in lower-class mother-child interactions is symptomatic of a parental control system which restricts the number and kinds of alternatives for action and thought left open to the child. A restricted verbal code and a constrictive control associated with it result in a passive, compliant reaction to challenge and a tendency to reach solutions impulsively and hastily. Conversely, an elaborate verbal code and open communication between parent and child foster the development of assertive and initiatory approaches to learning and a tendency to reflect and compare alternatives.

Hess and Shipman subjected their formulations to an empirical test by studying the prevalence of restricted and elaborate language communication in middle-class and lower-class mother-child pairs. One hundred and sixty-three mothers and their four-year-old children were the subjects in the study. The mothers were taught three simple tasks and then asked to teach these tasks to their children. The results of the study showed that middle-class mothers used significantly more elaborate verbal codes while lower-class mothers used significantly more restricted codes in teaching

these tasks to their children. Correspondingly, lower-class children were less successful in problem-solving and used more primitive, less differentiated categories to classify stimuli.

Brophy (1970) reanalyzed the data from the Hess and Shipman study to investigate differences in the preresponse instructions compared to postresponse feedback by the mothers in the teaching situation. He found that the major difference between middle- and lower-class mothers consisted in preresponse instructions; the middle-class mothers spent more time than the lower-class mothers on the initial orientation to the task and on helping the child focus his attention on the relevant aspects of the learning task. In contrast, lower-class mothers spent less time on preparing the child and more time on corrective feedback after the child had started responding to the initial instructions. By shifting the emphasis from reinforcement to structuring the learning situation, Brophy extended the implications of the distinction between different communications styles for the teaching process.

The role of elaborated language styles in the teaching process was investigated further by Gahagan and Gahagan (1968) and Smothergill et al. (1969). Gahagan and Gahagan attempted to apply Bernstein's theory of restricted and elaborated codes in language communication between adults and children in lower-class and middle-class families. The authors constructed four kinds of situations to modify language functioning in lower-class deprived children. The situations were built around conditions requiring explanation, fine distinction, making hypotheses, qualifications, descriptions, and the verbalization of feelings and intents.

As conditions requiring explanation, the author used situations in which children worked in pairs, separated by small screens, with one child having to instruct the other in how to assemble and arrange materials by verbal means alone. A second type of situation was one in which a teacher worked with a small group of children and helped them to explain and demonstrate to the class how to do things, how things worked, and why things happen.

Situations requiring descriptions were made up of guessing games in which children had to differentiate objects from each other in terms of such properties as color, shape, weight, size and texture. Situations requiring hypotheses utilized picture stories and drama. Children would take turns describing aloud one of the pictures until the turn came for one of the children to narrate the whole story, which was made up of all the individual pictures. For the drama situations, the children were given a theme and asked to organize a play around it. For situations requiring verbalization of feeling and intent, pictures were presented in which action was portrayed which did not make sense unless the intentions and feelings of the characters were verbalized. A technique used to improve the children's listening and remembering was to have the teacher tell a story in which the visual messages conflicted with the verbal messages and therefore required that the children ignore the visual messages in order to comprehend what the teacher was saying.

A major interest of the investigators was to determine whether the experimental techniques would result in an ability to generate a larger variety of verbs than in the control condition. To test this difference children were supplied with nouns and asked to make up sentences. A related prediction was that children who could generate a greater variety of verbs would reach criteria on a paired associate learning task more quickly than children who were more restricted in their ability to generate verbs.

The study included three groups of 18 children who were five years old at the onset of training. The program lasted for two years or four school semesters. The experimental group included nine boys and nine girls divided into three subgroups on the basis of pretest scores on the English

Picture Vocabulary Test. There were two control groups of equal size matched with the experimental group both on sex and English Picture Vocabulary Test scores. The experimental group received 20 minutes of special instruction daily. The first control group received an unrelated intervention program. The second control group received no intervention other than going to school.

The investigators found that children who received the experimental language training generated significantly more verbs than did the two control groups which did not differ significantly from each other. An important additional finding was that the major effect of training occurred with children who had the lowest vocabulary scores at the outset of the study. The latter applied both to the criterion of generating a larger variety of verbs and learning the paired associate task faster than control children.

Smothergill et al. (1969) also investigated effects of elaborate and nonelaborate verbal communications between teachers and children. Nonelaborate (directive) statements were those involving a minimum of information necessary for the teacher to direct the action or behavior of the child. Elaborate statements were those which conveyed more information than was essential for completing tasks, gave reasons for the request, and provided labels and descriptions. The teacher requested verbal feedback from the child and gave supportive statements to reward the child for responding verbally to the teacher.

The study was carried out with 24 white children from a local day-care center for children whose mothers were on welfare. The ages of the children ranged from 3.5 to 5.25 years. Each child was pretested, matched with another on the basis of his total score, and then put in the opposite group than his pair. The children were taught for 17 days, during which the teachers conducted four 20-minute sessions each day, two elaborate and two nonelaborate, with six children in each session. The same two teachers taught all sessions, modifying their styles according to the group they were instructing. During the sessions the experimenter made extensive recordings both through the use of microphones and observers. Investigators found that their elaborative method produced more elaborative statements on a posttest in the group receiving the elaborative language training. The authors also found that children trained with the elaborative method were significantly better on verbal problem-solving tasks on which they had received no training.

More supportive evidence for the importance of verbal communication as a component of teaching and its consequence for cognitive functioning in children has been forthcoming from studies which investigated teacher behaviors in ongoing educational programs for preschool children. Soar (1970, 1971) found that drill correlated negatively and effective personal communication positively with pupil gain scores on six abstract language measures. Eisenberg et al. (1966) studied the effects of teacher behavior on the verbal intelligence of Head Start children by observing 38 Head Start teachers over a four-day period. Eisenberg found that teachers who rated high on communication produced significantly more positive changes in Peabody Picture Vocabulary scores.

Blank and Solomon (1968, 1969) developed a tutorial approach to language development in which the emphasis was on helping the child verbalize and rewarding him at every opportunity. The child was made to recognize that information needed for understanding situations was not immediately evident but had to be sought from his previous experience. The use of language was further maximized by omitting gestures in the communication between adult and child. The program concentrated on developing specific areas of language functioning such as selective attention, imagery of future events, sustained sequential thinking, awareness of possessing language and the ability to categorize. To increase selective attention, an attempt was made to help the child respond to relevant characteristics of an array of stimuli rather than to the most obvious one, which may not have been the relevant one. To give the child the opportunity to develop the capacity for imagery of future events, he was asked to describe an object in a certain location, e.g., a block on the table, and then asked, "Where would the block be if it fell from the table?" To facilitate greater utilization of inner verbalization, a child might be asked to look at an object and say the name of the object to himself without speaking out loud, and, after the object was removed, tell the name to the teacher. Children were trained to sustain sequential thinking, which is necessary for the child to understand words and events in their complex context. To be able to perceive objects and words as located within their appropriate context, an attempt was made to teach the child to maintain concentration and to determine various courses of action. Finally, the authors emphasized that concepts were not taught as ends in themselves. Concepts were taught as necessary tools for thinking and for that reason simple labeling activities were avoided. The preferred approach was to select concepts which were suitable for stressing the more abstract functions of language, for instance number, speed, direction and emotion.

The program was carried out in a day-care setting with two experimental groups and two control groups matched on sex, age and Stanford-Binet pretest scores. One experimental group of six children was tutored five days a week, another experimental group of six children was tutored three days a week. One control group of seven children remained in the regular nursery program without any additional language training. A second control group, consisting of three children, had daily individual sessions with the same teacher and was exposed to the same materials as the experimental group, with the major difference that the children were permitted to choose their own activities in which the teacher did not initiate or expand interchange in the ways in which it was done in experimental groups. At the end of four months' training the first experimental group showed a mean gain of 14 IQ points. The second experimental group, which received three tutoring periods per week, gained 7 points, while the two control groups did not exceed a gain of 2 IQ points. In the light of their varied and extensive training one would have expected the authors to have measured a wider range of specific effects of their program than change in IQ.

INTERACTING EFFECTS
IN THE TEACHING PROCESSES

The other study, carried out by the present writer (Beller, 1967), investigated interacting effects of teaching and pupil variables by matching methods of training with cognitive styles of children. Ninety-three four-year-old children attending Head Start classes were first classified into three cognitive style groups and then assigned to methods of language training which had been modified to match cognitive styles. On the basis of Sigel's cognitive styles test (Sigel, Jarman, & Hanesian, 1967), the children were divided into three groups: one with a part-whole or descriptive-analytic style, a second group with a contextual-relational or functional style, and a third group in which children had not developed sufficient language to verbalize the basis for their classifications. Children from each of these three groups were then assigned randomly to three treatment groups: 1) a group in which language training corresponded to the child's cognitive style; 2) a group in which language training did not correspond to the child's cognitive style; and 3) a control group in which children received as much attention as children in the experimental training group without receiving language instruction. Instruction was carried out by six different experimenters who held 15 20-minute training sessions with two children per session. Training consisted of labeling objects and associating objects and labels on the basis of a given cognitive style, e.g., for the descriptive-analytic method of training, a box and button go together because they are both brown, for the relational or functional method of training, a box and a button go together because the button can be put into the box. The effectiveness of language training was assessed by obtaining pretest measures on the Illinois Test of Psycholinguistic Abilities and on a Paired Associate Learning task which was specially constructed to assess specific effects of the language training procedures.

The major findings of the study were as follows: children with language training gained significantly more on the Illinois Test of Psycholinguistic Abilities than children who did not receive training. On one of the subtests, children performed most poorly after they had been trained with a method which did not correspond with their own cognitive style. Children with poor language ability, that is, those who could not yet verbalize their choices on the cognitive style test, benefited most from language training generally, and specifically, from the functional-relational method of training. The salience of these training effects was evident from the fact that the posttesting of the Illinois Test of Psycholinguistic Abilities was carried out seven months after the completion of the experimental training. With regard to the paired associate learning method, it was found that children with language training were superior to control children in reaching criterion on the learning task. Moreover, it was found that specific methods of training affected different memory processes. Children trained with the descriptive-analytic method received the higher scores when learning involved recognition memory, while children trained with the functional or contextual-relational method received the higher scores when learning involved associative memory. The effectiveness of matching cognitive style and method of language training was supported by a very consistent empirical trend. Groups with matched cognitive style and language training in all instances were superior to groups in which the method of language training corresponded to the child's cognitive style.

We shall now turn to a discussion of studies which investigated motivational and cognitive components of teaching and their role in relationships between teacher variables and pupil achievement. With regard to the motivational component, it was found that approval and disapproval have to be further broken down to discern with greater precision their effect on cognitive performance. While neither verbal nor nonverbal praise by itself (Harris et al., 1968; Harris & Serwer, 1966; Perkins, 1965; Soar, 1966; Spaulding, 1965) was found to relate to pupil achievement, specific expressions and elaborations of praise did prove to be effective. For example, Wallen (1966) found that brief verbal expressions, such as "Aha" and "Right," related positively to improved cognitive performance. Probably such expressions have more distinct cue value than nonverbal expressions and are both more specific and less interfering than more elaborate verbal statements. However, certain types of elaborations, such as restating and analyzing the response of the child or explaining what was good about the response, were found to make praise more effective (Fortune, 1967; Morrison, 1966; Perkins, 1965; Soar, 1966). Possibly the greater effectiveness of the latter type of praise is due to interactional effects of motivational components of praise and cognitive clarification of the response being praised. While disapproval or criticism has been found to have a negative effect on cognitive behavior and learning, it appears that the intensity of criticism is crucial for its effect. Only strong criticism has shown a consistently negative effect on achievement. No negative effects have been found for mild criticism, which has sometimes shown positive effects on cognitive perform-

ance. The same qualification appears to apply to the intensity of praise and positive valuation of the pupil's achievement. For example, Eisenberg (1966) reported a positive relationship of moderate encouragement and moderately valued self-confidence in children with the child's performance on the Peabody Picture Vocabulary Test. Finally, combinations of praise and criticism have yielded positive relationships with cognitive performance as the proportion of praise increased and exceeded criticism.

With regard to the cognitive component, investigators have found specific patterns of probing and intellectual exercise to be very effective. For example, one study found equal mixtures of convergent and divergent questions to be most successful (Thompson & Bowers, 1968); another study (Soar, 1966) found a higher ratio of inquiry as opposed to drill activity to be most effective. Rosenshine (1971) concludes from his extensive review that the most successful interactional strategy may involve a moderate amount of structuring initially by the teacher to elicit responses from children, then reinforcing children for their cognitive reactions, and finally encouraging children to further elaborate their reactions. It is this last formulation which addresses itself to a more complete segment of the adult-child interaction affecting the cognitive development of the child. The fruitfulness of such an approach can be illustrated by a study which attempted to encompass a more complete segment of the complex interrelationships between motivational and cognitive factors in the interactions between teachers and children in Head Start programs (Beller, 1969a).

A central question of that study was whether intellectual gain from the program related to teacher-child transactions interacts with dependent behavior of children. It was found that preschool children who gained in their intellectual performance from a Head Start program when compared to nongaining children made more realistic dependency requests of the teacher, received more positive reactions to their requests, made more constructive use of the help they received, and reacted more constructively when the teacher failed to respond to the child's request. (Moreover, boys who gained from Head Start received twice as much unsolicited attention from teachers as boys who did not gain when they engaged in autonomous activities.)

Several other studies have reported similar relationships between teacher behaviors and academic achievement of pupils. In 1949 deGroat and Thompson found that children who received high approval from teachers were more intelligent, high on academic achievement, and scored higher on personality adjustment tests. Hoehn (1954) reported that teachers had more favorable contacts with children of high economic status and of high academic achievement. In a more recent study of observational techniques in preschool classrooms, Wilensky (1968) found that teachers spent more time with brighter children.

Beller (1969a, 1969b) also investigated links between teacher behavior and a child's success in learning a problem-solving task under conditions of intrinsic reinforcement. It was found that both teaching techniques and teaching styles affected the child's ability to learn the problem-solving task. Children who learned the problem-solving task best tended to come from teachers who used more diversified teaching techniques, a more flexible curriculum, more flexible arrangements of classroom space; they also made less distinction between work and play. Teacher style characteristics associated with success in problem-solving were greater closeness to the child, respect for the child's family, and an emphasis on consideration of the rights and idiosyncrasies of others. Finally, teachers who manifested respect for the child's family had more of the children who not only succeeded on the problem-solving task, but who gained in a variety of ways intellectually.

This work shows clearly the importance of a positive cycle in the teacher-child inter-

action. For the children who gained, the teacher responded positively not only to the child's dependency request but also to his uniqueness, his rights and his family. In turn, these children made more reasonable requests of the teacher, were more patient and reacted more constructively when the teacher could not meet their requests immediately. Clearly, emotional components and interpersonal attitudes play an important part in the impact of the teacher-child relationship on the cognitive development of the child. There is another important implication of these findings. The great similarity between certain behaviors of teachers and children who benefited most from the educational program suggests that a modeling process as well as reinforcement were at work in the situation. Both teacher and child were more accepting of each other, more sensitive to each other's needs, and more responsive to the autonomous needs of the other person. The child who succeeds in meeting the adult's expectation by growing intellectually, who waits patiently until the adult is ready to meet his request for help, who makes constructive use of the help he receives, and who copes constructively with the teacher's failure to help him or to pay attention to him evokes not only similar behavior on the part of the teacher but also reinforces the teacher to behave in a similar way. The subtle manner in which this benign cycle continues to function can be seen in the teacher's unsolicited and nonintrusive expression of interest in the child when he engages in solitary play or other autonomous activities. Supportive evidence for such an interpretation comes from a study by Battle (1957) which found that a high achiever and his teacher held more similar values than a low achiever and his teacher.

IN RETROSPECT

I have tried to present a multivaried approach to the study of teacher-child interactions. Such an approach leads to a preference for the question, "Who benefits from what?" or "How does a given technique of teaching affect child A differently from child B?" rather than "Does a given technique help?" or "Do children benefit from teaching technique A more than teaching technique B?" The issue can be illustrated by re-examining some findings on teacher behavior and their effects on learning in children, reported and interpreted by Sears and Dowley (1963) in their chapter "Research on Teaching in the Nursery School," to be found in the Gage *Handbook*. Sears and Dowley discussed the findings of several experimental studies to draw implications from research for the effect of variations of the teacher's warmth, nurturance and attentiveness on children attending nursery school. These laboratory studies very much fit what Stevenson (1963) has described as "short term studies of the effects of particular variables on child behaviors" (Stevenson, 1963, p. 2). Gewirtz and Baer (1958a, 1958b) and Hartup and Keller (1960) reported evidence from their experimental investigations that a condition variously referred to as nurturance withdrawal or social deprivation resulted in better performance on learning tasks in which the children received social reinforcement for the behaviors to be learned. A related finding was that attention seeking on the part of children is greater when adults are less available than when they are not available. Sears and Dowley (1963) interpreted these findings by stating that the strong positive effect of nurturance withdrawal on the learning of various tasks by children may be due to the child's interpretation of the withdrawal as a threat to the warm relationship and, hence, the motivation "to greater effort in an attempt to win back the rewarding warm interaction" (p. 828). These findings and their interpretation by Sears and Dowley led another writer (Burgess, 1965) to conclude that from her "basic nurturing relationship the teacher can and should indicate disapproval..." (p. 19).

The interpretations and conclusions from these early studies are reasonable against the backgrounds of the findings. However, very different conclusions are now indicated from more recent research in which the same questions and the same relationships have been re-examined in a more complex context. In a series of studies (Beller, Adler, Newcomer, & Young, 1972) the effects of nurturance and nurturance withdrawal before and during the learning period (social versus intrinsic reinforcement) on the child's learning were investigated when the task to be learned and the level of relevant motivation of the child were systematically varied. A major finding in these new studies was that the generalizations based on the earlier studies have to be limited to the learning of easy or noncognitive tasks such as marble dropping. When the task to be learned is more difficult and requires the type of learning challenge that a child encounters in school, more complex relationships are found. Nurturance withdrawal in the prelearning situation has opposite effects on the effectiveness of social reinforcement during learning in low and high dependent children. Low dependent children improve, whereas high dependent children tend to perform worse than they do when learning under conditions of social reinforcement is preceded by an experience of nurturance from an adult. In our latest study we discovered an additional link in these relationships by varying type of reinforcement in addition to type of task, nurturance deprivation and dependency motivation of children. We found that neither nurturance deprivation nor type of reinforcement were the decisive factors for the learning of difficult tasks by high dependent children. Each of these conditions was superseded by a third condition, namely, the consistency of the adult from the prelearning to the learning situation. It did not matter whether the adult was nurturant or detached as long as she was consistent. Moreover, these relationships did not hold for low dependent children, and not for simple learning tasks. Thus, the earlier generalizations concerning the effects of nurturance withdrawal on learning were oversimplified and incomplete without much qualification for the usual everyday teaching and learning situation in a nursery. The new evidence points to a more complex yet more meaningful relationship between teacher and child variables because it takes into account not only *how,* but also *what* and *who* is being taught. In short, the new relationship is more specific.

REFERENCES

Adkins, D. C., and others. Preliminary evaluation of a language curriculum for preschool children. Final report No. OEO-4219. Honolulu: University of Hawaii, Educational Research and Development Center, 1967. ED 021 618.

Appel, M. H. Aggressive behavior of nursery school children and adult procedures in dealing with such behavior. *Journal of Experimental Education,* 1942, 11, 185–199.

Banta, T. J. Is there really a Montessori method? Paper presented at the joint meeting of the Ohio Psychological and Ohio Psychiatric Associations, February 1966.

Battle, H. J. Relation between personal values and scholastic achievement. *Journal of Experimental Education,* 1957, 26, 38–41.

Beller, E. K. Methods of language training and cognitive styles in lower class children. Paper presented at the meeting of the American Educational Research Association, New York, February 1967.

Beller, E. K. The evaluation of effects of early educational intervention on intellectual and social development of lower-class disadvantaged children. In E. Grotberg (Ed.), *Critical issues related to disadvantaged children.* Princeton, N.J.: Educational Testing Service, 1969. (a)

Beller, E. K. Teaching styles and their effects on problem-solving behavior in Headstart programs. In E. Grotberg (Ed.), *Critical issues in research related to disadvantaged children.* Princeton, N.J.: Educational Testing Service, 1969. (b)

Beller, E. K. Adult-child interaction and personalized day care. In E. Grotberg (Ed.), *Day care: Resources for decisions.* Washington, D.C.: Office of Economic Opportunity, 1970. Pp. 229–264.

Beller, E. K. Teacher evaluation: Why, what, and how. *Peabody Journal of Education,* 1971, 48, 125–139.

Beller, E. K. Impact of early education on disadvantaged children. In S. Ryan (Ed.), *A report on longitudinal evaluation of preschool programs.* Washington, D.C.: Department of Health, Education and Welfare, Office of Child Development, 1972, in press.

Beller, E. K., Adler, P., Newcomer, A., & Young, A. Motivation reinforcement, and problem solving in children. In A. Pick (Ed.), *Minnesota symposium on child psychology.* Minneapolis: University of Minnesota Press, 1972, in press.

Beller, E. K., & Kurtz, M. The effect of two nursery environments on the development of conservation. Unpublished manuscript, Temple University, 1970.

Beller, E. K., Zimmie, J., & Aiken, L. Levels of play in different nursery settings. Paper presented at the meeting of the International Congress for Applied Psychology, Liege, Belgium, July 1971.

Bereiter, C., & Engelmann, S. *Teaching disadvantaged children in the preschool.* Englewood Cliffs, N.J.: Prentice-Hall, 1966.

Bernstein, B. Social class and linguistic development: A theory of social learning. In A. H. Halsey, J. Floud, & C. A. Anderson (Eds.), *Education, economy, and society.* New York: Free Press, 1961. Pp. 288-314.

Bissell, J. S. *Implementation of planned variation in Head Start.* Washington, D.C.: U.S. Department of Health, Education and Welfare, Office of Child Development, 1971.

Bittner, M. L., Rockwell, R. E., & Matthews, C. V. An evaluation of the preschool readiness centers program in East St. Louis, Illinois, July 1, 1967–June 30, 1968. Final report. East St. Louis, Ill.: Southern Illinois University, 1968. ED 023 472.

Blank, M., & Solomon, F. A tutorial language program to develop abstract thinking in socially disadvantaged preschool children. *Child Development,* 1968, 39, 379–389.

Blank, M., & Solomon, F. How shall the disadvantaged child be taught? *Child Development,* 1969, 49, 47–61.

Brophy, J. E. Mothers as teachers of their own preschool children: The influence of socioeconomic status and task structure on teaching specificity. *Child Development,* 1970, 41, 79–94.

Brown, M., & Precious, N. *The integrated day in the primary school.* London: Ward Lock, 1968.

Burgess, E. *Values in early childhood education.* Washington, D.C.: Department of Elementary-Kindergarten-Nursery Education of the National Education Association, 1965.

Caldwell, B. Impact of interest in early cognitive stimulation. Paper presented at the meeting of the National Association for the Education of Young Children, Boston, November 1970.

Caldwell, B., Moselle, C., & Honig, A. S. The implicit parental learning theory. Unpublished manuscript, University of Syracuse, 1968.

Caldwell, B., & Richmond, J. B. Programmed day care for the very young child—A preliminary report. *Journal of Marriage and the Family,* 1964, 26, 481–488.

Chittenden, G. E. An experimental study in measuring and modifying assertive behavior in young children. *Monographs on the Society for Research in Child Development,* 1942, 7 (1).

Cicirelli, B., et al. The impact of Head Start: An evaluation of the effects of Head Start on children's cognitive and affective development. Washington, D.C.: Office of Economic Opportunity, 1969.

Classen, R. E., Spear, J. E., & Tomaro, M. P. A comparison of the relative effectiveness of two types of preschool compensatory programming. *Journal of Educational Research,* 1969, 62, 401–405.

deGroat, A. F., & Thompson, G. G. A study of the distribution of teacher approval and disapproval among sixth-grade pupils. *Journal of Experimental Education,* 1949, 18, 57–75.

Di Lorenzo, L. T. Effects of year-long prekindergarten programs on intelligence and language of educationally disadvantaged children. *Journal of Experimental Education,* 1968, 36(3), 36–42.

Dreyer, A. S., & Rigler, D. Cognitive performance in Montessori and nursery school children. *Journal of Educational Research,* 1969, 62, 411–416.

Eisenberg, L., et al. Bibliography of papers covering work under OEO Contract No.

510. Final report. [Title supplied] Baltimore: Johns Hopkins University, 1966. ED 020 773.

Forrester, B. J., Harge, B. M., Outlaw, D. M., Brooks, G. P., & Boismeier, J. D. *The intervention study with mothers and infants.* Nashville: Peabody Demonstration and Research Center in Early Education, 1971.

Fortune, J. C. A study of the generality of presenting behaviors in teaching preschool children. Memphis, Tenn.: Memphis State University, 1967. ED 016 285.

Gahagan, G. A., & Gahagan, D. M. Paired-associate learning as partial validation of a language development program. *Child Development,* 1968, 39, 1119–1131.

Gardner, D. E. M. *Experiment and tradition in primary schools.* London: Methuen, 1966.

Gewirtz, J. L., & Baer, D. M. Deprivation and satiation of social reinforcers as drive conditions. *Journal of Abnormal and Social Psychology,* 1958, 57, 165–172. (a)

Gewirtz, J. L., & Baer, D. M. The effect of brief social deprivation on behaviors for a social reinforcer. *Journal of Abnormal and Social Psychology,* 1958, 56, 49–56. (b)

Goldfarb, W. Effects of psychological deprivation in infancy and subsequent stimulation. *American Journal of Psychiatry,* 1945, 102, 18–33.

Gordon, I. J. *Early childhood stimulation through parent education.* Final report to the Children's Bureau, Social and Rehabilitation Service, Department of Health, Education, and Welfare. Gainesville, Fla.: University of Florida, Institute for Development of Human Resources, 1969. ED 038 166.

Gordon, I. Infant intervention project: Progress report. 1972.

Gray, S., & Klaus, R. A. The early training project: A seventh-year report. *Child Development,* 1970, 41, 909–924.

Harris, A. J., Morrison, C., Serwer, B. L., & Gold, L. A continuation of the Craft Project comparing reading approaches with disadvantaged urban Negro children in primary grades. New York: Division of Teacher Education of the City University of New York, U.S. Office of Education, Project No. 5-0570-2-12-1, 1968. ED 020 297.

Harris, A. J., & Serwer, B. L. *Comparison of reading approaches in first-grade teaching with disadvantaged children (the Craft Project).* New York: City University of

New York Research Foundation, 1966. ED 010 037.

Hartup, W. W., & Keller, E. D. Nurturance in preschool children and its relation to dependency. *Child Development,* 1960, 31, 681–689.

Harvey, O. J., White, B. J., Prather, M. S., Alter, R. D., & Hoffmeister, J. K. Teachers' belief systems and preschool atmospheres. *Journal of Educational Psychology,* 1966, 57, 373–381.

Henry, N. B. (Ed.) *Development in and through reading.* Sixtieth Yearbook of the National Society for the Study of Education, Part I. Chicago: NSSE, 1961.

Herman, S. J. *The relationship between maternal variable scores and infant performance in a Negro experimental stimulation training population.* (Doctoral dissertation, University of Florida) Ann Arbor, Mich.: University Microfilms, 1971. No. 71-16, 791.

Hess, R. D., & Shipman, V. C. Early experience and the socialization of cognitive modes in children. *Child Development,* 1965, 36, 869–886.

Hodges, W. L., McCandless, B. R., & Spicker, H. H. The development and evaluation of a diagnostically based curriculum for preschool psycho-socially deprived children. Final report, Grant No. OEG-32-24-0210-1011, U.S. Office of Education. Bloomington, Ind.: Indiana University Press, 1967. ED 021 948.

Hoehn, A. J. A study of social status differentiation in the classroom behavior of nineteen third grade teachers. *Journal of Social Psychology,* 1954, 39, 269–292.

Holmes, M., & Holmes, D. Evaluation of two associated YM-YWHA Head Start Programs. In E. Grotberg (Ed.), *Review of research 1965 to 1969.* Washington, D.C.: Project Head Start (OEO), 1969. ED 014 318.

Honig, A. S., & Brill, S. A comparative analysis of the Piagetian development of twelve month old disadvantaged infants in an enrichment center with others not in such a center. Paper presented at the meeting of the American Psychological Association, Miami, 1970.

Hubbard, J. An exploratory study of oral language development among culturally different children, 1967. ED 000 828.

Hyman, I. A., & Kliman, D. S. First grade readiness of children who have had summer Head Start programs. *The Training School Bulletin,* 1967, 63, 163–167.

Irwin, O. Language and communication. In P. H. Mussen (Ed.), *Handbook of research methods in child development.* New York: John Wiley, 1960. Pp. 487–516.

Jack, L. M. An experimental study of ascendant behavior in preschool children. *University of Iowa Studies in Child Welfare,* 1934, 9, 7–65.

Karnes, M. B. Investigations of classroom and at-home interventions: Research and development program on preschool disadvantaged children. Final report, Bureau No. 5-1181, Bureau of Research, Office of Education, U.S. Department of Health, Education, and Welfare, 1969. ED 036 663.

Karnes, M. B., Teska, J. A., Hodgins, A. S., & Badger, E. D. Educational intervention at home by mothers of disadvantaged infants. *Child Development,* 1970, 41, 925–935.

Katz, L. G. *A study of the changes in behavior of children enrolled in two types of Head Start classes.* (Doctoral dissertation, Stanford University) Ann Arbor, Mich.: University Microfilms, 1968. No. 68-15, 064.

Katz, L. G. *Teaching in preschools; roles and goals.* ERIC Clearinghouse on Early Childhood Education, Contract No. OEC-3-7-70706-3118. Urbana, Ill.: National Laboratory on Early Childhood Education, 1969. ED 032 942.

Keister, M. E. The behavior of young children in failure. *University of Iowa Studies in Child Welfare, Studies in Preschool Education,* Vol. 1, 1937, 14, 27–82.

Keister, M. E. *The good life for infants and toddlers.* Washington, D. C.: National Association for the Education of Young Children, 1970.

Kessen, W. *The child.* New York: John Wiley, 1965.

Kohlberg, L. Early education; A cognitive-developmental view. *Child Development,* 1968, 39, 1013–1062. (a)

Kohlberg, L. Montessori with the culturally disadvantaged: A cognitive developmental interpretation and some research findings. In R. Hess, & R. M. Bear (Eds.), *Early education current theory, research and action.* Chicago: Aldine, 1968. Pp. 105–118. (b)

Kounin, J. S. *Discipline and group management in classrooms.* New York: Holt, Rinehart & Winston, 1970.

Kounin, J. S., & Gump, P. V. The comparative influences of punitive and nonpunitive teachers upon children's concepts of school misconduct. *Journal of Educational Psychology,* 1961, 52, 44–49.

Lally, J. R. Development of a day care center for young children. Progress Report P.R.–156 (C6). Office of Child Development. Syracuse, N.Y.: University of Syracuse, 1971.

Levenstein, P. Cognitive growth in preschoolers through verbal interaction with mothers. *American Journal of Orthopsychiatry,* 1970, 40, 3–17.

Levenstein, P. Mothers as early cognitive trainers: Guiding low income mothers to work with their preschoolers. Paper presented at the meeting of the Society for Research in Child Development, Minneapolis, April 1971.

Levenstein, P., & Levenstein, S. Fostering learning potential in preschoolers. *Social Casework,* 1971, 52, 74–78.

Levenstein, P., & Sunley, R. M. Aiding cognitive growth in disadvantaged preschoolers: A progress report. Freeport, N. Y.: Mother-Child Home Program, Family Service Association of Nassau County, 1968.

Lewin, K. *Dynamic theory of personality.* New York: McGraw-Hill, 1935.

Miller, L. B., & Dyer, J. L. *Two kinds of kindergarten after four types of Head Start.* Louisville, Ky.: University of Louisville Press, 1970.

Miller, L. B., Dyer, J. L., et al. Experiment variation of Head Start curricula: A comparison of current approaches. Progress Report No. 5. Research Grant #CG 8199, Office of Economic Opportunity. Louisville, Ky.: University of Louisville, 1969–1970. (a)

Miller, L. B., Dyer, J. L., et al. Experimental variation of Head Start curricula: A comparison of current approaches. Progress Report No. 7. Research Grant #CG 8199, Office of Economic Opportunity. Louisville, Ky.: University of Louisville, 1970. (b)

Miller, L. B., Dyer, J. L., et al. Experimental variation of Head Start curricula: A comparison of current approaches. Progress Report No. 9. Research Grant #CG 8199, Office of Economic Opportunity. Louisville, Ky.: University of Louisville, 1971.

Morrison, B. M. The reactions of external and internal pupils to patterns of teaching behavior. (Doctoral dissertation, University of Michigan) Ann Arbor, Mich.: University Microfilms, 1966. No. 66-14,560.

Page, M. L. The modification of ascendant behavior in preschool children. *University of Iowa Studies in Child Welfare,* 1936, 12(3).

Painter, G. The effect of a structured tutorial program on the cognitive and language development of culturally disadvantaged infants. *Merrill-Palmer Quarterly,* 1969, 15, 279–294.

Palmer, F. H. Concept training curriculum for children aged two and three years old and eight months, Institute for Child Development and Experimental Education, the City University of New York, N.Y., N.Y., October, 1968.

Palmer, F. H. Children under three—finding ways to stimulate development: II. Some current experiments: Learning at two. *Children,* 1969, 16, 55–57.

Palmer, F. H. Minimal interaction at age two and three and subsequent intellectual changes. In R. K. Parker (Ed.), *The preschool in action.* Boston: Allyn & Bacon, 1972. Pp. 437–465.

Perkins, H. V. Classroom behavior and underachievement. *American Educational Research Journal,* 1965, 2, 1–12.

Prather, M. Project Head Start teacher-pupil-parent interaction study. In E. Grotberg (Ed.), *Review of research 1965 to 1969.* Washington, D.C.: Project Head Start (OEO), 1969.

Prescott, E. et al. Group day care as a child-rearing environment: An observational study of day care programs. Pasadena, Calif.: Pacific Oaks College, 1967. ED 024 453.

Rosenshine, B. Teaching behavior related to pupil achievement: A review of research. In I. Westbury, & A. A. Bellack (Eds.), *Research into classroom processes.* New York: Teachers College Press, 1971. Pp. 51–98.

Rusk, B. An evaluation of a six-week Head Start program using an academically oriented curriculum: Canton, 1967. Toronto: Ontario Institute for Studies in Education. April, 1968.

Schaefer, E. S. Home tutoring, maternal behavior and infant intellectual development. In: Cognitive stimulation in infancy. Symposium presented at the meeting of the American Psychological Association, Washington, D.C., September 1969.

Schaefer, E. S. Need for early and continuing education. In V. H. Denenberg (Ed.), *Education of the infant and young child.* New York: Academic Press, 1970. Pp. 61–82.

Schoukert, R., & Kouchton, R. An experimental method of relating variations in teacher participation to measures of child fatigue in preschool training programs. *Journal of Educational Research,* 1968, 62(3), 123–125.

Scott, G., & Lally, J. R. A comparison of the scores of trained and untrained environmentally deprived male and female infants on the Griffiths' Mental Development Scale. In I. Gordon (Ed.), *Reaching the child through parent education, the Florida approach.* Gainesville, Fla.: University of Florida, Institute for Development of Human Resources, 1969. Pp. 57–67.

Sears, P. S., & Dowley, E. M. Research on teaching in the nursery school. In N. L. Gage (Ed.), *Handbook of research on teaching.* Chicago: Rand McNally, 1963. Pp. 814–864.

Sigel, I. E., & McBane, B. The relationship between cognitive competence and level of symbolization among five-year-old children. In E. Grotberg (Ed.), *Review of research 1965 to 1969.* Washington, D.C.: Project Head Start (OEO), 1969.

Sigel, J. E., Jarman, P., & Hanesian, H. Styles of categorization and their perceptual, intellectual and personality correlates in young children. *Human Development,* 1967, 10, 1–17.

Smothergill, N. L., et al. The effects of manipulation of teacher communication style in the preschool. Paper presented at the meeting of the Society for Research in Child Development, Santa Monica, Calif., March 1969. ED 034 598.

Soar, R. S. An integrative approach to classroom learning. Final report. Public Health Service Grant No. 5-R11 MH 01096 and National Institute of Mental Health Grant No. 7-R11 MH 02045. Philadelphia: Temple University, 1966. ED 033 749.

Soar, R. S. Follow through model implementation. Interim report on Project No. OEG-O-8-522471-4618(100), U.S. Office of Education. Gainesville, Fla.: University of Florida, Institute for Development of Human Resources, College of Education, 1970.

Soar, R. S. Follow through classroom process measurement. Institute for Development of Human Resources, contract OEG-0-8-522471-4618(100) to University of Florida, OEG-0-8-522384-3991(286) to Florida Educational Research and Development Council. Gainesville, Fla.: University of Florida, June 1971.

Spaulding, R. L. *Achievement, creativity, and self-concept correlates of teacher-pupil transactions in elementary schools.* Cooperative Research Project No. 1322, U.S. Office of Education. Hempstead, N.Y.: Hofstra University, 1965.

Spitz, R. Anaclitic depression. *The psychoanalytic study of the child.* Vol. II. New York: International Universities Press, 1946. Pp. 313–342.

Steglich, W. G., & Cartwright, W. J., Report of the effectiveness of Project Head Start, Lubbock, Texas. Parts I, II, and Appendices. Lubbock, Texas: Texas Technological College, 1965. ED 019 131.

Stern, C., & Keislar, E. Comparative effectiveness of echoic and modeling procedures in language instruction with culturally disadvantaged children. Paper presented at the meeting of the American Psychological Association, San Francisco, August 1968. ED 025 314.

Stevenson, H. W. Introduction. In H. W. Stevenson (Ed.), *Child psychology.* The Sixty-second Yearbook of the National Society for the Study of Education, Part I. Chicago: NSSE, 1963. Pp. 1–3.

Thompson, G. E. The social and emotional development of preschool children under two types of educational programs. *Psychological Monographs,* 1944, 56 (5, Whole No. 258).

Thompson, G. R., & Bowers, N. C. Fourth grade achievement as related to creativity, intelligence, and teaching style. Paper presented at the meeting of the American Educational Research Association, Chicago, February 1968.

Tuckman, B. W., Forman, N., & Hay, W. K. Teacher innovativeness: A function of teacher personality and school environment. *Proceedings of the 79th APA Annual Convention.* Washington, D.C.: American Psychological Association, 1971. Pp. 527–528.

Wallen, N. E. Relationships between teacher characteristics and student behavior—Part III. Cooperative Research Project No. 2628, Contract OEC-SAE-5-10-181, U.S. Office of Education. Salt Lake City: University of Utah Press, 1966. ED 010 390.

Weikart, D. P. Preschool progress preliminary finding. Adaptation for paper presentation at the University of Kansas Symposium on the Education of Culturally Disadvantaged Children, May 5–6, 1966.

Weikart, D. P. Early childhood special education for intellectually subnormal culturally different children. Paper prepared for the National Leadership Institute in Early Childhood Development, Washington, D.C., October 1971. (a)

Weikart, D. P. Organizational scheme for preschool curriculum models. Ypsilanti, Mich.: High/Scope Educational Research Foundation, 1971. (b)

Weikart, D. P. Relationship of curriculum, teaching, and learning in preschool education. Paper presented at the Hyman Blumberg Memorial Symposium on Research in Early Childhood Education, Baltimore, February 1971. (c)

Weikart, D. P., Deloria, D. J., Lawson, S. A., & Wiegerink, R. Longitudinal results of the Ypsilanti Perry Preschool Project. Final report. Ypsilanti, Mich.: High/Scope Educational Research Foundation, 1970. ED 044 536.

Wilensky, H. Observational techniques in preschool classrooms. Institute for Developmental Studies, School of Education, New York University. In ERIC Bibliography No. 3. Urbana, Ill.: University of Illinois, 1968. Pp. 15–23.

CHAPTER 19 Research and the Urban School: Implications for Educational Improvement[1]

ROBERT L. GREEN
Michigan State University

RITA F. BAKAN
Vancouver, B.C., Department of Health

JOSEPH H. McMILLAN
Michigan State University

LAWRENCE W. LEZOTTE
Michigan State University

THE PROBLEM

In 1968 the National Advisory Commission on Civil Disorders (Kerner, 1968) reported that for many minorities the schools had failed to provide the educational experiences needed to overcome the effects of discrimination and deprivation. Today the educational status of minority students in the United States has reached the proportions of a national dilemma.

At times people have believed the educational plight of disadvantaged youngsters to be linked only to the South. This is a misconception; children in all regions of the United States have experienced low academic achievement in our educational system. The educational system has not only failed black and Puerto Rican children in our large urban communities, but it has also failed Mexican American and American Indian children in the West and Southwest, and poor white children in Appalachia. The large urban communities, however, exhibit the most obvious educational problems. The low academic achievement of many urban youth, the reluctance on the part of many teachers to accept assignments in urban schools with large percentages of minority students, and the growing controversy over issues such as corporal punishment and community control of urban schools are all symptoms of a system that needs analyzing and restructuring (Green, 1969).

The Detroit High School Study Commission (Report, 1968), in a report to the Board of Education, concluded that the public schools are becoming symbols of society's neglect and indifference rather

[1] The authors wish to express their appreciation to Mrs. Eugenia Smith for her invaluable editorial and research assistance in the preparation of this chapter.

601

than institutions that serve the needs of society by providing upward and economic mobility.

Silberman (1970) shares this concern:

Our democracy . . . is in danger. Not the least of the reasons is the fact that the community has *not* wanted for all its children what the best parent wants for his own child. As a result, the public schools are failing dismally in what has always been regarded as one of their primary tasks—. . . to be 'the great equalizer of the conditions of men,' facilitating the movement of the poor and disadvantaged into the mainstream of American economic and social life. Far from being 'the great equalizer,' the schools help perpetuate the differences in condition, or at the very least, do little to reduce them (p. 53).

Urban parents have long been concerned with the quality of education their children receive. In Harlem, for example, there have been committees for better schools going back to the 1930s (Clark, 1965). Education is seen by urban parents as a concrete vehicle to enhance the status of their children and their community. Contrary to much popular thought, economically poor urban parents believe that through education their children will have the opportunity to lead a decent life. Public schools and their administrators have thus become targets in what is really a deep-seated struggle by minority groups for educational, political and economic equality. The record of public education in the United States demonstrates that despite previous conditions of economic or political deprivation and discrimination, people have been able to use education as one tool in overcoming those disadvantages (Clark, 1970).

Since the public school has always been essentially a middle-class institution (Silberman, 1970), urban parents believe that decentralized community schools would be optimally sensitive and responsive to the needs of their children (Smith & McGrail, 1969). When complaints are registered in middle-class communities regarding school curriculum, community groups are considered to be exercising their constitutional rights. Yet when people in Harlem, Detroit or Watts say "these are our schools, this is our community," they are accused of militant propagandizing and making trouble (Young, 1969). Opponents of community control frequently argue that inevitably it would mean having a less qualified educational staff, a poorer curriculum, and would produce an even lower achievement level for the children (Smith & McGrail, 1969). Yet urban schools presently have the lowest achievement levels, the highest dropout rates, and the least experienced and least competent staffs.

In the area of reading achievement, the basis for success in all other academic areas, the Kerner Commission (1968) reported that black students in the metropolitan Northeast are, on the average, 1.6 grades behind the national level, and by the twelfth grade they are 3.3 grades behind. Clark (1965) cited the achievement levels of Harlem children. Minority students at the third-grade level are one year behind the achievement levels of other New York City students; by the sixth grade they are two years behind, and by the eighth grade they are two and one-half years behind other New York City students and three years behind the national level.

In reading comprehension, 30 percent of the Harlem third-grade pupils are reading below grade level compared to 21.6 percent who are reading above. For sixth-grade pupils the story is even more dismal—80.9 percent of the pupils score below grade level in reading, while only 12 percent of the pupils score above (Clark, 1965). Between grades three and six, word knowledge test scores also alter; in third grade 38.9 percent score below grade level, 19 percent score above; in sixth grade 77.5 percent are below, 10.6 percent are above (Clark, 1965). Arithmetic shows a similar pattern of underachievement. In the sixth grade in the Harlem schools 57.6 percent are below grade level in computation and 66.6 percent are below in problems and concepts (Clark, 1965).

By the eighth grade, 75 percent of the Harlem junior high-school students score below grade level in reading comprehension and word knowledge, and in arithmetic 83.8 percent score below (Clark, 1965).

When Dr. Bernard E. Donovan announced his retirement as superintendent of the New York City schools in 1969, he said that although the schools were doing a creditable job in educating the children of the middle class, the schools had not found a way to provide a successful educational program for the disadvantaged.

The fact that the educational system has been middle-class–oriented and that teachers have helped to fulfill the prophecy of failure for black and poor youth (Vinter & Sarri, 1965) has had a great bearing on the dropout rates of minority students. Youngsters growing up in depressed neighborhoods become increasingly aware of an affluent society which exists for others but is out of reach for them. Often frustrated and bored by school and by a curriculum which seems void of relevance to his life and culture, the disadvantaged youngster may drop out of school early (Morlan & Ramonda, 1968). Coleman et al. (1966) showed that in the metropolitan North and West black students are more than three times as likely as white students to drop out of school by age 16–17.

When children are taught effectively without regard to economic disadvantage or social status they learn (Clark, 1970). But if children are placed in tracks or if certain judgments about their ability are made, the results tend to justify the assumptions that these children will fail (Clark, 1970).

The schools attended by the urban poor are usually staffed by teachers with less experience and lower qualifications than those attended by children from middle-income homes (Morlan & Ramonda, 1968). For example, a 1963 study ranking Chicago's public high schools by the socioeconomic status of surrounding neighborhoods found that in the 10 lowest ranking schools only 63 percent of all teachers were fully certified and the median level of teaching experience was 3.9 years. In three of these schools the median level was one year. Four of the lowest ranking schools were 100 percent black in enrollment and three were more than 90 percent black. By contrast, eight of the 10 highest ranking schools had nearly total white enrollments, and the other two were more than 75 percent white. In these schools 90.3 percent of the teachers were fully certified and the median level of teaching experience was 12.3 years (Kerner Report, 1968).

In testimony given to the Kerner Commission, Dr. Daniel Dodson, director of the New York University Center for Human Relations and Community Services, reported that between 1952 and 1962 almost half of the licensed teachers of New York City left the system. Almost two out of every five of the 50,000 teaching personnel of New York City did not hold regular permanent licenses for the assignments they had (Kerner Report, 1968).

Many teachers do not want to teach in urban schools, and those who are assigned to urban schools are not prepared to teach in them. Often the teachers begin with negative attitudes toward the children and these attitudes are aggravated by serious discipline problems. The disadvantaged child often loses interest in the classroom and then becomes a behavior problem to the teacher. The teacher, in turn, often resorts to punitive measures for control, further aggravating the situation (Morlan & Ramonda, 1968). The problems are compounded when the emphasis in low-income urban schools is on maintaining order rather than on teaching (Silberman, 1970). In one school, classroom procedures were studied and it was shown that teachers spent as much as 75 percent of their time trying to maintain order, leaving the remaining time for actual instruction (Deutsch, 1960). As the Coleman report (1966) indicated, there are many more dissatisfied teachers in urban schools than there are in other schools.

Since many minority children are at an economic and educational disadvantage, it is all the more important for them to gain the skills which will enable them to effectively function in a highly literate society. But the environmental conditions that relate to this disadvantage do not necessarily need to be completely altered before the school can teach urban children to read and write adequately. In other words, the educational system cannot use environmental (community) deprivation as an excuse not to provide urban children with quality education. Community deprivation should be used as the major criterion for providing urban disadvantaged youth with the best education possible. The educational know-how exists to do the job well right now (Cohen, 1969).

In order to review the factors that are related to increasing the educational performance of urban youth, the focus will be on four major areas. The effects of malnutrition and health care on the academic performance of children, particularly the urban poor, is discussed in the section, Learning and the Poor: Environmental Determinants. The need for relevant training programs for teachers of the urban poor is discussed in Teacher Training Programs. The concern for quality education and a decentralized educational system is examined in Community Control of Urban Schools. The fourth section on Implications for Improving Educational Research in Urban Schools looks at the need for social scientists to use their skills to aid society in solving its problems and to apply scientific methods to social problems in order to effect change.

LEARNING AND THE POOR: ENVIRONMENTAL DETERMINANTS

In the history of educational research the 1960s may well be characterized as the decade of the "discovery" of the disad-vantaged and the deprived whose children constitute an increasing proportion of the urban school population. One of the difficulties of reviewing research on the learning behavior of poor children is the lack of clarity and agreement among researchers in defining the terms which they use to discuss the nature of deprivation and disadvantage. As a result, one of the highest priorities in research design and program planning should be the development of a more adequate definition of the problem. As currently employed, these terms—generally used in reference to the lower-class ethnic poor—are regarded as euphemisms by some and insults by others (Birren & Hess, 1968). In addition, terms such as underprivileged, culturally different, working-class and inner-city children have also been used to refer to those who are perceived as suffering a lack of opportunity and who are relatively low in prestige, power and the resources basic to determining their own and their children's destinies.

Much confounding of information occurs when low SocioEconomic Status (SES) ethnic minority groups, the under-educated, and the mentally retarded are indiscriminately included under the rubric of 'disadvantaged' and studied as a homogeneous group. To properly understand the influences of social class variables, ethnic variables, etc., upon learning ability, precise descriptions for such variables must be developed and utilized to define the population of interest (Birren & Hess, 1968, p. 149).

While terms and constructs have varied from researcher to researcher, the assumption that the crucial determinants of behavior are environmental has been shared by most researchers. One of the earliest studies based on this assumption was that of Skeels, Updegraff, Wellman, and Williams (1938). They transferred a few young orphanage children who were showing retarded development to an institution for the mentally retarded, where they were cared for by adolescent and young adult mentally retarded girls. Most of the children, after receiving the intense attention of these surrogate mothers, became adoptable and when studied some 30 years later (Skeels, 1966) were found to have been functioning in the community and to have produced children who were also capable of normal function. In comparison, a group of children who had remained in the orphanage were, 30 years later, not economically independent and many were still receiving some form of institutional care.

In 1961, J. M. Hunt presented a detailed analysis of previous views concerning the nature of intelligence. On the basis of empirical evidence, he argued for the rejection of these views as they were based on the assumptions of fixed intelligence and predetermined development. During the following decade a large number of studies were carried out on the relationship of environmental variables to the development of intellectual functions.

In some of these studies the focus of attention was the interaction between broad social variables and individual cognitive and educational achievement (Hess & Bear, 1968; Kamii & Radin, 1967), particularly through behavior mediated by the family. In others the relationship of socioeconomic status to cognitive behavior was investigated (Bloom, Davis, & Hess, 1965; Deutsch, 1967; Hess & Bear, 1968).

A concurrent, and divergent, development of interest in the relationship of socioeconomic status to intelligence was that of William Shockley (1966) and Arthur Jensen (1969). Shockley, a Nobel Prize-winning physicist, argued for an expansion of research evaluating the relative effects of heredity and environment on human intelligence and performance. Underlying his proposal was the assumption that the relatively poor performance of blacks on intelligence tests was the result of inferior genetic inheritance rather than inferior environment. Jensen's position was similar; he concluded, after a lengthy review of the literature on testing and socioeconomic status, that environmental factors are not as important as

genetic factors in determining IQ. Jensen also presents data on the relationship of IQ to such prenatal environmental influences as nutrition, multiple birth, prematurity and low birth rate, all of which he concedes have a higher incidence among black, Mexican American and American Indian children (Jensen, 1969). One is hard put to explain how he can, with any degree of certainty, separate the influence of these variables from "purely genetic" ones on the learning ability of children. It becomes even more difficult to understand Jensen's notions of causality when one considers the early childhood experience of further malnutrition, parasitic infestation, and a host of other problems which many of these children experience. Given identical genetic constitutions, two organisms developing under different environmental conditions will differ from each other. According to Gottesman (1968) these environmental conditions must be defined in such a way as to include intrauterine and postnatal conditions as well as a multitude of molecular factors within and between embryonic cells. In view of the current incompleteness of our knowledge of environmental parameters and the lack of specificity in delineating these variables, Jensen's and Shockley's pleas for more research into *genetic* explanations of differences in IQ as a function of racial or ethnic membership are disingenuous at best.

From the data which Jensen himself presents and from data gathered from other sources, it would seem that separating the effect of genetics from that of environment —especially the prenatal environment—is impossible and, at best, speculative. If there are genetic differences related to race, it is highly unlikely that they correspond to the criteria developed for measuring school performance. In any case, our society is still committed to providing the opportunity for realizing potential, regardless of such a possible difference in genetic potential. Jensen's argument that he is merely attempting to provide the *right kind* of opportunities for "genetically handicapped" children is based on peculiar evidence. After indicating that socioeconomic status is a crucial variable, Jensen cites support for differences in level I (concrete) and level II (abstract) learning between two groups of children. He parenthetically indicates that race and socioeconomic status were confounded: "in this study all the level I children were black and lower-class, while all the level II children were 'white' and middle-class" (Jensen, 1969). It would seem, in view of his lengthy analysis of the contributions of racial, genetic and social-class factors to intelligence, that it is a fairly serious flaw in experimental design to have all of the white children in the middle-class group and all of the black children in the lower-class group. Even if it were difficult for Jensen to immediately identify a large middle-class black population from which to draw his sample, no such difficulty exists in finding lower-class whites. The majority of poor people in this country are not black, Mexican American or American Indian—they are white. The lack of precision in designing this study, as well as the carelessness with which much of the data concerning post- and prenatal environmental factors is presented, should cause one to question Dr. Jensen's vaunted objectivity.

His final plea for individualized instruction has little relevance to almost the whole of the preceding review of the literature—especially since he stresses that one cannot infer from group data what the performance of the individual will be (Jensen, 1969). Obviously, if one wishes to maximize one's impact, one chooses those who would seem most able to benefit from whatever treatment one plans to use. It is not that we have made *too much* of an effort at compensatory education but rather that our efforts have not been providing the right kinds of compensation, in the right amounts, at the right times, and for a long enough time. This is not a crime but a mistake. Obviously if we knew all the answers we would make no mistakes. But just as ob-

viously it is almost impossible to learn what the answers are until we start asking questions—and making mistakes. The kind of question that Dr. Jensen raises in the bulk of his paper—the relationship of genetics to learning—is not the kind that will lead us to finding answers that educators can deal with constructively.

In his response to Jensen's article, Brazziel (1969) points out that Jensen's position does not adequately account for the ravages of malnutrition and illness on the intellectual development of poor and black children. Jensen does, in fact, ignore much of the literature on the relationship of such variables as low birth weight, malnutrition and health care to cognitive development. He cites only those few studies which support his contention that variation produced by these variables is not great enough to account for differences in IQ. In his lack of awareness of the research on the relationship of biological variables to cognitive development he is not alone. The great bulk of studies of cognitive development and the majority of intervention programs have either ignored or made only superficial assessments of the effects of such variables as malnutrition and health care on the academic performance and IQ of the child.

It is well known that the risk of academic failure is higher for poor children than it is for middle-class children (Birren & Hess, 1968). What is not as well known is that the rate of infant and mother mortality, the incidence and severity of chronic and infectious diseases, and the occurrence of low birth weight and prematurity are also greater for the poor. All of these factors are in turn related to the disproportionate number of poor and black children who are mentally retarded (Kushlick, 1966).

The mortality rate of nonwhite infants in the United States is twice that of white infants. In addition (E. Hunt, 1966), the disparity between white and nonwhite rates is increasing since the rates for nonwhites have declined less than that for whites. Between 1950 and 1965 the white infant death rate declined 19.8 percent; the nonwhite rate dropped only 9.4 percent. Thus, while the nonwhite rate was 66 percent higher than the white rate in 1950, it was 87 percent higher by 1965. In absolute terms, the nonwhite rate of infant deaths in 1965 was at the level of white infant deaths prior to 1942.

Related to the high infant death rate is a correspondingly high maternal death rate. While there has been a large decline in absolute rates for both white and nonwhite mothers since 1940, the *disparity* between the two groups has been increasing. In 1967 the maternal death rate among nonwhite women was 69.5 per 100,000 live births, while the white rate was 19.5 (National Center for Health Statistics [NCHS], 1969), a ratio of about 3.5 to 1. While the rates (439.9 for whites and 875.5 for non-whites) were higher in 1950, the ratio between them was smaller, roughly 2:1.

These high rates of infant and maternal deaths among nonwhites are significant not only because they reflect a tragic waste of life but also because they are indicative of conditions which are hostile to healthy growth and development. Underlying these high maternal and infant mortality rates are the poor health, growth, medical care and nutrition of the mother (Food & Nutrition Board, 1970). According to Birch and Gussow (1970), "a high rate of infant death, in any population, indirectly suggests survival with increased risk of damage in the survivors.... Those children who have come through birth and infancy alive have not necessarily come through unscathed, and it is reasonable to anticipate that the condition of the survivors will surely reflect the relative hostility of the environments to which they have been exposed" (p. 13).

More than 100 years ago Little (1862) discussed the negative influence of reproductive complications and prematurity on the physical and cognitive development of children. Recently it has been shown that complications of pregnancy and delivery are more prevalent among the poor (Illsley,

1967) and especially among the nonwhite (Pasamanick, Knobloch, & Lilienfeld, 1956). Pregnancy and birth complications are hypothesized by Pasamanick and Knobloch (1969) to result in a continuum of reproductive casualty extending from death through varying degrees of neuropsychiatric disability and resulting in behavior disorders, reading disabilities and mental deficiency. Despite a number of statistical and methodological considerations (McMahon & Sowa, 1961) which preclude the inference of a direct cause and effect relationship, this hypothesis has been supported by a number of studies (McNeil, Wiegerink, & Doziers, 1970).

In addition, children who were premature at birth were found to be shorter and lighter at school age than were full-term controls (Wiener, Rider, Oppel, Fischer, & Harper, 1965), were more often hospitalized for illness, and suffered from a higher incidence of visual, hearing and other defects. Drillien (1964) found that 75 percent of a group of school-age children who had weighed three pounds or less at birth had some congenital defect or mental retardation. There is mounting evidence (Drillien, 1964; Harper, Fischer, & Rider, 1959; Weiner, Rider, Oppel, & Harper, 1968) to support the hypothesis that premature children achieve somewhat lower IQ scores than do full-term children and that as birth-weight decreases so do IQ scores.

There are data which also suggest an interaction of the effects of prematurity and social class on IQ scores. Illsley (1966) found that the measured intelligence of low birth-weight children from the lowest social classes was depressed, while in the upper classes birth weight appeared to have little effect on IQ scores. Similar findings in regard to the relationship of prenatal complications and socioeconomic status on IQ were reported by Werner, Simonian, Bierman, and French (1967). When tested on a variety of measures, including the Bender-Gestalt test, a positive correlation was found between birth weight and test performance of a group of prematurely born six- to seven-year-olds (Wiener et al., 1965). Subsequently reported data on the Wechsler Intelligence Scale for Children (WISC), administered to these children at ages eight to ten (Wiener et al., 1968), showed a greater effect of low birth weight on the abstract verbal reasoning and perceptual-motor integration subtests than on the total IQ score. School-age prematures have also been found to have more difficulty adjusting to school routine and are more likely to be judged "unsettled" or "maladjusted" by these teachers (Drillien, 1964). Drillien also found that twice as many prematurely born children were working below capacity in school as were the full-time controls (26 percent versus 13 percent) and these children were from the "best" homes.

For the educator, however, the crucial area of concern is the great number of low birth-weight children who are not obviously or severely damaged. Achievement in school may be diminished in children who suffer minor neurologic disorders which result in perceptual deficit or impulsivity or any of the other handicaps which have been found to be related to low birth weight.

The number of children in the United States who are born weighing less than 2500 grams is large and the rate is increasing among nonwhites. In 1967 the rate was 13.6 percent (87,836) for blacks, while for whites the rate was 7.1 percent (204,136) (National Center for Health Statistics, 1968). In 1951 the rate for whites was also 7.1 percent but for nonwhites it was 10.8 percent (National Center for Health Statistics, 1968).

Although this excess of low birth-weight babies among nonwhites has been explained as a "natural" ethnic difference, Crump (Crump & Horton, 1961; Crump, Horton, Masuoka, & Ryan, 1957; Crump, Payton, & Horton, 1959), in a series of studies, has shown that a more likely explanation is socioeconomic both within and between ethnic groups. Scott, Jenkins, and Crawford (1950) had found a similar relationship between economic status and birth weight

among Washington, D.C. blacks. Thomson (1963) and Drillien (1964), working in Scotland with a relatively homogeneous ethnic population, also found that the incidence of prematurity decreased as income and social status increased.

Further evidence of the interrelationship of poverty, malnutrition, illness and the development of the child is found in a study which identifies undernutrition of poor urban mothers as the cause of prenatal growth retardation (Naeye, Diener, Dellinger, & Blanc, 1969). In addition to being 15 percent smaller in body weight, the infants from poor families had multiple evidences, in terms of the relative weight of such organs as the thymus, spleen and liver, of prenatal undernutrition. The biggest difference between the babies of poor and nonpoor mothers was in the relative weight of the thymus. The offspring of nonpoor families had a mean thymus weight which was 104 percent of the normal weight while that of poor babies was only 66 percent of normal weight. The function of the thymus (Defendi & Metcalf, 1964) is not yet completely understood, although there is increasing evidence that it is involved in both growth and immunological functions. The higher incidence of illness and short stature characteristic of poor children may be a manifestation of the lack of adequate development of the thymus. In addition, there is increasing evidence (Cowley, 1968) that the effects of prenatal malnutrition span more than one generation.

Evidence that the nutrition of the mother is one of the important variables related to the intellectual performance of the child has also been increasing. Children whose mothers received a vitamin supplement during pregnancy had significantly higher IQs at three and four years of age than did children whose mothers received placebos (Harrell, Woodyard, & Gates, 1956). Erickson (1967), on the basis of a later study, also found that "when vitamin supplementation was given to a low socioeconomic group of pregnant and lactating women with poor nutritional environment, the offspring at 4 years of age had an average IQ score 8 points greater than the average score of the children of mothers given a placebo over the same period" (p. 1210). Kennedy's study (1967) of the effect of prenatal nutrition on the general measures of intellectual and physical health yielded similar results.

A significant negative correlation between the mother's nutritional status and the risk of prematurity and birth complications has been found by a number of researchers (Thomson, 1963; Thomson & Billewicz, 1963; Warkany, 1944). Wartime studies (Antonov, 1947; Duncan, Baird, & Thomson, 1952; Smith, 1947; Thomson, 1959; Toverud, 1950) supported this finding as well as demonstrated a positive relationship between nutrition and birth weight.

There is, then, an increasing amount of data which indicate that the poor and non-white suffer a higher rate of mortality, pregnancy and birth complications, low birth weight and prematurity. An observation that is supported by a great deal of data (Birch & Gussow, 1970) is that mothers of poor children have been less well fed, less cared for and have not grown as well as more affluent women. They start having children at a younger age and continue having children over a longer period of time, more often, and with less time between pregnancies. During pregnancy they receive poorer prenatal care and at delivery their care continues to be inadequate. Their poor health, lack of care, low income and inadequate education all interact to produce a negative influence on the health and growth of their children.

Available evidence from human studies, reinforced by the findings of experiments with animals, suggests that early infancy is a critical period for the development of the brain. This is also the time when the brain is extremely vulnerable to the effects of malnutrition. Since direct measurement of brain growth in humans is not possible with living children, an indirect measure widely employed has been the rate of increase in head circumference. Malnutrition, especially during the first year of life, will curtail the normal rate of increase in head circumference. This reduced head circumference of malnourished children during the first six months of life, according to Winick (1969), accurately reflects the reduced number of cells present in their brains. Monckeberg (1969) has demonstrated that the brain of a severely malnourished child may be even smaller than the head circumference would indicate. He has developed a "transillumination" test which reveals the presence of spinal fluid in the skull. The test is conducted by focusing a thousand-watt light on the top of the skull. As the light is diffused the surrounding area glows. In normal children this area is very small, but in the affected children the entire brain case from the forehead to the back of the head glows.

Malnourished human infants also exhibit abnormal brain-wave activity (Cravioto, Delicardie, & Birch, 1966; Nelson & Dean, 1959). Electroencephalographic (EEG) abnormalities have also been found in malnourished animals (Platt, Pampiglione, & Stewart, 1965). Whether these abnormalities of brain-wave pattern are permanent and whether they are related directly to nutritional deprivation and irreversible behavioral change has been demonstrated more often in animal (Birch & Gussow, 1970) than in human research. There is, however, some indirect evidence of the relationship of abnormality of EEG disorders of communication or perceptual integration and "pseudomental retardation" (Kellaway, Crawley, & Maulsby, 1965). Of more than 1,000 children failing in school, 40 percent were found to have significant EEG abnormalities. A number of clinical characteristics were consistently found. The poor school performance was out of proportion to the measured intelligence of the child and performance was variable, even within the same day. The attention span was short and distractibility was high. These children were also characterized by what may be considered a general disorder of sensorimotor integration which manifested itself in their reading, writing and number identification. Many of these EEG abnormalities, seen in patients whose measured intelligence was adequate but who had a specific disability such as failure in reading, appeared only in sleep or were greatly accentuated during sleep.

Since these abnormalities may be the only objective evidence of cerebral dysfunction and since they must be obtained when the child is asleep, it is not surprising that the relationship between poor school performance and organic brain dysfunction is often obscure. The recognition of certain subtle disturbances of cerebral dysfunction may have important implications in preventing punitive behavior on the part of parents and teachers toward the child with ensuing tension and emotional upset complicating the learning failure.

In general, hyperkinetic behavior has been treated by behavior-modifying drugs such as Ritalin. Cott (1970) has been treating children who are hyperkinetic and have specific learning disabilities with massive doses of Vitamins B_2, B_3, B_6, C and E, along with high protein diets. These substances have been associated with proper functioning of chemicals that conduct impulses between brain cells and are thus thought to be vital to mental processes.

Coursin (1965) has shown that deficiencies in the B-complex vitamins and in Vitamin C can produce abnormalities of nerve cell metabolism and function and impair mental development. Vitamin therapy has affected improvement in the mental functioning of such children.

The children in the Monckeberg study were restored to physical health, but follow-up intelligence tests showed that they achieved lower scores than children who had not suffered from malnutrition. Their greatest deficit was in the area of language development. Similarly, the malnourished children studied by Stoch and Smythe (1968) who exhibited reduced head circumference had lower IQs even after long-term

follow-up. Frisch (1970) questions, however, whether these deficits are truly irreversible and argues that the data thus far are not conclusive.

Using a wide battery of tests, Klein and Gilbert (1967) studied the performance of malnourished and normally nourished children from the same social class. On tests where the test stimulus was only available for a short period of time, the malnourished children did not perform as well as the normally nourished. There was no difference in performance when the duration of the test stimulus was not controlled. The deficit which the malnourished children exhibited seems to involve speed of perception or of information processing and impairment of short-term memory.

A number of other studies have demonstrated that nutritional therapy of the child may have a beneficial effect on intellectual performance. Kugelmass, Poull, and Samuel (1944) demonstrated an increase in the IQ of both retarded and mentally normal children as a result of prolonged nutritional rehabilitation. The children, ranging in age from two to 10, were divided into two groups, those who were malnourished and those who were well nourished. Each of these groups contained retarded and normal children. The *malnourished* retarded children showed a gain of 10 points and the normal children gained 18 points after a period of dietary improvement. In contrast, there was relatively little change in the scores of the well-nourished retarded and nomal children.

Harrell (1946) found that in closely matched groups of presumably normal orphanage children, the double-blind daily administration of a placebo versus a 2 milligram thiamine tablet for one year produced a superior mental response in the thiamine group. Muecher and Gruenwald (1962) demonstrated that improvement of intellectual functions can be extended even into the late teens. Students who received vitamin and mineral supplements showed a significant improvement in the performance of mental arithmetic as compared to students receiving a placebo.

A series of studies by Cravioto and his associates (1966) in Mexico and Guatemala has shown that the performance of children on psychological tests was related to nutritional factors and not to differences in personal hygiene, housing, cash income, or other social and economic variables. The performance of both preschool and school children in Mexico on the Terman-Merrill, Gesell, and Goodenough Draw-A-Man tests was positively correlated with body weights and body heights. A similar positive relationship between size and performance was found in Guatemala. The tests used in this study provided measures of visual, haptic and kinesthetic sensory integration. Children exposed to severe early malnutrition exhibited perceptual defects as well as smaller body size. The earlier the malnutrition the more profound the psychological retardation. The most severe retardation occurred in children admitted to the hospital under six months of age and did not improve on serial testing even after 220 days of treatment. Children admitted later, with the same socioeconomic backgound and the same severe malnutrition but a different time of onset, did recover with prolonged rehabilitation.

Cravioto et al. (1966) concluded that nutritional inadequacy may interfere with both the staging and the timing of development of the brain and of behavior. Their demonstration of delayed neurointegrative development in children who have grown poorly because of malnutrition has important implications for more complex psychological functioning.

Evidence already exists that the lag in the development of certain varieties of intersensory integrations have a high correlation with backwardness in learning to read .... studies of reading disability in British ... and ... American school children have shown that backwardness in reading is strongly associated with inadequacy in auditory-visual integration .... skill in visual-kinesthetic integration [is

found] to be highly and significantly correlated with design-copying in normal children. If it is recognized ... that such visual-motor control is essential in learning to write, [it becomes apparent that] the inadequacy in intersensory organization can interfere with a second primary educational skill—learning to write.

Thus, inadequacies of intersensory development can place the child at [the] risk of failing to establish an ordinary normal background of conditionings in his preschool years and at the risk of failing to profit from educational experience in the school years (p. 359).

In addition to the negative impact of malnutrition on the growth rate and intersensory development of children, Cravioto et al. (1966) also found a relationship between these aspects of development and infection. Eichenwald and Fry (1969) have shown that certain infections in malnourished children may produce severe and prolonged hypoglycemia, a condition which can by itself cause brain damage. In addition, various biochemical defects of children with malnutrition are accentuated by infection. There is the further possibility that many infectious diseases, or the treatment of these diseases, result in damage to the nervous system that is not necessarily evident during the acute state of the illness. Eichenwald concludes by stating that "infection and malnutrition thus act synergistically to produce a chronically and recurrently sick child less likely to react to sensory stimuli from his already inadequate social environment" (p. 644).

The goal of providing every child with the opportunity to fulfill his potential will not be met by simplifying the nature of the obstacles children of the poor have to overcome. Intervention, to be successful, must be sustained over a long period of time and must be multifaceted. Compensatory education programs which focus *only* on "cultural deprivation" will not help the child who is hungry. And it will not aid any child if the effort is not well timed, sustained over a sufficient period of time, and carried out by individuals who are aware of the complexity of their task.

TEACHER-TRAINING PROGRAMS

Compensatory education programs have proliferated in the past decade and have been accompanied by a wave of training programs for teachers of disadvantaged youth. Most of these training programs were designed as a response to the demands of minority-group parents and frustrated school officials who discovered that regular training programs did not adequately prepare teachers to teach urban youth. Educators have discovered that curriculum innovations and various compensatory programs cannot be successful until relevant teacher-training models for urban teachers are developed. Smith and Arnez (1969) write that the key to improved instruction for educationally deprived children is improved training for their teachers. Wilkerson (1965) concluded that even highly professional teachers commonly lack the insights, social attitudes and instructional skills which are essential for integrating social class and ethnic diversity in the classroom.

It is interesting to note that most of these special training programs have had little or no effect on existing teacher-training programs in colleges and universities. The typical training program for urban teachers is an annex to the regular program and reflects only slight, if any, modification over the established model of teacher training. Generally, training programs for teachers of urban youth may be categorized as either pre-service or in-service.

Pre-service Teacher-training Programs

Haubrich (1963), in an experimental project at Hunter College, demonstrated that placing pre-service student teachers in urban schools for a period of supervised teaching, which included community field experiences, would improve their skills and competencies and would also encourage them to select an urban school for their actual teaching.

The extension of the Haubrich model, Project True at Hunter College, is one of the more publicized training programs for urban teachers. Teacher candidates in this program received instruction centering around students who come from families with low income, low education backgrounds, and cultural-language diversity. Following a combination of study, observation, laboratory experiences and practice teaching, the candidates taught full time in the New York schools. The training covered a two-year period (Green, 1967).

Project Beacon at Yeshiva University exposed students to a pre-service teaching curriculum emphasizing the social, developmental and learning problems of the disadvantaged (Gordon & Wilkerson, 1966). This was coupled with field experience and practice teaching in the mobilization for youth project and its affiliated schools.

A similar teacher-training program was Project Y003, developed and implemented at Coppin State College in Maryland. This one-year experimental program was developed to determine if intercultural misunderstandings in urban schools could be eliminated by seeking out prospective teachers from among the ethnic and cultural groups served and then preparing these teacher candidates for work in urban schools. The 19 Coppin juniors and seniors who were selected for this program were perceived to have the academic and personal characteristics necessary for quality teachers. In addition to field experiences, the students were offered courses in the sociology of the city, minority people, history of the Negro in America, and education of the culturally different. The curriculum's objective was to deepen the understanding of the positive values that inhere in the subcultures of American life. Seminars held for prospective teachers featured lectures by members of minority groups who were from disadvantaged backgrounds and who had succeeded. Urban parents and leaders were invited to the lectures. Supervising teachers in the schools selected for student-teaching experiences were enrolled in a summer institute to insure that their attitude and behavior toward disadvantaged children were appropriate. The students who completed their training during this academic year were employed by the Baltimore Public Schools. The Baltimore schools, in cooperation with Coppin, Morgan, and Towson state colleges, established a pre-service training program (Project Mission) in which intern teachers work closely under the supervision of project professors and successful master teachers within the confines of the urban community (Green, 1967).

These are examples of the burgeoning pre-service training programs for urban teachers which grew out of rising concern and consternation regarding the education of disadvantaged children. Generally these programs lacked systematic evaluation components to assess their effectiveness. However, they reflected the trends in general teacher education programs. There is a similar pattern in most of these kinds of pre-service programs, many of which were started in urban universities. Internship experiences were an important aspect of each program and prospective teachers were trained in the urban schools in which they were to teach. Close association with teacher-training programs and various community agencies was stressed. An effort was made to integrate educational theory with practice. Theoretical preparation of teachers generally included courses in sociology, anthropology, black studies and psychology. A seminar for supervising teachers stressing sensitivity for disadvantaged children was almost always included.

With the advent of federally supported compensatory education programs under the Economic Opportunity Act of 1964 and the Elementary Secondary Education Act of 1965, several government teacher-education projects, falling under the rubric of pre-service teacher-training programs for urban

children, were developed and implemented. Perhaps the best known of these programs has been the National Teacher Corps begun in 1966.

The major objectives of the Teacher Corps were delineated in the enabling legislation for this program, which was initially funded by the U.S. Office of Economic Opportunity (OEO). The Teacher Corps was established to strengthen the educational opportunities available to children in areas having a high concentration of low-income families and to encourage colleges and universities to broaden teacher-preparation programs.

Teacher Corps programs were developed in colleges and universities around the country and followed the national guidelines. Typically, Teacher Corps interns were recent college graduates who had not prepared for careers in education.

In general, five or six interns were assigned a team leader from a college or a university or a local public-school system. This team worked in the participating school to assist regular faculty as teachers of disadvantaged students. The interns were involved in field trips, home visits, working with agencies, after-school tutoring, after-school recreation, agency referrals, developing new services, block club work, advising parent groups, and adult education programs. Professional courses focused on the disadvantaged child and his community. After a pre-service period of eight to 13 weeks, Teacher Corps interns usually became professional employees for the duration of the two-year program.

Because systematic research and evaluation were not done in the Teacher Corps Program there was little evidence to show its effectiveness. Most data collected on the Teacher Corps were limited to opinions, ratings and countings. A national report (Teachers Corps, 1968) on Teacher Corps suggests that a more systematic evaluation be an integral part of the program. This evaluation should provide measures of performance, identify and rank factors affecting performance, relate costs to design and performance variables, and analyze cost effectiveness and relationships.

An evaluation might also ask:

1. Are Teacher Corps graduates more effective than other teachers from myriad teacher-education programs?
2. Do Teacher Corps graduates stay in urban schools?
3. To what extent can a successful Teacher Corps program be transferred into a traditional teacher-training program?

A great deal of criticism has been directed at Teacher Corps because not all believe it to be a viable mechanism for meeting the need for teachers in urban schools. Much of this criticism is based on the premise that Teacher Corps did not live up to its goals, purposes and objectives.

In addition to the funding difficulties encountered by Teacher Corps officials and the lack of an adequate research component in this program, some evidence has demonstrated that Teacher Corps did not train the population of teachers it purported to serve (Watson, 1967). Although Teacher Corps has changed its direction and has been placed under the Education Professions Development Act, to date no significant research has been reported to demonstrate its increased effectiveness. The new thrust in Teacher Corps is based on a fundamentally different approach to training teachers commonly called "competency based education" (described later in this section in a brief discussion of the Model Elementary Teacher Education Program and of the Competency Based Personalized and Field Centered Model of an Elementary Teacher-Education Program, both of which are recent models of competency-based teacher education). Succinctly, it means that teachers will not be certified merely because they have acquired and demonstrated competence in a wide spectrum of teaching methods and skills.

In response to the need for more ade-quately trained teachers for urban school populations, another pre-service teacher-training model has emerged in several large teacher-training institutions. The Mott Institute for Community Improvement program is characteristic of such programs. This program was developed at Michigan State University in collaboration with school officials in the Michigan cities of Grand Rapids, Flint, Pontiac, Saginaw, Highland Park and Lansing.

The major purpose of this program is to prepare young teachers through an internship experience in an urban community to teach in such communities. To this extent it was merged with the Michigan State University Elementary Internship Program through which prospective teachers are involved in student teaching at a particular site while taking courses in methods of instruction. Although it had no specific research design, several subjective evaluations of this program have been made. Of the first 72 students who participated in the program at Flint, 44 had graduated at the time of the initial evaluation. Of those 44, 10 had contracted to teach in Flint; eight were teaching in schools in their husband's community (one of which was an urban school); seven returned to their home communities (one taught in an urban school); seven were teaching in urban schools other than Flint; seven were teaching in non-urban schools other than Flint or their home areas; two were working on advanced degrees and three were not teaching (Hickey, 1970).

Similar teacher-training models have been designed in many universities throughout the country. Except in a few instances most of these programs have been annexes to the regular teacher-training programs. Some universities have developed separate urban education departments which have been specifically established to train teachers of urban youth. Among these are Temple University in Philadelphia and the Bank Street College in New York City. To date no systematic research has been reported to demonstrate the effectiveness of these separate urban education programs, many of which are in their embryonic stages.

Shall urban teachers be trained in separate teacher-education programs or shall urban education programs be integrated into the regular teacher-training program? Again, there is insufficient research evidence available to teacher trainers to adequately answer this question definitively.

In a rather bold teacher-educational experiment, Antioch College (Fairfield, 1967), in conjunction with the District of Columbia Public Schools, developed and implemented a teacher-training program through which intern teachers, experienced teachers and supervisors were simultaneously trained. Working with a community council, Antioch was responsible for managing the total educational programs of the district's Adams-Morgan School. Although this teacher-training program was discontinued after one year, the Adams-Morgan School became one of the first community-controlled schools in the nation. Like so many other pre-service teacher-training programs for urban teachers, this unique effort lacked an adequate research and evaluation component.

There are many universities which now have developed pre-service urban teacher-training programs. These programs should become an integral part of the regular teacher-training program if enough skilled teachers are to be provided for our urban communities. Wisniewski (1969) corroborates this:

As we continue to flounder in our efforts to prepare teachers who can 'reach' the disadvantaged, we may well put into effect the reforms needed in teacher education in general. Putting it more bluntly, we have to move from the piecemeal, experimental, special project approach for small numbers of prospective teachers and must initiate relevant reforms for all the students in the mainstream of teacher preparation (p. 78).

In-service Teacher-training Programs

Because of the increasing demand for quality urban teachers, a plethora of urban in-service teacher-training programs has arisen. Many of these in-service programs for urban teachers were begun in conjunction with various federally funded projects such as Head Start, Follow Through and Adult Basic Education. In these cases, teachers already in school systems were retrained in programs consonant with the specific compensatory education project.

The Institutes for Advanced Study for Teachers of Disadvantaged Youth, under Title XI of the National Defense Education Act (NDEA), were started in 1964. These summer institutes were designed to shore up teacher skills and attitudes, particularly as they pertain to urban youth. They focused on the myriad problems of urban teaching. Usually there was some intern or extern experience built into the institute in an effort to link theory with practice. Heavy emphasis was placed on English as a second language, the social-psychological backgrounds of disadvantaged children, Negro history, and teaching reading to disadvantaged children. Again, there is a paucity of research to show the functionality or dysfunctionality of the institute as a means of retraining urban teachers.

Closely related to the NDEA Institute was the governmentally funded Experienced Teacher Fellowship Program. Through this program experienced teachers could spend an academic year bolstering their skills and competencies in a given discipline. The Center for Inner City Studies in Chicago was initially funded through this program. Smith and Arnez (1969), describing this in-service teacher education program, state its objectives:

1. To help students gain cultural and historical insight that will lead to more effective communications with poor people and their communities.

2. To give students an understanding and

appreciation of the cultures of minority groups, with special emphasis on the Afro-American, southern white migrant, Spanish-speaking American, and American Indian.

3. To focus on minority-group children and adults in a changing urban setting, illuminating such problems as population explosion, segregation, industrial changes, and employment, housing and family patterns.

4. To guide students in investigating the minority-group child's cognitive and affective experiences, his assets, his needs, the strengths and weaknesses of his culture, and the resources of his community.

5. To stimulate students who have instructional and school curricular responsibilities in their professional setting to discover creative and innovative techniques that will improve the learning experiences of children and adults.

Sonja Stone (1969) reports that the Center for Inner City Studies has developed a unique curriculum which

is designed not only to challenge historical socio-cultural deficits now blatant in urban education but also to stimulate radical research, to remodel social institutions, to provide technical assistance to depressed communities, to create a forum for the repressed masses; in essence, to exemplify the comm-university where the needs of the people are the ultimate concern of its scholars, where a scholarly community is accountable to its indigenous community (p. 530).

Though the center has been particularly effective in training urban teachers, no objective research regarding this program has been reported.

A similar program is Operation Fair Chance underway at two California state colleges. This program is designed to help prospective and experienced teachers develop empathy with the culturally deprived, to find more effective ways of teaching disadvantaged children and youth, and to

work with their parents and community leaders to emphasize realistic pupil orientation to the world of work (Olsen, 1967). Although rigorous evaluation of the project by the University of California was included in the proposal for this project, there is insufficient data to prove its effectiveness vis-a-vis the education of urban children.

As a response to the legion of critics who condemned pre-service and in-service training programs for teachers of urban youth, the Trainers of Teacher Trainers program was conceived. This program is primarily concerned with the pre-service and in-service development of the trainers of teacher trainers and their students. Utilizing certain aspects of the "clinical professor" approach to teacher education, as advanced by Conant (1964), this project proceeds on the premise that teacher training is not the sole responsibility of colleges of education. Teacher training for the contemporary society requires the resources of the total university along with contributions from school systems and community resources.

The program has been designed to involve the trainers of teacher trainers in training programs through cooperative planning and implementation by all personnel concerned with the preparation of elementary and secondary teachers. It was modeled after the Tri-University Project at the University of Nebraska, which was subsequently absorbed into it. Presently, this global federal effort in teacher education is being funded through the Education Professions Development Act. There is substantial research evidence to show the effectiveness of the Tri-University Project.

It will be difficult to adequately assess the national program because of its tremendous diversity from site to site, although instruments for program evaluation are presently being developed. Also, internal evaluations are being conducted in 13 Trainers of Teacher Trainers projects. Four large progress reports, which grew out of major conferences held in various cities, are, in effect, subjective evaluations of the program. The enterprise appears to be a program which has great potential for restructuring teacher-training programs in general, and preparation programs for teachers of urban youth in particular.

The concern for relevant teacher-training programs has recently resulted in the development of several models of instruction. Among these are the University of Massachusetts' Model Elementary Teacher Education Program and a Competency Based Personalized and Field Centered Model of an Elementary Teacher Education Program. Although these models are not specifically designed to train teachers of urban youth, each of them is an individualized instructional model. Couched in the tenets of behavioral psychology, each of them has a built-in research and evaluation component. At this juncture, however, these models are being tested in university and regional laboratories. Although each model has great potential for training teachers, it is much too early to tell if they can train teachers who can succeed in the present-day urban school. As these models are implemented in urban settings it is imperative that they be carefully researched. More importantly, they must be assessed in terms of their effectiveness in the training of teachers of urban youth.

Teacher training programs across the country are in a veritable state of flux. Relevant teacher-training programs for teachers of disadvantaged youth are in their embryonic stages of development. However, growing concern for relevant teacher-training programs for disadvantaged youth may lead to the overall improvement of teacher education. In the development and implementation of these teacher-training programs, a new kind of association among colleges and universities and public schools will be required.

With the burgeoning demand for community control, accountability, relevancy, and self-determination by ethnic minorities, particularly black people, has come a concern for adequate teacher-training programs for blacks and other minorities. At this juncture, few urban or ethnic studies programs in universities have been linked to teacher-training programs. However, the recent concern for community involvement has prompted several agencies of state and federal government to establish programs for the training of teachers and teacher aides, for example, the Career Opportunity Program which is funded through the Education Professions Development Act. A more ambitious proposal is the one advocated by J. C. Stone (1971) in which he outlines the Education Professions Institute. Succinctly, this institute would be a separate agency of higher education designed to provide professional training for teacher aides, associate teachers, intern teachers, regular teachers, master teachers, and teachers of teachers through the bachelor's and master's degrees. This model is based on the premise that teacher training for the disadvantaged must be planned and conducted at the grassroots level and must ultimately involve the local school neighborhood with responsibility lodged in an agency controlled by those client groups that comprise the community.

A modification of this model, a Black People's Institute of Teacher Education, has already been implemented in San Francisco in a consortium of representatives of the black community of Hunter's Point in San Francisco, the San Francisco Unified School District, and the University of California at Berkeley and Santa Cruz. James Stone (1971) describes this effort as a practical application—a blueprint of the theoretical model of the Education Professions Institute. Its purpose is to provide liberal and professional education needed to train people of minority backgrounds to become teachers. Trainers recruited to the Institute include hard-core dropouts, high-school graduates, parents from the community, returning black Vietnam veterans and students with four years of college who qualify for internship training. These kinds of teacher-training programs represent a new thrust in urban teacher-education programs and, while they seem to smack of abrasive and disruptive change, they are not unprecedented. In another era there was a shortage of teachers for rural America. In response to this acute shortage and demand for rural teachers, state departments of education established special institutions such as the "normal school" so rural people could be trained to teach.

Given the present failure of our teacher-training programs to adequately prepare teachers for urban communities, it is likely that such models will become widespread. Cuban (1970) suggests that a teacher-training model should be rooted in day-to-day, face-to-face experiences in the urban school and community, enriched by university support and producing the kinds of knowledge and skills that will be effective in the classroom. The major thrust, however, involves shifting the center of gravity from the university to the classroom and community.

Increased demands for self-determination by alienated minorities—the blacks, Chicanos, the American Indians and the poor rural whites—will push our teacher-training institutions in the direction of community-based programs. This will inevitably result in radical change and revamping of obsolete teacher-training programs designed to prepare teachers for another age.

Silberman (1970) states:

While the schools cannot be transformed unless colleges and universities turn out a new breed of teacher educated to think about purpose, the universities will be unable to do this unless they, working with the schools, create classrooms that afford their students live models of what teaching can and should be. At the moment, painfully few such classrooms exist, and painfully few schools of education are trying to create them (p. 473).

COMMUNITY CONTROL OF URBAN SCHOOLS

While educators must continue to devise new ways of training teachers, they must also recognize the need to develop new approaches to involve the community in the educational process. Involvement of parents in the decision-making process of the schools which their children attend is crucial to the development of effective educational programs in urban schools. This concept of community control evokes much opposition when it is mentioned. The proponents, however, see it as an innovative approach for changing the status of public education and as a more functional way of managing schools.

In the early beginnings of this nation's formal educational growth, local school control was a fact (Elsbery, 1969). Middle-class parents in the suburbs have long played a key role in determining how their children were to be educated. The level of their direct involvement ranged from sitting on school boards to utilizing established mechanisms for change such as Parent-Teacher Associations. Their indirect involvement was manifested in the fact that school-board members were usually white, middle-class parents who reflected the views of their constituency.

In urban communities, however, a different arrangement has emerged. The management and control of the decision-making process is often carried on by people who do not live in the community and who do not reflect its views. Teachers often come from a distance to instruct and administrators only see their constituency on the way to and from the office. As a result, urban parents have come to suspect and question whether these educators are genuinely interested in their children, and questions of accountability and control have emerged as major issues in the current upheaval in urban education.

In the mid-1960s it was believed that school integration was an efficient way to improve the quality of education in urban schools. It was perceived, especially by many black parents, that having white youngsters in classrooms with black youngsters was one way to bring the same kind of educational accountability to the black community that had always existed in the white community. Presently, however, there is much controversy in both the black and white communities concerning the practicality of desegregation. When this issue was linked with the question of decentralization in Detroit, Michigan, several school-board members who supported school desegregation subsequently lost their board positions. To a certain extent, this interest in quality education is being expressed in the concept of community control.

Some discussion is needed to define what is meant by community control. Already a complex issue, community control becomes even more complicated because of its association with the concepts of decentralization and desegregation. Decentralization is a term used to describe decision-making arrangements of organizations. It implies a total reorganization of a school system's administrative structure to bring decision making closer to the community and to give individuals more power to influence policy decisions. It also affects the number of bureaucratic channels and levels which one must negotiate before decisions are made.

In a centralized metropolitan school system most major decisions are made by higher level representatives or bureaucrats who have no direct personal tie to the neighborhoods involved. This usually means that lower status areas go unrepresented in such decision-making processes. It is conceivable, but not likely, that one could have a centralized school system with a relatively high degree of community control (Smith & McGrail, 1969).

More common, though, is the opposite tendency. Many school systems have kept the major decision-making power in the central boards while delegating only limited authority to district superintendents and setting up local boards that serve only advisory capacities (Ocean Hill-Brownsville, 1969). Thus, while the decision-making process has been decentralized, the degree of community control has either remained virtually constant or has diminished. It seems fair to say that in school systems in the large urban areas a decentralized decision-making process is a necessary, but not the only, condition needed for community control. A further consideration is whether the boards are advisory or have broad powers. This rationale is based on the theory that involvement of urban residents in the decision-making process of the schools will lead to greater pupil achievement. That theory has roots in the traditional middle-class model (Ocean Hill-Brownsville, 1969).

Decentralization of community school systems reaffirms the basic values regarding community control over the educational process. The most frequent argument against decentralization is the allegation that it hinders integration (Smith & McGrail, 1969) and that it is a step back to de facto segregation. This argument loses most of its force when it is noted that under the present centralized educational systems the percentage of blacks and other minorities in urban schools has been increasing steadily during this decade. Decentralization would not necessarily facilitate integration or segregation (Smith & McGrail, 1969).

If this trend is to continue, as demographers project it is, residents of core-city communities should have a say in the decisions affecting the education of their children. Decentralization is the base for this, as the late Whitney Young (1969) stated: "We've never had integration, and so long as black children are denied decent schools, and black families remain imprisoned in rotten tenements and grinding poverty, arguments about segregation take on an aspect of unreality" (p. 290).

A second common argument is that decentralization inevitably leads to the inefficient use of educational resources. Centralized purchasing power enables school systems to be economical in the acquisition and use of resources. While it may be necessary to sacrifice this economy for the sake of more important values, the central office could still be responsible for purchasing and maintenance (Smith & McGrail, 1969). It could also be responsible for allocating local district expenditures to principals and community school boards (Shedd, 1967).

A child needs to feel that there is a partnership between school and community if he is to develop a sense of self-worth and an awareness of his heritage. He needs to know that his school is committed to him, to his success and to his future. Black parents and community members have been convinced that only through community control of the schools will these educational benefits accrue to their children (Young, 1969).

Historically, large centralized bureaus have been noted for their insensitivity to the real needs of the local communities they purport to serve (Smith & McGrail, 1969). Today urban parents are rising up against the educational establishment. The concern is for decentralization and community involvement in the decision-making process (Young, 1969). Thus, out of desperation caused by the existing school systems, community leaders and parents feel that there is a greater chance to make important decisions responsive to their educational needs through decentralization. Community control, for its proponents, can provide opportunities for people to share in decisions that affect their children, and it can restore a sense of community and foster responsibility and accountability on the part of professional educators (Manning, 1969).

Community control may be described as the process of collective community self-determination where citizens are involved in the decision-making process. According to Wilcox (1969), urban communities are asking for:

1. Control over hiring, firing, training and programming of school staff. The local governing board should have the power to establish a staff with knowledge of the community and a commitment to the education of the children of that community. Evaluation of the staff should be based on pupil performance.

2. Control over site selection and naming of schools. The local governing board should have the power to determine school location with the community and have an effect on any associated relocation. In addition, schools serving large numbers of minority youth should allow them to name their schools after their own heroes.

3. Control over expenditure of funds— local, state and federal. The local governing board should have the power to employ local people, develop programs, and direct money toward locally owned businesses through its purchasing power.

4. Control over design and construction of schools. The local governing boards should have the power to award contracts permitting the employment of skilled minority people present within the community.

Urban educational institutions have received the greatest pressure for community control, not only because of the high concentration of minority people in urban areas, but also because the bureaucratic urban school systems have been found to be most unresponsive to the expressed interest of the urban dwellers. The sheer mass of urban school systems has created bureaucracies which convert instructional traditions, educational cliches, and general pedagogic inertia into a philosophical and procedural barrier to educational reform (Shedd, 1967).

Urban bureaucracies have tended generally to codify and enforce systemic values which divert attention from education in the classroom. Historically and symbolically, children and teachers rarely appear on organization tables. Centrally dictated curriculum and personnel assignments, central office monopoly of status positions, and centrally formulated rules and procedures which gain the force of moral dicta are the identifying marks of large school systems (Shedd, 1967).

In this scheme of things, centralized and rigid uniformity becomes an implicit goal; curriculum guidelines become psycho-social bulwarks; individual student learning and behavioral problems are handled by general precepts of objective counseling; and personnel caution and acquiescence are elements of survival and promotion. Students are provided with a woefully inadequate education. Effective personal communication is supplemented by directive; human intention is confused with convention; and administratively oriented student-personnel stability is equated with stolidity (Shedd, 1967). All of these factors provide a backdrop to the issues surrounding increased community control and greater community self-determination.

Urban parents want to make the educational system accountable to them. Then, if the system fails, the parents and the community can initiate changes to rectify the failure. Thus, the proponents of community control are rendering the diagnosis that the problem is not with the learner; the problem is with the system, with the institution. Parents want a system that is responsive to their children and to them. They want to build this new and relevant system (Fantini, 1969). Also, it is a well-accepted principle that parental involvement in the schools leads to favorable attitudes toward education in the children. Young (1969) noted that the accountability of the local schools to the communities which they serve has been compromised by the increasing size and complexity of the administration of large urban school systems. Parents have less ability to influence decisions which affect the education of their children. Communications have broken down between the ghetto schools and the community; the schools often seem unresponsive and the parents do not trust the officials responsible for formulating educational policy.

Community control proponents believe that parents would increase their involvement in the education of children. Moreover, there is a deep and abiding faith in minority communities that, in the face of all obstacles, a decent education can be obtained if the right decisions are made; those decisions will be made only if the community has major control over them. They are weary of being presented new packages that do not reflect the realities of life in the communities, the variety and beauty of their cultural heritage, or the complexity of upward mobility (Manning, 1969).

Community control can improve the academic achievement of youngsters. A study of decentralization in Washington, D.C., clearly illustrates this claim. After one year of community control, students in the Adams-Morgan community school showed considerable gains in reading proficiency. Only a handful of other public schools in the city exhibited such improvements, while most schools showed declines (Levin, 1970).

Although full integration has supposedly been the law of the land for 16 years, urban schools are becoming more segregated, and the current national administration has reduced the nation's commitment to integration. Proponents of community control argue that it is the best path to multiracial school communities. It leads to cohesive educational achievement, and, eventually, economic and political strength (Caughey & Caughey, 1969). The root issue here is equality. "People in disadvantaged areas are demanding their fair share of American life in terms of political and economic power and in terms of social position relative to the major ethnic groups" (Smith & McGrail, 1969, p. 5).

Hamilton (1968) notes that

Many black people are demanding more black principals in predominantly black schools, if only because they serve as positive role models for the children. Children should be able to see black people in positions of day-to-day power and authority. There is a demand to have the schools recognize *black* heroes with national holidays. There is concern for emphasizing group solidarity and pride which is crucial for the development of black Americans. And there is very serious question whether a predominantly white, middle-class ethos can perform this function (p. 678).

A growing number of black Americans are insisting that the schools begin to reflect this new concern. Likewise it is not only important that Afro-American, Chicano and American Indian history be taught in minority schools, but that it also be incorporated into the curriculum of white schools throughout this country. It is not sufficient to give an accurate historical picture of the ethnic groups only to minority children. All Americans must have this exposure in the city, the suburbs, the local schools (Hamilton, 1968).

Of utmost concern to the urban community is the desire for educational programs which are structured to facilitate the academic and social growth of their youngsters. The press for community control and decentralization did not occur as an isolated phenomenon in the urban community. It came about through the community's awareness that educational resources were in abundance in middle-class communities. Integration was seen as one way of providing minority youngsters with strong and positive educational options.

Decentralization and community control are basic approaches to providing minority members with decision-making power over education. To the large community, however, it means that those who are in power positions must share their power. Of course, there are many who are reluctant to do this. Minority communities, however, do not see power as an end in itself. Rather, it is seen as a means of facilitating positive educational programs for their children.

In considering decentralization and community control as one step toward quality education there are two crucial considerations: 1) resources must be reallocated on

a disproportionate basis, and 2) school districts must be limited in size. School districts which reach an unmanageable size in terms of pupil population should consider size as one criterion when considering decentralization of a district.

However, the basic concern of minority communities must be kept in mind as a prime consideration, that is, educational programs must be structured to facilitate the academic and social growth of urban youngsters. Community control and decentralization are viewed only as steps toward this end.

IMPLICATIONS FOR IMPROVING EDUCATIONAL RESEARCH IN URBAN SCHOOLS

The increased number of innovations being tried in teacher training, contract learning, and community control, and the overriding press for accountability, all highlight the need for improving educational research and evaluation generally, but in urban schools specifically. The improved research and evaluation strategies may well begin with a broadened definition of the concept of educational achievement. This definition should serve to move researchers away from the narrow definition of achievement generally reflected in most tests purporting to measure educational achievement. Such concepts of self-concept and willingness to use one's ability to read are suggestive of the broadened definition of educational achievement being advanced here.

During the decade of the 1960s, "contradiction" plagued educational institutions. While the proportion of the population that entered school earlier and stayed in school longer continued to grow, the worth of the school experience was being questioned at every level. As the level of five- to 34-year-olds enrolled in school increased from 56 to 60 percent (Genovese, 1969), the Coleman Report was questioning whether the school experience had any marked and significant effect on individuals at all (Light & Smith, 1970). Even as the greatest increase in percent of school attendance was experienced by preschool children, the Westinghouse Learning Corporation study of the Head Start Program declared this massive preschool program a failure. Finally, while some educators were advocating the Follow Through Program as an extension of the Head Start Program, Arthur Jensen was stating that all attempts at compensatory programs had failed.

The charge is clear: if the educational institutions are going to survive, the 1970s must be approached as the decade of clarification and conflict resolution. The basic thesis being suggested here is that the educational research and program evaluator must share an essential part of the burden for providing such clarification and conflict resolution. Metaphorically, the position assumes that the quality of the educational product or process will never exceed the capability of its "quality control department" to monitor and document changes in that quality. Education will never be able to clarify contradictions and respond effectively to the impending pressures unless precise procedures are developed and implemented to establish the worth of any educational innovation, be it as narrow as a new preschool reading-readiness program or as broad as an alternative model to public education as we know it.

The educational researcher-evaluator must resolve a number of issues if he is going to meet his responsibility. The first and possibly most fundamental issue facing the researcher-evaluator is that his work has become political. Where evaluators once bemoaned the neglect of their results by policymakers, they are now being given more and more of an active role in decision making. Evaluation reports are becoming front page news (Weiss, 1970). This politicization can be traced back to the passage of the 1965 Elementary and Secondary Education Act. A clause in the Act stipulated that evaluation must be a necessary building block in the design and construction of American educational reform. Provus (1969) suggests that this clause may prove to have greater impact on education than the Act itself. Individuals trained in the scientific method would be likely, at first glance, to applaud the wisdom of basing policy decisions on sound evaluation. The evidence suggests, however, that rather than transforming what was once political to an empirical base, the reverse is actually occurring. The scientific method as applied to program evaluation is slowly becoming a political process.

A second issue confronting the researcher-evaluator is represented in the relationship between the researcher and the researched subject. Historically, the constituent population for research studies has passively participated in various experimental programs. This passivity had been attributed to the fact that the participants shared the researcher's value that research was useful (Lorton, 1969). Today, however, constituent groups (blacks, poor whites, urban residents), finding themselves relegated to a marginal status in society, have begun to rise up and question the value of research. Marginal status groups are now demanding a "piece of the action." They are saying that the scientific community must allow them to define their own problems, set their own priorities, and develop their own innovative programs. This press for self-determination and control is going to increase rather than dissipate in the future. The researcher must realize this and decide whether he can conduct his research in cooperation with constituent populations. Should the researcher feel he needs autonomy in his work, he would be well advised to search for areas of scientific inquiry other than those found in innovative programs intended to affect marginal status groups in urban areas.

A third issue confronting the researcher-evaluator is that most of the research being funded by the federal government and foundations today is decision-oriented—inquiries designed to provide information to a decision-maker—rather than conclusion-oriented. In this case, the researcher is not free to develop his inquiry as he sees fit, as his activities are defined in terms of the decision-maker's requirements (Cronbach & Suppes, 1969). Conclusion-oriented research, on the other hand, is inquiries that take direction from the investigator's commitments and "hunches." The researcher is free to develop and test his own conceptions. The implications of this distinction transcend the entire research act. For example, in the conclusion-oriented research act involving tests of significance, the researcher is free to decide what level of risk he desires to take in setting his significance level for his decision rules about accepting or rejecting his hypotheses. In decision-oriented research involving similar hypotheses and significance tests, who has the responsibility or the right to set the decision rules or confidence levels? This may seem like a small point until one realizes that the generalizations of the Westinghouse Learning Corporation study of the Head Start Program, for example, could have been altered radically simply by readjusting the confidence levels and decision rules, and by an alternate emphasis on what differences were to be judged significant and what differences were to be judged chance fluctuation.

The distinction between research and evaluation continues to remain critical. If the practitioner fails to consider this issue he quickly finds himself experiencing a "methodological identity crisis."

A fourth issue confronting the researcher-evaluator comes from the fact that in the past some practitioners have felt that research and evaluation were essentially indistinguishable because the evaluator, like the researcher, could maintain his objectivity and let the data speak for itself. They would argue that someone other than the evaluator would make the final decision. Unfortunately, it is not that simple; to approach evaluation with this orientation will likely yield data which represent neither good research nor evaluation. The question is not who makes a decision, but rather what information ought to be gathered so as to facilitate the decision-making process. The question of what information will be collected emanates from the value questions which undergird the entire project (Hemphill, 1969).

Recent attempts to provide sound program evaluation have led to the realization that classical measurement techniques are not completely adequate (Glaser, 1963). Designed to assess the relative ordering of individuals with respect to test performance, this technique has been labeled as norm references measurement. Such measures are designed to maximize the discrimination among individuals within a group and minimize discriminations among groups. However, most innovative educational programs require just the opposite procedure. Glaser (1963) has described this measurement procedure as "criterion reference" measurement. With such measurements the emphasis is on minimizing the discriminations among individuals in a group, while at the same time maximizing the discriminations among groups.

Program evaluators must carefully examine the context in which they are operating. If the program is designed to improve the competency of groups relative to some other group or criterion, then priority should be given to those measuring devices which will be most sensitive to group differences.

Scholars involved in innovative program evaluation have come to realize that most of the problems with which they work are multifaceted and no program is likely to be all good or all bad. Evaluators have begun to approach the problems and programs as if they represent delicately balanced ecosystems. This orientation will improve the quality of the evaluations being done. The recent advances in multivariate research and analysis procedures have tended to strengthen the position of those who view the problem as complex and multidimensional. However, one should not be lulled into a false sense of security by such multivariate techniques because decisions will still involve human judgment and be based on some priorities (Hemphill, 1969). One of the most encouraging developments made in evaluation methodology is the realization that educational innovation is a dynamic process requiring evaluation of all the phases and stages of the innovation in addition to an assessment of the final product (Provus, 1969). This factor is extremely significant because in retrospect it appears that programs have been judged to be ineffective when, in fact, the programs went wrong in the early stage of the implementation process. Approaching innovation as a dynamic process which requires continuous monitoring and feedback will greatly reduce, if not preclude, erroneous judgments.

Politically inspired innovative programs will probably continue, and since such programs are likely to have a national scope, evaluators must find methodologies that will allow them to evaluate the entire program while protecting the idiosyncracies of the local units. This need rests on the obvious fact that selected programs and selected aspects of programs are going to be more or less successful in one location versus another. Unless the methodology makes provisions for this fact, treatment and location effects will be masked and relegated to the position of error variance.

Emphasis will continue to be placed on experimental and innovative programs designed to assist minority groups historically relegated to a marginal social status. This will be particularly apparent in the experimental activities centering on urban social institutions.

A failure to understand and be sensitive to the intricacies of conducting research involving minority groups has been cited by some authors (Baratz & Baratz, 1970; Coard, 1969; Lorton, 1969; Sroufe, 1970) as a basic reason why the research has led to equivocal results on the one hand and precipitated community revolt on the other. The common theme of most of these authors is that the researcher-evaluator tends to be characteristically middle class with all of the accompanying beliefs and values, and that the composition of those values transcends the scientific objectivity and interferes with the research activities. Excellent reviews of the nuances involved in this subtle yet significant phenomenon can be found elsewhere (Baratz & Baratz, 1970; Lorton, 1969). It is sufficient to say the concern is real and must be confronted by the researcher-evaluator if he hopes to successfully accomplish his task.

A number of suggestions have been made for overcoming this problem, and they vary from training researchers from marginal groups to supervising such research and to approaching the problem like the anthropologist approaches a different cultural setting. Each approach has validity. Since it seems reasonable to assume that for the immediate future the intervention-oriented research and evaluation studies will necessarily involve middle-class–oriented personnel, some immediate strategy is needed. Coard (1969) has suggested that members from the researched group, be it the black community, welfare mothers, etc., be meaningfully involved in the design and implementation of studies in which their groups are represented. This involvement may take the form of advisory groups, indigenous people trained as research assistants or community review committees. Such involvement, though not insuring success, will substantially increase the probability that the resultant research design will meet with less resistance from the communities involved. In addition, the procedure will assist the researcher in overcoming many of the language problems and will likely balance, if not eliminate, the presence of the middle-class values on nonmiddle-class populations. No one would deny that the defining characteristics of a ghetto, for example, are different if you are on the outside looking in or on the inside looking out. Since one view is no more real than another, at best, both views ought to be represented in the questions asked and definitions given in research studies.

When the researcher was in his laboratory conducting his science, his accountability rested with his scientific discipline and colleagues. When the researcher moved out of the laboratory utilizing federal and state revenues as a source of funds for his research, he implicitly entered into a consortium with an additional constituency—the public community. For example, research conducted in urban schools utilizing tax dollars which come from the parents of the children involved in the study makes that research open to public scrutiny from its inception to its termination.

Social scientists have been characterized by one black leader as "military," "mercenary" and "missionary"—military because they are seen as part of the control apparatus, mercenary because they get a "lion's share" of the money from programs like Head Start and use urban research for publications and job security, and missionary because they "co-opt the minds" of young black children (King, in Sroufe, 1970). If research and evaluation are going to be effective in the future, such perceptions, real or imagined, must be confronted and clarified.

The rising suspicion of the social scientist can be easily overcome to the betterment of society and social science if the research scientist is willing to commit himself and his skills to the service of the constituent groups—a level of commitment that has never been extended to disenfranchised groups.

The position offered here is that social scientists do have a responsibility to use their skills to aid society in solving its problems. Further, scientific methods can be applied to social problems so that changes can occur in society in a systematic, planned and orderly manner which is compatible with and indeed essential to humanitarian values (Fairweather, 1968).

If the social scientist is to meet his responsibility, significant changes must occur. If social innovative research procedures are going to be successful, changes in the mores and pathways of the American culture must also occur. Historically, cultural innovation and social science research have proceeded relatively independently, with neither one affecting the other to any great degree (Fairweather, 1967).

Education is at the hub of the social innovation which must necessarily occur if this nation is to survive. Educational researchers, like other constituent groups, must accept their full measure of responsibility in these difficult times. Anything less than full commitment will only result in another decade of contradiction.

SUMMARY

This chapter represents a partial review of many critical issues and related research in urban education as it is viewed in the 1970s. Because the educational system is so complex and because the urban context in which it is located is even more complex, partial treatment is necessary. No single work can attempt to cover all the research and all the issues.

The underlying theme is that urban schools are failing in what has always been regarded as one of their primary tasks, namely, to serve as the great equalizer of the conditions of men—black, white, rich and poor. The system has failed to meet the needs of long-standing American minorities —blacks, American Indians, and more recently, Mexican Americans and Puerto Ricans. A major reason for this is that the system reflects the biases that permeate the broader society; the term racism is appropriate in this context. The educational system has not made a major commitment nor has it established strategies to eradicate the various forms of racism that negatively impact on American minorities. A strong, white middle-class bias is reflected in the curriculum, i.e., social studies, humanities, and in the attitudes of many teachers toward minority-group children. Many of the tensions in urban school communities today are directly related to a system, long insensitive to the needs of America's ethnic minorities, that has failed to democratize itself. The authors have attempted to substantiate four beliefs which partly explain why today's urban educational institutions are in such a deplorable state.

1. Educational innovators have not given adequate attention to the environmental context from which urban youngsters come. This chapter places particular emphasis upon early health factors of urban children. Differential infant mortality and birth complications as a function of economic status are but two indices suggestive of the importance of environmental influences on learning. However, although the authors acknowledge the relationship between environmental factors—many of them community-based—and school performance, we strongly adhere to the point of view that the educational system cannot use this as an excuse for failing to provide strong educational programs for children in urban school communities. Rather, the system is obliged to overcome the deficiencies that exist in the educational system.

2. Teacher-training programs, which provide the essential element of the delivery system in the person of the teacher, remain rather unchanged and seemingly unresponsive to urban needs. The chapter emphasizes the critical need for imaginative in-service and pre-service programs for teachers. Programs must be in the mainstream of the total training process and not appendices.

3. Large urban school systems seem to be unresponsive to the needs of the individuals, the parents and the communities they serve. This state is understandable when one attempts to comprehend the magnitude of the "institutional inertia" driving these large systems. The authors support the point of view that new strategies must be found whereby urban systems can be decentralized and control over educa-

tional decisions will revert to the community.

4. Social scientists have not met their full responsibility as researchers in attempting to seek answers to the critical and conflicting problems facing urban education. The authors advocate training a new type of researcher who is socially concerned and who is, at the same time, well grounded in methodology. Somehow researchers must conduct their research in cooperation with the community. This research must have a direct link to educational improvement as it relates to urban and minority youngsters.

These are four points of view which the authors see as priority concerns if urban educational institutions are going to survive. Deprivation can no longer be used as an excuse for not providing strong, adequate education programs for urban and minority youth. Racism, racial discrimination, and other artificial man-made barriers prevent youngsters from learning and performing well in an educational setting. Education can and must be a leader; professional organizations such as the National Education Association and the National Committee to Support the Public Schools must all speak out and eliminate these barriers.

REFERENCES

Antonov, A. N. Children born during the siege of Leningrad in 1942. *Journal of Pediatrics,* 1947, 30, 250–259.

Baratz, S. S., & Baratz, J. C. Early childhood intervention: The social science base of institutional racism. *Harvard Educational Review,* 1970, 40, 29–50.

Birch, H. G., & Gussow, J. D. *Disadvantaged children.* New York: Harcourt Brace Jovanovich, 1970.

Birren, J. E., & Hess, R. D. Influences of biological, psychological and social deprivations upon learning and performance. *Perspectives on human deprivation: Biological, psychological and sociological.* Bethesda, Md.: Department of Health, Education and Welfare, National Institute of Child Health and Human Development, 1968. Pp. 91–183.

Bloom, B. S., Davis, A., & Hess, R. *Compensatory education for cultural deprivation.* New York: Holt, Rinehart & Winston, 1965.

Brazziel, W. F. A letter from the South. *Harvard Educational Review,* 1969, 39, 348–356.

Caughey, J., & Caughey, L. Decentralization of the Los Angeles schools: Front for segregation. *Integrated Education,* 1969, 8, 48–51.

Clark, K. B. *Dark ghetto.* New York: Harper & Row, 1965.

Clark, K. B. Answer for disadvantaged is effective teaching. *New York Times,* Annual Educational Review, January 12, 1970, p. 50.

Coard, R. M. Effective urban research: Problems and possibilities. *Urban and Social Change Review,* 1969, 3 (1), 21–22.

Cohen, S. A. Local control and the cultural deprivation fallacy. *Phi Delta Kappan,* 1969, 50, 255–259.

Coleman, J. S., et al. *Equality of educational opportunity.* Washington, D.C.: U.S. Government Printing Office, 1966.

Conant, J. B. *The education of American teachers.* New York: McGraw-Hill, 1964.

Cott, A. Learning to learn. *Wall Street Journal,* November 17, 1970, p. 1.

Coursin, D. B. Effects of undernutrition on central nervous system function. *Nutrition Reviews,* 1965, 23, 65–68.

Cowley, J. J. Time, place and nutrition: Some observations from animal studies. In N. S. Scrimshaw, & J. E. Gordon (Eds.), *Malnutrition, learning and behavior.* Cambridge, Mass.: MIT Press, 1968. Pp. 218–228.

Cravioto, J., Delicardie, E. R., & Birch, H. G. Nutrition, growth and neurointegrative development: An experimental and ecologic study. *Pediatrics Supplement,* 1966, 38, 319–372.

Cronbach, L. J., & Suppes, P. *Research for tomorrow's schools: Disciplined inquiry for education.* New York: Macmillan, 1969.

Crump, E. P., & Horton, C. P. Growth and development in Negro infants and children. *Lancet,* 1961, 81, 507–517.

Crump, E. P., Horton, C. P., Masuoka, J., & Ryan, D. Growth and development. I. Relation of birth weight in Negro infants to sex, maternal age, parity, parental care, and socioeconomic status. *Journal of Pediatrics,* 1957, 51, 678–697.

Crump, E. P., Payton, E., & Horton, C. P. Growth and development. IV. Relationship between prenatal maternal nutrition and socioeconomic index, weight of mother, and birth weight of infant. *American Journal of Obstetrics and Gynecology,* 1959, 77, 562–572.

Cuban, L. *To make a difference: Teaching in the inner city.* New York: Free Press, 1970.

Defendi, V., & Metcalf, D. (Eds.) *The thymus.* Philadelphia: Wistar Institute Press, 1964.

Deutsch, M. Minority group and class status as related to social and personality factors in scholastic achievement. *Society for Applied Anthropology Monograph,* 1960, No. 2.

Deutsch, M. & associates. *The disadvantaged child.* New York: Basic Books, Inc., 1967.

Drillien, C. M. *The growth and development of the prematurely born infant.* Baltimore: Williams & Wilkins, 1965.

Duncan, E. H. L., Baird, D., & Thomson, A. M. The causes and prevention of stillbirths and first week deaths. Part I. The evidence of vital statistics. *Journal of Obstetrics and Gynaecology of the British Empire,* 1952, 59, 183–196.

Eichenwald, H. F., & Fry, P. C. Nutrition and learning. *Science,* 1969, 163, 644–648.

Elsbery, J. W. Local school control in perspective. Paper presented at the meeting of the American Educational Research Association, Los Angeles, February 1969.

Erickson, M. T. Intelligence: Prenatal and preconception environmental influences. *Science,* 1967, 157, 1210.

Fairfield, R. P. Teacher education: What design? *The Antioch-Putney Graduate School Report,* Updating, Fall, 1967, No. 1.

Fairweather, G. W. *Methods for experimental social innovation.* New York: John Wiley, Inc., 1968.

Fantini, M. D. Participation, decentralization and community control. *National Elementary Principal,* 1969, 48 (5), 25–31.

Findings and Recommendations of the Citizens Advisory Committee on Equal Opportunities. Detroit: Detroit Board of Education, 1962.

Food and Nutrition Board's Division of Biology and Agriculture. *Maternal nutrition and the course of pregnancy.* Washington, D.C.: National Academy of Science, 1970.

Frisch, R. E. Present status of the supposition that malnutrition causes permanent mental retardation. *The American Journal of Clinical Nutrition,* 1970, 23, 189–195.

Genovese, E. D. Black studies: Trouble ahead. *The Atlantic Monthly,* 1969, 223(6), 37–41.

Glaser, R. Instructional technology and the measurement of learning outcomes: Some questions. *American Psychologist,* 1963, 18, 519–521.

Gordon, E., & Wilkerson, D. A. *Compensatory education for the disadvantaged.* Princeton, N.J.: College Entrance Examination Board, 1966.

Gottesman, I. I. Biogenetics of race and class. In M. Deutsch, I. Katz, & A. R. Jensen, (Eds.), *Social class, race and psychological development.* New York: Holt, Rinehart & Winston, 1968. Pp. 11–51.

Green, R. L. Crisis in American education: A racial dilemma. Paper delivered at the National Conference of Equal Educational Opportunity in America's Cities, U.S. Commission on Civil Rights, Washington, D.C., November 1967.

Green, R. L. (Ed.) *Racial crisis in American education.* Chicago: Follett, 1969.

Hamilton, C. V. Race and education: A search for legitimacy. *Harvard Educational Review,* 1968, 38, 669–684.

Harper, P. A., Fischer, L. K., & Rider, R. V. Neurological and intellectual status of prematures at three to five years of age. *Journal of Pediatrics,* 1959, 55, 679–690.

Harrell, R. F. Mental response to added thiamine. *Journal of Nutrition,* 1946, 31, 283–289.

Harrell, R. F., Woodyard, E. R., & Gates, A. J. The influence of vitamin supplementation of the diets of pregnant and lactating women on the intelligence of their offspring. *Metabolism,* 1956, 5, 555–562.

Haubrich, V. F. Teachers for big city schools. In A. H. Passow (Ed.), *Education in depressed areas.* New York: Columbia University Press, 1963. Pp. 243–261.

Hemphill, J. K. The relationships between research and evaluation studies. In R. W. Tyler (Ed.), *Educational evaluation: New roles, new means.* The Sixty-eighth yearbook of the National Society for the Study of Education, Part II. Chicago: NSSE, 1969. Pp. 189–220.

Hess, R. D., & Bear, R. M. (Eds.) *Early education.* Chicago: Aldine, 1968.

Hickey, H. Mid-point evaluation of the MICI five level inner-city teacher preparation program. Unpublished manuscript, Michigan State University, 1970.

Hunt, E. *Recent demographic trends and their effects on maternal and child health needs and services.* U.S. Department of Health, Education and Welfare. Washington, D.C.: U.S. Government Printing Office, 1966. Pp. 1–20.

Hunt, J. M. *Intelligence and experience.* New York: Ronald Press, 1961.

Illsley, R. Early prediction of perinatal risk. *Proceedings of the Royal Society of Medicine,* 1966, 59, 181–184.

Illsley, R. The sociological study of reproduction and its outcome. In S. A. Richardson, & A. F. Guttmacher (Eds.), *Childbearing: Its social and psychological aspects.* Baltimore: Williams & Wilkins, 1967. Pp. 75–135.

Jensen, A. R. How much can we boost IQ and scholastic achievement? *Harvard Educational Review,* 1969, 39, 1–123.

Kamii, C. K., & Radin, N. L. Class differences in the socialization practices of Negro mothers. *Journal of Marriage and the Family,* 1967, 29, 302–310.

Kellaway, P., Crawley, J., & Maulsby, R. The electroencephalogram in psychiatric disorders in childhood. In W. P. Wilson (Ed.), *Applications of electroencephalography in psychiatry.* Durham: Duke University Press, 1965. Pp. 30–53.

Kennedy, W. A. Addendum to "Intelligence: prenatal and preconception environmental influences," *Science,* 1967, 157, 1210.

Kerner, Otto, et al. *Report of the National Advisory Commission on Civil Disorders.* New York: E. P. Dutton, 1968.

Klein, R. E., & Gilbert, O. Malnutrition and intellectual development. Paper presented at the XI Inter-American Congress of Psychology, Mexico City, December 1967.

Kugelmass, I. N., Poull, L. E., & Samuel, E. L. Nutritional improvement of child mentality. *American Journal of the Medical Sciences,* 1944, 208, 631–633.

Kushlick, A. Assessing the size of the problem of subnormality. In J. E. Meade, & A. S. Parkes (Eds.), *Genetic and environmental factors in human ability.* New York: Plenum Press, 1966. Pp. 121–147.

Levin, H. M. Summary of conference discussion: Community control of schools. Washington, D.C.: Brookings Institution, 1970.

Light, R. J., & Smith, P. V. Choosing a future: Strategies for designing and evaluating new programs. *Harvard Educational Review,* 1970, 40, 1–28.

Little, W. J. On the influence of abnormal parturition, difficult labour, premature birth, and asphyxia neonatorum on the mental and physical conditions of the child, especially in relation to deformities. *Transactions of the Obstetrical Society,* 1862, 3, 293–344.

Lorton, P., Jr. Survey of literature on issues of research with low income and ethnic groups. Prepared for National Institute of Child Health and Human Development, 1969.

Manning, W. R. Decentralization: Problems and promises. *Bulletin of the National Association of Secondary School Principals,* 1969, 53(339), 116–123.

McMahon, B., & Sowa, J. M. Physical damage to the fetus. In Milbank Memorial Fund, *Causes of mental disorders: A review of epidemiological knowledge, 1959.* New York: Milbank Memorial Fund, 1961. Pp. 51–110.

McNeil, T. F., Wiegerink, R., & Doziers, J. E. Pregnancy and birth complications in the births of seriously, moderately, and mildly behaviorally disturbed children, I. *Journal of Nervous and Mental Disease,* 1970, 151, 24–34.

Monckeberg, F. Nutrition and mental development. Paper presented at the Conference on Nutrition and Human Development, East Lansing, Michigan, May 1969.

Morlan, J., & Ramonda, R. The disadvantaged child and his culture. In S. W. Tiedt (Ed.), *Teaching the disadvantaged child.* New York: Oxford University Press, 1968. Pp. 3–18.

Muecher, H., & Gruenwald, G. Pharmacological stimulation of arithmetic performance and graphomotor expansion. *Perceptual and Motor Skills,* 1962, 15, 101–102.

Naeye, R. L., Diener, M. M., Dellinger, W. S., & Blanc, W. A. Urban poverty: Effects of prenatal nutrition. *Science,* 1969, 166, 1026.

National Center for Health Statistics. Advance report. *Monthly Vital Statistics Report* 17:9: Supplements 1–8, December 4, 1968.

National Center for Health Statistics. Advance final mortality, 1967. *Monthly Vital Statistics Report,* March 25, 1969.

Nelson, G. K., & Dean, R. F. A. The electroencephalogram in African children: Effect of kwashiorkor and a note on the newborn. *Bulletin of the World Health Organization,* 1959, 21, 779–782.

Ocean Hill-Brownsville: The agony of decentralization. *Nation's Schools,* 1969, 83(1), 26–28, 94.

Olsen, E. G. Teacher education for the deprived: A new pattern. *School and Society,* 1967, 95, 232–234.

Pasamanick, B., & Knobloch, H. Epidemiologic studies on the complications of pregnancy and the birth process. In G. Caplan (Ed.), *Prevention of mental disorders in children.* New York: Basic Books, 1969. Pp. 74–94.

Pasamanick, B., Knobloch, H., & Lilienfeld, A. M. Socioeconomic status and some precursors of neuropsychiatric disorders. *American Journal of Orthopsychiatry,* 1956, 26, 594–601.

Platt, B. S., Pampiglione, G., & Stewart, R. J. C. Experimental protein-calorie deficiency: Clinical, electroencephalographic and neuropathological changes in pigs. *Developmental Medicine and Child Neurology,* 1965, 7, 9–26.

Provus, M. Evaluation of ongoing programs in the public school system. In R. W. Tyler (Ed.), *Educational evaluation: New roles, new means.* The Sixty-eighth yearbook of the National Society for the Study of Education, Part II. Chicago: NSSE, 1969. Pp. 242–283.

Report of the Detroit High School Study Commission. Detroit: Detroit Board of Education, 1968.

Scott, R. B., Jenkins, M. E., & Crawford, R. P. Growth and development of Negro infants. I. Analysis of birth weights of 11,818 newly born infants. *Pediatrics,* 1950, 6, 425–431.

Shedd, M. R. Decentralization and urban schools. *Educational Leadership,* 1967, 25, 32–35.

Shockley, W. Possible transfer of metallurgical and astronomical approaches to the problem of environment versus ethnic heredity. *Science,* 1966, 154, 428. (Abstract)

Silberman, C. E. *Crisis in the classroom: The remaking of American education.* New York: Random House, 1970.

Skeels, H. M. Adult status of children with contrasting early experiences. *Monograph, Society for the Research of Child Development,* 1966, 31, 3, Serial No. 105.

Skeels, H. M., Updegraff, R., Wellman, B. L., & Williams, H. M. A study of environmental stimulation; an orphanage pre-school project. *University of Iowa Studies in Child Welfare*, 1938, 15, 10–11.

Smith, C. A. Effects of maternal undernutrition upon the newborn infant in Holland. *Journal of Pediatrics*, 1947, 30, 229–243.

Smith, D. H., & Arnez, N. L. Inner city studies: Graduate training for teachers of the disadvantaged. *Journal of Teacher Education*, 1969, 20, 347–350.

Smith, D. H., & McGrail, R. F. Community control of schools, a review of issues and options. *Urban and Social Change Review*, 1969, 3, 2–3, 5.

Sroufe, L. A. A methodological and philosophical critique of intervention-oriented research. *Developmental Psychology*, 1970, 2, 140–145.

Stoch, M. B., & Smythe, S. M. Undernutrition during infancy and subsequent brain growth and intellectual development. In N. S. Scrimshaw, & J. E. Gordon (Eds.), *Malnutrition, learning and behavior*. Cambridge, Mass.: MIT Press, 1968. Pp. 278–289.

Stone, J. C. Training teachers of the disadvantaged: Blueprint for a breakthrough. In S. M. McMurrin (Ed.), *Resources for urban schools: Better use and balance*. New York: Committee for Economic Development, 1971. Pp. 49–75.

Stone, S. H. Chicago's Center for Inner-City Studies: An experiment in relevancy. *Social Education*, 1969, 33, 528–532.

Teachers Corps: Two full years of progress and plans for the future Teachers Corps. Washington, D.C.: Washington School of Psychiatry, October 1968.

Thomson, A. M. Diet in pregnancy. 3. Diet in relation to the course and outcome of pregnancy. *British Journal of Nutrition*, 1959, 13(4), 509–525.

Thomson, A. M. Prematurity: Socio-economic and nutritional factors. *Bibliotheca Paediatrica*, 1963, 8, 197–206.

Thomson, A. M., & Billewicz, W. Z. Nutritional status, maternal physique and re- productive efficiency. *Proceedings of the Nutrition Society*, 1963, 22, 55–60.

Toverud, G. The influence of nutrition on the course of pregnancy. *Milbank Memorial Fund Quarterly*, 1950, 28, 7–24.

Vinter, R. D., & Sarri, R. C. Malperformance in the public school: A group work approach. *Social Work*, 1965, 10(1), 3–13.

Warkany, J. Congenital malformations induced by maternal nutritional deficiency. *Journal of Pediatrics*, 1944, 25, 476–480.

Watson, B. C. *The taming of a reform: Co-optation of the National Teacher Corps.* Unpublished doctoral dissertation, University of Chicago, 1967.

Weiss, C. H. The politicization of evaluation research. *Journal of Social Issues*, 1970, 26(4), 57–68.

Werner, E., Simonian, K., Bierman, J. M., & French, F. E. Cumulative effect of perinatal complications and deprived environment on physical, intellectual and social development of preschool children. *Pediatrics*, 1967, 39, 490–505.

Wiener, G., Rider, R. V., Oppel, W. C., Fischer, L. K., & Harper, P. A. Correlates of low birth weight: Psychological status at six to seven years of age. *Pediatrics*, 1965, 35, 434–444.

Wiener, G., Rider, R. V., Oppel, W. C., & Harper, P. A. Correlates of low birth weight: Psychological status at eight to ten years of age. *Pediatric Research*, 1968, 2, 110–118.

Wilcox, P. The meaning of community control. *Foresight*, I, Vol. V, 1969.

Wilkerson, D. Quality integrated education. *IRCD Bulletin*, 1965, 5, 1–2.

Winick, M. Malnutrition and brain development. *Journal of Pediatrics*, 1969, 74, 667–679.

Wisniewski, R. Urban teacher preparation programs. *Social Education*, 1969, 33, 77–82.

Young, W. M., Jr. Minorities and community control of the schools. *Journal of Negro Education*, 1969, 38, 285–290.

CHAPTER **20**   Teaching the Mentally Retarded[1]

BURTON BLATT
Syracuse University

FRANK GARFUNKEL
Boston University

INTRODUCTION

Focus of this Chapter

Our central focus is concerned with research on teaching the mentally retarded. For reasons to be discussed in the next section, we adhere to a broad operational definition of empirical study that includes formal experimentation as well as other types of observational systems. Frankly, we have viewed with concern an almost total commitment to experimental and quasi-experimental approaches applied even to very complex and "dirty" field problems that cannot be studied satisfactorily in the laboratory—i.e., outside the natural setting. As Shulman (1970) remarked:

If the object of such research [educational] is the development of coherent and workable theories, researchers are nearly as far from that goal today as they are from controlling the weather. If the goal of educational research is significant improvement in the daily functioning of educational programs, I know of little evidence that researchers have made discernible strides in that direction (p. 371).

The problem of relevancy has been particularly troublesome in the field of mental retardation. With some rare exceptions—few of which might be called research on teaching (e.g., Edgerton, 1967; Goffman, 1961)—research in mental retardation has followed traditional lines of experimentation, survey analysis, and test construction and validation. With rare exceptions participant observation procedures and other phenomenological approaches to systematic data collection and analysis have not been applied to the general study of mentally retarded children or, specifically, to their school lives.

The above remarks are not meant to suggest antagonism to the value and promotion of formal experimentation in the field. Our concern is with the extent to

[1] The authors are grateful to Dr. Harriett Blank and Professors Arthur Blumberg, Thomas Green, Samuel Guskin, Samuel A. Kirk, Horace Mann, James J. McCarthy, Maynard Reynolds, Seymour B. Sarason, Paul R. Salamone and Howard Spicker for reading earlier drafts of this chapter and offering us valuable and constructive comments and suggestions. We are also indebted to Mrs. Virginia Andrews, Mrs. Mary Kishman, and Mrs. Nancy Spekman for their generous assistance in typing various manuscript drafts of this chapter.

which traditional models have determined the kind of research that is being conducted rather than, conversely, models determined by the nature of problems studied. Further, we are concerned that such traditional research models also determine the kinds of independent variables that are selected for study and influence the scaling of independent variations.[2] To state this another way, researchers are confronted by problems connected with the assignment of children to treatments and, to further complicate this, of teachers to treatments. This problem becomes formidable when the researcher attempts to deal effectively with triads of teachers, children and methods. Therefore, when one designs an experiment that includes children (who vary) and teachers and, possibly, some other adults (who vary) in classrooms, the notion of homogeneity of variance that assumes there is similarity in the way a treatment occurs in different classes with different teachers and different children is questionable. In attempting to deal with group comparability, some re-searchers have utilized random procedures (or substitute methods) to gain group comparability in the assignment of children, teachers and methods. Unfortunately, although this may solve certain theoretical problems if the randomization procedures are maintained—which they rarely are in field studies—other problems are hardly dealt with and certain new ones are created.[3]

Our review of recent literature relating to how and under what conditions the mentally retarded learn, reveals continued major emphasis on experimental studies that attempt to control various independent factors. This research has assessed differences among several independent methods of teaching the mentally retarded. Investigators have designed research utilizing randomization procedures in which groups of children learning to read under one method are equal to those assigned to another method. Further, the researcher randomly assigns teachers to each group, hopefully to insure that one teacher would be more or less as well adjusted to his group and method as any other teacher would be to any other group and method; and, lastly, to give greater assurance to the assumption of group equality, other pertinent variables would be measured to check the randomization. Consequently, the researcher is in a position to claim that these two variables, children and teachers, were held constant for all of the groups studied.

The above research strategy is based on the belief that the method of teaching (or the curriculum or the curriculum organization) is the most significant independent variable. In such studies the kinds of chil-

---

[2] Presenting a compelling argument, Shulman (1970) encouraged educational researchers to leave the safe and sterile atmosphere of the conventional laboratory for the classroom setting. Because the current "gap between such studies ('conclusion-oriented') and needed educational applications is simply too great," what is needed is another form of investigation "to bridge that gap and create the basis for educational theory" (p. 377). Shulman concluded that, in view of its complexity, "it might be in the long range interest of both psychological theory and education to ignore those theories for the moment and proceed along a relatively atheoretical path in the study of education" (p. 383).

In a personal communication, Samuel A. Kirk, pursuing a line of reasoning similar to Shulman's, speculated that "one of the research approaches that could get at process and some of the things that you are talking about is through idiographic studies. I always think of the report by Itard which has become a classic....I think that in our field we need more intensive studies of cases; how they learn, what obstacles there are to their learning, etc. in order to understand their learning processes. When we have enough hypotheses from this kind of approach, we could do better controlled research. As you indicated, we tend to jump on comparison of methods, without making a real analysis of what ought to be done."

[3] Accompanying the randomization strategy is the assumption that factors which do not interest the researcher, or with which he cannot deal, will "randomize out," i.e., will equalize across groups. Although, as we stated above, this may provide a theoretical solution for the researcher—if the randomization procedure does not break down—it is entirely possible that those variables with which the researcher has attempted to deal through randomization may be the very factors upon which the research might have profitably focused.

dren and the personalities of the teachers are considered to be intervening variables that have importance but are peripheral to the experimental comparison being made. Therefore controls are employed to equalize the other potentially independent variables. One objective of this chapter is to present a rationale that is a reversal of the above example. By this, we intend to discuss the possibilities and values that may obtain by specifically assigning—for the purposes of field research on teaching—major independent variables which relate directly to teachers and children, and intervening variables which relate to method and curriculum content. Although this approach is suitable for the study of classroom situations per se, it appears to be especially appropriate for the study of the educational environment of mentally retarded or most other disabled children.[4] In those special programs, the "usual" curriculum goals are generally subordinate to ones pertaining to interpersonal relationships. Emphasis is not primarily on achievement, and methods of teaching are not generally considered to be of greatest importance and are, in fact, de-emphasized. This is another way of saying that the independent variables which *should be* given most attention in such settings—teachers, children, and their interactions—*have not been* subjected to careful measurement and control.

There are several technical reasons for experimenting with only one or two fairly discrete variables at a time; on the other hand, there are as many reasons for analyzing the complex interactions of children in natural settings (Shulman, 1970, p. 383). In the latter case, classroom situations can be manipulated in order to provide the

observer with limited structure in a natural setting. Data obtained could then be used to compare programs and curricula for children in order to enhance the possibility of favorable behavioral changes which will depend upon prior maximization of the principal sources of variance—teachers and children. Through such study we begin to confront the following questions: What anomalous behaviors are displayed by the children and how are they connected to the evolving class atmosphere? What are the specific effects of various procedures upon individual and group behaviors?

To continue this line of reasoning, much attention has been given to the proposition that the teacher-child relationship is critical to the teaching process, suggesting the importance not only of the "how" of teaching, but the relationship that develops between the teacher, on the one hand, and both individual children and the total group on the other (Rosenthal & Jacobson, 1966). An example of this phenomenon is the "Hawthorn Effect," one that persistently appears in psychological and educational experiments and which seems to be more consistently related to improved performance than any particular method or curriculum. Stated another way, the excitement generated by a research project (e.g., the "Hawthorn Effect") is an experimental side effect that appears to have more research significance than so-called main effects. Therefore, one assumption the researcher might consider is that something like the "Hawthorn Effect" is necessary to the development of a significant interaction. Yet another way of stating this is to specifically design "Hawthorn Effects" as sources of independent variation in research on teaching.

Although we believe that something akin to the "Hawthorn" is necessary, we also believe that, in itself, such an effect is not sufficient. There are other questions to be answered. How do children spend their time in classrooms? Do they attend to what is going on? How is their attention moni-

---

[4] In personal communication, James J. McCarthy echoed support of the above assumption: "...during the past months, the thought has been occurring to me that the real differences in treatments have often hinged on affective variables (e.g., motivation) and, therefore, we ought to put our research effort there. To your view that most research on teaching the retarded ignores 'processes,' I can only say, amen!"

tored? How are they dealt with when they succeed and when they fail? What kinds of questions do they ask? What kinds of questions are asked of them? Questions such as these—and a good many others—must be studied and answered if we are to learn more about behavior and how it can be affected. Yet rarely do we pose such questions; rarely do we judge a teacher's effectiveness, for example, by other than an estimate of her acquisition of knowledge concerning her "subject" or her "teaching."

In spite of the neglect and ignorance we have mentioned, there is sufficient evidence to reconsider this particular pervasive focus on teaching. To begin, variables in the usual educational situation are of such a nature as to discourage the rigorous experimentalist from dealing with them. The classroom situation is antithetical to an experiment that demands rigid application of certain a priori determined conditions. Personalities of teachers and children, social interactions and creative processes are examples of difficult-to-measure factors that must be dealt with if we are to do more than produce sterile descriptions of curricula. As stated earlier, since these factors cannot be measured easily, or perhaps not at all with presently available techniques, they are not usually included in the design of an experimental study.[5] For purposes of clarification, we may discuss these factors in terms of the *process* and the *substance* of classroom life.

Process refers to the way in which relationships are initiated, develop and endure among individuals, and the extent to which they exist. *Substance* is concerned with that well-defined content of relationships which can be tested formally. In studies of children in school, substance has received consider-

ably more attention than process. Thus, in terms of what is here called substance, an extensive body of literature provides hypothetical and empirical constructs that describe how children differ from one another and how individual children's test scores change. However, the literature is not at all clear on how to produce changes most efficiently, especially in dealing with children who have cognitive or other disorders. In terms of the present discussion, process has received less attention because it is less amenable to study. This is to say that the measurement of children's abilities (substance) is less difficult than the measurement of their social interactions and motivations. It is understandable that psychologists and educators have concentrated on variables that are relatively easy to measure, even though such variables may be of trivial importance to learning.

For example, an intelligence quotient is a good predictor of academic success. However, academic success is a function of both substance and process variables. The latter, being difficult to measure, are more or less ignored. Why, then, is IQ such a good predictor of academic success if it measures essentially the substance and not the process? It is probable that process variables affect IQ in the same way that they affect academic success, and the predictive efficiency of the IQ is, to a greater or lesser extent, due to indirect measurement of the process. Therefore, it is important for those engaged in research on teaching to explore not only the components of the IQ but those of academic success as well. Such exploration calls for intensive investigation of the total field of child behavior with minimal attention to conventional aptitudinal criteria and maximal attention to processes. Although this is neither a new nor profound idea, it remains conspicuously absent from research and evaluation programs. Such a focus is clearly a reversal of what generally takes place in research on teaching.

In summary, the focus and rationale of this chapter suggest the development of

[5] In recent years the works of Amidon, Bales, Flanders, and Medley and Mitzel, among others, have developed interesting and potentially illuminating observational systems. However, with very rare exceptions, these newer observational approaches have been noticeably excluded from the design of research dealing with teaching the handicapped. What such exclusion suggests is impossible for us to determine.

research strategies that are in harmony with discovering and evaluating what actually occurs in classrooms. It is further concluded that such research should assign, as bases for comparison, the variability that exists among and between interactions rather than among and between either teachers or children. Possibly this orientation to research on teaching offers a solution to what Blackman (1969) described as the serious and ambivalent dichotomy between those so-called logical positivists who prefer experimentation as the method of proof and those who view education essentially as an art form, one which would lose its color and vitality if the movement to fractionate the teacher-pupil interaction achieves its apparent goal.

CHAPTER OVERVIEW

During the past decade, more textbooks, monographs, research studies, and journal articles concerning the mentally retarded have been published than in all the previous history of man's efforts to describe and understand this group of people. As in other fields, and in spite of valiant efforts by individuals and organizations to catalogue and retrieve information and to prepare bibliographies and reviews, it is impossible for even the most diligent scholar to keep up with all of the literature in this field. Fortunately, in recent years, a number of superior substantive reviews have been published. In the past *The Review of Educational Research* regularly devoted one of its issues to "exceptional children," and the reader will want to examine the still timely analyses of Dunn and Capobianco (1959) and Blackman and Heintz (1966). In 1963 the Council for Exceptional Children published Kirk and Weiner's *Behavioral Research on Exceptional Children*. The chapters by Heber on the educable retarded child, and Charney on the trainable retarded child, present a valuable collection of abstracts that have recently been updated

by the contribution of Spicker and Bartel in Johnson and Blank's (1968) *Exceptional Children Research Review*. Several other important reviews of research on teaching the mentally retarded should be noted for readers wishing to pursue the literature beyond this chapter's limits, dictated by the ever-present compromise between space allocations and chapter focus: Guskin and Spicker (1968), Kirk (1964), McCarthy and Sheerenberger (1966), and Quay (1963). Lastly, among the many related books that have been published in recent years, the following are particularly noteworthy in that each presents comprehensive reviews of literature that, in direct and tangential ways, are relevant to our central concern: Ellis (1966a, 1966b, 1968), Jordan (1966), Phillips (1966), Robinson and Robinson (1965), Sarason and Doris (1968), and Schiefelbusch, Copeland, and Smith (1967).

The review of literature to be presented in this chapter will not attempt to duplicate, or even elaborate upon, the aforementioned reviews. Rather, we will deal briefly with only recent literature pertaining to teaching the mentally retarded and, beyond that, discuss the general research in this area in terms of our hypotheses relative to the study of teaching and our theoretical formulations that have obtained from both the evaluation of prior work and our own research experiences.

The remainder of this chapter will be concerned with, first, the continuance and elaboration of our earlier discussion of research on teaching. Second, a selected critical review of the most recent relevant research has been divided into three sections: studies concerning variations in home and community settings, studies concerning variations in educational atmosphere, and studies dealing with variations in children and teachers. Lastly, the chapter will conclude with a discussion of the nature of research on teaching, the importance of hypothesis-generating studies, and possibilities for the development of new scientific traditions that may enable field researchers to deal with heretofore insuperable problems in the study of teaching and its effects.

RESEARCH ON TEACHING

A Polemic

Nearly all research on teaching-learning is plagued by a paradox: on the one hand there is the need to support generalizations about teachers, children and methodologies, and on the other hand lies the problem of individualization, i.e., which children work best with which teachers and under what methodological conditions (Vale & Vale, 1969). The need for generalizations produces research which attempts to structure supposedly categorical uniformity over qualitatively different inputs. Independent variation is assumed to exist a priori, as is the case with comparative studies of methodologies, curricula or teacher styles. Such propositions set forth the premise that, given discrete independent variation of particular teacher, methodological or curriculum variables, there will be measurable differences in output as inferred from either the later measurement of observed behavior or through the use of standardized or specially constructed tests which specifically measure independent variation that is a function of independent variables. This approach lends itself to the study of many different classes and teachers who may be assigned to points on a scale of independent variation. This assignment can be random or it can be ex post facto in terms of the given characteristics of a general environment, teacher, classroom, physical facility, curriculum or chosen pedagogy.

A second major approach implicitly assumes that class variation is secondary to individual variation and that the primary research unit should be either an individual child or an individual child with a specific teacher or class. Without doubt this leads to a far more tedious research procedure

and does not lend itself to the random assignment of children to treatments. This molecular approach suggests that the search for what promotes difference must center on the longitudinal dynamic interaction between specific children, their teachers and their peers; further, it implies that between-class differences will not be as important as variations of children within particular classes.

This is not to say that there will never be uniform class (i.e., classrooms of children) differences but, rather, that such differences will be relatively rare since they would be dependent upon uniform application of specific kinds of subject matter and goals across groups of children of widely varying abilities, interests, values and motivations. The factor that is brought into bold relief when we study the education of mentally retarded children, as opposed to children in regular classes, is the impossibility of applying uniform academic goals. This reasoning follows from those factors leading to the placement of mentally retarded children in special classes, the structure and continuity of those classes and the powerful variations —vis-a-vis the handicapped—that exist between different school systems, classes and teachers.[6] The extent to which within-class variation is trivial will depend upon the existence of powerful and uniform differences between classes, which is by way of saying that no matter what the differences are within classes they are not nearly as

---

[6] For example, an impressive literature fails to demonstrate the superiority of either special curricula, administrative organization or special methods in the educational treatment of the retarded (Blatt, 1958; Cain & Levine, 1963; Cassidy & Stanton, 1959; Goldstein, Moss, & Jordan, 1965; Hottel, 1958; Kirk, 1958; Mullen & Itkin, 1961; and Wrightstone, Forlano, Lepkowski, Sontag, & Edelstein, 1959). We speculate that these rather consistent findings are due, in part, to the nature of "special child" identification and, in part, to the pervasive effects of such identification, which together provide both extraordinary variation between and within each class *as well as* an equally extraordinary variation between those classes and so-called regular classes.

important as the commonality that exists over groups of children in their abilities, goals, and acceptance of basic educational assumptions regarding why they are in school, what they hope to achieve, what rules they have to attend to, and their sources of gratification.

Our argument is not that there is a categorical difference between regular and special education with regard to critical sources of variation; rather, the fact that special education consists largely of children who are rejects from the regular system suggests that greater within-variation and less uniformity of behaviors and attitudes than generally are encountered in typical academic situations will be found here. However, it should be added that gross models used to compare different teaching methods or curricula have failed as badly in studies of regular classes as they have in studies of special classes (Gage, 1963).

An illustration of this phenomenon (i.e., the effects and importance of within- and between-class differences) may be found in research related to home and community effects on learning. Where there is relatively little variation between homes and within a community with regard to academic progress, one can expect school inputs and processes to contribute strongly to output variances; and it may not be necessary to be specially concerned with out-of-school variables. (However, this assumes that variation in academic behavior of children includes success and failure. There are schools where there is no important variation— virtually everyone succeeds or everyone fails.) On the other hand, where there is significant effective variation—i.e., effective in the sense that what takes place in the home and in the community will alter school behavior significantly—it is necessary to consider out-of-school environmental factors seriously, to measure them carefully and, perhaps, to contribute to independent variation in them (i.e., to actively manipulate) in order to assess change more adequately.

It is our contention that special classes in general, and special classes for the mentally retarded in particular, are heavily loaded with effective sources of variation other than those pertaining to academic activities in the school. With regard to constitutional variation (including genetic factors) which is relatively constant within educationally relevant time periods, we must, at the present time, consider ourselves to be more or less ignorant and must, therefore, remain open-minded. The literature on stability and change in children from various social classes does not offer a solid foundation from which to theorize about educational programs. Consequently, our position about the potential and probability for change in children has to be derived from other than (or in addition to) a strictly experimentally designed empirical base. This has been incisively demonstrated in the debate that has taken place recently between Jensen (1969) and Deutsch (1969), Kagan (1969) and others.

If constitutional (physiological) variation is eliminated from a total input-process-output design for the study of teaching—and where the primary criteria for the appropriateness of input are based on the careful measurement and description of process rather than presumptions about capacity (IQ) or potential, and also where we can assume the importance of community, home and nonacademic school variables in the process of change—it becomes imperative to assess research on teaching the mentally retarded in terms of the aforementioned questions and assumptions.

Goodness of Fit

In numerous ways individuals function differently. Research attempts to record these ways and explain the whys. For some researchers description is an end in itself. However, the history of social science has at least one certainty about it: description always leads from and to something. There is no "unbiased description." For example, when several groups are given IQ tests, almost invariably they will have different means. Are these objectively derived differences? We believe not! A good deal went into the development of the IQ test, selection of items, and procedures for administering the test. The testing format is, itself, a very special structure for communication. Tests are validated in specific ways using specific criteria. They are developed to do *something*. The narrower that *something* is, the easier it is to validate the test; however, the test becomes more biased when used with other groups at other times.

We often talk about variability. What makes the greatest difference? Is it heredity or environment? Is it school or home? Latin or home economics? Discipline or therapy? If a child has a problem, what (or who) had most to do with it? What is the main, most significant, most pervasive cause? What is the best, very best, way of undoing the problem? Does the answer to the first question (cause) lead to the answer to the second (undoing)? Does what is wrong indicate what should be done?

Eventually the question is: What should we do? And, how do we obtain that answer? Does it depend on who does it, or where it is done, or how much time there is? It is wishful thinking to expect that there is a clear relationship between what exists, why it exists, and what to do about it. Useful reductions are impossible, at least in the usual sense. Prescriptive education is a reduction. Therapeutic education is a reduction. Montessori, Frostig, Kephart, Cruickshank, Bereiter and A. S. Neill all offer reductions. They say *this* is what to do with children who present or behave in *this* manner. Whatever *this* is, there is the assumption that *this* can be identified, described and distinguished from something other than *this*.

What contributes to difference? Children are poor, come from families who have inadequate housing, food, medical services, space—are crowded into cities (or rurally separated)—and they do not do well in

school!—or on tests!—or on the cello! Often, they are migrants, emigrants or immigrants. And they do not speak standard English. They are different. They do not fit well.

A lot of confusion exists about what people should do, how they should do it, and when it should be done. Who is to judge? Are the judges' values my values? Or yours? How can it all be put together: poverty, delinquency, migration, retardation, language, values, disability, learning? Or, can it be put together? Is it psychology, sociology, anthropology or epistemology? Some individuals in some groups do not fit. The first problem is to decide about fit: individuals who do not fit, groups that do not fit, and individuals who do not fit groups that do not fit.

There are several differences to being an individual who does not fit (I-no-fit) rather than in a group that does not fit (G-no-fit). Special education "rides" the I-no-fit local. Black power "rides" the G-no-fit express. The new field of learning disabilities has epitomized the I-no-fit way (Blatt, 1969a). Find out what is wrong, then treat it. The patient subsequently will get better. Mental retardation has always been in the I-no-fit category, but it was a strategic error to assign the retarded to it. Either in special classes, institutions or at home, many do not have the skills to make it on their own.

A G-no-fit means there is something wrong with the society, or the culture, or with the G, or with everything. What do you want your child to become? Or yourself? Or Lee Harvey Oswald? But whatever it is, it has little to do with the child, with you, or Lee Harvey.

With any problem there are I-no-fit and G-no-fit alternatives. For example, we can examine juvenile delinquency. According to the I-no-fit strategy, the delinquent can be treated individually (or in groups) as a sick, ill-advised or alienated person requiring rehabilitation, therapy, education, counseling or, possibly, vocational training. A G-no-fit policy leads to a dilemma. Do we categorically change G? Or the rest of society? Are delinquents to be understood and treated as a collection of individuals who have something superficially in common with each other? They all have done something illegal. Therefore, should we impose or prescribe a common treatment? Enter, G-no-fit analysis. It is absurd to talk about a thousand or 10 thousand adolescents getting the same treatment. The G is at issue. But that either leads backwards—lock them all up, vengeance, punishment, retribution—or to an examination of who does not fit what, and when. Whoever and whatever does not fit has to apply to the total G. Whatever is to be done has to apply to the total G. How can we speak in these terms without descending to an absurd reductionism? In other words, if the G-justifying generality cannot apply to G, maybe there is a generality that can uniformly be applied to non-G. What is it that can be said about non-G that connects it to G—that forces G to be G-no-fit? What does non-G do, think, believe, feel, worship or deny that operates on G? This is not simply a question of prevention versus treatment. The kind of prevention or treatment will depend on which no-fit track is being used.

The learning disabilities movement has pushed for the identification of a particular kind of child—perceptually impaired—who is supposed to be different from mentally retarded or emotionally disturbed children. Each of these children is to receive individualized assessment and treatment. This appears to be a bastard no-fit strategy. But, in reality, it is not. It is I-no-fit all the way. The G is supposedly identified, but it is always quite clear that it is really I that does not fit and must be dealt with. Again, we ask what makes a difference. Are children with learning disabilities going to be any different if we view them as different from mentally retarded or emotionally disturbed children? Or is the real difference going to center around the goodness or badness of fit? To what extent do we change individuals, or at least try to change them, and to what extent do we change

groups and structures? For example, programs that change the structure of services for mentally retarded children that go beyond the requirements of any given individual child or adult who has been designated as being mentally retarded are clearly G-no-fit programs. The greater the inclusiveness of the G—therefore, including diverse disability groupings—the more it leans in the direction of G-no-fit. The introduction of more refined diagnostic categories is a push in the I-no-fit direction. This is certainly justified, at times, by the special needs of some disabled individuals and some disability groups. For example, a special diet for a child who has been identified as being phenolketonuric is the appropriate I-no-fit strategy. However, in our view, this is a proper exception to, not regularity of, our philosophical and clinical orientation.

Curriculum and Learning

The preceding section leads to a primary concern: whether any particular educational strategy—be it related to methodology, teacher, peer group or curriculum—"takes" in more or less the same way as an inoculation does or does not take. It is easy to establish whether an inoculation was administered, but there is considerable uncertainty in knowing whether or not it accomplished its purpose, i.e., before its effects can be verified by long-term follow-up. Thus, in the case of our analogy, it is one thing to judge whether an inoculation has "taken" by examining the individual some time after it was given; it is another to analyze whether or not it "took" in terms of its effect. The latter circumstance involves questions about whether the inoculation influenced susceptibility or, on the other hand, whether the individual was susceptible but never in contact with the disease-producing germ.

Similar questions exist with regard to educational input, process and output. The input can be there for various groups of children and it might or might not "take" depending upon personnel, timing and method of application. If there is reasonable evidence that, in fact, it did "take," it still does not mean that it will affect output. For example, it might or might not generalize to other situations and materials. Or appropriate situations and materials may not present themselves and, therefore, although the process originally "took," follow-up will offer no evidence of this.

Most research on teaching the mentally retarded (and, for that matter, most research on teaching) tends to concern itself with input and output phases but to ignore process. At best this can seriously decrease the power of a study and, at worst, it can destroy entirely the meaning of such research because of the "noise" that exists in a system that results in an error-ridden process that often has an overwhelmingly negative effect on children for whom there is a misfit between their needs and the educational situation.

Teachers and Teaching

The model used here assumes that research on teaching covers a finite period of time where certain individuals and groups are exposed either naturally or through manipulation to ordinary or extraordinary interventions, with measurements taken at various points during this period. Criteria for effectiveness can consist of a sequence of measures, a final measure or a series of measures in the last phase of the period. Studies can concern themselves with any one or all of the following stages: input, process and output. These are not meant to be mutually exclusive but, rather, useful for raising provocative research questions.

Input includes teacher, child, facility, methodological and curriculum variables that are given sources of independent variation and that may or may not be affected by the interventional process. Input variables may or may not be measurable even though they can be conceptually described. They

may or may not include nonschool variables such as those concerned with home, community or other external conditions and processes which are operating upon children, teachers and schools at the time of the intervention. They necessarily include the choice of the sampling unit to be studied, whether it be individual children, teacher-child dyads, classrooms, schools, or other units either defined externally or in terms of in-put characteristics.

Process variables are concerned with what takes place during the intervention and the ways in which input variables are modified as a result of the intervention. They include the quantity and quality of verbal and social interactions, the ways in which materials and activities are used by children, the ways children and teachers spend their time, and the interrelationships that exist between school and nonschool activities. Process variables can be conceived both in terms of teaching and learning, or in terms of what we might call the teacher-learning process. They can be the end product of a study—namely, to affect process by certain input—or they can be a means to producing stipulated goals.

Output is the effect(s) produced by a given intervention, with given inputs, and with either certain assumptions made or certain conditions ascertained about processes. Output can be measured with standardized or specially constructed tests, observational scales, or by measuring behaviors in subsequent extra-experimental situations. The strength of inferences about the relationship between input and output will depend upon the extent to which processes are identified, measured, and included in the data analysis.

Studies of the effects of educational interventions must be concerned with the extent to which observed behaviors are child-specific or situation-specific. Child-specific behaviors will be relatively unchanged by situational variation, whereas situationally specific behaviors will vary for any given child as he enters into different kinds of situations. Inputs that do not attend to situational variance will necessarily have marginal effects on children. But it is unlikely that the differential effects of situations will be identified unless considerable attention is paid to process measurement and input variation which permit attention to specific and systematic situational variation.

This is not to say that child-specific behaviors are accepted as being immutable but, rather, the existence of situational variations suggests strategies of teaching which attempt to re-create elements of other situations in which desired behaviors are known to exist. If a child's behavior varies with different adults, and this information is critical for generating effective interventions, it is unwise to leave to chance the study of factors which are closely associated with, or cause, behavioral variation, particularly with children who have repeatedly demonstrated situational failures. To assume that all situational failures are also child failures is both dangerous and misleading. Similarly, an excessive preoccupation with child-specific behaviors without careful recognition of their implications for teaching can only reinforce the expectation that the total child is child-specific and that educational programs can be little more than holding operations which keep children occupied and, hopefully, happy.

REVIEW OF RESEARCH

As mentioned earlier in this chapter, this review has been arbitrarily divided into three sections. Further, it claims neither depth nor does it include all possible variables that deserve consideration. It is designed to augment more comprehensive reviews and, secondly, it is included to illustrate both the kinds of research programs currently receiving support and the status of the field with respect to the nature and correlates of teaching the mentally retarded. Lastly, because there have been several recent substantive reviews (e.g., Guskin & Spicker, 1968; Spicker & Bartel,

1968), this section will be brief and will focus on subsequently published literature —our purpose being to provide a basis for discussing research trends, interests and strategies.

Variations in Home and Community Settings

Review of recent literature indicates that little attention has been given to studying the effects of the home and community on learning ability and achievement. This is surprising in view of the enormous support to compensatory education and the documentation, during the last 10 years, of a strong, persistent and pervasive relationship between socioeconomic class and educational achievement. The authors' own research with so-called "high risk" children (Blatt & Garfunkel, 1969) found, on secondary analysis, a significant correlation (0.52) between family organization and family (sibs) school behavior. That finding is consistent with the Coleman report (1966), Hurley (1969), and unpublished follow-up data from our aforementioned study. With such modest exceptions as the few studies describing the effects of family counseling or community recreation programs (e.g., Pumphrey, Goodman, Kidd, & Peters, 1970), there appears to have been little research activity in this area. Further, there is an equal paucity of studies that seek to illuminate or modify the attitudes of community groups or individuals toward the handicapped. Although several studies did report parents' attitudes toward their mentally retarded children, only one recent study was located which attempted to assess general community beliefs (Meyers, Sitkei, & Watts, 1966).

The dearth of research dealing specifically with variables of home and/or community —especially those studies that bear directly on social, emotional and cognitive aspects of school behavior—is particularly discouraging in view of what we had thought to have been deep interest in this area. Most related research, little as it has been, was concerned with intelligence as the critical, and usually as the only, independent variable. There has been a growing acceptance of the importance of home and social class factors, but these are not taken very seriously. Witness the design of Coleman's survey on *Equality of Educational Opportunity* (1966) and of evaluations of compensatory education including Head Start. It is not that variables from home and community are not used. They are usually present in most current research studies but are visibly trivial. That is, they do not have particular meaning or importance and contribute very little to the researcher's understanding of the problems confronting him. Asking parents of Head Start children questions about how they feel toward their children, Head Start and their community does not deliver revealing data. It amounts to using a teaspoon to do the work of a steam shovel. Similarly, attention to socioeconomic status does not, in itself, attend to the relationship between poverty and the ways that poor families or families with mentally retarded children deal with schools.

Our review of literature indicates either the general belief that the home and community have little influence on school-related development or—as is more probably the case—the belief that current experimental research capacities and techniques do not lend themselves to the adequate examination of that multitude of interrelated variables connected with families and communities. To be sure, experimental methodologies have not been as useful or productive as the so-called "soft" approaches of Edgerton (1967), Glaser and Strauss (1967), or the general model of participant observation as described by Bruyn (1966). However, there are other reasons—perhaps more important—why scant research attention has been given to home and community variables:

1. It is easier to use well-established instruments, with known reliabilities, short administration times, and pre-

sumed conceptual clarity. As soon as one gets into other methodologies it usually requires months of observation.
2. Apparently there is a degree of satisfaction in doing relatively "clean" research, even if it may not have important meaning or relevancy.
3. Possibly a covert factor is related to whatever biases researchers have against the concept of "change." To discover that others can and have changed means that the researcher could have changed. He could be somebody other than what he is. Expectations for change are tied up with the lives of the expecters as much as with those for whom they have greater and lesser expectations. Designs, variables, procedures and analyses are certainly influenced by these expectations.
4. If retarded individuals (or any other group) are studied in environments that are maximally different from what they are used to (certainly not necessarily a special class), and criteria are selected that are tied up with that difference and, furthermore, if those criteria have not been operationalized to demonstrate reliability (short-term consistency) and stability (long-term consistency) as a major function, but rather have been intentionally constructed to get at change (even at the sacrifice of predictability), then we can expect to be able to document change (see Blatt & Garfunkel, 1969). Most special classes do not radically alter children's lives and most homes do not change very much. But there are variations between homes and between communities that are probably much more compelling than formal educational variation—including school, teacher, methodology and materials.

Variations in Educational Atmosphere

Our review confirms the continued popularity of so-called efficacy studies, curriculum studies and evaluations of teaching methodologies. The abundance of research of this type is disconcerting in light of frequent expressions in the literature relegating such research to positions of minor value with little possibility for shedding either new light on tired questions, or generating new hypotheses for the study of heretofore puzzling problems. Kirk (1964) expressed the belief of many educational researchers with his comment that research on efficacy of special classes will yield little return in relation to the effort and resources required. Insofar as studies of special methodologies or curricula are concerned, the literature discloses the near universal failure to reject the null hypothesis, i.e., no difference between various experimental and control groups of children (Blatt, 1967).

What have we learned from these efficacy and methodology studies? Or how may we interpret their relatively uniform findings? We have concluded that the accumulation of evidence leads to a clear rejection of even the legitimacy of the form and content of these two questions asked rhetorically. The special versus regular class dichotomy is not a defensible independent variable. Although there may be powerful exceptions to this hypothesis, the regularity of data findings suggests strongly that children's experiences are not systematically different in a consistent way if they are in one or the other class. A child can have individual attention, warmth, support, friends and an exciting program in either class. Furthermore, his home can vary independently of the kind of class he is in. For many children, the home contributes so potently to variance that it may well drown out any differences connected with educational programming.

The most recent efficacy studies are in the familiar tradition. Welch (1965) compared the effects of segregated and partially integrated school programs on self-concept and achievement of educable retarded children. She found that those educable children who remain in a regular classroom one-half day were significantly less self-derogatory than those who were completely segregated, i.e.,

had no contact with typical youngsters while in school. Further, the partially integrated children improved significantly in reading in contrast with the academic achievement of the comparison group. Grounded along similar theoretical lines, Zito and Bardon (1969) investigated differences in achievement motivation between two groups of Negro educable adolescents, one group in a special education program and a second group in a regular school program. A third group, adolescent Negroes of typical intelligence in regular classes, comprised the remainder of the study sample. The results indicated that retarded adolescents were more influenced by success than failure and, further, that their achievement motivation was comparable to that of typical subjects from similar socioeconomic backgrounds. Insofar as comparisons between special and regular class youngsters, the special class experience appears to have made these adolescents more cautious in setting goals and more likely to anticipate failure, while the regular class children anticipated success and, in fact, showed greater achievement. In a study similar to Johnson's (1950) now-classic sociometric research on friend selection, rejection and acceptance of mentally retarded children in public schools, Rucker, Howe, and Snider (1969) administered a sociometric instrument in 30 regular junior high-school classes. The results of their investigation, designed to measure the social acceptance of the educable mentally retarded participating in both academic and nonacademic regular classes, supported the conclusion that retarded children enrolled at least half time in regular junior high classes were less accepted than their nonretarded peers. Further, these children were equally rejected in nonacademic and academic classes.

Other recently reported "efficacy" research has dealt with such matters as the effectiveness of cooperative programs between special education and rehabilitation departments (Bloom, 1967), off-campus work placement for the educable retarded (Howe, 1968), the effectiveness of special education on perceptual-motor performance (Krop & Smith, 1969), and integration versus segregation as related to success expectation and achievement (Schwarz & Jens, 1969). Each of the above studies, although relatively well controlled, has added little more than new layers to the massive ambiguity surrounding such questions as they concern curriculum design, administrative organization, and the efficacy of special interventions or treatments.

Preschool studies are being reported with increasing frequency, due—at least in part—to the favorable conditions vis-a-vis federal and state support of both service programs and research in this area. Guskin and Spicker (1968), Spicker and Bartel (1968), and Blatt and Garfunkel (1969) have all reviewed this rather impressive literature. Since the work of Skeels and his associates to the most recent studies, several theoretical threads reappear and, if for no other reason than their consistency and frequency, may be noteworthy. There continues to be marked interest in the study of so-called "cultural-familial" mentally retarded children and their families. More broadly, there is a significant escalation of interest in studies concerning the correlates of social class and intelligence. However, whereas during the first decades of this century cultural-familial cases were viewed as a specific etiological grouping of genetic origin, they tend now to be viewed as part of that much larger group labeled "culturally deprived" (Blatt & Garfunkel, 1969).[7] Insofar as genetic processes are concerned, the argu-

ment of Jensen (1969) and his adherents is by no means original. Even before Goddard's infamous "Kallikak" study, and through all of the decades to the present, there has been general agreement in the psychological and educational communities that genetic processes represent an important source of influence on the biological foundations of intelligence (see Blatt & Garfunkel, 1969, or Sarason & Doris, 1968, for discussions of this history). However, there has also been recognition, which is now increasing remarkably, that far too little is known about the nature of intelligence—except, perhaps, that it is vastly more complex than what is indicated by the IQ score —to justify anything more than the formulation of hypotheses and sheer speculations about the role played by multiple genetic factors (Blatt, 1970, and Bodmer & Cavalli-Sforza, 1970). As we have stated elsewhere (Blatt & Garfunkel, 1969), the nature-nurture controversies of the past are being superseded by the realization that earlier positions (either nativist or environmental) were oversimplifications which served certain polemicists' personal opinions far better than they clarified the problem. This important shift in viewing the nature-nurture controversy as neither settled nor understood, together with the emergence of cultural deprivation as a major political, economic, social and educational problem in our society, seem to have set the stage for systematic research and social action on environmental changes that might prevent intellectual deficits.[8]

---

[7] Although the "technical" definition of cultural-familial mental retardation is stated somewhat differently (Heber, 1959, pp. 39–40), substantively it suggests at least five characteristics which have long been descriptive of these individuals: 1) by traditional methods of evaluation their intelligence is subnormal, 2) the intellectual level and social adequacy of at least one parent and one sibling appear also to be subnormal, 3) there is no discernible central nervous system pathology giving rise to the subnormality, 4) they were born into, and reared in, a cultural milieu which is "inferior" to other strata of our society, and 5) they represent a disproportionately large part of the case load of many social agencies.

[8] For a full discussion of classification and terminological problems in mental retardation, tied so intimately to each shifting nature-nurture "fashion," see Blatt and Garfunkel (1969) and Heber (1959). Traditionally, mental retardation was defined as a constitutional condition of the central nervous system existing from birth or early age, incurable, and irremediable, oftentimes resulting in the inability of the individual to profit from ordinary schooling. This traditional definition was joined to a classification system that utilized arbitrarily determined I.Q. scores to categorize levels of intellectual capacity; e.g., 25–50 IQ was in the "trainable" category; 50–75 IQ was in the "educable" category. More recently (Heber, 1959), a new and widely used definition and classification manual was de-

To date, relatively few well-controlled studies bear directly on the effects of planned intervention on the intellectual development of culturally deprived or cultural-familial mentally retarded children (see Sarason & Doris, 1968, for a perspective on this problem). The accumulated research in this area varies greatly in methodological sophistication and quantity of descriptive detail about sample selection, differences in contrasting environments, and control of bias in collection of data. Although findings generally tend to suggest that planned interventions have the predicted effect of increasing intelligence test scores, these studies have neither produced compelling data nor have they permitted us to draw other than the most cautious conclusions concerning the correlates of intelligence. The three most recent preschool studies, not previously discussed in the aforementioned reviews, have had little more success than their predecessors in contributing to either educational theory or practice. Using groups of disadvantaged children of average intelligence, Karnes, Hodgins, and Teska (1968) compared the effects of traditional and highly structured experimental preschools. Kodman (1970) observed the effects of a special enrichment program designed for Appalachian children, and the third study, conducted at the University of Washington's Experimental Education Unit, dealt with behavior modification procedures for Head Start children (Haring, Hayden, & Nolen, 1969). All three studies reported significant changes in the predicted directions. However, each employed very small samples

---

veloped by a committee of the American Association on Mental Deficiency. This new manual defined mental retardation as subaverage general intellectual functioning, originating during the developmental period and associated with impairment in adaptive behavior. This definition did not assume a constitutional condition as a necessary requirement for mental retardation (e.g., in "cultural-familial mental retardation," pp. 39–40). It referred to function rather than, as is traditional, to capacity, and it did not preclude possibilities for prevention, cure or amelioration of mental retardation and its associated consequences.

and, with the exception of Karnes and her associates, there was little attempt to deal with the harassing problems of internal validity. Of the three, Haring et al. was most encouraging, first because the investigators were able to meaningfully depart from the tradition of IQ change as the major dependent variable and, secondly, because their design permitted the systematic study of teacher-child interactions and the modifiability of behavior.

In spite of the educational community's current interest in programmed materials, textbooks and, further, in elaborate new "hardware" systems to promote pupil learning, only a handful of studies relating to the education of mentally retarded children has been reported in recent years that dealt with assessing the potentialities of these newer educational technologies. Of those reviewed, Blackman and Capobianco's (1965) —the most sophisticated in terms of research design and conduct—reported disappointing results with a carefully developed teaching machine program in reading and arithmetic. Other studies by Bradley and Hundziak (1965), Miller and Miller (1968), and Rainey and Kelley (1967) reported greater possibilities with time-telling programs, programmed textbooks, and a unique method for teaching word recognition and discrimination, respectively. However, both Bradley and Hundziak's research and the Millers' study of "symbol accentuation" should be considered exploratory in view of both their small samples and limited research objectives.

Several other methodology studies are worth mentioning. Cawley and Goodman (1969) hypothesized that trained teachers, employing a well-planned program, could effect significant improvement in the arithmetic problem solving of mentally retarded children. Utilizing two control and two experimental groups—three of these classes for the retarded and one a regular class—it was demonstrated that, when teachers were trained during a two-week workshop, mentally retarded children improved significantly. Rouse (1965) found significant gain scores resulting from the involvement of educable mentally retarded children in a training program designed to enhance their productive thinking. However, Budoff, Meskin, and Kemler (1968) were unable to improve productive thinking scores in a general replication of Rouse's experiment. Working with 30 institutionalized retarded children, Bradley, Maurer, and Hundziak (1966) demonstrated the effectiveness of milieu therapy and language training in incrementing psycholinguistic functioning. In a study of the effects of group counseling on educable boys, Mann, Beaber, and Jacobson (1969) found that those who received counseling exhibited anxiety reduction and improved self-concept, deportment and school grades. Lastly, Vergason (1966) compared the effects of a traditional and an auto-instructional method on retention of sight vocabulary. Although there were no differences between groups after one day, superior retention for words learned by the automated self-instructional procedure was found during several follow-up periods.

Elsewhere we have reviewed and discussed an almost endless sea of studies relating to physical performance and capacity of the retarded child (Blatt, 1957, 1958, 1969b). For good and sufficient reason, few of the traditional strength, motor ability and physical ability studies are currently being reported. Replacing the physical fitness comparison and survey research of three and four decades ago is a renewed interest in perceptual-motor training and performance. Certainly, this interest is a reflection of a major educational movement—learning disabilities—which is now literally sweeping the country and obviously has broad and important implications for the field of mental retardation (Blatt, 1969a). Kahn and Burdett (1967) found that, by utilizing practice and reward schedules, mentally retarded adolescents improved significantly in motor skills. Employing specially designed training programs, both Lillie (1968) and Ross (1969) reported similar results, i.e.,

with training, mentally retarded children improved in motor proficiency. Edgar, Ball, McIntyre, and Shotwell (1969) reported gains in adaptive behavior after a program of sensory-motor training with a small group of organically impaired retarded children. However, Alley (1968) was unable to demonstrate significant effects resulting from a systematic perceptual-motor training program. Lastly, both Corder (1966) and Solomon and Pangle (1967) found that physical education programs significantly influenced the development of retarded children. However, most of these studies suffer from one or more serious design problems: samples that are too small or ambiguous, very short-term treatments, and dependent variables that seem unrelated to the experimental treatment (e.g., Corder, 1966, with an experimental sample of eight boys, designed a 20-day program of physical education using the Wechsler Intelligence Scale for Children as a dependent variable).

Since the theoretical work of B. F. Skinner in the fifties, the field of behavior analysis and modification has gained increasing attention and importance. A perusal of the literature in mental retardation generously testifies to the prominence and influence the operant conditioning movement has had in this field. Although much of the work reported emanates from the laboratory, a growing literature, anchored in the field, can now be found regularly in journals dealing with the education and treatment of the mentally retarded. Much of this literature is concerned with the severely retarded and the modification of such self-help skills as toileting, dressing and eating. A number of other studies have been successful in extinguishing destructiveness, aggression and self-abuse. The following reports are examples of behavioral studies that have succeeded in modifying the performance of mildly and severely retarded children —some institutionalized and others in the community: Bensberg, Colwell, and Cassel (1965); Broden, Hall, Dunlap, and Clark (1970); Doubros (1966); Karen and

Maxwell (1967); McKenzie, Clark, Wolf, Kothera, and Benson (1968); and Siegel, Forman, and Williams (1967). Undoubtedly, a great deal more can be said concerning the influence of this movement on the development of theory and practice in the field. There appears to be almost no possibility for other than escalated activity in this area and prominence and support for its advocates, in spite of shortcomings and limitations inherent in the concept of behavior modification as well as increasing misuse of this potentially important area by its unsophisticated advocates (Macmillan & Forness, 1970). For example, the senior author served recently on an HEW panel reviewing proposals to improve conditions in state schools for the mentally retarded. With possibly one and no more than two exceptions, each of those 60 applications communicated neither a glimmer of interest nor even an awareness of other than one or another variation of behavior-modification programming. Again, we have come full circle; as psychotherapy was the mental aspirin of the forties and fifties, it seems certain that our current era will be noted for the influence of this rediscovered approach we term "behavior modification."

Variations in Children and Teachers

The preponderance of research dealing with the learning characteristics and behavior of mentally retarded children originates in the laboratory and emanates from the experimental tradition. Experimenters continue to be interested in the laboratory examination of: paired-associate learning (Baumeister, Hawkins, & Davis, 1966; Hawker & Keilman, 1969; Milgram & Riedl, 1969; Ring, 1965); short-term recall (Baumeister, Hawkins, & Holland, 1967; Gallagher, 1969); discrimination learning (Riese & Lobb, 1967); curiosity behavior (Morgan, 1969); learning transfer (Gerjuoy & Alvarez, 1969); and attention (Follini, Sitkowski, & Stayton, 1969).

The contrast between the great number of

basic research studies and the scarcity of field or applied studies is remarkable. Except for the organizational efficacy and methodology studies, there is almost no recent research to report in the latter area. Lovell and Bradbury (1967) observed the learning of English morphology in educable retarded children. Huber (1965) studied the relationship of anxiety to the academic work of retarded institutionalized children. Jacobs and Pierce (1968); Laing and Chazen (1966); and Levine, Elzey, and Paulson (1966) reported on the social status of retarded children in various in-school or school-excluded settings. Lastly, a number of personality-type studies—reminiscent of the familiar comparison and status reports of the thirties and forties—have appeared from time to time during recent years, neither adding to our knowledge nor worthy of further discussion here.

We found but four studies dealing with teachers, their prestige, turnover and characteristics: Knox (1968); Meisgeier (1965); Sharples and Thomas (1969); and Sparks and Younie (1969). Finally, we found only two studies (Jones, Marcotte, & Markham, 1968; Strauch, 1970) that dealt with the attitudes typical children have toward the retarded.

We have said little here beyond noting for the reader's attention references to a sample of the more recent reports dealing with characteristics and variations of children and teachers. We have said little because little deserves saying, not because these are poorly designed or poorly executed studies; on the contrary, there is at least equal overall research precision here as contrasted with research more comprehensively discussed in other sections of this chapter. We choose to merely list the above reports because, first, laboratory research has yet to offer more than a promise for useful application to classrooms, teachers and children (a promise that we believe will be realized one day) and, secondly, because much of the remaining research mentioned in this section reveals little that was not reported as long ago as the forties and fifties, and whose value might have been questioned then.

DISCUSSION

During the 1969–70 academic year, the Council for Exceptional Children asked both of the authors of this chapter to participate in a unique experience involving the organization of what they termed an "invisible college." Due to limitations of time and resources, and because the Council needed some fairly reliable data concerning the kind of research that is currently being conducted and who is doing it, a core of key researchers in special education were interviewed by telephone to ascertain their opinions concerning current research efforts, issues and controversies. Eventually, the consensus on several topics will form the base for convening the "invisible colleges." A total of 55 telephone interviews were conducted, the interviewers asking each participant to:

1. Identify projects they found interesting and significant;
2. Describe their own work;
3. Identify the "hottest" controversy in the field;
4. Identify technical or methodological problems delaying research efforts;
5. Name the creative mavericks.

In the general field called "special education," the categories of behavior modification, early childhood, strategies in special education, curriculum development in mental retardation and innovations in personnel training were the most frequently cited. Pupil characteristics, methods and materials, and speech, language, and communication disorders were mentioned with lesser, but impressive, frequency. Although the above survey assessed research interest in a much broader area than ours—mental retardation—these findings accurately reflect how we would respond to such questions as they might deal specifically with the field of mental retardation. Our brief critical litera-

ture survey revealed the great and increasingly influential position now enjoyed by those engaged in behavior modification research. When—for the purposes of categorization—reinforcement, applied behavior change and classical conditioning studies are grouped together, they probably constitute the greatest percentage of articles on mental retardation to be found in current major journals. Further, although the Council for Exceptional Children has a somewhat different constituency and mission than the American Association on Mental Deficiency or other organizations focused specifically on mental retardation, literature reviews in our field would, undoubtedly, disclose the majority of basic studies concerned with: verbal learning, discrimination, reinforcement and applied behavior change, and—to a lesser extent—generalization and motor learning. (See Gardner, Solomowitz, & Saposnek's paper, "Trends in Learning Research with the Mentally Retarded," unpublished but reproduced in the Council for Exceptional Children *Planning Report for Information Analysis Products,* 1969.)

Our literature survey and the results of the Council's telephone study have both indicated that the preponderance of published research in mental retardation is experimental. Most studies of teaching have used traditional designs, whether they were efficacy studies, follow-up studies of children in special and regular classes, studies of different reading approaches, or studies of different curriculum approaches. Although these kinds of studies are more amenable to design modifications which may account for dyadic variation, we believe that there are more appropriate ways to study teaching-learning in classroom or tutorial situations. Guskin and Spicker (1968) commented upon what, to us, is the most important lesson we could learn about the effects of our current style of research with the handicapped (i.e., our research has contributed almost nothing of value for the educational practitioner and, may we add, for the educational theoretician). It is well known that researchers, especially doctoral students, engage not in what they want to do but what they are able to do, not in what is important but what is possible, not in what is risky but what is safe and gives assurance of completion. People do what can be supported and most of us engage ourselves in activities that are comfortable and appreciated by others. Possibly the most accurate judgment we can make about the research in mental retardation now being published is that this is what the people in the field want or, possibly, there is not anything else known that they can or wish to substitute for their current mode of activity.

We conclude that:

1. There is nothing intrinsic in mental retardation—or in any disability—to produce handicap. Further, it is not the primary responsibility of the behavioral sciences to determine the validity of the aforementioned statement, but to make it become valid. We have supported far too many studies purporting to demonstrate differences between groups or the disorders of one type of child in contrast with another. All these years we should have promoted and encouraged research that sought to make it true that a child would learn after participation in a special program or curriculum. To state this another way, we are less than enthusiastic about the possibility that "all or nothing"—i.e., either we find something (significant) or we find nothing—research has anything to offer, either to our understanding of the handicapped or to pragmatic solutions to their learning problems. As an aside—we believe an important aside—in such "all or nothing" studies, one can see important and, perhaps, insidious relationships between the needs of research design and programming. That is, it is certainly seductive to randomly assign groups of children to treatments in order to see whether those treatments are effective, disregarding questions concerning the desirable way to develop educational programs for children.

2. The above leads directly to our second

recommendation, viz., the study of particular methods for the purpose of demonstrating their efficacy is rather fruitless and whatever is demonstrated will eventually be contradicted by subsequent research. Such "all or nothing" studies of methodologies prove little. By "all or nothing," we mean studies that compare the efficacy of one method with that of another or compare the superiority of one type of individual with that of another.[9] As methods do not exist outside of a psychoeducational setting, and as they are implemented by unique groups of human beings, only a naive researcher could conclude that the demonstrated superiority of his method has direct and specific transferability to other educational settings.[10] Our research preference is to study children and how they change in different educational environments. We believe it is more defensible, and will make a greater difference, to generalize about children interacting with each other and with adults in situations than it is to generalize about procedures. It is from evaluations of varieties of methods, with varieties of children in more or less formal and informal settings, utilizing teachers with heterogeneous backgrounds, that hypotheses will be generated that will lead to viable theories concerning human development and learning. It appears to us that, in this kind of strategy, theory construction shifts from methodological concerns to those involving human interactions.

[9] Or, as Campbell and Stanley (1963) incisively concluded, "we must increase our time perspective, and recognize that continuous, multiple experimentation is more typical of science than once-and-for-all [what the present writers term "all or nothing"] definitive experiments.... we should not expect that 'crucial experiments' which pit opposing theories will be likely to have clear-cut outcomes" (p. 3).

[10] On the other hand, we are not ready to suggest that there is *nothing but* uniqueness in an educational setting. There must be possibilities for building generalizations, for, if "knowledge" is an objective, we must be concerned with the degrees of nonuniqueness. Unfortunately, as we stated above, the numerous dimensions of child-teacher interactions have been neglected and, consequently, hardly understood.

3. Every researcher is confronted with a decision concerning the number of variables and sample size to be studied. Consequently, in light of limited resources, manpower, and time, to the degree that the researcher does not restrict variables of the study, he will have to restrict his sample, or vice versa. Our recommendation is to restrict—to the necessary degree—sample size rather than number of variables. In studying the complex problems of the handicapped on the one hand, and teaching them on the other hand, the restriction of variables to be studied and accounted for may lead to a distorted impression of results that either mislead the researcher or tell him very little about that which he has so diligently attempted to investigate. Therefore, although it is desirable to use as large, unbiased and representative a sample as possible—especially if one is interested in the generalizability that a study may provide—in respect to the aforementioned realities and compromises that must be made, we cannot help but recommend that the research payoff will be greater if compromises are made with sample size rather than number of variables.

4. Leading from the above discussion is our recommendation that a great deal more work is needed before we truly comprehend the varieties and natures of educational settings for the mentally retarded. Education and psychology are now just beginning to appreciate the dictum that before the researcher attempts to manipulate variables he should describe the natural setting. What are so desperately needed today are studies describing how and under what conditions handicapped children are admitted to school programs, how and under what conditions they perform in such programs, their attitudes and the attitudes of their instructors, and the interactive effects of such programs on those children, their families and other involved children.

5. Finally, the enormous current interest in specialized education strategies—e.g., Montessori, Bereiter, Special Classes, Head Start, token reinforcement, compensatory education, operant conditioning, and various learning disabilities programs—is testimony to the wide acceptance of a view of learning that places high value on teachers and learners rather than on teaching and learning. All of those strategies are attractive, in part because they are self-contained and can be discussed, described and set up as independent variables. Similarly, single-dimensional teacher differences as a factor in differential learning places us in a comparable trap. Such distinctions as structured versus nonstructured, directive versus permissive, child-centered versus teacher-centered, do not appear to make much of a difference other than that which is specifically tied to the behaviors under consideration. It would appear that other factors in teaching and learning are more important, that they cannot be simply described by the aforementioned methodologies or style labels, and that they are best studied by looking at differential process.

In this chapter we have presented the position that before we can adequately measure and understand quantitative differences in children and their teachers, we will first have to deal with and understand qualitative differences and processes. Our goal as educational researchers is to examine the components of the teaching-learning interaction. We conclude that, to accomplish this goal, individual components cannot be amputated; that is, as we amputate, we both change the natural setting and destroy much of any understanding we might have gained from a more holistic view. To extend this analogy further, the surgeon might more easily examine and operate on the brain if it could be removed from the skull. However, notwithstanding modern medicine and its miracle workers, that trick is not yet possible. We in the behavioral areas seem not to believe that the variables we study and manipulate are more complex and less well understood than the surgeon's.

REFERENCES

Alley, G. R. Perceptual-motor performances of mentally retarded children after systematic visual perceptual training. *American Journal of Mental Deficiency*, 1968, 73, 247–250.

Baumeister, A. A., Hawkins, W. F., & Davis, P. A. Stimulus-response duration in paired-associates learning of normals and retardates. *American Journal of Mental Deficiency*, 1966, 70, 580–584.

Baumeister, A. A., Hawkins, W. F., & Holland, J. M. Retroactive inhibition in short-term recall in normals and retardates. *American Journal of Mental Deficiency*, 1967, 72, 253–256.

Bensberg, G. J., Colwell, C. N., & Cassel, R. H. Teaching the profoundly retarded self-help activities by behavior shaping techniques. *American Journal of Mental Deficiency*, 1965, 69, 674–679.

Blackman, L. S. *A scientific orientation for special education.* New York: Teachers College, Columbia University, 1969.

Blackman, L. S., & Capobianco, R. J. An evaluation of programmed instruction with the mentally retarded utilizing teaching machines. *American Journal of Mental Deficiency*, 1965, 70, 262–269.

Blackman, L. S., & Heintz, P. The mentally retarded. *Review of Educational Research*, 1966, 36, 5–36.

Blatt, B. The physical, personality, and academic status of children who are mentally retarded attending special classes as compared with children who are mentally retarded attending regular classes. (Doctoral dissertation, The Pennsylvania State University) Ann Arbor, Mich.: University Microfilms, 1957. No. 57–425.

Blatt, B. The physical, personality, and academic status of children who are mentally retarded attending special classes as compared with children who are mentally retarded attending regular classes. *American Journal of Mental Deficiency*, 1958, 62, 810–818.

Blatt, B. A hypothesis of theories and methods in special education. In Jerome Hellmuth (Ed.), *Disadvantaged child.* Vol. 1. Seattle, Wash.: Special Child Publications, 1967. Pp. 65–76.

Blatt, B. (Ed.) Learning disabilities. *Seminars in Psychiatry*, 1969, 1, 237–361. (a)

Blatt, B. Time's passage—unchanging times. Keynote address in *Physical education and recreation for handicapped children.* Washington, D.C.: American Association of Health, Physical Education and Recreation, 1969, 50–56. (b)

Blatt, B. On the educability of intelligence. *Syracuse Scanner*, 1970, 15, 7–10.

Blatt, B., & Garfunkel, F. *The educability of intelligence.* Washington, D.C.: Council for Exceptional Children, 1969.

Bloom, W. Effectiveness of a cooperative special education vocational rehabilitation program. *American Journal of Mental Deficiency*, 1967, 72, 393–403.

Bodmer, W. F., & Cavalli-Sforza, L. L. Intelligence and race. *Scientific American*, 1970, 223(4), 19–29.

Bradley, B. H., & Hundziak, M. TMI-Grolier Time Telling Program for the mentally retarded. *Exceptional Children*, 1965, 32, 17–20.

Bradley, B. H., Maurer, R., & Hundziak, M. A study of the effectiveness of milieu therapy and language training for the mentally retarded. *Exceptional Children*, 1966, 33, 143–150.

Broden, M., Hall, R. V., Dunlap, A., & Clark, R. Effects of teacher attention and a token reinforcement system in a junior high school special education class. *Exceptional Children*, 1970, 36, 341–349.

Bruyn, S. T. *The human perspective in sociology: The methodology of participant observation.* Englewood Cliffs, N. J.: Prentice-Hall, 1966.

Budoff, M., Meskin, J. D., & Kemler, D. J. Training productive thinking of EMRs: A failure to replicate. *American Journal of Mental Deficiency*, 1968, 73, 195–199.

Cain, L. F., & Levine, S. *Effects of community and institutional school programs on trainable mentally retarded children.* Washington, D.C.: National Education Association, Council for Exceptional Children, 1963.

Campbell, D. T., & Stanley, J. C. *Experimental and quasi-experimental designs for research.* Chicago: Rand McNally, 1963.

Cassidy, V. M., & Stanton, J. E. *An investigation of factors involved in the educational placement of mentally retarded children.* Columbus, Ohio: Ohio State University Press, 1959.

Cawley, J. F., & Goodman, J. O. Arithmetical

problem solving: A demonstration with the mentally handicapped. *Exceptional Children,* 1969, 36, 83–88.

Charney, L. The trainable mentally retarded. In S. A. Kirk, & B. B. Weiner (Eds.), *Behavioral research on exceptional children.* Washington, D.C.: National Education Association, Council for Exceptional Children, 1963. Pp. 90–114.

Coleman, J. S., Campbell, E. Q., Hobson, C. J., McPartland, J., Mood, A. M., Weinfeld, F. B., & York, R. L. *Equality of educational opportunity.* Washington, D.C.: U.S. Government Printing Office, 1966.

Corder, W. O. Effects of physical education on the intellectual, physical, and social development of educable mentally retarded boys. *Exceptional Children,* 1966, 32, 357–364.

Deutsch, M. Happenings on the way back to the forum: Social science, IQ, and race differences revisited. *Harvard Educational Review,* 1969, 39, 523–557.

Doubros, S. G. Behavior therapy with high level, institutionalized, retarded adolescents. *Exceptional Children,* 1966, 33, 229–233.

Dunn, L. M., & Capobianco, R. J. Mental retardation. *Review of Educational Research,* 1959, 29, 451–470.

Edgar, C. L., Ball, T. S., McIntyre, R. B., & Shotwell, A. M. Effects of sensory motor training on adaptive behavior. *American Journal of Mental Deficiency,* 1969, 73, 713–720.

Edgerton, R. B. *The cloak of competence: Stigma in the lives of the mentally retarded.* Berkeley: University of California Press, 1967.

Ellis, N. R. (Ed.) *International review of research in mental retardation.* New York: Academic Press, Volume 1, 1966(a); Volume 2, 1966(b); Volume 3, 1968.

Follini, P., Sitkowski, C. A., & Stayton, S. E. The attention of retardates and normals in distraction and non-distraction conditions. *American Journal of Mental Deficiency,* 1969, 74, 200–205.

Gage, N. L. (Ed.) *Handbook of research on teaching.* Chicago: Rand McNally, 1963.

Gallagher, J. W. Short-term recall of sentences in normal and retarded children. *American Journal of Mental Deficiency,* 1969, 74, 57–61.

Gardner, J. M., Solomowitz, S., & Saposnek, D. T. *Trends in learning research with the mentally retarded.* Unpublished manuscript, Washington, D.C.: Council for Exceptional Children, 1969.

Gerjuoy, I. R., & Alvarez, J. M. Transfer of learning in associative clustering of retardates and normals. *American Journal of Mental Deficiency,* 1969, 73, 733–738.

Glaser, B. G., & Strauss, A. L. *The discovery of grounded theory: Strategies for qualitative research.* Chicago: Aldine, 1967.

Goffman, E. *Asylums: Essays on the social situation of mental patients and other inmates.* Garden City, N.Y.: Anchor Books, 1961.

Goldstein, H., Moss, J. W., & Jordan, L. J. *The efficacy of special class training on the development of mentally retarded children.* Cooperative Research Project No. 619. Urbana, Ill.: Institute for Research on Exceptional Children, University of Illinois, 1965.

Guskin, S. L., & Spicker, H. H. Educational research in mental retardation. In N. R. Ellis (Ed.), *International review of research in mental retardation.* Vol. 3. New York: Academic Press, 1968. Pp. 217–278.

Haring, N. G., Hayden, A. H., & Nolen, P. A. Accelerating appropriate behaviors of children in a Head Start program. *Exceptional Children,* 1969, 35, 773–784.

Hawker, J. R., & Keilman, P. A. Prompting and confirmation in paired-associate learning by retardates. *American Journal of Mental Deficiency,* 1969, 74, 75–79.

Heber, R. A manual on terminology and classification in mental retardation. Monograph supplement to the *American Journal of Mental Deficiency,* 1959, 64(2), 111.

Hottel, J. V. *An evaluation of Tennessee's day class program for severely mentally retarded children.* Nashville: George Peabody College for Teachers, 1958.

Howe, C. E. Is off campus work placement necessary for all educable mentally retarded? *Exceptional Children,* 1968, 35, 323–326.

Huber, W. G. The relationship of anxiety to the academic performance of institutionalized retardates. *American Journal of Mental Deficiency,* 1965, 69, 462–466.

Hurley, R. L. *Poverty and mental retardation: A causal relationship.* New York: Random House, 1969.

Jacobs, J. F., & Pierce, M. L. The social position of retardates with brain damage associated characteristics. *Exceptional Children,* 1968, 34, 677–681.

Jensen, A. R. How much can we boost IQ and scholastic achievement? *Harvard Educational Review,* 1969, 39, 1–123.

Johnson, G. O. A study of the social position of mentally-handicapped children in the regular grades. *American Journal of Mental Deficiency,* 1950, 55, 60–89.

Johnson, G. O., & Blank, H. (Eds.) *Exceptional children research review.* Washington D.C.: Council for Exceptional Children, 1968.

Jones, R. L., Marcotte, M., & Markham, K. Modifying perceptions of trainable mental retardates. *Exceptional Children,* 1968, 34, 309–315.

Jordan, T. E. *The mentally retarded.* (2nd ed.) Columbus, Ohio: Charles E. Merrill, 1966.

Kagan, J. S. Inadequate evidence and illogical conclusions. *Harvard Educational Review,* 1969, 39, 274–277.

Kahn, H., & Burdett, A. D. Interaction of practice and rewards on motor performance of adolescent mental retardates. *American Journal of Mental Deficiency,* 1967, 72, 422–427.

Karen, R. L., & Maxwell, S. J. Strengthening self-help behavior in the retardate. *American Journal of Mental Deficiency,* 1967, 71, 546–550.

Karnes, M. B., Hodgins, A., & Teska, J. A. An evaluation of two preschool programs for disadvantaged children: A traditional and a highly structured experimental preschool. *Exceptional Children,* 1968, 34, 667–676.

Kirk, S. A. *Early education of the mentally retarded.* Urbana, Ill.: University of Illinois Press, 1958.

Kirk, S. A. Research in education. In H. A. Stevens, & R. A. Heber (Eds.), *Mental retardation: A review of research.* Chicago: University of Chicago Press, 1964. Pp. 57–99.

Kirk, S. A., & Weiner, B. B. (Eds.) *Behavioral research on exceptional children.* Washington, D.C.: Council for Exceptional Children, 1963.

Knox, S. C. Turnover among teachers of the mentally retarded. *Exceptional Children,* 1968, 35, 231–235.

Kodman, F., Jr. Effects of preschool enrichment on intellectual performance of Appalachian children. *Exceptional Children,* 1970, 36, 503–507.

Krop, H. D., & Smith, C. R. Effects of special education on Bender-Gestalt performance of the mentally retarded. *American Journal of Mental Deficiency,* 1969, 73, 693–699.

Laing, A. F., & Chazan, M. Sociometric groupings among educationally subnormal children. *American Journal of Mental Deficiency,* 1966, 71, 73–77.

Levine, S., Elzey, F. F., & Paulson, F. L. Social competence of school and non-school trainable mentally retarded. *American Journal of Mental Deficiency,* 1966, 71, 112–115.

Lillie, D. L. The effects of motor development lessons on mentally retarded children. *American Journal of Mental Deficiency,* 1968, 72, 803–808.

Lovell, K., & Bradbury, B. The learning of English morphology in educationally subnormal special school children. *American Journal of Mental Deficiency,* 1967, 71, 609–615.

Macmillan, D. L., & Forness, S. R. Behavior modification: Limitations and liabilities. *Exceptional Children,* 1970, 37, 291–297.

Mann, P. H., Beaber, J. D., & Jacobson, M. D. The effect of group counseling on educable mentally retarded boys' self concepts. *Exceptional Children,* 1969, 35, 359–366.

McCarthy, J. J., & Sheerenberger, R. C. A decade of research on the education of the mentally retarded. *Mental Retardation Abstracts,* 1966, 3, 481–501.

McKenzie, H. S., Clark, M., Wolf, M. M., Kothera, R., & Benson, C. Behavior modification of children with learning disabilities using grades as tokens and allowances as back up reinforcers. *Exceptional Children,* 1968, 34, 745–752.

Meisgeier, C. The identification of successful teachers of mentally or physically handicapped children. *Exceptional Children,* 1965, 32, 229–235.

Meyers, C. E., Sitkei, E. G., & Watts, C. A. Attitudes toward special education and the handicapped in two community groups. *American Journal of Mental Deficiency,* 1966, 71, 78–84.

Milgram, N. A., & Riedel, W. Verbal context and visual compound in paired-associate learning of mental retardates. *American*

Journal of Mental Deficiency, 1969, 73, 755–761.

Miller, A., & Miller, E. E. Symbol accentuation: The perceptual transfer of meaning from spoken to printed words. *American Journal of Mental Deficiency,* 1968, 73, 200–208.

Morgan, S. B. Responsiveness to stimulus novelty and complexity in mild, moderate, and severe retardates. *American Journal of Mental Deficiency,* 1969, 74, 32–38.

Mullen, F. A., & Itkin, W. Achievement and adjustment of educable mentally handicapped children. Cooperative Research Project SAE 6529, 1961, Board of Education, City of Chicago, Chicago, Illinois.

Phillips, I. (Ed.) *Prevention and treatment of mental retardation.* New York: Basic Books, 1966.

Pumphrey, M. W., Goodman, M. B., Kidd, J. W., & Peters, E. N. Participation of retarded children in regular recreational activities at a community center. *Exceptional Children,* 1970, 36, 453–458.

Quay, L. C. Academic skills. In N. R. Ellis (Ed.), *Handbook of mental deficiency.* New York: McGraw-Hill, 1963. Pp. 664–690.

Rainey, D. S., & Kelly, F. J. An evaluation of a programed textbook with educable mentally retarded children. *Exceptional Children,* 1967, 34, 169–174.

Riese, R. R., & Lobb, H. Discrimination learning in retarded children: Non-reward vs. reward. *American Journal of Mental Deficiency,* 1967, 71, 536–541.

Ring, E. M. The effect of anticipation interval on paired-associate learning in retarded and normal children. *American Journal of Mental Deficiency,* 1965, 70, 466–470.

Robinson, H. B., & Robinson, N. M. *The mentally retarded child: A psychological approach.* New York: McGraw-Hill, 1965.

Rosenthal, R., & Jacobson, L. Teachers' expectancies: Determinants of pupils' IQ gains. *Psychological Reports,* 1966, 19, 115–118.

Ross, S. A. Effects of an intensive motor skills training program on young educable mentally retarded children. *American Journal of Mental Deficiency,* 1969, 73, 920–926.

Rouse, S. T. Effects of a training program on the productive thinking of educable mental retardates. *American Journal of Mental Deficiency,* 1965, 69, 666–673.

Rucker, C. N., Howe, C. E., & Snider, B. The participation of retarded children in junior high academic and nonacademic regular classes. *Exceptional Children,* 1969, 35, 617–623.

Sarason, S. B., & Doris, J. L. *Psychological problems in mental deficiency.* (4th ed.) New York: Harper & Row, 1968.

Schiefelbusch, R. L., Copeland, R. H., & Smith, J. O. *Language and mental retardation.* New York: Holt, Rinehart & Winston, 1967.

Schwarz, R. H., & Jens, K. G. The expectation of success as it modifies the achievement of mentally retarded adolescents. *American Journal of Mental Deficiency,* 1969, 73, 946–949.

Sharples, D., & Thomas, D. J. The perceived prestige of normal and special education teachers. *Exceptional Children,* 1969, 35, 473–479.

Shulman, L. S. Reconstruction of educational research. *Review of Educational Research,* 1970, 40, 371–396.

Siegel, P. S., Forman, G. E., & Willams, J. An exploratory study of incentive motivation in the retardate. *American Journal of Mental Deficiency,* 1967, 71, 977–983.

Solomon, A., & Pangle, R. Demonstrating physical fitness improvement in the EMR. *Exceptional Children,* 1967, 34, 177–181.

Sparks, H. L., & Younie, W. J. Adult adjustment of the mentally retarded: Implication for teacher education. *Exceptional Children,* 1969, 36, 13–17.

Spicker, H., & Bartel, N. The mentally retarded. In G. O. Johnson, & H. Blank (Eds.), *Exceptional children research review.* Washington, D.C.: Council for Exceptional Children, 1968. Pp. 38–189.

Strauch, J. D. Social contact as a variable in the expressed attitudes of normal adolescents toward EMR pupils. *Exceptional Children,* 1970, 36, 495–500.

Vale, J. R., & Vale, C. A. Individual differences and general laws in psychology: A reconciliation. *American Psychologist,* 1969 24, 1093–1108.

Vergason, G. A. Retention in educable retarded subjects for two methods of instruction. *American Journal of Mental Deficiency,* 1966, 70, 683–688.

Welch, E. A. *The effects of segregated and*

partially integrated school programs on self concept and academic achievement of educable mental retardates. Unpublished doctoral dissertation, University of Denver, 1965.

Wrightstone, J. W., Forlano, G., Lepkowski, J. R., Sontag, M., & Edelstein, J. D. *A comparison of educational outcomes under single-track and two-track plans for educa-*

ble mentally retarded children. Cooperative Research Project No. 144, 1959, Board of Education, Brooklyn, New York.

Zito, R. J., & Bardon, J. I. Achievement motivation among Negro adolescents in regular and special education programs. *American Journal of Mental Deficiency,* 1969, 74, 20–26.

CHAPTER 21 Teaching the Emotionally Disturbed[1]

FRANK M. HEWETT
University of California, Los Angeles

PHILLIP R. BLAKE
University of California, Los Angeles

Most children manifest disturbed behavior sometime while growing up. A surprisingly large number display problems of oversensitiveness, fearfulness, somberness, irritability, temper tantrums, destructiveness and hyperactivity from early childhood to adolescence (Macfarlane, Allen, & Honzik, 1954). But most children are not labeled *emotionally disturbed* because their disturbed behavior is moderate in degree, infrequent in occurrence and not definitely patterned. This chapter concerns those children who are candidates for the label because of the severity, frequency and clustering of their behavior problems in the school setting. We will discuss the definition and classification of emotional disturbance, incidence and identification, critical issues in the education of the emotionally disturbed, and related content and research evidence which has emanated from several contrasting approaches.

DEFINITION AND CLASSIFICATION

Emotionally disturbed children have been described, defined and classified from psychiatric, psychodynamic, psychoeducational, neurological, and behavioral-educational points of view.

Psychiatrically, Watson (1959) presents categories of emotional disturbance under three main headings: 1) primary behavior disorders including habit disturbances, conduct disturbances and neurotic traits, 2) psychosomatic disorders, and 3) psychoses. The inner life of the child is the focus of psychodynamic definitions: *impairment of emotional growth during some stage of development with resultant distrust toward the self and others and hostility generated from anxiety* (Moustakas, 1953, 1955). A definition in the direction of a psychosocial or psychoeducational approach has been proposed by Morse (1967): 1) socially defective children (semisocialized children, children arrested at a primitive level of socialization, children lacking capacity to socialize), 2) children with neurotic conflicts, and 3) children with psychotic processes. Neurologically based classifications of disturbed be-

[1] The authors are indebted to Mrs. Clara Lenert for her valuable assistance in compiling and organizing the references used in this chapter. Appreciation is also due Mrs. Mary Hunt and Mrs. Diane Trombi for their help in the preparation of this manuscript.

657

havior cover such problem behaviors as hyperactivity, impulsiveness, emotional liability, short attention span, and distractibility (Clements & Peters, 1962; Cruickshank, Bentzen, Ratzeburg, & Tannhauser, 1961). A behavioral-educational definition has emanated from the work of Quay, Morse, and Cutler (1966) who factor analyzed problem behavior trait ratings made by 60 classroom teachers for 441 children on a scale developed by Peterson (1961). The sample represented a wide range of geographic locus and placement and program philosophies. Three independent clusters of behaviors were found to account for about two-thirds of the variance of the interrelationships among the problem behaviors: 1) conduct disorder (defiant, impertinent, uncooperative, irritable, boisterous behavior), 2) inadequacy-immaturity (sluggishness, laziness, lack of interest, preoccupation, dislike for school, inattentiveness) and 3) personality problems (inferiority feelings, self-consciousness, lack of self-confidence, fearfulness, depression).

Dupont views the classification of emotional disturbance as *"a behavior disorder which consists of inadequate or inappropriate behavior that is learned and can therefore be changed through application of learning procedures"* (1969) as a current trend (Bandura & Walters, 1963; Milton, 1965; Quay, 1963; Ullmann & Krasner, 1965). Woody (1969) relates a behaviorally-oriented definition to classroom learning and defines the behavioral problem child as *"the child who cannot or will not adjust to the socially acceptable norms for behavior and consequently disrupts his own academic progress, the learning efforts of his classmates and interpersonal relations."*

The emotionally disturbed child has also been defined as a *"socialization failure"* whose behavior is maladaptive and deviates from what is expected for his age, sex and social status (Hewett, 1968). In terms of functioning in the classroom, the disturbed child is a problem because of his lack of attainment of one or more basic goals related to learning and school success: attention, response, order, exploratory, social, or mastery (Hewett, 1964).

In this chapter we will be primarily concerned with children with emotional disturbance and/or behavior disorders and will not attempt to cover the literature on social maladjustment and delinquency. Quay (1963) has questioned whether delinquent and socially maladjusted children are in fact emotionally disturbed since their behavior may be most appropriate in the real world of the street in which many of them live even though it is clearly deviant in other settings.

In a chapter oriented toward empirical research evidence regarding the education of emotionally disturbed children, the point must be made at the onset that while available content in the field has been largely obtained through experience and observation, it has generally not been verified by means of precise and controlled experimentation. The problem begins with the treatment and service orientation of the field which generally has considered disturbed children "mentally ill" and has placed psychiatric and therapeutic concerns ahead of learning and education. However, once the decision to do research has been made, the emotionally disturbed child is a difficult subject to pin down and study. How can you define the types of problems exhibited by disturbed children so that similar children receive similar labels? Woody (1969) has pointed out that "timidity" and "withdrawal" may be considered separate descriptive terms for one investigator and as synonymous by another and that the exact criteria for assigning such global terms as "introverted" may be impossible to ascertain.

INCIDENCE AND IDENTIFICATION

As we review studies relating to the incidence of emotional disturbance among children, the problems of definition just raised clearly relate to the discrepancies in population estimates which have been reported.

White and Harris (1961) reviewed studies relating to incidence of maladjustment from 1928 to 1953 and concluded that 4 to 7 percent of all school children were seriously maladjusted. They found estimates of mild maladjustment impossible to provide due to problems in definition, sampling techniques, and assessment. The American Psychiatric Association (1964) has estimated that 7 to 12 percent of the elementary-school population is disturbed. Boys are consistently found in greater numbers than girls. Estimates range from twice as many boys as girls (Bower & Lambert, 1962; McCaffrey & Cumming, 1967) to 80 percent boys (Quay, Morse, & Cutler, 1966).

The validity of incidence estimates arising from single surveys has been questioned by McCaffrey and Cumming (1967). In a longitudinal study which followed a group of children classified as emotionally disturbed in teacher ratings in the second-grade to the fifth-grade levels, they found that the majority of the children did not reappear among the population considered emotionally disturbed by teachers at that time. Such spontaneous improvement over time without special intervention has also been reported by Glavin (1968) and Clarizio (1968). If the majority of disturbed children are apt to improve when left alone, considerable research effort must go into demonstrating that approaches to the education of the emotionally disturbed 1) are more effective with the persistent cases and 2) hold promise for more efficiently alleviating the problems of the others than time alone.

In identifying emotionally disturbed children, the judgment of classroom teachers is a common criterion measurement and such judgments are often proved valid. Glidewell, Domke, and Kantor (1963) found a positive relationship between child-symptoms reported by mothers' and teachers' judgments of degree of maladjustment. The identification of emotionally disturbed children by teachers and peers was found by Bower (1960, 1961) to be surprisingly ac-

curate in relation to selections made by clinicians. Glavin and Quay (1969) concluded that the "widespread use of teacher judgment in screening for disturbed children is generally justifiable" but added they were not valid indexes of disturbance. They suggest that behavioral rating check lists and inventories (Pate & Webb, 1965; Pimm & McClure, 1967; Stevenson, Hill, Hale, & Moely, 1966; Walker, 1968; Werry & Quay, 1968) hold promise as screening devices in combination with teacher judgments.

The use of sociometric techniques in which peer ratings reveal positive and negative classroom status of children has been found useful in predicting school success (Cannon, 1958; Gronlund & Holmlund, 1958) and in screening maladjusted children without an exorbitant investment of time or money (Bowman, 1956). Bower and Lambert (1962) have developed a "Class Play" with a variety of negative and positive roles which children "cast," thereby revealing their perceptions of class members.

Research in the field of education of the emotionally disturbed child can be organized into three major areas: 1) classroom conditions including environmental design and classroom climate, grouping procedures, curriculum, instruction and management; 2) teacher competencies; and 3) supportive operations involving work with parents and psychotherapy.

Morse, Cutler, and Fink (1964) collected data through mail surveys from 117 educational programs for disturbed children throughout the United States and undertook site visitations to 74 classrooms representing 54 of these programs. Some 500 disturbed children from early elementary level through senior high school were represented in the study. The largest number of programs were at the upper elementary and junior high levels. The authors classified the points of view or program types found in their study into seven categories: psychiatric-dynamic, psychoeducational, psychological-behavioral, educational, naturalistic, primitive and chaotic. In our presentation of the literature relating to classroom conditions, we will, where possible, organize our discussion around four of these contrasting approaches or points of view: psychiatric-dynamic, psycho-educational, neurological and behavioral-educational. A brief review of the origin and educational goals of these points of view is in order before we proceed with research findings relating to classroom conditions which have emanated from them.

The Psychiatric-Dynamic Approach

The psychiatric-dynamic approach has been influenced by Freudian psychoanalytic theory in establishing its goals for education with emotionally disturbed children. It is concerned with the psychic origin and meaning of disturbed behavior and arrested intellectual and psychological functions during critical periods of personality development. High priority is given to accepting the child as he is without censure and to the development of a positive, trusting relationship between teacher and child before formal educational training is stressed. Thus, the teacher may assume in part the role of a therapist who attempts to understand the psychodynamics of the child's problem.

Aichhorn (1965) set up an early program in the twenties in a residential training school for delinquent boys which incorporated psychoanalytic principles. He attempted to counter the rigid and punitive approach prevalent in such schools in his day with total acceptance of disturbed behavior and continual expression of friendliness and warmth. This permissive approach resulted in many assaultive and destructive acts, but these reportedly diminished over time and Aichhorn found the boys more amenable to staff contact and formation of positive relationships. Bettelheim (1950, 1967) has published several books reporting on his work as director of the University of Chicago's Orthogenic School, a residential treatment center for severely disturbed children maintaining a psychoanalytic orientation. Pearson (1949) has stressed bringing

unconscious material into consciousness in treatment of emotionally disturbed children. He states that education has applied psychoanalytic principles incompletely in granting too much permissiveness, and he recommends that a psychoanalyst be assigned to every school. Axline (1947), Berkowitz and Rothman (1966), Devereux (1956), Ekstein and Motto (1969), Freud (1954), Moustakas (1953), and Rabinow (1961) are also proponents of a psychiatric-dynamic approach.

The Psychoeducational Approach

A related approach to the education of emotionally disturbed children preserves the emphasis on acceptance, understanding and relationship building with disturbed children seen in the psychiatric-dynamic approach but also is concerned with the child's adjustment to his total environment, particularly the school, and with devising and implementing more educationally oriented diagnostic and teaching procedures.

Redl and Wineman (1951, 1952) have reported on an extensive project with young delinquent boys in their Pioneer House study in Detroit. Their work has emphasized the difficulties in control and conformity exhibited by these boys in terms of faulty ego development. Limits were imposed in the group living situation and educational program, but many opportunities were provided for deviant behavior to be expressed as a means of studying these boys' problems. Newman (1959) has been associated with the development of public school programs for hyperactive, aggressive children and has emphasized accepting such children as they are, providing opportunities for self-expression and attempting to change their behavior only when the child evidences readiness for such a change.

Morse (1966) has described a psychoeducational approach which would bring the resources of a total mental health program including special education teachers, psychometrists, social workers, guidance workers, speech personnel, and psychiatric and psychological consultants into the schools.

Slavson (1954) has emphasized that emotional problems must be reduced before academic learning can take place. He advocates broadening disturbed children's interests through a wide range of activities, discontinuation of formal academic learning and a nonrigid, nonrestrictive school environment. Rogers (1942, 1951) has also stressed the need for self-expression of disturbed children and for arranging the social environment to fit their needs.

The Neurological Approach

The inclusion of a discussion regarding a neurological approach in this chapter may seem inappropriate since emotional disturbance more commonly implies a functional rather than organic disorder. Nevertheless, disturbed behavior such as impulsiveness, hyperactivity and distractibility commonly found with disturbed children appears frequently in the behavior of children considered neurologically impaired. Differential diagnosis between emotional and neurological causal factors is often extremely difficult to establish, and assignment of the label "emotionally disturbed" or "neurologically impaired" on a primary basis may sometimes be a matter of professional bias. The neurological approach aims at discovering the child's sensory and neurologically based deficits, often through extensive observation and diagnostic testing. Once these deficits are uncovered, training procedures are implemented to aid him in more accurately perceiving and comprehending stimuli and gaining motor proficiency as a prelude to complex learning. Clements and Peters (1962) have stated that most childhood psychoses are based on brain deviation. They cite as evidence to support the relation of minimal brain dysfunction to disturbed behavior: 1) the similarities of perceptual deficits and symptoms of children with questionable histories and adults with known brain damage, 2) the clustering of these symptoms into recognizable entities, 3) the positive correlation between complications of pregnancy and later behavior and learning problems, 4) the good response of children with suspected brain damage to drugs and training without psychotherapy, and 5) differences between siblings reared in similar environments.

Interest in the behavior and learning problems of children with suspected neurological impairment may be traced back to the work of Strauss (Strauss & Kephart, 1955; Strauss & Lehtinen, 1947), who conceived of special materials and training procedures to aid such children with problems of attention, discrimination and motor coordination. Cruickshank et al. (1961) have extended this work in designing public school programs for hyperactive, distractible children, and Kephart (1960) has formulated a developmental framework of perceptual-motor behaviors which are thought to underlie complex learning.

The National Advisory Committee on Handicapped Children, USOE (1968), places children whose learning problems cannot be accounted for on the basis of physical, sensory-intellectual, experiential or emotional factors into the category of "learning disabilities," and this classification has replaced reliance on previously established terms such as "brain damage," "brain injury," "cerebral dysfunction" and "neurological impairment." Yet many such children exhibit behavior problems whether on a primary or secondary basis and verification of the existence of actual brain dysfunction must largely be done by indirect behavioral measurement. Thus vigorous efforts to clearly separate emotional disturbance from neurological impairment are probably academic since remediation of learning and behavior problems, whatever their cause, is the major concern of special education.

The Behavioral-Educational Approach

In our earlier presentation of definition trends in the area of emotional disturbance, a shift was noted from traditional psychiatric and medical preoccupation with causation and disease to more recent concern with learning and behavioral deficits. This shift has come about due to introduction of a behavioral approach based on social learning theory (Rotter, 1954), operant and respondent conditioning (Bijou & Baer, 1961; Holland & Skinner, 1961; Skinner, 1953) and imitation modeling (Bandura, 1966, 1969) into special education. Rather than "disturbed," "ill" or "retarded," the child is viewed as a "learner" (Hewett, 1967) or "behaver" (Lindsley, 1970) with the emphasis on *what* he is ready to learn and *how* to teach him rather than *why* he has problems in the first place. This learning and education-oriented point of view moves the teacher from the role of therapist or diagnostician suggested by the approaches discussed earlier and establishes her clearly as a learning specialist.

The behavioral-educational approach is represented in the literature as behavior-modification (Becker, 1971; Homme, Csanyi, Gonzales, & Rechs, 1970; Meacham & Wiesen, 1970; Quay, 1966; Ulrich, Stachnik, & Mabry, 1970; Whelan, 1966), precision teaching (Haring & Lovitt, 1967; Haughton, 1970; Lindsley, 1966b) and educational engineering (Hewett, 1967, 1968). It focuses on the behavior of the child which is observable, can be measured, counted or quantified. Whelan (1966) emphasizes that the approach does not deny the reality of the central nervous system or the effect of cognition, thinking and conceptualization but that since these functions are not observable at present and are difficult to measure and quantify, we should concentrate our efforts on direct behavioral measurement.

Among the first to introduce the behavioral approach into special education were Birnbrauer, Bijou, Wolf, and Kidder (1965) with institutionalized retardates, and Haring and Phillips (1962) with emotionally disturbed children in the public schools. Because of the emphasis on observable behavior rather than inferred states and events in this approach, we might expect more controlled research studies to have emanated from it. This will be apparent as we begin our review of research findings in the field of education of the emotionally disturbed child.

Not all of the four approaches presented in our previous discussion are represented in the literature in equal measure, and not all investigators or all research can be clearly placed under one approach to the exclusion of the others. But because the emotionally disturbed child is such a difficult individual to define, and because he has been studied from such diverse points of view, some organization of position and content hopefully will be useful.

CLASSROOM CONDITIONS

The teacher waiting by the classroom door for her class of emotionally disturbed children to arrive is faced with a number of problems, as is the teacher in a regular classroom who recognizes that two or three of her pupils have emotional problems. How should the physical environment of the classroom be designed to facilitate improved learning and adjustment for these children? What type of classroom climate with respect to permissiveness and structure is desirable? How should they be grouped in the program to start with? What types of curriculum tasks and materials should be utilized? How can the teacher go about instructing and managing the class or individual children—motivating them to learn, setting limits on their behavior and maintaining discipline? Research in the field of education of the emotionally disturbed has considered these questions, and we shall examine some of the findings in the following sections on environmental design and climate, grouping procedures, curriculum, and instruction and management.

Environmental Design and Classroom Climate

When setting up a classroom for emotionally disturbed children most teachers must make the best of whatever physical facilities are available. Redl (1966) has suggested that the actual physical design of the classroom has been beyond the consideration of most special educators. More important may be how existing facilities are put to use and the "climate" for teaching and learning which is established. We shall first consider findings relating to physical facilities themselves and then review the settings or climates which have been explored.

Morse, Cutler, and Fink (1964), in their national survey of programs for emotionally disturbed children throughout the United States, observed that, in general, the physical facilities were adequate but "far from plush." Converted regular classrooms were the most frequent facilities, with converted music and art rooms next most common. At the extreme were programs conducted in factory buildings or repair shops. Specially designed facilities planned for educational programs for emotionally disturbed children were almost nonexistent. Investigators' ratings of the adequacy of physical facilities in the programs studied revealed the following: very poor—6 percent; adequate—52 percent; very good—36 percent; and outstanding—6 percent.

Hay and Cohen (1967) stressed the importance of examining every aspect of the classroom for the emotionally disturbed child. They advocate placement of such a class in a quiet location apart from large numbers of children. It should be close to an exit and not above the second floor. In terms of space, they suggest that 55 to 65 square feet be allowed for each child and that 450 square feet be available for even the smallest group. Chalkboards and bulletin boards for display of the children's work are also recommended.

Hewett (1968) has recommended a room of from 1200 to 1500 square feet for nine or 10 pupils to allow for placement of a number of learning and activity centers around the room at some distance from the student desk areas. Double desk tables with a two-by-four–foot working surface have been found useful for each child as they

separate students physically, provide a spacious work area for the child and permit the teacher to sit alongside the child in a comfortable and businesslike manner without crowding in or hovering over him.

One issue relating to physical facilities that has received considerable attention is the use of study booths or cubicles in classrooms for emotionally disturbed children. Such booths screen off the classroom from the child and provide a small, enclosed, independent working area. Concern with the effects of classroom stimuli on distractible, inattentive and hyperactive children stems from the work of Strauss and Lehtinen (1947) and Strauss and Kephart (1955), who may be considered within the neurological approach to children with learning and behavior problems.

Neutrally colored walls, frosted windows, considerable distance between desks, removal of bulletin boards, and even elimination of colorful teacher attire have been considered important by advocates of stimulus control in special education. A study which investigated the effects of stimulus controlled classroom environment including the use of cubicles on the academic and behavioral progress of hyperactive, distractible children was conducted by Cruickshank et al. (1961). Four small classes of brain injured children were followed for a two-year period. Two of the classes rigidly adhered to an experimental condition of reduction of environmental space, elimination of extraneous stimuli and a carefully planned routine. The teachers in the other classes had knowledge of the experimental condition but maintained a more traditional program. While there were no significant differences between the experimental and control classrooms, the children in all four classes were found to have made significant gains in achievement, visual perception, and social behavior at the end of the study.

Shores and Haubrich (1969) compared the effectiveness of assigning emotionally disturbed children to cubicles and found a significant increase in attending behavior as a result of such an assignment. Academic progress in reading, however, was not significantly related to working in a cubicle. The effect of cubicles on brain injured children's performance on a reaction time test was studied by Cruse (1962). Results indicated that children working under stimulus control conditions in a cubicle did not perform better than those working in cubicles with such extraneous stimuli as toys, moving balloons and mirrors.

As was suggested earlier, rigid classification of practices with emotionally disturbed children into the four approaches is not possible, but we can gain an organizational advantage by discussing research efforts within these three frameworks although individual authors might not view the theoretical premise of their work accordingly. An issue that is difficult to subject to research but which arises again and again when attempting to describe the nature of educational programs for emotionally disturbed children concerns the degree of permissiveness versus structure reflected in the classroom climate. The issue basically involves the degree of child-determined as compared with teacher- and environmentally determined limits and expectations operating in the program. It will be reflected in most of the remaining sections of this chapter.

Morse, Cutler, and Fink (1964) rated teachers' control styles in their national study, and these ratings reveal a broad range of structure and permissiveness. Four percent were seen as utilizing punitive overcontrol; 16 percent—rigid control; 28 percent—tolerant, patient control; 10 percent—planned permissiveness; 11 percent—loose, some confusion; and 3 percent—chaotic. In general, it can be stated that the psychiatric-dynamic and psychoeducational approaches to education of the emotionally disturbed child involve a more permissive and child-centered orientation, while the neurological and behavioral-educational approaches emphasize teacher- and environmentally determined limits.

The Summerhill program described by Neill (1960) includes a child-centered classroom for both disturbed and normal children in which pupils may at any time sit on the floor or stand. They may receive their instruction in or out of the classroom and there is no established place for furniture or class supplies. Bettelheim's (1955) classrooms at the Orthogenic School attempt to convey a homelike atmosphere with much freedom for individual exploration or engagement in academic learning if the child desires.

Phillips (1956) has suggested that attention-seeking children who are easily stimulated be seated in the front of the class near the teacher where they may receive immediate assistance while withdrawn children be placed nearer the center of the class. The aim of this arrangement is to enable the teacher to develop a "positive expectancy" in each child because he receives the help he needs and experiences success.

Haring and Phillips (1962), Rubin, Simson, and Betwee (1966), and Whelan (1966) have emphasized the usefulness of a structured classroom approach with emotionally disturbed children and some of their findings will be presented in the instruction and management section.

An engineered classroom design incorporating a behavioral-educational approach has been developed by Hewett, Taylor, and Artuso (1969). The emotionally disturbed child is viewed in terms of deficits according to a developmental sequence of educational goals which includes six levels: attention, response, order, exploratory, social and mastery. The physical facilities of the room provide learning and activity areas designed to strengthen functioning on all levels. An Order Center offers simple puzzles and games for teaching children to pay attention, respond and follow directions. The Exploratory Center provides arts and crafts and science activities. A Communication Center is used to engage two or more children in cooperative social interactions, and the Mastery Center consists of individual work tables and two study booths where academic work may be undertaken. In this room children are assigned to the work area offering tasks and activities which relate to their most critical problems on the developmental sequence of educational goals and are rewarded for their efforts by means of a check-mark system which will be described later.

The role of the physical environment in promoting behavioral and academic growth with emotionally disturbed children has yet to be clearly defined, as has the role of learning and teaching climates along the permissiveness-structure continuum. As we begin to suspect here and will see in our continuing discussion, separating out single variables from the complex interaction of emotionally disturbed children, teachers and educational programs poses a sizable problem for researchers in the field.

Grouping Procedures

The issue of grouping emotionally disturbed children so that they might receive the benefits of a good education involves two major questions: 1) should disturbed children be taken out of the regular classroom and placed in special self-contained classes? and 2) if special classes are set up, how many children should be included and should the nature of their behavior and learning problems be considered when assigning them?

The efficacy of a special class assignment for any exceptional child continues to be debated in the field of special education (Dunn, 1968). With respect to leaving emotionally disturbed children in the regular classroom or assigning them to special classes, opinion, observation, experience and research tend to create positions at both extremes as well as in the middle. At the one extreme special class placement in the public school is viewed as desirable in terms of a temporary assignment for children whose behavior is too disruptive to be maintained in a regular classroom (Pate, 1963), for aiding the child in attaching a more positive

meaning to school and self (Scheuer, 1966), for greater improvement when the child is also enrolled in a private school for educational therapy (Frostig & Maslow, 1969), and for promoting self-confidence, leadership, social adjustment and academic progress (Hay, 1953). Hewett, Taylor, Artuso, and Stillwell (1970) compared 30 educationally handicapped (California's classification for children with serious learning and behavior problems) children in a self-contained, engineered classroom with 30 matched children left in the regular classroom and 30 normals. The engineered classroom group improved significantly more (making beyond the expected one-year gain) than the educationally handicapped controls in reading and arithmetic and maintained superior task attention.

At the other extreme Knoblock (1966) has condemned "noxious social labeling" as "eroding" the child's self-concept, and Trippe (1963) has challenged establishment of special classes for disturbed children as an effort to make an inappropriate educational system work and calls for consideration of the circumstances in the child's total life situation which underlie emotional disturbance. Kanner (1948) cited the difficulty parents have in accepting special class placement for their child since it inevitably is viewed as the "dumb class." Safford and Watts (1967), in evaluating the academic progress of 27 disturbed pupils also considered minimally neurologically impaired in a special class program, found only one-third the expected academic growth rate during the course of a year. However, no information was provided regarding the teaching methods or management procedures utilized.

Rubin, Simson, and Betwee (1966) employed an impressive research design to test the efficacy of special class placement for emotionally disturbed children. Although the results showed no significant differences in academic gains between children left in regular classrooms and those given a special class assignment, greater improvement in social and emotional adjustment was reported for the latter group.

Bisgyer, Kahn, and Frazee (1964) have described a program in which the special class for emotionally disturbed children is located in the public school and assigned students participate part time in a regular classroom. Morse (1965) has described the use of a "crisis teacher" who is available in the school to assist regular teachers when a given child's behavior can no longer be tolerated in the classroom. Such a teacher might work on an individual basis with the child until he can be returned to his regular room. Hewett, Taylor, Quay, Soloway, Stillwell, and Artuso (1970) have developed an administrative and instructional program which aims at systematically moving both educable mentally retarded and emotionally disturbed children toward integration in the regular school program. This program, called the Madison School Plan, provides three supportive settings which focus on bolstering the child's pre-academic skills (paying attention, starting, working, taking part orally, following task directions, doing what you're told and getting along with others), his academic skills and his ability to profit from instruction in various groupings (teacher in front of class, child independent in class, teacher with small group, child independent in group, child in group interaction, child independent in study booth and teacher-child). It also attempts to bring the child under the control of traditional classroom reinforcers such as grades and praise. The goal of the Madison School Plan is to provide the best of both the special class and regular class worlds for the exceptional child. Mesinger (1965) has argued against combining retarded and seriously disturbed children since he thinks they will readily identify each other as deviant from the group and seriously impair the academic efforts of the teacher and others in the class. Eventual evaluation of the effectiveness of programs like the Madison School Plan will hopefully shed light on this issue.

Quay and Glavin (1970) undertook a four-year investigation of self-contained special classes and resource rooms which utilized principles of behavior modification with behaviorally disordered children in the public school. The results of their program indicated that social behavior and academic achievement definitely improved in these experimental classes and that the resource room concept in which the child participates part-time in the regular class program is the most cost-effective method for the education of behavioral problem children currently available in the public school.

Morse, Cutler, and Fink (1964) reported the commonest pattern for grouping found in their national survey of public school classes for emotionally disturbed children was the segregated pattern. Sixty-two percent of the classes visited did not attempt any integration of students in the regular class. With regard to class size, the average number of children specified by state legislation was 10 although class sizes of from four to 19 were found during the actual survey.

In establishing a special class, various criteria for grouping have been discussed in the literature. Wilderson (1967) studied the relationship of reading skill deficiencies and psychiatric symptoms in emotionally disturbed children and concluded educators should define their own parameters for grouping such children since educational and psychiatric characteristics often vary considerably. Patterson (1964) rejects the psychiatric classification model for grouping disturbed children and suggests homogeneous grouping according to dimensions of hyperactivity, aggressiveness, immaturity, anxiety and withdrawn behavior. Other criteria suggested include what the individual student can tolerate as well as how much he can be tolerated (Grossman, 1965), age rather than grade level (Berkowitz & Rothman, 1966), academic level rather than sociobehavioral functioning (Schroeder, 1965), and similar psychopathology (Devereux, 1956). Fenichel (1966) does not advocate any fixed formula for grouping emotionally disturbed children but avoids placing children in a group where problems might be intensified because of the presence of certain other children.

Rubin (1962) has stated that emotionally disturbed children should not be grouped by age or psychiatric diagnosis but according to readiness for school and classroom conditions. In the Madison School Plan mentioned earlier, the dimension of *readiness for regular classroom functioning* is utilized for assigning children to one of the three supportive settings which lead up to the regular classroom. These settings are labeled Pre-Academic I, Pre-Academic II, and Academic I with Academic II constituting the regular classroom itself. Each setting involves a degree of expectancy along the dimension of readiness for regular classroom functioning in relation to pre-academic and academic skills, types of instructional settings, and susceptibility to reinforcers. Pre-Academic I places the child in a pre-academically oriented program, with emphasis on individualized instruction and offers tangible and activity-time rewards. In Pre-Academic II the child enters an academically oriented program involving teacher–small-group instruction and activity-time rewards. The Academic I setting is a simulated regular classroom with intensive academic work, teacher–large-class instruction, and grades. An initial Placement Inventory is done on each child to identify his strengths and weaknesses in terms of the expectations described above and assignment is made on the basis of the resultant profile.

Although the special versus regular class controversy continues, middle-ground options are beginning to appear and educationally relevant dimensions rather than psychiatric nomenclature are beginning to be utilized for purposes of assessment and grouping. Little research evidence is available to settle the issues raised in this section, but when the somewhat recent trend for the field to move from a medical and psychiatric model to one concerned with learning and

teaching is considered, such evidence may begin to accumulate.

Emotionally disturbed children may be provided an educational program while residing in a 24-hour residential treatment center or a state mental hospital. Most of our discussion in this chapter concerns disturbed children in day or public school classes. However, one residential program of particular note is Project Re-ED (Hobbs, 1966; Lewis, 1967) which has aimed at altering the isolated nature of traditional institutional experience for the disturbed child and instead approaches him as an inseparable part of a small, ecological unit made up of himself and his family, school, neighborhood and community. The Project Re-ED school consists of 40 children from six to 12 years of age who are divided into five groups of eight children each. Each group is the responsibility of two teacher-counselors who have participated in a special nine-month training program. These counselors, along with a principal, assistant principal, and social workers, liaison teachers, consultants, and secretarial and housekeeping staff, constitute an around-the-clock school team which attempts to reestablish the child as quickly as possible in his home, school and community. The average stay per child is six months. Lewis (1967) reports a success rate of between 75 and 87 percent as determined by staff evaluation, parents' independent ratings of symptom decrease and community school teacher and peer ratings of improved school adjustment.

Curriculum

In this section we shall review studies relating to the intelligence and academic functioning level of emotionally disturbed children as well as curriculum emphasis and materials and methods found in programs for them.

Woody (1969) has reviewed the research literature related to the mean intelligence level of children who have emotional and behavior problems and concludes, in general, that such children score lower on intelligence or mental abilities tests than unselected or nonabnormal samples. Woody (1968) himself found "well-behaved" boys scoring significantly higher than "behavioral problem" boys on all three intelligence quotients derived from the Wechsler Intelligence Scale for Children—Verbal Scale IQ, Performance Scale IQ, and Full Scale IQ. A contradiction to this finding was reported by Vane, Weitzman, and Applebaum (1966), who found problem and nonproblem children had essentially the same mean intelligence quotients on the Stanford-Binet Intelligence Test. In view of the serious functioning problems of many disturbed children, particularly in stressful test-taking situations and the chaotic, fragmented experiences many of them have had, it is not surprising to find them, in general, scoring lower on intelligence tests. It does not permit us, however, to consider them basically less intelligent than normals and to reduce our expectations in efforts to teach them, for as resistance, avoidance withdrawal, and anxiety are reduced, many disturbed children may function well above their tested levels. With respect to academic achievement, Bower (1960) found emotionally disturbed children functioning significantly below other children in their classrooms in reading and arithmetic. Differences were greater in arithmetic than in reading, and, as might be expected due to continuing failure, overall academic differences between disturbed and normal children increased in the higher grades. Stone and Rowley (1964) found 116 hospitalized emotionally disturbed children functioning some 1½ years below expected level for age in both arithmetic computation and word pronunciation on the Wide Range Achievement Test. Balow (1966b) considers the belief that emotionally disturbed children as a group are deficient in school skills, a commonly held but still controversial view.

The priority ranking given academic as compared to nonacademic activities in educational programs for emotionally disturbed children relates to the differences among the four approaches: psychiatric-dynamic, psychoeducational, neurological and behavioral-educational discussed earlier. From the first two points of view, establishment of a therapeutic environment may take priority over formal academic training. Berkowitz and Rothman (1966) state that concern with skill and discipline should give way to a new concept of teaching focused on education of the emotions and complete acceptance of the child. Nonacademic activities such as creative arts are viewed as giving the disturbed child ways to externalize emotion and make contact with the environment in conflict-free areas. Hay (1953) and Cohen (1965) also recommend emphasis on nonacademic units. Morse (1967) views "fun" as much a subject to be offered emotionally disturbed children as arithmetic.

Cruickshank et al. (1961) indicate that the emotionally disturbed child can profit from the highly structured, planned routine in the classroom which has been successful with hyperactive and so-called brain injured children. They also see resolution of psychopathological aspects as secondary to the academic program. Here we see a distinct contrast between the psychiatric-dynamic and psychoeducational on the one hand and neurological approach on the other. The former may strive to place the therapeutic aspects of special education before the academic while the latter considers skill training the first order of business. Along with Cruickshank, Frostig and Maslow (1969) suggest perceptual-motor training as an area of preacademic emphasis.

From a behavioral-educational point of view, Goodwin (1968) considers the primary target for change with children who have learning and behavior problems acceleration of academic and social performance, with a secondary target the increase of problem-solving and decision-making skills. Quay (1966) places individualized academic instruction coupled with immediate and concrete reinforcement at the top of the list of program goals with emotionally disturbed children. In the engineered classroom (Hewett, Taylor, & Artuso, 1969) the Mastery or academic area constitutes a home base for disturbed children, but the Communication, Exploratory, and Order centers are available at all times for use as intervention assignments when it becomes apparent a child cannot succeed with an academic task.

In the Morse, Cutler, and Fink study (1964), public school teachers of disturbed children listed academics as occupying more than 50 percent of class time in some 70 percent of the programs evaluated. Teachers in the study also conceived of the primary problem of their students in educational and behavioral terms. Forty-six percent saw the problem as educational, 24 percent as symptomatic-descriptive, 18 percent as psychodynamic, 8 percent as mental hygienic, and 1 percent as complex psychoeducational.

A national network of Instructional Materials Centers has been established by the USOE Bureau of the Handicapped (McCarthy, 1969). These centers, located on a regional basis, are depositories of a wide range of teaching materials for all exceptional children including the emotionally disturbed and offer consultative assistance to special educators.

Berkowitz and Rothman (1966) have suggested the use of projective language arts techniques such as story writing and talking games as a means of allowing free expression and gaining a better understanding of the emotional problems of the child. Fairy tales and myths are seen as valuable as reading material because they disguise obvious realistic situations which the child might otherwise find emotionally upsetting. They describe a "phantasy booklet" made up of the child's own stories which are illustrated, typed and bound. However, Jacobson and Faegre (1959) caution against using subject matter that may stimulate conflictual and distracting fantasies and describe a technique of "neutralization" in selecting curriculum material for disturbed children. Newman (1959) has also considered the

effect of certain thematic material on such children. She views material concerned with happy family life, naughty pranks and tender emotional themes too threatening and best avoided. Devereux (1956) has discussed the use of bibliotherapy, which involves the use of selected readings with themes and characters of therapeutic value to the disturbed child.

Minuchin, Chamberlain, and Graubard (1967) conducted a project to teach learning skills to disturbed and delinquent children over a five-week period. Emphasis was on listening, taking turns, role playing and conceptual skill development. Cognitive growth was the main feature of the program rather than behavior change. However, most of the children regressed following the five-week program and withdrawal of the special conditions.

Fenichel (1966) emphasizes starting with simple tasks and activities in programs for disturbed children and teaching self-care skills in order to enable the child to master the realities of everyday living and reduce self-preoccupation. Curriculum should be reality oriented and include experiences offering continuity, stability, security and a sense of achievement. Fenichel recommends the use of educational techniques and materials found in programs for normal children where possible.

Quay (1966) and Eldred (1966) have advocated the use of automated teaching devices and programmed instructional materials with disturbed children. Additional suggestions for curricular approaches to teaching disturbed children have included kinesthetic and auditory emphasis in teaching (Talmadge, Anthony, & Laufer, 1963), presenting subject material requiring rote memory rather than conceptualization (Pearson, 1954), and creative dramatics for developing communication skills (Shapiro, 1965).

In general, the basic issues in grouping, curriculum, and teaching methods in programs for emotionally disturbed children are yet to be explored. While teachers may largely view the problems of disturbed children as educational as cited in the Morse, Cutler, and Fink study (1964), what actually transpires during the day in terms of activities chosen, subject matter presented, and techniques utilized probably is determined by previous experience, available materials and supplies, trial and error, and to some degree formal training of the teacher rather than a body of knowledge. When one considers the fact that emotional disturbance is a largely undefined category and that similar children can be viewed as mentally ill, neurologically impaired, behaviorally disordered, or academically deficient, the difficulties involved in doing cumulative research to create such a body of knowledge are considerable. It simply stands to reason that you must first know the nature of the problem you are attempting to resolve through an educational program before that program can be made optimal. Although emotionally disturbed children will continue to line up at classroom doors in probably increasing numbers and teachers will continue to do the best they can to teach them, the fundamental problem of definition must be dealt with before questions of grouping, curriculum and methods are answered.

INSTRUCTION AND MANAGEMENT

The issues of instruction and management are critical ones in the education of the emotionally disturbed child. Most such children are referred for special help because regular classroom teachers are unable to successfully teach them, motivate them to learn, or to set and enforce limits on their behavior. In actuality, academic problems may be of secondary importance if the child is able to function within the range of tolerance for behavioral differences which a given teacher maintains. In the Morse, Cutler, and Fink (1964) survey, teachers reported management of hostile-aggressive behavior and academic motivation their number one and two problems, respectively.

Much of what is reported in the literature regarding the management of the emotionally disturbed child represents a logical extension of some theoretical approach to the nature of disturbance rather than knowledge based on experimental findings. However, as we shall see, learning theory and studies centering on behavior modification which have emanated from it are beginning to provide such evidence. In this section we shall consider some general problems of instruction as well as motivation or the acceleration of desirable behavior in the classroom and discipline or the deceleration of undesirable behavior. We shall also find ourselves returning to consideration of the structure-permissiveness continuum in this regard.

The psychiatric-dynamic and psychoeducational approaches strive to promote self-expression and inner-determined motivation for learning in the disturbed child. Rogers (1942, 1951) views a completely permissive relationship as necessary for such expression and motivation and considers the school too punitive to provide an adequate setting for therapy. Axline (1947) believes in providing permissiveness, understanding, acceptance, and recognition and clarification of feelings to promote the emotional growth of the child. Hobbs (1966) considers "joy" a missing ingredient in motivating disturbed children and suggests that most psychological experiments rely on avoidance of pain or hunger for motivation. Such a motivational approach limits pleasure to that obtained from minute, discrete rewards and leads to "anemic" programming for children. He states there should be joy available daily and a joy-producing event anticipated by the child each day. While Slavson (1954) states orderliness and routine are important aspects of the school environment, he feels emotional problems can be reduced through broadening the child's interest and giving him more ways of expression through doing. The major problem, however, with accepting all behavior of a disturbed child in hopes of building a positive relationship is that it fails to provide opportunities for the child to learn to discriminate between appropriate and inappropriate behavior (Whelan, 1966).

Although terms like "total permissiveness" and "complete acceptance" may be used in describing ideal approaches to instructing and managing disturbed children, most special educators recognize the necessity of presenting the child with reality limits, particularly if he is going to participate in an organized school program. The ideal solution to this has been suggested by Nichtern, Donahue, O'Shea, Marans, Curtis, and Brody (1964), who have stated that the teacher must be able to help the child within identifiable and acceptable limits without destroying the basic relationship in the process. Fenichel (1966), for example, encourages permissiveness on the part of the teacher but finds disorganized children need someone to organize the world for them. Since such children may fear loss of control, they need protection against their impulses and they need limits set for them. According to Redl and Jacobson (1958), such limits should provide the child with considerable freedom in his choice of behavioral responses. Grimes and Allinsmith (1961) found that anxious children in unstructured settings appear to have the greatest difficulty achieving.

Pearson (1954) and Graubard and Miller (1968) have recognized the importance of helping the emotionally disturbed child delay gratification in the classroom. Since effective learning, particularly in the public school, requires engaging in sustained task-oriented behavior without the provision of immediate social or extrinsic rewards each step of the way, or continual opportunities to act out impulses, such a goal is essential. The behavioral-educational approach, to be discussed later, has aimed at increasing the child's tolerance for delay by initially offering immediate and even concrete rewards such as food and prizes for small units of

accomplishment and later moving to periodic reinforcement and more traditional rewards of social praise and grades. In terms of providing feedback to the disturbed child regarding the quality or accuracy of his work in school, Blom (1966) suggests responding in a neutral, mechanical manner since "correct" and "wrong" have strong connotations of good-bad and love-reject which may provoke strong emotional responses on the part of the child. This suggestion is in contrast to the behavioral approach, where positive and negative reinforcement are viewed as basic in aiding the child.

Morse, Cutler, and Fink (1964) surveyed teaching techniques and motivational methods in their national study of public school programs for disturbed children and compiled a frequency list of procedures mentioned by teachers. Indicated by 75 to 100 percent of the teachers was "work more highly individualized both in rate and level." Fifty to 74 percent claimed, "whole classroom group instruction seldom used." From 25 to 49 percent of the teachers utilized "strategic seating in classroom setting," "reward by self-interest activities after assignments completed," "less structure—more self-selection," "relaxed evaluation, errors minimized," "motivation through encouragement and deeper teacher support," "employment of more structure and demands," "work geared for success," "technique of neutralizing anxiety-producing material," "group projects," "less academic stress and lower expectations," and "manipulative materials and games methods." One to 24 percent mentioned such procedures as "use of progress charts and prizes for motivation," "less grouping for instruction, more individual activity and freedom to move about," "concrete rather than abstract materials," "reducing competition," "letting pupil decide what constitutes good work," "independent work and projects rather than large group," "food and treats as rewards," "stressing material with intrinsic pupil interest," and "grades as rewards." The authors report that "diversity was the keynote" and "there were few universal practices." In general, the actual class process was seen as resembling the regular classroom.

Rivlin (1958) suggests that the teacher strive to create a comfortable room and notes that even the way books are distributed and collected may set the "tone" of the class. Boocock and Coleman (1966) claim that games have valuable motivating potential and that they are more self-disciplinary than most forms of learning.

Learning–theory-based approaches to teaching the emotionally disturbed child, referred to in this chapter as behavioral-educational approaches, concentrate upon the child's observable behavior and the environmental consequences which may increase or decrease the frequency of future responses. They are not as global or psychotherapeutic in the traditional sense as those of the psychiatric-dynamic or psychoeducational approaches or as narrow in range as those associated with the perceptual-motor training of the neurological approach. Through techniques of response measurement, the behavioral approach lends itself to experimentation and research and while settling for overt behavior as a target rather than personality reorganization or ego strengthening, methodologies can be specified and studies replicated with a greater degree of certainty than those derived from more descriptive and intuitive approaches.

The use of operant conditioning techniques for teaching speech and academic skills to individual autistic children has been reported as effective by a number of investigators (Hewett, 1964, 1965; Lovaas, Berberich, Perloff, & Schaeffer, 1966). Selection of a discrete target behavior (e.g., eye contact), presentation of a stimulus to elicit the behavior (e.g., "Look at me"), setting of an expectation or contingency which must be met (e.g., direct eye contact for specified period of time), and provision of a positive reinforcement (e.g., food, verbal praise) according to the contingency are the key elements of such projects. The child's behavior is then shaped toward more complex levels by gradually increasing expectations and using the method of successive approximation.

Less severely disturbed children with behavior and learning problems have also been helped to modify their behavior in individual studies. Zimmerman and Zimmerman (1962) demonstrated that the spelling disability of a student who constantly misspelled words and received continual teacher attention as a result improved markedly when the teacher withheld such attention until the student correctly spelled a word. Patterson and Ebner (1965) rewarded a hyperactive child for paying attention in class by flashing a light on his desk and providing a piece of candy, thereby markedly increasing the child's attention span. Quay (1966) used a similar method to increase the listening attention of children with conduct disorders.

Walker and Buckley (1968) also increased the attending behavior of a nine-year-old, underachieving boy by first training him in an experimental situation, lengthening the delay of reinforcement from 30 to 600 seconds, and successfully transferring the effects of the training back into the child's regular classroom. Packard (1970) has demonstrated how a teacher alone can increase the attention of a class and individual members in it by making group privileges contingent on the class's maintaining a specified level of attending behavior.

The effects of teacher attention on the study behavior of pupils were studied by Hall, Lund, and Jackson (1968). One first-grade and five third-grade students given to disruptive or "dawdling" behavior were given teacher attention when they were working appropriately and were ignored when they were inattentive. This sharply increased the study rates of the children. A reversal procedure during which the teacher paid attention to nonstudy behavior produced low study rates. When the initial approach was reinstated, study rates again markedly increased and were maintained after the formal program terminated.

Haring and Phillips (1962) investigated the effectiveness of a structured, behaviorally oriented classroom approach with emotionally disturbed children in the public school. Their classroom design included stimulus reduction, clear-cut expectations and rewarding consequences for appropriate behavior and academic accomplishment. In a comparison of children placed in a structured classroom with others in a less structured learning environment, the experimental group showed significant academic gains although differences in ages and grade levels between the two groups tended to limit the validity of the findings.

The application of operant conditioning techniques to group instruction was demonstrated in a landmark study by Birnbrauer et al. (1965) with mentally retarded children in an institutional school. Small teacher-pupil ratio, careful programming of reading, written language and number concepts, systematic use of token and extrinsic rewards, and a high degree of structure resulted in a surprising increase in rate of academic learning and accomplishment of retardates. Extension of this to public and institutional schools for disturbed children was made in the engineered classroom design (Hewett, Taylor, & Artuso, 1969) described earlier. In this program the teacher did not present any group lessons and dealt on a strictly individual basis with each child. Also, the amount of teacher verbalization in the classroom was reduced because of the often negative association adult lecturing and direction-giving have for disturbed children. Central to the motivation method used was a check-mark system. Each child in the room carried around a work record card with some 200 ruled squares on it. Every 15 minutes the teacher or aide in the room acknowledged the

child's functioning in relation to the assigned task and classroom behavioral expectations. Completed cards could be traded for candy or inexpensive toys or 15 minutes of free activity time. Children assigned to engineered classrooms maintained a 5 to 20 percent task attention (defined as eye contact with assigned task) advantage over children in control classrooms. Gains in arithmetic fundamentals were significantly correlated with use of the engineered design, but reading and spelling gains were not significantly different between experimental and control conditions.

The use of free activity time as a rewarding consequence has been reported by Whelan (1966). Making a period of free choice time in a high interest area with intriguing games and activities contingent on completion of a specific academic assignment is based on the Premack principle (Premack, 1959) which states that behavior normally occurring at a low rate may increase in frequency when it is followed by activities which are highly desirable to the student. Haring and Lovitt (1967) have incorporated this principle in a precision-teaching approach. This approach is based on the work of Lindsley (1966a) and involves 1) pinpointing a specific behavior (e.g., number of arithmetic problems done correctly, 2) recording the occurrence of this behavior daily and charting it on a graph, 3) recording changes in the teaching program, 4) analyzing the child's performance to determine the relationship between the program and the child's behavior, and 5) systematically changing the program variable and reevaluating its effect on the child's performance. Walker, Mattson, and Buckley (1969) and Haughton (1970) have also applied a precision-teaching approach to the education of children with learning and behavior problems.

Lovitt and Curtiss (1969) found that the academic response rate of children with behavior disorders increased when pupils acted as their own contingency managers (selecting conditions under which activity time reinforcement in line with the Premack principle would be delivered) rather than the teacher. It was also found that amount of reinforcement was not the determining variable. The investigators concluded that self-controlling behavior is capable of being taught and learned by children with behavior disorders. McKenzie, Clark, Wolf, Kothera, and Benson (1968) used naturalistic classroom events as incentives for academic progress. When children's academic behaviors failed to reach optimal levels, parents were asked to provide allowances at home based on weekly grades, and a significant increase in academic behavior was reported.

Walker and Mattson (1969) explored the use of a learning-theory model in a classroom for emotionally disturbed boys from fourth to sixth grade. A variety of response-reinforcement contingencies and reinforcers were utilized in the program, and results indicated measurable reduction of deviant behavior and increase in task-oriented behavior. The authors also developed several reliable and valid screening and rating instruments in the study to describe the behavior of disturbed children, record the behavior of the teacher in the classroom, and measure the task-oriented behavior of the children.

Discipline

Since some degree of structure and establishment of reasonable limits is generally recognized as essential, what should happen when a given disturbed child's behavior exceeds such limits? We turn now to consideration of the issue of discipline.

Berkowitz and Rothman (1966) have echoed the permissive position of acceptance of inappropriate behavior regardless of how unacceptable that behavior may be and suggest that the aggressive child be permitted to express his aggression without harming himself or others. Devereux (1956) views the disciplinarian as being effective to the extent he is educator, guide, philosopher and friend and that therapeutic education is the reverse of interpersonal relations characteristic of punitive situations.

Colvin (1961) advocates interrupting the child's frustration-aggression cycle without retaliation, and Morse (1965) advises empathetic handling of an aggressive child but holding him if necessary to prevent destruction. The importance of avoiding power struggles has been stressed by Cohen (1965). Rebellious behavior is seen as best ignored with dangerous aggression halted instantly through minimal interference.

Klincewicz (1969) reports on a unique *social-modeling approach* with adolescents with behavior disorders. He employs the services of an actor who portrays various types of misbehavior and attempts to get the students to join him. In practice, the most frequent rule violators within the group are reluctant to escalate their misbehavior beyond a certain level and tend to disassociate from the inappropriate activities of the actor. Postinterviews with the students reveal an extremely critical attitude toward the actor's "poor" performance. Redl (1949), however, has described a reverse effect when children with behavior problems are exposed to acting out behavior on the part of a classmate in the classroom setting. He has labeled this *group contagion*. Blom (1966) refers to this as the *ripple effect* leading to group disorganization, and Kounin, Friesen, and Norton (1966) report that teachers who are successful in managing surface behavior lower the rate of such contagion.

The technique of *life-space interviewing* has been described by Morse (1963), Redl (1959), and Morse and Small (1959) as an intervention approach when the child's behavior exceeds tolerable limits. The life-space interview is a form of reality-oriented, therapeutic "first aid" in which the teacher discusses a given problem in the immediate context within which it has occurred rather than probing into past events as might be done by the professional psychotherapist.

A modification of the life-space interviewing technique has been utilized by Blom (1966) in a university laboratory day school for elementary age disturbed children. A "standby officer" drawn from members of the school staff may be called to the classroom to assist in dealing with a behavior problem which arises. The standby officer takes the child to a quiet room where conflicts and anxieties involved in the problem may be discussed. The main objective of this approach is to return the child to the school program as quickly as possible.

The national study conducted by Morse, Cutler, and Fink (1964) revealed three overall ways teachers attempted to maintain class limits. First, there was counseling, individual or group discussion, or some form of life-space interviewing following a problem. Second, individual and group responsibility was stressed with pupils who were excluded being allowed to return when they stated they were ready. The third was indirect and considered the best approach. It consisted of attempting to maintain a good program and reasonable routines. When these approaches failed, the teachers reported a variety of back-up methods. Academic problems might result in lowering of grades, make-up work, late dismissal, after-school work or being sent home. Behavior problems might be handled by verbal nagging, giving reminders, the teacher's "counting to five" as a warning, making students repair or make restitution for damages they caused, withholding pleasures such as recess, isolation, or removal to the office for discipline. Six of the 74 teachers included in the study mentioned physical punishment such as "unangry" swatting or paddling. Minimizing pressures and expectations when the child was obviously upset and adhering to "support, don't punish, give them another chance" was reported.

Ott (1958) has employed a four-step plan of acting out with adolescent students. Step one involves clearly re-stating the rule which is violated. Step two occurs if the violation happens again. The child is given the option of accepting disciplinary action now or returning to work with the understanding that next time he will be a three-time loser and automatically receive discipline. Step three is followed if the violation occurs again and the promised discipline used. Step four consists of considering the problem over and no more mention made of it at any time.

Whelan and Haring (1966) have reported success in getting a child to settle down by use of a "time-out" area of isolation, and Hewett (1968) suggests five points for consideration in assigning children to a time-out period of exclusion from class:

1. It should occur only after the child's behavior has exceeded the limits which have been clearly stated to him previously.
2. It should occur matter-of-factly rather than as the result of teacher exasperation.
3. It should be presented to the child as a constructive aid to learning rather than arbitrary punishment.
4. It should involve a specific period of time decided upon by the teacher rather than the child.
5. Once the time-out period has passed, the child should immediately return to class without any lecture or attempt to get him "to promise to be a good boy from now on."

Chapman (1962) suggests that systematic suspension of disturbed children from school is therapeutic in that it strengthens self-control and reduces anxiety.

In the engineered classroom design described earlier (Hewett, Taylor, & Artuso, 1969) a series of nine interventions was available when it became apparent that a given child was not able to function successfully in the classroom. Of course, the preferred intervention of "anticipation of the problem" would head the list. In order of suggested usage and in line with the developmental sequence of educational goals, the interventions were as follows:

1. Keep assignment but reassign child to a study booth or cubicle (Mastery)
2. Modify assignment (Mastery)
3. Restructure classroom expectations verbally (Social)
4. Send to Exploratory Center (Exploratory)
5. Send to Order Center (Order)
6. Take student outside room and agree on task such as punching a punching bag or running around building (Response)
7. Provide individual tutoring (Attention)
8. Place on "time-out" exclusion period
9. Send home.

Wolf, Hanley, King, Lachowicz, and Giles (1970) employed a game approach to the management of out-of-seat behavior with problem children in an elementary classroom. A bell rang every 20 minutes and students earned token reinforcements exchangeable for later privileges if they were in their seats at that time. Problems of out-of-seat and talking-out behavior were studied by Barrish, Saunders, and Wolf (1969) in a regular fourth-grade class which included several disturbed children. The class was divided into two teams "to play a game." Whenever a given child left his seat or talked out, a mark was placed on the chalkboard which meant possible loss of privileges by all members of his team. These privileges were natural reinforcers available in the class such as extra recess, first in line for recess, time for special projects, stars and name tags as well as winning the game itself. The approach was successful in improving individual student's behavior during arithmetic and reading periods. Schmidt and Ulrich (1969) successfully applied a group contingency approach in reducing the noise level of a regular classroom.

The use of social praise as reinforcement to motivate and control disturbed children's behavior has been explored by a number of investigators. In these studies praising appropriate behavior and ignoring disruptive behavior constituted the approach. In general, positive results were obtained (Becker, Madsen, Arnold, & Thomas, 1967; Thomas, Becker, & Armstrong, 1968; Walker & Buckley, 1968), but the approach was not always effective (Hall, Lund, & Jackson, 1968), the teachers had difficulty actually ignoring all disruptive behavior (Madsen, Becker, & Thomas, 1968), and praising appropriate and ignoring disruptive behavior actually created classroom pandemonium (O'Leary, Becker, Evans, & Saudargas, 1969).

A study by Levin and Simmons (1962) found praise ineffective in getting emotionally disturbed children to engage in a task of dropping marbles into a box. Food rewards were found to be superior to praise, and food rewards presented alone were superior to food paired with social praise. The results of this and other studies suggest that adult verbalization, even if positive in nature, may not have a predictable effect on the behavior of the disturbed child.

An interesting aspect of teacher attempts at verbal control with disruptive children in regular classrooms was studied by O'Leary, Kaufman, Kass, and Drabman (1970). An initial study revealed that most teacher reprimands were loud in nature and could be heard by many other children in the class. When the teachers were asked to use soft reprimands, audible only to the child in question, the frequency of disruptive behavior declined in most of the children. Reversal of the procedure again produced an increase of disruptive behavior and return to the "soft" condition caused such behavior to decline.

Cobb, Ray, and Patterson (1970) demonstrated that having a psychologist work with the teacher and the members of a class to create a total class environment in which appropriate behavior of hyperaggressive boys was positively reinforced was successful in maintaining the attention level of these boys (68 percent) close to the attention level of their peers (70 percent) after a five-month period.

A number of manuals which explain the principles of a behavioral approach to the management of the disturbed child have been prepared for classroom teachers (Becker, 1971; Buckley & Walker, 1970; Homme et al., 1970; Lindsley, in press; Meacham & Wiesen, 1970; Patterson & Guillion, 1970; Smith & Smith, 1966; Valett, 1969; Zifferblatt, 1970).

Although the use of corporal punishment may have greatly diminished in all education, Skinner (1965) cites the "astonishing" list of noncorporal punishments such as ridicule, scolding, sarcasm and incarceration (being kept after school) which are commonly accepted. The effect of punishing consequences has been described as exerting complex effects on behavior going far beyond the teacher's expectation and control (Haring & Lovitt, 1967), as only temporarily suppressing undesirable behavior and increasing maladaptive behavior including escape and avoidance (Whelan, 1966), as improving performance although many factors influence outcome (Marshall, 1965), as of use only after all other possibilities have been considered (Engelmann, 1969), and as a continuing research question (Nurnberger, Ferster, & Brady, 1963).

The matter of managing instructional and behavior problems through motivation and discipline in programs with disturbed children is difficult to summarize due to the almost limitless combination of approaches which result from the complex interaction of teacher experience and style, psychopathology of the children themselves, and conditions existing in the educational program. However, emphasis on individualization of instruction, flexible changing of expectations to fit child and situation, setting of fair and clearly stated limits, systematic provision of positive consequences when appropriate, and consistent but reasonable enforcement of rules seem to be reflected in the literature as a result of the observation or study of emotionally disturbed chil-

dren. Such a list might appear in relation to managing any classroom of normal children, and from our review we see that most of what is used with disturbed children is but an extension, simplification or solidification of practices commonly viewed as effective with most children.

TEACHER COMPETENCIES

If one were to compile a list of desirable personal qualities for teachers of emotionally disturbed children from recommendations appearing in the literature, the result might well resemble an excerpt from the canonization of a saint. Such qualities as "tender without being sentimental," "permissive without sanctioning," "profoundly aware without loss of spontaneity," "trusting in the intuitive, humane responsiveness of one's self and one's colleagues," and "self-actualized" have all at one time or another been suggested. In this section we shall review several studies relating to teacher competencies with disturbed children which have approached the problem in a systematic manner and reflect more than mere opinion.

A comprehensive attempt to survey the specific competencies viewed by teachers of socially and emotionally maladjusted children as important was made by Mackie, Kvaraceus, and Williams (1957) for the USOE. Eighty-eight competencies thought to be valuable for success in teaching disturbed children were compiled and teachers asked to rank them. Some 75 teachers throughout the country selected by state departments of education as outstanding special teachers with disturbed children participated in the study. Heading the list of important competencies was "knowledge of techniques adaptable to classroom situations for relieving tension and promoting good mental health" followed by "understanding the advantages of providing experiences in which pupils can be successful" and "understanding the advantages of flexibility of school programs and schedules to permit individual adjustment and development."

Dorward (1963) modified this competency check list and attempted to single out special competencies needed by teachers of disturbed children over and above those needed by the regular classroom teacher and found these two competencies to be significantly more important: "the ability to accept pupils who are violent," and "experience on a clinical team with psychiatrists, psychologists, and social workers."

The child who is disruptive and aggressive has long been of major concern to teachers. In an early study, Wickman (1928) revealed that teachers rated "acting out" children as having more serious problems than children who were timid and shy, in direct contradiction to the ratings of mental hygienists who placed withdrawn children at the top of the serious problem list. Recent attempts to replicate the Wickman study (Beilin, 1959; Bower, 1957) indicate that teachers at the present time are more aware of the significance of withdrawn behavior than their earlier counterparts, but the fact remains that disruptive children are far more difficult to tolerate and manage in a program of group instruction.

Hewett (1966) organized competencies needed by teachers of disturbed children in hierarchial order after conducting a training program in a psychiatric hospital over a seven-year period. From most basic to highest level these competencies were: 1) *objectivity*—knowledge of normal and deviant psychosocial development and professional literature, ability to communicate with other professionals and to define educational goals and evaluate success and failure; 2) *flexibility*—ability to shift teaching goals in line with student variability; 3) *structure*—capacity to set and maintain reasonable behavioral and academic expectations; 4) *resourcefulness*—ability to formulate innovative approaches to learning; 5) *social reinforcement*—capacity to establish one's self as a positive social reinforcer; 6) *curriculum expertise*—thorough knowledge of all basic curriculum content and methods; and 7) *ability to function as*

an intellectual model—skill in stimulating students' creativity and pursuit of learning in breadth and depth.

An interesting investigation of reasons teachers leave positions in classrooms of disturbed children was conducted by Bruno (1969). Teachers who remained in the field were rated significantly higher in "dominance," "autonomy," and "succorance" while those who left were significantly higher in "nurturance." The former also resembled social science teachers more closely while the latter more closely resembled psychologists. This study tends to suggest that a therapeutic, interpersonal orientation may lead to more difficulty in teaching satisfaction and success with the disturbed than a more educational, managerial approach. In this regard Eaton, Weathers, and Phillips (1957) found that problems of behavior management were primarily responsible for causing teachers to leave the field.

A competent teacher is essentially a competent teacher whether working with disturbed or normal children, and the critical elements in programs for disturbed children may revolve around the ability to extend good teaching practices in areas of motivation, discipline and individualization rather than the capacity to assume a truly unique professional role.

SUPPORTIVE OPERATIONS

Work with Parents

Since the emotionally disturbed child spends the largest part of his waking hours outside the classroom, efforts to help him improve his social-emotional adjustment often quite logically involve work with his parents. Inclusion of parents in total educational programs for the disturbed has been described by Bisgyer, Kahn, and Frazee (1964), Fenichel, Freedman, and Klapper (1960), Goodwin (1968), Haring and Phillips (1962), Hobbs (1966), and LaVietes, Hulse, and Blau (1960) among others. The parent may be included in a counseling group or seen on an individual basis by the school psychologist, social worker or teacher. In general, such an approach results in favorable comments from "helpful to parent and child" to "vital for both teacher and parent," although few actual studies have been done to evaluate the effects of such parent participation on the school adjustment and performance of the child. Slatoff (1968) reported strong resistance on the part of parents of disturbed children to get actively involved in therapeutic educational programs since they preferred to deny the existence of the child's problems.

D'Angelo and Walsh (1967) tried various short-term treatment approaches with parents and children, measuring child improvement by psychodiagnostic evaluations and teacher ratings. Children whose parents received group therapy exhibited a positive trend in improvement. Lisle (1968) found no difference on pupil adjustment among a variety of counseling approaches involving children, parents, and teachers or some combination of the three. However, treatment approaches without pupil involvement were found to be more effective for improving teacher-perceived pupil adjustment. Glavin and Quay (1969) conclude that therapeutic interventions are probably more effective if they involve the parent rather than the disturbed child.

The importance of positive parent support in educational programs for disturbed children is reflected in the national survey of Morse, Cutler, and Fink (1964). Twenty-five percent of the teachers in the survey stated that "lack of parent cooperation" was a source of major discouragement and 19 percent viewed parents as important allies in maintaining control with students.

Psychotherapy

The question of whether or not individual psychotherapy improves the emotionally disturbed's social-emotional adjustment in general and his school functioning in particular has long been debated. Lewis (1965) did a systematic review and synthesis of the literature concerned with the efficacy of therapeutic intervention procedures with disturbed children and concluded that approximately two-thirds of the cases improve whether they receive therapy or not. This conclusion is interesting to consider when the findings of McCaffrey and Cumming (1967) are reviewed. In their study the majority of children identified as disturbed in the early school years were not labeled as such in the fifth grade. Lewis suggests that maturation, not psychotherapy, is the central element responsible for improving adjustment.

Levitt, Beiser, and Robertson (1959) reviewed more than 1,000 cases treated in a Community Child Guidance Clinic and concluded the results of psychotherapy in effecting major adjustment changes among disturbed children were discouraging. Winn (1962) found no reading improvement after a 16-week play therapy program. Westendorp, Abramson, and Wirt (1962) reported slight improvement in grades and attendance among students receiving group therapy one-half hour weekly in the public school.

Phillips (1960) compared the results of short-term, nondepth therapy with traditional depth therapy in a Child Guidance Clinic setting with children from three to 11 years of age who were matched for IQ. Nondepth therapy divided treatment hours equally between parent and child, eventually decreased sessions to two per month, gave parents a "common sense" explanation of their child's behavior, and included the child's teacher in an information-giving and -taking role. It involved half the time of the depth therapy approach with its long-term treatment aimed at uncovering deep-seated, psychological conflicts of the child. Parents of children in both groups rated their children on improvement since original complaint, child's behavior at home, child's behavior in formal and informal groups, and child's behavior specifically at school. The nondepth therapy yielded significantly better results on all items judged by the parents, and the outcome success ratio was 92 percent for the nondepth group and 60 percent for the depth therapy group.

Other findings with respect to effectiveness of therapy on the adjustment of the disturbed child suggest that group therapy is better than individual therapy (Meyer, Borgatta, & Jones, 1965), group counseling is unproductive for underachieving students (Cohn, Ohlsen, & Proff, 1960), "open-door therapy" with students electing to see a counselor on a demand basis is effective with underachievers (Coleman & Hewett, 1962), therapy is more effective than tutoring in improving reading proficiency and personality adjustment (Tierney, 1957), and that group therapy with fifth- and sixth-graders is more effective in producing reading gains rather than improvement in adjustment (Seeman & Edwards, 1954).

Many of the above studies did not use control groups and, when the findings of Lewis (1965) that some two-thirds of the disturbed children improve over time regardless of involvement in psychotherapy of some type are considered, the relationship of treatment to the observed gain becomes questionable.

DISCUSSION AND SUMMARY

The field of special education which is concerned with the emotionally disturbed child is rich with inspiration, conviction and description but generally impoverished with respect to facts. In this chapter we have dealt with a melting pot of content, much of which is based on opinion and experience rather than research evidence. Beginning with definition and classification we find that the label assigned to a disturbed child often reflects the bias of the labeler and that if the child is seen as psychiatrically ill, neurologically impaired or behaviorally disordered, the descriptive terminology used will vary accordingly. Perhaps the most pressing need in the field at present is the establishment of a reliable system for defini-

tion and classification of emotional disturbance. The use of behavior trait ratings such as those developed by Quay, Morse, and Cutler (1966) may well be moving in that direction by linking what we "call" a child with what we "see" in the classroom. Once we have such a system, the long overdue major incidence studies can get underway using modern sampling techniques and follow-up procedures. These will increase our knowledge of the transient-persistent issue in relation to disturbed behavior and markedly improve efforts at prediction and identification.

Balow (1966a) has referred to the "dramatic return to learning theory" which has occurred in the sixties, specifically behaviorism, for the treatment of disturbed behavior. While the medical-psychiatric tradition of the field and the complexity of emotional disturbance will maintain psychiatric-dynamic and psychoeducational approaches, focus on observable behavior and specification and arrangement of environmental events in the education of the disturbed is probably here to stay. Indeed, what is likely to happen is a merging of points of view, honest recognition of the many similarities which exist, and a resultant psycho-behavioral-educational position established. The major program type found in the Morse, Cutler, and Fink (1964) study was "educational," and in practice it appears most teachers approach disturbed children as learning and behavior problems. It may well be that our professional biases are in actuality artificial with respect to the reality of school programs and are mainly useful for purposes of theoretical and scholarly discourse.

We know very little about the effects of the physical arrangement of the classroom on disturbed children, and research in this area would be useful. However, the issues of classroom climate, grouping, curriculum, instruction and management are probably of greater relevance in determining the quality of education provided. Much research is needed in relation to special versus regular class placement for disturbed children. If, as has been suggested by Kounin, Friesen, and Norton (1966), the critical skill in handling problem children in either the special or regular class setting relates to group management techniques, as such techniques are defined and emphasized in all teacher preparation programs, our dependence on the special class may lessen. Also, development of options between the regular and special class approach such as transitional settings (Hewett et al. 1970b), resource rooms with crisis teacher support (Morse, 1965), and consultative services (Knoblock & Garcea, 1965) appear promising.

While the teacher of the emotionally disturbed may be charged with "being all things at all times to all people," emphasis on managerial competence and sound academic teaching appears very important in training programs. Glavin and Quay (1969) suggest that since we cannot predict which children will spontaneously improve and those whose problems will persist, we should focus on problem behaviors of immediate concern and remediate learning problems rather than aim at "ambitious restructuring of personality." The issue of supportive operations such as psychotherapy with parents and disturbed children is far from settled in relation to education of the emotionally disturbed as it is unresolved in the counseling, guidance and therapy fields in general. Whatever the value of extraeducational therapeutic interventions, teachers of disturbed children will probably never be able to rely on these interventions to accomplish the job which the teachers must take the responsibility for in the classroom.

It can be stated that research evidence must be obtained in almost every phase of education of the disturbed child starting with the critical area of definition and classification mentioned earlier. The list of methodological inadequacies reflected in research efforts in the field is considerable. Balow (1966a) calls attention to inadequate criterion measures, lack of control groups, inadequate sampling, poorly defined differ-

ential treatments and retrospective designs. He also emphasizes the importance of research questions which will lend themselves to generalized results rather than to specific group or individual implications. Finally, there is an urgent need for planned, programmatic research which is cumulative and which moves systematically toward building a body of knowledge in the field.

REFERENCES

Aichhorn, A. *Wayward youth.* New York: Viking Press, 1965.

American Psychiatric Association. Planning psychiatric services for children in the community mental health program. Washington, D.C.: American Psychiatric Association, 1964.

Axline, V. M. *Play therapy.* Boston: Houghton Mifflin, 1947.

Balow, B. The emotionally and socially handicapped. *Review of Educational Research,* 1966, 36, 120–133. (a)

Balow, B. A program of preparation for teachers of disturbed children. *Exceptional Children,* 1966, 32, 455–460. (b)

Bandura, A. Behavioral modification through modeling procedures. In L. Krasner, & L. Ullmann (Eds.), *Research in behavior modification.* New York: Holt, Rinehart & Winston, 1966. Pp. 310–340.

Bandura, A. *Principles of behavior modification.* New York: Holt, Rinehart & Winston, 1969.

Bandura, A., & Walters, R. H. *Social learning and personality development.* New York: Holt, Rinehart & Winston, 1963.

Barrish, H. H., Saunders, M., & Wolf, M. M. Good behavior game: Effects of individual contingencies for group consequences on disruptive behavior in a classroom. *Journal of Applied Behavior Analysis,* 1969, 2, 119–124.

Becker, W. C. *Parents are teachers.* Champaign, Ill.: Research Press, 1971.

Becker, W. C., Madsen, C. H., Arnold, C. R., & Thomas, D. R. The contingent use of teacher attention and praise in reducing classroom behavior problems. *Journal of Special Education,* 1967, 1, 287–307.

Beilin, H. Teachers' and clinicians' attitudes toward the behavior problems of children:

A reappraisal. *Child Development,* 1959, 30, 9–12.

Berkowitz, P. H., & Rothman, E. P. *The disturbed child: Recognition and psychoeducational therapy in the classroom.* New York: New York University Press, 1966.

Bettelheim, B. *Love is not enough.* Glencoe, Ill.: Free Press, 1950.

Bettelheim, B. *Truants from life: The rehabilitation of emotionally disturbed children.* Glencoe, Ill.: Free Press, 1955.

Bettelheim, B. *The empty fortress.* New York: Free Press, 1967.

Bijou, S. W., & Baer, D. M. *Child development: A systematic and empirical theory.* New York: Appleton-Century-Crofts, 1961.

Birnbrauer, J., Bijou, S., Wolf, M., & Kidder, J. Programmed instruction in the classroom. In L. Krasner, & L. P. Ullmann (Eds.), *Case studies in behavior modification.* New York: Holt, Rinehart & Winston, 1965. Pp. 358–363.

Bisgyer, J. L., Kahn, C. L., & Frazee, V. F. Special classes for emotionally disturbed children. *American Journal of Orthopsychiatry,* 1964, 34, 696–704.

Blom, G. E. Psychoeducational aspects of classroom management. *Exceptional Children,* 1966, 32, 377–383.

Boocock, S. S., & Coleman, J. C. Games with simulated environments in learning. *Sociology of Education,* 1966, 39, 215–236.

Bower, E. M. A process for identifying disturbed children. *Children,* 1957, 4, 143–147.

Bower, E. M. *Early identification of emotionally handicapped children in school.* Springfield, Ill.: Charles C Thomas, 1960.

Bower, E. M. Primary prevention in a school setting. In G. Caplan (Ed.), *Prevention of mental disorders in children.* New York: Basic Books, 1961. Pp. 353–377.

Bower, E., & Lambert, N. A process for in-school screening of children with emotional handicaps. In *Manual for school administrators and teachers.* Princeton, N.J.: Educational Testing Service, 1962.

Bowman, P. H. *Mobilizing community resources for youth: Identification and treatment of maladjusted, delinquent, and gifted children.* Dept. of Education, Supplementary Education Monographs No. 85. Chicago: University of Chicago Press, 1956.

Bruno, F. Life values, manifest needs, and vocational interests as factors influencing

professional career satisfaction among teachers of emotionally disturbed children. Unpublished doctoral dissertation, Wayne State University, 1969.

Buckley, N. K., & Walker, H. M. *Modifying classroom behavior.* Champaign, Ill.: Research Press, 1970.

Cannon, K. L. Stability of sociometric scores of high school students. *Journal of Educational Research,* 1958, 52, 43–48.

Chapman, R. W. School suspension as therapy. *Personnel and Guidance Journal,* 1962, 40, 731–732.

Clarizio, H. Stability of deviant behavior through time. *Mental Hygiene,* 1968, 52, 288–293.

Clements, S. D., & Peters, J. E. Minimal brain dysfunctions in the school-age child. *Archives of General Psychiatry,* 1962, 6, 185–197.

Cobb, J. A., Ray, R. S., & Patterson, G. R. Direct intervention in the schools. Unpublished manuscript, Oregon Research Institute, September 1970.

Cohen, R. S. Therapeutic education and day treatment: A new professional liaison. *Exceptional Children,* 1965, 32, 23–28.

Cohn, B., Ohlsen, M., & Proff, F. Roles played by adolescents in an unproductive counseling group. *Personnel and Guidance Journal,* 1960, 38, 724–731.

Coleman, J. C., & Hewett, F. M. Open-door therapy: A new approach to the treatment of underachieving adolescent boys who resist needed psychotherapy. *Journal of Clinical Psychology,* 1962, 18, 28–33.

Colvin, R. W. The education of emotionally disturbed children in a residential treatment center. *American Journal of Orthopsychiatry,* 1961, 31, 591–597.

Cruickshank, W. M., Bentzen, F. A., Ratzeburg, F. H., & Tannhauser, M. T. *A teaching method for brain-injured and hyperactive children.* Syracuse, N.Y.: Syracuse University Press, 1961.

Cruse, D. The effect of distraction upon the performance of brain-injured and familial retarded children. In E. Trapp, & P. Himmelstain (Eds.), *Readings on the exceptional child.* New York: Appleton-Century-Crofts, 1962.

D'angelo, R. Y., & Walsh, J. F. An evaluation of various therapy approaches with lower socioeconomic group children. *Journal of Psychology*, 1967, 67, 59–64.

Devereux, G. *Therapeutic education*. New York: Harper & Brothers, 1956.

Dorward, B. A comparison of the competencies for regular classroom teachers and teachers of emotionally disturbed children. *Exceptional Children*, 1963, 30, 67–73.

Dunn, L. M. Special education for the mildly retarded—Is much of it justifiable? *Exceptional Children*, 1968, 35, 5–22.

Dupont, H. (Ed.) *Educating emotionally disturbed children*. New York: Holt, Rinehart & Winston, 1969.

Eaton, M. T., Weathers, G., & Phillips, B. N. Some reactions of classroom teachers to problem behavior in school. *Educational Administration and Supervision*, 1957, 43, 129–139.

Ekstein, R., & Motto, R. L. *From learning for love to love of learning*. New York: Brunner Mazel, 1969.

Eldred, D. M. *The use of programmed instruction with disturbed students*. Waterbury, Vt.: Vermont State Hospital, 1966.

Engelmann, S. *Preventing failure in the primary grades*. Chicago: Science Research Associates, 1969.

Fenichel, C. Psycho-educational approaches for seriously disturbed children in the classroom. In P. Knoblock (Ed.), *Approaches in educating emotionally disturbed children*. Syracuse, N.Y.: Syracuse University Division of Special Education and Rehabilitation, 1966. Pp. 5–18.

Fenichel, C., Freedman, A. M., & Klapper, Z. A day school for schizophrenic children. *American Journal of Orthopsychiatry*, 1960, 30, 130–143.

Freud, A. The relation between psychoanalysis and pedagogy. In *Psychoanalysis for teachers and parents* (trans. by B. Low). New York: Emerson Books, 1954.

Frostig. M., & Maslow, P. Treatment methods and their evaluation in educational therapy. In J. Hellmuth (Ed.), *Educational therapy*. Vol. 2. Seattle, Wash.: Special Child Publications, 1969. Pp. 415–431.

Glavin, J. P. "Spontaneous" improvement in emotionally disturbed children. (Doctoral dissertation, George Peabody College for Teachers) *Dissertation Abstracts*, 1968, 28, 3503A.

Glavin, J. P., & Quay, H. C. Behavior disorders. *Review of Educational Research*, 1969, 39, 83–102.

Glidewell, J. C., Domke, H. R., & Kantor, M. B. Screening in schools for behavior disorders: Use of mothers' reports of symptoms. *Journal of Educational Research*, 1963, 56, 508–515.

Goodwin, D. L. *The psychologist as an agent of behavioral change*. Paper presented at the meeting of the American Psychological Association, San Francisco, September 1968.

Graubard, P., & Miller, M. D. Behavioral disorders. In G. O. Johnson, & H. Black (Eds.), *Exceptional children research review*. Washington: Council for Exceptional Children, 1968. Pp. 262–303.

Grimes, J. W., & Allinsmith, W. Compulsivity, anxiety, and school achievement. *Merrill-Palmer Quarterly*, 1961, 7, 247–271.

Gronlund, N. E., & Holmlund, W. S. The value of elementary school sociometric status scores for predicting pupils' adjustment in high school. *Educational Administration and Supervision*, 1958, 44, 255–260.

Grossman, H. *Teaching the emotionally disturbed: A casebook*. New York: Holt, Rinehart & Winston, 1965.

Hall, R. V., Lund, D., & Jackson, D. Effects of teacher attention on study behavior. *Journal of Applied Behavior Analysis*, 1968, 1, 1–12.

Haring, N. G., & Lovitt, T. C. Operant methodology and educational technology in special education. In N. G. Haring, & R. L. Schiefelbusch (Eds.), *Methods in special education*. New York: McGraw-Hill, 1967. Pp. 12–48.

Haring, N. G., & Phillips, E. L. *Educating emotionally disturbed children*. New York: McGraw-Hill, 1962.

Haughton, O. Personal communication, 1970.

Hay, L. A. A new school channel for helping the troubled child. *American Journal of Orthopsychiatry*, 1953, 23, 676–683.

Hay, L., & Cohen, S. Perspectives for a classroom for disturbed children. *Exceptional Children*, 1967, 33, 577–580.

Hewett, F. M. A hierarchy of educational tasks for children with learning disorders. *Exceptional Children*, 1964, 31, 207–214.

Hewett, F. M. Teaching speech to an autistic child through operant conditioning. *American Journal of Orthopsychiatry*, 1965, 35, 927–936.

Hewett, F. M. A hierarchy of competencies for teachers of emotionally handicapped children. *Exceptional Children*, 1966, 33, 7–11.

Hewett, F. M. Educational engineering with emotionally disturbed children. *Exceptional Children*, 1967, 33, 459–467.

Hewett, F. M. *The emotionally disturbed child in the classroom.* Boston: Allyn & Bacon, 1968.

Hewett, F. M., Taylor, F. D., & Artuso, A. A. The Santa Monica project: Evaluation of an engineered classroom design with emotionally disturbed children. *Exceptional Children*, 1969, 35, 523–529.

Hewett, F., Taylor, F. D., Artuso, A. A., & Stillwell, R. The Santa Monica engineered classroom: Progress report I. Unpublished manuscript, Santa Monica Unified School District, Department of Special Services, Santa Monica, California, 1970.

Hewett, F., Taylor, F., Quay, H., Soloway, M., Stillwell, R., & Artuso, A. A. The Santa Monica Madison School plan. Unpublished manuscript, Santa Monica Unified School District, Department of Special Services, Santa Monica, California, 1970.

Hobbs, N. Helping disturbed children: Psychological and ecological strategies. *American Psychologist*, 1966, 21, 1105–1115.

Holland, J. G., & Skinner, B. F. *The analysis of behavior.* New York: McGraw-Hill, 1961.

Homme, L., Csanyi, A., Gonzales, M., & Rechs, J. *How to use contingency contracting in the classroom.* Champaign, Ill.: Research Press, 1970.

Jacobson, S., & Faegre, C. Neutralization: A tool for the teacher of disturbed children. *Exceptional Children*, 1959, 25, 243–246.

Kanner, L. *Child psychiatry.* Springfield, Ill.: Charles C Thomas, 1948.

Kephart, N. C. *The slow learner in the classroom.* Columbus, Ohio: Charles E. Merrill, 1960.

Klincewicz, W. Cybernetics and automation: Their impact on education. In J. Hellmuth (Ed.), *Educational therapy.* Vol. 2. Seattle, Wash.: Special Child Publications, 1969. Pp. 35–77.

Knoblock, P. (ED.) *Intervention approaches in educating emotionally disturbed children.* Syracuse, N.Y.: Syracuse University Press, 1966.

Knoblock, P., & Garcea, R. A. Toward a broader concept of the role of the special class for emotionally disturbed children. *Exceptional Children*, 1965, 31, 329–335.

Kounin, J. S., Friesen, W. V., & Norton, A. E. Managing emotionally disturbed children in regular classrooms. *Journal of Educational Psychology*, 1966, 57, 1–13.

LaVietes, R. L., Hulse, W. C., & Blau, A. A psychiatric day treatment center and school for young children and their parents. *American Journal of Orthopsychiatry*, 1960, 30, 468–482.

Levin, G., & Simmons, J. J. Response to praise by emotionally disturbed boys. *Psychological Reports*, 1962, 11, 10.

Levitt, E. E., Beiser, H. R., & Robertson, R. E. A follow-up evaluation of cases treated at a community child guidance clinic. *American Journal of Orthopsychiatry*, 1959, 29, 337–349.

Lewis, W. W. Continuity and intervention in emotional disturbance: A review. *Exceptional Children*, 1965, 31, 465–475.

Lewis, W. W. Project Re-ED: Educational intervention in discordant child rearing systems. In E. L. Cowen, E. A. Gardner, & M. Zax (Eds.), *Emergent approaches to mental health problems.* New York: Appleton-Century-Crofts, 1967. Pp. 352–368.

Lindsley, O. An experiment with parents handling behavior at home. *Johnstone Bulletin*, 1966, 9, 27–36. (a)

Lindsley, O. Personal communication, 1966. (b)

Lindsley, O. Precision teaching. Speech presented at Santa Monica Unified School District, Santa Monica, Calif., October 1970.

Lindsley, O. *Precision teaching* (a manual), in press.

Lisle, J. D. The comparative effectiveness of various group procedures used with elementary pupils with personal-social adjustment problems. (Doctoral dissertation, Kent State University) *Dissertation Abstracts* 28: 448A; No. 11, 1968.

Lovaas, O. I., Berberich, J. P., Perloff, B. F., & Schaeffer, B. Acquisition of imitative speech by schizophrenic children. *Science*, 1966, 151, 705–707.

Lovitt, T. C., & Curtiss, K. A. Academic response rate as a function of teacher- and self-imposed contingencies. *Journal of Applied Behavior Analysis*, 1969, 2, 49–53.

MacFarlane, J. W., Allen, L., & Honzik, M. *A developmental study of the behavior problems of normal children between 21 months and 14 years.* Berkeley, Calif.: University of California Press, 1954.

Mackie, R., Kvaraceus, W., & Williams, H. *Teachers of children who are socially and emotionally maladjusted.* Washington, D.C.: U.S. Department of Health, Education, and Welfare, 1957.

Madsen, C. H., Jr., Becker, W. C., & Thomas, E. R. Rules, praise, and ignoring: Elements of elementary classroom control. *Journal of Applied Behavior Analysis*, 1968, 1, 139–150.

Marshall, H. H. The effect of punishment on children: A review of the literature and a suggested hypothesis. *Journal of Genetic Psychology*, 1965, 106, 23–33.

McCaffrey, I., & Cumming, J. *Behavior patterns associated with persistent emotional disturbances of school children in regular classes of elementary grades.* Onondaga County: Mental Health Research Unit, New York State Department of Mental Hygiene, December 1967.

McCarthy, J. J. Instructional material centers in special education. In J. Hellmuth (Ed.), *Educational therapy.* Vol. 2. Seattle, Wash.: Special Child Publications, 1969. Pp. 14–31.

McKenzie, H. S., Clark, M., Wolf, M. M., Kothera, N., & Benson, C. Behavior modification of children with learning disabilities using grades as tokens and allowances as backup reinforcers. *Exceptional Children*, 1968, 34, 745–752.

Meacham, M. L., & Wiesen, A. E. *Changing classroom behavior: A manual for precision teaching.* Scranton, Pa.: International Textbook, 1970.

Mesinger, J. F. Emotionally disturbed and brain damaged children—Should we mix them? *Exceptional Children*, 1965, 32, 237–240.

Meyer, H. J., Borgatta, E. F., & Jones, W. C. *Girls at Vocational High.* New York: Russell Sage Foundation, 1965.

Milton, O. (Ed.) *Behavior disorders: Perspectives and trends.* New York: Lippincott, 1965.

Minuchin, S., Chamberlain, R., & Graubard,

P. A project to teach learning skills to disturbed, delinquent children. *American Journal of Orthopsychiatry*, 1967, 37, 558–567.

Morse, W. C. Working paper; Training teachers in life space interviewing. *American Journal of Orthopsychiatry*, 1963, 33, 727–730.

Morse, W. C. The crisis teacher. In N. J. Long, W. C. Morse, & R. G. Newman (Eds.), *Conflict in the classroom: The education of emotionally disturbed children.* Belmont, Calif.: Wadsworth, 1965. Pp. 251–254.

Morse, W. C. Public schools and the disturbed child. In P. Knoblock (Ed.), *Intervention approaches in educating emotionally disturbed children.* Syracuse: Syracuse University Press, 1966. Pp. 113–128.

Morse, W. C. The education of socially maladjusted and emotionally disturbed children. In W. M. Cruickshank, & O. Johnson (Eds.), *Education of exceptional children and youth.* (2nd ed.) Englewood Cliffs, N.J.: Prentice-Hall, 1967. Pp. 557–608.

Morse, W. C., Cutler, R. L., & Fink, A. H. *Public school classes for the emotionally handicapped: A research analysis.* Washington, D.C.: National Education Association Council for Exceptional Children, 1964.

Morse, W. C., & Small, E. R. Group life space interviewing in a therapeutic camp. *American Journal of Orthopsychiatry*, 1959, 29, 27–44.

Moustakas, C. E. *Children in play therapy.* New York: McGraw-Hill, 1953.

Moustakas, C. E. The frequency and intensity of negative attitudes expressed in play therapy: A comparison of well-adjusted and disturbed young children. *Journal of Genetic Psychology*, 1955, 86, 309–325.

National Advisory Committee on Handicapped Children. *Special education for handicapped children*, First Annual Report. Washington, D.C.: Department of Health, Education, and Welfare, Office of Education, January 31, 1968, 34.

Neill, A. S. *Summerhill: A radical approach to child rearing.* New York: Hart, 1960.

Newman, R. G. The assessment of progress in the treatment of hyperaggressive children with learning disturbances within a school setting. *American Journal of Orthopsychiatry*, 1959, 29, 633–643.

Nichtern, S., Donahue, G. T., O'Shea, J., Marans, M., Curtis, M., & Brody, C. A community educational program for the emotionally disturbed child. *American Journal of Orthopsychiatry*, 1964, 34, 705–713.

Nurnberger, J. I., Ferster, C. B., & Brady, J. P. *An introduction to the science of human behavior*. New York: Appleton-Century-Crofts, 1963.

O'Leary, K. D., Becker, W. C., Evans, M. B., & Saudargas, R. A. A token reinforcement program in a public school: A replication and systematic analysis. *Journal of Applied Behavior Analysis*, 1969, 2, 3–13.

O'Leary, K. D., Kaufman, K. F., Kass, R. E., & Drabman, R. S. The effects of loud and soft reprimands on the behavior of disruptive students. *Exceptional Children*, 1970, 37, 145–155.

Ott, J. F. Teaching the emotionally disturbed teenage student. *Bulletin of the National Assn. of Secondary School Principals*, 1958, 42(236), 164–181.

Packard, R. G. The control of "classroom attention": A group contingency for complex behavior. *Journal of Applied Behavior Analysis*, 1970, 3, 13–28.

Pate, J. E. Emotionally disturbed and socially maladjusted children. In L. M. Dunn (Ed.), *Exceptional children in the schools*. New York: Holt, Rinehart & Winston, 1963. Pp. 239–283.

Pate, J. E., & Webb, W. W. Screening beginning first graders for potential problems. *Exceptional Children*, 1965, 32, 111.

Patterson, G. R. An empirical approach to the classification of disturbed children. *Journal of Clinical Psychology*, 1964, 20, 326–337.

Patterson, G. R., & Ebner, M. Applications of learning principles to the treatment of deviant children. Paper presented at the meeting of the American Psychological Assn., Chicago, September 1965.

Patterson, G. R., & Guillion, M. E. *Living with children: New methods for parents and teachers*. Champaign, Ill.: Research Press, 1970.

Pearson, G. H. J. *Emotional disorders of children*. New York: W. W. Norton, 1949.

Pearson, G. H. J. *Psychoanalysis and the education of the child*. New York: W. W. Norton, 1954.

Peterson, D. R. Behavior problems of middle childhood. *Journal of Consulting Psychology*, 1961, 25, 205–209.

Phillips, E. L. *Psychotherapy: A modern theory and practice*. Englewood Cliffs, N.J.: Prentice-Hall, 1956.

Phillips, E. L. Parent-child psychotherapy: A follow-up study comparing two techniques. *Journal of Psychology*, 1960, 49, 195–202.

Pimm, J. B., & McClure, G. Working with emotionally disturbed children in a public school setting. Paper presented at the 44th Annual Convention, Council for Exceptional Children, Toronto, Canada, April 1966.

Pimm, J. B., & McClure, G. A screening device for early detection of emotional disturbance in a public school setting. *Exceptional Children*, 1967, 33, 647–648.

Premack, D. Toward empirical behavior laws: 1. Positive reinforcement. *Psychological Review*, 1959, 66, 219–233.

Quay, H. C. Some basic considerations in the education of emotionally disturbed children. *Exceptional Children*, 1963, 30, 27–31.

Quay, H. C. Dimensions of problem behavior in children and their interaction in the approaches to behavior modifications. *Kansas Studies in Education*, 1966, 16, 6–13.

Quay, H. C., & Glavin, J. The education of behaviorally disordered children in the public school setting. *Final Report Project No. 482207*, Department of Health, Education, and Welfare, U.S. Office of Education, Bureau of Education for Handicapped, 1970.

Quay, H. C., Morse, W. C., & Cutler, R. L. Personality patterns of pupils in special classes for the emotionally disturbed. *Exceptional Children*, 1966, 32, 297–301.

Rabinow, B. An agenda for educators working with the emotionally disturbed in residential settings. *American Journal of Orthopsychiatry*, 1961, 31, 584–90.

Redl, F. The phenomenon of contagion and "shock effect" in group therapy. In K. Eissler (Ed.), *Searchlights on delinquency*. New York: International Universities Press, 1949. Pp. 315–328.

Redl, F. Strategy and techniques of the life space interview. *American Journal of Orthopsychiatry*, 1959, 29, 1–18.

Redl, F. *When we deal with children*. New York: Free Press, 1966.

Redl, F., & Jacobson, S. The emotionally disturbed. *National Education Association Journal*, 1958, 47, 609–611.

Redl, F., & Wineman, D. *Children who hate.* New York: Free Press, 1951.

Redl, F., & Wineman, D. *Controls from within: Techniques for the treatment of the aggressive child.* Glencoe, Ill.: Free Press, 1952.

Rivlin, H. N. Classroom discipline and learning. In M. Krugman (Ed.), *Orthopsychiatry in the school.* New York: American Orthopsychiatric Association, 1958. Pp. 113–118.

Rogers, C. R. *Counseling and psychotherapy.* Boston: Houghton Mifflin, 1942.

Rogers, C. R. *Client-centered therapy.* Boston: Houghton Mifflin, 1951.

Rotter, J. B. *Social learning and clinical psychology.* New York: Prentice-Hall, 1954.

Rubin, E. Z. Special education in a psychiatric hospital. *Exceptional Children,* 1962, 29, 184–190.

Rubin, E. Z., Simson, C. B., & Betwee, M. C. *Emotionally handicapped children and the elementary school.* Detroit: Wayne State University Press, 1966.

Safford, A. L., & Watts, C. A. An evaluation of a public school program for educationally handicapped children. *California Journal of Educational Research,* 1967, 18, 125–132.

Scheuer, A. L. Certification, teacher preparation, and special classes for the emotionally disturbed and socially maladjusted. Report by states. *Exceptional Children,* 1966, 33, 120–121.

Schmidt, G. W., & Ulrich, R. E. Effects of group contingent events upon classroom noise. *Journal of Applied Behavior Analysis,* 1969, 2, 171–179.

Schroeder, L. B. A study of the relationships between five descriptive categories of emotional disturbance and reading and arithmetic achievement. *Exceptional Children,* 1965, 32, 111–112.

Seeman, J., & Edwards, B. A therapeutic approach to reading difficulties. *Journal of Consulting Psychology,* 1954, 18, 451–453.

Shapiro, M. I. The development of communication skills. Final report. Pittsburgh Child Guidance Center, Pennsylvania, October 19, 1965. *Exceptional Child Bibliography series. Emotionally disturbed research reports.* Abstract 19, 6, September 1969, Arlington, Va.

Shores, R. E., & Haubrich, P. A. Effect of cubicles in educating emotionally disturbed children. *Exceptional Children,* 1969, 36, 21–24.

Skinner, B. F. *Science and human behavior.* New York: Macmillan, 1953.

Skinner, B. F. Why teachers fail. *Saturday Review,* Oct. 16, 1965, 48, 80–81, 98–102.

Slatoff, J. A combined educational and psychiatric approach to early primary grade learning problems. *Research Relating to Children,* Bulletin No. 22, p. 84.

Slavson, S. R. *Re-educating the delinquent through group and community participation.* New York: Harper & Brothers, 1954.

Smith, J. M., & Smith, D. E. P. *Child management: A program for parents.* Ann Arbor, Mich.: Ann Arbor Publishers, 1966.

Stevenson, H. W., Hill, K. T., Hale, G. A., & Moely, B. E. Adult ratings of children's behavior. *Child Development,* 1966, 37, 929–941.

Stone, F. B., & Rowley, V. N. Educational disability in emotionally disturbed children. *Exceptional Children,* 1964, 30, 423–426.

Strauss, A. A., & Kephart, N. C. Psychopathology and education of the brain-injured child. Vol. II. *Progress in theory and clinic.* New York: Grune & Stratton, 1955.

Strauss, A. A., & Lehtinen, L. E. *Psychopathology and education of the brain-injured child.* New York: Grune & Stratton, 1947.

Talmadge, M., Anthony, D., & Laufer, M. W. A study of experimental methods for teaching emotionally disturbed, brain damaged, retarded readers. *Journal of Educational Research,* 1963, 56, 311–316.

Thomas, D. R., Becker, W. C., & Armstrong, M. Production and elimination of disruptive classroom behavior by systematically varying teacher's behavior. *Journal of Applied Behavior Analysis,* 1968, 1, 35–45.

Tierney, T. E. Psychotherapy and reading tutoring: Effect of psychotherapy and reading instruction on reading ability and personal and social adjustment. (Doctoral dissertation, New York University). *Dissertation Abstracts,* 1957, 17, 811–812.

Trippe, M. J. Conceptual problems in research on educational provisions for disturbed children. *Exceptional Children,* 1963, 29, 400–406.

Ullmann, L. P., & Krasner, L. (Eds.) *Case studies in behavior modification.* New York: Holt, Rinehart & Winston, 1965.

Ulrich, R. E., Stachnik, T. J., & Mabry, J. H. *The control of human behavior, Vol. II:*

From cure to prevention. Glenview, Ill.: Scott, Foresman, 1970.

Valett, R. E. *Modifying children's behavior: A guide for parents and professionals.* Palo Alto, Calif.: Fearon, 1969.

Vane, J. R., Weitzman, J., & Applebaum, A. P. Performance of Negro and white children and problem and nonproblem children on the Stanford-Binet Scale. *Journal of Clinical Psychology,* 1966, 22, 431–435.

Walker, H. M.. *Behavior checklist.* Los Angeles: Western Psychological Services, 1968.

Walker, H. M., & Buckley, N. K. The use of positive reinforcement in conditioning attending behavior. *Journal of Applied Behavior Analysis,* 1968, 1, 245–250.

Walker, H. M., & Mattson, R. Identification and treatment of social-emotional problems. Interim report. Emotionally Disturbed Research Report, *Council for Exceptional Children Abstract 23,* September 8, 1969.

Walker, H., Mattson, R., & Buckley, N. Special class placement as a treatment alternative for deviant behavior in children. In F. A. M. Benson (Ed.), *Modifying deviant social behavior in various classroom settings.* Eugene, Ore.: University of Oregon Press, 1969.

Watson, R. I. *Psychology of the child.* New York: John Wiley, 1959.

Werry, J. S., & Quay, H. C. A method of observing classroom behavior of emotionally disturbed children. *Exceptional Children,* 1968, 34, 389.

Westendorp, F., Abramson, B., & Wirt, R. D. Group psychotherapy in a public school setting. *Group Psychotherapy,* 1962, 15, 30–35.

Whelan, R. J. The relevance of behavior modification procedures for teachers of emotionally disturbed children. In P. Knoblock (Ed.), *Intervention approaches in educating emotionally disturbed children.* Syracuse, N.Y.: Syracuse University Press, 1966.

Whelan, R. J., & Haring, N. G. Modification and maintenance of behavior through systematic application of consequences. *Exceptional Children,* 1966, 32, 281–289.

White, M. A., & Harris, M. W. *The school psychologist.* New York: Harper & Row, 1961.

Wickman, E. K. *Children's behavior and teachers' attitudes.* New York: Commonwealth Fund, 1928.

Wilderson, F. B., Jr. An exploratory study of reading skill deficiencies and psychiatric symptoms in emotionally disturbed children. *Reading Research Quarterly,* 1967, 2(3), 47–73.

Winn, E. V. The influence of play therapy on personality change and the consequent effect on reading performance. (Doctoral dissertation, Michigan State University) *Dissertation Abstracts* 1962, 22, 4278–4279.

Wolf, M. M., Hanley, E. L., King, L. A., Lachowicz, J., & Giles, D. K. The timergame: A variable interval contingency for the management of out-of-seat behavior. *Exceptional Children,* 1970, 37, 113–117.

Woody, R. H. Diagnosis of behavioral problem children: Mental abilities and achievement. *Journal of School Psychology,* 1968, 6, 111–116.

Woody, R. H. *Behavioral problem children in the schools.* New York: Appleton-Century-Crofts, 1969.

Zifferblatt, S. M. *You can help your child improve study and homework behavior.* Champaign, Ill.: Research Press, 1970.

Zimmerman, E. H., & Zimmerman, J. The alteration of behavior in a special classroom situation. *Journal of the Experimental Analysis of Behavior,* 1962, 59–60.

CHAPTER 22 The Nature of Giftedness and the Education of the Gifted[1]

J. W. GETZELS
University of Chicago

J. T. DILLON
University of Chicago

No statement has better captured the significance of the study of giftedness than these opening words to Terman's (1925) monumental *Genetic Studies of Genius:*

> It should go without saying that a nation's resources of intellectual talent are among the most precious it will ever have. The origin of genius, the natural laws of its development, and the environmental influences by which it may be affected for good or ill, are scientific problems of almost unequaled importance for human welfare (p. vii).

If the phrase "intellectual talent" is taken to include "talent of all sorts," Terman's statement hardly permits of improvement, and its pertinence has become increasingly evident through the years. The conditions of modern life demand not only high intellectual ability in the traditional fields of learning, but also giftedness in all fields of human aspiration, the social as well as the technological, the artistic as well as the scientific, the humanistic as well as the economic.

Our review of the nature, recognition and education of the gifted is placed in the context of these circumstances. We begin by examining what is variously meant by the term *giftedness* and the significant historical and conceptual shifts in the scholarly study of superior human ability. We next consider in some detail three major conceptions of giftedness: superior intellectual ability, superior creative ability, and superior talent in a variety of human activities. We describe the neglect of talent among the disadvantaged and female populations and survey research on the education of the gifted. The chapter ends with a brief note on research and theory.

HISTORICAL CONTEXT

The term *gifted* became the standard designation for persons of superior ability during the early part of the twentieth century. It has since remained a designation rather than a definition, for it specifies neither the type of ability nor the degree of superiority. The ability with which the term came to be most commonly associated was intelligence, but circumstance rather than logic encour-

[1] A grant to the senior author from the Ford Foundation aided in the preparation of this chapter.

aged the widespread identification of giftedness with intellectual talent alone. It was the development of the intelligence test and its vigorous use in an early influential study of genius (Terman, 1925) that combined to give this conception of intellectual giftedness its central place in education and psychology, a place which it has held so long and honorably that only recently have conceptions of nonintellectual giftedness been gaining attention and acceptance. It is, however, the acceptance of these other conceptions, and not their origin, which is recent.

CONCEPTIONS OF GIFTEDNESS

At the time that giftedness was becoming associated with high intelligence, this association was already being questioned for excluding other abilities. It was early proposed not to use the term gifted without qualifying it with "mentally," "aesthetically," or "physically," or without including the social and moral as well as the mental development of the child (Baldwin, 1924); and it was argued that giftedness includes artistic and mechanical talents, and creative ability generally, besides intelligence (Osburn & Rohan, 1931). In advancing its definition, the 1931 White House Conference on children regretted that the word "gifted" was at that time "understood by most people to mean something quite different from that which is intended" (p. 537)—namely, to refer inappropriately to gifts in art, music, poetry and other areas—whereas the Conference meant "merely the child with exceptional intelligence" (p. 538). It was this conception of giftedness which became the dominant theme around which other conceptions have played obbligato.

One rightly speaks, then, of definitions of giftedness. Distinctions among them may be made with respect to the ability specified, whether intellectual or nonintellectual. Within the intellectual abilities, one may further distinguish between high IQ and high creativity; and within the nonintellectual, among various talents such as the so-

cial, aesthetic and mechanical. Definitions also distinguish between potential and demonstrated ability, its rate of development and its degree of exceptionality; they may place the gifted in the top 1 percent or 10 percent of a population, general or specific, or above a cut-off line arbitrarily drawn "at IQ 120, 130, 140, 150, or anywhere else in the superior range" (Terman, 1931, p. 570). Examples of these definitions are:

1. *Intelligence.* "Ability to make a high score on such intelligence tests as the National, the Terman Group, and the Stanford-Binet" (Terman, 1925, p. 631).

2. *Academic aptitude.* "The term 'gifted' will apply to those students who have a very high level of academic aptitude either demonstrated or potential" (Durr, 1964, p. 16).

3. *Creativity.* "The greatest characteristic of capability is the ability to create. This is the highest activity of man (p. 35)....the great heritage of the capable pupil and the chief reason why we can ill afford to neglect him" (Osburn & Rohan, 1931, p. 37).

4. *Development.* "An able or gifted child is one whose rate of development, with respect to time, on some personality variable of agreed social value is significantly larger than the generality" (Gowan & Demos, 1964, p. 7).

5. *Talent.* "The talented or gifted child is one who shows consistently remarkable performance in any worth-while line of endeavor" (Havighurst, Hersey, Meister, Cornog, & Terman, 1958, p. 19).

6. *Omnibus.* Giftedness may be defined as a superior general intellectual potential and ability (approximate IQ 120+); a high functional ability to achieve in various academic areas commensurate with general intellectual ability; a high-order talent in such special areas as art, music, mechanical ability, foreign languages, science, mathematics, dramatics, social leadership, and creative writing; and a creative ability to develop a novel event in the environment (Fliegler, 1961, p. 16).

Legislation providing for the education of the gifted has incorporated these definitions in all their variety. The legal definition of the gifted in one state is "a group intelligence quotient of 120 or higher"; another state provides for children of "such general intellectual capacity as to place them within the top 2 percent of all students having achieved his school grade throughout the state"; and another state provides for "children who have demonstrated outstanding leadership qualities and abilities or whose performance is consistently remarkable in mechanics, manipulative skills, the art of expression of ideas, orally or written, music, art, human relations or any other worthwhile line of human achievement" (Ackerman & Weintraub, 1969, p. 569).

The various definitions of giftedness are well established in the field and each is maintained by a significant corpus of studies and a cadre of investigators. Recent attempts have broadened notions of superior human ability while advancing definitions of such variety and sometimes of such unmanageable proportions that no one can entertain the hope of formulating a single satisfactory definition. The term "giftedness" is a rubric for several populations of children and for an increasing body of scientific knowledge about them. In doing a study one should specify the definition and the population to which it applies; in examining a study one should take careful note of these specifications; and in comparing the results of several studies one should accommodate their definitions and populations or refrain from comparing them.

SHIFTS IN RESEARCH EMPHASES

The first quantitative psychological study of giftedness was Galton's *Hereditary Genius: An Inquiry into Its Laws and Consequences,* published in 1869. This work not only touched off the familiar nature-nurture controversy over the source of superior human achievement, but also came to serve as a point of departure for virtually every issue which was to develop later. In the century since the appearance of Galton's study, the

field has shifted its emphasis from an examination of adult genius as defined by achievement to the study of childhood giftedness as defined by intelligence tests, from the study of giftedness to the study of creativity, and most recently from the study of general creative talent to the investigation of specific talents in a wide variety of human activities. Such is the development of the field and its shifts in emphases which are selected for review here with the understanding that research interests in these areas will overlap at any given period.

From Genius to Giftedness

The enduring interest engendered by Galton's early investigations of genius is reflected by the nearly 100 studies of genius contained in a review of the literature for the six years following the reissue of *Hereditary Genius* in 1914 (Terman & Chase, 1920). The major issues in studies of genius were questions of the demography, heredity and psychopathology of superior achievement. With the publication in the 1920s and 1930s of Terman's longitudinal studies of gifted children, interest in genius per se began to wane, and by World War II genius had ceased to be a focus of major interest (Albert, 1969). As interest in genius declined, interest in gifted children accelerated. The first encyclopedia article (Norris & Noonan, 1941) and the first research review in the *Review of Educational Research* (Newland, 1941) appeared at the beginning of the war, while the postwar period signaled the "growing curiosity as to just what giftedness is" (Newland, 1953, p. 417) and was marked by an extraordinary burgeoning of the literature. Two new journals appeared in the late 1950s, *Gifted Child Quarterly* and *The Superior Child.* Whereas the first major bibliography on giftedness (Henry, 1924) had listed some 450 references including all the literature appearing in the preceding three decades, a bibliography for the single decade of the 1950s listed nearly twice that number, and one for the first five years of the 1960s listed nearly three times that number (Gowan, 1961, 1965), despite its exclusion of popular articles, case studies, and reports of practices and programs.

The profusion of studies on giftedness was not matched by a profusion of findings; rather, many studies appear redundant in the light of the work of early investigators like Terman and Hollingworth. In the preface to the first volume of his *Genetic Studies of Genius* (1925), Terman stated that his conclusions were derived from experimental procedures which could be "repeated ad libitum for purposes of verification or refutation" (p. ix); the bulk of subsequent studies in intellectual giftedness have made this ad libitum repetition nearly ad infinitum. Despite the fact that the essential picture of the intellectually gifted child was drawn in the years 1925–1930 (Miles, 1954) and has not been substantially altered since, numerous investigations continue to discover and rediscover, to state and re-state what has already been known for decades.

From Giftedness to Creativity

In the late 1950s research emphasis began to turn from intellectual giftedness as defined by IQ to creativity, with which it is related. While giftedness continued to be of major concern, creativity rapidly became the dominant interest in the study of superior mental functioning. In 1931 a review of materials for the study of creative thinking could cite only "a mass of adjuvant material from other fields," and concluded that one could not speak of a literature on creativity, for no one had as yet made a direct impression in the field (Hutchinson, 1931, p. 404). One who was to make a direct impression, J. P. Guilford, summarized the history of the field as follows:

[Creativity] was almost entirely ignored by psychologists. Psychometric psychologists ruled creative potential out of intelligence, and behaviorism adopted a general viewpoint from which creativity could not be seen. Non-

psychologists made a few attempts to fill the gap, utilizing an anecdotal approach.... Almost nothing was learned about the nature of creative thinking itself (1967, pp. 5–6).

In his notable presidential address to the American Psychological Association, Guilford (1950) called attention to the circumstance that less than 0.2 of one percent of publications indexed in the *Pyschological Abstracts* for the preceding quarter-century had dealt with creativity, a figure he was later (1970) to revise as closer to only 0.1 of one percent. Guilford's remarks and his own work sparked an explosion of studies in creativity. In 1959 a separate section entitled "Creativity" was for the first time added to a review of research on giftedness (Fliegler & Bish, 1959); in 1962 the subject "Creativity" was shifted from the index to the table of contents of the *Psychological Abstracts;* and in 1967 *The Journal of Creative Behavior* was founded and rapidly gained more subscribers than all other related publications combined (Frierson, 1969). The growth of research literature in creativity was startling. The number of studies for the year and a half of 1965–1966 equaled that of the preceding five years, which in turn equaled that of the preceding 10 years, which in *its* turn equaled that of the preceding 100 years (Parnes & Brunelle, 1967). Much of the literature bore on areas other than education, such as industry, science, business or the arts; a bibliography of creativity studies in these areas lists some 350 studies from the early 1950s alone (Deutsch & Shea, 1958). While 6 percent of the references of a bibliography on giftedness for 1950–1960 dealt with creativity (Gowan, 1961), its successor for 1960–1964 listed 50 percent of its titles under creativity (Gowan, 1965).

From Creativity to Talent

The most recent emphasis emerging in the field, and in the nation as well in this regard, is that on talent. Although talent is no less ambiguous a concept than intelligence or creativity, it here refers to superior specific abilities valued by society but not necessarily included in the general conceptions of creativity or intelligence. Illustrative of this more recent emphasis in conceptions of giftedness is the definition in the National Society for the Study of Education 57th *Yearbook* on the gifted—the talented or gifted child is one who shows superior performance in *any* worthwhile line of endeavor including, besides the intellectual, academic, and creative, such areas as music, graphic arts, dramatics, mechanical skills and social leadership (Havighurst et al., 1958, p. 19). It is this very conception which some legislatures have adopted to distinguish between "gifted" children, who are identified by intelligence instruments, and "talented" children, who are not identified by such instruments, but who possess other abilities valuable to society (Ackerman & Weintraub, 1969).

Two events in the early 1950s illustrate the trend toward expanding the concept of giftedness to include specific nonintellectual talents: the founding of the prestigious annual Van Dyke Bingham lectures, later published as *The Discovery of Talent* (Wolfle, 1969), and the appointment of the Committee on the Identification of Talent by the Social Science Research Council (McClelland, Baldwin, Bronfenbrenner, & Strodtbeck, 1958). The Bingham lectures began, appropriately, with Terman on intellect (1954), and included one on creativity (MacKinnon, 1962); but there were also lectures on the diversity of talent (Wolfle, 1960), on managerial talent (Ghiselli, 1963), and on vocational talents (Paterson, 1957; Strong, 1958). The Committee on the Identification of Talent began its work by noting "a general ignorance" of criteria of talent other than the strictly academic or intellectual, and established as one of its first objectives the breaking of new ground in the field by investigating types of talented behavior other than those requiring "cognitively guided skills"; the Committee's report, *Talent and*

Society (McClelland et al., 1958), contained studies on social sensitivity, achievement motivation and occupational mobility.

Texts on the gifted may now be subtitled "Developing Total Talent," and may examine, besides intellectual talents, the kinesthetic, manipulative, psycho-social, performing arts and the mechanical (Rice, 1970). Studies have appeared on talent in social leadership (DeHaan & Havighurst, 1961), graphic arts (Getzels & Csikszentmihalyi, 1966a, 1966b), mechanics (*Vocationally Talented Pupils,* 1962), and morality (Getzels & Jackson, 1962). Efforts are being made to locate children with special nonacademic talents in the general population (Flanagan, Dailey, Shaycoft, Gorham, Orr, & Goldberg, 1962), and especially in the culturally and economically disadvantaged groups. Gallagher (1969) correctly summarizes what he calls the "distinct change" in current as compared to preceding work in giftedness:

There is less concern for the nature of giftedness and more concern for the role of the gifted in the classroom; less concern for administrative adjustments and greater concern for the nature of the program given to gifted students; less interest in the high-achieving gifted and more concern for the talent loss represented by the chronic underachiever and the talented student with low socioeconomic status; a greater interest in the multidimensional nature of talent and less interest in a single dimension of giftedness represented by the IQ score (p. 537).

Bibliographic Summary

Table 1 lists selected bibliographies and reviews from 1919–1970. In addition to summarizing the trends and shifts in the literature, it may serve as a convenient resource and guide for investigators faced with a nearly unmanageable volume of literature. Half of the bibliographies listed have appeared since 1960, but six early bibliographies have been included for reference to the beginnings of the field. The number of entries and the dates of the earliest and latest entry in each bibliography are recorded in order to provide a ready index to the literature, and special characteristics of each listing are noted. Comprehensive bibliographies for successive periods of years are Henry (1924) and Williams (1925), which include all the known literature to their time (Williams unfortunately remains unpublished); Martens (1951) for the years 1920–1950; Gowan (1961) for 1950–1960; and Gowan (1965) for 1960–1964. Major bibliographies on creativity are Razik (1965), with 4200 references for the two centuries to 1964; and Brunelle (n.d.) with 1200 for the succeeding two years. Period reviews of the research literature from the *Review of Educational Research* are Newland (1941), Woods (1944), Newland (1953), Fliegler and Bish (1959), Birch and Reynolds (1963), Gallagher and Rogge (1966), and Frierson (1969); those from the *Encyclopedia of Educational Research* are Norris and Noonan (1941), Norris, Hayslip, and Noonan (1950), Carter (1960), and Gallagher (1969).

MAJOR CONCEPTIONS OF GIFTEDNESS

The concept of giftedness has long been associated with high intellectual or academic ability. But if giftedness is taken to embrace superior human ability generally, then high-order achievement or potential in areas other than the academic may also usefully be included under the rubric of giftedness. Within the past two decades trends in research have borne increasingly upon other areas of high-order accomplishment, notably upon creativity and talent. This section reviews the three major conceptions of giftedness: superior ability in intelligence, in creativity, and in the variety of human talents.

INTELLIGENCE

By far the most important study of giftedness, and one of the most significant studies in all of developmental psychology, not to say of social science, is Terman's monu-

mental *Genetic Studies of Genius* (Burks, Jensen, & Terman, 1930; Cox, 1926; Terman, 1925; Terman & Oden, 1947, 1959). This massive longitudinal investigation (projected to continue until the year 2010) studied some 1500 children whose average Stanford-Binet IQ was approximately 150 in order to discover their characteristic traits as children and later as adults. Terman's work is here taken as prototypical of the study of giftedness as superior intelligence, for the innumerable studies which it has engendered illustrate its continuing influence and enduring achievement. Thirty years after beginning his study, Terman (1954) was able to say, "I take some pride in the fact that not one of the major conclusions we drew in the early 1920's regarding the traits that are typical of gifted children has been overthrown in the three decades since then" (p. 223). Nearly another two decades later, research into intellectual giftedness continues to identify and describe high-IQ children, confirming many of Terman's findings with a regularity bordering on redundancy.

Traits of the Highly Intelligent Child

"Great wits," said Dryden, "are sure to madness near allied." There is hardly a belief regarding superior human attainment that has had a longer life than that genius is either a pathologic condition in itself or is promoted by a pathologic condition (Getzels, 1968). The ancients believed that the genius was possessed by a god, muse or demon; the moderns not uncommonly believe that the "quiz kid" is a "queer kid," physically immature, socially maladjusted, emotionally unstable and morally untrustworthy. Early "scientific" support for such notions appeared in *The Insanity of Genius* (Nisbet, 1891), and Lombroso's influential *The Man of Genius* (1891), and was clearly expressed by Lange-Eichbaum (1932): "It may be a bitter pill for mankind to swallow, this recognition that in most instances genius and 'insanity' are inseparable" (p. 178). Freud (1922) pointed out that neurosis and

TABLE 1
SELECTED BIBLIOGRAPHIES AND REVIEWS ON GIFTEDNESS, 1919–1970

Compiler	Date	No. of entries	Earliest & latest entry	Special characteristics
Whipple	1919	124	1873/1918	12 non-English & 7 pre-1900 titles.
Henry	1920	157	1891/1919	11 non-English & 6 pre-1900 titles.
Terman & Chase	1920	95	1913/1919	14 non-English titles; reviews research on genius for 1913–1919.
Henry	1924	453	1891/1923	24 non-English & 206 pre-1920 titles; annotated.
Williams	1925	555	1869/1925	24 non-English & 223 pre-1920 titles; annotated & classified.
Cleeton	1926	24	1911/1924	Reviews research on originality.
Hutchinson	1931	152	1860/1931	43 non-English & 39 pre-1920 titles; reviews materials on creative thinking.
Terman & Burks	1933	126	1869/1932	12 non-English & 35 pre-1920 titles.
Noonan & Norris	1938	125	1916/1936	
Newland	1941	91	1930/1940	Reviews research for 1930–1940.
Norris & Noonan	1941	56	1916/1938	
Woods	1944	22	1940/1944	Reviews research for 1941–1943.
Norris & Hayslip	1950	79	1916/1947	Revision of Norris & Noonan, 1941.
Martens	1951	234	1921/1950	Annotated & classified.
Newland	1953	80	1943/1953	Reviews research for 1944–1953.
Miles	1954	414	1853/1953	42 non-English & 83 pre-1920 titles.
Deutsch & Shea	1958	621	1890/1958	Creativity in science, engineering, business & the arts.
Bristow	1959	303	1926/1959	Education of the gifted.
Fliegler & Bish	1959	251	1953/1959	Reviews research for 1953–1959.
Carter	1960	145	1924/1957	Emphasis on 1947–1957.
Holt	1960	718	1924/1960	Annotated & classified.
Pilch	1960–64	481	1938/1964	Education of the gifted.
Stein & Heinze	1960	340	1870/1959	Creativity; annotated & classified; emphasis on 1950–1959.
Gowan	1961	770	1945/1961	For 1950–1960; annotated & indexed.
Witty & DeBoer	1962	53	1925/1962	Annotated.
Birch & Reynolds	1963	57	1958/1962	Reviews research for 1959–1962.
Goldberg	1965	225	1920/1964	Education of the talented; classified.
Gowan	1965	1169	1940/1964	Giftedness & creativity for 1960–1964; annotated & indexed.
Razik	1965	4176	1744/1964	Creativity; classified; emphasis on 1950–1964.
Gallagher	1966	222	1925/1966	Emphasis on 1960–1966.
Gallagher & Rogge	1966	75	1962/1965	Reviews research for 1963–June 1965.
U.S. Office of Education	1966a	275	1957/1965	Education of the gifted; annotated.
Brunelle	n.d.	1199	1965/1966	Creativity.
Educator's ERIC Handbook	1967a, b	142	1960/1965	Education of the gifted; annotated; abstracts of each entry.
Grotberg	1967	53	1952/1966	Annotated.
Journal of Creative Behavior	1967	94	1966/1967	Creativity.
Parnes & Brunelle	1967	153	1956/1967	Creativity; annotated.
Parnes	1967	117	1954/1966	Creativity; annotated; continues Parnes & Brunelle, 1967.
Arasteh	1968	487	1900/1966	Creativity; annotated.
Frierson	1969	58	1960/1968	Reviews research for 1965–1968.
Gallagher	1969	85	1942/1965	Emphasis on 1958–1965.
Roweton	1970	311	1898/1969	Creativity; emphasis on 1950–1969.

genius have common sources in unconscious conflict, and Jung (1954) spoke of the "narrow margin between a gift and its pathological variant," and the difficulty of determining in some cases "whether it is the gift or the psychopathic constitution that predominates" (p. 141).

Terman's findings were diametrically opposed to these popular and scientific beliefs, which he labeled "superstitious in origin" (1925, p. vii). Instead of being inferior, his gifted children were superior to unselected children, not only intellectually, but also physically, socially, emotionally and morally. Their superior achievement in school, where they were typically two and sometimes four grades advanced beyond their age-group, applied so generally to the different school subjects that they refuted another traditional belief that gifted children are usually "one-sided." Numerous subsequent studies confirmed the developmental characteristics identified by Terman. As Gowan and Demos remark after having reviewed the literature, "The developmental patterns true of one group of the gifted usually apply to another" (1964, p. 36).

The Extremely Intelligent Child

Although the child with a high IQ may be accepted as "normal" and even superior in other respects, the child with a *very* high IQ often remains liable to certain suspicions; to rank somewhat high on an intelligence scale may be all right but to be all the way off the scale is too much. Is there indeed a point at which the very extremity of intelligence leads to a discontinuity or even a reversal in achievement? When Terman and Oden (1947) examined the 47 girls and 34 boys in the gifted group whose IQs were 170 or higher, they found that, contrary to common expectation, these children were as successful in their social adjustment as the gifted group in general. The very highly intelligent children learned to read at an earlier age and were more accelerated in school than the other children (but the child who

was recorded as reading earliest of all was in the lower group with an IQ of 144, barely four points above the cut-off for selection to the gifted group at all). The men in the high group were more likely to graduate from college, more likely to get high grades, and more likely to be successful occupationally; but about 25 percent of the *most* gifted subjects had college records that were only fair to poor, and there were both men and women in the group whose careers were much less satisfactory than might be expected from their IQs. Although there were a number of methodological difficulties that may have blurred existing variations, Terman and Oden (1947) concluded that "even when generous allowance is made for these factors, it is obvious that subjects of highest childhood IQ are not sharply differentiated in adult life from subjects who tested considerably lower" (p. 295).

The classic investigation of children at the highest level of intelligence as measured by available tests was performed by Hollingworth (1942). She identified 12 children with an IQ of 180 or above, and studied each child in depth. Ten of the children were first-born, five being only children. In most aspects of their physical development they were close to the norm, but in other aspects they were substantially, even astonishingly, earlier: the median age of talking was 14 months, and of reading 36 months. The children's school behavior ranged from truancy to enthusiasm, variations which seemed to depend upon the earliness of the identification of their giftedness—the earlier the identification, the more favorable the development. As compared to children with what Hollingworth called "optimum intelligence" (IQ 125/130 to 150/155), who have both the advantages of superiority and a sufficiency of equally superior companions to offer mutual esteem and understanding, the children of 170 or 180 IQ seem so far above others that they may suffer a personal isolation leading to problems of social development. They are too intelligent to be understood by their general company and too infrequent to find many congenial companions among themselves: "To have the intelligence of an adult and the emotions of a child combined in a childish body is to encounter certain difficulties" (Hollingworth, 1942, p. 282).

Growth of the Highly Intelligent Child

The periodic follow-ups of Terman's original gifted children showed that they had retained their early superiority. The incidence among them of ill health, mortality, insanity, delinquency and alcoholism was well below that of the general population of corresponding age. On subsequent adult level intelligence tests they scored about as far above the generality of adults as they had scored above the generality of children at the time they were selected. Indeed, they not only held their own but actually increased their superiority. Moreover, a group of the gifted subjects who did not go beyond high school obtained the same scores on these tests as did a group of candidates for advanced degrees at a leading university. And so another of the entrenched myths about giftedness, i.e., "early ripe, early rot," was found not to hold. As Terman put it, "So far no one has developed post-adolescent stupidity" (1954, p. 23).

Close to 90 percent of the gifted group entered college, and 70 percent graduated. Of those graduating, 30 percent were awarded honors and about two-thirds went on to graduate work. The achievement of the group at middle life was impressive and is best illustrated by the case histories of the 800 men in the sample (only a minority of the women had gone into professional careers). Included among the men were 78 who had taken a Ph.D. degree, 48 a medical degree, 85 a law degree, and 74 who were teaching or had taught in a four-year college or university. Of the scientists, 47 were listed in the 1949 edition of *American Men of Science*. Nearly all these numbers are from 10 to 30 times as large as would be found in 800 men of corresponding age

picked at random in the general population. By 1950, when the men were 40 years of age, they had published a total of 93 books (33 of them novels); 2000 scientific, technical and professional articles; more than 375 short stories, novelettes and plays; and some 275 articles of a miscellaneous sort. They had more than 230 patents to their credit (Terman, 1954; Terman & Oden, 1959).

Clearly, achievement in the gifted group was superior to achievement in the general population. But important, and at first inexplicable, differences in achievement appeared within the gifted group itself. In 1940, when the men were 25 years old, they were rated on the extent to which they had made use of their superior intellectual ability. The 150 men rated highest (group A) and the 150 rated lowest (group C) were compared on some 200 items of school, family and personal information obtained from childhood onward.

Although the A's tested a little higher in intelligence both in 1922 and 1940, the average score of the C's was high enough to permit brilliant college work; but while 97 percent of the A's entered college and 90 percent graduated, only 68 percent of the C's entered college and only 37 percent graduated. Of those graduated, 52 percent of the A's but only 14 percent of the C's received honors. Significant differences were found in the family backgrounds and personality characteristics of the two groups. Half of the A fathers but only 15 percent of the C fathers were college graduates; the estimated number of books in the A homes was nearly 50 percent greater than in the C homes; when the average age of the subjects was 16 years, more than twice as many of the C parents as of the A parents had been divorced. Of the 25 traits on which they had been rated by parents and teachers in 1922, only in health were the two groups equal in 1940. In all other traits they differed; the A's were significantly higher in such variables as prudence, self-confidence, desire to excel, leadership, popularity, and sensitivity to approval or disapproval. But the most telling differences emerged from three sets of ratings made in 1940 on a dozen personality traits. The A's were uniformly superior to the C's in each of the following: freedom from inferiority feelings, self-confidence, integration toward goals as contrasted with drifting, and persistence in the accomplishment of ends (Terman & Oden, 1947, pp. 311–352; Terman, 1954, p. 229). These characteristics recall Galton's observations, and those made by Cox (1926) in her study of historic genius: "High but not the highest intelligence, combined with the greatest degree of persistence, will achieve greater eminence than the highest degree of intelligence with somewhat less persistence" (p. 187).

Terman's (1954) conclusion with respect to such notions as Lange-Eichbaum's, viz., that intellectual superiority is related to emotional inferiority, may be put most simply in his own words:

Our data do not support the theory of Lange-Eichbaum that great achievement usually stems from emotional tensions that border on the abnormal. In our gifted group, success is associated with stability rather than instability, with absence rather than with presence of disturbing conflicts—in short with well-balanced temperament and with freedom from excessive frustrations (p. 230).

Creativity

Although it was believed that there were types of giftedness other than superior academic ability, for many years it was not seriously questioned that they too could be identified and explained by a high IQ. There can be no doubt about the signal usefulness of the IQ metric in identifying and measuring giftedness. But sharp questions have been raised recently about restricting the concept of giftedness to high intelligence and limiting the measure of giftedness to a high IQ. The crucial issue has become whether the intelligence test identifies all or

most of the factors contributing to superior human achievement of various types, including creative ability. In his presidential address to the APA, J. P. Guilford (1950) charged that not all the primary abilities measured by the intelligence test are important for creative behavior, while some of the primary abilities important for creative behavior are not to be found in the intelligence test at all. Guilford predicted that only low or moderate correlations would be obtained between intelligence tests and creativity, and concluded: "We must look well beyond the boundaries of the I.Q. if we are to fathom the domain of creativity" (1950, p. 448).

An outpouring of studies on creativity appeared in the decades following Guilford's remarks, as many each year as had appeared in the preceding century (Frierson, 1969, p. 34). Whereas the issues regarding giftedness as high intelligence and academic aptitude seem relatively settled—and in fact it has been said that "the age of the IQ is passing" (Gowan & Demos, 1964, p. 41)—the issues regarding giftedness as high creative ability are largely unsettled, the studies as yet fragmentary, and the findings to be discussed in this section necessarily more tentative than those reviewed in the preceding section.

Definitions and Identification

There is no universally agreed upon definition of creativity, and hence there are no measures of it which are in any degree as widely accepted or used as the IQ metric is for intelligence. Major conceptions of creativity may be classified according to the relative emphasis placed on the product, the process or the experience of creativity. Some definitions are formulated in terms of a novel and useful manifest *product* (MacKinnon, 1962); other definitions are in terms of a divergent but fruitful underlying *process* (Ghiselin, 1952); and still others are in terms of an inspired and immanent subjective *experience* (Maslow, 1963). One suggested omnibus definition of creative thinking is: the product has novelty and value for the thinker or the culture; the thinking is unconventional, highly motivated and persistent or of great intensity; the task involves a clear formulation of an initially vague and undefined problem (Newell, Shaw, & Simon, 1962). Omnibus definitions have the advantage of being inclusive, but of course the disadvantage of being an inventory without a unifying rationale.

Getzels and Csikszentmihalyi (1964) and Getzels and Madaus (1969) categorized the criteria and measures of creativity, suggesting that the criteria and measures are as varied as the conceptions and definitions. The categories include:

1. *Achievement.* Deeds or thoughts which bespeak manifestly superior achievement may be identified, especially if they are given recognition in form of prizes, awards or other marks of accomplishment (Ghiselin, 1952).

2. *Ratings.* Under the assumption that an observer can provide a sound judgment of another person's inventiveness or originality, evaluation by peers, superiors and teachers has been used as a criterion of creative ability (Drevdahl, 1964; MacKinnon, 1964).

3. *Intelligence.* As creativity is presumably a mental function, and as the best validated index of mental functioning is performance on intelligence tests, a superior IQ has been used as a criterion of creative potential (Terman, 1925).

4. *Personality.* Personality characteristics are evaluated in relation to an empirically derived or a priori profile of the "creative personality," and the closeness of the fit is used as a criterion (R. Cattell & Drevdahl, 1955; Domino, 1970).

5. *Biographical correlates.* Certain items in a person's history are related to his creative performance and are then used to predict others' future performance (Schaefer, 1969; Taylor & Ellison, 1964).

6. *Divergent thinking or "creativity" tests.* Among the many tests are: Remote

Associates Test (Mednick & Mednick, 1964); Ingenious Solutions to Problems Test (Flanagan, 1958); AC Test of Creative Ability (Buhl, 1960); Torrance Tests of Creative Thinking (Torrance, 1966); and numerous other devices such as ink-blots, block-construction, drawings, and so forth.

Creativity and Intelligence

Among the major issues—if not *the* major issue—in creativity research is the relation between creativity and intelligence. The IQ is without doubt the best single metric for predicting school achievement. Yet it often appears inadequate to account for originality and imaginative processes or for great artistic and creative accomplishment. Early studies, even before the advent of the IQ, reported that some persons of "intellectual type" and "logical power" performed poorly on indices of imagination and intellectual "spontaneity" (Colvin, 1902; Dearborn, 1898); and with the advent of the IQ, early studies also sporadically reported low correlations between the IQ proper and tests of originality and imagination (Andrews, 1930; McCloy & Meier, 1939). Individuals of outstanding creative accomplishment were by no means credited with equally high intelligence. Mill, Bentham and Macaulay, for example, were assigned IQs of 180 or above; Locke, Lavoisier and Bach, IQs of 130 or below (Cox, 1926). Nor did all children with high intelligence achieve equally. One-fourth of Terman's subjects with IQs of 170 and above had only fair to poor records (Terman & Oden, 1947), and Hollingworth (1942) reported that some of her children with the very highest possible IQ seemed entirely uncreative. Guilford's (1950) controversial hypothesis of a low or moderate correlation between intelligence test scores and many types of creative performance, which touched off the avalanche of more recent studies in this domain, was not without prior foundation.

Two problems in the more recent work, which regrettably are not always discriminated, must be distinguished if the relation between intelligence and creativity is to be clarified (Getzels & Madaus, 1969). One problem is the relation between intelligence and creativity represented by measures of recognized achievement; the other is the relation between intelligence and creativity represented by measures of divergent thinking or other creativity tests. Although the terms "creativity" and "divergent thinking" have come to be used synonymously, as if the measure of divergent thinking were already a measure of creative achievement, *the distinction as to what is actually being measured in a particular study must be borne in mind.*

A number of studies have dealt with the relationship between intelligence and creative achievement (MacKinnon, 1962; Roe, 1953). Creative individuals unquestionably perform better than the average on intelligence tests, but the correlation between their intelligence and their creativity tends to be low; indeed, MacKinnon (1962) reported that the correlation between the rated creativity of 60 eminent architects and their scores on an adult intelligence scale was —0.08. The bulk of research on children has dealt not with their creative achievement but with the relation between their performance on intelligence tests and on divergent thinking tests. Getzels and Jackson (1959, 1962) found positive but low correlations (about 0.26) between these two indices. The same results were found in studies using other instruments and a wider range of subjects (Torrance, 1962b); and essentially the same results were found with British children (Hudson, 1966). A review of the literature concluded that the greater number of investigations report positive but low correlations (0.20–0.40) for the general population and almost no correlation at the higher ability levels (Taylor & Holland, 1962).

Critical questions about this line of research have been raised by Burt (1962) and by Thorndike (1963), especially with respect to the dimension underlying the various creativity measures. The latter re-analyzed the Getzels-Jackson and Guilford data and suggested that although there might be a broad factor distinct from general intelligence (*g*), the factor is very much less closely formed than *g* and pooling the separate measures into a single score was inadvisable. A recent study of the Torrance Tests of Creative Thinking also called such a procedure "statistically unwarranted" (Harvey, Hoffmeister, Coates, & White, 1970). The issues remain controversial. Wallach and Kogan (1965) claimed that timed Guilford-type creativity measures used in studies preceding theirs did not constitute a domain independent of intelligence but that their own untimed creativity measures did. Cronbach (1968) re-analyzed their data and declared that their study "does not seem to shed light on 'creativity' and 'intelligence'" (p. 510). After a detailed factorial study, Madaus (1967) concluded that the relation between timed creativity tests and intelligence is "negligible" and that the claims for untimed as against timed tests must be questioned, but whether or not creativity tests "form a separate underlying dimension distinct from intelligence is not entirely clear" (p. 233). Hudson (1966), however, argued that the issue of dimensionality is not the crucial one for the school in any case, maintaining that what is crucial for the teacher is that a knowledge of the IQ alone seems to be of little help if he is faced with a "formful of clever boys," for the one among them with the lowest IQ is almost as likely to be creative as the one with the highest.

Development and Characteristics of Creative Persons

Galton (1869) stressed the importance of heredity in creative achievement; J. Cattell (1915) insisted on the significance of the environment. The heredity-environment issue remains an inveterate problem and, as stated in traditional terms, is not yet amenable to unambiguous resolution. Recent studies in the development of creativity have taken a somewhat different course and have revolved around such questions as the influence of age, culture, family background and child-rearing practices.

Lehman (1953) found that adult creativity matures early, reaches its highest point in the 30s, and then gradually declines, a view disputed by Dennis (1956). Since no systematic criteria of creative achievement have been established for children, Torrance (1962a) examined the development of performance on divergent thinking tests with age. He found the following generalized curve: an increase in divergent thinking abilities from age three to four and a half; a small drop upon entering kindergarten; a rise and then a sharp drop at about the fourth grade; and, except for a small decline at grade seven, a steady rise (with some sex and test variations) through grade 11. What is especially provocative in these observations is that each decrement seems to occur at a period marking the transition from one to another of Sullivan's (1953) stages of interpersonal development.

In order to study to what extent the developmental curve of creativity was culturally determined, Torrance (1962a) compared the performance of children in Australia, Germany, India, Samoa, and segregated black children in the United States, and found both similarities and sharp dissimilarities among the different cultures. The curve for the American black children showed a continuity of development second only to that of Samoan children. But the stipulated relation between ideational fluency and age was not duplicated in another study of lower-class southern white and black children where performance seemed to be a function of the specific test stimuli and the experience of the respondents (Iscoe & Pierce-Jones, 1964). The development of creative thinking of bilingual children, presumably with dual cultural influences on their growth, has also been studied (Janssen, 1969; Landry, 1968; Torrance, Wu, Gowan, & Aliotti, 1970). The conclusions generally are that the bilingual experience seems to result in the development of greater potential creativity, apparently because the dual linguistic or cultural experience provides the individual with varied views of the world, a more flexible approach to problems, and encouragement to express himself in several ways (Landry, 1968).

The major emphasis of research in the development of creativity has been on family influences and child-rearing practices. Eisenman and Schussel (1970) found striking birth-order effects on a variety of creativity tests: first-born males were significantly more creative than later-born males on all measures. Getzels and Jackson (1961, 1962) studied the family background of creative children and reported that mothers of high-IQ children expressed admiration for conventional qualities in children, were vigilant over their child's performance in school, and restricted their child's independence more often than mothers of high creative children. Children's conformity and lack of originality were found to be related to the mother's authoritarian child-rearing attitudes (Nichols, 1964), and adult creative achievement was found to be related to the granting of responsibility and independence during childhood (Drevdahl, 1964; MacKinnon, 1964). Domino's (1969) results may serve as a reasonably accurate summary of other reports in this area: the mothers of creative children, compared to mothers of control groups, showed greater self-assurance and initiative; preferred change and unstructured demands; valued autonomy and independent endeavor; were less sociable, conscientious, dependable, and inhibited; less concerned with creating a favorable impression, and less nurturant and obliging toward others—traits, that is, suggesting that mothers of creative children may well be more creative than the general population and foster creativity in their children through the force of their own unstereotyped behavior.

Torrance (1962b) surveyed a large number of investigations and compiled a list of

84 cognitive and affective characteristics which discriminated between creative and less creative subjects in one study or another. Although a number of the separate items were contradictory, *patterns* of characteristics seemed quite systematically to distinguish creative persons. Creative scientists (Taylor & Ellison, 1964), architects (MacKinnon, 1964) and art students (Getzels & Csikszentmihalyi, 1964) were all found to hold high theoretical and aesthetic values. Creative persons in a wide variety of fields shared a characteristic pattern of interpersonal relations, including high self-sufficiency, low extraversion, more concern with ideas than with people, and disinterest in social activities (R. Cattell, 1963; Drevdahl, 1956, 1964; Getzels & Csikszentmihalyi, 1964; Schaefer, 1969; Taylor & Ellison, 1964). Creative persons also seemed to share a common pattern of perception and cognition, preferring complexity, showing independent judgment and strongly resisting group pressure (Barron, 1963). They were "stimulus-free" rather than "stimulus-bound," humorous in their free associations, and they expressed ideas that were not consensual (Getzels & Jackson, 1962); they were willing to take risks (McClelland, 1963). In their self-ratings and in ratings by others, these adjectives typically appeared: creative, independent, uninhibited, iconoclastic, complicated and asocial (Schaefer, 1969, p. 238).

As has previously been noted, there is a long and apparently ineradicable tradition that superior intellectual or creative performance is in some way related to neuroticism. A number of studies with a variety of subjects and instruments found no relationship between measures of creativity and measures of anxiety or emotional disturbance (Feldhusen, Denny, & Condon, 1965; Flescher, 1963; Ohnmacht, 1966). However, in an ingenious investigation comparing students characterized by creative attitudes with those characterized by creative productivity, Taft and Gilchrist (1970) found that although the two groups held a number of the usual creative traits in common, they were also markedly different in others, especially with respect to neuroticism. Creative attitudes alone tended to correlate with extraversion, enthusiasm, quick-wittedness and high academic interests; creative production correlated with disorderliness, impracticality, lack of self-control, interest in intraceptive activities such as daydreaming, unhappiness in childhood and emotional disorders requiring medical attention. As the investigators say, the study has its limitations—it refers to artistic rather than scientific or other forms of creativity—but it does indicate the value of distinguishing between attitudes and creative performance, and it illustrates the necessity of carefully considering findings from present creativity research in light of the particular criterion used.

Creativity and School Performance

A multitude of studies followed the unexpected observation by Getzels and Jackson (1959, 1962) that, despite a 23 point difference in IQ, their High Creative and High IQ groups performed equally well on standard measures of achievement. These results were soon duplicated in six of eight attempted replications (Torrance, 1960, 1962b), and other investigations showed similar effects (Palm, 1959; Yamamoto, 1964a, 1965). However, generalizations from these studies must be made with caution in light of contrary findings. Flescher (1963) reported no evidence for the phenomenon, and questioned whether creativity should be related to scholastic achievement, which presumably requires convergent rather than divergent thinking. Ohnmacht (1966) found that although their creativity measures were related to achievement, the results were not independent of the commonality with intelligence. In a recent study of academic achievement, Feldhusen, Treffinger, and Elias (1970) concluded that both the "convergent variables represented by STEP and SCAT ... and the divergent measures of originality and flexibility are all valuable predictor variables" (p. 51).

Explanations for the diversity of these

findings have called attention to the possible effects of relative rigidity or permissiveness in the learning conditions in the schools (Torrance, 1962b); the systematic interaction effects in the classroom between convergent and divergent teachers and their students (Hudson, 1968); and J. E. Anderson's (1960) ability gradient hypothesis, suggesting that increments in IQ above 120 have no effect on achievement, whereas divergent thinking does—an effect proposed previously by work with creative scientists and architects (MacKinnon, 1962; Roe, 1953). The threshold hypothesis itself has been investigated with diverse results, one study finding some evidence for the presumed effect (Yamamoto, 1964b), another not (Flescher, 1963), and a third reporting some weak evidence without being able to determine the IQ point at which creativity affects achievement differentially (Cicirelli, 1965). An interesting and complicating observation was reported by Hudson (1968): "Divergers" may do better as they progress up the academic ladder; among English 15-year-olds, "the diverger is less academically successful than the average converger in a ratio of more than two to one. At the level of university entrance, the balance has begun to redress itself" (p. 76).

The school performance of the highly creative child as identified by "creativity" tests remains a complex issue. Two additional problems have been the object of some systematic inquiry. One problem is the relation of divergent thinking to different subject matters. British students specializing in the humanities were found relatively weak in IQ tests and better on divergent thinking tests, while those specializing in the sciences were the reverse (Hudson, 1966). High creatives have been found to perform better in reading and language skills than in arithmetic and work studies (Torrance, 1962b); the opposite has also been reported (Yamamoto, 1964a); and significant and similar correlations have been found for both reading and mathematics (Feldhusen, Denny, & Condon, 1965). Another problem is the relation of the high creative student to his teachers. Getzels and Jackson (1962) observed that teachers preferred the high creative but not the high-IQ students to the average group of students. Torrance (1962b) found that teachers preferred high-IQ over high creative students, and Holland (1959) reported that teacher preferences correlated more highly with leadership and academic achievement than with creativity. However, Richards, Cline, and Needham (1964) found that teacher ratings in originality did not favor the intelligent over the creative child, and Klausmeier, Harris, and Ethnathios (1962) obtained positive correlations between teacher ratings in creativity and performance on creativity tests. The relationships between students and teachers of different types are, of course, complicated in the extreme, and as Hudson's (1968) observations suggest, there may be systematic interaction effects between convergent and divergent teachers and convergent and divergent students. Although many of the issues in the domain of creativity are as yet unstated in manageable form, and many of the resolutions propounded by one study are overthrown by another, there is no doubt that if the volume of work and disputation is a valid index, this domain is at present, as the vernacular has it, where the action is (Parnes & Brunelle, 1967).

TALENT

While our society seems to value intelligence, and to a lesser degree, creativity, certain aspects of our technological age tend to narrow our view of the full range of human talent and to restrict the expression of giftedness in all its variety. Prevailing sentiment conceives of Man as Manpower (Boulding, 1954), and singles out for recognition and promotion those talents that will contribute visibly to technological and economic advancement: the measure of man becomes his potential contribution to the Gross National Product. From this point of view, children with exceptional talents are often seen as sources of Manpower to be trained and directed, if not conscripted, into the service of technological progress and economic advancement (Getzels, 1957). But it is possible to distinguish between the child as precursor of Manpower and as precursor of Man, a distinction of sharpest contrast. As Man, the child possesses a variety of talents for being as well as for doing, and these talents seek and indeed require expression not only for his own welfare but also for the welfare of everyone. Many of these talents have been neglected. In the first Bingham lecture on the "Discovery and Encouragement of Exceptional Talent," Terman (1954) observed the widespread emphasis on science and technology, and he rejoiced in their accomplishments, but he added a note of regret that the prevailing zeitgeist "is not equally favorable to the discovery and encouragement of potential poets, prose writers, artists, statesmen, and social leaders" (p. 228). The consequence has been that little is known about the variety of human talents which are not measurable in immediately utilitarian terms, although conceptions of the nature of giftedness have recently become broader, and increasing attention has latterly been paid to the *variety* of human talents.

The Variety of Talents

As is the case with intelligence and creativity, definitions of talent vary and the terms entail ambiguity. The difficulties in terminology are a function both of the variety of talents and the several ways in which talent may be conceived. Talent can refer to an ability or aptitude *in* a person or to talented performance or achievement *by* a person (McClelland et al., 1958, p. 1); it can refer to a capability or to an acquired behavior; to a latent process or to a manifest product; and it can be described in generic terms such as intelligence or creativity, or in specific terms such as manual dexterity or artistic technique. To illustrate a broad notion of the variety of talents, one may begin with the following propositions:

1. For each and every human activity there exists a corresponding talent.
2. If a thought, behavior or activity is possible to humans, some human somewhere has experienced it.
3. If a thought, behavior or activity can be experienced, someone somewhere can experience it superiorly.

These propositions appear to state the case in its broadest terms, allowing the greatest plurality of talents: one talent for every given activity. But not all activities are equally valued, however superior the performance. Society approves and rewards only those talents which contribute to its welfare or do not threaten its customary patterns of functioning. Furthermore, society may find a given talent acceptable or unacceptable under one circumstance or time and not under another, and may at once accept and reject one and the same talent. In periods of significant shifts in a culture's "core values," for example, the society may begin to reward scientific activity and cease rewarding religious activity; it may then "lose faith" in its scientists just as it had before lost faith in its priests; and it may center its cultural heart upon the poetical rather than the technological modes of existence. In wartime, the society tends to exalt and reward talents for killing and destroying and will legitimize allied talents otherwise thought criminal. In more pedestrian pursuits, the society will reward a talent for wheeling-and-dealing in a business executive or entrepreneur but will punish it in an accountant or bank examiner; it will value creative display in its advertising but not in its surgery. In school a student is punished for a display of talented behavior such as enhances his life in the street, is encouraged to develop talents which may subsequently prove of little use in his occupation or living, and withal must exhibit talents which the school wishes to foster or he risks not being considered talented in anything.

Several classifications of talent have been advanced. DeHaan and Havighurst (1961, pp. 18–19) list categories of intellectual ability, creative thinking, scientific ability, social leadership, mechanical skills and talents in fine arts. C. W. Taylor (1968, p. 27) categorizes talents into academic, creative, communication, planning, forecasting and decision-making sorts. Rice's (1970, pp. 44–45) "tentative taxonomy of talent" distinguishes the academic, creative, kinesthetic, manipulative, psycho-social, performing arts and mechanical talents.

What is striking about the talents listed is not their apparent diversity but their similarity; not that they are not useful and socially acceptable but that so many useful and socially acceptable talents are not included. The talents listed are utilitarian and operational; that is, they are talents of doing or performing in a strictly functional, not to say marketable, sense. Certain other talents which are readily and universally recognized in everyday life are almost wholly overlooked.

Everyone has had the experience of admiring someone with a great passion for life, a "life talent," a talent not so much for doing something as for being something or for "living" something. The conception here is manifestly humanistic, the reference being to those talents anciently thought virtuous: the talent to love, to understand, to empathize, to be compassionate, to be of service; the talent of coping, of surviving, of getting through and getting along with grace and authenticity. These, it would seem, are indisputably talents. One can discern such modes in others, and, further, one can remark that certain people live in these modes more fully than do others; that is, they have a talent for them, being gifted beyond most in these respects. These modes satisfy any definition of talent insofar as they are activities useful to the welfare of society and capable of being expressed or "done" in a superior way. Why then are they neglected in conventional conceptions of talent and educational objectives? The reason for their neglect cannot be that they are socially useless—for they are, par excel-

lence, useful; nor that they are not discernible—for they are evident; but that while useful they are not marketable, and while observable they are not testable—at least not by available psychometric methods. They win one neither high scores, nor money, nor certificates. They are nonetheless legitimate talents and they need as much as any other to be discovered and encouraged in our children in and out of school.

Identification of the Talented

It is clear that the problems of defining the specific talents to be recognized and of selecting who is to be regarded as talented are not yet solved to everyone's satisfaction. No matter what is done, someone may with justification ask why something else was not attempted. Nonetheless, the preceding observations regarding talent and technology, and the varieties of talent from the scientific to the poetic, from doing to being, do suggest certain procedures in addition to the current intelligence, achievement and creativity tests, for identifying and selecting different types of talented individuals, especially children.

Manifest talented accomplishments. Certain types of superior performance speak for themselves, and one may recognize as talented those children who, at their own level, win prizes in various competitions or exhibits, publish poetry, are consistently elected to positions of leadership, demonstrate marked enthusiasm for certain subjects, or receive outstanding marks of accomplishment in such activities as art, music or community service. The school, however, where such accomplishments are most likely to manifest themselves, tends to focus on academic performance as the regnant criterion of talent. This criterion, emphasized to the exclusion of others, may obscure certain talents and grossly miss genuinely talented students.

The schooling of some American novelists is instructive in this regard (Hattam, 1968).

James Fenimore Cooper was expelled from Yale for misconduct. Herman Melville left school before he was 15 years old. Hawthorne, who was graduated from Bowdoin, confessed, "I was an idle student, negligent of college rules and the Procrustean details of academic life, rather choosing to nurse my own fancies than dig into Greek roots and be numbered among the learned Thebans." Stephen Crane went to Lafayette College but did not graduate, preferring to hide away in his fraternity house to read and write. Mark Twain and Sherwood Anderson went to work at the beginning of their teens. William Faulkner's education was irregular after the fifth grade and he did not graduate from high school. Ernest Hemingway graduated from a high school where it was customary for two-thirds of the senior class to go to college, but he did not. F. Scott Fitzgerald wrote to the president of Princeton after publication of *This Side of Paradise,* "It was a book written with the bitterness of my discovery that I had spent several years trying to fit in with a curriculum that is after all made for the average student." While at Princeton, Fitzgerald had failed a third of his courses and had maintained a D— average in the rest. Had school achievement alone been used as the criterion of talent, these individuals would assuredly have been numbered among the untalented, as no doubt students in other fields have been; Einstein's headmaster, for example, told his father that Albert would "never make a success at anything," and Albert was expelled from the gymnasium with the admonition, "Your presence in the class is disruptive and affects the other students" (Clark, 1971, pp. 10, 12).

Observations of potential talent. At the childhood level there may not be opportunity to record talented accomplishment in any formal way in anything except academic endeavor. Yet serviceable judgments may be made regarding potential talent by individuals who have had an opportunity and have been sensitized to observe such behavior (Lowenfeld & Brittain, 1964). Evaluation by teachers, counselors and peers may be used as an index. Indeed, in the School of the Art Institute of Chicago, as an instance, students receive both grades for work done in class and ratings of artistic potential, the two by no means being identical (Getzels & Csikszentmihalyi, 1966b). Ratings are, of course, liable to the danger of unreliability, but helpful criteria can be set up, teachers trained in their use, and, at least at extremes, dependable consensus obtained. Kough (1960) provides a list of characteristics for identifying talent in art, science and leadership:

1. *Artistic talent.* The student a) fills extra time with drawing, painting and sculpture activities; b) takes art work seriously and seems to find satisfaction in it; c) uses art work to express personal experiences and feelings; d) is interested in other people's art work and takes time to appreciate and criticize it; etc.

2. *Scientific talent.* The student a) spends much time on special projects such as making collections, telescopes and rockets; b) reads freely in the scientific literature and discusses scientific affairs; c) wants to know the causes and reasons for things; d) is not easily discouraged by failure of his experiments or projects; etc.

3. *Leadership talent.* The student a) is liked and respected by most members of his class; b) is able to influence others to work toward given goals; c) can judge the ability of other students and find a place for them in the group's activities; d) is consulted by other students when something must be decided; etc.

Similar behavior characteristics can be established for literary, dramatic, musical, mechanical and other talents (Kough, 1960). In addition to the observation of such *unassigned* behavior reflecting specialized talents, observations of *assigned* "work samples" of behavior requiring specialized talent have been used with some success to identify potentially talented children (Bowman, Dietrich, DeHaan, Hackamack, Havighurst, Johnson, King, & Litler, 1953).

Tests of potential talent. Aptitude tests have been applied to predict certain specialized talents; for example, in music, the Seashore Measures of Musical Talents, and in graphic arts, the Meier Art Tests. Similar tests are available in mechanics, architecture, leadership and a number of other talents, and are discussed fully in *The Sixth Mental Measurements Yearbook* (Buros, 1965). Project TALENT, by far the most massive attempt to study talent, depends heavily on these types of instruments, using some 37 aptitude or talent variables such as leadership, social sensitivity, mechanical reasoning, creativity, and clerical and perceptual aptitudes (Flanagan et al., 1962, 1964). Tests designed to assess these aptitudes were given to some 440,000 students in 1350 secondary schools in all parts of the country. Followup studies planned for the next quarter-century will relate performance in adult life to these measures secured in adolescence. Because of the wide variety of aptitudes tested and the large size of the sample, Project TALENT promises to be a rich source of information pertaining not only to the various talents of the secondary-school population but also to the relation between aptitudes measured in adolescence and achievement recorded in adulthood.

What is noteworthy about this undertaking compared to Terman's of a half-century earlier is not merely the magnitude of the numbers involved (440,000 compared to Terman's 1500), but, more importantly, the change it represents in the conception of giftedness: "The simple concept of general intelligence which provided the focus of Terman's series of studies entitled, 'Genetic Studies of Genius,' has been replaced by a relatively wide array of important and fairly distinct aptitudes" (Flanagan et al., 1962, p. 207). It is in no sense to derogate the importance of the talents with which these

studies deal to call attention to the fact that they have omitted from consideration the humanistic talents—talents not merely for doing, but of being: talents for love and compassion, for empathy and altruism, for living life with grace and authenticity. Are these talents beyond psychological and educational purview?

Talent and Personality

It is well known that people of equal aptitude and talent are not equally successful. No observation or test of aptitude can tell how a student will eventually achieve, for his attitudes, motives and values are involved in the use which he makes of his talents. Time and again a relation has been found between the individual's value orientations and his cognitive and creative achievement. High intelligence and creativity have been found related to high aesthetic and theoretical values (Gee, 1959; MacKinnon, 1964; Warren & Heist, 1960), and low economic and religious values with lower intelligence and creativity (Gee, 1959; Warren & Heist, 1960). Theoretical values are related to "spontaneous" as against "deliberative" artistic processes (Burkhart, 1960), and fourth-year art students have significantly higher aesthetic and lower social values than first-year art students (Deignan, 1958).

The general relationships between values and cognitive and creative performance seem well established. In order to study the specific relations between values and achievements and the specific uses to which talent in the arts is put, Getzels and Csikszentmihalyi (1964, 1968a, 1968b), as part of a large study of artists, administered the Allport-Vernon-Lindzey Study of Values to more than 250 art students, with the following results: a) there were significant differences between the values of art students and the relevant norms for the population at large and for other professions; b) compared to students in other professions, the values of the art students were remarkably one-sided, as if their entire being revolved about aesthetic values and rejected economic and social values; c) students with similar technical skills but pursuing different specializations in art (e.g., fine art, advertising art, art education) held different values; d) the relations between values and performance were complex, differing by sex, by field of specialization, and by the particular value and criterion involved. In short, there seemed to be systematic relations between certain personal characteristics of art students, the use to which they chose to put their artistic talent, and their performance in art school—at least as fruitful suggestions for further inquiry. Additional studies of the relation between personality and artistic and scientific talent and achievement are provided by H. H. Anderson (1960), Barron (1969), Cattell and Drevdahl (1955), Cross, Cattell, and Butcher (1967), and Roe (1946).

Academic and Nonacademic Talents

The multiple talent approach to the identification and study of superior human attainment led to the question of whether or not the apparent variety of talents is correlated, and more especially whether academic aptitude, academic performance, and nonacademic achievement are related. The question here, as in the case of intelligence and creativity, has resulted in a statistically opulent argument between those who believe that talent is unidimensional and those who believe that it is multidimensional, and between those who believe that academic and nonacademic achievement are correlated, and those who do not.

Typical of the controversy is the series of studies by Holland and Richards (1965), the counterstudy by Werts (1967), and the counter to the counterstudy by Holland and Richards (1967). In the first study Holland and Richards correlated the scores of 7,262 freshmen attending 24 colleges and universi-

ties on a variety of measures of academic potential and performance, and on measures of nonacademic achievement including art, music, literature, dramatic arts, leadership and sciences. Their verdict was that "the results strongly suggest that academic and nonacademic accomplishment are relatively independent dimensions of talent" (p. 165). In a counterstudy Werts (1967) attacked the methods and views of work "typified" by Holland and Richards, and found that for a sample of 127,125 freshmen in 248 colleges and universities, there *was* a relation between academic performance and achievement in the scientific, literary, leadership, speech, drama, music and art areas. In a counter to this counterstudy, Holland and Richards (1967) defended their work against the methodological attack, stating that they had in fact done most of the things which Werts had cited as desirable in studies of academic and nonacademic achievement. They proceeded to reshuffle Werts's data and claimed that "Werts's own data do not support his hypotheses" (p. 205). They then reviewed the results from other studies contradicting him and refused to retreat from their previous position that "measures of academic potential are good predictors of academic success and measures of nonacademic potential are good predictors of nonacademic accomplishment—but not vice versa" (p. 205; see also Baird & Richards, 1968; Richards, Holland, & Lutz, 1967; Wallach & Wing, 1969). A later independent study (Elton & Shevel, 1969) found a slight but significant relationship between these two types of talent, and noted that any relationship depended upon the specific achievements chosen to define the talents.

The question, how are academic and nonacademic talents related? has not yet been answered to everyone's satisfaction. The most recent and complete review of work in this domain is by Richards (1970). But he warns that his conclusions may be biased since he has already taken the position that grades and typical multiple choice tests involve only academic achievement (in the pejorative sense of academic) and have little or no relationship to accomplishment in other important areas of human endeavor. He suggests that although the prevailing correlational methodology may somewhat exaggerate the degree of independence, "the consistency and meaningfulness of the results make it doubtful there is more than a low relationship between academic and non-academic accomplishment" (p. 10). Richards points out that the results further suggest that a single-minded pursuit of academic excellence may be destructive of other, perhaps more important, values, and that there is need for more diverse, though equally rigorous, ways of evaluating student talents. Fitzgerald need not have written *This Side of Paradise* with the "bitterness" of his discovery that he had "spent several years trying to fit in with a curriculum that is after all made for the average student," and, as Richards comments, "a student might be forgiven, say, failure to master French verbs if he were composing good music" (p. 10).

NEGLECTED GIFTEDNESS

Just as it is not enough to consider giftedness as applying only to one type of talent, so it is not enough to consider the gifted as belonging to only one type of population. Talents are distributed not only among many areas of human endeavor, but also among many people; and the notion of "talent loss" may refer not only to types of talent that go unrecognized or unencouraged, but also to the types of populations whose talents are ignored, dismissed, or overlooked. Two such populations which merit special attention are females and the urban and rural poor. It is clear that talent loss occurs in these groups out of proportion to other populations, less in the sense that their talents have been lost than in that they have not been found because they have not been looked for. Yet there are no grounds for supposing that the poverty of the poor

necessarily extends to their gifts and talents, or that low socioeconomic or sexual status must connote low intellectual status; or that, being less privileged, the poor or females must inevitably also be less gifted.

THE GIFTED DISADVANTAGED

The poor and culturally "disadvantaged" or "different" are thought of as belonging to a few major groups, notably the black and Hispano who live in large city slums or ghettoes. Although these two groups are surely disadvantaged, it can be both untrue and misleading to conceive of the poor as necessarily either nonwhite or slum dwellers, for they are distributed among all ethnic and racial groups—blacks, whites, Oriental- and Mexican-Americans, American Indians, Puerto-Ricans, Central- and South-American and European immigrants with rural backgrounds—and are found in city slums, on farms, and in nonfarm rural areas in all parts of the country. In fact, more of the poor are white than nonwhite, and more poor are found outside the central cities than within them. It is the *proportion* of poverty among nonwhites which is in all cases higher than among whites (United States Bureau of Census, 1969, p. 53; 1970b, pp. 328–331).

One must not assume that talent is to be found only in economically privileged environments, or that it is the exclusive possession of the propertied class. Terman (1925, pp. 64–65) reviewed studies of the origins of superior ability, showing that leading American men of science and letters, French members of scientific academies, and British men and women of genius have come from the lower socioeconomic classes, while in his own group of 1500 gifted children—sought without special effort to recruit from any one social class—some 20 percent came from families whose fathers engaged in "practically unskilled" occupations such as teamster, waiter and day laborer (pp. 62–63). More recently, one-fourth of the finalists in the first National Achievement Scholarship program for talented black students came from families with incomes under $4,000 (Roberts & Nichols, 1966); and Allison Davis (1968) estimates that "slum" and working-class children "comprise the majority of the children at the highest level of 'academic aptitude' in the United States" (p. 1).

If there is widespread failure to identify, develop and use the talents of gifted children generally, there is, *a fortiori,* a failure to provide for children who are both gifted *and* disadvantaged. Insofar as these children are gifted, they suffer the same specific lacks as do the gifted generally in measures, programs and encouragement; insofar as they are disadvantaged, they suffer the same general lack of opportunities and resources as do their less gifted fellows. It is especially among the urban and rural disadvantaged that neglect of the gifted and their gifts is most widespread.

The Urban Disadvantaged

It is relatively easy to give certain cold facts about slums, but it is more difficult to convey, supposing one understood, the experience of living there. What must it be like? And what must it be like more especially for the black child, to whom applies in extreme form whatever is true of the lower-class child's development in relation to education and intellectual attainment?

As Davis and Dollard (1940) pointed out long ago, caste status places the black in an inferior subculture even within the lowest socioeconomic class. In their study of black ego development, Ausubel and Ausubel (1963) found that well over half of black families live at the very lowest level of the lower-class standard: their physical surroundings are more likely to be inferior, intellectual stimulation less available, family life less stable; and whereas, like the white lower-class child, the black may yet hope to escape and surmount *class* barriers, he

finds the barriers of subordinate *caste* membership "inescapable and insurmountable" (p. 119). The black cannot realistically compete in the labor and professional market with whites of equal talent and education. Unfavorable socialization experiences, unequal school opportunities, and manifest occupational discrimination all conspire to depress the motivation and achievement of black children, especially boys, however talented; they attend school less regularly, they drop out in greater numbers, they learn less than they could, and their talents are more often lost to themselves and to society (Bloom, Davis, & Hess, 1965; Dreger & Miller, 1960; Pettigrew, 1964). In 1969 over 60 percent of the nation's nonwhite high-school graduates did not enter college; of nonwhites aged 25–29, only 9 percent had had four years of college; and blacks constituted only 4.32 percent of students working for degrees, and 3 percent of all graduate students (U.S. Office of Education, 1970, pp. 9, 74, 120, 134).

It is of course impossible to say what percentage of any population should have advanced education. Nonetheless, the percentage of doctorates granted to blacks is by any standards minute, and in certain fields so egregiously minute as to justify the assertion of substantial talent loss. In 1960–1962, of 32,675 doctorates granted in American universities, 480 or 1.4 percent went to blacks; from 1920–1962 the percentage of black doctorates in engineering was 0.03, in physics, 0.17, in mathematics, 0.46, in medical sciences, 0.73, and in humanities and business administration, 0.82; and the percentage of blacks practicing in the professions was: architects, 1.8; chemists, 2.01; dentists, 2.46; engineers, 0.56; physicians and surgeons, 2.05; lawyers and judges, 1.02 (Bond, 1966, pp. 564–569).

There is no way of estimating the number of black youth talented in the creative and the performing arts, but that there are such talents of the very highest order cannot be doubted. Though born in the ghetto, James

Baldwin is said to be among the best prose writers in America, and Ralph Ellison has written one of the most distinguished American novels of the first half of this century. Ellison's (1952) rendering of black anguish may be taken to reflect the plight of the gifted black:

I am an invisible man. No, I am not a spook. ...I am a man of substance, of flesh and bone, fiber and liquids—and I might even be said to possess a mind. I am invisible, understand, simply because people refuse to see me.... When they approach me they see only my surroundings, themselves, or figments of their imagination—indeed, everything and anything except me (p. 7).

A review of studies reporting incidence of giftedness among ethnic groups (Adler, 1967) found "little evidence that one ethnic or racial group is superior to another with respect to superior intellectual potential" (p. 105). But there seems to be little question that blacks score significantly lower than other groups, at least on intelligence tests (Dreger & Miller, 1960; Kennedy, Van De Riet, & White, 1961; Klineberg, 1963). A massive review (Shuey, 1966) of 382 studies using 81 different tests of intellectual ability reports that blacks score about 15 points below the white average, and concludes that indications "inevitably point to the presence of native differences between Negroes and whites *as determined by intelligence tests*" (p. 521; emphasis added). Jensen, advancing a hypothesis to explain social and racial differences in IQ, has provoked a spirited discussion, much of which may be found in *Environment, Heredity, and Intelligence* (1969). This discussion is not the issue here. The point is rather that since, as Jensen (1969) remarks, "as far as we know, the full range of human talents is represented in all the major races of man and in all socioeconomic levels" (p. 78), the problem at hand is not due to any lack of able lower-class or black children but to the failure to recognize and encourage them, not only in

intellectual abilities as measured by psychometric designs, but also in manifold other talents. The question of identifying and developing talents among the disadvantaged seems to lie less in the scarcity or paucity of their gifts or their numbers than it lies in the attitudes with which one approaches the issue both of neglected talents and neglected talented.

The Rural Disadvantaged

The rural disadvantaged are "a people left behind" in more ways than economically and educationally. As a recent survey of research points out, since rural youths tend to be removed from major research centers they have not been the object of sustained inquiry, and especially not of needed longitudinal and developmental studies; and, where they have been studied, they have been treated as if they comprise an integrated group about which generalizations could be made and similar programs suggested, instead of comprising a variety of different groups as they do (Edington, 1970). Differences exist not only between rural youths and urban youths, but also between groups of rural youths, e.g., between Appalachian whites and rural southern blacks, or between farming Mexican-Americans and Indians; and further, differences within the groups themselves. The variety of languages which Indians speak makes the variety of English and Spanish dialects seem a *lingua franca;* and, of course, language difficulties in school are experienced not only by the Indian- or Spanish-speaking children, but also by the rural black and Appalachian white children whose first language is a nonstandard form of English.

Among the most disadvantaged of these rural youths are unquestionably the migrant workers and the American Indians. In 1970, 16 percent of male migrant farm workers aged 25–44 had had less than four years of elementary schooling, and only 4 percent had completed the eighth grade (United

States Bureau of the Census, 1970a, p. 25). The Indian has the greatest cultural differences to overcome; he may belong to any one of 13 major Indian groups, and in a population of invisible disadvantaged, he is the most invisible. Compared to the general population, the Indian's income is two-ninths as much, his unemployment rate 10 times greater, his life expectancy seven years less, his years of schooling less than half, and his school drop-out rate twice as high (Bass & Burger, 1967).

The rural gifted may fare even worse than the urban gifted or their less gifted rural peers because of the inadequacy of appropriate educational and intellectual resources, and because of the community's negative attitude toward things intellectual (Edington, 1970). One consequence is that gifted children may leave the community, which then suffers further "intellectual erosion." In one rural community, of the 161 youngsters who had graduated from eighth grade over a nine-year period, all 10 of those with IQs of 130, including one with an IQ of 160, had left the area, some even for their secondary education. The community was marked by "provincialism, religious bigotry, and a suspicious distrust of the educated and of educational ideas" (Lee & Newland, 1966, p. 366). If one were to assume, on the basis of census data and the probability of distribution of superior aptitudes, that a significant number of the nation's gifted reside and attend school in small communities, one encounters in the rural no less than in the urban population a loss of talent to the individual and the society of no mean magnitude.

THE GIFTED FEMALE

That under present conditions differences exist between men and women in modes of cognition, personality and values seems fairly well agreed upon. There are more male geniuses, and there are also more male criminals, mental defectives, suicides, stutterers, and color-blinds (Heim, 1970, p. 136). It is evident that men have been both more prominent and more numerous than women in areas of high achievement, but they have been so by reason of differing opportunities rather than differing abilities. In any case, the issue is not the relative superiority of men or women, but the neglect of talent among those of the female population who are in fact gifted or who may be found to be so.

Education and Occupation

Of all degrees awarded in 1968–1969 (U.S. Office of Education, 1970, p. 89), women earned some 44 percent of the bachelor degrees, 37 percent of the master's degrees, and 13 percent of the doctorate degrees. While the proportion of total degrees awarded to women has been increasing since 1950, the proportion of master's and doctorate degrees awarded them has *decreased* compared to 1930, when women earned 40 percent of the master's and 15 percent of the doctorate degrees. In 1968–1969 the proportion of doctorate degrees awarded to women was: in business and commerce, 2 percent; engineering, 0.35 percent; mathematics, 6 percent; biological sciences, 15 percent; physical sciences, 5 percent; fine and applied arts, 17 percent; dentistry, 0.98 percent; medicine, 7.6 percent; and law, 4 percent of the LLBs and no JDs. With the exception of fine and applied arts, these may be thought to be traditionally masculine fields of endeavor. What is striking is that women do not go on to higher degrees even in "female fields," but seem to abandon them to men (with the sole exception of nursing, where women earn 99 percent of the bachelor's and master's and 100 percent of the doctorate degrees). The proportion of degrees which women earn in "female fields" *decreases* as the level of the degree increases: in education, from 76 percent bachelor's to 54 percent master's to 20 percent doctor's; fine and applied arts, 59 percent to 45 percent to 17 percent; foreign languages and literature, 73 percent to 58 percent to 34 percent; library science, 94 percent to 81 percent to 29 percent. Another striking occurrence is that while women earned less than 9 percent of the bachelor's and 2 percent of the doctorate degrees in business and commerce, they earned 75 percent of the bachelor's degrees in business and commerce *education* (U.S. Office of Education, 1970, p. 89).

Despite the presumed "liberation" of women, it is misleading to suppose that masses of them are entering the professions. In 1968–1969, only 13 women received higher degrees in business and commerce, 12 in engineering and 59 in mathematics; and while more of them received degrees in law (680) and medicine (610), their numbers have not appreciably increased in the past 20 years, while their proportion to men has in fact *decreased* since 1950 in medical degrees (U.S. Office of Education, 1970, p. 90). The proportion of women in the *practice* of professions such as medicine, engineering, mathematics, and physical and biological science has also decreased since 1950 (Rossi, 1965, p. 58). Furthermore, the proportion of women in medicine, law and engineering in the USA is lower than in the USSR, the United Kingdom, Japan, Sweden, West Germany, Denmark, Poland and India. Indeed, in the USSR, women account for 75 percent of the physicians (6.5 percent in the USA), 83 percent of the dentists (2 percent in the USA), and 28 percent of the engineers (1.2 percent in the USA) (Epstein, 1970, p. 12).

Career and Marriage

Terman and Oden (1959) found that of their 610 gifted females at midlife (average age: 44), fully one-half were housewives with no outside employment, 42 percent were employed full-time and 8 percent part-time. Asked how satisfied they felt with their occupations, nearly all expressed deep satisfaction or at least fair contentment, and more than half thought that their abilities were being lived up to reasonably well. Terman's gifted females could be satisfied and feel their abilities lived up to either by staying at home or pursuing a career. Yet despite the apparent satisfaction, the fact is that the professional achievement of these intellectually gifted women as compared with the no more intellectually gifted men was much inferior. Although some 70 percent of both the men and women were graduated from college, 13.8 percent of the men but only 4 percent of the women had taken a doctorate (Terman & Oden, 1959, p. 67). The occupational status of the women with full-time employment was very much lower—20 percent of them were secretaries or office workers. The earnings of the two groups were in sharpest contrast: 47.7 percent of the fully employed males but only 6 percent of the fully employed females earned $10,000 or more annually; the median earned income of the males was $9,640, of the females, $4,875. As Terman and Oden (1959) say:

Although the gifted women equaled or ex-celled the men in school achievement from the first grade through college, after school days were over the great majority ceased to compete with men in the world's work. This characteristic appears to be due to lack of motivation and opportunity rather than to lack of ability (p. 106).

Terman and Oden's study of gifted females may be compared with Watley's (1969) study of female National Merit Scholars. The Terman group of 610 were in their mid-40s in 1955 and reported actual behavior; the National Merit group of 883 were in their mid-20s in 1965 and reported planned behavior. Ten percent of the Terman group were unmarried while 6 percent of the Merit group planned no marriage; fully half of the Terman group had no career while only 8.6 percent of the Merit group planned no career. Clearly, more of the female Merit scholars planned to combine marriage and career than the Terman group succeeded in actually doing; more of the Merit group planned marriage, more planned a career, and more planned career-*cum*-marriage. They did not, however, plan to depart too far from traditional occupations of women, for the most part choosing careers in the humanities, fine arts and education; only a very few chose medicine, law, science or business.

It makes a difference whether talented women can have careers and a marriage and family; it also makes a difference which careers they can have. Although the percentage of women in the labor force increased by 244 percent from 1940 to 1964, it increased only in the lower-echelon occupations and not in the professional categories (Kaley, 1971). More women, and more talented women, may be entering careers, but it is of importance to note whether their careers have them exercising their talents upon the keyboards of a typewriter, a computer or a piano. No evidence is available to support any single claim as to why few contemporary women, despite their talents, pursue graduate education or enter professional occupations. But whatever the reason:

Until the education of men and women includes curriculums based on principles of individual need and fulfillment, and limitless career opportunities, few women will experience the personal fulfillment and satisfaction of a profession. Moreover, society will continue to suffer tremendous loss of women's potential contribution (Kaley, 1971, p. 305).

EDUCATION OF THE GIFTED

Whatever the controversy, ambiguity or outright ignorance about identifying the gifted child, programs for educating him have been increasing. In 1955, Havighurst, Stivers, and DeHaan (1955) surveyed and described some 50 such programs in various institutions including schools, an art museum, a public library and a symphony orchestra. For the years 1957 to 1965, the United States Office of Education (1966b) listed 275 state and local programs for the gifted. A compilation for the years 1962–1965 listed some 121 reports of funded projects for the gifted and noted that New York State experienced a sudden growth of programs for the gifted since 1957, such that within a decade approximately one-half of its schools outside the largest cities had some enterprise in this area (*Educator's Complete ERIC Handbook*, 1967b, p. 445). Gowan and Demos (1964, p. 127) estimated that between the years 1950 and 1962 programs for the gifted in public schools increased sixfold, but they hazard the guess that no provisions were made for about 80 percent of the gifted children, while some provisions were made for about 20 percent and fully adequate provisions for about 5 percent. Figures from the United States Office of Education (1942, 1963, 1969) show an increase in enrollment of children in programs for the gifted, from 3,000 in 1936 and 53,000 in 1958 to 312,000 in 1966; but the estimate of children in need of such programs in 1958 was fully 835,000. In view of the ambiguities as to who is a gifted child and what constitutes a bona fide program for him, these figures are only illustrative and suggest the problems involved in determining a precise census of gifted children and programs for their education.

Types of Programs

Programs for the gifted may be categorized according to their locus—whether in the school, shared by several schools, districts or systems, or outside the school, as in a museum or library; or according to the degree to which gifted children are segregated from other children—in separate schools, classes or groups. Gallagher (1966, p. 77) classifies programs within the school into the *administrative*—changing the educational world about the child; the *instructional*—changing the content of the subject matter or the style in which it is presented;

and the *adjunctive*—providing special services, such as counseling, beyond the usual school program. The variety of practices and programs for educating the gifted may be seen in the following representative list:

1. Summer institutes
2. Nongraded primary schools
3. Early admissions to college
4. College-level courses for high-school students
5. College credit for high-school courses
6. Special classes in a particular subject matter in the student's curriculum
7. Special classes in all subject matter in the student's curriculum
8. Saturday seminars
9. Ability grouping
10. Enrichment in regular classrooms
11. Itinerant resource teachers
12. Adding a course to the student's normal course load
13. Clubs and extracurricular projects for the gifted
14. Field trips
15. Special televised courses
16. Half-day regular program, half-day enriched program
17. Acceleration
18. Special schools for gifted students only
19. Counseling for the gifted
20. Individual tutoring
21. Independent study
22. Student exchange
23. Flexible progression (e.g., elementary-school students taking courses in high school; high-school students taking courses in college)
24. Advanced placement
25. Honors programs
26. Activities offered by nonschool institutions (museums, libraries, orchestras, etc.)
27. New curriculum (P.S.S.C., S.M.S.G., etc.)

The literature commonly groups the research in this area under headings of Enrichment, Grouping, and Acceleration; this practice will be followed here, noting that the categories inevitably omit some research and overlap with others. Schools adjust procedures to the requirements of the gifted by making special opportunities or materials available to them in the regular class situation, by grouping them into separate classes or schools, or by accelerating them through the hierarchy of grades and courses.

Enrichment

In a generic sense, all types of adjustments for gifted students are forms of *enrichment,* but the term will be used here specifically to designate those provisions of different learning experiences in the otherwise undifferentiated or heterogeneous classroom. Enrichment came into vogue during the early 1930s when Hollingworth and others decided that it was better to keep a child in his social age group than to segregate or accelerate him (Gowan & Demos, 1964, p. 14). Although the majority of gifted children are probably in regular classrooms with their own age groups, there appear to be few studies to support the efficacy of such a practice. Evaluations of enrichment programs in the heterogeneous class, while generally favorable, are based upon the opinions of teachers, administrators, parents and students rather than upon experimental evidence (Carter, 1960). The few research studies available, however, are favorable to enrichment. Early studies report achievement of the gifted in the regular classroom under the Winnetka Plan (Washburne, 1924), and superior achievement of gifted students in an enriched typical classroom as compared to matched gifted students in a nonenriched typical classroom (Dransfield, 1933). More recent studies at the elementary level (Ziehl, 1962) and junior high level (Arends & Ford, 1964) report that special provisions in the classroom increased the performance of gifted children. It is difficult to see how anyone can be against enrichment, for it essentially means adjusting instruction according to the needs and abilities of the individual child. The question is whether it is more advantageous to provide enrichment in a heterogeneous class, to group children into homogeneous classes, or to accelerate the brighter ones.

Grouping

Grouping—placing students in special classes, "tracks," or "streams" according to age, ability or preference—is the subject of a long and often sharp controversy, revolving as much around democratic and egalitarian issues as about the effectiveness of grouping for improving academic achievement. Some hold that only through ability grouping can the gifted be stimulated (Ward, 1962, p. 72); others argue that such a practice establishes an intellectual elite through an educational caste system reminiscent of Mandarin China (Bettelheim, 1958, p. 272).

The considerable amount of research on homogeneous versus heterogeneous grouping allows contradictory conclusions. On the one hand, a review (Passow, 1958) of a dozen comparative studies of gifted students in regular and special classes at all educational levels reports favorable outcomes for ability grouping, and a review of the literature (Carter, 1960) similarly concludes that the accumulated evidence is strongly in favor of ability grouping for gifted students. On the other hand, a study comparing the college records of high ability students from various secondary-level grouping programs with those from heterogeneous classrooms concluded that specialized high-school and homogeneous honors-class programs could claim no superiority in preparing their students for college over the comprehensive high school (Abramson, 1959). A series of investigations (Goldberg & Passow, 1962; Passow & Goldberg, 1961) examined the achievement of 2200 children with different IQ scores in 45 schools who had been systematically grouped in order to yield classes of high scorers, classes of low scorers, and classes of combined high, middle and low

scorers. The classes remained together for two years, and the effects of grouping were studied by giving pre- and posttests at the fifth and sixth grades. In general, the differences in achievement among students of like ability in the different classes varied little. Another study (Raph, Goldberg, & Passow, 1966) examined the effects of grouping on gifted underachievers in high school—those with a 120 or more IQ whose school grades were lower than average. No differences in performance at the end of grades 10, 11 and 12 were found for the two groups of bright underachievers who had been placed in special guidance and study-skill classes and the third group which had acted as control. Studies of "streaming" in English schools support the negative findings on "grouping" in American schools, and as Gold (1965) remarks, "It is curious to note new research which does not support policies of ability grouping that have been maintained for years" (p. 312).

The last word has not yet been said with regard either to the social desirability of grouping or its effects upon achievement. Borg (1964) provides useful tables summarizing the varying conclusions found in some 40 studies of grouping at the elementary- and secondary-school levels for 1922 to 1962. Grouping apparently is a helpful but not automatically effective instructional adjustment; achievement seems to improve only when grouping is accompanied by a differentiation in teacher quality, curriculum, guidance and method (Gold, 1965, pp. 312, 327).

Acceleration

Acceleration refers to modifications in the regular program which enable a student to complete the program in less time or at an earlier age than is usual. Such modifications include early entrance to kindergarten through college; combining two years' work into one; skipping a course or grade; taking extra courses or summer sessions to shorten total time in school; earning college credit for high-school work; and "placing out" of certain courses by examination (Passow, 1958, p. 212).

Research findings on acceleration are clearly favorable, and may be illustrated by noting some of the studies most often cited in the literature. Worcester (1956) studied reports of early admissions to elementary schools and found that the early entrants generally did better than the normally placed children throughout school and, contrary to popular belief, were less often referred for personality, emotional or social problems. Justman (1953, 1954) studied 95 matched pairs of secondary-school students with an IQ of 130 or above placed in accelerated or normal-progress classes. He found differences favoring the accelerates in mathematics, science and social studies, and no significant differences in reading, computation, creative writing, or in nonacademic factors such as social adjustment, attitudes and interests. Keys (1938) compared the performance of 348 students entering the university at age 16½ or less with a control group entering at age 17 or more. He found a significant superiority for the accelerates in academic achievement as reflected in grade point average, election to Phi Beta Kappa, and scholarships earned. In the 25-year follow-up of their gifted group, Terman and Oden (1947) concluded that the accelerates made a better record than the nonaccelerates in educational achievement, physical health, marital adjustment and vocational success, and suggested that the supposed influence of acceleration in causing social maladjustment had been greatly exaggerated, for such maladjustment as they found was a temporary feeling of inferiority which was later overcome (p. 275).

More evidence is available in favor of acceleration than of enrichment or grouping, yet acceleration is the least practiced device for educating the gifted. As Gold (1965) says, "No paradox is more striking in the education of the gifted than the inconsistency between research findings on acceleration and the failure of our society to reduce the time spent by superior students in formal education" (p. 328). Apparently the cultural values favoring a standard period of dependency and formal education are stronger than the social or individual need for achievement and independence. This is an instance of the more general case one remarks throughout education: when research findings clash with cultural values, the values are more likely to prevail.

FACILITATION OF TALENT AND CREATIVITY

Programs for the student with special talents like fine arts or leadership remain the exception. The Portland, Oregon, school system reports an extensive program for identifying and developing such abilities (Sanders, 1961, pp. 43–45). New York City has high schools of Performing Arts, of Science, and of Music and Art. The number of students enrolled in music classes in public secondary schools nearly doubled between 1949 and 1961, and tripled for those in art classes (U.S. Office of Education, 1965, p. 99). Such increases seem dramatic, but the figures count duplicate individuals and represent only a small proportion of total enrollment: while in 1961 some 1.6 million students grades 9–12 were enrolled in art classes and some 2.3 million in music, the total enrollment in grades 9–12 was nearly nine million students (U.S. Office of Education, 1966a, p. 24). Moreover, most classes in music and art include all manner of students and are not designed especially for the talented; they cannot be called special provisions for the talented. In short, "the arts simply are not an organized part of the general education of most public school students in the United States" (Goodlad, 1966, p. 83). This situation may be due to the difficulty of locating the artistically talented and to the cost and scheduling difficulties of providing for them (Brittain, 1961, p. 297). Another factor is that the school typically so loads the curriculum of a gifted student with the required "solid subjects" that he has little time left for work in his special talent area. Assigning courses in this manner is an educational practice "predicated upon armchair logic rather than upon research" (Gold, 1965, p. 284).

The greater part of education in the fine and performing arts probably proceeds outside of school grounds and hours—in museums, clubs and performing institutions, in apprenticeships with artists, in lessons with private tutors, or in special schools. Of special schools, those which grant a degree or diploma for specified programs of study number over 800 in art, over 600 in music, 165 in sculpture and 14 in ballet (Miller & Brown, 1967). The Chicago Yellow Pages alone list over a hundred various private schools and tutors of music, art, voice and dance. Little is known about the practices, quality or achievement of such agencies except that there is an apparent demand for them. Other extraschool efforts to provide for education in the fine and performing arts include the Arts and Humanities Program, established in 1964, which had by 1966 supported over 100 projects in art, theater, dance, etc. (Goodlad, 1966, p. 84); and the Projects to Advance Creativity in Education, which by 1969 had sponsored 46 activities in music education (Title III, ESEA Projects, 1969, p. 54). Efforts to promote development in the arts have not gone without sharp public criticism. One critic (Evett, 1971) remarked of music, drama and dance education, "the underlying theory, that All God's Chillun have a creative potential that can be realized, is one that will support no scrutiny at all.... Incompetence and pretentiousness, hand in hand, are the most conspicuous characteristics of the creative work being done in schools and colleges throughout the country" (p. 79).

Numerous strategies for teaching or at least facilitating or liberating creative thinking have been proposed, usually, however, without accompanying evidence of effectiveness (Getzels & Madaus, 1969). Mearns (1958) suggested that not only must a teacher shun drill but manifestly reinforce original behavior at every opportunity. Osborn (1953) proposed *brainstorming* as a strategy requiring groups to produce large quantities of ideas under conditions which suspend criticism. Gordon (1961) proposed "synectics," which amalgamates individual experiences in a group to arrive at creative solutions to problems through the use of metaphor. Parnes and Meadow (1960, 1963) reported that subjects who had taken courses in brainstorming produced significantly more good ideas than those who had not, and that the effects of the experience tended to persist. Conclusions of this kind were challenged by Taylor, Berry, and Block (1958), who found that individuals working alone produced more and better ideas than those brainstorming in groups. Maltzman and his colleagues carried out a series of laboratory experiments on the "training of originality" (Maltzman, Bogartz, & Breger, 1958; Maltzman, Simon, Raskin, & Licht, 1960). They found that training in the production of responses low in an individual's response hierarchy increased originality of verbal associations and that the effect of such training tended to endure, at least under the given experimental conditions.

Laboratory demonstrations are often not directly applicable to classroom practice, and increasingly research has turned to the school situation itself. Torrance (1961) found that pupils in the primary grades could be taught to use Osborn-type principles to enable them to produce more and better ideas. An intriguing technique for stimulating originality in a classroom was reported in studies by Covington and Crutchfield (1965), who devised autoinstructional programs comprised of detective and mystery study material, which they gave to fifth- and sixth-grade children. Subjects using the programs were markedly superior to control subjects on criterion problem solving, creativity and relevant attitude measures. At the secondary level, Reese and Parnes (1970) found that programmed materials could be used to yield significant gains in standard measures of creative behavior, although working through the same materials presented in conventional fashion by an instructor generally yielded larger gains. At the college level, Khatena (1970) found that the application of training instruments consisting of creative thinking strategies (breaking away from the obvious and commonplace, transposition, analogy, restructuring and synthesis) increased the students' probability of giving superior responses to subsequent measures of originality.

The most extensive work on classroom creativity is probably to be found in the volumes by Torrance (1965) and Torrance and Myers (1970). Among their numerous observations is that pupils permitted to practice without teacher evaluation were able to perform more creatively on subsequent occasions than were pupils who had practiced with teacher evaluation. White and Owen (1970) similarly found that a classroom setting in which evaluation was the responsibility of the student himself resulted in the development of greater creative potential than classroom settings in which evaluation was the responsibility of classmates or of the teacher. Although independent creative activity may at times lead to creative growth, the mere provision of such environments or exercises does not guarantee such growth. The teacher's attitude toward spontaneity and originality, and the degree of controlling behavior that he uses, contribute important effects (Wodtke & Wallen, 1965).

After reviewing the research on deliberate methods of facilitating creative behavior, Parnes and Brunelle (1967) concluded that the vast majority of the evidence indicates that creative ability, as measured by existing tests, can be increased through instruction. The question remains, however: do people with high scores on tests of creative thinking ability behave more creatively than those who scored low? In an attempt to answer this question for teachers, Torrance, Tan, and Allman (1970) examined the relation between the scores on a test of creative thinking administered at the time the subjects were juniors in an elementary teacher-preparation program, and self-reports on activities and achievements obtained six years later when they were teachers. The investigators report that the "teacher trainees identified as highly original in their thinking during their junior year appear to live more fully, be more fully involved in their teaching, and behave more creatively in the classroom than their less original counterparts" (p. 340). It need hardly be added that one such finding should not be interpreted as a conclusion of a more general order. The issues regarding the facilitation of creative thinking through teaching, and the relation between scores on creativity tests and other forms of creative behavior, are not foreclosed and require additional careful research.

TEACHERS OF THE GIFTED

Virtually no attention or systematic research has been given to the selection and preparation of teachers or, as Ward (1961) points out, to the conceptualization of teaching of the gifted. A 1951 survey of teacher education institutions reported that about 2 percent of the 400 institutions responding offered special courses on the gifted at the undergraduate level, and 5 percent offered such courses at the graduate level (Wilson, 1953); a follow-up study five years later reported the same findings (Wilson, 1958). Abraham (1958, p. 185) reports that of 4,601 persons majoring in the area of special education, only 27 majored in teaching the gifted, and only two of 1,549 degrees in special education were awarded to teachers specializing in the gifted.

The dearth of preparation of teachers of the gifted is matched by the dearth of research in this area. The few studies of worth are investigations of scientific talent. Knapp and Goodrich (1952) found that many American scientists had taken their undergraduate work in small liberal arts colleges, studying with dedicated and humane teachers who took a personal interest in them. Brandwein (1955) examined the characteristics of teachers whose students had won awards in the Westinghouse Science Talent Search, and found that the teachers were dedicated to their subject, had published articles and been active in professional organizations, were parental surrogates for their students, and exhibited some of the same characteristics as their gifted students: high intelligence, persistence and curiosity. MacCurdy's study (1956) of 600 National Science Talent Scholarship winners reported similar characteristics for the teachers. In a more recent study, Bishop (1968) compared 109 teachers who most influenced gifted secondary-school students with 97 teachers who were not influential. There were no differences between the two groups of teachers in sex, marital status, type of education or professional activity, but the "influential" teachers were intellectually superior, pursued more intellectual avocations, exhibited a higher need to achieve, held more favorable attitudes toward students, were more enthusiastic about their subject, and preferred to teach gifted students.

Such empirical studies of teachers of the gifted are unfortunately the exception. Most references in the literature are "still in the initial stage of armchair speculation about traits or qualities that teachers of the gifted should have" (Gowan & Demos, 1964, p. 383). Lists of such qualities for teachers have been drawn up from opinions of teachers (Wilson, 1958) and students (N. Davis, 1954). One summary of such lists (Abraham, 1958, p. 177) includes the following qualities: fairness, tolerance, modesty, personality, goodwill, alertness, intuition, resourcefulness, friendliness, understanding, consideration, impartiality, versatility, patience, sense of humor, common sense, democratic attitude, curiosity, imagination, flexibility, constructiveness, thoughtfulness, positiveness, decisiveness and vigor. Surely no one can object to these abilities and traits

as desirable in a teacher of the gifted. But are they not also entirely suitable for teachers of any pupils? It is said that good teachers are friendly, cheerful, sympathetic and morally virtuous rather than cruel, depressed, unsympathetic and morally depraved. However, as Getzels and Jackson (1963) pointed out, when this has been said, not very much that is useful for the understanding of teachers and teaching has been revealed, for what conceivable human interaction is not the better if the persons involved are friendly, cheerful, sympathetic and virtuous rather than otherwise? And which virtuous traits are fit only for teachers of the gifted and not also for teachers of the retarded as well? What is needed is theory and research leading to the discovery of specific and distinctive features, if there be such, of teacher personality and behavior which are related uniquely to special effectiveness with various groups of students. As of this writing no useful theory seems available within which to pose the fruitful problems and to guide widely applicable research in this domain.

CONCLUSION

The present conceptions and investigations of giftedness, creativity, and talent deal almost exclusively with superiority in problem solving; they say very little about superiority in problem finding. Yet the signal mark of the truly gifted or, for that matter, fully functioning person is not only the possession of the technical skills and information for solving problems but also the curiosity and imagination for finding problems. Indeed, there are those who argue that the supreme problem-solvers of the day are the information-processing machines, and that the rate and quality of new discoveries will depend upon the people who can find and formulate the significant problems to be solved (Mackworth, 1965, p. 52). In this sense, only discovering a problem may be a more significant human achievement than finding the solution to the problem once formulated. As Einstein and Infeld (1938) have put it:

The formulation of a problem is often more essential than its solution, which may be merely a matter of mathematical or experimental skill. To raise new questions, new possibilities, to regard old problems from a new angle, requires creative imagination and marks real advance in science (p. 95).

A crucial distinction must be made, both in research and in instruction, between problem solving and problem finding. In an effort to deal systematically with the indicated issues, Getzels (1964) distinguished between *presented* problem situations and *discovered* problem situations, and followed the initial analysis with descriptive and empirical studies in art (Getzels & Csikszentmihalyi, 1966a; Csikszentmihalyi & Getzels, 1970, 1971), science (Getzels & Csikszentmihalyi, 1967), and administration (Getzels, 1970). Presented and discovered problems differ according to the degree to which the problem, its formulation, its method of solution and its solution are known. In the presented problem situation, these elements are already determined; in the discovered problem situation, these elements, including the problem itself, still need to be determined.

Some individuals, like the copyist in art, the technician in science, the pedant in scholarship, deal with problems that have been identified for them, that is, they work with presented problems. Other individuals, like the fine artist, the inventive scientist, the creative scholar, do not wait for others to identify problems for them but are continually sensitive to new problems themselves, that is, they work with discovered problems. These "inquirers" or problem-finders differ from the "solvers" in that situations which appear already determined for the solver appear questionable to the inquirer, or are made questionable by him. The solver creates only the solution. The inquirer creates both the problem and the solution. He is, in Einstein and Infeld's (1938) metaphor, both the criminal and the detective: "For the detective, the crime is given, the problem formulated: Who killed Cock Robin? The scientist must, at least in part, commit his own crime as well as carry out the investigation" (p. 78).

It seems clear that traditional concepts and research in education and intellect have focused on presented problem situations, and have accordingly emphasized problem-solving abilities and orientations; they have tended to avoid discovered problem situations and accordingly have neglected problem-finding abilities and orientations. One readily visible effect of this may be seen in graduate study, which so frequently eventuates not in the Ph.D. but in the ABD (All But Dissertation). And one may detect in much current research the retreading of tired old questions which supply only the same twice-told barren answers.

Some 20 years ago the Committee on the Criteria of Teacher Effectiveness of the American Educational Research Association (Remmers, 1952, 1953) considered the shortcomings of research in teaching and observed that research in the field was conducted in a theoretical vacuum. The committee concluded that only by working within the context of sound theory can one hope to pose the heuristic problems that will result in useful, relevant and widely applicable research. No such powerful theory seems as yet available in the realm of teaching, and hence neither in the teaching of the gifted nor in research on the teaching of the gifted.

The vastness of the work on giftedness has already been noted, as has the disproportion between the multitude of studies and the fruitfulness of the results. The research has been severely criticized for its redundancy (Gallagher, 1966), its general lack of sophistication (Gowan & Demos, 1964), and its aimlessness and ambiguity (Newland, 1963). These judgments, unqualified, may be overly harsh, but in charging that research on the gifted has been ruled by "convenience rather than conscientiousness or psychological conceptualization" (1963, p. 392), Newland correctly identifies the limitations of much that has been done.

Thousands of able men and machines are prepared to solve problems and test theories. What is needed are the more fertile theories, the new and more heuristic problems, that will give direction and meaning to what will be done. In research as in instruction it is necessary to redress the current imbalance and attend not only to presented problem situations and problem-solving orientations and activities, but also to discovered problem situations and problem-finding orientations and activities.

REFERENCES

Abraham, W. Common sense about gifted children. New York: Harper & Brothers, 1958.

Abramson, D. A. The effectiveness of grouping for students of high ability. *Educational Research Bulletin,* 1959, 38, 169–182.

Ackerman, P. R., & Weintraub, F. J. Summary analysis of state laws for gifted children. *Exceptional Children,* 1969, 35, 569–576.

Adler, M. Reported incidence of giftedness among ethnic groups. *Exceptional Children,* 1967, 34, 101–105.

Albert, R. S. Genius: Present-day status of the concept and its implications for the study of creativity and giftedness. *American Psychologist,* 1969, 24, 743–753.

Anderson, H. H. The nature of creativity. *Studies in Art Education,* 1960, 1(2), 10–17.

Anderson, J. E. The nature of abilities. In E. P. Torrance (Ed.), *Education and talent.* Minneapolis: University of Minnesota Press, 1960. Pp. 9–31.

Andrews, E. G. The development of imagination in the preschool child. *University of Iowa Studies in Character,* 1930, 3 (Whole No. 4).

Arasteh, A. R. *Creativity in the life cycle. Vol. 1. An annotated bibliography.* Leiden, Netherlands: E. J. Brill, 1968.

Arends, R., & Ford, P. M. *Acceleration and enrichment in the junior high school: A follow-up study.* Research report 03-05. Olympia, Wash.: State Superintendent of Public Instruction, 1964.

Ausubel, D. P., & Ausubel, P. Ego development among segregated Negro children. In A. H. Passow (Ed.), *Education in depressed areas.* New York: Teachers College Bureau of Publications, Columbia University, 1963. Pp. 109–141.

Baird, L. L., & Richards, J. M., Jr. The effects of selecting college students by various kinds of high school achievement. *ACT Research Report,* 1968 (Whole No. 23).

Baldwin, B. T. Methods of selecting superior or gifted children. In G. M. Whipple (Ed.), *The education of gifted children,* The Twenty-third Yearbook of the National Society for the Study of Education, Part I. Bloomington, Ill.: Public School Publishing, 1924. Pp. 25–47.

Barron, F. X. *Creativity and psychological health: Origins of personal vitality and creative freedom.* Princeton, N.J.: Van Nostrand, 1963.

Barron, F. X. *Creative persons and creative process.* New York: Holt, Rinehart & Winston, 1969.

Bass, W. P., & Burger, H. G. *American Indians and educational laboratories.* Albuquerque, N.M.: Southwestern Cooperative Educational Laboratory, 1967. ED 014 369.

Bettelheim, B. Segregation: New style. *School Review,* 1958, 66, 251–272.

Birch, J. W., & Reynolds, M. C. The gifted. *Review of Educational Research,* 1963, 33, 83–98.

Bishop, W. E. Successful teachers of the gifted. *Exceptional Children,* 1968, 34, 317–325.

Bloom, B. S., Davis, A., & Hess, R. *Compensatory education for cultural deprivation.* New York: Holt, Rinehart & Winston, 1965.

Bond, H. M. The Negro scholar and professional in America. In J. P. Davis (Ed.), *The American Negro reference book.* Englewood Cliffs, N.J.: Prentice-Hall, 1966. Pp. 548–589.

Borg, W. R. *The evaluation of ability grouping.* Cooperative Research Project No. 577. Utah State University, 1964.

Boulding, K. E. An economist's view of the manpower concept. In National Manpower Council, *Proceedings of a conference on the utilization of scientific and professional manpower.* New York: Columbia University Press, 1954. Pp. 11–26.

Bowman, P. H., Dietrich, W. J., DeHaan, R. F., Hackamack, H., Havighurst, R. J., Johnson, L. A., King, R. D., & Litler, L. O. *Studying children and training counselors in a community program.* Supplementary Educational Monograph, No. 78. Chicago: University of Chicago Press, 1953.

Brandwein, P. F. *The gifted student as future scientist.* New York: Harcourt, Brace, 1955.

Bristow, W. H. *The gifted student in the New York city schools: A memorandum and bibliography.* New York: Board of Education of the City of New York, 1959.

Brittain, W. L. Creative art. In L. A. Fliegler (Ed.), *Curriculum planning for the gifted.* Englewood Cliffs, N. J.: Prentice-Hall, 1961. Pp. 272–302.

Brunelle, E. A. *1965–66 bibliography. Creativity and problem-solving.* Buffalo, N.Y.: Creative Education Foundation, n.d.

Buhl, H. R. *Creative engineering design.* Ames: Iowa State University Press, 1960.

Burkhart, R. C. The creativity-personality continuum based on spontaneity and deliberateness in art. *Studies in Art Education,* 1960, 2(1), 43–65.

Burks, B. S., Jensen, D. W., & Terman, L. M. *Genetic studies of genius.* Vol. 3. *The promise of youth: Follow-up studies of a thousand gifted children.* Stanford, Calif: Stanford University Press, 1930.

Buros, O. K. (Ed.) *The sixth mental measurements yearbook.* Highland Park, N.J.: Gryphon Press, 1965.

Burt, C. The psychology of creative ability. *British Journal of Educational Psychology,* 1962, 32, 292–298.

Carter, H. D. Gifted children. In C. W. Harris (Ed.), *Encyclopedia of educational research.* New York: Macmillan, 1960. Pp. 583–593.

Cattell, J. Families of American men of science. *Popular Science Monthly,* 1915, 86, 504–515.

Cattell, R. B. The personality and motivation of the researcher from measurements of contemporaries and from biography. In C. W. Taylor, & F. X. Barron (Eds.), *Scientific creativity: Its recognition and development.* New York: John Wiley, 1963. Pp. 119–131.

Cattell, R. B., & Drevdahl, J. E. A comparison of the personality profile (16 P. F.) of eminent researchers with that of eminent

teachers and administrators, and of the general population. *British Journal of Psychology,* 1955, 46, 248–261.

Cicirelli, V. G. Form of the relationship between creativity, IQ, and academic achievement. *Journal of Educational Psychology,* 1965, 56, 303–308.

Clark, R. W. *Einstein. The life and times.* New York: World Publishing, 1971.

Cleeton, G. U. Originality: A summary of experimental literature. *Journal of Abnormal and Social Psychology,* 1926, 21, 304–315.

Colvin, S. S. Invention versus form in English composition: An inductive study. *Pedagogical Seminary,* 1902, 9, 393–421.

Covington, M. V., & Crutchfield, R. S. Facilitation of creative problem solving. *Programmed Instruction,* 1965, 4(4), 3–5, 10.

Cox, C. M. *Genetic studies of genius.* Vol. 2. *The early mental traits of three hundred geniuses.* Stanford, Calif.: Stanford University Press, 1926.

Cronbach, L. J. Intelligence? Creativity? A parsimonious reinterpretation of the Wallach-Kogan data. *American Educational Research Journal,* 1968, 5, 491–511.

Cross, P. G., Cattell, R. B., & Butcher, H. J. The personality pattern of creative artists. *British Journal of Educational Psychology,* 1967, 37, 292–299.

Csikszentmihalyi, M., & Getzels, J. W. Concern for discovery: An attitudinal component for creative production. *Journal of Personality,* 1970, 38, 91–105.

Csikszentmihalyi, M., & Getzels, J. W. Discovery-oriented behavior and the originality of creative products: A study with artists. *Journal of Personality and Social Psychology,* 1971, 19, 47–52.

Davis, A. The able among the socially disadvantaged. Unpublished manuscript, The University of Chicago, Department of Education, 1968.

Davis, A., & Dollard, J. *Children of bondage: The personality development of Negro youth in the urban South.* Washington, D.C.: American Council on Education, 1940.

Davis, N. Teachers for the gifted. *Journal of Teacher Education,* 1954, 5, 221–224.

Dearborn, G. V. A study of imaginations. *American Journal of Psychology,* 1898, 9, 183–190.

DeHaan, R. F., & Havighurst, R. J. *Educating gifted children.* (Rev. & Enlarged ed.) Chicago: University of Chicago Press, 1961.

Deignan, F. J. Note on the values of art students. *Psychological Reports,* 1958, 4, 566.

Dennis, W. Age and achievement: A critique. *Journal of Gerontology,* 1956, 11, 331–333.

Deutsch & Shea, Inc. *Creativity: A comprehensive bibliography on creativity in science, engineering, business, and the arts.* New York: Industrial Relations News, 1958.

Domino, G. Maternal personality correlates of sons' creativity. *Journal of Consulting and Clinical Psychology,* 1969, 33, 180–183.

Domino, G. Identification of potentially creative persons from the adjective check list. *Journal of Consulting and Clinical Psychology,* 1970, 35, 48–51.

Dransfield, J. E. *Administration of enrichment to superior children in the typical classroom.* Contributions to Education No. 558. New York: Bureau of Publications, Teachers College, Columbia University, 1933.

Dreger, R. M., & Miller, K. S. Comparative psychological studies of Negroes and whites in the United States. *Psychological Bulletin,* 1960, 57, 361–402.

Drevdahl, J. E. Factors of importance for creativity. *Journal of Clinical Psychology,* 1956, 12, 21–26.

Drevdahl, J. E. Some developmental and environmental factors in creativity. In C. W. Taylor (Ed.), *Widening horizons in creativity.* New York: John Wiley, 1964. Pp. 170–186.

Durr, W. K. *The gifted student.* New York: Oxford University Press, 1964.

Edington, E. D. Disadvantaged rural youth. *Review of Educational Research,* 1970, 40, 69–85.

Educator's complete ERIC handbook. Compiled by the Prentice-Hall editorial staff. Curriculum guides for the gifted. Englewood Cliffs, N.J.: Prentice-Hall, 1967. Pp. 413–423. (a)

Educator's complete ERIC handbook. Compiled by the Prentice-Hall editorial staff. Programs for the gifted. Englewood Cliffs, N.J.: Prentice-Hall, 1967. Pp. 439–476. (b)

Einstein, A., & Infeld, L. *The evolution of physics: The growth of ideas from early concepts to relativity and quanta.* New York: Simon & Schuster, 1938.

Eisenman, R., & Schussel, N. R. Creativity, birth order, and preference for symmetry. *Journal of Consulting and Clinical Psychology,* 1970, 34, 275–280.

Ellison, R. *Invisible man.* New York: Random House, 1952.

Elton, C. F., & Shevel, L. R. Who is talented? An analysis of achievement. *ACT Research Report,* 1969 (Whole No. 31).

Environment, heredity, and intelligence. Compiled from the *Harvard Educational Review.* Cambridge, Mass.: *Harvard Educational Review* Reprint Series No. 2, 1969.

Epstein, C. F. *A woman's place: Options and limits in professional careers.* Berkeley, Calif.: University of California Press, 1970.

Evett, R. The anatomy of pretentiousness. *Atlantic,* 1971, 227 (1), 75–79.

Feldhusen, J. F., Denny, T., & Condon, C. F. Anxiety, divergent thinking, and achievement. *Journal of Educational Psychology,* 1965, 56, 40–45.

Feldhusen, J. F., Treffinger, D. J., & Elias, R. M. Prediction of academic achievement with divergent and convergent thinking and personality variables. *Psychology in the Schools,* 1970, 7, 46–52.

Flanagan, J. C. Definition and measurement of ingenuity. In C. W. Taylor (Ed.), *The second (1957) University of Utah research conference on the identification of creative scientific talent.* Salt Lake City: University of Utah Press, 1958. Pp. 109–118.

Flanagan, J. C., Dailey, J. T., Shaycoft, M. F., Gorham, W. A., Orr, D. B., & Goldberg, I. *Design for a study of American youth.* Boston: Houghton Mifflin, 1962.

Flanagan, J. C., Davis, F. B., Dailey, J. T., Shaycoft, M. F., Orr, D. B., Goldberg, I., & Neyman, C. A., Jr. *The American high-school student: The identification, development, and utilization of human talents.* Technical report for Cooperative Research Project No. 635, U.S. Office of Education. Pittsburgh: Project TALENT Office, University of Pittsburgh, 1964.

Flescher, I. Anxiety and achievement of intellectually gifted and creatively gifted children. *Journal of Psychology,* 1963, 56, 251–268.

Fliegler, L. A. (Ed.) *Curriculum planning for the gifted.* Englewood Cliffs, N.J.: Prentice-Hall, 1961.

Fliegler, L. A., & Bish, C. E. The gifted and talented. *Review of Educational Research,* 1959, 29, 408–450.

Freud, S. *Leonardo da Vinci; A psychosexual study of an infantile reminiscence.* London: Kegan Paul, 1922.

Frierson, E. C. The gifted. *Review of Educational Research,* 1969, 39, 25–37.

Gallagher, J. J. *Research summary on gifted child education.* Springfield, Ill.: Illinois Department of Program Planning for the Gifted, 1966. ED 026 753.

Gallagher, J. J. Gifted children. In R. L. Ebel (Ed.), *Encyclopedia of educational research.* (4th ed.) New York: Macmillan, 1969. Pp. 537–544.

Gallagher, J. J., & Rogge, W. The gifted. *Review of Educational Research,* 1966, 36, 37–55.

Galton, F. *Hereditary genius: An inquiry into its laws and consequences.* London: Macmillan, 1869.

Gee, H. H. Differential characteristics of student bodies—implications for the study of medical education. In *Selection and educational differentiation.* Berkeley: University of California Field Service Center and Center for the Study of Higher Education, 1959. Pp. 125–154.

Getzels, J. W. Social values and individual motives: The dilemma of the gifted. *School Review,* 1957, 65, 60–63.

Getzels, J. W. Creative thinking, problem-solving, and instruction. In E. R. Hilgard (Ed.), *Theories of learning and instruction,* The Sixty-third Yearbook of the National Society for the Study of Education, Part I. Chicago: NSSE, 1964. Pp. 240–267.

Getzels, J. W. The nature and nurture of the gifted child. In R. E. Cooke, & S. Levin (Eds.), *The biologic basis of pediatric practice.* Vol. 2. New York: McGraw-Hill, 1968. Pp. 1639–1648.

Getzels, J. W. Creative administration and organizational change: An essay in theory. In L. J. Rubin (Ed.), *Frontiers of school leadership.* Chicago: Rand McNally, 1970. Pp. 69–85.

Getzels, J. W., & Csikszentmihalyi, M. *Creative thinking in art students: An exploratory study.* Cooperative Research Project No. E008. Chicago, Ill.: University of Chicago, 1964.

Getzels, J. W., & Csikszentmihalyi, M. Portrait of the artist as an explorer. *Trans-action,* 1966, 3 (6), 31–34. (a)

Getzels, J. W., & Csikszentmihalyi, M. The study of creativity in future artists: The criterion problem. In O. J. Harvey (Ed.), *Experience, structure, and adaptability.* New York: Springer, 1966. Pp. 349–368. (b)

Getzels, J. W., & Csikszentmihalyi, M. Scientific creativity. *Science Journal,* 1967, 3 (9), 80–84.

Getzels, J. W., & Csikszentmihalyi, M. On the roles, values, and performance of future artists: A conceptual and empirical exploration. *Sociological Quarterly,* 1968, 9, 516–530. (a)

Getzels, J. W., & Csikszentmihalyi, M. The value-orientations of art students as determinants of artistic specialization and creative performance. *Studies in Art Education,* 1968, 10 (1), 5–16. (b)

Getzels, J. W., & Jackson, P. W. The creative adolescent: A summary of some research findings. In C. W. Taylor (Ed.), *The third (1959) University of Utah research conference on the identification of creative scientific talent.* Salt Lake City: University of Utah Press, 1959. Pp. 46–57.

Getzels, J. W., & Jackson, P. W. Family environment and cognitive style: A study of the sources of highly intelligent and of highly creative adolescents. *American Sociological Review,* 1961, 26, 351–359.

Getzels, J. W., & Jackson, P. W. *Creativity and intelligence: Explorations with gifted students.* New York: John Wiley, 1962.

Getzels, J. W., & Jackson, P. W. The teacher's personality and characteristics. In N. L. Gage (Ed.), *Handbook of research on teaching.* Chicago: Rand McNally, 1963. Pp. 506–582.

Getzels, J. W., & Madaus, G. F. Creativity. In R. L. Ebel (Ed.), *Encyclopedia of educational research.* New York: Macmillan, 1969. Pp. 267–275.

Ghiselin, B. (Ed.) *The creative process.* New York: New American Library, 1952.

Ghiselli, E. E. Managerial talent. *American Psychologist,* 1963, 18, 631–642.

Gold, M. J. *Education of the intellectually gifted.* Columbus, Ohio: Charles E. Merrill, 1965.

Goldberg, M. L. Selected bibliography on education of the talented. In M. L. Goldberg, *Research on the talented.* New York:

Teachers College Bureau of Publications, Columbia University, 1965. Pp. 63–72.

Goldberg, M. L., & Passow, A. H. The effects of ability grouping. *Education,* 1962, 82, 482–487.

Goodlad, J. I. *The changing school curriculum.* New York: Fund for the Advancement of Education, 1966.

Gordon, W. J. J. *Synectics: The development of creative capacity.* New York: Harper & Row, 1961.

Gowan, J. C. *An annotated bibliography on the academically talented.* Washington, D.C.: National Education Association, 1961.

Gowan, J. C. *Annotated bibliography on creativity and giftedness.* Northridge, Calif.: San Fernando Valley State College Foundation, 1965.

Gowan, J. C., & Demos, G. D. *The education and guidance of the ablest.* Springfield, Ill.: Charles C Thomas, 1964.

Grotberg, E. H. A selected bibliography on the gifted and creative child. *Education,* 1967, 88, 52–56.

Guilford, J. P. Creativity. *American Psychologist,* 1950, 5, 444–454.

Guilford, J. P. Creativity: Yesterday, today, and tomorrow. *Journal of Creative Behavior,* 1967, 1, 3–14.

Guilford, J. P. Creativity: Retrospect and prospect. *Journal of Creative Behavior,* 1970, 4, 149–168.

Harvey, O. J., Hoffmeister, J. K., Coates, C., & White, B. J. A partial evaluation of Torrance's tests of creativity. *American Educational Research Journal,* 1970, 7, 359–372.

Hattam, E. The school days of our novelists: The case for creativity. *Teachers College Record,* 1968, 69, 459–464.

Havighurst, R. J., Hersey, J., Meister, M., Cornog, W. H., & Terman, L. M. The importance of education for the gifted. In N. B. Henry (Ed.), *Education for the gifted,* The Fifty-seventh Yearbook of the National Society for the Study of Education, Part II. Chicago: NSSE, 1958. Pp. 3–20.

Havighurst, R. J., Stivers, E., & DeHaan, R. F. *A survey of the education of gifted children.* Supplementary Educational Monographs No. 83. Chicago: University of Chicago Press, 1955.

Heim, A. *Intelligence and personality: Their assessment and relationship.* Baltimore, Md.: Penguin Books, 1970.

Henry, T. S. Bibliography on the psychology and pedagogy of gifted children. In G. M. Whipple (Ed.), *Classroom problems in the education of gifted children,* The Nineteenth Yearbook of the National Society for the Study of Education, Part II. Bloomington, Ill.: Public School Publishing Company, 1920. Pp. 120–125.

Henry, T. S. Annotated bibliography on gifted children and their education. In G. M. Whipple (Ed.), *The education of gifted children,* The Twenty-third Yearbook of the National Society for the Study of Education, Part I. Bloomington, Ill.: Public School Publishing Company, 1924. Pp. 389–443.

Holland, J. L. Some limitations of teacher ratings as predictors of creativity. *Journal of Educational Psychology,* 1959, 50, 219–223.

Holland, J. L., & Richards, J. M., Jr. Academic and nonacademic accomplishment: Correlated or uncorrelated? *Journal of Educational Psychology,* 1965, 56, 165–174.

Holland, J. L., & Richards, J. M., Jr. The many faces of talent: A reply to Werts. *Journal of Educational Psychology,* 1967, 58, 205–209.

Hollingworth, L. S. *Children above 180 IQ, Stanford-Binet: Origin and development.* Yonkers-on-Hudson, N.Y.: World Book Co., 1942.

Holt, E. E. *A selected and annotated bibliography on the gifted.* Columbus, Ohio: Ohio State Board of Education, 1960.

Hudson, L. *Contrary imaginations: A psychological study of the English schoolboy.* London: Methuen, 1966.

Hudson, L. *Frames of mind: Ability, perception and self-perception in the arts and sciences.* London: Methuen, 1968.

Hutchinson, E. D. Materials for the study of creative thinking. *Psychological Bulletin,* 1931, 28, 392–410.

Iscoe, I., & Pierce-Jones, J. Divergent thinking, age, and intelligence in white and Negro children. *Child Development,* 1964, 35, 785–797.

Janssen, C. *A study of bilingualism and creativity.* Final report. Washington, D.C.: American Personnel and Guidance Association, 1969. ED 034 269.

Jensen, A. R. How much can we boost IQ and scholastic achievement? *Harvard Educational Review,* 1969, 39, 1–123.

Journal of Creative Behavior. Bibliography.

Journal of Creative Behavior, 1967, 1, 432–437.

Jung, C. G. The gifted child. In H. Read, M. Fordham, & G. Adler (Eds.), *The collected works of C. G. Jung.* Vol. 17. New York: Pantheon Books, 1954. Pp. 135–145.

Justman, J. Personal and social adjustment of intellectually gifted accelerants and non-accelerants in junior high schools. *School Review,* 1953, 61, 468–478.

Justman, J. Academic achievement of intellectually gifted accelerants and non-accelerants in junior high school. *School Review,* 1954, 62, 143–150.

Kaley, M. M. Attitudes toward the dual role of the married professional woman. *American Psychologist,* 1971, 26, 301–306.

Kennedy, W. A., Van De Riet, V., & White, J. C. *The standardization of the 1960 revision of the Stanford-Binet intelligence scale on Negro elementary-school children in the southeastern United States.* Tallahassee: Florida State University Human Development Clinic, 1961.

Keys, N. *The underage student in high school and college.* University of California Publications in Education. Berkeley: University of California Press, 1938.

Khatena, J. Training college adults to think creatively with words. *Psychological Reports,* 1970, 27, 279–281.

Klausmeier, H. J., Harris, C. W., & Ethnathios, Z. Relationships between divergent thinking abilities and teacher ratings of high school students. *Journal of Educational Psychology,* 1962, 53, 72–75.

Klineberg, O. Negro-white differences in intelligence test performance: A new look at an old problem. *American Psychologist,* 1963, 18, 198–203.

Knapp, R. H., & Goodrich, H. B. *Origins of American scientists.* Chicago: University of Chicago Press, 1952.

Kough, J. *Practical programs for the gifted.* Chicago: Science Research Associates, 1960.

Landry, R. G. *Bilingualism and creative abilities.* Fargo, N.D.: North Dakota State University, 1968. ED 039 602.

Lange-Eichbaum, W. *The problem of genius.* E. Paul, & C. Paul (Trans.). New York: Macmillan, 1932.

Lee, R. E., & Newland, T. E. A small community and its gifted school children. *Educational Forum,* 1966, 30, 363–368.

Lehman, H. C. *Age and achievement.* Princeton, N.J.: Princeton University Press, 1953.

Lombroso, C. *The man of genius.* London: W. Scott, 1891.

Lowenfeld, V., & Brittain, W. L. *Creative and mental growth.* New York: Macmillan, 1964.

MacCurdy, R. D. Characteristics and backgrounds of superior science students. *School Review,* 1956, 64, 67–71.

MacKinnon, D. W. The nature and nurture of creative talent. *American Psychologist,* 1962, 17, 484–495.

MacKinnon, D. W. The creativity of architects. In C. W. Taylor (Ed.), *Widening horizons in creativity.* New York: John Wiley, 1964. Pp. 359–378.

Mackworth, N. H. Originality. *American Psychologist,* 1965, 20, 51–66.

Madaus, G. F. Divergent thinking and intelligence: Another look at a controversial question. *Journal of Educational Measurement,* 1967, 4, 227–235.

Maltzman, I., Bogartz, W., & Breger, L. A procedure for increasing word association originality and its transfer effects. *Journal of Experimental Psychology,* 1958, 56, 392–398.

Maltzman, I., Simon, S., Raskin, D., & Licht, L. Experimental studies in the training of originality. *Psychological Monographs,* 1960, 74 (6), 1–23.

Martens, E. H. Annotated bibliography on gifted children. In P. Witty (Ed.), *The gifted child.* Boston: D. C. Heath, 1951. Pp. 277–323.

Maslow, A. H. The creative attitude. *Structurist,* 1963, 3, 4–10.

McClelland, D. C. The calculated risk: An aspect of scientific performance. In C. W. Taylor, & F. X. Barron (Eds.), *Scientific creativity: Its recognition and development.* New York: John Wiley, 1963. Pp. 184–192.

McClelland, D. C., Baldwin, A. L., Bronfenbrenner, U., & Strodtbeck, F. L. *Talent and society: New perspectives in the identification of talent.* Princeton, N.J.: Van Nostrand, 1958.

McCloy, W., & Meier, N. C. Re-creative imagination. *Psychological Monographs,* 1939, 51 (5), 108–116.

Mearns, H. *Creative power: The education of youth in the creative arts.* (2nd, Rev. ed.) New York: Dover Publishers, 1958.

Mednick, S. A., & Mednick, M. T. An associative interpretation of the creative process. In C. W. Taylor (Ed.), *Widening horizons in creativity*. New York: John Wiley, 1964. Pp. 54–68.

Miles, C. C. Gifted children. In L. Carmichael (Ed.), *Manual of child psychology*. (2nd, Rev. ed.) New York: John Wiley, 1954. Pp. 984–1063.

Miller, A. E., & Brown, B. I. *National directory of schools and vocations*. (3rd ed.) North Springfield, Pa.: State School Publications, 1967.

Newell, A., Shaw, J. C., & Simon, H. A. The processes of creative thinking. In H. E. Gruber, G. Terrell, & M. Wertheimer (Eds.), *Contemporary approaches to creative thinking*. New York: Atherton Press, 1962. Pp. 63–119.

Newland, T. E. The mentally gifted. *Review of Educational Research*, 1941, 11, 277–287.

Newland, T. E. The gifted. *Review of Educational Research*, 1953, 23, 417–431.

Newland, T. E. A critique of research on the gifted. *Exceptional Children*, 1963, 29, 391–398.

Nichols, R. C. Parental attitudes of mothers of intelligent adolescents and creativity of their children. *Child Development*, 1964, 35, 1041–1049.

Nisbet, J. F. *The insanity of genius and the general inequality of human faculty physiologically considered*. London: Kegan Paul, 1891.

Noonan, N., & Norris, D. E. Studies of gifted children. *Journal of Exceptional Children*, 1938, 4 (extra issue), 46–56.

Norris, D. E., Hayslip, M., & Noonan, N. I. Gifted children. In W. S. Monroe (Ed.), *Encyclopedia of educational research*. (Rev. ed.) New York: Macmillan, 1950. Pp. 505–510.

Norris, D. E., & Noonan, N. I. Gifted children. In W. S. Monroe (Ed.), *Encyclopedia of educational research*. New York: Macmillan, 1941. Pp. 75–81.

Ohnmacht, F. W. Achievement, anxiety and creative thinking. *American Educational Research Journal*, 1966, 3, 131–138.

Osborn, A. F. *Applied imagination: Principles and procedures of creative thinking*. New York: Scribner, 1953.

Osburn, W. J., & Rohan, B. J. *Enriching the curriculum for gifted children*. New York: Macmillan, 1931.

Palm, H. J. *An analysis of test-score differences between highly creative and high Miller Analogies members of the Summer Guidance Institute*. Minneapolis: Bureau of Educational Research, University of Minnesota, 1959.

Parnes, S. J. The literature of creativity (Part II). *Journal of Creative Behavior*, 1967, 1, 191–240.

Parnes, S. J., & Brunelle, E. A. The literature of creativity (Part I). *Journal of Creative Behavior*, 1967, 1, 52–109.

Parnes, S. J., & Meadow, A. Evaluation of persistence of effects produced by a creative problem-solving course. *Psychological Reports*, 1960, 7, 357–361.

Parnes, S. J., & Meadow, A. Development of individual creative talent. In C. W. Taylor, & F. X. Barron (Eds.), *Scientific creativity: Its recognition and development*. New York: John Wiley, 1963. Pp. 311–320.

Passow, A. H. Enrichment of education for the gifted. In N. B. Henry (Ed), *Education for the gifted*, The Fifty-seventh Yearbook of the National Society for the Study of Education, Part II. Chicago: NSSE, 1958. Pp. 193–221.

Passow, A. H., & Goldberg, M. L. *The talented youth project: A progress report, 1961*. Horace Mann-Lincoln Institute of School Experimentation. New York: Teachers College, Columbia University, 1961.

Paterson, D. G. The conservation of human talent. *American Psychologist*, 1957, 12, 134–144.

Pettigrew, T. F. *A profile of the Negro American*. Princeton, N.J.: Van Nostrand, 1964.

Pilch, M. M. *Bibliography of the education of the gifted*. State of Minnesota: Department of Education, 1960, 1961, 1962, 1963, 1964.

Raph, J. B., Goldberg, M. L., & Passow, A. H. *Bright underachievers*. New York: Teachers College Press, 1966.

Razik, T. A. *Bibliography of creativity studies and related areas*. Buffalo, N.Y.: State University of New York, 1965.

Reese, H. W., & Parnes, S. J. Programming creative behavior. *Child Development*, 1970, 41, 413–423.

Remmers, H. H. (Chairman) et al. Report of the committee on criteria of teacher effectiveness. *Review of Educational Research*, 1952, 22, 238–263.

Remmers, H. H. (Chairman) et al. Second report of the committee on criteria of teacher effectiveness. *Journal of Educational Research*, 1953, 46, 641–658.

Rice, J. P. *The gifted: Developing total talent.* Springfield, Ill.: Charles C Thomas, 1970.

Richards, J. M., Jr. *Assessing student performance in college.* Report 2. Washington, D.C.: ERIC Clearing house on Higher Education, 1970. ED 040 307.

Richards, J. M., Jr., Cline, V. B., & Needham, W. E. Creativity tests and teacher and self judgments of originality. *Journal of Experimental Education*, 1964, 32, 281–285.

Richards, J. M., Jr., Holland, J. L., & Lutz, S. W. Prediction of student accomplishment in college. *Journal of Educational Psychology*, 1967, 58, 343–355.

Roberts, R. J., & Nichols, R. C. Participants in the national achievement scholarship program for Negroes. *National Merit Scholarship Corporation Research Reports*, 1966, 2 (Whole No. 2).

Roe, A. The personality of artists. *Educational and Psychological Measurement*, 1946, 6, 401–408.

Roe, A. A psychological study of eminent psychologists and anthropologists, and a comparison with biological and physical scientists. *Psychological Monographs*, 1953, 67 (2), 1–55.

Rossi, A. S. Barriers to the career choice of engineering, medicine, or science among American women. In J. A. Mattfeld, & C. G. Van Aken (Eds.), *Women in the scientific professions.* Cambridge: MIT Press, 1965. Pp. 51–127.

Roweton, W. E. *Creativity: A review of theory and research.* Theoretical Paper No. 24. Madison, Wisc.: Wisconsin Research and Development Center for Cognitive Learning, University of Wisconsin, 1970. ED 044 012.

Sanders, D. C. *Elementary education and the academically talented pupil.* Washington, D.C.: National Education Association, 1961.

Schaefer, C. E. The self-concept of creative adolescents. *Journal of Psychology*, 1969, 72, 233–242.

Shuey, A. M. *The testing of Negro intelligence.* (2nd ed.) New York: Social Science Press, 1966.

Stein, M. I., & Heinze, S. J. *Creativity and the individual.* Glencoe, Ill.: Free Press, 1960.

Strong, E. K., Jr. Satisfactions and interests. *American Psychologist*, 1958, 13, 449–456.

Sullivan, H. S. *The interpersonal theory of psychiatry.* New York: W. W. Norton, 1953.

Taft, R., & Gilchrist, M. B. Creative attitudes and creative productivity: A comparison of two aspects of creativity among students. *Journal of Educational Psychology*, 1970, 61, 136–143.

Taylor, C. W. Multiple talent approach: A teaching scheme in which most students can be above average. *Instructor*, 1968, 77 (8). 27, 142, 144, 146.

Taylor, C. W., & Ellison, R. L. Predicting creative performances from multiple measures. In C. W. Taylor (Ed.), *Widening horizons in creativity.* New York: John Wiley, 1964. Pp. 227–260.

Taylor, C. W., & Holland, J. L. Development and application of tests of creativity. *Review of Educational Research*, 1962, 32, 91–102.

Taylor, D. W., Berry, P. C., & Block, C. H. Does group participation when using brainstorming facilitate or inhibit creative thinking? *Administrative Science Quarterly*, 1958, 3, 23–47.

Terman, L. M. *Genetic studies of genius.* Vol. 1. *Mental and physical traits of a thousand gifted children.* Stanford, Calif.: Stanford University Press, 1925.

Terman, L. M. The gifted child. In C. Murchison (Ed.), *A handbook of child psychology.* Worcester, Mass.: Clark University Press, 1931. Pp. 568–584.

Terman, L. M. The discovery and encouragement of exceptional talent. *American Psychologist*, 1954, 9, 221–230.

Terman, L. M., & Burks, B. S. The gifted child. In C. Murchison (Ed.), *A handbook of child psychology.* (2nd, Rev. ed.) Worcester, Mass.: Clark University Press, 1933. Pp. 773–801.

Terman, L. M., & Chase, J. M. The psychology, biology and pedagogy of genius. *Psychological Bulletin*, 1920, 17, 397–409.

Terman, L. M., & Oden, M. H. *Genetic studies of genius.* Vol. 4. *The gifted child grows up: Twenty-five years' follow-up of a superior group.* Stanford, Calif.: Stanford University Press, 1947.

Terman, L. M., & Oden, M. H. *Genetic studies of genius.* Vol. 5. *The gifted group at midlife: Thirty-five years' follow-up of the superior child.* Stanford, Calif.: Stanford

University Press, and London: Oxford University Press, 1959.

Thorndike, R. L. Some methodological issues in the study of creativity. In E. F. Gardner (Ed.), *Proceedings of the 1962 Invitational Conference on Testing Problems*. Princeton, N.J.: Educational Testing Service, 1963. Pp. 40–54.

Title III, ESEA projects in music: Where has all the money gone? *Music Educator's Journal*, 1969, 55 (5), 64–72.

Torrance, E. P. *Educational achievement of the highly intelligent and the highly creative: Eight partial replications of the Getzels-Jackson study*. Minneapolis: Bureau of Educational Research, University of Minnesota, 1960.

Torrance, E. P. Priming creative thinking in the primary grades. *Elementary School Journal*, 1961, 62, 34–41.

Torrance, E. P. Cultural discontinuities and the development of originality of thinking. *Exceptional Children*, 1962, 29, 2–13. (a)

Torrance, E. P. *Guiding creative talent*. Englewood Cliffs, N.J.: Prentice-Hall, 1962. (b)

Torrance, E. P. *Rewarding creative behavior: Experiments in classroom creativity*. Englewood Cliffs, N.J.: Prentice-Hall, 1965.

Torrance, E. P. *Torrance tests of creative thinking, Manual*. Princeton, N.J.: Personnel Press, 1966.

Torrance, E. P., & Myers, R. E. *Creative learning and teaching*. New York: Dodd, Mead, 1970.

Torrance, E. P., Tan, C. A., & Allman, T. Verbal originality and teacher behavior: A predictive validity study. *Journal of Teacher Education*, 1970, 21, 335–341.

Torrance, E. P., Wu, J., Gowan, J. C., & Aliotti, N. C. Creative functioning of monolingual and bilingual children in Singapore. *Journal of Educational Psychology*, 1970, 61, 72–75.

United States Bureau of the Census. *Current population reports,* Series P-23, Special Studies (formerly Technical Studies), No. 27, Trends in Social and Economic Conditions in Metropolitan Areas. Washington, D.C.: U.S. Government Printing Office, 1969.

United States Bureau of the Census. *Current population reports,* Series P-20, No. 207, Educational attainment: March 1970. Washington, D.C.: U.S. Government Printing Office, 1970. (a)

United States Bureau of the Census. *Statistical abstract of the United States 1970* (91st ed.) Washington, D.C.: U.S. Government Printing Office, 1970. (b)

United States Office of Education. *Statistics of special schools and classes for exceptional children 1939–40*. Washington, D.C.: U.S. Government Printing Office, 1942.

United States Office of Education. *Statistics of special education for exceptional children and youth, 1957–58. Final report*. Washington, D.C.: U.S. Government Printing Office, 1963.

United States Office of Education. *Subject offerings and enrollments in public secondary schools*. Washington, D.C.: U.S. Government Printing Office, 1965.

United States Office of Education. *Digest of educational statistics 1966*. Washington, D.C.: U.S. Government Printing Office, 1966. (a)

United States Office of Education. State and local provisions for talented students: An annotated bibliography. *Bulletin*, 1966 (Whole No. 5). (b)

United States Office of Education. *Digest of educational statistics 1969*. Washington, D.C.: U.S. Government Printing Office, 1969.

United States Office of Education. *Digest of educational statistics 1970 edition*. Washington, D.C.: U.S. Government Printing Office, 1970.

Vocationally talented pupils. Cooperative Research Project No. 1038. New Brunswick, N.J.: Division of Field Studies and Research, Rutgers, The State University, 1962.

Wallach, M. A., & Kogan, N. *Modes of thinking in young children*. New York: Holt, Rinehart & Winston, 1965.

Wallach, M. A., & Wing, C. W., Jr. *The talented student: A validation of the creativity-intelligence distinction*. New York: Holt, Rinehart & Winston, 1969.

Ward, V. S. *Educating the gifted: An axiomatic approach*. Columbus, Ohio: Charles E. Merrill, 1961.

Ward, V. S. *The gifted student: A manual for program improvement*. Southern Regional Education Board, 1962.

Warren, J. R., & Heist, P. A. Personality attributes of gifted college students. *Science,* 1960, 132, 330–337.

Washburne, C. W. The attainments of gifted children under individual instruction. In G. M. Whipple (Ed.), *The education of gifted children,* The Twenty-third Yearbook of the National Society for the Study of Education, Part I. Bloomington, Ill.: Public School Publishing Co., 1924. Pp. 247–261.

Watley, D. J. Career or marriage?: A longitudinal study of able young women. *National Merit Scholarship Corporation Research Reports,* 1969, 5 (Whole No. 7).

Werts, C. E. The many faces of intelligence. *Journal of Educational Psychology,* 1967, 58, 198–204.

Whipple, G. M. A partial bibliography on gifted children and their education. In G. M. Whipple, *Classes for gifted children.* Bloomington, Ill.: Public School Publishing Co., 1919. Pp. 148–151.

White, K., & Owen, D. Locus of evaluation for classroom work and the development of creative potential. *Psychology in the Schools,* 1970, 7, 292–295.

White House Conference on Child Health and Protection, Report of the Committee on Special Classes. Gifted children. In *Special education: The handicapped and the gifted. Education and training.* Section III. New York: Century, 1931. Pp. 537–550.

Williams, D. E. Bibliography on the gifted and special classes. In D. E. Williams, *The gifted child and the special class.* Unpublished master's thesis, Ohio State University, 1925. Pp. 124–249.

Wilson, F. T. Preparation—for teachers of gifted children in the United States. *Exceptional Children,* 1953, 20, 78–80.

Wilson, F. T. The preparation of teachers for the education of gifted children. In N. B. Henry (Ed.), *Education for the gifted,* The Fifty-seventh Yearbook of the National Society for the Study of Education, Part II. Chicago: NSSE, 1958. Pp. 362–376.

Witty, P. A., & DeBoer, D. L. A selected bibliography of studies and research on the gifted and on the creative individual. *Education,* 1962, 82, 496–499.

Wodtke, K. H., & Wallen, N. E. The effects of teacher control in the classroom on pupils' creativity-test gains. *American Educational Research Journal,* 1965, 2, 75–82.

Wolfle, D. Diversity of talent. *American Psychologist,* 1960, 15, 535–545.

Wolfle, D. L. (Ed.) *The discovery of talent.* Cambridge, Mass.: Harvard University Press, 1969.

Woods, E. L. The mentally gifted. *Review of Educational Research,* 1944, 14, 224–230.

Worcester, D. A. *The education of children of above-average mentality.* Lincoln, Neb.: University of Nebraska Press, 1956.

Yamamoto, K. Role of creative thinking and intelligence in high school achievement. *Psychological Reports,* 1964, 14, 783–789. (a)

Yamamoto, K. Threshold of intelligence in academic achievement of highly creative students. *Journal of Experimental Education,* 1964, 32, 401–405. (b)

Yamamoto, K. Multiple achievement battery and repeated measurements: A postscript to three studies on creative thinking. *Psychological Reports,* 1965, 16, 367–375.

Ziehl, D. C. *An evaluation of an elementary school enriched instructional program.* (Doctoral dissertation, State University of New York at Buffalo) Ann Arbor, Mich.: University Microfilms, 1962. No. 62–4644.

CHAPTER 23 Stage Transition in Moral Development

ELLIOT TURIEL
Harvard University

In this chapter I will discuss a body of recent theory and research on the development of moral thought and action. Several reviews and critiques covering the major psychological theories of moral development have appeared recently (e.g., Hoffman, 1970; Kohlberg, 1964; Maccoby, 1968; Zigler & Child, 1969). It is not my intent to provide another overview or evaluation of this work. Instead, I will consider moral development primarily from one theoretical viewpoint—the *structural-developmental* perspective. This approach stems from the work of a number of researchers in the areas of cognitive development (Kaplan, 1966; Langer, 1969b; Piaget, 1950, 1970a, 1970b; Piaget & Inhelder, 1969; Werner, 1948) and social development (Kohlberg, 1963, 1969; Kohlberg & Turiel, 1971; Turiel, 1969) who subscribe to similar conceptions of human development.

Basic to this framework are the following propositions: 1) development refers to the individual's progress through a series of organized structures of thought and action, which 2) are transformed in an ordered way in ontogenesis through 3) interaction with the social and physical environment,

and 4) that the process of developmental advance is self-constructed and self-regulated. A structural-developmental approach to the study of moral thought and action implies that such development takes place through a universal sequence of stages which represent forms of thinking and interacting with the environment. Such stages define the ways in which the child actively organizes his own experiences and it is out of efforts at active organization of experience that stage change occurs.

I have said that it is not my intent to review moral development research. It is also not my intent to review research stemming from the structural-developmental perspective, inasmuch as a comprehensive review of moral development theory and its implications for moral education (Kohlberg & Turiel, 1971) has recently appeared. This chapter will focus, in some depth, upon the process of change in moral development. This will include a consideration of both the individual's way of interacting with his social environment and what we mean by the self-constructed and self-regulated nature of development. However, first it is necessary to describe briefly the research on stages of moral development that provides the starting point for a consideration of the theoretical and experimental work regarding the child's transition from one stage to the next.

STAGES OF MORAL DEVELOPMENT

Our view of the child's growth is termed *structural-developmental* because it rests on an analysis of the organization of thought and action and the transformations these undergo in the process of development. Present knowledge of such transformations in children's thinking about moral values stems mainly from the work of Kohlberg (1958, 1963, 1969). He began his investigations by interviewing children and adolescents between the ages of 10 and 16. The procedure involved the presentation of several moral conflicts (in story form) and extensive questioning about these conflicts. (An example of such moral conflicts is the case of a man who must choose between breaking into a drugstore to obtain medication that he cannot afford for his wife or letting his wife die.) This work was then extended into longitudinal study (which included interviewing adults). Kohlberg's findings showed that children's thinking about right and wrong and their ways of making moral decisions form organized patterns. His studies indicated that children generate their values and conceptions out of their own active efforts to understand the world around them and organize their social experiences. Furthermore, the data showed that with increasing age the organization of moral thinking undergoes ordered step-by-step transformations. These investigations resulted in the formulation of a sequence of stages of moral development hypothesized to be universal. Table 1 presents a summary of the stages.

As can be seen in Table 1, the developmental progression that emerged from Kohlberg's analysis proceeds from an initial preconventional level through a conventional level to a principled level. In moving

TABLE 1

DEFINITIONS OF STAGES OF MORAL DEVELOPMENT

I. Preconventional Level.

At this level the child is responsive to cultural rules and labels of good and bad, right and wrong, but interprets these labels in terms either of the physical or the hedonistic consequences of action (punishment, reward, exchange of favors), or in terms of the physical power of those who enunciate the rules and labels. The level is divided into the following two stages:

Stage 1: *The punishment and obedience orientation.* The physical consequences of action determine its goodness or badness regardless of the human meaning or value of these consequences. Avoidance of punishment and unquestioning deference to power are valued in their own right, not in terms of respect for an underlying moral order supported by punishment and authority (the latter being Stage 4).

Stage 2: *The instrumental relativist orientation.* Right action consists of that which instrumentally satisfies one's own needs and occasionally the needs of others. Human relations are viewed in terms like those of the market place. Elements of fairness, of reciprocity and equal sharing are present, but they are always interpreted in a physical, pragmatic way. Reciprocity is a matter of "you scratch my back and I'll scratch yours," not of loyalty, gratitude or justice.

II. Conventional Level.

At this level maintaining the expectations of the individual's family, group or nation is perceived as valuable in its own right regardless of immediate and obvious consequences. The attitude is not only one of *conformity* to personal expectations and social order, but of loyalty to it, of actively *maintaining,* supporting and justifying the order and of identifying with the persons or group involved in it. At this level there are the following two stages:

Stage 3: *The interpersonal concordance or "good boy—nice girl" orientation.* Good behavior is that which pleases or helps others and is approved by them. There is much conformity to stereotypical images of what is majority or "natural" behavior. Behavior is frequently judged by intention—"he means well" becomes important for the first time. One earns approval by being "nice."

Stage 4: *Authority and social order maintaining orientation.* There is orientation toward authority, fixed rules and the maintenance of the social order. Right behavior consists of doing one's duty, showing respect for authority and

TABLE 1 (Continued)

DEFINITIONS OF STAGES OF
MORAL DEVELOPMENT

maintaining the given social order for its own sake.

III. Postconventional, Autonomous, or Principled Level.

At this level there is a clear effort to define moral values and principles which have validity and application apart from the authority of the groups or persons holding these principles and apart from the individual's own identification with these groups. This level again has two stages:

Stage 5: *The social-contract legalistic orientation.* Generally with utilitarian overtones. Right action tends to be defined in terms of general individual rights and in terms of standards which have been critically examined and agreed upon by the whole society. There is a clear awareness of the relativism of personal values and opinions and a corresponding emphasis upon procedural rules for reaching consensus. Aside from what is constitutionally and democratically agreed upon, the right is a matter of personal values and opinions. The result is an emphasis upon the legal point of view, but with an emphasis upon the possibility of changing law in terms of rational considerations of social utility (rather than freezing it in terms of Stage 4 law and order). Outside of the legal realm, free agreement and contract are the binding elements of obligation. This is the "official" morality of the American government and Constitution.

Stage 6: *The universal ethical principle orientation.* Right is defined by the decision of conscience in accord with self-chosen *ethical principles* appealing to logical comprehensiveness, universality and consistency. These principles are abstract and ethical (the Golden Rule, the categorical imperative); they are not concrete moral rules like the Ten Commandments. At heart these are universal principles of *justice* of the *reciprocity* and *equality* of the human *rights* and of respect for the dignity of human beings as *individual persons*.

through the stages, the child's moral judgments become increasingly differentiated and integrated. At the first stage, morality is defined on the basis of the consequences of actions; moral value is undifferentiated from the value of material objects or from the power to implement rules (see Kohlberg, 1963, for examples of moral judgments

made by children at these stages). At stage 2 there is differentiation of power, material value, etc., from the needs and wants of the self (and to a limited extent other individuals), but moral value is undifferentiated from individual desire or need. At stage 3 a consideration of the welfare of others and conventional role-expectations begin to appear. There is a differentiation of needs and desires from a globally defined "good person" role (based on the approval and disapproval which stem from adherence to—or violation of—conventional expectations). At stage 4 moral judgment is articulated into a concern for, and an understanding of, rules, authority and the social organizations that govern human relations. However, at this stage commitment to the institutional order (a commitment to custom and law for their own sake) is undifferentiated from the principles of universal rights, which can be defined independently of any given social order. At the most advanced level, that of principled morality, there emerges a differentiation of universal moral principles from the rules and conventions of a particular social order. At this level (stages 5 and 6), moral judgment is characterized by an understanding of (and commitment to) values having universal, prescriptive applicability (principles that are not limited to any particular social order), and a differentiation between these principles and values that are specific to a given social order. Therefore, change to this highest level includes a recognition of the arbitrary nature of conventional values in conjunction with greater understanding of the universality of moral principles. (For more detailed descriptions of these stages and their interrelationships, see Kohlberg, 1971, and Kohlberg & Turiel, in press.)

Experimental (Rest, Turiel, & Kohlberg, 1969; Turiel, 1966, 1969) and longitudinal (Kohlberg & Kramer, 1969; Kramer, 1968) research have demonstrated that the stages form a developmentally invariant sequence in which each stage is a reorganization of the previous stage. Development, therefore, does not represent an increasing knowledge of cultural values; rather, it represents the transformations that occur in the child's form of thought and action. As representing organized structures of thought, the stages describe *how* moral judgments are made and moral values defined. In contrast, a child's knowledge of the values of his culture or society does not, in itself, provide us with an understanding of how he reasons in moral situations, how he makes and acts upon moral decisions, or how he is going to develop.

Studies have been done which assess the child's moral thought by means of tests presumed to measure degree of knowledge of cultural values. "Moral knowledge" tests of this sort generally contain items concerning lying, stealing, cheating, maintaining promises, etc. Such tests present statements describing a transgression and the child is required to rate (for example, on a five-point scale) the degree of wrongness of the act. A number of studies using these tests have shown that a child's knowledge or awareness of the values espoused by his social environment does not reflect the means by which he makes moral decisions nor does it help to predict his actions. For example, studies of "moral character" (Hartshorne & May, 1928–1930; Jones, 1936) have shown that scores on moral knowledge tests do not predict behavior in experimental situations that provide the child with an opportunity to cheat.

In a recent study (Turiel, in press), we have also demonstrated that such tests do not assess a developmentally meaningful dimension. A moral knowledge test was administered to a group of boys and girls ranging in age from 10 to 16 years. Our results were initially somewhat surprising in that the test scores decreased with age. It turned out that, on the average, 10-year-olds obtained higher scores than 13-year-olds, who in turn obtained higher scores than 16-year-olds. High scores on these tests are achieved by the time children reach first grade, which indicates that they are rela-

tively aware of the moral cliches of their culture at an early age. The decrease in test scores we observed after age 10 does not mean, however, that these children forgot what they once knew about societal values. Rather, the items on the tests do not reflect the way in which moral judgment matures. The test scores decreased because as children grow older they think about the same issues in a different way. The moral judgment interview was also administered in this study, and we found that the stage of moral development increased with age. Considering these two findings from the same individuals—decrease in moral knowledge scores and increase in stage level—it becomes clear that with developmental changes in the *structure* or organization of the child's thought, he interprets the *content* of his social environment in new ways.

Although the content of values may vary from culture to culture, an understanding of how the child interacts or deals with his social environment cannot be based on his knowledge of the culture, but requires analysis of his developing moral judgment. Conceptualizing development in structural terms implies that the stages of development would be found in all cultures. Studies conducted in various cultures have empirically substantiated this proposition (Kohlberg, 1969; Turiel, Kohlberg, & Edwards, in press). We have interviewed children and adults from a Malaysian aboriginal village, a Turkish city and village, a Mexican city and a Mayan Indian village. In addition, some longitudinal work has been done with the children in the Turkish village. The basic finding from all of these investigations has been that the children progress through the same stages in the same invariant sequence no matter from which culture they come. These studies demonstrate, therefore, that there exists a universal sequence in the development of basic moral values.

Nevertheless, there are systematic differences among cultures. We found that these were only variations in developmental pace. Generally, the rate of development was slower among rural children than city children. For example, children in Mexican and American cities move somewhat more quickly through the stages than village children in Turkey or Mexico. Yet, we should not interpret this to mean that environments can be classified homogeneously as determinants of developmental rate, for similar systematic differences have also been observed within the same society. Recent data (Turiel, in press) have shown that although both boys and girls develop through the same sequence of stages, they sometimes do so at varying rates. In one type of school, which might be characterized as a "traditional" upper-middle-class private school, from age 13 on, boys progressed at a faster rate than girls. In another type of school which might be characterized as a "progressive" upper-middle-class school, no differences in rate of development were observed.

To understand both the universality of structures and the systematic variations in developmental rate requires consideration of how change from stage to stage occurs. This first entails a discussion and explanation of the nature of the individual's interaction with the environment.

INTERACTION WITH THE SOCIAL ENVIRONMENT

A conception of development as involving basic universal forms of thought and an invariant sequence of stages implies that moral values and judgments derive from the child's active attempts to organize social experience. Each stage represents a construction not originating in the social world but generated out of actions in that social world. Piaget (1970a) formulates this principle as follows: "Knowledge, at its origin, neither arises from objects nor from the subject, but from interactions...between the subject and those objects" (p. 704).

In positing universality, our position comes into direct contrast with many psychological and sociological explanations of

morality. In relativistic conceptions the relation of the individual to the social environment is assumed to be one in which the individual derives his moral values or judgments directly from the culture. For example, Durkheim (1961) proposed that moral development involves the acquisition, initially through group sanctions, of respect for the rules and institutions of society. Freud (1930, 1960), too, believed that the individual's morality (in the form of a superego) originates in society. Freud explained moral behavior as resulting from the clash of biological needs with societal demands which occurs during early life. Behavioristic or associationistic psychology (e.g., Aronfreed, 1968; Eysenck, 1960) theorizes that the social environment is the predominant force which shapes a malleable individual in accordance with its own patterns.

The social learning theorists (Bandura, 1969; Berkowitz, 1964; Maccoby, 1968) provide a contemporary formulation of the behavioristic approach to moral development. Their view that development is a process of learning or internalizing values through imitation, identification and conditioning can be seen in the following definition:

> moral behavior is behavior a social group defines as good or right and for which the social group administers sanctions. Moral values are beliefs, again shared in a social group, about what is good or right (Maccoby, 1968, p. 229).

The findings from our cross-cultural investigations of moral development do not support the proposition that moral values are acquired through the internalization of cultural content. If morality were a direct reflection of the specific values of a culture, we would expect to find a) more homogeneity within cultures rather than age-related sequential changes and b) greater dissimilarity among cultures rather than the same sequence of stages. Thus, our findings affirm the structural-developmental notion that the individual's active organization of experience determines the existing form of moral thought as well as any subsequent changes.

The problem, then, is to explicate the process by which interaction with the environment results in transformations in form of thought. Since we have said that internalization does not explain how change occurs, and yet stating that the individual is an active agent in his mental development, the problem is one of explaining constructions. The theoretical position here is based on the hypothesis that development is a process of self-regulated "progressive equilibration" (cf. Langer, 1969a; Piaget, 1967, 1970b; Turiel, 1969). This principle is an integral component of stage theory in that a stage describes the form of the individual's interaction with his environment, while interaction, in turn, is the source of progressive transformations in stage. We are hypothesizing that moral stage development is continually directed toward increasing equilibrium.

There are two interrelated aspects to the principle of equilibration. The first refers to equilibrium within structures that form coherent wholes: stages are defined as organized ways of thinking and relating to events. The second refers to equilibrium in the interaction of the individual with the environment. Stages in a developmental sequence are, then, successive levels of equilibrium in two respects. First, each stage is a more equilibrated form than the previous ones (e.g., there is more internal consistency). Second, each stage represents a more equilibrated means of interacting with the environment. That is, each new stage is a more adequate way of understanding moral problems and resolving the conflicts encountered.

The ideal equilibrium is not passive adjustment or conformity to external demands. Nor is the term equilibrium being used in the static sense of the organism acting to attain a state of rest, a decrease of discomfort or a balance of forces. In contrast, from a structural-developmental perspective, increases in disequilibrium are viewed as the conditions for development. That is, if the individual's existing structure is inadequate to deal with events encountered, the resulting state of heightened disequilibrium (manifested in conflict and confusion) could lead to compensatory activity. In such a case the feedback of new information could result in transition to a new stage.

The characteristics of disequilibrium in the process of transition from one stage of moral development to the next form the main focus in the remainder of this chapter. Disequilibrium may originate from several sources. We have seen that there exist systematic differences in rate of development from culture to culture. This suggests that the structure of social environments in which we found faster rates of development contain more conflicts and discrepancies. This points to the structure of the social environment itself as one important source of disequilibrium and indicates that social environments differ in the extent to which they stimulate development. We have also seen that among students in one traditional private school, the rate of progress tended to be slower for girls than for boys. It is likely that differential treatment resulted in boys having more experiences of structural disequilibrium than did girls. Within the same social environment, therefore, conflict between the individual's own structure and his experiences is another major source of disequilibrium.

There is a third source of disequilibrium we have observed. While stages have been defined as unitary wholes, it is almost always the case that children and adolescents use more than one stage in making moral judgments. Typically they show predominant usage of one stage and some usage of the adjoining stages. Such "stage mixture" represents structural inconsistencies which exist within the individual. We have determined (Turiel, 1969) that stage mixture affects the rate of developmental change;

periods of greater mixture are characterized by faster development. Thus, the conflicts inherent in structural mixture are a potential source of disequilibrium and, consequently, development.

Although the nature of the interrelations between these three sources of disequilibrium has not yet been adequately explored, stage transformations are affected by all three. The principles of equilibration outlined in this section can be made more concrete through examples from research focused on this process. Three types of studies will be considered: a) experimental and educational programs designed to stimulate developmental progress; b) the investigation of a transition between two specific stages of moral development; c) experiments concerning the relationship between moral reasoning and action.

STIMULATION OF DEVELOPMENTAL CHANGE

Earlier I discussed the theoretical differences between universalistic and relativistic conceptions of morality and pointed to distinctions between constructivist and internalization conceptions of development. In considering any given study on the stimulation of change, it is important to look at the way these conceptions have been combined.

Various combinations can be observed in the research discussed. One type of study has combined a nonstage but vaguely defined notion of universal moral maturity (in the form of character traits) with the view that morality is learned from others. A second type has combined internalization with a relativistic conception of morality. In still a third type, acceptance of the developmental notion of universal stages has been combined with the idea that the stages can be taught directly. In such a case, stages of moral development are seen as valid, and the attainment of the higher stages by large numbers of people is seen as desirable both from the point of view of the individual and

of society. It is thereby assumed that children can and should be taught the principles of the highest stages as soon as possible. This combination is inconsistent with the one we have proposed and with our research evidence, which demonstrates that an individual cannot be taught any stage directly because he must generate its principles himself. Our theoretical position combines universalism with a constructivist, equilibration view of development.

Educators and psychologists who assume that the form of morality (however defined) is acquired through direct instruction have implemented research designed to teach morality. Several programs of moral education (e.g., Hartshorne & May, 1928–1930; Jones, 1936) combine internalization with a loosely defined idea of desirable moral values. The goal of such programs is to improve the child's "character," which is seen as consisting of a set of traits and values. Although educators involved in such efforts do not always agree as to which specific traits are desirable (Kohlberg & Turiel, 1971), it is assumed that traits and values can be inculcated by providing proper examples, by giving children opportunities for practicing these traits and by rewarding and praising them for the expression of such traits.

However, the experimental programs designed to improve character have met with little success in changing children's moral behavior. An elaborate study undertaken by Jones (1936) can be seen as paradigmatic of both the methods utilized and the results obtained by character education programs. In this study more than 200 children from three seventh-grade and three eighth-grade classes were given instructions one and one-half hours per week during a nine and one-half month academic year. The training was implemented through a curriculum designed to provide instruction on a variety of rules, values, manners and virtues. Three teaching methods were employed. In the first, the children had firsthand experience in concrete situations, in the second only discussion of the situations was included, and in the third, firsthand experience was combined with discussion.

All of the children involved in the training, as well as a control group of children who received no training, were tested at the beginning and at the end of the year. These assessments included several tests of moral behavior, such as tests of honesty and cooperation, as well as a test of moral knowledge. The purpose of administering these tests was, of course, to determine the effect of the program on "character." It was found that the program had no appreciable effect on the honesty, cooperation or moral knowledge of the children who participated. The only method that proved to show any effect at all was the combination of firsthand experience with discussion. However, the effects of this method were extremely small, short-term gains that were not maintained over time. Teachers' inability to transmit to children a fixed set of values and character traits, as demonstrated by the Jones study, is quite consistent with other similar efforts (Hartshorne & May, 1928–1930).

An example of research that combines relativism with the assumption that moral values are acquired through direct instruction is provided by those psychologists (e.g., Bandura & Walters, 1963; Sears, Maccoby, & Levin, 1957) who define moral development as social learning. While in the programs of moral education just discussed it was generally assumed that mature moral values could be identified, social learning theorists have rejected this notion. Instead, they have proposed that morality is nothing but the values and traits that children happen to be taught by socializing agents such as parents and teachers. Experimental studies which derive from the social learning perspective have been undertaken, therefore, to a) demonstrate that children can be taught any form of value by adults and b) discover which methods provide for the most efficient learning. An illustrative example of an experiment designed to achieve

both of these aims is a study by Bandura and McDonald (1963). The purposes of the experiment performed by Bandura and McDonald were to a) demonstrate that children learn their moral judgments by observing others and imitating them, and to b) show that empirically observed stages of moral development represent, not a natural sequence, but a sequence determined by the way children are taught.

In their experiment, Bandura and McDonald used stages based on Piaget's (1932) preliminary studies of children's moral judgments. In that work Piaget proposed that a *heteronomous* stage of moral judgment is followed by a stage of *autonomous* moral judgment. While Piaget's stages were defined by several dimensions of judgment, Bandura and McDonald worked with only one (cf. Turiel, 1966). The dimension used was that of judging moral acts on the basis of consequences or intentions. Piaget had proposed that at the lower stages children judge the wrongness of an act on the basis of the amount of physical damage incurred (labeled "objective responsibility"), while at the higher stage children judge on the basis of the individual's intentionality (labeled "subjective responsibility").

Following assessment procedures developed by Piaget (1932), Bandura and McDonald first pretested children between the ages of five and eleven to distinguish between those judging on the basis of consequences and those judging on the basis of intentions. The children were tested on several pairs of stories. In each pair, one story always concerned an accidental or well-intentioned act that resulted in a large amount of material damage, while the other concerned an intentionally "naughty" or disobedient act that resulted in a small amount of damage. On the basis of responses to these stories, the children's judgments were categorized as objective (lower stage) or subjective (higher stage). Because it was generally the case that children did not judge solely on one basis or the other, they were categorized according to their most dominant mode of responding. Subsequent to the pretest an attempt was made to teach each child to judge on the basis of the orientation opposite to his dominant one. That is, children initially judging on the basis of consequences were given training on intentions, while children initially judging on the basis of intentions were given training on consequences. The training involved a short experimental session in which the child and an adult model alternately judged pairs of stories. The adult model always expressed judgments that were in opposition to the child's pretest orientation, and the experimenter always expressed approval of the model's judgments.

The effect of these training sessions was determined by assessing how much the child used the orientation opposite to his initial dominant orientation. Responses made during the training session as well as on the posttest immediately following the training were assessed. Bandura and McDonald report changes of a limited amount in both directions: a) children whose initial moral judgments were predominantly on the basis of intentions showed some increase in responses based on consequences, and b) children who initially judged on the basis of consequences increased in their responses based on intentions. While the increase in responses based on consequences was of the same magnitude during the training session and on the posttest, the increase in responses based on intentions diminished from the training session to the posttest.

Although a certain amount of immediate change was presumably induced by this procedure, the meaning of these results is ambiguous. First, it is uncertain whether the reported changes represent changes in mode of judging or changes in choices on the story pairs. Second, there is uncertainty as to the stability of the effects obtained (Turiel, 1966). In an effort to answer some of these questions, the Bandura and McDonald study was replicated (Cowan, Langer, Heavenrich & Nathanson, 1969) in more careful fashion.

Three aspects of the replication study are of interest. First, it was found that the amount of stable changes in children's mode of judging was relatively small. Second, changes in the direction of the higher stage were more stable over time than changes to the lower stage. Third, and most important, it was found that, in general, children's responses after the training were quite difficult to categorize (cf. Langer, in press). The findings of another similar study (Crowley, 1968), using Piaget's stages of moral judgment, were quite consistent with the results of Cowan et al. (1969). Again, children's responses after training were difficult to categorize, the meaning of the measured changes for the child's thinking was quite ambiguous, and the amount of change observed was relatively small.

No positive evidence that children's morality develops through internalization has been provided by studies undertaken from either the character education or social learning perspectives. Both approaches begin with the conception that the process of acquiring moral values is one of internalizing the values of the culture as transmitted by the school, teachers or parents. This view has led to laboratory and classroom experiments in which children are provided with examples to emulate and given approval for the expression of certain values and traits. In regard to the character education studies, it is clear that no changes in verbal and behavioral measures were effected by participation in the classes. In regard to social learning studies, the effects of experimental training were generally small, the significance of training for stable changes in the way the child thinks and acts is quite ambiguous, and results from study to study are inconsistent.

It is important that research into processes of developmental change be based on developmentally meaningful measures of the child's moral values. Both the character education studies and the social learning experiments we have described began with inadequate methods of assessing the child's initial state. Character education programs, such as the Jones study, have been carried out with no theoretical framework underlying the assessment of what was vaguely termed "character." It has been shown (Hartshorne & May, 1928–1930; Kohlberg, 1969) that the types of tests used by Jones for assessing honesty or cooperation are poor measures in that a) there is a low correlation among such tests in different situations, b) there is little individual consistency in performance on these tests, and c) there is a low correlation between performance on these tests and verbal measures of the values of honesty and cooperation. We have already demonstrated that the other measure used by Jones, the "moral knowledge test," is also not a valid means of assessing development.

In studies dealing with stage change two considerations are of importance. First, to be valid the stages used must meet theoretical and empirical criteria. Second, adequate methods must be used to assess the child's stage. Experiments like that of Bandura and McDonald (1963) are subject to criticism on both of these grounds. One reason for the ambiguous results from such studies is that they are based on stages formulated by Piaget after only very preliminary investigation. While Piaget greatly extended and systematized his earlier work on stages of cognitive development (Inhelder & Piaget, 1958, 1964; Piaget, 1952, 1970a, 1970b; Piaget & Inhelder, 1969), he did not further pursue or elaborate his work on moral development. Kohlberg (1963, 1964, 1969) has, on the one hand, pointed to the theoretical and empirical inadequacies of Piaget's moral judgment stages and, on the other hand, has provided a more adequate description of stages of moral development. In fact, Piaget's stages of moral development do not meet his own criteria (1954) for a developmental stage sequence, while Kohlberg's stages, which we detailed earlier, do meet these criteria (cf. Kohlberg & Turiel, in press). In studies like that of Bandura and McDonald (1963), this prob-

lem has been further compounded by the fact that only one dimension of Piaget's stage descriptions—objective and subjective responsibility—has been taken to represent the entire definition and only one method of assessing development along this dimension has been used.

In such experiments it has consistently been shown that judging the wrongness of an act in terms of consequences or intentions on the Piaget story pairs is age-related. Although this dimension is age-related in a general sense, it does not define a sequence of stages as there is no clear age shift from consequences to intentions across all situations. In some contexts judgments are based on intentionality by the age of 5 or 6, in other contexts intentionality is not applied until the age of 8 or 9, and in still other situations the use of intentionality in moral judgments increases between the ages of 10 and 14 (studies reviewed in Kohlberg & Turiel, in press).

The situational inconsistency of this dimension indicates that studies of the stimulation of developmental change using only one type of situation to assess children's initial stages can produce misleading results. This was clearly demonstrated in a study by Lickona (1971). In Lickona's study two types of stories were used to measure first-grade children's judgments on the dimension of consequences and intentions. The first set of stories was similar to the ones used by Bandura and McDonald (a well-intentioned act resulting in a large amount of material damage compared with an intentionally naughty act resulting in a small amount of damage). On the pretest, children who showed a majority (80–90 percent) of responses based on consequences were retained for an experimental training session. Using similar stories in the experimental training, different types of training conditions resulted in significant increases in responses based on intentionality. The most successful condition (increase to 80 percent or 90 percent intentionality responses) was one in which children were directly presented with judgments based on intentionality and told that they constituted the correct answer. These findings may be taken to mean that stage change was induced. However, other findings from this study demonstrate that this was not the case. All the children had also been pretested on a second set of story pairs, in which a non-intended deviation from the truth resulting in large negative consequences was contrasted with an intentional lie resulting in minor negative consequences. It turned out that on these pretest stories children responded on the basis of intentions 50 percent to 60 percent of the time. Therefore, the increase produced by the training did not constitute learning of a concept, but rather it reflected the extension of a concept they had already internalized. If only the first type of story had been used in the pretest (which was the case in the Bandura & McDonald, 1963; Cowan et al., 1969; and Crowley, 1968, studies), we would have been misled to believe that the training resulted in attainment of a new concept.

This study, along with the others reviewed thus far, demonstrates how important it is to begin with adequate conceptions of the way children develop and to use appropriate methods of assessing the child's level prior to experimental training. Further, none of these studies indicates that children develop morality through direct inculcation of virtues, social rules and values or social concepts. Both for theoretical and empirical reasons it is not surprising to us that no significant changes were produced as a result of direct teaching. Utilizing the stages of moral development formulated by Kohlberg which meet the necessary theoretical and empirical criteria, we have conducted a series of experiments on developmental change. These studies have demonstrated that a child's stage and the direction of his natural development place important limits on the type of change that can be stimulated. Several principles have emerged. First, an individual moves through the stages in a stepwise sequential fashion so that no

stage can be skipped. Second, there is a natural developmental progression. And third, a stage is not learned but constructed by the individual himself.

Before we elaborate on these principles and discuss experiments on the stimulation of development, it would be useful to consider some experiments concerning the comprehension of moral judgment statements that correspond to the stages above and below the child's own (Rest, 1968; Rest, Turiel, & Kohlberg, 1969). In these studies, each child was first interviewed individually in order to determine his stage of moral judgment. Generally, a child's responses to the interview questions were predominantly at one stage, with some usage of the adjoining stages. Then the child was presented with a series of statements representing each of the six stages. This was done in the context of providing possible answers for moral dilemmas. The child was asked a) to put into his own words the moral reasoning reflected by each of the statements, and b) to rate the adequacy of the statements as solutions for the moral conflict (i.e., to select which statement he thought "best," which he thought "smartest," etc.).

We found that all of the children were able to represent correctly all the statements at their own dominant stage and at the stages below. Most of the children, however, had difficulty in comprehending reasoning at the stages above their own. Some children were able to comprehend statements at the stage directly above their dominant stage. These were the ones who had shown a substantial amount of usage of that stage on the pretest and thus were already moving toward that next higher stage. Almost none of the children were able to comprehend statements at two or more stages above their dominant stage. Interestingly, however, although these children were unable to comprehend stages above their own, when asked to judge which statements were better, they repeatedly and emphatically preferred the higher stages to their own stage and the stages below. For the most part they stated that the reasoning at stages below their own was inadequate—an evaluation which they made from their own stage perspective.

These findings demonstrate the ways in which the child's natural direction of development and the limits set by his own stage will affect the changes that may be induced. We have found that statements at stages below a child's own stage are rejected as inadequate ways of making moral judgments, which suggests that any attempts to teach a child the principles of those stages would be ineffective. The inability shown by these children even to comprehend the reasoning of stages above also suggests that transformations in their own thinking are not likely to be induced by direct transmission of the principles of more advanced stages. This is precisely what we had found in an earlier experiment in which we studied the effects of presenting children with reasoning at stages other than their own (Turiel, 1966). In that study, too, we began by carefully assessing the stage level of seventh-grade boys by obtaining their responses to some of the hypothetical dilemmas in the moral judgment interview we described earlier. These children were assigned either to one of three experimental groups or to a control group. All of the children (with the exception of those in the control group) then role-played and discussed additional moral judgment stories with the experimenter. In this context, the experimenter first presented reasoning supporting one alternative in the dilemma (e.g., the husband should steal the drug) and then presented reasoning supporting the other alternative (e.g., the husband should not steal the drug). For one of the groups, the experimenter utilized moral reasoning one stage above the child's dominant stage. For a second group, the moral reasoning was two stages above the child's own. And for the third group, the reasoning was one stage *below* the child's own. All the children were reinterviewed a week later in order to determine the amount of change resulting from exposure to reasoning at a stage other than their own.

The results of the posttest interviews showed that insofar as any changes were induced by our experimental procedures, it was only a very small amount of progress to the stage one above on the part of the children exposed to that stage. It should be pointed out, however, that most of the increase in usage of the stage above was in response to the same stories that had been used to present the stage above reasoning. Children exposed to the stage below showed no change in the direction of that stage nor any progressive change. Those exposed to reasoning two stages above their own did not show any increase in usage of either that stage or the stage one above.

In these studies it was possible to stimulate very little change toward the next developmental stage and none at all to any more advanced stages. It may be argued, however, that such a small change was observed only because the exposure to new reasoning during the experimental sessions was of a rather short duration. Therefore, before discussing the theoretical significance of these findings, we will report another study (Blatt & Kohlberg, in press) obtaining similar results, a study in which children were presented with moral discussions for a much longer period of time. In that study, 11 twelve-year-old children in a Sunday school class were first pretested. The pretest interviews showed that initially the dominant stages of children in the class ranged from stage 2 to stage 4. The program consisted of discussions of moral conflict stories (different from those used in the pretest) one hour a week for a total of twelve weeks. During these sessions the children in the class discussed and argued about the moral dilemmas among themselves and with the experimenter. In discussing the dilemmas among themselves, it generally turned out that children at different stages argued with each other. The experimenter entered the discussions by encouraging the children at the higher stage to explain why they thought the arguments at the lower stage were inadequate. The experimenter also supported and clarified the arguments which were one stage above the majority of the children. These procedures resulted in a good deal of discussion of moral dilemmas and much conflict between children arguing at adjacent stages. Furthermore, for the majority of children, these sessions provided exposure to statements and solutions of other children and an adult at stages above their own stage.

Upon completion of the 12-week program, the children were once again given a moral judgment interview in order to assess the effects of the discussions upon their stage of moral development. An interview was also administered one year following the completion of the program to assess its long-term effects. A comparison of stage scores from the first posttest interviews with scores from the pretest interviews showed that some changes in stage level were effected by the classroom discussions. Four of the children progressed a small amount in the direction of the stage above their initial stage while four of the other children advanced somewhat more than one stage. The remaining three children showed no advance at all. On the one-year follow-up posttest, however, it was also found that those children who initially showed only a small amount of change to the stage above retained their advantage while those who had shown more than a one-stage change were back at about the initial pretest stage. In other words, the only form of long-term stable change was in the few children who moved in very small steps within the sequence.

This program of classroom discussion was replicated in a later study (Blatt, 1969) with essentially the same results. In both classroom programs a fair amount of time was spent discussing the moral conflicts. Yet the amount of stage change observed was relatively small and only somewhat larger than the changes observed in our short-term experimental studies. The findings from all these studies are of interest for our theoretical understanding of developmental change. First, our findings demonstrate the importance of the child's own stage of development as the basis from which change occurs. As we have seen, the stage at which the child is functioning sets significant limits on what he can comprehend and the types of changes that can be stimulated. The influence of presenting moral judgments is, in large part, determined by the *relation* of the level of those judgments to the child's own stage of development. It seems to be the case that judgments or ideas at the stage directly above a child's own stage may have some influence on his moral thinking, while ideas that are further above seem to have little influence.

Secondly, our studies have demonstrated that the sequence of moral development stages cannot be altered. Progress through the stages occurs in step-by-step fashion, without the skipping of any stage. Even in the one case in which it appeared that some children had advanced more than one stage immediately after training (Blatt & Kohlberg, in press), a year later these children were behind those who had shown smaller advances. It is possible that attempts to accelerate development can be premature and thereby serve to slow it down.

Finally, our studies demonstrate that the stage sequence defines the natural direction of development. We have seen that the children in our studies never reverted to a stage through which they had already passed. When children encounter concepts that are less developmentally advanced than their own, they do not acquiesce, even if these concepts are presented by an adult. Rather, lower-stage reasoning is actively considered from the child's own more advanced perspective, and exposure to such reasoning does not, therefore, constitute a change-inducing experience. In fact, those studies which directly assessed children's reactions to less advanced concepts showed that differences between those concepts and their own way of thinking were perceived and that the less advanced thinking was rejected as inadequate. Under normal conditions, therefore, regressive transformations do not occur as change must be in accordance with the child's natural direction of development.

We have said that the presentation of moral judgments at the stage directly above a child's stage may facilitate some change toward that stage. This may be incorrectly interpreted as meaning that the child incorporates into his repertoire some judgments from that stage, while he fails to incorporate judgments further above because of their difficulty. As we have said, our evidence indicates that the child cannot be taught directly the principles of any stage, but must generate them himself. Children fail to be influenced by judgments either at the stage below their own or two stages above their own because the attainment of a new stage represents a reorganization of the previous stage. Indeed, there is some indication (cf. Turiel, 1969) from both the classroom discussion programs and the experimental studies that the process of stage change is best explained by the principles of self-generated equilibration we discussed earlier. Currently, we are further investigating the ways in which discussion of moral conflicts and presentation of judgments at the stage above influences the child's own thinking. We have begun to formulate explanations of the equilibration process as it applies to some specific transitions of the moral development stages. However, to further clarify the principles of equilibration, we will discuss some recent experiments on transition in stages of cognitive development before presenting specific details of equilibration in regard to moral development.

The research on cognitive development that is relevant to an understanding of stage transformations in the moral domain is largely based on Piaget's (e.g., Inhelder & Piaget, 1958, 1964) formulations. He has delineated a series of stages of cognitive development that may be outlined as follows: 1) infant sensorimotor activity, 2) preoperational thought, 3) intuitive thought, 4) concrete operations and 5) formal operations. These stages were derived from investigations of children's physical and logical concepts, such as the conservation of quantity and matter (Piaget, 1952) and the classification and seriation of objects (Inhelder & Piaget, 1964).

Recently there has been an increased concern with the question of how the child progresses through the stages of cognitive development. In order to explore this problem, a number of experiments have been performed which focus on teaching children concepts they have not yet attained. Several studies (e.g., Smedslund, 1961a, 1961b; Sigel & Hooper, 1968) have attempted to teach conservation of substance and number directly. A variety of training methods has been used, including the reinforcement of responses (Smedslund, 1961a, 1961b), direct verbal instruction on the strategies used in solving conservation problems (Wallach & Sprott, 1964; Wallach, Wall, & Anderson, 1967; Wohlwill & Lowe, 1962) and training in the linguistic terminology associated with the more advanced concepts (Inhelder & Sinclair, 1969; Sinclair, 1969). In all of these studies, little developmental change was effected by these methods. Similar to the findings from studies concerning the direct teaching of moral judgments, these experiments have indicated that direct training does not facilitate the child's cognitive development.

Additional experimental work, however, has shown that those principles we have outlined for transition in moral development also apply to transition in the cognitive domain. One such study (Kuhn, 1969) dealt with the development of children's logical classification activities. Children between four and eight years of age were pretested to assess their initial stage. Employing the paradigm from our own experiments, they were then exposed to models who solved classification problems at one of the following levels in relation to their initial stage: the stage one below, the same stage, the stage one above or the stage two above.

Kuhn's findings paralleled some of our own in the area of moral development: a small amount of change to the stage above was displayed by the children's observing a model who solved problems at the stage one above. The only other children showing change were a few of those exposed to a model's solutions at the stage two above, but that change was solely to the stage one above their own.

Essentially the same results were obtained through the use of different procedures in the training of conservation concepts (Inhelder, Bovet, Sinclair, & Smock, 1966; Inhelder & Sinclair, 1969). Some of the children participating in the experiment were at a stage in which the concept had not yet been attained (intuitive thought), while the rest of the children were somewhat more advanced and showed some use of the concept (an intermediate level between the intuitive and concrete operational stages). It was found that the effect of training depended upon the initial cognitive level of the child. The training procedures resulted in progress only for those children already at the intermediate level and for whom, therefore, the change was relatively small.

Experiments in which change in cognitive development has been induced suggest that in this realm, too, the principles of equilibration apply. In Smedslund's (1961c) series of studies on conservation a variety of training methods was tried, including direct teaching procedures and conditions of conflict. The only procedure that proved to be at all effective was one that Smedslund labeled "cognitive conflict." Stated simply, this means that in the experimental condition the child is presented with contradictions and inconsistencies that lead him to be aware of the inadequacy of his concepts for solving the task. Presumably the cognitive conflict induced may lead the child to compensate with transformations in his thought at a more advanced stage.

The experience of conflict or disequilibrium as a condition for developmental change is consistent with equilibration the-

ory. However, this notion requires clarification and extension. Disequilibrium within this theoretical context refers to a process that goes beyond experiences of conflict or uncertainty, per se. To illustrate this point we will consider a study (Langer, 1969b) of conflict in the development class inclusion. One of the procedures for investigating the development of the concept of class inclusion is the following (Inhelder & Piaget, 1964). The child is presented with 10 round beads—seven of these may be one color (red) while three are of another color (blue). To ascertain the child's level of conceptualization, he is asked to solve a problem such as whether a necklace made of all the round beads or one made of all the red beads would be longer. Prior to the stage of concrete operations the child will say that a necklace made of red beads would be longer. Only children who have reached concrete operational thinking say that the necklace made of round beads would be longer. For it is not until this stage that the child is able to differentiate between a class (whole) and its subclasses (parts) and to coordinate the two.

In order to more clearly assess the child's internal experience of conflict and to specify the type of conflict that may be related to equilibration, Langer experimented with an interesting procedure. The child was presented with 10 round beads (seven red and three blue) and was told to place "the round beads on one side of the table and the red beads on the other" (Langer, 1969a, p. 31). Of course, it is impossible to perform this task correctly because all the red beads are also round. What happens, however, when children are presented with this impossible situation? The answer depends on the child's stage of cognitive development. Some children do not perceive the task as a problem at all, while others who do perceive a problem may attempt to understand its source. In Langer's study almost all of the kindergarten and third-grade children did not perceive the problem. A majority of the fifth-grade children, on the other hand, did perceive that something was wrong and attempted to solve the problem by altering some aspect of the situation, such as pointing to the need for a change in the instructions or in the nature of the materials.

Children's reactions to this "impossible" task demonstrate that conflicts or discrepancies presented to a child are not necessarily experienced as such. If the conflicts presented are not related to the child's existing stage as well as to the emerging stage, they are unlikely to have an effect on him. In the case of the impossible task, only children who were already close to attaining the concept of class inclusion could perceive what was wrong in the instructions. The child's realization that the insolubility of the problem is related to his thinking about the problem can provide a necessary basis for change.

The studies on conservation referred to earlier (i.e., Inhelder et al., 1966; Inhelder & Sinclair, 1969) support Langer's findings on the effects of presenting conflict to the child. In these studies children were faced with discrepancies between their predictions and the observed outcomes. Again, the effect of presenting such discrepancies depended upon the initial level of the child. The majority of nonconserving children did not change at all. The few nonconservers who showed change moved only to the intermediate stage. A majority of children initially at the intermediate stage did change as a result of the experimental procedure.

We see once again that the conflict presented and inherent to the situation did not affect all who "experienced" it. The experience itself must be of a special sort. It must be conflict involving tension about the existing way of thinking as related to an awareness of ideas at the next level. Actions to resolve the conflict may then lead to reorganization of thought and a new equilibrium. This entire process, even though it can be instigated by external events, is ultimately internally controlled and self-regulated.

We have made this brief mention of research in cognitive development to clarify principles of equilibration as they have been elucidated by that type of work. The findings of experiments on stage change in cognitive development have paralleled our own experimental findings on moral development. Consequently, it seems plausible to relate knowledge of developmental principles generated by experiments in the cognitive domain to the moral domain. Currently we are engaged in further research on processes of transition from one stage of moral development to the next. In the section that follows we will further elaborate on how principles of equilibration apply to one specific transition.

AN ANALYSIS OF STAGE TRANSITION

In this section we will consider the characteristics of disequilibrium as they apply to the transition from conventional to principled morality. Our current investigations of the mechanisms of transition from each stage to the next higher stage have led us to formulations regarding the restructuring involved in the movement from stage 4 to stage 5.

Earlier we listed the six stages of moral development (Table 1, pp. 733–734) and provided a brief description of the differentiations made at each of these stages. While the differentiations we described for stages 4 and 5 provide a conception of the thinking characteristic of these two levels, we are still left with the problem of explaining the transition from one mode to the next. Our understanding of the change requires consideration of the structure of both stage 4 and stage 5 thinking. In addition, it is necessary to determine the relationship between these two structures—i.e., to explicate how stage 5 thinking stems from stage 4 thinking. Those individuals in the process of moving from one stage to the next provide the appropriate data for analysis and verification of transitional processes.

What we have already said about developmental change suggests that the transition from stage 4 to stage 5 involves a phase of conflict or disequilibrium in which responses would not be clearly classifiable at either stage 4 or stage 5. Indeed, such anomolous responses have been observed in some studies (Haan, Smith, & Block, 1968; Kohlberg & Kramer, 1969; Kramer, 1968) of moral judgments made during the late adolescent years. Most informative was a longitudinal study (Kramer, 1968) in which moral judgment interviews were administered to a number of individuals at three-year intervals from age 14 to age 27. In general, progression through the moral development stages occurred in the usual sequence. A number of the individuals displayed predominantly stage 4 thinking by the end of high school and maintained that form of judgment throughout college and young adulthood. Some of the others displayed predominantly stage 4 thinking when interviewed during late high school but made many moral judgments that could not be clearly specified at any of the stages when they were interviewed during the second or third year of college. Three years later their responses showed a clear predominance of stage 5 thinking.

Our concern is with the characteristics of the "anomolous" thinking shown by these college students during what was apparently a transitional phase from stage 4 to stage 5. These responses were not readily classified in accordance with the stages because they involved a great deal of inconsistency, vacillation and internal contradiction. The most characteristic aspect of the vacillation was a fluctuation between, on the one hand, a view that all moral values are arbitrary, relative to one's society, and determined by individual inclination, and, on the other hand, a strong commitment to moral positions on specific issues. They will argue with fervor that all values are relative and, with equal vehemence, will argue in very absolutistic terms about such issues as civil rights, the Vietnam war, etc.

One subject (as reported by Kohlberg, 1970) seemed to experience these contradic-tions consciously, saying that he "questioned the whole terminology, the whole moral bag." He went on to say, however, "but then I am also an incredible moralist, a real puritan in some senses and moods. My moral judgment and the way I perceive things morally changes very much when my mood changes. When I am in a cynical mood, I take a cynical view of morals, but still, whether I like it or not, I am terribly moral in the way I look at things. But I am not too comfortable with it."

Indeed, his response to one of our dilemmas reflects the same vacillation. In considering whether a man should steal a drug to save his wife's life, he stated, "There's a million ways to look at it. Heinz had a moral decision to make. Was it worse to steal or to let his wife die? In my mind, I can either condemn him or condone him. In this case I think it was fine. But possibly the druggist was working on a capitalist morality of supply and demand."

When asked whether it would be wrong for the husband not to steal the drug, he replied: "It depends on how he is oriented morally. If he thinks it's worse to steal than to let his wife die, then it would be wrong what he did. It's all relative. What I would do is steal the drug. I can't say that's right or wrong or that it's what everyone should do."

The vacillation experienced so consciously in these examples often appears with less conscious awareness. Responding to the same dilemma, another subject (reported in Kohlberg, 1970) said, "I think he should steal it because if there is any such thing as a universal human value, it is the value of life and that would justify stealing it." When asked if there is any such thing as a universal human value, she replied, "No, all values are relative to your culture."

It is our hypothesis that these kinds of responses reflect the necessary disequilibrium in progressing from stage 4 to stage 5 (cf. Turiel, in press). The type of conflict and vacillation observed takes on the status of disequilibrium because of their relation to both of the stages in the transition. It is necessary, therefore, to review the progressive differentiations made at each of these two levels in order to see how these specific conflicts are part of the transition.

As we noted earlier, from the stage 4 perspective (*authority and social order maintaining orientation*) moral value is undifferentiated from rules, law, authority and the social organizations that govern human relations. At stage 4, therefore, rules and values are seen as fixed; right and wrong are determined by the rules and values of the existing social system. Thus, one of the salient characteristics of stage 4 thinking is that moral values and rules, norms and customs are all treated alike and serve to maintain the system; that is, there is a fusion of moral evaluation with conventionality. At stage 5, however, moral values and principles are differentiated from maintenance of authority and rules of any particular social order. At this level, moral judgment is characterized by distinctions between values having universal, prescriptive applicability (principles not limited to any particular society) and values such as norms and conventions that are specific to society. Within the organization of this higher level, a system of conventions is integrated into morality such that it is subordinate to a system of moral principles.

Therefore, in contrasting these two levels we see that stage 5 thinking includes a greater recognition of the arbitrariness of society's conventions; it implies greater relativism. At the same time, however, stage 5 includes greater recognition of universality in moral principles and, thereby, implies less relativism.

The transition between these stages generally does not occur until late adolescence and early adulthood. During this time, greater autonomy and exposure to a diversity of individual and cultural values may serve to provide experiences that may challenge the conventional moral orientation of stage 4. In particular there is increased awareness of actual differences that exist between societies. Often the diversity perceived is in connection with the very rules that are treated, from a stage 4 perspective, as fixed and necessary for the social structure.

An increased awareness of cultural relativism would be dealt with in different ways according to the individual's stage. At stage 2, for instance, cultural differences can be readily assimilated as consistent with the instrumental egoistic orientation—everybody does what he wants. It is also likely that these experiences would be assimilated into the stage 3 structure by categorizing people into stereotypes of good and evil. Relativism of values is, however, more likely to strain the limits of stage 4 thinking because it comes into conflict with the concern and respect for social order and for the role of fixed rules, laws and norms in its maintenance.

This may then lead to reconsideration of the adequacy of a system of moral evaluation that is so closely tied to a specific social order or group identification. Such a reconsideration represents a beginning in the attempt to construct principles that have more universal applicability. At the same time, it represents the beginning of a reordering of conceptions about the conventional aspects of the social system. Thus conventionality must be recast into a new mold through which moral judgments can be made on a broader basis (i.e., across individuals and societies).

The completed transition (to stage 5) is one in which the individual generates principles having universal applicability and develops ways of differentiating these from social conventions that are not applicable to all. The conflict observed in our subjects reflects the transition between the two stages. The process of reorganization leading to stage 5 includes an intuitive understanding of principles coupled with a sense of the relativity and arbitrariness of societal conventions. At stage 4 conventions and moral principles are fused into one undifferentiated system; in order to move to stage 5 the individual must become critical of the stage 4 fusion he had previously made. The vacillation and conflict, therefore, reflect a tension between the two stages, with stage 4 conventionality being judged from a perspective in which the understanding of moral principles is still intuitive and not yet entirely successful. Because of the interplay between two modes of thinking, it is inevitable that there will be inherent cognitive confusion.[1]

The tension between elements of stage 4 and stage 5 thinking is clearly illustrated by the paradoxical response we presented earlier. The subject had said that a drug should be stolen, "because, if there is any such thing as a universal human value, it is the value of life." On the other hand, when asked if there are universal human values, she responded, "No, all values are relative to your culture." Our explanation of these seemingly contradictory positions is that they reflect the separation of the conventional and the moral and her attempts to coordinate them. In essence, she is in the process of distinguishing between those "oughts" which ought to be "oughts" and those that have been treated as "oughts" which ought not be treated as "oughts."

From this analysis we can begin to formulate characteristics of developmental change.

It is now possible to further elucidate the principles of structural disequilibrium, which we postulated as the necessary condition for development. Any period of transition from one stage to the next includes the following characteristics:

a) A recognition of the inadequacies of the existing mode of thinking and a concomitant questioning of that mode.

b) An attempt to construct a new mode of thinking.

c) Still only an intuitive understanding of the new mode and, therefore, a tension existing between the old and the new which is manifested in conflict and fluctuation.

d) A consequent attempt to subordinate the earlier mode of thinking into the new mode which, ultimately, results in the integration of a new view of the earlier mode into the more advanced mode.

In the movement from stage 4 to stage 5, these general characteristics of transition take the following form:

a) A critical view of stage 4 absolutism is coupled with an awareness of the relativity of social conventions.

b) An intuitive understanding of the separability of universal principles from convention feeds back on the undifferentiated stage 4 conventionality.

c) The beginning of an integration of the conventional system with the moral system.

THE COORDINATION OF REASONING AND ACTION IN DEVELOPMENT

The research discussed so far has been limited to the reasoning component of moral development. However, from a structural-developmental perspective, as we have defined it, reasoning *is* related to action. The two are interrelated in the sense that the way an individual reasons relates to how he acts and the way he acts relates to how

---

[1] In analyzing the data from their longitudinal study, Kohlberg and Kramer (1969) categorized responses of the sort we are describing as stage 2. Since the subjects who responded in this way had previously passed through stages 3 and 4, Kohlberg and Kramer interpreted this finding as an example of regression in moral development. Elsewhere (Turiel, in press) we have maintained that it is incorrect to categorize this thinking at stage 2 or to view it as a regression. The theoretical framework used by Kohlberg and Kramer did not explain transitions from stage to stage. Therefore, their analysis could not account for the conflicts that constitute part of the disequilibrium in moving from stage 4 to stage 5. The concern with relativism on the part of subjects making this transition was mistaken for the relativism that is part of stage 2 thinking. The relativism we have described here, which forms a necessary part of the movement to the principled stages, serves different functions and has a very different meaning from the relativism of stage 2 judgments.

he reasons—theoretically a developmental stage reflects these two components and their interrelationship. A second way in which reasoning and action are interrelated is that the child's coordination of reasoning and action is a factor influencing developmental change.

The notion that reasoning and action are interdependent is not shared by all other theories of moral development. For example, in the social learning explanations of the internalization of moral values a distinction is made between verbal values and behavior. Verbal and behavioral responses are seen as distinct types of events whose acquisition and performance are not necessarily related (cf. Aronfreed, 1968). It is assumed, therefore, that what people say they would do and what they actually do are two different things. The empirical evidence for this position comes from research using behavioral measures of resistance to transgression of cultural values in situations that presumably tempt the child to transgress. In their studies of cheating behavior, Hartshorne and May (1928-1930) found that children's verbal evaluations of cheating did not correlate with how they actually behaved in experimental situations that provided them with the opportunity to cheat.

While our hypothesis that reasoning and behavior are interrelated would lead us to expect an empirical relation between reasoning, as structurally determined, and behavior, we would not necessarily expect behavior to be correlated with a content measure of verbal values. The Hartshorne and May findings are based on the type of "moral knowledge" test we described earlier as a content measure. Consequently, their findings do not really pertain to the interdependence of reasoning and action. In fact, studies in which a structural measure of reasoning was used have shown that the developmental stage is correlated with cheating behavior. It has been found (Krebs, 1967; Schwartz, Feldman, Brown, & Heingartner, 1969) that individuals at the two most advanced stages of moral development (stages 5 and 6) are less likely to cheat than individuals at the intermediate level (stages 3 and 4) who in turn cheat less than those at stages 1 and 2.

A fair amount of evidence from investigations of other forms of behavior further substantiates the interrelation of reasoning and action. In a study by Milgram (1963), subjects were ordered (under the pretext of a learning experiment) to administer increasingly severe electric shocks to another person (who was a confederate of the experimenter and did not receive any shock). The majority of subjects using stage 6 reasoning on the moral judgment interview refused to administer the electrical shocks, while the majority of subjects at the lower stages complied with the experimenter's demands (Kohlberg, 1969).

In another study (Haan, Smith, & Block, 1968) a sample of students attending the University of California at Berkeley during the 1964 Free Speech Movement were administered the moral judgment interview. A number of them had engaged in an act of civil disobedience which they believed necessary to preserve the right of free speech. It was found that a majority (80 percent) of students at stage 6 engaged in civil disobedience while half of the students at stage 5 and only a small percentage (10 percent) of those at stages 3 and 4 did so.

These studies support the view that a relationship exists between reasoning (as indicated by developmental stage) and action. However, correlational studies of this sort do not serve to specify the nature of this relationship. Further, they do not provide information regarding the coordination of reasoning and behavior in developmental change. Our present concern is with another set of experiments (Rothman, 1971; Turiel & Rothman, in press) that bear on this issue. Utilizing the paradigm of our previous experiments (Turiel, 1966), we investigated how children respond to reasoning at stages other than their own in making behavioral choices.

In one of these experiments (Turiel &

Rothman, in press) boys in the seventh and eighth grades were first administered a moral judgment interview to determine their dominant stages. A few of these boys were predominantly at stage 2 while the rest were distributed between stages 3 and 4. In a second session each subject was introduced to two adults and all three were told they would participate in an experiment to see if punishment facilitates learning. (In actuality the two adults were confederates of the experimenter and responded in predetermined ways.) They were instructed to serve as teachers for another person who was to learn the correct spelling of a list of words. Their task would be to present the words and administer a "punishment" for each mistake. The punishment consisted of taking back money supposedly earned by the "learner" (also a confederate) in a previous experiment.

The two adults served as teachers first while the subject observed (presumably awaiting his turn as a teacher). In accordance with a predetermined schedule, the "learner" complained when his money was taken away. One of the "teachers" then said he thought they should stop the experiment; the other disagreed and thought they should continue. The experimenter then asked each of the teachers to explain his position. By having them present arguments at a given stage, it was possible to expose the subject to reasoning in support of each alternative (stop or continue) at a stage other than his own. In one condition the reasons for stopping were one stage above ($+1$) the subject's dominant stage, while the reasons for continuing were one stage below (-1). In the other condition this was reversed. That is, subjects were assigned to one of two experimental conditions: a) *+1 Stop: −1 Continue,* or b) *+1 Continue: −1 Stop.* After being exposed to these arguments each subject was given the choice of continuing or stopping the "learning" experiment. This was a meaningful choice for the children because they felt they had the responsibility for deciding whether or not the ex-

periment would take place. The children viewed their decision as posing a conflict between the claims of the experimenter and the claims of the "learner."

In addition to assessing the subject's behavioral choice, we also obtained measures of the following: a) which reasoning was preferred, b) degree of comprehension of the reasoning, and c) amount of stage change from the pretest to a posttest administered one week after the experimental session.

One of our concerns in this study was to investigate the ways in which behavioral choice would be influenced by the reasoning presented. To determine this, however, it was first necessary to know how the subjects would have behaved without being exposed to reasoning at the stages above and below. An estimate of this comes from the control group in a similar study (Rothman, 1971) in which two adults disagreed with each other as to whether or not to continue the experiment, while the subjects observed without being presented with any moral reasoning. The majority of those subjects chose to continue with the experiment. Since the subjects in Rothman's (1971) study were comparable to the subjects in the study we are discussing (i.e., Turiel & Rothman, in press) in terms of age and stages, we can conclude in this situation, too, the initial tendency is to continue rather than stop. Rothman (1971) also replicated the Turiel and Rothman study and confirmed the findings.

The basic findings on behavioral choices that the subjects made after being exposed to the reasoning are presented in Table 2. It can be seen that subjects at stages 2, 3 and 4 responded differently to the experimental conditions. That is, in both experimental conditions almost all of the subjects at stages 2 and 3 chose to continue. On the other hand, subjects initially at stage 4 were influenced in their behavioral choices by reasoning at the stage above (all of these differences were statistically significant).

On the basis of Rothman's (1971) find-

TABLE 2

NUMBER OF SUBJECTS AT EACH STAGE CHOOSING TO
STOP OR CONTINUE IN EACH EXPERIMENTAL CONDITION

Initial Dominant Stage	Experimental Conditions			
	+ 1 Stop	− 1 Continue	+ 1 Continue	− 1 Stop
2	0	2	2	0
3	0	8	6	1
4	6	1	5	1
Totals	6	11	13	2

Note: From E. Turiel and G. R. Rothman, in preparation.

ing that subjects chose to continue when no reasoning was presented, it can be assumed that the initial tendency for all these subjects was to choose to continue. Subjects at stage 2 and stage 3 persisted in this choice regardless of the level of reasoning used to support either alternative. Subjects at stage 4 chose to stop when the reasoning supporting this choice was at the stage above. It appears, therefore, that higher stage reasoning influences the behavior of those who have attained stage 4 differently from those who have only attained stages 2 or 3.

Further, we found that, as in our other experiments which did not involve any behavioral decisions, the subjects in this study generally preferred the reasoning at the stage above to the reasoning at the stage below. The patterns of comprehension of reasoning at the stage above were also similar to what was found in previous experiments. These subjects showed only a small degree of comprehension of the stage above; those subjects at stage 3 showed a capacity for comprehending the stage above equal to stage 4 subjects. In this study, too, the amount of stage change, as measured by the posttest interview, was extremely small. Regardless of the initial stage or whether they chose the alternative argued at the stage above or below, there was only a slight increase in usage of the stage above and no change to the stage below.

Although no stage transformations were stimulated by what was experienced in the experiment, the finding that the reasoning had different influences on the behavior of subjects at stages 2 and 3 as compared to those at stage 4 suggests that the way an individual coordinates reasoning and action is an important factor in development. Comparisons of pretest stage distributions (Turiel & Rothman, in press) showed that the observed distinction between stages cannot be explained as due to stage 4 subjects having been initially closer to the attainment of the stage above than those at stages 2 or 3. Therefore, the most plausible explanation of the distinction between subjects at different stages lies in the means by which higher stage reasoning is related to behavioral choice. It was seen that both groups of subjects were responding to the higher stage reasoning in that they evaluated it positively and showed some comprehension. Yet those at stage 4 shifted in their own behavior, indicating that they considered the higher stage reasoning and the behavioral choice in relation to each other. In doing so, these subjects integrated the two domains by subordinating the behavioral choice to the reasoning. In contrast, the behavior of subjects at stages 2 and 3 did not shift in response to the more advanced reasoning. They kept the two domains segregated rather than integrating them, and behavioral choice thus remained uninfluenced by the higher stage reasoning.

These considerations suggest that in relating action decisions to new reasoning which is higher in stage (yet somewhat comprehensible), there is a developmental progression from the segregation of differentiated domains to their integration. The way in which the stage 4 subjects reacted represents the integration of action with new, higher stage reasoning—one in which the action choice is subordinated to the reasoning. The way in which the lower stage subjects reacted represents the failure to coordinate the new reasoning with action choices.

In the progression from the segregation of these domains to their integration there is also an intermediate, transitional phase that reflects awareness of a discrepancy between the positive evaluation of the higher stage reasoning on the one hand, and action that is not in accord with it on the other. The behavior of some of the stage 3 subjects choosing to continue in the $+1$ *Stop:* -1 *Continue* experimental condition included vacillation and conflict reflecting their transitional attempts at relating behavioral choice to higher stage reasoning. Of the eight stage 3 subjects in that condition, five of them displayed some form of vacillation. The most dramatic example was that of one boy who actually decided to stop the "learning" experiment in the middle of it. Another boy, after completing the experiment, stated that he regretted his decision and volunteered the information that he "cheated" sometimes by not taking money away when the learner made mistakes. Three other boys had great difficulty making their decision and went back and forth between the two alternatives before finally choosing to continue. In addition, this group of subjects was the only one that was inconsistent and indecisive when choosing which of the two arguments they preferred.

The conflict manifested by such inconsistency and indecision suggests that these subjects were at an intermediate level between those who did not relate the higher stage reasoning to their action and those who did so. The stage 4 subjects who coordinated their behavioral choice with the higher stage reasoning were, in effect, as-

similating reasoning at the stage one above their own by integrating it with their own actions. In this process, higher stage reasoning is being assimilated by means of an action associated with it and should, therefore, have consequences for transformations in the individual's own stage. That is, one transitional path may be through performance of actions that are guided by reasoning at the stage above. In such a case an individual's actions would not be, in his own mind, consonant with his level of reasoning and could provide feedback leading to a reorganization of his own reasoning.

While this notion has the status of a hypothesis that we are still exploring, there is some indication of its validity from Rothman's (1971) study. Two conditions in her study are of relevance. In one, the experiment we have just described was replicated. In the other, the subject was presented with the entire situation (including reasoning at the stages above and below) as a hypothetical dilemma and asked what he would do. He was not required to act on his choice. Subjects in both of these conditions made choices comparable to those we have reported. It was found, however, that subjects who were required to act on their choices showed some slight increase in usage of the stage above, while those in the hypothetical condition showed no such change.

Taken together, the results of these studies suggest that action can play an important role in the disequilibrium necessary for stage change. The following working hypothesis summarizes what we have said. In a behavioral situation there are three phases in responding to reasoning at the stage above (which is positively evaluated and partially comprehended). First, reasoning remains segregated from behavior. Second, an attempt is made to relate the reasoning to behavior—this is manifested in conflict and not a change in behavior. Third, reasoning and behavior are integrated so that the behavior is guided by the higher stage reasoning. This is a form of integration through which action can provide the conditions for stage reorganization.

The results of these studies also provide experimental validation for a basic proposition of our approach—that development involves transformations in organized structures of thought and action. The validity of the hypothesis of interdependence of thought and action in development was demonstrated in several ways. First, the studies showed that behavior can be dependent on the stage of development. Behavior changes in the experimental situation could be differentiated on the basis of an assessment of the subject's stage of moral judgment: stage 4 subjects responded differently from those at stages 2 and 3. Second, insofar as reasoning affected changes in behavior, it was reasoning at the stage one above, while reasoning at the stage below had no influence upon behavior. These findings on changes in behavior have been paralleled by findings regarding the effects of our experimental treatment on subjects' reasoning. Just as behavioral shifts were limited to the influence of the stage above, changes in subjects' reasoning were slight and limited to small increases in usage of the stage one above. Reasoning at the stage below did not influence behavior or reasoning. These studies demonstrated another form of parallelism between behavior and reasoning. In previous studies (Rest, Turiel, & Kohlberg, 1969; Turiel, 1966) subjects were exposed to reasoning at stages above and below in experimental situations involving no behavioral choice. In both types of experiments we found only small increases in usage of the stage above and no increase in usage of the stage below.

We find, therefore, that in experiments involving behavioral decisions, as well as experiments in which no behavior is involved, the same principles of sequential development emerge. Structures of thought and action form a developmental order through which the transitions occur in a step-by-step fashion.

REFERENCES

Aronfreed, J. M. *Conduct and conscience: The socialization of internalized control over behavior.* New York: Academic Press, 1968.

Bandura, A. Social-learning theory of identificatory processes. In D. A. Goslin (Ed.), *Handbook of socialization theory and research.* Chicago: Rand McNally, 1969. Pp. 213–262.

Bandura, A., & McDonald, F. J. Influence of social reinforcement and the behavior of models in shaping children's moral judgments. *Journal of Abnormal and Social Psychology,* 1963, 67, 274–281.

Bandura, A., & Walters, R. H. *Social learning and personality development.* New York: Holt, Rinehart & Winston, 1963.

Berkowitz, L. *The development of motives and values in the child.* New York: Basic Books, 1964.

Blatt, M. The effects of classroom discussion on the development of moral judgment. Unpublished doctoral dissertation, University of Chicago, 1969.

Blatt, M., & Kohlberg, L. The effects of classroom discussion upon children's level of moral judgment. In L. Kohlberg, & E. Turiel (Eds.), *Recent research in moral development.* New York: Holt, Rinehart & Winston, in press.

Cowan, P. A., Langer, J., Heavenrich, J., & Nathanson, M. Social learning and Piaget's cognitive theory of moral development. *Journal of Personality and Social Psychology,* 1969, 11, 261–274.

Crowley, P. M. Effect of training upon objectivity of moral judgment in grade-school children. *Journal of Personality and Social Psychology,* 1968, 8, 228–232.

Durkheim, E. *Moral education.* New York: Free Press, 1961.

Eysenck, H. J. Symposium: The development of moral values in children. VII—The contribution of learning theory. *British Journal of Educational Psychology,* 1960, 30, 11–21.

Freud, S. *Civilization and its discontents.* London: Liveright, 1930. (Republished, New York: W. W. Norton, 1961.)

Freud, S. *The ego and the id.* New York: W. W. Norton, 1960.

Haan, N., Smith, M. B., & Block, J. Moral reasoning of young adults: Political-social behavior, family background and personality correlates. *Journal of Personality and Social Psychology,* 1968, 10, 183–201.

Hartshorne, H., & May, M. A. *Studies in the nature of character.* Vol. 1: *Studies in deceit.* Vol. 2: *Studies in service and self-control.* Vol. 3: *Studies in organization of character.* New York: Macmillan, 1928–1930.

Hoffman, M. L. Moral development. In P. H. Mussen (Ed.), *Carmichael's manual of child psychology.* Vol. 2. New York: John Wiley, 1970. Pp. 261–359.

Inhelder, B., Bovet, M., Sinclair, H., & Smock, C. D. On cognitive development. *American Psychologist,* 1966, 21, 160–164.

Inhelder, B., & Piaget, J. *The growth of logical thinking from childhood to adolescence.* New York: Basic Books, 1958.

Inhelder, B., & Piaget, J. *The early growth of logic in the child: Classification and seriation.* New York: Harper & Row, 1964.

Inhelder, B., & Sinclair, H. Learning cognitive structures. In P. H. Mussen, J. Langer, & M. Covington (Eds.), *Trends and issues in developmental psychology.* New York: Holt, Rinehart & Winston, 1969. Pp. 2–21.

Jones, V. A. *Character and citizenship training in the public schools.* Chicago: University of Chicago Press, 1936.

Kaplan, B. The study of language in psychiatry. In S. Arieti (Ed.), *American handbook of psychiatry.* Vol. 3. New York: Basic Books, 1966. Pp. 689–704.

Kohlberg, L. The development of modes of moral thinking and choice in years ten to sixteen. Unpublished doctoral dissertation, University of Chicago, 1958.

Kohlberg, L. The development of children's orientations toward a moral order: 1. Sequence in the development of moral thought. *Vita Humana,* 1963, 6, 11–33.

Kohlberg, L. Development of moral character and moral ideology. In M. L. Hoffman, & L. W. Hoffman (Eds.), *Review of child development research.* Vol. 1. New York: Russell Sage Foundation, 1964. Pp. 383–431.

Kohlberg, L. Stage and sequence: The cognitive-developmental approach to socialization. In D. A. Goslin (Ed.), *Handbook of socialization theory and research.* Chicago: Rand McNally, 1969. Pp. 347–480.

Kohlberg, L. Relativity versus indoctrination in value-education. Paper presented at the Lecture for Values Symposium, Georgetown University, Washington, D.C., June 1970.

Kohlberg, L. From is to ought: How to commit the naturalistic fallacy and get away with it in the study of moral development. In T. Mischel (Ed.), *Cognitive development and epistemology.* New York: Academic Press, 1971.

Kohlberg, L., & Kramer, R. B. Continuities and discontinuities in childhood and adult moral development. *Human Development,* 1969, 12, 93–120.

Kohlberg, L., & Turiel, E. Moral development and moral education. In G. Lesser (Ed.), *Psychology and educational practice.* Chicago: Scott, Foresman, 1971. Pp. 410–465.

Kohlberg, L., & Turiel, E. (Eds.) *Recent research in moral development.* New York: Holt, Rinehart & Winston, in press.

Kramer, R. B. Changes in moral judgment response pattern during late adolescence and young adulthood: Retrogression in a developmental sequence. Unpublished doctoral dissertation, University of Chicago, 1968.

Krebs, R. L. Some relationships between moral judgment, attention, and resistance to temptation. Unpublished doctoral dissertation, University of Chicago, 1967.

Kuhn, D. Patterns of imitative behavior in children from 3 to 8: A study of imitation from a cognitive developmental perspective. Unpublished doctoral dissertation, University of California, Berkeley, 1969.

Langer, J. Disequilibrium as a source of development. In P. Mussen, J. Langer, & M. Covington (Eds.), *Trends and issues in developmental psychology.* New York: Holt, Rinehart & Winston, 1969. (a)

Langer, J. *Theories of development.* New York: Holt, Rinehart & Winston, 1969. (b)

Langer, J. Interactional aspects of mental structures. In C. B. Lavatelli (Ed.), *The natural curriculum of the child.* Urbana: University of Illinois Press, in press.

Lickona, T. E. The acceleration of children's judgment about responsibility: An experimental test of Piaget's hypotheses about the causes of moral judgmental change. Unpublished doctoral dissertation, State University of New York at Albany, 1971.

Maccoby, E. E. The development of moral values and behavior in childhood. In J. A.

Clausen (Ed.), *Socialization and society*. Boston: Little, Brown, 1968. Pp. 227–269.

Milgram, S. Behavioral study of obedience. *Journal of Abnormal and Social Psychology*, 1963, 67, 371–378.

Piaget, J. *The moral judgment of the child*. New York: Free Press, 1932. (Republished, New York: Free Press, 1965.)

Piaget, J. *The psychology of intelligence*. New York: Harcourt, Brace, 1950.

Piaget, J. *The child's conception of number*. London: Routledge & Kegan Paul, 1952.

Piaget, J. *The construction of reality in the child*. New York: Basic Books, 1954.

Piaget, J. *Six psychological studies*. New York: Random House, 1967.

Piaget, J. Piaget's theory. In P. H. Mussen (Ed.), *Carmichael's manual of child psychology*. Vol. 1. New York: John Wiley, 1970. Pp. 703–732. (a)

Piaget, J. *Structuralism*. New York: Basic Books, 1970. (b)

Piaget, J., & Inhelder, B. *The psychology of the child*. New York: Basic Books, 1969.

Rest, J. Developmental hierarchy in preference and comprehension of moral judgment. Unpublished doctoral dissertation, University of Chicago, 1968.

Rest, J., Turiel, E., & Kohlberg, L. Level of moral development as a determinant of preference and comprehension of moral judgments made by others. *Journal of Personality*, 1969, 37, 225–252.

Rothman, G. R. An experimental analysis of the relationship between level of moral judgment and behavioral choice. Unpublished doctoral dissertation, Columbia University, 1971.

Schwartz, S. H., Feldman, K. A., Brown, M. E., & Heingartner, A. Some personality correlates of conduct in two situations of moral conflict. *Journal of Personality*, 1969, 37, 41–57.

Sears, R. R., Maccoby, E. E., & Levin, H. *Patterns of child rearing*. Evanston, Ill.: Row, Peterson, 1957.

Sigel, I. E., & Hooper, F. H. (Eds.) *Logical thinking in children: Research based on Piaget's theory*. New York: Holt, Rinehart & Winston, 1968.

Sinclair, H. Developmental psycho-linguistics. In D. Elkind, & J. H. Flavell (Eds.), *Studies in cognitive development: Essays in honor of Jean Piaget*. New York: Oxford University Press, 1969. Pp. 315–336.

Smedslund, J. The acquisition of conservation of substance and weight in children: II. External reinforcement of conservation of weight and of the operations of addition and subtraction. *Scandinavian Journal of Psychology*, 1961, 2, 71–84. (a)

Smedslund, J. The acquisition of conservation of substance and weight in children: III. Extinction of conservation of weight acquired 'normally' and by means of empirical controls on a balance. *Scandinavian Journal of Psychology*, 1961, 2, 85–87. (b)

Smedslund, J. The acquisition of conservation of substance and weight in children: V. Practice in conflict situations without external reinforcement. *Scandinavian Journal of Psychology*, 1961, 2, 156–160. (c)

Turiel, E. An experimental test of the sequentiality of developmental stages in the child's moral judgments. *Journal of Personality and Social Psychology*, 1966, 3, 611–618.

Turiel, E. Developmental processes in the child's moral thinking. In P. Mussen, J. Langer, & M. Covington (Eds.), *Trends and issues in developmental psychology*. New York: Holt, Rinehart & Winston, 1969. Pp. 92–133.

Turiel, E. Equilibration and transition in moral development. In L. Kohlberg, & E. Turiel (Eds.) *Recent research in moral development*. New York: Holt, Rinehart & Winston, in press.

Turiel, E. Sex differences in the development of moral knowledge and judgment. In L. Kohlberg, & E. Turiel (Eds.), *Recent research in moral development*. New York: Holt, Rinehart & Winston, in press.

Turiel, E., Kohlberg, L., & Edwards, C. Cross-cultural studies of moral development. In L. Kohlberg, & E. Turiel (Eds.), *Recent research in moral development*. New York: Holt, Rinehart & Winston, in press.

Turiel, E., & Rothman, G. R. The influence of reasoning on behavioral choices at different stages of moral development. *Child Development*, in press.

Wallach, L., & Sprott, R. L. Inducing number conservation in children. *Child Development*, 1964, 35, 1057–1071.

Wallach, L., Wall, A. J., & Anderson, L. Number conservation: The roles of reversibility, addition-subtraction, and misleading perceptual cues. *Child Development,* 1967, 38, 425–442.

Werner, H. *Comparative psychology of mental development.* New York: International Universities Press, 1948.

Wohlwill, J. F., & Lowe, R. C. Experimental analysis of the development of the con-

servation of number. *Child Development,* 1962, 33, 153–167.

Zigler, E., & Child, I. L. Socialization. In G. Lindzey, & E. Aronson (Eds.), *The handbook of social psychology. Vol. 3. The individual in a social context.* Reading, Mass.: Addison-Wesley, 1969. Pp. 450–489.

CHAPTER 24 The Teaching of Affective Responses

S. B. KHAN
The Ontario Institute for Studies in Education

JOEL WEISS
The Ontario Institute for Studies in Education

If the school does not teach values, it will have the effect of denying them (Allport, 1961, p. 215).

The youth of today are living in a more complex society than their forefathers did. On the one hand they have experienced "man on the moon" phenomena made possible by advanced space technology and live television; on the other hand they have witnessed racial riots, war, poverty and ecological corruption. The audiovisual media have brought distant environmental and human problems to the comfortable living rooms of North American suburbia. How has this affected the outlook of our youngsters? Judging by the popular press, the present generation, unlike the youth of the fifties studied by Jacob (1957), seems to be more concerned about human conditions than they are about material acquisitions and status.

In terms of the formal responsibility for the development of appropriate human concerns and healthy social and educational attitudes, the school, along with the nuclear family, has been seen as the primary institution for teaching desirable affective tend-encies. However, students have begun to question the value and relevance of formal education insofar as it prepares them for coping with pressing social concerns and an increasingly more complex technological society. This trend has seemingly resulted in negative attitudes on the part of the youngsters toward school, teachers, education and academic learning. A crucial question that must be asked is whether the schools have met their responsibility, both in terms of a relatively clear idea as to their mission with regard to affective behaviors and deliberate strategies for teaching such behaviors.

An analysis of the statements of objectives for formal education may help in gaining a perspective of what has been seen by educators as the appropriate roles for the schools with regard to affective outcomes. Such statements (Dressel, 1960; Education Policies Commission, 1938; French & associates, 1957; Hand, 1948; Havighurst, 1953; Kearney, 1953; etc.) indicate that attitudes, values, beliefs and interests constitute important outcomes of education. The emphasis on affective outcomes of education has gained renewed impetus in writings concerned with the process of evaluating instructional programs and the pressures for social accountability (Allport, 1961; Messick, 1970; Scriven, 1966; Stake, 1970).

However laudable these objectives might be, the extent to which they are reflected in the actual operations of the school is a prime issue. In practice, most classroom teaching is concentrated on the realization of cognitive objectives. Often it is assumed that students will acquire relevant affective behaviors as a result of cognitive learnings. The belief that a student will develop positive attitudes toward subject matter, school, education, the teacher and others just by coming to school and interacting with curriculum materials, other students, and the teacher is an untenable assumption (Friedenberg, 1965; Holt, 1964; C. E. Silberman, 1970).

What happens in teaching situations is highly related to the affective responses acquired related to school, teachers and the subject-matter area. If desirable affective goals are to be realized as a result of the educational process, relevant formal learning situations have to be developed and the effects of such learning experiences will have to be systematically appraised. This chapter is devoted to a review of research on affective dispositions held by students toward school, teachers, school situations and subject-matter areas. In the process we will examine antecedents of school-related affective responses and the ways in which they are acquired. Implications for classroom teaching of these affective behaviors as well as areas for further research will be suggested.

THE CONCEPT OF ATTITUDE

A plethora of variables such as attitudes, values, interests, motivation, anxiety, appreciation, adjustment and other personality characteristics are generally subsumed under the rubric of affective behavior. The term noncognitive is also used to characterize these variables in order to distinguish them from the task-oriented cognitive variables such as aptitude and achievement. The term *affective* has an alternative usage in literature on attitudes: *the evaluative component of attitudes associated with a feeling core of liking or disliking for social and psychological objects.* It is this latter usage of the term in relation to classroom teaching and learning which will be the focus of this chapter.

As a research construct, attitude has occupied a central place in the domains of sociology and social psychology since the study of the Polish peasant by Thomas and Znaniecki (1918). An impressive body of theoretical and empirical literature has accumulated since that time. Although much of the discussion concerned with theories and research on attitude formation, change and measurement methodology has been presented in several places (e.g., Fishbein, 1967; Kiesler, Collins, & Miller, 1969; Rosenberg, Hovland, McGuire, Abelson, & Brehm, 1960), we will present a brief overview of these topics because of their relevance to research on the affective components of attitudes in the educational setting.

Definitions of Attitude

A variety of definitions of *attitude* representing different theoretical viewpoints has been offered: an affect for or against a psychological object (Thurstone, 1931b); a mental and neural state of readiness, organized through experience, exerting a directive and dynamic influence upon the individual's response to all objects and situations with which it is related (Allport, 1935); an implicit drive-producing response considered socially significant in the individual's society (Doob, 1947); a multidimensional construct consisting of cognitive, affective and conative components (M. B. Smith, 1947).

The affective component attached to a stimulus object, which includes emotions, feelings and values, was strongly emphasized in the studies of attitudes by Fishbein (1967a), Krech, Crutchfield, and Ballachey

(1962), and Osgood, Suci, and Tannenbaum (1957). While the importance of cognitive and conative components in the description of attitudes was recognized, subsequent research and measurement procedures were geared mainly to the affective components of attitudes (Ostrom, 1968). Despite the many ways in which attitudes are defined, the communality among the various definitions is illustrated by noting *that attitudes are selectively acquired and integrated through learning and experience; that they are enduring dispositions indicating response consistency; and that positive or negative affect toward a social or psychological object represents the salient characteristic of an attitude.*

Attitude Development and Change

Personality traits including attitudes develop quite early in childhood as a result of formal learning, experiences and interaction with others. By the age of one year an infant is capable of affective responses toward various stimulus objects. These responses are manifested in approach-avoidance tendencies toward objects, persons and situations. Baldwin (1960) has noted that children provide valuable experimental subjects for the study of affective responses because of their relatively greater impulsivity and spontaneity.

Many theories of personality hypothesize a rapid growth in different personality characteristics during early years of infancy and childhood with marked changes during adolescence, and a small change in the postadolescent period. Definitive studies, however, on stability and change of affective characteristics over time are scarce (Bloom, 1964). This paucity of longitudinal research is attributed to the numerous methodological problems that arise in developmental studies on affective components of human behavior (Ausubel, 1958).

During infancy the home environment through parent-child and other interactions is recognized as having pervasive influence on the development of the child's affective behavior. Parents, siblings, peers and other persons and situations with which the child comes into frequent contact form the major source of the origin and development of attitudes toward self (Weiss, 1970a) and toward the immediate physical and social environments (Mussen, Conger, & Kagan, 1969). By the time the child enters school, he has already acquired both desirable and undesirable attitudes. It therefore becomes one of the major tasks of the school to change undesirable attitudes, to strengthen existing desirable ones, and to work toward the development of new attitudes by providing appropriate learning experiences.

Krech, Crutchfield, and Ballachey (1962) have defined two types of attitude change. An attitude change is said to be congruent if the change occurs in the direction of the existing attitude. Conversely, if the change is in the direction opposite to the existing attitude, then it is said to be an incongruent change. They hypothesize that, other things being equal, it is easier to produce congruent change than incongruent change. Further, the modifiability of an attitude is a function of various characteristics of an attitude system (extremeness, complexity, consistency, etc.) and the personality and group affiliation of the individual.

Bloom (1964) has suggested that the extent to which one's attitudes are modifiable depends upon the way they are acquired and their relationship to one's self. He thinks that attitudes toward objects not immediately related to self may be easier to change than attitudes in the form of superstitions and prejudices and those based on early home or religious training. Attitudes acquired toward self in terms of self-evaluations and self-perceptions are generally more stable and relatively difficult to change.

Man's social behavior is largely determined by communication through the use of language, and any deliberate attempt to change the action tendencies of individuals will involve attitude change through some form of communication. McGuire (1968) has identified persuasive communication as one of the important factors which contribute to the development and stability of individual differences in attitudes. Extensive research has been done to study the effects of persuasive communication on the formation and change of attitudes (Cohen, 1964; Davis, 1965). Different psychological theories (e.g., learning, perceptual, cognitive consistency, functional) have been formulated to explain relationships between variables in a communication situation and changes in attitudes. Evaluating these different theories, McGuire (1968) and Kiesler, Collins, and Miller (1969) agree that although none fully explains the relationships between independent variables and attitude change, they have nevertheless led to productive research in the areas of attitude formation and attitude change.

Models of Affective Behavior in the Educational Setting

Few strategies concerned with affective behaviors have been conceptualized or developed for the formal educational setting. Two notable exceptions are the development of the affective domain of the taxonomy of educational objectives (Krathwohl, Bloom, & Masia, 1964) and the theoretical writings and practical procedures about values developed by Raths, Harmin, and Simon (1966).

The Taxonomy of Educational Objectives: Affective Domain (Krathwohl, Bloom, & Masia, 1964) is a handbook published as a companion volume to the earlier work for the cognitive area (Bloom, 1956). It offers a classification system for affective behaviors and was developed as an aid for both defining educational objectives and familiarizing teachers with the techniques available for evaluating learning in the affective area.

The organizing principle adopted by Krathwohl and his associates (1964) was that affective behaviors could be ordered along a continuum of internalization representing "a continuous modification of behaviour from the individual's being aware of a phenomenon to a pervasive outlook on life that influences all his actions" (p. 33). The continuum has been structured into stages of behavior which serve as a classification scheme for affective outcomes of instruction.

In addition to its use in stating educational objectives and providing ideas about evaluation, the authors hoped that the handbook would facilitate communication between various groups of educators and social scientists that would lead to "a somewhat more precise understanding of how affective behaviors develop, how and when they can be modified, and what the school can and cannot do to develop them" (Krathwohl, Bloom, & Masia, 1964, p. 23). These expectations may be unduly optimistic since the affective taxonomy has generated few research studies in comparison with the number conducted using the cognitive taxonomy (Cox & Unks, 1967). However, like its cognitive counterpart, the affective taxonomy has influenced many publications concerned with the practical considerations of stating objectives and developing evaluation items (Bloom, Hastings, & Madaus, 1971; Kibler, Barker, & Miles, 1970; Metfessel, Michael, & Kirsner, 1969; Senathirajah & Weiss, 1971).

An important exception to this lack of research is a study by Lewy (1968) which attempted to validate the properties of the affective taxonomy. Lewy set out to "(1) demonstrate the existence of empirical referents for its constructs, and (2) show that these empirical referents display the structure defined by the model" (p. 71), which were termed descriptive and dynamic validities, respectively. Tests of approximately 80 items were developed for the curricular areas of mathematics, music and reading. Items were developed to correspond to the taxonomic levels of receiving, responding, valuing and organization. Each of the tests was administered to 200–300 high-school and college students. Descriptive validity was tested in two ways: 1) by obtaining the extent of interrater agreement in classifying the test items, and 2) by predicting the emergence of factors congruent with the model. Two raters with previous experience in constructing affective items as well as familiarity with the affective taxonomy classified the test items with the following results: 74 percent agreement, 25 percent assigned to adjacent categories, and the remaining 1 percent to nonadjacent categories. An oblique transformation of the original factor solution developed: 1) approximately 80 percent of the items had higher correlations with the factor associated with the postulated taxonomic level than with the other factors; 2) the correlations among the factors ranged from 0.4 to 0.8 for each of the tests of mathematics and reading and from 0.7 to 0.9 for music. The results obtained by Lewy for two of the three tests indicated that the categories of the affective taxonomy possessed descriptive validity.

Lewy tested several hypotheses concerning the hierarchical nature of the taxonomy. Using frequency of choice of items by students as an index, the data supported the hypothesis that frequency of occurrence of behavior was inversely related to taxonomic level, i.e., the higher the taxonomic level, the fewer students chose an item as reflecting their behavior. Further evidence for the hierarchical structure was determined by displaying an adequate fit of the pattern of correlations for each of the levels to a simplex model. Additional information was sought with regard to sex differences at different levels of the taxonomy, but the results were in the intended direction for the mathematics test only.

While Lewy's work provided useful information about the properties of the affective taxonomy and might serve as an example for testing models in educational research, many more studies should be conducted. One important topic which should be researched is the relationship between cognitive and affective behaviors. While a logical rationale has been put forward by Krathwohl, Bloom, and Masia (1964, chapter 4), several empirical studies have reported independence between cognitive and affective behaviors (Johnson, 1967; Neidt & Hedlund, 1969). Since these studies have not specifically used behaviors based upon the affective taxonomy, the use of this classification system for future research is important. Perhaps the inevitable gap between application of the taxonomy for classroom purposes and research studies generated by it will become less obvious.

A very different approach has been developed by L. E. Raths, Harmin, and Simon (1966). While the affective taxonomy is mainly concerned with affective responses as outcomes or products, Raths, Harmin, and Simon postulate a theory which emphasizes the processes by which values may be acquired. Three processes are involved in the acquisition of affective responses: *choosing, prizing* and *acting*. The process of *choosing* requires that it be chosen freely, from among alternatives, and after thoughtful consideration of each alternative. *Prizing* includes being happy with a choice and a willingness to make it public. Finally, *acting* includes activity involved in using the choice and doing it repeatedly.

A variety of strategies is suggested by Raths, Harmin, and Simon (1966) for use by classroom teachers for clarifying the values of students. Included are materials for use with individual students as well as with groups. Raths and his associates see the materials being used for affective responses of a general nature as well as general lessons concerned with the development for specific subject-matter areas (e.g., literature, social studies).

Several studies have been made to test Raths's theory at the elementary, high-school and college levels, and have applied either to individual or group strategies (L. E. Raths, Harmin, & Simon, 1966, chapter 10). For instance, a study was made on students from grades five to eight, applying some of the techniques from the value theory. It was reported that 88 of 100 students showed gains on attitude toward school learning over the course of a year (J. Raths, 1962). Because of methodological shortcomings of these studies (e.g., lack of control groups), the empirical evidence is not as yet convincing about either the postulated theory or the classroom strategies. Further research work is necessary. Some especially important topics would be the validity of the seven criteria used to define a value and the relationships between cognitive and affective behaviors for different subject areas. Before turning to an extensive review of research on the acquisition of affective responses, it would be worthwhile to discuss the problems that arise in the measurement and quantification of affective variables.

METHODOLOGICAL ISSUES

Two types of methodological issues generally arise in research on affective behavior. The first pertains to techniques of data collection and the second to experimental design considerations and data analysis. We will attempt to review briefly the issues involved in collecting data on individuals, classroom settings and curriculum materials in the following section. Issues related to experimental design will emerge in the critique of the research in this area at the end of the chapter.

DATA COLLECTION TECHNIQUES

Different techniques of data collection on attitudes of individuals have been described in several sources (Cook & Selltiz, 1964; Fishbein, 1967b; W. A. Scott, 1968; Summers, 1970; Wight & Doxsey, 1972). We will discuss self-report, observational, and projective techniques with examples of studies in which instruments of one or the other kind have been used for assessment of affective behaviors of teachers and students and for measuring classroom climates. In addition, appropriateness of content analysis methodology for measuring affective content in curriculum materials will be discussed.

Self-Report Techniques

The most frequently used procedure for measuring attitudes toward a stimulus object has been the administration of a collection of questions or statements to individuals. A variety of methods for scaling attitude statements and scoring responses has been developed. These methods include paired comparisons (Thurstone, 1927), equal-appearing intervals (Thurstone & Chave, 1929), summated ratings (Likert, 1932), and scalogram analysis (Guttman, 1944). The scale-discrimination method (Edwards & Kilpatrick, 1948) combines Thurstone's and Likert's procedures for evaluating the discriminatory power of individual items and Guttman's criteria of scalability. The semantic differential technique (Osgood, Suci, & Tannenbaum, 1957), developed originally for measuring the meaning of concepts, has been strongly recommended for attitude measurement because of its ease of construction and versatility for measuring the affective components of attitudes (Fishbein, 1967a; Heise, 1970).

The majority of scales reported in the attitude literature have been developed by using the method of summated ratings. For instance, out of 176 scales reported by Shaw and Wright (1967) for measuring attitudes, nearly two-thirds are Likert-type scales while scale discrimination, scalogram, and the other techniques have been used in very few studies. The popularity of Likert's method has been attributed to its ease of construction and reliability (Barclay & Weaver, 1962; Edwards & Kenney, 1946; Seiler & Hough, 1970) and to the complexity of other procedures (Shaw & Wright, 1967).

Several self-report instruments have been developed for measuring teachers' and students' attitudes toward each other, toward education, toward school and toward courses. Two instruments, the Minnesota Teacher Attitude Inventory (MTAI) (Cook, Leeds, & Callis, 1951) and the Survey of Study Habits and Attitudes (Brown

& Holtzman, 1967), are briefly described below because of their extensive use in research on teachers' and students' attitudes.

The MTAI was developed to distinguish between good and poor teachers in terms of their relationships with pupils. It is assumed that teachers who score high on this instrument should be able to maintain better relations with their pupils than teachers who score low. Several studies involving the use of the MTAI have been summarized by Getzels and Jackson (1963) and Stern (1963). Factor-analytic studies (Horn & Morrison, 1965; Yee & Fruchter, 1971) have indicated that at least five factors representing different aspects of teachers' attitudes are measured by MTAI with "Traditionalistic versus Modern Beliefs about Child Control" representing the major dimension. Yee and Fruchter noted the similarity of this dimension to the factor, "understanding and democratic versus aloof, harsh and autocratic in dealings with pupils" of the Teacher Characteristic Schedule (Ryans, 1960), and the "progressive versus traditional" factor isolated by Kerlinger (1961, 1967). In summary, teachers' attitudes toward their pupils have been characterized mainly along such continua as progressive versus traditional, integrative versus dominative, and democratic versus autocratic.

The Survey of Study Habits and Attitudes, a Likert-type scale, was originally developed to measure study skills and attitudes of college students. Its frequent use led the authors to develop a high-school version of the survey consisting of four logically derived scales: Delay Avoidance, Work Methods, Teacher Approval, and Education Acceptance. Holtzman and Brown (1968) have reported on the reliability, stability and validity of scores on this survey and have recommended its use in prediction of future academic achievement and in the study of attitude change. In a study by Khan and Roberts (1971), it was found that six empirically derived scales of a modified version of the Survey of Study Habits and Attitudes varied in stability depending upon the number of items in each scale.

Observational Techniques

The major difference between self-report and observational techniques for measuring attitudes is that in the latter case affective dispositions held by individuals toward stimulus objects are inferred from their observable behaviors. In a recent article, Rosenshine (1970) has reviewed the use of observational instruments in studies on classroom behavior and classroom interaction between teachers and students. These instruments are classified into category or rating systems depending upon the amount of inference required in the judgments of the observer.

Measures in the category systems are usually employed in observations of specific behaviors which require minimum inference of the observer. Weick (1968) has discussed issues and problems that arise in the use of observational techniques in social and behavioral research. Medley and Mitzel (1963) have examined a variety of procedures that have been developed for systematically observing and recording classroom behavior of teachers and students. Observational schedules have been used in research on classroom social and emotional climate (Withall, 1949); on teachers' personality characteristics (Anderson, Brewer, Reed, & Wrightstone, 1946; Ryans, 1960); on the teacher-pupil interactions (Flanders, 1970; Fuller, 1969; Medley & Mitzel, 1958; Simon & Boyer, 1967); and on students' affective behavior (Bemis & Liberty, 1970).

When behavior categories are quite broad and lack specificity, high inference measures falling under rating systems are used for observation. Rating procedures for research on classroom teaching have been discussed by Remmers (1963) and their use as a criterion of teaching effectiveness has been evaluated by Stern (1963). The studies conducted by Callis (1953) and Leeds (1952, 1969) in connection with validation of MTAI, by Reed (1953) and Wandt (1954) on teacher effectiveness, by Harvey, White, Prather, Alter, and Hoffmeister (1966) and Harvey, Prather, White, and Hoffmeister

(1968) on teachers' beliefs, and by Walberg (1969b) on classroom learning environment represent the use of rating scales for data collection on students and teachers.

Students' academic achievement has been used as one of the major criteria for validating observational systems for teacher behavior. Rosenshine and Furst (1971) have reviewed past research and have isolated 11 categories of teacher behavior. Four categories, namely, enthusiasm, use of student ideas and general indirectness, criticism, and probing seem to be directly relevant to the acquisition of students' attitudes and have been shown to be favorably associated with students' school achievement.

Projective Techniques

This group includes procedures such as sentence completion, essays and ambiguous drawings that have been used for attitude measurement. D. T. Campbell (1950) has reported the use of the Thematic Apperception Test (TAT) and ambiguous pictures similar to TAT in several studies on social attitudes. Similar procedures have been used by Alexander (1950) for predicting teacher-pupil interactions, by Malpass (1953) for measuring attitudes toward school, and by G. B. Johnson (1955, 1957) for analysis and prediction of teacher effectiveness. Loree (1971) has summarized several studies on teachers' attitudes in which disguised measures have been used.

ATTITUDES AND BEHAVIOR

The discrepancy between professed attitude and overt behavior demonstrated by La Piere (1934) remains a perplexing issue in attitude measurement (Green, 1954). The self-report technique is often independent of observations of overt behavior and is susceptible to faking, response set and social desirability. The approach of indirect or disguised testing through unstructured situations has been offered as an alternative to paper and pencil measures although no evidence exists that disguised measures predict "real life" behavior better than undisguised measures (D. T. Campbell, 1950). In view of the difficulties associated with direct observation in natural settings (e.g., limited sampling, observer bias, complexity of behavior, cost) and the ethical and moral issues and scoring problems of disguised testing, self-report inventories will remain the major sources of collection of data on attitudes. It has been argued that responses to attitude statements will not be distorted if made without the fear of social disapproval and in nonthreatening situations (Edwards, 1957; Rosen, 1960). Measurement of attitudes through self-report inventories can be improved by use of the multiple-indicator approach suggested by Cook and Selltiz (1964) and the multitrait-multimethod approach of Campbell and Fiske (1959) along with other scaling and psychometric considerations (Tittle & Hill, 1967). Wang (1932) and S. L. Payne (1951) have offered suggestions and criteria for writing and evaluating items to construct better attitude scales.

AVAILABILITY OF ATTITUDE SCALES

The actual availability and documentation of psychometrically sound attitude scales is, however, far from satisfactory. There have been two recent attempts (Bonjean, Hill, & McLemore, 1967; Shaw & Wright, 1967) to report data on scales which have been used in previous attitude research. Although the approach to the inventory and classification of scales is different, the intent of both volumes is an emphasis on the use of existing scales in future research. Bonjean, Hill, and McLemore have discussed and included items of those measures in detail which were used five times or more in the sociological literature between 1954 and 1965. They have given bibliographic information on other measures including several for attitude toward and perceptions of education. Shaw and Wright have provided detailed psychometric and content descriptions of scales for measuring attitudes toward various concepts including education and educational practices, teaching and school courses.

We have listed some of the instruments that have been reported in the literature for measuring students' and teachers' attitudes toward education, including school and teacher, and toward mathematics, science and social studies in Table 1. The instruments have been further classified into Likert, Thurstone, Projective, Physiological, Guttman, and Semantic Differential categories. We have not employed any criteria for including scales in the list, and it is not by any means exhaustive either with respect to the coverage of the areas or the instruments in each area. For instance, quite a few instruments have been developed to measure attitudes toward physical education (e.g., Wear, 1955; Richardson, 1960). However, it is clear from Table 1 that the Likert technique has been widely used but that promising techniques such as projective and semantic differential have rarely been used. An investigator may evaluate the existing scales in terms of psychometric and other relevant criteria before embarking on the construction of a new scale.

CONTENT ANALYSIS

Content analysis methodology can be used for determining the attitudinal components of a variety of curriculum materials. Berelson (1954) has defined content analysis as a research technique for the objective, systematic and quantitative description of the manifest content of communication. Kerlinger (1964) has described content analysis in these terms: "It is . . . a method of observation. Instead of observing people's behavior directly, or asking them to respond to scales, or interviewing them, the investigator takes the communications that people have produced and asks questions of the communications" (p. 544). Holsti (1968) summarized the various definitions employed by researchers: "any technique for making inferences by systematically and objectively identifying specified characteristics of messages" (p. 601).

Content analysis procedures have been widely used in the fields of journalism, communications, political science, psychology and other social sciences (Budd, Thorp, & Donohew, 1967; Cartwright, 1953; Pool, 1959; Smith, Lasswell, & Casey, 1946). Barcus (1960) has estimated that more than 60 percent of the empirical studies in content analysis have been concentrated in five areas: social values, propaganda analyses, media inventories, journalistic studies, and psychological-psychoanalytic research. Although the educational field has lagged behind these other areas, there are signs that educational researchers are beginning to recognize the importance of content analysis (Fox, 1969; Kerlinger, 1964). Among the many uses for content analysis in education have been the analysis of textbooks for propaganda (McDiarmid & Pratt, 1971), determining readability of written materials (Flesch, 1948), analyzing children's language (Finn, 1969), analyzing readers for societal trends (DeCharms & Moeller, 1962), and evaluating curriculum materials (Weiss, 1971). Since attitudinal influences are usually present in various types of educational communications, researchers should become familiar with the variety of content analysis procedures summarized in Holsti (1968) and Webb (1967). For textbook analysis, the Evaluation Assertion Rating System (McDiarmid & Pratt, 1971) appears to be promising.

So far we have briefly reviewed the theoretical and methodological issues that arise in the research on affective behaviors. We now turn our attention to the review of studies on the antecedents of students' school-related attitudes.

ANTECEDENTS OF SCHOOL-RELATED AFFECTIVE BEHAVIORS

There are several influences which impinge upon students' school-related atti-

TABLE 1

SCALES FOR MEASURING ATTITUDES TOWARD EDUCATION AND SCHOOL COURSES

Area	Type					
	Likert	Thurstone	Projective	Physiological	Guttman	Semantic Differential
Education	The Education Scale (Rundquist & Sletto, 1936)	Attitude toward Teaching (Miller, 1934)				
	Attitude toward Education Scale (Mitchell, 1941)	Attitude toward any School Subject (Silance & Remmers, 1934)				
	Minnesota Teacher Attitude Inventory (Cooks, Leeds, & Callis, 1951)	A Scale for Measuring Attitude toward any Teacher (Hoshaw, 1936)				
	Opinionnaire on Attitude toward Education (Lindgren & Patton, 1958)	Attitude toward Education (Glassey, 1945)				
	Education Scale (Kerlinger & Kaya, 1959)					
	Survey of Study Habits & Attitudes, Form H (Brown & Holtzman, 1967)					
	The Clark High School Attitude Survey (Jeffs, 1967)					
	Pupil Opinion Questionnaire (Bowman & Havilicek, 1969)					

Mathematics	Revised Mathematics Attitude Scale (Aiken, 1963) Mathematics Attitude Questionnaire (Alpert, Stellwagon, & Becker, 1963) A. V. Scale (Adams & Von Brock, 1967) Pupils' Attitude toward Arithmetic (Dutton & Blum, 1968)	Inventory of Prospective Teachers' Attitudes (Dutton, 1951) Attitudes of Junior and Senior High School Students toward Mathematics (Malone & Freel, 1954) Attitudes of Junior High School Pupils toward Arithmetic (Dutton, 1956)	Mathematics Affect (Alpert, Stellwagon, & Becker, 1963) Pupil Attitude toward Mathematics (Nealigh, 1968)	Number Anxiety Test (Dreger & Aiken, 1957) Situational Anxiety Expression Test (Milliken & Spilka, 1962)	Students' Attitudes toward Arithmetic (Anttonen, 1968)
Science	An Attitude Scale (Allen, 1959) Generalized Attitude toward Science held by Secondary School Students (Vitrogan, 1967) Biology Attitude Assessment Scale (L. W. Glass, 1970)	Science Attitude Scale (Dutton & Stephens, 1963)	Attitude toward Scientists (Mead & Métraux, 1957) Projective Test of Attitudes (Lowery, 1966) Children's Attitude toward Science in Elementary School (Perrodin, 1966)		Science Attitude Scale (Geis, 1969)
Social Studies	Scale of Beliefs (Grim, 1936) Interest in Civic Attitude Scale (Trenfield, 1965) Social Studies Interest Inventory (Kehoe, 1970)				Semantic Differential Scales (Hoover, 1967)

tudes. Some of these influences are the learner's own characteristics and background factors such as sex, age, socioeconomic status, school achievement and personality characteristics. In addition, there are some influences related to the school environment such as the teacher, classroom climate, curriculum materials and instructional strategies. Figure 1 is an attempt to outline schematically what we consider to be some of the important influences on school-related attitudes and what is to follow in the next few sections. By using single and double arrows we have tried to indicate the directionality of influence. For example, we tend to think that the teacher and classroom climate have reciprocal relationships with school-related attitudes. In the case of socioeconomic status, sex and age, the influence is in the direction of school-related attitudes only. We have taken the position that instructional strategies, curriculum input, and the student's personality and achievement may influence a learner's attitudes which in turn may partially influence instructional strategies.

Figure 1 is neither an attempt to develop a theoretical model to account for these relationships nor exhaustive of all possible combinations. For instance, we have not taken into consideration the relationships among various antecedents (e.g., teacher, classroom climate). Our purpose has been to provide a schematic view of the various factors which have been found to influence school-related attitudes.

LEARNER CHARACTERISTICS

In this section we will review research on the relationships between students' attitudes and their academic performance and such background characteristics as sex, personality, age and socioeconomic status. Suggestions for further research will be offered wherever they seem appropriate.

Students' Attitudes and Achievement

The relationship between favorable scholastic attitudes and level of academic achievement is functional rather than causal—that is, academic successes help to promote satisfaction with school, which in turn increases the possibility of future successes (Bloom, 1971; Jackson, 1968). Aiken (1970) has reviewed studies indicating that if certain attitudes are held and reinforced consistently in the same direction they lead to a particular self-concept on the part of the pupil which influences his expectation of future achievement. One of the reinforcing conditions in such a situation is the type of evidence the pupil has regarding his achievement from his teacher, his parents and his peers.

Studies in this area have generally followed the form of ascertaining students' school-related attitudes and relating such attitudinal measures to subsequent academic achievement. The rationale for these studies appears to be that since attitudes lend themselves to modification, positive findings will provide the basis for devising treatments in order to bring about change in academic achievement. Such a change will not only

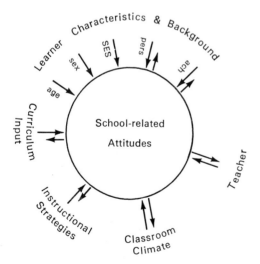

Fig. 1. A schematic representation of various effects on school-related attitudes (SES-Socioeconomic status; Pers-Personality; Ach-Achievement).

improve future attitudinal dispositions of students toward school and school learning but will also contribute to personal and social adjustment (Holtzman & Brown, 1968; Khan & Roberts, 1971).

The relationship between attitudes toward school and school achievement has been investigated in several studies. Malpass (1953) correlated measures of students' perception of school with their achievement after controlling for the effects of ability for 92 eighth-grade students. It was found that children's perception of school was significantly related to teachers' grades but unrelated to standardized achievement. Brodie (1964) classified 505 high-school students as "satisfied" and "dissatisfied" with school and compared their achievement. He reported that the satisfied group performed better on educational tasks and, in particular, on tests of academic skills than the dissatisfied group.

Several studies have been conducted at the high-school level which used scores on the Survey of Study Habits and Attitudes as predictors of academic performance. For instance, Holtzman & Brown (1968) reported correlations ranging from 0.32 to 0.66 between the total score on this survey and several achievement measures for a large sample of students in grades 7 through 12. Khan (1969) correlated scores on eight school-related attitudinal factors derived from an experimental version of this survey and six subtests of the Metropolitan Achievement Test Series for 428 male and 456 female ninth-grade students. The multiple correlations between the composite of affective variables and subtests ranged from 0.48 to 0.59 for males and 0.62 to 0.69 for females, all significant beyond the 0.01 level. When linear composites of both sets of variables were correlated, canonical correlations of 0.69 and 0.79 were obtained for males and females, respectively. In a follow-up study (Khan, 1970), the survey factor scores were related to standardized achievement for 142 male and 152 female students in the twelfth grade. The multiple cor-

relations between the attitudinal factors and each of the four achievement areas ranged from 0.51 to 0.59 for males and from 0.50 to 0.62 for females. In another study (Khan & Roberts, 1969), a multiple correlation of 0.56 was obtained between the linear composite of six factors measured by the Survey of Study Habits and Attitudes and teacher marks for 240 eighth-grade students. When standardized achievement scores in vocabulary, spelling and arithmetic computation were used as criteria, multiple correlations ranging from 0.44 to 0.54 were obtained. These findings are contrary to those reported by Malpass (1953) on the absence of relationship between attitudes and standardized achievement measures.

In contrast to the positive findings reported above, several studies have reported nonsignificant relationships between school-related attitudes and performance. For instance, Tenenbaum (1944) found no relationship between attitude toward school, attitude toward teachers, attitude toward other pupils, and performance measures including intelligence, school marks and school progress for a sample of 639 elementary-school children. Schultz and Green (1953) have reported nonsignificant correlations between attitudes and achievement for a sample of female high-school students. Jackson and Lahaderne (1967) and Lahaderne (1968) related scores on questionnaires measuring attitudes toward school and toward teachers to achievement for sixth-grade children. They found no relationship between these attitudes and school achievement.

Jackson (1968) has suggested that the relationship between attitudes and academic achievement may not be easily demonstrable by procedures followed in studies which have reported a lack of relationship between school-related attitudes and academic performance. The instruments used in these studies may not have been sensitive enough to reveal differences in the intensity of attitudes for a large group of students who have neutral or mixed feelings about school.

Another reason for a lack of relationship in these studies may be that attitudes and academic achievement are nonlinearly related.

In some studies attitudes have been treated as moderator variables—that is, individuals have been classified into several groups on attitude level for studying the relationship between ability and achievement. It has been hypothesized in these studies (see Aiken, 1970) that the correlation between ability and achievement may vary with the level of attitude. In one study at the college level (Cristantiello, 1962), it was found that ability and achievement correlated higher in a group with mild attitudes than in groups with extreme attitudes. In a recent study at the high-school level (Williams, 1970), it was found that students who were dissatisfied with school obtained significantly lower scores on tests of ability and achievement than students with positive orientation toward school.

The reason for nonsignificant relationship between attitudes and achievement may also be the use of an overall score to represent the multiplicity of attitudes toward the school situation. Recently Holtzman and Brown (1968) divided the Survey of Study Habits and Attitudes into four logically derived subscales, believing that the use of relatively homogenous scales may be more profitable in research and practice than one general score. Khan (1969) has provided evidence that a combination of several subscores on relevant attitude scales correlates higher with academic performance than a single score.

A somewhat different strategy has been to examine the contribution of attitudinal variables to the prediction of academic achievement beyond that which is realized by scholastic aptitude variables alone. The impetus for such research has come from a preoccupation with academic prediction and the inability of aptitude measures to account for more than half of the reliable variance in school achievement. From the methodology of multiple regression analysis,

it follows that affective variables will significantly increase the correlation between aptitude and achievement only if they have lower correlations with aptitude scores and higher correlations with achievement. Such evidence is interpreted to mean that affective measures have less in common with aptitudes and more in common with achievement. Holtzman and Brown (1968) have concluded from such evidence with regard to the Survey of Study Habits and Attitudes that it measures traits that are not tapped by standardized aptitude tests. Khan (1969, 1970) combined affective variables with scholastic aptitude to predict performance on standardized achievement tests in grades 9 and 12 for the same students and compared the resulting multiple correlations with those obtained between aptitude and achievement. It was found that affective variables significantly added to the prediction of performance in grade 9 but not in grade 12.

The findings of Cristantiello (1962) and the arguments of Jackson (1968) seem to be of benefit to research concerned with increasing the accuracy of academic prediction. For instance, affective variables will make significantly more contribution to prediction by aptitude variables in groups with extreme attitudes than in groups with middle attitude scores. Alternatively, Bloom (1971) believes that for students who are extreme in school achievement there is a relation between positive or negative attitudes toward school and indications of adequacy or inadequacy in school achievement.

Correlates of School Attitudes

Several studies have been conducted to ascertain the influence of such background characteristics as socioeconomic status, sex, age and personality on the quality of students' attitudes toward school and teachers. Social class differences have been assumed to operate in educational attitudes because socioeconomic status symbolizes a variety of values, attitudes and motivations (Lavin, 1965). The differing expectations from males and females in terms of social behavior are reflected in attitudes and dispositions toward social and psychological objects. Jackson (1968) points out that boys and girls differ in their reactions to teacher, school and learning situations which result in sex differences in classroom behavior. The nature of the experiences in school varies with age and grade level, and several studies have examined shifts in school-related attitudes of students as a function of increasing age and grade level.

Socioeconomic status. In general, studies have yielded results which show that students from lower socioeconomic backgrounds do not have favorable attitudes toward school and teachers. Neale and Proshek (1967) and Glick (1970) have reported that children in schools located in the upper socioeconomic status areas held more positive attitudes toward teachers and school than children in the schools located in the lower socioeconomic areas. Yee (1966, 1968) has suggested that since lower-class pupils often have fewer potent sources of adult warmth and support at home, they are influenced more by the teachers in school than students of middle-class background. Teachers' less positive attitudes toward students in lower-class schools tend to make pupils' attitudes toward teachers become less favorable. In a study on the influence of family income on attitudes, Coster (1958) reported no differences between three income groups in students' attitudes toward school and the value of education. However, significant differences were reported in attitudes toward other people, including peers and teachers.

Recently researchers have begun to question the use of gross indicators such as socioeconomic status and parental educational level and occupation for determining the effects of home environment upon children. It is felt that these indicators rarely provide

useful information about the most salient behavioral features of the sociopsychological environment. In addition, there is little that can be done about modifying these indicators in the expectation that concomitant changes in the child would result (Shulman, 1970; Weiss, 1970b).

Rather than use these relatively static indicators, Bloom (1964) has suggested the study of more dynamic processes of the home environment (e.g., achievement press, language models). Thus far this strategy has been applied mainly to the study of cognitive characteristics of students (Dave, 1963; Hanson, 1970; Marjoribanks, 1972; Wolf, 1966). However, one study (Weiss, 1970a) investigated the relationships between the home environment and two noncognitive characteristics—self-esteem and achievement motivation. It was found that process variables (e.g., standards of excellence and expectations, independence training, parent evaluation of child) were more meaningful than static indicators.

Sex. Significant sex differences in attitudes toward school and toward teachers have been reported in favor of girls. Leeds and Cook (1947) reported that female high-school students held more favorable attitudes towards teachers than did male students. Gregersen and Travers (1968) reported that boys reject their teachers more than girls do. There is an increase in rejection of teachers on the part of girls with increasing age while there is no such increase in rejection by boys. Jackson (1968) has summarized the results of a study in which teachers were asked to classify boys and girls into "satisfied" and "dissatisfied" groups. The teachers were able to classify satisfied girls and dissatisfied boys with greater accuracy than they were able to classify dissatisfied girls and satisfied boys.

Age. Results of studies on the relationship between students' age and their attitudes agree that school-related attitudes tend to become less favorable with increasing age or school experience (Demos, 1960; Dunn, 1968). After surveying 8,156 high-school boys and girls, Coleman (1959) found that adolescents were negatively oriented to scholastic matters irrespective of the wider differences in parental background, type of school and type of community.

Personality characteristics. Flanders, Morrison, and Brode (1968) reported that loss in positive attitude toward teacher and school was not related to intelligence, socioeconomic status or grade assignment but was due to the externability-internability dimension of personality. There was a greater negative shift in attitude of students who thought that their degree of success was determined by sources beyond their control (external) than students who believed that their success or failure was self-determined (internal). Goldberg (1968) investigated the extent to which students' perceptions of teachers' behavior are influenced by students' own attitudes. He found that highly compulsive students perceived teachers as less authoritarian than did less compulsive students, and those students who differed on measures of authoritarian and flexible attitudes did not perceive teachers differentially. Della Piana and Gage (1955) tested the hypothesis that pupils' liking of teachers is a function of the interaction between pupils' values and teachers' attitudes. They classified students into two groups—one liking teachers with "cognitive merit" and the other liking teachers with "affective merit." The results suggested that teachers with favorable attitudes (as measured by MTAI) were better liked by pupils who held strong affective values concerning teachers. Nelson (1964) reported that teachers and pupils in junior high school deviate significantly in terms of their attitudes toward each other. He found that teachers are cognitively oriented toward pupils while pupils are affectively oriented toward teachers.

It is evident that teachers are an impor-

tant influence on students' attitudes. In the next section, we review research on different aspects of teachers' attitudes and attitude change.

THE TEACHER

During the preschool period the child's interaction is limited mainly to his parents, and what happens in the home has significant effects on the personal, social and emotional growth of the child (Bloom, 1964; Kagan & Moss, 1962; Weiss, 1970a). When he enters school, his adult environment broadens to include the teacher as another important person who acquires a significant role in the child's development. The quality of the teacher-pupil relationship and the teacher's attitudes toward the child are two of the potentially important influences on the attitudes of the child toward the teacher and toward the objects or activities with which the teacher is related. For instance, it can be postulated from the theory of interpersonal perception (Heider, 1958) that a child's attitudes toward the teacher will affect his attitudes toward the courses taught by the teacher and toward the school. It is surprising, however, that very little direct evidence exists on the extent to which students' school-related affective behaviors are influenced by teachers' attitudes. Exceptions to this are two studies conducted during the evaluation of Harvard Project Physics. Rothman, Welch, and Walberg (1969) found no relationship between teachers' scores on MTAI and students' attitudes toward physics. In the other study (Rothman, 1969) attitudes toward physics were measured by the semantic differential technique and mostly weak relationships were found between teachers' and students' attitudes toward physics. Notwithstanding these studies, it would appear that the relationship between teachers' and students' attitudes has been regarded as axiomatic with no need for empirical research. It is likely that this premise has served as a basis for the large number of studies conducted on students' perceptions of teachers' attitudes, teachers' values and beliefs, and the effects of demographic characteristics and teacher education on teachers' attitudes.

Students' Perceptions of Teachers' Attitudes

Teachers' attitudes toward their students are reflected in teachers' classroom behavior as perceived by students or observed by experts. For instance, Seidman and Knapp (1953) reported a close agreement between teachers' statements of likes and dislikes regarding their students and students' predictions about teachers' attitudes. Silberman (1969) obtained a significant relationship between students' predictions about teachers' attitudes toward them and actual classroom behavior of teachers. In a somewhat different study, Murray (1969) investigated the influence of teachers' level of self-actualization and social values upon students' perceptions of the teachers' concern about them. He reported that teachers who were self-actualizing and those high on social values were perceived as more concerned about students than teachers who were non-actualizing and those low on social values. Reed (1953) investigated the hypothesis that the teacher who is more accepting of himself and his environment is the more effective teacher as perceived by students. He obtained a significant relationship between teachers' effectiveness in the classroom and teachers' level of self-acceptance.

Teachers' Values and Beliefs

Several investigations were conducted to study the general nature of teachers' values and belief systems about education because of their importance in determining teachers' attitudes toward children. Oliver and Butcher (1962) investigated whether or not teachers' attitudes toward education might be represented by the dimension of naturalism, radicalism and tendermindedness. A factor analysis of data collected on 300 teach-

ers provided support for the existence of three distinct categories of teachers' attitudes and beliefs. Wehling and Charters (1969) suggested that teachers' attitudes can be meaningfully described as a complex organization of beliefs. They developed a number of questionnaires to measure teachers' beliefs about classroom teaching behavior and, using factor analytic techniques, identified eight dimensions: subject-matter emphasis, personal adjustment, ideology, student autonomy versus teacher direction, emotional disengagement, consideration of student viewpoint, classroom management, student challenge, and integrative learning. Harvey et al. (1966) classified preschool teachers as either abstract or concrete after rating them on factors such as flexibility, attitude toward rules, encouragement of children's independence and activity, need for structure, and punitiveness. They found that the more abstract teachers differed from the more concrete teachers in an educationally favorable direction on all dimensions. In another study, Harvey et al. (1968) related teachers' level of abstraction to students' behavior in the classroom and found that children in classes of abstract teachers (who displayed more resourcefulness, less dictatorialness, and less punitiveness) were more involved, more active, higher in achievement, and less concrete than children in classes of concrete teachers.

Demographic Characteristics and Teachers' Attitudes

Several investigators have studied the differences in teachers' attitudes as a function of grade level taught and sex of both teachers and students. Wandt (1954) reported that elementary-school teachers held more positive attitudes toward students than secondary-school teachers. Lindgren and Patton (1958) obtained similar results and in addition found differences favoring female teachers. Kearney and Rocchio (1955) reported significant differences between the attitudes of elementary-school teachers of self-contained classrooms and teachers of special subjects. They remarked that teachers who have the same pupils throughout the day are concerned not only with the subject matter but also with pupils' interests and physical and mental health, while teachers of special subjects are interested only in subject-matter coverage.

Teachers' Attitudes Toward Students' Behavior Problems

Teachers' handling of behavior problems has been reported to have significant effects on students' behavior. Carlson (1935) reported that cheating decreased under teachers who were least in favor of blaming and shaming the students and who rated the greatest number of common behavior problems as having serious implications for the integrated development of the child. Kounin and Gump (1961) have reported that children who have punitive teachers are more unsettled, confused about misconduct in school, less concerned with learning and school values, and manifest more aggression in their misconduct than children with nonpunitive teachers.

Several studies have been conducted in the area of teachers' attitudes toward children with behavior problems since Wickman (1928) reported differences in teachers' and clinicians' ratings of the seriousness of behaviors. These studies were undertaken either to support or reject Wickman's findings or to discover reasons for shifts in the direction of agreement between teachers and clinicians. Peck (1935), Ellis, and Miller (1936), and Sparks (1952) contradicted Wickman's findings by reporting closer agreement between teachers and clinicians.

However, Morsh and Plenderleith (1949) supported Wickman's findings, and, in addition, reported that elementary-school teachers were more tolerant than secondary-school teachers and that female teachers were more severe in handling behavior problems than male teachers. Hunter (1957) reported congruence between ratings of

Wickman's teachers and teachers in his own study. Tolor, Scarpetti, and Lane (1967) found differences in teachers' and clinicians' ratings of behavior falling into the categories of aggressive, repressive, and affect experience. They further discovered that inexperienced teachers differed more from psychologists than experienced teachers.

Ample evidence exists, however, that there has been a genuine change in the attitudes of teachers toward students' behavior problems because of improvement in teacher education. There is far more emphasis on the study of mental hygiene, child growth and development, and dynamics of group behavior in teacher training than in the past (LaBue, 1959; Pinckney, 1962; Rocchio & Kearney, 1956; Schrupp & Gjerde, 1953; Stouffer, 1952). The review of research has, however, suggested consistent differences in attitudes of male and female teachers and elementary- and secondary-school teachers toward the behavior problems of children (Beilin, 1959; Stouffer, 1956).

Teachers' Attitude Change

In the realm of attitude change, teacher training is concerned with desirable changes in a student-teacher's attitude toward himself and his pupils (Loree, 1971). Several studies have reported positive changes in the attitudes of student-teachers as a result of education courses. Remmers, Dodds, and Brasch (1942) administered a 100-item questionnaire about educational practices and policies to 50 students before and after a course in principles of secondary education. They reported significant positive changes with regard to expansion and reorganization of curriculum, formal discipline, recognition of individual differences, and personality development. In other studies (Brim, 1966; Jacobs, 1968), significant changes toward more positive attitudes were observed as a result of theory courses in education. Attitudes of student-teachers toward young people became more favorable, liberal and democratic. However, actual practice teaching caused student-teachers' attitudes to become more negative, rigid and authoritarian (Day, 1959; Dutton, 1962; Harrison, 1967; Jacobs, 1968). Results of other studies (Callis, 1950; Ragsdale, 1967) revealed that teacher education does not influence the nature of the attitudes of student-teachers toward their pupils.

Kearney and Rocchio (1956) studied the relationship between the type of teacher-education institution attended by elementary-school teachers and their ability to maintain harmonious relationships with children. They found that teachers who had attended a university held more positive attitudes than those who had attended a liberal arts college. Comparing elementary- and secondary-school teacher-trainees, Weinstock and Peccolo (1970) reported that after practice teaching, elementary-school teachers were more logically consistent in their views and had more favorable attitudes than secondary-school teachers. In order to study differential change in student-teachers' attitudes as a result of practice teaching, D. E. Campbell (1967) classified MTAI statements into five categories: moral status of children, classroom management, child development and behavior, philosophy and curriculum, and teachers' reactions. The total scores both before and after practice did not change significantly, while scores in the child development and behavior category changed significantly when subscores were considered.

The influence of supervisors and cooperating teachers on change in attitudes of student-teachers was studied by several investigators. O. Scott and Brinkley (1960) reported that students who had a lower MTAI score than their supervisors showed a significant improvement while students who had a higher MTAI score than their supervisors did not change. Yee (1969) pre- and posttested 124 student-teachers, 124 cooperating teachers, and 12 college supervisors to test the hypothesis that cooperating teachers were a significant source of influence in student teaching. The results

showed that the attitudes of student-teachers toward young people were generally influenced by their cooperating teachers. However, Horowitz (1968) noted that cooperating teachers are not influential in bringing about change in student-teachers' expectations and perceptions about teaching.

In several studies, effects of specially designed treatments on attitude change of teachers were investigated. Shaw, Klausmeier, Luker, and Reid (1952) reported significant improvement in teachers' attitudes as a result of a two-week workshop in guidance. Watson (1968), however, did not obtain significant changes in attitudes of student-teachers as a result of 10 sessions in learning, counseling, and leadership. Maas (1950) found that relevant field-work programs improved student-teachers' attitudes toward themselves and toward young children. Hicks (1967) reported that apprentice teaching and additional information produced favorable attitudes toward self and the school in some Negro students.

There are many ways in which the teacher can influence students. Aside from the one-to-one relationship of the teacher with each of the students, the teacher influences the group atmosphere in the classroom as a whole. The teacher sets the tone of the classroom social climate through his/her philosophy about classroom conduct, educational beliefs and values, strategies of instruction, and methods of administering reward and punishment (Tuel & Shaw, 1966). We now turn to a review of research on the effects of classroom social climate upon students' attitudes.

CLASSROOM CLIMATE

School is more than a place where academic skills are taught and learned: it is a miniature community in itself where members interact and influence the behavior of each other (Shoben, 1962). The social relations among the students as a group and between the students and the teacher significantly influence the quality of the classroom social climate which, in turn, influences the cognitive and affective learning outcomes (Anderson, 1970; G. I. Brown, 1960; Buswell, 1953; Calvin, Hoffman, & Harden, 1957; E. E. Johnson, 1958; Porterfield & Schlichting, 1961). The classroom has been designated as one of the most important places for organizing children's attitudes and behavior (Henry, 1957). The nature of interactions and experiences in the classroom is an important factor in determining the learner's perceptions of school and his attitudes toward school-related persons and activities (Ehrlich, 1969; Finley, 1969).

Getzels (1969) has traced several influences of previous research on group dynamics and social interaction which have contributed to the study of classroom climate. The classic studies of Lewin, Lippitt, and White (1939) on the effects of democratic, laissez-faire, and authoritarian leadership styles on the subsequent social climate of the groups and behavior of individual members provided the basis for later work on teachers' attitudes and beliefs (Yee & Fruchter, 1971). Several studies (Kerlinger & Pedhazur, 1968; Lindgren & Singer, 1963; McGee, 1955; Sontag, 1968) have reported a close relationship between teachers' authoritarian or democratic, traditional or progressive attitudes and actual or perceived teacher classroom behavior related to students.

Based on global observations and ratings of social interaction, classroom climates have been characterized as teacher-centered versus student-centered, and the effects of such climates on the affective behavior of students have been studied (Getzels, 1969). Other terms such as authoritarian versus democratic, permissive versus restrictive, dominative versus integrative have also been used in the literature to describe classroom climates. Withall (1949) reported that more positive pupil reactions to teachers were made in student-centered classes than in teacher-centered classes. In two studies (Bovard, 1951a, 1951b), group-centered classes produced a higher level of interpersonal affect among its members who showed greater liking for each other as a

learning group than the leader-centered classes. Anderson and Kell (1954), in a study of four classes, found that students in group-centered classes held more positive attitudes toward themselves as participants in that group than students in leader-centered classes who had mixed feelings about their participation.

A series of studies was recently undertaken by Walberg and his associates (Walberg, 1969a, 1969b; Walberg & Ahlgren, 1970; Walberg & Anderson, 1968) to test hypotheses derived from a sociopsychological theory (Getzels & Thelen, 1960) of the classroom as a social system. The Getzels-Thelen model holds that institutional and individual characteristics interact in classrooms and determine school learning. In several of these investigations, the influence of classroom social climate and students' and teachers' characteristics on learning was studied. The general findings of these studies have been that affective aspects of classroom climate (e.g., satisfaction, intimacy and friction) predict both cognitive and affective learning. For instance, in one study (Walberg, 1969a), significant multiple correlations of 0.44 and 0.41 were obtained between 14 properties of classroom social climate and science interest and physics interest, respectively.

GROUP CHARACTERISTICS

The group serves as an important reference for the child because it provides appropriate social roles, norms, values and attitudes for group members for facilitating group conformity and peer acceptance (Jenkins, 1951; Lombardi, 1963). Group characteristics such as size, cohesiveness, composition and so on may have important effects on the nature of interactions and social climate.

Group Size

The study by Walberg (1969a) and the review of the literature by McKeachie (1963) have indicated that class size is not generally related to cognitive learning. At present there is no research evidence on the effects of class size on affective learning. Getzels (1969) is of the view that greater opportunities for interpersonal interaction and individual participation, which should facilitate a more favorable social climate, will exist in smaller groups than in larger groups.

Group Cohesiveness

Lott and Lott (1960) have noted that a favorable climate is more likely if there are numerous strong positive attitudes among the members of the learning class. This should lead to a group characterized by cohesiveness rather than friction. A person will more readily value membership in a cohesive group and subscribe strongly to group attitudes. For example, Kelley and Volkart (1952) and Kelley (1955) conducted experiments on changing of group-anchored attitudes in relation to importance that an individual places on group membership. They found that the amount of change was inversely related to saliency of group membership.

Group Composition

The extent of group cohesiveness depends upon the characteristics of the individuals in the group. The existing structure of schools allows for grouping based on age, grade level and curriculum programs. Several other factors such as sex, socioeconomic status, race and religion also influence the grouping of children either at the school or grade level. Students are frequently further grouped based on their scholastic ability or attainment. It is maintained that homogenous grouping by ability facilitates learning and instruction. Research evidence on the usefulness of homogenous grouping for improvement in academic learning is inconclusive (Yates, 1966). Research on affective aspects of ability grouping is practically nonexistent. A possible consequence of grouping on low-ability students may be damage to self-concept, which might result in a dis-

like for school and learning. Research is needed on the effects of ability grouping on the attitudes, values, anxiety and self-concept of students.

A group in which an individual's social, emotional and personality needs are met will seem to facilitate and encourage affective learning. Getzels (1969) has noted that the optimal group composition should allow for matching a person's dispositions and the role he is expected to play in the group. Yates (1966) has suggested that grouping procedures should achieve a better fit or congruence between the student and the teacher, the peer group, the task and a set of common purposes in order to facilitate both cognitive and affective learning.

TEXTBOOKS AND OTHER COMMUNICATIONS MATERIALS

In addition to the teacher and classroom environment, other major sources of influence on the development of affective behaviors are communication materials (such as textbooks and other software) used in schools. In this section we shall briefly review the literature on communications and textbook analysis.

Communications and Textbooks

The analysis of written materials has benefited from two lines of research in the social sciences: experimental communications research and analysis of textbooks by historians and social psychologists. The communications work has generally concerned itself with tightly designed experimental studies of the effects upon attitudes of type of communication or message (Gruner, 1965; Moan & Flick, 1968), length of communication (Ragsdale, 1968), characteristics of audience (Janis & Hovland, 1959; Payne, 1964). L. M. Smith and Hudgins (1965, ch. 14) present a useful integration of the more salient communications research in an attempt to account for attitude change in the educational setting.

One important finding of the communications research is that information given to an individual can be an influential determinant in modifying attitudes (Annis & Meier, 1934; Davis, 1965). An important source of information for students can be found in the textbooks and other software widely used in schools (Cronbach, 1955). The study of textbooks owes much to public agencies concerned with bias against minority groups or propaganda about world events. In a study sponsored by the Anti-Defamation League of B'nai Brith, Marcus (1961) analyzed 48 high-school social studies textbooks during the period 1949–60 for their treatment of Jews, Negroes, immigrants, and the Nazi persecution of minorities. The texts were evaluated using the criteria of inclusion, validity, balance, comprehensiveness, concreteness, unity and realism. Some of the findings were: 1) Jews are no longer referred to as a race, but, on the whole, are mentioned only incidentally; 2) Nazi atrocities against minorities are largely not presented; 3) the Negroes' position in society is largely ignored, but, when included, Negroes are depicted as simple and uneducated people; 4) recent immigrants such as Asians and Spanish-speaking people are either ignored or portrayed much less favorably than the earlier middle-European immigrants. Similar results about minority groups were obtained in a study of primary (grades one to three) social studies texts (Golden, 1965). The treatment of Negroes in texts is receiving increasingly more attention by social scientists (Carpenter, 1941; Elkin, 1965; Knowles & Prewitt, 1969).

Textbooks have also been analyzed for content related to international affairs and attitudes toward other countries. A fascinating account of the treatment of past wars in the history texts of both the United States and those of its former enemies is provided by Walworth (1938), where the same event is portrayed from completely opposite viewpoints. The importance of research leading to the improvement of textbooks is highlighted by the United Nations Educational,

Scientific, and Cultural Organization's *Handbook for the Improvement of Textbooks and Teaching Materials as Aids to International Understanding* (1949). A comprehensive summary of research in content analysis of textbooks is offered by McDiarmid and Pratt (1971, chapter 1).

INSTRUCTIONAL STRATEGIES

In addition to textbooks, there are many ways of structuring curricular experiences for students. (Teachers are usually quick to utilize new instructional media and strategies, often before any evidence is available about the effectiveness of the technique.) Because of the variety of media and instructional strategies, we have arrived at a somewhat arbitrary (and perhaps artificial) way of grouping them according to either *passive* or *active* involvement of the student with the strategy: students behave as passive recipients with no involvement of a physical nature expected of them with strategies such as records, radio, film and television; it is necessary for a student to be an active participant with programmed instruction, computer-assisted instruction, games, role-playing and simulation. The research can also be divided as to the outcome: either attitude toward the medium or strategy itself, or toward the content being presented.

Passive Participation Strategies

Most of the research has been conducted for television, with film running a distant second. Fewer studies involved the effects of radio on students, with virtually none reported for phonograph records.

The earliest research on media and attitudes was associated with the work of Thurstone and other social psychologists for changing students' social attitudes. For movies, several studies were conducted which used a pre- and posttest design with the showing of a film about Germans and war (Peterson & Thurstone, 1932), gambling (Thurstone, 1931a), the Works

Progress Administration, and soil erosion (Ramseyer, 1939). In general, these experiments resulted in more positive attitudes toward the intended concept. Also, follow-up studies indicated that the changes induced by the films remained stable at least several months after initial viewing (Peterson & Thurstone, 1932; 1933). However, in a study of racial attitudes of 540 Scottish children between the ages of eight and nine exposed to a series of films about different peoples, McFarlane (1945) found no differences between experimental and control groups in attitudes toward black and white groups.

One of the few studies using phonograph records for attitude change also was concerned with views about Germans and war (Rulon et al., 1944). A record series "Then Came War" was played for 864 students in 11 schools throughout the United States, and Thurstone instruments toward Germans and war were administered both before and after the treatment. Significant changes were reported for less favorable attitudes toward Hitler and Germans, and some change toward less favorable attitudes toward war. A study using radio reported no significant attitude changes resulting from the effects of the program, "Germans in the United States," heard by 21 eleventh-grade English classes (Haugh, 1952). The differential results of the foregoing two studies may reside less in either the medium or content than in the context of time, since the study reporting significant attitude changes toward Germans was conducted during the Second World War.

The extensive research on the effects of television can be categorized into two classes: attitudes toward the content of instruction and attitudes toward the medium itself. The group of studies concerned with the medium itself can be further divided since research has been conducted for both teachers and students. Teacher attitudes toward television have been studied because of the expectation that if teachers like the medium they will more readily and successfully use it. Several studies have reported that teachers with more experience using television have more positive attitudes toward the medium (Goetzinger & Valentine, 1963; Handleman, 1960; Karns, 1967). Westley and Jacobson (1962) found fourth-grade teachers less threatened than ninth-grade teachers by the use of television, while no differences were reported for teachers' education level or years of experience.

The findings on student attitudes toward television used in the school, as differentiated from the extensive and sometimes emotional literature on the effects of television viewing on childern (Himmelweit, Oppenheim, & Vince, 1958; Schramm, 1962; Schramm, Lyle, & Parker, 1961; Witty, 1964), are generally less positive than for teachers. McDaniel and Filiatreau (1965) reported that students enrolled in an elementary education course preferred conventional to television instruction. In another study college students had more positive attitudes toward small classes (30–35 students) than either large classes or television instruction (Siegel & Macomber, 1957).

The research evidence for the effects of television instruction upon attitude changes toward, or as a result of, instructional material is more positive than for attitudes toward the medium. In a study of the effects of televised mathematics instruction on ninth graders, Westley and Jacobson (1963) reported that participants rated mathematics course concepts more favorably than did nonparticipating pupils. In his study of the responses of high-school students to a CBS National Citizenship Test, Alper (1967) reported viewers had more positive attitudes toward rights and obligations of American citizens than nonviewers, but that no differences remained after a six-month follow-up. Elementary-school teachers exposed to a series of televised demonstrations of reading instruction developed more positive attitudes toward individualized reading instruction (Lottes, 1961). On the negative side, college students exposed to live teacher lessons had more significant attitude changes than those exposed to video-taped lessons (Croft, Stimpson, Ross, Bray, & Breglio, 1969). After reviewing the research on the effects of television and conventional teaching on attitude change, Schramm (1962) found that the higher the level of schooling, the less students think they learn from instructional television.

Active Involvement Strategies

In this category, programmed instruction is the strategy which has the most attitude research reported. Like the research on television, many of the studies on programmed instruction are concerned with attitudes toward the strategy. In a study relating attitude toward programmed instruction with achievement, Tobias (1969) found that attitudes toward instructional media accounted for a large proportion of achievement variance. In addition, students who preferred traditional devices such as textbooks did not learn effectively from programmed instruction. Another study (Frey, Shimabukuro, & Woodruff, 1967) reported a decline in attitudes of eighth-grade students during the second semester of a two-semester programmed instructional sequence in general science. In addition, there was a concomitant decline in subject-matter achievement.

Neidt and Meredith (1966) reported on changes in students' attitudes when a programmed instruction unit was presented between several weeks of initial lectures and another few weeks of conventional instruction. The results for 70 U.S. airmen studying radiation detection and 53 studying camera repair were significantly more favorable during the programmed units. Other studies should be conducted which look at affective achievement during the sequencing of different instructional strategies.

Fewer studies on attitudes have been reported for computer-assisted instruction than for programmed instruction. Mathis, Smith, and Hansen (1970) conducted a study which looked at the attitudes toward computer-assisted instruction of 64 college students instructed by that medium or with reading materials in general psychology. The following results were reported on attitudes toward computer-assisted instruction: 1) students exposed to it had more positive attitudes than the reading control group; 2) within the computer-assisted instruction group, a negative correlation ($r = -0.49$) was obtained with the number of errors made on performance measures. Brown and Gilman (1969) studied junior high-school students' attitudes toward computer-assisted instruction involving two strategies (contingent prompting with feedback and knowledge of the correct response) and programmed instruction involving the strategy of knowledge of the correct response only. Three groups used these strategies in learning a unit in physics: the two groups which used computer-assisted instruction had more positive attitudes toward that medium than the other group's attitudes toward programmed instruction.

Another area in which the learner is actively interacting with the instructional strategy includes games, simulation and role-playing. Since these have only recently been introduced into the classroom (particularly games and simulation techniques), few research studies are to be found. In one study (Boocock, 1963) the evaluation of the use of an election campaign game in four high-school classes revealed that more realistic attitudes toward politics had developed in the participating students. Other studies report on the "in-basket" technique (Frederiksen, 1962) and internation simulation (Alger, 1963). However, these studies are only tangentially related to attitudes. The interest with which these techniques are being adopted in schools may augur well for future research in this area.

Curriculum Focus Areas

For most of our students, school is a collection of different subjects since the major activities of schooling are usually categorized into subject-matter areas. (While these categories are somewhat different for each level of school—i.e., primary, secondary and university levels—the only differences can be found in the amount of specificity, e.g., language arts, English, English literature.)

In this section we will review studies which have reported upon the attitudes of students toward the different subject areas. Rather than be all-inclusive, we have tried to note trends in the type of research that has been conducted. Where possible, we have tried to provide information about the effects of some of the newer curriculum programs and materials. Although there has been much discussion about the differences between research and evaluation (G. V. Glass & Worthen, 1972) no attempt has been made to differentiate between the two types of studies here. Also, it has not been possible to cover all of the subject areas: missing are areas such as physical education, industrial arts, and the various curricula for professional training (e.g., medicine, law).

Mathematics

A recent review of this area underscores the importance of studying attitudes toward mathematics (Aiken, 1970). This comprehensive review covers the years 1960–1970 and includes topics such as methods of measuring attitudes toward mathematics, grade distribution and stability, relationship between attitude and achievement, teacher characteristics associated with student behaviors, developing positive attitudes and modifying negative attitudes, as well as a critique of the research studies. It should be noted that many of Aiken's criticisms of the research on mathematics attitudes apply equally to other curriculum areas, and indeed to all facets of attitude research.

Research studies have been conducted on several of the new curriculum programs. For the School Mathematics Study Group (SMSG), most studies reported no differences between SMSG and traditional programs on mean mathematics attitude test scores (Phelps, 1964; Woodall, 1967), and

the results of one study (Hungerman, 1967) favored the traditional program. Alpert, Stellwagon, & Becker (1963) found that an interaction of teacher and program was more important than the main effect of curriculum materials: theoretically oriented teachers in SMSG classes produced more positive attitudes than in non-SMSG classes. A study contrasting college students who had the University of Illinois Committee on School Mathematics (UICSM) program and those in a traditional high-school program showed that the UICSM students had significantly more favorable attitudes toward mathematics and took more mathematics courses in college (Comley, 1967) than traditional mathematics students. A comparison of three new programs (UICSM, SMSG, and Ball State) and a traditional course showed no differences between experimental and conventional programs on students' attitudes and interests (Ryan, 1968).

Other researchers have investigated the effects of diverse treatments such as homework (Maertens, 1968), games (Jones, 1968; Zschocher, 1965), and program-centered versus teacher-centered classes (Devine, 1967) on attitudes toward mathematics. Aiken concludes his review: "Of all the factors affecting student attitudes toward mathematics, teacher attitudes are viewed as being of particular importance" (Aiken, 1970, p. 592).

Science

With the introduction of the Physical Science Study Committee (PSSC) materials in 1957, the science area was catapulted onto the center stage of curricular change. In 1957 a poll taken of 2,000 students in grades 10, 11 and 12 in the United States reported that students generally had negative attitudes toward science and scientists (Heath, Maier, Remmers, & Rodgers, 1957). Since that time a wide variety of new materials and approaches have been developed (Goodlad, 1964, 1966). However, it is difficult to obtain a picture of the effects of more than a decade of intensive curriculum activity on the development of affective behaviors of students: while the number of research studies devoted to cognitive outcomes of science instruction has increased since 1957, the research on affective outcomes is disproportionately smaller.

Most of the research over the past three decades has been devoted to science interests. The science interests of 3,200 New York City students attending both private and public junior and senior high schools were reported in one of the earliest studies. It was found that students were most interested in aspects of science most related to their lives, e.g., anatomy, animal life, health (Zim, 1941). In a more recent study of science interests during high school (Wynn & Bledsoe, 1967), no differences were reported in mean scores on the scientific interest section of the Kuder Preference Record between freshmen and senior years. In addition, scientific interest scores of freshmen did not change from 1959 through 1963, an indication that despite the increasing status given to science in society, students were not viewing scientific interests as personally appealing.

Few research studies have been reported showing the effects of curriculum programs on attitudes of students. One of the most extensive evaluations of any new curricular materials was undertaken with Harvard Project Physics. In a comparison between Harvard Project Physics and other physics courses (Ahlgren, 1969), 53 teachers were randomly selected from a list of 16,000 high-school physics teachers, with 34 assigned to teach Harvard Project Physics materials (after attending a summer workshop) and the remaining 19 teaching what they ordinarily would. No significant differences were found between the groups on overall student attitudes (which included feelings about laboratory experiments, learning about science, and physics). With regard to feelings toward the physics course, Harvard Project Physics students scored significantly higher on a course satisfaction questionnaire. These comparative results must be interpreted cautiously since the control group was not homogenous (i.e., contained traditional and PSSC classes).

At the elementary-school level, a study was conducted on the effects of a fifth grade unit on animal coloration with the ordinary unit on animals (Lowery, 1967). Results of the study showed: 1) significantly greater attitude change toward science for the experimental groups; 2) boys changed more than girls; 3) greater changes associated with lower than middle or upper socioeconomic status of students; 4) attitude changes were independent of IQ levels, except for lower socioeconomic students where higher IQ was associated with positive change; and 5) attitude changes were independent of increases in knowledge of general science. Other studies have looked at the effects of strategies of inquiry (Raun & Butts, 1967–1968), filmed materials (Allison, 1967; Weisgerber, 1961), literary novels (Tatara, 1964), and television (Sheehan, 1961).

Social Studies

Of all the curriculum areas, social studies has the most extensive history of research studies on student attitudes. Aside from attitudes toward specific curriculum areas and course materials, responses toward such concepts as international understanding, prejudice, political persuasion, democracy and the like have been studied for many decades by both social studies educators and social scientists specializing in psychology and sociology.

The early research in this area had its impetus during the 1930s and 1940s when social scientists were concerned about world and societal events, and was aided by the methodological advances in attitude instrument construction. Most of the studies conducted during this period were attempts at surveying attitudes of a general nature rather than studying behaviors developed as a result of exposure to particular social studies courses or experiences. Research was reported on attitudes toward international relations (Eckert & Mills, 1935), prejudice (Guilford, 1931; Remmers & Wood, 1947), liberalism-conservatism (Breemes, Remmers, & Morgan, 1941; Fay & Middleton, 1939) and government (Fitch & Remmers, 1941).

Studies reporting the effects of social studies courses upon student attitudes have been few and have been conducted mainly at the college level. The criteria are usually of a general nature (e.g., liberal-conservative) rather than specifically for the course (e.g., attitude toward program X or toward social studies as an abstract concept). Of the research conducted for courses, studies are reported for sociology (Cuber, 1939; Gerberich & Jamison, 1934), economics (Kornhauser, 1930), social studies (Yivisaker & Pace, 1940) and political science (Somit, Tanenhaus, Wilke, & Cooley, 1958). In a three-year study comparing attitude changes toward personal political participation, Somit et al. found no significant differences between a traditional course in political science (which stressed American government) and participation-oriented courses covering psychology, sociology, economics and political science. This finding is interesting since students in the participation-oriented courses were exposed to practical politics and practicing politicians and were urged to attend political campaigns and workshops.

An area of social studies which has become more popular in the recent research literature is political socialization. Although concerns relevant to political science in the form of civics materials and courses have been a central feature of elementary- and secondary-school programs, few research studies were conducted at these levels. However, an increasing number of researchers have recently concentrated upon the acquisition of political attitudes by elementary-school children (Easton & Dennis, 1966; Greenstein, 1965; Hess & Torney, 1967).

Along with mathematics and science, social studies has shared in the post-Sputnik boom in new curriculum projects. A variety of large scale curriculum programs and packages have been developed during the last decade. New approaches and materials have been developed for geography, economics, anthropology and sociology, have focused upon humans, and controversial issues, and have adopted a variety of didactic approaches from "discovery" to "induction" (Goodlad, 1966; Michaelis, 1967). However, with all this development activity, research or evaluation studies concerned with either affective objectives or attitudes toward the programs are virtually nonexistent. This state of affairs may reflect "that the professional social studies writers have failed to come to grips with the issue of affective objectives in social studies" (Pratt, 1969, p. 33).

Other Curriculum Areas

A small number of attitude studies in the arts, humanities and language arts are available. Within these areas the subject which has generated the most research is reading. Much of the literature in reading pertaining to attitudes is concerned more with general hortatory material (e.g., Gray, 1951) or the use of reading passages as instructional material for changing attitudes toward specific objects—e.g., American Indians (Fisher, 1968). In addition, there have been several studies on reading interests which have reported on both class and outside reading habits of students. Some of the earliest work in surveying reading interests was conducted during the Eight Year Study (Smith & Tyler, 1942). A recent experimental study reported that students had more positive attitudes toward reading when paperbacks were used in class, compared with clothbound books available either in class or in the school library (Lowery & Grafft, 1968).

A number of recent studies have been concerned primarily with reading achievement and secondarily with attitudes toward reading. A variety of treatments were investigated: instructional materials and approaches (e.g., basal, linguistic, language experience, basal plus phonics), writing medium (initial teaching alphabet versus traditional orthography), and organizational arrangements (e.g., individual pupil-teacher conferences). While the studies on the whole showed no differences on attitude measures (Hahn, 1965–1966; Kendrick, 1966; Sheldon & Lashinger, 1965–1966; Stauffer, 1966–1967), significant results were obtained in those studies where students came into more contact with the teacher (Marita, 1966–1967; Macdonald, Harris, & Mann, 1965–1966). Also important are two British studies (Cashdan & Pumfrey, 1969; Dunham, 1960) which reported that even when reading achievement of remedial students was improved their attitude toward reading remained the same.

Other studies in the language arts area were concerned with literature (Whitehead, 1956) and poetry (Mosher, 1953). An interesting program for developing positive attitudes toward literature is described in *Hooked on Books: Program and Proof* (Fader & McNeil, 1968). With regard to learning second languages, few attitude studies have been conducted. Among the more interesting are studies looking at the effects of learning a second language on attitudes toward French people (Sutherland, 1946), toward Spanish-speaking countries (Riestra & Johnson, 1964), and toward the Welsh language (W. R. Jones, 1950). Recently there seems to be more interest on the part of researchers in this area. It has been reported in an interim report of a 10-year longitudinal survey (Burstall, 1970) that about half of the students included in the survey held favorable attitudes toward French, females more so than males. Other interesting studies have been reported by Lambert (1963) and Jakobovits (1970).

Even fewer studies have been conducted in the arts, with most of them confined to interests. Studies using the Kuder Preference Record have been conducted for music (Buegel & Billing, 1952) and art (Borg, 1950). Eisner (1965, 1966) has conducted studies which have examined students' attitudes toward art and artists. Given the increasingly greater emphasis on leisure time in our society, much more will have to be done about the role of the school in developing attitudes toward the arts.

IMPLICATIONS FOR EDUCATION

After such an extensive review of research, the reader might well be asking about the implications of this literature for the teaching situation. Much as we would like to, the research results render it difficult to piece together what types of educational experiences would most likely promote desirable affective responses. Rather than attempting to bridge the formidable chasm between an extensive but necessarily superficial overview and the reality of the classroom situation, we would like to present some of the more striking trends which have emerged from the literature.

One of the most important trends is that experiences in the classroom and school *do* influence students' feelings about school and school-related objects. Children who start school with a relatively neutral or positive attitude often develop negative attitudes toward school as they progress from grade to grade. It is likely that these negative affective responses are the result of the cumulative day-to-day encounters and experiences that a child has during the course of time spent in school (Jackson, 1968). Are there indications from the research that school-related attitudes can be altered in a positive direction?

It is clear that whatever else may transpire in the school, the teacher has the most central role in the development of students' affective responses. This role stems from the teacher's interaction with instructional strategies and curriculum materials, his attitudes toward the group and each child, and his educational values and beliefs. Since children accurately perceive the nature of the feelings that the teacher has toward them, teachers' attitudes become important in shaping the expectations of students. A warm, friendly, sympathetic and understanding teacher is more likely to have a positive influence on the students compared to one who is cold, unfriendly and autocratic. This seems to be consistent with the literature which suggests that democratic and student-centered classroom practices are more effective than authoritarian and teacher-centered practices in promoting positive affective behaviors. However, it is unrealistic to expect that one type of classroom climate will be optimal for all students and all kinds of learning.

The nature of feedback by significant adults, especially the teacher, to students regarding their performance in the educational setting has been shown to have significant influence on the self-evaluations of students and their affective dispositions toward school learning (Block, 1971). If a student is consistently evaluated negatively, it will result in negative affect toward the teacher and toward the learning skills in which he was evaluated. This may possibly be avoided by sequencing learning tasks in such a way that the student can successfully master skills in the sequence and thus have positive evidence of his achievement. The teacher should recognize such successes which, in turn, will help the student to build a positive concept of himself and to acquire desirable attitudes toward the school situation.

The teacher's own education during training is an important factor in determining how he or she will view the teaching of affective responses. Most teacher-training institutions have stated objectives regarding the development of desirable affective behaviors. Although evidence on the effects of teacher education on student-teachers' attitudes is inconclusive, several research studies have indicated that student-teachers' attitudes toward children become negative after coming into contact with the reality of the classroom during practice teaching.

Teacher-educators should make efforts to improve the conditions under which practice teaching is carried out in order to make it a meaningful rather than a traumatic experience.

A hidden source of influence upon attitudes lies in the textbooks and other software used by students. While content-analysis studies have been conducted with social studies materials, it is likely that materials in other subject areas are an important source of affective content. Teachers and curriculum specialists can determine whether software materials are promoting positive attitudes by paying attention to this dimension when making decisions about adopting materials for classroom use. At the very least, materials which may have an adverse effect upon attitudes can be eliminated. Instruments for analyzing instructional materials have recently become available for both research and practical use (Eash, 1972; Social Science Education Consortium, 1971).

Several instructional strategies such as games, role-playing and simulation hold much promise for cultivating desirable school-related attitudes (see Klausmeier & Ripple, 1971, chapter 14). These techniques seem specially suitable for young children since much of their social learning occurs through imitation and identification. However, follow-up studies which look at the transfer of these behaviors to real-life situations are crucial for determining the validity of these techniques.

Since films have become a way of life in contemporary society, it is likely that this medium can be utilized more fruitfully in the future. Indeed, the early research showed that attitudes learned through motion pictures tend to be retained over a period of time. Recently the strategy of students becoming involved in film production has become popular in schools. The expectations for this strategy are that students will have more positive attitudes toward the content of their film-making activity as well as knowledge of film-making techniques

(Katz, 1971). The literature on instructional television is less encouraging: students do not necessarily develop more positive attitudes as a result of being exposed to this medium. However, since the evidence is clear that exposure to any medium should be confined to short periods of time (lest boredom set in), television can be useful for providing varied experiences.

An important reason for the lack of specific implications that could be readily adopted into classroom practices is the paucity of well-conceptualized and designed research on attitudes in the educational setting. It is possible that systematic and well–thought-out research can lead to better classroom practices for teaching affective responses.

FUTURE RESEARCH

Many of the inadequacies in the research on the teaching of affective behaviors are those endemic to educational research in general. They include: inadequate explication of treatment, use of inappropriate indices of change (Cronbach & Furby, 1970; Harris, 1963), inappropriate use of the student rather than class as sampling unit, and fragmented instrumentation. Rather than dwelling upon these inadequacies we would like to turn to some suggestions for future research.

Follow-up Research and Longitudinal Studies

While little information is known about the stability of affective behaviors, even less is known about the long-term effects of various influences on these behaviors. Only a few of the hundreds of studies have built-in follow-up procedures for ascertaining if a treatment has had more than short-term effects. An example of this approach has been suggested by the literature which reports either on attitudes of student teachers toward teaching or on a subject-matter area.

While attitudes of student teachers may be useful information, it would be even more revealing if follow-up data were collected after the students had entered teaching and if information on their students was also collected. Also, more studies of a longitudinal nature are necessary for constructing an adequate base of knowledge about individual development and the effects of different environments (Bloom, 1964).

Evaluation of New Curriculum Programs and School Organizational Structures

Although there has been an influx of new curricular programs in almost all subject areas over the last decade, a very small proportion of research or evaluation studies related to affective outcomes has been reported. While the first wave of new curricula was concerned almost exclusively with cognitive outcomes, the most recent programs have been placing more emphasis on affective behaviors. Evaluators and researchers should be reporting on these outcomes of the programs. Researchers should pay special attention to those areas such as the social studies and humanities which have had the most glaring deficiencies in reports of evaluation. In addition to research on curricular materials and strategies, it would be useful to determine the effects that new arrangements for learning (e.g., individualized instruction, open-plan systems, flexible scheduling, free schools) have upon affective behaviors.

Research on Interaction Effects

One of the important findings has been that main effects by themselves may not be adequate for understanding affective phenomena. It is likely that interaction effects such as teacher-program, teacher-instructional strategy, student-program, student-instructional strategy, student-teacher, and student-classroom environment may prove to be important sources of information in trying to understand how affective responses develop and how they may prove useful in developing classroom strategies. We would like to see the concept of aptitude-treatment interaction (Cronbach & Snow, 1969; Gagné, 1967) broadened so that affective-treatment interactions become equally amenable for research. For example, a student's attitude toward an instructional strategy may prove to be more important for learning both cognitive and affective behaviors than either aptitude or past achievement.

Sequencing of Instructional Strategies

From the large body of literature collected on the effects of particular instructional strategies, it is clear that no one strategy represents the educational panacea. It is likely that the way media and strategies are used during the course of a school day help to either promote or hinder learning. Studies of the combinations and sequences of different instructional strategies may help in our understanding of the optimal conditions for affective learning.

"Education in Depth"

R. M. Jones (1968) calls for more emphasis on imagination, fantasy and feelings as part of the curriculum, and utilizing techniques such as analyses of dreams and free-association writings as part of curricular activities. He contrasts two contemporary trends in education: 1) education in depth which "seeks to enliven the educative process from inside the pupil out, by means of freeing his emotions and fantasies for service in his schoolwork..." (R. M. Jones, 1967, p. 1); and 2) the new curricula which "seeks to enliven the educative process from outside the pupil in, by means of streamlining the challenges that are carried to the intellect by classroom exercises and materials" (R. M. Jones, 1967, p. 1). In addition to making suggestions as to how the "education in depth" approach can be uti-

lized for curricular purposes, it is recognized that educational research will play a crucial role in trying to develop and sustain affective behaviors for increased subject-matter mastery. While examples of psycho-analytic research in education are available (e.g., R. M. Jones, 1960; Kingsbury, 1967), this area merits more extensive and systematic attention.

Identifying Crucial Affective Responses

Finally, perhaps the most crucial initial research question to be asked is concerned with the nature of the educational enterprise itself: what are the crucial affective responses that the schools should be promoting? With the increased emphasis on accountability, this question can no longer be ignored or assumed. Education cannot afford the luxury of having its most important affective outcomes occur as accidents or unintended effects of the curriculum and of school life in general.

Concluding Remarks

Lest the reader emerge from a reading of this chapter with a pessimistic view of the research on affective responses, it should be emphasized that this is a relatively new area in educational research and practice. A beginning has recently been made with the introduction of several new programs, for both students and teachers concerned with the development of favorable attitudes toward school, self, and subject-matter areas (e.g., G. I. Brown, 1970; Fagen & Long, 1970; Levin, 1972; Weinstein, 1971). It may also be equally true that the instrumentation and quantification procedures in the study of affective outcomes are perhaps more complex than they have been in the study of cognitive outcomes. The research on affective behavior is still in its infancy and it is our hope that this chapter may represent a timely effort for taking stock of the current situation in order to plan future endeavors.

REFERENCES

Adams, S., & Von Brock, R. C. The development of the A-V scale of attitudes toward mathematics. *Journal of Educational Measurement*, 1967, 4, 247–248.

Ahlgren, A. Evaluation of Harvard project physics: Interim report. Cambridge: Harvard University, 1969. (photo offset)

Aiken, L. R., Jr. Personality correlates of attitude toward mathematics. *Journal of Educational Research*, 1963, 56, 476–480.

Aiken, L. R., Jr. Attitudes toward mathematics. *Review of Educational Research*, 1970, 40, 551–596.

Alexander, T., Jr. The prediction of teacher-pupil interaction with a projective test. *Journal of Clinical Psychology*, 1950, 6, 273–276.

Alger, C. F. Use of the inter-nation simulation in undergraduate teaching. In H. Guetzkow, C. F. Alger, R. A. Brody, R. C. Noel, & R. C. Snyder, *Simulation in international relations: Developments for research and teaching*. Englewood Cliffs, N.J.: Prentice-Hall, 1963. Pp. 150–189.

Allen, H., Jr. *Attitudes of certain high school seniors towards science and scientific careers*. New York: Bureau of Publication, Teachers College, Columbia University, 1959.

Allison, R. W., Sr. *The effect of three methods of treating motivational films upon the attitudes of fourth-, fifth-, and sixth-grade students toward science, scientists, and scientific careers*. (Doctoral dissertation, The Pennsylvania State University) Ann Arbor, Mich.: University Microfilms, 1967. No. 67–11,176.

Allport, G. W. Attitudes. In C. A. Murchison (Ed.), *A handbook of social psychology*. Worcester, Mass.: Clark University Press, 1935. Pp. 798–844.

Allport, G. W. Values and our youth. *Teachers College Record*, 1961, 63, 211–219.

Alper, S. W. *The impact of the National Citizenship Test on the expressed attitudes and knowledge of high school students*. (Doctoral dissertation, Purdue University) Ann Arbor, Mich.: University Microfilms, 1967. No. 67–16,610.

Alpert, R., Stellwagon, G., & Becker, D. Psychological factors in mathematics education. *Newsletter*, No. 15, School Mathematics Study Group, Stanford University, 1963.

Anderson, G. J. Effects of classroom social climate on individual learning. *American Educational Research Journal*, 1970, 7, 135–152.

Anderson, H. H., Brewer, J. E., Reed, M. F., & Wrightstone, J. W. Studies of teachers' classroom personalities III. Follow-up studies of the effects of dominative and integrative contacts on children's behavior. *Applied Psychological Monographs*, 1946, Whole No. 11.

Anderson, R. P., & Kell, B. L. Student attitudes about participation in classroom groups. *Journal of Educational Research*, 1954, 48, 255–267.

Annis, A. D., & Meier, N. C. The induction of opinion through suggestion by means of "planted content." *Journal of Social Psychology*, 1934, 5, 65–81.

Anttonen, R. G. *An examination into the stability of mathematics attitude and its relationship to mathematics achievement from elementary to secondary school level*. (Doctoral dissertation, University of Minnesota) Ann Arbor, Mich.: University Microfilms, 1968. No. 68–1521.

Ausubel, D. P. *Theory and problems of child development*. New York: Grune & Stratton, 1958.

Baldwin, A. L. The study of child behavior and development. In P. H. Mussen (Ed.), *Handbook of research methods in child development*. New York: John Wiley, 1960. Pp. 3–35.

Barclay, J. E., & Weaver, H. B. Comparative reliabilities and ease of construction of Thurstone and Likert attitude scales. *Journal of Social Psychology*, 1962, 58, 109–120.

Barcus, F. E. *Communications content: Analysis of the research, 1900–1958*. (Doctoral dissertation, University of Illinois) Ann Arbor, Mich.: University Microfilms, 1960. No. 60–143.

Beatty, W. H. (Ed.) *Improving educational assessment and an inventory of measures of affective behavior*. Washington, D.C.: Association for Supervision and Curriculum Development, 1969.

Beilin, H. Teachers' and clinicians' attitudes toward the behavior problems of children: A reappraisal. *Child Development*, 1959, 30, 9–25.

Bemis, K. A., & Liberty, P. G. *Southwestern Cooperative Educational Laboratory interaction observation schedule (SCIOS): A system for analyzing teacher-pupil interaction in the affective domain*. Albuquerque, N.M.:

Southwestern Cooperative Educational Laboratory, 1970. ED 038 188.

Berelson, B. Content analysis. In G. Lindzey (Ed.), *The handbook of social psychology.* Vol. 1. Cambridge, Mass.: Addison-Wesley, 1954. Pp. 488–522.

Block, J. H. (Ed.) *Mastery learning: Theory and practice.* New York: Holt, Rinehart & Winston, 1971.

Bloom, B. S. (Ed.) *Taxonomy of educational objectives. Handbook I: Cognitive domain.* New York: David McKay, 1956.

Bloom, B. S. *Stability and change in human characteristics.* New York: John Wiley, 1964.

Bloom, B. S. Affective consequences of school achievement. In J. H. Block (Ed.), *Mastery learning.* New York: Holt, Rinehart & Winston, 1971. Pp. 13–28.

Bloom, B. S., Hastings, J. T., & Madaus, G. F. *Handbook on formative and summative evaluation of student learning.* New York: McGraw-Hill, 1971.

Bonjean, C. M., Hill, R. J., & McLemore, S. D. *Sociological measurement: An inventory of scales and indices.* San Francisco: Chandler Publishing, 1967.

Boocock, S. S. *Effects of election campaign game in four high school classes.* Unpublished manuscript, Department of Social Relations, The Johns Hopkins University, 1963.

Borg, W. R. The interests of art students. *Educational and Psychological Measurement,* 1950, 10, 100–106.

Bovard, E. W., Jr. The experimental production of interpersonal affect. *Journal of Abnormal and Social Psychology,* 1951, 46, 521–528. (a)

Bovard, E. W., Jr. The psychology of classroom interaction. *Journal of Educational Research,* 1951, 45, 215–224 (b)

Bowman, P., & Havilicek, L. Pupil opinion questionnaire. Reported by O. Glick in *The interdependence of sixth graders' school attitudes and academic performance.* Paper presented at the Annual Convention of the Western Psychological Association, Vancouver, B.C., 1969.

Breemes, E. L., Remmers, H. H., & Morgan, C. L. Changes in liberalism-conservatism of college students since the depression. *Journal of Social Psychology,* 1941, 14, 99–107.

Brim, B. J. Attitude changes in teacher-education students. *Journal of Educational Research,* 1966, 59, 441–445.

Brodie, T. A., Jr. Attitude toward school and academic achievement. *Personnel and Guidance Journal,* 1964, 43, 375–378.

Brown, B. R., & Gilman, D. A. Expressed student attitudes under several conditions of automated programmed instruction. *Contemporary Education,* 1969, 40, 286–289.

Brown, G. I. Which pupil to which classroom climate? *Elementary School Journal,* 1960, 60, 265–269.

Brown, G. I. *Human teaching for human learning.* New York: McGraw-Hill, 1970.

Brown, W. F., & Holtzman, W. H. *Survey of study habits and attitudes: Form H.* New York: Psychological Corporation, 1967.

Budd, R. W., Thorp, R. K., & Donohew, L. *Content analysis of communications.* New York: Macmillan, 1967.

Buegel, H. F., & Billing, P. S. Inventoried interests of participants in music groups. *Journal of Educational Research,* 1952, 46, 141–146.

Burstall, C. *French in the primary school: Attitudes and achievement.* London: National Foundation for Educational Research in England and Wales, 1970.

Buswell, M. M. The relationship between the social structure of the classroom and the academic success of the pupils. *Journal of Experimental Education,* 1953, 22, 37–52.

Callis, R. Change in teacher-pupil attitudes related to training and experience. *Educational and Psychological Measurement,* 1950, 10, 718–727.

Callis, R. The efficiency of the Minnesota Teacher Attitude Inventory for predicting interpersonal relations in the classroom. *Journal of Applied Psychology,* 1953, 37, 82–85.

Calvin, A. D., Hoffmann, F. K., & Harden, E. L. The effect of intelligence and social atmosphere on group problem solving behavior. *Journal of Social Psychology,* 1957, 45, 61–74.

Campbell, D. E. Dimensional attitude changes of student teachers. *Journal of Educational Research,* 1967, 61, 160–162.

Campbell, D. T. The indirect assessment of social attitudes. *Psychological Bulletin,* 1950, 47, 15–38.

Campbell, D. T., & Fiske, D. W. Convergent and discriminant validation by the multitrait-multimethod matrix. *Psychological Bulletin,* 1959, 56, 81–105.

Carlson, H. S. Teachers' attitudes in relation

to classroom morale and cheating. *Journal of Experimental Education,* 1935, 4, 154–213.

Carpenter, M. E. *The treatment of the Negro in American history school textbooks.* New York: Bureau of Publications, Teachers College, Columbia University, 1941.

Cartwright, D. P. Analysis of qualitative material. In L. Festinger, & D. Katz (Eds.), *Research methods in the behavioral sciences.* New York: Holt, Rinehart & Winston, 1953. Pp. 421–470.

Cashdan, A., & Pumfrey, P. D. Some effects of the remedial teaching of reading. *Educational Research,* 1969, 11, 138–142.

Cohen, A. R. *Attitude change and social influence.* New York: Basic Books, 1964.

Coleman, J. S. Academic achievement and the structure of competition. *Harvard Educational Review,* 1959, 29, 330–351.

Comley, R. E. *A study of mathematical achievement and attitudes of UICSM and non-UICSM students in college.* (Doctoral dissertation, University of Illinois) Ann Arbor, Mich.: University Microfilms, 1967. No. 67–6588.

Cook, S. W., & Selltiz, C. A multiple-indicator approach to attitude measurement. *Psychological Bulletin,* 1964, 62, 36–55.

Cook, W. W., Leeds, C. H., & Callis, R. *Minnesota Teacher Attitude Inventory.* New York: Psychological Corporation, 1951.

Coster, J. K. Attitudes toward school of high school pupils from three income levels. *Journal of Educational Psychology,* 1958, 49, 61–66.

Cox, R. C., & Unks, N. J. *A selected and annotated bibliography of studies concerning the taxonomy of educational objectives: Cognitive domain.* Pittsburgh: Learning Research and Development Center, 1967, No. 13.

Cristantiello, P. D. Attitude toward mathematics and the predictive validity of a measure of quantitative aptitude. *Journal of Educational Research,* 1962, 55, 184–186.

Croft, R. G., Stimpson, D. V., Ross, W. L., Bray, R. M., & Breglio, V. J. Comparison of attitude changes elicited by live and videotape classroom presentations. *Audiovisual Communication Review,* 1969, 17, 315–321.

Cronbach, L. J. (Ed.) Text materials in *Modern education: A comprehensive theory and platform for research.* Urbana, Ill.: University of Illinois Press, 1955.

Cronbach, L. J., & Furby, L. How we should measure "change": Or should we? *Psychological Bulletin,* 1970, 74, 68–80.

Cronbach, L. J., & Snow, R. E. *Individual differences in learning ability as a function of instructional variables.* Final Report. Contract No. OEC 4-6-061269-1217. Washington, D.C.: U.S. Office of Education, 1969. ED 029 001.

Cuber, J. F. The effect of an introductory sociology course upon students' verbalized attitudes. *Social Forces,* 1939, 17, 490–494.

Dave, R. H. The identification and measurement of environmental process variables that are related to educational achievement. Unpublished doctoral dissertation, University of Chicago, 1963.

Davis, E. E. *Attitude change: A review and bibliography of selected research.* Reports and papers in the social sciences, No. 19. Paris: UNESCO, 1965.

Day, H. P. Attitude changes of beginning teachers after initial teaching experience. *Journal of Teacher Education,* 1959, 10, 326–328.

DeCharms, R., & Moeller, G. H. Values expressed in American children's readers: 1800–1950. *Journal of Abnormal and Social Psychology,* 1962, 64, 136–142.

Della Piana, G. M., & Gage, N. L. Pupils' values and the validity of the Minnesota Teacher Attitude Inventory. *Journal of Educational Psychology,* 1955, 46, 167–178.

Demos, G. D. Attitudes of student ethnic groups on issues related to education. *California Journal of Educational Research,* 1960, 11, 204–206, 224.

Devine, D. F. *Student attitudes and achievement: A comparison between the effects of programed instruction and conventional classroom approach in teaching algebra 1 at Rich Township High Schools.* (Doctoral dissertation, Colorado State College) Ann Arbor, Mich.: University Microfilms, 1967. No. 67–9621.

Doob, L. W. The behavior of attitudes. *Psychological Review,* 1947, 54, 135–156.

Dreger, R. M., & Aiken, L. R., Jr. The identification of number anxiety in a college population. *Journal of Educational Psychology,* 1957, 48, 344–351.

Dressel, P. L. Measurement and evaluation of instructional objectives. In E. M. Huddleston (Ed.), *The 17th yearbook of the Na-*

tional Council on Measurements used in Education. Ames, Iowa: National Council on Measurements Used in Education, 1960. Pp. 1–6.

Dunham, J. The effects of remedial education on young children's reading ability and attitude to reading. *British Journal of Educational Psychology,* 1960, 30, 173–175.

Dunn, J. A. The approach-avoidance paradigm as a model for the analysis of school anxiety. *Journal of Educational Psychology,* 1968, 59, 388–394.

Dutton, W. H. Attitudes of prospective teachers toward arithmetic. *Elementary School Journal,* 1951, 52, 84–90.

Dutton, W. H. Attitudes of Junior High School pupils toward arithmetic. *School Review,* 1956, 64, 18–22.

Dutton, W. H. Attitude change of elementary school student teachers and anxiety. *Journal of Educational Research,* 1962, 55, 380–382.

Dutton, W. H., & Blum, M. P. The measurement of attitudes toward arithmetic with a Likert-type test. *Elementary School Journal,* 1968, 68, 259–264.

Dutton, W. H., & Stephens, L. Measuring attitudes toward science. *School Science and Mathematics,* 1963, 63, 43–49.

Eash, M. J. Developing an instrument for the assessment of instructional materials. In J. Weiss (Ed.), *Curriculum Theory Network Monograph Supplement,* 1972 8 (9), 193–220.

Easton, D., & Dennis, J. Political socialization of the elementary school child. *National Council for the Social Studies Yearbook,* 1966, 36, 216–235.

Eckert, R. E., & Mills, H. C. International attitudes and related academic and social factors. *Journal of Educational Sociology,* 1935, 9, 142–153.

Education Policies Commission. *The purpose of education in American democracy.* Washington, D.C.: National Education Association and the American Association of School Administrators, 1938.

Edwards, A. L. *Techniques of attitude scale construction.* New York: Appleton-Century-Crofts, 1957.

Edwards, A. L., & Kenney, K. C. A comparison of the Thurstone and Likert techniques of attitude scale construction. *Journal of Applied Psychology,* 1946, 30, 72–83.

Edwards, A. L., & Kilpatrick, F. P. A technique for the construction of attitude scales. *Journal of Applied Psychology,* 1948, 32, 374–384.

Ehrlich, V. Z. *The dimensions of attitude towards school of elementary school children in grades 3 to 6.* (Doctoral dissertation, Columbia University) Ann Arbor, Mich.: University Microfilms, 1969. No. 69–15,160.

Eisner, E. W. Graduate study and the preparation of scholars in art education. In W. R. Hastie (Ed.), *Art education.* The Sixtyfourth Yearbook of the National Society for Study in Education, Part II. Chicago: NSSE, 1965. Pp. 274–298.

Eisner, E. W. The development of information and attitude toward art at the secondary and college levels. *Studies in Art Education,* 1966, 8 (1), 43–58.

Elkin, S. M. Minorities in textbooks: The latest chapter. *Teachers College Record,* 1965, 66, 502–508.

Ellis, D. B., & Miller, L. W. Teachers' attitudes and child behavior problems. *Journal of Educational Psychology,* 1936, 27, 501–511.

Fader, D. N., & McNeil, E. B. *Hooked on books: Program and proof.* New York: Putnam, 1968.

Fagen, S., & Long, N. The American university. Hillcrest Children's Mental Health Center Research Report to the U.S. Office of Education, Bureau of Handicapped Children, 1970.

Fay, P. J., & Middleton, W. C. Certain factors related to liberal and conservative attitudes of college students: Sex, classification, fraternity membership, major subject. *Journal of Educational Psychology,* 1939, 30, 378–390.

Finley, R. E. *Environmental and experiential characteristics of students and attitudes toward school.* (Doctoral dissertation, Purdue University) Ann Arbor, Mich.: University Microfilms, 1969. No. 69–7439.

Finn, J. D. Patterns in children's language. *School Review,* 1969, 77, 108–127.

Fishbein, M. A consideration of beliefs, and their role in attitude measurement. In M. Fishbein (Ed.), *Readings in attitude theory and measurement.* New York: John Wiley, 1967. Pp. 257–266. (a)

Fishbein, M. (Ed.) *Readings in attitude theory and measurement.* New York: John Wiley, 1967. (b)

Fisher, F. L. Influences of reading and discussion on the attitudes of fifth graders toward

American Indians. *Journal of Educational Research,* 1968, 62, 130–134.

Fitch, L., & Remmers, H. H. What the college student thinks of government. *Journal of Social Psychology,* 1941, 14, 187–194.

Flanders, N. A. *Analyzing teaching behavior.* Don Mills, Ontario: Addison-Wesley, 1970.

Flanders, N. A., Morrison, B. M., & Brode, E. L. Changes in pupil attitudes during the school year. *Journal of Educational Psychology,* 1968, 59, 334–338.

Flesch, R. A new readability yardstick. *Journal of Applied Psychology,* 1948, 32, 221–233.

Fox, D. J. *The research process in education.* New York: Holt, Rinehart & Winston, 1969.

Frederiksen, N. In-basket tests and factors in administrative performance. In H. Guetzkow (Ed.), *Simulation in social science: Readings.* Englewood Cliffs, N.J.: Prentice-Hall, 1962. Pp. 124–137.

French, W., & associates. *Behavioral goals of general education in high school.* New York: Russell Sage Foundation, 1957.

Frey, S. H., Shimabukuro, S., & Woodruff, A. B. Attitude change in programmed instruction related to achievement and performance. *Audiovisual Communication Review,* 1967, 15, 199–205.

Friedenberg, E. Z. *Coming of age in America: Growth and acquiescence.* New York: Random House, 1965.

Fuller, F. F. *Fair system manual: Fuller affective interaction records.* Austin, Tex.: The Research and Development Center for Teacher Education, 1969.

Gagné, R. M. (Ed.) *Learning and individual differences.* Columbus, Ohio: Charles E. Merrill, 1967.

Geis, F., Jr. The semantic differential technique as a means of evaluating change in "affect." Unpublished doctoral dissertation, Harvard University, 1969.

Gerberich, J. R., & Jamison, A. W. Measurement of attitude changes during an introductory course in college sociology. *Journal of Educational Sociology,* 1934, 8, 116–124.

Getzels, J. W. A social psychology of education. In G. Lindzey, & E. Aronson (Eds.), *The handbook of social psychology,* Vol. V. Don Mills, Ontario: Addison-Wesley, 1969. Pp. 459–537.

Getzels, J. W., & Jackson, P. W. The teacher's personality and characteristics. In N. L. Gage (Ed.), *Handbook of research on teach-*

ing. Chicago: Rand McNally, 1963. Pp. 506–582.

Getzels, J. W., & Thelen, H. A. The classroom group as a unique social system. In N. B. Henry (Ed.), *The dynamics of instructional groups.* The Fifty-ninth Yearbook of the National Society for the Study of Education, Part II. Chicago: NSSE, 1960. Pp. 53–82.

Glass, G. V., & Worthen, B. R. Educational evaluation and research: Similarities and differences. In J. Weiss (Ed.), *Curriculum Theory Network Monograph Supplement,* 1972, 8 (9). Pp. 149–165.

Glass, L. W. *Assessment of affective outcomes of instruction with high school sophomore biology students and teachers.* Paper presented at the Forty-Third Annual Meeting of the National Association for Research in Science Teaching, Minneapolis, March 1970.

Glassey, W. The attitude of grammar school pupils and their parents to education, religion and sport. *British Journal of Educational Psychology,* 1945, 15, 101–104.

Glick, O. Sixth graders' attitudes toward school and interpersonal conditions in the classroom. *Journal of Experimental Education,* 1970, 38, 17–22.

Goetzinger, C., & Valentine, M. Faculty attitudes toward educational television: A survey report and preliminary analysis. *Speech Teacher,* 1963, 12, 127–130.

Goldberg, J. B. Influence of pupils' attitudes on perception of teachers' behaviors and on consequent school work. *Journal of Educational Psychology,* 1968, 59, 1–5.

Golden, L. *The treatment of minority groups in primary social studies textbooks.* (Doctoral dissertation, Stanford University) Ann Arbor, Mich.: University Microfilms, 1965. No. 64–13,549.

Goodlad, J. I. *School curriculum reform in the United States.* New York: The Fund for the Advancement of Education, 1964.

Goodlad, J. I. *The changing school curriculum.* New York: The Fund for the Advancement of Education, 1966.

Gray, W. S. (Ed.) *Promoting growth toward maturity in interpreting what is read.* Chicago: The University of Chicago Press, 1951.

Green, B. F. Attitude measurement. In G. Lindzey (Ed.), *Handbook of social psychology.* Vol. 1. Cambridge, Mass.: Addison-Wesley, 1954. Pp. 335–369.

Greenstein, F. I. *Children and politics.* New Haven, Conn.: Yale University Press, 1965.

Gregersen, G. F., & Travers, R. M. W. A study of the child's concept of the teacher. *Journal of Educational Research,* 1968, 61, 324–327.

Grim, P. R. A technique for the measurement of attitudes in the social studies. *Educational Research Bulletin,* 1936, 15, 95–104.

Gruner, C. R. An experimental study of satire as persuasion. *Speech Monographs,* 1965, 32, 149–153.

Guilford, J. P. Racial preferences of a thousand American university students. *Journal of Social Psychology,* 1931, 2, 179–204.

Guttman, L. A basis for scaling qualitative data. *American Sociological Review,* 1944, 9, 139–150.

Hahn, H. T. Three approaches to beginning reading instruction—ITA, language arts and basic readers. *The Reading Teacher,* 1965–66, 19, 590–594.

Hand, H. C. The case for the common learnings course. *Science Education,* 1948, 32, 5–11.

Handleman, S. D. *A comparative study of teacher attitudes toward teaching by closed-circuit television.* (Doctoral dissertation, New York University) Ann Arbor, Mich.: University Microfilms, 1960. No. 60–3746.

Hanson, R. A. The application of a general model of environmental assessment to longitudinal data on verbal ability and general intelligence. Paper presented at the meeting of the American Educational Research Association, Minneapolis, March 1970.

Harris, C. W. (Ed.) *Problems in measuring change.* Madison: The University of Wisconsin Press, 1963.

Harrison, A., Jr. *An analysis of attitude modifications of prospective teachers toward education before and after a sequence of teacher preparation experiences.* (Doctoral dissertation, University of Oklahoma) Ann Arbor, Mich.: University Microfilms, 1967. No. 67–11,473.

Harvey, O. J., Prather, M., White, B. J., & Hoffmeister, J. K. Teachers' beliefs, classroom atmosphere, and student behavior. *American Educational Research Journal,* 1968, 5, 151–166.

Harvey, O. J., White, B. J., Prather, M., Alter, R. D., & Hoffmeister, J. K. Teachers' belief systems and preschool atmospheres. *Journal of Educational Psychology,* 1966, 57, 373–381.

Haugh, O. M. The relative effectiveness of reading and listening to radio drama as ways of imparting information and shifting attitudes. *Journal of Educational Research,* 1952, 45, 489–498.

Havighurst, R. J. *Human development and education.* New York: Longmans, Ltd., 1953.

Heath, R. W., Maier, M. H., Remmers, H. H., & Rodgers, D. G. High school students look at science. *The Purdue Opinion Panel* (Report of Poll No. 50), Purdue University, November 1957.

Heider, F. *The psychology of interpersonal relations.* New York: John Wiley, 1958.

Heise, D. R. The semantic differential and attitude research. In G. F. Summers (Ed.), *Attitude measurement.* Chicago: Rand McNally, 1970. Pp. 235–253.

Henry, J. Attitude organization in elementary classrooms. *American Journal of Orthopsychiatry,* 1957, 27, 117–133.

Hess, R. D., & Torney, J. V. *The development of political attitudes in children.* Chicago: Aldine, 1967.

Hicks, L. B., Sr. Apprentice teaching and exposure to additional information as methods of attitude modification in Negro students. Unpublished doctoral dissertation, University of Illinois, 1967.

Himmelweit, H. T., Oppenheim, A. N., & Vince, P. *Television and the child: An empirical study of the effect of television on the young.* London: Oxford University Press, 1958.

Holsti, O. R. Content analysis (with the collaboration of J. K. Loomba, & R. C. North). In G. Lindzey, & E. Aronson (Eds.), *The handbook of social psychology.* Vol. II. Don Mills, Ontario: Addison-Wesley, 1968. Pp. 596–692.

Holt, J. *How children fail.* New York: Pitman, 1964.

Holtzman, W. H., & Brown, W. F. Evaluating the study habits and attitudes of high school students. *Journal of Educational Psychology,* 1968, 59, 404–409.

Hoover, K. H. Using controversial issues to develop democratic values among secondary social studies students. *The Journal of Experimental Education,* 1967, 36 (2), 64–69.

Horn, J. L., & Morrison, W. L. Dimensions of teacher attitudes. *Journal of Educational Psychology*, 1965, 56, 118–125.

Horowitz, M. Student-teaching experiences and attitudes of student teachers. *Journal of Teacher Education*, 1968, 19, 317–324.

Hoshaw, L. D. The construction and evaluation of a scale for measuring attitude toward any teacher. *Bulletin of Purdue University: Studies in Higher Education XXVII*, 1936, 37, 238–251.

Hungerman, A. D. Achievement and attitude of sixth-grade pupils in conventional and contemporary mathematics programs. *Arithmetic Teacher*, 1967, 14, 30–39.

Hunter, E. C. Changes in teachers' attitudes toward children's behavior over the last thirty years. *Mental Hygiene*, 1957, 41, 3–11.

Jackson, P. W. *Life in classrooms*. New York: Holt, Rinehart & Winston, 1968.

Jackson, P. W., & Lahaderne, H. M. Scholastic success and attitude toward school in a population of sixth graders. *Journal of Educational Psychology*, 1967, 58, 15–18.

Jacob, P. E. *Changing values in college*. New York: Harper & Row, 1957.

Jacobs, E. B. Attitude change in teacher education: An inquiry into the role of attitudes in changing teacher behavior. *Journal of Teacher Education*, 1968, 19, 410–415.

Jakobovits, L. A. *Foreign language learning: A psycholinguistic analysis of the issues*. Rowley, Mass.: Newbury House, 1970.

Janis, I. L., & Hovland, C. I. (Eds.), *Personality and persuasibility: Yale studies in attitude and communication*. Vol. 2. New Haven, Conn.: Yale University Press, 1959.

Jeffs, G. A. *Student attitude survey–Clark High School*. Las Vegas, Nev.: Clark County School District, 1967. ED 011 674.

Jenkins, D. H. Interdependence in the classroom. *Journal of Educational Research*, 1951, 45, 137–144.

Johnson, E. E. Student ratings of popularity and scholastic ability of their peers and actual scholastic performances of those peers. *Journal of Social Psychology*, 1958, 47, 127–132.

Johnson, G. B., Jr. An evaluation instrument for the analysis of teacher effectiveness. *Journal of Experimental Education*, 1955, 23, 331–344.

Johnson, G. B., Jr. An experimental technique for the prediction of teacher effectiveness. *Journal of Educational Research*, 1957, 50, 679–689.

Johnson, S. R. *Relationships among cognitive and affective outcomes of instruction*. (Doctoral dissertation, University of California, Los Angeles) Ann Arbor, Mich.: University Microfilms, 1967. No. 67–6179.

Jones, R. M. *An application of psychoanalysis to education*. Springfield, Ill.: Charles C Thomas, 1960.

Jones, R. M. (Ed.) *Contemporary educational psychology: Selected readings*. New York: Harper & Row, 1967.

Jones, R. M. *Fantasy and feeling in education*. New York: New York University Press, 1968.

Jones, T. The effect of modified programmed lectures and mathematical games upon achievement and attitude of ninth-grade low achievers in mathematics. *Mathematics Teacher*, 1968, 61, 603–607.

Jones, W. R. Attitude toward Welsh as a second language. *British Journal of Educational Psychology*, 1950, 20, 117–132.

Kagan, J., & Moss, H. A. *Birth to maturity*. New York: John Wiley, 1962.

Karns, E. A. *Teacher and pupil attitudes toward textbooks and instructional television as authoritative sources of information in sixth grade social studies*. (Doctoral dissertation, Kent State University) Ann Arbor, Mich.: University Microfilms, 1967. No. 67–9422.

Katz, J. S. Interaction and film study. In J. S. Katz (Ed.), *Perspectives on the study of film*. Boston: Little, Brown, 1971. Pp. 280–289.

Kearney, N. C. *Elementary school objectives*. New York: Russell Sage Foundation, 1953.

Kearney, N. C., & Rocchio, P. D. The relation between the Minnesota Teacher Attitude Inventory and subject matter taught by elementary teachers. *Educational Administration and Supervision*, 1955, 41, 358–360.

Kearney, N. C., & Rocchio, P. D. The effect of teacher education on the teacher's attitude. *Journal of Educational Research*, 1956, 49, 703–708.

Kehoe, J. Students' interests in the social studies. *Canadian Journal of History and Social Science*, 1970, 6, 34–39.

Kelley, H. H. Salience of membership and resistance to change of group-anchored attitudes. *Human Relations,* 1955, 8, 275–289.

Kelley, H. H., & Volkart, E. H. The resistance to change of group-anchored attitudes. *American Sociological Review,* 1952, 17, 453–465.

Kendrick, W. M. A comparative study of two first grade language arts programs. *The Reading Teacher,* 1966–1967, 20, 25–30.

Kerlinger, F. N. Factor invariance in the measurement of attitudes toward education. *Educational and Psychological Measurement,* 1961, 21, 273–285.

Kerlinger, F. N. *Foundations of behavioral research.* New York: Holt, Rinehart & Winston, 1964.

Kerlinger, F. N. The first- and second-order factor structures of attitudes toward education. *American Educational Research Journal,* 1967, 4, 191–205.

Kerlinger, F. N., & Kaya, E. The construction and factor analytic validation of scales to measure attitudes toward education. *Educational and Psychological Measurement,* 1959, 19, 13–29.

Kerlinger, F. N., & Pedhazur, E. J. Educational attitudes and perceptions of desirable traits of teachers. *American Educational Research Journal,* 1968, 5, 543–560.

Khan, S. B. Affective correlates of academic achievement. *Journal of Educational Psychology,* 1969, 60, 216–221.

Khan, S. B. Affective correlates of academic achievement: A longitudinal study. *Measurement and Evaluation in Guidance,* 1970, 3, 76–80.

Kahn, S. B., & Roberts, D. M. Relationships among study habits and attitudes, aptitude and grade 8 achievement. *Educational and Psychological Measurement,* 1969, 29, 951–955.

Khan, S. B., & Roberts, D. M. Factorial stability of academically relevant affective characteristics. *Measurement and Evaluation in Guidance,* 1971, 3, 209–212.

Kibler, R. J., Barker, L. L., & Miles, D. T. *Behavioral objectives and instruction.* Boston: Allyn & Bacon, 1970.

Kiesler, C. A., Collins, B. E., & Miller, N. *Attitude change: A critical analysis of theoretical approaches.* New York: John Wiley, 1969.

Kingsbury, D. An experiment in higher education. In R. M. Jones (Ed.), *Contemporary educational psychology: Selected readings.* New York: Harper & Row, 1967. Pp. 196–209.

Klausmeier, H. J., & Ripple, R. E. *Learning and human abilities: Educational psychology.* New York: Harper & Row, 1971.

Knowles, L. L., & Prewitt, K. (Eds.) *Instructional racism in America.* Englewood Cliffs, N.J.: Prentice-Hall, 1969.

Kornhauser, A. W. Changes in the information and attitudes of students in an economics course. *Journal of Educational Research,* 1930, 22, 288–298.

Kounin, J. S., & Gump, P. V. The comparative influence of punitive and nonpunitive teachers upon children's concepts of school misconduct. *Journal of Educational Psychology,* 1961, 52, 44–49.

Krathwohl, D. R., Bloom, B. S., & Masia, B. B. *Taxonomy of educational objectives. Handbook II: Affective domain.* New York: David McKay, 1964.

Krech, D., Crutchfield, R. S., & Ballachey, E. L. *Individual in society.* New York: McGraw-Hill, 1962.

LaBue, A. C. Teachers' classroom attitudes. *Journal of Teacher Education,* 1959, 10, 433–434.

Lahaderne, H. M. Attitudinal and intellectual correlates of attention: A study of four sixth-grade classrooms. *Journal of Educational Psychology,* 1968, 59, 320–324.

Lambert, W. E. Psychological approaches to the study of language, Part II: On second-language learning and bilingualism. *The Modern Language Journal,* 1963, 47, 114–121.

La Piere, R. T. Attitudes vs. actions. *Social Forces,* 1934, 13, 230–237.

Lavin, D. E. *The prediction of academic performance: A theoretical analysis and review of research.* New York: Russell Sage Foundation, 1965.

Leeds, C. H. A second validity study of the Minnesota Teacher Attitude Inventory. *Elementary School Journal,* 1952, 52, 398–405.

Leeds, C. H. Predictive validity of the Minnesota Teacher Attitude Inventory. *Journal of Teacher Education,* 1969, 20, 51–56.

Leeds, C. H., & Cook, W. W. The construction and differential value of a scale for determining teacher-pupil attitudes. *Journal of Experimental Education,* 1947, 16, 149–159.

Levin, M. N. Teacher preparation for affective education. Paper presented at the meeting of the American Educational Research Association Special Interest Group on Affective Education, Chicago, April 1972.

Lewin, K., Lippitt, R., & White, R. K. Patterns of aggressive behavior in experimentally created "social climates." *Journal of Social Psychology,* 1939, 10, 271–299.

Lewy, A. The empirical validity of major properties of a taxonomy of affective educational objectives. *Journal of Experimental Education,* 1968, 36 (3), 70–77.

Likert, R. A technique for the measurement of attitudes. *Archives of Psychology,* 1932, Whole No. 140.

Lindgren, H. C., & Patton, G. M. Attitudes of high school and other teachers toward children and current educational methodology. *California Journal of Educational Research,* 1958, 9, 80–85.

Lindgren, H. C., & Singer, E. P. Correlates of Brazilian and North American attitudes toward child-centered practices in education. *Journal of Social Psychology,* 1963, 60, 3–7.

Lombardi, D. N. Peer group influence on attitude. *Journal of Educational Sociology,* 1963, 36, 307–309.

Loree, M. R. Shaping teachers' attitudes. In B. O. Smith (Ed.), *Research in teacher education.* Englewood Cliffs, N.J.: Prentice-Hall, 1971. Pp. 99–118.

Lott, B. E., & Lott, A. J. The formation of positive attitudes toward group members. *Journal of Abnormal and Social Psychology,* 1960, 61, 297–300.

Lottes, J. J., Jr. *The effects of open-circuit television demonstrations of reading instruction on the observed classroom performances and attitudes of teachers.* (Doctoral dissertation, The Pennsylvania State University) Ann Arbor, Mich.: University Microfilms, 1961. No. 61–47.

Lowery, L. F. Development of an attitude measuring instrument for science education. *School Science and Mathematics,* 1966, 66, 494–502.

Lowery, L. F. An experimental investigation into the attitudes of fifth grade students

toward science. *School Science and Mathematics,* 1967, 67, 569–579.

Lowery, L. F., & Grafft, W. Paperbacks and reading attitudes. *The Reading Teacher,* 1968, 21, 618–623.

Maas, H. S. Attitudinal changes of youth group leaders in teacher training: A preliminary study. *Journal of Educational Research,* 1950, 43, 660–669.

Macdonald, J. B., Harris, T. L., & Mann, J. S. Individual versus group instruction in first grade reading. *The Reading Teacher,* 1965–1966, 19, 643–646, 652.

Maertens, N. Effects of arithmetic homework upon the attitudes of third grade pupils toward certain school-related structures. *School Science and Mathematics,* 1968, 68, 657–662.

Malone, W. H., & Freel, E. L. A preliminary study of the group attitudes of junior and senior high school students toward mathematics. *Journal of Educational Research,* 1954, 47, 599–608.

Malpass, L. F. Some relationships between students' perceptions of school and their achievement. *Journal of Educational Psychology,* 1953, 44, 475–482.

Marcus, L. *The treatment of minorities in secondary school textbooks.* New York: Anti-Defamation League, 1961.

Marita, M. Beginning reading achievement in three classroom organizational patterns. *The Reading Teacher,* 1966–1967, 20, 12–17.

Marjoribanks, K. Environment, social class, and mental abilities. *Journal of Educational Psychology,* 1972, 63, 103–109.

Mathis, A., Smith, T., & Hansen, D. College students' attitudes toward computer-assisted instruction. *Journal of Educational Psychology,* 1970, 61, 46–51.

McDaniel, E., & Filiatreau, W. K. A comparison of television and conventional instruction as determinants of attitude change. *Journal of Educational Research,* 1965, 58, 293–297.

McDiarmid, G., & Pratt, D. *Teaching prejudice: A content analysis of social studies textbooks authorized for use in Ontario.* Toronto: The Ontario Institute for Studies in Education, 1971.

McFarlane, A. M. A study of the influence of the educational geographical film upon the racial attitudes of a group of elementary school children. *British Journal of Educational Psychology,* 1945, 15, 152–153.

McGee, H. M. Measurement of authoritarianism and its relation to teachers' classroom behavior. *Genetic Psychology Monographs,* 1955, 52, 89–146.

McGuire, W. J. The nature of attitudes and attitude change. In G. Lindzey, & E. Aronson (Eds.), *The handbook of social psychology.* Vol. III. Don Mills, Ontario: Addison-Wesley, 1968. Pp. 136–314.

McKeachie, W. J. Research on teaching at the college and university level. In N. L. Gage (Ed.), *Handbook of research on teaching.* Chicago: Rand McNally, 1963. Pp. 1118–1172.

Mead, M., & Metraux, R. Image of the scientist among high school students—A pilot study. *Science,* 1957, 126, 384–390.

Medley, D. M., & Mitzel, H. E. A technique for measuring classroom behavior. *Journal of Educational Psychology,* 1958, 49, 86–92.

Medley, D. M., & Mitzel, H. E. Measuring classroom behavior by systematic observation. In N. L. Gage (Ed.), *Handbook of research on teaching.* Chicago: Rand McNally, 1963. Pp. 247–328.

Messick, S. The criterion problem in the evaluation of instruction: Assessing possible outcomes, not just intended outcomes. In M. C. Wittrock, & D. E. Wiley (Eds.), *The evaluation of instruction: Issues and problems.* New York: Holt, Rinehart & Winston, 1970. Pp. 183–202.

Metfessel, N. S., Michael, W. B., & Kirsner, D. Instrumentation of Bloom's and Krathwohl's taxonomies for writing educational objectives. *Psychology in the Schools,* 1969, 6, 227–231.

Michaelis, J. U. A directory of social studies projects. *Bulletin of the National Association of Secondary School Principals,* 1967, 51 (317), 77–80.

Miller, F. D. The validation of a generalized attitude scaling technique: Construction of an attitude scale toward teaching. *Bulletin of Purdue University: Studies in Higher Education XXVI,* 1934, 35, 98–110.

Milliken, R. L., & Spilka, B. Mathematical-verbal ability differentials and somatic expressions of situational anxiety. *Journal of Experimental Education,* 1962, 31, 3–26.

Mitchell, C. Do scales for measuring attitudes have any significance? *Journal of Educational Research,* 1941, 34, 444–452.

Moan, C. E., & Flick, G. L. Support and refutation of a threat-inducing communication in change of attitude toward cigarette smoking. *Psychological Reports,* 1968, 22, 1054.

Morsh, J. E., & Plenderleith, E. M. Changing teachers' attitudes. *Canadian Journal of Psychology,* 1949, 3, 117–129.

Mosher, H. H. Attitudes toward poetry. *English Journal,* 1953, 42, 33–34.

Murray, M. E. *Self-actualization and social values of teachers as related to students' perception of teachers.* (Doctoral dissertation, The Pennsylvania State University) Ann Arbor, Mich.: University Microfilms, 1969. No. 69–14,549.

Mussen, P. H., Conger, J. J., & Kagan, J. *Child development and personality.* New York: Harper & Row, 1969.

Neale, D. C., & Proshek, J. M. School-related attitudes of culturally disadvantaged elementary school children. *Journal of Educational Psychology,* 1967, 58, 238–244.

Nealeigh, T. R. *Development and validation of a non-verbal attitude and achievement index for mathematics.* (Doctoral dissertation, The Ohio State University) Ann Arbor, Mich.: University Microfilms, 1968. No. 68–3039.

Neidt, C. O., & Hedlund, D. E. Longitudinal relationships between cognitive and affective learning outcomes. *Journal of Experimental Education,* 1969, 37 (3), 56–60.

Neidt, C. O., & Meredith, T. F. Changes in attitudes of learners when programed instruction is interpolated between two conventional instruction experiences. *Journal of Applied Psychology,* 1966, 50, 130–137.

Nelson, C. C. Affective and cognitive attitudes of junior high school teachers and pupils. *Journal of Educational Research,* 1964, 58, 81–83.

Oliver, R. A. C., & Butcher, H. J. Teachers' attitudes to education: The structure of educational attitudes. *British Journal of Social and Clinical Psychology,* 1962, 1, 56–69.

Osgood, C. E., Suci, G. J., & Tannenbaum, P. H. *The measurement of meaning.* Urbana, Ill.: University of Illinois Press, 1957.

Ostrom, T. M. The emergence of attitude theory: 1930–1950. In A. G. Greenwald, T. C. Brock, & T. M. Ostrom (Eds.), *Psycholog-*

ical foundations of attitudes. New York: Academic Press, 1968. Pp. 1–32.

Payne, I. R. *Persuasibility and its relationship to affect, sex, and type persuasive appeal.* (Doctoral dissertation, The Pennsylvania State University) Ann Arbor, Mich.: University Microfilms, 1964. No. 64–1408.

Payne, S. L. *The art of asking questions.* Princeton, N.J.: Princeton University Press, 1951.

Peck, L. Teachers' reports of the problems of unadjusted school children. *Journal of Educational Psychology,* 1935, 26, 123–138.

Perrodin, A. F. Children's attitudes toward elementary school science. *Science Education,* 1966, 50, 214–218.

Peterson, R. C., & Thurstone, L. L. The effect of a motion picture film on children's attitudes toward Germans. *Journal of Educational Psychology,* 1932, 23, 241–246.

Peterson, R. C., & Thurstone, L. L. *Motion pictures and the social attitudes of children.* New York: Macmillan, 1933.

Phelps, J. *A study comparing attitudes toward mathematics of SMSG and traditional elementary school students.* (Doctoral dissertation, Oklahoma State University) Ann Arbor, Mich.: University Microfilms, 1964. No. 64–8942.

Pinckney, G. A. Changes in student teachers' attitudes toward childhood behavior problems. *Journal of Educational Psychology,* 1962, 53, 275–278.

Pool, I. D. (Ed.) *Trends in content analysis.* Urbana, Ill.: University of Illinois Press, 1959.

Porterfield, O. V., & Schlichting, H. F. Peer status and reading achievement. *Journal of Educational Research,* 1961, 54, 291–297.

Pratt, D. Affective objectives in social studies. *Curriculum Theory Network,* 1969, 3, 26–39.

Ragsdale, E. M. *Attitude changes of elementary student teachers and the changes in their classroom behavior during student teaching.* (Doctoral dissertation, Ball State University) Ann Arbor, Mich.: University Microfilms, 1967. No. 67–10,687.

Ragsdale, J. D. Effects of selected aspects of brevity on persuasiveness. *Speech Monographs,* 1968, 35, 8–13.

Ramseyer, L. L. Measuring intangible effects of motion pictures. *Educational Screen,* 1939, 18, 237–238, 261.

Raths, J. Clarifying children's values. *The National Elementary Principal,* 1962, 42 (2), 35–39.

Raths, L. E., Harmin, M., & Simon, S. B. *Values and teaching: Working with values in the classroom.* Columbus, Ohio: Charles E. Merrill, 1966.

Raun, C. E., & Butts, D. P. The relationship between the strategies of inquiry in science and student cognitive and affective behavioral change. *Journal of Research in Science Teaching,* 1967–1968, 5, 261–268.

Reed, H. J. An investigation of the relationship between teaching effectiveness and the teacher's attitude of acceptance. *Journal of Experimental Education,* 1953, 21, 277–325.

Remmers, H. H. Rating methods in research on teaching. In N. L. Gage (Ed.), *Handbook of research on teaching.* Chicago: Rand McNally, 1963. Pp. 329–378.

Remmers, H. H., Dodds, B. L., & Brasch, I. W. A study of changes in attitudes toward education. *School and Society,* 1942, 55, 593–596.

Remmers, H. H., & Wood, W. F. Changes in attitudes toward Germans, Japanese, Jews, and Nazis. *School and Society,* 1947, 65, 484–487.

Richardson, C. E. Thurstone scale for measuring attitudes of college students toward physical fitness and exercise. *Research Quarterly,* 1960, 31, 638–643.

Riestra, M. A., & Johnson, C. E. Changes in attitudes of elementary school pupils toward foreign speaking peoples resulting from the study of a foreign language. *Journal of Experimental Education,* 1964, 33, 65–72.

Rocchio, P. D., & Kearney, N. C. Does a course in mental hygiene help teachers? *Understanding the Child,* 1956, 25, 91–94.

Rosen, N. A. Anonymity and attitude measurement. *Public Opinion Quarterly,* 1960, 24, 675–679.

Rosenberg, M. J., Hovland, C. I., McGuire, W. J., Abelson, R. P., & Brehm, J. W. (Eds.) *Attitude organization and change: An analysis of consistency among attitude components.* New Haven, Conn.: Yale University Press, 1960.

Rosenshine, B. Evaluation of classroom instruction. *Review of Educational Research,* 1970, 40, 279–300.

Rosenshine, B., & Furst, N. Research on

teacher performance criteria. In B. O. Smith (Ed.), *Research in teacher education: A symposium.* Englewood Cliffs, N.J.: Prentice-Hall, 1971. Pp. 37–72.

Rothman, A. I. Teacher characteristics and student learning. *Journal of Research in Science Teaching,* 1969, 6, 340–348.

Rothman, A. I., Welch, W. W., & Walberg, H. J. Physics teacher characteristics and student learning. *Journal of Research in Science Teaching,* 1969, 6, 59–63.

Rulon, P. J., & others. The effect of phonographic recordings upon attitudes. *Harvard Educational Review,* 1944, 14, 20–37.

Rundquist, E. A., & Sletto, R. F. *Personality in the depression: A study in the measurement of attitudes.* Minneapolis: University of Minnesota Press, 1936.

Ryan, J. J. *Effects of modern and conventional mathematics curricula on pupil attitudes, interests, and perception of proficiency.* Final report. Minnesota National Laboratory, BR-5-1028, U.S. Office of Education, 1968. ED 022 673.

Ryans, D. G. *Characteristics of teachers, their description, comparison, and appraisal: A research study.* Washington, D.C.: American Council on Education, 1960.

Schramm, W. Learning from instructional television. *Review of Educational Research,* 1962, 32, 156–167.

Schramm, W., Lyle, J., & Parker, E. B. *Television in the lives of our children.* Toronto: University of Toronto Press, 1961.

Schrupp, M. H., & Gjerde, C. M. Teacher growth in attitudes toward behavior problems of children. *Journal of Educational Psychology,* 1953, 44, 203–214.

Schultz, D. G., & Green, B. F., Jr. Predicting academic achievement with a new attitude-interest questionnaire-II. *Educational and Psychological Measurement,* 1953, 13, 54–64.

Scott, O., & Brinkley, S. G. Attitude changes of student teachers and the validity of the Minnesota Teacher Attitude Inventory. *Journal of Educational Psychology,* 1960, 51, 76–81.

Scott, W. A. Attitude measurement. In G. Lindzey, & E. Aronson (Eds.), *The handbook of social psychology.* Vol. II. Don Mills, Ontario: Addison-Wesley, 1968. Pp. 204–273.

Scriven, M. Student values as educational objectives. In *Proceedings of the 1965 invitational conference on testing problems.* Princeton, N.J.: Educational Testing Service, 1966. Pp. 33–49.

Seidman, J. M., & Knapp, L. B. Teacher likes and dislikes of student behavior and student perceptions of these attitudes. *Journal of Educational Research,* 1953, 47, 143–149.

Seiler, L. H., & Hough, R. L. Empirical comparisons of the Thurstone and Likert techniques. In G. F. Summers (Ed.), *Attitude measurement.* Chicago: Rand McNally, 1970. Pp. 159–173.

Senathirajah, N., & Weiss, J. *Evaluation in geography: A resource book for teachers.* Toronto: The Ontario Institute for Studies in Education, 1971.

Shaw, J., Klausmeier, H. J., Luker, A. H., & Reid, H. T. Changes occurring in teacher-pupil attitudes during a two-week guidance workshop. *Journal of Applied Psychology,* 1952, 36, 304–306.

Shaw, M. E., & Wright, J. M. *Scales for the measurement of attitudes.* New York: McGraw-Hill, 1967.

Sheehan, A. C. *The interrelations of interests and attitudes and specified independent variables in the teaching of natural science by television in the fifth grade.* (Doctoral dissertation, Boston University) Ann Arbor, Mich.: University Microfilms, 1961. No. 60-5585.

Sheldon, W. D., & Lashinger, D. R. Effect of first grade instruction using basal readers, modified linguistic materials and linguistic readers. *The Reading Teacher,* 1965–1966, 19, 576–579.

Shoben, E. J., Jr. Potency in the schools. *Teachers College Record,* 1962, 63, 548–550.

Shulman, L. Reconstruction of educational research. *Review of Educational Research,* 1970, 40, 371–396.

Siegel, L., & Macomber, F. G. Comparative effectiveness of televised and large classes and of small sections. *Journal of Educational Psychology,* 1957, 48, 371–382.

Silance, E. B., & Remmers, H. H. An experimental generalized master scale: A scale to measure attitudes toward any school subject. *Bulletin of Purdue University: Studies in Higher Education XXVI,* 1934, 35, 84–88.

Silberman, C. E. *Crisis in the classroom.* New York: Random House, 1970.

Silberman, M. L. Behavioral expression of teachers' attitudes toward elementary school students. *Journal of Educational Psychology,* 1969, 60, 402–407.

Simon, A., & Boyer, E. G. (Eds.) *Mirrors for behavior: An anthology of classroom observation instruments.* Vols. 1–6. Philadelphia: Research for Better Schools, 1967.

Smith, B. L., Lasswell, H. D., & Casey, R. D. *Propaganda, communication, and public opinion.* Princeton, N.J.: Princeton University Press, 1946.

Smith, E. R., & Tyler, R. W. *Appraising and recording student progress.* Vol. III. New York: Harper & Row, 1942.

Smith, L. M., & Hudgins, B. B. *Educational psychology: An application of social and behavioral theory.* New York: Knopf, 1965.

Smith, M. B. The personal setting of public opinions: A study of attitudes toward Russia. *Public Opinion Quarterly,* 1947, 11, 507–523.

Social Science Education Consortium. *Curriculum materials analysis systems.* Publication Nos. 143, 144, 145. Boulder, Colo.: SSEC, 1971.

Somit, A., Tanenhaus, J., Wilke, W. H., & Cooley, R. W. The effect of the introductory political science course on student attitudes toward personal political participation. *American Political Science Review,* 1958, 52, 1129–1132.

Sontag, M. Attitudes toward education and perception of teacher behaviors. *American Educational Research Journal,* 1968, 5, 385–402.

Sparks, J. N. Teachers' attitudes toward the behavior problems of children. *Journal of Educational Psychology,* 1952, 43, 284–291.

Stake, R. E. Objectives, priorities, and other judgment data. *Review of Educational Research,* 1970, 40, 181–212.

Stauffer, R. G. The effectiveness of language arts and basic reader approaches to first grade reading instruction. *The Reading Teacher,* 1966–1967, 20, 18–24.

Stern, G. G. Measuring noncognitive variables in research on teaching. In N. L. Gage (Ed.), *Handbook of research on teaching.* Chicago: Rand McNally, 1963. Pp. 398–447.

Stouffer, G. A. W., Jr. Behavior problems of children as viewed by teachers and mental hygienists. *Mental Hygiene,* 1952, 36, 271–285.

Stouffer, G. A. W., Jr. The attitude of secondary-school teachers toward certain behavior problems of children. *School Review,* 1956, 64, 358–362.

Summers, G. F. (Ed.) *Attitude measurement.* Chicago: Rand McNally, 1970.

Sutherland, M. B. A study of the effects of learning French on attitudes toward the French. *British Journal of Educational Psychology,* 1946, 16, 44.

Tatara, W. T. Effects of novels on ideas about the scientist. *Journal of Educational Research,* 1964, 58, 3–9.

Tenenbaum, S. Attitudes of elementary school children to school, teachers and classmates. *Journal of Applied Psychology,* 1944, 28, 134–141.

Thomas, W. I., & Znaniecki, F. *The Polish peasant in Europe and America.* Vol. 1. Boston: Badger, 1918.

Thurstone, L. L. The method of paired comparisons for social values. *Journal of Abnormal and Social Psychology,* 1927, 21, 384–400.

Thurstone, L. L. Influence of motion pictures on children's attitudes. *Journal of Social Psychology,* 1931, 2, 291–305. (a)

Thurstone, L. L. The measurement of social attitudes. *Journal of Abnormal and Social Psychology,* 1931, 26, 249–269. (b)

Thurstone, L. L., & Chave, E. J. *The measurement of attitude.* Chicago: University of Chicago Press, 1929.

Tittle, C. R., & Hill, R. J. Attitude measurement and prediction of behavior: An evaluation of conditions and measurement techniques. *Sociometry,* 1967, 30, 199–213.

Tobias, S. Effect of attitudes to programed instruction and other media on achievement from programed materials. *Audio-Visual Communication Review,* 1969, 17, 299–306.

Tolor, A., Scarpetti, W. L., & Lane, P. A. Teachers' attitudes toward children's behavior revisited. *Journal of Educational Psychology,* 1967, 58, 175–180.

Trenfield, W. G. An analysis of the relationships between selected factors and the civic interests of high school students. *Journal of Educational Research,* 1965, 58, 460–462.

Tuel, J. K., & Shaw, M. C. The development of a scale to measure attitudinal dimensions of the educational environment. *Educational and Psychological Measurement,* 1966, 26, 955–963.

UNESCO. *A handbook for the improvement of textbooks and teaching materials as aids to international understanding.* Paris: UNESCO, 1949.

Vitrogan, D. A method for determining a generalized attitude of high school students toward science. *Science Education,* 1967, 51, 170–175.

Walberg, H. J. Predicting class learning: An approach to the class as a social system. *American Educational Research Journal,* 1969, 6, 529–542. (a)

Walberg, H. J. Social environment as a mediator of classroom learning. *Journal of Educational Psychology,* 1969, 60, 443–448. (b)

Walberg, H. J., & Ahlgren, A. Predictors of the social environment of learning. *American Educational Research Journal,* 1970, 7, 153–167.

Walberg, H. J., & Anderson, G. J. Classroom climate and individual learning. *Journal of Educational Psychology,* 1968, 59, 414–419.

Walworth, A. *School histories at war: A study of the treatment of our wars in the secondary school history books of the United States and in those of its former enemies.* Cambridge, Mass.: Harvard University, 1938.

Wandt, E. A comparison of the attitudes of contrasting groups of teachers. *Educational and Psychological Measurement,* 1954, 14, 418–422.

Wang, C. K. A. Suggested criteria for writing attitude statements. *Journal of Social Psychology,* 1932, 3, 367–373.

Watson, D. H. *A comparison of the effects of certain types of group work on the attitudes, opinions and pupil evaluations of student teachers.* (Doctoral dissertation, The University of New Mexico) Ann Arbor, Mich.: University Microfilms, 1968. No. 68-3487.

Wear, C. L. Construction of equivalent forms of an attitude scale. *Research Quarterly,* 1955, 26, 113–119.

Webb, E. J. *Unconventional uses of content analysis in social science.* Philadelphia: National Conference on Content Analysis, Annenberg School of Communications, 1967.

Wehling, L. J., & Charters, W. W., Jr. Dimensions of teacher beliefs about the teaching process. *American Educational Research Journal,* 1969, 6, 7–30.

Weick, K. E. Systematic observational methods. In G. Lindzey, & E. Aronson (Eds.), *The handbook of social psychology.* Vol. II. Don Mills, Ontario: Addison-Wesley, 1968. Pp. 357–451.

Weinstein, G. The trumpet: A guide to humanistic psychological curriculum. *Theory into Practice,* 1971, 10, 196–203.

Weinstock, H. R., & Peccolo, C. M. Do students' ideas and attitudes survive practice teaching? *Elementary School Journal,* 1970, 70, 210–218.

Weisgerber, R. A. Motivation for science. *The Science Teacher,* 1961, 28, 20–23.

Weiss, J. The development and measurement of home environmental models for personality characteristics. Paper presented at the meeting of the American Educational Research Association, Minneapolis, March 1970. (a)

Weiss, J. Fathers, the missing link: Some methodological implications for environmental research. *Generator* (American Educational Research Association Division G Newsletter), 1, No. 2, December 1970. (b)

Weiss, J. *Formative curriculum evaluation: In need of methodology.* American Educational Research Association 1971 annual meeting, Tape No. 7A. Washington, D.C.: AERA, 1971.

Westley, B. H., & Jacobson, H. K. Teacher participation and attitudes toward instructional television. *Audiovisual Communication Review,* 1962, 10, 328–333.

Westley, B. H., & Jacobson, H. K. Modern mathematics on TV: Its impact on pupils and teachers. *Research Bulletin* No. 15. Madison: University of Wisconsin Television Laboratory, 1963.

Whitehead, F. The attitudes of grammar school pupils towards some novels commonly read in school. *British Journal of Educational Psychology,* 1956, 26, 104–111.

Wickman, E. K. *Children's behavior and teachers' attitudes.* New York: Commonwealth Fund, 1928.

Wight, A. R., & Doxsey, J. R. *Measurement in support of affective education.* Salt Lake City, Utah: Interstate Educational Resource Service Center, 1972.

Williams, R. L. Personality, ability and achievement correlates of scholastic attitudes. *Journal of Educational Research,* 1970, 63, 401–403.

Withall, J. The development of a technique

for the measurement of social-emotional climate in classrooms. *Journal of Experimental Education*, 1949, 17, 347–361.

Witty, P. A. Effects of television on attitudes and behavior. *Education*, 1964, 85, 98–105.

Wolf, R. The measurement of environments. In A. Anastasi (Ed.), *Testing problems in perspective*. Washington, D.C.: American Council on Education, 1966. Pp. 491–503.

Woodall, P. G. *A study of pupils' achievements and attitudes in the School Mathematics Study Group and the traditional mathematics programs of the Lewiston school district: 1960–1965.* (Doctoral dissertation, University of Idaho) Ann Arbor, Mich.: University Microfilms, 1967. No. 67-5389.

Wynn, D. C., & Bledsoe, J. C. Factors related to gain and loss of scientific interest during high school. *Science Education*, 1967, 51, 67–74.

Yates, A. (Ed.) *Grouping in education*. New York: John Wiley, 1966.

Yee, A. H. *Factors involved in determining the relationship between teachers' and pupils' attitudes.* Austin, Tex.: University of Texas, 1966. ED 010 336.

Yee, A. H. Source and direction of causal influence in teacher-pupil relationships. *Journal of Educational Psychology*, 1968, 59, 275–282.

Yee, A. H. Do cooperating teachers influence the attitudes of student teachers? *Journal of Educational Psychology*, 1969, 60, 327–332.

Yee, A. H., & Fruchter, B. Factor content of the Minnesota Teacher Attitude Inventory. *American Educational Research Journal*, 1971, 8, 119–133.

Yivisaker, H., & Pace, R. Differential changes in college students' information and attitudes in social studies courses. *Social Education*, 1940, 4, 116–120.

Zim, H. S. Student interest in science. *School Science and Mathematics*, 1941, 41, 385–389.

Zschocher, S. Zur diagnostik und therapie von rechenschwierigkeiten bei hortkindern des 1. Schuljahres. (On the diagnosis and treatment of arithmetic difficulties in first grade students.) *Probleme und Ergebrisse der Psychologie*, 1965, 13, 47–63.

CHAPTER 25 Skill Learning[1]

MICHAEL I. POSNER
University of Oregon

STEVEN W. KEELE
University of Oregon

INTRODUCTION

What is a *skill*? The psychological use of the term is quite broad (Welford, 1968) and includes the study of those processes producing expert, rapid and accurate performance. This definition of skill may be applied not only to tasks which involve manual activity, but also to those which require the internal manipulation of symbols (Bartlett, 1958; Fitts & Posner, 1967) as in language and thought. In this chapter we shall limit the discussion almost entirely to the study of the control of skilled movements (Keele, 1968). In part this is done because the ordinary use of the term skill is typically confined to motor activity, but also because we believe that the study of motor control provides a good way of approaching issues of attention and the performance of mental operations in general (Keele, 1968; Posner & Boies, 1971). Thus we see the study of motor activity as an important vehicle for the development of a general theory of skill. Although it is generally supposed that manual skills are relatively simple in comparison with intellectual performance, Fitts (Fitts & Posner, 1967) has pointed out that the problem of programming a computer to hit a baseball is no less complex than programming it to play chess.

The teacher of skill must consider the qualifications and abilities of those who are to perform the skill, the characteristics of the skill which is to be taught, and the program which will best convey the skill to the learner. Maximization of skilled performance must involve, therefore, some combination of personnel selection, task design and training (Holding, 1965). For the learning of manual skills, a knowledge of how movements are planned, executed and corrected may help in the accomplishment of each of these goals.

This chapter relies primarily upon laboratory experiments. Despite the limitations of this approach, we hope to provide a frame-

[1] This chapter reports research supported by the National Science Foundation under grants 5960 and 21020 and by the Advanced Research Projects Agency of the Department of Defense monitored by the Air Force Office of Scientific Research under Contract No. F 44620-67-C-0099.

A preliminary version of the first part of the chapter was presented to the First Canadian Conference on Psychomotor Skill and Sports Psychology, October 1969 in Edmonton, Alberta, Canada.

work of established results and methods within which the reader can interpret his problem and define the necessary research which he needs to improve performance of the skill with which he is involved. We shall try to point to the great gaps in our current knowledge which provide much opportunity for the researcher and teacher to develop and expand the framework of this chapter. We realize that laboratory studies often do not in themselves provide an obvious or ready-made means of generalization to the myriad of situations in which skill is important. The task of applying laboratory analyses to the improvement of skills requires no less creativity than the design of the experiments and theories discussed here. However, it is possible that a systematic framework for viewing skills will aid the reader in conceptualizing his own problem and in thinking about its possible solution. In recent years the idea of direct applicability of basic research findings has given way increasingly to viewing such results as providing only a very general orientation for the creative designer of technologies (H. A. Simon, 1969).

Information Processing Approach

The view of humans developed in this chapter is one of an adaptive information processing system combining highly flexible conscious strategies and more specific unconscious control mechanisms. This is a view which has come to have increasing influence within experimental psychology (Broadbent, 1958; Fitts & Posner, 1967; Neisser, 1967; Simon & Newell, 1971). On the perceptual side, the problem is how the sensory systems interact with past learning to provide a stable, conscious world (Neisser, 1967). Studies of problem solving explore conscious and extremely flexible strategies which allow men to assemble information from their memories and from fresh observation in order to produce new inferences (Reitman, 1965; Simon & Newell, 1971). The information processing approach is no

less applicable to the study of skilled movements. Here the central issue becomes how the laborious, conscious movements of the novice come to be performed with a minimal involvement of attention. What changes as skill learning progresses and when and how are central attentional mechanisms brought into the control of highly skilled movements? It is primarily to these questions that this chapter is addressed.

The study of skilled movement is an old one in experimental psychology. At the turn of the century Woodworth (1899) studied the nature of a simple voluntary movement, and Bryan and Harter (1899) investigated the development of skill in telegraphy. These studies illustrated the principles of intermittent conscious control and increasing automation which are still the central themes in current research. However, this promising beginning was not, in general, followed up until rather recently.

A number of factors have converged to make the study of skilled movement once again of particular concern to psychologists. First, there is more known now about the physiological substrate of action (Eccles, Ito, & Szentágothai, 1967). In particular, work on the stretch receptors (Granit, 1970) and on the cerebellum (Eccles, Ito, & Szentágothai, 1967) has provided mechanisms which may serve to control movement. These developments suggest that studies of voluntary movement may rival vision and audition as a vehicle for studying the relationship of brain and behavior. Moreover, work with animals (Hinde, 1969) has served to emphasize the importance of central control of movement. Complex patterns of movement seem to appear even in the absence of sensory return (Taub & Berman, 1968). Thus, despite the importance of feedback information in the initial control of movement sequences there is ample reason to consider more central systems of control. Finally, the development of an information processing psychology has provided the framework for studies of the roles of attention, memory and perception in the control of movement. Already some of these ideas are being applied to the study of physical education (Whiting, 1967) and factory skills (Senders, 1964; Young, 1969).

It is this information processing framework which provides the basis for the present chapter. We have not tried to survey the entire literature, but have focused on certain experiments and techniques which illustrate the basic approach and seem fruitful for possible application to improvement of skills.

The next section of this chapter attempts to describe the psychological processes involved in the performance of a single skilled movement. A simple experimental task is chosen so as to illustrate the components of skill within a concrete context. The third section builds on the second by discussing the control of sequences of movements. The fourth section describes changes in the properties of these skill components as the learner masters the task. In the final section the use of these ideas in the selection, design and training of skills is briefly discussed.

DESCRIPTION OF A SINGLE MOVEMENT

REFERENCE TASK

Consider yourself as a subject in a simple experiment. Your hand grasps a stylus which is resting against a home button. There are two targets, one to your left and one to your right. The target distance is a few inches and the size of the target about a quarter of an inch. You first receive a warning signal in the form of an amber light. Three quarters of a second later either one of the two target lights comes on. You move as quickly as possible to one of the designated targets and touch it with the stylus. When you hit the target all lights extinguish and the room is in total darkness. You must reproduce the movement by reaching back to the home button and replacing the stylus.

s_1	s_2			Target
		Reaction Time	Movement Time	
Foreperiod		(RT)	(MT)	Storage

Fig. 1. Schematic of reference experiment.

This simple task carries many of the component skills which are present in familiar activities. The time between the warning signal (s_1) and the target light (s_2) represents a period of preparation not unlike that of the track man just prior to the sound of the gun. The target light (s_2) tells the subject where to go in somewhat the same way that an opponent's tennis return informs a player of where to move. The motion to the target is roughly analogous to the path of a football end in moving to a predesignated location to receive the pass from the quarterback. The storing and reproducing of the movement perhaps resembles what the bowler must do when he tries to repeat a particular set of movements to hit his mark. If our simple experimental task captures anything of the elements of skill, it seems worthwhile to ask how it is that a simple movement is controlled.

METHODS OF ANALYSIS

Such a movement sequence may be described at many levels. A motion picture of the movement would reveal something of its acceleration and deceleration, but such a picture would be useless in exploring the activities which occur during the warning or reaction time intervals. At another level the contractions of the muscles through time provide a dynamic picture of their activity (Basmajian, 1962). Recently more information has become available concerning electrical activity in the spinal cord, cerebellum and cortex in the process of movement (Eccles, Ito, & Szentágothai, 1967; Granit, 1970). However, the main problems of skill learning cannot be solved at the level of muscle contraction. The study of the electrophysiology of brain processes is useful, but it provides only a rather sketchy view of the role of attention and memory in the control of the movement. Our major focus will be on the study of the central processes which control movement as revealed by psychological experiments. It appears to us that this is the most important level for the teacher and educational researcher to concentrate their search for information which can improve skills.

According to Holding (1965), skilled behavior involves the integration of three kinds of information: first, information about what is to be achieved; second, information from the task itself; and third, information about the results of one's own action. The integration of these diverse sources of information must involve sensory systems, long- and short-term memory, and other central processes operating together in a very complex way. However, it is precisely in these areas of the central control of skill that physiological data are least available and for which objective information is difficult to collect. Like all analyses of internal process, the psychological understanding of the control of skill requires inferences from carefully designed experiments. While we cannot observe mental operations directly, we can study them because of two characteristics which can be measured. First, each operation involved in the control of movement requires time, and second, each operation may demand space within a limited capacity central attention system (Posner & Keele, 1970).

Following Helmholtz's (1853) demonstration of the time for neural conduction, Donders (1868) attempted to develop tasks to measure the time for such simple mental operations as discrimination and choice. The use of time measures to isolate and observe mental processes has undergone something of a revival in the last dozen years (Koster, 1969; Posner & Mitchell, 1967; Sternberg, 1969). This method can also be applied to the study of motor movements. Indeed, the measurement of reaction and movement time has had a long and fruitful history in the study of skill (Fitts & Posner, 1967; Keele, 1968; Welford, 1968).

Less well known is the use of interference techniques to study the requirements of certain components of task for access to a limited capacity attentional system. This method also has a long history in psychology (Welch, 1898; Welford, 1968) and in physical education (Henry & Harrison, 1961). A common way to demonstrate limited capacity is to present a signal to which the subject must respond. During the processing of that signal another signal is presented. If both signals require access to the same mechanism, the response time or processing time of the second signal will be somewhat delayed or retarded. If careful control is taken to make sure that the signals do not require conflicting receptor or effector processes, the delay may be attributed to competition in a central processor. This phenomenon has been widely studied in experimental psychology under the term *psychological refractory period* (Welford, 1968). It is this competition between signals for access to the limited capacity mechanism which provides our major method for studying the role of attention in processing signals.

Not all information impinging upon the organism needs to go through this system. For example, stimuli which control the heart or respiration may place no load on attention. Instead, this information is transmitted from receptors to effectors without going through the limited capacity system. It is an empirical question to determine whether or not such overlearned skills as walking place loads upon the central processing system.

COMPONENT INTERVALS

The central processing system is relatively late in the sequence of processing a signal (Posner & Keele, 1970) and thus the performer has a good deal of control over its operation. It is for this reason that studies of the attentional control of skill are particularly important for the educator. Presumably he can influence skill learning and performance by his instructions on how to allocate the students' attentional capacities. With this background we can ask how this attentional system operates and what information it deals with during the execution of our reference experiment. The overall time in the reference task can be broken down into several critical intervals (see Figure 1, p. 807). The time between the warning signal (s_1) and the target light is called the foreperiod. This is followed by a reaction time period which extends from the informative signal (s_2) until the subject's hand leaves the home key. The movement itself follows the reaction time and ends when the subject reaches the target. Following completion of the movement there is a brief time during which the memory of the movement is highly susceptible to loss. We will consider each of these intervals in turn.

Preparation

What is happening during the foreperiod? Subjectively you can feel yourself getting ready for the occurrence of the target light. Psychologists have called this process *preparation* (Bertelson, 1967). Providing a warning signal reduces reaction time to the target. If the foreperiod is kept constant for a series of trials and varied only between series, it is possible to show that a foreperiod of from 200–500 milliseconds is needed for reaction time to become optimal (Bertelson, 1967; Posner & Wilkinson, 1969). Once the optimal level of preparation is reached it can be maintained, but it appears to take considerable effort to do so. If variable foreperiods are used so that subjects are uncertain about when the signal will occur, they generally show optimal performance near the mean of the foreperiods (Bevan, Avant, & Lankford, 1966). The development and maintenance of preparation appears to be pretty much under voluntary control. In the high stress of competition it is likely that subjects can achieve optimal preparation well within the 500 millisecond figure suggested by laboratory studies and can probably maintain it for a considerable period.

Preparation appears to involve at least two major processes. One of these is a change in the level of alertness. The change in alertness is not peripheral because the time course of preparation found in reaction time experiments is quite similar to that found when the subject prepares only to detect a signal to which no overt response is required (Egan, Greenberg, & Schulman, 1961; Leavitt, 1969). For this reason it is doubtful that preparation involves *only* a change in the state of the responding muscle such as might be recorded as altered muscle potential, although such changes frequently accompany preparation.

The change in central alertness appears to conform to the older idea of a *sensory set* (Henry, 1960; Woodworth, 1938). The term *sensory set* suggests that the subject performs operations which increase the rate at which he can process the target signal when it occurs. One possible mechanism for central alertness is a reduction in the cortical threshold for sensory stimulation. Indeed, changes in brain wave activity (electroencephalogram [EEG]) which are present during preparation suggest this possibility. Another possible mechanism is an increase in the rate at which the limited capacity central attentional mechanism receives the signal. Experiments indicate that central alertness does not appear to be specific to any particular sensory modality. For example, if the subject is prepared for a visual stimulus, his processing of an infrequent auditory probe stimulus is improved or at least not diminished over what it would be if he were not alert (Näätänen, 1970; Posner & Boies, 1971). Such results suggest that alertness is not itself selective for a given modality but improves the handling of all incoming signals. Unfortunately, experiments have not yet provided a clear choice between the two mechanisms for alertness which have been outlined above.

There is a second process which occurs during the foreperiod. This process conforms more closely to the idea of a *motor set* (Henry, 1960; Woodworth, 1938). Consider the two possible movements which might occur when the target light comes on. Corresponding to each movement there is an internal motor program or plan which can serve to control the movement. At the time of the warning signal the threshold of these two motor programs can be altered by the subject. Thus, the two specific responses, out of all possible responses which might be made, are placed in a system of very high availability. Moreover, if the subject has reason to believe that one response is more likely than the other, that motor program can be given priority. One kind of evidence of such specific preparation of responses is the finding that the more probable of two responses shows a greater improvement in reaction time with an optimal warning interval than does the less probable (Bertelson & Barzeele, 1965). This finding indicates that the foreperiod involves a specific preparation of the responses as well as an increase in central alertness. It is possible that such specific preparation involves a peripheral adjustment in muscle potential. However, studies (Weiss, 1965; Botwinick & Thompson, 1966) show that the presence of a warning signal reduces the time between the signal and the muscle potential rather than the time between muscle potential and the overt response. This argues that the changes are occurring in the internal units which control the movements rather than only in the muscle.

Another reason for believing that preparation involves changes in brain processes and not merely peripheral changes comes from studies involving EEG recording. During the foreperiod of reaction time or signal detection tasks there develops a negative shift in the EEG (contingent negative variation) (Karlin, 1970) which has a time course very similar to behavioral preparation as discussed above (Posner & Wilkinson, 1969). Careful work has shown that this change is not due to peripheral artifacts such as eye movement or muscle changes (Karlin, 1970). Unfortunately, the negative EEG shift does not distinguish between sensory and motor sets. A very similar shift is present before any voluntary movement initiated by the subject, even when no warning signal is present. Thus, it appears that both changes in central alertness and specific activation of a motor program give rise to the negative EEG shift.

There is some evidence that the subjects can manipulate the relative emphasis which they place on these two kinds of preparation. If instructed to take a sensory set, subjects will give somewhat different reaction times than if instructed to take a motor set (Henry, 1960). However, recent experiments (Posner & Boies, 1971) have found evidence that with optimal warning intervals subjects can perform both the general alertness function and the specific activation of the internal motor programs simultaneously. The question of how well the two sets can be performed simultaneously is one of considerable interest both on theoretical and practical grounds. For example, a recent physiological model of brain activity proposed that stimulus processing and response execution involve two fundamentally different and mutually inhibitory physiological systems (Routtenberg, 1968). Moreover, the usual instruction given by many coaches to adopt a "motor set" also assumes mutual inhibition between these two systems. While current research is sufficient to provide clear evidence for separation of these two processes, the degree of their mutual inhibition is still in doubt.

Although the details of the process of preparation are not yet completely clear, we are beginning to develop techniques which reveal the time course and the brain changes involved in it. A combination of behavioral analysis of reaction times at varying foreperiods with the use of electromyogram (EMG) and EEG methods may allow us a more detailed analysis of this very important interval.

Decision

At the time the target light is presented the subject has reached an alert state. The set of possible responses has been activated and is held in readiness. When the target occurs it is necessary to locate the internal response or motor program which corresponds to the light and to initiate the response. The time to locate the internal response will depend upon the number of responses which have been placed in active readiness. It is known that the time to search material in active memory is a function of the number of items in storage (Sternberg, 1969). Experiments of the type we have been discussing usually show an increase in reaction time which is proportional to the logarithm of the number of possible targets (Hick, 1952; Hyman, 1953). It has also been found that a probable target will elicit a response more quickly than an improbable one. The search of active memory is biased toward the more probable or higher frequency alternatives. Such biases may be rearranged by the subject for each trial. For example, if the target lights alternate on successive trials, subjects will respond more rapidly to the one they expect to occur.

The time to begin the correct response is also affected by the tendency of a signal to activate competing motor programs. Consider our reference experiment. If the subject is instructed to move to the target which is lighted (compatible condition), the reaction time will be relatively short. However, if the target lights are spatially separate from the target which they signify, the light will have some tendency to activate both movement programs. If the instruction is to move in the direction opposite the target which is lighted (incompatible condition) the conflict will be even greater. In compatible assignment will frequently cause errors and will almost always produce a slowing in reaction time (Fitts & Posner, 1967). The ease with which the target locates the correct motor program is a func-

tion of the compatibility. Studies have shown (Posner, 1966) that the slope of the curve relating reaction time to a number of alternatives may be quite flat for highly compatible assignments and quite steep for incompatible ones. Thus, the relative disadvantage of an incompatible assignment will be greater as the number of possible targets increases.

Compatibility effects can have considerable practical importance. Assignments which are incompatible tend to reduce the level of performance even after many months of practice (Fitts & Posner, 1967). Moreover, under conditions of stress high compatibility responses which might have been inhibited with practice will tend to emerge (Fitts & Posner, 1967). One important compatibility condition is the tendency to react in the spatial direction of the stimulus (J. R. Simon, 1969). If the stimulus is located in the same direction as a subject must respond, he will be faster. Most of the evidence for this comes from studies where the subject has multiple response alternatives. However, if it applies where there is only one response, it suggests that times for sprint events in track or swimming might be improved if the starter's gun were sounded in front of rather than behind or to the side of the runners. Other examples of the applications of stimulus-response (S-R) compatibility, particularly in the design of equipment, are discussed later in this chapter.

During the reaction time interval the subject appears to search among his possible responses for the correct program for the particular target light. The search time is a function of the number of possible responses. The location of the motor program is not much affected by details of the program itself. This is in agreement with the idea that the reaction time involves the location of the correct response program while the movement time involves the execution of the program (Fitts & Peterson, 1964). We now turn to the process of executing the movement.

Movement

Perhaps the most interesting part of the reference task requires the least time. This is the movement itself, which in our reference experiment can be accomplished in less than 0.5 second. The length of time required to complete the movement is affected mainly by two things. These are the overall movement length and the required accuracy of its termination. The relationship of movement length and accuracy to time may be expressed by the equation

$$\text{Movement Time} = a + b \log_2 \frac{2A}{W}.$$

In this equation A is the movement length and W the width of the target while a and b are constants reflecting the type of movement and characteristics of the individual performing it. This equation has been called Fitt's Law (Keele, 1968), and it accounts for about 90 to 95 percent of the variance in speed of movement in situations of the type we have been discussing (Fitts & Peterson, 1964). There are a number of closely related formulations of this equation (Welford, 1968) and also several different ways in which it can be formally derived from underlying assumptions about control of the movement (Fitts & Posner, 1967; Keele, 1968).

Although the equation was originally derived from information theory (Fitts & Posner, 1967), probably the most interesting way to view Fitts's Law is as a consequence of the processing of feedback information. Exact derivations of the law from feedback considerations are provided elsewhere (Keele, 1968). However, basically the idea is that the overall movement to a target can be divided into an initial movement and a series of corrections which eventually reach the target. The corrections depend upon feedback information so that such corrections cannot be made until after a reaction time interval during which feedback can be processed. The derivation also assumes that each correction requires a constant time and leaves an error which is proportional to the remaining distance. This view suggests that in moving to a target the bulk of the overall movement time will be spent in corrections which are quite close to the target. Movies taken of such movements confirm this prediction (Annett, Golby, & Kay, 1958).

If the assumptions expressed above are correct, many fast movements must not involve feedback because they are too rapid for feedback to be processed. This means that visual feedback, for example, cannot be effective in a movement lasting less than some critical time. This view was first tested by Woodworth (1899) and Vince (1948), but in these experiments complex repetitive movements were used. In order to test this idea with a simple movement such as in our reference experiment, subjects were taught (Keele & Posner, 1968) to perform the movement at rates varying from 150 to 450 milliseconds. On half the trials the room lights were extinguished immediately after the subject left the home position and remained off until he hit or missed the target. This elimination of visual feedback only affected the accuracy of the movement if it lasted longer than about 200 milliseconds. Thus, for this method the minimum time for which a movement can be corrected by visual feedback is about 0.2 second. Several recent experiments have suggested that the value obtained by this method is reasonable (Keele, 1968). It is still possible for movements made more rapidly than this to be corrected by kinesthetic feedback, since measurements of the time to process kinesthetic return show it to require only 110 to 160 milliseconds (Higgins & Angel, 1970).

If a task lasts more than 0.25 second, subjects can use information from the task to make corrections. It is interesting to see how such feedback is utilized within a given task. Recently the task of catching a ball has been examined with this in mind (Whiting, 1967). Visual information about the ball's trajectory is manipulated by varying the time that light inside the ball is lit.

Results have suggested that subjects benefit from increased visual information but tend to rely less upon it as the skill increases (Whiting, Gill, & Stephenson, 1970). When information comes late in the trajectory, subjects seem to adopt strategies to increase its availability. For example, if light is available within the last 0.1 second of the ball's flight (less than the critical feedback processing period discussed above), Whiting found that his subjects moved their hands backward to extend the effective trajectory of the ball so as to be able to utilize the information.

One way to measure the attention demands of a primary task is to insert a probe stimulus at varying points in the task (Posner & Boies, 1971; Posner & Keele, 1969). Delays in the reaction time to the probe stimulus when it is performed together with the primary task provide a kind of dynamic picture of the attention demands of the primary task. In order for the probe reaction times to be simply interpreted it is necessary to insure that the primary task is being performed at full efficiency. Comparison of primary task performance with and without probes provides such a control.

A probe reaction time method can be used to separate the various components to which the subject might be attending when he moves. In order to study something about these sources of control a probe tone is presented under varying movement conditions (Posner & Keele, 1969). In one condition the subject was blindfolded and moved to a stop. In the second condition the subject was still blindfolded and had to move to a target which he had in memory. That is, he had to rely on a motor program obtained from his previous learning. The subjects were highly skilled and presumably knew quite well this particular movement which they had made many hundreds of times. These two conditions were compared with a sighted condition in which the subject was moving to either wide or narrow visual targets. We examined the attention demands required of these varying types of movements by measuring reaction time to the tone. When the subject was moving to a stop, he was the most rapid in response to the extraneous probe signal. When he was guided by internal memory, he was the slowest. The visual conditions were intermediate, with probe reaction times being greater with the smaller target. The movement to the stop gave no increase in reaction time over a no-movement control. Apparently when the subject has to make no corrections, although actual kinesthetic feedback is present, it is not attended to since the probe is not interfered with. However, a movement which requires control from memory or visual feedback interfered greatly with the probe reaction time.

There is evidence that feedback processing may interfere with performance when it is delayed or distorted, even when the task could be carried on perfectly well with no feedback at all. For example, speech which occurs with nearly normal fluency in the absence of feedback is greatly disturbed if the feedback is delayed or distorted (Smith & Smith, 1962; Yates, 1965). Indeed, delayed feedback has been suggested as a cause of some cases of impaired movement control such as in Parkinson's disease and stuttering (Angel, Alston, & Higgins, 1970; Dinnerstein, Frigyesi, & Lowenthal, 1962).

The relationship between a movement and its feedback is of great interest in current studies of motor skill. There is a very obvious difference between the first movement you make to a target and the movements which occur after considerable practice. The first movement is carefully constructed and you tend to be quite conscious of guiding your hand to the target. With practice the motor program is developed and the movement begins to drop from consciousness. This suggests that a motor program can guide a movement without requiring any attention. This view has had considerable support in experimental psychology. For example, it has been used to account for the outside world's appearing stable when you move your eyes from place to place (Hein & Held, 1962). If you move your eyes the outside world is swept across the retina. There is, however, no perception of movement—the world appears stable. If the eye is moved passively, as when poking it with the finger, the world does appear to jump suddenly. This has been used (Hein & Held, 1962) to suggest that a movement of the visual field does not come to the subject's attention unless the input disagrees with the motor plan.

The same basic principle appears to apply to the processing of feedback information from our reference experiment. When the movement requires no correction, as when moving to a stop, there are no greater reaction times to the probe than with a no-movement condition. This suggests that the movement is "automated" in the sense that it does not interfere with the subject's response to other signals. It might be suggested that movements also can be automated if the movement is proceeding in accordance with the internal motor program so that it gives rise to feedback which is highly predictable. Such predictable feedback might be ignored without coming to attention. However, if the movement produces feedback which is not in accord with the internal plan, either because the movement is incorrect or because the feedback itself is delayed or distorted, the subject's attention will be brought to bear upon the task. This idea is in accord with much of our everyday experience. Tasks like walking seem to take very little attention and normally we can perform other activities simultaneously; however, occasionally the movements of walking tend to intrude. These might be those occasions when the feedback from the movement is not in agreement with the program which controls it. Our probe experiments have not as yet shown movements made from memory to be free of attention. Further experimental work is needed to investigate this idea.

The importance of motor programs in the control of even very simple movements makes the problem of storing movements of great interest.

Storage

Now your hand has reached the target. In order to benefit from the experience of having made the movement you must retain some information about the movement. One way to test for retention is to have you reproduce the movement. The instruction in our reference task to return the stylus to the starting position in the dark is one way of testing your retention of the length and direction of the movement. If these two cues are perfectly retained you should be able to return to the starting position without error.

The study of memory for movements has been going on since the turn of the century. The importance of such experiments is that they tell us something about the development of a representation of a movement in memory. Such central representations are what we have been calling motor programs (Keele, 1968) and they must form the basis for performance of skills in the absence of feedback. Indeed, as we have seen, they also appear to regulate our processing of feedback. For this reason the study of memory for motor activity has become a very active field of investigation in the last several years.

The experimental results have shown several important factors about the system which stores the trace of previous movements. Many of these factors are common to all memory systems, others may be unique to the retention of motor movements. Of first importance is the remarkable range of information about a movement which might be stored. For example, in our reference experiment, you might store a visual representation of the experimental apparatus with the location of the start and end position. If such a visual code is stored, you may be able to reproduce the movement even in the dark, provided the internal representation is aligned with the outside world. Or you might have stored the rate of movement and the time required for the movement. Given these two factors, plus a movement direction, the movement can be reproduced. Or you might have a record of the amount of muscular effort required to reproduce the movement. Or some record of the pattern of innervation or instruction given to move the muscle may be retained. These are only some of the possibilities. There are also a number of physiological systems involved in movements which are related to these cues. For example, in kinesthesis, muscle spindles, Golgi tendon organs, skin receptors and joint receptors are all sources of cues about movement length and position. It is also known that outflow information (instructions to the muscles) can be used as the basis of judgment (Freedman, 1968; Howard & Templeton, 1966).

There is reason to suspect that all these mechanisms are used under various circumstances. For this reason the study of memory for motor movements has given a bewildering variety of results. It is likely that these results are due to the use of different cues in making and storing the movement. A few studies have tried to use conditions which allow for separation of these cues, and the results obtained by such studies are interesting although far from definitive.

For example, Festinger & Canon (1965) attempted to study the use of outflow information versus kinesthetic return as bases for retention. They compared head movements, where there is abundant kinesthetic information, with eye movements, where anatomical and physiological evidence suggest little kinesthetic return. They found that the two systems were equally accurate in storing movement information if the subject knew in advance where he was going, but when he had to track a moving object, and thus could not construct a motor program prior to his movement, retention of eye movements was inferior. This led the authors to conclude that outflow information could serve as a basis of retention.

Another example of separating cues for movement involves comparing blind with visually guided movements. In one such study (Posner, 1967), it was found that blind movements showed a spontaneous loss in retention with time between execution and reproduction but showed little effect of interference due to distracting the subject's attention. On the other hand, visually guided movements appeared to show no loss with time if the subject was left free to rehearse, but were greatly affected by demanding his attention. Moreover, it appeared that regardless of whether the movements were blind or sighted, remembering locations in space provided results resembling visual guidance, while remembering distance gave results more like blind movements. These results led the author to propose two distinct memory systems. Memories for locations in space involved a kind of visual code which could be rehearsed but was subject to interference from a task which blocked rehearsal. Memories for pure distance were not rehearsable and thus decayed spontaneously.

It is known that muscle spindles project directly to the cerebellum and not to the sensory cortex, while joint receptors project to the cortex (Howard & Templeton, 1966). If one identifies cortical information as available to the central processing system for rehearsal, then it might be supposed that judgments based on muscle spindles would show spontaneous decay. Such a view would account for Posner's finding that visual tasks are rehearsable (since information here would clearly be cortical) while kinesthetic distance tasks are not, since distance judgments might be considered to be based on spindle data.

It is difficult to take this speculation too seriously because of the difficulty of disentangling cues and the consequent conflicting results. For example, the difference between distance and location may be more apparent than real. It is always possible for subjects to code a distance as the difference between two locations. Moreover, the results obtained by Posner for kinesthetic distance appear to be true mainly for relatively long distances of movement (Posner & Keele, 1969). Recent work on reproducing the magnitude of a force exerted against a stationary knob (Pepper & Herman, 1970) has raised some cogent criticisms against models of the type discussed above. Still, it appears that there are important differences in the storage and retention characteristics of various cues made available by movements. If these can be tied in with underlying physiological systems, the understanding of motor retention will be greatly advanced. In many ways the multiple cue approach to the retention of motor movements is similar to recent models of memory for other kinds of material (Bower, 1967). All such models suggest that memory consists of a complex constellation of separable cues, each with its own storage and decay characteristics.

Another similarity between motor memory and memory in general is the tendency for a movement to resist forgetting when it is well practiced. If you were to move back and forth from the home button to the target, the ability to reproduce the movement accurately would increase (Adams & Dijkstra, 1966). Moreover, delay and distraction between any execution of the movement and its reproduction would have less and less effect. Indeed, it would begin to be possible to execute the movement in the presence of considerable distraction.

The ability to produce the movement without attention is what we call *automation* of the movement. However, efforts to develop automated movements by practice have not been entirely successful. You may recall that probe reaction times during movements to a mechanical stop were not longer than reaction times to probe when no movement was being made. It has also been shown that well-practiced movements, which are performed from memory (Noble & Trumbo, 1967; Posner & Keele, 1969) can be executed at the same time subjects do some other information processing without any interference with the movement. However, it has not yet been demonstrated that movements to a location held in memory can occur without delaying the response to a probe task. In addition, when subjects are instructed to give their primary attention to another task, even a very well-learned, repetitive movement shows a decrease in regularity (Posner, 1969). This may mean only that such movements require attention intermittently, such as when they get out of phase with the controlling program. However, convincing evidence in favor of this theory requires more experimental analysis than has so far been reported.

There are many other qualities which memory for motor movements shares with memory in general. Perhaps of greatest interest is the ability of a skilled movement to be performed under a variety of different conditions. For example, a quarterback can adjust the forward pass to changes in distance, velocity and movement pattern of his receiver, to differences in wind velocity and characteristics of the defense. This suggests that skill learning is not usually a matter of mere reproduction of a movement. The learning involves a general program, the parameters of which can be altered as conditions change (Young, 1969). This same flexible quality is found in studies of pattern recognition (Uhr, 1966) in which men are able to recognize a familiar pattern with amazing success despite changes in viewing conditions. The central question of pattern recognition is how a trace system that allows flexibility in the recognition of new forms is organized. In the context of motor skills, this means we cannot confine our study to the execution and reproduction of a single movement, but must go to the development of complex motor programs.

CONTROLLING SEQUENCES OF MOVEMENT

The preceding description has dealt for the most part with a single, isolated movement. Although much human activity does involve such isolated motions (e.g., reaching for an object), a good many motions are made in the context of a continuing sequence of motion. It is frequently useful to view the sequence as the stringing together of individual movements. Thus Craik (1947) has analyzed continuous tracking of a rapidly changing and unpredictable course in such terms. After each move the target being tracked has changed in position so a new decision and ensuing correction must be made. The overall level of performance in such a case is constrained by the limits of processing individual movements. Indeed, Crossman (1960) and Elkind and Sprague (1961) have shown that the rate of information transmission in continuous tracking typically does not reach the theoretical limit which would be imposed by the decision time and movement accuracy of individual moves. When each movement is relatively independent, the skill is said to be under *closed-loop* control because the feedback resulting from each movement becomes the input for the elicitation of the next movement.

Early in practice many skills probably are controlled in a closed-loop fashion. Frequently, visual observation of each movement may be necessary to control performance, as, for example, in the early stages of learning to type. However, with practice, the timing and sequencing of successive outputs may shift from external visual feedback control to an internalized control. Performance is said to be *open-loop* when there is at least temporary independence of the sequence from external feedback.

There are a number of sources of evidence for such a shift in mode of control with increased practice. Noble and Trumbo, with a number of coinvestigators (see Noble & Trumbo, 1967, for a review), have studied step-tracking tasks. Typically, a vertical line on an oscilloscope jumped to one of 15 different positions at the rate of one jump per second, and subjects tracked the target with an arm-controlled target follower. The

sequencing of steps could be either random or of varying degrees of predictability up to the situation in which the same sequence of steps repeated periodically. With a perfectly predictable sequence, subjects came to anticipate the next step by typically moving the follower in much less than the minimum reaction time (i.e., less than 150 milliseconds). Often the onset of movement slightly preceded the step of the target. Clearly the timing and sequencing of movements under such predictable circumstances had shifted from direct visual control and was under internal control. Of course, vision was still useful for calibrating the timing.

Somewhat the same point was made in an earlier study by Poulton (1957). He showed that when subjects were tracking a sinusoidal input, they often tracked as well with their eyes closed for periods of five seconds as with them open. The only real error with eyes closed was a gradual shift in the phase relationships of target and follower.

Perhaps the most interesting study indicating a shift in control was performed by Pew (1966). His work has indicated an alternative mode of control to both closed-loop and strictly open-loop modes. Subjects attempted to keep a spot centered on an oscilloscope by alternately tapping two keys, one of which caused acceleration to the left and the other to the right. Early in practice, subjects exhibited a quite irregular pattern of responding with relatively long times between successive responses, resulting in considerable movement away from the center target. With a few weeks' practice some subjects developed an open-loop mode of response. Very regular and rapid alternations in key pressing were obtained. After a gradual drift off the center target, a single large correction was made. It was as though visual feedback was used only intermittently for control. Other subjects also had a rapid, regular rate of responding. But as the spot moved gradually off target, instead of a single correction, the pattern of responding was *modulated* so that one key would be depressed slightly longer than the other, resulting in a slow drift to the other side of the target. Thus, those subjects, using what Pew called *modulation mode,* exhibited slow oscillations about the center upon which were superimposed the small, rapid fluctuations in position. Visual feedback was being used neither for control of individual movements nor for intermittent, single step corrections, but for modulating the patterning of movements.

CENTRAL MOTOR PROGRAMS

After much practice on predictable sequences of movement, visual feedback is not used for control of individual moves but for monitoring of progress toward a goal, resulting in modulations and occasional large-scale corrections in the pattern of responding (Miller, Galanter, & Pribram, 1960). The control of the actual sequencing and timing is primarily internal.

There are two general possibilities for the mechanism of internal control. One is a commonly accepted view that kinesthetic feedback from one movement of a sequence triggers the next, an S-R chaining notion. The other is that the patterning is centrally represented in memory, and sequencing and timing of neural impulses to the muscles is initiated independently of kinesthetic feedback. Much recent evidence has pointed toward the latter hypothesis of *central motor program control.*

The most impressive evidence supporting the motor program notion comes from de-afferentation studies of Rhesus monkeys. Taub and Berman (1968) severed the dorsal roots of the sensory fibers entering the spinal cord. Such an operation presumably eliminates the kinesthetic feedback emanating from the limbs but leaves the neural flow from brain to muscle intact. As in a classic study by Mott and Sherrington (1895), it was found that when one forelimb was de-afferented, the animal did not use it in walking and instead walked on three legs. Taub and Berman went further, however, and showed that when the good forelimb

was immobilized with a straight jacket, the monkey reverted to use of the de-afferented forelimb. The limb could be used without kinesthetic feedback!

In further studies it was shown that the animals could walk and even climb relatively normally with both forelimbs de-afferented. Good forelimb control remained even with the entire body de-afferented, presumably removing all kinesthetic feedback. Further, de-afferented animals were able to perform these skilled tasks when blindfolded.

The Taub and Berman studies strongly support the contention that the patterning of well-practiced sequences of motion can be centrally controlled. The representation in memory of the movement pattern is called the *motor program.* In discussing single movements, the term motor program was used to refer to the representation in memory of a single movement. At least for a minimum time such a movement must be free of feedback control because it takes some time for feedback to be processed. Now it is suggested that entire movement sequences can be stored and executed free of feedback.

Bossom and Ommaya (1968) have cautioned that severing the dorsal roots may be incomplete and leave some kinesthetic feedback. Although Taub and Berman reported that stimulation of exposed peripheral nerves resulted in no evoked cortical responses, Bossom and Ommaya suggest other techniques should be used as well. Using such cautionary techniques, they also found that de-afferented forelimbs of monkeys could be controlled even in the absence of visual feedback.

There are other sources of evidence for motor program control. Wilson (1961) has shown that a coordinated wing-beat in locusts can be maintained in the absence of kinesthetic feedback. Nottebohm (1970) has severed the nerves that supply part of the muscular apparatus used by birds in the control of songs. Consequently portions of the song dropped out, since some muscles were inoperative. The remainder of the song proceeded unimpaired, showing that feedback from the missing portions is not needed to trigger succeeding portions. It is also important to note that the birds in question had learned the songs to some extent. Motor programs, therefore, appear to be learnable.

For humans, Lazlo (1966) has shown that finger tapping can be performed when kinesthetic feedback is blocked by cutting off blood circulation. All sensations of touch and passive movement had dropped out, but tapping, although impaired, could still occur. With practice over additional sessions, tapping gradually improved (Lazlo, 1967). This latter observation is important in demonstrating again that motor programs are learnable. In a related study, Provins (1958) found that tapping was practically unimpaired when the index finger was anesthetized, but it is important to note that forearm muscles used in finger movements were not deadened.

One caution should be made with respect to the Lazlo and Provins studies. Even though any conscious awareness of kinesthetic feedback may be eliminated, it is still possible that some kinesthesis remains. Konorski (1970) has pointed out that there are two distinct kinesthetic systems, one having only indirect connection with the cortex via the cerebellum. It is possible that only one system is conscious and can be impaired without affecting the other.

As final evidence for motor program control, many years ago Lashley (1951) noted that in some cases successive movements (e.g., in piano playing) occur so fast that there is not time for the kinesthetic feedback from one movement to affect the next.

Functions of Feedback

After considerable practice on a complex sequence of motions, the control shifts from closed-loop dependence on vision to an internalized form of control. Although there are some weaknesses in the evidence, the preponderance of it suggests that the internalized control is by a motor program. Kinesthetic feedback from one portion of a movement is not needed for initiating the next.

A number of studies, however, have shown that kinesthesis is important in skilled performance. Fleishman and Rich (1963) found that as practice proceeded on a tracking task, subjects with a high degree of kinesthetic sensitivity came to outperform subjects lower on kinesthetic sensitivity. Briggs, Fitts, and Bahrick (1957) found that characteristics of the control stick (e.g., degree of spring loading and amplitude of movement) influenced tracking performance. Notterman and Page (1962) showed that it is the kinesthetic feedback from the control that is important and not just the control dynamics resulting from different control inertias that are important. Finally, some investigators (see Schmidt, 1968, for a general review) have found kinesthetic cues to be useful in timing of movements.

On the one hand it has been strongly suggested that kinesthesis is not needed for controlling sequences of movements. On the other hand evidence suggests that kinesthesis does aid performance. There are several possibilities for reconciling these seemingly contradictory sources of evidence. One possibility is that as control passes from direct visual control, it passes to kinesthetic control. Via a conditioning process the feedback from one portion of a movement sequence comes to initiate the next (Greenwald, 1970). This would be essentially a closed-loop system dependent on kinesthesis. Only at a quite late stage of development is control assumed by a motor program. Another possibility is that as control is shifted from a closed-loop visual mode, a motor program is established and kinesthesis plays other roles. What might those roles be?

For well-practiced sequences of movement, kinesthesis may serve as a *monitoring* device for periodic corrections or modulation much as Pew (1966) found for the visual system. Take walking as an example. The patterning of leg movements may well be controlled by a motor program. But suppose the foot hits an unexpected impediment. Obviously the motor program would need to be adjusted. In order to know that an adjustment is needed, feedback which tells the actual position of the foot must continually be compared with where the motor program says the foot should be. This idea was discussed previously with respect to a single movement (page 813). Hinde (1969) has reviewed models of the comparison process.

A related function has been suggested by Gibbs (1970). Most skills occur in a moderately changing environment. Thus, in walking, the terrain is often uneven with slight rises and depressions. According to Gibbs, the regular patterning of movements can be controlled by a motor program, and a peripheral feedback mechanism makes minor adjustments in the movements to fit slight changes in the terrain.

The changing view as to what role kinesthesis plays in skilled movements has great implications for skill training. The S-R chaining notion that feedback from one part of a complex sequence is conditioned to and elicits the succeeding part would suggest that the only way to learn a task is to perform it. Unless feedback is generated, conditioning cannot occur. But the notion that movement control is based on motor programs opens the possibility that at least in some stages of training, actual movements may not be needed at all. Rather, techniques of mental practice, loop films, observing models, and guidance might be useful in developing motor programs.

IMPROVING SKILLS BY TRAINING

Most psychologists studying skilled performance have been rather global in looking for training principles and did not really analyze the particular skills in detail. It has generally been accepted that distributing practice with intervening rests yields performance superior to massing of practice, although there are cases in which distribution has little advantage (McGeoch & Irion, 1952). Similarly, there has been much controversy on whether practice of parts of a task is superior to practice on the whole or whether a progressive part practice in which new parts are successively added is best (e.g., Naylor & Briggs, 1963). Much concern also has been with when and how knowledge of results should be presented (Bilodeau, 1966; Holding, 1965).

Although not contradictory to the traditional approach for improving skill, the approach adopted here is to analyze the skill of interest, determine what processing components are difficult about the task, and take specific steps to improve on the difficult portions. With respect to part versus whole practice, the question is, "What part?" Such an approach is very similar in principle to the long-established practice in industry of time and motion analysis (e.g., Niebel, 1962). Rather than having people practice and improve in a trial and error manner, time and motion analysts discovered the more efficient ways to perform a task (perhaps by observing the best performers) and then showed trainees how to do it.

Basically there appear to be two ways to improve skilled performance. One way is to improve on the components of a skill—namely, reduce reaction time and movement time or increase the precision of movements as reproduced from memory. A close analysis of a task may often reveal why those times are long or memory is poor, and steps can be taken to improve them (Crossman, 1959). The second basic way to improve on a skill is to develop a motor program. Skills which do not involve predictable sequences of movement cannot be programmed; for those skills that do, a program can be constructed and run off as a unit. Such a program bypasses the time-consuming decision component of closed-loop performance and may also reduce the attention required, leaving the person at least partly free to perform other tasks simultaneously. These two general approaches will be examined separately.

IMPROVING THE COMPONENTS OF SKILL

Performance on a skill which is not pre-programmed depends on the speed of decisions and the efficiency of the movements. In the second section of this chapter various factors that affect these processes were discussed, such as preparation, number of alternatives, compatibility, predictability due to sequential constraints or high probabilities, and the length and precision of movement. How can such components be improved? There follow some general speculations. For any particular skill much research would need to be done to determine whether these speculations would be useful.

Preparation

In some skills it is important not only to prepare for signals but to anticipate them and respond at about the same time as the signal. *Sports Illustrated* (Kane, 1969) measured simple reaction time and movement time of the famous boxer, Muhammed Ali. His reaction time, measured from the time a light came on until the fist began to move, was 190 milliseconds, which is only average. The time to move 16 inches and strike a punching bag was only 40 milliseconds, though. Quite clearly, movement time is so much faster than reaction time that the skilled boxer does not have time to react once an opponent's punch has begun. A large part of the skill of boxing, then, must consist in picking up cues that allow one to prepare for and anticipate events.

Realizing the importance of preparation, improvement can be gained either by introducing preparatory cues in situations that lack them, giving preview of coming events (Poulton, 1964), or by picking out and giving special emphasis to cues which naturally occur in advance of important events.

Good drivers are ones who not only know the mechanics of driving well but who are constantly looking ahead for cues (e.g., intersections, other cars that might change lanes, etc.) that might be followed by significant events requiring rapid decisions and responses. Any training program might well profit from thoroughly cataloging important cues and ensuring that trainees learn to use them. For instance, trainees on a driving simulator might press a key every time an important cue was presented. This would give a clear indication when a cue was or was not processed, and appropriate corrective action could then be taken.

Compatibility

Even with a high degree of alertness, the decision of what action is needed can take a relatively long time when the relationship between the stimuli and responses is unnatural. The decision time is compounded for incompatible relationships when there are also many alternative signals. In addition to increases in decision time, errors are likely to occur under stress (Fitts & Jones, 1961). Although much larger improvements occur with practice on incompatible relationships than with compatible ones (Keele, 1967), performance does not come to equal that with compatible arrangements even after very extensive practice (Fitts & Seeger, 1953).

The most reasonable solution to reducing decision time in the face of incompatibility is to redesign the task. More will be said about this later. In other cases, however, no simple redesign is apparent. In typing there is no natural correspondence between a letter and the key that should be pressed, although some advantage could be taken of the serial ordering of letters in mapping them into keys (Conrad & Longman, 1965). An alternative then would be to devise training programs which place special emphasis on reducing decision times due to incompatibilities.

One technique for emphasizing decision times to the exclusion of other components is mental practice. Considerable research has shown that mental practice is sometimes useful in task improvement, but little research has been analytic in determining what kind of situations are susceptible to mental practice. Perhaps such practice may be useful when there are incompatible S-R relationships.

Another approach for reducing decision times in incompatible situations is to devise simulators that have primary emphasis on the decision component. Consider the operation of a typical power shovel. There are three basic motions: a) hoist—the bucket is raised by releasing a foot brake and pressing forward one lever, and lowered by merely releasing a foot brake; b) crowd— the bucket is run forward by releasing a brake and pushing a lever forward and hauled back by releasing the brake and pulling the lever back; c) swing—the shovel is rotated left by pressing a lever forward and rotated right by pulling the lever back. Operation of a power shovel is quite difficult, indeed, since the movement of levers does not always mimic movement of the machine. An extensive period of mental practice would almost be mandatory before actual machine operation to prevent costly mistakes. A simulator could be constructed, however, using pursuit tracking on an oscilloscope display. The subject would follow movements of a target by controlling levers and brakes just as occur in the shovel. One lever could control right-left movement (swing) of the target follower, another lever and brake arrangement could cause an increase or decrease in size (to simulate the forward and back movement of crowd), and a final lever and brake could control up-down movement (hoist). The advantage of such a simulator would be that it could give extensive practice on relating lever and brake movements to rapidly changing targets (much more rapidly than on the actual machine). It would also allow the elimination of many other essential features of machine operation which take time but demand little skill. The main concentration would be on reducing the decision time intervening between the signal to where to move and the onset of the appropriate response. Undoubtedly, initial transfer to the real task would result in relatively poor performance because so many background cues are different in the two situations (Hammerton & Tickner, 1967), but perhaps rapid adaptation would occur.

Another example in which critical decision times could possibly be reduced is the use of driving simulators to present emergency situations very much more frequently than would occur in normal driving.

Sequential Dependencies

In most skilled tasks successive events typically occur in a partially predictable fashion. Many studies have shown that once these sequential dependencies are learned, decision time is very much reduced (e.g., Cattell, 1886; Hyman, 1953). Shaffer and Hardwick (1968) found typing speed to be much faster for words than for random, equally probable letters. Typing of nonwords constructed from syllables of actual words was also very fast, indicating that sequential predictability and not just meaning is important in decision speed.

Just because sequential dependencies are present in a task does not mean that a learner will pick them up easily. Keele (1967) found for a serial reaction-time task that subjects not instructed that sequential dependencies were present did no better than subjects performing on a random sequence. Moreover, just knowing that sequential dependencies are present may not lead to improvements until one learns to utilize them from actual experience.

Certainly more research on training to utilize sequential dependencies is needed. The point is that techniques which emphasize the dependencies (e.g., use of much higher probabilities in the training sequence than occur in the real task) might vastly facilitate improvement. In learning to type, for example, it might be beneficial to select vocabularies that emphasize the statistical structure of the English language. This would be much the same principle as is often used in teaching children to read, where initial vocabularies use only the regular features of the language (Bloomfield, 1933).

Movements

It was said (Gilbreth & Carey, 1948) that Frank Gilbreth, one of the founders of time and motion study, could lay bricks considerably faster than other bricklayers. How did he "learn" to do so? One aspect of his improvement was simply to construct a scaffold that maintained the bricks and mortar at working level, thereby reducing movement time. Much so-called learning in motor skills is like this. Over time, more efficient movements are selected. The insight of Gilbreth was that rather than having a trial and error improvement, the skill in question could be critically analyzed to determine just what movements were involved and then steps could be taken to optimize the skill.

As shown by Fitts (1954) and Fitts and Peterson (1964), movement time depends both on the distance of movement and the required precision. Reductions in movement time can consequently be gained by adjusting either factor.

In addition to requiring time, movements may also take attention (see page 807). Bruner (1968) has shown that an important aspect of learning to control movements in infants is to reduce attention demands. At very early ages infants may inhibit sucking when focusing their attention on other objects. Reaching for an object may also be impaired by viewing the arm.

Reducing the precision and distance of a movement, then, has a dual advantage: not only will it take less time but it may require less attention. In particular, other movements may occur simultaneously. Time

and motion analysts (e.g., Niebel, 1962) have repeatedly stressed that movements should be arranged so that both hands work simultaneously, and, where practical, the feet should be used as well as the hands. To do this the task often has to be arranged so that the hands and feet actually rest on the controls being operated. No precision should be required to find them.

THE ACQUISITION OF MOTOR PROGRAMS

When successive motions of a skill occur in fixed sequence, it is possible for the movement to be under programmed control. Considerable insight into the acquisition of motor programs has come from recent studies of bird song development (see Hinde, 1969; Marler & Hamilton, 1966; and Nottebohm, 1970, for reviews). Some birds, such as European chaffinches, white-crowned sparrows and Oregon juncos, exhibit flexibility in song development. Although they cannot learn the songs of other species, there are different dialects that develop out of a rudimentary song common to the species. Marler has shown that if young birds are raised in isolation never hearing an adult song, then an appropriate song does not develop as the young bird learns to sing. On the other hand, if isolated juvenile birds are exposed for only a few weeks in the summer to the adult song and then do not hear it again, the appropriate song is developed the following spring. The acquisition of a motor program appears to require storage in memory of a standard or model of the final skill.

In subsequent studies Konishi (1965) deafened young birds at different stages of development. If the young birds exposed to an adult song in the field were deafened, the appropriate song failed to materialize even though a model was presumably stored. When deafening was delayed until after the song had been established, however, the appropriate song persisted. Auditory feedback was no longer needed. And, as pointed out earlier, Nottebohm (1970) has shown that when portions of a well-developed song are eliminated by de-innervation of some muscles involved in song production, other portions of the song persist even though both auditory feedback and kinesthetic feedback are disrupted.

The view of skill learning that emerges from the above studies is as follows. First, a template corresponding to the skill must be established. Although in the bird song studies the template was auditory, it is also possible that a template could be visual or kinesthetic, the latter perhaps being established by passive guidance or mental practice. Once the template is established, the organism must begin to execute movements. It might be useful in this stage to develop at least approximate movements by instruction or demonstration. The feedback from those movements can then be compared to the standard template stored in memory. If discrepancies occur, the pattern of innervation to the muscles can be altered and feedback again compared to the template and so on until the correct pattern is established. It might be noted that, according to this theory, feedback is not conditioned to subsequent movements, eliciting them in an S-R chaining fashion. Rather, feedback is used for making alterations in the program. Once the program is established, feedback can be eliminated and the skill still performed. However, feedback still retains other functions mentioned earlier.

The Suzuki Method of Music Learning

As far as we know, there have been no explicit studies applying the theory of skill acquisition which has come from the studies of bird songs. This would be expected, since the theory of bird song development is itself very new. But in Japan more than 20 years ago Suzuki devised a teaching method for violin playing that bears a striking resemblance to bird song acquisition (Pronko, 1969).

The Suzuki technique calls for the playing of a single selection of great, high fidelity music to babies only a few months old. The same piece of music is played repeatedly for perhaps several months until the baby recognizes it as evidenced by the music's soothing effect. At that point another piece is selected. Further selections are gradually added to the growing child's repertoire until the age of three or four years, when he is sent to music school. The young child most certainly is not taught how to read music at that age. Rather, he learns by ear. The sounds that he produces on the instrument are presumably matched to auditory templates stored in memory since the time of infancy, and corrections in the pattern of movements are made. As the skill is acquired, students develop excellent playing abilities on other music. It is only at the age of five or six years that the child begins to read music.

According to reports, the Suzuki method produces extremely capable and occasionally internationally known musicians. Of course it is impossible to separate a motivational from a memory template explanation of success of the method.

Recent research (Kagan, 1970) has indicated that perceptual models developed in infancy may be very important to learning in general. Discrepancies that occur from models stored at the early ages are instrumental in directing attention.

General Implications for Skill Learning

If the memory template explanation of the Suzuki method is correct, it suggests that the general strategy of model development and matching to sample could be advantageous in learning some other skills. Rather than strictly following the old guideline, "practice makes perfect," it might be more important to instill in memory a perfect standard. Large periods of time during skill acquisition might be spent in observing skilled performers, perhaps on loop film (Gray & Brumbach, 1967; Rizk, 1969).

For some skills, observation of visual performance or listening to auditory products may not be appropriate. In swinging a golf club people watch the ball, not the swing, and the auditory accompaniments of the swing are probably minimal. Perhaps more important would be a kinesthetic model on how the swing should "feel." To this end, training on some skills might profitably use guidance devices that either passively move the limbs of the performer in the appropriate pattern over and over or mechanically restrict the allowed movements of the learner (Hoitsma, 1969; Holding, 1965). The use of such devices would not be to build a motor program but to build a template to which feedback resulting from execution of a motor program can be compared.

There are several problems that can be foreseen for attempts to establish internalized models of the skill to which feedback can then be compared. People may not have the patience to observe models for extended periods of time. Even when models are observed, critical movements may not be seen. The mode of observation may be very different from the mode of feedback available; people can see others perform but cannot see their own body in the same way.

An alternative to establishing an internal model in memory is to provide external models of performance. Films or tapes of correct performance can be alternated with the trainee's performance so that he can compare his results with a standard. Such an approach is quite common in language training. A difficulty here is that the learner must remember for a brief time just what he did and, depending on the nature of his feedback and the model, transform the feedback into a representation appropriate for comparison. For visual models, one promising technique to overcome the transformation and memory problems might be to use a video-tape recorder, showing a model and then replaying the model and the trainee's performance side by side on a split screen. We are aware of no research using simultaneous showing of model and trainee.

Even with side by side or nearly simultaneous display of model and performance, the learner may be unable to perceive critical differences. A classic example of the problem occurs in second language learning. Learners are notoriously unable to correct the motor programs needed for speaking certain sounds, because they are unable to perceive certain crucial distinctions (see Liberman, Cooper, Shankweiler, & Studdert-Kennedy, 1967, for evidence on categorical perception of speech sounds).

A very ingenious experimental program for training pronunciation has been developed by Kalikow and Klatt (1970). Spanish-speaking people learning English have difficulty in correct pronunciation of English vowels. Analyzing the sound spectrum of monosyllabic words, Kalikow and Klatt are able to use a computer to infer the height and front-back position of the tongue during vowel pronunciation. The deduced position can then be *visually* displayed on an oscilloscope along with a target area. The visual discrepancy between target and actual tongue position forms the basis for corrective action. This study is underway at present and its success as compared with the standard auditory feedback method is not yet known.

ALTERNATIVE PROCEDURES FOR IMPROVING PERFORMANCE

The thesis of this chapter has been that a thorough analysis and understanding of a skill can, at least in some cases, lead to a rational training program. A general framework has been attempted to aid in analyzing whatever task is of interest. When the framework is applied, the features that impede performance or that require a high degree of mastery before that task can be efficiently performed can be identified. The training program can then be specifically designed to overcome those bottlenecks.

Once the difficult components are identified, it becomes very apparent that there are alternate methods to training for many tasks. The task or machine can itself be redesigned (human engineered) to fit the information-processing limitations of man. When the task is properly engineered to reduce the demands on the operator, the problem of training becomes less acute. Another procedure, once the more difficult components of a task have been isolated, is to select individuals who are particularly facile on the components which are causing the primary problems.

In theory, therefore, the information-processing approach presents a unified way of looking at tasks and improving performance through training, human engineering or personnel selection.

HUMAN ENGINEERING

A vast literature on human engineering exists, and many recommendations and much data to be used in making design decisions are summarized in sources such as Morgan, Chapanis, Cook, and Lund (1963). The purpose here is merely to present some illustrations of how identification of information-processing difficulties might lead to design improvements.

It has been pointed out that in typing one major bottleneck is the decision time in translating a letter or word into an appropriate response. In addition, typing speed is limited by the necessity for making movements to target keys and the fact that only one letter can be typed at a time. Conrad and Longman (1965) studied a radically different keyboard design. Ten fingers rested on 10 keys. To type a letter, two keys had to be pressed simultaneously, one with the left hand and one with the right. There are 25 combinations of one finger from each of the two hands, allowing only 25 symbols to be typed. But for their purposes, 25 symbols were sufficient since they were designing a keyboard for postal coding. More symbols could be obtained by using com-binations of any two keys, regardless of hand, or by using a special key to shift the keyboard function from letters to numerals, for example.

The design studied by Conrad and Longman (1965) eliminated the need for moving the fingers off the keys, theoretically reducing movement time. In addition, the time to learn the associations between letters and keys was vastly reduced by assigning letters in a regular manner. Once the keyboard had been learned, actual typing speed was little different from a control group trained on a standard keyboard; the main time saving was in the initial training stage, which is important in itself. Nonetheless, this example is a good illustration of how, once processing limitations are identified, human engineering is an alternative to training.

Other ways of arranging keyboards could be considerably more effective. Levy (described in Conrad & Longman, 1965) devised a keyboard in which the five fingers of the left hand typed one letter and the right hand, another letter. There are 31 possible combinations of finger presses with five fingers on one hand, ranging from a single finger to all fingers at once. Thus, two letters can be typed simultaneously, the left hand always yielding the left of two letters and the right hand the right letter. Although formal experiments using the arrangement are lacking, there is some slight evidence that extremely fast rates of typing can be achieved with this design.

When an incompatible or variable relationship exists between stimuli and responses, the more attractive proposal is to reduce the source of incompatibility rather than design training programs to overcome the problem. Fitts and Jones (1961) studied critical errors made by pilots and found that many errors were due to unnatural control-display arrangements and lack of standardization across aircraft. Based on their recommendations, many changes were made in cockpit design to reduce decision time and errors. Similar recommendations could be made for automobile displays and controls.

Numerous other examples could be given, but the point should be clear: a full analysis of a task's information-processing demands may suggest ways to improve the task as well as suggest training programs.

Personnel Selection

In driving, many simultaneous demands are made on the operator in addition to the routine mechanical operations. There is a multiplicity of sounds and sights that may indicate danger, and there are often passengers to converse with. It has been seen that some components of skills require attention, resulting in lowered efficiency in dealing with other simultaneous signals. Perhaps a useful training device on a driving simulator would be to give extensive driving periods under conditions of information overload. But another possibility would be to select individuals who are particularly good at performing tasks together. Brown (1966) has found, in fact, that drivers who are successful in a bus-driver training school show less decrement, while driving, on a subsidiary memory task than unsuccessful trainees. Such a task can therefore be used as a selection device, although the selection process would probably be considerably improved by devising other information processing tasks as well.

In theory a person's potential ability to perform any task of interest could be predicted by a complete knowledge of his capacities on various information-processing components. In practice, however, there have been no systematic attempts to devise a battery of tests to tap information-processing capacities. Of course there have been many tests devised to select individuals, but such tests have typically been based on how well the tests predict a criterion task, and have not been selected to tap processing capacity. Presumably, if a complete inventory of capacities and a thorough task analysis were available, then an individual's ability to perform practically any task could be predicted.

Lacking a systematic study of individual differences in information processing, the researcher interested in selection needs to devise his own tests and use them for predicting performance on the task he is interested in. Such tests might be used to: deduce the reaction-time constants in the Hick-Hyman Law (Fitts & Posner, 1967); derive the constants in Fitts's Law of movement time (Fitts & Peterson, 1964); determine the accuracy of the motor system in the absence of visual feedback (Vince, 1948); scale the ability to utilize sequential dependencies (Rabbitt & Birren, 1967); find accuracy and decay rate of memory for movements (Posner, 1967); determine accuracy of visual and kinesthetic models stored in memory; and so on.

SUMMARY

In this chapter we have tried to give a broad outline of the way skills are seen from an information-processing viewpoint. The human is seen as interacting with the environment. The environment is continually changing, presenting new information to each person. The preparation and decision making with regard to the information from the environment constitutes information processing. Ultimately, as a result of the processing, a motor program for a single response is emitted. When a sufficient degree of predictability occurs in the environment, longer chains of output can be constructed in the form of a longer motor program, bypassing the time and attention demands of closed-loop performance.

In theory any task can be analyzed with respect to the processing demands made on the organism. Such demands are of two general types: demands of time and demands of attention. Although all the information processing components take a measurable amount of time, they may or may not require attention. As a result of a task analysis that identifies processing difficulties, three options become available for improving performance: 1) a training program designed to overcome the difficulties can be devised; 2) the machines or tools which interact with the environment can be redesigned to reduce processing demands; or 3) individuals with greater capacity on critical components can be selected.

REFERENCES

Adams, J. A., & Dijkstra, S. Short-term memory for motor responses. *Journal of Experimental Psychology*, 1966, 71, 314–318.

Angel, R. W., Alston, W., & Higgins, J. R. Control of movement in Parkinson's Disease. *Brain*, 1970, 93, 1–14.

Annett, S., Golby, C. W., & Kay, H. The measurement of elements in an assembly task—The information output of the human motor system. *Quarterly Journal of Experimental Psychology*, 1958, 10, 1–11.

Bartlett, F. C. *Thinking*. New York: Basic Books, 1958.

Basmajian, J. V. *Muscles alive: Their functions revealed by electromyography*. Baltimore: Williams & Wilkins, 1962.

Bertelson, P. The time course of preparation. *Quarterly Journal of Experimental Psychology*, 1967, 19, 272–279.

Bertelson, P., & Barzeele, J. Interaction of time-uncertainty and relative signal frequency in determining choice reaction time. *Journal of Experimental Psychology*, 1965, 70, 448–451.

Bevan, W., Avant, L. L., & Lankford, H. G. Serial reaction time and the temporal pattern of prior signals. *American Journal of Psychology*, 1966, 79, 551–559.

Bilodeau, I. M. Information feedback. In E. A. Bilodeau (Ed.), *Acquisition of skill*. New York: Academic Press, 1966. Pp. 255–296.

Bloomfield, L. *Language*. New York: Holt, 1933.

Bossom, J., & Ommaya, A. K. Visuo-motor adaptation (to prismatic transformation of the retinal image) in monkeys with bilateral dorsal rhizotomy. *Brain*, 1968, 91, 161–172.

Botwinick, J., & Thompson, L. W. Premotor and motor components of reaction time. *Journal of Experimental Psychology*, 1966, 71, 9–15.

Bower, G. A multicomponent theory of the memory trace. In K. W. Spence, & J. T. Spence (Eds.), *The psychology of learning*

and motivation, Vol. I. New York: Academic Press, 1967. Pp. 229–325.

Briggs, G. E., Fitts, P. M., & Bahrick, H. P. Effects of force and amplitude cues on learning and performance in a complex tracking task. *Journal of Experimental Psychology*, 1957, 54, 262–268.

Broadbent, D. E. *Perception and communication*. London: Pergamon, 1958.

Brown, I. D. Subjective and objective comparisons of successful and unsuccessful trainee drivers. *Ergonomics*, 1966, 9, 49–56.

Bruner, J. S. *Processes of cognitive growth: Infancy*. Worcester, Mass.: Clark University Press, 1968.

Bryan, W. L., & Harter, N. Studies on the telegraphic language: The acquisition of a hierarchy of habits. *Psychological Review*, 1899, 6, 345–375.

Cattell, J. McK. The time it takes to see and name objects. *Mind*, 1886, 11, 63–65.

Conrad, R., & Longman, D. J. A. Standard typewriter versus chord keyboard—An experimental comparison. *Ergonomics*, 1965, 8, 77–88.

Craik, K. J. W. Theory of the human operator in control systems. I. The operator as an engineering system. *British Journal of Psychology*, 1947, 38, 56–61.

Crossman, E. R. F. W. A theory of the acquisition of speed-skill. *Ergonomics*, 1959, 2, 153–166.

Crossman, E. R. F. W. The information capacity of the human motor system in pursuit tracking. *Quarterly Journal of Experimental Psychology*, 1960, 12, 1–16.

Dinnerstein, A. J., Frigyesi, T., & Lowenthal, M. Delayed feedback as a possible mechanism in Parkinsonism. *Perceptual and Motor Skills*, 1962, 15, 667–680.

Donders, F. C. On the speed of mental processes (1868). Translated in W. G. Koster (Ed.), *Attention and performance II*. Amsterdam: North-Holland Publishing Co., 1969.

Eccles, J. C., Ito, M., & Szentágothai, J. *The cerebellum as a neuronal machine*. New York: Springer Verlag, 1967.

Egan, J. P., Greenberg, G. Z., & Schulman, A. I. Interval of time uncertainty in auditory detection, *Journal of the Acoustical Society of America*, 1961, 33, 771–778.

Elkind, J. I., & Sprague, L. T. Transmission of

information in simple manual control systems. *IRE Transactions of the PGHFE*, 1961, 2, 58–60.

Festinger, L., & Canon, L. K. Information about spatial location based on knowledge about efference. *Psychological Review*, 1965, 72, 373–384.

Fitts, P. M. The information capacity of the human motor system in controlling the amplitude of movement. *Journal of Experimental Psychology*, 1954, 47, 381–391.

Fitts, P. M., & Jones, R. E. Analysis of factors contributing to 460 "pilot-error" experiences in operating aircraft controls. In H. W. Sinaiko (Ed.), *Selected papers on human factors in the design and use of control systems*. New York: Dover, 1961. Pp. 359–396.

Fitts, P. M., & Peterson, J. R. Information capacity of discrete motor responses. *Journal of Experimental Psychology*, 1964, 67, 103–112.

Fitts, P. M., & Posner, M. I. *Human performance*. Belmont, Calif.: Wadsworth, 1967.

Fitts, P. M., & Seeger, C. M. S-R compatibility: Spatial characteristics of stimulus and response codes. *Journal of Experimental Psychology*, 1953, 46, 199–210.

Fleishman, E. A., & Rich, S. Role of kinesthetic and spatial-visual abilities in perceptual-motor learning. *Journal of Experimental Psychology*, 1963, 66, 6–11.

Freedman, S. J. (Ed.) *The neuropsychology of spatially oriented behavior*. Homewood, Ill.: Dorsey Press, 1968.

Gibbs, C. B. Servo-control systems in organisms and the transfer of skill. In D. Legge (Ed.), *Skills*. Middlesex, England: Penguin, 1970.

Gilbreth, F. B., Jr., & Carey, E. G. *Cheaper by the dozen*. New York: Bantam Books, 1948.

Granit, R. *The basis of motor control*. New York: Academic Press, 1970.

Gray, C. A., & Brumbach, W. B. Effects of daylight projection of film loops on learning badminton. *Research Quarterly*, 1967, 38, 562–569.

Greenwald, A. G. Sensory feedback mechanisms in performance control: With special reference to the ideo-motor mechanism. *Psychological Review*, 1970, 77, 73–99.

Hammerton, M., & Tickner, A. H. Visual factors affecting transfer of training from a simulated to a real control situation. *Journal of Applied Psychology*, 1967, 51, 46–49.

Hein, A., & Held, R. A neural model for labile sensori-motor coordinations. In E. E. Bernard, & M. R. Kare (Eds.), *Biological prototypes and synthetic systems: Proceedings, Vol. I.* Proceedings of the 2nd Bionics Symposium, Ithaca, 1961. New York: Plenum Press, 1962. Pp. 71–74.

Helmholtz, H. On the methods of measuring very small portions of time and their application to physiological process. *Philosophical Magazine*, 1853, 4, 313–325.

Henry, F. M. Influence of motor and sensory sets of reaction latency and speed of discrete movements. *Research Quarterly*, 1960, 31, 459–468.

Henry, F. M., & Harrison, J. S. Refractoriness of a fast movement. *Perceptual and Motor Skills*, 1961, 13, 351–354.

Hick, W. E. On the rate of gain of information. *Quarterly Journal of Experimental Psychology*, 1952, 1, 175–179.

Higgins, J. R., & Angel, R. W. Correction of tracking errors without sensory feedback. *Journal of Experimental Psychology*, 1970, 84, 412–416.

Hinde, R. A. Control of movement patterns in animals. *Quarterly Journal of Experimental Psychology*, 1969, 21, 105–126.

Hoitsma, H. A. A study of the effectiveness of selected teaching methods on the ball throwing accuracy of primary grade children. (Doctoral dissertation, New York University) *Dissertation Abstracts*, 1969, 30, 2361A.

Holding, D. H. *Principles of training*. New York: Pergamon, 1965.

Howard, I. P., & Templeton, W. B. *Human spatial orientation*. New York: John Wiley, 1966.

Hyman, R. Stimulus information as a determinant of reaction time. *Journal of Experimental Psychology*, 1953, 45, 188–196.

Kagan, J. The determinants of attention in the infant. *American Scientist*, 1970, 58, 298–306.

Kalikow, D. N., & Klatt, D. H. Second-language learning. In *Information processing models and computer aids for human performance*, Semi-Annual Technical Report, No. 7, Contract F44620-67-C-0033, ARPA. Cambridge, Mass.: Bolt, Beranek, & Newman, 1970.

Kane, M. The art of Ali. *Sports Illustrated*, 1969, 30(18), 48–57.

Karlin, L. Cognition, preparation and sensory-evoked potentials. *Psychological Bulletin*, 1970, 73, 122–136.

Keele, S. W. Compatibility and time-sharing in serial reaction time. *Journal of Experimental Psychology*, 1967, 75, 529–539.

Keele, S. W. Movement control in skilled motor performance. *Psychological Bulletin*, 1968, 70, 387–403.

Keele, S. W., & Posner, M. I. Processing of visual feedback in rapid movements. *Journal of Experimental Psychology*, 1968, 77, 155–158.

Konishi, M. The role of auditory feedback in the control of vocalization in the white-crowned sparrow. *Z. Tierpsychologie*, 1965, 22, 770–783.

Konorski, J. The problem of the peripheral control of skilled movements. *International Journal of Neuroscience*, 1970, 1, 39–50.

Koster, W. G. (Ed.) *Attention and performance II*. Amsterdam: North-Holland Publishing Co., 1969.

Lashley, K. S. The problem of serial order in behavior. In L. A. Jeffress (Ed.), *Cerebral mechanisms in behavior: The Hixon symposium*. New York: John Wiley, 1951. Pp. 112–136.

Lazlo, J. I. The performance of a simple motor task with kinaesthetic sense loss. *Quarterly Journal of Experimental Psychology*, 1966, 18, 1–8.

Lazlo, J. I. Training of fast tapping with reduction of kinaesthetic, tactile, visual and auditory sensations. *Quarterly Journal of Experimental Psychology*, 1967, 19, 344–349.

Leavitt, F. Accuracy of report and central readiness. *Journal of Experimental Psychology*, 1969, 81, 542–546.

Liberman, A. M., Cooper, F. S., Shankweiler, D. P., & Studdert-Kennedy, M. Perception of the speech code. *Psychological Review*, 1967, 74, 431–461.

Marler, P. R., & Hamilton, W. J., III. *Mechanisms of animal behavior*. New York: John Wiley, 1966.

McGeoch, J. A., & Irion, A. L. *The psychology of human learning*. New York: Longmans, Ltd., 1952.

Miller, G. A., Galanter, E., & Pribram, K. H. *Plans and the structure of behavior*. New York: Holt, Rinehart & Winston, 1960.

Morgan, C. T., Chapanis, A., Cook, J. S., III, & Lund, M. W. *Human engineering guide to equipment design*. New York: McGraw-Hill, 1963.

Mott, F. W., & Sherrington, C. S. Experiments upon the influence of sensory nerves upon movement and nutrition of the limbs: Preliminary communication. *Proceedings of the Royal Society of London*, 1895, 57, 481–488.

Näätänen, R. Evoked potential EEG and slow potential correlates of selective attention. In A. F. Sanders (Ed.), *Attention and performance III*. Amsterdam: North-Holland Publishing Co., 1970.

Naylor, J. C., & Briggs, G. E. Effects of task complexity and task organization on the relative efficiency of part and whole training methods. *Journal of Experimental Psychology*, 1963, 65, 217–224.

Neisser, U. *Cognitive psychology*. New York: Appleton-Century-Crofts, 1967.

Niebel, B. W. *Motion and time study*. Homewood, Ill.: Richard D. Irwin, 1962.

Noble, M., & Trumbo, D. The organization of skilled response. *Organizational Behavior and Human Performance*, 1967, 2, 1–25.

Nottebohm, F. Ontogeny of bird song. *Science*, 1970, 167, 950–956.

Notterman, J. M., & Page, D. E. Evaluation of mathematically equivalent tracking systems. *Perceptual and Motor Skills*, 1962, 15, 683–716.

Pepper, R. L., & Herman, L. M. Decay and interference effects in the short-term retention of a discrete motor act. *Journal of Experimental Psychology Monograph*, 1970, 83(2), Part 2.

Pew, R. W. Acquisition of hierarchical control over the temporal organization of a skill. *Journal of Experimental Psychology*, 1966, 71, 764–771.

Posner, M. I. Components of skilled performance. *Science*, 1966, 152, 1712–1718.

Posner, M. I. Characteristics of visual and kinesthetic memory codes. *Journal of Experimental Psychology*, 1967, 75, 103–107.

Posner, M. I. Reduced attention and the performance of "automated" movements. *Journal of Motor Behavior*, 1969, 1, 245–258.

Posner, M. I., & Boies, S. J. Components of attention. *Psychological Review*, 1971, 78, 391–409.

Posner, M. I., & Keele, S. W. Attention demands of movements. **Proceedings of the**

XVIIth Congress of Applied Psychology. Amsterdam: Zeitlinger, 1969.

Posner, M. I., & Keele, S. W. Time and space as measures of mental operations. Invited address, Division 3, presented at the meeting of the American Psychological Association, Miami Beach, August 1970.

Posner, M. I., & Mitchell, R. F. A chronometric analysis of classification. *Psychological Review*, 1967, 74, 392–409.

Posner, M. I., & Wilkinson, R. T. On the process of preparation. Talk presented at the meeting of the Psychonomics Society, St. Louis, November 1969.

Poulton, E. C. On the stimulus and response in pursuit tracking. *Journal of Experimental Psychology*, 1957, 53, 189–194.

Poulton, E. C. Postview and preview in tracking with complex and simple inputs. *Ergonomics*, 1964, 7, 257–265.

Pronko, N. H. On learning to play the violin at the age of four, without tears. *Psychology Today*, 1969, 2(12), 52–53, 66.

Provins, K. A. The effect of peripheral nerve block on the appreciation and execution of finger movements. *Journal of Physiology*, 1958, 143, 55–67.

Rabbitt, P., & Birren, J. E. Age and response to sequences of repetitive and interruptive signals. *Journal of Gerontology*, 1967, 22, 143–150.

Reitman, W. R. *Cognition and thought.* New York: John Wiley, 1965.

Rizk, A. The relative effectiveness of a multimedia approach in learning soccer. (Doctoral dissertation, University of Kentucky) *Dissertation Abstracts*, 1969, 30, 1849A–1850A.

Routtenberg, A. The two arousal hypothesis: Reticular formation and limbic system. *Psychological Review*, 1968, 75, 51–80.

Schmidt, R. A. Anticipation and timing in human motor performance. *Psychological Bulletin*, 1968, 70, 631–646.

Senders, J. W. The human operator as a monitor and controller of multidegree of freedom systems. *IEEE Transaction of the Human Factors in Electronics Groups*, 1964, 5, 2–5.

Shaffer, L. H., & Hardwick, J. Typing performance as a function of text. *Quarterly Journal of Experimental Psychology*, 1968, 20, 360–369.

Simon, H. A., *The sciences of the artificial.* Cambridge: M.I.T. Press, 1969.

Simon, H. A., & Newell, A. Human problem solving. *American Psychologist*, 1971, 26, 145–159.

Simon, J. R. Reactions toward the source of stimulation. *Journal of Experimental Psychology*, 1969, 81, 174–176.

Smith, K. U., & Smith, W. M. *Perception and motion.* Philadelphia: Saunders, 1962.

Sternberg, S. The discovery of processing stages: Extension of Donder's method. In W. G. Koster (Ed.), *Attention and performance II.* Amsterdam: North-Holland Publishing Co., 1969. Pp. 276–315.

Taub, E., & Berman, A. J. Movement and learning in the absence of sensory feedback. In S. J. Freedman (Ed.), *The neuropsychology of spatially oriented behavior.* Homewood, Ill.: Dorsey Press, 1968. Pp. 173–192.

Uhr, L. M. (Ed.) *Pattern recognition: Theory, experiment, computer simulations, and dynamic models of form perception and discovery.* New York: John Wiley, 1966.

Vince, M. A. Corrective movements in a pursuit task. *Quarterly Journal of Experimental Psychology*, 1948, 1, 85–103.

Weiss, A. D. The locus of reaction time change with set, motivation, and age. *Journal of Gerontology*, 1965, 20, 60–64.

Welch, J. C. On the measurement of mental activity through muscular activity and the determination of a constant of attention. *American Journal of Physiology*, 1898, 1, 283–306.

Welford, A. T. *Fundamentals of skill.* London: Methuen, 1968.

Whiting, H. T. A. *Acquiring ball skill.* London: G. Bell, 1967.

Whiting, H. T. A., Gill, E. G., & Stephenson, J. M. Critical time intervals for taking in flight information in a ball-catching task. *Ergonomics*, 1970, 13, 265–272.

Wilson, D. M. The central nervous control of flight in a locust. *Journal of Experimental Biology*, 1961, 38, 471–490.

Woodworth, R. S. The accuracy of voluntary movement. *Psychological Review*, 1899, 3 (2, Whole No. 13).

Woodworth, R. S. *Experimental psychology.* New York: Holt, Rinehart & Winston, 1938.

Yates, A. J. Delayed auditory feedback and shadowing. *Quarterly Journal of Experimental Psychology*, 1965, 17, 125-131.

Young, L. R. On adaptive manual control. *Ergonomics*, 1969, 12, 635–675.

CHAPTER 26 Instrumentation for Teaching and Instructional Management[1]

ROBERT GLASER
University of Pittsburgh

WILLIAM W. COOLEY
University of Pittsburgh

INTRODUCTION

The character of various epics in history has been determined in large part by the tools available in the period: fire, bows and arrows, pottery, domesticated animals, iron working and the alphabet. In an analogous way, the character of teaching is determined by available tools. Such obvious examples as textbooks and blackboards immediately come to mind; less obvious tools as bells demarking instructional periods and report cards also affect the instructional process. The number of available tools for teaching is increasing daily in this age of "multimedia technology," and a concern for their rational and appropriate use is becoming increasingly important in terms of economy and teacher effectiveness. Certainly inadequate attention has been given to the underlying principles which tools do or could utilize or which their utilization implies.

At the outset we should dispel any fears and misconceptions about the spectre of en-croaching mechanisms. To a great extent the evils of mechanisms are a function of the way in which they are used. Humanity and appropriate values do not necessarily result from eschewing civilized developments. Instruments used by the physician for healing can be used humanely or not. The important point is that, as tools and practices become increasingly complicated, understanding of them and experience in their use is required by the practitioner in order to use them wisely.

Some distinction in terms is also necessary at the outset. The word *technology* is frequently used to refer to tools in the form of *hardware*. We prefer to use the word technology, however, in its broadest sense, as the application of science to practice. The word *instrumentation* will be used to refer to tools and procedures developed for use by the teacher and to such recent examples as teaching machines, programmed textbooks, teacher-training techniques that use microteaching and television feedback, television used for instruction in general, and computer-assisted procedures for testing, guidance and instruction.

The use of technology as the application

[1] The research reported herein was supported by a grant from the National Science Foundation to the Learning Research and Development Center (GJ540X).

of science calls attention to the fact that scientific knowledge thought to be useful in educational practice has been distributed primarily through journal articles, textbooks, teacher-training courses and administrative channels. This effort to convert new knowledge regarding learning into teacher actions has been a slow route to follow. A new and exciting development that could hasten progress is the recognition that scientific principles can be designed into teaching instruments and systems which can then become available to the teacher to use in guiding the learning of students. Thus, one objective of this chapter on instrumentation and the application of instructional technology is to describe ways in which instrumentation might facilitate the distribution of scientific knowledge to teachers and students regarding how learning proceeds most effectively.

A second objective is to define, through an analysis of the functions to be served by the instruments, how the school environment must change if the instruments are to be used effectively. Experience has shown that new instrumentation will be effective only to the extent that school environments are designed to take maximum advantage of it.

A third objective of the chapter is to point out that anyone who would improve education through technological applications of science must consider instructional means in the context of the aims of education that are directly *and* indirectly affected by the implementation of those means. For example, if one goal of elementary-school education is to have each child learn the basic skills involved in arithmetic computation, one could implement instructional procedures for efficiently teaching these skills which would make it extremely unlikely that the student would have an appreciation for the mathematical principles involved in computation. It is also possible that one might teach arithmetic skills in a way which would make it unlikely that the child would apply these skills in novel situations, i.e., in

solving problems he had not encountered before. In addition, one might provide instruction which would decrease the probability of the student's electing to learn more mathematics when his required mathematical training was complete.

SOME GENERAL PRINCIPLES IN THE DESIGN OF INSTRUMENTATION

DISPLAY, RESPONSE AND FEEDBACK

Consideration of the potential of new tools for teaching and learning leads us to look at the ways in which subject matter can be presented to the learner and the ways in which he can respond to it and work with it in the course of learning. Despite all the service that printed materials and traditional aids have provided, it is appropriate to examine new possibilities for providing interaction between the student and his subject matter. For example, by means of a cathode-ray tube, which looks like a television screen, alphabetic and numeric characters and graphic displays can be computer-generated, and the student can control these with a standard typewriter keyboard or a "light pen." On such a display, a youngster might manipulate a number line or trace letter patterns to learn handwriting. He might learn about the geometric representation of an algebraic equation by manipulating different parameters on a keyboard, thereby changing the slope and intercept of a line displayed on the screen.

In broad outline, teaching instrumentation can be conceptualized in terms of the display of the subject matter, the manipulanda (e.g., pencil, crayon or controls of a teaching machine) by which the student works with the subject matter, and some logical process between the display and manipulanda. If a teaching sequence requires the manipulation of numbers and words, then consideration should be given to questions such as how these stimuli are to be presented, i.e., in what form and through what sense modality; how the student should manipulate the stimuli and in what contexts; and what sort of information should be fed back to the student as a result of his actions. This feedback requirement is an integral part of the design of teaching instrumentation. Characteristics of the feedback are dictated by the intervening logic that is established between the student's response to the display and a change in the display that results from his actions.

The responsive relationship between subject-matter display and manipulation of it by the learner is one of the essential aspects of the design of instruction. A student learns by manipulating the objects and concepts of his environment: the environment is responsive to his manipulation and in some way the student is informed of the results of his subject-matter operations. A basic premise is that the manipulation of subject-matter events is the primary means by which the student learns, and that this manipulation should take place on the basis of a wide range of display and response modes. These modes are dictated by subject-matter characteristics and requirements of the learning process, and are made possible by the application of modern engineering developments in display and response technology. Instructional environments, as a result, can be less limited and less impoverished than is the case with traditionally available instructional materials and procedures.

The relationships between display, response and feedback determine the characteristics of a teaching tool; the nature of these relationships is a function of the properties and structure of the subject matter and the teaching strategy or instructional logic required by the kind of behavior being taught. These relationships are built into a properly designed workbook, into a programmed textbook, or into the program of a teaching machine or computer-connected console. Because of their importance in instrumentation, some further aspects of display, response and feedback must be considered.

Display

Good displays should present subject-matter stimuli in a form and sense modality appropriate to the subject matter. This is a nontrivial statement if one considers that it is not always possible to do this when subject-matter dimensions are restricted by conventional tools used for teaching. For example, learning to listen demands an auditory stimulus and a listening response which is measured in some way by determining the results of having listened.

A human's capabilities and limitations in various sensory modalities have been reasonably documented by research on the sensory characteristics of visual and auditory displays (Morgan, Cook, Chapanis, & Lund, 1963). For example, with respect to visual displays, much information is available about the factors affecting visual acuity such as depth perception, color discrimination, brightness contrast and ambient light; cathode-ray tube visibility has been carefully studied in terms of signal size and its duration and brightness. The design of letter shape and print size has been carefully investigated. The perception of auditory displays, sound signals and speech has been studied with respect to the factors affecting the detection of loudness, pitch and intelligibility. Human beings can discriminate differences and changes in these properties of objects and sounds much more keenly than they can identify them in isolation. For example, a person can hear very small differences between tones and, under certain conditions, can make some 400 to 500 discriminable steps in frequency. In contrast, when the same person is asked to assign different identifying labels to tones displayed singly over his range of hearing, he can accurately assign only six or seven identifying categories. The ability of humans to discriminate has been found to be especially effective in teaching young children to identify and make fine distinctions between such stimuli as numerals and letters.

Of parallel importance to these human

engineering aspects of displays are the aspects of sensory input that facilitate or inhibit learning. This can be illustrated by pointing out what seems to be an undocumented truism among elementary-school teachers and audio-visual promoters—multimedia and multisensory stimulation enhances learning because the learner experiences the same thing through different sensory channels. While there may be good reasons for presenting certain subject matters in a variety of ways, sheer multiple stimulation is not reason enough. In addition, it has been suggested that the human organism at any moment in time is best conceived of as only a single channel system (Broadbent, 1958; Travers, 1964). Experiments have shown that when redundant information is presented over audio and visual channels, there is no facilitation over audio or visual transmission alone; at low transmission speeds the learner time-shares the channels, and at high speeds he attempts to block out one channel. It should be pointed out, however, that a different effect might prevail when the information presented over the two channels is not redundant but rather involves a relationship between auditory and visual stimuli, such as there is in learning the correspondence between printed letters and spoken words. In these cases the relationship must be systematically examined in order to determine the conditions of presentation that are relevant to learning.

One of the fundamental means by which new modes of behavior are acquired and existing behavior modified entails the process called *observational learning or modeling* (Bandura, 1969). Modeling influences behavior in several ways. First, an observer may acquire response patterns that did not previously exist in his behavioral repertoire and, in this way, learn new or novel responses. Second, through observation of the consequences of modeled actions, the behavior of the observer can be strengthened or weakened. This comes about as a result of the observer's witnessing that, as a consequence of a behavior, the model is either rewarded or punished. Third, modeled behavior serves to alert the observer to discriminate and attend to cues on the basis of which an already-learned behavior can be used when it is appropriate. In general, the factors that govern modeling and observational learning have been extensively studied; this research suggests ways in which behavior can be modeled in instructional displays in order to guide the behavior of the learner.

A final aspect to be considered in this section on displays concerns written text material as instructional displays. Research (Frase, 1970; Rothkopf, 1970) has indicated that the behavior of a reader can be influenced in specific ways by embedding testlike questions in text material. Changes in the position, frequency and type of question influence how the learner studies the text and processes the information in it. For example, more careful inspection of the text occurs when questions are placed after a text passage than when questions are placed before the passage. Apparently prequestions orient the learner to attend only to particular parts of a passage, whereas postquestions establish a general set which results in more careful reading of the entire passage. In general, embedded questions, before and after reading, result in better retention of text information than when such features are not incorporated in the text display. There is a good deal of current research of this kind (e.g., Carroll, 1968) on both written and spoken material; the results should eventually influence the design of verbal material used for instructional purposes.

Response

In considering displays, certain things about response have been implied, but some other aspects must be further discussed, namely, response detectability, realism and learner capability. *Response detectability* refers to the fact that effective teaching requires close attention to the behavior of the learner, so that information about this behavior can be stored and then summarized for the teacher or the student as the basis for presenting further learning activities. Instrumentation such as teaching machines offers the possibility of assessing response components that are useful in guiding instruction but that are difficult for a teacher to detect or keep track of. For example, small differences in the speed or latency with which a student responds may be difficult for a teacher to detect, but there is some evidence (Judd & Glaser, 1969; Suppes, Groen, & Schlag-Rey, 1966) that a very small change in response speed is indicative of the strength of learning, and this change can be detected by instrumentation. As another example, the motor responses involved in handwriting can be monitored and displayed to the student by certain arrangements in chemically treated workbooks.

In many instances, the nature of the media through which instructional information is presented forces restraints on realism —realism in the sense of reproducing characteristics of the task eventually to be learned. A significant example of a restriction on realism, although no value judgment is implied in these remarks, is the use of multiple-choice responses, which limit other forms of response so that answers on a test can be automatically detected. The appropriate use of instrumentation may reduce this kind of artificiality. On the other hand, work on the design of simulators has taught us that realism in instructional devices may be a much overemphasized notion (Gagné, 1965). When simulators are used, it is often obvious that to foster learning, simulation needs to omit and control aspects of a real situation. In the early stages of learning a subject matter, artificiality may be a necessary requirement; at more advanced stages, the necessity for efficient performance measures may introduce artificiality. What is required is an analysis of the component tasks involved so that behavior is taught which insures transfer to

situations that will be encountered in real life. If anything, insistence on realism too early in learning may be a disservice to the learner.

A major aspect of the response requirements of instrumentation is *learner capability*. For example, young children can speak and point to things before they have developed the fine motor skills for manipulating a pencil or typewriter keys. Current activity in early learning is much concerned with the design of appropriate materials for the very young learner. A computer terminal has recently been developed which allows a child to touch a screen with his fingers; the screen detects the position and sequences of touches and, as a result of certain patterns of touches, presents new displays (Fitzhugh & Katsuki, 1971). The limited capabilities of handicapped individuals, with muscular dystrophy, for example, suggest another significant area for instrument design (e.g., Blackhurst, 1965).

Feedback

The effective display of information and response detection can be of little consequence in insuring learning without a third component—feedback appropriate to and contingent upon the learner's responses. The fundamental principle of feedback is that an environment that is highly responsive and adaptive to the behavior of the learner will facilitate learning. That is, the study of learning has indicated that feedback contingent upon the consequences of the student's response is a powerful force in guiding and maintaining learning. It is this necessary responsive aspect of a learning situation which makes traditional methods of instruction appear inefficient and outmoded; it is this responsive aspect of instrumentation which is a key notion considered in its design. In practice, this leads to the demanding requirement that instrumentation systems provide, with little delay, information to students and teachers about the results of their actions, and that this information result in an appropriate change in the display presented to the student.

The nature of the feedback display as it relates to the reinforcement of behavior has been studied extensively. Feedback can be extrinsic to the subject matter being learned, as when a teacher says "good" or when the student is assigned an "A," but what seems of special interest in newly designed systems is feedback intrinsic to the subject matter, intrinsic being defined as a change in the subject-matter display which comes about as a result of the student's manipulation or processing of it. This gives the student a feeling of a high degree of control and self-management with respect to the body of knowledge and skills with which he is interacting. The learner can produce changes in the subject matter as a result of his behavior, and it is these changes that are reinforcing and motivating and which foster effective learning. The effectiveness of stimulus change has undergone an increasing amount of research over the past decade. Highly responsive learning environments can result in highly curious and exploratory individuals (Fowler, 1965). Investigations have repeatedly demonstrated that new behavior is efficiently learned if it leads to a change in the stimulus display with which the individual is interacting. In addition, this stimulus change elicits side effects which can be labeled as curiosity and inquisitiveness. With highly responsive educational systems, it should be possible to add a significant dimension to education.

In addition to a consideration of the principles of learning relevant to the design of the display, response and feedback mechanisms, it is also important to illustrate the general principles of learning which need to be designed into the environment in which instruments are used as well as into the instruments themselves. The purpose of the next section of this chapter is to illustrate that the design of instrumentation for educational environments is a way of building psychological knowledge into what happens in those environments.

INSTRUMENTATION AND PRINCIPLES OF LEARNING

The design of instrumentation involves two primary considerations. One is the incorporation of available knowledge about the learning process. The second is tryout, evaluation and redesign in order to determine that the principles of learning which have been incorporated in the instrumentation work appropriately in the specific implementation or application at hand. The purpose of this section is to describe some of the learning principles that can be considered in the design of instruments and the environments in which they are used.

It is naive to assume that principles of learning can be applied directly and literally after reading a treatise in which they are discussed. As with most knowledge, specific application requires a careful analysis of the situation in which the knowledge is to be applied, and adjustment with respect to the details and parameters of that situation. However, as psychological knowledge becomes more precise and as more experience is gained in the application of psychological principles to instructional design, it should be possible to make applications more directly, i.e., with less tryout and evaluation than is possible at the present time.

The Analysis of Tasks

In the design of instruction, analysis of the subject matter to be learned is an essential preliminary step. Detailed analysis of what is to be learned facilitates instruction by defining what an expert in the subject-matter domain has learned; for example, what distinguishes a skilled reader from an unskilled one. When this analysis identifies classes of behaviors whose properties as learning tasks are known or can be systematically studied, then inferences about optimal instructional procedures and assisting instrumentation can be devised and tested.

Task-analysis procedures essentially involve, or are characterized by, a description of tasks in terms of the demands they place on psychological processes such as discrimination, attention, concept formation, and linguistic ability or processing. Further, since an individual's capacity changes over time, task analysis reflects knowledge of the processes available at different stages of learning or development.

An important point to bear in mind in the analysis of tasks is the distinction between subject-matter structure as it is organized by scholars of that discipline and the way in which the subject matter needs to be structured or formulated for students acquiring knowledge about it. The organizations employed by the expert are not necessarily the structures most useful in facilitating learning at a particular development level of the learner. Since advanced knowledge structures may not be good structures for elementary learning, task analysis needs to concentrate on the determination of units and sequences which facilitate learning for the novice.

Categories of learning. One way to describe tasks is through the use of a taxonomy of behavior categories into which tasks can be sorted. A set of such categories is useful in identifying instructionally similar tasks, tasks that, although differing in certain subject-matter content, share similar characteristics with respect to optimal conditions for learning. Taxonomies can be established on the basis of the different learning conditions required for different classes of tasks and on the basis of inferred processes which underlie the performance of the task. A recent major effort in categorizing tasks according to learning requirements or the conditions under which tasks are learned has been accomplished in a book by Gagné (1970) entitled *The Conditions of Learning.* In this book, eight varieties of learning are described, ranging from conditioned response learning to the learning of concepts and rules, to problem-solving. Each of the varieties of learning is differentiated from the others in terms of the conditions required to bring it about. A detailed presentation is made which shows that each variety of learning begins with a different set of abilities in the learner and ends with a different capability for performance as defined by the category named. The categories described are: conditioned responses, the chaining of responses, verbal associations, sets of discriminations, concept formation, rule learning, and the ability to use discriminations, rules and concepts to solve problems. This taxonomy offers useful leads for the design of instruction.

Learning hierarchies. The concept of learning hierarchies (Gagné, 1968, 1970; Resnick, Wang, & Kaplan, 1970) has been seen as a useful tool in instructional design, particularly in connection with curriculum sequences and the ordering of learning tasks. A hierarchy of component learning tasks is constructed by beginning with a desired instructional objective and then asking in effect, "To perform this behavior, what prerequisite or component behaviors must a learner be able to perform?" For each behavior so identified, the same question is asked, thus generating a hierarchy of objectives based on observable prerequisites. The analysis can begin at any level and always specifies what is hypothesized to come earlier in the curriculum. The major importance of this backward analytical procedure for instructional design is that it provides a method for identifying critical prior behaviors—behaviors whose absence not only may be difficult to diagnose, but also may be significant impediments to future learning. In practical application, a component task analysis can stop when the behaviors identified are the ones that the course designer believes can be safely assumed in the student population. Thus, this kind of analysis attempts to provide an ordered set of tasks for inclusion in a curriculum learning sequence, and also attempts to specify the skills a student needs to enter a curriculum successfully. The hierarchies generated through such a process are frequently represented in the form of tree diagrams such as those shown in Figures 1 and 2, which illustrate hierarchies for pre-kindergarten mathematics and beginning reading, respectively.

Such learning hierarchies provide useful information for designing instruction and its accompanying instrumentation. First, a learning hierarchy observes a basic constraint that no objective is taught to the learner until he has, in one way or another, met the prerequisites for that objective. The prerequisite objectives, however, can be attained in a variety of ways. They can be learned one at a time, several at a time, or all of them can be learned at once. The learning process can be optimized by continuous identification of the educational objective farthest along the hierarchy that a student could perform at any moment, or if a student is unsuccessful at a particular objective, by determining the most immediate subobjective at which he is unsuccessful.

Once such hierarchies have been validated by empirical data so that tasks are reliably placed in subordinate and superordinate relationships, the hierarchical structure provides a basis for sequential or adaptive testing. Since individuals can be ordered with respect to their level of attainment, each sequential objective can define a test exercise which an individual can pass or fail and by which his placement at the appropriate point in an instructional sequence can be determined. Passing an objective implies that the individual should be further tested on the next superordinate objective; failing implies that he should be tested on subordinate objectives in order to determine whether lack of competence is a result of inadequate learning of prerequisite subobjectives, or the result of inadequate instruction on the new objective. Such a structure provides a decision tree for the applica-

tion of tailored testing procedures where an individual's prior performance determines his next test exercise (Ferguson, 1971; Green, 1970; Lord, 1970).

As a final comment on learning hierarchies, different task structures suggest differences as to what a prerequisite relationship between tasks might mean. In general, the lower-order task is said to be a component of the higher-order task. However, there are several possible relationships that might exist between component tasks. The lower-order task might be one of a number of components of the more complex task, each of which can be acquired independently of the others, but all of which must be combined to produce the higher-order performance. Alternatively, the lower-order tasks may themselves be hierarchically related to one another, constituting a sequenced progression leading to increasingly complex performance. Lower-order tasks may also be competencies which facilitate the learning of the more complex task but are dropped out in the more "skillful" performance, or the lower-order tasks might be employed as heuristics for discovering or inventing the more complex task.

Individualizing Mechanisms

An important principle of learning is that an instructional environment should be designed so that information about the student is provided to the student, the teacher and the teaching device so that each can appropriately use this information for the design of subsequent instructional activities. At the beginning of a course of learning, information is usually obtained for appropriate placement of the student in the curriculum. This information includes present level of knowledge and skill, and the individual's preferred styles of learning. The learning hierarchies described in the last section indicated how individual students can be placed and adaptively assessed with respect to a learning sequence as they progress through it.

840

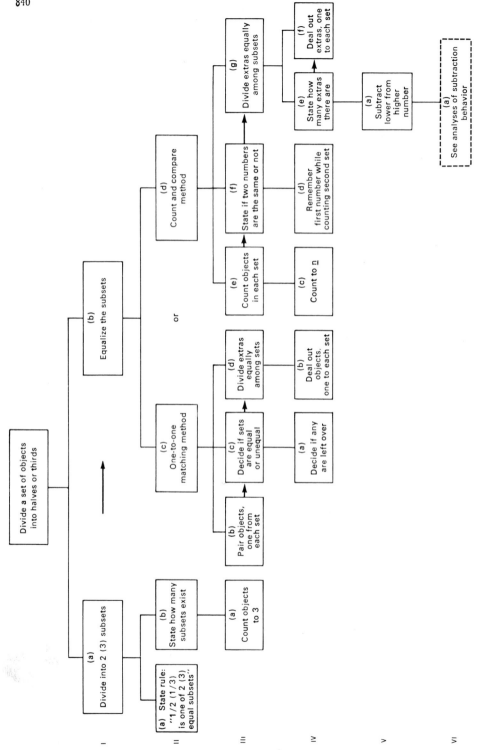

Fig. 1. Learning hierarchy for a pre-kindergarten mathematical skill (from Resnick, 1967).

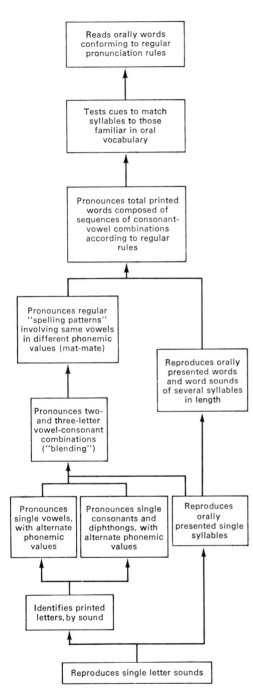

In addition to initial placement in a curriculum, instrumentation can serve to monitor students as they proceed to learn. Measures of performance can be summarized and indexed at appropriate intervals, and this information can be supplied to the student, the teacher and teaching devices for appropriate instructional decisions. The essential problem in setting up individualizing mechanisms is to determine what to measure about student performance in order to obtain the most diagnostic information, and then relate this diagnostic information to instructional alternatives. Detailed analysis of student responses, if provided as feedback immediately responsive to student performance, can effectively guide the course of learning. An important task is to design instructional instrumentation that is responsive to the learner's performance so that information is supplied with minimum delay.

For the individualizing of instruction, indexes of a student's performance can be obtained as he proceeds through a course of learning. These indexes, together with instructional assignments and alternatives, are interlinked in a series of adaptive stages so that instruction consists of a continuous pattern of assessment of progress (and learning style) and means for learning. This involves careful analysis of the kinds of errors students make, the ways in which they go about solving problems, and the ways in which they relate their ideas to the ideas of others. Appropriate instrumentation can provide feedback to the student on these matters more effectively and with less delay than has been the case in the past.

In the design of instrumentation for this purpose, development of ways of assessing how students learn is required. This might include the extent to which particular students can and cannot rely on their memory, the way in which they organize material so it can be effectively retrieved from memory, the degree of anxiety they generate over their errors, the way they distribute their attention, their vulnerability to distraction,

Fig. 2. A learning hierarchy for a basic reading skill ("decoding") (from Gagné, 1970).

etc. If effective means for assessment can be developed and utilized on a relatively immediate basis for making instructional decisions, then it seems that significant facilitation of learning for individual students could occur.

Motivational Variables

Reinforcement has long been considered a key variable in the instructional process. The principle of reinforcement stems from the observation that environmental consequences can increase or decrease the probability with which behavior occurs. Furthermore, the particular kind of behavior that an individual learns or the kind of performance that he exhibits often depends on the details of these environmental consequences. A reinforcing consequence is defined as an event or state of affairs that changes subsequent behavior when it temporally follows an instance of that behavior. Throughout all the various theoretical interpretations of how the mechanisms of reinforcement work, the operational description of reinforcing situations is clear. Behavior is acquired and its occurrence regulated as a result of a contingent relationship between the response of an individual and a consequent event. The pervasiveness of the influence of reinforcement in our daily lives leaves little doubt of the significance of the management of reinforcing operations for educational and instructional practice.

Principles of reinforcement have been applied with increasing frequency in the context of clinical psychology and in education in the classroom (Bandura, 1969; Wolf & Risley, 1971). A number of guidebooks for teachers interested in applying behavior modification techniques have appeared (Buckley & Walker, 1970; Homme, Csanyi, Gonzales, & Rechs, 1969), as well as some recent collections of readings on behavioral modification in education (Fargo, Behrns, & Nolen, 1970; Roden, Klein, & Hapkiewicz, 1971). The effective application and scheduling of reinforcing events, such as

the results of one's work, praise, social approval, attention or leadership have been established as important variables to be considered in the design of educational environments.

Of special interest with respect to the design of instrumentation is the kind of reinforcement that is referred to as *sensory reinforcement*. Sensory reinforcement appears to result from the presentation or removal of stimulus displays that serve to introduce changes into the environment following some activity of the individual. When individuals perform some activity and the results of that activity are fed back to them, the observation of this change is highly motivating, particularly if the change that is produced shows that some novel feature or additional complexity has been introduced into the situation. This is a particularly exciting aspect in the design of instructional instrumentation, particularly instrumentation using the capabilities of computer processing and computer-controlled displays.

An additional dimension of reinforcement is its relativistic character (Premack, 1965, 1971). The effects of reinforcement can be formulated in terms of the preference value for certain activities, or the probability of occurrence of these activities in a person's repertoire. A more preferred activity can be used to reinforce a less preferred activity. Access to a more preferred behavior which has a high probability of occurrence can be used to reinforce a less preferred activity that has a lower probability of occurrence. Common sense examples of this phenomenon occur when parents permit their children to watch television only after they have eaten dinner or permit the eating of dessert only after other food has been eaten. This phenomenon suggests that a useful technique in designing classroom procedures might be to determine a student's preferred activity for learning, establish a hierarchy of these activities, and then employ one activity to reinforce the other in the course of learning. In this case the reinforcing event is the activity that becomes possible once certain knowledge and skills have been attained.

Learning Processes

In addition to analyzing the tasks involved in a subject matter and situational aspects influencing motivation for learning, there is a third class of learning principles which relate to the conditions under which learning occurs. Motivational variables, on the one hand, determine whether an individual engages in and maintains his activity in certain kinds of performance; on the other hand, the procedural variables discussed in this section are more concerned with insuring that learning takes place in a way that optimizes retention and transfer. An exhaustive account of learning variables cannot be presented here. Thus, this section presents a sample useful in the design of instrumentation, and the reader is referred elsewhere for broader coverage (DeCecco, 1968; Gagné, 1970; Glaser, 1969; Glaser & Resnick, 1972; Hilgard & Bower, 1966; Travers, 1972).

Generalization and discrimination. When a learner has acquired a response to a particular stimulus situation, it is evident that other similar situations will also elicit the behavior that has been learned. Once behavior has been reinforced in one situation, the probability that the response will occur in other similar situations is increased. This fact of behavior is referred to as generalization. Generalization refers to making the same kind of responses to different stimuli or performing similar behavior in similar situations; it involves learning common elements and disregarding differences so that behavior occurs in new situations which are in some way similar to the situations in which previous learning occurred. Whether or not generalization is desirable or undesirable, appropriate or inappropriate, depends upon the particular task being taught.

Discrimination learning can be described as a contrast to generalization. Discrimina-tion learning is the process by which particular situations set the occasion for the occurrence of particular behaviors in that situation. A learner is said to have learned to discriminate between stimulus situations when he responds differently in different situations and does so reliably. In a simple two-choice discrimination, an individual learns to behave in one way if an instance of stimulus A occurs and to choose another response if stimulus B occurs. In most real-life situations, individuals learn multiple discriminations involving more than two kinds of responses and more than two kinds of stimuli. Learning the alphabet, for example, is a multiple discrimination involving making 26 kinds of responses to 26 kinds of stimuli.

In the course of learning new knowledges and skills, an individual may overgeneralize, that is, assume that certain situations are similar when they are not. In this case what has occurred is that he has recognized certain similarities with situations he has responded to in the past but has failed to discriminate the critical aspects of the new situation. A playful example is that of a young child who learns to respond "doggie" to the dog at home and then proceeds to use the term "doggie" to classify all four-footed creatures. As learning proceeds, the critical differences among different animals are learned. In the design of instrumentation, the critical dimensions of the subject matter being learned can be analyzed and errors of over- or undergeneralization can be identified; appropriate learning sequences can then be selected which can assist a learner in detecting the subtle similarities and differences that are necessary to learn.

Concept learning. Concepts are learned by experience with appropriate or inappropriate instances or exemplars of class. The properties common to all the instances are abstracted and become the bases according to which an instance is classified as a member or nonmember of a concept class. The special properties of "rivers" as compared with the properties of "lakes" permit appropriate instances of these to be responded to as a class. Rivers have different characteristics from lakes, and the general concept is what is responded to when one deals with a particular instance.

Concepts are of different kinds; lakes and rivers are defined by the presence or absence of certain properties and the joint presence of certain properties and absence of others. Other concepts involve relational propositions, such as the concepts of "many," "few" and "average"; these require the learner to think in terms of relationships between a base quantity and a reference quantity in order to understand the rule or abstraction that defines a concept class. For many complex concepts, such as "justice" and "gravity," the process of abstraction is probably never complete, and as new instances are encountered by the learner, the concepts constantly undergo revision.

Concept learning involves generalizing within classes and discriminating between classes. For example, given three sets of geometric figures—e.g., triangles, quadrilaterals and circles—the student learns these three concepts when he generalizes among the various kinds of triangles and categorizes them correctly as "triangles," and when he discriminates among the three classes of figures and labels them as belonging to different categories. Knowledge of whether concept learning has taken place is obtained when the learner makes the appropriate category responses and is able to apply the "classification rule" (verbalizable or not) to a new set of instances involving the concept attributes. The kind of rule by which attributes are combined to form a particular concept determines, to a large extent, the complexity and nature of the concept. When a rule is not too complex, it is possible that a student can memorize the instances that belong to that category without learning the rule; such a possibility leads to the concern in school learning about whether the student has "just memo-

rized" or "really learned" the concept. In general, concepts are taught well when a range of instances is presented which permits the learner to recognize the presence of the concept attributes in a wide variety of situations in which the presence of the concept rule must be detected out of existing irrelevant features. This permits the individual to transfer his knowledge to a wide variety of situations.

Attention. The extent to which certain features of a situation fail to control or direct the learner's behavior is often referred to as a "failure of attention." Attention is generally conceived of as activity which must occur before a stimulus will be associated with a response. Attention is considered to be a set of preparatory responses which orient a learner to observe critical features in a situation. As such, attentional or orienting responses consist of learned behavior which can be taught and which can be reinforced and extinguished. As a result, individuals learn to pay attention to particular attributes of a stimulus situation and the attentional responses are reinforced because they produce or clarify a stimulus which serves to elicit a discriminative response. Previous reinforcement, with respect to particular features in one situation, will transfer to other situations and the learner's history can serve to make that aspect of the situation predominant as a cue for learning. When this learned cue is relevant it can facilitate learning, and where it is irrelevant it can inhibit learning. In certain learning situations it has been found that asking the learner to label certain features of a complex stimulus serves to draw attention to the particular properties that are important to discriminate. If, in the course of learning, a stimulus pattern varies on many attributes, then during learning, different responses are tried until the relevant attribute is established and the subject learns to attend to that aspect of the stimulus as being relevant in this particular situation. In a variety of learning tasks, learning to pay attention occurs before further learning can take place.

Attentional responses can take on a key role in preparing instructional materials. For example, certain studies have compared the nature of discrimination learning between bright and retarded children (Zeaman & House, 1963). These studies indicate that learning discrimination involves two processes: 1) an attentional response to the relevant features of the stimulus display, and 2) the correct response to the appropriate feature of the relevant dimension. The differences in learning between the brighter and duller children indicate that it is not the rate of learning to associate the correct response with the correct stimulus dimension that distinguishes bright and dull, but rather it is how long it takes the attentional response to discriminate the relevant stimulus features; after this occurs, improvement is uniformly fast for both groups. A difficult discrimination task would be one in which the relevant dimensions involved have a low probability of being attended to; in an easy task, both bright and dull subjects have a high probability of paying attention. Retarded learners can be slow learners in the attentional phase, but once attention does occur, they might learn in one or two trials. It follows from this, then, that an important aspect in instructional design is the development of materials that facilitate attentional learning on the part of the learner. Variables that influence the selection of stimulus features during learning have been discussed by Berlyne (1960). Attentional responses during observational and imitative learning have been described by Bandura (1969), and the activities involved in eliciting attention to verbal materials have been described by Rothkopf (1970) and by Frase (1970).

TEACHING MACHINES AND PROGRAMMED INSTRUCTION

In the light of the previous discussion of some general learning principles, we can

point to the work of B. F. Skinner as a clear-cut instance in the history of education of the translation of learning principles into instrumentation for the classroom. In an article entitled "The Science of Learning and the Art of Teaching," Skinner (1954) pointed out that some promising advances had been made in the field of learning that had implications for instruction. He referred to laboratory research on the contingencies of reinforcement and feedback that are involved in the acquisition of complex behavioral repertoires. He described research in which arrangements of feedback of the consequences of behavior enable the experimenter to produce dramatic instances of learning and the maintenance of this learning in the context of appropriate environmental conditions. It was also shown that complex repertoires could be established by beginning with the reinforcement of simpler behaviors occurring in response to simpler environmental stimuli (displays).

On the basis of his laboratory work, Skinner turned his attention to the "Technology of Teaching" (Skinner, 1968). Analyzing the teaching of complex repertoires in reading, writing and arithmetic that a child learns in elementary school, Skinner raised a number of questions: How can reinforcement contingencies occur in establishing and learning these complex repertoires? What kind of reinforcements are used by the teacher or are present in the school environment? How effective are these reinforcements? How frequently does the child work to avoid punishment as a behavioral consequence rather than to attain a positive outcome? How are the contingencies of reinforcement arranged? Are there long delays between the occurrence of the behavior and the reinforcing consequence? How systematic and conscious is the teacher's arrangement of these contingencies? How effective are workbooks and other aids to learning in providing successive and frequent enough reinforcement to enable the student to learn complex tasks without frustration and easy ones without boredom?

The answers to these and related questions indicated that careful arrangements of instructional materials and of the consequences of behavior in the instructional environment were required—arrangements that seemed to be beyond the capacity of the human teacher to arrange. Even if a single teacher devoted all her time to a single child, this would be true, and this is multiplied manyfold when many children must be attended to at one time.

Consequently, Skinner invented his teaching machines and programmed textbooks. The important features of these devices were: 1) reinforcement for certain kinds of responses could be immediate; 2) manipulation of the material was possible and reinforcing to the student; 3) a student was not forced into the general class schedule but could progress at his own rate, taking time out to investigate some interesting bypaths; 4) the material could be designed so that one problem could depend upon the answer to preceding problems; and 5) the material could be modified where, for example, many pupils tended to have trouble. In addition, the instructional environment could be designed so that reinforcers available from the teacher or present in the school could be made contingent upon work on the teaching machines.

Following Skinner's first public paper in 1954, the teaching machine "movement" had its ups and downs. One reason for this was that teaching machines were taken as a technology that could be applied following a few simple rules of program development and device construction. Although the field was in the state where developers and scientists needed to work carefully together so that underlying behavioral processes could be understood and both theory and practice revised and advanced accordingly, popularizers of the movement maintained little contact with the scientific principles involved. There was a general lack of real understanding of the subtleties of reinforcement contingencies, of the techniques of bringing behavior under stimulus control,

and of the necessity of detailed trial and error similar to the kind required in the long-term validation of psychological tests. In general, use of the early machines could be compared to immediately applying all the external characteristics of the first airplane without further interaction between the development of flying machines, the principles of aerodynamics, and extensive developmental testing. The overall lesson seems to be that a careful balance in educational research and development must be maintained and relationships must be kept that preserve the interaction of both theory and development. The rapid forcing of developments based on superficially abstracted notions is hardly the way new technological developments should proceed, especially in the case of the behavioral and social sciences.

A second lesson comes from the way in which new teaching aids such as programmed instructional materials were introduced into the school. This can be illustrated by an interesting case study reported by Carlson (1966) of the effects of introducing short-term programmed materials into a school system. While the results of using the programs were satisfactory as far as teaching effectiveness was concerned, there were at least three unanticipated consequences that resulted from the lack of accommodation of the school to the impact of these new programs.

First of all, the programs created a classroom situation with which principals apparently could not deal in terms of observing and assessing teacher performance. Carlson reported that when programmed instruction was used in the classroom, principals abandoned their usual procedure of observing teachers, on the grounds that implementation of the programs was of such an experimental nature that they should not disturb it. The observing they did do consisted of interrogating students about how the teacher was doing, noting whether the teacher was sitting at a desk or moving about the room, and determining her orderliness in storing and making available the materials. Clearly, principals did not know what to look for and assess in a teacher's handling of programmed instruction.

Secondly, although programmed instruction permitted students to perform at widely varying rates, various forces operated to minimize these differences. Carlson observed that teachers paced students, restricting the output of swift students and prodding the slower students. The teacher's understandable rationale was to keep the students in groups so that when problems arose, small-group instruction could be given. In addition, the solutions devised to solve the problem of scheduling students who completed a program before the end of the allotted term and those who never completed it tended to return to the familiar practices of the conventional classroom and limited the individualized spread of progress which the programmed instructional aids attempted to foster.

The third unanticipated consequence had to do with the teacher's need to perform. What teachers seemed to define as teaching was capturing the attention of students and serving as a mediator between the student and the information. In the eyes of many teachers, programmed instruction did not provide them the opportunity to do these things; therefore, using programmed instruction was not teaching. Carlson observed that the teachers introduced their own innovations, such as review and discussion periods, in order to recapture some of the role that they felt they had lost to programmed instruction.

Carlson's case study illustrates that the process of education involves multiple interacting components—the student, the teacher, the learning environment, and instructional materials and devices—and the management of all these things. Each component has implications for the others, and the effective design of instruction must treat all the components so that the rigidity of one aspect of the system does not stultify the contributions of other components.

Instrumental aids like teaching machines and programmed materials can encourage changes in school practices—changes such as individual student pacing, revised classroom structures, more self-management by the student, more effective use of teacher time, and greater specificity of achievement standards. However, the effect of any innovative device must be considered in the context of the environment and conditions in which it is used. New instruments can have only very limited success if they are accepted only as devices to be plugged into existing educational procedures and school operations. In contrast, they should be considered as enabling devices around which redesign can take place, and the school system employing them needs to accommodate to their operational implications.

The case of teaching machines and programmed instruction is instructive in education's quest for instrumental aids to the teacher. It illustrates the importance of the interaction between science, technology, and practice and the too early separation of these three entities. Second, it is instructive in pointing out that instruments can only be effective if the implications of their use for redesigned practices and teacher education are considered.

It is with respect to this latter point that the remainder of this chapter proceeds. If one assumes that current educational needs for change center around the concept of adapting educational environments to the individual student, then what kind of instrumentation, in the broad sense of this term, can be developed to assist teachers and students?

INSTRUMENTS FOR INDIVIDUALIZATION

It is now platitudinous to say that instructional systems need to adapt to the requirements of the individual learner, but how to bring this about in schools overwhelmingly geared to mass group instruction is a fundamental question for educational change.

There is a general awareness of several problems facing schools today which may facilitate this change process, however. Five examples of such problems are:

1. Ability grouping or tracking, which has become quite commonplace in elementary schools, tends to separate students of different ability and socioeconomic status. The research on the negative side effects of this practice suggests that alternative ways of adjusting instruction for individual differences should be found.

2. The mobility of families in this country is producing a hardship on schools and children, as children are forced to move into a different school and begin with a new class at that point in the curriculum where the teacher is with that class. Alternatives need to be found which allow children to enter the curriculum at a point appropriate to the child's previous learning.

3. Our rapidly changing society produces demands on the graduates of our schools that our schools cannot anticipate. New skills and knowledges must be learned after leaving school. Therefore, a system of education needs to be developed which teaches students how to learn on their own. Learning to learn must be an important ingredient of any new educational program.

4. As educational costs appear to be outstripping resources, people look for new ways of utilizing schools year-round and providing teacher employment for 12 rather than nine months. To achieve this yet allow flexibility for summer vacation schedules that parents seem to demand, a year-long school would be facilitated by an educational program that permits students and teachers to take leaves on a staggered basis without their absence producing the kinds of hardships that occur with a teacher-led class.

5. Schools, especially elementary schools, seem unable to keep their good teachers. Thus, a consideration in developing a new model for schools is to better utilize the professional talents of teachers and to allow them to grow professionally. In the typical classroom the teacher's responsibilities are essentially the same on the first day of teaching as on the last. An instructional system that allows for differential staffing patterns seems to be necessary if we are to improve the professional lot of the teacher.

These and other problems facing schools, together with the possibility of applying the results of science to the technology of instruction, have led several organizations to a consideration of the instrumentation required to operate individualized instructional systems in our schools. An example of such an organization is the Learning Research and Development Center (LRDC) at the University of Pittsburgh. In the discussion which follows, we draw our illustrations from LRDC because we are most familiar with its work.

LRDC's first approximation to an individualized instructional system is called Individually Prescribed Instruction (IPI) (Lindvall & Bolvin, 1967). The IPI development was based upon an instructional model which is best summarized in terms of the following six components (Glaser, 1970):

1. Outcomes of learning are specified in terms of the competencies to be attained and the conditions under which they are to be exercised. The foreseeable outcomes of instruction are described, insofar as possible, in terms of certain measurable performances and assessable student projects. Depending upon what is being taught and what the goals of instruction are, prior specification is more or less possible. However, analysis and definition should be made of the performance domain intended to be taught and learned. The "structure" of the domain is specified in terms of its subgoal competencies and possible paths along which students can progress to attain learning objectives.

2. Detailed diagnosis is made of the initial state of a learner entering a particular instructional situation. A description of student performance characteristics relevant to the instruction at hand is necessary to

pursue further education. Without the assessment of initial learner characteristics, carrying out an educational procedure is a presumption. It is like prescribing medication for an illness without first examining the symptoms. In the early stages of a particular educational period, instructional procedures will adapt to the findings of the initial assessment, generally reflecting the accumulated performance capabilities resulting from the long-term history and background of the learner. The history that is specifically measured is relevant to the next immediate educational step that is to be taken.

3. Educational alternatives are provided that are adaptive to the classifications resulting from the initial student educational profiles. These alternative instructional procedures are assigned selectively to the student or made available to him for his choice. They are available through the teacher and/or through materials or automated devices with which the student works.

4. As the student learns, his performance is observed and repeatedly assessed at longer or shorter intervals appropriate to what is being taught. In early skill learning, assessment is almost continuous. Later, as competence grows, problems grow larger; as the student becomes increasingly self-sustaining, assessment occurs less frequently. This monitoring serves several purposes: it provides a basis for knowledge of results, appropriate reinforcement contingencies to the learner, and a basis for adaptation to learner demands. This learning history accumulated in the course of instruction is called short-term history and, in addition to information from the long-term history, provides information for choice of the next instructional unit. These observations also provide information about the effectiveness of the instructional material itself.

5. Instruction and learning proceed in a cybernetic fashion, tracking the performance and selections of the student. Assessment and performance are interlinked, one determining the nature and requirement for the other. Instruction proceeds as a function of the relationship among measures of student performance, available instructional alternatives, and learning criteria that are chosen to be optimized. The outcomes of learning measured at any point in instruction are referenced to and evaluated in terms of competence criteria and the values to be optimized; provision is always made for the ability of humans to surpass expectations.

6. The system collects information in order to improve itself; inherent in the system's design is its capability for doing this. A major defect in the implementation of educational innovations has been the lack of the cumulative attainment of knowledge on the basis of which the next innovation is better than the one that preceded it.

The original instruments developed for mathematics in accordance with this model of individualization for an elementary-school program included: an inventory of about 385 objectives for mathematics instruction organized into 85 units; placement tests indicating with which unit the child should begin instruction; pretests for each unit to indicate the objectives the child needs to master; lessons for each objective which are largely self-instructional; tests for each objective as the child moves through the unit; a posttest for the unit to allow the child to demonstrate mastery on all objectives in the unit; and manuals for the teacher on how to manage an IPI classroom and how to prescribe lessons for children given results on placement, pre- and posttests. When all of this was put together, the following picture emerged of an operating classroom in the Oakleaf School in the Pittsburgh, Pennsylvania suburb of Baldwin-Whitehall, the first place IPI was tried.

At the beginning of each mathematics period, the children got their folders. Each folder contained information on the child's past performance and his current work assignment: a continuation of work already begun, perhaps with teacher assistance; the assignment of additional workpages; or a test. For first- and second-graders, assigned workpages were in the folders; older children got their own pages from a storage area immediately outside the classroom where they could, if they wished, discuss their assignments with one another before returning to the classroom. If a child needed help while he was working, he raised his hand and the teacher came to his desk. If a new assignment was needed, the teacher may have made the assignment immediately or suggested that the child work on something else that he was interested in. In grades 1 to 3, children took their completed workpages to a clerk for scoring. If an instructional problem was indicated the child was referred to the teacher. Students in grades 4 to 6 generally scored their own work from keys kept in looseleaf notebooks. These older children had to decide for themselves if they needed teacher assistance. If a test was the assignment, the child went to a testing area or an adjoining room to be tested by an aide and receive immediate information about his performance.

At the end of class, each child put his folder in a box in the classroom for review and evaluation by the teacher. If a test had been required, it was just inserted into the folder. If a new assignment was needed, the student's immediate past work and his entire record were examined. Based on this information as well as on the teacher's general assessment of the student's ability, a new work assignment—either individual work, tutoring or small group work—was indicated. If no additional work was required, the teacher decided whether the student was making sufficient progress or if personal attention was needed during the next class.

Experience with this first approximation to individualization led to the design of a new LRDC program called the Primary Education Project (PEP), which began in the Frick School in Pittsburgh (Resnick, 1967). Although the basic model of pretesting, individual lessons and posttesting was retained, the PEP curriculum more closely approximated a hierarchical structuring of objectives, instructional activities included more manipulative and gamelike activities, and the classroom was more open in terms of alternative possibilities for student activities. Exploratory activities were introduced which the children could freely select and which were openended in character, i.e., there was no one right answer or right way of doing something. In addition, teacher practices were established for adapting to each child's needs for motivation and reinforcement.

Current work at LRDC is concerned with developing a third approximation to an individualized school. It includes a merger of IPI and PEP with both prescriptive and exploratory curricula, as well as an additional form of instrumentation which has been under investigation in the LRDC laboratory for the past several years—computer assistance for adapting to individual requirements and preferences. We will now turn to this aspect of instrumentation for individualization.

The Computer as an Instructional Tool

Even the critics of the present status of educational technology admit that the computer will eventually have a large impact on education. Opinions differ, however, as to when this will take place or what is needed to bring it about. Some argue that the big task is to bring hardware costs down. Certainly that will help, but costs did not prevent the computer's growth in areas such as business, engineering and scientific computation, where applications have been so successful. Also, even where special educational grants to school systems have made costs essentially irrelevant, the computer's contributions to primary and secondary education have not been dramatic except in supporting the business-related administrative functions of large school systems. Even in these school systems with computers for administrative purposes, where many of these business functions could be performed at night, computer power is not being used for instructional uses during the school day to any significant degree.

There are several reasons why the great computer revolution is considered to be somewhere in the future, at least as far as direct support of instruction is concerned. One reason is that computer implementation requires rather precise definition of what is to be accomplished. It is easier to establish goals for accounting procedures, airline reservations or matrix algebra solutions than for teaching Johnny to read or helping him determine what science lesson he should study next. Detailed specification of instructional objectives relevant to each student's requirements has not been typical of educational practice.

The computer requires specification of how to teach as well as what is to be taught. Although there is more knowledge about human learning than is presently being used in most instructional settings, a great deal more needs to be learned before the unqualified success of the computer can be established. The computer itself can help here, however.

Research on instruction in the schools has proceeded at a snail's pace. This is partly a result of the difficulty of adequately controlling the instructional processes in a school. The computer now makes it possible to have instructional procedures selected systematically and the resultant learning observed in the school context. The history of science is full of examples of how the availability of a new instrument has affected the rate of development of a science. At this time the computer should be viewed as much a device for increasing our ability to acquire psychological knowledge about learning *in* the school as a device for delivering psychological knowledge, for facilitating learning, *to* schools.

Another reason for the computer revolution's delay is the fear that computers will control the educational process. Psychologists see the computer as an opportunity for building sound psychological principles into the design of instruction. They, along with educators, are concerned about the question of "control," although an analysis of the aims of education suggests that schools are successful only insofar as they affect the behavior of the children in their charge. What needs to be sorted out is who needs to be in control of what and when. If one aim of the school is to help each student see that he can exert considerable control over what happens to him, the computer (as one kind of learning experience in coordination with many other kinds) can serve as a device for helping the student to explore and control his environment rather than a device for controlling him in that environment. However, once the student is engaged in a particular instructional task which he has selected, with or without the help of a teacher and/or computer, the computer can be useful in controlling the manner in and rate at which that particular lesson proceeds.

An additional problem to be solved before the computer revolution will be upon us is to design educational environments which are able to take advantage of the computer's availability. Even the most ardent computer advocates do not suggest that the computer can ever assume the entire instructional burden. Thus there remains the problem of determining how the computer can perform a finite set of instructional functions and how these functions should relate to the other ("off-line") instructional resources in the school. At LRDC this problem is being attacked by analyzing the individualized program in operation at the Oakleaf Elementary School, and by identifying functions which the computer can perform well that would improve that system of individualized instruction.

There are three main functions required in an individualized elementary school that the computer could help support: management, testing and instruction. Although these are separate aspects of the problem of individualizing instruction, a given computer program might serve all three functions. That is, a child's session at a computer terminal might begin by exploring instructional options currently available to the student (management), proceed to determining his competency on prerequisite behaviors to be sure he is ready for the lesson (testing), then proceed to the lesson (instruction).

In terms of management functions, the computer can provide information to both teacher and student on the nature and structure of the objectives in the various curricula available at the school. Sass (1971) has shown how directed graph procedures are efficient ways of storing hierarchical structures in computer memory. Another information storage and retrieval function is the inventory of instructional resources available for each objective in the curriculum.

Another management function is data acquisition—collecting information on student progress. The resulting student files would make it possible to display information on student progress along with curricular structure and instructional resources, thus allowing the teacher and student to interact with the information required for planning the child's educational development. The data collected for management purposes can also be useful to curriculum developers in evaluating the various instructional resources and procedures used in the school. We have previously (Cooley & Glaser, 1969) described a working model of such a computer management system.

A by-product of having student progress data is teacher self-evaluation. Programs can allow teachers to evaluate their performance in terms of the accomplishments of their students.

As indicated earlier, testing is a key component to any individualized program. The computer is well suited to the peculiar requirements of testing in that context. Given a hierarchical structure of the curriculum and the need to know what the student has and has not mastered, branching is an important timesaving device, as Ferguson (1971) has shown. Also, the number of test items required to determine mastery of a given objective varies considerably from child to child. Thus, preprinted tests may include too few or too many items for providing a reliable estimate of the child's abilities. In computer-administered testing, after the child's response to each item it can be determined whether it is possible to make a decision regarding mastery for that child at some predetermined level of reliability or whether additional testing is required. A third important feature of computer-administered testing is the possibility of sampling from item forms stored in the computer as a means of generating a unique parallel test for each administration.

Computer-administered tests not only reduce the amount of student time required for testing, but they also eliminate the clerical time required for scoring the tests as well as the delay between completion of the test and the availability of the test results. Thus, there is great promise for the computer in an individualized environment for assistance in locating and monitoring a student's progress through the curriculum.

The third main function of the computer in an individualized school is to provide actual instruction. Here the computer is viewed as another instructional resource to be used for particular lessons. One important consideration in the design of computer-assisted instruction (CAI) is to make sure that the computer-administered lessons are related to and integrated with the curriculum and are supplementing the other instructional resources available for achieving the objectives of that curriculum. Wherever CAI has been brought into the school by sticking a few terminals in a "back room," more problems are created than are solved if what goes on in the classroom remains the same. Teachers frequently resist "pulling kids out" of their teacher-led classroom lessons "just to play at a computer terminal" or even to work on CAI lessons if those lessons seem unrelated to what the teacher is currently teaching in the classroom. If, however, CAI lessons have been built to be part of an individualized curriculum, and if the teacher sees them as performing instructional functions for which the computer is uniquely qualified, then teachers will in fact welcome computer support and use it to advantage.

There are three kinds of computer lessons which LRDC is building into its individualized program in the Oakleaf Elementary School—tutorial, exploratory and skill maintenance. Tutorial lessons are designed to teach new skills or concepts which the child has not previously learned, generally in a programmed instruction format. The computer is particularly useful here if branching is likely to be a requirement of such lessons.

Exploratory lessons are open-ended experiences in which the child is free to manipulate the subject matter in a variety of ways. An example of this is the LOGO language (Feurzeig & Papert, 1968), which is a computer language designed to teach young children mathematical concepts through computer programming. Since LOGO is easily learned, very young children can soon be making a complex machine do simple or complex things for them. Children soon learn mathematical notions of function and variable, and gain insights into arithmetical functions by writing computer programs for operations such as multiply and divide with only addition and subtraction commands available. Other kinds of exploratory computer experiences include games and simulations. An example of the latter would be a simulated baseball game which fifth graders could write in LOGO and which would give them important experience in how statistics such as batting averages can be interpreted as probabilities and how the manipulation of those probabilities can affect the outcome of a game.

A third kind of instructional program being tried out in the context of the LRDC individualized program at Oakleaf is the skill maintenance programs. These are designed to provide drill and practice on skills previously learned, but in which spaced

practice is required for retention. Lessons in such subjects as spelling and basic arithmetic skills are available for this purpose.

A Scenario

It is easier to describe the various functions which a computer might perform in an individualized educational environment than to provide the reader with a feel of what that environment might be like for the child. One approach is to write a scenario which illustrates how the computer fits in with the rest of the educational setting.

To do this, let us turn to a day in the life of a student in such a school—Warren, age ten. When he arrived one morning he went to his homeroom and greeted his friends and his teacher and got out his folder of planning sheets. There was one sheet for each of the areas in which he was currently doing work: mathematics, social studies, science, language arts, music and art. He noticed that he was running behind schedule on what he had hoped to accomplish in mathematics this month. He was having trouble with decimal fractions, and this was something he particularly wanted to be able to do because of his interest in baseball statistics. The workbook pages he had been studying in this area did not seem to help, so he decided that today would be a good time to take the diagnostic test in the unit on decimal fractions.

He noticed that the cathode-ray tube in his homeroom was being used by the teacher in a student planning session, so he went down the hall to the testing room and found an empty terminal. The scope was in a "ready" position with the usual numbered list of available options. He typed a "4," indicating that he wanted to take a diagnostic test. The scope then came back with a request for his name, which he entered on the keyboard. Next was a display for selecting the subject matter, and he typed a "2" for mathematics. He then typed "G-Fractions" to indicate the level and area with which he was concerned. A set of numbered test items then appeared on the screen with a question of where he wanted to begin. He next typed in a "5" because he thought he could easily work the items numbered one through four and thought he would begin to have trouble with item five. A test item then appeared on the screen with a flashing line after the word "answer." After working out his answer on a pad of paper, he entered it on the keyboard and discovered that he was correct. He then proceeded through a series of items, some of which he answered correctly and some incorrectly. After about 10 minutes the computer, after analyzing the kinds of errors he was making, came back with the code numbers for work pages and a cassette tape with a suggestion that he try these.

He went to the resources center and picked up the tape cartridge and the work pages and went to the tape-playback room. Following the tape instructions, he was able to work through the work pages in about 30 minutes and began to feel that he was finally seeing why he was having problems in the unit. He returned the cartridge and went back to his homeroom, put his new work pages with the ones he had been working on, and entered the page numbers on his planning sheet so that when the teacher reviewed his math work with him they would have both the computer record of the prescription and the results of his having found the work useful. He then looked over his other math and decided that tomorrow he would try the posttest on the unit.

He next went over to see what his friend Ben was up to. Ben had just finished a book report; so they decided to work on their mural on oceanography. They had both gotten interested in oceanography while watching a Jacques Costeau TV special and decided to do some oceanography units in science. When they had completed that work a few days ago, they had asked the art teacher if they could do a mural showing the different kinds of plant and animal life that are found in the ocean. When they came back from the art room, Ben went to work on his math and Warren indicated to the teacher that he wanted to talk with her. He then went back to his desk to read the biography on Willie Mays that he was doing for reading.

As soon as the teacher was free, she called him to her desk. He had not started any new work in science since finishing the oceanography unit, and he needed to develop some new plans. Warren told the teacher that his electric car set had made him interested in electricity and he was wondering if he could learn more about how the little motor works. The teacher turned to the scope, which was in its normal ready position, and she entered a "1" because that was the option for planning. The next display in the sequence was the list of subject areas, and she entered a "3" for science. Back came a display of the science content areas available, and she entered a "12" for electricity. The next display was a list of topics available under electricity, and she entered a "7," indicating electric motors. The cathode-ray tube then asked for the student's name. She entered Warren's name, and back came two lists on the scope: on the left were the science units available on electric motors, and on the right the following information was indicated: 1) Warren had not studied any of the available units; 2) his reading level made all available units appropriate; and 3) his previous studies of electricity and magnetism indicated he had achieved mastery on the necessary prerequisites for the available units. However, the teacher knew that Warren's dad often worked with him on science, so rather than starting him on the first unit in the series, she thought it might save a little time if he took the pretest on the first two units to make sure he had not already mastered the objectives for those units. She ended the planning session by indicating that he could probably start with unit three but that the test results would help him decide where to begin.

Since the teacher had no more planning slips, she decided to move about the classroom. This meant that Warren could use the classroom terminal for his science tests. The teacher typed in "DONE," indicating they were finished with the planning sequence, and the scope went back to the ready position with the different possible functions enumerated. Warren entered a "5" to indicate pretesting, a "3" to indicate science, a "10" to indicate electricity, and a "12" to indicate electric motors—these code numbers being determined from each list in the display sequence. He thought it was fun moving through these display sequences and always marveled at how fast he could get to where he wanted to be. He made a note to ask the teacher about studying computers next after he finished his work on motors. After only eight test items, the computer was able to indicate that he ought to begin with the first unit on motors, so he noted that result on his science planning sheet, entered "DONE" at the keyboard, and went off to the science room to get the kit and the tape for that first unit. He listened to the taped directions for the first experiment, which involved a compass, a battery and a wire, but since it was lunch time, he decided to ask his dad to try it with him that night and went off to lunch with his friend Bill, who had just finished his science unit.

After lunch Warren had a trombone section meeting with the music teacher. They reviewed the numbers they were going to perform as a brass choir for the Christmas program. After that, he met with his social studies committee and discussed the ways in which school elections were handled. His job had been to interview a sample of students in his homeroom to determine how they felt students should be nominated for school president.

After the committee meeting was over, he joined the teacher and five other students who were scheduled to give book reports. He hadn't finished his biography of Willie Mays yet, so he hoped it wouldn't

be his turn today. He figured that if he worked on science a little that night he could spend more time finishing the biography the following day and be ready for a report on it when the group met the next time. Just as it was his turn to make his book report, buses began to arrive at the school. His teacher said he was "saved by the bell." He wondered why the teacher always used that expression. He had never heard any bells in his school.

SOME CAUTIONS

In this chapter on instrumentation for teaching and instructional management we deliberately chose not to survey the variety of hardware aids such as slides, movie and overhead projectors, TV, audio devices, teaching machines, computers, etc. We decided that a more profitable approach would be to consider how the design and use of such instrumentation could become a vehicle for making available to schools what psychologists have learned about learning. To do this it was first necessary to illustrate learning principles that could be the basis for such instrumentation, and then provide examples of how those principles can be built into instructional materials, devices and procedures which are then designed into a total, individualized, educational environment. We have attempted to illustrate here the search for a technology which will truly extend the power of the teacher in facilitating student learning.

In any enthusiasm for this approach it is important also to remember that there are frequently indirect consequences of technological applications of science, and that the developers of such technologies must consider the possible side effects. As Miller (1970) has pointed out so well in his assessment of psychotechnology, the major task of such assessment is not only to determine whether the technology actually works but whether the possible indirect consequences have been adequately determined. Indirect consequences can only be foreseen if the technologist has a broad view of his task, broader than is needed for the solution of the immediate problem. Miller's principles for assessing psychotechnology are directly applicable to the assessment of instrumentation designed for use in the schools. His assessment principles, as applied here to instrumentation for education, can be summarized as follows: the instrument should accomplish what it is claimed to accomplish; it must be intelligible, that is, we must be able to understand how and why it works; it should be reliable—always giving the same result under the same conditions; it should contribute to the solution of problems that are of wide concern; it should not endanger the physical, mental or social well-being of those to whom it is applied; the person (or institution) who employs the instrument should be identifiable and held responsible for his actions; the instrument should not be used without the knowledge and permission of the individual to whom it is applied; the true intent of the instrument should be clear to the student and clear to the teacher, i.e., no deception should be involved.

The positive potential of educational technology will only be realized if the technologists who would bring the results of their science to bear on educational problems are actively concerned with the broad goals of education and make a concerted effort to fully assess the effects of that new technology.

REFERENCES

Bandura, A. *Principles of behavior modification*. New York: Holt, Rinehart & Winston, 1969.

Berlyne, D. E. *Conflict, arousal, and curiosity*. New York: McGraw-Hill, 1960.

Blackhurst, A. E. Technology in special education—Some implications. *Exceptional Children*, 1965, 31, 449–456.

Broadbent, D. E. *Perception and communication*. New York: Pergamon Press, 1958.

Buckley, N. K., & Walker, H. M. *Modifying classroom behavior: A manual of procedure for classroom teachers*. Champaign, Ill.: Research Press, 1970.

Carlson, R. O. Programmed instruction: Some unanticipated consequences. In R. Glaser et al., *Studies of the use of programmed instruction in the classroom*. Pittsburgh: Learning Research and Development Center, 1966. Pp. 121–131.

Carroll, J. B. On learning from being told. *Educational Psychologist*, 1968, 5, 5–11.

Cooley, W. W., & Glaser, R. The computer and individualized instruction. *Science*, 1969, 166, 574–582.

DeCecco, J. P. *The psychology of learning and instruction: Educational psychology*. Englewood Cliffs, N.J.: Prentice-Hall, 1968.

Fargo, G. A., Behrns, C., & Nolen, P. (Eds.) *Behavior modification in the classroom*. Belmont, Calif.: Wadsworth, 1970.

Ferguson, R. L. *Computer assistance for individualizing measurement*. Pittsburgh: Learning Research and Development Center, 1971. ED 049 608.

Feurzeig, W., & Papert, S. Programming languages as a conceptual framework for teaching mathematics. In *Proceedings, NATO Conference on Computers and Learning*, Nice, France, May 1968.

Fitzhugh, R. J., & Katsuki, D. The touch-sensitive screen as a flexible response device in CAI and behavioral research. *Behavioral Research Methods and Instrumentations*, 1971, 3, 159–164.

Fowler, H. *Curiosity and exploratory behavior*. New York: Macmillan, 1965.

Frase, L. T. Boundary conditions for mathemagenic behaviors. *Review of Educational Research*, 1970, 40, 337–347.

Gagné, R. M. Simulators. In R. Glaser (Ed.), *Training research and education*. New York: John Wiley, 1965. Pp. 223–246.

Gagné, R. M. Learning hierarchies. *Educational Psychologist*, 1968, 6, 1–9.

Gagné, R. M. *The conditions of learning*. (2nd ed.) New York: Holt, Rinehart & Winston, 1970.

Glaser, R. Learning. In R. L. Ebel (Ed.), *Encyclopedia of educational research*. (4th ed.) New York: Macmillan, 1969. Pp. 706–733.

Glaser, R. Evaluation of instruction and changing educational models. In M. C. Wittrock, & D. E. Wiley (Eds.), *The evaluation of instruction.* New York: Holt, Rinehart & Winston, 1970. Pp. 70–86.

Glaser, R., & Resnick, L. B. Instructional psychology. *Annual Review of Psychology,* 1972, 23, in press.

Green, B. F., Jr. Comments on tailored testing. In W. H. Holtzman (Ed.), *Computer-assisted instruction, testing, and guidance.* New York: Harper & Row, 1970. Pp. 184–197.

Hilgard, E. R., & Bower, G. H. *Theories of learning.* (3rd ed.) New York: Appleton-Century-Crofts, 1966.

Homme, L., Csanyi, A. P., Gonzales, M. A., & Rechs, J. R. *How to use contingency contracting in the classroom.* Champaign, Ill.: Research Press, 1969.

Judd, W. A., & Glaser, R. Response latency as a function of training method, information level, acquisition, and overlearning. *Journal of Educational Psychology Monograph,* 1969, 60(4), Part 2.

Lindvall, C. M., & Bolvin, J. O. Programed instruction in the schools: An application of programing principles in "Individually Prescribed Instruction." In P. C. Lange (Ed.), *Programed instruction,* The Sixty-sixth Yearbook of the National Society for the Study of Education, Part II. Chicago: NSSE, 1967. Pp. 217–254.

Lord, F. M. Some test theory for tailored testing. In W. H. Holtzman (Ed.), *Computer-assisted instruction, testing, and guidance.* New York: Harper & Row, 1970. Pp. 139–183.

Miller, G. A. Assessment of psychotechnology. *American Psychologist,* 1970, 25, 991–1001.

Morgan, C. T., Cook, J. S., Chapanis, A., & Lund, M. W. *Human engineering guide to equipment design.* New York: McGraw-Hill, 1963.

Premack, D. Reinforcement theory. In D. Levine (Ed.), *Nebraska symposium on motivation.* Lincoln: University of Nebraska Press, 1965. Pp. 123–180.

Premack, D. Catching up with common sense or two sides of a generalization: Reinforcement and punishment. In R. Glaser (Ed.),

The nature of reinforcement. New York: Academic Press, 1971. Pp. 121–150.

Resnick, L. B. *Design of an early learning curriculum.* Pittsbugh: Learning Research and Development Center, 1967. (Working Paper 16)

Resnick, L. B., Wang, M. C., & Kaplan, J. *Behavior analysis in curriculum design: A hierarchically sequenced introductory mathematics curriculum.* Pittsburgh: Learning Research and Development Center, 1970. (Monograph 2) ED 047 954.

Roden, A., Klein, R., & Hapkiewicz, W. (Eds.) *Behavior modification in educational settings.* Springfield, Ill.: Charles C Thomas, 1971, in press.

Rothkopf, E. Z. The concept of mathemagenic activities. *Review of Educational Research,* 1970, 40, 325–336.

Sass, R. E. *A computer-based instructional management program for classroom use.* Pittsburgh: Learning Research and Development Center, 1971. (Publication 1971/13)

Skinner, B. F. The science of learning and the art of teaching. *Harvard Educational Review,* 1954, 24, 86–97.

Skinner, B. F. *The technology of teaching.* New York: Appleton-Century-Crofts, 1968.

Suppes, P., Groen, G., & Schlag-Rey, M. A model for response latency in paired-associate learning. *Journal of Mathematical Psychology,* 1966, 3, 99–128.

Travers, R. M. W. The transmission of information to human receivers. *AV Communication Review,* 1964, 12, 373–385.

Travers, R. M. W. *Essentials of learning: An overview for students of education* (3rd ed.). New York: Macmillan, 1972.

Wolf, M. M., & Risley, T. R. Reinforcement: Applied research. In R. Glaser (Ed.), *The nature of reinforcement.* New York: Academic Press, 1971. Pp. 310–325.

Zeaman, D., & House, B. J. The role of attention in retardate discrimination learning. In N. R. Ellis (Ed.), *Handbook of mental deficiency.* New York: McGraw-Hill, 1963. Pp. 159–223.

CHAPTER 27 The Analysis and Application of Media

W. HOWARD LEVIE
Indiana University

KENNETH E. DICKIE
Western Michigan University

One decision facing a communicator is the selection of the means he will use to present his message. Should some form of print be used or would an audio presentation be better? Would pictures help? If so, should they be realistic photographs or simplified line drawings? What about a motion picture or television? There are many ways to present information. Choosing the most effective medium from among these many alternatives is one of the communication practitioner's most perplexing problems.

While the problem of media choice has long been a matter of some concern in education, its importance is becoming more apparent. At the time when almost all instruction was presented by classroom lecture or the printed page and other media were used for "enrichment" purposes only, the problem of media selection received little attention. Ideas, if not practice, are changing. New procedures for instructional development place emphasis upon the need to consider alternative means of providing instruction and choosing from these alternatives on the basis of criteria which will maximize learning. With the increasing use of various forms of mediated instruction in which large numbers of students receive instruction via the same message materials, the demand for valid information upon which to base media choice decisions will become more pressing.

How are media choice decisions made? In practice, considerations such as equipment availability for production and presentation, the skills and preferences of the producers, and economic constraints often take precedence. While such pragmatic determinants are crucial and often legitimate, they will not be treated in this chapter. This chapter is a selected review of the empirical evidence and scholarly literature which appeared prior to 1971 dealing most directly with the relative effectiveness of various instructional media in various learning contexts. Emphasis is given to the analysis of pictorial media and to applications related to the attainment of cognitive learning objectives.

MEDIA SELECTION STRATEGIES

Gerlach (1966), Briggs, Campeau, Gagné, and May (1967), and Tosti and Ball (1969) are among those who have proposed models for making instructional decisions with particular relevance to media selection. These procedures may be contrasted with many earlier media utilization practices as being response-oriented rather than stimulus-oriented. The focus is upon what the learner does rather than upon what is done to the learner. In these behavioral approaches, media selection begins not with questions regarding the nature of various types of stimuli but with questions regarding what is to be learned and who is to do the learning. Task analysis and learner analysis are activities which precede decisions about the design of the learning environment.

What are the relationships between types of learning tasks and media? First it should be noted that most objectives may be attained through instruction presented by any of a variety of different media. A great many studies have shown no significant difference between one medium and another in facilitating the attainment of a wide range of objectives. Second, it should be noted that most media may be used effectively to present information instrumental to the attainment of numerous different objectives. In fact, Tosti and Ball (1969) claim that almost anything can be taught to literate learners using only printed text and illustrations. The question, however, is one of efficiency. Some types of objectives and learning tasks have been shown to be particularly congruent with certain media characteristics. Pictorial media are suited to presenting concrete information while print media are better for communicating abstractions. Film and television are particularly useful for showing motion and change. The identification of such relationships is one focus of this chapter. While many of these relationships are presently generic and tentative, a basic postulate for a technology of media selection is that the nature of the learning task and the nature of the objectives associated with a unit of instruction should be determinants of the medium used to provide the instruction.

The characteristics of the learner should also be analyzed prior to media selection. Glaser (1966) notes four classes of prein-structional learner behavior that deserve attention: 1) the extent to which the terminal behavior has already been learned, 2) the extent to which the necessary prerequisites for learning have been acquired, 3) the presence of learning sets which might facilitate or hinder the attainment of the learning objectives, and 4) aptitudelike variables such as cognitive style. The last area holds the greatest relevance for media selection. Learner variables which have been shown to interact with media variables include differences in communication skills such as reading ability and visual literacy, cognitive factors such as IQ and learning rate, and personality characteristics such as ascendancy and responsibility (see Briggs, 1968; Snow & Salomon, 1968). While the use of research designs which will allow interactions between learner variables and media variables to emerge has been widely advocated, it has been infrequently practiced. Even so, the identification of relationships between learner characteristics and media characteristics is another focus of this chapter.

While only task-media relationships and learner-media relationships are discussed in this chapter, several other aspects of the systems approach to instruction hold implications for media selection, including the analysis of the utilization context (e.g., media differ in terms of the ease with which they may be adapted to large group or individual instruction), the evaluation procedures employed (e.g., media differ in terms of the ease with which developmental evaluation and revision may be accomplished), and dissemination and adoption conditions (e.g., media differ in terms of the ease with which they may be utilized and in their acceptability to potential adopters).

DEFINITIONS OF "MEDIA" AND MEDIA-COMPARISON STUDIES

While the term *media* is widely used, very few definitions have been provided.

Some writers have attempted definitions by enumeration which include categories such as *projected materials* (slides, filmstrips, overhead transparencies, motion pictures, microfilm, etc.), *nonprojected materials* (books, photographs, drawings, charts, maps, posters, chalkboards, flannel boards, etc.), *audio materials* (lectures, audio tapes, compressed speech, phonograph records, radio, telephone, etc.), and *real* or *3-D materials* (models, globes, sculpture, demonstrations, field trips, museums, dance, games, live human beings, etc.). Those who have attempted explicit definitions of the term often employ the word "means." The *means* (or medium) is differentiated from the *content* (or message) of a communication. More restricted but equally vague definitions have been provided for terms such as "audiovisual media" and "educational media." Meredith (1965) calls for a taxonomy of educational media, and Salomon (1970) proposes that media be defined in terms of unique presentation modes which fulfill unique psychological functions. Finally, the general frustration is epitomized by Hayman and Dawson (1968) with their melancholy conclusion that media can be defined only in terms of "gestalts" formed by combinations of various elements which result in "particular modes" of communication.

An unfortunate handmaiden of this conceptual imprecision has been a host of poorly conceptualized research studies. Hundreds of studies have been conducted to compare the effectiveness of one medium with another medium without having carefully defined what is being compared. Stickell (1963) analyzed 250 studies which compared television instruction with face-to-face instruction and judged only 10 of them to be interpretable. While such "media comparison" studies typically suffer from a variety of theoretical and methodological inadequacies (see Lumsdaine, 1963), only one such problem will be dealt with here. Consider the question, "Are motion pictures more effective than textbooks?" One matter that must be considered before the question can be approached is, "What is a motion picture?" Clearly the things called "motion pictures" are not all of one sort. They may be either silent or sound films, color or black and white, animated or live action. They may or may not employ high-speed or time-lapse photography or they may not depict motion at all. Motion pictures are usually regarded as being fixed-pace and fixed-sequence presentations, but even these characteristics are only artifacts of traditional utilizations and standard projection equipment. Thus, for research purposes, the concept "motion picture" is far too inexact to be useful as an experimental construct.

MEDIA ATTRIBUTES

A more productive conceptualization of research related to media selection is one that specifies the relevant variables in terms of the attributes of media rather than in terms of the media themselves. Media attributes are properties of stimulus materials which are manifest in the physical parameters of media. The attributes of a medium, then, are the capabilities of that medium— to show objects in motion, objects in color, objects in three dimensions; to provide printed words, spoken words, simultaneous visual and auditory stimuli; to allow for overt learner responses or random access to information. Some attributes, such as the capacity to provide pictorial stimuli, are shared by many media. Other attributes, such as the capacity to show objects in three dimensions, are properties of relatively few media.

Media attributes which are important to the problem of media selection are those which relate to psychological response. For example, a medium which has the attribute of providing pictorial stimuli may elicit psychological responses which are not possible with a medium that does not have this attribute. However, the same picture presented on a piece of paper, on a television monitor, or projected on a screen will result in viewer responses which are identical in most important respects. As another example, suppose a filmstrip consisting of 10 pictures projected for 10 seconds each were compared with a motion picture showing exactly the same pictures for the same time durations. Logically no important differences in learner response would be expected. But what if, with all other parameters still equal, the scenes in the motion picture showed movement? Differences in response might logically now be expected, but these differences should be attributed to the motion attribute, not to the medium of motion pictures as compared with the medium of filmstrips.

Hence the process of media selection may be usefully conceptualized as one of matching media *attributes* to task-learner-situation characteristics. The first question is not, "What medium is appropriate for the given task-learner situation?" but, "What media attributes are appropriate for the given task-learner situation?" After the appropriate media attributes have been specified, the medium which incorporates these attributes is identified. If more than one medium is capable of providing the required attributes, the further choice may be made on the basis of pragmatic determinants such as cost.

A comprehensive and detailed taxonomy of media attributes which are critical in media selection has not yet appeared in the literature. Tosti and Ball (1969) come the closest, offering six "dimensions of presentation": 1) encoding form (pictorial, symbolic, verbal, or environmental structure), 2) duration (transience or permanence of presentation), 3) response-demand characteristics (the type of learner response required), 4) response-demand frequency, 5) presentational management frequency, and 6) management purpose.

The attributes which are treated in this review were chosen on the basis of the amount and the quality of empirical evidence relating them to instructional problems. Two areas are reviewed in some detail: a) sign type (typically represented as the question of the relative effects and uses of words versus pictures), and b)

sense modality (typically represented as the audio versus visual versus audiovisual question). Two other areas, c) realism-abstraction cues and d) response-feedback characteristics, are reviewed in less detail. Other attributes, such as referability (the ease with which repeated exposure to material may be accomplished) and fixedness versus flexibility of pace, are mentioned at various points throughout the discussion.

SIGN TYPES

When a communicator wishes to make reference to an object, he may do so either by actually presenting the object in the presence of his audience or by producing a sign that stands for the object. A sign is a stimulus intentionally produced by a communicator for the purpose of making reference to some other object, event or concept. The words "Eiffel Tower" are a sign for a famous Parisian structure. A photograph of the tower would be another sign for this referent. Most human communication is heavily dependent on the use of signs and, hence, an understanding of the characteristics of signs is important in the effective use of media. Key attributes of any medium are the sign types it employs.

Any sign—with trivial exceptions—may be classified as being either an iconic sign or a digital sign. An iconic sign is one which in some way resembles the thing it stands for. Photographs, drawings, sculpture and maps are iconic signs because they in some way look like their referents. Iconic signs never resemble their referents in all respects. In fact, they may resemble their referents in very few respects. For example, a mere silhouette of George Washington is often all that is required to denote our first president. However, an iconic sign must be like its referent in enough critical respects so that the viewer can make the connection between the display and the referent.

A digital sign is one which in no way resembles its referent; it is arbitrary. Words, numbers, Morse code and semaphore are examples. To interpret the sign the receiver must know the code. The word "okunnig" is not a sign for most Americans, but it is for most Swedes. There are cases (an example would be TALL) which include both iconic and digital characteristics, but their occurrence in instruction is relatively infrequent.

(Strictly speaking, stimulus objects such as pictures and words are sign vehicles. Signs are the internal responses evoked by sign vehicles. However, for simplicity's sake the term "sign" will be used to refer to classes of sign vehicles such as words and pictures.)

The Nature of Iconic Signs and Digital Signs

Langer (1942), Morris (1946), and Knowlton (1964, 1966) are among those who have discussed the distinctions between iconic and digital signs. Digital signs are trivial in and of themselves. They are intrinsically uninteresting. They are transparent. You have been unaware of the particular physical appearance of the words you have been reading, but have been "going right through to the idea." Iconic signs, on the other hand, are more likely to be viewed as objects of interest in their own right. This characteristic of iconic signs may be an advantage—as in the case in which a communicator employs pictures to gain and maintain attention to his message as well as to communicate his ideas; or it may be a disadvantage—as the case in which the receiver is distracted from the communicator's intended message by the nonsign characteristics of the picture. The nonsign characteristics of a picture are those features that are unnecessary to the communication of the intended message. Realistic pictures, as Knowlton (1964) puts it, sometimes "say too much." Realistic iconic signs which are rich in detail may act to reduce fidelity of communication because they provide the viewer with cues that are irrelevant to the communicator's purposes. Digital signs are much less subject to this effect.

Another difference between digital and iconic signs is the ease with which they may be used to refer to concrete objects and abstract concepts. A single picture of a complex object, e.g., an elephant, may do the work of many words; but it would take many pictures to communicate an abstract concept, e.g., "mammal." While a picture may be worth a thousand words in some cases, a single word is worth a thousand pictures in other cases. Knowlton (1964) makes the point by noting that iconic signs give knowledge *of* the world by providing sensory data whereas digital signs give knowledge *about* the world by providing conceptual information. Pictures are successfully used in subject-matter areas such as the biological sciences where objects are important. For example, pictures are very helpful in learning to discriminate breeds of dogs. When the learner has discriminated an Irish Setter from other spaniels and associated the term, the words "Irish Setter" will then be a more convenient and economical sign for that concept. Thus, in considering the relative merits of words and pictures, it is important to distinguish between cases in which words or pictures are being used to *teach* a concept and cases in which words or pictures are being used to *communicate* a concept that has already been learned. There are, however, concepts which are not easily coded in verbal terms. When asked the question, "What does your friend Charlie look like?" a photograph would be a much more satisfying response than a verbal description of Charlie's physiognomy. Thus, a notable instructional use of iconic signs occurs when language is referentially insufficient—either because the receiver has not learned the concept or because the concept has not been adequately coded in language.

A related distinction between digital and iconic signs concerns the elements present in each and the ways in which these elements are combined to make statements. English words are constructed from a limited number of elements—phonemes—

which are combined in certain grammatical structures. The system known as the English language includes a syntax that specifies how signs will be related to make statements. In iconic signs, elements analogous to phonemes are not apparent, and it makes little sense to talk about an "alphabet of lines and shapes" or a "grammar of picturing." Consequently, the tools of linguistic analysis cannot be applied to the study of how (or even if) pictures make statements. In any event, pictures appear to be more limited than words in conveying certain types of expressions. The propositional potential of pictures seems to be limited to the verbal equivalent of "it exists" or "it looks like this." The meanings "is not," "could be," "should be," "will be," and "was" are not directly picturable. Also, as Gropper (1963) notes, pictures are poor signs for communicating generalizations and qualifications such as "all," "many" or "most." It is for reasons such as these that iconic signs are inadequate vehicles for communicating abstractions.

Another distinction between digital and iconic signs relates to the temporal presentation of elements. Digital signs such as spoken language present elements sequentially. While language is not interpreted in totally linear fashion—individual words are retained until they may be interpreted in a context—digital signs often exercise greater response control in the temporal dimension. An iconic sign such as a single picture presents all its parts simultaneously, allowing the perceiver greater control of the order in which the parts are "taken in." Eye movement studies have revealed a few indications about the ways in which people scan visual displays, but as yet the generalizations are sparse and weak (see Fleming, 1969). Hence, when the order in which ideas are encountered is critical, digital signs may be preferred over some types of iconic signs. However, when the learning task involves understanding a large number of relationships, a visual display which presents all the relationships simultaneously in a structure

(such as a map or schematic diagram) may help overcome man's limited capacity to retain a sequence of ideas (see Knowlton's 1966 discussion of "logical pictures").

The nonlinear nature of iconic signs also appears to be facilitative when learner behaviors such as divergent thinking, hypothesis formation and creative activity are desired. Pictures have received heavy use in inquiry approaches to education. Langer (1942) discusses the inhibiting effects of linear symbolism on intellectual activity, suggesting that language is sometimes a poor vehicle for the generation and expression of new ideas which often "break in upon the mind" in nonlinguistic idioms. It is in this sense that McLuhan's cryptic statement, "the medium is the message," may be best appreciated.

Experimental Studies of Words and Pictures

Many researchers have studied the relative merits of words and pictures in simple learning tasks. Rohwer, Lynch, Levin, and Suzuki (1967), Jenkins (1968), and several others have found that pictures are superior to words as stimulus items in paired-associate learning. This finding has implications for learning foreign vocabulary (see Kopstein & Roshal, 1954) or for any task which requires learning names of objects. Jenkins, Neale, and Deno (1967) found greater recognition for pictures than for corresponding nouns. People have an extraordinary recognition memory for pictures. Shepard (1967) exposed subjects to 612 pictures and found that when later presented with pairs of pictures, one from the original set and one they had not previously seen, subjects were able to identify the picture they had previously seen with a median accuracy of more than 98 percent. In a similar study Nickerson (1965) obtained 95 percent accuracy. Haber (1970) exposed subjects to 2,560 photographic slides at a rate of one every 10 seconds over a two- or four-day period. When later shown pairs of pictures, one previously seen and one not, subjects were able to identify the previously seen picture 85 to 95 percent of the the time. Standing, Conezio, and Haber (1970) obtained like results even when the presentation time was reduced to one second per picture and even when the pictures were reversed in orientation from left to right in the presentation and test conditions. While comparisons of free recall for verbal versus pictorial material are complicated by the fact that a recall response for a picture would consist of something like drawing the picture, Lieberman and Culpepper (1965), and Dallett and Wilcox (1968) have attempted rough approximations of recall conditions, finding a superiority for pictorial material.

Why are pictures usually found to be superior to words in these experimental comparisons? Several researchers have offered logical explanations centering upon the notion that pictures typically provide more cues for recall and recognition than do words. It is thought that more information is taken in from pictures than from words, providing a richer storage from which to retrieve. Other researchers have produced evidence that fails to support this view. Wicker (1970) compared simple line drawings and color photographs (presumably richer in cues than the drawings) with corresponding nouns as stimulus items in paired-associate learning. While recall was greater with pictorial stimuli, there was no difference between photographs and drawings, suggesting that richness of cues is not an adequate explanation for word-picture differences. Paivio, Rogers, and Smythe (1968) provide similar evidence and hypothesize that the superiority of pictures in such tasks is due to the possibility that pictures are encoded in both verbal and nonverbal storage, and retrieval from both stores is possible. Sampson (1969) also favors this double encoding-retrieval hypothesis and offers other supporting arguments.

Under certain circumstances recognition memory is also high for words. Kintsch (1970) reviews studies in which recognition

for words and sentences approached 90 percent, and draws attention to an interesting aspect of Shepard's (1967) study. Shepard exposed subjects to 540 words, 270 of which appear with high frequency in standard prose material, and 270 of which appear very infrequently. Recognition was greater for the infrequently appearing words. This suggests that the high recognition value of pictures may be due in part to their uniqueness in the past experience of the viewer. This hypothesis is presently untested. Noting the pervasiveness of real life experiences such as, "I never forget a face, but can't remember names," Gropper (1963) observes that in practice visual displays are normally available for inspection for longer periods than their verbal counterparts, allowing for greater response practice. In any event, the conditions that favor differential recall or recognition for word and pictorial stimuli require more study and the theoretical question remains open.

Imagery and Verbal Elaboration

Related to the picture-word question is the fast growing body of literature dealing with the scientific study of mental imagery and verbal elaboration. In one line of research, subjects in paired-associate learning tasks are instructed to associate stimulus and response items by forming mental images of them interacting in some way. If, for example, the task is to associate the word "cat" with the word "apple," the image of a cat biting into an apple might be formed. Compared with whatever methods people use when left to their own devices, such procedures have resulted in dramatically improved performance on paired-associate learning tasks (see, for example, Ross & Lawrence, 1968). Words may also be employed effectively as mediators in learning tasks. For example, Bower and Clark (1969) gave subjects lists of words and asked them to construct stories using them. After having done this for 12 lists of 10 words each, subjects could recall 93 percent of the original words as compared with a 14 percent recall rate for subjects who simply memorized the 12 lists in succession. Paivio and Foth (1970) found an interaction between the effectiveness of imaginal and verbal mediators and noun concreteness and abstractness in paired-associate learning. Imagery is more effective than verbal mediation for associating concrete noun pairs, whereas verbal mediation is more effective for abstract noun pairs. This interaction is in agreement with the generalization that words are preferred for teaching abstractions while pictures are superior for teaching about concrete objects and events.

One outcome of imagery studies which has surprised researchers is that the use of imagery has a greater facilitating effect for older children than for younger children. Dilley and Paivio (1968) found that the efficacy of pictures in paired-associate tasks increased significantly with age for nursery school, kindergarten and first-grade children, and Rohwer (1968) obtained corresponding results with kindergarten, first-grade and third-grade children. Davidson and Adams (1970) found that provision of a minimal language cue such as a connective preposition between stimulus and response items facilitated learning in paired-associate tasks more than an imagery technique for second-graders. The generalization that the superiority of pictures over words increases with age during early childhood has received varying interpretations. Reese (1970) offers six plausible explanations, preferring the explanation that younger children are not able to "read" pictures. He suggests that, for young children, pictures do not arouse meanings that facilitate learning.

Rohwer (1970) suggests some implications of imagery research for instruction. Cues for eliciting desired responses should be concrete rather than abstract, pictorial rather than verbal, and associated in a meaningful linguistic context which is depicted in some kind of spatial relationship or meaningful interaction. Children should be taught how to employ both verbal and imaginal elaborative techniques for learning.

Children's Responses to Pictures

In communicating with words it is obvious that if the receiver does not know the language he will not be able to decode the message. It is obvious that reading is a skill that must be learned. It is not so obvious—indeed it is sometimes completely unnoticed—that a parallel condition exists in the case of pictures. All people cannot correctly interpret pictures. Children must learn how to "read" pictures.

Several researchers (e.g., Oh, 1968) have found that young children are unable to interpret depth cues in pictures. Kilbride, Robbins, and Freeman (1968) found that the ability of Baganda children to perceive depth in pictures was related to the amount of formal education they had. Elkind, Koegler, and Go (1964) presented children with pictures such as an arrangement of fruits that form a human figure, and found that while young children could identify the smaller elements (the fruits) they could not integrate them into a perception of the whole figure. Travers and Alvarado (1970) discuss the problems young children have in interpreting action elements in still pictures, as implied by structural cues, e.g., dynamic relationships between objects, the blurring which occurs when moving objects are photographed, and the graphic addition of trailing edges; they suggest that it is unreasonable to expect many children to recognize such cues much before the third grade. Jenkins, Stack, and Deno (1969) found, in contrast to the results of studies using older subjects, that second-grade students did not recall more picture than word stimuli.

Analogous findings have obtained from studies of illiterate adults' responses to pictures. Spaulding (1956) studied the failures of poorly educated adults in Costa Rica and

Mexico to correctly interpret pictures, and presents some of his findings in a way which illustrates similarities between problems in interpreting pictures and problems in reading textual material. When subjects were unfamiliar with the objects pictured in an illustration, communication effectiveness suffered in much the same way that vocabulary level affects reading comprehension. He also observes that pictorial complexity may reduce the "readability" of a picture in much the same way that idea density reduces the readability of printed material. Little is known about how people learn to interpret pictures. The emphasis placed upon the importance of learning how to read has not been matched with concern for visual literacy (a selected bibliography on visual literacy appears in the February, 1971, issue of *Audiovisual Instruction*). Finally it should be noted that changing media consumption patterns may have altered young children's responses to pictures and other media forms. Some of the generalizations based on studies of children conducted in the past may be invalid for the post-Sesame Street generation.

Words and Pictures in Combination

The interacting effects of words and pictures have received little study. Samuels (1967) showed that pictures may be used as prompts for the recognition of unfamiliar words in textual material, but that pictures may also miscue or divert attention from textual material. Reviewing evidence related to the effects of pictures upon children's acquisition of sight-vocabulary, Samuels (1970) concludes that pictures often interfere with learning how to read by providing distracting stimuli, particularly for poorer students. This evidence, combined with findings from the study of imagery indicating that young children have trouble in decoding pictures into verbal responses, casts doubt upon the instructional virtue of the widespread practice of heavily illustrating children's textbooks.

With older learners, Allen (1967) found that pictorial illustrations increased learning from printed programmed sequences only when the subject-matter content consisted of material having concrete referents. Baker and Popham (1965) found that adding pictorial embellishments to verbal material did not increase learning, but resulted in higher ratings for interest and enjoyment. Gropper (1966) concluded that a visual/verbal order of presentation is appropriate for concept-learning tasks (which agrees with findings in paired-associate learning that a pictorial stimulus with a verbal response is a highly successful combination) and that the addition of words to pictures facilitates the formation of longer verbal chains and the use of more sophisticated technical language. Among studies investigating the effects of words upon responses to pictures, Steinfeld (1967) demonstrated that verbal material may have a marked effect upon the interpretation of ambiguous pictorial stimuli, and Chan and Travers (1966) found that recognition of simple ambiguous figures was facilitated when they were accompanied by a meaningful, relevant word label. Smith (1960) has discussed some principles of textbook design and illustration, and Fleming (1967) has provided a taxonomy of instructional illustrations and verbal modifiers.

Summary

Pictures and words are different sign types that are differentially useful in various learning tasks and for various learners. Pictures are examples of iconic signs—signs that resemble their referents and are inherently interesting and syntactically limited. Words are examples of digital signs—signs that bear no physical resemblance to their referents and are presented sequentially according to a set of conventions. Pictures are usually superior for eliciting recall and recognition responses, for mediating learning of concrete subject matter, and for a learner lacking a verbal equivalent. Words are better for abstract subject matter and probably channel the learner's thought processes more narrowly and predictably. Young and poorly educated children are typically unable to interpret many types of pictorial cues and learn better from aural language.

Research in imagery has led Bower (1970) and Paivio (1969) to add nonverbal imagery to verbal symbolic processes as a second major component of thinking. Neisser (1967) has provided provocative speculations regarding iconic memory—the short-term storage of visual input. A key to further progress in understanding word-picture relationships lies in the convergence of research findings from studies that manipulate sign types as an independent variable, and theory in human information processing which is applicable to both verbal and nonverbal information.

SENSORY MODALITY

A second media attribute is the sensory modality used. People receive external stimulation through several senses, but since almost all instruction of nonhandicapped learners is presented through sight and sound, the following discussion will be limited to vision and audition. The terms *modality* and *channel* will be used synonymously to refer to the entire visual or auditory perceptual systems. Basically, this section is directed toward two questions: 1) under what conditions is seeing superior to hearing and vice versa, and 2) when is seeing plus hearing superior to either seeing alone or hearing alone?

Characteristics of the Visual and Auditory Channels

Wulfeck and Zeitlin (1962), McCormick (1964), and Travers (1970) are among those who have discussed the characteristics of the visual and auditory channels. Several of these characteristics are functions of the physics of light and sound. Auditory signals are omnidirectional whereas visual displays require spatial orientation. The perception of a visual sign requires spatial scanning and adequate illumination, while auditory signals are received by all within hearing range regardless of the receiver's field of view and are consequently useful for eliciting immediate attention. Auditory signals are finite in duration and are relatively difficult to preserve. Visual displays are normally long-lasting and have high referability, that is, they are available for long periods so that they can be referred to repeatedly. Instructional materials such as printed matter which allow the learner to control the pace, sequence and occasion of his exposure and reexposure have advantages over instructional presentations such as lectures, which have low referability.

In auditory transmissions elements are presented sequentially. Visual transmissions may present elements simultaneously, facilitating the making of comparisons. Pattern recognition appears to be superior in the visual channel (see Baker & Alluisi, 1962; Baker & Payne, 1969; Rosenbusch & Gardner, 1968). For verbal material, transmission rate is usually sender-determined in audition and receiver-determined in vision. In normal verbal communication this results in slower transmission rates for audition since speaking rates average about 150 words per minute while adult reading rates are commonly in excess of 300 words per minute. However, the technique of compressed speech (see Foulke & Sticht, 1969) may be used to speed up auditory transmission.

Experimental Comparisons of Auditory Versus Visual Presentation

Comparisons of auditory and visual presentation become meaningful only when the same information may be coded in both channels. Consequently, modality comparison studies almost always use words as experimental material. Even so, researchers have noted that the same word presented auditorily and visually is equivalent only referentially and that differences which are available in speech such as loudness and inflection may be only approximated by visual differences in typography.

Most modality comparison studies may be placed in one of three categories: 1) studies comparing reading versus listening to textual material, 2) studies employing experimental tasks such as paired-associate learning or serial learning, and 3) studies conducted by researchers whose primary interest is in the area of short-term memory. Studies in each of these three areas are reviewed in turn, after which some findings related to individual differences are presented.

Studies comparing the auditory versus visual presentation of textual materials to literate audiences have usually shown a superiority of reading over listening. Gulo and Baron (1965) presented prose material via print, lecture, television lecture and radio to college students. Reading was superior to the other three presentations on a multiple-choice retention test. Thalberg (1964) found that with moderately difficult and highly difficult material, reading was superior to listening for college students of all ability levels. Haugh (1952) found that reading was superior to listening for eleventh-grade students on a test of immediate recall. James (1962), Harwood (1951), and Cody (1962) are among those who report similar findings. While such studies may be biased toward visual presentation due to the fact that test instruments were administered visually rather than auditorily, the preferred explanation for the superiority of reading relates to the greater referability of print combined with the fact that during the equated time periods in which listening subjects were receiving only one exposure, reading subjects (who were receiving information at a faster rate because reading is faster than speaking) could obtain more than one learning opportunity by re-reading.

A smaller number of studies have been conducted employing experimental tasks typically used in verbal learning experiments. Schulz and his associates (Schulz, 1969) conducted 17 comparisons of auditory versus visual presentation in a variety of experimental tasks including serial learning, paired-associate learning, free recall, verbal discrimination and word association. The majority of these studies showed no significant difference for modality. In other studies, auditory superiority was found about as frequently as visual superiority. One fairly consistent interaction emerged between modality and the meaningfulness of the material to be learned. Schulz and Kasschau (1966) found visual presentation to be superior for items low in meaningfulness (defined by the Montana Scale of Meaningfulness, Noble & Parker, 1960), while auditory presentation was superior when items were high or medium in meaningfulness. In a verbal discrimination task, Schulz and Hopkins (1968) found visual superiority for low meaningful material and auditory superiority for high meaningful material. Consistent with these findings, Williams and Derks (1963) in paired-associate learning, and Van Mondfrans and Travers (1964) in serial learning found visual superiority in learning nonsense syllables (low in meaningfulness). Cooper and Gaeth (1967) also found visual superiority in paired-associate learning of nonsense syllables across five learner grade levels and audio superiority for words (high meaningfulness) for tenth- and twelfth-grade students but, unexpectedly, visual superiority for learning words for fourth-, fifth- and sixth-grade students. This interesting interaction between age and modality for meaningful material has not been followed up with further research. Reviewing studies of this kind, Schulz has concluded that modality input variables are not particularly potent in such tasks and that, in general, the same laws operate on the learning of verbal material in both channels.

Most workers in the area of human memory distinguish between short-term memory (sometimes called primary memory or immediate memory) and long-term memory (sometimes called secondary memory) (see Norman, 1970). Long-term memory is characterized as being extremely large in capacity, relatively permanent in duration, and encoded in numerous, unknown ways. Short-term memory is usually viewed as small in capacity (seven plus or minus two), short in duration (a matter of seconds, though capable of longer holding through rehearsal), and encoded, at least insofar as verbal material goes, auditorily. It is postulated that items are coded and held in short-term memory in an acoustic or articulatory fashion. For example, a telephone number may be encoded by "hearing it in the mind." If it is necessary to wait a few seconds before dialing, the number may be retained by "saying it" over and over subvocally. Several researchers (e.g., Craik, 1969; Margrain, 1967; Murdock, 1968) have studied the relative effects of auditory versus visual presentation of verbal information on short-term retention. Two generalizations that have emerged from such studies are that auditory presentation is superior to visual presentation for short-term learning tasks, and that there is a recency effect in which the superiority of the auditory mode is more pronounced for material presented last in a learning task. Studies which have manipulated the rate of information presentation (e.g., Mackworth, 1964) have shown that auditory presentation is superior at fast presentation rates while recall of visual information improves with slower rates of presentation. Such evidence indicates that processing and storage mechanisms for material received visually or auditorily are fundamentally different. Models of short-term memory and theory regarding differences in memory for iconic versus verbal information may well develop into the bridges which relate media characteristics to human psychological processes.

Comparisons of affective response to auditory and visual messages are rare. Crane, Dieker, and Brown (1970) found that arousal as measured by galvanic skin response is greater for listening than for reading. In the area of opinion change, McGuire (1969) cites a series of studies that lead to the generalization that the spoken word has greater persuasive impact than the printed word. However, the results of these studies may be due not to the modality variable, but to the physical presence of the communicator in spoken communication and the consequent heightened social pressure to conform.

Individual Differences

When a child enters school his systems for processing and responding to spoken language are fairly well developed and are far superior to his reading ability. Once concentrated instruction on reading begins, his ability to learn from visually presented verbal material improves rapidly. Perceptual processes tend to decrease in relative importance while meaning factors become relatively more important. On a word recognition task, Carterette and Jones (1967) found that the superiority of auditory over visual presentation for first-grade children diminished with age, so that by the fifth grade, subjects' performances were essentially as good as adults' performances. Van Valkenburg (1968) found that culturally deprived children profited more from listening than from reading relative to high socioeconomic status children.

A few researchers have demonstrated individual differences among adults in channel efficiency. On a paired-associate learning task with 262 college students, Kay (1958) found 31 subjects who displayed marked visual superiority and 11 subjects who displayed marked auditory superiority. Westover (1958) found that some students showed consistent differences in performance on similar tests administered by listening or by reading, and Klemmer (1958) found individual differences in responses to visual and auditory stimuli on a manual key-pressing task.

Ingersoll (1970) identified "visual attenders" and "aural attenders" by their performance on a bisensory auditory-visual digit-span task. On a series of later tasks in which information was presented simultaneously through both channels, "visual attenders" were found to recall more visual stimuli whereas "aural attenders" recalled more auditory stimuli. As Ingersoll notes, students who have developed such stable response characteristics may be at a disadvantage in learning from audiovisual presentations when information in both channels is not redundant. Those who have a preference for attending to the visual component will suffer when demands are made for information from the auditory channel, and aural attenders will suffer when recall of visual information is required. It should be noted, however, that channel efficiency may not be related to the stated preferences of students. James (1962) obtained individual preferences of Air Force personnel for learning from lecture or print. Each group was subdivided so that half received instruction from their preferred mode and half did not. No differences in learning were found between the two groups. James concluded that receiving instruction in the favored channel appears to have little influence on learning.

Two-channel versus Single-channel Presentation

What are the possible outcomes of presenting information to more than one sense modality simultaneously? First, consider the case in which the information presented in one channel is unrelated to the information being presented simultaneously in a second channel. Mowbray (1953) asked subjects to read a prose passage presented by a visual pacer and simultaneously listen to a different prose passage being presented auditorily. His results, which are consistent with other studies, indicate that people cannot pay attention to two different things at the same time. Broadbent (1954), however, presented two sets of three digits each simultaneously

to different ears, one set to the right ear and another set to the left ear. He found that subjects could reproduce both sets, but invariably did so by first naming one set in its entirety and then the second set in its entirety rather than by mixing digits from the two sets. He obtained similar results (Broadbent, 1957) when two sets of digits were simultaneously presented visually and auditorily. To account for the finding that man can pay attention to only one thing at a time, Broadbent (1958) proposes a human information-processing system that can process only one piece of information at any given moment. To account for the finding that different information presented simultaneously may be processed sequentially, he proposes another system which is capable of storing information for brief periods so that it may be input into the second system should the second system be freed. This short-term memory model consisting of a single channel utilization system preceded by a momentary storage system has been elaborated by Travers (1967) as a model for information transmission by means of audiovisual materials.

In the Travers-Broadbent model, incoming information is compressed (redundancy is reduced) by the sense organs and peripheral nervous systems and by categorization, that is, some bits of information are treated as being equivalent and are "chunked together" into fewer bits of information. This compressed information enters a central processing system which can handle sequential but not simultaneous information. If the central processing system is overloaded, some information may be stored briefly, but if it must remain in storage for more than a second or so, it fades and is lost. This model predicts that the simultaneous, bimodal presentation of redundant information affords no advantage over the unimodal presentation of the same information since all information must ultimately pass through a sequential utilization system.

Van Mondfrans and Travers (1964) compared recall of common words presented simultaneously by vision and audition with recall of words presented by vision alone and by audition alone. No differences in the three presentation conditions were found. In similar studies, Hartman (1961) and Severin (1967) found no advantage for the combined audiovisual presentation of words over printed words alone. Haygood (1965) found that adding redundant auditory information in a concept identification task resulted in no improvement over only visual presentation. Hsia (1968), however, compared presentation of prose material of six difficulty levels under audio, visual and audiovisual conditions, with and without the introduction of noise—a 25 percent white noise in the auditory channel and random black dots scattered over 25 percent of the visual display. He found a general overall audiovisual superiority which was most predominant with easy material under the noise condition. The introduction of noise affected the audiovisual presentation less than either audition or vision alone. Audiovisual presentation of verbal material may also have an overall advantage for groups of learners taken as a whole when some learners are more proficient visually and other learners are more proficient auditorily, resulting in better group data scores than would be attained by either print or speech alone.

The conclusion of Travers and his associates that the use of two sensory modalities has no advantage over the use of a single modality pertains only to the condition in which the information in both channels is redundant—when the same *words* are presented in both channels. When the visual channel consists of pictorial material, the effects of two-channel communication are more complex. In a paired-associate learning task using simple geometrical figures and/or their names as stimulus items, Van Mondfrans and Travers (1965) found no advantage for audiovisual presentation. However, they found that simultaneous presentation of stimulus and response pairs was superior to sequential presentation of

stimulus and response items. The simultaneous presentation of paired-associates is analogous to the common audiovisual practice of simultaneously picturing an object and providing its label auditorily. Research dealing with motion picture variables has generally shown an advantage for sound plus picture combinations (see Hoban & VanOrmer, 1950; Ketcham & Heath, 1962). May and Lumsdaine (1958) analyzed learning from two sound films and concluded that learning was enhanced by word-picture combinations. They suggest that under certain conditions nonverbal stimuli may act as reinforcers of responses elicited by words, thereby increasing learning.

Drawing hypotheses based upon the concepts of 1) cue summation, which predicts that learning will increase as the number of relevant cues are increased, and 2) stimulus generalization, which predicts improved performance with increasing similarity between learning and testing conditions, Severin (1967) found that when testing for recognition was provided in the channel or channels in which information was presented, a word plus a related picture combination was superior to either alone, and that a combination of an unrelated picture plus a word was inferior to either alone. Accordingly, Baldwin (1968) found that recall of both audio and visual elements presented simultaneously in a film was positively related to the redundancy in the audiovisual relationships. Contrary to Severin's findings, Conway (1968) found recognition accuracy for pictures alone better than for word related picture combinations independent of testing mode. Conway argues that the concern with stimulus variables should shift to consideration of the ways in which signs are internally coded and retrieved. Indeed, researchers such as Posner and Keele (1967) and Tversky (1969) have demonstrated that recognition responses based upon verbal and nonverbal aspects of stimulus presentations are dependent upon complex patterns of information processing.

If people can attend to only one source at

a time (Tulving & Lindsay, 1967, offer evidence that the nonattended source in simultaneous presentations is not completely blocked out but only "attenuated"), learning from audiovisual presentations such as sound motion pictures may require learners to switch their attention back and forth from channel to channel. Channel switching may result in inefficiency since switching takes time. Reid and Travers (1968) found a decrement in learning nonsense syllables when switching between visual and auditory channels was required, and they calculated the time lost in switching to be about one-fifth of a second per switch. In a different situation, Kolers (1968) found that the time required to switch from handling messages in one language to handling them in another was on the order of seconds. The time necessary to switch between an auditory-verbal message and a visual-iconic message is not known. While the problem of channel switching becomes critical only when numerous switches are required at high rates of information presentation, producers of audiovisual materials should be aware of the frequency and speed with which they are asking their audience to engage in channel-switching.

When nonredundant information is presented simultaneously in both channels, are people more likely to attend to the visual channel or the auditory channel? Studies of short-term memory using only verbal material show a superiority for auditory stimuli (see, for example, Dornbush, 1970), while short-term memory studies using nonverbal material indicate greater attention to visual stimuli (Tulving & Lindsay, 1967). Studies by Mowbray (1953, 1954) using verbal material on longer-term tasks indicate greater attention to the visual channel, and Chan, Travers, and Van Mondfrans (1965) found greater learning with the visual channel, which was further accentuated by the addition of color and embellishment. Hence, while the factors that determine which channel will be attended to are numerous, there may be a tendency to prefer

attention to the visual, particularly when complex pictorial stimuli are presented.

Another type of task which has relevance to the multisensory question involves cases where incoming stimuli are difficult to detect, recognize or discriminate. Loveless, Brebner, and Hamilton (1970) cite a number of signal detection or vigilance experiments which demonstrate that bisensory presentations may yield higher detection rates than unimodality presentations.

Summary

Channel comparison studies have dealt with a variety of stimulus variables (such as sign type, meaningfulness and referability of verbal material, rate of presentation, the presence or absence of noise, and the degree of redundancy in audiovisual presentations), task variables (such as learning of textual material, paired-associate learning and short-term memory tasks, pattern recognition, and signal detection), dependent variables (such as recall and recognition assessed by techniques such as forced-choice test, trials to criterion, and measurement of errors), stimulus-response interactions (such as the degree of correspondence between presentation, test and response conditions), and subject differences (such as age, preferences and individual differences in channel utilization efficiency). While many of the interactions between these variables have not been investigated and other experimental conditions require study (e.g., tasks involving relearning and higher order cognitive responses), the following generalizations seem warranted on the basis of present evidence.

In learning from textual material, reading is superior to listening when the learner may take advantage of the greater referability of print. Auditory presentation is superior in short-term learning tasks, particularly at high rates of presentation, due to the acoustic nature of human encoding in short-term memory. In many experimental tasks typically used in verbal learning experiments, presentation modality is not a very potent variable, except that auditory presentation is usually superior for meaningful material and visual presentation is better for nonsense syllables. Children learn better from spoken language until about the fifth grade, and individual differences among adults in channel utilization efficiency have been found. Simultaneous audiovisual presentation of words is not superior to learning from print alone, but when pictures are presented in the visual channel, more learning may result from audiovisual presentation under certain conditions which are not fully defined or understood. When information presented in one channel of an audiovisual presentation is not redundant with the information in the second channel, some information will be lost at high presentation rates due to people's inability to pay full attention to more than one source at a time and due to losses caused by channel switching.

Realism and Abstraction

A recurring question in the audiovisual literature involves the relative merits of realism and abstraction in instructional materials. In an early influential audiovisual textbook, Dale (1946) presented a model called the "cone of experience" which classified ways to present information on an abstract-to-concrete continuum ranging from abstract symbols to "direct, purposeful experience." Some writers have interpreted such models to mean that concrete, realistic materials are somehow better than abstract signs. Writing in the first issue of *AV Communication Review,* Carpenter (1953) expresses this viewpoint as the "sign similarity hypothesis," the proposition that materials which are highly similar to the objects and situations they refer to are more effective for most instructional purposes than materials which have little similarity to their referents. More recently writers such as Travers (1967) have taken issue with this viewpoint, observing that human re-

ceivers are capable of processing only a portion of the information available in complex realistic events, and that learning may be enhanced when presentations are reduced in complexity so that only the cues relevant to the learning task are provided.

The following discussion is limited to attributes which relate to realism and abstraction in *pictorial* media only. Gibson (1954) defined the fidelity of a picture as being the degree to which a sheaf of light rays reflected by the picture is identical to those reflected by its referent from the same point of view. The dimensions of pictorial realism which have received the most study are the amount of detail shown (line drawings versus detailed drawings versus photographs), chroma (color versus black and white), and the presence or absence of motion cues.

Amount of Detail

When pictures varying in amount of detail are compared, the most common finding is one of no differences. Wicker (1970), for example, found no differences when photographs or line drawings were used as stimulus items in paired-associate learning, and Wheelbarger (1970) found no differences between line drawings and shaded drawings for several kinds of learning. In instances where differences have been observed, Travers (1969) found that the addition of interior detail and shading to outline drawings increased the recognizability of tachistoscopically presented pictures. Cobun (1961) compared photographs, perspective drawings and outline drawings in teaching fish anatomy, finding that while outline drawings were best for teaching nomenclature of external anatomy, photographs were best for internal structure.

The most extensive research in this area has been done by Dwyer. In a series of studies (summarized in Dwyer, 1970), which exhibits a rare and commendable continuity, pictorial cues were varied (simple line drawings, detailed drawings, models, photographs, in color or black and white) in a unit of instruction presented in various ways to learners of several grade levels tested on several criteria. While the effectiveness of the type of picture interacted with each of the other variables in complex ways, one general outcome is of particular interest. In cases where the pace of presentation was fixed (slides, television), visuals containing little detail tended to be more effective. Visuals high in realism tended to be more effective when the individual learner could control his rate of exposure (programmed booklets). Dwyer speculates that in fixed-pace presentations learners do not have time to take advantage of the added information available in realistic visuals and may be distracted from important verbal information. When learners can take as much time as they wish, realistic detail may provide additional learning experiences.

Color versus Black and White

Numerous researchers have compared color with black and white versions of motion pictures. Usually no differences in learning are found, although occasional results favor one or the other with about equal frequency. Kanner (1968) reviewed 18 studies dealing with the effectiveness of color in television and concluded that the addition of color does not result in greater learning, even though color is almost always preferred by learners. Color may enhance learning when it is used to emphasize relevant cues and aid in making appropriate discriminations (see, for example, Norman & Rieber, 1968). In an interesting pair of studies, Scanlon (1967, 1970) asked subjects who viewed color or black and white versions of television programs to make written reports of what they saw. Subjects in the black and white group wrote longer, more detailed accounts and referred to information in the audio more frequently. The color group made more references to color and included more emotional content in their descriptions. McCoy (1962) found

that color films were not rated as being more realistic than black and white films. Finally, Travers (1969) found that color facilitated young children's perception of movement and the understanding of themes in still pictures.

Motion

Comparisons of motion pictures with equivalent static versions of pictorial material usually show no differences in learning except when the concept to be learned deals with motion or change, in which case the motion version is superior (see, for example, Silverman, 1958). The same result was obtained in an abstract context by Houser, Houser, and Van Mondfrans (1970), in which the task was to associate nonsense syllables with concepts defined by simple geometric shapes. When motion was a defining attribute of a concept, motion picture presentation was superior to slide presentation. In other studies where differences have been observed, Roshal (1949) found that using a subjective "over the shoulder" viewpoint in a realistic setting which included motion was superior to static presentation in learning a perceptual-motor skill. Allen and Weintraub (1968) found an overall superiority for motion pictures as compared with equivalent still pictures over a range of subject-matter content and instructional objectives, but particularly in instances where the content entailed motion itself and when motion helped separate an important figure from the ground. This last example suggests that the functions which motion can perform to enhance learning have not been fully identified.

Because motion pictures (and television) combine many of the attributes available in other media, theoreticians concerned with cinematic communication are particularly aware that when media attributes are used in combination they do not operate independently. The use of an additional attribute such as motion may alter the functions which other attributes may perform.

Pryluck (1968) has proposed a symbol system describing the relationships obtainable from the simultaneous and sequential juxtaposition of filmic elements. While Pryluck's model and the writings of scholars who approach film from an aesthetic viewpoint (e.g., Kracauer, 1960) are of interest to instructional developers and media technicians, they have failed to stimulate research directed toward understanding the unique ways in which experience may be represented by film.

Preferences and Individual Differences

Spaulding (1955), Allen (1960), and Travers (1967) have reviewed studies of children's preferences for pictures. Generally children prefer large, colored, realistic pictures that relate to previous experience. Early preferences for bright colors and simplicity of design soon shift in the direction of adult preferences for more subtle coloration and design complexity. Adults as well as children generally prefer moving presentations to static presentations, although Miller (1969) found no overall difference in emotional reaction (as measured by galvanic skin response) to equivalent motion and nonmotion presentations. As previously mentioned, young children may have difficulty in interpreting complex pictures. Guba, Wolf, DeGroot, Knemeyer, Van Atta, and Light (1964) studied children's eye movements in television viewing and found differences in the viewing patterns of high and low IQ children. While low IQ viewers tended to fixate on one portion of the screen —often the mouth of the television teacher —high IQ viewers shifted their gaze more frequently to other portions of the scene.

Summary

Visual perception is a selective process. Everything "out there" is not taken in. The process of interpreting a picture entails a sampling procedure, and the communicator's intent will be achieved only if the viewer gets the "right" sample. Researchers such as Black (1962) have shown that learning is facilitated by increasing the redundancy of relevant cues and reducing the number of cues that are irrelevant to the learning task. Hence, when a cue that contributes to realism is itself a critical attribute of the concept to be learned, or when such a cue is used to emphasize a relevant cue or to increase the redundancy of relevant cues, learning will be more predictable and replicable. Realism cues which are not relevant to the learning task may produce divergent responses, especially under conditions of high information loads. However, learners usually express preferences for realistic presentations, and, if given adequate time, may learn more from them when they provide more complete information.

PROVISIONS FOR ACTIVE RESPONDING AND FEEDBACK

Two important attributes of programmed materials are provisions for learner response and immediate feedback. It seems reasonable that giving the learner practice in what he is expected to do and informing him of his success or failure should facilitate learning. While these attributes have found their greatest utilization in printed programs, they may also be incorporated into many other media forms. Programmed instruction is the name of a technique, not a medium. Two key issues that have concerned researchers interested in response and feedback variables involve the relative effectiveness of overt responding versus covert responding, and the effectiveness of providing the learner knowledge of results about the correctness of his responses.

Since Lumsdaine's (1963) coverage of these issues in the first Handbook, several excellent reviews have appeared, including those by Schramm (1964), Holland (1965), May (1966), Anderson (1967), Popham (1969), and Gagné and Rohwer (1969). The following brief discussion may be considered to be a summary of these reviews, and the reader is referred to them for the studies that support the generalizations that are presented below.

Overt versus Covert Responding

In the six reviews noted above, 61 different studies are cited which have compared overt responding (usually writing answers or selecting from multiple-choice alternatives) with covert responding ("thinking" answers or merely reading). Of these 61 studies, 33 resulted in no differences in posttest achievement, 18 showed overt responding to be superior, four studies favored covert responding, and six studies revealed interactions with other variables. The fact that more than one-half of these studies showed no differences should not lead one to conclude that overt responding is of little value, but only that there are many circumstances in which response mode makes little difference. What are the conditions under which either overt or covert responding is differentially effective?

Overt responding facilitates learning only when the prescribed responses are relevant to the criterion objectives. Requiring the learner to produce irrelevant or "trivial" responses will not help and may interfere with the learning of relevant material. Overt responding is particularly effective when the required response is not already in the learner's repertory. Recall of new technical terms, learning foreign language vocabulary, and performing motor skills is aided by overt responding, while it appears to make little difference in recognition tasks, forming associations and recalling already familiar material. Overt responding facilitates learning more for difficult material than for easy material, and more for long programs wherein the learner may be inclined to skim when responding covertly. Overt responses provide proof that the learner has, in fact, responded. However, overt responding takes time. Almost all studies have shown covert response to be more efficient than overt responding. Covert responding is better at fast presentation rates which will not allow time for overt responses. There is a suggestion that more incidental material (material for which no response is asked) is learned under conditions of covert responding.

More study is needed in this area which seeks interactions between response mode and other important variables. A good example of such a study is that done by Tobias (1969), who compared overt with covert responding to material varying in familiarity (overt responding was superior for unfamiliar material but no better than covert responding for familiar material) for learners varying in creativity (no interactions were found). A number of studies dealing with individual differences are now appearing, but as yet no generalizations seem warranted.

Knowledge of Results

Most researchers have found that knowledge of results is of little value following correct responses, casting doubt on the proposition that the confirmation of correct responses has rewarding properties and acts as a reinforcer. Feedback may aid when the learner has responded correctly but is not certain about the correctness of his response. Knowledge of results does facilitate learning when it follows wrong responses. Such feedback permits the learner to correct his mistakes and will lessen the likelihood that he will recall wrong responses as being correct. Feedback which provides the correct answer is better than merely telling the learner he was wrong. Generally, knowledge of results is beneficial to the degree that it adds to information. Guthrie (1970) found that feedback consisting of both stimulus and response was superior to no feedback, whereas feedback consisting of only the response did not differ from no feedback. Researchers have generally found that knowledge of results is most effective when provided immediately following the response. However, two studies by Sassenrath and Yonge (1968, 1969) showed that delayed feedback resulted in superior delayed recall, and More (1969) found that feedback provided two and one-half hours or one day after responding resulted in better delayed recall than feedback provided immediately or after a four-day delay. Few studies dealing with learner variables have been reported.

FINAL COMMENT

Early research dealing with media attributes sought main effects—spoken versus printed words, color versus black and white, overt versus covert responding, and so forth. Invariably the emerging generalization has been that no single level of the independent variable is consistently superior and that often the variable is, in fact, inoperative. The question then turns to the more complex problem of discovering the conditions under which different levels of attributes are differentially effective. What media attributes will facilitate learning for what kinds of learners in what kinds of tasks? The shift of focus from main effects to interactions is typically accompanied by a shift of focus from the physical parameters of stimulus attributes to concern with inferences about the internal human processes that may be aroused or facilitated by media attributes. Researchers cease to be satisfied with discovering what happens but seek to explain why it happens in varying contexts.

These two foci are critical to the development of a technology for media selection. The medium through which instruction is presented is but one aspect of the teaching-learning situation, and a theory of media selection would be subsumed by a theory of instruction. If improved theory is to be a goal of research, independent variables must relate to the constructs which are central to the theory—in this case, the implicit human processes which mediate instructional stimuli and learning outcomes.

Understanding media may be furthered by 1) specifying media in terms of attributes, 2) defining these attributes in terms which relate to the ways in which information is processed internally, and 3) discovering relationships between these attributes and other important instructional variables.

REFERENCES

Allen, W. H. Audio-visual communication. In C. W. Harris (Ed.), *Encyclopedia of educational research.* (3rd ed.) New York: Macmillan, 1960. Pp. 115–137.

Allen, W. H. *Visual and audio presentation in machine programed instruction.* Final report. Los Angeles: University of Southern California, 1967. ED 016 400.

Allen, W. H., & Weintraub, R. *The motion variables in film presentations.* Final report. Los Angeles: University of Southern California, 1968. ED 027 750.

Anderson, R. C. Educational psychology. *Annual Review of Psychology,* 1967, 18, 129–164.

Baker, E. J., & Alluisi, E. A. Information handling aspects of visual and auditory form perception. *Journal of Engineering Psychology,* 1962, 1, 159–179.

Baker, E. J., & Payne, M. C., Jr. Pattern recognition by audition and vision. *Perceptual and Motor Skills,* 1969, 29, 129–130.

Baker, E. L., & Popham, W. J. Value of pictorial embellishments in a tape-slide instructional program. *AV Communication Review,* 1965, 13, 397–404.

Baldwin, T. F. *Redundancy in simultaneously presented audiovisual message elements as a determinant of recall.* East Lansing: Michigan State University, 1968.

Black, H. B. *Improving the programming of complex pictorial materials: Discrimination learning as affected by prior exposure to and relevance of components of the figural discriminanda.* Final report, NDEA Title VII, Project No. 688. Washington, D.C.: U.S. Office of Education, 1962.

Bower, G. H. Analysis of a mnemonic device. *American Scientist,* 1970, 58, 496–510.

Bower, G. H., & Clark, M. C. Narrative stories as mediators for serial learning. *Psychonomic Science,* 1969, 14, 181–182.

Briggs, L. J. Learner variables and educational media. *Review of Educational Research,* 1968, 38, 160–176.

Briggs, L. J., Campeau, P. L., Gagné, R. M., & May, M. A. *Instructional media: A procedure for the design of multimedia instruction, a critical review of research, and suggestions for future research.* Pittsburgh: American Institutes for Research, 1967. ED 024 278.

Broadbent, D. E. The role of auditory localization in attention and memory span. *Journal of Experimental Psychology,* 1954, 47, 191–196.

Broadbent, D. E. Successive responses to simultaneous stimuli. *Quarterly Journal of Psychology,* 1957, 9, 1–11.

Broadbent, D. E. *Perception and communication.* New York: Pergamon Press, 1958.

Carpenter, C. R. A theoretical orientation for instructional film research. *AV Communication Review,* 1953, 1, 38–52.

Carterette, E. C., & Jones, M. H. Visual and auditory information processing in children and adults. *Science,* 1967, 156, 986–988.

Chan, A., & Travers, R. M. W. The effect on retention of labeling visual displays. *American Educational Research Journal,* 1966, 3, 55–67.

Chan, A., Travers, R. M. W., & Van Mondfrans, A. P. The effect of colored embellishment of a visual array on a simultaneously presented audio array. *AV Communication Review,* 1965, 13, 159–164.

Cobun, T. C. *The relative effectiveness of three levels of pictorial presentation of biological subject matter on the associative learning of nomenclature by sixth grade students.* (Doctoral dissertation, Indiana University) Ann Arbor, Mich.: University Microfilms, 1961. No. 61-3196.

Cody, M. I. *An investigation of the relative effectiveness of four modes of presenting meaningful material to twelfth-grade students.* (Doctoral dissertation, Fordham University) Ann Arbor, Mich.: University Microfilms, 1962. No. 62-3759.

Conway, J. K. Information presentation, information processing, and the sign vehicle. *AV Communication Review,* 1968, 16, 403–414.

Cooper, J. C., Jr., & Gaeth, J. H. Interactions of modality with age and with meaningfulness in verbal learning. *Journal of Educational Psychology,* 1967, 58, 41–44.

Craik, F. I. M. Modality effects in short-term storage. *Journal of Verbal Learning and Verbal Behavior,* 1969, 8, 658–664.

Crane, L. D., Dieker, R. J., & Brown, C. T. The physiological response to the communication modes: Reading, listening, writing, speaking, and evaluating. *The Journal of Communication,* 1970, 20, 231–240.

Dale, E. *Audio-visual methods in teaching.* New York: Dryden Press, 1946.

Dallett, K., & Wilcox, S. G. Remembering pictures vs. remembering descriptions. *Psychonomic Science,* 1968, 11, 139–140.

Davidson, R. E., & Adams, J. F. Verbal and imagery processes in children's paired-associate learning. *Journal of Experimental Child Psychology,* 1970, 9, 429–435.

Dilley, M. G., & Paivio, A. Pictures and words as stimulus and response items in paired-associate learning of young children. *Journal of Experimental Child Psychology,* 1968, 6, 231–240.

Dornbush, R. L. Attention in bisensory simultaneous short-term memory. *Perception and Psychophysics,* 1970, 7, 244–246.

Dwyer, F. M., Jr. Exploratory studies in the effectiveness of visual illustrations. *AV Communication Review,* 1970, 18, 235–249.

Elkind, D., Koegler, R., & Go, E. Studies in perceptual development: II. Part-whole perception. *Child Development,* 1964, 35, 81–90.

Fleming, M. Classification and analysis of instructional illustrations. *AV Communication Review,* 1967, 15, 246–258.

Fleming, M. Eye movement indices of cognitive behavior. *AV Communication Review,* 1969, 17, 383–398.

Foulke, E., & Sticht, T. Review of research on the intelligibility and comprehension of accelerated speech. *Psychological Bulletin,* 1969, 72, 50–62.

Gagné, R. M., & Rohwer, W. D., Jr. Instructional psychology. *Annual Review of Psychology,* 1969, 20, 381–418.

Gerlach, V. S. Selecting an instructional medium. In W. C. Meierhenry (Ed.), *Media competencies for teachers.* Lincoln, Nebr.: Teachers College, University of Nebraska, 1966. Pp. 70–100.

Gibson, J. J. A theory of pictorial perception. *AV Communication Review,* 1954, 2, 3–23.

Glaser, R. Psychological bases for instructional design. *AV Communication Review,* 1966, 14, 433–449.

Gropper, G. L. Why *is* a picture worth a thousand words? *AV Communication Review,* 1963, 11(4), 75–95.

Gropper, G. L. Learning from visuals: Some behavioral considerations. *AV Communication Review,* 1966, 14, 37–69.

Guba, E., Wolf, W., De Groot, S., Knemeyer, M., Van Atta, R., & Light, L. Eye movements and TV viewing in children. *AV Communication Review,* 1964, 12, 386–401.

Gulo, E. V., & Baron, A. Classroom learning of meaningful prose by college students as a function of sensory mode of stimulus presentation. *Perceptual and Motor Skills,* 1965, 21, 183–186.

Guthrie, J. T. *Feedback and sentence learning.* Report No. R-71. Washington, D.C.: Office of Education, Bureau of Research, 1970. ED 040 484.

Haber, R. N. How we remember what we see. *Scientific American,* 1970, 222(5), 104–112.

Hartman, F. R. Recognition learning under multiple channel presentation and testing conditions. *AV Communication Review,* 1961, 9, 24–43.

Harwood, K. A. An experimental comparison of listening comprehensibility with reading comprehensibility. *Speech Monographs,* 1951, 18, 123. (Abstract)

Haugh, O. M. The relative effectiveness of reading and listening to radio drama as ways of imparting information and shifting attitudes. *Journal of Educational Research,* 1952, 45, 489–498.

Haygood, D. H. Audio-visual concept formation. *Journal of Educational Psychology,* 1965, 56, 126–132.

Hayman, J. L., Jr., & Dawson, M., Jr. Development and modification of attitudes through educational media. In R. A. Weisgerber (Ed.), *Instructional process and media innovation.* Chicago: Rand McNally, 1968. Pp. 40–61.

Hoban, C. F., & Van Ormer, E. B. *Instructional film research 1918–1950.* Technical report no. SDC 269-7-19, NAVEXOS P-977. College Park, Pa.: Pennsylvania State College, 1950.

Holland, J. G. Research on programing variables. In R. Glaser (Ed.), *Teaching machines and programed learning, II: Data and*

directions. Washington, D.C.: National Education Association, 1965. Pp. 66–117.

Houser, R. L., Houser, E. J., & Van Mondfrans, A. P. Learning a motion and a nonmotion concept by motion picture versus slide presentation. *AV Communication Review,* 1970, 18, 425–430.

Hsia, H. J. Effects of noise and difficulty level of input information in auditory, visual, and audiovisual information processing. *Perceptual and Motor Skills,* 1968, 26, 99–105.

Ingersoll, G. M. *The effects of presentation modalities and modality preferences on learning and recall.* (Doctoral dissertation, Pennsylvania State University) Ann Arbor, Mich.: University Microfilms, 1970. No. 71-16,615.

James, N. E. Personal preference for method as a factor in learning. *Journal of Educational Psychology,* 1962, 53, 43–47.

Jenkins, J. R. Effects of incidental cues and encoding strategies on paired-associate learning. *Journal of Educational Psychology,* 1968, 59, 410–413.

Jenkins, J. R., Neale, D. C., & Deno, S. L. Differential memory for picture and word stimuli. *Journal of Educational Psychology,* 1967, 58, 303–307.

Jenkins, J. R., Stack, W. B., & Deno, S. L. Children's recognition and recall of picture and word stimuli. *AV Communication Review,* 1969, 17, 265–271.

Kanner, J. H. *The instructional effectiveness of color in television: A review of the evidence.* Stanford, Calif.: Stanford University, 1968. ED 015 675.

Kay, B. R. Intra-individual differences in sensory channel preference. *Journal of Applied Psychology,* 1958, 42, 166–167.

Ketcham, C. H., & Heath, R. W. Teaching effectiveness of sound with pictures that do not embody the material being taught. *AV Communication Review,* 1962, 10(2), 89–93.

Kilbride, P. L., Robbins, M. C., & Freeman, R. B., Jr. Pictorial depth perception and education among Baganda school children. *Perceptual and Motor Skills,* 1968, 26, 1116–1118.

Kintsch, W. *Learning, memory, and conceptual processes.* New York: John Wiley, 1970.

Klemmer, E. T. Time sharing between frequency-coded auditory and visual channels.

Journal of Experimental Psychology, 1958, 55, 229–235.

Knowlton, J. Q. *A socio- and psycho-linguistic theory of pictorial communication.* Bloomington, Ind.: Indiana University Division of Instructional Systems Technology, 1964.

Knowlton, J. Q. On the definition of "picture." *AV Communication Review*, 1966, 14, 157–183.

Kolers, P. Bilingualism and information processing. *Scientific American*, 1968, 218(3), 78–86.

Kopstein, F. F., & Roshal, S. M. Learning foreign vocabulary from pictures vs. words. *American Psychologist*, 1954, 9, 407–408. (Abstract)

Kracauer, S. *Theory of film.* New York: Oxford University Press, 1960.

Langer, S. K. *Philosophy in a new key: A study in the symbolism of reason, rite and art.* Cambridge, Mass.: Harvard University Press, 1942.

Lieberman, L. R., & Culpepper, J. T. Words versus objects: Comparison of free verbal recall. *Psychological Reports*, 1965, 17, 983–988.

Loveless, N. E., Brebner, J., & Hamilton, P. Bisensory presentation of information. *Psychological Bulletin*, 1970, 73, 161–199.

Lumsdaine, A. A. Instruments and media of instruction. In N. L. Gage (Ed.), *Handbook of research on teaching.* Chicago: Rand McNally, 1963. Pp. 583–682.

Mackworth, J. F. Auditory short-term memory. *Canadian Journal of Psychology*, 1964, 18, 292–303.

Margrain, S. A. Short-term memory as a function of input modality. *Quarterly Journal of Experimental Psychology*, 1967, 19, 109–114.

May, M. A. *The role of student response in learning from the new educational media.* Final report, USOE Contract OE-5-16-006. Washington, D.C.: U.S. Dept. of Health, Education and Welfare, 1966.

May, M. A., & Lumsdaine, A. A. Patterns of words and pictures. In M. A. May, & A. A. Lumsdaine (Eds.), *Learning from films.* New Haven: Yale University Press, 1958. Pp. 150–167.

McCormick, E. J. *Human factors engineering.* New York: McGraw-Hill, 1964.

McCoy, E. P. Influence of color on audiences' rated perception of reality in film. *AV Communication Review*, 1962, 10, 70–72.

McGuire, W. J. The nature of attitudes and attitude change. In G. Lindzey, & E. Aronson (Eds.), *The handbook of social psychology.* (2nd ed.) Reading, Mass.: Addison-Wesley, 1969. Pp. 136–314.

Meredith, P. Toward a taxonomy of educational media. *AV Communication Review*, 1965, 13, 374–384.

Miller, W. C. Film movement and affective response and the effect on learning and attitude formation. *AV Communication Review*, 1969, 17, 172–181.

More, A. J. Delay of feedback and the acquisition and retention of verbal materials in the classroom. *Journal of Educational Psychology*, 1969, 60, 339–342.

Morris, C. W. *Signs, language and behavior.* Englewood Cliffs, N.J.: Prentice-Hall, 1946.

Mowbray, G. H. Simultaneous vision and audition: The comprehension of prose passages with varying levels of difficulty. *Journal of Experimental Psychology*, 1953, 46, 365–372.

Mowbray, G. H. The perception of short phrases presented simultaneously for visual and auditory reception. *Quarterly Journal of Experimental Psychology*, 1954, 6, 86–92.

Murdock, B. B., Jr. Modality effects in short-term memory: Storage or retrieval? *Journal of Experimental Psychology*, 1968, 77, 79–86.

Neisser, U. *Cognitive psychology.* New York: Appleton-Century-Crofts, 1967.

Nickerson, R. S. Short-term memory for complex meaningful visual configurations. A demonstration of capacity. *Canadian Journal of Psychology*, 1965, 19, 155–160.

Noble, C. E., & Parker, C. V. C. The Montana scale of meaningfulness. *Psychological Reports*, 1960, 7, 325–331.

Norman, C., & Rieber, M. Facilitation of concept formation in children by the use of color cues. *Journal of Experimental Psychology*, 1968, 76, 460–463.

Norman, D. A. (Ed.) *Models of human memory.* New York: Academic Press, 1970.

Oh, C. Y. *A study of the development of children's ability to perceive depth in static two-dimensional pictures.* (Doctoral dissertation, Indiana University) Ann Arbor, Mich.: University Microfilms, 1968. No. 69-4793.

Paivio, A. Mental imagery in associative learning and memory. *Psychological Review*, 1969, 76, 241–263.

Paivio, A., & Foth, D. Imaginal and verbal

mediators and noun concreteness in paired-associate learning: The elusive interaction. *Journal of Verbal Learning and Verbal Behavior,* 1970, 9, 384–390.

Paivio, A., Rogers, T. B., & Smythe, P. C. Why are pictures easier to recall than words? *Psychonomic Science,* 1968, 11, 137–138.

Popham, W. J. Curriculum materials. *Review of Educational Research,* 1969, 39, 319–338.

Posner, M. I., & Keele, S. W. Decay of visual information from a single letter. *Science,* 1967, 158, 137–139.

Pryluck, C. Structural analysis of motion pictures as a symbol system. *AV Communication Review,* 1968, 16, 372–402.

Reese, H. W. Imagery and contextual meaning. *Psychological Bulletin,* 1970, 73, 404–414.

Reid, I., & Travers, R. M. W. Time required to switch attention. *American Educational Research Journal,* 1968, 5, 203–211.

Rohwer, W. D., Jr. Socioeconomic status, intelligence and learning proficiency in children. Paper presented at the meeting of the American Psychological Association, San Francisco, September, 1968.

Rohwer, W. D., Jr. Images and pictures in children's learning: Research results and educational implications. *Psychological Bulletin,* 1970, 73, 393–403.

Rohwer, W. D., Jr., Lynch, S., Levin, J. R., & Suzuki, N. Pictorial and verbal factors in the efficient learning of paired associates. *Journal of Educational Psychology,* 1967, 58, 278–284.

Rosenbusch, M. H., & Gardner, D. B. Reproduction of visual and auditory rhythm patterns by children. *Perceptual and Motor Skills,* 1968, 26, 1271–1276.

Roshal, S. M. *Effects of learner representation in film-mediated perceptual-motor learning: Rapid mass learning.* Pennsylvania State College. Instructional film research program. Technical report, Port Washington, N.Y.: Office of Naval Research, Special Devices Center, 1949.

Ross, J., & Lawrence, K. A. Some observations on memory artifice. *Psychonomic Science,* 1968, 13, 107–108.

Salomon, G. What does it do to Johnny? A cognitive-functionalistic view of research on media. In G. Salomon, & R. E. Snow (Eds.), *Commentaries on research in instructional*

media: An examination of conceptual schemes. Bloomington, Ind.: Indiana University, 1970. Pp. 33–62.

Sampson, J. R. Further study of encoding and arousal factors in free recall of verbal and visual material. *Psychonomic Science,* 1969, 16, 221–222.

Samuels, S. J. Attentional process in reading: The effect of pictures on the acquisition of reading responses. *Journal of Educational Psychology,* 1967, 58, 337–342.

Samuels, S. J. Effects of pictures on learning to read, comprehension and attitudes. *Review of Educational Research,* 1970, 40, 397–407.

Sassenrath, J. M., & Yonge, G. D. Delayed information feedback, feedback cues, retention set, and delayed retention. *Journal of Educational Psychology,* 1968, 59, 69–73.

Sassenrath, J. M., & Yonge, G. D. Effects of delayed information feedback and feedback cues in learning on delayed retention. *Journal of Educational Psychology,* 1969, 60, 174–177.

Scanlon, T. J. Color television: New language? *Journalism Quarterly,* 1967, 44, 225–230.

Scanlon, T. J. Viewer perceptions on color, black and white TV: An experiment. *Journalism Quarterly,* 1970, 47, 366–368.

Schramm, W. L. *The research on programed instruction.* Washington, D.C.: U.S. Government Printing Office, 1964.

Schulz, R. W. *Learning of aurally received verbal material.* Iowa City: Iowa University Press, 1969. ED 027 591.

Schulz, R. W., & Hopkins, R. H. Presentation mode and meaningfulness as variables in several verbal-learning tasks. *Journal of Verbal Learning and Verbal Behavior,* 1968, 7, 1–13.

Schulz, R. W., & Kasschau, R. A. Serial learning as a function of meaningfulness and mode of presentation with audio and visual stimuli of equivalent duration. *Journal of Experimental Psychology,* 1966, 71, 350–354.

Severin, W. The effectiveness of relevant pictures in multiple-channel communications. *AV Communication Review,* 1967, 15, 386–401.

Shepard, R. N. Recognition memory for words, sentences, and pictures. *Journal of Verbal Learning and Verbal Behavior,* 1967, 6, 156–163.

Silverman, R. E. *The comparative effectiveness*

of animated and static transparencies. Technical report No. SDC 78-1. Port Washington, N.Y.: U.S. Naval Training Device Center, 1958.

Smith, K. U. The scientific principles of textbook design and illustration. *AV Communication Review*, 1960, 8, 27–49.

Snow, R. E., & Salomon, G. Aptitudes and instructional media. *AV Communication Review*, 1968, 16, 341–357.

Spaulding, S. Research on pictorial illustration. *AV Communication Review*, 1955, 3, 34–45.

Spaulding, S. Communication potential of pictorial illustration. *AV Communication Review*, 1956, 4, 31–46.

Standing, L., Conezio, J., & Haber, R. N. Perception and memory for pictures: Single-trial learning of 2500 visual stimuli. *Psychonomic Science*, 1970, 19, 73–74.

Steinfeld, G. J. Concepts of set and availability and their relation to the reorganization of ambiguous pictorial stimuli. *Psychological Review*, 1967, 74, 505–522.

Stickell, D. W. *A critical review of the methodology and results of research comparing televised and face-to-face instruction.* (Doctoral dissertation, The Pennsylvania State University) Ann Arbor, Mich.: University Microfilms, 1963. No. 64-1419.

Thalberg, S. P. *An experimental investigation of the relative efficiency of the auditory and visual modes of presentation of verbal material.* (Doctoral dissertation, State University of Iowa) Ann Arbor, Mich.: University Microfilms, 1964. No. 64-7949.

Tobias, S. Effect of creativity, response mode, and subject matter familiarity on achievement from programmed instruction. *Journal of Educational Psychology*, 1969, 60, 453–460.

Tosti, D. T., & Ball, J. R. A behavioral approach to instructional design and media selection. *AV Communication Review*, 1969, 17, 5–25.

Travers, R. M. W. *Research and theory related to audiovisual information transmission.* (Rev. ed.) U.S.O.E. Contract No. 3-20-003. Washington, D.C.: U.S. Department of Health, Education, and Welfare, Office of Education, 1967.

Travers, R. M. W. *A study of the advantages and disadvantages of using simplified visual presentations in instructional materials.* Final Report, Grant N. OEG-1-71070144-5235. Washington, D.C.: U.S. Office of Education, 1969. ED 031 951.

Travers, R. M. W. *Man's information system.* Scranton, Pa.: Chandler, 1970.

Travers, R. M. W., & Alvarado, V. The design of pictures for teaching children in elementary school. *AV Communication Review*, 1970, 18, 47–64.

Tulving, E., & Lindsay, P. H. Identification of simultaneously presented simple visual and auditory stimuli. *Acta Psychologica*, 1967, 27, 101–109.

Tversky, B. Pictorial and verbal encoding in a short-term memory task. *Perception and Psychophysics*, 1969, 6, 225–233.

Van Mondfrans, A. P., & Travers, R. M. W. Learning of redundant material presented through two sensory modalities. *Perceptual and Motor Skills*, 1964, 19, 743–751.

Van Mondfrans, A. P., & Travers, R. M. W. Paired-associate learning within and across sense modalities and involving simultaneous and sequential presentations. *American Educational Research Journal*, 1965, 2, 89–99.

Van Valkenburg, J. *Learning through listening: Implications for reading.* (Doctoral dissertation, The University of Rochester) Ann Arbor, Mich.: University Microfilms, 1968. No. 68-15,881.

Westover, F. L. A comparison of listening and reading as a means of testing. *Journal of Educational Research*, 1958, 52, 23–26.

Wheelbarger, J. J. *An investigation of the role of pictorial complexity in visual perception.* (Doctoral dissertation, University of Virginia) Ann Arbor, Mich.: University Microfilms, 1970. No. 71-6636.

Wicker, F. W. Photographs, drawings, and nouns as stimuli in paired-associate learning. *Psychonomic Science*, 1970, 18, 205-206.

Williams, J. M., & Derks, P. L. Mode of presentation and the acquisition of paired associates that differ in pronunciability and association value. *Journal of Verbal Learning and Verbal Behavior*, 1963, 2, 453–456.

Wulfeck, J. W., & Zeitlin, L. R. Human capabilities and limitations. In R. M. Gagné (Ed.), *Psychological principles in system development.* New York: Holt, Rinehart & Winston, 1962. Pp. 115–156.

CHAPTER 28 Reading Research[1]

GABRIEL M. DELLA-PIANA
University of Utah

GEORGE T. ENDO
University of Utah

This chapter does not attempt a comprehensive review of the field but rather focuses on selected topics with an emphasis on highlighting studies and sources which appear to be productive for methodological,

theoretical or practical values in developing a body of generalizable knowledge about reading and in improving reading instruction. The chapter is divided into three major sections: comparative treatment studies of beginning reading programs, reading processes, and the technology of reading instruction.

COMPARATIVE TREATMENT STUDIES

Method comparisons of complex treatments have produced significant controversy as research paradigms. The controversy exists primarily because when complex treatment conditions are compared, the specific characteristics of the treatments which produced the results are said to be unknown (e.g., Travers, 1962, p. 520; Samuels, 1969a). Others (e.g., Stolurow, 1960) see no utility in such studies. Some (e.g., Cronbach, 1966) have argued that the best treatment comparison is one in which there is optimization of each treatment within a fixed time so that the best example of each treatment is compared even if the content itself is not held constant. Even though ex-

[1] Readers desiring to survey the field are referred to some major sources: The *Reading Research Quarterly* which includes periodic summaries of investigations in reading; the ERIC-CRIER basic references (Summers & Siffin, 1970); summaries coming out of the Southwest Regional Laboratory (e.g., Desberg & Berdiansky, 1968); *The Reading Teacher; The Journal of Reading;* and *Journal of Reading Behavior*. In addition, a comprehensive review of research in reading is under way in connection with the U.S. Office of Education-supported Targeted Research and Development Program on Reading (Ellson, 1970; Gephart, 1970). The first phase of this proposed twenty-year program is to conduct a literature search and synthesis on the reading process, the learning to read process, and language development related to reading. The objective of this search is to delineate models for these processes. The second literature search will focus on instructional practice. Funding for the program may not continue, but several reports are forthcoming. For an overview of the total program and a critique of the program see Gephart (1970) and Ellson (1970). For a report on two of the massive literature reviews already completed see Davis (1971) and Corder (1971). For reports on current developments in the National Assessment Survey of Reading, see Education Commission of the States (undated).

perimental controls may be hampered in comparisons of complex treatments, statistical controls (e.g., covariance) can be used to exclude some of the alternative interpretations. And, of course, as in any type of research, generality can be demonstrated through direct and systematic replications.

In spite of the limitations noted, treatment comparisons do have value. Promising hypotheses can be generated concerning treatment-aptitude interactions so that further work can be pursued to verify the hypotheses and optimize a treatment for a given aptitude pattern (Marks, 1964). If concurrent observation of teacher or pupil behavior is conducted, variables or relationships not previously or clearly identified might be uncovered (Reid, 1968). And hunches could be generated for a theory of information processing which could be programmed for computer simulation and tested by comparing the behavior of the computer with the behavior of subjects when both are given the same problem (Newell & Simon, 1961).

This section reports on some comparative treatment studies of beginning reading under the following headings: Chall's Conclusions, The USOE-sponsored first-grade reading studies, treatments relevant to neurological deficiencies, and aptitude-treatment interactions.

Chall's Conclusions

Chall's (1967) study entitled *Learning to Read: The Great Debate* presents a number of major conclusions and observations, among which are the following:

1. Methods which have a code emphasis (earlier, heavier, or more direct emphasis on teaching the sound values of the letters) produced better overall reading achievement by the beginning of fourth grade than methods with a meaning emphasis (phonics introduced later, more moderate in amount or through a process of analyzing known sight words or by use of context).

2. The child reads faster in the early stages of learning by meaning-emphasis methods, but the advantage is lost by third or fourth grade. Also, the meaning emphasis is associated with poorer comprehension and vocabulary in about the third grade, probably because of poorer word recognition.

3. Under a code emphasis the child reads more slowly at the beginning because he is stressing accuracy, but by grade three or four his rate is at least equal to that produced under a meaning emphasis. Also, the early advantage in word recognition accuracy produces better vocabulary and comprehension on silent reading tests by grade two.

4. Teaching the code can be done by a variety of methods. The direct teaching of letter-sound correspondences is as successful or more successful than the "discovery" approach of the so-called linguistic methods.

5. Modified alphabet schemes (such as Initial Teaching Alphabet) may of course be used with code emphasis or meaning emphasis. When these methods are used with control of words or spelling patterns so that the child may discover the letter-sound correspondence, children master the code more effectively than when exposed to high frequency irregularly spelled words with late and little phonics.

6. Children of average or below average general scholastic aptitude and lower socio-economic background probably perform better under a code emphasis than a meaning emphasis although the differences do not show up immediately. The differences between a code emphasis and a meaning emphasis are not as great for high scholastic aptitude children because they tend to discover sound-letter relationships even though not directly taught (e.g., Gibson's work in a later section of this chapter entitled, "Experimental Analysis of Graphic Perception and Decoding").

7. Ability to give the names of letters of the alphabet prior to learning to read helps the child whether under a code or meaning emphasis (but see Samuels, 1969b, 1970a in

the section on Experimental Approach below). This also holds for being able to produce the sound values for written letters and hearing similarities and differences in spoken words. Also, letter and phonics knowledge is more highly correlated with reading achievement than is mental age or IQ.

The USOE-Sponsored First-Grade Studies

Many of the findings of the USOE-sponsored first-grade reading studies (Bond & Dykstra, 1967) and the second-grade follow-up of the USOE-sponsored first-grade studies (Bond & Dykstra, 1967; Dykstra, 1967) are similar to those reported by Chall for earlier studies. Meaning emphasis methods (the Basal Approach) were less effective in general than code emphasis methods such as the Initial Teaching Alphabet and phonic linguistic programs. But no one program or method was superior for all outcomes and types of pupils. The Basal Approach in these studies included all sets of materials possessing most of the following characteristics: vocabulary, based on frequency of usage rather than regularity of sound-symbol relationships, was introduced slowly and repeated often; phonic analysis, introduced after some sight words, was gradually taught and was only one of the word-attack approaches among others such as use of context, structural analysis and picture clues; comprehension and interpretation of what was read was emphasized from the beginning; and silent reading was emphasized early. The Initial Teaching Alphabet approaches had in common a novel 44 character alphabet representing the major 44 sounds of the English language. A transition to traditional orthography using the conventional alphabet was part of the method. The Phonic/Linguistic program (Lippincott materials) was included as a separate treatment because, although it controlled vocabulary on the basis of sound-symbol correspondences and introduced vocabulary rapidly (and thus was similar to

the linguistic programs), it used a unique set of filmstrips correlated with reading to facilitate word recognition, meaning and motivation. The other major approach used was the Language Experience approach which emphasized using the child's own writing as the material for teaching reading and provided fewer highly structured instructional materials. Also, vocabulary control was handled by using the child's own language produced in an environment to stimulate language production.

The major results for the first year of the study were as follows: There were many treatments by project interactions. Treatment variances were very similar whereas treatment means were not. The Phonic/Linguistics program was superior to the Basal in word reading, paragraph meaning, spelling and word-study skills. Adding a supplementary phonics program to the Basal produced results superior to the Basal. There were very few significant interpretable treatment by aptitude (intelligence, auditory discrimination, letter knowledge) interactions. The Linguistics group outperformed Basals on word recognition tests while the Basal groups evidenced greater speed and accuracy in reading, and there were no differences in comprehension for this comparison.

For the second year the above results were confirmed. The Phonic/Linguistics group was superior to Basals in word reading, paragraph meaning, vocabulary and spelling.

In one of the better designed USOE-sponsored projects involving multiple methods comparisons, the Phonic/Linguistics program (Lippincott) was compared with Initial Teaching Alphabet, Basals (Scott, Foresman), and a Basal supplemented by phonics (Scott, Foresman plus *Phonics and Word Power*) in a third-year follow-up (Hayes & Wuest, 1969). There was a systematic attempt to monitor and train teachers to maintain fidelity to the assigned treatment. Treatment IQ means and the teacher-effectiveness ratings were similar. The results showed that the number of classes with 50 percent or more pupils achieving at least one-half grade above the predicted levels of word meaning, word-study skills and paragraph meaning by the end of third grade were four out of five (4/5), 4/5, 3/5, 2/5, and 2/4 for the Lippincott, Initial Teaching Alphabet, Merrill, Scott, Foresman plus *Phonics and Word Power,* and Scott, Foresman, respectively. Also, Lippincott was significantly superior to Initial Teaching Alphabet, Scott, Foresman, and *Phonics and Word Power* for high IQ pupils on paragraph meaning, but not significantly different for middle and low IQ groups. On Gilmore Oral Reading Comprehension, Initial Teaching Alphabet was superior. The Initial Teaching Alphabet and Lippincott were superior on word recognition measured by the Gates and Fry word lists, but by April of grade 3 the differences were no longer significant. Most Initial Teaching Alphabet pupils made the transfer to traditional orthography by grade 2 and the Initial Teaching Alphabet group was superior to Scott, Foresman and Lippincott on Gilmore Comprehension by April of grade 3. Finally, although the formal study ended in grade 3 and all pupils were taught by Scott, Foresman in grade 4, in February of grade 4 the Lippincott evidenced significantly greater performance than the other three groups on word meaning.

The reader is directed to a series of studies by Gillooly (1966a, 1966b, 1967, 1968, and 1969), who argued that the Initial Teaching Alphabet is not superior to most traditional orthography reading series. Gillooly cited as reasons for his argument a variety of methodological shortcomings in the studies reviewed in addition to the findings that Initial Teaching Alphabet children exhibited more spelling errors (although these might be transient) and more difficulty transferring to traditional orthography.

The difficulties in interpreting the USOE-sponsored beginning reading studies cannot be ignored. Nevertheless, the past decade has produced some convincing experimental support for earlier and more intense programs of word-analysis instruction than was common in the 1940s and 1950s, more rapidly introduced vocabulary, and more emphasis initially on words with regular symbol-sound relationships. Our own work using the McGraw-Hill Programmed Reading Series (Reid, 1968) confirmed this conclusion along with the well-designed, significant studies by Bliesmer and Yarborough (1965) and Tanyzer and Alpert (1965). But the lack of consistent superiority of results with the phonic-linguistic materials across both projects and ability levels and the occasional superiority of other approaches for specific outcomes warrant more systematic investigation of aptitude-treatment interactions (see next section). Additionally more studies are needed which utilize refined, curricular-relevant, molecular measures of reading outcome, as are more studies which evaluate the treatment selected against criterion-referenced, curricularly relevant measures which are revised until the treatment effectiveness is maximized (Della-Piana, Hogben, & Anderson, 1969). For hints as to variables affecting maintenance of early gains in reading skills see Durkin (1966) and McKee and others (1966).

Methods Relevant to Neurological Deficiencies

Reed, Rabe, and Mankinen (1970) reviewed 42 articles dealing with methods of training brain-damaged children indexed under the terms "dyslexia," "perceptually handicapped child," "brain-injured child," "minimal cerebral dysfunction," etc. Only nine articles representing seven studies were considered honest efforts to investigate experimentally the efficacy of the methods used. The reviewers focused primarily upon the adequacy of criteria for establishing the neurological condition of subjects. A criterial shortcoming due to a lack of specification was noted for establishing the diagnosis. Also, there was a noticeable lack of detailed information on neurological examinations. Because of the inadequacies noted, the authors were unable to examine the efficacy of the reading methods used for impaired children. They concluded from their findings that there is no empirical basis for recommending specific techniques of instruction for specific types of difficulties, such as those proposed by Cruickshank (1966) and Kephart (Cruickshank, 1966), that would not be equally appropriate for nonimpaired children with similar kinds of learning disabilities. This criticism, of course, does not extend to the effectiveness of the methods for teaching children with specific learning disabilities, but simply states that on the basis of current data there is no recommended preferred treatment based on differential diagnosis of specific neurological impairment.

A set of 15 experiments relevant to Delacato's (1959, 1963, 1966) theory and treatment with respect to neurological organization and reading performance has been reviewed by Glass and Robbins (1967). Delacato argues that some reading problems are a result of impairment of neurological growth at some stage prior to the achievement of complete neurological organization. The appropriate treatment for such cases is the determination of the stage at which neurological growth was impaired and the initiation of training or therapy to foster the complete neurological organization from that point on. For example, the diagnosis of neurological organization at the level of the midbrain is determined in part by observing eye movement during tracking of objects moved by the child in his own hand. If indeed the visual tracking is not smooth, then training is initiated to teach proper performance of the visual tracking task.

Glass and Robbins (1967) wrote a highly critical analysis of the evaluative attempts of 15 studies dealing with the Delacato approach. Four major criticisms were given. These included failure to control for up-ward regression effect due to lack of control group, failure to use adequate matching techniques and methods of randomization, failure to use the appropriate data (i.e., unit of analysis), and failure to control for experimenter's bias. Taking together the criticisms of the studies reviewed and the negative results of more well-controlled studies (e.g., Robbins, 1966), the authors argued that current data support neither the Delacato theory nor the therapy presented for improving reading performance.

Aptitude-Treatment Interactions

The search for aptitude-treatment interactions represented in the Cronbach and Snow (1969) report is a significant line of research for more productive method comparisons. Not many studies of this type have been methodologically sound. Some pilot studies by Snow and Stallings (Cronbach & Snow, 1969, pp. 111–113) are illustrative of the methodology and data generated by this line of research. They compared alternative instructional methods in initial reading. The aptitude measures were the auditory and visual sequencing tests of the Illinois Test of Psycholinguistic Abilities (ITPA). The Auditory-Vocal Sequential Test requires the child to respond to items such as "Listen. Say 6-8-9." The Visual-Motor Sequential Test requires responses to items in which the examiner places on a tray before the child a sequence of a square, a triangle and a circle. The child is given five seconds to examine them and then they are dumped off and the examiner says, "Now make one just like mine." Experimental versions of the Auditory-Vocal and Visual-Motor Sequencing Tests were developed to eliminate the nonlinguistic portions of the tests. Twenty first-graders were divided randomly to form two comparable groups on the basis of an aptitude battery. For the first two months of school one group received a phonics treatment using Fry's material and the other received a look-say treatment using Scott, Foresman materials. Two teachers unaware of subjects' aptitude scores alternated daily to balance treatments. Dependent variables included the California Achievement Test in reading and the Murphy-Durrell Readiness Analysis, both given after two months. Another dependent variable was observations of avoidance (e.g., excessive fidgeting, distracting others) during reading instruction. The avoidant behavior correlated 0.82 with similar observations by teachers in children's other classes. The frequency of avoidance of learning behavior was differently related to visual sequencing skill in the two treatments. In the Look-Say Treatment, high visual sequencers showed little avoidance behavior and low sequencers showed much avoidance behavior. In the Phonics Treatment the relationship was reversed, with high visual sequencers showing much avoidance behavior. The phonics method served poor visual sequencers best, perhaps because it provides a substitute for the poor sequencing ability and short memory in its analytical structured drill. The more able visual sequencers were better off in reading achievement under the look-say method. Phonics yielded poorer results on reading achievement for more able subjects, probably because of boredom (see results for avoidance behaviors above).

In a follow-up study with seven classes of first-grade children using the whole word approach and six classes using a linguistic approach, there was a significant interaction between the two treatments on the auditory vocal sequencing test of the Illinois Test of Psycholinguistic Abilities and all five achievement test scores (Stallings, 1970). In sum, auditory sequencing ability is necessary to perform well in the linguistic method of reading. However, children with low ITPA auditory vocal scores on the Illinois Test of Psycholinguistic Abilities (below 15) did better with a whole word method while those with scores above 15 achieved more in the linguistic method. Likewise, high visual sequencing scores (experimental version) were more closely related to high achievement test scores in the linguistic treatment. Also, if a pupil scored high on either a visual or auditory sequencing pretest, he also scored high on the opposite mode in the posttest if he was in the linguistic treatment. For the whole word treatment the pretest sequencing scores were unrelated to posttest sequencing scores. Also, children who scored low on avoidance of learning behavior in September also scored high on the achievement test scores in January if they were in the linguistic treatment. This seems reasonable when one notes that identifying small units (letters) and putting them together in predetermined sequences (word) would positively influence the sequencing abilities of pupils who were low on avoidance behavior and therefore could pay attention to the task.

Also, pupils in the linguistic treatment scoring high on avoidance of learning behavior in September scored low in January. But in the whole word treatment those scoring high on the first observation also scored high later, and children scoring low in visual sequencing tests were likely to show more avoidance behavior in the whole word treatment.

In summary, the linguistic method of teaching reading is superior to the whole word method for most children, particularly higher sequencing ability children. Below a certain level of sequencing ability (15 on the Illinois Test of Psycholinguistic Abilities auditory sequential test and eight on the experimental visual sequential test), a child could be placed in a whole word method to maximize his chances of success. However, an alternate solution for the low sequencer not yet investigated may be training in sequencing in preschool.

Cronbach and Snow reported some intriguing findings here and there but stated that none of it has been pursued with enough replication and validity generalization studies to be impressive. They concluded that there are no solidly established aptitude-treatment interaction relations or even hypotheses ready for application and development. The arguments they gave are, in addition to lack of replications, in part that conceptualizations of treatment dimensions are too gross, that conceptualizations of aptitude variables are also inadequate, and that the methodology appropriate to predicting from differential aptitudes to high performance on differential vocational assignments appears to be abortive in predicting from differential aptitudes to high performance on the same tasks. Thus, they see this as a high-risk research area which ought to be encouraged because of the tenability of the expectations in spite of the methodological problems of the research (see also Shulman, 1970).

In a stimulating volume on early experience and visual information processing in relation to perceptual and reading disorders (Young & Lindsley, 1970), the reader will find considerable attention to more molecular measures of processes related to reading performance ranging from Young's suggestion for refinements in the measurement of visual acuity (p. 377f) to Kagan's approach to assessing reflection-impulsivity (p. 347f). Perhaps this literature from disciplines working on reading-related phenomena will help in suggesting the variables called for by Cronbach and Snow (1969).

THE CONCEPTUAL, EMPIRICAL, AND EXPERIMENTAL ANALYSES OF THE READING PROCESSES

One of the most compelling, potentially fruitful domains of reading research is the little understood phenomenon referred to as the reading process. The reading process is said to consist of unobservable events which putatively mediate between the initial visualization of graphic symbols and the terminal behavior of reading which it produces. The questions as to how the process works and what elements and mechanisms are involved have received no definitive answers. Recent studies generated within the frameworks of various methodological approaches may provide a relatively

better understanding of reading skills. The three major approaches to the analysis of reading processes considered here are the conceptual approach, the empirical approach and the experimental approach.

CONCEPTUAL APPROACH

This classification includes a range of studies from various methodological approaches which merit attention because of their potential value as models and microtheories of reading analysis. The common feature shared by the studies in this section is the attempt made in each to formalize the reading process even though the basis for each may differ, e.g., inductive, deductive, empirical. Of course, in evaluating such studies, heuristic, predictive and explanatory powers should be the principal concerns.

Wolf, Huck and King (1967) began with a definition and a three-factor construct described in the literature. This was elaborated into detailed behavioral terms and submitted to "experts" for a critique including ratings of importance of the skills and notations as to skills omitted. The revised list was then checked for completeness in elementary-school classrooms by including in the list any critical reading behaviors observed which were not already on the list. The test was then developed and subsequently submitted to factor analysis.

Otto (1968) presented a hierarchically arranged set of behavioral objectives in reading at the elementary level. The scope and sequence of the skills were developed by consensus among teachers, unit leaders and reading consultants. The list is intended to be prototypic rather than dogmatic. It is not clear from the report exactly in what sense the list is hierarchical and thus it is not possible to compare the hierarchy with the findings of the relative effectiveness of different emphases on meaning or phonic analysis in beginning reading programs. One of the limitations of such an approach is that it might include more skills than are necessary for achievement of the major objectives of reading instruction. Thus, an empirical approach to reducing the list to the minimum or optimum subset would be desirable.

A taxonomy of concepts and critical abilities related to the assessment of verbal arguments has also been developed by Allen, Feezel, and Kauffeld (1967). This comprehensive taxonomy is based on Stephen Toulmin's *The Uses of Argument* (1958) and is a practical set of definitions of concepts necessary for critical evaluation of everyday discourse and a set of tests for assessing abilities for such evaluation.

Sample: Indicate whether you think the person or group cited is an acceptable source for the information cited.
Football Coach: After the lights went out, I heard three boys boxing two others at the far end of the lockers.
State Department of Education: Most of the public high schools in our state have less than 3,000 students.

This is a test of the evaluation of testimony; other parts of this test assess comparisons of two pieces of testimony for the better of the two and for the effect of a second testimony on a previous one.

"Reading is a psycholinguistic process by which the reader (a language user) reconstructs, as best he can, a message which has been encoded by a writer as a graphic display" (Goodman, 1970b, p. 103). Goodman (1970b) identifies three cue systems in the reading process: graphophonic—responds to graphic sequences with sounds utilizing correspondences between the graphic and phonological systems of his English dialect; syntactic—uses pattern markers such as function words and inflectional suffixes which are cues to predict structures; semantic—feeds into the reading process his own experience and conceptual background.

He sees readers as making predictions from which they may recover when producing miscues which change meaning, syntax or sound in unacceptable ways. It is puzzling that far less success is achieved in learning to read than in learning to speak since the former is learned in school and the latter is not taught in an organized fashion.

Goodman states six generalizations about learning to read which are basically hypotheses derived from his own research analysis. In brief these hypotheses are:

1. If a child has oral language he can learn to read.
2. If a child has oral language it will assist him in comprehending written language.
3. Reading instruction should center on comprehension strategies.
4. The reading process cannot be broken up into subskills to be taught nor can it be subdivided into categories like code-breaking and comprehension without making a qualitative change in the process.
5. Reading instruction should be carried out with text material using natural, meaningful language within the conceptual grasp of learners.
6. Initial literacy should be achieved in reading material representing the child's own oral language.

Goodman (1969), on the basis of taped oral reading behavior, developed a taxonomy of cues and miscues in reading through the analysis of natural language. Goodman uses the term *miscues* rather than *reading errors* to avoid the connotation of errors. Not all miscues are bad; good reading is not free from miscues. Suppose the text sentence, "He was *folding* the check," was read as, "He was *holding* the check," by a child named Daniel. Goodman's taxonomy provides an analysis including observations such as: he did not correct it, *folding* and *holding* are both verbs, a substitution was made, it was a word substitution, there was one grapheme difference in observed and expected response, syntax was acceptable and unchanged, and meaning was acceptable but changed. A further analysis of Daniel's miscues indicated that there was little relationship between miscues and comprehension, some miscues did not change meaning, miscues were corrected more often when meaning was affected and/or syntax was unacceptable, and dialect-related miscues did not cause meaning change. The significance of Goodman's taxonomy is not merely in its utility for interpreting reading errors (i.e., miscues), but in its verification of a theoretical view of reading as more than matching letters or sounds or naming words, a view of reading as a complex psycholinguistic process in which responses are cued or miscued by a variety of graphophonic, syntactic and semantic events.

Kirk (1966, pp. 180–196) and Bateman (1967) discussed the contributions made by the Illinois Test of Psycholinguistic Abilities to reading diagnosis and treatment. The test was based on a communication model of Osgood (1957), Osgood and Miron (1963), and Wepman, Jones, Bock, and Pelt (1960). The value of these tests and experimental modifications of them for research on aptitude-treatment interactions is illustrated in the Cronbach and Snow (1969) and Stallings (1970) studies reported earlier in this chapter.

Hively (1966) presented the basic elements in a taxonomy for the analysis of reading behavior. He specifies six elements: A = nonverbal stimuli (taste, touch, color, design, nonlinguistic sounds), A = nonverbal and nonlinguistic responses (copying designs, matching to design), a = written verbal stimuli or responses and a = spoken verbal stimuli or responses. He also distinguishes between multiple-choice association tasks and free-response association tasks. For example, A: a, b in a multiple choice association task signifies that the subject is to select the appropriate spoken symbol (a or b) to fit the nonverbal referent (A). Also, for the pattern $a \rightarrow$ a, in a free response association task the "a" signifies that the subject is to write a symbol and "$a \rightarrow$" signifies that it be written in response to a spoken stimulus. Likewise A: A, B, in a multiple-choice matching task signifies that the subject is to match-to-sample with nonverbal stimuli. The pattern $a \rightarrow a$ in a free re-

sponse matching task signifies that the subject is to repeat the spoken verbal stimulus (i.e., make an echoic response).

Hively provides illustrations of nine tasks in reading based on these elements as follows:

1. Nonlinguistic responses: A-A, a-A, a-A
2. Spoken responses: A-a, a-a, a-a
3. Written responses: A-a, a-a, a-a

The categories of behavior represented by A-a and a-A (silent reading and writing or reading for the deaf) and a-a, and a-a (transcription) are descriptive of what is considered criterion behavior in reading. The categories of behavior represented by a-A and A-a (speaking and listening or first language learning) are descriptive of behaviors assumed to be prerequisite to reading. The model proposed is intended as a framework to assist in the analysis of reading behavior and the development of programs for reading instruction.

It is clear that the approaches to understanding the reading process derived from psycholinguistics are not taxonomic in the traditional sense, although Goodman uses that term for some of the schemes he has developed. Rather, they provide a more complex and presumably more accurate and useful model for analyzing word recognition and comprehension skills. For a fairly comprehensive review of some of these approaches see the article by Calfee and Venezky (1969) and other reports in the volume edited by Goodman and Fleming (1969) (see also Burke & Goodman, 1970, and McNeil, 1970).

EMPIRICAL APPROACH

Some correlational design studies are discussed in this section. Readers who are interested in the use of some types of correlation designs as a method of causal analysis are referred to Cattell (1966).

Hall and Robinson (1945) analyzed 25 reading and study-skills tests. Out of the 25 tests in the battery, only five distinct abilities were clearly identified: carefulness in reading, inductive reasoning rate, verbal or word meaning, rate for unrelated facts and chart reading.

C. W. Harris (1948) investigated the distinctness of the ability to understand poetry and ability to understand prose. He found that with seven tests assessing comprehension of prose and poetry there was little evidence for two different abilities.

Olson, Simpson, Rosen, and Rentz (1968), using data gathered from first grades, identified four oblique factors of reading readiness. These included auditory-visual discrimination, verbal comprehension, perceptual organization and verbal association. Similar factors were again identified by Olson and Rosen (1971) using first-grade students.

Holmes (1970) identified a number of factors accounting for variance in reading speed and power and proposed a *Substrata-Factor Theory* of reading which states in part that reading is a complex process in which a hierarchy of abilities is brought into play according to the purpose of the reader (see also Holmes & Singer, 1964).

Singer (1970) hypothesized a developmental model and tested it by determining whether substrata-factors at successively higher grade levels (3 through 6) have systematic changes in magnitude or composition associated with the improvement of speed of reading. Singer's data yielded factors accounting for 47 percent of the variance in speed of reading at grade 3 and 69 percent at grade 4. Speed of word perception (ability to recognize words and phrases quickly) and visual verbal meaning (ability to recognize a word and match it with a synonym) together accounted for 37 percent of the variance at grade 3 and at grade 6.

The Primary Test Level II of the *Ohio State University Critical Reading Tests* was administered to 341 third-graders and then submitted to factor analysis by Wolf and Mehrotra (1969). Four minor group factors identified were literary analysis, comprehension of underlying elements, logical analysis, and inference, each having specific factors which accounted for most of the variance.

While the studies surveyed are not exhaustive, it is clear that different factor structures are often reported. In fact a recent review of factor-analytic studies of reading (Farr, 1969) revealed considerable disparity in results. With different tests, subjects, and factor-analytic techniques it is not surprising that some studies yield one factor and others six and that the factors are different (see also Furst, 1950).

It is suggested that careful consideration be given to the reliability and validity of tests used whenever factor analyses or regression analyses are performed. Additionally, direct and systematic replications are essential before much can be imputed to the findings. Nevertheless, empirical research has as its main value the ability to reduce massive amounts of data to a few significant factors. It is thus possible to evaluate and include many variables on the basis of communality and orthogonality. Correlational techniques are valuable tools when viewed within a framework as one step in a total research strategy. They can be used to generate new measures (see Shores & Saupe, 1953). It would be most desirable to subsequently submit to behavioral and linguistic analyses and experimental tests the possible sources of variance discovered by the empirical methods.

EXPERIMENTAL APPROACH

Experimental analysis can lead us to the development of more elemental measures of reading behavior. It is quite possible that the development of purer measures of micro-skills will result in more significant payoffs in basic research on reading. Behavior theory and neurochemical theories might then generate experimental studies which produce consistently lawful relationships between independent variables and reading behavior.

Some of the significant attempts to submit the reading process to experimental investigation are discussed below. Studies from other approaches are also included when deemed necessary. The topical headings are arranged on a hierarchical basis. Hopefully the topic order presented will provide a look at the reading process from the most elemental precursors to the most complex behaviors.

Experimental Analysis of Graphic Perception and Decoding

Examples of how the perceptual process and the development of percepts might occur are provided by the following studies.

Haber and his associates concluded that primitive percepts develop as a function of repeated exposures. The conclusion was based on the fact that the subject's ability to perceive all letters of tachistoscopically presented words exhibited a similar type of development regardless of whether the words used were common English words (Haber & Hershenson, 1965; Hershenson & Haber, 1965), rare words (Haber, 1965), nonsense words (Hershenson & Haber, 1965), or words of which the subject had prior knowledge (Haber, 1965). Prior knowledge did facilitate initial perception but the later development of the percept assumed growth functions similar to percepts for which the subject had no prior knowledge. Standing, Sell, Boss, and Haber (1970) concluded that perceptual development as a function of repeated exposure is a purely perceptual process which is akin to Hebb's notion of growth of cell assembly, a neurophysiological process. And repeated exposure results in more than facilitation of simple sensory discrimination (Haber, Standing, & Boss, 1970). Haber, Standing, and Boss (1970) concluded that repetition represents a mediated process since percepts of uppercase letters facilitated the perception of their lowercase counterparts. The reason for the mediated process is said to result because of some feature other than the physical form of the letter's identity.

The research of Gibson (1970) and her students provides another interpretation of the analysis of graphic perception and decoding. She reasons that there is an internal motivation for the reduction of uncertainty or the discovery of structures that reduce information processing. While the evidence for the conclusion with respect to motivation is at present sketchy, it is a significant, plausible hypothesis. A brief resumé of her studies is presented here based on her recent review (Gibson, 1970). Children given a stylus that leaves a trace spent significantly more time in voluntary scribbling (mean of 72 seconds) than children with a nontracing tool (mean of 21 seconds) (Gibson & Yonas, 1968). This was interpreted as evidence for visual stimulation as a reinforcer or source of motivation. Gibson, Schapiro, and Yonas (1968) and Gibson and Yonas (1968) reported that letters are distinguished from one another by virtue of their distinctive patterns. What has emerged is error and latency data showing the significance for discriminability of dimensions such as verticality, horizontality, diagonality, curvature, openness, or closeness. The latter study included adult subjects and seven-year-olds.

Confusion matrices were developed for two sets of nine Roman capitals and a set of nine artificial graphemes. The letter pairs in which Ss made same-different judgments were based on actual errors in differentiating letters as well as an intuitive pairing. Latencies and errors yielded high intercorrelations. In a replicated study, latencies for discriminating artificial graphemes were nearly the same as for letters, suggesting that the same set of distinctive features was probably successfully built in. In hierarchical cluster analysis of latency data for children, the first split separated out clean curves (CGPR) from straight letters (EFMNW). On the second split the round letters (CG) are branched off from P and R and the square letters (EF) from those with diagonality (MNW).

If rulelike information in *orthography* provides the structuring of units for reading, are these patterns learned as invariant patterns or as a search for regularities? Gibson (1970) concluded that children can discriminate the presence or absence of two specific letters that are pointed out to them (so**ng**, **r**i**ng**, **t**eam, **r**ea**d**, **ch**op, **ch**in) but that this is not the ability that leads to detecting common spelling patterns among items. Instead, she proposed that a child learns to search for invariant patterns and a discovery of them is necessary for transfer to new problems. The evidence comes from a series of studies, one of which included a searching set condition in which pairs of words were presented to children, along with instructions which induced a general hint, specific hint, or no hint. The result was that it is better (in terms of fewer errors and shorter latencies) to get only a general hint to search for invariant features in a stimulus array than it is to get "specific" help. A study by Lott, Smith, and Cronnell (1968) appears to support the notion of search for invariant patterns or regularities.

But how about the process of decoding written symbols to speech? "Pronounceable" letter strings (e.g., glurck) produced **more** accurate recall of the letters with short **exposures** than "unpronounceable" ones (e.g., ckurgl) where pronounceability was defined in terms of regularity of mapping of clusters of phonemes onto clusters of letters (Gibson, Pick, Osser, & Hammond, 1962). But if it was pronounceability that made these strings easier to read, deaf subjects should not perform as well as hearing subjects on the pronounceable combinations. This was not true (Gibson, Shurcliff, & Yonas, 1972). Gibson interpreted this as meaning that there is a kind of grammar of letter sequences in which certain combinations are permissible for certain structures (e.g., gl for beginning a word). Another possibility of unit-forming principles is that of morphological rules. For example, if endings that mark tenses or forms carry over as units, one might expect that a five-letter word (start) transformed to a six- or eight-letter word by a regular ending (starts, starting) may be read with greater accuracy **and** shorter latency than nontransformed

words of equal length. Errors in responding to transformed words did not occur in the endings as frequently as they did for nontransformed words of the same length. Also, when an error did occur it tended to be substitution of another regular ending (e.g., -ing for -ed). Thus, it appears that the ending is detected as a marker or feature added to a stem word prior to specifically identifying it.

Another method for determining the perceptual decoding processes stems from the following studies. Gibson (1965) conducted a study in which the introspective data were perhaps more significant than the experimental data. She identified three phases of learning as a child begins his progression from spoken to written language: 1) differentiating graphic symbols (logically precursive to reading); 2) decoding letters to sounds; and 3) using progressively higher-order units of structure. Phase 2 is the process of "associating a graphic stimulus with the appropriate spoken response...." As a test of phase 2, adult subjects were taught Arabic words to try to simulate the child's process of learning to read. Gibson found that the letter-training group performed better on transferring skills to new words than the word-training group. But the significant finding came out of her asking each subject to explain how he tried to learn the transfer words. Most of the letter-trained subjects reported using knowledge of component letter-to-sound correspondences. But so did 12 of the 20 subjects in the word-trained group. And the scores of the 12 on the transfer test were similar to the letter-trained subjects, whereas the remaining eight subjects performed no better than the control group. Gibson's data raise serious questions about assumptions that treatments can be defined in terms of what the experimenter does to the subject rather than what the subject does in response to the experimenter's manipulations. Further, the study points up the problems in translating a reading process (phase 2) into procedures for training.

Reitman (1970) used information processing and computer-simulation concepts and techniques as a basis for the development of a *model of memory behavior and memory processes in reading*. The general approach makes use of "protocol collection methods" to generate tentative hypotheses which are later submitted to experimental tests.

In spite of the limitations of such data, there is evidence that it may contain significant clues as to what is going on. The subjects *do* improve their own performance. Protocol reports *are* predictive of other behavioral data. And giving subjects instructions to use procedures similar to those they generate *does* result in significant improvement in performance. One thing is obvious. The data generated by the experiments described suggest that the experimental procedure does not decouple a distinct simple memory subsystem and inactivate the rest of the subject's cognitive system. The evidence is that the subject's behavior is much more complicated and involves the development and provisional try of a variety of strategies for coding and retrieving the information presented. Identifying these strategies and relating them to individual and task variables as well as seeing how they are built up or developed certainly comes closer to the complex phenomena involved in memory.

This approach to isolating reading and recall process has the value of recognizing the complexity involved but would most likely benefit from analysis of protocol data from a psycholinguistic framework.

Predictors of Beginning Reading Performance

The child's ability to name letters has been regarded as one of the best predictors of beginning reading performance (Bond & Dykstra, 1967). In Dykstra's (1966) review he confirmed letter naming as a good index of reading achievement. A study by DeHirsch, Jansky, and Langford (1966), using a battery of 37 tests, yielded similar results. While the studies involved a small sample (N = 53 children aged about 5.2 to 6.5), they illustrated the value of cutting scores on tests measuring a variety of processes so that prediction can lead to treatment decisions on component processes of reading.

That letter-naming is a valid predictor is not without controversy. Samuels (1969b) differed with the import assigned to letter-naming and argued instead that knowledge of letter sounds is the more relevant variable. Indeed, research by Ohnmacht (Samuels, 1969b) demonstrated that letter-trained subjects performed no better on transfer tasks than control subjects and that the letter- and sound-trained group performed significantly better than either group. R. J. Johnson (1970) and Samuels (1970b) both reported the relative ineffectiveness of letter-naming knowledge on transfer tasks. Knowledge of both letter names and letter sounds is indispensable for further acquisition and development of hierarchical reading skills. Unless there is a tremendously high correlation between knowledge of letter names and letter sounds, both should be taught by the practitioner. Of course, the question remains as to why either or both variables are predictors and what other variables contribute to performance. It is quite likely that some of the psycholinguistic variables assessed by Goodman (1969, 1970b) and by Holden and MacGinitie (1969) may contribute to accounting for variance in beginning reading performance.

Holden and MacGinitie (1969) investigated the relationship of kindergarten children's awareness of lexical units to reading readiness and beginning reading performance. The technique involved presenting tape-recorded utterances which the child was to repeat. When the child had repeated an utterance correctly (several tries if necessary) he was asked to tap one poker chip (from a line of eight in front of him) for each word. The score was based on this final repetition with tapping, with one point for each correctly identified word boundary.

The most common error made by the children was compounding a function word with the following content word but the compounding depended on the context. Common compounds were have-to (in "you have to go home"), to-eat (in "the dog wanted to eat"), is-drinking (in "Bill is drinking soda"), the-men (in "houses were built by the men"). Of course, at the end of grade 1 most able children made almost no errors. But since current readiness tests account for only ⅓ to ½ of the variance in end of first-year reading achievement, other indices are worth exploring. There are low correlations between scores on this instrument for assessing ability to identify lexical boundaries and readiness test scores. If there is a high correlation with reading achievement in the beginning stages of reading, we may have a significant contribution to prediction of beginning reading success and possibly to programming preventive treatments.

Oakland (1969) investigated the relationship between social class and phonemic and nonphonemic auditory discrimination ability among first-graders. He found that in no case did a lower socioeconomic group perform significantly better than a higher socioeconomic group on either phonemic or nonphonemic measures. Since children with poor auditory discrimination are more likely to be poor readers (Christine & Christine, 1964) and since nonphonemic assessment overcomes problems associated with dialect differences and permits analysis of frequency, intensity and pattern dimensions of auditory signals, it appears a profitable direction for diagnosis and research with respect to prediction of beginning reading performance and treatment programs.

The studies reviewed by Farquhar (1965) on home factors in predicting reading achievement must be interpreted cautiously if one is to explain the correlation of 0.80 between home factors and fourth-grade achievement. The home environment measures used in the studies included pupil reports of their own school performance.

While the efficacy of television as an educational medium is not clear, it is interesting to note that the amount of viewing of the program "Sesame Street" was significantly related to the amount learned as reported by the Educational Testing Service (Today's McGuffy, 1971). The amount viewed overrode such variables as age, sex, IQ and socioeconomic status. Of course, what was learned was the materials stressed (e.g., naming, recognizing and matching letters). In the final analysis, the most important outcome of the project would be to determine academic success based on the amount viewed, amount learned, and what was learned.

Schiffman (1964), in a four-year survey of 10,000 children, found that early intervention (grade 2 versus grade 9) with children having reading problems yielded considerably greater success but that many children who showed significant gains did not maintain them. Early prediction with diagnostic utility could lead to the construction of better curricula with appropriate research and developmental validation processes.

For a review of research on reading readiness tests for prediction and diagnosis of reading performance see Dykstra (1966). Harckham's (1970) report also contains a comprehensive summary of readiness tests. The major deficiency in current data is on the use of such information for differential treatment. The work on Aptitude-Treatment Interaction studies cited above is a move to provide data in this direction.

Experimental Analysis of Transfer and Word Recognition Processes

What is the process of visual word recognition or differentiation of graphic symbols? It is after all not clear from the gross comparative methods studies *why* it is that the phonic-linguistic programs yield generally superior performance in word recognition. In the late 1800s Cattell concluded that whole words (if not too long or unfamiliar) can be read with as short a latency as a single letter. While this finding led many educators to conclude that reading should be taught by some kind of "whole word" approach, the method was not clearly indicated by the data. Indeed, children taught that way could not recognize many new words nor analyze words into their more elemental components (Bowden, 1911). There is also impressive clinical evidence that extreme "whole word" methods and extreme word-analysis methods each yield their own kinds of casualties. Durrell (1960, p. 197) noted that in 1930, 90 percent of the children with severe reading disability attending the Boston University Educational Clinic evidenced signs of overintensive work in phonics of the type where each grapheme was sounded and blended with the next. The symptoms were slow recognition of words and phrases, difficulty in synthesizing sounds, and lack of higher level syllabication skills. But six years later, when there was a shift to newer reading methods, 90 percent were so weak in word analysis that they could not discriminate words of similar form, guessed aimlessly at words, and made no attempt at word analysis. Thus, a clear specification of optimum methods for teaching word recognition requires research on the process and technological developmental work on the techniques.

The previously cited works (Gibson, 1970; Gibson et al., 1962; Gibson, Osser, Schiff, & Smith, 1963; Gibson, Schapiro, & Yonas, 1968; Gibson, Shurcliff, & Yonas, 1972; Gibson & Yonas, 1968) have thrown some light on the matter. Gibson (1970) reasoned that knowledge of component relationships within words is necessary for transfer of word recognition strategies to the recognition of new words. While Gibson argues that the motivation for reducing massive inputs of data through search for invariant patterns or regularities is internal, and while her research has provided some compelling findings, many questions remain unanswered. For example, should

children be taught the alphabet based on distinctive and configural aspects of the letters? Provided that meaningful groups of letters can be found, what method of teaching will best facilitate learning and transfer? Some (Karraker & Doke, 1970) have argued for errorless discrimination training of the type proposed by Terrace (1963a, 1963b). Errorless discrimination training involves fading techniques of the nondiscriminative stimulus which is paired with the discriminative stimulus during the initial or later part of the discrimination training. Others such as Samuels (1971) believe that a matching to sample technique presents the best method of alphabet training and that training should occur on groups of letters based on their distinguishing characteristics. Once the alphabet is learned, what method will best suggest meaningful psychological and psycholinguistic and linguistic groupings of phonemes which will best promote word attack skills? Such questions can be extended throughout each level of the reading process. Certainly the research of Gibson and her associates has opened up a new trend in the analysis of word-attack skills as well as the entire area of reading processes.

Sullivan, Okada, and Niedermeyer (1971) investigated the effectiveness of the single-letter approach and letter-combination approach of word-attack instruction for beginning first-graders of three different ability levels. The single-letter approach involved a letter-by-letter sounding out of new words, and the letter-combination approach involved a technique in which children were taught ending vowel-consonant and vowel-consonant-consonant combinations as single grapheme-phoneme units. The criterion measures were 1) words and letter sounds given during training and 2) transfer words composed of the original grapheme-phoneme units. The two treatment groups did not differ significantly on the criterion measures. There was a significant treatment by ability interaction, however. The high-ability, letter-combination trained group performed higher than the high-ability, single-letter trained group, whereas the reverse was true for low-ability subjects.

The effects of four language units upon subsequent recall and transfer of training of kindergarten children were assessed by Skailand (1971). The four units were the grapheme/phoneme approach (synthetic), the morpheme approach (similar spelling pattern), the morphophoneme/morpho-grapheme approach (contrastive spelling pattern), and the whole word approach (sight). The transfer words contained the same correspondence as words and syllables which had been taught, but each differed in one letter. Skailand found that spelling-pattern treatment groups were able to recall significantly more items than the remaining groups. No significant differences were found among the groups with respect to transfer, although the direction of results favored the spelling groups.

Otto and Pizzillo (1971) investigated the effects of three levels of intralist similarity (number of similar letters in words—none to all) upon acquisition rate, word recognition and generalization among kindergarten children. The groups differed significantly on acquisition rate in this order from fastest to slowest: no similarity, medium similarity and high similarity. Word recognition among the three groups did not differ significantly. For transfer, the no-similarity group outperformed the combined performances of the remaining groups. A perusal of the words used in the generalization (transfer) task revealed some puzzling task characteristics. In terms of the number of different letters used in the transfer task and not used in the initial set of words, it was discovered that for the no-similarity group there was one different letter, for the medium similarity group three different letters, and for the high similarity group four different letters. Whether such differences constitute an adequate test for generalization is open to question.

Marsh and Sherman (1970) conducted a study of transfer of word components to words and vice versa. They had three word lists: W (whole words such as pat, men), SO (sounded-out words such as p-a-t, m-e-n) and L (isolated letter sounds such as a, e, m, n, p, t). Six major groups were formed to study the transfer effects of learning one task to performance on another. The six groups were W-SO, W-L, SO-W, SO-L, L-W, and L-SO. Subjects were prekinder-garten and kindergarten children. The first list was learned in two successive errorless trials and the second in a single correct trial or a maximum of 10 trials. Study trials alternated with recall trials. There were two major outcomes. First, direction of training did not make a difference in transfer. That is, none of the following comparisons reached significance: W-SO versus SO-W; W-L versus L-W; and L-SO versus SO-L. Second, the greatest amounts of transfer were between sounded-out words and isolated letter sounds and between sounded words and whole words.

As is evident, not too much is clear about the factors which produce transfer from one situation to the next. It cannot be argued that the sole reason for the failure of various instructional methods to yield clear transfer effects was because of inadequate control of various subject characteristics, tasks used and so forth. An analysis of the methodological approach may yield some suggestions for the resulting lack of transfer. In typical designs as used by the previously mentioned studies, transfer effects were assessed immediately following training. Some math-learning models (e.g., three-state Markov process) postulate a relatively regularly appearing plateau effect following a certain amount of learning. Could this be the reason why transfer of training fails to occur? A longitudinal assessment could provide the answer. Other clues regarding the transfer problem could possibly be obtained if the types of errors emitted during criterion testing were recorded. Unfortunately such data are seldom gathered. While methods of error classifications such as those produced by Goodman (1969), cited earlier, and by Dunn-Rankin (1970) may not be totally applicable; some relevant ideas may be generated by them to produce a taxonomy of errors which occur during criterion testing.

A comprehensive survey of the literature on visual word-recognition was reported from Southwest Regional Laboratory (Lott, 1969). Before children can translate alphabetic symbols into meaning they must be able to discriminate the alphabetic symbols. On the basis of her comprehensive literature review Lott hypothesizes six stages of training: perceptual training (direction of scan and attention to relevant cue dimensions in nonsense figures), training in the use of distinctive features of letters and words (letter learning by discrimination training), training in the use of critical features sets of letters and words (configurations of curves, diagonals, etc.), training in the use of alternative criterial sets, training in the use of functionally equivalent criterial sets of features (different type styles and cases) and training in the use of redundancy (frequently occurring spelling patterns).

Richardson and Hiniker (1970) presented developmental testing data on an attempt to individualize instruction in decoding skills in a regular classroom situation. Other investigators who have accomplished similar tasks in individual tutoring situations were cited by the authors (Gotkin, McSweeney, & Richardson, 1969; Silberman, 1963). Subjects were 36 kindergarteners who had two hours per week of reading in a regular program. The experimental program ran for five months daily including 39 six-minute group lessons and 18 ten-minute group games plus individual remedial sessions varying from zero to 38 depending on the child's performance. The significance of this type of study is not that the program worked but that it could be managed in a regular classroom and that a generalized word-analysis skill was learned. Generalized blending was not successfully learned. The blending procedure was not described in detail, but the techniques described by Cole-man (1970) and Engelmann (SRA, 1969) are likely to get better results.

Fairchild (1967) used a sequential cue presentation procedure to assess the effect of various clues as aids in identification of unknown words in a group of fifth-graders of average or above average reading achievement and word-analysis skills. If a subject could not by use of context alone produce the word which was replaced by a blank, additional cues provided were initial elements, final elements and remaining vowels. High performers in identifying words by use of context and word element cues were superior to low performers in sight-word vocabulary, listening-meaning vocabulary and reading achievement. Context clues without additional word elements produced meaningful substitutions more than exact words.

For a comprehensive summary of recent research on word attack see Desberg and Berdiansky (1968). In their summary they focus on the work of a half dozen investigators: Marchbanks and Levin (1965), Bishop (1964), Samuels and Jeffrey (1966), Gibson et al. (1962), Gibson, Schapiro, and Yonas (1968), Gibson, Shurcliff, and Yonas (1972), the Stanford group (Wilson & Atkinson, 1967), and Venezky and Weir (1966). Desberg and Berdiansky assessed the work of Venezky and Weir as the most complete investigation of English orthography and corresponding pronunciation to date. Their spelling-to-sound rules for reading instruction and vocabulary selection make use of the morphophonemic levels of rules (mediating between grapheme sequences and phonemes) and thereby account for more regularity in the language than depicted by traditional investigators.

Dialect and Reading

For a dramatic introduction to the issues in the effect of dialect on training in reading see Rystrom (1970), who attempted to train black pupils in approximating white speech and found that there was no significant effect of such training on reading achievement. Then read Goodman's (1970a) response to the Rystrom study in which he takes issue with attempts to drill on a few selected features of a language in a way that introduces uncertainties for order and confusion for confidence. According to Goodman, even if black pupils actually learned to produce final /s/ or other ending sounds whenever they saw certain letters, they would be hearing themselves produce unfamiliar sound sequences foreign to their own dialects. Goodman argued that reading instruction should not reject the child's language but build on it. He stated that using language-experience approaches and personalized reading programs will yield better results. But the data are not yet in.

On the basis of a literature survey, several experiments, and analysis of preprimers and primers, Hatch (1969a; 1969b) concluded that there is a mismatch between language used in reading books and that used by the kindergarten child. Also, even where children have used some structures, comprehension and production problems are still evident and such structures do appear in beginning reading books. In one study children moved markers on a four-column bead abacus in response to taped commands. A sample command was, "Move a *yellow* one before you move a green one." In another study children pushed a lever to indicate which of two pictures projected on a screen correctly represented the taped stimulus sentence. Sample sentences are: "*If* it's red, raise your hand," "*Unless* it's red, raise your hand." Misinterpreted sentence meanings occurred in various *if-then* clauses for kindergarten subjects, in *unless* clauses followed by an affirmative for second-grade subjects, and in *before/after* time clauses with reversed temporal order for kindergarten subjects. Shuy (1968), Goodman (1965), Baratz (1968) and Baratz and Shuy (1969) recommended changing materials to correspond with the child's language whereas Bereiter and Engelmann recommended increasing the child's lan-

guage ability in standard English. Some of the research directions that would help clarify the issue are proposed by Hatch (1969b) (see also Brown & Deutsch, 1965; Donoviel, 1966; Hawkridge & others, 1968).

A comprehensive review of literature on social dialects and their implications for beginning reading instruction has come out of the Southwest Regional Laboratory (Legum, Williams, & Lee, 1969). The authors suggest gathering sociolinguistic data on black English as a basis for four kinds of action: developing a formal phonics-based reading program for black English-speakers; demonstrating that black English is as regular and general as Anglo-English; teaching black English as a second dialect for teachers; and teaching Anglo-English as a second dialect for black ghetto children.

Another contribution to the problems of nonstandard dialects and reading has been made by the Upper Midwest Regional Laboratory (Hess, 1970; Hess & Maxwell, 1969). Among other things this group has developed a survey instrument to determine the degree of social acceptability of specific dialect features. For example, in one area the usage of "don't got" may be considered strongly unacceptable whereas "in" for "ing" may be thought acceptable. The Laboratory project staff is working on means for training teachers to recognize and transcribe nonstandard utterances, create an individual dialect-usage curriculum for each student, and organize a bank of materials for use. Whatever the theoretical point of view, value orientation or practical concerns of those dealing with dialect, the projects would seem to have value for adapting materials to dialect or modifying dialect to suit the material.

Some of the observations of Garcia, Blackwell, Williams, and Simpkins (1969) are also relevant here. They analyzed the deficiencies in research in the black community. They cited observations by Bereiter and others to the effect that culturally deprived or disadvantaged children have not learned the language rules necessary for mature thinking, definition of concepts, making inferences, asking questions or explaining. And they cited Labov's data refuting this position. They argued for self-determination by blacks on what is researched, for applied research rather than obtaining knowledge for the sake of knowledge, for design and delineation of how the results of the research can be of use to the subjects, for commitments to report in communicable language, and for commitment of white researchers to get acquainted with the black experience prior to attempting research with blacks. The moral problems in research are discussed elsewhere in this volume. Some of the concerns leading to the statement by Garcia et al. (1969) are due to problems of validity of criterion measures, data obtained, and interpretation of data as discussed above in the work of Goodman, Hatch, and Legum.

Experimental Analyses of Factors Affecting Comprehension Processes of Connected Discourse

Mosberg and Shima (1969) view reading comprehension as a complex information-processing event and they reviewed the literature relevant to the topic. Comprehension is seen as a system of processes involving linguistic, psychological and perceptual events. Generally they see comprehension as the extraction and recall of new information from a language stimulus. The goal of the review is the development of a comprehension curriculum. To this end they consider how they will go about measuring information gain, what stimulus characteristics of passages may affect comprehension, and the theoretical issues relevant to the construction of a model of comprehension.

But what is meant when it is said that a child comprehends or does not comprehend? What skills are included in the concept of comprehension and how are these to be analyzed and eventually used for instructional purposes? Research findings are not too clear on any of the questions although the efforts are not new (Gray, 1958). Many focal points exist in attempting to determine what the relevant factors are concerning comprehension. Some of these are discussed below.

Linguistic factors. One of the most significant conceptual and methodological attempts at the analysis of comprehension has been generated by Bormuth (1969a; 1969c; 1970b) and Bormuth, Carr, Manning, and Pearson (1970). Disenchanted with past comprehension research because it has neither contributed to a general body of knowledge nor provided for a sound instructional theory, Bormuth (1969c) has reconceptualized the concept of comprehension and developed a unique methodological approach in an attempt to clarify the area. Bormuth begins with the following definition: "Comprehension skills are a set of generalized knowledge acquisition skills which permit people to acquire and exhibit information gained as a consequence of reading printed language" (1969c, p. 3). A taxonomy of comprehension skills has been described by Bormuth (1970b). From the definition given the following characteristics were derived: 1) that language is a stimulus, and language features (syntactical structures, semantics and so forth) signal information in an infinite number of forms; 2) that there is a unit of comprehension instruction which can be analyzed into its component parts and these include the language stimulus, types of test questions, and overt responses; 3) that comprehension is an increase in gain as a *direct result* of reading a passage. Thus, comprehension processes are viewed as corresponding to observable features, most of which can be manipulated both instructionally and experimentally. More specifically, a child can be taught the skills or rules required to decode information which is encoded in language features and he can be taught skills which will allow him to respond to various test questions.

Bormuth's research strategy can be seen in the following studies. His initial attempt (Bormuth, 1969a) was to identify linguistic features which may be causally related to comprehension processes. Bormuth identified five sets of linguistic features contained in 330 passages taken from 10 subject-matter areas taught to students from first grade to college level. The five sets of linguistic features provisionally identified as stimuli related to comprehension processes were vocabulary variables (features of words), parts of speech, number of transformationally derived syntactic structures, syntactic complexities as determined by various theories of sentence processing, and complexity and frequency of anaphoric structures. An *anaphora* is a word or phrase which shortens or substitutes (such as a pronoun) for an antecedent expression. The rationale underlying Bormuth's strategy to identify linguistic stimuli was that variables were causally related to comprehension processes only if such variables correlated with comprehension difficulty (as measured by cloze procedures[2]). Students in grades 4 to 12 were given cloze tests on passages appropriate to their age levels. Most of the variables assessed correlated with passage difficulty. Further attempts to reduce the number of possible variables through correlational analyses were not successful since a large number of variables exhibited correlation with passage difficulty but exhibited little common variation within most of the sets of the variables defined. There are a large number of manipulable features of language which may be involved in the comprehension processes. However, not all linguistic variables are causally related to comprehension even though they relate to difficulty since some of the variables cannot be independently varied. Bormuth excluded as causal variables language features such as parts of speech, sentence length and vocabulary. The exclusion was based on the

---

[2] See section on "Readability Factors" for definition of cloze technique.

reasoning that such variables can be varied only through operations which change sentence structures which in turn produce variation in parts of speech, sentence length and so forth. Thus, only transformational operations and not the effects of the operations can be held as causal. In the light of the reasoning stated, Bormuth concluded that only sentence structures, anaphora, and syntactic complexity variables are related to comprehension processes since they can be independently varied.

Bormuth et al. (1970) used fourth-grade subjects to assess the factual comprehension skills of three categories of linguistic structure in an effort to determine whether the skills represent homogeneous classes of behavior and are hierarchically related. The linguistic structure categories consisted of syntactic relationships within sentences, anaphoric expressions and intersentence syntax. Four types of questions were used to assess factual comprehension: rote questions, transform questions, semantic substitute questions and compound questions (the reader is referred to Bormuth, 1969c, for a detailed analysis and rationale for the types of questions used). The findings indicated significant within-class difficulties for each of the linguistic structure categories as well as significant differences exhibited among linguistic structure categories. The mean percentages of students responding correctly to the comprehension questions of each class of structure were as follows: syntactic relationship within sentence, 73 percent; anaphoric expressions, 77 percent; and intersentence syntax, 58 percent. The conclusion was that the skills are homogeneous but may be hierarchically related.

Hatch, Sheff, and Chastain (1969) studied five-year-old prereaders on a 10-minute task in which sentences had undergone a number of transformations and expansions of conjoined sentences. A stimulus sentence was presented (e.g., John ate a sandwich and Mary ate a hotdog) to the child to read and then the child was queried (e.g., What did Subject 2 do? Tell me about **Subject 1** and Subject 2). Two response measures were used in the study: accuracy and latency of response. The data show that transformation type was related to comprehension. Specifically, subject-verb order proved significantly better than verb-subject order. Deletion (reducing redundancy) made sentences more difficult. It is not yet clear whether the problem areas in sentence comprehension are due to permutations as a process or to a specific permutation such as the subject-verb order change.

Of relevance here is the finding of Rosenthal and Resnick (1971) concerning the facilitation of problem-solving of one step arithmetical (addition and subtraction) word problems. Third-grade subjects were given two sequences of information (parallel and reverse). Information sequence was referred to as the order in which the problem was stated. These examples were cited: "If John started out with 3 coins and he found 2 coins, how many coins did he end up with? How many coins did John end up with if he found 2 coins and he started out with 3 coins?" The first problem was considered to be parallel to the event sequence (actual order of events) and the second was considered to be the reverse. Significantly more parallel problems were solved than reverse problems.

R. E. Johnson (1970) devised a method of partitioning linguistic subunits. College students were asked to divide complex textual narratives (folktales) into pause-acceptability units. The subjects were told that the function served by pausing might be to catch a breath, give emphasis to the story, or enhance meaning. The rationale for devising the pause-acceptability units was that functional boundaries would be delineated and such boundaries might be used in encoding written passages. Additional raters were then asked to eliminate $\frac{1}{4}$, $\frac{1}{2}$ or $\frac{3}{4}$ of the subunits with the restriction that in each case the essence of the story would remain intact (structural importance). A series of three experiments suggested that even following various retention intervals and intra-trial intervals of presentation, structural importance of the linguistic units was related to amount of recall. R. E. Johnson (1971) applied the same techniques to textual prose again using college students as subjects. The findings were that recall was related to structural importance but the relationship was curvilinear. Johnson's rationale for pause-acceptability units to which he attributes psychological significance appears to parallel closely the notion of the previously cited works of Gibson and her associates concerning the subject's search for invariant patterns or regularities within passages. It would be interesting to know the frequencies and the types of syntactic structures within each of the structural importance categories. Such information would definitely add to the findings of the studies cited above which dealt with linguistic units (for an introspective research methodology on the problem see Ames, 1966).

Personality variables. Samuels (1970a) reviewed studies on the effects of pictures on learning to read, comprehension and attitudes. He found evidence that pictures interfere with acquisition of sight vocabulary, do not facilitate comprehension and can influence attitudes. The data on attitudes are not clear and there is no systematic research on how pictures may be used to develop attitudes (make texts and reading less aversive) and build comprehension and sight vocabulary through cueing responses and fading the picture cues away in the final stages of mastery.

Groff (1962) demonstrated that attitude toward content type of material influences reading comprehension. But the relationships in studies of this type are not easy to generalize as demonstrated by J. C. Johnson's study (1966) in which total recall was not related to attitude but other specific types of comprehension were related to specific attitudes. For example, literal comprehension of material with a culturally alien theme was related to culturally alien attitudes. Schnayer (1967) demonstrated that high reading interest produces reading performance beyond the mean reading performance of low interest stories for most students but that high ability students are less affected. But more analytic studies are needed in this area of research.

The relationships between various personality variables and reading comprehension are unclear. For example, Eysenck and Cookson (Farley & Truog, 1971) reported that extroverts were superior to introverts on reading performance and that subjects who scored either high or low on a neuroticism scale performed better than subjects who scored in the middle range. Farley and Truog (1970–1971), however, failed to replicate the above findings. Similarly, Johnson, Dunbar, and Hohn (1971) found no relationship between high and low anxiety groups and reading performance. While the conflicting results may be due to the tests used because of questions of reliability and validity, a more important question is what implications would such findings have for either remedial or instructional purposes. If personality inventories were supplemented with behavioral observations, a finding such as a high positive correlation between neuroticism and avoidance behaviors (similar to that described by Cronbach & Snow, 1969) might provide a viable approach in working with pupils classified as anxious or high in neuroticism.

Vocabulary factors. Shima (1970) studied the effects of associative strength (high, low-related and low-unrelated), trials (one or two readings of the material prior to testing) and retention interval (immediate or 24-hour delay) in recall of specific content words or sequences and recall of substance or main point of a passage. Contrary to other studies (Rosenberg, 1968), no associative facilitation was found. As a matter of fact, there was greater recall of both specific content and the main idea among subjects in the low-associative condition, i.e., where low-associative stimulus-response

(S-R) word pairs were embedded in the passages. The author reasoned that the differences in results may be due to the population (grade 5 children in this study, adults in other studies) and the use of S-R word pairs rather than S-R, R, R triads. Substance learning (main idea) was greater than content word recall (50 percent versus 32 percent) as in previous studies cited by Shima (1970) such as that of Yavuz. However, retention loss (the drop from short- to long-term) is not consistent with previous studies. Also, recall of chunks of information for connected discourse (3.23 word average) was greater than for single sentences (2.75 word average).

Samuels (1968) has experimentally isolated word-association strength and related it to reading speed and recall of paragraphs containing the words but equated for other characteristics such as semantic content and word length. As predicted, elementary-school and college students had significantly faster mean times and comprehension in reading paragraphs with words having high-associative relationships than in similar paragraphs with words having low-associative relationships. Studies of this sort open the way for experimental studies of other determinants of rate and comprehension since they allow selecting materials and subjects on the basis of excluding some determinants of the performance deficiencies. The problems of this associative approach for understanding retention of connected discourse are analyzed by Shima (1970). It is easy to see that selecting words for embedding in passages turns out quite differently if it is based on child norms for S-R associations rather than adult ratings of semantic communality.

Another promising line of comprehension process research with both methodological and substantive significance is that of Bloomer (1961a, 1961b) who found that emotional intensity of words was related to stimulus strength of meaning and investigated the relationship between accuracy of meaning and the number of meanings possessed by a word.

Reading rate. It is doubtful that gross rate of reading as such provides major theoretical or practical problems in the analysis of reading. In most skill learning, accurate performance with good form is usually followed by rapid gains in rate with a dropping off of unnecessary movements as a result of practice and simple motivation. That it is possible to make significant increases in reading rates through instruction is clear. But perhaps the more important issue is that of maintaining higher rates and of flexibility in rates of comprehension for different purposes.

Spache (1962) analyzed the speed of silent reading issue because of the considerable attention it has received in the press. He argues that 800 to 900 words a minute is the maximum silent reading speed physiologically possible if "reading" is defined in terms of discriminating most of the words on a page. The estimate is based on the fact that to read a 10-word line of four inches requires about 0.66 seconds because the shortest time for one fixation is 0.20 seconds, the time for a sweep to the next fixation is 0.05 seconds, the return sweep to the next line is 0.04 seconds and the maximum number of words that can be seen in continuous reading at a single fixation is three words.

Wark, Raygor, and Summers (1967) briefly cited studies and reviews of reading-rate research indicating that average increases in reading rates doubling preinstruction rate are commonly achieved without loss of comprehension, and that no one particular method is uniquely effective for all readers. Harris (1970) presents similar evidence together with data showing that rate increases may be achieved without expensive equipment. His students simply timed themselves and worked to beat their previous performances. Wark, Raygor, and Summers (1967) have demonstrated another efficiency; they produced mean gain

in reading rate equivalent to more typical instruction through a correspondence course. The mean rate difference from pre- to posttest in 19 previous studies was 238 words per minute (with final rate at 499 words per minute) and in the Wark, Raygor, and Summers study it was 223 words per minute (with final rate at 484 words per minute). Comprehension results were similar with final rates of 81 percent for the 19 previous studies and 87 percent for the Wark, Raygor, and Summers study.

Since rates should be adjusted to reading purpose it is important to know whether in fact reading rates do vary according to purpose and whether this variability is trainable. A paper from the Laboratory for Research in Basic Skills at the University of Wisconsin reported evidence that individual variability in adjusting reading speed to reading purpose (fact, main idea, sequence) was demonstrated by good readers at the fourth-grade level. Speed was defined as words per minute to reach full comprehension for a given purpose. Within individual speed, variability according to purpose of reading was greater for narrative than expository style. The findings on effects of training hold primarily for pupils who already possess well-developed reading skills. Specifically, training increases within individual variability, and fastest rates were for specific fact followed by main idea and sequence. Also, expository passage styles were read faster than narrative materials for sequence measures, but the reverse was true for main idea and fact.

Harris (1968, 1970) reviewed research on rates of reading comprehension and flexibility of rate. He cites evidence that most readers do not vary rate of reading according to purpose, that flexibility in rate can be developed, that conventional emphasis on rate generally improves rate moderately but does not change comprehension, that extreme emphasis on rate as in some of the new techniques can produce large gains in rate of reading (skimming) but at the expense of comprehension, and that study-skills training without rate training can produce significant gains in comprehension and grade-point average.

Readability factors. Readability of a passage has typically been associated with the lower and upper boundaries within which the maximum amount of comprehension occurs. A common practice is to select for supervised reading materials in which students can answer 75 percent or more of the questions, and to select for unsupervised reading materials in which students can answer 90 percent of the questions. Presumably materials below 75 percent comprehension condition aversive and avoidance responses to the reading tasks because of frequent failures.

The cloze technique (Taylor, 1953, 1956) for assessing readability of material has received considerable attention both for research and as a practical procedure which may overcome the limitations of earlier readability formulas (Chall, 1958). The essential feature of the technique is the deletion of randomly selected words in a passage which the reader is to fill in on the basis of context clues. Thus, highly redundant texts are very readable since deleted words are easy to fill in on the basis of remaining context. Tightly written texts would lose much in readability if every fifth word (excluding conjunctions and prepositions) were eliminated. The possible variation and uses of the technique are limitless. Schneyer (1965) suggested constructing cloze tests which eliminate words related to different kinds of content. Thus, if a student makes completions more effectively when deleted words are "concepts" than when they give clues to "relationships among concepts," the nature of his comprehension difficulty becomes clearer to the teacher. There is currently little evidence that cloze technique assesses anything other than what is assessed by conventional multiple-choice comprehension tests (Bormuth, 1969b), but the technique provides useful procedures for research (see also Mosberg, Potter, & Cornell, 1969).

For a comprehensive review of research on the cloze technique see Potter (1968). Potter hypothesizes that cloze scores based on function word deletions are likely to be related to syntactic complexity, and cloze scores based on content deletions are likely to be related to information load. Studies of hypotheses of this type are likely to yield more generalizable results than gross cloze scores.

Bloomer (1966) found that training of from three to 12 weeks in completing blanks in cloze exercises did not improve reading comprehension of students in grades 5, 7, 9, and 11. Schneyer (1965) obtained similar results for sixth-graders.

In earlier studies (Bormuth, 1967, 1969b) it was found that cloze readability test scores of 44 and 57 percent were comparable to the traditional difficulty levels of 75 and 90 percent, respectively. Thus it appears that the traditional 75 percent comprehension level for instructional material is supported by the Bormuth data. Of course, replication is needed on a variety of material with known syntactic characteristics and using tests constructed by other experimenters.

Bormuth is engaged in a series of studies designed to investigate information gain and affective responses in relation to materials of varying difficulty. In this particular study, Bormuth assessed further the relationship between cloze difficulty levels, information gains and readability levels as determined by other techniques. The general strategy of the study is as follows: students are matched (Students A and B) on the basis of the initial cloze test performance, then the difficulty level of another passage is ascertained by giving a cloze test to Student A of each pair. Next Student B is given two identical multiple-choice tests before and after reading the passage. Information gain for the pair of students on that particular passage is defined as the difference in scores between the two multiple-choice tests. The findings were that studying materials with a cloze readability of 22 percent yielded information gain of 13 percent. Studying materials with a cloze readability score of 37 percent yielded information gain of about 40 percent and reached asymptote.

Comprehension measures. The adequacy of typical measures of comprehension (e.g., achievement tests) has been questioned by two independent sources (Bormuth, 1969c, 1970a; Tuinman, 1970, 1971). Both investigators expressed concern that typical comprehension measures contain two components: questions which students can answer without having read the passage, and questions which students could answer only if the passage was read. Only the latter should be viewed as a gain in comprehension. Bormuth (1969c) argued further that serious interpretative errors of validity may result without further clarification of the problem. Bormuth recommended that all test constructors should specify not only the linguistic features used in the passages but also the population from which passages were derived (Bormuth's Theory of Comprehension Questions is contained in his 1969c article).

Tuinman (1970, 1971) cited a series of studies which demonstrated that subjects were able to answer passage questions without having read that passage and conducted a study in which his experimental passages yielded a mean score under the no-passage condition below or at the level which would occur by chance (0.25).

Still another method of measuring comprehension gain or information gain was devised by Coleman and Miller (1968) whose technique is an adaptation of Shannon's (1951) "Guessing Game Technique." The subject was asked to guess the first word in a passage and, if incorrect, given the right answer by *E*. Then the next word was guessed and so on. The passage was then given a second time. Information gain was defined as the difference between the correct number of guesses per 100 words be-

tween the first and second administrations. Mean guesses between the first and second test administrations were 33.73 and 72.66, respectively. Passages that maximized information gain for college subjects were at about the fifth-grade level. But if any one word was deleted from a 150-word passage at this level subjects were able to insert the correct word only 65 percent of the time.

Mathemagenic factors. Mathemagenic activities (Rothkopf, 1970) are those activities which "give birth to learning" according to the literal translation of the term coined by Rothkopf. Rothkopf has distinguished three classes of activity with mathemagenic significance for the use of written instructional material: orientation (getting subjects into the instructional situation), object acquisition (selecting and procuring appropriate instructional objects), translation into internal speech or representation, and the mental accompaniments of reading (including discrimination, segmentation, processing, etc.). Translating and processing is what is commonly called reacting. Rothkopf cites three studies of directly observable components of the reading process. Carmichael and Dearborn's study (1947) demonstrated that adjunct questions delayed the onset of *regressive eye-movement* patterns in prolonged reading. Schroeder and Holland (1968) demonstrated that *eye movement* patterns in search can be modified by consequences and brought under stimulus control. McGuigan and Rodier (1968) demonstrated that reading produced *respondent behaviors* measured by electromyographic potentials from the throat and face.

Hypothetical components of mathemagenic behaviors have also been demonstrated and are the focus of Rothkopf's own research. Vague hortatory directions affect subjects' mathemagenic activities enough to raise postreading test performance (Rothkopf, 1966). Specific search directions along with text characteristics also produce predictable forms of incidental learning (Frase, 1969). Adjunct questions presented after inspecting the text materials to which they are relevant affect mathemagenic activities more than no-question control groups and groups who saw the questions before inspecting the text segment (Rothkopf, 1966; Frase, 1967). Rothkopf sees this research as leading to a consideration of less attention to development of instructional materials and more to manipulations of the instructional environment to influence mathemagenic inspection activities of students. For a review of research on mathemagenic behaviors see Frase (1970).

Excellent materials get developed, but unless students attend to, inspect, search, discriminate—in short, respond to the material, there will be no learning. Rothkopf and Bloom (1970), in two separate experiments, have demonstrated confirmation of previous studies indicating that adjunct questions embedded within text materials resulted in higher performance than reading without questions, that some kind of periodic contact with a teacherlike person during reading resulted in higher performance than written adjunct questions embedded in the text, and that these two conditions (periodic contact with a person and adjunct questions within the materials) produce longer inspection of the written material. This latter result, of course, may be direct evidence of changes in mathemagenic activities brought about by the experimental manipulations.

Attentional determinants of performance such as those investigated by Rothkopf are more likely to be productive in identifying manipulable variables than the typical studies of affective factors in reading reviewed by Athey (1969).

But there are questions which remain such as: What factors modify mathemagenic behaviors? What causes positive mathemagenic behaviors to deteriorate? What are the most critical student activities affecting what is learned in instructional settings? Additionally, Rothkopf's (1966) contention that mathemagenic research findings are leading to more consideration

of manipulation of the instructional environment than to instructional materials assumes that all readers are capable of comprehension. Bormuth (1970a) would definitely challenge such an assumption based on his analysis of reading literacy. Moreover, since there is evidence that comprehension problems exist, other approaches (e.g., linguistics, psycholinguistics) also warrant much consideration.

Carver (1970) reviewed several studies dealing with mathemagenic behaviors, especially those by Frase and by Rothkopf, and argued that their complete disregard for two variables relevant to retention (amount of time reading and the subject's learning strategy) negates much of their findings. Specifically, Carver argued that testlike events produce a longer reading time and it is the longer reading time rather than the questions which is related to greater retention. Additionally, Carver stated that the use of vague instructions concerning the testlike events changes a subject's strategy, thus differences in strategy may also affect amount of retention. In addition to the criticisms cited, Carver also criticized the vagueness of Rothkopf's concept of mathemagenics.

Psychological factors. Anderson and his associates conducted a series of studies to see if recall of specific words and sentences was facilitated by semantic encoding rather than auditory or phonological encoding. Their reasoning was that semantic encoding provides meaningful representation of events contained within written discourse and thus facilitates recall. However, articulatory and phonological encoding simply stresses sound and therefore poorer recall is expected. Anderson, Goldberg, and Hidde (1971) found that asking a subject to fill in a blank facilitated more recall (presumably because filling a blank forces semantic encoding) than no blank conditions. Anderson and Hidde (1971) demonstrated that asking a subject to rate imagery-evoking value of sentences (assumed to be a part of meaningful representation) enhanced more recall than asking a subject to rate the pronounceability of sentences. Due to the results of another study, however, Anderson (1971) hypothesized that the ability to store and recall subject nouns of sentences may be a function of other long-term storage processes which are different from the one postulated to occur for semantic encoding. Anderson's results are not surprising since the works of Haber and his group, cited previously, revealed that frequent exposure leads to greater recognition and recall.

Amount of learning and time spent in reading prose passages of college subjects were assessed as a function of immediate, delayed or no feedback conditions and immediate, delayed or no-test conditions by Guthrie (1971). The main findings were that delayed feedback produced more learning than immediate feedback on the original learning material, but immediate feedback produced more perseverance on a continuation passage than delayed feedback. The results were discussed in terms of positive and negative affective responses due to type of feedback. Specifically, immediate feedback was postulated to evoke positive affect toward some aspect of the test situation such that the affect would generalize to similar passages and induce perseverance. The reverse was posited for the delayed feedback condition. Guthrie's study has direct bearing on programmed texts since immediate feedback is one of the key features assumed to promote learning. Additional studies independently varying types of materials, the ideas or facts to be comprehended, and various feedback conditions are warranted.

Clark and Walberg (1966) reported a significant effect on reading achievement by simply increasing the use of rewards such as social approval. But although general approaches to locating reinforcers are clearly prescribed (Addison & Homme, 1966), there are problems in applications of these general principles for specific children (Kerr, Meyerson, & Michael, 1965). One example of differential reinforcement for specific children from different socioeconomic status is Koos's work (1971). With the use of social and token reinforcement, Koos facilitated reading gains as well as other academic gains. The reader is also referred to an article by Ferritor, Buckholdt, Hamblin, and Smith (undated) which argued for designing specific contingencies for specific target behaviors.

Maroon, Washington, and Frase (undated) tested comprehension processes of students in grades 2, 4, and 6. The subjects were required to read prose passages based on three types of organization (concept, attribute, and scrambled), and then were tested on three levels of problem difficulty which required that for the subject to respond correctly he either had to relate one, two or three sentences. A binary response system was used to measure comprehension. All children experienced the most difficulty if the sentences had to be related rather than taken singly, especially for the poorly organized prose. Concept-organized sentences were comprehended the best, followed by attribute-organized and scramble-organized.

PRODUCT DEVELOPMENT

The distinguishing characteristics of research and development in education are outlined in a paper by the Director of the Southwest Regional Laboratory for Educational Research and Development (Schutz, 1970). The outcome of research is generalizable knowledge about human behavior and the outcome of development is a replicable set of techniques for producing behavior change. This section will include descriptions of product development efforts of the Southwest Regional Laboratory and other producers. Specifically we shall review the following: Coleman's Educational Engineering, the Stanford CAI project, the Computer and Instructional Management, Project PLAN and IPI, programmed tutoring, and the Southwest Regional Laboratory Kindergarten Reading and Support

Programs. There are no doubt other approaches such as the Wisconsin Design for Reading Skill Development (Quilling, 1971) not discussed here.

Coleman's Educational Engineering

The technology of education is in its infancy but there is powerful potential in the techniques and systems currently under development. Coleman's (1970) research strategy for educational engineering is based on the assumption that scientific knowledge must be transformed into numerical form in tables of measures which are useful for making engineering decisions. He discussed how the appropriate data base can be generated in a series of transforming experiments, that is, experiments which transform some of the laboratory generalizations about learning into useful tables. The transforming experiments reported yielded tables which scaled the most commonly occurring words for ease in reading (saying), scaled letter-sound associations for ease of learning, scaled phonic blendability of consonant-vowel and vowel-consonant syllables, and scaled letters for ease of discriminability. The research strategy is to begin with scaling studies (using subjects from target population) which rank-order materials according to rather gross or molar reading subskills. Later the materials under study are to be rank-ordered according to each of the more analytic stages of paired-associate learning.

Data for scaling are collected basically by the paired-associates anticipation method with a prespecified criterion of learning. The words used are carefully selected according to some relevant factors (e.g., regularity in spelling, frequency of usage).

Such tables are not only of immediate use for constructing a beginning reading program but are also of value in suggesting narrowband studies to isolate the specific variables which determine rank-order. Concerning the latter, for example, one might investigate the relationship between stimulus characteristics and discriminability, or the determinants of response availability or a set of rankings based upon meaningfulness or association values.

Many useful applications are associated with Coleman's general strategy. An instructional program can be developed more efficiently and effectively with such data. If beginning reading is sequenced according to ease of learning there will surely be gains in motivation and time to criterion, and teaching of phonic blending should be easier if it begins with that small number of words for which scaling studies found components that sound almost identical whether pronounced in isolation or blended (at, is, up, us) as opposed to words like too (tuh-oo). Thus there is significant value in this approach to the transformation of data into systematic tables which suggest immediate practical applications and productive research hypotheses.

The Stanford CAI Project

Since its experimental beginnings in 1965, the Stanford project has been committed to the development of a computer-assisted instruction (CAI) reading program with the dual purpose of developing models for instructional research and producing practical learning systems. One of the most successful efforts of the project is that of individualization. For example, at the end of the first year of the project the difference between the fastest and slowest students was more than 4,000 main line problems completed (Atkinson, 1968). A main line problem is a task on which a student exhibits mastery, such as identifying the letter "t" by typing "t" when it is presented as a visual display with the audiosignal, "type t." There are, of course, more complex problems. Extremely interesting is the fact that the differences in rate of progress through the curriculum were not correlated with response rate. The average response rate was about four per minute with small variation among students. Optimization schemes and other individualization procedures were said to be the reason for student success. Thus, it was found that presenting items equally often in a fixed order is less efficient and yields less variability in rate of getting through the program than an optimization routine in which the item presented fewest times previously and having the lowest count (add one to count if response is correct and set to "O" if it is incorrect) was the item presented at a given trial after the first run through all items in any order.

Other impressive results were that sex differences in achievement have been virtually eliminated, and by the use of CAI adjunct programs, for a 12-minute daily session a child can maintain at least a year's growth for each of the first three years of school as measured by standardized test performance.

The current Stanford CAI reading program emphasis is on decoding aspects of reading and leaves the emphasis on meaning to the regular classroom. Thus the program assumes that learning to read is facilitated by acquiring a large number of automatic or rapid phoneme-grapheme associations such as /aeb/ with *ab* or /eyb/ with *abe*. The procedure is CAI short drills. The CAI program can be an adjunct to any initial reading program. Their initial curriculum (in 1968) was linked with the commonly used basal readers in the local school district. The current curriculum is based on word lists from the major basic reading texts as well as common sightword lists. The vocabulary chosen was generated by computer scanning of these two lists to identify common occurrences and order of introduction (Atkinson, Fletcher, Chetin, & Stauffer, 1970).

A discussion of the Stanford CAI Reading Program is presented in relation to implications for a psychology of instruction (Atkinson & Paulson, 1970). A recent evaluation is presented in Fletcher and Atkinson (1971).

The Computer and Instructional Management

The computer has been used successfully for instructional management systems (Coulson & others, 1968). No experimental data are reported yet in terms of effects on pupil performance. The present report deals with data generated in getting the system operational. Preliminary post hoc analysis is encouraging, although much more work needs to be done. Teacher variability was evident in the use of the computerized materials and prescriptions. The one teacher who followed most of the instructions (e.g., changed children from one group to another based on the print-out, giving instructions for independent work) produced appreciable gains in students on reading skills. All participating students were divided according to three ability levels (high, medium and low) and according to three skills (phonic analysis, sentence comprehension and paragraph comprehension). Most teachers made few queries via teletype to find out the objectives for which a low achieving child needed help. All teachers, however, failed to follow up such information by asking for a prescription for low achievement. The data presented indicate the kinds of information provided to teachers to aid them in making decisions. The low level of teacher use of the total system suggests the need for a behavioral analysis to determine whether the data are of value, to identify incompatible responses which interfere with teacher use, to design a check list or guidance system to remind teachers to use the data, and to determine whether reinforcement must be provided for the teacher contingent on use of the system or production of pupil achievement gain.

Project PLAN and IPI

Flanagan (1970) reviewed selected research on variables relevant to individualizing education and described the beginnings of Project PLAN (Program for Learning in Accordance with Needs). The system can be briefly described in relation to five major decision points.

1. Students select their own objectives which were generated for grades 1–12 with teacher's assistance. Five objectives, each requiring two or three hours to achieve, are grouped into a module intended for about two weeks.

2. Teaching-learning units are developed for each module. A teaching-learning unit lists objectives, materials and alternative study routes.

3. Mastery of objectives is evaluated to determine subsequent student learning moves (e.g., placement, study routes).

4. Guidance and individual planning for students are provided by giving the student feedback on relevant intellectual and non-intellectual factors relevant to performance along with indications of probability of success in specific endeavors (e.g., engineering as a major). The student is familiarized with all available opportunities, aided in accepting and formalizing goals, and assisted in managing his own development.

5. Student development is managed by microteaching, modeling and practice followed by inservice training. Finally the computer is used as a clerical teacher support management device.

Current evaluation and research activities of Project PLAN were reported by Wright (1970a, 1970b). One feature reported was the attempt to recommend teaching-learning units on the basis of student characteristics. Rahmlow (1970) discussed how individualized teaching-learning units based on student performances improved learning.

The effects of Project PLAN on independent learning activities (e.g., starting assignments without reminders, unusually thorough job on assignments) of PLAN students and control students were compared (Jung, 1970). The critical incidents technique was used to help translate global objectives into more specific behavioral

terms. Fifth- and sixth-grade PLAN students exhibited more independent learning activities than control students. However, generalizability is limited because of the restricted sample of control students as opposed to PLAN students and the use of a self-report method of data collection.

Beck and Bolvin (1969) described the first four years of the individually prescribed instruction program (IPI) of the Learning Research and Development Center at the University of Pittsburgh. The major dimensions of individualization that are the current focus are:

1. Provision of opportunity for differential rates of progress through a sequenced set of objectives;

2. Mastery prior to moving to the next objective;

3. Self-direction, self-evaluation, and self-initiation on the part of the students; and

4. Development of individualized techniques and materials of instruction.

The curriculum contains about 400 behavioral objectives including 13 areas of study (e.g., literal comprehension, vocabulary development) and 11 levels of difficulty. Recordings which students can select and listen to are used to introduce sounds, new words, dictation exercises, etc. The basic material is Sullivan Associates *Programmed Reading* published by McGraw-Hill. The Individually Prescribed Instruction adaptation reduced by 50 percent the amount of work assigned in the first 14 books.

The lack of consistently significant superior reading performance of experimental PLAN and Individually Prescribed Instruction pupils over controls has been defended in terms of students being required to achieve mastery of a unit before going on and therefore not having exposure to as many skills as the controls who, however, have not mastered the skills. This is a strange defense since it is also assumed that individualized programs produce students who proceed at their own rate and are not held back by others. Data on these programs are at present quite limited, but since they are both now operational, it will be instructive to see whether the initial high cost of production and high cost of operation can be reduced and justified in terms of outcomes produced. For a discussion of the role of evaluation in such programs see Lindvall and Cox (1969).

PROGRAMMED TUTORING

Ellson, Barber, Engle, and Kanpwerth (1965), and Ellson, Harris, and Barber (1968) have developed a technique of programmed tutoring applied to the teaching of beginning reading. The first report detailed the initial development and field testing of the technique on 400 children of various ability levels. No tutored children in the group failed to read except one "normal" first-grader and some of a group of children with below 50 IQs. There are three significant values of the studies. First, a research strategy is demonstrated in which program development took priority initially and later yielded to experimental design requirements when the treatment technique was fairly well developed. Second, the treatment may be used as a supplement to any regular classroom program and therefore is consonant with approaches in which one may select a treatment out of several that proves generally effective and develop procedures to maximize its effectiveness. Third, the treatment technique yields individual and group data which are helpful for corrective instruction and program evaluation.

The authors began with an attempt to automate the teaching of sight-reading vocabulary to retarded children. Because of the need for a live person to discriminate correct and incorrect oral responses for instructional purposes, the program was not completely automated and is thus termed programmed tutoring. The studies are, of course, extensive, as are the methods. The method includes sight-reading, comprehen-

sion, and word analysis. Some of the basic methodology may be illustrated by the sight-reading program described in the first and second reports.

The teaching technique included identification of each word in a list and in a sentence and asking the child to read it before telling him the word. Five steps were involved. Step one tested the child's initial knowledge and steps three and five tested acquisition following training for incorrect responses on steps two and four. Immediate reinforcement, prompts and other procedures were used to promote learning.

The first report (Ellson et al., 1965) indicated that programmed tutoring alternated daily with classroom teaching was optimally effective and more effective than classroom teaching alone. The tutors were trained for about 12 hours and no effects of different tutors were detected. Word analysis was recommended to be moved to later in the instructional sequence since it appeared to benefit from sight-reading and comprehension. A shift toward more reading in context and less paired-associates learning was indicated.

The second report (Ellson, Harris, & Barber, 1968) yielded data on first-graders in 20 schools which included 16 low economic level schools and four lower middle-class schools. Two daily sessions of programmed tutoring were more effective than one, and directed tutoring ("individual attention" in completing reading-related activities) did not have significant effects. The major limitations in the reports are the lack of specification of results in criterion-referenced form (except for sections completed) or in terms of norm-referenced data.

SOUTHWEST REGIONAL LABORATORY KINDERGARTEN READING AND SUPPORT PROGRAMS

The comprehensive development procedures as cited by Schutz (1970) used by the Southwest Regional Laboratory are illustrated in their development and research process for the kindergarten reading program, the teacher-training component, the tutor-training component, and the parent-assisted learning component.[3]

The Kindergarten Reading Program

Baker (1969) described the Southwest Regional Laboratory kindergarten reading program and presented some data on its developmental testing. The term *program* is given the specific denotation of "a system of instruction in which the procedures used to achieve stated objectives are reproducible from classroom to classroom." The program is objectives-based, and development is based on continual trial and revision. Program objectives generally stated include: sight-recognition skills (ability to recognize a set of 90 words, name letters and read sentences with the words at a minimum criterion level of 80 percent), word-attack skills (letter-to-sound correspondences, blending phonemes, and reading previously unencountered printed combinations of phonemes in their letter-to-sound repertoire at an average criterion level of 75 percent), and comprehension skills (responding to questions about the actors or action in sentences at a criterion level of 80 percent). The program covers 30 weeks at 20 minutes a day. Materials include pupil booklets and 60 paperback reading books at the rate of two a week. Preliminary data are presented on formative evaluation of the program. For many objectives the criterion level has not been reached, and the program is undergoing revision such as programming of phonics material rather than relying on teacher presentation exclusively and developing more extensive teacher training. One weak area in the current program is the blending of previously unencountered com-

binations of printed letters (average percentage correct was 39). However, children up to this point had produced only oral blendings of printed letters and none of the uninstructed children could blend unfamiliar printed combinations when only letter-to-sound correspondences were learned with no direct blending practice. Other evaluation data on the program were reported by Sullivan (1969) and Berger (1969) and an adaptation of the program for Spanish-speaking children was described by McNeil (1969). Sullivan's report illustrated how detailed formative evaluation leads to program revision. Thus it was found that book reading was motivationally more successful than word attack, that teachers spent more time at it, and that word-attack skills suffered as a result. Also, in situations where choral responding or repetitive questioning occurred, it was found that students were echoing responses of others rather than responding to printed materials or teacher stimulus. Also, girls were given more opportunities to respond than boys. In an earlier study McNeil demonstrated that poorer reading performance of boys was associated with the "opportunity to read" phenomenon. Procedures for remedying these defects are being instituted (e.g., use of video tapes for teacher training, use of audio tapes and response sheets for pupils who do not meet criterion, use of criteria for teachers on pupil performance during instruction, etc.) and necessary research is being conducted (e.g., the relative effectiveness of choral aloud responses, choral whispered, group subvocal, individual aloud). For another report of data-based revision of a reading program see Quilling's (1971) report of the Wisconsin Design for Reading Skill Development.

The Teacher-training Component

As personalized, individualized, objectives-based, instructional programs become increasingly available to the schools the

---

[3] Only the kindergarten reading program is discussed in some detail to show the systematic approach of feedback and revision used by SWRL. The remaining SWRL programs are given only brief mention.

teacher's role is changing. The success of these programs (such as PLAN, Individually Prescribed Instruction, McGraw-Hill Programmed Reading, etc.) depends on the teacher's effectiveness as a teacher-manager. We have noted that there is considerable variance in performance of pupils using the same program in different classes and that this variance is attributable in part to teacher differences. The Southwest Regional Laboratory has attacked the problem directly. Niedermeyer (1970) reported data to support the need for specific teacher training for criterion-referenced instructional programs and also reported on the development of a four-hour teacher-training session for one such program, the Southwest Regional Laboratory's First-Year Communication Skills Program.

Initially there was not systematic teacher training. The results of pupil performance yielded considerable variability between classes, some of which could not be easily attributable to student differences. Systematic observation of approximately half of the teachers indicated the following: anticipated outcome of a particular lesson did not coincide with pupil responses; some pupils (40 percent) never made individual responses; and there were inappropriate feedback sequences and lack of appropriate reinforcement. Data from other sources (teacher questionnaires, field visits) supported these observations and the need for a more systematic teacher-training program. Preliminary data following revisions suggested the invaluableness of the overall SWRL approach.

Individualized instructional programs that have effectively produced a system where a computer or manager can handle the instruction should now give attention to other variables or roles for the teacher. Thus, the work of Guszak (1967) has demonstrated that more than 70 percent of teacher questions about reading assignments involve recall and recognition of a literal comprehension type.

The Tutor-training Component

Niedermeyer and Ellis (1970) presented the rationale, development, evaluation and revision of the program for training non-professionals (in this case fifth- and sixth-grade students) to be effective tutors for kindergarten reading instruction. Specification of objectives for tutor behaviors was based on literature reviews and later modified on the basis of a four-week tryout of the program. The program was subsequently put into effect for one year. Continual analyses of all facets of the program suggested the need for still other changes based on such findings as, "if the child was unresponsive, the tutors rephrased the questions only 25 percent of the time," and "teachers were superior to tutors in teaching students in sounding-out new words." The program was again revised to overcome the limitations.

The Parent-assisted Learning Component

For a review of parent variables and reading performance see Della-Piana, Stahmann, and Allen (1968). One of the most systematic and successful approaches to parent-assisted learning is contained in a report by Niedermeyer (1969). Careful experimental procedures were used in both parent selection and parent placement into the experimental group and the two comparison groups. Following the initial announcement that participation in the parent-assisted learning program was contingent on attendance at the 90-minute sessions, three devices were introduced to insure parent attendance. The devices included late afternoon and evening sessions, free baby-sitting and movies at school during session, and a written indication signifying intent to attend or not attend session. The training sessions provided structural role-playing in which parents practiced procedures for working with their children. The procedures included practicing appropriate feedback, reinforcement contingencies, and scheduling the session. Also, carefully programmed materials with clear instructions for each item were sent home. The two treatment variables included school-to-home feedback (weekly feedback to parents on the effects of home exercises on school performance) and parent accountability (parent signatures on record cards signifying completion of exercise).

The results were impressive. The parent-assisted group pupil performance on a post-test averaged 83 percent compared to the two comparison groups' performances of 55 and 50 percent. Pre-post gain for the parent-assisted pupils was 23 percent.

Even among parents not under feedback and accountability conditions, the parent participation was so high (above 90 percent) that variations in these treatment variable effects were small. One major value of this study appears to be in its provision of a model for designing and implementing a treatment appropriate to the determinants of performance deficiencies. For example, where training was necessary it was provided—as in the role-playing training sessions to get parents to provide feedback, praise and correct responses to the child. But where a simple guidance or prompting system was appropriate it was used, as in providing specific reading exercises for the parent with instructions written in the margin telling the parent what to do. Another major value of the study is in its provision of a model for criterion-referenced evaluation relevant to the objectives of instruction. The comprehensive approach of the Southwest Regional Laboratory is likely to reduce the loss of early gains and capitalize on the out-of-school potential in reading improvement documented by these investigators.

CONCLUSIONS

It would be difficult and unnecessarily redundant to briefly summarize the major conclusions or implications of the chapter. Yet there are a few observations that should be made with respect to research and development and current practice.

Schutz (1969) has documented and pungently highlighted many of the methodological issues underlying and interfering with educational research and development. Schutz's analysis is directly relevant to the status of reading research. The major observations are: many innovative programs are not producing the outcomes expected nor even administering the treatments specified; curriculum research is characterized by static methodologies as opposed to a methodology in which there is a systematic use of alternative explanations of the available data, a series of experiments which successively exclude as many alternatives as possible and a repetition of the process on the outcome of the previous studies; improvement of performance of students is dependent on development and technology (the application of organized knowledge); and the methodological contributions of other disciplines are directly relevant in the areas of organizational research, program budgeting, determination of values and success indicants to guide production, policy formulation and program-planning techniques, and the politics of science and education. The reader is directed to the review by Schutz (1969) and to his discussion of the characteristics of education development in his own organization (Schutz, 1970). The present chapter includes some work not highly subject to the criticisms of Schutz. His own organization's developmental work is certainly a model for using the contribution of other methodologies to organize a tightly articulated team effort in producing technologically efficient and effective products (i.e., see the Southwest Regional Laboratory Kindergarten Reading and Support Programs above) and, as contrasted with development, the research work of Gibson and others previously described is an example of research in which the investigator makes systematic use of alternative explanations of data which are then tested and become the focus of another set of alternative explanations. There are other examples, but these suffice to illustrate the methodological points made.

As for current practice, it may be unlikely that we will "find" one best method of instruction but it is not unlikely that we will *develop* best methods for specific outcomes, populations, personnel and time-cost factors. That is the promise of the evolving technologies. Meanwhile, practitioners (persons or institutional teams) should develop the expertise to be able to identify and evaluate products so as to find the "best" for their outcome-population-personnel-time-cost complex. They should also develop the expertise in a staff that can make maximum use of the technologies for installing, monitoring and adapting these best products.

REFERENCES

Addison, R. M., & Homme, L. E. The reinforcing event (RE) menu. *NSPI Journal,* 1966, 5(1), 8–9.

Allen, R. R., Feezel, J. D., & Kauffeld, R. M. Occasional Paper No. 9. A taxonomy of concepts and critical abilities related to the evaluation of verbal arguments. Madison, Wis.: Research and Development Center for Cognitive Learning, 1967.

Ames, W. S. A study of the process by which readers determine word meaning through the use of verbal context. Unpublished manuscript, University of Missouri, 1966.

Anderson, R. C. Encoding processes in storage and retrieval of sentences. Unpublished manuscript, University of Illinois, 1971.

Anderson, R. C., Goldberg, S. R., & Hidde, J. T. Meaningful processing of sentences. *Journal of Educational Psychology,* 1971, 62, 395–399.

Anderson, R. C., & Hidde, J. T. Imagery and sentence learning. *Journal of Educational Psychology,* 1971, 62, 526–530.

Athey, I. Affective factors in reading. Paper presented at the International Reading Association Conference, Kansas City, Missouri, April 1969.

Atkinson, R. C. Computerized instruction and the learning process. *American Psychologist,* 1968, 23, 225–239.

Atkinson, R. C., Fletcher, J. D., Chetin, H. C., & Stauffer, C. M. Instruction in initial reading under computer control: The Stanford project. Technical Report 158. Stanford, Calif.: Institute for Mathematical Studies in the Social Sciences, 1970.

Atkinson, R. C., & Paulson, J. A. An approach to the psychology of instruction. Technical Report 157. Stanford, Calif.: Institute for Mathematical Studies in the Social Sciences, 1970.

Baker, E. L. Developing a research-based kindergarten reading program. *Experiments in kindergarten reading.* Inglewood, Calif.: Southwest Regional Laboratory, 1969.

Baratz, J. C. *Linguistic and cultural factors in teaching reading to ghetto children.* Washington, D.C.: Center for Applied Linguistics, 1968.

Baratz, J. C., & Shuy, R. W. (Eds.) *Teaching black children to read.* Washington, D.C.: Center for Applied Linguistics, 1969.

Bateman, B. Reading: A controversial view—research and rationale. Curriculum Bulletin, No. 278. Eugene, Ore.: University of Oregon, The School of Education, 1967.

Beck, I. L., & Bolvin, J. O. A model for nongradedness: The reading program for individually prescribed instruction. *Elementary English,* 1969, 46, 130–135.

Bereiter, C., & Engleman, S. *Teaching disadvantaged children in preschools.* Englewood Cliffs, N.J.: Prentice-Hall, 1966.

Berger, R. J. Pupil performance in a kindergarten program. *Experiments in kindergarten reading.* Inglewood, Calif.: Southwest Regional Laboratory, 1969. Pp. 23–28.

Bishop, C. H. Transfer effects of word and letter training in reading. *Journal of Verbal Learning and Verbal Behavior,* 1964, 3, 215–221.

Bliesmer, E. P., & Yarborough, B. H. A comparison of ten different beginning reading programs in first grade. *Phi Delta Kappan,* 1965, 46, 500–504.

Bloomer, R. H. Concepts of meaning and the reading and spelling difficulty of words. *Journal of Educational Research,* 1961, 54, 178–182. (a)

Bloomer, R. H. Connotative meaning and the reading and spelling difficulty of words. *Journal of Educational Research,* 1961, 55, 107–112. (b)

Bloomer, R. H., & others. Nonovert reinforced cloze procedure. USOE Cooperative Research Project 2245. Storrs, Conn.: University of Connecticut, 1966.

Bond, G. L., & Dykstra, R. The cooperative research program in first-grade reading instruction. *Reading Research Quarterly,* 1967, 2(4), 5–142.

Bormuth, J. R. Comparable cloze and multiple-choice comprehension test scores. *Journal of Reading,* 1967, 10, 291–299.

Bormuth, J. R. Development of readability analysis. Final Report, Project No. 7-0052. Chicago, Ill.: University of Chicago, 1969. (a)

Bormuth, J. R. Factor validity of cloze tests as measures of reading comprehension ability. *Reading Research Quarterly,* 1969, 4, 358–365. (b)

Bormuth, J. R. An operational definition of comprehension instruction. In K. S. Goodman, & J. T. Fleming (Eds.), *Psycholinguistics and the teaching of reading.* Newark, Del.: International Reading Association, 1969. Pp. 48–60. (c)

Bormuth, J. R. Empirical determination of instructional reading level. Unpublished manuscript, University of Chicago, 1970. (a)

Bormuth, J. R. Reading literacy: Its definition and measurement. Unpublished manuscript, University of Chicago, 1970. (b)

Bormuth, J. R., Carr, J., Manning, J., & Pearson, D. Children's comprehension of between- and within-sentence syntactic structures. *Journal of Educational Psychology,* 1970, 61, 349-357.

Bowden, J. H. Learning to read. *Elementary School Teacher,* 1911, 12, 21–33.

Brown, B. R., & Deutsch, M. Some effects of social class and race on children's language and intellectual abilities: A new look at an old problem. Paper presented at the meeting of the Society for Research in Child Development, Minneapolis, March 1965.

Burke, C. L., & Goodman, K. S. When a child reads: A psycholinguistic analysis. *Elementary English,* 1970, 47, 121–129.

Calfee, R. C., & Venezky, R. L. Component skills in beginning reading. In K. S. Goodman, & J. T. Fleming (Eds.), *Psycholinguistics and the teaching of reading.* Newark, Del.: International Reading Association, 1969. Pp. 91–110.

Carmichael, L., & Dearborn, W. F. *Reading and visual fatigue.* Boston: Houghton Mifflin, 1947.

Carver, R. P. A critical review of mathemagenic behaviors and the effect of questions upon the retention of prose materials. Paper presented at the meeting of the American Psychological Association, Miami Beach, September 1970.

Cattell, R. S. (Ed.) *Handbook of multivariate experimental psychology.* Chicago: Rand McNally, 1966.

Chall, J. S. Readability: An appraisal of research and application. Bureau of Educational Research Monograph, No. 34. Columbus, Ohio: Ohio State University, 1958.

Chall, J. S. *Learning to read: The great debate.* New York: McGraw-Hill, 1967.

Christine, D., & Christine, C. The relationship of auditory discrimination to articulatory defects and reading retardation. *Elementary School Journal,* November, 1964, 65, 97–100.

Clark, C. A., & Walberg, H. The effect of increased rewards on reading achievement and school attitudes of potential dropouts. Paper presented at the Annual Convention of the American Psychological Association, New York City, September 1966.

Coleman, E. B. Collecting a data base for a reading technology. *Journal of Educational Psychology Monographs,* 1970, 61 (No. 4, part 2) 1–23.

Coleman, E. B., & Miller, G. R. A measure of information gained during prose learning. *Reading Research Quarterly,* 1968, 3, 369–386.

Corder, R. The information base for reading. Final report, project No. 0-9031. Office of Education, National Center for Research and Development. Berkeley, Calif.: Educational Testing Service, 1971. ED 054-922.

Coulson, J. E., & others. *Progress report for the instructional management system.* A report to the Southwest Regional Laboratory for Educational Research and Development. Santa Monica, Calif.: Systems Development Corporation, 1968.

Cronbach, L. J. The logic of experiments on discovery. In L. S. Shulman, & E. R. Keislar (Eds.), *Learning by discovery: A critical appraisal.* Chicago: Rand McNally, 1966, Pp. 76–92.

Cronbach, L. J., & Snow, R. E. *Individual differences in learning ability as a function of instructional variables.* Final Report. United

States Office of Education, Contract No. OEC 4-6-061269-1217. Stanford, Calif.: Stanford University, 1969.

Cruickshank, W. M. (Ed.) *The teacher of brain-injured children.* Syracuse, N.Y.: Syracuse University Press, 1966.

Davis, F. B. (Ed.) *Final report: The literature of research in reading with emphasis on models.* New Brunswick, N.J.: Rutgers University Press, 1971.

DeHirsch, K., Jansky, J. J., & Langford, W. S. *Predicting reading failure.* New York: Harper & Row, 1966.

Delacato, C. H. *The treatment and prevention of reading problems.* Springfield, Ill.: Charles C Thomas, 1959.

Delacato, C. H. *The diagnosis and treatment of speech and reading problems.* Springfield, Ill.: Charles C Thomas, 1963.

Delacato, C. H. *Neurological organization and reading.* Springfield, Ill.: Charles C Thomas, 1966.

Della-Piana, G., Hogben, M., & Anderson, D. R. A scheme for maximizing program effectiveness. *Educational Product Report,* 1969, 2(6), 6–9.

Della-Piana, G., Stahmann, R. F., & Allen, J. E. Parents and reading achievement: A review of research. *Elementary English,* 1968, 45, 190–200.

Desberg, P., & Berdiansky, B. *Word attack skills: Review of literature.* Inglewood, Calif.: Southwest Regional Laboratory, 1968.

Donoviel, S. J. Responsiveness to maternal reinforcement in middle and low socioeconomic children. Unpublished doctoral dissertation, University of Utah, Department of Psychology, 1966.

Dunn-Rankin, P. Analyzing the development of reading skills using an error-word preference inventory. Unpublished manuscript, University of Hawaii, Education Research and Development Center, 1970.

Durkin, D. The achievement of pre-school readers: Two longitudinal studies. *Reading Research Quarterly,* 1966, 1(4), 5–36.

Durrell, D. D. *Improvement of basic reading abilities.* New York: Harcourt, Brace & World, 1960.

Dykstra, R. The use of reading readiness tests for prediction and diagnosis: A critique. Unpublished manuscript, University of Minnesota, 1966.

Dykstra, R. Continuation of the coordinating center for first-grade reading instruction programs. Final Report. Minneapolis: University of Minnesota, 1967.

Education Commission of the States. Reports on National Assessment Survey of Reading. Suite 300, 1860 Lincoln Street, Denver, Colorado 80203.

Ellson, D. G. A critique of the targeted research and development program on reading. *Reading Research Quarterly,* 1970, 5, 524–533.

Ellson, D. G., Barber, L., Engle, T. L., & Kanpwerth, L. Programmed tutoring: A teaching aid and a research tool. *Reading Research Quarterly,* 1965, 1(1), 77–127.

Ellson, D. G., Harris, P., & Barber, L. A field test of programed and directed tutoring. *Reading Research Quarterly,* 1968, 3, 307–367.

Fairchild, F. E. A study of the extent to which selected clues serve as aids to the identification of unknown words. Unpublished doctoral dissertation, University of Missouri, 1967.

Farley, F. H., & Truog, A. L. Individual differences in reading comprehension. *Journal of Reading Behavior,* Winter 1970–1971, 3(1), 29–35.

Farquhar, R. H. Home influences on achievement and intelligence: An essay review. *Administrator's Notebook,* 1965, 13(5).

Farr, R. *Reading: What can be measured?* Newark, Del.: International Reading Association Research Fund, 1969.

Ferritor, D. E., Buckholdt, D., Hamblin, R. L., & Smith, L. Effects of contingent reinforcement for attending behavior on work accomplished. Unpublished manuscript. Central Midwestern Regional Educational Laboratory, Inc. (undated)

Flanagan, J. C. Individualizing education. *Education,* 1970, 90, 191–206.

Fletcher, J. D., & Atkinson, R. C. An evaluation of the Stanford CAI program in initial reading (grades 1 through 3). Unpublished manuscript, Stanford University, 1971.

Frase, L. T. Learning from prose material: Length of passage, knowledge of results, and position of questions. *Journal of Educational Psychology,* 1967, 58, 266–272.

Frase, L. T. Cybernetic control of memory while reading connected discourse. *Journal of Educational Psychology,* 1969, 60, 49-55.

Frase, L. T. Boundary conditions for mathemagenic behaviors. *Review of Educational Research*, 1970, 40, 337–347.

Furst, E. J. Effect of the organization of learning experiences upon the organization of learning outcomes. *Journal of Experimental Education*, 1950, 18, 215–228.

Gagné, R. M. Contributions of learning to human development. *Psychological Review*, 1968, 75, 177–191.

Garcia, S. J., Blackwell, A., Williams, C. E., & Simpkins, G. *Research in the black community: A need for self-determination.* Inglewood, Calif.: Southwest Regional Laboratory, 1969.

Gephart, W. J. The targeted research and development program on reading: A report on the application of the convergence technique. *Reading Research Quarterly*, 1970, 5, 505–523.

Gibson, E. J. Learning to read. *Science*, 1965, 148, 1066–1072.

Gibson, E. J. The ontogeny of reading. *American Psychologist*, 1970, 25, 136–143.

Gibson, E. J., Osser, H., Schiff, W., & Smith, J. An analysis of critical features of letters, tested by a confusion matrix. In *A basic research program on reading* (Cornell University and United States Office of Education Cooperative Research Project No. 639). Ithaca, N.Y.: Cornell University, 1963.

Gibson, E. J., Pick, A., Osser, H., & Hammond, M. The role of grapheme-phoneme correspondence in the perception of words. *American Journal of Psychology*, 1962, 75, 554–570.

Gibson, E. J., Schapiro, F., & Yonas, A. Confusion matrices for graphic patterns obtained with latency measure. In *The analysis of reading skill: A program of basic and applied research* (Cornell University and United States Office of Education, Final Report, Project No. 5-1213). Ithaca, N.Y.: Cornell University, 1968.

Gibson, E. J., Shurcliff, A., & Yonas, A. Utilization of spelling patterns by deaf and hearing subjects. In H. Levin, & J. P. Williams (Eds.), *Basic studies in reading*. New York: Basic Books, 1972. Pp. 57–73.

Gibson, E. J., & Yonas, P. M. A new theory of scribbling and drawing in children. In *The analysis of reading skill: A program of basic and applied research* (Cornell University and United States Office of Education Final Report, Project No. 5-1213). Ithaca, N.Y.: Cornell University, 1968.

Gillooly, W. B. Mr. Gillooly replies. *Phi Delta Kappan*, 1966, 47, 552–553. (a)

Gillooly, W. B. The promise of i.t.a. is a delusion. *Phi Delta Kappan*, 1966, 47, 545–550. (b)

Gillooly, W. B. The use of I.T.A. in special education: A critical review. *Journal of Special Education*, 1967, 1, 127–134.

Gillooly, W. B. The Boston reading experiment (1866–1879): The evaluation of an early educational innovation which was a forerunner to the initial teaching alphabet. In J. R. Beock (Ed.), *ITA as a language arts medium*. Hempstead, N.Y.: ITA Foundation at Hofstra University, 1968. Pp. 47–53.

Gillooly, W. B. The effectiveness of ITA in reading instruction. In N. B. Smith (Ed.), *Current issues in reading*. Newark, Del.: International Reading Association, 1969. Pp. 245–253.

Glass, G. V., & Robbins, M. P. A critique of experiments on the role of neurological organization in reading performance. *Reading Research Quarterly*, 1967, 3, 5–51.

Goodman, K. S. Dialect barriers to reading comprehension. *Elementary English*, 1965, 42, 853–860.

Goodman, K. S. Analysis of oral reading miscues: Applied psycholinguistics. *Reading Research Quarterly*, 1969, 5, 9–30.

Goodman, K. S. Dialect rejection and reading: A response. *Reading Research Quarterly*, 1970, 5, 600–603. (a)

Goodman, K. S. Psycholinguistic universals in the reading process. *Journal of Typographic Research*, 1970, 4, 103–110. (b)

Goodman, K. S., & Fleming, J. T. Psycholinguistics and the teaching of reading. Newark, Del.: International Reading Association, 1969.

Gotkin, L. G., McSweeney, M., & Richardson, E. The development of a beginning reading program. New York: Institute for Developmental Studies, 1969.

Gray, W. S. New approaches to the study of interpretation in reading. *Journal of Educational Research*, 1958, 52, 65–67.

Groff, P. J. Children's attitudes toward reading and their critical reading abilities in four content-type materials. *Journal of Educational Research*, 1962, 55, 313–317.

Guszak, F. J. Teacher questioning and reading. *The Reading Teacher,* 1967, 21, 227–234.

Guthrie, J. T. Feedback and perseverance in reading. Unpublished manuscript, Johns Hopkins University, 1971.

Haber, R. N. Effect of prior knowledge of the stimulus on word-recognition processes. *Journal of Experimental Psychology,* 1965, 69, 282–286.

Haber, R. N., & Hershenson, M. Effects of repeated brief exposures on the growth of a percept. *Journal of Experimental Psychology,* 1965, 69, 40–46.

Haber, R. N., Standing, L., & Boss, J. Effects of position and typeface variation on perceptual clarity. *Psychonomic Science,* 1970, 18, 91–92.

Hall, W. E., & Robinson, F. P. An analytical approach to the study of reading skills. *Journal of Educational Psychology,* 1945, 36, 429–442.

Harckham, L. D. Development of teacher evaluation scales to predict reading success of pupils in primary grades. Final Report. Project No. 9-B-087. Bronx, N.Y.: Fordham University, 1970.

Harris, A. J. Research on some aspects of comprehension: Rate, flexibility, and study skills. *Journal of Reading,* 1968, 12, 205–210.

Harris, A. J. *How to increase reading ability.* New York: David McKay, 1970.

Harris, C. W. Measurement of comprehension of literature. *School Review,* 1948, 56, 332–342.

Hatch, E. Four experimental studies in syntax of young children. TR No. 11. Inglewood, Calif.: Southwest Regional Laboratory, 1969. (a)

Hatch, E. The syntax of four reading programs compared with language development of children. TR No. 21. Inglewood, Calif.: Southwest Regional Laboratory, 1969. (b)

Hatch, E., Sheff, J., & Chastain, D. The five-year-old's comprehension of expanded and transformed conjoined sentences. Inglewood, Calif.: Southwest Regional Laboratory, 1969.

Hawkridge, D. G., Tallmadge, G. K., Larsen, J. K., & Michaels, D. D. Foundations for success in educating disadvantaged children. Palo Alto, Calif.: American Institute for Research in the Behavioral Sciences, 1968.

Hayes, R. B., & Wuest, R. C. A three year look at ITA, Lippincott, phonics and word power, and Scott Foresman. Paper presented at American Educational Research Association Annual Conference, Los Angeles, California, February 1969.

Hershenson, M., & Haber, R. N. The role of meaning in the perception of briefly exposed words. *Canadian Journal of Psychology,* 1965, 19, 42–46.

Hess, K. M. Creating individualized usage curriculum. Minneapolis: Upper Midwest Regional Laboratory, 1970.

Hess, K. M., & Maxwell, J. C. What to do about nonstandard dialects: A review of the literature. Minneapolis: Upper Midwest Regional Laboratory, 1969.

Hively, W. A framework for the analysis of elementary reading behavior. *American Educational Research Journal,* 1966, 3, 89–103.

Holden, M. H., & MacGinitie, W. H. Children's conceptions of word boundaries as a function of different linguistic contexts. Paper presented at the meeting of the American Educational Research Association, Los Angeles, California, February 1969.

Holmes, J. A. The substrata-factor theory of reading: Some experimental evidence. In H. Singer, & R. B. Ruddell (Eds.), *Theoretical models and processes of reading.* Newark, Del.: International Reading Association, 1970. Pp. 187–197.

Holmes, J. A., & Singer, H. Theoretical models and trends toward more basic research in reading. *Review of Educational Research,* 1964, 34, 127–155.

Johnsen, E. P., Dunbar, K., & Hohn, R. L. The effects of trait anxiety and task difficulty on prose learning. Paper presented at the meeting of the American Educational Research Association, New York, February 1971.

Johnson, J. C., II. A study and analysis of the relationships at the intermediate grade levels between attitude as reflected in certain thematic content and recalled comprehension of that content. Unpublished doctoral dissertation, University of Virginia, 1966.

Johnson, R. E. Recall of prose as a function of the structural importance of the linguistic units. *Journal of Verbal Learning and Verbal Behavior,* 1970, 9, 12–20.

Johnson, R. E. Remembering of textual prose as a function of structural importance. Paper presented at the meeting of the American

Educational Research Association, New York, February 1971.

Johnson, R. J. The effect of training in letter names on success in beginning reading for children of differing abilities. Paper presented at the meeting of the American Educational Research Association, Minneapolis, February 1970.

Jung, S. M. Evaluative uses of unconventional measurement techniques of an educational system. Paper presented at the Annual Convention of the American Psychological Association, Miami, Florida, September 1970.

Karraker, R. J., & Doke, L. A. Errorless discrimination of alphabet letters: Effects of time and method of introducing competing stimuli. *The Journal of Experimental Education*, 1970, 38(4), 29–35.

Kephart, N. C. The needs of teachers for specialized information on perception. In W. M. Cruickshank (Ed.), *The teacher of brain-injured children*. Syracuse, N.Y.: Syracuse University Press, 1966. Pp. 169–180.

Kerr, N., Meyerson, L., & Michael, J. A procedure for shaping vocalization in a mute child. In L. P. Ullman, & L. Krasner (Eds.), *Case studies in behavior modification*. New York: Holt, Rinehart & Winston, 1965. Pp. 366–370.

Kirk, S. A. The diagnosis and remediation of psycholinguistic disabilities. Urbana, Ill.: University of Illinois, Institute for Research on Exceptional Children, 1966.

Koos, E. M. Future time perspective change in institutionalized mental retardates under token or social reinforcement of language and number learning. Paper presented at the meeting of the American Educational Research Association, New York, February 1971.

Legum, S. E., Williams, C. E., & Lee, M. Social dialects and their implications for beginning reading instruction. Inglewood, Calif.: Southwest Regional Laboratory, 1969.

Levin, H., & Watson, J. The learning of variable grapheme-to-phoneme correspondences: Variations in the initial position. New York: Cornell University Cooperative Research Project No. 639, 1963.

Lindvall, C. M., & Cox, R. C. The role of evaluation in programs for individualized instruction. In R. W. Tyler (Ed.), *Educational evaluation: New roles, new means*. The

Sixty-eighth yearbook of the National Society for the Study of Education, Part II. Chicago: NSSE, 1969. Pp. 156–188.

Lott, D. *Visual word recognition: Its implications for reading research and instruction.* Inglewood, Calif.: Southwest Regional Laboratory, 1969.

Lott, D., Smith, F., & Cronnell, B. Functional equivalence of feature combinations in the visual identification of words. Inglewood, Calif.: Southwest Regional Laboratory, 1968.

Marchbanks, G., & Levin, H. Cues by which children recognize words. *Journal of Educational Psychology,* 1965, 56, 57–61.

Marks, M. R. How to build better theories, tests, and therapies: The off-quadrant approach. *American Psychologist,* 1964, 19, 793–798.

Maroon, S., Washington, E. D., & Frase, L. T. Text organization and its relationship to children's comprehension. Unpublished manuscript, Rutgers University, undated.

Marsh, G., & Sherman, M. *Transfer from word components to words and vice-versa in beginning reading.* Inglewood, Calif.: Southwest Regional Laboratory, 1970.

McGuigan, F. J., & Rodier, W. I., III. Effects of auditory stimulation on covert oral behavior during silent reading. *Journal of Experimental Psychology,* 1968, 76, 649–655.

McKee, P., Brzeinski, J. E., & Harrison, M. L. *The effectiveness of teaching reading in kindergarten.* Final Report, Cooperative Research Project 5-0371, Department of Health, Education and Welfare, U.S. Office of Education. Denver, Colo.: Colorado State Department of Education, 1966.

McNeil, D. *Developmental psycholinguistics.* New York: John Wiley, 1970.

McNeil, J. D. Adapting a beginning reading program for Spanish-speaking children. *Experiments in kindergarten reading.* Inglewood, Calif.: Southwest Regional Laboratory, 1969. Pp. 17–22.

Mosburg, L., Potter, T. C., & Cornell, R. K. The relation between cloze and multiple choice test scores as a function of relative paragraph difficulty and grade level. Inglewood, Calif.: Southwest Regional Laboratory, 1969.

Mosburg, L., & Shima, F. Comprehension of connected discourse. Inglewood, Calif.: Southwest Regional Laboratory, 1969.

Newell, A., & Simon, H. A. Computer simulation of human thinking. *Science,* 1961, 134, 2011–2017.

Niedermeyer, F. C. *Parent-assisted learning.* Inglewood, Calif.: Southwest Regional Laboratory, 1969.

Niedermeyer, F. C. *Developing exportable teacher training for criterion-referenced instructional programs.* Inglewood, Calif.: Southwest Regional Laboratory, 1970.

Niedermeyer, F. C., & Ellis, P. A. *Development of a tutorial program for kindergarten reading instruction.* Inglewood, Calif.: Southwest Regional Laboratory, 1970.

Oakland, T. Relationships between social class and phonemic and nonphonemic auditory discrimination ability. Paper presented at the meeting of the American Educational Research Association, Los Angeles, California, February 1969.

Olson, A. V., & Rosen, C. L. Exploration of the structure of selected reading readiness tests. Paper presented at the meeting of the American Educational Research Association, New York, February 1971.

Olson, A. V., Simpson, H., Rosen, C. L., & Rentz, R. A multivariate analysis of first grade reading achievement, reading readiness and intelligence. Research and Development Center and the General Research Foundation at University of Georgia, Athens, Georgia, 1968.

Osgood, C. E. Motivational dynamics of language behavior. *Nebraska Symposium on Motivation.* Lincoln, Nebr.: University of Nebraska Press, 1957. Pp. 339–424.

Osgood, C. E., & Miron, M. S. (Eds.) *Approaches to the study of aphasia.* Urbana, Ill.: University of Illinois Press, 1963.

Otto, W. Practical Paper No. 5. Overview of the Wisconsin prototypic system of reading instruction in the elementary school. Madison, Wis.: Wisconsin Research and Development Center for Cognitive Learning, 1968.

Otto, W., & Pizzillo, C. Effect of intralist similarity on kindergarten pupils' rate of word acquisition and transfer. Paper presented at the meeting of the American Educational Research Association, New York, February 1971.

Parker, R. K., Ambron, S., Danielson, G. I., Halbrook, M. C., & Levine, J. A. *An overview of cognitive and language programs for 3, 4, and 5 year old children.* Atlanta,

Ga.: Southeastern Education Laboratory, 1970.

Potter, T. C. *A taxonomy of cloze research, part I: Readability and reading comprehension.* Inglewood, Calif.: Southwest Regional Laboratory, 1968.

Quilling, M. R. The reading achievement of primary age pupils using the Wisconsin design for reading skill development: A comparative study. Paper presented at the meeting of the American Educational Research Association, New York, February 1971.

Rahmlow, H. Some results of using student performance data for improvement of individualized instructional units. Paper presented at the meeting of the American Psychological Association, Miami, Florida, September 1970.

Reed, J. C., Rabe, E. F., & Mankinen, M. Teaching reading to brain-damaged children: A review. *Reading Research Quarterly,* 1970, 1, 379–401.

Reid, E. Evaluation of teacher training in a title III center. *Proceedings of the Invitational Conference on Testing Problems.* Princeton, N.J.: Educational Testing Service, 1968. Pp. 31–44.

Reitman, W. What does it take to remember? In D. A. Norman (Ed.), *Models of human memory.* New York: Academic Press, 1970. Pp. 470–508.

Richardson, E., & Hiniker, M. A developmental test of a classroom program to teach decoding skills in reading. *NSPI Journal,* 1970, 9(8), 5–9.

Robbins, M. P. A study of the validity of Delacato's theory of neurological organization. *Exceptional Children,* 1966, 32, 517–523.

Rosenberg, S. The source of facilitation in the recall of context words that accompany associatively related words in connected discourse, 1968. ED 021 226.

Rosenthal, D. J., & Resnick, L. B. The sequence of information in arithmetic word problems. In preparation, 1971.

Rothkopf, E. Z. Learning from written instructive materials: An exploration of the control of inspection behavior by test-like events. *American Educational Research Journal,* 1966, 3, 241–249.

Rothkopf, E. Z. The concept of mathemagenic activities. *Review of Educational Research,* 1970, 40, 325–336.

Rothkopf, E. Z., & Bloom, R. D. Effects of interpersonal interaction on the instructional value of adjunct questions in learning from written material. *Journal of Educational Psychology*, 1970, 61, 417–422.

Rothkopf, E. Z., & Coke, E. U. Variations in phrasing, repetition intervals, and the recall of sentence material. *Journal of Verbal Learning and Verbal Behavior*, 1966, 5, 86–91.

Rothkopf, E. Z., & Thurmer, R. D. Effects of written instructional material on the statistical structure of test essays. *Journal of Educational Psychology*, 1970, 61, 83–89.

Rystrom, R. Dialect training and reading: A further look. *Reading Research Quarterly*, 1970, 5, 581–599.

Samuels, S. J. Effect of word associations on reading speed, recall and guessing behavior on tests. *Journal of Educational Psychology*, 1968, 59, 12–15.

Samuels, S. J. Research design in reading. *The Reading Teacher*, 1969, 22, 346–349. (a)

Samuels, S. J. Word recognition and beginning reading. *The Reading Teacher*, 1969, 23(2), 159–161. (b)

Samuels, S. J. Effects of pictures on learning to read, comprehension and attitudes. *Review of Educational Research*, 1970, 40, 397–407. (a)

Samuels, S. J. Letter names versus letter-sound knowledge as factors influencing learning to read. Paper presented at the meeting of the American Educational Research Association, Minneapolis, February 1970. (b)

Samuels, S. J. Facilitating letter-name learning by training on noting distinctive features of letters. Paper presented at the meeting of the American Educational Research Association, New York, February 1971.

Samuels, S. J., & Jeffrey, W. E. Discriminability of words, and letter cues used in learning to read. *Journal of Educational Psychology*, 1966, 57, 337–340.

Schiffman, G. Early identification of reading disabilities: The responsibility of the public school. *Bulletin of the Orton Society*, 1964, 14, 42–44.

Schnayer, S. Some relationships between reading interests and reading comprehension. Unpublished doctoral dissertation, University of California, Berkeley, 1967.

Schneyer, J. W. Use of the cloze procedure for improving reading comprehension. *The Reading Teacher*, 1965, 19, 174–179.

Schroeder, S. R., & Holland, J. G. Operant control of eye movements. *Journal of Applied Behavior Analysis*, 1968, 1, 161–166.

Schutz, R. E. Methodological issues in curriculum research. *Review of Educational Research*, 1969, 39, 359–366.

Schutz, R. E. The nature of educational development. *Journal of Research and Development in Education*, 1970, 3(2), 39–64.

Science Research Associates (SRA). *What is the proof? The Distar Reading System.* Chicago: Science Research Associates, 1969.

Shannon, C. E. Prediction and entropy of printed English. *Bell System Technical Journal*, 1951, 30, 50–64.

Shima, F. *Research on word association in connected discourse.* Inglewood, Calif.: Southwest Regional Laboratory, 1970.

Shores, J. H., & Saupe, J. L. Reading for problem-solving in science. *Journal of Educational Psychology*, 1953, 44, 149–158.

Shulman, L. S. Reconstruction of educational research. *Review of Educational Research*, 1970, 40, 371–396.

Shuy, R. W. Some considerations for developing beginning reading materials for ghetto children. Unpublished manuscript, Washington, D.C.: Center for Applied Linguistics, 1968.

Silberman, H. F. *Reading and related verbal learning.* Santa Monica, Calif.: System Development Corporation, 1963.

Singer, H. A developmental model for speed of reading in grades three through six. In H. Singer, & R. B. Ruddell (Eds.), *Theoretical models and processes of reading.* Newark, Del.: International Reading Association, 1970. Pp. 198–218.

Skailand, D. B. A comparison of four language units in teaching beginning reading. Paper presented at the meeting of the American Educational Research Association, New York, February 1971.

Spache, G. D. Is this a breakthrough in reading? *The Reading Teacher*, 1962, 15, 258–263.

Stallings, J. A. Reading methods and sequencing abilities: An interaction study in beginning reading. Unpublished doctoral dissertation, Stanford University, 1970.

Standing, L., Sell, C., Boss, J., & Haber, R. N. Effect of visualization and subvocalization on perceptual clarity. *Psychonomic Science,* 1970, 18, 89–90.

Stolurow, L. M. Teaching machines and special education. *Educational and Psychological Measurement,* 1960, 20, 429–448.

Sullivan, H. J. Variables affecting the success of a beginning reading program. *Experiments in kindergarten reading.* Inglewood, Calif.: Southwest Regional Laboratory, 1969. Pp. 3–8.

Sullivan, H. J., Okada, M., & Niedermeyer, F. C. Learning and transfer under two methods of word instruction. *American Educational Research Journal,* March 1971, 8(2), 227–239.

Summers, E. G., & Siffin, C. F. (Compilers) Portfolio of information on reading available from ERIC/CRIER. November 1970. ERIC/CRIER, 200 Pine Hall, School of Education, Indiana University, Bloomington, Indiana 47401.

Tanyzer, H. J., & Alpert, H. *Effectiveness of three different basal reading systems on first grade reading achievement.* Cooperative Research Project No. 2720. Hempstead, N.Y.: Hofstra University, 1965.

Taylor, W. L. Cloze procedure: A new tool for measuring readability. *Journalism Quarterly,* 1953, 30, 415–433.

Taylor, W. L. Recent developments in the use of cloze procedures. *Journalism Quarterly,* 1956, 33, 42–48.

Terrace, H. S. Discrimination learning with and without "errors." *Journal of the Experimental Analysis of Behavior,* 1963, 6, 1–27. (a)

Terrace, H. S. Errorless transfer of a discrimination across two continua. *Journal of the Experimental Analysis of Behavior,* 1963, 6, 223–232. (b)

Today's McGuffey: The street where letters live and children learn. *Carnegie Quarterly,* 1971, 19 (1), 5–6.

Toulmin, S. E. *The uses of argument.* Cambridge: Cambridge University Press, 1958.

Travers, R. M. W. A study of the relationship of psychological research to educational practice. In R. Glaser (Ed.), *Training research and education.* Pittsburgh, Pa.: University of Pittsburgh Press, 1962. Pp. 525–558.

Tuinman, J. J. Assessment of the acquisition of information from reading prose passage. Paper presented at the Annual Conference of the National Reading Conference, St. Petersburg, Florida, December 1970.

Tuinmann, J. J. Passage related reading comprehension questions. Paper presented at the meeting of the American Educational Research Association, New York, February 1971.

Venezky, R. L., & Weir, R. H. A study of selected spelling-to-sound correspondence patterns. Final report. Cooperative Research Project No. 3090. Palo Alto, Calif.: Stanford University, 1966.

Wark, D. M., Raygor, A. L., & Summers, E. G. Reading rate increase through the mail. *Journal of Reading,* 1967, 10, 393–398.

Wepman, J. M., Jones, L. V., Bock, R. D., & Pelt, D. V. Studies in aphasia: Background and theoretical formulations. *Journal of Speech and Hearing Disorders,* 1960, 25, 323–332.

Wilson, H. A., & Atkinson, R. C. Computer-based instruction in initial reading. A progress report on the Stanford project. Technical Report No. 119. Palo Alto, Calif.: Stanford University, Institute for Mathematical Studies in the Social Sciences, 1967.

Wolf, W., Huck, C. S., & King, M. L. *Critical reading ability of elementary school children.* U.S. Office of Education Project No. 5-1040. Columbus, Ohio: Ohio State University Research Foundation, 1967.

Wolf, W., & Mehrotra, C. A factor analytic study of the Ohio State University Critical Reading Tests. *Journal of Research and Development in Education,* 1969, 3, 100–110.

Wright, C. E. Evaluation data and their uses in an individualized education program. American Institutes of Research. Paper presented at the meeting of the American Psychological Association, Miami, Florida, September 1970. (a)

Wright, C. E. Project PLAN progress report. *Education,* 1970, 90, 261–269. (b)

Young, F. A., & Lindsley, D. B. (Eds.) *Early experience and visual information processing in perceptual and reading disorders.* Washington, D.C.: National Academy of Science, 1970.

CHAPTER 29 Gaming and Simulation

F. L. GOODMAN
University of Michigan

Games are analogous to schools in that they involve their participants with rules which apply to them only during the time they are participants. In this sense a game like soccer, played by millions of children and adults throughout the world, is similar to a game like "Equations," a relatively new game designed to promote the learning of mathematics. In playing both games the particular activities involved constitute playing those games only when there is adherence to rules which restrict their participants from doing otherwise plausible things—like catching a ball in one's hands or taking two steps in a row to move rapidly toward a particular solution to a mathematical problem (Suits, 1967, explicates this conception of a game). Soccer does differ from "Equations," however, in that the rules of soccer are not rules which incorporate another set of rules which apply outside the game of soccer. By contrast, the rules of "Equations" do incorporate another set of rules which apply to people not playing the game, namely, the rules of mathematics. Soccer is an example of a large set of games which do not formally relate to other sets of rules which are learned and utilized in their own right

outside the game. Chess, bridge, darts, baseball and many other familiar games are thus distinguishable from games which are designed to relate to some existing set of rules (some quite formal and precise, others quite informal and imprecise)—games which are variously called academic games, learning games, instructional games and any number of other names designed to indicate their nontrivial nature.

Since these academic games place upon their participants some restrictions which do not apply outside the game, there is some question as to when the added game rules facilitate and when they detract from the learning which might come from a direct attempt to study the subject-matter rules. When does the added formalization of the exercise, the process of turning it into a game, help learning and when does it hinder learning, and why? This question parallels a question suggested by the opening analogy. When does the formalization of learning in schools, the process of bringing learning into an environment characterized by rules which do not apply outside school, help learning and when does it hinder learning, and why? The return to this analogy may warrant some illustrative examples of the point. A rule requiring students to learn to read by proceeding from one book to another in a required sequence may promote learning, or it may not. Such a rule does, however, apply to students only when in school, not when they are out of school. A similar statement can be made about rules requiring certain groups of people to associate with each other while attempting to learn certain things. More or less elaborate codes of behavior are associated with people who are in any school buildings or on any school grounds. Indeed, it is now the rare student who is asked to leave school because of his failure to learn; it is not so rare to ask a student to leave school if he fails to conform to the rules which govern the operation of the school.

But the analogy between games and schools is just that—an analogy—and no more. Schools may be like games in some important ways, but they are not games. The rules which govern games are generally much more explicit and precise than the rules governing schools. Of perhaps even greater importance, the success or failure of a given person's choice in a game is a function of choices made by opponents who are players and thus subject to the same game rules that apply to that person. Success or failure is not interpreted solely by teachers who are part of the authority system which makes and enforces the rules.

The point is that those who are concerned with formalizing learning have a relatively unique opportunity to learn about formal learning when they study the relationship between games and learning because games are, by definition, nothing but sets of formal rules. To turn learning into a game, in the technical sense of the word, is to add rules, to formalize the exercise in a precise way.

BASIC DEFINITIONS

A rigorous definition of games has been available for about 30 years since the publication of Von Neumann and Morgenstern's *Theory of Games and Economic Behavior* (1947).

Several general distinctions drawn by Von Neumann are of fundamental importance. A *game* is the "totality of the set of rules which describe it," whereas a *play* of a game is a "particular instance at which the game is played—in a particular way—from beginning to end." Similarly a *move* is "the occasion of a choice between various alternatives, to be made either by one of the players, or by some device subject to chance, under conditions precisely prescribed by the rules of the game" (an abstract component of a *game*), whereas a *choice* is "the specific alternative chosen in a concrete instance—i.e., in a concrete *play*" (Von Neumann & Morgenstern, 1947, p. 49).

The rules of a game are, in a general sense, of two types: the rules governing the *moves* which may be made and the rules governing the *termination* of a play which "must specify what the outcome of the play is for each player" (Von Neumann & Morgenstern, 1947, p. 50).

It becomes immediately apparent from just these initial considerations that interaction in a game departs from most everyday interaction in that the range of choices open to a person in the normal conduct of his affairs is not precisely limited by explicit rules, and the typical human endeavor is not oriented toward a specific, predetermined, unambiguous outcome. The questions under consideration are how and why is learning affected by the vigorous specification of when one may choose and what constitutes one's range of choices, how and when one is to cease an activity and what his payoffs will be. Put this way, the questions sound like questions asked by educators in connection with many other kinds of attempts to improve learning. At first glance the work of every textbook author, programmed instruction designer, and perhaps even any careful teacher, sounds like it could be cast in the mold of a game. This is not an uncommon claim, and the word is used very widely in a loose sense. More careful use of the word rests on two distinctions.

First, are the rules of the activity stated with sufficient rigor so that any violation of the rules will conspicuously constitute a termination of the activity? This would not be true of a textbook. What rule specifies when a textbook stops being a textbook and becomes something else? A programmer may depart from his objectives and write a bad program, a teacher may wander from stated objectives and teach poorly, but the activities go on. It should be recalled that a game is that game only so long as the players honor the rules. A person (other than a goalie) who catches a soccer ball, runs with it and throws it is indulging in a healthy activity, but he is not playing soccer.

Second, are there at least two players governed by the same set of rules, engaging in the activity together, each with a chance of making choices in response to the other's choices, each with the chance to be paid off as having had success? A teacher and a student could indeed constitute such a twosome, but if a teacher and a student are engaged in a play of a game, the "authority" which the teacher has over the student while playing the game is derived from superior performance with that activity, not by virtue of her role as teacher. If the teacher employs her general authority to gain an advantage over the student and a game rule is broken, the game ends immediately. Thus a person taking a test is not playing a game. The question designer and answer interpreter is not governed by the same set of move rules or terminal rules as the test taker.

In game theory the question of "one player games," sometimes referred to as "games against nature," is handled in a relatively simple fashion. It is acknowledged that one of two players may be fictitious. To be a bona fide "fictitious player," the construct must both make choices and receive payoffs (thus honoring the two basic kinds of rules,

move rules and termination rules). If the fictitious player only makes choices or only receives payoffs he is referred to as a *dummy*. One cannot have a bona fide game without two bona fide players. A dummy player, however, may play an extremely important role in a bona fide game if there are at least two other players, both of whom are bona fide players (see Rapoport, 1966, pp. 18–21).

When these criteria are applied to activities frequently called academic, learning or instructional games, not all such activities qualify for the formal label of *game*. The intention here is not to exclude such activities from further consideration but to clarify the situation and to pose reasons for valuing *gamelike* activities over *games* for some purposes. The following categories can now be identified.

Activities which have explicit rules governing moves and termination can properly be referred to as *games,* subject to the additional qualification that the rules call for the involvement of two bona fide players (one of whom might be fictitious). If all these conditions apply to an activity except for the presence of rules governing the termination of the activity (which, it will be recalled, include the specification of payoffs to those involved), that exercise can be usefully referred to as gamelike. That is, if at least two people are engaged in an activity which is governed by rules specifying their moves, when they may or must choose and what the range of choices is, it is reasonable to say that the activity is "like a game" even though it does not have all the technical attributes of a game (it is not possible for an exercise to have *terminal* rules but no move rules, for terminal rules involve move rules; that is, they specify what the final moves are).

The class of activities which are games or gamelike is here referred to as the class of *gaming activities*. Thus, *nongaming activities* is a term which can be used to refer to activities which are not governed by rules specifying moves or activities, and which do not have at least two persons engaged in making choices governed by move rules and receiving payoffs governed by termination rules.

The terminology *gaming* and *nongaming, game* and *gamelike* was not developed by Von Neumann and Morgenstern (1947). It is, however, derived from the kinds of distinctions drawn by Von Neumann. The following distinctions, necessary for a clarification of the diverse exercises which employ the word "game" in their titles, are not based upon ideas dealt with by Von Neumann.

The words "simulation" and "nonsimulation" are frequently used in conjunction with the word "game" (Twelker, 1970). It is useful to return to some distinctions alluded to at the outset to clarify the situation. Some games have rules which incorporate other sets of rules by reference. As suggested above, the incorporated rules may be quite informal and imprecise, to the point that it might be more reasonable to say that there are some games with rules which incorporate by reference sets of "principles." If the principles incorporated by reference in game rules are in fact an explicitly developed set of rules, indeed a set of rules such as mathematics which constitute a body of subject matter, the exercise is usefully termed a *nonsimulation* game. The rules by which such a game is played—in addition to the special game rules added—*are* the rules of mathematics; they do not simulate the rules of mathematics. The implications of this set of rules incorporated by reference in the game rules are not *like* the implications of the rules of mathematics, they *are* the implications of the rules of mathematics. This situation can be viewed as the end of a continuum, or, more precisely, the ends of two closely related continuums.

To the extent that the set of principles incorporated by reference in a game's rules are clear rules on which there is a high degree of *consensus,* one is dealing with a *nonsimulation* exercise. As one moves away from this position, either along a continuum involving the degree of *clarity* of the rule-set (moving toward general "modes of action," perhaps, rather than formal "codes of action") or along a continuum involving the degree of *consensus* on the incorporated subject-matter rule-set (moving toward some individual's idiosyncratic view of the principles governing some phenomena, no matter how clearly developed those principles), one is moving in the direction of activities which properly bear the label *simulation*. It cannot be said of simulation games dealing with political science that players are asked to cope with a clear, precise set of existent rules which constitute the science of political behavior. Instead, in such simulation games, the participants are involved with principles which are not so well defined and on which there is not widespread consensus among political science experts. To the extent to which players are presented with a set of clearly specified rules which allege to relate precisely to political behavior, there is likely to be lack of consensus on that allegation.

The distinction which Von Neumann and Morgenstern (1947) make between a game and a play of a game is also useful to illustrate further the distinction between games designed to promote learning and games which may incidentally promote learning. It is entirely conceivable that the play of a game, the rules of which do not formally incorporate the principles of some subject matter, can nevertheless deal with that subject matter. A soccer player may utilize principles of geometry or principles of psychology in his play and one might say that in that play of the game something happened which involved the rules of geometry or principles of psychology and, indeed, something was learned about such subjects. In this sense a play of soccer may be said to simulate some other activity which is valued from a subject-matter point of view. One might even argue that the play did not simulate the activity, it *was* the activity in question. But such relationships between a play of a game and subject matter exist as subjective states in the minds of players; there is no relationship between the game, viewed as a set of rules, and the rules of the subject matter. Thus it is possible to distinguish clearly between two categories of games, games with rules which refer to subject-matter principles and games with rules which do not. If the distinction between a game and a play is blurred, distinctions between games designed to promote learning and games which may incidentally promote learning are likely to become blurred and depend solely on subjective impressions of participants.

Convenient labels for the two classes of games just described are hard to find. The former class, games with rules which do incorporate subject-matter principles, will be characterized here as "formal learning games" with respect to the incorporated subject matter. All other games, although formal activities in the sense that they are rule-governed, can then be thought of as "informal learning games," a label which may sound strange but which has the proper connotation in that it indicates that learning of some subject matter may occur in the play of any game, but that some games' rules are designed to formalize the learning of a particular subject.

THE DYNAMICS OF GAMING EXERCISES

The emphasis given by the phrase "formal learning games" is exactly the emphasis which holds promise for educational researchers and others interested in learning for a variety of reasons. When does the formalization of a learning activity, in this case the addition of game rules, help learning, and when does it hinder learning? What light can explicit attempts to formalize the learning process shed upon learning and other forms of behavior—rule-governed behavior, contingency management and so forth?

A more thorough development of the concept of rules which incorporates, by reference, rules or principles which apply, or

are alleged to apply, in subject-matter areas is dependent upon a presentation of some additional ideas employed in the theory of games.

Von Neumann and Morgenstern's (1947, p. 50) discussion of the rules which govern moves identifies two basic kinds of moves, *personal moves* and *chance moves*. Recalling the distinction between a move and a choice, these two categories also give rise to the terms *personal choices* and *chance choices*, for a *move* is the abstraction, the occasion for choosing, the *choice* is the particular alternative selected from among those specified by the rules as permissible, during a particular play.

A *personal choice* is one which depends entirely on the free decision of the player. A *chance choice* is that which depends on the "device subject to chance" referred to in the passage above which introduced the concept of a move. Although Von Neumann does not provide names for a further breakdown of chance choices, he does indicate the following distinctions: some chance choices are totally dependent on chance as is the case with the roll of a die or the deal of a card from a well-shuffled deck. Some *chance choices* depend partially on the free decision of a player and partially on the behavior of the "device subject to chance." An example of this category would be the throw of a dart, an act which involves both the thrower's decision to aim at a particular target and chance in the form of the dart's performance (in the language of game theory, "the dart's choice") on its way to the target. It is reasonable to distinguish between these two types of chance choices by referring to the first type as *total chance choices* and the second type as *partial chance choices*.

Rules governing moves also specify the information available to players on the occasion of a choice. Precisely formalizing what a person may or may not know in conjunction with a specific range of choices allows some interesting ways of exploring behavior. A dramatic way of illustrating the possibilities is to note that Von Neumann and Morgenstern (1947, p. 53) characterize bridge as a two-player game in which each player has a "split personality." Thus persons playing each "half" of the player signal their intentions to each other in a more or less explicit fashion, thus giving rise to some very interesting problems of communication, the development of mutual trust, and so on.

These concepts developed by game theorists are quite useful in describing the process of formalizing the principles inherent in a subject-matter area, the process of incorporating such principles into the rules of games. If the task is to incorporate a set of rules like the rules of mathematics into the rules of a game, the problems are of one kind. If the task is to incorporate loosely conceived principles into the game by way of the game rules, the problems are different. Techniques associated with chance choices and restrictions on information are most helpful in clarifying problems of the latter type.

Most (or, if liberties are taken with the word, all) simulation games as well as gamelike simulations involve role playing. A *role,* according to Gould and Kolb's *A Dictionary of the Social Sciences* (1964), "can be referred to as a patterned sequence of actions, set in an environment characterized by interactions, which has been learned by a person" (p. 609). Viewing such a patterned sequence as a kind of *principle,* it is sometimes the case that the *principles incorporated by reference* in a simulation game are the *roles incorporated by reference.* This approach can be developed along two lines.

First, simulation games frequently require that a player make the moves allowed by the game rules according to the principles that would guide a politician, a resident in a black ghetto, a landlord, or whatever. Of course, the legitimacy of such choices can only be determined insofar as one can tell whether the choices made are legitimate according to the game rules. The legitimacy

of choices cannot be determined if they are claimed to be legitimate only according to the vague principles which constitute someone's understanding of a role. Thus players, to conform to the game rules, must consider the principles of the role as they have learned about it (inside or outside the play of the game) in a way which is *formalized by the game rules.* The implications of the highly general, patterned sequence of actions which is the learned role are rendered precise by the restrictions added by the move rules.

Again, care must be taken to distinguish between moves and choices. It is reasonable to say that the relationship between the play of a role to a role is somewhat similar to the relationship between the play of a game and a game. To play a role is to make specific choices within a range of choices. That the range of choices is not as precisely defined by the concept of role as is the range of choices specified by the rules governing moves in a game is what makes the two situations only somewhat similar rather than the same. It is in just this sense that games "formalize" learning about roles by making precise what is otherwise defined in only a general way.

For example, a father in a given instance may choose to play his role in a number of ways, with the range of choices of how to play the role at a particular juncture being roughly analogous to a move. But a person playing the role of father in a simulation game must compare the choices open to him according to the move rules with the choices he is aware of in terms of his understanding of the role of father, the choices which would be open to him if he were *not* limited by the game rules. This kind of comparison illustrates the potential of games as aids to learning. As asked before, when do the restrictions placed upon one's considerations by game rules help one's learning and when do they hinder one's learning when the learning is dealing with one's awareness of options open to him outside the game? *Why* does such a formalization of one's options produce the effects it does? At a speculative level a possible answer to the question of "why" begins to emerge.

Gaming adds rules which formalize the choices open to a person studying roles. These may be roles which he might not be able to play or might not choose to play in actuality. In studying the role as opposed to actually playing it, one could also read about it, observe, listen or talk about it. One could also play it in a nongaming sense. Of all these options, including the latter (nongaming role playing), only gaming attempts to relate vague rules or principles of the role to precise rules about the role. Among other things this permits personal experiments with the role, experiments which can be analyzed in terms of formal choices made and the consequences thereof.

In addition to this generalization, the distinctions provided by game theory suggest some clues as to why the formalizing of choices may promote useful study of roles. The normal notion of role-playing in the context of a game simply means that individuals can experiment with different, but precisely prescribed, personal choices and relate these choices to the partial chance choices and total chance choices which occur as specified by formal rules. The rules also govern precisely what information is and is not available at different times to different participants. The crux of the research problem associated with formal learning games is to ascertain if participants do draw relationships between the precise game rules and the precise choices they occasion and the much more vague subject-matter rules (which also deal with the freedom one has to choose, the impact of chance events, and the certainty or uncertainty derived from information about the environment) and the choices in which such vague principles result. This exposition merely suggests why learning might occur—it is not an argument that learning does occur in such settings. It would appear that researchers will have to give attention to what

actually goes on in games and how participants perceive this rather than to the fact that people have participated in a play of a game if they are to develop and verify hypotheses capable of explaining any learning which occurs.

The line of analysis just presented is the first of two ways of dealing with the way simulation games incorporate roles by reference. Other dimensions of the research implications of simulation games are linked to the second set of arguments.

In addition to the normal concept of role-playing in simulation games, or perhaps in some cases in place of it, the concept of an *operating model* is frequently present in such activities (Hermann, 1967, pp. 216–231). Although this is the language frequently used to discuss simulation techniques, the concept of "model" has a number of difficulties associated with it. That which is called an "operating model," an algorithm in a computer game, a notebook in which "results" are looked up in simpler games, can also be referred to as a "fictitious player," to employ the language of game theory.

In other words, the designer of a simulation game often sees fit to provide the players of his game with a fictitious player, frequently a dummy player that only makes choices rather than a bona fide player who both makes choices and receives payoffs. The designer not only specifies by his rules a mix of moves—personal, partial chance and total chance—which relate to his view of the subject matter in question, he frequently incorporates a role via a dummy player which makes specific *choices* that affect the play of other players. The game rules specify when the dummy may or must choose. The construct may be a limited one that always plays the role the same way, or it may be more complex and more nearly analogous to a role than a play of a role in that the choice that dummy makes may be made from a range of choices precisely specified by the designer. The dummy may make personal choices, partial chance choices, or total chance choices. In effect, the designer has the opportunity to play a role interpreting his view of the vague principles of that role, subject to the constraints of the game rules, just as live players do.[1] This simply represents a higher level of formalization of the learning exercise. Not only can students interact with two precisely different views of a role by engaging in games with different dummy players, students can express their views of the way the role is or should be played in a more formal fashion than by playing roles "live" by designing their own dummy. This is an even more demanding task than designing the rules of one's own game, which is frequently recommended in gaming literature as the most fruitful dimension of learning afforded by gaming.

In either case, the act of designing rules—game rules or rules governing the behavior of a dummy—becomes the kind of exercise which calls for explicit formalization of vague principles. If games are similar to schools, as is being suggested here, then this is a specific way of operationalizing the maxim that one learns more by teaching than by merely studying. The assumption is that he who makes the rules learns more than he who follows them. The assumption is testable in this context without giving up the generalized authority that schools seem reluctant to give up. (The student-as-game-designer's task is also more profound than the student-as-teacher's task precisely because he does not inherit the teacher's generalized authority. Players of games have not proved reluctant to challenge the authority of game designers, a point to be developed later.)

Before further expanding the comments on the notion of dummy as role player, it is reasonable to acknowledge that the dummy might better be viewed as being "in the na-ture of a play of a role" rather than as an actual play of a role. If the dummy represents "the economy" rather than, say, "a banker" or some other "person," it may stretch the concept of "role" beyond acceptable limits. In the definition of "role" given by Gould and Kolb (1964), the term was said to apply to "a patterned sequence of learned actions performed by *a person* [emphasis added] in an interaction situation" (p. 610). But the concept of a player in game theory is not a personal one, as indicated by language asserting that dice and darts "make choices" as "players" in games. The problems here are very much the problems of not having consensus on clear ways of defining things in some subject areas. Whether the "principles" incorporated by the rules of simulation games are "roles" or "rolelike," "rules" or "rulings," is hard to determine. The point is precisely that the game rules formalize the constructs involved, stripping them of their ambiguity at the level of the move in the game, leaving them open to interpretation and argument at the level of criticism of the way a play of the game developed or criticism of the game itself.

To refer to an operating model as a dummy player making the choices the game designer would have it make as it plays its role in the game has the advantage of reminding everyone that the model is nothing but a mix of some designer's personal choices along with his view of the way chance choices appropriately intervene.

It must be remembered that what players learn about subject-matter rules or roles can be learned either inside the game or outside the game. This is extremely important for two reasons. In the first place, much of what a player learns about his role and the roles of others transpires during the course of a play of a game. The assumption is that this learning intermixes with what the player had already learned about the role he finds himself playing in the game. One reads things into the actions of others, derives understandings of rules (game and

---

[1] The concept of a fictitious player in a formal learning game is not limited to simulation games. L. E. Allen and Ross (1971) have developed a number of bona fide fictitious players who play "Equations" with people in the form of what are called "Imp-Kits."

subject matter) by interpreting choices. Thus, much of what is learned by players about a dummy player's performance may have little or nothing to do with what the dummy's designer had in mind as he designed the dummy role.

A powerful technique is suggested by this observation. If, instead of designing a dummy to express one's personal choices, the designer provides chance devices to serve as a dummy, it can be said that the dummy makes no purely personal choices but only chance choices. If devices which a game rule refers to as representing some general phenomenon in the subject-matter area are viewed as a dummy, players are likely to project details into the "behavior" of the dummy and learn about and from it. In this way a designer can stay relatively free of introducing his personal choices into the exercise, yet provide for learning which might not take place if the behavior involved only the *personal choices* of the potential learners.[2]

RESEARCH PROBLEMS

The other consequence of the observation that learning related to games takes place both inside and outside games serves to obscure the problem of doing research on games. Not only is learning in a game likely to be a function of what players had learned prior to the game, it is quite conceivable that it affects what is learned and what transpires in the learning environment after a game. To choose an example from the same nonsimulation game used before, "Equations," a child who loses several times in a row because he does not understand a mathematical concept may proceed to learn that concept after the game precisely because of what he learned in the game, namely, that someone found useful something which he did not know. Much of the literature on simulation games refers to the importance of postgame "de-briefing" discussions. The rationale developed here explicitly supports the idea that learning is likely to be a function of efforts to relate the formalized game choices to the less structured choices which must be made outside the game. There is no reason to believe that reflections on this process terminate when the game terminates and much reason to believe that they should not and in fact do not.

The problem for researchers is to develop a broad enough research paradigm to permit the analysis of the way games may "infect" a total learning environment. Do children who have played "Equations" after school behave differently in mathematics classes, thus affecting the conduct of the class and the learning of children who did not play "Equations"? Does participation in simulation games, perhaps by the way children relate to authority while playing, affect school attendance?[3] Is the attitude of a teacher toward a particular child changed by observing him in a game, with concomitant implications for the teacher's relations with that child in the future?

The question of the context in which games take place and the implications for learning within that context is another example of a question which at first glance is similar to questions which can be asked

---

[2] A series of marble games dealing with subjects like police-community relations, developed at the University of Michigan, is based on this approach. In such exercises marbles stand for means of gaining employment, jobs, difficulties, police, and many other things. As these devices subject to chance do or do not behave the way one wishes, the marbles, as dummy, make choices which allow the players to learn about the implications of some of their own choices, or to shoot or not to shoot, to aim for this target or that, etc.

[3] Cohen (1970) declares that a group of uninterested, unmotivated truants were motivated to attend school by playing the "Consumer Game," even though the experiment was conducted under far from ideal conditions. Cohen's report is one of an interesting series emanating from attempts by researchers associated with the Johns Hopkins gaming group to evaluate the use of simulation games in schools. The work springs from the early insights of James S. Coleman relating the motivational power of athletic competition to the academic goals of schools (cf. Coleman, 1961, especially chapter 11).

about any pedagogical innovation. This may be the case, but there is something about the nature of games which suggests a unique approach to the context problems. Whereas move rules have been discussed with respect to various types of choices and information restrictions, little attention has been given to termination rules. Many of the interesting characteristics of games spring from the fact that there are definite ways of bringing the activity to a conclusion and specific payoffs to players associated with the conclusion. One of these characteristics is that when a specific play of a game ends, an ambivalent state exists. On the one hand, the payoffs awarded the winner cannot be taken away from him, the victory is not erasable. On the other hand, an extremely poor performance is held against the loser no more than a marginal loss, and in this sense the performance is erasable. One can begin a new play with little or no legacy from past performance. Another way of putting the second point is to say that games are games because they are not real, they do not "count," and in this sense they are erasable. But a discussion of this kind is sure to raise questions of what becomes of payoffs, what is done with any score that results from a particular play? Is it accumulated in such ways that the margin of victory is important? Are scores used for or against the players, thus negating the erasability point?

These questions suggest that a specific play can be embedded in a context such that it is part of a larger game, or gamelike activity. An individual play can be part of a tournament, for example. The rules of the tournament can specify what the ultimate payoffs are. Options concerning who may or must play which of several games are specified by the tournament's move rules, for example. The pedagogical implications of tournament rules, the rules governing the context in which a play occurs, are enormous. L. E. Allen's work with mathematics games suggests that an absolutely critical variable in the formalized learning game

environment is to get the right mix of players interacting in each play of the game. This is accomplished by a specific set of rules governing how tournaments are to be run (see R. W. Allen, 1965; also L. E. Allen, 1971). But the point is not only significant in terms of getting learners of similar achievement (in terms of game performance) together to provide just the right level of challenge for each other. The analogy between game and school is again called to mind. Certainly school can be viewed in terms of rules of the large-scale game or tournament it represents. The rules of school do not apply outside the school, each specific formalized learning setting in a school is conducted with rules which do not apply outside of school, but when one's schooling terminates he does receive payoffs as a relative winner or loser of the overall activity (or some large portions thereof). There is a tendency to treat these payoffs in a very generalized way, to accord them a kind of "liquidity" in the economic sense of that word. Even though the activity called schooling differs from nonschooling in the same general way that gaming differs from nongaming, winners of the limited exercises are accorded wide benefits outside school. Whether those who do well in school will do well out of school, when their activities really count, when the moves are not formalized, when payoffs are not formalized, is a moot point—and one which researchers find hard to handle because of the privileges school success brings quite apart from privileges accorded as a function of what one has learned. The problems faced by those who would do research on gaming are almost exactly analogous to the problems associated with research on schooling —and vice versa. Certainly the distinctions between nonsimulation and simulation activities are relevant when considering schooling. If the rules incorporated by the rules of school are the rules which apply out of school, the situation is quite different from the situation when the principles incorporated by the rules of school are more or less like the unclear principles which people may or may not agree upon out of school. But in both cases, the question is whether formalizing the rules, converting the principles into specific rules, helps or hinders learning.

By virtue of the termination rules of games there is a potential for creating hierarchies of games (represented by the outcome of a single performance in a game—local tournament—involved in a general tournament, etc.). When generalized, informal behavior is rendered formal, there can be unambiguous winners and losers. One of the direct consequences of formalizing learning is that those responsible for so doing must be prepared to be responsible for the competition which will inevitably ensue. The way to minimize the potential adverse effects of competition is to see that "nothing becomes of scores," which is to say to avoid the creation of hierarchies of games. This amounts to emphasizing the erasability of each play. Obviously there are advantages and disadvantages to this. At some points in time with some learners or groups of learners there are advantages to emphasizing that performance will count, advantages to emphasizing the competitive nature of the activity. At other times, there are advantages to emphasizing that one's performance will not count. It cannot both count and not count at the same time. Thus researchers must accept the burden of attempting to specify not only when a game should or should not be advocated as an advantageous learning environment, but also when the game should or should not be played as an element in a larger game. In any event, there is a burden which falls on all of those who would introduce gaming into a learning environment, the burden to see that competition is handled in a responsible fashion.

Game hierarchies, "games-within-games," have several other implications. The phrase has been used to indicate that a given exercise can be divided in such a way that a portion of the players engage in playing a "core game" and another group or groups attempt to improve the performance of those participating in the core game.[4] In this sort of activity one has the opportunity to formalize the act of coaching, teaching and helping in general. As such it represents an opportunity to do research on the teaching-learning process in general as well as on the way games are played and how to improve players' performances.

Still another way of exploiting the hierarchical potential of games is to focus on learning by designing games rather than learning by playing games. Cherryholmes's (1966, especially p. 7) much-cited summary of the effectiveness of simulations concludes that one of the best ways of getting students to relate the formalizations of a game to the constructs formalized is to have them engage in design and redesign efforts.[5] This represents a technique of formalizing the typically informal "de-briefing" session recommended for most simulation games. Actually the process can be built into the gaming exercise instead of being considered as outside (prior to or after) the exercise. The marble game referred to earlier is designed to place the task of game rule design, interpretation and enforcement into the hands of a "government" which must satisfy its constituency within the context of the gaming exercise. The general rules of the exercise begin to approach the "meta-rule" stage and the whole question of rules for generating useful rules begins to emerge as the kind of concept which might interest theorists in

[4] Nathan S. Caplan of the University of Michigan has embedded "Prisoner's Dilemma" type games as core games in situations designed to study how individuals may improve their ability to affect social change. Funded by the Public Health Service of the U.S. Department of Health, Education and Welfare, the research is entitled, "Definitional Processes in Planning for Social Change." For a general discussion of the research done on the Prisoner's Dilemma type of game, see Rapoport and Chammah (1965) and Guyer (1967).

[5] The October and November 1966 special issues of the *American Behavioral Scientist* are of considerable value in relation to this problem.

behavioral science (see Goodman & Parnes, 1971).

Any discussion which is linked to the notion of termination rules is on the borderline that runs between games and gamelike exercises. If the termination rule is vague, or if there simply is no attempt to incorporate one, the activity is what is referred to here as a gamelike exercise rather than a game. There are clear reasons for and distinct advantages to gamelike activities.

With no termination rule there can be no clearcut agreement as to winners and losers, thus mitigating some of the problems of competition. In addition, the intensely complex problem of payoffs, that is, the whole issue of "utilities," the process of assigning numbers to subjective preferences, is avoided. The question is whether there is more to be gained than lost by having a termination rule.

Basically gamelike activities throw the issue of winning and losing and what payoffs should or should not be assigned into the "de-briefing" arena. One of the clearest claims for the pedagogical advantage of game-like activities is that they seem to promote discussions of quite predictable types. (It would probably be useful for researchers to start with the assumption that discussions of a certain type are useful, and then design experiments to discern the circumstances under which such discussions did or did not take place after a gaming exercise.)

The nature of a postexercise discussion may be profoundly influenced by whether payoffs are specified or not. If there are outcomes (payoffs), the "ends" of the exercise have been formalized. Discussions of strategies, "means," can be conducted rigorously. If there are no technical *outcomes,* the question of ends and means is blurred. The state which exists when players stop playing in a gamelike exercise, as distinct from the termination of a play of a game, can be discussed in terms of what the implications of the points, pegs, marbles or whatever the coin of the realm is, might mean in terms of their future consequences. Instead of

being anchored by the taste and subjective preferences of the game designer, the discussion is free to explore what might be termed the "pragmatic" implications of the various strategylike principles that were guiding players.

Such considerations return one's attention to the two dimensions of simulation games, the degree of clarity involved in the representations of the subject matter incorporated and the degree of consensus on the representations utilized. Any gamelike activity can become a game if players agree to add a termination rule. Thus if players wish to give a pretense of clarity and consensus to their activities they can do so by prior agreement.

What must be guarded against is the notion that the termination rules, or for that matter the move rules or the dummy player if one exists, must yield a relatively "accurate" representation of the subject matter in question to promote learning. As suggested above, all kinds of learning might occur if one experimented with pretenses of clarity and/or pretenses of consensus. As Hermann (1967) has stressed, however, students should be made aware of the pretense. The point cannot be emphasized too much. Perhaps the game-school analogy is again useful. The assumption on the part of the general public is that the primary purpose of schooling may be to promote clarity, in the sense that students should be taught to think clearly. The history of mass education suggests that the primary purpose of schooling may be just as much an effort to promote consensus, in the sense that students should be taught to agree upon a set of principles incorporated by the rules of school.

The formalization of learning that occurs in simulation games and gamelike activities may be a very powerful technique for promoting consensus on the part of participants. Since there are so many variables associated with the enormous number of plays which could occur at different times in different learners' careers, and since the good-

ness of fit between the exercise and the subject simulated may be a function of the play
rather than the game, and the nature of the
learning involved may be a function not only
of the play but the way the play is handled by the game director, a policy of "defensive research" is not plausible.[6] That is,
it does not seem reasonable to suggest that
researchers attempt to specify how plays of
games do or do not relate to intended reference systems in order to warn users of possible distortions or to alert them to possible
advantages. The most reasonable posture on
this front is for researchers to attempt to
design research paradigms which students
can work with themselves in determining
the way a particular play of a game affects
the way they view the subject matter involved.

This approach does not speak to the comparative aspect of gaming research, the question of how formal learning of the gaming
variety, in both nonsimulation and simulation areas, compares with informal learning
(or, perhaps, with formalized, rule-governed learning of other types). Here researchers can focus on games rather than
plays in the sense that some games may give
rise to enough useful plays to "infect" a
learning environment in a manner which
can be shown to be advantageous. They can
focus on the formalized nature of the exercises to produce data which might give
some indications of what is actually going
on as learners make one choice or another.

As stated repeatedly, the choices which a
person makes while playing a game are

more limited than the choices he could
make if he were not playing a game. Researchers need to learn if participants in
these formal, restricted activities even understand the options open to them in such
restricted activities, let alone the implications of their choices outside the game.
Armed with this insight, the researcher
might then go on to see if participants understand the implications of such restricted
choices by removing the restrictions of the
game. This could be accomplished by
comparing discussions of some subject-matter area based on plays of a game with discussions based on some other pedagogical
technique. Although it may not be easy to
validate the impact of the discussions on
the participants, such an approach would at
least bring research on gaming into an area
where expectations are reasonable. Perhaps
for the present we shall have to settle for
evidence of the ability to critically discuss
how much clarity and how much consensus
exist in a subject area as evidence of learning rather than insist on measuring the effects of such discussions.

Of course nonsimulation games will probably be easier to do research on precisely
because the subject-matter rules incorporated by their game rules are clearer and
there is more consensus on them than is the
case with simulation games. Thus studies of
transfer between in-game and out-of-game
performance can be made more directly. Instead of relying on evidence of critical discussion of the incorporated subject-matter
rules as evidence of learning, one can look
to see if the understanding of the subject
matter, as indicated by the choices made on
conventional tests, is affected by the playing
of games.

But the appropriate research posture
seems to be to determine when formalization of learning helps and when it hinders
learning, not a posture calculated to demonstrate the overall superiority of one or the
other. It would appear to be far more exciting and profitable to follow efforts to
determine when (under what circumstances) gaming "works" with efforts to

---

[6] Inbar (1968, especially p. 185) calls for better-mea-
sured game variables at both the individual and group
levels if a greater amount of variance is to be explained. He also stresses the importance of the game
director in general and in particular his performance in
the introductory stages of the game. The research
implications are formidable, for the number of variables
present in a classroom setting are considerable, even
when a highly programmed teaching technique is to
be employed. When the teaching technique permits,
and even encourages, a wide variety of developments
within the learning activity, as does a play of a game,
the range of hypotheses which it might be useful to
explore may simply become unmanageable.

discover why it works, rather than to move toward producing ever more convincing evidence that there are times when it does seem to work.

In particular, research efforts should not neglect to consider the impact of gaming on the noninstrumental dimension of learning. For decades educators have advocated an approach to learning that recognizes the consummatory side of problem solving, the sense of satisfaction that is "consumed" at the moment of doing, quite apart from the residual, instrumental benefits which may accrue from having solved the problem. The sense of closure that is possible in a formal learning activity such as a game may be of great value in bringing a student to an appreciation of the joys of learning in its own right.

Lest these "joys of learning" be merely the satisfaction of dominating another person, researchers have the additional obligation to search for harmful side effects of irresponsible competition. Since activities that have termination rules which specify winners and losers do tend to promote intensive competition, policy considerations in this area must be based on what can be learned about the structure and processes of tournaments as well as the structure and processes of games. One of the most hopeful avenues of gaming research lies in the direction of getting people to understand what they have learned when they lose and to be able to distinguish between the advantages and disadvantages of learning on the one hand, and the advantages and disadvantages of winning or losing on the other.

REFERENCES

Allen, L. E. Some examples of programmed non simulation games: Wff'n Proof, On-sets, and Equations. In P. J. Tansey (Ed.), *Educational aspects of simulation.* Maidenhead, Berkshire, England: McGraw-Hill, 1971. Pp. 72–77.

Allen, L. E., & Ross, J. K. *Instructional math play (IMP) kits.* New Haven, Conn.: Autotelic Instructional Materials Publishers, 1971.

Allen, R. W. *One teacher's guide to equations.* New Haven, Conn.: Autotelic Instructional Materials Publishers, 1965.

Cherryholmes, C. H. Some current research on effectiveness of educational simulations: Implications for alternative strategies. *American Behavioral Scientist,* 1966, 10(2), 4–7.

Cohen, K. C. *Effects of the "Consumer Game" on learning and attitudes of selected seventh grade students in a target-area school.* Report No. 65 of the Center for the Study of Social Organization of Schools. Baltimore: Johns Hopkins University, 1970. ED 038 733.

Coleman, J. S. *The adolescent society.* New York: Free Press, 1961.

Goodman, F. L., & Parnes, R. *They shoot marbles, don't they?* Ann Arbor, Mich.: Learning Games Associates, 1971.

Gould, J., & Kolb, W. L. (Eds.) *A dictionary of the social sciences.* New York: Free Press, 1964.

Guyer, M. *A review of the literature on zero-sum and non-zerosum games in the social sciences.* Ann Arbor, Mich.: University of Michigan, Mental Health Research Institute, 1967. Communication No. 220.

Hermann, C. F. Validation problems in games and simulations with special reference to models of international politics. *Behavioral Science,* 1967, 12, 216–231.

Inbar, M. Individual and group effects on enjoyment and learning in a game simulating a community disaster. In S. S. Boocock, & E. O. Schild (Eds.), *Simulation games in learning.* Beverly Hills, Calif.: Sage Publications, 1968. Pp. 169–190.

Rapoport, A. *Two-person game theory: The essential ideas.* Ann Arbor, Mich.: University of Michigan Press, 1966.

Rapoport, A., & Chammah, A. M. *Prisoner's dilemma: A study in conflict and cooperation.* Ann Arbor, Mich.: University of Michigan Press, 1965.

Suits, B. What is a game? *Philosophy of Science,* 1967, 34, 148–156.

Twelker, P. A. A basic reference shelf on simulation and gaming. In D. W. Zuckerman, & R. E. Horn (Eds.), *The guide to simulation games for education and training.* Cambridge, Mass.: Information Resources Press, 1970. Pp. 313–328.

Von Neumann, J., & Morgenstern, O. *The theory of games and economic behavior.* (2nd ed.) Princeton, N.J.: Princeton University Press, 1947.

CHAPTER 30 Research on Teacher Education[1]

ROBERT F. PECK
The University of Texas at Austin

JAMES A. TUCKER
The University of Texas at Austin

STATE OF THE ART, 1971

In 1964 Collier reviewed the strengths and weaknesses of the methods used in studies of teacher education up to that time. He noted that very few of the studies were experimental in nature (Collier, 1964). In the same year, Cyphert and Spaights (1964) came to essentially the same conclusion in their study of the literature. They also compiled an excellent collection of critical and forward-looking essays on the state of the art and how it could be improved. In 1967 Wilk, Edson, and Wu (1967) found only one experimental study in their review of the literature on "Student Personnel Research in Teacher Education." They remarked on the variegated sources that had to be ferreted out to find any true research reports. They also noted that even journal articles "often lacked adequate reporting of basic data."

Also writing in 1967, Denemark and Macdonald found the available research on teacher education to be extremely scanty, and in many areas nonexistent (Denemark & Macdonald, 1967). For example, they noted that although the liberal arts portion of a teacher's training is said to be crucial to effective teaching, they could find no empirical research at all bearing on this proposition. There was widespread agreement that supervised classroom practice is a good thing for prospective teachers, but almost no research to find out how, why or what specific kinds of practice actually do have demonstrably good effects. They observed that "the large grants for teacher education have been given for program development, not for theory or research." Indeed, they noted that it was almost impossible to identify the theoretical basis for most of the studies reported. They concluded the most needed next step would be to put large resources (concentrated, by implication) into theory-based, complex programs of research and development in teacher education.

In surveying for this present review the journals, books, dissertation abstracts, and final reports of contract research which constitute the literature for the period 1955–

[1] The research discussed herein was supported in part by the U.S. Office of Education Contract OE 6-10-108, The Research and Development Center for Teacher Education. The opinions expressed do not necessarily reflect the position or policy of the Office of Education, and no official endorsement by the Office of Education should be inferred.

1971, we found all too many examples, still, of inadequate research design or inadequate reporting. One 1968 journal article, for example, ended with the tantalizing information that the experimental group differed significantly from the control group on 80 percent of the variables. Since the study was on an interesting issue, it was frustrating that the editors failed to note that no information was given about the *nature or direction* of the differences that were found. Nonetheless, since 1964 there has been a great deal more empirical research performed on one or another operation in the education of teachers than in all the decades before that date.

Moreover, it is our strong impression that a quantum leap occurred, somewhere between 1963 and 1965, in the quality of both the design and the reporting of research in this field. One can only speculate about possible causes, but the most likely one would appear to be the influx of substantial federal monetary support for graduate training and research in education, for the first time in American history, starting in the early 1960s. While good individual research has come from many parts of the country, the majority of seminal studies since that time have come out of a relatively few places. Most, if not all, of these places won substantial research grants in the 1960s from such sources as the U. S. Office of Education, the National Institutes of Mental Health and the National Science Foundation. Since 1964 a number of these places have begun to receive larger-scale, programmatic support as National Research and Development Centers, or as Regional Educational Laboratories, under the National Center for Educational Research and Development of the U. S. Office of Education.

The highly influential work Flanders began at Michigan, for example (drawing on the very first pioneer studies by Harold Anderson in the 1930s), is now being continued at the Far West Regional Laboratory in Berkeley, where Flanders recently moved. That laboratory also picked up the tech-nique of microteaching which Allen and others first generated at Stanford University. The Far West Laboratory has developed complete training systems ("mini-courses") in this technique, and has been able to subject them to somewhat more rigorous, detailed experimental testing than had been possible at Stanford in earlier years.

Amidon and others at Temple University carried forward and expanded the studies of classroom interaction which Flanders had inspired. One of the highly productive members of the Temple team, Rosenshine, has recently moved to the University of Illinois. It is undoubtedly no coincidence that Illinois has been one of the strong centers of research on teaching for the past decade.

The work initiated by Gage, Macdonald and others at Stanford won long-term, programmatic support when the Stanford Center for Research and Development in Teaching was created as one of the national R & D Centers in Education.

Studies of in-service teacher education are currently being conducted by the Northwest Regional Educational Laboratory; and at least one major report comes from the Mid-Continent Regional Educational Laboratory.

Researchers like Good from Indiana University, and Emmer from Flanders's program at the University of Michigan, were recruited in recent years to the R & D Center for Teacher Education at The University of Texas. That center grew out of a series of interlocked studies initiated by Peck in 1956 and funded by the Hogg Foundation for Mental Health, the National Institute for Mental Health ("Mental Health in Teacher Education," "Computer Analysis of Personality"), the National Science Foundation (Butts's program on teacher education and the development of teacher trainers) and the U. S. Office of Education ("Teacher Personality, Teacher Education and Teaching Behavior," "Cross-National Study of Coping Styles and Achievement"). The research work, to be discussed later, of Bown, Butts, Davis, Emmer, Fuller, Good, Menaker, Peck, Veldman and others has grown out of that program.

This is certainly not a complete list of productive research centers and people. Instances of outstanding research by one individual are visible, such as the series of studies by Sandefur at Kansas State Teachers College at Emporia; and a whole series of well-designed dissertation studies which were stimulated by Bledsoe at the University of Georgia at Athens. Nonetheless, most of the continuing, effective research tends to be concentrated in a few places. (It must be emphasized that we are only discussing *experimental research* on *the process of teacher education*. These observations say nothing about the excellent research on the classroom teaching process or the other kinds of educational research which are proceeding in many other places.)

The reason for this concentration is not hard to see. It explains the present state of the art and indicates quite simply what it will take to continue and strengthen the empirical base for making sound, major decisions about teacher education. The reason for the relatively explosive growth of sound research on the education of teachers, in just the last eight to 10 years, can be summed up in one word: money.

The recent influx of increased brainpower into educational research that followed this influx of money must undoubtedly be given ample credit. Without any more talent than existed before the 1960s, however, it could have been predicted that an infusion of fairly large-scale funding would produce more and better research than had ever been done previously.

The reason for this is the inherently complex nature of the phenomenon to be studied. "Teacher education" is a long, complicated series of operations. Each operation is, itself, an extremely complex set of steps, most of which have never been carefully identified, let alone measured. In these respects teacher education resembles psychotherapy as a process which cries out for precise, microscopic analysis. Psychotherapy, in the past 25 years, has received many times the research dollars that have gone into teacher education; yet only a few solidly established principles have been empirically validated in that field so far.

Indeed, teacher education involves many more factors which interact simultaneously: the pupils' aptitudes, interests, readiness and attitudes toward learning; their parents' and their subcultures' attitudes toward schooling; the administrative policies and the interpersonal organization of the schools; similar characteristics of the teacher-training institutions; the individual, personal characteristics of the teachers; these, and even more factors, are constantly at work in the real settings we too briefly sum up with the simple sounding phrase, "teacher education."

Research designs, to be adequate, must accurately identify, measure and account for all of these factors and their complex, interacting effects. A simple design may be appropriate if just one or two factors can genuinely be isolated and studied; but then it is certain that a great many such studies would have to be performed before they would add up to an adequate map of the total process of teacher education—even of just one kind in one setting. Such a program necessarily costs a great deal of money.

Conversely, a programmatic attempt to study at once many parameters operating as a totality requires an extremely complex, multifaceted research operation which is inherently expensive to perform correctly. It appears quite understandable, therefore, why very few good empirical studies of teacher education were ever carried out before the middle 1960s.

On the positive side it is pleasant to be able to report a substantial number of sound studies which have appeared recently. Furthermore, although even this amounts to bits and pieces of a far-from-finished plan for effective teacher education—perhaps 10 percent of it—there do appear to be some major lines of convergence in the research evidence. The rest of this review is organized around the converging lines which we think we see. We may or may not be seeing clearly. We may have missed important studies or important implications of the studies we have discovered.

WHAT THE AVAILABLE RESEARCH APPEARS TO DEMONSTRATE

There is a good deal of overlap and logical interconnectedness among the conceptual themes we have used to group the studies. Many studies illustrate two or more themes. It is an arbitrary choice to put a study in one cluster rather than another. Such choices have been made purely as a practical expedient. As much to arouse thought as to settle the evidence, therefore, here are some themes which seem to emerge from this recent, but growing, body of research:

1. A "systems" approach to teacher education, often called "instructional design," substantially improves its effectiveness. There are a number of studies illustrating that this works equally well to induce desirable teaching behavior in cognitive and in affective respects. A good deal of research is clustered around three special cases of this general model: training teachers in interaction analysis, microteaching, and behavior modification.

2. Teacher educators should practice what they preach. When teachers are treated in the same way they are supposed to treat their pupils, they are more likely to adopt the desired style of teaching behavior.

3. Direct involvement in the role to be learned, or such close approximations as sensitivity-training laboratories or classroom simulation laboratories, produce the desired teaching behavior more effectively than remote or abstract experiences such as lectures on instructional theory.

4. Using any or all of the techniques just mentioned, it is possible to induce a more self-initiated, self-directed, effective pattern of learning, not only in teachers but, through them, in their pupils.

5. Traditional ways of educating teachers have some of the intended effects, but they also have some quite undesired effects.

6. The training of teachers of teachers is a current concern at numerous places in the United States. At this point in time there is *no* empirical research whatever on this aspect of teacher education. Some would seem indicated. (In fact, there is no discernible research on training for college teaching in *any* field.)

7. One long-needed methodological advance is beginning to appear in the research: the use of pupil-gain measures as the ultimate criteria of the effectiveness of any given process of teacher education. These include affective and behavioral gains as well as gains in subject mastery.

THE VIRTUES OF THE "SYSTEMS" APPROACH

This approach consists of a series of steps which recur in cyclical fashion:

1. Precise specification of the behavior which is the objective of the learning experience;

2. Carefully planned training procedures aimed explicitly at those objectives;

3. Measurement of the results of the training in terms of the behavioral objectives;

4. Feedback to the learner and the instructor of the observed results;

5. Reentry into the training procedure (a trial-teaching experience, for example);

6. Measurement, again, of the results following the repeated training.

It is much, much easier to talk about these steps than to put them into practice, as many educators have discovered. Only in the past few years has this process been rigorously applied to the education of teachers, even in relatively small segments. Nonetheless, where it has been applied, the research reports testify almost unanimously to its superiority to older, more diffusely focused kinds of instruction.

There is a cluster of studies, for example, which test the effect of precisely stating teacher-behavior objectives and training directly for those objectives. Aubertine studied the effect of training student teachers to induce an initial learning set in high-school students. As compared with a traditionally instructed control group, these teachers were judged by their pupils to be significantly more effective in their instruction (Aubertine, 1965). When Peace Corps trainees were instructed to aim at specified behavioral objectives selected to be appropriate to their individual abilities and readiness, they induced significant gain in their pupils' achievement (Baker, 1969). Breit and Butts (1969) used an instructionally designed program in "Science: A Process Approach." The teachers receiving this training significantly increased in their knowledge of the processes of science. They also improved their instructional decision-making behavior by comparison with control samples who did not receive the instruction. In a workshop conducted by the Northwest Regional Educational Laboratory to improve "inquiry" teaching, the use of instructional design in conducting the workshop led to highly significant gains directly in line with the stated objectives (Butman, 1970). Greif (1961) found that specifying and emphasizing the desirability of fostering creative and critical thinking in educational methods courses and in student teaching produced highly significant gains in the students' ability to think critically, to think creatively and to implement such thinking in their pupils. Kaya (1969) trained teachers to set sharply specified, cognitive pupil-behavior outcomes as objectives for themselves and to modify their own instructional techniques to achieve these objectives. The children in the experimental groups gained significantly more in cognitive skills than children in control classes over the period of the school year. Kaya underlined the important observation that such gain appeared to be contingent on the teacher practicing such instruction for a full year. No significant improvement was observed when the new technique was used by the teachers for only one unit. Millett (1969) compared the effectiveness of four

procedures for training secondary social studies teachers: unstructured discussion, oral instruction on how to teach the material, video-tape demonstration of how to teach the material, and a combination of oral instruction and video-tape demonstration. Analysis of later classroom operations showed that the demonstration plus discussion was significantly the most effective treatment, with unstructured discussion the least effective. Wallen and Utsey (1969) trained teachers to identify a word recognition task requiring a pupil response to judge which pupil responses would be considered adequate and to judge when pupil performance matched the response criterion. Before the instruction very few of the subjects attained the three criteria, but after the program most of them did. An additional finding of some interest was that experienced teachers were no more able to determine child achievement of specified reading objectives than were inexperienced student teachers prior to the instructional program. Wedberg (1963) compared traditional classroom observational experience, largely unstructured, with two experimental treatments. In the first case the students had 10 hours of on-campus study of films, tape recordings and other samples of classroom teaching, plus 10 hours of off-campus classroom observation. The second experimental group had only 10 hours of the on-campus film and tape training. Both experimental groups were statistically superior to the traditional observation group in their acquisition of information and in their attitude toward the training experience. The more specifically structured nature of the on-campus training appears to have made the chief difference.

Wittrock (1962) studied the effect of telling student teachers that their own grades would be based on the achievement gains of their high-school pupils. When compared with the results achieved by the pupils of a control group of similar student teachers, the pupils of the experimental teachers made significantly higher scores on standardized tests in social studies and English at the end of the experiment. Wittrock explained the increase in pupil achievement as an effect of the explicit "set" given the student teachers to press for pupil gain. He also underlined, however, the fact that the pupils in the experimental English classes expressed a significantly greater amount of negative feeling toward the experience than did the pupils in the control classes. Thus, in this instance the gain in information was somewhat offset by an undesirable side effect.

Hough and Revsin (1963) compared the effects of several kinds of programmed instruction for prospective teachers. Overall there were no systematic differences in achievement between students using electromechanical teaching machines, programmed textbooks, or programmed textbooks with the reinforcement frames removed. The students did tend to prefer the machine over the book, but in view of the differential in cost, the findings would suggest that programmed text materials are preferable to the more costly teaching machines.

In the affective realm, Hoover and Schutz (1968) made a systematic effort to alter the attitudes of education students by explicitly teaching them to recognize and evaluate their own value assumptions. From pre- to posttest, 10 concepts showed significant change: 1) dirty, lazy students (plus—plus meaning a change to a less negative or more positive attitude); 2) being proved wrong (plus); 3) Negro (plus); 4) lower-class values (plus); 5) middle-class values (minus—minus meaning a change to a less positive attitude); 6) conformity (minus); 7) fixed, absolute facts (minus); 8) competition (minus); 9) keeping up with the Joneses (minus); 10) Marxism (plus). The shifts apparently were not from a middle-of-the-road position to a radically liberal position, but rather from a quite conservative initial position to a more moderate stand (there is a discrepancy between Hoover and Schutz's text and their table as to the direction of these shifts).

Burge (1967) did the kind of study which is much needed and which seldom is done: he studied the effects of a traditional student-teaching experience on the classroom behavior of teachers as measured by Flanders's Interaction Analysis System. The student teachers were *not* instructed to try to teach in the desired style represented by Flanders's system. The consequence was that they showed no change during their student teaching on any of these dimensions.

In short, there is a substantial amount of evidence that specifying objectives and teaching to them is effective. The one study which explored the converse proposition confirmed the virtues of specificity in the sense that a lack of specificity led to a lack of improvement in teaching performance.

Effects of Performance Feedback

The next cluster of studies tests the proposition that feedback to teachers about their style of performance and about the effects on pupils will tend to increase their mastery of teaching skills. MacGraw (1966) found that feedback based on 35mm time-lapse photography could be effective in changing the behavior of student teachers, in contrast to another group which did not receive such feedback. Heinrich and McKeegan (1969) compared the effects of immediate and delayed feedback in modifying student-teaching behavior. The experimental treatment was very immediate, indeed. It consisted of having a supervisor raise color-coded cards each time the student teacher showed a desirable or undesirable kind of teaching behavior. The control group received feedback by the supervisor after the classroom teaching session was completed. It was hypothesized that, in both groups, the discrepancy should be reduced between the teachers' beliefs about how they were acting and how they were observed to act. A greater reduction in discrepancy was expected for the immediate feedback group. The results verified both hypotheses. Ishler (1967), using Withall's Social-Emotional Climate Index, tested the effects of feedback versus no feedback in two comparable groups of student teachers. The teachers who received feedback became significantly more learner-centered than did the teachers in the group who received no feedback. Joyce (1967) likewise found that feedback could be effective; but he also found that supervisors need extensive training if they are to give effectively constructive feedback. There was a tendency for supervisors to discuss hypothetical examples of teaching rather than stick to the filmed and taped samples of the students' own teaching. James (1970) found that a combination of supervision with self-confrontation via video-taped feedback was significantly superior to traditional supervision alone in getting student teachers to move toward indirect teaching strategies.

Morse and Davis (1970) found significant gains from a teaching laboratory experience which lasted only two weeks. In the first meeting the general approach was introduced. In the second meeting each student taught a 10-minute lesson to peers, and the other students completed an evaluation form on his use of a questioning strategy. The lesson was audio-taped and before the next class meeting the students listened to this recording using a structured listening guide. In the third meeting the class discussed the behaviors observed by the instructor in their teaching effort. In the fourth meeting each student participated in a 10-minute "re-teach" which also was taped. A control group received three classroom periods of discussion and instruction on the questioning strategies at issue. In their fourth class, they also taught a 10-minute class to peers which was taped. A comparison of the final teaching tapes of the two groups showed that the teaching laboratory group asked more questions of a cognitive nature rather than an affective or procedural nature, and their reactions to pupils were more positive, accepting and supportive.

Steinbach and Butts (1968) studied the relationships of teaching practice with peers or with children, and the presence or absence of feedback about this teaching to the achievement of specific teaching competencies. There were several significant differences between the students who taught children and those who taught peers, suggesting that at the elementary level, at least, some skills can only be learned by teaching children. With regard to feedback, students who received it were better able to gear the lesson to pupil needs. They also were better able to use their plans so that their presentations were logical and coherent.

Steinen (1967) found that any one of three methods of providing feedback to student teachers of mathematics increased their skill, as compared to a control group. Feedback from fellow student teachers working in pairs, and feedback from pupils were both found to be more successful than self-appraisal feedback by the student teachers themselves as they modified and re-taught lessons.

Several studies appear to say the same thing: solitary self-confrontation with feedback information is ineffectual, or much less effectual than when a second person participates in the feedback process. Fuller, Veldman, and Richek (1966) found that listening to tape recordings alone did not reduce the discrepancies between student teachers' self-ratings and ratings by observers of their teaching performance. There was a significant reduction in these discrepancies when this playback was accompanied by instructor and peer commentary. In a similar vein, Morse, Kysilka, and Davis (1970) found that audio-tape feedback, with or without a listening guide, was not effective in improving the teaching competence of students unless the feedback included a personal conference with their instructor. Acheson (1965) found that the presence of a supervisor during the feedback of video-taped teaching led to significantly more reduction in teacher monologue than did viewing of the video tapes by the student alone. He also found that the combination of the video tape with the student-supervisor conference was more effective than a conference alone. Ranson (1969) tested the efficacy of a self-instructional program in Flanders's System of Interaction Analysis. While experienced teachers showed a moderate gain in their knowledge of interaction analysis after using this program, no significant changes took place in their classroom behavior. The results were not any better in a comparison group which also received a weekly television lecture on the system.

Tuckman, McCall, and Hyman (1969) also found that merely knowing the system of interaction analysis was not sufficient to induce change in teachers' classroom behavior. Verbal feedback from another person had to be added to the self-observation before changes were achieved. They found, too, that the more a teacher's self-perception disagreed with the facts about his actual teaching behavior, the more likely the teacher was to change his self-perception to match the observed facts (teachers *are* reality-oriented). Tuckman and Oliver (1968) found that feedback from pupils led to improved teaching behavior, whereas feedback from the student teacher's supervisor produced no additional effect when combined with pupil feedback, and actually had a negative effect when used alone. Young (1968) found that video-taped feedback during a microteaching experience was a much more effective treatment if accompanied with specific comments about the teaching skills at issue, as compared with viewing the video tape alone. Similarly, the effects of viewing a model performance by an experienced teacher were also significantly enhanced when the presentation of the model was accompanied by a focused commentary.

Confirmation for this principle may also be found in Morgan and Woerdehoff's (1969) study, where teaching behavior over the period of student teaching was carefully measured and where the student teachers received no feedback about their specific teaching behavior relative to the dimensions of the Interaction Analysis System. There was no significant change in their behavior from the first to the last week of student teaching. Lacking any effective intervention, the best predictors of their classroom behavior were found to be four personality factors derived from the Guilford-Zimmerman Temperament Survey and the Creativity Self-Rating Scale.

All in all, the research evidence looks quite consistent in confirming the utility of giving teachers objective feedback about specific aspects of their teaching behavior. Furthermore, the available evidence all indicates that teachers use such feedback to make instructive changes in their teaching style only if another person participates in the feedback session. Apparently, simply looking at one's own performance does not lead to much new insight into what one is doing, or else it does not provide adequate motivation to alter that pattern. The presence of another human being adds a potent factor which does induce positive change (*when* that influence is beneficially exercised). Clearly, there is a need for further research to determine exactly how and why this human influence is essential to the feedback process if positive change is to occur. It may introduce a degree of objectivity that is lacking in solitary self-confrontation; it may provide a motivating incentive to change one's behavior; or it may have some other, as yet unidentified, influence.

Interaction Analysis as a Training Device

Flanders's Interaction System is a concise set of dimensions for describing the way a teacher interacts with his class. The dimensions contain a strong emphasis on affective elements of the classroom atmosphere, although cognitive issues are also represented. When used as a training device to give feedback to teachers about their observable patterns of action, the system has a very explicit set of objectives. Its intent is to get teachers to maximize the frequency with which they foster more self-starting, self-directed, actively inquiring patterns of learning behavior in their pupils. The system is used to help the teacher achieve this objective by adopting more "indirect" methods of reacting to pupils: more questioning and less lecturing; more positive reinforcement for pupils' responses rather than critical or negative comments; etc.

There is one set of studies which directly tests the proposition that using this system for recording teaching behavior and feeding it back to teachers will get them to engage in more and more "indirect" behavior toward their pupils. Amidon (1970) reported the results of a two-and-a-half–year study of this question. He not only studied the effects of interaction analysis training on student teachers but also studied the effects on student teacher behavior of training the cooperating teachers in the system. Those student teachers who were taught interaction analysis were significantly more indirect at the end of their student-teaching experience on nearly all of the 20 indices used than were student teachers who were not taught the system. Similarly, Bondi (1970) found that student teachers who had received instruction in interaction analysis prior to student teaching were significantly more indirect in their behavior than students who had not received the training and feedback about their own teaching earlier in their training. The number of students was only 20 in each of the two samples but the differences were quite large enough to be highly significant. In an even smaller-scale study, with nine pairs of student teachers, Finske (1967) found that student teachers who were given training and feedback using the Interaction Analysis System were more flexible throughout student teaching, used more extended, indirect methods in discussion lessons, used more lecturing in lessons which were intended to exert a direct influence, and elicited more pupil-initiated talk.

Before going on to cite the other studies on interaction analysis, it should be said that some educators emphatically espouse a very different model of "desirable" teaching behavior. Bereiter and Englemann, for example, forcefully urge that the teacher be highly directive. The pupil's role is to follow orders in this model. No proponent of

this model has reported any empirical research, however, which describes an organized plan of teacher training and measures its effects on either teachers or pupils. Flanders's review of a large body of research, moreover, demonstrated that most classrooms are overwhelmingly dominated by teacher talk, with most of the remaining time taken up by brief, rote answers to teacher questions (Flanders & Simon, 1969). Consequently, to propose that teachers be trained to allow somewhat more scope for pupil-initiated exploration and trial solution of problems seems no more than a modest redressing of the balance.

Moreover, there is a certain kind of built-in validation in the studies using interaction analyses. In the course of recording the amounts and kinds of pupil behavior, almost all of these studies have demonstrated that when teachers actually try to elicit more independent thinking in their pupils, they get it. Pupils do respond with more self-initiated, thoughtful behavior.

It seems doubtful that educators who counsel clear, firm, purposeful direction by teachers would rule out the desirability of pupil initiative. What the interaction studies do appear to show is that the teacher has to act in ways that specifically allow and encourage such pupil initiative, or it does not occur to any great extent.

The very small numbers in many of these studies would severely limit the generalizability of the findings, if it were not that essentially the same research design has been replicated in a sizable number of different places, with students of varying backgrounds, in institutions with quite different characteristics. The small research samples are eloquent testimony, of course, to the great amount of time, energy and money it takes to carry out objectified measures on even a carefully condensed handful of behavioral dimensions. In none of these studies was it possible to find the resources to measure other influential factors such as pupil characteristics, the administrative climate of the schools, personal characteristics of the teachers, the constraints imposed by different curricular materials, or the like.

Hough, Lohman, and Ober (1969) tried two different methods of instruction to help students achieve an effective pattern of teaching behavior. In the first group, 168 students learned the Flanders system and used it repeatedly in pairs who coded each other's early teaching efforts. Another group of 252 students listened to tape recordings of classroom incidents and analyzed the behaviors used by the teachers. During class discussions, categories of role behaviors similar to those of the Flanders system were identified and discussed. However, students in this second group did not create a formal conceptual system for observational purposes, nor did they engage in specific matrix analysis such as the Flanders system involves. They did do microteaching and got feedback from their partners in an unsystematized way. Except for this difference, all other instructional experiences were the same in the two groups. At the close of the course, all students taught a 20- to 30-minute lesson which was coded by the instructor, using a modification of the Flanders system. The experimental students were found to use significantly more praise and encouragement, more acceptance and clarification of student ideas, fewer directions, less criticism, less justification of authority, less feedback and less solicitation of student talk in response to the teacher. In a follow-up study, 30 students from each group were observed in student teaching during the next year. The experimental teachers were found to be significantly more receptive to and more prone to clarify student feelings and ideas, more given to praising and encouraging students, less prone to lecture, less prone to give directions and more inclined to stimulate student-initiated talk. Kirk (1967) studied student teachers in the elementary grades and concluded that interaction analysis training led to a more relaxed, conversational teaching style. The student teachers who were trained in this method were more indirect and were more

aware of what they did in the classroom. In a study of 18 trained and 18 untrained experienced secondary teachers, Parrish (1969) found that the interaction-trained teachers were more indirect, more acceptant of student feelings, more given to praise, made use of pupil ideas and were less critical of these ideas. Furthermore, their pupils talked more, integrated their ideas into discussions more freely, and talked for longer intervals. In still another study of this type, Simon (1967) found that student teachers trained in interaction analysis used more praise, less criticism, and used more extended indirect influence than student teachers who were trained in learning theory but not interaction analysis. She compared 14 trained with 14 untrained teachers.

In one of the few studies in this field with a sizable sample, Sandefur, Pankratz, and Couch (1967) studied 231 teacher-education students from five different colleges and universities in Kansas. They were taught the Flanders system and compared with a control sample of untaught students. The experimental students were significantly more positive toward video-tape recording after viewing tapes of classroom situations than were the control students. Indeed, those who did not receive interaction analysis training became more negative in their attitudes toward being video-taped.

Recently the Far West Educational Laboratory developed Mini-course Four to facilitate training in the Flanders system of interaction analysis. They started a field test with 24 teachers, but, because of the usual "unexpected administrative problems" encountered, "nineteen carried out the course assignment at a level which made posttaping meaningful in some respect" (Langer & Allen, 1970).

Langer and Allen found that teachers taking the mini-course achieved coding accuracy between 60 and 70 percent. This was stated to be "satisfactory," although not as high as had been hoped. Furthermore, teachers who had had previous experience at being video-taped did not differ in their behavior in the initial lesson from those who had no previous experience. Finally, teachers who took the mini-course did increase their use of praise, their acceptance of student ideas and their use of questioning, and the amount of lecturing they did decreased.

Lest an overly simple conclusion be drawn from this assembled evidence, it is important to note the study by Luebkemann (1966). He divided 176 student teachers into three groups. Group One substituted instruction in Flanders's Interaction Analysis for the usual course material concerned with motivating student interest and eliciting student participation. Group Two got neither the interaction analysis training nor the content on student motivation. Group Three did get experience in writing analyses of pupil observations and in panel discussions about how to motivate pupil participation. Since Group One only got a descriptive discussion of the Flanders system, without using it in any active way or getting any feedback on their own teaching performance in terms of these dimensions, it is not too surprising that Group One showed less tendency to use indirect procedures in their student teaching than did the students in Group Three. The direct, active attention which the latter student teachers gave to specific examples of pupil behavior, and teaching intervention, led them to use the kinds of skills which Flanders would prefer teachers to employ to a greater degree than the students who merely had an intellectual discussion of the Flanders categories.

Another set of studies takes up the effects of combining interaction analysis with other training procedures, or considers the interacting effects of teacher characteristics with the training treatment. Flanders (1963), for example, conducted a nine-week training course for 51 experienced teachers, designed to compare the effects of using a direct (lecture) method of instruction and an indirect method of instruction. In both cases the content of the course was instruction in interaction analysis. Observations of teach-

ing taken prior to the course were used to identify the teachers as either direct or indirect in their overall teaching pattern. Teachers initially classified as indirect became significantly more indirect when taught by the indirect method than when taught by the lecture method. This was the only significant difference between the two methods of teacher training, however. Flanders concluded that the final position of the teachers in terms of their average indirect-direct ratio "seems to be more directly associated with their initial style of teaching than with the style of in-service training."

Hough and Amidon (1965) administered the Rokeach D-Scale and the Teaching Situation Reaction Test to 40 students at Temple University just prior to student teaching. Subsequently, half the group were trained in interaction analysis while the other half were not so trained. Student teachers with low dogmatism scores who learned interaction analysis showed significantly greater change toward the use of indirect teaching methods than did either equally open-minded student teachers who had not learned interaction analysis, or more closed-minded students who had learned interaction analysis. Previously, Hough and Amidon (1964) had studied another group of 40 student teachers, half of whom got a combination of interaction analysis training with an experimental human relations laboratory. Supervisors rated this experimental group as more effective in their student teaching. Supervisors also judged the students with low dogmatism scores as more effective in their teaching than those with more closed-minded attitudes. The students with low dogmatism scores made significantly more positive changes on the Teaching Situation Reaction Test. In three other studies (Hough & Amidon, 1967; Hough & Ober, 1966; Lohman, Ober, & Hough, 1967), training in interaction analysis was combined with a relatively personalized examination of these students' experiences in teaching. By comparison with a group of students taking a traditional, methods-oriented program, these students were found to be more empathic with students, more objective in using data about students, and more experimental in their use of methodology. Still another group of students trained in the same way were found to use more praise and encouragement in their instruction, accept and use student ideas more, give fewer directions, and spend less time criticizing or giving corrective feedback. (The authors noted that it was impossible to tell which of the two or more elements in the training had the observed effects.) Subsequently, student teachers who were followed four to 12 months later were found to maintain their difference from the control students, still being more indirect in their teaching.

In this field of study of the interactions of teachers and pupils, a powerful new tool has recently been added (Brophy & Good, 1969; Good & Brophy, 1970). The Teacher-Child Dyadic Interaction System captures the specific pattern of interaction between a teacher and each separate child in the class. This not only makes it possible, for the first time, to study differences in teacher behavior toward different individual pupils; it also permits the study of teacher behavior toward different *types* of pupils, such as high achievers and low achievers (Good & Brophy, 1970).

Micro-Teaching

Micro-teaching is a combination of a conceptual system for identifying precisely specified teaching skills with the use of videotape feedback to facilitate growth in these teaching skills. It was developed in the early 1960s by Allen and others at Stanford at about the same time that Fuller, Peck and others were developing the use of 8mm sound movies for personalized feedback to student teachers at Texas, and teacher educators in a number of other places were beginning to experiment with the crude, early video-tape equipment which was just becoming available.

At Stanford, and more recently at the Far West Regional Laboratory, micro-teaching has generated a more persistent, cumulative body of research than is available in most other systems. Allen and Fortune (1967) analyzed the results of the Stanford micro-teaching clinics in 1963 and 1964. They found that students trained in this way for an eight-week period, spending less than 10 hours a week at it, performed at a higher level of teaching competence than a comparable group of student teachers who spent 20 to 25 hours a week receiving traditional instruction with an associated experience as teacher aides. Further, they found that performance in the micro-teaching situation significantly predicted subsequent practice teaching grades. Interns trained through micro-teaching showed significant improvement in six specific skills of teaching. Subsequently, Fortune, Cooper, and Allen (1967) conducted a micro-teaching clinic for 140 teacher trainees. The clinic consisted of a series of six five-minute micro-teaching sessions, each followed by a 10-minute supervisory conference with the instructor who had observed the preceding session. In addition, twelve 20- to 25-minute lessons were taught by each student under the direction of a supervisor, and each lesson was followed by a conference of about the same duration. On nine of 12 aspects of teaching the students showed significant gains. Cooper and Stroud (1967) reported on the 1966 Stanford summer micro-teaching clinic, which started with 145 teaching interns. The Stanford Teacher Competence Appraisal Guide showed significant gains for the interns in their teaching competence, from first to last micro-teaching session. One curious finding provokes some unanswered questions. Supervisors who had made specific suggestions to individual students between their "teach" lesson and "reteach" lesson reported seeing significant differences between these two pairs of lessons. A panel of students that rated the pairs of lessons, however, saw no significant difference between teach and reteach across the short intervals which intervened. Whether the supervisors were "seeing" what they hoped to see, or whether some other factor accounts for it, the discrepancy remains unexplained.

Emmer and Millett (1968) studied the effects of a sequence of micro-teaching units on the teaching behavior of secondary education students. In the experimental group of 27 students, each taught a total of 10 lessons during the semester, 10 to 15 minutes each, one for each of the eight instructional and learning tasks, one reteach after the first four tasks, and one final performance lesson. Seven to nine fellow students acted as students for these lessons. Regular feedback was given by fellow students and by instructors in the form of discussions and ratings about the particular teaching task at issue and about the impact of the lesson on the students. The comparison group, of equal size, did not have this laboratory experience but had one micro-teaching experience at the beginning of the semester and one at the end. Their preparation consisted of a traditional curriculum and instruction course. The final lessons taught by students in both groups were audio-taped and coded. The experimental group performed significantly better than the control group on three of the four dimensions measured: determining readiness, motivating students, and evaluating student responses. There was no difference on the dimension of clarifying objectives. The experimental group also showed significantly greater use of student ideas, used more questioning, and elicited more student response and more student initiation.

Davis and Smoot (1969) found that 85 students going through a micro-teaching laboratory, as compared with a control group of 55, showed significantly more desirable patterns of teaching behavior. They used more divergent questions, did more probing, less information giving, and elicited more pupil questions and statements. They were more supportive, more clarifying, less procedural and less nonsubstan-

tive in their remarks. The variety of their teaching methods increased significantly, as well.

Limbacher (1969) found that pupils of student teachers who had earlier participated in micro-teaching experiences rated their student teachers significantly higher than did pupils of student teachers who had not had micro-teaching. At the same time, however, the cooperating teachers reported no significant difference between the two sets of students in their "readiness to assume full responsibility for a class." Further, contrary to expectation, the control group turned out to be more indirect than the experimental group in their teaching behavior. Since the specific content of the micro-teaching units was not given, it is not possible to tell whether the stress on teacher skills may have caused the student teachers in the experimental group to focus on more direct teaching methods.

Kallenbach and Gall (1969) replicated Allen and Fortune's earlier study to determine the effectiveness of micro-teaching with elementary interns. Contrary to previous findings, micro-teaching was not found to result in significantly higher ratings of teacher effectiveness, either immediately or after training, as compared with ratings of interns who did not have micro-teaching. They concluded, nonetheless, that micro-teaching is an effective training strategy since it achieves similar results when compared with conventional training methods, at one-fifth the cost in time and with fewer administrative problems. They noted that the discrepancy with earlier results might come from the fact that this study involved elementary interns whereas the earlier studies involved secondary interns. Moreover, they reported that the subjects in this study comprised a "less highly selected" group than the interns in the earlier studies. An incidental but significant finding was that ratings of teaching performance based on a brief, video-taped lesson, in advance of the micro-teaching program, significantly predicted later ratings of effectiveness in student teaching (in short, if people are not trained to act differently, they will keep doing what they already know how to do, rightly or wrongly).

Perhaps the most completely developed form of micro-teaching instruction is described in *The Mini-Course: A Micro-Teaching Approach to Teacher Education* (Borg, Kelley, Langer, & Gall, 1970). In this book a series of mini-courses is described in detail, and the results of empirical field tests are reported.

Mini-course One deals with teacher skills in conducting class discussions. Forty-eight teachers took part in the field test. They averaged nine years of full-time teaching experience. Pre- and postvideo tapes were scored on each of the 13 variables at issue, with reliability from 0.60 to 0.98. The teachers who took the Mini-course made very significant improvements in all but two of the 13 variables. They used more redirection, more prompting, more clarification, less repetition of their own questions, less repetition of student answers, less answering of their own questions, and allowed longer pauses after their questions. The length and number of multiword student responses increased. The percentage of teacher talk decreased, and the cognitive level of student questions increased. Two months later a refresher course was given. Two months after that (four months after the original study), the 38 teachers still available were again video-taped to see what loss, if any, had occurred. There was only one significant loss—prompting, but there were two significant additional gains—using further clarification and avoiding repetition of own questions. Furthermore, it was established that this maintenance of skills was not due to the intervening refresher course. At the outset of this refresher course the teachers were asked to perform on video tape in the same way they had during the earlier training. In all but one behavior area no loss occurred as compared with the immediate, postcourse video tape two months earlier. The teachers maintained the high level of

skill performance that they had shown immediately after the mini-course. Consequently, there was not much room for them to score higher on the video tape taken four months after the mini-course was completed.

Mini-course Two deals with skills in language instruction. It was tested with 47 kindergarten teachers. Substantial gains in skill were found for 10 of the 14 skills involved.

Mini-course Three concerns "Effective Questioning in a Classroom Discussion—Secondary Level." The 74 high-school teachers who took the mini-course significantly increased their use of cognitively complex questions and the use of clarification techniques. They decreased the number of factual questions, repeated their own questions less frequently, answered their own questions less frequently, and repeated pupil answers to questions less frequently. Their percentage of teacher talk decreased, the average length of pupil response increased and the percentage of pupil talk increased. The quality of pupil responses also increased very significantly.

Mini-course Five concerns tutoring in mathematics. Forty-seven experienced teachers took the mini-course, most of whom had had considerable previous in-service instruction. Through the mini-course they became more economical in their use of tutoring time, requiring less time to accomplish the same tasks. They used more praise and more effective questioning skills. They also increased the number of different techniques that they used in demonstrating mathematical concepts.

Mini-course Eight concerns meeting individual learning needs at the kindergarten level. Nine teaching skills were defined and measured by trained observers on video tapes. Pupil reactions to the teaching were also measured in the same manner. In all but one of the nine areas the teachers in the sample improved significantly. In all nine areas the pupils responded significantly better. The authors concluded that the teachers learned to utilize new techniques for instruction, and that the mini-course fostered independent learning in pupils.

Perhaps it is not unfitting to end this parade of studies, testifying to the utility of micro-teaching, by citing a study which points up a risk that may be inherent in this kind of tactical coaching in highly specified skills. Emmer, Good, and Oakland (1970) found that a teacher's preference for a particular teaching style can be significantly influenced by the kind of feedback the teacher expects to receive. When the student teachers in this study expected to receive feedback based on the appropriateness of their behavior for the style they chose to practice, they tended to abandon the discovery style of teaching and shift their preferences toward an expository style. Eighty-eight students took part in a series of micro-teaching experiences. Four feedback conditions were arranged: 1) feedback concerning the extent to which the student teacher's behavior matched the style he chose to practice; 2) feedback about the extent to which students learned from the micro-teaching lesson; 3) feedback focused on the student's interest and motivation in a lesson; and 4) no feedback at all. Students were assigned to one of the four kinds of treatment. Only those who were informed that their feedback would be of the first type made any significant change in their preference for teaching style. Apparently, they gravitated toward the style which they thought they "understood better" than another style. The authors raised the caveat that when student teachers come to expect this type of feedback in a micro-teaching program, it can be detrimental to their willingness to experiment with less familiar patterns of instruction. (May it, indeed, make them more rigid and more directive, unless this risk is perceptively circumvented?)

Training Teachers in Behavior Modification Techniques

Still another relatively recent instructional technique which stresses careful specifying of behavioral objectives, reinforcement of desirable behaviors, and rapid feedback of the effects of such reinforcements, is the system variously called behavior modification, behavioral intervention or the like. What follows here is condensed from an excellent review of the literature by Patterson (1971). He summarizes the research, almost all of it within the last five or six years, finding numerous studies which have trained teachers to use behavioral modification procedures in order to alter the classroom behavior of children (more often than not, problem children). Most investigators, he reports, report successful outcomes for their teacher-training efforts although some report equivocal findings.

Teachers vary greatly, it appears, in their readiness and willingness to use positive reinforcers. Even more pressing is the problem of providing social reinforcers that will maintain the behavior of the teacher. A good many studies appear to indicate that it is possible to train teachers to use positive social reinforcers to alter the behavior of children. The problem is, how is the behavior of the *teacher* to be maintained over the lengthy period of time it takes to establish lasting changes in child behavior? Research by Brown, Montgomery, and Barclay (1969) suggests that unless a great deal of reinforcement is supplied to the teacher, the teacher may not maintain the desired behavior modification strategy with the child. In one case study, the rate of positive reinforcement supplied by two teachers for a deviant boy was graphed. In the first phase, their natural style of reinforcement was recorded. In a second phase, a psychologist reinforced the teachers for *their reinforcing behavior*. For a subsequent third period the psychologist stopped reinforcing the teachers. In a fourth phase, he again supplied reinforcement to the teachers. A graph of these four stages shows a dramatic drop in the teachers' use of positive reinforcement with the child, precisely during the stage when the psychologist stopped reinforcing them. Subsequently, there was a dramatic resurgence in reinforcement of the child when the teachers were again given positive reinforcement by the psychologist. In turn, the child's incidence of deviant behavior was a mirror image of the teachers' behavior. As the psychologist reinforced the teachers, they gave much more positive reinforcement to the boy, and his deviancy plummeted. As soon as the psychologist stopped reinforcing the teachers, they stopped reinforcing the boy's positive behavior, and his deviancy rate climbed. As soon as the psychologist resumed rewarding the teachers, they rewarded the boy for good behavior and his deviancy fell off dramatically.

It should be noted that most of the experiments with this strategy have dealt only with "problem children." Little research is reported with normal children. Consequently, generalization of the method to most school situations remains an untested proposition.

The whole pattern of Skinnerian reinforcement, which stresses positive rewards for desirable behavior but sturdily ignores all other behaviors, flies in the face of traditional "common sense." It certainly contravenes the behavior pattern most teachers and parents have learned to use with children. It is all very well to cite scientific evidence in support of this new strategy, but it is a severe wrench for either teachers or parents to depart from their age-old custom of punishing undesirable acts in order to adopt this strategy. Just this one element, alone, might be sufficient to account for a great deal of the difficulty in getting adults to deal with children by using predominantly positive reinforcement. Proposing this new approach may create a good deal of anxiety in a conscientious adult, thereby interfering with its adoption and maintenance.

Patterson remarks that alterations in child behavior are simply not all that reinforcing for the teacher, even when the new strategy is successful, and that many teachers probably will not maintain the strategy after the termination of training. He has the unusual practicality to suggest that the permanence of such training might be considerably more effective if teacher salaries were contingent on their ability to maintain the desired behavior. Patterson cites a report by Koenig (1967) in which student teachers' course grades were contingent on their effectiveness in achieving pupil gains. Wittrock's study, cited earlier (Wittrock, 1962), suggests that this approach might have some undesirable side effects, however. In any case, Patterson makes a highly valid point when he notes that the problem of effective reinforcers for teachers has gone almost totally unconsidered and that it is a crucial problem in designing programs of this kind that will actually work and *keep on working*.

The Virtues of Practicing What We Preach

"Do as I say, not as I do" is a notoriously poor formula for getting people to act the way you want them to. Nonetheless, teacher education has largely followed that formula for centuries. Generations of student teachers in America have sat through unnumbered hours of lectures on the virtues of educating children through democratic discussion. Other examples could be cited, much more numerous and varied than anyone would care to review in detail. In every generation there have been outstanding educators who have not succumbed to this ineffectual procedure, but only recently has this problem been remedied in a systematic, reproducible way. Whatever innovative practices may have been mounted in the past, it is only within the past few years that such efforts have been specified in detail and empirically tested to demonstrate their relative efficacy.

Several converging lines of progress are evident in the recent literature. One of these is the active involvement of pre-service teachers in the teaching act as early as possible in their professional training. There has been an increasing movement in this direction in numerous places in America. Research which carefully defines this process, however, and which measures its effects, is just now in progress, as far as we have been able to determine (Mazer, 1969; Veldman, Menaker, & Newlove, 1970).

Next to firsthand experience at responsible teaching in the classroom might come direct, personal interaction with small samples of the people whom the students will later teach (Emmer, 1970; Gordon, 1966; Holmes, 1968).

Perhaps equally relevant to actual teaching are such activities as interpersonal training experiences that are aimed directly at the kinds of interpersonal skills to be used in subsequent teaching (Bierman, Carkhuff, & Santilli, 1968; Dysart, 1953; Gregg, 1969; Krafft, 1968; Lee, 1970). There is a little parallel evidence that teachers can be made more creative by training experiences which directly employ creativity-fostering techniques (Buckeye, 1968; Compton, 1968).

Just a little further removed from actual teaching experience, but still quite potent, judging by the modest available evidence, is the use of simulation experiences which bring the prospective teacher into vicarious contact with classroom experience by way of films, tapes and other samples (Kelly, 1968; Koran, 1969; Vicek, 1965).

Almost all the studies of micro-teaching which were cited earlier include this element of an early trial experience of actual teaching. In the original model this might be considered more a simulation experience than a completely realistic sample of school performance, since the student teachers either taught each other or taught small, usually paid, samples of high-school students. Nonetheless, the prospective teachers were keenly aware that they were on the "firing line" and that their teaching was going to undergo a searching yet constructive scrutiny.

A quite similar experiment was carried on at Kansas State Teachers College in Emporia (Sandefur, 1970). In the beginning, students observed classrooms through closed circuit television and by direct visits. These observations were freely discussed in seminars each week, along with issues raised by assigned writings in the behavioral sciences and in pertinent educational fields. This was followed by participation experiences and then by graduated instructional responsibilities, climaxed in the final year by student teaching. The structure of the experiences is less notable than some of the principles which were used as guidelines throughout the project. Only informal informational statements were made by the instructors, spontaneously, if this answered an expressed need of a particular student. There were no formal lectures at any time. Since tests were considered to overemphasize memorization of facts, and also to introduce an extraneous threat, no tests were given throughout the project. Instead, there was continuous recording and discussion of each student's observable performance in the instructional tasks he was carrying out. Since the classes were intended to be as nearly threat-free as possible, there was a firm rule against sarcasm or ridicule. The classes were "dedicated to both cognitive and affective development of the students through the teacher education process." As compared with a control sample who received a more traditional form of education, the experimental students earned higher grades in their eventual student teaching, they gained an equal amount on the General Education section of the National Teachers Examination, and they showed greater gain on the Professional Education section of that exam. When their teaching was recorded and analyzed by observers using the Classroom Observation Record and by another set of observers using a 16-category system of interaction analysis, the experimental group showed many more desirable behaviors than the control group: they were fairer, more democratic, more responsive, more understanding, more stimulating, more original, more alert, more responsible, steadier, more poised, more confident, more systematic, etc. Also, the pupils of these experimental student teachers showed a large number of more desirable kinds of classroom behavior. The experimental teachers used significantly more indirect activity, and their pupils showed considerably more self-initiated activity and more thoughtfully inquiring action. Sandefur concluded that directly involving a prospective teacher in the teaching-learning process is a far more potent way to effect behavioral changes than giving theoretical training in advance of firsthand experience.

In a somewhat similar study at The University of Texas (Veldman, Menaker, & Newlove, 1970), prospective teachers served as teacher aides at a junior high school from the time of their first professional course. This included occasional tutoring of individual pupils and occasional instructional presentations to the entire class. They also received the assessment feedback consultation and the video-tape feedback consultation which are parts of the Texas R & D program of Personalized Teacher Education. A control section was taught by the same instructors, but the students did not receive the teacher-aide experience or the personalized-feedback experiences. A complex battery of nine instruments, ranging from an exit interview, through various psychological measures, to the Fuller Affective Interaction Records system of interaction analysis, was used to compare the experimental and control group gains across the training period. Some of the significant differences showed the experimentals increasing their verbal fluency and coherence on the Directed Imagination Instrument. The experimental students became more confidently oriented toward establishing their own families with a lessened dependence on their own homes and parents, whereas the control group lost some ground in this respect. In the exit interview the experimental students expressed many more kinds of satisfaction with their supervising professors. They were more satisfied with their own teaching style. Finally, they expressed, in several ways, a much stronger interest in a teaching career. There were some variables on which the control students improved more than the experimental students, but the researchers report that the results support the basic hypothesis that the experimental treatment would have beneficial effects.

Emmer (1970) took 44 secondary education students through a three-stage process. First, they participated in simulated teaching experiences where they taught lessons using their college classmates as pupil stand-ins. Next, four to seven Negro or Mexican-American volunteer students were substituted for the college classmates. In the second stage, not only was there no significant drop in the skills the prospective teachers exhibited, but there was a slight increase on some dimensions. Finally, when college classmates were again used as "pupils" following the real teaching experience, there was substantial carry-over of the increased abilities which had been demonstrated in the second stage. Significant improvements were shown on all five dimensions measured: determining pupil readiness, clarifying objectives, motivating students, evaluating students, and using indirect methods of teaching.

Mazer (1969) mounted a summer graduate training program with 53 novice teachers who were preparing to teach disadvantaged youth. They engaged in paid internships either in elementary school or in a summer camp serving disadvantaged children. The ones serving in the schools worked with predominantly Spanish-speaking children of migrant families. The group also had daily group discussions and weekly group therapy, intended to increase both their understanding and their acceptance of the children with whom they were working. These teachers came to evaluate the children more favorably in a number of respects. On the Personal Orientation Inventory they became more like self-actualized adults in their personal orientation. In another "involvement" study, Gordon

(1966) had 14 white student teachers conduct value clarification interviews with black elementary-school pupils. Another group of 14 student teachers was trained to give individual tutoring help to pupils on subject-matter problems, and a third group of 14 experienced regular student teaching in a black school setting. The MTAI, the California Behavior Preference Record and two case-study tests were used to measure differences among the three groups. Both groups who dealt with individual black children made significantly greater gains in their understanding of these pupils. The control group made no significant gains at all. Feelings of social distance from the blacks were significantly reduced only in the first group, who engaged in the individual interviews with black children.

Holmes (1968) gave 76 future secondary teachers a community field experience designed to reduce their prejudice against Negroes. There was a significant reduction of prejudice, as measured by an instrument designed for this study.

Clothier and Lawson (1969) introduced 22 teacher trainees to an intensive array of inner-city experiences in and out of school. Compared with 13 students who were simply put into these schools as student teachers, the experimental sample showed more gains in teaching skill (indirectness), in attitude toward the children, and in democratic style of teaching preference. Most impressive, perhaps, were the simple facts that of 40 students completing this program in its first year, 31 took urban school jobs, another seven took analogous teaching jobs and only one did not teach.

Moving to the more vicarious level of training, Koran (1969) demonstrated that the presentation of a model of a specific teaching skill, by way of a filmed portrayal, produced highly significant improvements in the acquisition of this skill by 121 intern teachers at Stanford. Kelly (1968) presented a simulated experience program to experienced teachers. One group of teachers

went through the simulation training prior to the start of the school year; another group went through the program later in the year, after they had assigned basal readers to pupils. The first group became significantly more aware of the reading levels of pupils in their classrooms than did the teachers who took the simulation training after they had already assigned basal readers to pupils. Vicek (1965) presented teacher trainees with a simulated classroom by means of sound motion pictures projected at life size. The trainees responded to each problem and immediately thereafter observed the class behavior elicited by their response. Problems and feedback sequences were presented repeatedly until the teacher trainee elicited the desired response from the simulated class. A guided discovery technique of instruction was employed. Students who went through this training showed greater skill at identifying and reacting effectively to representative problems than did student teachers who did not receive the simulated experience. Furthermore, the students were later able to identify and react to actual classroom problems more effectively when placed in student teaching. Finally, the students with the classroom simulated experience exhibited a higher level of self-confidence about their teaching ability than did the comparison group.

Two studies which attempted to train teachers to be more creative in their thinking reported similar results. Buckeye (1968) taught an experimental group of 95 future elementary teachers by the discovery method and a control group by lecture method. On the AC Test of Creative Ability, the experimental group increased significantly in their demonstrated creativity while the controls actually lost a significant amount of ground. Compton (1968) used a brainstorming technique to increase the creative-thinking ability of a group of Florida teachers. Thirty-six teachers were randomly assigned either to this brainstorming group or to a group using a round-table discussion approach to solving problems. Three of

Guilford's tests showed significant gains by the experimental group in spontaneous flexibility and in originality of thinking. Ten to 14 weeks later, on retest, the experimental group maintained their superiority on originality of thinking and showed a new superiority at seeing deficiencies. In short, the use of a training technique which embodies the active encouragement of originality and idiosyncratic thought appears to induce these kinds of intellectual behavior upon later measurement.

In the realm of affective experience, five studies were found, all of which supported the proposition that training which includes modeling and direct experience dealing with people, with attention focused on specific aspects of affective interaction, would significantly improve people's feelings toward other people and their ways of relating to others. Bierman, Carkhuff, and Santilli (1968) conducted a brief empathic communication training program for preschool teachers in a Head Start Program. Practice was focused on shaping trainee behavior toward increasingly emphatic levels of communication. A model of highly empathic communication was provided and the trainees were given opportunities to pursue self-explorations with the trainer about difficulties they encountered in learning the empathic skills. Both professional teachers and social workers as well as nonprofessional teacher aides and family assistants benefited significantly from the training. They increased their empathic sensitivity and their responsiveness, from an average starting level where they essentially ignored others' feelings to an average posttraining level where they achieved a high degree of reflective responsiveness to others' feelings. When the trainees compared the communication workshop with a seminar on preschool program content, they reported feeling that the communication training made a significantly greater contribution both to their work effectiveness and to their conceptual development.

Dysart (1953) found that teacher-pupil rapport improved significantly when the teachers received in-service training in sociometry and sociodrama. Gregg (1969) found that sensitivity training was an effective means of developing empathic understanding in student teachers. Lee (1970) used a Q-sort and the MTAI to compare 18 teachers who received sensitivity training, 10 teachers who received instruction in good classroom principles and 21 teachers who received no treatment. The Q-sort measured such characteristics as empathy, flexibility, communication skill, and self-perceptions on these dimensions. The sensitivity training group showed more gain in MTAI scores than did the control group. There were also significant changes on the Q-sort, favoring the sensitivity training group. The teachers in this group also increased significantly more in self-esteem than did those in the control group. Finally, the pupils of teachers who received sensitivity training were absent significantly less often than were pupils in the control classes.

Krafft (1968) found that a 10-day workshop in human relations, using an undefined "laboratory" procedure, significantly improved the instructional and interpersonal behavior of the participants. Thirty-four high-school teachers were drawn from around the country, two from each of 17 schools. An equal number of teachers from the same schools served as the control group. Six months later a team of interviewers consulted all experimental and control subjects. The interviews were taped and scored by independent coders. The coding reliability was 0.98. The workshop participants showed significant improvement, in contrast to the control group, on 18 characteristics. They were more willing to share information, made an increased effort to listen better and with more understanding, they were less irritating to others, less commanding, more cooperative and more willing to try new ideas. They were more conscious of and sensitive to the feelings, the needs and the reactions of other people. Moreover, their pupils expressed increased satisfaction with the atmosphere in small group seminars instructed by the experimental trainees. Interestingly, the best predictor of change was a composite prediction by the members of the sensitivity training group (0.55). In addition, the participants showed increased intellectual understanding of human behavior and also of such important aspects of group process as subcurrents of attitude, hidden group agendas, and the roles different members play in a group. Overall, this training appeared to generate both emotional and intellectual gains which had a beneficial impact on the trainees' co-workers, superiors and pupils after they returned to their jobs.

PROMOTING SELF-DIRECTED LEARNING

Almost all of the strategies for teacher education which have been discussed so far share one major, central theme. Either implicitly or explicitly they try to foster teacher behavior which will have the effect of engendering an actively inquiring, independent style of learning in students. The skills of micro-teaching embody this objective in a variety of ways. Equally, the whole thrust of Flanders's interaction analysis and its descendants is to generate increasingly self-starting, self-correcting learning. The "teaching laboratories" at many places usually make this philosophy an explicit part of their practice. While there may be genuine room for doubt that such an approach is the most efficient way to induce memorization and playback of information, it would be hard to argue that autonomy of thought and responsible independence of action are not major parts of the American ideal (Peck, 1970).

A number of studies have converged on this issue, training experienced teachers to maximize their pupils' growth in self-reliance, objectivity and emotional poise in coping with life. Burrell (1951) found that when teachers were trained to identify and meet the emotional needs of individual pupils, positive changes in the achievement

and in the social acceptance of those pupils resulted. Furthermore, concentration on a few selected pupils at the beginning eventually led to significant increases in the achievement and the social acceptability of the total class, by contrast with a comparable group of pupils and teachers. The study was done in two New York City schools with pupils from the lowest socioeconomic class in grades 4 through 6. Other, similar schools were used for control purposes. In 16 weeks of in-service training, the teachers studied the emotional needs of children through discussion, lecture and films, and participated in numerous informal discussions. Following this, each teacher identified five pupils who were having learning difficulties and social problems and then tried to work out tailored instructional tactics in conference with a consultant. In addition to the gains shown on the Ohio Social Acceptance Scale and on the Stanford Achievement Test, Burrell reports that truancy was reduced, the attitudes of some parents were bettered, teacher attitudes improved, pupils' interest in school increased and the work habits of the pupils improved. While only three teachers and their classes made up the experimental group, and three other classes the control group, the differences were large enough to be meaningful.

It would be unsafe to generalize from such a tiny sample if it were not that several similar studies report similar results. For example, Fleming (1951) trained teachers to meet the emotional needs of selected pupils who were prone to exhibit psychosomatic symptoms regularly. This produced a significant reduction in the frequency and intensity of such symptoms. In addition, the pupils' school attendance improved significantly in the experimental group and their academic achievement was maintained.

Trione (1967) studied the effects of having a school psychologist serve as an in-service consultant to teachers, promoting a "do it yourself" style of diagnostic evaluation and instructional invention on the part of the teachers. The psychologist worked with nine teachers who had 229 fourth-grade pupils. Eight other teachers, with 162 pupils, constituted a control group. The two groups were similar in IQ scores. Controlling for years of experience in the teachers, it was found that the experimental pupils made significantly greater improvement in reading achievement.

Currently, the Personalized School Program of the Texas R & D Center is engaged in a somewhat larger-scale study of this kind (Peck, 1971). Behavioral consultants work with teachers at both the elementary and secondary level, starting with intensive diagnostic study and modified, individualized instruction for selected pupils in each class. The aim of the program is to increase the generalized coping skills of the children so that they will tend to confront problems more actively, generate their own trial solutions and work persistently to achieve effective outcomes. Preliminary findings indicate similar effects to those found in the studies just cited.

By far the most impressive completed research of this kind is described in a final report which arrived just as this chapter was being completed. It reports on a five-year, longitudinal study of the effects of early educational intervention in the lives of disadvantaged children in Durham, North Carolina (Spaulding, 1971). This report, condensed though it is, occupies three volumes. Goals were set for the teachers in terms of the experimental treatments they were to apply in their dealings with pupils. The goals included discovery pedagogy in several subject fields: direct instruction in motor skill development; programmed learning when there were materials consistent with the first two goals; individualized, ungraded, noncompetitive instruction; procedures for reinforcing effective coping behavior by individual pupils; avoidance of negative reinforcement wherever possible; fostering of problem-oriented, self-directed learning; and several other consonant goals. A complex training program was worked out for the teachers, always including ex-

perimental work with a few selected children at any one time. Where verbal and graphic feedback to the teachers about their classroom behavior did not seem to be working, video tapes and micro-teaching techniques were invoked.

Reminiscent of the first theme of this chapter is the finding that teacher learning increased greatly and reached greatest stability when the teacher was equipped with a wireless, transistorized audio-receiver (with ear speaker) so that she could be prompted during classroom activities by an observer who was behind a one-way glass window. The complex, ingenious set of treatments needs to be read in the original.

The results of this five-year study were positive and impressive. In the group of 154 children, those whose teachers applied the experimental procedures showed the following improvements, as contrasted with control pupils: 1) when the intent of the class was to pursue teacher-directed activities, the experimental children became more conforming and cooperative in their behavior; 2) when the intent of the class was to have the children operate productively on their own, they did, in fact, increase their independence, their assertiveness and their productivity. With respect to intellectual performance, the experimental children made significant gains in Stanford-Binet IQ scores. These gains were sustained throughout the period of treatment. The IQs of the children in the matched control groups declined slightly during the period of the study.

There was a special finding of particular interest concerning the IQ scores of the black children in the experimental sample. Over the period of the study, the original bimodal distribution changed to a normal distribution, without the excessive frequency of children at the low end of the IQ range which had appeared in the beginning. The mean IQ for the group moved up to approximate the mean for the local white children. The authors point out the serious question this throws on any recommendation that low-income black children should be trained primarily in associative skills. This experimental program tried to teach the children problem-solving skills without teaching anything like the test items per se. Spaulding believes the findings indicate that teachers *can* teach young children to think, and that restricting the early instruction of poor black children to associative learning, as some have suggested, would simply institutionalize a pattern of intellectual deficit which does *not* stem from innate differences in capability.

Moreover, the younger a child was when he entered the program, the higher he was likely to score on the Stanford-Binet at exit. The authors interpret this as a result of less decline in IQ *prior* to school for the younger children. Length of time within the experimental program did not relate to gain in IQ.

The experimental program proved significantly more effective in generating language skills if continued for two or more school years rather than only one year.

Regarding academic performance, the experimental children did not perform as well as the control sample at the end of the first year. By the end of the second or third year of ungraded experience, however, they scored slightly higher than the control pupils on the Metropolitan Achievement Test. After departure from the program and entry into regular classes of the public schools, experimental pupils lost ground relative to Metropolitan Achievement Test norms, but so did the control children of similar background.

The authors believe the study demonstrates that teachers can be taught to use differentiated reinforcement treatments which develop desirable social skills in their pupils as well as enhance their intellectual development.

A quite different program for pre-service teachers has been developed at the Texas R & D Center, but it is conceptually linked quite closely with the studies just cited from in-service education. This Personalized Teacher Education Program is an integrated assemblage of a number of different instructional strategies. All of the procedures are designed to maximize the personal relevance of the experiences the prospective teacher undergoes. Special techniques have been invented and tested for facilitating self-discovery, individualized pacing and selection of learning experiences, and the encouragement of increasingly independent, self-correcting thought and professional action. This is an instructionally designed system, modularized as far as possible. Many of the learning experiences consist of self-study units with carefully stated objectives, a complete set of learning materials, and exit measures of mastery. In a larger sense, all of the instructional operations are moving toward the state where their objectives are precisely identified, the procedures and processes are spelled out in detail, and appropriate evaluative measures are provided for both the student and the instructor to gauge individual progress.

There is direct, early involvement in the teaching process. Instruction is done by a multidisciplinary team of college and public school instructors who play multiple, differentiated roles (Butts, Carter, Colton, Gibb, Hall, & Rutherford, 1970).

One phase of this program consists of a complex system of assessment procedures, including psychological, behavioral and observational measures which are used sequentially throughout training. At the outset the psychological assessment battery is used as the basis for self-confrontation, feedback counseling. This technique was originally developed for executive training (Peck, 1954) and applied experimentally to teacher education. In two studies of the effects of such counseling (Fuller & Bown, 1967; Fuller, Menaker, Peck, & Bown, 1967), it was found that student teachers who had been counseled showed significantly fewer self-protective concerns and more concern with pupil learning than did a comparable, noncounseled group. The counseled group also showed greater openness to feedback from pupils when their classroom behavior was filmed.

In precursor studies, 8mm sound movies were used to give personalized feedback to individual student teachers. More recently, video tape has been used for the same purpose. Video tapes are also used at other points in the program in an adaptation of micro-teaching to coach students individually on skills which they need to increase. Even such conferences, however, are informed by the instructor's knowledge of the student as a person, gained from appropriate input from the assessment counseling experience and from reciprocal discussions throughout the training among the student, the counselor and the other instructors on the team.

Another major part of the program consists of learning modules on the teaching of various kinds of subject matter by "discovery" processes, wherever this is applicable (Butts, 1971). By no means all of the content of the teacher education sequence has yet been cast in this form, but a number of subsystems of such modules are now available (Thomas, 1969; York, 1971).

Still another aspect of the program combines independent study with guided, individual conferences in a self-paced, proctored instruction program. In this program a senior professor supervises 10 senior undergraduate proctors who, in turn, guide junior level undergraduates through self-paced instructional units and monitor the testing at the end of each unit. The students are free to take a unit test at any time. A score of 100 percent is necessary to proceed to a following unit. Less than 100 percent mastery means additional readings and a discussion of possible remedies with the proctor, followed by an alternate form of the exit test. When a comparison was made with conventionally taught control sections, no significant difference was found on the unit test scores. However, 33 percent of the students in the self-paced group completed the course work earlier than the control classes. In exit interviews, the experimental students

indicated very positive feelings about the method and expressed a strong desire to have other courses conducted in the same manner. What is more, the senior proctors became intensely involved with the idea of individualized instruction. They talked freely of their feelings about the different forms of education they had experienced. In addition, they regarded the proctoring as an extremely valuable practicum in diagnosis and prescription for learning. The authors of the report pointed out that instructional cost is considerably less with this self-paced format. Seven hundred and twenty undergraduates could be managed by only five faculty members and two full-time secretaries, with 90 senior proctors working in the program for course credit (Bunderson, Hereford, & Stenning, 1968).

Several of the major components of this personalized teacher-education program were tested in a five-year experimental study (Fuller, Peck, Bown, Menaker, White, & Veldman, 1969). The results demonstrated that the personalized intervention treatment had measurable, desirable effects on both the attitudes and the teaching behavior of students in the experimental program, six to 12 months after the intervention treatments. By contrast with control students, they spent less time lecturing and more time questioning students. Their pupils engaged in a considerably greater amount of in-class talk. On the Directed Imagination Test the experimental students showed superiority to the control students in the sharpness of focus of their thinking, the organization of their thinking, their imaginativeness, their optimism and their self-confidence in their own abilities. The experimental students expressed a more positive attitude toward assessment feedback and film feedback, although they were quite discriminating in reacting to the specific nature of the feedback they individually received. The authors summarized the behavioral results by saying that the experimental students became more receptive to feedback from pupils in their teaching and

showed a number of positive gains in attitudinal and intellectual characteristics. Finally, they became more firmly committed
to teaching as a career than did the control
students.

Before leaving this subject, it must be observed that many of the current innovative
systems for promoting learning do *not* provide for training teachers to involve pupils
in the decision-making process in an active,
self-directing way. For example, the creators
of the Individually Prescribed Instruction
program at the University of Pittsburgh
R & D Center have frequently stated a wish
that this could be done, but the actual operation of the Individually Prescribed Instruction system does not currently give pupils
much opportunity to make decisions of any
degree of cognitive complexity. Indeed, most
of the new systems of "individualized" curricula either build the decisions into the materials themselves in a programmed way, or
they put the decision making firmly in the
hands of the teacher. In many cases the developers of these systems have been the first
to say that more room for pupil initiative
needs to be built into the systems; so far,
however, there has not been the scale of support that would bring about the marriage of
curricular materials, arduously developed in
one institution with a strategy of teacher
training developed in another institution
that would give pupils continuing, graduated experience in thinking for themselves
and learning how to check their own thinking.

Human Factors Make a Difference

Lest overly simple generalizations about
educational strategies go unchallenged, a
number of researchers have studied differences in training which stem from differences in the characteristics of the participants: the teacher himself, the college
supervisor and the cooperating teacher.

There have been many studies showing
significant differences in values and styles
of teaching between elementary teachers

and secondary teachers. For the purposes of
this review, four studies were found which
measured the effects of such grade-level
preference on response to a teacher-training
process. Butts and Raun (1968a) trained 60
elementary teachers to adopt the method of
"Science: A Process Approach." Teachers of
primary grades showed a very positive
change in their attitude toward the teaching
of science, whereas teachers of intermediate
grades showed no change or a negative
change in their attitude. In another study
(Butts & Raun, 1968b), the researchers concluded that such an innovative program for
science teaching produced the greatest
change in teachers who have considerable
teaching experience but who have not had
a great deal of formal training in science.
The longer a teacher has taught, they
found, the more value she placed on this
curriculum innovation, the greater was its
impact on her and the more she saw herself
being actively involved in it. Wilk (1964)
found that students who preferred to teach
the upper grades created a better climate in
the classroom when placed at that level than
they did when teaching in lower grades.
Student teachers who preferred the lower
grades performed equally well when placed
first in one and then the other grade level.

Out of 138 student teachers, Coody and
Hinely (1967) had their college supervisors
pick the 12 most dominant and the 12 most
submissive students. The Edwards Personal
Preference Schedule differentiated significantly between these two groups. The dominant group had significantly higher scores
on the scales of aggression, autonomy and
dominance, whereas the submissive groups
scored significantly higher on abasement
and succorance. Both groups showed some
common characteristics, such as avoidance
of routine, a lack of endurance and avoidance of positions of leadership and responsibility. Not too surprisingly, perhaps, both
of these extremely deviant groups received
significantly lower grades in student teaching than did the average teacher in the total
sample.

Feshbach (1969), studying 240 female student teachers, found that they preferred pupils whose behaviors reflected control, caution and conformity over pupils whose behavior reflected independence, challenge and flexibility, even though they felt that the latter pupils were probably more intelligent. There was an important difference in sex-typed perceptions. The student teachers found girls more desirable than boys if they showed control, caution and conformity, whereas they rated girls less desirable than boys if they showed independence, challenge and flexibility.

Gall, Borg, Kelley, and Langer (1969) studied the relationship of 17 personality variables to six kinds of teaching behavior, before and after an in-service mini-course in micro-teaching. Among female teachers they found no significant correlation between personality characteristics and teaching behavior, either before or after the training. With male teachers, however, they found that the more the males talked in class discussion before the training, the more likely they were to be achievement-oriented, autonomous, nonaffiliative, aggressive, authoritarian and seeking consistency. After the mini-course, however, this influence of personality almost disappeared.

As in several of the studies reported earlier, this suggests that good training does make a difference. Teaching skills can be taught. If they are not taught, teachers are apt to do whatever they happen to have learned through earlier life experiences, but training can override these accidental effects of unguided experience if it is well done.

Musella (1969) studied the relationship between dogmatism and self-evaluation during student teaching, and the relationship between dogmatism and students' evaluations of their supervisors. He found that dogmatic students tended to rate themselves higher in teaching than did open-minded student teachers, and that they tended to rate supervising teachers lower than did the more open-minded student teachers. They described themselves in more positive terms than the less dogmatic teachers, and they displayed less differentiation and variability in their perception of teaching. Hunt and Joyce (1967) found that student teachers who thought at a high conceptual level were more flexible, more capable of invoking alternate solutions and, in general, helped children think for themselves more effectively. This was by contrast with students whose conceptual level, as measured by a special sentence completion instrument, was appreciably lower. In one other study of cognitive effects of teacher preparation, Rouse (1968) found that there was actually a slight negative correlation between the amount of college mathematics which elementary teachers had studied and the arithmetic achievement of their pupils. Students of teachers who had less college preparation in mathematics actually learned more arithmetic. Whether too much college preparation puts teachers out of step with the simpler levels of mathematics, whether teachers who elect more mathematics in college tend to relate less well to children, or whether some other reason could be found, the author did not speculate.

Cicirelli (1969) studied the relationship of the creativity of university supervisors to the nature of the evaluative thinking they applied to their observations of student teachers. He found that more creative supervisors were aware of a greater number of factors in the student teachers' performances, tended to use broad, general factors in assessing performance rather than minutely detailed ones, and were more sensitive to factors involving teacher-pupil relationships than were their less creative colleagues. The measures of creativity ability were the Torrance Test of Creative Thinking and the Mednick Remote Associates Test.

The largest group of studies concerns the influence of the cooperating teacher on the performance and growth of the student teacher. Haberman (1970) found that neither cooperating teachers nor student teachers were unrealistically gullible. He informed the cooperating teachers that an experimental group of students was "decidedly above average in ability." At the close of student teaching, the supervisors did not rate these particular students any higher than they rated a control group. Similarly, when the student teachers were informed that they were working with "one of the finest teachers in the state," their end-of-term ratings of the cooperating teachers were no higher than the ratings given teachers by students who were not given this rosy picture in advance. Johnson (1969) studied whether the degree of dogmatism of the supervising teacher affects the change in dogmatism of the student during the student-teaching experience, using Rokeach's scale. The population consisted of 80 student teachers and their 80 supervising teachers. A significant influence on student change was observed. By the end of the semester, of the 80 pairs, 53 showed a change in the student toward the position of the supervising teacher on the dogmatism scale.

Sanford (1960) found a complicating factor in the attitudinal interaction of students under supervisors. Using the MTAI, he found that student teachers who shared the same basic attitudes toward pupils at the beginning as their cooperating teachers tended to change further toward the cooperating teacher's position. On the other hand, student teachers who initially held attitudes opposed to those of their cooperating teacher tended to change even farther away from the teacher's position.

Underhill (1969) studied the factor of empathy. He found that student teachers tended to change toward the empathy level of their cooperating teacher; but, if a student teacher who had a low empathy score was placed with a cooperating teacher with a high empathy score, the student teacher tended to become even less empathic. Empathy was measured by viewing video-taped excerpts of real counseling sessions and selecting statements to describe the counselee's feelings.

Veldman (1970), on the other hand, after studying 55 seventh-grade classes where pupils described their student teachers with the Pupil Observation Survey Report (Veldman & Peck, 1964), concluded that the cooperating teachers did tend to set the structure of class activities which the student teachers thereafter followed, but that they did not shape the individual teaching style which the pupils saw the student teacher display. The individual personality of the student teacher came through quite strongly in these evaluations. Hayes (1969) used several attitude scales and concluded that the beliefs student teachers held prior to their field experience had a greater effect on their later beliefs than did the external influence of the cooperating teacher or the college supervisor. Nonetheless, he did find a number of influences at work, such as the tendency of student teachers to gravitate toward the dogmatism score of their cooperating teachers, particularly in the case of highly open-minded students.

Sorenson and Halpert (1968) studied 248 student teachers at UCLA, measuring the amounts and kinds of stress reported throughout the student teaching. They concluded that it was not so much the interaction between the student teacher and individual people in the school as the organizational climate of this school which affected students' senses of stress. There was an interesting overall finding: 70 percent of the subjects reported considerable stress at the beginning of the period while only 20 percent of them still experienced strong discomfort by the end of student teaching.

Moskowitz (1967) found that when both cooperating teachers and student teachers were trained in interaction analysis, they both showed more variability in their teaching patterns than did similar people who were not trained in this manner. Such training did not affect the attitudes of cooperating teachers toward their students, although students showed very positive attitudes toward cooperating teachers who had been trained in interaction analysis, whether or not the students had been so trained. Trained student teachers showed negative attitudes toward cooperating teachers who were not so trained.

Finally, Yee (1968) applied a sophisticated statistical technique to study the interacting effects of cooperating teachers and student teachers (124 of each) on MTAI change scores in each group. He concluded that the cooperating teachers did, indeed, influence their student teachers' attitudes, largely in the direction of the attitudes held by the cooperating teachers. He found little evidence of student teachers' influencing the attitudes of their supervising teachers. In an even more complex study, Yee (1969) analyzed the triadic relationships of the student teacher, the cooperating teacher and the college supervisor over a semester student-teaching period. He found that during the semester coalitions were formed, particularly between the college supervisors and the cooperating teachers. The consequence was that the relationships between students and supervisors strongly tended to become more negative as the semester wore on.

Desirable and Questionable Effects of Traditional Teacher Education

There is ample and impressive testimony that student teaching tends to be the most practical and useful part of pre-service education in the minds of prospective teachers. This being said, it must next be recognized that there is also a substantial body of evidence suggesting that undefined or ill-defined student teaching is by no means beneficial in its effects.

To begin on a positive note, Bradtmueller (1964) found that student teaching improved student teachers' skills in the teaching of reading. As it happens, the author reports enough other facts to make it clear that someone had done a good job of selecting the supervising teachers of these students. The supervisors did significantly better on a test of skill in the teaching of reading than did a random sample of other elementary classroom teachers who were taking a graduate class at the university. Thus, in this case, it looks as though the students' growth in skills was a direct result of careful selection and planning of the supervision they received. Howard (1966) also found a large number and variety of gains by teachers who were taking a special fifth-year program. Their classroom behavior, their attitudes and many other characteristics showed improvement over the year's training. Even so, he found that teacher aptitude, verbal ability and critical thinking significantly predicted child gains and that various estimations of teacher classroom behavior also predicted child gains. Unfortunately, the report included no details on the nature of the teacher-education program which might explain the systematic improvements.

Lantz (1964) found that student teaching improved the self-evaluations of 36 female student teachers. In a rather similar study, however, Dumas (1969) found that among the 94 student teachers he studied, only those specializing in English showed any gain in self-appraisal. Student teachers in other subjects showed no such improvement in self-confidence. In short, undefined "student teaching" does not have uniformly good effects.

From this point on, all of the discoverable studies came together in one large cluster. What they indicate is that, at least by the end of student teaching, there are some almost universally reported decrements in attitude and in teaching behavior, as compared with the starting position of the students prior to their field experience. Gewinner (1968), as so many have, used the MTAI to study attitude changes. He found that 150 student teachers tended to change strongly in the direction of more authoritarian attitudes. Muuss (1969) found a pattern that is repeated frequently in other studies. During a period of academic courses in education on the college campus, MTAI scores increased significantly among 52 students in a fifth-year graduate program. During a following internship, however, their attitudes declined strongly. He attributed this to their reports of frustration in the internship, although placement in an inner-city school was not significantly correlated with a decrease in MTAI scores. Osmon (1959) found a significant loss in MTAI score during student teaching among 222 secondary student teachers. The students associated this negative change in attitude with problems of motivating pupils, difficulty with pupil control and discipline, a belief that the pupils were achieving commensurate with their abilities, beliefs that the pupils had cooperated very poorly, and a belief that their cooperating teacher's supervision had not been adequate. Many of those who declined in their scores decided not to seek a teaching position the following year.

Scott and Brinkley (1960) found an interaction effect with the attitudes of the cooperating teachers. Student teachers whose supervisors' attitudes toward pupils were superior to their own made significant improvements in their attitudes toward pupils. On the other hand, those who worked with cooperating teachers whose MTAI scores were lower than their own showed no significant change in their scores by the end of student teaching. Teigland (1966) separated 45 subjects who changed most positively on their MTAI scores from 45 who changed most negatively. He found that the group with the positive change scored significantly higher on a measure of deference and also received higher course grades. He suggested that the MTAI may measure something other than the students' actual attitudes (apple-polishing?). Indeed, when Ragsdale (1967) compared the changes in the attitudes of 49 elementary student teachers with changes in their classroom behavior, he found that changes on the MTAI, the F Scale of Authoritarianism and the Ryans Teacher Characteristics Schedule, all self-report instruments, did not show changes that corresponded to actual changes in classroom behavior as measured by the Flanders Interaction Analysis System and by Ryans's

Teacher Characteristics Classroom Record. In short, he raised some doubts about the validity of the self-report measures, including the MTAI.

Lest the highly consistent set of studies just reported be dismissed too easily, however, on grounds of lack of validity in the questionnaire, some other evidence is available which points in exactly the same direction. Jacobs (1967) studied the attitude changes of 1,007 education students during their initial academic preparation and during the student-teaching phase of their training. The Valenti-Nelson Survey of Teaching Practices was the instrument used. In the initial training phase, the students changed away from more rigid and formal types of responses to more informal and personal styles. In the student-teaching phase, however, the changes were exactly the opposite: toward a more rigid and impersonal style of response. Similarly, Hoy (1967), in studying 282 student teachers, found that they changed significantly from a "humanistic" approach to a "custodial" approach which stressed the virtues of bureaucratic order and control.

In a study where 64 student teachers in suburban, middle-class schools were compared with 77 similar students who were tutoring inner-city children, the attitude changes over the experience, as measured by two semantic differential instruments and a condensed version of the MTAI, were decidedly in favor of the tutoring experience. The student teachers became more controlling and less pupil-centered while the tutors became less controlling and more pupil-centered. The authors suggest that there are considerable advantages in the tutoring situation as it helps teachers learn to see pupils as individuals (Walberg, Metzner, Todd, & Henry, 1968).

Two other studies did not take the relatively easy way out of administering questionnaires but made objective measures of classroom behavior in order to study changes in teaching behavior during student teaching. Iannaccone (1963) analyzed the daily logs of 25 education students written throughout their student-teaching semester. Twenty-four of the 25 students initially showed the characteristic pattern of shock and "horror" at the "incorrect" methods employed by their cooperating teachers. There was much disagreement expressed between what the student teachers had learned in their university courses and what they observed the cooperating teachers doing. When actually faced with the task of teaching, however, they too began to use these formerly unacceptable methods. Their logs showed a tendency to justify their actions on the basis of the fact that "it works." When faced with children who were not discipline problems, for example, but who did not openly show responsive reactions to the teacher during instruction, the student teachers reclassified them simply as "slow learners." Their expressed concern at the beginning for the individual pupil and his learning dropped out of their logs as they moved into teaching. It was replaced by concern for "getting the class through the lesson." They no longer saw remedial work with the individual pupils as teaching. "Teaching means taking the class through the lesson."

While there is undoubtedly some degree of realism in this change of attitude, it sounds even more like a cry of despair when faced with many simultaneous demands without adequately precise, constructive guidance in techniques which would *both* maintain orderly operation and facilitate growth in pupil thinking and skill. Matthews (1967) applied interaction analysis to the measurement of 52 student teachers over a period of three years. He found that by the end of student teaching the student teachers became more restrictive of student behavior, that they devoted an increasing proportion of their time to stating facts or their own opinions, that they showed less acceptance and less clarification of student ideas, and that the frequency and length of student response to their questions decreased. When this study is put alongside

the group of MTAI studies, it suggests that the negative changes in student teachers may be quite real.

One study, happily, was found which makes it possible to end these remarks on a positive note. Perrodin (1961) found that student teachers made significant improvements in professional attitudes, as measured by the MTAI, when they were placed with cooperating teachers who had received a special preparation program in supervising student teachers. Apparently when cooperating teachers are trained to supervise beginners, the beginners finish their student teaching with much more learner-centered values than do most beginners at the end of their student teaching.

The Training of Teachers of Teachers: A Research Vacuum

Heiss (1970) surveyed higher education to find out what is being done to improve college teaching. She concluded that very little, indeed, is being done. Furthermore, practically no research of any kind is being carried out in this field. Our own efforts found exactly the same result: nothing.

This is not to say that there is not a good deal of activity in this field. For several years there was a national program under the auspices of the U. S. Office of Education which went by the Triple-T designation. It sponsored action programs at numerous places. A number of the national R & D Centers and Regional Laboratories collaborated in these efforts. Both the Stanford Center and the Texas Center are collaborating with other institutions in projects of this kind. As yet, probably because these programs are just getting organized and because they are hard to mount, let alone to research, neither evaluative nor basic research can be reported from these efforts.

Progress in Using Pupil Gain Criteria

Until fairly recently, for perfectly good practical reasons in most cases, most studies of teacher education tended to end in mid-air, so to speak. The terminal criterion was stated in terms of teacher behavior. No connection was made to the consequences of that behavior in terms of pupil gains. This left a great many decisions about teacher education to be based on sheer, untested assumptions—scarcely a desirable state of affairs (Peck & Dingman, 1968).

There is an accelerating trend, however, toward linking teacher education to its consequences in the cognitive, affective or behavioral learning of the teachers' pupils (Aubertine, 1964; Baker, 1969; Borg et al., 1970; Brophy & Good, 1970; Burger, 1961; Davis & Smoot, 1969; Emmer & Millett, 1968; Howard, 1966; Kaya, 1969; Krafft, 1968; Lee, 1970; Limbacher, 1969; Parrish, 1969; Sandefur, 1970; Spaulding, 1971; Trione, 1967; Wittrock, 1962). Studying such linkages is not just an academic exercise for intellectual purists. It is essential to gather empirical evidence which will indicate precisely what kinds of teachers, using what kinds of procedures, most effectively foster healthy mental and behavioral skills in different kinds of children who have greatly differing backgrounds, needs and future careers. If only because so much variation in learning is due to the many social, intellectual, emotional and motivational differences among children, any technique which purports to be appropriate for teachers to use must be assessed for its impact on different kinds of children. In a larger sense, it simply is not good science, nor good empirical practice, to recommend a way of training teachers without knowing, in fact, how it will affect those teachers' students. That, after all, is the only criterion by which the ultimate worth of any educational system can be measured.

Our past collective failure to subject teacher education to this test was not because we did not understand this. We simply could not afford to do it in most cases. Now a growing number of studies attest to the feasibility of doing it, at least in a limited way. In some cases, the judicious design of data-collecting procedures (such as interaction analysis, of several kinds) makes it possible to capture not only what the teacher does after a specified kind of training, but some useful part of the students' reactions to that teaching. Most of the studies cited here have conducted this kind of formative evaluation. Summative evaluation, particularly of important long-term effects on student learning, attitudes and behavior, largely remains to be done in future studies.

SOME POSITIVE IMPLICATIONS OF THE AVAILABLE RESEARCH

Just within the past 10 to 15 years the operational skills of teaching have become better defined and measured than ever before. Traditional teacher education, with its frequently lengthy stays in the semantic stratosphere, has not done a very effective job of developing these skills, particularly at the pre-service level. Accumulating evidence does suggest, however, that a genuine revolution in the nature and quality of teacher education is already visible on the horizon. It may not be implemented effectively in very many places, as yet, but the direction of movement does seem rather clear. That direction is indicated by the themes reviewed here, if we have read the evidence correctly.

Teacher education seems likely to become a far more systematized process in the years ahead. Its objectives seem likely to be much better stated in terms of concrete, observable and trainable teaching behaviors. Methods for capturing objective records of teaching behavior and feeding them back to teachers seem likely to win rapidly spreading adoption. At the pre-service level, well-planned, early involvement in actual teaching seems likely to be available to more and more students. The influence of the most widely favored systems for conceptualizing effective teaching, and the emergence of more effective techniques for training teachers in this direction, both seem likely to accelerate the move toward more active, self-directed learning, both for teachers and for their pupils.

Meanwhile, skilled manpower and improved technology are becoming available on an increasing scale, to make possible more penetrating and more adequately comprehensive studies of alternative training procedures. The national level of support for such research showed encouraging growth from 1963 to 1968. Since then the slowing, almost to a halt, of growth in support for this work postpones somewhere into the future any great advance in the complexity and power of research which can be mounted. Even so, the improved quality of the research capability which the past few years has brought should make it more possible to secure resumed growth in the funding for educational research and development.

Teacher education can no longer remain in a happily ignorant, ineffectual state consisting of romanticized lectures, on the one hand, and fuzzy or unplanned "practical" experience on the other. We are genuinely in sight of the theoretical principles, the operational measures, and even the developmental technology for moving onto a performance-based method of appraising teaching. A great deal of research remains to be done to discover additional theoretical principles which would lead to more effective training. Even more extensive and more expensive evaluative research will be absolutely necessary in order to test and refine instructional systems so that we can be sure they will have beneficial effects under carefully specified, differentiated conditions of application. The day is still quite a long way off, but it is no longer merely wishful thinking to foresee a performance-based system for the certification of teachers. More importantly, we can foresee an objective, extremely helpful system of continuing, lifelong development for all members of the profession who want to keep improving their skills.

REFERENCES

Acheson, K. A. *The effects of feedback from television recordings and three types of supervisory treatment on selected teacher behaviors.* (Doctoral dissertation, Stanford University) Ann Arbor, Mich.: University Microfilms, 1965. No. 64-13,542.

Allen, D. W., & Fortune, J. C. An analysis of micro-teaching: A new procedure in teacher education. In *Micro-teaching: A description.* Stanford, Calif.: School of Education, Stanford University, 1967. Section III, pp. 1–11.

Amidon, E. (Ed.) *Project on student teaching: The effects of teaching interaction analysis to student teachers.* U. S. Department of Health, Education and Welfare project number 2873 under the provisions of the Cooperative Research Program. Philadelphia: Temple University, 1970.

Aubertine, H. E. *An experiment in the set induction process and its application in teaching.* (Doctoral dissertation, Stanford University) Ann Arbor, Mich.: University Microfilms, 1965. No. 64-13,544.

Baker, E. L. Relationship between learner achievement and instructional principles stressed during teacher preparation. *The Journal of Educational Research,* 1969, 63, 99–102.

Bierman, R., Carkhuff, R. R., & Santilli, M. Efficacy of empathic communication training groups for inner city preschool teachers and family workers. Unpublished manuscript, University of Waterloo, Waterloo, Ontario, 1968. Report available from the authors. (mimeograph)

Bondi, J. C., Jr. Feedback from interaction analysis: Some implications for the improvement of teaching. *Journal of Teacher Education,* 1970, 21, 189–196.

Borg, W. R., Kelly, M. L., Langer, P., & Gall, M. *The minicourse: A micro-teaching approach to teacher education.* Beverly Hills, Calif.: Macmillan Educational Services, 1970.

Bradtmueller, W. G. *An investigation of the development of problem solving skills related to teaching reading during student teaching.* (Doctoral dissertation, Indiana University) Ann Arbor, Mich.: University Microfilms, 1964. No. 64-1671.

Breit, F. D., & Butts, D. P. *A comparison of*

the effectiveness of an inservice program and a preservice program in developing certain teaching competencies. R & D Report Series Number 11. Austin, Tex.: The University of Texas, The Research and Development Center for Teacher Education, 1969.

Brophy, J. E., & Good, T. L. Teacher-child dyadic interaction: A manual for coding classroom behavior. R & D Report Series No. 27. Austin, Tex.: The University of Texas, The Research and Development Center for Teacher Education, 1969.

Brophy, J. E., & Good, T. L. Teachers' communication of differential expectations for children's classroom performance: Some behavioral data. Journal of Educational Psychology, 1970, 61, 365–374.

Brown, J. C., Montgomery, R., & Barclay, J. An example of psychologist management of teacher reinforcement procedures in the elementary classroom. Psychology in the schools, 1969, 6, 336–340.

Buckeye, D. A. The effects of a creative classroom environment on the creative ability of prospective elementary mathematics teachers. (Doctoral dissertation, Indiana University) Ann Arbor, Mich.: University Microfilms, 1968. No. 68-17,256.

Bunderson, C. V., Hereford, C., & Stenning, W. Computer-assisted instruction in self-paced teacher education. Paper presented at the meeting of the American Educational Research Association, Chicago, February 1968.

Burge, E. W. The relationship of certain personality attributes to the verbal behavior of selected student teachers in the secondary school classroom. (Doctoral dissertation, North Texas State University) Ann Arbor, Mich.: University Microfilms, 1967. No. 67-8079.

Burger, E. The use of television for in-service teacher training. (Doctoral dissertation, University of Virginia) Ann Arbor, Mich.: University Microfilms, 1961. No. 60-4629.

Burrell, A. P. Facilitating learning through emphasis on meeting children's basic emotional needs: An in-service training program. Journal of Educational Sociology, 1951, 24, 381–393.

Butman, J. Memorandum to participants in the facilitators of inquiry workshop, Anchorage, Alaska. Portland, Ore.: Northwest Regional Educational Laboratory, 1970.

Butts, D. P. The design of self-directed learning guides. R & D Report Series No. 57. Austin, Tex.: The University of Texas, The Research and Development Center for Teacher Education, 1971.

Butts, D. P., Carter, H., Colton, T., Gibb, E. G., Hall, G. E., & Rutherford, W. The block program: A personalized teacher education professional program. R & D Report Series No. 54. Austin, Tex.: The University of Texas, The Research and Development Center for Teacher Education, 1970.

Butts, D. P., & Raun, C. E. A study in teacher attitude change. R & D Report Series No. 6. Austin, Tex.: The University of Texas, The Research and Development Center for Teacher Education, 1968. (a)

Butts, D. P., & Raun, C. E. A study in teacher change. R & D Report Series No. 5. Austin, Tex.: The University of Texas, The Research and Development Center for Teacher Education, 1968. (b)

Cicirelli, V. G. University supervisors' creative ability and their appraisal of student teachers' classroom performance: An exploratory study. The Journal of Educational Research, 1969, 62, 375–381.

Clothier, G. M., & Lawson, J. H. Innovation in the inner-city. Kansas City, Mo.: Mid-Continent Regional Educational Laboratory, 1969.

Collier, R. O., Jr. Some strengths and weaknesses of research methodology in teacher education. In F. R. Cyphert, & E. Spaights (Eds.), An analysis and projection of research in teacher education. U.S.O.E. Cooperative Research Project No. F-015. Columbus, Ohio: The Ohio State University Research Foundation, 1964. Pp. 123–148.

Compton, M. F. An attempt to foster creative thinking in teachers. (Doctoral dissertation, University of Florida) Ann Arbor, Mich.: University Microfilms, 1968. No. 68-9463.

Coody, B. E., & Hinely, R. T. A validity study of selected EPPS subscales for determining need structure of dominating and submissive student teachers. The Journal of Educational Research, 1967, 61, 59–61.

Cooper, J. M., & Stroud, T. The Stanford Summer Micro-teaching Clinic, 1966. In Micro-teaching: A description. Stanford, Calif.: School of Education, Stanford University, 1967. Section I, pp. 1–22.

Cyphert, F. R., & Spaights, E. An analysis and

projection of research in teacher education. U.S.O.E. Cooperative Research Project No. F-015. Columbus, Ohio: The Ohio State University Research Foundation, 1964.

Davis, O. L., Jr., & Smoot, B. R. *Effects on the verbal teaching behaviors of beginning secondary teacher candidates' participation in a program of laboratory teaching.* R & D Report Series No. 2. Austin, Tex.: The University of Texas, The Research and Development Center for Teacher Education, 1969.

Denemark, G. W., & Macdonald, J. B. Preservice and in-service education of teachers. *Review of Educational Research,* 1967, 37, 233–247.

Dumas, W. Factors associated with self-concept change in student teachers. *The Journal of Educational Research,* 1969, 62, 275–278.

Dysart, J. M. *A study of the effect of in-service training in sociometry and sociodrama on teacher-pupil rapport and social climate in the classroom.* (Doctoral dissertation, New York University) Ann Arbor, Mich.: University Microfilms, 1953. No. 4542.

Emmer, E. T. *Transfer of instructional behavior and performance acquired in simulated teaching.* R & D Report Series No. 50. Austin, Tex.: The University of Texas, The Research and Development Center for Teacher Education, 1970.

Emmer, E. T., Good, T. L., & Oakland, T. D. *The effect of feedback expectancy on teacher trainees' preferences for teaching styles.* R & D Report Series No. 29. Austin, Tex.: The University of Texas, The Research and Development Center for Teacher Education, 1970.

Emmer, E. T., & Millett, G. B. An assessment of terminal performance in a teaching laboratory: A pilot study. Austin, Tex.: The University of Texas, The Research and Development Center for Teacher Education, 1968. (mimeographed)

Feshbach, N. D. Student teacher preferences for elementary school pupils varying in personality characteristics. *Journal of Educational Psychology,* 1969, 60, 126–132.

Finske, C.S.C., Sister M. Joanice. *The effect of feedback through interaction analysis on the development of flexibility in student teachers.* (Doctoral dissertation, The University of Michigan) Ann Arbor, Mich.: University Microfilms, 1967. No. 67-15,621.

Flanders, N. A. (Ed.) *Helping teachers change*

their behavior. Ann Arbor, Mich.: University of Michigan, 1963.

Flanders, N. A., & Simon, A. Teacher effectiveness. In R. L. Ebel (Ed.), *Encyclopedia of educational research.* (4th ed.) New York: Macmillan, 1969. Pp. 1423–1437.

Fleming, R. S. The effects of an in-service education program on children with symptoms of psychosomatic illness. *Journal of Educational Sociology,* 1951, 24, 394–405.

Fortune, J. C., Cooper, J. M., & Allen, D. W. The Stanford summer micro-teaching clinic, 1965. *Journal of Teacher Education,* 1967, 18, 389–393.

Fuller, F. F., & Bown, O. H. The influence of feedback on empirically derived student teacher concerns. Paper presented at the meeting of the American Educational Research Association, New York, February 1967.

Fuller, F. F., Menaker, S., Peck, R. F., & Bown, O. H. Influence of counseling and film feedback on openness to pupil feedback in elementary teachers' filmed behavior. Paper presented at the meeting of the American Psychological Association, Washington, D. C., September 1967.

Fuller, F. F., Peck, R. F., Bown, O. H., Menaker, S. L., White, M. M., & Veldman, D. J. *Effects of personalized feedback during teacher preparation on teacher personality and teaching behavior.* R & D Report Series No. 4. Austin, Tex.: The University of Texas, The Research and Development Center for Teacher Education, 1969.

Fuller, F. F., Veldman, D. J., & Richek, H. G. Tape recordings, feedback and prospective teachers' self evaluation. *Alberta Journal of Educational Research,* 1966, 12, 301–307.

Gall, M. D., Borg, W. R., Kelley, M. L., & Langer, P. The relationship between personality and teaching behavior before and after inservice microteaching training. Berkeley, Calif.: Far West Laboratory for Educational Research and Development, 1969. (mimeographed)

Gewinner, M. N. *A study of the results of the interaction of student teachers with their supervising teachers during the student teaching period.* (Doctoral dissertation, Mississippi State University) Ann Arbor, Mich.: University Microfilms, 1968. No. 68-9413.

Good, T. L., & Brophy, J. E. Teacher-child dyadic interactions: A new method of classroom observation. *Journal of School Psychology,* 1970, 8, 131–138.

Gordon, J. E., Jr. *The effects on white student teachers of value clarification interviews with Negro pupils.* (Doctoral dissertation, New York University) Ann Arbor, Mich.: University Microfilms, 1966. No. 66-5778.

Gregg, D. B. *An investigation of the development of empathic communication through a sensitivity training experience.* (Doctoral dissertation, Lehigh University) Ann Arbor, Mich.: University Microfilms, 1969. No. 69-7337.

Greif, I. P. *An investigation of the effect of a distinct emphasis on creative and critical thinking in teacher education.* (Doctoral dissertation, Wayne State University) Ann Arbor, Mich.: University Microfilms, 1961. No. 60-2324.

Haberman, M. The relationship of bogus expectations to success in student teaching (or Pygmalion's illegitimate son). *Journal of Teacher Education,* 1970, 21, 69–72.

Hayes, A. P. *Effects of cooperating teachers and college supervisors on student teachers' beliefs.* (Doctoral dissertation, The University of Florida) Ann Arbor, Mich.: University Microfilms, 1969. No. 69-17,027.

Heinrich, D., & McKeegan, H. F. Immediate and delayed feedback procedures for modifying student teaching behavior according to a model of instruction. Paper presented at the meeting of the American Educational Research Association, Los Angeles, February 1969.

Heiss, A. M. The preparation of college and university teachers. Berkeley, Calif.: University of California, The Center for Research and Development in Higher Education, 1970. (mimeographed)

Holmes, F. E. *The effect of a community field study on the tolerant-prejudice attitude of prospective secondary teachers toward Negroes.* (Doctoral dissertation, University of Denver) Ann Arbor, Mich.: University Microfilms, 1968. No. 68-6117.

Hoover, K. H., & Schutz, R. E. Student attitude change in an introductory education course. *The Journal of Educational Research,* 1968, 61, 300–303.

Hough, J. B., & Amidon, E. J. *Behavioral change in pre-service teacher preparation: An experimental study.* Philadelphia: Temple University, College of Education, 1964.

Hough, J. B., & Amidon, E. J. The relationship of personality structure and training in interaction analysis to attitude change during student teaching. Paper presented at the meeting of the American Educational Research Association, Chicago, February 1965.

Hough, J. B., & Amidon, E. J. Behavioral change in student teachers. In E. J. Amidon, & J. B. Hough (Eds.), *Interaction analysis: Theory, research, and application.* Reading, Mass.: Addison-Wesley, 1967. Pp. 307–314.

Hough, J. B., Lohman, E. E., & Ober, R. Shaping and predicting verbal teaching behavior in a general methods course. *The Journal of Teacher Education,* 1969, 20, 213–224.

Hough, J. B., & Ober, R. The effect of training in interaction analysis on the verbal teaching behavior of pre-service teachers. Paper presented at the meeting of the American Educational Research Association, Chicago, February 1966.

Hough, J. B., & Revsin, B. Programed instruction at the college level: A study of several factors influencing learning. *Phi Delta Kappan,* 1963, 44, 286–291.

Howard, J. L. *An analysis of change in teacher and pupil behavior: A study of the fifth-year program in teacher education at the University of North Carolina, 1963–1964.* (Doctoral dissertation, The University of North Carolina at Chapel Hill) Ann Arbor, Mich.: University Microfilms, 1966. No. 65-14,351.

Hoy, W. K. Organizational socialization: The student teacher and pupil control ideology. *The Journal of Educational Research,* 1967, 61, 153–155.

Hunt, D. E., & Joyce, B. R. Teacher trainee personality and initial teaching style. *American Educational Research Journal,* 1967, 4, 253–259.

Iannaccone, L. Student teaching: A transitional stage in the making of a teacher. *Theory into Practice,* 1963, 2, 73–80.

Ishler, R. E. An experimental study using Withalls' Social-Emotional Climate Index to determine the effectiveness of feedback as a means of changing student teachers' verbal behavior. *The Journal of Educational Research,* 1967, 61, 121–123.

Jacobs, E. B. *Personal and instructional variables as related to changes in educational attitudes of prospective elementary school teachers during two phases of the teacher education program, 1965–1966.* (Doctoral dissertation, Northern Illinois University) Ann Arbor, Mich.: University Microfilms, 1967. No. 67-12,898.

James, H. H. Differential efficacy of three supervisory methods for development of a teaching strategy. Paper presented at the meeting of the American Educational Research Association, Minneapolis, March 1970.

Johnson, J. S. Change in student teacher dogmatism. *The Journal of Educational Research,* 1969, 62, 224–226.

Joyce, B. R. *Exploration of the utilization of personnel in the supervision of student teachers when feedback via films and systems for the analysis of teaching are introduced into the student teaching program. Final report.* New York: Teachers College, Columbia University, 1967. ED 202 575.

Kallenbach, W. W., & Gall, M. D. Microteaching versus conventional methods in training elementary intern teachers. *The Journal of Educational Research,* 1969, 63, 136–141.

Kaya, E. Improving the cognitive functioning of pupils through teacher-training in process objectives: A field experiment. Paper presented at the meeting of the American Educational Research Association, Los Angeles, February 1969.

Kelly, D. *Effects of an in-service education program utilizing simulated classroom procedures on classroom teachers' awareness of pupils' instructional reading levels in the classroom.* (Doctoral dissertation, Case Western Reserve University) Ann Arbor, Mich.: University Microfilms, 1968. No. 68-3315.

Kirk, J. Elementary school student teachers and interaction analysis. In E. Amidon, & J. B. Hough (Eds.), *Interaction analysis: Theory, research, and application.* Reading, Mass.: Addison-Wesley, 1967. Pp. 299–306.

Koenig, C. H. Precision teaching with emotionally disturbed pupils. Research Training Paper, No. 17, University of Kansas Medical Center, Special Education Research, Children's Rehabilitation Unit, 1967.

Koran, M. L. *The effects of individual differences on observational learning in the acquisition of a teaching skill.* (Doctoral dissertation, Stanford University) Ann Arbor, Mich.: University Microfilms, 1969. No. 69-17,435.

Krafft, L. J. *The influence of human relations laboratory training upon the perceived behavioral changes on secondary school seminar instructors.* (Doctoral dissertation, Michigan State University) Ann Arbor, Mich.: University Microfilms, 1968. No. 68-4165.

Langer, P., & Allen, G. E. The minicourse as a tool for training teachers in interaction analysis. Paper presented at the meeting of the American Educational Research Association, Minneapolis, March 1970.

Lantz, D. L. Changes in student teachers' concepts of self and others. *Journal of Teacher Education,* 1964, 15, 200–203.

Lee, W. S. Human relations training for teachers: The effectiveness of sensitivity training. *California Journal of Educational Research,* 1970, 21, 28–34.

Limbacher, P. C. *A study of the effects of microteaching experiences upon practice teaching classroom behavior.* (Doctoral dissertation, University of Illinois) *Dissertation Abstracts International,* 1969, 30, 189.

Lohman, E. E., Ober, R., & Hough, J. B. A study of the effect of pre-service training in interaction analysis on the verbal behavior of student teachers. In E. J. Amidon, & J. B. Hough (Eds.), *Interaction analysis: Theory, research, and application.* Reading, Mass.: Addison-Wesley, 1967. Pp. 346–359.

Luebkemann, H. H. *The effects of selected student teaching program variables on certain values and certain verbal behaviors of student teachers.* (Doctoral dissertation, The Pennsylvania State University) Ann Arbor, Mich.: University Microfilms, 1966. No. 66-8737.

MacGraw, F. M., Jr. *The use of 35mm time lapse photography as a feedback and observation instrument in teacher education.* (Doctoral dissertation, Stanford University) Ann Arbor, Mich.: University Microfilms, 1966. No. 66-2516.

Matthews, C. C. *The classroom verbal behavior of selected secondary school science student teachers and their cooperating classroom teachers.* (Doctoral dissertation, Cornell University) Ann Arbor, Mich.: University Microfilms, 1967. No. 67-1394.

Mazer, G. E. Attitude and personality change

in student teachers of disadvantaged youth. *The Journal of Educational Research,* 1969, 63, 116–120.

Millett, G. B. *Comparison of training procedures for promoting teacher and learner translation behavior.* Technical Report No. 9. Stanford, Calif.: Stanford University, Center for Research and Development in Teaching, 1969.

Morgan, J. C., & Woerdehoff, F. J. Stability of student teacher behaviors and their relationship to personality and creativity factors. *The Journal of Educational Research,* 1969, 62, 251–254.

Morse, K. R., & Davis, O. L., Jr. *The effectiveness of teaching laboratory instruction on the questioning behaviors of beginning teacher candidates.* R & D Report Series Number 43. Austin, Tex.: The University of Texas, The Research and Development Center for Teacher Education, 1970.

Morse, K. R., Kysilka, M. L., & Davis, O. L., Jr. *Effects of different types of supervisory feedback on teacher candidates' development of re-focusing behaviors.* R & D Report Series Number 48. Austin, Tex.: The University of Texas, The Research and Development Center for Teacher Education, 1970.

Moskowitz, G. The attitudes and teaching patterns of cooperating teachers and student teachers trained in interaction analysis. In E. J. Amidon, & J. B. Hough (Eds.), *Interaction analysis: Theory, research and application.* Reading, Mass.: Addison-Wesley, 1967. Pp. 271–282.

Musella, D. Perceptual-cognitive style as related to self-evaluation and supervisor rating by student teachers. *The Journal of Experimental Education,* 1969, 37(3), 51–55.

Muuss, R. E. Differential effects of studying versus teaching on teachers' attitudes. *The Journal of Educational Research,* 1969, 63, 185–189.

Osmon, R. V. *Associative factors in changes of student teachers' attitudes during student teaching.* (Doctoral dissertation, Indiana University) Ann Arbor, Mich.: University Microfilms, 1959. No. 59-4279.

Parrish, H. W. *A study of the effects of inservice training in interaction analysis on the verbal behavior of experienced teachers.* (Doctoral dissertation, University of Oregon) Ann Arbor, Mich.: University Microfilms, 1969. No. 69-38.

Patterson, G. R. Behavioral intervention procedures in the classroom and in the home. In A. E. Bergin, & S. L. Garfield (Eds.), *Handbook of psychotherapy and behavior change: An empirical analysis.* New York: John Wiley, 1971. Pp. 751–775.

Peck, R. F. The use of individual assessments in a management development program. *Journal of Personnel Management and Industrial Relations,* 1954, 1, 79–98.

Peck, R. F. Personalized education: An attainable goal in the seventies. In *Needs of elementary and secondary education for the seventies.* A compendium of policy papers compiled by the General Subcommittee on Education of the Committee on Education and Labor, U.S. House of Representatives. Washington, D.C.: U.S. Government Printing Office, 1970.

Peck, R. F. Promoting self-disciplined learning: A researchable revolution. In B. O. Smith (Ed.), *Research in teacher education.* New York: Prentice-Hall, 1971. Pp. 82–98.

Peck, R. F., & Dingman, H. F. Some criterion problems in evaluation of teacher education. *Psychological Reports,* 1968, 23, 300.

Perrodin, A. F. In support of supervising teacher education programs. *Journal of Teacher Education,* 1961, 12, 36–38.

Ragsdale, E. M. *Attitude changes of elementary student teachers and the changes in their classroom behavior during student teaching.* (Doctoral dissertation, Ball State University) Ann Arbor, Mich.: University Microfilms, 1967. No. 67-10,687.

Ranson, J. T. (Ed.) *The effectiveness of two interaction analysis instructional modules within an inservice setting.* Charleston, W. Va.: Appalachia Educational Laboratory, 1969.

Rouse, W. M., Jr. *A study of the correlation between the academic preparation of teachers of mathematics and the mathematics achievement of their students in kindergarten through grade eight.* (Doctoral dissertation, Michigan State University) Ann Arbor, Mich.: University Microfilms, 1968. No. 68-4205.

Sandefur, J. T. Kansas State Teachers College experimental study of professional education for secondary teachers. *The Journal of Teacher Education,* 1970, 21, 386–395.

Sandefur, J. T., Pankratz, R., & Couch, J. *Observation and demonstration in teacher edu-*

cation by closed-circuit television and video-tape recordings. Final Report of Research Project No. 5-1009, Title VII-A, NDEA, PL. 85-864. Emporia, Kans.: Kansas State Teachers College, 1967. ED 014 904.

Sanford, A. *The practice teaching experience and its effect on cadet teacher attitudes toward pupils.* (Doctoral dissertation, Boston University School of Education) Ann Arbor, Mich.: University Microfilms, 1960. No. 59-6957.

Scott, O., & Brinkley, S. G. Attitude changes of student teachers and the validity of the Minnesota Teacher Attitude Inventory. *Journal of Educational Psychology,* 1960, 51, 76–81.

Simon, A. *The effects of training in inter-action analysis on the teaching patterns of student teachers in favored and non-favored classes.* (Doctoral dissertation, Temple University) Ann Arbor, Mich.: University Microfilms, 1967. No. 67-6258.

Sorenson, G., & Halpert, R. Stress in student teaching. *California Journal of Educational Research,* 1968, 19, 28–33.

Spaulding, R. L. *Educational intervention in early childhood,* Vols. I, II, & III. Durham, N.C.: Duke University, 1971.

Steinbach, A., & Butts, D. P. *A comparative study of the effect of practice with elementary children or with peers in the science methods course.* R & D Report Series Number 10. Austin, Tex.: The University of Texas, The Research and Development Center for Teacher Education, 1968.

Steinen, R. F. *An exploratory study of the results of providing increased feedback to student teachers of mathematics.* (Doctoral dissertation, The Ohio State University) Ann Arbor, Mich.: University Microfilms, 1967. No. 67-2544.

Teigland, J. J. The relationship between measured teacher attitude change and certain personality characteristics. *The Journal of Educational Research,* 1966, 60, 84–85.

Thomas, M. P., Jr. *Cooperation and competition in problem solving.* Austin, Tex.: The University of Texas, R & D Center for Teacher Education, October 1969.

Trione, V. The school psychologist, teacher change and fourth grade reading achievement. *California Journal of Educational Research,* 1967, 18, 194–200.

Tuckman, B. W., McCall, K. M., & Hyman,
R. T. The modification of teacher behavior: Effects of dissonance and coded feedback. *American Educational Research Journal,* 1969, 6, 607–619.

Tuckman, B. W., & Oliver, W. F. Effectiveness of feedback to teachers as a function of source. *Journal of Educational Psychology,* 1968, 59, 297–301.

Underhill, R. G. *The relation of elementary student teacher empathy (affective sensitivity) change to supervising teacher empathy and student teaching success.* (Doctoral dissertation, Michigan State University) Ann Arbor, Mich.: University Microfilms, 1969. No. 69-5980.

Veldman, D. J. Pupil evaluation of student teachers and their supervisors. *Journal of Teacher Education,* 1970, 21, 165–167.

Veldman, D. J., Menaker, S. L., & Newlove, B. The Porter Project: Teacher aides in a secondary school. A preliminary report. Austin, Tex.: The University of Texas, The Research and Development Center for Teacher Education, 1970. (mimeographed)

Veldman, D. J., & Peck, R. F. The influence of teacher and pupil sex on pupil evaluations of student teachers. *Journal of Teacher Education,* 1964, 15, 393–396.

Vicek, C. W. *Assessing the effect and transfer value of a classroom simulator technique.* (Doctoral dissertation, Michigan State University) Ann Arbor, Mich.: University Microfilms, 1965. No. 66-450.

Walberg, H. J., Metzner, S., Todd, R. M., & Henry, P. M. Effects of tutoring and practice teaching on self-concept and attitudes in education students. *The Journal of Teacher Education,* 1968, 19, 283–291.

Wallen, C., & Utsey, J. Training teachers to determine learner achievement of objectives in reading instruction. Paper presented at the meeting of the American Educational Research Association, Los Angeles, February 1969.

Wedberg, D. P. *A comparative investigation of the instructional and administrative efficiency of various observational techniques in the introductory course in education.* (Doctoral dissertation, University of Southern California) Ann Arbor, Mich.: University Microfilms, 1963. No. 63-5065.

Wilk, R. E. An experimental study of the effects of classroom placement variables on student teacher performance. *Journal of Ed-*

ucational Psychology, 1964, 55, 375–380.

Wilk, R. E., Edson, W. H., & Wu, J. J. Student personnel research in teacher education. *Review of Educational Research,* 1967, 37, 219–232.

Wittrock, M. C. Set applied to student teaching. *Journal of Educational Psychology,* 1962, 53, 175–180.

Yee, A. H. Interpersonal relationships in the student-teaching triad. *The Journal of Teacher Education,* 1968, 19, 95–112.

Yee, A. H. Do cooperating teachers influence the attitudes of student teachers? *Journal of Educational Psychology,* 1969, 60, 327–332.

York, L. J. *An individualized multi-media approach to the study of team teaching.* A series of seven instructional units. Dallas: Leslie Press, 1971.

Young, D. B. The effectiveness of self-instruction in teacher education using modeling and video tape feedback. Paper presented at the meeting of the American Educational Research Association, Chicago, February 1968.

CHAPTER **31** Educational Technology and Related
Research Viewed as a Political Force

ROBERT M. W. TRAVERS
Western Michigan University

Many reviews of educational technology have been written—some with enthusiastic support and some with skepticism. This chapter attempts an entirely different task. Here we will examine the contemporary attempt to expand educational invention as a process deeply rooted in the politics of the times and, like all technological developments, having unwanted side effects that may even be of disastrous proportions unless steps are taken to counteract them. An attempt will be made here to show that the trend in the development of educational technology parallels closely the development that other technologies have taken in past centuries, but with potential consequences that need to be studied rather than ignored as they are at present. Our concern will not be with particular devices but with the broad trend of technological development in education as it has emerged under the sponsorship of the federal government during the past decade. Although a certain amount of gadgetry has been produced by private enterprises during that time, the main impetus for educational technological development in the United States has come from the U.S. Office of Education and the

very substantial sums of money that the Congress has provided to support the programs of the Office.

Since a chapter such as this one is easily misinterpreted as being antitechnology, the point must be made at the outset that my position, like that of others who have written on the subject, is that the human lot has gained rather than suffered by the development of technology. The latter position was taken by the panel convened by the National Academy of Sciences and reported by Brooks and Bowers (1970). This position does not mean that all technologies have such a balance in their favor, but only that an overall evaluation of technology comes out with a balance on the credit side. Educational technology has much to offer, but it is as likely as any other technology to have contributions on the negative side of the ledger. The possibility of such a negative contribution seems to have been hardly considered until recently and, at the time of writing, neither the American Psychological Association nor the American Educational Research Association (AERA) has any committees considering that possibility.

The concept that a revolution could be

brought about in education through the development of an educational technology appears to have originated in the writing of Pressey (1932) nearly 50 years ago. Pressey drew a colorful picture of an industrial revolution in education that would parallel in significance the revolution that took place earlier in the manufacturing world. The industrial revolution that Pressey foresaw in the schools was imagined to be a mechanical one, with machinery being introduced to aid in the task of teaching much as the introduction of machinery into industry had facilitated the task of manufacturing. Pressey wrote as a scientist and took the view that what he called the coming industrial revolution in education would be a revolution based on scientific knowledge. The new technology of education was to be a science-based technology and the scientific foundation was to be provided by the emerging behavioral sciences. Pressey overlooked the fact that the industrial revolution took place in Europe before science had had any significant impact on technology, and he viewed the emergence of an educational technology as being the outgrowth of a science of behavior. Nearly a quarter of a century later, when Skinner began writing on the same topic (see his collected papers on this subject, 1961), he took the position that a technology had not emerged, as Pressey had predicted it would, because the science of learning had not, until near mid-century, provided the foundation on which a technology of education could be built. Skinner believed that a science of learning had, at last, advanced to the point where it could be used as a guide in the development of a technology of education. Pressey had viewed the schools as needing the efficiency of a factory, but Skinner saw the schools as needing a more effective control over behavior like that which the psychologist can exercise in the laboratory. Skinner (1961) thought that the problem would be a quite simple one to solve and, writing of the need to reform education, wrote that "the technical prob-

lem of providing the necessary instrumental aid is not particularly difficult" (p. 154). Such an optimistic view turned out to be quite unjustified. Skinner's view that a body of psychological knowledge is there, awaiting application, is not shared by many other scientists who investigate learning phenomena. Mackie and Christensen (1967), who studied the views of research psychologists on this matter, concluded that these psychologists doubted that any simple, direct translation could be made from laboratory findings to practical applications. The general view expressed was that such translations were highly hazardous and had not had a marked history of success.

The basic idea propounded by both Pressey and Skinner was that technology was a result of scientific development and that technology would not develop until the necessary underlying sciences had progressed to the point where related technologies could be based upon them. This is a modern, and parochial, view of technology, for the fact is that technology has had a history of development at least back to the time of cave men, and probably before. Only in recent times have there emerged technologies that are based on advanced scientific knowledge, of which perhaps the pharmaceutical industry would be an example. Much of modern technology, if not most technology, is based on inventions made prior to the scientific era. Although the development of scientific knowledge has had enormous impact on some aspects of technology in recent times, history shows that technology has had growth independent of scientific knowledge.

The government sponsorship of educational research and development has been based largely on the concepts of Pressey and Skinner. The Cooperative Research Act of 1954 implied that there is a close relationship between scientific research and educational technology of the kind of which the latter two authors wrote. The Cooperative Research Act implied that what needed to be done was to develop the necessary knowledge and demonstrations of that knowledge, and the industrial revolution in education was bound to take place. During the next decade, some disillusionment concerning the validity of this position became evident. When the Elementary and Secondary Education Act of 1965 was written, the legislation implied that much more was needed than a body of research knowledge and some demonstration concerning its utility, but that definite machinery had to be developed for making applications of knowledge. The latter act proposed that a network of dissemination centers and laboratories be established which would hold the key to educational change. These organizations, in the form of research and development centers and regional laboratories, were to provide the machinery that was to build the new educational technology. The act specifically mentions "dissemination" as a function of the new organizations, implying that there was some kind of knowledge in need of widespread distribution. Like many innovations, these centers were set up without too much thought about the conditions under which a technology can best be developed, and absolutely no thought about the possibility that the new technology might have as disastrous side effects as most of the other technologies have had. Indeed, one suspects that the new organizations were set up in an atmosphere of political opportunism and inadequate planning.

The wide acceptance of the viewpoint that technology has to be a science-based enterprise led psychologists and educational technologists to look for bodies of knowledge that offered the possibility of quick application. For many, the greatest promises were offered by the findings of operant psychology. For this reason the new educational technology showed a profound influence of the operant approach. The Learning Research and Development Center at the University of Pittsburgh was influenced considerably in its early work by the concepts of operant psychology. The Regional Laboratory at Minneapolis, now defunct, was influenced more by operant psychology

than by any other area of knowledge, and the Southwest Regional Laboratory in Los Angeles has also shown considerable impact from the operant area. The ill-conceived performance contract venture was also largely operant-oriented and was pushed by an opportunistic alliance of operant psychologists and businessmen.

As the plan for revolutionizing education through the development of a federally sponsored technology emerged, the Research and Development Centers were seen as the sources of the packaged technology, and the Regional Laboratories were viewed as the dissemination centers for the technology that had been developed. The Research and Development Centers were to have contact with both the basic sciences and the schools, and through such dual contacts the application of the behavioral sciences could be sculptured to the needs of the schools. There seems to have been the assumption that scientific work had produced a body of knowledge that was just awaiting application, and that such application would necessarily be beneficial.

It is now becoming quite evident that the development of an educational technology that will benefit the people is far from being the simple matter of applying readily available scientific knowledge. Also, even if such direct applications could be made easily, there is no reason for supposing that the results would necessarily be beneficial. Although the blue-ribbon government committees that established such programs of education may have lived in an age when people believed that the mere development of a technology was necessarily beneficial, such a simplistic view can no longer be maintained. Even the schoolchild now understands that technology may have disastrous consequences.

Much can be learned about the dangers to be avoided in, and the benefits to be gained from, the development of an educational technology by searching the pages of history of technological development. An exploration of this history changed my entire conception of the role of technical inventions in social change. As a result of engaging in study in this historical area, I found myself taking a view of contemporary educational technology which I could not have imagined myself taking a decade ago. The next section of this chapter shares with the reader some of the significant ideas that emerge from this study of history.

SOME POINTS FROM THE HISTORY OF TECHNOLOGY

Histories of technology fortunately are available and provide an extraordinarily detailed description of the inventions and developments that have had enormous impact on the emergence of culture. The Singer, Holmyard, and Hall five-volume work (1954) and the Daumas volumes (translated 1969) are the classic reference works in the field, but other less comprehensive works provide detailed descriptions of particular phases of technological development. For example, Lilley (1966) has written a fine history of the development of man's use of energy other than that provided by man's own muscles. Lilley's book emphasizes the medieval period. Giedion's history of technology (1969) is of particular value in tracing the history and emergence of modern inventions. He appropriately subtitles his work, *A Contribution to Anonymous History*. White (1962) has provided a book which examines the role played by technology in the rise to power of various social groups.

Anyone who fingers through the pages of these works cannot but be impressed with the extraordinary achievements of technology that have taken place in the past without the help of scientific knowledge and the recency of the close tie between science and technology. One is surprised to find, for example, that already in Roman times there were metal smelting plants producing more than 1,000 tons of metal a year. The men who developed the large-scale production of iron from ore in Roman times

were brilliant and knowledgeable people. Their knowledge was not scientific knowledge, but their work was so effective that it permitted the arming of the Roman legions and, through the development of iron rivets, the building of large ships. The technology of the Romans was highly tied to the development of their military system and much less to the building of their cities and the life that was led there. Lilley has pointed out that, outside of the military, the ruling class of Roman citizens had little incentive for inventing ways to make life easier, for a large slave class was exploited to provide all the comforts that the Roman citizen might want. By the end of the Roman era, it was already quite apparent that the trend in the development of any technology is closely related to the needs of the ruling class by whom it is sponsored.

White (1962) has shown in his remarkable book how the power of the European nobility in the early Middle Ages was made possible through certain inventions related to the horse which made mounted warfare possible. Two inventions were necessary before the horse could be used by the mounted, armed man in Europe. One was the development of the horseshoe. Although the hoof of the horse protects the animal in the dry Middle Eastern countries where the horse was first used by man on a large scale, the hoof does not stand up well in wet climates, where it becomes soft, much as a toenail becomes soft after taking a bath. The horse was virtually useless in most European countries until man developed the iron horseshoe, which protected the foot from prolonged exposure to the wet ground. Even with the invention of the horseshoe, the armed nobility would have had difficulty in using the animal for warfare and internecine strife without the development of the stirrup. Until the stirrup arrived in Europe in the early part of the eighth century, the armed warrior had to descend from horseback to engage in combat, for the horsebacked knight who swung his sword at a target and missed was likely to be dismounted by the inertia of his swing. The arrival of the stirrup in Europe resulted in the development of cavalry as a highly mobile and effective military unit that became the source of power for many centuries. One should note that technological developments related to the horse that benefited the people seem to have taken place quite independently of the developments in which the nobles were interested. The noble bred horses for warfare, and this prevented them from being bred in a form that would make them useful for agricultural purposes. The development by the so-called barbarian of the use of the horse for working in the fields and the invention of a suitable harness was much slower than the corresponding development for warfare purposes. Indeed, White concludes that horses did not become generally used by the peasants until the eleventh century. By that time, the collar had been developed and the iron plow had replaced the pointed pole as a plowing device, and the combination of the harnessed horse and iron plow began to revolutionize food production.

The point I am making here is that technology, when its development is sponsored by a government or by the group in power, tends to develop only those ideas and devices that are of particular value to the government or power group. Technology developed under these conditions is likely to be reactionary and far removed from the welfare of the people. Indeed, it is likely to be detrimental to the people, for it has commonly been used to maintain the power of the particular government or power group. This has been true not only of governments but also of other groups which have wielded great political power, such as church, nobility or industrial complex.

The promotion of technology by the power structure has generally limited the scope of what it accomplished. This was as true in Roman times as it is today. The Roman slave state, with its great preoccupation with war, accomplished virtually nothing in the direction of producing a technology that would improve the general lot of man; but while the Romans were preoccupied with the development of the technology underlying their war machine, those who were rudely referred to as barbarians were engaged in a completely different line of development. The barbarians, unlike the Roman ruling class, needed new sources of energy to extend that of the human muscle so that the amount of work that a single person could undertake could be increased. The invention that filled this role was that of the waterwheel, which became important in many domestic operations, particularly producing ground grains and processing crude fabric. The waterwheel became a common piece of equipment and, according to Lilley (1966), by the time of the Norman conquest near the middle of the eleventh century, several thousand of these wheels were in use in southern England.

Of particular significance in the present context is the history of the development of printing, which ultimately became man's prime invention in the field of educational technology. Daumas (translated 1969), Singer, Holmyard, and Hall (1954), and other historians of technology have pointed out that although early printing from wooden blocks had been largely a monastic activity, the printing press of the Middle Ages with movable type was a development of the new artisan class that began to form the new "democratic capitalism" (White, 1962, p. 78) of urban life. Although Gütenberg is commonly given credit for inventing movable type, there is considerable evidence that Dutch printers before him had already made the invention. Credit to Gütenberg seems to be largely a result of his visibility as a character in Mainz, Germany, and the recognition given him by the Catholic Church for his work in producing a Bible that could be widely disseminated. Although the development of printing with movable type was brought about by an emerging new political force, the urban artisans, the invention could not have achieved success had it not become the servant of the great religious political estate. As the servant of the religious estate it flourished, but the religious estate was also immensely strengthened by the control it could now exercise over the ideas disseminated by this new invention. The control that the religious estate exercised in this respect is well known, but the important point to note in the present connection is that the technology of printing promoted by the Church gave the Church power that paralleled the power the nobility had been given by the development of technology related to the horse. Early printing is just another example of how technology becomes harnessed to the maintenance and enhancement of particular power groups and, thereby, very often prevents any significant contribution to the welfare of the people. However, before leaving this matter, one should note that the printing press ultimately became the main instrument through which the political power of the religious estate became eroded and reduced and, in fact, eventually became the tool that overthrew much of the power and teaching of traditional Christianity.

This brief discussion of the history of technology serves to bring out the important relationship that has existed between sources of political power and the development of particular technologies. Power groups have always exploited those aspects of technology that appeared to be instruments for maintaining power, and the resulting technologies have always been important sources of political power. Let us now turn again to educational technology as it has been nurtured and developed through the sponsorship of the federal government and consider the relationship of that enterprise to the sources of power that promote it.

THE EMERGING
GOVERNMENT-SPONSORED
EDUCATIONAL TECHNOLOGY

The new machinery for improving education that emerged as a result of federal legislation soon acquired a distinctive character reflecting the new federal emphasis on cost-benefit analysis. The new technology was to be the instrument of achieving the traditional goals of education more efficiently, in more people, and, ultimately, at less cost to the government. Although the hope was clearly expressed that through such programs education could be so designed that it would produce more learning in the affluent at less cost, considerable emphasis was placed on the development of procedures for educating along traditional lines the children of minority groups in whom the traditional goals were not being achieved. Programs were set up to help the academic achievement of ghetto children, Mexican children, the children of Eskimos, and the children of other underprivileged groups. The problems of society, as seen through government agencies, were produced by the inability of certain groups to fit the pattern of culture approved by the majority-elected government. The schools, as they had existed, had failed to produce in the minority groups the uniform pattern of human behavior that would fit the majority's concept of civilized life. Perhaps a new educational technology, highly oriented to producing such a uniform pattern of adult behavior, might succeed where the older system had failed. In addition, the new technology was expected to provide more effective education for the same expenditure, or the same quality of education for less expenditure. Like all earlier technologies, the new one in education was to become focused on what the political sources of power viewed as the main threats to the status quo. The political goals to be achieved by the new venture in education were to be much like the political goals of earlier power-group sponsored technologies, namely that of maintaining the status quo. But the nature of these goals becomes even more apparent when one examines some of the materials that these programs have produced.

The new machinery for educational

change modeled itself after other contemporary industrial enterprises and sought to change the school, and hence society, by delivering packaged products. The concentration on the packaged product seems to stem largely from the fact that there exists machinery for distributing such materials. The idea of packaged reform in education fits well with the way in which other sections of our society operate. The doctor prescribes packaged medicines. The home-owner who wishes to improve his bathroom can buy a packaged shower door complete with installation instructions. The housewife covers up her culinary limitations by buying the packaged main dish which only needs heating. With the aid of federal programs, the expectation was that the teacher could hand out packaged education backed up by some kind of guarantee concerning utility. Implicit in these packaged educational materials are political goals that have been largely ignored by both producer and user alike. Occasionally the implicit goals seep to the surface, as when one notes that Haga's book (1967), *Automated Educational Systems,* has an introduction by Max Rafferty.

Consider, for example, *The Alaskan Readers* developed under the auspices of the Northwest Regional Educational Laboratory. The descriptive pamphlet describing *The Alaskan Readers* (*The Alaskan Readers,* 1970) outlines some of the problems involved in teaching traditional academic skills to members of minority groups and presents criticisms of the usual Dick and Jane approach to the study of reading. The author of the pamphlet points out that the activities of suburban Dick and Jane are not likely to be understood at all by children living in an Eskimo village. The proposal is that the readers be based on the common experiences these children have in their natural habitat, and that knowledge be imparted in Herbartian manner, beginning with that which is familiar to them. Other publications and materials related to *The Alaskan Readers* (Jones, 1968, 1969) de-

scribe in much greater detail the design of the readers and the sophisticated linguistic and analytic approach through which they were developed. The development of the readers was based on the analysis of the skills to be learned, a theory of the development of grapheme-phoneme relationships, the identification of culturally relevant materials, the careful selection of decoding exercises, and so forth. The materials were designed and planned with all the technical skills available for such a task. One must accord those who designed them the credit they deserve for the technical competence with which they went about their task. Those who have prepared these new materials are the first to admit that the gross appearance of the material is not too different from the Dick-and-Jane style material, but the claim is also made that the materials are more efficient than those which were replaced. The goals of the Dick-and-Jane type readers and *The Alaskan Readers* are essentially the same, but the cultural bias has been altered and vastly greater care has been exercised in the details of design. The materials are not designed to achieve anything radically new but have been prepared to increase the efficiency of conservative and traditional education.

Before contrasting the educational products of the new technology with those of a different nature, the political character of the present technology must be noted. The materials are developed upon the assumption that if minority groups can be trained to fit into the system, all will be well. The emerging educational technology is intensely conservative in that it is designed to preserve the world of the establishment, just as all government-sponsored technologies have done in the past. This point will become clearer as the materials of the present technology are contrasted with others that have been developed and as we consider alternative directions in which such a technology might develop. Another example of the characteristics of materials that have been developed is found in Jones's (1970) charming book for Eskimo children entitled *Benjamin Beaver's Box,* a delightful, romantic story about the beaver. Like all works of this character, it contains a smattering of correct information and, because it is a fantasy, contains a heavy emphasis on incorrect information, such as that beavers talk. The material is almost certainly enjoyable for children, as good literary material has to be. One can present strong arguments that the material can well be described as escapist rather than as carrying a message about how to produce a better world. As literature, it does not fall into the category of John Steinbeck's *Grapes of Wrath* or Erskine Caldwell's *Tobacco Road,* for it is devoid of any message about how to correct the deficiencies in life. The mastery of reading skill alone is presumed to be the channel through which a better world is to be reached.

What has been said about *The Alaskan Readers* could be stated in parallel terms about the materials produced by other regional laboratories. The materials produced by the Southwest Regional Laboratory (SWRL) for kindergarten and the lower elementary grades, for example, develop concepts related to "color, shape, amount, position, and comparison" (SWRL, *The Instructional Concepts Program,* 1970; also from the same source, *Sizes,* undated) through illustrations of such materials as dogs balancing on balls, clowns walking on stilts, and stylized figures of various kinds. The material could also well be described as escapist. It has absolutely nothing to do with the improvement of quality of life of the people involved except for the vague hope that through the learning of these concepts a better world may evolve.

A notable example of an alternative approach to the development of such packaged materials for an elementary-school reading program is found in the work of Seay and Meece (1944) of nearly a quarter century ago. The latter work was also directed toward the development of an elementary-school curriculum that would help a minority group, that group being Appalachian children. The project, sponsored by the Sloan Foundation, was designed to produce reading materials that would help children solve some of the economic and social problems of their community. The initial step in the development of the materials was to send a team of economists, physicians, agronomists and nutritionists into the Appalachian communities in order to determine the changes that the people themselves could and should make in their handling of their affairs in order to improve the quality of life in their community. As a result of this analysis of community needs, readers and related materials were prepared with materials designed to bring about improvement in the food, clothing and housing in the community.

The details of these materials cannot be described here, but an example of the kind of findings derived from the community survey that influenced the design of the readers will stress the main point to be made. A survey of the community showed that the main food was corn and a small amount of pork; the nutritional deficiencies of the people in the experimental communities were evident. In order to improve their diet the people had to learn that they would do much better to raise goats rather than pigs. The goats could live well off the hillsides and, apart from providing a source of meat, could also give milk, some of which could be made into cheese. Their diet of corn was highly deficient in vitamins, but the people could easily learn to raise tomatoes and other vegetables and preserve some of them for winter use. One of the first programs undertaken by the project was a series of readers for the lower elementary grades entitled *Food From Our Land.* In this series, children learned, from the first reader in the first grade, how they could improve their diet by growing appropriate vegetables in their gardens. The underlying idea was that the children would take home information that they might discuss with their parents, and that the parents in turn would heed the advice given. The materials were designed to use every accessible resource to improve the people's lives. Some of the first-grade materials, as well as those for higher grades, dealt with the matter of how to combat pests that might interfere with the growth of the garden produce. Children in school performed such tasks described in the readers as those of constructing rabbit traps. In some cases the initial work on planting was undertaken in frames in the school building, and the task became a lesson in biology as well. The materials were designed to have impact on the quality of life in the community and were not limited to materials of literary interest alone.

The original plan of the Appalachian project, which is also known as the Sloan Experiment in Kentucky, was to evaluate the effectiveness of the materials in terms of community change. Health records of the children were kept in order to determine whether the long-term effects of the readers would be to improve nutrition and reduce the incidence of nutritional deficiencies. The plans for evaluating the educational approach have been described by Seay and Meece (1944) and by Clark (1943). The plans would have been a credit even to today's scientists, who live in an age that has seen the development of sophistication in the field of evaluation. Unfortunately, the plans for the evaluation study were never carried through to any degree of completion, because the war years not only limited what could be done but also did much to bring new influences into the lives of the people of the experimental communities.

The school materials described in the *Sloan Experiment in Kentucky* bring out, by contrast, the basic limitations of the materials that have been developed by the federally sponsored enterprises of recent times. In the Kentucky experiment, materials of great significance to the quality of life of the people were introduced from the start. The materials of the new educational technology are escapist and recreational.

The new readers are essentially Dick and Jane readers, but the characters are in different cultural settings. The materials are developed to produce, in those exposed to them, the step-by-step development of skills, much as a car is assembled step by step on the production line. The content of the new materials is not uninteresting to the young readers, but it does shield them from a single new idea that might improve their community or the quality of life which they enjoy.

The new materials are the inevitable products of a government-sponsored technology and are designed largely to maintain a smoothly running industrialized society in which the skills supposedly needed by workers are systematically built into them in schools run along lines very much like those of the modern assembly plant. Just as in the industrial setting, behavior is almost completely controlled by the situation, as when a person installs a front wheel on a car every 50 seconds, so in the new type of educational program are the behaviors of the pupils controlled by the educational paraphernalia that confronts them. Both systems are designed to produce a uniform product that will fit into a smoothly running system, but the manufacturer is at least making some change in the models he produces each year, while the technologically operated schools seem to be designed on the assumption that the basic skills will always be basic and the only problem is that of finding out how to teach these eternal skills effectively. Improvement of education as it appears in much of the contemporary literature produced by the new technologists means improvement along any of the dimensions of "utility and reliability effect, time, and cost" (Schutz, 1970). The typical emphasis is on time and cost, items that appropriations committees of the Congress readily understand but which may have little relevance for the improvement of the quality of life of the future generations that are involved. The point made here assumes, as Mumford has done (1970), that quality of life has little to do with fitting the individual neatly into a slot in the great industrial mega-technic machine. One can state with some assurance that the closer man comes to fitting all of his species into the megatechnic machine, the less happy man is likely to be. Mumford also points out that the new technology of education is producing in schools conditions similar to those in other aspects of the culture against which the younger generation is so vigorously pro-testing. Such an education does not enhance the human spirit and makes no contribution to what has been called the humaneness of man.

The conservative in education seeks to develop the traditional skills at less cost to the taxpayer. The radical seeks to change the content of the educational program to improve the quality of life by seeking new patterns of living. The radical is not against improving the efficiency with which basic skills can be acquired, but he would not view any particular skill as necessarily being an essential component of education for all time. The radical cannot be preoccupied with mere problems of cost in an affluent society, for a change in society brought about by education may be of priceless value. He wants to produce basic changes in society and not just remachine some of the badly fitting components.

Federally sponsored educational tech-nology is undertaking the task that power structure technology has always undertaken, namely that of maintaining the base of power of the governmental structure. It is inevitably conservative, cost-conscious, blind to the social issues of the day, and creative only within very narrow limits. It is hardly surprising that the suggestions for bold changes in education are coming largely from outside the federal power structure. High impact proposals, such as those of Silberman (1970), have to come from out-side the system, much as the barbarians of Roman times were making important tech-nological developments while the Romans were exploiting technological development only for the purpose of maintaining and developing Roman imperialism. Some read-ers will, at this point, come up with a counterargument to the one presented here and point to the fact that some of the more radical changes in education in the world today are taking place in the state-operated schools in England. This would appear to support the position that a government-sponsored technology may help free man from the machine of which he is a part. However, what has to be recognized is that the state-supported schools of England are probably freer of government control than are the state schools in any country of the world. The head executive of such a school is not the servant of a political system, as he is in the United States, but he has extraordinary freedom to plan, re-organize and create a program, and is answerable only to other professional people in his field.

The main message that this section has attempted to communicate is that educa-tional technology does not necessarily have to be oriented around the development of educational environments that will retain the status quo in society. However, tech-nology is likely to do so if it remains under the control of a government bureaucracy. Educational inventions could be made that might have the effect of developing men and women with greater freedom and greater independence of the control that the industrial machine and the government bureaucracy exercise over them. Socrates' invention of his method of teaching was of that character, and so too were the inven-tions of Pestalozzi, Froebel and Montessori. The kind of educational technology that modern governments sponsor is not de-liberately reactionary, but the emphasis of legislators is inevitably on finding some balm that will heal the sore spots in society, for that is often the reason for which they were elected to office. Any solution that seeks to solve social ills through the develop-ment of a uniform educational product by technological means is unlikely to produce the smoothly running social machine it is designed to produce, for it includes features that are highly abrasive to the spirit of man.

EDUCATION AND RESISTANCE TO SUBSEQUENT STIMULUS CONTROL

The present trend in educational technology is clearly to bring the pupil under the identifiable stimulus control to the highest degree possible. Presumably this kind of training, for one can hardly call it education, is surely designed to fit individuals into an industrial system in which they will show the same passive acceptance of control as they did in their days in the classroom. Programs such as that of Individually Prescribed Instruction, developed in the Oakleaf School by the Research and Development Center of the University of Pittsburgh, represent an extreme form of the phenomenon to which reference is made. In such a program the student has an independence of the teacher, obtaining new materials for himself as he completes each assignment. Such behavior should not be confused with autonomy, for the term autonomy implies that the individual makes real decisions for himself. In the Individually Prescribed Instruction program the pupil makes only the most trivial decisions for himself, the kind that the economist Shackle (1961) refers to as empty decisions and that he contrasts with decisions that have real significance in a person's life which make an important change in the direction of his subsequent life. Such children are required to make empty decisions for themselves within the confining controls of the educational materials. When a child finishes unit number 78 in the mathematics curriculum, he obtains the materials for unit number 79. There are no significant alternatives offered to him. If he were making decisions of real importance, the pupil would have several distinct alternatives open to him, and the choice of one of these might make a difference in some phase of his future life.

A child who asks his teacher to help him undertake an experiment that he found described in a magazine may have made an important decision in so doing, for the experience might lead to a career in science. The decision is vastly different from that of the child who decides to obtain the materials for unit 79 after completing unit 78.

The emerging new school programs are of the kind that one would design to teach children to become passively controlled by the immediate circumstances in which they are placed. The programs are education's answer to the problems created by the fact that the human components turned out by the schools do not fit easily and precisely with the mechanical components of the machine age. One can view such programs as the nonthinking man's solution to the problem of creating a nonthinking world. Yet one can build a strong case, as Mumford does (1970), that the orderly society, in which much of the control of human behavior is exercised by machines, is likely to be a society in which little of value in the human spirit can survive. The devastating effects of such control are already quite evident in the lives of those who can escape from them only by joining a drug society. Schools with programs directed toward producing uniform human components for the great production megamachine are probably contributing to this kind of social devastation. Perhaps the machinery of government is such that it cannot sponsor any other kind of educational technology, but that is an unnecessarily pessimistic point of view. The governments of many free countries have given money to enterprises over which they claim no political control.

Now evidence is accumulating from a number of different sources indicating that individuals can learn to achieve autonomy of behavior, in the sense that they can become relatively immune to much of the controlling influence of immediate circumstances. Of course, behavior cannot be completely divorced from immediate circumstances, for, if it were, it would be out of touch with reality, much as it is in the case of many psychotics. Nevertheless, in some respects independence can be acquired. One example of an adaptive type of relinquishment of immediate stimulus control is where the individual disregards immediate rewards offered in order to work for more remote rewards to be delivered at a future date. Some studies of this phenomenon have been reviewed by Walls and Smith (1970), who also point out that the ability to do this is associated with a middle-class education. The disadvantaged have not learned to detach themselves from the controlling effects of immediate stimuli and, hence, seek immediate rewards rather than long-term goals. The point to note is that the middle-class children have been able, to some degree, to detach themselves from the influence of immediate circumstances. The data are highly suggestive that education can instill the potential for achieving this important goal, the achievement of which would be one step toward becoming what has been termed here an autonomous individual. There are other sources of evidence that such autonomy can be learned. Any of the many recent reviews of attitude research, such as that provided by McGuire (1969), also provide evidence that some degree of autonomy can be achieved with respect to influences that might have immediate impact in changing attitudes. An individual can learn to relate to such influences with caution and to avoid coming under their immediate spell. The individual can learn to regard with skepticism those influences that would take over his thinking for him and deprive him of his autonomy.

The area of the development of autonomy is one that merits careful investigation. One does not know, for example, the extent to which the techniques for controlling behavior that have been introduced into some aspects of education in the last two decades result in the relinquishment of autonomy in out-of-school activities. The assumption here is that they do, and it is hardly reasonable to assume that they could do otherwise.

They might, of course, result in a heightened rebelliousness and hostility to society.

One should note, in passing, that Skinner (1971b), in his book *Beyond Freedom and Dignity*, takes a whack at medieval concepts of autonomy and disposes of them as easily as he disposes of nineteenth century psychology. He shows little disposition to contest the positions of modern psychologists who differ from his own position, and he completely disregards modern concepts of autonomous man. The choice he offers his readers is a trivial choice, and the technique he uses in presenting the alternatives is that of the politician. Like most political documents, the book ignores genuine alternatives.

The kind of education directed toward the development of what has been termed here the autonomous individual would surely have to be entirely different from that which is being developed by the federally sponsored new technology of education. Indeed, the new technology of education appears to be directed in the opposite direction. It is an extension of the machine's control over man that is evident in every factory. It embodies the worst features of the tyranny over the intellect of man that man has invented. Education should be the means of escaping from that tyranny. To do this, education has to depart from the search for ways of the step-by-step acquisition of particular skills. What is said here is not antitechnology but rather suggests that the direction of educational technology needs to be altered. Educational technology needs to become preoccupied with the development of rich and interesting environments in which children can make real decisions about what to explore. It needs to bring out the importance of significant intellectual relationships between people and the significance of intellectual interaction. It needs to encourage self-initiated exploration. It needs to demonstrate the importance of remaining relatively detached from the megamachine described by Mumford, and the school itself should be a model of such detachment.

The education provided should be truly liberal, for never was there a greater need for attempting to achieve the ideals implicit in such education.

SOME UNCONSIDERED SIDE EFFECTS OF EDUCATIONAL TECHNOLOGY

Up to this point consideration has been given to the thesis that educational technology is following the typical trend of government-sponsored technologies and is placing a strong emphasis on the immediate political goals of the times. The widely held view that the development of such a technology is surely beneficial lacks credibility in view of the harm that has resulted from other aspects of technological development. Skinner's view, expressed in public lectures (1971a) and in his book (1971b), that all that needs to be done to solve the remaining problems of the times is to develop a technology of human behavior, is likely to stimulate naive enthusiasm for social reform, already rampant in the behavioral sciences, rather than a thoughtful consideration of what techniques should be applied to the solution of our social problems with a watchful eye for harmful side effects. Let us consider some of the more obvious side effects.

If any reader does not fully appreciate the immense harm that may be done through the misapplication and misdevelopment of a technology of behavior, he should read the article by Wolf and Jorgensen (1970) which presents the frightening role that social scientists have played in the war in Southeast Asia during the sixties. As an example of the latter enterprise, one can cite the proposal that came out of one research project which was that if food was to be used to control the behavior of Southeast Asians, then the first step would have to be that of destroying all the crops and food supplies of the people to be controlled. As the population would begin to feel the effects of starvation, then doling out food could

be used to control behavior. In addition, the Wolf and Jorgensen report presents evidence that anthropological research was undertaken on tribesmen in Thailand so that means could be found for controlling their behavior as a part of the military counter-insurgency program in that part of the world. The cooperation and friendship of these people were sought so that data could be collected to be used later for controlling their behavior.

Wolf and Jorgensen (1970) point out that anthropology came into being in an era in which one part of mankind believed that it had some special right to control the destiny of the other part of mankind. In such an atmosphere the anthropologist who identified himself with the controlling portion of mankind came to view the rest of mankind as consisting of objects to be studied objectively. Later, when these objects began to assert their independence, the data collected became instruments of political power on the part of the would-be controllers. The viewpoint that divides the world into the categories of controllers and controlled is a political relic of the past that some modern behavioral scientists are using as the basis of their work and are perpetuating as a part of an obsolete political system.

Not much is known at this time about the long-term effects of treating individuals as though they were objects to be manipulated, largely because psychologists typically conduct only very short-term experiments. There are some classic examples of experimental procedures in psychology having long-term results. The best known of these are those reported by Pavlov on the effects of discrimination learning through classical conditioning techniques in which the discriminations become very difficult for the animal to make. Under such conditions a disorganization of behavior occurred, and the resulting behavior pathology had effects lasting for months. In such cases Pavlov found that the behavior pathology was not only durable, but also difficult to cure. One would like to know what are the long-term effects of treating a child as an object to be manipulated when there is otherwise no particular mistreatment of the child. Psychologists have neglected to study this important matter, much as detergent manufacturers failed to explore the possibility that detergents might damage the balance of life in the waterways. My guess is that the long-term consequences of treating a child as a manipulandum might be dramatic and culturally disastrous. Throughout history the treatment of people in this manner has led to revolt and revolution. Both the church and the nobility of the Middle Ages were able to treat people as objects to be controlled through the judicious use of rewards and punishments. The church and the nobility had absolute power, but the absolute power did not give them ultimate absolute control, for those whom the power group sought to control ultimately became the controllers. Attempts to treat children as objects to be controlled may well lead later to rebellion against this system of control and move toward an educational system in which there are participants and partisans rather than controllers and controlled and in which emphasis is placed on each person acquiring some degree of autonomy from the technological controlling system.

What seems clear is that the human does not like, and will not accept, obvious sources of control. When he can identify a person or an institution that has this power over him, then he seeks to regain, for himself, the control exerted by the outside source. The present popularity of a grass-roots participatory democracy is, to some degree, a rebellion against the power of centralized bureaucracy and centralized decision-making functions. When pupils come to realize that the new technology of education is taking all significant decision-making functions from them, then they surely are going to rebel against the system, perhaps by apathy, perhaps by rejection of education and educational goals, perhaps by disruptive behavior or other means.

SCIENCE AND EDUCATIONAL TECHNOLOGY

The belief that the development of technology is necessarily an outgrowth of the scientific enterprise leads to the belief that technology is quite remote from politics. Now there can be no doubt that the scientist does play a highly important role in the development of modern technology, even though this has not been so in the past. However, the nature of the scientific work applied may be highly dependent upon the power politics of the day. It is quite beyond the scope of this chapter to document such a statement in detail, but consideration can be given to the present impact of the behavioral sciences on education.

It is easy to see the influence of operant psychology as the impact of a pure scientific enterprise on a developing technology, much like the relationship that has evolved between biochemistry and pharmacology, but much more seems to be involved in this relationship. One of the interesting features of operant psychology is that it can be described to an extraordinary degree by a statement of the assumptions that underlie the workings of a modern capitalistic society. In such a society behavior is widely believed to be controlled by the reward system and, indeed, rewards are believed to be the only practical source of behavior control and political power. Welfare is kept at a starvation level on the basis of the belief that any rewards for doing nothing will institutionalize unemployment. The reason given by the government that a person should not indulge in crime is that "crime doesn't pay." Presumably, if crime did pay, then the occupation of the criminal would be commendable. Operant psychology reflects at least as much the modus operandi of American capitalism as it does the laboratory behavior of pigeons and rats. One can hardly be surprised that such a branch of psychology would be warmly embraced both by many American academicians and by programs sponsored by the federal government. Operant psychology has a certain American apple pie flavor to it that has given it a home in America. For the same reason, operant psychology has not received a particularly warm welcome in most countries of Western Europe, for it hardly fits the atmosphere of these other cultures. The sponsorship of operant psychology by highly influential components of the American civilization represents a political tie similar to that which has typically occurred in the past between the power structure and the intellectual forces in the community. A parallel example from history is found in the ties between the European nobility and the alchemists. The interests of the alchemists and the nobility were closely tied at one point, for both sought new sources of control. The conversion of base metals into gold was a point of common interest. Both operant psychologists and influential sources of power in the American culture seek new techniques of exerting improved control over human behavior. Whether operant psychology can or cannot deliver is as irrelevant to our present concern as is the issue of whether alchemy could deliver. Such political alliances are made in terms of expectancies—not in terms of established capabilities. The existence of this political alliance should not be taken as a disparagement of the research underlying operant psychology. Such research has been productive even though the limits of the generalizability of the findings remain controversial.

The relationship of operant psychology to the developing federally sponsored educational technology is an alliance of forces having a common value base and in which each can use the other for political advantage. Whether a healthier relationship between technology and science can exist within the structure of federally sponsored projects related to human development remains to be seen. One might hope that there is some possibility of technological development in education being undertaken outside of the control of government agencies, for under such conditions a healthier relationship with the scientific enterprise might emerge.

What would be an ideal relationship of scientific capability to technological development in education is controversial. Technologies have generally developed a long way before a scientific base was necessary for further advancement. In their early stages all other technologies have developed without a scientific foundation, but whether a new technology of behavior requires or does not require a scientific base remains to be seen. Also, there is controversy whether the behavioral sciences are sufficiently developed to provide such a scientific foundation. Although much of the new educational technology is believed by many to have emerged from research on learning, the relationship is often remote and difficult to discern. The development of most of the educational products of the regional laboratories is a result of the ability of the developers to make a systematic analysis of the problem involved rather than a product of scientific principles. Some scientific training may be useful to those who are engaged in the development of the new technology, but history also seems to indicate that the real accomplishments in the development of technologies at basic levels are made by people of considerable genius who do not necessarily make any specific use of scientific knowledge. The effort involved is also long and concentrated. Furthermore, advances made by one generation are typically just a new chapter in a long history of advances. Lilley (1966) notes that Watt first became intrigued with the problem of designing a useful steam engine when he was called in to repair a Newcomen engine in 1763. The Newcomen engine was the predecessor of the Watt-type steam engine, as we know it today, and was quite an inefficient and cumbersome device. It took Watt the next six years to completely redesign the Newcomen engine and another 10 years to produce the first engines for commercial use, though some of the latter delay must be attributed to Watt's financial difficulties. Also, one must note that the initial six years of Watt's development work, which taxed his genius, were not on work involving the development of a steam engine as such, but on the elimination of certain technical difficulties in the Newcomen engine. The steam engine did not suddenly come into being, but the Watt engine was the culmination of slow and continuous development from the waterwheel of the Roman era to the double-acting steam engine of the late eighteenth century. So impressive was the waterwheel as a device for extending the useful energy available to man that the first inventors of steam engines in Europe designed their engines on the waterwheel principle. The famous Savery steam engine, patented in 1668, was simply a device that used heat to raise water so that it could be used to operate a waterwheel. The steam engine slowly evolved from the waterwheel, though ultimately steam was used not to push water to a higher level, but to push a piston. Although Watt was a scientist and engineer, his scientific knowledge played only a very indirect role in the redesign of the Newcomen engine. The basic difficulties that had to be overcome required inventiveness rather than scientific sophistication.

Government programs tend to embrace those aspects of the scientific enterprise that share with them a common value base, and then the programs search for applications. This conception of the nature of scientific resources is based on the same fallacy as is the idea that the planet Earth contains a certain fixed amount of natural resources that are there to be discovered and used. Natural resources are a product of man's genius to invent uses for objects in his environment. They are not there in fixed amounts to be discovered and used. Also, nobody can predict what will be considered natural resources in the future, for what will become a natural resource will depend upon the future inventiveness of man. Knowledge that has been developed in the behavioral sciences is also not there waiting to be used. Uses of that knowledge have to be invented by persons of genius. Now this is quite the reverse of what psychologists have so often done when, armed with some neat package of what they believe to be truths, they have gone forth to change society. Thus, operant psychologists have scanned the world for situations in which somebody's behavior can potentially be controlled by some kind of reinforcement. Such behavior reflects what Kaplan (1964) has called the law of the hammer. The law, in essence, says give a child a hammer and he will find things to hit with it. I would submit that the law of the hammer does not provide a useful formula for the development of an educational technology. The development of a technology does require inventors who will produce solutions to problems, drawing where they can upon scientific knowledge but using whatever other knowledge is available in developing creative solutions. Technology, in its more advanced stage, also requires that there be scientific knowledge available to contribute to the solution of particular aspects of the problem. Watt's engines would have remained limited if there had not been later developments in the chemistry and physics of metal structures. A strong scientific body of information will always be one of the important resources to which the educational technologist should have access, but not the only resource. The behavioral sciences must be well supported to provide the backing that the educational technologist will need, and much greater contact is needed between the behavioral scientist and the educational inventor than there has been in the past. The problem of this relationship needs to be examined and studied as a basis for future federal programs. The formula involving discovery, then application and finally dissemination has little rationale to it. One can see the virtue in the parallel development of technology and scientific research, with technology borrowing as opportunities arise.

This leads to a consideration of the question of whether a culture oriented toward the development of technology should encourage particular lines of scientific development rather than let the scientific enterprise develop in whatever directions the whims of scientists might make it drift. The policy of the United States Office of Education, since the mid-sixties, has been that of choosing areas of scientific development that seemed to offer promise for educational advancement. This is a superficially attractive position, but who would ever have thought that Faraday's experiments with wires and solutions would have led to a whole new source of power? Who would have expected 25 years ago that research on perception, or what Piaget calls genetic epistemology, would later become one of the most influential points of impact of psychological research on applied theory of learning in the classroom?

A close intellectual proximity between the scientist and the developer of educational technology would appear to be desirable. The present arrangement in which behavioral scientists undertaking basic research are congregated in liberal arts departments and the developers of technology are found elsewhere is far from desirable. Although the developers of the new education may still be able to accomplish much on their own initiative, particularly when they are politically free, one must presume that the area of educational development will follow the same pattern of growth as have other areas of development and will show an increasing dependence of technology on scientific research, even though that day does not yet seem to have arrived. The close contact of scientists and educators in schools of education might be of special benefit, especially in that the basic behavioral sciences are quite obviously providing the language in terms of which problems are defined for the educational technologist to solve.

REFERENCES

The Alaskan Readers. Portland, Ore.: Northwest Regional Educational Laboratory, 1970.

An Act to Authorize Cooperative Research in Education. P. L. 83-531. 83rd United States Congress, July 26, 1954.

Brooks, H., & Bowers, R. The assessment of technology. *Scientific American,* 1970, 222(2), 13–21.

Clark, H. F. Schools can change a community. *Teachers College Record,* 1943, 44, 408–416.

Daumas, M. (Ed.) *A history of technology and invention.* (Translated by Eileen B. Hennessey) New York: Crown, 1969. 2 vols.

Elementary and Secondary Education Act of 1965. P. L. 89–10. 89th United States Congress, April 11, 1965.

Giedion, S. *Mechanization takes command: A contribution to anonymous history.* New York: W. W. Norton, 1969.

Haga, E. J. (Ed.) *Automated educational systems.* Elmhurst, Ill.: The Business Press, 1967.

Jones, V. W. *The Alaskan holiday book.* Portland, Ore.: Northwest Regional Educational Laboratory, 1968.

Jones, V. W. *Reading and language development.* Portland, Ore.: Northwest Regional Educational Laboratory, 1969.

Jones, V. W. *Benjamin beaver's box.* Portland, Ore.: Northwest Regional Educational Laboratory, 1970.

Kaplan, A. *The conduct of inquiry.* San Francisco: Chandler, 1964.

Kuhn, T. S. *The structure of scientific revolutions.* (2nd ed., enlarged) Chicago: University of Chicago Press, 1970.

Lilley, S. *Men, machines, and history.* New York: International Publishers, 1966.

Mackie, R. R., & Christensen, P. R. Translation and application of psychological research. Contract report, Office of Naval Research, Nonr 4337(11), ONR Authority Identification, NR 154-247 and 145-183X. 1967.

McGuire, W. J. The nature of attitudes and attitude change. In G. Lindzey, & E. Aronson (Eds.), *The handbook of social psychology.* Vol. 3. Reading, Mass.: Addison-Wesley, 1969. Pp. 136–314.

Mumford, L. *The myth of the machine: The*

pentagon of power. New York: Harcourt Brace Jovanovich, 1970.

Pressey, S. L. A third and fourth contribution toward the coming "industrial revolution" in education. *School and Society,* 1932, 36, 668–672.

Saettler, P. *A history of instructional technology.* New York: McGraw-Hill, 1968.

Schutz, R. E. The nature of educational development. *Journal of Research and Development in Education,* 1970, 3(2), 39–64.

Seay, M. F., & Meece, L. E. *The Sloan experiment in Kentucky.* Lexington, Ky.: University of Kentucky, Bureau of School Service, 1944.

Shackle, G. L. S. *Decision, order, and time in human affairs.* Cambridge, England: Cambridge University Press, 1961.

Silberman, C. E. *Crisis in the classroom.* New York: Random House, 1970.

Singer, C. J., Holmyard, E. J., & Hall, A. R. (Eds.) *A history of technology.* Oxford: Clarendon Press, 1954–1958. 5 vols.

Skinner, B. F. *Walden two.* New York: Macmillan, 1948.

Skinner, B. F. *Cumulative record.* New York: Appleton-Century-Crofts, 1961.

Skinner, B. F. Beyond freedom and dignity. Address given at Kalamazoo College, Kalamazoo, Michigan, March 11, 1971. (a)

Skinner, B. F. *Beyond freedom and dignity.* New York: Knopf, 1971. (b)

Southwest Regional Laboratory. *Sizes.* Inglewood, Calif.: Southwest Laboratory for Educational Research and Development, undated.

Southwest Regional Laboratory. *The instructional concepts program.* Inglewood, Calif.: Southwest Regional Laboratory for Educational Research and Development, 1970.

Walls, R. T., & Smith, T. S. Development of preference for delayed reinforcement in disadvantaged children. *Journal of Educational Psychology,* 1970, 61, 118–123.

White, L. T., Jr. *Medieval technology and social change.* Oxford: Clarendon Press, 1962.

Wolf, E. R., & Jorgensen, J. G. Anthropology on the warpath in Thailand. *New York Review of Books,* 1970, 15(9), 26–35.

CHAPTER **32**   Research on Teaching
in Higher Education[1]

JAMES W. TRENT
University of California, Los Angeles

ARTHUR M. COHEN
University of California, Los Angeles

PROLOGUE

In response to two forces, the form and content of teaching in higher education shifted markedly in the 1960s. The most obvious force was the dissident students who demanded and received a greater role in the teaching process both within and without traditional institutional formats. This had several effects.

Within the institutions students increasingly received the right to sit on committees, evaluate instructors and otherwise take active roles in the deliberations of the academy. Outside the walls free universities and experimental colleges were organized by students and sympathetic faculty members, marking a resurgence of the theme—if not the name—of general education. And, perhaps of most far-reaching importance, public belief in the university as a singularly beneficial element was severely shaken.

The second force impinging on teaching in higher education was the further incur-

sion of technology. As the 1960s opened, high claims were made for the efficiency to be derived from television, programmed instruction and a host of other devices frequently lumped together under the term "new media." Much of the research reported in the decade compared results obtained in courses using two or more different media. By the end of the decade the educational researcher had discovered that television, for example, could "teach" as well (or as poorly) as the professor. And the professor himself had made an accommodation with the new media, using them for some purposes and not for others.

The research reflected the impact of these forces. Studies comparing the effects of different media peaked in mid-decade and then began to decline in number. The methodology became more rigorous as researchers attempted to uncover subtle effects of media and study the fascinating problem of why professors in particular frequently tended to resist changed instructional formats. In addition, a great deal of study on student and faculty militancy in higher education was launched. The student activist and the instructor demanding a greater part in the

[1] The collaboration of Clare Rose is acknowledged in portions of the chapter. Parts of the bibliography were prepared by the staff of the ERIC Clearinghouse for Junior Colleges.

997

governance of the institution both became the subjects for a variety of investigations. However, much of the research lagged behind the needs of the decade as traditional methods of educational study proved inadequate to cope with either the narrow questions of teaching as related to learning or the broad issues of student and community disaffection.

This report considers the literature of the decade pertinent to the teaching-learning function in higher education under five main headings: 1) teaching environments; 2) student characteristics and the learning process; 3) teaching technology and methods; 4) teaching recruitment, training and resources; and 5) evaluation of teaching.

The first two sections consider the contemporary climate and clientele of college teaching. Students' backgrounds, goals, disposition toward learning, attitudes and values have a bearing on what they will gain from a teaching situation. Student characteristics also combine to form a major component of the college environment which, in turn, affects the educational process. Therefore, a review of research on college teaching necessitates the inclusion of the relation of college-student characteristics to teaching. The characteristics of student activism have been singled out for special consideration in this context.

The third area of research, teaching technology and methodology, is in part an updating of McKeachie's (1963) earlier summary of research on teaching in higher education. The current thrust toward innovation is considered through an examination of old and new media forms. Particular attention is given to the problems associated with the introduction, maintenance and assessment of varied teaching techniques.

The section on teaching recruitment and training includes studies of the instructor as a person, his professional situation and the way he relates to his work. Also reviewed here are the assessments of college-teacher preparation programs. Of particular note in this section is the growing body of litera-

ture on instruction in the junior college—the most rapidly growing segment of higher education.

The section on evaluation of teaching, currently a critical, sensitive issue in higher education, treats correlates of teaching competency: practices, problems and results of student rating of faculty effectiveness; the interaction of faculty-student characteristics and behavior related to the teaching-learning function; the nagging question of appropriate criteria for teaching effectiveness; and the faculty's perception of their teaching role.

Student activism was the cause—or effect —of several important shifts during the 1960s. Although much of the writing on activism was more speculative and hortatory than deliberate, several lines of research on related issues evolved. The free university or experimental college is one of these related results. In many areas of the country disaffected students and disenchanted faculty members organized courses and programs outside the academy. The course emphases and the teaching methodologies both reflected students' desires to turn away from traditional patterns in order to find more relevant experiences. Even though the methodologies of educational research have proved inadequate to treat these variant forms of education satisfactorily, a summary of research on teaching in higher education cannot ignore this significant development.

A variety of criteria are important to consider in research on teaching, including students' mastery of subject content, appreciation of knowledge and ideas, disposition toward learning, development of social awareness, self-concept and personality development generally. It is rare, if ever, that a single factor will be found as the sole contributor to any criterion. Interrelated and interacting contributing factors include elements of students' socioeconomic environment, student characteristics, teacher characteristics, peer influence and school environments. Critical to this review, therefore, is the identification of key combinations of factors that predict or contribute in important ways to the criteria considered. We will also evaluate the means used to assess these factors and investigate possible reasons for both convergence and divergence of the research in this context.

TEACHING ENVIRONMENTS
by
James W. Trent and Clare Rose

There has been considerable interest in the sixties in assessing and describing the college environment. This interest reflects the underlying assumption that the kinds of changes that take place in the student during his college years often depend upon the environment to which he is exposed. Indeed, the teaching-learning function cannot conceivably be separated from the interacting environment in which this function takes place. Therefore administrators and instructors who are responsible for educational policy and practice should have comprehensive and comparative information about the environments of different colleges.

The development of the College Characteristics Index to measure environmental press, the corresponding Activities Index to measure psychological needs (Pace, 1963; Stern, 1963) and the College and University Environment Scales (Pace, 1963) have stimulated research on the interaction of student and environmental characteristics. Pace (1962) identified four factorial dimensions of the College Characteristics Index representing environmental presses for: 1) the intellectual, humanistic and aesthetic; 2) independence, change and science; 3) personal and interpersonal status coupled with a practical or vocational orientation; and 4) group welfare, social responsibility and a well-mannered community. He also demonstrated the capability of indicating similarities and differences in the profiles of various colleges on these dimensions. In the process he enumerated several methodological approaches to the study of college environments:

1. Educational approaches based on inventories of resources from the U.S. Office of Education, the American Council on Education, accreditation agencies, as well as case histories, alumni studies and evaluation studies emphasizing students' attainment of educational objectives.

2. Sociological approaches viewing the college as a social system emphasizing peer groups, role behavior, communication networks and other organizational characteristics.

3. Psychological approaches concerned with the personality development of students, individual differences between and within student bodies, and students' perceptions of the college environment.

Differences in methods and measurement used in assessing the environment of the teaching-learning function can be critical. This is true since quite different conclusions can be drawn about the environment depending upon the method or measurement employed. Pace illustrated this point by describing how students at San Francisco State College, in terms of their response to items in the College Characteristics Index, held a perception of the intellectual climate at their campus that was quite different from that formulated by Riesman and Jencks (1962) in their commentary on the culture of this college. In their "case study" approach, Riesman and Jencks concluded that not only was the primary orientation of the student body at San Francisco State College vocational, but that there was a general lack of group cohesion in the student culture. However, the College Characteristics Index data Pace obtained from San Francisco State College at approximately the same time led him to conclude that although there was an apparent relative weakness in the student culture, the data did not confirm Riesman and Jencks's judgment about the dominance of vocationalism in the students or in the college. Rather, the data indicated that the environment was more intellectual and scholarly than most colleges.

Stern's (1962a, 1962b, 1963) descriptions

of the College Characteristics Index and the Activities Index point out the key differences between the two measurements. The latter consists of 30 scales of 10 items each to which the respondent indicates his like or dislike for each item. The items consist of statements about college life (e.g., rules and procedures, curricula, faculty, features and facilities, students' interests and values) reflecting various psychological needs of students pertinent to their college experiences.

The College Characteristics Index is similarly designed but the items are concerned with policies, procedures, impressions, attitudes and activities that may be characteristic of various types of undergraduate settings. Moreover, rather than reflecting student needs, the scales indicate aspects of the college environment which likely influence or "press" on the students' lives. Boyer and Michael (1965) derived several conclusions from their comparison of the research conducted by Pace and by Stern based upon the two indices:

1. Significant relationships have been found between needs scale profiles of the Activities Index and other forms of overt behavior, such as academic performance, study habits, reading skills, attitudes and values, deviant behavior, other personality processes, career choice and social background.

2. Student bodies have been described by needs scale profiles that clearly have been seen to represent the personalized versions of the existing presses at their institution, although there has been greater variability among students as they described themselves on the Activities Index than there has been in the College Characteristics Index descriptions of their institutional press.

3. Significant relationships have been determined between profiles on press scales and types of institutions sampled. Specifically, three distinct types of colleges have been identified in those sampled: denominational colleges emphasizing conformity, constraint and dependence; small private liberal arts colleges having the highest standing on the intellectual press as well as personal autonomy; and colleges described by their students as sources of social pleasure though lacking academic strength.

In addition, Stern (1963) identified six environmental factors extracted from the intercorrelations of the College Characteristics Index scales based on the responses of 1,076 students at 23 institutions: 1) intellectual orientation, 2) social effectiveness, 3) play, 4) friendliness, 5) constraint and 6) dominance-submission. Eleven institutions that ranked high in intellectual disposition were compared to 11 institutions which ranked low on this measurement on the following characteristics: size and composition of student bodies, regional representation, type of institutional control (public versus private); type of program (liberal arts, professional, etc.); highest degree offered; student activities; financial assets; and tuition. Personality characteristics of students in the colleges of high and low intellectual climates were also compared and evaluated. Students in colleges high in intellectual climate compared to those in institutions low in intellectual climate possessed stronger intellectual interests, had a greater desire to understand themselves as well as others, had a better understanding of political and social problems, were more able to find solutions to learning problems, exhibited lower dependence needs, showed less self-indulgence, and demonstrated more spontaneity in emotional expression.

The development of the College Characteristics Index and Activities Index encouraged a number of researchers to consider the total learning context. Lawlor (1970) analyzed College Characteristics Index data for 207 students enrolled in a College of Business Administration to determine institutional press by comparing the findings with data from 104 students enrolled in the College of Arts and Sciences. Comparisons were made of the means and variances of the scores of both groups to determine the degree of institutional press. No significant difference in variance appeared for the groups in work-play, group life and academic organization. On the scales measuring nonvocational climate and student dignity, however, significant differences appeared favoring the arts and sciences sample. Mean scores for all the other factors favored the business administration students. Data were further treated statistically to determine whether the College Characteristics Index mean scores for the College of Business Administration sample differed significantly from the normative sample of universities. The results indicated that the normative data deviated more in the intellectual than in the nonintellectual area. One major interpretation of this research is that evaluative research on the teaching-learning function must take into account influential environmental differences both within and among institutions.

Subsequent to this work on the College Characteristics Index, Pace (1963, 1969) developed and has since revised a new, standardized 150-item instrument, the College and University Environment Scales. Pace's development of this scale resulted in part from his having demonstrated a lack of parallelism in the organization of factors in the Activities Index with those of the College Characteristics Index. The scales, based on students' perception of their environment, measure five factors of the college environment which Pace originally identified as Practicality, Community, Awareness, Propriety and Scholarship. The revised version of the College and University Environment Scales includes, in addition, two ad hoc scales, one labeled "Campus Morale" and the other "Teaching and Faculty-Student Relationships."

Relative to the 30 scales of the Activities Index, each of which consists of only 10 items, the 20-item scales of the new instrument have three important advantages: 1) they provide a more parsimonious evaluation of the institutional differences in educational environments; 2) they possess greater reliability; and 3) the scores can be related to normative data more representative of colleges generally.

Astin has taken still a different approach to the study of college environments. The Environmental Assessment Technique developed by Astin and Holland (1961), described and further validated in a number of research papers and experimental studies (Astin, 1962a, 1962b, 1962c, 1963a, 1963b, 1964a, 1964b, 1964c, 1965, 1967), is based on the assumption that the dominant features of an environment are dependent upon the typical characteristics of its members. If, then, we know the characteristics of the people in the group, we should know the climate that group creates.

Since the Environmental Assessment Technique illustrates a concerted effort to obtain independent measures of student and environmental characteristics and is the subject of so much of the research on college environments, an in-depth analysis of its application and methodological problems seems pertinent. The Astin instrument measures eight characteristics of college environments: size, average intelligence, and six personal orientations classified as realistic, intellectual, social, conventional, enterprising, and artistic. In a sample of 36 colleges, the variables were found to have a substantial correlation with many scales of the College Characteristics Index (Astin & Holland, 1961). The advantages of the eight variables of the Astin scales, however, are that they are relatively simple and inexpensive to administer and score. Astin (1962a, 1962b, 1962c) also found that his device predicts students' ratings of the college environment, as well as the perceived "effects" of the college as reported by the student.

In addition, Astin developed a variety of other measurements of the college environment. A factor analysis of 33 college attributes based on a sample of 335 institutions yielded six principal dimensions: affluence, size, private versus public, masculinity, realistic emphasis, and homogeneity of the environment (Astin, 1962a). Affluence was the factor of largest proportion of variance.

Two other studies (Astin, 1964b, 1964c) investigated student input variables. A factor analysis of 52 student input variables yielded six major dimensions: Intellectualism, Aestheticism, Status, Leadership, Pragmatism, and Masculinity. A comparison was made of the presumably independent estimates of student and institutional characteristics derived from the above studies. In summary, Astin reported that characteristics of entering freshman classes were highly related to institutional characteristics: high-ability students were exercising a high degree of self-selection in deciding where to attend college and in general the aspirations of the entering students appeared to be well suited to the curricular offerings of the particular institution. Multiple-regression analyses indicated that five of the six freshman input factors (intellectualism, aestheticism, status, masculinity, and pragmatism) can be estimated with substantial accuracy from known characteristics of the institution.

An attempt was made to identify differential college effects on the students' motivations to seek Ph.D. degrees (Astin, 1963a). Ph.D. aspiration was negatively affected by the size of the student body, the percentage of males in the student body and the conventional orientation of the college environment.

The extent to which academic programs adequately serve the goals of college students was researched indirectly through studies of college withdrawals (Astin, 1964a). Astin discovered no significant relationship between the characteristics of an institution and the rate of attrition among male students. Women's chances of withdrawing, however, were found to increase if they attended a college with a relatively high proportion of men in the student body.

A 1965 study by Astin was undertaken to determine if there are consistent differences related to the various fields of study in the classroom environments of different college courses. More specifically, the objective was to see if the behavior of the instructor, the behavior of the student, and the types of instructor-student interaction that occur in classes in various fields differ systematically from one another in such a way that various fields of study could be classified on the basis of the similarities and differences found. Ratings of introductory undergraduate courses in 19 different fields were obtained from 4,100 students majoring in these fields at 246 colleges and universities. Students in each field were selected from a larger sample of 31,000 students so as to reduce differences among institutions. Differences among the 19 fields on all 35 ratings were highly significant statistically. An inverse factor analysis of the 19 fields yielded three bipolar factors, foreign language versus social science, natural science versus English and fine arts, and business versus history. These findings support the hypothesis that the college environment is affected by the relative proportions of students and faculty in various fields of study.

Creager and Astin (1968) examined the interrelations among 70 administrative and environmental variables used in describing 244 four-year colleges and universities. Astin postulated that although there is a logical distinction between variables that describe an institution's structure (e.g., public versus private) and variables that describe its environment, it is reasonable to suppose that these two types of variables are statistically related to each other and functionally related to outcomes. Further, if one assumes that environmental variables are more strongly influential in student development, then it is important to determine if the commonly used administrative variables (e.g., geography and size) have negligible relationships with these environmental variables. If so, administrative variables will be of limited value in studying differential college influence on student development.

Several alternative ways of describing institutional and college environments were represented in this study by groups of variables that form logical blocks in terms of their sources and the ways in which they were developed. One block consisted of 17 dichotomous administrative characteristics measuring such elements as the demographic features of student bodies and the geographical locations of institutions. A second block was composed of Environmental Assessment Technique variables. A third block of variables represented student inputs. A fourth block consisted of stimuli variables such as those identified in still another study by Astin (1967), and a fifth block consisted of variables derived from the College and University Environment Scales (Pace, 1964).

Intercorrelations among the 70 variables were computed across 244 institutions and three separate factor analyses were performed. The results showed that many of the variables provide relatively unique ways of describing institutions. For example, Factor 1 is a large bipolar group factor that cuts across the various blocks of variables. Its primary definer is the drinking (negative) versus religiousness (positive) stimulus factor from the peer environment. It is also closely associated with three measures from the administrative environment which measure the severity of administrative policy against drinking, sexual and aggressive behaviors. Other loadings include intellectualism and Protestant church affiliation, all of which suggest a "Protestant ethic" atmosphere.

College administrators, especially in those institutions affiliated with Protestant denominations, may find it useful to know that admissions policies favoring intellectual qualities in the students may be inconsistent with admissions or administration policies designed to foster a conservative, moralistic atmosphere. Where the purpose of the college is to maintain certain behavioral values, the institution may either have to accept a less intellectual student body or compensate in some way through special curricular adjustments. Similarly, the college that tries to upgrade the intellectual level

of its student body must be prepared to cope with student demands for greater behavioral freedom. The results of this study are consistent with McConnell's (1961) findings that institutions are differentially selective with respect to such student characteristics as aptitude, interests, values, social background and intellectual disposition.

Two methodological problems underlie Astin's research. Certain institutional or environmental attributes are based on the characteristics of past student bodies (e.g., percent graduated in realistic fields) whereas student characteristics are defined in terms of the characteristics of present student bodies (e.g., percent enrolled in realistic fields). This means that Astin is basing present assessment of the environment on previous student inputs. Rather than providing independent estimates of student and environmental characteristics, Astin's methodology may be a way of estimating the extent to which the processes of formal selection, self-selection or both remain relatively constant from one generation of students to another. A second problem results from the confounding of input, environmental and outcome variables.

Several other approaches to the study of college environments have been used. An anthropological approach has been taken by Boroff (1961), Bushnell (1962), Jencks and Riesman (1962), and Keeton and Hilberry (1969). These studies are concerned with the patterns of values, beliefs and prescribed modes of behavior of various student and faculty groups at different colleges. The personal observations and hypotheses contained in these studies can be instructive. Yet as Boyer and Michael (1965) state, "This period of research has been more successful in challenging old assumptions regarding the outcomes of college than it has been in establishing new generalizations" (p. 289).

An investigation of the effects of various college characteristics on student aptitudes was undertaken by Nichols (1964), who compared the effects of different colleges on student ability as measured by Graduate Record Examination aptitude scores and found that college influence was impressively less than might have been expected. The size of the college effects was small relative to the variability attributable to differences between students which existed before the students entered college.

Going from Astin's assumption that institutions of higher learning are characterized by variations in the teacher-learning climate, an exploratory study (Lacognata, 1966) sought to determine whether college-student academic role expectations differ across educational institutions. The instrument used was a questionnaire scale containing 33 pretested role statements. Seventeen role items revealed significant differences existed in academic expectations between private and state college students (representing 52 percent of the role items). Of these, seven items were concerned primarily with differences in degrees of agreement in expectations. Two other items dealt with differences between crystallized versus ambiguous role expectations, and the remaining eight reflected student academic role dissensus. These findings suggest that organizationally different types of institutions of higher learning contain student bodies manifesting different academic expectations.

In his rationale for the development of a questionnaire—the Transactional Analysis of Personality and Environment (TAPE)— Pervin (1967) suggests that human behavior can best be understood in terms of the interactions or transactions between the individual and the environment, and that the assessment instruments developed by Pace, Stern and Astin do not provide for an analysis in terms of individual-environment interaction. Pervin also proposes that it is not clear that the need and press scales on the instruments are comparable and that while these instruments include items relevant to various parts of a college environment, analysis in terms of the interactions or transactions among these parts has not been reported.

The Transactional Analysis of Personality and Environment is an instrument which uses the semantic differential technique to study the various interactions and transactions that occur within a college environment and their relevance to institutional strain and student satisfaction. In Pervin's study 3,000 students from 21 colleges rated the following concepts on 52 scales: my college; my self; students, faculty, administration, and ideal college. Ratings of satisfaction of college life were also made on 16 scales. In general, discrepancies between student perceptions of themselves and their college were found to be related to dissatisfaction with college.

The data were interpreted as supporting the theoretical model of student-college interaction and the utility of the instrument in this area of research. Pervin concluded that this research should be useful in suggesting the transactions within the college, or between students and parts of the college, that might be influenced in the direction of fostering student development. The particular data obtained in this study show that significant areas of discrepancy and dissatisfaction vary from college to college and the relationship between perceptions may vary within the same area. For example, dissatisfied students at one school viewed the college as more conservative, less equalitarian and less scholarly and viewed themselves as more liberal, equalitarian and scholarly than did satisfied students. The opposite held true for dissatisfied students at a second school.

Most of the studies of college environments are restricted to four-year colleges. The approximately 1,000 accredited junior colleges in the United States have been for the most part neglected, although there have been several treatments of junior colleges (Blocker, Plummer, & Richardson, 1965; Medsker, 1960; Thornton, 1966; Trent & Medsker, 1968); sociological studies of a single junior college (Clark, 1960); studies of the articulation between two- and four-year colleges (Kintzer, 1970; Knoell &

Medsker, 1964); and studies of the performance and characteristics of students (Hills, 1965; Koos, 1970; Trent, in press).

Richards, Rand, and Rand (1966), in a population of 581 accredited two-year colleges, replicated Astin's (1962a) study of four-year colleges. Measures of 36 major institutional variables were intercorrelated. Factor analyses were performed and six factors were identified: cultural affluence, technological specialization, size, age, transfer emphasis, and business orientation. The junior college factors were not congruent with the factors for four-year colleges, where affluence, realistic orientation, masculinity, homogeneity, and public versus private control were found to be dominant environmental factors. Only the factor of size overlapped between the two types of institutions. The findings indicate that junior colleges are different from four-year colleges, and it is inappropriate to apply a classification scheme developed for one type of college to the other.

Problems and limitations of research aside, researchers such as Astin, Pace, Pervin and Stern have provided a significant contribution to the literature dealing with the student in higher education. Their pioneering studies have shifted the research emphasis from a descriptive to a dynamic model. Findings to date suggest that a productive line of research would be to do much more to apply this dynamic model to the development and evaluation of the teaching-learning function.

STUDENT CHARACTERISTICS AND THE LEARNING PROCESS
by
Clare Rose and James W. Trent

Considerable attention has been given to research concerning students' social-psychological adjustment in college and the relationship between their adjustment and scholastic success. The issue is important because, just as is the environment, the social-psychological characteristics of students are inextricably bound in the teaching-learning function. The inconsistencies, however, perhaps best characterize the results of the research in much of this area.

A review of the research indicates that most studies of social-psychological characteristics may be organized under the following headings: 1) student characteristics related to academic achievement, 2) personality development, 3) minority students, 4) women and 5) student activists. These classifications, particularly the latter three, reflect the times. A substantive portion of the research done during the decade focuses on those issues perceived as most pressing.

Student Characteristics Related to Academic Achievement

In reference to studies relating scholastic success, two investigators (Burgess, 1956; Davie, 1961) reported that the socially passive and introverted students do better in scholastic matters than active students. They characterized successful students as having more trouble adjusting to the nonacademic aspects of college life, being less likely to belong to fraternal organizations, having difficulty making friends and getting along well with others and being less responsive to outside diversions. The findings of other studies, however, seem to be in direct conflict (Corlis, 1963; Dana & Baker, 1961; Holland, 1961; Rosenberg, McHenry, & Rosenberg, 1962). They found high achievement to be related to social ease, extraversion and popularity with peers.

Studies of emotional adjustment also appear to have inconsistent findings. One group of researchers reported that unstable, maladjusted and anxious students do less well in scholastic competition than do other students (Dana & Baker, 1961; Powell & Jourard, 1963; Spielberger, Weitz, & Denny, 1962; Whiteis, 1962). Other studies found that emotionally anxious students do as well or better than other students (Anderson & Spencer, 1963; Baymur & Patterson, 1960).

A study by Coombs and Davies (1967)

utilized peer ratings of adjustment by student leaders who were familiar with 186 freshmen at Washington State University. Rating forms which were completed by student leaders, who resided in the subjects' places of residence and thus were familiar with the subjects, consisted of statements designed to give measures of sociability, emotional balance, motivation, conformity and organizational effort. The response scale consisted of five points ranging from much above average to much below average.

The results were consistent with the consensus of earlier studies in that a pronounced difference in scholastic achievement was found to exist between students who were rated high and those rated low on organizational effort. Similarly, a large difference was found when high and low groups were compared on motivation ratings. Conformity was only slightly related, and emotional balance and sociability were not related at all.

Several studies have dealt with the relationship of attitudes toward school or toward a specific subject matter and achievement, and some have found significant, although small relationships (L. R. Aiken & Dreger, 1961; Garverick, 1964). One exception is Teigland's (1966) study in which groups of students enrolled in an educational psychology course who showed changes in the direction of a more positive attitude toward the course, scored significantly higher on a deference scale and received significantly higher grades. Apparently, although attitude is an important variable in learning, no instruments have been developed which adequately measure it in relation to a specific learning experience.

To explore the relationship between change in students' attitudes toward a class in which they were participating and final achievement in that class, five equivalent forms of a 26-item attitude scale were administered by Neidt and Hedlund (1967) at two-week intervals to 573 university students in three courses. Coefficients of correlation between the various sequential attitude scores and final achievement, with aptitude held constant, were computed in the three situations. Some evidence was found to support the hypothesis that attitudes progressively become more closely related to final achievement throughout the period of instruction.

In a study by Gulo (1966), a modified semantic differential scale of 166 items ranging over four concepts (professor, university administration, student organization, and campus atmosphere) was administered to 600 students representing 20 percent of the total population of an eastern university, a sample considered to be representative of the university's classes and sex distribution. Results were reduced to four 27 x 27 matrices and separately factor analyzed. In the analysis of the fourth concept, a structure involving eight separate factors emerged, indicating the complexity involved in evaluation, assessment, and the attitudinal components of the students' concepts of their professors. Although the semantic differential has great potential for reflecting the complexity of multidimensional concepts, this study raises questions of a validational nature as to how its results would compare with studies at other similar universities.

Potter (1962) conducted a preliminary descriptive study to discover the extent to which graduate students felt that they possessed certain characteristics, abilities and attitudes that are thought to be related to the achievement of the scholar and researcher. Potter obtained the anonymous self-ratings of graduate students which indicated that they perceived themselves to be comparatively well fitted for graduate study and research as far as their physical qualifications and ethics were concerned; the traits receiving the top three ranks for all groups were nonintellectual, consisting of moral attitude, health and cooperation.

A replication of Potter's study was undertaken by Mehrens (1967). Ratings were obtained from 142 graduate students enrolled in two educational psychology courses concerning the extent to which they perceived themselves possessing selected characteristics. Students rated themselves on a six-point scale from very poor to superior on the following 10 traits: reasoning power, originality, memory, alertness, accuracy, application, cooperation, moral attitude, health, and zeal for investigation. Half of these students were requested to sign their names; half remained anonymous. Analysis of the results indicated that:

1. Students rated themselves higher on nonintellectual than on intellectual traits.

2. There was no significant difference in ratings between the anonymous group and the group who signed their names.

3. Self-ratings were independent of both the sex and the number of graduate credits earned by the subject.

The self-ratings obtained were essentially the same as in Potter's study and suggest the possibility of using signed self-ratings in an attempt to improve prediction of graduate school achievement. A possible factor that could contribute to an accurate prediction of achievement in graduate school is a student's self-concept—how he perceives himself with respect to various traits.

Previous grades, of course, remain the predominant variable for predicting future academic achievement. Holland and Astin (1962), among many others, have found the best predictor of academic achievement in college is high-school grade-point average. They found this particularly true when students also had high self-ratings of scholarship. In fact, many investigators have been moving away from the old model of predicting intellective criteria such as grades from intellective predictors (e.g., ability tests) and have displayed an interest in nonintellective predictors or correlates of grades such as self-ratings of achievement potential. Heist and Webster (1960), for example, presented data to illustrate that attitudes, values and interests of students should not be overlooked as supplements to the more traditional selective criteria. They argued that the intellectual climates

provided by student attitudes and values must be understood and taken into account before institutional objectives can be realized.

Goodstein and Heilbrun (1962) studied the contribution of scores on the Edwards Personal Preference Schedule to achievement at three levels of ability. They found that personality factors contribute most to the prediction of the academic achievement of the average college male. Heist and Williams (1961) reported a significant difference among three achievement levels in terms of a system used to classify Strong Vocational Interest Blank profiles for degree of intellectual disposition. The high achievers were described as being more strongly oriented toward inquiry and speculative and creative thought than the other two achievement groups. Within their homogeneous sample of bright science majors, however, most other differences were slight.

Several other studies challenged the use of grades as either the only criterion for or predictor of academic success. Holland (1961) developed an achievement scale based on the number of original papers published, prizes won and inventive projects completed by the student and found that these creative achievements were unrelated to grades. In parallel findings, Locke (1963) reported that academic success as judged by self-initiated activities performed outside the classroom did not correlate with academic performance in the structured classroom situation.

Ramsey (1962) found that although differences in academic behavior among Harvard Law School freshmen drawn from five types of undergraduate colleges could be correlated primarily with undergraduate grade-point average, differences in academic performance were also strongly related to father's occupation, family income, type of secondary school attended, religious affiliation and region of residence. Ramsey concluded that individuals with contrasting cultural orientations perceived academic roles in different ways and that these perceptions shifted during the student's academic career. Lavin (1965), however, analyzed studies to determine the validity of ability, personality and sociological variables as predictors of grade-point average. None of these variables accounted adequately for the variance in grade-point average.

After conducting an extensive review, Hoyt (1965) concluded that college grades have no more than a modest correlation with adult success no matter how success is defined. Hoyt suggests the use of a profile of student growth and development instead of grades. And, as a matter of fact, there are increasing questions about the use of grades, as such, in higher education. The questions center particularly on the use of grades as an incentive to learning.

Critics of competitive grading systems contend that students will learn more when the deleterious effects of competitive grading are reduced or eliminated and that encouraging learning through grades as incentives is contrary to the contemporary educational philosophy which says a student should study because he is interested in the subject, not the grade (see, e.g., A. M. Cohen, 1969). These assumptions are also congruent with the psychological notion of intrinsic motivational correlates of learning.

Many institutions have established a pass-fail alternative to the traditional grading systems and there have been some investigations designed to justify the above assumptions. Karlins, Kaplan, and Stuart (1969), for example, investigated the differential performance by students at Princeton taking courses with competitive and less competitive grading systems concurrently. Each student at Princeton has the option of taking one course per year on a pass-fail basis. Instructors were not informed which members were taking the course pass-fail and graded all students taking the course in the traditional manner. Only when the grades were turned into the registrar's office were the numerical grades of the pass-fail students transformed into a pass or fail. The results of student-attitude questionnaires indicated that students believed they learned more, worked closer to their capacity, were motivated to learn and more actively participated in the regularly graded courses than the ones marked pass-fail. These beliefs, in addition, were reflected in the actual performance. Students received significantly better grades in their competitively graded courses than in their pass-fail courses.

The weakness in these findings, of course, is apparent. It is not unreasonable to expect that a student's course load which creates time pressures in his study schedule will result in the student's withdrawing time from a pass-fail class to invest in a dividend-paying course. A system in which all courses are taken pass-fail should be evaluated in order to determine more realistically the effects of nongraded performance. As a matter of fact, an evaluation of this kind has been conducted to some degree at Pennsylvania State University's experimental CREATION College, where total elimination of grades has been found to contribute to students' academic interests and motivation.

Personality Development

Another way of conceptualizing student achievement is in terms of personality development or attitudinal change, matters that go beyond the issue of grades in subject areas. Although most researchers in the fifties and a few in the sixties studied changes in student attitudes and opinions about social, religious, economic or political issues, or studied particular personality characteristics, several studies in the 1960s dealt with the total impact of college on a variety of personality characteristics.

The interpretations of several studies of personality change during college have been that the college experience has been a liberalizing one in terms of personality development (Dellas & Gaier, 1969; Dressel & Lehmann, 1965; Feldman & Newcomb, 1969; Freedman, 1960; Lehmann, 1963; Lehmann & Dressel, 1963; Lehmann, Sinka,

& Hartnett, 1966; McConnell, 1961; L. B. Murphy & Raushenbush, 1960; Parkes, 1962; Plant, 1965; Plant & Minium, 1967; Ritter, 1969; Telford & Plant, 1963; Trent & Medsker, 1968; Webster, Freedman, & Heist, 1962). These studies noted changes at intervals of one to four years, compared changes of those remaining for a full four years with changes in individuals withdrawing after various periods of time, and compared changes of students who attended colleges for varying lengths of time with those of peers who did not enter college. The studies were based on a combination of objective evidence obtained from a number of cognitive and affective instruments and tests of critical thinking such as the Omnibus Personality Inventory, Rokeach's Dogmatism Scale, Prince's Differential Values Inventory, and a number of questionnaires developed specifically in relation to student experiences, current student language, and interviews from both students and faculty.

Major findings from these studies, in summary, reveal that:

1. College students generally became significantly less stereotypic in their beliefs, less dogmatic and more receptive to new ideas.

2. Generally the most positive change of all occurred in autonomy—open-mindedness, independence and flexibility of thinking. Relatively nominal change occurred on measurements of intellectual disposition indicating such traits as interest in abstract ideas, intellectual curiosity, tolerance for ambiguity and aesthetic interests.

3. Seniors were more "outer-directed" than they had been as freshmen.

4. While in college, students developed a greater sense of social responsibility, confidence in personal relationships, and a clearer idea of self.

5. Students showed significant improvement in critical thinking ability.

6. Students generally changed toward the peer norm, so that seniors were more alike in attitudes and values than freshmen, the norm usually being in a more liberal direction.

7. Students who remained in college for four years changed significantly more in measurable traits of autonomy and intellectual disposition after four years than students who withdrew from college before obtaining a baccalaureate degree. Both groups of college students changed significantly more on these traits than high-school graduate peers who did not enter college, the latter tending to regress on these traits over a period of four years.

8. There is some evidence that the greatest amount of change in students' values and attitudes took place during their first two years of college, although they continued to change significantly during their third and fourth years of college.

9. "Student input" variables such as academic aptitude and socioeconomic status were found to interact with students' changes in personality dimensions on occasion. Students of high academic aptitude have been found to change more than those of lower aptitude. However, measurable change continued to exist independently of these "input" variables.

10. There is some but not entirely consistent evidence that college women generally changed more than men on personality traits after a four-year period regardless of the amount of time spent in college. On measurements having to do with liberal versus conservative issues, however, men generally became more liberal than women.

11. Not all changes were in a positive direction. A small but significant proportion of students regressed on measurable personality traits, becoming more authoritarian and close-minded rather than autonomous and intellectually disposed.

12. Changes of values and attitudes varied by major area of study both within and among colleges.

13. Tentative evidence suggests that faculty had influence on individual student's career decisions but had relatively little on students' changes in values and attitudes generally.

14. Some indications were that changes in students' attitudes and values were more prevalent in small, residential colleges where

there were greater opportunities for faculty-student interaction within and outside class.

Although these studies have demonstrated that significant changes occur in the attitudes, values, interests and beliefs of college students between the freshman and senior years, because of the absence of a noncollege control group in most cases, these changes cannot be directly related to college education. Exceptions are the research of Plant (1965), Plant and Minium (1967), Telford and Plant (1963), and particularly Trent and Medsker (1968). Problems exist with the authors' interpretations of the differences in difference scores in the Telford and Plant research. For example, these researchers found statistically significant t ratios across groups when comparing pre- and posttest scores of students who attended college for varying lengths of time. They concluded, therefore, that length of exposure is not related to personality change of students. However, they ignored the fact that the differences in the magnitude of the t ratios suggested differences in the rate of change among the groups. In any event, the evidence based on pre- and posttest scores obtained from thousands of college and noncollege peer groups over a period of two to four years indicated that college students changed considerably more than their peers who did not enter college. This was true when controlling for academic aptitude and socioeconomic status as well (Trent & Medsker, 1968).

In spite of the changes in students' attitudes and values uniquely associated with a college education, questions remain regarding the amount colleges actually contribute to these changes. Plant concluded that the reported changes in personality characteristics resulting from college attendance may well be developmental changes in personality characteristics for bright young adults regardless of their higher educational attainment during a given period of time.

Trent and Medsker (1968) concluded that college might only be a facilitating agency, providing the opportunities for change for those students already predisposed to change. Likewise, Lehmann, Sinka, and Hartnett (1966) suggested that college education per se is not instrumental in bringing about personality changes, although attendance might facilitate this development. Therefore, college faculties and administrators must realize that they are not necessarily providing a unique experience for their students, but that maturation and the social environment might have more impact on personality development than courses and formal academic experiences.

Feldman and Newcomb (1969) posit the principle of accentuation. They state that those characteristics which impel a person toward a particular educational setting are the characteristics which are reinforced and strengthened by that setting. Processes of attraction are similar to processes of impact.

Feldman and Newcomb suggest that this process can be delimiting: if colleges, departmental majors and peer groups apply ever more restrictive criteria of selection, the student's world may be narrowed to students and teachers like himself.

Problems in the interpretation of the amount and process of college impact are illustrated in the research of Chickering (1969), Eddy (1959), J. Katz and associates (1968), and Lehmann, Sinka, and Hartnett (1966). The study by Eddy (1959) examined the part played by the "campus climate" in changing the attitudes and values of college students. Eddy found that experiences outside the classroom were a significant factor in the development of character and that particular aspects of the environment (e.g., attitudes, surroundings, extra activities, manners and morals) have the power to reinforce or negate all that the college has to offer. Eddy concluded that an environment best suited for the development of character is the result of unity in common goals. Eddy also found that the "level of expectancy" in all matters concerning the student in the college environment is a highly important determinant of what happens to him.

In interviews with sophomores and juniors, Lehmann, Sinka, and Hartnett (1966) found that the informal, nonacademic experiences such as friends and bull sessions have as great or greater impact upon personality development as do the formal, academic experiences of courses and instruction.

Katz and associates (1968) presented the results of a five-year longitudinal study of changes in students at Stanford and the University of California at Berkeley. Interviews, analyses of freshman-senior personality scales and case studies were carried out on selected samples of 250 students. These researchers found that college had little impact on student development and concluded that the answer to the present dilemma lies in changing several components of the educational environment and in particular the focus of education which should be on the student and his development rather than on the accumulation of course credits.

Somewhat contradictory findings were obtained by Chickering (1969). In his study the Omnibus Personality Inventory was administered to entering freshmen at 13 small colleges (the student population varying from 91 to 703) and again after the first year and the second year. Institutional differences were measured by a College Goals Rating Sheet, the College and University Environment Scales, and campus visits. The test-retest data indicated that most student change was found in Autonomy, Impulse Expression, Aestheticism and Practical Orientation, while least change was found in Intellectual Interests, Social Extroversion and Altruism.

These findings were the same for both men and women, were irrespective of their mean scores at entrance, and the changes were highly consistent for all colleges. That is, the change occurred among many different kinds of students attending many different institutions. However, the evidence does not support the assumption of campus-wide impact. The colleges sampled ranged from a student-centered school with a highly flexible curriculum to a college with a highly structured curriculum. Whether or not the institution had a traditional approach to curriculum and teaching or a flexible and innovative approach stressing independent study and student-centered courses, there was little increase in intellectual difference. Not one of the 13 exerted sufficient force to retard, accelerate or deflect the general developmental trends shared by their diverse entering student populations.

In another of Chickering's studies (1968) the frequency distribution of difference scores on the Omnibus Personality Inventory scales was examined, and institutional variability was found to be substantial. In one college where the scores reflected a significant mean change, almost all students changed in the same direction in varying amounts. At another institution, 25 percent changed in the opposite direction even when difference scores were pooled across six scales reflecting significant differences. Upon reexamination of difference scores for scales that reflected no significance, substantial institutional differences were noted.

Clearly, the impact of college is not simple or clear-cut. More complex studies are needed. There has been little evidence that any one factor explains changes in attitudes and values. And, although most research on this subject indicates that college students change in some areas, very little is known about how or why. Significant subgroups within each institution must be explored and measured. Moreover, particular relationships among institutional characteristics, student characteristics and student change must be explored. More attention needs to be given appropriate multivariate analyses simultaneously taking into account student input characteristics, educational experiences and environmental factors, noncollege control groups, and carefully delineated outcomes. Much more attention needs to be given to the independent effects of specific courses and programs in this context versus the cumulative effects of the total college experience.

Whatever the individual propensity or the environmental press, the interaction of personality factors with external demands must be observed in any concern with student development. Attempting to look at qualities not usually examined in community college students, A. M. Cohen and Brawer (1970) noted a tendency toward homogeneity among entering freshmen. Although no major differences in personality factors were identified between students who persisted and those who withdrew before completion of their initial college semester, withdrawals tended to be enrolled for fewer than 12 units and to be employed more hours out of school than persisters. Further, nonpersisters had mothers with less education, had lower mean scores on a test measuring ego strength (Brawer, 1967), and had attended more schools before the tenth grade than had persisters. These variables, then, in apparent contrast to findings for college students generally, appeared more significant than the personality factors measured by the Omnibus Personality Inventory (cf. Feldman & Newcomb, 1969). In *A Constant Variable* (A. M. Cohen & associates, 1971), Brawer further delineated studies of students in community junior colleges, making a plea against the collection of more of the same types of data and emphasizing the need for new ways of observing students at all institutions of higher education.

Other studies have found personality traits to be important distinguishing characteristics of persisters and nonpersisters over a four-year period. Trent (1970a, in press), for example, found that differences in disposition related to academic pursuit also existed between students who withdrew from college with grade point averages of C or better versus below a C average. More specifically, multivariate analysis of a wide array of background, educational experience, value and personality variables revealed the three greatest predictors of persistence in college to be, in order of importance, the student's stress on the importance of college, the certainty of the student's plans, and Social Maturity (an early Omnibus Personality Inventory measure of autonomy). Omnibus

Personality Inventory measurements of Complexity (intellectual curiosity and tolerance for ambiguity), Thinking Introversion (preference for reflective, abstract thought, particularly in the area of the humanities), and Nonauthoritarianism also were among the greatest predictors of persistence in college.

In addition, the nonpersisters, compared with persisters, manifested a greater need for rules and regulations. One interpretation of the findings is that it corroborates the greater authoritarianism found among the nonpersisters, which would be expected to be reflected in a greater need for reliance upon authoritatively structured regulation and specification. Implications are that students of this kind are unhappy with unstructured learning situations which depend upon their self-initiation and independent judgments.

Trent drew upon the multivariate analyses of his data to establish a model as a start in the development of a framework designed to promote the use of data of this kind in assisting students to understand and make the most of their potential as they move through the educational process. H. A. Rose (1965) and H. A. Rose and Elton (1966) have actually substantiated the usefulness of aspects of the model. They used scales and items of the Omnibus Personality Inventory to predict withdrawals among entering University of Kentucky freshmen. Subsequent examination of experimental and control groups showed not only the validity of the prediction technique, but that attrition can be significantly arrested through group counseling dealing with students' adjustment and learning problems.

SPECIFIC GROUPS IN HIGHER EDUCATION

Black students, women and student activists were the subjects of separate lines of research—and controversy—in the sixties which have great implications for the teaching-learning function in higher education. Higher education, heretofore unprepared to deal with the culturally disadvantaged student in its traditional curriculum, has been having difficulties meeting the demands for a new curriculum for a new clientele. For example, according to Korn's review of the research (1969), the discrepancy between individual needs of blacks and institutional requirements reaches tragic proportions.

Black Students

Blacks are demanding courses that emphasize Afro-American culture and in general are challenging the traditional and accepted academic procedures. A book of essays edited by Parsons and Clark (1966) spelled out the dimensions of the Afro-American experience. At the present time the most significant dimension can be described in terms of the polar concepts of integration and separatism. Integration into American society seems to be too slow and too disappointing for many blacks. The sense of identity and basis for self-respect are being pursued through their demand for Afro-American cultural studies.

All levels of education felt the pressure to offer particularized programs to aid black students in enhancing their self-image; hence, black studies courses were introduced widely. The community colleges were especially sensitive to these needs and enrolled sizeable proportions of black students in higher education. Lombardi (1971) documented the extent of black studies programs in community colleges including numbers and types of courses, teaching techniques, and patterns of curriculum modification. Black studies in the university was the subject of numerous articles in *Phi Delta Kappan* (Cleveland, 1969), *Journal of Negro Education* (Black Studies in American Education, 1970), *Ebony* (Which Way Black America, 1970), and elsewhere. The book by Robinson, Foster, and Ogilvie (*Black Studies in the University,* 1969) reviewed the scope of these special programs with particular emphasis on their goals.

Although empirical studies are few, there is growing awareness and recently consid-erable evidence to support the hypothesis that some differences in the psychological functioning between black and white subjects may be due to a great extent to the situational variables within the social setting of the experiment rather than a difference inherent in the race (I. Katz, 1964; Katz, Epps, & Axelson, 1964; Katz & Greenbaum, 1963; Katz, Roberts, & Robinson, 1965).

Baratz (1967) investigated the effect of race of the examiner on the level of reported anxiety of black subjects through the administration of the Test Anxiety Questionnaire to 120 undergraduates under eight experimental conditions. Black subjects tested by a black examiner reported less anxiety than those tested by a white examiner, and Baratz concluded that the level of reported anxiety was dependent upon the stress characteristics of the immediate social situation.

Harris and Reitzel (1967) explored differences in freshman grade-point average, the verbal and mathematics forms of the Scholastic Aptitude Test (SAT), and rank in high-school graduating class in order to assess the comparative value of black students' high-school rank versus the high-school rank of the total freshman population as a predictor of freshman grade-point average.

The black freshmen in a predominantly white university obtained lower SAT scores on both forms and obtained lower than average freshman grade-point averages although their high-school rank was above average. The blacks' academic achievement was best predicted when the forecast was made for them as a group rather than as undifferentiated members of the freshman class. To the extent that the small analysis sample (45) compared to the relatively large normative sample (3,895) was indicative, the data suggested that either the pre-college education of these black students was less adequate than that of the total freshman population or that grading standards in high schools from which the blacks came were more lenient. Current sociological and psychological theory supports the former possibility and suggests the latter possibility may also hold true.

N. E. Bradley (1967) found that the American College Test scores were not equally predictive of grade-point average for black and white students in predominantly white state colleges and universities in Tennessee. Bradley saw the problem as primarily the need for improved interracial education at elementary- and secondary-school levels. Cherdack (1971) arrived at similar results and conclusions in his comparative study of black, Mexican-American and Anglo students at different income levels enrolled at two University of California campuses.

A comprehensive treatment of the problems of the black student in higher education is the subject of the Summer 1967 issue of the *Journal of Negro Education*. Charles H. Thompson (1967), Dean Emeritus of the graduate school of Howard University, presented a critical summary of the issue which emphasized the need for adequate higher educational opportunities for blacks. Thompson stated that such opportunities could be provided by greatly improved predominantly black institutions and increased enrollment of Negroes in predominantly white higher education institutions. He urged "that each of the four-year PDN [predominantly Negro] colleges engage in a self-study...which will eventuate in a long-range plan for the development of each institution" (1967, p. 314).

The response by higher education to the challenge presented by the black students may well be the key to its readiness to respond to a wide variety of problems and issues, including those related to the vast majority of white students—a point explored by Lombardi and Quimby (1971). Fundamental to this response is systematic evaluative research into the conditions underlying teaching effectiveness pertinent to blacks, Mexican-Americans and other minority students. For the most part, however, research of this kind does not yet appear to be forthcoming.

Mexican-American Students

Apart from the relatively nominal research on black students, systematic research is essentially nonexistent on Mexican-American or other minority students in higher education. One reason for the lack of research on Mexican-Americans may be their very low representation in higher education. Possible reasons for this situation are suggested by the research of Schwartz (1969) and Gordon and associates (1968) which compared Anglo and Mexican-American ninth- and twelfth-graders from 13 schools in the Los Angeles area. A majority of both groups aspired to formal education after high school, but nearly twice the proportion of Anglo students compared with Mexican-Americans desired to continue their education. Moreover, among those students who desired post–high-school education the Anglos tended toward four-year institutions and subsequent graduate work whereas the Mexican-Americans tended toward trade school and two-year institutions.

Although the Anglo and Mexican-American students in the Gordon-Schwartz research were from the same neighborhoods, the academic achievement level of the Anglos was average, while that of the Mexican-Americans was low. Desired occupational levels of the two groups were similar when controlling for level of achievement; differences in educational aspiration, however, were reduced but not eliminated.

No doubt the language problems and other handicaps enter into this finding. But it is just as likely that patterns of family values are also relevant. In examining the values of the students and their parents, Gordon and Schwartz found that the dominant cultural values of the Mexican-Americans precluded some orientations which are highly related to achievement in middle-class American society, including willingness to exercise control over others, independence from parental control, an optimistic orientation toward the future, a generalized confidence in mankind and a nonrational orientation toward activity. According to Schwartz:

One can conclude from this analysis that as opportunities are presented to Mexican-American youth for some acculturation of Anglo values, so are opportunities presented for greater educational achievement. While the deliberate modification of value orientation through indoctrination is and should be beyond the ken of any public educational system, such modification which occurs through normal social processes is not.

With the firm conviction that some form of cultural adaption to the larger society by Mexican-American youngsters is necessary if the already apparent grim consequences of educational failure are to be avoided, this study recommends that educational systems make a formal effort to structure the social context of education so that achievement values which may not be derived from the home can be developed at school, through informal social processes. Through deliberate encouragement and through manipulation of attendance boundaries, school officials must be permitted and, indeed, required to develop school environments which are most positive for academic achievement and for values which support it (1969, pp. 53–54).

Much of what Schwartz recommends for the educational system generally might be applied to higher education specifically, and should be assisted by research indicating productive methods to encourage Mexican-American and other minority students to enter and progress in college.

Women

The separate needs and problems of women in higher education also received increased study. This research is particularly pertinent in light of the well-documented historical and existent discrimination against women in the labor force and in the educational process. Ever since Betty Friedan's 1963 treatise on the feminine mystique, a proliferation of books, research studies, journals and magazine articles has been devoted to the study of women and particularly to the cultural stereotypic definition of women which characterizes them as passive and subordinate. At the same time, armed with this increasing body of damaging evidence, the Women's Liberation movement has attempted to change the cultural definition of women's roles in society. Nondiscriminatory legislation has been passed by Congress; a woman ran for the Democratic presidential nomination of the United States in 1972. Yet the impact of the educational process, a potentially powerful source of influence on the lives of young women, seems to be negligible.

In 1963, 24 million women, representing more than $\frac{1}{3}$ of the labor force, were employed, and proportionately more women are entering employment today. Moreover, many of these women, particularly those who have completed college, do not have to work for financial reasons but rather are working because of career interests and self-fulfillment. Mary D. Keyserling (1967), Director of the Women's Bureau, U.S. Department of Labor, reported a study made by the Women's Bureau of the activities of alumnae of the class of 1945, 15 years after graduation. One-third of the group was employed; five out of six of the remaining $\frac{2}{3}$ indicated an interest in future employment. She also reported a 1957 study of women graduates seven years after graduation which revealed that more than half of the women were employed. Because women who wish to enter employment many years after they have attended or graduated from college may need to update their skills, Mrs. Keyserling describes the need for continuing educational programs for women, courses that update the basic information women received in their fields of interest as undergraduates, flexible scheduling of hours, liberal provision for transfer of credits, educational and employment counseling, and special programs for women who wish to resume an interrupted college education on a part-time basis.

One implication to be drawn from **Keyser-**

ling's paper is that a very large proportion of women college graduates are actively pursuing careers or at least some type of employment. This situation leaves major questions unanswered, however—that is, to what extent does the pre-college educational system facilitate and stimulate women's desire to enroll in college? to what extent do women's college educational experiences contribute to the attainment of satisfying careers and life-styles? The review of the literature suggests an even more basic question: to what extent must our entire educational system act as a counterforce to those societal and parental pressures that tend to restrict women's development?

For many years psychiatrists and psychologists have stressed the importance of early childhood experiences in the development of behavior patterns and attitudes that, in turn, influence adult behavior, attitudes and outcomes. Only recently, however, psychologists have become more attentive to sex-linked differences in these early childhood behaviors and to the differential impact of both early childhood family and school experiences on the sexes. Not only are sex differences manifest in early childhood abilities and behaviors, but these early childhood sex-linked behaviors are also predictors of similar adult behaviors (Jones, Bayley, MacFarlane, & Honzik, 1971; Kagan & Moss, 1963).

Berelson and Steiner's (1964) review of behavioral science literature presents substantial evidence that opinions, attitudes and beliefs are "inherited from parents"; they are learned in early childhood and persist into adulthood. Certainly parents are the first significant influences in the individual's life, and, as "significant others," determine more than anyone else the individual's self-perception, including that person's conception of his or her position in society and the role he or she is to play in that position (Trent, 1970). Bronfenbrenner (1961) found in this respect that parents make significantly fewer demands of girls than they do of boys.

Research has also shown that parents and adults in general exert greater influence upon girls than boys (Crandall, 1964), and that family attitudes and social relationships are fully developed for women by grade 9 and persist, unchanged, to college age (Berdie, 1968). On the basis of a synthesis of four research studies, Cross (1963) found that 55 percent of the females compared to 39 percent of the males questioned said it was "very important" to satisfy their parents' wishes. These findings gain in relevance in view of the fact that parental encouragement has been found to be a key variable distinguishing between those who go to college and those who do not. At the same time, according to students' self-reports, parents expect their sons to get more education than their daughters. This parental encouragement for education is greater for boys than girls, particularly among the lower socioeconomic groups (Trent & Medsker, 1968). These findings suggest that perhaps parents, by reinforcing the traditional sex stereotypes and the "college is for men" attitude, may, as a result, affect females' achievement behavior as well as their role-orientation and educational and vocational aspirations.

Apparently schools further contribute to this situation. Boys are more strongly encouraged to enroll in mathematics and science courses; girls are encouraged to enroll in home economics and literature courses. Girls are rewarded for being passive and well behaved while boys are expected to be aggressive and noisy, and they both behave as they are expected to behave. In fact, high-school girls, including those who do not go on to college, have been found to be considerably more involved in their studies and activities than are boys over the four-year period of high school. Girls are better behaved, better mannered, more social, and they take their school assignments more seriously. In addition, they have significantly higher grade-point averages (Flanagan et al., 1964; Jones et al., 1971; Tillery et al., 1972). This achievement differential continues during college: according to Cross's (1963) review, 43 percent of the women and only 30 percent of the college men graduated in the top 10 percent of their high-school classes.

In spite of women's potential, few expect or are encouraged by school personnel to enter traditionally masculine careers. The evidence is that this lack of encouragement is true even among counselors, who, by nature of their role and training, might be expected to be receptive to women's fullest exploration of educational and career possibilities. Karman (1972) found that college women with "nontraditional" career aspirations had requested assistance with vocational plans from counselors significantly less often than women planning to enter a traditionally feminine occupation. Thomas (1967) studied the reactions of male and female counselors to college women who had "traditional" feminine career goals and to those holding "nontraditional" career goals. He observed that all, but particularly male, counselors perceived the traditional feminine goals as more appropriate for women.

It is not surprising, then, in light of these findings, that females are less prone than males to go to college and/or choose occupations of a professional nature (Astin, 1963a; Astin & Panos, 1969; Flanagan et al., 1964; Thistlethwaite, 1965; Tillery et al., 1972; Trent & Medsker, 1968). In 1962 more women than men graduated from high school—966,000 women and 872,000 men. At high-school graduation, 67 percent of the females and only 45 percent of the males had a "B" average or better. However, women constituted only 42 percent of the 1962 college enrollment. Of the brightest 40 percent of high-school students, only ½ went to college; of the half who did not go, ⅔ were women (Cross, 1963; Epstein, 1970).

Once in college, sex is a dominant predictor of students' final major fields and career choices—college men move toward traditionally defined "masculine" majors and careers, women toward more "feminine"

careers and majors (Astin, 1968; Astin & Panos, 1965; Karman, 1972). Women indicate preferences for careers in nursing, teaching and business (Bruemmer, 1969; Trent & Medsker, 1968). In general, women report negative feelings about jobs requiring assertive or competitive characteristics, particularly where the competition is with men (Epstein, 1970; Wright, 1967). Of the 1,646 upper-class women surveyed nationally by the University of California at Los Angeles's Center for the Study of Evaluation, only 109 (or 6.6 percent) expressed career aspirations in nontraditional fields; 1,537 aspired to careers in occupational fields where women represent the large majority of the work force (Karman, 1972).

Moreover, throughout the college years the conflict between the drive for academic achievement and the pressure to conform to traditional feminine role behavior continues. For example, according to J. Katz and associates (1968), the relative importance of "husband-hunting" increases in direct proportion to the proximity of graduation. In addition, many career-oriented women change their preference from male-dominated careers (Schwartz, 1969), or they seek feminine specialties within these fields (Bruemmer, 1969). In fact, two studies found that some college women even deliberately prostitute their achievements in order to increase their appeal to men. These studies revealed that 40 percent of the college women on two very different campuses admitted to "playing dumb" occasionally, to concealing academic honors or to pretending ignorance (Komarovsky, 1953). Even Vassar women who valued achievement were reluctant to develop their potential in such a way that would threaten the status or security of men by their exceptional accomplishments (Freedman, 1969).

Sex is also a strong predictor of subsequent doctoral degree aspirations among college undergraduates. Although more women than men have been found to increase their desire during their undergraduate years to do graduate work, the vast majority of women aspiring to graduate school plan to work for a master's degree only; most students with interest in and plans to obtain doctoral degrees are males (Astin, 1963a; Astin & Panos, 1965; Flanagan et al., 1964; Tillery et al., 1972; Trent & Medsker, 1968). Moreover, there is a greater discrepancy between the aspirations to enter and the actual entry of women into graduate school than there is for men. The results of a study of academically talented students revealed that 78 percent of the women questioned aspired to graduate school but only 27 percent actually enrolled, whereas 89 percent of the males aspired to graduate school and 62 percent actually entered within one year after college graduation (Thistlethwaite, 1965). Of the upper-class students recently surveyed nationally by the Higher Education Project of the Center for the Study of Evaluation, 70 percent of the men indicated they planned to enroll in graduate school compared to 57 percent of the women, and 27 percent of the men planned to earn a doctoral degree compared to less than 9 percent of the women (Morey, Pace, & Trent, 1970).

In 1966 women received only 34 percent of the master's degrees awarded as opposed to 19 percent in 1900, 40 percent in 1930 and 38 percent in 1958. Women earned only 12 percent of the doctorates in 1966, a decrease from the 1930 figure of 15 percent and the 1920 figure of 16 percent (Painter, 1971). Although the absolute number of women receiving Ph.D.s increased from 93 in 1920 to 885 in 1956, their relative proportion has shown a marked decline. More specifically, according to the National Manpower Council in 1959, female doctorate holders represented only 1/300th of the women capable of earning such a degree (Newcomer, 1959).

One reason for this decline may be the Ph.D. explosion which occurred in the fields of engineering and business administration (Sexton, 1969). Another likely reason is discrimination. Women have only a small chance of becoming professors or administrators. According to one survey of 30 leading colleges and universities, only 20 percent of the professors were women. Women rarely constituted more than 10 percent and never more than 20 percent of the full professors. In addition, women never held more than 30 percent of the associate or assistant professorships. These inequities were also reflected in committee appointments and salaries (Bird, 1968; Robinson, 1971). Of course, the lack of women doctorates at the outset probably accounts for part of this situation. The problem, then, is to encourage women to attain advanced degrees as much as it is to encourage their subsequent professional advancement.

The statistics on women are particularly disappointing since significant differences were found in favor of females, particularly in the areas of personality and cognitive development. At college entry, for example, females compared to males were significantly less stereotypic in their attitudes and values, less dogmatic and less authoritarian. With few exceptions, although college students of both sexes showed an increase over the four-year period in critical-thinking ability and a decrease in stereotypic beliefs, dogmatism, authoritarianism and unreceptivity to new ideas, for females, the more college completed, the more they became oriented to emergent values and the less they adhered to stereotypic beliefs (Lehmann & Dressel, 1962, 1963). In fact, college women showed the greatest growth in autonomy. Females who entered homemaking immediately after high school changed the least and generally regressed both in intellectual disposition and autonomy compared to their employed peers and particularly to their college-attending peers (Trent & Medsker, 1968). Interviews with Vassar women revealed similar changes: greater independence, increased sophistication, complexity, relativism of outlook, greater expression of critical attitudes and more independence from family values (Freedman, 1969). Personality factors such as these may warrant further consideration if for no other reason than because of their relevance to educational experience and career outcomes of college women. For example, Rand (1968) found that career-oriented women had higher masculine personality and ability characteristics as well as higher feminine ability characteristics. Homemakers, on the other hand, had higher feminine personality and social interest characteristics. Differences between two groups of freshman women were also found by Hoyt and Kennedy (1958). The career-oriented women were higher on achievement, intraception and endurance while those oriented toward homemaking were higher on heterosexuality and succorance. Hoyt and Kennedy suggest that career-oriented women are motivated by one or more of four relatively independent needs: 1) need to establish worth through competitive behavior or achievement; 2) need to know and understand intellectually (intraception); 3) need to accomplish concrete goals (endurance); and 4) need to avoid relations with the opposite sex (heterosexuality). Homemakers, on the other hand, are motivated by needs for affection and acceptance (succorance) which can be satisfied by marriage.

Using multiple regression analysis to determine which variables were most predictive of nonstereotypic career choice among upper-class college women, Karman (1972) found that, regardless of type of college attended, women with nonstereotypic career aspirations came from higher socioeconomic levels; had mothers who attained higher levels of education; held more liberal attitudes toward the role of women in society and toward international relations among governments; expressed a stronger liking for science and mathematics; maintained higher academic records in college; saw their college experiences more in terms of vocational and liberal education benefits; participated in college to a greater degree in social service and academically oriented activities; were less involved in artistically creative activities such as creative writing,

dance, art, theater, and music; were more likely to come from Jewish homes; and particularly were more theoretically oriented. In fact, the most differentiating variable was theoretical orientation—the propensity for logical, analytical and critical thinking.

The fact that the proportions, characteristics and outcomes of these women did not differ among the types of colleges they attended suggests that the higher educational experiences commonly offered women are not designed for their fullest development as defined in this context. The evidence is that this is as true for the select liberal arts college or university as it is for nonselective, general colleges and universities. An illustration of this point appears in a study of 129 undergraduate women attending nine different colleges and universities where they were majoring in physical science (Dement, 1962). The findings revealed that those women who could meet the scholastic competition and were able to withstand the social pressures and cope with their special problems had certain common characteristics: strong scholastic ability and emotional security, very high motivation and strong ambitions. More significant, however, were the findings that in addition to all of the threats encountered by men in highly competitive courses with difficult subject matter, these women had to cope with the negative attitudes of peers, personal prejudices of many professors, an increased sense of loneliness and isolation from other members of their sex, and the objections of parents. Dement suggests that more encouragement be given to women by the institution and that special living arrangements be available so that women with special interests such as studies in the sciences can live together and share their work, interests and problems. But Dement's suggestion about living arrangements, however well meaning, may be self-defeating. The suggestion's implementation might only serve to further isolate women, making it all the more difficult for them to interact with and contribute to the social, educational and professional world around them which is currently dominated by men.

Certainly more effort must be made to develop programs in higher education to counteract the myth of the "feminine mystique," the glorification of the homemaker and the denigration of the career-woman that has psychologically straitjacketed so many women.

Federal legislation has begun tearing down the discriminatory job barriers for women and affirmative action programs encouraging women to seek higher education have been implemented in many colleges. In addition to removing all discrimination, however, the stigma of the "masculine" versus "feminine" career must be eliminated. Of course, the place to begin is in the elementary schools where young children should be reading books which depict women in all kinds of role-models, not just that of wife, mother, nurse or teacher. But it is equally important that the entire educational system systematically help redefine the role of women and encourage their development so that women are completely free to pursue or not to pursue any career or life-style of their choosing.

Student Activists

Student activism was much in the mind of the educational researcher during the latter half of the sixties. Although most studies of student activists sought to investigate and describe the characteristics peculiar to this group, several studies indicated that student activist movements really involved only a very few select students in a very few select colleges and universities. Peterson (1965) reported that at most only 9 percent of any student body was involved in protest movements. Similar findings were obtained by Heist (1965; 1966) and Trent (1970b).

The several studies that investigated the social-psychological characteristics of the student activists reported consistent findings and seem to represent at least one area of research in which there appear to be few disagreements (see, e.g., M. Aiken, Demerath, & Marwell, 1966; Bay, 1967; Flacks, 1967; Haan, Smith, & Block, 1968; Heist, 1965, 1966; Kornhauser, 1967; Lyonns, 1965; Selvin & Hagstrom, 1960; Somers, 1965; Trent, 1970b; Trent & Craise, 1967; Watts & Whittaker, 1966). The conclusions of the studies are summarized below.

1. Student activists were exceptionally high in measured intellectual disposition, autonomy, flexibility and liberalism, as well as in level of ability. They exhibited marked qualities of individuality, social commitment and intellectuality not observed among more random samples of college students. In fact, they represented some of higher education's most able and intellectually dedicated students.

2. Activists represented humanities and especially social science majors in disproportionately high numbers.

3. Jews were also highly overrepresented among activists.

4. Nonactivists and their parents tended to express conventional orientations toward achievement, material success, sexual morality and religion; the activists and their parents tended to place greater stress on involvement in intellectual and aesthetic pursuits, humanitarian concerns, and opportunities for self-expression, while de-emphasizing or disvaluing personal achievement, conventional morality and religiosity.

5. Activists tended to come from upper middle-class families; their fathers tended to be professional (doctors, lawyers, professors) rather than lower-level business, white-collar or working-class men. Their mothers were likely to be employed in "career" types of employment with many holding advanced academic degrees.

6. Fathers of activists were disproportionately liberal in their political views. Contrary to popular belief, most of these activists were not rebelling against parental authority or their fathers' political views

and values; rather, the great majority of these students were attempting to fulfill and renew the political traditions of their family, acting out the values which their parents explicitly believed but did not have the courage or opportunity to practice or fight for.

Although the findings from the above research indicate that activists are relatively good students in terms of academic achievement and intellectual interests, whether conforming students achieve higher grades than nonconforming students has not been resolved. The consensus of findings from several studies early in the 1960s investigating general student populations (e.g., Davie, 1961; Erb, 1961; Gill & Spilka, 1962; Powell & Jourard, 1963) is contrary to findings obtained in the studies of activists in that they characterize successful students as being conventional, docile and willing to conform to academic requirements, routine and regulation, manifesting less hostility toward authority and reflecting a lifelong pattern of conventional behavior.

Although the contradiction between the findings of these studies and data concerning activists may be a result of differences in study design, measurement or sample, it is also possible that the difference in findings reflects not only college students' growing social awareness but their willingness to work actively toward bringing about what they consider to be a better society.

A number of researchers have considered the relation of institutional characteristics to student activism, including D. R. Brown (1967), Cowan (1966), Keniston (1967a, 1967b), Lipset (1965), Sampson (1967) and Sampson, Korn, and associates (1970). The consensus of their conclusions is that student protest is associated with the following interrelated elements:

1. Institutional size and particularly the congregation of large numbers of protest-prone students in close proximity to one another.

2. The presence of a ready body of persons with unusual qualities of leadership including a disproportionate number of teaching assistants.

3. Institutions noted for academic excellence such as selective and progressive private liberal arts colleges, major state universities which have long traditions of excellent undergraduate teaching, high admissions policy and prestige (e.g., the University of Michigan, the University of Wisconsin and the University of California at Berkeley) which tend to congregate large numbers of potentially protesting students.

4. Institutions which command little institutional allegiance from large numbers of highly capable graduate students.

5. Institutions which have a tradition of conflict within the institution.

6. Conflicting perspectives in large institutions concerning research versus teaching.

7. The presence of a para-institutional environment such as the underground community of perpetual students, part-time students and nonstudents that exist within the academic community.

8. The active participation of admired faculty members in activities such as protests, teach-ins and peace marches.

A study by Lipset and Ladd (1970) is particularly relevant to the final point (8) above. The study was based upon a national survey of 60,000 professors in 307 colleges and universities and investigated the relationships between faculty attitudes and support for student activism. Principal findings were that:

1. Faculty support varies distinctly by discipline, with social science professors being the most sympathetic to activism.

2. Professors whose views on national issues are liberal or left give much more support to student activism than do middle-of-the-roaders or conservatives. About half the faculty described themselves as generally left or liberal, while one-quarter described themselves as conservative.

3. The more productive academics, as

measured by involvements in research or extent of publications or similar indices, are likely to favor left-liberal policies and approve of student activism.

4. In each discipline, as age increases, support for student activism decreases; the greatest effect of age was among political scientists.

5. Jewish professors are more supportive of activism than gentiles and they constitute a significant part of the faculty—10 percent of the total, 17 percent in the elite universities, and 25 percent of the social science faculties in elite universities.

Not only do activists receive support from a number of academics in the "system," but they themselves largely remain engaged with the system: rather than being part of a subculture of "alienation," most activists are relatively well satisfied with their undergraduate education, as are most students. However, more than other students they are dissatisfied with the "civil-libertarian" defects of their college administration and tend to be more responsive than other students to deprivations of civil rights on campus as well as off campus.

This new wave of radicalism—or at least its activistic elements—contradicts all early studies pertaining to the determinants of disaffection among intellectuals. Historical surveys of radical movements of the intelligentsia are reviewed by Flacks (1967) in an effort to find a rationale for the student protest movements of the sixties. He cites Aaron (1965), Eisenstadt (1956) and Lasch (1965), who indicate that the radical movements at the turn of the century came about when values such as gentility, laissez faire, naive optimism, naive rationalism and nationalism seemed increasingly inappropriate due to the impact of large-scale industrial organizations intensifying class conflict, economic crises and the emergence of total war.

The student generation of the 1960s, however, did not look forward to occupational insecurity but each individual could hope for and expect increased opportunity for occupational advance and the maximum demand for and prestige given to his skills. In addition, according to Flacks, there was no evident erosion of the legitimacy of established authority. Although there are current signs of changing values, mores and morals, Flacks considered that we are not in a period of rapid disintegration of traditional values any more now than 10 years ago when sociological studies observed the exhaustion of opportunity for radical social movements in America (see Bell, 1962; Lipset, 1960). Moreover, current college students on the whole are found to be basically satisfied with their college experience and show major concern for their vocational advancement (cf. Cook, 1971).

At the same time the personal orientation of the activist students represents a sharp contrast to the orientation of the post-World War II "silent generation." Jacob (1960) and Goldsen (1960) describe the orientation of the college students of the fifties as an absorbing self-interestedness directed toward satisfying the desires for material well-being, privacy within one's male-oriented family domain, and group dependence; social and political indifference, irresponsibility and an instrumental approach to reason and morality were also the norm.

Several explanations for the existence of the student activist movement have been offered. Parsons (1965) and Eisenstadt (1956) developed the argument that self-conscious subcultures and movements among adolescents tend to develop when there is a sharp distinction between the values and expectations embodied in the traditional families in a society and the values and expectations prevailing in the occupational sphere. The greater the disjunction, the more self-conscious and oppositional the youth culture. Keniston (1970) analyzed the power of the youth culture to effect change and attributed some of its potential force to contradictions inherent in society. Great economic wealth permits the development of a class of young adults free to pursue idealistic goals, but the very factors producing this wealth incur conditions antithetical to human values, thus inciting idealists to seek change.

Peterson (1966) suggests the presence of a protest-prone personality which, according to Keniston (1970), raises several questions for further research because of its implications. Peterson's protest-prone personality is one which will probably involve a high grade-point average, a high achievement motive, a family with liberal values, a pacifist orientation, a liberal religious or nonreligious orientation, professional parents and high social status. The fact that these conditions are fulfilled most often in Jewish families raises the question that there may still be other factors associated with social class and religion that independently promote activism. For example, being in a Jewish minority group that has preserved its culture in the face of opposing community pressures for centuries may in some way prepare or permit the individual to take controversial positions as a student. Conservative religious affiliation can have the opposite effect not only on issues of this kind but disposition to learning generally (see Trent & Golds, 1967). Have we been studying the determinants of radical beliefs, of activism in general, or of the interaction between a particular set of radical beliefs and a particular type of radical action?

Not all answers to such questions will be consistent. Nor are all preceding assumptions universally accepted. Surely Roszak (1969) and Reich (1970), among others, would argue that we are indeed in the throes of a cultural revolution that is leading to a restructuring of our values and mores. To all appearances, college youth represent much of the forefront of this revolution. The revolution on college campuses was quieter in 1971 than it had been in the recent past. The state of the economy made funds from parents and scholarship loan resources no longer so readily available and also made it clear that college graduates could not necessarily expect employment security, let alone a satisfying, prestigious career. Perhaps these events caused students to think more seriously about both their present and future financial situations.

But the indications are that current events are not diminishing youths' development of a "new consciousness" which, as represented by the activists, continues to act as a press on higher education to change. Major concerns of youths are that they participate in educational policy and practice affecting them, that their education relate to them personally and be flexible enough to take their individual needs and desires into account, that their education relate to the issues of the world around them, and that there be some form of accountability for the educational process.

In reflecting upon Flack's (1967) study discussed above, Miles and Charters (1970) suggested the possibility that,

Colleges and high schools (and elementary schools?) will be the primary interaction arenas where revised value and belief systems for our "post-industrial" society will be developed, reinforced and diffused. If so, the question for educators is will this happen in spite of us, or with our aid? (p. 500).

In light of many of the findings enumerated above, Miles and Charters's question is a good one to bear in mind in assessing the implications of the following material on teaching techniques, training and effectiveness.

TEACHING TECHNOLOGY AND METHODS
by
Arthur M. Cohen, Clare Rose and James W. Trent

Serious questioning of the system of higher education has resulted in a thrust toward innovation and experimentation in colleges. Unfortunately, however, when compared with the reported claims of colleges having embraced nongrading, team teaching, and the use of a great diversity of instructional methods and materials, relatively few of the educational innovations developed during the 1960s with great hope for widespread usefulness are found in operation. Moreover, the word "innovation" has lost much of its meaning through misuse and overuse. For example, educational programs were labeled "innovative" if they employed forms of media and multimedia such as instructional television, programmed materials, audio tapes and filmstrips, or if they used various instructional techniques and methods such as simulations, independent study, discussion groups, laboratory experiences and team teaching singly or in combination. The term "innovative" was also applied to new forms of colleges such as cluster colleges and experimental colleges. Because of the almost relentless demand for educational innovations during the 1960s, however, the common tendency was to equate innovation with improvement without rigorously evaluating the effectiveness of each new educational program or instructional procedure.

Media Studies

The 1960s began with vast claims for, and ended with equally vast disillusionment with, new instructional media. The journalists, hardware salesmen, and those educators who might be called "professional innovators" argued that media such as television, auto-instructional programs and dial access information systems would release the teacher for creative interaction with his students. As initial enthusiasm wore off, however, the innovator left the campus, or the funds ran out, and disillusionment set in, with attendant abandonment of the media form. This pattern recurred in numerous colleges and with a variety of "new media."

Specific media. Several researchers attempted to identify the problems associated with media. Murphy and Gross (1966) documented the problems associated with the introduction and continued use of instructional television, difficulties that ranged from faculty antagonism to improper use of the medium. Evans and Leppman (1967) traced faculty resistance to television in a well-documented study of 10 institutions and found numerous problems in maintaining the changed instructional form. Using survey forms and interview schedules within a research design that stemmed from social-psychological theory, they discerned resistance based on both the personal characteristics of faculty members and the characteristics of the traditional college as a social system. They concluded that the reasons for terminating an innovation were extremely varied but that most seemed to relate to the idiosyncracies of instructors and the basic tendency to resist change that is inherent in most types of social structures. At "Metro University," the pro-TV professors were found to be more experimental in their teaching, less recondite, and more related to student activities than those professors who opposed TV. Yet the instructional TV program was abandoned.

J. W. Brown and Thornton (1963) had anticipated the problems of introducing and maintaining reproducible media in higher education when they pointed out that problems will arise when proposed uses are viewed favorably by trustees and administrators but with suspicion by professors who see them as threatening to job security, individual freedom, rewards or conditions of work.

The difficulties attendant upon introducing and maintaining changed media forms led researchers to concern themselves more and more with students' and instructors' preferences for particular forms. F. N. Moore (1969) arranged for 1,630 students to regulate and evaluate their own progress in supplemental instruction in basic and intermediate mathematics classes. The students seemed to prefer the television programs with no difference found between students who intensively used the programs and those who were casual users.

A study of students' attitudes toward

computer-assisted instruction (CAI) was undertaken by Mathis, Smith, and Hansen (1970). Attitude scales were given to a small (and not necessarily representative) sample of 64 students before and after they worked through CAI programs. The findings indicated that students were generally favorable toward CAI before experiencing the program and that their attitudes remained unchanged subsequent to their experience.

During this same time there was a proliferation of studies undertaken in an attempt to establish the effectiveness of instructional technology. The reports were contradictory. Chambers (1969) and Roderick and Anderson (1968) compared programmed materials with conventional materials and found that students who used programmed materials performed significantly better on recognition test materials but not on the section of the test that sought transfer of learning from the given materials to other situations. Roderick and Anderson found the program to be of greatest advantage with the seniors and on the delayed achievement test.

Other studies which compared reproducible media-based programs with conventional instructional methods found no significant results (R. Davis, Johnson, & Dietrich, 1969; Erickson, 1967; Menne, Hannum, Klingensmith, & Nord, 1969; Orr, 1968; D. R. Taylor, Lipscomb, & Rosemier, 1969; White, 1970). These researchers compared the effectiveness of media to conventional methods, most commonly the lecture, and found no significant difference between experimental and control groups on standardized achievement tests or final examinations. A summary of 100 studies of the effectiveness of television reviewed by Schramm (1964) indicated that 84 of the investigations reported no significant differences in achievement between televised and conventional instruction.

Several of the findings, however, did indicate significant differences in attitudes (R. Davis, Johnson, & Dietrich, 1969; Deeming, 1966; Menne et al., 1969). Students liked the freedom and flexibility the method

allowed them, although the student attitudes toward the televised lectures were related to the individual lecturer and the type of course being televised. Classes which did not involve writing on the blackboard were generally better received. An interesting finding in Menne et al. was the comparison of the number of students in the experimental group who dropped the course (5 out of 290) with the number of students in the control group who dropped the course (58 out of 408), or 0.02 percent compared to 14 percent. A possible explanation, according to the investigators, is that students drop a course when they feel they are hopelessly behind. This situation does not occur as readily if the material is always available to them on tape.

The effectiveness of a TV college program designed to give students maximum freedom with respect to their college education was assessed over an extended period by Stecklein, Ringo, and Macdonald (1966). The TV College at Minnesota was designed to enable students to complete the freshman and sophomore years via television. Stecklein concluded that the population responding to the televised instruction (lower middle-age) differed from the college-age group originally sought. No evidence was found to support the notion that college-age students would spontaneously select TV as a vehicle for the first two years of college.

In these and most other "media" studies, no attempts were made to control for type of auto-instructional program, type of conventional instruction, instructor effect, or appropriateness of random-selection procedures.

Multimedia. Multimedia studies were even more complex. *Multimedia instruction* is the generic term used for courses or programs in which various auto-instructional devices are used in combination. Frequently the components include programmed workbooks, audio tapes alone or with film strips, TV presentations, and laboratory exercises. Occasionally institutions in which multimedia instruction has been introduced use the term *instructional systems*. This term is misused, however, because systematic controls, feedback mechanisms and evaluative devices—essential components of "systems"—are almost always lacking.

Information about multimedia takes several forms. Rationales for the development of multimedia instructional sequences have been presented by Briggs, Campeau, Gagné, and May (1967); extant multimedia programs have been described by J. W. Brown and Thornton (1963) and Johnson (1969); procedures for constructing multimedia sequences have been presented by R. E. Banister (1970) and Postlethwait, Novak, and Murray (1964); and descriptions of instructional systems have been presented by Banathy (1968), Oettinger (1969) and Trzebiatowski (1968).

Implementation of multimedia instruction on a college-wide basis was rarely found although some institutions became rather heavily committed to the process. St. Louis Junior College District introduced a multimedia instructional approach in English, chemistry and psychology at one of its campuses (Hunter, 1970). The program was developed in four phases: planning, preparing the components of the system, demonstration and evaluation. Components included a variety of individually paced learning activities built around several different media forms. Preliminary evaluations showed a significant increase in student achievement; the rate of failure in the chemistry course dropped 10 percent, and dropout rates were lower in English and psychology.

The tendency to adopt new techniques of instruction in the junior college was identified by Johnson (1969) who visited and/or corresponded with staff in more than 250 institutions. He found junior college instructors taking a lead in utilizing programmed instruction, audio-tutorial teaching, television and other mechanical devices. In addition, he reported the use of a variety of innovative techniques that were not "hardware-based," for example, simulation exercises, independent study and

the use of students as teachers. Johnson's conclusions were that the junior college as an institution was quite receptive to the use of different forms of instruction and was, in fact, the segment of higher education most responsive to changed instructional practices. However, he cautioned that innovation without evaluation of the usefulness of the technique seemed prevalent and suggested that the colleges do more to assess the effects of their varied teaching methods. Although large-scale program evaluation was undertaken in some instances, most institutions (four-year colleges included) continued to adopt or reject varied instructional forms without attempting rigorous program evaluation.

For example, in the late 1960s Mt. San Jacinto College and Harrisburg Area Community College began using taped lessons and programmed workbooks to teach shorthand and typing. The instructors at Fullerton Junior College used tapes, filmstrips and worksheets in seminars in several mathematics courses, and Golden West College adopted Postlethwait's (1966) audio-tutorial system for teaching its biology courses and prepared slides and tapes for remedial English. In most of these installations the instructors put together the multimedia sequences themselves, taking ideas from various sources, making local adaptations and preparing the requisite materials.

Less concerned with evaluating the effects of their efforts than with maintaining and revising their projects, the instructors usually allowed evaluations to be made by institutional research offices. Hence the level of sophistication of program evaluation depended on whether a college had a knowledgeable research director or a liaison with a neighboring research group. Most colleges collected information on students' preferences for particular forms. Some compared costs and only a few assessed student learning related to the objectives set up by the program directors.

For example, two industrial arts classes in beginning electronics were assessed (total students, 44) to evaluate the effects of multimedia. The investigator concluded that multimedia may not be suitable for all learners (Harmon, 1969). General education science and physical science students took part in studies which respectively investigated lecture-demonstration and an auto-tutorial laboratory. Eighty students who experienced lecture-demonstrations were contrasted with 82 who individually completed their laboratory work (R. L. Bradley, 1965). Class examinations and final grades reflected no differences. Final examinations and an American College Testing Program test of science reasoning and understanding were administered to evaluate the effects of the auto-tutorial laboratory with an open schedule which was used in place of the traditional laboratory for the physical science students (Rowbotham, 1970). Although no significant differences were found, the author noted that the lower-ability students did better with the auto-tutorial lab.

Trent (1970c) evaluated the effects of auto-tutorial techniques on a sample representing a cross section of engineering students at the University of California at Berkeley. Three classes of students taking a course in engineering properties were administered pre- and posttests at the beginning and end of the fall, winter and spring quarters, 1968–1969. The tests' variables included input or "control" variables such as socioeconomic background, engineering aptitude, personality characteristics, study habits and attitudes toward learning, perceptions of the field of engineering, course achievement factors and ratings of the course experience.

One class did not have access to the auto-tutorial techniques designed to explicate complex models of engineering properties. The second class had access to the materials only during class sessions. The third class had unlimited access to the materials and opportunity to discuss them during class time.

The three groups of students did not differ in their total final examination scores, scores on laboratory problems or grades.

The scores of the three groups were significantly different on 19 out of 35 of the final examination's media-related items, however, or in a little more than half (54 percent) of the cases. Eleven out of the 19 significant differences (60 percent) were in the predicted, desirable direction. Five differences were in reverse of the predicted direction, and three were curvilinear. To state the propositions in another way, out of the 35 media-related items the three groups differed significantly in the predicted direction in 31 percent of the total cases, in the reverse direction in 14 percent of the cases, and scored curvilinearly in 9 percent of the cases. Only nominal differences were apparent between the two groups exposed to the media. Both these groups were also alike in generally evaluating their course experience more positively on a variety of items compared with the "control" group.

The evidence indicated some trend toward a positive relationship between multimedia instruction and performance on media-related examination tasks and attitudes toward course experiences. The relationships were far from perfect, however, and exceptions to the expected outcome warrant close scrutiny.

Trent did discover one contaminating factor. Each class comprised three units, each unit taught by a different instructor. The same instructor taught the same unit in all three classes. Students in the two media-access classes characteristically performed more poorly on the media-related items that pertained to the unit of one instructor compared with the others. Prior interview data revealed that that was the one instructor who was sceptical of the media techniques and their evaluation. Quite possibly this attitude affected his approach in class, which in turn affected his students' reactions. Although the evidence does not demonstrate the fact, it does suggest that the teacher's attitude is important to the effects of media on other instructional techniques.

Beyond this type of generalized study, research on the effects or influence of multimedia instruction per se was rarely found.

Moreover, where researchers assessed the media forms, they assessed them separately while the colleges put them together in various ad hoc combinations. The effects of the combinations remain essentially unevaluated.

Teaching Methods

Lecture versus discussion. Not all of the research on methods and technology was concerned with "new media." Attempts to compare various teaching styles and techniques continued. The old lecture-discussion treatment came in for its share of attention with classroom interactions and the congruence of student characteristics and teaching styles adding a changed dimension to studies comparing groups and treatments.

Haines and McKeachie (1967) divided 82 students in introductory psychology into two groups. Each group participated in two weeks of cooperative and two weeks of competitive class discussions. With the aid of graduate student observers, the amount of tension produced, student performance and student satisfaction were measured for both discussion methods. The data implied that the competitive method results in higher tension, poorer achievement and less satisfaction.

Learner characteristics have most commonly been studied with respect to the content or difficulty level of instruction. Several studies were designed to determine the relationship between student characteristics and the teaching method. Tallmadge and Shearer (1967) found no significant interactions between instructional method and student characteristic variables but speculated that the nature of the material to be learned was critical and needed to be examined as a separate, independent experimental variable.

They did so in their study involving 231 Navy enlisted men who had completed basic training (Tallmadge & Shearer, 1969). Two separate subject-matter areas, logistics and aerial reconnaissance, were selected, and two separate courses developed for each.

One consisted of an inductive and the other a deductive instructional approach. One subject was governed by logically consistent rules and the second subject matter was governed by arbitrary rules such as grammar and consisted of the identification of aircraft from aerial photographs. Four tests were administered to each of the men. Twenty-eight measures of aptitudes, interests and personality were obtained on each subject. The primary finding of the study was the significant interaction among instructional methods, learner characteristics and subject matters. That is, the results strongly supported the existence of learning styles, an attribute of an individual which interacts with instructional circumstances in such a way as to produce differential learning achievement as a function of these circumstances. The findings also supported the hypothesis that the nature of the content of the learning experience is a critical factor affecting the magnitude and direction of the relationships existing between learner characteristics and instructional methods.

Similar investigations concerning the interaction between teaching method and student characteristics indicated that students who achieved most in conventional lecture situations were characterized by moderate achievement and social needs and low creativity (Doty, 1967; Hovey, Gruber, & Terrell, 1963). Students characterized by high creativity or by high social needs tended to perform best in small discussion groups. These findings are consistent with the findings that highly creative students may be characterized by a high level of curiosity which is not satisfied in classes taught by conventional methods. Perhaps this phenomenon helps explain the substantial evidence that the most creative students are those who are most likely to withdraw from college before obtaining their baccalaureate degree (Heist, 1968).

G. S. Bigelow and Egbert (1968) compared the personality development and achievement of students in an independent study group and a traditional study group, each of which was dealing with the same subject matter. Results indicated that students in the traditional study group performed as well on the examination as the independent study group students but that the independent study students developed more in terms of intellectual efficiency and responsibility. Within the group of independent study students who received high grades, those with the higher social needs tended to be less satisfied with completely autonomous study.

In the course of an experiment with small self-directed learning groups in a social psychology course at Hope College, Beach (1970) studied the interactions in the groups to determine what types of activities were helpful and which were harmful to learning and to assess other possible desirable outcomes which might result from this approach to learning. "Experimental" students in the small learning groups were compared with "control" students who were not assigned to such groups. Data were gathered from questionnaires answered by the students at the beginning and end of the course, course tests, the Brown-Holtzman Survey of Study Habits and Attitudes, the Watson-Glaser Critical Thinking Appraisal Test and observation of the small groups from behind a one-way mirror. There was a significant difference in achievement test scores, the control group doing slightly better than the experimental group. However, results of the Watson-Glaser Critical Thinking Appraisal Test showed a significant improvement in critical thinking among the students in the class who had participated in the small groups. There were also indications from self-reports of students with lower grade-point averages that they profited considerably from the independent study groups—they reported consulting more books in preparing their papers than did the control students and they had a greater increase in their interest in social psychology.

The Bales (1950) interaction analysis employed indicated that interaction among group members in the small group meetings was positive. But Beach suggested that in general learning was inhibited when students were too oriented to their own personal knowledge or viewpoint to interact with another person or did not understand how best to lead another person to a new insight. Learning was enhanced when group members were "other-oriented."

Several studies were concerned with courses emphasizing student participation in contrast to straight lectures (Creiger, 1968; French & Cooper, 1967; Jason, 1969). Some considered the effects of manipulating class size in this respect (Feldhusen, 1963; Hoover, Baumann, & Shafer, 1970); others assessed students' attitudes toward class size (Stones, 1969).

Hoover's study, for example, investigated the influence of class size variables on both the cognitive and affective learning of college freshmen. For this purpose two groups, together consisting of 320 college freshmen, were compared on a 15-concept semantic differential scale and a teacher-made test. After attending a weekly lecture, half the students were divided into 8 permanent discussion sections of 20 students each which met twice each week. The small group discussions emphasized critical examination of feelings and their impact on evaluation of personal, social and professional problems. The remaining 160 students were divided into 3 conventional classes which comprised the control group. Analysis of covariance failed to reveal any significant difference between the groups. Apparently large group lectures combined with small group discussions were just as effective as conventional classes of 50 or 60 students. The teacher variable was not controlled, however, and the instructional procedures varied as each discussion leader pursued the course objectives in a slightly different manner.

Additional attempts to find differences in self-concept and personality adjustment variables, attitudes toward a subject, and class involvement or participation met with no more success. Typical of these efforts was a study by Grozier (1969) in which two large lecture groups, one with and the other without laboratory experience in their general education science course, were compared to determine the effects of laboratory experiences on attitudes toward science. Although attitudes did not appear to differ in relation to the treatment, the author noted that the laboratory experience did help in the interpretation of scientific data. Findings might also differ depending upon the type of laboratory experience involved.

Green (1969) did obtain positive results along these lines, within the limits of his study. He compared T-group sensitivity training, group discussions of filmed classroom experiences, and in-school observation experiences of students in human development and education classes. The comparison group sizes were 21, 19 and 24. The variables of concern—human understanding and self-understanding—were measured with the Personality Orientation Inventory, the Tennessee Self-Concept Scale, an interpersonal orientation inventory, and an objective check list. Results indicated that the students in the T-groups saw their experience as promoting greater changes in regard to the variables of concern. Interpretation is difficult, though, since Green did not examine control group differences and other possible contributing variables.

Team teaching. Other specific instructional approaches were investigated with particular attention paid to team teaching. The hypotheses common to most of the studies were that students participating in team-taught classes would score higher on examinations than students in traditionally taught classes and that student attitudes toward the team-teaching method would be positive.

Yuker (1966) compared team-taught and individually taught English sections on grammatical usage and punctuation using scores on the Cooperative English Test as the criterion variable. Two other reports also described experimental-control group comparisons with English composition classes constituting the groups. An oral language laboratory was used for the experimental treatment for one of the studies (Kivits, 1969); an increased number of assigned themes served as the condition for the other (Christiansen, 1965). Both of the latter studies used theme scores for statistical comparisons. However, none of the three studies attained significant results.

Fraenkel (1967) found no significant differences between two groups on questions requiring factual recall but found significant differences favoring the team-taught group on questions requiring thought and reflection. The author concluded that teaching teams may be more effective than conventional classroom arrangements in producing certain types of learning. Significant differences between an experimental group taught by a team and a control group were also found by Cornett and Butler (1967) and Fugate (1966). Although no formal evaluations have yet been made, preliminary reports indicate that team teaching was successful in freshman English classes at Central Missouri State College, where students felt they had a greater understanding of each assignment (Burns & Jones, 1970), and at Federal City College in Washington, D.C. (Gunstone & Hatton, 1969).

Independent study and tutorials. Independent study is a catchall term for tutorials, interactional machines, and procedures that simply allow the student to select the type of project that he wishes to pursue and the means he prefers to use. These practices are widespread. Felder (1964) reported that of 520 four-year, degree-granting institutions with enrollments exceeding 2,000, 68 percent offered some form of independent study. In the most prevalent types of independent study, the students chose their areas of study with the consent of their advisors. These could be laboratory, library or field work along with original presentations. Testing was usually at the students' requests, and evaluations of student performance were based on written papers, comprehensive written or oral examinations, and conferences with the instructor.

Investigation of the effects of independent study has proceeded along several lines. Studies of tutorials have produced significant results with undergraduate students in their first year of college, in core college courses, and in freshman engineering. Parsons College conducted a supplementary tutorial program which provided bachelor level instructors with 30 minutes of assistance once a week (Etters, 1967). This assistance was available for 345 students enrolled in core classes and large lecture classes with discussion sections. Expectations were confirmed statistically that tutoring would help the low achiever. Statistical tests also supported the fact that grade-point average is related inversely to course load for low achievers.

Similarly, H. Taylor (1969) concluded that tutored students made substantially more progress over three quarters than nontutored students. Taylor's study included two groups of 43 students in freshman engineering. The students were on probation, except for a few with grade-point averages of 2.00 (on a 4.00 point system), and were matched across groups on the basis of high-school rank. A *t* test comparing the means of the cumulative grade-point averages for three quarters indicated a significantly higher mean grade-point average for the tutored group.

In a second study of tutored students compared with a control group of nontutored students, R. G. Taylor, Cartwright, and Hanson (1970) attempted to determine the effect tutoring would have on specific subjects—such as English, mathematics and physics—as well as on cumulative grade-point averages. Taylor also examined the long-range effects of tutoring on persistence and attrition. The most observable effects of tutoring were seen in physics, where four comparisons of tutored and nontutored groups favored the tutored group. In English

and mathematics the tutored groups obtained adjusted mean grade-point averages that were significantly higher. Three other tutored versus nontutored comparisons approached significance in favor of the tutored group, and the decreasing attrition rate of tutored students when compared with comparable nontutored students of similar ability favored the tutored program. Future research might also examine the extent to which findings of this sort are the result of increased attention and support given students versus tutoring as such.

A dissertation study by Shafer (1969) also supported the use of tutoring for low-ability freshmen. The subjects were 351 women who lived in residence halls at Madison College and scored within the lowest third on the Scholastic Aptitude Test. Tutoring was accompanied with counseling, and the third of the subjects who received both tutoring and counseling were more successful academically during their first year at college than the others. Again, these findings raise questions regarding the relative effect of increased attention and support (in this case through counseling) as opposed to teaching in the form of tutoring.

Several researchers investigated the relative merit of independent programs. The results of several experimental studies showed little difference between the experimental (independent study) students and the control groups without independent study in their grades on examinations or in retention of knowledge two years later (Baskin, 1961; Hamilton, 1967). Independent study was nevertheless viewed favorably by most authors, many of whom, however, did not evaluate the effects of independent study on the students' achievements or attitudes (see Alexander & Myers, 1970; Alpern, 1966; Epperson, 1963; Faw, 1969; Leuba, 1964; Young, 1969).

This bias in favor of independent study is notable in itself because study findings vary according to the criteria used. Faw, for example, showed that the students taking independent studies as a group achieved both more products (papers, reports, etc.) and a greater variety of products compared with students who did not participate in independent studies. The kinds of products in the experimental group were more original and less stereotyped than those in the control group. Criteria of this kind, of course, can be even more important than grades earned and information memorized.

Upon considering a variety of criteria, Beach (1970) concluded that beyond the content learning achieved, there are other desirable outcomes of the self-directed and small-group experience such as critical thinking, grasping of applications and implications of the material, increased interest in the subject field, the amount of study and reading done for the course and general satisfaction with the course experience.

Cognitive approaches to instruction. Attempts to show the superiority of particular instructional approaches on cognitive achievement resulted in a standoff. An investigation of the inquiry or discovery method in a laboratory was explored for beginning college chemistry students (Richardson & Renner, 1970). The inquiry-discovery materials were commercially prepared and used with half of a group of 202 students who had the same instructor. According to pre- and posttest scores on the American College Test's composite and natural science tests and on the final laboratory examinations, the inquiry-discovery group was statistically superior.

Knowledge of concepts and application of concepts to new situations were the dependent variables for comparing two instructional methods in mathematical analysis (Levine, 1968). Two classes of mathematics majors were used, one for a theory-to-application sequencing of materials. Results indicated that student ability to handle and generalize concepts was higher for those who had the experience-to-theory approach.

Another study that demonstrated increased cognitive achievement investigated the use of case histories for a general education course in science (Peterson, 1969). The students in the experimental group were presented case histories of scientific research on the topic of atomic-molecular concepts. For the same topic, control students were presented conventional textbooks and materials. The students were divided according to high, medium and low intelligence levels; also, each was pre- and posttested on a test of scientific facts, scientific methods and scientific attitudes. A two-way analysis of covariance produced findings that favored case histories for increasing scores in the areas of scientific methodology and attitudes.

Nonmathematics and nonscience majors did not score higher on standardized tests when a guided discovery method of teaching, including class discussions, was substituted for the exposition method (Reimer, 1969). A total of 104 students was divided into ability groups that provided the second dimension for a two-way analysis of variance design. None of the ratios was significant.

Curricular studies. Studies in the area of curriculum are equally disappointing. Most studies are naturalistic studies which merely note trends and describe what is being done throughout the country but ignore the relationship of the trend to the goals of the college or the relative effectiveness of the courses. In other words, disappointingly few attempts at evaluating the effectiveness of the curriculum have been undertaken.

For example, Lindvall and Cox (1969) describe the Bucknell system of individualized interdisciplinary instruction in five departments—biology, psychology, philosophy, religion and physics. Mastery of the subject as evidenced by test performance was the criterion, but overall evaluation of the program was not reported. Interdisciplinary courses at Beloit, Amherst, University of California at Irvine, St. Mary's College at Notre Dame, Raymond College, Mills College and Nasson College are described by Baskin, Watson, Dixon, and Manion

(1967). The interdisciplinary programs are designed to widen students' perspectives while emphasizing certain underlying themes. The goals are laudable but, again, the programs have not been evaluated.

A relatively few studies have attempted to measure the actual impact of a particular curriculum. Fahey and Ball (1960) evaluated the general education program at the University of Pennsylvania and found that experimental students enrolled in core courses in English, humanities, social sciences and natural sciences did as well as the control students and more of them were graduated. Brinker (1960) studied courses taken by liberal arts students in four colleges in the Southwest with the assumption that a graduate in arts and sciences should have a balanced familiarity with humanities, social science and natural science. Brinker reported that humanities and social science majors did not receive an adequate introduction to disciplines outside their area of speciality. However, neither study provided sufficient substance to evaluate fully its conclusions. The fact is that no substantial relationship between institutional research and curriculum planning or practice can be found. In his review of the literature, Boyer (1967) concluded, "As a result of this neglect, the questions of what should be taught, and how and when, are still more a matter of mythology than of rational judgment" (p. 14).

Experimental colleges. The lack of evaluative studies is noticeable even in the most ambitious area of innovative programs—the cluster colleges and the experimental colleges. Cluster colleges are small, semi-independent units which have been created in an effort to combat the impersonality of the multiversity. Although the promise inherent in the idea of cluster colleges is apparent, implementation of the idea has presented many problems, from petty departmental jealousies to fundamental questions relating to the philosophy of education. These problems, moreover, often result in the very characteristics for which the multiversity has been criticized (Kells & Stewart, 1967; Martin, 1968).

The positive feature of the cluster colleges is that they provide some of the advantages of a large college while retaining the advantages traditionally accepted as resulting from the interaction of relatively small groups of students and faculty members. This advantage has yet to be demonstrated, however. But the need for this demonstration was underscored at the Conference on the Cluster College held in 1967, which focused attention on the need to assess systematically the impact on students of the different types of cluster colleges. A participant at the Conference, Paul Dressel (1967), commented that although cluster colleges, such as those at Claremont or at the Atlantic University Center, have better facilities and libraries and a wider choice of instructors than at the more typical institutions, yet these institutions do not seem to differ in the quality or nature of the curriculum nor in the kind of instruction provided. He suggests that the difference is more in the size of the hive than in the quality of the honey.

Astin (1967) made a similar comment and also suggested longitudinal evaluative studies that could systematically assess the impact of cluster colleges on different types of students.

Clearly, experimental studies designed to assess the cluster colleges are needed. Moreover, research will not be able to provide any definitive answers to the problems confronting the cluster colleges unless the administrators of the institutions are willing to participate in longitudinal studies. According to Astin (1967), "Such studies would seem to require two minimal ingredients: a taxonomy of practices, so that the 'independent variables' will be adequately described and measured; and longitudinal studies of student change over time in the various cluster arrangements" (p. 397).

Although most experimental college programs remain unevaluated as far as the literature is concerned, a few colleges have attempted to validate systematically their programs, or at least portions of their programs. One such study was that undertaken by Schoen (1966) to evaluate certain aspects of an experimental New College at Hofstra University. The population consisted of the third class of New College students entering in September 1962. An individually matched control group was chosen from the entering freshman class in the regular or main college on the basis of sex, major area of academic interest, and secondary-school achievement data.

The College and University Environment Scales were administered to students in each group at the conclusion of the first year of attendance to determine whether students in the experimental college perceived the social and intellectual climate of the New College in a significantly different way from the perception the other students had of the regular program. The five scales measured interpersonal status and practical benefit; friendliness, group welfare and loyalty; reflectiveness and aesthetic appreciation; propriety and consideration; and scholarship and academic attainment. A group of 35 key faculty and administrative members were also given the instrument and asked to identify the desired campus climate.

The results indicated that New College students did not perceive the social and intellectual climate of the experimental college in a significantly different manner from the way in which the main college students perceived their climate, despite the relative isolation of the New College, the close student-faculty relationships, and a hoped-for orientation more closely geared to the intellectual objectives of the college. Both the experimental (New College) and control group (main college) students perceived their respective campus climates in significantly different ways from the atmosphere and climate desired by the faculty.

Another evaluative study was that undertaken at the experimental college

CREATION (Cultural and Recreational Education Achieved Through Investigations Ordinarily Neglected) at Pennsylvania State University. At enrollment time the age, term and academic average of each student was recorded. Two approaches to instruction were adopted in CREATION; three classes were student-oriented, that is, the courses were structured to discover where the students were in their thinking and development and to move with them from that point. Three other courses were more academic or knowledge-oriented. Attitude inventories administered to the students prior to the instruction revealed that the students were planning to spend as much time "as the course was worth" and that they would not waste time or attend class except when they were so inclined. Their attitudes indicated that they were serious about their education even in the absence of exams and credits, and some students indicated that the lack of pressure was the motivating factor for their enrollment in CREATION.

Results of the evaluation study indicated that the student-oriented courses had significantly better attendance than the knowledge-oriented courses throughout their duration. The knowledge-oriented courses showed the most rapid and drastic decline in attendance. There was no correlation between the characteristics of students in courses (age, term, academic accomplishment) and the failure or success of these courses as judged by attendance drops. Furthermore, the students involved in the program were average in most respects, contradicting the popular notion that the intellectually superior student is the one often attracted to and most in need of experimental education. The authors concluded that the success or failure of the experimental course depended more on the approach of the individual instructor than the nature of the content of the course.

An example of research designed to test strategies for the improvement of the college climate has been undertaken at the

University of Michigan, where a pilot program served as a test for opening an experimental residential college for 1,200 students (D. R. Brown, 1967). Six hundred entering freshmen of both sexes in the College of Literature, Science and Arts volunteered and were assigned to special houses within the larger dorms known as Pilot Houses. They enrolled in regular introductory courses reserved for members of the Pilot Houses only and chose their own curriculum within the structure of the college rules. Each student's development was constantly evaluated from a variety of viewpoints, with particular emphasis on evaluating the implications of the programs with respect to student stress and unrest. The study compared the pilot students with nonpilot students in the Literature, Science and Arts College and indicated that the pilot students tended to self-select themselves into the program on the basis of a greater need for contact with faculty. These students expressed greater satisfaction with the nature of residential life at the university and the quality of the residential staff.

On the basis of this pilot study and the committee's evaluation of the courses given in the pilot program, special courses were designed for the residential college. The main thrust of the residential college program was to align the college closer with students' expectations of it, the assumption being that a large part of student stress and unrest comes from the discrepancy between students' expectations of and preparations for college and the reality of the institution. In the experimental program intimate faculty and peer contact was stressed in order to satisfy the students' hope for deep interpersonal and intrapersonal communication and need for true intellectual stimulation. The program was unique in that a concerted effort was made to apply the knowledge of student development and evaluation techniques directly to the continuing evaluation of the institution. Evaluation of the program indicated that the program as designed had a great impact on the students

in terms of reducing student stress and loneliness while increasing the students' sense of dignity and competence as measured by the Student Activities Index and the College Characteristics Index.

The entire line of comparative methods studies was criticized by Dubin and Taveggia (1968). Reanalyzing the data from 96 investigations carried out over the previous 40 years, they found that the studies canceled one another out. That is, for each study that identified a learning advantage in lecture over discussion, another found the reverse. They concluded that the time had come for a reconceptualization of the entire problem.

Further investigation is necessary—not only to determine the many different kinds of learning styles, instructional methods and subject-matter variables but also to determine which differences between subject matters are responsible for the reversal of relationships between learner characteristics and instructional methods found in the research. This information pertains, as well, to faculty recruitment, training and evaluation.

TEACHING RECRUITMENT, TRAINING AND RESOURCES
by
Arthur M. Cohen

Recruitment of Faculty

The story of faculty recruitment in the 1960s is a study in the inexact science of demography. Early in the decade dire predictions of severe faculty shortages by the year 1970 were heard (e.g., Brown & Tontz, 1966; Rogers, 1965a, 1965b). These predictions stemmed from the disparities among the number of doctorates being granted, the number of degree holders who were available for college teaching, and projected student enrollments.

Using NEA figures, Rogers (1965a, 1965b) foresaw 141,300 doctorates being conferred in the decade. It was anticipated that seven million students would be enrolled in American colleges and universities in 1970. Thus, assuming a constant student-faculty ratio of approximately 14 to 1, 500,000 total faculty members would be needed. Ph.D. production during the 1960s, although expanding rapidly, would not keep up with enrollment increases. And, because fewer than half of those who received the Ph.D. between 1961 and 1963 had remained in college teaching, the gap between supply and demand would actually widen. Accordingly, Rogers concluded that 335,000 college positions would have to be filled with nondegree-holders. Predictions of faculty shortages in particular subject fields were even more dire. The instructional staff for engineering, mathematics and physics was expected to be 89 percent higher in 1970 than in 1960—this as compared with a 65 percent increase in fields other than science (Projections of College Faculty, 1963).

Many recommendations for coping with the anticipated college teacher shortage were made. Austin (1966) suggested that colleges and universities identify prospective instructors early in their undergraduate work, open up more teaching assistant positions, and provide information about college teaching as a career. Singletary (1967) insisted that if liberal arts colleges were to maintain favorable teacher-student ratios, they would have to set up a variety of procedures to keep their qualified instructors and to recruit additional staff members. Other recommendations included employing part-time staff, raising salaries so that Ph.D. awardees would be enticed to remain in academia, expanding degree-granting programs, and diverting students to the two-year institutions where work loads and student-faculty ratios were higher.

It is somewhat inappropriate to talk of faculty "shortages" per se because problems in faculty recruitment vary from one type of institution to another. The supply of qualified instructors follows trends in institutional desirability based on geographical location, salary and fringe benefits offered, and institutional prestige. Some subject-field areas may be in oversupply, while others are short. And the fact that most institutions tend to employ someone—regardless of qualifications—to fill every budgeted position makes it difficult to assess the magnitude of the faculty recruitment problem.

Because they were less prestigious and offered lower salaries than the major universities, the two-year colleges and the state colleges particularly felt the press of finding qualified instructors during the 1960s. Many recruiting "tips" were advanced, with college leaders being encouraged to spread their recruitment nets nationwide, to employ more women, members of minority groups, and part-time instructors, to establish liaisons with graduate-training institutions, and generally to enhance orientation and interview procedures so that instructors would be encouraged to stay at the institutions. A statewide group that would publicize junior college teaching and coordinate and facilitate recruitment of instructors was recommended for Michigan (Vaccaro, 1964). Community colleges in New York were urged to articulate precisely their hiring policies, to develop strong links with university placement offices, and to share data on applicants as a way of attracting better-qualified instructors (Kelly, 1968). And the state colleges were admonished to seek highly qualified master's degree holders rather than less well-suited instructors who had obtained Ph.D.s (Dunham, 1969).

By 1970, perhaps partially because of these factors, the anticipated shortage of college instructors had failed to materialize. The reasons that supply met demand varied. For example, the number of students receiving doctoral degrees rose more than had been anticipated. The actual figures exceeded the projections by more than 25 percent (Hooper & Chandler, 1969). A second reason was that the percentage of graduate degree-holders seeking college positions increased as the opportunities for alternative employment decreased toward the end of the decade. Cutbacks in research-related activities in defense industries and health laboratories had reduced the nonteaching market, and people with master's degrees were in plentiful supply in many geographic areas.

The fact that two-year community colleges and state colleges took the brunt of the expansion in college enrollments is a third reason that the expected shortage failed to develop. The community colleges, expanding from 640,000 students in 1959 to more than 2.2 million in 1969, were more inclined to employ—and be perfectly satisfied with —people with masters degrees. In fact, the research-oriented Ph.D. was seen as being particularly undesirable for junior-college teaching (Gleazer, 1967). Only 6 percent of beginning community-college faculty members held Ph.D. degrees in 1969, a figure that had remained constant for more than a decade. Thirty-seven percent of state-college faculty members held doctorates (compared to 42 percent in all higher education). Hence, as both these types of institutions expanded in enrollment, their acceptance of less than doctoral level people and their less favorable student-faculty ratios helped to mitigate the expected shortages.

Teacher Preparation

Although the anticipated crisis in "qualified" instructors for colleges did not materialize, the threat of a shortage, coupled with such issues as student cries for teachers who would attend to their needs and the press for instructors representative of minority groups, led to the reexamination of teacher-preparation sequences. Fellowship programs, such as those supported by the Danforth and Ford Foundations, were useful in attracting people to undergraduate teaching, but the problem was seen in a broader context than the recruitment and selection of instructors. The various types of pre-service experiences enjoyed by college teachers came under question.

Heiss (1968) surveyed 450 graduate institutions that listed courses or programs of instruction designed to assist beginners in college teaching. Eighty percent of the programs were directed toward the student's attainment of a doctorate degree, but few of the institutions reported specialized sequences for instructors of particular subject matters. Most relied primarily on the award of teaching assistantships with minimal or no supervision provided to the neophyte instructor.

A study of 279 state colleges and regional universities done for the Carnegie Commission on Higher Education (Dunham, 1969) reviewed faculty backgrounds along with other aspects of the institutions. The preparation sequences leading to teaching in the state colleges were found to be inappropriate in the opinion of some educators because research-oriented Ph.D.s from graduate schools attempt to transform their employing institutions into what they have just left as students. Dunham proposed radical revisions in faculty recruitment and training—particularly the employment of people with Doctor of Arts degrees.

The teaching assistantship as the vehicle for phasing students into college teaching at any level continued to dominate faculty training. Hagiwara (1970) surveyed language departments in 92 universities and found most institutions awarding fellowships or assistantships to students who had good academic records and a command of the target language. The teaching assistants were typically put in charge of first- and second-year language courses with group supervision provided by the senior faculty members. But this pattern of the teaching assistantship as the accepted apprenticeship in undergraduate instruction was challenged by students who claimed that an unsupervised graduate assistant, intent upon his own studies, was a less-than-ideal instructor. Although many faculty members shared these opinions, most saw no reason to change the pattern. As an example, a survey of 1600 faculty members found nearly half of them *opposed* to a doctorate in college teaching (Heiss, 1968). The assistantship was not universally applauded, but it was accepted as better than anything that might replace it.

Where the teaching assistant was supervised at all, the nature of the association between him and other members of the department was usually rather loosely structured. A lower-ranking department member with no additional compensation was assigned to maintain contact with the assistant. He "evaluated" the trainee by visiting his classes and checking his distribution of grades. In courses with multiple classes and more than one assistant, each assistant contributed items to a pool from which the supervising instructor drew the final examination (Hagiwara, 1970). There were many variations on this pattern, but the general theme remained as it had for generations.

In an attempt to break the pattern, the Danforth Foundation (1970), beginning in 1964, supported efforts to strengthen the teaching assistantship by making funds available to a limited number of colleges and universities. The proposals were designed to alleviate the practice of awarding teaching assistantships as consolation prizes where sequenced teaching experiences beginning with limited responsibility and progressing to more substantive roles were not established. The teaching-intention programs developed under auspices of the Foundation helped at least the few universities that were funded to develop more carefully articulated sequences for phasing new instructors into college teaching. However, there were also findings that "many teaching interns reject the prospect of careers which replicate those of the senior professors with whom they are associated" (Danforth, 1970, p. 7). This type of strained relationship was impossible to overcome within the context of the Danforth grants.

The preparation of junior-college instructors received a considerable amount of attention as those institutions showed tremendous growth in enrollments and consequently in numbers of faculty. Most surveys found that new junior-college instructors

had not participated in specialized training programs but had served as teaching assistants or had been prepared in programs designed to train teachers for secondary schools. The paucity and/or inadequacy of special programs led to demands for the junior colleges to build highly structured faculty-orientation programs and for the universities to develop new forms for junior-college teacher preparation (A. M. Cohen & Brawer, 1968; Gleazer, 1968; Kelly & Connolly, 1970).

Specialized teacher-preparation programs were sought for a variety of reasons—particularly at the junior-college level, where administrators called for programs that would aid new instructors in gaining a broader picture of curriculum and the needs of students than that usually afforded in a graduate school, subject-matter–centered sequence (American Association of Junior Colleges, 1969). The administrators wanted their instructors to have more training in the areas of general education, curriculum and student learning, and they sought changed sequences that would improve training in the occupational fields. Instructors who would be responsive to current student concerns and who could teach "remedial courses" were also demanded, as were instructors who could serve well in courses where minority students predominated. The administrators also felt the need for continuing in-service training but recognized the difficulty in arranging these types of programs without the intervention of sympathetic graduate schools. Some administrator-dominated groups called for separate training institutions in which junior-college instructors might be prepared outside the "contaminating influence" of the research-dominated universities (E. Cohen, 1970; Singer, 1968).

Specialized programs for preparing teachers in particular subject areas received a certain amount of attention, with many academic disciplinary associations conducting their own surveys in an attempt to determine the types of preparation experienced by instructors in their own subject fields. The preparation of junior-college English instructors was reviewed in a study done under the auspices of the Modern Language Association (A. L. Davis, 1968). The chairmen of 53 departments of English in graduate institutions in which specialized programs for junior-college instructors were found responded to the survey instrument. Their programs tended to consist of master's degrees in English sequences combined with education courses. Most programs were the joint responsibility of the English and education departments; however, of the 53 departments, only 26 had training programs particularly for junior-college instructors, and of these, only eight allowed supervised teaching in the junior college. An additional two schools had "paid internship" programs. Nevertheless, although the numbers of specialized programs were small, the trend was clearly in the direction of more such programs with field experience in the junior college becoming a requisite.

Some academic associations polled junior-college instructors to assess their recommendations for specialized training programs. The Advisory Council on College Chemistry collected responses from 507 administrators of chemistry departments and 649 individual faculty members (Mooney & Brasted, 1969). These chemistry instructors and department administrators recommended special master's degree programs for junior-college chemistry instructors, the use of industrial personnel as part-time instructors, reduced teaching loads, more specialized training and continued opportunity for professional upgrading.

Science education in the junior colleges was reviewed by a congresssional subcommittee because the problems of preparing college students in the sciences were seen as being most acute (Haworth, 1967). This comprehensive study provided a useful status report but reached few conclusions regarding the quality of science education in the two-year colleges. Staff quality was found to be improving, but the question of whether scarce faculty resources were being dissipated remained open.

Junior-college administrators sought especially trained instructors; university undergraduate students demanded teachers responsive to their needs; faculty associations sought programs that would aid their members in coping with the varied demands of teaching. These calls coalesced in renewed and growing support for programs leading to doctoral-level degrees other than the Ph.D. First promulgated at the turn of the century, the specialized degree for college teaching had never attained widespread support, but by the end of the 1960s it received increased attention.

Guidelines for special degrees in college teaching follow a typical pattern: the equivalent of a master's degree in a subject area; three or four courses in professional education; some practice teaching under supervision; and a special curriculum project to be written up, tested and evaluated by the candidate. These degrees carry such titles as "Candidate in College Teaching" or "Doctor of Arts in College Teaching," and graduates of these programs are seen as being qualified to teach in two-year colleges and in the lower divisions of four-year colleges and universities. By the end of the decade nearly 100 graduate-training institutions either had such programs established or were actively establishing them (National Faculty Association, 1968; University of Miami, 1969).

Whether or not the Doctor of Arts would prove to be an answer to questions of adequate undergraduate teaching remains to be seen. Nevertheless, Dunham (1969) advised the state colleges to devise programs leading to the Doctor of Arts and to employ graduates of such programs in preference to Ph.D.s. And the degree was seen as answering the needs of junior-college instructors as well (Wortham, 1967).

Considering the anticipation some educational leaders have for these programs, there is a critical need to evaluate their effectiveness compared with the teaching effectiveness of college faculty who have gone through traditional doctoral programs. Needless to say, research of this kind must take into account that a great deal, if not the greater part, of the teaching-learning function is realized outside of the classroom. There is also the unresolved matter of the extent to which faculty research contributes to teaching.

The Teaching Situation

Several surveys undertaken by professional associations and other groups assessed the working situation of professors in colleges and universities. These surveys usually included separate data on instructors in two-year and four-year colleges, with some being further subdivided into categories based on professors' spending the major portion of their time on either undergraduate or graduate students.

Under the auspices of the Modern Language Association, the National Council of Teachers of English, and the American Association of Junior Colleges, Shugrue (1970) surveyed teachers of English in junior colleges. More than 4,000 instructors and department chairmen responded to the inquiry regarding class size and teaching load, course content, and personal data on the instructors themselves. In the junior colleges 57 percent of the English instructors averaged 13 to 15 class-hours per week with half the time spent on freshman composition and the remainder on courses in literature and remedial reading and composition. The English faculty was young—two-thirds of the staff members had not yet reached age 40—and included a heavy representation of women (44 percent). This latter figure, incidentally, was twice the percentage of women found in four-year college English departments. In common with the instructors in other departments of junior colleges, a sizable percent had previous teaching experience in the secondary schools. The most serious problems faced by the instructors related to the large classes and heavy work-loads, with little released time available for professional upgrading.

A different set of problems was identified by psychology instructors in junior colleges (Daniel, 1970). The psychology instructors were usually among only three instructors in a department, and many of them taught other subjects in addition to introductory psychology and personality courses. The numbers of students and teaching loads were not nearly as heavy as for the English instructors. However, in common with the English faculty, the lack of continuing professional currency was indicated. The psychology instructors indicated they felt isolated from the larger professional community by virtue of their teaching psychology in an institution that demanded no research or broader professional involvements.

The problem of professional isolation was also reported by Garrison (1967), who talked with nearly 1,000 instructors in junior colleges throughout the country. He found individual faculties feeling separated from one another both as groups and as individuals within their disciplinary fields. The problems associated with large classes and long hours of student contact were also cited as constraints on junior-college instructors' keeping up with the latest developments in their teaching fields. Nevertheless, the instructors did seem to be aware of the recent developments in the use of reproducible media in teaching and were willing to "innovate" by trying all sorts of techniques in the hope that some would prove more effective than others. In general, the two-year college teacher was seen as more involved with instruction as a discipline than was his counterpart at the university (A. M. Cohen, 1969); however, there was some question about the depth of his commitment (Cohen, 1970).

Resources

In addition to some special doctoral programs directed toward teaching rather than research, the "center for teaching" type of organization developed. Generally established on campuses with funds obtained intramurally, these groups attempted to diffuse innovation within the university teaching staffs. The activities of these centers include describing various teaching techniques employed elsewhere, publicizing local professors' efforts to create new types of courses, offering test-scoring services, providing the means for evaluating teaching, initiating intramural dialogues on teaching and learning, and, in a few cases, offering programs designed to improve teaching.

Information bulletins and developments in teaching were published by such enterprises as the Center for Learning and Development at McGill University, the Center for Research and Teaching at the University of Michigan, and similar groups at other institutions. Beginning in 1965 the Educational Resources Information Center, operating through a network of federally supported clearinghouses, began to publish materials designed to aid practitioners in all aspects of the field of education. However, the academic mill grinds slowly, and evience has yet to be brought to bear that these efforts have materially changed instructional practices other than in a few isolated instances.

EVALUATION OF TEACHING[2]
by
Arthur M. Cohen, James W. Trent and Clare Rose

The criteria for merit advancement and the proper process for advancement has been a perennial issue in the teaching profession. But it became a paramount issue in higher education in the late 1960s following the wave of student protest. Increasingly, research-oriented universities and colleges have been engaged in the perplexing search

[2] Portions of this section were adapted from *Measuring Faculty Performance* by Arthur M. Cohen and Florence B. Brawer (1969).

for criteria and techniques for the evaluation of teaching effectiveness. The search for the "good teacher" encompasses a threefold problem: first, defining appropriate criteria for judging teacher effectiveness; second, developing and administering the necessary assessment devices; and third, getting faculties to incorporate the procedures and act on the results.

Correlates of Teaching Competence

Some progress seems to have been made in the last decade in providing an operational definition of teacher competence as reflected by pupil growth, but researchers have avoided using this criterion because of the methodological difficulties inherent in measuring pupil gain. A bibliography of research studies through 1967 revealed that out of 1,000 studies there were only 20 in which the criterion of teacher effectiveness was student growth (Burkhart, 1969). Nine hundred and eighty studies rated teachers in accordance with the impressions or judgments made by supervisors, independent observers and, more commonly in secondary education, by principals. More frequently, researchers have correlated particular teachers' behavioral characteristics with pupil gain measured on achievement tests or by self-reports. They analyzed teacher behavior in the classroom in order to find the "good teacher."

Several criticisms of this method of teacher evaluation have been made. G. Sorenson and Gross (1967) point out that, "to attempt to define teaching success in terms of some single fixed teacher-ideal is both untenable and inappropriate.... teachers are bound to be regarded differently by persons with varying concepts of the teacher's role" (pp. 1–2). An earlier study by A. G. Sorenson, Husek and Yu (1963) attempted to develop an instrument that would assess teacher-role expectations in order to deal with the problem of the fixed ideal. A preliminary form administered to 284 students was designed to measure six role dimensions: information giver, disciplinarian, advisor, counselor, motivator and referrer.

A factor analysis confirmed these six factors and provided a basis for a revised form, the Teacher Practices Questionnaire, which was administered to a second sample. The questionnaire consists of 30 problem situations typical of those encountered by teachers in their daily routine. For each problem, four alternative solutions were presented representing different role dimensions. The subjects were instructed to rate each of the alternative courses of action on a five-point scale as to the degree of appropriateness. Such a procedure permits the prediction of teacher effectiveness, not in terms of a set of absolute characteristics but in terms of the traits regarded as significant by judges of differing educational philosophies, differing personal preferences and in differing situations.

Ryans (1960) noted that "two very important reasons why effective and ineffective teachers cannot be described with any assurance are the wide variation in the value concepts underlying the descriptions of desirable teaching objectives and the differences in teacher role at different educational levels, in different subjects, and with different pupils" (p. 371). Consistent with this conclusion are the findings reported by D. Solomon, Rosenberg, and Bezdek (1964), who reported that teachers in the social sciences differ from their counterparts in other areas with respect to certain behavioral dimensions such as permissiveness, clarity and control.

Popham (1967), commenting on the classroom observation approach to teacher assessment, concludes that "the quality of learning which transpires in a given instructional situation is a function of *particular* instructional procedures employed by a *particular* instructor for *particular* students with *particular* goals in mind" (p. 2).

Other disadvantages of using rating systems are summarized by Mouly (1969). They include the halo effect, the error of central tendency, generosity or leniency error, and the lack of a common referent for scoring calibrations such as "excellent" or "seldom." Furthermore, instead of evaluating teaching by the *results* it produces, evaluation of the characteristics of the *act* of teaching or the personal qualities of the teacher represent subjective ratings of performance or of personality, not measures of effectiveness, and the standards employed are often obscured within the minds of the individual raters.

These difficulties form the basis of much of the criticism of student rating of instruction, currently the predominant means of evaluating teaching effectiveness in higher education. According to A. M. Cohen and Brawer (1969), "there have been few studies to date ascertaining the empirical relationship between student ratings of 'teacher effectiveness' in the classroom and subsequent student attainment on objective educational criteria" (p. 18). Nevertheless, researchers continue attempting to find clusters of faculty characteristics and behaviors that either are related to various notions of effectiveness or to good ratings by students. Their efforts have met with mixed success.

Sorey (1968) administered the Purdue Rating Scale for Instructors, the Guilford-Zimmerman Temperament Survey and a staff rating scale to 50 instructors in an attempt to measure the accuracy of their self-concept. In addition, students rated the instructors. A discrepancy score was obtained between the instructor's self-rating and the Temperament Survey. Inferior and superior teachers conceived of themselves very much in the same ways; yet the characteristics commonly valued by teachers were associated with those instructors the students rated as inferior.

Two studies with contradictory results investigated the relationship between instructors' publications output, their success in obtaining government awards, and their teaching effectiveness as assessed by student opinion and student performance.

Bresler (1968) found that faculty members who received grants and who published widely were also rated as better teachers by their students than those who did less of both. Voeks (1962), however, found no relationship between the total number of publications and teacher effectiveness in any academic area as determined by the students' performances on achievement tests, evaluations by colleagues and student opinion. The only comparison that approached statistical significance was that associate and assistant professors who published most included more mediocre than poor teachers whereas nonpublishers had a higher proportion of the poorest teachers than of the mediocre teachers. The ghost of "teaching versus research" apparently was not laid to rest, but clearly research productivity could not be ascribed to poor teaching.

Classroom behaviors were analyzed by D. Solomon, Rosenberg, and Bezdek (1964). Twenty-four teachers and their students served as the sample which provided four categories of data for analysis: tape recordings of lectures, student ratings of teachers, teacher questionnaires regarding objectives and motives, and student performance. A factor analysis of classroom behaviors resulted in eight factors related to students' learning (on pre- to posttests) and to student evaluations. Achievement was viewed as knowledge of facts and comprehension. Learning of facts related significantly to teacher "clarity and expressiveness" whereas gains in comprehension related significantly to such teacher traits as energy and flamboyance. Positive evaluations also related significantly to teacher clarity, expressiveness and warmth.

Isaacson, McKeachie, Milholland, Lin et al. (1964) also factor-analyzed student responses to a questionnaire regarding dimensions of their instructors' behavior and found that student responses generally clustered around six factors: skill, overload, structure, feedback, group interaction and student rapport. These factors appeared consistently in two administrations of the questionnaire in different semesters with different students and instructors as subjects.

An attempt to obtain from students and/or professors a composite picture of the ideal outstanding teacher was the focus of several studies (Ahern, 1969; Hall, 1970; McGrath, 1962; McKeachie, 1969; Rayder, 1968b; Yamamoto & Dizney, 1966). The findings were contradictory. Proportionately more outstanding teachers in Ahern's study were mature, tenured, married males who had published one or more articles compared to the less outstanding instructors. Rayder and McKeachie's findings, however, indicated that the older, more educated, experienced, published instructors were rated lower than the younger and less experienced, often unpublished instructors. The younger faculty were consistently rated friendlier, more understanding, systematic, responsible, stimulating, imaginative and enthusiastic.

Variations of institutional, departmental and student characteristics need to be examined in this context. The contradictory results could also be a direct function of the specific professor description employed but more likely they reflect the findings of J. Katz (1962), Rayder (1968b), and D. Solomon, Rosenberg, and Bezdek (1964) that students' perceptions of teachers are more a function of internal frames of reference or value systems than of concrete teacher characteristics.

There is no universal set of expectations in our society which defines a teacher's role; instead, an unknown number of sets are held by people from different cultural and socioeconomic backgrounds. In order to predict how a particular observer or even sets of observers will judge a given teacher, it is necessary to discover first what the observer's expectations are with respect to the teacher role.

A number of teacher typologies were identified by Brawer (1968), whose extensive study reviewed personality assessment and roles and images of faculty as well as typological schemes. Brawer sought patterns in Gusfield and Riesman's (1968) pioneer settlers, pioneer adventurers and jobholders; Adelson's (1962) shamans, priests and mystic healers; and Friedman's (1965) subject matterists and disciplinarians. Combining elements of these, she evolved her own typology comprised of end-of-the-roaders, ladder climbers, job holders, and defined-purpose routers.

Student's preferences for different types of college professors was the subject of Yamamoto and Dizney's study (1966). Four roles were described (in order of students' preference)—teacher, researcher, socialite and administrator. Researcher was the only type of role to gain in preference from junior to graduate status.

Evidence that student perceptions as well as personalities correlate with teacher ratings is available from a variety of sources (see Carter, 1969; P. L. Crawford & Bradshaw, 1968; Freehill, 1967; Gulo, 1966; Langen, 1966; Rees, 1969; Renner, 1967; Yonge & Sassenrath, 1968). A summary of the results of these studies indicates that: 1) certain student characteristics significantly correlate with student ratings of certain instructors, but these characteristics are not the same for each teacher; and 2) identifiable factors which represent different points of view and perceptions in rating college teachers are socioeconomic, racial, class in school, masculinity, sophistication, social disposition and emotional instability.

Student Ratings of Teacher Effectiveness

Despite the fact that many instructors and researchers deny the reliability and value of student ratings, this method is receiving considerable attention. As previously indicated, student evaluations administered by faculty or student organizations gained attention and support during the 1960s perhaps as a result of the clamorous demand that students have a say in the evaluation of their instruction as well as in the selection of their instructors.

The most common method employed in student ratings is the questionnaire. Most questionnaires used require the student simply to rate his instructor on various attributes relevant to teaching ability; some, however, include open-ended questions or invite suggestions and comments. Several studies have investigated the nature of these instruments.

A number of characteristics have been consistently identified as comprising effective teaching, at least in terms of approach or style. Eble (1970) summarizes three major sets of such characteristics which are highly comparable with one another although obtained from independent research. Hildebrand and Wilson (1970) offer another set of characteristics to be included in students' rating forms obtained from a factor analysis of traits found to distinguish professors at the University of California at Davis, who were nominated as outstanding teachers. Hildebrand and Wilson's (1970) results were comparable to those summarized by Eble. Major factors consistent to the four studies were:

1. Clarity of organization, interpretation and explanation;
2. Encouragement of class discussion and the presentation of diverse points of view;
3. Stimulation of students' interests, motivation and thinking;
4. Manifestation of attentiveness to and interest in students;
5. Manifestation of enthusiasm.

Support for the use of student evaluations is provided by J. Bannister et al. (1961), who noted that student evaluations, when carefully and properly handled, provide the best criterion of the quality of instruction. Research conducted by Rayder (1968b) demonstrates that student ratings of instructors are not substantially related to the student's age, sex, grade-point average or grades previously received from the instructor being rated. Moreover, Rayder contends that students, unlike administrators or colleagues, have the opportunity to view the instructor in his day-to-day teaching activities and therefore should not be ignored as evaluators.

A contradictory finding was obtained in a study by Spaights (1967). Students who responded to a student-rating sheet were classified according to grade-point average as high achieving (GPA of 2.44 or more on a 4.00 system) and low achieving (below 2.44). Only 12 percent of the high achievers felt instructors were impersonal or aloof, whereas over 94 percent of the low achievers felt so.

Personality dimensions in teachers' ratings were added by Issacson, McKeachie and Milholland (1963). A peer group nomination procedure, a descriptive adjective inventory and the Institute for Personality and Ability Testing Sixteen Personality Factors Questionnaire were administered to two groups of teaching fellows in an introductory psychology course at the University of Michigan. These personality scores were related to the teaching fellows' teaching effectiveness ratings made by their students and to the factor scores obtained from factor analyses of the separate items of the student-rating instrument. The teacher variable most consistently correlated with good ratings by students was the peer group evaluation of the teaching fellows' general "cultural attainment." Because this was a peer nomination procedure, however, there is no information as to whether the teachers with superior student evaluations were really more artistically sensitive or intellectually oriented. Perhaps students tend to see teachers they judge to be effective as possessing high cultural attainment.

Although most of the research in this area has focused on gathering student opinions of teaching as a source of data on teaching effectiveness, more recently researchers

have been concerned with determining the validity of the ratings in terms of criteria of student achievement. Previous data on validity in terms of the criterion of student change satisfy neither the proponents nor the opponents of student evaluation of teaching. Studies by Bendig (1953a, 1953b), S. H. Cohen and Berger (1970), Elliott (1949), McKeachie and Solomon (1958) and H. E. Russell (1951), in addition to those described previously, provide the greatest support.

In a comprehensive project by McKeachie, Lin, and Mann (1971), all items that had previously been used for student ratings of instructors and instruction were factor analyzed in a series of studies. Six stable factors that emerged were skill, overload (difficulty), structure, feedback, group interaction and student-teacher rapport (warmth). What these dimensions have to do with effective teaching was then investigated in a series of studies to determine the validity of the students' ratings. Several indices of student learning were used as the criterion for teaching effectiveness. These included the mean score of the students on the Introductory Psychology Criteria Test (Milholland, 1964), the mean score of students on a test of knowledge consisting of items taken from old final examinations, a departmentally administered test of oral expression, a test of grammar, a test of reading French and a test designed to measure students' level of aptitude sophistication in economics. The findings of the five studies indicated that:

1. In four of the five studies, teachers rated high on "skill" tended to be effective with women students.
2. In all five studies, teachers rated high in "structure" tended to be more effective with women than with men; in fact, on the whole, the more structured instructors were generally ineffective for men.
3. The students of teachers who were

high in "rapport" (warmth) performed better on measures of critical thinking versus lower-order knowledge than did the other students.

4. Teachers whom students rated as having an impact on beliefs were effective in changing attitudes.

These results taken together with the earlier studies do not invalidate the use of student ratings as one source of evidence about teacher effectiveness, but indicate they are less convincing than was expected. The conclusion drawn by McKeachie, Lin, and Mann from their study was that the major slippage in the validity studies was due to the differing goals of teachers and students. Students come to class with many different personal objectives for that class. Some of these objectives may coincide with those of the instructor, but the overlap between instructor and student goals or among the goals of differing students is certainly far from perfect. Moreover, the extent to which tests measure achievement of these goals is also limited. Thus, even if each student's rating of the instructor's effectiveness in helping that student achieve his own goals was perfectly valid, low validity coefficients in studies such as this would still be found. Instead of asking which teachers are most effective, we need to ask which teachers are most effective for which objectives and for which students. Only with these additions can student evaluations really provide fully useful evidence of teaching effectiveness.

The use of student rating forms, however, does have some demonstrated merit. In a study conducted at St. Johns River College and reported by Overturf and Price (1966), students rated their instructors on a scale of one to five on five separate characteristics. A comparison of scores achieved by the full-time teaching faculty for the two years 1964–65 and 1965–66 indicated that faculty members who made significant improvement had taken the students' ratings seriously, particularly their written comments. These findings are consistent with the

findings of several other studies that investigated the influence of student feedback on teachers. Most of these studies involved written student feedback. In an investigation using pre- and postquestionnaires of teacher self-perceptions and student descriptions of their ideal teacher, Gage (1963) concluded that if teachers learned how the students wanted them to behave they would become more like the student ideal. Tuckman and Oliver (1968) used student ratings to determine changes in teacher behavior and found that teachers changed their behavior positively according to suggestions received from their students. Other studies which support the notion that certain teacher responses are influenced by written student feedback include Jenkins and Deno (1969), Soar (1966), and Turner (1967); studies indicating the effects of nonwritten student feedback include Rosenfeld (1967) and Sarbin and Allen (1968); student influence on the behavior of counselors is reported by Bandura, Lipsher, and Miller (1960), Gamsky and Farwell (1966), Heller, Myers, and Kline (1963), and P. D. Russell and Snyder (1963).

The dangers of relying solely on student ratings, however, are pointed out by Gage (1961). He cites a study in the College of Education at the University of Illinois where teachers of lower-level courses consistently received less favorable mean ratings than did those of more advanced courses. Teachers in courses with 30 to 39 students received consistently lower ratings than did those in courses with more or fewer students; instructors and assistant professors received lower ratings than did associate professors and full professors; teachers of on-campus courses received significantly lower ratings than did those of off-campus courses, and teachers of elective courses received consistently more favorable ratings than did instructors of required courses.

These differences were not only statistically significant but also substantively different. As a result they raise several questions. Are students in very small and very large classes better taught because such sections are easier to teach or are the students more lenient? Are teachers of higher academic rank better teachers or are they assigned to more generous and lenient students? Do teachers operate more effectively in elective courses or are the students in such courses easier to please, perhaps because they are better motivated?

For all the limitations and inconsistencies revealed by the research on student ratings of teaching effectiveness, there is enough promising and convergent data to suggest possible directions for improving college teaching. A composite professor profile based on student ratings can be compared with the combined profile of his peers and provide valuable feedback to the professor insofar as determining if his teaching was generally adequate, superior or inferior in relation to that of his colleagues, in which respects and in what courses. Certainly, some characteristics of effective university teachers may be isolated and measured quantitatively. Valid ratings, however, require knowledge of which personality traits influence ratings and which personality and value factors characterize the student group. In other words, judgments of these ratings must be interpreted in light of who is doing the judging.

The belief that college teaching can—and should—enhance the instructor's own growth was advanced by A. M. Cohen and Brawer (1972). Using the concept of identity as defined by Erikson (1963), they outlined procedures for self-evaluation as the core of teacher-evaluation processes. In their scheme each instructor would assess himself on the basis of his students' learning, his service to college and community and his advancement in professional knowledge. Inputs would be obtained from colleague, administrator and student ratings. The result would be the mature, professional instructor.

In summation, the consensus of relatively plentiful research indicates that student evaluation, if conducted systematically, provides useful and reliable information about at least three aspects of college teaching:

1) The skill of a teacher in terms of his personal effectiveness;
2) The rapport between the teacher and his students;
3) The organization and management of a particular course.

Interaction of Faculty and Student Characteristics

Research in college teaching varies from comparisons of the overall effects of different teaching methods to investigations of the effectiveness of different methods upon various kinds of students, and the interactions between student characteristics and teacher cues as they affect student achievement. However, most reports of research on group characteristics or teaching effectiveness describe the subjects as students or group members without reference to sex. More recently it has become apparent that if the interactions between social-psychological variables and individual difference variables are to be studied, sex is an important individual difference variable and should be studied. Little data appear to be available on the actual interactions between sex and social-psychological variables. In addition, most groups studied involved college males only.

McKeachie, Lin, Milholland, and Isaacson (1966) reported that interactions between teacher warmth and need for affiliation did not consistently affect the achievement of women students. McKeachie's assumption was that as a group women respond well to interpersonal warmth.

Another study by McKeachie and Lin (1971) revealed that with male teachers, high teacher warmth results in relatively high achievement for women students but not for men. For women instructors, high warmth teachers seem to be more effective with both sexes of students than teachers with low warmth. Low-warmth women with low-achievement standards were the least effective of any of the teachers in the study.

The subjects sampled were the freshmen-sophomore students of experienced teachers of five multisection courses in French, mathematics and general psychology. The measure of teacher warmth in the first three samples was the mean student rating of a teacher by his students on three items: 1) the instructor takes a personal interest in the students, 2) the instructor calls the students by name, and 3) students in the class are friendly. In the second and third sample, one additional item, "the teacher is friendly," was added. Course grades were used as a criterion measure for all courses, and achievement tests were available for the French and psychology students. The consistency of the differences in all five studies was statistically significant. There was no evidence that women students performed better with women instructors.

Faculty-Student Influence

The evidence from a number of the studies cited above strongly suggests that students influence their instructors beyond the feedback of their ratings. There is also some indication that the direction of the influence may be predicted: positive student behaviors (i.e., accepting and encouraging) correlate with positive teacher behaviors and negative student behaviors (i.e., rejecting and criticizing) are associated with negative teacher behaviors. Likewise, positive teacher behaviors are associated more frequently with student growth than are negative teacher behaviors (see Amidon & Flanders, 1967; Flanders & Simon, 1969; Rosenshine, 1971).

Despite recognition of the importance of studying classroom interactions, little attention has been focused on whether or not particular student behaviors can promote specified positive or negative teacher behaviors. That is, just as there may be some

identifiable effective teacher behaviors that contribute to improved student achievement or attitudes, there may be such a thing as "pupil effectiveness" wherein the students are able to help their teachers improve their teaching behavior.

This particular line of inquiry was undertaken by Klein (1971). Twenty-four college teachers served as subjects in 24 experiments while students in the classes assumed the role of experimenters. The teachers ranged from graduate teaching assistants to full professors in six universities. All were guest teachers and not the regularly assigned teachers of the classes in which the experiments took place.

Before each experiment the students in the class were directed to behave normally during the control periods and to follow particular experimental specifications for positive and negative behaviors during the appropriate treatment periods. Some of the positive student behaviors included smiling, looking at the teacher and answering the teacher's questions quickly and correctly. Examples of negative student behaviors were frowning, looking out the window and talking to classmates. During each experiment, the verbal behaviors of the teacher and students were recorded by observers. The tapes were later analyzed using Flanders's Interaction Analysis (Amidon & Flanders, 1967).

The major findings of this study augment and agree with the research discussed previously. Student behavior did influence the verbal and nonverbal behaviors of the teachers and the direction of the influence was predictable. When the students behaved positively the teachers were positive, and when the students behaved negatively the teachers were negative.

The findings of this study may have important implications for educational practices. For example, taking into account student behavior may enable studies of student achievement to become more consistent in the identification of effective teacher behavior. In fact, student behavior may prove to be as important a measure of teacher effectiveness as student achievement and attitudes. Conversely, it may be that a class may become more productive if students are taught how their behavior influences the behavior of their teachers. Thus the students may be encouraged to assume responsibility for their own behavior and purposely elicit more positive teacher behavior. Additional research might profitably test these possibilities.

Objective-based Criteria for Teaching Effectiveness

In the last decade increased attention has been given to student growth as a major criterion for teacher effectiveness (A. M. Cohen & Shawl, 1970; Popham, 1968; Rose, 1971). This, in turn, has led educators to give increased attention to the consequences of instruction. In a summary of seventy-five doctoral studies undertaken at the University of Wisconsin, Barr, Worcester, Abell, Beecher, Jensen, Peronto, Ringness, and Schmid (1961) concluded that pupil growth or achievement is "the primary criterion against which all other criteria should be validated" (p. 13).

Perhaps the problem has been not so much blind adherence to rating forms but the absence of objective and reliable measures of effective teaching based on student gain which would be practical for use in the schools. A. M. Cohen and Brawer (1969) contend that although the stated purpose of evaluation is to improve instruction, the methods seldom relate to instructional practice and even less often to the results of instruction. They suggest that student achievement of learning objectives is the main criterion on which studies of faculty and of instructional efforts should be based. In their view the use of student gain on short-range objectives as a measure of teacher effectiveness is generally acknowledged as being more valid than the use of

such criteria as, for example, the teacher's effort expended or the various perceptions of observers. Of course, both the latter criteria as well as "short-range objectives" are limited compared with lasting, long-range effects of teaching which are seldom considered and less often examined.

A rigorously controlled experiment in an Air Force school examined student gain as a measure of instructor's effect. As described by Morsh, Burgess, and Smith (1955), multiple sections of an aircraft mechanics course were used in which 121 instructors taught to the same objectives and administered the same examination. Results of the investigation indicated that student gain can be reliably measured and that students' ratings of their instructor's verbal facility correlated significantly with student learning.

Several studies have been conducted in which evaluation of student teachers has been based on the degree to which their students attain prespecified instructional objectives. In Moffett's 1967 study, student teachers were assigned at random to one of two treatment groups. Teachers in the experimental group used the course content, results of a pretest, and knowledge of pupils to arrive at appropriate instructional objectives. The student teacher and his supervisor arrived at an agreement on both the behavioral objectives and on acceptable evidence that the objectives had been achieved. It was also agreed that the degree of successful pupil achievement of the objectives would have an effect on the student teacher's grade.

The results indicated that the pupils of teachers in the experimental group not only achieved the goals of instruction, but the teachers themselves expressed more satisfaction with their student-teaching grade and considered the supervision more helpful than the student teachers in the control group.

McNeil's (1966) method, described as "supervision by objectives," is based on the results of several studies and consists of a process by which a supervisor and a teacher agree in advance as to what they will accept as evidence of the teacher's success in changing the students' behavior. This method provides the teacher-training coordinator with a practical means for comparing concurrently the relative effectiveness of several student teachers. There is evidence that student gains are greater when the teacher expects to be evaluated on the basis of those gains.

A new approach to the development of more precise tools for assessing teacher competence uses behavioral objectives in an attempt to deal with the very basic question of what is being evaluated. Performance tests of teaching proficiency are developed and teachers are given sets of explicit instructional objectives and asked to teach specifically to them. Instructional effectiveness is then assessed in terms of the teacher's ability to produce the student behavior changes prescribed by the objectives. Although most of the reported research pertains to elementary and secondary schools, efforts of the kind reported are also being incorporated in higher education, particularly in junior colleges (see, e.g., A. M. Cohen, 1969; Johnson, 1969; Roueche & Pitman, 1972). The unique and long-range effectiveness of this system in higher education has yet to be fully evaluated. However, the need for such evaluation is evident from Popham's research.

Popham (1967) attempted to validate a series of performance-test instruments by hypothesizing that these instruments would discriminate between teachers and nonteachers. In one study he compared the ability of teachers and nonteachers to achieve prespecified social science objectives. Thirteen experienced high-school teachers and thirteen upper-division college students were given a social studies resource unit and directed to achieve as many of the behaviorally stated objectives as possible in a four-hour period of instruction. A test designed to measure achievement of the objec-

tives was administered on the day following instruction.

The test results indicated that the experienced teachers did not perform significantly better than the nonteachers. The probable explanation for the failure of the experienced teachers to out-perform the nonteachers, according to Popham, was the teachers' lack of experience in helping learners achieve behaviorally stated objectives. In other words, teachers, too, must be trained to bring about changes in students. Popham (1967) concludes that "the general performance test strategy for the assessment of teacher competence still seems more than an acceptable method, it seems to be *the* acceptable method" (p. 19). Granting the difficulties of validating such a strategy, demonstration of its being "the acceptable method" is yet forthcoming. No doubt this demonstration will be especially difficult at the higher-education level where, as A. M. Cohen and associates (1971, pp. 112–114) point out, definitions of "good teaching" lack both particularity and consistency.

Performance tests are based on the assumption that if subject knowledge and general teaching ability combine to produce specific changes in students and if the students' content knowledge and ability level can be held constant, then a teacher's general teaching ability can be measured by testing his students for the skills specified by the teacher's instructional objectives (Popham, 1971). Although this approach poses certain serious methodological problems (e.g., finding topics of instruction unfamiliar to the students that can be taught in a relatively short time but not confined to simply low level behaviors), several studies indicate that performance tests may detect at least a minimum performance level of teaching proficiency and should be researched further.

O'Conner and Justiz (1970) applied the procedures developed in a previous study by Justiz to junior-college instructors. Justiz (1968) identified more or less effective teachers on the basis of their ability to produce low-order problem-solving skills in two different subject areas. Student teachers were given packets containing an objective, related subject matter and instructions. Each student teacher randomly selected 18 experimental pupils from his training teacher's class who were given instruction for 30 minutes followed by a criterion test. The control group was pretested with the post-test given to the experimental group. The difference between the mean scores of the experimental and the control students provided evidence of increased learning in each experimental group.

O'Conner and Justiz concluded that teacher effectiveness can be measured reliably by the two performance tests developed by Justiz, and that these measures can be used as an indicator of general teaching ability in different subject fields as well as a teacher's ability to produce achievement of the particular objectives specified by the performance test. Again, long-range effects and applicability of the method have yet to be ascertained.

An attempt to develop even more precise performance-test instruments was undertaken by C. A. Rose (1971). In this study, performance tests were developed that were domain-oriented, that is, cognitive performance tests, affective performance tests and psychomotor performance tests. These instruments were designed to test the hypothesis that teacher effectiveness varies; and that this variation can be isolated and measured by sensitive performance tests. In other words, some teachers might be more effective in teaching cognitive skills than affective or psychomotor skills, while other teachers might be more effective in changing attitudes or stimulating students' interest in a subject than in teaching cognitive skills.

The findings did not support the hypothesis, but Rose concluded the deficiencies in the design of the instruments themselves accounted for the findings, and that the study should be replicated in order to properly test this hypothesis. Apparently much more is to be learned about the effectiveness and proper mix of instructional objectives, performance tests and teacher characteristics at all educational levels.

Faculty Perception of Teaching

Regardless of the problems of assessing the effectiveness of different teaching methods in higher education, or of the evaluation of any teaching method, there are, at least, strong indications that college and university teachers take their teaching seriously. Recent evidence to this effect was obtained by Gaff and Wilson (1971), who surveyed 1,085 faculty members at six institutions—a large state university, a large state college, a medium-sized public junior college, a medium-sized private university, a small selective liberal arts college and a small Protestant college. The majority of faculty members tended not only to have contact with students in prescribed capacities such as teacher and adviser, but also in ways above and beyond what is formally required, as friend and counselor.

At every school most of the faculty reported that the quality of teaching actually was given less weight than they thought it should be. Nine out of 10 faculty members said they felt teaching should be a very important criterion in pay and promotion decisions. Also, nine out of 10 faculty members said teaching was the "major source of satisfaction in their lives." In addition, all but a handful said their students viewed them as effective teachers. The findings indicated a greater faculty interest in teaching than was expected, even allowing for the self-report nature of the data.

Substantial majorities of faculty members favored such educational reforms as increases in the proportion of students from minority groups, in the amount of informal interaction between faculty and students, in the proportion of interdisciplinary courses, in the use of independent study, in the proportion of courses directed at contemporary social problems and in the granting of academic credit for work in community action programs.

In general, faculty members who favored reform had more contact with students outside the classroom and were more likely to be from junior ranks, politically liberal and nonreligious. Such faculty members, according to the investigators, were more likely to see the purpose of a college education as promoting self-development of the student and were more likely to emphasize personalization in the educative process. In addition, such faculty members were more likely to be discursive, analytic and integrative, and were more attuned to encouraging student participation and to employing less structured evaluation of procedures in the classroom. The opposite was generally true of faculty members who opposed educational change.

Yet, regardless of the faculty's sentiments regarding their teaching, Gustad's (1961) position of a decade ago seems warranted. After surveying policies and practices of faculty evaluation in 584 institutions during the 1950s, he noted that the majority of institutions studied claimed they placed great weight on teaching ability even though no effective method of evaluating this appeared to be in use. They evaluated other factors on a hit-or-miss basis. Gustad emphasized that higher education needs to get its own house in order.

The literature surveyed herein at least represents an attempt by higher education to "get its house in order," and while far from precise, represents a positive step forward.

CONCLUSION

Changing populations, increased technology, advancement in communications and the culture-wide upheaval in value systems are all factors which have placed increasing demands on higher education in the last decade. At the same time colleges and universities, which should be preparing young men and women to take their places in a world of social and intellectual change, have themselves resisted change. The paradox has resulted in an increased demand that individual campuses as well as the community of higher education collectively become more responsive to the problems of the world.

Such demands could have produced significant research and great theoretical formulations, and there has certainly been a marked and steady growth in the literature on higher education in recent years. However, while it is evident from the studies just reviewed that some studies were well designed, relatively sophisticated and based on substantial empirical findings, the greater majority of studies gives evidence of being only slightly more imaginative in conception, and only somewhat more rigorous in design than those reviewed in earlier years. In general, the research has been disappointing. While a few excellent studies have emerged, educators lack carefully planned and cumulative research to guide decisions. The curricular and instructional dimensions of higher education have remained fixed without sufficient guiding research.

The questions that remain unanswered proliferate. Research during this period has been more successful in challenging old assumptions than it has been in establishing new generalizations, and much of the research lacks critical appraisal. Many studies have been limited to correlating assessment variables with some other criterion where neither the validity of the assessment, the meaningfulness of the criterion or the significance of the question under attack has been critically reviewed by the researcher. Experimental studies in which significant variables have been systematically manipulated are exceedingly rare.

Moreover, the impact of research on higher education is questionable. No firm relationship between research and actual decision making has been established. As Baskin (1964) points out:

Despite recent developments in higher education, the change agent is still badly needed.... Something has been missing for far too long, which I suspect relates to our own unwillingness to examine our assumptions about teaching and learning, and to our unreadiness to ask ourselves some questions about how we go about the educational process. Someone needs to take hold. Why not the researcher? (p. 1).

Organizational change in educational settings, its causes, characteristics and results are presently being studied through the Environment for Teaching program of Stanford's Center for Research and Development in Teaching (Baldridge, 1970). This research focuses on a number of issues, including: 1) the link between the school's decision structure and the degree of participation in decision making by professional teachers; 2) the type of "professionalization" that academics display and how this affects their role in policy making; 3) the educational impact of including the professionals in the decision process; 4) the type of activity in which teachers participate in order to influence policy; and 5) how teachers' policy-influencing activities are linked to their satisfaction with working conditions, trust in the administration of the institution, and involvement in unions or professional organizations. In short, the project examines the "political" activities as they tend to influence deliberate policy decisions in the institution. After a period of planning and theoretical development, the project is beginning to collect data in the schools. A representative national sample of 321 colleges and universities has been selected, and questionnaires that ask about the teacher's role in important policy decisions in his school will be mailed to more than 17,000 teachers in these institutions.

This research is important for teaching because teachers' perceptions of their effec-tiveness in influencing policies greatly affect their teaching, work satisfaction and willingness to continue in the teaching profession. Most important, these teacher attributes affect student behavior, learning patterns and satisfaction with their educational experience. The results should be one of the most complete analyses ever conducted on academic governance and policy making. Moreover, the analyses should reveal the links between "political" decision activities in institutions and the teaching that occurs in them.

Another central issue concerns the relevance of research to the fundamental goals of higher education. To what extent are the colleges' stated objectives understood and supported by components of the campus community? What are major similarities and differences among colleges in this respect? In situations that are comparable, do different changes occur on various campuses over a period of time? What factors can be isolated to account for variable change in given situations? Can concepts and techniques that have been productive on one campus be incorporated usefully on other campuses?

Researchers have not generally interpreted their studies in terms of their implications, or evaluated existing programs and agencies in light of their data. Nor have they offered recommendations concerning what the data mean and how they should be used. Research is needed that not only describes the characteristics of the college and its population, but also tests strategies for the improvement of the college climate in ways that will help all members of the college community understand rather than merely react to the forces that bear on them.

A wide range of innovation and experimentation is currently being undertaken in colleges and universities throughout the country. This includes increased student participation in course curriculum planning, independent study, new technologies, change or elimination of grades, and restructuring of curricula. Yet these innovations are rarely evaluated. Even when evaluation is attempted, most of the research is poorly designed. Measures are often not congruent with the experimental objectives because the most important goals are difficult to measure. Results are often not immediately apparent but innovators are reluctant to wait long enough. Evaluation of teaching *must* go beyond a particular teacher or class. It depends upon an examination and understanding of the accumulative effects of the many aspects of the college environment that bear on the teaching-learning function. This, in turn, requires assessing the interaction of the many variables contributing to their cumulative effects. Yet very rarely is this issue recognized, let alone dealt with. And this is particularly true at the institutional level.

Methodology is difficult. Since it is so very hard to match colleges or even classes, researchers do not usually employ control groups nor do they generally take into account the interactions of influencing contextual variables. One annotated bibliography cites almost 150 articles dealing with the problems of change in higher education (Watson, 1967). Only a few of the studies reported sought to evaluate in any way the reforms that were undertaken. Educators must evaluate the effects of change, and gain through research a better understanding of the strategies involved in the change. To do this, researchers must be willing to ask critical questions: How did this change come about? What are the dynamics of this particular innovation? To what degree has it been planned? To what degree has it been successful in accomplishing its goals as well as the broader goals of higher education? In other words, more research is needed on the innovative process itself.

It seems more imperative than ever before that educators explicate their goals, establish their own educational priorities, determine what changes are needed and how they can best be brought about. Through research

structured in this way, colleges may understand the extent to which their programs and climates promote or prevent the fulfillment of their stated goals. Analysis of research data could offer the college the kind of information needed to make defensible decisions.

There seems to be no body of literature that examines the extent to which institutional research actually has helped improve academic life or whether it has at all. We are only able to hope that such research has had some constructive impact, but the paucity of rigorous empirical studies would suggest that institutional research has had only minor impact on the academic process. Once again, this may well be the result of the circumscribed nature of the research rather than its potential usefulness.

There have been, of course, some positive changes. Probably the most obvious changes have been in the area of management, and a strong link exists between institutional research activities and the efforts to make colleges and universities more efficient. Several studies dealt with college and university facilities, state-wide systems, and data-processing systems. For example, Walker and Coffelt (1964) studied the needs of 21 colleges and universities in Oklahoma, examined the existing land and building facilities, and evaluated the use of the present space and projected physical plant needs and costs. As a result of their comprehensive study, local administrators could easily determine what campus space was needed, what could be saved and what should be added or replaced. Comparisons were made between institutions, and state-wide projections were simplified, clearly illustrating the role research should take in facilitating decision making and systematic and orderly change.

Institutional research played a significant role in altering enrollment and transfer practices. Lins's (1960) and Fincher's (1965) papers are examples of researchers helping colleges decide how many students will apply and which students should be admitted. Richards, James, and Holland's study (1965) and Trent's (1970a, in press) indicate the degree of sophistication that can be reached by researchers to help administrators understand why students choose particular colleges or choose to attend college at all. Important factors in college choice such as intellectual emphasis, practicality, advice of others, personality factors, motivation, peer relations and social emphases were identified and models developed as an initial step to apply this information. Such research could have a major impact on the university's recruitment practices as well as significantly altering its counseling programs.

Although no major breakthroughs were effected in educational and psychological testing, the research studies reviewed reflected a continued and expanding use of factor analysis and a concern for measurement of process objectives in achievement examinations as well as evaluation of affective objectives in the curriculum. While two publications by Tucker (1963a, 1963b) devoted to the development of a formal prediction system and to the factor analysis of three-dimensional matrices were noteworthy advances in statistical methodology, the critical need in educational and psychological testing is not for additional statistical sophistication as much as for the formulation of a comprehensive and workable theory of the teaching and learning process to which measurement and evaluation procedures can be meaningfully related (see Michael, 1965; Popham & Husek, 1969).

The measure of good teaching still remains complex and unclear. The actual development of teaching theories, moreover, remains in its infancy. Clearly, the many comparisons made using ambiguously defined experimental and control methods have added little to our knowledge of teaching and perhaps are not the most profitable lines to pursue.

The academic community still cleaves tenaciously to theories which have not found support in data. Why must administrators, for example, continue to admonish faculty about disproportionate student-teacher ratios when research data support the view that instruction can be equally effective in large classes and small groups depending on the nature of the students and course? Why do faculty members not reexamine course content when research data indicate that not very much has been learned?

The general climate for learning in a given college unquestionably affects student and instructor performance. However, no studies have systematically related this factor to the nature and quality of college instruction, and only occasional studies have explored the significance of student and teacher traits in influencing learning, even though these may account for much of the unexplained variance in achievement. Little has been determined beyond what was reported in the late 1950s regarding faculty members' personal characteristics and the meaning of these for their teaching.

Findings from the studies reported herein, for example, those by Solomon, Rosenberg, and Bezdek (1964) and the work done by McKeachie and his associates, suggest that teaching styles do influence learning. But much more needs to be discovered about how teachers' personal traits influence their choice of methods and students' success and satisfactions in learning. To the extent that faculties do influence student development and aspirations, this almost neglected area of research is essential to an understanding of college environment interactions.

McKeachie's framework, which studies the complex interactions of the college environment, personal traits of teachers and students, instructional methods and instructional outcomes, is a most promising line of research. Process-descriptive studies such as the Solomon, Rosenberg, and Bezdek (1964) study aimed at finding out what actually transpires in the classroom might well be elaborated. The experimental application of theoretically derived variables as in Lumsdaine and May (1965) and McKeachie and his associates should be continued in an effort to sharpen the definition of experimental variables. Further work along both these lines should aid in setting up meaningful experiments and in developing better theories of teaching.

Perhaps the most salient and important research trend to emerge has been the systematic investigation of the interaction between student and environmental characteristics. These studies focus on the correlations among measured student and environmental characteristics as well as on student selection of colleges and the impact of college education on the students. Major studies such as those we have already described suggest that student change occurs in the direction of decreased authoritarianism and commitment to orthodox religious beliefs, increased independence, increased openness to impulses and readiness to express them, increased intellectual interests and increased liberal sociopolitical attitudes and beliefs. The conditions contributing to such development still are not clearly defined and more evidence is needed.

The case for campus-wide impacts which are systematically related to differential educational practices or institutional conditions is even more unclear. These studies do represent, however, a shift from a predominantly descriptive to a more dynamic level of analysis which may be considered a major breakthrough in the social-psychological study of the student in higher education.

In general, recent studies of teaching methods and materials have, like their predecessors, yielded no clear-cut evidence of the superiority of any one approach. Of course this may partially reflect problems in definition, design and instrumentation. Another reason, however, may be that often the methods or materials have been considered in the abstract, without reference to the particular subject content involved. As more

knowledge is gained about the structure of individual disciplines, both teaching methods and methods for evaluating their effectiveness may require modification.

Still other important issues embody such questions as: What are the conditions under which one learns to learn, and what educational ingredients encourage learning? How can the practice of continuous learning be developed effectively? How can students be helped to develop attitudes, habits and skills conducive to lifelong learning? What factors are responsible for positive educational changes? What characteristics of educational programs elicit positive learning responses from those students with different perceptions, different learning patterns and different goals?

We also need to know more about the determinants of teacher role-expectations, the stability of teacher role-expectations, the conditions under which change occurs, the relationship between an individual teacher's role-expectation and other personality variables, the relationship between teacher characteristics and student characteristics, the relationship between the teachers' goals and the students' goals, and finally, the relationship between a teacher's concept of the teaching role and his performance as it is observed by others and as it affects student performance.

As an agent of academic change, research depends not only on the willingness of educators to experiment and innovate in seeking change, but upon their willingness to evaluate and make use of their research studies. Sanford's remark in 1962 is pertinent to the 1970s: "The colleges will change only when more knowledge of what they do and of what they might do has been produced and made available to educators. The need for theory is apparent but what is more striking is the paucity of empirical studies" (p. 1012).

The great need, therefore, is for more comprehensive and sophisticated research, for more evaluation based on the research, for better dissemination of its results, and for the institutions to make use of these results.

REFERENCES

Aaron, D. *Writers on the left.* New York: Avon Books, 1965.

Adelson, J. The teacher as a model. In N. Sanford (Ed.), *The American college.* New York: John Wiley, 1962. Pp. 396–417.

Ahern, J. *Characteristics of teachers who have received an "outstanding teacher" award from New England institutions of higher education in the five-year period beginning with the academic year 1963–1964.* (Doctoral dissertation, University of Massachusetts) Ann Arbor, Mich.: University Microfilms, 1969. No. 69-22,079.

Aiken, L. R., Jr., & Dreger, R. M. The effect of attitudes on performance in mathematics. *Journal of Educational Psychology,* 1961, 52, 19–24.

Aiken, M., Demerath, N. J., & Marwell, G. Conscience and confrontation: Some preliminary findings on summer civil rights volunteers. Unpublished manuscript, University of Wisconsin, 1966. (mimeo)

Alexander, W. B., & Myers, A. F. *Evaluation of an experiment in off-campus independent study at Bard College.* Washington, D.C.: U.S. Department of Health, Education and Welfare, 1959. ED 000 373.

Alpern, D. K. In place of recitations: An experiment in teaching. *Teachers College Record,* 1966, 67. 589–594.

American Association of Junior Colleges. *Inservice training for two-year college faculty and staff: A survey of junior and community college administrators.* Faculty Development Project. Washington, D.C.: AAJC, 1969. ED 034 519.

Amidon, E. J., & Flanders, N. A. *The role of the teacher in the classroom.* (Rev. ed.) Minneapolis: Association for Productive Teaching, 1967.

Anderson, L. B., & Spencer, P. A. Personal adjustment and academic predictability among college freshmen. *Journal of Applied Psychology,* 1963, 47, 97–100.

Apt, M. H. *A measurement of college instructor behavior.* (Doctoral dissertation, University of Pittsburgh) Ann Arbor, Mich.: University Microfilms, 1967. No. 67-4558.

Astin, A. W. An empirical characterization of higher educational institutions. *Journal of Educational Psychology,* 1962, 53, 224–235. (a)

Astin, A. W. Influences on the student's motivation to seek advanced training: Another look. *Journal of Educational Psychology,* 1962, 53, 303–309. (b)

Astin, A. W. "Productivity" of undergraduate institutions. *Science,* 1962, 136, 129–135. (c)

Astin, A. W. Differential college effects on the motivation of talented students to obtain the Ph.D. *Journal of Educational Psychology,* 1963, 54, 63–71. (a)

Astin, A. W. Further validation of the environmental assessment technique. *Journal of Educational Psychology,* 1963, 54, 217–226. (b)

Astin, A. W. Distribution of students among higher educational institutions. *Journal of Educational Psychology,* 1964, 55, 276–287. (a)

Astin, A. W. Personal and environmental factors associated with college dropouts among high aptitude students. *Journal of Educational Psychology,* 1964, 55, 219–227. (b)

Astin, A. W. Some characteristics of student bodies entering higher educational institutions. *Journal of Educational Psychology,* 1964, 55, 267–275. (c)

Astin, A. W. Classroom environment in different fields of study. *Journal of Educational Psychology,* 1965, 56, 275–282.

Astin, A. W. The conference on the cluster college concept: Students. *Journal of Higher Education,* 1967, 38, 396–397.

Astin, A. W., & Holland, J. L. The environmental assessment technique: A way to measure college environments. *Journal of Educational Psychology,* 1961, 52, 308–316.

Astin, A. W., & Panos, R. J. *The educational and vocational development of college students.* Washington, D.C.: American Council on Education, 1969.

Austin, C. G. Recruiting college teachers. *Journal of Higher Education,* 1966, 37, 513–515.

Baldridge, J. V. Images of the future and organizational change. *Research and Development Memorandum No. 58.* Palo Alto, Calif.: Stanford Center for Research and Development in Teaching, 1970. ED 037 184. (a)

Bales, R. F. *Interaction process analysis*. Cambridge, Mass.: Addison-Wesley, 1950.

Banathy, B. H. *Instructional systems*. Palo Alto, Calif.: Fearon, 1968.

Bandura, A., Lipsher, D. H., & Miller, P. E. Psychotherapists' approach-avoidance reactions to patients' expressions of hostility. *Journal of Consulting Psychology*, 1960, 24, 1–8.

Banister, R. E. *Case studies in multi-media instruction*. ERIC Clearinghouse for Junior Colleges, Topical Paper No. 13. Los Angeles: UCLA, 1970. ED 044 098.

Bannister, J., et al. Evaluating college teaching. *Curriculum Reporter Supplement*, December 1961, No. 1.

Baratz, S. S. Effect of race of experimenter, instructions, and comparison population upon level of reported anxiety in Negro subjects. *Journal of Personality and Social Psychology*, 1967, 7, 194–196.

Barr, A. S., Worcester, D. A., Abell, A., Beecher, C., Jensen, L. E., Peronto, A. L., Ringness, T. A., & Schmid, J., Jr. *Wisconsin studies of measurement and prediction of teacher effectiveness: A summary of investigations*. Madison, Wis.: Dembar Publications, 1961.

Baskin, S. Experiment in independent study, 1956–1960. *Antioch College Reports*, 1961, 2, 1–4.

Baskin, S. A conceptual framework for institutional research. In Proceedings of the Fourth Annual National Institutional Research Forum, St. Paul, Minn., May 17–20, 1964. Pp. 1–3.

Baskin, S., Watson, G., Dixon, J., & Manion, P. Innovation in higher education: Developments, research, and priorities. *New Dimensions in Higher Education*, April 1967, No. 19.

Bay, C. Political and apolitical students: Facts in search of theory. *Journal of Social Issues*, 1967, 23(3), 76–91.

Baymur, F. B., & Patterson, C. H. A comparison of three methods of assisting underachieving high school students. *Journal of Counseling Psychology*, 1960, 7, 83–89.

Beach, L. R. Learning and student interaction in small self-directed college groups. Final report. Washington, D.C.: U.S. Department of Health, Education, and Welfare, 1970. ED 026 027.

Bell, D. *The end of ideology: On the exhaus-* tion of political ideas in the fifties. New York: Free Press, 1962.

Bendig, A. W. The relation of level of course achievement to students' instructor and course ratings in introductory psychology. *Educational and Psychological Measurement*, 1953, 13, 437–448. (a)

Bendig, A. W. Student achievement in introductory psychology and student ratings of the competence and empathy of their instructors. *Journal of Psychology*, 1953, 36, 427–433. (b)

Berdie, R. Personality changes from high school entrance to college matriculation. *Journal of Counseling Psychology*, 1968, 15, 376–380.

Berelson, B., & Steiner, G. A. *Human behavior: An inventory of scientific findings*. New York: Harcourt, Brace, 1964.

Bigelow, G. S., & Egbert, R. L. Personality factors and independent study. *Journal of Educational Research*, 1968, 62(1), 37–39.

Bird, C. *Born female: The high cost of keeping women down*. New York: David McKay, 1968.

Black studies in American education. *Journal of Negro Education*, Special Issue, 1970, 39(3).

Blocker, C. E., Plummer, R. H., & Richardson, R. C., Jr. *The two-year college: A social synthesis*. Englewood Cliffs, N.J.: Prentice-Hall, 1965.

Boroff, D. *Campus USA*. New York: Harper & Row, 1961.

Boyer, E. L. *Institutional research and the academic program*. New Dimensions in Higher Education, No. 20. Durham, N.C.: Duke University, April 1967. ED 013 381.

Boyer, E. L., & Michael, W. B. Outcomes of college. *Review of Educational Research*, 1965, 35(4), 277–291.

Bradley, N. E. The Negro undergraduate student: Factors relative to performance in predominantly white state colleges and universities in Tennessee. *Journal of Negro Education*, 1967, 36, 15–23.

Bradley, R. L. Lecture demonstration versus individual laboratory work in a general education science course. *Journal of Experimental Education*, 1965, 34(1), 33–42.

Brawer, F. B. *The concept of ego strength and its measurement through a word association technique*. (Doctoral dissertation, University of California, Los Angeles) Ann Arbor,

Mich.: University Microfilms, 1967. No. 67-14,251.

Brawer, F. B. *Personality characteristics of college and university faculty: Implications for the community college.* ERIC Clearinghouse for Junior Colleges, Monograph No. 3. Washington, D.C.: American Association of Junior Colleges, 1968. ED 026 048.

Bresler, J. B. Teaching effectiveness and government awards. *Science,* 1968, 160, 164–167.

Briggs, L. J., Campeau, P. L., Gagné, R. M., & May, M. A. *Instructional media: A procedure for the design of multi-media instruction, a critical review of research, and suggestions for future research.* Pittsburgh: American Institutes for Research, 1967.

Brinker, P. A. Our illiberal-arts colleges: The dangers of undergraduate overspecialization. *Journal of Higher Education,* 1960, 31, 133–138.

Bronfenbrenner, U. The changing American child. In E. Ginzberg (Ed.), *Values and ideals of American youth.* New York: Columbia University Press, 1961. Pp. 73–84.

Brown, D. G., & Tontz, J. L. The present shortage of college teachers. *Phi Delta Kappan,* 1966, 47, 435–436.

Brown, D. R. Student stress and the institutional environment. *Journal of Social Sciences,* 1967, 23(3), 92–107.

Brown, J. W., & Thornton, J. W., Jr. *College teaching.* New York: McGraw-Hill, 1963.

Bruemmer, L. The condition of women in society today: A review. Part I. *Journal of the National Association of Women Deans and Counselors,* 1969, 33, 118–125.

Burgess, E. Personality factors of over- and under-achievers in engineering. *Journal of Educational Psychology,* 1956, 47, 89–99.

Burkhart, R. C. (Ed.) *The assessment revolution: New viewpoints for teacher evaluation.* New York State Education Department, Albany. Buffalo, N.Y.: State University of New York, Division of Teacher Education and Certification, 1969. ED 036 485.

Burns, R. S., & Jones, R. C. *Two experimental approaches to freshman composition—lecture-tutorial and team teaching.* Washington, D.C.: U.S. Department of Health, Education and Welfare, 1970. ED 015 214.

Bushnell, J. H. Student culture at Vassar. In N. Sanford (Ed.), *The American college: A psychological and social interpretation of the higher learning.* New York: John Wiley, 1962. Pp. 489–514.

Carter, R. E. *The effect of student characteristics on three student evaluations of university instruction.* (Doctoral dissertation, Indiana University) Ann Arbor, Mich.: University Microfilms, 1969. No. 69-4735.

Chambers, W. M. *A comparison of programed and conventional materials for study in introductory psychology.* (Doctoral dissertation, University of Kentucky) Ann Arbor, Mich.: University Microfilms, 1969. No. 69-18,244.

Cherdack, A. N. *The predictive validity of the scholastic aptitude test for disadvantaged college students enrolled in a special educational program.* (Doctoral dissertation, University of California, Los Angeles) Ann Arbor, Mich.: University Microfilms, 1971. No. 71-10,636.

Chickering, A. W. FD's and SD's—Neglected data in institutional research. Proceedings, 1968 Forum, Association for Institutional Research. Athens: AIR, 1968.

Chickering, A. W. *Education and identity.* San Francisco: Jossey-Bass, 1969.

Chickering, A. W., McDowell, J., & Campagna, D. Institutional differences and student development. *Journal of Educational Psychology,* 1969, 60, 315–326.

Christiansen, M. A. *The relative effectiveness of two methods of teaching composition in freshman English at Metropolitan Junior College—Kansas City.* (Doctoral dissertation, University of Kansas) Ann Arbor, Mich.: University Microfilms, 1965. No. 65-7639. ED 034 549.

Clark, B. R. *The open door college.* New York: McGraw-Hill, 1960.

Cleveland, B. Black studies and higher education. *Phi Delta Kappan,* 1969, 51, 44–46.

Cohen, A. M. *Dateline '79: Heretical concepts for the community college.* Beverly Hills, Calif.: Glencoe Press, 1969.

Cohen, A. M. Technology: Thee or me? Behavioral objectives and the college teacher. *Educational Technology,* 1970, 10(11), 57–60.

Cohen, A. M., & associates. *A constant variable: New perspectives on the community college.* San Francisco: Jossey-Bass, 1971.

Cohen, A. M., & Brawer, F. B. *Focus on learning—preparing teachers for the two-year college.* Junior College Leadership Program.

Los Angeles: University of California, 1968. ED 019 939.

Cohen, A. M., & Brawer, F. B. *Measuring faculty performance.* ERIC Clearinghouse for Junior Colleges, Monograph No. 4. Washington, D.C.: American Association of Junior Colleges, 1969. ED 031 222.

Cohen, A. M., & Brawer, F. B. *Student characteristics: Personality and dropout propensity.* ERIC Clearinghouse for Junior Colleges, Monograph No. 9. Washington, D.C.: American Association of Junior Colleges, 1970. ED 038 130.

Cohen, A. M., & Brawer, F. B. *Confronting identity: The Community College Instructor.* Englewood Cliffs, N.J.: Prentice-Hall, 1972.

Cohen, A. M., & Shawl, W. F. Coordinating instruction through objectives. *Junior College Journal,* October 1970, 41(2), 17–19.

Cohen, E. Faculty for teaching-learning: Proposed new graduate centers for the systematic preparation of community college teachers. February 1970. ED 038 133. (mimeo)

Cohen, S. H., & Berger, W. G. Dimensions of students' ratings of college instructors underlying subsequent achievement on course examinations. *Proceedings of the Annual Convention of the American Psychological Association,* 1970, 78, 605–606.

Cook, R. *Upperclassmen's satisfaction with college.* Unpublished doctoral dissertation, University of California, Los Angeles, 1971.

Coombs, R. H., & Davies, V. Socio-psychological adjustment in collegiate scholastic success. *Journal of Educational Research,* 1967, 61, 186–189.

Corlis, R. B. *Personality factors related to underachievement in college freshmen of high intellectual ability.* (Doctoral dissertation, University of Florida) Ann Arbor, Mich.: University Microfilms, 1963. No. 63-5804.

Cornett, J. D., & Butler, W. *The effect of a team approach in achieving the objectives of an introductory course in education.* Washington, D.C.: Department of Health, Education and Welfare, 1967. ED 025 489.

Cowan, J. L. Academic freedom, protest and university environments. Paper presented at the meeting of the American Psychological Association, New York, September 1966.

Crandall, V. Parents' attitudes and behaviors and grade school children's academic achievements. *Journal of Genetic Psychology,* 1964, 104, 53–56.

Crawford, P. L., & Bradshaw, H. L. Perception of characteristics of effective university teachers: A scaling analysis. *Educational and Psychological Measurement,* 1968, 28, 1079–1085.

Creager, J. A., & Astin, A. W. Alternative methods of describing characteristics of colleges and universities. *Educational and Psychological Measurement,* 1968, 28, 719–734.

Cregier, D. M. Direct involvement of students. *Improving College and University Teaching,* 1968, 16, 26–27.

Cross, K. P. College women: A research description. *Journal of the National Association of Women Deans and Counselors,* 1969, 33, 118–125.

Dana, R. H., & Baker, D. H. High school achievement and the Bell Adjustment Inventory. *Psychological Report,* 1961, 8, 353–356.

Danforth Foundation. Teaching improvement grants. *Danforth News and Notes,* 1970, 6(2), 1–7.

Daniel, R. S. Teaching psychology in the community and junior college. *American Psychologist,* 1970, 25, 537–543.

Davie, J. S. Some observations on superior students. *Journal of Educational Sociology,* 1961, 35, 172–177.

Davis, A. L. *Dialect research and the needs of the schools.* Champaign, Ill.: National Council of Teachers of English, 1968. ED 022 153.

Davis, R., Johnson, C., & Dietrich, J. Student attitudes, motivations shown to influence reception to televised lectures. *College and University Business,* 1969, 46(5), 59–63.

Deeming, J. D. Experimental use of a modified programmed lecture preview technique for teaching freshman gross anatomy. *Journal of Educational Research,* 1966, 60, 8–9.

Dellas, M., & Gaier, E. L. Modes of conformity of freshmen women at differently oriented colleges. *Journal of Educational Research,* 1969, 62, 370–374.

Dement, A. L. The college woman as a science major. *Journal of Higher Education,* 1962, 33, 487–490.

Doty, B. A. Teaching method effectiveness in relation to certain student characteristics. *Journal of Educational Research,* 1967, 60, 363–365.

Dressel, P. L. The conference on the cluster college concept: Curriculum and instruction. *Journal of Higher Education*, 1967, 38, 393–396.

Dressel, P. L., & Lehmann, I. J. The impact of higher education on student attitudes, values, and critical thinking abilities. *The Educational Record*, 1965, 46, 248–258.

Dubin, R., & Taveggia, T. C. *The teaching-learning paradox: A comparative analysis of college teaching methods.* Eugene, Ore.: University of Oregon, Center for the Advanced Study of Educational Administration, 1968.

Dunham, E. A. *Colleges of the forgotten Americans: A profile of state colleges and regional universities.* New York: McGraw-Hill, 1969.

Eble, K. E. The recognition and evaluation of teaching. Salt Lake City, Utah: The Project to Improve College Teaching, 1970. ED 046 350.

Eddy, E. D., Jr. *The college influence on student character.* Washington, D.C.: American Council on Education, 1959.

Eisenstadt, S. N. *From generation to generation: Age groups and social structure.* Glencoe, Ill.: Free Press, 1956.

Elliott, D. N. *A study of various criteria in predicting teaching success in higher education.* (Doctoral dissertation, Purdue University) New York: H. W. Wilson, 1950. No. 17.

Epperson, D. C. Accommodating for individual differences. *Improving College and University Teaching*, 1963, 11, 47–50.

Epstein, C. F. *Women's place.* Berkeley and Los Angeles: University of California Press, 1970.

Erb, E. D. Conformity and achievement in college. *Personnel and Guidance Journal*, 1961, 39, 361–366.

Erickson, R. J. Programmed learning and personality styles at the college level. *Journal of Educational Research*, 1967, 60(7), 330–333.

Erikson, E. H. *Childhood and society.* (2nd ed.) New York: W. W. Norton, 1963.

Etters, E. M. Tutorial assistance in college core courses. *Journal of Educational Research*, 1967, 60, 406–407.

Evans, R. I., & Leppmann, P. K. *Resistance to innovation in higher education.* San Francisco: Jossey-Bass, 1967.

Fahey, G. L., & Ball, J. M. Objective evaluation of a program in general education. *Journal of Educational Psychology*, 1960, 51, 144–151.

Faw, V. Undergraduate education in psychology. An unpublished paper described in C. R. Rogers, *Freedom to learn*, Chapter 2. Columbus: Charles E. Merrill, 1969.

Felder, D. Independent-study practices in colleges and universities. *Journal of Higher Education*, 1964, 35, 335–338.

Feldhusen, J. F. The effects of small and large group instruction on learning of subject matter, attitudes, and interests. *Journal of Psychology*, 1963, 55, 357–362.

Feldman, K. A., & Newcomb, T. M. *The impact of college on students.* San Francisco: Jossey-Bass, 1969.

Fincher, C. *Probabilistic versus deterministic models on college admissions.* Athens, Ga.: University of Georgia, Institute of Higher Education, 1965.

Flacks, R. The liberated generation: An exploration of the roots of student protest. *The Journal of Social Issues*, 1967, 23(3), 52–75.

Flanagan, J. C., et al. *The American high school student.* Technical Report to the U.S. Office of Education, Cooperative Research Project No. 635. Pittsburgh, Pa.: University of Pittsburgh, Project TALENT Office, 1964.

Flanders, N. A., & Simon, A. Teacher effectiveness. In R. L. Ebel (Ed.), *Encyclopedia of educational research.* (4th ed.) New York: Macmillan, 1969. Pp. 1423–1437.

Fraenkel, J. R. A comparison of achievement between students taught by a teaching team and students taught in traditional classes on a standardized examination in United States history. *The Journal of Educational Research*, 1967, 61, 43–46.

Freedman, M. B. *Impact of college.* New Dimensions in Higher Education, No. 4, U.S. Department of Health, Education & Welfare, Office of Education (OE-50011). Washington, D.C.: U.S. Government Printing Office, 1960.

Freedman, M. B. *The college experience.* San Francisco: Jossey-Bass, 1969.

Freehill, M. F. Authoritarian bias and evaluation of college experiences. *Improving College and University Teaching*, 1967, 15, 18–19.

French, S. J., & Cooper, R. M. Pilot project for improving college teaching—the Florida

College Teaching Project. Tampa: University of South Florida, 1967. ED 013 083.

Friedan, B. *The feminine mystique.* New York: Dell, 1963.

Friedman, N. L. *The public junior college teacher in unified public school system junior colleges: A study in the sociology of educational work.* (Doctoral dissertation, University of Missouri) Ann Arbor, Mich.: University Microfilms, 1965. No. 65-9109.

Fugate, J. K. Two heads are better than one—report on an experiment. Washington, D.C.: Department of Health, Education and Welfare, 1966. ED 013 549.

Gaff, J. G. & Wilson, R. C. The teaching environment. *AAUP Bulletin,* 1971, 57 (4), 475–493.

Gage, N. L. The appraisal of college teaching: An analysis of ends and means. *Journal of Higher Education,* 1961, 32, 17–22.

Gage, N. L. A method for "improving" teacher behavior. *Journal of Teacher Education,* 1963, 14, 261–266.

Gamsky, N. R., & Farwell, G. F. Counselor verbal behavior as a function of client hostility. *Journal of Counseling Psychology,* 1966, 13, 184–190.

Garrison, R. H. *Junior college faculty: Issues and problems, a preliminary national appraisal.* Washington, D.C.: American Association of Junior Colleges, 1967. ED 012 177.

Garverick, C. M. Retention of school learning as influenced by selected affective tone variables. *Journal of Educational Psychology,* 1964, 55, 31–34.

Gill, L. J., & Spilka, B. Some nonintellectual correlates of academic achievement among Mexican-American secondary school students. *Journal of Educational Psychology,* 1962, 53, 144–149.

Gleazer, E. J., Jr. Preparation of junior college teachers. *Educational Record,* 1967, 48(2), 147–152. ED 016 489.

Gleazer, E. J., Jr. *This is the community college.* Boston: Houghton Mifflin, 1968. ED 026 063.

Goldsen, R. K., Rosenberg, M., Williams, R., Jr., & Suchman, E. A. *What college students think.* Princeton, N. J.: Van Nostrand, 1960.

Goodstein, L. D., & Heilbrun, A. B., Jr. Prediction of college achievement from the Edwards Personal Preference Schedule at three

levels of intellectual ability. *Journal of Applied Psychology,* 1962, 46, 317–320.

Gordon, C. W., Schwartz, A. J., Wenkert, R., & Nasatir, D. *Educational achievement and aspirations of Mexican-American youth in a metropolitan context.* CSE Report No. 36. Los Angeles: University of California, Center for the Study of Evaluation, 1968.

Green, J. G. A study of expressed behavior changes occurring as a result of exposure to filmed classroom situations and t-group sensitivity training. Unpublished manuscript, Washington State University, 1969.

Grozier, J. E., Jr. *The role of the laboratory in developing positive attitudes toward science in a college general education science course for nonscientists.* (Doctoral dissertation, East Texas State University) Ann Arbor, Mich.: University Microfilms, 1969. No. 69-21, 167.

Gulo, E. V. University students' attitudes as measured by the semantic differential. *The Journal of Educational Research,* 1966, 60(4), 152–158.

Gunstone, B. J., & Hatton, B. R. Involving students in the teaching-learning process. *Journal of the National Association of Women Deans and Counselors,* 1969, 32, 80–82.

Gusfield, J., & Riesman, D. Faculty culture and academic careers. In K. Yamamoto (Ed.), *The college student and his culture: An analysis.* Boston: Houghton Mifflin, 1968. Pp. 271–291.

Gustad, J. W. *Policies and practices in faculty evaluation.* Washington, D.C.: American Council on Education, 1961.

Haan, N., Smith, M. B., & Block, J. Moral reasoning of young adults: Political-social behavior, family background, and personality correlates. *Journal of Personality and Social Psychology,* 1968, 10, 183–201.

Hagiwara, M. P. *Leadership in foreign-language education: Trends in training and supervision of graduate assistants.* ERIC Clearinghouse on the Teaching of Foreign Languages. New York: Modern Language Association, 1970. ED 041 523.

Haines, D. B., & McKeachie, W. J. Cooperative vs. competitive discussion methods in teaching introductory psychology. *Journal of Educational Psychology,* 1967, 58, 386–390.

Hall, D. T. The effect of teacher-student congruence upon student learning in college classes. *Journal of Educational Psychology,* 1970, 63, 205–213.

Hamilton, R. H. An experiment with independent study in freshman history. *Liberal Education,* 1967, 53, 271–278.

Harmon, J. S. *Effects of a multi-media environment in college level electronics.* (Doctoral dissertation, Colorado State College) Ann Arbor, Mich.: University Microfilms, 1969. No. 69-19,216.

Harris, J., & Reitzel, J. Negro freshman performance in a predominantly non-Negro university. *The Journal of College Student Personnel,* 1967, 8, 366–368.

Haworth, L. J. *The junior college and education in the sciences.* Third report in a series prepared for the Subcommittee on Science, Research, and Development of the Committee on Science and Astronautics of the U.S. House of Representatives. Washington, D.C.: National Science Foundation, 1967. ED 015 733.

Heiss, A. M. *The preparation of college and university teachers.* Berkeley: Center for Research and Development in Higher Education, 1968. ED 029 844.

Heist, P. Intellect and commitment: The faces of discontent. In O. A. Knorr & W. J. Minter (Eds.), *Order and freedom on the campus; The rights and responsibilities of faculty and students.* Boulder, Colo.: Western Interstate Commission for Higher Education, 1965. Pp. 61–69.

Heist, P. The dynamics of student discontent and protest. Paper presented at the meeting of the American Psychological Association, New York, September 1966. ED 025 214.

Heist, P. Creative students: College transients. In P. Heist (Ed.), *The creative college student: An unmet challenge.* San Francisco: Jossey-Bass, 1968. Pp. 35–55.

Heist, P., & Webster, H. A research orientation to selection, admission, and differential education. In H. T. Sprague (Ed.), *Research on college students.* Boulder, Col.: Western Interstate Commission for Higher Education, 1960. Pp. 21–40.

Heist, P., & Williams, P. A. Variation in achievement within a select and homogeneous student body. *Journal of College Student Personnel,* December 1961, 3, 50–59.

Heller, K., Myers, R. A., & Kline, L. V. Interviewer behavior as a function of standardized client roles. *Journal of Consulting Psychology,* 1963, 27, 117–122.

Hildebrand, M., & Wilson, R. C. Effective university teaching and its evaluation. Berkeley: University of California, Center for Research and Development in Higher Education, 1970. ED 039 860.

Hills, J. R. Transfer shock: The academic performance of the junior college transfer. *Journal of Experimental Education,* 1965, 33, 201–215.

Holland, J. L. Creative and academic performance among talented adolescents. *Journal of Educational Psychology,* 1961, 52, 136–147.

Holland, J. L., & Astin, A. W. The prediction of the academic, artistic, scientific, and social achievement of undergraduates of superior scholastic aptitude. *Journal of Educational Psychology,* 1962, 53, 132–143.

Hooper, H. E., & Chandler, M. O. *Earned degrees conferred, 1967–68: Part A—summary data.* Washington, D.C.: U.S. Government Printing Office, 1969.

Hoover, K. H., Baumann, V. H., & Shafer, S. M. The influence of class-size variations on cognitive and affective learning of college freshmen. *The Journal of Experimental Education,* 1970, 38(3), 39–43.

Hovey, D. E., Gruber, H. E., & Terrell, G. Effects of self-directed study on course achievement, retention, and curiosity. *Journal of Educational Research,* 1963, 56, 346–351.

Hoyt, D. P. The relationship between college grades and adult achievement—a review of the literature. Research Report No. 7. Iowa City, Iowa: American College Testing Program, 1965. ED 023 343.

Hoyt, D. P., & Kennedy, C. E. Interest and personality characteristics of career-motivated and homemaker-motivated college women. *Journal of Counseling Psychology,* 1958, 5, 44–48.

Hunter, W. E. A systems approach to the instructional process. St. Louis, Mo.: Meramec Community College, 1970. ED 040 696.

Isaacson, R. L., McKeachie, W. J., & Milholland, J. E. Correlation of teacher personality variables and student ratings. *Journal of Educational Psychology,* 1963, 54, 110–117.

Isaacson, R. L., McKeachie, W. J., Milholland, J. E., Lin, Y. G., Hofeller, M., Baerwaldt,

J. W., & Zinn, K. L. Dimensions of student evaluations of teaching. *Journal of Educational Psychology*, 1964, 55, 344–351.

Jacob, P. Social change and student values. *The Educational Record*, 1960, 41, 338–342.

Jason, M. H. A comparison between lecture and small group discussion methods at the college level. *Illinois School Research*, 1969, 5(2), 10–14.

Jencks, C., & Riesman, D. Patterns of residential education: A case study of Harvard. In N. Sanford (Ed.), *The American college*. New York: John Wiley, 1962. Pp. 731–773.

Jenkins, J. R., & Deno, S. L. Influence of student behavior on teacher's self-evaluation. *Journal of Educational Psychology*, 1969, 60, 439–442.

Johnson, B. L. *Islands of innovation expanding: Changes in the community college*. Beverly Hills, Calif.: Glencoe Press, 1969.

Jones, M. C., Bayley, N., MacFarlane, J. W., & Honzik, M. P. (Eds.) *The course of human development*. Waltham, Mass.: Xerox College Publishing, 1971.

Justiz, T. B. A method for identifying the effective teacher. *Dissertation Abstracts*, March 1969, Vol. 29, No. 9. P. 3022-A, order # 69–5321.

Kagan, J., & Moss, H. A. *Birth to maturity*. New York: John Wiley, 1962.

Karlins, M., Kaplan, M., & Stuart, W. Academic attitudes and performance as a function of differential grading systems: An evaluation of Princeton's pass-fail system. *The Journal of Experimental Education*, 1969, 37(3), 38–50.

Karman, F. J. Women: Personal and environmental factors in sole identification and career choice. Unpublished doctoral dissertation, University of California, Los Angeles, 1972.

Katz, I. Review of evidence relating to effects of desegregation on the intellectual performance of Negroes. *American Psychologist*, 1964, 19, 381–399.

Katz, I., Epps, E. G., & Axelson, L. J. Effect upon Negro digit-symbol performance of anticipated comparison with whites and with other Negroes. *Journal of Abnormal and Social Psychology*, 1965, 2, 53–59.

Katz, I., & Greenbaum, C. Effects of anxiety, threat, and racial environment on task performance of Negro college students. *Journal of Abnormal and Social Psychology*, 1963, 66, 562–567.

Katz, I., Roberts, S. O., & Robinson, J. M. Effects of task difficulty, race of administrator, and instructions on digit-symbol performance of Negroes. *Journal of Personality and Social Psychology*, 1965, 2, 53–59.

Katz, J. Personality and interpersonal relations in the college classroom. In N. Sanford (Ed.), *The American college*. New York: John Wiley, 1962. Pp. 365–395.

Katz, J., & associates. *No time for youth*. San Francisco: Jossey-Bass, 1968.

Keeton, M., & Hilberry, C. *Struggle and promise: A future for colleges*. New York: McGraw-Hill, 1969.

Kells, H. R., & Stewart, C. T. The conference on the cluster college concept—A summary of the working sessions. *Journal of Higher Education*, 1967, 38, 359–363.

Kelly, M. F. Job-seeking strategies of public two-year college faculties in New York state. Buffalo: State University of New York, 1968. ED 022 440.

Kelly, M. F., & Connolly, J. *Orientation for faculty in junior colleges*. ERIC Clearinghouse for Junior Colleges, Monograph No. 10. Washington, D.C.: American Association for Junior Colleges, 1970. ED 043 323.

Keniston, K. An analysis of dissent. In Proceedings, Council of Graduate Schools in the United States, San Francisco, 1967. Pp. 120–128. (a)

Keniston, K. Deans and dissenters. *National Association of Student Personnel Administrators*, 1967, 5, 183–193. (b)

Keniston, K. Sources of student dissent. In E. E. Sampson, H. A. Korn, & associates. *Student activism and protest*. San Francisco: Jossey-Bass, 1970. Pp. 158–190.

Keyserling, M. D. Continuing education for women—A growing challenge. Paper presented at the twenty-second National Conference on Higher Education, Chicago, March 1967. ED 015 281.

Kintzer, F. C. Nationwide pilot study on articulation. Topical Paper No. 15. ERIC Clearinghouse for Junior Colleges. Los Angeles: University of California, Los Angeles, 1970. ED 045 065.

Kivits, V. M. An experiment in teaching English composition using an oral laboratory approach. Minneapolis: University of Minnesota, General College, 1969. ED 032 871.

Klein, S. S. Student influence on teacher behavior. *American Educational Research Journal*, 1971, 8, 403–421.

Knoell, D. M., & Medsker, L. L. *Factors affecting performance of transfer students from two to four-year colleges.* Berkeley, Calif.: Center for the Study of Higher Education, 1964.

Komarovsky, M. *Women in the modern world: Their education and their dilemmas.* Boston: Little, Brown, 1953.

Koos, L. V. *The junior college.* Minneapolis: University of Minnesota, 1924.

Koos, L. V. *The community college student.* Gainesville, Fla.: The University of Florida Press, 1970.

Korn, H. A. Higher education programs and student development. *Review of Educational Research,* 1969, 39, 155–171.

Kornhauser, W. Alienation and participation in the mass university. Paper presented at the meeting of the American Orthopsychiatric Association, Washington, D.C., March 1967.

Lacognata, A. A. A comparative analysis of private and state college student academic expectations. *The Journal of Educational Research,* 1966, 60, 32–34.

Langen, T. D. F. Student assessment of teaching effectiveness. *Improving College and University Teaching,* 1966, 14, 22–25.

Lasch, C. *The new radicalism in America, 1889–1963; the intellectual as a social type.* New York: Alfred A. Knopf, 1965.

Lavin, D. E. *The prediction of academic performance: A theoretical analysis and review of research.* New York: Russell Sage Foundation, 1965.

Lawlor, G. F. An analysis of institutional press in a college of business administration. *The Journal of Experimental Education,* 1970, 38(3), 48–53.

Lehmann, I. J. Changes in critical thinking, attitudes, and values from freshman to senior years. *Journal of Educational Psychology,* 1963, 54, 305–315.

Lehmann, I. J., & Dressel, P. L. *Changes in critical thinking ability, attitudes, and values associated with college attendance.* U.S. Department of Health, Education and Welfare, Office of Education Cooperative Research Project #1646. East Lansing, Mich.: Michigan State University, 1963. ED 003 296.

Lehmann, I. J., Sinka, B. K., & Hartnett, R. T. Changes in attitudes and values associated with college attendance. *Journal of Educational Psychology,* 1966, 57, 89–98.

Leuba, C. Using groups in independent study. *Improving College and University Teaching,* 1964, 12, 26–30.

Levine, J. L. *A comparative study of two methods of teaching mathematical analysis at the college level.* (Doctoral dissertation, Columbia University) Ann Arbor, Mich.: University Microfilms, 1968. No. 68-5542.

Lindvall, C. M., & Cox, R. C. The role of evaluation in programs for individualized instruction. In R. W. Tyler (Ed.), *Educational evaluation: New roles, new means.* The Sixty-eighth Yearbook of the National Society for the Study of Education, Part II. Chicago: NSSE, 1969. Pp. 156–188.

Lins, L. J. *Methodology of enrollment projections for colleges and universities.* Washington, D.C.: American Council on Education, 1960. ED 025 919.

Lipset, S. M. *Political man; the social bases of politics.* Garden City, N.Y.: Doubleday, 1960.

Lipset, S. M. University student politics. In S. M. Lipset, & S. S. Wolin (Eds.), *The Berkeley student revolt.* New York: Anchor Books, 1965. Pp. 1–9.

Lipset, S. M., & Ladd, E. C., Jr. And what professors think about student protest and manners, morals, politics and chaos on the campus. *Psychology Today,* November 1970, 4(6), 49–51, 106.

Locke, E. A. The development of criteria of student achievement. *Educational and Psychological Measurement,* 1963, 23, 299–307.

Lombardi, J. Black studies as a curriculum catalyst. In A. M. Cohen & associates, *A constant variable: New perspectives on the community college.* San Francisco: Jossey-Bass, 1971.

Lombardi, J., & Quimby, E. A. *Black studies in the community college: A survey.* Final report. ERIC Clearinghouse for Junior Colleges, Monograph No. 13. Washington, D.C.: American Association of Junior Colleges, 1971. ED 048 851.

Lumsdaine, A. A., & May, M. A. Mass communication and educational media. *Annual Review of Psychology,* 1965, 16, 475–534.

Lyonns, G. The police car demonstration: A survey of participants. In S. M. Lipset, &

S. S. Wolin (Eds.), *The Berkeley student revolt.* New York: Anchor Books, 1965. Pp. 519–530.

Martin, W. B. *Alternative to irrelevance: A strategy for reform in higher education.* Nashville: Abingdon Press, 1968.

Mathis, A., Smith, T., & Hansen, D. College students' attitudes toward computer-assisted instruction. *Journal of Educational Psychology,* 1970, 61, 46–51.

McConnell, T. R. Problems of distributing students among institutions with varying characteristics. *North Central Association Quarterly,* 1961, 35, 226–238.

McGrath, E. J. Characteristics of outstanding college teachers. *Journal of Higher Education,* 1962, 33, 148–152.

McKeachie, W. J. Research on teaching at the college and university level. In N. L. Gage (Ed.), *Handbook of research on teaching.* Chicago: Rand McNally, 1963. Pp. 1118–1172.

McKeachie, W. J. *New developments in teaching.* New Dimensions in Higher Education, No. 16. Report No. BR-6-1722-16. Durham, N.C.: Duke University, April 1967. ED 013 341.

McKeachie, W. J. Student ratings of faculty. *AAUP Bulletin,* 1969, 55, 439–444.

McKeachie, W. J., & Lin, Y. Sex differences in student response to college teachers: Teacher warmth and teacher sex. *American Educational Research Journal,* 1971, 8, 221–226.

McKeachie, W. J., Lin, Y., & Mann, W. Student ratings of teacher effectiveness: Validity studies. *American Educational Research Journal,* 1971, 8, 435–445.

McKeachie, W. J., Lin, Y., Milholland, J., & Isaacson, R. Student affiliation motives, teacher warmth, and academic achievement. *Journal of Personality and Social Psychology,* 1966, 4, 457–461.

McKeachie, W. J., & Solomon, D. Student ratings of instructors: A validity study. *Journal of Educational Research,* 1958, 51, 379–382.

McNeil, J. D. Antidote to a school scandal. *Educational Forum,* 1966, 31(1), 69–77.

McNeil, J. D. Concomitants of using behavioral objectives in the assessment of teacher effectiveness. *Journal of Experimental Education,* 1967, 36(1), 69–74.

Medsker, L. L. *The junior college: Progress and prospect.* New York: McGraw-Hill, 1960.

Mehrens, W. A. Self-concepts of graduate students. *Journal of Educational Research,* 1967, 61, 112–113.

Menne, J. W., Hannum, T. E., Klingensmith, J. E., & Nord, D. Use of taped lectures to replace class attendance. *Audiovisual Communication Review,* 1969, 17, 42–46.

Michael, W. B. A short evaluation of the research reviewed in educational and psychological testing. *Review of Educational Research,* 1965, 25(1), 92–99.

Miles, M. B., & Charters, W. W., Jr. *Learning in social settings.* Boston: Allyn & Bacon, 1970.

Milholland, J. E. Measuring cognitive abilities. In W. McKeachie, R. Isaacson, & J. Milholland, *Research on the characteristics of effective college teaching.* Final report, Cooperative Research Project No. OE 850, Office of Education, Department of Health, Education and Welfare. Ann Arbor, Mich.: University of Michigan, 1964. Part II, Sec. A, pp. 1–15.

Moffett, G. M. *Use of instructional objectives in the supervision of student teachers.* (Doctoral dissertation, University of California, Los Angeles) Ann Arbor, Mich.: University Microfilms, 1967. No. 67-446.

Mooney, W. T., Jr., & Brasted, R. C. *A report on the education and training of chemistry teachers for two-year colleges.* Palo Alto: Stanford University, Department of Chemistry, Advisory Council on College Chemistry, 1969. ED 034 523.

Morey, A. I., Pace, C. R., & Trent, J. W. *Institutional profiles: Normative report for upperclassmen.* Los Angeles: University of California, Center for the Study of Evaluation, 1970.

Moore, F. N. *A comparative study of teaching strategies involving closed-circuit TV and programmed instruction.* Columbus, Ohio: Ohio State University, 1969.

Morsh, J. E., Burgess, G. G., & Smith, P. N. Student achievement as a measure of instructor effectiveness. Project No. 7950, Task No. 77243. San Antonio, Texas: Air Force Personnel and Training Research Center, Lackland Air Force Base, 1955.

Mouly, G. J. Research methods. In R. L. Ebel (Ed.), *Encyclopedia of educational research.* (4th ed.) New York: Macmillan, 1969. Pp. 1144–1152.

Murphy, J., & Gross, R. *Learning by television.*

New York: Fund for the Advancement of Education, 1966.

Murphy, L. B., & Raushenbush, E. (Eds.) *Achievement in the college years.* New York: Harper & Brothers, 1960.

National Faculty Association of Community and Junior Colleges. Guidelines for the preparation of community/junior college teachers. Washington, D.C.: National Faculty Association of Community and Junior Colleges, 1968. ED 031 205.

Neidt, C. O., & Hedlund, D. E. The relationship between changes in attitudes toward a course and final achievement. *Journal of Educational Research,* 1967, 61, 56–58.

Newcomer, M. *A century of higher education for American women.* New York: Harper & Brothers, 1959.

Nichols, R. C. Effects of various college characteristics on student aptitude test scores. *Journal of Educational Psychology,* 1964, 55, 45–54.

O'Connor, E. F., Jr., & Justiz, T. B. *Identifying the effective instructor.* Los Angeles, Calif.: ERIC Clearinghouse for Junior Colleges, 1970.

Oettinger, A. G. *Run, computer, run: The mythology of educational innovation.* Cambridge, Mass.: Harvard University Press, 1969.

Orr, W. C. Retention as a variable in comparing programmed and conventional instructional methods. *Journal of Educational Research,* 1968, 62, 11–13.

Overturf, C. L., & Price, E. C. *Student rating of faculty at St. Johns River Junior College, with addendum for Albany Junior College.* Palatka, Fla.: St. Johns River Junior College, 1966. ED 013 066.

Pace, C. R. Methods of describing college cultures. *Teachers College Record,* 1962, 63, 267–277.

Pace, C. R. *College and University Environment Scales (CUES): Preliminary technical manual.* Princeton, N.J.: Educational Testing Service, 1963.

Pace, C. R. The influence of academic and student subcultures in college and university environments. U.S. Office of Education, Cooperative Research Project No. 1083. Washington, D.C.: U.S. Office of Education, 1964. ED 003 037.

Pace, C. R. *CUES technical manual.* (2nd ed.)

Princeton, N.J.: Educational Testing Service, 1969.

Painter, E. G. Women: The last of the discriminated. *Journal of the National Association of Women Deans and Counselors,* 1971, 34, 59–63.

Parkes, J. C. Impact of an experimental curriculum upon students at Austin College. In R. L. Sutherland, & others (Eds.), *Personality factors on the college campus: Review of a symposium.* Austin, Tex.: Hogg Foundation for Mental Health, 1962. Pp. 136–141.

Parsons, T. Youth in the context of American society. In E. H. Erikson (Ed.), *The challenge of youth.* Garden City, N.Y.: Anchor Books, 1965. Pp. 110–141.

Parsons, T., & Clark, K. B. (Eds.) *The Negro American.* Boston: Houghton Mifflin, 1966.

Pervin, L. A. A twenty-college study of student college interaction using TAPE (transactional analysis of personality and environment): Rationale, reliability and validity. *Journal of Educational Psychology,* 1967, 58, 290–302.

Peterson, R. E. The scope of organized student protest in 1964–65. Report to the meeting of the American Psychological Association, Chicago, September 1965.

Peterson, R. E. *The scope of organized student protest in 1964–1965.* Princeton: Educational Testing Service, 1966.

Peterson, R. E. Reform in higher education—demands of the left and right. *Liberal Education,* 1969, 55(1), 60–77.

Plant, W. T. Longitudinal changes in intolerance and authoritarianism for subjects differing in amount of college education over four years. *Genetic Psychology Monographs,* 1965, 72, 247–287.

Plant, W. T., & Minium, E. W. Differential personality development in young adults of markedly different aptitude levels. *Journal of Educational Psychology,* 1967, 58, 141–152.

Popham, W. J. *Development of a performance test of teaching proficiency.* Final report, U.S. Office of Education Project No. 5-0566-2-12-1. Washington, D.C.: U.S. Office of Education, 1967. ED 013 242.

Popham, W. J. The performance test: A new approach to the assessment of teaching proficiency. *Journal of Teacher Education,* 1968, 19(2), 216–222.

Popham, W. J. Performance tests of teaching proficiency: Rationale, development, and validation. *American Educational Research Journal,* 1971, 8, 105–117.

Popham, W. J., & Husek, T. R. Implications of criterion-referenced measurement. *Journal of Educational Measurement,* 1969, 6(1), 1–9.

Postlethwait, S. N. *Plant science: A study guide with an audio tutorial approach.* Minneapolis: Burgess, 1966.

Postlethwait, S. N., Novak, J., & Murray, H. *An integrated experience approach to learning, with emphasis on independent study.* Minneapolis: Burgess, 1964.

Potter, W. H. Self-appraisal of advanced degree candidates. *Journal of Educational Research,* 1962, 55, 279–281.

Powell, W. J., & Jourard, S. M. Some objective evidence of immaturity in underachieving college students. *Journal of Counseling Psychology,* 1963, 10, 276–282.

Projections of college faculty, 1950–70. *Higher Education,* 1963, 9, 22–23.

Ramsey, R. R., Jr. A subcultural approach to academic behavior. *Journal of Educational Sociology,* 1962, 35, 355–376.

Rand, L. Masculinity or femininity? Differentiating career-oriented and homemaking-oriented college freshman women. *Journal of Counseling Psychology,* 1968, 15, 444–450.

Rayder, N. F. *College student ratings of instructors.* East Lansing: Michigan State University, Office of Evaluation Services, 1968. ED 021 527. (a)

Rayder, N. F. College student ratings of instructors. *Journal of Experimental Education,* 1968, 37(2), 76–81. (b)

Rees, R. D. Dimensions of students' points of view in rating college teachers. *Journal of Educational Psychology,* 1969, 60, 476–482.

Reich, C. A. *The greening of America.* New York: Random House, 1970.

Reimer, M. K. J. *A proposed curriculum for the University of Minnesota Technical College.* (Doctoral dissertation, University of North Dakota) Ann Arbor, Mich.: University Microfilms, 1969. No. 69-8545.

Renner, R. R. A successful rating scale. *Improving College and University Teaching,* 1967, 15, 12–14.

Richards, J. M., Jr., & Holland, J. L. A factor analysis of student "explanations" of their choice of a college. *ACT Research Report,* No. 8. Iowa City, Iowa: American College Testing Program, 1965.

Richards, J. M., Jr., Rand, L. M., & Rand, L. P. Description of junior colleges. *Journal of Educational Psychology,* 1966, 57, 207–214.

Richardson, V., & Renner, J. W. A study of the inquiry-discovery method of laboratory instruction. *Journal of Chemical Education,* 1970, 47, 77–79.

Riesman, D., & Jencks, C. The viability of the American college. In N. Sanford (Ed.), *The American college.* New York: John Wiley, 1962. Pp. 74–192.

Ritter, C. American college student values: Relationship to selected personal and academic variables. Unpublished manuscript, Colorado State College, 1969.

Robinson, A. L., Foster, C. C., & Ogilvie, D. H. *Black studies in the university: A symposium.* New Haven: Yale University Press, 1969.

Robinson, L. H. *The status of academic women.* Washington, D.C.: ERIC Clearinghouse on Higher Education, 1971.

Roderick, M., & Anderson, R. C. Programmed introduction to psychology vs. textbook style summary of the same lesson. *Journal of Educational Psychology,* 1968, 59, 381–387.

Rogers, J. T. *Retired military personnel as junior college instructors: An analysis conducted in Florida public colleges.* (Doctoral dissertation, Florida State University) Ann Arbor, Mich.: University Microfilms, 1965. No. 65-336. ED 012 578. (a)

Rogers, J. T. Staffing our colleges in the present decade. *Teachers College Record,* 1965, 67, 134–139. (b)

Rose, C. A. The development of precision instruments for assessing teacher effectiveness. Unpublished master's thesis, University of California at Los Angeles, 1971.

Rose, H. A. Prediction and prevention of freshman attrition. *Journal of Counseling Psychology,* 1965, 12, 399–403.

Rose, H. A., & Elton, C. F. Another look at the college dropout. *Journal of Counseling Psychology,* 1966, 13, 242–245.

Rosenberg, L. A., McHenry, T. B., & Rosenberg, A. M. Sociometric ratings as predictors of academic performance. *Journal of Applied Psychology,* 46, 1962, 265–268.

Rosenfeld, H. M. Nonverbal reciprocation of approval: An experimental analysis. *Journal of Experimental Social Psychology*, 1967, 3, 102–111.

Rosenshine, B. Teaching behavior related to pupil achievement: A review of research. In I. Westbury, & A. A. Bellack (Eds.), *Research into classroom processes*. New York: Teachers College Press, 1971. Pp. 51–98.

Roszak, T. *The making of a counter-culture*. Garden City, N.Y.: Doubleday, 1969.

Roueche, J. E., & Pitman, J. C. *A modest proposal: Students can learn*. San Francisco: Jossey-Bass, 1972.

Rowbotham, N. D. *The comparison of an auto-tutorial laboratory and a traditional laboratory in physical science*. (Doctoral dissertation, University of Arkansas) Ann Arbor, Mich.: University Microfilms, 1970. No. 70-405.

Russell, H. E. Interrelations of some indices of instructor effectiveness: An exploratory study. Unpublished doctoral dissertation, University of Pittsburgh, 1951.

Russell, P. D., & Snyder, W. U. Counselor anxiety in relation to amount of clinical experience and quality of affect demonstrated by clients. *Journal of Consulting Psychology*, 1963, 27, 358–363.

Ryans, D. G. *Characteristics of teachers, their description, comparison, and appraisal*. Washington, D.C.: American Council on Education, 1960.

Sampson, E. E. Student activism and the decade of protest. *Journal of Social Issues*, 1967, 23(3), 1–33.

Sampson, E. E., Korn, H. A., & associates. *Student activism and protest*. San Francisco: Jossey-Bass, 1970.

Sanford, N. Research and policy in higher education. In N. Sanford (Ed.), *The American college*. New York: John Wiley, 1962. Pp. 1009–1034.

Sarbin, T. R., & Allen, V. L. Increasing participation in a natural group setting: A preliminary report. *The Psychological Record*, 1968, 18, 1–7.

Schoen, W. T., Jr. The campus climate: Student perception and faculty idealism. *Journal of Educational Research*, 1966, 60, 3–7.

Schramm, W. *The research on programmed instruction. An annotated bibliography*. U.S. Office of Education Bulletin No. 35. Washington, D.C.: Government Printing Office, 1964.

Schwartz, A. J. *Comparative values and achievement of Mexican-American and Anglo pupils*. CSE Report No. 37. Los Angeles: University of California, Center for the Study of Evaluation, 1969.

Schwartz, J. Medicine as a vocational choice among undergraduate women. *Journal of the National Association of Women Deans and Counselors*, 1969, 33, 13–18.

Selvin, H., & Hagstrom, W. Determinants of support for civil liberties. *British Journal of Sociology*, 1960, 11, 51–73.

Sexton, P. C. *The feminized male: Classrooms, white collars and the decline of manliness*. New York: Vintage Books, 1969.

Shafer, E. G. *Academic effectiveness of ability grouping and a student tutorial-counseling program at Madison College*. (Doctoral dissertation, Florida State University) Ann Arbor, Mich.: University Microfilms, 1969. No. 69-11,329.

Shugrue, M. F. *The national study of English in the junior college*. A joint project of the Modern Language Association, the National Council of Teachers of English, and the American Association of Junior Colleges. New York: ERIC Clearinghouse on the Teaching of English in Higher Education, The Modern Language Association, 1970. (Funded by the Carnegie Corporation of New York, 1968–69.) ED 037 480.

Singer, D. S. Do we need a community college institute? *Junior College Journal*, 1968, 39(2), 36–40.

Singletary, O. A. Faculty recruitment and retention in the liberal arts college. *Liberal Education*, 1967, 53, 336–343.

Soar, R. S. *An integrative approach to classroom learning*. Grant No. 5-R11 MH 01096 and Grant No. 7-R11 MH 02045. Philadelphia: Temple University, 1966. ED 033 749.

Solomon, D., Rosenberg, L., & Bezdek, W. E. Teacher behavior and student learning. *Journal of Educational Psychology*, 1964, 55, 23–30.

Somers, R. H. The mainsprings of the rebellion: A survey of Berkeley students in November, 1964. In S. M. Lipset, & S. S. Wolin (Eds.), *The Berkeley student revolt*. New York: Anchor Books, 1965. Pp. 530–557.

Sorenson, A. G., Husek, T. R., & Yu, C. Divergent concepts of teacher role: An approach to the measurement of teacher effectiveness. *Journal of Educational Psychology*, 1963, 54, 287–294.

Sorenson, G., & Gross, C. F. Teacher appraisal —a matching process. An Occasional Report. Los Angeles: University of California, Los Angeles, Graduate School of Education, Center for the Study of Evaluation, 1967. ED 016 299.

Sorey, K. E. *A study of the distinguishing personality characteristics of college faculty who are superior in regard to the teaching function.* (Doctoral dissertation, Oklahoma State University) Ann Arbor, Mich.: University Microfilms, 1968. No. 68-8502.

Spaights, E. Students appraise teachers' methods and attitudes. *Improving College and University Teaching,* 1967, 15, 15–17.

Spielberger, C. D., Weitz, H., & Denny, J. P. Group counseling and the academic performance of anxious college freshmen. *Journal of Counseling Psychology,* 1962, 9, 195–204.

Stecklein, J. E., Ringo, E. N., & Macdonald, J. D. Students enrolled in the T. V. College General Extension Division, Fall, 1965. *University of Minnesota T. V. College Research Report* No. 3. Minneapolis: University of Minnesota, Minnesota Bureau of Institutional Research, 1966.

Stern, G. G. Environments for learning. In N. Sanford (Ed.), *The American college.* New York: John Wiley, 1962. Pp. 690–730. (a)

Stern, G. G. The measurement of psychological characteristics of students and learning environments. In S. Messick, & J. Ross (Eds.), *Measurement in personality and cognition.* New York: John Wiley, 1962. Pp. 27–68. (b)

Stern, G. G. Characteristics of the intellectual climate in college environments. *Harvard Educational Review,* 1963, 33, 5–41.

Stones, E. Students' attitudes to the size of teaching groups. *Educational Review,* 1969, 21, 98–108.

Tallmadge, G. K., & Shearer, J. W. Study of training equipment and individual differences. Technical Report NAVTRADEVCEN 66-C-0043-1. Orlando, Fla.: Naval Training Device Center, March 1967.

Tallmadge, G. K., & Shearer, J. W. Relationships among learning styles, instructional methods, and the nature of learning experiences. *Journal of Educational Psychology,* 1969, 60, 222–230.

Taylor, D. R., Lipscomb, E., & Rosemier, R. Live versus videotaped student-teacher inter-action. *Audio-visual Communication Review,* 1969, 17, 47–51.

Taylor, H. *Students without teachers: The crisis in the university.* New York: McGraw-Hill, 1969.

Taylor, R. G., Cartwright, P., & Hanson, G. R. Tutorial programs for freshman engineering students: Effect on grades and attrition. *Journal of Experimental Education,* 1970, 38(3), 87–92.

Teigland, J. J. The relationship between measured teacher attitude change and certain personality characteristics. *The Journal of Educational Research,* 1966, 60, 84–85.

Telford, C. W., & Plant, W. T. The psychological impact of the public two-year college on certain non-intellectual functions. U.S. Office of Education, Cooperative Research Project No. 914. San Jose, Calif.: San Jose State College, 1963. ED 002 985.

Thistlethwaite, D. L. *Effects of college upon student aspirations.* Technical Report to the U.S. Office of Education, Cooperative Research Project No. D-098. Nashville, Tenn.: Vanderbilt University, 1965.

Thomas, A. H. Counselor response to divergent vocational goals of a female client in terms of acceptance appropriateness and need for further counseling. Unpublished doctoral dissertation, Michigan State University, 1967.

Thornton, J. W. *The community junior college.* (2nd ed.) New York: John Wiley, 1966.

Tillery, D. et al. *SCOPE: School to college: Opportunities for post-secondary education.* Berkeley, Calif.: University of California, Center for Research and Development in Higher Education, 1972.

Trent, J. W. The decision to go to college: An accumulative multivariate process. Report No. 64. Los Angeles: University of California, Los Angeles, Center for the Study of Evaluation, November 1970. ED 047 651. (a)

Trent, J. W. Revolution, reformation, and reevaluation. In E. E. Sampson, H. A. Korn, & associates, *Student activism and protest.* San Francisco: Jossey-Bass, 1970. Pp. 23–59. (b)

Trent, J. W. Toward educational improvement: Engineering 45. Report No. 61. Los Angeles: University of California, Los Angeles, Center for the Study of Evaluation, 1970. (c)

Trent, J. W. *In and out of college: Processes and patterns of college attendance.* San Francisco: Jossey-Bass, in press.

Trent, J. W., & Craise, J. L. Commitment and conformity in the American college. *Journal of Social Issues,* 1967, 23(3), 34–51.

Trent, J. W., & Golds, J. *Catholics in college: Religious commitment and the intellectual life.* Chicago: University of Chicago Press, 1967.

Trent, J. W., & Medsker, L. L. *Beyond high school.* San Francisco: Jossey-Bass, 1968.

Trzebiatowski, G. (Ed.) *Guide to audiovisual terminology. Product information supplement No. 6.* New York: Educational Products Information Exchange Institute, 1968. ED 021 440.

Tucker, L. R. Formal models for a central prediction system. *Psychometric Monograph No. 10.* Richmond, Va.: Psychometric Society, 1963. (a)

Tucker, L. R. Implications of factor analysis of three-way matrices for measurement of change. In C. W. Harris (Ed.), *Problems in measuring change.* Madison: University of Wisconsin Press, 1963. Pp. 122–137. (b)

Tuckman, B. W., & Oliver, W. F. Effectiveness of feedback to teachers as a function of source. *Journal of Educational Psychology,* 1968, 59, 297–301.

Turner, R. L. Pupil influence on teacher behavior. *Classroom Interaction Newsletter,* 1967, 3, 5–8.

University of Miami. Diplomate in collegiate teaching: Preliminary information. Coral Gables, Fla.: University of Miami, 1969. ED 029 828.

Vaccaro, L. C. Faculty recruitment by community colleges. *Michigan Education Journal,* 1964, 41(9), 11–14.

Voeks, V. W. Publications and teaching effectiveness: A search for some relationship. *Journal of Higher Education,* 1962, 33, 212–218.

Walker, C. R., & Coffelt, J. J. Physical facilities for higher education in Oklahoma. *Self-study report No. 5.* Oklahoma City, Okla.: Oklahoma State Regents for Higher Education, 1964.

Watson, G. Annotated bibliography. In S. Baskin, G. Watson, J. Dixon, & P. Manion (Eds.), *Innovation in higher education: Developments, research and priorities.* Durham, N.C.: Duke University, 1967. Pp. 87–121. ED 013 380.

Watts, W. A., & Whittaker, D. Free speech advocates at Berkeley. *Journal of Applied Behavioral Science,* 1966, 2(1), 41–62.

Webster, H., Freedman, M. B., & Heist, P. Personality changes in college students. In N. Sanford (Ed.), *The American college.* New York: John Wiley, 1962. Pp. 811–846.

Which way black America? Separation? Integration? Liberation? *Ebony,* Special Issue, August 1970.

White, C. C. *The use of programed texts for remedial mathematics instruction in college.* (Doctoral dissertation, Utah State University) Ann Arbor, Mich.: University Microfilms, 1970. No. 70-2445.

Whiteis, U. E. Poor scholarship in college. *Harvard Educational Review,* 1962, 32, 3–38.

Wortham, M. The case for a Doctor of Arts degree: A view from junior college faculty. *AAUP Bulletin,* 1967, 53, 372–377.

Wright, D. M. Junior college students' view of women's roles. *Journal of the National Association of Women Deans and Counselors,* 1967, 30, 71–77.

Yamamoto, K., & Dizney, H. F. Eight professors—A study on college students' preferences among their teachers. *Journal of Educational Psychology,* 1966, 57, 146–150.

Yonge, G. D., & Sassenrath, J. M. Student personality correlates of teacher ratings. *Journal of Educational Psychology,* 1968, 59, 44–52.

Young, D. D. The effects of instruction through team learning on achievement in a general education college course in physical science. Buffalo: State University of New York, 1969. ED 041 777.

Yuker, H. E. A comparison of the performances of team-taught and individually-taught classes in freshman English. Hempstead, N.Y.: Hofstra University, Office of Instructional Research, 1966. ED 036 279.

CHAPTER **33** Research on Teaching Literature, Language and Composition

NATHAN S. BLOUNT
University of Wisconsin

By and large, the research cited in this chapter was reported during the decade 1960–1970. Other sources, named under each main heading, review the research of earlier decades.

This chapter is bound by the constraints of the categories literature, language and composition, none of them being mutually exclusive. Certain topics which members of the profession might wish to see as main headings remain for the most part empty categories: research in the study of oral expression, creative dramatics, humanities, multimedia. Discussion of the research in reading appears as Chapter 28 in this volume.

The decade 1960–1970 was marked by considerable effort to maintain and enhance a tradition of research in the teaching of English. The U. S. Office of Education funded such meetings as the conference on research design and the teaching of English (Russell, Early, & Farrell, 1964), the conference on needed research in the teaching of English (Steinberg, 1963) and the Allerton Park Conference (Wasson, 1962). It sponsored curriculum study centers from which research evolved (Bennett, 1966b; Shugrue, 1966). It funded research projects (e.g.,

Hook, Jacobs, & Crisp, 1969; Mellon, 1967) to be cited in the pages to follow. The National Council of Teachers of English made research available to its membership through issues of *Elementary English* and *English Journal*, and through *Research in the Teaching of English*. It published a series of distinguished research monographs (e.g., Hunt, 1965; Loban, 1963; Squire, 1964). It used its committees to synthesize the results of research (Braddock, Lloyd-Jones, & Schoer, 1963; Petty, Herold, & Stoll, 1968). It presented annual awards to distinguished researchers in English. The National Council of Teachers of English/ Educational Resources Information Center published summaries of research in National Council of Teachers of English journals, prepared indexes of documents relating to English teaching which had been processed into the Educational Resources Information Center system, and commissioned state-of-the-art papers (e.g., Hoetker, 1969; Odland, 1969). The universities produced an increasing number of Ph.D.s in Education–English, and the numbers of dissertations, including many experimental studies, grew steadily.

The studies to be cited hereafter are selected, not exhaustive. It is possible that because of problems of theoretical foundation, design or analysis the studies are not uniformly excellent in quality, but when less than excellent they suggest the hypotheses and techniques of the recent past which will be scrutinized by a new generation of researchers.

LITERATURE

The scope of the research in the teaching of literature is wide. However, the number of visible, as opposed to fugitive, experimental studies is few; many of the contributions are descriptive. The discussion here deals with the general areas curriculum and instruction, responses to literature, measurement, and teacher preparation.

Curriculum and Instruction

Comprehensive reviews which include information on the history of teaching literature in the United States have been written by Meckel (1963), Mersand (1960), Pooley (1960), and Squire (1969). Squire (1969) also provides valuable sections on recent research involving objectives, curriculum, instruction, reading interests, response, evaluation and teacher preparation. Shane and Mulry (1963) and Odland (1969) have synthesized knowledge on current practices and on research and development in teaching literature in the elementary school.

Observers in the National Study of High School English Programs (Squire & Applebee, 1966) found class time emphasizing literary study to be 46 percent in tenth grade, 61.5 percent in twelfth grade and 40.8 percent in classes of terminal students. Data showed representative current objectives in teaching literature as ranked by selected English department chairmen, from most to least importance, to be: the student's intellectual and emotional development through literature, the student's acquaintance with literary tradition, the student's ability to comprehend the meaning and development

of a particular work, the student's aesthetic response and appreciation. Data from a check list indicated that 95 percent of all students in the study were instructed in such concepts as alliteration, allusion, blank verse, connotation, epic, paradox and satire. Observers found the teaching of literature integrally related to the teaching of composition and to other aspects of the English curriculum. Data showed 22 percent of classroom time spent in recitation and 21 percent in lecture; 19.5 percent of classroom time was devoted to class discussion and 2.2 percent to Socratic questioning. Outstanding literature programs combined intensive analytical study with wide personal reading of worthwhile selections.

Surveys of titles used in high-school literature study suggest both unity and diversity. Anderson (1964) obtained responses from 22 public, 192 independent, 54 urban and 223 Catholic schools to a questionnaire on works taught in each grade of secondary schools. Over 1000 titles were being taught; *Macbeth* headed all lists, with *Julius Caesar* next. Squire and Applebee (1966), too, found *Macbeth* ranked first and *Julius Caesar,* second, but they went on to list many other titles being taught. Whitman (1964), reporting on the impact of books read in high school on recent graduates, listed 416 titles cited by 975 students as significant in shaping their attitudes, values or thoughts.

To help the classroom teacher with a burgeoning list of titles, specialists helped analyze various selections and their values for teaching and for learning. D. V. Smith (1963) analyzed developments in 50 years of children's books. Kingston (1969) reported on 53 books exemplifying the best examples of the tragic mode currently available in realistic fiction for eight- to twelve-year-old children. Kochant (1969) investigated the image of the American elementary-school experience as portrayed in contemporary realistic fiction for eight- to twelve-year-old children. Lynch and Evans (1963) criticized secondary-school literature anthologies for lack of clear purpose, for altering selections, and for letting organization dictate content, among other things. Comparing objectives for the study of literature expressed by national professional groups with content of secondary-school textbooks, Berberi (1966) found predominantly traditional views in the thirties, some modern approaches in the fifties, and a reemphasis on traditional content and approaches in the sixties. Agee (1967) used archetypal analysis to examine the initiation theme in selected contemporary American novels dealing with adolescents. Dedmond (1969) examined the maturation theme in recent American drama. Analyzing 30 junior novels suggested by expert librarians on the basis of popularity with teenagers, Dunning (1959) presented titles valuable for theme-centered units, providing for individual differences in extensive reading programs. Hipple (1969) used H. S. Broudy's value categories (economic values; health, body, and recreational values; social values; moral values; aesthetic values; intellectual values; and religious values) to discover values in selected American novels and to suggest uses of these values in high-school English classes.

Hoetker and Robb (1969) compared objectives for teaching drama as held by English teachers, school administrators and drama teachers. While they found differences in attitudes toward problems of school-theatre projects, differences which were functions of occupational groupings, the investigators found general agreement as to the relative importance of various objectives for drama.

Use of contemporary literature has created problems of censorship. On the basis of responses to a questionnaire sent to members of the National Council of Teachers of English secondary section, Ahrens (1966) found that ⅔ of the books receiving complaints appear on well-known standard lists of books for use in high school. Of the 616 teachers responding, 78 (12.6 percent) reported censorship incidents. Studying senior

high-school libraries, Farley (1965) found that a majority of librarians interviewed had known attempts at censorship by members of the communities which they served; however, voluntary censorship was more prevalent than involuntary censorship. The National Council of Teachers of English Committee to Report on Case Studies on Censorship (Hove, 1967) published case studies on dealing with efforts at censorship.

A factor-analytic study by Rees and Pedersen (1965) suggested that students experiencing a broad range of poetry early in the school years will give positive evaluations to later poetic experiences.

Monson (1967) investigated the responses of fifth-grade children to humor in literature. Different techniques of questioning—structured and nonstructured—resulted in different responses. Males viewed selections as humorous more frequently than females when items were presented in a structured situation.

Research in the uses of audio-visual materials in the teaching of literature is rare. Studying the effects of a film version of selected short stories on the responses of junior high-school students, Levinson (1964) reported that viewing films based on short stories, either before or after reading, improved responses of both good and poor readers. C. E. White (1968) reported that students studying American literature in experimental television classes learned as well as students studying in conventional American literature classes.

R. J. Smith (1968) found that assignment to students of a creative writing task preparatory to their reading a short story is effective in stimulating creative thinking about that story. He also reported that the kind of writing task assigned prior to reading a short story makes a difference in student attitudes toward the story.

Several studies have considered the effect of literature on divergent thinking. In an experiment with fourth- and fifth-grade students, Casper (1965) found a statistically significant effect of Junior Great Books on divergent thinking. Hackett, Brown, and Michael (1968) reported an investigation directed toward determining possible difference in the average level of achievement between a) an experimental group of students exposed to a method involving a minimum threat to self-esteem, student participation in the development of cognitive understandings and divergent thinking and b) a control group of students taught by a method involving acquisition of factual information using routine questions with potential threat-inducing properties and convergent thinking. As measured by both an essay and an objective examination, experimental subjects given the treatment facilitating divergent processes performed significantly better than did subjects in the control group. Grindstaff (1969) reported responses to the novel of tenth-grade students assigned to three groups: a group studying by a structural-analysis method, a group studying by an experiential-reflective-analysis method, and a control group. Both treatment groups demonstrated more divergent responses and fewer difficulties in reading than did the control group. The experiential-analysis approach seemed superior to the structural-analysis approach as a method of teaching the novel to teenagers.

Evidence on the utility of team teaching is conflicting. For ninth-grade students Scott (1966) found a traditional approach more effective than a team-teaching approach for progress in analyzing and interpreting literature. Studying twelfth-grade students, Waters (1969) reported that team teaching and traditional self-contained classroom teaching produced the same achievement in literary comprehension and appreciation. Lester (1966) suggested that team teaching was significantly more effective than departmental organization in influencing scholastic achievement in English for eighth-grade students.

Three investigators have studied inquiry approaches in the literature program. Using Essay Question 2, Grade 11, End-of-Year Examinations in English for College-Bound

Students as an instrument to measure students' ability to interpret literature, Hopkins (1968) found no significant differences in scores between a group taught by a deductive method and a group taught by an inductive discovery methodology. LaRocque (1966) conducted an experimental study to determine differences in student learning attributable to inductive and deductive methods of teaching figurative language to eigthth-grade students. Results of tests of retention and transfer indicated a) that mean scores were higher ($p < 0.01$) for both inductive and deductive groups than for a control population, b) that inductive method was consistently less effective with students of low mental ability, and c) that the deductive method tended to greater overall effectiveness in teaching figurative language ($p < 0.01$). Weiss (1969) compared the effects of two methods of teaching poetry—inductive and programmed—on the responses of urban eleventh-grade students. Analyses of a transfer test did not show that programmed instruction altered the fundamental approach or quantity of responses to poetry. However, there was evidence that the inductive method produced significant quantitative gains.

Appleby (1968) sought to investigate what differences, if any, result when high-school students who have experienced an individualized reading approach to the study of literature (experimental subjects) are compared with students who have not had an individualized approach (control groups). Data collected at the end of one semester of treatment were through Test 7, Form Y-3, "Ability to Interpret Literary Materials" of the Iowa Tests of Educational Development and the Inventory of Satisfactions Found in Reading Fiction. Experimental subjects had fewer dislikes of fiction than control subjects and found more satisfaction in reading fiction for characterization, style and technique. Experimental subjects were also more inclined to find satisfaction in the possible contributions of literature to their self-improvement. Appleby concluded that students in a one-semester English elective using an individualized reading approach are more inclined to derive satisfaction from literature study than are students in a required English program.

Fader and McNeil (1968) reported research on the effects of a "saturation" and "diffusion" program in which every classroom contains abundant magazines, paperbacks and newspapers and in which every teacher is an English teacher. The individualized reading approach used with the treatment population was compared with a more conventional approach used with a control group on teachers' perceptions of students' attitudes (toward literacy, school and self), performance and personality. Findings suggested that the experimental program produced significant improvement in such factors as attitude by the student toward his own literary efforts and toward reading newspapers, magazines and books.

Milgrim (1968) compared the effects of classics and contemporary works of literature on the attitudes of twelfth-grade students in urban areas toward selected moral values. Data from Havighurst and Taba's Students' Beliefs Test suggested that contemporary works proved at least as effective as classics in affecting attitudes toward such values as friendliness, honesty, loyalty and moral courage.

Reading interests surveys have played a role in the research used in curriculum development and in teaching practices for a number of decades. Studies of interests and tastes of elementary-school children have been analyzed by Odland (1969), studies of secondary-school students by Squire (1969) and by McKay (1969). Researchers have often employed checklists and questionnaires to determine interests and have analyzed data on correlates of reading—sex, age, mental ability, race, aspects of personality, socioeconomic factors—and data on the characteristics of the material read—its content, readability, etc.

A recent example of research on the char-acteristics of literature read is a study (Nelms, 1968) which examined preferences of a selected group of adolescents in poetry. Students tended to prefer poems with a narrative interest rather than the brief lyric poem. Modern poems fared better than "classics." Clarity and comprehension were important factors; there was a negative relationship between students' evaluations and complex syntax. Appeal of subject matter was a considerable factor: students' favorable evaluations were highly related to a combination of masculine interest, realism, and emotional versus rational appeal.

Some of the findings on the effects of literature study reported by various researchers may be accounted for in small part by studies involving observation and classification of language interaction and cognitive goals in classroom teaching and testing.

According to observers in the National Study on High School English (Squire & Applebee, 1966), 43 percent of classroom time was devoted to lecture or recitation, 19.5 percent to discussion. Observers in the study found many teachers unable to ask consistently appropriate questions which might stimulate discussion and lead to generalizations.

Hoetker (1968) reported on teacher-questioning behavior in junior high-school English classes. The mean teacher questioning rate per minute of substantive talk was 5.17 questions per minute or one teacher question every 11.8 seconds. This questioning rate appeared unrelated to grade level or to ability level. These verbal behavior patterns in observed classrooms revealed patterns similar to those described by Bellack, Kliebard, Hyman, and Smith (1966).

Pfeiffer (1967) studied verbal interaction and cognitive goals at different ability levels in eleventh-grade English classes. Using Flanders's Interaction Analysis, the investigator found that English teachers did not differentiate patterns of teacher-pupil interaction in classes of differing levels of ability. Most teachers observed used direct influence (criticism, directions, or lecture) more than indirect influence (praise, questions, use of students' ideas). Using the six major categories from Bloom's *Taxonomy*, Pfeiffer also analyzed teacher-constructed tests and found that teachers indicated a given category of cognitive goals to be important but then tested for another category. Another study (Hirshfield, 1967) using Bloom's *Taxonomy* (1956) examined teacher questioning in class and in the testing program. The English teachers observed devoted more classroom time to knowledge than to comprehension. Analysis of objective-type test questions revealed heavy concentration on knowledge and light concentration on comprehension.

Responses to Literature

Squire (1969) summarized research on the ways in which readers respond to a literary work, the studies mentioned including the important work of Loban (1954), Richards (1929) and Taba (1955).

A method of studying the responses of adolescent readers to literature was reported by Squire (1964), who analyzed the reactions of ninth- and tenth-grade students to four short stories. He recorded responses of 27 males and 25 females to the stories and coded and classified the responses into seven categories: literary judgments, interpretational responses, narrational reactions, associational responses, self-involvement, prescriptive judgments, and miscellaneous. Responses coded in interpretational response (a response in which the reader generalizes and tries to find the story's meaning, its motivational forces and the nature of its characters) occurred more frequently than any other response category. The investigator found a strong positive relationship between the number of responses in literary judgment and the number of responses indicating self-involvement. He reported that literary judgments occur early in responding to a story or after completion of reading of a story, but that such judgments decline perceptibly while the student is involved in reading the story. Squire also identified six sources of difficulty in literary appreciation which create problems for adolescents reading fiction: failure to grasp meaning, reliance on stock responses, happiness binding, critical predispositions, irrelevant associations, and search for certainty.

Using Squire's seven categories of student responses to literature to classify responses of 54 college students to three novels, J. R. Wilson (1966) examined college students' study of the novel. Data were responses written before and after group discussion. The investigator reported study of the novel to result in more interpretation, less retelling of the story and fewer self-involvement responses.

An important contribution to a theory of response to literature is the work of Purves with Rippere (1968), who have reported a controlling point of view or framework for inspecting students' responses to literature. Incorporating examination of student papers, responses of teachers and responses of a number of critics, Purves has categorized the elements of writing about a literary work to be the elements a) engagement-involvement, b) perception, c) interpretation and d) evaluation. Each of the four categories contains subheadings which help account for every sentence in a critical essay. He makes two disclaimers—that the elements are not exhaustive and that the elements are not taxonomical.

Incorporating a version of Purves's response categories, Cooper (1969) sought to determine the preferred modes of literary response among eleventh-grade students in relation to the consistency of their reactions to three dissimilar short stories. He found that the students had a preferred way of responding to the short story: interpretation was more prevalent than the other three Purves categories. He also reported that neither story type nor teacher-stated methods and goal result in a significant effect on the student's preferred mode of response.

Ring (1969) described the interpretive processes employed by twelfth-grade students to three short stories. Data were from free written responses, structured responses, and responses to a questionnaire on reading behavior. Ring found free responses limited in scope—often to giving personal preference, and to describing and repeating details. He found students to be dealing with the short stories as objective reports of human behavior rather than as literature. Ring identified four reading and interpreting difficulties: egocentrism, failure to maintain aesthetic distance from the stories, failure to perceive the focus of the stories, and invention. Analysis of structured responses revealed no characteristic process of interpretation or pattern of perception. Analysis of a questionnaire showed students' statements of their own behavior in reading and interpreting to be fairly accurate descriptions.

Measurement

Squire (1969) has suggested that instruments for evaluation of instruction in literature have not yet achieved expected standards of reliability and validity.

Typical of the attempts to develop instruments during the sixties are the following studies. Andresen (1969) designed a scale to evaluate the profundity of themes in literature, a scale with five levels of literary profundity: physical plane, mental plane, moral plane, psychological plane and philosophical plane. He determined validity through the opinions of experts in literature and reliability through coefficient of correlation and through item analysis; and stopped questioning the validity of his instrument. Using semantic differential scales, Rees and Pedersen (1965) constructed the Poetic Evaluation Scale to measure individual differences in the evaluation of poetry. Lawson (1969) developed two equivalent forms of a poetry test for grades 11 and 12 to measure students' ability to understand and appreciate poetry, and he reported reliability and validity coefficients, and indices of item difficulty and discrimination, all within ranges

suggested by various testing authorities. Zais (1969) developed a scale to measure sophistication of reading interests but suggested further testing and revision to improve reliability and construct validity.

In addition to using several standardized tests of intelligence to determine the impact of reading, Fader and McNeil (1968) developed several research instruments in terms of psychological and behavioral phenomena: a Teacher's Behavior Rating Sheet, a Teacher's Evaluation Form, a "How Much Do You Like?" Form, a Behavioral Rating Form, a "How Do You Feel About Things in Class?" a Literary Attitude Scale and a Verbal Proficiency Test.

At the time of the writing of this chapter the tests on literature prepared for the National Assessment of Education in the United States are still a year away.

Teacher Preparation

The National Council of Teachers of English Committee on the National Interest (1961) reported state requirements for teaching in an elementary school to range from 16 to 46 (median 21) semester hours of professional education, and to range from 0 to 18 (median 6) in English and the related areas dramatics, journalism and speech. While 73.1 percent of elementary teachers were required to complete a course in children's literature prior to certification, the average number of semester hours devoted to literature study averaged not more than six to eight. The Committee also reported state requirements to teach English in secondary schools to include 12 to 30 (median 18) semester hours of college credits in English and the related areas of dramatics, journalism and speech. In a second published report, this Committee (1964) found that only half (51.9 percent) of secondary-school English teachers considered themselves well prepared to teach literature.

Hook, Jacobs, and Crisp (1969) reported teachers of English better prepared in literature than in composition or language but noted deficiencies in preparation in applied criticism, literature written for young people, literary backgrounds and world or comparative literature. The investigators also noted that while high-school English teachers are expected to teach reading in the English classroom, they are poorly prepared to teach it.

LANGUAGE

Curriculum, language development, teaching grammar, language variations and teacher preparation have all provided areas of investigation for research scholars in recent years. However, the amount of work conducted in any of these areas varies substantially and, again, there are empty subsets (i.e., research in the teaching of rhetoric, of language geography, etc.).

Curriculum

Searles and Carlsen (1960) provide a comprehensive summary on the history of teaching language and grammar in American schools. Markwardt (1970) has edited a definitive volume on linguistics in present school programs that includes reports of historical surveys, experimental studies, and theoretical discussions of the structure and geography of language, the sociology of education, history of the language, and rhetorical perspectives; it contains articles that discuss linguistics as related to literature, reading and spelling as well as surveys of language development. In this same volume Douglas (1970) summarizes the history of language instruction in the schools.

Descriptive data on the teaching of language in secondary schools is provided by Squire and Applebee (1966), who reported language the least well-taught component of English. Language study involved minimal attention to the systematic study of grammar and almost no attention to dialectology, history of the language, lexicography, phonology or semantics. Few of

the 438 teachers interviewed mentioned the teaching of language as a strength. In the 1,609 classes visited by the project staff, observers reported class time emphasizing language study to be 21.5 percent in tenth grade, 8.4 percent in twelfth grade and 19.9 percent in classes of terminal students. Data from a concept check list indicated comparative absence of agreement over concepts associated with the study of language. Observers reported that in no area of language were misunderstandings greater, differences more apparent and standards more variable than in the teaching of usage. Teachers were reported to confuse the study of grammar and of usage, to talk about "functional grammar," by which they meant an error-based approach to assigning drills based on student writing, and to provide instruction in a most haphazard way. The investigators found no attention given to the linguistic aspects of literary study.

Language Development

Comprehensive reviews of recent language development studies have been written by Carroll (1960), Ervin and Miller (1963), MacGinitie (1969), Hodges (1970) and John and Moskovitz (1970). The latter authors complement the earlier reviews by providing summaries of research on the social context of language acquisition and the role of language in learning and thought, and by presenting a description of preschool intervention programs with a language focus.

Drawing from structural linguistics, Strickland (1962) identified the phonological unit to analyze the oral language of children. Besides calculating the average length of phonological units, Strickland observed the patterns of syntactic units and the kinds of subordinate structures found within units. She reported that with advance in grade there was increased flexibility in placing moveables and that 10-sentence patterns used by older children did not appear in the speech of first-grade students.

Riling (1965) used a system of analysis similar to Strickland's to examine oral and written language collected from fourth- and sixth-grade children. Sixth-grade students were reported to speak with greater clarity and to write more complex sentences than did fourth-grade students. Examining the writing of fourth-graders, Riling noted some structural patterns which seldom appeared in speech.

In a report of the first seven years of a 13-year longitudinal study (kindergarten through twelfth grade), Loban (1963) employed the phonological unit, a unit based on structural data, and the communication unit, a unit employing semantic information. Oral language samples were obtained each year by having the children discuss a series of still pictures. As well as making a two-level analysis of communication units for 338 students, Loban also compared the language production of 30 children high in general language ability and of 24 children exceptionally low in language ability. Results of the study showed that as the children grew older they increased the number and length of their communication units. The high-ability group used more communication units and more subordination within the units than did the low-ability group.

Using data collected on students in grades 10, 11 and 12, Loban (1967) reported that students characterized by high language proficiency used both a larger number of optional transformations and more accurate transformations than did students of lesser ability. High language proficiency students used more adverbial clauses of cause, concession and condition. They used relational words more accurately. They developed language skills earlier and to a greater degree of competence than did students from below-average socioeconomic groups.

Menyuk (1969) applied Chomsky's generative model of grammar to describe the structure of the sentences produced and comprehended by children two to seven years old. She found that the structures used in the language samples could be accommo-dated and described by the Chomsky model. She reported outstanding developments occurring in sentences produced by children of the age range four to seven years old. These developments were expansions of base structure nodes; observation of selectional constraints on the occurrence of members of a class; and application of operations of addition, deletion, permutation and substitution both to items in a single underlying string and to underlying sentences.

Using paired samples of oral and written composition obtained from 55 eleventh-grade students, Golub (1968) investigated 35 linguistic structures which might differ in oral and written composition or which might receive high or low teacher ratings. Nine of the linguistic items analyzed showed significant differences. There was significantly greater negation in low-oral than in low-written, high-oral or high-written. There were greater linking verb plus adjective structures in low-oral than in high-written. There were significantly greater relative clauses in high-oral than in high-written. There was significantly more present tense in the low-oral than there was in the low-written, the high-oral or the high-written. There were more transitive verbs followed by direct objects in the high-written than in the low-oral. There were significantly fewer prepositional phrases in low-oral than in low-written, high-oral or high written. There were significantly more transitionals and connectors in high-oral than in either high-written or low-written. There was more content-specific vocabulary in low-written than in low-oral. And there were fewer interpretive statements in high-written than in low-written.

Hunt (1964, 1965, undated) conducted a series of studies of the syntactic structures found in the written composition of students at various grade levels, of students in two ability groups and of skilled adults. He developed measures which he found more reliable means of measuring syntactic growth than sentence length: these measures were

T-unit length, number of short T-units, and clauses per T-unit (Hunt defined a T-unit as a main clause plus any subordinate clauses attached to it). Hunt reported that T-unit length, for example, increased from 8.6 words at grade 4 to 11.5 words at grade 8 and 14.4 words in grade 12, and that adult writers publishing in *Harper's* and *Atlantic* averaged 20.3 words per T-unit. He reported that the increase in T-unit length resulted from two factors: an increase in subordinate clause length, which develops early, and an increase in the number of subordinate clauses, which develops later. He found that the frequency of adjectival and adverbial clauses increases with maturity but that only the increase for adjectival clauses is statistically significant, with the number doubling from grade 4 to grade 12. The increase in clause length was attributed to such factors as use of adjectives, genitives, prepositional phrases, infinitives, participles to modify nouns, near-clause nominals, auxiliary verbs and coordination within T-units.

O'Donnell, Griffin, and Norris (1967) used the measures developed by Hunt with samples of discourse of 180 children in grades K, 1, 2, 3, 5 and 7. The language samples analyzed were responses to two films. The children were asked to tell the story orally, to answer specific questions, and in grades 3, 5 and 7 to write the story and the answers to the same questions. An increasing use of syntactic resources was shown by the number of transformations per T-unit, a number which rose markedly in the speech samples and even more dramatically in the writing samples. Especially noteworthy were the increases in nominal and adverbial transformational constructions and in frequency of coordination in nominals and predicates. The data suggested to the investigators that although the use of syntactic resources in speech increases so that at grade 3 speech is more mature than the newly learned writing skills, a shift in emphasis occurs by grade 5 which causes writing to catch up and to surpass skills in

speech. Seventh grade showed another spurt in speech development in nearly all constructions. Writing development improved markedly in grade 5 and in grade 7—in adverbial clauses, complex structures functioning as direct objects, coordination within T-units, genitive forms and relative clauses. There was no major preference trend in the use of sentence patterns; even the younger children used all patterns.

Teaching Grammar

One issue which is illuminated by some of the recent research is the issue as to whether students in a normal school setting can learn concepts of structural and transformational grammar, or whether these concepts are too formidable because of their high level of generalization and abstraction.

Using the Sequential Tests of Educational Progress Writing Tests as one dependent variable, R. H. White (1965) found that seventh-grade students studying structural grammar scored higher ($p < 0.05$) than groups exposed to traditional or to no grammar. Students seemed to learn introductory material from structural grammar well. White reported that the use of the test frames of the form classes and the composing of a variety of sentences using the form classes and basic sentence patterns were sound instructional approaches. Klauser (1965) conducted a treatment, grades 7, 8 and 9, utilizing structural grammar. STEP, Forms 3A and 3B, Writing, were used as pretest and posttest measurements. Klauser found that in seven months structural grammar produced results as good as traditional grammar, that students mastered the concepts of structural grammar, and that eighth- and ninth-grade students showed enthusiasm about structural grammar when given a questionnaire.

Goddin (1969) produced evidence that students at grades 3 and 7 learned generative grammar linguistic concepts and gained as much in achievement as measured by a standardized test as did students working with a traditional language series. Using data consisting of T-unit analyses of 1000-word composition samples written at the beginning and end of the school year, Gale (1968) conducted research on fifth-grade children studying concepts from structural and generative grammar. She reported that the fifth-graders of her study understood the concepts relatively easily.

A similar finding was reported at the high-school level by Bateman and Zidonis (1966), who found that principles of generative grammar were learned relatively easily because of the grammar's consistency, specificity and relevance to the notion of well-formedness. Using a textbook written for his experiment, Mellon (1969) found seventh-grade students able to learn simple and complex transformations in a program of transformational sentence combining. Davis (1967) presented evidence that transformational-generative grammar, when taught to junior high students, offered promise to the adolescent's understanding of "matured" syntactic structures of the English language. MacLeish (1967) reported that structural and transformational grammar can be taught successfully in the secondary school, both to students thoroughly indoctrinated in traditional grammar and to students who know little grammar. Knowledge of the grammars seemed to make adolescents increasingly sensitive to the structure of language and to their own communication problems. The grammars seemed to motivate students to further English language study.

Studying seventh- and eighth-grade students, Behmer (1965) reported results of analysis of variance leading to the inference that there was no significant difference between scores of a group instructed in traditional grammar by television and a group instructed in traditional grammar in the usual self-contained classroom.

Research evidence is conflicting about the effectiveness of programmed materials in teaching grammar. Fillmer (1963) reported finding no significant difference between two groups of fourth-grade children studying verbs, one group studying programmed materials and another group studying the customary expository textbook. Three investigators (Bennett, 1966a; Kahler, 1966; Munday, 1966) examined the effects of *English 3200* (a commercial programmed textbook presenting traditional grammar) on learning. Bennett reported that programmed learning and lecture/textbook presentation were equally effective as measured by objective test items administered to eleventh-grade students. Kahler found some evidence that low and middle achievement tenth-grade students, as measured by the Sequential Tests of Educational Progress Writing Test, scored higher than students conventionally taught. Studying twelfth-grade students, Munday concluded that group achievement with programmed materials was not higher than group achievement of students without programmed materials.

Language Variations

H. R. Wilson (1970) has published on the geography of language, including a statement on implications for research in the classroom. McDavid (1970) has described a language program based on concepts from the sociology of language.

Analyzing interviews of members of different age groups, sexes, ethnic groups and social classes, Shuy, Wolfram, and Riley (1967) reported that each social dialect has a structure adequate for its users and that differences are in certain linguistic forms rather than in the structure of the varieties of language.

The early work of Labov (1966) on social stratification in New York City suggests methods for systematic analysis of stylistic and social variation, and provides valuable pedagogical data such as his findings on the incoming prestige form -r or on the phonological variables th- and -ing. Labov and Cohen (1967) reported that native speakers of nonstandard dialect possess ability to perceive, abstract and reproduce the meaning of many standard forms which they do not produce themselves. They hypothesized that a single pan-dialectical grammar could be constructed which could account for the syntactic variations found in oral language of subjects from the urban ghetto. In a later publication, Labov (1970) has drawn on his scholarship in sociolinguistics for principles, educational implications and research models which might assist English teachers working in the urban ghettos. Labov's hypotheses and models for sociolinguistic research within the school should generate considerable data to influence the teaching and learning of language in both elementary and secondary schools.

Loban (1966) analyzed data on social class dialect using samples of oral speech from a representative group of 338 subjects for whom spoken responses had been recorded from kindergarten through ninth grade. He categorized problems in oral language as verb problems, pronoun problems, syntactic confusion and other. All children continued to experience difficulties involving the factors' coherence and effectiveness. The most troublesome language problem among students speaking a social class dialect was difficulty with verbs, especially the verb "to be." Blacks showed improvement through grade 5 but then experienced difficulties such that they did not achieve fifth-grade level again until grade 9.

Graves (1968) studied language differences among upper- and lower-class black and white eighth-graders. Upper-class students produced a significantly larger number of words and significantly longer T-units than did lower-class students in both oral and written language. The usage analysis revealed lower-class students to have a greater frequency of double negatives, to use a singular subject with an uninflected verb, and to use the present tense form of the verb for the nonpresent, among other characteristics.

Using a corpus of papers from black students $(N = 30)$ in grades 9, 10 and 11,

Briggs (1969) followed categories for classifying deviations from standard English set forth in earlier research by Loban (1966): verb problems, pronoun problems, syntactic confusion and other problems. At each grade level Briggs found consistently high numbers of deviations in each area. Total deviations per 1000 words were almost constant for each grade: 79.46 in ninth grade, 73.44 in tenth grade, and 76.51 in eleventh grade.

Teacher Preparation

The National Council of Teachers of English Committee on the National Interest (1961) reported that more than 94 percent of colleges failed to require work in the English language in the preparation of elementary teachers; half of the colleges did not require a course on teaching the English language. Examining the English language preparation of secondary teachers of English, the Committee found that only 25 percent of colleges required a course in the history of the English language and only 17.4 percent required a course in modern English grammar. In a second report this Committee (1964) found that only 53.5 percent of secondary-school English teachers felt well prepared to teach English language.

Pearson and Reese (1969) headed a two-year national study of the linguistic and language preparation of secondary-school English teachers. Data and opinions were from questionnaires and from interviews with linguists, language specialists, curriculum specialists, teachers and students. There was high agreement among the respondents that present preparation for secondary-school English teachers in the area of language is grossly inadequate.

Information on language attitudes of a stratified random sample of elementary- and secondary-school English teachers in Minnesota was reported by Hess (1969). Attitudes were determined by responses to a 100-item questionnaire. When measured by a criterion of at least 50 percent agreement with linguists on at least 50 percent of the items, 647 elementary teachers did not have informed language attitudes; 786 secondary English teachers showed only minimum evidence of possessing informed language attitudes and beliefs.

Frogner (1969) developed and administered a two-part Language Inquiry. Part I consisted of 100 items validated against the judgments of 10 linguists. Part II required the respondent to select three items from Part I for discussion and to justify the selection. The instrument was used with three groups: college students ($N = 597$), cooperating teachers ($N = 202$) and recent graduates ($N = 83$). Analysis of those Part I items eliciting differing responses between linguistics and each of the three groups revealed what Frogner termed an unrealistic approach by members of the three groups to many details of language: the attitude of respondents in the three groups often seemed to be that of following a rigid classification or a traditional rule without attention to the particular language situation involved. Examination of responses to Part II of the Language Inquiry suggested to the investigator a lack of awareness by the respondents as to the possibility of an answer other than their own.

COMPOSITION

An indispensable source of information on research in written composition is a work by Braddock, Lloyd-Jones, and Schoer (1963). The document grows out of the screening of a list of 504 references on the teaching of composition. Most of the references surveyed left important variables uncontrolled or undescribed. However, the authors selected five soundly based (but not perfect in all respects) studies to describe at length. In one section of the volume the authors treat methods of research—rating compositions, frequency counts, general considerations; in a second section they describe the state of knowledge about compo-

sition—instructional and environmental factors influencing composition, rhetorical considerations, objective tests versus actual writing as measures, and so on. They conclude that composition research is not highly developed.

Shane and Mulry (1963) surveyed research studies on written expression in the elementary-school years. Petty (1967) edited a bulletin on research in oral language, including the relationship of oral communication to other language skills. Sherwin (1969, pp. 109–168) reported on studies dealing with increasing the student's skill in writing: through writing practice, through study of traditional grammar, and through study of linguistics.

The sections below are, in part, an attempt to supplement the sources above.

Curriculum

Judy (1967) studied the history of curriculum in composition in American secondary schools, 1850–1893. Other information on the history of composition curriculum is to be found in Searles and Carlsen (1960), Meckel (1963) and Braddock (1969). Braddock (1969) also affords invaluable information on recent research on environmental factors affecting writing, on rhetoric, on grammar, on instruction and on evaluation.

Observers in the National Study of High School English Programs (Squire & Applebee, 1966) reported only 15.7 percent of class time, at all levels in all schools, emphasizing composition. Most of the instruction included in the 15.7 percent total occurred after the papers had been written. The bulk of comments and corrections appearing on students' papers had to do with proofreading rather than with teaching.

Interrelationship of Grammar and Writing

Several investigators concerned themselves with studying the effects of instruction in grammar—traditional grammar, structural grammar or transformational grammar—on student composition. R. H. White (1965) questioned the effects on writing of teaching structural and traditional grammar and of teaching no grammar. Fifty minutes a week during one semester an experimental group of seventh-grade students studied structural grammar. For the same period Control Group I studied traditional grammar; Control Group II was involved in free reading. Comparing the scores of the three effectiveness groups on the Sequential Tests of Educational Progress Writing Tests, White found that the experimental group studying structural grammar scored higher ($p < 0.05$). Evaluation of themes assigned before and after treatment revealed greater mean improvement by the structural grammar group. There was no significant difference in writing between Control Groups I and II.

Davis (1967) investigated the effects of instruction in the kernel sentences of transformational-generative grammar and in parallel concepts from traditional school grammar upon four sentence variables: average length of clauses, noun-phrase element, predicate expansion element and verb-phrase element. Experimental and control groups were equated on the basis of achievement test scores, chronological age and IQ. Treatment was for a period of 14 weeks. Both groups wrote pre- and posttreatment. The experimental group (studying transformational grammar) obtained statistically significant increases for predicate expansions (the mean increased from 36.51 to 40.07) and for total numbers of clauses (from 26.18 to 29.78).

A two-year experiment in teaching transformational grammar was conducted by Bateman and Zidonis (1966), who asked questions on the effect of the grammar on the writing of ninth- and tenth-grade students. The students were randomly assigned to two sections taught by two teachers also randomly assigned. The experimental class (transformational grammar) studied phrase structure rules the first year and transformational rules the second year. Writing collected from both experimental and control groups early in the first year and late in the second year exceeded 70,000 words. Analysis of the sentences in the sample utilized three component measures: proportion of well-formed sentences, structural complexity score and error change score. Comparisons between experimental and control classes were made by analysis of variance. The investigators reported that knowledge of selected concepts from transformational grammar enabled the student to increase significantly the proportion of well-formed sentences. Knowledge of transformational grammar enabled the student to increase sentence complexity without sacrificing sentence grammaticality. Knowledge of transformational grammar enabled the student to reduce the occurrence of certain errors in his writing.

Mellon (1969) investigated the hypothesis that practice in transformational sentence-combining (an a-rhetorical, intensive and structured experiencing of mature sentences) would enhance students' normal growth of syntactic fluency. He tested this hypothesis with seventh-grade students in an experiment lasting one year. Students were assigned to three groups: a) an experimental group ($N = 100$) receiving sentence-combining problems, b) a control group ($N = 100$) receiving traditional parsing exercises, and c) a placebo group ($N = 47$) receiving extra instruction in composition and in literature rather than in grammar. Students were in four schools. All students wrote in-class compositions during the normal course of the school year. Basic data for the dependent variable, syntactic fluency, were from a 90 T-unit paper written by each student early in the school year and from another 90 T-unit sample written at the end of the school year. The investigator looked at 12 factors of syntactic fluency—ranging from mean T-unit length to embedded kernel sentences per 100 T-units to mean maximum depth level. The experimental group (studying sentence-combining problems) experienced significant pre–post growth on all 12 factors. The control group experienced no significant growth. While the control group and the experimental group were similar in pre-writing, analysis of covariance showed that the experimental group surpassed the control group on every measure ($p < 0.01$) in postwriting. The experimental group was significantly above the placebo group on eight of 12 measures. There were few significant differences between control and placebo groups. The investigator cautioned teachers not to conclude from his research that grammar study "improves" sentence structure, saying that it was the sentence-combining practice associated with grammar study, not the grammar study itself, which influenced the growth rate of syntactic fluency of students used in the research.

Vocabulary

Petty, Herold, and Stoll (1968) sought to identify knowledge about the teaching of vocabulary. Some 565 titles relating to the investigation were screened; of these some 80 items served as the principal bases for the report. The authors focused on studies concerned with pedagogical method (the teaching of vocabulary rather than the acquiring of vocabulary). The volume contains an overview of vocabulary studies, a review of selected studies and a section on linguistic considerations in vocabulary teaching and research. A chapter growing out of observed strengths and deficiencies includes suggestions for designing vocabulary research. The investigators close with the statement that the profession knows little of substance about the teaching of vocabulary and then list questions which should be answered if vocabulary is to be taught adequately.

Student Characteristics

One of the objectives of a project by Maloney (1968) was to identify qualities differentiating performance in expository composition between superior and poor ninth-grade writers. Evaluators used an analytic method of rating papers, considering organization, maturity of insight, style and word choice. The greatest differences between superior and poor writers, in the areas listed above, occurred in maturity of insight and in organization. For the most part superior writers were female, white, relatively committed to a future career and frequent readers. Superior students either had high mental ability or, if they were of average ability, were taught in challenging, homogeneously grouped English classes. Superior students made fewer mechanical errors on their themes, earned higher and more consistent grades in English, and scored high in reading comprehension, verbal reasoning, and vocabulary tests.

The findings of Maloney are, to some extent, supported by Barbig (1969) who reported on the relationship of selected variables to poor writing in grades 9 and 12. In this study the good writer tended to be the academic female; the poor writer, the non-academic male. Good writers did more voluntary reading and had a better self-concept and attitude toward writing. Females in all writing categories did more reading and more voluntary writing than did males.

In a national study Lacampagne (1969) examined approaches and attitudes toward composition of twelfth-grade students with superior writing performance and students of average writing performance. Superior students were National Council of Teachers of English Achievement Award winners or runners-up; average students were selected by teachers or administrators. Data were from a 40-item questionnaire on which Lacampagne had a 65 percent return. Results suggested that superior writers had developed a more conscious and structured approach to composition than had average writers. Superior writers had more positive attitudes toward composition and their profiles differed from average writers' profiles in writing interests and in amounts of time devoted to writing. There was some correlation between superior performance in composition and extensive reading experiences.

Measurement

During the 1960s the rating of compositions continued to be one of the important topics for research in the teaching of composition. Investigators conducted research advancing information on such facets as the rater variable, the assignment variable and objective tests versus actual compositions as measures of writing.

Godshalk, Swineford, and Coffman (1966) reported studies investigating the relative validity of different approaches to measuring written composition skills. During a three-week period 646 students, approximately half in grade 11 and half in grade 12, wrote on five topics, took tests containing six classes of objective items (usage, sentence correction, paragraph organization, prose groups, error recognition and construction shift), and wrote two interlinear exercises (weak prose requiring the student to locate and correct deficiencies). Objective tests and interlinear exercises were scored following standard procedures. Compositions were assigned to 25 readers who were asked to make a global or holistic rather than an analytical judgment of each paper, assigning scores of three, two or one to each essay. Each reader scored at least one essay written by each student. The total of the scores assigned by the 25 readers was the criterion for evaluating objective tests and interlinear exercises. Estimates of reading reliability resulted in a correlation coefficient of 0.92; estimate of score reliability was 0.84. From the data the investigators generalized that if students can write on as many as five different topics, and if each topic can be read by five different readers, reliability per unit of reading time for short topics read holistically is high. They reported that objective questions designed to measure writing skills prove highly valid when evaluated against a reliable criterion of writing skills. Finally, they reported that an efficient predictor of a reliable direct measure of writing ability includes interlinear exercises or essay questions in combination with objective questions.

The Follman and Anderson study (1967) compared five methods of rating compositions. Five groups of five raters, education-English majors, were paid to assign grades to 10 themes. The themes, each about 370 words long, were from students of a wide range of high-school and college writing ability. Each rater graded the same 10 themes but used one of five methods. The five methods were: a) the California Essay Scale, in which 25 questions about content, organization, style and mechanics are asked; b) the Cleveland Composition Rating Scale, in which content, conventions and style are rated on 10 scales such as "organized" versus "jumbled"; c) the Diederich Rating Scale, in which points are given in eight topics ranging from ideas and organization to spelling and handwriting; d) the Follman English Mechanics Guide, a checklist concerned with punctuation, sentence structure, paragraphing, diction and usage; and e) Everyman's Scale, in which the rater's own particular criteria are used. After determining that the rater groups did not differ in English skills, Follman and Anderson tested the rating methods for significance. The essays received substantially the same scores from all five rating groups. The correlations between four of the rating scales ranged from 0.93 to 0.99. Correlations for the Diederich Scale ranged from 0.51 to 0.61. A measure of reliability showed four of the scales above 0.93 and the Cleveland scale at 0.81. The investigators inferred that rating scales measure many common elements and that the usual unreliability of theme evaluation occurs because of the heterogeneity of the experiential and academic backgrounds of raters.

Wood and Pooley (1967) surveyed a number of currently published tests which are used to measure success in English. Their survey revealed no evidence to support the hypothesis that composition can be measured by any objective test or any combination of objective tests. The investigators cautioned school administrators and educational test directors to interpret results of objective tests as being measures of a limited number of English skills such as spelling, punctuation, capitalization and usage.

Teacher Preparation

The National Council of Teachers of English Committee on the National Interest (1964) reported that two-thirds of secondary English teachers did not feel confident of their preparation in composition, and that four-fifths of the institutions preparing elementary-school teachers did not require a course in composition beyond freshman English.

Squire and Applebee (1966) reported questionnaire data showing that English teachers felt more deficient, by a considerable margin, in composition than in language, literature, reading and speech.

SUMMARY AND EVALUATION

In his classic monograph on investigations relating to grammar, language and composition, Lyman (1929) was able to provide infrequent end-of-chapter conclusions, many of them wise and farsighted. For example, he cited accord in usage investigations on two principles: a) the emphasis of the instruction should be placed on the student's immediate needs rather than on deferred needs and b) remedial work which follows diagnosis must be largely, if not exclusively, individual. While Lyman spoke of the investigators listed in his references as pioneers, it still seemed clearly possible in 1929 to solve significant educational problems in the teaching of English by quantitative evidence rather than by authority or by historical precedent.

Braddock, Lloyd-Jones, and Schoer (1963), in their soon-to-be classic monograph, could only conclude that the state of knowledge about the teaching of composition was not highly developed; Petty, Herold, and Stoll (1968) concluded that very little was known about the teaching of vocabulary. As this chapter is being written Alan Purves, University of Illinois, is working under a National Endowment for the Humanities grant to report on the state of knowledge about the teaching of literature; perhaps this project will unearth further research with implications for teaching practices. But end-of-chapter statements on specifics from research in English/language arts which might lead to improved teaching and learning were infrequent in the sixties. Generalizations from research studies conducted over a period of 50 years seemingly could not be unified.

In an apparently timeless generalization, Lyman said at the end of the chapter dealing with research on curriculum, "The objectives of instruction in English are as yet vague, uncertain, and far from agreed upon" (1929, p. 69). In the sixties curriculum theory and objectives in English/language arts vacillated among being ponderous, humanistic, rigorous and academic, spiraled and structured, and the champion of a tentative language and personal growth anticurriculum. Though it often seemed imbalanced, the language/literature/composition tripod might have served as a model guiding research in teaching English in secondary schools. Research on the talk/engage-in-drama/write/read model might have done much to interrelate the literature, language, composition, popular culture and the elementary- and secondary-school compartments. But agreement on theoretical foundations for curriculum did not characterize the profession. There being no unifying theory, the researcher sometimes tested hypotheses which now seem insignificant. Since it would be naive to imagine that there might ever be unity or harmony as to a definition or delimitation of the subject matter of English, future end-of-chapter generalizations could only occur as the result of a considerable bulk of research contained in several constellations.

Lyman congratulated most of the investigators in the field because in general they avoided elaborate statistical treatment of their data and shunned "heavy barrages of statistics and intricate mathematical formulas" (1929, p. 4). No one in the sixties would argue that investigations must employ complicated statistics and design. However, considering the overwhelming number of complex interacting relationships identified in school settings, it is hardly a matter for congratulation that there hasn't been greater use of multivariate designs and of recent methodological contributions in statistics.

Much of the recent research consisted of descriptive and status studies (e.g., teacher preparation, reader interest, the censor in the community). Status studies are invaluable. But they may account for too much of the research literature in the teaching of English. Empirical research in which variables are manipulated and in which the effect of these variables is observed and reported has been rare. The intelligence invested in collecting normative data for studies with an emphasis on practicality has been at the expense of examining hypotheses and alternative hypotheses on instructional/learning variables which might generate ideas affecting English/language arts classrooms.

In an era of great advances in analytical tools and of revolutionary changes in computer applications, the value of much of the experimental research was its being a model of deficiencies in conception, in execution or in reporting. Inferences which might lead to unity were suspect because of the nature of the questions, the sample, the collection of data and the processing of data. Considering even the best of the studies, one investigator was censured for not describing the treatment for a control group and another criticized for having studied atypical students in a university demonstration school.

Requisite large-scale federal and private foundation funding of investigators was short-lived. Some of the most highly sophisticated, visible, high-impact, valuable research (Bateman & Zidonis, 1966; Loban, 1963, 1966; Mellon, 1967; O'Donnell, Griffin, & Norris, 1967) was made possible, at least in part, through federal funds. With cessation of federal grants, long-range programs on transformational sentence-combining, the effect of transformational grammar on writing, problems in oral English, etc. became somewhat less likely.

Little effort went into developing tests and other measuring instruments. Based as they were on instruments lacking validity or reliability, the generalizations of some of the studies were suspect.

Scholars were reluctant to conduct longitudinal studies. Replication was rare.

Much of the research in the teaching of English came from Ph. D. candidates. Some doctoral investigations were incorporated into products which were quite significant, visible and influential (e.g., Labov, 1966; Squire, 1964). However many of the studies suffered from having to be conducted quickly and inexpensively. A few journal articles resulted, but by and large the men and women who authored doctoral dissertations did not establish national reputations as researchers.

Research in the teaching of English often seemed to have little effect on classroom practices. Even if the teacher had the training in statistics and research design to be an intelligent reader of research, the flaws in many of the investigations made findings suspect. The reports were often very abstruse and dull and contained too little on treatments, subjects or dependent variables to be very usable. Hypotheses were sometimes on such molecular aspects of English/language arts that inferences had little import for daily teaching.

If the teacher was not a consumer, neither was he a producer. There were almost no reports of attempts by the English/language arts teachers to solve professional problems using the methods of science—an action research approach to the solution of practical problems. Problem-solving seemed to come from resorting to custom and tradition, to authority, to personal experience or to syllogistic reasoning rather than from action research in school buildings and systems.

Research findings were often contradictory. Even if one wanted to teach traditional school grammar in a programmed format, results of the experimental studies were not in accord. Evidence on divergent thinking and team teaching was conflicting, as were language development studies on such matters as occurrence or nonoccurrence of given sentence patterns at an early grade level.

Change seemed to be increasing in speed. New grammars of English, new theory for rhetoric, new critical methods in literature study and so on made earlier pedagogical research antique and irrelevant except for hints to be gathered of research methodology. What remained from the never-to-be-unified earlier research was clearly more research process than pedagogical precept; but research process had changed too.

Research had focused on subject matter —which had or would soon change. Little was done with comparisons of instructional methods (inquiry, tutorial, discussion, lecture) as they facilitate a host of objectives. Little or nothing was learned of the English/language arts/communications teacher's cognitive/affective style, or of the student's cognitive/affective style. Little attention was given to concepts—their instances, their complexity, their mode of presentation—as found in audio-visual/printed materials. Scant attention was given horizontal and vertical organization as it affects the learner in the English/language arts classroom, or the effects of the size of schools, or the comparative effects of urban, suburban or rural environments. Little was done on the effects of hardware. By and large it was the effects of content, not process, which were quantified.

Change and flux cast doubt on some of the studies that had been well executed. Did boys in 1970 in grades 7 through 12 still prefer books dealing with sports, animals and patriotism as had boys in 1950? Did boys dislike stories of love, the didactic, the philosophical? There were hints in the sixties of vast teen-age audiences for *Demien, Steppenwolf, Stranger in a Strange Land.* The findings of reading-interest studies may have become outdated. If adolescents in 1970 were reading *Malcolm X, Soul on Ice, Manchild in a Promised Land, The Painted Bird, I Never Promised You a Rose Garden,* research findings on reader responses might need to be reexamined; hypotheses that children and adolescents reading out of the canon might be responding to literature in what had been shortly before termed "more adult" ways need to be tested.

This cataloging of the trivial, the dated, the fragmented and uncoordinated, the small facts, the unreliable, the insignificant words, and the flaws and inadequacies does not constitute an indictment of all of the research of the sixties. The references cited as Cooperative Research Reports are valuable. The references from National Council of Teachers of English journals represent firm judgments of worth by outstanding editors. The Educational Resources Information Center Clearinghouse on the Teaching of English has carefully screened the items which have been stored in its systems. First-rate universities have produced some first-rate doctoral dissertations. The studies listed in the references as National Council of Teachers of English Research Reports have been screened by experts in the profession and pronounced excellent. The classroom teacher might profitably engage students in transformational sentence-combining if mature sentence structure is an objective (Mellon, 1969). The classroom teacher or researcher can measure a student's entering and terminal behavior in manipulating elements within the sentence (Hunt, 1964; Loban, 1963; O'Donnell, Griffin, & Norris, 1967) and compare this writing behavior with that of skilled adults (Hunt, n.d.). The teacher or researcher can categorize responses to literature in a relatively molecular way and can pose questions based on differing categories of responses to promote differing interaction of teacher and student, student and student (Purves, 1968). The teacher can be reassured that the double negative or negative concord is a stylistic marker, as is deletion of forms of *be* and certain other auxiliary verbs (Labov, 1970; Loban, 1966). Teachers and researchers can gain high reliability for reading short papers holistically if a student writes on as many as five different topics and if each topic is read by five different readers (Godshalk, Swineford, & Coffman, 1966). The profession has rather clear descriptions of the preparation of secondary-school English teachers and of their teaching of literature, composition, language, reading and speech, their evaluation of learning, and their innovations (Hook, Jacobs, & Crisp, 1969; Squire & Applebee, 1966). These investigations remove some of the obstacles to unions, junctions and connections. In 1970 it seems clearly possible to solve significant educational problems in the teaching of English by research.

Even if research in the teaching of English in 1970 should prove to be as much the work of the pioneer as the research of which Lyman wrote in 1929, another decade of research might hopefully be characterized by long-range research programs of co-ordinated studies, by unity of theoretical foundations within constellations, by imaginative uses of recent methodological contributions in statistics and research design, by experimental as well as status studies, by requisite public and private funding, by its correspondence with current scholarship in the subject matter, and by the development of more sophisticated measuring instruments. The studies would be authored by doctoral candidates, professors, agencies, career researchers, elementary- and secondary-school teachers, business, and teams of experts in varying areas. Such studies would be of educational significance to those who teach and to those who learn to use the English language and its literature.

REFERENCES

Agee, W. H. *The initiation theme in selected modern American novels of adolescence.* (Doctoral dissertation, The Florida State University) Ann Arbor, Mich.: University Microfilms, 1967. No. 67-282.

Ahrens, N. H. *Censorship and the teacher of English: A questionnaire survey of a selected sample of secondary school teachers of English.* (Doctoral dissertation, Columbia University) Ann Arbor, Mich.: University Microfilms, 1966. No. 65-14,958.

Anderson, S. B. *Between the Grimms and "the group": Literature in American high schools.* Cooperative Test Division Reports. Princeton, N.J.: Educational Testing Service, 1964.

Andresen, O. The significance of profundity in literary appreciation. *Reading Research Quarterly,* 1969, 5, 100–118.

Appleby, B. C. *The effects of individualized reading on certain aspects of literature study with high school seniors.* (Doctoral dissertation, The University of Iowa) Ann Arbor, Mich.: University Microfilms, 1968. No. 67-16,771.

Barbig, E. V. *An exploration of growth in written composition to determine the relationship of selected variables to poor writing in grades nine and twelve.* (Doctoral dissertation, The University of Tennessee) Ann Arbor, Mich.: University Microfilms, 1969. No. 69-1231.

Bateman, D. R., & Zidonis, F. J. *The effect of a study of transformational grammar on the writing of ninth and tenth graders.* National Council of Teachers of English Research Report No. 6. Champaign, Ill.: National Council of Teachers of English, 1966.

Behmer, D. E. *An experiment in teaching a unit of English grammar by closed-circuit television with a visual technique for teaching syntax as a variable.* (Doctoral dissertation, Western Reserve University) Ann Arbor, Mich.: University Microfilms, 1965. No. 65-2311.

Bellack, A. A., Kliebard, H. M., Hyman, R. T., & Smith, F. L., Jr. *The language of the classroom.* New York: Teachers College Press, 1966.

Bennett, R. A. *A comparison of the effects of programed instruction and lecture-textbook instruction on English language learning of eleventh grade students.* (Doctoral dissertation, The Florida State University) Ann Arbor, Mich.: University Microfilms, 1966. No. 65-5568. (a)

Bennett, R. A. (Ed.) *Summary progress report of English curriculum study and demonstration centers.* Champaign, Ill.: National Council of Teachers of English, 1966. (b)

Berberi, E. A. W. *A descriptive analysis of anthologies for the tenth grade as the texts are related to the objectives for the study of literature as expressed by national professional groups.* (Doctoral dissertation, Indiana University) Ann Arbor, Mich.: University Microfilms, 1966. No. 65-14,031.

Bloom, B. S. (Ed.) *Taxonomy of educational objectives.* New York: David McKay, 1956.

Braddock, R. English composition. In R. L. Ebel (Ed.), *Encyclopedia of educational research.* (4th ed.) New York: Macmillan, 1969. Pp. 443–461.

Braddock, R., Lloyd-Jones, R., & Schoer, L. *Research in written composition.* Champaign, Ill.: National Council of Teachers of English, 1963.

Briggs, D. G. *Deviations from standard English in papers of selected Alabama Negro high school students.* (Doctoral dissertation, University of Alabama) Ann Arbor, Mich.: University Microfilms, 1969. No. 69-6528.

Carroll, J. B. Language development. In C. W. Harris (Ed.), *Encyclopedia of educational research.* New York: Macmillan, 1960. Pp. 744–752.

Casper, T. P. *Effects of the junior great books program at the fifth grade level on four intellectual operations and certain of their component factors as defined by J. P. Guilford.* (Doctoral dissertation, St. Louis University) Ann Arbor, Mich.: University Microfilms, 1965. No. 64-13,453.

Cooper, R. C. Preferred modes of literary response: The characteristics of high school juniors in relation to the consistency of their reactions to three dissimilar short stories. Unpublished doctoral dissertation, University of California, Berkeley, 1969.

Davis, M. W. *A comparative analysis of sentences written by eighth grade students instructed in transformational-generative grammar and traditional grammar.* (Doctoral dissertation, Boston University) Ann Arbor, Mich.: University Microfilms, 1967. No. 66-14,776.

Dedmond, F. The maturation theme in contemporary American drama. Unpublished doctoral dissertation, Florida State University, 1969.

Douglas, W. W. The history of language instruction in the schools. In A. H. Marckwardt (Ed.), *Linguistics in school programs.* The Sixty-ninth Yearbook of the National Society for the Study of Education, Part II. Chicago: NSSE, 1970. Pp. 155–166.

Dunning, A. S. A definition of the role of the junior novel based on analyses of thirty selected novels. Unpublished doctoral dissertation, Florida State University, 1959.

Ervin, S. M., & Miller, W. R. Language development. In H. W. Stevenson et al. (Eds.), *Child psychology.* The Sixty-second Yearbook of the National Society for the Study of Education, Part I. Chicago: NSSE, 1963. Pp. 108–143.

Fader, D. N., & McNeil, E. B. *Hooked on books: Program & proof.* New York: Berkley Medallion Books, 1968.

Farley, J. J. *Book censorship in the senior high school libraries of Nassau County, New York.* (Doctoral dissertation, New York University) Ann Arbor, Mich.: University Microfilms, 1965. No. 65-969.

Fillmer, H. T. Programmed instruction in elementary English. *Elementary English,* 1963, 40, 833-837.

Follman, J. C., & Anderson, J. A. An investigation of the reliability of five procedures for grading English themes. *Research in the Teaching of English,* 1967, 1, 190–200.

Frogner, E. A. *A study of the responses to the Language Inquiry.* USOE Contract No. OEC-5-10-029, Champaign, Ill.: Illinois State-Wide Curriculum Study Center in the Preparation of Secondary School English Teachers, 1969.

Gale, I. F. *An experimental study of two fifth-grade language arts programs: An analysis of the writing of children taught linguistic grammar compared to those taught traditional grammar.* (Doctoral dissertation, Ball State University) Ann Arbor, Mich.: University Microfilms, 1968. No. 68-3242.

Goddin, M. A. P. *A comparison of the effects on student achievement of a generative approach and a traditional approach to the teaching of English grammar at grades three and seven.* (Doctoral dissertation, West Virginia University) Ann Arbor, Mich.: University Microfilms, 1969. No. 69-6702.

Godshalk, F. I., Swineford, F., & Coffman, W. E. *The measurement of writing ability.* College Entrance Examination Board Research Monograph, No. 6. New York: College Entrance Examination Board, 1966.

Golub, L. S. *Syntactic and semantic elements of students' oral and written discourse: Implications for teaching composition.* (Doctoral dissertation, Stanford University) Ann Arbor, Mich.: University Microfilms, 1968. No. 67-17,427.

Graves, R. L. *Language differences among upper- and lower-class Negro and white eighth graders in East Central Alabama.* (Doctoral dissertation, The Florida State University) Ann Arbor, Mich.: University Microfilms, 1968. No. 68-2917.

Grindstaff, F. L. *The responses of tenth-grade students to four novels.* (Doctoral dissertation, Colorado State College) Ann Arbor, Mich.: University Microfilms, 1969. No. 69-12,486.

Hackett, M. G., Brown, G. I., & Michael, W. B. A study of two strategies in the teaching of literature in the secondary school. *The School Review,* 1968, 76, 67–83.

Hess, K. M. *The language attitudes and beliefs of Minnesota elementary and high school English teachers.* (Doctoral dissertation, University of Minnesota) Ann Arbor, Mich.: University Microfilms, 1969. No. 69-11,402.

Hipple, T. W. *The values in four selected American novels and suggested uses of these values in high school English classes.* (Doctoral dissertation, University of Illinois) Ann Arbor, Mich.: University Microfilms, 1969. No. 69-10,724.

Hirshfield, G. *A taxonomic approach to the evaluation of secondary school English programs.* (Doctoral dissertation, the University of New Mexico) Ann Arbor, Mich.: University Microfilms, 1967. No. 67-11,759.

Hodges, R. E. Language development: The elementary school years. In A. H. Marckwardt (Ed.), *Linguistics in school programs.* The Sixty-ninth Yearbook of the National Society for the Study of Education, Part II. Chicago: NSSE, 1970. Pp. 215–228.

Hoetker, J. Teacher questioning behavior in nine junior high school English classes. *Research in the Teaching of English,* 1968, 2, 99–106.

Hoetker, J. *Dramatics and the teaching of literature.* Champaign, Ill.: National Council of Teachers of English, Educational Resources Information Center, Clearinghouse on the Teaching of English, 1969.

Hoetker, J., & Robb, R. Drama in the secondary school: A study of objectives. *Research in the Teaching of English,* 1969, 3, 127–159.

Hook, J. N., Jacobs, P. H., & Crisp, R. D. *Illinois state-wide curriculum study center in the preparation of secondary school English teachers: Final report.* USOE Contract No. OEC-5-10-029. Champaign, Ill.: Illinois State-Wide Curriculum Study Center in the Preparation of Secondary School English Teachers, 1969.

Hopkins, K. H. *The relative effectiveness of two methodologies in high school senior English in the development of composition skills.* (Doctoral dissertation, North Texas State University) Ann Arbor, Mich.: University Microfilms, 1968. No. 68-2774.

Hove, J. (Ed.) *Meeting censorship in the school: A series of case studies.* Champaign, Ill.: National Council of Teachers of English, 1967.

Hunt, K. W. *Sentence structures used by superior students in grades four and twelve, and by superior adults.* Cooperative Research Project No. 5-0313. Tallahassee, Fla.: Florida State University, n.d.

Hunt, K. W. *Differences in grammatical structures written at three grade levels.* Cooperative Research Project No. 1998. Tallahassee, Fla.: Florida State University, 1964.

Hunt, K. W. *Grammatical structures written at three grade levels.* National Council of Teachers of English Research Report No. 3. Champaign, Ill.: National Council of Teachers of English, 1965.

John, V. P., & Moskovitz, S. Language acquisition and development in early childhood. In A. H. Marckwardt (Ed.), *Linguistics in school programs.* The Sixty-ninth Yearbook of the National Society for the Study of Education, Part II. Chicago: NSSE, 1970. Pp. 167–214.

Judy, S. N. *The teaching of English composition in American secondary schools, 1850-1893.* (Doctoral dissertation, Northwestern University) Ann Arbor, Mich.: University Microfilms, 1967. No. 67-15,256.

Kahler, A. D., Jr. *The effects of programmed grammar and journal writing on student writing ability: An exploratory study.* (Doctoral dissertation, Oklahoma State University) Ann Arbor, Mich.: University Microfilms, 1966. No. 66-4029.

Kingston, C. T. *Exemplifications of the tragic mode in selected realistic fiction for eight-to-twelve-year-old children.* (Doctoral dissertation, Columbia University) Ann Arbor, Mich.: University Microfilms, 1969. No. 69-665.

Klauser, E. L. *A comparison of a structural approach and a traditional approach to the teaching of grammar in an Illinois junior high school.* (Doctoral dissertation, University of Colorado) Ann Arbor, Mich.: University Microfilms, 1965. No. 65-4252.

Kochant, H. E. H. *The image of the American elementary school experience as portrayed in contemporary realistic fiction for eight-to-twelve-year-old children.* (Doctoral dissertation, Columbia University) Ann Arbor, Mich.: University Microfilms, 1969. No. 69-666.

Labov, W. *The social stratification of English in New York City.* Washington, D.C.: Center for Applied Linguistics, 1966.

Labov, W. *The study of nonstandard English.* Champaign, Ill.: National Council of Teachers of English by special arrangement with the Center for Applied Linguistics, 1970.

Labov, W., & Cohen, P. *Systematic relations of standard and non-standard rules in the grammars of Negro speakers.* Project Literacy Reports No. 8. Ithaca, N.Y.: Cornell University, 1967.

Lacampagne, R. J. *A national study of selected attitudes and approaches to writing of twelfth-grade students with superior writing performance versus those with average writing performance.* (Doctoral dissertation, University of Illinois) Ann Arbor, Mich.: University Microfilms, 1969. No. 69-10,757.

LaRocque, G. E. *The effectiveness of the inductive and deductive methods of teaching figurative language to eighth grade students.* (Doctoral dissertation, Stanford University) Ann Arbor, Mich.: University Microfilms, 1966. No. 66-2581.

Lawson, J. H. *The development of a poetry test for grades eleven and twelve.* (Doctoral dissertation, University of Kansas) Ann Arbor, Mich.: University Microfilms, 1969. No. 69-11,271.

Lester, J. F., Jr. A comparative study of the effects of team teaching and departmental-ized teaching on the scholastic achievement of eighth-grade students in social studies and language arts. Unpublished doctoral dissertation, University of Kansas, 1966.

Levinson, E. *Effects of motion pictures on the response to narrative: A study of the effects of film versions of certain short stories on the responses of junior high school students.* (Doctoral dissertation, New York University) Ann Arbor, Mich.: University Microfilms, 1964. No. 63-6669.

Loban, W. D. *Literature and social sensitivity.* Champaign, Ill.: National Council of Teachers of English, 1954.

Loban, W. D. *The language of elementary school children.* National Council of Teachers of English Research Report No. 1. Champaign, Ill.: National Council of Teachers of English, 1963.

Loban, W. D. *Problems in oral English.* National Council of Teachers of English Research Report No. 5. Champaign, Ill.: National Council of Teachers of English, 1966.

Loban, W. D. *Language ability: Grades ten, eleven, and twelve.* Project No. 2387. Berkeley: University of California, Berkeley, 1967.

Lyman, R. L. *Summary of investigations relating to grammar, language, and composition.* University of Chicago Supplementary Educational Monographs, No. 36. Chicago: University of Chicago, 1929.

Lynch, J. J., & Evans, B. *High school English textbooks: A critical examination.* Boston: Little, Brown, 1963.

MacGinitie, W. M. Language development. In R. L. Ebel (Ed.), *Encyclopedia of educational research.* (4th ed.) New York: Macmillan, 1969. Pp. 686–699.

MacLeish, A. *Materials and methods for teaching structural and generative grammar to high school students and their teachers.* Project No. H-144. DeKalb, Ill.: Northern Illinois University, 1967.

Maloney, H. B. *An identification of excellence in expository composition performance in a selected 9A population with an analysis of reasons for superior performance.* (Doctoral dissertation, Columbia University) Ann Arbor, Mich.: University Microfilms, 1968. No. 68-2432.

Marckwardt, A. H. (Ed.) *Linguistics in school programs.* The Sixty-ninth Yearbook of the National Society for the Study of Education, Part II. Chicago: NSSE, 1970.

McDavid, R. I., Jr. The sociology of language. In A. H. Marckwardt (Ed.), *Linguistics in school programs*. The Sixty-ninth Yearbook of the National Society for the Study of Education, Part II. Chicago: NSSE, 1970. Pp. 85–108.

McKay, J. W. *A summary of scientific research and professional literature on reading interests of secondary school students—grades 7-12, 1889-1965*. (Doctoral dissertation, University of Pittsburgh) Ann Arbor, Mich.: University Microfilms, 1969. No. 69-8578.

Meckel, H. C. Research on teaching composition and literature. In N. L. Gage (Ed.), *Handbook of research on teaching*. Chicago: Rand McNally, 1963. Pp. 966–1006.

Mellon, J. C. *Transformational sentence-combining: A method for enhancing the development of syntactic fluency in English composition*. Final Report, Cooperative Research Project No. 5-8418. Cambridge, Mass.: Harvard University, 1967.

Mellon, J. C. Transformational sentence-combining: A method for enhancing the development of syntactic fluency in English composition. *National Council of Teachers of English Research Report No. 10*. Champaign, Ill.: National Council of Teachers of English, 1969.

Menyuk, P. *Sentences children use*. Cambridge, Mass.: The M.I.T. Press, Press Research Monographs No. 52, 1969.

Mersand, J. The teaching of literature in American high schools, 1865-1900. In R. C. Pooley (Ed.), *Perspectives on English*. New York: Appleton-Century-Crofts, 1960. Pp. 269–302.

Milgrim, S. *A comparison of the effects of classics and contemporary literary works on high-school students' declared attitudes toward certain moral values*. (Doctoral dissertation, New York University) Ann Arbor, Mich.: University Microfilms, 1968. No. 68-4785.

Monson, D. L. *Children's responses to humorous situations in literature*. (Doctoral dissertation, University of Minnesota) Ann Arbor, Mich.: University Microfilms, 1967. No. 67-869.

Munday, R. G. *The effects of the use of English 3200, a programed textbook, on achievement in English grammar at the twelfth-grade level in a large metropolitan high school*. (Doctoral dissertation, North Texas State University) Ann Arbor, Mich.: University Microfilms, 1966. No. 65-15,120.

National Council of Teachers of English, Committee on the National Interest. *The national interest and the teaching of English*. Champaign, Ill.: National Council of Teachers of English, 1961.

National Council of Teachers of English, Committee on the National Interest. *The national interest and the continuing education of teachers of English*. Champaign, Ill.: National Council of Teachers of English, 1964.

Nelms, B. F. *Characteristics of poetry associated with preferences of a panel of tenth grade students*. (Doctoral dissertation, The University of Iowa) Ann Arbor, Mich.: University Microfilms, 1968. No. 68-963.

Odland, N. *Teaching literature in the elementary school*. Champaign, Ill.: National Council of Teachers of English, Educational Resources Information Center, Clearinghouse on the Teaching of English, 1969.

O'Donnell, R. C., Griffin, W. J., & Norris, R. C. *Syntax of kindergarten and elementary school children: A transformational analysis*. National Council of Teachers of English Research Report No. 8. Champaign, Ill.: National Council of Teachers of English, 1967.

Pearson, J. R., Jr., & Reese, J. R. *Project grammar: The linguistic and language preparation of secondary school teachers of English*. Interim Report, USOE Contract No. OE-5-10-029. Champaign, Ill.: Illinois State-Wide Curriculum Study Center in the Preparation of Secondary School English Teachers, 1969.

Petty, W. T. (Ed.) *Research in oral language*. Champaign, Ill.: National Council of Teachers of English, 1967.

Petty, W. T., Harold, C. P., & Stoll, E. *The state of knowledge about the teaching of vocabulary*. Cooperative Research Project 3128. Champaign, Ill.: National Council of Teachers of English, 1968.

Pfeiffer, I. L. Teaching in ability grouped English classes: A study of verbal interaction and cognitive goals. *Journal of Experimental Education*, 1967, 36(1), 33–38.

Pooley, R. C. English—literature. In C. W. Harris (Ed.), *Encyclopedia of educational research*. (3rd ed.) New York: Macmillan, 1960. Pp. 470–478.

Purves, A. C., with Rippere, V. *Elements of writing about a literary work: A study of response to literature*. National Council of Teachers of English Research Report No. 9. Champaign, Ill.: National Council of Teachers of English, 1968.

Rees, R. D., & Pedersen, D. M. A factorial determination of points of view in poetic evaluation and their relation to various determinants. *Psychological Reports*, 1965, 16, 31–39.

Richards, I. A. *Practical criticism: A study of literary judgment*. New York: Harcourt, Brace, 1929.

Riling, M. E. *Oral and written language of children in grades 4 and 6 compared with the language of their textbooks*. Cooperative Research Project No. 2410. Durant, Okla.: Southeastern State College, 1965.

Ring, J. W. *A study of the interpretive processes employed by selected adolescent readers of three short stories*. (Doctoral dissertation, The Ohio State University) Ann Arbor, Mich.: University Microfilms, 1969. No. 69-4959.

Russell, D. H., Early, M. J., & Farrell, E. *Research design and the teaching of English*. Champaign, Ill.: National Council of Teachers of English, 1964.

Scott, C. L. *A comparison of achievement of students in a team teaching and a traditional approach to ninth grade English*. (Doctoral dissertation, Arizona State University) Ann Arbor, Mich.: University Microfilms, 1966. No. 66-9823.

Searles, J. R., & Carlsen, G. R. English— language, grammar, and composition. In C. W. Harris (Ed.), *Encyclopedia of educational research*. (3rd ed.) New York: Macmillan, 1960. Pp. 454–466.

Shane, H. G., & Mulry, J. G. *Improving language arts instruction through research*. Washington, D.C.: National Education Association, Association for Supervision and Curriculum Development, 1963.

Sherwin, J. S. *Four problems in teaching English: A critique of research*. Scranton, Pa.: International Textbook Company, 1969.

Shugrue, M. F. New materials for the teaching of English: The English program of the USOE. *Publication of the Modern Language Association of America*, 1966, 41, 1–36.

Shuy, R., Wolfram, W., & Riley, W. K. *Linguistic correlates of social stratification in Detroit speech*. Cooperative Research Project No. 6-1347. East Lansing, Mich.: Michigan State University, 1967.

Smith, D. V. *Fifty years of children's books, 1910–1960: Trends, backgrounds, influences*. Champaign, Ill.: National Council of Teachers of English, 1963.

Smith, R. J. *The effects of reading a short story for a creative purpose on student attitudes and writing*. (Doctoral dissertation, The University of Wisconsin) Ann Arbor, Mich.: University Microfilms, 1968. No. 67-12,158.

Squire, J. R. *The responses of adolescents while reading four short stories*. National Council of Teachers of English Research Report No. 2. Champaign, Ill.: National Council of Teachers of English, 1964.

Squire, J. R. English literature. In R. L. Ebel (Ed.), *Encyclopedia of educational research*. (4th ed.) New York: Macmillan, 1969. Pp. 461–473.

Squire, J. R., & Applebee, R. K. *A study of English programs in selected high schools which consistently educate outstanding students in English*. Cooperative Research Project No. 1994. Urbana, Ill.: University of Illinois, 1966.

Steinberg, E. R. *Needed research in the teaching of English*. U.S. Office of Education Cooperative Research Monograph, No. 11. Washington, D.C.: U.S. Department of Health, Education, & Welfare, Office of Education, 1963.

Strickland, R. G. The language of elementary school children: Its relationship to the language of reading textbooks and the quality of reading of selected children. *Indiana University School of Education Bulletin*, 1962, 38 (4), 1–131.

Taba, H. *With perspective on human relations: A study of peer group dynamics in an eighth grade*. Washington, D.C.: American Council on Education, 1955.

Wasson, R. *Proceedings of the Allerton Park Conference on research in the teaching of English*. Cooperative Research Project No. G-1006. Urbana, Ill.: University of Illinois, 1962.

Waters, J. C. *An investigation of the effects of team teaching in English at Central High*

School. (Doctoral dissertation, Arizona State University) Ann Arbor, Mich.: University Microfilms, 1969. No. 68-15,022.

Weiss, J. D. *The relative effects upon high school students of inductive and programmed instruction in the close reading of poetry.* (Doctoral dissertation, New York University) Ann Arbor, Mich.: University Microfilms, 1969. No. 69-11,775.

White, C. E. *A case study: American literature as taught on television in Detroit public schools from 1957 to 1963.* (Doctoral dissertation, Wayne State University) Ann Arbor, Mich.: University Microfilms, 1968. No. 68-13,448.

White, R. H. *The effect of structural linguistics on improving English composition compared to that of prescriptive grammar or the absence of grammar instruction.* (Doctoral dissertation, University of Arizona) Ann Arbor, Mich.: University Microfilms, 1965. No. 65-188.

Whitman, R. S. Significant reading experiences of superior English students. *Illinois English Bulletin,* 1964, 51 (5), 1–23.

Wilson, H. R. The geography of language. In A. H. Marckwardt (Ed.), *Linguistics in school programs.* The Sixty-ninth Yearbook of the National Society for the Study of Education, Part II. Chicago: NSSE, 1970. Pp. 64–84.

Wilson, J. R. *Responses of college freshmen to three novels.* National Council of Teachers of English Research Report No. 7. Champaign, Ill.: National Council of Teachers of English, 1966.

Wood, S., & Pooley, R. C. *An evaluation of published English tests.* Department of Public Instruction, Bulletin No. 144. Madison, Wis.: Wisconsin State Department of Public Instruction, 1967.

Zais, R. S. A scale to measure sophistication of reading interests. *Journal of Reading,* 1969, 12, 273–276, 326–335.

CHAPTER 34 Research on Teaching in the Natural Sciences

LEE S. SHULMAN
Michigan State University

PINCHAS TAMIR
Hebrew University of Jerusalem

INTRODUCTION

Some words are used so indiscriminately by writers that they lose their communicative impact. Yet no term other than "revolutionary" can adequately describe the changes and developments undergone by the field of science education during the 10 years since the Gage *Handbook of Research on Teaching*. We have been inundated by revolutionary waves of funding, new curricula, texts and tests, evaluations, denunciations and dissertations. Hurd's (1961) statement that "it is harder to change the curriculum than it is to move a cemetery" no longer applies. H. Grobman (1968a) testified that "by 1967, there were over 70 [curriculum] projects in science alone." It would appear that in the interim our curricular cemeteries have become jet-propelled.

Where does such a wave begin? The wave first became visible at the end of the 1950s. PSSC had already been funded, Sputnik had orbited, Explorer had aborted, mathematicians had gathered steam under the banners of UICSM and SMSG, BSCS was underway and the National Academy of Sciences had decided to commission the deliberations of a group of experts on the teaching of science. A conference under its auspices was convened at Woods Hole and chaired by Jerome Bruner of Harvard; out of this conference emerged a book of barely 90 pages, *The Process of Education* (Bruner, 1960).

This book was surely neither the beginning of the wave nor was it the crest, but it provided an unmistakable sign to the rest of the educational community that radical changes in the teaching of science were imminent. For Silberman (1970), Bruner's book was the most influential piece of writing to emerge from the curriculum reform movement. We concur in that judgment.

Lawrence Cremin has quoted Lloyd Morris's observation that "Great books... are either reservoirs or watersheds; they sum up and transmit the antecedent past or they initiate the flow of the future" (Cremin, 1965). Bruner's small book served as both reservoir and watershed, both recapitulation and prophecy. Whether an accurate representation of the deliberations of that conference or not, the report emphasized four conceptions which, in their respective ways, can serve to characterize much of the ferment of the sixties in science education.

The first such conception was the *structure* of the subject matter. Questions of structure have been central to the reorientation of science education. Discussions of conceptual schemes, substantive and syntactic structures, learning hierarchies, scientific literacy and the like all reflect the desire to redefine the content and objectives of science teaching in terms better articulated with modern ideas of the structures of disciplines and the processes of science.

A second reconception dealt with the learner, his capabilities, his readiness and his motives. *The Process of Education* introduced the provocative proposition that "the foundations of any subject may be taught to anybody at any age in some form." This peculiarly Brunerian version of Piagetian theory has had a more dramatic impact on the teaching of mathematics than on the teaching of science. But the Piagetian concept of the developing child nevertheless pervaded science education. His view of learning as an active process involving manipulation and discovery is easily as important to the science educator as the more dramatic or provocative notion of early readiness. This characterization of the learner as capable of conceptual discovery through active manipulation of the environment that is motivated intrinsically by the need constantly to re-establish equilibrium with that environment has become one of the basic tenets of the educational theories underlying science education.

A third theme that emerged from Bruner's book dealt with conceptions of teaching and learning. Implicit here were notions of intuition, intellectual risk, discovery and inquiry. The focus was on the processes by which students cope with problems presented to them and the importance of those processes as educational ends in themselves. The notions of discovery and inquiry have been recurring themes in the science education of the sixties and will deserve a great deal of our attention in the pages to come.

Clearly, the respective emphases on structure, early readiness, and intuition or discovery are not arbitrary and independent. They fit together to form a coherent instructional theory. Important knowledge can be envisioned as composed of fairly simple structures generally taking the form of relations among fundamental concepts or principles. In fact, as Szent-Györgyi (1964) pointed out, the growth of knowledge in science is characterized by simplification of structures and invention of new concepts which synthesize previously distinct systems. Hence, what is to be grasped by "any child at any age" can be fairly simple, thus capable of translation into an "honest" representation in the learner's frame of reference. This representation will not be in formal symbolic terms but in more concrete form where it can be intuitively discovered and assimilated by the learner. This theoretical framework for subject matter, learning and teaching had great influence on the science and mathematics curriculum developers (Shulman, 1968, 1970a).

A fourth theme in *The Process of Education* dealt with the technology of teaching, the hardware and software of pedagogy. The variety of new instructional media that could serve as transmitters, transducers, magnifiers, amplifiers or accelerators of knowledge were perceived as presenting to the educator an unparalleled instructional arsenal. William James had long ago characterized the classroom as a battlefield wherein teachers and students engaged in their academic combat. Here, in the form of teaching machines, film loops, television, computers and the like, a marvelous electronic weaponry would be introduced into the fray to aid in the pursuit of knowledge.

We will repeatedly encounter these themes in the present chapter as we deal with the theoretical and empirical research efforts that accompanied the science education revolution. We will emphasize theoretical and empirical studies more than polemics or homiletics although the past decade has seen an ample amount of the latter in science teaching publications. We will not attempt a comprehensive review of the voluminous research literature in science education. Many excellent reviews already exist (e.g., Belanger, 1969; Ramsey & Howe, 1969a, 1969b, 1969c; H. Smith, 1969; Welch, 1969b). Nor will we be able to give equal time to each of the roughly six dozen new curricula that have been created. Instead we will selectively review a variety of contributions that illustrate or characterize the scope of educational research in the teaching of science; we will emphasize the individuals and the issues that have served as foci for those inquiries; and we will critically examine their findings and implications for science teaching.

Not surprisingly, many of the issues, polemics and personalities that will dominate this chapter are not exclusively or even primarily identified with science education. Many of the leading figures of research in science teaching play a central role on the stage of pedagogical and psychological theory, "writ large." It is to the lasting benefit of science education that they chose to devote some of their efforts specifically to this field. We will continually refer to these more general theoretical and methodological issues in the course of the present chapter. A problem in science education becomes more meaningful when seen in the context of the broader set of issues from which it has emerged and to which it contributes. In this manner we hope to make this chapter more a "narrative of enquiries" than a "rhetoric of conclusions."

The important thing to recognize is that the controversies that characterized the debates in science education in the 1960s were not matters of taste concerning the use of new media or the inclusion of a particular topic in the curriculum. These controversies were rooted in fundamental issues of *epistemology* (what knowledge is of most worth? how is knowledge acquired and verified?), *psychology* (how does learning take place? what constitutes readiness for learning?), *philosophy of science* (what is the influence of theory upon observations in science? what is "scientific objectivity"?), *policy science* (what do our country and society need from science?), and *educational theory* (how should objectives be expressed? do new curricula matter?). It is only by reference to these broader issues that their particular manifestations in science education can be understood.

Overview of Chapter

We will turn first to an issue that has dominated the research literature—the *subject matter* of science education with special reference to the concept of *structure*. Consideration of how the subject matter is viewed and how structures can be defined and measured will lead us to examine the goals of science education as reflected in controversies over *educational objectives*—their values, forms, and characters.

It will be seen that the debates on the objectives of science education rapidly spill over into the general domain of *psychological and pedagogical theory*. Using the critical albeit ambiguous concepts of *inquiry* and *discovery* as focal points, we will examine the major theoretical positions that have influenced science education and its research literature.

With these more theoretical discussions as background, we will then turn to a highly selective and critical review of two bodies of empirical research in science education: *comparative learning experiments* and *curriculum evaluation studies*. In the former, we will focus especially on studies of the laboratory and on the problem of instruments for measuring the outcomes of science curricula.

In a final section of the chapter we will attempt to draw conclusions, criticize current trends and suggest strategies for continued inquiry.

SUBJECT MATTER AND THE CONCEPT OF STRUCTURE

The most visible aspects of the revolution in science education have been in the very subject matter of the programs themselves —their content, organization and emphases. In an important contribution to the evaluation literature in science teaching, Klopfer (1971) characterized the contrast of the traditional and the modern in these terms:

the traditional science courses concentrate on the knowledge of scientific facts, laws, theories, and technological applications, while the newer courses put emphasis on the nature, structure, and unity of science and on the processes of scientific inquiry. The traditional programs attempt to cover a great number of topics, while modern programs prefer depth to breadth. The traditional courses are taught largely by the lecture and recitation method and see confirmation in laboratory exercises which are not essential to the course, whereas the modern programs employ discovery investigations as the basis of course development (p. 565).

The new programs have generally attempted to be more accurate and up-to-date scientifically than their predecessors, most of which had been written by men substantially removed from the contemporary scientific enterprise (Brownson & Schwab, 1963). They strove for greater sophistication from a philosophy and history-of-science perspective, avoiding the naiveté of older texts and their presentation of "the scientific method." The new programs tried to portray the fluidity and dynamism of science in contrast to its image as a collection of immutable truths. These objectives can be summarized as directing instruction toward the students' understanding of the "revisionary nature of science," possibly the focal element of "scientific literacy" (Robinson, 1968).

A recurring theme in the discussion of the content and organization of the new curricula has been the "structure of the subject matter." We are accustomed to thinking of educational research as an endeavor consisting mainly of empirical data-gathering, experimental manipulations or statistical analyses. We typically reserve pejoratives like "mere armchairing" for activities characterized mainly by careful historical or philosophical thought unbuttressed by quantitative data. Examination of research efforts in science teaching should disabuse us of that naive misconception. Philosophical and historical inquiries into the variety of meanings assigned to the concept of structure are likely to have a greater long-term impact on science education than the plethora of empirical studies that fill our journals and the spools of microfilmed dissertations on file at the University of Michigan. Robinson (1969) has reviewed this body of work for the *Review of Educational Research*.

Although Bruner brought the attention of the education establishment to the problem of structure, it is Joseph Schwab who has explicated and extended the concept most significantly for science education. Bruner had advocated teaching the structure of a discipline as a defense against the explosion of informational minutiae and as a guarantor of future relevance. Hence, for Bruner the importance of structure is based less on philosophy than on psychology. Generalizations are more easily retained and transferred than are facts; therefore our emphasis in teaching ought to be on structure.

What is this structure Bruner would have us teach? It consists of those generalizations or principles so basic that the fundamental facts of a discipline can be encompassed by or reconstructed from them. As Lukinsky (1970) has observed, these structures are described by most curriculum theorists as if they were solid and permanent cornerstones of a discipline. In contrast, for Schwab, "the structure of a discipline consists, in part, of a body of imposed conceptions which define the investigated subject-matter of that discipline and control its inquiries" (1962a, p. 199). Thus the structures not only precede the facts of a discipline, they even determine what will be considered a fact.

Schwab has addressed himself to the question of structure in a series of papers (Schwab, 1951, 1960, 1962a, 1962b, 1964a, 1964b). He has distinguished three different ways in which the concept of structure is used. First, the manner in which the various disciplines are defined and organized with respect to each other involves questions of structure. This level of analysis is most relevant to the broadest questions of curriculum design. In what sequence should disciplines be taught? Which subjects can suitably be combined and which ought to be taught separately? Schwab has shown how different philosophical starting points —Comtian, Platonic, Aristotelian—can generate contrasting "right" organizations leading to vastly different curriculum structures.

Within a discipline Schwab distinguishes between two closely related and interdependent aspects of structure—the *substantive* and the *syntactic*. The substantive structure of a discipline consists of "a body of concepts—commitments about the nature of a subject matter functioning as a guide to inquiry" (1962a, p. 203). This sense of structure is most similar to what Bruner had in mind, though Schwab explicates the concept much more clearly, emphasizes its transitional status and generally explores it in the context of the philosophy of science rather than the psychology of learning.

The syntactic structure of a discipline involves "the pattern of its procedures, its method, how it goes about using its conceptions to attain its goals" (Schwab, 1962a, p. 203). Schwab's two meanings of structure are interrelated, capable of distinction in theoretical discourse but never in practice. Nevertheless, many science educators have chosen to emphasize either the conceptual schemes of science or its inquiry processes as nearly separate systems. Schwab summarizes his discussion of structure with the admonition that

truth is a complicated matter. The conceptual structure of a discipline determines what we shall seek the truth about and in what terms that truth shall be couched. The syntactical structure of a discipline is concerned with the operations that distinguish the true, the verified, and the warranted in that discipline from the unverified and unwarranted. Both of these —the conceptual and the syntactical—are dif-

ferent in different disciplines (Schwab, 1962a, p. 205).

Schwab thus concludes with an observation systematically ignored by the science teaching establishment in its quest for a set of structures, whether conceptual schemes or science processes, that will be universally applicable to "science." In this matter we find him in surprisingly full agreement with Ausubel, who has repeatedly argued that the general conceptual schemes or process approaches to science are vain quests for uniformity in a world characterized by systematic diversity (Ausubel, 1963b).

As noted above, an important aspect of Schwab's work is his emphasis upon the substantive structure of a discipline as an imposed construction, not an organization inhering in that subject matter. It is no coincidence that the Schwab-influenced Biological Sciences Curriculum Study (BSCS) alone among the new curricula was produced in three versions, each reflecting a different way of conceiving the substantive structure of biology. For Schwab, not only is the positing of a set of conceptual schemes that cut across disciplines a futile exercise, but so is the attempt to capture *the* structure of any single subject matter.

In discussing syntactic structures, Schwab distinguishes the short-term syntax of *stable enquiry* from the long-term syntax of *fluid enquiry*. This contrast of Schwab's is similar to Kuhn's (1962) *normal science* and *revolutionary science* and Robinson's (1968) *completive* and *generative* inquiries. Ironically, although the major theme of many modern science educators has been the fluid, revolutionary, generative aspects of scientific work, the curriculum materials themselves have tended to stress the stable or normal aspects of scientific inquiry. For critics such as Ausubel, both the syntax of fluid inquiry and its substantive consequence—the fragility of scientific truth—have been grossly oversold. Ausubel (1963b) argues that "any science curriculum worthy of the name must be concerned with the systematic presentations of an organized body of knowledge as an explicit end in itself." He further asserts that there has been far more stability to the teachable content of science than the reformers have been prepared to admit.

The investigations of structure have been carried out in a disciplined scholarly manner. The work of Schwab was based on his careful analyses of more than 4,000 research reports in a variety of disciplines. In his "What Do Scientists Do?" (Schwab, 1960), he reports in detail the nature of the evidence marshaled to support his conceptions of science. The subsequent investigations of Robinson (1968), Connelly (1968), Herron (1971) and others have involved similar methods of criticism and analysis using original research reports or the works of philosophers as their primary data. Their work unquestionably represents a too-long overlooked genre of educational research. To discuss the teaching of science is to imply that one possesses a definition of science that he can employ in his discourse. The methods of philosophical, critical and historical inquiry are indispensable in avoiding the slipshod, sloppy reasoning that so frequently characterizes educational writings.

It is not only at the philosophical level that studies of structure have been conducted. We noted earlier that Bruner's emphasis when discussing structure was on the psychological implications of the concept. Gagné's theory of learning hierarchies (Gagné, 1962, 1970) revolves around the design of "learning structures." Ausubel's subsumption theory of learning has the concept of "cognitive structures" as a central facet. His preeminent concern is with the ways in which the materials of instruction can be organized to facilitate integration into the learner's organized structure of knowledge. Similarly, Piaget's formulations regarding schema of cognitive organization reflect his interest in the developing relations among the elements of knowledge.

There are several approaches to assessing the acquisition of structured knowledge by learners. In the Gagné approach, given a well-articulated learning hierarchy for a topic, a test can be constructed to measure each capability in the hierarchy. The resulting pattern of passed and failed items could be used to describe the structures or partial structures that have been mastered by the learner. Gagné has demonstrated repeatedly (e.g., Gagné, 1962) that the lower levels of a hierarchy generally serve as prerequisites to the higher-level capabilities. Science—A Process Approach (American Association for the Advancement of Science [AAAS], 1965) has used this notion of structure in both curriculum design and evaluation activities (Walbesser, 1966; Walbesser & Carter, 1968).

Ausubel's conception of structure, though highly developed theoretically, has not yielded to direct attempts to assess or describe the structure per se. In science education the work of Novak (1965) has been influenced by Ausubel's position. O. R. Anderson (1966) is pursuing a promising line of research into the assessment of structure within a modified S-R framework. In the associative structure tradition of Deese (1965), Johnson (1964, 1967) has conducted word association studies aimed at generating precise descriptions of learned structures so that any changes in such structures as a function of a course or lesson can be adequately measured.

The crucial question for science educators has been how one transmits a particular conception or structure of knowledge to students so that it becomes an enduring component of the learners' cognitive structure (O. R. Anderson, 1966; Novak, 1965, 1966). We shall examine several of the approaches to this topic in the section on psychological theory. When we shift our discussion from definitions of the object of knowledge (what is science?) to the changes desired in learners, we have moved over into the neighboring realm of educational objectives.

OBJECTIVES OF SCIENCE EDUCATION

We have observed that two important ways in which the new science differed from its predecessors were in the emphasis on structure and conceptual schemes which students were to understand, and the emphasis on the processes of science, which students were both to understand and frequently to perform. When controversies arose involving these goals of science teaching, they inevitably became enmeshed in a web of issues that stretched far beyond science education into the realm of epistemology, curriculum theory and the transfer-of-training. Herbert Spencer's famous query, "What knowledge is of most worth?" remained a central concern. Content or process? Which content? Which processes? In what combinations or sequences?

Schwab's conception of the "teaching of science as enquiry"[1] (1962b) is a good place to begin this discussion. Schwab recognized that:

> The phrase "the teaching of science as enquiry" is ambiguous. It means, first, a process of teaching and learning which is, itself, an enquiry, "*teaching* as enquiry." It means, second, instruction in which science is seen as a process of enquiry, "*science* as enquiry." The ambiguity is deliberate. Both of these meanings are parts of the idea in its complete form. The complete enquiring classroom would have two aspects. On the one hand, its materials would exhibit science as enquiry. On the other hand, the student would be led to enquire into these materials. He would learn to identify their component parts, detect the relations among these parts, note the role played by each part, detect some of the strengths and weaknesses of the enquiry under study. In short, the classroom would engage in an *enquiry into enquiry* (Schwab, 1926b, p. 65).

Schwab's distinction between "science as enquiry" and "teaching-learning as enquiry" is an important one. The first defines the

___
[1] Schwab prefers the British spelling of "enquiry" and has used it consistently in his more recent writings. In the balance of this chapter we shall use enquiry whenever referring directly to Schwab's work or to work which reflects his influence (such as the BSCS Invitations to Enquiry). In all other cases the more common inquiry spelling will be used.

substantive focus of the classroom, *what* is taught and learned. The second refers to the syntax of the classroom and its consequences, the nature of the transactions that will be conducted, the enquiry skills that will be mastered, the attitudinal "metalessons" that will be learned.

In this definition of teaching-learning as enquiry, it should be noted that the activity in which the student participates is not scientific enquiry per se but the critical analysis, interpretation and evaluation of reports of scientific enquiry. Although this surely simulates many of the processes in which the scientist engages himself reflectively as he sorts out his decisions during enquiry, it does not require the student to conduct original enquiries in a laboratory.

Schwab proceeds to contrast the "dogmatic classroom" and the "enquiring classroom" in terms of the ends they seek and the means they employ to achieve those ends. The aim of the enquiring classroom "is not only the clarification and inculcation of a body of knowledge but the encouragement and guidance of a process of discovery on the part of the student" (1962b, p. 66).

After Schwab characterizes the full range of activities and purposes of the enquiring classroom, he observes that it is

> by no means the only version nor necessarily the most desirable version in all schools for all students. Of the two components—science as enquiry and the activity of enquiring—it is the former which should be given first priority as the objective of science teaching in the secondary school (1962b, p. 71).

This objective, similar to Robinson's emphasis on scientific literacy, is summarized by Schwab when he states that the learner should "become cognizant of science as a product of *fluid enquiry,* understand that it is a mode of investigation which rests on conceptual innovation, proceeds through uncertainty and failure, and eventuates in knowledge which is contingent, dubitable, and hard to come by" (1962b, p. 5). Such an understanding of "science as enquiry" rather than as a "rhetoric of conclusions" is the most important goal of science education.

Ausubel disagrees with Schwab's diagnosis of current ills and his prescription for change. He argues that the fluidity of the scientific enterprise which Schwab emphasizes is exaggerated and distorted out of all proportion. There are organized bodies of knowledge that are worth teaching and learning as such. He contends that "although the specifics of science change rapidly, basic principles tend to manifest impressive longevity" (Ausubel, 1968, p. 489). He further argues that the basic objective of a high-school biology course should be the teaching of "those broad biological ideas that constitute part of general education" (Ausubel, 1968, p. 355). In contrast, Gagné would accept Schwab's observations on the transient nature of scientific *knowledge* but would argue that modes of *knowing* in science are more permanent. Thus, the Gagné-influenced AAAS curriculum aims to teach the student the processes of science and to develop his science-relevant intellectual skills, since both remain constant even as scientific conceptions change.

The issues are drawn at a number of levels. In an abrupt turnabout from his earlier theoretical stance, Gagné (1968) took the position that a strict distinction had to be made between bodies of organized content and intellectual skills as educational objectives. They had different psychological antecedents, were acquired via different learning conditions, were of contrasting transferability and, perhaps most important, were of substantially different long-term value to the learner. Gagné argued that intellectual skills, not organized subject-matter content, could be represented structurally in learning hierarchies, were most effectively transferable and were of most permanent worth to the learner. The content, after all, could always be looked up in a reference book while the intellectual skill had to be reinstatable as needed.

Here again, the discord over objectives in science education took place against the background of the general controversies among educationists. It is enormously difficult to distinguish among the three levels of those disagreements—the *normative* (what ought students to know? what knowledge is most useful to the citizen in a democracy?); the *cognitive* (what are the learnings that can best be retained? what types of learning are most effectively transferred?); and the *technical* (how should objectives be stated or formulated?).

The *normative* questions can be further subdivided into a series of problems that have been addressed by science educators. Since theorists of every stripe are at least in agreement that something called "science" is to be conveyed to students, the question, "What is science?" becomes quite central. This question can be answered philosophically, historically, sociopolitically, etc. When Schwab (1960) copes with the question, "What do scientists do?" he is engaging the fundamental premise of science education. Similarly Robinson (1968), Elkana (1970), Bridgham (1969) and Herron (1971) are attempting to clarify the domain that students are to understand. The works of general philosophers and historians of science such as Kuhn (1962) are frequently cited for the same purposes. Far more than in any previous period, philosophical studies of this sort are used to justify a particular choice of educational objectives.

The *cognitive* level of discourse examines science subject matter from the psychological perspectives of what is most learnable under given conditions, what is most readily retained and transferred to new situations, what is most involving or motivating to students. From this perspective, rather than the nature of science or of social policy dictating the content and form of the instruction, the potentials and limitations of learning and teaching play that role.

It may be noted that our normative category subsumes both the *subject-matter* and *milieu* levels of the Tyler-Schwab-Dunkel model, while our cognitive category subsumes much of their *teacher* and *learner* dimensions (Schwab, 1962b, pp. 32–38). Controversies at the normative level occur when educators disagree on the essential conceptual schemes of science (or whether such a notion is even viable), on the relative emphases on content or process as goals, on the rudimentary understandings constituting *scientific literacy,* or on whether high-school science courses ought to be directed toward producing scientists or scientifically literate citizens.

Controversies at the cognitive level occur when educators disagree on the relative transferability of content or process learnings, on whether a learning hierarchy is the appropriate form for science subject matter, on what achievements can be expected of pupils at different ages. Most often these disagreements are traceable to the choice of psychological theory that has directed the educator's conception of what is to be taught and learned.

Issues about objectives drawn at the *technical* level of discourse generated more heat than most others during the sixties even though the questions raised were often rather trivial. Here again, the problems are not independent of the normative and cognitive dimensions. Whether or not you advocate the stating of all objectives in behavioral terms will depend, partly at least, on your commitment to a behavioristic view of human learning. Additionally, one's willingness to make explicit statements of objectives will be contingent on one's normative stance. Thus Atkin (1963), Eisner (1969) and Ebel (1970) have strongly criticized the behavioral objectives approach on the grounds that ultimate educational ends are not foreseeable, nor ought they to be in good learning situations. Furthermore, returning to the technical dimension, even were it theoretically possible, Atkin (1963), Eisner (1969) and Ebel (1970) see a great deal of wasted time and effort in laboriously making explicit every desired behavior in

a learning situation. Although some of the technical discussion over educational objectives may have verged on the trivial, the implications of these debates are far from unimportant in a decade in which the watchword may well turn out to be "accountability."

Objectives—The Normative Level

The major debates at the normative level have already been reviewed in the previous section. It need only be added that the way one chooses to define the nature of science will also have important implications for the general expectations one has for science education and hence the manner in which science curricula are evaluated. Bridgham (1969) has observed that three contrasting ways of characterizing science—*rational empiricism, systematic empiricism* or *paradigmatic research*—each lead to vastly different conceptions of what the teaching of science can accomplish.

Science viewed as either rational or systematic empiricism leads to the expectation that the successful student of science will be an all-purpose "critical thinker," "problem solver" and general troubleshooter. Although this is a transparently overblown claim, we will observe how frequently evaluators choose to measure the outcomes of a science program with a general test of critical thinking such as the Watson-Glaser.

When science is conceived as paradigmatic research, however, the claims for learning science are much more modest and realistic. Consistent with the position of Schwab, Bridgham sees this conception as composed of two parts. Students will come to understand the natural world as it is understood by science and they will understand scientific research efforts in the sciences. Bridgham's critical analysis of the meanings assigned to science and the consequent educational claims that are made for learning science exemplifies the type of inquiry that ought to precede the definition of objectives for a science program and the selection of measuring instruments to evaluate that program.

Objectives—The Cognitive Level

What sort of knowledge is most learnable, transferable and therefore valuable to the student? This is the crux of the cognitive level of analysis. Bruner observed that at the heart of this question lay "the classic problem of transfer." Bruner's emphasis on general structures and heuristics of discovery as objectives, Gagné's concern with intellectual skills, Ausubel's commitment to the teaching of organized bodies of subject-matter knowledge, all are rooted in their contrasting views of the psychology of transfer-of-training. In order better to grasp the rationale for their contrasting conceptions of the most important objectives, we shall have to review their respective positions on the transfer-of-training.

The major theorists differ in their respective emphases upon *what* is transferred in learning. Bruner stresses the lateral transfer of broad principles and strategies from one domain or topic to another. Broad transfer-of-training occurs when one can identify in the structures of subject matters basic, fundamentally simple concepts, principles or strategies which, if learned well, can be transferred to other disciplines. He gives examples such as the concept of conservation or balance. Is it not possible to teach balance of trade in economics so that, when ecological balance is considered, pupils see the parallel? This could then be extended to balance of power in political science or to balancing equations. Of equal if not greater importance for Bruner is the broad transferability of the knowledge-getting processes —strategies, heuristics, investigatory methods, and the like.

Gagné considers himself a conservative on matters of transfer. To the extent that an element which has been learned (be it association, concept or principle) can be directly employed in a new situation, transfer will occur. If the new context requires a behavior substantially different from the specific capability mastered earlier, there will be no transfer. He thus clearly identifies himself with the "identical elements" position of Thorndike, a point of view in clear contrast to Bruner.

Gagné is concerned primarily with the conditions for *vertical* transfer. His theory of learning hierarchies is clearly a theory of positive vertical transfer. Though not denying the possibility of lateral transfer—he goes so far as to describe the theoretical conditions for lateral transfer—such as practicing the capability to be transferred in as wide a variety of contexts as is feasible—his massive body of theoretical and empirical work is directed at the vertical transfer problem.

Gagné distinguishes between the learning of "verbalizable knowledges" and "intellectual skills or strategies," which are parallel to what are sometimes referred to as contents and processes. He asserts that his hierarchical model of learning is only appropriate to the acquisition of intellectual skills. Furthermore, like Bruner he finds the acquisition of such processes far more important for learners than the acquisition of knowledge.

Ausubel asserts that *what* is transferred is subject-matter knowledge. This places him in clear contrast to the positions of Bruner and Gagné. With respect to the breadth of transfer, he maintains an intermediate position between Bruner and Gagné—less conservative than Gagné's insistence on identical elements, yet more moderate than Bruner's claims of the most far-reaching process transfer. He compares his position to that of Judd, who spoke of transfer by generalization.

In summary, the three theorists we have reviewed each rests his preference for particular types of educational objectives mainly on the conception of *transfer* to which he subscribes. Their debates serve as much of the basis for the controversies in science education concerning objectives.

Objectives—The Technical Level

Controversies at the technical level in this area were unique in that they were aired not only in professional journals and association meetings but through the medium of automobile bumper stickers as well. The message, "Help stamp out non-behavioral objectives" (later tempered to "....some non-behavioral objectives"), took its place in the vicinity of some college campuses and regional laboratories alongside stickers hailing the virtues of favorite political candidates. With the publication of Robert Mager's (1962) book on objectives, the techniques of objective writing had become a fashionable concern. Mager, following Gagné and the programmed instruction approach, insisted that an adequate statement of objectives must include a description of the terminal *performance* sought (the desired *response*), the specific *conditions* under which the performance could be observed (the *stimulus* situation), and the *criteria* by which the adequacy of performance could be judged. These specifications were in the operational definitions of objectives tradition of Tyler (1950) and Bloom (1956) but went well beyond them in the degree of precision demanded. Mager's standards were much more consonant with the experimental work of Gagné. This may be attributable to the fact that Tyler and Bloom were concerned much more with evaluation while Gagné and Mager focused on instructional design and training.

In the field of science teaching, one of the earliest debates was between the behavioral objectives approach of AAAS and the firm demurrer of Atkin (1963). Although often couched in the terms of the technical level of discourse (e.g., just how specific need an objective be to provide ample guidance to planners, evaluators, teachers and students?), the disagreements

nearly always contained elements of other levels (e.g., will you not hamstring the creative, spontaneous teacher with an overly precise, prescriptive and restrictive set of behavioral objectives?). Although these technical issues were faced in science education, they typically failed to stimulate empirical studies of the relative educational values of the various ways of stating objectives. The bulk of the technical-level dialogues were conducted in the general educational forum among participants such as Eisner (1969), Popham (1969) and Ebel (1970).

Objectives and Programs

More important than some of the debates were the actual statements of objectives written for science teaching programs. Only three will be considered here. In the AAAS project (Walbesser, 1966), the entire program pivots around the behavioral objectives and the learning hierarchies in which they are arranged. Similarly, the Individually Prescribed Instruction science program (Learning Research and Development Center, 1969; cited in Klopfer, 1971) employs precise behavioral statements of objectives as the basis for designing their materials and generating their formative, curriculum-embedded tests. Examples of such objectives, drawn from the Individually Prescribed Instruction A-level lessons, are:

Given one sound at a time, the student identifies the object or event which makes that sound.
Using a color-coded thermometer, the student measures the change in temperature of an object over a period of time.

A relative newcomer to the behavioral objectives approach has been BSCS. While they were not heavily emphasized in the first edition of the Biology Teachers' Handbook (BSCS, 1963), the second edition (BSCS, 1970) contains an imposing 27-page set of "Objectives for Teaching Enquiry Processes in Biology." These were the product of a collaborative venture involving BSCS and the Mid-Continent Regional Educational Laboratory. Although cast in the same general grammatical form as the AAAS or Individually Prescribed Instruction objectives, they remain at a more general level of precision. This may indicate that the goals of secondary science teaching are more abstract and general than those of lower grades, and different standards of specificity must be exercised for judging the adequacy of objectives at the higher grades. It is conceivable that as one progresses to more advanced levels of science teaching, the relative proportions of *instructional* and *expressive* objectives (Eisner, 1969) shift radically until, when reaching the levels of doctoral education, most of the objectives are expressive in form.

A major contribution to the teaching of science, in which educational objectives play a central role, is Klopfer's (1971) chapter in the Bloom, Hastings, and Madaus (1971) handbook. This handbook attempts to synthesize the earlier work of Tyler (1950) on curriculum development and evaluation, the taxonomies of educational objectives in the cognitive (Bloom, 1956) and the affective (Krathwohl, Bloom, & Masia, 1964) domains, and the more recent mastery learning model (Bloom, 1968; Block, 1971b).

There are several noteworthy characteristics in the new approach. The emphasis on precise behavioral statements of objectives is significantly greater than in Tyler or in the taxonomies but less doctrinaire than in Mager.

The original taxonomies had attempted to employ a single set of behavioral categories to encompass the objectives of all subject-matter areas. This tactic is clearly at odds with Schwab's repeated admonitions about the distinctive syntactic structures of the disciplines. In the new handbook each discipline modifies (often radically) the cognitive and affective taxonomy categories to capture more accurately the objectives of its subject-matter area. In Table 1 we re-produce a portion of the taxonomy written by Klopfer (1971) to reflect the objectives of science education relevant to processes of scientific inquiry. Although even a set of behaviors unique to science learning would not go far toward satisfying Schwab, the new approach surely makes the taxonomy-mastery learning model more readily applicable to evaluation in science education.

Another attribute of both Klopfer and the BSCS objectives is the attention devoted to the affective, attitudinal domain. This is unquestionably an important component of scientific literacy in its full sense, and deserves far more attention from science education researchers.

The arguments over the objectives of science teaching carried out at the normative level must be resolved using the methods and canons of evidence of the appropriate domains—philosophy of science, logic, history of science, political science, economics. The debates at the cognitive level rest on investigations in the psychology of learning and instruction. We would guess that the technical questions will be resolved relatively painlessly as the normative and cognitive problems are clarified. We shall now turn to an analysis of the psychology of teaching and learning in science with special reference to the twin concepts of discovery and inquiry around which so much of the discourse has revolved.

PSYCHOLOGICAL ANALYSES OF PEDAGOGICAL METHOD

The planning, conducting, evaluating and revising of instruction in science have not been done on a purely ad hoc or intuitive basis. During the period of its recent boom, the field of science education has been intimately bound up with issues of psychological theory. Like their colleagues in mathematics education, science educators have found psychological rationales both useful weapons for supporting already present predispositions and fruitful sources of new ideas (Shulman, 1970a). We have

TABLE 1

KLOPFER TABLE OF SPECIFICATIONS
(Excerpt)

Processes of Scientific Inquiry

B.0 I. Observing and Measuring
1. Observation of objects and phenomena
2. Description of observations using appropriate language
3. Measurement of objects and changes
4. Selection of appropriate measuring instruments
5. Estimation of measurements and recognition of limits in accuracy

C.0 II. Seeing a Problem and Seeking Ways to Solve It
1. Recognition of a problem
2. Formulation of a working hypothesis
3. Selection of suitable tests of a hypothesis
4. Design of appropriate procedures for performing experiments

D.0 III. Interpreting Data and Formulating Generalizations
1. Processing of experimental data
2. Presentation of data in the form of functional relationships
3. Interpretation of experimental data and observations
5. Evaluation of a hypothesis under test in the light of data obtained
6. Formulation of generalizations warranted by relationships found

E.0 IV. Building, Testing and Revising A Theoretical Model
1. Recognition of the need for a theoretical model
2. Formulation of a theoretical model to accommodate knowledge
3. Specification of relationships satisfied by a model
4. Deduction of new hypotheses from a theoretical model
5. Interpretation and evaluation of tests of a model
6. Formulation of a revised, refined, or extended model

H.0 Attitudes and Interests
H.1 Manifestation of favorable attitudes toward science and scientists
H.2 Acceptance of scientific inquiry as a way of thought.
H.4 Enjoyment of science learning experiences
H.5 Development of interests in science and science-related activities

TABLE 1 (Continued)

KLOPFER TABLE OF SPECIFICATIONS
(Excerpt)

I.0 Orientation
I.2 Recognition of the philosophical limitations and influence of scientific inquiry
I.5 Awareness of the social and moral implications of scientific inquiry and its results

Note: Excerpt from the Klopfer Table of Specifications, Klopfer, 1971, pp. 562–563.

already seen how the controversies over educational objectives in science teaching can in part be understood in terms of underlying differences in theories of transfer-of-training. In the recent years of the science teaching revolution, decisions about instruction have most often been explicitly rooted in, or at least rationalized by reference to, some form of psychological theory.

These theories were sufficiently diverse to justify programs as contrasting as AAAS Science, Individually Prescribed Instruction Science or Mastery Learning, all more or less rooted in a psychology of learning expounded by Robert M. Gagné; BSCS and its commitment to Schwab's conception of teaching as enquiry; the more nearly Piagetian emphasis of Elementary Science Study, Science Curriculum Improvement Study, and Macmillan Science, among others; and the general attractiveness of "discovery methods" as propounded by Bruner. Ausubel's subsumption theory, though admirably suited to the new science's emphasis on structure and conceptual themes, gained few advocates among the curriculum makers, perhaps because of his often difficult and pedantic writing style. One notable exception is the audiotutorial approach which is consonant with Ausubel's theory (Postlethwait, Novak, & Murray, 1969).

In this section we will first subject the key concept of *discovery* to critical analysis since it has served as the focal point for so much of the psychologically relevant discourse on instruction. We shall then turn to a brief review of the ways in which specific psychological theories have been translated into pedagogical prescriptions.

Discovery and Inquiry in Science Teaching

The concept of discovery has been replete with ambiguities as it is used in both the research literature and the more inspirational writings of science education.

A useful way of discussing an instructional situation (Wittrock, 1966) is in terms of the familiar trichotomy of independent, dependent and intervening variables: *independent variables* include the methods, materials or media of instruction, the characteristics of teachers or students, etc. The *dependent variables* are the goals of instruction: knowledge, understanding, skills, strategies, attitudes. The *intervening variables* are those processes, activities or events, usually not directly observed, whose presence is inferred to explain why a particular set of independent variables effectively leads to the observed values of the dependent variables.

Probably the major problem with the concept of discovery has been its use in different contexts to describe variables of each kind. The "discovery method of teaching" is a frequent descriptor for modes of instruction that are usually contrasted with other forms of instruction called "traditional," "expository," "guided," "didactic," "teacher-centered," "deductive" or "dogmatic." The latter terms usually carry with them a thinly veiled pejorative connotation. Alas, there is ambiguity enough just within the range of meaning assigned to discovery as an independent variable.

Discovery is also used to refer to the goals of instruction. "Learning to discover" as an objective of instruction can refer to almost any of the process objectives frequently cited as the most important goals of science education. Those associated with AAAS are good examples. In these cases discovery as an objective is contrasted with "content," "knowledge," "structure" and the like. Yet another way in which discovery is used to denote an instructional goal is when the instruction is directed toward achievement of a *particular* discovery.

Learning *by discovery* frequently refers to an internal process in the learner. This is the sense in which discovery is used as an intervening variable. Certain instructional conditions are designed to lead to the learning of some concept, principle and/or attitude via an intervening discovery process. Such a process is distinguished from learning by "reception," "being told" or "passively." Thus, an "act of discovery" (Bruner, 1961) may be seen as necessary to ensure that the learner integrates the material learned into his cognitive structure, develops the capacity to transfer what has been learned to novel problem situations, and acquires a positive concept of himself as an autonomous problem solver. The emphasis here is clearly on neither the method of instruction nor the ultimate instructional goals but on the ostensive intervening discovery processes that make successful attainment of the goals possible.

Wittrock has emphasized that no necessary isomorphism can be assumed between methods labeled "discovery" and learning outcomes similarly named. That is, a provocative, well-constructed lecture presentation (unlikely to be classified as a discovery method by even the most ecumenical of categorizers) could evoke internal discovery processes in members of the audience which in turn might lead to outcomes of a process type. For example, a narrative of enquiry approach to biology instruction might well teach students to use some of the strategies and processes of inquiry. Conversely, not even the most inductively sequenced or minimally guided instruction necessarily will teach students to discover.

With such considerable ambiguity in the use of the term "discovery" across the independent-intervening-dependent variable categories, not to mention the within-category confusions to be discussed presently, there is little wonder that Ramsey and Howe (1969a, 1969b) see the first priority in research on science teaching as cleaning up the language of discourse.

METHODS OF INSTRUCTION

The most widespread use of the term "discovery" has been in reference to teaching method. The research literature abounds with experimental contrasts between discovery teaching and its usually demeaned alternative. But pinning down what is generally meant by a "discovery method" is far from easy. We will examine only three frequently used (though practically orthogonal) conceptions of discovery teaching.

The Dimension of Guidance

The most intuitively meaningful conception of discovery teaching is teaching that is minimally guided or directed by the teacher—teaching that is not "merely telling." Clearly, however, there is a variety of levels at which guidance can be provided or withheld and these must be specified.

A useful framework for viewing this question of guidance has been provided by Schwab (1962b) and elaborated by Herron (1971). In describing the use of an enquiring laboratory for the teaching of biology, Schwab first distinguishes among three components of the learning situation: 1) problems, 2) ways and means for discovering relations and 3) answers. As can be seen in Table 2, there are a number of possible ways to permute these components to arrive

TABLE 2

LEVELS OF OPENNESS IN THE TEACHING OF INQUIRY

	Problem	Ways & Means	Answers
Level 0	Given	Given	Given
Level 1	Given	Given	Open
Level 2	Given	Open	Open
Level 3	Open	Open	Open

at different levels of guidance or "openness and permissiveness" in Schwab's terms.

The manual can pose problems and describe ways and means by which the student can discover relations he does not already know from his books. At a second level, problems are posed by the manual but methods as well as answers are left open. At a third level, problem, as well as answer and method, are left open: the student is confronted with the raw phenomenon . . . (Schwab, 1962b, p. 55).

Herron added the most highly guided dimension where all three levels are given in order to fill out the analysis. It is apparent that the more a program is committed to enquiry or discovery, the less guided the curriculum will be. The new science curricula were ostensibly so committed, hence we would expect that an analysis of their teaching methods would reveal a preponderance of minimally guided experiences. This has not been the case, however.

Herron (1971) analyzed the proposed laboratory exercises in the manuals of our two oldest and most distinguished secondary science programs, Physical Science Study Curriculum (PSSC) and BSCS, using the framework proposed by Schwab. He reports that of the 52 PSSC laboratory activities, 39 (nearly 80 percent) are at the zero level of total guidance. Eleven are at Level 1, two at Level 2 and none at Level 3.

The data for BSCS are hardly more impressive. The BSCS Blue version laboratory materials show 45 out of 62 lab exercises at the zero level, 13 at Level 1, four at Level 2 and, once again, none at Level 3. Table 3 summarizes Herron's data for the two curricula.

Thus, although reading their theoretical literature would surely lead us to anticipate that the new curricula would be filled with discovery teaching, Herron's analysis finds that there is a massive difference between philosophy and practice—this despite the claim that the laboratory had changed from a "demonstration" activity under traditional

TABLE 3

ANALYSIS OF PSSC AND BSCS (BLUE) LABORATORY EXERCISES BY DEGREE OF DISCOVERY OR ENQUIRY IN METHOD

Level of Discovery	BSCS	PSSC
0	45	39
1	13	11
2	4	2
3	0	0

programs to an inquiry activity in the new programs.

Quite similar analytic frameworks have also been advanced by Getzels (1964) and Shulman (1970a) in slightly different contexts. None of these, however, had ever been applied in the critical analysis of existing programs.

It should perhaps be reemphasized at this point that Schwab was well aware of the inherent ambiguity of the phrase *"teaching of science as enquiry"* and gave first priority to the concept of enquiry as a property of the science-to-be-learned (the dependent variable) and lower priority to enquiry as a method of instruction (independent variable). Thus, as long as the conception of science conveyed to the students reflects the proper role of enquiry, perhaps the relative infrequency of enquiry activities in the lessons need not be cause for alarm.

We may also observe the importance of Herron's contribution. It is so often taken for granted by investigators that a curriculum always teaches as advertised even if it does not always attain all the results it may claim. When the publicity announces a "ten-transistor radio that reproduces sound like a Fisher receiver," we would at least expect to find the number of transistors as advertised, even if the sound fidelity falls somewhat short of the claims. Herron has demonstrated that we had better count our curricular transistors as well. This is one of the few studies in science teaching in which the comparison of intention and reality at the level of antecedents of instruction (Stake, 1967) is carried out.

Sequence of Instruction

Although degree of guidance or openness in instruction is the most intuitively sensible meaning for discovery, it is by no means the most widely employed in studies of discovery teaching. Most often the more easily manipulated experimental dimension of *instructional sequence* serves as independent variable. An *inductive sequence,* wherein examples or observations precede generalizations, is inevitably dubbed the discovery treatment, while a *deductive sequence,* in which generalizations are provided first to be followed by illustrations, is labeled the expository or nondiscovery treatment.

The facile manner in which inductive sequencing is identified with discovery reflects a prevalent misunderstanding of how science is conducted. It reflects the pervasive influence of a tradition usually attributed to Bacon and Mill with a little help from generations of science textbook writers who managed to compound the problem by badly misinterpreting Dewey on scientific method. The essence of the position is that modern science was created by breaking away from Aristotelian rationalism and syllogistic reasoning. These were replaced by the objective, inductive and experimental methods of modern science. Hence, deduction is arcane, pre-Gallilean rationalism while induction is truly modern science. Since the new science curricula valued the way scientists make discoveries as a model for student activity, this conception of how scientific discovery takes place would lead to equating "discovery teaching" with inductive teaching.

It should be emphatically noted that contemporary philosophy and history of science has clearly rejected this way of characterizing science as an objective inductive process. The analyses of scientific thought by Popper (1935), Schwab (1960), Kuhn (1962), Medawar (1969) and others have amply demonstrated the hypothetico-deductive character of modern science. This implicit allegiance to the Baconian inductive myth may reflect how far from current thinking about science are many of those who conduct empirical studies of teaching and learning science.

Table 4 illustrates the independence of the *guidance* and *sequence* versions of discovery as independent variable. A guided sequence can be inductive or deductive. An inductive presentation can be highly guided or very open.

frames had formerly been treated as the most significant of variables, repeated studies demonstrated that even random scrambling of the sequence had little or no effect on learning outcomes (e.g., Payne, Krathwohl, & Gordon, 1967).

One of the reasons that sequence has been such a disappointing variable may be the very limited way in which it has been experimentally manipulated. There are at least four different levels at which one can

TABLE 4
VARIATIONS OF GUIDANCE AND SEQUENCE IN SCIENCE INSTRUCTION

	Inductive	Deductive
Guided	Examples of different organisms are given before names of phyla and principles of classification are given (example-rule sequence).	Names of phyla and principles of classification are given. Subsequently, specific organisms are given as illustrations (rule-example sequence).
Unguided	Examples of organisms are left to students to characterize and then classify. After students have done their own classifications they may be given conventional phyla.	Principles of classification are given. Students are then confronted with an array of organisms which they must classify (see Atkin & Karplus, 1962).

It is easy to imagine the very same guided inductive sequence being labeled "discovery" in one study and "expository" in another. How then is one to interpret the research literature when names are used interchangeably while meaning different things? Would it not make more sense to index any experimental treatment precisely in terms of a set of dimensions or distinctive features (Shulman, 1970b)? For example, a particular instructional treatment could be classified at a specific level of guidance or openness *and* an index of sequence rather than simply being labeled "discovery" and leaving the reader to guess what is meant.

Serious questions can be raised over the continued usefulness of sequence as an independent variable of concern. When used as the experimental variable of interest in learning studies, inductive sequencing has rarely been shown to have major advantages over alternatives. Most discouraging of all have been the programmed learning studies. In an area where sequence of

look at the educational consequences of instructional sequence:

1. The order in which the elements of instruction are presented *within a single lesson;*

2. The order in which lessons are sequenced *within an instructional unit;*

3. The order in which units are sequenced *within an instructional term* (may be of several months, half-year, full academic year or even several years' duration);

4. The order in which instructional *programs* are sequenced and/or correlated across a multiyear curriculum.

The experimental studies of sequence in science learning (in fact, school learning generally) have been almost exclusively of the first type, manipulations of within-lesson sequence. The remaining three levels remain relatively innocent of empirical trammeling albeit extremely important for educational planning and curriculum development.

The questions raised by Atkin and

Karplus (1962) on the combining of invention and discovery in teaching units could be studies at both levels 1 and 2. We have seen no examples of such research. Level 3 questions are similarly hard to find although some of Gagné's longer-term studies may fit that category. The audio-tutorial method lends itself rather easily to studies in which different instructional methods are used in predetermined sequences (e.g., Gallagher, 1970). Level 4 studies would involve the optimal sequencing of, say, particular science and math topics or subjects across grade levels. This is a topic of serious debate, especially between the Piagetians and their adversaries, but few studies have dealt with it (e.g., Collagham, 1969).

Source and Direction of Classroom Transactions

A quite different quality often attributed to the enquiring classroom or the discovery method of teaching is the active and initiatory role of the learner. Though this role may be influenced by the degree of guidance, it can be more readily indexed by identifying who initiates and controls the transactions in a learning situation, the teacher or the student.

An example of a student-controlled transaction is the inquiry-training approach to the teaching of science (Suchman, 1961). After being shown a very brief film clip of an intrinsically anomalous event, the students must conduct the ensuing inquiry through interrogation of the teacher in a format much like "Twenty Questions."

This is quite different from what is classically called the "Socratic method." In Socratic teaching students are encouraged to formulate principles to account for some phenomenon or to resolve an apparent problem. The teacher then takes control through a series of skillful questions to confront the student with contradictions or internal inconsistencies in the student's position. The teacher usually makes use of a variety of examples, analogies or metaphors in So-

cratic teaching. The control of the transaction is clearly in the hands of the teacher.

Ironically, although the control and direction of communications are exactly opposite in the two examples, both are usually classified toward the discovery/inquiry end of the pedagogical continuum. This is probably because both methods employ a great deal of discussion and this characteristic is usually associated with the enquiring classroom. Schwab has always made a great deal of the role of discussion as an instructional technique, both in his earlier "Eros and Education" (Schwab, 1954) and in his later work on science teaching (Schwab, 1962b). The lecture, characterized by high levels of guidance (problems, ways and means, and answers all given), typically deductive sequencing and teacher control of transactions with little or no pupil participation, stands firmly as the epitomization of traditional teaching method. Its diametric opposite would be minimum guidance (problems, methods and answers all left to student invention or discovery) and undetermined sequences left to student control in a classroom in which pupils determine what to do and when to do it while the teacher plays the role of benevolent, supportive resource for inquiry. Considering Herron's findings, about the only place we would currently find that "instruction-complex" is in one of the Elementary Science Study's activities characterized as "messing around" by David Hawkins (1966) and in some of the BSCS approaches such as the Laboratory Blocks or the BSCS Second Course (BSCS, 1965).

If current interest in open classrooms and free schools continues, however, unguided types of instruction are likely to proliferate, leaving the educational researcher with the responsibility for understanding what is taking place and developing approaches to the assessment of learning outcomes. This is consistent with Hawkins's (1966) observation that the best teaching is usually well ahead of the theoretical models that purport to explain and prescribe instruction. Hence Hawkins recommends an educational research strategy of identifying outstanding exemplars of effective teaching and studying what it is about those approaches that make them so successful. Shulman (1970b) advocates a similar research strategy for ultimately developing theoretical statements more consonant with the best of pedagogical practice.

Between the extremes of method just delineated lie an imposing variety of potentially useful (and undoubtedly well-employed) pedagogical procedures. For example, Atkin and Karplus (1962) describe an instructional procedure which combines the excitement and heuristic emphasis of minimally guided approaches with the efficiency and lack of ambiguity of expository methods. They distinguish between *invention,* where a concept must be constructed (usually by the teacher) to account for a particular puzzling phenomenon, and *discovery,* where, given a concept invented for them, students must discover ways to apply that concept to the anomalous events they confront. Although no systematic empirical evidence is marshaled to support their claims, the authors claim that this type of teaching is highly effective.

Psychological theories

Several psychological theories of learning and cognition have effectively dominated program development and research in science teaching. We shall now briefly review three of these theories. They are described in greater detail in the context of mathematics teaching in Shulman (1970a).

Robert M. Gagné—Learning Hierarchies

Gagné begins with the task analysis of the instructional objectives. He asks the question, "What is it you want the learner to be able to do?" This capability, he insists, must be stated specifically and behaviorally (Gagné, 1970).

By capability he means the ability to perform certain specific functions under specified conditions. A capability could be the ability to classify a group of plants into the appropriate phyla. It might be the ability to calculate the amount of work done in lifting an object to a specified height.

A capability can be thought of as a terminal behavior and placed at the top of what will eventually be a complex pyramid of prerequisites leading to the objective which is the desired capability. Gagné has developed a model for describing the different levels of such a hierarchy. If the final capability desired is a problem-solving capability, the learner first must know how to use certain rules or principles. To employ these principles he must be capable of using certain concepts. But prerequisite to these are particular simple associations or facts differing from each other in a distinctive manner. He continues such an analysis until he reaches the fundamental building blocks of learning—classically or instrumentally conditioned responses.

After completing the whole map of prerequisites, Gagné advocates the administration of pretests to determine which objectives have already been mastered. The pattern of responses to these diagnostic tests identifies precisely what must be taught (e.g., Okey & Gagné, 1970). This model serves as the theoretical foundation for much of Bloom's work on mastery learning (Bloom, 1968).

Gagné repeatedly points out that the learning hierarchy or learning structure which results from a task analysis by no means describes the universally necessary single pathway to a terminal objective. Instead it is a theoretical description of the average pathway taken by an average group of students. Specific individuals may vary from the derived learning hierarchy by skipping specific stages, by interpolating other stages that were not specified by those who constructed the hierarchy, or by reordering the sequence in which they traverse the stages. Although it is possible to achieve the terminal capability via alternate routes, Gagné would argue that the pathway identified in a well-constructed learning hierarchy will be the optimal plan for most students. If there is a predominant direction to Gagné's thinking, it is from the simple to the complex, from the initial building of associations and concepts through the inculcation of more complex rules and problem-solving capabilities.

Jerome S. Bruner—Learning by Discovery

For Bruner the focal point of student learning is a process called discovery. In discovery the learner is confronted by problems. These problems may take the form of a) goals to be achieved in the absence of readily discernible means for achieving those goals, b) contradictions among sources of information of apparently equal credibility, or c) the quest for structure or symmetry in situations where such order is not readily apparent.

The first step of discovery is a sensed incongruity or contrast. Bruner is always attempting to build potential or emergent incongruities into the materials of instruction. Such contradictions are used to engage the child, because of the resulting intellectual discomfort, in an attempt to resolve this disequilibrium by making some new discovery in the form of a reorganization of his understanding—what the Gestalt psychologists would have called "cognitive restructuring."

This discovery may require forming a new distinction, thus creating a new category of experience which will account for the now-recognized complexity of the situation. Or the discovery may involve a higher-order synthesis whereby the two apparently discrepant events—the previous understanding and some unexpected counter example—are now seen as jointly accounted for through some more abstract concept or rule. The essence of discovery for Bruner is something which takes place inside the learner through the eduction of new relations and the creation of new structures. For Bruner, discovery is not synonymous with looking up new material in the encyclopedia.

It can be argued that the dialectical quality of discovery learning sequences, wherein what the learner was previously confident of suddenly evaporates in the face of new data not assimilable in that old structure, simulates the manner in which new knowledge is actually discovered in the sciences. Such a model would be consistent with several contrasting contemporary characterizations of the dynamics of theoretical changes in science (e.g., Kuhn, 1962; Toulmin, 1970). Thus Bruner can argue not only for the cognitive effectiveness of learning by discovery but also, in the teaching of science, its effective simulation of what scientists do.

David P. Ausubel—Meaningful Verbal Learning

Ausubel, like Gagné, emphasizes the importance of systematically guided exposition in the process of education. The key is the careful sequencing of instructional experiences so that any unit taught is clearly related to those that preceded. It is this continuity between the learner's existing cognitive structure and the new material to be learned that makes the new material meaningful. Ausubel insists that there is certainly no basis for the assertion that anything learned through reception in that manner has been learned by rote.

In contrast to Bruner, Ausubel sees no reason why problem-solving activity (discovery) must precede the internalization of new facts, concepts or principles. If the material can be meaningfully organized by the instructor the need for student discovery is removed and the process of learning rendered far more efficient.

Ausubel begins the instructional sequence with a set of organizing statements at a level of abstraction higher than what must be learned subsequently. He calls such statements *advance organizers*. He uses these to establish an "ideational scaffolding" which both links what is to be learned with what the learner already knows and creates an organization or structure within which the new learning will be embedded. These organizers are expositorily taught to the learners as the first step in a unit of instruction. They are not to be discovered, as would be the initial stage of a Bruner program of instruction.

It is interesting to note that for many years Ausubel and Gagné were considered to be in fundamental agreement about the process of learning, although Gagné tended to view it as a process where meaningfulness occurred through movement from the simple to the complex, that is, from the concrete to the abstract, while Ausubel tended to view meaningfulness as a function of embedding specifics into the already assimilated context of more complex generalizations. In more recent years Gagné's assertion that the learning of processes and skills is far more important and fundamental than that of subject-matter mastery has made the two positions far more distinctive. One possible synthesis of the two positions may be to view Gagné's theory of learning hierarchies as a reasonable account of how *intellectual skills* are best acquired while treating Ausubel's subsumption theory of meaningful verbal learning as our most viable account for how organized bodies of subject-matter knowledge can best be acquired.

Where does this leave Bruner's theory of learning by discovery? It has repeatedly been noted that no firm evidence in support of the superiority of discovery learning exists (Belanger, 1969; Shulman, 1970a). But there are enough suggestive studies and strong advocates, such as Schwab, to maintain the seriousness of the hypothesis that under certain conditions, such as those in which highly transferable problem-solving proficiencies and attitudes toward inquiry in science are the objectives of instruction, those sorts of activities advocated by Bruner or Schwab are more likely to be fruitful than those so strongly supported by Gagné or Ausubel.

COMPARATIVE LEARNING RESEARCH

The theoretical discussions over psychological theories and teaching methods must ultimately be translated into carefully constructed empirical studies if they are to be useful to educators. In this section we shall begin to examine some of these studies. Thorough reviews of this research literature have been written by Belanger (1969) and Ramsey and Howe (1969a; 1969b; 1969c). Rather than redo their excellent reviews, we shall concentrate on three topics in this section: experimental studies of the laboratory in science education, the variety of tests used to assess the effectiveness of science instruction, and studies of instructional alternatives to the laboratory.

The Laboratory

The laboratory has always been the most distinctive feature of science instruction. It continues to occupy a central role in all of the new science curricula (BSCS, 1963; Chemical Bond Approach Project, 1964; Chemical Education Material Study, 1963; Earth Science Curriculum Project, 1967; Nuffield, 1965).

Three major rationales are generally advanced for this emphasis on the laboratory:

1. Science involves highly complex and abstract subject matter. Even high-school students may fail to grasp such concepts without the concrete props and opportunities for manipulation afforded in the laboratory.

2. Student participation in enquiry, in actual collection of data and analysis of real phenomena, is an essential component of the enquiring curriculum (Schwab, 1962b). It gives students an appreciation of the spirit and methods of science, it promotes problem-solving, analytic and generalizing ability (Ausubel, 1968) and it provides a real image of science.

3. Students enjoy activities and practical work (Selmes, Ashton, Meredith, & Newal, 1969).

With the advent of the new curricula important changes have taken place in the role assigned to the laboratory. The laboratory had traditionally been viewed as an organizational setting where science students observed and manipulated materials which demonstrated certain aspects of the subject matter which had been learned in class primarily through textbooks, lectures and discussions. Over the years many studies had been made to assess the relative effectiveness of laboratory and demonstration approaches for achieving those goals. Most of these studies failed to establish any superiority of the laboratory, as measured by paper and pencil achievement tests (Chester, 1938; Coulter, 1966; Cunningham, 1946; Goldstein, 1937; Mallinson, 1947). However, with the shift of emphasis from acquisition of knowledge to other objectives which stress the processes of science, the laboratory acquired a central role, not as a means for demonstration and confirmation but rather as the core of the science learning process.

This shift in the role of the laboratory has not been based on empirical evidence but rather on opinions of leading personalities, often scientists who took part in the design of the new curricula. At present this has become one of the major controversies in science education. While some educators feel that "at least half of the class time should be spent on activities and laboratory exercises" (Romey, 1969), others will demand a third of the class time be devoted to the laboratory (Organization for Economic Cooperation and Development, 1962) and still others will contend that "a reasonable objective and also a minimum objective is to plan for one laboratory period or field trip each week" (Novak, 1970a). Ausubel (1968) believes that since the laboratory is very time consuming and inefficient it should typically carry the burden of conveying the methods and spirit of science whereas the teacher and the textbook assume the burden of transmitting subject-matter content. Clearly, considering the state of current knowledge, debates over the distribution of hours to laboratory work are premature. The important question now is, given the new roles assigned to the laboratory, how effectively are these being carried out?

What are the objectives now sought via laboratory teaching? We have reviewed various lists of laboratory objectives (Bingman, 1969; BSCS, 1963; Glass, 1960; Lee, Lehman, & Petersen, 1967; A. Novak, 1963; J. D. Novak, 1970a; Romey, 1969; Wilson, 1962) and they are remarkably coextensive with the objectives generally adduced for science learning per se (Bingman, 1969; Pella, 1961). The stated objectives fall into one or more of the following areas:

Skills: e.g., manipulative, inquiry, investigative, organizational, communicative;

Concepts: e.g., hypothesis, theoretical model, taxonomic category;

Cognitive abilities: e.g., critical thinking, problem solving, application, analysis, synthesis, evaluation, decision making, creativity;

Understanding the nature of science: e.g., the scientific enterprise, the scientists and how they work, the existence of multiplicity of scientific methods, the interrelationship between science and technology and among the various disciplines of science;

Attitudes: e.g., curiosity, interest, risk-taking, objectivity, precision, confidence, perseverance, satisfaction, responsibility, consensus and collaboration, liking science.

Fortunately recent investigations of laboratory teaching have attempted to assess changes in many of these types of variables in addition to the more conventional measures of science achievement. We have chosen a study which reflects many desirable characteristics in terms of questions posed, experimental design employed and actual execution to exemplify the best research in this area. This study (Yager, Englen, & Snider, 1969) used a variety of measures which cover the cognitive as well as the affective and the psychomotor domains. In addition, the researchers were very careful to control for many possible sources of contamination so as to keep internal validity appreciably high. They were especially careful to ascertain that the "no laboratory" group would not experience a lecture approach where premium was placed upon fact mastery as had been true in many of the studies reported earlier in the literature. Like the two other groups, the "no laboratory" group experienced science as inquiry, although this was not experienced in the laboratory sense.

The subjects were 60 students in the eighth grade (mean IQ 117.3) who studied an adaptation of the BSCS Blue version. They were divided into three groups.

In the *laboratory group* the students performed individually or in groups, as specified in the Teacher's Guide, 50 out of 57 laboratories of the BSCS Blue Version. They were also the only ones who had the benefit of comparing results with other individuals or groups in the classroom.

The *demonstration group* was handled in the same manner and used the same 50 experiments except that only one experiment was performed at one time in the class, either by the teacher or by one of the students. Here most students were observers. Although one set of results was secured, conflicting data were occasionally provided by the teachers for discussion purposes.

In the *discussion group* no experiments were performed and the students neither used nor saw any of the usual materials that characterize the laboratory. However research results of the same 50 experiments were available and the students did interpret results and draw conclusions from them and related such conclusions to other situations. They also discussed experimental design and alternative experiments.

The teacher's approach with each of the three groups was one of attempting to do the best job possible within the framework described. The three sections were treated as a single group for purposes of grading and general evaluation. The teacher variable was controlled by having the teachers shift from section to section at natural intervals about every four weeks. The teachers involved were similar in terms of experience, education and dedication, and were judged to practice "science as inquiry" in the classroom.

A series of pre- and posttests was administered using the following instruments: Test on Understanding Science Form W, Watson-Glaser Critical Thinking Appraisal, Silance Attitude Scale, Prouse Subject Preference Scale, Read Science Test, Nelson Biology Test, BSCS Comprehensive Final, and a practical laboratory test developed for this particular study. This practical test consisted of the following:

1. ability to focus a microscope at low and high power;

2. time involved in constructing a manometer;

3. ability to set up a workable manometer;

4. ability to make coacervates.

On the basis of the research findings it was concluded that the laboratory approach provided no measurable advantages over other modes of instruction except in the development of laboratory skills.

Strong support for this conclusion has been found in a similar study with Introductory Physical Science eighth-graders where again the only advantage of the laboratory method was the development of certain manipulative skills (Pella & Sherman, 1969).

On the basis of their results, Yager, Englen, & Snider (1969) suggested four implications, each of which must be regarded at this stage as a hypothesis which requires much more research in order to be either substantiated or rejected. These implications follow:

A. Since desirable outcomes in science are obtained even though the laboratory is limited, the role of the laboratory as a central activity for individual students which characterizes all new curricula should be questioned.

B. For certain students and certain teachers a verbal nonlaboratory approach may be the best means of stimulating them to understand and to appreciate science.

C. Some students (especially at advanced levels) may find the laboratory to be a waste of time and merely a means of slowing their pursuit of new theories and concepts.

D. Structuring of some new courses that would de-emphasize the laboratory per se while still emphasizing the nature of the scientific enterprise may well be a worthwhile effort.

Several critical comments are warranted. Yager, Englen, and Snider suggest that "for certain students and certain teachers" a nonlaboratory approach may be more effective. They are strongly implying the existence of aptitude-treatment interactions (Cronbach & Snow, 1969) in this area of science learning. Yet such studies are thus far nearly nonexistent. When they have been conducted in other domains the findings have generally not reflected the anticipated interaction. What sorts of student or teacher variables are hypothesized to interact with laboratory teaching? We have little idea.

In their observation concerning the appropriateness of the laboratory for more advanced students, Yager, Englen, and Snider introduce another aspect of the aptitude-treatment interaction issue. An aptitude, for Cronbach and Snow, is any characteristic of a learner that is likely to make him more *apt* to learn something in one way than in some other. Such characteristics include general intelligence, specific intellectual aptitudes (e.g., verbal ability, spatial relations, mathematical reasoning), personality characteristics and *prior levels of achievement* in the learning areas of concern. It is thus reasonable to suggest that the effectiveness of the laboratory may be partially a function of when it is introduced during the development of scientific understanding by students. Such research on the effectiveness of particular teaching methods at different stages of learning a topic has not been conducted (cf. our discussion of the meanings of "sequence" in an earlier section).

Finally, the Yager, Englen, and Snider (1969) study lacks classroom process measures to ascertain what sorts of interactions are in fact taking place under the label "enquiry." Herron's (1971) analysis of the BSCS (Blue) laboratories revealed little open-ended inquiry even possible with the instructions given. If this be the case, perhaps the "no difference" findings should be less surprising than the finding that all three groups showed significant gains in critical thinking.

There is no doubt that before any far-reaching conclusions can be generally accepted, replications of the study with different students and different teachers in different schools and different age groups using different subject matter should be carried out. But even more important than that are the following questions: Have we succeeded in measuring all possible outcomes? Have we not fallen into the trap of using available standardized instruments which have not been designed specifically to test the outcomes of laboratory work and therefore have failed to discriminate and to indicate existing although hitherto unnoticeable differences?

These are fundamental questions not only with regard to the laboratory but to any problem in science education. It will, therefore, be worthwhile to stop and examine the dependent variables and the instruments used for assessment in this study since they are characteristic of typical research in the field.

ACHIEVEMENT IN SCIENCE AND BIOLOGY

Three standardized multiple-choice paper and pencil tests were used by Yager, Englen, & Snider (1969). The lack of any significant differences among the groups is not surprising at all since similar results concerning achievement have been obtained in hundreds of studies comparing Method A with Method B, even when these methods were much more distinctive than the ones employed in the Yager research. The tests used here, like most standardized science achievement tests, can no doubt be criticized for their preoccupation with "knowledge" objectives, the lowest common denominator of science achievement. Hopefully such contributions to the measurement of science achievement as Klopfer (1971) will help to remedy that problem.

UNDERSTANDING THE SCIENTIFIC ENTERPRISE

In order to measure this outcome, Yager's study, like many others, used the Test on Understanding Science (Cooley & Klopfer, 1961). Since this test has been so widely used in research in science education, "findings in this area stand or fall on how well changes in scores on this particular instrument measure growth in understanding the scientific enterprise" (Ramsey & Howe, 1969a). A review of studies done between 1960 and 1969 led Ramsey and Howe to conclude that a "multireference, laboratory centered approach to biology will produce greater student growth in understanding the scientific enterprise." Yet in the Yager study and in several others (e.g., Jungwirth, 1970; Trent, 1965) no such difference could be detected.

Connelly (1969) has noted that of 24 curriculum or method evaluation studies reported in the *Journal of Research in Science Teaching* during 1965 and 1966, nine used the Test on Understanding Science to measure student understanding of science. He appropriately criticizes the uncritical use of this test in all these studies, since the Cooley-Klopfer test reflects only one of the possible conceptions of enquiry. This criticism is echoed by Welch (1969b).

Few studies were located in which the Test on Understanding Science was compared with other measures on understanding the nature of science or related abilities and attitudes. In those studies (Tamir, 1968; Troxel & Snider, 1970), correlations were low to moderate between this test and the Welch Science Process Inventory, the Vitrogan Attitude Scale and several critical thinking tests.

CRITICAL THINKING

The Watson-Glaser Critical Thinking Appraisal has been almost the only instrument used to measure critical thinking ability. Most of the discussion in the previous paragraph concerning the Test on Understanding Science will hold for the Critical Thinking Appraisal. In addition, "the items on this instrument do not refer specifically to science, so changes in scores may as readily be attributed to the social studies or English courses as to a particular science course. For this reason gains on the test can only validly be attributed to a particular instructional procedure in science if both the experimental and control groups have identical teachers and courses in all other subjects, and this is a difficult requirement to attain in practice" (Ramsey & Howe, 1969a, p. 65). Still another problem is that preparation, background and philosophy of the teacher were found to be extremely important. If the above statements are kept in mind, one can hardly be surprised that laboratory-centered instruction seems to enhance the development of critical-thinking skills in some studies (Johns, 1966; Sorensen, 1966) while not in others (George, 1965; Pella & Sherman, 1969; Yager, Englen, & Snider, 1969). Connelly's (1969) sensitivity to the fine distinctions among ways of conceiving of enquiry, cited above, is not applied to distinctions among kinds of cognitive processes. He observes that some of the reviewed papers, "of course, deal with such matters as critical thinking and use the appropriate standardized tests." We would point out that a standardized instrument to measure an undifferentiated ability called critical thinking surely has no more validity than an all-purpose test of understanding science.

Unquestionably the global category of "critical thinking" must be broken down and redefined operationally into a series of science-oriented measurable capabilities. Only when this is done can we expect to find replicable differences of educationally relevant magnitude attributable to particular approaches to the teaching of science. We should also remember Bridgham's (1969) admonition against overblown claims that science instruction transfers broadly to general, nonscience thinking processes and abilities.

Attitudes

Ramsey and Howe sum up the current state of affairs when they observe that "the evidence is mounting that ... teaching procedures can be devised to bring about attitude change.... There is still a large question mark over the relation between actual behavior and scores on pencil-and-paper tests, .." (1969a, p. 68). It is doubtful whether the instruments used by Yager, Englen, and Snider (1969)—the *Silance Scale for Measuring Attitudes Toward Any School Subject* and the *Prouse Subject Preference Survey*—are immune to that criticism. It would require attitude measures far more sensitive than we currently possess to tap such laboratory-related attitudes as habits of accuracy, curiosity, readiness to experience and accept repeated failures, perseverance, the satisfaction and excitement of discovery, responsibility, collaboration and consensus, and reliance on the observables of experience rather than on the dogmas of textbooks.

Additional techniques used to measure attitude change are adaptations of the semantic differential (Geis, 1968; Rothman, 1968) and development of a multi-attitude self-report inventory (Moore & Sutman, 1970). Klopfer's (1971) work on science-learning evaluation in the affective domain is also both relevant and promising.

Laboratory Skills: Manual and Investigative

The superiority of the laboratory group in practical manual performance, observed in both the Yager, Englen, and Snider (1969) and Pella and Sherman (1969) studies, may not deserve the subtle contempt in which it appears to be held by some writers. "The development of psychomotor skills has been almost completely ignored in science education" (Ramsey & Howe, 1969a, p. 68) without good justification. Jeffrey's (1967) study which employed special tests using slides and movie films to assess the development of communicative, observational and investigative competencies in chemistry laboratory work is a step in the right direction.

Practical examinations need not be designed to meet such narrow objectives as reported by Yager, Englen, and Snider (1969) or Pella and Sherman (1969). A practical examination can be devised to allow the appraisal of outcomes much more important than manipulative skills. Investigative, inquiry, reporting, communicative and creative abilities, problem identification, problem solving, response to failure, overcoming of unpredicted obstacles and interrelating reasoning and action are some of the outcomes which can be well appraised by properly designed practical examinations (Tamir & Glassman, 1970; 1971a).

Similarly, sequential decision-making examinations are being developed (Koos, 1971) which assess the student's capability for conducting an inquiry. In addition, the work of Butts (e.g., Butts & Jones, 1967) has been the source of an exciting attack on the sequential problem-solving aspects of science.

It is foreseeable that with progress in educational technology and computerized retrieval devices, simulation of laboratory situations can be devised where many laboratory-related objectives can be evaluated more efficiently. Even then we shall not be able to overlook the broadly oriented practical examination, presenting science problems for students to solve, as an important vehicle for evaluation of achievement. This statement is supported by the finding that when the performance of students in paper and pencil tests is compared with their performance in laboratory tests, the practical appears to be a unique and distinct mode of performance (Tamir, 1972).

Dynamics of the Laboratory

The laboratory continues to occupy its central role in most science courses. Yet research on alternative ways of conducting and organizing a laboratory, the teacher and student roles, and the relations between the laboratory and other learning modes remains scarce. Hurd and Rowe (1966) studied the group dynamics within the laboratory setting and identified important differences between college-bound and non-college-bound students. The more active role of students in laboratory situations may be inferred from the relatively low percentage of teacher talk (50 percent) during the laboratory period as compared to 75 percent in the regular classroom (Parakh, 1968). The relative effectiveness of four types of laboratory reports (essay, report sheet, question report, no written report) was studied by Torop (1969). The findings favored the structured type of written report in terms of achievement in chemistry and of performance on the Test on Understanding Science. However the lack of an instrument to measure the criterion directly was justifiably recognized to be one of the limitations of this study.

A "content-centered" laboratory where activities revolved around explicit directions of the manual and/or instructor was compared with a "process-centered" laboratory where students were engaged in solving problems which had been defined by their teacher or themselves (Murphy, 1967). The subjects were college freshmen, and a variety of instruments were used to assess the outcomes after a year of study. Findings led to the conclusion that while neither the content-centered nor the process-centered general biology laboratory was categorically more effective than the other, the factors contributing to student success were not the same for the two approaches.

The entire area appears to be open to research. Some of the problems described need replication and elaboration. Many others await their turn. If anything remains nearly certain about the laboratory as both planned and practiced, it is that the laboratory is still far from becoming a center of inquiry in the typical science teaching program (Brandwein, 1969; Herron, 1971). A notable exception may be the well-conducted laboratory block. We need more evidence that laboratory blocks can be consistently administered in the enquiring mode and subsequent research to assess the results of such programs.

Vicarious Instruction

While the conventional classroom engages the learner in face-to-face contact with a live teacher and the laboratory involves direct tactile encounters with objects and instruments of scientific investigation, there also exist a host of other devices with which the student can learn. We shall refer to these media as means of *vicarious instruction*. They include films and film loops, television, slides, programmed instruction and combinations of these.

Watson (1963) concluded that in general there were no significant differences in achievement between students who studied by films and television and those who studied by conventional methods. Students who studied exclusively by film or television for longer periods experienced significant loss of interest and developed negative attitudes toward science. It seems unlikely that filmed or television courses can take over the entire instructional role. A more promising approach is to use television, films and other audiovisual aids as an integral part of the teaching process. Several studies have shown that effective integration of audiovisual aids into the instructional sequence may result in improved achievement of high-school as well as elementary students (e.g., Clegg, 1966; Nasca, 1965).

An important innovation in science teaching has been the development of single topic loops, each lasting four minutes. These short films have been widely used for various purposes: to review, motivate, establish a concept, set a problem, emphasize a skill, depict a situation and describe an environment. Gibbs (1968) found that the ability to construct relevant hypotheses in biology was improved significantly in classes using the BSCS single topic loops.

PROGRAMMED INSTRUCTION

While 10 years ago programmed materials dealing with science were rare (Watson, 1963), today many such programs which cover specific topics in science are available for elementary, secondary and college levels. In elementary grades programmed instruction was found to be as efficient or better than traditional instruction in terms of acquisition of concepts and performance in achievement tests (Hedges & MacDougall, 1965; Taylor, 1960). Thus it appears that programmed instruction can be successfully used in elementary schools, encouraging individual work and freeing the teachers for tasks other than direct instruction. Similar results were obtained with high-school science students. Young (1968) found that students achieved under programmed instruction as well as controls but in less time, while Carnes's (1966) experimental group achieved in the same time better than the controls. Programmed self-instruction also constitutes a major component of Individually Prescribed Instruction Science (Klopfer, 1971) in the form of multimedia packages.

Programmed materials have been used successfully at the high-school level as part of a course (BSCS, 1966) to combine reading and laboratory work (Nasca, 1965), to teach science students the elements of statistics (Benson & Howell, 1968) and for many other purposes. Programmed materials seem to be especially helpful for topics with which students encounter difficulties, like population genetics, energy relationships or the structure of DNA. In an evaluation of a program on population genetics for BSCS, tenth-graders in program classes had a significantly higher (53 percent) gain than nonprogram classes. The highest gains were achieved by students who possessed the

necessary entering behavior skills and who completed the program without shortcuts. Both teachers and students liked the program (R. C. Anderson, Faust, & Roderick, 1969).

Research in this area should move away from feasibility studies to the problem of how programmed material can be best incorporated and applied in the classroom. One such example is a study by Reynolds and Glaser (1964). It is interesting to note that the BSCS invitations to enquiry (BSCS, 1963) may be viewed as a special variant of programmed instruction. One has only to glance at the teacher's guide for any of these invitations, such as the BSCS single topic loops, to recognize the frames of the program. However, what occurs in the classroom between any pair of frames depends on the initiative, ideas and activities of both the teacher and his students, many of which cannot be anticipated. Moreover, these programmed materials are not aimed at individualized but rather at group instruction and are at the same time programmed and open-ended. Analysis of basic issues of programmed instruction within the framework of invitations to enquiry should prove to be a very interesting research project.

AUDIO-TUTORIAL INSTRUCTION

This type of programmed instruction was begun in 1961 by S. N. Postlethwait at Purdue University and soon became the core of the introductory botany course there. Audio-taped programs are used by individual students in specially arranged carrels located in the learning center. The tape commentary is supplemented with textbook, laboratory manual, specimens, experimental equipment, etc. The learning center is open from 7:30 a.m. to 10:30 p.m. Monday through Friday and the student may run through the program at his convenience. He may proceed at his own rate and is free to leave any time (Postlethwait, Novak, & Murray, 1964). The system claims to possess many advantages (Sanderson, Postlethwait, & Sanderson, 1968). The most important advantage is the opportunity given to the individual learner to integrate experiences by bringing together related learning activities so that they complement and enhance each other. The audiotutorial system attempts to provide an opportunity for individualized study while retaining the important ingredients of inquiry (Postlethwait, 1970).

While audio-tutorial instruction is being used at all levels—elementary, secondary and college—evaluation reports are only beginning to appear. The rate of failure of college botany students was reported to decrease and the percentage of A's and B's to increase. In general, students who spend more time working in the learning center achieve higher scores on tests. However students with high analytic ability gained more knowledge in nine hours of study than students with low analytic ability acquired in 20 hours (Postlethwait, Novak, & Murray, 1969). This finding should be carefully replicated as a possible aptitude-treatment interaction. Novak (1970b) observes that "since it becomes increasingly apparent that most normal students are capable of learning the subject matter, the time variable is by far the most important. In audio-tutorial instruction, learning time can be monitored systematically."

Audio-taped programs in the lower grades of elementary school were pioneered by Novak (1970b). These programs may be especially important for first- and second-graders where reading is a persistent handicap. It also helps many elementary teachers overcome their reluctance to introduce science into their classrooms. Three years of experimentation with these programs in the U. S. and in Israel have been very encouraging. More definite evaluation is in progress.

Gallagher (1970) found that third-grade pupils instructed in the individual audio-tutorial mode were distracted overtly for a smaller proportion of instructional time than pupils who were instructed in the teacher-directed group mode. He also found

that pupils who were instructed individually were better able to generalize across several exemplars.

MULTIMEDIA APPROACHES

A teaching situation which incorporates a variety of instructional modes and media is becoming more and more popular, especially at the college level. This multimedia approach is based on the assumption that while certain objectives can be best achieved by self-instruction, others will require group discussion and still others will favor large group assemblies (Postlethwait, 1970; Siemankowsky, 1969). Another assumption is that students differ in their learning styles—some learn better by one medium while others will prefer another. Since we know very little about what medium under what conditions will best suit a particular student in his pursuit of a certain objective, the most we can do is to provide a variety of media until more definite guidance is offered by research. This approach was adopted by some of the new curricula. With Harvard Project Physics students the multimedia approach seemed to benefit both high and low achievers and to increase student interest in physics (Poorman, 1968). Employment of the multimedia approach in introductory college physics increased the interest of students and enrollment in physics went up more than 100 percent as compared to an all-university increase of only 11 percent (Black & Poorman, 1970). The multimedia approach was superior to conventional methods in teaching physical science to nonscience majors in college (Siemankowsky, 1969). The multimedia approach made physics more attractive and interesting for students and more satisfying to teach, and it promoted acquisition of concepts and understanding of processes (M. D. Smith, 1969).

Another advantage of this approach, especially for nonscience majors, may lie in the development of more favorable attitudes toward science. In a recent study in England, high-school graduates were asked to account for the fact that the number of students wishing to study arts and social sciences at universities is increasing more rapidly than the number wishing to study natural sciences. The main reasons given by most students, both girls and boys, for rejecting the natural sciences were: high level of intelligence required, less scope for self-expression, more boredom in lessons and lack of practical application (Selmes et al., 1969). The multimedia approach is typically less routine and offers a variety of experiences to and demands greater initiative from the learner. There already exists some evidence that this approach indeed results in a more positive attitude toward science and scientists (Siemankowsky, 1969).

Elementary Science

One of the major developments in science education within the last 10 years has been the inclusion of science as an integral part of almost any elementary-school curriculum. That this is a rather major development is indicated by the fact that elementary science was not even mentioned in the Research On Science Teaching chapter of the Gage *Handbook* (Watson, 1963). Although many good reasons have been offered for introducing science to elementary schools, such as building concepts, developing skills, laying the basis for subsequent learning, developing intellectual potential, and motivating and raising interest, few have been based on research evidence. No doubt, however, Piaget's work and Bruner's emphasis on early readiness played an important role.

Ramsey and Howe (1969c) reviewed 132 studies related to instructional procedures in elementary-school science in the last decade. They show that various objectives can be attained such as developing reading skills, concepts, critical thinking, problem-solving ability, creativity and inquiry skills (see their paper for specific references). They also demonstrated that various instructional means may be effective in elementary science such as programmed

instruction, films, television and individualized instruction. However, 95 percent of these studies involved grades 4 through 6, and even with these grades it is rather difficult to assess what would be lost if science were completely removed from the curriculum.

To date, research dealing with the value of elementary science is almost nonexistent, and what is available is not very encouraging. For instance, Price (1968) investigated whether pupils who gathered data by manipulating materials would transfer this behavior outside the classroom. He designed appropriate test situations outside the classroom but the pupils failed to use any manipulative processes in seeking data under outside conditions. Raun (1967) found that fifth- and sixth-graders, as compared to fourth-graders who studied Science—A Process Approach, showed regressive tendencies in inquiry performance.

The findings of these two studies may support those who doubt the utility of teaching processes and skills devoid of content. Although Science—A Process Approach has succeeded in building into its materials specific objectives to be matched by individual task tests, the huge evaluation reports (Walbesser, 1966) do not yet provide answers to the more fundamental questions of elementary science.

Critique of Experimental Studies

The disappointing harvest gleaned from the body of comparative experimental research in science teaching presents serious problems. In the most incisive of recent reviews of learning research in science, Belanger (1969) makes a number of rather pessimistic observations. After noting that descriptions of experimental treatments are usually so brief or obscure that generalization to other teaching situations is most often precluded, he observes that comparative experiments contrasting "method X vs. method Y" do little more than demonstrate the obvious or add to our confusion; that no evidence for the superiority of discovery methods exists; and that generally the learning studies conducted were too simplistic for the nature of the phenomena studied. At best the experimental studies are "suggestive." Even on those relatively rare occasions when a significant difference is observed and replicated, the magnitude of the difference appears trivial indeed.

R. C. Anderson (1969) argues that the most useful kind of curriculum-related research is the comparative field experiment in which portions of two actual curricula are contrasted under more-or-less natural conditions. He demonstrates how such research can be conducted using his own comparative field testing of a self-instructional unit in genetics as an example. Such research is very different from the type of learning experiment typically undertaken in educational research.

Thus, Anderson suggests we turn our attention from the learning laboratory to the broader arena of curriculum evaluation. Even if we fail to answer successfully questions like "what type of instruction works best?" perhaps we can cope with the question of how well the new programs developed during the period of science curriculum reform have performed.

CURRICULUM EVALUATION

The obvious question to ask about the new curricula is "Did they work?" No less an educational critic than Charles Silberman (1970) declared that the new programs had been a dismal failure. He supported his assertion with several types of evidence.

In a chapter of *Crisis in the Classroom* entitled "The Failures of Educational Reform," Silberman (1970) states that "the reform movement has produced innumerable changes, and yet the schools themselves are largely unchanged." The curriculum reform had been "blunted on the classroom door." First he cites evidence that only a small proportion of high-school seniors have actually studied new programs in physics,

biology or chemistry (Fornoff, 1969; Kastrinas, 1969; Thompson, 1969; Watson, 1967). If they are not adopted, he reasons, how can they succeed? Second, even when adopted they are not effectively used. Here he simply declares that "one need only sit in classrooms...to know that...the curriculum reform movement has made a pitifully small impact on classroom practice."

Most science educators would doubtless wish to argue that Silberman's report of the new curricula's demise is grossly exaggerated. Yet how does one refute the claims of the critics? Consideration of the problems of evaluating science curricula quickly brings us to the heart of a number of substantive and methodological issues in research on the teaching of science.

Evaluation Research

In spite of the huge investment in efforts and money, large- and small-scale studies have substantiated that students of the new curricula typically perform as well as those of so-called conventional curricula on traditional tests and achieve somewhat better on tests especially designed for the new curricula. Reviews and summaries of these studies were provided by Ramsey and Howe (1969b) and Welch (1969b). Some are disappointed with these findings and argue that following such massive efforts students in the new curricula should achieve far better rather than approximate the achievements of students in the old curricula (Ausubel, 1968; Easley, 1966). It can be argued, however, that the success of "new" students on conventional tests is a favorable characteristic since the new curricula de-emphasize factual knowledge and devote larger proportions of time to the pursuit of other objectives.

It appears safe to assert that massive comparisons generally fail to yield useful information and research should therefore focus on careful study of more specific questions. Additionally, rather than concentrate on narrow conceptions of academic achievement usually summarized by a single test score, emphasis should be on the measurement of multidimensional outcomes including both intended and unintended consequences.

We have chosen to classify evaluation studies into five categories, each of which will be discussed in turn:

a. Evaluation of programs through studies of adoption and use;
b. Studies of the "impact" of new programs;
c. Comparative evaluation studies;
d. Long-term follow-up studies;
e. Transaction studies focusing on actual classroom processes rather than exclusively on outcomes.

Each of the above has its merits and limitations, yet each can play an important role in evaluation and research. The most comprehensive evaluation will incorporate a variety of such approaches. We shall discuss briefly some selected studies which represent each of the mentioned approaches.

Adoption of New Curricula

The extent to which a certain curriculum has been adopted may serve as a reflection of its success. Silberman (1970) leans heavily on such studies to support his argument that the new curricula have failed. Available information is incomplete, conflicting and unreliable (Tamir, 1970; Welch, 1968b). However, even with this situation, some important findings could be secured. First, the Yellow Version was the most widely used in comparison to other BSCS versions (Blight & Bila, 1968; Psychological Corporation, 1967; Tamir, 1968). Second, there was no correlation between the quality of high school, as defined in the studies, and the adoption of the new curricula (Cawelti, 1967; H. Grobman, 1968b; Tamir, 1970). Third, enrollment in physics departments of high schools has continued to drop even after the introduction of PSSC physics

(Bridgham & Welch, 1969; Krieger, 1968; V. J. Young, 1965). Fourth, the BSCS, as compared to other National Science Foundation programs, is the most widely used in the United States (McCurdy, 1969; NCA Today, 1967). And fifth, BSCS has been adopted with local adaptations by nearly 50 countries all over the world (Mayer, 1970).

In contrast to the disappointing data on adoption and use of new curricula cited by Silberman, Conant (1967) had reported wide adoptions of new physics, biology and chemistry courses. Silberman argues, however, that Conant's questionnaires were worded so ambiguously that the findings are misleading. This is further evidence that data on adoptions, which would appear so simple and reliable, are also full of potentially misleading errors.

Impact of the New Curricula

Another somewhat indirect way of evaluating the outcomes of a new program is through assessing its spin-offs—the activities or products spawned under its influence. At least two types of influence can be identified, influence on other programs and teachers and influence on the development and use of new approaches to testing and evaluation.

Program and Teaching Impacts

Atkin (1967–1968) suggests that the most important substantive changes in the schools over the past two decades have been a result of the curriculum development projects supported primarily by the National Science Foundation. The impact of the new curricula is being felt not only because they produce an abundance of instructional materials, but also because they influence commercial writers to update their materials and motivate considerable improvements in teaching methods and facilities (Dawson, 1964). Moreover, many students, teachers, colleges and teacher-training courses not officially committed to the new curricula have made extensive use of the instructional materials of the new curricula. In this way new programs have had direct or indirect influences on most of the science teaching programs in the country. Undoubtedly most existing commercially produced "conventional" curricula have also been heavily influenced by the new curricula.

Testing and Evaluation

Testing and measurement is another area where the impact of the new curricula has been conspicuous. "Old" instruments such as the Dunning Physics Test, the Nelson Biology Test, the Read Science Test and the American Chemical Society Chemistry Test have continued to be widely used, but, in addition, standardized achievement tests especially designed to meet the new curricula's content and process objectives were published by the BSCS, PSSC, Chemical Education Material Study, Harvard Project Physics, Earth Science Curriculum Project and others. With regard to more general objectives, the Test On Understanding Science has been quite popular.

The development of instruments to measure a variety of objectives in the cognitive, affective and psychomotor domains is a major requirement in multidimensional evaluation. Most of the initial research efforts of Harvard Project Physics have been invested in developing instruments (Welch, 1968b) such as the Science Process Inventory (Welch & Pella, 1967–1968) which was designed to measure knowledge of the assumptions, activities, products and ethics of science, or the Science Related Semantic Differential Instrument (Rothman, 1968) which has been used to assess attitudes of students. The Pupil Activity Inventory has been used to assess the degree of participation of students in various activities in learning science (Welch, 1968a). Other individuals and groups have developed a variety of instruments. Unfortunately, at this stage relatively little information is available on these instruments because of rather limited use.

Although Harvard Project Physics was a leader in the field, a variety of additional instruments have been developed by other workers. A critical thinking test for grades 4 to 6 was designed by Maw (1959) and used by George and Dietz (1968). Cornell Critical Thinking Test Form Z (Ennis & Millman, 1961) is much more related to science than is the Watson-Glaser. The Tab Inventory of Science Processes (Butts & Jones, 1967) attempts to sample pupil behavior as he solves a problem. The Cognitive Preference Test was developed by Heath (1964) and used to assess outcomes of the PSSC physics course (Atwood, 1969) and, with adaptation, the Chemical Bond Approach and Chemical Education Material Study chemistry courses (Atwood, 1967–1968; Marks, 1967). Of a more general nature is the Test of Science Processes (Tannenbaum, 1971). A scale to measure a generalized attitude toward science was developed by Vitrogan (1969). The Understanding the Nature of Science test (Kimball, 1967–1968) and the Inventory of Scientific Attitudes (Moore & Sutman, 1970) add to the list of instruments that purport to measure this crucial but undefined cognitive-attitudinal attribute. It would be an important contribution to pool items of all these instruments (Test on Understanding Science, Science Process Inventory, Vitrogan Scale, Kimball Test, Inventory of Scientific Attitudes, and perhaps some items from related general instruments of known character such as the Rokeach Dogmatism Scale). This collection of items could be used for convergent and discriminant validation studies (Campbell & Fiske, 1959) under a variety of population and instructional conditions in order to define more accurately the constructs which bear the name "understanding the nature and processes of science" or "possessing scientific attitude."

A number of instruments were developed outside the United States. Standardized achievement tests which include items provided by many countries, as well as interest and attitude instruments, were developed for the International Education Association studies (International Education Association, 1969). Understanding in Science is an instrument which yields the stage of mental operations as defined by Piaget (Tisher, 1962). A practical laboratory test for BSCS students was developed in Israel and has been used to assess inquiry, problem-solving and intellectual skills within the laboratory setting (Tamir & Glassman, 1971b).

Another related area where the impact of the new curricula is steadily increasing is in external examinations such as the Nuffield O and A level examinations (e.g., Kelly, 1970), the New York Regents (Osborn, 1969; Van Deventer, 1969) and the Israeli matriculation examinations (Jungwirth & Dreyfus, 1972; Tamir, 1972). These examinations can be looked upon as a reflection of the changes in content, methodology and philosophy in the teaching of science in secondary schools.

Still another recent and rather encouraging development which may be considered a result of the new curricula is the commitment of commercial publishers, such as Ginn or McGraw-Hill, to trial test their new programs and revise them accordingly (Welch, 1968a).

Comparative Evaluation Studies

"Science 5-13" in Britain, the Israeli BSCS project and Harvard Project Physics in the United States are all examples of new curricula which have incorporated comparative evaluation as an integral part of program development. All three have found the use of control classes of great help in the interpretation of results and in making judgments as to the validity of certain gains in achievement, understanding science and the acquisition of inquiry skills (Jungwirth, 1970; Science 5–13, 1970; Welch, 1968b).

A pretest-posttest design with comparative groups can be quite useful as shown by the following study. In 1964 the introduction of the Unified Natural Science course in the ninth grade at the University of Chicago High School called for a study which would compare the new course with the Time, Space and Matter course then being offered. In contrast to most studies comparing method X with method Y, student responses to *individual items* of the test used (Test on Understanding Science Form Jx and a specially designed subject-matter test) were analyzed. The detailed analysis allowed the pinpointing of areas of success and failure within each of the courses compared. For example, the new course appeared to be very effective in teaching graph interpretation and drawing correct inference from data, but rather ineffective in teaching students to distinguish interpretation from observation (Klopfer & McCann, 1969). On the other hand, another study which found that the upper $\frac{2}{3}$ of students who studied unified science did better than students in traditional programs on a test measuring one's rational universe image (Slesnick, 1963) was criticized for failing to equate the training of teachers in the controls with that of the experimental ones (Troost, 1968). Such a criticism can be leveled at most other curriculum evaluations with some notable exceptions. Welch (1969b) calculated that of 46 science curriculum projects reviewed, only 18 used any sort of control group. Of that number, four projects specified that their controls had been randomly selected.

The Harvard Project Physics evaluation program represents an exemplary approach to the use of evaluation in course development. Formative, summative and exploratory research evaluation studies were all conducted. Multiple measures were employed at all levels of analysis—learning outcomes (both cognitive and affective), student-entering characteristics, teacher attributes, analyses of the learning environment and both student and teacher reactions to the course. In terms of the independent-intervening-dependent variable framework discussed earlier, the Harvard Project Physics evaluation activities were sensitive to variations in all these aspects of the instructional setting. Furthermore, this program employed a randomly assigned control group design in their evaluations.

The characteristics of the Harvard Project Physics evaluation design allow far more useful conclusions to be derived from their studies than is typically the case. Ahlgren (1970) has summarized these findings. He points out that achievement gain in Harvard Project Physics was much less dependent on prior physics achievement than it was for other courses. Previously less able students were able to gain more in this program than in other programs. Course satisfaction was much higher than in other courses. Such teacher variables as teacher knowledge of physics, teacher personality and teacher attitudes toward science and teaching generally bore no relation to student achievement. Reflecting the goals and orientation of Harvard Project Physics, students in this program saw physics as more historical, philosophical and social, and less mathematical and applied than did those in other programs (which included PSSC). Finally, students recruited into the course who under normal circumstances never would have taken secondary-school physics gained as much or more from the course than regular physics students. Considering that this project was organized in response to the falling numbers of students electing physics courses, this finding was especially relevant.

The present authors have reviewed a large number of studies reported during 1968 and 1969 from the perspective of the *magnitude of gain* observed between pretest and posttest irrespective of experimental or control group membership. Criterion instruments used have included specially constructed achievement tests, general science achievement tests such as Read or Nelson, several forms of the Test On Understanding Science, and the Watson-Glaser Critical Thinking Appraisal among others. In the studies reviewed, the magnitudes of the learning gains, though often significant statistically, were strikingly small. Part of the problem may lie with inadequately sensitive instruments, an issue we discussed in the previous section. Relatively simple methods for estimating the amount of overall variance accounted for by the experimental method in comparative studies, such as Omega squared, were never employed.

The difficulties of assessing the absolute value of a learning gain from the magnitudes of test scores have further stimulated the development of those programs or approaches to science teaching based on behaviorally defined instructional objectives. These programs include AAAS (Walbesser, 1966), Individually Prescribed Instruction (Lindvall & Cox, 1969) and mastery learning (Airasian, 1970). Evaluation studies in each of these programs has been criterion-referenced in terms of the set of objectives which define the goals of the course. Even in such evaluations, however, we cannot ignore the fact that the selection of particular objectives over others, the determination of minimum acceptable passing levels as criteria, and the design of instruments suitable for assessing those objectives are all acts of very human judgment carefully calibrated when possible and arbitrarily reckoned when necessary (Block, 1971a; Ebel, 1971).

All the studies discussed in this section have tested achievement immediately after a course experience. The next section examines long-term evaluation studies.

Long-Term Evaluation

Most available studies may be characterized as short-term. Such short-term studies are necessary and useful in the formative evaluation of developing projects. However, in the long run they are of limited value and may even be misleading. For example, in comparing students who studied different BSCS versions in high school, Blue version students excelled and males consistently outscored females (Psychological Corporation, 1967). However, when BSCS students reached college, only exceptionally high ability Blue version graduates had maintained their excellence while most Blue version graduates (SAT 500–575) achieved and gained significantly less than any other group. Females achieved in college biology as well as males (Tamir, 1969). There is no doubt that the more important objectives such as the development of scientific literacy, retention, transfer, attitudes and interests are cumulative in nature. Therefore follow-up studies should constitute a major component of any respectable summative evaluation (Ausubel, 1963b; Cronbach, 1963; Tamir, 1970).

One obvious type of follow-up study traces student success in a course as related to previous work in ostensibly prerequisite courses. It is commonly believed that a certain physical science background is prerequisite for the successful study of modern biology (Matala, 1960; Robinson, 1960). In an increasing number of schools, ninth-grade physical science courses have been developed at least partially for the purpose of fulfilling this need. Yet a study especially designed to test this problem concluded that students who had completed a previous physical science course did not achieve significantly more in biology than students who had not taken physical science (Gray, Fullerton, & Yale, 1969). One possible explanation is that previous science courses had provided the necessary background. Since the biology course utilized a traditional textbook (the 1965 edition of *Modern Biology* by Otto & Towle) the results might have been different with a BSCS course. However, this type of study points at the need to refrain from recommendations based on untested assumptions.

A most important question is that of the relationship between high school and college. Many college professors are still reluctant to change their courses and contend that their introductory courses will remain what they have been regardless of the new curricula in high school (e.g., Rozolis, 1967b). This approach sharply contradicts the view of most high-school teachers and administrators who believe that the new courses provide the students with a more profound understanding of science, thereby enabling them to excel in meeting the requirements of the university (Rozolis, 1967a).

Research has established that freshmen entering college in the 1960s were superior in their high-school preparation when compared to those of the 1950s (Kruglak, 1969). However, comparison of the achievement of students of the old high-school curricula with those of the new high-school curricula in introductory college science courses consistently failed to reveal significant differences between the two groups (Finger, Dillon, & Corbin, 1965; A. Grobman, 1966; Kruglak, 1969; Rozolis, 1967b; Tamir, 1968). One reason may be the conventionality and conservatism of college courses. Students may have acquired excellent concepts, intellectual skills and inquiry strategies in high school, but if the college course fails to build on them, the effect of past experience may be negligible (Tamir, 1970). Another explanation for the lack of differences is the impact of the new curricula on the traditional ones. Students of the traditional programs have improved significantly (Kruglak, 1969) and some of them have been using innovations of the new curricula such as the BSCS laboratory blocks even without fully and officially committing themselves to the new curricula (Tamir, 1969).

Follow-up studies may serve not only as a delayed measure of success or failure but also as a means for detecting cause and effect relationships. Thus it was established that a major reason for the continuing decline of enrollment in physics is the students' fears that their grade-point average will suffer and college admission chances be damaged because of severe grading practices of physics teachers. Evidence does indicate that on the average a high-school student may expect to receive a physics grade two letter grades lower than his chemistry grade (Krieger, 1968). These findings are supported by Bridgham and Welch (1969). Elective courses taken in college and career choices may be another long-term indication of success. It has repeatedly been found that success in certain subjects in high school results in positive attitudes and more satisfaction, thereby increasing the probability of electing these subjects for subsequent learning. There is no study available as yet to show whether the new curricula have had any stronger effect in this respect.

National Assessment and International Evaluation

Surely the largest-scale study of achievement in science was conducted in the context of the National Assessment Program (Merwin & Womer, 1969; National Assessment of Educational Progress, 1970). National assessment can be viewed as a form of curriculum evaluation. Since a scientifically literate citizenry is clearly the concern of most contemporary science educators (Robinson, 1968; Schwab, 1962b), a continuously performed national assessment should reflect any changes in the public's understanding of science.

The first assessment, which included science, tested approximately 100,000 individuals. These included about 28,000 subjects from each of the nine-, thirteen- and seventeen-year-old age groups and approximately 10,000 adults. Although inappropriate for evaluating specific programs or individuals, this continuing project will provide guidance to curriculum developers and educators generally in their planning.

The extension of the International Education Association's comparative studies of mathematics achievement to other disciplines including science will provide further national data for science curriculum planners. Husen (1967, 1969) and his collaborators have reported on their twelve-nation study of mathematics achievement,

describing their methods, findings, interpretations and implications. As new findings are published related to science achievement, they will be of great use.

Transaction Studies

Traditionally most attention in formal evaluation has been given to outcomes. Very little has been done with respect to what is really going on in the classroom and how new curricula and new objectives affect the daily activities of teachers and students. Stake (1967) has referred to these events that intervene between the planned goals and curricula and the ultimate outcomes as "transactions."

Teachers' responses to questionnaires indicated that there was a marked difference in the amount of time spent in laboratory work by different chemistry teachers and that quantitative and discovery approaches were emphasized more by teachers of newer chemistry than by teachers of conventional chemistry (Hein, 1970). A representative sample of teachers in one state reported their use of various instructional media in the year 1966–1967 (McCurdy, 1969). Only 10 percent of the teachers used other than four media, namely textbooks, bulletin boards, workbooks, graphs and diagrams. Very few teachers reported using reference books, periodicals, models, overhead projectors, films or slides. None used any of the other available media such as single-concept loops, tape recordings, educational television, teaching machines or programmed instruction.

Studies such as those described yield important information; nevertheless they are based on inferences and post-factum analysis. If an accurate assessment of what is actually happening in the classroom is desired, direct observations and careful interaction analyses may be the only answer. The last decade has witnessed the rapid development of a variety of instruments using direct observations as well as audio and video tapes to collect the data for detailed analysis of transactions and inter-actions in the classroom and the laboratory.

Harris and McIntyre (1964) designed the Teacher Question Inventory for the purpose of analyzing the types of questions asked by the teachers in terms of Bloom's (1956) taxonomy. By using this observation instrument Wilson (1969) found that "not only are the new science teachers asking questions of the higher cognitive type, they are asking more questions in general."

The absence of the desired forms of interaction cannot be explained merely as a function of teacher unwillingness or ineptitude. It may also be that the materials of instruction contribute to the problem. Another form of study, similar in some ways to analyses of classroom transactions, takes the written material of instruction, whether student text, laboratory guide or teacher's manual, and evaluates its congruence with the planned goals and methods of instruction. Herron's (1971) critique of the laboratory exercises of BSCS (Blue) and PSSC is of this sort. His findings, reported in detail in our section on psychological analyses, clearly demonstrate the incongruence between plan and program in the projects studied. Similar analyses are in order for other curriculum projects as well.

Parakh (1968) made audio-tape recordings of verbal communications between teachers and students in biology classes which were later analyzed according to an especially developed category system. He found that in the normal classroom, teacher talk accounted for 75 percent of communications as compared to only 15 percent pupil talk. In the laboratory teacher talk was 50 percent, nonverbal, pedagogically relevant teacher activities 40 percent, and pupil talk 10 percent. He also found that explicit statements about the nature and processes of science occurred less than 0.5 percent of the time. Balzer (1969) and Evans (1968) categorized all verbal and nonverbal activities in the classroom and in the laboratory. BSCS and non-BSCS

teachers were equally represented. They found that of all teacher behaviors encoded, 47 percent were teacher-centered content development and about 3 percent were student-centered content development. The other 50 percent of the teacher behaviors did not pertain to content development or inquiry. Only 6 percent of the time was devoted to scientific process behavior, most of which pertained to data interpretation, prediction of results, formation of conclusions and specific questions that posed problems. Behavior requiring experimental design was rare, while problem identification and hypothesis formulation were virtually nonexistent.

Similar results were obtained with somewhat different instruments in interaction analyses of physics classes (Matthews, 1967; Pankratz, 1966; Snider, 1966). In a five-year period Brandwein (1969) investigated the teaching of science in 1,112 school systems, in 259 of which direct observations were made. His findings were that high-school teachers lectured 80–90 percent of the time, junior high-school teachers 80 percent, and teachers in grades 4, 5 and 6 up to 60 percent of the time. In addition, in 95 percent of the cases where the laboratory was used, the materials were prepared in advance so that satisfactory conclusions would be reached within the limit of the laboratory period. The inevitable conclusion of such studies is that inquiry is preached far more widely than practiced.

The differential effect of the teacher on the degree of content achievement, critical thinking, understanding the nature of science and attitudes has been repeatedly asserted (e.g., Yager, 1966). However there is still very little research which may answer the question: what are the specific behavior patterns which make a given teacher strong in stimulating a certain outcome in his students and weak in stimulating another outcome?

The Gallagher study of teacher variation in concept presentation (Gallagher, 1967) is an example of interaction analysis which yields information regarding instructional styles, levels of conceptualization and the relative emphasis on content and skills. The design was careful to avoid any contamination which might be caused by different subject matters by limiting its investigation to classes studying the same topic (photosynthesis as presented by the BSCS Blue version). The classes of six biology teachers were observed for three days. Recordings were made and analyzed according to a classification system developed by Aschner and others (1965). The following were the most important conclusions:

a) There was no such thing as BSCS curriculum presentation. Rather, every teacher presented his own interpretation of the curriculum.

b) Different teachers possessed different styles of presentation.

c) The different approaches resulted in different ideas and concepts being presented to the students.

d) The actual biological concepts were presented with different emphases.

e) Several of the classes showed little in their discussions that resembled a substantial interchange of intellectual ideas and the enquiring approach.

f) Girls tended not to participate in general discussions as much as boys although achievement measures indicated that they were equal to boys.

g) Those students who were constant participants in class discussion were superior in knowledge as well as in thinking ability. A substantial number of students in every class remained mute or nearly so.

An analysis of this kind not only provides an accurate description of what is actually going on in class discussion but may be effectively used as a means for teacher self-evaluation. McLeod (1967) found that student teachers stimulated to analyze their own classroom behavior tended to engage in more indirect behavior in their teaching. The implications of this and similar findings for teacher training are discussed by Bruce (1969). Such self-evaluation may also be useful for practicing teachers, but there is no empirical evidence for this notion.

Interaction analysis may be used for other purposes. For example, interesting results were obtained about group efficiency and degree of participation of students in BSCS laboratory blocks (Hurd & Rowe, 1966). Observation of BSCS laboratory groups in four high schools for two years indicated that while most groups operated smoothly, every classroom had 15 percent to 50 percent incidence of groups who suffered from organizational disturbances and failed to complete their tasks satisfactorily. Using the 12 categories developed by Bales (1950), it was found that goal achievement was positively correlated with compatibility of college-bound groups. However, with noncollege-bound students the goal achievement of incompatible groups tended to exceed that of compatible groups. Other studies dealing with interaction analysis in science classrooms were reported by Fox (1965) and Ferrance and Anderson (1969).

The virtues of direct observation transaction studies are apparent from the studies reviewed. Such studies also possess several disadvantages. They are expensive in both man-hours and monetary cost whether using human observers or electronic eavesdroppers. The impact on behavior of observation itself is uncertain though not likely to be great under typical circumstances. More important, it may be that the way in which students *perceive* the learning environment accounts for achievement better than an apparently objective description of the classroom activities.

It was in response to such concerns for both economy and validity that the Harvard Project Physics group developed the Learning Environment Inventory (G. Anderson, Walberg, & Welch, 1969; Walberg & Ahlgren, 1970; Walberg & Anderson, 1968). Their studies demonstrated that different curricula, such as Harvard Project Physics and PSSC, affected the perception of classroom climate in different ways; that such perceptions of classroom climate measured at midyear predicted changes in a variety of cognitive and noncognitive criterion measures for the school year; and that the perceptions of classroom environment could themselves be predicted from a battery of cognitive and noncognitive predictors. These findings are impressive evidence that measures of student perception of a learning environment can serve as useful adjuncts to, if not substitutes for, direct observations.

Many important questions remain to be asked. What are the relations between observed teacher behavior and perceived learning environment—between the *nominal* and *effective* stimulus value of a teaching-learning setting, to borrow a distinction from experimental psychology. Which components of the setting—teacher behavior and personality, nature of instructional materials, quality of interaction among pupils, compatibility of classroom groups—have the greatest impact on perception of the environment and subsequent learning? Studies of this sort are not characteristic of what has traditionally been viewed as curriculum evaluation, but they will undoubtedly constitute a major portion of evaluation programs in the future.

This section opened with Charles Silberman's assertion that the curriculum reform movement had failed. We would now argue that the Silberman obituary is premature. Although evidence for undeniable success cannot be adduced for the new curricula, neither can support for the claim of morbidity. The judgments will have to be long-term and multidimensional. Programs have been changing constantly in response to formative feedback and summative shock. Promising new programs like Harvard Project Physics were themselves responses to disappointments with the effects of earlier innovations, such as PSSC. Ultimate evaluation may await increasingly sensitive national assessment studies as this generation passes into adulthood. Without question the available evaluation instruments and techniques must be improved if either short- or long-term evaluation is to be fruitful.

SOME CONCLUSIONS AND IMPLICATIONS

Having reviewed the complex web of issues and investigations that characterize the field of research on science teaching, it is now our responsibility to reflect on the investigations that have been conducted, to summarize and extend the criticisms that have been made, and to suggest both models and directions for future inquiries.

Earlier in this chapter we discussed the relevance of different conceptions of the organization of the disciplines for the study of science teaching. We observed that there were many alternative ways of organizing the disciplines in relation to one another. It was apparent that the disciplines could be characterized by contrasting substantive structures (usually several alternatives for any one discipline) as well as by discipline-specific syntactic structures. Hence an obvious question must be, what are the limits of generalizability from instructional research on one scientific discipline to another? Can a general field of "research in science teaching" exist?

If, as Robinson so cogently argues, the structures of biology and of physics are respectively so disparate, what business have we to generalize from the results of experiments on the use of the laboratory in BSCS to speculations concerning the use of the laboratory in physics? Furthermore, if Robinson's characterization of the biological sciences "as having predominantly descriptive explanations and physics predominantly predictive explanations" (1969, p. 461) is a reasonable contrast of one aspect of their respective syntactic structures, does this suggest that the appropriate model for biology might be research in some other discipline, whether humanistic or social scientific, having a similar syntactic structure?

Cronbach and Snow (1969) have urged us to extend our conception of experimental research on instruction from the simple treatment to the aptitude-treatment interaction. Walberg (1970) argues that an adequate research model must also include a factor representing the learning environment. We are now adding that the structure of the *subject matter* taught and learned must also become an explicit facet of research design in the field of instructional research. But that facet may *not* be well represented by characterizing subject matters in traditional discipline terms (science, mathematics, English, etc.). Instead, we may have to develop ways of characterizing the dynamic pedagogical structure of a discipline, the types of cognitive processes that particular disciplines or subdisciplines require from learners. We may already see an indication of how such research will be conducted in the recent work of G. J. Anderson (1971), who is investigating the relationships between learning environments and other school-related variables across a variety of subject-matter areas.

Although it is convenient to analyze various programs in science education in terms of the theoretical consistencies of their authors, the quest for theoretical consistencies remains one of the salient weaknesses of this area of instruction. Psychological theories of learning and cognition remain far too weak a foundation to support any entire curricular program. No single theoretical formulation has yet demonstrated sufficient comprehensive validity to be trusted to this task. Thus the ease with which we were able to relate programmatic approaches to the teaching of science to commitments to single theoretical models may itself be symptomatic. In his "The Practical—A Language for Curriculum," Schwab (1969) suggests that the curriculum field has fallen on evil times because it has failed to recognize that it is a discipline in the practical domain, not in the theoretical (*theoretical* and *practical* are used in the Aristotelian sense). He then proceeds to lay the framework for a practical approach to curriculum in which a variety of theories and experiences are used eclectically and deliberately by curriculum developers in their practical inquiries. We find Schwab's observations particularly meaningful to the field of science education at this time.

One important characteristic of much of the literature in science education is the vast disparity between the profound and truly important nature of the questions raised by the philosophers working in the field and the too-frequently trivial empirical studies conducted by the empirical researchers in the field. For example, the enormous emphasis placed upon the importance of the structure of the subject matter should have generated far more empirical research studying the understanding of structure as a criterion variable. Instead we have a proliferation of theoretical pieces on this topic but precious little empirical study.

A general critique of most of the published research in the period since the Gage *Handbook* would be that the typical experimental studies continue to be short-term, poorly analyzed statistically and ambiguously reported. Far too little attention is given to the detailed descriptions of experimental instructional treatments and far too much attention is given to overly detailed descriptions of typically simple statistical procedures. This observation is similar to that made by Eisner in his chapter in the present volume. It should be acknowledged that in recent volumes the quality of the *Journal of Research in Science Teaching* has improved markedly, both in substantive relevance and methodological adequacy.

Several research areas appear worthy of serious consideration by investigators. The first would be characterized by intensive comparative field studies such as R. C. Anderson's (1969), or overall curriculum comparisons but with far more sensitive indicators of specific areas of strength and weakness than is characteristic of past work. Employment of experimental multivariate-longitudinal designs (Shulman,

1970b) would be appropriate for such research.

There should also be an increase in a genre of basic research that is science-specific rather than experiments to test aspects of psychological theories where science content happens to be a convenient subject matter to use for research material. Such science-relevant basic research would be on a topic like the cognitive development of science-relevant concepts in young children, e.g., cause and effect, space, time, mass, momentum. This sort of research is clearly in the tradition of Piaget. The purpose would be to identify some general normal expectancies for the evolution of particular concepts around which curriculum developers and program writers could plan their creative endeavors. It would not really matter whether such conceptual developments were the products of ontogenetic cognitive development or of learning. The importance would be to provide general maps that would be useful for the activities of the curriculum developers.

A third kind of research which would be extremely useful would involve direct studies of criterial members of the scientific community to serve as operational models on the basis of which objectives for science teaching could be established. That is, if the working scientist is to serve as a useful model for the development of certain aspects of the science curriculum, much better empirical data are needed about how the working scientist actually conducts his inquiries, what his characteristics are and how they developed. These sorts of descriptive studies would be very useful for those who would plan and evaluate science programs. The work of Arthur Koestler (1964) on thought among creative scientists, Hadamard (1954) on the analyses of mathematical discovery, and Elstein and Shulman (1971) and Elstein, Kagan, Shulman, Jason, and Loupe (1972) on the medical reasoning of expert physicians can serve as models for such work.

A parallel emphasis well worth pursuing would evolve from the suggestion of David Hawkins (1966) that if one wants to know what the elements of good science teaching are, one finds good science teachers and studies what they do. These descriptive studies would consist of careful analysis of the characteristics of their teaching processes.

Finally, the science education research community must be prepared to develop centers of research in which groups of investigators coordinate their efforts in joint attacks on common problems. The bulk of research in science teaching during the past decade appeared to be dissertation-related one-shot studies by investigators for whom this would be their last research effort. We must move away from using the individual investigator as our model and more toward the research group, as exemplified by the Harvard Project Physics efforts, or the work of the Science Education Center of the University of Texas.

We are entering an era when we will be asked to acknowledge the importance of affect, imagination, intuition and attitude as outcomes of science instruction that are at least as important as their cognitive counterparts. We are entering the age of the open classroom, the free school, and a host of other educational approaches that stress the feelings of the student as necessary adjuncts to cognitive learning and as co-equal consequences. We are simultaneously entering an age of accountability with emphasis placed on expressing the contents of our curriculum in terms of long lists of highly specific behavioral objectives, a demand that some may see as antithetical to the quest for affect and attitude development. Science educators must avoid the all-too-seductive temptation to toss in their lot exclusively with the behavioral-objective writers, thus giving short shrift or none at all to those whose concern is with the much less easily measured affective components of learning. Science without feeling will be a mere skeleton of the science that is practiced by the disciplined inquirer. Both aspects must be kept alive in our approaches to science instruction, and especially in our research and evaluation efforts.

REFERENCES

AAAS Commission on Science Education. *The psychological bases of science—a process approach.* Washington, D.C.: AAAS, 1965.

Ahlgren, A. *Some evaluation findings from Harvard Project Physics.* Unpublished manuscript, Harvard University, April 1970.

Airasian, P. W. The use of hierarchies in the analysis and planning of chemistry instruction. *Science Education,* 1970, 54(1), 91–95.

Anderson, G. J. Effects of course content and teacher sex on the social climate of learning. *American Educational Research Journal,* 1971, 8, 649–663.

Anderson, G. J., Walberg, H. J., & Welch, W. W. Curriculum effects on the social climate of learning: A new representation of discrimination functions. *American Educational Research Journal,* 1969, 6, 315–328.

Anderson, K. E., & Montgomery, F. S. An evaluation of the introductory physics course on film. *Science Education,* 1959, 43, 386–394.

Anderson, O. R. A refined definition of structure in teaching. *Journal of Research in Science Teaching,* 1966, 4(4), 289–291.

Anderson, R. C. The comparative field experiment: An illustration from high school biology. *Proceedings of the ETS invitational conference on testing, 1968.* Princeton, N.J.: Educational Testing Service, 1969.

Anderson, R. C., Faust, G. W., & Roderick, M. C. A brief report of the field test of a program in population genetics. *BSCS Newsletter,* No. 35, 1969.

Aschner, M. J., & others. *A system for classifying thought processes in the context of classroom verbal interaction.* Urbana, Ill.: University of Illinois, Institute for Research on Exceptional Children, 1965.

Atkin, J. M. Some evaluation problems in a course content improvement project. *Journal of Research in Science Teaching,* 1963, 1, 129–132.

Atkin, J. M. Research styles in science educa-

tion. *Journal of Research in Science Teaching,* 1967–1968, 5, 338–345.

Atkin, J. M., & Karplus, R. Discovery or invention? *The Science Teacher,* 1962, 29(5), 45–51.

Atwood, R. K. CHEM study achievement among groups classified by cognitive preference scores. *Journal of Research in Science Teaching,* 1967–1968, 154–159.

Atwood, R. K. Change in cognitive preferences of high school physics students, *School Science and Mathematics,* 1969, 69, 697–699.

Ausubel, D. P. *The psychology of meaningful verbal learning.* New York: Grune & Stratton, 1963. (a)

Ausubel, D. P. Some psychological considerations in the objectives and design of an elementary-school science program. *Science Education,* 1963, 47, 278–284. (b)

Ausubel, D. P. An evaluation of the BSCS approach to high school biology. *American Biology Teacher,* 1966, 28, 176–186.

Ausubel, D. P. *Educational psychology.* New York: Holt, Rinehart & Winston, 1968.

Bales, R. F. *Interaction process analysis.* Cambridge, Mass.: Addison-Wesley, 1950.

Balzer, L. Nonverbal and verbal behaviors of biology teachers. *American Biology Teacher,* 1969, 31, 226–229.

Balzer, L. Teacher behaviors and student inquiry in biology. *American Biology Teacher,* 1970, 32, 27–28.

Belanger, M. Learning studies in science education. *Review of Educational Research,* 1969, 39, 377–395.

Benson, B. W., & Howell, J. E. A programmed unit in statistics for secondary science students. *School Science and Mathematics,* 1968, 68, 691–698.

Bingman, R. M. (Ed.) *Inquiry objectives in the teaching of biology.* Mid-Continent Regional Educational Laboratory and BSCS, 1969.

Biological Sciences Curriculum Study. *Biology teacher's handbook.* New York: John Wiley, 1963.

Biological Sciences Curriculum Study. *Biological science: Interaction of experiments and ideas.* New York: Prentice-Hall, 1965.

Biological Sciences Curriculum Study. *Patterns and processes.* New York: Holt, Rinehart & Winston, 1966.

Biological Sciences Curriculum Study. *Biology*

teacher's handbook. (2nd ed.) New York: John Wiley, 1970.

Black, H. T., & Poorman, L. G. Multimedia systems approach in college physics laboratories. *School Science and Mathematics,* 1970, 70, 277–280.

Blight, H. F., & Bila, J. S. Curriculum patterns in high school science courses. Paper presented at the meeting of the National Association for Research in Science Teaching, Chicago, February 1968.

Block, J. H. Criterion-referenced measurements: Potential. *School Review,* 1971, 79, 289–298. (a)

Block, J. H. (Ed.) *Mastery learning.* New York: Holt, Rinehart & Winston, 1971. (b)

Bloom, B. S. (Ed.) *Taxonomy of educational objectives. Handbook I: Cognitive domain.* New York: David McKay, 1956.

Bloom, B. S. Learning for mastery. *Evaluation Comment,* May 1968. University of California, Los Angeles, Center for the Study of Evaluation of Instructional Programs.

Bloom, B. S., Hastings, J. T., & Madaus, G. F. *Handbook on formative and summative evaluation of student learning.* New York: McGraw-Hill, 1971.

Brandou, J. R. Single concept films: A pilot study based on CHEM Study films. *Journal of Research in Science Teaching,* 1966, 4, 187–191.

Brandwein, P. F. Observations on teaching: Overload and "the methods of intelligence." *The Science Teacher,* 1969, 36(2), 38–40.

Bridgham, R. G. Conceptions of science and learning science. *School Review,* 1969, 78, 25–40.

Bridgham, R. G., & Welch, W. W. Physics enrollments and grading practices. *Journal of Research in Science Teaching,* 1969, 6, 44–46.

Brownell, W. A. The evaluation of learning under different systems of instruction. *Educational Psychologist,* 1965, 3, 3–7.

Brownson, W. E., & Schwab, J. J. American science textbooks and their authors, 1915 and 1955. *School Review,* 1963, 71, 170–180.

Bruce, M. H. Teacher education in science. *Review of Educational Research,* 1969, 39, 415–427.

Bruner, J. S. *The process of education.* Cambridge, Mass.: Harvard University Press, 1960.

Bruner, J. S. The act of discovery. *Harvard Education Review,* 1961, 31, 21–32.

Butts, D. P., & Jones, H. L. The development of the TAB science test. *Science Education,* 1967, 51, 463–473.

Cain, R. W., & Lee, E. C. An analysis of the relationship between science and mathematics at the secondary school level. *School Science and Mathematics,* 1963, 63, 705–713.

Campbell, D. T., & Fiske, D. W. Convergent and discriminant validation by the multitrait-multimethod matrix. *Psychological Bulletin,* 1959, 56, 81–105.

Carnes, P. E. *An experimental study in the use of programmed materials for seventh-grade open-ended laboratory experiences.* (Doctoral dissertation, University of Georgia) Ann Arbor, Mich.: University Microfilms, 1966. No. 66-13,592.

Carre, C. G. Audiotutorials as adjuncts to formal lecturing in biology teaching at the tertiary level. *Journal of Biology Education,* 1969, 3, 57–64.

Cawelti, G. Innovative practices in high schools: Who does what—and why—and how. *Nation's Schools,* 1967, 79(4), 56–58.

Chemical Bond Approach Project. *Teacher's guide to investigating chemical systems.* New York: McGraw-Hill, 1964.

Chemical Education Material Study. *Chemistry: An experimental science.* San Francisco: W. H. Freeman, 1963.

Chester, W. Laboratory by demonstration. *Journal of Higher Education,* 1938, 9, 32–36.

Clegg, F. E. An experiment on the retention of matter presented in a sound film. *Journal of Research in Science Teaching,* 1966, 4, 244–245.

Collagham, R. B. The construction and evaluation of a programmed course in mathematics necessary for success in collegiate physical science. *Journal of Research in Science Teaching,* 1969, 6(4), 358–365.

Conant, J. B. *The comprehensive high school: A second report to interested citizens.* New York: McGraw-Hill, 1967.

Connelly, F. M. Conceptual structures in ecology with special reference to an enquiry curriculum in ecology. Unpublished doctoral dissertation, University of Chicago, 1968.

Connelly, F. M. Philosophy of science and the

science curriculum. *Journal of Research in Science Teaching,* 1969, 6, 108–113.

Cooley, W. W., & Klopfer, W. *Test on understanding science.* Princeton, N.J.: Educational Testing Service, 1961.

Cossman, G. W. The effects of a course in science and culture for secondary school students. *Journal of Research in Science Teaching,* 1969, 6, 274–283.

Coulter, J. C. The effectiveness of inductive laboratory, inductive demonstration, and deductive laboratory in biology. *Journal of Research in Science Teaching,* 1966, 4, 185–186.

Cremin, L. A. *The wonderful world of Ellwood Patterson Cubberley.* New York: Columbia University, Teachers College, Bureau of Publications, 1965.

Cronbach, L. J. Course improvement through evaluation. *Teachers College Record,* 1963, 64, 672–683.

Cronbach, L. J., & Snow, R. E. *Individual differences in learning ability as a function of instructional variables.* Final Report, U.S. Office of Education Contract No. OEC-4-6-061269-1217. Stanford, Calif.: Stanford University, School of Education, 1969. ED 029 001.

Cunningham, H. A. Lecture demonstration versus individual laboratory method in science teaching—a summary. *Science Education,* 1946, 30, 70–82.

Dawson, J. R., Jr. Impact of new curricula on facilities for biology. *American Biology Teacher,* 1964, 26, 601–604.

Deese, J. E. *The structure of associations in language and thought.* Baltimore: Johns Hopkins, 1965.

Earth Science Curriculum Project. *Investigating the earth.* Boston: Houghton-Mifflin, 1967.

Easley, J. A., Jr. The natural sciences and educational research—a comparison. *The High School Journal,* 1966, 50, 39–50.

Ebel, R. L. Knowledge vs. ability in achievement testing. In *Invitational Conference on Testing Programs.* Princeton, N.J.: Educational Testing Service, 1969. Pp. 66–76.

Ebel, R. L. Behavioral objectives: A close look. *Phi Delta Kappan,* 1970, 52, 171–173.

Ebel, R. L. Criterion-referenced measurements: Limitations. *School Review,* 1971, 79, 282–288.

Eisner, E. W. Instructional and expressive objectives: Their formulation and use in curriculum. In J. Popham (Ed.), *Instructional objectives.* Monograph No. 3. Washington, D.C.: American Educational Research Association, 1969. Pp. 1–31.

Elkana, Y. Science, philosophy of science and science teaching. *Educational Philosophy and Theory,* 1970, 2, 15–35.

Elstein, A. S., Kagan, N., Shulman, L. S., Jason, H., & Loupe, M. J. Methods and theory in the study of medical inquiry. *Journal of Medical Education,* February 1972, 47, 85–92.

Elstein, A. S., & Shulman, L. S. *Analysis and interpretation of medical inquiry protocols.* Paper presented at the meeting of the American Educational Research Association, New York, February 1971.

Engelman, M. D. Construction and evaluation of programmed materials in biology classroom use. *American Biology Teacher,* 1963, 25, 212–214.

Ennis, R. H., & Millman, J. Cornell Critical Thinking Test, Form Z.

Evans, T. P. *An exploratory study of the verbal and non-verbal behaviors of biology teachers and their relationship to selected personality traits.* (Doctoral dissertation, The Ohio State University) Ann Arbor, Mich.: University Microfilms, 1968. No. 68-15,317.

Ferrance, G. M., & Anderson, H. O. *Measuring small group interaction in the science laboratory.* Unpublished manuscript, Indiana University, Science Education Center, 1969.

Finger, J. A., Jr., Dillon, J. A., Jr., & Corbin, F. Performance in introductory college physics and previous instruction in physics. *Journal of Research in Science Teaching,* 1965, 3, 61–65.

Fornoff, F. J. *A survey of the teaching of chemistry in secondary schools.* Princeton, N.J.: Educational Testing Service, 1969.

Fox, F. W. Levels of performance in teaching. *The Science Teacher,* 1965, 32(4), 31–32.

Gagné, R. M. The acquisition of knowledge. *Psychological Review,* 1962, 69, 355–365.

Gagné, R. M. Learning hierarchies. *Educational Psychologist,* 1968, 6, 1–9.

Gagné, R. M. *The conditions of learning.* (2nd ed.) New York: Holt, Rinehart & Winston, 1970.

Gallagher, J. J. Teacher variation in concept

presentation in BSCS programs. *BSCS Newsletter*, 1967, No. 30, 8–19.

Gallagher, J. J. A comparison of individualized and group instruction in science: Effects on third grade pupils. *Journal of Research in Science Teaching*, 1970, 7(3), 253–264.

Geis, F., Jr. The semantic differential technique as a means of evaluating changes in "affect." Unpublished doctoral dissertation, Harvard University, 1968.

George, K. D. The effect of BSCS and conventional biology on critical thinking. *Journal of Research in Science Teaching*, 1965, 3, 293–299.

George, K. D., & Dietz, M. The relationship of teacher-pupil critical-thinking ability. *Science Education*, 1968, 52, 426–432.

Getzels, J. W. Creative thinking, problem-solving, and instruction. In E. R. Hilgard (Ed.), *Theories of learning and instruction*. The Sixty-third Yearbook of the National Society for the Study of Education, Part I. Chicago: NSSE, 1964. Pp. 240–267.

Gibbs, R. K. *An analysis of the effectiveness of the Biological Sciences Curriculum Study single topic films in teaching hypothesis construction to high school biology students.* (Doctoral dissertation, Indiana University) Ann Arbor, Mich.: University Microfilms, 1968. No. 67-16,399.

Glass, B. H. Revolution in biology. *BSCS Newsletter*, 1960, 9, 12–15.

Glass, B. H. A new high school biology program. *American Scientist*, 1961, 49, 524–531.

Goldstein, P. Student laboratory work versus teacher demonstration as a means of developing laboratory resourcefulness. *Science Education*, 1937, 21, 185–193.

Gray, R. C., Fullerton, B. J., & Yale, F. G. Student achievement in high school biology. *School Science and Mathematics*, 1969, 69, 708–714.

Grobman, A. National Science Foundation role in the improvement of science education in the American schools. *BSCS Newsletter*, 1965, 27, 7–10.

Grobman, A. Statement of results and conclusions of an informal study on the performance of BSCS students in freshman biology courses, 1966. (mimeo)

Grobman, H. G. *Evaluation activities of curriculum project.* American Educational Research Association Monograph Series on Curriculum Evaluation, No. 2. Chicago: Rand McNally, 1968. (a)

Grobman, H. Some factors in the adoption of new science curricula. Paper presented at the meeting of the National Association for Research in Science Teaching, February, 1968. (b)

Hadamard, J. S. *An essay on the psychology of invention in the mathematical field.* New York: Dover, 1954.

Harris, B. M., & McIntyre, K. E. *Teacher questions inventory.* Austin, Tex.: University of Texas, 1964.

Hawkins, D. Learning the unteachable. In L. S. Shulman, & E. R. Keislar (Eds.), *Learning by discovery: A critical appraisal.* Chicago: Rand McNally, 1966. Pp. 3–12.

Heath, R. W. Comparison of achievement in two physics courses. *Journal of Experimental Education*, 1964, 32, 348–354.

Hedges, W. D., & MacDougall, M. A. Teaching fourth-grade science by means of programed science materials with laboratory experiences. *Science Education*, 1965, 49, 348–358.

Hein, H. C. The role of laboratory instruction in high school chemistry. *School Science and Mathematics*, 1970, 70, 245–249.

Herron, M. D. Nature of science: Panacea or Pandora's box. *Journal of Research in Science Teaching*, 1969, 6, 105–107.

Herron, M. D. The nature of scientific enquiry. *School Review*, 1971, 79, 171–212.

Hurd, P. D. *Biological education in American secondary schools, 1890–1960.* BSCS Bulletin No. 1. Washington, D.C.: American Institute of Biological Sciences, 1961.

Hurd, P. D., & Rowe, M. B. A study of small group dynamics and productivity in the BSCS laboratory block program. *Journal of Research Science Teaching*, 1966, 4, 67–73.

Husen, T. (Ed.) *International study of achievement in mathematics: A comparison of twelve countries.* Vols. I and II. New York: John Wiley, 1967.

Husen, T. International impact of evaluation. In R. W. Tyler (Ed.), *Educational evaluation: New roles, new means.* The Sixty-eighth Yearbook of the National Society for the Study of Education, Part II. Chicago: NSSE, 1969, Pp. 335–350.

International Education Association Science Tests. Wenner Gren Center, Sveavagen 166, Stockholm, 1969.

Jeffrey, J. C. *Identification of objectives of the chemistry laboratory and development of means for measuring student achievement of some of these objectives.* (Doctoral dissertation, The University of Texas) Ann Arbor, Mich.: University Microfilms, 1967. No. 66-1928.

Johns, K. W. *A comparison of two methods of teaching eighth grade general science: Traditional and structured problem-solving.* (Doctoral dissertation, University of Arizona) Ann Arbor, Mich.: University Microfilms, 1966. No. 66-10,201.

Johnson, P. E. Associative meaning of concepts in physics. *Journal of Educational Psychology,* 1964, 55, 84–88.

Johnson, P. E. Some psychological aspects of subject-matter structure. *Journal of Educational Psychology,* 1967, 58, 75–83.

Jungwirth, E. An evaluation of the attained development of the intellectual skills needed for "understanding of the nature of scientific inquiry" by BSCS pupils in Israel. *Journal of Research in Science Teaching,* 1970, 7, 141–151.

Jungwirth, E., & Dreyfus, A. The Israeli Bagrut Examination in BSCS biology. *Journal of Research in Science Teaching,* 1972, 9, in press.

Kastrinos, W. *A survey of the teaching of biology in secondary schools.* Princeton, N.J.: Educational Testing Service, 1969.

Kelly, P. J. Implications of Nuffield A Level Biological Science. *School Science Review,* 1970, 52, 272–285.

Kimball, M. E. Understanding the nature of science: A comparison of scientists and science teachers. *Journal of Research in Science Teaching,* 1967–1968, 5, 110–120.

Klopfer, L. E. Evaluation of learning in science. In B. S. Bloom, J. T. Hastings, & G. F. Madaus (Eds.), *Handbook on formative and summative evaluation of student learning.* New York: McGraw-Hill, 1971. Pp. 559–642.

Klopfer, L. E., & McCann, D. C. Evaluation in Unified Science: Measuring the effectiveness of the natural science course at the University of Chicago High School. *Science Education,* 1969, 53(2), 155–164.

Koestler, A. *The act of creation.* New York: Macmillan, 1964.

Koos, E. M. *Developmental studies of a series of measures of inquiry skill in biology:*

"Explorations in biology." Paper presented at the meeting of the American Educational Research Association, New York, February 1971.

Krathwohl, D. R., Bloom, B. S., & Masia, B. B. *Taxonomy of educational objectives. Handbook II. Affective domain.* New York: David McKay, 1964.

Krieger, A. G. A comparative study of grades received by students in chemistry and physics. *School Science and Mathematics,* 1968, 68, 828–833.

Kruglak, H. Pre- and post-Sputnik physics background of college freshmen. *Journal of Research in Science Teaching,* 1969, 6, 42–43.

Kuhn, T. S. *The structure of scientific revolutions.* Chicago: University of Chicago Press, 1962.

Lee, A. D., Lehman, D. L., & Peterson, G. E. (Eds.) *Laboratory blocks in teaching biology.* BSCS Special Publication No. 5. Boulder, Colo.: University of Colorado, 1967.

Lindvall, C. M., & Cox, R. C. The role of evaluation in programs for individualized instruction. In R. W. Tyler (Ed.), *Educational evaluation: New roles, new means.* The Sixty-eighth Yearbook of the National Society for the Study of Education, Part II. Chicago: NSSE, 1969. Pp. 156–188.

Lukinsky, J. S. The term Structure in recent educational theory. *Educational Philosophy and Theory,* 1970, 2, 15–31.

Mager, R. F. *Preparing instructional objectives.* Palo Alto, Calif.: Fearon, 1962.

Mallinson, G. G. The individual laboratory method compared with the lecture-demonstration method in teaching general biology. *Science Education,* 1947, 31, 175–179.

Marks, R. L. CBA high school chemistry and concept formation. *Journal of Chemical Education,* 1967, 44, 471–474.

Matala, D. The biology course: When to teach it? *American Biology Teacher,* 1960, 22, 270–271.

Matthews, C. C. *The classroom verbal behavior of selected secondary school science student teachers and their cooperating classroom teachers.* (Doctoral dissertation, Cornell University) Ann Arbor, Mich.: University Microfilms, 1967. No. 67-1394.

Maw, E. W. *An experiment in teaching critical thinking in the intermediate grades.* (Doctoral dissertation, University of Pennsylvania) Ann Arbor, Mich.: University Microfilms, 1959. No. 59-4646.

Mayer, W. V. The view from here. *BSCS Newsletter,* 1970, 39, 1.

McBurney, W. F. Individualized instruction: A case for the independent student investigation in science. *School Science and Mathematics,* 1969, 69, 827–830.

McCurdy, D. W. Are science teachers making adequate use of their instructional resources? *School Science and Mathematics,* 1969, 69, 323–330.

McLeod, R. J. *Changes in verbal interaction patterns of secondary science student teachers who have had training in interaction analysis and the relationship of these changes to the verbal interaction of their cooperating teachers.* Final report USOE. Report No. BR-6-8078. Ithaca, N.Y.: Cornell University, 1967. ED 015 148.

Medawar, P. B. *Induction and intuition in scientific thought.* London: Methuen, 1969.

Merwin, J. C., & Womer, F. B. Evaluation in assessing the progress of education to provide bases of public understanding and public policy. In R. W. Tyler (Ed.), *Educational evaluation: New roles, new means.* The Sixty-eighth Yearbook of the National Society for the Study of Education, Part II. Chicago: University of Chicago Press, 1969. Pp. 305–334.

Moore, R. W., & Sutman, F. X. The development, field test and validation of an inventory of scientific attitudes. *Journal of Research in Science Teaching,* 1970, 7, 85–94.

Murphy, G. W. A study of the relative effectiveness of content and process centered biology laboratories for college freshmen. Unpublished doctoral dissertation, University of Kentucky, 1967.

Nasca, D. *Effect of varied presentations of laboratory exercises within programed materials on specific intellectual factors of science problem solving behavior.* Washington, D.C.: U.S. Office of Education, 1965. ED 010 292.

National Assessment of Educational Progress. *Report 1: 1969–1970 Science.* Education Commission of the States, July 1970.

NCA Today: Innovation study of the nation's high schools reveals important changes in recent years. *North Central Association Today,* 1967, 11, 3–4.

Novak, A. Scientific inquiry in the laboratory. *American Biology Teacher,* 1963, 25, 342–346.

Novak, J. D. A model for the interpretation and analysis of concept formation. *Journal of Research in Science Teaching,* 1965, 3, 72–83.

Novak, J. D. The role of concepts in science teaching. In H. J. Klausmeier, & C. W. Harris (Eds.), *Analyses of concept learning.* New York: Academic Press, 1966. Pp. 239–254.

Novak, J. D. *The improvement of biology teaching.* New York: Bobbs-Merrill, 1970. (a)

Novak, J. D. Relevant research on audio-tutorial methods. *School Science and Mathematics,* 1970, 70, 774–784. (b)

Nuffield A-level biology. Project aims and outline scheme. London: The Nuffield Foundation, 1965.

Okey, J. R., & Gagné, R. M. Revision of a science topic using evidence of performance on subordinate skills. *Journal of Research in Science Teaching,* 1970, 7(4), 321–326.

Organization for Economic Cooperation and Development. *New thinking in school biology.* Paris: Organization for Economic Cooperation and Development Publication, 1962.

Osborn, G. Influence of the Chemical Bond Approach and the Chemical Educational Materials Study on the New York Regents Examination in high school chemistry. *School Science and Mathematics,* 1969, 69, 53–58.

Otto, J. H., & Towle, A. *Modern biology.* New York: Holt, Rinehart & Winston, 1965.

Pankratz, R. S. *Verbal interaction patterns in the classrooms of selected science teachers: Physics.* (Doctoral dissertation, The Ohio State University) Ann Arbor, Mich.: University Microfilms, 1966. No. 66-10,034.

Parakh, J. S. A study of teacher-pupil interaction in BSCS Yellow Version biology classes. *American Biology Teacher,* 1968, 30, 841–848.

Payne, D. A., Krathwohl, D. R., & Gordon, J. The effect of sequence on programmed instruction. *American Educational Research Journal,* 1967, 4, 125–132.

Pella, M. O. The laboratory and science thinking. *The Science Teacher,* 1961, 28, 20–31.

Pella, M. O., & Sherman, J. A comparison of two methods of utilizing laboratory activities in teaching the course IPS. *School Science and Mathematics,* 1969, 69, 303–314.

Poorman, L. E. *A comparative study of the effectiveness of a multimedia systems approach to Harvard Project Physics with traditional approaches to Harvard Project Physics.* (Doctoral dissertation, Indiana University) Ann Arbor, Mich.: University Microfilms, 1968. No. 68-4745.

Popham, J. (Ed.) *Instructional objectives.* American Educational Research Association Monograph Series on Curriculum Evaluation, No. 3. Chicago: Rand McNally, 1969.

Popper, K. R. *The logic of scientific discovery.* Vienna: Springer, 1935.

Postlethwait, S. N. The audio-tutorial system. *American Biology Teacher,* 1970, 32, 31–33.

Postlethwait, S. N., Novak, J., & Murray, H. *An integrated experience approach to learning.* Minneapolis: Burgess, 1964.

Postelthwait, S. N., Novak, J., & Murray, H. T., Jr. *The audio-tutorial approach to learning: Through independent study and integrated experiences.* Minneapolis: Burgess, 1969.

Price, L. *An investigation of the transfer of an elementary science process.* (Doctoral dissertation, University of Southern California) Ann Arbor, Mich.: University Microfilms, 1968. No. 68-10,246.

Psychological Corporation. *A report of the Biological Sciences Curriculum Study end-of-year evaluation program 1964–1965.* BSCS Newsletter No. 30, 1967.

Ramsey, G. A., & Howe, R. W. An analysis of research on instructional procedures in secondary school science, Part I: Outcomes of instruction. *The Science Teacher,* 1969, 36(3), 62–70. (a)

Ramsey, G. A., & Howe, R. W. An analysis of research on instructional procedures in secondary school science, Part II: Instructional procedures. *The Science Teacher,* 1969, 36(4), 72–81. (b)

Ramsey, G. A., & Howe, R. W. An analysis of research related to instructional procedures in elementary school science. *Science and Children,* 1969, 6(7), 25–36. (c)

Raun, C. E. *The interaction between curriculum variables and selected classroom student characteristics.* (Doctoral dissertation, The University of Texas) Ann Arbor, Mich.: University Microfilms, 1967. No. 67-14,878.

Reynolds, J. H., & Glaser, R. Effects of repetition and spaced review upon retention of a complex learning task. *Journal of Educational Psychology,* 1964, 55, 297–308.

Robinson, J. T. Developing a science sequence. *School Science and Mathematics,* 1960, 60, 685–692.

Robinson, J. T. *The nature of science and science teaching.* Belmont, Calif.: Wadsworth, 1968.

Robinson, J. T. Philosophical and historical bases of science teaching. *Review of Educational Research,* 1969, 39, 459–471.

Romey, W. D. Inquiry techniques for teaching science. Englewood Cliffs, N.J.: Prentice-Hall, 1969.

Rothman, A. I. The factor analysis of a science-related semantic differential instrument. *Journal of Educational Measurement,* 1968, 5, 145–149.

Rozolis, J. T. An evaluation of the Biological Sciences Curriculum Study program from the professional viewpoint and implications for the university. *Bio Science,* 1967, 17, 452–460. (a)

Rozolis, J. T. An evaluation of the newer university biology core curriculum from the professional viewpoint and implications for secondary schools. *Bio Science,* 1967, 17, 703–707. (b)

Sanderson, R. A., Postlethwait, S. N., & Sanderson, S. E. Individualized instruction through audio-tape: Why, how, what. *Pacific Speech,* 1968, 2(3), 49–58.

Schwab, J. J. Dialetical means vs. dogmatic extremes in relation to liberal education. *Harvard Educational Review,* 1951, 21, 37–64.

Schwab, J. J. Eros and education. *Journal of General Education,* 1954, 8, 51–71.

Schwab, J. J. What do scientists do? *Behavioral Science,* 1960, 5, 1–27.

Schwab, J. J. The concept of the structure of a discipline. *Educational Record,* 1962, 43, 197–205. (a)

Schwab, J. J. The teaching of science as enquiry. In J. J. Schwab, & P. F. Brandwein, *The teaching of science.* Cambridge, Mass.: Harvard University Press, 1962. Pp. 1–103. (b)

Schwab, J. J. Problems, topics, and issues. In

S. Elam (Ed.), *Education and the structure of knowledge.* Chicago: Rand McNally, 1964. Pp. 4–43. (a)

Schwab, J. J. Structure of the disciplines: Meanings and significances. In G. W. Ford, & L. Pugno (Eds.), *The structure of knowledge and the curriculum.* Chicago: Rand McNally, 1964. Pp. 6–30. (b)

Schwab, J. J. The practical: A language for curriculum. *School Review,* 1969, 78, 1–23.

Science 5–13. Evaluation of metals unit. *Schools Council Publication,* 1970.

Selmes, C., Ashton, B. G., Meredith, H. M., & Newal, A. B. Attitudes to science and scientists. *The School Science Review,* 1969, 51, 7–22.

Shulman, L. S. Psychological controversies in the teaching of science and mathematics. *The Science Teacher,* 1968, 35 (6), 34–38, 89–90.

Shulman, L. S. Psychology and mathematics education. In E. G. Begle (Ed.), *Mathematics education.* The Sixty-ninth Yearbook of the National Society for the Study of Education, Part I. Chicago: University of Chicago Press, 1970. Pp. 23–71. (a)

Shulman, L. S. Reconstruction of educational research. *Review of Educational Research,* 1970, 40, 371–396. (b)

Siemankowsky, F. T. An auto-paced teaching process in physical science for elementary teacher preparation: A pilot report. *Journal of Research in Science Teaching,* 1969, 6, 150–156.

Silberman, C. E. *Crisis in the classroom.* New York: Random House, 1970.

Slesnick, I. L. *The effectiveness of a unified science in the high school curriculum.* (Doctoral dissertation, Ohio State University) Ann Arbor, Mich.: University Microfilms, 1963. No. 63–4702.

Smith, H. A. Curriculum development and instructional materials. *Review of Educational Research,* 1969, 39, 397–413.

Smith, M. D. Response to a multi-media system. *Journal of Research in Science Teaching,* 1969, 6, 322–332.

Snider, R. M. *A project to study the nature of physics teaching using the Flanders method of interaction analysis.* (Doctoral dissertation, Cornell University) Ann Arbor, Mich.: University Microfilms, 1966. No. 66–6078.

Sorensen, L. L. *Change in critical thinking between students in laboratory centered and lecture-demonstration-centered patterns of instruction in high school biology.* (Doctoral dissertation, Oregon State University) Ann Arbor, Mich.: University Microfilms, 1966. No. 66-3939.

Stake, R. E. The countenance of educational evaluation. *Teachers College Record,* 1967, 68, 523–540.

Suchman, J. R. Inquiry training: Building skills for autonomous discovery. *Merrill-Palmer Quarterly of Behavior and Development,* 1961, 7, 147–169.

Szent-Györgyi, A. Teaching and the expanding knowledge. *Science,* 1964, 146, 1278–1279.

Tamir, P. *An analysis of certain achievements and attitudes of Cornell students enrolled in introductory biology with special reference to their high school preparation.* (Doctoral dissertation, Cornell University) Ann Arbor, Mich.: University Microfilms, 1968. No. 69-5034.

Tamir, P. High school preparation and college biology. *Bio Science,* 1969, 19, 447–449.

Tamir, P. Long-term evaluation of BSCS. *American Biology Teacher,* 1970, 32, 354–358.

Tamir, P. The Practical Mode—a distinct mode of performance in biology. *Journal of Biological Education,* 1972, 6, in press.

Tamir, P., & Glassman, F. A practical examination for BSCS students. *Journal of Research in Science Teaching,* 1970, 7, 107–112.

Tamir, P., & Glassman, F. A laboratory test for BSCS students—a progress report. *Journal of Research in Science Teaching,* 1971, 8, 332–341. (a)

Tamir, P., & Glassman, F. Laboratory test for BSCS students. *BSCS Newsletter,* 1971, 42, 9–13. (b)

Tannenbaum, R. S. The development of the Test of Science Processes. *Journal of Research in Science Teaching,* 1971, 8, 123–136.

Taylor, A. L. The influence of teacher attitudes and individual differences on pupil achievement with programed science materials. *Journal of Research in Science Teaching,* 1966, 4, 38–39.

Thompson, R. E. *A survey of the teaching of physics in secondary schools.* Princeton, N. J.: Educational Testing Service, 1969.

Tisher, R. P. The development of some science concepts: A replication of Piaget's studies.

Unpublished doctoral dissertation, University of New England, 1962.

Torop, W. The relative effectiveness of four types of laboratory reports in CHEM Study chemistry. *Journal of Research in Science Teaching,* 1969, 6, 335–339.

Toulmin, S. E. Does the distinction between normal and revolutionary science hold water? In I. Lakatos, & A. Musgrave (Eds.), *Critisism and the growth of knowledge.* London, Eng.: Cambridge University Press, 1970. Pp. 39–47.

Trent, J. H. *The attainment of the concept "understanding science" using contrasting physics courses.* (Doctoral dissertation, Stanford University) Ann Arbor, Mich.: University Microfilms, 1965. No. 65-6262.

Troost, C. J. A critique of Unified Science. *School Science and Mathematics,* 1968, 68, 845–846.

Troxel, V. A., & Snider, B. F. Correlations among student outcomes on the Test on Understanding Science, Watson Glaser Critical Thinking Appraisal, and the American Chemical Society Cooperative Examination —General Chemistry. *School Science and Mathematics,* 1970, 50, 73–76.

Tyler, R. W. *Basic principles of curriculum and instruction.* Chicago: University of Chicago Press, 1950.

Van Deventer, W. C. Toward the teaching of modern biology in high school. *School Science and Mathematics,* 1969, 69, 811–816.

Vitrogan, D. Characteristics of a generalized attitude toward science. *School Science and Mathematics,* 1969, 69, 150–158.

Walberg, H. J. A model for research on instruction. *School Review,* 1970, 78, 185–200.

Walberg, H. J., & Ahlgren, A. Predictors of the social environment of learning. *American Educational Research Journal,* 1970, 7, 153–167.

Walberg, H. J., & Anderson, G. J. Classroom climate and individual learning. *Journal of Educational Psychology,* 1968, 59, 414–419.

Walbesser, H. H., Jr. Science curriculum evaluation: Observations on a position. *Science Teacher,* 1966, 33 (2), 34–39.

Walbesser, H. H., Jr., & Carter, H. Some methodological considerations of curriculum evaluation research. *Educational Leadership,* 1968, 26, 53–64.

Watson, F. G. Research on teaching science. In N. L. Gage (Ed.), *Handbook of research on teaching.* Chicago: Rand McNally, 1963. Pp. 1031–1059.

Watson, F. G. Why do we need more physics courses? *The Physics Teacher,* 1967, 5, 212–214.

Welch, W. W. Curricular decisions—How can evaluation assist science teachers? *The Science Teacher,* 1968, 35 (8), 22–25. (a)

Welch, W. W. The impact of national curriculum projects—The need for accurate assessment. *School Science and Mathematics,* 1968, 68, 225–234. (b)

Welch, W. W. Correlates of course satisfaction in high school physics. *Journal of Research in Science Teaching,* 1969, 6, 54–58. (a)

Welch, W. W. Curriculum evaluation. *Review of Educational Research,* 1969, 39, 429–443. (b)

Welch, W. W., & Pella, M. O. The development of an instrument for inventorying knowledge of the processes of science. *Journal of Research in Science Teaching,* 1967–1968, 5, 64–68.

Wilson, J. H. The "new" science teachers are asking more and better questions. *Journal of Research in Science Teaching,* 1969, 6, 49–53.

Wilson, R. The grading of laboratory performance in biology courses. *American Biology Teacher,* 1962, 24, 196–199.

Wittrock, M. C. The learning by discovery hypothesis. In L. S. Shulman, & E. R. Keislar (Eds.), *Learning by discovery: A critical appraisal.* Chicago: Rand McNally, 1966. Pp. 33–75.

Yager, R. E. Teacher effects upon the outcomes of science instruction. *Journal of Research in Science Teaching,* 1966, 4, 236–242.

Yager, R. E., Englen, H. B., & Snider, B. C. Effects of the laboratory and demonstration methods upon the outcomes of instruction in secondary biology. *Journal of Research in Science Teaching,* 1969, 6, 76–86.

Young, P. A. *An experiment in the use of programmed materials in teaching high school biology.* (Doctoral dissertation, University of Georgia) Ann Arbor, Mich.: University Microfilms, 1968. No. 67-16,246.

Young, V. J. Survey of enrollment in physics. *The Physics Teacher,* 1965, 3, 117.

CHAPTER **35** Research on the Teaching of
Elementary-School Mathematics

C. ALAN RIEDESEL
State University of New York at Buffalo

PAUL C. BURNS
University of Tennessee

PERSPECTIVES

Interest in elementary-school mathematics instruction has steadily increased in recent years as has the number of research studies dealing with the field. In fact, it is probable that the 1960s will go down in history as the decade in which elementary mathematics programs developed, while the 1970s will be recorded as a time of great study on the teaching of elementary-school mathematics.

Research concerned with teaching elementary-school mathematics has always reflected the tenor of the times and has been strongly influenced by forces outside the field. Thus, as a prelude to a discussion of the research concerned with elementary-school mathematics instruction that has been conducted, we feel it important to sketch briefly the historical development of contemporary elementary-school mathematics.

In early colonial days mathematics, if taught, usually consisted simply of learning to count and to perform fundamental operations with whole numbers. The early textbooks were imported from England and were single copies for the "master." The early American textbooks were published in the 1700s and consisted of an approach of 1) state a rule and 2) give several worked examples with explanations (steps in computation, not meaning).

In the century between 1820 and 1920, American educators began to revise their methods of teaching mathematics. Early reform was based on the philosophy of Joseph Pestalozzi, a Swiss educator. The most influential author on mathematics in America was Warren Colburn. His book, *First Lessons in Intellectual Arithmetic upon the Inductive Method of Instruction,* printed in 1821, was very important for the next 50 years. Colburn used a set of leading questions rather than the rule-response approach. During the mid 1800s the book of Joseph Ray was quite popular and emphasized the study of mathematics for business use and mental discipline. The first book dealing specifically with the teaching of elementary-school mathematics was written by Edward Brooks and appeared in 1880. The book was well written, remarkably up-to-date, and in keeping with the Colburn philosophy.

The turn of the century writing of David

Eugene Smith was very influential. Smith (1913) made these suggestions:

(1) that pupils begin with content (having first felt some sensible reason for approaching the subject); (2) that they then pass to a use of symbols, to be handled automatically when expediency demands it, employing a particular form of expression only because that form best expresses the thought held; (3) that they be encouraged in flexibility of expression as well as of thinking, the former, however, always being controlled by the latter; and (4) that they be given many opportunities to exercise choice and judgment in applying the knowledge gained in life situations.

Following the demise of mental discipline, the stimulus-response (S-R) psychology of Thorndike dominated the approach to teaching. Extreme and often faulty application of this theory caused many elementary mathematics programs to be little more than endless drill exercises.

From the 1920s through the middle 1950s two theories predominated. The theory of social utility in curriculum selection was emphasized, and large numbers of research studies conducted by Guy Wilson (1939) focused on the topics in mathematics necessary for adult business use. Also the extreme S-R theory was giving way to varieties of field theory. One of the chief spokesmen for the "meaning theory," a field orientation, was William Brownell. He conducted studies which helped to establish the concept that pupil achievement in mathematics is better when children understand the mathematical principles.

The 1950s saw the emergence of "modern mathematics" programs. The majority of these programs emphasized the logical or pure mathematics basis for curriculum development. The first such project to develop an entire mathematics program for the elementary school was the School Mathematics Study Group. Wooten (1965) has reviewed the work of this group in detail. Other projects of major concern in the "mathematics revolution" were the Greater Cleveland Mathematics Program, Minnesota School Mathematics Center, University of Illinois Arithmetic Project, The Madison Project, and several Stanford projects. These and other smaller projects have been reviewed by Deans (1963), Corle (1964), Riedesel (1967) and The National Council of Teachers of Mathematics (1961, 1963).

Studies such as the National Longitudinal Study in Mathematics Assessment (1969) and those carried out by Ruddell (1962), Payne (1965), Hungerman (1967) and Friebel (1967) have evaluated modern programs and made comparisons with traditional programs. Evaluation has been difficult because of the task of developing instruments appropriate for both modern and traditional programs. In general, findings suggest slight differences favoring modern mathematics programs. However it should be noted that it is difficult to assess the effectiveness of modern programs in general since there are many types and varieties of such programs.

In 1963 the Cambridge Conference on School Mathematics compiled the recommendations of 29 mathematicians for future reform. This report has been the basis for a great deal of discussion and review. Stone (1965) points up some weaknesses in the report while Adler (1966) suggests a number of positive ideas developed by the group. The Central Mississippi Regional Laboratory is developing a mathematics curriculum following some of the Cambridge Conference's suggestions.

At this time research and development are taking several directions. There is interest in exploring the "laboratory approach" (Biggs & MacLean, 1969; R. B. Davis, 1967a), instructional sequencing (Heimer, 1969), individualization of instruction (Gibb, 1970) and Piagetian-type studies (Rosskopf, Steffe, & Taback, 1971).

THE LEARNER

Three topics are given major attention within this section: attitudes, Piaget-type explorations and individual differences. The amount of research reported for other aspects associated with the learner was considerably smaller.

Attitudes

Attitudes toward elementary-school mathematics have been investigated most frequently by the use of some type of attitude scale. Sometimes various school subjects have been ranked by order of preference, or pupils have been asked how they feel about mathematics. Obviously there are many problems which plague the study of attitudes, not the least of which is to find a way to improve the accuracy of attitude measures.

Surveys (Herman, 1963) report mathematics to be at least average or above as a preferred subject. There is evidence that very definite attitudes toward arithmetic may be formed as early as the third grade (Fedon, 1958), and that the intermediate grades are highly influential in the development of attitudes (K. J. Smith & Heddens, 1964). Using a revised form of the *Dutton Attitude Scale,* Stright (1960) found that in general pupils' attitudes toward mathematics improved from grade 3 through grade 6. While more researchers report that boys seem to prefer mathematics slightly more than do girls, especially in the upper elementary-school years, Capps and Cox (1969) found fourth-grade girls favoring arithmetic significantly more than fourth-grade boys.

Pupil attitudes have been thought to affect performance in some way. Although some research findings have not been in agreement (Cleveland, 1961), a general trend or a low positive relationship between pupil attitudes toward mathematics and pupil achievement in mathematics has been noted (Bassham, Murphy, & Murphy, 1964; Lindgren, Silva, Faraco, & Da Rocha, 1964; Anttonen, 1969). At this time there is no body of research evidence indicating that these two factors are correlated in a signifi-cantly positive manner and, furthermore, such a correlation would not imply causation.

One outcome of a modern mathematics program anticipated by some advocates would be an improvement in pupils' attitudes toward the subject, but this has not been established. According to Hungerman's findings (1967), pupils' attitudes were similarly positive both for contemporary and conventional programs. But for each type of program there was a low positive relationship between intelligence quotients and attitude, and also between attitude and achievement. Reasons given by 346 sixth-, seventh- and eighth-graders for disliking "new math" include: word problems, outside assignments, and rules to learn. Reasons for favorable attitudes include: useful, practical applications; logical concepts; and fun or challenging work with numbers (Dutton & Blum, 1968).

In terms of what forces affect attitudes, Shapiro (1961) suggested peer attitudes may be influential, especially in the case of girls. From a well-designed study of third-grade pupils Maertens (1968) concluded that arithmetic homework (teacher-prepared, experimenter-prepared, or none at all) does not uniformly affect pupils' attitudes toward the subject.

In order to study the effects of ability grouping on attitudes, Lerch (1961) compared the changes in attitudes toward arithmetic of fourth-grade pupils taught intermittently in ability groups with the changes in attitudes of pupils taught in traditional, nongrouped classes. The average change in attitude of the ability-grouped classes was not significantly different from that of the nongrouped classes. Socioeconomic status (Hungerman, 1967) or the type of school system attended (McDermott, 1956) have been reported to be noninfluential factors upon attitudes. Kaprelian (1961) found that arithmetic presented by television seemed to help fourth-grade pupils develop more favorable attitudes toward arithmetic.

For the interested reader, critical discussions of research on attitudes have been prepared by Feierabend (1960), Aiken (1969) and Neale (1969).

Piagetian-type Studies

Piaget has long been involved in studies dealing with the young child's conception of number, space and geometry (Piaget, 1952; Piaget & Inhelder, 1956; Piaget, Inhelder, & Szeminska, 1960) as well as areas other than mathematics. Considerable attention has been directed again toward his developmental psychology.

The Piagetian theory proposes four stages: sensori-motor (first 18 months), pre-operational (up to 7 years), concrete operations (about age 7 to about age 11) and formal operations (beginning at about 11 or 12 years of age). Operations most frequently researched are: a) conservation (recognition that certain aspects of an object or group of objects remain unchanged in the face of transformation) of substance, length, number, weight, distance and volume; b) transitivity (recognizing that if a R b [a is related to b] and b R c, then a R c); c) perception (size-weight illusion); and d) classification (sorting by attribute) and seriation (placing objects in order determined by some characteristic of the objects).

Piaget hypothesizes that children advance through certain sequences of concept development as determined by a) maturation, b) experience, c) social transmission and d) equilibration. For example, Piaget found the following typical, age-related emergence of various conservations: substance, age 7–8; length, 7–8; number, 6–7½; weight, 9–10; distance, 6½–12; and volume, 11–12. Such a stage of emergence has been supported on the whole by replication studies by Wohlwill (1960), Coxford (1963), Uzgiris (1964), Shantz and Smock (1966), and Lovell, Healey, and Rowland (1968). Smedslund (1963) found transitivity of length to be achieved by most of his subjects between the ages of 7 and 8 (Piaget's

finding was about age 8). Piaget's proposition that discrimination, seriation and numeration follow in that order in the child's development of number concepts has been upheld in a study by Elkind (1964) which involved 90 children ranging in age from four to six.

Some researchers, while supporting a general sequence of developmental stages, have found difficulty in assigning any given child to a particular stage of development (Dodwell, 1968) or in defining definite age barriers (Feigenbaum, 1963). Sister Gilmary (1964) has reviewed the experimental replications dealing with Piaget's work.

There is some evidence that gains in stage placement may be induced by instruction. For example, Wallach and Sprott (1964) provided first-graders with either no practice or practice in manipulation of objects to develop conservation of number (to understand that the number of elements in a group does not change no matter how they are rearranged). None of the no-training group achieved growth in conservation, while 14 of the 15 trained children evidenced growth on one test, and 13 of 15 on another test. This effect was not diminished after two to three weeks.

As to what training procedure appears to be most effective in inducing conservation, Palmer (1968) produced gains in children's ability to conserve number by producing cognitive conflict in two ways: expressing verbal surprise whenever a child responded as a conserver and exposing nonconservers to the contradictory conclusions of their own peers who were already conservers. Gruen (1965) found a combination of verbal pertaining (involving terms like "more" and "same") and cognitive conflict experiences to be superior to direct, reinforced practice in inducing number conservation of length and substance. Other training procedures (direct observation, social reinforcement, nonverbal, etc.) have been tested, but no single training procedure appears to have been equally effective for all cases. In brief, inducing conservation-type behavior earlier than typically would be expected has not met with a great deal of success regardless of the type of training procedure used, and particularly the direct training procedure.

Obviously assessment of conceptual development would be of less concern if it were not thought to affect performance in some way. Several studies of this type will be cited in a following section on pre-number mathematics.

For further reading, Duckworth (1964) and Adler (1966) give thoughtful listings of suggested teaching implications from Piaget-type findings. Harrison (1969) carefully reviewed 80 studies and attempted an extrapolation of the findings to mathematics learning and instruction. Furthermore, some mathematics projects which have been closely associated with Piagetian ideas include: The Madison Project (R. B. Davis, 1967b), Mathematics Laboratories (E. Biggs & MacLean, 1969); and the Nuffield Mathematics Teaching Project (1967).

Individual Differences

To date little substantial evidence has appeared to suggest that programs of individualized mathematics instruction will lead to higher levels of pupil achievement when compared with nonindividualized programs. Bartel (1965) compared achievement among fourth-graders under two treatments: a program of individualized instruction with content from the new mathematics and a traditional program which was not individualized. No significant difference was observed between students undergoing the two treatments on standardized tests. In a Progress Report (1969) on Individually Prescribed Instruction (IPI) (a cooperative venture of the University of Pittsburgh's Learning Research and Development Center and Oakleaf Elementary School) it was concluded that IPI pupils do as well as non-IPI pupils on the standard achievement tests. No significant differences in computation or problem-solving scores were found between different ability groups using the

IPI program (Deep, 1966). At the third-, fourth- and fifth-grade levels, Fisher (1967) found no significant achievement differences under three instructional treatments: IPI, programmed instruction and standard classroom instruction.

Programmed instruction has been considered one means of freeing teachers for greater individualization. Goebel (1966) found that teachers using programmed instructional material devoted 68 percent of their time to work with individuals while traditional class teachers devoted only 3 percent of their time to individuals. Computer-assisted instruction is another facet of individualizing instruction. Suppes and Morningstar (1969) have reported on use of both tutorial and drill-and-practice computer-assisted programs. They found the latter materials result in at least equivalent achievement in less time than would be taken by the classroom teacher and that the computer readily collects data on how children are responding, thus facilitating diagnosis of their difficulties. In the 1967–1968 Report of the Computer-Assisted Instruction Laboratory of the University of Texas, Gibb (1968) reported the results of three studies involving elementary-school mathematics pupils. For additional references the reader is referred to Hatfield's review (1969) on the topic of computers in mathematics education and the March 1969 issue of *The Arithmetic Teacher*, which is devoted to computer-assisted instruction.

Provisions for individualization are conditioned in part by class patterns of grouping. Evidence on the effectiveness of intraclass grouping for mathematics instruction is conflicting. Comparing performance of 11 *ability*-grouped classes with that of eight classes not grouped, Provus (1960) saw bright pupils profiting most from the grouping. In the same year, Wallen and Vowels had each of four sixth-grade teachers use both ability grouping and nongrouping procedures for one year each. No significant difference was found, though a significant interaction was exhibited between teachers and the procedures used. This interaction may be a major reason for differences in findings.

While not restricted to mathematics, perhaps the most substantial study of the effects of ability grouping in recent years is that of Goldberg, Passow, and Justman (1966). About 2,200 fifth- and sixth-grade children in 45 elementary schools in the New York City area were studied over two school years. This study reported that simply narrowing the ability range does not necessarily result in better adjustment of method or content and does not necessarily result in increased achievement.

The findings of research on *achievement* grouping have been more variable. Dewar (1963) concluded that establishing three intraclass sixth-grade groups benefited high and low achieving groups more than did whole-class instruction, while Koontz (1961) found that fourth-graders who were heterogeneously grouped achieved significantly higher scores than those homogeneously grouped. A summary of findings of studies of the 1950s and early 1960s dealing with intraclass grouping has been reported by O. L. Davis and Tracy (1963). Their analysis leads to the conclusion that there appears to be no one grouping plan which is best.

Attempts to isolate and measure the effects of organizational patterns such as nongradedness, departmentalization or specialization, multigradedness, or team teaching are extremely difficult since so many other factors interact with the patterns, and achievement differences are affected by many variables, particularly the teacher. Wolff (1968) found no significant differences in arithmetic achievement among third-year pupils in individualized graded or nongraded classrooms. On the other hand, Hart (1962) compared the arithmetic achievement of 50 beginning fourth-grade pupils who had spent three years in a nongraded primary school with the achievement of 50 matched pairs who had spent three years in a graded primary program. The difference, which favored the nongraded sample, was significant at the 0.02 level. Price, Prescott, and Hopkins (1967) investigated the relative efficiency of using special subject teachers in grade 5. This study uses a more comprehensive statistical approach than has often been used in research dealing with this question. There was no evidence that children learned mathematics more effectively in a departmentalized classroom than in a self-contained classroom. Achievement did not differ significantly between multigraded and single-graded groups (Finley & Thompson, 1963; Metfessel, 1960) or between children assigned to self-contained classrooms and those taught by team teaching (J. Jackson, 1964; Lindgren et al., 1964). No general conclusions can be drawn but the suggestion can be made that good teachers are effective regardless of the nature of organization. The effectiveness of various organizational procedures for the teaching of mathematics at the elementary-school level was last reviewed by Weaver (1966a), whose summary contained 92 references.

Numerous studies have dealt with a variety of instructional techniques for use with high achieving or with low achieving pupils. In general, acceleration has been reported to be effective for some children. Ivey (1965) found that fifth-graders who were given an accelerated and enriched program in the fourth grade gained significantly more than those receiving regular mathematics instruction. Klausmeier (1963) detected no unfavorable academic, social, emotional or physical correlates of acceleration from second to fourth grade, a conclusion which has been supported by findings from follow-up studies of accelerated pupils at the intermediate grade levels. Many topics have proven effective with accelerated bright pupils—sets, coordinate systems, geometry, signed integers, logic and symmetry (Suppes & Ihrke, 1967).

Diagnostic and remedial studies represent a refined extension of the analysis of individual differences. Early work in diagnosis was largely limited to determining the kinds and frequency of errors in computational skills, with the exception that if typical or characteristic errors can be identified, teachers might anticipate and prevent trouble spots. Such studies were done with whole numbers (Buswell & John, 1926), fractions and decimals (Brueckner, 1928a, 1928b). A more recent example of a diagnosis-remediation program would be L. F. Harvey and Kyte's sixth-grade study (1965) of zero difficulties in multiplication. Ross (1964) presented a case study report involving 20 sixth- and seventh-grade pupils, suggesting the importance of affective factors and stating that arithmetic underachievement appeared to be a complex and multiple-factored disability. Few experiments have attempted to use some of the statistical innovations of the sixties that try to assess individual improvement rather than merely look at a mythical average or norm.

Bernstein (1959) reviewed the research on remedial teaching of mathematics, noting that every cited experiment used lesson plans based on individual diagnosis as a basic teaching approach. A historical summary statement has been prepared by Gibb (1970) relating the efforts which have been made to individualize instruction through the years.

CURRICULUM

This section discusses pre-number experiences and teaching of whole numbers, fractions, problem solving and other content.

Sources of Curriculum

The research reported in this section is primarily concerned with the teaching of specific topics in the elementary mathematics curriculum. However, as a prelude to this approach the writers feel that a short reference to the theoretical sources of elementary mathematics curriculum should be discussed. Glennon and Callahan (1968) identify three major themes that can be the basis of curriculum:

1. The psychological basis for curriculum. There are several psychological theories on which curriculum can be developed. One approach views curriculum selection on the basis of the development of cognitive learning by analysis of the nature of the learner and his developmental stages in learning in connection with the subject matter to be learned. Research conducted by Piaget, Brownell, Ausubel, Bruner and Gagné is representative of this approach. Another psychological approach is that of A. S. Neill (1960), who takes the position that a pre-planned program in elementary mathematics is not appropriate. Neill would have all of the curriculum based upon the needs of the child as expressed by that child.

2. The sociological basis for curriculum. This theory of curriculum development was very prevalent in the United States during the 1930s. In this approach the content of the elementary mathematics program would be the content most useful to adults in daily life and in the adult business world. Wilson (1939) conducted large numbers of studies in an attempt to determine these topics.

3. The logical or pure mathematics basis for curriculum. Following this approach the curriculum would be determined only by the logical mathematical sequencing of a topic and would be taught in a "pure" form.

Certainly few of the researchers noted above have only subscribed to one point of view. However the importance of individual research findings can vary depending upon the relative emphasis given to each of the three approaches.

Pre-mathematics

Earlier studies, mostly concerned with an inventory of the number knowledges and abilities of young children, are typified by the research of Buckingham and MacLatchy (1930). Brownell's is another memorable study (1941) for all who are interested in the early school years. More recent studies have provided additional information about the number abilities and concepts possessed by preschool children (Holmes, 1963; McDowell, 1962). Dunkley (1965) has provided information about number concepts of disadvantaged children.

One ability of particular importance as a foundation for developing mathematical operations such as addition and subtraction is the ability to count. Surveys report that almost all kindergarten children can count by ones, with many children counting both rotely and rationally to at least 19 (Bjonerud, 1960). Fewer children can also count by twos, fives and 10's or understand a sequence of odd numbers. It has been assumed that the preschool child learns to say the number names and then begins to say them (rotely) in order before he associates the name (rationally) with sets of objects (Brace & Nelson, 1965), but some investigators have detected a rather strong relationship between the ability to rotely and rationally count (Rea & Reys, 1970). Most five-year-olds can recognize a group of three or four items. The concepts of ordinal and cardinal numbers do not necessarily develop concurrently. Some first-grade entrants can write and recognize numerals to five or 10.

Gunderson and Gunderson (1957) found that at least 50 percent of the children entering school can recognize halves, fourths and thirds and have acquired some facility in using these fractions. Many recognize circles and squares. Four- and five-year-olds exhibit wide differences in familiarity with ideas of time, linear and liquid measures and money, with little mastery evident. Some children can solve addition and subtraction examples in an oral context. The wide range of variability found in young children's number concepts has been associated with such factors as age, previous education and socioeconomic status. An 81-item paper-and-pencil test devised by Schwartz (1969) for assessing mathematical concepts of five-year-olds, with a reported reliability of 0.94, represents work in the development and testing of measurement instruments in pre-mathematics education.

Dutton (1963) administered the Metropolitan Readiness Test to 236 kindergarten entrants. He concluded that at least one-third of each entering class is mature enough and ready for systematic work involving the use of counting, enumeration, grouping, reproducing numerals and extending other mathematical concepts of size, shape, form and measurements. He also found that after a year in kindergarten without systematic instruction, 78 percent were above a norm he considered necessary for beginning systematic instruction. Roberts and Bloom (1967) reported no significant differences for type of program (formal versus informal) at the kindergarten level as measured by tests of mathematical skills, concepts and general readiness, while Stephens and Dutton (1969) found kindergarten children developed more concepts of telling time through a planned program plus incidental teaching than when concepts were presented only incidentally.

Unanswered questions at this time include: What is mathematics readiness? What activities can be used to prepare the pupil? Perhaps some of the answers will come from findings of the Piaget-oriented research in relation to developmental stages which have implications for ascertaining teaching stages.

Almy's (1966) longitudinal and cross-sectional studies of the emergence of conservation of number, using children from two kinds of cultural backgrounds, point up the importance of experience in the development of Piaget's stages. Steffe (1968) suggests that one type of ability possessed by children who do better in first-grade addition problems is the ability to "conserve numerousness" (is able to specify that if two sets are matched one to one, the number of objects in each is the same regardless of the arrangement or rearrangement of the two sets). Tests of addition facts and word problems were administered to 132 end-of-the-year first-graders who were of similar general intelligence but, with respect to the ability to conserve numerousness, were at four different levels. Children at the lowest level of number conservation performed significantly less well on both tests than did children in the upper three levels of conservation. LeBlanc (1968) reported similar results on a parallel study with subtraction problems and facts and suggested that a test of conservation of numerousness would provide a basis for a readiness test for first-graders. Pace (1968) found that kindergarten and first-grade nonconservers instructed in principles of equivalency (one-to-one correspondence) achieved significantly more than those not instructed and accelerated their attainment to the concept of number. Harper, Steffe, and VanEngen (1969) reported success in teaching conservation of numerousness, including one-to-one correspondence and equivalent and nonequivalent sets, to children at the first-grade level through 12 weekly 30-minute lessons. The teaching sequence involved a progress from physical action of children to manipulation of concrete materials to observation of semiconcrete illustrations.

Evidence is not strong for any one way of developing foundational number concept though there has been much writing and production of materials which have influenced modern programs. For example, Suppes and McKnight (1961) stated that working with sets is more meaningful than operations on numbers since sets are concrete objects; this finding is not in agreement with that by Holmes (1963). Crowder (1965) reported that a group of first-graders using the Cuisenaire program learned more mathematical concepts and skills than pupils taught by a conventional program. Lucas (1966) studied the use of Dienes's attribute blocks in the first grade. He found that children so trained showed greater ability to conserve cardinally and to conceptualize addition-subtraction relations than those taught more conventionally.

Discussion of other approaches to mathematical foundation experiences for young children is available (Lovell, 1961; Montessori, 1964; Stern, 1949). When comparing relative effectiveness of different systems of instruction, the reader will profit by keeping in mind such ideas as those proposed by Brownell (1968).

Numbers

Some early research efforts focused upon the relative difficulty of addition and subtraction facts when the drill method of teaching was popular (MacLatchy, 1933; Washburne & Vogel, 1928; Wheeler, 1939). In 1944 Swenson substantiated that difficulty appears to be at least in part a function of teaching method, and suggested a need to reconsider difficulty level in terms of the more meaningful methods in use at that time. More recently Suppes and Groen (1967), using computer-assisted instruction, have presented some evidence of the difficulty of the basic facts in terms of analysis of error types and conditions of their occurrence in children's work.

Based on a very few studies, there is mild support for the ideas that stress on the relationship between addition and subtraction facilitates understanding and that teaching two operations simultaneously promotes some increase in achievement, although some intertask interference may occur (Brownell, 1928; Spencer, 1967).

Subtraction. Gibb (1956) found that the highest degree of pupil attainment in subtraction was on take-away problems; the lowest on comparison problems. She also found that addition problems took longer to complete. For introductory work, Osborne (1966) reported that using set-partitioning-without-removal resulted in greater understanding than the take-away problem situation. While Gibb (1956) concluded that semiconcrete representation was better than concrete or abstract representation in her subtraction experiment, Ekman (1966) found that with third-graders the use of manipulative materials increased under-standing of addition concepts (number facts) more than the use of only pictures before introduction of the addition algorithm.

The question of the method of teaching subtraction involving renaming has received much attention—particularly whether to teach by decomposition or equal additions. In two well-executed educational experiments, Brownell (1947a) and later Brownell and Moser (1949) compared the effectiveness of these two methods when they were taught in two ways—meaningfully and mechanically. They found that the decomposition method when taught meaningfully was the most successful if the criteria were understanding and transfer, while mechanical teaching using equal additions produced greater accuracy and rate, but possibly at the expense of understanding. Brownell considered equal additions difficult to rationalize. More recently Cronbach (1965) pointed out the development of a technique of using the number line which may make the rationalization of the equal-additions algorithm more meaningful. This, combined with some of the newer emphasis on properties (e.g., compensation), suggests that the equal addition methods can be presented with meaning. There may be a shift toward wider use of this procedure in the future.

Multiplication. Hervey (1966) compared the equal-additions approach with the use of Cartesian products. She reported that for her second-grade subjects, equal-additions multiplication problems were less difficult to solve and conceptualize, and that Cartesian-product problems were more readily solved by high achievers than by low achievers. At the third-grade level Schell (1964) investigated achievement of pupils who used array representations exclusively for their introductory work with multiplication as compared with pupils who used a variety of representations. He found no conclusive evidence of a difference in achievement levels. Studying the use of mathematical properties to teach multiplication, K. D. Hall (1967) found that stress on the commutative property was effective. In an excellently designed study, Gray (1965) observed the use of the distributive property in teaching multiplication. He found that the use of the property was effective for such measures as comprehension, transfer and retention.

Division. VanEngen and Gibb (1956) compared the subtractive algorithm of division with the distributive (conventional or standard) algorithm. While the results were mixed, the suggested advantages of the subtractive algorithm were: greater transfer to unfamiliar division situations, less difficulty for children of low intellectual ability, and greater understanding of the division operation. Such studies and suggestions have led to the current wide use of the subtractive algorithm.

Zweng (1964) studied measurement, partitive and rate concepts of division, finding that partitive division problems were significantly more difficult for second-graders than measurement problems. In a small exploratory study, Scott (1963) made use of two algorithms for division, using the subtractive form for measurement situations and the distributive form for partitive situations. He found this procedure to be effective with third-grade children.

The question of how to estimate quotient digits has been the subject of many rather extensive investigations. The two methods usually compared in such investigations have been the apparent (or round down) and the increase-by-one (round both ways or round up only). In the former, the tens number of the two-digit divisor is used in estimating the quotient. In the second there is rounding down and rounding up (round both ways) to the next higher multiple of the tens number in the quotient, or rounding up always. Earlier studies attempted primarily to determine by which of these methods the smallest number of errors would occur (Grossnickle, 1932; Morton, 1947; Osburn, 1946). Hartung (1957) critically reviewed these and other analytic division studies which provide background and support for many of the procedures devised for estimating quotient digits. When success on the first trial is the criterion, then "round both ways" would be recommended, but other factors may be more important considerations in the instructional program. There are very few experimental investigations on this topic and little firm evidence to verify which is the most effective method of teaching pupils to estimate quotient digits.

Fractions. Gunderson and Gunderson (1957) suggested that second-graders could understand fractions when they used manipulative materials. Many studies support the importance of using meaningful methods of work with fractions (Krich, 1964; Shuster & Pigge, 1965).

R. C. Anderson (1965) compared the use of the procedures of either a) setting up classes of equivalent fractions or b) factoring the denominators for finding the common denominator for addition and subtraction with unlike, unrelated fractions. She found no achievement differences.

Brooke (1954) and Capps (1963) studied the use of the common denominator method for division with fractions as compared with the inversion method. Immediate results showed these methods to be equally effective; however retention tests favored the common denominator method. Capps (1963) also found that the use of the inversion method aided in achievement on multiplication with fractions. This retroactive effect on multiplication was also reported by Bidwell (1968). Where the inversion algorithm has been accompanied by explanation of the reciprocal principle, above average pupils understand the principle and retention seems to be higher

(Krich, 1964; Sluser, 1962). Some investigators have found use of the complex fraction algorithm effective for division with fractions (Bergen, 1966).

Some earlier studies were concerned with the specific errors made by pupils in dealing with fractions. Major errors reported for all operations were: a) difficulty with renaming in simplest form, b) inadequate understanding of the process involved, and c) computational errors (Brueckner, 1928b; Morton, 1947). More recently, Aftreth (1958) concluded that systematic practice in identifying and correcting errors in addition and subtraction with fractions had no appreciable effect upon achievement. Scott (1962) found fifth-graders made more errors in fraction subtraction involving renaming, suggesting that current emphasis on the decimal system resulted in pupils tending to relate the process to the decimal scale.

R. C. Anderson (1969) has provided a comprehensive list of suggestions for instruction in fractions based on 74 selected references which she has cited.

Decimals. Difficulty in placing the decimal point in the quotient has been the subject of a number of studies (Brueckner, 1928a). Grossnickle (1932) found 21 kinds of errors in division with decimals. He urged meaningful teaching regardless of which of the following methods of locating the decimal point is used: a) inserting a caret; b) subtracting the number of decimal places in the divisor from the number of places in the dividend; or c) multiplying both divisor and dividend by a power of 10 in order to make the divisor a whole number. He recommended the third way as the best one to make the placing of the decimal point meaningful. F. Flournoy (1959) found that multiplying by a power of 10 resulted in greater accuracy than the subtraction method.

Willson (1969) compared decimal-common fraction sequence with conventional sequence of common-decimal fractions for fifth-graders and found no significant differences between the two sequences. Pupils achieved significantly with each, suggesting that emphasis should continue to be placed both on relating decimals with common fractions and also on place value.

Percentages. Kenny and Stockton (1958) found a method combining emphasis on drill and understanding more effective in teaching percentage than emphasis on either alone. Tredway (1959) reported that emphasis in instruction of seventh-grade pupils on the relationships between the elements of percent (usually named *number, percent* and *part*) was more effective than the usual textbook presentation. Tredway and Hollister (1963) reported that teaching the three "cases" of percentage as related parts of a whole process provided for better retention. In comparing three methods of teaching percentage, Wynn (1966) found no significant difference in achievement or retention between unitary analysis, formula or decimal methods. McCarty (1966) reported success in teaching ratio and percentage at grades 4, 5 and 6.

Problem Solving

The improvement of problem-solving skills has been the topic for more research studies than any other single topic. The quality of this research has been generally low in research design. However, even with limitations considered, there are probably more practical answers from research to help the improvement of problem solving than for any other area of the elementary-school mathematics curriculum.

In addition to the following cited studies, several published reviews and/or analyses concerned with problem solving are available. Johnson (1944b) analyzed studies preceding 1944. Gorman (1967) analyzed research on word problems conducted between 1925 and 1965 and identified 37 studies that were of acceptable quality.

Riedesel (1969) lists several procedures for improving problem solving based on research. Kilpatrick (1969) reports on the problem-solving research from 1964 to 1969.

Several researchers have examined the structure of problems and the effect of reading skills upon the solution of problems. Burns and Yonally (1964) found that pupils made significantly higher scores on problems in which the numerical data were in proper solution order, and Suppes, Loftus, and Jerman (1969) reported that structural variables such as number operations were less important in determining problem difficulty than similarity of a problem to the previous problem. Steffe (1967) found that problems with a common name for sets (cookies, cookies) were easier for first-grade children to solve in an oral context than problems with different names for the sets (kittens, goldfish). Further, Steffe concluded that first-graders had significantly more difficulty with problems that had no accompanying aids (physical or pictorial) than with problems with aids, regardless of the level of conservation. Williams and McCreight (1965) report that pupils achieve slightly higher scores when the question is asked first in problems. They suggest that some problems be developed in which the question is presented first, since the question is normally presented last in textbook series. Several studies have revealed that direct teaching of reading skills and vocabulary directly related to problem solving improves achievement (Dresher, 1934; Johnson, 1944a; Robertson, 1931; Treacy, 1944; Vanderlinde, 1964).

A number of other factors contribute to problem-solving achievement. Studies by Stevenson (1925) and Corle (1958) reveal that pupils often give little attention to the actual problems; instead, they almost randomly manipulate numbers. K. J. Smith and Heddens (1964) and Heddens and Smith (1964) found that experimental materials and commercial textbook materials were at a reading difficulty higher than that prescribed by reading formula analysis.

Several researchers have identified factors associated with high achievement in problem solving. Some of these traits are: intelligence, computational ability, ability to analyze problems, arithmetic vocabulary, ability to use quantitative relationships that are social in nature, ability to note irrelevant detail, and knowledge of arithmetical concepts (Alexander, 1960; Babcock, 1954; Balow, 1964; Beldin, 1960; Butler, 1956; Chase, 1960; W. M. Cruickshank, 1948; Hansen, 1944; Klausmeier & Loughlin, 1961; Kliebhan, 1955).

Problem setting has also been found to be important to problem-solving achievement (Bowman, 1929, 1932; Brownell, 1931; Evans, 1940; Hensell, 1956; Lyda & Church, 1964; Sutherland, 1941; Wheat, 1929). Their findings are mixed. However the generalizations that problems should be of interest to the children and relevant to lives are justifiable conclusions.

For many years researchers have explored methods of improving verbal problem solving. Evidence by Hanna (1930), Burch (1953) and Chase (1960) indicated that informal procedures are superior to following rigid steps such as the following: "Answer each of these questions: 1) What is given? 2) What is to be found? 3) What is to be done? 4) What is a close estimate of the answer? and 5) What is the answer to the problem?" J. W. Wilson (1967) compared a "wanted-given" approach with an "action-sequence" in which children write the mathematical sentence that conveys the action of the problem. His findings strongly support the "wanted-given" approach; however it should be noted that Wilson's "wanted-given" approach was not the formal analysis method described above. Studies by Stevenson (1924), Washburne and Osborne (1926), Thiele (1938), Luchins (1942), Bemis and Trow (1942), J. V. Hall (1942), Klausmeier (1964), Riedesel (1964) and Sekyra (1969) suggest that a number of specific techniques will aid in improving pupils' problem-solving abilities. These techniques include: 1) using drawings and diagrams; 2) following and discussing a model problem; 3) having pupils write their own problems and solve each others' problems; 4) using problems without numbers; 5) using orally presented problems; 6) emphasizing vocabulary; 7) writing mathematical sentences; 8) using problems of proper difficulty level; 9) helping pupils correct problems; 10) praising pupil progress; and 11) sequencing problem sets from easy to hard.

Other Topics

In recent years there have been a number of topics that have received increased emphasis in the elementary mathematics curriculum. The topics considered below are: geometry, sets, logic and nondecimal numeration systems. The research in each of these areas is limited in scope; therefore it is very difficult to draw many conclusions.

Dealing with geometry, D'Augustine (1964) identified topics that could be taught using programmed instruction. His list included: congruency; interior, exterior and boundary points; simple closed curves; triangle properties and definition; collinearity; finite and infinite points; and properties of lines and line segments. Shah (1969) found that children in elementary school could learn concepts of plane figures, symmetry, reflection, rotation, translation, networks and nets of figures. Neatrour (1969) reported on the amount of geometry contained in contemporary textbooks in the middle school. Herbst (1968) determined that some topics from coordinate geometry were effective topics for fifth-grade children. Weaver's (1966b) inventory of geometric understandings revealed no significant differences between conventional and modern classes. Gagné and Bassler (1963) found that groups having the smallest variety of task examples to perform in nonmetric geometry materials retained less than those with a greater variety of tasks. Jencks (1969) experimented with geoboard usage.

While sets have been incorporated into

the elementary mathematics curriculum, there are few studies which have been designed to analyze the contribution made by the study of sets. H. K. Smith (1968) reported that students who received instruction in set theory showed significant superiority in logical reasoning. Suppes and McKnight (1961) report success with the use of sets in introductory work in elementary mathematics.

Suppes and Binford (1965) investigated the teaching of mathematical logic to academically talented fifth- and sixth-grade children. They compared these pupils with college students and found that the upper quartile of elementary-school children can achieve at a level approaching college students. McAloon (1969) found that groups at the third- and sixth-grade level having been instructed in logic scored significantly higher on mathematics achievement and reasoning tests than groups not taught logic. Allen (1965) reported that the game of WFF'N Proof aids in logic achievement. Scott (1965) indicated that the School Mathematics Study Group (SMSG) program aided in the improvement of logic scores.

A feature of the majority of new mathematics programs at the elementary level is the study of nondecimal numeration systems. This topic was included in the belief that exploration into another system would improve the child's understanding of the decimal system. As yet this transfer cannot be substantiated. In a careful study Schlinsog (1968) reported no significant differences from nondecimal instruction on basic understanding, computational ability and preference when compared with regular decimal instruction. On the other hand, R. L. Jackson (1966) indicated that pupils receiving instruction in nondecimal numeration systems did significantly better than those studying the decimal system on tests of understanding and problem solving. There were no significant computational differences. It should be noted that there is agreement that nondecimal numeration

systems can be effectively taught (Hollis, 1964; Trueblood, 1970). D. E. Cruikshank and Arnold (1969) provide a summary of five studies on nondecimal instruction.

TEACHING

This section deals with the use of class time, sequencing, teaching approaches and materials. The topics are interrelated and it is necessary to interpret the findings from research in light of each.

Use of Class Time

Shipp and Deer (1960), Shuster and Pigge (1965), Zahn (1966) and Hopkins (1966) explored the optimum ratio between amount of class time devoted to developmental activities and the amount of class time devoted to practice. While there are some differences in the methodology used in the various studies, the findings all point to improved pupil achievement when between 50 and 75 percent of the class time is devoted to developmental activities. M. F. Flournoy (1954) suggests that a portion of the mathematics class time be devoted to non-pencil-and-paper computation.

Sequencing

As the emphasis upon making decisions based upon research increases, the need for information concerning the structuring of content and ordering the instructional tasks becomes more essential. While there is little substantive knowledge concerning proper sequencing in elementary mathematics, several investigators have begun major study on efficient sequencing. Gagné (1967) has suggested that any human learning task may be analyzed into a set of component tasks which are distinct from each other in terms of the experimental operations needed to produce them. Thus, the presence or absence of these task components effects positive transfer to the final performance. Following this reasoning it is necessary to:

a) identify the component tasks of a final performance, b) ensure achievement of each of the tasks, and c) arrange the total learning situation in a sequence which insures optimal mediational effects from one component to another. Programs such as Individually Prescribed Instruction rely heavily on these ideas. Following a somewhat different tack, Suppes (1967) has developed sets of mathematical models dealing with variables important in the presentation of sequences. Also, Scandura and Wells (1967) have developed approaches to sequencing variables.

It should be noted that a discussion of sequencing has been purposely omitted for two reasons: first, it is our belief that the topic is more thoroughly covered in several of the psychologically oriented chapters; second, the findings with implications toward classroom practice are at present limited. For further information it is suggested that the reader see the review and analysis of sequencing by Heimer (1969).

Teaching Strategies

There are numbers of identifiable teaching strategies that could be the basis for research studies. At the present time the majority of studies have contrasted "discovery" or "guided discovery" teaching with didactic or "expository" teaching. Interest in these approaches is evident in the literature (Shulman, 1970; Shulman & Keislar, 1966). In addition, there is a growing amount of research concerned with a "laboratory" approach or laboratory strategies.

Discovery learning has appeared in educational literature from Plato through present-day writing. Early research by McConnell (1934), Thiele (1938) and Swenson (1944) indicated some superiority in discovery-type teaching. Carlow (1967) provides a concise list of a priori claims for and against discovery learning distilled from the literature. Researchers favoring discovery learning have suggested that it: a) is the natural and preferred way of learning for man; b) builds motivation; c) promotes better learning and retention; and d) leads the learner to be a constructionist and thus avoids the information drift that fails to keep account of the uses to which information might be put. On the other hand, other researchers suggest that discovery learning: a) requires a vastly increased expenditure of time; b) causes frustration and superstition when children fail to discover; c) without adequate consolidation is likely to be a vain pursuit because it is incomplete and may lead to frustrating perplexities as the learners are unaware of restrictions that logic imposes on possibility and reality; and d) is not equally appropriate for all children; thus the teacher may underestimate the cost in loss of communication for the pupils who do not discover.

A recent study by Worthen (1968), conducted with fifth- and sixth-grade children, compared a discovery-oriented teaching approach and an expository presentation. Based on the evidence of the study, he suggests that if pupil abilities to retain mathematical concepts and to transfer the heuristics of problem solving are valued outcomes of education, then discovery sequencing should be an integral part of the methodology used in teaching mathematics to elementary-school pupils. On the other hand, if immediate recall is a valued outcome of education, then expository sequencing should be continued as the typical instructional practice used in elementary classrooms.

Scandura (1964) has conducted several related studies concerned with type of discovery teaching. He reports that: a) discovery pupils were better able to handle problem tasks; b) discovery pupils took longer to reach the desired level of facility; and c) expository pupils generally used the algorithm taught while discovery subjects varied in the algorithm used. Armstrong (1969) suggested that an inductive mode aided in the learning of mathematical operations while the deductive mode resulted in greater learning of mathematical properties.

In addition to studies related to discovery in the typical classroom setting, there have been numerous research studies which have focused on "activity" or "laboratory" teaching over the years. During the 1930s informal research on activity programs was conducted. Such research is typified by the study of Harap and Mapes (1934) which favored activity programs. Using observational methods, R. B. Davis (1966, 1967b), Dienes (1967), E. E. Biggs (1965), J. Biggs (1968), and E. E. Biggs and MacLean (1969) provide insights into children's learning using laboratory activities. Kieren (1969) has reviewed the recent research on activity learning in mathematics.

Also, for many years researchers have studied "meaningful" versus "mechanical" teaching. The results of such studies suggest: 1) rote rule and meaning produce about the same results when immediate computational ability is used as a criterion; 2) when retention is used as a criterion, the meaning method is superior to the rote-rule method; 3) greater transfer is facilitated by the meaning method; and 4) the meaning method produces greater understanding of mathematical principles and comprehension of complex analysis (Brownell & Moser, 1949; Dawson & Ruddell, 1955; Greathouse, 1966; Krich, 1964; G. H. Miller, 1957; Rappaport, 1958, 1963).

Materials

Studying textbooks, H. L. Smith and Eaton (1942a, 1942b, 1943a, 1943b) and H. L. Smith, Eaton, and Dugdale (1945) analyzed textbooks published over a 150-year period and found that there was a trend toward inclusion of more inductive method, increased "real-life" emphasis, and greater importance of learner interest. Dooley (1960, 1961) studied the content of textbooks in light of research findings. She found that research recommendations were incorporated into textbooks within five years. Folsom (1960) found that only about ½ of the teachers she surveyed used the teacher's

manual. Durr (1958) found workbooks in grades 4 and 5 to be an effective aid.

G. H. Miller (1957) found that significantly higher gains in multiplication with fractions were made by pupils using programmed practice materials than by pupils using conventional textbook materials. Fincher and Fillmer (1965) also found the programmed materials were more effective on achievement posttests—but not on retention tests—in teaching addition and subtraction with fractions than conventional classroom instruction. Greatsinger (1968) found no significant difference between the programmed instruction group and the textbook instruction group (grade 6) in division with fractions. There are few findings from studies which explore programmed instruction variables (but use some aspect of mathematics as the content) which give definitive direction to curriculum decision making, but one often-mentioned conclusion —equivalent results can be achieved with less time—could be a possible fruitful area of further research.

Studies concerning the use of desk calculators were made by Fehr, McMeen, and Sobel (1956) and Triggs (1966). They reported that use of a calculator for work with fundamental operations resulted in increased achievement scores. Lucas (1966) found attributive blocks to compare very favorably with use of a textbook series. Plank (1950) reported Montessori materials to be helpful for remedial work. In general, the materials seemed to be more effective for slow and average learners than for above average learners.

Studying the use of rods, Brownell (1963) found mixed results. Hollis (1965), Nasca (1966) and Lucow (1963, 1964) found that children using rods achieved less than other groups. Harshman, Wells, and Payne (1962) found that teacher-made materials were as effective as either expensive or inexpensive purchased materials. In contrast, Reddell and DeVault (1960) reported that two commercial aids increased some aspects of achievement more than teacher-made aids.

G. R. Anderson (1957), Trueblood (1970) and Howard (1950) report effective use of audio-visual devices.

With the increased interest in the "math lab" approach to teaching, one would expect that the next few years will see an even greater number of studies concerned with the use of manipulative materials.

FUTURE DIRECTIONS

Research related to elementary-school mathematics instruction has steadily improved; however, there is a great need for still further improvement. There are several approaches to research and topics for research that we feel should be emphasized in coming years. Inclusion of an idea in this list does not mean that there has been no research in the area but that there is need for further research and/or refinement of research in the area.

1. There is much current discussion on developing a theory or theories of instruction (Bruner, 1966). The type of thinking required to develop and test such a theory or theories is very desirable to the improvement of the teaching of elementary mathematics. There is a great need to determine and investigate the complex variables such as content, teacher behavior, student aptitudes, etc., and to determine the specific teacher behavior that is most appropriate for each distinct set of mathematical content and pupil population. Such studies probably would focus first on identifiable teaching strategies and determine the effectiveness of each for specific types of children and specific types of mathematical content. Also, it may well be that specific teacher types are more effective using one type of strategy. If proper instrumentation can be developed to validly and reliably conduct such studies, hopefully it will be possible to make statements such as: for content material X, taught by teacher Q to pupil Z, the best strategy is A.

2. There have been great numbers of attitude studies concerned with pupils, teachers and elementary-school mathematics. At the present time work is being conducted and may continue to differentiate the components of attitude so that it will be possible to a) get a measure of a child's general attitude; b) if the attitude is low give "diagnostic" type attitude measures that will determine specific reasons for the lack of positive attitude (this might require a host of specific measures of effect of content, teacher, instructional materials, peer, home, etc.); and c) on the basis of the specific information provide the child with a "package" of mathematical learning materials that will improve his attitude toward mathematics. The whole area of the affective domain (Krathwohl, Bloom, & Masia, 1964; Mueller, 1970) and mathematics teaching and learning needs to be explored. This will require a major effort in the development of proper instruments and materials.

3. Fruitful attacks upon the proper sequencing of and within mathematical topics have begun (Suppes, 1967; Gagné, 1968). There is a need to further develop a systematic program of research and development to construct, evaluate and refine instructional sequential algorithms (Heimer, 1969).

4. In recent years there has been increasing interest in the studies of Piaget. A growing number of researchers have engaged in replications, extensions and new studies using the technique of interview task in a manner similar to Piaget. Further work is needed in this area, and a great deal of information is needed concerning the thinking of children before, during and after particular types of mathematics instruction. It seems reasonable to think that instructional procedures in mathematics could be guided by appropriate utilization of information of cognitive differences, but this is not yet the case—at least as based upon research data.

5. Many experiments in elementary mathematics instruction raise the question, "Which approach is better—Approach A or Approach B?" This question is important

to the development of proper mathematical curricular materials; however, on many occasions it is equally important to ask the questions, "Is method A effective? Is method B effective?" Also, an important independent variable missing from such studies is the efficiency or time variable. The typical procedure is to hold time constant over treatment groups. It may be quite possible that achievement on two different treatments is the same when time is held constant, but that when time is used as a manipulated variable, one treatment may be more efficient than the other.

6. With a renewed emphasis upon the use of activity materials and procedures, the question arises as to the relationships between laboratory learning and a planned, sequential and structured mathematics program. There seems to be little profit from an "either-or" position on this issue. Research is needed for evaluation checkups of activity components and will perhaps assist in finding the best "fit" within the mathematics curriculum.

7. Also, study is needed concerning the contribution of the other curricular areas. For one set of suggestions see the report of the Cambridge Conference on the Correlation of Science and Mathematics in the Schools (1969).

8. While there is a great need to develop better basic and programmatic research, there is always the need to provide well-documented answers to specific problems concerned with teaching mathematics to children. In fact, many of the studies which have had the greatest impact on elementary mathematics teaching have been of this type (Brownell & Moser, 1949; VanEngen & Gibb, 1956).

9. It is axiomatic that for research to be worthwhile (mathematics education research as an applied field) the results must be used. There is a continued need to find ways of putting research findings to use. The question, "How can we get valid research findings applied in classrooms?" is of major importance.

We have suggested several avenues of research that we believe to be fruitful. There are certainly others. Recently the editor of an elementary-school mathematics textbook series said, "I don't believe that there really are any research findings of importance in elementary-school mathematics." While such a statement can certainly be questioned today, we hope that in the near future such a statement would automatically brand the speaker as uninformed.

REFERENCES

Adler, I. Mental growth and the art of teaching. *The Arithmetic Teacher,* 1966, 13, 576–584.

Aftreth, O. B. The effect of the systematic analysis of errors in the study of fractions at the sixth grade level. *Journal of Educational Research,* 1958, 52, 31–34.

Aiken, L. R. Attitudes towards mathematics. In J. W. Wilson, & L. R. Carry (Eds.), *Studies in mathematics, Vol. 19. Reviews of recent research in mathematics education.* Stanford: School Mathematics Study Group, 1969. Pp. 1–49.

Alexander, V. E. Seventh graders' ability to solve problems. *School Science and Mathematics,* 1960, 60, 603–606.

Allen, R. W. The fourth "R." *California Journal of Educational Research,* 1965, 16, 75–79.

Almy, M. *Young children's thinking.* New York: Teachers College Press, 1966.

Anderson, G. R. Visual-tactual devices and their efficacy. *The Arithmetic Teacher,* 1957, 4, 196–201.

Anderson, R. C. A comparison of two procedures for finding the least common denominator in the addition of unlike, unrelated fractions. Unpublished doctoral dissertation, University of Iowa, 1965.

Anderson, R. C. Suggestions from research—fractions. *The Arithmetic Teacher,* 1969, 16, 131–135.

Anttonen, R. G. A longitudinal study in mathematics attitude. *Journal of Educational Research,* 1969, 62, 467–471.

Armstrong, J. R. Curricular and instructional factors which facilitate mathematical learning. *Journal of Experimental Education*, 1969, 38 (2), 5–15.

Babcock, H. An analysis of problem solving in arithmetic. Unpublished doctoral dissertation, University of California at Berkeley, 1954.

Balow, I. H. Reading and computation ability as determinants of problem solving. *The Arithmetic Teacher*, 1964, 11, 18–22.

Bartel, E. V. A study of the feasibility of an individualized instructional program in elementary school mathematics. Unpublished doctoral dissertation, University of Wisconsin, 1965.

Bassham, H., Murphy, M., & Murphy, K. Attitude and achievement in arithmetic. *The Arithmetic Teacher*, 1964, 11, 66–72.

Beldin, H. O. A study of selected arithmetic verbal problem solving skills among high and low achieving sixth grade children. Unpublished doctoral dissertation, Syracuse University, 1960.

Bemis, E. O., & Trow, W. C. Remedial arithmetic after two years. *Journal of Educational Research*, 1942, 35, 443–452.

Bergen, P. M. Action research on division of fractions. *The Arithmetic Teacher*, 1966, 13, 293–295.

Bernstein, A. Library research—a study in remedial arithmetic. *School Science and Mathematics*, 1959, 59, 185–195.

Bidwell, J. K. A comparative study of the learning structure of three algorithms for the division of fractional numbers. Unpublished doctoral dissertation, University of Michigan, 1968.

Biggs, E. E. Research in the children's method of learning. *Mathematics in Primary School in Curriculum Bulletin*, 1965, 1, 5–9.

Biggs, E. E., & MacLean, J. R. *Freedom to learn: An active learning approach to mathematics.* Reading, Mass.: Addison-Wesley, 1969.

Biggs, J. *The teaching of mathematics in the primary school.* London: Commonwealth Secretariat, 1968.

Bjonerud, C. E. Arithmetic concepts possessed by the preschool child. *The Arithmetic Teacher*, 1960, 7, 347–350.

Bowman, H. L. The relation of reported preference to performance in problem solving. *University of Missouri Bulletin*, 1929, 30, 1–52.

Bowman, H. L. The relation of reported pref-

erence to performance in problem solving. *Journal of Educational Psychology*, 1932, 23, 266–276.

Brace, A., & Nelson, L. D. The preschool child's concept of number. *The Arithmetic Teacher*, 1965, 12, 126–133.

Brooke, G. M. The common denominator method in the division of fractions. Unpublished doctoral dissertation, State University of Iowa, 1954.

Brooks, E. *The philosophy of arithmetic.* Lancaster, Pa.: Normal Publishing Co., 1880.

Brownell, W. A. The development of children's number ideas in the primary grades. *Supplementary Educational Monographs*, No. 35. Chicago: University of Chicago, 1928.

Brownell, W. A. *The effect of unfamiliar settings on problem solving.* Duke University research studies in education, No. 1. Durham, N.C.: Duke University Press, 1931.

Brownell, W. A. *Arithmetic in grades 1 and 2: A critical summary of new and previously reported research.* Duke University research studies in education, No. 6. Durham, N.C.: Duke University Press, 1941.

Brownell, W. A. An experiment on "borrowing" in third grade arithmetic. *Journal of Educational Research*, 1947, 41, 161–171. (a)

Brownell, W. A. The place of meaning in the teaching of arithmetic. *Elementary School Journal*, 1947, 47, 256–265. (b)

Brownell, W. A. Arithmetical abstractions—progress toward maturity of concepts under differing programs of instruction. *The Arithmetic Teacher*, 1963, 10, 322–329.

Brownell, W. A. Conceptual maturity in arithmetic under differing systems of instruction. *Elementary School Journal*, 1968, 69, 151–163.

Brownell, W. A., & Moser, H. E. *Meaningful vs. mechanical learning: A study in grade III subtraction.* Duke University research studies in education, No. 8. Durham, N.C.: Duke University Press, 1949.

Brueckner, L. J. Analysis of difficulties in decimals. *Elementary School Journal*, 1928, 29, 32–41. (a)

Brueckner, L. J. Analysis of errors in fractions. *Elementary School Journal*, 1928, 28, 760–770. (b)

Bruner, J. S. *Toward a theory of instruction.* Cambridge, Mass.: Belknap Press, 1966.

Buckingham, B. R., & MacLatchy, J. The number abilities of children when they enter grade one. In G. M. Whipple (Ed.), *Research in arithmetic*. Twenty-ninth Yearbook of the National Society for the Study of Education, Part II. Bloomington, Ill.: Public School Publishing Co., 1930. Pp. 473–524.

Burch, R. L. Formal analysis as a problem-solving procedure. *Journal of Education*, 1953, 136, 44–47, 64.

Burns, P. C., & Yonally, J. L. Does the order of presentation of numerical data in multi-steps arithmetic problems affect their difficulty? *School Science and Mathematics*, 1964, 64, 267–270.

Buswell, G. T., & John, L. *Diagnostic studies in arithmetic*. Supplementary educational monographs, No. 30. Chicago: University of Chicago Press, 1926.

Butler, C. C. A study of the relation between children's understanding of computational skills and their ability to solve verbal problems in arithmetic. *Dissertation Abstracts*, 1956, 16, 2400.

Cambridge Conference on School Mathematics. *Goals for school mathematics*. Boston: Published for Educational Services Inc., by Houghton Mifflin, 1963.

Cambridge Conference on School Mathematics. *Goals for the correlation of elementary science and mathematics: The report of the Cambridge conference on the correlation of science and mathematics in the schools*. Boston: Houghton Mifflin, 1969.

Capps, L. R. A comparison of the common denominator and inversion method in teaching division of fractions. *Journal of Educational Research*, 1963, 56, 516–522.

Capps, L. R., & Cox, L. S. Attitude toward arithmetic at the fourth- and fifth-grade levels. *The Arithmetic Teacher*, 1969, 16, 215–220.

Carlow, C. D. A study of variables within the method of individually guided discovery in secondary school mathematics: The experimental comparison of conceptual structures, consolidations, and learner personality with learning, retention, and transfer by ninth-grade college preparatory males. Unpublished doctoral dissertation, Syracuse University, 1967.

Chase, C. I. The position of certain variables in the prediction of problem-solving in arithmetic. *Journal of Educational Research*, 1960, 54, 9–14.

Cleveland, G. A. A study of certain psychological and sociological characteristics as related to arithmetic achievement. Unpublished doctoral dissertation, Syracuse University, 1961.

Colburn, W. *First lesson*. Boston: Houghton Mifflin, 1821.

Corle, C. G. Thought processes in grade six problems. *The Arithmetic Teacher*, 1958, 5, 193–203.

Corle, C. G. *Teaching mathematics in the elementary school*. New York: Ronald Press, 1964.

Coxford, A. F., Jr. Piaget: Number and measurement. *The Arithmetic Teacher*, 1963, 10, 419–427.

Cronbach, L. J. Issues current in educational psychology. *Monographs of the Society for Research in Child Development*, 1965, 30, 109–126.

Crowder, A. B., Jr. *A comparative study of two methods of teaching arithmetic in the first grade*. Unpublished doctoral dissertation, North Texas State University, 1965.

Cruickshank, W. M. Arithmetic work habits of mentally retarded boys. *American Journal of Mental Deficiency*, 1948, 52, 318–330.

Cruikshank, D. E., & Arnold, W. R. Nondecimal instruction revisited. *Elementary School Journal*, 1969, 70, 108–11.

D'Augustine, C. H. Topics in geometry and point set topology—a pilot study. *The Arithmetic Teacher*, 1964, 11, 407–412.

Davis, O. L., Jr., & Tracy, N. H. Arithmetic achievement and instructional grouping. *The Arithmetic Teacher*, 1963, 10, 12–17.

Davis, R. B. Discovery in the teaching of mathematics. In L. S. Shulman, & E. R. Keislar (Eds.), *Learning by discovery: A critical appraisal*. Chicago: Rand McNally, 1966. Pp. 114–128.

Davis, R. B. *The changing curriculum: Mathematics*. Washington, D.C.: Association for Supervision and Curriculum Development, National Education Association, 1967. (a)

Davis, R. B. (Ed.) *A modern mathematics program*. Cooperative Research Project No. D-233. Syracuse, N.Y.: Syracuse University, 1967. (b)

Dawson, D. T., & Ruddell, A. K. An experimental approach to the division idea. *The Arithmetic Teacher*, 1955, 2, 6–9.

Deans, E. *Elementary school mathematics: New directions.* Washington, D.C.: U.S. Government Printing Office, 1963.

Deep, D. The effect of an individually prescribed instruction program in arithmetic on pupils at different ability levels. Unpublished doctoral dissertation, University of Pittsburgh, 1966.

Dewar, J. A. Grouping for arithmetic instruction in sixth grade. *Elementary School Journal,* 1963, 63, 266–269.

Dienes, Z. P. Some basic processes involved in mathematics learning. In J. Scandura (Ed.), *Research in mathematics education.* Washington, D.C.: National Council of Teachers of Mathematics, 1967. Pp. 21–34.

Dodwell, P. C. Children's understanding of spatial concepts. In I. E. Sigel, & F. H. Hooper (Eds.), *Logical thinking in children: Research based on Piaget's theory.* New York: Holt, Rinehart & Winston, 1968. Pp. 118–140.

Dooley, (Mother) M. C. The relationship between arithmetic research and the content of arithmetic textbooks (1900–1957). *The Arithmetic Teacher,* 1960, 7, 178–183, 188.

Dooley, (Mother) M. C. The relation between arithmetic research and the content of arithmetic textbooks, 1900–1957. *Journal of Experimental Education,* 1961, 29, 315–318.

Dresher, R. Training in mathematics vocabulary. *Educational Research Bulletin,* 1934, 13, 201–204.

Duckworth, E. Piaget rediscovered. *The Arithmetic Teacher,* 1964, 11, 496–499.

Dunkley, M. E. Some number concepts of disadvantaged children. *The Arithmetic Teacher,* 1965, 12, 359–361.

Durr, W. K. The use of arithmetic workbooks in relation to mental abilities and selected achievement levels. *Journal of Educational Research,* 1958, 51, 561–571.

Dutton, W. H. Growth in number readiness in kindergarten children. *The Arithmetic Teacher,* 1963, 10, 251–255.

Dutton, W. H., & Blum, M. P. The measurement of attitudes toward arithmetic with a Likert-type test. *Elementary School Journal,* 1968, 68, 259–264.

Ekman, L. G. A comparison of the effectiveness of different approaches to the teaching of addition and subtraction algorithms in the third grade. Unpublished doctoral dissertation, University of Minnesota, 1966.

Elkind, D. Discrimination, seriation, and numeration of size and dimensional differences in young children: Piaget replication study VI. *Journal of Genetic Psychology,* 1964, 104, 275–296.

Evans, J. E. A study of the effect of unfamiliar words in problem solving. Unpublished master's thesis, State University of Iowa, 1940.

Fedon, J. P. The role of attitude in learning arithmetic. *The Arithmetic Teacher,* 1958, 5, 304–310.

Fehr, H. F., McMeen, G., & Sobel, M. Using hand-operated computing machines in learning arithmetic. *The Arithmetic Teacher,* 1956, 3, 145–150.

Feierabend, R. L. Review of research on psychological problems in mathematics education. In *Research problems in mathematics education,* U.S. Office of Education, Cooperative Research Monograph No. 3, 1960. Pp. 3–46.

Feigenbaum, K. D. Task complexity and IQ as variables in Piaget's problem of conservation. *Child Development,* 1963, 34, 423–432.

Fincher, G. E., & Fillmer, H. T. Programmed instruction in elementary arithmetic. *The Arithmetic Teacher,* 1965, 12, 19–23.

Finley, C. J., & Thompson, J. M. A comparison of the achievement of multi-graded and single-graded rural elementary school children. *Journal of Educational Research,* 1963, 56, 471–475.

Fisher, J. R. An investigation of three approaches to the teaching of mathematics in the elementary school. Unpublished doctoral dissertation, University of Pittsburgh, 1967.

Flournoy, F. A consideration of pupils' success with two methods for placing the decimal point in the quotient. *School Science and Mathematics,* 1959, 59, 445–455.

Flournoy, M. F. The effectiveness of instruction in mental arithmetic. *Elementary School Journal,* 1954, 55, 148–153.

Folsom, M. Teachers look at arithmetic manuals. *The Arithmetic Teacher,* 1960, 7, 13-18.

Friebel, A. C. Measurement understandings in modern school mathematics. *The Arithmetic Teacher,* 1967, 14, 476–480.

Gagné, R. M. Training and principles of learning. In E. A. Fleishman (Ed.), *Studies in personnel and industrial psychology.* Homewood, Ill.: Dorsey Press, 1967. Pp. 175–181.

Gagné, R. M. Learning hierarchies. *Educational Psychologist*, 1968, 6 (1), 3–6, 9.

Gagné, R. M., & Bassler, O. C. Study of retention of some topics of elementary nonmetric geometry. *Journal of Educational Psychology*, 1963, 54, 123–131.

Gibb, E. G. Children's thinking in the process of subtraction. *Journal of Experimental Education*, 1956, 25, 71–80.

Gibb, E. G. Report of the University of Texas computer-assisted instructional laboratory, 1967–1968. Austin, Tex.: The University of Texas, 1968.

Gibb, E. G. Through the years: Individualizing instruction in mathematics. *The Arithmetic Teacher*, 1970, 17, 369–402.

Gilmary, S. M. Examination of some of Piaget's principles in application to psychology of arithmetic. *Catholic Educational Review*, 1964, 62, 369–375.

Glennon, V. J., & Callahan, L. G. *Elementary school mathematics: A guide to current research.* Washington, D.C.: Association for Supervision and Curriculum Development, National Education Association, 1968.

Goebel, L. G. An analysis of teacher-pupil interaction when programed instruction materials are used. Unpublished doctoral dissertation, University of Maryland, 1966.

Goldberg, M. L., Passow, A. H., & Justman, J. *The effects of ability grouping.* New York: Teachers College Press, 1966.

Gorman, C. J. A critical analysis of research on written problems in elementary school mathematics. Unpublished doctoral thesis, University of Pittsburgh, 1967.

Gray, R. F. An experiment in the teaching of introductory multiplication. *The Arithmetic Teacher*, 1965, 12, 199–203.

Greathouse, J. J. An experimental investigation of relative effectiveness among three different arithmetic teaching methods. *Dissertation Abstracts*, 1966, 26, 5913.

Greatsinger, C. An experimental study of programed instruction in division of fractions. *AV Communication Review*, 1968, 16, 87–90.

Grossnickle, F. E. Classification of the estimations in two methods of finding the quotient in long division. *Elementary School Journal*, 1932, 32, 595–604.

Gruen, G. E. Experiences affecting the development of number conservation in children. *Child Development*, 1965, 36, 963–979.

Gunderson, A. G., & Gunderson, E. Fraction concepts held by young children. *The Arithmetic Teacher*, 1957, 4, 168–173.

Hall, J. V. Oral aids to problem-solving. *Elementary School Journal*, 1942, 43, 220–224.

Hall, K. D. An experimental study of two methods of instruction for mastering multiplication facts at the third-grade level. Unpublished doctoral dissertation, Duke University, 1967.

Hanna, P. R. Methods of arithmetic problem solving. *The Mathematics Teacher*, 1930, 23, 442–450.

Hansen, C. C. Scholastic achievement of Indian pupils. *Journal of Genetic Psychology*, 1937, 50, 361–369.

Hansen, C. W. Factors associated with successful achievement in problem solving in sixth grade arithmetic. *Journal of Educational Research*, 1944, 38, 111–118.

Harap, H., & Mapes, C. E. The learning of fundamentals in an arithmetic activity program. *Elementary School Journal*, 1934, 34, 515–525.

Harper, E. H., Steffe, L. P., & VanEngen, H. An evaluation of teaching conservation of numerousness. *School Science and Mathematics*, 1969, 69, 287–296.

Harrison, D. B. Piagetian studies and mathematics learning. In J. W. Wilson, & L. R. Carry (Eds.), *Studies in mathematics, Vol. 19, Reviews of recent research in mathematics education.* Stanford: School Mathematics Study Group, 1969. Pp. 93–127.

Harshman, H. W., Wells, D. W., & Payne, J. N. Manipulative materials and arithmetic achievement in grade 1. *The Arithmetic Teacher*, 1962, 9, 188–192.

Hart, R. H. The nongraded primary school and arithmetic. *The Arithmetic Teacher*, 1962, 9, 130–133.

Hartung, M. L. Estimating the quotient in division. *The Arithmetic Teacher*, 1957, 4, 100–111.

Harvey, L. F., & Kyte, G. C. Zero difficulties in multiplication. *The Arithmetic Teacher*, 1965, 12, 45–50.

Harvey, M. A. Children's responses to two types of multiplication problems. *The Arithmetic Teacher*, 1966, 13, 288–292.

Hatfield, L. L. Computers in mathematics instruction. In J. W. Wilson, & L. R. Carry Eds.), *Studies in mathematics, Vol. 19,*

Reviews of recent research in mathematics education. Stanford: School Mathematics Study Group, 1969. Pp. 129–152.

Heddens, J. W., & Smith, K. J. The readability of elementary mathematics books. *The Arithmetic Teacher,* 1964, 11, 466–468.

Heimer, R. T. Conditions of learning in mathematics: Sequence theory development. *Review of Educational Research,* 1969, 39, 493–508.

Hensell, K. C. Children's interests and the content of problems of arithmetic. *Dissertation Abstracts,* 1956, 16, 1857.

Herbst, L. A. The effect of teaching coordinate geometry on the understandings of selected geographic concepts in the fifth grade. *Dissertation Abstracts,* 1968, 28, 2599A–2600A.

Herman, W. L., Jr. How intermediate children rank the subjects. *Journal of Educational Research,* 1963, 56, 435–436.

Hervey, M. A. Children's responses to two types of multiplication problems. *The Arithmetic Teacher,* 1966, 13, 288–292.

Hollis, L. Y. Why teach numeration? *The Arithmetic Teacher,* 1964, 11, 94–95.

Hollis, L. Y. A study to compare the effects of teaching first and second grade mathematics by the Cuisinaire-Gattegno method with a traditional method. *School Science and Mathematics,* 1965, 65, 683–687.

Holmes, E. E. First graders' number concepts. *The Arithmetic Teacher,* 1963, 10, 195–196.

Hopkins, C. D. An experiment on use of arithmetic time in the fifth grade. *Dissertation Abstracts,* 1966, 26, 5291–5292.

Howard, C. F. Three methods of teaching arithmetic. *California Journal of Educational Research,* 1950, 1, 25–29.

Hungerman, A. D. Achievement and attitude of sixth grade pupils in conventional and contemporary mathematics programs. *The Arithmetic Teacher,* 1967, 14, 30–39.

Ivey, J. O. Computation skills: Results of acceleration. *The Arithmetic Teacher,* 1965, 12, 39–42.

Jackson, J. Analysis of a team teaching and of a self-contained homeroom experiment in grades five and six. *Journal of Experimental Education,* 1964, 32, 317–331.

Jackson, R. L. Numeration systems: An experimental study of achievement on selected objectives of mathematics education resulting from the study of different numeration systems. *Dissertation Abstracts,* 1966, 26, 5292–5293.

Jencks, S. M. The construction and validation of geoboard investigations: A programmed approach to laboratory materials in elementary mathematics. *Dissertation Abstracts,* 1969, 29, 2975B.

Johnson, H. C. The effect of instruction in mathematical vocabulary upon problem solving in arithmetic. *Journal of Educational Research,* 1944, 38, 97–110. (a)

Johnson, H. C. Problem-solving in arithmetic: A review of the literature, I & II. *Elementary School Journal,* 1944, 44, 396–403, 476–482. (b)

Kaprelian, G. Attitudes toward a television program—patterns in arithmetic. *The Arithmetic Teacher,* 1961, 8, 408–412.

Kenney, R. A., & Stockton, J. D. An experimental study in teaching percentage. *The Arithmetic Teacher,* 1958, 5, 294–303.

Kieren, T. E. Activity learning. *Review of Educational Research,* 1969, 39, 509–522.

Kilpatrick, J. Problem solving in mathematics. *Review of Educational Research,* 1969, 39, 523–534.

Klausmeier, H. J. Effects of accelerating bright older elementary pupils: A follow up. *Journal of Educational Psychology,* 1963, 54, 165–171.

Klausmeier, H. J. Using research: Improving problem solving. *Wisconsin Journal of Education,* 1964, 96 (8), 15–16.

Klausmeier, H. J., & Loughlin, L. J. Behaviors during problem solving among children of low, average, and high intelligence. *Journal of Educational Psychology,* 1961, 52, 148–152.

Kliebhan, Sister M. C. An experimental study of arithmetic problem-solving ability of sixth grade boys. Unpublished doctoral dissertation, Catholic University of America, 1955.

Koontz, W. F. A study of achievement as a function of homogeneous grouping. *Journal of Experimental Education,* 1961, 30, 249–253.

Krathwohl, D. R., Bloom, B. S., & Masia, B. B. *Taxonomy of educational objectives: The classification of educational goals, Handbook II: Affective domain.* New York: David McKay, 1964.

Krich, P. Meaningful vs. mechanical method, teaching division of fractions by fractions.

School Science and Mathematics, 1964, 64, 697–708.

LeBlanc, J. F. The performances of first grade children in four levels of conservation of numerousness and three IQ groups when solving arithmetic subtraction problems. Unpublished doctoral dissertation, University of Wisconsin, 1968.

Lerch, H. H. Arithmetic instruction changes pupils' attitudes toward arithmetic. *The Arithmetic Teacher,* 1961, 8, 117–119.

Lindgren, H. C., Silva, I., Faraco, I., & Da-Rocha, N. S. Attitudes toward problem solving as a function of success in arithmetic in Brazilian elementary schools. *Journal of Educational Research,* 1964, 58, 44–45.

Lovell, K. *The growth of basic mathematical and scientific concepts in children.* London: University of London Press, 1961.

Lovell, K., Healey, D., & Rowland, A. D. Growth of some geometrical concepts. In I. E. Sigel, & F. H. Hooper (Eds.), *Logical thinking in children: Research based on Piaget's theory.* New York: Holt, Rinehart & Winston, 1968. Pp. 140–157.

Lucas, J. S. The effect of attribute-block training on children's development of arithmetic concepts. Unpublished doctoral dissertation, University of California, 1966.

Luchins, A. S. Mechanization in problem solving: The effect of Einstellung. *Psychological Monographs,* 1942, 54(6), Whole No. 248.

Lucow, W. H. Testing the Cuisenaire method. *The Arithmetic Teacher,* 1963, 10, 435–438.

Lucow, W. H. An experiment with the Cuisenaire method in grade three. *American Educational Research Journal,* 1964, 1, 159–167.

Lyda, W. J., & Church, R. S. Direct, practical arithmetical experiences and success in solving realistic verbal "reasoning" problems in arithmetic. *Journal of Educational Research,* 1964, 57, 530–533.

MacLatchy, J. H. Another measure of the difficulty of addition combinations. *Educational Research Bulletin,* 1933, 12, 57–61.

Maertens, N. Effects of arithmetic homework upon the attitudes of third grade pupils toward certain school-related structures. *School Science and Mathematics,* 1968, 68, 657–662.

McAloon, Sister M. D. An exploratory study on teaching units in logic to grades three and six. *Dissertation Abstracts,* 1969, 30, 1918A–1919A.

McCarty, T. P. The relative effectiveness of introducing percentage in grades four, five, and six. Unpublished doctoral dissertation, University of California, 1966.

McConnell, T. R. *Discovery vs. authoritative identification in the learning of children.* Iowa City, Iowa: University of Iowa Studies in Education, 1934, 9, 11–62.

McDermott, L. A. A study of some factors that cause fear and dislike of mathematics. Unpublished doctoral dissertation, Michigan State University, 1956.

McDowell, L. K. Number concepts and pre-school children. *The Arithmetic Teacher,* 1962, 9, 433–435.

Meconi, L. J. Concept learning and retention in mathematics. *Journal of Experimental Education,* 1967, 36(1), 51–57.

Metfessel, N. S. The Saugus experiment in multi-grade grouping. *California Journal of Educational Research,* 1960, 11, 155–158.

Miller, G. H. How effective is the meaning method? *The Arithmetic Teacher,* 1957, 4, 45–49.

Miller, J. W. An experimental comparison of two approaches to teaching multiplication of fractions. *Journal of Educational Research,* 1964, 57, 468–471.

Montessori, M. *The Montessori method.* New York: Schocken Books, 1964.

Morton, R. L. Estimating quotient figures when dividing by two-place numbers. *Elementary School Journal,* 1947, 48, 141–148.

Mueller, F. J. Affective components of mathematical learning in elementary school, Part I. Conceptualization of research problems, final report. U.S. Office of Education Bureau of Research, Project No. 0-8001, 1970. (mimeo)

Nasca, D. Comparative merits of a manipulative approach to second grade arithmetic. *The Arithmetic Teacher,* 1966, 13, 221–226.

National Council of Teachers of Mathematics. *The revolution in school mathematics.* A report of the regional orientation conference in mathematics. Washington, D.C.: National Council of Teachers of Mathematics, 1961.

National Council of Teachers of Mathematics. *An analysis of new mathematics programs.*

Washington, D. C.: National Council of Teachers of Mathematics, 1963.

National Longitudinal Study of Mathematics Assessment. *NLSMA Reports, Nos. 1 through 18.* Edited by J. W. Wilson, L. S. Cahen, & E. G. Begle. Stanford: Stanford University School Mathematics Study Group, 1969.

Neale, D. C. The role of attitudes in learning mathematics. *The Arithmetic Teacher,* 1969, 16, 631–640.

Neatrour, C. R. A status survey of the geometric content in the mathematics curriculum of the middle school. *School Science and Mathematics,* 1969, 69, 610–614.

Neill, A. S. *Summerhill: A radical approach to child rearing.* New York: Hart, 1960.

Nuffield Mathematics Project (Teacher Guides). Published for the Nuffield Foundation by W. Chambers, R. Chambers, & J. Murray. New York: John Wiley, 1967.

Osborne, A. R. The effects of two instructional approaches on the understanding of subtraction by grade two pupils. Unpublished doctoral dissertation, University of Michigan, 1966.

Osburn, W. J. Levels of difficulty in long division. *Elementary School Journal,* 1946, 46, 441–447.

Pace, A. The effect of instruction upon the development of the concept of number. *Journal of Educational Research,* 1968, 62, 183–189.

Palmer, E. L. The equilibration process: Some implications for instructional research and practice. Paper presented at the Annual Meeting of the American Educational Research Association, Chicago, February 1968.

Payne, H. What about modern programs in mathematics? *The Arithmetic Teacher,* 1965, 58, 422–424.

Piaget, J. *The child's conception of number.* New York: Humanities Press, 1952.

Paiget, J., & Inhelder, B. *The child's conception of space.* New York: Humanities Press, 1956.

Piaget, J., Inhelder, B., & Szeminska, A. *The child's conception of geometry.* New York: Basic Books, 1960.

Plank, E. N. Observations on attitudes of young children toward mathematics. *The Mathematics Teacher,* 1950, 43, 252–263.

Price, E. B., Prescott, A. L., & Hopkins, K. D. Comparative achievement with depart-mentalized and self-contained classroom organization. *The Arithmetic Teacher,* 1967, 14, 212–215.

Progress report: Individually prescribed instruction. Philadelphia, Pa.: Research for Better Schools, September 1969.

Provus, M. M. Ability grouping in arithmetic. *Elementary School Journal,* 1960, 60, 391–398.

Rappaport, D. Understanding meanings in arithmetic. *The Arithmetic Teacher,* 1958, 5, 96–99.

Rappaport, D. The meanings approach in teaching arithmetic. *Chicago Schools Journal,* 1963, 44, 172–174.

Ray, J. *Practical arithmetic, Ray's arithmetic, part third.* (Rev. ed.) Cincinnati: Winthrop B. Smith, 1853.

Rea, R. E., & Reys, R. E. Mathematical competencies of entering kindergartners. *The Arithmetic Teacher,* 1970, 17, 65–74.

Reddell, W. D., & DeVault, M. V. In-service research in arithmetic teaching aids. *The Arithmetic Teacher,* 1960, 7, 243–246.

Riedesel, C. A. Verbal problem solving: Suggestions for improving instruction. *The Arithmetic Teacher,* 1964, 11, 312–316.

Riedesel, C. A. *Guiding discovery in elementary school mathematics.* New York: Appleton-Century-Crofts, 1967.

Riedesel, C. A. Problem solving: Some suggestions from research. *The Arithmetic Teacher,* 1969, 16, 54–58.

Roberts, D. M., & Bloom, I. Mathematics in kindergarten—formal or informal? *Elementary School Journal,* 1967, 67, 338–341.

Robertson, M. S. Problem solving in arithmetic. *Peabody Journal of Education,* 1931, 9, 176–183.

Rosskopf, M. F., Steffe, L. P., & Taback, S. *Piagetian cognitive-development research and mathematical education.* Washington, D. C.: National Council of Teachers of Mathematics, 1971.

Ross, R. A description of twenty arithmetic underachievers. *The Arithmetic Teacher,* 1964, 11, 235–241.

Ruddell, A. K. The results of a modern mathematics program. *The Arithmetic Teacher,* 1962, 9, 330–335.

Scandura, J. M. An analysis of exposition and discovery modes of problem solving instruction. *Journal of Experimental Education,* 1964, 33, 148–159.

Scandura, J. M., & Wells, J. N. Advance organizers in learning abstract mathematics. *American Educational Research Journal,* 1967, 4, 295–301.

Schell, L. M. Two aspects of introductory multiplication: The array and the distributive property. Unpublished doctoral dissertation, State University of Iowa, 1964.

Schlinsog, G. W. The effects of supplementing sixth-grade instruction with a study of nondecimal numbers. *The Arithmetic Teacher,* 1968, 15, 254–260.

Schwartz, A. N. Assessment of mathematical concepts of five-year-old children. *Journal of Experimental Education,* 1969, 37(3), 67–74.

Scott, L. Children's concept of scale and the subtraction of fractions. *The Arithmetic Teacher,* 1962, 9, 115–118.

Scott, L. A study of teaching division through the use of two algorithms. *School Science and Mathematics,* 1963, 63, 739–752.

Scott, L. Children's perception of mathematical inconsistencies. *The Arithmetic Teacher,* 1965, 12, 617–624.

Sekyra, F., III. The effects of taped instruction on problem-solving skills of seventh grade children. *Dissertation Abstracts,* 1969, 29, 3473A–3474A.

Shah, S. A. Selected geometric concepts taught to children ages seven to eleven. *The Arithmetic Teacher,* 1969, 16, 119–128.

Shantz, C. U., & Smock, C. D. Development of distance conservation and the spatial coordinate system. *Child Development,* 1966, 37, 943–948.

Shapiro, E. W. Attitudes toward arithmetic among public school children in the intermediate grades. Unpublished doctoral dissertation, University of Denver, 1961.

Shipp, D. E., & Deer, G. H. The use of class time in arithmetic. *The Arithmetic Teacher,* 1960, 7, 117–121.

Shulman, L. S. Psychology and mathematics education. In E. G. Begle (Ed.), *Mathematics education.* The Sixty-ninth Yearbook of the National Society for the Study of Education, Part I. Chicago: NSSE, 1970. Pp. 23–71.

Shulman, L. S., & Keislar, E. R. (Eds.) *Learning by discovery: A critical appraisal.* Chicago: Rand McNally, 1966.

Shuster, A. H., & Pigge, F. L. Retention

efficiency of meaningful teaching. *The Arithmetic Teacher,* 1965, 12, 24–31.

Sluser, T. F. A comparative study of division of fractions in which an explanation of the reciprocal principle is the experimental factor. Unpublished doctoral dissertation, University of Pittsburgh, 1962.

Smedslund, J. Development of concrete transitivity of length in children. *Child Development,* 1963, 34, 389–405.

Smith, D. E. *The teaching of arithmetic.* Boston: Ginn & Co., 1913.

Smith, H. K. The effects of instruction in set theory upon the logical reasoning of seventh-grade students and subsequent effects upon their learning to solve percentage problems. *Dissertation Abstracts,* 1968, 28, 4963A.

Smith, H. L., & Eaton, M. T. An analysis of arithmetic textbooks (first period—1790 to 1820). *Indiana University School of Education Bulletin,* 1942, 18(1), 1–52. (a)

Smith, H. L., & Eaton, M. T. An analysis of arithmetic textbooks (second period—1821 to 1850, and third period—1851 to 1880). *Indiana University School of Education Bulletin,* 1942, 18(6), 1–108. (b)

Smith, H. L., & Eaton, M. T. An analysis of arithmetic textbooks (fourth period—1881 to 1910). *Indiana University School of Education Bulletin,* 1943, 19(4), 1–58. (a)

Smith, H. L., & Eaton, M. T. An analysis of arithmetic textbooks (fifth period—1911 to 1940). *Indiana University School of Education Bulletin,* 1943, 19(6), 1–41. (b)

Smith, H. L., Eaton, M. T., & Dugdale, K. One hundred fifty years of arithmetic textbooks. *Indiana University School of Education Bulletin,* 1945, 21(1), 1–149.

Smith, K. J., & Heddens, J. W. The readability of experimental mathematics materials. *The Arithmetic Teacher,* 1964, 11, 391–394.

Spencer, J. E. Intertask interference in primary arithmetic. Unpublished doctoral dissertation, University of California, 1967.

Steffe, L. P. The effects of two variables on the problem-solving abilities of first grade children, Teaching Report #21. Madison, Wis.: Wisconsin Research & Development Center for Cognitive Learning, University of Wisconsin, 1967.

Steffe, L. P. The relationship of conservation of numerousness to problem-solving abilities of first-grade children. *The Arithmetic Teacher,* 1968, 15, 47–52.

Stephens, L., & Dutton, W. H. The development of time concepts by kindergarten children. *School Science and Mathematics,* 1969, 69, 59–63.

Stern, C. *Children discover arithmetic.* New York: Harper & Row, 1949.

Stevenson, P. R. Increasing the ability of pupils to solve arithmetic problems. *Educational Research Bulletin,* 1924, 3, 267–270.

Stevenson, P. R. Difficulties in problem solving. *Journal of Educational Research,* 1925, 11, 95–103.

Stone, M. H. Goals for school mathematics. *The Mathematics Teacher,* 1965, 58, 353–360.

Stright, V. M. A study of the attitudes toward arithmetic of students and teachers in the third, fourth, and sixth grades. *The Arithmetic Teacher,* 1960, 7, 280–286.

Suppes, P. The ability of elementary-school children to learn the new mathematics. *Theory into Practice,* 1964, 3, 57–61.

Suppes, P. Some theoretical models for mathematics learning. *Journal of Research and Development in Education,* 1967, 1, 5–22.

Suppes, P., & Binford, F. Experimental teaching of mathematical logic in the elementary school. *The Arithmetic Teacher,* 1965, 12, 187–195.

Suppes, P., & Groen, G. Some counting models for first-grade performance data on simple addition facts. In *Research in mathematics education,* Washington, D.C.: National Council of Teachers of Mathematics, 1967.

Suppes, P., & Ihrke, C. Accelerated program in elementary-school mathematics—the third year. *Psychology in the Schools,* 1967, 4, 293–309.

Suppes, P., Jerman, M., & Groen, G. Arithmetic drills and review on a computer-based teletype. *The Arithmetic Teacher,* 1966, 13, 303–309.

Suppes, P., Loftus, E., & Jerman, M. Problem solving on a computer-based teletype. *Technical Report #131, Psychological Series.* Stanford: Institute for Mathematics Studies in the Social Sciences, 1969. (mimeo)

Suppes, P., & McKnight, B. A. Sets and numbers in grade one, 1959–1960. *The Arithmetic Teacher,* 1961, 8, 287–290.

Suppes, P., & Morningstar, M. *Computer-assisted instructions: the 1966–1967 Stanford arithmetic program.* New York: Academic Press, 1969.

Sutherland, J. An investigation into some aspects of problem solving in arithmetic. *British Journal of Educational Psychology,* 1941, 11, 215–222; 1942, 12, 35–46.

Swenson, E. J. Difficulty ratings of addition facts as related to learning method. *Journal of Educational Research,* 1944, 38, 81–85.

Thiele, C. L. *The contribution of generalization to the learning of the addition facts.* Contributions to Education, No. 763. New York: Columbia University Teachers College, Bureau of Publications, 1938.

Treacy, J. P. The relationship of reading skills to the ability to solve arithmetic problems. *Journal of Educational Research,* 1944, 38, 86–96.

Tredway, D. C. A statistical comparison of two methods of teaching percentage. Unpublished doctoral dissertation, University of Wyoming, 1959.

Tredway, D. C., & Hollister, G. E. An experimental study of two approaches to teaching percentage. *The Arithmetic Teacher,* 1963, 10, 491–495.

Triggs, E. The value of a desk calculating machine in primary school maths. *Educational Research,* 1966, 9, 71–73.

Trueblood, C. R. A comparison of two techniques for using visual-tactual devices to teach exponents and nondecimal bases in elementary school mathematics. *The Arithmetic Teacher,* 1970, 17, 338–340.

Uzgiris, I. C. Situational generality of conservation. *Child Development,* 1964, 35, 831–841.

Vanderlinde, L. F. Does the study of quantitative vocabulary improve problem-solving? *Elementary School Journal,* 1964, 65, 143–152.

VanEngen, H., & Gibb, E. G. General mental functions associated with division. Educational Service Studies, No. 2. Cedar Falls: Iowa State Teachers College, 1956.

Wallach, L., & Sprott, R. L. Inducing number conservation in children. *Child Development,* 1964, 35, 1057–1071.

Wallen, N. E., & Vowles, R. O. The effect of intraclass ability grouping on arithmetic achievement in the sixth grade. *Journal of Educational Psychology,* 1960, 51, 159–163.

Washburne, C. W., & Osborne, R. Solving

arithmetic problems, I. *Elementary School Journal*, 1926, 27, 219–226.

Washburne, C., & Vogel, M. Are any number combinations inherently difficult? *Journal of Educational Research*, 1928, 17, 235–255.

Weaver, J. F. Differentiated instruction and school-class organization for mathematical learning within the elementary grades. *The Arithmetic Teacher*, 1966, 13, 495–506. (a)

Weaver, J. F. Levels of geometric understanding: An exploratory investigation of limited scope. *The Arithmetic Teacher*, 1966, 13, 322–332. (b)

Wheat, H. G. *The relative merits of conventional and imaginative types of problems in arithmetic.* Contributions to education, No. 359. New York: Columbia University Teachers College, Bureau of Publications, 1929.

Wheeler, L. R. A comparative study of the difficulty of the 100 addition combinations. *Journal of Genetic Psychology*, 1939, 54, 295–312.

Williams, M. H., & McCreight, R. W. Shall we move the question? *The Arithmetic Teacher*, 1965, 12, 418–421.

Willson, G. H. A comparison of decimal-common fraction sequence with conventional sequence for fifth grade arithmetic. Unpublished doctoral dissertation, University of Arizona, 1969.

Wilson, G. M., Stone, M. B., & Dalrymple, C. O. *Teaching the new arithmetic.* New York: McGraw-Hill, 1939.

Wilson, J. W. The role of structure in verbal problem solving. *The Arithmetic Teacher*, 1967, 14, 486–497.

Wohlwill, J. F. A study of the development of the number concept by scalogram analysis. *Journal of Genetic Psychology*, 1960, 97, 345–377.

Wolff, B. R. An analysis and comparison of individualized instructional practices in arithmetic in graded and nongraded elementary classrooms in selected Oregon school districts. Unpublished doctoral dissertation, University of Oregon, 1968.

Wooten, W. *School mathematics study group: The making of a curriculum.* New Haven, Conn.: Yale University Press, 1965.

Worthen, B. R. Discovery and expository task presentation in elementary mathematics. *Journal of Education Psychology Monograph Supplement*, 1968, 59(1), Part 2.

Wynn, R. S. A study of the relative efficiency of three methods of teaching percentage in grade seven. (Doctoral dissertation, Colorado State College) Ann Arbor, Mich.: University Microfilms, 1966. No. 65-14,842.

Zahn, K. G. Use of class time in eighth-grade arithmetic. *The Arithmetic Teacher*, 1966, 13, 113–120.

Zweng, M. J. Division problems and the concept of rate. *The Arithmetic Teacher*, 1964, 11, 547–556.

CHAPTER 36 Research on Teaching Secondary-School Mathematics

DONALD J. DESSART
The University of Tennessee

HENRY FRANDSEN
The University of Tennessee

This chapter identifies and summarizes empirical studies important to secondary mathematics education and attempts to provide some insights concerning the educational conditions which initiated them. Other reviews and discussions have been provided by Atkin and Mayor (1964), Atkin and Romberg (1969), K. E. Brown and Abell (1965), Dessart and Burns (1967), Fehr (1966), Higgins (1972), Hooten (1967), Suydam (1972), Weaver (1970), Willoughby (1969) and Wilson and Carry (1969).

MODERN MATHEMATICS IN AN AGE OF DISSEMINATION AND EVALUATION

As the impact of the curriculum reform of the fifties and early sixties was beginning to permeate the schools of the United States, and before evaluation of the new curricula could be completed, there was a call for further revision. *Goals for School Mathematics,* commonly called the Cambridge Report, which appeared in 1963, was put forth by a small group of distinguished mathematicians and educators to stimulate discussion and experimentation on the shape and content of the precollege mathematics curriculum as it might appear 30 years later. The impact of the Cambridge Report was difficult to judge. At the very least it put an end to any hopes of seeing the curriculum stabilized in the foreseeable future. It also brought forth some interesting responses. A critical review was written by Stone (1965) and a complimentary appraisal by Adler (1966a). There was very little public discussion of the Cambridge Report, but it stands as a landmark in the history of mathematics education curriculum development.

The rate at which the use of modern mathematics curricula spread is probably one of the most remarkable features of mathematics education during the past decade. A survey of seniors who had taken a College Board achievement test in mathematics, reported by Williams (1969), indicated that several topics which were sometimes considered exemplary of modern mathematics curricula had been studied by well over half the students surveyed. Some people felt that the newer materials had been disseminated much too quickly and were in widespread use before they could be properly evaluated.

The most extensive evaluation project was a five-year study begun in 1961 by the Minnesota National Laboratory (Rosenbloom & Ryan, 1968). The latter enterprise, referred to as the Secondary Mathematics Evaluation Project, was designed to determine the differences in achievement between pupils in grades 7 through 11 who were instructed with conventional materials and those instructed with one of the modern programs—either the School Mathematics Study Group (SMSG), the University of Illinois Committee on School Mathematics (UICSM), the Ball State Indiana Teachers College Project (Ball State), or the University of Maryland Mathematics Project (UMMaP). Volunteer teachers from a five-state area were each asked to participate for a period of two years, teaching a class with conventional materials during the first year and two classes, one with conventional and the other with experimental materials, during the second year. Their students were tested in September, May, and again the following September to measure initial levels of achievement, final achievement, and retention, respectively.

The tests used were the Sequential Tests of Educational Progress (STEP) series, a four-level series which was constructed by the investigators, and the Cooperative Mathematics Tests (COOP), the latter two being introduced at the end of the fourth and fifth years of the project, respectively. The results did not show that the experimental programs had a strong influence on increasing (or reducing) student achievement in mathematics as measured by these tests. There were exceptions within one or more individual years; the seventh-grade UMMaP and eighth-grade Ball State programs were singled out as those for which students' superior performances on the structure of the number system were most generalizable. In a companion study of the effects of mathematics curricula on pupil attitudes, interests and perceptions of pro-

ficiency reported by Ryan (1968), no unequivocal differences were found between the modern and conventional curricula. A conclusion which might have been drawn from these projects was that the experimental materials tested were not worth the vast resources that had gone into their development. The project reporters suggested that such a conclusion should be tempered because of possible lack of validity of the achievement tests for measuring significant objectives of the experimental programs or because of possible lost impact due to poor teacher performance with experimental materials. Another serious procedural fault cited was that of not obtaining random assignment of pupils to classes in which alternate treatments were given. This project was an ambitious one which should pave the way for future investigations of the effects of modern programs.

Many empirical studies comparing traditional and modern curricula of a smaller duration or scope than the Secondary Mathematics Evaluation Project were reported. While none of these had reported significant differences favoring the traditional curricular materials, there were very few which reported significant differences favoring the modern materials. One such study (Friebel, 1967) avoided two of the problems of the Secondary Mathematics Evaluation Project by making random assignments of students to experimental and control classes and by administering an investigator designed test to measure what was called "measurement understandings" as well as the standardized California Achievement Test. This study concluded that SMSG materials maintained growth in general arithmetic achievement but promoted significantly superior growth in arithmetic reasoning at the seventh-grade level.

Davidson and Gibney (1969) measured differences in achievement in mathematics and science following modern mathematics in the eighth grade and found significant differences favoring modern mathematics in eight out of 10 high-school subjects. A comparison of SMSG with traditional materials with respect to students' performances in college calculus was reported by Flanagan (1969). He found no significant differences for students with Scholastic Aptitude Test (SAT) scores of 600 or above, but that students who scored below 600 on their SAT mathematics tests (and above 442) and had had four or more semesters of study from SMSG materials had an advantage over students with similar abilities and conventional mathematics backgrounds. A report by Beckmann (1969) indicated that ninth-grade mathematical competence for students in 42 schools in Nebraska using modern curricular materials in the school year 1965–1966 made sizable gains over comparable results for students of 1950–1951.

One of the newest and most extensive programs of development of new curricula is the Secondary School Mathematics Curriculum Improvement Study described by Fehr and Fey (1969). This project, which is located at Columbia University Teachers College, was begun in 1965 and was planned to continue beyond the school year 1971–1972. The goal was to produce a six-year unified secondary-school curriculum for college-capable students, grades 7 through 12, and the plans included procedures for writing textbooks, preparing teachers, and evaluation. The evaluation included direct observation of classes, conferences involving teachers and consultants, and testing of student achievement in both traditional and modern topics of the curriculum. A unique aspect of this project was its attempt to remove the boundaries of arithmetic, algebra, geometry, etc. that had been the hallmark of most curricula.

The Geometry Curriculum

There was very little empirical research reported on questions related to the geometry curriculum. A report by Quast (1968) of a historical analysis of geometry in the high schools of the United States indicated that the geometry curriculum had been receiving heavy criticism and re-evaluation almost continually since 1890 with very little actual change taking place. One reason for this lack of progress was probably the lack of consensus on the objectives of a geometry course. Adler (1968) delineated the changes that had been tried recently throughout the world. He proposed teaching a unit on isometries of the plane and another on hyperbolic geometry. Secondary School Mathematics Curriculum Improvement Study materials described by Fehr and Fey (1969) included the former in courses I and II. The approach to geometry taken by curriculum writers of the School Mathematics Project in England, as described by Thwaites (1966), emphasized "motion geometry" and apparently de-emphasized axiomatics. An experimental course, highly algebraic in content, which was evaluated both when it was given and six years later in a follow-up questionnaire to the students, was reported by Willoughby (1966). Some students were surprisingly critical of the experimental course in the follow-up study, but 10 of the 19 responding to the survey were apparently favorably impressed with the course even after six years.

The Placement of Additional Topics in the Curriculum

Although formal logic had generally been excluded from secondary mathematics curricula, a considerable amount of research had been carried out to determine the extent to which it could be taught. An interesting study reported by Retzer and Henderson (1967) supported the conjecture that a formal unit on logic which included the concepts of variable, open sentence, universal quantifier, and others, will help students who are taught by guided discovery to state their discoveries precisely. Studies by Hrabi (1968) for grades 7 and 9, and Miller (1968) for grades 8, 10 and 12 supported the feasibility of teaching logic in grades 9 through

12. Platt (1968) made similar observations for tenth-grade geometry.

Another topic which was studied for possible inclusion in curricula is probability and statistics. A report by Smith (1966) concluded that at least some aspects of probability and statistics were appropriate for seventh-graders. Shulte (1970) developed a unit on probability and statistics for a ninth-grade general mathematics course and tested the effects of the unit on students' performances and student and teacher attitudes. The surprising conclusion of this report was that while students seemed to be capable of learning the concepts of probability and statistics, their attitudes as measured on the Aiken-Dreger scale (Attitude toward Mathematics) showed a significant decline.

The effects of calculus taught in secondary school was the topic of two research reports. McKillip (1966) reported that one semester of high-school calculus had no significant effects on the grades of students taking calculus in college; two semesters of high-school calculus did improve the grades of students who had not attained advanced placement. A subsequent study in a different part of the country which obtained similar findings with regard to two semesters of high-school calculus was reported by Robinson (1970). These findings gave mild support to the teaching of calculus in high school for the purpose of attaining better performance, as measured by grades, in calculus when it is repeated in college.

VARIATIONS IN ORGANIZATIONAL PATTERNS OF THE CLASSROOM

Certain variables of teaching might be called administratively controlled variables. Among these are the allotment of time and space for instruction and the organization of students and staff. The amount of research reported in these areas was surprisingly small. If these variables have any effects on educational outcomes, those effects are more important to know than others,

e.g., the effects of teacher attitudes, because these variables are more easily modified by administrative actions.

Grouping Students by Ability

Homogeneous grouping, which has gained widespread acceptance in the schools, may in fact be based upon a myth. In a fine review of the literature which preceded a research report, Willcutt (1969) pointed out that individual student abilities may change so rapidly that it is perhaps impossible to obtain homogeneous grouping. Willcutt had studied the effects of a flexible grouping procedure on achievements and attitudes at the seventh-grade level. The grouping procedures permitted teachers to regroup their students in experimental classes into three levels for instruction at eight different times during the year. Control classes were not grouped according to ability and were taught as typical self-contained classes. No differences in achievement were noted at the end of the year, but attitudes, measured by responses to a questionnaire, showed a general positive change among students in the experimental classes. Another experiment in flexible grouping with seventh-graders was reported by Stevenson (1967). With a similar set of three ability groups and 10 units between which regrouping could take place, it was reported that an average of 44 percent of 142 students changed group levels at each of 10 junctures during the year.

A different type of grouping experiment was reported by Campbell (1965). Students were grouped in two different ways: whole classes of a homogeneous nature were compared with heterogeneous classes which provided in-class grouping into three ability levels. The whole-class grouping method was reported to have resulted in greater gains in achievement than the within-class method.

An interesting related study considered the effects of using "easy" or "difficult" textbooks on achievements of homogeneous classes of fast learners. Nelson (1965) reported a carefully devised experiment in which the SMSG texts for college-capable students were used in control classes and the SMSG texts modified for slower learners were used in experimental classes. There were six pairs of seventh-grade and eight pairs of ninth-grade classes involved, all of which were classified as advanced or fast learner classes by their schools. The findings showed a tendency for the low-achieving students among the high-ability classes to perform better on both mathematics achievement tests and the unit tests when they studied the easier texts. There was a slight hint that the use of the modified text might have had an adverse effect on the most capable students in the experimental classes.

Class Sizes and Classroom Staffing

An important question, especially when enrollments are high, is whether large group instruction is as valuable as it seems in light of the obvious savings which accrue through reduced staff needs. Two reports claimed that it was. Bhushan, Jeffryes, and Nakamura (1968) reported that large group (69 students) instruction did not have unfavorable results on achievement. Madden (1968) reported achievement significantly higher when students were taught in large groups. Unfortunately neither of these studies was rigorously designed. A study involving 7500 seventh- and eighth-grade pupils, reported by M. Johnson and Scriven (1967), found no significant differences in performances on the Iowa Test of Basic Skills between small classes (18–24 students) and large classes (34–35 students) in mathematics and English.

Even without changing student-teacher ratios, there are alternatives in class size and staffing patterns. Many schools experimented with team teaching. Typical of these experiments was one reported by Klinkerman and Bridges (1967) in which geometry classes were combined to form classes of 50

students with two teachers. No statistical evidence was gathered, but the results of an opinionnaire indicated both students and teachers favored team teaching. In a more classical experiment, Paige (1967) combined classes to form new sets of 90 students with three teachers at both the seventh- and eighth-grade levels. Control groups were taught in the typical manner with classes of 30 students and one teacher. No significant differences were found in mathematical achievement, mathematical retention, or ability to relearn and use mathematical knowledge, but there were signs which indicated that the eighth grade was more suitable for team teaching than the seventh. Paige concluded that more research should be done by school systems before they adopt team teaching.

The Use of Students' and Teachers' Time

The classroom teacher usually makes most decisions regarding the use of classroom time and the assignment of study activities for outside the classroom. The amount of time the teacher spends in grading papers and determining students' grades is also under the control of the teacher. Research should constantly be applied toward assisting the teacher in making these decisions.

A research effort with direct implications for teachers was reported by Zahn (1966). He investigated the results of four different treatments which ranged from dividing classroom time in a ratio of 2 to 1 favoring developmental over practice activities to the opposite ratio of 2 to 1 favoring practice over developmental activities. The results supported the conclusion that students learned arithmetic skills better by spending less time on practice work in class and more time on developmental activities; this conclusion generally held for all three ability levels considered.

The question of the use of homework is an important one for teachers. Small, Holtan, and Davis (1967) reported no significant differences in achievement arising from having homework spot-checked rather than graded carefully each day. Two other reports, Hudson (1965) and Ten Brinke (1967), suggested that no significant differences in achievement will arise as a result of assigning no homework at all. So perhaps with more evidence to support it, we may see a future abandonment of homework in the secondary schools sanctioned by mathematics educators.

Another time-saving innovation which seemed less likely to be accepted was supported in a report by Christensen (1968). When the grading of students was suspended for one semester there were no significant differences in student achievement. This experiment was too short in duration and small in scale to be of significant value, but it delved into an important problem which should be investigated.

PEDAGOGICAL TECHNIQUES

The Learning by Discovery Controversy

The use of discovery as a method of teaching has been vigorously discussed among mathematics educators during the past decade. Genuine progress in such discussions was often hampered by a fundamental lack of agreement concerning a precise definition of the discovery method. If one reviewed the plethora of suggested definitions, it could be reasonably concluded that collective research will contribute little toward definitive answers concerning the efficacy of discovery teaching until such time as agreement is reached among researchers concerning a definition.

Following an extensive examination of tasks which had been called "discovery learning," Glaser (1966) noted that a basic confusion seemed to exist between two types of events: a) learning by discovery and b) learning to discover. In the former, the teacher employs strategies in which her objective is to have the student acquire particular concepts, whereas in the latter case

the terminal objective of instruction is manifested in the student by a capability to make his own discoveries. Glaser further observed that learning by discovery is usually defined as teaching a concept, a rule or an association in such a manner that "discovery" of the concept, rule or association is done by the student as opposed to being carefully pointed out by the teacher in a more direct expository fashion. In conclusion, Glaser felt that learning by discovery seemed to be most frequently characterized by two properties. First, the teacher employs an inductive approach, that is, exemplars of a more general case are presented and the pupils are expected to induce a more general proposition involving the exemplars. Second, the teacher imposes a minimum of structured sequences in which the students are permitted to pursue trial and error approaches in various degrees.

After a careful analysis of recorded tapes of verbal behavior of mathematics teachers in the classroom, Henderson (1969) defined discovery teaching as a particular pattern or strategy of teacher moves. Four basic types of moves were identified: a) the statement of a principle; b) the clarification of a principle; c) the justification of a principle; and d) the application of a principle. If the initial move of the teacher is the statement of a principle or the referring of a student to a principle in a textbook followed by clarification and application or justification moves, the sequence of moves is defined as an expository strategy; however, if the statement move is not the initial move, but appears, if at all, near the conclusion of a sequence, the sequence is then called a guided discovery strategy.

Research studies designed to shed light on the learning by discovery controversy were typified by an investigation conducted by Price (1967). Three classes of tenth-grade general mathematics students were formed randomly from pupils enrolled in a large city high school. One class was taught by a teacher employing the traditional, deductive, textbook-lecture approach (the control class); a second class was taught by an inductive-intuitive procedure designed to promote student discovery of mathematical principles; and a third class was taught by use of the discovery approach in addition to supplementary materials designed to enable the student to transfer mathematical concepts to problems of the real world. Each of the three groups was administered standardized measures to determine gains in mathematical achievement, in mathematical reasoning and in critical thinking. Results of the investigation revealed that the two classes taught by procedures designed to promote discovery had slight but nonsignificant gains over the control class in achievement, had greater increases in mathematical reasoning, and had positive attitude changes toward mathematics; the control class showed negative changes. Furthermore, as had been demonstrated in other studies, students using specially designed transfer materials gained significantly in critical thinking over students not using such materials.

Findings in studies similar to the one conducted by Price were often confounded by the interactive effects of the inherent and varying teaching capabilities of instructors and the various types of materials and procedures employed by these instructors. Some investigations have partially remedied this problem by removing the effects of teachers almost entirely through the use of programmed materials. Frequently these studies led to inconclusive results which seemed strongly to suggest that the capability of the teacher is the critical variable in research on learning by discovery.

Investigations using such programmed procedures were reported by Meconi (1967) and Henderson and Rollins (1967). In the Meconi study, 45 high-ability eighth- and ninth-grade students were randomly assigned to three groups employing programmed materials prepared according to one of three designs: a) rule and example, b) guided discovery, and c) pure discovery. The rule-and-example design was similar in nature to an expository-lecture procedure

employed by teachers; the guided discovery program was similar to an inductive approach in which students are led to generalizations by considering examples; and the pure discovery design was similar to a classroom procedure in which students learn concepts without the guidance of a teacher except for the presentation of terms and references. After all three groups had studied a common introductory program, each was exposed to one of the three specially designed programs. Following an analysis of variance on test results, no significant differences among the three approaches could be found in a problem-solving test of immediate transfer or on a retention test administered four weeks later. The pure discovery group required significantly less time to complete their studies than either of the other two groups.

Henderson and Rollins (1967) attempted to determine the relative efficacy of three discovery-type learning programs in which the primary approach was one of presenting instances of a generalization to be learned. In the first program, named the *stratagem of agreement,* only instances in which the generalization held true were given; in the two other programs a *stratagem of difference* (instances in which the generalization was not satisfied) was used as well as the agreement stratagem. Two variations of this composite approach were used: a) the paired instances stratagem of agreement and difference in which each instance of agreement was followed immediately by one obtained by difference; and b) the nonpaired instances stratagem of agreement and difference in which all instances of each were presented separately. Results were quite conclusive that students were able to learn generalizations by each of the methods. However, comparisons of the relative efficacy of the three proved to be inconclusive.

Techniques for Teaching Atypical Students

Numerous studies dealt with a variety of instructional techniques for use with low-achieving or with high-achieving students. Techniques such as providing students with aids to lessen the burdens of computation, using modified programmed materials and mathematical games, and employing special tutorial teachers were among many procedures reported as being advantageous for motivating the low achiever, while acceleration and enrichment were among the primary means promoted for use with the academically talented.

A three-year study (1965–1968) to ascertain the effects upon the mathematical achievements and attitudes of low-achieving junior high-school students of study materials specially designed to minimize the burdens of computation was reported by DeVenney (1969). The computational burdens were lessened through the use of such aids as computational tables, and the necessity for memorizing procedures for examinations was minimized by using "open-book" tests. An experimental group consisting of 10 classes and a control group of six classes were pretested in the fall of 1966 with the SMSG Opinion Inventory, Form SC, and the Stanford Achievement Test (Intermediate) and posttested in the spring of 1968 with the opinion inventory and the advanced portion of the Stanford Achievement Test.

Over the two-year period (1966–1968) substantial gains were realized by both the experimental and control groups in achievement but, surprisingly, significantly greater gains were made by the control groups. Perhaps more importantly, the experimental group showed favorable changes whereas the control group did not on the following attitude scales: Mathematics Easy versus Hard, Mathematics Fun versus Dull, Actual Mathematics Self-Concept and Debilitating Anxiety. In comparing these scores with a five percent stratified random sample of students from the National Longitudinal Study of Mathematical Abilities, it was found that initially both the experimental and control groups were significantly different from National Longitudinal Study of

Mathematics Abilities students, but at the conclusion of the study the experimental group compared favorably with the National Longitudinal Study of Mathematics Abilities sample, whereas the control group did not.

A major three-year investigation involving at the onset 25 school systems, 51 classes and about 1500 able junior high-school students was designed by Goldberg, Passow, Camm, and Neill (1966) to compare the relative effectiveness of six programs: a) Standard Enriched—the social applications content for grades 7 and 8, popular prior to 1957, and traditional algebra topics of grade 9 were enriched with the addition of special units based on more advanced topics; b) Standard Accelerated—the pre-1957 content for grades 7 and 8 was completed in one year and a pre-1957 type algebra course was studied during the second year; c) SMSG Normal—*Mathematics for Junior High School, Volumes I and II*, and the *First Year Course in Algebra* were studied in grades 7, 8 and 9 at the pace intended by SMSG; d) SMSG Accelerated—the SMSG materials for a four-year sequence concluding with *Intermediate Mathematics* were studied in three years; e) UICSM 8—the same materials as were studied by SMSG Accelerated in grade 7 were completed during the seventh year, after which the UICSM program for the ninth grade was begun; and f) UICSM 7—the UICSM materials were begun two years earlier than usual, resulting in the completion of one year's work in geometry at the end of grade 9. At the conclusion of the three-year period a 40 percent attrition in data had resulted through a variety of unavoidable occurrences so that only 37 classes and 868 students were analyzed through the entire period.

At the end of each of the three junior high-school years all students were tested on the applicable forms of the Developed Mathematical Abilities Test (ETS-I) and the Mathematics Achievement Test (ETS-II) prepared by the Educational Testing Service expressly for this study. At the conclusion of grade 9 all students in the study were given the Ability Self-Rating Scale and the Questionnaire on Mathematics. Following an extensive statistical treatment in which the results for ETS-I and ETS-II were combined and the individual pupil differences in abilities and attitudes were partially controlled, it was found that SMSG Accelerated ranked highest, followed by UICSM 8, UICSM 7, SMSG Normal, Standard Accelerated and Standard Enriched in that order. It was further revealed that in the analyses of cross-program scores, the accelerated programs generally exceeded the enriched programs, and the contemporary programs usually outdistanced the standard or traditional ones.

ROLE OF MEDIA IN MATHEMATICS INSTRUCTION

The role of media in secondary mathematics education had not been as significant as in many other fields of educational endeavor. Programmed instruction, after a spurt of interest, became an important research tool for learning studies but had not entered the instructional arena of the secondary schools in any major ways. The use of computers had been highly restricted but a steady growth seemed possible for the future. Television and films had been utilized to a limited degree, but there was an extreme dearth of available research pertaining to their effectiveness. Mathematical laboratories, which were quite popular in the elementary grades, had not enjoyed rapid growth at the secondary level and had had few research studies such as Higgins (1970) to determine their usefulness.

Programmed Instruction

In the early 1960s programmed instruction created a flood of interest not only as a convenient research tool for learning studies but also as a medium for classroom instruction. Unfortunately, as Lange (1967, p. 319)

observed, the early proponents of programs and teaching machines frequently permitted their claims to outdistance reality with the inevitable consequence that criticism which mounted was often quite severe; however it was felt that this disillusionment would gradually give way to a period of solid growth for this medium of learning (Lange, 1967, p. 286).

Mathematics became a popular subject for researchers in programmed learning with a great deal of effort being expended on the determination of its effectiveness. A frequently tested and debated question was whether programmed instruction or teacher-directed instruction was superior. The results of this research did not settle the question of the superiority of either; in fact, the results were highly contradictory (Fey, 1969, p. 68).

Zoll (1969), for example, reviewed 13 comparative studies designed to determine the superiority of either programmed instruction or teacher-directed instruction and reported that three of the studies showed significant findings in favor of teacher-directed instruction, another three showed significant findings in favor of programmed instruction, and seven found no significant differences between the two approaches. However, in all cases it was revealed that students did, in fact, learn using this medium, but a basic question remained concerning the types of learning and the quality of the learning that were possible.

Although many investigations comparing programmed instruction with teacher-directed learning were of relatively short duration, a much longer study ($2\frac{1}{2}$ years) revealed that no significant differences existed between the mean achievements of students taught through the two approaches (Biddle, 1967). An experimental group of 54 students studied a linear program in geometry during one school year, and a control group of 74 students studied a geometry textbook of comparable material for the same length of time. The teachers of the control group taught their classes using their normal teaching styles, whereas the teachers of the experimental group only interacted with the students by answering questions raised by the students. Posttesting was conducted immediately at the conclusion of the year and again at periods of 12 and 18 months following the end of the experiment.

In a thoroughly provocative article, May (1966) conjectured that the teacher should and will remain a central and vital component in mathematics instruction at all levels of education. He urged that vigorous research should be directed toward the best teacher utilization of many kinds of media, including films, transparencies, tapes and programmed sequences. In fact, he argued that students should not be limited to learning by programmed materials but should be given varied opportunities including both reading and writing of extended pieces of mathematical exposition.

Some educators felt that programmed materials were adequate for teaching certain factual information of mathematics but could not meet the challenge of teaching more complex types of outcomes, e.g., the ability to write logical proofs (May, 1966, p. 449). A study completed by Beane (1965) was related to this issue. In reporting the results of a two-week experiment in secondary-school geometry involving geometrical proof, Beane suggested that even though the low-ability students of the experiment enjoyed an error rate of only eight percent, they were able to master neither the logical sequence nor the overall plan of a geometrical proof.

An investigation designed to study a flexible use of programmed materials in teacher-directed classrooms was conducted by the UICSM Programmed Instruction Project (O. R. Brown, Jr., 1967) over a six-week period. The text covered the basic elements of solid geometry in a program which was essentially linear but was filled with illustrations, inductive-type sequences and optional problems. The program, which had undergone revisions on the basis of study

with 250 tenth-grade students prior to the experimental period, was used by the teachers in a highly flexible manner. Each teacher was instructed to use the program as if it were an ordinary textbook. Full class discussions, small group discussions, lectures or any other teaching procedures felt necessary by the teachers were encouraged.

The classes were tested with the Cooperative Solid Geometry Test, Form P; the Space Visualization Test, Forms A and B; and tests especially prepared by UICSM. The results of the testing showed that the ability of the students to visualize and to draw spatial relationships had been increased, that the time required for study and final achievement scores had nonsignificant correlations, and that significant achievement (when compared with normed groups as no control groups were used) occurred during the study period as evidenced by the solid geometry test. Although the results of this study were very encouraging, one should note that good secondary-school students frequently outperform normed groups on standardized tests under very traditional instructional procedures.

The Emergence of Computers in Mathematics Instruction

Hatfield (1969) identified three major areas of computer innovation: a) computer-assisted instruction (CAI); b) computer-assisted problem solving (which we have assigned the acronym, CAPS); and c) instructional management, frequently called computer-managed instruction (CMI). Within the category of CAI may be included drill and practice systems, tutorial systems and dialogue systems. In CAPS, students write computer programs to solve selected problems and in this way gain insights into mathematical concepts, whereas in CMI the computer is used to assist the teacher in effectively administering and guiding instruction.

Research at the frontiers of the development of CAI was reported. In describing the Programmed Logic for Automatic Teaching Operations, Alpert and Bitzer (1970) described a strategy for teaching the concept of proof. A glowing report of progress of students from deprived areas in learning logic through CAI was provided by Suppes and Morningstar (1969). Both of these efforts represented research at the frontiers of the development of this innovation so that classical evaluation studies were not possible because of extremely limited availability of data (Alpert & Bitzer, 1970, p. 1584; Suppes & Morningstar, 1969, p. 350). In spite of this lack of evaluation, it did seem clear from these studies that CAI had emerged as a viable means of instruction.

Kemeny (1966) described CAPS as a most promising future use of the computer. One of the pioneer research projects designed to study CAPS in secondary-school instruction was conducted at the University of Minnesota High School in grades 7, 9 and 11 during a two-year period (D. C. Johnson, 1966). This project, known as the Computer-Assisted Mathematics Project, had as a primary purpose the identification of materials in the curriculum which students might learn through designing computer programs. In connection with this project, a two-year study was conducted (Kieren, 1969) in which 36 students from the first year and 45 from the second year were randomly assigned to either a computer or a noncomputer group. In the computer group the students learned much of their mathematics by writing BASIC (an elementary programming language) programs involving concepts, problems and skills from the mathematics course of the eleventh grade, whereas the noncomputer group did not use the computer in any way. Although results of this study were somewhat inconclusive, it appeared that students of the computer classes were able to master such complex skills as organizing data and drawing valid conclusions from data.

In a comprehensive and thought-provoking article, Brudner (1968) predicted that CMI will revolutionize the field of education at a relatively minor increase in cost. In CMI, teachers are provided a flow of stored information to enable them to monitor, evaluate, test and direct the progress of students who in turn receive a variety of learning materials tailored to fit their individual abilities and learning styles. Although still in its infancy, CMI appears to offer one of the most promising means of combining the personal warmth and attention of the teacher with the impersonal efficiency of the machine.

PSYCHOLOGICAL STUDIES RELATED TO LEARNING AND TEACHING

There is a certain affinity between psychology and mathematics which produced a set of psychologists whose research deals with mathematical learning and a set of mathematics education researchers who specialize in psychological types of problems. While this section is concerned mainly with the works of the latter, the former set, including such prominent scholars as Thorndike, Bruner, Gagné and Piaget, should not be disregarded by the serious student. Excellent surveys of the concepts and controversies of psychologists (Shulman, 1970) and educational psychologists (Cronbach, 1965) which are related to research in mathematics education are available.

The Study of Problem Solving

Mathematical problem solving was studied rather extensively from several points of view and probably deserves a designation as a "branch" of mathematics education as much as any other topic which might be named. At the secondary-school level, where problem solving would seem to come into its most important role, few empirical studies were found. An excellent report on the state of the art at all grade levels including an extensive bibliography was given by Kilpatrick (1969).

Seventh-grade students did not significantly increase problem-solving achievement as a result of being exposed to the structure of the problem-solving process in a study reported by Post (1968). A strong positive gain in problem-solving ability at the eleventh-grade level was reported by Wills (1967) to be the result of an experience of learning by discovery. On the posttest covering general mathematical topics, the experimental group doubled their pretest performance while the control group made only slight gains. Travers (1967) developed an instrument for testing for problem preferences and found no significant difference in success between preferred and nonpreferred problems. Sheehan (1968), using a multivariate analysis of covariance on data obtained from 107 high-school freshmen, reported a sex difference which favored boys in higher level cognitive processes. His use of a clever step-down procedure gave some insight into how test results may be masked by the influence of concomitant variables.

Variations in Student Abilities and Perception Patterns

The fact that the abilities and perception patterns of preadolescent children are a function of their age and other factors is well known and documented by the works of Piaget and his many followers. Piaget's theories are the crux of an extensive body of studies in mathematics education which were reviewed by Harrison (1969). It was therefore surprising to find so few Piagetian studies of secondary–school-age children.

In a study of students in grades 4, 6, 8, 9, 10 and 12 which tested students' understanding of the mathematical axioms for a field, a pattern of increase in mean scores from one even-numbered grade to the next persisted through grade 12. On the other hand, in an experiment in which 72 students from grades 8, 10 and 12 were tested on their ability to predict the shapes of plane sections of solid figures, Boe (1968) reported that an analysis of variance indicated five sources of significant variation among which grade

level did not appear. Of the 72 students in the sample, only 10 achieved success, so one might conclude that ability to perceive plane sections had not developed at grade 12.

There is need for substantially more research into the variations of secondary-school students' mathematical abilities and perception patterns. Motivation for this research can be gained through reading a review of Piaget's ideas and some of their implications by Adler (1966b) and also by reading the proceedings of a Piagetian conference held in 1970 at Columbia University (Rosskopf, Steffe, & Taback, 1971).

Measurements of Achievements and Attitudes

Mental tests and pupil classification have had a long and varied history (Cronbach & Suppes, 1969, pp. 73–88) and may be regarded as a major branch of educational research. A portion of the recent research specifically related to mathematics education was reviewed by Romberg (1969), who pointed out the unfortunate time lag between changes in instructional programs in mathematics and the development of appropriate tests.

Another major area of research activity was that of attitudes toward mathematics. Aiken (1970) gave an exhaustive review of the recent literature dealing with methods of measuring attitudes toward mathematics, the distribution and stability of attitudes and the effects of attitudes on achievement in mathematics, and influences of other factors such as the school curriculum on student attitudes toward mathematics.

COMPREHENSIVE ASSESSORIAL STUDIES

A promising dimension of research in mathematics education was represented by a set of comprehensive assessorial-type studies of longer duration and of greater complexity than the many restricted, limited studies of the past. The increased availability of research funds and the improved analyses made possible by high-speed computers produced such significant studies as the International Study of Achievement in Mathematics and the National Longitudinal Study of Mathematical Abilities.

International Study of Achievement in Mathematics

A monumental advance in mathematics education research was represented by the International Study of Achievement in Mathematics completed in 1966 (Husén, 1967). This study, which included nearly 133,000 students and more than 13,000 teachers in approximately 5300 schools of 12 different nations, was concerned with achievement and attitudes of students from four populations: a) 1A (13-year-olds), b) 1B (the grade group containing the largest fraction of 13-year-olds), c) 3A (students of mathematics in the final year of secondary education), and d) 3B (nonmathematical students in the final year of secondary education).

As noted by Astin (1967, p. 1722), the project accomplished not only a major technical achievement but perhaps a diplomatic one as well. Beberman (1967, p. 68) lauded the researchers because of the procedural accomplishments and particularly for their development of an international code for converting questionnaire responses. Carnett (1967, p. 586) was impressed with an outstanding cooperative spirit as evidenced by the fact that the data were processed in the United States; a sampling expert was supplied by England; mathematical experts from Belgium and Sweden assisted test editors from England, France and the United States; and additional resources were supplied by each of the 12 nations.

Although the study was not meant to be an international contest, comparisons among nations arose. When the national means of total mathematics test scores were compared (Husén, 1967, Volume II, p. 27) across the four populations, Japan, Israel and Ger-

many ranked highest and the United States and Sweden ranked lowest. A closer examination of the study revealed that the United States educated 70 percent of its children through high school and that 18 percent studied mathematics through the senior year whereas England, for example, educated 12 percent through high school but only five percent completed mathematics study through the senior year. Willoughby (1968, p. 625) made the somewhat facetious but nevertheless penetrating observation that if he were conducting a foot race in which the average time required for a team of runners from each country to run a certain distance was determined, he would expect the fastest five percent from England to be a great deal faster than the fastest 18 percent from the United States! Willoughby concluded that an examination of the top four percent of students from each nation was far more pertinent, in which case many of the earlier differences in achievement were negligible. An additional concern was expressed by Astin (1967, p. 1721), who felt it was most unfortunate that the samples were not examined independently for representativeness in light of the fact that the students were frequently selected by local school officials.

Neale (1969) analyzed three of the attitudinal measures of the study: a) attitudes toward mathematics as a process in which a low score indicated a viewpoint of mathematics as a fixed, formal system but a high score indicated a view of mathematics as a developing field; b) attitudes toward the difficulty of learning mathematics in which a low score indicated a belief that mathematics is only for an elite, whereas a high score indicated a belief that mathematics can be learned by many; and c) attitudes toward the place of mathematics in society in which scores ranged from a viewpoint that mathematics is only a luxury for national development to a viewpoint that it is essential for such development.

In statistics for population 1B it was found that the United States ranked tenth in achievement, second in "mathematics as a process," second in "difficulty of mathematics," eighth in "the place of mathematics in society," and that the correlation between the attitudes and achievement measures was nearly zero. Consequently, it was reasonable to conclude from these data that the United States placed high in two of the attitudinal measures, but that those students who scored high in achievement were not necessarily those who also scored high on the attitudinal measures.

Aspects of this report will occupy the attention of mathematics educators for many decades to come, and the results will certainly influence educational theory and practice. Although an extensive set of critiques of the study was completed (Wilson & Peaker, 1971), it will be many years before a complete assessment of the study can be made. In spite of this delay in complete appraisal, a significant place for the International Study in the history of mathematics education seems certain.

National Longitudinal Study of Mathematical Abilities

The National Longitudinal Study of Mathematical Abilities was a five-year investigation (1962–1967) sponsored by SMSG for the purpose of identifying and measuring variables associated with the development of abilities in mathematics (Begle & Wilson, 1970). Such variables as attitudes, textbook effects and teacher backgrounds were studied. More than 110,000 students from 1500 schools in 40 states were members of the study when it began. Three populations, designated X, Y and Z, were examined in the fall and spring of each year. The X population, consisting of fourth-graders in 1962, and the Y population, consisting of seventh-graders, were tested for the full five years, whereas the Z population, composed of tenth-graders, was tested for three years and then inventoried by questionnaire after graduation from high school. An attrition rate of approximately 15 percent for each

year of the study occurred but had been anticipated in the initial design of the study.

An enormous amount of information was collected over the five-year period. Measuring instruments included tests for IQ, logical thinking, numerical reasoning, spatial visualization, attitudes toward mathematics, attitudes toward school and numerous others. The design and development of the NLSMA instruments represented a significant accomplishment (Becker, 1968; Romberg & Wilson, 1968). The tests of mathematical achievement were developed according to a model containing a dimension of content (number systems, geometry and algebra) and a dimension of cognition (computation, comprehension, application and analysis).

A thorough examination of the NLSMA results would require a very lengthy analysis. A brief review of the findings in regard to textbook effects revealed three interesting observations: a) the variability of means associated with textbook groups seemed to decrease as grade levels increased; b) the SMSG textbook groups often outperformed conventional textbook groups on the comprehension, application and analysis levels but not on the computational level; and c) some of the modern texts, particularly those that were extremely formal and rigorous (such as those containing a strong emphasis upon axiomatics and deduction instead of understanding of basic concepts), seemed to produce poor results on all cognitive levels from computation through analysis (Begle & Wilson, 1970, pp. 400–402).

The NLSMA project illustrated to mathematics educators that curricular evaluation is an extremely complex task requiring an examination of many variables over an extended period of time, and even after such lengthy observations and analyses, few really clear-cut generalizations can be made.

SUMMARY

Research on teaching secondary-school mathematics has been discussed in six main sections. In each of these sections an attempt has been made to identify the primary thrusts of research and to discuss some of the issues which have not been resolved. The chapter would not be complete without an attempt to summarize the current state of affairs and to provide some indications of what the future may hold for research in this area.

Mayor, Henkelman, and Walbesser (1965) observed that the decade ending with 1965 was marked by intensive work in curriculum innovation, whereas the following 10-year period would be dominated by research efforts in the learning and teaching of mathematics. While research work in content innovation has slackened somewhat since the massive efforts of SMSG, novel teaching procedures have not made significant appearances. The slow rate at which programmed learning, computers and television have entered the classroom exemplify this lack of significant progress. It would seem wise for innovators to expend greater efforts in these directions; in fact, Davis (1967) predicted that the revolution in technology, particularly computers, should overshadow the curriculum work of the 1950s and 1960s in its real impact on the schools.

In spite of the predicted growth in technology, it seems clear that there will also be continuing efforts in curricular revision for at least the next generation. Efforts are being made to integrate topics, add new topics and completely revise the viewpoint of some subjects such as geometry. It is strange to find a product being replaced before it has been evaluated, and it is not a healthy state of affairs since it breeds innovation for its own sake.

Innovation all too frequently forges ahead with evaluation lagging far behind, whereas evaluation should be an early phase of every developmental project. But evaluation is difficult to conduct because secondary mathematics education is in need of a firmer theoretical foundation upon which to build innovation. A search for learning principles, however crude, would provide the beginnings of such a foundation. In contrast to the wealth of such materials which have been written about the mathematical development of children of primary-school age, very little has been done for secondary-school youth. The major question of how problems are solved, and the many abstract concepts involving space perception, logic and the all-pervasive concept of function, are among the topics for which a more intensive search for fundamental principles might begin in hopes of building foundations to support valid research.

REFERENCES

Adler, I. The Cambridge Conference report: Blueprint or fantasy? *The Mathematics Teacher,* 1966, 59, 210–217. (a)

Adler, I. Mental growth and the art of teaching. *The Mathematics Teacher,* 1966, 59, 706–715. (b)

Adler, I. What shall we teach in high school geometry? *The Mathematics Teacher,* 1968, 61, 226–238.

Aiken, L. R., Jr. Attitudes toward mathematics. *Review of Educational Research,* 1970, 40, 551–596.

Alpert, D., & Bitzer, D. L. Advances in computer-based education. *Science,* 1970, 167, 1582–1590.

Astin, A. W. Learning mathematics: A survey of 12 countries. *Science,* 1967, 156, 1721–1722.

Atkin, J. M., & Mayor, J. R. (Eds.) Natural sciences and mathematics. *Review of Educational Research,* 1964, 34, 259–393.

Atkin, J. M., & Romberg, T. A. (Eds.) Science and mathematics education. *Review of Educational Research,* 1969, 39, 377–551.

Beane, D. G. A comparison of linear and branching techniques of programed instruction in plane geometry. *Journal of Educational Research,* 1965, 58, 319–326.

Beberman, M. Measuring academic productivity. *Saturday Review,* July 15, 1967, 50, 68–69.

Becker, J. P. Geometry achievement tests in NLSMA. *American Mathematical Monthly,* 1968, 75, 532–538.

Beckmann, M. W. Ninth grade mathematical competence—15 years ago and now. *School*

Science and Mathematics, 1969, 69, 315–319.

Begle, E. G., & Wilson, J. W. Evaluation of mathematics programs. In E. G. Begle (Ed.), *Mathematics education.* The Sixty-ninth Yearbook of the National Society for the Study of Education, Part I. Chicago: NSSE, 1970. Pp. 367–404.

Bhushan, V., Jeffryes, J., & Nakamura, I. Large-group instruction in mathematics under flexible scheduling. *The Mathematics Teacher,* 1968, 61, 773–775.

Biddle, J. C. Effectiveness of two methods of instruction of high school geometry on achievement and retention: A two and one-half year study. *School Science and Mathematics,* 1967, 67, 689–694.

Boe, B. L. A study of the ability of secondary school pupils to perceive the plane sections of selected solid figures. *The Mathematics Teacher,* 1968, 61, 415–421.

Brown, K. E., & Abell, T. L. *Analysis of research in the teaching of mathematics.* Washington, D. C.: United States Office of Education, 1965.

Brown, O. R., Jr. Using a programmed text to provide an efficient and thorough treatment of solid geometry under flexible classroom procedures. *The Mathematics Teacher,* 1967, 60, 492–503.

Brudner, H. J. Computer-managed instruction. *Science,* 1968, 162, 970–976.

Campbell, A. L. *A comparison of the effectiveness of two methods of class organization for the teaching of arithmetic in junior high school.* (Doctoral dissertation, The Pennsylvania State University) Ann Arbor, Mich.: University Microfilms, 1965. No. 65-6726.

Carnett, G. S. Is our mathematics inferior? *The Mathematics Teacher,* 1967, 60, 582–587.

Christensen, D. J. The effect of discontinued grade reporting on pupil learning. *The Arithmetic Teacher,* 1968, 15, 724–726.

Cronbach, L. J. Issues current in educational psychology. *Monographs for the Society for Research in Child Development,* 1965, 30, 109–126.

Cronbach, L. J., & Suppes, P. (Eds.) *Research for tomorrow's schools: Disciplined inquiry for education.* London: Macmillan, 1969.

Davidson, W. W., & Gibney, T. C. Evaluation of a modern mathematics program. *School Science and Mathematics,* 1969, 69, 364–366.

Davis, R. B. *The changing curriculum: Mathematics.* Washington, D.C.: National Education Association, Association for Supervision and Curriculum Development, 1967.

Dessart, D. J., & Burns, P. C. A summary of investigations relating to mathematics in secondary education: 1965. *School Science and Mathematics,* 1967, 67, 135–144.

DeVenney, W. S. Final report on an experiment with junior high school very low achievers in mathematics. SMSG Reports, No. 7. Stanford, Calif.: Stanford University, 1969.

Fehr, H. F. (Ed.) *Needed research in mathematical education.* New York: Columbia University, Teachers College Press, 1966.

Fehr, H. F., & Fey, J. The secondary school mathematics curriculum improvement study. *American Mathematical Monthly,* 1969, 76, 1132–1137.

Fey, J. T. Classroom teaching of mathematics. In J. W. Wilson, & L. R. Carry (Eds.), *Studies in mathematics, Vol. 19. Reviews of recent research in mathematics education.* Stanford, Calif.: School Mathematics Study Group, 1969. Pp. 51–92.

Flanagan, S. S. The effects of SMSG texts on students' first semester grade in college mathematics. *School Science and Mathematics,* 1969, 69, 817–820.

Friebel, A. C. Measurement understandings in modern school mathematics. *The Arithmetic Teacher,* 1967, 14, 476–480.

Glaser, R. Variables in discovery learning. In L. S. Shulman, & E. R. Keislar (Eds.), *Learning by discovery: A critical appraisal.* Chicago: Rand McNally, 1966. Pp. 13–26.

Goldberg, M. L., Passow, A. H., Camm, D. S., & Neill, R. D. A comparison of mathematics programs for able junior high school students, Volume 1. Final report, Project No. 5-0381. New York: Columbia University, 1966.

Harrison, D. B. Piagetian studies and mathematics learning. In J. W. Wilson, & L. R. Carry (Eds.), *Studies in mathematics, Vol. 19. Reviews of recent research in mathematics education.* Stanford, Calif.: School Mathematics Study Group, 1969. Pp. 93–127.

Hatfield, L. L. Computers in mathematics instruction. In J. W. Wilson, & L. R. Carry

(Eds.), *Studies in mathematics, Vol. 19. Reviews of recent research in mathematics education.* Stanford, Calif.: School Mathematics Study Group, 1969. Pp. 129–152.

Henderson, K. B. *What research says to the teacher. Vol. 9. Teaching secondary school mathematics.* Washington, D.C.: Association of Classroom Teachers, 1969.

Henderson, K. B., & Rollins, J. H. A comparison of three stratagems for teaching mathematical concepts and generalizations by guided discovery. *The Arithmetic Teacher,* 1967, 14, 583–588.

Higgins, J. L. Attitude changes in a mathematics laboratory utilizing a mathematics-through-science approach. *Journal for Research in Mathematics Education,* 1970, 1, 43–56.

Higgins, J. L. (Ed.) *Investigations in mathematics education.* Vol. 5. Columbus, Ohio: Ohio State University, Center for Science and Mathematics Education, 1972.

Hooten, J. R., Jr. (Ed.) Mathematics. *Journal of Research and Development in Education,* 1967, 1 (1), 1–142.

Hrabi, J. S. *An experimental study of a unit on logic and proof strategy in the grades seven and nine mathematics curriculum.* (Doctoral dissertation, University of Colorado) Ann Arbor, Mich.: University Microfilms, 1968. No. 67-15,040.

Hudson, J. A. *A pilot study of the influence of homework in seventh grade mathematics and attitude toward homework in the Fayetteville public schools.* (Doctoral dissertation, University of Arkansas) Ann Arbor, Mich.: University Microfilms, 1965. No. 65-8456.

Husén, T. (Ed.) *International study of achievement in mathematics: A comparison of twelve countries, Vols. I and II.* New York: John Wiley, 1967.

Johnson, D. C. *Preliminary reports 1 and 2, computer assisted mathematics project.* Minneapolis: University of Minnesota, 1966.

Johnson, M., & Scriven, E. Class size achievement gains in seventh- and eighth-grade English and mathematics. *School Review,* 1967, 75, 300–310.

Kemeny, J. G. The role of computers and their application in the teaching of mathematics. In H. F. Fehr (Ed.), *Needed research in mathematical education.* New

York: Columbia University, Teachers College Press, 1966. Pp. 10–11.

Kieren, T. E. *The computer as a teaching aid for eleventh grade mathematics: A comparison study.* (Doctoral dissertation, University of Minnesota) Ann Arbor, Mich.: University Microfilms, 1969. No. 68-17,690.

Kilpatrick, J. Problem-solving and creative behavior in mathematics. In J. W. Wilson, & L. R. Carry (Eds.), *Studies in mathematics, Vol. 19. Reviews of recent research in mathematics education.* Stanford, Calif.: School Mathematics Study Group, 1969. Pp. 153–187.

Klinkerman, G., & Bridges, F. Team teaching in geometry. *The Mathematics Teacher,* 1967, 60, 488–492.

Lange, P. C. Future developments. In P. C. Lange (Ed.), *Programed instruction.* Chicago: The National Society for the Study of Education, 1967. Pp. 284–325.

Madden, J. V. An experimental study of student achievement in general mathematics in relation to class size. *School Science and Mathematics,* 1968, 68, 619–622.

May, K. O. Programming and automation. *The Mathematics Teacher,* 1966, 59, 444–454.

Mayor, J. R., Henkelman, J. H., & Walbesser, H. H., Jr. An implication for teacher education of recent research in mathematics education. *Journal of Teacher Education,* 1965, 16, 483–490.

McKillip, W. D. The effects of high school calculus on students' first-semester calculus grades at the University of Virginia. *The Mathematics Teacher,* 1966, 59, 470–472.

Meconi, L. J. The mathematically gifted student and discovery learning. *The Mathematics Teacher,* 1967, 60, 862–865.

Miller, W. A. *The acceptance and recognition of six logical inference patterns by secondary students.* (Doctoral dissertation, The University of Wisconsin) Ann Arbor, Mich.: University Microfilms, 1968. No. 68-13,651.

Neale, D. C. The role of attitudes in learning mathematics. *The Arithmetic Teacher,* 1969, 16, 631–640.

Nelson, L. D. Textbook difficulty and mathematics achievement in junior high school. *The Mathematics Teacher,* 1965, 58, 724–729.

Paige, D. D. A comparison of team versus traditional teaching of junior high mathematics. *School Science and Mathematics,* 1967, 67, 365–367.

Platt, J. L. *The effect of the use of mathematical logic in high school geometry: An experimental study.* (Doctoral dissertation, Colorado State College) Ann Arbor, Mich.: University Microfilms, 1968. No. 68-7158.

Post, T. R. *The effects of the presentation of a structure of the problem-solving process upon problem-solving ability in seventh grade mathematics.* (Doctoral dissertation, Indiana University) Ann Arbor, Mich.: University Microfilms, 1968. No. 68-4746.

Price, J. Discovery: Its effect on critical thinking and achievement in mathematics. *The Mathematics Teacher,* 1967, 60, 874–876.

Quast, W. G. *Geometry in the high schools of the United States: An historical analysis from 1890 to 1966.* (Doctoral dissertation, Rutgers, The State University) Ann Arbor, Mich.: University Microfilms, 1968. No. 68-9162.

Retzer, K. A., & Henderson, K. B. Effect of teaching concepts of logic on verbalization of discovered mathematical generalizations. *The Mathematics Teacher,* 1967, 60, 707–710.

Robinson, W. B. The effects of two semesters of secondary school calculus on students' first and second quarter calculus grades at the University of Utah. *Journal for Research in Mathematics Education,* 1970, 1, 57–60.

Romberg, T. A. Current research in mathematics education. *Review of Educational Research,* 1969, 39, 473–491.

Romberg, T. A., & Wilson, J. W. The development of mathematics achievement tests for the national longitudinal study of mathematical abilities. *The Mathematics Teacher,* 1968, 61, 489–495.

Rosenbloom, P. C., & Ryan, J. J. *Secondary mathematics evaluation project: Review of results.* St. Paul, Minn.: Minnesota National Laboratory, 1968.

Rosskopf, M. F., Steffe, L. P., & Taback, S. (Eds.) *Piagetian cognitive-development research and mathematical education: Proceedings of a conference conducted at Columbia University, October 1970.* Washington, D.C.: National Council of Teachers of Mathematics, 1971.

Ryan, J. J. *Effects of modern and conventional mathematics curricula on pupil attitudes, interests, and perception of proficiency.* Washington, D.C.: United States Department of Health, Education and Welfare, Bureau of Research, 1968.

Sheehan, T. J. Patterns of sex differences in learning mathematical problem-solving. *Journal of Experimental Education,* 1968, 36, 84–87.

Shulman, L. S. Psychology and mathematics education. In E. G. Begle (Ed.), *Mathematics education.* The Sixty-ninth Yearbook of the National Society for the Study of Education, Part I. Chicago: NSSE, 1970. Pp. 23–71.

Shulte, A. P. The effects of a unit in probability and statistics on students and teachers of ninth-grade general mathematics. *The Mathematics Teacher,* 1970, 63, 56–64.

Small, D. E., Holtan, B. D., & Davis, E. J. A study of two methods of checking homework in a high school geometry class. *The Mathematics Teacher,* 1967, 60, 149–152.

Smith, M. A. *Development and preliminary evaluation of a unit on probability and statistics at the junior high school level.* (Doctoral dissertation, University of Georgia) Ann Arbor, Mich.: University Microfilms, 1966. No. 66-13,620.

Stevenson, R. L. *The achievement gains in mathematics of seventh grade pupils when achievement grouping and flexible scheduling are employed in a team teaching program.* (Doctoral dissertation, New York University) Ann Arbor, Mich.: University Microfilms, 1967. No. 67-4911.

Stone, M. H. Review of "Goals for school mathematics." *The Mathematics Teacher,* 1965, 58, 353–360.

Suppes, P., & Morningstar, M. Computer-assisted instruction. *Science,* 1969, 166, 343–350.

Suydam, M. N. Annotated compilation of research on secondary school mathematics, 1930–1970. Final report, Project No. 1-C-004. University Park, Pa.: The Pennsylvania State University, 1972. 2 vols.

Ten Brinke, D. P. *Homework: An experimental evaluation of the effect on achievement in mathematics in grades seven and eight.* (Doctoral dissertation, University of Minnesota) Ann Arbor, Mich.: University Microfilms, 1967. No. 65-15,326.

Thwaites, B. Mathematical reforms in English secondary schools. *The Mathematics Teacher,* 1966, 59, 42–52.

Travers, K. J. A test of pupil preference for problem solving situations in junior high school mathematics. *Journal of Experimental Education,* 1967, 35 (4), 9–18.

Weaver, J. F. (Ed.) *Investigations in mathematics education.* Stanford, Calif.: Stanford University School Mathematics Study Group, Vols. 1 and 2, 1969, Vol. 3, 1970, Vol. 4, 1971.

Willcutt, R. E. Individual differences—Does research have any answers for junior high mathematics teachers? *School Science and Mathematics,* 1969, 69, 217–225.

Williams, S. I. *A survey of the teaching of mathematics in secondary schools.* Princeton, N.J.: Educational Testing Service, 1969.

Willoughby, S. S. Algebraic geometry for high school pupils. *American Mathematical Monthly,* 1966, 73, 650–654.

Willoughby, S. S. Who won the international contest? *The Arithmetic Teacher,* 1968, 15, 623–629.

Willoughby, S. S. Mathematics. In R. L. Ebel (Ed.), *Encyclopedia of educational research.*

4th ed. New York: Macmillan, 1969. Pp. 766–777.

Wills, H., III. *Transfer of problem solving ability gained through learning by discovery.* (Doctoral dissertation, University of Illinois) Ann Arbor, Mich.: University Microfilms, 1967. No. 67-11,937.

Wilson, J. W., & Carry, L. R. (Eds.) *Studies in mathematics, Vol. 19. Reviews of recent research in mathematics education.* Stanford, Calif.: School Mathematics Study Group, 1969.

Wilson, J. W., & Peaker, G. F. (Eds.) Special issue: International study of achievement in mathematics. *Journal for Research in Mathematics Education,* 1971, 2, 65–176.

Zahn, K. G. Use of class time in eighth-grade arithmetic. *The Arithmetic Teacher,* 1966, 13, 113–120.

Zoll, E. J. Research in programmed instruction in mathematics. *The Mathematics Teacher,* 1969, 62, 103–110.

CHAPTER 37 Research on Teaching the Visual Arts

ELLIOT W. EISNER
Stanford University

This chapter deals with research on teaching the visual arts. It does not examine research in the areas of music, drama or literature although surely these areas of human activity also come under the general heading of art.

PERVADING PROBLEMS

At the outset it should be noted that two general types of problems pervade research on teaching the visual arts. One type of problem is characteristic of empirical research in education in general. The other problem deals with the particular difficulties indigenous to research in teaching the visual arts. Both of these types of problems will be discussed prior to analyzing the empirical studies that have been undertaken in the field, but even before doing that I shall identify certain issues and developments in the field of art education in order to provide the reader with a context for the material that follows.

The field of art education within which most of the studies are drawn does not have a long heritage of empirical research. Empirical work in the field began to develop

and take on a distinct character in the early 1950s. Since that time both research journals and graduate programs have been started which have contributed to the life of research in art education (Eisner, 1965). But to say that empirical research in art education has not had a long history is only a part of the story. For years, indeed even today there is a substantial number of individuals who claim that scientific inquiry has no proper place in the field. Still others believe that scientific inquiry is not merely irrelevant for understanding artistic growth but that it is likely to be pernicious (D'Amico, 1966; Kaufman, 1959). It will, in the eyes of some, take the mystery out of art and thereby rob it of its special charm and peculiar power.

The reasons for holding such views are easy to understand when one realizes that the background from which many art educators come is one which provides little training in the methods of science. For men to fear what they do not understand is a story long told in man's history. For those sophisticated to the methods and assumptions of science, objections are sometimes raised on epistemological grounds. Art, it is claimed, discloses a mode of reality that is fundamentally different from that disclosed by science. Art must be known through art. The argument holds, a fortiori, with respect to understanding growth in art or its teaching.

There is one other factor of no small importance which also needs to be considered when reviewing research in teaching the visual arts. That factor deals with the philosophic orientation of a vast segment of the field. Since the birth of the child-study movement in the late 1880s there has been an important naturalistic, neo-Rousseauian orientation in the field. This orientation holds, in general, that art is not so much taught as it is caught. It argues that the primary responsibility of the teacher of art is to provide the stimulation and environmental conditions that will allow the child's latent potentialities to unfold. The image of the teacher is that of a gardener, one who brings forth what the child possesses. It does not conceive of the teacher as an instructor.

Examples of this view are found in two of the most influential books in the field of art education. *Creative and Mental Growth* by Viktor Lowenfeld was first published in 1947 and has undergone five editions since that time. The book has been published in seven languages and is perhaps the most widely used textbook in the field. *Education Through Art* by Sir Herbert Read was first published in 1945 and has undergone three editions. Read's book is a byword in art education in England as well as in this country, and a society called the International Society for Education Through Art, which emphasizes the ideals set forth in Read's works, has been formed and is now operating. Both Lowenfeld and Read view the child naturistically. But let them speak for themselves. Lowenfeld writes,

If children developed without any interference from the outside world, no special stimulation for their creative work would be necessary. Every child would use his deeply rooted crea-

tive impulse without inhibition, confident in his own kind of expression. We find this creative confidence clearly demonstrated by those people who live in the remote sections of our country and who have not been inhibited by the influences of advertisements, funny books, and "education." Among these folk are found the most beautiful, natural, and clearest examples of children's art. What civilization has buried we must try to regain by recreating the natural base necessary for such free creation. Whenever we hear children say, "I can't draw that," we can be sure that some kind of interference has occurred in their lives (1947, p. 12).

Read follows by saying,

Generally speaking, the activity of self-expression cannot be taught. Any application of an external standard, whether of technique or form, immediately induces inhibitions, and frustrates the whole aim. The role of the teacher is that of attendant, guide, inspirer, psychic midwife (1945, p. 206).

What we see here are views of the child as an organism that develops best from the inside out. The concepts of teaching or instruction are not central to this conception. Indeed, neither of the indexes to these major books in the field contains listings under "teaching." Similarly, the concept of teaching art has not been popular in the field. While art educators would agree that mathematics, spelling, social studies and reading can and should be taught, many would disagree that teaching has an important place in the art program—especially for elementary-school children.

Given this context it becomes a bit easier to understand why research in the teaching of the visual arts has been both a late development and a scarce one. The conception of what art education should be, the view of the child's nature, and the conception of the appropriateness of scientific inquiry in the field militated against the kinds of studies to be dealt with here.

Regarding the two types of problems I identified earlier, one dealing with general problems of empirical research in education and the other with problems peculiar to research in art education, several observations can be made.

The problems that plague educational researchers in general also plague those in art education. What are those problems? And what is their importance?

First is the general tension between reliability and educational significance. Art educators doing research on teaching have not been immune to the expectations and standards that have influenced the conduct of research in education in general. One important standard is the expectation that judgments and measurements made be both objective and reliable. The quest for objectivity and reliability has too often led to experiments that are educationally trivial. In the desire to achieve precision in measurement, criterion measures have been used that do indeed provide precision but at the same time deal with forms of behavior that may be generously regarded as educationally peripheral. Furthermore, in their effort to control variables that might confound the results of experiments, researchers have employed experimental treatments that are extremely brief in duration. Short periods for experimental treatments are more manageable than long ones and researchers in education have been lured to use brief periods so that control is possible. Indeed, the modal amount of experimental time per subject reported in experimental studies in the *American Educational Research Journal* for 1968–1969, 1969–1970 was about 45 minutes per subject. The likelihood that significant educational outcomes will occur in 45 minutes is extremely small and can be achieved only if the experimental treatment is quite powerful. The ability to measure changes when powerful treatments are not available requires very sensitive instruments. Those familiar with educational research will be quick to realize that neither of these conditions is characteristic of educational research today.

What this all adds up to is that some of the assumptions and traditions in educational research have, in my view, hindered research in art education. The ability to generalize findings and treatments to educational settings is small when the conditions needed for control in such settings are not likely to be obtained.

A second problem characteristic of educational research and also prevalent in art education is the tendency of researchers to skimp on the amount of descriptive material provided on the characteristics of the experimental treatment. In an analysis of the amount of space devoted to describing experimental treatments compared to describing results of experimental studies reported in 1968–1969, 1969–1970 issues of the *American Educational Research Journal,* I found that about four times as much space was devoted to reporting findings as to describing the treatment. Researchers apparently believe that what is done to achieve results is not as important as the results themselves. But of course a paucity of information regarding the treatment reduces the possibility of replicating the study. Hence credence in findings must often rest upon one-shot research studies. Ironically, emphasis on results and neglect of methods used in the treatment contribute little to the aspirations of those in the schools who are looking for ways of making educational practice more effective.

A third problem peculiar to empirical research in education and other normative enterprises emanates from the fact that the educational values of educators change; hence, what was once considered important as a method or a finding may be considered trivial today. Indeed, the more rapidly educational values change, the shorter tenure findings are likely to have. When, for example, the development of creativity through art was considered the major goal of the field of art education, research on creativity was considered of paramount importance. Today, however, values in the field which emphasize the development of visual sensitivity and the understanding of art as a human contribution to man's cultural experience have tended to place creativity research on the periphery of research concerns. The journals and conventions reflect such shifts. A content analysis of the titles of papers published and delivered in the field would provide good evidence of such shifts in what is considered significant or useful research.

Another source of tenuousness in educational research in general as well as in art education is the fact that conclusions secured from populations of, say, 20 years ago might not hold true today. Unlike other aspects of the natural world, men change attitudes and dispositions at a comparatively rapid rate. The uses and forms of television and motion pictures, the rate of mobility, and the wars that have plagued the country over the past quarter century have affected what people believe and how they feel. Studies of human behavior can have concurrent and predictive validity only if population characteristics remain reasonably stable. Given the rate of change in the life-styles of the young over the past decade one can only treat conclusions from studies executed before that period with the utmost judiciousness.

Such characteristics imply that unless researchers can do the type of basic research on human behavior that is so fundamental in character as to be able to withstand altered educational values and changed people, the likelihood of securing conclusions on human behavior which will endure will probably be small.

Thus far I have identified some of the problems that are characteristic of educational research in general. Research in art education, being a subcategory of the latter, shares these problems. But research in the teaching of art also has some problems that are peculiarly its own. Some of these have already been identified. Perhaps the most significant of those that have been identified is the epistemological dispositions of a substantial number of those working in the field. Many believe that science cannot, in principle, yield insights into art or its teaching. In art education itself one finds the "two cultures" side by side.

But there are other problems. For one, in rule-governed fields, what constitutes a satisfactory criterion level of performance is subject to little dispute and to even less ambiguity. In developing more effective ways of teaching spelling, arithmetic, geography and some aspects of reading, the criterion to be achieved can be formulated with clarity and applied with precision. Indeed, a machine can do it. But what about appraising achievement in art? To be sure, there is a variety of skills which can be formulated and assessed with precision, but these are peripheral rather than central desired outcomes in the field. Determining the artistic outcomes of instruction requires the making of a judgment rather than the application of a standard, for there are *no* necessary and sufficient conditions for producing a work of art, appreciating it or understanding its place in history. Thus the problem of appraising effective art teaching, insofar as it is based upon the character and quality of student artwork, student response to art and student comprehension of its significance, is fraught with much difficulty, much more difficulty, in my opinion, than one finds in other fields.

Related to this problem is the fact that the qualities that constitute excellence in art and hence some of the objectives of art teaching are ineffable. Discursive language is in no way adequate to describe what the eyes can see and what emotions one can feel (Polanyi, 1966). Perceptive critics who are poetically competent employ metaphor, simile, analogy and tempo in their use of language to provide a verbal rendering of visual work. But even here the adequate comprehension of such critical language requires sensitivity to language as an art form.

This reality—one which can be avoided only at the cost of using art for research purposes other than artistic ones—places the researcher in art education in peculiarly difficult circumstances, especially when he attempts to employ research paradigms originally designed to assess the effects of fertilizer on corn yield per acre. Psychological paradigms for research in education have been dominant since the child-study movement. Such paradigms—paradigms which attempt to imitate those used in the natural sciences—often reduce educational questions to questions that the paradigm can handle. In the study of artistic learning as well as in the study of the qualitative aspects of teaching in general, new models are desperately needed. Progress in the study of teaching in general and the teaching of art in particular might move more rapidly than it has in the past if some of the procedures of cultural anthropology and art criticism were used. A type of research which I have called "clinical criticism" (Eisner, 1969) might provide one of the needed alternatives for the study of educational practice.

One other comment before moving to the research in the field—the use of psychological paradigms for doing research in the teaching of art has often led to the formation of questions that have greater psychological than artistic import. For example, research on the social values of art students is an interesting area of investigation, but it has only marginal utility for improving the teaching of art. Two of the central goals of the field of art education are to develop the student's ability to experience the visual world aesthetically and to develop his ability to form visual images in some material that expresses his personal experience. Using these objectives as criteria with which to assess the significance of research in teaching the visual arts, the field of candidates becomes even smaller.

THE STUDIES

One of the more interesting studies of the teaching of art appreciation was conducted by Brent Wilson in 1962 (Wilson, 1966). Wilson's problem was to determine if the fifth- and sixth-grade students' perceptions of reproductions of works of art could be improved through the use of systematic instructional programs.

What Wilson did was to provide an experimental treatment consisting of having students view the development of sketches Picasso had produced in preparation for his large black and white mural, *Guernica*. After having viewed these sketches, students were gradually provided with increasing amounts of information and commentary about them, and they were helped to acquire a variety of technical terms referring to aspects of visual art that they normally would not see. During the experimental period, which consisted of two or three half-hour sessions extending over a period of 12 weeks, the students were asked to compare and contrast the variety of Picasso's sketches that were available. At the end of the 12-week experimental period the experimental group and the control group, which consisted of one fifth- and two sixth-grade classes, were compared on performance on the Wilson Aspective Perception Test, an instrument especially designed by Wilson for this study.

This instrument, which was given as a pretest as well as a posttest, consisted of 34 slides of well-known twentieth century paintings. The slides were used as stimuli to elicit verbal responses from the students. The comments that students made were then analyzed through the use of a 28-category taxonomy.

This instrument, which has an interjudge reliability in the mid-90s, was used to determine the effectiveness of the instruction.

Wilson found that the experimental treatment was effective in increasing the use of technical language in describing the works shown. Wilson concludes by observing that, "Careful attention to the language and perceptual activities with which students are confronted hold [sic] promise as effective means by which students might develop a more aspective perceptual mode with regard to works of art" (Wilson, 1966, p. 41).

What is significant about Wilson's study is not only its rarity as a type of experimental research in art education, but the fact that he realized that linguistic categories concerning visual qualities can be taught and learned. Qualities such as hue, intensity, value, composition and so forth do not wear their labels on their sleeves. There is no good reason to assume that students will generate such concepts themselves. Most college students are ignorant of their meaning unless they have been immersed in art prior to college (Eisner, 1966).

Now what should be emphasized over and over again is that the verbal categories are not ends but means. Any teacher who merely helps children acquire words without helping them perceive their referents is engaged in meaningless verbal teaching. The important point is that the verbal categories function as a starting point for reminding students of what can be attended to in a work of art. Verbal categories do not exhaust the work since they are considerably more gross than the amount of information that can be obtained through vision. They do function in much the same way that theories of art function. Morris Weitz has pointed out (1966) that the great contributions of theories of art lie not in their definitions of art, but what they lead the viewer to see. Each theory, because it highlights an aspect of art, reminds the viewer of what to look for. For example, formalism directs the viewer's attention to the relationships among the component forms of the work; emotionalism directs the viewer's attention to the expressive qualities of the form; organicism points out the relationship between the forms of art and the forms of nature. Thus, Weitz asserts, the great theorists of art have been the greatest teachers, since they help us to see art more completely by illuminating what other theorists have neglected.

It is interesting to note that while the type of research Wilson did is rare, a similar although less sophisticated study was reported by Waymack and Hendrickson in 1932. Working with fourth-, fifth- and sixth-grade students, Waymack and Hendrickson (1932) gave children a variety of reproductions and asked them to rank the pictures in order in terms of preference. Following this the children were asked to keep the one they most liked and to write why they liked it. With this information the researchers were able to determine what the children said they responded to about the work—its subject matter, its technique, its form and so forth.

Following this, Waymack and Hendrickson provided a program through which they enabled the children to learn how to look at reproductions of works of art with respect to qualities such as color contrast, color repetition and other formal aspects of the work. The experience they provided the students enabled them to expand the range of visual qualities students were able to perceive. Like the Wilson study, the Waymack and Hendrickson study provides some evidence that instruction in the perception of art can increase what students are able to perceive in art—at least as evidenced in the way in which they talk about it.

In an effort to find out how paintings are judged, that is, the factors that influence judgment, James Doerter (1966) studied college art instructors' influence on the painting style of their students. What Doerter did was to randomly select eight painting students from each of five painting classes in three colleges. Each instructor in each class furnished two personal paintings and each student furnished the first and last painting he had done during the course of a semester's work with that instructor. After having constructed a scale by which to rate the student painting, and after having selected judges to do so, Doerter was able to determine whether or not the instructor's style of painting "appeared" in his students' work. Doerter found that not only did this influence occur, but that the vast proportion of students did in fact move toward their instructor's style during the course of the semester.

What is interesting about this study is not only the question itself, but the findings, especially since there has been such a great tendency among college teachers of art to espouse stylistic freedom in their teaching. The Doerter study suggests that the maintenance of stylistic independence on the part of the student might be more difficult than previously anticipated. It is not unlikely that art teachers use as criteria for judging and talking about student work qualities related to their own work. What the teacher likes in his own work he probably prefers in the work of others; what he dislikes in his own he probably dislikes in others. If, in fact, such preferences are exercised in teaching, it is little wonder that the works of the student look like those of his teacher.

This condition, however, need not be seen as inevitable. It is possible for teachers to find out from students what they, the students, are after and to help them achieve it. This will require the teacher to use himself more consciously in the classroom, especially when he is engaged in talking with students about their work. It will require the teacher to enter the student's frame of reference, to understand the territory that he wants to travel and to help him learn how to cope with the terrain.

Do the preferences people have for styles of art relate to the personality characteristics they possess? To answer this question Bernard Pyron (1966) studied the relationships between personality and the acceptance of popular, classical and avant-garde styles in literature, painting and music. There has been some research to indicate that people who prefer complex forms to simple ones are likely to be more flexible and more creative. The ability to tolerate, indeed to seek the ambiguous and the complex, has been considered a personality trait related to creative ability. Pyron hypothe-

sized that people who have a high need for simple order would reject avant-garde art significantly more than those who have a high need for complexity.

To test the hypothesis, Pyron asked college students to evaluate four examples of avant-garde, popular and classical art in each of three art forms; painting, literature and music. Their evaluations of the work were made on a semantic differential, an instrument used to relate bipolar adjectives such as nice-awful, clear-dirty, and so forth, to each of the works. In addition, each of the subjects in the study was administered a variety of personality tests. Pyron found "that those people who are highest in attitudinal rigidity and highest in simplicity of perceptual organization would reject avant-garde art more than those who accept change and tolerate a wider range of social stimuli . . . (1966)." This suggests to me that art education might be able to perform a most important function in helping people who tend to be rigid in their expectations open up and become more receptive to change. Indeed, a desire to seek perceptual surprise might be an important consequence of effective art programs, especially if such an attitude developed within the realm of the visual arts extended to other human activities. Of course, the need to eventually distinguish between the search for the merely bizarre and the search and recognition of the significant is crucial here. Yet without an inclination to search it is hardly likely that much will be found. In principle and in practice, teachers can encourage exploration, speculation and inventiveness. The history of art is in an important sense a record of the products of such inclinations.

In the realm of the productive there is a variety of studies which are related to the problems of teaching art. One of the most influential of these is research by Beittel and Mattil (1961) on the effects of breadth and depth in curriculum on students' skills and attitudes toward art.

What Beittel and Mattil did was to develop a depth and breadth curriculum and to offer it to ninth-grade pupils over the course of an academic year. In the study the depth and breadth approach was defined as follows:

Depth. A teaching program which allows a sustained long-term concentration in one specific area of study. There may be variety within this area but the different activities are such that they permit an easy transition from one problem to another. This approach stimulates both sequential and cumulative learning.

Breadth. A teaching program in which a variety of well-chosen subjects and activities are dispersed in such a way as to accommodate differences in the interests and experiences of the pupils (Beittel & Mattil, 1961, p. 75).

The criteria for achievement were identified as spontaneity and aesthetic quality in students' paintings. Spontaneity is described as "freedom or ease in movement in the use of materials and rendering of forms." Deliberateness, its opposite, is defined as "stiffness of handling forms and materials in the total work."

Aesthetic quality was determined on a global or overall basis by judges using a five-point scale to rate the work produced. What did the study reveal about the effects of these different curriculum emphases? Did they have differential effects?

Beittel and Mattil found that the students who worked in the depth program produced paintings judged to have higher degrees of spontaneity and aesthetic quality than those students who worked in the breadth-oriented program. However, when the students were asked which type of program they preferred, it was the breadth rather than the depth program that came out on top.

What this study suggests is that spontaneity is a product of both control and confidence and that such abilities and attitudes are more likely to develop in programs that provide for intensive work in a limited range of media than in those which shift quickly from media to media. It is when

skill is absent that confidence diminishes and tightness and rigidity enter. At the same time it reminds us that children develop expectations for art courses as a function of what they have experienced in the past.

If past courses have emphasized variety, they will come to expect it and may be disappointed if they do not find it. This should not be taken to mean that their desires should be catered to. Art educators should, I believe, understand what children want but should make judgments using such information as *part* of the data to be considered. If current practices dictate future practices, the future looks bleak indeed. Instead, I suggest that we let our visions of the desirable enter into our decisions for practice and that we scrutinize the consequences of those decisions to determine if that vision is being realized.

The problem of determining how children's drawing and painting skills can be improved has been of interest to a variety of investigators. What these investigators have in common is their desire to improve children's abilities to draw or to paint and their belief that methods can be found which will have this effect. One of the earlier studies attempting to influence and improve children's art abilities was carried out in 1944 by Elizabeth Dubin (1946). Working with children of nursery-school age, Dubin identified from the literature describing stages of child art a series characteristic for children of nursery-school age. Categories such as scribble-unnamed, scribble-named, diagram, design and representation were used to classify children's art and to determine whether or not artistic development had taken place. What Dubin did was to identify the particular stage at which children in her experimental group performed and, through discussion about their work and through questions of various types, attempted to move them "one stage up" from where they were. Dubin found that by talking with nursery-school children about their work and by helping them begin to see more advanced possibilities she was able to increase significantly the group's development in art.

Although the Dubin study was completed in 1944 and although by present research standards it lacks some of the controls we now consider desirable, the study was a pioneering effort to facilitate growth in art. What is important about the study is not only the fact that it succeeded in facilitating artistic learning among nursery-school children, but also that it represented an intentional and explicit rejection of a laissez-faire approach to art teaching.

Other attempts to develop drawing skills are represented by the more recent efforts of R. H. Salome (1965).

The Salome study was based upon theoretical ideas concerning the way in which humans secure visual information from the environment. One of the tenets of this theory argues that in any visual form there are certain contours which provide maximum information about it. For example, the points at which a form changes direction provide such information. One does not have to look at the total form to secure an understanding of its visual character; one can acquire such information by attending to areas of change.

Using this assumption Salome attempted to teach children how to attend to form, that is, to attend to points that theoretically provide the most visual information. Since perception of form is a necessary condition for drawing a form realistically, Salome hypothesized that the quality of children's drawing with respect to closure-clarity, proportion and realism would increase.

Salome found that children in the fourth and fifth grades who received instruction in the perception of form achieved higher levels of drawing performance than a comparable control group. Salome also found that "perceptual training relevant to the utilization of visual cues located along contour lines does increase the amount of visual information fifth grade children in-

clude in drawings of visual objects..." (1965, pp. 31–32).

The relationship between one's feelings and one's work in the visual arts has intrigued art educators for years. Do children express their feelings through art? If so, how? Do children display their frustrations in the art they produce? To answer some of these questions R. Murray Thomas (1951) conducted an experiment dealing with the effects of frustration on children's drawing. In this experiment 40 nursery-school children from ages two to four were divided into control experimental groups. In the experimental group the children were put into a potentially frustrating situation. This situation consisted of being shown toys and large colored boxes that they were not allowed to open or play with. The control group, however, was shown the same items but was allowed to open and play with the toys and the contents of the boxes. After the experimental and control conditions the children were allowed to paint using tempera, brushes and an easel.

Now according to one psychological theory frustration tends to breed regression. That is, people who become frustrated are likely to revert to forms of behavior characteristic of a period of development earlier than their own. Thus, a child of seven or eight when frightened might revert to sucking his thumb, an adolescent when frustrated might act out as a seven- or nine-year-old, and so on. In the area of art it was hypothesized that the character of what children paint when frustrated would reflect an earlier stage of artistic development and would reveal qualities of frustration described in the work of Alschuler and Hattwick (1947), who provide some evidence on the relationship of art to personality at the nursery-school level.

The paintings that were produced by children in the experimental and control groups were analyzed to determine whether regression had occurred, and Thomas was able to find none of the differences he theoretically expected to find between the paintings made by children in the two groups. The children who were frustrated did not regress to an earlier stage of visual expression as he had anticipated they would.

Now it might be that the children in the experimental group were not sufficiently frustrated or perhaps not frustrated at all. If this was indeed the case, then the hypothesis that Thomas put forth was not really tested. If indeed they were frustrated, the psychological theory which argues that frustration affects the level, type and style of expression must be revised or qualified.

In another inquiry related to the effects of feelings and beliefs on artistic expression, an effort was made to find out how hypnotically induced change in a person's self-image affected his ability to draw.

In this study David Manzella (1963) hypothesized that drawing ability is influenced by a person's self-image and that reinforcement of an artist's belief in his talent and creativity would be reflected in his work. Manzella theorized further that such reinforcement will tend to free the individual to use techniques and aesthetic insights that were only partly employed when working in normal conscious states. What Manzella did was to select 10 artists and to interview them concerning their own conceptions of this ability in art. These individuals were then asked to draw from a nude model in the normal waking state of consciousness. Following this they were put into a hypnotic state and were told such phrases as, "You are talented; you are very, very talented and creative; you are going to draw as the talented and creative artist you are; you are going to draw only to please yourself." Following these post-hypnotic suggestions they again drew from the model. Upon completion of both drawings their work was evaluated with respect to its inventiveness and aesthetic quality. Manzella (1963) found that the quality of the drawings the artists made under a hypnotic state did not differ significantly

from those they made under normal circumstances.

There was general agreement among the judges that while one or more of each subject's drawings made under hypnosis was aesthetically more significant than those made in the waking state, they in no instance indicated an unexpected or unusual extension of the normal expressive range of the artist (Manzella, 1963, pp. 64, 67).

The Thomas and Manzella studies share a common quality: both represent efforts to determine whether abnormal mental states affect the quality and character of expression. They also share a common conclusion: no significant differences due to such states were found.

To what extent do drawings provide an index to an individual's general intelligence? Since its publication in 1926, the Draw a Man Test has been used by psychologists and educators as a nonverbal measure of general intelligence. This test consists of asking a child to draw a man or a woman on a standard size paper using a pencil. The drawing that is made is then evaluated by applying a variety of visual criteria to the various parts of the human body. Validation of the Draw a Man Test has been made by comparing scores acquired on that test to those acquired on standard group and individual intelligence tests. Correlations between the Draw a Man Test scores and scores on the latter tests are far better than chance—ranging from $+0.50$ to $+0.70$ (Harris, 1963). Thus the Draw a Man Test has been considered by many in psychometrics as a useful instrument, easy to administer, brief in time of administration and not too difficult to score.

But can scores on the Draw a Man Test be experimentally manipulated? To answer this question Medinnus, Bobitt, and Hullett (1966) selected 14 kindergarten and 20 first-grade students and divided them into two groups. The experimental and control groups were asked to make a drawing of a man using the standard procedures suggested by the test-makers. The experimental group was then asked to assemble a jigsaw puzzle of a male figure made from plywood. The figure consisted of 14 separate pieces: hair, head, neck, trunk, shoulders, arms, hands, legs and feet. Over the course of a two-week period the children had four sessions in which they had an opportunity to put the jigsaw puzzle together. Then, after the last experimental session, the Draw a Man Test was readministered to both groups and comparisons of the scores received on pre- and posttests made. Medinnus, Bobitt and Hullett found upon analysis of the scores that the experimental group received a significantly higher score than did the control group. In other words, because of the experience of working on the jigsaw puzzle of the man, the degree of complexity of their drawings was significantly increased.

What is theoretically interesting about this study is that the Draw a Man Test is designed to assess intelligence, yet practice in putting a puzzle of a man together was apparently responsible for increasing Draw a Man scores. The researchers rightfully point out that while they have no evidence that the children in the experimental group did not in fact increase their intelligence through the puzzle-solving experience, it is unlikely that this would happen. Thus they raise some questions about what it is that the Draw a Man Test actually measures—in light of the fact that its scores can be manipulated through brief training sessions with a puzzle.

In an interesting article on "What Copying Requires," Eleanor Maccoby (1968) advances the hypothesis that for the discrimination of simple geometric forms wholistic perception is adequate, but in order to make an accurate copy of what is seen such a mode of perception is inadequate. Maccoby then goes on to argue that since drawing is temporal and sequential it is necessary for children to learn how to fractionate the stimulus into its respec-

tive parts in order to match the drawing to the model. In addition to fractionating the model the child has to be able to relate the various parts to each other in a way that is isomorphic to the model, a most difficult task, as she concedes.

To provide evidence regarding the validity of this hypothesis, Maccoby then reports the experimental work of one of her students, Jonathan Goodson. Goodson worked with 80 children ages three to five and divided them into four groups—three experimental and one control. Experimental group 1 was asked to draw four figures—a cube, a square, a triangle and a diamond—by first having an opportunity to draw on a board a figure that had been constructed in the form of a deep groove. The child mastered tracing the figure by moving his pencil along the groove. Five minutes of experimental time was allocated.

Group 2 was helped to learn to attend to aspects of the same figures—corners, slanted lines and so forth.

Group 3 did not only what group 2 did, but also was allowed to practice drawing *parts* but not all of the figure.

The control group received no treatment.

Results of the experimental treatment were determined by rating the posttest drawings the students in each group produced. The investigation revealed that the experimental treatment was effective in groups 2 and 3 but not in groups 1 and 4. No differences were found between groups 2 and 3. Thus, the additional practice that students in group 3 had did not increase their ability to copy better than that which was achieved by simply learning to attend to aspects of the form.

This study, one related to that done by R. H. Salome, provides some additional evidence that the skills needed to create verisimilitude in drawing can be both taught and learned. However, one must not forget that one swallow does not make a summer—there is much, much more to drawing than being able to copy.

One of the few studies of teacher discourse in art was conducted by Robert Clements in 1964. In this study Clements attempted to identify the types and patterns of questions teachers asked of their students when teaching art. Classrooms were examined at the first-grade, seventh-grade and college levels. Specifically, the objectives of the study were four: to determine if different kinds of questions were asked at different instructional levels; to determine if teachers' questions were constant in type over different classes or days; to determine if patterns of questions emerged; and to determine if certain questions provided larger, more thoughtful answers than others.

Through the use of tape recordings which were then used to produce typed transcripts, Clements (1964) was able to analyze classroom discourse with the categories he developed for this purpose. This system contained the following categories: 1) experience questions, 2) judgment questions, 3) intent questions, 4) beginning questions, 5) process result questions, 6) identification questions, 7) suggestion-order questions, 8) rule questions, and 9) o.k. questions.

The use of these categories for analyzing the transcripts revealed that among first-grade teachers experience questions, intent questions and beginning questions were asked at least six times as often as they were at the seventh-grade and college levels. Judgment type questions, however, were asked at least three times as often at the seventh-grade and college levels as at the first-grade level. No significant differences were found among grade levels for the other question types that constitute the categories Clements used. In addition to these findings Clements calculated time allowed for students to respond, interruptions by the teacher and duration of response. He found that teachers rarely give students much chance to think before answering: "In the average 50 minute art lesson in which 59 questions were asked, a total of only five seconds of pausing were [sic] given." It was also found that five percent of the students' answers were interrupted and that college teachers interrupted most frequently. One of the striking findings of the study is that more than half of the questions received answers of one second duration or less and that 90 percent of the questions received answers of less than four seconds.

Clements's study of classroom discourse in art only scratches the surface, but in a field where that surface has not been scratched it is important. The field of art education badly needs further and more comprehensive studies of what goes on in the teaching of art. Clements's major contribution is that he has been among the first to do so in art education.

The foregoing studies represent those that I have considered to be important in the field. There are others, of course, which could have been included. But these even more than the studies reported leave a host of problems unresolved. What are those areas of concern to art teachers and curriculum developers in art education to which research might address itself?

First, there is the general problem of identifying in a careful, descriptive way the kinds of teaching practices that teachers do in fact employ in the teaching of art. In the field of art education we need studies of practice at both elementary and secondary levels. Although descriptive studies of teaching in discursive fields are available (Bellack, Kliebard, Hyman, & Smith, 1966; Flanders, 1970; Smith & Meux, 1970), study of the ways in which art is taught in classrooms has been neglected, with the exception of Robert Clements's (1964) work. Thus no one, I believe, knows with confidence what teachers of art do in the classroom beyond those general practices that are obvious. Yet an understanding, even a careful description of practice, could prove to be an important first step in improving teacher education in art and in developing curriculum.

A second area that needs attention emanates from the interest of most art teachers in developing attitudes and sensibilities that transfer to the visual world outside the class-room. Few teachers would be so parochial as to be content with teaching effects that terminate with the parameters of their class-room. What kinds of teaching techniques and curriculum activities are likely to facilitate transfer? How can teachers determine the extent to which the transfer of artistic learning has occurred?

This question bears upon a more generic concern regarding the validity of criterion measures used in educational research. The field of education desperately needs measures that have demonstrated predictive or concurrent validity. The vast majority of achievement measures assess circumscribed outcomes often directly related to the program of instruction—the curriculum. Yet in one sense these criterion measures are more appropriately viewed as independent variables which provide limited data predictive of more significant and enduring attitudes and skills. For the most part, the next step—one of determining predictive or concurrent validity—is not taken. Thus what constitutes experimental success in educational research are significant gains of a statistical sort at the end of an experimental period. The *educational* significance of the statistically significant remains to be demonstrated.

A third type of problem that warrants scientific inquiry in art education deals with the effects of different types of motivation on the content and form of artwork produced by children. In informal studies some of my students have found that the amount of detail and ingenuity displayed in children's art after they have had an opportunity to role play is greater than when other motivational procedures are used. Thus role playing such as acting like a wave crashing upon the shore or a bird lofting through the sky tends to increase the presence of certain artistically valued properties in children's work.

What about other types of motivational experience? For example, how does the analysis of expressionistic works of art prior to painting or sculpting affect the form and content of art in the classroom? This question is, of course, related to the larger question of how set and vicarious experience influence image formation and visual expression. If, in fact, different approaches to motivation yield different outcomes, teachers might have an expanded repertoire with which to influence what children create.

Perhaps one of the most important areas that warrants further study in the teaching of art deals with the extent to which systematic and sustained instruction at the elementary level improves the child's ability to see and respond to visual form, to produce visual form and to secure gratification and potency in this aspect of human activity. The experimental studies of teaching that have been undertaken in the field have most often been short term and have focused upon rather narrow segments of outcomes that are significant in the visual arts. What I believe the field needs are studies that extend over considerably longer periods of time—perhaps several months—and that intensively attempt to develop both technical and expressive skills. Programs systematically organized and sensitively taught might provide conclusions that would illuminate what can be achieved in the visual arts through the aegis of the school.

Regarding methodology for the study of teaching, I would hope that some new paradigms for inquiry would be developed. The critical-clinical model seems to me to hold considerable promise for illuminating the phenomenology of classroom life. As Dewey said so well, "The function of criticism is the reeducation of perception of works of art" (1934, p. 324). The tools of criticism include an understanding of the work in its historical and contemporary context, a sensitive eye and an ability to articulate linguistically the qualities that constitute the work. Through language the critic helps us see, and through seeing to feel. Through the exercise of criticism in the study of teaching we might come to vicariously participate in the qualities and life of teaching and learning and thus be better able to appreciate what such life means for both students and teachers.

REFERENCES

Alschuler, R., & Hattwick, L. *Painting and personality: A study of young children.* Chicago: University of Chicago Press, 1947. 2 vols.

Beittel, K., & Mattil, E. The effect of a "depth" versus a "breadth" method of art instruction at the ninth grade level. *Studies in Art Education,* 1961, 3, 75–87.

Bellack, A., Kliebard, H. M., Hyman, R. T., & Smith, F. L., Jr. *The language of the classroom.* New York: Teachers College Press, 1966.

Clements, R. *Question types, patterns, and sequences used by art teachers in the classroom.* Cooperative Research Project No. S-161, 1964.

D'Amico, V. Art education today: Millennium or mirage. *Art Education,* 1966, 19, 27–32.

Dewey, J. *Art as experience.* New York: Minton Blach, 1934.

Doerter, J. Influences of college art instructors upon their students' painting styles. *Studies in Art Education,* 1966, 7(2), 46–53.

Dubin, E. R. The effect of training on the tempo of development of graphic representations in preschool children. *Journal of Experimental Education,* 1946, 15, 166–173.

Eisner, E. W. Graduate study and the preparation of scholars in art education. In W. R. Hastie (Ed.), *Art education,* Sixty-fourth Yearbook of the National Society for the Study of Education, Part II. Chicago: NSSE, 1965. Pp. 274–298.

Eisner, E. W. The development of information and attitudes toward art at the secondary and college levels. *Studies in Art Education,* 1966, 8(1), 43–58.

Eisner, E. W. Instructional and expressive educational objectives: Their formulation and use in curriculum. In R. E. Stake (Ed.), *Instructional objectives,* AERA Monograph Series on Curriculum Evaluation, No. 3. Chicago: Rand McNally, 1969. Pp. 1–31.

Flanders, N. A. *Analyzing teacher behavior.* Reading, Mass.: Addison-Wesley, 1970.

Harris, D. B. *Children's drawings as measures of intellectual maturity.* New York: Harcourt Brace & World, Inc., 1963.

Kaufman, I. Some reflections on research in art education. *Studies in Art Education,* 1959, 1, 9–18.

Lowenfeld, V. *Creative and mental growth.* New York: Macmillan, 1947.

Maccoby, E. What copying requires. *Ontario Journal of Educational Research,* 1968, 10, 163–170.

Manzella, D. The effects of hypnotically induced change in the self image on drawing ability. *Studies in Art Education,* 1963, 4, 59–67.

Medinnus, G. R., Bobitt, D., & Hullett, J. Effects of training on the "Draw-a-Man Test." *Journal of Experimental Education,* 1966, 35, 62–63.

Polanyi, M. *The tacit dimension.* New York: Doubleday, 1966.

Pyron, B. Rejection of avant-garde art and the need for simple order. *Journal of Psychology,* 1966, 63, 159–178.

Read, H. *Education through art.* New York: Pantheon Books, 1945.

Salome, R. A. The effects of perceptual training upon the two dimensional drawings of children. *Studies in Art Education,* 1965, 7(1), 18–33.

Smith, B. O., & Meux, M. *A study of the logic of teaching.* Urbana, Ill.: University of Illinois, Bureau of Educational Research, 1970.

Thomas, R. M. Effects of frustration on children's paintings. *Child Development,* 1951, 22(2), 123–132.

Waymack, E., & Hendrickson, G. Children's reactions as a basis for teaching picture appreciation. *Elementary School Journal,* 1932, 33, 268–276.

Weitz, M. The nature of art. In E. W. Eisner, & D. W. Ecker, *Readings in art education.* Waltham, Mass.: Blaisdell, 1966. Pp. 49–56.

Wilson, B. G. An experimental study designed to alter fifth and sixth grade students' perception of paintings. *Studies in Art Education,* 1966, 8(1), 33–42.

CHAPTER 38 Research on Teaching Physical Education

JOHN E. NIXON
Stanford University

LAWRENCE F. LOCKE[1]
University of Massachusetts

Children are not taught how to move, they are prewired for movement at birth. Under the impetus of environmental stimulation, children acquire goal-directed movement behaviors. They do so through the selective inhibition of diffuse motor outflow into organized patterns of muscular contraction.

The natural and untutored expansion of motor ability produces a substantial movement repertoire before the child's first encounter with formal physical education. Further, during the ensuing school years, physical education classes will represent a relatively minor portion of his total daily practice in motor development.

Thus the pedagogical efficiency with which the physical education instructor intervenes to facilitate the addition of a few specialized skills might appear to be a relatively unimportant matter. It might seem so unless two additional facts are taken into account: 1) the social sanctions assigned these additional skills can give them an awesome valence in the child's world, and 2) an unacceptably large number of children who attend physical education classes are not able to acquire the sanctioned skills in sports and games satisfactorily.

Learning, and thus teaching, the tasks of the physical education class are important because the entire culture conspires to make them important to the children who attend those classes. So long as the skills of sports and games remain part of the heritage transmitted by the schools, children deserve to encounter those skills under optimum conditions for successful mastery.

ORIGINS OF PRACTICE

In theory, research on teaching is one source of information that can be used in designing optimum conditions for learning motor skills. In practice, teaching physical education has little to do with scientific knowledge about learning and even less to do with knowledge drawn from research on teaching. The traditional model of the well-taught physical education lesson remains essentially the same everywhere: explanation, demonstration, drill on basic skills,

[1] We wish to express our appreciation to W. G. Anderson and W. E. Kroll for their generous and effective assistance in reviewing this chapter.

practice in leadup activities, and game participation—all dispatched with much concern for organizational efficiency, discipline and a high level of teacher control.

The origins of the modal description given above are not in science, in theory, or even in ideology. The wellsprings of traditional teacher behaviors in physical education lie, as Hoffman (1971) concluded, "...in the unglamorous realities of life" (p. 9). It is easier to explain what happens in the gymnasium in terms of social expectations, the influence of traditional "method" textbooks, the logistics of class size and composition, and the personal traits of individuals drawn to careers in physical education, than it is to attempt an account which presumes teaching to be directed rationally by feedback from student learning or by some set of scientifically derived principles of instruction.

This review gives primary attention only to that portion of available research which is concerned with teaching as a means of facilitating the acquisition of motor skills. The area of central interest may be described as "what the teacher does to help children learn movement skills related to sports and games." As a consequence of this necessary restriction, many areas of research interest in physical education have been excluded. One of these, motor learning, has received special emphasis in the last decade and will be considered briefly at this point.

Motor Learning

The most obvious single event that might be related to changing what teachers do in the gymnasium is the explosion of research activity by physical educators in the area of motor learning.[2] Growing interest and the accumulation of research have produced

a group of new motor-learning textbooks primarily directed to the practitioner (Cratty, 1967; Lawther, 1968; Oxendine, 1968; Singer, 1968a). Two particularly strong additions from England (Knapp, 1963; Whiting, 1970) further extend the list.

Most of the new texts contain a single chapter purporting to describe instructional procedures based on the evidence from motor-learning research. Several weaknesses limit the utility of such guides for teaching. As the body of knowledge in motor learning remains a recondite tangle of fragments unrelated by unifying theory, it is impossible to generate implications for method that consist of other than lists of hints for the teacher. Such guidelines, as they often are called, represent little more than speculative leaps from isolated bits of data.

A second problem in extrapolating from motor-learning research is the limitation imposed by the absence of an adequate understanding of teaching. Without sound models to describe the teaching process, the usefulness of knowledge about motor learning is limited to commentary on specific, isolated variables. Ordinarily it is necessary to use experimental procedures to extract the desired variable from the jumble of real teaching and learning. Yet the reality of teaching skills is not just the total sum of all possible motor-learning variables—it is something else and something more, an event that demands its own explanations. Knowing how children learn simply is not the same thing as knowing how to help them learn.

Thus, this chapter reviews only a small and selected portion of the motor-learning literature. For the most part, citations are limited to instances in which motor-learning research is directly relevant to an aspect of teaching under discussion.

Quality in Perspective

Research on teaching physical education suffers from a variety of persisting problems that range from methodological, at the level

[2] Argument that a truly nomothetic science of psychology will find it unnecessary to distinguish between cognitive and motor learning here is a non sequitur. Teaching operations will continue to reflect what are perceived to be the unique demands of motor tasks for the foreseeable future.

of experimental design, to logistical, at the level of organization for the profession's entire research enterprise. Careful exposition of these problems, their precise nature, their etiology, their impact on the generation of knowledge, and suggestions for their amelioration would demand a separate chapter. In the absence of an opportunity to provide such an extended analysis, we feel obliged to indicate something of the degree to which qualitative standards were exercised in selecting research for review. The following is intended to provide both a caveat for the reader and a general statement of our position concerning qualitative standards.

At this time, and specifically for research on teaching, we regard the only useful posture concerning quality to be one of "rational relativism." Research on teaching physical education cannot simply be categorized into good or bad, useful or worthless. For the present purpose each study must be regarded as methodologically better or poorer than other studies. This is not to say that quality does not matter. Indeed, that is one issue on which progress will hinge. Fewer than half of the items reviewed were worthy of citation here by any standard of quality. This *is* to say, however, that physical education must begin where it is. Pretension to the grandeur of absolute standards would be of small service.

A LEARNING FRAMEWORK FOR TEACHING AND RESEARCH

Presentation of research on teaching physical education poses a problem of appropriate format. First, any attempt to define teaching reveals its inherent indeterminacy—the chameleon-like quality of presenting a different appearance on successive occasions. At best, the boundary between teaching and learning is indistinct, as is the terminator between teaching and curriculum. Further, much of what teachers do in the gymnasium is unrelated to educational objectives in any systematic fashion. Second, the vast bulk of research on teaching represents what graduate students find

interesting or expedient to investigate—regardless of actual events in the gymnasium. Hence there are serious gaps in the existing literature. Taken together, the two problems make it unreasonable to define the domain of teaching research either in terms of what teachers are thought to do or in terms of what researchers have undertaken to date.

The format used for this review is based on *the learner*. A schema has been created by Gentile (1970) which contains the salient events in learning a motor skill.[3] A rough translation of the sequence for student learning presented in Figure 1 is as follows: 1) the student grossly perceives what is to be learned and desires to try; 2) he makes general note of the important elements in the task; 3) he envisions the rough form of his first attempt; 4) he gives it a go; 5) he attends to the results; 6) he decides how to try to do it next time; and 7) he tries a second time.

A parallel part of the model in Figure 1 presents a concurrent sequence of teacher decisions and potential interventions. Available research can be distributed into the seven major subsets of teacher behavior that appear relevant to the student's progress through the learning sequence.

Thus, Figure 1 links the three principals: teachers, learners and researchers. It also functions to underscore one relationship that too often is obscured. It is the *student* who must do the learning. No set of acts by the teacher can ever substitute for that wonderfully inexorable fact.

A REVIEW OF RESEARCH

Preactive Decisions

To the degree that teachers engage in planning, almost all decisions could be con-

---

[3] The model of skill acquisition used here, as well as elements in the parallel model of teacher functions, is the work of A. M. Gentile, Teachers College, Columbia University. We extend our appreciation for her generous assistance and advice, both here and throughout the chapter.

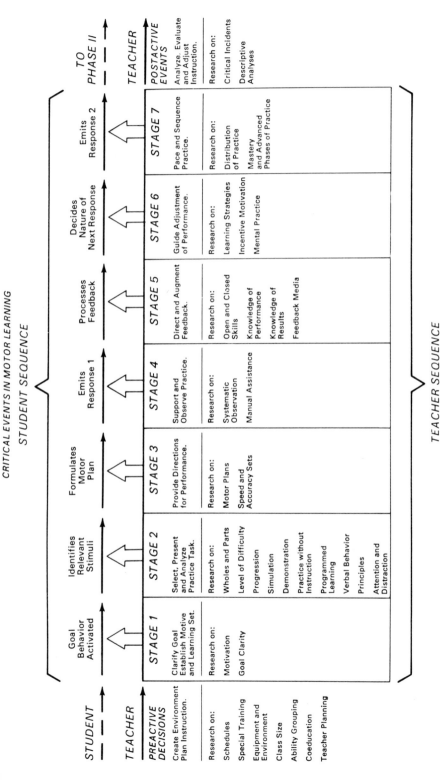

Fig. 1.   Sequences of critical events in student learning and concurrent teacher intervention.

sidered preactive. It is probable, however, that relatively few decisions about teaching, as distinct from curriculum, are made until the class is under way. The few items with a direct relation to teaching that demand preplanning are classified broadly as administrative: schedule, staff, equipment, and grouping.

Schedules. The most elementary question here appears to have been settled. Some instruction and practice is better than none, as indicated by the significantly inferior performance of "pure" control groups in a variety of studies (for example, see Mitchellette, 1960, or Sweeney, 1966). An increase in class time means more practice, which is reflected in greater learning (L. C. Johnson, 1968; Maxey, 1967; Sexton, 1965; Sloan & Liba, 1966).

Although studies of schedule patterns commonly are labeled as investigations of massed versus distributed practice, they may better be considered contrasts of varying degrees of distribution. Not surprisingly then, when total practice time is held constant, it appears to make little difference how class hours are distributed through the school week (Beal, 1965; Breeding, 1958; Cronan, 1968; Deutsch, 1960; Keough, 1963; Moncrieff, Morford, & Howell, 1962; Morris, 1967). One reservation is that unusual skills (Johansson, 1965), special criterion measures (Stull, 1962), or contrasts between very different kinds of skills (O. G. Young, 1954) may produce results that favor one schedule over another. The fact that discontinuous schedules (Miller, 1964) or schedules which alternate the content of instruction (Matthews, 1946; Nelson, 1957) yield inferior learning is explained on the basis of presumptions about transfer.

The innovations of modular scheduling have been little studied, probably because their use in physical education is not widespread (Garcia, 1965; Schmuck, 1968). Work by Snyder (1966) with flexible schedules and the earlier investigation of Keller (1964) involving the use of time blocks for independent study, indicate both some rea-

son for optimism and a need for further research.

Teacher training. A number of studies confirm that when the measure of learning is physical performance, elementary and junior high students taught by trained physical education specialists display significant superiority over children taught by untrained classroom teachers (Kenzie, 1963; Ross, 1960; Workman, 1968; Yeatts & Gordon, 1968; Zimmerman, 1959). Hallstrom (1966) demonstrated that even combinations of specialists and classroom teachers are to be preferred to a nonspecialist working alone. It is not surprising to find that despite a generally positive attitude toward physical education (M. B. Phillips, 1967), many classroom teachers have inadequate backgrounds in the specifics of physical education (Baker, Annis, & Bontz, 1952, 1954; N. D. Smith, 1964).

Although correlates of teacher success are notoriously difficult to find (Dawson, 1969), work by Hult (1968) suggests that student achievement in skill covaries directly with the teacher's level of skill and knowledge, the correlation rising as the complexity of the subject matter increases.

Equipment and environment. Few useful generalizations can be made about mechanical learning aids. Many ingenious and theoretically sound aids fail to produce the desired result under experimental conditions (Chui, 1965; Dailey, Wessel, & Nelson, 1963; Gensemer, 1969; Rohland, 1960; M. P. Ryan, 1964). Alternately, simple aids such as a chalked target on the basketball backboard (T. Anderson, 1942), or an incongruous invention such as an elbow splint for learning the tennis backhand (Pye, 1964) may produce significant advantage for the learner.

Equipment which increases the volume and quality of practice is likely to influence the rate of learning. In beginning tennis classes, for example, Solley and Borders (1965) found that the use of automated ball delivery was superior to the usual practice condition. Riccio (1963) failed to find significant advantage in a similar device. In the latter case, however, the contrasting condition was wall rallying which in itself provides a high volume of practice.

Equipment which reduces psychological hazards may work well, as illustrated by studies of flotation devices in swimming instruction (Hodapp, 1967; Kaye, 1965). Even here, however, age, sex, degree of student fear and the criterion of learning may influence the result (McCatty, 1968). Work by Bruce (1961) suggests that nonsignificant contrasts of grouped data are obtained in some studies because the security provided by safety aids exerts a critical influence on learning in only a small number of subjects.

Little is known about environmental manipulations involving color, light, sound or temperature. Music, as a background adjunct to practice, has failed to influence learning (Leslie, 1967; McLellan, 1964). Rhythmic accompaniment might produce more hopeful results when used to provide an external source of temporal patterning for specific learning tasks. Such may be the case with basic movement skills for very young learners (Beisman, 1967; Bowers, 1966) and with more complex skills, such as swimming, which contain rhythmic cycles of movement important to the production of good form (Dillon, 1952).

Class size. Perennial complaints about the difficulties of teaching large physical education classes are given substantial support in studies by Verducci (1969) and Overstreet (1968). Larger class size generally means less practice for each child, less teacher-student interaction, and consequent lower skill achievement, although the degree of loss may vary with specific skills (Hicks, 1965) or with the teaching tactics employed (M. G. Scott, 1954).

Ability grouping. Despite the substantial enthusiasm of teachers and supervisors (Feely, 1961; Reams & Bleier, 1968), there is little support for ability grouping when measures of physical performance are the standard for judgment (Gravett, 1969;

Jesseph, 1956; S. L. Moore, 1966; J. L. Phillips, 1961; Wilson, 1966). In general, homogeneous grouping appears to be no better than ordinary methods of assignment to classes, despite the considerable expenditure of time and resources involved. The possibility that achievement may be improved for high ability students placed in homogeneous groups has been raised by a number of investigators and received some confirmation in an early study by Lockhart and Mott (1951).

Coeducation. Although coeducational physical education has been sanctioned in theory for some time (McCann, 1954), it is far from common in the schools. Evidence from studies employing a variety of measures indicates little difference in results obtained from sex-segregated and combined classes (Bracken, 1964; Brightwell, 1969; Burks, 1966). The only exception appears to be a distinct advantage in skill learning for women who attend coeducational classes and some smaller disadvantage for men (Evaul, 1961; Ladner, 1969).

Stage I: Clarify Goal, Establish Motive and Set to Learn

Although the assignment of a specific practice task functions to establish the immediate goal for learning, the teacher may first present the larger objective, such as a game or an area of motor competence. In doing so, expectations and rewards for learning also may be communicated.

Motivation, in the sense of attempting to establish an initial set for student effort, has been subject to some examination. If it is allowed that arousal is related to at least some conditions controlled by the teacher, then it is of practical significance that, up to moderate levels, arousal is positively correlated with both the learning and the performance of motor skills (E. D. Ryan, 1962). The difficulties involved in translating this fact into classroom operations, however, are well known.

In most experiments, perceived expectations and self-instruction make it nearly impossible to study any given motive treatment in contrast to a true no-motive condition. A host of subject variables, including initial ability (Fleishman, 1958), age (Wilkinson, 1965) and sex (Caskey, 1968) act to further confound results. Only a few tentative conclusions may be set forth. Competition has a significantly greater positive influence on learning than no external incentive at all, and self-competition differs little from team competition in this respect (Hesse, 1955; Stitt, 1964). Teacher-established learning goals work well with younger children (Dudley, 1966) but not well at all with college-age subjects where self-imposed goals are more powerful influences on skill learning (Clawson, 1965). Finally, there is evidence that the common tactic of placing stress on grades can influence achievement in at least some subject groups (Trafton, 1965).

Apparently a number of teacher strategies can be employed to encourage motivational states that will favorably influence learning. Research conducted by Read (1969), however, underscores continuing concern with the less desirable consequences of methods involving competitive conditions. The impact of persistent losing in a competitive class situation may be reflected in a significant decline in both positive self-concept and favorable body-image.

Stage II: Select, Present, and Analyze the Practice Task

Next the teacher selects a particular skill to practice, communicates the task to the learner, and determines what, if anything, he will say about the nature of the skill.

Whole and part. In many instances the first decision faced is whether to begin instruction with practice on the skill or game as a whole or on a subcomponent. The literature on whole and part instruction is large, undisciplined by theory, and a morass of potentially relevant but largely uncontrolled variables. In a review of the whole-part concept in research on teaching, M. L. Johnson (1970) has argued that the dichotomy itself is defective and might better be replaced by a continuum based upon more clearly defined elements.

Research involving contrasts of various forms of whole and part practice presents one simple conclusion. If the learner is familiar and comfortable with the method of practice involved, neither parts nor wholes are likely to afford extreme advantage or disadvantage. To that basic conclusion, the following points are worthy of addition. In the 30 whole-part studies reviewed, not one showed unambiguous superiority for experimental treatments involving the part or progressive part methods of instruction. In the majority of studies, some permutation of the whole method was associated with superior learning (for example, see Knapp & Dixon, 1952; Lewellen, 1951; Purdy & Stallard, 1967; Shay, 1934; E. Young, 1965).

Individual skills with tightly integrated structure, such as diving or driving a golf ball, seem more amenable to whole practice. Even where pure wholes are inappropriate, beginning with wholes and shifting to parts as needed seems a reasonable teaching strategy (Welser, 1958).

Sports with a combination of difficult skill components and complex game structures often require some attention to the individual parts, even if combined with whole practice. Skills that fall between the two extremes permit a variety of practice forms, their effectiveness depending upon such factors as complexity of the sport (Niemeyer, 1958), unique demands of particular skills (O'Donnell, 1956), criterion test employed (Cross, 1937), intelligence of the subjects (McGuigan & MacCaslin, 1955), stage of learning (Arnold, 1960; Theunissen, 1955) and a host of other variables.

Level of difficulty. One obvious reason teachers use part practice is to reduce perceptual-motor demands on the student in the hope of facilitating learning. A reverse kind of logic sometimes is employed at higher levels of skill learning by making the practice task more difficult in the hope of stimulating greater competence. Although the degree of modification might be a critical factor (Lindeburg & Hewitt, 1965), changing the nature of the task could alter the course of learning, just as altering equipment influences the quality of performance (Knuttgen, 1959).

Unfortunately, the results of experimental studies give scant support to such reasoning. Whether the teacher modifies the equipment to make it easier to use (Briwa, 1967; Cione, 1962; Kurth, 1966; Roberts, 1967; Van Oteghen, 1968) or reduces spatial dimensions of the task and progressively returns them to normal (Cotten & Nixon, 1968), the result is of no significant advantage to the learner. Manipulating perceptual-motor demands to make the skill more difficult for advanced learners produces the same finding (King, 1959; Takacs, 1965; Winningham, 1966).

Nearly all of the studies in which initial practice on an easy motor skill is contrasted with initial practice on a more difficult version of the same task yield nonsignificant results. Whether the manipulated variable is target distance (Cooper, 1968; Girouard, 1967; Goldman, 1963; Singer, 1966; Slayden, 1966; Stevenson, 1967), target size (Kite, 1965; Scannell, 1968), or weight of equipment (Jable, 1965), practice on the actual skill to be learned appears to be as valuable as mastering modifications of the task.

-The few studies that yield significant positive results for altered tasks are of particular interest. Wright (1967) found that while regular weight equipment generally provided the best learning, lightweight equipment did help children of very limited strength. Likewise, in women's tennis where wrist strength is an important problem early in learning, Rhodes (1963) found that shorter and lighter rackets were superior to standard equipment in the first weeks of instruction.

Progression. The underlying assumption of specially devised progressions (particular sequences of skills for practice) involves another form of simplification. Tasks to be learned are ordered from simple to complex, from easy to difficult. Progression is a near-sacred principle in physical education and is taken most seriously in teacher training. Evidence indicates that the faith, at least in some instances, may be misplaced. Although results vary somewhat with the kind of criterion involved (Sprague, 1968), particular progressions generally appear not to be significant factors in learning many motor skills (Bevacque, 1964; Ford, 1958; Hodapp, 1967; Keth, 1968; Loftin, 1957; Singer, 1968b).

Simulation. While simulated practice sometimes is employed for reasons of logistics—lack of equipment or space—more often it is used on the assumption that simulation provides a simplified practice task by reducing the number of variables present. Unfortunately, when simulation is contrasted with equivalent practice on the real task (Buck, 1967; Chui, 1965; Clayton, 1963; Lewis, 1966; D. J. Phillips, 1964), no advantage is apparent. Only when the contrast is between simulation and no practice at all does a significant difference favoring the treatment appear (Minaert, 1950).

Generally, then, it may be concluded that the teacher is likely to be on safe ground if he chooses the real skill as a practice task. One clear exception lies in the area of modifications for special learner characteristics. The very young and the low strength subjects mentioned earlier fall in this category. Swimming instruction provides another example. Some students fear the water and the ensuing anxiety has a direct bearing on learning (Behrman, 1967; Daugert, 1967; Karbe, 1968; Whiting & Stembridge, 1965). Teaching methods designed to confront problems of this kind have significantly improved the acquisition of skill (Broomell, 1967; Bruce, 1961; Foster, 1963; Lerch, 1969; Ribet, 1957).

Demonstration. Having selected a skill for practice, the teacher must now communicate the task to the learner. The message may be as explicit as a demonstration to be imitated, or as general as a problem to be solved. In either case the limits and demands of the task must be described.

While it is possible that children differ in their ability to utilize demonstration as a model for performance (Berlin, 1959), it generally is accepted that some form of demonstration is the most direct and economical method of communicating the practice task to the learner. It is possible to learn many skills without the use of demonstration if verbal models are substituted (Jones, 1965), although surprisingly little is known about the subject. It does seem certain that film or television media can substitute for direct demonstration without significant impairment of learning (Church, 1963; Karsner, 1953; Maynard, 1962; Montgomery, 1968; Winslade, 1963). For reasons that are not yet clear, there is an indication that demonstration becomes more critical in complex tasks (Hill, 1958; Worthington, 1958).

A study of Friedrichsen (1956) raises the issue of whether initial demonstrations should include negative examples (common errors in performance) as well as a correct model. The subjects in Friedrichsen's study who viewed loop films of incorrect performance were significantly more advanced in learning gymnastic skills than subjects who had viewed only correct loops.

Some research has indicated that learners have difficulty in providing accurate judgments about their competence and in detecting their errors (DeBacy, 1970; Robb & Teeple, 1969; Sloan & Liba, 1966). On the other hand, research by Girardin & Hanson (1967) shows a substantial and direct relationship between the ability to diagnose errors and the ability to perform skills. Thus, if the perception of incorrect performance is both difficult and important, Friedrichsen's suggestion of error demonstration gains further support.

Whatever form of demonstration is used, once the model has been provided, the further use of illustration, correct or incorrect, direct or via film, seems to yield little useful impact on learning (Berlin, 1959; Douglas, 1963; Dressen, 1961; Drury, 1959; Irwin, 1958; Nelson, 1958; Spencer, 1961; Watt, 1954). A single exception is Rizk's (1969) recent experimental use of a multimedia approach to instruction.

Practice without instruction. Having selected and set the task for the learner, the teacher must now decide what further comment may be of use. The first possibility is to say nothing further. That is, in the traditional sense of the word, to give no "instruction." Such a decision could, of course, be made at any one of the remaining stages in the learning process, but it first occurs as an alternative at this point.

The notion of practice without instruction sounds unusual to most people, and foolish to many physical educators because of the common assumption that teaching and learning are causally related. Learning does occur in the presence of instruction, but the possibility is rarely considered that it sometimes (or often) may occur despite rather than because of the instruction. Given the typically high motivational level of children engaged in learning the skills of sports and games, and given the prompt, unambiguous information feedback provided by practice on most skills, there is good reason to believe that autotuition not only is possible but that sometimes it may be a superior alternative to instruction.

Beginning with the pioneer studies of Kulcinski (1931) and Davies (1945), a line of respectable studies has shown that groups allowed to practice without instruction may do surprisingly well when acquisition of skill is the criterion. Some studies show that groups given only the benefit of orientation and demonstration do roughly as well as instructed groups (Bowers, 1966; Rivenes, 1961; Sweeney, 1966) and some suggest that such groups can have a significant advantage in learning (Berlin, 1959). It must be a shock to discover that a class exposed to 12 weeks of uninstructed "recreational" bowling shows a level of achievement not significantly different from that observed in classes receiving instruction over the same period, but it can happen (Lewis, 1966).

Most teachers would respond, as does B. Knapp (1963), that in some skills the learner encounters a point where the available feedback is neither as prompt nor as clear as further progress demands. This argument is well supported by facts revealed in several studies (B. D. Anderson, 1969; Cugini, 1959), as well as by common observation, and will be discussed in the section dealing with feedback.

A small amount of preparation apparently makes it possible for the student to accept a range of substitutes for instruction, including his own judgment (Keller, 1964), the group's judgment (Whilden, 1956; Whitaker, 1954), or even a sheet of written instructions (Jones, 1965; Mariani, 1970).

Programmed learning. What most physical education teachers attempt to do is shape movement responses through small steps of successive approximation using the tools of correction and reinforcement. Programmed learning is an instructional agency that can perform the same function at an infinitely more systematic and individualized level. This gives an entirely new meaning to "practice without teacher instruction."

Research concerning the use of general written materials to supplement skill practice has yielded uneven results reflecting different content and patterns of use (Jarvis, 1967; Malone, 1960; Prybylowski, 1960). In contrast, the use of programmed instruction for the transmission of knowledge about skills is well supported by research (Lutz, 1967; Mariello, 1968; B. J. Neuman, 1965). This aspect of teacher behavior can be relegated confidently to auto-instruction whenever suitable materials are available.

Far more impressive and significant, however, are the studies in which practice itself is regulated through the use of programmed materials. All of the studies to this date have shown that groups using programmed practice learn as much or more than groups given traditional teacher-mediated instruction (Adler, 1967; Farrell, 1970; Hosinski, 1966; M. J. E. Johnson, 1969; B. J. Moore, 1968; Neuman & Singer, 1968; Stutters, 1969). Further, there is indication that motor ability and academic aptitude do not produce significant interactions with programmed instruction.

In confronting the usually high level of heterogeneity found in class composition, programmed learning offers the advantage of much needed individualization of learning rate. A number of studies also have underscored the fact that programming provides exceptional freedom for the instructor to move about the class giving special help where it is most needed. In this sense, programming increases rather than decreases the importance of the teacher's role as a source of instruction.

Problems do exist in devising effective learning programs for motor skills. It is difficult, for example, to provide for accurate feedback with regard to correct and incorrect responses. Comprehensive programs may prove to be uneconomical or impossible for some sport skills. Nevertheless, early indications are that programmed learning deserves further exploitation in the gymnasium and careful development and evaluation through research.

Verbal description. If the teacher decides to give direct, personal instruction, he has many alternatives. A common choice is to accompany demonstration with supplemental verbal description. There is a small but informative body of research concerning that method. So long as the ultimate test lies in the skill achieved by beginning students, the chances seem good that verbal descriptions of performance will have little if any influence on learning (Rivenes, 1961; Sampson, 1967; Schaafsma, 1968). Should the teacher's discussion impinge on practice time, it may well have a negative effect on learning (Berlin, 1959; Frey, 1947).

Principles. Another topic about which teachers often choose to talk is the structure of the task, the basic principles which explain the mechanics of performance. This has long been a popular area for professional emphasis. For half a century professors and textbook writers have urged teachers to tell children "why" rather than "just how." The underlying thesis is not that such information is interesting or inherently valuable as knowledge, but that it will facilitate the acquisition of skill.

The research literature on the use of principles in instruction has not been encouraging. So long as acquisition of skill has been the measure, it has proved difficult to devise a sound experiment showing the teaching of principles to be superior to an equivalent period of actual practice (Callaway, 1968; Cobane, 1960; Colville, 1956; Dehnert, 1962; Farley, 1967; Fath, 1968; Graves, 1963; Halverson, 1949; Kearns, 1960; Mikesell, 1962; Reed, 1968; Toth, 1969). Only M. E. Barrett (1959), Mohr and Barrett (1962), and Papcsy (1969) have found positive results.

Research on the use of principles has been beset by a host of methodological problems. Two recent studies are notable in their attempts to overcome some of these impediments. An investigation by Love (1967) found no significant effects from the use of principles. Through the use of more sophisticated experimental procedures, the study did demonstrate, however, what has long been suspected: 1) many children already know the principle; 2) some children who are not given the principle acquire it anyway; 3) some children who do know the principle do not apply it in practice; and 4) some children who are exposed to a treatment involving principles do not learn them. Papcsy (1969) set out systematically to confront many of the traditional difficulties in research on the use of principles. Careful pilot studies were used to establish criteria for learning; verbal, written and performance assessments were made for knowledge of the principle at various stages of the experiment; and placebo treatments were devised for the "no principle" groups. The results showed clear superiority in learning and retention for subjects who understood specific mechanical principles. Further, Papcsy found the greatest advantage was displayed by the subjects of lower intelligence.

A final fact for teachers to consider with regard to verbal behavior is provided by the literature bearing upon the relationship between performance and conceptual knowledge (principles, rules and strategies). The verdict from research is unanimous. There is little or no relation between abstract knowledge and the ability to perform motor skills (Annarino, 1962; Casady, 1964; Cobane, 1960; Girardin & Hanson, 1967; B. J. Neuman, 1965; O'Neil, 1967; Welser, 1958; Yingling, 1968).

For the purpose of facilitating the acquisition of skill, there appears to be some definite limit (in the early stages of learning, at least) to the usefulness of understanding principles, just as there is a limit to the learner's curiosity for knowing "why" rather than "just how."

Attention and distraction. Another broad alternative for further teacher talk is the identification of critical elements in performance, the regulatory stimuli. In simple terms, the teacher may point out what the learner must pay attention to while attempting the skill. The elements emphasized by the teacher may be external, as in watching the ball, or internal, as in attending to specific parts of the skill being performed.

A recent review by Whiting (1970) underscored the surprising absence of research concerning the teacher's role in directing the learner's attention to specific cues in the environment. A small group of studies, however, have been concerned with the learner's attention to his own performance. Some authorities (Lawther, 1968; Lawther & Cooper, 1952, 1955) have suggested that the learner's attention should be diffused over the general framework of the task and under no condition directed to the details of his intended movements. Using a variety of instructional strategies to direct attention in the early stages of learning, Foster (1963), Sampson (1967) and Thomas (1961) have given at least limited support to the diffusion hypothesis. A recent study by Neil (1968), however, shows no difference between specific and general sets.

Two laboratory studies have employed techniques designed to distract the learner's attention from the details of his performance. Berlin (1947) found significant learning advantages associated with the distraction strategy. Cugini (1959) failed to confirm the distraction hypothesis but did provide clear evidence of differential subject response to the treatment. Some students appear to be assisted by the distractions that serve as impediments to others. At the very least, research suggests that the teacher might well delay emphasis on the details of performance until the learner is past the early trials.

In the same vein, it has been suggested that some learners may profit by directing their attention to kinesthetic feedback (Phillips & Summers, 1954). Methods of teaching that put deliberate emphasis on awareness of the sensations generated by movement are no longer popular. One legacy of the kinesthetic hypothesis, however, is a group of studies in which vision, the dominant form of feedback in early learning, was restricted by blinders (Bush, 1961) or eliminated through the use of blindfolds (Gellinger, 1965; Gephart, 1954; Griffith, 1931; Rollo, 1959) or practice in darkened rooms (Frazier, 1952; Walters, 1952). In these investigations subjects were forced to utilize sources of feedback other than the details normally provided by vision. The

frequency of success through such strategies has been high enough to invite further and more sophisticated research.

Stage III: Provide Directions For Performance

The task having been set, the learner must formulate his plan for action—his "vision" of the desired response. The teacher may, and often in fact does, now proceed to specify particular movements as part of the performance. In some cases, details of execution are provided in the discussion of principles or in an analysis of critical stimuli. At this stage, however, the intent of the teacher is to tell the learner "how to do it" as distinct from discussing the nature of the skill.

The motor plan. Of particular relevance here are results from several experiments involving mental practice. It appears possible that there is a distinct advantage for learning when the subject is free to form his own image of the task with a minimum of verbal or visual imposition from the teacher (Jones, 1965; Surburg, 1968). The failure of Stebbins (1968) to find significant advantage for practice when the subject's motor imagery is directed by an external model thus gains new significance.

It is a fact of more than academic significance that the central emphasis of traditional instruction is exerted at this stage in learning—"telling how to do it"—where the only suggestion from research is that having performed the prior functions of identifying the goal and clarifying the general framework, the teacher may serve best by allowing the student to decide exactly how to do it *for himself.*

Sets for speed and accuracy. As the learner envisions the form of his initial attempt, the teacher may impose a final set for action, the instruction being for either speed or accuracy or both in combination. Nowhere in the literature is research in more perfect and happy agreement. Instructions for either speed or accuracy produce the intended effects. Tasks that demand equal emphasis profit from equal emphasis throughout the learning process. Whenever the teacher feels that a choice must be made between the alternatives, it would be well to remember that gains made under a speed set transfer well to multiple sets, while gains made under an accuracy set do not. Certainly the natural proclivity of the teacher to stress accuracy in early trials is contraindicated (Jordan, 1966; McCoy, 1968; Solley, 1952; Woods, 1967).

Stage IV: Support and Observe Practice

The learner now emits his first response. The teacher may function to support the effort by providing supplemental cues, direct physical assistance or special safety precautions. A second function for the teacher is to observe the response and gather information that may be used as augmentation to feedback.

There has been little investigation of practice-concurrent teacher behaviors. For example, the entire matter of the teacher's role as a systematic observer is unexplored. Only Girardin and Hanson (1967) have interested themselves in the teacher's capacity to observe and analyze motor performance. At best, the relationship between what the teacher does during practice and how well the student learns is poorly understood.

Stage V: Directing and Analyzing Feedback

The response ends and within a few seconds residual traces of the act are welded into the stuff of learning or are lost in the confusion of sensate experience. The teacher's behavior here may be critical in directing attention to particular traces in the pool of feedback and in aiding the consolidation of temporary traces into more permanent storage. Unfortunately, however, only the teacher's role as a potential source of additional feedback has been subject to intensive investigation.

The motivational and corrective influences of feedback ensure that it will be the strongest and most important variable controlling motor performance (Bilodeau & Bilodeau, 1961). With the stimulus provided by Ammons's (1956) brilliant review and theoretical formulation, physical educators have focused on the role of feedback in learning the skills of sports and games. It is now well demonstrated that manipulation of feedback produces a direct influence on the course of learning (Malina, 1969), and that external sources of feedback such as vision are the more powerful inputs during the early stages of acquisition (Morford, 1966; Robb, 1968).

Common observation reveals that the learner often encounters a limit to his capacity to discriminate available feedback (Fitts, 1964). Given this fact, it is inevitable that physical education research should turn its attention to methods for augmenting feedback. The advent of video tape and Land photographic techniques have turned interest into a stampede.

Open and closed skills. To understand research on feedback two concepts are critical. The first, the distinction between open and closed types of skill, was introduced by Poulton (1957). In open skills the performer responds to the spatial and temporal demands that occur in the environment, such as movement of the ball or another player. The performer is, in a sense, externally driven. Skill in the open type of performance lies in the appropriateness of the response when taken in the context of a dynamic situation rather than in the particular nature of the movements produced.

In the closed type of skill the performer attempts only to reproduce a particular movement pattern. The environment is a constant factor, as in diving, weight lifting or high jumping. The performer is, in a sense, internally driven, and skill lies in the exact details of execution.

Knowledge of performance and knowledge of results. The second important concept distinguishes two broad categories of feedback: knowledge about performance and knowledge about results (Annett & Kay, 1957). The contrast here is between information concerning how the learner moved and information concerning the consequences of that movement.

Often the teacher is in a position to augment information available to the learner for either performance or results. Logic dictates that the most powerful influence should be exerted by augmented knowledge of performance in closed types of skill when form is used as the criterion measure. In contrast, augmented knowledge of results should have a maximum impact on the learning of open types of skill when accuracy is the criterion measure.

A common presumption is that form and accuracy are directly related, thus making it possible, for example, to interchange criterion measures in the paradigm above. Unfortunately, little is known about the interaction of form and accuracy. Empirically there is good reason to believe that they are unrelated in many open skills. The unfortunate consequences of presuming that supplements to the learner's knowledge of performance should result in improved accuracy are scattered throughout the physical education literature on feedback.

The uses of augmented feedback. It is impossible here to review the large number of studies involving augmented feedback. A morass of contradiction has resulted from inadequacies in method of investigation and improper use of theory to generate design. Most of the nonsignificant results occur when: 1) augmented knowledge of performance is used with open skills; 2) augmented knowledge of results is used with closed skills; 3) augmented knowledge of performance is used with closed skills but its impact measured by an accuracy criterion; 4) results are attenuated by extensive delays in providing feedback to the subjects; 5) results are attenuated by allowing the feedback treatment to reduce total practice time for the experimental group; 6) obfuscation occurs through the contamination of feedback treatments with teacher correction and analysis; 7) there is inadequate provision for the control of subject attention during feedback treatment; and 8) augmented knowledge of results is used when high levels of knowledge of results already are available to the subject.

Persistent positive results have been obtained with combinations of augmented knowledge of performance involving closed skills and form criteria (Del Rey, 1970; Hawthorne, 1964; Plese, 1968). Even when learning is measured by criteria other than form, research involving such closed skills as shot putting (Hampton, 1970) and golf (Thompson, 1969) may yield significant results favoring the use of augmented knowledge of performance.

Beginning with the influential work of Howell (1956), attempts have been made to increase the potency of augmented feedback by providing a concurrent model of ideal performance. In theory, by comparing real with ideal the learner should more quickly come to approximate the desired form. Available evidence indicates, however, that the use of models either alone, as supplements to practice, or in combination with augmented knowledge of performance, provides little advantage in the early stages of learning (B. D. Anderson, 1969; DeBacy, 1970; Gray & Brumbach, 1967; Paulat, 1970).

Given the present state of knowledge, it is possible to speculate that in the case of closed skills the teacher's provisions for augmented knowledge of performance may be rewarded by improved learning. Likewise, both augmented knowledge of results and assistance in untangling the meaning of available information should assist students engaged in learning open skills. The latter should be particularly true in competitive team games and high speed dual contests where the consequences of a given action are obscured so easily for the participant.

Stage VI: Guide Adjustment of Performance

Having assimilated available feedback, the learner must now decide upon the nature of his next response. Once again a paradox is revealed. At this juncture traditional methods place great emphasis on a critical form of intervention—correction—yet there is no equivalent body of research dealing with this subject.

Given feedback concerning whether or not he executed the intended movements and whether or not he achieved the intended result, the learner is confronted with complex decisions concerning alternative possibilities for the form of the next trial. It seems certain that at this point the teacher's guidance is an important factor in the learning process. Teachers do in fact provide such guidance as well as they can but completely without the help of knowledge derived from research.

Learning strategies. Research tells us little about the learner's own attempts to cope with the problems presented in a series of practice trials. Intensive examination of the learning strategies used by a single subject engaged in a series of practice trials is one potential source of insight into modes of self-correction (Lindquist, 1969). It does appear that the learner's method of attack in mastering a skill is specific to particular tasks (Rice, 1968).

Incentive motivation. As the learner moves through a series of trials with all of the attendant difficulties, teachers often attempt to provide incentive motivation through verbal reinforcement. Results of research vary according to subject age,

treatment schedule and criterion measure. Generally, studies reveal a situation familiar in classroom research—anything is better than being completely ignored. As might be expected, mixtures of praise and criticism are the most powerful incentive treatment (Hanley, 1968; Sparks, 1963; Wilkinson, 1965).

Finally, several studies have shown that the teacher's inclination to give positive verbal reinforcement on a relatively fixed schedule can have negative consequences. This seems to be particularly true for highly skilled subjects engaged in complex motor tasks (Cummiskey, 1963). The reinforcing effects of clear information feedback may produce better results than encouragement from the teacher (Caskey, 1968). Apparently simple extrinsic rewards used in operant conditioning procedures can have a significant advantage over traditional forms of verbal reinforcement (Rushall, 1969).

Mental practice. Another form of intervention open to the teacher is to substitute a formal version of "stop and think about what you're doing" for some portion of active practice. It is well established that mental practice can facilitate the acquisition of motor skills, although how it does so is not at all clear. Fortunately this is an area in which a recent and competent critical review exists (A. Richardson, 1967a, 1967b). Attention here will thus be limited to developments since 1965.

Problems of experimental bias effects (Gephart & Antonoplos, 1969) and inadequate control over treatment procedures have plagued research on mental practice. However, results continue to associate various conditions of imaginary performance with significantly improved learning. Truly negative results are rare enough to attract considerable attention (Conly, 1969; B. J. Wills, 1967).

The most common patterns of results show that 1) mixtures of mental practice and physical practice are superior to mental practice alone (E. L. Arnold, 1965; Corbin,

1966; Stebbins, 1968), and 2) mixtures of mental practice and physical practice are as effective though never more effective than an equivalent period of physical practice (Bissonnette, 1965; Doyle, 1968; J. D. Johnson, 1965; Swartzendruber, 1965; K. C. Wills, 1965; Witker, 1968).

Work by Corbin (1966, 1967) suggests that some previous experience with the task improves the utility of mental practice. This is reinforced by Schramm's (1967) finding of greater electromyographic activity during mental practice preceded by physical trials.

In contrast, other studies have demonstrated that in early learning there is a significant advantage in mental practice unaccompanied by overt trials (Phipps & Morehouse, 1969) or by demonstration (Jones, 1965). An experiment by Surburg (1968) further underscores the possibility that the learner may be better off without an explicit model to imitate in his imagined practice. Once again it appears possible that in the early stages of learning it may be wise for the teacher to impose less detail and to allow the student to work things out for himself, in mental as in physical practice.

Two additional points may be of import for teaching physical education: the placement of mental practice just prior to a practice trial and the use of overt verbalization. Nearly all skilled athletes report some form of covert rehearsal just prior to performance. The use of more formal and systematic pre-trial review has not attracted interest among teachers, although at least one study yielded affirmative results (Waterland, 1961). The use of overt verbalization, either in rehearsal or concurrent with practice, also appears to deserve investigation (Brassie, 1969).

Stage VII: Pace and Sequence Practice

Distribution of practice. However the learner may grapple with revising his motor plan, the next trial must come, and with it the next decision for the teacher. Decisions pertaining to the interval between trials and the length of the practice session are the practical version of the experimental variable called distribution of practice. As was the case with part and whole practice, research on distribution of practice in motor skills has been burdened by the impediment of inadequate and inconsistent definitions. When the rules of the game are sufficiently loose, one man's massed practice can serve as another man's distributed practice to the detriment of both logic and knowledge.

It is interesting to note that it is often the studies of distribution conducted under field conditions that produce nonsignificance (Brassie, 1965; Dixon, 1968; Howard, 1960; Kahn, 1959; Robertson, 1969). More discrete skills, practiced under tighter controls and more refined definitions of "distribution," persistently favor distributed over massed practice (Baines, 1962; Knapp & Dixon, 1950; Knapp, Dixon, & Lazier, 1958; Massey, 1959; Singer, 1965). The few field studies that have found significant results also tend to favor distributed regimens (Johansson, 1965; Niemeyer, 1958; Schroeder, 1968).

Another persistent finding favors relative massing early in learning followed by subsequent distribution of practice (Harmon & Miller, 1950; Harmon & Oxendine, 1961; Oxendine, 1960; Wagner, 1962). Recent work by Fox (1968) indicates the possibility that such progressive distribution schedules may interact with the type of skill involved to produce a variety of results.

Postactive Teaching Events

The events that occur after the lesson have drawn little scientific consideration. Nothing is known about the roles of review and evaluation in the modification of teaching method. Nothing is known about the strategies used by the physical educator in confronting the fact that some children fail to learn. Nothing is known about the assimilation of critical feedback and its impact on teacher behavior.

There is some evidence that teachers have great difficulty in consistently evaluating the effectiveness of their own lessons (Heitmann, 1966). It may be that in practice teachers give little credence to the importance of teaching method. Despite the fact that supervisors and administrators rate the ability to provide instruction as the most significant element in teacher success (Coombe, 1952; Roundy, 1967; Shuford, 1963; Yinger, 1962), physical education teachers themselves may not. C. A. Moore (1965) demonstrated that some teachers believe the greatest impediments to teaching success lie in areas external to their competence as instructors. Matters such as facilities, class size and student attitudes are commonly cited factors influencing teaching success when the respondent is himself a teacher. More directly, there was no evidence from the teachers in Moore's sample to indicate that they considered successful teaching to be under their control. This is reflected in studies that show physical education teachers to be far more concerned with problems of class discipline, equipment supply and grading than with teaching methods per se (Brown, 1940; Roundy, 1967).

Two kinds of research do offer some important promise in the area of feedback for teachers: critical incident technique and descriptive analytic methods.

Critical incident research. Studies involving the analysis of critical teaching incidents in physical education are not common. Logistical problems in gathering data, the scarcity of sponsors with adequate technical background, the need for a high order of sophistication in handling the subjective steps in categorizing data, and widespread misunderstanding of the technique as a "mere survey of opinion" all conspire to discourage critical incident research. The handful of studies that have been done in physical education (Arnsdorff, 1960; Barclay, 1969; Benton, 1960; Blank, 1958; Crawford, 1961; Garis, 1967; Pestolesi, 1969)

offer a mirror for the teacher in an area of teaching where feedback often is ambiguous or all too easy to ignore—the effectiveness of specific instructional tactics in helping students to learn. A point repeatedly underscored by critical incident studies is the sometimes devastating difference between the student's assessment of what matters most in learning motor skills and what the teacher (or the theoretician) considers to be important.

Descriptive analytic research.[4] Descriptive research in physical education is in its infancy. The pioneering efforts of W. G. Anderson (1971) in encouraging descriptive research in the gymnasium will only begin to bear fruit over the next decade.

Three studies have devised and tested methods for the systematic recording of events in motor skill learning. Each of the three studies utilizes combinations and modifications of techniques developed for use in the classroom. Dougherty (1970) has made successful revision and application of Interaction Analysis in an evaluation of Mosston's (1966) command, task and individual styles of teaching. In an exceptional study of teacher behavior in movement education, K. R. Barrett (1969) developed a category-type system for descriptive research. The first successful use of The Observation Schedule and Record (Medley & Mitzel, 1963) in physical education was made by Bookhout (1967) in an examination of social-emotional climate in physical education classes.

MOVEMENT EDUCATION, EXPLORATION AND PROBLEM SOLVING

It is impossible to undertake here a discussion of these conceptually elaborate

---

[4] Readers who are unfamiliar with this technique may wish to refer to Medley & Mitzel (1963) as well as to Chapter 5 of this volume.

schemes for instruction and curriculum in physical education. Readers who may be interested in background material should see J. C. Smith (1966) for problem solving, K. R. Barrett (1964) for exploration, K. R. Barrett (1969) for movement education, or Locke (1969) for a review of all three methods.

The pattern of results from experimental evaluations of movement education programs is quite consistent. At the elementary-school level, with standardized motor skill tests as the most common criterion, the results are generally nonsignificant (Howard, 1960; Kenzie, 1963; Scott, 1967; Shochat, 1966) or uneven (Gravlee, 1965). At high-school and college levels the results are the same: nonsignificant (Berendsen, 1967; Coleman, 1967; LaPlante, 1965; Ritchie, 1966; Russell, 1967; M. E. Smith, 1966; Ziegler, 1965) or uneven (Garland, 1960).

A host of methodological difficulties attend these studies. The central problem appears to lie with the selection of criterion measures. Four studies that utilized dependent variables consisting of psychosocial factors rather than skill achievement produced significant results favoring the programs. Ball (1968), Deelman (1968) and Vitalone (1964) found a significant and positive impact on behavior traits of elementary-school children. A study of college women by D. A. Richardson (1967) suggests that movement education might narrow the difference between self and ideal-self concepts.

METHODS BASED ON THEORY

The general absence of theory as a tool in designing research on teaching physical education is a problem that lies at the heart of the entire enterprise. With appropriate deference to Travers's (1966) dour account of the important distinctions between engaging rhetoric and scientific theory, the fact remains that only through the creation and testing of theory can sense and order be brought to research on teaching physical education. The development and use of even modest micro-theory would exert a powerful influence toward selecting significant questions, making sense out of tangled results and welding facts into higher order generalizations.

The strongest argument for the use of theory is seen in the few studies that have attempted to employ a theoretical base in the design of teaching method—and the consequent design of an investigation. Even though some are overly ambitious in terms of experimental resources and the present understanding of teaching and learning, they make exciting reading, evoking hosts of new possibilities for physical education. Sheehan (1966) has devised a successful teaching model drawn from theory in social psychology. Marburger (1966), Mudra (1966) and Hussey (1967) have examined methods based on Gestalt Theory. Blatnick (1969) and Rushall & Pettinger (1969) have employed operant conditioning in behavior-modification techniques suggested by reinforcement theory.

Mosston's spectrum of teaching styles (1966), the most significant advance in the theory of physical education pedagogy in recent history, has yet to undergo full experimental testing. Early results have confirmed the power of the theory to predict both teaching events (Dougherty, 1970) and consequences in student learning (Mariani, 1970).

SUMMARY AND CONCLUSION

Research does not tell the physical education teacher how to teach motor skills—no matter how attentively he listens. The research we now have contains: 1) some suggestions that the teacher may pursue with confidence, as in the cases of demonstrations through film and augmented knowledge of performance for closed skills; 2) some suggestions for experimental alterations to traditional practice, as in the cases of programmed learning and the use of distraction; 3) some strong suggestions about what is not effective, as in the case of progressive part practice, extended verbal analysis for beginners, and task simplification; 4) some information, as yet so incomplete and subject to qualification that it can mean little more than "it all depends," as in the case of mental practice and distribution of practice; 5) some great voids where the teacher's operations must now depend on tradition, chance, intuition and native wit, as in the cases of teacher observation and the guidance of student response to feedback; and 6) some suggestions for the improvement of pedagogy through the development and use of empirically based models, as in the few studies that utilize the power of learning theory or the control over treatment provided by systematic description of teaching.

Perhaps it is too optimistic, but we have gained the strong impression that physical education research is now at the threshold on which the wider world of educational research was poised a decade ago with the advent of the first *Handbook of Research on Teaching*. In our judgment it will not be technical, financial or purely intellectual resources that determine whether physical education now falters or moves forward. Progress will hinge first on how thoroughly research is understood as a tool, then on how strongly physical educators are committed to the task of finding their own way through the mazes of teaching and learning, and finally on whether physical educators care enough about providing the best possible teaching—for all children.

REFERENCES

Adler, J. D. *The use of programed lessons in teaching a complex perceptual-motor skill.* (Doctoral dissertation, University of Oregon) Eugene, Ore.: Microcard Publications, 1967. No. PSY 341.

Ammons, R. B. Effects of knowledge of performance: A survey and tentative theoretical formulation. *Journal of General Psychology,* 1956, 54, 279–299.

Anderson, B. D. *The influence of model performances and feedback on the learning of a complex motor skill.* (Doctoral dissertation, University of Minnesota) Ann Arbor, Mich.: University Microfilms, 1969. No. 69-6789.

Anderson, T. A study of the use of visual aids in basket shooting. *Research Quarterly,* 1942, 13, 532–537.

Anderson, W. G. Descriptive-analytic research on teaching. *Quest,* 1971, 15, 1–8.

Annarino, A. A. *A comparison of the relative effectiveness of two methods of soccer instruction.* (Doctoral dissertation, Indiana University) Ann Arbor, Mich.: University Microfilms, 1962. No. 62-2292.

Annett, J., & Kay, H. Knowledge of results and "skilled performance." *Occupational Psychology,* 1957, 31, 69–79.

Arnold, D. E. The effect of four part-whole ratio in learning soccer. (Master's thesis, University of Illinois) *University of Illinois Abstracts of Graduate Theses in Physical Education, Recreation and Health Education.* Urbana, Ill.: University of Illinois, College of Physical Education, 1960. (abstract)

Arnold, E. L. *The relationship between physical and mental practice and initial ability in learning a simple motor skill.* (Doctoral dissertation, Indiana University) Ann Arbor, Mich.: University Microfilms, 1965. No. 65-11,106.

Arnsdorff, D. *Perceptions of critical behaviors for women physical education teachers at the secondary school level.* (Doctoral dissertation, Stanford University) Ann Arbor, Mich.: University Microfilms, 1960. No. 59-6866.

Baines, W. E. *An experimental study to determine the effect of various practice period patterns on the achievement levels of two motor skills.* (Doctoral dissertation, Boston University) Ann Arbor, Mich.: University Microfilms, 1962. No. 62-4803.

Baker, G. M., Annis, E., & Bontz, J. Supervision of physical education in the elementary school. *Research Quarterly,* 1952, 23, 379–390.

Baker, G. M., Annis, E., & Bontz, J. Supervision of physical education in the elementary school. *Research Quarterly,* 1954, 25, 379–386.

Ball, B. A. *The primary school child's self-concept: The influence of the child-centered program of physical education.* (Doctoral dissertation, Ohio State University) Ann Arbor, Mich.: University Microfilms, 1968. No. 68-2947.

Barclay, R. E. *Critical incidents in the instruction of beginning swimming.* (Doctoral dissertation, Columbia University) Ann Arbor, Mich.: University Microfilms, 1969. No. 69-10,534.

Barrett, K. R. An analysis of exploration as a method for teaching movement. Unpublished master's thesis, University of Wisconsin, 1964.

Barrett, K. R. A procedure for systematically describing teacher-student behavior in primary physical education lessons implementing the concept of movement education. Unpublished doctoral dissertation, University of Wisconsin, 1969.

Barrett, M. E. A study of the effects of a knowledge of mechanical principles on learning to perform specific swimming strokes. Unpublished master's thesis, University of Maryland, 1959.

Beal, J. C. *The effect of two different practice distributions on acquisition of skill in the tennis forehand and backhand drives by college women.* (Master's thesis, University of Oregon) Eugene, Ore.: Microcard Publications, 1965. No. PSY 214.

Behrman, R. M. Personality differences between nonswimmers and swimmers. *Research Quarterly,* 1967, 38, 163–171.

Beisman, G. L. Effect of rhythmic accompaniment upon learning of fundamental motor skills. *Research Quarterly,* 1967, 38, 172–176.

Benton, C. W. *Critical requirements for effective teaching in professional preparation courses in physical education at California state colleges.* (Doctoral dissertation, University of Southern California) Ann Arbor, Mich.: University Microfilms, 1960. No. 60-2066.

Berendsen, C. A. *The relative effectiveness of descriptive teaching and structured problem solving in learning basic tennis skills.* (Master's thesis, University of Washington) Eugene, Ore.: Microcard Publications, 1967. No. PSY 294.

Berlin, P. An experimental study of the learning of a fine motor skill under conditions of diffused attention. Unpublished master's thesis, Pennsylvania State University, 1947.

Berlin, P. *Effects of varied teaching emphases*

during early learning on acquisition of selected motor skills.* (Doctoral dissertation, Pennsylvania State University) Ann Arbor, Mich.: University Microfilms, 1959. No. 59-5095.

Bevacque, Y. A. A comparison of the influence of two club progressions on the ability of beginning golf students to hit a golf ball. Unpublished master's thesis, University of Colorado, 1964.

Bilodeau, E. A., & Bilodeau, I. McD. Motor skills learning. *Annual Review of Psychology,* 1961, 12, 243–280.

Bissonnette, R. The relative effects of mental practice and physical practice in improving speed of forward skating. Unpublished master's thesis, Springfield College, 1965.

Blank, L. B. Critical incidents in the behavior of secondary school physical education instructors. *Research Quarterly,* 1958, 29, 1–6.

Blatnik, A. M. *An experimental study in selected required college physical education courses to determine the effect of a teaching model structured to produce positive attitudes toward participation in lifetime sports and conditioning activities for physiological and psychological well-being throughout life.* (Doctoral dissertation, West Virginia University) Ann Arbor, Mich.: University Microfilms, 1969. No. 69-6700.

Bookhout, E. C. Teaching behavior in relation to the social-emotional climate of physical education classes. *Research Quarterly,* 1967, 38, 336–347.

Bowers, I. W. The effectiveness of instruction and the use of music as an aid in teaching rope jumping skills to first grade children. Unpublished master's thesis, University of Iowa, 1966.

Bracken, D. The values of college coeducational badminton. Unpublished master's thesis, Springfield College, 1964.

Brassie, P. S. Effectiveness of intermittent and consecutive methods of practicing free throws. Unpublished master's thesis, State University of Iowa, 1965.

Brassie, P. S. *Acquisition and retention of a motor skill as a function of overt self-verbalization and physical or mental practice.* (Doctoral dissertation, University of Iowa) Ann Arbor, Mich.: University Microfilms, 1969. No. 69-8710.

Breeding, B. A. A study of the relative effectiveness of two methods of spacing archery practice. Unpublished master's thesis, University of Colorado, 1958.

Brightwell, D. S. Effect of coeducational and segregated classes on tennis achievement. *Research Quarterly,* 1969, 40, 262–265.

Briwa, H. H. *A study of the comparative effectiveness of five-foot skis and skis of regular length in teaching beginning skiers.* (Doctoral dissertation, Ohio State University) Ann Arbor, Mich.: University Microfilms, 1967. No. 67-2421.

Broomell, E. W. *The relative effectiveness of two methods of teaching the American crawl stroke to beginning swimmers.* (Master's thesis, University of Washington) Eugene, Ore.: Microcard Publications, 1967. No. PSY 296.

Brown, M. C. Learning problems in student teaching. *Research Quarterly,* 1940, 11(4), 25–32.

Bruce, P. J. *The effects of conscious relaxation and a flotation device on learning beginning swimming skills.* (Doctoral dissertation, Indiana University) Ann Arbor, Mich.: University Microfilms, 1961. No. 61-5207.

Buck, M. C. *The effects of two practice techniques on selected swimming strokes.* (Doctoral dissertation, University of Iowa) Ann Arbor, Mich.: University Microfilms, 1967. No. 67-9046.

Burks, A. W. *Gains in social adjustment of coeducational classes and segregated classes in physical education.* (Doctoral dissertation, University of Arkansas) Ann Arbor, Mich.: University Microfilms, 1966. No. 66-7031.

Bush, J. J. *The effect on early motor learning of forcing hypothetically correct visual behavior on the learner.* (Master's thesis, Pennsylvania State University) Eugene, Ore.: Microcard Publications, 1961. No. PSY 147.

Callaway, C. R. *The effect of five different approaches in teaching the overhand throw for accuracy to junior high school girls.* (Master's thesis, University of North Carolina at Greensboro) Eugene, Ore.: Microcard Publications, 1968. No. PE 1056.

Casady, D. R. Relationship between written test scores and performance skill in sports. *Proceedings of the National College Physical Education Association for Men* (67th Annual Meeting) Washington, D.C.: American Association of Health, Physical Education & Recreation, 1964. Pp. 43–46.

Caskey, S. R. Effects of motivation on standing broad jump performance of children. *Research Quarterly,* 1968, 39, 54–59.

Chui, E. F. A study of golf-o-tron utilization as a teaching aid in relation to improvement and transfer. *Research Quarterly,* 1965, 36, 147–152.

Church, K. R. *The effect of different teaching methods and spot of aim techniques on bowling achievement of college men.* (Doctoral dissertation, Indiana University) Ann Arbor, Mich.: University Microfilms, 1963. No. 63-5783.

Cione, J. S. The effect of a modified basketball size on the performance of selected basketball skills by senior high school girls and college women. (Master's thesis, University of Illinois) *University of Illinois Abstracts of Graduate Theses in Physical Education, Recreation and Health Education.* Urbana, Ill.: University of Illinois, College of Physical Education, 1962. (abstract)

Clawson, A. L. The effect of three types of competitive motivating conditions upon scores of archery students. Unpublished doctoral dissertation, Texas Woman's University, 1965.

Clayton, R. D. *The efficacy of the land-drill, implicit rehearsal and water-practice methods in teaching the breast stroke and crawl stroke to college men.* (Doctoral dissertation, University of Oregon) Eugene, Ore.: Microcard Publications, 1963. No. PSY 164.

Cobane, E. *A comparison of two methods of teaching selected motor skills.* (Doctoral dissertation, Syracuse University) Ann Arbor, Mich.: University Microfilms, 1960. No. 59-6299.

Coleman, D. M. The effect of a unit of movement education upon the level of achievement in the specialized skill of bowling. Unpublished doctoral dissertation, University of Texas, 1967.

Colville, F. M. *The learning of motor skills as influenced by knowledge of general principles of mechanics.* (Doctoral dissertation, University of Southern California) Eugene, Ore.: Microcard Publications, 1956. No. PSY 80.

Conly, A. G. *A comparative study of the effects of pre-test and mental practice on the ability of athletes and non-athletes to perform a post-test of a motor skill.* (Doctoral dissertation, University of New Mexico) Ann

Arbor, Mich.: University Microfilms, 1969. No. 69-9239.

Coombe, E. M. *Functions and competencies of physical education teachers.* (Doctoral dissertation, Stanford University) Eugene, Ore.: Microcard Publications, 1952. No. PE 156.

Cooper, T. L. Effects of initial practice distance on the transfer of skill and ultimate success in archery. Unpublished master's thesis, Pennsylvania State University, 1968.

Corbin, C. B. *The effects of mental practice on the development of a specific motor skill.* (Doctoral dissertation, University of New Mexico) Ann Arbor, Mich.: University Microfilms, 1966. No. 66-3092.

Corbin, C. B. Effects of mental practice on skill development after controlled practice. *Research Quarterly,* 1967, 38, 534–538.

Cotten, D. J., & Nixon, J. A comparison of two methods of teaching the tennis serve. *Research Quarterly,* 1968, 39, 929–931.

Cratty, B. J. *Movement behavior and motor learning.* (2nd ed.) Philadelphia: Lea & Febiger, 1967.

Crawford, M. *Critical incidents of instructional methods in physical education in southern secondary schools.* (Doctoral dissertation, University of Texas) Ann Arbor, Mich.: University Microfilms, 1961. No. 60-6642.

Cronan, J. C. A comparison of two methods of teaching and scheduling beginning bowling. Unpublished master's thesis, Louisiana State University, 1968.

Cross, T. J. A comparison of the whole method, the minor game method, and the whole part method of teaching basketball to ninth-grade boys. *Research Quarterly,* 1937, 8(4), 49–54.

Cugini, E. D. *The effect on gross motor skill attainment of varying the degree of attention focus during the learning process.* (Master's thesis, Pennsylvania State University) Eugene, Ore.: Microcard Publications, 1959. No. PSY 239.

Cummiskey, J. K. *The effects of motivation and verbal reinforcement upon performance of complex perceptual-motor tasks.* (Doctoral dissertation, Stanford University) Ann Arbor, Mich.: University Microfilms, 1963. No. 63-4591.

Dailey, L., Wessel, J. A., & Nelson, R. C. Effectiveness of a bowling aid to university bowling instruction. *Research Quarterly,* 1963, 34, 136–143.

Daugert, P. J. *The relationships of anxiety and the need for achievement to the learning of swimming.* (Doctoral dissertation, University of Michigan) Ann Arbor, Mich.: University Microfilms, 1967. No. 67-8236.

Davies, D. R. The effect of tuition upon the process of learning a complex motor skill. *The Journal of Educational Psychology,* 1945, 36, 352–365.

Dawson, W. P. *The relation of personal data to teaching competence of male physical education majors.* (Doctoral dissertation, University of Utah) Ann Arbor, Mich.: University Microfilms, 1969. No. 69-4593.

DeBacy, D. Effect of viewing video tapes of a sport skill performed by self and others on self-assessment. *Research Quarterly,* 1970, 41, 27–31.

Deelman, M. J. *An investigation into the effects of two different programs of physical education on certain aspects of behavior of first grade children.* (Master's thesis, University of Wisconsin) Eugene, Ore.: Microcard Publications, 1968. No. PSY 319.

Dehnert, A. E. A comparison of the effects of two methods of instruction upon free throw shooting ability. Unpublished master's thesis, University of Wisconsin, 1962.

Del Rey, P. The effects of video-taped feedback and environmental certainty on form, accuracy and latency during skill acquisition. Unpublished doctoral dissertation, Teachers College, Columbia University, 1970.

Deutsch, H. The effect of two selected distributions of practice on the acquisition of skill in basketball. (Master's thesis, University of Illinois) *University of Illinois Abstracts of Graduate Theses in Physical Education, Recreation and Health Education.* Urbana, Ill.: University of Illinois, College of Physical Education, 1960. (abstract)

Dillon, E. K. A study of the use of music as an aid in teaching swimming. *Research Quarterly,* 1952, 23, 1–8.

Dixon, C. J. Massed and distributed practice in beginning gymnastics for college women. Unpublished master's thesis, North Texas State University, 1968.

Dougherty, N. J. A comparison of the effects of command, task, and individual program styles of teaching in the development of physical fitness and motor skills. Unpublished doctoral dissertation, Temple University, 1970.

Douglas, J. G. The value and limitations of loop movies in the teaching of wrestling at the University of Massachusetts. Unpublished master's thesis, Springfield College, 1963.

Doyle, J. F. The effects of two types of practice on motor learning at two skill levels. Unpublished master's thesis, Pennsylvania State University, 1968.

Dressen, C. J. The value of a loop film in teaching the crawl stroke. Unpublished master's thesis, University of Colorado, 1961.

Drury, F. A. *An evaluation of visual aids in the teaching of tumbling.* (Doctoral dissertation, State University of Iowa) Ann Arbor, Mich.: University Microfilms, 1959. No. 59-3792.

Dudley, H. A comparison of two methods of motivation on the learning of motor skills. Unpublished master's thesis, University of Iowa, 1966.

Evaul, T. W., Jr. *The effect of all male, all female, and coeducational classes on skill development in badminton.* (Doctoral dissertation, Indiana University) Ann Arbor, Mich.: University Microfilms, 1961. No. 61-6575.

Farley, W. E. *The effects of instruction and use of a mechanical device based upon a scientific principle as applied to basketball shooting.* (Doctoral dissertation, Colorado State College) Ann Arbor, Mich.: University Microfilms, 1967. No. 67-13,674.

Farrell, J. E. Programed vs. teacher-directed instruction in beginning tennis for women. *Research Quarterly,* 1970, 41, 51–58.

Fath, J. A. A study of the effects of two different methods of teaching gymnastics. Unpublished master's thesis, North Carolina College at Durham, 1968.

Feely, M. J. Ability grouping. *Journal of Health, Physical Education and Recreation,* 1961, 32(8), 18, 66–67.

Fitts, P. M. Perceptual-motor skill learning. In A. W. Melton (Ed.), *Categories of human learning.* New York: Academic Press, 1964. Pp. 243–285.

Fleishman, E. A. A relationship between incentive motivation and ability level in psychomotor performance. *Journal of Experimental Psychology,* 1958, 56, 78–81.

Ford, C. *A comparison of the relative effectiveness between two methods of teaching the whipkick to college women enrolled in beginning swimming classes.* (Master's thesis, Woman's College, University of North Car-

olina) Eugene, Ore.: Microcard Publications, 1958. No. PSY 93.

Foster, M. V. *The development of a method of swimming instruction based on efficiency of propulsion including a comparative study of fear reduction.* (Master's thesis, University of Wisconsin) Eugene, Ore.: Microcard Publications, 1963. No. PSY 199.

Fox, E. R. *The effects of progressively changing duration of practice periods on the learning of two gross motor skills.* (Doctoral dissertation, Temple University) Ann Arbor, Mich.: University Microfilms, 1968. No. 68-14,133.

Frazier, V. The effects of visual limitations on the rate of learning of the tennis serve. Unpublished master's thesis, Pennsylvania State College, 1952.

Frey, B. G. *A study of teaching procedures in selected physical education activities for college women of low motor ability.* (Doctoral dissertation, State University of Iowa) Eugene, Ore.: Microcard Publications, 1947. No. PE 68.

Friedrichsen, F. W. *A study of the effectiveness of loop films as instructional aids in teaching gymnastic stunts.* (Master's thesis, State University of Iowa) Eugene, Ore.: Microcard Publications, 1956. No. PSY 49.

Garcia, F. J. An investigation of the utilization of independent study time in the physical education program of selected high schools utilizing flexible scheduling. Unpublished master's thesis, Sacramento State College, 1965.

Garland, I. L. Effectiveness of problem solving method in learning swimming. Unpublished master's thesis, University of California, Los Angeles, 1960.

Garis, R. A. *Critical incidents in the instruction of gymnastic activities for girls.* (Doctoral dissertation, Columbia University) Ann Arbor, Mich.: University Microfilms, 1967. No. 67-2797.

Gellinger, T. J. The effect of blindfold and instructed practice on pitching control. (Master's thesis, University of Illinois) *University of Illinois Abstracts of Graduate Theses in Physical Education, Recreation and Health Education.* Urbana, Ill.: University of Illinois, College of Physical Education, 1965. (abstract)

Gensemer, R. E. *The effectiveness of the golf-lite as a practice device on learning to drive a golf ball straight.* (Doctoral dissertation, Ohio State University) Ann Arbor, Mich.: University Microfilms, 1969. No. 69-11,638.

Gentile, A. M. The nature of motor skill and skill acquisition: A working model. Paper delivered at the Post-Doctoral Invitational Seminar in Motor Learning, Columbia University, Teachers College, New York, June 1970.

Gephart, G. C. The relative effect of blindfold, sighted and no practice on free throw accuracy. (Master's thesis, University of Illinois) *University of Illinois Abstracts of Graduate Theses in Physical Education, Recreation and Health Education.* Urbana, Ill.: University of Illinois, College of Physical Education, 1954. (abstract)

Gephart, W. J., & Antonoplos, D. P. The effects of expectancy and other research-biasing factors. *Phi Delta Kappan,* 1969, 50, 579–583.

Girardin, Y., & Hanson, D. Relationship between ability to perform tumbling skills and ability to diagnose performance errors. *Research Quarterly,* 1967, 38, 556–561.

Girouard, J. E. The effect of practice position on accuracy in goal shooting in basketball. Unpublished master's thesis, Springfield College, 1967.

Goldman, H. *The effect of variations of methods of shooting and of distance on the achievement in archery for male college beginners.* (Doctoral dissertation, Indiana University) Ann Arbor, Mich.: University Microfilms, 1963. No. 63-3573.

Graves, O. C. *The effects of initial testing and knowledge of mechanical principles upon the performance of a motor skill.* (Doctoral dissertation, Colorado State College) Ann Arbor, Mich.: University Microfilms, 1963. No. 63-1108.

Gravett, B. L. *A comparison of the effects of four selected programs of physical education with regard to physical fitness and attitude toward physical education.* (Doctoral dissertation, North Texas State University) Ann Arbor, Mich.: University Microfilms, 1969. No. 69-13,217.

Gravlee, G. *A comparison of the effectiveness of two methods of teaching a four-week unit on selected motor skills to first grade children.* (Master's thesis, University of North Carolina at Greensboro) Eugene, Ore.: Microcard Publications, 1965. No. PSY 284.

Gray, C. A., & Brumbach, W. B. Effect of day-light projection of film loops on learning badminton. *Research Quarterly,* 1967, 38, 562–569.

Griffith, C. R. An experiment on learning to drive a golf ball. *The Athletic Journal,* 1931, 11(10), 11–13.

Hallstrom, T. L. *An exploratory study of the effect of special teacher, combination special-classroom teacher, and classroom teacher instruction upon certain aspects of physical fitness and motor skill development.* (Doctoral dissertation, Colorado State College) Ann Arbor, Mich.: University Microfilms, 1966. No. 65-14,812.

Halverson, L. E. *A comparison of three methods of teaching motor skills.* (Master's thesis, University of Wisconsin) Eugene, Ore.: Microcard Publications, 1949. No. PSY 126.

Hampton, J. E. The effects of manipulating two types of feedback, knowledge of performance and knowledge of results, in learning a complex motor skill. Unpublished doctoral dissertation, Columbia University Teachers College, 1970.

Hanley, T. F. The effect of two motivational techniques on the performance of a gross motor skill by female subjects. Unpublished master's thesis, Springfield College, 1968.

Harmon, J. M., & Miller, A. G. Time patterns in motor learning. *Research Quarterly,* 1950, 21, 182–187.

Harmon, J. M., & Oxendine, J. B. Effect of different lengths of practice periods on the learning of a motor skill. *Research Quarterly,* 1961, 32, 34–41.

Hawthorne, M. E. A study of the effectiveness of the slow-motion picture in teaching golf. Unpublished master's thesis, Louisiana State University, 1964.

Heitmann, H. M. *Teacher effectiveness in relationship to motor effectiveness and temperament grouping.* (Doctoral dissertation, Springfield College) Eugene, Ore.: Microcard Publications, 1966. No. PSY 267.

Hesse, B. P. *A study of the effects of self competition and team competition upon motor performance of sixth, eighth, and ninth grade girls.* (Master's thesis, University of Wisconsin) Eugene, Ore.: Microcard Publications, 1955. No. PSY 51.

Hicks, D. E. *The relationship of learning efficiency to class size in badminton, beginning swimming, and volleyball classes.* (Doctoral dissertation, University of Tennessee) Ann

Arbor, Mich.: University Microfilms, 1965. No. 65-1434.

Hill, F. E. The comparison of verbal and visual instruction with trial and error method in learning certain skills of balance. Unpublished master's thesis, Pennsylvania State University, 1958.

Hodapp, M. L. *Effects of variations in progression and use of a flotation device on teaching beginning swimming.* (Doctoral dissertation, Indiana University) Ann Arbor, Mich.: University Microfilms, 1967. No. 66-15,269.

Hoffman, S. J. Traditional methodology: Prospects for change. *Quest,* 1971, 15, 51–57.

Hosinski, J. P. *An investigation of the use of computer assisted instruction in teaching the shuffle offense in basketball.* (Doctoral dissertation, Florida State University) Ann Arbor, Mich.: University Microfilms, 1966. No. 66-2094.

Howard, S. *A comparison of two methods of teaching ball handling skills to third grade students.* (Doctoral dissertation, University of Iowa) Ann Arbor, Mich.: University Microfilms, 1960. No. 60-4377.

Howell, M. L. Use of force-time graphs for performance analysis in facilitating motor learning. *Research Quarterly,* 1956, 27, 12–22.

Hult, J. S. *Relationships among selected levels of attainment of physical education teachers and students.* (Doctoral dissertation, University of Southern California) Ann Arbor, Mich.: University Microfilms, 1968. No. 67-17,677.

Hussey, R. W. *A comparison of two methods of teaching a specific motor activity to youngsters in relation to intelligence and motor ability measures.* (Doctoral dissertation, Colorado State College) Ann Arbor, Mich.: University Microfilms, 1967. No. 67-6076.

Irwin, J. The effect of selected audio-visual aids on teaching beginning tennis skill and knowledge to college women. Unpublished doctoral dissertation, Indiana University, 1958.

Jable, J. T. The relative effects of training with basketballs of varying weights upon free throw shooting accuracy. Unpublished master's thesis, Pennsylvania State University, 1965.

Jarvis, L. Effects of self-instructive materials in learning selected motor skills. *Research Quarterly,* 1967, 38, 623–629.

Jesseph, M. J. *The effect of motor ability classification in physical education on achievement and attitude of high school girls.* (Master's thesis, University of California, Berkeley) Eugene, Ore.: Microcard Publications, 1956. No. PE 377.

Johansson, G. E. The relative effectiveness of massed and distributed practice in the learning of beginning folk dance. Unpublished master's thesis, University of California, Santa Barbara, 1965.

Johnson, J. D. *The effect of selected conceptualizing techniques upon the early learning of a gross movement.* (Doctoral dissertation, University of Southern California) Ann Arbor, Mich.: University Microfilms, 1965. No. 65-6910.

Johnson, L. C. *The effects of a five-day-a-week versus a two- and three-day-a-week physical education program on physical fitness, activity skill, subcutaneous adipose tissue, and physical growth.* (Doctoral dissertation, University of Utah) Ann Arbor, Mich.: University Microfilms, 1968. No. 67-17,384.

Johnson, M. J. E. *The effectiveness of programmed instruction in teaching basic gymnastics.* (Doctoral dissertation, University of Michigan) Ann Arbor, Mich.: University Microfilms, 1969. No. 69-12,145.

Johnson, M. L. Gestalten practice pattern selection: Methodology and task structure. *Quest,* 1970, 14, 56–63.

Jones, J. G. Motor learning without demonstration of physical practice, under two conditions of mental practice. *Research Quarterly,* 1965, 36, 270–276.

Jordan, W. L. *The results of speed and accuracy emphases on the learning of a selected motor skill in golf.* (Doctoral dissertation, University of Minnesota) Ann Arbor, Mich.: University Microfilms, 1966. No. 66-1666.

Kahn, J. S. A comparison of various patterns of practice in bowling achievement. Unpublished master's thesis, University of California, Los Angeles, 1959.

Karbe, W. W. *The relationship of general anxiety and specific anxiety concerning the learning of swimming.* (Doctoral dissertation, New York University) Ann Arbor, Mich.: University Microfilms, 1968. No. 66-9459.

Karsner, M. G. *An evaluation of motion-pic-*

ture loops in group instruction in badminton. (Doctoral dissertation, State University of Iowa) Ann Arbor, Mich.: University Microfilms, 1953. No. 6522.

Kaye, R. A. The use of a waist-type flotation device as an adjunct in teaching beginning swimming skills. *Research Quarterly,* 1965, 36, 277–281.

Kearns, N. J. A study of an analytical and kinesiological approach to teaching bowling. Unpublished master's thesis, University of North Carolina, Woman's College, 1960.

Keller, R. J. *A comparison of two methods of teaching physical education to secondary school boys.* (Doctoral dissertation, University of Illinois) Ann Arbor, Mich.: University Microfilms, 1964. No. 64-2911.

Kenzie, L. P. A comparison of the effectiveness of two methods of instruction on the performance of first grade children in selected motor activities. Unpublished master's thesis, University of Wisconsin, 1963.

Keough, B. J. *The effects of a daily and two day per week physical education program upon motor fitness of children.* (Doctoral dissertation, University of Iowa) Ann Arbor, Mich.: University Microfilms, 1963. No. 63-935.

Keth, E. K. *An experimental study of the relative merits of initial training clubs used for group golf instruction.* (Doctoral dissertation, University of Missouri) Ann Arbor, Mich.: University Microfilms, 1968. No. 68-3621.

King, R. M. The effect of increasing the weight of the racket on the tennis ability of beginners. (Master's thesis, University of Illinois) *University of Illinois Abstracts of Graduate Theses in Physical Education, Recreation and Health Education.* Urbana, Ill.: University of Illinois, College of Physical Education, 1959. (abstract)

Kite, J. C. *The effects of variations in target size and two methods of practice on the development of accuracy in a motor skill.* (Doctoral dissertation, Louisiana State University) Ann Arbor, Mich.: University Microfilms, 1965. No. 65-3382.

Knapp, B. *Skill in sport.* London: Routledge & Kegan Paul, 1963.

Knapp, C. G., & Dixon, W. R. Learning to juggle: I. A study to determine the effect of two different distributions of practice on

learning efficiency. *Research Quarterly,* 1950, 21, 331–336.

Knapp, C. G., & Dixon, W. R. Learning to juggle: II. A study of whole and part methods. *Research Quarterly,* 1952, 23, 398–401.

Knapp, C. G., Dixon, W. R., & Lazier, M. Learning to juggle: III. A study of performance by two different age groups. *Research Quarterly,* 1958, 29, 32–36.

Knuttgen, H. G. *The effects of varying tennis racket dimensions on stroke performance.* (Doctoral dissertation, Ohio State University) Ann Arbor, Mich.: University Microfilms, 1959. No. 59-5910.

Kulcinski, L. Comparative effectiveness of formal, informal and combination methods of instructing university freshmen in fundamental muscular skills. *Research Quarterly,* 1931, 2(2), 18–26.

Kurth, S. J. The acquisition of shooting skill in basketball using balls of different weight. Unpublished master's thesis, Washington State University, 1966.

Ladner, M. J. *A comparison of bowling achievement in coeducational and non-coeducational college classes.* (Doctoral dissertation, University of Tennessee) Ann Arbor, Mich.: University Microfilms, 1969. No. 69-1248.

La Plante, M. *A study of the problem solving method of teaching bowling.* (Master's thesis, University of North Carolina at Greensboro) Eugene, Ore.: Microcard Publications, 1965. No. PSY 287.

Lawther, J. D. *The learning of physical skills.* Englewood Cliffs, N.J.: Prentice-Hall, 1968.

Lawther, J. D., & Cooper, J. M. Methods and principles of teaching physical education (Report of the Curriculum Research Committee: Sub-Committee IV). *Proceedings of the National College Physical Education Association for Men* (55th Annual Meeting), Washington, D.C.: American Association of Health, Physical Education & Recreation, 1952, 127–131.

Lawther, J. D., & Cooper, J. M. Methods and principles of teaching physical education (Report of the Curriculum Research Committee: Sub-Committee IV). *Proceedings of the National College Physical Education Association for Men* (58th Annual Meeting). Washington, D.C.: American Association of Health, Physical Education & Recreation, 1955. Pp. 25–29.

Lerch, H. A. *An analysis of the personal constructs of beginning swimmers using the repertory grid.* (Doctoral dissertation, Ohio State University) Ann Arbor, Mich.: University Microfilms, 1969. No. 69-4927.

Leslie, J. J. The effect of music on the development of speed in running. Unpublished master's thesis, University of Washington, 1967.

Lewellen, J. O. *A comparative study of two methods of teaching beginning swimming.* (Doctoral dissertation, Stanford University) Eugene, Ore.: Microcard Publications, 1951. No. PE 89.

Lewis, A. E. *A comparison of three methods of teaching bowling to college women.* (Doctoral dissertation, George Peabody College for Teachers) Ann Arbor, Mich.: University Microfilms, 1966. No. 66-4428.

Lindeburg, F. A., & Hewitt, J. E. Effect of an oversized basketball on shooting ability and ball handling. *Research Quarterly,* 1965, 36, 164–167.

Lindquist, E. L. *An information processing approach to the study of a complex motor skill.* (Doctoral dissertation, University of Michigan) Ann Arbor, Mich.: University Microfilms, 1969. No. 69-12,170.

Locke, L. F. Movement education: A description and critique. In R. C. Brown, Jr., & B. J. Cratty (Eds.), *New perspectives of man in action.* Englewood Cliffs, N.J.: Prentice-Hall, 1969.

Lockhart, A., & Mott, J. A. An experiment in homogeneous grouping and its effect on achievement in sports fundamentals. *Research Quarterly,* 1951, 22, 58–62.

Loftin, A. *Effects of variations in method and club progression on golf achievement of college women.* (Doctoral dissertation, Indiana University) Eugene, Ore.: Microcard Publications, 1957. No. PSY 115.

Love, A. M. The relationship of knowledge of a principle and knowledge of a movement cue to the acquisition of a gross motor skill by upper elementary school students. Unpublished doctoral dissertation, Teachers College, Columbia University, 1967.

Lutz, L. L. *The influence of programed instruction on the achievement of specific knowledge in a selected physical education activity.* (Doctoral dissertation, Colorado State College) Ann Arbor, Mich.: University Microfilms, 1967. No. 67-1122.

Malina, R. M. Effects of varied information

feedback practice conditions on throwing speed and accuracy. *Research Quarterly,* 1969, 40, 134–145.

Malone, J. P. The effectiveness of the use of a textbook in the teaching of physical education. Unpublished master's thesis, University of Iowa, 1960.

Marburger, D. R. *The effect of two methods of teaching beginning tennis on the development of tennis skill and knowledge, and on attitude toward physical education.* (Doctoral dissertation, Colorado State College) Ann Arbor, Mich.: University Microfilms, 1966. No. 65-14,823.

Mariani, T. A comparison of the effectiveness of the command method and the task method of teaching the forehand and backhand tennis strokes. *Research Quarterly,* 1970, 41, 171–174.

Mariello, F. A comparison of the effect of ordered and scrambled sequential techniques in programed tennis rules for beginning classes. Unpublished master's thesis, University of North Carolina at Greensboro, 1968.

Massey, M. D. The significance of interpolated time intervals on motor learning. *Research Quarterly,* 1959, 30, 189–201.

Matthews, J. *Effects of limited numbers of class periods upon performance in track and field events.* (Doctoral dissertation, University of Missouri) Eugene, Ore.: Microcard Publications, 1946. No. PE 109.

Maxey, J. A. *An investigation of the effects of class attendance on learning efficiency in selected physical education activity classes.* (Doctoral dissertation, University of Tennessee) Ann Arbor, Mich.: University Microfilms, 1967. No. 67-7485.

Maynard, J. T. A comparison of two methods of teaching fencing. Unpublished master's thesis, Smith College, 1962.

McCann, J. V. *A study of the factors affecting the values of coeducational physical education and corecreation in the public high schools of California.* (Doctoral dissertation, University of Southern California) Eugene, Ore.: Microcard Publications, 1954. No. PE 183.

McCatty, C. A. M. Effects of the use of a flotation device in teaching nonswimmers. *Research Quarterly,* 1968, 39, 621–626.

McCoy, K. W. *The effect of varied speed and accuracy training upon a gross motor skill.*

(Doctoral dissertation, University of Wyoming) Eugene, Ore.: Microcard Publications, 1968. No. PSY 326.

McGuigan, F. J., & MacCaslin, E. F. Whole and part methods in learning a perceptual motor skill. *American Journal of Psychology*, 1955, 68, 658–661.

McLellan, M. I. A study of the use of music as an aid in teaching the beginning badminton serve. Unpublished master's thesis, University of Iowa, 1964.

Medley, D. M., & Mitzel, H. E. Measuring classroom behavior by systematic observation. In N. L. Gage (Ed.), *Handbook of research on teaching.* Chicago: Rand McNally, 1963. Pp. 247–328.

Mikesell, D. J. *The effect of mechanical principle centered instruction on the acquisition of badminton skills.* (Master's thesis, University of Illinois) Eugene, Ore.: Microcard Publications, 1962. No. PSY 220.

Miller, S. E. *The relative effectiveness of high school badminton instruction when given in two short units and one continuous unit involving the same total time.* (Master's thesis, University of Washington) Eugene, Ore.: Microcard Publications, 1964. No. PSY 222.

Minaert, W. A. An analysis of the value of dry-skiing in learning selected skiing skills. *Research Quarterly*, 1950, 21, 47–52.

Mitchellette, J. L. The effect of instruction on the improvement made by upper elementary school children in selected tennis skills. Unpublished master's thesis, University of Colorado, 1960.

Mohr, D. R., & Barrett, M. E. Effect of knowledge of mechanical principles in learning to perform intermediate swimming skills. *Research Quarterly*, 1962, 33, 574–580.

Moncrieff, J., Morford, W. R., & Howell, M. L. Acquisition of elementary swimming skills. *Research Quarterly*, 1962, 33, 405–409.

Montgomery, M. A. P. *The effects of various rates of presentation in combination with massed and spaced, concurrent and nonconcurrent practice modes on film-mediated perceptual motor performance.* (Doctoral dissertation, Indiana University) Ann Arbor, Mich.: University Microfilms, 1968. No. 68-7221.

Moore, B. J. The construction and evaluation of a written self-instruction program for teaching the jump shot. Unpublished master's thesis, Southern Illinois University, 1968.

Moore, C. A. *A study of some psychological characteristics of selected male physical education teachers as revealed through problem analysis.* (Doctoral dissertation, University of Alabama) Ann Arbor, Mich.: University Microfilms, 1965. No. 64-12,787.

Moore, S. L. *The effect of homogeneous and heterogeneous grouping on motor skill learning of college women in elementary archery.* (Master's thesis, University of Oregon) Eugene, Ore.: Microcard Publications, 1966. No. PSY 270.

Morford, W. R. The value of supplementary visual information during practice on dynamic kinesthetic learning. *Research Quarterly*, 1966, 37, 393–405.

Morris, N. J. Effectiveness of distribution of practice on underhand volleyball serve skill achievement and retention. Unpublished master's thesis, Washington State University, 1967.

Mosston, M. *Teaching physical education.* Columbus, Ohio: Charles E. Merrill, 1966.

Mudra, D. E. *A critical analysis of football coaching practices in light of a selected group of learning principles.* (Doctoral dissertation, Colorado State College) Ann Arbor, Mich.: University Microfilms, 1966. No. 65-14,827.

Neil, G. I. *Attention and individual difference factors relative to efficiency in motor skill learning.* (Doctoral dissertation, University of Oregon) Eugene, Ore.: Microcard Publications, 1968. No. PE 974.

Nelson, D. O. Studies of transfer of learning in gross motor skills. *Research Quarterly*, 1957, 28, 364–373.

Nelson, D. O. Effect of slow-motion loopfilms on the learning of golf. *Research Quarterly*, 1958, 29, 37–45.

Neuman, B. J. The effect of a self-instructional program of badminton rules on the knowledge and playing ability of beginning badminton players. Unpublished master's thesis, University of North Carolina, 1965.

Neuman, M. C., & Singer, R. N. A comparison of traditional versus programed methods of learning tennis. *Research Quarterly*, 1968, 39, 1044–1048.

Niemeyer, R. Part versus whole methods and massed versus distributed practice in the learning of selected large muscle activities.

College Physical Education Association Proceedings, 1958, 61, 122–125.

O'Donnell, D. J. *The relative effectiveness of three methods of teaching beginning tennis to college women.* (Doctoral dissertation, Indiana University) Eugene, Ore.: Microcard Publications, 1956. No. PSY 57.

O'Neil, S. M. *The relationship between knowledge of performance and level of performance.* (Doctoral dissertation, University of Michigan) Ann Arbor, Mich.: University Microfilms, 1967. No. 66-14,565.

Overstreet, E. L. *Effect of class size on achievement in physical education.* (Doctoral dissertation, West Virginia University) Ann Arbor, Mich.: University Microfilms, 1968. No. 68-2688.

Oxendine, J. B. *A study of the significance of varying lengths of practice periods on the growth of a motor skill.* (Doctoral dissertation, Boston University) Ann Arbor, Mich.: University Microfilms, 1960. No. 59-6756.

Oxendine, J. B. *Psychology of motor learning.* New York: Appleton-Century-Crofts, 1968.

Papcsy, F. E. *The effect of understanding a specific mechanical principle upon learning a physical education skill.* (Doctoral dissertation, New York University) Ann Arbor, Mich.: University Microfilms, 1969. No. 69-21,196.

Paulat, J. G. *The effects of augmented videotaped information feedback and loop film models upon learning of a complex motor skill.* (Doctoral dissertation, Stanford University) Ann Arbor, Mich.: University Microfilms, 1970. No. 70-1638.

Pestolesi, R. A. *Critical teaching behaviors effecting attitude development in physical education.* (Doctoral dissertation, University of Southern California) Ann Arbor, Mich.: University Microfilms, 1969. No. 69-640.

Phillips, D. J. *The effectiveness of land-drill exercise in teaching young male children to swim.* (Master's thesis, University of Oregon) Eugene, Ore.: Microcard Publications, 1964. No. PE 634.

Phillips, J. L. Homogeneous grouping and its effects upon learning in volleyball. (Master's thesis, University of Illinois) *University of Illinois Abstracts of Graduate Theses in Physical Education, Recreation and Health Education.* Urbana, Ill.: University of Illinois, College of Physical Education, 1961. (abstract)

Phillips, M., & Summers, D. Relation of kinesthetic perception to motor learning. *Research Quarterly,* 1954, 25, 456–469.

Phillips, M. B. An investigation of elementary classroom teachers' perceptions of their role in teaching physical education. Unpublished master's thesis, Kent State University, 1967.

Phipps, S. J., & Morehouse, C. A. Effects of mental practice on the acquisition of motor skills of varied difficulty. *Research Quarterly,* 1969, 40, 773–778.

Plese, E. R. *A comparison of videotape replay with a traditional approach in the teaching of selected gymnastic skills.* (Doctoral dissertation, Ohio State University) Ann Arbor, Mich.: University Microfilms, 1968. No. 68-3054.

Poulton, E. C. On prediction in skilled movements. *Psychological Bulletin,* 1957, 54, 467–478.

Prybylowski, F. A comparative study of the relative effectiveness of two methods of teaching beginning swimming to children. Unpublished doctoral dissertation, Colorado State College, 1960.

Purdy, B. J., & Stallard, M. L. Effect of two learning methods and two grips on the acquisition of power and accuracy in the golf swing of college women. *Research Quarterly,* 1967, 38, 480–484.

Pye, J. G. *An experimental study of the value of a device designed to restrict elbow-bend in teaching tennis forehand and backhand drives.* (Doctoral dissertation, University of Houston) Ann Arbor, Mich.: University Microfilms, 1964. No. 64-1524.

Read, D. A. *The influence of competitive and non-competitive programs of physical education on body-image and self-concept.* (Doctoral dissertation, Boston University) Ann Arbor, Mich.: University Microfilms, 1969. No. 69-7871.

Reams, D., & Bleier, T. J. Developing team teaching for ability grouping. *Journal of Health, Physical Education, Recreation,* 1968, 39(7), 50–54.

Reed, J. A. An investigation of the effectiveness of prerequisite instruction of the principle of rebound upon the learning of rebound tasks. Unpublished master's thesis, Central Missouri State College, 1968.

Rhodes, W. M. *Effects of variations and number of strokes taught and equipment used on tennis achievement by college women.* (Doctoral dissertation, Indiana University) Ann Arbor, Mich.: University Microfilms, 1963. No. 63-883.

Ribet, E. C. *Teaching techniques used with fear cases in beginning swimming for college women.* (Master's thesis, University of North Carolina, Woman's College) Eugene, Ore.: Microcard Publications, 1957. No. PSY 87.

Riccio, M. A. The relative effectiveness of two types of practice devices on learning the forehand and backhand tennis drives. Unpublished master's thesis, University of Colorado, 1963.

Rice, S. D. *The rate of learning motor tasks.* (Doctoral dissertation, University of Southern California) Ann Arbor, Mich.: University Microfilms, 1968. No. 68-7197.

Richardson, A. Mental practice: A review and discussion. Part I. *Research Quarterly,* 1967, 38, 95–107. (a)

Richardson, A. Mental practice: A review and discussion. Part II. *Research Quarterly,* 1967, 38, 263–273. (b)

Richardson, D. A. *A study of the effect of different approaches to gymnastics on movement concept.* (Master's thesis, University of North Carolina at Greensboro) Eugene, Ore.: Microcard Publications, 1967. No. PE 1099.

Ritchie, G. H. A comparison of the problem-solving and explanation-demonstration method of teaching basketball. Unpublished master's thesis, University of Massachusetts, 1966.

Rivenes, R. S. *Effect on motor skill acquisition and retention of teaching by demonstration with and without accompanying verbal explanation.* (Master's thesis, Pennsylvania State University) Eugene, Ore.: Microcard Publications, 1961. No. PSY 154.

Rizk, A. *The relative effectiveness of a multimedia approach in learning soccer.* (Doctoral dissertation, University of Kentucky) Ann Arbor, Mich.: University Microfilms, 1969. No. 69-15,513.

Robb, M. Feedback and skill learning. *Research Quarterly,* 1968, 39, 175–184.

Robb, M., & Teeple, J. Videotape and skill learning: An exploratory study. *Educational Technology,* 1969, 9(11), 79–82.

Roberts, J. A. *The effect of a particular practice technique on the golf swing.* (Doctoral dissertation, State University of Iowa) Ann Arbor, Mich.: University Microfilms, 1967. No. 67-2669.

Robertson, J. A. *The effect of varying short time intervals between repetitions upon performance of a motor skill.* (Doctoral dissertation, University of Southern California) Ann Arbor, Mich.: University Microfilms, 1969. No. 69-19395.

Rohland, D. A. *Instructional aids in tennis.* (Master's thesis, University of California, Los Angeles) Eugene, Ore.: Microcard Publications, 1960. No. PSY 177.

Rollo, E. T. A comparison of two methods of teaching selected golf strokes. Unpublished master's thesis, State University of Iowa, 1959.

Ross, B. M. A study of the performance of boys and girls taught by the specialist and the nonspecialist. *Research Quarterly,* 1960, 31, 199–207.

Roundy, E. S. Problems of and competencies needed by men physical education teachers at the secondary level. *Research Quarterly,* 1967, 38, 274–282.

Rushall, B. S. Some applications of psychology to swimming. Paper presented at the 6th Annual Swimming Clinic of the Illinois Swimming Association, Champaign, May 1969.

Rushall, B. S., & Pettinger, J. An evaluation of the effect of various reinforcers used as motivators in swimming. *Research Quarterly,* 1969, 40, 540–545.

Russell, M. R. E. *Effectiveness of problem solving methods in learning a gross motor skill.* (Master's thesis, University of Washington) Eugene, Ore.: Microcard Publications, 1967. No. PSY 332.

Ryan, E. D. Relationship between motor performance and arousal. *Research Quarterly,* 1962, 33, 279–287.

Ryan, M. P. The effect of a head stabilizer on the learning of the golf swing. Unpublished master's thesis, University of North Carolina at Greensboro, 1964.

Sampson, O. *Attention and learning selected motor skills.* (Doctoral dissertation, University of Oregon) Eugene, Ore.: Microcard Publications, 1967. No. PSY 312.

Scannell, R. J. Transfer of accuracy training when difficulty is controlled by varying target size. *Research Quarterly,* 1968, 39, 341–350.

Schaafsma, F. M. *The effects of varied amounts of verbal instruction upon the learning and performance of selected tasks of accuracy.* (Doctoral dissertation, University of Southern California) Ann Arbor, Mich.: University Microfilms, 1968. No. 68-10,252.

Schmuck, D. A. *Modular scheduling as related to the physical education program in secondary schools.* (Master's thesis, South Dakota State University) Eugene, Ore.: Microcard Publications, 1968. No. PE 1103.

Schramm, V. An investigation of electromyographic responses obtained during mental practice. Unpublished master's thesis, University of Wisconsin, 1967.

Schroeder, P. J. Massed vs. distributed practice on the learning of the forehand and backhand tennis drives. Unpublished master's thesis, University of North Carolina at Greensboro, 1968.

Scott, M. G. Learning rate of beginning swimmers. *Research Quarterly,* 1954, 25, 91–99.

Scott, R. S. A comparison of teaching two methods of physical education with grade one pupils. *Research Quarterly,* 1967, 38, 151–154.

Sexton, C. N. *The development of physical fitness and sports skills of high school boys in two-year and four-year physical education programs.* (Doctoral dissertation, Indiana University) Ann Arbor, Mich.: University Microfilms, 1965. No. 65-8822.

Shay, C. T. The progressive-part vs. the whole method of learning motor skills. *Research Quarterly,* 1934, 5(4), 62–67.

Sheehan, T. J. *The construction and testing of a teaching model for attitude formation and change through physical education.* (Doctoral dissertation, Ohio State University) Ann Arbor, Mich.: University Microfilms, 1966. No. 65-13,280.

Shochat, E. A study of the effect on balance of two methods of teaching physical education. Unpublished master's thesis, Springfield College, 1966.

Shuford, D. F. *An analysis and comparison of critical qualities of the beginning physical education teacher.* (Doctoral dissertation, University of Tennessee) Ann Arbor, Mich.: University Microfilms, 1963. No. 63-1627.

Singer, R. N. Massed and distributed practice effects on the acquisition and retention of a novel basketball skill. *Research Quarterly,* 1965, 36, 68–77.

Singer, R. N. Transfer effects and ultimate success in archery due to degree of difficulty of the initial learning. *Research Quarterly,* 1966, 37, 532–539.

Singer, R. N. *Motor learning and human performance.* New York: Macmillan, 1968. (a)

Singer, R. N. Sequential skill learning and retention effects in volleyball. *Research Quarterly,* 1968, 39, 185–194. (b)

Slayden, J. An experimental investigation of the effect of sequence of distances on the achievement in archery for female college beginners. Unpublished master's thesis, University of Colorado, 1966.

Sloan, M. R., & Liba, M. R. Effects of participation in physical education on achievement in selected characteristics. *Research Quarterly,* 1966, 37, 411–423.

Smith, J. C. Problem solving in movement education. Unpublished master's thesis, Wayne State University, 1966.

Smith, M. E. A study of two methods of teaching beginning bowling to college women. Unpublished master's thesis, University of North Carolina, 1966.

Smith, N. D. *A study of first year classroom teachers' competence in teaching elementary physical education.* (Doctoral dissertation, New York University) Ann Arbor, Mich.: University Microfilms, 1964. No. 64-8481.

Snyder, G. P. The effects of flexible scheduling on the achievement of male eleventh grade physical education students. Unpublished master's thesis, University of Washington, 1966.

Solley, W. H. The effects of verbal instruction of speed and accuracy upon the learning of a motor skill. *Research Quarterly,* 1952, 23, 231–240.

Solley, W. H., & Borders, S. Relative effects of two methods of teaching the forehand drive in tennis. *Research Quarterly,* 1965, 36, 120–122.

Sparks, J. L. *Relative effects of various verbal incentives on learning and retention of a gross motor skill.* (Master's thesis, Pennsylvania State University) Eugene, Ore.: Microcard Publications, 1963. No. PSY 178.

Spencer, P. M. Movies, slides and demonstrations as aids in teaching. Unpublished master's thesis, University of Colorado, 1961.

Sprague, H. A comparison of two different sequences in teaching the ground strokes in tennis to tenth grade girls. Unpublished master's thesis, California State College at Long Beach, 1968.

Stebbins, R. J. A comparison of the effects of physical and mental practice in learning a motor skill. *Research Quarterly,* 1968, 39, 714–720.

Stevenson, C. L. The effect of practice task difficulty on transfer of training in target archery. Unpublished master's thesis, Pennsylvania State University, 1967.

Stitt, E. A. *The effect of competitive type incentives upon the learning and performance of gross motor tasks.* (Doctoral dissertation, University of Southern California) Ann Arbor, Mich.: University Microfilms, 1964. No. 64-13,509.

Stull, G. A. *Relationship of quantity and distribution of practice to endurance, speed, and skill development by beginners.* (Doctoral dissertation, Pennsylvania State University) Ann Arbor, Mich.: University Microfilms, 1962. No. 61-6817.

Stutters, D. G. *The influence of programed instruction on the achievement of specific skills in a selected physical education activity.* (Doctoral dissertation, University of Colorado) Ann Arbor, Mich.: University Microfilms, 1969. No. 69-4321.

Surburg, P. R. Audio, visual, and audio-visual instruction with mental practice in developing the forehand tennis drive. *Research Quarterly,* 1968, 39, 728–734.

Swartzendruber, L. T. A comparison of physical and mental practice on the performance of basketball shooting. Unpublished master's thesis, Pennsylvania State University, 1965.

Sweeney, J. M. *The effects of instruction and practice and of practice only on the motor learning of elementary school children.* (Doctoral dissertation, Ohio State University) Ann Arbor, Mich.: University Microfilms, 1966. No. 66-1847.

Takacs, R. A comparison of the effect of two methods of practice on basketball free throw shooting. Unpublished master's thesis, Arkansas State College, 1965.

Theunissen, W. *"Part"-teaching and "whole"-teaching of beginning group-golf classes for male college students.* (Doctoral dissertation, Indiana University) Eugene, Ore.: Microcard Publications, 1955. No. PSY 39.

Thomas, P. *Economy of learning at beginning levels of gross motor performance.* (Doc-

toral dissertation, University of Southern California) Ann Arbor, Mich.: University Microfilms, 1961. No. 61-3808.

Thompson, D. H. Immediate external feedback in the learning of golf skills. *Research Quarterly,* 1969, 40, 589–594.

Toth, J. *The effect of knowledge of mechanical principles on transfer of learning selected gymnastic movements.* (Doctoral dissertation, Colorado State College) Ann Arbor, Mich.: University Microfilms, 1969. No. 69-12,506.

Trafton, D. C. The effect of grades as incentives on junior high school girls in the learning and performing of skills in a selected team sport. Unpublished master's thesis, University of Illinois, 1965.

Travers, R. M. W. Towards taking the fun out of building a theory of instruction. *Teachers College Record,* 1966, 68, 49–60.

Van Oteghen, S. L. A comparison of two methods of teaching tennis to college women. Unpublished master's thesis, University of Iowa, 1968.

Verducci, F. Effects of class size upon the learning of a motor skill. *Research Quarterly,* 1969, 40, 391–395.

Vitalone, G. E. *A study of certain behavior traits and the physical performance of a selected group of first grade children participating in a program of movement experiences.* (Doctoral dissertation, New York University) Ann Arbor, Mich.: University Microfilms, 1964. No. 64-8483.

Wagner, C. G. *The effect of different lengths of practice on learning certain basketball skills among junior high school boys.* (Doctoral dissertation, Temple University) Eugene, Ore.: Microcard Publications, 1962. No. PSY 231.

Walters, C. E. A perceptual approach to the teaching of bowling. *Perceptual and Motor Skills Research Exchange,* 1952, 4, 75–79.

Waterland, J. C. The effect of mental practice combined with kinesthetic perception when practice precedes each overt performance of a motor skill. Unpublished master's thesis, University of Wisconsin, 1961.

Watt, M. A. *Meaningfulness of audio-visual instruction at different stages of learning in bowling.* Doctoral dissertation, State University of Iowa) Ann Arbor, Mich.: University Microfilms, 1954. No. 10,253.

Welser, P. An experimental study of a whole and a whole-part method of teaching volleyball. Unpublished master's thesis, Pennsylvania State University, 1958.

Whilden, P. P. Comparison of two methods of teaching beginning basketball. *Research Quarterly*, 1956, 27, 235–242.

Whitaker, P. H. *A comparative study of teaching methods in physical education.* (Doctoral dissertation, University of Southern California) Eugene, Ore.: Microcard Publications, 1954. No. PSY 41.

Whiting, H. T. A. *Acquiring ball skill.* Philadelphia: Lea & Febiger, 1970.

Whiting, H. T. A., & Stembridge, D. E. Personality and the persistent non-swimmer. *Research Quarterly*, 1965, 36, 348–356.

Wilkinson, R. E. Effect of motivational conditions upon the muscular performance of boys of different age levels. Unpublished doctoral dissertation, Springfield College, 1965.

Wills, B. J. *Mental practice as a factor in the performance of two motor tasks.* (Doctoral dissertation, University of Wisconsin) Ann Arbor, Mich.: University Microfilms, 1967. No. 66-9988.

Wills, K. C. The effect of mental practice and physical practice on learning a motor skill. Unpublished master's thesis, Arkansas State College, 1965.

Wilson, K. S. The effects of ability grouping upon learning volleyball skills. Unpublished master's thesis, Northeast Missouri State Teachers College, 1966.

Winningham, S. N. *Effect of training with ankle weights on running skill.* (Doctoral dissertation, University of Southern California) Ann Arbor, Mich.: University Microfilms, 1966. No. 66-5498.

Winslade, D. K. The effect of 8mm. slow motion color film on the learning of specific motor skills. Unpublished master's thesis, University of British Columbia, 1963.

Witker, J. E. The relative effects of variations of combined mental and physical practice on learning a novel task. Unpublished master's thesis, Illinois State University, 1968.

Woods, J. B. The effect of varied instructional emphasis upon the development of a motor skill. *Research Quarterly*, 1967, 38, 132–142.

Workman, D. J. Comparison of performance of children taught by the physical education specialist and by the classroom teacher. *Research Quarterly*, 1968, 39, 389–394.

Worthington, R. M. *Factors affecting the delayed imitation of a demonstrated psychomotor skill.* (Doctoral dissertation, University of Minnesota) Ann Arbor, Mich.: University Microfilms, 1958. No. 58-3562.

Wright, E. J. Effects of light and heavy equipment on acquisition of sports-type skills by young children. *Research Quarterly*, 1967, 38, 705–714.

Yeatts, P. P., & Gordon, I. J. Effects of physical education taught by a specialist on physical fitness and self-image. *Research Quarterly*, 1968, 39, 766–770.

Yinger, H. L. *Evaluation of criteria for selection and the determination of success of male physical education teachers, by selected Missouri superintendents.* (Doctoral dissertation, Indiana University) Ann Arbor, Mich.: University Microfilms, 1962. No. 62-3994.

Yingling, H. E. *The effect of teaching of concepts upon attitudes and general motor performance of ninth grade girls in physical education.* (Doctoral dissertation, New York University) Ann Arbor, Mich.: University Microfilms, 1968. No. 68-6188.

Young, E. *A comparison of two methods of teaching field hockey to college women.* (Master's thesis, Arkansas State College) Eugene, Ore.: Microcard Publications, 1965. No. PSY 265.

Young, O. G. Rate of learning in relation to spacing of practice periods in archery and badminton. *Research Quarterly*, 1954, 25, 231–243.

Ziegler, Y. P. *A comparison of two methods of teaching gymnastics.* (Master's thesis, University of Wisconsin) Eugene, Ore.: Microcard Publications, 1965. No. PSY 247.

Zimmerman, H. Physical performance of children taught by special teachers and by classroom teachers. *Research Quarterly*, 1959, 30, 356–362.

CHAPTER 39 Research on Teaching Social Studies

JAMES P. SHAVER
Utah State University

A. GUY LARKINS
University of Georgia

The intent behind this chapter is *not* to provide a comprehensive review of the research in social studies education. Reviews are available elsewhere (Cox & Cousins, 1965; Dimond, 1960; Fair, 1965; Grannis, 1970; Gross & Badger, 1960; Massialas, 1969; McPhie, 1964; Metcalf, 1963; Penix, 1965; Shaver, 1962; Skretting & Sundeen, 1969), including a series of annual articles in *Social Education* (Cox, Girault, & Metcalf, 1966; Cox, Johnson, & Payette, 1968; Girault & Cox, 1967; Harrison & Solomon, 1964, 1965; Johnson, Payette, & Cox, 1969; Payette, Cox, & Johnson, 1970).

Although it would be instructive to be able to provide a summary of the major findings upon which these reviews agree, it is not possible to do so in any satisfactory way. In the first place, the reviews tend to be little more than annotated bibliographies. With few exceptions, they do not attempt to interpret findings or pull them together in general conclusions. Grannis (1970) was analytic in his review of research related to the education of social studies teachers. Metcalf (1963) did note the lack of studies based on the reflective theory of teaching. Shaver (1962) stated that the available re-

search suggested that defining one's objectives and teaching for them directly was more effective than the incidental teaching of critical thinking—a conclusion shared by Cox and Cousins (1965, p. 100)—but conclusions could not be drawn as to which method was best for that explicit teaching. Massialas (1969) provided an excellent list of conclusions in regard to political socialization, some of which are directly relevant to teaching social studies; Patrick (1969) drew implications from political socialization research for the social studies curriculum. And the annual reviews of research in *Social Education* have moved in recent years (Johnson, Payette, & Cox, 1969; Payette, Cox, & Johnson, 1970) toward the limited drawing of conclusions, but these are restricted by the focus on one year's research.

In addition, the reviews of research on teaching social studies are almost totally lacking in the critical evaluation of research design—such as Rosenshine (1970) has done in the area of teaching effectiveness—that is vital if one is to use them as the basis for drawing one's own conclusions. At least one set of reviewers (Cox, Johnson, & Payette, 1968, p. 557) has disclaimed any attempt to make such judgments; most simply do what Metcalf (1963, p. 932) has chided them for doing—they ignore the question and report brief capitulations of findings seriatim as if all were of equal validity. Some of the reviewers (Cox, Girault, & Metcalf, 1966, p. 348; Harrison & Solomon, 1964, p. 277; 1965, p. 281) claim to have been selective in terms of design, reviewing only studies meeting rigorous standards. But the criteria are not spelled out or applied explicitly to the individual studies reviewed. Finding that such "selective" reviews (e.g., Harrison & Solomon, 1965) refer to studies whose reports indicate little other than casual classroom observation to commend them as "research" does not bolster one's confidence in the character of the other studies that have passed the "rigorous" standards for inclusion in the review.

Providing another compendium of research studies hardly seems worthwhile. At the same time, the critical review of research on teaching social studies has been neglected for so many years and the accumulated number of reports is so great that it did not seem feasible to try to "catch up" in one article. Instead, we have directed our efforts toward what Payette and his associates (1970, p. 933) have also identified as a lack of continuity and a failure to attack "broad and fundamental problems" in research on teaching social studies. This chapter is an attempt to highlight some basic considerations for the graduate student or other researcher who is trying to develop viable research plans with potential for making a contribution to the knowledge about teaching social studies.

WHAT IS SOCIAL STUDIES?

Writing about research on teaching social studies is a difficult task in part because of the ambiguous nature of the field. Other curricular areas, such as mathematics or science, are more obviously tied to specific academic disciplines. Although each has its problems of defining a role vis-à-vis general education, the content, if not the methods of teaching the content, is considered to be legitimately defined by academic scholars. The "new math," for example, did not represent a break from the academicians but an attempt to bring the elementary- and secondary-school curriculum in line with the thinking of mathematicians.

No such clear mandate is apparent in the social studies. Growing out of a base of history and geography instruction in the schools in the 1800s, the rubric *social studies* came into use in the early 1900s. At the same time that the various social sciences have been competing for time in the elementary and secondary schools, social studies educators have taken on much of the school's responsibility for citizenship education. This can be seen in the statements of goals commonly made in curriculum guides. Yet much of the curriculum appears based on the predilections of academic scholars rather than on any careful consideration of the requirements of citizenship education. Of the original so-called New Social Studies Projects (see the April 1965 issue of *Social Education*), only one—the Harvard Social Studies Project—was primarily centered on citizenship education.

In looking over the writings about teaching social studies, one is struck by the lack of a body of systematic, empirically based knowledge. The research, frequently involving surveys of "expert" opinion, has not been significant in terms of affecting classroom practice, building a body of knowledge upon which decisions about classroom practice could be made, or laying a foundation for further research.

In part, the problem is due to a lack of relevant research. For example, Martorella (1971) and Price (1964, p. 19) have pointed out that despite the commitment of social studies educators to the importance of teaching concepts, there is little research on the effectiveness of specific instructional procedures for teaching concepts in social studies. To a great extent, however, the problem arises because research studies on teaching social studies—primarily the theses of graduate students because practitioners and professors of social studies education seem to have little commitment to research —tend to lack a clear conception of what is meant by "social studies education." Careful attention to defining the scope of the field rather than simply perpetuating the potpourri of practices which occur in the schools or the predilections of university scholars would help to sharpen the focus of research.

In light of the disparity of opinion within the field, this chapter does not assume any one definition (e.g., Shaver, 1967, or Wesley & Wronski, 1958, p. 3) of social studies. We are, however, assuming that social studies is not limited to social science education, that research on teaching social studies involves more than how to best teach the social science disciplines.

The social sciences are definitely a very important part of the conglomeration contemplated and taught under the social studies rubric. But the concerns of social studies educators with value inculcation and clarification, with attitudes (for example, toward minority groups), and with encouraging students to explore the meaning of the dignity of man through materials from the humanities also raise significant research questions.

Research on teaching social studies *must be based on some definition of social studies education,* hopefully taking into account the variety of concerns noted above, *if there is to be a fruitful accumulation of knowledge.* Certainly a more comprehensive scheme than any now available relating the social sciences to citizenship education is badly needed. The absence of such a well-developed rationale probably accounts in large part for the lamentable lack of research to determine whether and how social science courses contribute to the oft-stated goals of citizenship education—an area where research is badly needed so that much of the current rhetoric based on supposition can be replaced by discourse based on evidence.

Various approaches to conceptualizing social studies could be taken. Barth and Shermis (1970) have, for example, proposed that a trichotomy be used in identifying traditional approaches to social studies— citizenship transmission, social studies as social science, and social studies as reflective inquiry. Their approach forces much social studies curriculum work into uncomfortable categories. Other attempts to define social studies have focused on the assumption of citizenship education as the central goal of social studies education, relating social science knowledge, the transmission of values, and the teaching of inquiry to that goal (e.g., Hunt & Metcalf, 1968; Oliver, 1957; Oliver & Shaver, 1966; Shaver, 1967; Tom, 1970).

WHAT RESEARCH IS WORTH DOING?

Examination of the philosophical and empirical assumptions of various approaches to social studies education would, then, help to alleviate a major problem with the research on teaching social studies—the failure to deal with questions that have intellectual significance or are closely related to pressing human needs. Researchers should view their choice of research topics as an ethical matter involving important questions about the allocation of scarce resources of time, money, and energy. Choosing between trivial and significant research topics presents ethical problems which ought to be faced explicitly.

Typically, discussions of ethics in research with humans revolve around the treatment of subjects (see, e.g., *The American Psychologist,* No. 5, Vol. 22, 1967). The moral treatment of subjects is an important question, but perhaps a more obvious point than the one we want to make here—that the decision to carry out research on a particular problem is an ethical one, demanding moral justification. This is a topic which researchers are wary of raising because justifying research on moral grounds is fraught with perils, not the least of which is that the search for dependable knowledge may be subverted to the propagation of dogma or the undergirding of political "truths." There is no sense, however, in pretending that research does not have social relevance (Caldwell, 1970), although the dangers involved are clearly indicated by the reactions (see, e.g., Scriven, 1970, Whitten & Kagan, 1969) to Arthur Jensen's (1969b) research on the relationship of genetic factors to racial differences in intelligence. In one reply to his critics, however, Jensen (1969a, p. 6) has clearly indicated the importance of the moral justification of research:

If social-class intelligence differences within the Negro population have a genetic component, as in the white population, the condition I have described could create and widen the genetic intelligence difference between Negroes and whites. The social and educational implications of this trend, if it exists and persists, are enormous. The problem obviously deserves thorough investigation by social scientists and geneticists....The possible consequences of our failure seriously to study these questions may well be viewed by future generations as our society's greatest injustice to Negro Americans (p. 6).

In a curricular area as frequently identified with citizenship education as is social studies, tests of social significance are particularly relevant for the researcher. Research in the teaching of the social studies is basically applied. That is, it is concerned with applying the theories and findings of other fields to the teaching act. It must take much of its direction, then, from the concerns of the society and of the profession. Questions that appear trivial, such as how to best use graphs along with textual material, may be considered significant by some researchers because they are being asked by many teachers. Investigations of the effects of factors such as socioeconomic status or race on teaching social studies, or on the best ways to accomplish specified

goals in black history, take on significance because they reflect the concerns of the society. Although the importance of intellectual curiosity and interest as motivators of research cannot be ignored, it is hoped that a researcher who had the options, for instance, of investigating children's perceptions of form and space as a problem in geographic education or studying the factors affecting children's attitudes toward their own and other ethnic groups would not make his choice on the basis of intellectual interest alone. Obviously, the call to heed social relevance and moral justification should not be taken as an argument that scientific objectivity must or should be broken down (see, e.g., Jensen, 1969a, p. 6).

The Role of Theory

The investigation of professionally and socially pressing matters will be more meaningful if done in the context of theory —frameworks of propositions about the teaching-learning process. There are too few examples of research studies on the teaching of social studies based on theory, and this antitheoretical, or perhaps more appropriately atheoretical, nature of so much of the research accounts in large part for the lack of cumulative findings. The failure to apply theory is indicated by the lack of hypotheses in many research reports. When hypotheses are required of graduate students, null hypotheses—which have their value as a basis for statistical inference—are frequently stated because the research is not grounded on a theory (or the careful review of past research) that could serve as the basis for formulating directional hypotheses.

When novice researchers—the students whose dissertations constitute the bulk of research in teaching social studies (Fair, 1965, p. 15; Girault & Cox, 1967, p. 388; Payette, Cox, & Johnson, 1970, p. 933)—do not have the benefit of the propositions in a theory, it often appears that there is a dearth of worthy research topics, or the only apparent ones are those growing out of their own limited experiences. Frequently seeing the dissertation as a hurdle to be overcome as quickly and easily as possible, the budding researcher clutches at any plausible, even if barely so, idea that he can come up with. Many researchers never get beyond the "budding" stage because they have picked a trivial topic for their first try at research. They recognize that the research is not worth pursuing further and are not able to generate other research problems of sufficient importance to motivate them to once again encounter the agonies of carrying out a research project.

Definition and Rationale as Theory. Our definition of theory includes such things as systematic attempts to define and build a rationale for social studies education, including the explication of assumptions about how people learn (see Shaver & Berlak, 1968, pp. 1–3). Despite the controversy and confusion about what social studies is, schema for identifying the philosophical and empirical assumptions underlying an approach to the social studies can provide helpful guidelines for the researcher in identifying significant research problems. For example, are questions about value education of importance, and if so, which questions? The person who sees social studies education as basically social science education—i.e., teaching the methodologies and findings of the social sciences—is likely to be more concerned with research on the teaching of concepts than on the teaching of values. On the other hand, a person who considers the major role of social studies to be the transmission of the knowledge and affective bases for citizenship is likely to be concerned with research on value acquisition. A person operating on a reflective citizen model of social studies education is likely to see as significant questions about how to teach students to identify and resolve value conflicts in the context of making decisions about public issues.

A curricular rationale not only suggests significant research, but, as with any theory, gives meaning to data. An example is available from the "public issues" approach

to social studies (Oliver & Shaver, 1966) based on the premise that the social studies curriculum should be organized around helping students to gain the value base, the intellectual skills, and the knowledge necessary to deal rationally with the major issues facing the society. One assumption of this approach is that students are more likely to learn and retain material that is useful to them in construing their reality, and that public issues are a part of that reality. Operating from this position, one would predict that information taught in a public issues context as compared, for example, to a typical chronological American history context, would be learned in less time and/or retained better. A test of this assumption was made (Oliver & Shaver, 1966, pp. 278–282) and the results supported the hypothesis. A finding that students scored as high on an American history test when only a third of the time in a two-year U.S. history sequence was devoted to the direct teaching of history might be of interest in itself; it takes on significance, however, in its relationship to a curricular rationale that proposes organizing social studies instruction around the analysis of public issues.

Theory of Teaching. Metcalf (1963), in criticizing research on teaching social studies, posited a theory of teaching as a focal point for research on teaching social studies. Rejecting the notion that variety of technique for its own sake is an adequate approach to social studies instruction, he proposed as a focal point for evaluating research the "reflective theory of teaching," based on the writings of Dewey (1910), as expanded by Bayles (1950), Hullfish and Smith (1961), and elaborated in theoretical and practical terms by Griffin (1942). He concluded:

Since Dewey's influence on social studies has been pervasive, research should have been expected to emphasize the testing, clarification, and refinement of his theory. Yet, only a few studies have attempted to do so, and the rest cast no light on his, or any other, theory of how a teacher might expect to perform his chief intellectual function, the direction of a process by which to assist students in concept attainment (p. 933).

Whether Metcalf's assumption (that researchers should have been testing the reflective theory of teaching) is justifiable is open to question. The sad fact, however, is that in the meantime no other theory of teaching the social studies was being systematically tested.

Theory of Learning and Development. Tying one's research into a curricular rationale or a theory of instruction is, then, one way to help ensure its significance. Another way is to relate one's research to a theory of cognitive functioning that has strong implications for social studies instruction.

Because so much of social studies instruction is concept oriented, research based specifically on theoretical work such as that of Piaget and Bruner, and more recently Kohlberg (1968), on the development of concepts and moral reasoning (see, e.g., McKeachie, 1964) is badly needed. Middle-level research (McKeachie, 1964, p. 79) utilizing psychological theory but carried out in the classroom setting is needed. But this will require an attention to theory that is frequently not present among educators who tend to be oriented toward practical classroom wisdom.

Because there is so much emphasis in social studies education on discussion as a means to objectives concerned with the application of learning in a political-social context, theorizing which relates theories of learning and personality to various teaching strategies and techniques is badly needed as a basis for research. The research by Uhes (1968; Uhes & Shaver, 1970) which indicated a relationship between convergent-divergent thinking and dogmatism (Rokeach, 1960), as well as that by Kemp (1962, 1963) indicating negative relationships between open-closed mindedness and critical thinking, indicates that those interested in increasing students' inquiry or reflective

thinking skills would do well to relate a theory of teaching to theories of conceptual functioning. Relationships between personality and learning must also be taken into account. This is suggested by Oliver and Shaver's (1966, p. 319) finding that when interviews and discussions were scored as a means of assessing thinking ability, the exhibition of intellectual skills was correlated with the personality traits of persistence and ascendance.

In addition, a broader conception of "learning" theory, going beyond pupil-teacher or pupil-media interaction, is needed if research on teaching the social studies is to be more productive. Learning-teaching theories for the social studies cannot be cast solely in terms of the classroom setting because so many of the goals of instruction are affected by other aspects of the environment. This is poignantly illustrated by the general recognition, even among social studies educators, that social studies education apparently has little effect on adult citizenship behavior. Researchers have too often ignored the obvious fact that much, if not most, of the student's learning takes place outside the social studies classroom, and that much of what the student learns in the classroom is conditioned by his out-of-classroom experiences. If a teacher is interested in instilling in his students a commitment to involvement in the society's political decision-making process, what are the effects of variations in the commonly authoritarian nature of the school's decision-making process? If a goal of social studies instruction is the development of a belief in the equality of man, in the sense of deserving equal respect, what are the effects of tracking systems in which students with different orientations toward college or with varying predicted academic abilities are put in separate programs?

RESEARCH METHODOLOGY AND DESIGN

We have argued that theorizing about teaching and learning is needed that takes into account the effects of factors that are environmental (for example, the decision-making climate of the school), sociological (such as socioeconomic and racial background), and psychological (such as openness to new beliefs). This sort of argument has obvious implications for research design. McKeachie (1961), for example, has noted the truism that the same teaching method will have varying effects on different subgroups of students, and averaging scores and comparing means are likely to obscure these effects. The statistical analysis capabilities of the computer make multivariate experiments practicable, and it is difficult to conceive of any reason for simple designs that only compare one teaching method against another. Yet research on teaching social studies still tends to ignore the possible effects on learning of interactions between student and teacher characteristics and teaching methods.

The selection of method and design often seems not to be a logical extension of the process of stating a research problem and generating hypotheses to get at the problem. Instead of methods being dictated by the problem and hypotheses, problems end up being construed to fit a research tradition—usually the classical statistical one. Even worse, many beginning researchers seem to turn to an approach, often survey research, because it seems less threatening than more "sophisticated" approaches. Often the hope is to avoid statistical analysis. The survey data are claimed to be descriptive of a total population so that inferential statistics can be avoided. Yet the researcher generalizes beyond his data, for instance, to social studies professors not included in the study. The results of such surveys frequently are data with little validity and more studies that contribute little to the profession.

The following pages contain some comments about the need to use traditional research methods in ways appropriate to building knowledge on teaching social studies. Classroom ethnography is also discussed as one alternative to the classical statistical research approach to highlight the importance of choosing research strategies according to the function to be served.

Verifying the Independent Variable

In research on teaching social studies, the independent variable most frequently has been teacher behavior, and the results of various studies have not been fruitful in the sense of building solid knowledge about teaching. We have already noted some reasons for this unproductive history. As Wispé (1953) pointed out some time ago, the failure of teaching-methods researchers to produce consistent cumulative findings may also be due in large part to the failure to confirm that the independent variable of teacher behavior did indeed occur as assumed.

One cannot assume that because he has prepared special materials for his experimental and control teachers, or has given them instructions about how to behave, the anticipated differences in experimental and control instruction will occur. Gathering teachers' opinions about the extent to which they succeeded in modeling the desired behaviors is also not a reliable way to confirm an independent variable (see Medley & Mitzel, 1963, pp. 249–250). In social studies, where there is so much interest in the effects of discussion techniques, systematic observation—in which the anticipated behaviors are carefully defined and the observed behavior then coded in the resulting categories—is an especially fruitful means for verifying an independent variable.

The independent variable which is the subject of investigation should be rooted in theory, thereby providing a theoretical basis for the categories in the observation system. On the other hand, the desirability of continuity in findings dictates that available observational instruments should be used when possible. When no extant system is appropriate to his theoretical frame, the researcher is faced with a difficult choice between validity and generalizability.

Although the proliferation of instruments is not likely to lead to cumulative findings, theoretical validity is the more important concern. If the available observational instruments (e.g., Medley & Mitzel, 1963; Simon & Boyer, 1967) do not provide an adequate description of the independent variable, it is better to construct a new system rather than use an invalid one. The Michigan Social Issues Cognitive Category System (Massialas, Sprague, & Sweeney, 1970) is an example of a recently developed system, as is the observational system developed for the Harvard Project (Oliver & Shaver, 1966), building on the previous work of Bales (1950). The same system was later used in a research project at Utah State University (Shaver & Larkins, 1969).

Validity of Dependent Variables

Dependent variables present particular challenges to the researcher of social studies teaching. The achievement of objectives sought in social studies instruction is typically difficult to measure—either because of their nature or because of the setting in which they are expected to occur. An example of the first would be objectives having to do with positive attitudes toward minority groups. How does one assess them? Certainly asking the student how he feels is inadequate, and the intent of many attitude questionnaires is so obvious that one cannot be certain what the students' responses mean. An example of the second difficulty involves a setting and time-lapse problem—the concern of social studies educators with citizenship behavior, much of which (such as voting) is not expected to occur in this culture until the student has left school. When one is concerned with objectives such as teaching students to think reflectively about public issues as an adult voter, the problem is compounded—the end desired is difficult to define and measure (Berlak, 1966), the setting is difficult to produce, and the time lapse before the criterion period presents extreme difficulties. One reaction to the difficulty of measuring commonly espoused social studies ob-

jectives has been a regressive tendency for researchers to fall back on that which is easily measurable—knowledge—ignoring attitudes, values and thought processes. Consequently, much of what is measured in research on teaching social studies is not relevant to many of the common objectives of the curriculum area.

A definition of and rationale for social studies should serve as the basis for the objectives sought via the curriculum, and therefore as a major basis for assessing a curriculum by a piece of research. Given the importance attached to teaching students to think as a social studies objective, such a rationale should include a model of thinking appropriate to the problems with which the students will be dealing as adult citizens (Berlak, 1965). This would provide the basis for asking the validity question: Does the test measure the concepts considered essential to critical thinking?

Lacking a well-explicated conception of critical thinking, researchers too often make their judgments of test validity by default, simply accepting a test because it is published and available. The Watson-Glaser Critical Thinking Appraisal has on many occasions been cast in the role of "available performer." Research supposedly conducted in the context of citizenship education but making exclusive use of published tests, none of which assesses the ability to analyze values and apply them in the decision-making process, suggests that the researcher either lacks an adequate concept of critical thinking or has ignored it in selecting his tests.

Aside from the problem of model-test correspondence, Berlak (1966) has discussed a related concern with published and other tests of thinking—that is, the general lack of validity data in the form of evidence that scores on the tests correlate with behavior outside the testing situation. This criticism, which is a serious one, reflects the difficulties, mentioned earlier, of assessing many social studies objectives because of their nature (complex thought processes) and the settings in which it is desired they will occur (e.g., adult discussions of public issues).

Researchers have tended to rely on paper-and-pencil tests, but they are hardly adequate to the measurement of thinking (Berlak, 1966; Oliver & Shaver, 1966), even when adequate models underly them. For example, paper-and-pencil tests fragment the thinking process (each item deals with only one aspect of the process) and do not get at the student's ability to follow a sequence of reasoning; they identify the relevant concepts for the student (an item asks a student to evaluate the relevance of a statement, and we do not know whether the student would recognize on his own that questions of relevance needed to be raised); they are structured in an unrealistic way (in the "real" life with which social studies instruction is concerned, people do not sit at desks responding to test items which frequently—as in the case of multiple-choice tests—lay out the acceptable alternatives). Furthermore, published tests frequently deal with trivia (e.g., advertisements for storm windows), not the citizenship education concerns of social studies.

Some of these shortcomings can be avoided even in paper-and-pencil tests. The Social Issues Analysis Tests developed by the Harvard Project (Oliver & Shaver, 1966, chapter 10) were an attempt to overcome some of these problems by focusing test content on public issues and making some variations from the typical test format. For example, questions were based on page-long dialogues about public issues presented to the students as part of the test. But these tests still provide the students with a set and a structure that obscure whether he could apply the critical thinking abilities in an unstructured "real life" setting.

A promising approach to assessing the student's learning in a more natural setting is a technique already discussed—the systematic observation of discussions. Using observational categories to code the content of ongoing (or recorded) discussions, it is not necessary to fragment and structure the thought process for the student; aspects of the discussion are not selected for the student to analyze (at least not in discussions not led by a teacher), nor is he provided with a set of responses from which to choose. As one example, the Harvard Project developed and used an observational system—the Social Issues Analysis Test No. 4 (Oliver & Shaver, 1966, chapter 11) for assessing thinking as evidenced by behavior in discussions. It was later modified so that it would be valid for a refined model of critical thinking and used in the Utah State University Project as the Analytic Content Analysis System (ACAS) (Shaver & Larkins, 1969; Slater, 1970).

The use of systematic observation to assess critical thinking does not circumvent validity questions. The specification of the behaviors to be categorized and valued should be based on a carefully developed model of thinking. In addition, scores obtained should be related to other criteria as a means of validation. The criteria may involve extraclassroom behavior or the judgments of "experts," such as lawyers and philosophy professors, as to the intellectual quality of the discussions (Berlak, 1964).

However, adequate measurement of the objectives of social studies instruction calls for more than the use of systematic observation. Other imaginative approaches to assessment are needed. One important source of potential stimulation is the work on unobtrusive measures by Webb, Campbell, Schwartz, and Sechrest (1966), which should be read if only for the perspectives on measurement which it provides. Is a unit supposed to develop interest in minority group problems? Check on the number of books dealing with such topics checked out of the library before and after instruction. Is tolerance toward minority group members the variable to be assessed? Quietly observe patterns of interaction on the playground or who sits with whom in the classroom before and after instruction. Is instruction intended to increase interest in local government? Ask the students a few weeks after instruction how many have been to a city council meeting, or leave government books "lying around" and tally their use. The opportunities are many, but a different conception of measurement is needed than is typically stressed in tests and measurement courses.

Replication

One other aspect of research design deserves special treatment in light of our concern for the noncumulative nature of the research on teaching social studies. We have already noted that much of the research in this area is carried out by graduate students. As Cox and Cousins (1965) have noted, persons doing dissertations usually "attempt to be unique in their experimentation in as many ways as possible" (p. 90). Part of the myth of graduate study is that one's study must be "original" to be a worthwhile (i.e., "scientific") contribution. In fact, one of the major shortcomings of research on teaching social studies is the lack of replication.

Sidman (1960) refers to two types of replication: 1) direct and 2) systematic. The former involves "performing the experiment again with new subjects or by making repeated observations on the same subjects under each of several experimental conditions" (p. 73), while the latter involves "performing new experiments and obtaining additional related data" (p. 111). There has been little of either in most educational research, and in research on teaching social studies in particular.

The importance of systematic replication is indicated by the extent to which scores on personality measures vary from subculture to subculture, even, for example, within the same religious groups (Shaver & Richards, 1968), and by the shifts in the results of data analyses depending upon the cultural variables included as covariates in an analysis of covariance (Low & Shaver, 1971).

Direct replication might not often be possible, but systematic replication, or a varia-

tion of it, is. Pure systematic replication calls for more control over the sampling process than is typically possible in educational research. Ironically, however, a variation of systematic observation can help to alleviate a related problem that confronts educational researchers—the difficulty of obtaining random samples from defined populations. Reports of research on teaching social studies indicate few attempts to define a population and then select a sample from it. Undoubtedly random samples could be obtained more frequently if researchers were willing to put in the time and effort necessary to do so. For example, if students and/or teachers cannot be sampled randomly, more schools could be used and classrooms sampled (see, e.g., Larkins, 1968). Instead of the extra effort, available samples are used. The report usually presents a brief description of the school and the students (perhaps reporting socioeconomic status and I.Q.), as if this justifies the lack of adequate sampling, and then goes on to generalize illegitimately to an implicit nationwide population.

As a consequence of the lack of random sampling and other forms of experimental control, such as random assignment, most research into teaching social studies has been at best quasi-experimental rather than experimental (Campbell & Stanley, 1963). However, as Campbell and Stanley (1963) indicated in their landmark chapter, the difficulty of setting up perfect experimental designs should not keep one from doing research. What the researcher should do is:

design the very best experiment which the situation makes possible.... deliberately seek out those artificial and natural laboratories which provide the best opportunities for control.... go ahead with experiment and interpretation, *fully aware of the points on which the results are equivocal* (authors' emphasis) (p. 204).

But more can be done through replication. As Stanley (1966) has pointed out, the problem is to determine how you can "whittle at the true experiment most effectively to produce a practicable design for teasing out 'if-then' causal relationships, probably *in a series of studies* rather than in just a one-shot attempt" (authors' emphasis) (p. 84). In the same vein, Campbell and Stanley (1963, p. 173) have called for "multiple studies" and Flanders and Simon (1969) have advocated "long-term" research.

Although the researcher may not be able to conduct a series of studies himself, he can fit his study into a series. And although he may not be able to control the experimental situation and systematically vary the variables from one study to the next as in pure systematic replication, he can ferret out and report the differences in samples and contexts from one study to the next—doing what we call *post hoc replication*. That is, an individual study can be carried out within a theoretical framework with as much control as possible over the experimental setting, but with the explicit recognition of variations in theoretically important variables that cannot be controlled. These variations are measured as part of the experiment and described afterwards. This is similar to the reporting of such characteristics as I.Q. and socioeconomic status for nonrandom samples. However, for post hoc replication the variables to be described are selected on theoretical grounds or because they provide continuity with earlier studies, not on the basis of what is readily available, for instance in the school records. If potentially important studies on teaching social studies were replicated in this way, with the researchers explicitly aware of a theoretical base and of the variations from one study to the next, a body of verified knowledge about teaching social studies could accumulate.

Systematic replication should be used when possible; but if not, post hoc replication presents a reasonable alternative to despair. In the use of either, however, it must be kept in mind that as Sidman (1960, pp. 111–112) has noted, certain risks are involved. If the replication attempt fails to produce results consistent with the earlier research, it is usually difficult, if not impossible, to determine whether the failure was due to inadequacies in the previous research or the introduction of new, uncontrolled variables in the replication study. Nevertheless, the potential rewards for building knowledge about teaching social studies are great. As a finding is reproduced under different conditions, confidence in its generality is enhanced.

An example of the potentially frustrating and rewarding results of replication also illustrates the lack of a clear distinction between systematic and post hoc replication. The Harvard Project (Oliver & Shaver, 1966), after confirming the independent variable of teaching style using systematic observation (Shaver, 1964), found no significant differences between Socratic and recitation teaching styles in affecting learning as measured by a number of tests. However, significant interactions between teaching style and student personality traits were found (Shaver & Oliver, 1968).

The Harvard study was carried out with seventh- and eighth-grade students in a Boston suburb. The research of the Utah State University Project (Shaver & Larkins, 1969) was planned as a systematic replication of the Harvard Project's research. The major variable of concern was teaching style, and the same styles (plus a third—called *seminar* teaching) were used and confirmed with the same systematic observation system. In addition, the same measures of learning (plus others) and the same personality measures were administered. The conditions varied were the students—juniors in a Utah high school in the latter study—and content—a modified critical thinking scheme and different curricular materials.

The lack of significant treatment affects was replicated, but the significant teaching style-student personality interactions were not. The confirmation of the lack of differential effectiveness of confirmed teaching styles across different populations of students and with similar, but modified, content and curricular materials indicated the general validity of rejecting simple Method A versus Method B studies. On the other hand, the failure to replicate the interaction findings—which was a disappointment—raised questions about the original Harvard Project findings. There was, however, no way, except further research, to determine the cause of the discrepancy in findings.

This example of replication highlights a deficiency in research already mentioned—the failure to operationally define and empirically describe the independent variable (as well as other aspects of the experimental setting). Without such definition and description, provided for in the Harvard and Utah State University Projects by the use of systematic observation, adequate replication is impossible.

Note that in the above example, the variable of major concern—teaching style—was controlled from one study to the next with other variables varied. By the same token, the same tests of learning and personality were used. Such control makes this an instance of systematic replication. On the other hand, if a researcher was interested in studying the effects of teaching style but, rather than controlling style, measured teacher behavior while the second project was in process in order to have data available on differences that might have occurred, the research would be what we call post hoc replication—clearly a matter of degree rather than of kind.

A BROADER VIEW

Selection of method should follow from, or at least be consistent with, the definition of the research problem. It is unfortunate when one type of research is generally preferred and researchers tend to fit every problem to that approach. At this point in educational research, the preference seems to be for statistical analysis of group data.

That some shift toward a broader conception of appropriate research methods may be occurring is illustrated by a comparison of the contents of the December 1966 and December 1969 issues of the *Review of Educational Research* dealing with research methodology. In contrast to the 1966 issue, seven of the 10 chapters in the 1969 issue were devoted to research methods related to history, aesthetics, anthropology, philosophy, political science, economics and sociology, with statistics restricted to a single chapter. Of the various nonstatistical approaches, a methodology from anthropology, *ethnography,* presents a promising alternative to research which relies on the statistical analysis of group data.

Classroom Ethnography

The commonly stated goals of instruction, and therefore the dimensions of the instructional setting, are more complex for social studies than for some areas of the curriculum—such as mathematics and the exact sciences. This is because social studies, particularly if defined in terms of citizenship education, has interrelated cognitive, affective, and interpersonal behavior objectives. Students are to learn knowledge and develop thinking competencies for dealing with the difficult issues facing the society. Commitments to the basic ideals of a democratic society are to be strengthened and clarified. How to behave during the discussion of emotion-laden topics is of concern. And the knowledge, the competencies, the commitments, and the behavior bear complex supportive relationships to one another as they are hopefully interwoven into the "complete" citizen.

We know little about the intricate interrelations among teachers, pupils, their environment, and the ends sought which make up the tangled web of instruction and learning in the social studies. And a different conception of research from the classical, statistical approach may be needed to tease out the complicated relationships.

New theory may be called for. As a minimum, available theories of learning and teaching will need to be related to definitions and rationales for social studies and to a realistic view of the classroom in order that meaningful hypotheses can be formulated about the teaching process and its effects. To accomplish the necessary theoretical work, researchers must distinguish between theory generation and theory verification and adopt methods appropriate to each. *Classroom ethnography*, particularly as developed by Louis Smith, presents a viable alternative for theory generation.

Smith's first major study as a classroom ethnographer was reported in *The Complexities of an Urban Classroom* (Smith & Geoffrey, 1968). The study was an attempt to find out how middle-class teachers cope with lower-class elementary-school children. Chapter One contains a general description of ethnography as applied in the study.

The first task of the ethnographer is to observe and gather data. Smith was in the classroom (or, on occasion, elsewhere in the school) observing during the total school day nearly every day for a semester. His data consisted of extensive longhand notes describing classroom events, interpretative comments interspersed in the notes, daily summaries dictated into a tape recorder, classroom documents (such as messages brought in to the teacher, assignment sheets, and announcements sent home to parents), and brief field notes kept by the classroom teacher.

The two data sources (researcher and teacher) are important. The nonparticipant observer provides an "outside" view that emphasizes objectivity and allows for the collection of detailed data. The "inside" view of the participant observer (the teacher) is helpful for such things as identifying teacher intentions. Students could also be used as participant observers, reporting on their observations and reactions.

Smith used his raw data, the descriptions of and reactions to classroom interactions over time, to generate concepts such as *pupil esteem*—positive feelings by students toward the teacher—and *teacher awareness*—infor-

mation about the students' lives that is important to them and which they know the teacher possesses (Smith & Geoffrey, 1968, pp. 102–103; Smith & Kleine, 1969a, 1969b). Such concepts were joined as propositions hypothesizing causal links—for example, "Increased teacher awareness leads to increased pupil esteem." And such propositions can be linked to other concepts in further propositions, such as, "Increased pupil esteem leads to increased classroom control." These sets of interrelated propositions Smith calls *mid-range* theory, and the hypothesized relationships can be tested using methods we have grouped under the label "statistical tradition" (including experiments and quasiexperiments, as well as correlational studies) in what has been referred to as "verification" research.

Smith has added an ironic twist to the criticism that research has not been related to theory. He claims that high-level theories —for instance, theories of learning—are difficult to apply to teaching. They are too abstract and do not translate easily to the solution of specific teaching problems. In contrast, he claims, the application of mid-range theory generated from the observation of specific teaching behaviors is more obvious. Although the propositions in a mid-range theory of teaching may seem too homey or even simple-minded to some, well-founded propositions of this sort might do more to improve teaching than grand sounding, complex theories. Of course, if high-level and mid-range theories are well grounded, they should be compatible (Smith & Brock, 1970, p. 73).

Contrasting Statistical and Ethnographic Research. A quick comparison of the orientations of the statistical researcher and the ethnographer makes it evident why the latter's approach is particularly appropriate for generating theory about teaching social studies. The drive of the statistical researcher is toward objectivity, the removal of the researcher's influence from his data and findings. There is a strong concern, supported by some evidence (Orne, 1962; Rosenthal, 1966), that the researcher may even unintentionally influence the results of the study. So he tries to separate himself from the object of his investigation, venturing into classrooms and meeting teachers and students only incidentally. He frequently becomes better acquainted, on a firsthand basis, with the library—the source of his intensive review of literature—and the computer center—the caretaker of his data—than with the children, the social context of the school, or the daily struggle to implement a curriculum.

The concern for objectivity is also evident in the area of measurement. If systematic observation is used, the principal investigator rarely serves as an observer because his expectations might affect his observations (Shaver, 1966). All important variables are reduced to scores on tests or frequencies in observation categories—hopefully little influenced by the test administrator, observer, or scorer, and readily replicated under similar circumstances.

The statistical researcher, then, tends to take a close look at a very limited sample of behavior—that which can be precisely measured, controlled, manipulated and analyzed. This tendency to limit the size and number of slices of reality under investigation may be unfortunate. As L. M. Smith and Brock (1970) have noted:

Classroom research has acted as though there were only one sequence of events going on at a time. It were as though none of us in classroom research had ever ... participated in a social situation in which there was a latent as well as manifest agenda. Our position now suggests that classrooms have these multiple strands or streams and that we must attend to them theoretically and empirically (p. 12).

Not only does the slicing of reality result in the observation of only a small amount of behavior, but teaching is not observed in flux over time. Pretests and posttests are administered and the two static samples

compared. Even if the treatment variable is verified through observation (a rarity, as we have already noted), observation takes place with set categories and on a few sample days.

The strategy is to state a research problem specifically in advance, formulate hypotheses, identify relevant variables, and then build control, manipulation, and objective measurement into the design. The predetermined procedures are not always followed, but deviations from them are usually viewed as concessions that weaken the study.

The contrast with the ethnographer's approach is great. A cardinal rule of his method is immersion—direct, continuous, daily contact with the objects of investigation, perhaps for months if not years. It is assumed that nearly every one of these contacts will produce data, primarily in the form of extensive field notes. The ethnographer may collect quantified data, but his observations and notes are not assumed to be free of his frame of reference, as are scores on paper-and-pencil tests or the frequencies of systematic observation.

Moreover, the ethnographer's approach is holistic. Even studies that anthropologists would regard as stringently restricted in scope attempt to examine schooling behavior in a much broader context than is true of most traditional, statistical research. And the ethnographer's continuous involvement in the setting is more conducive to looking at process than is the measurement of static chunks of behavior sliced off prior to, during, and after treatment.

The ethnographer is also more open-ended in his approach. He does delineate a research problem. He knows that he wants to study a certain social system and its relations to other systems, or certain types of individuals and how they function within a social system. But he does not design a study with a fixed set of hypotheses to be tested, nor with a predetermined set of variables to which he will attend. The matter of structure is, of course, one of degree, and the ethnographer does enter his study with questions in mind, with the intent of probing problems he deems important. Because these questions, identified *prior* to the study, do, in a sense, cast shadows that guide and restrict the researcher's view, Smith calls them *foreshadowed* problems:

Foreshadowed problems are those knotty questions, the toughest ones you can find, which you keep asking the data to answer....

The central thrust of the foreshadowed problem is that it selectively guides one's perception and thought while one is in the field. For instance, in our Washington School study (Smith & Geoffrey, 1968) I was continuously asking myself, How does one manage them? How do you get them to listen to you? (L. M. Smith, 1968, p. 33).

Foreshadowed problems provide a focus for observation. For instance, researchers interested in different trends within social studies education—teaching the structures of the disciplines or teaching the analysis of public issues—might deliberately approach the classroom with different questions in mind. But these problems are not used to structure the research setting or to screen out unanticipated data as are formal hypotheses in statistical research.

Function. The characteristics of the statistical tradition—the stress on a carefully narrowed scope of inquiry, predetermined variables, and precise, objective instrumentation—make it well suited for hypothesis testing and theory verification. On the other hand, the ethnographer's immersion in the object of study, his deliberate attempts to be sensitive to many things, and his open searching for unanticipated relationships between persons and systems are well suited to the identification of important variables and their antecedents and consequences—the basis of theory generation. Of course, the same researcher may at one time use one methodology for generating theory and at another time use a different one for verify-

ing propositions. For instance, Smith and Kleine (1969b) used correlational methods in an attempt to verify hypotheses about teacher awareness and pupil esteem that came out of Smith and Geoffrey's (1968) earlier study.

The demands of formative and summative evaluation (Scriven, 1967) are also sufficiently different that different research strategies will often be appropriate. Formative evaluation requires attention to unanticipated student or teacher reactions to the curriculum, as well as quick feedback to the developers. Ethnography fits with what Scriven (1967) refers to as "seat of the pants" research necessary in the formative stage of curriculum development. However, once the researcher is called upon to determine in summative evaluation the worth of a finished product, the rigorous research designs and objectivity of statistical research are appropriate.

Again, absolute, exclusive prescriptions cannot be made. In well-planned and directed formative evaluation, tryouts of lessons may entail the rigorous but quick gathering and statistical analysis of data, allowing for revisions without unduly interrupting the development process. Or the researcher might want to include in a summative evaluation design a broader set of variables and settle for a lower probability of a correct decision about the effects of the curriculum (Larkins & Shaver, 1969b). A more open approach such as ethnography would then be acceptable. In some cases a combination of approaches might be used for either formative or summative evaluation (Smith & Pohland, 1969).

Ethnography and Significant Research. In research on social studies, as in other fields (Smith & Brock, 1970, p. 42), trivial studies are frequently conducted because of overemphasis on objectivity, quantification, and experimentation. If tests are not available which get at important variables, those variables are often abandoned in favor of less important but more readily measured behavior. If important behavior is exhibited in settings which make experimentation difficult, tidier if less significant research topics are frequently selected.

The assessment of the impact of a new curriculum in elementary social studies (Larkins, 1968; Larkins & Shaver, 1969a; Shaver & Larkins, 1966) serves as a case in point. The cognitive impact of the curriculum was researched because of the traditional concern of school people for assessing cognitive objectives and because putting together a respectable statistical study of affective variables would have taken more monetary and human resources than were readily available. Construing the need, however, as the generation of propositions rather than verification of hypotheses could have led to a different approach. A profitable semester or two might have been spent observing children interacting with the target curriculum. Children might have been observed in their homes, neighborhoods, on the playground, and in the classroom in an attempt to generate propositions about how socioeconomic background interacted with the values favored in the curriculum in question. The groundwork might have been laid for a series of manageable and worthwhile verification studies.

A Caveat

Ethnography entails intellectual involvement and risk taking, especially when the intent is not just to describe a setting but to generate theory. There is too frequently a tendency in statistical research to assume that the computer can do one's thinking. Of course, computers cannot provide the basic reasoning in any kind of study, but research aimed at developing explanatory propositions in particular demands that the researcher himself come to grips with his data.

The intellectual demands of theory generation through classroom ethnography are challenging—and threatening. Entering into a study without being able to anticipate a precise end result can be anxiety provoking for even self-assured researchers. In carrying out a traditional statistical study, there is the assurance that data will be obtained and analyzed with statistical findings to report. The ethnographer must face the specter of spending months in data gathering without being able in the end to build worthwhile concepts and draw them together into powerful explanatory propositions. Although the researcher in the statistical tradition can counteract disappointing results by pointing out that he followed a generally approved, rigorous research design, it would be of little comfort to the ethnographer to point out that he had faithfully observed the social setting and had taken fully comprehensive notes but could do little with them.

Classroom ethnography is new to research on teaching social studies, and it may be comforting to know that research using the approach is in progress. Seif (1970) is studying the issue discussion lessons from the Washington University Elementary Social Science Curriculum Project. Applegate (1970) is describing and analyzing role playing as it is used in some units of the same project. Solomon (1969) is investigating a series of lessons in the fourth grade portion of the Washington University Social Science Curriculum.

CONCLUSION

This chapter has focused on suggestions for moving toward a body of cumulative research knowledge on teaching social studies. The need to carry out research from a clear definition of and rationale for social studies education was stressed as part of a general emphasis on the need to relate research on teaching social studies to theory. More careful attention to research methodology—to the verification of independent variables, the valid assessment of dependent variables, and the use of replication to build interrelated findings—was called for. In addition, an opening of research perspectives to include approaches such as classroom ethnography when appropriate to tasks such as theory generation and formative evaluation was urged.

There are a number of ways in which research on teaching social studies can be sharpened and made more fruitful. In addition, there are viable research alternatives available in the research strategies of the various social sciences—to which one would expect researchers on teaching social studies to be particularly in tune. The point has been to suggest modifications in the traditional approach to research on teaching social studies and to suggest that there are alternative research strategies, such as ethnography, which may be more appropriate to certain research tasks.

REFERENCES

Applegate, J. R. A description and analysis of role playing as a student activity in an elementary classroom. Proposal for doctoral dissertation, Washington University, 1970.

Bales, R. F. *Interaction process analysis.* Cambridge, Mass.: Addison-Wesley, 1950.

Barth, J. L., & Shermis, S. S. Defining the social studies: An exploration of three traditions. *Social Education,* 1970, 34, 743–751.

Bayles, E. E. *The theory and practice of teaching.* New York: Harper & Brothers, 1950.

Berlak, H. The construct validity of a content analysis system for the evaluation of critical thinking in political controversy. Paper presented at the annual meeting of the American Educational Research Association, Chicago, February 1964.

Berlak, H. The teaching of thinking. *The School Review,* 1965, 73, 1–13.

Berlak, H. New curricula and the measurement of thinking. *Educational Forum,* 1966, 30, 303–311.

Borg, W. R. *Educational research: An introduction.* New York: David McKay, 1963.

Caldwell, C. Social science as ammunition. *Psychology Today,* September 1970, 4, 38–41, 72–73.

Campbell, D. T., & Stanley, J. C. Experimental

and quasi-experimental designs for research on teaching. In N. L. Gage (Ed.), *Handbook of research on teaching.* Chicago: Rand McNally, 1963. Pp. 171–246.

Cox, C. B., & Cousins, J. E. Teaching social studies in secondary schools and colleges. In B. G. Massialas, & F. R. Smith (Eds.), *New challenge in the social studies: Implications of research for teaching.* Belmont, Calif.: Wadsworth, 1965. Pp. 89–120.

Cox, C. B., Girault, E. S., & Metcalf, L. E. Review of research in social studies: 1965. *Social Education,* 1966, 30, 348–359.

Cox, C. B., Johnson, W. D., & Payette, R. F. Review of research in social studies: 1967. *Social Education,* 1968, 32, 557–571.

Dewey, J. *How we think.* Boston: D. C. Heath, 1910.

Dimond, S. E. Citizenship education. In C. W. Harris (Ed.), *Encyclopedia of educational research.* (3rd ed.) New York: Macmillan, 1960. Pp. 206–210.

Fair, J. Research in the education of social studies teachers. *Social Education,* 1965, 29, 15–19.

Flanders, N. A., & Simon, A. Teacher effectiveness. In R. L. Ebel (Ed.), *Encyclopedia of educational research.* (4th ed.) New York: Macmillan, 1969. Pp. 1423–1437.

Girault, E. S., & Cox, C. B. Review of research in social studies: 1966. *Social Education,* 1967, 31, 388–396.

Grannis, J. C. The social studies teacher and research on teacher education. *Social Education,* 1970, 34, 291–301, 315.

Griffin, A. F. A philosophical approach to the subject-matter preparation of teachers of history. Unpublished doctoral dissertation, Ohio State University, 1942.

Gross, P. E., & Badger, W. V. Social studies. In C. W. Harris (Ed.), *Encyclopedia of educational research.* (3rd ed.) New York: Macmillan, 1960. Pp. 1296–1319.

Guilford, J. P. *The nature of human intelligence.* New York: McGraw-Hill, 1967.

Harrison, S. E., & Solomon, R. J. Review of research in the teaching of social studies: 1960–1963. *Social Education,* 1964, 28, 277–292.

Harrison, S. E., & Solomon, R. J. Review of research in the teaching of social studies: 1964. *Social Education,* 1965, 29, 281–290.

Hullfish, H. G., & Smith, P. G. *Reflective*

thinking: The method of education. New York: Dodd, Mead, 1961.

Hunt, M. P., & Metcalf, L. E. *Teaching high school social studies.* (2nd ed.) New York: Harper & Row, 1968.

Jensen, A. R. Arthur Jensen replies. *Psychology Today,* October 1969, 3, 4, 6. (a)

Jensen, A. R. How much can we boost IQ and scholastic achievement? *Harvard Educational Review,* 1969, 39, 1–123. (b)

Johnson, W. D., Payette, R. F., & Cox, C. B. Review of research in social studies: 1968. *Social Education,* 1969, 33, 965–989.

Kemp, C. G. Critical thinking: Open and closed minds. *American Behavioral Scientist,* 1962, 5(5), 10–15.

Kemp, C. G. Improvement of critical thinking in relation to open-closed belief systems. *Journal of Experimental Education,* 1963, 31, 321–323.

Kohlberg, L. The child as a moral philosopher. *Psychology Today,* September 1968, 2, 25–30.

Larkins, A. G. Assessing achievement on a first-grade economics course of study. Unpublished doctoral dissertation, Utah State University, 1968.

Larkins, A. G., & Shaver, J. P. Economics learning in grade one: The USU assessment studies. *Social Education,* 1969, 33, 958–963. (a)

Larkins, A. G., & Shaver, J. P. Hard-nosed research and the evaluation of curricula. Paper presented to a symposium at the meeting of the American Educational Research Association, Los Angeles, February 1969. (b)

Low, W. B., & Shaver, J. P. *Open-closed mindedness of students in teacher education and in other college fields.* Final report to USOE on Project No. O-H-011. Logan, Utah: Utah State University, Bureau of Educational Research, 1971.

Martorella, P. A. Classroom concept learning: Issues and research perspectives. *Social Education,* 1971, 35, 888–892.

Massialas, B. G. Citizenship and political socialization. In R. L. Ebel (Ed.), *Encyclopedia of educational research.* (4th ed.) New York: Macmillan, 1969. Pp. 124–141.

Massialas, B. G., Sprague, N. F., & Sweeney, J. A. C. *Structure and process of inquiry into social issues in secondary schools.* Vol. I. *Inquiry into social issues.* Final report to

USOE. Ann Arbor, Mich.: University of Michigan, 1970.

McKeachie, W. J. Motivation, teaching methods, and college learning. In M. R. Jones (Ed.), *Nebraska Symposium on Motivation,* 1961, 9, 111–142.

McKeachie, W. J. Needed research on psychological factors in learning as related to the social studies. In R. A. Price (Ed.), *Needed research in the teaching of the social studies.* Washington, D.C.: National Council for the Social Studies, 1964. Pp. 79–92.

McPhie, W. E. *Dissertations in social studies education: A comprehensive guide.* Research Bulletin No. 2. Washington, D.C.: National Council for the Social Studies, 1964.

Medley, D. M., & Mitzel, H. E. Measuring classroom behavior by systematic observation. In N. L. Gage (Ed.), *Handbook of research on teaching.* Chicago: Rand McNally, 1963. Pp. 247–328.

Metcalf, L. E. Research on teaching the social studies. In N. L. Gage (Ed.), *Handbook of research on teaching.* Chicago: Rand McNally, 1963. Pp. 929–965.

Mouly, G. W. *The science of educational research.* (2nd ed.) New York: Van Nostrand-Reinhold, 1970.

Oliver, D. W. The selection of content in the social studies. *Harvard Educational Review,* 1957, 27, 271–300.

Oliver, D. W., & Shaver, J. P. *Teaching public issues in the high school.* Boston: Houghton Mifflin, 1966.

Orne, M. T. On the social psychology of the psychological experiment: With particular reference to demand characteristics and their implications. *American Psychologist,* 1962, 17, 776–783.

Patrick, J. J. Implications of political socialization research for the reform of civic education. *Social Education,* 1969, 33, 15–21.

Payette, R. F., Cox, C. B., & Johnson, W. D. Review of research in social studies: 1969. *Social Education,* 1970, 34, 933–954.

Penix, F. C. Teaching social studies in elementary schools. In B. G. Massialas, & F. R. Smith (Eds.), *New challenges in the social studies: Implications of research for teaching.* Belmont, Calif.: Wadsworth, 1965. Pp. 63–88.

Price, R. A. (Ed.) *Needed research in the teaching of the social studies.* Washington,

D.C.: National Council for the Social Studies, 1964.

Rokeach, M. *The open and closed mind*. New York: Basic Books, 1960.

Rosenshine, B. The stability of teacher effects upon student achievement. *Review of Educational Research*, 1970, 40, 647–662.

Rosenthal, R. *Experimenter effects in behavioral research*. New York: Appleton-Century-Crofts, 1966.

Scriven, M. The methodology of evaluation. In R. W. Tyler, R. M. Gagné, & M. Scriven, *Perspectives of curriculum evaluation*. Chicago: Rand McNally, 1967.

Scriven, M. The values of the academy (Moral issues for American education and educational research arising from the Jensen case). *Review of Educational Research*, 1970, 40, 541–549.

Seif, E. A description and analysis of issue discussion lessons from the Washington University Elementary Social Science Curriculum Project. Proposal for doctoral dissertation, Washington University, 1970.

Shaver, J. P. Educational research and instruction for critical thinking. *Social Education*, 1962, 26, 13–16.

Shaver, J. P. The ability of teachers to conform to two styles of teaching. *Journal of Experimental Education*, 1964, 32, 259–267.

Shaver, J. P. Experimenter bias and the training of observers. *Utah Academy of Sciences, Arts and Letters Proceedings*, 1966, 43, Part I, 143–152.

Shaver, J. P. Social studies: The need for redefinition. *Social Education*, 1967, 31, 588–592.

Shaver, J. P., & Berlak, H. *Democracy, pluralism and the social studies—Readings and commentary*. Boston: Houghton Mifflin, 1968.

Shaver, J. P., & Larkins, A. G. *SRA economics materials in grades one and two*. Report to Salt Lake City School District. Logan, Utah: Utah State University, Bureau of Educational Research, 1966.

Shaver, J. P., & Larkins, A. G. *The analysis of public issues: Concepts, materials, research*. Final report to USOE, Project No. 6-2288. Logan, Utah: Utah State University, Bureau of Educational Research, 1969.

Shaver, J. P., & Oliver, D. W. The effect of student characteristic-teaching method interactions on learning to think critically. Paper presented at the annual meeting of the American Educational Research Association, Chicago, 1968.

Shaver, J. P., & Richards, H. E. *Open-closed mindedness of college students in teacher education*. Final report to USOE, Project No. 7-8056. Logan, Utah: Utah State University, Bureau of Educational Research, 1968.

Sidman, M. *Tactics of scientific research: Evaluating experimental data in psychology*. New York: Basic Books, 1960.

Simon, A., & Boyer, E. G. *Mirrors for behavior: An anthology of classroom observation instruments*. Philadelphia, Pa.: Research for Better Schools, 1967. 7 vols.

Skretting, J. R., & Sundeen, J. E. Social studies education. In R. L. Ebel (Ed.), *Encyclopedia of educational research*. (4th ed.) New York: Macmillan, 1969. Pp. 1231–1241.

Slater, R. D. Teaching style and student use of analytic concepts in discussions of controversial issues. Unpublished doctoral dissertation, Utah State University, 1970.

Smith, L. M. *Classroom social systems in teacher education*. St. Ann, Mo.: Central Midwestern Regional Educational Laboratory, 1968.

Smith, L. M., & Brock, J. A. M. *"Go, bug, go!": Methodological issues in classroom observational research*. St. Ann, Mo.: Central Midwestern Regional Educational Laboratory, 1970.

Smith, L. M., & Geoffrey, W. *The complexities of an urban classroom*. New York: Holt, Rinehart & Winston, 1968.

Smith, L. M., & Kleine, P. F. *Minor studies in teacher-pupil relationships*. St. Ann, Mo.: Central Midwestern Regional Educational Laboratory, 1969. (a)

Smith, L. M., & Kleine, P. F. Teacher awareness: Social cognition in the classroom. *The School Review*, 1969, 77, 245–256. (b)

Smith, L. M., & Pohland, P. A. Participant observation of the CAI program. In H. Russell (Ed.), *Evaluation of computer assisted instruction program*. St. Ann, Mo.: Central Midwestern Regional Educational Laboratory, 1969.

Solomon, W. A description and analysis of a sequence of innovative social studies lessons taught in an elementary school classroom. Proposal for doctoral dissertation, Washington University, 1969.

Stanley, J. C. A common class of pseudo-experiments. *American Educational Research Journal,* 1966, 3, 79–87.

Tom, A. *An approach to selecting among social studies curricula.* St. Ann, Mo.: Central Midwestern Regional Laboratory, 1970.

Uhes, M. J. The open-closed cognitive dimension and divergent-convergent abilities. Unpublished doctoral dissertation, Utah State University, 1968.

Uhes, M. J., & Shaver, J. P. Dogmatism and divergent-convergent abilities. *The Journal of Psychology,* 1970, 75, 3–11.

Webb, E. J., Campbell, D. T., Schwartz, R. D., & Sechrest, L. *Unobtrusive measures: Nonreactive research in the social sciences.* Chicago: Rand McNally, 1966.

Wesley, E. B., & Wronski, S. P. *Teaching social studies in high schools.* (4th ed.) Boston: D. C. Heath, 1958.

Whitten, P., & Kagan, J. Jensen's dangerous half-truth. *Psychology Today,* August 1969, 3, 8, 66, 68.

Wispé, L. G. Teaching methods research. *American Psychologist,* 1953, 8, 147–150.

CHAPTER 40

Research on Teaching
Business Subjects

LEONARD J. WEST
City University of New York
Office of Teacher Education

The term *business education* has several meanings. At collegiate levels the term refers, on the one hand, to preparation for professional careers in the broad area of business management or in the specializations that serve management (e.g., economics, statistics) and, on the other hand, to the preparation of teachers of business subjects, mainly for the secondary schools. In the junior or community college there has been increasing attention to individually owned small business operation, side by side with the traditional focus on specific vocational training for office, retailing and services occupations. In the secondary schools the term covers specific preparation for office and retailing occupations as well as "general education" objectives relating to business, consumer, and economic information and understandings applicable to all people.

The office occupations embrace general clerical skills, typewriting and other office machines, stenographic and secretarial skills, bookkeeping and accounting, and the operation of data-processing equipment. Retailing occupations run the gamut from wrapping packages and operating a cash register to the operation of an individually owned small business, the latter at community college rather than at high-school levels.

The principal but not exclusive focus of this chapter is on relationships between teaching acts and learning outcomes. Attention is largely confined to investigations that permit generalizations about the consequences for learning of specifiable instructional behaviors bearing on the materials and methods of instruction. Reviews and syntheses of the entire spectrum of business-education research are available elsewhere.[1]

The extent to which there exists in business-education research a basis for descrip-

---

[1] See the descriptive reviews by Lanham and Trytten (1966) covering 257 studies, and by Price and Hopkins (1970) covering 260 studies mostly completed during the 1966–1968 period. More analytical and chiefly focused on instructional variables is the review by West (1969b) covering 111 investigations. Research bibliographies have been provided by Rahe for typewriting (1963) and for stenographic and secretarial skills (1965). Research bibliographies are also included in doctoral theses completed at Indiana University in bookkeeping and accounting (Devine, 1962), general business (Sluder, 1966), office practice (Prewitt, 1961) and economics (G. G. Green, 1965).

tion and analysis of relationships between teaching acts and learning outcomes varies with the several meanings or foci of business education given above. In the area of collegiate education for management, the overwhelming concern has been with objectives rather than with means of achieving objectives. Two major foundation-supported studies (Gordon & Howell, 1959; Pierson & others, 1959) have advocated an analytical treatment of subject matter aimed at long-term preparation for management careers, while Gallagher (1963) is a representative spokesman for the more conventional focus on a descriptive treatment of subject matter aimed at immediate job preparation as proper for undergraduate collegiate education for business.

Equally little on the effects of teacher behavior is to be found in the business–teacher-education literature. Studies of generalized teacher traits, as reviewed by Crunk (1960), and of credit and course allocations abound. Nineteen guidelines for the preparation of office-occupations teachers (Cook, 1966), representing a consensus among business-education leaders, cover the major concerns, but each is so global, e.g., "A teacher should have an understanding of and competency in the teaching-learning process" (p. 69), that nothing that relates instructional acts to learning outcomes is provided.

With hardly an exception, reliable information that could serve as a basis for identifying superior patterns of teacher behavior lies in studies that are task-specific, relating to the office and retailing skills and knowledges of the business curriculum.[2] Accordingly, the major instructional variables are treated on a subject-matter basis.

Concerning task-specific investigations, there is a substantial body of evidence for the typing task, somewhat less for stenographic skills, and not more than a few items for each of the other subject-matter or occupational areas within business education.[3] The large body of behavioral information on typing and stenographic skills probably arises from their distinctiveness as well as from their novelty. In contrast to the millenial concern with educational matters of universal interest, from Plato onward, the typewriter is an invention of the 1870s, and the shorthand system most widely used in this country (Gregg) dates from the 1890s. School training for business occupations is largely a twentieth-century phenomenon. Given two entities (the typewriter and shorthand systems) without a long history in the schools, it is not surprising that they should have been viewed as having distinctive characteristics, this view leading to the development of an edifice of training materials and methodological practices and to research on training variables pertinent to these tasks. Bookkeeping has almost as long a large-scale school history as typewriting and shorthand but seems not to have been perceived as having unique features calling for intensive methodological inquiries. The little that has been done in that and other lightly investigated business-education areas will be treated in turn.

THREE GENERAL PHENOMENA

A number of phenomena broadly applicable across vocational business education deserve brief mention before attention is given to details on a task basis. First is the concern with the development of character and personality traits thought to be associated with obtaining and retaining a job. In that connection, "the exhortations of hundreds of businessmen speakers at educational meetings over the preceding fifty years" (Lanham & Trytten, 1966, p. 57) are redundantly paralleled in the many surveys that report employer dissatisfaction

---

[2] The business-education research literature contains a small number of studies of teacher-education techniques (e.g., microteaching), but the information provided is not unique to business-teacher education.

[3] General clerical skills (aside from typewriting) are not treated in the present chapter because the research in that area has no pertinence to patterns of teacher behavior.

with employees for reasons of deficiencies in conscientiousness, initiative, dependability, common sense and ability to follow directions—not to mention grooming, speech, courtesy, and language and arithmetic fundamentals. As an extreme instance, secretaries, executives and secretarial teachers were reported to consider personal qualities more important for secretarial success than either fundamental or specialized skills and knowledges (Weber, 1969). To put such a finding in proper focus, one need only ask whether a person with exemplary character and personality traits, but who could not type, would be hired as a typist. Other studies (e.g., Cook & Lanham, 1966) report deficiencies in specific job skills, rather than in personal attributes, as the primary cause of dismissal from jobs among 16- to 21-year-olds. The pertinent generalization refers to "the failure to find clear-cut relationships between personality . . . and occupational choice or success," so that "our current knowledge of the role of personality . . . in work is impressionistic or, when quantitative, largely superficial" (Super & Crites, 1962, pp. 516–517). That characterization, the little that is known about how teachers might bring about the desired personal attributes in students, and the difficulties of reliable assessment of personal attributes of students by teachers suggest that instructional attention should preferably be addressed to less recalcitrant objectives.

A second general phenomenon is the impact of technology on office occupations. The advent in recent years of data-processing equipment has led to the establishment of training programs for data-processing occupations in some high schools and in many two-year colleges and proprietary schools. Bangs and Hillestad (1968) have estimated personnel needs in the field and the requirements for entry positions.

A third general phenomenon of recent years, common to many educational areas, is the development of instructional materials in programmed form. Those cited in the canvasses of business education research (Lanham & Trytten, 1966; Price & Hopkins, 1970) in the areas of shorthand, business mathematics, English fundamentals, business communications, economics, and bookkeeping and accounting have been tested against conventional instruction. The usual but not universal finding has been of superiority for the programmed materials. However, these studies do not, and were not intended to, provide useful generalizations about the controllable properties of that instructional medium. The extent to which the many commercially published programs are in routine use, as contrasted with those constructed by graduate students for thesis purposes, is not known.

OFFICE OCCUPATIONS

The most ambitious program of current research on training for office occupations is embodied in the New Office and Business Education Learning Systems (NOBELS) project. NOBELS is an outgrowth of dissatisfaction with high-school business education as "an aggregate of courses rather than a curriculum" (Lanham & Trytten, 1966, p. 26), rather than as integrated programs of learning. The project is self-described as a systems approach to curriculum analysis and modification following the constructs of behaviorists (Lanham, Herschelmann, Weber, & Cook, 1970). The outcomes of the earlier stages of the NOBELS program are summarized in the report of the development of an inventory of 375 performance goals derived from large-sample interviewing of office employees and their supervisors in large firms in metropolitan areas (Lanham et al., 1970). The report makes apparent the inadequacy of job title as an indicator of job duties, and it organizes its goals in 11 functional categories (e.g., accounting, production, sales, communications). The goal statements start with a "given" (e.g., "Given a request for credit information") followed by a specification of the action taken, each specification using one or more of 57 "action verbs" (e.g., the worker "compiles and delivers" the information to the requester). Statements of the kind quoted have some analogies with job analysis, but they have no psychological content and stop short of measures of employee proficiency at the various tasks covered by the performance goals. However, the investigators consider the performance goals to represent a marked improvement (in specificity) over what was formerly available and to provide a beginning basis for examination of current instructional materials and their modification when indicated.

The next phases of NOBELS are aimed at selection from the goal inventory of those goals pertinent to high-school and community college training, the preparation of relevant learning experiences, their classroom trial, assessment of trial results, and modification based on results. It is at the stage of "preparation of learning experiences" that the opportunity to bring instruction into closer accord with a psychology of learning and teaching exists. Before that, the goals may have to be rewritten with greater behavioral specificity than is denoted by "action verbs" such as adjust, arrange, check, correct, proofread. In some difficult instances (e.g., proofread), the mediating responses will have to be specified, as will means of bringing them under stimulus control, before an "effective learning experience" can be designed.

Typewriting

Typewriting instruction can conveniently be dichotomized into a) the early stages devoted to stroking techniques, keyboard learning, and the development of ordinary copying skills, and b) subsequent attention to the application of stroking skills to realistic personal and vocational typing tasks (e.g., correspondence, tables, manuscripts, forms), "production typing," as it is called.

There have been three major treatments of learning to typewrite. The first was the pioneer investigation of Book (1908), wholly devoted to stroking skills and followed by his advice to teachers (1925) based on his earlier study. Second was *Typewriting Behavior* (Dvorak, Merrick, Dealey, & Ford, 1936), a monumental treatise primarily devoted to ordinary stroking skills and based on a vast array of experimental evidence and the then-existing psychology of skill. Third was *Acquisition of Typewriting Skills* (West, 1969a), an exhaustive treatment of typewriting learning, based on the experimental and correlational evidence, that analyzes and makes recommendations for instructional materials and procedures for copying skills and for production typing in the light of that evidence. In *Acquisition of Typewriting Skills* five general principles are applied as yardsticks for evaluating instructional issues (reinforcement, contiguity, individual differences, transfer, and guidance versus confirmation techniques). Most of the particular studies mentioned below are discussed in West (1969a). On a narrower scale, Lindsay, in a doctoral thesis (1967), has treated motor-skill development in typewriting in the light of psychological concepts and theories, deducing three performance phases (familiarization and response orientation, refinement, fixation and automatization). Leonard and Newman (1966) also refer to the first two of those three phases in an inquiry into augmented feedback, and numerous human factors principles for keyboard design and operation are contained in a summary review prepared for the Post Office Department by Alden, Daniels, and Kanarick (1970).

Aptitude. In the light of Porter's estimate (1966) that 35 million Americans use the typewriter, it is clear that the typewriter has become even more an ordinary writing tool than a vocational device. This is not to minimize its vocational importance, however; 85 percent of all office positions for other than the unskilled require typing skill as a prerequisite (Cook & Lanham, 1966). Fortunately for the sake of widespread diffusion of typewriter use in the population, and to some extent accounting for it, ordinary stroking or copying skill has been shown in dozens of studies to be virtually independent of measured intelligence. However, kinesthetic sensitivity might be an important predictor of stroking skills (Fleishman & Rich, 1963). For production typing, the evidence on relationships with intelligence (from a small number of studies summarized in West, 1969a) is ambiguous: the obtained correlations range between 0.10 and 0.50, the lower values reflecting restriction of range in one or both variables. Martin (1956) reviewed the literature on aptitude tests for typing, suggesting that a task as near as possible to the criterion task might have some predictive value; Flanagan, Fivars, and Tuska (1959) have developed a "tapping" test. It may be concluded from the available evidence that beginning typewriting should be available to all, but possibly not advanced training for higher-level vocational skills.

Copying Skills. Stroking techniques, concurrent with keyboard learning, precede instructional attention to building copying speed and accuracy. Despite the conventional reference to "touch" typewriting and the heavy insistence on nonvisual techniques from the start of learning, West (1967) has shown the unavailability of kinesthetic feedback to beginners and has recommended large amounts of visual work at the start: as a source of feedback for responses in keyboard learning, for the sake of facilitating ballistic stroking in place of the pressing motions that often accompany early nonvisual work, and for its motivational and anxiety-reducing effects. Speed-forcing procedures that deny the learner the time to look back and forth from his copy to his machine provide a response-competition condition that is recommended as the primary means of accomplishing the transition to nonvisual operation; finer details for accomplishing the transition remain to be worked out by teachers.

Findings about the extent of chaining of responses among typists support a general principle for practice materials for building copying skills: ordinary, unselected English prose over a wide vocabulary. It was originally supposed (Book, 1908, 1925) that there exists a hierarchy of stroking habits corresponding to language units (letters, syllables, words, phrases). The consequence for years was a heavy focus on contrived keyboard drills (for keyboard learning and perfecting of "letter" habits) and, even now, on a relatively narrow vocabulary of common words to be typed "on the word level" (for skill building). Later evidence (Fendrick, 1937; an unpublished study summarized by West, 1969a, pp. 57–60) showed that up through the levels of skill commonly developed in school training (about 60 words per minute) much of the typing is still letter by letter and that chaining is largely restricted to a modest number of 2- and 3-letter sequences that have no necessary correspondence with syllables or words. A wide vocabulary of practice materials will contain the variety of letters and letter sequences in the language in their various positions in words and should thus be expected to have better transfer value than would a narrow vocabulary containing fewer letter sequences. H. H. Green (1932) showed equal proficiency at a common-word vocabulary by those trained on a common-word vocabulary and by those trained largely on a low-frequency vocabulary.

Concerning keyboard presentation order (finger by finger, row by row, "skip around"), all orders are equally effective provided they quickly permit the typing of normal language, rather than nonsense materials. Concerning rate of keyboard presentation, the typing textbooks vary between about five to about fifteen lessons (days) for the alphabet keys, although devoting two days per lesson and five to six weeks to alphabetic-keyboard presentation is not uncommon for so-called slow learners. The slow-but-sure rate of keyboard presentation is apparently based on the supposition that for the 26 letters of the alphabet there are

26 responses to be learned. Consider, however, that the "r" of "brush" brings the left index finger over a different distance at a different angle than is involved in the "r" of "from" or "cream" or "erase." There is not one "r," but several "r's"; likewise for the other letters of the alphabet. Keyboard learning involves hundreds of responses (motion paths), not merely 26, and the variety of motion paths should make apparent that the letter sequence, not the single stroke, is the proper focus of attention. The sooner the keyboard is presented, the sooner the wide vocabulary containing the letter sequences of the language and the motion paths that go with them can be used.

Keyboard presentation accomplished, in whatever number of lessons, the subsequent attention to building copying speed and accuracy is based on the uniform finding in numerous studies (reviewed by West, 1969a, p. 238) of an essentially zero correlation between speed and accuracy among students at all stages of training. With the low correlation suggesting that the two features of performance are based on different underlying factors, speed practice at forced rates is commonly conducted with tolerant error limits; separate practice is given to accuracy, preferably in the form of typing at comfortable rates. The effects of speed-accuracy programs depend on the amount and distribution of practice toward each objective, on the degree of emphasis (how fast? how accurate?), and on the extent to which practice goals are individualized. Accuracy practice has also commonly invoked a torrent of specially contrived practice materials that focus on specified types of motion sequences. These practice materials, as well as "rhythm drills," have never been shown to have the desired effects. Accuracy is not a function of materials or of equal interresponse intervals but of stroking at a comfortable speed.

External pacing of responses—at comfortable rates for the sake of accuracy and at uncomfortably high rates for the sake of the contiguity conditions that lead to chaining of responses and higher speeds—should theoretically be expected to have the desired effects. However, the several investigations of external pacing of responses (reviewed by Lanham & Trytten, 1966; Price & Hopkins, 1970; discussed in more detail by West, 1969a) have had varying outcomes. It seems probable that the effects of external pacing depend heavily on such variables as distribution of paced speed and accuracy practice, individualization of practice goals and pacing rates, and for some people a temperamental resistance to imposed response rates. The pacing, incidentally, is not metronomic, not stroke by stroke, with equal time intervals between strokes. That hallowed concept of typewriting rhythm (Book, 1908) was long ago shown to be wrong (Coover, 1923; Harding, 1933). Instead, easy stroking sequences (e.g., *th*) involve short latencies, while more difficult sequences (e.g., *az*) require longer interresponse times. Accordingly, in recent years pacing materials and devices have been designed and engineered for line-by-line pacing units or by quarter-minutes. Stroke-by-stroke pacing is confined to the earliest stages of learning and is handsomely implemented, using audiovisual techniques, in the electronic display panels for keyboard learning used in some proprietary school training (see the July 1969 issue of *The Office,* the June 1967 issue of *Personnel Management,* and the June 15, 1964, issue of *Steel* for examples).

A final issue on copying skills relates to the virtual dogma about repetitious practice. One small-scale study (Temple, 1963) addressed to the question found no advantages to it in contrast to nonrepetitious practice over a more varied body of materials. For speed-building routines that consist of repeating a piece of copy until it is completed in a given time before attempting a new piece of copy that sets a slightly higher speed goal, there is no alternative to repetitious practice. For untimed activities, on the other hand, there would seem to be little merit in the typical "type each word (or line) two (or three) times" tactics. This is because the pertinent response units for typing are the letter and the letter sequence. Since letters and letter sequences appear and reappear in various positions in a wide vocabulary of words, nonrepetitive practice at varied materials should be expected to have better effects than repetitious practice narrowly confined to the letters and letter sequences of a smaller practice vocabulary.

Production Typing. Conventional instruction focuses largely on copying skills, especially on stroking accuracy, through the first semester of instruction, with periodic attention to such skills thereafter. The supposition has been that copying skills make an important contribution to proficiency at realistic personal and vocational typing tasks. The evidence (Muhich, 1967; West, 1969a, Chap. 13) demonstrates, instead, that among trainees with up to 2+ years of instruction, decision-making about the placement of materials on the page (e.g., margins, table arrangement) plays a larger role in production proficiency than does stroking skill, increasingly so as amount of training increases. Copying speed has a moderate correlation with speed at production tasks, whereas copying accuracy is only slightly related to production accuracy. Apparently the typist's "set" for production typing differs from his perception of the copying task; accordingly, his stroking habits differ. Production-typing errors are greatly below copying errors, and typists at all levels of copying accuracy are found at all levels of production accuracy. Less attention to copying skills and earlier attention to production tasks and to the placement features of such tasks before executing them at the typewriter have indeed led to terminal proficiency greatly superior to that following the reversed, conventional tactics (West, 1971).

For production-typing training, the established generalization about guidance or "show how" versus confirmation techniques (Bugelski, 1956; Stolurow, 1959) is applicable: guidance is valuable if provided in small doses confined to the early stages of instruction; in large amounts or if continued too long, it is harmful. In contravention of that principle, current typewriting textbooks provide the learner with page-placement information (e.g., location of the date line in a business letter, side margins and tabular stops in a table) even at late stages of training. Other changes in the production-typing materials of selected typing textbooks that would bring them into better accord with the work of employed typists have been identified by Wise (1968): decreases in business letters, increases in tables and in numbers, and a wider spread of vocabulary.

A number of studies (e.g., Crawford, 1960; Hill, 1957; West, 1971) support the various inferences drawn here, and there is no contrary experimental evidence. Even so, conventional practices too often rely on the opinions of teachers, solicited via questionnaire (Robinson, 1967a). As one might expect, the experimental evidence sometimes shows these opinions to be correct, sometimes wrong.

Measurement of Proficiency. Copying skills are measured by "straight copy" tests —the line for line copying of perfectly printed prose, without error correction, usually for five minutes. These tests are scored for speed (words per minute) and for number of errors or, more commonly, by a composite score involving subtracting a penalty for errors from the speed score. Gross speed scores show high reliability (routinely in the 0.80s and 0.90s) even over long intertest intervals, whereas error reliabilities rarely exceed the 0.30s to 0.40s (West, 1969a, p. 296). Composite scores inevitably have intermediate levels of reliability (West & McLean, 1968). These data on score reliability, together with the earlier mentioned finding of low relationships between copying accuracy and production-typing accuracy, argue for separate speed and error scoring and for giving more weight to copying speed than to copying errors.

Once stroking speeds of about 20–25 words per minute have been attained—not before—the vocabulary of the straight-copy materials influences stroking speed but not accuracy (Robinson, 1967b; a number of studies summarized in West, 1969a, pp. 528–536). Copy difficulty is expressed in measures of syllabic intensity (mean number of speech syllables per dictionary word), stroke intensity (mean number of typewriter strokes per dictionary word, including punctuation and spacing), and percentage of common words (within the 1,000 most common words). Although for years it has been assumed that 1.40 represents mean syllabic intensity and 5.0 mean stroke intensity—with practice and test materials constructed accordingly—a reputable vocabulary of written business communication (Silverthorn, 1955) was found to have a weighted-for-frequency mean syllabic intensity of 1.54 and a mean stroke intensity of 6.0 (West, 1968). Despite the conventional underestimates of copy difficulty, copying tests have such a long history that well-established proficiency standards exist, as reflected, for example, in Civil Service typing tests.

The slighting of production typing in favor of copying skills has led to the virtual absence of national standards and norms for the genuine objectives of instruction. Normative data are confined to commercially published tests, as given in the series of Mental Measurements Yearbooks (Buros, 1972), none of which has been administered to samples of examinees sufficient for national extrapolation. However, a pioneer attempt to provide indices of production-task difficulty (McLean, 1971) as a necessary precondition for interpretable norms and standards, is a promising development.

Stenographic Skills

A brief description of stenographic skills in stimulus-response terms has been sup-

plied by West (1963). Dickinson (1966) examined methodological practices in stenographic instruction (e.g., Leslie, 1953) in the light of the writings of learning theorists, finding numerous practices to be without theoretical support. Research findings on several major instructional issues will be detailed following discussion of aptitudes and shorthand-system characteristics in relation to stenographic requirements.

Aptitude. Instruction in the two major symbolic systems of shorthand taught in this country (Gregg and Pitman) has characteristically been accompanied by failure rates approximating 30 percent (Frink, 1961). During the years when stenographic instruction in the high schools was typically for two years, only 40 percent of first-year enrollees took a second year of shorthand (Wright, 1965). Business teachers have continually complained that the business subjects have been made a "dumping ground" for low-ability, nonacademic students. For stenographic training the complaint is justified. There seems to have been little awareness among educational administrators that stenographic skills are on a par with the more difficult academic subjects in their demands on intelligence, showing correlations in numerous studies of 0.50 to 0.60 with measured IQ (Frink, 1961). These demands are created not only by a complex system of symbolic notation, but also by the requirement of high verbal skills (vocabulary, spelling, punctuation, word division, "word sense") for the correct transcription of shorthand outlines on the typewriter.[4] The problem of attrition has been aggravated by the trend in recent years toward reduction of stenographic training in the high schools to one year, often followed, however, by up to a full year of "secretarial practice" partly devoted to stenographic skills per se. In one study, the findings of which may well be typical of general ex-

---

[4] An *outline* is a shorthand word or phrase written without lifting the pen. *Transcription* refers to the conversion of the dictated shorthand notes (outlines) into standard English orthography on the typewriter.

perience (Smith, 1967), one year of training was found insufficient for attaining the traditional minimum standard of a shorthand writing speed of 80 words per minute. Numerous simpler, largely nonsymbolic shorthand systems have been developed, and some of them have been compared to Gregg shorthand in their effects on stenographic proficiency, sometimes under less than ideal experimental conditions. Lanham and Trytten (1966) are not optimistic about the fruitfulness of comparative studies and suspect that, whatever their outcomes, there is little hope of dislodging the more difficult symbolic systems.

In any event, an IQ below 110 appears to promise less than a 50-50 chance of success in stenographic training (Freiberg, 1968); grade-point average and grades in selected English courses are also pertinent predictors; the variables judged to underlie stenographic skills are represented in a number of validated prognostic tests reviewed in the various editions of The Mental Measurements Yearbooks. By whatever method, the screening of applicants for stenographic training is clearly desirable.

Stenographic Requirements and Shorthand System Characteristics. One avenue toward the reduction of attrition, besides the development of nonsymbolic systems, has been the reduction of system complexities in Gregg shorthand. The changes have been in the direction of making that system more fully phonetic and eliminating some shorthand theory rules found to have been confusing. However, Iannizzi's (1967) finding of no differences in dictation or transcription error rates as between learners of the 1949 and 1963 revisions of Gregg shorthand would appear to call into question the sufficiency of the system changes. Even so, the greater importance of variables external to the shorthand system is suggested by Iannizzi's finding that more than 80 percent of incorrectly written outlines were correctly transcribed, while more than half the transcript errors were from correctly written notes. Comparable results were found in studies by Lusk (1959) and Frye (1965). What might be called "word sense" (size of vocabulary and the ability to infer missing words or to interpret poorly written shorthand outlines from contextual clues) is probably the dominating factor, as shown by the findings of Hillestad (1961) and Uthe (1967) that the vocabulary level of the dictated materials, not shorthand-system characteristics, was highly correlated with errors in the shorthand notes. The generality of poorly written shorthand is reflected in the finding that about 18 percent of the shorthand outlines written from 80–words-per-minute dictation by those completing two years of high-school Gregg shorthand training were incorrect (Hillestad, 1961). The findings on errors in the typed transcript of Farmer (1962) for Pitman shorthand and of Baggett (1964) confirm the preeminence of verbal over shorthand-system skills.

Nonetheless, system features that reduce the demand on verbal skills must be helpful. Analysis of Gregg and Pitman shorthand reveals numerous instances of unwanted stimulus generalization and response generalization, of convergent and divergent associations, rather than one-to-one relationships between sound and symbol. It is probable that these difficulties are almost unavoidable in complex symbolic systems capable of sustaining court reporting speeds of 200+ words per minute. Only the simpler nonsymbolic systems, with their greatly lower speed ceilings, are largely free of such complexities. Moreover, the better nonsymbolic systems are no doubt adequate for some stenographic positions, as suggested by the dictation speeds found among employers (H. H. Green, 1950).

Instructional Variables. Attention is confined here to those variables that are exclusively stenographic: the encoding process of taking dictation in a symbolic shorthand system and the decoding process that mediates transcription of shorthand notes on the typewriter. Teachers necessarily give much attention to spelling, punctuation, word division, letter style and other verbal skills. But these latter features characterize all writing; they are not unique to the stenographic act.

Several of the leading issues in shorthand instruction are well represented in the several global "approaches" to shorthand learning, each comprised of many variables. The features of these various approaches, together with their purported advantages and disadvantages, have been summarized by Russon (1968), based on the personal judgment of the summarizer. The issues are:

1. Writing of shorthand at the outset versus devoting at least several weeks to reading of perfectly written textbook shorthand before writing is begun.

2. Deliberate teaching of the theory or rules of the shorthand system (and frequent testing for knowledge of theory) versus reading and copying of perfect textbook shorthand, without whys and wherefores, as a basis for taking dictation.

3. Early versus late introduction of new-matter dictation. *New matter* refers to materials not earlier practiced as such, that may or may not contain at least a few individual words the learner may never before have read or written in shorthand.

4. Early versus late introduction of transcription of shorthand notes on the typewriter.

Not a feature of the various global approaches, but important, is:

5. Extensive drill on the most common words in the language versus practice at them proportional to their frequency of occurrence in the language.

There are, of course, many ancillary issues—e.g., spread of vocabulary in the training materials, optimum dictation rates, increments in dictation rates for repetitive practice purposes, and so on.[5] Because dependable research evidence is in short supply on some issues, derivation of desirable patterns of teacher behavior sometimes requires recourse to inferences from the principles of a psychology of learning.

Concerning early writing versus reading, recognition is easier than reproduction; reading shorthand is simpler than writing it. How much reading might profitably precede writing is an empirical question not yet satisfactorily answered. Although practitioners do not put the issue in such terms, reading furnishes mediators for writing. Accordingly, it is common early instructional practice in Gregg shorthand to have learners vocalize the component sounds represented in a shorthand outline while looking at it (e.g., *s-a, say*; *s-e-d, said*). When "say" is later dictated by the teacher, the learner can spell its two component sounds to himself as he writes its two corresponding parts in shorthand. Pitman shorthand does not easily lend itself to vocalization techniques because, in it, vowels are inferred rather than directly represented.

Concerning focus on shorthand rules, since none of the leading symbolic systems of shorthand is fully phonetic, with undeviating one-for-one correspondence of sound to symbol, numerous shorthand outlines require adherence to a specified rule if they are to be correctly written. In early years there was much recitation of rules. In more recent years attention has focused on whether or not accurate transcripts depend on correctly written shorthand and whether correct shorthand, in turn, depends on an instructional focus on shorthand theory leading to technical correctness of outlines, as measured by frequent word-list tests.[6] The findings discussed earlier of

---

[5] See Frink (1961), Lanham and Trytten (1966), and Price and Hopkins (1970) for the spectrum of research on stenographic and secretarial skills. The present discussion is mostly confined to the five major issues itemized above.

[6] The typical word-list tests do *not* test knowledge of shorthand theory because they tend to consist of words and phrases earlier subjected to heavy practice. A proper test of theory knowledge requires the application of system rules to new words. Another objection is that the word-list tests are typically dictated and the outlines are later transcribed, thus confounding two other variables (writing speed and shorthand reading) with theory knowledge.

much incorrect transcription of correct out-lines and much correct transcription of in-correct outlines would seem to deny an important role to knowledge of shorthand theory and to technical correctness of short-hand outlines. Still, dealing with the issue of its own terms, one inquiry (Pullis, 1966) showed positive correlations between word-list scores and dictation and transcription scores, as did Danielson (1960) between word-list scores and dictation rates. How-ever, the conditions of word-list testing and of dictation-transcription testing are vastly different, and there is nothing whatever to show that correct shorthand in word-list tests was accompanied by correct shorthand in the dictation tests. Besides, the three phenomena (word lists, dictation, transcrip-tion) have no evident causal interrelation; instead, they are probably all related to general intelligence. The role of knowledge of shorthand theory and, in turn, of correct shorthand in relation to the criterion of accurate transcripts must be characterized as uncertain. The best that can be suggested is that correct shorthand is preferred to incorrect shorthand and that immediate feedback via prompt checking of outlines written under dictation conditions against model shorthand may be the most effective and economical way to handle the matter.

Concerning early versus late new-matter dictation, in the several studies "late" was taken to mean after completion of system theory, usually some time during the second semester of instruction. Neither Persing (1966), Baird (1967), or McKenna (1967), in a study that combined introduction of new-matter dictation with other variables, could find advantages for it in relation to deferred new-matter dictation. However these studies were not very explicit in de-tailing the tactics that accompanied new-matter dictation. The incidence of words never written before is not given, nor is it determinable whether immediate feed-back for the correctness of outlines was given. Since much incorrect shorthand seems to follow whether or not shorthand

theory is stressed, and since the potential vocabulary of occupational use of shorthand greatly exceeds the spread of vocabulary contained in standard instructional ma-terials, there would seem to be no option but to give students substantial amounts of practice in constructing new outlines under the press of dictation, amounts that can-not be sufficient unless begun relatively early in training. As between automatizing a high-frequency vocabulary and acquiring a method of coping with new outlines under dictation conditions, Hillestad's find-ing (1961) of a 2.6 percent error rate on the very high frequency words represented by the arbitrarily abbreviated "brief forms" of Gregg shorthand, in contrast to a 15.6 percent error rate on all other words, lends force to the recommendation made here. Prince (1967) found that intensive drill on the 500 most-used words led to better tran-scription performance on those words and on other words than did the nonuse of intensive drills. However, a more pertinent contrast would be between such drills and an equal amount of time devoted to new-matter dictation over a varied vocabulary deliberately including a reasonable number of words never before practiced.

The conventional deferring of typewritten transcription of dictated notes until rela-tively late stages of training has led to dis-appointing transcription speeds. No uncon-founded test of early transcription has been conducted. However, Condon (1945), in combining early transcription with other features, found the combination generally to be superior to a combination of more conventional instructional procedures that did not include early transcription. There is no apparent reason why plentiful practice at the criterion task of transcribing one's dictated notes at the typewriter should not be furnished. To do so, it must be started somewhat earlier than is typical.

Conventional instruction may be char-acterized as one that focuses on a high-frequency vocabulary, that continues guid-ance into late stages of training (e.g., "previewing" of selected outlines prior to dictation), and that defers practice at the criterion task until relatively late stages of training. The unimpressive consequences of such tactics suggest that they be reversed and that appropriately designed studies bearing on the reversed tactics would be desirable.

Measurement of Proficiency. There are, in principle, three criteria of stenographic proficiency: shorthand writing rate, transcription speed, and transcript quality or accuracy. In practice, evaluation of terminal proficiency in high-school training has tended to consist solely of a minimum requirement of 95 percent accuracy in transcribing business letter materials dictated for three to five minutes at 80 words per minute. It is not common practice to test at a variety of dictation speeds and to grade, in part, on the basis of the dictation speed at which the notes can be acceptably transcribed; at least there are no distributions of terminal dictation speeds in the research literature. Similarly, since it is not common practice to time the transcript, no transcription-speed standards exist. However, one fairly large-scale but old study (Wanous, 1940) found a median transcription speed in California high schools after two years of training of 14 words per minute. Possibly the mechanics of test-administration conditions that measure all three criteria are too burdensome for teachers. Also, no one has worked out a scoring scheme and a means of weighting the three criteria to arrive at an overall assessment of demonstrated reliability and validity, let alone one for which the arithmetic would be feasible for all teachers. The measurement of stenographic proficiency remains an important area for research.

The difficulty of test materials has been exclusively controlled in terms of syllabic intensity, with 1.40 assumed to represent average difficulty. Dictation is based on "standard" words; 80 words per minute means 112 speech syllables per minute

(80×1.40), not 80 dictionary words. Aside from the fact that 1.54 is the true mean syllabic intensity for a vocabulary of 11,055 different words of written business communication—so that 80 words per minute means 123, not 112, syllables per minute—West (1968) also found that syllabic intensity is virtually uncorrelated $(r = -0.11)$ with word frequency. The latter finding, and Hillestad's comparable one (1961), demonstrate that percentage of words in the dictation within the 1,500 or 2,000 most common words is a necessary additional index of the difficulty of dictation materials. The conventional 1.40 syllabic intensity index underestimates true average difficulty, overestimates student proficiency, and is additionally weak when unaccompanied by the index of percentage of common words in the materials.

Bookkeeping and Data Processing

Devine's (1963) descriptive compendium of the bookkeeping and accounting research is virtually devoid of inquiries bearing on patterns of teacher behavior. He found the "balance sheet" approach to be more popular than the "journal" approach—the bird's eye view to the worm's eye view; and he found "practice sets" to be popular. However, the evidence for the merits of working through an entire bookkeeping cycle, in contrast to piecemeal activities, is ambiguous. The large-scale NOBELS survey concluded that "...the functional classification of accounting and computing might well have been relabeled numerical data handling.... The number of tasks collected requiring application of 'principles of accounting' as taught in schools or 'double entry bookkeeping' as a system of financial transaction analyses was minimal" (Lanham et al., 1970, p. 27). Spanswick (1968) found that employers considered the one-year bookkeeping training that predominates in the high schools to be inadequate for initial employment in manual bookkeeping positions and its content unrealistic. Fairbank

(1968), on the basis of a 36 percent response to a mailed questionnaire survey of former bookkeeping students in New York State, found them to consider their training useful, although some instructional content was identified as having low job utility. Except for the small office in which the bookkeeper does other things as well, manual bookkeeping is expected to be taken over to a rather large degree by electronic data-processing techniques (Diebold, 1963).

Inquiries into data processing are exemplified in a national survey of data-processing managers (Bangs & Hillestad, 1968) which found that beginning positions in computer installations are available to high-school graduates in the majority of operator and clerical classifications (e.g., keypunch operator, unit records operator, tape librarian, computer operator). The community college is the locus for training as programmer and other higher-level positions. For entry positions, on-the-job training is often available and selection tests for operators are often used (Carter, 1965).

RETAILING AND DISTRIBUTIVE OCCUPATIONS

The research in this area has not been aimed at instructional variables. In a study of two groups of workers in distributive occupations who did and did not receive formal high-school training for such occupations, small and probably not significant differences were found in the workers' self-reports of the extent to which their jobs required or involved knowledge and experience, judgment, initiative and ingenuity, supervisory activities, and responsibility for sales volume (Mason, 1962). Entry positions in retailing occupations appear to have no apparent prerequisites other than high-school graduation (Cook & Lanham, 1966). The community college has increasingly become the locus for higher-level programs aimed at middle management and individually owned small-business operation. For small-business operation, the educa-

tional research has tended to be oriented toward traits and generalized abilities: communications skills, human relations sensitivity, thinking ability, technical knowledge and drive (Pickle, 1964). Kunsemiller (1961) interviewed and tested independent retail store owners in 66 California cities and concluded that the qualities that distinguish successful from unsuccessful owners are analytic ability, discriminating thinking, problem solving and decision making. The same qualities no doubt apply to success in hundreds of occupations.

GENERAL BUSINESS SUBJECTS

The general or social business subjects are considered part of general education. The research in the field has been descriptively summarized by Sluder (1966), revealing little pertinent to patterns of teacher behavior. The Joint Council on Economic Education, in a national survey of students and adults, found disappointingly low knowledge of "extremely elementary" economic understandings developed through the social studies curriculum (Bach & Saunders, 1965) and, as reported by Price and Hopkins (1970, pp. 17–18), has undertaken a three-year project (1969–72) aimed at the business curriculum that will focus intensively on teacher education, course structure, development of study materials, and evaluation.

STATUS OF RESEARCH

Lanham and Trytten (1966) have pointed out that the research in business education "has been almost exclusively produced by graduate students, motivated by degree requirements" (p. 95), as amply shown by the research listings in the spring issues of *The National Business Education Quarterly.*[7] The *Quarterly,* however, tends to con-

[7] As of 1971, abstracts of selected research studies, formerly published regularly in the *Quarterly,* now appear in the *Business Education Forum* (National Business Education Association, Washington, D.C.).

fine its listings to theses and dissertations furnished by department chairmen in institutions that grant graduate degrees. In these listings, master's theses greatly outnumber doctoral dissertations, and questionnaire studies that solicit opinions and judgments or that determine current status vastly outnumber experimental studies of the effects of instructional behaviors on student achievement. Although the productions of graduate students have displayed more statistical sophistication in recent years, much of their research suffers from the theoretical naiveté of which Wallen and Travers (1963) complain. Little of the business-education research reveals an understanding, on other than a superficial level, of the findings of a psychology of learning.

In recent years federal funding has made it possible to undertake more ambitious research enterprises under more sophisticated direction. It remains to be seen what impact these efforts will have on the instructional behavior of practicing teachers and on teacher-education programs.

REFERENCES

Alden, D. G., Daniels, R. W., & Kanarick, A. F. *Human factors principles for keyboard design and operation—A summary review.* Washington, D.C.: Post Office Department, Bureau of Research and Engineering, 1970.

Bach, G. L., & Saunders, P. Economic education: Aspirations and achievements. *American Economic Review,* 1965, 55, 329–356.

Baggett, H. W., Jr. *The validity of a measure of the difficulty of Gregg shorthand dictation materials.* (Doctoral dissertation, University of Minnesota) Ann Arbor, Mich.: University Microfilms, 1964. No. 64–9471.

Baird, S. J. *The effectiveness of introducing regular dictation of unpracticed material before the completion of Gregg shorthand theory.* (Doctoral dissertation, Oregon State University) Ann Arbor, Mich.: University Microfilms, 1967. No. 67-9681.

Bangs, F. K., & Hillestad, M. C. *Curricular implications of automated data processing for educational institutions.* Boulder, Colo.: University of Colorado, 1968.

Book, W. F. *The psychology of skill.* Missoula, Mont.: University of Montana, 1908. (Republished: New York: McGraw-Hill, 1925.)

Book, W. F. *Learning to typewrite.* New York: Gregg Publishing Co., 1925.

Bugelski, B. R. *The psychology of learning.* New York: Holt, Rinehart & Winston, 1956.

Buros, O. K. (Ed.) *The seventh mental measurements yearbook.* Highland Park, N.J.: Gryphon Press, 1972.

Carter, D. M. *A study of office training programs for data processing personnel in selected businesses in metropolitan Denver, Colorado, with implications for business education in the secondary schools.* (Doctoral dissertation, State University of Iowa) Ann Arbor, Mich.: University Microfilms, 1965. No. 65-11,601.

Condon, A. A comparative study of the transcription and functional methods of teaching elementary shorthand. Unpublished doctoral dissertation, New York University, 1945.

Cook, F. S. *Office and business education teacher training clinics.* U.S. Office of Education, Project No. 6-1522-1-32. Wayne State University, 1966.

Cook, F. S., & Lanham, F. W. *Opportunities and requirements for initial employment of school leavers with emphasis on office and retail jobs.* U.S. Office of Education, Project No. 2378, 1966.

Coover, J. E. A method of teaching typewriting based on a psychological analysis of expert typing. National Education Association, *Addresses and Proceedings,* 1923, 61, 561–567.

Crawford, T. J. *The effect of emphasizing production typewriting, contrasted with speed typewriting, in developing production typewriting ability.* Monograph 97. Cincinnati, Ohio: South-Western Publishing, 1960.

Crunk, D. E. *Guiding the teacher trainee's development of the qualifications of an effective teacher—with special application to the business teacher.* Vol. I and Vol. II. (Doctoral dissertation, Indiana University) Ann Arbor, Mich.: University Microfilms, 1960. No. 60-1263.

Danielson, H. A. *The relationship between competency in shorthand vocabulary and achievement in shorthand dictation.* (Doctoral dissertation, Indiana University) Ann Arbor, Mich.: University Microfilms, 1960. No. 59-6593.

Devine, J. W. *A comprehensive analysis, classification, and synthesis of research findings and thought on the teaching of bookkeeping and accounting, 1950–1960*. In two volumes. (Doctoral dissertation, Indiana University) Ann Arbor, Mich.: University Microfilms, 1963. No. 63-3816.

Dickinson, J. A. *The role of practice in shorthand skill development as related to selected classical theories of learning*. (Doctoral dissertation, University of Oklahoma) Ann Arbor, Mich.: University Microfilms, 1966. No. 66-14,205.

Diebold, J. When will your husband be obsolete? *McCall's*, 1963, 90, 64–65, 118–119.

Dvorak, A., Merrick, N. L., Dealey, W. L., & Ford, G. C. *Typewriting behavior*. New York: American Book, 1936.

Fairbank, R. E. A followup of New York State high school bookkeeping students. Albany, N.Y.: State Education Department, Bureau of Occupational Education Research, 1968.

Farmer, G. M. *An experiment to test the validity of a measure of the difficulty of shorthand dictation materials*. (Doctoral dissertation, University of Minnesota) Ann Arbor, Mich.: University Microfilms, 1962. No. 62-1777.

Fendrick, P. Hierarchical skills in typewriting. *Journal of Educational Psychology*, 1937, 28, 609–620.

Flanagan, J. C., Fivars, G., & Tuska, S. A. Predicting success in typing and keyboard operation. *Personnel and Guidance Journal*, 1959, 37, 353–357.

Fleishman, E. A., & Rich, S. Role of kinesthetic and spatial-visual abilities in perceptual-motor learning. *Journal of Experimental Psychology*, 1963, 66, 6–11.

Freiberg, F. A. A study to determine the validity of administering a stenographic aptitude test at Medford High School. Unpublished master's thesis, Wisconsin State University (Eau Claire), 1968.

Frink, I. *A comprehensive analysis and synthesis of research findings and thought pertaining to shorthand and transcription; 1946–1957,* Vol. I and Vol. II. (Doctoral dissertation, Indiana University) Ann Arbor, Mich.: University Microfilms, 1961. No. 61-3206.

Frye, C. F. An error analysis of dictation notes of second-semester high school students of Gregg Shorthand Simplified. Unpublished master's thesis, University of Tennessee, 1965.

Gallagher, B. G. One president's views on schools of business. *Collegiate News and Views* (South-Western Publishing), 1963, 16(3), 1–6.

Gordon, R. A., & Howell, J. E. *Higher education for business*. New York: Columbia University Press, 1959.

Green, G. G. *The teaching of economics: A comprehensive analysis and synthesis of research findings and thought*. Vol. I and Vol. II. (Doctoral dissertation, Indiana University) Ann Arbor, Mich.: University Microfilms, 1965. No. 65-2371.

Green, H. H. The relative effectiveness of the thousand commonest words in the teaching of typewriting. *University of Iowa Monographs in Education, Research Studies in Commercial Education*, 1932, 5, 167–178.

Green, H. H. The nature of business dictation. Unpublished doctoral dissertation, University of Pittsburgh, 1950.

Harding, D. W. Rhythmization and speed of work. *British Journal of Psychology,* 1933, 23, 262–278.

Hill, D. J. A study of the effects of drill upon typewriting. Unpublished master's thesis, University of Michigan, 1957.

Hillestad, M. C. *Factors which contribute to the difficulty of shorthand dictation materials*. (Doctoral dissertation, University of Minnesota) Ann Arbor, Mich.: University Microfilms, 1961. No. 61-567.

Iannizzi, E. *Transcription and shorthand errors among elementary and advanced high school writers of Simplified and Diamond Jubilee Gregg Shorthand*. (Doctoral dissertation, New York University) Ann Arbor, Mich.: University Microfilms, 1967. No. 67-11,107.

Kunsemiller, C. F., III. *Recognized educational needs of independent retail store owners in selected cities in California*. (Doctoral dissertation, University of Southern California) Ann Arbor, Mich.: University Microfilms, 1961. No. 61-6293.

Lanham, F. W., Herschelmann, K. M., Weber, C. P., & Cook, F. S. *Development of performance goals for a new office and business education learnings system (NOBELS)*. Project No. 8-0414. U.S. Office of Education, Bureau of Research, 1970. ED 041 139.

Lanham, F. W., & Trytten, J. M. *Review and synthesis of research in business and office occupations education.* Columbus, Ohio: Ohio State University, Center for Research and Leadership Development in Vocational and Technical Education, 1966.

Leonard, J. A., & Newman, R. C. On the acquisition and maintenance of high speed and accuracy in a keyboard task. *Ergonomics,* 1966, 8, 281–304.

Leslie, L. A. *Methods of teaching Gregg shorthand.* New York: McGraw-Hill, 1953.

Lindsay, V. J. *Psychological concepts germane to efficient motor skill development in typewriting.* (Doctoral dissertation, Indiana University) Ann Arbor, Mich.: University Microfilms, 1967. No. 67-4019.

Lusk, N. M. A study of the comparison between construction of shorthand outlines according to theory and the accuracy of transcription. Unpublished master's thesis, University of Washington, 1959.

Martin, A. Predicting keyboard trainability. *Occupational Psychology,* 1956, 30, 216–227.

Mason, R. E. *An analysis of related instruction for cooperative part-time programs in distributive education in Illinois.* (Doctoral dissertation, University of Illinois) Ann Arbor, Mich.: University Microfilms, 1962. No. 62-647.

McKenna, M. A. *An experiment to determine the effect of the early introduction of new-matter dictation in the teaching of beginning shorthand to college students.* (Doctoral dissertation, Michigan State University) Ann Arbor, Mich.: University Microfilms, 1967. No. 67-1656.

McLean, G. N. Difficulty indices and performance standards for office-typing tasks. Project 8-B-113, U.S. Office of Education. City University of New York, Division of Teacher Education. *Research Report 71-2,* January 1971. ED 047 160.

Muhich, D. M. Key-stroking versus decision-making factors in proficiency at office-typing tasks. Unpublished master's thesis, Southern Illinois University (Carbondale), 1967.

Persing, B. S. *A classroom investigation of when to begin new-matter dictation in Gregg shorthand.* (Doctoral dissertation, University of Oklahoma) Ann Arbor, Mich.: University Microfilms, 1966. No. 66-14,240.

Pickle, H. B. *An inquiry into the characteristics of successful small business managers.* (Doctoral dissertation, University of Arkansas) Ann Arbor, Mich.: University Microfilms, 1964. No. 64-10,073.

Pierson, F. C., and others. *The education of American businessmen.* New York: McGraw-Hill, 1959.

Porter, S. Typewriter boom. *New York Post Magazine,* June 22, 1966, 2.

Prewitt, L. V. B. *A comprehensive analysis, classification, and synthesis of research findings and thought in the area of office practice instruction, 1951–1959.* Vol. I and Vol. II. (Doctoral dissertation, Indiana University) Ann Arbor, Mich.: University Microfilms, 1961. No. 61-3221.

Price, R. G., & Hopkins, C. R. *Review and synthesis of research in business and office education.* (2nd ed.) Columbus, Ohio: Ohio State University, ERIC Clearinghouse on Vocational and Technical Education, 1970.

Prince, D. J. An experiment comparing the achievement in transcription of students when the 500 most used words were emphasized with the achievement of students when these words were not emphasized in beginning shorthand. Unpublished master's thesis, University of Maryland, 1967.

Pullis, J. M. *The relationship between competency in shorthand accuracy and achievement in shorthand dictation.* (Doctoral dissertation, North Texas State University) Ann Arbor, Mich.: University Microfilms, 1966. No. 66-10,953.

Rahe, H. *Typewriting research index.* New York: McGraw-Hill, 1963.

Rahe, H. *Shorthand-secretarial research index.* New York: McGraw-Hill, 1965.

Robinson, J. W. (Ed.) *Practices and preferences in teaching typewriting.* Monograph No. 117. Cincinnati, Ohio: South-Western Publishing, 1967. (a)

Robinson, J. W. The relation of copy difficulty to typewriting performance. *Delta Pi Epsilon Journal,* 1967, 9(2), 9–24. (b)

Russon, A. R. *Methods of teaching shorthand.* Monograph No. 119. Cincinnati, Ohio: South-Western Publishing, 1968.

Silverthorn, J. E. *The basic vocabulary of written business communication.* (Doctoral dissertation, Indiana University) Ann Arbor, Mich.: University Microfilms, 1955. No. 55-386.

Sluder, L. I. *An analysis and synthesis of research findings pertaining to general business.* Volumes I–III. (Doctoral dissertation, Indiana University) Ann Arbor, Mich.: University Microfilms, 1965. No. 65-14,070.

Smith, E. R. *A comparison of the learning difficulty of Forkner alphabet shorthand and Gregg shorthand* (DJ). (Doctoral dissertation, Ohio State University) Ann Arbor, Mich.: University Microfilms, 1967. No. 67-2540.

Spanswick, R. S. *An investigation to determine the qualifications and skills desired, accepted, and actually used in manual bookkeeping jobs which were listed in Chicago and New York City newspapers during the months of May and August, 1966.* (Doctoral dissertation, Northern Illinois University) Ann Arbor, Mich.: University Microfilms, 1968. No. 68-1120.

Stolurow, L. M. The psychology of skills—Part II: Analysis and implications. *Delta Pi Epsilon Journal*, 1959, 2(3), 16–31.

Super, D. E., & Crites, J. O. *Appraising vocational fitness by means of psychological tests.* (Rev. ed.) New York: Harper & Row, 1962.

Temple, P. A comparison of two methods of teaching typewriting. Unpublished master's thesis, University of Minnesota, 1963.

Uthe, E. F. *An evaluation of the difficulty level of shorthand dictation material.* (Doctoral dissertation, University of Minnesota) Ann Arbor, Mich.: University Microfilms, 1966. No. 67-14,686.

Wallen, N. E., & Travers, R. M. W. Investigation and analysis of teaching methods. In N. L. Gage (Ed.), *Handbook of research on teaching.* Chicago: Rand McNally, 1963. Pp. 448–505.

Wanous, S. J. Transcription standards in business correspondence. Unpublished doctoral dissertation, University of Pittsburgh, 1940.

Weber, W. C. *A Q-sort study of curriculum priorities in secretarial education.* (Doctoral dissertation, Arizona State University) Ann

Arbor, Mich.: University Microfilms, 1969. No. 69-12,567.

West, L. J. The acquisition of stenographic skill: A psychological analysis. *Business Education Forum*, 1963, 18(1), 7–8.

West, L. J. Vision and kinesthesis in the acquisition of typewriting skill. *Journal of Applied Psychology*, 1967, 51, 161–166.

West, L. J. The vocabulary of instructional materials for typing and stenographic training—research findings and implications. *Delta Pi Epsilon Journal*, 1968, 10(3), 13–25.

West, L. J. *Acquisition of typewriting skills.* New York: Pitman, 1969. (a)

West, L. J. Business education. In R. L. Ebel (Ed.), *Encyclopedia of educational research.* (4th ed.) New York: Macmillan, 1969. Pp. 105–106. (b)

West, L. J. Effects of programed versus conventional instruction on proficiency at office-typing tasks. *Research Report 71–8.* City University of New York, Office of Teacher Education, 1971. ED 055 420. (See also: *Delta Pi Epsilon Journal*, 1972, 14 [2], 28–36.)

West, L. J., & McLean, G. N. Evaluation of error-cutoff scoring in straight copy typewriting tests. *Business Education Forum*, 1968, 23(2), 10–12.

Wise, E. L. *A comparative study of the materials typed by beginning typists in representative business offices of metropolitan Denver, Colorado, with production materials contained in selected high school typewriting textbooks including the development of a scale of difficulty for typing similarly constructed materials in different forms.* (Doctoral dissertation, University of Colorado) Ann Arbor, Mich.: University Microfilms, 1968. No. 68-14,409.

Wright, G. S. *Subject offerings and enrollments in public secondary schools.* United States Office of Education, OE-24015-61. Washington, D.C.: Government Printing Office, 1965.

CHAPTER 41 Research on Teaching Foreign Languages

EMMA M. BIRKMAIER
University of Minnesota

In the 1950s business and government asked to have foreign languages taught in the way communication of the future would require. Carroll's (1969a) comprehensive article on the status of foreign language instruction from 1960 to 1967 indicated what can be done with plentiful financial support from the federal government. Enrollments grew, language-learning materials emphasizing oral communication were developed, institutes trained teachers for the new approach, and research in learning and teaching accelerated.

However, the past few years have seen society challenging the educational establishment. Cuts in federal spending caused the virtual elimination of support for foreign language programs. Researchers were uncomfortable with their findings. Negative publicity did not help. Students challenged the singleness of method prevalent in the 1960s which did not recognize the individual's idiosyncratic approach to learning nor his needs for foreign language study.

This chapter will be limited to the trends and research findings of 1967–1970 with an occasional reference to earlier studies.

BIBLIOGRAPHICAL SOURCES

The American Council on the Teaching of Foreign Languages, founded in 1967, in its quarterly, *Foreign Language Annals,* and other publications, devotes itself to language learning problems and publishes an annual bibliography (Birkmaier & Lange, 1968; Harmon, 1968; Lange, 1969, 1970b). Bibliographical aid is also provided by two Educational Resources Information Center clearinghouses, one for foreign language teaching in general operated by the Modern Language Association (MLA), the other for linguistics, uncommonly taught languages, and English as a second language, at the Center for Applied Linguistics.

The *Review of Educational Research* devotes a chapter to foreign language education every three years (Birkmaier, 1958; Johnston, 1961; Sawyer, 1964; Birkmaier & Lange, 1967); the *Encyclopedia of Educational Research,* an article every 10 years (Birkmaier, 1960; Carroll, 1969a). Surveys of research update the preceding chapters (Carroll, 1963, 1966; Ornstein & Lado, 1967). Periodic abstract coverage in America is provided by *Language and Language Behavior Abstracts;* in Britain, by *Language Teaching Abstracts.*

In 1968 the American Council on the Teaching of Foreign Languages began publishing an annual assessment of trends, issues and research in *The Britannica Review of Foreign Language Education* (Birkmaier, 1968). The chapters cover the theory and practice as well as the context and organization of foreign language teaching and learning. Volume 2 (Lange, 1970a) focuses on individuated instruction and reviews work in the teaching of English as a second language.

ENROLLMENT TRENDS

A National Education Association (NEA) survey (1967) indicated that foreign languages were offered to elementary-school students by approximately 95 percent of large public school systems, 75 percent of average school systems, 60 percent of low average school systems, and 50 percent of small school systems.

Modern Language Association surveys on foreign language enrollment in public secondary schools, grades 7–12, showed the impact of the 1958 National Defense Education Act on foreign language study. Whereas public secondary-school enrollment increased by 50 percent in eight years, the foreign language enrollment grew 70 percent (Kant, 1970). The largest spurt in foreign language enrollment occurred from 1960 to 1965. From 1965 to 1968 the growth was only 5.7 percent whereas secondary-school enrollment increased 7 percent. Spanish grew 15 percent, German 27 percent, Italian 10 percent, French 6 percent, and other languages 92 percent. Russian and Latin suffered a serious decline of 10.7 percent and 37 percent, respectively. Apparently modern languages grew at the expense of Latin. As a result, Latin teachers are re-examining their goals and innovating interdisciplinary programs (Erickson, 1970, chapter 10; Kovach, 1968, chapter 14).

Teitelbaum (1969), comparing 1966 with 1968 data on foreign language programs in 64 Long Island school districts, found an alarming decrease in Russian, Latin and marginal programs despite increased language enrollment. Spanish and French showed an increase of 70 percent to 90 percent. The study also indicated an abandonment of language laboratories and advanced placement programs.

While college foreign language enrollments grew faster (31 percent) than total college enrollment (25.5 percent) between 1960 and 1963, they barely kept pace from 1963 to 1965 and from 1965 to 1968 had only a 10 percent growth as compared with a 36 percent increase in college enrollment (Brod, 1970, chapter 12). The less widely taught languages such as Hebrew, Chinese, Japanese and Portuguese increased by 40 percent between 1965 and 1968 (Kant, 1970).

In a sampling of 275 colleges, Richards and Salas (1969) noted an erosion of the foreign language requirement with 29 percent reporting a downward trend, outright abolition, reduction or an expansion of options. Very few institutions are reaffirming entrance requirements (Association of Departments of Foreign Languages, 1969, 1970). This trend probably will have an impact on language study in the public schools.

The abolishment of requirements reflects student rejection of prescribed curricula in general. It necessitates a re-examination of college language curricula, especially their purpose in higher education.

Enrollment surveys have been put to little diagnostic use. Dusel (1968, chapter 15) suggests careful periodic sampling as a better source of information about hidden causal factors for the results obtained. National and community attitudes, administrative policy, budget priorities and the quality of teaching all affect growth and decline of elective subjects. Attitude, interest and aptitude assessments are needed in developing relevant foreign language programs (Jakobovits, 1970, chapter 5). If not done, the "liberating experience" of foreign language programs in the schools and liberal arts colleges could become a memory.

LINGUISTIC AND PSYCHOLOGICAL THEORY

Linguists and psychologists are concerned with the design of language, better explications of *competence* (the speaker-hearer's knowledge of his language), *performance* (the application of that capacity), and the processes occurring in the speaker-hearer when he produces sentences and perceives them when spoken by others (Bach & Harms, 1968; Chomsky, 1968; DiPietro, 1968; Postal, 1968). The study of deep and surface grammar and the role of semantics are of paramount interest. Lenneberg (1967) supports the contemporary theorist's idea of language universals when he concludes from his studies on physiological and psychological aspects of language acquisition and disorders that "language is a manifestation of species-specific cognitive propensities" (p. 374), and that cognitive function categorizes and extracts from the environment.

The vigorous expansion of contrastive studies reveals much, theoretically and pedagogically, about language (Alatis, 1968). Procedures used to contrast the languages of the world with one another are presently closely allied with the search for universals and the recognition of deep and surface structures. Contrastive studies are now oriented toward competence (Ritchie, 1968). Their real contribution is to show how the second language differs from the learner's native language. The interlanguage differences cover syntax, semantics and phonology, and they point out the new ranges of competence the student needs that have to be built into the learner wherever discrepancies occur (DiPietro, 1970). Contrastive studies do not tell us when and in what way a student makes a mistake. There are too many other variables that affect student performance—e.g., attention span, personal motivation and instructional techniques.

The modern theoretical linguists' development of the semantic component of language learning runs parallel to the applied linguist's attempt to add semantic depth to existing audiolingual instructional strategies. The inadequacies of structural drills not accompanied by meaningful situational contexts illustrate the importance of the semantic component. Oller and Obrecht (1968) report teaching two groups of students the same set of instructional exercises. One group had meaning given once, then proceeded to listen, repeat and manipulate drills. The second group emphasized meaning, extending the situation by questions and answers and directed dialogue activities. Analysis of response latency and accuracy indicated that relating practice exercises to live communication caused earlier attainment of the goals. The experimenters neatly isolated a variable which has hindered both competence and performance in foreign language learning.

If the language teaching profession accepts the transformationalist's views that operant conditioning, overlearning and reinforcement are not enough for language acquisition, and that ordinary linguistic behavior also involves the formation of new sentences according to abstract rules, language teachers will have to take another look at the audiolingual approach which has not been able to help students attain the linguistic competence expected. Most certainly the training of the future teacher will have to include more work in grammatical theory and cognitive psychology (Chomsky & Halle, 1968).

Although historical linguistics yielded to synchronic studies, the new approaches to historical linguistics offer new insights to the student (Chomsky & Halle, 1968; Postal, 1968). Labov (1966) deals with the role played by social stratification in language change. The sizable body of data on linguistic performance and its societal features relates to the linguist's theory of competence and performance. For the language teacher a close communication between psycholinguist and sociolinguist in the description of speech communities and individual members of these communities is imperative for effective foreign language teaching. Few foreign language texts present social levels of style in a systematic way (Fishman, 1968a; Jakobovits, 1970; Rosenberg & Koplin, 1968).

Psycholinguists and foreign language pedagogues now have the opportunity to experiment within the framework of several linguistic models. If these are to aid language learning, they need psychological support for the way the linguist orders his rules, the way the foreign language teacher presents them, and the way the speaker-hearer applies them in processing the speech act.

STUDENT CHARACTERISTICS

Research on student aptitude, attitude, and motivation and their relationship to success in foreign language learning have been given considerable attention recently. According to Carroll (1962), foreign language aptitude consists of auditory ability, inductive language learning ability, grammatical sensitivity, and ease of rote memorization. Intelligence, motivation and general scholastic ability are independent of language aptitude. However, all contribute to success in language learning.

Three most-used aptitude batteries are the Carroll-Sapon Modern Language Aptitude Test, the Carroll-Sapon Elementary Modern Language Aptitude Test and the Pimsleur Language Aptitude Battery. Pimsleur (1966) improved the correlation of his battery with success in foreign language study by considering the grade-point average (a perseverance factor) and a student's statement of interest in learning a language.

For prognosis, aptitude tests should be used only where budget and time factors demand that individuals who show the greatest chance of succeeding be found. They should not be used to exclude students from foreign language study in public schools since aptitude is only one factor contributing to success in foreign language learning. Any individual able to speak his

native language can attain competence in a foreign language if given time, quality of instruction and motivation.

The diagnostic function of aptitude tests still remains to be exploited. Components in the tests which measure grammatical sensitivity and auditory ability can be used to achieve the kind of grouping recommended in underachievement studies (Pimsleur & Struth, 1969; Pimsleur, Sundland, & McIntyre, 1966). The subtests can also provide controls in language learning research.

In investigations of the values American students hold with regard to foreign language study, it is clear that achievement is not a central goal. Two surveys of college students' interest in foreign languages indicated that ⅓ to ½ have no interest in their specific foreign language. Fifty percent take a foreign language primarily to attain a reading knowledge. Most disapprove of it as a college requirement. In the Pennsylvania Project (P. D. Smith, 1970) highschool students' attitudes declined during the two years of their language experience. College requirement was the primary objective and one in four, even at the end of four years of study, saw no real use for his language skills. The challenge for the teacher is to perceive his role clearly as an "interest director" teaching language as a code of a different and interesting social group (Feenstra, 1967; Jakobovits, 1970, chapter 2; Politzer, 1953–1954; P. D. Smith, 1970).

In their investigations of the roles of attitude and motivation, Lambert and his associates found that students with low aptitudes can learn a foreign language if attitude and motivation are strong. Even those with unfavorable attitudes succeed if aptitude is high. Aptitude is needed for learning grammar and vocabulary. However, attitude, motivation and orientation contribute to the rapid acquisition of listening and speaking. Certainly these factors affect the learner's perseverance in his language study and his reactions to contact with a foreign culture. There is also evidence that becoming bilingual usually carries with it the tendency to become bicultural. Students' orientation toward other linguistic-cultural groups is largely developed within the family. The relationship between sociocultural factors and success in foreign language performance is so important that a systematic examination of such variables must be incorporated into the design of foreign language programs if they are to be successful (Fishman, 1968a; Jakobovits, 1970; Lambert, 1968; Lambert, Gardner, Barik, & Tunstall, 1963; Tursi, 1970).

OBJECTIVES AND EVALUATION

Foreign language learning goals fall into four broad categories: speaking, reading, communicating, and cultural awareness. The implementation of these goals is dependent upon an articulated, precise description of objectives and accompanying evaluation techniques (Steiner, 1970). Valette (1969a) developed a taxonomy in which the total language learning experience is reduced to 1) areas of competence and 2) categories of behaviors in the cognitive, psychomotor and affective domains. The former includes listening, speaking, reading, writing, kinesics (body language), an acquaintance with the culture, a familiarity with the literature and communication. The behaviors in the cognitive domain ascend from knowledge to comprehension, application, analysis, synthesis and evaluation; in the psychomotor domain, from perception to mimicry-memorization to manipulation to internalization and free production. In the affective domain the student moves from receiving through responding to valuing. With the assistance of grids (1969a, pp. 24, 32), Valette illustrates the interrelationships among objectives and domains. The framework enables teacher and researcher to develop test items evaluating the total language experience. The grids show lacunae in kinesics, deep culture, the higher literary aims, the affective domain and communication, thus indicating a need for curriculum development and evaluation in these areas.

Standard or Norm-referenced Tests

In foreign languages achievement tests are norm-referenced and criterion-referenced. The former compares student performance with national samples; the latter reports student proficiency in absolute terms where the student is graded on a mastery/nonmastery basis.

A classification of commercial tests measuring a variety of skills and knowledge has been undertaken by the Center of Bilingual Studies at Laval University (Mackey, 1967a; Savard, 1968). Most widely used are the California Common Concepts Test, the MLA-Cooperative Foreign Language Classroom Tests, the MLA-Foreign Language Proficiency Tests for Teachers and Advanced Students, the Pimsleur Proficiency Tests, and the College Entrance Examination Board Achievement Tests (see Buros, 1965; Valette, 1967, 1969a). These tests are normally used to provide comparative data. According to the Valette taxonomy the tests are limited in scope and contain biases. The reading tests unduly emphasize vocabulary knowledge, most speaking tests focus only on accurate production of phonemes, and listening tests are not nearly comprehensive enough. None accurately test real communication. These inadequacies make their indiscriminate use in research projects questionable (P. D. Smith, 1970).

Criterion-referenced Tests

In studies on underachievement Pimsleur, Sundland, and McIntyre (1966) pointed out the cumulative nature of language learning. Less than 50 percent of first year "A" students get the same grade in the second year; more than 50 percent of first year "B" students get a lower grade in the second. Unless a student masters the material for the first year, he stands very little chance of success in his second year.

Innovative work is occurring in the field of criterion-referenced testing. G. Newmark and Sweigert (1966) demonstrated the feasibility of using criterion-referenced testing in research when comparing the effectiveness of three elementary-school Spanish programs only to find students attaining a small percentage of the stated objectives. Present methods of testing a sample of linguistic objectives obscure deficiencies in learning conditions and materials (Valette, 1969a).

Mastery learning utilizes formative testing which covers a brief unit of instruction and is graded on a mastery/nonmastery basis. Banathy (1968a) states that an objective in speaking proficiency contains: 1) the context in which the student operates, 2) the kind of language features he acquires, 3) the degree of accuracy and fluency he attains, and 4) the types of tasks the learner is expected to perform. The student is given as many opportunities as he needs to attain the objective successfully. The criterion-based test not only diagnoses but also prescribes remedies (Bloom, 1968).

M. I. Smith (1968) experimented with sixth-grade students of Spanish. Group I had to answer 80 percent of the items on a formative test before proceeding to the next unit; Group II was informed of test results but continued with the next unit; Group III, the control group, was not given the results of the unit tests. At the end of the year, although covering less material, Group I showed significantly greater gains on unit pretests and posttests and performed significantly better than the other groups in the final test. Smith concludes that teachers held responsible for *specific* objectives can be at least 1.6 times more effective than those not held responsible.

Since criterion-referenced tests require prior establishment of the language items to be measured, the difficulty lies in determining the sequencing of the structures and selection of vocabulary. Assuming that structurally languages have a closed system, Damore (1968) developed a system of classifying structures in categories. However, in the area of vocabulary, sampling techniques are still required. Valette (1968b) presents

a core-test concept in which all students master core vocabulary, core structures, and the phonemic and morphophonemic systems. Those who finish first do supplementary work in reading and listening. Since all students work on the same core material, group work in speaking and writing is facilitated. Grades are replaced with report cards indicating the number of units mastered.

Techniques for formative evaluation not only enable students to achieve success but could eliminate the attrition rate in foreign languages. Tests based on a taxonomy of objectives could solve problems of articulation and placement.

The profession is exploring better ways of testing listening comprehension (Belasco, 1967; Brière, 1967; Spolsky, Sato, Walker, & Arterburn, 1968; Valette, 1964, 1968a), administering and scoring speaking tests (Carton, 1964; J. D. Clark, 1967; Stack, 1966), and developing new types of items and new approaches (Pimsleur, 1961; Roy, 1967). Some experts suggest that the message communicated in composition work is of prime importance. Errors and spelling mistakes which do not interfere with the understanding of the message should be graded less severely or overlooked and expressions highly appropriate to the message given extra credit.

Little testing has been done in kinesics. Green (1968) categorized the gestures of Spanish natives. Filmclips make it possible to measure whether a student perceives certain movements, understands their significance and analyzes the conditions under which they are used. Simulation techniques are also used.

In the area of deep culture Lado (1964) and Seelye (1968) have been working on testing techniques ranging from the cognitive to the affective domain. Seelye (1966) described difficulties in validating deep culture items in a macroculture which contains a variety of microcultures. Yousef (1968) found students knowing a foreign language and its culture refusing to apply this knowledge in situations where behavior patterns of the foreign culture ran counter to the student's native culture. In the affective domain, attitude scales have been developed specifically for research projects but are now becoming available to the profession (Jakobovits, 1970, chapter 5; Snider & Osgood, 1969).

Testing real communication cuts across all areas—language, kinesics, culture. The total behavior of the student is evaluated in a situation in the target country, face to face with its speakers, or in structured simulations where the burden of performance and comprehension is placed on the student. It is obvious that precise definitions of the cultural, communicative and affective components are needed before refined and effective tests can be devised.

Davies (1968), Harris (1968), Lado (1964), Paquette and Tollinger (1968) and Valette (1967) discuss testing problems and illustrate them with copious item types. A chapter by Carroll (1968) in Davies's *Language Testing Symposium* (1968) develops a system for classifying items. Teachers and researchers will find each volume relevant.

CURRICULA AND INSTRUCTION

Curricula

Ways in which foreign language programs can efficiently make use of modular scheduling, team teaching, paraprofessionals, grouping, individuated instruction, new types of learning tasks and resource centers are dependent upon the model and the goals of a particular foreign language program. Arendt (1970), Banathy (1968a), JeKenta and Fearing (1968) and Logan (1970) report curricular innovations at the elementary, secondary and college levels. Most are pilot programs with little or no research results on language competence, student attitude toward language, and culture and language learning.

Elementary School Foreign Language Programs. Foreign languages in the ele-

mentary school got off to a bad start in the 1950s, but just recently good programs have begun to flourish and various patterns are emerging (Otto, 1968). Elementary foreign language teachers are collaborating with teachers in other disciplines to enrich the learning environment, especially in the inner-city schools (Paquette & Allen, 1969). Good instruction elicited an increasing mental maturity, motivation, and advancement in the pupils' language progress (Donoghue, 1969; W. H. Smith, 1967). Foreign languages in the elementary school programs also resulted in broader and more comprehensive achievement when students continued with the language in high school (Oneto, 1968; Vocolo, 1967). Short daily sessions of instruction were found to be most effective, especially in increasing speaking skills (Cornfield, 1965; Muller & Muller, 1967). Training in speaking preceding training in listening seemed to cause better results (Mace, 1966). Physical involvement in learning tasks produced greater listening comprehension (Asher & Price, 1967; Humphrey, 1965).

Secondary-school Programs. The variation in programs in secondary schools is as great as that of the elementary school. Although the profession speaks of 9-, 6- and 4-year sequences, few schools have them. The nongraded school (Fearing, 1969), the maintenance of skills program (Grittner, 1968), innovative short courses (Arendt & Fearing, 1971), intensive summer language programs (Elkins, 1968), and more programs for foreign language study abroad (R. A. Clark, 1968) attempt to maintain continuity of the foreign language at the advanced levels. Greater flexibility is provided by humanities and other subject-matter aspects taught within the study of the foreign language (Ort & Smith, 1969). The program is no longer a college-preparatory program. Rather it is beginning to serve the learner in attaining his own objectives in crosscultural communication.

The learning carrel in the materials resource center plus an electronically equipped classroom has replaced the laboratory of the 1960s (Fearing, 1970). Optical equipment is incorporated in both carrel and classroom. Thus the language laboratory concept is fulfilling its original purpose—helping to individuate instruction by giving the student a chance to learn languages at his own pace and in his own manner (Arendt, 1970; Dodge, 1968; W. F. Smith, 1970).

Methods

Although present methods or approaches to language learning are roughly classified as audiolingual or traditional, to differentiate between them is difficult. By devising an analysis technique, Mackey (1967a) was able to identify 15 different methods. Hayes, Lambert, and Tucker (1967) are developing techniques by which to ascertain whether course design, program administration and individual teaching performance conform to certain principles and procedures that seem to play a role in successful language learning. Thus far the authors have analyzed ratings which 364 instructors at National Defense Education Act institutes gave 324 features believed to be significant in developing language proficiency. The consensus strongly favors the practices assumed to be effective in an audiolingual approach.

The Pennsylvania Foreign Language Project

Design. Comparative studies on different approaches are numerous. The most challenging was the Pennsylvania Foreign Language Project, a well-designed, large-scale, longitudinal investigation conducted from 1965 to 1969 (P. D. Smith, 1970). It undertook to determine the effectiveness of three teaching strategies and three laboratory systems as used in typical American classrooms. Complete data on age, intelligence and foreign language aptitude were gathered for 2,171 typical high-school students in 104 beginning French and German classes from a sample of schools throughout the state. Thirty-eight measures were obtained on

1,190 students in 50 classes at the end of the second year. A 10 percent random sample of students was given speaking and writing tests at the end of each of the two years. Standardized tests were used. The 104 Project teachers were considered representative of urban, suburban and rural schools, and of selective academic and lower socioeconomic areas. Twenty-four intact classes were carried through French III and French IV, and data were obtained on 92 students who completed level IV classes during the school year 1968–1969 to assess the long-range effect of the methods and laboratory treatments, the motivation which prompted students to continue, and the achievement levels that could be attained in a four-year language sequence.

Teaching methods were defined by a panel of experts. The strategies were defined as 1) traditional, with emphasis on reading, writing, translation and grammar analysis; 2) functional skills or audiolingual, stressing controlled vocabulary and language structures with emphasis on listening and speaking; and 3) functional skills plus grammar, corresponding to 2 above but including grammatical analysis.

The laboratory systems complementing strategies 2 and 3 above were a) audio-active, with two 25-minute sessions per week during which a 10-minute drill tape was played twice; b) audio-record, with two 25-minute sessions per week with recording of student responses to a 10-minute drill tape; and c) tape recorder in the classroom with daily 10-minute tape-guided practice. In systems a and b the groups received guided practice in the classroom via tape recorder during 1/5 of each class period.

Results. The Pennsylvania Foreign Language Project was to provide empirical support for the audiolingual approach and to validate an assumption that the language laboratory helps students acquire language more efficiently. Results showed no differences among the three teaching strategies on any skills except reading, where the traditional group performed significantly better than the audiolingual groups. No differences were observed among the three laboratory systems with respect to achievement, and no effective strategy-system combination could be detected. At the end of the fourth year, students from the traditional group performed significantly better in both listening and reading than did those from the audiolingual groups.

The best overall predictors of foreign language achievement were scholastic success and the Modern Language Aptitude Test. Student attitudes toward foreign language study indicated a downward shift and were independent of teaching strategy or language laboratory treatment. And no relationship existed between any teacher variable and class attitude toward language study. Females had a significantly higher foreign language aptitude than males. No significant relationship existed between teacher scores on the MLA Proficiency Tests and class achievement. On the standardized tests students did not achieve up to the national norms for their grade and experience in language learning. Coverage of the materials in the audiolingual groups was less than indicated by the authors of the textbooks.

The success of the traditional group in reading is understandable. The traditional students covered twice as much material as the audiolingual students. Valette (1969b) indicated that coverage corresponded to 525–650 words for the latter group as opposed to 1400–1500 words for the former. Although the difference was significant, it was small. The small spread may be related to better vocabulary retention by the audiolingual groups. The Project points out that size of vocabulary is directly related to success in reading.

Critique. Reviews have been critical of sampling and design (J. D. Clark, 1969), difficulty and insensitivity of criterion measures (Valette, 1969b), lockstep use of equipment (Martin, 1969), nonadherence to guidelines (W. F. Smith, 1970), and the unspecified weighting of laboratory performance and laboratory maintenance problems (Hocking, 1969).

In his extensive review Carroll (1969b) concluded that the Pennsylvania Foreign Language Project did not infer the abandonment of the audiolingual approach since the traditional method incorporated considerable spoken language. Nor did the Project indicate the abandonment of language laboratories. It did not reveal what machine-aided instruction could do in conjunction with traditional texts nor the degree of interaction between teacher proficiency and laboratory use. With audiolingual teachers more proficient in oral skills than the traditional teachers, the laboratory was not given an opportunity to show its advantages under *less* proficient teachers, which is one reason for installing laboratories.

The study disclosed the vastness of foreign language instructional content—vocabulary, grammar, phonological and graphemic systems—which must be taught and which were more successfully taught by traditional method materials. Apparently audiolingual methods place too little emphasis on content with too much emphasis on *habit-formation* techniques which *could retard* the learning process. This became apparent at the end of the third year when the traditional group led the audiolingual groups significantly in both reading and listening skills (Carroll, 1969b).

There is a need for clearer definition of objectives and methods. Effective strategies cannot be encapsulated in *a method*. Teachers tend to cross methodologies. Materials and techniques in machine-aided instruction need to incorporate motivational power and student involvement. Only then can the profession know its real capabilities.

Problems of Instruction

Most comparative studies find no significant difference between the audiolingual and cognitive-code approaches in listening and speaking. If there is, it will be slight and in favor of the audiolingual approach. However, in reading and writing, the cognitive-code approach achieves significantly more at the college, senior and junior high-school levels (Chastain & Woerdehoff, 1968; Lusetti, 1968; P. D. Smith, 1970). The assumption seems to be that the cognitive-code and the audiolingual approaches are mutually exclusive when in reality they may be highly integrated. If language learning is developing psychomotor skills, then semantic, structural and cultural understanding of the language to be mastered helps to manipulate and generate language skills. Thus cognitive processes seem to be necessary to make efficient use of the time allowed for foreign language learning in formal education (Rivers, 1964).

Reviews by Carroll (1953, 1963, 1965), Birkmaier (1960) and Birkmaier and Lange (1967) discuss large comparative studies as contrasted with the small, discrete studies which focus on a specific contribution to learning. Such small studies are ineffective if not placed within the framework of different learning models which provide more precise information for determining the strategies to be used for attaining predetermined objectives.

At the college level Chastain and Woerdehoff (1968) found the deductive presentation of language structures superior to the inductive, with analysis superior to analogy. Meaning was found to be fundamental in language practice and the multisensory approach seemed more effective than the natural order of presentation. The experimenters found low aptitude students achieved greater success with the audiolingual approach than with other approaches.

One of the principal tenets of the audiolingual approach is the *time lag* between the presentation of oral and written language to prevent interference of the two language systems in cases where both use similar graphic systems.

Lange (1966), working with high-school students of French, exposed two groups to

a 12-week prereading treatment. The other two groups used a multisensory approach where all four language skills were used simultaneously in the introduction of a unit of work. Using standard tests, at the end of 12 weeks both approaches were found to be equally effective in listening, reading and writing with the prereading group more effective in speaking. However, at the end of the year this difference in the speaking skill no longer existed.

Muller and Muller (1968) developed techniques for determining whether exposure to Portuguese written symbols comparable to those of English interferes with the formation of pronunciation habits in Portuguese. The experiment contrasted a group not allowed to see the written symbols of Portuguese for four weeks with one that used the written symbols as a visual prop for oral work. The group not using the written symbols had a distinct pronunciation advantage at the end of the four weeks. The situation was analyzed to see which letters caused the difficulties. Interference was shown to be due to the difference of pronunciation represented by the same orthographic symbols used in both languages. The development of a predicting formula to examine sound-symbol association in both English and Portuguese can be applied to other languages to predict points of interference and thus anticipate the interference with appropriate analysis and drill before it actually occurs.

Spaced and Massed Learning. Few studies have been done in this area. Williamsen (1968) evaluated an intensive learning experience with the usual paced program at the college level. Nineteen students living in a dormitory during summer session studied Spanish for an eight-week period with a daily program of four 55-minute instruction periods, four half-hour laboratory sessions and two hours of homework. The experimental group was compared to a control group completing two years of Spanish from 1965 to 1967. After their eight weeks the experimental group equaled the control group after one year of instruction; 12 students achieved the level of the control group after two years of instruction. With the changing scheduling patterns in high schools and colleges that incorporate modules of six to eight weeks for concentrated study in a particular field, intensive language programs like the one described above can be a possible boon for language teaching (Elkins, 1968).

Listening, Reading, Speaking, Writing. There is a paucity of empirical research on listening and reading. Most of the literature involves theorizing and conjecture. A substantial part of the reported research is extrapolated from seemingly related native language investigations. A genuine drought of scientifically graded listening and reading materials at the beginning and intermediate stages prevents the profession from making progress in these fields (Jarvis, 1970; Rivers, 1968). A. N. Smith (1970), reviewing the literature on speaking and writing, describes pilot programs exploring the adaptability of individuated instruction. These programs are in need of careful evaluation as to their effectiveness in bringing about better skills, communication and attitudes.

The attainment of truly liberated communication at the advanced levels in formal school situations was the topic of a Northeast Conference Report (Edgerton, 1968). The lack of good evaluating techniques at this level of instruction has hindered the profession from determining its effectiveness in bringing about liberated expression. Using each of the four language skills, Rivers (1968) outlines a series of procedures to attain this freedom in communication. In the most neglected area—listening comprehension—she outlines four stages: identification; identification and selection without retention; identification and guided selection with short-term retention; identification, selection and long-term retention. She describes various techniques to use for each stage.

Drills. Although practice drills play a significant role in instruction in the new methodologies, they have been found to be dull and ineffective in promoting language communication. In the study by Oller and Obrecht (1968) and corroborated by L. Newmark and Reibel (1968) and Politzer (1968), it is during the contextual drill, where meaning and context are emphasized, that students attain most success in generating language.

Situations in which languages are taught are unpredictable. Teaching strategies effective with children do not necessarily work with adolescent and adult groups. The individual's learning style will not always adapt to a method. Goals as well as attitudinal factors, the teacher, motivation and materials used play an important part in language learning.

Long-term effects of exposure to foreign language study cannot be determined from short-term studies such as those conducted by the profession at the present time. A wait of as much as five to 10 years, perhaps even longer, may be needed to note the full effect on the life-styles, attitudes and actions of people exposed to language study.

Since no theoretical models of foreign language pedagogy have as yet been established and with no empirical data to test their implications if the models should be forthcoming, there seems to be room for eclecticism. New materials and strategies of instruction show this (Finocchiaro, 1969; Rivers, 1964, 1968; Rutherford, 1968). How to teach still remains an open question left to the practitioner rather than to the linguistic theorists of a few years ago.

Machine-Aided Language Learning

Chapters by Arendt (1970), Dodge (1968) and W. F. Smith (1970) give valuable information on new electromechanical equipment and its potential in foreign language programs. The 1969 Northeast Conference Report (Edgerton, 1969) covered nonprojected visuals, sound recordings, slides and filmstrips, transparencies, motion pictures and video tape in foreign language learning, with uses illustrated by demonstration films (Dodge, 1969).

Although the language laboratory still represents a continuum of equipment from simple tape recorder through audio-active-record capabilities to remote-control, dial-access and video-complemented student positions, with the reduction of federal funds the rather inexpensive electronic classroom has again become popular. Teachers committed to electromechanical equipment continue to use it despite the negative publicity on the Pennsylvania Project.

However, language laboratories need greater flexibility for more interaction with the student. Chomei and Houlihan (1968–1969) assessed the effectiveness of short-delayed, long-delayed and simultaneous feedback (audio-active) equipment on auditory memory. The study was done on three groups of high-school students, each using programmatic tapes in one of the treatments. After two months of intensive study students performed best on the listening and speaking tests when using short-delayed feedback. Long-delayed and simultaneous feedback were less effective. After retraining the last two groups with short-delayed feedback equipment, the differences disappeared. Apparently short-delayed feedback promoted motivation by reducing the time interval in discovering correctness of response and by demanding greater attention. It more nearly simulated real communication. The students became accustomed to correct listening habits and responses. Brown (1968) described two simulation strategies which provide more life-like communication. The first strategy involves recording a teacher's voice as he interacts with a live student (the foil). Only the teacher's remarks are recorded. The foil's responses give feedback on the approximate time-lapse for the answer. Students have the illusion of interacting with a live tutor. The simulated

conversation strategy involves the student in a situation in which he is confronted with a somewhat unpredictable communication. He acquires the structures and vocabulary needed to understand the communication. However, he cannot predict the possible recombinations needed. This exercise does not confirm the responses the student might generate. Its value lies in manipulated freedom. Brown advises having students go through the conversation several times with suggested responses given before they are on their own. Such tutorial exercises can teach language competence, audiolingual performance, and with the aid of optical equipment could eventually involve the student in interacting with selected cultural concepts.

Grittner (1969) holds that for visual and audio learning materials to play an effective role they must be totally integrated into a language learning system. He gives 18 criteria for developing such a system. Obviously strategies used in machine-aided learning must also contain an instructional component. A sophisticated use of an electronic classroom, the Classroom Laboratory Instructional System, was tested by Banathy and Jordan (1969) at the Defense Language Institute. The purpose was to involve students actively in learning a greater quantity of linguistically and pedagogically well-organized materials than is possible in the normal classroom. The program made intensive use of electronic equipment. The teacher, as manager of the learning process, determined when the student was to use the semiprogrammed materials of the system. The long-range experiment (starting in 1962) showed the average Classroom Laboratory Instructional System student's language production to be seven times greater than that of a member of the control group. The experiment needs replication in schools and colleges to see whether the same results will eventuate.

The studies that have been mentioned reveal machine-aided instruction to be effective in semi-individualized and highly-motivated intensive language learning. Electro-mechanical-optical equipment has an unlimited capacity to assist the teacher. *But,* emphasis must be on content and organization of the instructional materials used and what combinations of teaching strategies and equipment promote effective and efficient learning for the *individual* student. More research is needed to test the effectiveness of the innovative equipment and the new audiovisual language programs so profusely described by Arendt (1970), Dodge (1968) and W. F. Smith (1970).

Programmed Learning. Programmed instruction helps students learn language at their own rates (Mueller, 1968b). Detailed descriptions of the principles of programmed learning in foreign languages exist (Lane, 1964; Mueller, 1968a; Spodak, 1966). Fiks (1969) gives detailed information on 48 programs. Although Arendt (1970) maintains that in a formal school situation existing programmed courses lack motivation, Shulze, Arendt, and Rainey (1966) found the pairing of students at the high-school level to be beneficial. Valdman (1968) and Morton (1968) found that display sessions where small groups of students (4 or 5) would practice their communications skills with each other facilitated and kept the interest of the college students. The trend seems to be toward programming certain elements of language such as discrimination training or the control of morpho-syntactic patterns. Such partial programming becomes an instructional component of a foreign language course that incorporates various media and instructional techniques (Marty, 1968; Sweet, 1968).

Computer-Assisted Instruction. Despite arguments against it (Ornstein, 1968), computer-assisted instruction (CAI) can attain a true Socratic dialog (Adams, Morrison, & Reddy, 1968). Studies by Ruplin and Russell (1968) and elaborated by

Morrison and Adams (1968) suggest that CAI provides for the teaching of partial skills, especially those aspects of foreign language learning which are the mechanics of language. Poulter (1969) describes a means by which daily listening comprehension quizzes can be administered providing both student and teacher a continuous record of achievement. The feedback increases student motivation. Several years of experimentation using CAI as an alternative to regular instruction indicated that the student using CAI experienced 10 times more interaction than a student in a single student-teacher interaction situation during a typical 50-minute class (Rosenbaum, 1969). Although the CAI laboratory emphasized written rather than aural exercises, there was little difference in speaking and listening comprehension between the CAI and non-CAI group. In reading and writing, the CAI group significantly outperformed its counterpart, probably due to the fact that it had received more systematic practice in syntax and vocabulary. Gains from CAI treatment were proportionately larger in the case of students who did poorly than for the very best students. Final achievement scores of the CAI group were more homogeneous.

The strength of CAI lies in remediation which can be given with exactitude so that the learner will know where to focus attention when faced with a similar situation. Total supervision is exercised in the learning process. Once criterion performance is attained the student skips over redundant material and uses his time more effectively, an aspect missing in foreign language programmed learning courses. Many psychologists look toward CAI as a key to better understanding of the process that takes place within the individual as he acquires another language.

The technical aspects of CAI such as machines used, programming, preparation of materials, execution, pedagogical control, and evaluation are discussed by Adams (1969), Adams, Morrison, and Reddy

(1968) and Morrison and Adams (1968). CAI at the present is highly experimental, controversial and costly.

THE FOREIGN LANGUAGE TEACHER

In the 1960s teachers were trained to be competent in audiolingual skills. New curricula of the 1970s demand further changes. In reviewing teacher-training programs since the publication of Paquette's guidelines (1966), Altman and Weiss (1970) and McArdle (1968) found few innovative programs. Although National Defense Education Act institutes provided an excellent model for preservice and inservice training (Axelrod, 1967), college departments did little about changing curricula to implement the work of the institutes.

Video-taping and interaction analysis are frequently used in teacher-training programs. By applying a systems approach Banathy (1968b) focuses on in-class performance that identifies specific behaviors. Longer periods of teaching and longer professional exposure beginning as early as the college freshman level, study abroad, moving methods courses into the schools to be taught concurrently with practice teaching, and performance-oriented microteaching have become part of the training programs. Few programs provide experiences with several teachers, with groups of students with different characteristics, or with different organizational patterns in the school. Training programs for teaching foreign languages to the disadvantaged are scarce (Dugas, 1967; Mackey, 1967b; Politzer & Bartley, 1967; Sheehan & Willis, 1969).

The profession is not clear as to the content of methods courses (Altman, 1970; Strasheim, 1967). Strasheim advocates a team-teaching approach involving personnel from each language. Prospective teachers, when involved in the teaching situation, are deficient in giving clear, simple explanations and demonstrations of structure, and in pre-

senting literature in a relevant way (Horner, 1970). Contemporary literature and an increased emphasis on culture and area studies are recommended subject matter (Keppeler, 1969; Rabura, 1969).

Graduate Teaching Assistants. In a recent survey Hagiwara (1970) studied the training of graduate assistants. Of 191 supervisory personnel, over 35 percent had no doctorate and 71 percent held the rank of assistant professor or below. Those charged with the supervision of lower-level courses tended to be young and held insecure positions. Fifty percent had literature as their specialty; only 17 percent specialized in methodology. Thirty percent of the supervisors received no released time for supervisory duties. Unfortunately, supervision is assigned to persons not particularly qualified for the job. Hagiwara listed the duties of a supervisor at the University of Michigan that go beyond class visitation: an introductory workshop for new teaching assistants, workshops on reading, a course in applied linguistics, checking tests and quizzes, evaluating new teaching fellows, class visits to teaching fellows in line for promotion, personal supervision of those deficient in teaching techniques, individual conferences with instructors whenever necessary, and checking departmental grade reports.

Elementary Foreign Language Teachers. Training foreign language teachers for elementary schools has received little attention. According to Gefen (1969) they must be elementary-school teachers, preferably regular classroom teachers. He presents an inservice training model with two components: a part-time course with 100 hours of instruction and a full-time intensive course of three months most profitably spent in the foreign country.

Prospective Teacher Competency. Few studies have been done on the influence of teacher behavior, knowledge and skills on student achievement. Using the MLA Foreign Language Proficiency Tests in a nationwide testing program of 2,782 college seniors majoring in foreign languages, Carroll (1967) provided evidence on a number of issues important in training prospective teachers. Listening and speaking skills were generally low; time spent abroad had a potent effect on language skills; students who had begun foreign language in the elementary school or who spoke it at home had an advantage. Aptitude was related to degree of skill attained. However, low aptitude students, through diligent study or study abroad, were able to compensate for deficiencies. Men and women were equal in language-learning ability. Students at large institutions did better than those at small ones, and those at private institutions better than those at public colleges and universities.

Teacher Competency and Student Achievement. The Pennsylvania Project found teacher proficiency correlating highly with scores on the MLA Foreign Language Proficiency Tests but not with teacher self-ratings. There was no significant relationship between teacher scores in all seven parts of the MLA test battery and achievement scores of first-year classes in the foreign language skills. Seemingly teachers' language proficiency at the beginning levels of instruction was not as important as assumed. However it did play a singular role at the advanced levels. After the second level, student listening ability correlated highly with teacher scores on the speaking test.

To determine the effects of interaction analysis, Moskowitz (1968) taught a category system for describing student-teacher interaction to prospective teachers in training. Questionnaires and observations indicated that prospective teachers with such training were most positive toward teaching, used more indirect teaching in grammar and conversation lessons, and were perceived more favorably by students in their classes. Moskowitz taught in-service teachers three systems of interaction analysis. Using these instruments teachers analyzed tape recordings of their teaching prior to the course and compared them with a video tape of themselves microteaching part way through their training. Activities were aimed at sensitizing teachers to the influence their behavior had on students. Teachers felt that studying observational systems changed their behavior, gave them confidence and more competency in working with students. Politzer and Weiss (1970) tried to identify teachers successful in terms of student achievement and to compare their behaviors and characteristics with a group identified as less successful. Each of 17 high-school French teachers was recorded on video tape in four 15-minute segments over a five-month period. They taught in districts which serviced a broad socioeconomic area. Audiolingual materials were used. Data from criterion tests, questionnaires, the MLA Foreign Language Proficiency Tests, systematic observation and rating of classroom techniques yielded 40 variables. Class means on the criterion tests were adjusted for aptitude. The intercorrelation matrix indicated a series of interrelated teacher behaviors correlating significantly with student achievement. The use of free response drills, visual aids, frequency of switching from one type of drill to another, residence in France and optimum performance in aural comprehension were characteristic of the successful language teacher.

To what extent study abroad and teacher competence in audiolingual skills supersede flexibility and innovativeness is not clear. Certainly teachers' sensitivity to adjust to student needs does play an important part in the success of their students.

Teacher Certification. Surveys on teacher certification show such complexity in procedures as to make inter- and intrastate standardization almost an impossibility. Teachers are still certified by number of hours in approved programs rather than by performance (Perkins, 1968; Sheppard, 1970).

The emphasis has been on the evaluation of teacher competence in the language skills. What the profession needs is an analysis of teacher performance in the new type foreign language programs translated into behaviors which can be objectively described and evaluated. A classification of teacher competencies has been made in a study already mentioned (Hayes, Lambert, & Tucker, 1967).

New graduate-school programs in foreign language education are now providing the personnel capable of training elementary-school foreign language teachers, secondary-school teachers, supervisors and college teachers rather than literary scholars (Altman & Weiss, 1970; Thomsen, 1970; Van Abbé, 1968).

CONCLUSION

There are no simple answers to language teaching. In spite of decades of innovation and research, the continuous questioning of our efforts and the persistent dissatisfaction among learners are still with us.

Methods fanaticism must yield to inquiry. We need intense empirical study of language acquisition in order to do justice to the complexities of the language problem. We need to determine what aspects of language are to be taught, their relative importance, when and how they can be taught most effectively, and how to adequately test for them. Attention needs to be focused particularly on the *learner,* with an eye to adapting teaching to his specific needs.

Language learners differ in their objectives and specialized needs. Therefore the range, objectives and techniques of language teaching will vary in accordance with specific requirements. One of the most surprising things about language is that the native language is acquired by *all* humans almost without fail, whereas a foreign language is rarely learned efficiently in a formal school situation.

Besides educational, linguistic and psycholinguistic research, there is an equal need for sociolinguistic and sociocultural research. The sociocultural component is essential to language learning. A theoretical framework is needed to identify and select appropriate cultural data relevant to the learning and use of any language.

Research and practice in teaching and learning native and foreign languages should be closely linked. Joshua Fishman (1968b) writes, "Native as well as foreign language teaching should benefit from the concept of a speech community with a repertoire of varieties" (p. 11).

The extreme complexity of language learning makes teaching an undertaking of interlocking activities involving the schools at all levels, the education of teachers, the producers of materials and the community. Lack of stress on linguistic and cultural aspects of the contemporary language at the university level can affect the quality of language teaching at all levels.

Language can be taught and learned in school settings. These include direct field experience, simulated environments, provisions for varied activities and the teaching of subjects in the foreign language. Much can be learned from a systematic evaluation of bilingual and multilingual schools.

Foreign languages and their teaching are in jeopardy where no national language policy exists. The question of where to place a given language in an educational system depends upon the importance attributed to that language by the particular society in which it is taught. The United States needs a social milieu in which foreign languages are accepted, promoted and used if language teaching is to succeed. It is only on such a basis that one can plan according to explicit priorities and objectives.

By concentrating on limited aspects of

language teaching we endanger the overall enterprise. The content, techniques and technology must have continued imaginative attention. Especially urgent is a perspective on language learning in its broadest social and educational context.

REFERENCES

Adams, E. N. Field evaluation of the German CAI lab. In R. C. Atkinson, & H. A. Wilson (Eds.), *Computer-assisted instruction: A book of readings.* New York: Academic Press, 1969. Pp. 205–208.

Adams, E. N., Morrison, H. W., & Reddy, J. M. Conversation with a computer as a technique of language instruction. *Modern Language Journal,* 1968, 52, 3–16.

Alatis, J. E. (Ed.) *Report of the nineteenth annual round table meeting on linguistics and language study.* Georgetown University Monograph Series in Languages and Linguistics, No. 21, 1968.

Altman, H. B. Preparation of high school German teachers: Practical training. *Die Unterrichtspraxis,* 1970, 3, 66–78.

Altman, H. B., & Weiss, L. Recent developments in the training and certification of the foreign language teacher. In D. L. Lange (Ed.), *The Britannica review of foreign language education.* Vol. 2. Chicago: Encyclopaedia Britannica, 1970. Pp. 239–273.

Arendt, J. D. Media in foreign language teaching. In D. L. Lange (Ed.), *The Britannica review of foreign language education.* Vol. 2. Chicago: Encyclopaedia Britannica, 1970. Pp. 157–189.

Arendt, J. D., & Fearing, P. *The extended foreign language sequence: With emphasis on new courses for levels IV and V.* Code No. xxxviii-A-8. Minnesota: State Department of Education, Division of Instruction, 1971.

Asher, J. J., & Price, B. S. The learning strategy of the total physical response: Some age differences. *Child Development,* 1967, 38, 1219–1227.

Association of Departments of Foreign Languages. The foreign language requirement: Status reports. *Bulletin of the Association of Departments of Foreign Languages,* 1969, 1(1), 7–10; 1(2), 9–11; 1970, 1(3), 5–10.

Axelrod, J. National Defense Education Act foreign language institute programs: The development of a new educational model. *Publications of the Modern Language Association of America,* 1967, 82(4), 14–18.

Bach, E., & Harms, R. T. (Eds.) *Universals in linguistic theory.* New York: Holt, Rinehart & Winston, 1968.

Banathy, B. H. Current trends in college curriculum: A systems approach. In E. M. Birkmaier (Ed.), *The Britannica review of foreign language education.* Vol. 1. Chicago: Encyclopaedia Britannica, 1968. Pp. 105–140. (a)

Banathy, B. H. The design of foreign language teacher education. *Modern Language Journal,* 1968, 52, 490–500. (b)

Banathy, B. H., & Jordan, B. A classroom laboratory instructional system (CLIS). *Foreign Language Annals,* 1969, 2, 466–473.

Belasco, S. The plateau; or the case for comprehension: The "concept" approach. *Modern Language Journal,* 1967, 51, 82–88.

Birkmaier, E. M. Foreign languages. *Review of Educational Research,* 1958, 28, 127–139.

Birkmaier, E. M. Modern languages. In C. W. Harris (Ed.), *Encyclopedia of educational research.* (3rd ed.) New York: Macmillan, 1960. Pp. 861–888.

Birkmaier, E. M. (Ed.) *The Britannica review of foreign language education.* Vol. 1. Chicago: Encyclopaedia Britannica, 1968.

Birkmaier, E. M., & Lange, D. L. Foreign language instruction. *Review of Educational Research,* 1967, 37, 186–199.

Birkmaier, E. M., & Lange, D. L. A selective bibliography on the teaching of foreign languages, 1920–1966. *Foreign Language Annals,* 1968, 1, 318–353.

Bloom, B. S. Learning for mastery. *UCLA Evaluation Comment,* 1968. Pp. 1–12.

Brière, E. J. Phonological testing reconsidered. *Language Learning,* 1967, 17, 163–171.

Brod, R. I. Trends in foreign language enrollments. In D. L. Lange (Ed.), *The Britannica review of foreign language education.* Vol. 2. Chicago: Encyclopaedia Britannica, 1970. Pp. 341–362.

Brown, G. H. *Providing communication experiences in programmed foreign language instruction.* Professional paper 35–68. Alexandria, Va.: George Washington University, Human Resources Research Office, 1968.

Buros, O. K. (Ed.) *Sixth mental measurements yearbook.* Highland Park, N.J.: Gryphon Press, 1965.

Carroll, J. B. *The study of language: A survey of linguistics and related disciplines in America.* Cambridge, Mass.: Harvard University Press, 1953.

Carroll, J. B. The prediction of success in intensive foreign language training. In R. Glaser (Ed.), *Training research and education.* Pittsburgh, Pa.: University of Pittsburgh Press, 1962. Pp. 87–136.

Carroll, J. B. Research on teaching foreign languages. In N. L. Gage (Ed.), *Handbook of research on teaching.* Chicago: Rand McNally, 1963. Pp. 1060–1100.

Carroll, J. B. Contributions of psychological theory and educational research to the teaching of foreign languages. *Modern Language Journal,* 1965, 49, 273–281.

Carroll, J. B. Research in foreign language teaching: The last five years. In R. Mead, Jr. (Ed.), *Language teaching: Broader contexts.* (Northeast Conference on the Teaching of Foreign Languages. Reports of the Working Committees.) New York: Modern Language Association/American Council on the Teaching of Foreign Languages Materials Center, 1966. Pp. 12–42.

Carroll, J. B. Foreign language proficiency levels attained by language majors near graduation from college. *Foreign Language Annals,* 1967, 1, 131–151.

Carroll, J. B. The psychology of language testing. In A. Davies (Ed.), *Language testing symposium: A psycholinguistic approach.* London: Oxford University Press, 1968. Pp. 46–69.

Carroll, J. B. Modern languages. In R. L. Ebel, (Ed.), *Encyclopedia of educational research.* (4th ed.) New York: Macmillan, 1969. Pp. 866–878. (a)

Carroll, J. B. What does the Pennsylvania Foreign-Language Research Project tell us? *Foreign Language Annals,* 1969, 3, 214–236. (b)

Carton, A. S. *Rating speech: Many considerations, some data.* New York: New York University, School of Education, Experimental Teaching Center, 1964.

Chastain, K. D., & Woerdehoff, F. J. A methodological study comparing the audio-lingual habit theory and the cognitive code-learning theory. *Modern Language Journal,* 1968, 52, 268–279.

Chomei, T., & Houlihan, R. An experimental study of the effectiveness of a newly devised short-delay playback system in a language laboratory. *Audio-Visual Language Journal,* 1968–1969, 6, 59–72.

Chomsky, N. *Language and mind.* New York: Harcourt, Brace & World, 1968.

Chomsky, N., & Halle, M. *The sound pattern of English.* New York: Harper & Row, 1968.

Clark, J. D. *Empirical studies related to the teaching of French pronunciation to American students.* Cambridge, Mass.: Harvard University, Graduate School of Education, Laboratory for Research in Instruction, 1967.

Clark, J. D. The Pennsylvania project and the "audio-lingual" versus "traditional" question. *Modern Language Journal,* 1969, 53, 388–396.

Clark, R. A. The Aachen program: "From I to Ich." *Die Unterrichtspraxis,* 1968, 1, 92–100.

Cornfield, R. R. FLES: How much time? *DFL Bulletin,* October, 1965, 5, 3.

Damore, A. P. *Teaching Spanish by being responsible for specific objectives.* Modesto, Calif.: Stanislaus County Schools Office, 1968.

Davies, A. (Ed.) *Language testing symposium: A psycholinguistic approach.* London: Oxford University Press, 1968.

DiPietro, R. J. Linguistics. In E. M. Birkmaier (Ed.), *The Britannica review of foreign language education.* Vol. 1. Chicago: Encyclopaedia Britannica, 1968. Pp. 15–36.

DiPietro, R. J. Competence and performance. In B. H. Banathy (Ed.), Proceedings of the 1969 Modern Language Association section on applied linguistics. *Modern Language Journal,* 1970, 54, 594–599.

Dodge, J. W. Machine-aided language learning. In E. M. Birkmaier (Ed.), *The Britannica review of foreign language education.* Vol. 1. Chicago: Encyclopaedia Britannica, 1968. Pp. 311–341.

Dodge, J. W. *Sight and sound: Media in foreign language teaching.* Madison, Conn.: Northeast Conference, Box 881, 1969. (Film series)

Donoghue, M. R. Foreign languages in the elementary school: Effects and instructional arrangements according to research. *ERIC focus reports on the teaching of foreign languages,* No. 3. New York: Modern Language Association/American Council on the Teaching of Foreign Languages Materials Center, 1969.

Dugas, D. G. Micro-teaching: A promising

medium for teacher retraining. *Modern Language Journal,* 1967, 51, 161–165.

Dusel, J. P. Surveys and reports on foreign language enrollments. In E. M. Birkmaier (Ed.), *The Britannica review of foreign language education.* Vol. 1. Chicago: Encyclopaedia Britannica, 1968. Pp. 415–438.

Edgerton, M. F. Liberated expression. In T. E. Bird (Ed.), *Foreign language learning: Research and development: An assessment.* (Northeast Conference on the Teaching of Foreign Languages. Reports of the Working Committees.) New York: Modern Language Association/American Council on the Teaching of Foreign Languages Materials Center, 1968. Pp. 75–118.

Edgerton, M. F. (Ed.) *Sight and sound: The sensible and sensitive use of audio-visual aids.* (Northeast Conference on the Teaching of Foreign Languages. Reports of the Working Committees.) New York: Modern Language Association/American Council on the Teaching of Foreign Languages Materials Center, 1969.

Elkins, R. J., Jr. *An evaluation of an intensive summer language program for secondary school students and suggestions for the improvement of future intensive programs.* (Doctoral dissertation, University of Kansas) Ann Arbor, Mich.: University Microfilms, 1968. No. 68-6913.

Erickson, G. M. Classics: The teaching of Latin and Greek and classical humanities. In D. L. Lange (Ed.), *The Britannica review of foreign language education.* Vol. 2. Chicago: Encyclopaedia Britannica, 1970. Pp. 275–321.

Fearing, P. Nongraded foreign language classes. *ERIC focus reports on the teaching of foreign languages,* No. 4. New York: Modern Language Association/American Council on the Teaching of Foreign Languages Materials Center, 1969.

Fearing, P. *Foreign language facilities workbook.* Code no. xxxviii-A-6. Minnesota: State Department of Education, Division of Instruction, 1970.

Feenstra, H. J. Aptitude, attitude, and motivation in second language acquisition. Unpublished doctoral dissertation, University of Western Ontario, 1967.

Fiks, A. I. Foreign language programmed materials: 1969. *ERIC focus reports on the teaching of foreign languages,* No. 7. New

York: Modern Language Association/American Council on the Teaching of Foreign Languages Materials Center, 1969.

Finocchiaro, M. *Teaching English as a second language.* (2nd ed.) New York: Harper & Row, 1969.

Fishman, J. A. (Ed.) *Readings in the sociology of language.* The Hague: Moulton, 1968.(a)

Fishman, J. A. Sociolinguistics and national development. *Language development.* Selected papers from a foundation conference on the state of the art. New York: Ford Foundation, 1968. Pp. 3–14. (b)

Gefen, R. Initial and in-service training for second language teaching in the primary school. In H. H. Stern (Ed.), *Language and the young child.* London: Oxford University Press, 1969.

Green, J. R. *A gesture inventory for the teaching of Spanish.* Philadelphia, Pa.: Chilton, Center for Curriculum Development, 1968.

Grittner, F. M. Maintaining foreign language skills for the advanced-course dropout. *ERIC focus reports on the teaching of foreign languages,* No. 1. New York: Modern Language Association/American Council on the Teaching of Foreign Languages Materials Center, 1968.

Grittner, F. M. *Teaching foreign languages.* New York: Harper & Row, 1969.

Hagiwara, M. P. *Leadership in foreign-language education: Trends in training and supervision of graduate assistants.* New York: Modern Language Association/American Council on the Teaching of Foreign Languages Materials Center, 1970.

Harmon, J. T. (Ed.) 1967 American Council on the Teaching of Foreign Languages bibliography. *Foreign Language Annals,* 1967, 1, 85–90; 178–181; 1968, 1, 270–280; 371–387.

Harris, D. P. *Testing English as a second language.* New York: McGraw-Hill, 1968.

Hayes, A. S., Lambert, W. E., & Tucker, G. R. Evaluation of foreign language teaching. *Foreign Language Annals,* 1967, 1, 22–44.

Hocking, E. The laboratory in perspective: Teachers, strategies, outcomes. *Modern Language Journal,* 1969, 53, 404–410.

Horner, L. T. Broader participation in foreign language teacher training. *Modern Language Journal,* 1970, 54, 250–254.

Humphrey, J. H. Comparison of the use of active games and language workbook exercises as learning media in the development of language understandings with third grade children. *Perceptual and Motor Skills,* 1965, 21, 23–26.

Jakobovits, L. A. *Foreign language learning: A psycholinguistic analysis of the issues.* Rowley, Mass.: Newbury House, 1970.

Jarvis, G. A. Strategies of instruction for listening and reading. In D. L. Lange (Ed.), *The Britannica review of foreign language education.* Vol. 2. Chicago: Encyclopaedia Britannica, 1970. Pp. 79–111.

JeKenta, A. W., & Fearing, P. Current trends in curriculum: Elementary and secondary schools. In E. M. Birkmaier (Ed.), *The Britannica review of foreign language education.* Vol. 1. Chicago: Encyclopaedia Britannica, 1968. Pp. 141–178.

Johnston, M. C. Foreign language instruction. *Review of Educational Research,* 1961, 31, 188–196.

Kant, J. G. Foreign language registrations in institutions of higher education, fall 1968 and summer 1969. New York: Modern Language Association, 1969. (Reprinted in part in *Foreign Language Annals,* 1969, 3, 247–304; 1970, 3, 459–476.)

Kant, J. G. Foreign language offerings and enrollments in public and non-public secondary schools, fall 1968. New York: Modern Language Association, 1970. (Reprinted in part in *Foreign Language Annals,* 1970, 3, 400–458.)

Keppeler, F. Literature in teacher education. Unpublished paper read at the Modern Language Association Convention, Denver, December 1969.

Kovach, E. M. A. Classics: The teaching of Latin and Greek. In E. M. Birkmaier (Ed.), *The Britannica review of foreign language education.* Vol. 1. Chicago: Encyclopaedia Britannica, 1968. Pp. 389–414.

Labov, W. *The social stratification of English in New York City.* Washington, D.C.: Center for Applied Linguistics, 1966.

Lado, R. *Language testing: The construction and use of foreign language tests.* New York: McGraw-Hill, 1964.

Lambert, W. E. Motivation and language learning: Psychological aspects. In S. Newell (Ed.), *Dimension: Languages 68.* Spartanburg, S. C.: Southern Conference on Language Teaching, 1968. Pp. 6–14.

Lambert, W. E., Gardner, R. C., Barik, H. C.,

& Tunstall, K. Attitudinal and cognitive aspects of intensive study of a second language. *Journal of Abnormal and Social Psychology,* 1963, 66, 358–368.

Lane, H. Programmed learning of a second language. *International Review of Applied Linguistics in Language Teaching,* 1964, 2, 249–301.

Lange, D. L. An evaluation of pre-reading instruction in beginning French instruction in secondary schools. Unpublished doctoral dissertation, University of Minnesota, 1966.

Lange, D. L. (Ed.) 1968 American Council on the Teaching of Foreign Languages annual bibliography. *Foreign Language Annals,* 1969, 2, 483–525.

Lange, D. L. (Ed.) *The Britannica review of foreign language education.* Vol. 2. Chicago: Encyclopaedia Britannica, 1970. (a)

Lange, D. L. (Ed.) 1969 American Council on the Teaching of Foreign Languages annual bibliography. *Foreign Language Annals,* 1970, 3, 629–668. (b)

Lenneberg, E. *Biological foundations of language.* New York: John Wiley, 1967.

Logan, G. E. Curricula for individualized instruction. In D. L. Lange (Ed.), *The Britannica review of foreign language education.* Vol. 2. Chicago: Encyclopaedia Britannica, 1970. Pp. 133–155.

Lusetti, W. I. A comparison of approaches to beginning Spanish instruction in grade seven. Unpublished doctoral dissertation, University of Oregon, 1968.

Mace, L. Sequence of vocal response-differentiation training and auditory stimulus-discrimination training in beginning French. *Journal of Educational Psychology,* 1966, 57, 102–108.

Mackey, W. F. *Language teaching analysis.* Bloomington, Ind.: Indiana University Press, 1967. (a)

Mackey, W. F. The new technology of teacher training. Unpublished paper, Université Laval, Quebec, 1967. (b)

Martin, W. A report on a discussion-conference on the West-Chester Pennsylvania Study. *National Association of Language Laboratory Directors Journal,* 1969, 4(1), 64–67.

Marty, F. *Teaching French.* Roanoke, Va.: Audio-Visual Publications, Box 5497, 1968.

McArdle, R. J. Teacher education, qualifications, and supervision. In E. M. Birkmaier (Ed.), *The Britannica review of foreign language education.* Vol. 1. Chicago: Encyclopaedia Britannica, 1968. Pp. 261–280.

Morrison, H. W., & Adams, E. N. Pilot study of a CAI laboratory in German. *Modern Language Journal,* 1968, 52, 279–287.

Morton, F. R. Four major problem areas in programmed instruction for modern language learning. In T. H. Mueller (Ed.), *Proceedings of the seminar on programmed learning.* New York: Appleton-Century-Crofts, 1968. Pp. 18–37.

Moskowitz, G. The effects of training foreign language teachers in interaction analysis. *Foreign Language Annals,* 1968, 1, 218–235.

Mueller, T. H. (Ed.) *Proceedings of the seminar on programmed learning.* New York: Appleton-Century-Crofts, 1968. (a)

Mueller, T. H. Programmed language instruction—Help for the linguistically "underprivileged." *Modern Language Journal,* 1968, 52, 79–84. (b)

Muller, D. H., & Muller, T. V. The problem of interference in beginning Portuguese. *Modern Language Journal,* 1968, 52, 201–205.

Muller, T. V., & Muller, D. H. A comparison of two time spacing arrangements in elementary school foreign language classes. *California educational research summaries.* Burlingame, Calif.: California Education Research Association, 1967.

National Education Association. Public school programs and practices: Foreign language programs. *NEA Research Bulletin,* 1967, 45, 111–114.

Newmark, G., & Sweigert, R. L. *A field test of three approaches to the teaching of Spanish in elementary schools.* Sacramento, Calif.: State Department of Education, 1966.

Newmark, L., & Reibel, D. A. Necessity and sufficiency in language learning. *International Review of Applied Linguistics in Language Teaching,* 1968, 6, 145–161.

Oller, J. W., & Obrecht, D. H. Pattern drill and communicative activity: A psycholinguistic experiment. *International Review of Applied Linguistics in Language Teaching,* 1968, 6, 165–174.

Oneto, A. J. *FLES evaluation: Language skills and pupil attitudes in Fairfield, Connecticut, public schools.* Bulletin No. 106. Hartford, Conn.: Connecticut State Department of Education, 1968.

Ornstein, J. Programmed instruction and educational technology in the language field: Boon or failure? *Modern Language Journal,* 1968, 52, 401–410.

Ornstein, J., & Lado, R. Research in foreign language teaching methodology. *International Review of Applied Linguistics in Language Teaching,* 1967, 5, 11–25.

Ort, B. A., & Smith, D. R. The language teacher tours the curriculum: New horizons for foreign language education. *Foreign Language Annals,* 1969, 3, 28–74.

Otto, F. Alternative approaches to staffing the elementary foreign language program: Cost and time versus achievement and satisfaction. *Modern Language Journal,* 1968, 52, 293–301.

Paquette, F. A. (Ed.) Guidelines for teacher education programs in modern foreign languages—An exposition. *Modern Language Journal,* 1966, 50, 323–425.

Paquette, F. A., & Allen, V. G. *New dimensions in the teaching of FLES.* New York: American Council on the Teaching of Foreign Languages, 1969.

Paquette, F. A., & Tollinger, S. (Eds.) *Handbook on foreign language classroom testing: French, German, Italian, Russian, Spanish.* New York: Modern Language Association, 1968.

Perkins, J. A. State certification and proficiency tests: The experiences in Pennsylvania. *Foreign Language Annals,* 1968, 2, 195–199.

Pimsleur, P. A French speaking proficiency test. *French Review,* 1961, 34, 470–479.

Pimsleur, P. Testing foreign language learning. In A. Valdman (Ed.), *Trends in language teaching.* New York: McGraw-Hill, 1966. Pp. 175–214.

Pimsleur, P., & Struth, J. F. Knowing your students in advance. *Modern Language Journal,* 1969, 53, 85–87.

Pimsleur, P., Sundland, D., & McIntyre, R. *Under-achievement in foreign language learning.* New York: Modern Language Association, 1966.

Politzer, R. L. Student motivation and interest in elementary language courses. *Language Learning,* 1953–1954, 5, 15–21.

Politzer, R. L. The role and place of explanation in the pattern drill. *International Review of Applied Linguistics in Language Teaching,* 1968, 6, 315–331.

Politzer, R. L., & Bartley, D. *Practice-centered teacher training, Spanish: A syllabus for the training or retraining of teachers of Spanish.* Stanford, Calif.: Stanford Center for Research and Development in Teaching, 1967.

Politzer, R. L., & Weiss, L. *The successful foreign-language teacher.* Philadelphia, Pa.: Chilton, Center for Curriculum Development, 1970.

Postal, P. M. *Aspects of phonological theory.* New York: Harper & Row, 1968.

Poulter, V. L. Computer-assisted laboratory testing. *Modern Language Journal,* 1969, 53, 561–564.

Rabura, H. M. The preparation of language teachers. In J. L. Mordaunt (Ed.), *Proceedings: Pacific-Northwest conference on foreign languages: Twentieth annual meeting, April 11–12, 1969.* Vol. 20. Victoria, B.C.: University of Victoria, 1969. Pp. 154–158.

Richards, H. J., & Salas, T. C. The erosion of foreign language requirements in college and university curricula: Some observable trends. *Bulletin of the Association of Departments of Foreign Languages,* 1969, 1(2), 37–40.

Ritchie, W. G. On the explanation of phonic interference. *Language Learning,* 1968, 18, 183–197.

Rivers, W. M. *The psychologist and the foreign language teacher.* Chicago: University of Chicago Press, 1964.

Rivers, W. M. *Teaching foreign-language skills.* Chicago: University of Chicago Press, 1968.

Rosenbaum, P. S. The computer as a learning environment for foreign language instruction. *Foreign Language Annals,* 1969, 2, 457–465.

Rosenberg, S., & Koplin, J. (Eds.) *Developments in applied psycholinguistic research.* New York: Macmillan, 1968.

Roy, R. R. Complexity—A factor of oral proficiency. *Manitoba Journal of Educational Research,* 1967, 3, 45–52.

Ruplin, F. A., & Russell, J. R. A type of computer-assisted instruction. *German Quarterly,* 1968, 41, 84–88.

Rutherford, W. E. *Modern English: A textbook for foreign students.* New York: Harcourt, Brace & World, 1968.

Savard, J. A proposed system of classifying language tests. In J. Upshur, & J. Fata (Eds.), *Problems in foreign language testing. Language Learning,* 1968, Special Issue No. 3, 167–177.

Sawyer, J. O. Foreign language instruction.

Review of Educational Research, 1964, 34, 203–210.

Seelye, H. N. Field notes on cross-cultural testing. *Language Learning,* 1966, 16, 77–85.

Seelye, H. N. Analysis and teaching of the cross-cultural context. In E. M. Birkmaier (Ed.), *The Britannica review of foreign language education.* Vol. 1. Chicago: Encyclopaedia Britannica, 1968. Pp. 37–81.

Sheehan, J., & Willis, R. Demonstration of the use of television in the training of foreign language teachers. In M. R. Edgerton (Ed.), *Sight and sound: The sensible and sensitive use of audio-visual aids.* (Northeast Conference on the Teaching of Foreign Languages. Reports of the Working Committees.) New York: Modern Language Association/American Council on the Teaching of Foreign Languages Materials Center, 1969. Pp. 109–112.

Sheppard, D. C. Certifying teachers of modern foreign languages for American public schools—1969. *Foreign Language Annals,* 1970, 3, 609–623.

Shulze, S., Arendt, J., & Rainey, R. G. *A two year study of the use of programmed materials for the instruction of French in high school.* Minnesota: Minneapolis Public Schools, 1966.

Smith, A. N. Strategies of instruction for speaking and writing. In D. L. Lange (Ed.), *The Britannica review of foreign language education.* Vol. 2. Chicago: Encyclopaedia Britannica, 1970. Pp. 113–131.

Smith, M. I. *Teaching to specific objectives.* Modesto, Calif.: Stanislaus County Schools Office, 1968.

Smith, P. D. *A comparison of the cognitive and audiolingual approaches to foreign language instruction: The Pennsylvania Foreign Language Project.* Philadelphia, Pa.: Chilton, Center for Curriculum Development, 1970.

Smith, W. F. Language learning laboratory. In D. L. Lange (Ed.), *The Britannica review of foreign language education.* Vol. 2. Chicago: Encyclopaedia Britannica, 1970. Pp. 191–237.

Smith, W. H. *Linguistic and academic achievement of elementary students studying a foreign language.* (Doctoral dissertation, Colorado State College) Ann Arbor, Mich.: University Microfilms, 1967, No. 67-6086.

Snider, J. G., & Osgood, C. E. (Eds.) *Semantic differential technique.* Chicago: Aldine, 1969.

Spodak, R. *Selected bibliography in programmed instruction.* Washington, D.C.: Center for Applied Linguistics, 1966.

Spolsky, B., Sato, M., Walker, E., & Arterburn, C. Preliminary studies in the development of techniques for testing overall second language proficiency. In J. A. Upshur, & J. Fata (Eds.), *Problems in foreign language testing. Language Learning,* 1968, Special Issue No. 3, 79–101.

Stack, E. M. *The language laboratory and modern language teaching.* (Rev. ed.) New York: Oxford Press, 1966.

Steiner, F. Behavioral objectives and evaluation. In D. L. Lange (Ed.), *The Britannica review of foreign language education.* Vol. 2. Chicago: Encyclopaedia Britannica, 1970. Pp. 35–78.

Strasheim, L. A. *Target: Methods.* Bloomington, Ind.: Indiana Language Program, 1967.

Sweet, W. E. Integrating other media with programmed instruction. *Modern Language Journal,* 1968, 52, 420–423.

Teitelbaum, S. L. *The foreign language instructional program in Long Island: 1969 survey.* East Meadow, N.Y.: Foreign Language Association of Chairmen and Supervisors, 1969.

Thomsen, E. V. Graduate programs in foreign language education in United States universities. Unpublished doctoral dissertation, University of Texas, 1970.

Tursi, J. A. *Foreign languages and the "new" student.* (Northeast Conference on the Teaching of Foreign Languages. Reports of the Working Committees.) New York: Modern Language Association/American Council on the Teaching of Foreign Languages Materials Center, 1970.

Valdman, A. Problems in the definition of learning steps in programmed foreign language materials. In T. H. Mueller (Ed.), *Proceedings of the seminar on programmed learning.* New York: Appleton-Century-Crofts, 1968. Pp. 50–62.

Valette, R. M. The use of the dicteé in the French language classroom. *Modern Language Journal,* 1964, 48, 431–434.

Valette, R. M. *Modern language testing: A handbook.* New York: Harcourt, Brace & World, 1967.

Valette, R. M. Evaluating oral and written communication: Suggestions for an integrated testing program. In J. A. Upshur, & J. Fata (Eds.), *Problems in foreign language testing. Language Learning,* 1968, Special Issue No. 3, 111–124. (a)

Valette, R. M. Testing and motivation. In S. Newell (Ed.), *Dimension: Language 68.* Spartanburg, S.C.: Southern Conference on Language Teaching, 1968. Pp. 65–69. (b)

Valette, R. M. *Directions in foreign language testing.* New York: Modern Language Association, 1969. (a)

Valette, R. M. The Pennsylvania Project, its conclusions and its implications. *Modern Language Journal,* 1969, 53, 396–404. (b)

Van Abbé, D. M. A new type of language degree course—A report from the United Kingdom. *Foreign Language Annals,* 1968, 1, 301–311.

Vocolo, J. M. The effect of foreign language study in the elementary school upon achievement in the same foreign language in the high school. *Modern Language Journal,* 1967, 51, 463–469.

Williamsen, V. G. A pilot program in teaching Spanish: An intensive approach. *Modern Language Journal,* 1968, 52, 73–78.

Yousef, F. S. Cross-cultural testing: An aspect of the resistance reaction. *Language Learning,* 1968, 18, 227–234.

CHAPTER 42   Research on Teaching Vocational Skills

CARL J. SCHAEFER
Rutgers University

GORDON F. LAW
Rutgers University

It is not surprising to find that research related to vocational teaching is still in a formative stage. A major portion of all such activities has taken place as recently as the past six years, since federal funds authorized by the Vocational Education Act of 1963 have been available.

Public Law 88-210, known as the Vocational Education Act of 1963, brought a dramatic change. According to David Bushnell, former Director of the Division of Comprehensive and Vocational Research, U.S. Office of Education, more than 60 million federal dollars have been spent on vocational education research since 1964. This rapid acceleration of research activity quickly precipitated a critical shortage of competent research personnel, especially those who combined advanced skills in research method with experience in vocational teaching. As a result, some of the initial efforts supported by federal research funds suffered, for time was needed to develop a new generation of vocational education researchers (*Proceedings*, 1969).

The rapid recent growth of vocational education research is in part a testimony to the efficacy of concerted effort through national committees that have had a sense of mission and dedication. A case in point is the research committee of the American Vocational Association (AVA). In 1961 the AVA Research Committee chose as its major objective the encouragement of a positive acceptance of the need for research and the promotion of the desire and ability of individuals to engage in research activities (Hill, 1966). The first step toward the achievement of this objective was a one-week vocational education research seminar in the spring of 1963. Planned and conducted by the AVA Research Committee together with the U.S. Office of Education and the Purdue University staff, the seminar gave primary concern to research design. In 1964 a series of three one-week vocational education research seminars was conducted. One seminar at Pennsylvania State University dealt with research design; a second emphasized the contributions of social sciences and was conducted by the University of Illinois. The Ohio State University was the site of the third seminar, which was planned to generate interest and increased involvement of state directors of vocational education and university department heads. Again in 1965 the leadership of the AVA Research Committee helped initiate seminars at various university settings. By this time federal funds were becoming available for such activities, and a virtual flood of new programs and projects relating to vocational education research was initiated.

Important steps in building a nationwide system of vocational education research have been the establishment of national centers for Vocational Technical Education at The Ohio State University and North Carolina State University and the authorization of funds for the formation of research coordinating units (RCUs) in each of the states. The national center in Columbus also serves as the Education Resources Information Center Clearing House for Vocational and Technical Education. The major objectives of the center are:

1. To provide continuing reappraisal of the role and function of vocational and technical education in our democratic society;
2. To stimulate and strengthen state, regional and national programs of applied research and development directed toward the solutions of pressing problems in vocational and technical education;
3. To encourage the development of research to improve vocational and technical education in institutions of higher education and other appropriate settings;
4. To conduct research studies directed toward the development of new knowledge and new applications of existing knowledge in vocational and technical education;
5. To upgrade vocational educational leadership (state supervisors, teacher educators, research specialists and others) through an advanced study and in-service education program;
6. To provide a national information retrieval, storage and dissemination system for vocational and technical education linked with the Education Re-

sources Information Center located in the U.S. Office of Education.

The establishment of research coordinating units in each of the states, a process which was begun in June 1965, has led to a growing commitment to vocational education research on the local scene. Although there is a wide disparity among state RCUs in terms of their organization and function, all have a degree of common identity and purpose, as derived from guidelines set forth by their parent organization and financial sponsor, the United States Office of Education.

The location of state RCUs has been a topic for debate ever since their inception. Persuasive arguments have been given by proponents for having them housed in state education department offices. Equally eloquent are statements that a university campus is the only suitable location. The Minnesota RCU Report (Moss, 1966) speaks in favor of a university setting. Ready access to scholars, computers and libraries, and the availability of advanced graduate students to assist in research activities are given as arguments to justify the university locus. On the other hand, the Illinois RCU Report (Bergener, 1967) states that an RCU which is an integral component of the state office of vocational instruction is in a better position to generate experimental programs in local schools.

Publications produced by the national centers for vocational and technical education represent a prime source of information relating to research on vocational education. Most informative is the series of review and synthesis publications growing out of the Ohio center. These "state of the art" reports are designed to provide researchers and practicing vocational educators with authoritative analyses of literature in the field. Those who wish to examine primary sources of information will find their bibliography invaluable. Nineteen review and synthesis reports have been produced since 1966. Recent releases which in some cases update earlier publications are in the following areas of interest: curriculum development; business and office education; industrial arts education; technical education; trade and industrial education; administration of vocational and technical education; distributive education; home economics education; placement and follow-up of vocational education students; vocational education in rural areas; and cooperative education.

Priorities for Research

In addition to the obvious need for training vocational education researchers, there has been considerable attention given to the identification of other priorities for research in vocational-technical education. Organizations and institutions which have been involved in such activities include the U.S. Office of Education, the Research Committee of the American Vocational Association (later the Research Division of the AVA), the centers for vocational and technical education and various state and university groups.

Participants at the National Conference on Research (*Proceedings,* 1969) listed the following items as critical problem areas for most states: 1) the methodology of curriculum development; 2) the formation of broad manpower policies; 3) the relative efficiency of various organizational structures for guiding occupational education; 4) building curriculum for the disadvantaged; 5) teacher education processes; 6) student selection procedures and devices; 7) the development of an information system which will keep practicing teachers up to date; 8) the indexing of staff and personnel throughout the state who are competent in research techniques; and 9) the extent of vocational education in the private sector.

The National Conference on Research also generated a set of implications for national research and development (*Proceedings,* 1969). Here the report states that one of the most critical priority areas appears to be the development of a common base for reporting information from state programs of vocational-technical education. Stating that such a system would require the stan-

dardization of terminology, the conference report predicted that immediate and reasonably comprehensive information disseminated to the states could prevent duplication and overlap of research efforts throughout the country.

The AVA publication on Research and Implementation (*Research and Implementation in Vocation Education,* 1969) has identified six topics relating to vocational teaching that call for investigation. These are: philosophical foundations of vocational education; the process of vocational instruction; the preparation of professional personnel; reorganizing the high-school curriculum; postsecondary vocational development; and vocational guidance and career development. Among the philosophical concepts discussed are six which had been generated by the M.I.T. Summer Study of Vocational Education (Frank, 1965). These concepts relate to accessibility of quality vocational education opportunities, programs to meet the full spectrum of capabilities of youth and adults, coupling vocational and general education, open-ended continuous vocational education and training opportunities, early orientation to vocational education through exploratory experiences, and instructional flexibility to prepare students for adaptation to constantly changing employment patterns.

Although the effort has been significant, the fruits of the research endeavor have by no means exceeded expectations. The remainder of this chapter reviews some of the outputs with clear admission that the input selections have possibly ignored many significant and worthy research undertakings.

ORGANIZATION OF VOCATIONAL INSTRUCTION

School and College Delivery Systems

The matching of vocational programs with appropriate manpower needs always has been a major challenge. Such a system, if properly functioning, reflects the delivery of youth and adults ready and willing to take existing jobs. The now annual *Manpower Report of the President* (U.S. Department of Labor, 1970) with its overall picture of the employment problems facing the nation serves in a global way to focus attention on the need for an adequate delivery system; national, state and local. Studies of a placement (employment) and follow-up nature have been carried on for some time by those engaged in vocational education. The U.S. Office of Education (1968) reported that 80 percent of those completing vocational-technical offerings and available for placement had been placed in their field of training or related training. Twelve percent were placed in a field unrelated to their training and 4 percent were placed part-time while 4 percent were unemployed.

Probably one of the most sorely needed areas of study is that of follow-up of vocational graduates over a longitudinal period. What happens to graduates when they become employees and citizens? Coe and Zanzalari (1964) did one of the few such studies by following up the graduating class of 1953 10 years later. Of the 108 graduates representing 13 different trade areas in the class of 1953, 91 percent took part in the study. Findings included: 1) in 1953 81 percent of the graduates were placed in trades for which they were trained and 10 years later 60 percent were still working in their trade; 2) the wage earned ranged from $2.40 per hour to $5.00 per hour with a mode of $3.00 per hour; 3) approximately 25 percent had reached the foreman or supervisor level; 4) graduates tended to live in the county and 75 percent of the group had spent the entire 10 years in the county; and 5) 8 percent of the graduates had attended postsecondary schools and 32 percent indicated that they had had some higher education.

Stromsdorfer (1969), an economist, has made some observations of occupational mobility and its relation to planning state vocational education programs. He is of the opinion that mobility must be taken into account in terms of: 1) mobility existing in an area and 2) mobility introduced by firms leaving an area. Obviously the school's occupational preparation programs must take into account such fluctuations.

Existing delivery systems mainly at the secondary level of education have been explored both on a regional and state level by Kaufman, Schaefer, Lewis, Stevens, and House (1967) and Schaefer and Kaufman (1968). The regional study compared the occupational preparation of graduates from vocational, general and college preparation (those who did not go on to college) programs in a stratified sample of large, medium and small cities. Included in the data were more than 5,000 interviews, 1,600 questions completed by teachers, and on-site visits to some 25 schools by a team of experts. The results of this study generally confirmed the notion that vocational education is an unrealized potential of education even though it possesses a number of weaknesses as presently being offered. In the Schaefer and Kaufman (1968) study of a single state, many of the same conclusions were reached—that the potential of vocational education has not been and cannot be reached fully under the prevailing pattern. Consequently, a plan of organization and implementation including state legislative changes was proposed. Among other things the plan proposed the establishment of shared-time school centers for the vocationally talented student and the development of an occupational preparation program based on the cluster concept in each local high school for less motivated but occupationally bound students.

Atttempts are constantly being made to innovate and bring about curriculum change. The work of Bottoms and Matheny (1969), Meyer (1969), Fuller and Phipps (1968), Berkey, Kelly, and Brown (1969) and others has focused on this goal. Obviously, innovation has been given impetus by the Vocational Education Amendments of 1968, Part D—Exemplary Programs and Projects. As stated in Section 141:

The Congress finds that it is necessary to reduce the continuing seriously high level of youth unemployment by developing means for giving the same kind of attention as is now given to the college preparation needs of those young persons who go on to college, to the job preparation needs of the two out of three young persons who end their education at or before completion of the secondary level, too many of whom face long and bitter months of job hunting or marginal work after leaving school. The purposes of this part, therefore, are to stimulate, through Federal financial support, new ways to create a bridge between school and earning a living for young people... (Conference Report, 1968, p. 19).

The evaluation of vocational education programs has plagued the field for some years. More and more, attention is being turned to ascertaining the quality of programs at the input and output sides of the picture. Kievit (1970) has looked at the characteristics of students at a community college and technical institute in terms of environmental press and found that the community college has greater holding power than the technical institute. This is in spite of the fact that freshmen entering both institutions had much the same demographic backgrounds.

Horowitz and Herrnstadt (1969) conducted an in-depth study of the training of tool and die makers in an attempt to develop a model to determine the combination of education, training and experience which would be most likely to yield highly qualified workers in a specific occupation. Among important findings were: 1) a worker's competency is more a result of the type of person he is than the type of training he received, and no important differences were produced by various paths of training; 2) there were differences in the time spent in training and in the time needed to become a craftsman and to be hired as one; 3) the combination of vocational high school and apprenticeship was the only path to scoring well on most measures of effectiveness.

An extensive investigation into the qual-

ity of secondary-school trade and industrial education offerings was conducted by Eninger (1965) in what he termed "the product and process." This two-year study of public vocational education in the United States had a stratified random sample of 100 high schools with three or more trade and industrial courses. Data were collected in areas of curriculum, methods, facilities, student services, teachers and administration. Pre- and postgraduate data from a sample of 10,000 vocational program graduates were investigated, and local and regional vocational opportunities were assessed. Relationships between vocational outcomes and school characteristics, student characteristics and regional characteristics were studied.

The work of Coster and Morgan (1969, 1970) has focused on the role of evaluation in the decision-making process. They have presented a model to provide a way of examining the complex activities which are involved in program planning and evaluation, a model which demonstrates the positions of the decision maker and program manager within the model and indicates in broad terms the information that must be provided by the program evaluator to the decision maker if appropriate alternatives are to be selected, objectives obtained and goals realized.

Although much more could be reported on the topic of "delivery systems," it should be apparent that substantial study is being directed toward this end.

Occupational Analysis for Curriculum Planning

It could be said that vocational education has used occupational or task analyses as a means of curriculum planning from its very conception. Texts have been written solely on this subject, and courses of trade and occupational analysis have been taught as part of almost every teacher-education program, especially for teachers of trade and industrial education. Nevertheless there have been some recent attempts to refine the process and to give it new meaning, especially from the behavioral objective point of view. The work of Mager and Beach (1967) and Tuckman (1968a) has focused the behavioral objective technique directly on the various areas of vocational education.

Mager and Beach (1967) advocate that curriculum construction should start with a detailed job description followed by a specific task analysis. They identified a task as, "...a logically related set of actions required for the completion of a job objective. ...One part of the salesman's job is writing orders; that is *one task* that makes up the salesman's *job*" (p. 10). The technique of "task listing" is suggested by Mager and Beach to include: tasks (by number), frequency of performance, importance (rated on a 1–5 scale), and learning difficulty (easy, moderate, difficult).

Tuckman (1968a) goes a step further through what he calls a structured analysis, which is a technique by which ultimate curriculum objectives, stated in behavioral terms, are sequentially analyzed to identify and specify each of the competencies which students must acquire if the terminal objectives are to be achieved. In its use for preparing instructional materials this technique involves six steps: 1) goal statements, 2) definitions, 3) recall of subordinate competencies, 4) integration of previous material, 5) demonstration, and 6) practice (Tuckman, 1968a, p. 15).

Varying applications of occupational analyses have been applied to almost every area of vocational education. Brandon (1960) conducted a U.S. Office of Education–sponsored study into the curricula of technicians. The result was a matrix model of value in the determination of understandings needed by technicians. With 472 firms drawn from a master list of 2,952, Loreen (1967) used a survey form to gather data on nonfarm agricultural jobs in the state of Washington. From the list it was felt that new programs of agricultural education could be con-

structed. Among most important needed competencies were: 1) employee relationships with supervisors; 2) employee relationships with fellow workers; 3) communications, and 4) salesmenship and customer relations. A similar study by Drake and Tom (1968) involved a task analysis of entry-level off-farm occupations in New York State, and Ertel (1966) identified the major tasks performed by merchandising employees working in three standard industrial classifications of retail establishments. Some 33 firms and more than 900 employees were included in the study sample and 332 tasks in 12 different categories were identified.

Huffman and Gust (1970) conducted a task-analysis–type investigation into the business education needed for emerging office occupations. They attempted to identify the high-priority abilities needed for new office occupations and the level of performance goals needed. Six hundred seventy-five companies took part in the analysis of emerging office occupations.

In 1970 a small group of outstanding vocational educators convened in a seminar sponsored by the Minnesota Research Coordinating Unit for vocational education to consider the topic, "Processes and Techniques of Vocational Curriculum Development" (Smith & Moss, 1970). It was their consensus that curriculum development for students preparing for immediate entry or reentry into the work force should follow six steps: 1) specify the role, 2) identify the tasks in the specified role, 3) select the tasks to be taught, 4) analyze each of the selected tasks, 5) state the performance objectives, and 6) specify the instructional sequence. It was the final conclusion of the seminar that,

...changes seen as desirable by the seminar members included: a) increasing attention paid to the products of instruction, b) making education more task oriented, with the tasks having validity for students and actual relevance to out of school behavior, and c) permitting nonverbal behavior in the learning process, essentially at the earlier stages of schooling, in order to provide the concrete experiences necessary for later abstract conceptual development (Smith & Moss, 1970, p. 7).

Even though much material has been written about occupational and task analysis, and though vocational educators periodically reaffirm their belief in the use of the method for curriculum development, much remains to be accomplished in this area. It seems that changes in occupations are occurring so rapidly that the job is too great for the limited though expanding efforts; consequently, it cannot be said that the situation is well in hand. A major research effort should be aimed at finding a way to systematize and synthesize the entire process.

Cooperative Education and Use of Community Resources

In terms of community utilization, cooperative education as an educational means has long been practiced in vocational education. At the same time relatively little has been accomplished in its study.

Wooldridge (1966), an advocate of cooperative education at the postsecondary as well as the secondary level, indicates that there are more than 125 institutions of higher education offering some work-study programs for their students. He also proposed that the acceptance of cooperative education into many professional fields reflects educators' concurrence that work experience should be part of a student's total education. Further acceptance is indicated at the secondary-school level where there are some sixty-five hundred cooperative programs reported nationally (U.S. Office of Education, 1968).

The notes and working papers of The National Conference on Cooperative Vocational Education (1969) discuss the implications for cooperative education of the Vocational Education Amendments of 1968. As a result, a guide to cooperative vocational education was developed covering such specific aspects as: cooperative vocational education and what it will do; what form and type is best for a specific school system; meeting student and manpower needs through cooperative vocational education; and staffing cooperative vocational education programs.

Gallington and Sievert (1966) studied the efficacy of four high-school pilot programs of cooperative education. They determined that: students seemed to handle their earnings fairly well; some students worked more hours than was wise; as hours worked increased so did absenteeism from school; those students who worked extra hours and missed school were about as successful in school as other students; cooperative students did not improve or lower their grade averages after entering the program; a large percentage made a satisfactory transfer from school to work; and cooperative students earned as much as other graduates from the school after graduation. Vocational agriculture personnel have been concerned about cooperative education. A study by Williams (1967) attempted to determine why teachers were not equally successful in implementing cooperative agricultural-occupations curricula. It was concluded that there was a relationship between innovativeness of the teacher and the degree of program adoption. Fink and Wenrich (1964) presented the history and the current status of the cooperative vocational industrial teacher-education program in the School of Education at the University of Michigan. Since the program was started in 1951, 65 students had enrolled over the years and 21 had successfully completed the program and were engaged in the teaching profession. The Rutger's Cooperative Occupational Pre-teaching Experience (COPE) Program was started in 1966 and has had a similar modest experience with this type of education on the college level (Cooperative Occupational Pre-teaching Experience Program, 1970).

Although much appears to be happening in cooperative education, not a lot is being accomplished in its study that might bring about improvements. Perhaps all that needs to be known about this form of vocational education has already been learned; this, however, is doubtful.

Systems Approach to Planning and Budgeting

It is not surprising to find work being done on planning and budgeting and especially on cost-benefit analysis. For quite some time educators have been aware of the high cost of providing vocational education. But cost is a relative term and to have a true measure it must be compared with benefit gain. Therefore, studies of cost-benefit, although not abundant, have been looked upon with favor in the vocational education field. In the main, these studies have been conducted by economists and have shown that there is a "pay-off" to vocational education. Kaufman, Stromsdorfer, Hu, and Lee (1969) report probably the most complete work thus far in their study of cost-effectiveness of secondary-school vocational education. They concluded that:

...additional public funds should be spent on vocational-technical education curricula rather than non-vocational-technical senior high school curricula. Yet, as it is currently constituted, there is no specific information on how much more should be spent. However, by comparing the costs of the different curricula with benefits measured in terms of earnings, the returns to investment in vocational-technical education was shown to be considerably greater than that returned to investment in the alternative curricula (p. 224).

In this study both cost and benefit measurements were used. Conceptional difficulties found by the researchers in cost evaluation included: joint costs of more than a single program; explicit costs paid out of tuition as compared to implicit costs

of foregoing earnings while taking training; services of capital plant, equipment, site acquisition and improvements.

In an earlier study by Kaufman, Schaefer, Lewis, Stevens, and House (1967) it was found that, "...while no pay-off in the form of a wage increment was immediately obtained by recipients of high-school level skill-training, subsequent advantages in the form of pay increases on the first job may accrue to the vocationally trained graduates ..." (p. 6–25). Then in 1968, in a study of *Occupational Education in Massachusetts,* Schaefer and Kaufman (1968) found that when comparing the hourly wages by groups (vocational, general education, college preparatory) over a span of the first, second and third jobs held,

In each case the vocational student, both male and female, received as high if not a higher hourly wage rate than did students from the other programs. Especially in the second job held, the vocational pay rate appears to be significantly higher. It is interesting to note that the pay differential is quite constant over all groups for the first three jobs with the exception of the third position for the college prep group... (p. 74).

However, Kaufman and Lewis (1968) caution:

Although the indices of employment experience, in terms of employment and earnings, showed an advantage for vocationally prepared graduates, one can not speak of the extra "payoff" of vocational education without relating it to the extra costs of this type of education ... (p. 110).

* * *

it is known that the drop out rate for vocational education is relatively high (it may well be that the drop out rate would be higher if the vocational curriculum were not available) and there is, at present, no accurate knowledge of the earnings differentials between graduates and drop outs (p. 113).

The work of Corazzini (1966) compared the starting wages of graduates of vocational high schools with those of post-high-school vocational programs as well as starting wages of those graduates of nonvocational high-school programs. He found the differential slight and suggested that post-high-school training costs were high when compared to high school because of the costs of two added years of schooling and two years of forsaken wage earnings. Moreover, the need for occupationally bound students to make an early decision concerning vocational training was implied purely on a cost basis.

Obviously more studies need to be conducted in terms of the systems approach to cost and planning. The whole notion of program, planning and benefit analysis is not only intriguing, but necessary for ascertaining the value of providing vocational education both from an economic and sociological point of view. Studies delving into the cost of providing vocational or skilled training through other paths such as apprenticeship, cooperative education, job corps and manpower centers are sorely needed for comparison of the relative merits of each model.

TEACHING AND LEARNING TECHNIQUES

Psychomotor, Cognitive and Affective Learning

Studies of a psychomotor, cognitive and affective learning nature are not abundant in vocational education. It appears that assessment of the "end-product" of vocational learning just does not receive as much emphasis as it should.

In an attempt to identify the relevant work in the psychomotor domain, Carlson and Griggs (1966) compiled an extensive annotated bibliography. This was then utilized by Simpson (1966) in her year-long study of the classification of psychomotor educational objectives. She considered this effort only a beginning, with more study needed in the psychomotor area and its

relation to the cognitive and affective domains. Some work has been done in terms of cognitive learning. The Ohio Achievement Tests in Trade and Industrial Education (Ohio Trade and Industrial Education Service, 1964) have made a major contribution in this area. These tests are instruments to measure success in machine trades, auto mechanics, electricity, electronics, drafting and printing. Since 1963, Kentucky, West Virginia, Illinois and Indiana have participated in this program on a statewide basis.

The Ohio Division of Vocational Education (Ohio Trade and Industrial Education Service, 1966) also conducted an in-depth study of the factors contributing to student achievement in trade and industrial education programs. The teacher's personality was found to be among the significant indicators of student achievement and quality learning situations. Teacher's age, grade level completed, years of teaching experience and degree held at a certain career point appeared to be insignificant factors. The study also showed that "the money spent per student... was a significant contributor to students' success programs" (p. 97).

Miller (1968) and Moss (1966) have carried on predictive-type studies to ascertain future success for advanced vocational work. Cognitive learning served as the basis for predicting success in post-high-school trade and technical curriculums in the Moss study. Using 27 variables, he found that no difference in scholastic achievement on certain post–high-school trade and technical curriculums could be attributed to differences in amounts of senior high-school industrial arts experience. Miller (1968) concentrated on determining the validity of a pre-selection battery of standardized tests as predictors of success in secondary-school trade programs. His tentative conclusion was that a reduced number of selective variables would yield almost as high a correlation with success as the total number of variables.

Mehaffey (1969) attempted to validate the hierarchies of the cognitive-domain taxonomy with social science subject matter. Data resulting from a sample of 112 eighth-grade students did not support the hypothesis that one class of behaviors is likely to make use of and be built on behaviors found in preceding classes of proposed hierarchies. Hughes (1968) undertook a more expanded study in this area and found strong support for the cumulative nature of the cognitive domain.

Research in the affective domain (changes in interest, attitudes and values, the development of appreciations, adequate adjustments) has been conspicuously absent in vocational education research. Obviously more has to be known about attitudinal change as well as the manipulative or motor-skill area.

Classroom Methods

In recent years several attempts have been made to study the effects of teaching methods in the vocational shop or laboratory. Unlike the formal classroom setting, the shop or laboratory provides a learning environment of diverse potentials. The teacher in this setting has come under study in terms of individualized instruction (Finch, 1969), direct detailed versus direct discovery methods (Tuckman, 1968b), and the utility of feedback in effecting teacher change (Oliver, 1967).

The Finch (1969) study purports to have developed an instrument that will measure student attitude toward individualized shop and laboratory instruction accurately. The results of a series of field trials indicated that the instrument was unidimensional in nature and contained sufficient validity and reliability for the intended purposes. The author believes that the use of this instrument in future research and development activities will enable an accurate assessment of student attitude toward individualization of instruction and will also enable the examination of student attitude as a potential

contributor to learning outcomes. If this is the case, teachers will be able to assess individualized instruction and utilize it in various ways and with those students whose attitude is favorably inclined toward individualization.

The work of Oliver (1967) compared the relative effectiveness of informational feedback to instructors from three sources: supervisors, students, and supervisors and students combined. Subjects were students from grades 10, 11 and 12 and vocational teachers from schools in New Jersey and three neighboring states. It was found that: 1) teachers exposed to informational feedback from students and students and supervisors combined changed more than those who were not so exposed; 2) feedback from students has an effect on teachers while feedback from supervisors alone has no effect either by itself or as an increment above and beyond the effect of student feedback; 3) sensitivity to feedback and years of teacher experience are inversely related; 4) there are no significant differences due to feedback interval, and 5) teacher effectiveness as perceived by students could be improved generally through the use of student feedback during the first 10 years of teaching.

Tuckman (1968b) tested the hypothesis that directive teachers would be more effective with concrete, authoritarian students, and nondirective teachers more effective with abstract, nonauthoritarian students. In testing this hypothesis the study compared two types of vocational high-school teachers (directive and nondirective) and the effect they have on students of different personalities in different subject areas. The design involved 12 directive and 12 nondirective teachers in two vocational high schools with half the subjects teaching vocational and half teaching nonvocational. Students were classified by two personality measures as abstract or concrete and authoritarian or nonauthoritarian. Results showed that students were more satisfied with, preferred and earned higher grades from nondirective teachers in both vocational and nonvocational subjects. The primary finding of the study was that abstract and non-authoritarian students showed differentiation between directive and nondirective teachers while concrete and authoritarian students did not. As predicted, abstract and non-authoritarian students preferred, were more satisfied with, and obtained higher grades from nondirective teachers as opposed to directive teachers, while the concrete and authoritarian students reacted similarly to the authoritarian styles. Although students showed a marked preference for vocational teachers, their higher grades were earned from nonvocational teachers. The inter-action effects were neither as frequent nor as long as expected. Implications and recommendations were made as a result of these findings and among them was the suggestion that teachers can be helped to develop the capability to use alternative teaching styles and to choose among them as the situation requires.

Vocational teachers are at liberty to employ a number of classroom methods of instruction. Among them have been the sometimes controversial project and problem-solving methods. At one time the project method was held as the best means of individualized instruction. Today the class or group project is being used more and more. In a study of effectiveness of group project training in distributive education, Coakley (1968) found that high-school students reacted favorably to the project 1) because projects gave students better understanding for working in marketing and distribution, 2) because projects were well managed by teachers, 3) because student attitudes were favorable, 4) because there was considerable student involvement, and 5) because projects were related to classroom instruction and the occupational interests of the students.

Birchenall (1969) attempted to relate the problem-solving method to instructing practical nurses. Her study of early exposure to the hospital setting and patient care in an attempt to stimulate future learning caused no significant difference as a result of the treatment on a paper and pencil test; however, those students introduced to a hospital setting early did receive a significantly higher performance rating than those who did not receive such indoctrination.

Folley (1964) evaluated and restructured a new course in electronics fundamentals in light of recognized educational and psychological principles. The new course: 1) presented each student with a complete or whole electronic system—a gestalt; 2) developed many joblike situations; 3) presented no circuit theory or principles until after the electronic system had been used or tested on actual equipment; 4) started students with the easy material and progressed to the complex; 5) did not present new information found in different equipment but presented a similar circuit contained in equipment previously worked on. As a result of this study it was found that: 1) the revised course would successfully train more trainees with average electronics aptitude; 2) students taught by the revised procedure mastered more knowledge; 3) students taught by the new course acquired more skill in troubleshooting. Moreover, it was concluded that by presenting the student with the whole system he could develop a realistic frame of reference on which to base abstract principles. Once this realistic frame of reference is established, the abstract principles would be retained longer.

Vocational Systems Packages

Probably the singularly most concentrated effort in improving vocational instruction has been brought about by 17 state instructional materials laboratories. These laboratories package materials for classroom use. Through this effort, which is estimated to involve an expenditure of close to a million dollars a year, it would seem that instructional materials for almost every occupational area would be refined into an instructional system. This definitely is not the case, however, and the task of keeping teaching systems and learning packages for the several hundred vocational occupational areas up-to-date is simply overwhelming. After many abortive attempts, those engaged in vocational curriculum development have organized within the American Vocational Association (1970) in a separate section—the Organization of Curriculum Specialists—dealing with their common interests. The one hundred plus members of this national group are determined to coordinate their efforts and to maintain a linkage so as to exchange information and eliminate much duplication of work.

Paramount in the task of disseminating instructional materials produced by the State Instructional Materials Laboratories is the quarterly publication, *Abstracts of Instructional Materials in Vocational and Technical Education*. In the Spring 1970 issue 284 different materials are listed (*Abstracts of Instructional Materials,* Spring 1970). The total cost of all 10 issues of microfiche collection (fall 1967 to winter 1969) was approximately $500 which, if produced separately in hard copy, would have cost several thousand dollars. Not to be confused with the efforts of the State Instructional Materials Laboratories are those of individual researchers who have attempted to package materials in various ways to facilitate instruction and learning. Among these are Pratzner and Hanson (1969), Schemick (1964), and Swets, Feurzeig, Harris, and Marill (1963). Although some of these studies used audiovisual devices as a means of delivering the packaged system, all were concerned with some type of program. Abma (1964) summed up the past, present and future of programmed instruction— which has had relevance to most studies involving a systems approach—as the adjunct autoinstruction of Sidney L. Pressey, the intrinsic programming of Norman A. Crowder and the linear programming of B. F. Skinner. He further pointed out that the most current research is centering on linear programming and that the future may see an integration of programmed instruction

and other teaching techniques within a systems approach to training and education.

An attempt to tie the systems approaches developed by individuals together with those of the State Instructional Materials Laboratories reveals that the potential of the two efforts appears quite unrelated. Larson (1964) proposed the creation of a physical facility called a Technology Resource Center which would serve as a focal point for maximizing and expanding such work. The center would be developed through an Office of Education contract and would include a technology facility, a resource facility and a computer center. The technology facility would capitalize on the expertise of business and industry in upgrading vocational teachers in technology; the resource facility would record the technology in terms of instructional packages, and the computer center would be used to individualize the package content for the student learner through computer-assisted instruction. Moreover, an evaluation component would be built into the system to provide a closed loop-effort to assure assessment of the output. Such a technology resource center has not been implemented in any state or region, however, perhaps because it is too advanced in concept or because it would be too expensive to create.

The Use of Materials and Devices

It is not surprising to find that the study of audiovisual aids for teaching manipulative skills and individualizing instruction is uppermost in the minds of vocational researchers. The mere limitation of teaching hardware in most shops and laboratories requires that some form of individualization be considered by the teacher. In other words, rarely can students be instructed on the same type of equipment at the same time simply because there is not enough equipment.

The early work of Vandermeer (1945) on the use of sound films to train engine lathe operators stimulated much thought on the use of teaching devices for imparting skills

(Finch, 1970; Folley, 1961; Folley and Bouck, 1964; Marovich and Campbell, 1968; Moeller, 1967; Moeller, 1968; Shemick, 1964; Sommer, 1970).

A little-known study of instructor-operated educational TV, but one which rather thoroughly tested this aspect of television, was conducted by Stout (1963). The television system employed was a low-cost, fixed-camera type installation. The instructor operated the entire system without a production staff. The purposes were to determine whether selected parts—mathematics, electron theory, general physics, and slide rule operation—of the electronics technology course could be taught by television, and to make a complete and detailed analysis of low-cost television that would be feasible for operation in a local school system. It was concluded that 1) the uses of an educational television program depend on thoughtful and detailed planning; 2) educational television systems need not always include the use of sophisticated equipment; 3) the maintenance cost can be kept low; 4) low-cost, fixed-camera TV seems feasible if at least 50 additional students can be taught with the system; 5) there should not be students in the room from which the program is emanating, and 6) students learn mathematics, slide rule, general physics and electron theory as well by TV as by having the instructor in the room.

The variety of approaches represented by the studies focusing on materials and devices ranges from the consideration of programmed texts for teaching foods-science to the incorporation of tutorial devices using sound film. The early work of Vandermeer (1945) was supported by Moeller's studies (1967, 1968) which found that films are not a substitute for individual demonstrations but are a supplement to a well-integrated instructional program. From his study on the use of single-concept loop films, Sommer (1970) concluded that: 1) teacher plus films (single-concept loop) was more effective than teacher only or films only; 2) the films-only group learned as much as the teacher-only group; 3) repetition of demonstrations was substantially reduced with the films; and 4) boys and girls did not differ significantly on any of the measures. Hensel and Johnson (1967) in an attempt to ascertain the utilization and worth of materials for off-farm agricultural occupations used by some 373 teachers concluded that: 1) teachers were using the materials as the developers had intended and 2) a lack of the time needed to adapt materials to local programs was a major reason for not using the materials. Collofello, Henrie, and Whiteford (1970) concluded that in microteaching situations high-school students were not more effective as the class participants than college students. However, student teachers' subjective reactions indicated a preference for working with high-school students mainly because the situation was more real in terms of students to be taught after becoming a full-time teacher. The use of video-recording for micro-teaching was the subject of the Third National Vocational-Technical Education Conference held in Miami and sponsored by The Center for Vocational and Technical Education (Cotrell & Brice, 1970). Results of 10 studies assessing micro-teaching and video-recording served as the basis of the conference. Folley (1961) proposes that, when designing performance aids, four steps must be considered: 1) identification of task elements for which aids should be provided; 2) determination of approximate functional characteristics of aids for these task elements; 3) specification of the physical design characteristics of the aids to carry out the functions, and 4) evaluation, modification and updating of aids.

TOWARD A THEORY OF VOCATIONAL TEACHER EDUCATION

The first major stimulus for the education of vocational teachers was the passage of the Smith-Hughes Act of 1917. This milestone in federal aid to education authorized the use of federal funds for ancillary services which specifically included the training of vocational subject teachers (*Administration of Vocational Education,* 1949). Programs were established to prepare teachers in vocational agriculture, home economics, and trade and industrial occupations. The George-Barden Act of 1946, its subsequent amendments, and the National Defense Education Act of 1958 made further provisions for the preparation of teachers, especially in fields of distributive education, practical nursing and various technical occupations (Swanson, 1962). The Vocational Education Act of 1963 broadened the definition of vocational education and specifically stated that business and office education were eligible for federal aid (Public Law 88-210, 1963).

In spite of the great expansion of programs to prepare teachers of vocational subjects, the preparation of vocational teachers still awaits a legitimate theoretical base founded on research and study. Other than occupational analyses by Fryklund (1965) and Bollinger (1955), and status surveys of vocational teacher characteristics (Allen, 1963), the development of various vocational teacher-educational curricula may be said to be operating primarily on a basis of tradition, convention, wisdom and personal experience (Moss, 1967).

By working toward a theoretical framework for the preparation of vocational teachers, some progress has been made in identifying who vocational teachers are and how they are recruited and admitted to various kinds of teacher-education programs. Barlow's (1968) descriptive profile of the trade and technical teacher in California showed that for a person who has developed a trade or technical competence a career in education means a transition to another world. The unique problem of assimilating the trade and technical teacher into that other world stems from the fact that he obtained his distinctive competence on the job instead of in school. This uniqueness, according to Barlow, is at once an asset and a liability. His vocational knowledge and skill provide him with the opportunity to enter the education profession. But a vocational background together with a lack of academic credentials generally relegates him to a lower social and professional ranking. In a similar study of trade and industrial teachers in New Jersey, House (1970) found the situation to be much the same.

Teacher-Learning Techniques

Surveying the opinions held by beginning high-school business teachers, McCullough (1966) found that student teaching was considered a very valuable aspect of their professional preparation but that they felt that additional time should be given to observation and to conferences with the college coordinator. McEwin (1968) sought to determine whether educational-methods courses and student teaching effect a change of attitudes in students. Employing the Minnesota Teacher Attitude Inventory and a questionnaire designed to reveal the relationship of selected factors to attitudinal change, McEwin concluded that there were significant differences in attitudinal change among a number of groups studied. The most influential factor considered in the study proved to be the personality of the cooperating teacher.

According to Ashmun and Larson (1970) the roles of teacher-education institutions and teacher educators are badly in need of clarification, especially in terms of: responsibilities of undergraduate and graduate education; pre-service and in-service education, teaching, research, counseling and advising; working with state departments of education; student recruitment; and follow-up of graduates.

Measuring Occupational Competency

A well-established raison d'être of vocational education is that it has an important mission in the preparation of youth and adults for gainful employment. A logical corollary is the widely accepted assumption that employment experience and competency in a recognized occupation or cluster of closely related fields are primary qualifications for teachers of vocational subjects.

Although competency testing of prospective vocational teachers has long been employed, there has been no uniform system for test development or application. Some state education departments have produced sets of written and performance tests; others employ written tests only. But the majority of states have no established plan for assessing skills and knowledge in various occupations.

Impellitteri's paper entitled "Constructing Valid Occupational Competency Examinations" was given as part of the Rutgers Feasibility Study (Griess, 1967) and focused on three questions: 1) What considerations should be given to reliability and validity in constructing nationwide occupational competency examinations? 2) How should valid and reliable occupational competency examinations be constructed? 3) How should the validity and reliability of occupational competency examinations be measured? When discussing the method of establishing norms, Impellitteri expressed the view that selection of individuals to be included in the norm group is a primary concern.

Shimberg's paper (Griess, 1967) gave particular emphasis to the performance phase of trade proficiency examinations. Citing the U.S. Navy's experience during World War II, Shimberg stated that it is generally conceded that written tests of trade knowledge cannot provide very dependable evaluations of shop performance, that without some type of direct or indirect performance measure it is unlikely that we can make an accurate assessment of an individual's trade competency.

The New York State Investigation of Reliability and Validity of Selected Occupational Competency Examinations (Koenigsberg & Reilly, 1968) helps to confirm Shimberg's position that written tests are incomplete measures. There was virtually a zero correlation between written and performance scores in auto mechanics, cosmetology and machine shop in examinations taken by candidates for vocational teaching positions. The considerable cost of the Koenigsberg-Reilly study, even though it dealt with a very small proportion of the potential number of occupations that could use proficiency examinations, gives evidence of the need for national or multistate regional centers of occupational test development. Support for this position is found in the National Competency Testing Project (Panitz & Olivo, 1970) which discovered the existence of severe restrictions for any one state or private organization to produce quality examinations.

The organization of a National Occupational Competency Institute or Center for Vocational Competency Testing with an incorporated association of states to provide advice and counsel was recommended.

IN RETROSPECT

The combined national resources to provide vocational-technical education, including the essential component of teacher education, is diverse and confused. At no time has there ever been an abundance of teachers of vocational-technical subjects, and the fact remains that diverse organizational patterns of school organization do not prescribe a uniform role for all vocational-technical teachers. Therefore, the administrative organization itself causes confusion among teacher-preparation efforts and techniques. The recent recognition of the need to assess the value of occupational experience (as measured by examination) in order to meet the requirements of subject-matter expertise and obtain college credit is encouraging.

Although the implementation of internship-externship programs is not unique to the vocational-technical teacher-preparation effort, it is a positive step for vocational education. Neither teacher-education institutions nor business and industry can be solely responsible for the preparation of teachers of vocational-technical subjects. The better plan would be to combine institutional and work-world settings through cooperative education programs and then to measure the results of such ventures against the results of traditional programs now in operation.

It should be obvious that vocational education research is not abundant. At the same time the mechanics of dissemination are functioning well, mainly through the *Abstracts of Research and Related Materials in Vocational and Technical Education* as published by the Educational Resources Information Center Clearing House on Vocational and Technical Education at The Ohio State University. All of the research done from 1960 through 1970 can be purchased on microfiche for $400. Such a collection would cost several thousand dollars in hard copy. In addition, The Center for Vocational and Technical Education has published two generations of the review and synthesis of research series in a number of areas of Vocational-Technical Education. The first of these covers materials from 1960 through 1969 and the second from 1969 to the present (*Review and Synthesis Series,* 1969).

What appears to be lacking is a systematic and planned program of research. The fragmentation of effort leaves the accumulation of an adequate body of knowledge to mere chance. The fact remains that vocational-technical education is still doing things the same old way and asking the same old questions with no better results and answers than were available over half a century ago. Somehow, a system that once and for all provides solid solutions to the problems of teaching vocational skills must be established.

REFERENCES

Abma, S. Programed instruction—past, present and future. Ohio: Wright-Patterson Air Force Base, Behavioral Science Laboratory, 1964.

Abstracts of instructional materials in vocational and technical education. Educational Resources Information Center Clearing House on Vocational and Technical Education. Columbus: The Ohio State University, The Center for Vocational and Technical Education, Spring 1970.

Abstracts of research and related materials in vocational and technical education. Educational Resources Information Center Clearing House on Vocational and Technical Education. Columbus: The Ohio State University, The Center for Vocational Technical Education, Summer 1970.

Administration of vocational education. Vocational Education Bulletin No. 1, General Series No. 1, Revised 1948. Washington, D.C.: United States Government Printing Office, 1949.

Agriculture Education and Distributive Education Staffs of Vocational Education Department, Virginia Polytechnic Institute. Preliminary report of a survey to determine the opportunities and training needs for career persons in agriculturally related-distributive businesses in the geographical area served by George Wythe High School, Wytheville, Virginia. Blacksburg, Va.: Virginia Polytechnic Institute, 1963.

Allen, D. A story of trade and technical teachers who received first credentials July 1955–June 1962. Los Angeles: University of California, Division of Vocational Education, 1963.

American Vocational Association. *Convention Proceedings Digest,* Boston, Dec. 6–10, 1969. Washington, D.C.: American Vocational Association, 1970.

Ashmun, R. D., & Larson, R. A. *Review and synthesis of research on distributive education.* (2nd ed.) Columbus: The Ohio State University, The Center for Research and Development in Vocational-Technical Education, 1970.

Barlow, M. L., & Reinhart, B. *Profiles of trade and technical teachers.* Los Angeles: University of California, Los Angeles, in cooperation with Bureau of Industrial Education, California State Education Department, 1968.

Bergener, V. E. Illinois vocational education occupational research and development coordinating unit. Springfield, Ill.: State Board of Vocational Education and Rehabilitation, 1967.

Berkey, A. L., Kelly, W. H., & Brown, D. W. The relevance of secondary occupational training in agriculture to occupational patterns and images. Ithaca, N.Y.: Cornell University, 1969.

Birchenall, J. M. A study of the value of student health agencies during the pre-clinical portion of the practical nursing program. Trenton, N.J.: The Research Coordinating Unit for Vocational-Technical Education, 1969.

Bollinger, E. W., & Weaver, G. G. *Trade analysis and course organization for shop teachers.* New York: Pitman, 1955.

Bottoms, G., & Matheny, K. B. *A guide for the development, implementation, and administration of exemplary programs and projects in vocational education.* Atlanta, Ga.: Georgia Department of Education, 1969.

Brandon, G. L. (Director) Explorations in research design: Curricula for technicians. East Lansing, Mich.: Michigan State University, 1960.

Carlson, N. W., & Griggs, M. B. The psychomotor domain—a selective bibliography with annotations. Urbana, Ill.: University of Illinois, 1966.

Coakley, C. B. The effectiveness of profit training in distributive education. Unpublished master's thesis, University of Wisconsin, 1968.

Coe, B. D., & Zanzalari, H. J. After ten years —a follow-up of Middlesex County vocational and technical high school graduates. New Brunswick, N.J.: Middlesex County Vocational and Technical High Schools, 1964.

Collofello, P., Henrie, H., & Whiteford, E. The relative effectiveness of two sources of feedback on teachers in the micro-teaching situation. Minneapolis: University of Minnesota, Minnesota Research Coordinating Unit for Vocational Education, 1970.

Conference Report. Vocational education amendments of 1968. Report No. 1938. Washington, D.C.: House of Representatives, 90th Congress, October 2, 1968.

Cooperative occupational pre-teaching experience program, third annual report. New Brunswick, N.J.: Rutgers University, De-partment of Vocational-Technical Education, University College, 1970.

Corazzini, A. J. Vocational education: A study of benefits and costs. Princeton, N.J.: Princeton University, Industrial Relations Section, 1966.

Coster, J. K., & Morgan, R. L. The role of evaluation in the decision making process. Raleigh, N.C.: North Carolina State University, 1969.

Coster, J. K., & Morgan, R. L. A holistic approach to evaluating occupational education with implications for accreditation. Raleigh, N.C.: North Carolina State University, 1970.

Cotrell, C. J., & Brice, G. R. (Eds.) *Third annual national vocational-technical education seminar proceedings—Micro teaching and video recording.* Columbus: The Ohio State University, The Center for Vocational and Technical Education, 1970.

Drake, W. E., & Tom, F. K. T. Entry occupations in off-farm agriculture—A survey and task analysis of entry level off-farm agricultural occupations in New York state. Ithaca, N.Y.: Cornell University, 1968.

Eninger, M. U. *The process and product of T & I high school level vocational education in the United States.* Pittsburgh, Pa.: American Institutes for Research, September, 1965. (abstract)

Ertel, K. H. Identification of major tasks performed by merchandising employees working in those standard industrial classifications of retail establishments. United States Office of Education Project No. ERD-257-65. Moscow, Idaho: University of Idaho, 1966.

Finch, C. R. The development of an instrument to measure student attitude toward individualized shop and laboratory instruction. Research Series, No. 2. University Park, Pa.: Pennsylvania State University, Department of Vocational Education, January 1969.

Finch, C. R., assisted by Gustilo, T., & Wiersteiner, S. R. Instructional resources for vocational-technical education: Teacher attitude, resource availability and resource utilization. University Park, Pa.: Pennsylvania State University, February 1970.

Fink, A. W., & Wenrich, R. C. The history and current status of the cooperative vocational-industrial teacher education program. Unpublished manuscript, University of Michigan, 1964.

Folley, J. D., Jr. A preliminary procedure for systematically designing performance aids. Ohio: Wright-Patterson Air Force Base, Behavioral Sciences Laboratory, Aerospace Medical Laboratory, Aeronautical Systems Division, Air Force Systems Command, U.S. Air Force, October 1961.

Folley, J. D., Jr. Functional fundamentals training for electronic maintenance personnel. Ohio: Wright-Patterson Air Force Base, Behavioral Sciences Laboratory, 1964.

Folley, J. D., Jr., & Bouck, A. J. A field experimental study of programmed instruction on a manipulative task. Ohio: Wright-Patterson Air Force Base, Behavioral Sciences Laboratory, 1964.

Frank, N. H. *The summer study of occupational, vocational, and technical education.* Cambridge, Mass.: Massachusetts Institute of Technology, 1965.

Fryklund, V. C. *Analysis technique for instructors.* New York: Bruce Publishing, 1965.

Fuller, G. R., & Phipps, L. J. Development of human resources through a vocationally oriented educational program for disadvantaged families in depressed rural areas. Interim Report No. 1. Urbana, Ill.: University of Illinois, September, 1968.

Gallington, R. O., & Sievert, N. W. Cooperative supervised job training—The final report and evaluation. Springfield, Ill.: Board of Vocational Education and Rehabilitation in cooperation with Southern Illinois University, School of Technology, 1966.

Griess, G. Feasibility of providing trade competency examinations on a national basis. New Brunswick, N.J.: Rutgers University, 1967.

Hensel, J. W., & Johnson, C. H., Jr. An evaluation of the off-farm agricultural occupations materials. Columbus, Ohio: The Ohio State University, October 1967.

Hill, C. W. *The further development of research competencies of personnel in vocational education research and development.* Ithaca, N.Y.: Cornell University, 1966.

Horowitz, M. A., & Herrnstadt, I. L. *The training of tool and die makers.* Boston, Mass.: Northeastern University, Department of Economics, September 1969.

House, E. W. Selected factors relating to the work cycle of vocational skill subject teachers. Unpublished doctoral dissertation, Rutgers University, 1970.

Huffman, H., & Gust, D. D. *Business education for the emergent office.* Columbus, Ohio: The Ohio State University, The Center for Vocational-Technical Education, 1970.

Hughes, R. P. *Measuring relationships during and between cognitive and affective behavior in a controlled learning situation.* New York: State Department of Education, Bureau of Occupational Education Research, 1968.

Kaufman, J. J., & Lewis, M. V. *The potential of vocational education.* University Park, Pa.: The Pennsylvania State University, The Institute for Research on Human Resources, 1968.

Kaufman, J. J., Schaefer, C. J., Lewis, M. V., Stevens, D. W., & House, E. W. *The role of the secondary schools in the preparation of youth for employment.* University Park, Pa.: The Pennsylvania State University, Institute for Research on Human Resources, 1967.

Kaufman, J. J., Stromsdorfer, E. W., Hu, T., & Lee, M. L. *A cost-effectiveness study of vocational education.* University Park, Pa.: The Pennsylvania State University, Institute for Research and Human Resources, 1969.

Kievit, M. B. A comparison of environmental press and selected characteristics of students at a community college and technical institute. New Brunswick, N.J.: Rutgers University, 1970.

Koenigsberg, L. A., & Reilly, R. R. An investigation of the reliability and validity of selected occupational competency examinations and their use in evaluating prospective trade and industrial teachers. Oswego, N.Y.: State University of New York, Division of Vocational Technical Education, 1968.

Larson, M. Technology resource center for vocational-technical education. New Brunswick, N.J.: A research study supported by a United States Office of Education grant under provisions of Section (4)c of the Vocational Education Act of 1963, 1964.

Loreen, C. O. Occupational opportunities and training needs for youth for non-farm agricultural jobs in Washington state. Pullman, Wash.: Washington State University, February, 1967.

Mager, R. F., & Beach, K. M., Jr. *Developing vocational instruction.* Palo Alto, Calif.: Fearon, 1967.

Marovich, P. E., & Campbell, A. M. Programmed instruction in teaching food service science. *Journal of American Dietetic Association,* 1968, 52, 421–426.

McCullough, E. L. Opinions of beginning high school business teachers regarding their college preparation for teaching. Unpublished doctoral dissertation, University of Southern California, 1966.

McEwin, T. Attitudinal changes of students during methods courses and student teaching. Unpublished doctoral dissertation, East Texas State University, 1968.

Mehaffey, B. J. Validity of the taxonomy of education objective: Cognitive domain tested in a controlled teaching situation with social science subject matter. Unpublished master's thesis, Cornell University, 1969.

Meyer, M. P. Workshop on program development for training homemaker-home health aides. New Brunswick, N.J.: Rutgers University, July 1969.

Miller, J. G. (Director) Predictive testing for entrance in vocational-technical schools. New York: New York University, Center for Field Research and School Services, August 1968.

Moeller, C. A. A comparison of selected audiovisual methods and lecture demonstration methods in teaching manipulative skills related to metal working operations. *Journal of Industrial Teacher Education,* 1967, 4(3), 20–29.

Moeller, C. A. The relationship of pre-study of factual materials prior to skill of performing selected manipulative operations on the engine lathe. Raleigh: North Carolina State University, 1968.

Moss, J., Jr. The influence of industrial arts experience on grades earned in post-high school trade and technical curriculums. Minneapolis: University of Minnesota, Minnesota Research Coordination Unit in Occupational Education, 1966.

Moss, J., Jr. Review of research in vocational technical teacher education. Minneapolis: University of Minnesota, College of Education, Department of Industrial Education, 1967.

The National Conference on Cooperative Vocational Education—Notes and working papers. Minneapolis: University of Minnesota, College of Education, 1969.

Nelson, H. E. National institutes on innovative curriculums in vocational-technical education. University Park, Pa.: The Pennsylvania State University, August 1969.

Ohio Trade and Industrial Education Service. A five state statistical analysis. Columbus, Ohio: State Department of Education, Division of Vocational Education, 1964.

Ohio Trade and Industrial Education Service. Factors contributing to student achievement. Columbus, Ohio: The Ohio State University, Industrial Materials Laboratory, Trade and Industrial Education, 1966.

Oliver, W. F. The relative effectiveness of informational feedback about supervisory and student reactions with beginning and experienced vocational teachers. U.S. Department of Health, Education, and Welfare, Office of Education, Bureau of Research. New Brunswick, N.J.: Rutgers University, October 1967.

Panitz, A., & Olivo, C. T. National occupational competency testing project, Vol. 2: The state of the art of occupational competency testing. Research Project No. 8-0474. New Brunswick, N.J.: Rutgers University, Department of Vocational-Technical Education, 1970.

Pratzner, F. C., & Hanson, M. The relative effectiveness of two ways of structuring and presenting pre-service and initial in-service vocational-industrial teacher education lessons. Minneapolis: University of Minnesota, Minnesota Research Coordinating Unit in Occupational Education, April, 1969.

Proceedings: National Conference on Research: 1968 Vocation Education Amendments. Stillwater, Okla.: Oklahoma State University, Research Coordinating Unit, 1969.

Public Law 88-210. 88th Congress, H. R. 4955, December 18, 1963.

Research and implementation in vocation education. Washington, D.C.: American Vocational Association, 1969.

Review and synthesis of research (series). Columbus, Ohio: The Ohio State University, The Center for Vocational-Technical Education, 1969.

Schaefer, C. J., & Kaufman, J. J. *Occupational education for Massachusetts.* Boston: Advisory Council on Education, 1968.

Shemick, J. M. A study of the relative effectiveness in teaching a manipulative skill—multi media teaching program versus classroom demonstration with printed instruction sheets. Project No. 1597. Washington, D.C.: United States Office of Education, supported by NDEA Funds, Title VII, 1964.

Simpson, E. J. The classification of educational objectives, psychomotor domain. Urbana, Ill.: University of Illinois, July 1, 1965–May 31, 1966.

Smith, B. B., & Moss, J., Jr. (Eds.) Process and techniques of vocational curriculum development. Minneapolis: University of Minnesota, Minnesota Research Coordinating Unit in Occupational Education, 1970.

Sommer, S. A. The use of silent single concept loop films to facilitate the acquisition of occupational skills. Unpublished doctoral dissertation, Rutgers University, 1970.

Stout, J. K. Instructor operated educational TV. Williamsport, Pa.: Williamsport Technical Institute, 1963.

Stromsdorfer, E. W. Aspects of geographic and occupational mobility in planning for state vocational education programs. In R. C. Young, (Ed.) Manpower information for vocational education planning. Columbus, Ohio: The Ohio State University, The Center for Vocational-Technical Education, November 1969. Pp. 137–158.

Swanson, J. C. (Compiler) Development of federal legislation for vocational education. Chicago, Ill.: American Technical Society, 1962.

Swets, J. A., Feurzeig, W., Harris, J. R., & Marill, T. The Socratic system: A computer system to aid in teaching complex concepts. Ohio: Wright-Patterson Air Force Base, Behavioral Sciences Laboratory, June 1963.

Tuckman, B. W. Structural analysis as an aid to curriculum development. Incidental Report No. 1. New Brunswick, N.J.: Rutgers University, Graduate School of Education, 1968. (a)

Tuckman, B. W. A study of the effectiveness of directive versus non-directive vocational teachers as a function of student characteristics and course format. U.S. Department of Health, Education, and Welfare, Office of Education, Bureau of Research. New Brunswick, N.J.: Rutgers University, September 1968. (b)

U.S. Department of Labor. Manpower report of the President. Washington, D.C.: U.S. Government Printing Office, March 1970.

U.S. Office of Education. Vocational and technical education. Annual report, fiscal year 1966. Washington, D.C.: U.S. Government Printing Office, 1968.

Vandermeer, A. W. The economy of time in industrial training: An experimental study of the use of sound films in the training of engine lathe operations. Journal of Educational Psychology, 1945, 25, 65–90.

Williams, D. L. Variables influencing adoption of cooperative agricultural occupations curricula. In W. L. Hull, & W. W. Stevenson (Eds.), Change in agriculture education. Proceedings of the Seventeenth Annual Southern Research Conference in Agricultural Education. Stillwater, Okla.: Oklahoma State University, 1967. Pp. 42–58.

Wooldridge, R. L. Cooperative education and the community colleges in New Jersey. A supplementary report prepared for the governor's committee on New Jersey higher education. New York: National Commission for Cooperative Education, April 2, 1966.

Credits and Acknowledgements

Acknowledgement is made to the following for their kind permission to reprint material from copyrighted sources:

Chapter 1

Houghton Mifflin Company (*Public Education in the United States* by E. P. Cubberley, 1919).

Chapter 3

American Educational Research Association (*Handbook of Research on Teaching* edited by N. L. Gage, 1963); American Psychological Association ("Of Models and Men" by W. K. Estes, *American Psychologist,* 1957, 12, 609–617); Cambridge University Press (*Axiomatic Method in Biology* by J. H. Woodger, 1937); Chandler Publishing Company (*The Conduct of Inquiry: Methodology for Behavioral Science* by A. Kaplan, 1964); Cornell University Press (*Models and Metaphors: Studies in Language and Philosophy* by M. Black, 1962); Prentice-Hall (*Theory Construction* by H. M. Blalock, Jr., 1969).

Chapter 4

Liveright Publishing Corporation (*The Sources of a Science of Education* by John Dewey, New York, copyright © 1929 by Horace Liveright).

Chapter 5

G. Nuthall ("Teacher Verbal Behavior and Pupil Learning," unpublished manuscript, 1971); *Theory Into Practice* ("The Model in Use" by S. S. Lail, 1968, 7, 176–180).

Chapter 6

Holt, Rinehart and Winston (*Discipline and Group Management in Classroom* by J. S. Kounin, 1970); L. Katz ("A Study of the Changes in Behavior of Children Enrolled in Two Types of Head Start Classes" by L. Katz, 1968); Society for Research in Child Development and J. Brophy ("Mothers as Teachers of Their Own Preschool Children: The Influence of Socio-Economic Status and Task Structure" by J. Brophy, *Child Development,* 1970, 41, 79–94).

Chapter 7

The Macmillan Company (*Encyclopedia of Educational Research* edited by R. L. Ebel, 1969); *The New York Times* ("The Problem of Weeding Out the Unfit Teacher" by L. Buder, © 1969 by The New York Times Company. Reprinted by permission); *Phi*

Delta Kappan ("Interaction Analysis: A Tardy Comment" by B. Rosenshine, Vol. 51).

Chapter 8

The Center for Urban Education ("Educational Development" by J. K. Hemphill, *The Urban Review*, 1969, 4(2), 23–27); *Journal of Research & Development in Education* ("The Nature of Educational Development" by R. E. Schutz, 1970, 3(2), 39–64); National Society for the Study of Education (*Theories of Learning and Instruction* edited by E. R. Hilgard, 1964).

Chapter 11

Society for the Experimental Analysis of Behavior ("The Control of the Content of Conversation through Reinforcement" by N. H. Azrin, W. Holz, R. Ulrich, & I. Goldiamond, *Journal of the Experimental Analysis of Behavior*, 1961, 4, 25–30).

Chapter 18

Society for Research in Child Development ("The Early Training Project: A Seventh-Year Report" by S. Gray & R. A. Klaus, *Child Development*, 1970, 41, 909–924).

Chapter 19

American Academy of Pediatrics ("Nutrition, Growth and Neurointegrative Development: An Experimental and Ecologic Study" by J. Cravioto, E. R. Delicardie, & H. G. Birch, *Pediatrics Supplement*, 1966, 38, 319–372); American Association for the Advancement of Science, H. F. Eichenwald, and P. C. Fry ("Nutrition and Learning" by H. F. Eichenwald & P. C. Fry, *Science*, 14 February 1969, 163, 644–648. © 1969 by the American Association for the Advancement of Science); Harcourt Brace Jovanovich (*Disadvantaged Children* by H. G.

Birch & J. D. Gussow, 1970); *Harvard Educational Review* ("Race and Education: A Search for Legitimacy" by C. V. Hamilton, 38(4), 1968); National Council for the Social Studies ("Chicago's Center for Inner City Studies: An Experiment in Relevancy" by S. H. Stone, *Social Education*, May 1969, 33, 528–532; "Urban Teacher Preparation Programs" by R. Wisniewski, *Social Education*, January 1969, 33, 77–82); Random House (*Crisis in the Classroom: The Remaking of American Education* by C. E. Silberman, 1970).

Chapter 20

American Educational Research Association ("Reconstruction of Educational Research" by L. S. Shulman, *Review of Educational Research*, 1970, 40(3), 371–396); S. A. Kirk (a personal communication); J. J. McCarthy (a personal communication).

Chapter 22

American Psychological Association ("The Discovery and Encouragement of Exceptional Talent" by L. M. Terman, *American Psychologist*, 1954, 9, 221–230); American Psychological Association and M. M. Kaley ("Attitudes toward the Dual Role of the Married Professional Woman" by M. M. Kaley, *American Psychologist*, 1971, 26, 301–306); Creative Education Foundation and J. P. Guilford ("Creativity: Yesterday, Today, and Tomorrow" by J. P. Guilford, *Journal of Creative Behavior*, 1967, 1, 3–14); Estate of Albert Einstein (*The Evolution of Physics: The Growth of Ideas from Early Concepts to Relativity and Quanta* by A. Einstein & L. Infeld, 1938); The Macmillan Company (*Encyclopedia of Educational Research*, 4th edition, edited by R. L. Ebel, 1969); Prentice-Hall (*Curriculum Planning for the Gifted* edited by L. A. Fliegler, 1961); Random House (*Invisible Man* by R. Ellison, 1952); Stanford University Press (*Genetic Studies of Genius. Vol. 1. Mental and Physical Traits of a Thousand Gifted Children,* 2nd edition, by L. M. Terman, 1926; *Genetic Studies of Genius. Vol. 5. The Gifted Group at Midlife: Thirty-five Years' Follow-up of the Superior Child* by L. M. Terman & M. H. Oden, 1959).

Chapter 26

Holt, Rinehart & Winston (*The Condition of Learning,* 2nd edition, by R. M. Gagne, © 1965, 1970).

Chapter 34

American Council on Education ("The Concept of the Structure of a Discipline" by J. J. Schwab, *Educational Record,* 1962, 43, 197–205); Harvard University Press (*The Teaching of Science* by J. J. Schwab, 1962); McGraw-Hill Book Company (*Handbook on Formative and Summative Evaluation of Student Learning* edited by B. S. Bloom, J. T. Hastings, & G. F. Madaus, 1971); National Science Teachers Association ("An Analysis of Research on Instructional Procedures in Secondary School Science, Part I" by G. A. Ramsey & R. W. Howe, *The Science Teacher,* 1969, 36(3), 62–70).

Chapter 37

The Macmillan Company (*Creative and Mental Growth* by V. Lowenfeld, 1947); National Art Education Association, K. Beittel, and E. Mattil ("The Effect of a 'Depth' Versus a 'Breadth' Method of Art Instruction at the Ninth Grade Level" by K. Beittel & E. Mattil, *Studies in Art Education,* 1961, 3, 75–87).

Chapter 39

American Educational Research Association (*Handbook of Research on Teaching* edited by N. L. Gage, 1963); Central Midwestern Regional Educational Laboratory (*Classroom Social Systems in Teacher Education* by L. M. Smith, 1968; *"Go, Bug, Go!": Methodological Issues in Classroom Observational Research* by L. M. Smith & J. A. M. Brock, 1970); *Psychology Today* ("Arthur Jensen Replies" by Arthur Jensen, October 1969, 3, 4, 6).

Chapter 42

Fearon Publishers (*Developing Vocational Instruction* by R. F. Mager & K. M. Beach, Jr., 1967); The Ohio State University, Instructional Materials Laboratory, Trade and Industrial Education (Factors Contributing to Student Achievement by the Ohio Trade and Industrial Education Service, 1965); The Pennsylvania State University, Institute for Research on Human Resources (*A Cost-effectiveness Study of Vocational Education* by J. J. Kaufman, E. W. Stromsdorfer, T. Hu, & M. L. Lee, 1969; *The Potential of Vocational Education* by J. J. Kaufman & M. V. Lewis, 1968); University of Minnesota, Minnesota Research Coordinating Unit in Occupational Education (Process and Techniques of Vocational Curriculum Development by B. B. Smith & J. Moss, Jr., 1970).

Name Index

Subject Index